On Cooking
SIXTH EDITION

Approach and Philosophy of
On Cooking

The sixth edition of *On Cooking* follows the model established in previous editions, which have prepared thousands of students for successful careers in the culinary arts by building a strong foundation based on sound fundamental techniques. Students and instructors alike have praised *On Cooking* for its comprehensive yet accessible coverage of culinary skills and cooking procedures. Chapters **focus on six areas** that are essential to a well-rounded culinary professional:

1 Professionalism Background chapters introduce students to the field and feature material on food history, food safety and menu planning. Updated food safety information reflects the most recent regulations. A new chapter on the basics of nutrition emphasizes the nutritional impact of cooking.

2 Preparation Chapters cover the core subjects all culinary students should be familiar with before stepping into the kitchen. Equipment, basic knife skills and mise en place concepts are explained and illustrated. Staple ingredients, such as dairy products, herbs and spices as well as flavor profiles are also presented in this section.

3 Cooking These chapters explain and then demonstrate fundamental cooking techniques with a wide range of recipes. Individual chapters focus on different categories of key ingredients such as meats, poultry, fish, eggs and vegetables.

4 Garde Manger These chapters cover kitchen preparations including salads, sandwich making, charcuterie and hors d'oeuvre preparations. Material is of sufficient depth to support a complete unit on garde manger skills.

5 Baking These chapters cover a range of classic and contemporary breads and pastries that every culinary student should know. The material is sufficient to support a stand-alone unit on breads and dessert preparation.

6 Presentation Revised chapters on plate and buffet presentation demonstrate traditional and contemporary techniques for enhancing the visual presentation of food. The basics of buffet setup and management are also included in this section.

UPDATES

More than 225 new photographs and illustrations clearly show core techniques, equipment and foods.

A new Nutrition chapter complements the revised Healthy Cooking and Special Diets chapter, which now includes expanded information on health-related and vegetarian diets.

Content updates, including new recipes, reflect current trends while a new Basic Procedure feature helps students understand and compare core cooking techniques. Expanded coverage of curing and smoking, *sous vide* cooking and principles of vegetable cookery show students modern cooking techniques widely used in professional kitchens.

New discussions on sustainability and environmental concerns encourage students to consider the impact of their food choices.

Learning objectives, end-of-chapter Questions for Discussion and margin definitions are fully linked to competencies required by the American Culinary Federation.

At-a-glance cooking technique callouts highlight core principles, equipment, ingredients and steps. Function of Ingredients sidebars reinforce the science of cooking and baking and explain the uses for certain bakery ingredients.

A greatly enhanced support package includes MyLab Culinary®, an online instructors' manual featuring performance-based learning activities, an improved text bank and lecture-based PowerPoint slides.

Visual Guide for the Reader

Easy to navigate, *On Cooking* is broken down into bite-size subsections as reflected in the table of contents. We invite you to take the guided tour to capture the flavor of *On Cooking*.

HALLMARK FEATURES

Learning Objectives

Each chapter begins with clearly stated objectives that enable you to focus on what you should achieve by the end of the chapter.

Chapter Introduction

Chapter introductions summarize the main themes in each chapter and help reinforce topics.

After studying this chapter, you will be able to:

‣ name key historical figures responsible for developing food service professionalism and describe the contributions of each

‣ list and describe the key stages in the development of the modern food service industry

‣ explain the organization of classic and modern kitchen brigades

‣ identify the attributes a student needs to become a successful culinary professional

‣ describe the importance of professional ethics for chefs and list the specific behaviors that all culinary professionals should follow

cookery the art, practice or work of cooking

cooking (1) the transfer of energy from a heat source to a food; this energy alters the food's molecular structure, changing its texture, flavor,

---

Like any fine art, great **cookery** requires taste and creativity, an appreciation of beauty and a mastery of technique. Like the sciences, successful cookery demands knowledge and an understanding of basic principles, and like any successful leader, today's professional chef must exercise sound judgment and be committed to achieving excellence in all endeavors.

This book describes foods and cooking equipment, explains culinary principles and **cooking** techniques and provides recipes using these principles and techniques. No book, however, can provide taste, creativity, commitment and judgment. For these, chefs and other culinary professionals must rely on themselves. This chapter explores the rich history of the restaurant industry and the individuals who influenced the development of the profession. It also outlines the attributes of the professional chef. As you begin your culinary studies, we hope that you find inspiration in the history of the food service industry as you learn about the qualities that will guide you in your chosen career.

CHEFS AND RESTAURANTS

Cooks have produced food in quantity for as long as people have eaten together. For millennia, chefs, whether they be Asian, Native American, European or African, have catered to the often elaborate dining needs of the wealthy and powerful; and for centuries, vendors in China, Europe and elsewhere have sold foods to the public that they prepared themselves or bought from others.

But the history of the professional chef is of relatively recent origin. Its cast is mostly French, and it is intertwined with the history of restaurants—for only with the

---

Margin Definitions ▶

Important terms appear in the margins to help you master new terminology. There is a helpful phonetic pronunciation guide for non-English terms.

stage [stahzh] a brief, unpaid internship or training session in a professional kitchen; from the French *stagiaire*, meaning apprentice or intern

Safety Alerts ▶

Brief notes remind you of safety concerns and encourage you to incorporate food safety and sanitation into your regular kitchen activities.

⚠ Safety Alert

The Temperature Danger Zone

The temperature danger zone is a broad range of temperatures in which most of the bacteria that cause food-borne illnesses multiply rapidly. The 2013 Food Code of the U.S. Food and Drug Administration (FDA), July 2015 supplement, indicates that the temperature danger zone begins at 41°F (5°C) and ends at 135°F (57°C). Regulations in some localities and with some organizations may vary. This text uses the range recommended by the FDA.

From Your Grocer's Shelf

Even the most sophisticated food service operation occasionally uses some prepared condiments or flavorings. The products listed here are widely used and available from grocery stores or wholesale purveyors. Some are brand-name items that have become almost synonymous with the product itself; others are available from several manufacturers. When there is a choice, select brands with all natural ingredients, few thickeners and no preservatives.

Barbecue sauce: Commercial barbecue sauce is a mixture of tomatoes, vinegar and spices used primarily for marinating or basting meat, poultry or fish. A tremendous variety of barbecue sauces are available, with various flavors, textures and aromas. Sample several before selecting the most appropriate for your specific needs.

Chile sauce: Asian chile sauce, also known as *sambol* or *sambol oelek*, varies somewhat depending on the country of origin or style, but all are thick, reddish-orange and extremely pungent and spicy. They usually contain ground chiles with garlic or onion and with less vinegar than Louisiana-style hot

sauce. Asian cuisines incorporate these bottled sauces in curries, soups, stews and other dishes and as table condiments. One of the most popular and widely available brands is the Vietnamese-style chile garlic sauce with a rooster logo on its label, made in California by Huy Fong Foods. Various imported **Sriracha** sauces, named for a port town in southern Thailand, are also widely available.

Hoisin sauce: Hoisin sauce is a dark, thick, salty-sweet sauce made from fermented soybeans, vinegar, garlic and caramel. It is used in Chinese dishes or served as a dipping sauce.

Old Bay brand seasoning: Old Bay is a dry spice blend containing celery salt, dry mustard, paprika and other flavorings. It is widely used in shellfish preparations, especially boiled shrimp and crab.

Oyster sauce: Oyster sauce is a thick, dark sauce made from oyster extract. It has a salty-sweet flavor and a rich aroma. Oyster sauce is often used with stir-fried meats and poultry in Chinese cuisine.

Pickapeppa brand sauce: Pickapeppa sauce is a dark, thick, sweet-hot blend of tomatoes,

onions, sugar, vinegar, mango, raisins, tamarind and spices. Produced in Jamaica, it is used as a condiment for meat, game or fish and as a seasoning in sauces, soups and dressings.

Tabasco brand sauce: Tabasco sauce is a thin, bright-red liquid blended from vinegar, chiles and salt. Its fiery flavor is widely used in sauces, soups and prepared dishes; it is a popular condiment for Mexican, southern and southwestern cuisines. Tabasco sauce has been produced in Louisiana since 1868. Other "Louisiana-style" hot sauces (containing only peppers, vinegar and salt) may be substituted.

Worcestershire sauce: Worcestershire sauce is a thin, dark brown liquid made from a variety of fermented ingredients including anchovies, malt vinegar, tamarind, molasses and spices. It is used as a condiment for beef and as a seasoning for sauces, soups, stews and prepared dishes. Its flavor should be rich and full, but not salty. Vegetarian and kosher versions made without anchovies are also available.

◀ Flavor Sidebars

These sidebars show how flavoring ingredients may be used to change the character of a dish.

Procedure for Rolling and Shaping Pie Dough

① Dough for a typical pie crust or tart shell should be rolled to a thickness of approximately ⅛ inch (3 millimeters); it should be at least 2 inches (5 centimeters) larger in diameter than the baking pan.

② When you have rolled the dough to the desired thickness, carefully roll the dough up onto a rolling pin. Position the pin over the pie pan or tart shell and unroll the dough, easing it into the pan or shell.

③ Press the dough into the pan. For a single crust pie, trim the edge. Use the index finger and thumb on one hand and the index finger on the other to create a scalloped edge. Bake or fill as desired.

◀ Procedures

Step-by-step color photographs of various stages in the preparation of ingredients and dishes help you visualize unfamiliar techniques and encourage you to review classroom or kitchen activities whenever necessary.

Herbs

Fragrant herbs are available fresh or dried. Because drying alters their flavors and aromas, fresh herbs are generally preferred and should be used if possible. **Micro herbs** are the first true leaves of virtually any edible herb, such as basil or chervil. Micro greens are very fragile and must be hand-picked and carefully packaged for delivery. They are bursting with intense flavor; chefs use them as garnishes, especially on entrées and canapés.

Basil (Fr. *basilic*) is one of the great culinary herbs. It is available in a variety of "flavors"—cinnamon, garlic, lemon, even chocolate—but the most common is sweet basil. Sweet basil has light green, tender leaves and small white flowers. Its flavor isn't actually sweet, but rather strong, warm and slightly peppery, with a hint of anise and cloves. Basil is used in Mediterranean and some Southeast Asian cuisines and has a special affinity for garlic and tomatoes. When purchasing fresh basil, look for bright green leaves; avoid flower buds and wilted or rust-colored leaves. Dried sweet basil is readily available but has a decidedly weaker flavor than fresh.

Opal basil is named for its vivid purple color. It has a tougher, crinkled leaf and a medium-strong flavor. Opal basil may be substituted for sweet basil in cooking, and its appearance makes it a distinctive garnish.

Thai sweet basil (Th. *bai borapha*) has a narrow leaf and purple stem. It has a slight licorice flavor and is used in both raw and cooked dishes in Southeast Asian cuisines.

Bay (Fr. *laurier*), also known as sweet laurel, is a small tree that produces tough, glossy leaves with a sweet balsamic aroma and

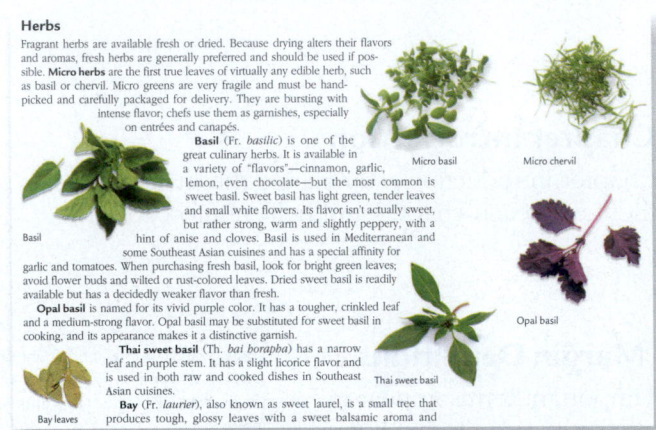

Micro basil Micro chervil

Basil

Opal basil

Thai sweet basil

Bay leaves

Product Identification ▶

Hundreds of original color photographs help you recognize and identify ingredients. You can explore a huge variety of items such as fruits, berries, chocolates, fresh herbs, fish, dried spices, game, meats and fine cheeses.

MISE EN PLACE
- Cut beef shank into pieces.
- Peel and chop onions, carrots and celery for mirepoix.
- Wash and peel turnips and leeks and chop into medium dice.
- Wash, peel, seed and dice tomatoes.
- Prepare herb sachet.

◀ Mise en Place

French for "put in place," this feature accompanying in-chapter recipes provides a list of what you must do before starting a recipe, such as preheating the oven, chopping nuts or melting butter.

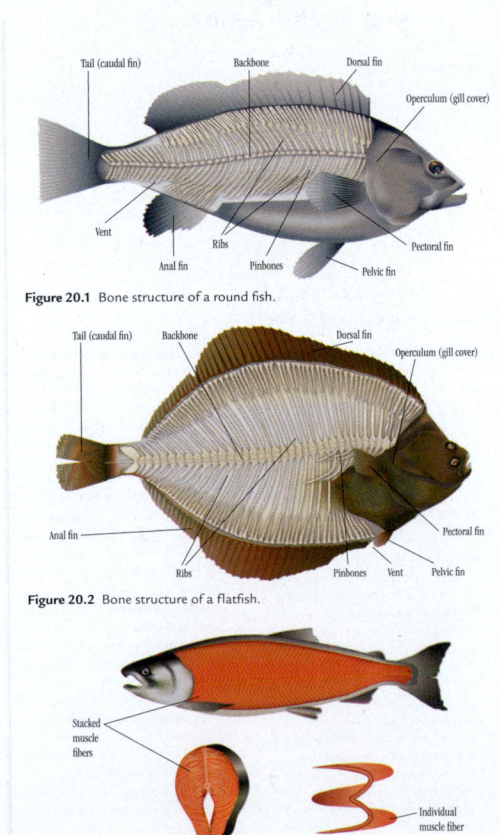

Tail (caudal fin) Backbone Dorsal fin Operculum (gill cover) Vent Ribs Pinbones Pectoral fin Anal fin Pelvic fin

Figure 20.1 Bone structure of a round fish.

Tail (caudal fin) Backbone Dorsal fin Operculum (gill cover) Anal fin Ribs Pinbones Vent Pelvic fin Pectoral fin

Figure 20.2 Bone structure of a flatfish.

▼ Icons

Icons identify recipes that are vegetarian, vegan or good choices for health-conscious diners.

 Good Choice    Vegan

Vegetarian

Line Drawings ▶

Detailed line drawings illustrate tools and equipment without brand identification. Other drawings depict the skeletal structure of meat animals, fish and poultry.

Stacked muscle fibers

Individual muscle fiber

Figure 20.3 Muscle fibers in a round fish.

Recipes

Measurements

All recipes include both U.S. and metric measurements. To aid in teaching scaling and consistent baking practices, we also provide metric equivalents for all temperatures, pan sizes and length measurements throughout the text. Baking recipes also include measurements in baker's percentage.

Illustrations

Recipes are illustrated with both sequential photos showing the preparation of dishes and many finished-dish photos that show you the authors' finished food created while testing the recipes.

Variations

Recipe variations show you how to modify recipe ingredients to create new dishes.

Nutritional Analysis

All recipes include a nutritional analysis prepared by a registered dietician.

Finished dish photos illustrate ways to present the recipe.

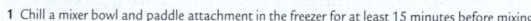

Chocolate Cherry Scones
Houston Community College, Houston, TX
Pastry Chef Eddy Van Damme

YIELD 24 Scones, approx. 4¼ oz. (130 g) each		METHOD Biscuit	
Unsalted butter, cold	14 oz.	420 g	44%
Granulated sugar	4 oz.	120 g	12.5%
Buttermilk	8 fl. oz.	240 ml	25%
Sour cream	1 lb.	480 g	50%
Salt	0.6 oz. (1 Tbsp.)	18 g	2%
Vanilla extract	0.5 fl. oz. (1 Tbsp.)	15 ml	1.5%
All-purpose or pastry flour	2 lb.	960 g	100%
Baking powder	2 oz.	60 g	6%
Dried cherries	1 lb.	480 g	50%
Chocolate chunks	9 oz.	270 g	28%
Powdered sugar	as needed	as needed	
Total dough weight:	6 lb. 6 oz.	3063 g	319%

1 Chill a mixer bowl and paddle attachment in the freezer for at least 15 minutes before mixing.
2 Cut the butter into 1-inch (6-millimeter) cubes. Set aside in the refrigerator.
3 Whisk together the sugar, buttermilk, sour cream, salt and vanilla extract in a bowl until smooth. Set aside in the refrigerator.
4 Put the flour and baking powder in the chilled mixer bowl. Place the butter on top. Mix on low speed using the paddle attachment until the mixture resembles coarse meal.
5 Add the buttermilk mixture to the dry ingredients and mix very briefly, until just combined. Mix in the cherries and chocolate until just combined.
6 Scale the dough into three uniform pieces. On a lightly floured surface, press each piece of dough out into an 8-inch (20.5-centimeter) disk using a metal torte ring or other form as a guide.
7 Cut each disk of dough into eight wedges. Position the wedges of dough spaced 2 inches (5 centimeters) apart on parchment-lined baking sheets. Bake at 375°F (190°C) until light golden brown, approximately 18–24 minutes. When cool, dust with powdered sugar if desired.

Variation:

Cinnamon Orange Scones—Omit the sun-dried cherries and chocolate chunks. Add 0.5 ounce (2 tablespoons/15 grams/1.5%) ground cinnamon and 0.2 ounce (1 tablespoon/6 grams/0.6%) grated orange zest in Step 3. Yield is reduced to 4 pounds 15 ounces (2313 grams).

Approximate values per 4¼-oz. (130-g) scone: **Calories** 430, **Total fat** 21 g, **Saturated fat** 13 g, **Cholesterol** 45 mg, **Sodium** 550 mg, **Total carbohydrates** 58 g, **Protein** 6 g, **Vitamin A** 25%, **Calcium** 20%, **Iron** 15%

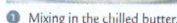
① Mixing in the chilled butter.

② Adding the chilled buttermilk mixture.

③ Placing the portioned dough on baking sheets.

Sidebars

Sidebars present information on food history, food in culture and the background of professional foodservice. These sidebars help you understand the culinary arts in a wider social context.

Questions for Discussion

Questions for Discussion, which appear at the end of each chapter, encourage you to integrate theory and technique into a broader understanding of the material.

Comprehensive Learning and Teaching Package

MyLab Culinary

FOR THE STUDENT

MyLab Culinary, a dynamic online tool, supports the many ways students learn. MyLab Culinary enables the student to study and master the content online on their own time and at their own pace. Media-rich personalized study plans are based on the student's performance using the site's interactive testing and games.

- UPDATED! Pearson Kitchen Manager has been redesigned and rebuilt for an improved customer experience and better connection to the Learning Objectives. With this collection of *On Cooking* recipes, you can quickly perform simple tasks such as recipe scaling, recipe costing and recipe conversions.
- NEW! Chapter 0, Culinary Math Fundamentals, with one model problem for 20 identified math concepts, with 10 practice problems for each concept (220 total problems).

The following updated chapter resources are included:

- Short Writing Assignments for each chapter build critical analysis and problem solving skills and send students to Pearson Kitchen Manager (when appropriate).
- Multiple Choice Questions in the form of Chapter Quizzes and Tests are in alignment with each Learning Objective, reinforcing the content in *On Cooking*.
- Videos align with *On Cooking* or current American Culinary Federation Standards.
- Video Assessment Questions are included with each video.
- Culinary Rubrics and Correlation Guides align with current American Culinary Federation Standards.

FOR THE INSTRUCTOR

Manage Your Course with MyLab Culinary

MyLab Culinary is an easy-to-use online resource designed to supplement a traditional lecture course. It provides instructors with basic course management capabilities in the areas of course organization, grades, communication and personalization of content. Instructors benefit from course management tools such as a robust grade book, integrated course email and reporting tools. MyLab Culinary also includes grading rubrics; these downloadable documents that can be used to grade and assess kitchen skills. Reporting features include data tracking and reporting for students.

Qualified adopters can download the following instructor supplements by registering at our Instructors' Resource Center at **www.pearsoned.com**.

Online Instructor's Manual

The Instructor's Manual includes chapter outlines, examination questions and answers, performance-based learning activities, answers to end-of-chapter questions for discussion and maps to ACF skill standards and competencies. (**ISBN-10:** 0-13-445365-4)

PowerPoint Lecture Presentations

This comprehensive set of slides can be used by instructors for class presentations or by students for lecture preview or review. There is a presentation for each chapter, including a selection of full-color photographs from the book. (**ISBN-10:** 0-13-444293-8)

TestGen (Computerized Test Bank)

TestGen contains text-based questions in a format that enables instructors to choose questions in order to create their own examinations. (**ISBN-10:** 0-13-444297-0)

For additional information on media resources or instructor materials, please contact Pearson Education faculty services at 1-800-526-0485.

On Cooking

A TEXTBOOK OF CULINARY FUNDAMENTALS | SIXTH EDITION

SARAH R. LABENSKY | ALAN M. HAUSE | PRISCILLA A. MARTEL

Photographs by **Richard Embery and Debby Wolvos**

Drawings by **Stacey Winters Quattrone and William E. Ingram**

330 Hudson Street, NY, NY 10013

Vice President, Portfolio Management: Andrew Gilfillan
Portfolio Manager: Pamela Chirls
Editorial Assistant: Lara Dimmick
Development Editor: Erin Mulligan
Senior Vice President, Marketing: David Gesell
Field Marketing Manager: Bob Nisbet
Marketing Coordinator: Elizabeth MacKenzie-Lamb
Director, Digital Studio and Content Production: Brian Hyland
Managing Producer: Cynthia Zonneveld
Manager, Rights Management: Johanna Burke
Operations Specialist: Deidra Smith
Creative Digital Lead: Mary Siener

Managing Producer, Digital Studio: Autumn Benson
Content Producer, Digital Studio: Leslie Brado
Full-Service Management and Composition: iEnergizer Aptara®, Ltd.
Full-Service Project Manager: Kelly Ricci
Interior Design: John Christiana
Cover Design: John Christiana
Cover Image: Topseller/Shutterstock
Printer/Binder: LSC/Willard
Cover Printer: Phoenix Color/Hagerstown
Text Font: ITC Garamond Std Light

Library of Congress Cataloging-in-Publication Data
Names: Labensky, Sarah R., author. | Hause, Alan M., author. | Martel, Priscilla, author.
Title: On cooking : a textbook of culinary fundamentals/Sarah R. Labensky, Alan M. Hause, Priscilla A. Martel; photographs by Richard Embery and Debby Wolvos; drawings by Stacey Winters Quattrone, William E. Ingram.
Description: Sixth edition. | Hoboken : Pearson, [2018] | Includes bibliographical references and index.
Identifiers: LCCN 2017050522| ISBN 9780134441900 | ISBN 0134441907
Subjects: LCSH: Cooking.
Classification: LCC TX714 .L29 2018 | DDC 641.5—dc23 LC record available at https://lccn.loc.gov/2017050522

16 2021

ISBN 10:   0-13-444190-7
ISBN 13: 978-0-13-444190-0

About the Authors

SARAH R. LABENSKY

Chef Sarah is a culinary educator and academic administrator with an extensive background as a restaurateur and caterer, textbook author and dedicated advocate for culinary professionalism. She is currently a professor at Woosong University's Sol International Culinary Arts School in Daejeon, Korea. Previously Chef Sarah was Founding Director of the Culinary Arts Institute at Mississippi University for Women (MUW) in Columbus, Mississippi. While living in Mississippi, she also owned two restaurants and worked as food and beverage director for a country club. Chef Sarah has also taught culinary arts at Scottsdale (Arizona) Community College and before teaching she spent many years as a working pastry cook and caterer.

In addition to *On Cooking*, Sarah Labensky is also co-author of *On Baking, Webster's New World Dictionary of Culinary Arts* and *Applied Math for Food Service*. She is a past president of the International Association of Culinary Professionals (IACP).

Sarah's passions include travel and mentoring young people to develop their own professional paths. To combine those interests, she has conducted culinary training programs in Russia, Korea, Moldova and Jamaica.

ALAN M. (SKIP) HAUSE

Chef Skip is a graduate of the Culinary Institute of America in Hyde Park, New York. Upon graduation, Chef Skip worked in both restaurants and hotels before settling in Arizona. For the past 20 years, he has owned and operated Fabulous Food Fine Catering and Events. He also launched and operates Gertrude's restaurant at the Desert Botanical Garden in Phoenix, Arizona. Chef Skip is involved in day-to-day food production, planning and execution of catered events as well as overseeing restaurant operations. A longtime member of the American Culinary Federation, Chef Skip is passionate about all aspects of food and cooking. He enjoys teaching and mentoring students and cooks, is active in the Careers through Culinary Arts Program (C-Cap) and is a board member of the East Valley Institute of Technology Culinary Program.

When not working in the kitchen, Chef Skip pursues his passions entertaining friends, traveling, hiking, biking (both motor and pedal) and, of course, anything to do with food. Chef Skip resides in Scottsdale, Arizona and summers in Kalispell, Montana, with his wife, Chantal, and sons, Logan and Grayson.

PRISCILLA A. MARTEL

Priscilla Martel is a professional chef, educator and food writer with a special interest in Mediterranean cuisines and artisan baking. She honed her cooking skills at Restaurant du Village, a country French restaurant she opened in Chester, Connecticut, in 1979. Today she operates All About Food, which holds several baking patents and collaborates with food manufacturers and restaurants to create innovative products, menus and marketing programs.

She is a visiting instructor at Boston University's certificate program in the culinary arts and in the Hospitality Management Program at Gateway Community College in New Haven, Connecticut. She is also a contributing writer for *Gourmet Retailer* among other food trade publications and the culinary director of American Almond, a leading baking-industry ingredient manufacturer. To honor her commitment to help young people prepare for their culinary careers, Priscilla Martel advises Pro Start Culinary teams in Connecticut. She is co-author of *On Baking* and *Math for Bakers* (DVD).

Contents

Recipes

Preface

Learning to cook is much more than simply learning to follow a recipe. Consequently, *On Cooking,* Sixth Edition, is not a cookbook or a collection of recipes. It is a carefully designed text intended to teach you the fundamentals of the culinary arts and to prepare you for a rewarding career in the food service industry.

The goal of *On Cooking* is to focus your attention on general procedures, highlighting fundamental principles and skills, whether it be for preparing a yeast bread or grilling a piece of fish. Both the how and why of cooking are discussed, emphasizing culinary principles first, not recipes. Only after the principles are introduced and explained are specific applications and sample recipes given. The content is extensively illustrated with photographs and line drawings to help you identify foods and equipment. Most recipes include photographs of the finished dish ready for service. Many procedures are illustrated with step-by-step photographs as well.

In order to provide you with a sense of the rich traditions of cookery, informative sidebars on food history, chef biographies and other topics are located throughout the book. Sidebars that relate to flavors and flavorings also appear throughout the material to enhance your understanding of key cooking ingredients and possible variations. Safety Alerts are shown in red, to remind you of conditions or situations that might pose a danger to you or to diners. Electronic resources accompanying this text enhance the learning experience while encouraging your use of computer technology in contemporary kitchens.

We wish you much success in your future career and hope that this text will continue to inform and inspire you long after graduation.

A NOTE ON RECIPES

Recipes are important and useful as a means of standardizing food preparation and recording information. In *On Cooking,* Sixth Edition, recipes are designed primarily to reinforce and explain techniques and procedures presented in the text. Many recipe yields are intentionally low in order to be less intimidating to beginning cooks and more useful in small schools and kitchens.

All ingredients are listed in both U.S. and metric measurements. The metric equivalents are rounded off to even, easily measured amounts. You should consider the ingredient lists as separate recipes or formulas; do not measure some ingredients according to the metric amounts and other ingredients according to the U.S. amounts or the proportions will not be accurate and the intended result will not be achieved. Throughout this book, unless otherwise noted:

- *mirepoix* refers to a preparation of 2 parts onion, 1 part celery and 1 part carrot by weight
- *pepper* refers to ground black pepper, preferably freshly ground
- *butter* refers to whole unsalted butter
- *milk* refers to whole or reduced fat (not nonfat) milk
- *yogurt* refers to whole plain (unsweetened) yogurt
- *TT* means "to taste"

Detailed procedures for standard techniques are presented in the text and generally are not repeated in each recipe (e.g., in a recipe, the instruction will be simply "deglaze the pan" or "monté au beurre"). Variations appear at the end of selected recipes. These variations illustrate how one set of techniques or procedures can be used to prepare different dishes with only minor modifications.

A mise en place feature is included for recipes that appear in the front sections of each recipe chapter. Ingredients that require preparation before the recipe is begun are listed in the margin under the Mise en Place heading. Consult this brief checklist after you read the recipe but before you begin to cook. Some recipes also include headnotes that describe the cultural or historical background of a dish or the unique techniques used in its preparation. This short text will enhance your understanding of a cuisine or cooking technique.

No matter how detailed the written recipe, however, we assume that you are acquiring certain knowledge, skills and judgment. It becomes a judgment call to know, for example, when a loaf of bread or a casserole is properly cooked. Ovens and cookware may vary in efficiency. For these reasons, recipes and formulas describe alternate tests for doneness, requiring you to use your developing skills to determine when a dish is fully cooked. You should also rely upon the knowledge and skills of your instructor for guidance. Although some skills and an understanding of theory can be acquired through reading and study, no book can substitute for repeated hands-on preparation and observation.

A registered dietician analyzed all the recipes in this book using nutritional analysis software that incorporates data from the U.S. Department of Agriculture, research laboratories and food manufacturers. The nutrient information provided here should be used only as a reference, however. A margin of error of approximately 20 percent can be expected because of natural variations in ingredients. Preparation techniques and serving sizes may also significantly alter the values of many nutrients. For the nutritional analysis, if a recipe offers a choice of ingredients, the first-mentioned ingredient is the one used. Ingredients listed as "to taste" (TT) and "as needed" are omitted from the analysis. It is assumed that corn oil and whole milk are used when a recipe calls for "vegetable oil" and "milk," respectively. In cases of a range of ingredient quantities or numbers of servings, the average is used.

 **Good Choice**

Throughout this book various recipes are marked with a Good Choice icon. This symbol identifies dishes that are particularly low in calories, fat, saturated fat or sodium; they may also be a good source of vitamins, protein, fiber or calcium.

 **Vegetarian**

Vegetarian dishes are indicated with a green leaf symbol. These recipes do not contain meat, fish, shellfish or poultry, but may contain dairy products and/or eggs. (This symbol is not used in the baked goods recipes in Chapters 31–35, however, because none of them contains meat, fish, shellfish or poultry.)

 **Vegan**

Vegan dishes are indicated with the blue V symbol. These recipes do not contain any animal products. Vegetarian and vegan dishes are not necessarily low in calories, fat or sodium; nor are they necessarily good sources of vitamins, protein, fiber or calcium.

Acknowledgments

This book would not have been possible without the assistance and support of many people. Special thanks to our photographers, Richard Embery, Debby Wolvos and Debby's assistants, Elizabeth Barry and Jenelle Bonifield, for their talent, professionalism and commitment to quality. The nutritional analysis for this edition was prepared by Mindy Hermann, MS, RD, whose thoroughness and prompt replies were greatly appreciated. Thanks also to Bill Ingram for his artistry.

Alan thanks his wife, Chantal, for her patience and guidance not only with this edition but since the book's conception 25 years ago, and his sons, Logan and Grayson, for pulling him away from work and reminding him that it's okay to just play and goof off sometimes. He is blessed to work with Priscilla Martel. She is not only a partner, but a friend. She is knowledgeable in all things food and cooking and she writes like a fiend. He thanks Sarah for working so hard on the project from halfway around the world. Her strong opinions and attention to detail have kept the text consistent through every edition.

Alan also acknowledges his many friends and coworkers who have been invaluable to the success of the text: Gregory Reynolds, Reynalda Montes, Davie Gabayan, Mark Bookhamer, Bob Tam, Declan Spears, Christina Brogan, Rosalino Morales, Estella Morales, Juan Soto, Jimmy Curry, Stephanie Bookhamer, Emily Phillips, Devin Rogers, Toni Connor, Luis Montes, Damian Montes and Raul Cinceros.

Sarah welcomes portfolio manager Pamela Chirls to the team with this edition. Pam, who is an icon in the world of cookbook publishing, added fresh insights and steady guidance to this revision. Sarah sends many thanks to Steve Labensky, Richard Embery and Robin Baliszewski for their hard work and participation over the years. She especially thanks Skip for always producing gorgeous and delicious food, and Priscilla for being the leader who pulls everything together with her breadth of knowledge and attention to detail. Finally Sarah thanks Woosong University and its Sol International Culinary Arts program in Daejeon, Korea for their support during this revision. The many wonderful students she has worked with over the years, both in Korea and the United States are the real reason that books such as this are written.

Priscilla would like to acknowledge the contributions of Carole Pierce and J. Patrick Truhn, two fine writers and editors, and the support of Chef Jeffrey Lizotte, Present Company, Chef Bryan Miller and the staff at On20 Restaurant, Chef Michel Nischan and Chef Eddy Van Damme. Special thanks go to Sheila Bowman, Seafood Watch Manager of Culinary and Strategic Initiatives at the Monterey Bay Aquarium, who provided key insights incorporated in this revision. She would like to sincerely thank Sarah and Skip for the extra effort it took to refresh this book, which honors our commitment to provide fundamental culinary knowledge to our student readers in a clear and inspiring manner.

The authors wish to thank the following companies for their generous donations of equipment and supplies: Zwilling J.A. Henckels AG and Parrish's Cake Decorating Supplies, Inc. We also wish to thank Demarle USA, Shamrock Foods Company, Peddlers Son Produce, KitchenAid Home Appliances, Taylor Environmental Instruments, Hobart Corporation, James Fagan, Degrenne North America, LLC., Elizabeth Jones of ISF International, Fairtrade International and Kristine Cueto, Manager Hotel Operations of Rosenthal USA, Ltd.

We also wish to thank everyone involved in this project at Pearson Education, including, Pamela Chirls, portfolio manager; Elizabeth Mackenzie-Lamb, marketing coordinator; Bob Nisbet, field marketing manager; Kelly Ricci, senior project manager; John Christiana, manager of design development; Erin Mulligan, developmental editor; and, Julianna Scott Fein, copy editor.

We are grateful for the outstanding quality of the responses to our review questionnaires and surveys. The excellent suggestions for improving the text and refining the recipes played a critical role in the preparation of this revision as well as previous revisions of

On Cooking. The following reviewers provided many excellent suggestions and ideas for improving the text:

G. Allen Akmon, Sullivan University
Karin Allen, Utah State University
Chris Argento, Nassau Community College
Mike Artlip, Kendall College
Victor Bagan, Odessa College
Jeff Bane, Clearly University
Todd Barrios, Stephen F. Austin State University
David Barrish, Reynolds Community College
Leslie Bartosh, Alvin Community College
Bea Beasley, Santa Rosa Junior College
Erica Beirman, Iowa State University
Carol Bennett, Central Arizona College
Frank Benowitz, Mercer County Community College
Paul John Bernhardt, Diablo Valley College
Ben Black, Culinary Institute of Charleston at Trident Technical College
LeRoy Blanchard, Los Angeles Trade Technical College
Patricia Bowman, Johnson & Wales University
Eric Breckoff, Piedmont Virginia Community College
Scott Bright, Quest Food Management Services
Tracey Brigman, University of Georgia
Stephen Burgeson, Buffalo State College
Angelo Camillo, Woodbury University
Kristina Campbell, Columbus Technical College
Mary Ann Campbell, Trenholm State Community College
Michael Carmel, Trident Technical College
Paul Carrier, Milwaukee Area Technical College
Melinda Casady, Portland's Culinary Workshop
Dorothy Chen-Maynard, California State University, San Bernardino
Susan Ciriello, Art Institute of Washington
Jeffrey Coker, Salt Lake Community College
Jerry Comar, Johnson & Wales University
Matt Cooper, Mott Community College
Anne Corr, Cook Like A Chef Camp
Sylvia Crixell, Texas State University, San Marcos
Chris Crosthwaite, Lane Community College
Cathy Cunningham, Tennessee Technological University
Chris Currier, Sandhills Community College
Jacqueline deChabert-Rios, East Carolina University
Richard Donnelly, East Stroudsburg University
Michael Downey, St. Louis Community College at Forest Park
Charles Drabkin, Edmonds Community College
Jodi Lee Duryea, University of North Texas
Tuesday Eastlack, Northwest Arkansas Community College
Sari Edelstein, Simmons College
Kimberly Emery, SUNY-Plattsburgh
Thom England, Ivy Tech Community College
Naomi Everett, University of Alaska
Melanie Ewalt, Kirkwood Community College
Richard Exley, Scottsdale Culinary Institute
Stephen Fernald, Lake Tahoe Community College
Edward Fernandez, Kapiolani Community College
Doug Flick, Johnson County Community College
Deborah Foster, Ball State University

Thomas Gaddis, Pellissippi State Community College
Wendy Gordon, SUNY Rockland Community College
Debra Gourley, Ivy Tech Community College
Clarke Griffin, St. Louis Community College
Lauri Griffin, Ivy Tech Community College
Kristen Grissom, Daytona State College
Marian Grubor, West Virginia Northern Community College
Jeff Hamblin, Brigham Young University-Idaho
Lois Hand, Bob Jones University
Brandon Harpster, Southeast Community College
Joe Harrold, Florida State College at Jacksonville
Kathleen Hassett, Horry-Georgetown Technical College
Ed Hennessy, Delaware Technical and Community College
Michael Herbert, Northern Virginia Community College
Travis Herr, Pensacola State College
Vern Hickman, Renaissance Culinary Center
Martina Hilldorfer, Kauai Community College
Carol Himes, Pueblo Community College
David Hoffman, Mohawk Valley Community College
David Horsfield, Kirkwood Community College
Thomas Hosley, Carteret Community College
John Hudoc, Robert Morris College
Robert Hudson, Pikes Peak Community College
Robert "Miles" Huff, Culinary Institute of Charleston at Trident Technical College
Sharon Hunt, Fort Valley State University
Barry Infuso, Pima Community College
Bruce Johnson, Salt Lake City Community College
Dorothy Johnston, Erie Community College
Melodie Jordan, Keystone College
Wendy Jordan, Rosemary's Restaurant
Thomas Kaltenecker, McHenry County College
Deborah Karasek, Bob Jones University
Debbie Kern, Delgado Community College
Mary Ann Kiernan, Syracuse University
Linda Kinney, University of Massachusetts
Kathy Knight, University of Mississippi
Chris Koch, Cooking or Whatever
Christopher Koch, Drexel University
Cindy Komarinski, Westmoreland County Community College
Julie Hosman Kulm, Boise State University
Jackson Lamb, Metropolitan State University of Denver
Claude Lambertz, University of Nevada-Las Vegas
Steve Lammers, Olympic College
Barbara Lang, Cornell University College of Agriculture and Life Sciences
Heinz Lauer, Culinaria Cuisine
Joseph LaVilla, San Francisco State University
Julie Lee, Western Kentucky University
Peter Lehmuller, Johnson & Wales University
Warren Leigh, Holyoke Community College
Larry Lewis, San Diego Culinary Institute
Dean Louie, University of Hawaii Maui College
Beth Lulinski, Northern Illinois University

George Macht, College of DuPage
Sylvia H. Marple, University of New Hampshire
Nicole Martinelli, Keiser University
Dean Massey, Clover Park Technical College
Lawrence Matson, The Art Institute of Dallas
Mark Mattern, M & M Enterprises, Inc.
James McGuiness, Keiser University
Paula McKeehan, Tarleton State University
Fiona McKenzie, Sandhills Community College
Ken Mertes, Robert Morris College
Brenden Mesch, The Art Institute of San Antonio
Deborah Miller, Keiser University
Maria Montemagni, College of the Sequoias
Judy Myhand, Louisiana State University
Andrea Nickels, Robert Morris College
Adrienne O'Brien, Luna Community College
Darla O'Dwyer, Stephen F. Austin State University
Lisa O'Neill, East Central Community College
Erich Ogle, Hinds Community College
Charlie Olawsky, Grand Rapids Community College
Shelly Owens, Metropolitan State College of Denver
Clarence Pan, Daytona State College
Joel Papcun, Great Lakes Culinary Institute
Patrick Parmentier, L'Ecole Culinaire, Kansas City
Jayne Pearson, Manchester Community College
Donna Pease, Technical College of the Lowcountry
Sean M. Perrodin, San Jacinto College-North Campus
Ellen Piazza, Saint Louis Community College
Christine Piccin, Santa Rosa Junior College
Tony Pisacano, Ogeechee Technical College
Toussaint Potter, AT&T
Joan E. Quinn, Northern Illinois University
Charles Robertson, Illinois Central College
Colin Roche, Johnson & Wales University
Linda Rosner, Lexington College
Charles Rossi, Atira Hotels
Scott Rudolph, California State Polytechnic University-Pomona
Carl Sandberg, Gwinnett Technical College
Janet Saros, Montgomery College
Craig Schmantowsky, Lynn University

Jules Schmitz, Cascade Culinary Institute
David Schneider, Indian River State College
Bridget Schwartz, George Washington University
Janet Shaffer, Lake Washington Technical College
Jeffrey Sheldon, Midwest Culinary Institute at Cincinnati State
Gregg Shiosaki, Seattle Central Community College
Cherie Simpson, The University of Alabama
Curtis Smith, Spokane Community College
Wayne Smith, Western Colorado Community College
Rupert Spies, Rupert Spies Consulting
Brian Stahlsmith, Mercyhurst College
Wendy Stocks, Purdue University-Calumet
Linda Sullivan, Indiana University of Pennsylvania
James Swenson, MilitaryChefs.com
Jim Switzenberg, Harrisburg Area Community College
Janis Taylor, Freed-Hardeman University
Klaus Tenbergen, Columbia College
Katie Thomas, Blackhawk Technical College
George Thompson, Oregon Culinary Institute
Peter Tobin, Inland Northwest Culinary Academy at Spokane Community College
Arthur Tolve, Bergen Community College
James Trebbien, The Institute for the Culinary Arts at Metropolitan Community College
Mary G. Trometter, Pennsylvania College of Technology
Armando Trujillo, Northern Arizona University
Anna Turner, Bob Jones University
Katrina Warner, Tarrant County College
Diana Watson-Maile, East Central University
Boo Wells, Jefferson Community College
Seunghee Wie, California State University-Sacramento
Brenda Wilkening, Estrella Mountain Community College
Lorna Williams, Bob Jones University
Josef Wollinger, Blackhawk Technical College
Chris Woodruff, Lake Michigan College
Louis Woods, Anne Arundel Community College
Mark Wright, Erie Community College-State University of New York
Kimberly Youkstetter, Worcester Technical High School
Charles Ziccardi, Drexel University

Professionalism 1

After studying this chapter, you will be able to:

▶ name key historical figures responsible for developing food service professionalism and describe the contributions of each

▶ list and describe the key stages in the development of the modern food service industry

▶ explain the organization of classic and modern kitchen brigades

▶ identify the attributes a student needs to become a successful culinary professional

▶ describe the importance of professional ethics for chefs and list the specific behaviors that all culinary professionals should follow

cookery the art, practice or work of cooking

cooking (1) the transfer of energy from a heat source to a food; this energy alters the food's molecular structure, changing its texture, flavor, aroma and appearance; (2) the preparation of food for consumption

professional cooking a system of cooking based on a knowledge of and appreciation for ingredients and procedures

Like any fine art, great **cookery** requires taste and creativity, an appreciation of beauty and a mastery of technique. Like the sciences, successful cookery demands knowledge and an understanding of basic principles, and like any successful leader, today's professional chef must exercise sound judgment and be committed to achieving excellence in all endeavors.

This book describes foods and cooking equipment, explains culinary principles and **cooking** techniques and provides recipes using these principles and techniques. No book, however, can provide taste, creativity, commitment and judgment. For these, chefs and other culinary professionals must rely on themselves. This chapter explores the rich history of the restaurant industry and the individuals who influenced the development of the profession. It also outlines the attributes of the professional chef. As you begin your culinary studies, we hope that you find inspiration in the history of the food service industry as you learn about the qualities that will guide you in your chosen career.

CHEFS AND RESTAURANTS

Cooks have produced food in quantity for as long as people have eaten together. For millennia, chefs, whether they be Asian, Native American, European or African, have catered to the often elaborate dining needs of the wealthy and powerful; and for centuries, vendors in China, Europe and elsewhere have sold foods to the public that they prepared themselves or bought from others.

But the history of the professional chef is of relatively recent origin. Its cast is mostly French, and it is intertwined with the history of restaurants—for only with the development of restaurants during the late 18th and early 19th centuries were chefs expected to produce, efficiently and economically, different dishes at different times for different diners.

The 18th Century—Boulanger's Restaurant

The word *restaurant* is derived from the French word *restaurer* ("to restore"). Since the 16th century, the word *restorative* had been used to describe rich and highly flavored soups or stews capable of restoring lost strength. Restoratives, like all other cooked foods offered and purchased outside the home during this period of history, were made by guild members. Each guild had a monopoly on preparing a category of food items. For example, during the reign of Henri IV of France (r. 1589–1610), there were separate guilds for *rôtisseurs* (who cooked *la grosse viande*, the main cuts of meat), *pâtissiers* (who cooked poultry, pies and tarts), *tamisiers* (who baked breads), *vinaigriers* (who made sauces and some stews, including some restoratives), *traiteurs* (who made meat stews) and *porte-chapes* (caterers who organized feasts and celebrations).

The French claim that the first modern restaurant opened one day in 1765 when a Parisian tavern keeper, a Monsieur Boulanger, hung a sign advertising the sale of his special restorative, a dish of sheep feet in white sauce. His establishment closed shortly thereafter as the result of a lawsuit brought by a guild whose members claimed that Boulanger was infringing on their exclusive right to sell prepared dishes. Boulanger triumphed in court and later reopened.

Boulanger's establishment differed from the inns and taverns that had existed throughout Europe for centuries. These inns and taverns served foods prepared (usually off premises) by the appropriate guild. The food—of which there was little choice—was offered by the inn or tavern as incidental to the establishment's primary function: providing sleeping accommodations or drink. Customers were served family style and ate at communal tables. Boulanger's contribution to the food service industry was serving a variety of foods prepared on premises to customers whose primary interest was dining.

Several other restaurants opened in Paris during the succeeding decades, including the Grande Taverne de Londres in 1782. Its owner, Antoine Beauvilliers (1754–1817), was the former steward (chief of the household staff) to the Comte de Provence, later King Louis XVIII of France. Beauvilliers advanced the development of the modern restaurant by offering his wealthy patrons a menu listing available dishes during fixed hours. Beauvilliers's impeccably trained wait staff served patrons at small, individual tables in an elegant setting.

The French Revolution (1789–1799) had a significant effect on the budding restaurant industry. Along with the aristocracy, the revolution generally abolished guilds and their monopolies. The revolution also allowed the public access to the skills and creativity of the well-trained, sophisticated chefs who previously had worked exclusively in the aristocracy's private kitchens. Although many of the aristocracy's chefs either left the country or lost their jobs (and some their heads), a few opened restaurants catering to the growing urbanized middle class.

The Early 19th Century—Carême and *Grande Cuisine*

As the 19th century progressed, more restaurants opened, serving a greater selection of items and catering to a wider clientele. By midcentury, several large, grand restaurants in Paris were serving elaborate meals, reminiscent of the *grande cuisine* (also known as *haute cuisine*) of the aristocracy. **Grande cuisine**, which arguably reached its peak of perfection in the hands of Antonin Carême was characterized by meals consisting of

grande cuisine the rich, intricate and elaborate cuisine of the 18th- and 19th-century French aristocracy and upper classes; it was based on the rational identification, development and adoption of strict culinary principles; by emphasizing the how and why of cooking, *grande cuisine* was the first to distinguish itself from regional cuisines, which tend to emphasize the tradition of cooking

Marie-Antoine (Antonin) Carême (1783–1833)

Antonin Carême, known as the "cook of kings and the king of cooks," was an acknowledged master of French *grande cuisine*. Abandoned on the streets of Paris as a child, he worked his way from cook's helper in a working-class restaurant to become one of the most prestigious chefs of his (or, arguably, any other) time. During his career, he was chef to the famous French diplomat and gourmand Prince de Talleyrand, the Prince Regent of England (who became King George IV), Tsar Alexander I of Russia and Baron de Rothschild, among others.

Carême's stated goal was to achieve lightness, grace, order and perspicuity in the preparation and presentation of food. As a pâtissier, he designed and prepared elaborate and elegant pastry and confectionery creations, many of which were based on architectural designs. (He wrote that "the fine arts are five in number, namely: painting, sculpture, poetry, music, architecture—the main branch of which is confectionery.") As a showman, he garnished his dishes with ornamental *hâtelets* (skewers) threaded with colorful ingredients, such as crayfish and intricately carved vegetables, and presented his creations on elaborate *socles* (bases). As a saucier, he standardized the use of the flour and butter mixture called *roux* as a thickening agent, perfected recipes and devised

A poultry illustration from Carême showing *hâtelets* (skewers) used as a garnish.

a system for classifying sauces. As a garde-manger, Carême popularized cold cuisine, emphasizing molds and aspic dishes. As a culinary professional, he designed kitchen tools, equipment and uniforms.

As an author, Carême wrote and illustrated important texts on the culinary arts, including *Le Maitre d'hotel français* (c. 1822), describing the hundreds of dishes he personally created and cooked in the capitals of Europe; *Le Pâtissier royal parisien* (c. 1825), containing fanciful designs for *les pieces montées*, the great decorative centerpieces that were the crowning glory of grand dinners; and his five-volume masterpiece on the state of his profession, *L'Art de la cuisine française aux XIXe siècle* (1833), the last two volumes of which were completed after his death by his associate, Plumerey. Carême's writings almost single-handedly refined and summarized five hundred years of culinary evolution. But his treatises were not mere cookbooks. Rather he analyzed cooking, old and new, emphasizing procedure and order and covering every aspect of the art known as *grande cuisine*.

Carême died before age 50, burnt out, according to French poet and essayist Laurent Tailhade, "by the flame of his genius and the coal of the spits."

restaurateur a person who owns or operates an establishment serving food, such as a restaurant

gourmand a connoisseur of fine food and drink, often to excess

gastronomy the art and science of eating well

gourmet a connoisseur of fine food and drink

gourmet foods foods of the highest quality, perfectly prepared and beautifully presented

classic cuisine a late 19th- and early 20th-century refinement and simplification of French *grande cuisine*. Classic (or classical) cuisine relies on the thorough exploration of culinary principles and techniques and emphasizes the refined preparation and presentation of superb ingredients.

dozens of courses of elaborately and intricately prepared, presented, garnished and sauced foods. Other **restaurateurs** blended the techniques and styles of *grande cuisine* with the simpler foods and tastes of the middle class (*cuisine bourgeoise*) to create a new cuisine simpler than *grande cuisine* but more complex than mere home cooking, which often centered around bread.

The Late 19th Century—Escoffier and *Cuisine Classique*

Following the lead set by the French in both culinary style and the restaurant business, restaurants opened in the United States and throughout Europe during the 19th century. Charles Ranhofer (1836–1899) was the first internationally renowned chef of an American restaurant–Delmonico's in New York City. In 1893, Ranhofer published his "Franco-American" encyclopedia of cooking, *The Epicurean*, which contained more than 3500 recipes.

One of the finest restaurants outside France was the dining room at London's Savoy Hotel, opened in 1898 under the directions of César Ritz (1850–1918) and Auguste Escoffier (1846–1935). There they created a restaurant that attracted royalty and aristocratic women, a group rarely seen dining in public at the time. Escoffier is generally credited with refining the *grande cuisine* of Carême to create *cuisine classique* or **classic cuisine**. He invented such dishes as *Suprêmes de soles à l'aurore* (or "fillet of sole at dawn") in a blushing pink sauce and *Pêche Melba* (or "Peach Melba"), named after Austrian singer Nellie Melba, a guest at the hotel. By doing so, he brought French cuisine into the 20th century.

Auguste Escoffier (1846–1935)

Auguste Escoffier's brilliant culinary career began at age 13 in his uncle's restaurant and continued until his death at age 89. Called the "emperor of the world's kitchens," he is perhaps best known for defining French cuisine and dining during La Belle Époque (also referred to as the "Gay Nineties").

Unlike Antonin Carême, Escoffier never worked in an aristocratic household. Rather he exhibited his culinary skills in the dining rooms of the finest hotels in Europe, including the Place Vendôme in Paris and the Savoy and Carlton hotels in London.

Escoffier did much to enhance *grande cuisine* as defined by Carême. Crediting Carême with providing the foundation for great—that is, French—cooking, Escoffier simplified the profusion of flavors, dishes and garnishes typifying Carême's work. For example, Carême would present elaborate displays of as many as 150 dishes for guests at a private function. In contrast, Escoffier would offer 11 dishes served tableside to each guest individually. Escoffier also streamlined some of Carême's overly elaborate and fussy procedures and classifications. For example, he reduced Carême's elaborate system of classifying

Tournedos Rossini, a dish created by Escoffier, as it might be served today.

sauces into the five families of sauces still recognized today. Escoffier sought simplicity and aimed for the perfect balance of a few superb ingredients. Some consider his refinement of *grande cuisine* to have been so radical as to credit him with the development of a new cuisine referred to as *cuisine classique* (classic or classical cuisine).

Escoffier's many writings include *Le Livre des menus* (1912), in which, discussing the principles of a well-planned meal, he analogizes a great dinner to a symphony with contrasting movements that should be appropriate to the occasion, the guests and the season, and *Ma cuisine* (1934), surveying *cuisine bourgeoise*. But his most important contribution is a culinary treatise intended for the professional chef titled *Le Guide culinaire* (1903). Still in use today, it is an astounding collection of more than 5000 classic cuisine recipes and garnishes. In it, Escoffier emphasizes the mastery of techniques, the thorough understanding of cooking principles and the appreciation of ingredients— attributes he considered to be the building blocks professional chefs should use to create great dishes.

The Mid-20th Century—Point and *Nouvelle Cuisine*

The mid-20th century witnessed a trend toward lighter, more naturally flavored and more simply prepared foods. Fernand Point was a master practitioner of this movement. But this master's goal of simplicity and refinement was carried to even greater heights by a generation of French chefs Point trained: principally Paul Bocuse, Jean and Pierre Troisgros, Alain Chapel, François Bise and Louis Outhier. They, along with Michel Guérard and Roger Vergé, were the pioneers of *nouvelle cuisine* in the early 1970s. Their contemporary, Gaston Lenôtre, modernized the classic pastries of *grande cuisine*, infusing them with the bright, fresh flavors of *nouvelle cuisine*.

Their culinary philosophy was principled on the rejection of overly rich, needlessly complicated dishes and an emphasis on healthful eating. The ingredients must be absolutely fresh and of the highest possible quality; the cooking methods should be simple and direct whenever possible. The accompaniments and garnishes must be light and contribute to an overall harmony; the completed plates must be elegantly designed and decorated. Following these guidelines, traditional cooking methods were applied to nontraditional ingredients, and ingredients were combined in new and previously unorthodox fashions.

The Late 20th and Early 21st Centuries—An American Culinary Revolution

During the last 30–40 years, broad changes launched in the United States have affected the global culinary landscape. Two such trends are bold, ethnic flavors and fresh food, simply prepared.

The popularity of **ethnic cuisine** is due, in large part, to an unlikely source: the Immigration and Nationality Act of 1965. Under its provisions, a large number of Asians immigrated to the United States. They brought with them their rich culinary traditions and ignited America's love affair with fiery hot cuisines. By the late 1970s many Americans were no longer content with overly salty pseudo-Chinese dishes. They demanded authenticity and developed cravings for spicy dishes from the Szechuan and Hunan provinces of China, Vietnam and Thailand. In the 1970s Mexican food also left the barrio and became mainstream. Now authentic regional Mexican dishes are commonplace throughout America.

During this same time period, restaurateurs and chefs began Americanizing the principles of French *nouvelle cuisine*. When Alice Waters opened Chez Panisse in Berkeley, California, in 1971, her goal was to serve fresh food, simply prepared. Rejecting the growing popularity of processed and packaged foods, Waters used fresh, seasonal and locally grown produce in simple preparations that preserved and emphasized the foods' natural flavors. Chez Panisse and the many chefs who passed through its kitchen launched a new style of American cuisine that became known as **California** or **New American cuisine**. As the culinary movement launched by Waters's philosophy spread across the United States, farmers and chefs began working together to make fresh, locally grown foods available, and producers and suppliers began developing domestic sources for some of the high-quality ingredients that were once available only from overseas.

These chefs ushered in a period of bold experimentation. American chefs and chefs working in America, such as Wolfgang Puck, began to combine ingredients and preparation methods from a variety of cuisines. Their work resulted in **fusion cuisine**. Fusion cuisine combines ingredients or preparation methods associated with one ethnic or **regional cuisine** with those of another. A fillet of Norwegian salmon might be grilled over hickory wood and then served on a bed of Japanese soba noodles, for example, or a traditional French duck confit may be seasoned with lemongrass, ginger and chiles. Pizzas with untraditional toppings, such as smoked salmon and caviar, which had never been conceived of before, launched Wolfgang Puck's career in Los Angeles, California, in the early 1980s. Today such fusion is commonplace from the creations of Kogi BBQ's Korean Mexican tacos in Southern California to the subtle use of Asian seasonings in the classic sauces prepared by Jean-Georges Vongerichten at his restaurant Jean-Georges in New York City. But in the 1970s and 1980s, fusion represented a breakthrough in cooking and helped establish Puck as the first celebrity chef.

nouvelle cuisine French for "new cooking"; a mid-20th-century movement away from many classic cuisine principles and toward a lighter cuisine based on natural flavors, shortened cooking times and innovative combinations

ethnic cuisine the cuisine of a group of people having a common cultural heritage, as opposed to the cuisine of a group of people bound together by geography or political factors

California or **New American cuisine** a late 20th-century movement that first became popular in California and spread across the United States; it stresses the use of fresh, locally grown, seasonal produce and high-quality ingredients simply prepared in a fashion that preserves and emphasizes natural flavors

fusion cuisine the blending or use of ingredients and/or preparation methods from various ethnic, regional or national cuisines in the same dish; also known as transnational cuisine

regional cuisine a set of recipes based on local ingredients, traditions and practices; within a larger geographical, political, cultural or social unit, regional cuisines are often variations of one another that blend together to create a national cuisine

global cuisine foods (often commercially produced items) or preparation methods that have become ubiquitous throughout the world; for example, curries and French-fried potatoes

national cuisine the characteristic cuisine of a nation

Smoked salmon and caviar pizza, a dish created by Wolfgang Puck in the early 1980s.

A dish composed of olive oil poached turnips and mushrooms, potatoes and red cabbage from the vegetable menu of Charlie Trotter's, a Michelin-starred restaurant that operated in Chicago from 1987 to 2012.

Sauce spooned over a dish at a meal prepared in New York City by Thomas Keller and his staff.

farm-to-table or **locavore movement** an awareness of the source of ingredients with an emphasis on serving locally grown and minimally processed foods in season

molecular gastronomy a contemporary scientific movement that investigates the chemistry and physics of food preparation

modernist cuisine a term that refers to science-inspired techniques for food preparation; an avant-garde approach to food preparation, sanitation and health concerns based on science-inspired techniques

Roast foie gras with almond fluid gel cherry chamomile prepared by Heston Blumenthal at The Fat Duck in Bray, England.

Other chefs who were instrumental in changing the way Americans dine imported the exacting standards and culinary techniques of European chefs. In so doing these chefs elevated the style and quality of food served in the United States. Charlie Trotter opened his eponymous restaurant in Chicago in 1987 after several apprenticeships in France. Trotter is noteworthy for introducing the multicourse tasting menus that are a signature of fine dining today. Among the first to dedicate as much attention to vegetables as to meat or fish, Trotter also explored raw food preparations, writing a book on raw foods in 2003. Chef Thomas Keller, who started cooking in restaurants in his teens, worked at renowned restaurants Guy Savoy and Le Taillevent in Paris before opening his own restaurant in 1994. Today experts regard Keller's restaurants, The French Laundry in Yountville, California, and Per Se in New York City among the finest in the world. His cuisine, based on traditional French and modern cooking techniques, utilizes only foods in season, many grown on premises or sourced from local farmers. Known for producing lengthy tasting menus of food with clean flavors as well as his obsessive attention to detail, Keller develops professionalism in his staff who are encouraged to be mindful, organized and "work clean."

The fluidity of international borders, the accessibility of global travel and the Internet have radically changed the way we cook and the foods we eat. Today the world's pantries are available to chefs and home cooks everywhere. Chefs are sourcing ingredients globally as well as working in tandem with farmers to supply their diners with fresh flavors while preserving local agriculture and heirloom varieties. As we discuss in detail later in this chapter, the concern for locally raised ingredients, referred to as the **farm-to-table** or **locavore movement**, has influenced chefs to serve fresh seasonal foods, such as wild greens or seafood from day boat fishermen, that is grown or harvested within a few miles of their restaurants.

Modernist Cuisine

During the 1990s scientists, particularly in the United States, England, France and Spain, began to see food preparation as a distinct and worthy field of exploration. Chefs and scientists wanted to understand why food behaved as it did, why traditional cooking techniques sometimes failed and how to improve culinary methods. Scientists began seeking answers to these questions under the umbrella of **molecular gastronomy**, a term coined by the British physicist Nicholas Kurti and French chemist Hervé This in 1988. Inspired by the experiments of molecular gastronomy, early 21st-century chefs reinvented the notion of cooking by employing ingredients and machinery more common in industrial food manufacturing than in restaurant kitchens. This offshoot of molecular gastronomy is now referred to as **modernist cuisine**, first defined by Nathan Myhrvold (former Chief Technology Officer at Microsoft, co-founder of Intellectual Ventures and the principal author of *Modernist Cuisine*). Among those following modernist techniques is a group of daring, innovative chefs practicing a form of *haute cuisine* that integrates classic French cuisine with the highest-quality ingredients and previously unthinkable presentations such as liquids solidified into spheres and powders.

The founding chef of this movement is Ferran Adrià of elBulli in Spain (1962–). Current practitioners include Heston Blumenthal at The Fat Duck in Bray, England, Gaggan Anand at Gaggan in Bangkok and Grant Achatz at Alinea in Chicago. The hallmarks of this high-tech cuisine include dehydrators, edible menus, gels and spheres, intensely flavored smoke and –30°F antigriddles that "cook" liquefied food. These chefs produce foods that look like one thing, taste like something totally different and smell like childhood memories. Take Heston Blumenthal's bacon and egg ice cream as one example. It is a plated dessert consisting of ice cream made from a bacon-infused custard. All the elements of the savory breakfast appear on the plate including a cup of tea, served as a sweet jelly, and toast in the form of sweet, caramelized brioche. As Blumenthal says, his goal is to make food exciting by overturning expectations. Although few restaurants are going to the extreme of replacing their cooktops with water baths and chemical freezers, many of the tools and techniques that these avant-garde chefs perfected are now being used and appreciated on a smaller scale by chefs who may add a gelled garnish or spheres of sauce to a traditional dish.

Ferran Adrià (1962–)

Cooking is a language through which all the following properties may be expressed: harmony, creativity, happiness, beauty, poetry, complexity, magic, humor, provocation and culture.
—Ferran Adrià

Ferran Adrià is an experimental Spanish chef called the Salvador Dalí of the kitchen. Adrià's prestigious restaurant elBulli (slang for "the bulldog"), was voted number one on The World's 50 Best Restaurants™ list four times. ElBulli also earned three Michelin stars, the highest Michelin rating, an award it maintained from 1997 until it closed in 2011.

Born near Barcelona, this food futurist planned a business career before a temporary dishwashing job redirected his path. Inspired by classic cuisine and an encouraging chef, Adrià began his self-education, reading *El Práctico*, a cooking manual edited by a Spanish chef heavily influenced by Auguste Escoffier, from cover to cover. A month working at elBulli was an experience so stimulating that he returned there upon completion of his military service in 1984.

At the time, the cuisine at elBulli was heavily influenced by *nouvelle cuisine*, then at its height of popularity. Working alongside the restaurant's chef, Adrià created new versions of acclaimed French dishes, earning the restaurant its first star in the influential Michelin Guide.

Liquid olives, created by Chef Ferran Adrià.

He enhanced his skills and knowledge of classic technique through brief apprenticeships in top kitchens in France. But in 1987 Adrià heard an expression that was to change his direction as a chef; "Creativity means not copying," said Jacques Maximin, then chef of Le Chantecler in Nice, France. At that moment Adrià and his team committed themselves to reinventing cuisine as we know it.

The food served at elBulli engaged all of one's senses. Dinner was a tasting menu of up to 35 bite-sized dishes. What appeared to be cooked may actually have been flash frozen. An herb clipped to a spoon allowed guests to smell the aroma before tasting the herb in the dish. Warm foam that tasted of carrots or mushrooms, hot gelatin, encapsulated mango purée that resembled egg yolks and ravioli filled with liquid were some of the show-stopping techniques for which Adrià became known. At the vanguard of experimental cooking, Adrià and staff spent six months each year working with food technologists, industrial designers and artists experimenting with new techniques. The chef and his staff documented their style of cooking in a 23-point style guide, "Synthesis of elBulli Cuisine." Using the freshest ingredients and mastery of technique are givens, they write. But also all foods are of equal gastronomic value, with a preference for vegetables and seafood to create a "light, harmonic cuisine" based on classic and modern technologies.

Adrià continues his experimentation and research into gastronomy, sharing his knowledge through the Internet and at elBulli Foundation.

MODERN FOOD SERVICE OPERATIONS

From Monsieur Boulanger's humble establishment, a great industry has grown. Today more than one million public dining facilities operate in the United States alone. The dramatic growth and diversification of the food service industry is due in part to the Industrial Revolution in the 19th century and the social and economic changes it brought, including the introduction of new culinary technologies, food supplies and consumer concerns.

Culinary Technologies

Technology has always had a profound effect on cooking. For example, the development of clay and, later, metal vessels that could contain liquids and withstand and conduct heat offered prehistoric cooks the opportunity to stew, make soups and porridge, pickle and brine foods and control fermentation. But it was not until the rapid technological advances fostered by the Industrial Revolution that anything approaching the modern kitchen was possible.

One of the most important advancements was the introduction of the cast-iron stove. Prior to the 19th century, most cooking was done on spits or grills or in cauldrons or pots set on or in a wood- or coal-burning hearth. Hearthside cooking did not lend itself well to the simultaneous preparation of many items or to items requiring constant and delicate attention. With the introduction of cast-iron stoves during the 1800s, cooks could more comfortably and safely approach the heat source and control its temperatures. On the new cook stoves, they could also prepare foods in the small quantities needed to serve individual diners on demand.

Also of great importance were developments in food preservation and storage techniques. For thousands of years food had been preserved by sun-drying, salting, smoking, pickling, sugar-curing or fermenting. Salt-cured codfish and salmon have been staples in Scandinavia for millennia, and the earliest household records and cookery manuscripts from medieval Britain include inventories of bacon and salted meats. Although useful, these ancient procedures dramatically change the appearance and flavor of most foods. By the early 19th century, preserving techniques began to emerge that had minimal effect on appearance and flavor. For example, by 1800 the Frenchman Nicolas François Appert successfully "canned" foods by subjecting foods stored in sterilized glass jars to very high heat. An early mechanical refrigerator was developed by the mid-1800s; soon reliable iceboxes, refrigerators and, later, freezers were available. During the 20th century freeze-drying, vacuum-packing and irradiation became common preservation techniques.

Developments in transportation technology were also underway. During the 19th century steam-powered ships and railroads brought foods quickly to market from distant suppliers. Since the mid-20th century temperature-controlled cargo ships, trains, trucks and airplanes have all been used as part of an integrated worldwide food transportation network. Combined with dependable food preservation and storage techniques, improved transportation networks freed chefs from seasonal and geographic limitations in their choice of foods and expanded consumers' culinary horizons.

Advancements in technology also facilitated or even eliminated much routine kitchen work. Since the 19th century chefs have relied increasingly on mechanical and motorized food processors, mixers and cutters as well as a wealth of sophisticated kitchen equipment from high-carbon stainless steel knife blades to infrared thermometers and ultrasonic homogenizers.

Food Supplies

Modern food preservation, storage and transportation techniques have made both fresh and exotic foods regularly available to chefs and consumers. Because of advances in packaging and transportation, foodstuffs grown or made virtually anywhere in the world are now available to restaurants regardless of season or location.

Last century's advancements in agriculture, such as the switch from organic to chemical fertilizers and the introduction of pesticides and drought- or pest-resistant strains, increased yields of healthy crops. Traditional hybridization techniques and, more recently, genetic engineering have produced new varieties of grains, such as soybeans, corn, rapeseeds and rice, which are resistant to herbicides or insects. Although scientists may argue that such engineering simply speeds up the process of natural selection, consumers are often more concerned about the unforeseen impact on consumer health and unintended consequences to the environment. Governments around the world regulate, restrict or outright ban the sale of foodstuffs containing **genetically modified organisms (GMOs)** on a case-by-case basis.

Additionally, advancements in animal husbandry and aquaculture have led to a more reliable supply of leaner meat, poultry and fish. Foods found traditionally only in the wild (for example, game, wild rice and many mushrooms) are now being raised commercially and are routinely available. The commercialization of foodstuffs has created a backlash among some consumers and chefs, however. New concerns about sustainability and support for local farmers and food producers present the industry with new challenges and new opportunities for chefs to revise their menus and adopt ecologically-based business practices.

genetically modified organism (GMO) refers to a plant, microorganism or animal in which genetic material (segments of DNA) have been modified or engineered in a laboratory in order to change inheritable characteristics, such as resistance to insects or herbicides

Consumer Concerns

Consumer concerns about nutrition and diet have fueled changes in the food service industry. Obviously what we eat affects our health. Adequate amounts of certain nutrients promote good health by preventing deficiencies; studies show that good nutrition also helps prevent chronic diseases and increases longevity. Chefs must now understand human nutritional needs and the various special diets followed by customers. Beyond simply reducing fat and sugar for weight control, chefs must accommodate customers' allergies, specialized diets due to illnesses and ethical or social dining concerns of groups such as vegetarians and locavores.

The public is also rightfully concerned about food safety. Federal, state and local governments help promote food safety by inspecting and grading meats and poultry, regulating label contents for packaged foods and setting sanitation standards. The last line of defense, however, are the restaurant workers who prepare and serve food. It is up to you, as a culinary professional, to follow sanitation and food safety guidelines to protect others from injury or illness.

As noted earlier in this chapter, concerns about nutrition and food safety have also resulted in renewed interest in local and organically grown fruits and vegetables and free-range-raised animals. The local food movement and the concern for sustainable food production are leading chefs to find new sources for ingredients and expand their community involvement.

Local Production

Fresh foods travel from the producer to the consumer by two basic methods: 1) the industrial, commercial system, which operates huge, consolidated farms and global transportation networks; and 2) small local or regional systems. One key difference is how far the food travels from where it is grown or produced to the end consumer. Local systems distribute food items over short distances. These local farms are often family farms, which are defined by the United States Department of Agriculture (USDA) as those operated by the people who own the land or the animals and have sales of less than $350,000 per year.

While the word *local* indicates that the food item is being sold close to where it was grown or produced, there is no consistent definition for it. Many consumers and organizations working in this field, such as farmer's markets, cite a radius of 50–100 miles (80–160 km) from production to point of sale as the determining factor. Weather conditions, urbanization or production capacity of the area also have an impact on the definition of *local*, sometimes extending the acceptable zone into a larger regional area. In 2010 the USDA began using a definition that implies food can be marketed as local or regional if the total distance the product was transported is less than 400 miles (640 km) from where it originated.

Chefs are using the public's interest in eating locally produced foods to create restaurant menus featuring such products. Some chefs, like their pre-industrial predecessors, now grow their own produce, raise their own pigs or chickens and forage from nearby forests for ingredients. They may contract with local farmers, beekeepers, cheese makers or fishermen to supply products, building their menus according to product availability, rather than serving out-of-season items or those transported long distances. In its purest version, farm-to-table means that the foods served come directly from a local farm, without passing through a market, distributor or grocery store. It implies a relationship between the chef and the farmer, with the chef serving the farm's products at their peak of freshness, ripeness and flavor. Farm-to-table menus may change daily due to product availability, and preparation techniques focus on retaining nutrients and freshness.

Sustainability

It is important to keep in mind that coming from nearby or being produced on a small farm does not necessarily mean the foods themselves are healthier, organic or in any

Chef Raymond Blanc samples radishes grown in the greenhouse at Belmond Le Manoir aux Quat'Saisons, Oxford, England.

The farm at Fäviken, a restaurant in Järpen, Sweden, supplies much of the food prepared by chef Magnus Nilsson and his staff.

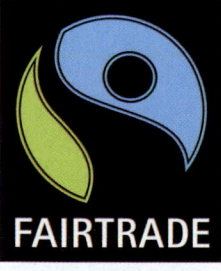

fairtrade a global social movement that helps commodity producers in developing countries obtain a fair deal for their export goods (such as fruit, coffee beans and cacao beans), supports sustainable farming practices and discourages the use of certain pesticides and bans child labor

way more natural. Sustainable and local are related concepts, but not necessarily the same thing. The term **sustainability** refers to the practices used to minimize human impact on the environment and protect natural resources. Sustainability is an integrated and systematic approach to what and how we consume. Energy and water consumption, land use, building construction and waste disposal all have an impact on sustainability. In the realm of food service, sustainability refers to growing or harvesting foodstuffs in an environmentally and socially responsibility manner. Sustainable farming practices include avoiding or minimizing the use of herbicides and pesticides, dry farming without irrigation and reducing the consumption of fossil fuels. Reducing packaging, composting and reducing transportation time by selling directly to consumers, all help farmers lessen their environmental impact. Such practices can also improve the socioeconomic conditions of the community and the health of farm workers.

For food service establishments, sustainability can begin with some simple steps. Minimize the **food miles**, the distance food travels to reach the establishment, by purchasing foodstuffs grown locally. Growing herbs and produce onsite also reduces fuel consumed by transportation. Incorporate more diverse local crops into your menu, and educate your staff so that they can explain these items to customers in a positive manner. Compost vegetable trimmings and coffee grounds to share with a local farm that recycles waste into nourishment. Install a water filtration system and replace bottled water with your own filtered water for customers, served in reusable glass. Use green cleaning products and biodegradable paper products; recycling cardboard, metal, glass and other trash are easily adopted sustainable practices.

Chefs can also use the principles of sustainability to foster their creativity. Two Scandinavian chefs have received worldwide renown for using only local products to create exciting new cuisines. Chefs René Redzepi of Noma and Restaurant 108 in Copenhagen, and Magnus Nilsson of Fäviken in Järpen, Sweden, rely on local ingredients to create ever-changing, highly unusual seasonal menus and award-winning restaurants. In Charleston, South Carolina, chef Sean Brock serves not only locally produced foods, but also researches and grows heirloom produce such as peas, corn, tomatoes and farro to serve in his restaurant Husk. Brock works with seed banks to bring back indigenous crops and even raises an heirloom breed of pigs that he uses in traditional dishes from the antebellum South. Instead of creating a new cuisine, Husk offers patrons historic recipes and dishes made with authentic, fresh and locally grown and raised ingredients.

Even without planting a restaurant garden, almost any chef can participate in these movements by buying as many seasonal, locally produced products as possible and using imported items, such as coffee, bananas and chocolate, that are **fairtrade** certified.

Social Changes

Demographic and social changes have contributed to the diversification of the food service industry by creating or identifying new consumer groups that each have their own desires or preferences. The needs of dual income households, single-parent families and an aging population, as well as other market segments, impact the places and ways in which foods are sold and consumed. By tailoring their menu, prices and décor accordingly, food service operators cater to consumers defined by age, type of household, income, education, geography and many other factors.

The number and types of institutions providing food services is also increasing. These include hospitals, schools, retirement centers, sports facilities, cruise ships, private clubs, hotels and resorts (which may in turn have fine dining, coffee shop, quick service, banquet and room service facilities), supermarkets, factories and office buildings. The lines between restaurant meals and at-home dining have blurred, as food is now prepared and consumed in a greater number of environments than ever before.

At the same time, consumers are becoming better educated and more sophisticated through travel or exposure to the many television programs, websites, books and magazines about food. Educated consumers provide a market for new cuisines as well as appreciation for innovative quality food service.

Chefs Work toward a Sustainable Future

An individual chef working in a specific restaurant may seem to have only a limited impact in the sustainably movement. Chefs can, however, lead this movement in a way that other public figures, government officials and environmental activists cannot.

Chef Alice Waters is now a world-renowned restaurateur, author and culinary activist. In 1995 she founded the Edible Schoolyard Project, which funds kitchens and organic gardens as interactive classrooms in public schools. Teaching children about food and the environment can transform their attitudes and behavior. In a 2014 essay for the *Wall Street Journal*, Waters said, "The reality is that the sustainable-food movement's reach will . . . ultimately be limited to those with access, means and education—unless legislators dramatically change food and agriculture policy." She noted that government officials and decision makers must realize that "the most sensible way to have a lasting impact is with a program of 'edible education'" for children. The Edible Schoolyard has expanded to Yale University and the American Academy in Rome and is a model for similar eco-education programs nationwide.

Another leader in the field is Dan Barber, chef of Blue Hill in New York City and Blue Hill at Stone Barns in upstate New York. A prolific writer and public speaker, Barber is one of today's leading proponents for local, farm-based cuisines. Barber supplies both restaurants from the Stone Barns Center for Food and Agriculture, a working farm and educational center. What the farm doesn't provide, he sources from local green markets

The Edible Schoolyard teaching garden in New Orleans, Louisiana, a project based on the program founded by Alice Waters in Berkeley, California.

and one-to-one relationships with other farms. Stone Barns Center also educates and encourages consumers—children and adults—about food choices and the ethical treatment of animals.

The focus of Barber's current work is to encourage appreciation and use of secondary or rotation crops, crops that farmers must plant intermittently to ensure healthy soil. Cover and rotation crops such as buckwheat, millet, kidney beans and clover produce little revenue but keep the soil fertile. Rotation crops are essential for production of the higher profit margin, more culinarily desirable crops. For farmers, the expense of planting rotation crops is a significant cost of doing business in an organic system. These foods may not be trendy or even recognizable to diners, but they can be delicious and offer chefs a forum for creativity and an opportunity to practice true sustainability. "Where farm-to-table gets it wrong," Barber states, "is in cherry-picking ingredients that are often ecologically

demanding and expensive to grow. Ingredients such as tomatoes, peas and asparagus are . . . luxuries that allow us to ignore the bigger picture of the whole farm and what is needed to sustain it." True sustainability allows the land to dictate the menu, instead of creating a menu and then sourcing products.

Chefs throughout the world strive to provide ethically sourced ingredients and operate businesses under a model of sustainability. The U.K.-based Sustainable Restaurant Association (SRA), led by chef Raymond Blanc, provides member restaurants with advice on improving sustainability practices. SRA also accredits restaurants that meet specific standards in three areas—sourcing, society and environmental impact—and evaluates establishments chosen for The World's 50 Best Restaurants™ awards for sustainability. Recent winners in the sustainability category include Relæ in Copenhagen; Septime in Paris; D.O.M. in São Paulo and Narisawa in Tokyo, showing that sustainability and environmental concerns are important to chefs throughout the world.

For the efforts of these chefs to have a real impact on our global environment, however, consumers must also adopt sustainable, eco-friendly practices. Being sustainable does not mean knowing the name of the farmer who grew your pork or buying tomatoes at the local farmer's market. Focusing on heirloom crops and heritage breeds of livestock is nostalgia, not a solution. The solution lies in moving away from industrially produced foods and single repetitive crops towards local food producers and a wider range of less well-known products.

THE MODERN KITCHEN BRIGADE

To function efficiently, a food service operation must be well organized and staffed with appropriate personnel. This staff is traditionally called a **brigade**. See Figure 1.1. Escoffier is credited with developing the classic kitchen brigade system used in large restaurant kitchens; modern kitchens use a simplified version of this brigade in order to reduce labor costs and streamline operations. Although a chef will be most familiar with the back-of-the-house or kitchen brigade, he or she should also understand how the dining room or front of the house is organized.

Today's food service operations are generally led by an **executive chef**, who coordinates kitchen activities and directs the kitchen staff's training and work efforts. The executive chef plans menus and creates recipes. He or she sets and enforces nutrition, safety and sanitation standards and participates in (or at least observes) the preparation and

brigade a system of staffing a kitchen so that each worker is assigned a set of specific tasks; these tasks are often related by cooking method, equipment or the types of foods being produced

presentation of menu items to ensure that quality standards are rigorously and consistently maintained. He or she is also responsible for purchasing food items and, often, equipment. In some food service operations, the executive chef may assist in designing the menu, dining room and kitchen. He or she trains the dining room staff so that they can correctly answer questions about the menu. He or she may also work with food purveyors, catering directors, equipment vendors, financial consultants, the media, sanitation inspectors and dietitians. In some operations, a chef with some or all of these responsibilities may be referred to as a **chef de cuisine**.

The executive chef is assisted by a **sous-chef** or **executive sous-chef**, whose primary responsibility is to make sure that the food is prepared, portioned, garnished and presented according to the executive chef's standards. The sous-chef may be the cook principally responsible for producing menu items and supervising the kitchen.

The Classic Kitchen Brigade

From the chaos and redundancy found in the private kitchens of the 19th century's aristocracy, Auguste Escoffier created a distinct hierarchy of responsibilities and functions for food service operations.

At the top is the *chef de cuisine* or *chef*, who is responsible for all operations, developing menu items and setting the kitchen's tone and tempo.

The chef's principal assistant is the *sous-chef* (the under chef or second chef), who is responsible for scheduling personnel and replacing the chef and station chefs as necessary. The sous-chef also often functions as the *aboyeur* (expediter or expo), who accepts the orders from the dining room, relays them to the various station chefs and then reviews the dishes before service. In large kitchens, a *communard* prepares meals for the staff.

The *chefs de partie* (station chefs) produce the menu items under the direct supervision of the chef or sous-chef. Before the brigade system was common, whenever a cook needed an item, assistants produced it; thus several cooks could be making the same sauce or basic preparation. Under Escoffier's system, each station chef is assigned a specific task based on either the cooking method and equipment or the category of items to be produced. They include the following:

- The *saucier* (sauté station chef), who holds one of the most demanding jobs in the classical kitchen, is responsible for most sauces and all sautéed items.
- The *poissonier* (fish station chef) is responsible for fish and shellfish items and their sauces.
- The *grillardin* (grill station chef) is responsible for all grilled items.

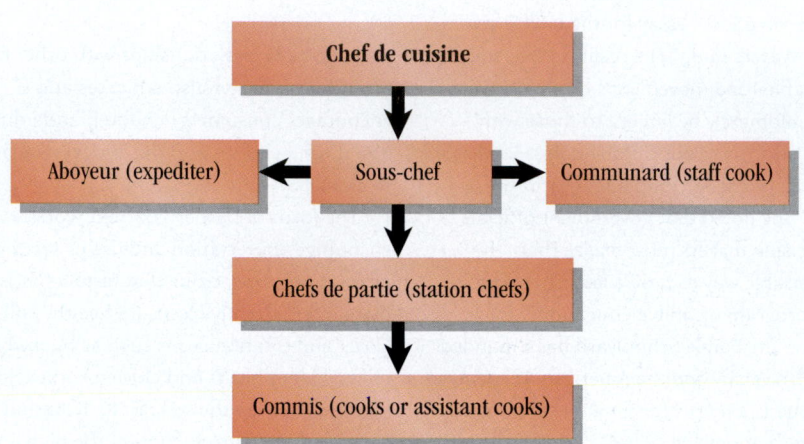

Figure 1.1 The Classic Kitchen Brigade

- The *friturier* (fry station chef) is responsible for all fried items.
- The *rôtisseur* (roast station chef) is responsible for all roasted items and jus or other related sauces.
- The *potager* (soup station chef) is responsible for soups and stocks.
- The *légumier* (vegetable station chef) is responsible for all vegetable and starch items.

The *potager* and *légumier* functions are often combined into a single vegetable station whose chef is known as the *entremetier*. *Entremets* were the courses served after the roast; they usually comprised vegetables, fruits, fritters or sweet items (the sorbet served before the main course in some contemporary restaurants is a vestigial *entremet*).

- The *garde-manger* (pantry chef) is responsible for cold food preparations, including salads and salad dressings, cold appetizers, charcuterie items, pâtés, terrines and similar dishes. The *garde-manger* supervises the

boucher (butcher), who is responsible for butchering meats and poultry, as well as the chefs responsible for hors d'oeuvre and breakfast items.

- The *tournant*, also known as the roundsman or swing cook, works where needed.
- The *pâtissier* (pastry chef) is responsible for all baked items, including breads, pastries and desserts. The *pâtissier* supervises the *boulanger* (bread baker), who makes the breads, rolls and baked flaky dough containers to hold savory dishes; the *confiseur*, who makes candies and petit fours; the *glacier*, who makes all chilled and frozen desserts; and the *décorateur*, who makes showpieces and special cakes.

Depending on the size and needs of any station or area, there may be one or more *demi-chefs* (assistants) and *commis* (second year cooks) as well as *apprentis* (student cooks) who work with the station chef or pastry chef to learn the area.

The Dining Room Brigade

Like the back-of-the-house (kitchen) staff, the front-of-the-house (dining room) staff is also organized into a brigade. A traditional dining room brigade is led by the **dining room manager** (*maître d'hotel* or *maître d'*), who generally trains all service personnel, oversees wine selections and works with the chef to develop the menu. He or she organizes the seating chart and may also seat the guests. The dining room manager's subordinates are the following:

- The **wine steward** (*sommelier*), who is responsible for the wine service, including purchasing wines, assisting guests in selecting wines and serving the wines

- The **headwaiter** (*chef de salle*), who is responsible for service throughout the dining room or a section of it. In smaller operations, this role may be assumed by the *maître d'* or a captain

- The **captains** (*chefs d'étage*), who are responsible for explaining the menu to guests and taking their orders. They are also responsible for any tableside preparations

- The **front waiters** (*chefs de rang*), who are responsible for assuring that the tables are set properly for each course, foods are delivered properly to the proper tables and the needs of the guests are met

- The **back waiters** (*demi-chefs de rang* or *commis de rang*, also known as dining room attendants or buspersons), who are responsible for clearing plates, refilling water glasses and other general tasks appropriate for new dining room workers

Whether a restaurant uses this entire array of staff depends on the nature and size of the restaurant and the type of service provided.

Line cooks (or section cooks) are responsible for preparing menu items according to recipe specifications. They may be assigned to a specific area, such as the broiler or pantry station. A **roundsman** or **swing cook** is capable of working several stations and is assigned to the area where the need is greatest during each shift.

The **pastry chef** is responsible for developing recipes for and preparing desserts, pastries, frozen desserts and breads. He or she is usually responsible for purchasing the food items used in the bakeshop.

Prep cooks, **assistants** and **apprentices** are employed as entry-level workers throughout modern kitchens.

New styles of dining have created new positions since Escoffier's days. The most notable is the **short-order cook**, who is responsible for quickly preparing foods to order in smaller operations. He or she will work the broiler, deep-fat fryer and griddle as well as make sandwiches and even some sautéed items. Another is the **institutional cook**, who generally works with large quantities of packaged or prepared foods for a captive market, such as a school, hospital or prison.

A restaurant may employ a **master chef** (*maître cuisinier*), **master pastry chef** (*maître pâtissier*) or a **master baker** (*maître boulanger*, or *bäckermeister* in German). These titles recognize the highest level of achievement; only highly skilled and experienced professionals who have demonstrated their expertise and knowledge in written and practical exams are entitled to use them. These titles recall the European guild tradition still alive in many countries today. In France and Germany, for example, a chef, pastry chef or baker must pursue many years of classroom and job training, work as an apprentice and pass numerous examinations before acquiring the right to the title "master." In the United States, professional organizations administer programs that certify the professional experience of chefs, pastry chefs and bakers.

THE PROFESSIONAL CHEF

Although there is no one recipe for producing a good professional chef, with knowledge, skill, taste, judgment, dedication and pride, a student chef will mature into someone who understands the importance of ethical, professional behavior in and out of the kitchen, and who is prepared to change jobs or career paths according to personal or industry needs.

Knowledge

Chefs must be able to identify, purchase, utilize and prepare a wide variety of foods. They should be able to train and supervise a safe, skilled and efficient staff. To do all this

successfully, chefs must possess a body of knowledge and understand and apply certain scientific and business principles. Schooling helps. A professional culinary program should, at a minimum, provide the student chef with a basic knowledge of foods, food styles and the methods used to prepare foods. Student chefs should also understand sanitation, nutrition and business procedures such as food costing.

In this way we follow the trail blazed by Escoffier, who wrote in the introduction to *Le Guide culinaire* that his book is not intended to be a compendium of recipes slavishly followed, but rather a tool that leaves his colleagues "free to develop their own methods and follow their own inspiration; . . . the art of cooking . . . will evolve as a society evolves . . . only basic rules remain unalterable."

Skill

Culinary schooling alone does not turn a student into a chef. Nothing but practical, hands-on experience will provide even the most academically gifted student with the skills needed to produce, consistently and efficiently, quality foods or to organize, train, motivate and supervise a staff.

Many food service operations recognize that new workers, even those who have graduated from culinary programs, need time and experience to develop and hone their skills. Therefore many graduates start in entry-level positions. Do not be discouraged; advancement will come, and the training pays off in the long run. Today culinary styles and fashions change frequently. What does not go out of fashion are well-trained, skilled and knowledgeable chefs. They can adapt.

Taste

In addition to being knowledgeable or skilled, a chef must be able to produce foods that taste great or the consumer will not return. Chefs can do this only if they are confident about their own perceptions of flavor and taste.

The human perception of taste is a complex combination of smell, taste, sight, sound and texture. All the senses are involved in the enjoyment of eating; all must be considered in creating or preparing a dish. The chef should develop a flavor memory by sampling foods, both familiar and unfamiliar. Chefs should also think about what they taste and the flavor they perceive, making notes and experimenting with flavor combinations and cooking methods. But a chef should not be inventive simply for the sake of invention. Rather a chef must consider how the flavors, appearances, textures and aromas of various foods will interact to create a total taste experience.

Judgment

Selecting menu items, determining how much of each item to purchase, deciding whether and how to combine ingredients and approving finished items for service are all matters of judgment. Although knowledge and skill play a role in developing judgment, sound judgment comes only with experience; and real experience is often accompanied by failure. Do not be upset or surprised when a dish does not turn out as you expected. Learn from your mistakes as well as from your successes; this is the only way to develop sound judgment.

Dedication

Becoming a chef is hard work; so is being one. The work is often physically taxing, the hours are usually long and the pace is frequently hectic. As a new cook, you may be expected to work nights, weekends and holidays. In the world of restaurants and hotels, these are the busiest times that require the most staff. Work hours may include early mornings, late nights and back-to-back shifts. Depending on your personality, you may find the adrenalin rush of a hectic restaurant dinner service exciting, or you may prefer quiet, early morning bakery preparations. In either situation, cooks must generally perform in close quarters, stand for several hours at a time, lift heavy pans of food and work around hot stoves and deep fryers. Despite these pressures, the chef is expected to efficiently produce consistently good food that is properly prepared, seasoned, garnished and presented. To do so, the chef must be dedicated to the job.

The food service industry is competitive and depends on the continuing goodwill of an often fickle public. One bad dish or one off night can result in a disgruntled diner and lost business. The chef should always be mindful of the food prepared and the customer served. The chef must also be dedicated to his or her staff. Virtually all food service operations rely on teamwork to get the job done well. Good teamwork requires a positive attitude and dedication to a shared goal, which is as impressive to a prospective employer as well-honed technical skills.

Chefs should demonstrate their dedication to the profession itself and to their peers as well. Numerous regional, national and international organizations provide services, educational seminars and networking opportunities for members. By joining and participating in relevant associations, chefs may encounter new job opportunities, new products and new ideas to expand their horizons.

Professional Ethics

As a professional culinarian, you are expected to be honest, responsible and ethical. Professional organizations, such as the American Culinary Federation (ACF), the International Association of Culinary Professionals (IACP), the World Association of Chefs' Societies (Worldchefs) and others, require their members to adhere to codes of ethics. These codes generally include specific behaviors that all professionals, in any industry, should follow, such as:

- Conducting yourself with honesty, fairness and integrity
- Avoiding conflicts of interest, or misuse of monies
- Not discriminating against others or engaging in sexual harassment
- Accurately representing yourself, your work experiences and your education
- Supporting the growth and professional activities of colleagues
- Cooperating with coworkers in a fair, considerate manner
- Respecting team members and supervisors
- Complying with local and national laws and regulations

Two chefs pictured in the frontispiece of Antonin Carême's c. 1822 book *Le Maître d'hotel francais* wear the classic double-breasted chef's jacket still worn today.

Pride

Not only is it important that the job be well done, but the professional chef should have a sense of pride in doing it well. Pride should also extend to personal appearance and behavior in and around the kitchen. The professional chef should be well-groomed and in a clean, well-maintained uniform when working.

The professional chef's uniform consists of comfortable shoes, trousers (often solid black or black-and-white checked), a white double-breasted jacket and an apron. (Some establishments also require a neckerchief usually knotted or secured with a metal ring.) The uniform has certain utilitarian aspects: Checked trousers disguise stains; the double-breasted white jacket can be rebuttoned to hide dirt, and the double layer of fabric protects from scalds and burns; and the apron protects the uniform and insulates the body. This uniform should be worn with pride. Shoes should be polished; trousers and jacket should be pressed. The crowning element of the uniform is the **toque**, the tall white hat worn by chefs almost everywhere.

Careers

Young adults entering the working world now can look forward to several different careers during their working lifetimes. Luckily, the choices available to well-trained culinary professionals now extend far beyond the kitchen. A culinary education prepares you for entry-level positions in hotel, catering and restaurant kitchens, but it can also lead to a wide range of other employment opportunities following graduation and for many years into the future. As a working chef, you may choose to focus in a specific area of food preparation, such as garde-manger, pastry, butchery, or any other station in the kitchen. You may also choose to be a generalist—a tournant or roundsman—able to work at virtually any station.

A culinary professional may enjoy cooking, developing recipes and producing food for others without working in a traditional hotel or restaurant kitchen, however. For example, personal chefs work in private homes cooking for a family or an individual. International cruise lines and private yachts also employ many cooks and chefs, as do corporate office buildings, factories and college food service operations. Experienced culinary professionals may be employed by food manufacturers or large restaurant groups in test kitchens, product research and development, sensory evaluation labs and marketing departments. Grocery stores hire chefs to develop and prepare home-meal replacement foods and conduct in-store demonstrations. Hospitals and assisted-living residences now hire trained chefs, in addition to registered dietitians and nutrition specialists, to accommodate the needs and interests of their clients.

Alternative careers for culinary graduates include working for food publications, including books, magazines and digital media, which need culinarians as writers, critics, recipe developers, food stylists and editors. You might even move into restaurant consulting, or open your own culinary business as an entrepreneur. With the proper advanced education and experience, you may find opportunities to teach in a professional culinary school, or for avocational or community classes.

Advanced education is available in gastronomy, hospitality, tourism, restaurant management, culinary entrepreneurship and related fields. Many non-degree programs offer specific training for cooks in subjects as diverse as international cuisines, wine and spirits, financial management and pâtisserie. A culinarian, even one with many years of experience, may work an unpaid **stage**, lasting from a few days to a few months, in a world-class kitchen simply for the opportunity to increase knowledge and skills. Self-education should continue by reading industry publications, attending conferences and trade shows and traveling locally and abroad. International travel allows you to experience different cuisines first-hand, perhaps by taking classes in the local cuisine and food culture.

In short, graduation from culinary school is just the beginning of your education. Your specific occupation may change or evolve depending on personal desires and abilities, family needs and unexpected opportunities. But, wherever you work, you must continue learning and developing your skills. A true professional never stops learning.

stage [stahzh] a brief, unpaid internship or training session in a professional kitchen; from the French *stagiaire*, meaning apprentice or intern

QUESTIONS FOR DISCUSSION

1 Summarize the contributions that chefs Carême and Escoffier made to advance the culinary arts during the 19th century.

2 Discuss two recent culinary movements and their impact on the way food is served in restaurants today.

3 List and explain three technological advances affecting food preparation.

4 How can a food service operation address customer concerns about where their food was grown or raised and participate in the sustainability movement?

5 Discuss the societal changes that have contributed to diversification in the modern food service industry.

6 Describe the kitchen brigade system. What is its significance in today's professional kitchens?

7 What are the roles of a chef, sous-chef and line cook in a modern kitchen?

8 Describe the key attributes of a culinary professional and things you can do to develop the skills, taste and judgment required in your chosen career?

9 List and explain the benefits that you can enjoy by belonging to a professional culinary organization.

10 Why do professional culinary organizations ask their members to adhere to a code of ethics?

11 The James Beard Foundation recognizes and honors outstanding American chefs each year. Use outside resources to learn who James Beard was. Which chefs are currently considered some of the most outstanding in the United States? Why?

Food Safety and Sanitation

► explain the importance of sanitation in the restaurant industry and identify the three major types of contaminants that cause food-borne illnesses

► identify and understand how to work with time and temperature controlled for safety (TCS) foods to prevent biological intoxications and infections

► identify chemical contaminants and ways to prevent direct chemical contamination when handling foods

► identify physical contaminants and ways to prevent direct physical contamination when handling foods

► list and follow the proper procedures to prevent cross-contamination and food-borne illnesses when handling foods

► identify the eight major food allergens and guidelines for protecting allergic guests

► explain and follow a HACCP system

► take appropriate actions to create and maintain a safe and sanitary working environment

microorganisms single-celled organisms and tiny plants and animals that can be seen only through a microscope

biological hazard a danger to the safety of food caused by disease-causing microorganisms such as bacteria, molds, yeasts, viruses or fungi

chemical hazard a danger to the safety of food caused by chemical substances, especially cleaning agents, pesticides or toxic metals

physical hazard a danger to the safety of food caused by particles such as glass chips, metal shavings, bits of wood or other foreign matter

The U.S. Department of Health and Human Services (HHS) identifies more than 250 diseases that can be transmitted through food. Many can cause serious illness; some are even deadly. Providing consumers with safe food is the food handler's most important responsibility. Unfortunately, food handlers are also the primary cause of food-related illnesses. Understanding what causes food-borne illnesses and what can be done to prevent them will help you be better able to protect your customers.

This chapter is not meant to be a complete discussion of sanitation in food service operations. Its primary goal is to alert you to practices that can result in food-borne illnesses. Federal, state, county and municipal health, building and other codes are designed in part to ensure that food is handled in a safe and proper manner. Chefs should consult the local health department for information and guidance and always be conscious of what they can do to create and maintain a safe product as well as a safe environment for their customers, their fellow employees and themselves.

SANITATION

Every food business must take sanitation seriously. **Sanitation** refers to the creation and maintenance of conditions that will prevent any contamination that might lead to a food-borne illness. It involves removing or reducing harmful substances to a level that is deemed safe by federal, state, county or municipal health agencies. Proper sanitation requires following time and temperature standards, avoiding cross-contamination and consistently following established safe food handling protocols. Failure to do so can lead to a variety of injuries or illnesses. Even as few as two or three sick customers can be enough to cause major financial loss, negative media attention, lawsuits and irreparable damage to a business's reputation. Local government health inspectors are responsible for issuing licenses and conducting periodic inspections to ensure that regulations are being followed. It is your responsibility as a cook or food server to make sure that sanitation techniques are being followed properly in order to avoid contamination on behalf of every customer, every day.

Contamination refers to the presence, generally unintended, of harmful organisms or substances, called **contaminants**. Contaminants can be biological, chemical or physical. When consumed in sufficient quantities, food-borne contaminants can cause illness or injury, long-lasting disease or even death. Contamination occurs in two ways: direct contamination and cross-contamination.

Direct contamination is the contamination of raw foods or the plants or animals from which they come, in their natural settings or habitats. Chemical and biological contaminants, such as bacteria and fungi, are present in the air, soil and water. This means that foods can be easily contaminated by their general exposure to the environment. For example, grains can be contaminated by soil fumigants in the field, or shellfish can become contaminated by ingesting toxic marine algae.

Chemicals and microorganisms generally cannot move on their own, however. Contaminants need to be transported, a process known as **cross-contamination**. The major cause of cross-contamination is people. Food handlers can transfer biological, chemical and physical contaminants to food while processing, preparing, cooking or serving. Sanitation is the correction of problems caused by direct contamination and the prevention of problems caused by cross-contamination during processing and service.

DIRECT BIOLOGICAL CONTAMINANTS

Several **microorganisms**, primarily bacteria, parasites, viruses and fungi, are **biological hazards**, contaminants that can cause biologically based food-borne illnesses. By understanding how these organisms live and reproduce, you can better understand how to protect food from them.

Bacteria

Bacteria, which are single-celled microorganisms, are the leading cause of food-borne illnesses. See Figure 2.1. Some bacteria are beneficial, such as those that aid in digesting food or decomposing garbage. Certain beneficial bacteria are used to make cheese, yogurt and sauerkraut. Other bacteria spoil food without rendering it unfit for human consumption. These bacteria, called **putrefactives**, are not a sanitation concern. (Indeed, in some cultures, they are not even a culinary concern. Cultures differ on what constitutes "bad" meat, for example. In some cultures, for instance, game is sometimes hung for a time to allow bacteria to grow.) The bacteria that are dangerous when consumed by humans are **pathogens**. These bacteria must be destroyed or controlled in a food service operation.

Most bacteria reproduce by binary fission: Their genetic material is first duplicated and the nucleus then splits, each new nucleus taking some of the cellular material with it. See Figure 2.2. Under favorable conditions each bacterium can divide every 15–30 minutes. Within 12 hours, one bacterium can become a colony of 72 billion bacteria, more than enough to cause serious illness. In instances when the bacterial count is high enough, a person may get sick within as little as 4 hours.

Some rod-shaped bacteria are capable of forming spores, which may not be destroyed by heating or sanitizing the cooking environment. Spores are thick-walled structures used as protection against a hostile environment. The bacteria essentially hibernate within their spores, where the bacteria can survive extreme conditions that would otherwise destroy them. When conditions become favorable, the bacteria return to a viable state. Dirt frequently contains bacterial spores. This is one reason why it is essential to properly wash fruit and produce thoroughly before use.

Bacterial Intoxications and Infections

Pathogenic bacteria can cause illnesses in humans in one of three ways: by intoxication, infection or toxin-mediated infection. Some of the more common food-borne illnesses and their characteristics are listed and described in Table 2.1.

Botulism is a well-known example of an **intoxication**. Certain bacteria produce **toxins**, by-products of their life processes. People cannot smell, see or taste toxins. Ingesting these toxin-producing bacteria by themselves does not cause illness. But the toxins the bacteria produce that are ingested can poison the consumer.

pathogens any organisms that causes disease; usually refers to bacteria; undetectable by smell, sight or taste, pathogens are responsible for as many as 95 percent of all food-borne illnesses

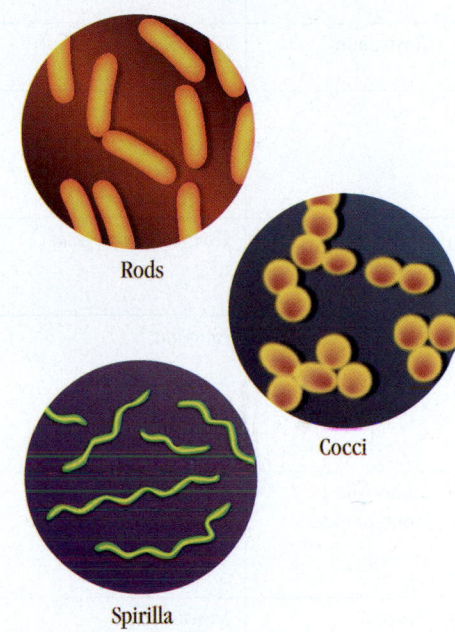

Rods

Cocci

Spirilla

Figure 2.1 Bacteria can be classified by shape: Rods are short, tubular structures; cocci are discs, some of which form clusters; and spirilla are corkscrews.

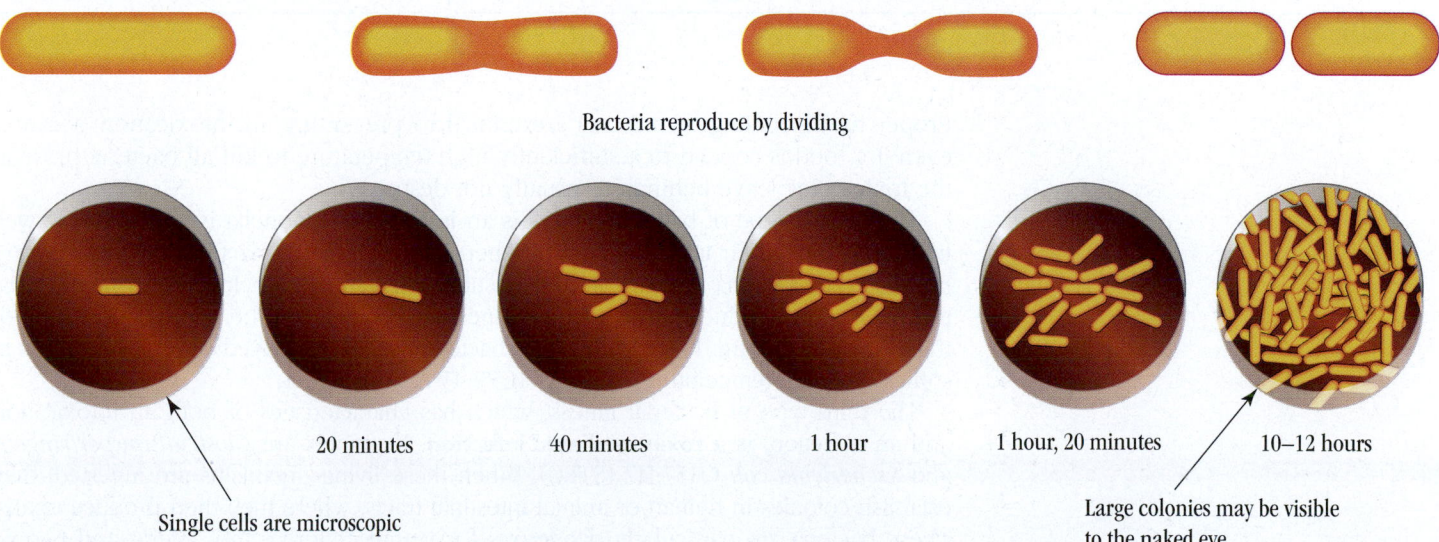

Bacteria reproduce by dividing

20 minutes   40 minutes   1 hour   1 hour, 20 minutes   10–12 hours

Single cells are microscopic

Large colonies may be visible to the naked eye

Figure 2.2 One bacterium divides into two; the two bacteria each divide, creating four; the four become 16 and so on. It takes only a very short time for one bacterium to produce millions more.

TOP CAUSES OF FOOD-BORNE ILLNESS   TABLE 2.1

COMMON NAME	ORGANISM	FORM	COMMON SOURCES	PREVENTION
Botulism	*Clostridium botulinum*	Intoxication	Improperly canned or packaged foods, prepared foods, raw garlic mixtures	Thoroughly cook or reheat items; discard damaged canned or packaged foods
Campylobacter	*Campylobacter jejuni*	Bacterial infection	Raw poultry, raw milk products, contaminated water	Thoroughly cook poultry; avoid raw milk products; maintain good personal hygiene
Clostridium	*Clostridium perfringens*	Intoxication	Raw poultry and meat, dirt, humans	Thoroughly cook and reheat poultry and meat
E. coli	Shiga toxin-producing *Escherichia coli O157:H7* (STEC) (and other enter-opathogenic strains)	Bacterial infection or toxin-mediated infection	Any food, especially raw milk products, raw fruits or vegetables, raw or rare beef, humans	Exclude food handlers with symptoms or diagnosis of an illness; thoroughly cook or reheat items; use only pasteurized milk products and fruit juices
Listeria	*Listeria monocytogenes*	Bacterial infection	Raw meat, raw milk products, prepared foods, deli meats	Thoroughly cook or reheat items; use only pasteurized milk products; avoid cross-contamination with raw foods
Norovirus	*Norovirus*	Viral infection	Contaminated fruits, vegetables or seafood, humans, fecal contamination	Exclude food handlers with symptoms or diagnosis of an illness; wash hands, utensils and equipment with approved sanitizers; maintain good personal hygiene; purchase shellfish from approved waters
Salmonella (nontyphoidal)	*Salmonella*	Bacterial infection	Raw eggs, fish, meat, poultry or produce, fecal contamination	Thoroughly cook all meats, poultry, fish and eggs; wash produce well; avoid cross-contamination with raw foods; maintain good personal hygiene
Shigella	*Shigella ssp.*	Bacterial infection	Greens, salads, prepared food, milk, poultry, contaminated water, infected food handlers	Exclude food handlers with symptoms or diagnosis of an illness; maintain good personal hygiene; prevent flies
Vibrio	*Vibrio vulnificus*	Bacterial infection	Raw or undercooked shellfish, especially oysters, contaminated water	Purchase shellfish from approved waters; keep all shellfish tags; avoid raw oysters and other raw seafood
Yersinia	*Yersinia enterocolitica*	Bacterial infection	Raw or undercooked pork, raw or contaminated milk products, tofu, nonchlorinated water	Thoroughly cook pork; use only pasteurized milk products; use only chlorinated water

Proper food-handling techniques are critical to preventing an intoxication because, even if a food is cooked to a sufficiently high temperature to kill all bacteria present, the toxins they leave behind are usually not destroyed.

The second type of bacterial illness is an **infection**. Salmonella is an especially well known example. An infection occurs when live pathogenic bacteria (**infectants**) are ingested. The bacteria then live in the consumer's intestinal tract. It is the living bacteria, not their waste products, that cause an illness. Infectants must be alive when eaten for them to do any harm. Fortunately these bacteria can be destroyed by cooking foods at sufficiently high temperatures, such as 165°F (74°C) or higher.

The third type of bacterial illness, which has characteristics of both an intoxication and an infection, is a **toxin-mediated infection**. Examples are *Clostridium perfringens* and *Escherichia coli* O157:H7 (STEC). When these living organisms are ingested, they establish colonies in human or animal intestinal tracts, where they then produce toxins. These bacteria are particularly dangerous for young children, the elderly and people with weakened immune systems.

Preventing Bacterial Intoxications and Infections

All bacteria need certain conditions in order to complete their life cycles. Like humans and other living things, they need food, a comfortable temperature, moisture, the proper pH, the proper atmosphere and time. The best way to prevent bacterial intoxications and infections is to attack the factors bacteria need to survive and multiply.

The following six conditions, which we will discuss in some detail in this section, affect the growth of bacteria:

- Food
- Acidity
- Time
- Temperature
- Oxygen
- Moisture

Food

Bacteria need food for energy and growth and thrive on foods that are referred to as **time and temperature controlled for safety (TCS)** foods. These foods are generally high in protein and include animal-based products, cooked grains and some raw and cooked vegetables. These foods, and items containing these foods, must be handled with great care.

Acidity

Bacteria thrive in an environment where the acidity and alkalinity are in balance. **pH** is a measurement of the acid or alkali content of a solution, expressed on a scale of 0 to 14.0. A pH of 7.0 is considered neutral or balanced. The lower the pH value, the more acidic the substance. The higher the pH value, the more alkaline the substance.

Although they can survive in a wider range, bacteria prefer a neutral environment with a pH of 6.6–7.5. Growth is usually halted if the pH is 4.6 or less. Acidic foods such as lemon juice, tomatoes and vinegar, which have lower pH values, create an unfavorable environment for bacteria. Simply adding an acidic ingredient to foods should not, however, be relied upon to destroy bacteria or preserve foods. The amount of acidity appropriate for flavoring is not sufficient to ensure the destruction of bacteria.

Time

Bacterial growth takes place in four phases. See Figure 2.3. When bacteria are moved from one place to another, they require time to adjust to new conditions. This resting period, during which very little growth occurs, is known as the **lag phase** and may last from 1 to 4 hours. The lag phase is followed by the **log phase**, a period of accelerated growth, and then by the **stationary phase**, which lasts until the bacteria begin to crowd within their colony, creating competition for food, space and moisture. This crowding signals the beginning of the **decline** or **negative-growth phase**, during which bacteria die at an accelerated rate.

Because of the lag phase, foods can be in the temperature danger zone for very short periods during preparation before bacterial growth increases to an unacceptable level. Exposure to the temperature danger zone is cumulative, however, and should not exceed 4 hours total. The less time food is in the temperature danger zone, the less opportunity bacteria have to multiply.

Temperature

Temperature is the most important factor in the pathogenic bacteria's environment because it is the factor food service workers can most easily control. High temperatures destroy most microorganisms. Freezing slows but does not stop growth, nor does it destroy bacteria.

FAT TOM

The words *FAT TOM* can be useful in helping you remember the six conditions that affect bacterial growth, as follows:

Food

Acidity

Time

Temperature

Oxygen

Moisture (water activity)

---

pH a measurement of the acid or alkali content of a solution, expressed on a scale of 0–14.0. A pH of 7.0 is considered neutral or balanced. The lower the pH value, the more acidic the substance. The higher the pH value, the more alkaline the substance.

⚠ Safety Alert

The Temperature Danger Zone

The temperature danger zone is a broad range of temperatures in which most of the bacteria that cause food-borne illnesses multiply rapidly. The 2013 Food Code of the U.S. Food and Drug Administration (FDA), July 2015 supplement, indicates that the temperature danger zone begins at 41°F (5°C) and ends at 135°F (57°C). Regulations in some localities and with some organizations may vary. This text uses the range recommended by the FDA.

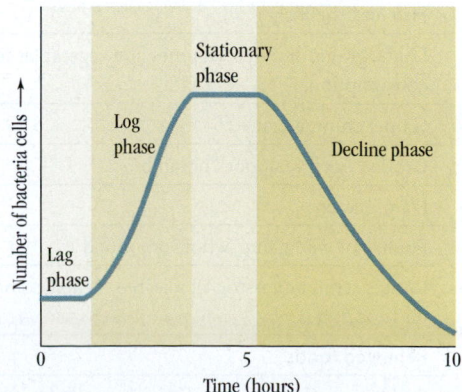

Figure 2.3 Bacterial growth curve.

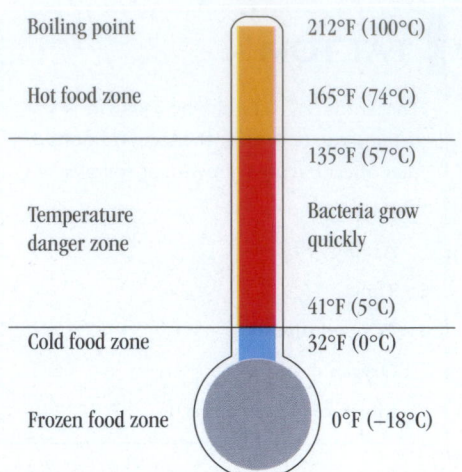

Figure 2.4 The temperature danger zone.

Most bacteria that cause food-borne illnesses multiply rapidly at temperatures between 70°F and 125°F (21°C and 52°C). Therefore the broad range of temperatures between 41°F and 135°F (5°C and 57°C) is referred to as the **temperature danger zone**. See Figure 2.4. To control the growth of any bacteria that may be present, it is important to maintain the internal temperature of food at 135°F (57°C) or above or 41°F (5°C) or below. Keeping foods out of the temperature danger zone reduces the bacteria's ability to thrive and reproduce.

Simply stated: Keep hot foods hot and cold foods cold. Time and temperature controlled for safety (TCS) foods should be heated or cooled quickly so that they are within the temperature danger zone as briefly as possible. This is known as the **time-and-temperature principle**.

Keep hot foods hot. The high internal temperatures reached during proper cooking kill most of the bacteria that can cause food-borne illnesses. Foods must be cooked to specific internal temperatures and held there for the time specified in Table 2.2. When foods are reheated, the internal temperature should quickly reach or exceed 165°F (74°C) in order to kill any bacteria that may have grown during storage. Once properly heated, hot foods must be held at temperatures of 135°F (57°C) or higher. (Holding food at 140°F/60°C offers an additional safeguard.) Foods that are to be displayed or served hot must be heated rapidly to reduce the time within the temperature danger zone. To facilitate this, when heating or reheating foods:

- Heat small quantities at a time.
- Stir frequently.
- Heat foods as close to service time as possible.
- Use preheated ingredients whenever possible to prepare hot foods.
- Never use a steam table for heating or reheating foods. Bring reheated food to an appropriate internal temperature (at least 165°F/74°C) before placing it in the steam table for holding.

RECOMMENDED INTERNAL COOKING TEMPERATURES	TABLE 2.2
PRODUCT	**TEMPERATURE**
Beef, pork, veal or lamb steaks or chops	Cook to 145°F/63°C for 4 minutes
Beef, pork, veal or lamb, roasts	Cook to 145°F/63°C for 4 minutes
Egg dishes	Cook to 155°F/68°C; if the dish is uncooked, use only pasteurized eggs
Eggs	Cook until the yolk and white are firm or cook to 145°F/63°C for 15 seconds if prepared for a customer's immediate order
Fish and shellfish	Cook to 145°F/63°C for 15 seconds; shells should open
Fruits, grains and rice, legumes and vegetables for immediate consumption	Cook to 135°F/57°C
Game, commercial	Cook to 145°F/63°C for 15 seconds
Ground beef, veal, pork or lamb	Cook to 155°F/68°C for 15 seconds
Ham, bacon	Cook to 155°F/68°C for 15 seconds
Poultry or wild game, whole or ground	Cook to 165°F/74°C for 15 seconds
Ratites (emu and ostrich), injected meats (commercially flavored with marinade or brine)	Cook to 155°F/68°C for 15 seconds
Reheated foods	Heat to 165°F/74°C for 15 seconds, use within 2 hours
Stuffing, stuffed meat, stuffed fish, stuffed pasta, casseroles	Cook to 165°F/74°C for 15 seconds
Any TCS food cooked in a microwave	Cook to 165°F/74°C, then let stand for 2 minutes

(*Sources:* USDA Food Safety and Inspection Service; FDA 2013 Food Code, July 2015 supplement.)

Keep cold foods cold. Foods that are to be displayed, stored or served cold must be cooled rapidly. When cooling foods:

- Refrigerate semisolid foods at 41°F (5°C) or below in containers that are less than 2 inches deep. (Increased surface area decreases cooling time.)
- Avoid crowding the refrigerator; allow air to circulate around foods.
- Vent hot foods in an ice-water bath, as illustrated in Chapter 11, Stocks and Sauces, p. 206.
- Prechill ingredients such as mayonnaise before preparing cold foods.
- Store cooked foods above raw foods to prevent cross-contamination.

Keep frozen foods frozen. Freezing at 0°F (–18°C) or below essentially stops bacterial growth but will not kill the bacteria. Do not place hot foods in a standard freezer. This will not cool the food any faster, and the release of heat can raise the temperature of other foods in the freezer. Only a special blast freezer can be used for chilling hot items. If one is not available, cool hot foods as mentioned earlier before freezing them. When frozen foods thaw, bacteria that are present begin to grow. Therefore:

- Never thaw foods at room temperature.
- Thaw foods gradually under refrigeration to maintain the food's temperature at 41°F (5°C) or less. Place thawing foods in a container to prevent cross-contamination from dripping or leaking liquids.
- Thaw foods under running water at a temperature of 70°F (21°C) or cooler. Place thawing foods in a clean container and then in a clean, sanitized prep sink.
- Thaw foods in a microwave only if the food will be prepared and served immediately.

Oxygen

Bacteria and pathogens can grow with or without oxygen. **Aerobic bacteria** thrive on oxygen, whereas **anaerobic bacteria** cannot survive in its presence. Still other bacteria, known as **facultative bacteria**, can adapt and will survive with or without oxygen. Unfortunately most pathogenic bacteria are facultative.

Canning, which creates an anaerobic atmosphere, destroys bacteria that need oxygen, but it creates a favorable atmosphere for anaerobic and facultative bacteria. A complete vacuum need not be formed for anaerobic bacteria to thrive. A tight foil covering, a complete layer of fat or even a well-fitting lid can create an atmosphere sufficiently devoid of oxygen to permit the growth of anaerobic bacteria.

Moisture

Bacteria need a certain amount of moisture to grow. The moisture in food that is not bound to food molecules and is available for bacteria to grow is expressed as **water activity** or A_w. Water itself has an A_w of 1.0. Any food with an A_w of 0.85 or greater is considered TCS food. Bacteria cannot flourish where the A_w is too low, usually below 0.85. This explains why dry foods such as flour, sugar and crackers are rarely subject to bacterial infestations. A low A_w only halts bacterial growth, however; it does not kill the microorganisms. When dried foods, such as beans or rice, are rehydrated, any bacteria present can flourish and the food may become a TCS food, requiring time and temperature control for safety.

Parasites

Like bacteria, parasites can be contaminants as well. **Parasites** are tiny organisms that depend on nutrients from a living host to complete their life cycle. Animals, poultry, fish, shellfish and humans can all play host to parasites. Several types of very small parasitic worms can enter an animal through contaminated feed, then settle in the host's intestinal tract or muscles, where they grow and reproduce. Parasites can also be found in the water that is used to irrigate produce.

Trichinosis is caused by eating undercooked meat (usually game or pork) infected with parasitic trichina larvae. Although trichinosis has been virtually eradicated by

⚠ **Safety Alert**

Time and Temperature Control for Safety (TCS) Food

Foods that may require time and temperature controls for safety are referred to as TCS foods. A TCS food is any food or food ingredient that will support the rapid growth of infectious or toxigenic microorganisms, or the slower growth of *Clostridium botulinum*. (TCS replaces the term *potentially hazardous food*.) TCS foods include the following:

- Food from an animal source (e.g., meat, fish, shellfish, poultry, milk and eggs)
- Food from a plant that has been heat treated (e.g., cooked rice, beans, potatoes, soy products, vegetables and pasta)
- Raw seed sprouts
- Cut melons
- Cut leafy greens
- Cut tomatoes or mixtures of cut tomatoes that are not acidified or otherwise appropriately modified at a processing plant
- Garlic-in-oil mixtures that are not acidified or otherwise appropriately modified at a processing plant
- Foods containing any of the preceding items (e.g., custards, sauces and casseroles)

grain-feeding hogs and testing them before slaughter, some cases still occur each year. Traditionally it was thought that pork must be cooked to internal temperatures of 170°F (77°C) or higher to eradicate the trichina larvae. This generally resulted in a dry, tough product. Scientists have now determined that trichina larvae are killed if held at 137°F (58°C) for 10 seconds. The FDA currently recommends cooking pork products to an internal temperature of 145°F (63°C) or above with a 3-minute rest time.

Anisakiasis is another illness caused by parasitic roundworms. Anisakis worms reside in the organs of fish, especially bottom feeders or those taken from contaminated waters. Raw or undercooked fish are most often implicated in anisakiasis. Fish should be thoroughly cleaned immediately after being caught so that the parasites do not have an opportunity to spread. Thorough cooking to a minimum internal temperature of 135°F (57°C) is the only way to destroy the Anisakis larvae, as they can survive even highly acidic marinades.

Cyclospora infections are caused by a single-celled parasite found in water or food contaminated by infected feces. Produce from undeveloped countries is a common source of cyclospora parasites, as is untreated water. Avoiding such products is the best prevention method.

Viruses

Viruses cause other biologically based food-borne illnesses such as hepatitis A and norovirus (formerly called the Norwalk virus) and are the leading cause of food-borne illnesses. **Viruses** are among the smallest known forms of life. They invade the living cells of a host, take over those cells' genetic material and cause the cells to produce more viruses.

Viruses do not require a host to survive, however. They can survive—but not multiply—while lying on any food or food contact surface. Unlike bacteria, viruses can be present on any food, not just a TCS food. The food or food contact surface simply becomes a means of transportation between hosts.

Also unlike bacteria, viruses are not affected by the water activity, pH or oxygen content of their environment. Freezing temperatures do not destroy viruses. Some viruses, however, can be destroyed by temperatures higher than 176°F (80°C). Even so, the only sure way to prevent food-borne viral illnesses is to prevent contamination in the first place. Foods most likely to transmit viral diseases are those that are not heated after handling. These include salads, sandwiches, milk, baked products, uncooked fish and shellfish and sliced meats. The best techniques for avoiding viral food-borne illnesses are to observe good personal hygiene habits, avoid cross-contamination and use foods only from reputable sources.

Hepatitis A enters the food supply through shellfish harvested from polluted waters. The virus is carried by humans, some of whom may never know they are infected, and is transmitted by poor personal hygiene and cross-contamination. The actual source of contamination may be hard to establish because it sometimes takes months for symptoms to appear.

Norovirus causes more than half of all food-borne illnesses in the United States. The virus is found in shellfish, human feces and contaminated water or vegetables fertilized by manure. This virus passes easily among infected people, contaminated food and contaminated work surfaces. It is spread almost entirely by poor personal hygiene among infected food handlers. The virus can be destroyed by high cooking temperatures, but not by sanitizing solutions or freezing.

Because norovirus is highly contagious, it is important to recognize the symptoms. Diarrhea, vomiting, nausea and stomach pain are common, but fever, headache and body aches may also be present. The virus is passed through contact with minute amounts of stool or vomit, as few as 10–100 virus particles. Contact may come directly from an infected person or through food contact surfaces that may be contaminated. If you are infected with norovirus, avoid contact with other people. Wait 3 days after you have stopped having symptoms before preparing food. Use proper handwashing techniques and wash frequently. When the presence of norovirus is suspected, clean and sanitize all food contact surfaces, floors, walls and equipment with a sanitizing solution that is registered as effective against norovirus. Wash napkins, table linens, side towels and uniforms thoroughly.

Fruits and vegetables may be contaminated with norovirus in the field. Shellfish can become contaminated from tainted water. Wash fruits and vegetables properly and cook shellfish thoroughly to prevent the spread of this illness.

Fungi

Fungi are a large group of plants ranging from single-celled organisms to giant mushrooms. Fungi are everywhere: in the soil, air and water. The toxins in poisonous mushrooms, a type of fungus, can cause illness or death if consumed. The most common fungi, however, are molds and yeasts.

Molds

Molds are algae-like fungi that form long filaments or strands. These filaments often extend into the air, appearing as cottony or velvety masses on food. Large colonies of mold are easily visible to the naked eye. Although many food molds are not dangerous, and some are even very beneficial, rare types known as mycotoxicoses form toxins that have been linked to food-borne illnesses. For the most part, however, molds affect only the appearance and flavor of foods. They cause discoloration, odors and off-flavors.

Unlike bacteria, molds can grow on almost any food at almost any temperature, moist or dry, acidic or alkaline. Although mold cells can be destroyed by heating to 135°F (57°C) for 10 minutes, their toxins are heat resistant, however, and are not destroyed by normal cooking methods. Therefore foods that develop mold should be discarded, and any container or storage area cleaned and sanitized.

Yeasts

Yeasts require water and carbohydrates (sugar or starch) for survival. As the organisms consume carbohydrates, they expel alcohol and carbon dioxide gas through a process known as **fermentation**. Fermentation is very beneficial in making breads and alcoholic beverages.

Although naturally occurring yeasts have not been proven to be harmful to humans, they can cause foods to spoil and develop off-flavors, odors and discoloration. Yeasts are killed at temperatures of 136°F (58°C) or above.

DIRECT CHEMICAL CONTAMINANTS

Contamination of foods by a wide variety of chemicals is a very real and serious danger in which the public has shown a strong interest. Chemical contamination is usually inadvertent and invisible, making it extremely difficult to detect. The only way to avoid such chemical hazards is for everyone working in a food service operation to follow proper procedures when handling foods or chemicals.

Chemical hazards include contamination with (1) residual chemicals used in growing the food supply, (2) food service chemicals and (3) toxic metals.

Residual Chemicals

Chemicals such as antibiotics, fertilizers, insecticides and herbicides have brought about great progress in controlling plant, animal and human diseases, permitting greater food yields and stimulating animal growth. The benefits derived from these chemicals, however, must be contrasted with the adverse effects when they are used indiscriminately or improperly. Some studies have shown that long-term, low-dose exposure to pesticides may result in respiratory, memory and neurological conditions as well as allergies and skin disorders.

The danger of these chemicals lies in the possible contamination of human foods, which occurs when chemical residues remain after the intended goal is achieved. Fruits and vegetables must be washed and peeled properly to reduce the risk of consuming residual chemicals.

Food Safety of Fruits and Vegetables

More than half of all food-borne illnesses are linked to fresh produce. The Centers for Disease Control and Prevention (CDC) estimates leafy greens are responsible for one in five cases of food-borne illness. Fruits and vegetables may be contaminated in the field from animal waste and harvesters, or during transportation, processing and packaging. Many large-scale produce farmers have adopted Good Agricultural Practices (GAPs) and Good Handling Practices (GHPs), general guidelines farms and food producers must follow to ensure food safety, and processors are developing and evaluating new produce washes to reduce surface contamination. However, there is no way to guarantee that produce will be pathogen-free, and the fact that these foods are most often eaten uncooked increases the risk of them passing along a pathogenic organism.

That said, there are some things you can do to reduce the likelihood of serving contaminated produce. Wash all whole produce well before cutting it. Clean and sanitize your equipment frequently, taking care not to contaminate your cutting board with field soil that may cling to the box or plant. Refrigerate any produce immediately after washing and cutting it.

Cut vegetables deteriorate much faster than intact produce. Cutting breaks the plant's cell walls, allowing microorganisms to invade the material. This accelerates spoilage and the growth of pathogenic organisms. Use cut produce as soon as possible. If you purchase prewashed bagged salad, mixed salad greens or fresh-cut produce, inspect the packages upon delivery. Reject any that are above 41°F (5°C) or those that show signs of decomposition. Always use bagged salad, mixed salad greens and fresh-cut produce by the "use by" date. Discard any decomposed prewashed greens; rewashing risks spreading contamination.

Food Service Chemicals

A more prevalent contamination problem involves the common chemicals found in almost every food service operation. Cleaners, polishes, pesticides and abrasives are often poisonous to humans. Illness and even death can result from foods contaminated by such common items as bug spray, drain cleaner, oven cleaner or silver polish. These chemicals pose a hazard if used or stored near food supplies. Even improperly washing or rinsing dishes and utensils can leave a soap residue that can be consumed by anyone eating from the item.

To avoid food service chemical contamination, make sure all cleaning chemicals are clearly labeled and stored well away from food preparation and storage areas. Always use these products as directed by the manufacturer; never reuse a chemical container or package. Properly wash and rinse all dishes used to prepare or serve food.

Toxic Metals

Another type of chemical contamination occurs when metals such as lead, mercury, copper, zinc and antimony are dispersed in food or water. For example:

- Metals can accumulate in fish and shellfish living in polluted waters or in plants grown in soil contaminated by the metals.
- Acidic foods, such as tomatoes or wine, can cause metal ions from zinc (galvanized) or unlined copper containers to be released into the food.
- Antimony (used in bonding enamelware) can be released into food when the enamel is chipped or cracked. For this reason, the use of enamelware is prohibited in food service facilities.
- Lead enters the water supply from lead pipes and solder, and it is found in the glaze on some imported ceramic items.

Consuming any of these metals can cause poisoning.

To prevent metal contamination, use only approved food service equipment and utensils and re-tin copper cookware as needed. Never serve fish or shellfish that was illegally harvested or obtained from uninspected sources.

DIRECT PHYSICAL CONTAMINANTS

Physical contaminants are foreign objects that find their way into foods by mistake. Examples of these physical hazards include metal shavings created by a worn can opener, pieces of glass from a broken container, hair or dirt. Physical contaminants may be created by intentional tampering, but they are more often the result of poor safety and sanitation practices or a lack of training. To prevent direct physical contamination, observe good personal hygiene as described on pages 27–28. Upon delivery inspect all foods for foreign objects, such as insects, pebbles, stickers, rubber bands or twist ties. Keep small objects such as pens, pencils and paper clips out of kitchen work areas. Discard any food product that may have come into contact with broken china, glass or plastic.

CROSS-CONTAMINATION

Generally microorganisms and other contaminants cannot move by themselves. Rather they are carried to foods and food contact surfaces by humans, rodents or insects. This transfer is referred to as cross-contamination. Cross-contamination is the process by which one item, such as your finger or a cutting board, becomes contaminated and then contaminates another food or tool. For example, suppose a chef's knife and cutting board are used in butchering a TCS food such as a chicken and the chicken was directly contaminated with salmonella at the hatchery. If the knife and board are not cleaned, washed, rinsed and sanitized properly, anything that touches them can also become contaminated. Even though cooking the chicken to an appropriate internal temperature may destroy the salmonella in the chicken, the uncooked salad greens cut on the same

Steps to Prevent Cross-Contamination

- Wash hands frequently:

  Before and after touching raw food

  After touching anything that may contaminate the hands (after removing the garbage, using the restroom, coughing, eating, smoking or touching dirty clothes or kitchen towels)

  Before putting on single-use gloves and when changing to a new pair

- Properly wash, rinse, sanitize and air dry all knives, cutting boards and equipment after each task.

- Use color-coded cutting boards for poultry, meats and produce.

- Discard soiled side towels. (Don't use kitchen side towels to wipe the floor, then your hands.)

- Use single-use gloves and change them frequently.

- Use clean tongs and bakery tissue paper when handling foods for immediate service.

- Use the two-spoon method (see sidebar on page 27) when tasting foods.

cutting board or with the same knife can contain live bacteria. You must properly clean, wash, rinse and sanitize all tools when preparing different types of foods and when switching from preparing raw to cooked foods.

Cross-contamination can occur with bacteria or other microorganisms, chemicals, dirt and debris. Side towels or kitchen towels are an especially common source of cross-contamination. If a cook uses a side towel to wipe a spill off the floor, then uses that same towel to dry his hands after visiting the restroom, he has recontaminated his hands with whatever bacteria or dirt was on the floor. Cross-contamination also occurs when raw foods come in contact with cooked foods. Never store cooked food below raw food in a refrigerator, and never return cooked food to the container that held the raw food. Cross-contamination also occurs easily from smoking, drinking or eating, unless hands are properly washed after each of these activities.

In addition to proper hand washing, food service workers should strive to minimize direct contact with prepared food by using single-use gloves, clean tongs, tasting spoons, bakery tissue paper and other appropriate tools. Disposable gloves can prevent cross-contamination only when used properly to prevent microbial contamination. Check your local regulations; some health departments require the use of disposable gloves when handling any ready-to-eat foods.

Cross-contamination can be reduced or even prevented by (1) personal cleanliness, (2) dish and equipment cleanliness, (3) proper food storage, (4) food labeling and (5) pest management.

Personal Cleanliness

To produce clean, sanitary food, all food handlers must maintain high standards of personal cleanliness and hygiene. This begins with good grooming. Humans provide the ideal environment for the growth of microorganisms. Everyone harbors bacteria in the nose and mouth. These bacteria are easily spread by sneezing or coughing, by not disposing of tissues properly and by not washing hands frequently and properly. Touching your body and then touching food or utensils transfers bacteria.

Hands should be washed before and after handling raw food; after smoking, drinking or eating; after coughing or sneezing; after removing the garbage; and after touching dirty clothes, side towels or anything that may contaminate the hands. Human waste carries many dangerous microorganisms, so it is especially important to wash your hands thoroughly after visiting the restroom. An employee who is ill should not be allowed in the kitchen. If during work an employee develops symptoms such as fever, diarrhea, vomiting, sore throat with fever or jaundice, he or she must report to a manager and request to be dismissed until recovered.

Current research shows that the human immunodeficiency virus (HIV), the causative agent of AIDS, is not spread by food. According to the Centers for Disease Control and Prevention (CDC), food service workers infected with HIV should not be restricted from work unless there is another infection or illness.

You can do several things to decrease the risk of an illness being spread by poor personal hygiene:

- Wash your hands frequently and thoroughly. Gloves are not a substitute for proper hand washing.
- Keep your fingernails short, clean and neat. Do not bite your nails or wear nail polish or artificial nails.
- Keep any cut or wound antiseptically bandaged. An injured hand should also be covered with a disposable glove.
- Bathe daily, or more often if required.
- Keep your hair clean and restrained. Wear approved head and beard covering if required.
- Wear work clothes that are clean and neat. Avoid wearing jewelry or watches.
- Remove aprons before leaving the kitchen.
- Do not eat, drink, smoke or chew gum in food preparation areas.

Procedure for Proper Hand Washing

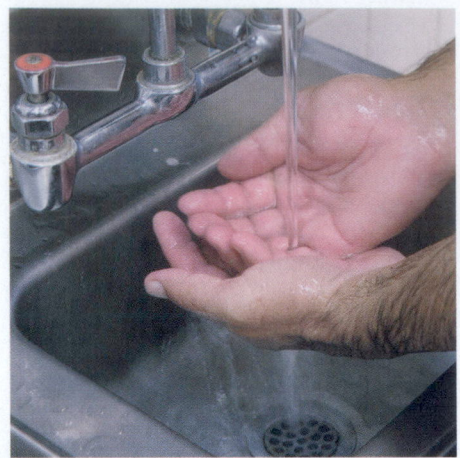

① Use hot water (100°F/38°C) to wet hands and forearms.

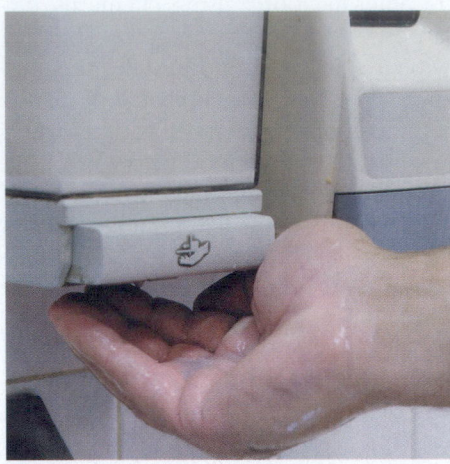

② Apply an antibacterial soap.

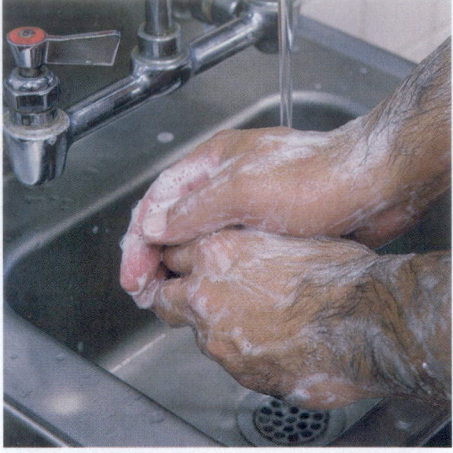

③ Rub hands and arms briskly with soapy lather for at least 20 seconds.

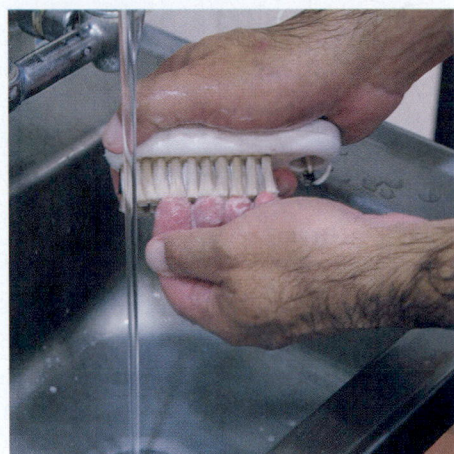

④ Scrub between fingers and clean nails with a clean nail brush.

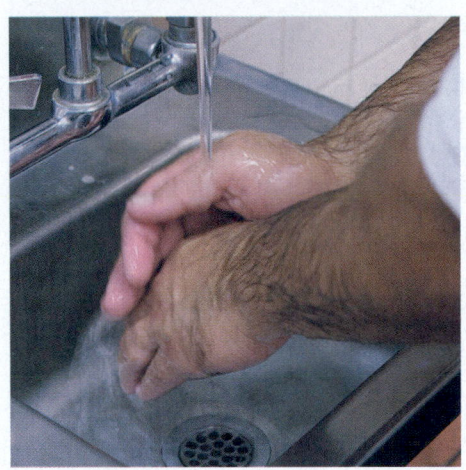

⑤ Rinse thoroughly under hot running water. Reapply soap and scrub hands and forearms for another 5–10 seconds. Rinse again.

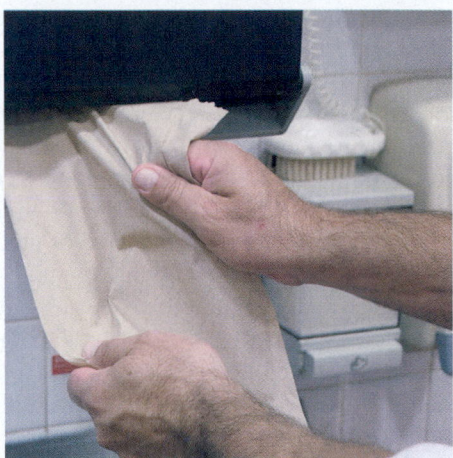

⑥ Dry hands and arms with a single-use towel or appropriate automatic hand dryer; use a clean towel to turn off the water. Discard the towel in a trash receptacle.

clean to remove visible dirt and soil

sanitize to reduce pathogenic organisms on clean surfaces to safe levels

sterilize to destroy all living microorganisms

Dish and Equipment Cleanliness

A requirement for any food service facility is cleanability. Note that there is an important difference between *clean* and *sanitary*. **Clean** means that the item has no visible soil on it. **Sanitary** means that harmful substances are reduced to safe levels. Thus something may be clean without being sanitary. The visible dirt can be removed, but disease-causing microorganisms can remain.

The cleaning of dishes, pots, pans and utensils in a food service operation involves both removing soil and sanitizing. Soil can be removed manually or by machine. Sanitizing can be accomplished with heat or chemical disinfectants. Heating to the proper temperatures **sterilizes** food contact surfaces by killing microorganisms. To sterilize using heat, wash water in the sink must be kept at 171°F (77°C) or higher. Dishwasher water must reach at 180°F (82°C) or higher.

There are three types of chemicals commonly used to sanitize and disinfect: chlorine, iodine and **quaternary ammonium compounds (quats)**. Each option has it pros and cons.

Food-grade chlorine bleach diluted in water is one commonly used sanitizing agent. It is inexpensive and kills a wide range of microorganisms. However bleach has a strong smell and is corrosive, unlike quats, which can be used on surfaces that may rust. Quats are colorless, odorless and non irritating but are more expensive and are less effective in the presence of dirt than bleach. Iodine sanitizers are useful but may leave a brown stain on contact surfaces. Whichever sanitizing product you use, follow the manufacturer's instructions for each product. Temperature, strength and contact time vary with each product.

When sanitizing tools, equipment and work surfaces, be sure to clean and remove all food and debris. Wash with detergent then rinse before applying sanitizing solution. Leave the solution undisturbed for the amount of time the manufacturer's directions recommend.

Procedures for manually washing, rinsing and sanitizing dishes and equipment generally follow the three-compartment sink setup shown in Figure 2.5. Food service items, dishes, silverware and utensils should always be allowed to air-dry, as towel drying may recontaminate them. Any cracked or chipped china should be discarded, as it can harbor bacteria that pose a food safety hazard.

Procedure for Manually Washing, Rinsing and Sanitizing Dishes and Equipment

1 Scrape and spray the item to remove soil.
2 Wash the item in the first sink compartment using 110°F (43°C) water and an approved detergent. Use a brush or cloth to remove any remaining soil.
3 Rinse or spray the item in the second sink compartment using clear, 110°F (43°C) water.
4 Sanitize the item in the third sink compartment by either:
   a. immersing it in 171°F (77°C) water for at least 30 seconds, or
   b. immersing it in an approved chemical sanitizing solution according to the manufacturer's directions.
5 Empty, clean and refill each sink compartment as necessary, and check the water temperature regularly.
6 Allow the items to air dry.

Figure 2.5 The three-compartment sink procedure: scrape, spray, wash, rinse, sanitize and air-dry each item.

Sanitizing Solution

Use a clean cloth dipped in sanitizing solution when wiping off your knives, utensils or cutting board during work. An acceptable solution can be made by combining 1 gallon (3.8 liters) lukewarm water with 1 tablespoon (15 milliliters) regular strength food-grade chlorine bleach. A designated container for sanitizing solution should be filled and placed at each work station. Cloths used to sanitize equipment should stay in the bucket of liquid when not in use. To sanitize, allow the solution to sit on the surface for one minute then wipe with clean paper towels. Store sanitizing solution below work areas to prevent accidentally spilling it onto food or food preparation areas. Replace solution when it becomes cloudy, dirty or after every 2 hours of use.

Machine-washing dishes or utensils follows a similar procedure. The person washing the dishes should first scrape and rinse items as needed, then load the items into dishwasher racks so that the spray of water will reach all surfaces. The machine cleans the items with a detergent, then sanitizes them with either a hot-water rinse (at least 180°F/82°C) or a chemical disinfectant. When the machine cycle is complete, items should be inspected for residual soil, allowed to air-dry and stored in a clean area.

Work tables and stationary equipment must also be cleaned and sanitized properly. Equipment and surfaces, including floors, walls and worktables, should be easily exposed for inspection and cleaning and should be constructed so that soil can be removed effectively and efficiently with normal cleaning procedures. A thorough cleaning schedule should be implemented and closely monitored. The following points are important to the safety and cleanliness of any food service facility:

- Equipment should be disassembled for cleaning; any immersible pieces should be cleaned and sanitized like other items.
- All worktables or other food contact surfaces should be cleaned with detergent, then sanitized with a clean cloth dipped in a sanitizing solution. Combining 1 gallon (3.8 liters) lukewarm water with 1 tablespoon (15 milliliters) regular strength food-grade chlorine bleach makes an acceptable sanitizing solution. Other chemical sanitizers should be prepared and used according to health department and manufacturer's directions.
- Surfaces, especially work surfaces with which food may come in contact, should be smooth and free of cracks, crevices or seams in which soil and microorganisms can hide.
- Floors should be nonabsorbent and should not become slippery when wet.
- Walls and ceilings should be smooth and light-colored so that soil is easier to see.
- Light should be ample throughout food preparation and storage areas. All lightbulbs should be covered with a sleeve or globe to protect surroundings from shattered glass.

A kitchen's design can also affect food safety and sanitation. Food preparation equipment should be arranged in such a way as to decrease the chances of cross-contamination. The workflow should eliminate crisscrossing and backtracking. Employees should be able to reach storage, refrigeration and cleanup areas easily. Dish- and pot-washing areas and garbage facilities should be kept as far from food preparation and storage areas as possible. Cleaning supplies and other chemicals should be stored away from foods.

Food Storage

Proper food storage prevents cross-contamination and ensures food safety. Freezers, refrigerators and dry goods storage facilities should have effective temperature, humidity and light controls in order to properly and safely maintain the stored items. Not only must food be purchased from approved suppliers, it must be physically inspected when it arrives. Upon delivery, the condition and internal temperature of foods should be verified. Use a thermometer to check TCS foods. Reject and return any unacceptable foods. Save labels and origin tags for foods such as shellfish in case there is a recall or an issue arises with the product.

Dry goods, such as flour, sugar, dried legumes, crackers and rice, are foods that will not promote the growth of hazards at room temperature. They should be stored least 6 inches (15 centimeters) off the floor and 6 inches (15 centimeters) away from walls on shelving or storage racks that are clean, sanitized and dry.

Store refrigerated foods appropriately to prevent cross-contamination and the growth of harmful bacteria. Foods must be kept at temperatures below the temperature danger zone 41°F (5°C). Wrap and cover food to prevent leakage. Store food in cleaned and sanitized food-grade containers. Raw meat, poultry and fish should be stored separately from prepared foods and produce. Refrigerate produce on separate storage racks or in a

⚠ Safety Alert

Chemical Storage

- Never store cleaning supplies or other chemicals with or near foods.
- Never store chemicals in a container that originally held food; never store food in a container that once held a chemical.
- Keep chemicals and cleaners in properly labeled containers.

Top shelf:
Ready-to-eat and cooked foods

Second shelf:
Cooked meats, fish and poultry, such as cold cuts

Third shelf:
Raw fish, seafood and shell eggs

Fourth shelf:
Raw whole cuts of beef, pork and veal

Next to lowest shelf:
Raw ground meat and ground fish

Bottom shelf:
Raw, whole and ground poultry

Figure 2.6 Storage of TCS foods in a refrigerator.

Sustainable Food Safety

Lessening a restaurant's environmental impact is of growing concern to chefs and their customers. Cleaning and sanitizing activities consume large quantities of water and chemicals. Systems can be put in place to reduce this consumption. Run dishwashers only when full. When feasible, replace older dishwashers with energy- and water-efficient models. To reduce the use of harsh chemicals, select cleaning products made from renewable plant-based ingredients such as corn or soybeans. Choose trash bags, single-use plates and utensils made from recycled and biodegradable materials.

Even without the latest technology, a restaurant can reduce its environmental impact by instituting a sustainable cleaning program. The Green Restaurant Association and the National Restaurant Association's Conserve program provide resources to assist food service operations with implementing such plans.

separate refrigerator. Certain fruits and vegetables such as citrus, root vegetables and onions, may be stored in cool dry areas.

This order is based on the minimum internal cooking temperature of each food. Refrigerated food should be stored so that cooked foods are stored above raw foods to prevent cross contamination. And items that will be cooked to a lower internal temperature must be placed above foods that will be cooked to a higher internal temperature. Store refrigerated food in the order shown in Figure 2.6.

Food Labeling

Accurate food labeling and consistent record keeping are as important as safe food-handling practices to prevent cross-contamination and food spoilage. Use food labels to date all foods that are made for kitchen use as well as leftovers. Systems for labeling foods vary in every operation but must be followed consistently to be effective. Once placed in clean, sanitized storage containers, food prepared for later use should be labeled with the product name and the date and time it was made. See Figure 2.7. Ready-to-eat TCS food that will be held for longer than 24 hours must be labeled with the day or date by which the food must be consumed on premises, sold or discarded. Once labeled, refrigerated or frozen products are easily identifiable by the entire kitchen staff.

Pest Management

Food can be contaminated by insects (e.g., roaches and flies) and rodents (e.g., mice and rats). These pests carry many harmful bacteria on their bodies and contaminate any surface with which they come in contact. An insect or rodent infestation is usually considered a serious health risk and should be dealt with immediately and thoroughly. Pests must be controlled by building them out of the facility, creating an environment in which they cannot find food, water or shelter, and relying on professional extermination.

FRI
Viernes

Item: _____
Shelf
Life: _____ Qty: _____ Emp: _____
☐ AM
Date: _____
☐ PM
☐ AM
Use By: _____
☐ PM

Temp: _____ _____ _____

Figure 2.7 A label used to identify and date foods after preparation.

The best defense against pests is to prevent infestations in the first place by building them out. Any crack—no matter how small—in door frames, walls or windowsills should be repaired immediately, and all drains, pipes and vents should be well sealed. Inspect all deliveries thoroughly, and reject any packages or containers found to contain evidence of pests.

Flies are a perfect method of transportation for bacteria because they feed and breed on human waste and garbage. Use screens or "fly fans" (also known as air curtains) to keep them out of food preparation areas. Controlling garbage is also essential because moist, warm, decaying organic material attracts flies and provides favorable conditions for eggs to hatch and larvae to grow.

Pest management also requires creating an inhospitable environment for pests. Store all food and supplies at least 6 inches (15 centimeters) off the floor and 6 inches (15 centimeters) away from walls. **Rotate stock** often to disrupt nesting places and breeding habits. Provide good ventilation in storerooms to remove humidity, airborne contaminants, grease and fumes. Do not allow water to stand in drains, sinks or buckets, as cockroaches are attracted to moisture. Clean up spills and crumbs immediately and completely to reduce pest food supply.

Even while making the best efforts to build pests out and maintain proper housekeeping standards, it is still important to watch for the presence of pests. For example, cockroaches leave a strong, oily odor and feces that look like large grains of pepper. Cockroaches prefer to search for food and water in the dark, so seeing any cockroach on the move in the daylight is an indication of a large infestation.

Rodents (mice and rats) also tend to hide during the day, so an infestation may be rather serious before any creature is actually seen. Rodent droppings, which are shiny black to brownish gray, may be evident, however. Rodent nests made from scraps of paper, hair or other soft materials may be visible evidence of an infestation.

Should an infestation occur, consult a licensed pest control operator immediately. With early detection and proper treatment, infestations can be eliminated. Employees should be very careful in attempting to use pesticides or insecticides themselves. These chemicals are toxic to humans as well as to pests. Great care must be taken to prevent contaminating food or exposing workers or customers to the chemicals.

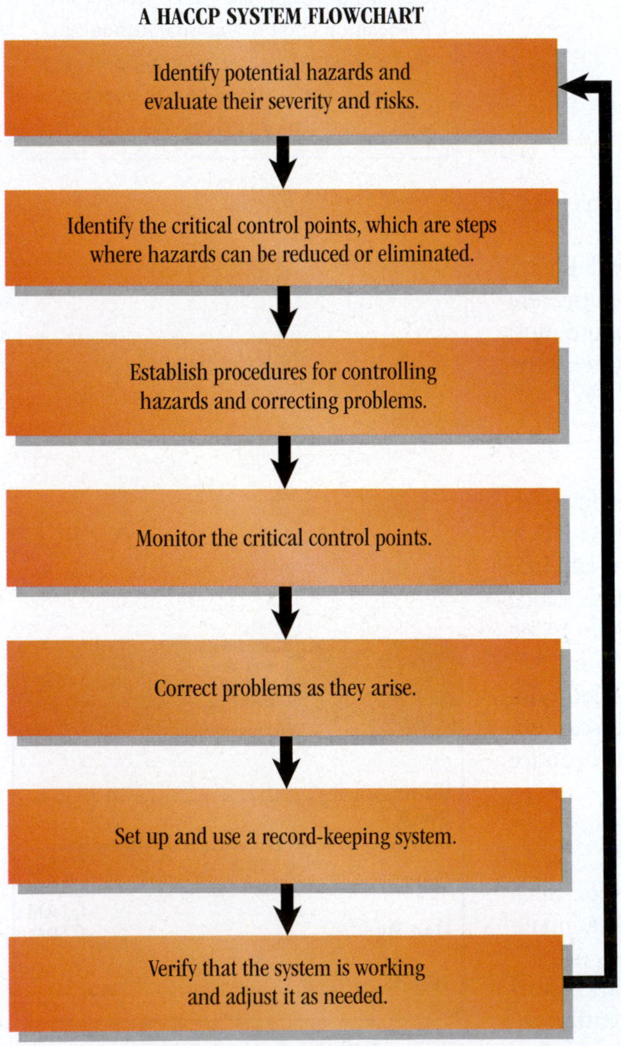

HAZARD ANALYSIS CRITICAL CONTROL POINTS (HACCP) SYSTEMS

Now that you understand what contaminants are and how they can be destroyed or controlled, it is necessary to put this information into practice during day-to-day operations. Although local health departments regularly inspect all food service facilities, continual self-inspection and control are essential for maintaining sanitary conditions.

Food service operations regularly put into place food safety management systems to prevent the spread of food-borne illnesses and to prevent cross-contamination from allergens. **Hazard Analysis Critical Control Points (HACCP)**, which is one of these systems, is an effective and efficient system for managing and maintaining sanitary conditions in all types of food service operations. HACCP [HASS-ip] is a rigorous system of self-inspection that must be in place in food manufacturing settings, although it is voluntary for most restaurants. It focuses on the flow of food through the food service facility, from the decision to include an item on the menu through service to the consumer. A **critical control point (CCP)** in that flow is any step during the processing of a food when a mistake can result in the transmission, growth or survival of pathogenic bacteria. The seven principles of a HACCP plan are illustrated in Figure 2.8.

rotate stock when receiving new deliveries; all perishable and semiperishable goods, whether fresh, frozen, canned or dry, should be used in the order in which they were received, known as the first in, first out (FIFO) principle

critical control point (CCP) a point, step or procedure at which control can be applied and a food safety hazard can be prevented, eliminated or reduced to an acceptable level

A HACCP SYSTEM FLOWCHART

Identify potential hazards and evaluate their severity and risks.

↓

Identify the critical control points, which are steps where hazards can be reduced or eliminated.

↓

Establish procedures for controlling hazards and correcting problems.

↓

Monitor the critical control points.

↓

Correct problems as they arise.

↓

Set up and use a record-keeping system.

↓

Verify that the system is working and adjust it as needed.

Figure 2.8 A HACCP system flowchart.

The HACCP process begins by identifying the steps and evaluating the type and severity of hazard that can occur when preparing food for service. It then identifies what actions can be taken to reduce or prevent each risk. See Table 2.3. The activities that present the highest risk of hazard should be monitored most closely. For example, a cook's failure to wash his or her hands before handling cooked food presents a greater risk of hazard than a dirty floor. In other words, hazards must be prioritized, and critical concerns take priority.

Note that the standards (or what some might call boundaries) applied in a formal HACCP system are no different from those that should be rigorously followed in any food service operation. HACCP does not impose new or different food safety standards; it is merely a system for ensuring that those standards are actually followed.

HACCP ANALYSIS: THE FLOW OF FOOD			TABLE 2.3
CONTROL POINT	**HAZARDS**	**STANDARDS**	**CRITICAL ACTIONS**
Selecting the menu and recipes	TCS foods; human hands involved in food preparation	Analyze menus and recipes for control points; wash hands frequently; use single-use gloves as appropriate	Plan physical work flow; train employees
Receiving	Contaminated or spoiled goods; TCS foods in the temperature danger zone	Do not accept torn bags, dented cans, broken glass containers or leaking or damaged packages; frozen food should be received at 0°F (−18°C) or below and refrigerated food at 41°F (5°C) or below	Inspect all deliveries and reject as necessary
Storing	Cross-contamination to and from other foods; bacterial growth; spoilage; improper holding temperatures	Avoid crowding and allow air to circulate in freezers and refrigerators; rotate stock and keep storage areas clean, dry and well lit; store frozen food at 0°F (−18°C) or below and refrigerated food at 41°F (5°C) or below	Maintain proper temperatures and other storage conditions; discard if necessary
Preparing	Cross-contamination; bacterial growth	Keep TCS foods at 41°F (5°C) or below or 135°F (57°C) or above; thaw frozen foods under refrigeration or under cold running water (70°F/21°C) for no more than 2 hours; microwave only if the food is to be cooked immediately once thawed	Avoid the temperature danger zone; maintain good personal hygiene; use sanitary utensils
Cooking	Bacterial survival; physical or chemical contamination	Heat foods to the appropriate internal temperature; reheat leftover foods to at least 165°F (74°C)	Cook foods to their proper temperatures
Holding and service	Bacterial growth; contamination	Maintain hot holding temperatures at 135°F (57°C) or above and cold holding temperatures at 41°F (5°C) or below; do not mix new product with old; discard food after 2 hours of being held at room temperature	Maintain proper temperatures; use sanitary equipment
Cooling leftovers	Bacterial growth	Spread food into clean, shallow, metal containers; use an ice bath; stir periodically during cooling; cool to 70°F (21°C) within 2 hours, then cool to 41°F (5°C) or below within 4 additional hours; cover and refrigerate; store cooked food above raw	Cool foods quickly; label and store foods properly
Reheating	Bacterial survival and growth	Use leftovers within 4 days; heat leftovers to 165°F (74°C) for 15 seconds within 2 hours; do not mix old product with new; discard secondary leftovers	Reheat food quickly (do not use a steam table to reheat foods) and as close to serving time as possible; reheat smaller quantities as needed; discard if necessary

BEEF STROGANOFF

Yield 8 Servings, 8 oz. (240 g) each	Method Sautéing	
Tenderloin tips, émincé	2 lb.	960 g
Clarified butter	3 Tbsp.	45 ml
Onion, medium dice	4 oz.	120 g
Mushrooms, halved	1 lb.	480 g
Demi-glace	10 fl. oz.	300 ml
Heavy cream	10 fl. oz.	300 ml
Sour cream	8 oz.	240 g
Dijon mustard	1 Tbsp.	15 ml
Fresh dill, chopped	1 Tbsp.	15 ml
Fresh parsley, chopped	1 Tbsp.	15 ml
Salt and pepper	TT	TT
Egg noodles, cooked	24 oz.	720 g

PRE-PREPARATION

A. Wash hands before handling food, after handling raw foods and after any interruptions in work.

B. Cut the beef tenderloin using a clean, sanitized knife and cutting board. Place the émincé into a clean container, cover and refrigerate until ready to use. If work is interrupted, return the beef to refrigerated storage during the interruption.

C. Measure the demi-glace, cream and sour cream, cover and keep refrigerated until ready to use.

D. Chop the onions and herbs using a clean, sanitized knife and cutting board.

PREPARATION

CCP 1. Sauté the tenderloin tips in the butter, searing on all sides. Remove the meat **to a clean container and hold at 135°F (57°C) or higher for no more than 2 hours.**

2. Add the onion to the pan and sauté lightly. Add the mushrooms and sauté until dry.

3. Add the demi-glace. Bring to a boil, reduce to a simmer and cook for 10 minutes.

CCP 4. Add the cream, sour cream, mustard and any meat juices that accumulated while holding the meat. **Cook until an internal temperature of 145°F (63°C) is maintained for at least 15 seconds.**

CCP 5. Return the meat to the sauce. **Cook until the meat reaches an internal temperature of 145°F (63°C).** Stir in the dill and parsley. Adjust the seasonings and serve over hot egg noodles.

HOLDING

CCP   Transfer the sauce to a clean steam table pan and cover. Hold for service in a preheated steam table at **135°F (57°C) or higher. Use within 4 hours.**

LEFTOVERS

CCP   Place in shallow metal pans with a product depth of no more than 2 inches. **Cool from 135°F (57°C) to 70°F (21°C) within 2 hours and from 70°F (21°C) to 41°F (5°C) or lower within 4 additional hours,** for a total cooling time of not more than 6 hours. Cover and store in a refrigerator so that the internal product temperature is 41°F (5°C) or less. Use leftovers within 4 days.

REHEATING

CCP   Reheat Stroganoff to an internal temperature of **165°F (74°C) or higher for 15 seconds within 2 hours;** discard any product that is not consumed within 4 hours.

NOTES:
Measure all internal temperatures with a clean, sanitized thermocouple or thermometer.
Once cooked, egg noodles are a TCS or potentially hazardous food and should be held and stored accordingly.

Figure 2.9 A recipe with embedded critical control points (CCPs).

One way to ensure compliance is to frequently check and record the temperature of TCS foods during cooking, cooling and holding. Maintaining written time-and-temperature logs enables management to evaluate and adjust procedures as necessary. Whatever system is followed, all personnel must be constantly aware of and responsive to risks and problems associated with the safety of the food they serve.

A food service operation can make workers aware of potential hazards and the actions that are necessary to avoid those hazards by including detailed safety information in every recipe. Figure 2.9 is a recipe for Beef Stroganoff, with all critical control points noted. The inclusion of this much detail in all of an operation's standardized recipes is a constant reminder to employees of both the specific actions necessary and the importance of food safety to the operation.

FOOD ALLERGIES AND INTOLERANCES

A **food allergy** occurs when the body's immune system reacts to a substance in a food, usually a protein. This sets off a chain reaction within the body. Symptoms, which may occur within minutes, range in severity from mild to life-threatening. The only way to prevent an allergic reaction is to avoid the food and any items that contain it. Protecting the allergic guest from exposure to **allergens** through direct contact or cross-contamination is the responsibility of every chef and food service worker.

According to the CDC, an estimated 4–6 percent of Americans have food allergies. More than 160 foods are known to cause food allergies from spices and seeds to meats and fruit. However, the following eight foods account for 90 percent of all food-allergic reactions:

1 Milk and milk products

2 Eggs

3 Fish (e.g., bass, flounder, cod)

4 Crustacean shellfish (e.g., crab, lobster, shrimp)

5 Tree nuts (e.g., almonds, pecans, walnuts)

6 Peanuts

7 Wheat

8 Soybeans

In the case of peanut, tree nut, milk, fish and shellfish allergies, the reactions can be severe. The consumption or contact with any of these ingredients can cause a potentially fatal, allergic reaction called anaphylaxis.

Many allergy-causing ingredients or allergens hide in unexpected places. Eggs, for example, may be used in the topping on specialty coffee drinks. Even pastas that don't contain eggs may be processed on equipment used for egg-containing pastas. Products made from soybeans are widely used in processed foods as well as vegetarian prepared meals. Wheat may be used in glucose syrup, soy sauce and some modified food starches. The **Food Allergen Labeling and Consumer Protection Act (FALCPA)** requires food manufacturers to label food products that contain a major food allergen. FALCPA specifies that the type of tree nut (e.g., almonds, pecans, walnuts), the type of fish (e.g., bass, flounder, cod) and the type of crustacean shellfish (e.g., crab, lobster, shrimp) be declared. Labeling makes it easier for consumers and chefs to identify foods that contain major allergens.

A **food intolerance** is an abnormal response to a food or additive. An intolerance occurs when the body is unable to digest a certain component of a food. Though symptoms of intolerance may be unpleasant, including abdominal cramping or diarrhea, they are not life-threatening. The reaction to a food intolerance, unlike an allergic reaction, does not involve the immune system.

Every food service establishment should provide food allergy training for its employees. Service staff should be able to provide customers with a list of ingredients

food allergy an immune system response to a substance in food; the response may be digestive discomfort, breathing difficulties, rashes and other physical reactions, some of which may be fatal

allergens substances that may cause allergic reactions in some people

for each menu item. They should be trained to recommend ingredient substitutions. In the kitchen, strict controls to avoid cross-contamination should be observed. The equipment and methods used when preparing food for an allergic guest must be considered to prevent allergenic food from coming into contact with other food preparation surfaces.

Pans and utensils used to prepare foods for an allergic customer must be cleaned thoroughly between uses. Even a trace of food on a spoon, spatula or cutting board can cause an allergic reaction. Wash your hands and change your gloves before preparing food for a guest with allergies.

Segregate preparation of food for allergic guests. When preparing several dishes at the same time, cook the allergen-free meal first. Then keep it covered and away from any splatter caused by other foods that are cooking. If you have handled an allergenic food, wash your hands with soap and warm water before serving the allergen-free meal. Some kitchens designate an allergen-free cooking station that is stocked with separate utensils and equipment. Many food service establishments use purple knives, cutting boards and cookware for this purpose. Treat any customer having an allergic reaction as an emergency. Call 911 and seek medical help immediately.

THE SAFE WORKER

Kitchens are filled with objects that can cut, burn, break, electrocute, crush or sprain the human body. The best ways to prevent work-related injuries are proper training, good work habits and careful supervision. The federal government enacted legislation designed to reduce hazards in the work area, thereby reducing accidents. The **Occupational Safety and Health Act (OSHA)** covers a broad range of safety matters. Employers who fail to follow its rules can be severely fined. Unfortunately human error is the leading cause of accidents, and no amount of legislation can protect someone who doesn't work in a safe manner.

Personal Safety

Safe behavior on the job reflects pride, professionalism and consideration for fellow workers. The following list of activities is aimed at preventing accidents and injuries:

- Clean up spills as soon as they occur.
- Learn to operate equipment properly; always use guards and safety devices. Turn off or unplug electrical equipment before cleaning.
- Wear clothing that fits properly; avoid wearing jewelry, which may get caught in equipment.
- Knives may be the chef's most important kitchen tool but they are also a potential source for serious personal injury. Observe the knife safety precautions listed on page 94.
- Use knives and other equipment for their intended purposes only. When walking in the kitchen, carry knives close to your side with the point down.
- Keep exits, aisles and stairs clear and unobstructed.
- Always assume pots and pans are hot; handle them with dry towels.
- Position pot and pan handles out of the aisles so that they do not get bumped.
- Get help or use a cart when lifting or moving heavy objects.
- Avoid back injury by lifting with your leg muscles; stoop, don't bend, when lifting.
- Use an appropriately placed ladder or stool for climbing; do not use a chair, box, drawer or shelf.

- Keep breakable items away from food storage or production areas. Never place knives or glassware in the pot sink.
- Never leave a pan of oil unattended; hot fat can ignite when overheated.
- Warn people when you must walk behind them, especially when carrying a hot pan.

All food service establishments should have procedures in place to ensure the safety of all workers and guests. When an unsafe situation arises, immediately report it to the manager on duty or appointed person in charge.

Fire Safety

From grease flare-ups on cooktops to major fires caused by dirty ventilation hoods, fires can develop into serious threats in busy professional kitchens. Understanding the danger posed by fires and having a proper fire safety program in place is of utmost importance in a professional kitchen. Fire extinguishers contain different types of chemicals that are effective for various types of fires (see Chapter 5, Tools and Equipment, page 90). Learn which types of fire extinguishers to use for specific combustible materials. Regulations require that commercial kitchens be outfitted with ventilation hoods and professional sprinkler systems. Grease fires in ventilation hoods are the primary cause of restaurant fires; thorough and regular cleaning prevents hazardous grease buildup. All fire suppression systems should be inspected regularly. When faced with a serious fire, do not waste time. Immediately call for help. Shut off all exhaust fans and turn off kitchen equipment if time permits. Close the kitchen doors and evacuate the premises.

Deep-fat fryers also pose a serious fire threat, and employee training should include instruction on the proper operation and cleaning of such equipment. In addition, large quantities of hot fat can cause severe burns if not properly handled. When liquids come into contact with the heated fat, hot steam is released. Take care when adding foods to all deep-fat fryers to prevent getting burned. The threat is most extreme when a large quantity of liquid hits the hot grease. Keep containers of liquids away from deep-fat fryers to avoid accidentally spilling liquid into the hot fat and causing a hazardous steam explosion.

Chef uniforms were designed with comfort and safety in mind; the double front panels and long sleeves help prevent burns. Clothing and towels can catch on fire, however. If an employee's garments catch on fire, use a safety blanket to wrap the person and smother the flames. Although it is generally best to use an appropriate fire extinguisher to douse kitchen fires, some simple measures can be useful for extinguishing a small flame in a pan. Immediately cover a pan in which a small oil flare-up occurs; lack of oxygen will extinguish the flame. To extinguish a small grease flare-up in a pan or on a cooktop, douse it quickly with a generous amount of baking soda or salt.

First Aid

Some accidents will inevitably occur, and it is important to act appropriately in the event of an injury or emergency. This may mean calling for help or providing first aid. Every food service operation should be equipped with a complete first aid kit. Municipal regulations may specify the exact contents of the kit. Be sure that the kit is conveniently located and well stocked at all times.

The American Red Cross and local public health departments offer training in first aid, cardiopulmonary resuscitation (CPR) and the Heimlich maneuver used for choking victims. All employees should be trained in basic emergency procedures. A list of emergency telephone numbers should be posted by each telephone.

QUESTIONS FOR DISCUSSION

1 Foods can be contaminated in several ways. Explain the differences between biological, chemical and physical contamination. Give an example of each.

2 Under what conditions do bacteria thrive? Explain what you can do to alter these conditions.

3 What is the temperature danger zone? What is its significance in food preparation?

4 In what ways can you ensure that residual chemicals do not contaminate food?

5 Explain how improper or inadequate pest management can lead to food-borne illnesses.

6 Define HACCP. How is this system used in a typical food service facility?

7 What systems can a food service operation put into place to protect guests who may have food allergies?

Nutrition 3

- identify the major categories of nutrients and explain their importance in a healthy diet

- identify the key characteristics of a nutritious diet for healthy adults

- describe the effects of storage and preparation techniques on the nutritional value of food

- describe diet-planning tools available to consumers and chefs

- evaluate recipes and dishes using recommended dietary guidelines and food labels

- apply dietary guidelines to plan and prepare menus and recipes

nutrition the science that studies nutrients

Since the days of prehistoric hunters and gatherers, people have understood that some animals and plants are good to eat and others are not. For thousands of years, cultures worldwide have attributed medicinal and beneficial effects to certain foods, particularly plants, such as olives and olive oil, revered by ancient Greeks. For just as long, people have recognized that foods that might otherwise be fine to eat may be unhealthy if improperly prepared or stored. Historical evidence dating back to 12,000 BCE indicates that food was preserved by air drying or curing with salt and sugar in Asian and Middle Eastern cultures. But in the past few decades, people have become increasingly concerned about how foods affect their health and which foods promote good health and longevity.

Because of national health concerns about over-consumption leading to obesity, cardio-vascular disease and diabetes, Americans are interested in dining out in a healthier way. At the same time people with certain health conditions that restrict or prohibit the intake of specific foodstuffs, such as sugar, fat or wheat, are looking for foods that will taste good and meet their diet regimens. These concerns lead us to address the study of nutrition and the role nutrition plays in healthy eating habits.

This chapter cannot provide an in-depth study of the nutritional sciences. Rather it sets forth basic information about nutrients and guidelines for planning a healthy diet. In Chapter 24, Healthy Cooking and Special Diets, we will discuss specific techniques for preparing foods for customers with special dietary concerns.

NUTRITION BASICS

The foundation of cooking is an understanding of ingredients, culinary techniques and the nutritive values of foods. All foods are composed of **nutrients**, the (chemical) substances that promote the growth, maintenance and repair of the body. Some nutrients also provide energy (calories).

There are six categories of nutrients: carbohydrates, lipids (fats and cholesterol), proteins, vitamins, minerals and water. Essential nutrients are those that must be provided by food because the body does not produce them in sufficient quantities to satisfy the needs of the body or cannot make them at all. See Table 3.1. Some nutritional components are considered nonessential because healthy, well-nourished bodies can make them in sufficient quantities to satisfy their needs. Scientists, however, are beginning to

ESSENTIAL NUTRIENTS	TABLE 3.1

Essential nutrients are those that must be provided in our diets because the human body does not produce them in sufficient quantities.

Carbohydrates	Starches and sugars
Fats	Linoleic and linolenic acids
Proteins	The amino acids: histidine, isoleucine, leucine, lysine, methionine, phenylalanine, threonine, tryptophan and valine
Vitamins	Thiamine, riboflavin, niacin, pantothenic acid, biotin, vitamin B_6, vitamin B_{12}, folate, vitamin C, vitamin A, vitamin D, vitamin E and vitamin K
Minerals	Calcium, chloride, magnesium, phosphorus, potassium, sodium, sulfur, selenium, zinc, chromium, copper, fluoride, iodide, iron, manganese and molybdenum
Water	

understand that our bodies may need more of some nonessential nutrients such as calcium, magnesium and potassium in order to provide protection against chronic diseases such as cancer, diabetes and heart disease.

The human body depends on the various nutrients for different purposes and requires different amounts of each depending on age, gender and health status. In addition, some nutrients depend on one another for proper functioning. For example, calcium and vitamin D work together in the body: Vitamin D promotes the absorption of the calcium that the body utilizes for proper bone growth. A deficiency of one nutrient thus affects the working of the other. Because foods differ with regard to their nutritional content, it is important to eat a variety of foods in order to achieve proper nutritional balance.

Essential Nutrients

Three of the essential nutrients provide calories or energy needed in larger quantities than other nutrients. These three, known as essential **macronutrients**, are carbohydrates, certain lipids and proteins.

The **calorie** (often abbreviated as kcal) is the unit that describes the amount of energy in a food. Different nutrients supply different amounts of energy. One gram of pure fat supplies 9 kcal; one gram of pure carbohydrate supplies 4 kcal, as does one gram of pure protein. Most foods are a combination of carbohydrates, proteins and fats; hence their calorie content may not be easily determined unless we know how much of each nutrient the food contains. Calorie tables help provide that information. Foods that have a high proportion of nutrients in relation to their calories are considered **nutrient dense**. Such foods have a concentrated amount of nutrients. The calories from some foods are considered **empty calories** because they have a low proportion of nutrients in relation to their calories. Consuming nutrient dense foods and avoiding foods that provide empty calories is the foundation of healthy eating.

Vitamins and minerals, sometimes referred to as **micronutrients** because they are needed in small quantities, are also essential nutrients. They must be provided through the diet because the body cannot manufacture them in quantities adequate to ensure good health. Although they provide no calories, vitamins and minerals are important to the body because they generate energy from the foods we eat.

Carbohydrates

In the human diet, essential carbohydrates are primarily obtained by consuming plant foods and the sugar in milk (lactose.) **Simple carbohydrates** include monosaccharides (single sugars such as glucose, fructose and maltose) and disaccharides (double sugars such as sucrose, galactose and lactose). See Table 3.2. Simple carbohydrates are found in the naturally occurring sugars in fruit, vegetables and milk, as well as in sweeteners such as honey, corn syrup and table sugar. See Figure 3.1. **Complex carbohydrates** are long chains of simple carbohydrates. Starch and fiber are complex carbohydrates. Complex carbohydrates are found in fruits, vegetables and cereal grains, such as wheat, barley and oats. See Figure 3.2.

The body digests or breaks down sugars and starches into the single sugar, glucose. Glucose, also known as blood sugar, is an important source of energy for the body. Carbohydrates are the body's major source of energy. A diet rich in complex carbohydrates

Energy from Essential Nutrients

1 gram pure fat = 9 calories

1 gram pure carbohydrate = 4 calories

1 gram pure protein = 4 calories

1 gram pure alcohol = 7 calories

calorie the unit of energy measured by the amount of heat required to raise 1000 grams of water one degree Celsius; also written as kilo-calorie or kcal

Figure 3.1 Sources of simple carbohydrates: refined sugars, such as brown sugar, granulated sugar, powdered sugar and sugar cubes, as well as honey, corn syrup and other sweeteners.

Figure 3.2 Sources of complex carbohydrates: vegetables, such as potatoes and corn, bread, grains, pasta and cereals, as well as fruits.

SUGARS	TABLE 3.2
MONOSACCHARIDES	DISACCHARIDES
Glucose (blood sugar)	Lactose (milk sugar composed of glucose and galactose)
Fructose (fruit sugar)	Maltose (malt sugar composed of two glucose molecules)
Galactose (part of milk sugar)	Sucrose (table sugar composed of glucose and fructose)

Figure 3.4 Whole grains: whole wheat flour (left), brown rice (center) and oats (right).

Figure 3.3 Sources of dietary fiber: the seeds and cell walls of fruits, such as raspberries, and in cereal grains, vegetables, beans, peas, lentils and chickpeas.

cholesterol a fatty substance found in foods derived from animal products and in the human body; it has been linked to heart disease

provides energy as well as minerals, vitamins and fiber. The simple carbohydrates found in foods that are high in added sugar, such as candy, cookies and sweetened soft drinks as well as in refined flour, provide empty calories. Consuming them in excess may contribute to weight gain.

Dietary fiber, which generally comes from the seeds and cell walls of fruits, vegetables and cereal grains, also plays an important role in health. See Figure 3.3. There are two types of fiber: **soluble** and **insoluble**. Fiber-containing foods are usually composed of both kinds, with one kind predominating. Fiber is a unique carbohydrate because humans cannot digest fiber, so they do not derive calories from it. Because the body cannot digest dietary fiber, it passes through the digestive system almost completely unchanged. This helps keep the digestive tract running smoothly. Insoluble fiber, such as that found in certain fruits and vegetables and whole grains, encourages proper elimination of waste products from the large intestines and helps prevent some forms of gastrointestinal distress. Soluble fiber, which forms a gel-type substance in the digestive tract, reduces serum **cholesterol** by helping to remove the cholesterol from the body, thereby lessening the risk for heart disease.

Whole grains are considered good sources of dietary fiber. Unfortunately what constitutes a whole grain is often misunderstood. Whole grains retain their bran, endosperm and germ. According to the Food and Drug Administration (FDA), in order to be labeled *whole grain*, a product must be composed of at least 51 percent whole grain by weight. The grain may be cracked, flaked or ground. Whole wheat, oatmeal, whole-grain cornmeal, brown rice, whole-grain barley, whole rye and buckwheat are whole-grain foods. See Figure 3.4. Foods labeled with the words *multigrain, stone-ground, 100% wheat, cracked wheat, seven-grain,* or *bran* are not necessarily whole-grain products. Color does not indicate a product's whole-grain content. Read the ingredient list to determine whether a product is indeed made with whole-grain ingredients.

Lipids

Fats and cholesterol are lipids. See Figure 3.5. Fats are found in both animal and plant foods, although fruits, vegetables and grains contain very little fat. Fats provide calories; pure fat provides more than twice as many calories by weight as carbohydrates or protein. Fats help our bodies process certain vitamins (called fat-soluble vitamins) and give food a creamy, pleasant mouth feel. A healthy diet contains a moderate amount of fat; in fact some forms of fat are considered essential.

Cholesterol, also a lipid, is found only in foods of animal origin, such as beef, pork, poultry, eggs, dairy products and fish. Cholesterol is not considered an essential nutrient, however, it is important to many body functions. It is not necessary to eat foods containing cholesterol because the body can manufacture all it needs from the fat in a normal healthy diet.

The fats in foods are classified as saturated or **unsaturated** (whether monounsaturated or polyunsaturated), depending on their structure. **Saturated fats** are found mainly in animal products such as milk, eggs and meats, as well as in tropical oils such

unsaturated fat fats with one (mono) or more (poly) double bonds, which eliminate hydrogen atoms from the molecule; found in plants and plant foods such as avocados, corn, cottonseed, olives, rapeseed (canola), safflower and sunflower, as well as fatty fish; liquid at room temperature

saturated fat fats found mainly in animal products, such as milk, butter, cheese, eggs and meat, as well as in tropical oils, such as coconut and palm; usually solid at room temperature. Research suggests that diets high in saturated fat may be linked to heart disease, obesity and certain forms of cancer.

as coconut and palm. **Monounsaturated fats** come primarily from plants and plant foods such as avocados and olives and the oils made from them. **Polyunsaturated fats** are found in plants (e.g., soy and corn) and fatty fish. Vegetable oils, such as rapeseed (canola) and olive, are high in monounsaturated fat. Cottonseed, sunflower, corn and safflower oils are high in polyunsaturated fat. All oils, however, are a combination of the three kinds of fat, and all vegetable oils are cholesterol-free because cholesterol is not found in plants.

Saturated fats such as butter, lard and other animal fats are usually solid at room temperature. Monounsaturated and polyunsaturated fats are usually soft or liquid at room temperature. Hydrogenation is a process by which a liquid fat is made more solid (or saturated) by the addition of hydrogen atoms. Hydrogenation also reduces the tendency to rancidity, thus increasing shelf life. Because the process results in these positive properties, **hydrogenated fats** have been widely used in the food manufacturing industry.

Unfortunately the hydrogenation process also results in the formation of unsaturated fatty acids called **trans fats**. The FDA has banned the use of artificial trans fats in processed food. (Natural trans fats occur in butter, cheese, milk and other animal products.) The food service industry has until 2018 to comply. Food manufacturers have eliminated trans fats in most widely produced products. Lower-trans-fat cooking oil is now standard at fast-food restaurants, and cities such as New York and Philadelphia have banned the use of artificial trans fats in restaurants.

Research suggests that high-fat diets, especially diets high in saturated fat and trans fats, are linked to heart disease, obesity and certain forms of cancer. Saturated fats are also linked to high levels of blood cholesterol, which is associated with arteriosclerosis (hardening of the arteries). The combination of a diet high in saturated fat and a diet high in dietary cholesterol may increase the risk of heart disease.

Figure 3.5 Some sources of lipids in the diet: butter, cheese and other dairy products, lard, vegetable oil and olive oil.

Proteins

Proteins are found in both animal and plant foods. See Figures 3.6 and 3.7. Protein chains consist of **amino acids**, the building blocks of protein. There are 20 amino acids, nine of which are essential for healthy adults but are not produced by the human body. People need to consume these essential amino acids in the form of protein-rich foods. Proteins are necessary for manufacturing, maintaining and repairing body tissues. They are essential for the periodic replacement of the outer layer of skin as well as for blood

Figure 3.6 Sources of protein in the diet: meat, poultry, fish, beans, legumes, eggs and grains.

hydrogenated fat unsaturated, liquid fats that are chemically altered to remain solid at room temperature, such as solid shortening or margarine

trans fats a type of fat created when vegetable oils are solidified through hydrogenation

Figure 3.7 Non-animal sources of protein in the diet: beans, grains, legumes, nuts and seeds.

clotting and scar tissue formation. Hair and nails, which provide a protective cover for the body, are composed of proteins. One special type of protein, known as **enzymes**, performs functions within cells such as assisting in the breakdown of foods to make them digestible. People who eat a varied diet with adequate calories and protein can easily get all the essential amino acids even if they do not eat any animal foods.

Vitamins

metabolism all the chemical reactions and physical processes that occur continuously in living cells and organisms

Vitamins are essential dietary substances needed for regulation of **metabolism** and for normal growth and body functions. They are noncaloric and needed in the body in small amounts.

There are 13 vitamins divided into two categories: **fat-soluble** and **water-soluble**. See Table 3.3. The fat-soluble vitamins are A, D, E and K and are found in foods containing fat. Excess supplies of these vitamins may be stored in the body in fatty tissues and the liver. Water-soluble vitamins are vitamin C and the B-complex vitamins, including thiamine (B_1), riboflavin (B_2), niacin (B_3), B_{12}, B_6, pantothenic acid, biotin and folate. Water-soluble vitamins are not stored in the body to the extent that fat-soluble vitamins are, and excesses may be excreted in the urine. Because of these differences, deficiencies in water-soluble vitamins develop more rapidly when intake is not sufficient.

Virtually all foods contain some vitamins. Nuts, such as almonds, hazelnuts and peanuts, and sunflower seeds are excellent sources of Vitamin E, for example. In addition to citrus fruits, broccoli, Brussels sprouts, papayas and red bell peppers are good sources of Vitamin C. Many factors contribute to a particular food's vitamin concentration. An animal's feed; the manner in which produce is harvested, stored or processed; and even the type of soil, sunlight, rainfall and temperature have significant effects on a food's vitamin content. For example, tomatoes have a higher concentration of vitamin C when picked ripe from the vine than when picked green. Furthermore different varieties of fruits and vegetables have different vitamin contents. A Wegener apple, for example, has 19 milligrams of vitamin C, whereas a Red Delicious has only 6 milligrams. Because freshness has an impact on vitamin retention, many chefs prioritize purchasing **organically farmed**, locally-grown ingredients and storing them properly.

organic farming a method of farming that does not rely on synthetic pesticides, fungicides, herbicides or fertilizers; organic practices require that animals have access to outdoors, sunlight and clean water and that they are raised without antibiotics and hormones on organically grown feed.

In cooking, the chef can control vitamin concentration and retention through careful food preparation:

- Prepare vegetables as close to service time as possible; vegetables that are peeled or cut in advance lose more vitamins than those cut immediately before cooking.

- Whether a vegetable is boiled, steamed or microwaved impacts the amount of vitamins it retains. Because the B-complex vitamins and vitamin C are water-soluble, they are easily leached (washed out) or destroyed by food processing and preparation techniques involving high temperatures and water. Steaming and microwaving help retain nutrients (when steaming, keep the water level below the vegetables).

- In general, roasting and grilling meats, poultry, fish and shellfish preserve more vitamins than stewing and braising. The temperatures to which foods are cooked and the length of time they are cooked may affect vitamin retention as well.

- Storage affects vitamin concentrations. For example, long exposure to air may destroy vitamin C. Using airtight containers prevents some of this loss. Vitamin C is also lost when fruits or vegetables become shriveled from water loss during long or improper storage. Riboflavin is sensitive to light, so milk products (which are good sources of riboflavin) should be stored in opaque containers.

Cooking does not always make a food less nutritious. Cooking, besides making the food more palatable in many cases, can help make foods more digestible, thereby making nutritious substances in the food more readily available to the body. Heating foods to appropriate temperatures also makes them safer to eat by destroying harmful bacteria.

VITAMINS: THEIR FUNCTIONS, SOURCES AND TECHNIQUES FOR RETAINING MAXIMUM NUTRIENT CONTENT

TABLE 3.3

VITAMIN	KNOWN FUNCTIONS IN THE HUMAN BODY	SOURCES	TECHNIQUES FOR NUTRIENT RETENTION
Fat Soluble			
Vitamin A	Keeps skin healthy; protects eyes; protects mouth and nose linings; supports immune functioning	Deep yellow and orange vegetables, leafy green vegetables, deep orange fruits, egg yolks, liver, fortified milk	Serve fruits and vegetables raw or lightly cooked; store vegetables covered and refrigerated; steam vegetables; roast or broil meats
Vitamin D	Helps body absorb calcium; regulates calcium and phosphorus in the bones; assists bone mineralization	Fortified milk, butter, some fish oils, egg yolks (exposure to sunlight produces vitamin D in the body)	Stable when heated and insoluble in water, therefore unaffected by cooking
Vitamin E	Antioxidant; protects membranes and cell walls	Vegetable oils, whole grains, dark leafy vegetables, wheat germ, nuts, seeds, whole grains	Use whole-grain flours; store foods in airtight containers; avoid exposing food to light and air
Vitamin K	Assists blood-clotting	Liver, dark green leafy vegetables (bacteria in the intestinal tract also produce some vitamin K)	Steam or microwave vegetables; do not overcook meats
Water Soluble			
Vitamin C (ascorbic acid)	Supports immune system functioning; repairs connective tissues; promotes healing; assists amino acid metabolism	Citrus fruits, green vegetables, strawberries, cantaloupes, tomatoes, broccoli, potatoes	Serve fruits and vegetables raw; steam or microwave vegetables
Thiamine (vitamin B_1)	Assists energy metabolism; supports nervous system functioning	Meats (especially pork), legumes, whole grains	Use enriched or whole-grain pasta or rice; do not wash whole grains before cooking or rinse afterward; steam or microwave vegetables; roast meats at moderate temperatures; do not overcook meats
Riboflavin (vitamin B_2)	Assists energy metabolism	Milk, cheese, yogurt, fish, enriched grain breads and cereals, dark green leafy vegetables	Store foods in opaque containers; roast or broil meats or poultry
Niacin (vitamin B_3)	Promotes normal digestion; supports nervous system functioning; assists energy metabolism	Meats, poultry, fish, dark green leafy vegetables, whole-grain or enriched breads and cereals, nuts	Steam or microwave vegetables; roast or broil beef, veal, lamb and poultry (pork retains about the same amount of niacin regardless of cooking method)
Vitamin B_6	Necessary for protein metabolism and red blood cell formation	Meats, fish, poultry, shellfish, whole grains, dark green vegetables, potatoes, liver	Serve vegetables raw; cook foods in the least amount of water possible and for the shortest possible time; roast or broil meats, poultry and fish
Vitamin B_{12}	Helps produce red blood cells; assists metabolism	Animal foods only, particularly milk, eggs, poultry, fish	Roast or broil meats, poultry and fish
Folate	Necessary for protein metabolism and red blood cell formation	Orange juice, dark green leafy vegetables, organ meats, legumes, seeds	Serve vegetables raw or steam or microwave for the shortest possible time; store vegetables covered and refrigerated
Biotin	Assists energy metabolism, glycogen synthesis and fat metabolism	Widespread in various foods; deficiency is unlikely	Serve fruits and vegetables raw or cooked in the least amount of water possible
Pantothenic acid	Assists energy metabolism	Widespread in various foods; deficiency is unlikely	

Healing Foods

Those who first think of food as a pleasurable experience may be averse to also thinking of it as medicine or having curative powers, yet there is scientific evidence to support that idea. Interestingly, scientific findings suggest that positive benefits may be derived from many foods considered to be potentially harmful to the body. The findings, although preliminary, hold out some hope for those who do not want to give up the pleasures of the table. Some of the findings include the following:

Avocados, although very high in fat, are good sources of antioxidants.

Beer consumption may increase bone density.

Dark chocolate contains antioxidants that may be beneficial in preventing heart disease.

Coffee may offer some beneficial effects in reducing the risk of cancer and diabetes.

Eggs are a source of lutein, a phytochemical implicated in reducing the incidence of degenerative eye diseases.

Drinking red wine may reduce the incidence of heart disease.

Avocados

flavonoids plant pigments that dissolve readily in water; they are found in red, purple and white vegetables such as blueberries, red cabbage, onions and tea

Figure 3.8 Sources of calcium in the diet: dark leafy greens, such as escarole, spinach and broccoli, as well as dairy and soy products, canned fish and almonds.

Minerals

Our bodies cannot produce minerals. We obtain minerals by eating plants that have drawn minerals from the ground or by eating the flesh of animals that have consumed such plants. See Figure 3.8. Minerals are a critical component in hard and soft tissues. For example, calcium, magnesium and phosphorus are minerals that are present in bones and teeth. Minerals also regulate certain necessary body functions. Nerve impulses, for example, are transmitted through an exchange of sodium and potassium ions in the nerve cells.

Minerals are divided into two categories: **major minerals** and **trace minerals**. See Table 3.4. Major minerals, such as calcium, are needed in relatively larger quantities. Trace minerals, such as iron, are needed in only very small amounts. As with vitamins, food processing and preparation can reduce a food's mineral content. Soaking or cooking in large amounts of water can leach out small quantities of water-soluble minerals. Processing or refining grains, such as the wheat used to make white flour, also removes important minerals.

Water

The human body is approximately 60 percent water. Water is necessary for transporting nutrients and waste throughout the body. It cushions the cells, lubricates the joints, maintains stable body temperatures and assists in waste elimination. Water also promotes functioning of the nervous system and muscles. Indeed virtually every process of the human body uses water. Although the principal sources of water are beverages, water is also the predominant nutrient by weight in most foods. Some foods such as tomatoes, oranges, watermelon and iceberg lettuce are particularly high in water. Others such as dried fruits, nuts and seeds are lower, but even dried fruits and foods such as chicken and bread still contain some water. The body produces water when other nutrients are metabolized for energy.

Phytochemicals

Scientific research has identified nonnutritive components of plant foods called **phytochemicals**, which may be important in preventing some forms of cancer, diabetes, Alzheimer's disease, heart disease and other degenerative diseases and slowing down the aging process. More than 900 of these chemicals have been identified, including phytoestrogens, carotenoids and flavonoids. The health benefits of these substances appear to depend on consumption of a varied diet that includes plenty of grains, fruits and vegetables. The importance of phytochemicals to human health and well-being should not be minimized even though they do not constitute a nutrient category. Phytochemicals such as **flavonoids** and other compounds found in blueberries, pomegranates, green tea and cooked tomato products may act as **antioxidants** in the body to help eliminate **free radicals** (unstable, potentially harmful substances produced naturally in the body during metabolism). See Figure 3.9.

MINERALS: THEIR FUNCTIONS AND SOURCES   TABLE 3.4

MINERAL	KNOWN FUNCTIONS IN THE HUMAN BODY	SOURCES
Major Minerals		
Calcium	Helps build bones and teeth; helps blood clot; promotes muscle and nerve functions	Dairy products, canned salmon and sardines, broccoli, kale, tofu, turnips
Magnesium	Muscle contraction; assists energy metabolism, bone formation	Green leafy vegetables, whole grains, legumes, fish, shellfish, cocoa, fruit
Phosphorus	Helps build bones and teeth; assists energy metabolism; formation of DNA	All animal tissues, milk, legumes, nuts
Potassium	Maintains electrolyte and fluid balance; promotes normal body functions; assists protein metabolism	Meats, poultry, fish, fruits (especially bananas, oranges, cantaloupes), legumes, vegetables
Sodium	Maintains normal fluid balance; necessary for nerve impulse transmission	Salt, soy sauce, processed foods, MSG
Chloride	With sodium, involved in fluid balance; a component of stomach acid	Salt, soy sauce, meats, milk, processed foods
Sulfur	A component of some proteins, insulin and the vitamins biotin and thiamine	All protein-containing foods
Trace Minerals		
Iron	Part of hemoglobin (the red substance in blood that carries oxygen); prevents anemia	Liver, meats, shellfish, enriched breads and cereals, legumes
Zinc	A component of insulin; enhances healing; a component of many enzymes; involved in taste perception; bone formation	Protein foods, whole-grain breads and cereals, fish, shellfish, poultry, vegetables
Selenium	Antioxidant	Fish, shellfish, meats, eggs, grains (depends on soil conditions)
Iodine	Involved in thyroid function	Iodized salt, fish, shellfish, bread, plants grown in iodine-rich soil
Copper	Facilitates iron absorption; part of enzymes	Meats, fish, shellfish, nuts, seeds
Fluoride	Necessary for bone and teeth formation; helps teeth resist tooth decay	Fluoridated drinking water, fish, shellfish
Chromium	Involved in insulin regulation	Liver, whole grains, brewer's yeast, nuts, oils
Molybdenum	Assists in metabolism	Legumes, cereals
Manganese	Assists in metabolism	Whole grains, nuts, organ meats
Cobalt	Component of vitamin B_{12} (cobalamin)	Liver, shellfish, lean beef, seafood, eggs, dairy, poultry, fermented soybeans (miso)

Figure 3.9 The phytochemicals called flavonoids in intensely colored fruits and vegetables such as blueberries and pomegranates may reduce the potential for developing debilitating diseases.

TOOLS FOR HEALTHY EATING

A nutritious diet is an important component of a healthy lifestyle. Eating well and exercising, getting adequate sleep and living moderately all can contribute to a longer, healthier life. Diet and lifestyle planning is made simpler with recommendations from organizations such as the American Heart Association, the American Cancer Society, the U.S. Department of Agriculture (USDA), the U.S. Food and Drug Administration (FDA) and the U.S. Department of Health and Human Services (HHS), to name a few. These organizations stress the importance of controlling the amount and type of fat in the diet; consuming plant foods, such as vegetables, fruits and whole grains, in greater quantities; and moderating the amount of salt, sugar and alcohol consumed.

Daily Calorie Requirements

Most adults need approximately 1800–2500 calories each day to maintain weight. To lose one pound of body weight per week, calorie intake should be reduced by approximately 500 calories per day.

Here are the nutrients needed per day for weight maintenance:

Calories	1800–2500
Fat	60–80 g
Protein	70–100 g
Carbohydrate	250–375 g
Sodium	Less than 2300 mg
Cholesterol	Less than 300 mg
Fiber	25–30 g

A typical calorie breakdown might look like this:

Breakfast	400–600 calories
Lunch	500–700 calories
Dinner	700–1000 calories
Snacks	Max. 200 calories per day

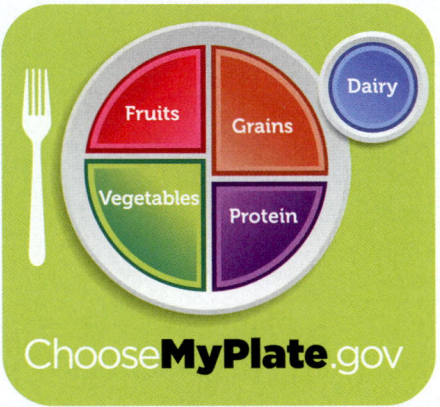

Figure 3.10 MyPlate food guidance system.

Figure 3.11 Dietary guidelines recommend obtaining half on one's daily calories from whole fruits and vegetables.

Dietary Guidelines for Americans

One useful diet planning tool is the Dietary Guidelines for Americans, jointly published every 5 years by the USDA and HHS. The *2015–2020 Dietary Guidelines for Americans* emphasizes adopting healthy eating habits to prevent chronic diseases. The combination of foods that one eats are called "eating patterns," which can adapt to one's lifestyle, cultural traditions, income level and flavor preferences. The most recent dietary guidelines take into account different eating patterns based on ethnicity and personal taste.

The *2015–2020 Dietary Guidelines for Americans* emphasizes five major goals for Americans:

1 Follow a healthy eating pattern that helps maintain a healthy body weight, reduces risk of disease and supports your nutritional needs throughout your life.

2 Consume a variety of nutrient-dense foods from all food groups including fruits, vegetables, whole grains, fat-free and low-fat dairy products, oils, lean meats and other protein-rich foods. Eat fruits, especially whole, unprocessed ones. Eat a variety of vegetables, from all groups: dark green, red and orange vegetables and beans and peas. Eat grains, half of which should be whole grains. Choose proteins from a variety of sources, including seafood, lean meat and poultry, eggs, beans and peas, soy products, and unsalted nuts and seeds.

3 Restrict the calories you consume from foods and beverages that contain sodium (salt), saturated fats, trans fats and added sugars.

4 Make healthy food and beverage choices taking into consideration your personal preferences. Make nutrient-dense foods and beverages the main part of your diet.

5 Maintain a healthy eating pattern at all times and help support others to do the same.

The guidelines also encourage everyone to participate in regular physical activity as outlined in the *Physical Activity Guidelines*, released by the HHS.

MyPlate

MyPlate is an educational tool developed by the Center for Nutrition Policy and Promotion (CNPP), an organization of the USDA. The MyPlate food guidance system is designed to promote the healthy eating recommendations from the *2015–2020 Dietary Guidelines for Americans*. MyPlate uses the familiar image of a dinner plate to illustrate the five food groups considered the building blocks for a healthy diet: fruits, vegetables, grains, protein and dairy. See Figure 3.10. Half of a plate of food should consist of fruit and vegetables, the other half grains and proteins. See Figure 3.11. Dairy is represented as a smaller circle. The MyPlate guidance system encourages consumers to choose unprocessed, whole fruits and vegetables, whole grains and low fat dairy products. It recommends that consumers vary the vegetables they eat and the sources of protein in their diets, and it recommends that consumers reduce the amount of sodium, saturated fats and added sugar in their diets. An interactive website helps consumers select foods and includes a diet and physical activity tracking program.

Nutrition Labeling

In an effort to provide consumers with greater information about the nutritional values of foods they purchase, the FDA requires that most food products be clearly labeled. All packaged food products must include the Nutrition Facts label. See Figure 3.12.

The FDA closely regulates the language used on all food labels. Terms such as *low fat*, *lite*, or *a good source of* have specific legal definitions. The FDA also closely monitors health claims on food labels. A breakfast cereal, for instance, may claim that its fiber content may reduce the incidence of heart disease only if it meets the criteria set forth by the FDA. The FDA has approved a number of qualified health claims that may legally be used on food labels and in the advertising of certain foods. One example of a qualified health claim that is acceptable concerns nuts: "Scientific evidence suggests, but does not prove, that eating 1.5 ounces per day of some nuts, as part of a diet low in saturated fat and cholesterol, may reduce the risk of heart disease."

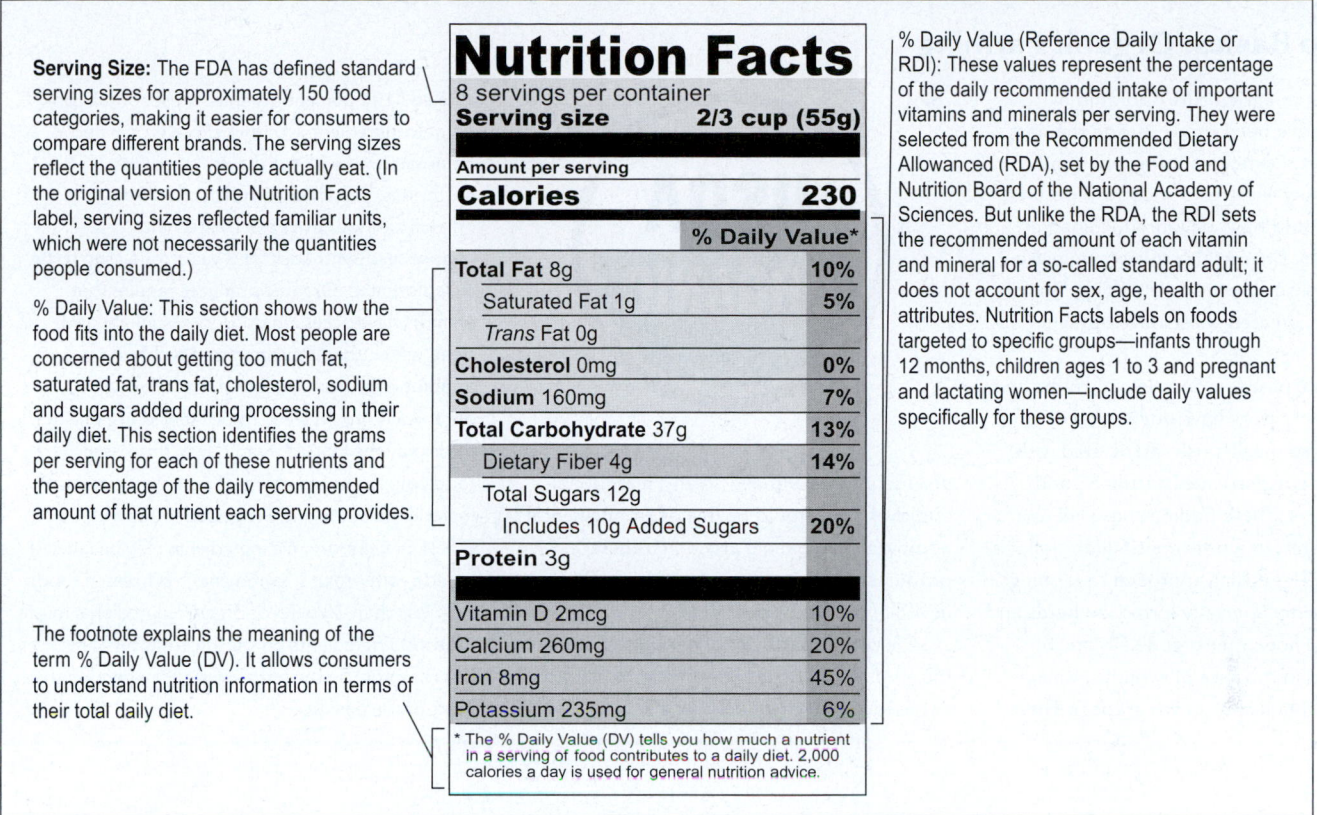

Serving Size: The FDA has defined standard serving sizes for approximately 150 food categories, making it easier for consumers to compare different brands. The serving sizes reflect the quantities people actually eat. (In the original version of the Nutrition Facts label, serving sizes reflected familiar units, which were not necessarily the quantities people consumed.)

% Daily Value: This section shows how the food fits into the daily diet. Most people are concerned about getting too much fat, saturated fat, trans fat, cholesterol, sodium and sugars added during processing in their daily diet. This section identifies the grams per serving for each of these nutrients and the percentage of the daily recommended amount of that nutrient each serving provides.

The footnote explains the meaning of the term % Daily Value (DV). It allows consumers to understand nutrition information in terms of their total daily diet.

% Daily Value (Reference Daily Intake or RDI): These values represent the percentage of the daily recommended intake of important vitamins and minerals per serving. They were selected from the Recommended Dietary Allowanced (RDA), set by the Food and Nutrition Board of the National Academy of Sciences. But unlike the RDA, the RDI sets the recommended amount of each vitamin and mineral for a so-called standard adult; it does not account for sex, age, health or other attributes. Nutrition Facts labels on foods targeted to specific groups—infants through 12 months, children ages 1 to 3 and pregnant and lactating women—include daily values specifically for these groups.

Figure 3.12 Nutrition Facts label. (The label illustrated reflects changes that take effect in 2018.)

The FDA sets standards for the nutrition claims that can be made on restaurant menus too. The language for menus is the same as that for product labels. Restaurateurs, however, are required to supply nutrition information only if they make a claim about a specific dish. (Some jurisdictions such as New York City require that nutritional information be supplied when a restaurant is part of a group of 15 or more restaurants bearing the same name.) For example, if a menu selection is described as "low fat," the dish must have 3 grams or less of fat per serving and the nutrition information (nutrient analysis) must be available to anyone who requests it.

Menu Labeling

Numerous health experts believe that menu labeling will promote better health and help stop the spread of obesity. A provision of the Affordable Care Act of 2010 requires that restaurants or similar retail food establishments with 20 or more locations doing business under the same name list calories on their menus. The regulations require that calories be listed on menus, menu boards and packaged foods on display. For self-service foods, such as a salad bar, calories must be listed per serving or per item on a sign next to the food. Menus are also required to contain the following statement concerning suggested daily caloric intake: "A 2,000-calorie diet is used as the basis for general nutrition advice; however, individual calorie needs may vary." In addition, nutritional information for standard menus must be available to patrons in written form. Many states and cities have already enacted similar laws and many chain restaurants currently comply.

Government Oversight

In addition to helping consumers follow healthy eating patterns, the federal government plays an important role in the way various foodstuffs are grown, raised, slaughtered, processed, marketed, stored and transported. The principal agencies are the **Food and Drug Administration (FDA)** of the **U.S. Department of Health and Human Services (HHS)** and the **U.S. Department of Agriculture (USDA)**.

Back to Basics: Organic Farming

Great strides in agriculture and animal husbandry have been made during the past two centuries. Pesticides, fungicides and herbicides now eliminate or control pests that once would have devoured, ruined or choked crops. Chemical fertilizers increase yields of many of the world's staples. But not everyone has greeted these developments with open arms.

During the past few decades, scientific and medical investigators have documented, or at least suggested, health risks associated with certain synthetic pesticides, fertilizers and other products. These findings have led to a renewed interest in a now multibillion-dollar-a-year back-to-the-basics approach to farming: organic farming. Specialty farms, orchards and even wineries now offer organically grown products (or, in the case of wineries, wines made from organically grown grapes). These

products come with few, if any, intentional additives and should be free of any incidental additives. Proponents argue that these products are better for you and better for the health of the farm workers.

The U.S. Department of Agriculture regulates the production and labeling of organically grown or raised foods. It requires that any natural food

labeled "100 percent organic" must contain only organic ingredients—that is, those grown and manufactured without the use of added hormones, pesticides, synthetic fertilizers, and so on; soil cannot have been treated with unapproved synthetics for 3 years for a crop to be called organic. Organic practices require that animals have access to outdoors, sunlight and clean water, that they are raised without antibiotics or hormones and that they eat organically grown feed. To be labeled organic or to display the USDA organic seal, processed foods must contain at least 95 percent organic ingredients by weight. Processed foods with 70–95 percent organic ingredients may be labeled "made with organic ingredients"; processed foods with less than 70 percent organic ingredients may list those ingredients on the information panel but may not use the term *organic* anywhere on the front of the package.

The FDA's activities are directed toward protecting the nation's health against impure and unsafe foods, as well as drugs, cosmetics, medical devices and other things. It develops and administers programs addressing food safety. For example, the FDA must approve any new food additive before a manufacturer markets the additive to food producers and processors. The FDA also sets standards for labeling foods, including nutrition labels. Labeling regulations not only address the type of information that must be conveyed, but also the way it is presented.

The USDA's principal responsibility is to make sure that individual food items are safe, wholesome and accurately labeled. It attempts to meet these responsibilities through inspection and grading procedures. For example, the U.S. Department of Agriculture regulates the production and labeling of organically grown or raised foods. The USDA also provides consumer services. It conducts and publishes research on nutrition and assists those producing our food to do so efficiently and effectively.

Other federal agencies that have a role in the nation's health and food supply include the U.S. Centers for Disease Control and Prevention (CDC), which tracks illnesses, including those caused by food-borne pathogens; the National Institutes of Health (NIH), which does basic biological and nutritional research; and the U.S. Department of the Interior (DOI), which sets environmental and land-use standards.

NUTRITION, EATING OUT AND THE CHEF

On a typical day, almost half of all American adults eat at least one meal in a food service establishment. Portion size and menu choices offered by many restaurants have been blamed for the epidemic of obesity in this country. Restaurant meals typically have more calories, sodium, fat and cholesterol but less fiber, vitamins and minerals than meals prepared at home. Studies have found that people who eat out most often tend to weigh more than those who usually eat at home.

Many Americans follow eating patterns specifically designed to reduce body weight and/or prevent disease states associated with excess body weight. Consequently, chefs may be called on to make modifications to the dishes they serve. Patrons concerned with calories and fat may choose to order appetizers in place of entrées to control quantity and thereby reduce calories and fat. They may request half-orders or split a full order with a companion. They may ask that dressings and sauces be served on the side or that a different cooking method be used—for instance, that a fish be broiled or baked instead of deep-fried or sautéed. Consumers who are concerned about ingredient allergies may ask for detailed information on how a dish is prepared. Waiters, cooks and other food service workers should take guests' inquiries seriously. Failure to do so could result in severe illness or death. Chefs and restaurateurs should be flexible and willing to accommodate these patrons. Throughout this book, we feature preparation techniques and recipes that can be adapted for special requests. In Chapter 24, Healthy Cooking and Special Diets, you will find procedures for cooking for gluten-free, vegan, vegetarian and other special eating patterns.

Healthful Cooking Techniques

Healthful cooking is based on the same principle employed in any fine professional kitchen: Cook quality ingredients skillfully using sound cooking techniques. Vegetables, fruits, whole grains, beans, nuts and seeds, fish and seafood, lean meats, healthful oils and low-fat dairy products are the key ingredients of a healthful menu. Fruits, vegetables and whole grains are rich in vitamins, minerals, phytochemicals and fiber, and they are relatively low in calories, fat and sodium. See Figure 3.13. As the health recommendations suggests, meat need not always be at the center of the plate. The MyPlate guidance system strongly suggests that a variety of breads, pasta and grains be included on the menu along with an interesting selection of vegetable dishes, and it cautions against the use of too much fat and sugar.

Crafting a healthy menu can begin with the health recommendations discussed in the previous section of this chapter. Often existing menu items already offer a healthy balance between portion size, ingredient selection and cooking techniques. For example, pasta with marinara sauce may be healthful as long as the serving size conforms to the portion size recommended by MyPlate and the *Dietary Guidelines for Americans*. Choose recipes that emphasize healthful ingredients. Look for those that contain beans, whole grains, vegetables, fruits, lean meats, poultry or fish. Select dishes that feature healthful cooking techniques such as poaching, steaming, broiling, grilling or roasting.

Important guidelines for preparing healthy meals and menus include the following:

- Start with fresh, minimally processed ingredients.
- Use proper purchasing and storage techniques in order to preserve nutrients.
- Offer a variety of foods so that customers have a choice.
- Offer entrées that feature healthful ingredients such as whole grains, vegetables, fruits, lean meats or poultry, fish, low-fat dairy products and vegetable oils. Emphasize plant instead of animal foods.
- Use minimal amounts of fat, only the amount that is necessary to provide flavor and texture. Choose healthful fats such as olive oil, canola oil, nut oils and the fat

Figure 3.13 Fruits are sources of dietary fiber, carbohydrates, vitamin A, vitamin C, folate, potassium and magnesium.

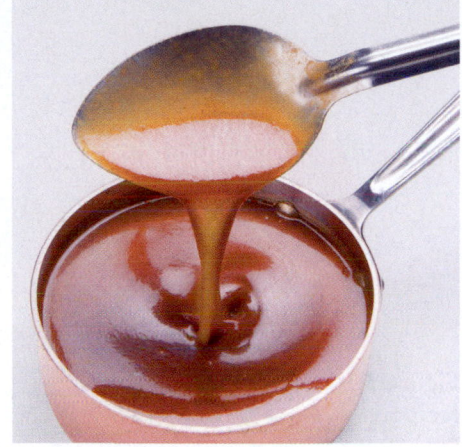

Intensely-flavored sauces made without fats or starches are healthier alternatives to traditional sauces.

A white bean salad with fresh vegetables and cheese provides a good balance of nutrient-dense foods.

Steaming is a healthy cooking method that does not require added fat.

Fresh fruit salad is a healthy dessert option.

from avocados when possible. Minimize the use of saturated fats such as butter and cheese.

- Keep sauces light in calories and fat. Intensify the flavor of sauces so that less sauce is required to add a memorable taste to a dish.
- Use cooking procedures that remove or avoid the use of fat (e.g., stocks, sauces and soups can be cooled and the congealed fats removed; foods can be browned in the oven instead of being sautéed in hot fat). Use equipment that minimizes the need to use added fat (e.g., non-stick pans).
- Use minimal amounts of added sugar and salt. Limit the amount of sodium from other sources such as soy sauce or prepared flavorings.
- Offer a selection of desserts that incorporate fresh fruit.
- Select cooking techniques that build flavor without using fat such as roasting, grilling, baking, poaching and steaming.
- Cook all foods with care to preserve their nutritional value, flavor, texture and visual appeal.
- Serve appropriately-sized portions.
- Train wait staff to respond properly to nutritional questions diners may have about menu items.

Nutritional Analysis of Recipes

Throughout this book various recipes are marked with the symbol illustrated in Figure 3.14. This symbol identifies dishes that are particularly low in calories, fat, saturated fat or sodium. These dishes may also be a good source of vitamins, protein, fiber or calcium that are indicated in the nutritional information.

A registered dietitian has analyzed all of the recipes in this book using nutritional analysis software that incorporates data from the USDA, research laboratories and food manufacturers. The nutrient information provided here should be used only as a reference, however. A margin of error of approximately 20 percent can be expected because of natural variations in ingredients; the federal government permits food manufacturers and other suppliers to use this same margin of error in their food labeling efforts. Preparation techniques and serving sizes may also significantly alter the values of many nutrients. For the nutritional analysis, if a recipe offers a choice of ingredients, the first-mentioned ingredient was the one used. Ingredients listed as "to taste" (TT) and "as needed" were omitted from the analysis. Corn oil and whole milk were used throughout for "vegetable oil" and "milk," respectively. When given a range of ingredient quantities or numbers of servings, the average was used.

Figure 3.14 Symbol for a healthy recipe.

QUESTIONS FOR DISCUSSION

1 Identify the six categories of nutrients and list two sources for each.

2 What are the differences between saturated fats and unsaturated fats? Identify two sources for each.

3 Identify three sources of empty calories and explain the meaning of that term.

4 List four ways to reduce mineral and vitamin loss when storing or preparing foods.

5 Describe the key messages in the *2015–2020 Dietary Guidelines for Americans*.

6 Describe the MyPlate guidance system. Explain how a chef can use it to plan well-balanced meals and how a consumer can use it to establish a healthful diet. What other diet-planning tools can be used along with MyPlate?

7 Consult the nutritional information panel on a jar of prepared mayonnaise or salad dressing. Compare this with the nutritional information provided with a similar recipe in this book. Discuss the differences.

8 Create a three-course dinner following the health guidelines discussed in this chapter. Discuss the ways you might use or adapt recipes in this book to conform to these guidelines.

Menus and Recipes

4

After studying this chapter, you will be able to:

▶ compare and contrast different types and styles of menus

▶ explain the purpose of standardized recipes

▶ use and write standardized recipes

▶ measure correctly and convert from one measurement system to another

▶ convert recipe yield and portion size amounts

▶ calculate unit costs, recipe costs and selling prices

▶ explain the need for and describe best practices for cost controls in food service operations

▶ describe the elements of a recipe for publication and the process for producing a recipe for publication

entrée the main dish of a meal in the United States and Canada, usually meat, poultry, fish or shellfish accompanied by a vegetable and starch; in France, the term entrée refers to the first course, served before the fish and meat courses

Professional chefs must master more than the basics of béchamel, butchering and bread baking. They must be equally skilled in the business of food services. They must know what ingredients cost and how to control and maintain food costs. They must also understand how accurate measurements, portion control and proper food handling directly affect the food service operation's bottom line. This chapter introduces various types and styles of menus. It explains a standardized recipe format and presents information on measurements and techniques for changing or converting recipe yields. It describes methods for determining unit and recipe costs and concludes with a discussion of methods for controlling food costs.

THE MENU

Whether it lists Spanish dishes, hamburgers, just desserts or classic cuisine and whether the prices are inexpensive or exorbitant, the menu is the soul of every food service operation. The purposes of the menu are to identify for the consumer the foods and beverages the operation offers and to create consumer enthusiasm and to increase sales. When combined with good food and good service, a good menu helps ensure success.

Most menus offer diners sufficient selections to build an entire meal. A typical meal in the United States and Canada consists of three courses, which are served in sequence one at a time. The first course is usually a hot or cold appetizer, soup or a small salad. The second course is the **entrée** or main dish, usually meat, poultry, fish or shellfish accompanied by a vegetable and starch. The third course is dessert, either a sweet preparation or fruit and cheese. For a more formal meal, there may be a progression of first courses, including a hot or cold appetizer and soup, as well as a fish course served before the main dish (which, in this case, is not fish). For a meal served in the European tradition, the salad would be presented as a palate cleanser after the main dish and before the dessert.

Types of Menus

Menus are classified according to the regularity with which the foods are offered:

Static or fixed menu: All patrons are offered the same foods every day. Once a static menu is developed and established, it rarely changes. Static menus are typically found in fast-food operations, restaurants serving the cuisines of local immigrant populations and steakhouses. Static menus can also be used in institutional settings. For example, a static menu at an elementary school could offer students, along with a vegetable and dessert, the same luncheon choices every school day: a cheeseburger, fish sticks, chicken tacos, pizza slices or a sandwich.

Cycle menu: A cycle menu is developed for a set period; at the end of that period it repeats itself. For example, on a seven-day cycle, the same menu is used every Monday. Some cycle menus are written on a seasonal basis, with a new menu for each season to take advantage of product availability. Cycle menus are used commonly in schools, hospitals, summer camps, on cruise ships and in other institutions. Although cycle menus may be repetitious, the repetition is not necessarily noticeable to diners because of the length of the cycles.

Market menu: A market menu is based on product availability during a specific period; it is written to feature foods when they are in peak season or readily available. Market menus are increasingly popular with chefs (and consumers) because they challenge the chef's ingenuity in using fresh, seasonal products. Market menus are typically short-lived because of limited product availability and perishability. In fact, they often change daily.

Hybrid menu: A hybrid menu combines a static menu with a cycle menu or a market menu of specials.

Food service operations may have separate menus for breakfast, lunch and dinner, often referred to as **day parts**. If all three meals are available all day and are listed on the same menu, the menu is known as a **California menu**; California menus are typically found in 24-hour restaurants. Depending on the food service operation's objectives, separate specialty menus for drinks, hors d'oeuvre, desserts, brunch or afternoon tea are used.

Whether the menu is static, cycle, market or hybrid, it can offer consumers the opportunity to purchase their selections à la carte, semi à la carte, table d'hôte, menu dégustation or some combination of the three.

À la carte: Every food and beverage item is priced and ordered separately.

Semi à la carte: With this popular menu style, some food items (particularly appetizers and desserts) are priced and ordered separately, while the entrée is accompanied by and priced to include other items, such as a salad, starch or vegetable.

Table d'hôte or prix fixe: This menu offers a complete meal at a set price. (The term *table d'hôte* is French for "host's table" and is derived from the innkeeper's practice of seating all guests at a large communal table and serving them all the same meal.) A table d'hôte meal can range from very elegant to a diner's blue-plate special. A *prix fixe* menu may offer limited choices at a fixed price, whereas a table d'hôte menu usually offers no choice.

Menu dégustation or *tasting menu:* It is increasingly common for restaurants to offer small portions served in four, five or more courses for a fixed price. This *menu dégustation* or tasting menu allows diners the opportunity to sample a wider range of dishes than would normally be eaten in one meal. Chefs carefully craft such menus so that each dish complements the next dish served. Chefs frequently design tasting menus with a theme such as "spring asparagus" in which each course highlights an ingredient in a new guise. A selection of wines can accompany a tasting menu. For ease of service, restaurants usually require that the entire table order the tasting menu.

Many menus combine à la carte, semi à la carte and table d'hôte choices as well as a tasting menu. For example, appetizers, salads and desserts may be available à la carte; entrées may be offered semi à la carte (served with a salad, starch and vegetable); while the daily special is a complete (table d'hôte or *prix fixe*) meal.

Menu Language

The menu is the principal way in which the food service operation, including the chef, communicates with the consumer. A well-designed menu often reflects the input of design, marketing, art and other consultants as well as the chef and management. The choice of folds, cover, artwork, layout, typefaces, colors and paper are all important considerations, but the most important consideration is the language.

The menu should list the foods offered. It may include descriptions such as the preparation method, essential ingredients and service method as well as the quality, cut and quantity of product. For example, the menu can list "Porterhouse Steak" or "Wood-Grilled 16-oz. Angus Beef Porterhouse Steak."

Truth in Advertising

Federal as well as some state and local laws require that certain menu language be accurate. Areas of particular concern include statements about quantity, quality, grade and freshness. Accurate references to an item's source are also important. If brand names are listed on the menu, those brands must be served. If the restaurant claims to be serving "Fresh Dover Sole," it must be just that, not frozen sole from New England. (On the other hand, like French or Russian dressing, "English mint sauce" is a generic name for a style of food, so using that geographical adjective is appropriate even if the mint sauce is made in Arizona.) A reference to "our own fresh-baked" desserts means that the restaurant regularly bakes the desserts on premises, serves them soon after baking and does not substitute commercially prepared or frozen goods.

recipe a set of written instructions for producing a specific food or beverage; also known as a formula

standardized recipe a recipe producing a known quality and quantity of food for a specific operation

Nutritional Statements

The Food and Drug Administration (FDA) carefully regulates the language used on packaged food labels. In 1997 the FDA extended its nutrition labeling regulations to restaurant menus. These regulations are intended to prevent restaurants from making misleading health or nutrition claims. For example, terms such as *light*, *healthy* and *heart-healthy* must be accurate and documented. The standards for calculating and presenting that information on menus are far less stringent than the regulations for packaged foods, however. Restaurants may support their claims with data from any "reasonable" source and may present that information in any format, including verbally. As discussed in Chapter 3, Nutrition, the federal government has passed legislation requiring that nutritional information be posted on menu boards and printed menus in chain restaurants with 20 or more locations. The regulations require that calories be listed on menus, menu boards and on packaged foods on display.

STANDARDIZED RECIPES

Menu writing and **recipe** development are mutually dependent activities. Once the menu is created, **standardized recipes** should be prepared for each item. A standardized recipe produces a known quality and quantity of food for a specific operation. It specifies (1) the type and amount of each ingredient, (2) the preparation and cooking procedures and (3) the yield and portion size.

Standardized recipes are not found in books or provided by manufacturers; they are recipes customized to a specific operation—cooking time, temperature and utensils should be based on the equipment actually available. Yield should be adjusted to an amount appropriate for that operation. A recipe must be tested repeatedly and adjusted to fit the facility and the chef's needs before it can be considered standardized.

Chefs and management use standardized recipes as tools to train cooks, educate service staff and control finances. Standardized recipes help ensure that customers receive a consistent quality and quantity of product, and they are essential for accurate recipe costing and menu pricing. Each recipe should be complete, consistent and simple to read and follow. Standardized recipe forms should be stored in a readily accessible place. Index cards, notebook binders or a computerized database may be used, depending on the size and complexity of the operation.

MEASUREMENTS AND CONVERSIONS

The quantity of ingredients in each dish must be measured accurately to achieve the same results consistently. There are different ways of measuring food and different systems for recording such measurements. Chefs need to know how to measure correctly and how to convert from one system to another.

Measurement Formats

Accurate measurements are among the most important aspects of food production. The chef must be able to prepare a recipe the same way each time, and portion sizes must be the same from one order to the next. In a kitchen, measurements can be made in three ways: weight, volume and count.

Weight refers to the mass or heaviness of a substance. Weight is expressed in terms such as grams, ounces, pounds and tons. Weight may be used to measure liquid or dry ingredients (e.g., 2 pounds of eggs for a bread recipe) and portions (e.g., 4 ounces of sliced turkey for a sandwich). Because weight is generally the most accurate form of measurement, portion scales or balance scales are commonly used to weigh ingredients in kitchens.

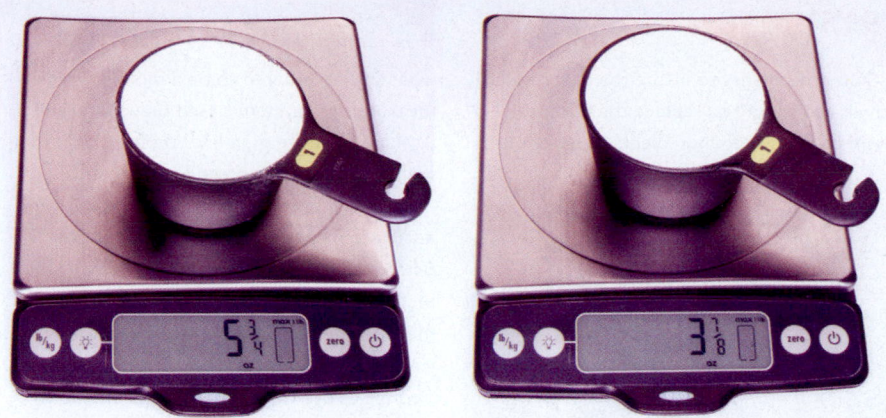

Figure 4.1 The weight of many ingredients, such as flour, varies when measured by volume. These two photos illustrate how flour that is packed into a measuring cup (left) weighs significantly more than flour sifted then spooned into a measuring cup (right).

Volume refers to the space occupied by a substance. Volume is calculated mathematically as *height* × *width* × *length*. It is expressed in terms such as cups, quarts, gallons, teaspoons, fluid ounces, bushels and liters. Volume is most commonly used to measure liquids. It may also be used for dry ingredients when the amount is too small to be weighed accurately (e.g., ¼ teaspoon of salt). Although measuring by volume is somewhat less accurate than measuring by weight, volume measurements are generally quicker to do.

Frequently mistakes are made in food preparation by chefs who assume wrongly that weight and volume are equal. Do not be fooled! One cup does not always equal 8 ounces. Although it is true that 1 standard cup contains 8 fluid ounces, it is not true that the contents of that standard cup will weigh 8 ounces. For example, the weight of 1 cup of diced apples will vary depending on the size of the apple pieces. Errors are commonly made in the bakeshop by cooks who assume that 8 ounces of flour is the same as 1 cup of flour. (In fact, 1 cup of all-purpose flour weighs only approximately 4½ ounces.)

Furthermore the weight of flour and other ingredients when measured by volume varies depending upon the type of flour and how it is placed in the measuring cup. See Figure 4.1.

It is not unusual to see both weight and volume measurements used in a single recipe. When a recipe ingredient is expressed in weight, weigh it. When it is expressed as a volume, measure its volume. Like most rules, however, there are exceptions to this one. The weight and volume of water, butter, eggs and milk are nearly identical. When measuring small quantities of these ingredients you may use whichever measurement is most convenient. Some common abbreviations for weight and volume measurements are listed in Table 4.1.

Count refers to the number of individual items. Count is used in recipes (e.g., 4 eggs) and in portion control (e.g., 2 fish fillets or 1 ear of corn). Count is also commonly used in purchasing to indicate the size of the individual items. For example, a "96 count" case of lemons means that a 40-pound case contains 96 individual lemons; a "115-count" case means that the same 40-pound case contains 115 individual lemons. Each lemon in the 96-count case is larger than those in the 115-count case. Shrimp is another item commonly sold by count. One pound of shrimp may contain from eight to several hundred shrimp, depending on the size of the individual pieces. When placing an order, the chef must specify the desired count. For example, when ordering one pound of 21–25-count shrimp, the chef expects to receive at least 21 but not more than 25 pieces.

COMMON ABBREVIATIONS		TABLE 4.1
teaspoon	=	tsp.
tablespoon	=	Tbsp.
cup	=	c.
pint	=	pt.
quart	=	qt.
gram	=	g
milliliter	=	ml
liter	=	lt
ounce	=	oz.
fluid ounce	=	fl. oz.
pound	=	lb.
kilogram	=	kg

Fannie Merritt Farmer (1857–1915)

Fannie Farmer was an early, vigorous and influential proponent of scientific cooking, nutrition and academic training for culinary professionals. At age 30 Farmer enrolled in the Boston Cooking School. The school's curriculum was not designed to graduate chefs, but rather to produce cooking teachers. After graduating from the two-year course, Farmer stayed on, first as assistant principal and then as principal.

During her years there (and, indeed, for the rest of her career) Farmer was obsessed with accurate measurements. She waged a campaign to eliminate the use of imprecise measurements such as a "wineglass" of liquid, a "handful" of flour, a chunk of butter the "size of an egg" or a "heaping spoonful" of salt. For, as she once wrote, "correct measurements are

absolutely necessary to insure the best results." Farmer also sought to replace the European system of measuring ingredients by weight with

Fannie Merritt Farmer, an early proponent of scientific cooking, offers her student a measuring cup full of flour.

what she considered to be a more scientific measurement system based on volume and level measures (e.g., a level tablespoon). To a great degree, she succeeded.

Farmer's writings reflect her concern for accurate measurements. Her first book, *The Boston Cooking School Cookbook* (1896), includes clearly written recipes with precise measurements. Later editions included recipe yields, oven temperatures and baking times. Farmer wrote other cookbooks, including *A New Book of Cookery* (first published in 1912 and republished in several revised versions). Her writings never address the joys of cooking and eating; rather, they reflect a scientific approach to cooking and rely on concisely, accurately measured recipes for good, solid food.

Note on Measurements

All ingredients in this text are listed in both U.S. and metric measurements. The metric equivalents are rounded off to even, easily measured amounts. Treat the two ingredient lists as separate complete recipes or formulas. Do not measure some ingredients according to the metric amounts and other ingredients according to the U.S. amount or the proportions will not be accurate and the intended result will not be achieved.

Measurement Systems

Weight, volume and count are used in both the U.S. and metric measurement systems. Both U.S. and metric systems are used in modern food service operations, so chefs should be able to prepare recipes written in either one.

The U.S. system, with which most students probably are familiar, is actually the more difficult system to understand. It uses pounds for weight and cups for volume. The metric system is the most commonly used system in the world. Developed in France during the late 18th century, it was intended to fill the need for a mathematically rational and uniform system of measurement. The metric system is a decimal system in which the gram, liter and meter are the basic units of weight, volume and length, respectively. Adding a prefix to the words gram, liter and meter forms larger and smaller units of weight, volume and length. Some of the more commonly used prefixes in food service operations are *deca-* (10), *kilo-* (1000), *deci-* (1/10) and *milli-* (1/1000). For example, a kilogram is 1000 grams; a decameter is 10 meters; a milliliter is 1/1000 of a liter. Because the metric system is based on multiples of 10, it is easy to increase or decrease amounts.

The most important thing for a chef to know about the metric system is that one does not need to convert between the metric system and the U.S. system in recipe preparation. If a recipe is written in metric units, use metric measuring equipment; if it is written in U.S. units, use U.S. measuring equipment. Luckily, most modern measuring equipment is calibrated in both U.S. and metric increments. The need to convert amounts arises only if the proper equipment is unavailable.

Converting Grams and Ounces

As you can see in Table 4.2, 1 ounce equals 28.35 grams and 1 fluid ounce equals 29.57 milliliters. To convert ounces/fluid ounces to grams/milliliters, multiply the number of dry ounces by 28 or the number of fluid ounces by 29, using a number that is rounded for convenience.

$$8 \text{ oz.} \times 28 = 224 \text{ g}$$

$$8 \text{ fl. oz.} \times 29 = 232 \text{ ml}$$

Likewise to convert grams/milliliters to ounces/fluid ounces, divide the number of grams/milliliters by 28 or 29 (rounded for convenience).

$$224 \text{ g} \div 28 = 8 \text{ oz.}$$

$$224 \text{ ml} \div 29 = 7.72 \text{ fl. oz.}$$

COMMON EQUIVALENTS   TABLE 4.2

dash	=	⅛ teaspoon
3 teaspoons	=	1 tablespoon
2 tablespoons	=	1 fluid ounce
4 tablespoons	=	¼ cup (2 fl. oz.)
5⅓ tablespoons	=	⅓ cup (2⅔ fl. oz.)
16 tablespoons	=	1 cup (8 fl. oz.)
2 cups	=	1 pint (16 fl. oz.)
2 pints	=	1 quart (32 fl. oz.)
4 quarts	=	1 gallon (128 fl. oz.)
2 gallons	=	1 peck
4 pecks	=	1 bushel
1 gram	=	0.035 ounce (¹⁄₃₀ oz.)
1 ounce	=	28.35 grams (often rounded to 30 for convenience)
454 grams	=	1 pound
2.2 pounds	=	1 kilogram (1000 g)
1 teaspoon	=	5 milliliters
1 tablespoon	=	15 milliliters
1 fluid ounce	=	29.57 milliliters (often rounded to 30 for convenience)
1 cup	=	0.24 liter
1 gallon	=	3.80 liters

To help you develop a framework for judging conversions, remember that:

A kilogram is about 2.2 pounds.

A gram is about ¹⁄₃₀ ounce.

A pound is about 460 grams.

A liter is slightly more than a quart.

A centimeter is slightly less than ½ inch.

0°C (32°F) is the freezing point of water.

100°C (212°F) is the boiling point of water.

These approximations are not a substitute for accurate conversions, however. Appendix I contains additional information on equivalents and metric conversions. There is no substitute for knowing this information and it should become second nature to you.

RECIPE CONVERSIONS

Whether it produces 6 servings or 60, every recipe is designed to produce or **yield** a specific amount of product. A recipe's yield may be expressed in volume, weight or servings (e.g., 1 quart of sauce, 8 pounds of bread dough or 8 half-cup servings). If the yield in a standardized recipe does not meet the chef's needs, he or she must convert (i.e., increase or decrease) the ingredient amounts. Recipe conversion is sometimes complicated by portion size conversion. For example, it may be necessary to convert a recipe that initially produces 24 8-ounce servings of soup into a recipe that produces 62 6-ounce servings.

You can change yields by uneven amounts just as you can double or halve recipes. The mathematical principle is the same: Each ingredient is multiplied by a **conversion factor (C.F.)**. Do not take shortcuts by estimating recipe amounts or conversion factors. Inaccurate conversions lead to inedible foods, embarrassing shortages or wasteful excesses. Take the time to learn and apply proper conversion techniques.

yield the total amount of a product made from a specific recipe; also, the amount of a food item remaining after cleaning or processing

conversion factor (C.F.) a number used to increase or decrease ingredient quantities and recipe yields

Converting Total Yield

When portion size is unimportant or remains the same, recipe yield is converted by a two-step process:

Step 1 Divide the desired (new) yield by the recipe (old) yield to obtain the conversion factor (C.F.):

$$\text{New Yield} \div \text{Old Yield} = \text{Conversion Factor}$$

$$\frac{\text{New Yield}}{\text{Old Yield}} = \text{C.F.}$$

Step 2 Multiply each ingredient quantity by the conversion factor to obtain the new quantity:

$$\text{Old Quantity} \times \text{Conversion Factor} = \text{New Quantity}$$

$$\text{Old Quantity} \times \text{C.F.} = \text{New Quantity}$$

EXAMPLE 4.1 Converting Total Yield

You need to convert a recipe for cauliflower soup that yields 1½ gallons. You want to make only ¾ gallon.

Step 1 Determine the conversion factor:

$$0.75 \text{ gallon} \div 1.5 \text{ gallons} = 0.5$$

Note that any unit can be used, as long as the same unit is used with both the new and the old recipes. In this example, the same conversion factor is obtained if the recipe amounts are converted to fluid ounces:

$$96 \text{ fluid ounces} \div 192 \text{ fluid ounces} = 0.5$$

Step 2 Apply the conversion factor to each ingredient in the soup recipe:

CAULIFLOWER SOUP

	Old quantity	×	C.F.	=	New quantity
Cauliflower, chopped	5 lb.	×	0.5	=	2½ lb.
Celery stalks	4	×	0.5	=	2
Onion	1	×	0.5	=	½
Chicken stock	2 qt.	×	0.5	=	1 qt.
Heavy cream	3 pt.	×	0.5	=	1½ pt.

Converting Portion Size

Sometimes you need to change the amount of food served in one portion. For example, the new soup bowls at your institution may hold less than the bowls now being used, or a banquet menu may require a smaller entrée portion than is normally served à la carte. You need to take a few additional steps to convert recipes when portion sizes must also be changed. This is easier to understand if you think in terms of the total amount of an item that is needed in relation to the total yield produced by the current recipe. The key is to find a common denominator for the new and old recipes: ounces, grams, cups, servings and so on. Again, any unit can be used, as long as the same unit is used with both the new and the old recipes.

Step 1 Determine the total yield of the existing recipe by multiplying the number of portions by the portion size:

$$\text{Original Portions} \times \text{Original Portion Size} = \text{Total (Old) Yield}$$

$$\text{No. of Portions} \times \text{Portion Size} = \text{Yield}$$

Step 2 Determine the total yield desired by multiplying the new number of portions by the new portion size:

$$\text{Desired Portions} \times \text{Desired Portion Size} = \text{Total (New) Yield}$$

Step 3 Obtain the conversion factor as described earlier:

$$\text{Total New Yield} \div \text{Total Old Yield} = \text{Conversion Factor}$$

$$\frac{\text{New Yield}}{\text{Old Yield}} = \text{C.F.}$$

Step 4 Multiply each ingredient quantity by the conversion factor:

Old Quantity × Conversion Factor = New Quantity

Old Quantity × C.F. = New Quantity

EXAMPLE 4.2 Converting Portion Size

For the cauliflower soup in Example 4.2, the original recipe produced 1½ gallons or 48 4-ounce servings. Now you need 72 6-ounce servings.

Step 1 Total original yield is 48 × 4 = 192 ounces.

Step 2 Total desired yield is 72 × 6 = 432 ounces.

Step 3 The conversion factor is calculated by dividing total new yield by total old yield:

432 ÷ 192 = 2.25

Step 4 Old ingredient quantities are multiplied by the conversion factor to determine the new quantities.

CAULIFLOWER SOUP

	Old quantity	×	C.F.	=	New quantity
Cauliflower, chopped	5 lb.	×	2.25	=	11.25 lb.
Celery stalks	4	×	2.25	=	9
Onion	1	×	2.25	=	2.25
Chicken stock	2 qt.	×	2.25	=	4.5 qt.
Heavy cream	3 pt.	×	2.25	=	6.75 pt.

Additional Conversion Problems

When making large recipe changes—for example, converting from 5 to 25 portions or 600 to 300 portions—you may encounter additional problems. The mathematical conversions described here do not consider changes in equipment, evaporation rates, unforeseen recipe errors or cooking times. Chefs learn to use their judgment, knowledge of cooking principles and skills to compensate for these factors. In the material that follows these factors are discussed.

Equipment

When the size of a recipe changes, the equipment necessary to produce it must change as well. Problems arise when the production techniques previously used no longer work with the new quantity of ingredients. For example, a small muffin recipe can be mixed by hand, but an increased batch size may require the use of a mixer. But if you use the same mixing time for the small and large batches, the batter may become overmixed, resulting in poor-quality muffins. Trying to prepare a small amount of product in equipment that is too large for the task can also affect its quality.

Evaporation

Equipment changes can also affect product quality because of changes in evaporation rates. Increasing a soup recipe's yield may require substituting a larger cooking vessel such as a tilt skillet for a saucepan. However a tilt skillet provides more surface area for evaporation than does a saucepan. In other words when substituting a skillet for a saucepan, reduction time must be decreased to prevent over-thickening the soup. The increased evaporation caused by increased surface area may also alter the strength of the seasonings.

Recipe Errors

A recipe may contain errors in ingredients or techniques that are not obvious when it is prepared in small quantities. When increased, however, small mistakes often become bigger (and more obvious) ones, and the final product suffers. The only way to prevent this is to test recipes carefully and rely on your knowledge of cooking principles to compensate for unexpected problems.

Time

Do not multiply time specifications given in a recipe by the conversion factor used with the recipe's ingredients. All things being equal, cooking time will not change when recipe size changes. For example, a muffin requires the same amount of baking time whether you prepare 1 dozen or 14 dozen. Cooking time will be affected, however, by changes in evaporation rate or heat conduction caused by equipment changes, and an oven filled to capacity may lose more heat, thus slowing the baking time. Mixing time may also change when recipe size changes. Different equipment may perform mixing tasks more or less efficiently than previously used equipment. Again, rely on experience and good judgment.

CALCULATING UNIT COSTS, RECIPE COSTS AND SELLING PRICES

To ensure profitability, food service operations need accurate recipes that include ingredient costs. Some ingredients are sold in units, such as a can of tomato paste or a case of apples, but are then used in smaller units, such as 2 tablespoons of tomato paste or 6 pounds of diced apples. Some ingredients, such as meats, vegetables and fruits, require preparation that results in waste. The cost of the wasted peels and trim must be accounted for in the final cost of the food item. Calculating the unit costs of ingredients allows you to determine the cost to prepare a recipe and the price to charge for a finished dish.

Unit Costs

Food service operations purchase most foods from suppliers in bulk or in wholesale packages. For example, food service operations purchase canned goods by the case; produce by the flat, case or lug; and flour and sugar in 25- or 50-pound bags. Fish and meats are often purchased in large cuts, not individual serving-sized portions. The purchased amount is rarely used for a single recipe. It must be broken down into smaller units such as pounds, cups, quarts or ounces.

In order to allocate the proper ingredient costs to the recipe being prepared, it is necessary to convert **as-purchased (A.P.) costs** to **unit costs**. To find the unit cost in a package containing multiple units (e.g., 1 egg in a 30-dozen case), divide the A.P. cost of the package by the number of units in the package:

$$\text{A.P. Cost} \div \text{Number of Units} = \text{Cost per Unit}$$

as purchased (A.P.) the condition or cost of an item as it is purchased or received from the supplier

unit cost the price paid to acquire one of the specified units

$$\frac{\text{A.P. Cost}}{\text{\# of Units}} = \text{Cost per Unit}$$

EXAMPLE 4.3 Calculating Unit Cost

A case of #10 cans contains 6 individual cans. If a case of tomato paste costs $23.50, you can use the formula just discussed to determine that each can costs $3.92:

$$\text{\$23.50 A.P. case cost} \div \text{6 cans per case} = \text{\$3.92 cost per can}$$

If a recipe requires less than the total can, you must continue dividing the cost of the can until you arrive at the appropriate unit amount in the specific recipe. If you need only 1 cup of tomato paste, divide the can price ($3.92) by the total number of cups contained in the can to arrive at the cost per cup (unit). The list of canned-good sizes in Appendix I indicates that a #10 can contains approximately 13 cups. Using the same formula, you can determine that each cup costs $0.30:

$$\text{\$3.92 cost per can} \div \text{13 cups per can} = \text{\$0.30 cost per cup}$$

The cost of 1 cup can be reduced even further if necessary. If the recipe uses only 1 tablespoon of tomato paste, divide the cost per cup by the number of tablespoons in a cup. The cost for 1 tablespoon of this tomato paste is $0.018.

$$\text{\$0.30 cost per cup} \div \text{16 tablespoons per cup} = \text{\$.018 cost per tablespoon}$$

Therefore when you calculate the total cost of a recipe containing a tablespoon of tomato paste, the unit cost is $.018 or 1.8¢.

Cost information is usually provided to the chef or manager from purchase invoices. It may also be necessary to examine a product's label or package to determine some information such as actual weight of the contents or size of ingredients contained within a package.

Yield Percentage

Many ingredients, such as fruit and vegetables, require cleaning and trimming before they are ready for use in a recipe. For example, you must remove excess fat from a piece of beef before slicing it into individual steaks, or you must peel a potato before boiling it to make mashed potatoes. Once the potato is peeled, the peels are discarded and what remains is the **edible portion (E.P.)**. (In the case of baked potatoes, the whole potato is used and the edible portion is the same as the purchased quantity.) To determine the actual cost of the edible portion of an ingredient, chefs conduct a **yield test** to determine the **yield percentage**, which is used to determine the as-purchased (A.P.) quantity for the recipe as well as the actual cost per pound of the ingredient. The edible portion (E.P.) or the weight of the ingredient after it is prepared for cooking divided by the weight of the ingredient as purchased (A.P.) gives the yield percentage for that food item.

> E.P. Weight ÷ A.P. Weight = Yield Percentage

To determine yield percentage follow these steps:

Step 1   Weigh the ingredient as purchased before cleaning, trimming and peeling.

Step 2   Peel, trim and clean the ingredient as required in the standardized recipe.

Step 3   Weigh the trimmed product to obtain the E.P.

Step 4   Divide the E.P. weight by the A.P. weight to obtain the yield percentage.

EXAMPLE 4.4 Calculating Yield Percentage

The weight of 5 pounds of potatoes (A.P.) after peeling is 4 pounds (E.P.). By dividing 4 pounds peeled potatoes (E.P.) by 5 pounds unpeeled potatoes (A.P.) you can determine that the yield percentage is 80%:

> 4 pounds peeled potatoes (E.P.) ÷ 5 pounds unpeeled potatoes (A.P.)
> = 80% Yield Percentage

Using Yield Percentage to Calculate A.P. Quantity

Often recipes are written listing the edible portion of an ingredient. You must then calculate the A.P. quantity required. To find the A.P. quantity needed for a recipe, divide the E.P. quantity in the recipe by the yield percentage:

> E.P. Quantity ÷ Yield Percentage = A.P. Quantity

EXAMPLE 4.5 Using Yield Percentage to Calculate A.P. Quantity

A recipe calls for 12 pounds of peeled potatoes with an 80% yield percentage. Using the formula, you can determine that 15 pounds of potatoes is required to produce 12 pounds of edible potatoes:

> 12 pounds (E.P.) ÷ 0.80 (Yield Percentage) = 15 pounds (A.P.)

Because trimming decreases the usable quantity of an ingredient, the cost of the ingredient must be increased by the amount that is discarded. Chefs can use the yield percentage to accurately calculate the cost of an ingredient after trimming:

> A.P. Cost per Pound ÷ Yield Percentage = E.P. Cost per Pound

---

edible portion (E.P.) the amount of a food item available for consumption or use after trimming or fabrication; a smaller, more convenient portion of a larger or bulk unit

yield test measuring and weighing an ingredient before and after trimming to determine the usable portion; used to determine the quantity of an ingredient to purchase as well as actual ingredient cost

yield percentage the ratio of the usable weight of an ingredient after cleaning and trimming to the quantity purchased; calculated by dividing the trimmed weight by the as-purchased weight of the ingredient

$$\frac{\text{E.P. Weight}}{\text{A.P. Weight}} = \text{Yield Percentage}$$

$$\frac{\text{E.P. Quantity}}{\text{Yield Percentage}} = \text{A.P. Quantity}$$

$$\frac{\text{A.P. Cost per Pound}}{\text{Yield Percentage}} = \text{E.P. Cost per Pound}$$

EXAMPLE 4.6 Using Yield Percentage to Calculate E.P. Cost per Pound

Potatoes cost $0.41 per pound and have a yield percentage of 80%. Using the formula, you can determine that the true cost of the edible portion of peeled potatoes is $0.51 per pound:

$0.41 per pound (A.P.) ÷ 0.80 (Yield Percentage) = $0.51 per pound (E.P.)

Chefs periodically conduct yield tests on items requiring fabrication and trimming to ensure that they are properly costing ingredients. Tables listing average yields of common ingredients are also available in books and from meat, poultry and fish purveyors. The butchering of meats, poultry and fish as well as other foods is complicated by the fact that these ingredients can yield trim and bones usable in other preparations. The calculation of E.P. cost must take this into consideration.

Recipe Costs

A standardized recipe, listing the ingredients and their amounts, as well as the number and size of the portions, must be established in order to determine the cost of a completed menu item. Once an accurate recipe is written, the **total recipe cost** is calculated with the following two-step process:

total recipe cost the total cost of ingredients for a particular recipe; total recipe cost does not reflect overhead, labor, fixed expenses or profit

cost per portion the amount of the total recipe cost divided by the number of portions produced from that recipe; the cost of one serving

$$\frac{\text{Total Recipe Cost}}{\text{\# of Portions}} = \text{Cost per Portion}$$

Step 1 Determine the cost for the given quantity of each recipe ingredient with the unit costing procedures described earlier.

Step 2 Add all the ingredient costs together to obtain the total recipe cost.

The total recipe cost can then be broken down into the **cost per portion**, which is the most useful figure for food cost controls. To arrive at cost per portion, divide the total recipe cost by the total number of servings or portions produced by that recipe.

Total Recipe Cost ÷ Number of Portions = Cost per Portion

The recipe costing form in Figure 4.2 is useful for organizing recipe-costing information. It provides space for listing each ingredient, the quantity of each ingredient needed, the cost

RECIPE COSTING FORM

Menu Item _____ Turkey Cheddar Sandwich _____ Date _____

Total Yield _____ 1 sandwich _____ Portion Size _____ 1 sandwich _____

| INGREDIENT | QUANTITY | COST | | | RECIPE COST |
		A.P. ($)	YIELD %	E.P. ($)	
Multigrain roll	1 3-oz. roll	6.48 doz.		0.54 each	0.54
Sliced turkey breast	4 oz.	3.89/lb.		0.24/oz.	0.97
Cheddar cheese, sliced	2 oz.	3.79/lb.		0.24/oz.	0.48
Cranberry relish	1.5 oz.	11.06/117 oz.		0.09/oz.	0.13
Mayonnaise	1 oz.	7.89/gal.		0.06/oz.	0.06
Salt	TT				-0-

Subtotal $ _____ 2.17

Q Factor $ _____ 0.10

Total recipe cost $ _____ 2.28

Number of servings _____ 1

Cost per portion $ _____ 2.28

Figure 4.2 Recipe costing form for a single-serving sandwich.

RECIPE COSTING FORM

Menu Item ___Beef Stew___　　　Date _____

Total Yield ___200 fl. oz.___　　　Portion Size ___12.5 fl. oz.___

| INGREDIENT | QUANTITY | COST | | | RECIPE COST |
		A.P. ($)	YIELD %	E.P. ($)	
Beef, cubes	6 lb.			$3.79/lb.	$22.74
Corn oil	4 Tbsp.	13.43/gal.		0.83/c.	0.21
Flour	1.5 oz.	13.50/50 lb.		0.27/lb.	0.03
Beef stock	2 qt.	2.50/gal.		0.62/qt.	1.25
Carrots, diced	1 lb.	0.56/lb.	70%	0.80/lb.	0.8
Potatoes, diced	2 lb.	0.41/lb.	80%	0.51/lb.	1.02
Onions	2	0.15 each	89%	0.17 each	0.34
Salt	TT				-0-

Subtotal $ _____26.39_____

Q Factor $ _____1.60_____

Total recipe cost $ ___27.99___

Number of servings ___16___

Cost per portion $___1.75___

Figure 4.3 Recipe costing form for a dish that produces more than one portion.

of each unit (E.P.) and the total cost for the ingredient. Some ingredients such as salt, pepper and spices that are used as needed in small amounts may be accounted for by assigning a fixed cost to them in each recipe. Called the **Q Factor** (for questionable ingredients), it is added to the total recipe cost after all ingredients are calculated. The Q Factor for an individual recipe may be as little as five or 10 cents and is established by management.

Total yield, portion size and cost per portion are listed at the bottom of the form. Note that there is no space for recipe procedures, because these are generally irrelevant in recipe costing.

In the example in Figure 4.2, the recipe produces one sandwich, which is also the portion. Because there are no fabrication requirements when assembling the ingredients for this sandwich, there are no yield percentages to calculate. The recipe costing form in Figure 4.3 shows the ingredients in a dish that serves more than one person. Calculating the yield percentages on the carrots and potatoes in this recipe requires an additional step. It is also necessary to calculate the final cost per portion.

Selling Prices

The cost of a portion of food is just one factor used to determine the selling price of a dish on the menu. Each item served on the plate, such as the buttered noodles and green beans that may accompany the Beef Stew in Figure 4.3, contributes to the total **plate cost** for that item, as shown in Figure 4.4. The portion cost of several recipes may need to be calculated in order to determine what it costs to serve a finished dish. A meal may include a roll and butter as well as condiments such as mayonnaise or mustard. The cost of these items may also be tracked using a Q Factor in the total plate cost calculation or an actual cost as shown in this example. In addition, as in any business, a food service operation incurs kitchen and dining room labor costs and numerous **overhead costs** in

overhead costs expenses related to operating a business, including but not limited to costs for advertising, equipment leasing, insurance, property rent, supplies and utilities

PLATE COSTING FORM

Menu Item Beef Stew with Parsley Buttered Noodles and Green Beans

INGREDIENT	QUANTITY
Beef Stew	$1.75
Parsley Buttered Noodles	0.32
Green Beans	0.62
Roll and butter	0.41
Total plate cost	$3.10
Desired food cost percentage	35%
Proposed menu selling price	$8.857

Figure 4.4 Plate costing form.

food cost percentage the ratio of the cost of foods used to the total food sales during a set period; calculated by dividing the cost of food used by the total sales in a restaurant

the preparation and service of a menu. Typically these include the cost of utilities, rent, supplies, linens, advertising and promotional expenses along with myriad other expenses necessary for the business to operate successfully. Working closely with its chef, restaurant management determines the **food cost percentage** it needs to achieve to be profitable. This percentage represents the cost of all food used divided by the total sales in a restaurant. Kitchen waste, inefficient trimming of meats and inconsistent portion sizes all contribute to increases in food cost and decreased profitability.

The food cost percentage is one of many methods used to determine selling prices of each individual menu item in the following manner:

Step 1 Determine the total cost of all components in a finished plate.

Step 2 Divide the total plate cost by the desired food cost percentage.

$$\frac{\text{Plate Cost}}{\text{Desired Food Cost \%}} = \text{Selling Price}$$

Plate Cost ÷ Desired Food Cost % = Selling Price

EXAMPLE 4.7 Calculating Selling Price

To determine the selling price for the Beef Stew in Figure 4.4, if management wants to achieve a 35% food cost, divide the total plate cost of $3.10 by 35%:

$3.10 Plate Cost ÷ 35% (Desired Food Cost %) = $8.857 (Proposed Selling Price)

Management may adjust selling prices to fit a particular pricing format. For example, institutions may round cents to the nearest dollar or add a flat sum to cover additional costs. Chefs work closely with food service managers to keep the food cost percentage within established guidelines. Taking periodic physical **inventory** helps management verify that the proper quantities of food are being used.

inventory the listing and counting of all foods in the kitchen, storerooms and refrigerators

CONTROLLING FOOD COSTS

Many things affect food costs in any given operation; most can be controlled by the chef or manager. These controls do not require mathematical calculations or formulas, just basic management skills and a good dose of common sense. Chefs tend to focus their control efforts in the area of kitchen preparation. Although this may seem logical, it is not adequate. A good chef is involved in all aspects of the operation to help prevent problems from arising or to correct those that may occur.

The menu, purchasing/ordering, receiving, storing, issuing, portions, waste and sales and service all have an impact on the operation's bottom line.

Menu

A profitable menu is based on many variables, including customer desires, physical space and equipment, ingredient availability, cost of goods sold, employee skills and competition. All management personnel, including the chef, should be consulted when planning the menu. Menu changes, though possibly desirable, must be executed with as much care as was taken in planning the original menu.

Purchasing and Ordering

Purchasing techniques have a direct impact on cost controls. On the one hand, **parstock (par)** must be adequate for efficient operations; on the other hand, too much inventory wastes space and resources and may spoil. Before any items are ordered, purchasing specifications should be established and communicated to potential purveyors. Specifications should precisely describe the item, including grade, quality, packaging and unit size. Each operation should design its own form to best meet its specific needs. A sample specification form is shown in Figure 4.5. The information in the form can be used to obtain price quotes from several purveyors. Update quotes periodically to ensure that you are getting the best value for your money.

MEAT PURCHASING SPECIFICATIONS	
Product:	
Menu Item:	
Grade/Quality:	NAMP/IMPS#:
Packaging:	
Pricing Unit:	
Delivery Conditions:	
Comments:	

Figure 4.5 Specification form.

Receiving

Whether goods are received by a full-time clerk, as they are in a large hotel, or by the chef or kitchen manager, certain standards should be observed. The person signing for merchandise should first confirm that the items were actually ordered. Second, confirm that the items listed on the invoice are the ones being delivered and that the price and quantity listed are accurate. Third, the items, especially meats and produce, should be checked for quality, freshness and weight. The temperature of all perishable items should be carefully checked at the time of delivery to ensure compliance with food safety standards. Established purchase specifications should be made readily available for anyone responsible for receiving goods. If an item does not meet any of these purchase specifications or is not within acceptable temperature ranges on arrival, the product should be refused.

parstock (par) the amount of stock necessary to cover operating needs between deliveries

Storing

Proper storage of foodstuffs is crucial in order to prevent spoilage, pilferage and waste. Stock must be rotated so that the older items are used first. Such a system for rotating stock is referred to as **FIFO (first in, first out)**. Dry storage areas should be well ventilated and lit to prevent pest infestation and mold. Freezers and refrigerators should be easily accessible, operating properly and kept clean and organized.

FIFO (first in, first out) a system of rotating inventory, particularly perishable and semiperishable goods, in which items are used in the order in which they are received

Issuing

It may be necessary, particularly in larger operations, to limit storeroom access to specific personnel. Maintaining ongoing inventory records helps the ordering process. Controlling when products are issued or taken from storage to be used in the kitchen eliminates waste caused by multiple opened containers and ensures proper stock rotation.

Kitchen Procedures: Establishing Standard Portions

Standardizing portions is essential to controlling food costs. Unless portion quantity is uniform, it will be impossible to compute portion costs accurately. Portion discrepancies can also confuse or mislead customers. To determine if portion sizes are appropriate, chefs can check plates that have been cleared from the table. Large quantities of waste could suggest a serious and costly problem.

   Actual portion sizes depend on the food service operation itself, the menu, the prices and the customers' desires. Some items are generally purchased preportioned for convenience (e.g., steaks are sold in uniform cuts, baking potatoes are available in uniform sizes, butter comes in preportioned pats and sandwich bread comes sliced for service).

Other items must be portioned by the establishment before service. Special equipment makes consistent portioning straightforward. There are machines to slice meats, cutting guides for cakes and pies and portion scales for weighing quantities. Standardized portion scoops and ladles are indispensable for serving vegetables, soups, stews, salads and similar foods. Many of these items are discussed and illustrated in Chapter 5, Tools and Equipment.

Once acceptable portion sizes are established, employees must be properly trained to present them. If each employee of a sandwich shop prepared sandwiches the way he or she would like to eat them, customers would probably never receive the same sandwich twice. Customers may become confused and decide not to risk a repeat visit. Obviously carelessness in portioning can also drastically affect food cost.

Kitchen Procedures: Managing Waste

The chef must control waste from overproduction or failure to use leftovers. With an adequate sales history, the chef can accurately estimate the quantity of food to prepare for each week, day or meal. An organized kitchen staff works from lists prepared by the head chef or station chefs, referred to as **prep lists**, outlining the type and quantities of products to be made. A well-planned prep list keeps workflow organized and waste to a minimum. The less waste generated in food preparation, the lower the overall food cost will be.

If the menu is designed properly, the chef can use leftovers and trim from product fabrication. When planning the menu, the chef should identify all trim and create uses for it before putting the menu into service. The chain muscle trimmed from beef tenderloin, for example, can be used for kebabs. Food items should be purchased in the most efficient way. For example, whole chickens should not be purchased if the menu only features recipes that use boneless breasts. Unless other dishes using the legs and carcass are on the menu, boned chicken breasts should be purchased. Anticipating uses for leftovers helps reduce waste. Leftover roast turkey from a holiday menu can be used on a turkey club sandwich at the next service. Including highly perishable items, that have limited use on a menu or such expensive garnishes as edible flowers, can also increase waste and overall costs.

Sales and Service

An improperly trained sales staff can undo even the most rigorous food cost controls. Front-of-the-house personnel are ultimately responsible for the sales portion of the food cost equation. Waiters and other sales staff must make sure that the business receives the correct amount of money as revenue. Prices charged must be accurate and complete. Waiters must record all orders correctly to ensure that everything served is paid for by the guest. Inattentive and impolite servers who provide poor service can lead to the need to "comp" (serve for free) food if customers are unhappy. Dropped or spilled foods do not generate revenues. Proper training is critical. The dining room manager and the chef should work together to educate servers about menu items and techniques for increasing sales and revenue. Chefs should use the time before each service to introduce new menu items to the service staff. Regular tastings of new menu items and daily specials educate the dining room staff and build their enthusiasm.

RECIPE WRITING 101

Chefs are frequently called upon to craft recipes to share with the public and their customers. Unlike the standardized recipes used in a specific restaurant operation, recipes to share with the public, whether in print or for electronic publication on a website, have different conventions. Various publications use different formats for presenting these directions, depending on their own style and layout decisions, but the directions themselves—the actual recipe—should follow certain conventions. The goal with all recipe writing is to guide the user to produce a dish accurately, efficiently and consistently.

Elements of a Recipe Written for Publication

The primary parts of a recipe written for publication are its name, number of servings, a headnote, a list of ingredients, and procedures. Each of these are described in the following material.

Name of the Recipe

Although some creativity is certainly permitted in naming a dish, be sure that the name is relevant and meaningful to potential users. "Chef's Surprise" tells the reader nothing. "Uncle Dan's Venison Sauce" may be slightly more meaningful but is still ambiguous. Is this a sauce made from venison or served with venison? Is the sauce spicy? Sweet? Fruity? Can it only be served on venison? And, unless the recipe is being written for use only by family members, "Uncle Dan" is irrelevant. In this case, a title such as "Spicy Blackberry Sauce for Game" would be more informative and useful.

Yield/Servings

Servings or yield, the term generally used in a professional context, refers to the total amount of the finished dish produced by the quantity of ingredients stated. This may be stated as "serves 8" or "makes 1 quart" or "one 9-inch pie." Greater detail can be added by phrasing the yield as "36 4-oz. cookies" or "six 8-oz. servings." Providing the total quantity produced by the recipe helps the reader know what to expect and clarifies the cooking experience.

Headnote

A headnote is an optional comment that explains the background or development of the dish. It could provide other information that might be nice to know but is not essential to preparing the recipe. Some publications require headnotes; others decline to use them entirely.

Ingredients

List ingredients in the order used. The quantity listed should be as specific as possible, with the exception of seasoning items, such as salt and pepper, which may be simply stated as "to taste." The reason for listing an ingredient with a range of quantity (3–4 cups all-purpose flour) should be further explained in the recipe procedures. If the amount of flour needed to make a loaf of bread varies depending on the brand used, for example, explain this in the recipe instructions. If you are developing recipes for a food producer, be careful to list name-brand items accurately. Use standard measurement terms and abbreviations, as discussed on page 57 and shown throughout this text.

Procedures

Procedures provide step-by-step explanations for preparing, cooking and assembling the ingredients. List each step in the order in which it should be performed. Include as much detail as necessary to ensure that the reader understands what is to be done and obtain the desired results from each step. Procedures may offer more or less detail depending on your audience. Within your own restaurant kitchen, it may be sufficient to use culinary shorthand (e.g., sauté, deglaze and reduce au sec), but this professional jargon would be inadequate in a recipe being published by your local newspaper. For a general audience, you might be more specific: "Sauté the minced shallots over medium heat for 5 to 6 minutes, until they are translucent and soft; add the wine and swirl to remove food particles from the pan. Reduce the heat and simmer until the wine is almost completely evaporated."

Procedures should include times, temperatures and visual clues that the user can follow. Offer as much information as necessary to make the reader feel comfortable and confident. Proofread written instructions carefully. Make sure that every ingredient listed is specifically used in the procedures and that every item mentioned in the procedures is listed with the ingredients. Double-check quantities and verify that they are stated clearly. Ensure that temperatures, cooking times and quantity produced are accurate. Does the recipe include enough detail to make the cooking experience a success, or will the new user end up frustrated and confused?

Other Considerations When Crafting a Recipe for Publication

When you think you have the written recipe finished, ask others to read and test the recipe in their own kitchens. Do they have any problems or questions? Is the final dish what they expected? Is it what you intended? Prepare the dish yourself, referring only to your written recipe, not your previous experience. Is the finished product what you intended? Did you encounter anything that needs to be changed? Do not assume that the newspaper, magazine or book publisher will test your recipe. In most cases, publications do not have the staff or the time to test and retest recipes. The obligation falls to you to produce a written recipe that is clear and accurate.

Finally a note about plagiarism: Don't plagiarize. If you are submitting a recipe for publication or distributing it to your customers upon request and that recipe was derived from another source, say so and credit the original in writing on any printed or online materials you share as well. The maxim that changing three ingredients makes a recipe your own is false. While it is true that a recipe cannot be copyrighted, ethically you should acknowledge the original source, noting that the recipe "is adapted from so and so." No one wants to see someone else taking credit for his or her hard work and creativity.

QUESTIONS FOR DISCUSSION

1   Describe the four types of menus. Can each type of menu offer foods à la carte, semi à la carte and/or table d'hôte? Explain your answer.

2   Chefs use standardized recipes to ensure that restaurants produce consistent results and that food costs are controlled. Identify and explain the three features of a standardized recipe.

3   Discuss three factors in food preparation that affect successful recipe yield or portion changes.

4   Why is it important to calculate the portion cost of a recipe in professional food service operations? Why is the full recipe cost inadequate?

5   Explain how to convert the weight of an ingredient measured in ounces to grams.

6   Calculate the recipe cost of the mayonnaise recipe on page 742. Then calculate the selling price of the Turkey Cheddar Sandwich on page 64 using the cost of the mayonnaise you calculated and a food cost of 35%.

7   List several factors, other than kitchen procedures, that a chef should examine when looking for ways to control food costs.

8   Describe the requirements when writing a recipe for publication. What must a chef consider when preparing a recipe to be used by home cooks?

Tools and Equipment 5

- list NSF safety standard requirements and explain safe and sanitary equipment design

- select and care for knives

- identify a variety of professional kitchen tools and equipment including hand tools, measuring and portion devices, cookware, strainers and sieves, heavy equipment, specialized equipment for emerging culinary techniques and buffet equipment

- identify the types of fire extinguishers available and understand their use in professional kitchens

- list and discuss ways to conserve energy in professional kitchens

Figure 5.1 The NSF mark.

The proper tools and equipment for a particular task may mean the difference between a job well done and one done carelessly, incorrectly or even dangerously. This chapter introduces the tools and equipment typically used in a professional kitchen. Items are divided into the following categories according to their functions: knives, hand tools, measuring and portioning devices, cookware, strainers and sieves, processing equipment, storage containers, heavy equipment, specialized equipment for emerging culinary techniques, buffet equipment and safety equipment.

A wide variety of specialized tools and equipment is available to today's chef. For example, breading machines, croissant shapers and doughnut glazers are designed to speed production by reducing handwork. Other devices, such as a duck press or a couscousière, are used only for unique tasks in preparing a few menu items. Much of this specialized equipment is quite expensive and found only in food manufacturing operations or specialized kitchens; a discussion of it is beyond the scope of this chapter. Brief descriptions of some of these specialized devices are, however, found in the Glossary. Baking pans and tools are discussed in Chapter 30, Principles of the Bakeshop.

Before using any equipment, study the operator's manual or have someone experienced with the particular item instruct you on proper procedures for its use and cleaning. And remember, always put safety first.

STANDARDS FOR TOOLS AND EQUIPMENT

NSF International (NSF), previously known as the National Sanitation Foundation, promotes and oversees consensus standards for the design, construction and installation of kitchen tools, cookware and equipment. Many states and municipalities require that food service operations use only NSF-certified equipment. Although NSF certification is voluntary, most manufacturers submit their designs to NSF for certification to show that they are suitable for use in professional food service operations. Certified equipment bears the NSF mark shown in Figure 5.1.

NSF standards reflect the following requirements:

1 Equipment must be easily cleaned.
2 All food contact surfaces must be nontoxic (under intended end-use conditions), nonabsorbent, corrosion resistant and nonreactive.
3 All food contact surfaces must be smooth (i.e., free of pits, cracks, crevices, ledges, rivet heads and bolts).
4 Internal corners and edges must be rounded and smooth; external corners and angles must be smooth and sealed.
5 Coating materials must be nontoxic and easily cleaned; coatings must resist chipping and cracking.
6 Waste and waste liquids must be easily removed.

In general, only commercial food service tools and equipment should be used in a professional kitchen. Look for tools that are well constructed. For example, joints should be welded, not bonded with solder; handles should be comfortable, with rounded borders; plastic and rubber parts should be seamless.

Before purchasing or leasing any equipment, you should ask the following questions:

1 Is this equipment necessary for producing menu items?
2 Will this equipment perform the job required in the space available?

3 Is this equipment the most economical for the operation's specific needs?

4 Is this equipment easy to clean, maintain and repair?

5 Does the equipment operate efficiently and meet energy conservation standards?

KNIVES

Knives are the most important items in the chef's tool kit. With a sharp knife, the skilled chef can accomplish a number of tasks more quickly and efficiently than any machine. Good-quality knives are expensive but will last for many years with proper care. Select easily sharpened, well-constructed knives that are comfortable and balanced in your hand. Knife construction and commonly used knives are discussed here; knife safety and care as well as cutting techniques are discussed in Chapter 6, Knife Skills.

Knife Construction

A good knife begins with a single piece of metal, stamped, cut or—best of all—forged and tempered into a blade of the desired shape. The following metals are generally used for knife blades:

Carbon steel: An alloy of carbon and iron, carbon steel is traditionally used for blades because it is soft enough to be sharpened easily. It corrodes and discolors easily, however, especially when used with acidic foods.

Stainless steel: Stainless steel will not rust, corrode or discolor and is extremely durable. A stainless steel blade is much more difficult to sharpen than a carbon steel one, although once an edge is established on a stainless steel blade, it lasts longer than the edge on a carbon steel blade.

High-carbon stainless steel: An alloy combining the best features of carbon steel and stainless steel, high-carbon stainless steel neither corrodes nor discolors and can be sharpened almost as easily as carbon steel. It is now the most frequently used metal for blades.

Ceramic: A ceramic called zirconium oxide is now used to make knife blades that are extremely sharp, very easy to clean, rustproof and nonreactive. With proper care, ceramic blades will remain sharp for years, but when sharpening is needed, it must be done professionally on special diamond wheels. Although ceramic is highly durable, it does not have the flexibility of metal, so never use a ceramic knife to pry anything, to strike a hard surface (e.g., when crushing garlic or chopping through bones), to cut frozen food or to cut against a china or ceramic surface.

A portion of the blade, known as the **tang**, fits inside the handle, as shown in Figure 5.2. On most knives, pins or rivets hold the two sides of the handle to the tang. The best knives are constructed with a full tang running the length of the handle; they also have a **bolster** where the blade meets the handle (the bolster is part of the blade, not a separate collar). Less expensive knives may have a ¾-length tang or a thin "rattail" tang. Neither provides as much support, durability or balance as a full tang.

Knife handles are often made of hard woods infused with plastic and riveted to the tang. In contrast to wooden handles, molded polypropylene handles are permanently bonded to a tang without seams or rivets. Stainless steel handles welded directly to the blade are durable but very lightweight. Any handle should be shaped for comfort and ground smooth to eliminate crevices where bacteria can grow.

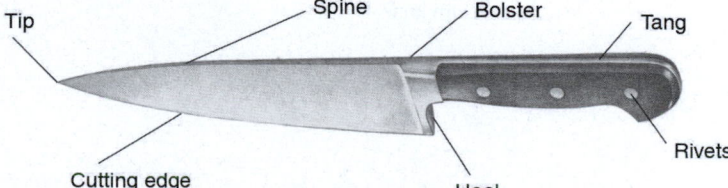

Figure 5.2 The parts of a chef's knife.

Knife Shapes and Sharpening Equipment

Many knives have specialized functions not described here. This list includes only the most basic knives and sharpening equipment.

French or chef's knife

Utility knife

Rigid boning knife

Paring knife

Cleaver

Flexible slicer

Serrated slicer

Butcher knife or scimitar

Oyster knife

Clam knife

Steel

Three-sided sharpening stone

French or Chef's Knife

A **French** or **chef's knife** is an all-purpose knife used for chopping, slicing and mincing. Its rigid 8- to 14-inch-long blade is wide at the heel and tapers to a point at the tip.

Utility Knife

A **utility knife** is an all-purpose knife used for cutting fruits and vegetables and carving poultry. Its rigid 6- to 8-inch-long blade is shaped like a chef's knife but narrower.

Boning Knife

A **boning knife** is smaller with a thin blade used to separate meat from bone. The blade is usually 5–7 inches long and may be flexible or rigid.

Paring Knife

A **paring knife** is short and used for detail work or cutting fruits and vegetables. The rigid blade is from 2 to 4 inches long. A **bird's-beak knife** or **tourné knife** is similar to a paring knife but with a curved blade; it is used to cut curved surfaces or to turn vegetables.

Cleaver

A **cleaver** has a large, heavy rectangular blade used for chopping or cutting through bones.

Slicer

A **slicer** has a long, thin blade used primarily for slicing cooked meat. The tip may be round or pointed, and the blade may be flexible or rigid. A similar knife with a serrated edge is used for slicing bread or pastry items.

Butcher Knife

Sometimes known as a **scimitar** because the rigid blade curves up in a 25-degree angle at the tip, a **butcher knife** is used for fabricating raw meat and is available with 6- to 14-inch blades.

Oyster and Clam Knives

The short, rigid blades of **oyster** and **clam knives** are used to open oyster and clam shells. The tips are blunt; only the clam knife has a sharp edge.

Steel

A **steel** is a scored, slightly abrasive steel rod used to hone or straighten a blade immediately after and between sharpenings.

Sharpening Stone

Also known as a **whetstone**, a **sharpening stone** is a flat brick of synthetic abrasives that is used to put an edge on a dull blade. Various grit sizes are available. The most practical sets include both coarse- and fine-grit stones.

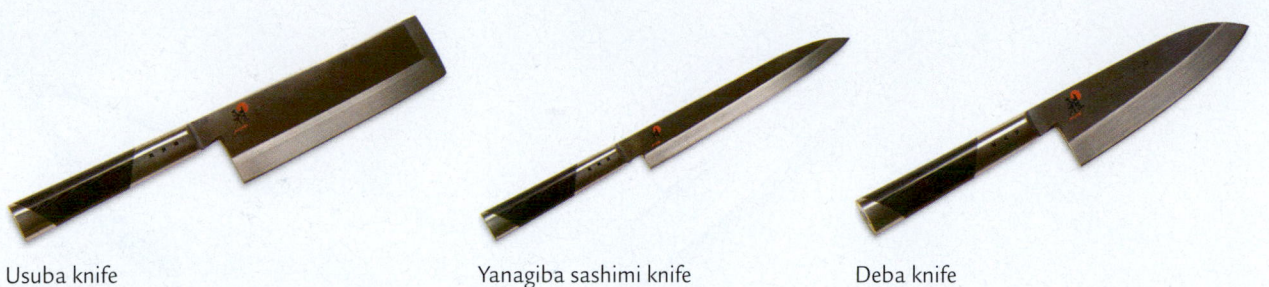

Usuba knife   Yanagiba sashimi knife   Deba knife

Japanese Knives

Specialized knives used in Japanese cooking are popular additions to a chef's toolkit. Traditional Japanese knives have an asymmetrical blade like a chisel, flat on one side and beveled to a sharp edge on the other side, which facilitates precise cutting. The **usuba** has a rectangular blade and is used to cut thin vegetable garnishes. The **yanagiba** has a thin 8- to 14-inch-long straight blade traditionally used to cut translucent slices of raw fish fillets called sashimi and sushi rolls. The **deba** has a wide, sturdy 5- to 7-inch-long wedge-shaped blade used for butchering and boning fish. The santoku resembles the deba in shape but it has a thinner symmetrical 6- to 7-inch long blade. Sharper than a European chef's knife, the santoku is considered an all-purpose knife.

HAND TOOLS

Hand tools are designed to aid in cutting, shaping, moving or combining foods. They have few, if any, moving parts. Sturdiness, durability and safety are the watchwords when selecting hand tools. Choose tools, such as the ones illustrated here, that can withstand the heavy use of a professional kitchen and are easy to clean.

Chef's fork

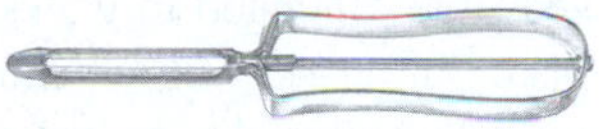

Vegetable peeler

Zester

Table-mounted can opener

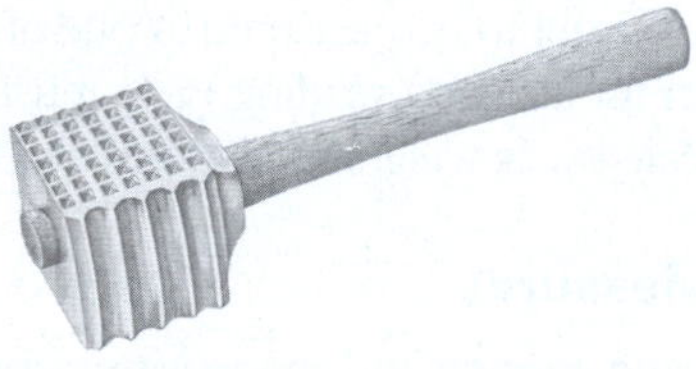

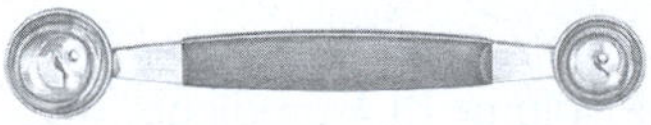

Melon ball cutter

Meat mallet

Straight spatula (cake spatula)

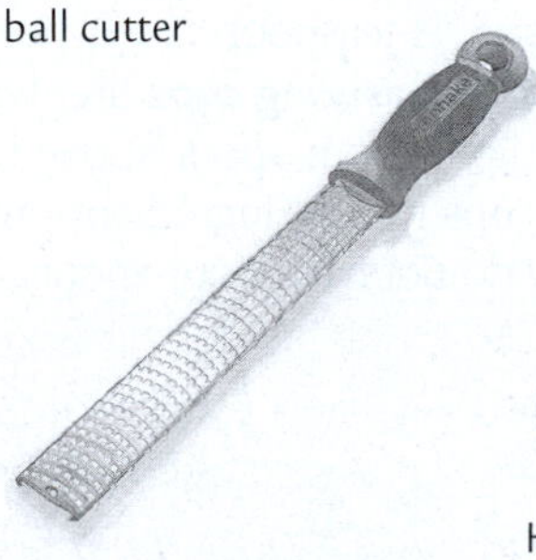

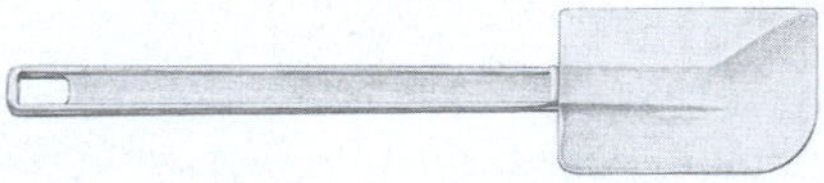

Heat-resistant plastic or silicone spatula

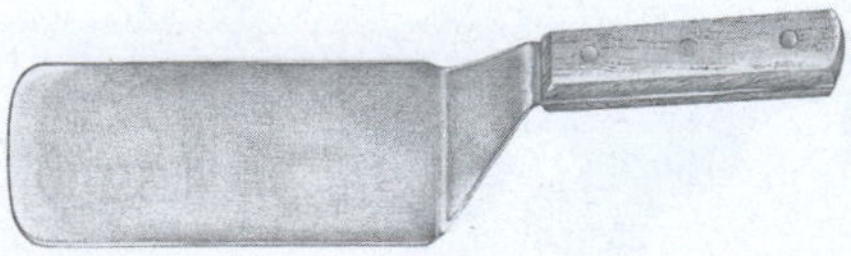

Rasp-style grater

Grill spatula

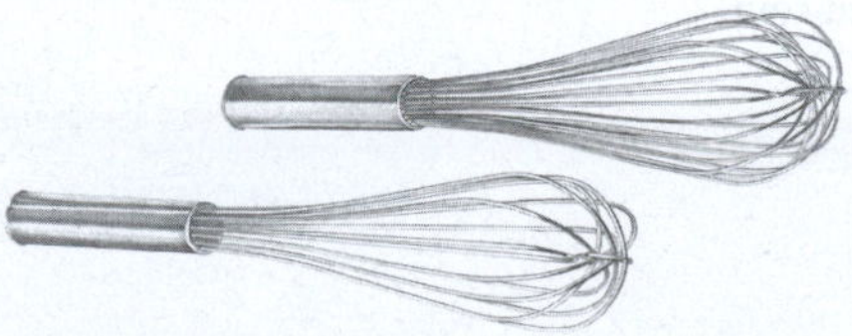

Balloon and rigid whisks

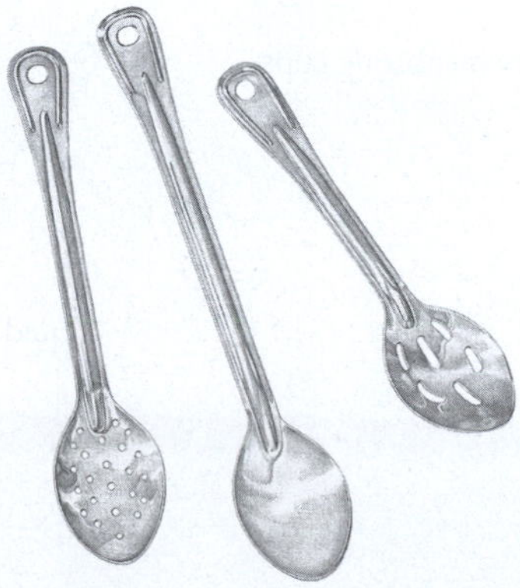

Perforated, plain and slotted spoons

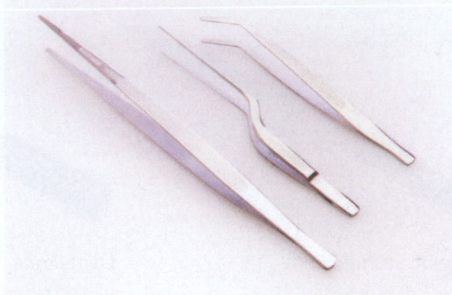

Plating tweezers

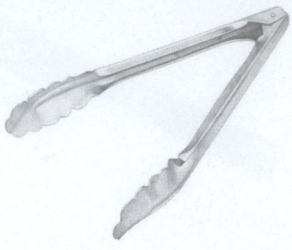

Straight tongs

MEASURING AND PORTIONING DEVICES

Ingredients must be measured precisely, especially in the bakeshop. Foods should also be measured when served to control portion size and cost. Most of the devices used to measure and portion foods are hand tools. These hand tools are designed to make food preparation and service easier and more precise. The accuracy they afford prevents costly mistakes.

Measurements may be based on weight (e.g., grams, ounces, pounds) or volume (e.g., teaspoons, cups, gallons). Therefore it is necessary to have available several measuring devices, including liquid and dry measuring cups and a variety of scales. Thermometers and timers are also measuring devices and are discussed here. When purchasing measuring devices, look for quality construction and accurate markings.

Scales

Scales measure the weight of an ingredient or a portion of food (e.g., the sliced meat for a sandwich). **Portion scales** feature a spring mechanism, round dial and single flat tray. They are available calibrated in grams, ounces or pounds. **Electronic scales** also use a spring mechanism but provide digital readouts. Electronic scales are often required where foods are priced for sale by weight. An automatic tare feature conveniently allows the user to disregard the weight of the container used to hold loose ingredients on the scale. **Balance scales** (also known as baker's scales) use a two-tray, free-weight counterbalance system. A balance scale allows more weight to be measured at one time because it is not limited by spring capacity.

To obtain an accurate reading, you must accurately use and maintain all scales. Never pick up a scale by its weighing platform, as this can damage the balancing mechanism.

Volume Measures

Use **measuring spoons** and **measuring cups** to measure the volume of ingredients. Measuring spoons sold as a set usually include ¼-teaspoon, ½-teaspoon, 1-teaspoon and 1-tablespoon units (or the metric equivalent). **Liquid measuring cups** are available in capacities from 1 cup to 1 gallon. They have a lip or pour spout above the top line of measurement to prevent spills. Measuring cups for dry ingredients are usually sold in sets of ¼-, ⅓- ½- and 1-cup units. They do not have pour spouts, so the

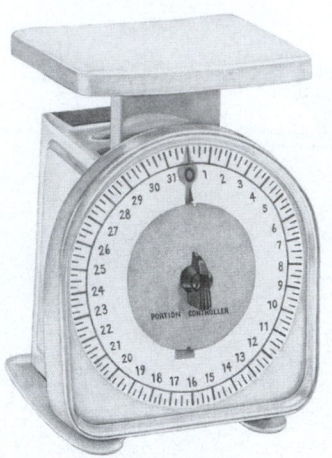

Portion scale

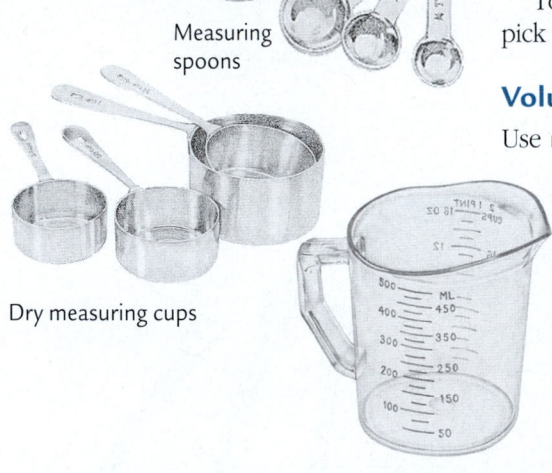

Measuring spoons

Dry measuring cups

Liquid measuring cup

Balance or baker's scale

top of the cup is level with the top measurement specified. Glass measuring cups are not recommended because they can break. Avoid using bent or dented measuring cups, as the damage may distort the measurement capacity.

Ladles

Long-handled **ladles** are useful for portioning liquids such as stocks, sauces and soups. Ladle capacity, in ounces or milliliters, is stamped on the ladle handle.

Portion Scoops

Portion scoops (also known as dishers) resemble ice cream scoops. They come in a range of standardized sizes and have a lever-operated blade for releasing their contents. Scoops are useful for portioning salads, vegetables, muffin batters or other soft foods. A number, stamped on either the handle or the release mechanism, indicates the number of level scoopfuls per quart. The higher the scoop number, the smaller the scoop's capacity. See Table 5.1.

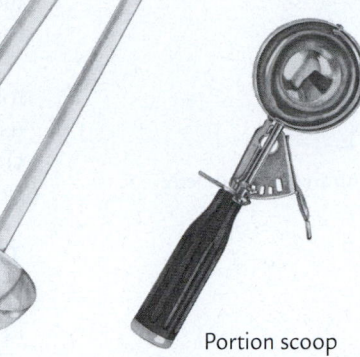
Portion scoop

Ladles

Thermometers

Various types of **thermometers** are used in the kitchen to check the temperature of foods and of equipment such as ovens, refrigerators and freezers. Stem-type thermometers, including instant-read models, are inserted into foods to obtain temperature readings. Temperatures are shown on either a dial or a digital readout. An **instant-read thermometer** is a small stem-type model, designed to be carried in a pocket and used to provide quick temperature readings. An instant-read thermometer should not be left in foods that are cooking because doing so damages the thermometer. Sanitize the stem of any thermometer before use in order to avoid cross-contamination.

Candy and fat thermometers measure temperatures up to 400°F (204°C) using mercury in a column of glass. A back clip attaches the thermometer to the pan, keeping the chef's hands free. Be careful not to subject glass thermometers to quick temperature changes, as the glass may shatter.

Electronic probe thermometers are reasonably priced and commonly used in food service facilities. These thermometers provide immediate, clear, digital readouts from a handheld unit attached to a metal probe (some are conveniently designed so that the probe is embedded in the tines of a long-handled fork or the bowl of a ladle). A detachable probe is especially useful inside an oven and for deep-frying and grilling. Digital

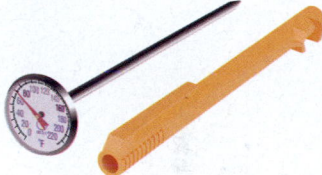
Instant-read thermometer

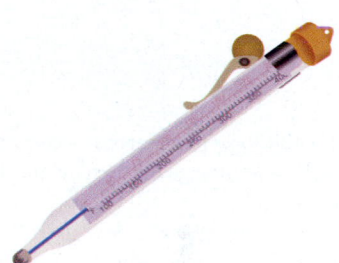
Candy thermometer

PORTION SCOOP CAPACITIES				TABLE 5.1
	APPROXIMATE VOLUME		APPROXIMATE WEIGHT*	
SCOOP NUMBER	U.S.	METRIC	U.S.	METRIC
6	⅔ c.	160 ml	5 oz.	160 g
8	½ c.	120 ml	4 oz.	120 g
10	3 fl. oz.	90 ml	3–3½ oz.	85–100 g
12	⅓ c.	80 ml	2½–3 oz.	75–85 g
16	¼ c.	60 ml	2 oz.	60 g
20	1½ fl. oz.	45 ml	1½ oz.	45 g
24	1⅓ fl. oz.	40 ml	1⅓ oz.	40 g
30	1 fl. oz.	30 ml	1 oz.	30 g
40	0.8 fl. oz.	24 ml	0.8 oz.	24 g
60	½ fl. oz.	15 ml	½ oz.	15 g

*Weights are approximate because they vary by food.

How to Calibrate a Stem-Type Thermometer

All stem-type thermometers should be calibrated at least weekly and whenever they are dropped. To calibrate a stem-type thermometer, fill a glass with shaved ice, then add water. Place the thermometer in the ice slush and wait until the temperature reading stabilizes. Following the manufacturer's directions, adjust the thermometer's calibration nut until the temperature reads 32°F (0°C). Check the calibration by returning the thermometer to the slush. Then repeat the procedure, substituting boiling water for the ice slush, and calibrate the thermometer at 212°F (100°C).

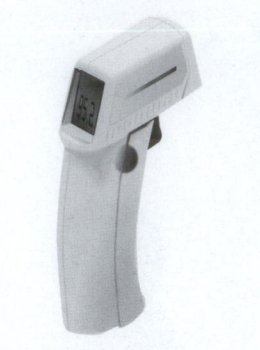

Digital infrared thermometer

probe thermometers with alarms are used when it is critical that steady temperatures be maintained (e.g., when smoking meats).

Infrared thermometers employ infrared sensors with laser sightings to instantly monitor the surface temperature of foods during cooking or holding. They can also be useful to monitor the temperature of goods at receiving and in storage. These infrared thermometers allow staff to instantly monitor a wide range of temperatures without actually touching the food, thus avoiding any risk of cross-contamination.

Oven and refrigerator thermometers are also useful to ensure constant temperatures for holding and storing foods. Some thermometers are equipped with alarms to alert the user when refrigerator temperature rises above levels that will ensure food safety. When choosing thermometers, select instruments with easy-to-read dials or clearly marked divisions on the column of mercury.

Timers

Portable kitchen timers are useful for any busy chef. Small digital timers can be carried in a pocket; some even time three functions at once. Select a timer with a loud alarm signal and long timing capability.

COOKWARE

Cookware includes the sauté pans and stockpots used on the stove top as well as the roasting pans, hotel pans and specialty molds used inside the oven. Select cookware for its size, shape, ability to conduct heat evenly and overall quality of construction.

Cookware Metals and Heat Conduction

Cookware that fails to distribute heat evenly may cause hot spots that burn foods. Because different metals conduct heat at different rates, and thicker layers of metal conduct heat more evenly than thinner layers, the most important considerations when choosing cookware are the type and thickness (known as the **gauge**) of the material. No single cookware or material suits every process or need, however; always select the most appropriate material for the task at hand.

gauge the thickness of a material such as aluminum; the lower the gauge number, the thicker the material

Copper

Copper is an excellent conductor: It heats rapidly and evenly and cools quickly. Unlined copper pots are unsurpassed for cooking sugar and fruit mixtures, but copper cookware is extremely expensive. It also requires a great deal of care and is often quite heavy. Because copper may react with some foods, traditional copper cookware usually has a tin lining, which is soft and easily scratched. Because of these problems, copper is now lined with stainless steel. Copper may also be sandwiched between layers of stainless steel or aluminum in the bottom of pots and pans to enhance their conductivity.

Aluminum

Aluminum is the metal used most commonly in commercial cookware. It is lightweight and, after copper, conducts heat best. Aluminum is a soft metal, though, so it should be treated with care to avoid dents. Do not use aluminum containers for storage or for cooking acidic foods because aluminum reacts chemically with many foods. Light-colored foods, such as soups or sauces, may be discolored when cooked in aluminum, especially if stirred with a metal whisk or spoon. Anodized aluminum has a hard, dark, corrosion-resistant surface that helps prevent sticking and discoloration.

Stainless Steel

Although stainless steel conducts and retains heat poorly, it is a hard, durable metal particularly useful for holding foods and for low-temperature cooking in which hot spots and scorching are not problems. Stainless steel pots and pans are available with aluminum or copper bonded to the bottom or with an aluminum-layered core. Although expensive, such cookware combines the rapid, uniform heat conductivity of copper or aluminum with the strength, durability and nonreactivity of stainless steel. Stainless steel is also ideal for storage containers because it does not react with foods.

Cast Iron

Cast-iron cookware distributes heat evenly and holds high temperatures well. It is often used for griddles and large skillets. Although relatively inexpensive, cast iron is extremely heavy and brittle. It must be kept properly conditioned and dry to prevent rust and pitting.

Carbon Steel

A lighter weight cousin of cast iron, **carbon steel** is an alloy of iron and carbon that is an excellent conductor of heat. Because it heats rapidly, carbon steel is often used to make frying pans; such slope-sided pans are standard in France for sautéing and searing foods. Like cast iron, carbon steel must be kept conditioned and dry. But with proper seasoning, carbon steel pans develop a non-stick surface.

Other Cookware Materials

Glass

Glass retains heat well but conducts it poorly. It does not react with foods. Tempered glass is suitable for microwave cooking provided it does not have any metal decoration. Commercial operations rarely use glass cookware because of the danger of breakage.

Ceramics

Ceramics, including earthenware, porcelain and stoneware, are used primarily for baking dishes, casseroles and baking stones, because they conduct heat uniformly and retain temperatures well. Ceramics are nonreactive, inexpensive and generally suitable for use in a microwave oven (provided there is no metal in the glaze). Ceramics are easily chipped or cracked, however, and should not be used over a direct flame. Also, quick temperature changes may cause ceramic cookware to crack or shatter.

Plastic

Plastic containers are frequently used in commercial kitchens for food storage or service, but they cannot be used for heating or cooking except in a microwave oven. Plastic microwave cookware is made of phenolic resin. It is easy to clean, relatively inexpensive and rigidly shaped, but its glasslike structure is brittle, and it can crack or shatter.

Enamelware

Pans lined with enamel should not be used for cooking; in many areas, their use in commercial kitchens is prohibited by law. The enamel can chip or crack easily, providing good places for bacteria to grow. Also, the chemicals used to bond the enamel to the cookware can cause food poisoning if ingested.

Silicone

Silicone is a heat-resistant polymer (plastic) used to make flexible bakeware and kitchen tools. While it is a poor conductor of heat, this light material resists sticking and can withstand temperatures from freezing to 485°F (251°C). Baking pan liners made from silicone materials rarely require greasing and are useful for baking as well as making candy and chocolate work. Sheets of baking molds made from silicone are used to form individual cakes, petit fours and desserts, as well as ice cream and frozen desserts. Heat-resistant silicone spatulas and pot holders are also effective and popular.

Muffins baked in silicone molds

Nonstick Coatings

A polymer (plastic) known as polytetrafluoroethylene (PTFE), which is marketed under the trade names Teflon and Silverstone, is applied to many types of cookware. It does not affect a metal's ability to conduct heat and it provides a slippery, nonreactive finish that prevents food from sticking and allows the use of less fat in cooking. (Newer nonstick coatings made from ceramic, silicone and titanium are also in use.) Cookware with nonstick coatings requires a great deal of care, however, because the coatings can scratch, chip and blister. Do not use metal spoons or spatulas in cookware with nonstick coatings. To prevent the surface from deteriorating, do not use cookware with nonstick coatings over high heat. Such temperatures may cause the release of unhealthy or toxic vapors from the pans' surface. Most cookware with nonstick coatings should be used below 500°F (260°C). (Verify the temperature limits of your cookware with the manufacturer.)

Common Cookware

The most common cookware in the professional kitchen are the pots and pans used every day to cook and store foods. Shape, diameter and depth determine which pots or pans to choose for your cooking task.

Pots

Pots are large round vessels with straight sides and two loop handles. Available in a range of sizes based on volume, pots are used on the stove top for making stocks or soups, or for boiling or simmering foods, particularly when rapid evaporation is not desired. Flat or fitted lids are available.

Pans

Pans are round vessels with one long handle and straight or sloped sides. They are usually smaller and shallower than pots. Pans are available in a range of diameters and are used for general stove top cooking, especially sautéing, frying or reducing liquids rapidly.

Stock pot with spigot

Sauce pot

Saucepan

Rondeau/braiser

Sauteuse (sloped sides)

Sautoir (straight sides)

Cast-iron skillet (Griswold)

Lead: from Roman Pots to Southern Stills

Lead is poisonous. Ingesting it can cause severe gastrointestinal pains, anemia and central nervous system disorders, including intelligence and memory deficits and behavioral changes.

The unwitting and dangerous consumption of lead is not limited to children eating peeling paint chips. Some historians suggest that the use of lead cookware and lead-lined storage vessels and water pipes may have caused pervasive lead poisoning among the elite of the Roman Empire and thus contributed to the empire's decline. There is also ample evidence from ancient times until just a few hundred years ago that wine was heated in lead vessels to sweeten it. This had disastrous effects on drinkers and, for several centuries in countries throughout Europe, on wine purveyors as well. The former could be poisoned, and the latter could be punished by death for selling adulterated wine. More recently it was found that much of the moonshine whiskey produced in the American South contained lead in potentially toxic ranges. The source of the lead in moonshine was the lead solder used in homemade stills, some of which even included old repurposed lead-containing car radiators as condensers.

Although commercially available cookware does not contain lead, be careful of imported pottery and those lovely hand-thrown pots found at craft fairs—there may be lead in the glaze.

Woks

Originally used to prepare Asian foods, **woks** are now found in many professional kitchens. Their round bottoms and curved sides diffuse heat and make it easy to toss or stir contents. Large domed lids retain heat for steaming vegetables. Woks are useful for quickly sautéing strips of meat, simmering a whole fish or deep-frying appetizers. Stove top woks range in diameter from 12 to 30 inches; larger built-in gas or electric models are also available.

Wok

Hotel Pans

Hotel pans (also known as steam table pans) are rectangular stainless steel pans designed to hold food for service in steam tables. Hotel pans are also used for baking, roasting or poaching inside an oven. Perforated pans, which are useful for draining, steaming or icing down foods, are also available. The standard full-size hotel pan is 12 × 20 inches; pans one-half, one-third, one-quarter, one-sixth and other fractions of this size are also available. Hotel pan depth is standardized at 2 inches (referred to as a "200 pan"), 4, 6 and 8 inches.

Hotel pans

Molds

Molds of all shapes, sizes and materials are used to form foods for serving or as vessels in which foods will be served. **Timbale molds** are small (about 4 ounces) metal or ceramic containers used for molding aspic or baking individual portions of mousse, custard or vegetables. Their slightly flared sides allow the contents to release cleanly when the mold is inverted. Small ceramic molds called **ramekins** (about 5–7 ounces) may be used for molding foods or for serving individual portions of mousse, custards and spreads. Molds used to form pâtés and terrines are discussed in Chapter 28, Charcuterie.

Timbale molds

STRAINERS AND SIEVES

Strainers and **sieves** are used primarily to aerate and remove impurities from dry ingredients and to drain or purée cooked foods. Strainers, **colanders**, drum sieves, china caps and chinois are each nonmechanical devices that have a stainless steel mesh or screen through which food passes. The size of the mesh or screen varies from extremely fine to several millimeters wide. Select the fineness best suited for the task at hand. Mechanical devices such as the food mill and flour sifter perform similar functions with the aid of a mechanical hand-crank.

Colander

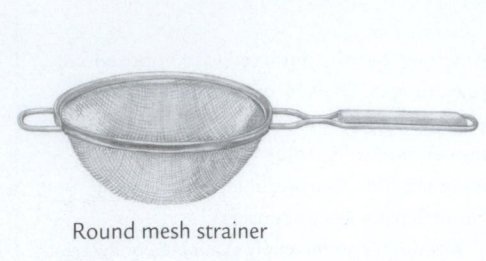

Round mesh strainer

Drum sieve (tamis)

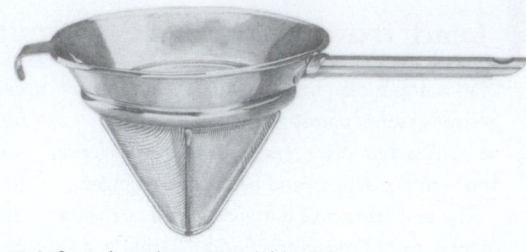

Reinforced mesh strainer (chinois)

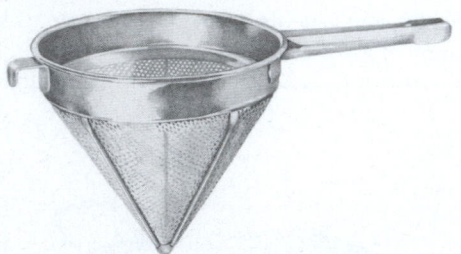

Perforated metal strainer (china cap)

Chinois and China Cap

Both the **chinois** and **china cap** are cone-shaped metal strainers. The conical shape allows liquids to filter through small openings. The body of a chinois is made from a very fine mesh screen. In contrast, a china cap has a perforated metal body. Both are used for straining stocks and sauces, with the chinois being particularly useful for consommé. A china cap can also be used with a pestle to purée soft foods.

Skimmer and Spider

Both the **skimmer** and **spider** are long-handled tools used to remove foods or impurities from liquids. The flat, perforated disk of a skimmer is used to skim stocks or remove foods from soups or stocks. The spider has a finer mesh disk, which makes it a better tool for retrieving items from hot fat. Wooden-handled spiders are available but are less sturdy and harder to clean than all-metal spiders.

Skimmer

Cheesecloth

Cheesecloth is loosely woven cotton gauze used for straining stocks and sauces and wrapping poultry or fish for poaching. Cheesecloth is also indispensable for making sachets, packets of herbs and spices used to flavor soups, stocks and other liquids. Always rinse cheesecloth thoroughly before use; this removes lint and prevents the cheesecloth from absorbing other liquids.

Food Mill

A **food mill** purées and strains food at the same time. Food is placed in the hopper and a hand-crank mechanism turns a blade in the hopper against a perforated disk, forcing the food through the disk. Most models have interchangeable disks with various-sized holes. Choose a mill that can be taken apart easily for cleaning.

Spider

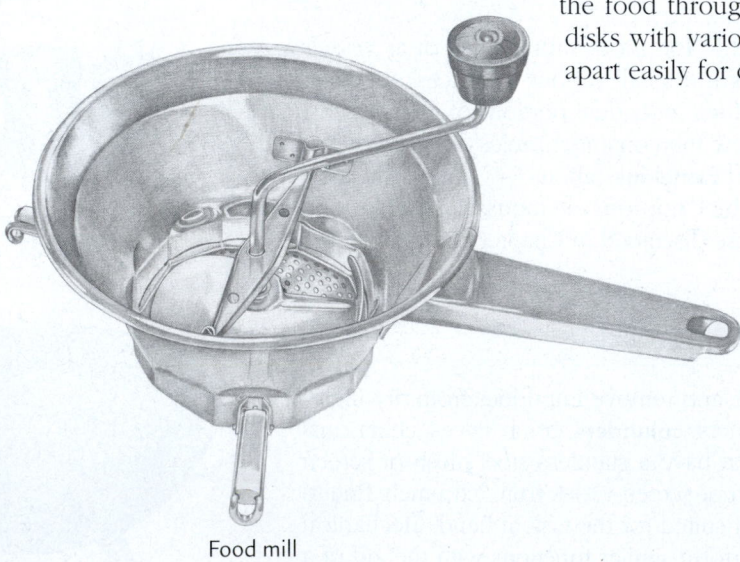

Food mill

Cheesecloth

Flour Sifter

A **sifter** is used for aerating, blending and removing impurities from dry ingredients such as flour, cocoa and leavening agents. The 8-cup hand-crank sifter uses four curved rods to brush the contents through a curved mesh screen. Choose a sifter with a medium-fine screen and a comfortable handle. The French **tamis** is a drum-shaped sieve useful for sifting ingredients as well as for straining thick purées to remove lumps and seeds.

Flour sifter

PROCESSING EQUIPMENT

Processing equipment includes both electrical and nonelectrical mechanical devices used to chop, purée, slice, grind or mix foods. Before using any such equipment, be sure to review its operating procedures and ask for assistance if necessary. All processing equipment must be cleaned and sanitized after using. Always turn the equipment off and disconnect the power before disassembling, cleaning or moving the appliance. Report any problems or malfunctions immediately. *Never place your hand into any machinery when the power is on. Processing equipment is powerful and can cause serious injury.*

Slicer

An electric **slicer** cuts meat, bread, cheese or raw vegetables into uniform slices. It has a circular blade that rotates at high speed. Food is placed in a carrier, then passed (manually or by an electric motor) against the blade. Slice thickness is determined by the distance between the blade and the carrier. Because of the speed with which the blade rotates, foods can be cut into extremely thin slices very quickly. An electric slicer is convenient for preparing moderate to large quantities of food, but the time required to disassemble and clean the equipment makes it impractical when slicing only a few items.

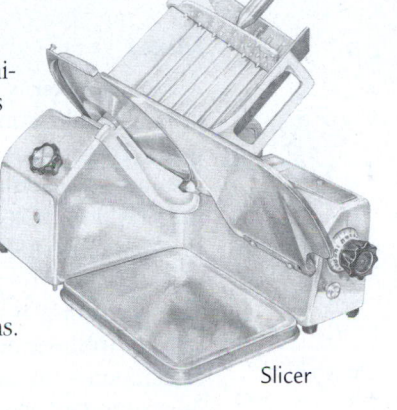

Slicer

Mandoline

A **mandoline** is a manually operated slicer made of stainless steel with adjustable slicing blades. It is also used to make julienne and waffle-cut slices. Its narrow, rectangular body sits on the work counter at a 45-degree angle. Foods are passed against a blade to obtain uniform slices. It is useful for slicing small quantities of fruits or vegetables when using a large electric slicer would be unwarranted. To avoid injury, always use a hand guard or steel glove when using a mandoline.

Mandoline

Food Chopper or Buffalo Chopper

A **food chopper** is used to process moderate to large quantities of food to a uniform size, such as chopped onions or bread crumbs. The food is placed in a large bowl that rotates beneath a hood and curved blades chop the food in the bowl. The size of the cut depends on how long the food is left in the machine. **Buffalo choppers** are available in floor or tabletop models. The motor of the chopper can usually be fitted with a variety of other tools such as a meat grinder or a slicer/shredder.

Food Processor

A **food processor** has a motor housing with a removable bowl and S-shaped blade. It is used for many tasks, including puréeing cooked foods, chopping nuts, preparing compound butters and emulsifying sauces. Special disks can be added that slice, shred or julienne foods. Bowl capacity and motor power vary; select a model large enough for your most common tasks.

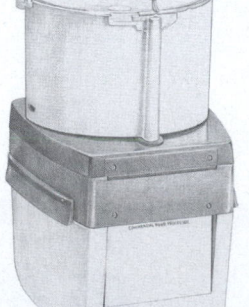

Food processor

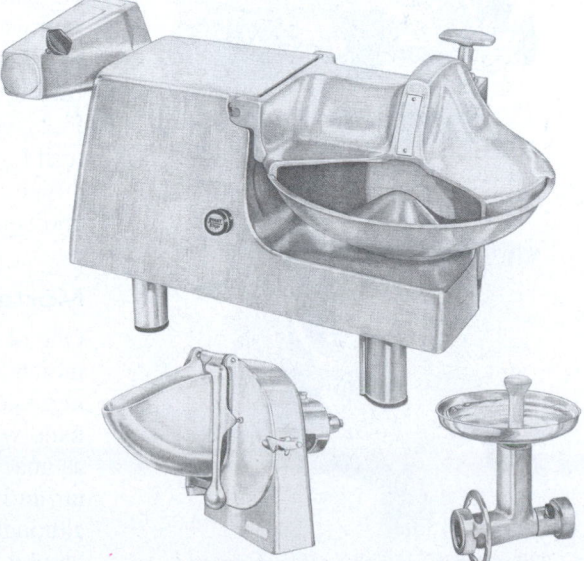

Buffalo chopper with slicer and meat grinder attachments

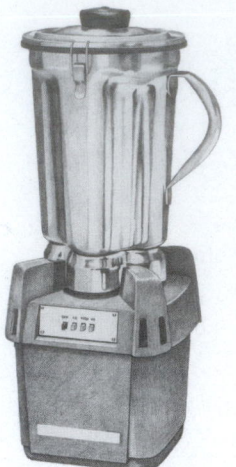

Heavy-duty blender

Blender

Though similar in principle to a food processor, a **blender** has a tall, narrow food container and a four-pronged blade. Its design and whirlpool action are optimal for processing liquids or liquefying foods quickly. A blender is used to prepare smooth drinks, purée soups and sauces, blend batters and chop ice. A **vertical cutter/mixer (VCM)** operates like a very large, powerful blender. A VCM is usually floor-mounted and has a capacity of 15–80 quarts.

Immersion Blender

An **immersion blender**—like its household counterpart the hand blender or wand—is a long shaft fitted with a rotating four-pronged blade at the bottom. An immersion blender is used to purée a soft food, soup or sauce directly in the container in which it was prepared, eliminating the need to transfer the food from the cooking container to a blender or food processor. This is especially useful when working with hot foods. Small cordless, rechargeable immersion blenders are convenient for puréeing or mixing small quantities or beverages, but larger heavy-duty electric models are more practical in commercial kitchens.

Immersion blender

Mixer

A vertical **mixer** is indispensable in the bakeshop and most kitchens. The U-shaped arms hold a metal mixing bowl in place; the selected mixing attachment fits onto the rotating head. The three common mixing attachments are the **whip** (used for whipping eggs or cream), the **paddle** (used for general mixing) and the **dough hook** (used for kneading bread). Most mixers have several operating speeds. Bench models range in capacity from 4.5 to 20 quarts, whereas floor mixers can hold as much as 140 quarts. To prevent injuries, larger mixers are fitted with a moveable metal or plastic **safety guard** that protects hands, clothing and other objects from coming into contact with the rotating head and mixer attachments. Some mixers can be fitted with shredder/slicers, meat grinders, juicers or power strainers, making the equipment more versatile.

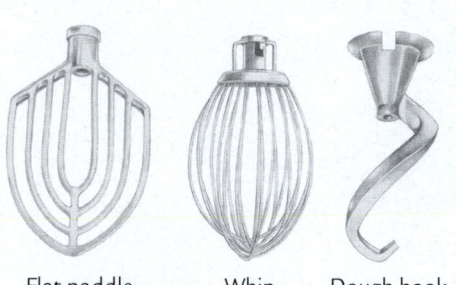

Flat paddle   Whip   Dough hook

Juicer

Two types of juicers are available: reamers and extractors. **Reamers**, also known as citrus juicers, remove juice from citrus fruits. They can be manual or electric. Manual models use a lever arm to squeeze the fruit with greater pressure. They are most often used to prepare small to moderate amounts of juice for cooking or beverages. **Juice extractors** are electrical devices that create juice by liquefying raw fruits, vegetables and herbs. **Centrifugal extractors** use centrifugal force to filter out fiber and pulp. **Masticating juicers** are a type of juice extractor that crushes then presses the fruits and vegetables to extract juice.

Citrus juicer

Mortar and Pestle

One of the oldest and most widely used processing tools is the mortar and pestle. The **mortar** is a bowl-shaped vessel in which ingredients can be pulverized, ground, mashed or blended by hand with a club-shaped **pestle**. Herbs and spices, sauces such as guacamole, even meats can be prepared this way. The mortar and the pestle are usually made from the same material, although that material varies depending on the culture and geographic region. Marble, granite, volcanic stone, hardwood and ceramic mortar and pestles are available in a variety of sizes.

Mortar and pestle

20-quart mixer with a safety guard and attachments

Whipping Siphon

A **whipping siphon** is designed to aerate and dispense whipped cream. It is composed of a stainless steel canister to hold the cream and a tight-fitting lid with a single-use cartridge or charger of nitrous oxide gas. Once discharged into the canister, the gas dissolves in the fat of the cream, pressurizing its contents. When dispensed, the gas turns into air bubbles and the cream expands and lightens. A whipping siphon can also be used to create and dispense cold or hot foams made from smooth and light soups, stocks or purées.

STORAGE CONTAINERS

Proper storage containers keep leftovers and opened packages of food safe for consumption. Proper storage can reduce the costs incurred by waste or spoilage. Although stainless steel pans such as hotel pans are suitable and useful for some items, the expense of stainless steel and the lack of airtight lids makes these pans impractical for general storage purposes. Aluminum containers are not recommended because the metal can react with even mildly acidic items such as cut citrus fruits or salad dressing made with vinegar. Glass containers are generally not allowed in commercial kitchens because of the hazards of broken glass. The most useful storage containers are those made of high-density plastic such as polyethylene and polypropylene.

Storage containers must have well-fitting lids and an operation must have a variety of sizes, including some that are small enough to hold even minimal quantities of food without allowing too much exposure to oxygen. Round and square plastic containers are widely available. Flat, snap-on lids allow containers to be stacked for more efficient storage. Containers may be clear or opaque white, which helps protect light-sensitive foods. Larger containers may be fitted with handles and spigots, making them especially suited for storing stock. Some storage containers are marked with graduated measurements so that content quantity can be determined at a glance.

Large quantities of dry ingredients, such as flour and rice, can be stored in rolling bins. The bins should be seamless with rounded corners for easy cleaning. They should have well-fitting easy-to-open lids and should move easily on well-balanced casters.

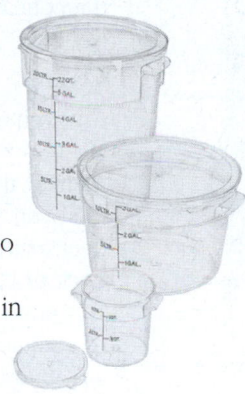

Storage containers

HEAVY EQUIPMENT

Heavy equipment includes the gas-, electric- or steam-operated appliances used for cooking, reheating or holding foods. It also includes dishwashers and refrigeration units. These items are usually installed in a fixed location determined by the kitchen's traffic flow and space limitations.

Heavy equipment may be purchased or leased new or used. Used equipment is most often purchased in an effort to save money. Although the initial cost is generally less for used equipment, the buyer should also consider the lack of a manufacturer's warranty or dealership guarantee and how the equipment was maintained by the prior owner. Functional used equipment is satisfactory for back-of-the-house areas, but it is usually better to purchase new equipment if it will be visible to the customer. Leasing equipment may be appropriate for some operations. The cost of leasing is less than purchasing, and if something goes wrong with the equipment, the operator is generally not responsible for repairs or service charges.

Stove Tops

Stove tops or **ranges** are often the most important cooking equipment in the kitchen. They have one or more burners powered by gas or electricity. The burners may be open or covered with a cast-iron or steel plate. Open burners supply quick, direct heat that is easy to regulate. A steel plate, known as a **flat top**, supplies even heat that is less intense. Although it takes longer to heat than a burner, the flat top supports heavier

Flat top range

weights and makes a larger area available for cooking. Many stoves include both flat tops and open burner arrangements.

Griddles are similar to flat tops except they are made of a thinner metal plate. Foods are usually cooked directly on the griddle's surface, not in pots or pans, which can nick or scratch the surface. The griddle surface should be properly cleaned and conditioned after each use. Griddles are popular for short-order and fast-food-type operations.

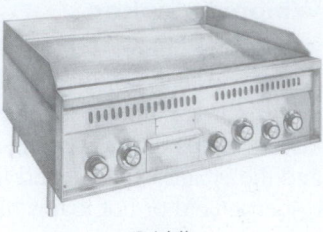

Griddle

Induction cooktops uses special conductive coils, called inductors that are below the stove top's surface, in combination with flat-bottomed cookware made of cast iron or magnetic stainless steel. The coil generates a magnetic current so that the cookware is heated rapidly with magnetic friction. Heat energy is then transferred from the cookware to the food by conduction. The cooking surface, which is made of a solid ceramic material, remains cool. Only the cookware and its contents get hot. Induction systems are extremely energy efficient. They feature instant response time because power is directed into the cooking utensil, not the surrounding air.

Induction cooktop

Induction cooking offers speed, by heating foods quickly, and easy cleanup. Portable **induction burners** are useful in the bakeshop, where there may be a limited need for direct-heat cooking because they maintain a safer, cooler cooking environment.

Ovens

An oven is an enclosed space where food is cooked by being surrounded with hot, dry air. Conventional ovens are often located beneath the stove top. There is a heating element at the unit's bottom or floor, and pans are placed on adjustable wire racks inside the oven. See Figure 5.3. Conventional ovens may also be separate, freestanding units or decks stacked one on top of the other. In **stack ovens**, pans are placed directly on the deck or floor, not on wire racks.

Stack oven

Convection ovens use internal fans to circulate the hot air. This tends to cook foods more quickly and evenly. **Convection ovens**, which are used in most commercial kitchens, are almost always freestanding units, powered by either gas or electricity. Because convection ovens cook foods more quickly, temperatures may need to be reduced by 25–50°F (10–20°C) from those recommended for conventional ovens. **Combination** or **combi ovens** combine steam and convected heat into one device. Such ovens perform several functions; they bake, poach, roast and steam. Programmable electronic controls precisely regulate oven temperatures. Foods such as bread can be baked with steam to develop a crisp crust. Roasts can be cooked in the oven then automatically held at lower temperatures to preserve them for service. Combination ovens are popular in large food service operations, which can bear the cost of these versatile and labor-saving devices.

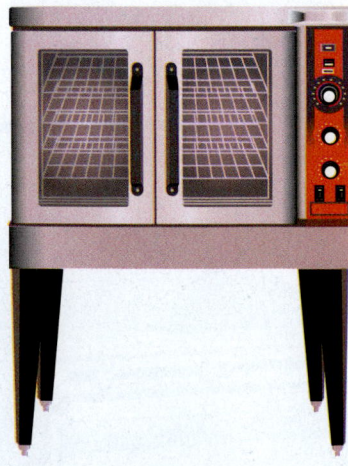

Convection oven

Wood-Burning Ovens

The ancient practice of baking in a retained-heat masonry oven has been revived in recent years, with many upscale restaurants and artisan bakeries installing adobe or **brick ovens** for baking pizzas and breads as well as for roasting fish, poultry and vegetables. These ovens have a curved interior chamber that is usually recessed into a wall. Although gas-fired models are available, wood-firing is more traditional and provides the aromas and flavors associated with brick ovens. A wood fire is built inside the oven to heat the brick chamber. The ashes are then swept out and the food is placed on the flat oven floor. Breads and pizzas baked in direct contact with the hot masonry rise better than in a conventional oven and develop a unique crisp crust. The combination of high heat and wood smoke adds distinctive flavors to foods.

Wood-burning oven

Gas grill

Rotisserie

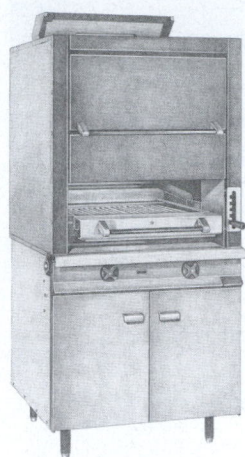

Overhead broiler

Microwave Ovens

Microwave ovens are electrically powered ovens used to cook or reheat foods. They are available in a range of sizes and power settings. A microwave oven will not brown foods unless the oven is fitted with a special browning element. Microwave cooking is discussed in more detail in Chapter 10, Principles of Cooking.

Broilers and Grills

Broilers and grills are generally used to prepare meats, fish and poultry. In a grill, the heat source is beneath the rack on which the food is placed. In a broiler, the heat source is above the food. Most broilers are gas powered; grills may be gas or electric powered or may burn wood or charcoal. A **salamander** is a small overhead broiler primarily used to finish or top-brown foods. See Figure 5.3. A **rotisserie** is similar to a broiler except that the food is placed on a revolving spit in front of the heat source. The unit may be open or enclosed like an oven; it is most often used for cooking poultry or meats. An enclosed rotisserie with a solid door is generally more energy efficient to operate than its open counterpart.

Steam Tables

Steam tables are large counter-height tables where foods are kept hot at food safe temperatures. Hotel pans or other containers are inset into a frame suspended over the heat source, which may be circulating steam or hot water. Steam tables ease the flow of meals from the kitchen to the guest. Hot soups, sauces and other moist foods are ready to be served at any time. Cafeterias and buffet restaurants are dependent on the use steam tables.

Figure 5.3 Gas burner and griddle with dual ovens and an overhead broiler (salamander).

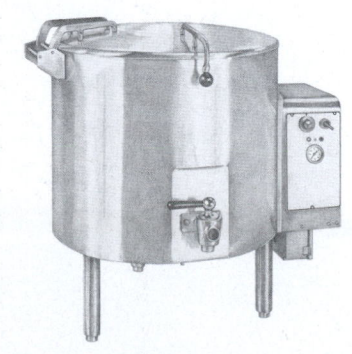

Tilting skillet

Tilting Skillets

Tilting skillets are large, freestanding, flat-bottomed pans about 6 inches deep with an internal heating element below the pan's bottom. They are usually made of stainless steel with a cover and have a hand-crank mechanism that turns or tilts the pan to pour out the contents. Tilting skillets can be used as stockpots, braziers, fry pans, griddles or steam tables, making them one of the most versatile of commercial appliances.

Steam Kettles

Steam kettles (also known as steam-jacketed kettles) are similar to stockpots except they are heated from the bottom and sides by steam circulating between layers of stainless steel. The steam may be generated internally or from an outside source. Because steam heats the kettle's sides, foods cook more quickly and evenly than they would in a pot sitting on the stove top. Steam kettles are most often used for making sauces,

Steam kettle

Convection steamer

soups, custards and stocks in large quantities. Steam kettles are available in a range of sizes, from a 2-gallon tabletop model to a 100-gallon floor model. Some models have a tilting mechanism that allows the contents to be poured out; others have a spigot near the bottom through which liquids can be drained.

Steamers

Pressure and convection steamers cook foods rapidly and evenly, using direct contact with steam. **Pressure steamers** heat water above the boiling point in sealed compartments; the high temperature and sealed compartment increase the internal pressure in a range of 4–15 pounds per square inch. The increased pressure and temperature cook the foods rapidly. **Convection steamers** generate steam in an internal boiler, then release it over the foods in a cooking chamber. Both types of steamers are ideal for cooking vegetables with minimal loss of flavor or nutrients.

Deep-Fat Fryers

Deep-fat fryers cook foods in a large amount of hot fat. Fryers are sized by the amount of fat they hold. Most commercial fryers range between 15 and 82 pounds. Fryers can be either gas or electric and are thermostatically controlled for temperatures between 200°F and 400°F (90°C and 200°C).

When choosing a fryer, look for a fry tank with curved, easy-to-clean sloping sides. Some fryers have a cold zone (an area of reduced temperature) at the bottom of the fry tank to trap particles. This prevents particles from burning, creating off-flavors and shortening the life of the fryer fat.

Deep-fryers usually come with steel wire baskets to hold the food during cooking. Fryer baskets are typically lowered into the fat and raised manually, although some models have automatic basket mechanisms. The most important factor when choosing a deep-fryer is **recovery time**. Recovery time is the length of time it takes the fat to return to the desired cooking temperature after food is submerged. When food is submerged, heat is immediately transferred to the food from the fat. This heat transfer lowers the fat's temperature. The more food added at one time, the greater the drop in the fat's temperature. Recovery time is important because if the temperature drops too much or does not return quickly to the proper cooking temperature, the food may absorb excess fat and become greasy.

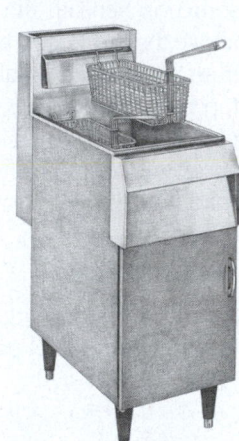

Deep-fat fryer

Refrigerators and Freezers

Proper refrigeration space is an essential component of any kitchen. Many foods must be stored at low temperatures to maintain quality and safety. Most commercial refrigeration is either walk-in units or reach-in upright units.

A **walk-in** is a large, room-sized box capable of holding hundreds of pounds of food on adjustable shelves. A separate freezer walk-in may be positioned nearby or even inside a refrigerated walk-in.

Reach-ins may be individual units or parts of a bank of units, each with shelves approximately the size of a full sheet pan. Reach-in refrigerators and freezers are usually located throughout the kitchen to provide quick access to foods. Small reach-in units may also be beneath the work counters. Freezers and refrigerators are available in a wide range of sizes and door designs to suit any operation.

Other forms of commercial refrigeration include chilled drawers, which are located beneath a work area and are just large enough to accommodate a hotel pan, and display cases used to show foods to the customer. **Blast chillers** and **blast freezers** rapidly and uniformly reduce the temperature of foods below 40°F (4°C) by circulating cold air at high speeds. Also called shock chillers, these devices are important tools in production kitchens where HACCP programs (see Chapter 2, Food Safety and Sanitation) are required to ensure food safety.

Dishwashers

Mechanical dishwashers wash, rinse and sanitize dishware, glassware, cookware and utensils. Small models clean one rack of items at a time, whereas larger models can handle several racks simultaneously on a conveyor belt system. Sanitation is accomplished either with extremely hot water (180°F/82°C) or with chemicals automatically dispensed during the final rinse cycle. Any dishwashing area should be carefully organized for efficient use of equipment and employees and to prevent recontamination of clean items.

Racks

Rolling racks are metal frames designed to hold a number of sheet trays in a space-saving manner. They are useful for storing trays of items waiting to be placed in the oven or for receiving hot pans directly from an oven.

SPECIALIZED EQUIPMENT FOR MODERN CULINARY TECHNIQUES

In today's kitchens, chefs are adopting new tools and cooking equipment to facilitate many modern and experimental cooking techniques. Often these new tools allow for more precision than it is possible to achieve with traditional equipment. One of the more widely discussed techniques is **sous vide** (French for "under vacuum"), a type of low-temperature cooking in which foods are vacuum-sealed in pouches, then cooked for an extended period in a temperature-controlled water bath. Chefs have discovered that this method produces tender, flavorful fresh meat, fish and seafood. *Sous vide* techniques are also useful for preparing delicate sauces, eggs and vegetables. The reduced oxygen environment of foods packaged under vacuum concentrates flavors and extends shelf life. In addition, the temperatures for *sous vide* cooking, which range from 125°F (51°C) to 195°F (90°C), rarely exceed the desired temperature of the finished dish, resulting in foods that are precisely cooked but not overcooked. Food safety is ensured by cooking the foods the proper length of time at a constant temperature.

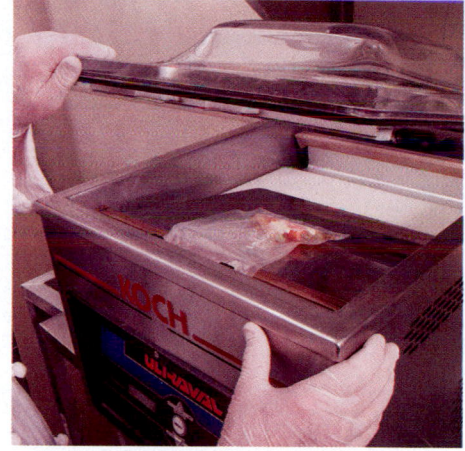

Chamber vacuum machine

Two essential pieces of equipment are required for *sous vide* cooking: a chamber vacuum machine and a thermal circulator or immersion circulator. The **chamber vacuum machine** allows solids and liquids to be packaged in food-grade polyethylene bags without oxygen. The packaging seals in flavor and prevents water from touching the food during cooking.

A **thermal circulator** is attached to a vessel of water, where the pouched foods are cooked in the warm circulating water bath. The heating element and temperature controls on the circulator maintain the precise and constant temperatures required for *sous vide* cooking. A pump ensures that the heated water circulates continuously. Because foods cooked *sous vide* resemble poached or braised foods, they are often finished for service by browning conventionally in a pan or using a **handheld propane torch** like those used in the plumbing trade.

Accurate temperature control and proper cooking time is essential when cooking foods *sous vide* at the low temperatures in which bacteria can thrive. The FDA's 2013 Food Code (see Chapter 2, Food Safety and Sanitation) requires that a detailed HACCP program, including time and temperature monitoring, be in place in any food service operation using *sous vide* cooking methods. Before employing *sous vide* techniques in any food service operation, consult local health authorities to learn what technical training, licensing and record keeping is required.

Among the tools migrating from the chemistry laboratory to the kitchen are microscopically fine **heat-resistant filters**. With perforations a mere 100 microns (0.004 inch) thick, these filters can be used for clarifying stock and making clear colorless consommé. The **vacuum rotary evaporator**, a costly lab instrument used to distill mixtures, has been adapted for kitchen use to reduce liquids without applying heat and to impregnate foods with flavors. Another device inspired by the science lab

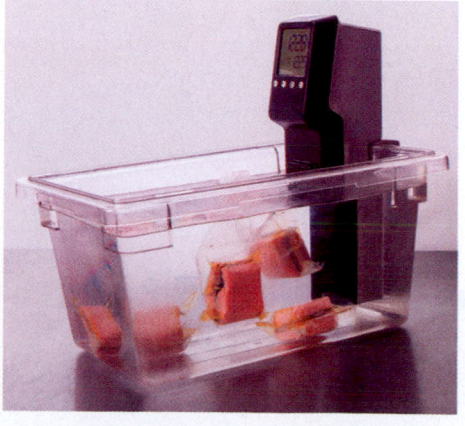

Thermal circulator and water bath

is the **anti-griddle**, which resembles a flat top on which food is frozen, not heated. The surface of the anti-griddle, chilled to –30°F (–34°C), "sears" food with cold. Hot purées and liquids can be sealed on the outside by freezing, yet still be warm or liquid inside.

BUFFET EQUIPMENT

Food service operations that prepare buffets or cater off-premise events need a variety of specialized equipment to ensure that food is handled safely and efficiently and displayed appropriately. Although many of these items can be rented, operations that regularly serve buffets may prefer to invest in their own transportation and serving equipment. Proper temperatures must be maintained during transportation, display and service.

Insulated carriers hold food at its current temperature for a time. They are designed to hold hotel pans or sheet pans and are available with wheels for easy movement. Some are available with a spigot for serving hot or cold beverages. Any carrier should be easy to clean and of a convenient size for the space available and the type of operation.

Temperature remains a concern when arranging food on a buffet table. **Chafing dishes** are commonly used for keeping hot foods hot during service. In chafing dishes, cans of solid fuel are placed under a deep hotel pan of hot water. Like a double boiler or *bain marie*, the hot water helps maintain the temperature of food placed in a second hotel pan suspended over the first. Chafing dishes should never be used to heat food—only to maintain the temperature of already-heated foods. Chafing dishes are available in several sizes and shapes, but the most convenient are those based on the size of a standard hotel pan. Round, deep chafing dishes are useful for serving soups or sauces. Exteriors can be plain or ornate and made of silver, copper or stainless steel.

Roast beef, turkey, ham and other large cuts of meat are sometimes carved on a buffet in front of guests. **Heat lamps** can be used to keep these foods warm. Heat lamps are also useful for maintaining the temperature of pizza or fried foods, which may become soggy if held in a chafing dish.

Pastries, breads and cold foods can be arranged on a variety of platters, trays, baskets and serving pieces, depending on the size and style of the buffet. Some of the most elegant and traditional serving pieces are flat display mirrors. These may be plastic or glass and are available in a wide variety of shapes and sizes. The edges should be sealed in easy-to-clean plastic to prevent chipping.

Insulated carrier

Chafing dish

Heat lamp

SAFETY EQUIPMENT

Safety devices, many of which are required by federal, state or local law, are critical to the well-being of a food service operation although they are not used in food preparation. Failing to include safety equipment in a kitchen or failing to maintain it properly endangers workers and customers.

Fire Extinguishers

Fire extinguishers are canisters of foam, dry chemicals (such as sodium bicarbonate or potassium bicarbonate) or pressurized water used to extinguish small fires. They must be placed within sight of and easily reached from the work areas. Different classes of extinguishers use different chemicals to fight different types of fires. See Table 5.2. The appropriate class must be used for the specific fire type. Fire extinguishers must be recharged and checked from time to time to ensure that sure they have not been discharged, tampered with or otherwise damaged.

FIRE EXTINGUISHERS		TABLE 5.2
CLASS	SYMBOL	USE
Class A		Fires involving ordinary combustibles such as wood, paper, cloth or plastic
Class B		Fires involving grease or flammable liquids such as gasoline, paint or alcohol
Class C		Fires involving electrical equipment or wiring
Class K		Fires involving cooking oils or fat and fats in commercial cooking equipment

Combination extinguishers—AB, BC and ABC—are also available.

Remember the acronym **PASS** for the four steps to follow when using any fire extinguisher:

Pull the safety pin on the extinguisher.

Aim the extinguisher hose at the base of the fire.

Squeeze the handle to discharge the material.

Sweep the hose from side to side across the base of the fire.

Ventilation Systems

Ventilation systems (also called ventilation hoods) are commonly installed over cooking equipment to remove vapors, heat and smoke. Some systems include fire extinguishing agents or sprinklers. A properly operating hood makes the kitchen more comfortable for the staff and reduces the danger of fire. The system should be designed, installed and inspected by professionals, then cleaned and maintained regularly.

First Aid Kits

First aid supplies should be stored in a clearly marked box, conspicuously located near food preparation areas. State and local laws may specify the kit's exact contents. Generally they should include a first aid manual, bandages, gauze dressings, adhesive tape, antiseptics, scissors, cold packs and other supplies. The kit should be checked regularly and items replaced as needed. Cards with emergency telephone numbers should be placed inside the first aid kit and near a telephone.

Protective Gear

All kitchens should be equipped with high quality heat-resistant gloves or pot holders to be used when handling hot pans and other equipment. In kitchens where a large quantity of shellfish is opened or a meat slicer is used, steel-mesh safety gloves may be required. Made from stainless steel woven into a fine fiber, these gloves recall medieval armor and are effective at preventing puncture or slicing wounds.

> **⚠ Safety Alert**
>
> *Storage*
>
> - Never store cleaning supplies or other chemicals with or near foods.
> - Never store chemicals in a container that originally held food; never store food in a container that once held a chemical.
> - Keep chemicals and cleaners in properly labeled containers.

Mesh safety gloves

ENERGY CONSERVATION IN THE PROFESSIONAL KITCHEN

The kitchen is the heart of a food service operation. It also consumes an enormous amount of natural resources, including water, electricity, natural gas and propane. In one year, a single electric deep-fat fryer uses more kilowatts of electricity than the average U.S. home. According to the U.S. Environmental Protection Agency's *ENERGY STAR®* *Guide for Cafés, Restaurants, and Institutional Kitchens*, 59 percent of the energy used in a food service operation comes from the kitchen: food preparation (35 percent), sanitation (18 percent) and refrigeration (6 percent).

Energy conservation is of concern to food service operators because of the monetary and environmental costs associated with wasteful practices. Although purchasing energy-efficient equipment may be beyond your immediate responsibility, there are many things you can do to help conserve energy including the following:

- Keep ovens, refrigerators, dishwashers, ice machines, exhaust vents and other equipment clean and maintained.
- Observe good water use practices. Thaw frozen food in the refrigerator instead of under running water. Repair leaky faucets and dishwashing equipment. Soak dirty cookware and dishes before washing under clean running water. Offer water to guests only when asked.
- Preheat equipment only when necessary. Preheat ovens only long enough to reach the required temperature before they are needed.
- To reduce heat loss during operation, open ovens only when needed. Reduce time when ovens are idle; turn off backup ovens when not in use.
- Turn off gas burners when not in use.
- Turn off interior oven lights when not needed.
- Turn off exhaust hoods and kitchen fans as soon as it is safe to do so at the end of service.
- Select the proper size and type of pot or pan for the task. A small pan placed over a large burner wastes gas. Select cookware that heats efficiently.
- Select the right kind of cooking device for the job. Review your menu to determine whether the most efficient cooking methods are being used. Cooking over open burners for example may be more efficient that using a hot top, which takes longer to heat.
- Report maintenance problems when you observe them. Leaking sinks and dishwashers, dripping faucets, and torn gaskets on refrigerators and ice machines, waste water and energy.
- Review energy conservation practices with your team.

QUESTIONS FOR DISCUSSION

1 What is NSF International? What is its significance with regard to commercial kitchen equipment?

2 List the parts of a chef's knife and describe the knife's construction.

3 List six materials used to make commercial cookware and describe the advantages and disadvantages of each.

4 Describe six pieces of equipment that can be used to slice or chop foods.

5 List four classes of fire extinguishers. For each one, describe its designating symbol and identify the type or types of fire it should be used to extinguish.

6 Discuss five ways to conserve energy when using equipment in a professional kitchen.

Knife Skills 6

After studying this chapter, you will be able to:

- use knives safely
- care for knives properly
- sharpen knives
- grip and control knives while cutting foods into a variety of classic shapes
- identify classic knife cuts
- understand when to use the classic knife cuts

fabricate to cut a larger portion of raw meat (e.g. a primal or subprimal), poultry or fish into smaller portions

fabricated cuts individual portions cut from a subprimal of raw meat, poultry or fish

Because the knife is the most commonly used tool in the kitchen, good knife skills are critical to a chef's success. Every chef spends countless hours slicing, dicing, mincing and chopping. Learning to perform these tasks safely and efficiently is an essential part of a chef's training.

At first, professional knives may feel large and awkward and the techniques discussed in this chapter may not seem efficient. Some techniques help make precise cutting easier. Others help stabilize awkwardly shaped food items to help you cut efficiently. As you become familiar with knives and practice your knife skills, using knives correctly will become second nature.

Knives are identified in Chapter 5, Tools and Equipment. Here we show how knives are used to cut vegetables. The techniques presented, however, can be used for almost any food that, like vegetables, holds their shape when cut. Knife skills for butchering and **fabricating** meat, poultry, fish and shellfish are discussed in Chapter 13, Principles of Meat Cookery, through Chapter 20, Fish and Shellfish.

USING KNIVES SAFELY

The first rule of knife safety is to be mindful and focus on what you are doing. Other basic rules of knife safety are as follows:

- Use the correct knife for the task at hand.
- Always cut away from yourself.
- Always cut on a cutting board. Do not cut on glass, marble or metal.
- Place a damp towel underneath the cutting board to keep it from sliding as you cut.
- Keep knives sharp; a dull knife is more dangerous than a sharp one.
- When carrying a knife, hold it point down, parallel and close to your leg as you walk.
- A falling knife has no handle. Do not attempt to catch a falling knife; step back and allow it to fall.
- Never leave a knife in a sink of water; anyone reaching into the sink could be injured or the knife could be dented by pots or other utensils.

CARING FOR AND SHARPENING YOUR KNIVES

With proper care and storage, your professional knives will last many years. Proper sanitation of knives is essential to prevent cross-contamination. Always sanitize, rinse and dry knives by hand immediately after each use. Do not wash knives in commercial dishwashers. The heat and harsh chemicals can damage the edge and the handle. In addition, do not leave your knives in a sink full of water, where a knife could injure an unsuspecting worker.

To prevent dulling, store knives so that their blades never touch other knives or tools. Slotted knife holders or magnetized strips can be wall-mounted near work stations. Portable knife kits, made from flexible washable material, are designed to hold each knife in an individual protective sleeve.

A sharp knife cuts smoothly. It will cut through the slippery skin of an onion with ease. When a knife is sharp, its edge is in alignment. A sharpening stone called a **whetstone** is used to put an edge on a dull knife blade. During this process you are grinding away minute amounts of metal on your knife, one side at a time. To use a whetstone, place the heel of the blade against the whetstone at a 15- to 20-degree angle. See Figure 6.1. Maintaining the angle throughout the sharpening process is key. With your fingers on top of the blade, press down on the blade while pushing it away from you in one long arc, as if to slice off a thin piece of the stone. The entire length of the blade should come in contact with the stone during each sweep. Repeat the procedure on both sides of the blade until

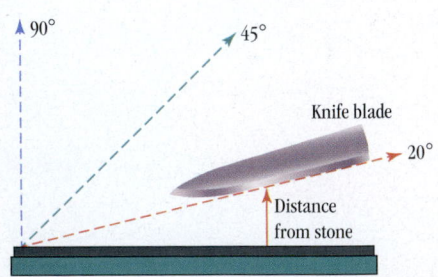

Figure 6.1 Blade angle when sharpening a knife on a whetstone.

it is sufficiently sharp. With a triple-faced whetstone, such as the one shown in the nearby photo, progress from the coarsest to the finest surface. Any whetstone can be moistened with either water or mineral oil, but not both. Do not use vegetable oil on a whetstone because it will soon become rancid and gummy.

Procedure for Using a Sharpening Stone

① Place the heel of the knife blade against the whetstone at a 15- to 20-degree angle. With your fingers on top of the blade, press down on the blade while pushing it away from you.

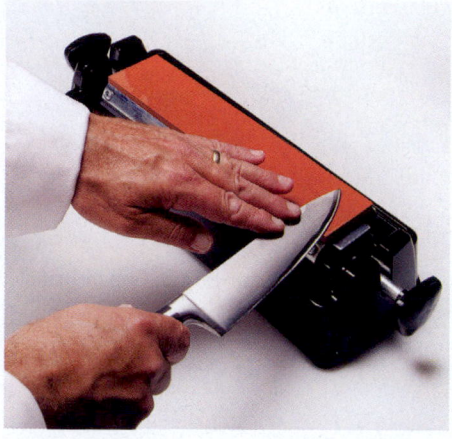

② Press and push away so that the entire length of the blade comes into contact with the stone.

③ Turn the knife over. Repeat the procedure on both sides of the blade until it is sufficiently sharp.

The constant force of cutting with your knife causes its fine sharp edge to dull. On a microscopic level, the edge comes out of alignment, wears and bends. A **steel** does not sharpen a knife nor does it remove any metal from the blade. Rather it is used to straighten the edge of the blade immediately after and between sharpenings. This restores the cutting edge of the blade and maintains the knife's sharpness. Using a steel on your knife every day before starting to use it, the knife should hold its edge without the constant need for sharpening. To use a steel, hold it in your non-dominant hand with your fingers behind the guard. Place the blade against the steel at a 15- to 20-degree angle. Draw the blade along the entire length of the steel using steady, even, light pressure and uniform strokes. Repeat the technique several times on each side of the blade. After using the steel, wash and sanitize the knife, then wipe off the blade with a clean towel before using.

Procedure for Using a Steel

① Place the base of the knife blade against the steel at a 15- to 20-degree angle.

② Using a steady, even, light pressure, draw the blade along the entire length of the steel in one smooth motion.

③ Draw the entire knife blade, including the tip, across the steel. Repeat on the other side of the knife blade.

GRIPPING YOUR KNIFE

There are several different ways to grip a knife. Use the grip that is most comfortable for you or the one dictated by the job at hand. Whichever grip you use should be firm but not so tight that your hand becomes tired. Gripping styles are shown here.

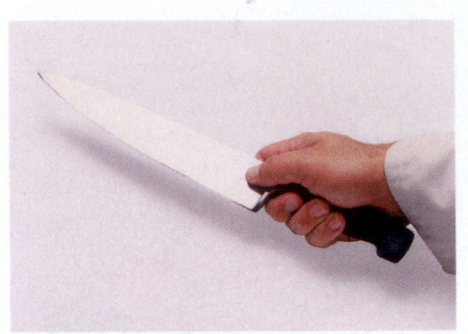

The most common grip: Hold the handle with three fingers while gripping the blade between the thumb and index finger.

A variation on the most common grip: Grip the handle with four fingers and place the thumb on the front of the handle.

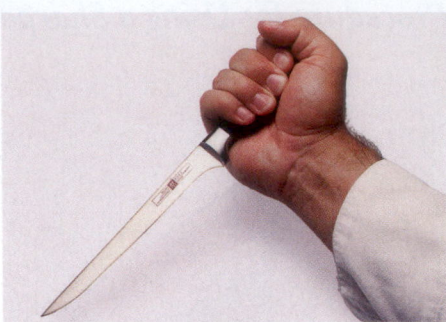

The underhand grip for a rigid boning knife: Grip the handle in a fist with four fingers and thumb. This grip allows you to use the knife tip to cut around joints and separate flesh from bone when boning meat and poultry.

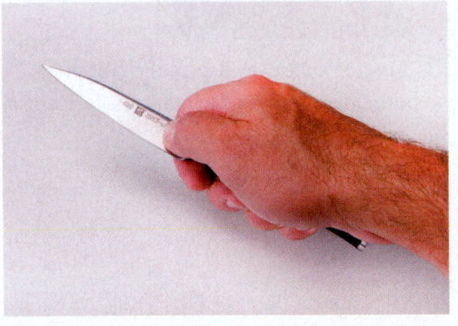

The most common grip for holding a paring knife: Grip the handle with four fingers and place the thumb on the front of the handle.

CONTROLLING YOUR KNIFE

To safely produce even cuts, control your knife with one hand and hold the item being cut with the other. Use smooth, even strokes. Never force the blade through the item being cut; allow its sharp edge to do the cutting. Using a dull knife or excessive force with any knife produces poor results and a significant safety risk. Two safe methods for controlling your knife are shown here.

Procedure for Controlling Your Knife: Method A

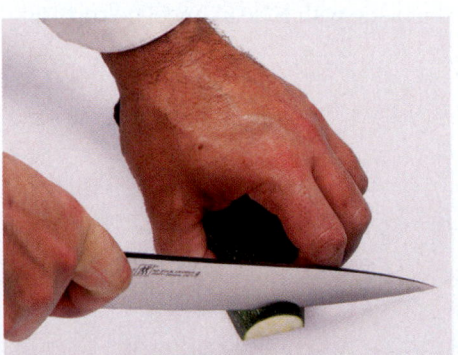

❶ Keeping your fingertips curled back, grip the item being cut with three fingertips and your thumb. Hold the knife in the other hand. While keeping the knife's tip on the cutting board, lift the heel of the knife.

❷ Using the second joint of your index finger as a guide, cut a slice using a smooth, even, downward stroke. Adjust the position of the guiding finger to produce even slices. After a few cuts, slide your fingertips and thumb down the length of the item and continue slicing. For this technique, the knife's tip acts as the fulcrum, the point from which the knife moves up or down.

Procedure for Controlling Your Knife: Method B

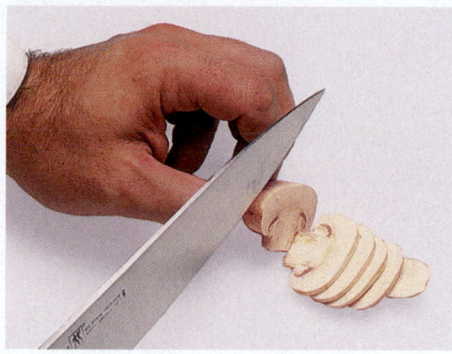

1 Grip the item as described in Method A. Using the second joint of your index finger as a guide, lift the knife's tip and slice by drawing the knife slightly back toward you and down through the item, cutting the item to the desired thickness.

2 The motion of the knife should come almost entirely from the wrist, not the elbow. Allow the weight of the knife to do most of the work; very little downward pressure needs to be applied to the knife. For this slicing technique, your wrist should act as the fulcrum, the point from which the knife pivots.

USING YOUR KNIFE

Chefs use knives to shape items and reduce their size. Uniformity of size and shape ensures even cooking and enhances the appearance of the finished product. A knife can shape items by slicing, chopping, dicing, mincing and other special cutting techniques. Many of the classic cuts are known by their French names: *julienne*, for example. Although these words are nouns and entered the English language as nouns (e.g., a julienne of carrot), they are also used as verbs (to julienne a carrot) and adjectives (julienned carrots).

Slicing

To slice is to cut an item into relatively broad, thin pieces. Slices may be either the finished cut or the first step in producing other cuts. Slicing is typically used to create three specialty cuts: chiffonade, rondelle and diagonal. Slicing skills are also used to produce oblique or roll cuts and lozenges. For most applications, vegetables and fruit are peeled before slicing except when you see a rustic appearance in a garnish or ingredient.

A **chiffonade** is a preparation of finely sliced or shredded leafy vegetables used as a garnish or a base under cold presentations. As shown here, slicing spinach en chiffonade is a relatively simple process.

> ### ⚠ Safety Alert
>
> *Handling Knives*
>
> Knives are perhaps the most dangerous of kitchen tools, both for the risk of cross-contamination they present and the inherent sharpness of their blades. Always clean, sanitize and dry knives by hand immediately after each use to prevent the transfer of pathogenic organisms (see Chapter 2, Food Safety and Sanitation) from one product to the next. Do not wash knives in commercial dishwashers or leave them to soak underwater as the knife blade can be damaged by other tools or can injure an unsuspecting worker.
>
> When walking with a knife, hold it by the handle, near your side, with the point facing downward. Store knives properly in slotted knife holders or on a wall-mounted magnetic strip, not in drawers or containers where the blades can be dulled by contact with other knives or tools.

chiffonade [shif-uh-NAHD] to finely slice or shred leafy vegetables or herbs

1 Wash and destem the leaves if necessary. Stack several leaves on top of each other and roll them tightly like a cigar.

2 Make fine slices moving the knife down and forward across the leaves while holding the leaf roll tightly.

rondelles [ron-DELLZ] disk-shaped slices

Rondelles or **rounds** are disk-shaped slices of cylindrical vegetables or fruits used in salads, side dishes, soups and stews.

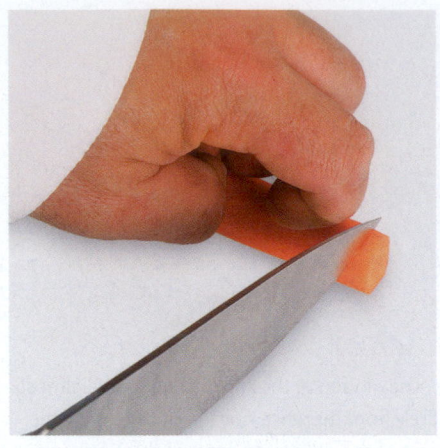

Place the peeled item on a cutting board. Make even slices perpendicular to the item being cut.

diagonals oval-shaped slices

Diagonals or bias cuts are elongated or oval-shaped slices of cylindrical vegetables or fruits. They are produced with a cut similar to that used to cut rondelles except that the knife is held at an angle to the item being cut. Because diagonals have more exposed cut sides, they cook more quickly that other cuts. They are used in Asian stir-fried dishes and for sautéed vegetables.

Place the peeled item on a cutting board. Position the knife at the desired angle to the item being cut and slice it evenly.

oblique cuts [oh-BLEEK] small pieces with two angle-cut sides

Oblique-cut or **roll-cut** items are small pieces with two angle-cut sides. It is a relatively simple cut most often used on carrots and parsnips in rustic dishes such as soups and stews.

Place the peeled item on a cutting board. Holding the knife at a 45-degree angle, make the first cut. Roll the item a half turn, keeping the knife at the same angle, and make another cut. The result is a wedge-shaped piece with two angled sides.

Lozenges are diamond-shaped cuts prepared from firm vegetables such as carrots, turnips, rutabagas and potatoes used in salads, side dishes, soups and stews.

lozenges diamond-shaped pieces, usually of firm vegetables

❶ Peel the item and square off the sides to create a block. Slice the item into long slices of the desired thickness. Then cut the slices into strips of the desired width.

❷ Cut the strips at an angle to produce diamond shapes.

Horizontal slicing is sometimes used to **butterfly** or make a pocket in meat, poultry or fish. It is also used to thinly slice soft vegetables, such as onions, for sautéeing.

butterfly to slice boneless meat, poultry or fish nearly in half lengthwise so that it spreads open like a book

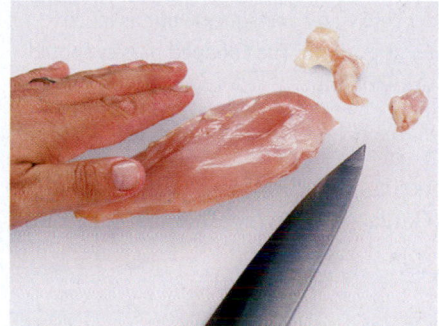 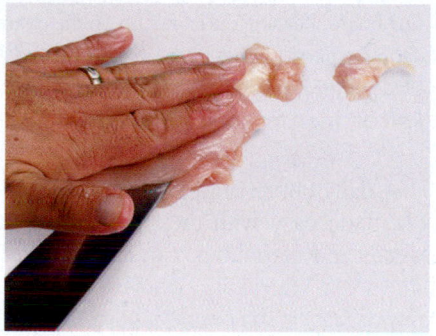

❶ With your hand open and your fingers arched upward, hold the item to be cut firmly in the center of your palm.

❷ Holding the knife parallel to the table, slice a pocket to the desired depth, or cut through the item completely.

Chopping

To **chop** is to cut an item into small pieces when uniformity of size and shape is neither necessary (e.g., coarsely chopped onions that will be strained out of a stock before service) nor feasible (e.g., parsley).

Coarse chopping is a procedure identical to that used for slicing but without the emphasis on uniformity. Coarsely chopped pieces should measure approximately ¾ inch × ¾ inch × ¾ inch (2 cm × 2 cm × 2 cm).

Grip the knife as for slicing. Hold the item being chopped with your other hand. It may not be necessary to use your finger as a guide because uniformity is not crucial.

Parsley and similar items are often **fine chopped** for use in recipes. As shown here, the procedure for properly chopping fresh herbs and similar foods is quick and efficient and the fineness can be adjusted as needed.

Procedure for Chopping Parsley and Similar Foods

1 Wash the parsley in cold water; drain well. Remove the parsley sprigs from the stems.

2 Grip the knife in one hand. With the other hand spread flat, hold the knife's tip on the cutting board. Keeping the knife's tip on the board, chop the parsley sprigs by rocking the curved blade of the knife up and down while moving the knife back and forth over the parsley.

3 Place the chopped parsley in a clean kitchen towel or a double layer of cheesecloth. Rinse it under cold water and squeeze out as much water as possible. The chopped parsley should be dry and fluffy.

A daily chore in many food service facilities, peeling and chopping garlic is a simple job made easy with the procedure shown here. Garlic paste, which blends easily into sauces and marinades, can also be made from chopped garlic.

Procedure for Chopping Garlic

1 Break the head of garlic into individual cloves with your hands. Lightly crush the cloves using the flat edge of a chef's knife or a mallet. The cloves will break open and the peel can be separated easily from the garlic flesh.

2 With a flat hand, hold the knife's tip on the cutting board. Using a rocking motion, chop the garlic cloves to the desired size. Garlic is usually chopped very finely.

3 To make garlic paste, first finely chop the garlic and then turn the knife on an angle and repeatedly drag the edge of the knife along the cutting board, mashing the garlic.

Cutting Sticks and Dicing

dice to cut into cubes with six equal-sized sides

To **dice** is to cut an item into cubes with six equal-sized sides. The techniques described here are most often used when uniformity of size and shape is important (e.g., julienned carrots for a salad or brunoised vegetables for a garnish). Before an item can be diced, it must be cut into a uniform block then into sticks such as juliennes and bâtonnets. These sticks are then reduced through dicing into the classic cuts known as brunoise, small dice, medium dice, large dice and paysanne. Although most cooks have some notion of what size and shape "small diced" potatoes or julienne carrots may be, there are specific sizes and shapes for these cuts. They are as follows:

Bâtonnet [bah-toh-NAY]: a stick-shaped item with dimensions of ¼ inch × ¼ inch × 2 inches (6 mm × 6 mm × 5 cm).

Julienne [joo-lee-EN]: a stick-shaped item with dimensions of ⅛ inch × ⅛ inch × 2 inches (3 mm × 3 mm × 5 cm). When used with potatoes, this cut is sometimes referred to as an **allumette** [al-yoo-MET]. A fine julienne has dimensions of ⅟₁₆ inch × ⅟₁₆ inch × 2 inches (1.5 mm × 1.5 mm × 5 cm).

Brunoise [BROON-wahz]: a cube-shaped item with dimensions of ⅛ inch × ⅛ inch × ⅛ inch (3 mm × 3 mm × 3 mm). A ⅟₁₆-inch (1.5-mm) cube is referred to as a fine brunoise.

Small dice: a cube-shaped item with dimensions of ¼ inch × ¼ inch × ¼ inch (6 mm × 6 mm × 6 mm).

Medium dice: a cube-shaped item with dimensions of ½ inch × ½ inch × ½ inch (1.2 cm × 1.2 cm × 1.2 cm).

Paysanne [pay-ZAHN]: a flat, square, round or triangular item with dimensions of ½ inch × ½ inch × ⅛ inch (1.2 cm × 1.2 cm × 3 mm).

Large dice: a cube-shaped item with dimensions of ¾ inch × ¾ inch × ¾ inch (2 cm × 2 cm × 2 cm).

Procedure for Cutting Julienne and Bâtonnet

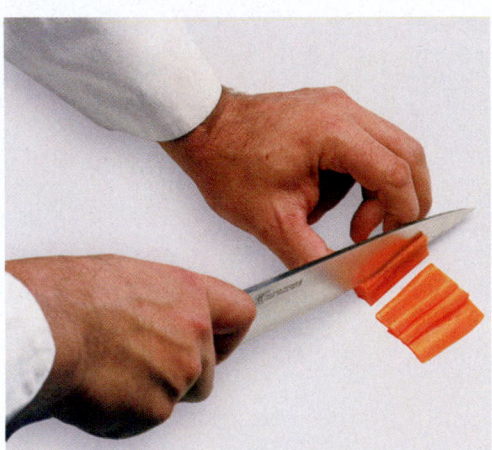

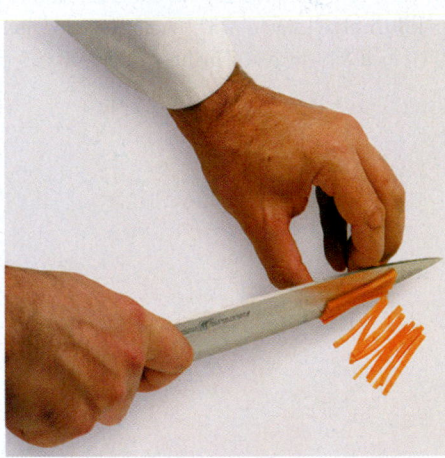

❶ Peel the item and square off the sides to create a block. Trim the block so that the slices cut from it will be the proper length.

❷ Cut even slices of the desired thickness from each block, ⅛ inch (3 millimeters) for julienne or ¼ inch (6 millimeters) for bâtonnet.

❸ Stack the slices and cut them evenly into sticks that are the same thickness as the slices.

Brunoise as well as small, medium and large dice are made by first cutting the item into sticks following the procedure for cutting julienne or bâtonnet, then making cuts perpendicular to the length of the sticks to produce small cubes. Making a ⅛-inch (3-millimeter) cut perpendicular to the length of a julienne produces a brunoise. Similarly a fine julienne (1/16 inch × 1/16 inch × 2 inches) is used to produce a fine brunoise. Making a ¼-inch (6-millimeter) cut perpendicular to the length of a bâtonnet produces a small dice. A ½-inch (1.2-centimeter) cut from a ½-inch (1.2-centimeter) stick produces a medium dice, and a ¾-inch (1.8-centimeter) cut from a ¾-inch (1.8-centimeter) stick produces a large dice.

Paysanne is a classic vegetable cut for garnishing soups and other rustic-style dishes. It could be described as a very thin ½-inch cube. Paysanne is produced by following the procedures for dicing, but in the final step the ½-inch × ½-inch (1.2-centimeter × 1.2-centimeter) sticks are cut into slices ⅛-inch (3 millimeters) thick. The terms *paysanne* and *fermière*, which mean "peasant" and "farmer" in French, are also used to refer to similarly sized round or triangular pieces. Regardless of the shape, when cutting *paysanne* and *fermière*, the pieces must be the same size.

When cutting paysanne, peel the item and square off the sides to create a block. Cut it into ½-inch × ½-inch (6-millimeter × 6-millimeter) sticks. Slice each stick into ⅛ inch (3-millimeter) slices.

Procedure for Dicing an Onion

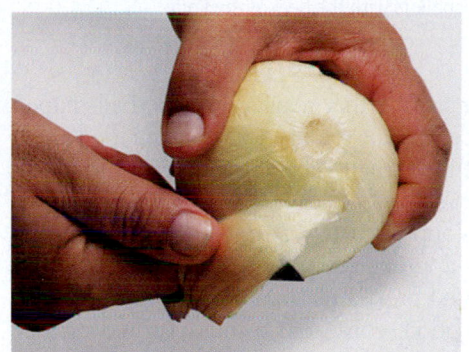

❶ Using a paring knife, remove the stem end. Trim the root end but leave it nearly intact (this helps prevent the onion from falling apart while dicing). Peel away the outer skin; be careful not to remove and waste too much.

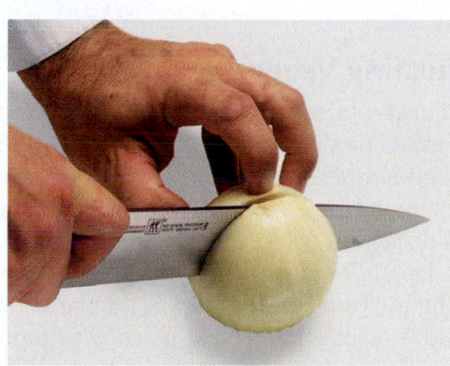

❷ Cut the onion in half through the stem and root. Place the cut side down on the cutting board.

❸ Cut parallel slices of the desired thickness vertically through the onion from the root toward the stem end without cutting completely through the root end.

❹ Make a single horizontal cut on a small onion or two horizontal cuts on a large onion through the width of the onion, again without cutting through the root end.

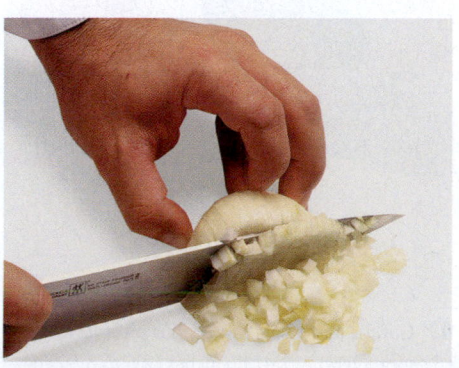

❺ Turn the onion and cut slices perpendicular to the other slices to produce diced onion.

Mincing

To **mince** is to cut an item into very small pieces. The terms *finely chopped* and *minced* are often used interchangeably and are most often used when referring to garlic, shallots, herbs and other foods that do not have to be uniform in shape.

Procedure for Mincing Shallots

① Peel and dice the shallots, following the procedure for peeling and dicing an onion.

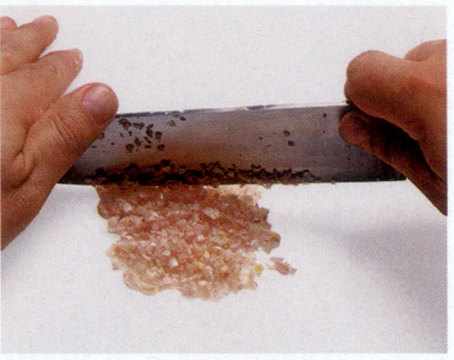

② With a flat hand, hold the knife's tip on the cutting board. Using a rocking motion, mince the shallots with the heel of the knife.

Turning Vegetables

tourner [toor-NAY] to cut into football-shaped pieces with seven equal sides and blunt ends

Tourner, or turning vegetables, is a cutting technique that results in a football-shaped finished product with seven equal sides and flat ends. The term is derived from the French word *tourner* ("to turn" in French). The size of the turned vegetable may vary, the most common being 2 inches (5 centimeters) long and 1 to 1½ inches (2.5 to 3.5 centimeters) in diameter. (*Cocotte* refers to turned vegetables approximately 1½ inches/3.5 centimeters in length. *Château* refers to turned vegetables approximately 2 inches/5 centimeters in length.) Turning vegetables is a more complicated procedure than producing other cuts, and it takes considerable practice to produce good, consistent results. Turned carrots, parsnips, potatoes, zucchini can be used as side dishes or to garnish entrées and stews.

Procedure for Turning Vegetables

① Cut the item being turned into pieces 2 inches (5 centimeters) × 1 to 1½ inches (2.5 to 3.5 centimeters). Each piece should have flat ends. (Potatoes, turnips and beets may be cut into as many as six or eight pieces; carrots can simply be cut into 2-inch lengths.) Peeling is optional because in most cases the item's entire surface area is trimmed away.

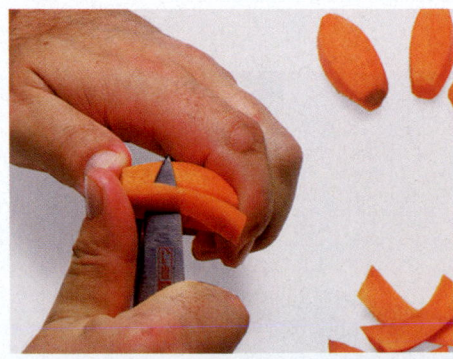

② Holding the item between the thumb and forefinger, use a curved or a bird's beak paring knife to cut seven curved sides on the item, creating a flat-ended, football-shaped product.

Making Parisiennes

A melon ball cutter or Parisienne scoop can be used to cut fruits and vegetables into uniform spheres, also referred to as **Parisiennes**. Small balls or spheres of fresh melon can be used in fruit salad, while tiny spheres of carrot, turnip, squash and so on can be used as a side dish or to garnish soup or an entrée. Melon ball cutters are available in a range of sizes, the smallest of which has an approximately ⅜-inch (9-millimeter) diameter and is known as a Parisienne (or Parisian) scoop.

Parisienne (pah-ree-zee-EN) spheres of fruits or vegetables cut with a small melon ball cutter

Procedure for Making Parisiennes

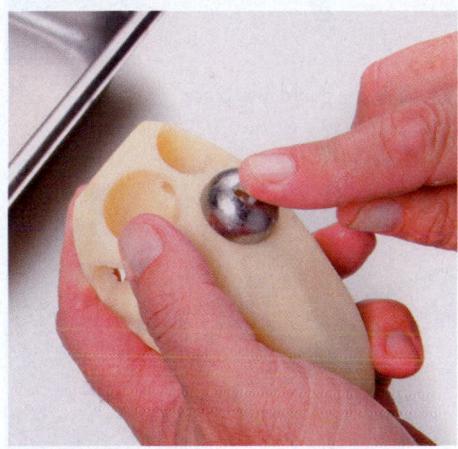 

❶ Press the scoop into the vegetable while twisting to form a sphere.

❷ Twist the handle to remove the sphere. Continue making spheres, placing them as close together as possible in order to minimize trim loss.

USING A MANDOLINE

The mandoline is a nonmechanical cutting tool. It does jobs that can also be done with a chef's knife, such as very thinly sliced apples or large quantities of julienned vegetables, quickly, easily and very accurately. It can also produce cuts such as a ridged slice or **gaufrette**, which a conventional chef's knife cannot produce.

When using the mandoline, always use the guard or a steel-mesh glove to protect your hand and follow the procedure illustrated on page 106.

gaufrette (goh-FREHT) a thin lattice or waffle-textured slice of vegetable cut on a mandoline

Using a Spiral Slicer

Specialized devices such as the spiral slicer shown here are used to make cuts that are difficult to produce with a knife. Firm fruits such as apples and pears and firm vegetables such as beets, carrots, parsnips, potatoes and zucchini can be sliced into spirals or ribbons using such devices. When using these tools, always follow manufacturer's directions. Use the guard or steel-mesh gloves to protect your hands.

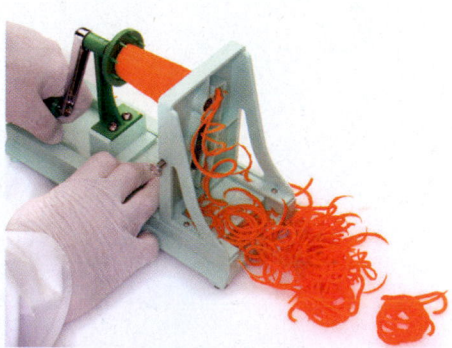

Using a spiral slicer to cut carrots.

Procedure for Using a Mandoline

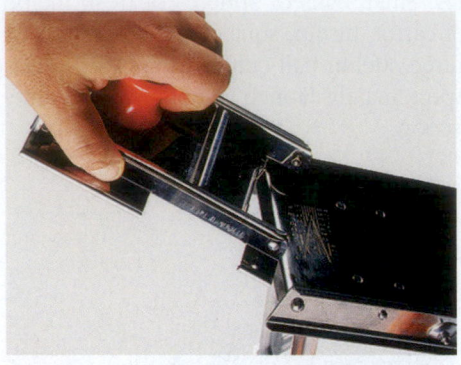

❶ To use a mandoline, position the legs and set the blade to the desired shape and thickness.

❷ Slide the guard into place.

❸ To slice, slide the item against the blade with a single, smooth stroke.

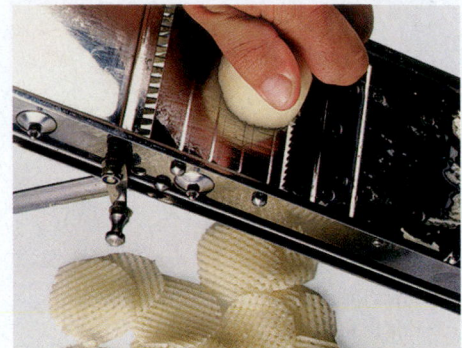

❹ To cut gaufrette, select the ridged blade and set it to the desired thickness. Make the first slice, turn the item 60–90 degrees and make a second slice. Turn the item back to the original position and make another slice, and so on.

QUESTIONS FOR DISCUSSION

1   What are the key rules for using knives safely?

2   Explain the step-by-step procedures for sharpening a knife using a three-sided whetstone.

3   What is the purpose of a steel? How is it used?

4   Why is it necessary to cut vegetables into uniform shapes and sizes?

5   Describe the following cutting procedures: slicing, chopping and dicing.

6   Identify the dimensions of the following cuts: julienne, bâtonnet, brunoise, small dice, medium dice, large dice and paysanne.

7   Describe the procedure for turning vegetables.

8   Describe three preparations for which a mandoline would be useful.

Flavors and Flavorings

7

condiment traditionally, any item added to a dish for flavor, including herbs, spices and vinegars; now also refers to cooked or prepared flavorings such as prepared mustards, relishes, bottled sauces and pickles

flavor an identifiable or distinctive quality of a food, drink or other substance perceived with the combined senses of taste, touch and smell

taste the sensations we detect when food, drink or other substances come in contact with our taste buds; the basic tastes include sweet, sour, salt, bitter and umami

mouthfeel the sensation created in the mouth by a combination of a food's taste, smell, texture and temperature

aroma the sensations we detect when a substance comes in contact with certain receptors in the nose

palate (1) the complex of smell, taste and touch receptors that contribute to a person's ability to recognize and appreciate flavors; (2) the range of an individual's recognition and appreciation of flavors

Honey, a sweetener

t is the chef's role to consistently present well-flavored foods—to excite the diner's brain and palate. This can be accomplished by simply sprinkling a bit of salt over a ripe watermelon to enhance the melon's natural sweetness or by using a long-simmered stock made from wild mushrooms to enrich a sauce flavored with herbs and wine. In either case, the chef must be able to recognize flavoring ingredients and know how to use them. This chapter discusses the sense of taste and smell and the flavoring ingredients used in the professional kitchen to enhance foods. Flavorings—the herbs, spices, salt, oils, vinegars, **condiments**, wines and other alcoholic beverages typically used to create, enhance or alter the natural flavors of a dish—are featured. The flavorings that are used primarily for baked goods and desserts are discussed in Chapter 30, Principles of the Bakeshop.

FLAVOR AND TASTE

From the simplest grunt of pleasure upon biting into a chunk of grilled steak to the most sophisticated discourse on the fruity top notes of a full-bodied Cabernet Sauvignon, people have long attempted to describe the flavors of food. Often this is done by describing physical perceptions ("it tastes sugary" or "it feels greasy") or the recognition of a flavor ("I can sense the rosemary" or "there is a hint of strawberries"). In either case, the terms *flavor* and *taste* are often confused. Although often used interchangeably, they are not synonymous.

Flavor is a combination of the tastes, aromas and other sensations caused by the presence of a foreign substance in the mouth. **Tastes**, such as sweet, sour, salt, bitter and umami, are the sensations we perceive when a substance comes in contact with the taste buds, which are sensory organs on the tongue. Some substances stimulate or irritate other nerves on the tongue or embedded in the fleshy areas of the mouth. These nerves respond to sensations of pain, heat or cold, or sensations that our brain interprets as spiciness, pungency or astringency. **Mouthfeel** refers to the sensation created in the mouth by a combination of a food's taste, smell, texture and temperature. **Aromas** are the odors that enter the nose or float up through the back of the mouth to activate smell receptors in the nose. Whenever we detect a particular taste, sensation and/or aroma, a set of neurons (specialized cells that transmit nerve impulses) in the brain is excited and, with experience, we learn to recognize the pattern of these sensations as the flavor of bananas, grilled lamb or sour cream. Each person has a unique ability to recognize and appreciate thousands of these patterns. This compendium of flavors and the ability to recognize them is sometimes referred to as the **palate**.

Tastes: Sweet, Sour, Salty, Bitter and Umami

Taste is the sensation we experience when substances come in contact with the taste buds on the tongue. For many years, western cultures have identified four tastes:

Sweet: For most people, sweetness is the most pleasurable and often sought-after taste. The fewer sweet-tasting foods we consume, the more enhanced our ability to recognize sweetness becomes. A food's sweetness derives from naturally occurring sugars (e.g., sucrose and fructose) or sweeteners added to it. Chefs can enhance the natural sweetness in foods by adding a small amount of a sour, bitter or salty taste. Adding too much sourness, bitterness or saltiness, however, lessen our perception of the food's sweetness.

Sour: Considered the opposite of sweet, a sour taste is found in acidic foods. Like sweetness, sourness can vary greatly in intensity. Many foods with a dominant sour taste, such as red currants or sour cream, also contain a slight sweetness. A sour taste can sometimes be improved by adding a little sweetness or it can be negated by adding a large amount of a sweet ingredient.

Salty: With the notable exception of oysters and other shellfish and seaweed, the presence of a salty taste in a food is the result of the cook's decision to add the mineral sodium chloride, known as salt, or to use a previously salted ingredient such as salt-cured fish, salt-cured meat, soy sauce or some cheese. Salt helps finish a dish, heightening or enhancing its other flavors. Dishes that lack salt often taste flat. Adding a small amount of salt or something salty corrects something that is overly sweet. Like the taste of sweetness, if we consume less salt on a regular basis, we are more able we to detect saltiness in foods.

Bitter: Although the bitter taste caused by alkaloids and other organic substances may occasionally be appreciated in foods such as beer, dark chocolate, fermented cheese or coffee, most people dislike a bitter-flavored ingredient that is not balanced by sour or salty flavors. Bitter is an acquired taste in all cultures. The natural human aversion to bitterness is believed to function as a survival mechanism, warning us of inedible or toxic foods. Many foods that are good for us, such as herbs and vegetables, especially those in the cabbage family, are bitter. But when used as a side note in a dish, these foods go from mouth-puckering to delicious. The sour taste in citrus juice or vinegar can offset bitterness, as does the addition of salt or sugar,

Umami: Long recognized as the fifth taste in Japanese cuisine, **umami** (from the Japanese word *umai*, meaning "delicious"), does not have a simple English translation. For some people it refers to a food's **savory** characteristic; for others to the richness or fullness of a dish's overall taste, and still others, the meatiness or meat taste of a dish. The umami sensation is caused by the naturally occurring amino acid glutamate and is abundant in aged or fermented foods and glutamate's commercially produced counterpart, monosodium glutamate (MSG). Glutamate is present in many foods and can be detected in cheeses, meats, rich stocks, soy sauce, shellfish, fatty fish, mushrooms, tomatoes and wine, which are all high in this amino acid.

Scientists have recently discovered that **fat**, which has long been known to carry or enhance flavors, is actually a sixth taste that can be detected by the human tongue. Research has established that receptors on taste buds can detect the presence of fat in foods. This finding is about more than just the creamy, juicy or silky texture associated with fat. **Oleogustus** refers to the actual taste of fatty acids, which although unpleasantly bitter in high concentrations can, in lower quantities, add an appealing contrast similar to the bitterness found in chocolate, wine, coffee or tea. Research is still ongoing, but the finding that some people are genetically more sensitive than others to the taste of fat may help us to better understand obesity and food cravings.

Often food professionals and others refer to tastes in addition to sweet, sour, salty, bitter, umami and fat. Typically, they describe foods as pungent, hot, spicy or piquant or astringent, sharp or dry. None of these terms, however, fit the definition of a taste, as none are detected solely by taste buds. Rather these sensations are detected by nerve endings embedded in the fleshy part of the mouth. When irritated by the presence of compounds such as piperine (the active ingredient in black peppercorns) or capsaicin (the active ingredient in chiles), these nerves register a burning sensation that the brain translates as the hot and spicy "taste" of a dish.

Lemon, an acidifier

Sodium chloride, the source of saltiness

Quinine, adds bitterness

Flakes of fermented bonito, adds umami

umami the taste sensation caused by the naturally occurring amino acid glutamate; gives food a savory richness or meatiness; found primarily in fermented foods and those to which monosodium glutamate has been added

savory a food that is not sweet

How We Experience Taste and Smell

The smallest functional unit of taste is the taste bud. These specialized sensory organs are found on the tongue within three different kinds of small bumps, known as **papillae**, as well as the back of the throat and the roof of the mouth. See Figure 7.1. Each taste bud contains several **taste receptor cells**. **Taste compounds** in the foods we eat interact with the tops of these specialized receptor cells, which transmit taste information through nerves to the brain. The process of tasting begins when a substance is placed in the mouth and the substance's taste compounds begin to dissolve in saliva. Chewing further breaks down the substance and increases the concentration of taste compounds dissolved in the saliva. The taste compounds stimulate taste receptors and ultimately elicit taste sensations. Because taste compounds must dissolve in the saliva in order to reach the taste receptors, they must be water-soluble.

The process of smelling begins when odor compounds reach the olfactory neurons, the specialized sensing organs of smell. Olfactory neurons at the top of the nasal cavity are clustered together in the **olfactory bulb**. See Figure 7.2. One olfactory bulb rests at the bottom of each hemisphere of the brain and at the top of each nasal cavity. Odor compounds reach these receptors through two different pathways: orthonasally or retronasally. When we sniff or experience odors that are external to our bodies via our **nostrils**, we are smelling **orthonasally**. Once we place a substance in our mouth, the aromas are delivered through the **retronasal path**. Regardless of route, in order for odor compounds to reach the olfactory receptors they must be able to volatilize– to dissolve in air. In contrast to taste compounds, odor compounds do not dissolve well in water; they dissolve better in oils.

A pervasive myth (based upon misinterpretation of an article written in German in the 1800s) is that you experience certain taste qualities on only certain areas of the tongue (sweet on the tip, bitter in the back, salt on the front sides and sour on the back sides). In fact you can taste all taste compounds everywhere on your tongue. You can prove this to yourself by placing various items representative of sweet, sour, salty, bitter and even umami on the tip of your tongue. You can immediately perceive any taste at the tongue tip (or anywhere else you have taste buds) and do not need to wait for bitter compounds to diffuse to the back, sour to the back sides, or salt to the sides.

—JEANNINE DELWICHE, PH.D., Certified Food Scientist, is an expert in sensory science and chemosensory psychophysics, editor-in chief of Chemosensory Perception and founder of TastingScience.org.

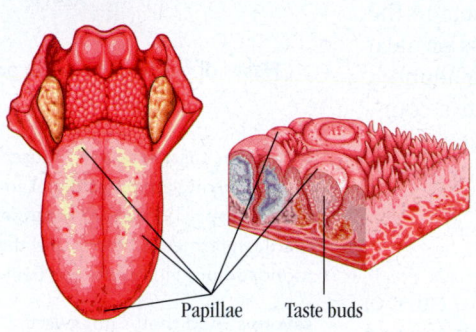

Figure 7.1 The human tongue and taste buds.

Papillae   Taste buds

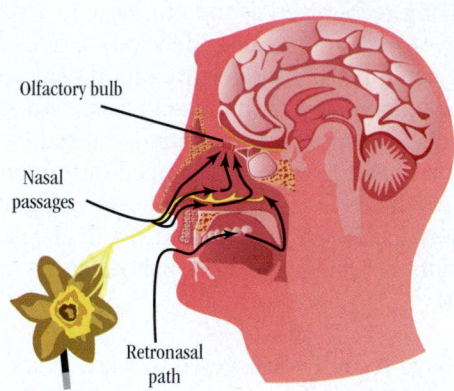

Olfactory bulb

Nasal passages

Retronasal path

Figure 7.2 The human olfactory system.

Factors Affecting Perception of Flavors

The most important factors affecting the flavor of a dish are the quantity, quality and concentration of the flavoring ingredients. (With practice, a chef gains a feel for the proper proportions.) Other factors that affect our perception of flavors include the following:

Temperature: The higher the temperature of the food, the stronger it's taste. Hot tea expresses more flavor compounds than iced tea or room temperature tea. Heating foods releases volatile flavor compounds, which intensifies our perceptions of odors. This is why fine cheese is served at room temperature to improve its eating quality and flavor. Foods tend to lose their sour or sweet tastes both the colder and the hotter they become. Saltiness, however, is perceived differently at extreme cold temperatures; the same quantity of salt in a solution is perceived more strongly when very cold than when merely cool or warm. For these reasons, it is best to adjust a dish's final flavors at its serving temperature. *S*eason food that will be served hot when they are hot and foods that will be served cold when they are cold.

Consistency: Consistency affects a food's flavor. Two items with the same amount of taste and smell compounds that differ in texture differ in perceived flavor intensity; the thicker item will take longer to reach its peak intensity and will have a less intense flavor. For example, two batches of sweetened heavy cream made from the same ingredients in the same proportions may taste different if one is whipped and the other is unwhipped; the whipped cream has more volume and therefore a milder flavor.

Contrasting taste: Sweet and sour are considered opposites, and often the addition of one to a food dominated by the other will enhance the food's overall flavor. For example, adding a little sugar to vinaigrette reduces the dressing's sourness; adding a squeeze of lemon to a broiled lobster reduces the shellfish's sweetness. Similarly, adding something sweet, sour or salty to a dish with a predominantly bitter flavor will cut the bitterness, but add too much contrasting flavor and the dominant taste will be negated.

Fat: Many of the chemical compounds that create tastes and aromas are dissolved in the fats that natural occur in foods or are added to foods during preparation. As these fat compounds are slowly released by evaporation or saliva, they provide a sustained taste sensation. If there is too little fat, the flavor compounds may not be released efficiently, resulting in a dish with little sustained flavor. This is one reason that low-fat and reduced-fat products, such as salad dressings, yogurt or sour cream can seem tasteless. Too much fat poses another problem; it can coat the tongue and interfere with the ability of taste receptors to perceive flavor compounds.

Color: A food's color affects how we perceive flavor before we even taste the food. When foods or beverages lack their customary color, we are less able to correctly identify them than when they are appropriately colored. As color level changes to match our expectations, our perception of taste and flavor intensity increases. A miscue created by color can have an adverse impact on the consumer's appreciation of flavor. For example, if the predominant flavor of a dessert is lemon, the dessert or some component of the dessert should be yellow. A green color triggers an expectation of lime and possible disappointment of the consumer. Similarly, the dark ruby-red flesh of a blood orange looks different from the more common bright orange flesh of a Valencia orange. This tonal difference can create the expectation of a different, non-orangey flavor, even though the blood orange's flavor is similar to that of other orange varieties. Likewise, a sliced apple that has turned brown may suggest an off-flavor, although there is none.

Of special note is the perception and appreciation of saltiness, which varies from one person to another. What one person perceives as highly salted, may taste ideal to someone else. And, over time, taste adapts to the level of saltiness in food. Continual exposure to highly salted foods increases salt tolerance. Similarly, a person can develop an appreciation over time for less salty food by decreasing the amount of salt consumed.

The sense of taste can be challenged by factors both within and beyond one's control. Age and general health can diminish one's perception of flavor, as can fatigue and stress. As we age, our sense of taste and smell naturally declines, although this varies from person-to-person. One's health impacts our ability to taste perceptions too. A cold can suppress our ability to smell because mucus prevents the flow of aromas to our receptors but the ability to perceive basic tastes on the tongue may be unaffected. Some medications may interact with basic tastes increasing or decreasing one's ability to taste salt or bitter compounds. Smoking has an immediate negative effect on one's ability to taste and smell foods, but scientific evidence suggests that taste perception may be restored after a few hours. Chefs need to be aware of the age and health of their clientele, adjusting the seasoning of foods served according to their needs.

Supertasters, Medium Tasters and Nontasters

Recent research into the physiology of taste has shown that some people detect a greater degree of a taste in foods than others. Labeled as **supertasters** by Professor Linda Bartoshuk of the University of Florida's Center for Smell and Taste, these people may have more taste buds than average, possibly twice as many as other people. Supertasters perceive the compound 6-n-propylthiouracil (PROP), which is found in foods such as coffee, broccoli, Brussels sprouts, grapefruit juice and green tea, as intensely bitter. In addition, they detect strongly bitter flavors where other people (referred to as nontasters) do not. Supertasters also tend to perceive artificial sweeteners as sweeter than the rest of the population does and also note a bitter aftertaste that most people miss. Similarly, supertasters find the spicy heat generated by the capsaicin in chile peppers to be more pronounced, sometimes unbearably so. Being a supertaster is an inherited genetic trait; it cannot be changed by experience or effort. Nontasters do not carry these genes.

An individual's responsiveness to tastes appears to influence food choices. Supertasters tend to avoid strong-tasting foods such as coffee, rich or very sweet desserts, greasy or spicy meats and green leafy vegetables. They also tend not to crave fats or sugars. Cooks who are not supertasters may not realize when a food would be too sweet or too bitter to medium tasters or supertasters who carry this genetic trait. Supertaster cooks may unconsciously avoid using foods that would be perfectly delicious to diners who are not supertasters. It is easy to determine your taste level with chemically treated tasting papers, known as PTC (phenylthiourea) test strips.

flavoring an item that adds a new taste to a food and alters its natural flavors; flavorings include herbs, spices, vinegars and condiments; the terms seasoning and flavoring are often used interchangeably

seasoning an item added to enhance the natural flavors of a food without dramatically changing its taste; salt is the most common seasoning

FLAVORING FOOD

The judicious use of **flavorings** and **seasonings** transforms raw ingredients such as beef chuck into the aromatic stew Boeuf Bourguignon or plain noodles into a fragrant bowl of pasta with pesto sauce. Mastery of flavoring and seasoning foods is the hallmark of a true culinary professional.

When you start to start to cook professionally and develop your chef's palate, keep the following general guidelines in mind:

- Start with simple combinations of ingredients until you build your knowledge and understand how flavors and ingredients interact.
- Select fresh foods that are in season whenever possible. During transportation and storage, foods can lose moisture, nutrients and volatile aromas.
- Match the flavoring used to both the ingredient and cooking technique. Cooking techniques affect the appearance, aroma, taste and texture of foods. Techniques such as roasting and caramelizing intensify foods' flavor while boiling and blanching may dilute it.
- Preparation techniques also impact the flavor of foods. The size of the cut affects the perception of the taste and texture of a vegetable, for example. Depending on how long they are cooked, vegetables cut into small pieces absorb more flavors in a dish than larger cuts.
- The temperature of foods impacts taste perception of their flavors.

Flavor Profiles

A food's **flavor profile** describes its flavor from the moment the guest gets the first whiff of its aroma until he or she swallows that last morsel. It is a convenient way to articulate and evaluate a dish's sensory characteristics as well as identify contrasting or complementing items that could be served with it. Chefs use the concept of flavor profiles as a tool to develop new dishes.

A food's flavor profile consists of one or more of the following elements:

Top notes or high notes: The sharp, first flavors or aromas of foods such as citrus, herbs, spices and many condiments. These top notes provide instant impact and dissipate quickly.

Middle notes: The second wave of flavors and aromas. More subtle and more lingering than top notes, middle notes come from dairy products, poultry, some vegetables, fish and some meats.

Low notes or bass notes: The most dominant, lingering flavors. These flavors consist of the basic tastes (especially sweetness, sourness, saltiness and umami) and come from foods such as anchovies, beans, chocolate, dried mushrooms, fish sauce, tomatoes, most meats (especially beef and game) and garlic. Alternatively, low notes can be created by smoking or caramelizing a food's sugars during grilling, broiling and other dry-heat cooking processes.

Aftertaste or finish: The final flavor that remains in the mouth after swallowing; for example, the lingering bitterness of coffee or chocolate or the pungency of black pepper or strong mustard.

Roundness: The unity of the dish's various flavors achieved through the judicious use of butter, cream, coconut milk, reduced stocks, salt, sugar and the like; these ingredients cause the other flavorings to linger without necessarily adding their own dominant taste or flavor.

Depth of flavor: The broad range of flavor notes in a dish.

These expressions can be applied to any dish to describe its sensory characteristics. For example, Lavender and Spice-Crusted Duck Breast with Apricot Compote (page 459) has a flavor profile with a top note of lavender, coriander and fennel. Its middle notes are the predominant flavors contributed by the duck breast, and its low notes are from the crisp skin. There is an aftertaste of the combined flavors. The sauce adds acidic and sweet notes to the duck, thus creating a dish with a fine depth of flavor.

An experienced chef is able to taste and evaluate a dish, adjusting flavorings, ingredients and cooking technique as needed to create an appealing balance of flavors.

Describing Aromas and Flavors in Food

Food scientists and professional tasters make their living describing the smell and taste of foods. Many have attempted to standardize the language used to describe both positive and negative aromas and flavors. Frequently they employ flavor wheels or other charts to identify and organize the flavors and tastes found in specific food items. For example, there are flavor wheels devoted to chocolate, wine, catfish, Italian cheese, coffee, citrus fruits and just about every other category of food and beverage on the market. These charts help food scientists, product developers and **culinarians** to speak a common language when describing the flavors they encounter.

Table 7.1 is one list used by chemists to describe 16 broad categories of tastes and smells that correspond to the major chemicals found in aromas and tastes. Such a list is helpful when trying to analyze and describe the flavors in a dish.

Classic Flavor Combinations

Culinary tradition provides chefs with myriad flavor combinations to use when preparing dishes. What would apple pie be without cinnamon? Or a hot dog without mustard? The recipes in this text use classic and traditional flavor combinations as well as such modern flavor pairings as coffee in a sauce for beef. It is helpful, as you begin to cook, to learn some classic flavor combinations, those that have become well-regarded matches due to decades, even centuries, of development and service. (See Table 7.2.)

Foods from the same botanical family often complement each other. Chile peppers, eggplants, potatoes and tomatoes, members of the *Solanaceae* or nightshade family, are often combined. The French vegetable casserole called ratatouille is one example of a dish that brings members of this botanical family together; it consists of chile peppers,

culinarian someone who is skilled in preparing food, generally a professional cook or chef

FLAVOR DESCRIPTIONS	TABLE 7.1
TYPE OF FLAVOR OR AROMA	FOODS WITH SUCH CHARACTERISTICS
Green, grassy	Green bell peppers, raw apple skins
Fruity, esterlike	Bananas, apples
Citrus, terpenic	Lemons, limes
Minty, camphoraceous	Fresh mint, rosemary
Floral, sweet	Roses, violets, honey
Spicy, herbaceous	Allspice, cinnamon, nutmeg
Woody, smoky	Smoked foods
Roasty, burnt	Coffee, toasted bread
Caramel, nutty	Burnt sugar, molasses
Bouillon, protein	Meat stock
Meaty, animalic	Roasted meat
Fatty, rancid	Old or stale shortening or fryer oil
Sulfurous, alliaceous	Onions, garlic, rotten egg
Mushroom, earthy	Cooked mushrooms, yeasty bread; popcorn
Celery, soupy	Celery, parsnip
Dairy, buttery	Cheese

CLASSIC FLAVOR COMBINATIONS	TABLE 7.2
MAIN INGREDIENT	**FLAVORINGS**
Beef	Fresh or dried herbs such as rosemary, sage, thyme
	Spices such as black pepper, chiles
	Spices and spice blends such as peppers, chilli powder, curry powder, garam masala, jerk seasoning
	Pungent seasonings such as anchovies, garlic, horseradish, mustard
Lamb	Fresh or dried herbs such as rosemary, herbes de provence,
	Spices and spice blends such as curry powder, garam masala, za'atar, ras el hanout
	Condiments such as chutney, mint jelly or sauce
	Sweet flavors such as dried fruits, apricots, raisins
	Pungent seasonings such as anchovies, garlic, mustard
Pork	Fresh or dried herbs such as rosemary, sage, tarragon
	Spices and spice blends such as black pepper, chili powder, Chinese five spice powder, curry powder, garam masala, jerk seasoning
	Acid flavors such as orange juice and rind, vinegar, wine
	Sweet flavors such as dried fruits, apricots, prunes and raisins, ginger, brown sugar, honey
	Pungent seasonings such as garlic, gochojang, mustard
Poultry	Fresh or dried herbs such as thyme, rosemary, coriander, marjoram, sage, tarragon
	Spice blends such as chilli powder, curry powder, garam masala, herbes de provence, jerk seasoning
	Acid flavors such as citrus fruits, juice and rind, vinegar, wine
	Pungent seasonings such as garlic, mustard
Fin fish	Fresh herbs such as chervil, chives, cilantro, dill, tarragon
	Spices and spice blends such as chile flakes, coriander, jerk seasoning
	Acid flavors such as lemon or lime juice and rind, vinegar, wine
	Condiments such as miso paste, mustard
	Pungent seasonings such as mustard, ginger, sherry, pesto
Shellfish	Fresh herbs such as chervil, chives, cilantro, dill, tarragon
	Spices and spice blends such as chile flakes, jerk seasoning
	Acid flavors such as citrus fruits, juice and rind, vinegar, wine
	Pungent seasonings such as garlic, horseradish, mustard
Eggs	Fresh or dried herbs such as chives, *fines herbes*, parsley, tarragon
Vegetables	Lemon, toasted nuts, fresh herbs such as rosemary and garlic

eggplants, tomatoes and zucchini with garlic, onions and thyme. Herbs, spices and flavorings that enhance one member of botanical family usually enhance another. For example, any combination of the ingredients and seasonings used in ratatouille would be delicious together. Similarly, herbs from one family are often interchangeable. Member of the *Lamiaceae* or mint family—basil, mint, oregano, sage, savory and thyme—share flavor characteristics that may make suitable substitutes. A pot of white beans or an aromatic vegetable or lamb stew could be simmered with any of the herbs in the group.

The section on international flavor principles on page 116 provides more specific information on flavor combinations common in various regions of the world, as do the green sidebars in this chapter and in other chapters in this text.

Amplifying Flavors

Chefs combine ingredients to enhance the flavor profile of the foods they prepare. Which ingredients they use and how they use them determine the effect on a dish. To intensify a particular taste or aroma in a dish, variations of the same flavoring or ingredient can be used. The addition of lemon rind, lemon juice and lemon basil to the dressing for a chicken salad, for example, layers the dish with flavors that amplify its lemony taste.

Chefs accent dishes, especially in the last moments before they are served, with herbs, spices, condiments, vinegars and other ingredients to add to the diner's eating experience. Take, for example, the act of sprinkling a small amount of large flake salt on a piece of grilled meat or vegetables before serving. The guest experiences the light crunchy texture of the salt as well as a burst of salinity in their first bites. Similarly, chopped garlic, lemon zest and parsley scattered over the Italian braised veal dish called Osso Buco enlivens the diner's palate. The bold, raw garnish contrasts with the rich flavors of the long-braised stew. A splash of acid on something sweet enhances the sweet tastes in the dish. That's why chefs squeeze lemon juice over fresh strawberries immediately before serving to highlight the sweetness of the ripe fruit.

Often the application of an herb, spice, condiment, vinegar or other ingredients harmonize a dish, bringing disparate ingredients together into a pleasing whole. Adding a swirl of butter or other fat to a pan sauce stabilizes the liquids and blends the flavors. A creamy soup benefits from fresh pepper, which both seasons the liquid and balances the fatty, creamy notes with a burst of resinous, pine-like flavor.

When working to layer, accent or harmonize the flavors in a dish, also consider the other elements that will be served with it. The chicken salad with layered lemon flavors described above requires an accompaniment that balances its tart assertive tastes. Serving it with a creamy potato salad would balance the acidic flavors, but serving it with vinegar-dressed coleslaw would not. Remember that all of the flavors on a plate must be agreeable and in balance.

Experimenting with Flavor

Creating dishes with appealing and complex flavors comes with practice and a solid understanding and appreciation of flavoring ingredients. Although some flavoring combinations are timeless—rosemary with lamb, dill with salmon, nutmeg with spinach, caraway with rye bread—less common pairings can be equally delicious and exciting. You must be willing and able to experiment with new flavors, but first you must become familiar with the distinctive flavors and aromas of various herbs, spices, condiments, vinegars and other ingredients. When considering a new flavor such as a new herb or spice combination in a dish, test it on a small portion of food. Then cook and taste this small portion before seasoning the entire dish. Even in a well-tested recipe, the quantity of flavorings may need to be adjusted because of a change in brands or the condition of the ingredients. You should strive to develop your palate to recognize and correct subtle variances as necessary. When you experiment, always bear in mind the following guidelines:

- Flavorings should not hide the taste or aroma of the primary ingredient.
- Flavorings should be combined in balance, so as not to overwhelm the palate.
- Flavorings should not be used to disguise poor quality or poorly prepared products.
- Flavorings should be added sparingly when foods are to be cooked over an extended period of time. During cooking, flavorings can intensify and overpower a dish.
- Always add flavorings and seasonings a small amount at a time. Taste and season foods frequently during cooking.

INTERNATIONAL FLAVOR PRINCIPLES

To thoroughly study world cuisines requires many years of reading, traveling and tasting. Luckily for both culinary students and working chefs, the essence of the world's many cuisines can be distilled into an evaluation of six general components: primary ingredients (protein and starches), religious influences, typical cooking methods, cooking liquids, fats and flavorings. Many of the ingredients used in a cuisine are the result of climate and geography. For example, the climate and landscape of northern Italy is good for grazing cattle, so beef, veal, butter and dairy products are more common there than in southern Italy, where seafood and olive oil prevail. Religious proscriptions against consuming certain meats, such as beef or pork, or drinking alcoholic beverages also impact cuisine.

But the key factor contributing to the characteristics of many cuisines is the herbs and spices used to flavor the primary ingredients. Whether a cuisine utilizes tomatoes, chiles, lemon, basil or fennel may be the result of indigenous foodstuffs or may linger from long-ago trade practices. For example, the primary ingredients of a Thai dish might be seafood, rice and vegetables. These items would generally be cooked quickly by sautéing or stir-frying with water or fish sauce as a liquid component. Thai cuisine relies on palm or coconut oil, rather than butter or olive oil, which affects that cuisine's distinctive taste as well. Flavoring ingredients such as chiles (from the New World), fresh herbs, fish sauce or curry-like spice blends (from Thailand's neighbor India) complete the picture, and result in a dish that is recognizably Thai.

Although this six-part framework offers an almost stereotypically broad description of a cuisine, it presents a profile that most diners would recognize on their plate. This approach can also be useful for you in deconstructing dishes or imparting ethnic flavors to your own preparations.

In *Ethnic Cuisine: The Flavor Principle Cookbook*, Elisabeth Rozin writes: "Every culture tends to combine a small number of flavoring ingredients so frequently and so consistently that they become definitive of that particular cuisine" (page xiv). She calls these defining flavors "flavor principles" and notes that they are "designed to abstract what is absolutely fundamental about a cuisine and, thus, to serve as a guide in cooking and developing new recipes" (page xvii). She identifies the following flavor principles:

- Central Asia: cinnamon, fruit, nuts
- China: generally—soy sauce, rice wine, fresh ginger
  Northern China (Mandarin/Peking)—miso and/or garlic and/or sesame
  Western China (Szechuan)—sweet, sour, hot
  Southern (Canton)—black beans, garlic
- Eastern Europe (Jewish): onion and chicken fat
- Eastern and northern Europe: sour cream and dill or paprika, allspice or caraway
- France: generally—olive oil, garlic and basil or wine and herb or butter and/or sour cream and/or cheese plus wine and/or stock
  Provence—olive oil, thyme, rosemary, marjoram, sage plus tomato as a variation
  Normandy—apple, cider, Calvados
- Greece: tomato, cinnamon or olive oil, lemon, oregano
- India: Northern—cumin, ginger, garlic
  Southern—mustard seed, coconut, tamarind, chile
- Italy: generally—olive oil, garlic, basil
  Northern Italy—wine vinegar, garlic
  Southern Italy—olive oil, garlic, parsley, anchovy, tomato
- Japan: soy sauce, sake, sugar
- Mexico: tomato and chile or lime and chile
- North Africa: cumin, coriander, cinnamon, ginger, onion and/or tomato and/or fruit
- Spain: olive oil, garlic, nut or olive oil, onion, pepper, tomato
- Thailand: fish sauce, curry, chile
- West Africa: tomato, peanut, chile

Like music, clothing, architecture, language and basic belief systems, food is a deeply ingrained factor in the culture of any group of people. Flavor principles may be a good phrase for explaining the differences among various global cuisines, as the words "ethnic" or "foreign" may be seen as insensitive, or even offensive, terms for non-western cultures and cuisines. Because of modern access to ingredients and increased international travel and migration, today's cooks are exposed to a greater variety of cuisines than at any time in history. But exposure is not expertise. Culinarians should strive to understand the heritage and history of cuisines that are different from their own and should work with these various cooking methods, ingredients and presentations in a thoughtful, respectful manner.

HERBS AND SPICES

Herbs and spices are used as flavorings, an item that adds a new taste to a food and alters its natural flavors. **Herbs** are members of the large group of **aromatic** plants whose leaves, stems or flowers are used in dried and fresh form to add flavors to other foods. **Spices** are strongly flavored or aromatic portions of plants used as flavorings, condiments or aromatics. Spices are the bark, roots, seeds, buds or berries of plants that usually grow naturally only in tropical climates. Spices are almost always used in their dried form, rarely fresh, and can usually be purchased whole or ground. Some plants—dill, for example—can be used as both an herb (its leaves) and a spice (its seeds). Some herbs and spices are rich in aromatic oils that may easily overpower a dish. Know which herbs and spices may overwhelm and use them sparingly.

In the sections that follow, we discuss common herbs and spices and show photos of them to help familiarize you with them. Herbs, spices and blends are listed alphabetically and pictured in three separate lists in the following sections.

herb any of a large group of aromatic plants whose leaves, stems or flowers are used as a flavoring; used either dried or fresh

aromatic (1) having a characteristic and pleasant odor or smell; (2) a food added to enhance the natural aromas of another food; aromatics include most flavorings, such as herbs and spices, as well as some vegetables, especially celery, carrots and onions

spice any of a large group of aromatic plants whose bark, roots, seeds, buds or berries are used as a flavoring; usually used in dried form, either whole or ground

Herbs

Fragrant herbs are available fresh or dried. Because drying alters their flavors and aromas, fresh herbs are generally preferred and should be used if possible. **Micro herbs** are the first true leaves of virtually any edible herb, such as basil or chervil. Micro greens are very fragile and must be hand-picked and carefully packaged for delivery. They are bursting with intense flavor; chefs use them as garnishes, especially on entrées and canapés.

Micro basil

Micro chervil

Basil (Fr. *basilic*) is one of the great culinary herbs. It is available in a variety of "flavors"—cinnamon, garlic, lemon, even chocolate—but the most common is sweet basil. Sweet basil has light green, tender leaves and small white flowers. Its flavor isn't actually sweet, but rather strong, warm and slightly peppery, with a hint of anise and cloves. Basil is used in Mediterranean and some Southeast Asian cuisines and has a special affinity for garlic and tomatoes. When purchasing fresh basil, look for bright green leaves; avoid flower buds and wilted or rust-colored leaves. Dried sweet basil is readily available but has a decidedly weaker flavor than fresh.

Basil

Opal basil is named for its vivid purple color. It has a tougher, crinkled leaf and a medium-strong flavor. Opal basil may be substituted for sweet basil in cooking, and its appearance makes it a distinctive garnish.

Opal basil

Thai sweet basil (Th. *bai horapha*) has a narrow leaf and purple stem. It has a slight licorice flavor and is used in both raw and cooked dishes in Southeast Asian cuisines.

Thai sweet basil

Bay leaves

Bay (Fr. *laurier*), also known as sweet laurel, is a small tree that produces tough, glossy leaves with a sweet balsamic aroma and

Chervil

peppery flavor. In cooking, dried bay leaves are often preferred over the more bitter fresh leaves. Essential in French cuisine, bay leaves are part of the traditional bouquets garni and court bouillon. Whole dried bay leaves are usually added to a dish at the start of cooking, then removed when sufficient flavor has been extracted.

Chervil (Fr. *cerfeuil*), also known as sweet cicely, is native to Russia and the Middle East. Its lacy, fernlike leaves can be used as a garnish. Chervil's flavor is delicate, similar to parsley but with the distinctive aroma of anise. It should not be heated for long periods. Chervil is commonly used in French cuisine especially in fish dishes where its subtle flavor can be appreciated. Chervil is one of the traditional ingredients in *fines herbes*, a classic French blend that consists of chives, chervil, parsley and tarragon.

Chives (Fr. *ciboulettes*) are perhaps the most delicate and sophisticated members of the onion family. Their hollow, thin grass-green stems grow in clumps and produce round, pale purple flowers, which are used as a garnish. Chives may be purchased dried, quick-frozen or fresh. They have a mild onion flavor and bright green color. Chives make an excellent garnish when snipped with scissors or carefully chopped and sprinkled over finished soups or sauces. Chives complement eggs, poultry, potatoes, fish and shellfish. They should not be cooked for long periods or at high temperatures.

Garlic chives or Chinese chives have flat, solid (not hollow) stems and a mild garlic flavor. Although they belong to another plant species, they may be used in place of regular chives if their garlic flavor is desired.

Chives

Garlic chives

Cilantro (Fr. *coriandre*; Sp. *culantro*) is the green leafy portion of the plant that yields seeds known as coriander. The flavors of the two portions of this plant are very different and cannot be substituted for each other. Cilantro, also known as Chinese parsley, is sharp and tangy with a strong aroma and an almost citrus flavor. It is widely used in Asian, Mexican and South American cuisines, especially in salads and sauces. Cilantro should not be subjected to heat, and its flavor is completely destroyed by drying. Do not use yellow or discolored leaves or the tough stems. When used in excess, cilantro can impart a soapy taste to foods.

Curry leaves (Hindi *kitha neem*) are the distinctively flavored leaves of a small tree that grows wild in the Himalayan foothills, southern India and Sri Lanka. These small shiny leaves have a strong curry-like fragrance and a citrus-curry flavor. Often added to a preparation whole, then removed before serving, they can also be minced or finely chopped for marinades and sauces. Choose fresh bright green leaves, if possible, or frozen leaves; dried leaves have virtually no flavor. Although used in making southern Indian and Thai dishes, curry leaves (also known as neem leaves) must not be confused with curry powder, which is discussed later.

Cilantro

Curry leaves

Dill (Fr. *aneth*), a member of the parsley family, has tiny, aromatic, yellow flowers and feathery, delicate blue-green leaves. The leaves taste similar to parsley, but sharper, with a touch of anise. Dill seeds are flat, oval and brown, with a bitter flavor similar to caraway. Both the seeds and the leaves of the dill plant are used in cooking. Dill is commonly used in Scandinavian and central European cuisines, particularly with fish and potatoes. Both leaves and seeds are used in pickling and sour dishes. Dill leaves are available fresh or dried but lose their aroma and flavor during cooking, so they should be added after the dish is removed from the heat. Dill seeds are available whole or ground and are used in fish dishes, pickles and breads.

Dill

Epazote, also known as wormseed or stinkweed, grows wild throughout the Americas. It has a strong aroma similar to kerosene and a wild flavor. Fresh epazote is used in salads and as a flavoring in Mexican and Southwestern cuisines. It is often cooked with beans to reduce their gaseousness. Dried epazote is brewed to make a beverage.

Lavender is an evergreen with thin leaves and tall stems bearing spikes of tiny purple flowers. Although lavender is known primarily for its aroma, which is widely used in perfumes, soaps and cosmetics, the flowers are also used as a flavoring, particularly in Middle Eastern and Provençal cuisines. These flowers have a sweet, lemony flavor and can be crystallized and used as a garnish. Lavender is also used in jams and preserves and to flavor teas and tisanes.

Lemongrass (Fr. *herbe de citron*), also known as citronella grass, is a tropical grass with the strong aroma and flavor of lemon. It is similar to scallions in appearance but with a woody texture. Only the lower base and white leaf stalks are used. Available fresh or quick-frozen, lemongrass is widely used in Southeast Asian cuisines.

Lime leaves from a species of thorny lime trees (*Citrus hystrix*) are used much like bay leaves to flavor soups and stews in Thai and other Asian cuisines. These small, dark green leaves have a bright citrus floral aroma. The limes have very little juice and are rarely used in cooking. The fragrant lime leaves should be used fresh or frozen, not dried.

Lovage (Fr. *céleri bâtard*, "false celery") has tall stalks and large dark green celery-like leaves. The leaves, stalks and seeds (commonly known as celery seeds) have a strong celery flavor. The leaves and stalks are used in salads and stews and the seeds are used as a spice.

Marjoram (Fr. *marjolaine*), also known as sweet marjoram, is a flowering herb native to the Mediterranean used since ancient times. Its flavor is similar to thyme but sweeter; it also has a stronger aroma than thyme. Marjoram is used in many European cuisines. Although it is available fresh, marjoram is one of the few herbs whose flavor increases when dried. Wild marjoram is more commonly known as oregano.

Mint (Fr. *menthe*), a large family of herbs, includes many species and flavors (even chocolate). Spearmint is the most common garden and commercial variety. Mint has soft, bright green leaves and a tart aroma and flavor. It does not blend well with other herbs, so its use is confined to specific dishes, usually fruits or fatty meats such as lamb. Mint has an affinity for chocolate. It can also be brewed into a beverage or used as a garnish.

Peppermint has thin, stiff, pointed leaves and a sharper menthol flavor and aroma. Fresh peppermint is used less often in cooking or as a garnish than spearmint, but peppermint oil is a common flavoring in sweets and candies.

Oregano (Fr. *origan*), also known as wild marjoram, is a pungent, peppery herb used in Mediterranean cuisines, particularly Greek and Italian, as well as in Mexican cuisine. Mexican varieties of oregano tend to be mild with citrus aromas, while Mediterranean varieties are more pungent and peppery. Oregano's thin, woody stalks bear clumps of tiny, dark green leaves, which are also available dried and crushed.

Epazote

Lavender

Lemongrass

Fragrant lime leaves

Marjoram

Spearmint

Oregano

Peppermint

Italian parsley

Parsley

Parsley (Fr. *persil*) is probably the best known and most widely used herb in the world. It grows in almost all climates and is available in many varieties. The most common type in the United States and Northern Europe is **curly parsley**. It has small curly leaves and a bright green color. Its flavor is tangy and clean. Other cuisines use a variety sometimes known as **Italian parsley**, which has flat leaves, a darker color and coarser flavor. Curly parsley is a ubiquitous garnish. Both curly and Italian types can be used in virtually any savory dish. Parsley stalks have a stronger flavor than the leaves and are part of standard bouquets garni. Chopped parsley forms the basis of any *fines herbes* blend.

Rosemary (Fr. *romarin*) is an evergreen bush that grows wild in warm, dry climates worldwide. It has stiff, needlelike leaves; some varieties bear pale blue flowers. It is highly aromatic, with a slight odor of camphor or pine. Rosemary is best used fresh. When dried, it loses flavor and its leaves become very hard and unpleasant to chew. Whole rosemary stems may be added to a dish such as a stew and removed when enough flavor has been imparted. They may also be added to bouquets garni. Rosemary has a great affinity for roasted and grilled meats, especially lamb, but it must be used sparingly because its strong flavor can easily overwhelm.

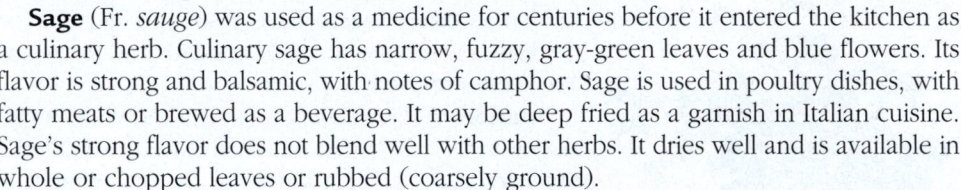

Rosemary

Sage

Sage (Fr. *sauge*) was used as a medicine for centuries before it entered the kitchen as a culinary herb. Culinary sage has narrow, fuzzy, gray-green leaves and blue flowers. Its flavor is strong and balsamic, with notes of camphor. Sage is used in poultry dishes, with fatty meats or brewed as a beverage. It may be deep fried as a garnish in Italian cuisine. Sage's strong flavor does not blend well with other herbs. It dries well and is available in whole or chopped leaves or rubbed (coarsely ground).

Savory (Fr. *sariette*) has also been used since ancient times. Its leaves are small and narrow, and it has a sharp, bitter flavor, vaguely like thyme. It dries well and is used in bean dishes, sausages and *fines herbes* blend. Although the variety called summer savory is most common and popular, a variety called winter savory is also available.

Savory

Tarragon (Fr. *estragon*), another of the great culinary herbs, is native to Siberia. It is a bushy plant with long, narrow, dark green leaves and tiny gray flowers. Tarragon goes well with fish, poultry and tomatoes and is essential in many French dishes such as béarnaise sauce and *fines herbes* blend. Its flavor is strong and diffuses quickly through foods. Tarragon is available dried, but drying may cause hay-like flavors to develop.

Tarragon

Thyme (Fr. *thym*) has been popular since 3500 BCE, when Egyptians used it as a medicine and in embalming. Thyme is a small, bushy plant with woody stems, tiny green-gray leaves and purple flowers. Its flavor is strong but refined, with notes of sage. Thyme dries well and complements virtually all types of meat, poultry, fish, shellfish and vegetables. It is often included in bouquets garni or added to stocks.

Thyme

Spices

Aleppo pepper

Aleppo pepper [ah-LEHP-oh] is made from bright red chiles grown in Turkey and northern Syria. The sun-dried Aleppo chiles are seeded and crushed, then used as a condiment. Also known as Halaby pepper, Aleppo pepper adds an authentic Mediterranean

Spice History

Spices have been used for many purposes for thousands of years. Egyptian documents dating back to 2800 BCE identify several spices native to the Middle and Far East that were used by the ruling and priestly classes for therapeutic, cosmetic, medicinal, ritualistic and culinary purposes. By 300 CE the Romans were regularly importing spices for use as perfumes, medicines, preservatives and ingredients from China and India via long, difficult journeys over sea and land. Spices were extremely expensive and unavailable to all but the wealthiest citizens.

After Rome fell in the second half of the fifth century CE, much of the over-land trade route through southern Europe became prey to bandits; after Constantinople fell in 1453, the Ottoman Turks controlled the spice routes through the Middle East. Spice costs soared and economies based on the spice trade, such as that of Venice, were at risk.

By then highly spiced food had become common, especially in wealthier households. In part to maintain their culinary norm, the Europeans set out to break the Ottoman Turk monopoly. These efforts led to Columbus's exploration of the Americas and Vasco da Gama's discovery of a sea route to India. Although the New World contained none of the spices for which Columbus was searching, it also provided many previously unknown foods and flavorings that subsequently changed European tables forever, including chiles, vanilla, tomatoes, potatoes and chocolate.

Formation of the Dutch East India Company in 1602 marked the start of the Dutch colonial empire and made spices from what is now Indonesia, whose Molucca Islands were once referred to as the "Spice Islands," widely available to the growing European middle classes. The transplantation and cultivation of spice plants eventually weakened the once-powerful trading empires until, by the 19th century, no European country could monopolize spice trade. Prices fell dramatically.

flavor and fragrance to foods. It has a sharp, but sweet, fruity flavor, with only mild heat. Although it is a member of the *Capsicum* or hot chile pepper family, Aleppo pepper is used more like ground peppercorns (*Piper nigrum*) in cooking.

Allspice (Fr. *quatre-épices*), also known as Jamaican pepper, is the dried berry of a tree that flourishes in Jamaica. It is one of the few spices still grown exclusively in the New World. Allspice is available whole; in berries that look like large, rough, brown peppercorns and ground. Ground allspice is pure allspice not a mixture of spices, although it does taste like a blend of cinnamon, cloves and nutmeg. Allspice is now used throughout the world, in everything from cakes to curries, and is often included in peppercorn blends.

Anise (Fr. *anis*) is native to the eastern Mediterranean, where it was widely used by ancient civilizations. Today it is grown commercially in warm climates throughout India, North Africa and southern Europe. The tiny, gray-green egg-shaped seeds have a distinctively strong, sweet flavor, similar to licorice and fennel. When anise seeds turn brown, they are stale and should be discarded. Anise is used in pastries, as well as fish, shellfish and vegetable dishes, and is also commonly used in alcoholic beverages (e.g., Pernod and ouzo). The green leaves of the anise plant are occasionally used fresh as an herb or in salads.

Star anise, also known as Chinese anise, is the dried, star-shaped fruit of a Chinese magnolia tree. Although it is botanically unrelated, its flavor is similar to anise seeds but more bitter and pungent. Used both whole and ground, it is an essential flavor in many Chinese dishes and one of the components of Chinese five spice powder.

Annatto seeds are the small, brick-red triangular seeds of a shrub grown in South America and the Caribbean. Annatto seeds add a mild, peppery flavor to rice, fish and shellfish dishes and are crushed to make Mexican achiote paste. Because they impart a bright yellow-orange color to foods, annatto seeds are commonly used as a natural food coloring, especially in cheeses and margarine.

Asafetida [ah-sah-FEH-teh-dah; also spelled asafoetida] is a pale brown resin made from the sap of a giant fennel-like plant native to India and Iran. It has a garlicky flavor and a strong unpleasant fetid aroma (the aroma does not transfer to food being flavored). Available powdered or in lump form, it is used—very sparingly—as a flavoring in Indian and Middle Eastern cuisines.

Capers (Fr. *capres*) come from a small bush that grows wild throughout the Mediterranean basin. The bushes' unopened flower buds have been pickled and used as a condiment for thousands of years. Fresh capers are not used, as the

Allspice

Anise seeds

Star anise

Annatto seeds

Capers

sharp, salty-sour flavor develops only after curing in salt or strongly salted white vinegar. The finest capers are the smallest, known as **nonpareils**, which are produced in France's Provence region. Capers are used in a variety of sauces (e.g., tartare, rémoulade) and are excellent with fish and game. Capers keep for long periods in their original curing liquid. Do not add or substitute vinegar, however, as this causes the capers to spoil. Soak salted capers in several changes of water before using.

Caraway (Fr. *carvi*) is perhaps the world's oldest spice. Its use has been traced to the Stone Age, and seeds have been found in ancient Egyptian tombs. The caraway plant grows wild in Europe and temperate regions of Asia. It produces a small, crescent-shaped brown seed with an earthy, peppery and anise-like flavor. Caraway seeds may be purchased whole or ground. (The leaves have a mild, bland flavor and are rarely used in cooking.) Caraway is used extensively in German and Austrian dishes, particularly breads, meats and cabbage. It is also used in alcoholic beverages and cheeses.

Cardamom (Fr. *cardamome*) is one of the most expensive spices, second only to saffron in cost. Cardamom seeds are encased in ¼-inch- (6-millimeter-) long light green or brown pods. Cardamom is highly aromatic. Its flavor, lemony with notes of camphor, is quite strong and is used in both sweet and savory dishes. Cardamom is common in foods from India and the Middle East, where it is also used to flavor coffee. Scandinavians use cardamom to flavor breads and pastries. Ground cardamom loses its flavor rapidly and is easily adulterated, so it is best to purchase whole seeds and grind your own as needed.

Chiles, including paprika, chile peppers, bell peppers and cayenne, are members of the *Capsicum* plant family. Although cultivated for thousands of years in the West Indies and Americas, capsicum peppers were unknown in the Old World prior to Spanish explorations during the 15th century. Capsicum peppers come in all shapes and sizes, with a wide range of flavors, from sweet to extremely hot. Some capsicums are used as a vegetable; others are dried, ground and used as a spice. Fresh chiles and bell peppers are discussed in Chapter 22, Vegetables. Capsicums are botanically unrelated to *Piper nigrum*, the black peppercorns discussed on page 124.

Cayenne, sometimes simply labeled "red pepper," is ground from a blend of several particularly hot types of dried red chile peppers. Its flavor is extremely hot and pungent; it has a bright orange-red color and fine texture.

Paprika, also known as Hungarian pepper, is a bright red powder ground from specific varieties of red-ripened and dried chiles. Paprika's flavor ranges from sweet to pungent; its aroma is distinctive and strong. It is essential to many eastern European and Spanish dishes in which an oak-smoked version called *pimentón* is used. Mild paprika is often used generously and may be sprinkled on prepared foods as a garnish.

Chile powders are made from pure dried chiles that are simply roasted, ground and sieved. A wide variety of dried chile peppers are processed this way, creating powders that range from sweet and mild to extremely hot and pungent. Commercial chilli powder, an American invention, is actually a combination of spices—oregano, cumin, garlic and other flavorings—intended for use in Mexican dishes. Each brand of commercial chilli powder is different and should be sampled before using.

Crushed chiles, also known as chile flakes, are blended from dried, crushed chiles. They are quite hot and are used in sauces, soups and meat dishes and sprinkled on pizza for an extra spiciness.

Cinnamon (Fr. *cannelle*) and its cousin **cassia** are among the oldest known spices: Cinnamon's use is recorded in China as early as 2500 BCE, and the Far East still produces most of the cinnamon and cassia consumed worldwide. Both cinnamon and cassia come from the bark of small evergreen trees, peeled from branches in thin layers and dried in the sun. High-quality cinnamon should be pale brown and thin, rolled up like paper into sticks known as quills. Cassia is coarser and has a stronger, less subtle flavor than cinnamon. Consequently it is cheaper than true cinnamon. Cinnamon is usually purchased ground because it is difficult to grind. Cinnamon sticks are used when long cooking times allow for sufficient flavor to be extracted (e.g., in stews or curries). Cinnamon's flavor is most often associated with pastries and sweets, but it also has a great affinity for lamb and spicy dishes.

Caraway seeds

Cardamom seeds

chile refers to the plant, **chili** refers to the stew-like dish containing chiles and **chilli** refers to the commercial spice powder

Cayenne pepper

Paprika

Chilli powder

Crushed chiles

Ground cinnamon and cinnamon sticks

Cloves (Fr. *clous de girofle*) are the unopened buds of evergreen trees that flourish in muggy tropical regions. When dried, whole cloves have hard, sharp prongs that can be pushed into other foods, such as onions or fruit, in order to provide flavor. Cloves are extremely pungent, with a sweet, astringent aroma. A small amount provides a great deal of flavor. Cloves are used in desserts, meat dishes, preserves and liquors. They may be purchased whole or ground.

Coriander (Fr. *coriandre*) seeds come from the cilantro plant. They are round and beige, with a distinctive sweet, spicy flavor and strong aroma. Unlike other plants in which the seeds and the leaves share the same flavor and aroma, coriander and cilantro are very different. Coriander seeds are available whole or ground and are frequently used in Indian cuisine and pickling mixtures.

Cumin is the seed of a small delicate plant of the parsley family that originally grew in North Africa and the Middle East. The small seeds are available whole or ground and look (but do not taste) like caraway seeds. Cumin has a strong earthy flavor and tends to dominate any dish in which it is included. It is used in Indian, Middle Eastern, Mexican and Latin American cuisines, and also in European sausages.

Fennel (Fr. *fenouil*) is a perennial plant with feathery leaves and tiny flowers long cultivated in India and China as a medicine and cure for witchcraft. Its seeds are greenish brown with prominent ridges and short, hairlike fibers. Their taste and aroma are similar to anise, though not as sweet. Whole fennel seeds are widely used in Italian stews and sausages; central European cuisines use fennel with fish, pork, pickles and vegetables. Ground seeds can also be used in breads, cakes and cookies. The same plant produces a bulbous stalk used as a vegetable.

Fenugreek (Fr. *fenugrec*), grown in Mediterranean countries since ancient times, is a small, bean-like plant with a tiny flower. Fenugreek seeds, available whole or ground, are pebble shaped and transfer their pale orange color to the foods with which they are cooked. Their flavor is bittersweet, like burnt sugar or maple syrup with a bitter aftertaste. Fenugreek is a staple in Indian cuisines, especially curries and chutneys.

Filé powder [fee-LAY] is the dried, ground leaf of the sassafras plant. Long used by Choctaw Indians, it is now most commonly used as a thickener and flavoring in Cajun and Creole cuisines. Filé is also used as a table condiment to add a spicy note to stews, gumbo and the like. The powder forms strings if allowed to boil; to prevent this, it should be added during the last minutes of cooking.

Galangal [guh-LANG-guhl] is the rhizome of a plant native to India and Southeast Asia. The rhizome has a reddish skin, an orange or whitish flesh and a peppery, ginger-like flavor and piny aroma. Also known as galanga root, Thai ginger and Laos ginger, it is peeled and crushed for use in Thai and Indonesian cuisines. Fresh ginger is an appropriate substitute.

Ginger (Fr. *gingembre*) is obtained from the rhizome of a tall, flowering tropical plant. Fresh ginger (also known as ginger root) is known as a "hand" because it looks vaguely like a group of knobby fingers. It has grayish-tan skin and a pale yellow, fibrous interior. Fresh ginger should be plump and firm with smooth skin. It should keep for about a month under refrigeration. Its flavor is fiery but sweet, with notes of lemon and rosemary. Fresh ginger is widely available and is used in Indian and Asian cuisines. It has a special affinity for chicken, beef and curries. Ginger is also available peeled and pickled in vinegar, candied in sugar or preserved in alcohol or syrup. Dried, ground ginger is a fine yellow powder widely used in pastries. Its flavor is spicier and not as sweet as fresh ginger.

Grains of paradise are the seeds of a perennial reedlike plant indigenous to the West African coast. Related to cardamom, grains of paradise have a spicy, warm and slightly bitter flavor, similar to peppercorns. In fact grains of paradise were traditionally used in place of black pepper and are also known as Guinea pepper or Melegueta pepper. Now enjoying a resurgence in popularity and increased availability, they are ground and used primarily in West African and Maghreb dishes, and in the spice blend known as ras el hanout.

Horseradish (Fr. *raifort*) is the large off-white taproot of a hardy perennial (unrelated to radishes) that flourishes in cool climates. Fresh roots should be firm and plump; they

Cloves

Coriander seeds

Cumin

Fennel

Fenugreek

Filé powder

Galangal

Ginger root

Grains of paradise

Horseradish root

Juniper berries

Ground mustard

Mustard seeds

Whole nutmegs with ground mace (left) and ground nutmeg (right)

Black pepper (left) and white pepper (right)

Green peppercorns

Pink peppercorns

do not have the distinctive horseradish aroma unless cut or bruised. The outer skin and inner core of a fresh horseradish root can have an unpleasant flavor and should be discarded. Typically used in Russian and central European cuisines, especially as an accompaniment to roasted meats and fish and shellfish dishes, horseradish is usually served grated, creamed into a sauce or as part of a compound butter or mustard preparation. If horseradish is cooked, heat can destroy its flavor and pungency, so any horseradish should be added near the end of cooking.

Juniper (Fr. *genièvre*), an evergreen bush grown throughout the Northern Hemisphere, produces round purple berries with a sweet flavor similar to pine. Juniper berries are used for flavoring gin and other alcoholic beverages and are crushed and incorporated in game dishes, particularly venison and wild boar.

Mustard seeds (Fr. *moutarde*), available in black, brown and yellow, are the seeds of three different plants in the cabbage family. The small, hard seeds have no aroma, but their flavor is sharp and fiery hot. Yellow seeds have the mildest and black seeds the strongest flavor. All are sold whole and can be crushed for cooking. Mustard seeds are a standard component of pickling spices and are processed and blended for prepared mustards, which we discuss on page 133. Ground or dry mustard is a bright yellow powder made from a blend of ground seeds, wheat flour and turmeric.

Nutmeg (Fr. *muscade*) and **mace** come from the yellow plumlike fruit of a large tropical evergreen. These fruits are dried and opened to reveal the seed, which is known as nutmeg. A bright red lacy coating, or *aril*, surrounds the seed; the aril is the spice mace. Whole nutmegs are oval and look like a piece of smooth wood. The flavor and aroma of nutmeg are strong and sweet, and a small quantity provides a great deal of flavor. Nutmeg should be grated directly into a dish as needed; once grated, flavor loss is rapid. Nutmeg is used in many European cuisines, mainly in pastries and sweets, but is also important in meat and savory dishes.

Mace

Mace is an expensive spice, with a flavor similar to nutmeg but more refined. It is almost always purchased ground and retains its flavor longer than other ground spices. Mace is used primarily in pastry items.

Peppercorns (Fr. *poivre*) are the berries of a vine plant (*Piper nigrum*) native to tropical Asia. Peppercorns should not be confused with the chile (*Capsicum*) peppers discussed earlier. Peppercorns vary in size, color, pungency and flavor. Many of these differences are the result of variations in climate and growing conditions. Good-quality pepper is expensive and should be purchased whole and ground fresh in a peppermill as needed. Whole peppercorns will last indefinitely if kept dry. They should be stored well-covered in a cool, dark place.

Black and **white peppercorns** are produced from the same plant but are picked and processed differently. For black peppercorns, the berries are picked when green and simply dried whole in the sun. Black pepper has a warm, pungent flavor and aroma. Tellicherry peppercorns from the southwest coast of India are generally considered the finest black peppercorns in the world and are priced accordingly. For white peppercorns, the berries are allowed to ripen until they turn red. The ripened berries are allowed to ferment, then the outer layer of skin is washed off. Alternatively white pepper may be produced by mechanically removing the outer skin from black peppercorns. This is not true white pepper, and the resulting product should be labeled "decorticated." White pepper has fewer aromas than black pepper but is useful in white sauces or when the appearance of black speckles is undesirable.

Green peppercorns are unripened peppercorn berries that are either freeze-dried or pickled in brine or vinegar. Pickled green peppercorns are soft, with a fresh, sour flavor similar to capers. They are excellent in spiced butters and sauces or with fish.

Pink peppercorns (Fr. *baies roses*) are the berries of a South American tree in the cashew nut family, not a true peppercorn. Consequently people with tree nut allergies may also have an allergic reaction to pink peppercorns. Pink peppercorns are available dried or pickled in vinegar. They are attractive in peppercorn blends and their flavor is sweet and pine-like, with less spiciness than true pepper.

Szechuan pepper, also spelled *Szechwan* and *Sichuan*, is made from the dried red berries of the prickly ash tree native to China. Also known as anise pepper and Chinese pepper, the berries have a numbing effect on the tongue and an extremely hot, peppery, spicy flavor with citrus overtones. They are used in Chinese cuisines and as part of Chinese five-spice powder. In Japanese cuisine, a green variety called sancho is used to season grilled fish and meats.

Poppy seeds (Fr. *pavot*) are the ripened seeds of the opium poppy, which flourishes in the Middle East and India. (When ripe, the seeds do not contain any of the pain relieving medicinal properties found elsewhere in the plant.) The tiny blue-gray seeds are round and hard with a sweet, nutty flavor. Poppy seeds are used in pastries and breads.

Saffron (Fr. *safran*) comes from the dried stigmas of the saffron crocus. Each flower bears only three threadlike stigmas, and each must be picked by hand. It takes about 250,000 flowers to produce 1 pound of saffron, making it the most expensive spice in the world. Beware of bargains; there is no such thing as cheap saffron. Luckily, a tiny pinch is enough to color and flavor a large quantity of food. Good saffron should be a brilliant orange color, not yellow, with a strong aroma and a bitter, honey-like taste. Saffron produces a yellow dye that diffuses through any warm liquid. Valencia or Spanish saffron is considered the finest. It is commonly used in fish and shellfish dishes, such as bouillabaisse, and rice dishes, such as paella and risotto. When using saffron threads, first crush them gently, then soak them in hot liquid from the recipe. Powdered saffron may be added directly to the other ingredients when cooking. It is less expensive but more easily adulterated.

Sesame seeds, also known as benne seeds, are native to India. They are small, flat ovals, with a creamy white color. Their taste is nutty and earthy, with a pronounced aroma when roasted or ground into a paste (known as tahini). Sesame seeds are the source of sesame oil, which has a mild, nutty flavor and turns rancid easily. Sesame seeds are roasted and used in or as a garnish for breads and meat dishes. They are popular in Indian and Asian cuisines. A black variety of seeds is particularly popular in Korean and Japanese cuisines.

Sumac is a red powder made from the dried petals and berries of a shrub native to Turkey. It has a sour, citric flavor and is used throughout the Middle East, especially in the spice blend known as za'atar. Early colonists made a beverage similar to lemonade from a variety of sumac they found in North America. The poisonous form of sumac is unrelated to the variety used as a seasoning.

Tamarind (Fr. *tamarin*; Sp. and It. *tamarindo*), also known as an Indian date, is the brown, bean-shaped pod of the tamarind tree, which is native to Africa. Although naturally sweet, tamarind also contains 12 percent tartaric acid, which makes it extremely tart. It is commonly used in Indian curries and Mediterranean cooking as a souring agent and in the West Indies in fruit drinks. Tamarind is sold as a concentrate or in sticky blocks of crushed pods, pulp and seeds, which should be soaked in warm water for about 5 minutes, then squeezed through a sieve. Tamarind's high pectin content is useful in chutneys and jams, and it is often included in barbecue sauces and marinades. It is a key ingredient in Worcestershire sauce.

Turmeric (Fr. *curcuma*), also known as Indian saffron, is produced from the rhizome of a flowering tropical plant related to ginger. It has a mild, woodsy aroma. It is most often available dried and usually ground although fresh turmeric is becoming more widely available. Turmeric is renowned for its vibrant yellow color and is used as a food coloring and dye. Turmeric's flavor is distinctive and strong; it should not be substituted for saffron. Turmeric is a traditional ingredient in Indian curries, to which it imparts color as well as flavor.

Wasabi is a pale green root similar, but unrelated, to horseradish. It has a strong aroma and a sharp, cleansing flavor with herbal overtones that is a bit hotter than that of horseradish. Fresh wasabi is rarely found outside Japan, but tins of powder and tubes of paste are readily available. It is commonly served with sushi and sashimi and can be used to add a spicy Asian note to other dishes, such as mashed potatoes or a compound butter.

Szechuan pepper

Poppy seeds

Saffron

Sesame seeds

Sumac

Tamarind pods

Tamarind paste

Turmeric

Wasabi

Chinese five-spice
powder

Curry powder

Herbes de Provence

Pickling spice

Shichimi togarashi

Herb and Spice Blends

Many cuisines feature recognizable combinations of flavors that are found in a variety of dishes. Although many of these blends are available ready-prepared for convenience, most can be mixed by the chef as needed. This can be a healthier option as commercial herb and spice blends can contain large amounts of salt. A few common herb and spice blends are described here.

Chinese five-spice powder is a combination of equal parts finely ground Szechuan pepper, star anise, cloves, cinnamon and fennel seeds. This blend is widely used in Chinese and some Vietnamese foods and is excellent with pork and in pâtés.

Curry powder is a European invention that probably took its name from the Tamil word *kari*, meaning "sauce." Created by 19th-century Britons returning from colonial India, it was meant to be the complete spicing for a "curry" dish. There are as many different formulas for curry powder as there are manufacturers, some mild and sweet (Bombay or Chinese style), others hot and pungent (Madras style). Typical ingredients in curry powder are black pepper, cinnamon, cloves, coriander, cumin, ginger, mace and turmeric.

Fines herbes [feenz AIRB] is a combination of parsley, tarragon, chervil and chives widely used in French cuisine. The mixture, which translates to "fine herbs" in English, is available dried, or it can be created from fresh ingredients.

Jamaican jerk seasoning is a powdered or wet mixture from the Caribbean island of Jamaica. It is a combination of spices that typically includes thyme, ground spices. such as allspice, cinnamon, cloves, and ginger, as well as onions and garlic. Chicken and pork are rubbed or marinated in the blend, then grilled.

Herbes de Provence [airb duh pro-VAWNS] is a blend of dried herbs commonly grown and used in southern France. Commercial blends usually include thyme, rosemary, bay leaf, basil, fennel seeds, savory and lavender. The herb blend is used with grilled or roasted meat, fish or chicken; in vegetable dishes; on pizza; and even in steamed rice and yeast breads.

Italian seasoning blend is a commercially prepared mixture of dried basil, oregano, sage, marjoram, rosemary, thyme, savory and other herbs associated with Italian cuisine.

Masala [mah-SAH-lah] is a flavorful, aromatic blend of roasted and ground spices used in Indian cuisines. A **garam masala** [gah-RAHM] is a masala made with hot spices (*garam* means warm or hot). A dry garam masala usually contains peppercorns, cardamom, cinnamon, cloves, coriander, nutmeg, turmeric, bay leaves and fennel seeds and is added toward the end of cooking or sprinkled on the food just before service. Adding coconut milk, oil or sometimes tamarind water to a dry garam masala makes a wet garam masala. A wet garam masala is typically added at the start of cooking.

Pickling spice, as with other blends, varies by manufacturer. Most pickling spice blends are based on black peppercorns and red chiles, with some or all of the following added: allspice, cloves, ginger, mustard seeds, coriander seeds, bay leaves and dill. These blends are useful in making cucumber or vegetable pickles as well as in stews and soups.

Quatre-épices [kah-tray-PEES] literally "four spices" in French, is a peppery mixture of black peppercorns with lesser amounts of nutmeg, cloves and dried ginger. Sometimes cinnamon or allspice is included. Quatre-épices is used in charcuterie and long-simmered stews.

Ras el hanout [rass al ha-NOOT] is a common Moroccan spice blend that varies greatly from supplier to supplier. It typically contains 20 or more spices, such as turmeric, cinnamon, cloves, grains of paradise, coriander, cumin, cardamom, peppercorns, dried chiles, dried flower petals and, allegedly, an aphrodisiac or two. It is sold whole and ground by the cook as necessary to flavor stews, rice, couscous and game dishes.

Seasoned salts are commercially blended products containing salt and one or more natural flavoring ingredients such as garlic, spices or celery seeds and, often, monosodium glutamate (MSG).

Shichimi togarashi is a chile pepper-based blend used as a condiment in Japanese cuisine. In addition to chile flakes, it usually contains six other seasonings (*shichimi* means "seven tastes"), depending on brand and regional preference. White sesame seeds, seaweed (nori) flakes, chopped dried citrus peel, garlic, ginger, sansho and white poppy seeds are typical ingredients. Hot, medium or mild versions are available.

Za'atar [ZAH-tar] is a blend of dried thyme, wild oregano, Aleppo pepper, sumac and sesame seeds used through the Middle East on flatbreads or mixed with olive oil as a condiment.

Za'atar

Storing Herbs and Spices

Fresh herbs should be kept refrigerated at 34°–40°F (2°–4°C). Large bouquets can be stored upright, their leaves loosely covered with plastic wrap and their stems submerged in water. Smaller bunches should be stored loosely covered with a damp towel. Excess fresh herbs can be dried in an electric dehydrator or spread out on baking sheets in a 100°F (38°C) oven.

Dried herbs and spices should be stored in airtight, opaque containers in a cool, dry place. Avoid light and heat, both of which destroy delicate flavors. If stored properly, dried herbs should last for 2 to 3 months.

As noted spices are often available whole or ground. Once ground, they lose their flavors rapidly, however. Whole spices should keep their flavors for at least 6–9 months if stored properly. To evaluate the freshness of spices, smell and taste them. Fresh spices should have a pronounced fresh scent. The flavor may be harsh or even unpleasant but it will be easily discernible. Stale spices lose their spicy aroma and develop a bitter or musty aftertaste. Discard them.

Using Herbs and Spices

Herbs and spices are a simple, inexpensive way to bring individuality and variety to foods. They add neither fat nor sodium and virtually no calories to foods; most contain only 3–10 calories per teaspoon. Table 7.3 lists just a few uses for some of the more common herbs and spices.

USES FOR COMMON HERBS AND SPICES		TABLE 7.3
FLAVORING	**FORM**	**SUGGESTED USES**
Allspice	Whole or ground	Fruits, relishes, braised meats, quick breads, spice cookies
Anise	Whole or ground	Asian cuisines, pastries, breads, cheeses
Basil	Fresh or dried	Tomatoes, salads, eggs, fish, chicken, lamb, cheeses, savory breads, pizza
Caraway	Whole or ground	Rye bread, cabbage, beans, pork, beef, veal
Cardamom	Ground	Sweet dough, cookies
Chervil	Fresh	Chicken, fish, eggs, salads, soups, vegetables
Chives	Fresh or dried	Eggs, fish, chicken, soups, potatoes, cheeses
Cilantro	Fresh leaves	Salsa, salads, Mexican cuisine, fish, shellfish, chicken
Cinnamon	Whole or ground	Infused in syrups for compotes, fruit, pies, pastries, breads, ice cream
Cloves	Whole or ground	Marinades, baked goods, braised meats, pickles, fruits, beverages, stocks
Cumin	Whole or ground	Chili, sausages, stews, eggs
Dill	Fresh or dried leaves; whole seeds	Leaves or seeds in soups, salads, fish, shellfish, vegetables, breads; seeds in pickles, potatoes, vegetables
Fennel	Whole seeds	Sausages, stews, sauces, pickling, lamb, eggs
Ginger	Fresh or powder	Asian, Caribbean, Indian cuisines; pastries, curries, stews, meats
Mace	Ground	Pâtés, sausage, spice breads, cookies
Marjoram	Fresh or dried	Sausages, pâtés, meats, poultry, stews, green vegetables, tomatoes, game
Mint	Fresh or dried	Infused in sauces, soups
Nutmeg	Ground	Curries, relishes, rice, eggs, custards, beverages
Rosemary	Fresh or dried	Lamb, veal, beef, poultry, game, marinades, stews
Saffron	Threads or ground	Rice, breads, potatoes, soups, stews, chicken, fish, shellfish
Sage	Fresh or dried	Poultry, charcuterie, pork, stuffings, pasta, beans, tomatoes
Tarragon	Fresh or dried	Chicken, fish, eggs, salad dressings, sauces, tomatoes
Thyme	Fresh or dried	Fish, chicken, meats, stews, charcuterie, soups, tomatoes
Turmeric	Fresh or powder	Curries, relishes, rice, eggs, breads

Substituting Dried Herbs for Fresh Herbs

In general, use only *one-half to one-third* as much dried herb as fresh in any given recipe. For example, if a recipe calls for 1 tablespoon of fresh basil, substitute only 1 teaspoon of dried basil. More can usually be added later if necessary.

Although the flavors and aromas of fresh herbs are generally preferred, dried herbs are widely used because they are readily available and convenient. Use less dried herb than you would fresh herb. The loss of moisture strengthens and concentrates the flavor in dried herbs. The delicate aroma and flavors of fresh herbs is volatile. Most fresh herbs such as chives, parsley, cilantro, basil and tarragon are best when added at the end of cooking.

Most dried spices need to be added early in order for their flavor to develop during cooking. Whole spices take the longest; ground spices release their flavor more quickly. In some preparations, Indian curries, for example, ground spices are first cooked in oil to release their aromas before being added to a dish. Some dried spices such as black pepper may become bitter when cooked for an extended period of time, however. In uncooked dishes that call for ground spices (e.g., salad dressings), the mixture should be allowed to stand for several hours to develop good flavor.

SALT

Salt (Fr. *sel*) is the most basic seasoning, and its use is universal. It preserves foods, heightens their flavors and provides the distinctive taste of saltiness. The presence of salt can be tasted easily but not smelled. Salt suppresses bitter flavors, making the sweet and sour ones more prominent. The flavor of salt does not evaporate or dissipate during cooking, so it should be added to foods carefully, in small amounts, according to taste. Remember, more salt can always be added to a dish, but too much salt cannot be removed nor can its flavor be hidden. Vegetables cooked in overly salted water may be improved by simmering them longer in fresh unsalted water but in most instances, excess salt cannot be removed from a food.

Be deliberate in your use of salt and consider the following:

- Salt does not evaporate during cooking. But, as liquids reduce, salt becomes more concentrated. Salt foods sparingly to start.
- Salt foods in small increments as you cook.
- Cooks can perspire in the kitchen and therefore need more salt. Be beware of this and do not add too much salt to a dish to satisfy your own craving for salt. Customers can add more salt at table.
- The temperature of food changes its perceived saltiness. A cold dish tastes less salty than when the dish is served hot. More salt may be needed in a dish that will be served cold.

Culinary or **table salt** is sodium chloride (NaCl), one of the minerals essential to human life. Salt contains no calories, proteins, fats or carbohydrates. It is available from several sources, each with its own flavor and degree of saltiness.

Rock salt, mined from underground deposits, is available in both edible and nonedible forms. It is used in ice cream churns, for thawing frozen sidewalks and, in edible form, in salt mills.

Common **kitchen salt**—often referred to as table salt—is produced by pumping water through underground salt deposits, then bringing the brine to the surface to evaporate. This process leaves behind crystals. Chemicals are usually added to prevent table salt from absorbing moisture and keep it free-flowing. Iodized salt is commonly used in the United States. The iodine has no effect on the salt's flavor or use; it is added as an easily available source of iodine, an important nutrient that the body requires in small amounts.

Kosher salt has large, irregular crystals and is used in the "koshering" or curing of meats. It is purified rock salt that contains no iodine or additives. It can be substituted for common kitchen salt in recipes. Some chefs prefer it to table salt because they prefer its flavor and it dissolves more easily than other salts.

Sea salt is obtained by evaporating seawater. The evaporation can be done by drying the salt in the sun (unrefined sea salt) or by boiling the salty liquid (refined sea salt).

Rock salt

Kosher salt

Unlike other table salts, unrefined sea salt contains additional mineral salts such as magnesium, calcium and potassium, which give it a stronger, more complex flavor and a grayish-brown color. The region where unrefined sea salt is produced can also affect its flavor and color. For example, salt from the Mediterranean Sea tastes different from salt from the Indian Ocean or the English Channel. Sea salt is considerably more expensive than other table salts and is often reserved for finishing a dish or used as a condiment.

Sel gris is a sea salt harvested off the coast of Normandy, France. It is slightly wet and takes its gray color from minerals in the clay from which it is collected. **Fleur de sel**, which means "flower of salt," is salt that collects on rocks in the sel gris marshes. It forms delicate crystals and has little color because it has not come into contact with the clay.

Some **specialty salts** are actually mined from the earth, such as that from the foothills of the Himalayan Mountains. The presence of iron and copper along with other minerals gives **Himalayan salt** a pink hue and distinct flavor. **Black salt** (*kala namak*), common in traditional Indian recipes, is mined rock salt; minerals and other components in the salt impart a dark color and sulfurous taste. **Smoked salt** is a flavored salt made by smoking the salt over a smoldering fire. It can also be made by adding liquid smoke to a salt solution. With their distinctive appearance and texture, specialty salts are often used to finish dishes before serving and may be referred to as finishing salts.

Salt keeps indefinitely. It will, however, absorb moisture from the atmosphere, which prevents it from flowing properly. Salt is a powerful preservative. Its presence stops or greatly slows down the growth of many undesirable microorganisms, and it is used to preserve meats, vegetables and fish. It is also used to develop desirable flavors in bacon, ham, cheeses and fish products, as well as pickled vegetables.

Fleur de sel

Himalayan pink salt

Black salt

OILS

Oils (Fr. *huiles*) are fats that remains liquid at room temperature. Cooking oils are refined from various seeds, plants and vegetables. (Other fats, such as butter and margarine, are discussed in Chapter 8, Dairy Products; fats for deep-frying are discussed in Chapter 10, Principles of Cooking.) They are included here as flavorings because each oil, along with its cooking properties, has specific flavor and aroma characteristics that should be considered when choosing an oil as a cooking medium or as an ingredient.

Cooking fats, including oils and **shortenings**, are manufactured for specific purposes such as deep-frying, cake baking, dressing salads and sautéing. Most food service operations purchase different fats for each of these needs. Fats break down at different temperatures. When fats break down, their chemical structure is altered; the molecules that make up fat are converted into individual fatty acids. These acids add undesirable flavors to the fat and can ruin the flavor of the food being cooked. The temperature at which a given fat begins to break down and smoke is known as its **smoke point**. When purchasing oils, consider their use, smoke point and cost. Choose fats with higher smoke points for high-temperature cooking such as deep-frying and sautéing.

In addition to its smoke point, the flavor and cost of each oil must be considered. For example, both corn oil and walnut oil can be used in a salad dressing. Their selection may depend on balancing cost (corn oil is less expensive) against flavor (walnut oil has a stronger, more distinctive flavor).

When fats spoil, they are said to go **rancid**. Rancidity is a chemical change caused by exposure to air, light or heat. It results in objectionable flavors and odors. Different fats turn rancid at different rates, but all fats benefit from refrigerated storage away from moisture, light and air. (Some oils are packaged in colored glass containers because certain tints of green and yellow block the damaging light rays that can cause an oil to go rancid.) Although oils may become thick and cloudy under refrigeration, this is not a cause for concern. The oils will return to their clear, liquid states at room temperature. Stored fats should also be covered to prevent them from absorbing odors.

Vegetable oils are extracted from a variety of plants, including corn, cottonseed, peanuts, grape seeds and soybeans, by pressure or chemical solvents. The oil is refined—cleaned to remove unwanted colors, odors or flavors. Vegetable oils are virtually odorless

shortening (1) a white, flavorless, solid fat formulated for baking or deep-frying; (2) any fat used in baking to tenderize doughs by shortening protein strands (gluten)

smoke point the temperature at which a fat begins to break down and smoke

flash point the temperature at which a fat ignites and small flames appear on the surface of the fat

and have a neutral flavor. Because they contain no animal products, they are cholesterol-free. If a commercial product contains only one type of oil, it is labeled "pure" (as in "pure corn oil"). Products labeled "vegetable oil" are blended from several sources. Products labeled "salad oil" are highly refined blends of vegetable oil.

Canola oil is processed from rapeseeds. It is a healthful cooking oil because it contains no cholesterol and has a high percentage of monounsaturated fat. Canola oil is useful for frying and general cooking because it has no flavor and a high smoke point.

Nut oils are extracted from a variety of nuts and are almost always packaged as "pure" products, never blended. A nut oil should have the strong flavor and aroma of the nut from which it was processed. Popular examples are walnut and hazelnut oils. These oils are used to give flavor to salad dressings, marinades and other dishes. But heat diminishes their flavor, so nut oils are not recommended for frying or baking. Nut oils tend to go rancid quickly and therefore are usually packaged in small containers.

Olive oil (Fr. *huile d'olive*) is the only oil that is extracted from a fruit rather than a seed, nut or grain. Olive oil is produced primarily in Spain, Italy, France, Greece and North Africa; California produces a relatively minor amount of olive oil. Like wine, olive oils vary in color and flavor according to the variety of tree, the ripeness of the fruit, the type of soil, the climate and the producer's preferences. Colors range from dark green to almost clear, depending on the ripeness of the olives at the time of pressing and the amount of subsequent refining. Color is not a good indication of flavor, however. Flavor is ultimately a matter of personal preference. Stronger-flavored oil may be desired for some foods, whereas milder oil is better for others. Good olive oil should be thicker than refined vegetable oils, but not so thick that it has a fatty texture.

The label designations—extra virgin, virgin and pure—refer to the percentage of free fatty acid in the oil (a low acid content is preferable) and the extent of processing used to extract the oil. The first cold-pressing of the olives results in virgin oil. (The designation "virgin" is used only when the oil is 100 percent unadulterated olive oil, unheated and without any chemical processing.) Virgin oil may still vary in quality depending on the level of acidity. Extra virgin oil is virgin oil with not more than 0.8% acidity; virgin oil may have up to 3%. Pure olive oil is processed using heat and chemicals from the pulp left after the first pressing. Pure oil is lighter in flavor and less expensive than virgin oil.

Sesame oil is produced from the seeds of a large annual herb native to India. The tiny seeds range from white to tan to black, depending on the variety. The oil has a nutty, slightly bitter flavor, which becomes even more pronounced when the seeds are toasted prior to pressing for oil. Toasted sesame oil is used as a condiment or flavoring oil in China, Japan and Korea. The milder oil pressed from raw seeds is used for baking and cooking in Mediterranean, Jewish and Indian cuisine.

Flavored oils, also known as **infused oils**, are an interesting and increasingly popular condiment. These oils may be used as a dip for breads, a cooking medium or a flavoring accent in marinades, dressings, sauces or other dishes. Flavors include, garlic, citrus, spices, basil and other herbs. Flavored oils are generally prepared with olive oil (for additional flavor) or canola oil, which are both considered more healthful than other fats. Top-quality commercially flavored oils are prepared by extracting aromatic oils from the flavoring ingredients and then blending them with a high-grade oil; any impurities are then removed. Aromatic oils yield a more intense flavor than oils in which a flavoring ingredient is simply steeped. Flavored oils should be stored like any other high-quality oil.

Canola oil

Hazelnut oil

Extra virgin olive oil

Toasted sesame oil

VINEGARS

Vinegar (Fr. *vinaigre*) is a thin, sour liquid used for thousands of years as a preservative, cooking ingredient, condiment and cleaning solution. Vinegar is obtained through the fermentation of wine, beer, fruits or grains. Bacteria attack the alcohol in the solution, turning it into acetic acid. No alcohol remains when the transformation is complete. The quality of vinegar depends on the quality of the wine or other fermented liquid. Vinegar flavors are as varied as the liquids from which they are made.

Vinegars should be clear and clean-looking, never cloudy or muddy. Commercial vinegars are pasteurized, so an unopened bottle should last indefinitely in a cool, dark place. Once opened, vinegars should last about 3 months if tightly capped. Any sediment that develops can be strained out, but if mold develops, discard the vinegar. The acid in vinegar reacts with metal. When cooking with vinegar, use nonreactive cookware lined with stainless steel. Store foods made with vinegar in stainless steel, glass, enamel or plastic containers.

Wine vinegars are as old as wine itself. They may be made from white or red wine, sherry or even Champagne, and should bear the color and flavor hallmarks of the wine used. Wine vinegars are preferred in French and Mediterranean cuisines.

Malt vinegar is produced from malted barley. It has a slightly sweet, mild flavor and is used as a condiment, especially with fried foods.

Distilled vinegar, made from grain alcohol, is completely clear with a stronger vinegary flavor and higher acid content than other vinegars. It is preferred for pickling and preserving.

Cider vinegar is produced from unpasteurized apple juice or cider. It is pale brown in color with a mild acidity and fruity aroma. Cider vinegar is particularly popular in the United States for salad dressings and pickling.

Rice vinegar is a clear, slightly sweet product brewed from rice wine. Its flavor is clean and elegant, making it useful in a variety of dishes, especially in Asian cuisines.

Flavored vinegars are vinegars in which herbs, spices, fruits or other foods are steeped. Flavored vinegars are easily produced from commercial wine or distilled vinegars, using any desired herb, spice or fruit. Inferior flavored vinegars are made by adding flavoring to low-grade vinegar.

Balsamic vinegar (It. *aceto balsamico*) has been produced in Italy for more than 800 years. To produce traditional balsamic vinegar, red or white wine made from specially cultivated grapes (white Trebbiano and red Lambrusco grapes among others) is reduced, then aged in a succession of wooden barrels made from a variety of woods—oak, cherry, locust, ash, mulberry and juniper—for at least 4, but sometimes up to 50, years. The resulting liquid is dark reddish-brown and sweet. Balsamic vinegar has a high acid level, but the sweetness covers the tart flavor, making it very mellow. True balsamic is extremely expensive because of the long aging process and the small quantities available. Most of the commercial products imported from Italy are now made by a quick caramelization and flavoring process. (White balsamic vinegar is cooked under pressure and aged for a shorter period in order to retain a light color and flavor.) Balsamic is excellent as a condiment or seasoning and has a remarkable affinity for tomatoes and strawberries.

Balsamic vinegar, raspberry vinegar and cider vinegar

CONDIMENTS

Strictly speaking, a condiment is any food added to a dish for flavor, including herbs, spices and vinegars. Today, however, condiments more often refer to cooked or prepared flavorings, such as prepared mustards, **relishes**, bottled sauces and **pickles** served to accompany foods. We discuss several frequently used condiments in this section. These staples may be used to alter or enhance the flavor of a dish during cooking or added to a completed dish at the table by the diner.

Chipotle in adobo is a Latin American seasoning made from smoked jalapeño peppers cooked in a tomato, onion and spice purée. It is used as a rub or as an ingredient in sauces.

Chutney (from the Hindi word for "catnip") is a pungent relish made from fruits, spices and herbs that is frequently used in Indian cuisine.

Chipotle in adobo

Chutney

relish a cooked or pickled sauce usually made with vegetables or fruits and often used as a condiment; can be smooth or chunky, sweet or savory, and hot or mild

pickle (1) to preserve food in a brine or vinegar solution; (2) food that has been preserved in a seasoned brine or vinegar, especially cucumbers

From Your Grocer's Shelf

Even the most sophisticated food service operation occasionally uses some prepared condiments or flavorings. The products listed here are widely used and available from grocery stores or wholesale purveyors. Some are brand-name items that have become almost synonymous with the product itself; others are available from several manufacturers. When there is a choice, select brands with all natural ingredients, few thickeners and no preservatives.

Barbecue sauce: Commercial barbecue sauce is a mixture of tomatoes, vinegar and spices used primarily for marinating or basting meat, poultry or fish. A tremendous variety of barbecue sauces are available, with various flavors, textures and aromas. Sample several before selecting the most appropriate for your specific needs.

Chile sauce: Asian chile sauce, also known as *sambol* or *sambol oelek*, varies somewhat depending on the country of origin or style, but all are thick, reddish-orange and extremely pungent and spicy. They usually contain ground chiles with garlic or onion and with less vinegar than Louisiana-style hot

sauce. Asian cuisines incorporate these bottled sauces in curries, soups, stews and other dishes and as table condiments. One of the most popular and widely available brands is the Vietnamese-style chile garlic sauce with a rooster logo on its label, made in California by Huy Fong Foods. Various imported **Sriracha** sauces, named for a port town in southern Thailand, are also widely available.

Hoisin sauce: Hoisin sauce is a dark, thick, salty-sweet sauce made from fermented soybeans, vinegar, garlic and caramel. It is used in Chinese dishes or served as a dipping sauce.

Old Bay brand seasoning: Old Bay is a dry spice blend containing celery salt, dry mustard, paprika and other flavorings. It is widely used in shellfish preparations, especially boiled shrimp and crab.

Oyster sauce: Oyster sauce is a thick, dark sauce made from oyster extract. It has a salty-sweet flavor and a rich aroma. Oyster sauce is often used with stir-fried meats and poultry in Chinese cuisine.

Pickapeppa brand sauce: Pickapeppa sauce is a dark, thick, sweet-hot blend of tomatoes,

onions, sugar, vinegar, mango, raisins, tamarind and spices. Produced in Jamaica, it is used as a condiment for meat, game or fish and as a seasoning in sauces, soups and dressings.

Tabasco brand sauce: Tabasco sauce is a thin, bright-red liquid blended from vinegar, chiles and salt. Its fiery flavor is widely used in sauces, soups and prepared dishes; it is a popular condiment for Mexican, southern and southwestern cuisines. Tabasco sauce has been produced in Louisiana since 1868. Other "Louisiana-style" hot sauces (containing only peppers, vinegar and salt) may be substituted.

Worcestershire sauce: Worcestershire sauce is a thin, dark brown liquid made from a variety of fermented ingredients including anchovies, malt vinegar, tamarind, molasses and spices. It is used as a condiment for beef and as a seasoning for sauces, soups, stews and prepared dishes. Its flavor should be rich and full, but not salty. Vegetarian and kosher versions made without anchovies are also available.

Fermented black bean paste

Fish sauce

Fermented black bean sauce is a Chinese condiment and flavoring ingredient made from black soybeans that have been heavily salted, then fermented and either slightly mashed (whole bean sauce) or puréed (paste). Both versions usually include hoisin, chile sauce or minced garlic and feature an intense, pungent, salty flavor. Yellow bean sauces are similar, but milder and sweeter.

Fish sauce (Viet. *nuoc mam*; Th. *nam pla*) is the liquid drained from fermenting salted anchovy-like fish. It is a thin, golden to light brown liquid with a very pungent odor and salty flavor. There is no substitute for the savory richness that it adds to food and it is considered an essential flavoring and condiment throughout Southeast Asia, where it is used in and served with most every sort of dish.

Gochujang [go-choo-JANG] is a paste made from finely ground dried Korean red peppers, glutinous (sticky) rice flour, fermented soy bean flour, salt and a bit of sugar or honey. It is used in stews, in marinades, as a condiment for simple rice and noodle dishes and as a dipping sauce, sometimes mixed with Korean fermented bean paste (doenjang), for grilled meats. Considered one of the primary flavors of Korean cuisine, gochujang is fiery hot with sweet, rich, mildly fermented notes. No other chile paste can be substituted for its distinctive flavor. Many commercial varieties are widely available; the best do not contain any artificial colors, MSG, cornstarch or other thickeners.

Gochujang

Tomato ketchup (also known as catsup or catchup) originally referred to any salty extract from fish, fruits or vegetables. Prepared tomato ketchup is a sauce, created in America and used worldwide as a flavoring ingredient or condiment. It is bright red and thick, with a tangy, sweet-sour flavor. Ketchup can be stored either in the refrigerator or at room temperature; it should keep well for up to 4 months after opening. Ketchup does not turn rancid or develop mold, but it does darken and lose flavor as it ages.

Prepared mustard is a mixture of crushed mustard seeds, vinegar or wine and salt or spices. It can be flavored in many ways—with herbs, onions, peppers and even citrus zest. It can be a smooth paste or coarse and chunky, depending on how finely the seeds are ground and whether the skins are strained out. Prepared mustard gets its tangy flavor from an essential oil that forms only when the seeds are crushed and mixed with water. Prepared mustard is used as a condiment, particularly with meat and charcuterie items, and as a flavoring ingredient in sauces, stews and marinades.

Dijon mustard takes its name from a town and the surrounding region in France that produces about half of the world's mustard. French mustard labeled "Dijon" must, by law, be produced only in that region. Dijon and Dijon-style mustards are smooth with a rich, complex flavor.

English and Chinese mustards are made from mustard flour and cool water. They are extremely hot and powerful. American "ballpark" mustard is mild and vinegary with a bright yellow color. Unless it contains a high percentage of oil, mustard never really spoils; its flavor just fades away. Because of its high acid content, mustard is not prone to rancidity, but it does oxidize and develop a dark surface crust. Once opened, mustard should be kept well-covered and refrigerated.

Soy sauce is a thin, dark brown liquid fermented from cooked soybeans, wheat and salt. Available in several flavors and strengths, it is ubiquitous in most Asian cuisines. Light soy sauce is thin, with a light brown color and a very salty flavor. Dark soy sauce is thicker and dark brown, with a sweet, less salty flavor. **Tamari** is a Japanese-style soy sauce made without wheat, although its name may be applied to a variety of Japanese-style soy sauces. Necessary for preparing many Asian dishes, soy sauce is also used in marinades and sauces and as an all-purpose condiment. Other common soy-based condiments include teriyaki sauce and fermented bean paste (miso), made by fermenting soybeans with a grain such as rice or barley.

Tahini is a thick, oily paste made of ground sesame seeds. It is thick and slightly grainy, with an ivory to grayish-tan color. Tahini can be bland or salty, depending on the manufacturer. Its toasted, nutty flavor is common in Middle Eastern and Mediterranean cuisine, especially in sauces and spreads such as hummus. Tahini is also useful in vegetarian dishes and is relatively high in protein and vitamins.

Yellow mustard

Dijon mustard

Whole-grain mustard

Brown mustard

Soy sauce

Tahini

WINES, BEERS AND DISTILLED SPIRITS

Wines, **beers**, **brandies**, **liquors** and **liqueurs** are frequently used in the kitchen, most often as flavorings, but also as primary ingredients. In some dishes, an alcoholic beverage can even serve as a cooking medium (e.g., pears poached in red wine). Fermented beverages—wines and beers—are often used to flavor and tenderize foods in marinades, to add flavor during or at the end of cooking, and to deglaze the pan for a sauce.

Distilled spirits are made by heating a fermented liquid to evaporate the water, thus **distilling** or concentrating the alcohol content. Distilled liquors such as rum, brandy, bourbon and whiskey, can be used for their own distinctive flavors or to blend with other flavors such as chocolate and coffee. Liqueurs, which are distilled and sweetened are selected for their specific flavors: amaretto for almond, Kahlúa for coffee, crème de cassis for black currant. They are used either to add flavors or to enhance other flavors in a dish. For example, brandy, especially the classic orange-flavored Grand Marnier, is a common bakeshop flavoring that can complement fruit and round off the flavors of custards and creams.

Because alcoholic beverages are used as flavorings, general information about them is included in the following sections. Brief guidelines for choosing appropriate wines or other alcoholic beverages as flavorings as well as guidelines on how to use them in the

wine an alcoholic beverage made from the fermented juice of grapes or other fruits; may be sparkling (effervescent) or still (non-effervescent) or fortified with additional alcohol; wine's alcohol content is 10–15%

beer an alcoholic beverage made from water, hops and malted barley, fermented by yeast; beer's alcohol content is 3–12%

brandy an alcoholic beverage made by distilling wine or the fermented mash of grapes or other fruits; brandy's alcohol content is 35–60%

liquor an alcoholic beverage made by distilling grains, fruits, vegetables or other foods; includes rum, whiskey and vodka; most distilled spirits' alcohol content is 40–60%

liqueur a strong, sweet, syrupy alcoholic beverage made by mixing or redistilling neutral spirits with fruits, flowers, herbs, spices or other flavorings; also known as a cordial; liqueur's alcohol content is 15–30%

kitchen are also included. The art of pairing wine and beer with food, or creating beverages with spirits is beyond the scope of this text. As with other flavoring ingredients, patience, research, experimentation and practice will help develop your feel for which alcoholic beverage—and how much—will best enhance a specific dish.

Wines

Wine is naturally fermented fruit juice. Its history spans over 8,000 years and its use and production has affected ancient and modern societies and cultures around the world. Most wine is made from one or more of the many varieties in the *Vitis vinifera* family of grapes. The most popular red wine varietals, or types, of grapes are Cabernet Sauvignon, Merlot, Nebbiolo, Pinot Noir, Syrah and Sangiovese. Popular white wine varietals include Chardonnay, Riesling, Pinot Grigio and Sauvignon Blanc. Other fruits and honey are used for making wine as well, however, these wines are generally sweeter and are not as popular today as those made from the classic wine grapes.

fermentation the metabolic process by which certain bacteria and yeasts (fungi) convert carbohydrates into enzymes, carbon dioxide and ethyl alcohol

To make wine, freshly harvested grapes are gently crushed to release their juices. If the **wine maker** is making a **red wine**, both the crushed red or black grapes and their juice are transferred to a fermentation tank and allowed to ferment. **Fermentation** is a natural process in which yeasts eat sugars and produce carbon dioxide and ethyl alcohol. As the red wine ferments, the grape skins color the juice, provide complex fruity flavors and release **tannins**, which give red wines their distinctive astringent characteristic and slightly bitter taste.

If the wine maker is making a **white wine**, the grape skins are removed and only the juice is fermented. If the vintner is making a **rosé wine** [ro-ZAY] or a blush wine, red grape skins are left in contact with the juice just long enough to add the desired amount of color.

Next the wine maker adds yeast to start the fermentation process, which creates alcohol and many of the wine's flavors and aromas.

Once fermentation is complete, the wines are filtered and stored in either stainless steel tanks or oak barrels for aging. Although more expensive, aging wines in oak barrels mellows the wine and adds vanilla, butter, caramel and oak flavors. When the wine maker determines that the wine has aged sufficiently, it is removed from the tank or barrel, bottled and labeled for sale.

White, rosé and red wine

Sparkling Wines

Sparkling wines are wines that undergo a second fermentation to generate carbon dioxide, which results in effervescence or bubbles. Champagne [shahm-PAHN] and other sparkling wines are classified by their degree of sweetness. From driest to sweetest, they are: Natural or Au Sauvage, Brut, Extra Dry, Dry or Sec, Demi-Sec and Doux. It is important to note that only a sparkling wine from the Champagne region of France can legally be called Champagne.

Sparkling wines are often served for special occasions; they also find their way into sorbet, mousse, custard and other pastry products. Heating or flambéing removes the carbonation and may destroy some of the more delicate aromas that make sparkling wine popular.

Sparkling wines in three styles of glasses

Fortified Wines

Wines typically have an alcohol content of 10–15%. Fortified wines are wines with an alcohol content that has been increased to 18–22% by the addition of neutral grape spirits or grape brandy. If the brandy is added before fermentation is complete, the fortified wine will be sweet because the extra alcohol stops the fermentation process before the yeast can digest all the sugars. If the brandy is added after fermentation is complete, the fortified wine will be drier. The best-known fortified wines—and the ones most often used in cooking—are listed here.

Port, traditionally produced in the Duoro valley of Portugal is divided into three categories. **Tawny** ports are pale brown and mellow, with a less fruity flavor than other ports. They are aged in wooden casks, sometimes for 20 or 30 years, before bottling.

Vintage ports have a deep, dark brick or burgundy color and a rich, sweet flavor. Vintage ports are aged 15–18 months in wood, then bottled and aged further, sometimes as long as several decades, before being consumed. They are considered the finest of ports and are too rare and expensive to use in cooking. **Ruby ports** are blends of younger ports of lesser quality than those used in vintage ports. They tend to have a bright, almost crimson color and a sweet, fruity flavor. Several reasonable priced domestic ports suitable for kitchen use are widely available.

Sherry is a fortified white wine traditionally from the Jerez region of southern Spain. Sherries can range from pale golden yellow and very dry to amber colored, thick and sweet with a pronounced nutty or dried fruit flavor. True aged Spanish sherries can be extremely expensive, but several domestic producers make both dry and sweet (also known as cream sherry) versions that are suitable for cooking use. Products labeled "cooking sherry" should be avoided as these are inferior-quality, highly salted products.

Madeira is a fortified wine from the island of Madeira. Its characteristic light brown color and toffee-caramel flavor are produced when the developing wine is placed in wooden barrels and heated for a period of time. Madeira is sometimes used in desserts and in several classic meat dishes.

Marsala, a fortified wine from western Sicily, is made from grapes that are dried prior to fermentation. This increases the wine's sugar content. Marsala is aged in wooden barrels to mellow its flavors. It is brown-colored and available in two styles, dry and sweet; both styles are used in baked goods, pastries and veal and chicken dishes.

Sherry wines

Wine Labeling

Most wines sold in the United States are labeled according to the grape varieties from which they are made. For example, if a wine is made from at least 75 percent Chardonnay grapes, then its label can simple say "Chardonnay." This makes it easy for buyers to select the type of wine that they prefer.

Wines may be labeled by their place of origin, and the names given to many European wines actually refer to specific locations where the wine is produced. For example, Chablis, a popular white wine from the district of Chablis in France's northern Burgundy region, is made from Chardonnay grapes. Likewise, Chianti is a locale in Italy's Tuscany region and refers to wine produced in that region from the Sangiovese grape.

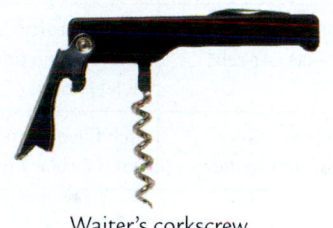

Waiter's corkscrew

Tasting Wines

Each grape varietal has certain hallmark aroma and flavor characteristics. See Tables 7.4 and 7.5.) This does not mean, however, that all wines made from the same grape varietal have exactly the same aromas and flavors. Take, for example, a Merlot wine from Australia and one from California. They may share a certain smooth, juicy, mellow flavor with strong plum, black currant, black cherry and herbal or minty notes, but they will not be identical beverages. Differences in the conditions under which the grapes are grown or the techniques the vintners use to make the wines create noticeable differences. Often vintners blend two or more grape varietals in order to create a wine with the best attributes of different grapes. The infinite possible combinations account for the wide number of wines available and the vast differences between them.

When tasting wine, three basic attributes should be considered: aroma, taste and body.

Aroma is the collection of different scents detected by the nose. With practice, individual aromas can often be distinguished from a complex aroma. The wine's aroma should remind you of some other scent, usually that of a fruit, flower, herb, spice or other easily distinguished item. For example, when evaluating the characteristic scent of a wine made with Cabernet Sauvignon grapes, many people recognize the aromas of black currants, chocolate, mint, cedar or fruit jam. Likewise the hallmark aromas of a Sauvignon Blanc are cut grass, fresh green herbs, asparagus and other vegetables. **Bouquet** refers to other aromas a wine develops as it matures such as the woody and toasted notes derived from the wood casks in which the wine is aged.

PRINCIPAL RED WINE GRAPES					TABLE 7.4
GRAPE VARIETALS	HALLMARK FLAVOR AND AROMA CHARACTERISTICS	ACIDITY	TANNINS	BODY	COMMON FOOD PAIRINGS
Cabernet Sauvignon [KA-bair-nay so-veen-yawn]	Assertive, rich, full flavor with fruity, black currant, chocolate, green bell pepper, mint or spice notes; notes of jams when young, cedar and tobacco when older	Moderate	Moderate to prominent	Medium to full	Lamb and beef, especially if grilled; game, especially venison; strong cheeses
Merlot [mer-low]	Soft, smooth, juicy, mellow flavor with strong plum, black currant, black cherry and herbal or minty notes	Low	Low to moderate	Medium	Highly spiced dishes; savory foods with a hint of sweetness; grilled meats; fish and shellfish; strong cheeses; chocolate
Pinot Noir [pee-noe nwahr]	Rich, complex flavor with cherry, raspberry and smoky or earthy notes and a velvety, silky texture	Moderate to high	Low to moderate	Light to medium	Game birds; rich, fatty fish or shellfish; roast beef; cheese
Zinfandel [zin-fahn-DELL]	Robust, ripe, fruity, spicy flavors with blackberry or raspberry jam and black pepper notes	Low to moderate	Moderate to substantial	Medium to full	Roast lamb; dishes with garlic, black pepper and other strong flavorings; chili con carne and other hearty, spicy dishes; vegetable dishes; cheese
Sangiovese [sahn-joe-VAY-zeh]	Earthy, hearty flavor with black cherry, raisin or floral (especially violet) notes	Moderate to high	Moderate	Light to medium	Veal; beef; lamb; hearty chicken dishes; tomato-based dishes
Syrah [see-rah] or Shiraz [shih-RHAZ]	Rich flavor with sweet fruity, spice, floral or black pepper notes	Low to moderate	Moderate to prominent	Medium	Peppery, tangy, spicy foods; grilled meats; game

Taste refers to the balance between the sugars and acids in the wine. These sugars and acids interact, exciting the taste buds to recognize the wine as sweet, dry or somewhere in between. The resulting taste attributes are usually described with words based on a sweet/sour continuum (e.g., syrupy, sweet, crisp, tart or dry) or a reference to an attribute more like mouthfeel than flavor: smooth, velvety, silky and so on. **Finish** is how long the aromas and taste last after the wine is swallowed.

Body refers to the weight of the wine in the mouth and is generally related to the amount of alcohol it contains. A wine's body is usually described as light, medium or full.

Selecting Wines to Use as Flavorings

For cooking purposes, choose good-quality wines at cost-effective prices. As with any other flavoring, you should evaluate wines before using them. Wines that are not suitable for drinking are also not suitable for cooking purposes. Here are some suggestions for when a recipe calls for only a general type of wine:

White wine or dry white wine: Try a simple, fruity Chardonnay or a dry, herby Sauvignon Blanc. Avoid wines with a sharp, acidic flavor and those with an excessive oaky or woody flavor.

Sweet or slightly sweet white wine: Try a Riesling or Chenin Blanc. When a dessert calls for white wine, such as for poached pears, a sweet wine might be appropriate.

Red wine or dry red wine: Try a simple, fruity red wine with a low tannin content. A Pinot Noir or a medium-bodied Merlot or red Zinfandel is usually a good choice.

Sweet red wine: Try the rich flavor of a ruby port or possibly substitute a red Zinfandel.

PRINCIPAL WHITE WINE GRAPES				TABLE 7.5
GRAPE VARIETALS	HALLMARK FLAVOR AND AROMA CHARACTERISTICS	ACIDITY	BODY	COMMON FOOD PAIRINGS
Chardonnay [shar-doe-nay]	Full, rich flavor with a buttery texture and apple, green apple or tropical fruit notes; if aged in oak, may have vanilla or spicy notes	Moderate to high	Light to medium	Fish; shellfish, especially lobster; veal; chicken; dishes flavored with herbs; foods served with rich or creamy sauces
Chenin Blanc [sheh-nan blahn]	Somewhat muted, tart acidic flavor with pine, melon or citrus notes; the name chenin blanc is also used in the United States for a slightly sweet wine with similar notes	Very high	Light to medium	Light, summer dishes; sweet or delicately flavored shellfish or fish; chicken; cheeses; Asian dishes
Pinot Grigio [pee-noe GREE-joe] or Pinot Gris [pee-noe GREE]	Crisp, dry, somewhat muted flavor with pine, orange rind and earthy or metallic notes	Moderate	Medium	Vegetables; fish; shellfish; pasta dishes; chicken
Riesling [REESE-ling]	Usually sweet but balanced by a strong steely acidity; apricot, citrus, peach or floral notes	Moderate to high	Light; medium to heavy as a dessert wine	Spicy foods; Asian dishes; highly seasoned chicken dishes; shellfish; cheese
Sauvignon Blanc [so-veen-yawn blahn]	Bright, crisp, green, tangy flavor with grassy, herb or citrus notes	High	Medium	Spicy foods; tomato-based dishes; rich or fatty fish, especially salmon; cheese

Sparkling wine: Try a sweet, fruity option as more delicate flavors may be destroyed by heat.

Dessert wine: Try one labeled "Late Harvest" as the grapes will have a higher sugar content.

Beers

Beer is an alcoholic beverage containing from 3–12% alcohol by volume. It is made from water, hops and malted barley or other grains, fermented by yeast (like wine) to produce alcohol and carbon dioxide.

Beers may be divided into two broad groups: **ales** and **lagers**. Ales are made with yeast that rises to the top during the fermentation process, producing an aromatic, cloudy brew; porter and stout are the darkest and most potent ales. Lagers are made with yeast that falls to the bottom during fermentation and are characteristically light, clear and crisp. Pilsner is a popular style of pale, light lager associated with the ancient brewing center of Plzen in the Czech Republic. Most of the mass-market beer produced today is lager, but small local breweries and microbreweries often specialize in ales.

Brewing Beers

To brew beer, the barley or other grain is first **malted** by steeping it in cool water for several days. This causes the grain to germinate and produce the sugar-producing enzymes required for fermentation. Then it is dried with warm air to establish color and flavor. The longer the drying period, the darker the resulting malt. A slow, gentle drying produces pale malts and a light-colored and light-bodied brew, whereas more intense heat develops dark malts that may be described as "caramelized," "chocolate" or "toasted." In the next stage, the ground malt is "mashed," which means it is soaked in hot water, producing a brown liquid called the wort. **Hops,** the cone-shaped flowers of the vine *Humulus lupulus,* provide bitterness and aroma. Hops are added to the wort to flavor the brew.

Ale

Irish stout

Pilsner

malting steeping barley or other grain until it germinates then drying it with warm air to develop its color and flavor

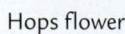

Hops flowers

CHARACTERISTICS OF BEER					TABLE 7.6
TYPE OF BEER	COLOR	ALCOHOL CONTENT	BODY	FLAVOR	COMMON FOOD PAIRINGS
American pilsner	Light	Very low	Light	Little aroma or bitterness	Spicy foods
Belgian lambic	Light	Moderate	Light	Sour	Sharp cheese; fruit desserts; dark chocolate
Brown ale	Red to brown	Low	Full-bodied	Sweet, nutty	Sausages; smoked fish; game; salad
European lager	Light	Moderate	Moderate	Bitter, floral finish	Meat and fish dishes; German sausage; pretzels
Pale ale	Light	Low	Moderate	Bitter, fruity, floral	Spicy foods; smoked or fried seafood; beef; lamb; game
Porter	Dark	Moderate	Full-bodied	Bitter	Barbecue; hearty meat dishes; oysters; shellfish; smoked salmon; strong cheeses
Stout; bock	Very dark	High	Full-bodied	Sweet; malty	Chocolate, nut or fruit desserts; heavy meat dishes; goulash; spicy desserts

Fermentation yeasts, selected according to the type of beer produced, are then added to the cooled wort and hops mixture. When fermentation is complete, the beer is transferred to storage vats for conditioning, a process that removes unwanted flavors and develops natural carbonation. This stage can last from a few days to a few months before the beer is filtered and bottled.

Beer does not improve with age and is best consumed as soon as possible after production. Light and heat both adversely alter beer's flavor. Colored glass bottles or aluminum cans are generally used to block damaging light. Beer is best stored between 50°F and 55°F (10°C and 13°C).

Selecting Beers to Use as Flavorings

Many characteristics influence the final outcome of the brewing process: the quality of the water, the type of malt, the hops used, any additives, the species of yeast selected for fermentation and the length of the fermentation and conditioning stages. The combined effects of these elements determine the color, body, astringency, taste, alcohol content and aroma of the finished product.

Beer is frequently used as a flavoring in the cuisines of northern France and Belgium, where it appears in such dishes as carbonnade, a stew flavored with beer. Because of beer's slight bitterness, sugar or brown sugar is often added to the dish to balance the flavor. Beer can also be used in marinades and to deglaze and prepare sauces in the same manner as wine. Beer is frequently used in batters for deep-fried fish or vegetables such as Beer-Battered Onion Rings (page 624). Beer can be used to leaven as well as flavor breads. As with wine, do not cook with any beer that is not of drinkable quality.

Although all beers share certain general characteristics, within each group there are immense variations, as noted in Table 7.6.

Distilled Spirits

Distilled spirits include all types of brandy, liquor and liqueur, which are made by distilling or concentrating the ethyl alcohol (ethanol) from a fermented liquid such as wine or

distillation the separation of alcohol from a liquid (or, during the production of alcoholic beverages, from a fermented mash); it is accomplished by heating the liquid or mash creating a gas that contains alcohol vapors; this vapor is then condensed into the desired alcoholic liquid (beverage)

beer made from grains, vegetables or other plants. By boiling the fermented liquid in a special cooking vessel known as a **still**, alcohol vapors condense and the liquid is collected and converted into a beverage. Distilled spirits contain at least 20% alcohol by volume, although most are at least 40%. These beverages are used to add flavors to all types of foods and are especially popular in bakeshop products.

Brandy

Brandy is an alcoholic beverage made by distilling fermented wine or fruit pulp. Brandies are divided into two general categories: grape brandy or fruit brandy.

Grape brandy is distilled from white wine or fermented grape pulp and skins. It is aged in wooden casks, which contributes to its rich, amber-brown colors and imparts additional mellowing flavors and aromas. **Cognac**, one of the best-known grape brandies, is made in France's Cognac region (and only brandy made there can be called Cognac). Cognac is twice distilled from blends of various wines. After distillation, the brandy is aged in oak casks. Traditionally Cognacs are labeled according to their age. Some common grades are V.S. (Very Special, at least 2½ years old), V.S.O.P. (Very Superior Old Pale, at least 4½ years old) and XO, Napoleon or Extra, at least 6 years old. **Armagnac** is another well-known French grape brandy from southwestern France; it is slightly drier and heavier than Cognac and is traditionally used in dishes containing pork or game birds, and with dried fruits, especially plums.

Fruit brandy is made from fermented fruits other than grapes. Do not confuse fruit brandy with **fruit-flavored brandy**, which is grape brandy that has been flavored with the extract of another fruit. Well-known true fruit brandies include **Calvados**, an apple brandy from Normandy, France; **Kirschwasser**, a cherry brandy from Bavaria, Germany; **Framboise**, a raspberry brandy from Alsace, France; **Poire**, a pear brandy from Alsace, France; and **Slivovitz**, a plum brandy from eastern Europe and the Balkans.

As with wines, when choosing a brandy for culinary purposes, do not skimp on quality. The brandy does not have to be the most expensive brand, but it should have a rich, full, mellow flavor. Try, for example, an inexpensive but genuine Cognac (one that is graded V.S.). If the recipe calls for a fruit brandy, do not use a fruit brandy with added artificial flavors, a fruit-flavored brandy or a fruit-flavored liqueur. The flavor, body, degrees of sweetness and alcohol content will be different from true fruit brandies.

Cognac

Liquors

Liquors are alcoholic beverages distilled from fermented grains, vegetables or other plants. After distillation the resulting clear liquid can be colored or flavored during aging. The alcohol content of liquors ranges from 20% to 75% by volume, which is also expressed as "proof." Proof is double the amount of alcohol by volume; for example, a vodka that is 80 proof is 40% alcohol by volume. Because of this higher alcohol content, liquors can be used to **flambé** or finish a dish with a splash of flaming alcohol. Rum, tequila and whiskey may be used to flavor dessert items, especially mousse, ice cream, custards and confections, while gin adds interest to meat and game marinades. Flavorless vodka is used less often in the kitchen, but is still essential to some cream-based pasta sauces and cured seafood dishes.

Gin is a clear spirit distilled from grains and flavored with juniper berries, citrus peels and spices.

Rum is distilled from fermented sugar cane juice or molasses. Its character varies according to its color: **White rums**, which are clear and colorless, are relatively dry and light; **amber** or **gold rums** have a slightly stronger flavor and a pale golden color; **dark rums** have a strong molasses flavor, a dark brown color and a heavy body.

Tequila is a clear to amber-colored spirit made in the Tequila region of Mexico from the fermented sap of agave bulbs. Its production is regulated by Appellation of Origin standards.

flambé [flahm-BAY] food served flaming; produced by igniting brandy, rum or other liquor

Vodka, whiskey and dark rum

neutral spirits or **grain spirits** pure alcohol (ethanol or ethyl alcohol); they are odorless, tasteless and a very potent 190 proof (95% alcohol)

Liqueurs in a range of colors

Vodka is traditionally a flavorless and colorless liquor distilled from potatoes, fruits, grains and other plant products. Most of the world's vodka is actually made from wheat. Many newer types of vodka are flavored, either by including the flavorings in the mash during distillation or by adding flavors afterward.

Whiskey (the English, Scots and Canadians spell it without the *e*) is distilled from various fermented grains. After distillation, whiskey is aged in oak barrels until the flavors are mellow and smooth. There are many types of whiskies. **Scotch whisky** is distilled from malted barley and has a range of flavors from sweet and nutty to smoky or peaty. **Irish whiskey** resembles Scotch, but without the smoky flavor. **Bourbon** is produced primarily in Kentucky and is distilled from a mash containing at least 51% corn and then aged in charred new oak barrels. **Rye whiskey** is an American whiskey made from rye.

Liqueurs

Liqueurs are traditionally made from herbs, fruits, nuts, spices, flowers or other flavorings infused into an alcohol base and sweetened with sugar. The base can be **neutral spirits**, brandy, rum or whiskey. Many newer liqueurs, especially less expensive products, are made with flavoring extracts, essential oils and even artificial flavors. **Cream liqueurs** are liqueurs blended with cream for a mild, rich flavor. They do not keep well once opened, so they need to be stored in the refrigerator. Oddly enough, **crème liqueurs**, such as crème de cacao, crème de menthe and crème de cassis, contain no cream. Rather additional sugar gives them a thick, syrupy, creamy texture and a very sweet flavor.

When using a liqueur as a flavoring, look for products with rich, true, natural flavors. Also keep in mind that a liqueur and a crème liqueur of the same flavor are not the same products and should not be used interchangeably. If a recipe calls for the coffee-flavored liqueur Kahlúa, use it, not a crème de café product; the latter will taste sweeter with a more syrupy texture. Similarly if a recipe calls for a proprietary blend such as Cointreau or Chambord, do not skimp on some lesser-quality generic product; customers may discern the difference. Some liqueurs commonly used as flavorings are listed in Table 7.7.

Guidelines for Cooking with Alcoholic Beverages

- *Use quality products:* Heating a mediocre wine, beer, liqueur or liquor tends to bring out the worst characteristics of the product, especially its acidic properties. Do not use "cooking" wines or liquors as these products contain a large amount of added salt, which can ruin the finished dish.

- *Pay attention to cooking time:* The longer a dish cooks, the more alcohol evaporates, thus concentrating its flavors, especially acidic flavors. Because alcohol evaporates at a lower temperature than water (172°F/86°C), the flavorings suspended in the alcohol concentrate faster than flavorings suspended in water.

- *Brown foods before adding wine or other alcoholic beverages:* Especially in dishes such as pan sauces or stews, browning allows the surface of the foods to caramelize before liquid is added. As the wine is reduced, all of the flavors blend together.

- *Do not pour alcohol directly from the bottle into a hot pan:* When the alcohol ignites, the flame may enter the bottle and cause an explosion or a fire. Pour the wine or spirit into a cup first, then into the cooking pan.

- *Do not use aluminum or cast-iron cookware:* Alcohol and acids in wine may react with aluminum or cast-iron so it is best to use nonreactive cookware when working with wine or other alcoholic beverages.

Cooking with Alcohol

For many, the consumption of alcohol is a concern. The amount of alcohol left after an alcoholic beverage has been added as a flavoring depends on cooking method and time. A dish flambéed tableside with Cognac that is allowed to burn out before being served, for example, may retain very little of its original alcohol content. In contrast, a chicken breast that has been marinated in white wine and then quickly sautéed could retain as much as 75 percent of the alcohol from the marinade. If, however, the same chicken breast is cooked over medium heat for 15 minutes, as much as 60 percent of the alcohol will evaporate. Simmering the same chicken breast over low heat for approximately 2 hours or more will reduce the alcohol content to 10 percent or even less. If you wish to avoid the use of alcoholic beverages entirely, try substituting an appropriate natural fruit juice, or even water, for the same volume of liquid in the recipe.

LIQUEURS COMMONLY USED AS FLAVORINGS — TABLE 7.7

LIQUEUR	ALCOHOL BASE	FLAVORINGS
Amaretto	Grape brandy	Almonds, apricots
Cassis	Neutral spirits	Black currants, herbs, roots, plants, peels
Chambord	Grape brandy	Black raspberries
Cointreau	Grape brandy	Bitter orange peel
Crème de cacao	Neutral spirits	Chocolate
Crème de cassis	Neutral spirits	Black currants
Crème de violette	Grape brandy	Violet flowers
Crème de menthe	Neutral spirits	Peppermint
Curaçao (clear or blue)	Neutral spirits	Bitter orange
Frangelico	Neutral spirits	Hazelnuts
Grand Marnier	Grape brandy	Bitter oranges
Kahlúa	Neutral spirits	Coffee
Kirsch	Neutral spirits	Cherries
Limoncello	Neutral spirits, vodka	Lemons
Pernod	Neutral spirits	Anise seed, licorice
St. Germain	Neutral grain spirits	Elderflower blossoms
Tia Maria	Cask-aged rum	Coffee beans, spices
Triple Sec	Grape brandy	Bitter orange peel

QUESTIONS FOR DISCUSSION

1 Describe factors that can affect our perception of flavors. Discuss the ways this relates to preparing certain foods.

2 What is a flavoring? Does every kitchen stock the same flavoring ingredients? Explain your answer.

3 What are the differences between an herb and a spice? Give an example of a plant that is used as both an herb and a spice.

4 If a recipe calls for a fresh herb and you only have the herb dried, what do you do? Explain your answer.

5 List three or four commonly used condiments and describe how they are used by chefs.

6 Cooking oils are made from many different plants. What factors should you consider when deciding which oil to use for a particular recipe?

7 Describe ways in which wines and other alcoholic beverages are used to flavor foods.

8 Research the typical foods of the region of the world in which your great-grandparents were born. Discuss how the climate and geography affected the most popular dishes from those regions.

Dairy Products **8**

After studying this chapter, you will be able to:

▶ identify, store and cook with a variety of milk and milk-based products

▶ describe basic cheese-making processes

▶ classify the characteristics of the five categories of fine cheeses: fresh or unripened, soft, semisoft, firm and hard

▶ describe the characteristics of goat's-milk cheeses

▶ identify, store and serve fine cheeses

ewe's milk produced by a female sheep; it has approximately 7.9% milkfat, 11.4% milk solids and 80.7% water

goat's milk produced by a female goat; it has approximately 4.1% milkfat, 8.9% milk solids and 87% water

water buffalo's milk produced by a female water buffalo; it has approximately 7.5% milkfat, 10.3% milk solids and 82.2% water

D airy products include cow's milk and foods produced from cow's milk such as butter, yogurt, sour cream and cheese. The milk of other mammals, namely, goats, sheep (ewe) and buffalo, is also made into cheeses that are used in commercial food service operations. Dairy products are extremely versatile and are commonly served both alone and as ingredients in foods as varied as soups, salads, breads and desserts.

MILK AND MILK PRODUCTS

Milk is not only a popular beverage, it is also an ingredient in many dishes. Milk and products derived from milk provide texture, flavor, color and nutritional value to cooked and baked items. Milk is one of the most nutritious foods available, providing proteins, vitamins and minerals (particularly calcium). Because milk, cream, cultured dairy products and butter are animal products, they do contain cholesterol. Overall fat content varies among dairy products and depends on the amount of milkfat left after processing. Milk is also highly perishable and an excellent bacterial breeding ground. Care must be exercised when handling and storing milk and other dairy products. Whole milk—that is, milk as it comes from the cow—consists of water primarily (about 88%). It contains approximately 3.5% milkfat and 8.5% other milk solids (proteins, milk sugar [lactose] and minerals).

Because of its relatively low fat content, in the presence of an acid or when heated, milk **curdles**. This means that the proteins solidify or coagulate and separate from the liquid. Coagulation of the milk proteins is beneficial in cheese making, discussed later, but it ruins custards, sauces and other dishes.

Milk-Processing Techniques

Whole milk is graded A, B or C according to standards recommended by the U.S. Public Health Service. Grades are assigned based on bacterial count, with Grade A products having the lowest count. Grades B and C, though still safe and wholesome, are rarely available for retail or commercial use. Milk must be processed before consumers can purchase it. By law, all Grade A milk must be pasteurized prior to retail sale.

Pasteurization is the process of heating milk to a sufficiently high temperature for a sufficient length of time to destroy pathogenic bacteria. Pasteurization typically involves holding milk at a temperature of 161°F (72°C) for 15 seconds. In addition to eliminating bacteria, the pasteurization process also destroys enzymes that cause spoilage, thus increasing shelf life. Although milk's nutritional value is not significantly affected by pasteurization, milk is often fortified with additional vitamins and minerals, especially vitamins A and D during processing.

Raw milk, which is not pasteurized, may host disease-causing organisms that can cause foodborne illness. **Certified milk** is milk, pasteurized or unpasteurized, produced in dairies that operate under the rules and regulations of an authorized medical milk commission. Though certified raw milk may be sold to consumers in some states, its use in food service establishments violates the FDA's 2013 Food Code, which requires that food service operations use Grade A milk. The FDA does, however, permit food service operations to use raw milk in cheeses that are then aged at least 60 days at not less than 35°F (2°C).

Ultra-pasteurization is a process in which milk is heated to a very high temperature (280°F/135°C) for a very short time (2–4 seconds) in order to destroy virtually all bacteria. The process may give the milk a noticeable cooked flavor. Ultra-pasteurization is most often used with whipping cream and individual creamers. Although the process may reduce cream's whipping properties, it extends its shelf life dramatically.

Ultra-high-temperature (UHT) processing is a form of ultra-pasteurization in which milk is held at a temperature of 280–300°F (138–150°C) for 2–6 seconds. It is then packed in sterile containers under sterile conditions and sealed to prevent bacteria from entering the container. Unopened UHT milk can be stored without refrigeration for at least 3 months. Although UHT milk can be stored unrefrigerated, it should be chilled before serving and stored like fresh milk once opened. UHT processing may give milk a slightly cooked taste, but it has no significant effect on milk's nutritional value.

Homogenization is a process in which the fat globules in whole milk are reduced in size and permanently dispersed throughout the liquid. This prevents the fat from clumping together and rising to the surface as a layer of cream. Although homogenization is not required, milk sold commercially is generally homogenized because the process ensures a uniform consistency, a whiter color and a richer taste.

Whole milk can be processed in a centrifuge to remove all or a portion of the milkfat, resulting in reduced-fat, low-fat and nonfat milks. According to the FDA, all reduced-fat milks must be nutritionally equivalent to full-fat milk and must provide at least the same amounts of the fat-soluble vitamins A and D as full-fat milk. **Reduced-fat** or less-fat milk is whole milk from which sufficient milkfat has been removed to produce a liquid with 2% milkfat. **Low-fat** or little-fat milk contains 1% milkfat. In **nonfat** milk, also referred to as fat-free, no-fat or skim milk, as much milkfat has been removed as possible. To be sold as nonfat milk, its fat content must be below 0.5%.

Concentrated Milks

Concentrated or condensed milk products are produced by removing all or part of the water from whole milk with a vacuum. The resulting products have a high concentration of milkfat and milk solids and an extended shelf life.

Evaporated milk is produced by removing approximately 60% of the water from whole, homogenized milk. The concentrated liquid is canned and heat-sterilized. This results in a cooked flavor and darker color. Evaporated skim milk, with a milkfat content of 0.5%, is also available. A can of evaporated milk requires no refrigeration until opened, although the can should be stored in a cool place. Evaporated milk can be reconstituted with an equal amount of water and used like whole milk for cooking or drinking.

Sweetened condensed milk is similar to evaporated milk in that 60% of the water has been removed. But unlike evaporated milk, sweetened condensed milk contains large amounts of sugar (40–45%). Sweetened condensed milk is also canned; the canning process darkens the color and adds a caramel flavor. Sweetened condensed milk cannot be substituted for whole milk or evaporated milk because of its sugar content. Its distinctive flavor is most often found in desserts and confections such as fudge.

Dry milk powder is made by removing virtually all the moisture from pasteurized milk. Dry whole milk, nonfat milk and buttermilk are available. The lack of moisture prevents the growth of microorganisms and allows dry milk powders to be stored for extended periods without refrigeration. Powdered milks can be reconstituted with water and used like fresh milk. Milk powder may also be added to foods directly, with additional liquid included in the recipe. This procedure is typical in bread making and does not alter the effect milk has on the dough or the flavor in the finished product.

Cream

Cream is a rich, liquid milk product containing at least 18% fat. Like milk, cream must be pasteurized or ultra-pasteurized and may be homogenized. Cream has a slight yellow or ivory color and is thicker and stickier than milk. Cream gives flavor and body to sauces, soups and desserts. Whipping cream, containing not less than 30% milkfat, can be whipped into a stiff foam and used in pastries and desserts. Cream is marketed in several forms with different fat contents.

Half-and-half is a mixture of whole milk and cream containing between 10% and 18% milkfat. It is often served with cereal or coffee, but it does not contain enough fat to whip into a foam.

Light cream, **coffee cream** and **table cream** are all products with more than 18% but less than 30% milkfat. These products are used in baked goods or soups as well as served with coffee, fruit and cereal.

Light whipping cream or, simply, **whipping cream**, contains between 30% and 36% milkfat. It is generally used for thickening and enriching sauces and making ice cream.

Imitation and Artificial Dairy Products

Coffee whiteners, imitation sour cream, whipped-topping mixes and some whipped toppings in pressurized cans are made from nondairy products. These products usually consist of corn syrup, binding agents, vegetable fats, coloring agents and artificial flavors. These products are generally less expensive and have a longer shelf life than the real dairy products they replace, but their flavors are no match. Imitation and artificial products may be useful, however, for people who have allergies or are on a restricted diet. If you choose to use these products, you cannot legally claim to be using real dairy products on menus or labels.

It is whipped into a foam and used as a dessert topping or folded into custards or mousses to add flavor and lightness.

Heavy whipping cream or, simply, **heavy cream**, contains not less than 36% milkfat. It whips easily and holds its whipped texture longer than other creams. It must be pasteurized but is rarely homogenized. Heavy cream is used in the same ways as light whipping cream. Both light and heavy creams, when heated gently, can withstand boiling. Milk on the other hand will separate into congealed curds and liquid.

Cultured Dairy Products

Cultured dairy products, such as yogurt, buttermilk and sour cream, are produced by adding specific bacterial cultures to fluid dairy products. The bacteria convert the milk sugar **lactose** into lactic acid, giving these products their body and tangy, unique flavors. The acid content also retards the growth of undesirable microorganisms; cultured products have been used for centuries to preserve milk.

Buttermilk originally referred to the liquid remaining after cream was churned into butter. Today buttermilk is produced by adding a culture (*Streptococcus lactis*) to fresh, pasteurized skim or low-fat milk. This results in tart milk with a thick texture. Buttermilk is most often used as a beverage or in baked goods.

Sour cream is produced by adding the same culture used to make buttermilk to pasteurized, homogenized light cream. The resulting product is a white, tangy gel. It is used as a condiment or to enrich soups and sauces or give baked goods a distinctive flavor. Sour cream must have a milkfat content of not less than 18%.

Crème fraîche is a cultured cream popular in French cuisine. Although thinner and richer than sour cream, it has a similar tart, tangy flavor. It is used extensively in soups and sauces, especially with poultry, rabbit and lamb dishes. It is easily prepared from the following recipe. Thinner than sour cream and crème fraîche, Mexican **crema** is a slightly salty and tangy cultured cream used in Mexican and Latin cooking. Crème fraîche and crema have a high fat content and can be boiled without curdling.

lactose a disaccharide that occurs naturally in mammalian milk; milk sugar

---

Buttermilk in a Pinch

To make a buttermilk substitute, combine 8 fluid ounces (240 milliliters) whole milk with ½ fluid ounce (15 milliliters) white vinegar or lemon juice. The mixture should begin to separate (curdle) in 15 minutes. Stir well before using. A mixture of 2 fluid ounces (60 milliliters) whole milk and 6 fluid ounces (180 milliliters) plain yogurt also works as a buttermilk substitute.

🌿 Vegetarian

Crème Fraîche

YIELD 16 fl. oz. (480 ml)

Heavy cream, not ultra-pasteurized	16 fl. oz.	480 ml
Buttermilk, with active cultures	1 fl. oz.	30 ml

1 Heat the cream to approximately 100°F (43°C).

2 Remove the cream from the heat and stir in the buttermilk.

3 Allow the mixture to stand in a warm place, loosely covered, until it thickens, approximately 12–36 hours.

4 Chill thoroughly before using. Crème fraîche will keep for up to 10 days in the refrigerator.

Approximate values per 1-fl.-oz. (30-ml) serving: **Calories** 90, **Total fat** 10 g, **Saturated fat** 6 g, **Cholesterol** 35 mg, **Sodium** 10 mg, **Total carbohydrates** 1 g, **Protein** 1 g, **Vitamin A** 10%, **Claims**—very low sodium

Yogurt is a thick, tart, custard-like product made from milk (either whole, low-fat or nonfat) cultured with *Lactobacillus bulgaricus* and *Streptococcus thermophilus*. Though touted as a health or diet food, yogurt is not necessarily low in fat or calories; it contains the same amount of milkfat as the milk from which it is made. Yogurt may also contain a variety of sweeteners, flavorings and fruits. Greek yogurt is a creamier and denser style of yogurt, made by straining additional **whey** from the product or by adding additional milk protein solids. (Authentic Greek yogurt is often made with sheep's milk.) Yogurt is generally eaten alone but is also used in baked products, salad dressings and frozen desserts.

Chefs who make yogurt and other fresh cheese in-house often reserve the whey for other uses such as a liquid in which to cook fish, meat or vegetables. Whey's acidity and tangy flavor make it a good option to use in place of a squeeze of lemon when finishing sauces or on top of seafood.

whey the watery liquid remaining after milk proteins coagulate into curds during the cheese making process. It contains vitamins, minerals, proteins and trace amounts of fat and is used in making whey cheese, such as ricotta, and as a substitute for non-fat milk

Butter

Butter is a fatty substance produced by agitating or churning cream. The flavor butter adds to sauces, breads and pastries is unequaled. Butter contains at least 80% milkfat, not more than 16% water and 2–4% milk solids. It may or may not contain added salt. Butter is firm when chilled and soft at room temperature. It melts into a liquid at approximately 93°F (33°C) and reaches the smoke point at 260°F (127°C).

Sweet butter is another name for unsalted butter. **Salted butter**, as the name implies, is butter with salt added. Typically 1.7% salt is used, although exact amounts vary from producer to producer. Salt not only changes the butter's flavor, it also extends its shelf life. When using salted butter in cooking or baking, the salt content must be considered in the total recipe.

European-style butter contains more milkfat than regular butter, usually 82–86%, and very little or no added salt. It is often churned from cultured cream, giving it a more intense, buttery flavor. It may be used in lieu of any regular butter in cooking or baking.

Whipped butter is made by incorporating air into the butter. This increases its volume and spreadability but also shortens its shelf life. Because of the change in density, whipped butter should not be substituted in recipes calling for regular butter.

Clarified butter is butter that is melted so that the water and milk solids can be removed by a process called clarification. **Ghee** is a form of clarified butter in which the milk solids remain with the fat and are heated until light brown. It originated in India but is now used worldwide as an ingredient and cooking medium. Although **whole butter** can be used for cooking or sauce making, sometimes a more stable and consistent product will be achieved by using clarified butter. The clarification process is described in Chapter 9, Mise en Place.

Margarine

Margarine is not a dairy product but is included in this section because it is frequently substituted for butter in cooking, baking and table service. Margarine is manufactured from vegetable fats and may contain milk products. Flavorings, colorings, **emulsifiers**, preservatives and vitamins are added, and the mixture is firmed or solidified by exposure to hydrogen gas at very high temperatures, a process known as **hydrogenation**. Generally the firmer the margarine, the greater the degree of hydrogenation and the longer its shelf life. Like butter, margarine is approximately 80% fat and 16% water but even the finest margarine cannot match the flavor of butter.

Margarine packaged in tubs is softer and more spreadable than solid products and generally contains more water and air. For example, diet margarine is approximately 50% water. Because they are less dense, these soft products should not be substituted for regular butter or margarine in cooking or baking.

Specially formulated and blended margarine is available for commercial use in making puff pastry, croissant doughs, frostings and related products.

Grading Butter

Although government grading is not mandatory for butter, most processors submit their butters for testing. The USDA label on the package assures the buyer that the butter meets federal standards for the grade indicated:

- *USDA Grade AA:* Butter of superior quality, with a fresh, sweet flavor and aroma, a smooth, creamy texture and good spreadability.

- *USDA Grade A:* Butter of very good quality, with a pleasing flavor and fairly smooth texture.

- *USDA Grade B:* Butter of standard quality, made from sour cream; has an acceptable flavor but lacks the flavor, texture and body of Grades AA and A. Grade B is most often used in industrial food manufacturing.

whole butter butter that is not clarified, whipped or reduced-fat

emulsifier a substance added to a mixture to assist in the binding of unmixable liquids such as oil and water. Chemicals may be used as emulsifiers, but naturally occurring soy and egg lecithin are commonly used in processed foods

Margarine: From Laboratory Bench to Dinner Table

Margarine was invented by a French chemist in 1869 after Napoleon III offered a prize for the development of an inexpensive synthetic edible fat that could be supplied to his military forces. Originally produced from beef fat and milk, margarine is now made almost exclusively from vegetable fats.

In *On Food and Cooking: The Science and Lore of the Kitchen*, Harold McGee recounts the history of margarine. He explains that margarine caught on quickly in Europe and America, with large-scale production underway by 1880, but the American dairy industry and the U.S. government put up fierce resistance. Under federal law it was taxed and its sale restricted to licensed stores. The U.S. government refused to purchase it for use by the armed forces. And, in an attempt to hold it to its true colors, some states did not allow margarine to be dyed yellow (animal fats and vegetable oils are much paler than butter); the dye was sold separately and mixed in by the consumer. World War II, which brought butter rationing, probably did the most to establish margarine's respectability. However, it was not until 1967 that yellow margarine could be sold in Wisconsin.

rancidity the decomposition of fats by exposure to oxygen, resulting in off-flavors and destruction of nutritive components

Storage of Milk and Milk Products

Fluid milk and cultured dairy products require time and temperature control for safety (TCS) and should be kept refrigerated at or below 41°F (5°C). The shelf life of fluid milk is reduced by half for every 5-degree rise in temperature above 41°F (5°C). Keep milk containers closed to prevent absorption of odors and flavors. Freezing is not recommended, although whole milk that has been frozen can be used to make simple cheeses, such as ricotta. Ultra-pasteurized cream will keep for 6 to 8 weeks if refrigerated at or below 41°F (5°C). Unwhipped cream should not be frozen. Keep cream away from strong odors and bright lights, as they can adversely affect its flavor. Under proper conditions, sour cream will last up to 4 weeks, yogurt up to 3 weeks and buttermilk up to 2 weeks. Freezing is not recommended for these products, however, dishes prepared with cultured products generally can be frozen.

Due to its high fat content, butter is extremely prone to **rancidity**. Butter that is rancid develops a harsh bitter taste and deep yellow to brown color. To preserve its freshness, butter should be well wrapped and stored at temperatures between 32°F and 35°F (0°C and 2°C). Unsalted butter is best kept frozen until needed. If well wrapped, frozen butter will keep for up to 9 months at a temperature of 0°F (–18°C).

Unlike butter, margarine is not prone to rancidity, but like butter it should be kept refrigerated at or below 41°F (5°C). Wrap it well to prevent it from absorbing odors. Well wrapped frozen margarine will keep for up to 9 months at a temperature of 0°F (–18°C).

CHEESE

Cheese (Fr. *fromage*; It. *formaggio*) is one of the oldest and most widely used foods known to humankind. It is served alone or as a principal ingredient in or an accompaniment to countless dishes such as cheese fondue and soufflé. Cheese is commonly used in everything from breakfast to snacks to desserts. It is popular as a standalone course, first course or dessert.

Natural Cheeses

Hundreds of natural, unprocessed cheeses are produced worldwide. Although their shapes, ages and flavors vary according to local preferences and traditions, all natural cheeses are produced in the same basic fashion that has been used for centuries. Each starts with a mammal's milk; cows, goats and sheep are the most commonly used. The milk proteins (known as *casein*) are coagulated with the addition of an enzyme, usually **rennet**, which is found in calves' stomachs. As the milk coagulates, it separates into solid (curds) and liquid (whey). After draining off the whey, either the curds are made into fresh cheese, such as ricotta or cottage cheese, or the curds are further processed by cutting, kneading and cooking. The resulting substance, known as "green cheese," is packed into molds to drain. Salt or special bacteria may be added to the molded cheeses, which are then allowed to **ripen** (age) under controlled conditions. The method used to ripen a cheese, the location where the ripening takes place, whether in a cave or temperature-controlled chamber, for example, and the length of time a cheese is allowed to ripen determine the texture, color and flavor of the final product.

Cheeses are a product of their environment, which is why most fine cheeses cannot be reproduced outside their native locale. The breed and feed of the milk animal, the wild spores and molds in the air and even the wind currents in a storage area can affect the manner in which a cheese develops. (Roquefort, for example, develops its distinctive flavor from aging in particular caves that are filled with crosscurrents of cool, moist air.) The interior, referred to as the **paste**, of a cheese changes texture as it ages, becoming creamy and flowing or firm and sometimes crunchy depending on the type of cheese being made.

Some cheeses (soft-ripened) develop a natural rind or surface called bloomy rind because of the application of bacteria–a mold, yeast or yeast-like fungus–that grows into a downy white coating. Repeated washing with brine, beer, brandy or wine also encourages the formation of surface mold on other types of cheese (washed rind). The pronounced aroma on washed rind cheese gives their paste distinctive flavors. Both soft-ripened and washed rind cheeses ripen from the outside into the center. Most natural rinds may be eaten if desired. Other cheeses are coated with an inedible wax rind to prevent moisture loss. (Cheeses that are smoked are frequently coated with a brown wax rind.) Fresh cheeses do not have rinds.

Most cheeses contain high percentages of fat and protein. Cheese is also rich in calcium, phosphorus and vitamin A. As animal products, natural cheeses contain cholesterol. Today many low-fat and even nonfat processed cheeses are available. Sodium has also been reduced or eliminated from some modern products.

Moisture and fat contents are good indicators of a cheese's texture and shelf life. The higher the moisture content, the softer the product and the more perishable it will be. Low-moisture cheeses may be used for grating and keep for several weeks if properly stored. (Reduced water levels prohibit bacterial growth.) Fat content ranges from low fat (less than 20% fat) to double cream (at least 60% fat) and triple cream (at least 72% fat). Cheeses with a high fat content are creamier and have a richer flavor and texture than low-fat products.

Cheese Varieties

Cheeses can be classified by country of origin, ripening method, fat content or texture. Here we classify the varieties of fine cheeses by texture and have adopted five categories: fresh or unripened, soft, semisoft, firm and hard. A separate section on goat's-milk cheeses is also included.

Many of the finest cheeses originated in European countries. Government regulations in those countries and in the European Union protect certain cheeses, by ensuring that they are made only in specific locations using traditional methods and by protecting their names (e.g., Roquefort, Parmigiano-Reggiano, Cabrales) from imitation or misuse. Cheese makers in the United States and elsewhere may succeed in producing a high-quality cheese similar to the original, but they cannot use the legally protected name. Hence there are many Emmental cheeses, but only one *Emmentaler Switzerland AOP*. Large commercial cheese producers worldwide may approximate the general characteristics of a style of cheese to produce less expensive substitutes. This accounts for the wide variety of cheddars, mozzarellas, Goudas and Parmesans on the market. The cheese descriptions here explain the original source and method of production, unless otherwise noted, and indicate cheese names that are legally protected.

Fresh or Unripened Cheeses

Fresh cheeses are uncooked and unripened. They are generally mild and creamy with a tart tanginess. A good fresh cheese does not taste acidic or bitter. Fresh cheeses have a moisture content of 40–80% and are highly perishable. A number of fresh cheeses can be easily made in a food service kitchen. When space and time permit, making fresh cheese ensures a quality product and may offer cost savings as well.

Cream cheese is a soft cow's-milk cheese containing approximately 35% fat. It is available in solid white blocks or whipped and sometimes flavored. It is used in baking, dips, dressings and confections and is popular as a spread for bagels. **Fromage blanc** and **fromage frais** are unripened soft cheeses from France made from cultured cow's milk. Mildly acidic and tangy, their fat content ranges from 0% to 40%. The texture of fromage blanc resembles yogurt although it can be purchased in molds that drain off some of the whey and firm the cheese. Fromage frais, which must contain live cultures, tends to be firmer than fromage blanc. Both cheeses are served at breakfast, as dessert or in sauces. Fromage frais is often blended with herbs and spices to make a cheese spread that is sold commercially or can be made from the following recipe.

Making Mozzarella

In Italy, mozzarella is made every day; it is meant to be consumed just as often. Before there was refrigeration, the balls of mozzarella were stored in well water to keep them cool, which is where the tradition originated of storing fresh mozzarella in liquid.

Once the milk coagulates and the curds are cut, the mass is slowly stirred to enhance the whey's expulsion. A few hours later, when the curds are mature, they are removed from the whey, chopped or shredded and then mixed with hot water.

To test the exact amount of maturity, a handful of curds is dipped into a bucket of hot water for 10 seconds. When the curds are removed, they should be kneaded briefly and then, holding the mass with two hands, it should be pulled and stretched out to determine its maturity. When it can be stretched as thin and opaque as tissue paper, it is exactly ready to be strung. At this point, small amounts of curd are dumped into a small vat and stirred with hot water using a paddle. This is known as "stringing" the cheese because as the curds are mixed with the water they begin to melt somewhat and become stringy. The more the cheese is stirred, the longer the strings are stretched. Eventually all the strings come together to make a large mass of satiny-smooth cheese. In Italian the word *filare* means "to string"; therefore all cheeses that are strung are members of the *pasta filata* family.

When stringing is complete, the cheese is ready to be shaped and hand-formed into balls. The balls are tossed immediately into vats of cool water so they will maintain the desired shapes. When cool, the balls are immersed in brine solution and then wrapped in parchment paper.

—PAULA LAMBERT, owner of the Mozzarella Company in Dallas, Texas.

🌿 Vegetarian

Herb Cheese Spread

YIELD 1 lb. 4 oz. (600 g); 5 Molds, 4 oz. (120 g) each

Unsalted butter, softened	4 oz.	120 g
Cream cheese, softened	1 lb.	480 g
Fine sea salt	½ tsp.	2 ml
Heavy cream	1 Tbsp.	15 ml
Fresh garlic, minced	1 Tbsp.	15 g
Fresh chives, minced	2 Tbsp.	30 ml
Fresh parsley, minced	1 Tbsp.	15 ml
White pepper, ground	¼ tsp.	1 ml

1 Blend the butter and cream cheese in the bowl of a mixer fitted with the paddle attachment on medium speed until smooth.

2 Dissolve the salt in the cream. Add the cream and remaining ingredients to the cheese. Scrape down the bowl and blend thoroughly.

3 Pack the cheese mixture into five 4-ounce molds lined with plastic wrap.

4 Chill thoroughly before using. This herb cheese will keep for up to 4 days in the refrigerator.

Approximate values per 1-oz. (30-g) serving: **Calories** 90, **Total fat** 10 g, **Saturated fat** 6 g, **Cholesterol** 35 mg, **Sodium** 10 mg, **Total carbohydrates** 1 g, **Protein** 1 g, **Vitamin A** 10%

Feta

Queso Oaxaca

Feta is a semisoft cheese popular in Mediterranean cuisines. Traditionally made from sheep's and/or goat's milk, it is a white, flaky cheese that is pickled (but not ripened) and stored in brine water, giving it a shelf life of 4–6 weeks. Feta's flavor becomes sharper and saltier with age. Feta is ideal for snacking and in salads and fillings for breads, pastries and other foods.

Mascarpone [mas-cahr-POHN-ay] is a soft cow's-milk cheese originally from Italy's Lombard region. It contains 70–75% fat and is extremely smooth and creamy. Mascarpone is highly perishable and is available in bulk or in 8- or 16-ounce tubs. It has a characteristic pale ivory color and rich, sweet flavor and is incorporated into both sweet and savory sauces as well as desserts. It is also eaten plain, with fresh fruit or spread on bread and sprinkled with cocoa or sugar.

Mascarpone

Mozzarella [maht-suh-REHL-lah] is a firm Italian cheese traditionally made with water buffalo's milk (today cow's milk is more common) and containing 40–45% fat. Mozzarella becomes elastic when melted and is well known as "pizza cheese." Fresh mozzarella is excellent in salads or topped simply with olive oil and herbs. It is a very mild white cheese best eaten within hours of production. Factory-made mozzarella is rather bland and rubbery and is best reserved for cooking, for which it may be purchased already shredded. When the fresh mozzarella is still warm, its center may be filled with cream, butter or another soft cheese to make **burrata**. This highly perishable semisoft cheese is served fresh with tomatoes, salad greens or fresh fruit.

Mozzarella

Queso Oaxaca [KEH-soh wah-HA-kaa], also known as Quesillo or Asadero, is one of the most popular cheeses of Mexico. It is a cow's-milk *pasta filata* or stretched-curd cheese that is kneaded and wound into balls, then soaked in brine for several minutes. It is pulled apart into thin strings before being used to fill tortillas or melted over cooked dishes. Queso Oaxaca is a good melting cheese with a smooth semisoft texture, white color and 45% fat content. It is invaluable in preparing Mexican and Mexican-American dishes, such as quesadillas, nachos and tacos, and is also available blended with herbs, spices or chiles.

Ricotta [rih-COH-tah] is a soft Italian cheese, similar to American cottage cheese, traditionally made from the whey leftover after other cow's-milk cheeses are produced. It contains only 4–10% fat. It is white or ivory in color and fluffy, with a small grain and sweet flavor. Ricotta is an important ingredient in many pasta dishes and desserts. Ricotta is best when freshly made; it can be made easily with the following recipe.

Ricotta

Ricotta Cheese

🌿 Vegetarian

YIELD 8 oz. (240 g)

Milk	28 fl. oz.	840 ml
Heavy cream	4 fl. oz.	120 ml
Fresh lemon juice or distilled white vinegar	3 fl. oz.	90 ml

1 Combine the milk and cream in a container with a cover. Cover and allow the milk and cream mixture to reach room temperature.

2 In a stainless steel saucepan, slowly heat the milk and cream to 180°F (82°C), stirring often. Hold the heated milk at 180°F (82°C) for 5 minutes.

3 Remove the milk from the heat and gently stir it while adding the lemon juice or vinegar. Continue to stir gently until curds begin to form. Stop stirring and allow the milk mixture to sit at room temperature, uncovered until a solid mass of curds forms, approximately 20 minutes.

4 Gently pour or ladle the curds into a strainer or china cap lined with new, rinsed cheesecloth. Allow the whey (liquid) to separate and drain away from the curds (solids). Discard the whey or reserve it for another use.

5 Allow the cheese to rest covered and undisturbed for 30 minutes to an hour.

6 Unwrap the cheese. Season it with salt if desired. Use the cheese as you would use commercially produced ricotta.

Dry ricotta cheese

Variation:

For a firm, dry ricotta, in Step 4 lift the corners of the cheesecloth and tie them together with twine. Suspend the bag in a tall, covered container, place it in the refrigerator and allow the cheese to drain for 4 hours or overnight. (Or line perforated cheese molds with cheesecloth. Pack the cheese into the molds. Fold up the cheesecloth, then top them with weights. Refrigerate overnight.)

Approximate values per 1-oz. (30-g) serving: **Calories** 80, **Total fat** 4 g, **Saturated fat** 2.5 g, **Cholesterol** 15 mg, **Sodium** 60 mg, **Total carbohydrates** 7 g, **Protein** 4 g, **Calcium** 15%

❶ Heating the milk to 180°F (82°C).

❷ Gently stirring in the lemon juice.

❸ Straining the mixture through cheesecloth.

Soft Cheeses

Soft cheeses are characterized by their thin skins and creamy centers. They are among the most delicious and popular of cheeses. They ripen quickly, from the rind toward the center, and are at their peak for only a few days, sometimes less. Moisture content of soft cheeses ranges from 50% to 75%.

Brie [bree] is a soft-ripened French cheese made with cow's milk and containing about 60% fat. Brie is made in round, flat disks weighing 2 or 4 pounds (1 or 2 kilograms) coated with a bloomy white rind and has a texture that oozes.

Brie de Meaux is a legally protected version made with unpasteurized milk in the town of Meaux. Selecting a properly ripened Brie is a matter of judgment and experience. Select a cheese that is bulging a bit inside its rind; there should be just the beginning of a brown coloring on the rind. Underripe Brie is bland with a hard, chalky core. Once the cheese is cut, it does not ripen any further. Overripe Brie has a brownish rind that may be gummy or sagging and smells strongly of ammonia.

Brie rind is edible but can be trimmed off if preferred. The classic after-dinner cheese, Brie is also used in soups, sauces and hors d'oeuvre. Small wheels of Brie may be wrapped in pastry, baked and served warm.

Brie

Camembert [kam-uhm-BAIR] is a soft-ripened cow's milk cheese traditionally from France containing approximately 45% fat. Camembert is creamy, like Brie, but milder. It is sold in small round or oval disks that have a white bloomy rind. Selecting a properly ripened Camembert is similar to selecting a Brie, but Camembert becomes overripe and ammoniated even more quickly than Brie. Camembert is an excellent dessert or after-dinner cheese and goes particularly well with fruit. Many fine Camembert-style cheeses, made from cow or goat's milk, are now produced in the United States.

Taleggio [tahl-EH-gee-oh] is a semisoft cheese that has been produced since the 10th century in a small town near Bergamo in the Lombardy region of Italy. Made with pasteurized or unpasteurized cow's milk, it contains 48% fat and is aged for 1 to 2 months. Taleggio has an orange-colored washed rind that is edible but pungent. It is molded in a distinctive 8-inch square, approximately 2 inches thick. Its nutty, salty flavor and strong aroma become softer, creamier and more piquant with age. Serve as a dessert cheese with a strong red wine, crusty bread and fruit, or with a salad at the end of a meal.

Taleggio

Semisoft Cheeses

Semisoft cheeses include many mild, buttery cheeses with smooth, sliceable textures. Some semisoft cheeses are also known as monastery or Trappist cheeses because their development is traced to monasteries, with some recipes having originated during the Middle Ages. The moisture content of semisoft cheeses ranges from 40% to 50%.

Cabrales [kah-BRAH-layss] is a blue-veined Spanish cheese made from a blend of raw goat's, ewe's and cow's milks and containing 45–48% fat. Its distinctive easily recognizable wrapper is made from large maple, oak or sycamore leaves. The outer foil wrapper is marked with the *Denominación de Origen* (D.O.) logo, and each 5- to 9-pound (2.5- to 4.5-kilogram) wheel is stamped with a unique number. It is aged for 3–6 months under the cold, humid and breezy conditions in natural caves found in the Asturias region. Cabrales has a moist, crumbly interior with purple-blue veins and a rough, salt-cured rind. It has a thick, creamy texture, a strong aroma and a complex sour, piquant flavor. Cabrales is especially good with salami and a full-bodied red wine or for dessert with a sweet sherry such as Pedro Ximénez.

Cabrales

Fontina

Fontina [fon-TEE-nah] is a cow's-milk cheese from Italy's Piedmont region containing approximately 45% fat. The original legally protected version, known as **Fontina Val D'Aosta**, has a dark gold, crusty rind; the pale gold, dense interior has a few small holes. It is nutty and rich. The original must have a purple trademark stamped on the rind. Imitation Fontinas (properly known as **Fontal** or **Fontinella**) are produced in Denmark, France, Sweden, the United States and other regions of Italy. They tend to be softer, with less depth of flavor, and may have a rubbery texture. Real Fontina is a good after-dinner cheese; the imitations are used in sauces, soups or sandwiches.

Gorgonzola [gohr-guhn-ZOH-lah] is a blue-veined cow's-milk cheese traditionally from Italy containing 48% fat. Gorgonzola has a white or ivory interior with bluish-green veins. It is creamier than other blues such as Stilton or Roquefort, with a somewhat more pungent, spicy, earthy flavor. White Gorgonzola has no veins but a similar flavor, while aged Gorgonzola is drier and crumbly with a very strong, sharp flavor. The milder Gorgonzolas are excellent with fresh peaches or pears or crumbled in a salad. Gorgonzola is also used in sauces and pasta dishes.

Gorgonzola

Gouda

Gouda [GOO-dah] is a Dutch cheese containing approximately 48% fat. Gouda is sold in various-sized wheels covered with red or yellow wax. The cheese is yellow with a few small holes and a mild, buttery flavor. Gouda may be sold soon after production, or it may be aged for several months up to two years, resulting in a firmer, more flavorful cheese. Cheese crystals in long-aged Gouda, a popular cheese board item, give the cheese a crunchy texture. Gouda is widely popular for snacking and sandwiches.

Havarti [hah-VAHR-tee] is a cow's-milk monastery-style cheese from Denmark containing 45–60% fat. Havarti is also known as Danish **Tilsit**. Pale yellow with many small, irregular holes, it is sold in small rounds, rectangular blocks or loaves. Havarti has a mild flavor and creamy texture. It is often flavored with dill, caraway seeds or peppers. Havarti is very popular for snacking and in sandwiches.

Havarti

Port du Salut [por doo suh-LOO] is a monastery cow's-milk product from France containing approximately 50% fat. Port du Salut (also known as Port Salut) is smooth, rich and savory. It is shaped in thick wheels with a dense, pale-yellow interior and an edible, bright orange rind. The Danish version is known as Esrom. One of the best and most authentic Port du Saluts has the initials S.A.F.R. stamped on the rind. Lesser-quality brands may be bland and rubbery. It is popular for breakfast and snacking, especially with fruit.

blue cheese (1) a generic term for any cheese containing visible blue-green molds that contribute a characteristic tart, sharp flavor and aroma; also known as a blue-veined cheese or bleu; (2) a group of Roquefort-style cheeses made in the United States and Canada from cow's or goat's milk rather than ewe's milk and injected with molds that form blue-green veins; also known as blue mold cheese or blue-veined cheese

Port du Salut

Roquefort [ROHK-fohr] is a blue-veined sheep's-milk cheese from France containing approximately 45% fat. The cheese, which has a storied history dating back to the 15th century, is intensely pungent with a rich, salty flavor and strong aroma. It is a white paste with veins of blue mold and a thin natural rind shaped into thick, foil-wrapped cylinders. Roquefort is always aged for at least 3 months in the limestone caves of Mount Combalou. Since 1926 no producer outside this region can legally use the name Roquefort or even "Roquefort-style." Roquefort is an excellent choice for serving before or after dinner and is essential in Roquefort dressing.

Roquefort

Stilton

Stilton is a blue-veined cow's-milk cheese from Great Britain containing 45% fat. One of the oldest and grandest cheeses in the world, with a name protected by the European Union, Stilton has a white or pale-yellow interior with evenly spaced blue veins. Stilton's distinctive flavor is pungent, rich and tangy, combining the best of blues and cheddars. It is aged in cool ripening rooms for 4–6 months to develop the blue veining; it is then sold in tall cylinders with a crusty, edible rind. Stilton should be wrapped in a cloth dampened with salt water and stored at cool temperatures, but not refrigerated. It is best served alone or with plain crackers, dried fruit or vintage port.

Firm Cheeses

Firm cheeses are not hard or brittle. Some are close-textured and flaky, like Cheddar; others are dense, holey cheeses like Emmenthaler. Most firm cheeses are actually imitators of these two classics. Their moisture content ranges from 30% to 40%.

Cheddars are widely produced in North America, Australia and Great Britain. **American Cheddar** is a cow's-milk cheese made primarily in New York, Wisconsin, Vermont and Oregon, containing from 45% to 50% fat. The best cheddars are made from raw milk and aged for several months. (Raw milk may be used in the United States provided the cheese is then aged at least 60 days.) They have a dense, crumbly texture. Cheddars are white or colored orange with vegetable dyes, depending on local preference. Flavors range from mild to very sharp, depending on the age of the cheese. **Colby** and **Longhorn** are two well-known mild, soft-textured Wisconsin Cheddars. Canadian and **English Cheddars** are also cow's-milk cheeses containing approximately 45–48% fat. They tend to be dryer and more sharply flavored than American Cheddars because of additional aging and are popular for snacking and in soups. Aged raw milk Cheddars are welcome additions to any cheese board.

American Cheddar: Wisconsin Sharp, Vermont Cabot, Canadian Black Diamond

fondue a Swiss specialty made with melted cheese, wine and flavorings; diners dip pieces of bread into the hot mixture with long forks

Emmenthaler [EM-en-tah-ler] is a cow's-milk cheese from Switzerland containing approximately 45% fat. Emmenthaler accounts for more than half of Switzerland's cheese production. It is mellow, rich and nutty with a natural rind and a light-yellow interior full of large holes. The holes or "eyes" in Emmenthaler and other cheeses are caused by gases expanding inside the cheese during fermentation. Authentic Emmenthaler is sold in 200-pound (90-kilogram) wheels with the word *Switzerland* stamped on the rind like the spokes of a wheel. Emmenthaler, one of the basic **fondue** cheeses, is also popular for sandwiches, snacks and after dinner with fruit and nuts.

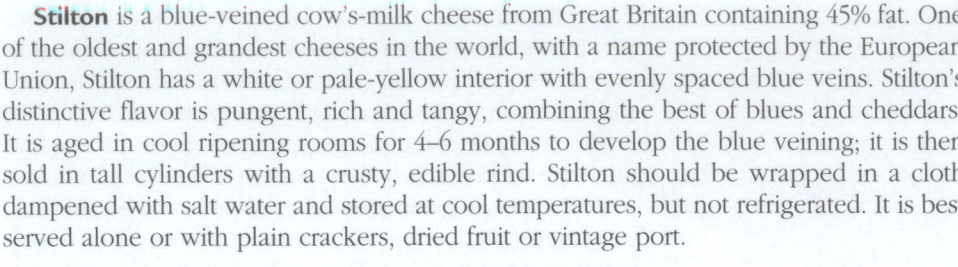

Emmenthaler

Gruyère [groo-YAIR] is a cow's-milk cheese made near Fribourg in the Swiss Alps that contains approximately 45–50% fat. Gruyère is often imitated, as the name is not legally protected. True Gruyère is moist and highly flavorful, with a sweet nuttiness similar to Emmenthaler. Gruyère is aged for up to 12 months and then sold in huge wheels. It should have small, well-spaced holes and a brown, wrinkled rind. Gruyère melts easily and is often used with meats in sandwiches and in sauces, but it is also appropriate before or after dinner. A similar cheese is **Comté** [con-TAY], also called Gruyère de Comté. It is cow's-milk cheese from the Jura Mountain region of France made from raw milk of the red and white Montbeliard breed.

Gruyère

Jarlsberg [YAHRLZ-behrg] is a Swiss-type cow's-milk cheese from Norway containing approximately 45% fat. Jarlsberg closely resembles Emmenthaler in both flavor and appearance. It is mild with a delicate, sweet flavor and large holes. Jarlsberg has a pale-yellow interior; it is coated with yellow wax and sold in huge wheels. It has a long shelf life and is popular for sandwiches and snacking and in cooking.

Manchego [mahn-CHAY-goh] is the best-known and most widely available Spanish sheep's-milk cheese. Its ivory to pale-yellow interior is firm and compact with a few small air pockets. It has a buttery and slightly piquant flavor with an aftertaste of sheep's milk. The inedible rind is black, gray or beige with a very distinctive zigzag pattern imprinted by the traditional esparto grass molds.

Jarlsberg

Manchego

There are two types of Manchego: farmhouse style, made with unpasteurized sheep's milk, and industrial, made with pasteurized milk. For both, only milk from Manchega sheep raised in the La Mancha region is used. Manchego is aged from 2 months (*fresco*) to 1 year (*curado*) to 2 years (*añejo* or *viejo*) and contains 45–57% fat. Its intense flavor and crumbly texture make it excellent for eating with bread or fruit or as the focal point of antipasto with a robust red wine or a dry sherry.

Monterey Jack

Monterey Jack is a cheddar-like cow's-milk cheese from California containing 50% fat. It is very mild and rich, with a pale ivory interior. It is sold in wheels or loaves. "Jack" is often flavored with peppers or herbs and is good for snacking and sandwiches. Dry-aged Jack develops a tough, wrinkled brown rind and a rich, firm yellow interior; it has a nutty, sharp flavor and is dry enough for grating.

Provolone [pro-voh-LOH-neh] is a cow's-milk cheese originally from southern Italy now widely made in the United States containing approximately 45% fat. Provolone *dolce*, aged only 2 months, is mild, with a smooth texture. Provolone *piccante*, aged up to 6 months, is stronger and somewhat flaky or stringy. Smoked provolone is also popular, especially for snacking. Provolone is shaped in various ways, from huge salamis to plump spheres shaped by hand. It is excellent in sandwiches and for cooking and is often melted in pizza and pasta dishes.

Provolone

Hard Cheeses

Hard cheeses are carefully aged for extended periods and have a moisture content of about 30%. Hard cheeses are most often used for grating; the best flavor results from cheeses grated as needed. Even the finest hard cheeses begin to lose their flavor within hours of grating. The most famous and popular hard cheeses are those from Italy, where they are known as *grana*. A high quality hard cheese can also be served as a table cheese or with a salad.

Asiago [ah-zee-AH-go] is a cow's-milk cheese from Italy containing approximately 30% fat. After one year of aging, Asiago is sharp and nutty with a cheddar-like texture. If aged for 2 years or more, Asiago becomes dry, brittle and suitable for grating. Either version should be a consistent white to pale yellow in color with no dark spots, cracks or strong aromas. Asiago melts easily and is often used in cooked vegetable dishes, on sandwiches and salads and in sauces.

Asiago

Grana Padano [gran-ah pa-DAN-o] is produced throughout Northern Italy from partly skim raw cow's milk. It is formed into large cylinders, salted and aged for at least 270 days. This process produces a cheese with a hard, dark beige crust and a firm white to straw-yellow interior with a granular texture and the aroma of almonds. It is excellent for grating, and its sweet yet salty flavor is also enjoyed with fruit and wine.

Parmigiano-Reggiano [pahr-me-ZHAN-no reg-gee-AH-no] is a cow's-milk cheese made exclusively in the region near Parma, Italy, containing from 32% to 35% fat. Parmigiano-Reggiano or **Parmesan** as it is called in English, is one of the world's oldest and most widely

Parmigiano-Reggiano
(Parmesan)

Pecorino Romano

imitated cheeses. Used primarily for grating and cooking, it is rich, spicy and sharp with a golden interior and a hard, oily rind. Parmigiano-Reggiano is not overly salty or bitter. Reggiano, as it is known, is produced only from mid-April to mid-November. It is shaped into huge wheels of about 80 pounds (36 kilograms) each, with the name stenciled repeatedly around the rind. Imitation Parmesan is produced in the United States, Argentina and elsewhere, but none match the distinctive flavor of true Reggiano.

Pecorino Romano [peh-coh-REE-no roh-MAH-no] is a sheep's-milk cheese tradition-ally made in central and southern Italy containing approximately 35% fat. Romano is very brittle, saltier and sharper than other grating cheeses, with a "sheepy" tang. Its light, grainy interior is whiter than Parmesan or Asiago. It is packed in large cylinders with a yellow rind. Romano is often substituted for, or combined with, Parmesan in dishes, but it is also good eaten with olives, sausages and red wine.

🌿 Vegetarian

Fromage Fort

Famously frugal, the French have a delicious way to repurpose bits of leftover cheese. Small pieces, dry ends and crumbles of hard and soft cheeses are puréed into a flavorful spread. Moistened with stock and a little wine, seasoned with garlic and herbs, this pungent mixture, called fromage fort, is served cold or slightly melted under the broiler. Any variety of cheese may be used to make this pungent spread. Using hard cheeses may require more butter and less wine or stock. Using creamy cheeses may require cutting back on the additional liquid.

YIELD 1 lb. 4 oz. (600 g); 5 Ramekins, 4 oz. (120 g) each

Fresh garlic cloves, peeled	2	2
Green onions, sliced	2	2
Assortment of hard and soft cheeses, grated	10 oz.	300 mg
Unsalted butter or cream cheese, softened	3 oz.	90 g
White wine	3 fl. oz.	90 ml
White stock, optional	3 fl. oz.	90 ml
Black pepper	¼ tsp.	2 ml
Fresh parsley, chopped	1 Tbsp.	15 ml
Fresh chives, sliced	1 Tbsp.	15 ml
Dried thyme	pinch	pinch

1 Blend the garlic and green onions in a food processor fitted with the metal blade until finely chopped.

2 Add the grated cheese and butter. Process until well blended.

3 Add the white wine, half of the stock and the pepper, parsley, chives and thyme. Process until the mixture reaches a smooth and creamy texture adding more stock as needed to make a smooth spread.

4 Pack the spread into ramekins. Cover and refrigerate or freeze until needed.

5 Present the molded cheese on a platter or press into a serving bowl. Garnish as desired and serve with toast points, crackers or raw vegetables.

Approximate values per 1-oz. (30-g) serving: **Calories** 90, **Total fat** 8 g, **Saturated fat** 4.5 g, **Cholesterol** 25 mg, **Sodium** 90 mg, **Total carbohydrates** 1 g, **Protein** 3 g

Goat's-Milk Cheeses

Because of their increasing popularity, cheeses made from goat's milk deserve a few words of their own. Although goats produce less milk than cows, their milk is higher in fat and protein and richer and more concentrated in flavor. Cheeses made with goat's milk have a sharp, tangy flavor. They range in texture from very soft and fresh to very hard, depending on age.

Assorted French soft cheeses and French goat's-milk cheeses (clockwise starting from the top right): log of herb-coated goat's cheese, Banon wrapped in leaves, cinder-coated Sainte Maure, Chabichou goat's cheese, Chabichou marinated in olive oil, herbs and peppercorns and, in the center, Camembert

Chèvre [shehv; French for "goat"] refers to small, soft, creamy cheeses produced in a variety of shapes: cones, disks, pyramids or logs. Chèvres are often coated with ash, herbs or seasonings. (Ash protects the surface of the cheese as it ages and enhances the development of beneficial surface mold.) They are excellent for cooking and complement a wide variety of flavors. Unfortunately they have a short shelf life, as brief as 2 weeks. Cheese labeled *pur chèvre* must be made with 100% goat's milk; other chèvres may be a mixture of cow's and goat's milk.

The finest goat's-milk cheeses traditionally come from France. Preferred brands include Bûcheron, exported from France in 5-pound (2-kilogram) logs; Chevrotin, one of the mildest; and Montrachet, a tangy soft cheese from the Burgundy wine region. Numerous North American cheese makers produce excellent goat's-milk cheeses in a wide variety of shapes and styles.

Cheese Terminology

The following terms often appear on cheese labels and may help you to identify or appreciate new or unfamiliar cheeses:

Affiné: French term for a cured or properly ripened cheese

Bleu: French for "blue"

Brique or *briquette:* Refers to a group of French brick-shaped cheeses

Brosse: French term for cheeses that are brushed with liquid or oil during ripening

Capra: Italian term for goat's-milk cheese

Carré: French term for square, flat cheeses

Cendré: French term for cheeses ripened in ashes

Coulant: French for "flowing," used to describe ripe Brie, Camembert and other cheeses with interiors that ooze or flow

Ferme or *fermier:* French adjective used to indicate farm-produced as opposed to factory-produced cheeses

Fromage: French for "cheese"

Kaas: Dutch for "cheese"

Käse: German for "cheese"

Lait cru: French term for raw milk

Laiterie or *laitier:* French for "dairy"; appears on factory-made cheeses

Matières grasses: French term for fat content

Mi chèvre: A French product containing at least 25% goat's milk

Ost: Scandinavian for "cheese"

Pecorino: Italian term for all sheep's-milk cheeses

Queso: Spanish for "cheese"

Râpé: French term applied to cheeses that are suitable for grating

Tome or *tomme:* Term used by the French, Italians and Swiss to refer to mountain cheeses, particularly from the Pyrénées or Savoie regions

Tyrophile: One who loves cheese

Vaccino: Italian term for cow's-milk cheese

Vache: French term for cow's-milk cheese

American Cheese Production

The first cheese factory in the United States was built in 1851 in Oneida County, New York. Neighboring Herkimer County soon became the center of the American cheese industry and remained so for the next 50 years. During this time, the largest cheese market in the world was at Little Falls, New York, where farm-produced cheeses and cheeses from more than 200 factories were sold.

Although New York still produces some outstanding cheddar cheeses, the bulk of the American cheese industry gradually moved westward, eventually settling in Wisconsin's rich farmlands, which now produce 25% of the country's cheese. In 2013 the United States produced over 5 million metric tons of cheese, mostly mozzarella, cheddar and Colby-Jack.

A movement to return to traditional, artisanal cheese making began in the 1980s. According to the American Cheese Society, as of 2016 there were more than 900 artisan cheese producers in the United States and 740 cheese professionals certified by the organization. **Artisan cheeses** are mostly handmade in small batches using as little mechanical assistance as possible. Almost 60% of these producers claim to employ organic practices, although barely 10% obtain organic certification. A subcategory referred to as **farmstead cheese** must be made on the producer's property with milk from the producer's own herd or flock. Artisan cheese makers generally use milk from cows or goats, but sheep and buffalo milk is also employed. These cheeses may be sold fresh or aged and are often flavored with herbs, fruits or other seasonings. Artisan cheeses are now made in virtually every state and are widely available at farmers markets and through online and specialty retailers.

Processed Cheeses

Pasteurized processed cheese is made from a combination of aged and unaged cheeses mixed with emulsifiers and flavorings, pasteurized and poured into molds to solidify. In this way, manufacturers produce cheeses with consistent textures and flavors. Processed cheeses are commonly used in food service operations because they are less expensive than natural cheeses. And, because processed cheeses will not age or ripen, their shelf life is much longer than natural cheeses. Nutritionally, processed cheeses generally contain less protein, calcium and vitamin A and more sodium than natural cheeses.

Processed cheese food contains less natural cheese (but at least 51% by weight) and more moisture than regular processed cheese. Often vegetable oils and milk solids are added, making cheese food soft and spreadable.

Imitation cheese is usually manufactured with dairy by-products and soy products mixed with emulsifiers, colorings and flavoring agents and enzymes. Although considerably less expensive than natural cheese, imitation cheese tends to be dense and rubbery, with little flavor other than that of salt.

Serving Cheeses

Cheeses may be served at any time of day. In Northern Europe, they are common for breakfast; in Great Britain, they are a staple at lunch. Cheeses are widely used in sandwiches, snacks and cooking in America, and they are often served following the entrée or instead of dessert.

The flavor and texture of natural cheeses are best at room temperature. All cheeses except for fresh cheeses should be removed from the refrigerator 30 minutes to an hour before service to allow them to come to room temperature. Fresh cheeses, such as cottage and cream, should be eaten chilled.

Chefs follow some general guidelines when preparing a cheese board or cheese plate to be served in a food service operation.

1   Any selection of fine cheeses should include a variety of flavors and textures: from mild to sharp, from soft to creamy to firm.

2   A variety of shapes and colors provide visual appeal.

3   Do not precut the cheeses, as this causes them to dry. When portioning cheese for a cheese board or cheese plate, choose the right knife or tool for the task. Soft and semisoft cheeses can be cut with a knife dipped in hot water then dried before using. Hard cheeses may require a two-handled knife. Often hard cheeses, such as aged Gouda, are shaved into thin slices.

4 A round soft or semisoft cheese should be cut through the center into wedges. A rectangular soft cheese may be cut into wedges or thin strips. Regardless of the shape of a soft cheese, each portion should include some of the rind and some of the paste so that the diner experiences all of the flavors in the cheese.

5 Fine cheeses are best appreciated with plain bread such as slices of a French baguette and crackers. Salted or seasoned crackers can mask the cheese's flavor. Stronger cheeses such as ripe blue cheese can stand up to breads made with nuts and dried fruit.

6 Condiments such as honey, quince paste and fruit preserves pair well with cheese as do nuts and dried or fresh non-citrus fruits.

Storing Cheeses

Most cheeses are best kept in the refrigerator, well wrapped to keep odors out and moisture in. Firm and hard cheeses can be kept for several weeks; fresh cheeses will spoil in 7–10 days because of their high moisture content. Some cheeses that have become hard or dry may still be grated for cooking or baking. Freezing cheese is possible but not recommended because it changes the cheese's texture, making it mealy or tough.

Cooking with Cheese

When heated, cheese can melt into a tough, stringy mass because of its high protein content. Long exposure to heat can also cause cheese mixtures to curdle and separate. Lower-fat cheeses, such as cottage, feta and factory-made low-fat products, are especially difficult to heat. Therefore it is important to use low temperatures and short cooking times. Cheeses can be incorporated into sauces and soups by first grating the cheese while cold. The resulting small pieces melt quickly and evenly. Add cheese toward the end of cooking, and do not allow cheese mixtures to boil. Hold cheese mixtures warm over a bain marie or indirect heat.

When melting a cheese topping, place the dish 4–6 inches from the heating element or broiler and broil only until the cheese melts. Cheese can taste scorched and the fats can separate if overheated. Dry, high-fat cheeses such as Parmesan and Pecorino can tolerate heat better and are good choices for toppings.

A cheese plate composed of American soft cheeses with garnishes (clockwise starting from the top): Crottin goat's-milk cheese from Vermont, Camembert from California, a raw cow and goat's-milk blue cheese from Oregon and a triple cream cow's-milk cheese from California

---

Classic Cheese Fondue

 Vegetarian

YIELD 1 Quart (960 ml)

Emmenthaler cheese, grated coarse	1 lb.	480 g
Gruyère cheese, grated coarse	1 lb.	480 g
Flour or cornstarch	1 ½ oz.	45 g
Dry white wine	24 fl. oz.	720 ml
Fresh lemon juice	2 fl. oz.	60 ml
Black pepper	TT	TT
Nutmeg, ground	TT	TT
Paprika	TT	TT
Kirsch	3 fl. oz.	90 ml
Garlic clove, halved	1	1
French bread, cut into 1-in. (2.5-cm) cubes	as needed	as needed

MISE EN PLACE

- Grate cheeses.
- Peel and cut garlic in half.
- Cut French bread into cubes.

1 Toss the grated cheesed in a bowl with the flour or cornstarch.

2 Heat the wine and lemon juice in a nonreactive saucepan over medium high heat. When the wine just starts to boil, add the cheese. Stir with a wire whisk until the cheeses melt. Add the pepper, nutmeg and paprika to taste. Stir in the Kirsch.

3 Rub a fondue pot with the cut clove of garlic. Add the cheese mixture and serve with cubed French bread.

Approximate values per 2-oz. (60-g) serving: **Calories** 140, **Total fat** 9 g, **Saturated fat** 5 g, **Cholesterol** 30 mg, **Sodium** 130 mg, **Total carbohydrates** 2 g, **Protein** 8 g, **Calcium** 25%

Wine and Cheese: Classic Combinations

Some cheeses are delicious with beers or ales. Others are best with strong coffee or apple cider, and nothing accompanies a Cheddar cheese sandwich as well as ice-cold milk. For most cheeses, however, the ultimate partner is wine. Wine and cheese bring out the best in each other. The proteins and fats in cheeses take the edge off harsh or acidic wines, whereas the tannins and acids in wines bring out the creamy richness of cheeses.

Because of their natural affinity, certain pairings are universal favorites: Stilton with port,

Camembert with Bordeaux, Roquefort with Sauternes and English Cheddar with Burgundy. Although taste preferences are an individual matter, cheese–wine marriages follow two schools of thought: pair likes or pair opposites.

Pairing like with like is simple: Cheeses are often best served with wines produced in the same region. For example, a white Burgundy such as Montrachet is an excellent choice for cheeses from Burgundy; goat cheeses from the Rhone Valley go well with wines of that region. Hearty Italian wines such as Chianti, Barolo

and Valpolicella are delicious with Italian cheese—Gorgonzola, Parmigiano-Reggiano, Provolone, Taleggio. And a dry, aged Monterey Jack is perhaps the perfect mate for California Zinfandel.

Opposites do attract as well. Sweet wines such as Riesling, Sauternes and Gewürztraminer go well with sharp, tangy blues, especially Roquefort. And light, sparkling wines such as Champagne or Spanish Cava are a nice complement to rich, creamy cheeses such as Brie and Camembert.

QUESTIONS FOR DISCUSSION

1 What is milkfat, and how is it used in classifying milk-based products?

2 If a recipe calls for whole milk and you have only dried milk, what do you do? Explain your answer.

3 Explain how rennet is used in the cheese-making process.

4 The texture and shelf life of cheese depends on what two factors? Which cheeses should be stored in a brine solution or with salt-water soaked cheesecloth?

5 Cheeses are categorized as fresh, soft, semisoft, firm and hard. Give two examples of each, and explain how they are generally used.

6 What are the flavor characteristics of goat's milk cheeses?

7 The FDA and many states currently ban the sale of raw milk or products such as cheese, made from raw milk. Several groups, including the American Cheese Society, A Campaign for Real Milk, Slow Food USA and some organic dairy farmers are fighting to legalize the sale of these products. Use outside resources to learn about the sale of raw milk products. What arguments are used in support of and in opposition to the sale of raw milk products?

8 Describe the guidelines to follow when choosing cheeses for a cheese plate for a restaurant menu.

Mise en Place 9

After studying this chapter, you will be able to:

▶ create and use a prep list

▶ measure and prepare items needed prior to cooking

▶ identify and gather the tools and equipment necessary to prepare a recipe properly or to work a station efficiently

▶ prepare and apply various flavoring or seasoning mixtures to food before they are cooked

▶ set up and apply the standard breading procedure

The French term *mise en place* [MEEZ ahn plahs] loosely translates as "to put in place" or "everything in its place." But in the culinary context, it means much more. Auguste Escoffier, the creator of *cuisine classique*, defined the phrase as "those elementary preparations that are constantly resorted to during the various steps of most culinary preparations." Essentially it is the gathering and preparation of the ingredients to be cooked as well as assembling the tools and equipment necessary to cook them.

In this chapter, we discuss the basics that must be in place before cooking begins: these preparatory steps include creating bouquets garni, clarifying butter, making bread crumbs, toasting nuts and battering foods. Chopping, dicing, cutting and slicing—important techniques used to prepare foods as well—are discussed in Chapter 6, Knife Skills; specific preparations, such as roasting peppers and trimming pineapples, are discussed in various other chapters.

MISE EN PLACE

The concept of mise en place is that a chef should have at hand everything needed to prepare and serve food in an organized and efficient manner.

Proper mise en place can consist of just a few items—for example, those needed to prepare a small quantity of chicken soup or Beef Stroganoff. Or it can be quite extensive—for example, the items that make up the hot line for a busy restaurant with a large menu. To prepare a proper mise en place, the chef must consider work patterns, ingredient lists and tool and equipment needs, and it requires mental concentration and focus so that the tasks at hand are prepared before the start of service. Taking the time to properly plan and prepare ensures success during the meal service to come. A well-executed mise en place is the sign of an experienced professional chef.

Proper mise en place is required for each recipe that comprises a dish or plate (main course, vegetable, starch, sauce, garnish) and for each item on the menu. The thought process and organizational skills required for effective mise en place are the same, however, no matter the dish or the setting. Regardless of the number of items used or the complexity of the recipes being prepared, completing a proper mise en place requires careful planning, efficient organization and attention to detail.

Coordination of multiple tasks is also important. An organized cook will think about everything that needs to be done and the most efficient way to complete those tasks before beginning the actual work. Taking the time to first plan the day's activities can conserve resources and eliminate unnecessary steps. Proper mise en place requires a good sense of timing. Knowing how long before service to begin a task, or how far in advance of service some preparations can be made, allows you to better plan for the efficient execution of your duties. In this type of planning, it is also important to consider food safety issues, such as those relating to time and temperature controls. (See Chapter 2, Food Safety and Sanitation.)

Mise en place for a kitchen work station must include all of the items that are required to serve the menu items prepared at that station. Take the example of a hypothetical salad station where the cook prepares three entrée salads. See Figure 9.1. The mise en place needed for each meal service must include every ingredient necessary to make these items in the quantity appropriate for the volume of anticipated business. Lettuce and other produce for the salads must be washed and stored at the station. Dressings must be prepared and stored in containers that help the cook dispense the proper quantity of dressing on each salad. The egg salad must be made fresh on a daily basis. It is the responsibility of the cook manning that station to have these items prepped on time for service.

MISE EN PLACE – SALAD STATION
MENU ITEMS
Caesar Salad
Romaine lettuce leaves, washed
Caesar salad dressing
Toasted croutons
Grated parmesan cheese
Egg Salad Platter
Curried egg salad
Cherry tomatoes, washed
Lettuce leaves, washed
Spinach Salad
Baby spinach leaves, washed
Sliced red onion rings
Sliced button mushrooms
Cooked bacon
Mustard vinaigrette salad dressing

Figure 9.1 Mise en place for a salad station includes all the ingredients required to prepare the items from the menu.

Mise en place differs from one restaurant and one kitchen station to another. The order of production and the holding times and temperatures differs depending on whether preparation is for à la carte service, buffet service or a plated banquet. A banquet chef's mise en place may include organizing large quantities of meats, vegetables, salad ingredients, breads, condiments and pastries for several dinners, all with different menus. Banquet mise en place may also include gathering plates, chafing dishes, tongs, spoons and ladles, and setting up the dish-up line. The mise en place for the broiler station at a steakhouse may include properly storing raw steaks and chops that will be cooked to order, as well as gathering the salt, pepper, prepared sauces and accompaniments that are used during cooking or served with the finished items. The broiler cook's mise en place could involve gathering plates, building a charcoal fire for the grill and stocking the work area with hand tools, towels and sanitizing solution. A waiter's mise en place may include brewing tea, cutting lemon wedges and refilling salt and pepper shakers—preparations that make work go more smoothly during actual service.

Creating a Prep List

A prep list is a road map for the day's kitchen work before service. It assures that all of the ingredients necessary for the day's food service will be on hand when needed. The prep list also identifies what kind of teamwork will be required to prepare a menu item. It helps the chef determine who will prepare certain dishes or their components so that no single workstation is overburdened.

Chefs prepare prep lists for each service. These may be informal handwritten notes or formalized into production charts. Whether preparing a single recipe or the components for an entire menu, successful chefs follow similar steps to devise their prep lists. Keep these steps in mind when preparing your prep list:

1   Familiarize yourself with the menu items required for your station. Read any recipes required for that station from start to finish. Become familiar with the ingredients and any advance preparation they may require. Verify the recipe yields and the number of portions each recipe will produce. Compare this to ingredients on hand and projected needs for that day's service. Adjust the recipe yield accordingly.

2   Identify the ingredients called for in each menu item. For speed and efficiency, gather everything you need for each item to prevent losing time by repeatedly walking to storage areas. Some ingredients may need to be thawed. Others many need to be fabricated before the recipes can be prepared. Plan accordingly.

3   Plan and prioritize workflow. Identify components that take longer to prepare. Stock, for example, takes hours of simmering and is often prepared days in advance. Identify items that can be made ahead and held for service. Many sauces and salad dressings can be made a day ahead.

4   Write the prep list. Schedule the order in which different tasks need to be done. Decide at what time of the day to prepare the different components in the recipe for best results. Chopping herbs to be used as garnish, for example, should be done as close to service as possible.

Figure 9.2 is a prep list for the salad station described in Figure 9.1. Note that preliminary steps, such as cooking the eggs in order to make the curried egg salad, are listed before

PREP LIST—SALAD STATION	QUANTITY
Cook and chill eggs for curried egg salad	2 dozen
Make Caesar salad dressing	1 pt.
Make mustard vinaigrette salad dressing	1 qt.
Cut and toast croutons for Caesar salad	1 loaf bread
Wash romaine lettuce leaves for Caesar salad	6 heads
Wash lettuce leaves for egg salad platter	1 head
Wash baby spinach leaves	2 lb.
Wash and stem cherry tomatoes for egg salad platter	3 pt.
Cook bacon for spinach salad	1 lb.
Prepare curried egg salad	4 lb.
Grate parmesan cheese for Caesar salad	½ lb.
Slice red onion rings for spinach salad	1 large onion
Slice button mushrooms for spinach salad	1 lb.

Figure 9.2 Salad station prep list.

making the finished egg salad. Tasks that are similar, such as making the two salad dressings required for this station, are grouped together. Quantities are determined by anticipated volume of business or past history from the chef or from other cooks who work the station. Writing down the prep list prevents mistakes. A written prep list, one that is not simply committed to memory, also allows others in the kitchen brigade to lend a hand when help is needed.

Quantity Planning

Determining how much of each item to prepare before service begins is critically important to efficient mise en place. The term **par** is used to indicate a standard amount that should always be on-hand or prepped before each day or meal. For example, the par stock for lunch salad prep might include 1 liter of each salad dressing, 3 liters of cleaned cherry tomatoes and 2 liters of blanched broccoli florets. Determining the proper par quantities requires knowledge of sales history and sound judgment.

The ideal par or daily prep amount is the number of guests expected times the average percentage of customers who order each item. If, for example, you know from sales history that 12–14% of customers will order veal scaloppini, and that there are 300 guests expected today, then you know to prep at least 36–42 portions of veal. Three hundred guests times 12–14% equals 36–42. Decisions about prep quantities are generally the responsibility of a sous chef or chef de cuisine and the person making the prep list should take directions from them and observe how accurately the prep quantities are estimated over a period of time. If the kitchen frequently runs out of an item, it may be that the par quantity should be increased. Likewise, par should be decreased to avoid waste if leftovers become excessive.

Chefs often write a prep schedule that takes into account par requirements for each station. In the prep list for a hypothetical grill station shown in Figure 9.3, the cook is responsible for preparing six menu items. It is the cook's responsibility to speak to the manager or chef about anticipated business and prepare these items accordingly. When few customers are anticipated, the cook prepares a par quantity for the slow service (slow par). When a busy evening is anticipated, the cook prepares the par for busy service (busy par). At the end of the service, the cook counts what remains and writes this on the prep sheet as the closing quantity on hand. Keeping track gives the kitchen management a record of what is selling and forms the basis for what to prepare the next day.

PREP LIST - GRILL STATION

Day __Monday__

ITEM	ON HAND	SLOW PAR	BUSY PAR	AMOUNT TO PREP	CLOSING
London Broil		15 orders	25 orders		
8 oz. Flank steak, bias cut	7	15 ea	25 ea	8	5
Marinade	1 pt.	1 qt.	2 qt.	1 pt.	0
Teriyaki Salmon		8 orders	16 orders		
6 oz. Salmon fillet, skin off	0	8 ea	16 ea	8	2
Salmon Caesar Salad		10 orders	20 orders		
3 oz. Salmon filets, skin off	4	10 ea	20 ea	6	2
Pork Chimichurri Kabobs		15 orders	25 orders		
4 oz. Pork loin skewer	9	15 ea	25 ea	6	10
Turkey Burgers		10 orders	20 orders		
5 oz. Turkey patties	8	10 ea	20 ea	2	6
Chicken Caesar Salad		10 orders	20 orders		
3 oz. Boneless chicken breast	4	10 ea	20 ea	6	0

Figure 9.3 Grill station prep list.

Furthermore the difference between the sum of the amount on hand plus the amount prepared minus the closing amount should equal the evening's sales. The form shown in Figure 9.3 may be used by management to track waste for the most expensive items in this example, the beef, salmon, pork, turkey and chicken.

SELECTING TOOLS AND EQUIPMENT

An important step in creating the proper mise en place is to identify and gather all of the tools and equipment necessary to prepare a recipe properly or to work a station efficiently. The tools and equipment used to prepare, cook and store foods are discussed in Chapter 5, Tools and Equipment. The following are a few general rules to bear in mind:

- Clean and sanitize all tools, equipment and work surfaces.
- Sharpen and hone knives.
- Check measuring scales and thermometers periodically for accuracy.
- Preheat ovens and cooking surfaces as necessary.
- Gather mixing bowls, saucepans and storage containers that are the correct size for the task at hand.
- Gather serving plates, cookware, utensils, hand tools and other necessary small-wares and store close at hand.
- Gather and store foods conveniently at the proper temperatures.
- Check expiration dates on foods periodically.
- Conveniently locate sanitizing solution, hand towels, disposable gloves, containers for trim and waste material collected during prep and trash receptacles.

MEASURING INGREDIENTS

In order to reproduce recipes consistently and for the same cost day after day, it is important that the ingredients be measured accurately each time. As explained in more detail in Chapter 4, Menus and Recipes, ingredients may be measured by weight, volume or count. Weight refers to the mass or heaviness of an item and is measured using a scale. Volume refers to the space occupied by a substance and is measured with graduated measuring cups and spoons. Count refers to the number of individual items. It is important to remember that foods do not weigh their volume. In other words, although 1 cup contains 8 fluid ounces, 1 cup of flour, honey, cinnamon, and so on does not *weigh* 8 ounces.

Measure liquids in liquid measuring cups, which may be marked in U.S. and/or metric units. Choose measuring cups that are marked with the units used in the recipe.

Measure small amounts of dry ingredients by overfilling the appropriate measuring spoon, then leveling the ingredient.

Procedure for Using a Digital Scale

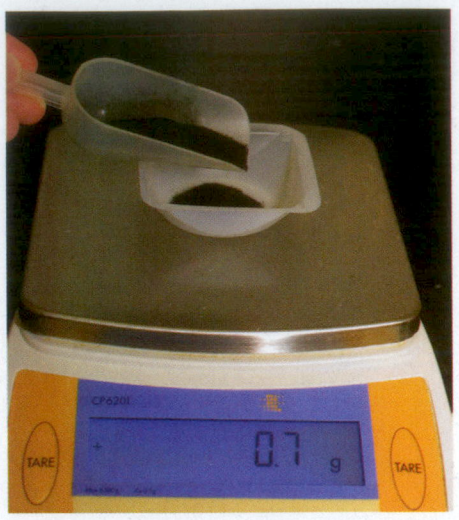

1 To use a digital scale to weigh an ingredient, place an empty container on the platform. Press the tare button, which sets the scale to zero.

2 Add the ingredient to (or remove it from) the container as necessary until the desired weight is reached.

PREPARING INGREDIENTS

Some ingredients that are used frequently throughout the kitchen are often prepared in large quantities so that they are ready when needed. For example, dry bread crumbs can be made and stored whenever a supply of bread is available. Large quantities of butter can be clarified on a back burner while other operations proceed on the line. These chores may be simple, but they are time-consuming and important. Consider the negative impact of running out of a simple item just when it is needed during service. An entry-level cook may be assigned responsibility for this type of key mise en place.

Clarifying Butter

Unsalted whole butter is approximately 80% fat, 16% water and 4% milk solids. Although whole butter can be used for cooking or sauce making, sometimes a more stable and consistent product is desirable. Butter is more stable once its water and milk solids are removed by a process called **clarification**.

Procedure for Clarifying Butter

1 Slowly warm the butter in a saucepan over low heat without boiling or agitation. As the butter melts, the milk solids rise to the top as a foam and the water sinks to the bottom.

2 When the butter is completely melted, skim the milk solids from the top.

3 When all the milk solids have been removed, ladle the butterfat into a clean saucepan, being careful to leave the water in the bottom of the pan.

4 The clarified butter is now ready to use. One pound (454 grams) of whole butter will yield approximately 12 ounces (340 grams) of clarified butter—a yield of 75%.

Skimming milk solids from the surface of melted butter.

Ladling the butterfat into a clean pan.

Clarified butter will keep for extended periods in either the freezer or refrigerator. **Ghee** is a form of clarified butter originating in India in which the milk solids remain with the fat and are allowed to brown. It cooks longer than clarified butter. Ghee can be used like clarified butter as an ingredient and cooking medium when its nutty, caramel-like flavor is desired.

Toasting Nuts and Spices

Nuts are often toasted lightly before being used in baked goods, breadings, salads and sauces. Whole spices are sometimes toasted before being ground for a sauce or used as a garnish. Toasting not only browns the food, it brings out its flavor and makes it crispier and crunchier. To toast nuts in the oven, spread them in one layer on a sheet pan so they cook evenly. Place them in an oven heated to a moderate temperature, 325–350°F (162–176°C). Watch them closely, checking them for doneness at five-minute intervals. Their color should darken slightly and the nuts should emit a delicate aroma. (The time required will depend upon the type of nut, its freshness and size.) To toast spices on the stovetop, spread them out into an even layer in a dry sauté pan. Place the pan over low heat. Shake the pan in a circular motion to keep the spices from burning. Watch them closely as spices can develop bitter scorched flavors and burn easily. A light color and fragrant aroma indicates spices that are toasted not burnt.

Toasting sesame seeds in a dry sauté pan on the stove top.

Making Bread Crumbs

Almost any bread can be used to make crumbs; the choice depends on how the crumbs will be used. **Fresh bread crumbs** are made from fresh bread that is slightly dried out, approximately 2–4 days old. If the bread is too fresh, the crumbs will be gummy and stick together; if the bread is too stale, the crumbs will taste stale as well. **Dry bread crumbs** are made from bread that has been lightly toasted in a warm oven. Do not make crumbs from stale or molding bread, as these undesirable flavors are apparent when the crumbs are used.

To make crumbs, cube or tear the bread into pieces and grind in a food processor. Dried bread can be processed to a finer consistency than fresh bread. After processing, the crumbs should be passed through a drum sieve (tamis) and stored in a tightly closed plastic container in a cool, dry place. For additional flavors, dried herbs and spices may be mixed into the crumbs.

> ### Convenience Products
>
> Convenience products have now replaced many of the chores that were typically part of a cook's routine mise en place. For example, stock and sauce bases eliminate the time and labor necessary to make these products from scratch. Fresh onions and garlic can be purchased peeled, chopped and ready to use. Bread crumbs are available in bulk, and ready-to-use clarified butter is sold in refrigerated tubs. All this convenience comes at a price, of course. A chef must carefully consider whether the savings in employee time, along with the quality and consistency of available products, justify the higher cost of some of the convenience products now on the market.

Procedure for Making Bread Crumbs

❶ Grind bread in a food processor.

❷ Pass the crumbs through a drum sieve or tamis so that they are uniform in size.

FLAVORING FOODS

Foods are often flavored with herbs or spices, marinades or rubs before they are cooked. The chef may prepare and apply various flavoring or seasoning mixtures and wait for a period of time between steps in a recipe.

Bouquets Garni and Sachets

Bouquets garni and sachets introduce flavorings, seasonings and aromatics into stocks, sauces, soups and stews.

A **bouquet garni** is a selection of herbs (usually fresh) and vegetables tied into a bundle with twine. A standard bouquet garni consists of parsley stems, celery, thyme, leeks and carrots.

A **sachet** (also known as a *sachet d'épices*) is seasonings tied together in cheesecloth. A standard sachet consists of peppercorns, bay leaves, parsley stems, thyme, cloves and, optionally, garlic. The exact quantity of these ingredients is determined by the amount of liquid the sachet is meant to flavor.

Bouquet garni

Sachet

Bouquets garni and sachets can be easily removed from a dish when their flavors have been extracted. A similar technique, although less commonly used, is an **onion piqué** (also known as an *oignon piqué*). To prepare an onion piqué, peel the onion and trim off the root end. Attach one or two dried bay leaves to the onion using whole cloves as pins. Simmer the onion piqué in milk or stock to extract flavors.

An **onion brûlé** (also known as *oignon brûlé*, French for "burnt onion,") is used to flavor and color stocks, sauces and soups such as consommé. To prepare an onion brûlé, peel the onion, trim off the root end and cut it in half. Place the onion halves cut sides down in a dry skillet over medium-high heat. Cook until the onion halves char and darken. Simmered in stocks or soups, the onion brûlé imparts a clear caramel color.

Onion brûlé

Onion piqué

Marinades

Marinating is the process of soaking meat or poultry in a seasoned liquid to flavor and tenderize. Marinades can be a simple blend (herbs, seasonings and oil) or a complicated cooked recipe (red wine, fruit and other ingredients). Mild marinades should be used on more delicate meats, such as veal. Game and beef require strongly flavored marinades. Salt, salty ingredients such as soy sauce and mildly acidic dairy products such as buttermilk or yogurt tenderize meat proteins. Highly acidic marinades, such as those containing lemon juice, vinegar or wine, also alter animal proteins and can toughen the surface of foods that marinate for too long. Certain fruits such as raw papayas and pineapples contain enzymes that also break down animal proteins. These fruits are effective tenderizers, but leaving foods in enzyme-based marinades for too long can make them unpleasantly soft and pulpy.

Poultry, veal and pork generally require less time to marinate than game, beef and lamb. Smaller pieces of meat take less time than larger pieces. More tender cuts of meat require less marinating time than tougher cuts of meat. When marinating, be sure to cover the meat or poultry completely and keep it refrigerated. The quantity of marinade needed varies depending on the size and form of the product; 2 pounds of boneless chicken breasts require less marinade to cover than 2 pounds of whole Cornish game hens. Stir or turn foods frequently so that the marinade can penetrate evenly.

Some chefs prefer to marinate food in heavy-duty plastic food storage bags. These are useful for smaller quantities and allow for easy disposal of leftover marinades with less risk of cross-contamination. Label the bags properly and be sure to seal them tightly to prevent leaks.

Marinating chicken breasts.

Brines

Brines are salty marinades used on meats such as ham or bacon that will be smoked for long preservation; this process is discussed in Chapter 28, Charcuterie. Lean cuts of pork or poultry can also benefit from a light brining before grilling, roasting or sautéing. Soaking the cuts in a 3–5% brine solution for a few hours or overnight increases moisture retention and tenderizes the meat. Because the meat and pan drippings can become salty after brining, never salt brined meat before cooking. Avoid making pan gravy from brined meats. Most brine recipes include sweeteners and other seasonings to counterbalance the saltiness. The ratios of salt to water for light brine are as follows:

3% solution: 0.5 oz. (15 g) salt per 16 fl. oz. (480 ml) water
5% solution: 0.8 oz. (24 g) salt per 16 fl. oz. (480 ml) water

Rubs and Pastes

Additional flavors can be added to meat, fish and poultry by rubbing them with a mixture of fresh or dried herbs and spices ground together with a mortar and pestle or in a spice grinder. The flavoring blend, called a **rub**, can be used dried, or it can be mixed with a little oil, lemon juice, prepared mustard or ground fresh garlic or ginger to make a **paste** (also known as a **wet rub**). Rubs and pastes add flavor and, often, a bit of crispy crust. They do not, however, generally act as a tenderizer unless they contain salt. They are most often used on foods that will be cooked with dry heat, especially by grilling, broiling, baking or roasting.

Applying a dry rub to beef.

To apply a rub or paste, slather the mixture over the entire surface of the food to be flavored. Use enough pressure to make sure that the rub or paste adheres. (Pastes tend to adhere better than rubs.) It is best to wear disposable gloves when applying a rub or paste. Some spices can irritate or stain the skin, and cross-contamination can occur from handling raw meats. The thicker the covering or the longer it remains on the food before cooking, the more pronounced the flavor. If the rubbed food is to be left for some time so that the flavors can be absorbed, it should be covered, refrigerated and turned from time to time.

Steeping

Steeping is the process of soaking dry ingredients in a liquid (usually hot) in order to either soften a food or **infuse** its flavor into the liquid. The steeping mixture is generally covered and removed from the heat to avoid evaporation or reduction of the liquid.

Spices, coffee beans and nuts are often steeped in hot milk to extract their flavors. The milk is then used to flavor other foods during cooking. For example, coffee beans can be steeped in hot milk and then strained out with the coffee-flavored milk used to make a custard sauce or ice cream.

infuse to flavor a liquid by steeping it with ingredients such as tea, coffee, herbs or spices

Steeping is also used to rehydrate dried fruits and vegetables, such as raisins and mushrooms. Typically the softened fruits or vegetables will be used in a recipe and the liquid discarded. Additional flavors can be achieved by using wine, spirits, stock or other flavored liquids as the rehydrating liquid.

Steeping a vanilla bean and cinnamon sticks in warm milk to extract their flavors.

Steeping raisins in hot water to rehydrate.

PREPARING TO COOK

Some mise en place techniques are completed very close to or almost as a part of the final preparation of a dish. However, the ingredients used in these techniques must still be prepared in advance as part of standard mise en place.

Breading

meal (1) the coarsely ground seeds of any edible grain such as corn or oats; (2) any dried, ground or powdery substance, such as cracker meal or almond meal

A breaded item is any food that is coated with bread crumbs, crushed crackers, cornmeal or other dry **meal** to protect it during cooking and add flavor and texture. Breaded foods can be seasoned before the breading is applied, or seasonings may be added to the flour, bread crumbs or meal before the food is coated. Breaded foods are generally cooked by deep-frying or pan-frying. The breading makes a solid coating that seals during cooking and prevents the fat from coming in direct contact with the food, which would make it greasy.

Standard Breading Procedure

For breading meats, poultry, fish, shellfish or vegetables, a three-step process is typically used. Called the **standard breading procedure**, it gives foods a relatively thick, crisp coating.

1 Pat the food dry and dredge it in seasoned flour. The flour adds seasoning to the food, helps seal it and allows the egg wash to adhere.

2 Dip the floured food in an egg wash. The egg wash should contain whole eggs whisked together with approximately 1 tablespoon (15 milliliters) milk or water per egg. The egg wash allows the crumbs or meal to completely coat the item and form a tight seal.

3 Coat the food with bread crumbs, cracker crumbs or other dry meal. Shake off excess crumbs and place the breaded item in a pan. As additional breaded items are added to the pan, align them in a single layer; do not stack them or the breadings will get soggy and the foods will stick together.

4 To ensure that breading adheres after cooking, refrigerate breaded foods for at least 30 minutes before frying.

Product to   Flour   Egg wash   Bread crumbs   Pan to hold
be breaded   breaded product

Figure 9.4 Setup for the standard breading procedure.

Figure 9.4 illustrates the proper mise en place setup for the standard breading procedure. The key to efficient breading is using one hand for the liquid ingredients and the other hand for the dry ingredients. This prevents your fingers from becoming coated with layer after layer of breading. The following process will help you to bread foods more efficiently:

1 Assemble the mise en place as shown in Figure 9.4.

2 With your left hand, place the food to be breaded in the flour and coat it evenly. With the same hand, remove the floured item, shake off the excess flour and place it in the egg wash.

3 With your right hand, remove the item from the egg wash and place it in the bread crumbs or meal.

4 With your left hand, cover the item with crumbs or meal and press lightly to make sure the item is completely and evenly coated. Shake off the excess crumbs or meal and place the breaded food in the empty pan for finished product.

Battering

Batters, like breading, coat the food being cooked, giving it flavor and texture while keeping it moist and preventing it from becoming excessively greasy. Batters consist of a liquid, such as water, milk or beer, combined with a starch, such as flour or cornstarch. Many batters also contain baking powder or whipped egg whites to give them a light texture after frying. Two common batters are beer batter, which uses beer for leavening as well as for flavor and is illustrated in the recipe for Beer Battered Onion Rings (page 624), and tempura batter, which is used in Tempura Vegetables with Dipping Sauce (page 645). Items coated with a batter are cooked immediately, usually by deep-frying or pan-frying. Figure 9.5 shows the proper mise en place setup for the standard battering procedure.

> ⚠ **Safety Alert**
>
> *Batters and Breading*
>
> Batters and breading are time and temperature control for safety (TCS) foods when eggs or milk are used in their preparation. Make small batches of batter, then discard after each use. Store fresh batter at or below 41°F (5°C). Discard crumbs, flour and eggs after each use. To prevent cross-contamination when coating different foods, such as vegetables and poultry, use separate batter or breading for each product.

Procedure for Battering Foods

1 Prepare the batter.

2 Pat the food dry and dredge in flour if desired. (Chopped fruits, vegetables or other chopped ingredients being battered do not need to be dredged.)

3 Dip the item in the batter.

4 Place the battered item directly in the hot fat.

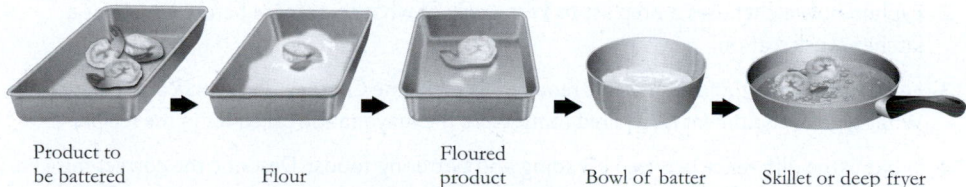

Product to   Flour   Floured   Bowl of batter   Skillet or deep fryer
be battered   product

Figure 9.5 Setup for the standard battering procedure.

Blanching and Parboiling

Some foods, especially vegetables, are **blanched** or **parboiled** before being used in a recipe. Items to be blanched or parboiled are immersed in a large quantity of a boiling or simmering liquid—oil or water—and partially cooked. This **parcooking** assists preparation

blanching very briefly and partially cooking a food in boiling water or hot fat; used to assist preparation, as part of a combination cooking method or to remove undesirable flavors

parboiling partially cooking a food in boiling or simmering liquid; similar to blanching but the cooking time is longer

parcooking partially cooking a food by any cooking method

shocking also called refreshing; the technique of quickly chilling blanched or parcooked foods in ice water to prevent further cooking and set colors

(e.g., it loosens peels from vegetables), removes undesirable flavors, softens firm foods, sets colors and shortens final cooking times. The only difference between blanching and parboiling is cooking time. Blanching is done quickly, usually only a few seconds. Parboiling lasts longer, usually several minutes. Foods that are blanched or parboiled in water (rather than fat) are often **shocked** or **refreshed** in ice water to halt the cooking process.

Procedure for Blanching and Parboiling

❶ Place the food in boiling water. Blanch or parboil as desired.

❷ Remove the food from the cooking liquid and submerge it in ice water to refresh.

Making an Ice Bath

Because of the risk of food-borne illness (see Chapter 2, Food Safety and Sanitation), it is important to cool hot foods quickly to a temperature below 41°F (5°C) before storing them in the refrigerator. An ice bath is an easy, efficient way to do so. An ice bath is also necessary for shocking or refreshing blanched or parcooked vegetables and for stopping the cooking of delicate mixtures such as custards.

An ice bath is equal parts ice cubes and cold water. The combination of ice and water chills foods more rapidly than a container of only ice. Adding a generous amount of salt to the ice bath will lower its temperature further as salt lowers the freezing point of water. The food being chilled will also cool faster if it is in a metal container, rather than one made of plastic or glass. The container of items to be chilled should be submerged into the ice bath so that the level of ingredients is at or below the level of liquid in the ice bath. Constant stirring speeds the cooling process.

Chilling Vanilla Custard Sauce in an ice bath.

QUESTIONS FOR DISCUSSION

1   Discuss how to create a prep list at the start of each day. Describe how the prep list can make work flow more smoothly.

2   Explain how a chef uses a prep list to keep track of what to prepare before service at a kitchen work station.

3   List the equipment and ingredients required to make the Chutney Chicken Salad on page 748. What type of equipment is required to measure the mayonnaise called for in the recipe?

4   What is the difference between breading and battering foods? Describe the correct mise en place for the standard breading procedure.

5   Discuss when it would be appropriate to use brine and when it would be appropriate to use a marinade when preparing meat for cooking.

6   Choose a dessert recipe from the baking chapters of this text and describe the proper mise en place for preparing that dish.

7   How can the concepts of mise en place be applied to activities outside the kitchen?

Principles of Cooking 10

conduction the transfer of heat (energy) from one item to another through direct contact

Cooking is the transfer of energy from a heat source to a food. The energy alters the food's molecular structure, changing its texture, flavor, aroma and appearance. But why is food cooked at all? The obvious answer is that cooking makes food taste better. Cooking also destroys undesirable microorganisms and makes foods easier to ingest and digest.

Understanding the ways in which heat is transferred—conduction, convection and radiation—helps you to cook food successfully. It is also helpful to understand what heat does to the proteins, sugars, starches, water and fats in foods.

To be a chef, you must master the cooking methods used to transfer heat: broiling, grilling, roasting, baking, barbecuing, smoking, sautéing, pan-frying, stir-frying, deep-frying, poaching, simmering, boiling, steaming, braising, stewing and cooking *sous vide*. Each method is used for many types of food, so you apply one or more of them every time you cook. The cooking method you select gives the finished product a specific texture, appearance, aroma and flavor. A thorough understanding of the basic procedures of each cooking method helps you produce consistent, high-quality products.

HEAT TRANSFER

Heat is a type of energy. When a substance gets hot, its molecules absorb energy. This causes the molecules to vibrate rapidly, expand and bounce off one another. As the molecules move, they collide with nearby molecules, transferring heat energy. The faster the molecules within a substance move, the higher its temperature. This is true whether the substance is air, water, an aluminum pot or a sirloin steak.

Heat energy may be transferred *to* foods via conduction, convection or radiation as shown in Figure 10.1. Heat then travels *through* foods by conduction. Only heat is transferred—cold is simply the absence of heat, so cold cannot be transferred from one substance to another.

Conduction

Conduction is the most straightforward means of heat transfer. It is the movement of heat from one item to another through direct contact. For example, when the flame of a gas burner touches the bottom of a sauté pan, heat is conducted to the pan. The metal of the pan then conducts heat to the surface of the food in the pan.

Some materials conduct heat better than others. Water is a better conductor of heat than air. This explains why a potato cooks much faster in boiling water than in an oven, and why you cannot place your hand in boiling water at a temperature of 212°F (100°C), but can place your hand, at least very briefly, into a 400°F (200°C) oven. Generally metals are good conductors (as discussed in Chapter 5, Tools and Equipment, copper and aluminum are the best conductors), and liquids and gases are poor conductors.

Conduction is a relatively slow method of heat transfer because physical contact must occur to transfer energy from one molecule to adjacent molecules. Consider what happens when a metal spoon is placed in a pot of simmering soup. At first the spoon handle remains cool. Gradually, however, heat travels up the handle, making it warmer and warmer, until it becomes too hot to touch.

Conduction is important in all cooking methods because it is responsible for the movement of heat from the surface of a food to its interior. As the molecules near the food's exterior gather energy, they move more and more rapidly. As they move, they conduct heat to the molecules nearby, transferring heat through the food (from the exterior of the item to the interior).

Figure 10.1 Arrows indicate heat patterns when using various heating methods (clockwise from top left): conduction to the pan from a heated gas burner; conduction to the pan from a heated gas burner and convection within a heated liquid; radiation from microwaves; radiation from a heated broiler.

In conventional heating methods (nonmicrowave), food cooks from the surface inward so that layers of molecules heat in succession. This produces a range of temperatures within the food, which means that the outside may brown and form a crust long before the interior is noticeably warmer. That is why a steak can be fully cooked on the outside but still rare on the inside.

Convection

Convection refers to the transfer of heat through a fluid, which may be a liquid or gas. Convection is actually a combination of conduction and circulation of energy. During convection, the molecules in a fluid (whether air, water or fat) move from a warmer area to a cooler one. There are two types of convection: natural and mechanical.

Natural convection occurs because of the tendency of warm liquids and gases to rise while cooler ones fall. This tendency causes a constant natural circulation of heat. For example, when a pot of stock is placed over a gas burner, the molecules at the bottom of the pot are warmed. These molecules rise while cooler, heavier molecules sink. Upon reaching the pot's bottom, the cooler molecules are warmed and begin to rise in turn. Meanwhile the molecules that rose to the top are cool enough to sink again. This ongoing cycle creates currents within the stock, and these currents distribute the heat throughout the stock.

Mechanical convection relies on fans or stirring to circulate heat more quickly and evenly. This explains why foods heat faster and more evenly when stirred. Convection ovens are equipped with fans to increase the circulation of air currents, thus speeding up the cooking process. But even conventional ovens (i.e., not convection ovens) rely on the natural circulation patterns of heated air to transfer heat energy.

Radiation

Unlike conduction and convection, **radiation** does not require physical contact between the heat source and the food being cooked. Instead energy is transferred by

convection the transfer of heat (energy) through a fluid (such as water or air) by natural or mechanical circulation

radiation the transfer of heat (energy) by electromagnetic waves of energy or light spreading out from a central source, such as a ceramic toaster element or a magnetron in a microwave oven electromagnetic waves of energy or light striking the food. Two kinds of radiant heat are used in the kitchen: infrared and microwave.

Infrared cooking uses an electric or ceramic element heated to such a high temperature that it gives off waves of radiant heat that cook the food. Radiant heat waves travel at the speed of light in any direction (unlike convection heat, which only rises) until they are absorbed by a food. Infrared cooking is commonly used with toasters and broilers. The glowing coals of a fire are another example of radiant heat.

Microwave cooking relies on radiation that is generated by a special oven. The radiation penetrates the food, where it agitates the water molecules contained within the food, creating friction and heat. This energy then spreads throughout the food by conduction (and by convection in liquids). Microwave cooking is much faster than other methods because energy penetrates the food up to a depth of several millimeters, setting all water molecules in the food in motion at the same time. Less energy is wasted in microwave cooking because the oven space itself is not heated. Instead heat is generated quickly and uniformly throughout the food. Microwave cooking does not brown foods and often gives meats a dry, mushy texture, making microwave ovens unacceptable as a sole replacement for traditional ovens. Microwave ovens are useful, however, for melting fats or chocolate and for quickly reheating foods.

Because microwave radiation affects only water molecules, a completely waterless material (such as a plate) does not get hot in a microwave. Any warmth felt in a plate used for microwaving food results from heat being conducted from the food to the plate.

Microwave cooking requires the use of certain types of utensils, usually heat-resistant glass or microwavable paper or plastic. But even heat-resistant glass can shatter in a microwave and is not recommended for professional use. Most of the aluminum and stainless steel utensils common in professional kitchens cannot be used in microwave ovens because metal deflects the microwave radiation, which can damage the oven.

THE EFFECTS OF HEAT

Foods are composed of proteins, carbohydrates (starches and sugars), water and fats, plus small amounts of minerals and vitamins. Changes in the shape, texture, color and flavor of foods occurs when heat is applied to each of these nutrients. See Table 10.1. The rate at which a substance changes when cooled or heated varies according to its composition. By understanding these changes and learning to control them, you will be able to prepare foods with the characteristics desired.

Proteins Coagulate

coagulation the irreversible transformation of proteins from a liquid or semiliquid state to a solid state

The heating of protein during cooking changes its structure, causing it to **coagulate** (change from a semiliquid state to a solid state). **Proteins** are large, complex molecules found in every living cell, plant as well as animal. They are formed from amino

TEMPERATURES AT WHICH PHYSICAL CHANGES TAKE PLACE IN FOODS	TABLE 10.1
TEMPERATURE	**PHYSICAL CHANGE**
250°F (121°C)	Sugars begin to brown. Products darken.
212°F (100°C)	Water boils and evaporates.
150°F (65°C)	Starches begin to gelatinize. Products thicken.
140°F (60°C)	Proteins begin to coagulate. Products firm.
70°F (21°C)	Fats begin to melt.
32°F (0°C)	Water freezes and solidifies.

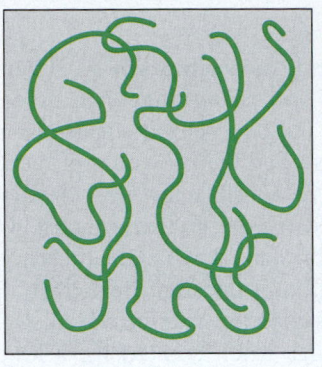

Figure 10.2 Protein coagulation, from left: loosely folded protein chain, denatured protein and coagulated protein.

acids that are chemically bonded into long, loosely folded chains. In the presence of heat, the protein chains unfold (or denature). As they are heated, the protein chains then rebond and solidify into a solid mass. In other words, as proteins cook, they lose moisture, shrink and become firm. See Figure 10.2. Common examples of protein coagulation are the firming of meat fibers during cooking, egg whites changing from a clear liquid to a white solid when heated and the setting of the structure of wheat proteins in bread during baking. The process of coagulation begins as proteins are heated to 140°F (60°C). Most proteins complete coagulation at 160–185°F (71–85°C). When heated for too long or above 185°F (85°C), most proteins dry out and toughen. Proteins also denature in the presence of an acid or salt. When an acid such as citrus juice, vinegar or wine is added to proteins as in a marinade or cooking liquid, it helps to tenderize them.

Starches Gelatinize

Gelatinization is the term for the cooking of starches. Starches are complex carbohydrates present in plants and grains such as potatoes, wheat, rice and corn. When a mixture of starch and liquid is heated, remarkable changes occur. The starch granules absorb water, causing them to swell, soften and clarify (become slightly clear). The liquid visibly thickens because of the water being absorbed into the starch granules and the granules themselves swell and occupy more space.

Gelatinization occurs gradually over a range of temperatures—150–212°F (66–100°C)—depending on the type of starch. Starch gelatinization affects not only sauces or liquids to which starches are added for the express purpose of thickening, but also any mixture of starch and liquid that is heated. For example, the flour (a starch) in cake batter gelatinizes by absorbing the water from eggs, milk or other ingredients as the batter bakes. This causes part of the firming and drying associated with baked goods. See Figure 10.3. Gelatinization of starch also takes place when beans or pasta absorb water, swell and soften during cooking.

gelatinization the process by which starch granules are cooked; they absorb moisture when placed in a liquid and heated; as the moisture is absorbed, the product swells, softens and clarifies slightly

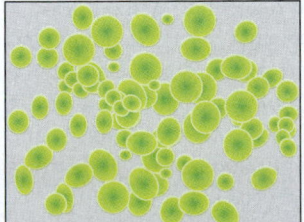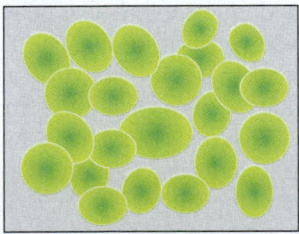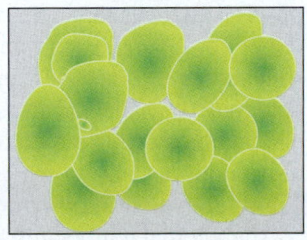

Figure 10.3 Gelatinization of starch, from left: uncooked starch granules floating in a liquid; starch beginning to swell when heated; fully gelatinized starches binding into a solid mass.

caramelization the process of cooking sugars; the browning of sugar enhances the flavor and appearance of foods

Maillard reaction the process whereby sugar breaks down in the presence of protein

Enzymatic Browning

A different type of browning occurs when some fruits and vegetables are cut or bruised. A molecular reaction between enzymes and natural acids (antioxidants) takes place, releasing a dark pigment called melanin. Known as enzymatic browning, this molecular reaction is undesirable in a sliced apple or potato, but it is desirable for creating the flavor in black tea. To prevent it from occurring, many sliced fruits or vegetables are tossed with lemon juice or soaked in acidulated water after cutting.

Sugars Caramelize

The process of cooking sugars is **caramelization**. As sugars cook, they gradually darken from golden to deep brown and change flavor. Caramelized sugar is used in many sauces, candies and desserts. But caramelized sugars are also partly responsible for the flavor and color of bread crusts and the browning of meats and vegetables. In fact, the process of caramelization is responsible for most flavors we associate with cooking. The **Maillard reaction**, named for the French scientist who discovered this principle, describes the process of sugar breaking down in the presence of protein. Maillard browning occurs when proteins and carbohydrates are heated to 250°F (121°C) and above. The product darkens and develops complex, meaty and baked flavors. (Higher alkaline foods and certain foods such as eggs when cooked for a long period of time will brown at lower temperatures.) Some of the aromas and flavors of roasted nuts, chocolate and coffee derive from Maillard browning. When we talk about browning, we are referring to this process of caramelization.

Sucrose (common table sugar) begins to decompose and brown starting at 290°F (143°C) or at higher temperatures when heated more quickly. The naturally occurring sugars in other foods, such as maltose, lactose and fructose, also caramelize, but at varying temperatures. Because high temperatures are required for browning (i.e., caramelizing), most foods will brown only on the outside and only through the application of dry heat. Foods cooked with dry-heat methods, including those using fats, reach the high temperatures at which browning occurs. Because water cannot be heated above 212°F (100°C), foods cooked with moist-heat methods do not get hot enough to caramelize.

Water Evaporates

All foods contain some water. Some foods, especially eggs, milk and leafy vegetables, are almost entirely water. As much as 75 percent of raw meat is water. As the internal temperature of a food increases, water molecules move faster and faster until the water turns into a gas (steam) and vaporizes. This **evaporation** of water is responsible for the drying of foods during cooking.

Fats Melt

Fat is an energy source for the plant or animal in which it is stored. Fats are smooth, greasy substances that do not dissolve in water. Their texture varies from very firm to liquid. Oils are simply fats that remain liquid at room temperature. Fats **melt** when heated; that is, they gradually soften, then liquefy. Butter begins to melt at temperatures as low as 70°F (21°C). Fats will not evaporate. Most fats can be heated to very high temperatures without burning, so they can be used as a dry-heat cooking medium to fry or brown (caramelize) foods.

DETERMINING DONENESS

When heated, foods undergo a complex set of chemical and physical reactions that result in improved flavor, aroma, texture and digestibility. Knowing when a food is cooked appropriately and ready to serve is determined by many factors. Observing the physical changes that take place during cooking will help you determine when a food is done. For example, you may use your sense of touch to feel that a baked potato has softened or a fork to test the tenderness of a piece of stewed meat. Doneness may be determined by specific visual clues such as clear juices running from poultry. Fish firms, becoming opaque, and flakes. The surface of a loaf of bread develops a crisp crust and turns an appealing brown color from caramelization. With experience, you will learn to control the application of heat and the length of time it takes to cook foods.

The internal temperature of food is another way to gauge doneness. Some foods, particularly animal proteins cooked using dry-heat cooking methods must be cooked to specific internal temperatures to ensure food safety. See Chapter 2, Food Safety and Sanitation. Chicken, for example should be cooked to 165°F (74°C) to destroy pathogenic bacteria. Internal temperature also correlates to desirable flavor characteristics in meats such as grilled steak or lamb. The difference between a medium rare lamb chop and a well done one is only 25°F (14°C), but that difference has a huge impact on the texture and flavor of the finished dish.

The speed of heat transfer effects the time it takes for food to reach the desired degree of doneness. Carrots cooked in boiling water will be tender in a few minutes. They may take two or three times longer to become tender when roasted in an oven, however, because water conducts heat more efficiently than air. Boiled carrots do not have the same dry, crisp exterior as roasted carrots, which is a factor to consider when choosing cooking methods.

The equipment used to prepare food, from the size and metal of a sauce pan to the type of oven, also affects cooking time. As described in Chapter 5, Tools and Equipment, a copper pan heats more quickly than an aluminum one. Variables in cookware from different manufacturers will also affect cooking efficiency and heat transfer. The size and temperature of the food itself affect the speed with which it cooks. A three-pound chicken cooks more quickly than a five-pound one. Food at room temperature cooks more quickly than chilled items.

Foods continue to cook after they are removed from a heat source. This **carryover cooking** is accomplished by the residual heat remaining in the food. When applying any cooking method, cook the foods to the appropriate temperature but keep in mind that the internal temperature of the food may rise 5–25 degrees after cooking, depending on the size of the item and the temperature used. Because food absorbs more heat when cooked at a higher temperature, carryover cooking is greater in an item cooked at 450°F (232°C) than one cooked at 325°F (162°C).

> **carryover cooking** the cooking that continues to occur after a food is removed from a heat source; it is caused by the residual heat remaining in the food

Timing alone is insufficient for determine doneness. In the sections that follow and in subsequent chapters, we include doneness characteristics to help you determine by sight, smell and touch when a food is correctly cooked.

INTRODUCTION TO COOKING METHODS

Foods can be cooked in air, fat, water or steam, which are collectively known as **cooking media**. There are two general types of cooking methods: dry heat and moist heat. See Table 10.2.

Dry-heat cooking methods use air or fat. They are broiling, grilling, roasting and baking, barbecuing and smoking, sautéing, pan-frying, stir-frying and deep-frying. Foods cooked using dry-heat cooking methods have a rich flavor caused by the browning that occurs when moisture on the surface of the food evaporates and sugars caramelize.

Moist-heat cooking methods use water or steam. They are poaching, simmering, boiling, steaming and cooking *sous vide*. Moist-heat cooking methods tenderize and emphasize the natural flavors of food.

Other cooking methods employ a combination of dry- and moist-heat cooking methods. The two most significant **combination cooking methods** are braising and stewing. A third combination cooking method, called **sous vide**, resembles both braising and poaching.

> **sous vide** a cooking technique that uses low temperature, moist-heat cooking methods similar to braising or poaching; the food item may be seared or browned before service to add color and flavor from caramelization

Each cooking method can be applied to a wide variety of foods—meats, fish, fruits, vegetables and even pastries. In the following material, we describe and show each of the cooking methods. Detailed procedures and recipes applying these methods to specific foods are found in later chapters.

DRY-HEAT COOKING METHODS

Cooking by dry heat involves applying heat either directly, by subjecting the food to the heat of a flame, or indirectly, by surrounding the food with heated air or heated fat. Even though fat is used in some of these techniques, they are dry-heat cooking techniques because liquid fat does not contain water. Fat can be used to cook at higher temperatures than water-based liquids, resulting in differences in the final product's taste, color and texture.

COOKING METHODS   TABLE 10.2

METHOD	MEDIUM	TECHNIQUE	EQUIPMENT	USE
Dry-Heat Cooking Methods				
Broiling	Air	Food is placed on a pre-heated grate or heatproof platter under an overhead radiant heat source.	Overhead broiler or salamander	Quick browning, melting and cooking.
Grilling	Air	Food is placed on a grill over heat produced by electricity, gas, charcoal or wood.	Electric, gas, charcoal or wood-burning grill	Achieving crusty exterior, grill marks and aromatic flavors.
Roasting	Air	Food is placed in a closed chamber filled with hot dry air.	Oven	Cooking and caramelizing meats, poultry and vegetables.
Baking	Air	Food is placed in a closed chamber filled with hot dry air.	Oven	Cooking and caramelizing bread, fish, starches and pastry items.
Barbecuing	Air	Food is placed in an oven, a covered grill or semi-enclosed chamber (pit) and cooked over a hardwood fire at low temperatures.	Oven, covered grill or pit	Cooking food while adding smoked flavor.
Smoking	Air	Food is placed in a closed chamber filled with hot dry air and smoke to cook at low temperatures.	Smoker oven	Smoking adds flavor more quickly than barbecuing.
Sautéing	Fat	Small pieces of food are browned and cooked in a small amount of fat over moderate to high heat.	Sauté pan on stove top	Quickly browning and cooking tender cuts of meat, poultry, fish, fruit and vegetables over high heat.
Stir-frying	Fat	Small pieces of food are browned and cooked in a moderate amount of fat while tossing over high heat.	Wok on stove top	Quickly browning and cooking tender cuts of meat, poultry, fish and vegetables.
Pan-frying	Fat	Food is partially submerged in hot fat.	Sauté pan on stove top, tilting skillet	Forming a caramelized crust on foods at lower temperatures than sautéing.
Deep-frying	Fat	Food is fully submerged in hot fat; batter or breading is generally used.	Deep-fat fryer	Forming a caramelized crust on foods.
Moist-Heat Cooking Methods				
Poaching	Water, stock, wine or other liquid	Food is submerged in a water-based liquid kept at 160–180°F (71–82°C).	Stove top, oven, steam kettle, tilting skillet, thermal bath	For delicate foods; flavor of liquid affects finished product.
Simmering	Water, stock, wine or other liquid	Food is submerged in a water-based liquid kept at 185–205°F (85–96°C).	Stove top, steam kettle, tilting skillet, thermal bath	For poultry, beef, fish, pork, fruit, grains and vegetables; flavor of liquid affects finished product.
Boiling	Water or other liquid	Food is submerged in a water-based liquid kept at a full boil 212°F (100°C).	Stove top, steam kettle, tilting skillet	For starchy foods, such as pasta and potatoes; flavor of liquid affects finished product.
Steaming	Steam	Food is surrounded and cooked by steam.	Stove top, convection steamer	For delicate foods and vegetables; helps retain nutrients.
Combination Cooking Methods				
Braising	Fat, then liquid	Large pieces of food are browned in fat; liquid is added, then food is covered and cooked at low heat.	Stove top, oven, tilting skillet	Tenderizing tough cuts of meat or poultry or softening fruit and vegetables after surface browning.
Stewing	Fat, then liquid	Small pieces of food are browned in fat; liquid is added, then food is covered and simmered.	Stove top, oven, tilting skillet, thermal bath	Tenderizing tough cuts of meat, poultry or fish, fruit and vegetables; liquid becomes sauce.
Sous vide	Liquid, then air or fat	Vacuum-sealed pouch of seasoned food is submerged in temperature-controlled water bath.	Chamber vacuum machine, thermal bath or water oven	Cooking at a precise, steady temperature for tenderness and uniformity without caramelization. Food may be browned after cooking.

Broiling

Broiling uses infrared radiant heat from an overhead source such as an overhead broiler or salamander to cook foods. The temperature at the heat source can be as high as 2000°F (1093°C). The food to be broiled is placed on a preheated metal grate. Radiant heat from overhead cooks the food, while the hot grate below creates attractive crosshatch marks. Broiled shrimp, for example, displays the crosshatch marks from the broiler on the **presentation side**, the surface that faces up when the plate is served to the guest.

Delicate foods that may be damaged by being placed directly on a metal grate or foods on which crosshatch marks are not desirable may be placed on a preheated heatproof platter and then placed under the broiler. For example, fillets of tender fish such as flounder, which could fall apart during cooking, are broiled on a heatproof platter. Only relatively firm and dry fruits and vegetables are suitable for broiling. Cooking takes place through indirect heat from the preheated platter as well as by direct heat from the broiler's overhead heat source. Broiling is considered a healthy cooking method when used to prepare leans cuts of meat, poultry or fish, fruits and vegetables as long as little or no fat is added.

BASIC PROCEDURE

Equipment: Overhead broiler or salamander
Method: Uses high temperatures and radiant heat from overhead source. Place food on a pre-heated grate or heatproof platter.
Use: Quick browning, melting and cooking.

Procedure for Broiling Foods

1   Heat the overhead broiler or salamander to its highest setting.

2   If necessary, use a wire brush to remove any charred or burnt particles stuck to the broiler grate. The grate can be wiped with a lightly oiled towel to remove any remaining particles and to help season it.

3   Cut, trim or otherwise prepare the food to be broiled. (Foods should be cut to an even thickness. Thicker pieces of food take longer to cook.) Marinate, rub or season food, as desired. Many foods can be brushed lightly with oil to keep them from sticking to the grate.

4   Pull out the broiler grate and place the food on it, presentation side down. Slide the grate back under the broiler. If necessary, use a chef's fork or tongs to turn or flip the item without piercing its surface.

5   Cook the food to the desired degree of doneness while developing the proper surface color. To do so, adjust the position of the item on the broiler grate, or adjust the distance between the grate and heat source. If practical, rotate the food 90 degrees to produce attractive crosshatch marks. Doneness is often determined by touch, internal temperature or specific visual cues (e.g., clear juices running from poultry).

❶ Preheat and clean the broiler grate. Place the food on the hot grate presentation side down. Slide the grate back under the broiler and cook until the food develops the proper color where it touches the grate.

❷ Pull the grate out to turn the food over as necessary in order to cook it evenly. Note the handle visible on the right, which can be used to adjust the distance between the food and the heat source. Smaller pieces of food can often be cooked closer to the source of heat.

❸ Remove the cooked item from the broiler grate.

Grilling

BASIC PROCEDURE

Equipment: Electric, gas, charcoal or wood-burning grill

Method: Uses radiant heat generated below the food

Use: Achieving crusty exterior, grill marks and aromatic flavors.

Although similar to broiling, grilling uses a heat source located below the cooking surface. Heat is transferred to the food through infrared radiant heat and conduction between the food and the grill rack itself. Grills may be electric or gas, or they can burn wood or charcoal. (Solid metal pans with ridged surfaces may also be used to pan-grill foods.) Grilled foods are characterized by their crusty exterior and aromatic flavors, and are often identified by crosshatch markings on the presentation side. With a gas or electric grill, the cooking temperature is controlled by adjusting a dial. The flame and heat decrease or increase almost immediately when the dial is turned. With a charcoal or wood-burning grill, you must control the fire itself to change the cooking temperature. There is a delay in the time it takes for the fire to die down (or build up) when cooking over a live fire. Grilling is considered a healthy cooking method when used to prepare leans cuts of meat, poultry or fish and vegetables if little or no fat is added. **Griddling** is a dry heat cooking method closely related to grilling in which foods are cooked on the heated surface of a flat solid metal griddle (Sp. *plancha*). Techniques and procedures for griddling are discussed further in Chapter 21, Eggs and Breakfast.

Procedure for Grilling Foods

1 Heat the grill.

2 If necessary, use a wire brush to remove any charred or burnt particles stuck to the grill grate. The grate can be wiped with a lightly oiled towel to remove any remaining particles and to help season it.

3 Cut, trim or otherwise prepare the food to be grilled. Marinate, rub or season it, as desired. Many foods can be brushed lightly with oil to keep them from sticking to the grate.

4 Place the food on the grill, presentation side down. If practical, rotate the food 90 degrees to produce the attractive crosshatch marks associated with grilling. Then use a fork or tongs to turn or flip the item without piercing its surface.

5 Cook the food to the desired degree of doneness while developing the proper surface color. To do so, adjust the position of the item on the grill, or adjust the distance between the grate and heat source. Doneness is often determined by touch, internal temperature or specific visual cues (e.g., clear juices running from poultry).

❶ Decide which side of the grilled food will be presented face up to the customer. Place the food on the hot grill with this side facing down. If the item is oblong, place it at a 45-degree angle to the bars on the cooking grate. Cook long enough for the food to develop dark charred lines where it touches the grate.

❷ Rotate the food 90 degrees and allow it to cook long enough for the grates to char it to the same extent as in Step 1.

❸ Turn the food over and finish cooking it. It is usually unnecessary to create the cross-hatch markings on the reverse side because the customer will not see this side.

Roasting and Baking

During roasting and baking, a food is surrounded with dry, heated air in a closed environment such as an oven. The term *roasting* is usually applied to meats, poultry and vegetables whereas *baking* applies to fish, fruits, starches, breads and pastry items. Heat is transferred by convection to the food's surface and then penetrates the food by conduction. The surface dehydrates and the food browns from caramelization, completing the cooking process.

During roasting, foods may be **basted** or moistened with melted fat, pan drippings, wine or other liquids to improve the surface appearance and texture. Lean meats, such as chickens and turkeys, which may dry out, are usually basted while they roast. Drippings that collect in the pan during roasting are the basis for gravy and sauces that are served with the food and are discussed in Chapter 11, Stocks and Sauces. Roasting and baking are considered healthy cooking methods when used to prepare lean cuts of meat, poultry or fish and vegetables if little or no fat is added.

BASIC PROCEDURE

Equipment: Oven
Method: Food is placed in a closed chamber filled with hot dry air.
Use: Cooking and caramelizing meats, poultry, vegetables, bread, fish, starches and pastry items.

baste to moisten foods during cooking (usually grilling, broiling or roasting) with melted fat, pan drippings, a sauce or other liquids to prevent drying and to add flavor

Procedure for Roasting or Baking Foods

1 Preheat the oven.

2 Cut, trim or otherwise prepare the food to be roasted or baked. Marinate or season as desired. Brush with oil or butter, as appropriate.

3 Place the food on a rack or directly in a roasting pan or baking dish.

4 Roast the food, generally uncovered, at the desired temperature. Baste as necessary.

5 Cook to the desired internal temperature or doneness, remembering that many foods will undergo carryover cooking after they are removed from the oven.

6 Allow the food to **rest** for anywhere from 10 to 30 minutes before carving or serving to allow the internal juices to redistribute themselves.

❶ Season the item to be roasted, arrange it in an uncovered roasting pan and place it in a preheated oven.

❷ Use a thermometer to check the internal temperature of the item being roasted.

Cooking with Fire

Grilling over a charcoal or wood fire requires experience building and tending a live fire and its embers. The radiant heat given off by glowing embers cooks the food, not the flames. Food burns quickly when in contact with flames. Oxygen in the air ignites causing the fire to burn. To lower the cooking temperature, decrease the amount of available oxygen. Controlling the flow of air to the heat source controls the fire. To burn fast and hot, increase the air flow under the charcoal or wood. Dampening or reducing the air flow reduces the flame creating the kind of steady heat used to prepare properly grilled items. Chefs often set a grill or build a fire so that different sections will be at different temperatures. They can then move foods from a hotter to a cooler section as needed to control the cooking temperature. On some equipment, temperature is adjusted by opening or closing a vent near the base of the fire. You can also use tongs to reposition burning coals or wood to improve air circulation.

When cooking over a gas, electric or charcoal grill, juice and fat from the meat drips onto the heat source, burning and sending flavor compounds into the smoke that surrounds the food. When wood is used, aroma molecules in the wood also contribute unique flavors to the smoke. Specific woods such as mesquite, hickory or vine clippings will create special flavors. You can add wood flavor notes to grilled foods by tossing wood chips into a charcoal fire. Some electric and gas grills allow wood or wood chips to be added for flavor. Electric smoker boxes can also be used to burn wood chips in order to add smoke to a conventional oven.

Barbecuing and Smoking

Barbecue

BASIC PROCEDURE

Equipment: Oven, covered grill or pit

Method: Food is placed in a closed or semi-enclosed chamber (pit) and cooked over a hardwood fire at low temperatures.

Use: Cooking food while adding smoked flavor.

Barbecue and smoking are dry-heat cooking methods related to baking or roasting. In traditional barbecue, large, usually tough, cuts of meat are cooked by natural convection in a semi-enclosed oven (called a pit) with the smoke from a hardwood fire at low temperatures, generally below 225°F (107°C). True barbecue is a slow process, requiring many hours of low temperature heat and smoke to tenderize tough cuts or whole carcasses. Doneness is not determined by internal temperature, but by tenderness and feel. The meat should be fall-off-the-bone tender. In the case of pork, the meat is torn or shredded rather than sliced when served.

Although many grilled foods are referred to as "barbecue," real barbecue is never produced over gas or electric grills. Hardwood charcoal and embers are required for the long, slow burn necessary. Because authentic barbecue relies on fatty cuts of meat and poultry, it is not usually considered a healthy cooking method. Techniques and procedures for barbecue cooking are discussed further in Chapter 13, Principles of Meat Cookery.

Smoking

BASIC PROCEDURE

Equipment: Smoker oven, wood chip smoker inserted in a traditional oven

Method: Food is placed in a closed chamber filled with hot dry air and smoke and cooked at low temperatures.

Use: Cooking meats, poultry or fish while adding smoked flavor.

Smoking is a dry-heat cooking method used to cook, color and flavor foods for immediate service or to preserve foods for later use. When smoking, heat is transferred by convection to the food's surface and then penetrates the food by conduction. Smoking involves burning wood or wood chips to create smoke vapors, which contain compounds that help preserve and flavor foods. Smokey flavors can also be added to uncooked items such as cheese and nuts by exposing them to smoke without heat. Techniques and procedures for hot and cold smoking are discussed further in Chapter 28, Charcuterie.

Sautéing

BASIC PROCEDURE

Equipment: Sauté pan on stove top

Method: Heat small amount of fat over moderate to high heat; add item to be cooked; turn or toss to develop proper browning.

Use: Quickly browning and cooking tender cuts of meat, poultry, fish, fruit and vegetables over high heat.

Sautéing is a dry-heat cooking method that uses conduction to transfer heat from a hot sauté pan to food. Heat then penetrates the food through conduction. High temperatures are used to sauté, and the foods are usually cut thinly or into small pieces to promote even cooking.

To sauté foods properly, begin by heating a sauté pan on the stove top, then add a small amount of fat. The fat should just cover the bottom of the pan. Heat the fat to the point just before it begins to smoke. The food to be cooked should be as dry as possible when it is added to the pan to promote browning and to prevent excessive spattering. Remove excess surface moisture from food using clean paper towels. Moist foods such as filets of fish or pieces of chicken are dredged in flour before sautéing.

Place the food in the pan in a single layer. (The pan should be just large enough to hold the food in a single layer; a pan that is too large may cause the fat to burn.) Adjust the heat so that the food cooks thoroughly; it should not be so hot that the outside of the food burns before the inside is cooked. The pan should be hot enough so that any surface moisture on the food evaporates quickly. The food should be turned or tossed periodically to develop the proper color. Larger items should be turned using a chef's fork or tongs that won't pierce the surface. Smaller items can be turned by shaking the sauté pan and using the pan's sloped sides to flip items back on top of themselves. When tossing sautéed foods, keep the pan in contact with the heat source as much as possible to prevent it from cooling. Sautéing sometimes includes the preparation of a sauce directly in the pan after the main item has been removed. See Chapter 11, Stocks and Sauces.

When a small amount of fat is used as the cooking medium, sautéing can be a healthy way to prepare lean cuts of meat, poultry and fish and vegetables. Using non-stick or well-seasoned cast iron cookware to sauté foods reduces the need for added fat.

Sweating is related to sautéing. It is used to cook food in a pan (usually covered), without browning, over low heat until the item softens and releases moisture. Sweating allows the food to release its flavor more quickly when cooked with other foods. Diced vegetables such as carrots, celery, mushrooms or onions are often sweated before they are browned or added to soups and stews for further cooking.

Procedure for Sautéing Foods

1 Cut, pound or otherwise prepare the food to be sautéed. Season it and dredge it in flour, if desired.

2 Heat a sauté pan and add enough fat (typically oil or clarified butter) to just cover the pan's bottom.

3 Add the food to the sauté pan in a single layer, presentation side down. Do not crowd the pan.

4 Adjust the temperature so that the food's exterior browns properly without burning and the interior cooks. The heat should be high enough to complete the cooking process before the food begins to stew in its own juices.

5 Turn or toss the food as needed. Avoid burns by not splashing hot fat.

6 Cook until done. Doneness is usually determined by timing or touch.

❶ Heat a sauté pan and then heat a small amount of fat in the sauté pan before adding the food.

❷ The sloped edge of the sauté pan can be used to toss the food.

❸ Items being sautéed should be cooked quickly.

Stir-Frying

Stir-frying is an Asian cooking technique that is a variation of sautéing. A wok is used instead of a sauté pan; the curved sides and rounded bottom of the wok diffuse heat efficiently and facilitate tossing and stirring. When stir-frying, the heat is kept at a constant high temperature. The wok must be heated until it appears to smoke. When the wok is properly heated, a few drops of water will evaporate within a few seconds when added to the pan. The fats used for stir-frying must have a high smoke point, such as peanut oil. The foods for stir-frying, are usually cut thinly or into small pieces to promote even cooking. When different foods are cooked together, such as shredded carrots, cabbage and snow peas, those that require the most cooking are added first. The ingredients must be dry before adding them to the pan. As when sautéing, a sauce is often made in the pan when stir-frying foods. Use a flat metal spatula to move the food up the sides of the pan before adding the sauce ingredients then stir and toss the foods into the sauce.

Stir-frying often requires a significant amount of fat. When a small amount of fat is used to stir-fry lean meats, poultry and fish or vegetables, stir-frying is considered a healthy cooking technique.

Procedure for Stir-Frying

1 Cut the food to be stir-fried into pieces as called for in the recipe.

2 Heat a wok over high heat until it is so hot that a few drops of water will evaporate within a few second when added to the pan.

3 Add enough fat (typically oil) to just cover the pan's bottom. Carefully swirl the fat around the wok.

4 Add any aromatics to the pan and fry, tossing the ingredients in the oil, to release their aromas for approximately 15–30 seconds.

5 Add the main ingredients; those requiring the longest cooking first followed by those that require less time. Cook, tossing the food with a metal spatula continuously. The constant motion keeps the foods from burning.

6 Cook until done. Doneness is usually determined by timing or touch.

7 Add sauce ingredients and thickeners. Cook while stirring until the sauce thickens. Serve immediately.

① Heat a wok over high heat. Add fat and stir so that the fat coats the bottom and halfway up the sides of the pan. Add items to the pan and cook while constantly stirring and tossing the food against the sides of the wok.

② When the items being stir fried are tender, add sauce ingredients, cooking until thickened.

Pan-Frying

Pan-frying shares characteristics with both sautéing and deep-frying. It is a dry-heat cooking method in which heat is transferred by conduction from the pan to the food, using a moderate amount of fat (i.e., more than sautéing; less than deep-frying). Heat is also transferred to the food from the hot fat by convection. Foods to be pan-fried, such as slices of eggplant or pieces of bone-in chicken, are usually coated in breading. This forms a seal that keeps the food moist and prevents the hot fat from penetrating the food and causing it to become greasy. (Breading procedures are explained in Chapter 9, Mise en Place.)

To pan-fry foods properly, first heat the fat in a sauté pan. Use enough fat so that when the food to be cooked is added, the fat comes one-third to halfway up the item being cooked. The fat should be at a temperature somewhat lower than that used for sautéing; it should not smoke but should be hot enough so that when the food is added it crackles and spatters from the rapid vaporization of moisture. If the temperature is too low, the food will absorb excessive amounts of fat; if it is too high, the food will burn on the outside before the interior is fully cooked. When the food is properly browned on one side, use a fork or tongs to turn it without piercing. Always turn the food away from you to prevent being burned by any fat that may splash. When the food is fully cooked, remove it from the pan, drain it on absorbent paper and serve it immediately. Pan-frying adds a significant amount of fat to foods. Healthy alternatives to pan-frying include roasting and oven-frying.

BASIC PROCEDURE

Equipment: Sauté pan on stove top, tilting skillet

Method: Food is cooked partially submerged in hot fat.

Use: Cooking temperatures below sautéing form a caramelized crust on foods.

Procedure for Pan-Frying Foods

1 Cut, pound or otherwise prepare the food to be pan-fried; then bread, batter or flour it as desired.

2 Heat a moderate amount of fat or oil in a heavy pan—usually enough to cover the item one-third to halfway up its sides.

3 Add the food to the pan, being careful not to splash the hot fat.

4 Fry the food on one side until brown. Using tongs, turn and brown the other side. Generally pan-fried foods are fully cooked when they are well browned on both sides.

5 Remove the food from the pan and drain it on absorbent paper before serving.

① Use tongs to carefully place the item being pan-fried into a moderate amount of hot oil, taking care not to get splashed by the hot fat in the pan.

② Fry the food on one side until browned. Turn the item to brown the other side.

③ When the food is browned on both sides, remove it from the pan. Drain the cooked item on absorbent paper.

Pan-basting by spooning hot fat over food while it sautés.

BASIC PROCEDURE

Equipment: Deep-fat fryer
Method: Food is cooked fully submerged in hot fat; batter or breading is generally used.
Use: Forming a caramelized crust on foods.

recovery time the length of time it takes a cooking medium such as fat or water to return to the desired cooking temperature after food is submerged in it

Pan-basting is a variation of pan-frying and sautéing. Portions of meat, poultry or fish are cooked in a generous amount of butter, oil or a combination. Fresh herbs and spices may be added to the melted fat for flavor. Once the portion of food is seared, hot butter from the pan is spooned over it. Pan-basting, although labor intensive, enhances the appearance, flavor and surface texture of foods cooked in this manner. This technique is also known as butter-basting. Like pan-frying, pan-basting adds a significant amount of fat to foods.

Deep-Frying

Deep-frying is a dry-heat cooking method that uses conduction and convection to transfer heat to food submerged in hot fat. Although conceptually similar to boiling, deep-frying is not a moist-heat cooking method because liquid fat contains no water. A key difference between boiling and deep-frying is the temperature of the cooking medium. The boiling point, 212°F (100°C), is the hottest temperature at which food can be cooked in water. At this temperature, most foods require a long cooking period and surface sugars cannot caramelize. With deep-frying, temperatures up to 400°F (200°C) can be reached. These high temperatures cook food more quickly and allow the food's surface to brown. In contrast to the partially submerged method of pan-frying, foods are completely submerged in hot fat when they are deep-fried. Unlike sautéing, foods are not moved as they cook and are left undisturbed in the hot fat when deep-frying.

Foods to be deep-fried are usually first coated in batter or breading. This preserves moisture and prevents the food from absorbing excessive quantities of fat. Foods to be deep-fried should be of a size and shape that allows them to float freely in the fat. Foods that are to be deep-fried together should be of uniform size and shape. Delicately flavored foods should not be deep-fried in the same fat used for more strongly flavored ones. The former could develop an odd taste from residual flavors left in the fat. Deep-fried foods should cook thoroughly while developing an attractive deep golden-brown color.

Today, most deep-frying is done in specially designed commercial fryers. These deep-fat fryers have built-in thermostats, making temperature control more precise. Deep-frying foods in a saucepan on the stove top is discouraged because it is both difficult and dangerous. The fat can spill easily, leading to injuries or creating a fire hazard. **Recovery time** is usually very slow, and temperatures are difficult to control.

To deep-fry food, first heat the fat or oil to a temperature between 325°F and 375°F (160°C and 190°C). The cooking medium's temperature can be adjusted within this range to allow the interior of thicker foods or frozen foods to cook before their surfaces become too dark. The fat must be hot enough to quickly seal the surface of the food so that it does not become excessively greasy, yet it should not be so hot that the food's surface burns before the interior is cooked.

There are two methods of deep-frying: the basket method and the swimming method. The **basket method** uses a basket to hold foods that will not tend to stick together during cooking. Typically these foods are breaded or are individually quick-frozen. The basket is removed from the fryer and filled as much as two-thirds full of product. (Do not fill the basket while it is hanging over the fat, as this allows excess salt and food particles to fall into the fat, shortening the usable life of the fat.) The filled basket is then submerged in the hot fat. When cooking is completed, the basket is used to remove the foods from the fat and hold them while excess fat drains off.

A variation on this procedure is the **double-basket method**. It is used because many foods float as they deep-fry. This may produce undesirable results because the portion of the food not submerged may not cook. To prevent this and to promote even cooking, a second basket is placed over the food held in the first basket, keeping the food submerged in the fat.

Most battered foods initially sink to the bottom when placed in hot fat, then rise to the top as they cook. Because they would stick to a basket, the **swimming method** is used for these foods. With the swimming method, battered foods are carefully dropped directly into the hot fat. (Baskets are not used.) They rise to the top as they cook. When the surface that is in contact with the fat is properly browned, the food is turned over with a spider or a pair of tongs so that it can cook evenly on both sides. When done, the product is removed with a spider or tongs and drained.

Procedure for Deep-Frying Foods

1 Cut, trim or otherwise prepare the food to be deep-fried. Bread or batter it, as desired.

2 Heat the oil or fat to the desired temperature.

3 Using either the basket method or the swimming method, carefully place the food in the hot fat.

4 Deep-fry the food until done. Doneness is usually determined by timing, surface color or sampling.

5 Remove the deep-fried food from the fryer and hold it over the cooking fat, allowing the excess fat to drain off.

6 Transfer the food to a hotel pan either lined with absorbent paper or fitted with a rack. Immediately season the food with salt so that it will adhere to the caramelized surface before it cools.

7 If the deep-fried items are to be held for later service, place them under a heat lamp; steam tables do not keep fried foods properly hot.

The basket method of deep-frying.

The double-basket method of deep-frying.

The swimming method of deep-frying.

Choosing Fats for Deep-Frying

Many types of fats can be used for deep-frying. Although animal fats, such as rendered beef fat, are sometimes used to impart their specific flavors to deep-fried foods, their low smoke points generally make them unsuitable for deep-frying unless they are blended with vegetable fats. By far the most common fats used for deep-frying are vegetable oils, such as soybean, peanut and canola oil, all of which have high smoke points and are relatively inexpensive. See Table 10.3.

Specially formulated deep-frying compounds are also available. These are usually composed of a vegetable oil or oils to which antifoaming agents, antioxidants and preservatives have been added. These additives increase the oil's usable life and raise its smoke point.

Deep-fryer fats may also be hydrogenated. **Hydrogenation** is a chemical process that adds hydrogen to oil, turning the liquid oil into a solid (margarine is hydrogenated vegetable oil). Hydrogenated fats are more resistant to oxidation, development of off flavors and foaming, all indications of chemical breakdown of the fat.

To choose the right fat, consider flavor, smoke point and resistance to chemical breakdown. High-quality frying fat should have a clean or natural flavor and a high smoke point and, when properly maintained, should be resistant to chemical breakdown.

Figure 10.4 Clean fat for frying (left) is clear, free from off-odors and light in color. Fat that has darkened (right) should be discarded.

REACTION TEMPERATURES OF FATS

TABLE 10.3

FAT	MELT POINT	SMOKE POINT	FLASH POINT
Butter	92–98°F/33–36°C	250°F/121°C	Possible at any temperature above 300°F/150°C
Butter, clarified	92–98°F/33–36°C	335–380°F/168–193°C	Possible at any temperature above 300°F/150°C
Lard	89–98°F/32–36°C	370°F/188°C	n/a
Deep-fryer shortening, heavy-duty, premium	102°F/39°C	440°F/227°C	690°F/365°C
Canola oil	n/a	430–448°F/221–230°C	553–560°F/289–293°C
Corn oil	40–50°F/4–7°C	450°F/232°C	610°F/321°C
Cocoa butter	88–93°F/31–34°C	n/a	n/a
Cottonseed oil	55°F/13°C	450°F/232°C	650°F/343°C
Margarine	94–98°F/34–36°C	410–430°F/210–221°C	Possible at any temperature above 300°F/150°C
Olive oil, extra virgin	32°F/0°C	325–410°F/165–210°C	n/a
Olive oil, pure or pomace	32°F/0°C	410–440°F/210–227°C	437°F/225°C
Peanut oil	28°F/–2°C	450°F/232°C	540°F/282°C
Shortening, vegetable, all-purpose	120°F/49°C	410°F/210°C	625°F/329°C
Soybean oil	–5°F/–20°C	495°F/257°C	540°F/282°C
Walnut oil	n/a	350–400°F/177–204°C	620°F/326°C

n/a = not available

This compilation of data is a guideline only. Because reaction temperatures depend on the exact type and ratio of fatty acids present, the actual temperatures will vary depending on the brand or manufacturer of the fat in question. Temperatures are for clean, unused fats. Heating a fat, even one time, can lower the smoke and flash points dramatically.

TABLE 10.4

FRYER FAT CAN BE DAMAGED BY
Salt and food particles
Water
Overheating
Oxygen
Detergent

CHANGE FRYER FAT WHEN IT
Becomes dark
Smokes or foams
Develops off-flavors and off-aromas
Becomes full of sediment
When cooking different types of animal proteins

Handling Fats for Deep-Frying

Properly maintaining deep-fryer fat greatly extends its useful life. See Figure 10.4 and Table 10.4. To do so:

1 Store fat in tightly sealed containers away from strong light; cover the deep fryer when not in use. Prolonged exposure to air and light turns fat rancid.

2 Skim and remove food particles from fat's surface during frying. Food particles cause fat to break down; if they are not removed, they accumulate in the fryer and burn.

3 Do not salt food over fat. Salt causes fat to break down chemically.

4 Prevent excessive water from coming into contact with fat; pat-dry moist foods as much as possible before cooking and dry the fryer, baskets and utensils well after cleaning. Water, like salt, causes fat to break down.

5 Do not overheat fat (turn the fryer down or off if not in use). High temperatures break down fat.

6 Filter fat each day or after each shift if the fryer is heavily used. Best results are obtained by using a filtering machine designed specifically for this purpose. Many large commercial fryers even have built-in filter systems. Less well-equipped operations can simply pour the hot fat through a paper filter.

The fat used to cook fish or shellfish should not be used to cook vegetables, meat or other foods in order to prevent an exchange of flavors and exposure to allergens.

Deep-fat fryers consume a large amount of fat but these fats may be recycled. Yellow grease, the term for used cooking fat, can be recycled for conversion into biodiesel fuel, animal feed, cosmetics and soaps.

Oven-Frying

Oven-frying is a dry-heat cooking method that uses conduction and convection to transfer heat to foods cooked in an oven. The technique is a reduced-fat alternative to deep-frying.

Oven-frying uses high temperatures, 400–425°F (204–218°C), to quickly cook the food while crisping its surface. Oven-fried foods are cut into small pieces and may be breaded and sprayed lightly or tossed with a cooking oil. Thus, the food's surface is lightly coated with oil before baking, not submerged in hot fat.

MOIST-HEAT COOKING METHODS

Cooking with moist heat involves applying heat to food by submerging it directly into a hot liquid or by exposing it to steam. The liquid may be plain water, but stock, wine or a seasoned liquid is often chosen to add flavor to the item being cooked. When heating liquids for moist heat cooking methods, cover the pot to prevent heat loss and evaporation. During cooking, keep the lid on or remove it as directed in the recipe. Each of the following moist-heat cooking methods can be applied to a variety of foods. See Table 10.5.

Poaching

Poaching is a moist-heat cooking method that uses convection to transfer heat from a liquid to a food. It is most often associated with delicately flavored foods that do not require lengthy cooking times to tenderize them, such as eggs, fruit or fish.

For poaching, the food is placed in a liquid held at temperatures between 160°F and 180°F (71°C and 82°C). The surface of the liquid should show only slight movement, but there should be no bubbles. It is important to maintain the desired temperature throughout the cooking process. Do not allow the liquid to reach a boil; the resulting agitation will cause meats to become tough and stringy and will destroy tender foods such as fresh fruit or fish.

BASIC PROCEDURE

Equipment: Stove top, oven, steam kettle, tilting skillet, thermal bath

Method: Food is submerged in a water-based liquid at 160–180°F (71–82°C).

Use: For delicate foods; flavor of liquid affects finished product.

MOIST-HEAT COOKING METHODS			TABLE 10.5
METHOD	LIQUID'S TEMPERATURE	LIQUID CONDITION	FOOD ITEMS
Poaching	160–180°F/71–82°C	Liquid moves slightly but no bubbles	Eggs, fish, fruits
Simmering	185–205°F/85–96°C	Small bubbles break through the surface	Meats, stews, chicken
Boiling	212°F/100°C	Large bubbles and rapid movement	Vegetables, pasta
Steaming	212°F or higher/100°C or higher	Food is in contact only with the steam generated by a boiling liquid	Vegetables, fish, shellfish

Poaching (160–180°F/71–82°C).

Simmering (185–205°F/85–96°C).

Boiling (212°F/100°C).

court bouillon *a liquid in which fish or vegetable are poached; made by simmering vegetables and seasonings in water and an acidic liquid such as vinegar or wine*

The flavor of the poaching liquid strongly affects the ultimate flavor of the finished product, so stock, **court bouillon** or broth is generally used. The liquid used to poach a food is sometimes used to make an accompanying sauce.

There are two methods of poaching: submersion poaching and shallow poaching. For **submersion poaching**, the food is completely covered with the cooking liquid. There should not be too much excess liquid, however, as additional liquid can leach away much of the food's flavor. Nor should there be too little liquid, as that could leave a portion of the food exposed, preventing it from cooking.

cuisson [kwee-sohn] *the liquid used for shallow poaching*

For **shallow poaching**, the food is placed in just enough liquid to come approximately halfway up its sides. The liquid for shallow poaching, called a **cuisson**, is brought to a simmer on the stove top. The pan is then covered with a piece of buttered parchment paper or a lid, and cooking is completed either on the stove top or in the oven. Shallow poaching combines aspects of poaching and steaming.

Both submersion and shallow poaching are healthy cooking methods as no fat is added. Any fat that is released into the cooking liquid from meat or fish during poaching should be removed if the cooking liquid will be used to make a sauce served with the dish. Any time food is submerged in water or other liquids during cooking, vitamins and minerals are removed by leaching into the liquid, which may be reserved for use as a sauce or stock.

Procedure for Poaching Foods

1   Cut, trim or otherwise prepare the food to be poached.

2   Bring an adequate amount of cooking liquid to the desired starting temperature. (For some items, such as eggs, the cooking liquid is first brought to a boil and then reduced to the poaching temperature.) Place the food in the liquid.

3   For submersion poaching, the liquid should completely cover the food.

4   For shallow poaching, the liquid should come approximately halfway up the side of the food. If shallow poaching, cover the pan with a piece of buttered parchment paper or a lid.

5   Maintaining the proper temperature, poach the food to the desired doneness in the oven or on the stove top. Doneness is generally determined by timing, internal temperature or tenderness.

6   Remove the food and hold it for service in a portion of the cooking liquid or, using an ice bath, cool it in the cooking liquid.

7   The cooking liquid can sometimes be used to prepare an accompanying sauce or reserved for poaching other foods.

❶ Season the poaching liquid as desired and bring it to the correct temperature.

❷ Carefully place the food item into the poaching liquid.

❸ Remove the cooked food from the poaching liquid.

Simmering

Simmering is another moist-heat cooking method that uses convection to transfer heat from a liquid to a food. It is often associated with foods that need to be tenderized through long, slow, moist cooking, such as less tender cuts of meat. Properly simmered foods should be moist and very tender. For simmering, the food is submerged in a liquid held between 185°F and 205°F (85°C and 96°C). Because simmering temperatures are slightly higher than those used for poaching, there should be more action on the liquid's surface, with a few air bubbles breaking through (see photo on page 191).

As with poaching, the liquid used for simmering has a great effect on the food's flavor. Be sure to use a well-flavored stock or broth and to add mirepoix (see page 203), herbs and seasonings as needed. Simmering is a healthy cooking method as no fat is added. Any fat that is released into the cooking liquid from meat or fish during simmering should be removed if the liquid will be used to make a sauce served with the dish. Any time food is submerged in water or other liquids during cooking, vitamins and minerals are leached into the liquid.

BASIC PROCEDURE

Equipment: Stove top, steam kettle, tilting skillet, thermal bath

Method: Food is submerged in a water-based liquid at 185–205°F (85–96°C).

Use: Used for poultry, beef, fish, pork, fruit, grains and vegetables; flavor of liquid affects finished product.

Procedure for Simmering Foods

1 Cut, trim or otherwise prepare the food to be simmered.

2 Bring an adequate amount of the cooking liquid to the appropriate temperature (some foods, especially smoked or cured items, are started in a cold liquid). There should be enough liquid to cover the food completely.

3 Add the food to the simmering liquid.

4 Maintaining the proper cooking temperature throughout the process, simmer the food to the desired doneness. Doneness is generally determined by timing or tenderness.

5 Remove the item and hold it for service in a portion of the cooking liquid or, using an ice bath, cool the food in its cooking liquid.

❶ Fully submerge the item being simmered in the seasoned liquid.

❷ Remove the cooked item from the liquid.

Boiling

Boiling is another moist-heat cooking method that uses the process of convection to transfer heat from a liquid to a food. Boiling relies on large amounts of rapidly bubbling liquid to cook foods. The turbulent waters and the relatively high temperatures cook foods more quickly than do poaching or simmering. Few foods, however, are cooked by true boiling. Most "boiled" meats are actually simmered. Even "hard-boiled" eggs are really only simmered. Blanching and par boiling, discussed in Chapter 9, Mise en Place, rely on boiling water to partially cook foods to assist in their preparation. Starches such as pasta and potatoes are among the only types of food that are truly boiled.

BASIC PROCEDURE

Equipment: Stove top, steam kettle, tilting skillet

Method: Food is submerged in a water-based liquid kept at a full boil, 212°F (100°C).

Use: For starchy foods such as pasta and potatoes; flavor of liquid affects finished product.

At sea level, water boils at 212°F (100°C). As altitude increases, the boiling point decreases because of the drop in atmospheric pressure. For every 1000 feet above sea level, the boiling point of water drops 2°F (1°C). In the mile-high city of Denver water boils at 203°F (95°C). Because the boiling temperature is lower, it takes longer to cook foods in Denver than in sea-level Miami.

The addition of alcohol also lowers the boiling point of water because alcohol boils at about 175°F (80°C). In contrast, the addition of salt, sugar or other substances raises water's boiling point slightly. This means that foods cooked in salted water cook faster because the boiling point is one or two degrees higher.

Use as much water as practical when boiling food. Whenever food is added to boiling water, it lowers the water's temperature. The greater the amount of water, however, the faster it returns to a boil. Boiling is a healthy cooking method as no fat is used. Any time food is submerged in water or other liquids during cooking, vitamins and minerals are leached into the liquid. Liquid in which food has been boiled may be reserved for cooking other foods as long as it has not picked up strong flavors.

Procedure for Boiling Foods

1 Bring an appropriate amount of a liquid to a boil over high heat. Add seasonings as desired.
2 Add the food to be boiled to the rapidly boiling water. Bring the liquid back to a boil and adjust the temperature to maintain the boil.
3 Cook until done. Doneness is usually determined by timing or texture.
4 Remove the boiled food from the cooking liquid, draining any excess liquid.
5 Serve the boiled food immediately. Some boiled foods can be refreshed in cold water and held for later service.

① Bring the cooking liquid to a full boil. When the item being cooked is added to the liquid, the temperature of the liquid decreases.

② After a boiled item, such as pasta, is cooked, it may be drained through a colander.

Steaming

Steaming is a moist-heat cooking method that uses the process of convection to transfer heat from the steam to the food being cooked. It is most often associated with tender, delicately flavored foods, such as fish and vegetables, which do not require long cooking times. Steaming can enhance a food's natural flavor and help to retain its nutrients. Properly steamed foods should be moist and tender. Additional flavor can be introduced by adding wine, stock, aromatics, spices or herbs to the liquid used as the steaming medium. The steaming liquid can also be used to make a sauce to be served with the steamed food.

Anytime food is enclosed and steam is created, such as when a potato is wrapped in foil before baking, steaming is part of the cooking method. Most often, however, the food to be steamed is usually placed in a basket or rack above a boiling liquid. In general, the food should not touch the liquid; it should be positioned so that the steam can circulate around it. Some foods, such as shellfish and ears of corn, however, can be placed directly in a shallow pool of boiling water. A lid should be placed on the steaming pot to trap the steam and also create a slight pressure within the pot, which speeds the cooking process.

Another type of steaming uses a convection steamer. Convection steamers use pressurized steam to cook food very quickly in an enclosed chamber. Convection steamer cooking does not produce a flavored liquid that can be used to make a sauce.

Steamed foods should be served immediately. If held for later service, they should be refreshed in ice water and refrigerated, then reheated for service. Steaming is considered a healthy cooking method as it uses no fats and vitamins and minerals do not leach into the cooking liquid.

Procedure for Steaming Foods

1 Cut, trim or otherwise prepare the food to be steamed.

2 If a convection steamer is not being used, prepare a steaming liquid and bring it to a boil in a covered pan or double boiler.

3 Place the food to be steamed on a rack, in a basket or on a perforated hotel pan in a single layer. Do not crowd the items. Place the rack, basket or pan over the boiling liquid.

4 Alternatively, place the food in a shallow pool of the cooking liquid.

5 Cover the cooking assemblage and cook to the desired doneness. Doneness is usually determined by timing, color or tenderness.

❶ Trim items before steaming them so that they cook evenly.

❷ A perforated hotel pan can be set over a deeper pan of boiling water, covered and used as a steamer.

COMBINATION COOKING METHODS

Some cooking methods employ both dry-heat and moist-heat cooking techniques. The two most common combination methods are braising and stewing. In both methods, the first step is usually to brown the main item using dry heat. The second step is to complete cooking by simmering the food in a liquid. Combination methods are often used for less tender but flavorful cuts of meat as well as for poultry and some vegetables. Depending upon the cuts of meat, fish or poultry used, and the accompanying sauce ingredients, braising can be a healthy cooking technique. Stews that include a starch-thickened cooking liquid are considered less healthy.

BASIC PROCEDURE

Equipment: Stove top, oven, tilting skillet

Method: Large pieces of food are browned in fat;
liquid is added, then food is covered and cooked
at low heat.

Use: Tenderizes tough cuts of meat or poultry or
softens firm fruits and vegetables after surface
browning.

Braising

Braised foods benefit from the best aspects of both dry- and moist-heat cooking methods. Foods to be braised are usually large pieces that are first browned in a small amount of fat at high temperatures. As with sautéing, heat is transferred from the pan to the food mainly by the process of conduction. Vegetables and seasonings are added, and enough sauce or liquid is added to come one-third to halfway up the item being cooked. The pan is covered, and the heat is reduced. The food is then cooked at low heat, using a combination of simmering and steaming to transfer heat from the liquid (conduction) and the air (convection) to the food. This can be done on the stove top, in a tilting skillet or in the oven. A long, slow cooking period helps tenderize the item. Braised foods are usually served with a sauce made from the cooking liquid.

Procedure for Braising Foods

sear to brown food quickly over high heat; usually done as a preparatory step for combination cooking methods

1   Cut, trim or otherwise prepare the food to be braised. Dredge it in flour, if desired.

2   Heat a small amount of fat in a heavy pan or tilting skillet.

3   **Sear** the food on all sides. Some foods—notably meats—should be removed from the pan and kept warm after they are seared.

4   Add vegetables, seasonings or any other ingredients and sauté.

5   Add flour or thickener, if desired, to thicken the sauce.

6   Add cooking liquid to partially cover the food being braised.

7   Add aromatics and seasonings.

8   If the principal item was removed, return it to the pan.

9   Cover the pan and bring the cooking liquid to a simmer. Cook slowly, either on the stove top or in an oven at 250–300°F (120–150°C). Baste and turn the food as needed.

10   Doneness is usually determined by texture and tenderness. When the principal item is cooked, remove it from the pan and hold it in a warm place.

11   Prepare a sauce from the braising liquid if desired. This may be done by cooking the liquid on the stove top to intensify its flavors. If the food was braised in an unthickened stock, the stock may now be thickened using a roux, arrowroot or cornstarch. Strain the sauce or, if desired, purée the mirepoix and other ingredients and return them to the sauce. Adjust the sauce's consistency as desired.

❶ Sear the item in fat.

❷ Add cooking liquid to the pan.

❸ Baste the item with liquid during cooking.

BASIC PROCEDURE

Equipment: Stove top, oven, tilting skillet, thermal
bath

Method: Small pieces of food are browned in fat; liquid is added, then food is covered and simmered.

Use: Tenderizes tough cuts of meat, poultry or fish, softens fruits and vegetables; liquid becomes sauce.

Stewing

Stewing also uses a combination of dry- and moist-heat cooking methods. Stewing is most often associated with smaller pieces of food that are first browned in a small amount of fat or oil or blanched in a liquid. Cooking is then finished in a liquid or sauce, which is served as part of the finished dish. Stewed foods have enough liquid added to cover them completely and are simmered at a constant temperature until tender. Cooking time is generally shorter for stewing than for braising because the items are smaller.

Procedure for Stewing Foods

1 Trim and cut the food to be stewed into small, uniform-sized pieces. Dredge the pieces in flour, if desired.

2 Heat a small amount of fat in a heavy pan. Sear the food on all sides, developing color as desired.

3 Add vegetables, seasonings or any other ingredients and sauté.

4 Add flour or roux to thicken the liquid during cooking.

5 Gradually add the cooking liquid, stirring to prevent lumps. The liquid should completely cover the principal items.

6 Bring the stew to the appropriate temperature. Cover and place in the oven at 250–300°F (120–150°C) or continue to simmer on the stove top until the principal items of meat, fish fruit or vegetables are tender. Doneness is usually determined by texture and tenderness.

7 Remove the principal items and hold them in a warm place.

8 Thicken the sauce as desired.

9 Return the principal items to the stew. If not added during the cooking process, vegetables and other garnishes may be cooked separately and added to the finished stew. Degrease the stew as necessary.

1 Brown food in a small amount of fat.

2 Add flour to make a roux.

3 Gradually add cooking liquid to the pan.

4 Degrease the finished stew as necessary.

Sous Vide

Sous vide, a French term that means "under vacuum," is a low-temperature, combination cooking method that resembles braising or poaching. Foods are vacuum sealed in heavy-gauge plastic pouches and cooked in a temperature-controlled water bath. Because pouches are completely sealed, flavorful juices stay within the foods. The temperature of the food will not exceed the temperature of the water bath. This cooking method, which uses conduction to convey heat from the hot water bath to the food, has been in use for several decades in commercial food production. It is of increasing interest to restaurant chefs for its precise and specific results.

To prepare foods *sous vide* in the restaurant kitchen, individual portions or small quantities of meat, poultry, fish, vegetables or other foods are trimmed and seasoned and placed in food grade, heat-resistant plastic pouches. The pouches are then sealed in a chamber vacuum machine. The chamber vacuum machine, which removes air and increases the pressure on the food, ensures that heat transfers efficiently from the water to the food in the pouch during cooking. Removing most of the oxygen also increases the shelf life of the food, both before and after it is cooked *sous vide.* (Once packaged, the food may be chilled below the temperature danger zone in a water bath, refrigerator or blast chiller to be cooked later.) Pressure is adjusted according to the food being cooked; firmer cuts of meat with low moisture content are packed at a higher pressure than fragile, moist cuts, for example.

Sous vide is used to cook fish, vegetables and tender cuts of poultry and meat, such as beef tenderloin. Tougher cuts of beef, veal, lamb and other meats that benefit from

BASIC PROCEDURE

Equipment: Chamber vacuum machine, thermal bath or water oven

Method: Vacuum-sealed pouch of seasoned food is submerged in temperature-controlled water bath.

Use: Cooking at a precise, steady temperature for tenderness and uniformity without caramelization. Food may be browned after cooking.

⚠ Safety Alert

Cooking Foods Sous Vide

When preparing foods to be packaged in plastic pouches for *sous vide* cooking, observe the following food safety practices:

1   Learn and follow the local health codes and requirements for preparing foods *sous vide*. Prepare a detailed HACCP plan for each *sous vide* item. (See page 32.)

2   Work in a clean and sanitized environment using professional vacuum packaging machinery. Wear clean single-use gloves and change them as needed during food preparation. To take the internal temperature of meat in a sous vide pouch, apply a piece of **closed cell foam tape** to the top of a bag. Then pierce the tape with a **needle probe thermometer** designed for use with sous vide bags. The tape will seal itself after the probe is removed.

3   To prevent the growth of microorganisms, chill any food to be cooked *sous vide* below the temperature danger zone (41°F/5°C) before cooking. Thoroughly chill any pre-cooked foods, such as meat that is browned for a stew, before sealing them in the pouches.

4   Be mindful of the temperature danger zone 41–135°F (5–57°C) when cooking *sous vide*. If the cooking temperatures are within the temperature danger zone, food cannot be held in the water bath for longer than 4 hours.

5   Foods prepared *sous vide* but not intended for immediate service must be chilled below the temperature danger zone (41°F/5°C) before refrigerating. Chilling the packages in a salted ice bath can lower the temperature to 32°F (0°C) or below rapidly.

braising are also ideal for *sous vide* cooking. Meats for stews or braises that would conventionally be browned before simmering may be browned before sealing in a pouch.

Sous vide cooking takes place in a precisely regulated hot water bath or water oven at temperatures between 122°F (50°C) and 185°F (90°C) for anywhere from one to 72 hours. Fish, tender cuts of meat and vegetables cook more quickly than tough cuts of meat that have more connective tissue. The temperature and the length of time in the water bath vary depending upon the type of food being cooked and the desired results. (Because of the many variables when cooking sous vide, follow the recommended cooking temperatures and times in the recipes provided in the book.) When cooking tender cuts of fish, poultry or meat such as beef tenderloin, the temperature is determined by the desired core temperature of the finished food item. When roasted conventionally, a beef tenderloin, for example, is seared and then roasted at 375–450°F (191–232°C) until its internal temperature reaches the desired degree of doneness. During the conventional dry-heat cooking process, the exterior layers of the meat cook more than the center and the final product may be overcooked and dry around the edges. When cooking beef tenderloin *sous vide,* the meat is vacuum packed then cooked in a water bath set to the desired final temperature (e.g., 125°F/51°C for rare meat). *Sous vide* cooking achieves a uniformly rare piece of meat with less shrinkage. To add the flavor and eye appeal of a browned surface, the surface of the meat may be seared at the time of service.

When braising tougher cuts of meats or poultry, cooking for several hours at a temperature from 148°F (64°C) to 160°F (71°C) may be recommended. This temperature range is hot enough to dissolve connective tissues and collagen without squeezing all the moisture and fat from the meat. The cooking temperature and the length of time used for braising foods *sous vide* depends on the desired results. A briefer cooking time at a higher temperature may be all that is needed to produce fork-tender meat as with a conventional braise. But cooking the food longer at a lower temperature may result in meat that retains its shape and pink color resembling rare meat yet is fully cooked and juicy. One benefit chefs cite for *sous vide* cooking is precision. Once food cooked *sous vide* reaches the temperature of the water bath, it cannot overcook and it can be held at the desired temperature for several hours in the water bath before service. Although holding a food in the water bath for too long does not alter its temperature, it may soften its texture. Foods cooked *sous vide* may also be chilled below the temperature danger zone (41°F/5°C) then held under refrigeration or frozen for later service. When refrigerating pouches of food cooked *sous vide*, store them covered with ice.

Food safety is of utmost concern when using *sous vide* techniques because of the low cooking temperatures and low oxygen atmosphere in the vacuum-sealed pouches. Such pathogens as *Clostridium botulinum, Escherichia coli (E. coli), Listeria monocytogenes* and *Salmonella* can multiply in the low cooking temperatures used. The 2013 Food Code requires that a detailed HACCP program, including time and temperature monitoring, be in place in any food service operation using *sous vide* cooking methods. Before using *sous vide* techniques consult local health authorities to learn what technical training, licensing and recordkeeping are required. Some communities may prohibit the use of *sous vide* cooking entirely. Consult the Bibliography for books on the subject. Equipment for *sous vide* cooking is discussed in Chapter 5, Tools and Equipment.

Procedure for Preparing Foods Sous Vide

1   Assemble the proper equipment–single-use gloves, digital thermometer, ice and water bath with salt and sanitizing solution–for preparing the food in a sanitary manner. Use an immersion circulator to bring a thermal bath to the desired temperature, or use a water oven.

2   Cut, trim or otherwise prepare food to be cooked *sous vide*. Immediately chill the food in a refrigerator or blast chiller. It must be chilled below the temperature danger zone (41°F/5°C) within 4 hours before proceeding.

3   Wearing single-use gloves, place the chilled foods to be cooked *sous vide* in a single layer in plastic pouches. Add fat, seasonings and cooking liquids as desired.

4 Vacuum seal the pouches using a chamber vacuum machine adjusted to the proper setting for the food. At this point, the pouches of food may be chilled below the temperature danger zone to be cooked later.

5 When ready to cook, place the pouches in the thermal bath heated to the desired cooking temperature of the food allowing enough space for the water to flow freely around them without overcrowding. Doneness is determined by temperature or texture of the food. Check the temperature with a pointed-tip digital probe thermometer. (Reseal the bag before returning it to the circulator if necessary.)

6 Serve the food immediately, or transfer the pouches of cooked food to an ice bath with salt added to reduce its temperature. The food must be chilled to below 41°F/5°C or lower within 4 hours.

7 To serve food previously cooked and chilled, reheat the pouch in a thermal bath set to the desired temperature. Check the temperature with a pointed-tip digital probe thermometer. (Reseal the bag before returning it to the circulator if necessary.) Reheating a ½-inch- (1.25-centimeter-) thick steak may take 30 minutes while a 2-inch- (5-centimeter-) thick one may take 2 or more hours to reheat. Plate the food. For a browned surface on foods cooked *sous vide*, reheat the item, remove it from the pouch, then sear it quickly and serve immediately.

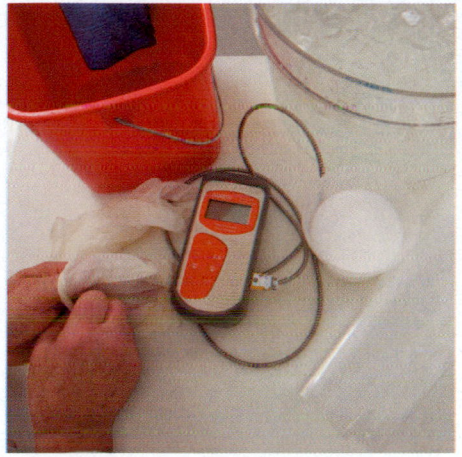

❶ Assemble the safety equipment—single-use gloves, digital probe thermometer with pointed tip, ice and water bath with salt and sanitizing solution—for preparing food *sous vide*.

❷ Wearing clean single-use gloves, place foods and seasonings in a single layer into plastic pouches.

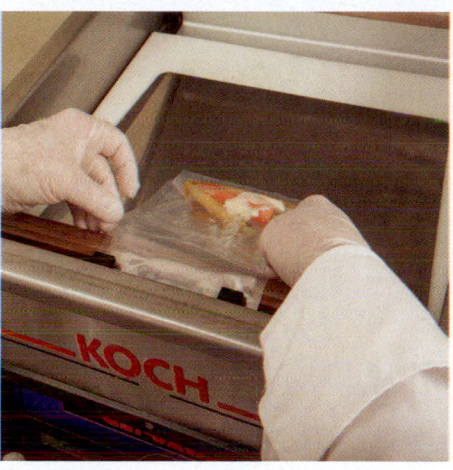

❸ Vacuum seal the pouches of food in a chamber vacuum machine.

❹ Place sealed pouches in a pre-heated thermal bath with a circulator.

❺ Unless being served immediately, use an ice bath to quickly chill pouches of food prepared *sous vide* below the temperature danger zone.

QUESTIONS FOR DISCUSSION

1 Describe the differences between conduction and convection. Identify four cooking methods that rely on both conduction and convection to heat foods. Explain your choices.

2 Identify two cooking methods that rely on infrared (radiant) heat. What is the principal difference between these methods?

3 At the same temperature, will a food cook faster in a convection oven or a conventional oven? Explain your answer.

4 Describe the process of caramelization and its significance in food preparation. Will a braised food have a caramelized surface? Explain your answer.

5 Name and describe two styles of deep-frying.

6 Compare and contrast poaching and simmering. Describe what makes them healthy cooking techniques.

7 Explain how cooking *sous vide* raises food safety issues and how you can avoid potential food borne illnesses when using the *sous vide* method.

Stocks and Sauces 11

- describe the principles of making stock
- prepare a variety of stocks
- prepare and use various types of mirepoix
- recognize and classify sauces
- explain the proper use of thickening agents
- prepare a variety of classic, traditional and contemporary sauces

fond (1) French for "stock" or "base"; (2) the concentrated juices, drippings and bits of food left in a pan after a food is roasted or sautéed; *fond* is used to flavor sauces made directly in the pans in which foods were cooked

A stock is a flavored liquid. A good stock is the key to a great soup, sauce or braised dish. The French appropriately call a stock *fond* ("base"), as stocks are the basis for many classic and modern dishes.

A **sauce** is a thickened liquid used to flavor and enhance other foods. A good sauce adds flavor, moisture, richness and visual appeal. A sauce should complement food; it should never disguise it. A sauce can be hot or cold, sweet or savory, smooth or chunky.

Although the thought of preparing stocks and sauces may be intimidating, the procedures are really straightforward. Carefully follow the basic procedures outlined in this chapter, use high-quality ingredients and, with practice and experience, you will soon be producing fine stocks and sauces.

This chapter addresses traditional hot sauces as well as coulis, contemporary broths, foams, flavored oils, salsas and relishes. Cold sauces, generally based on mayonnaise and vinaigrettes, are discussed in Chapter 25, Salads and Salad Dressings; dessert sauces are discussed in Chapter 35, Custards, Creams, Frozen Desserts and Dessert Sauces.

STOCKS

There are several types of stocks. Although all stocks are made from a combination of bones, vegetables, seasonings and liquids, each type is made using specific procedures to give it distinctive characteristics.

A **white stock** is made by simmering chicken, veal or beef bones in water with vegetables and seasonings. The stock remains relatively colorless during the cooking process. A **brown stock** is made from chicken, veal, beef or game bones and vegetables, all of which are caramelized before being simmered in water with seasonings. The stock has a rich, dark color. Both a **fish stock** and a **fumet** are made by slowly cooking fish bones or crustacean shells and vegetables without coloring them, then simmering them in water with seasonings for a short time. For a fumet, wine and lemon juice are also added. The resulting stock or fumet is a strongly flavored, relatively colorless liquid. A **court bouillon** is made by simmering vegetables and seasonings in water and an acidic liquid such as vinegar or wine. It is used to poach fish or vegetables.

The quality of a stock is judged by four characteristics: body, flavor, clarity and color. Body develops when collagen proteins dissolve in protein-based stock. Vegetable stocks have less body than meat stocks because they lack animal protein. Aromatic vegetables, herb sachets and the proper ratios of ingredients to liquid give stocks their flavor. Clarity is achieved by removing impurities during stock making. Many ingredients contribute to a stock's color. Vegetables such as leeks and carrots give white stock a light color. Browned bones and tomato paste color dark stocks. Improper uses of coloring ingredients can overwhelm the color and flavor of a stock.

Quality stock is made using the proper ingredients in the right ratios. To ensure that a stock has a consistent flavor each time it is prepared, do not use random pieces of meat, poultry, fish and vegetables. Instead use any random meat, poultry, fish and vegetable trimmings you have on hand to make one-of-a kind soups or liquids for cooking beans or grains.

INGREDIENTS FOR STOCKS

The basic ingredients of any stock are bones, mirepoix (a mixture of coarsely chopped onions, carrots and celery used to flavor stocks discussed below), seasonings and water.

Bones

Bones are the most important ingredient in protein-based stock; they add flavor, richness and color. Traditionally the kitchen or butcher shop saved the day's bones to make stock. But because food service operations now buy meats and poultry items precut or portioned, bones are purchased specifically for stock making.

Different bones release their flavor at different rates. Even though the bones are cut into 3- to 4-inch (8- to 10-centimeter) pieces, a stock made entirely of beef and/or veal bones requires 6–8 hours of cooking time, whereas a stock made entirely from chicken bones requires only 5–6 hours.

Beef and Veal Bones

The best bones for beef and veal stock are from younger animals. They contain a higher percentage of **cartilage** and other **connective tissue** than do bones from more mature animals. Connective tissue has a high **collagen** content. Through the cooking process, the collagen is converted into **gelatin** and water. Gelatin adds richness and body to finished stock.

The best beef and veal bones are back, neck and shank bones, as they have high collagen contents. Beef and veal bones should be cut with a meat saw into small pieces, approximately 3–4 inches (8–10 centimeters) long, so that they can release as much flavor as possible while the stock cooks.

Chicken Bones

The best bones for chicken stock are from the neck and back. If a whole chicken carcass is used, it can be cut up for easier handling.

Fish Bones

The best bones for fish stock are from lean fish such as sole, flounder, whiting or turbot. Bones from fatty fish (e.g., salmon, tuna and swordfish) do not produce good stock because of their high fat content and distinctive flavors. The entire fish carcass can be used, but it should be cut up with a cleaver or heavy knife for easy handling and even extraction of flavors. After cutting, rinse the pieces in cold water to remove blood, loose scales and other impurities.

Other Bones

Lamb, turkey, game and ham bones can be used for white or brown stocks. Although mixing bones is generally acceptable, be careful of blending strongly flavored bones, such as those from lamb or game, with beef, veal or chicken bones. The former's strong flavors may not be appropriate or desirable in the finished product.

Mirepoix

A **mirepoix** is a mixture of onions, carrots and celery added to a stock to enhance its flavor and aroma. Although chefs differ on the ratio of vegetables, generally a mixture of 50 percent onions, 25 percent carrots and 25 percent celery, by weight, is used. (Unless otherwise noted, any reference to mirepoix in this text refers to this ratio.) For a brown stock, onion skins may be used in mirepoix to add color. Although washing is essential, it is not necessary to peel the carrots or celery because flavor, not aesthetics, is important.

The size into which the mirepoix is chopped is determined by the stock's cooking time: The shorter the cooking time, the smaller the vegetables must be chopped to

cartilage also known as gristle; a tough, elastic, whitish connective tissue that helps give structure to animal's body

connective tissue tissue found throughout an animal's body that binds together and supports other tissues such as muscles

collagen a protein found in nearly all connective tissue; collagen dissolves when cooked with moisture

gelatin a tasteless and odorless mixture of proteins (especially collagen) extracted from simmering bones, connective tissue and other animal parts; when dissolved in a hot liquid and then cooled, gelatin forms a jellylike substance used as a thickener and stabilizer

mirepoix [meer-pwa] a mixture of coarsely chopped onions, carrots and celery used to flavor stocks, stews and other foods; generally, a mixture of 50 percent onions, 25 percent carrots and 25 percent celery, by weight, is used

matignon a standard mirepoix plus diced smoked bacon or smoked ham and, depending on the dish, mushrooms and herbs; sometimes called an edible mirepoix, it is usually cut more uniformly than a standard mirepoix and left in the finished dish as a garnish

Formula for standard mirepoix
= 50% onions + 25% carrots
+ 25% celery by weight

Mirepoix ingredients

ensure that all possible flavor is extracted. For white or brown stocks made from beef or veal bones, the vegetables should be coarsely chopped into large, 1- to 2-inch (2.5- to 5-centimeter) pieces. For chicken and fish stocks, the vegetables should be more finely chopped into ½-inch (1.2-centimeter) pieces.

A **white mirepoix** is made by replacing the carrots in a standard mirepoix with parsnips and adding mushrooms and leeks. Some chefs prefer to use a white mirepoix when making a white stock, as it produces a lighter product. Sometimes parsnips, mushrooms and leeks are added to a standard mirepoix for additional flavors.

The uses for mirepoix extend beyond stock making. Many braised dishes, sauces, soups and stews begin with gently sautéed mirepoix. Cuisines throughout the world have their own variations of this flavor base. The "holy trinity" in Cajun cooking, for example, is a mixture of diced onions, celery and green bell peppers that are gently sautéed as a base for many dishes such as gumbo and jambalaya. Similarly Asian cuisines often start with a mixture of chopped garlic, ginger and scallions to flavor stir-fried and simmered dishes.

Seasonings

Principal stock seasonings are peppercorns, bay leaves, thyme, parsley stems and, optionally, garlic. These seasonings generally can be left whole. A stock is cooked long enough for all of their flavors to be extracted, so there is no reason to chop or grind them. Seasonings generally are added to the stock at the start of cooking. Some chefs do not add seasonings to beef or veal stock until midway through the cooking process, however, because of the extended cooking times. Seasonings can be added as a sachet d'épices or a bouquet garni. (See Chapter 9, Mise en Place.)

Salt, an otherwise important seasoning, is not added to stock. Because a stock has a variety of uses, it is impossible to know how much salt to add when preparing it. If, for example, the stock was seasoned to taste with salt, you could not reduce it later; salt is not lost through reduction, and the concentrated product would taste too salty. Similarly seasoning the stock to taste with salt could prevent you from adding other ingredients that are high in salt when finishing a recipe. Unlike many the flavor of many seasonings, which must be incorporated into a product through lengthy cooking periods, salt can be added at any time during the cooking process and effect flavor in the same way.

PRINCIPLES OF STOCK MAKING

Quality stocks are made using the proper ingredients and by taking the proper steps. The principles of making stocks described here and outlined in Figure 11.1, apply to all stocks. Follow them in order to achieve the highest-quality stocks possible. Consult Table 11.1 when problems arise.

Always start the stock in cold water. When bones are covered with cold water, blood and other impurities dissolve. As the water heats, the impurities coagulate and rise to the surface, where they can be removed easily by skimming. If the bones were covered with hot water, the impurities would coagulate more quickly and remain dispersed in the stock without rising to the top, making the stock cloudy. Stocks made from vegetables should also be started in cold water so that the vegetables cook slowly. Gentle simmering allows their flavors to be fully extracted. If the water level falls below the bones or vegetables during cooking, add cold water to cover them. Flavor cannot be extracted from bones that are not under water, and bones exposed to the air will darken and discolor a white stock.

The stock should be brought to a boil and then reduced to a simmer, a temperature of approximately 185°F (85°C). Gentle simmering allows the ingredients to release their flavors into the liquid. If kept at a simmer, the liquid will remain clear as it reduces and the stock develops. Never boil a stock for any length of time. Rapid boiling of a stock, even for a few minutes, causes impurities and fats to blend with the liquid, making it

Start the stock in cold water.
Simmer the stock gently.
Skim the stock frequently.
Strain the stock carefully.
Cool the stock quickly.
Store the stock properly.
Degrease the stock.

Figure 11.1 Principles of stock making.

cloudy. A stock should be skimmed often to remove the fat and impurities that rise to the surface during cooking. If they are not removed, fat and impurities may make the stock cloudy. Even vegetable stocks should be skimmed should any fat or scum rise to the surface.

Once a stock finishes cooking, the liquid must be separated from the bones, vegetables and other solid ingredients. In order to keep the liquid clear, it is important not to disturb the solid ingredients when removing the liquid. This is easily accomplished if the stock is cooked in a steam kettle or stockpot with a spigot at the bottom. Open the spigot and allow the stock to drain through a mesh strainer lined with several layers of damp cheesecloth. Dampening the cheesecloth with clean water helps prevent it from absorbing the stock.

If the stock is cooked in a standard stockpot, follow these steps to strain it:

1   Skim as much fat and as many impurities from the surface as possible before removing the stockpot from the heat.

2   After removing the pot from the heat, carefully ladle the stock from the pot without stirring it.

3   Strain the stock through a china cap lined with several layers of damp cheesecloth.

Procedure for Making Stock

1   Start the stock in cold water. Place the bones for the stock in a large stock pot. Cover the bones with cold water making certain that all of the bones are completely submerged.

2   Simmer the stock gently. Bring the stock to a boil and then reduce to a simmer, a temperature of approximately 185°F (85°C), for the time specified in the recipe for the particular type of stock you are making. (Fish stock may simmer for as little as 30 minutes while brown beef stock may require 8 hours of gentle simmering.) Do not allow the stock to boil. If the water level falls below the bones during cooking, add cold water to cover them.

3   Skim the stock frequently. While the stock simmers, skim off the fat and impurities that rise to the surface of the stock.

4   Strain the stock carefully. Once the stock finishes cooking, carefully strain out the bones, vegetables and other solid ingredients then strain the stock through a china cap lined with several layers of damp cheesecloth.

❶ Covering bones with cold water.

❷ Skimming the fat and the impurities from stock as it simmers.

❸ Straining stock through a cheesecloth-lined china cap

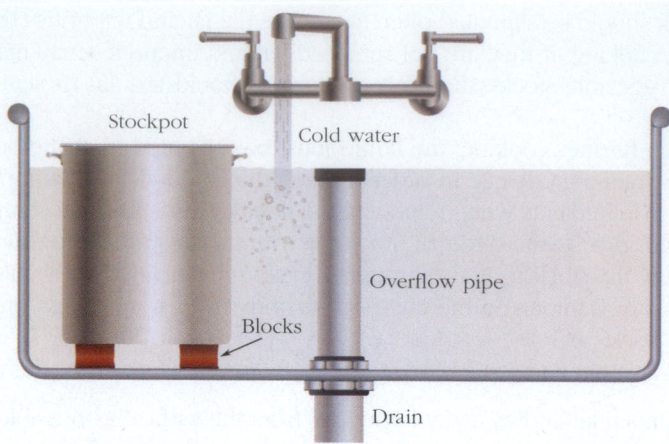

Figure 11.2 Venting a stockpot.

Most stocks are prepared in large quantities, cooled and held for later use. Great care must be taken when cooling a stock to prevent food-borne illnesses or the development of a sour, off-taste. To cool a stock below the temperature danger zone quickly and safely, several steps must be followed. One critical step is **venting** the stockpot by elevating it in a deep sink then filling the sink with cold water. The water circulates on all sides of the pot speeding cooling. See Figure 11.2. In addition to this venting procedure, **cooling wands** can be used to speed the cooling of stocks, soups, sauces and other liquids. These wands (also known as ice paddles) are hollow plastic containers that can be filled with water or ice, sealed, frozen and then used to stir and cool liquids. Clean and sanitize the wand after each use to prevent cross-contamination.

Procedure for Cooling Stock Quickly

Lifting fat from the surface of a cold stock.

degrease to remove fat from the surface of a liquid such as a stock or sauce by skimming, scraping or lifting congealed fat

1 Keep the stock in a metal container. A plastic container is a poor choice because it insulates the stock and delays cooling.

2 Vent the stockpot in an empty sink by placing it on blocks or a rack. This allows water to circulate on all sides and below the pot when the sink is filled with water. See Figure 11.2.

3 Install an overflow pipe in the drain and fill the sink with cold water or a combination of cold water and ice. Make sure that the weight of the stockpot is adequate to keep it from tipping over.

4 Let cold water run into the sink and drain out the overflow pipe. Stir the stock frequently to facilitate even, quick cooling.

Once the stock is cooled, transfer it to a sanitized covered container (either plastic or metal) and store it in the refrigerator. As the stock chills, fat rises to its surface and solidifies. If left intact, this layer of fat helps preserve the stock. Stocks can be stored for up to 1 week under refrigeration or frozen for several months.

Before the stock can be used, the fat that has solidified on its surface must be removed. This is referred to as **degreasing** a stock. To degrease the stock, remove the congealed fat from the surface of the stock using a spoon. Discard the fat.

White Stock

A white or neutral stock is made from beef, veal or chicken bones. The finished stock should have a good flavor, good clarity, high gelatin content and little or no color. Veal bones are most often used, but any combination of beef, veal or chicken bones may be used. Chefs disagree on whether the bones for a white stock should be blanched to remove impurities. Some chefs argue that blanching keeps the stock as clear and colorless as possible; others argue that blanching removes nutrients and flavor.

Procedure for Blanching Bones

If you choose to blanch the bones:

1 Wash the cut-up bones, place them in a stockpot and cover them with cold water.

2 Bring the water to a boil over high heat.

3 As soon as the water boils, skim the rising impurities. Drain the water from the bones and discard it.

4 Refill the pot with cold water and proceed with the stock recipe.

White Stock

 **Good Choice**

YIELD 2 gal. (7.6 lt)

Bones, veal, chicken or beef, rinsed and cut into 3 to 4-in. (8- to 10-cm) pieces	15 lb.	7.2 kg
Cold water	3 gal.	11.5 lt
Mirepoix	2 lb.	960 g
Sachet:		
Bay leaves	2	2
Dried thyme	½ tsp.	2 ml
Peppercorns, crushed	½ tsp.	2 ml
Parsley stems	8	8

MISE EN PLACE

- Cut up and wash bones.
- Peel and chop onions, carrots and celery for mirepoix.
- Prepare herb sachet.

1 Place the bones in a stockpot and cover them with cold water.

2 If blanching, bring the water to a boil, skimming off the scum that rises to the surface. Drain off the water and the impurities. Then add the 3 gallons (11.5 liters) cold water and bring to a boil. Reduce to a simmer. If not blanching the bones, bring the cold water to a boil. Reduce to a simmer and skim the scum that forms.

3 Add the mirepoix and sachet to the simmering stock.

4 Continue simmering and skimming the stock for 6–8 hours. (If only chicken bones are used, simmer for 3–4 hours.)

5 Strain, cool and refrigerate.

Approximate values per 1-fl.-oz. (30-ml) serving: **Calories** 4, **Total fat** 0.1 g, **Saturated fat** 0.1 g, **Cholesterol** 0 mg, **Sodium** 5 mg, **Total carbohydrates** 0 g, **Protein** 0.2 g, **Claims**—fat free; very low sodium

1 Adding water to bones for white stock.

2 Skimming the white stock.

3 Adding mirepoix to the white stock and seasonings.

Brown Stock

A brown stock is made from chicken, veal, beef or game bones. The finished stock should have a good flavor, rich dark brown color, good body and high gelatin content. The primary differences between a brown stock and a white stock are that for a brown stock, the bones and mirepoix are caramelized before being simmered and a tomato product is added. These extra steps provide the finished stock with a rich dark color and a more intense flavor. Recall from Chapter 10, Principles of Cooking, that caramelization is the process of browning the sugars found on the surface of most foods. Caramelization gives brown stock its characteristic flavor and color.

Procedure for Caramelizing Bones

If caramelizing bones, do not wash or blanch them as this retards browning. To caramelize:

1 Place the cut-up bones in a roasting pan one layer deep. It is better to roast several pans of bones than to overfill one pan.
2 Roast the bones for approximately 1 hour in a hot oven (375°F/190°C). Stirring occasionally, brown the bones thoroughly, but do not allow them to burn.
3 Transfer the roasted bones from the pan to the stockpot.

deglaze to swirl or stir a liquid (usually wine or stock) in a pan to dissolve cooked food particles remaining on the bottom; the resulting mixture often becomes the base for a sauce

After the bones are caramelized, the excess fat should be removed and reserved for future use. The caramelized and coagulated proteins remaining in the roasting pan are very flavorful. To utilize them, **deglaze** the pan.

Procedure for Deglazing the Pan

1 Place the roasting pan on the stove top over medium heat and add enough water to cover the bottom of the pan approximately ½ inch (1.2 centimeters) deep.
2 Stir and scrape the pan bottom to dissolve and remove all the caramelized materials while the water heats.
3 Pour the deglazing liquid (also known as the deglazing liquor) over the bones in the stockpot.

Caramelizing the mirepoix used in brown stock gives it a rich flavor and color. The mirepoix may be caramelized along with the bones in the oven or it may be caramelized using the following procedure.

Procedure for Caramelizing Mirepoix

1 Add a little of the reserved fat from the roasted bones to the roasting pan after it has been deglazed (or use a sautoir large enough to contain all the mirepoix without crowding).
2 Sauté the mirepoix, browning all the vegetables well and evenly without burning.
3 Add the caramelized mirepoix to the stockpot.

Almost any tomato product can be used in a brown stock: fresh tomatoes, canned whole tomatoes, crushed tomatoes, tomato purée or paste. If using a concentrated tomato product such as paste or purée, use approximately half the amount by weight of fresh or canned tomatoes. It is traditional to brown the tomato paste with the mirepoix to reduce any acidity and bitterness, although this step is often omitted. When using fresh tomatoes, canned whole tomatoes, crushed tomatoes or tomato purée, add the tomato product to the stockpot with the mirepoix.

Brown Stock

YIELD 2 gal. (7.6 lt)

Bones, veal or beef, cut in 3- to 4-in. (8- to 10-cm) pieces	15 lb.	7.2 kg
Cold water	3 gal.	11.5 lt
Mirepoix	2 lb.	960 g
Tomato paste	8 oz.	240 g
Sachet:		
Bay leaves	2	2
Dried thyme	½ tsp.	2 ml
Peppercorns, crushed	½ tsp.	2 ml
Garlic cloves, crushed	3	3
Parsley stems	12	12

MISE EN PLACE

- Cut up and wash bones.
- Peel and chop onions, carrots and celery for mirepoix.
- Prepare herb sachet.

1 Place the bones in a roasting pan, one layer deep, and caramelize them in a 375°F (190°C) oven. Turn the bones occasionally to brown them evenly.

2 Remove the bones and place them in a stockpot. Pour off the fat from the roasting pan and reserve it.

3 Deglaze the roasting pan with part of the cold water.

4 Add the deglazing liquor and the rest of the cold water to the bones, covering them completely. Bring to a boil and reduce to a simmer.

5 Add a portion of the reserved fat to the roasting pan and sauté the mirepoix until evenly caramelized. Add the tomato paste and continue cooking until the tomato paste and mirepoix are a deep brown color. Add the mixture to the simmering stock.

6 Add the sachet to the stock and continue to simmer for 6–8 hours, skimming as necessary.

7 Strain, cool and refrigerate.

Approximate values per 1-fl.-oz. (30-ml) serving: **Calories** 3, **Total fat** 0 g, **Saturated fat** 0 g, **Cholesterol** 0.3 mg, **Sodium** 105 mg, **Total carbohydrates** 0 g, **Protein** 0 g, **Claims**—fat free; low sodium

❶ Caramelizing the bones.

❷ Deglazing the pan with water.

❸ Caramelizing the mirepoix in the deglazed roasting pan.

❹ Adding water to cover the bones completely as they cook.

Remouillage

Remouillage is a French term for "rewetting" that refers to a second batch of stock made by reusing the bones from making your first batch of stock. After draining the original stock from the stockpot, add fresh mirepoix, a new sachet and enough water to cover the bones and mirepoix, to make a second stock. A remouillage is treated like the original stock; allow it to simmer for 4–5 hours before straining. A remouillage is not as clear or as flavorful as the original stock, however. It is often used to make glazes or in place of water when making stocks.

Fish Stock and Fish Fumet

A fish stock and a fish fumet [foo-MAY] are similar and can be used interchangeably in most recipes. Both are clear with a pronounced fish flavor and very light body. A fumet, however, is more strongly flavored and aromatic than a fish stock and contains an acidic ingredient such as white wine and/or lemon juice.

Only the bones and heads of lean fish and crustacean shells are used to make fish stock. Oily fish such as mackerel, salmon or tuna are not used because their pronounced flavor would overwhelm the stock. The fish bones and shells used to make a fish stock or fumet should be washed but never blanched. Blanching removes too much flavor. They may be **sweated** without browning if desired, however. Because of the size and structure of fish bones and crustacean shells, stocks and fumets made from them require much less cooking time than even a chicken stock; 30–45 minutes is usually sufficient to extract full flavor. Mirepoix or other vegetables should be cut small so that all of their flavors can be extracted during the short cooking time.

The procedure for making a fish stock is very similar to that for making a white stock.

sweat to cook a food in a pan (usually covered), without browning, over low heat until the item softens and releases moisture; sweating allows the food to release its flavor more quickly when cooked with other foods

♥ Good Choice

MISE EN PLACE

- Peel and chop onions, carrots and celery for mirepoix.
- Slice mushrooms.
- Wash fish bones or shells.
- Prepare herb sachet.

Adding cold water to bones and mirepoix.

Fish Stock

YIELD   1 gal. (3.8 lt)

Mirepoix, small dice	1 lb.	480 g
Clarified butter	2 fl. oz.	60 ml
Mushrooms, sliced	8 oz.	240 g
Fish bones or crustacean shells	10 lb.	4.8 kg
Water	5 qt.	4.8 lt
Sachet:		
Bay leaves	2	2
Dried thyme	½ tsp.	2 ml
Peppercorns, crushed	¼ tsp.	1 ml
Parsley stems	8	8

1 Sweat mirepoix in butter until tender for 1–2 minutes.

2 Combine all ingredients in a stockpot. Add enough water to cover the bones completely.

3 Bring to a simmer and skim impurities as necessary.

4 Simmer uncovered for 30–45 minutes.

5 Strain, cool and refrigerate.

Approximate values per 1-fl.-oz. (30-ml) serving: **Calories** 5, **Total fat** 0 g, **Saturated fat** 0 g, **Cholesterol** 0 mg, **Sodium** 100 mg, **Total carbohydrates** 0 g, **Protein** 1 g, **Claims**—fat free; low sodium

A fish fumet is flavored with white wine and lemon juice. When making a fumet, sweat the bones and vegetables before adding the cooking liquid and seasonings. A fish stock is sometimes used to make a fish fumet. The resulting product is more strongly flavored than a fish fumet made with water.

Fish Fumet

 **Good Choice**

YIELD 1 gal. (3.8 lt)

Whole butter	1 oz.	30 g
Onions, small dice	8 oz.	240 g
Parsley stems	6	6
Fish bones	5 lb.	2.4 kg
Dry white wine	12 fl. oz.	360 ml
Lemon juice	1 fl. oz.	30 ml
Cold water or fish stock	3½ qt.	3.3 lt
Mushroom trimmings	1 oz.	30 g
Fresh thyme	1 sprig	1 sprig
Lemon slices	5	5

1 Melt the butter in a stockpot.
2 Add the onions, parsley stems and fish bones. Cover the pot and sweat the bones over low heat for 5–10 minutes.
3 Sprinkle the bones with the wine and lemon juice.
4 Add the cold water or stock, mushroom trimmings, thyme and lemon slices. Bring to a boil, reduce to a simmer and cook approximately 30 minutes, skimming frequently.
5 Strain, cool and refrigerate.

Approximate values per 1-fl.-oz. (30-ml) serving: **Calories** 5, **Total fat** 0.7 g, **Saturated fat** 0.2 g, **Cholesterol** 0.5 mg, **Sodium** 90 g, **Total carbohydrates** 0 g, **Protein** 1 g, **Claims**—fat free; low sodium

- Peel onions and chop into small dice.
- Cut up and wash bones.

1 Sweating the onions, parsley stems and fish bones.

2 Adding cold water and seasonings.

Vegetable Stock

A good vegetable stock should be clear and light-colored. Because it contains no animal products, vegetable stock has no gelatin content and little body. A vegetable stock can be used instead of a meat-based stock in most recipes. This substitution is useful when preparing vegetarian dishes. Vegetable stock is also a lighter, more healthful alternative to use when preparing sauces and soups. Although almost any combination of vegetables can be used for stock making, more variety is not always better. Sometimes a vegetable stock made with one or two vegetables that complement the finished dish particularly well produces better results than a stock made with many vegetables. Strongly flavored vegetables such as asparagus, broccoli and other cruciferous vegetables, spinach and bitter greens, should be avoided when making an all-purpose vegetable stock. Potatoes and other starchy vegetables cloud the stock and should not be used unless clarity is not a concern. As with meat or fish stocks, vegetable stock should be started with cold water to extract all of the flavor from the ingredients used. Any fat or scum that rises to the surface should be skimmed off. A recipe for basic vegetable stock follows. A recipe for a more boldly flavored Rich Brown Vegetable Stock appears on page 244.

Good Choice   Vegan

MISE EN PLACE

- Peel and chop onions, carrots and celery for mirepoix.
- Clean, peel and chop leek and garlic cloves.
- Wash and dice fennel, turnip and tomato.
- Prepare herb sachet.

Adding cold water to sweated vegetables.

Vegetable Stock

YIELD 2 gal. (7.6 lt)

Vegetable oil	4 fl. oz.	120 ml
Mirepoix, small dice	4 lb.	1.9 kg
Leek, white and green parts, chopped	1 lb.	480 g
Garlic cloves, chopped	8	8
Fennel, small dice	8 oz.	240 g
Turnip, diced	4 oz.	120 g
Tomato, diced	4 oz.	120 g
White wine	1 pt.	480 ml
Water	2 gal.	7.6 lt
Sachet:		
Bay leaf	2	2
Dried thyme	1 tsp.	5 ml
Peppercorns, crushed	1 tsp.	5 ml
Parsley stems	16	16

1 Heat the oil. Add the mirepoix, leek, garlic, fennel, turnip and tomato and sweat for 10 minutes.

2 Add the wine, water and sachet.

3 Bring the mixture to a boil, reduce to a simmer and cook for 45 minutes, skimming the stock if necessary.

4 Strain, cool and refrigerate.

Approximate values per 1-fl.-oz. (30-ml) serving: **Calories** 5, **Total fat** 0 g, **Saturated fat** 0 g, **Cholesterol** 0 mg, **Sodium** 0 mg, **Total carbohydrates** 0 g, **Protein** 0 g, **Claims**—fat free; low calorie

Court Bouillon

A court bouillon [bool-yawn], is not actually a stock. However, it is prepared in much the same manner as stocks, so we include it here. A court bouillon (French for "short broth") is a flavored liquid, usually water and wine or vinegar, in which vegetables and seasonings have been simmered to impart their flavors and aromas.

Court bouillon is most commonly used to poach foods such as fish and shellfish. Recipes vary depending on the foods to be poached. Although a court bouillon can be made in advance and refrigerated for later use, its simplicity lends itself to fresh preparation whenever needed.

 Good Choice   Vegan

MISE EN PLACE

- Peel and chop onions, carrots and celery for mirepoix.
- Crush peppercorns.

Straining court bouillon.

Court Bouillon

YIELD 1 gal. (3.8 lt)

Water	1 gal.	3.8 lt
Vinegar	6 fl. oz.	180 ml
Lemon juice	2 fl. oz.	60 ml
Mirepoix	1 lb. 8 oz.	720 g
Bay leaves	4	4
Peppercorns, crushed	1 tsp.	5 ml
Dried thyme	1 pinch	1 pinch
Parsley stems	1 bunch	1 bunch

1 Combine all ingredients and bring to a boil.

2 Reduce to a simmer and cook for 45 minutes.

3 Strain and use immediately or cool and refrigerate.

Note This recipe can be used for poaching almost any fish, but it is particularly well suited to salmon, trout and shellfish. When poaching freshwater fish, replace the water and vinegar with equal parts white wine and water.

Approximate values per 1-fl.-oz. (30-ml) serving: **Calories** 3, **Total fat** 0 g, **Saturated fat** 0 g, **Cholesterol** 0 mg, **Sodium** 0 mg, **Total carbohydrates** 0 g, **Protein** 0 g, **Claims**—fat free; low sodium

Nage

An aromatic court bouillon is sometimes served as a light sauce or broth with fish or shellfish. This sauce or broth accompaniment is known as a **nage** [nahj], and dishes served in this manner are described as *à la nage* (French for "swimming"). After the fish or shellfish is cooked in court bouillon, additional herbs and aromatic vegetables are added to the cooking liquid, which is then reduced slightly and strained.

Glaze

A glaze (Fr. *glace*) is the dramatic reduction and concentration of a stock. One gallon (4 liters) of stock produces only 8–16 fluid ounces (240–480 milliliters) of glaze. Meat glaze (Fr. *glace de viande*) is made from brown stock, reduced until it becomes dark and syrupy. Poultry glaze (Fr. *glace de volaille*) is reduced chicken stock, and fish glaze (Fr. *glace de poisson*) is reduced fish stock. Glazes are added to soups or sauces to increase and intensify flavors. They are also used as a source of intense flavoring for several of the small sauces discussed in the following section.

Procedure for Reducing a Stock to a Glaze

1 Simmer the stock over very low heat. Be careful not to let it burn, and skim it often.

2 As it reduces and the volume decreases, transfer the stock into progressively smaller saucepans. Strain the liquid each time it is transferred into a smaller saucepan.

3 Strain the glaze a final time, cool and refrigerate. A properly made glaze keeps for several months under refrigeration.

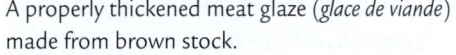

A properly thickened meat glaze (*glace de viande*) made from brown stock.

Chilled meat glaze (*glace de viande.*)

Commercial Bases

Commercially produced flavor (or convenience) bases are widely used in food service operations. They are powdered or paste flavorings added to water to create stocks or, when used in smaller amounts, to enhance the flavor of sauces and soups. These products are also sold as bouillon cubes or granules. Although inferior to well-made stocks, flavor bases do reduce the labor involved in the production of stocks, sauces and soups. Used properly, they also ensure a consistent product. Because most bases do not contain gelatin, stocks and sauces made from them do not benefit from reduction. (Frozen *glace de viande* and demi-glace are increasingly available from meat and other food service suppliers.)

Bases vary greatly in quality and price. Sodium (salt) is the main ingredient in many bases. Better bases are made primarily of meat, poultry or fish extracts. To judge the quality of a flavor base, prepare it according to package directions and compare the flavor to that of a well-made stock. A flavor base can be improved by adding a mirepoix, a standard sachet and a few appropriate bones to the mixture, then simmering for 1 or 2 hours. It can then be strained, stored and used like a regular stock. Although convenience bases are widely used in the industry, it is important to remember that even the best base is a poor substitute for a well-made stock.

Infusion

An **infusion** is a light flavorful stock made from dried fruits or vegetables, herbs, spices or other ingredients steeped in very hot water. Infusing is similar to the method used to make tea or coffee. Perhaps the most well-known culinary infusion is *dashi*, the traditional Japanese broth made from dried fish and dried seaweed that is used to make miso and other soups (see recipe below). Almost any aromatic ingredient can be steeped in water to make an infusion. Umami-rich dried mushrooms, dried shrimp or dried tomatoes make especially flavorful infusions, as do dried anchovies and the rind of hard aged cheese such as Parmesan and Romano.

A well-made infusion has an appealing color and the concentrated flavor of the ingredients used to prepare it. Some infusions, such as saffron infusion, are clear while others, like Parmesan cheese infusion, are cloudy. Although most lack the intensity of flavor of a traditional meat, fish or vegetable stock, infusions can be used in much the same way as stock. Chefs treat infusions as lighter, more healthful alternatives to stock for cooking and flavoring foods.

♥ Good Choice

Straining the dashi.

kombu an edible kelp or seaweed, usually the species *Laminaria japonica*, which grows wild in East Asian oceans; kombu's long, thin strips can be eaten raw, but are generally preferred frozen, pickled or dried

bonito (*katsuobushi*) thin flakes of dried fermented bonito fish, used in many Japanese dishes as a seasoning or topping

Dashi

Although referred to as a Japanese-style stock, **dashi** *is a quick infusion that is used in soups, sauces and as a simmering liquid. Do not overcook or steep the broth too long, or it will become bitter and cloudy.*

YIELD   1 gal. (3.8 lt)

Kombu	2 oz.	60 g
Cold water	1 gal.	3.8 lt
Bonito flakes (*katsuobushi*)	3 oz.	90 g

1 Combine the kombu and cold water in a medium sauce pan and soak for 15 minutes.

2 Bring the kombu and water to just below a simmer over medium heat. Immediately remove the pan from the heat and sprinkle the bonito flakes onto the broth. Allow this mixture to steep for 4 minutes.

3 Strain the stock through a china cap lined with cheesecloth. The dashi may be used at this point or cooled, covered and refrigerated for service at a later time.

Approximate values per 1-fl.-oz. (30-ml) serving: **Calories** 5, **Total fat** 0 g, **Saturated fat** 0 g, **Cholesterol** 0 mg, **Sodium** 0 mg, **Total carbohydrates** 0 g, **Protein** 0 g, **Claims**—fat free; low calorie

TROUBLESHOOTING CHART FOR STOCKS		TABLE 11.1
PROBLEM	**REASON**	**PREVENTION/REMEDY**
Cloudy	Impurities Stock boiled during cooking	Start stock in cold water. Strain through layers of cheesecloth.
Lack of flavor	Not cooked long enough Inadequate seasoning Improper ratio of bones to water	Increase cooking time. Add more flavoring ingredients. Add more bones.
Lack of color	Improperly caramelized bones and mirepoix Not cooked long enough	Caramelize bones and mirepoix until darker. Increase cooking time.
Lack of body	Wrong bones used Insufficient reduction Improper ratio of bones to water	Use bones with a higher content of connective tissue. Increase cooking time. Add more bones.
Too salty	Commercial base used Salt added during cooking	Change base or make own stock. Do not salt stock during preparation.

SAUCES

With a few exceptions, a sauce is a liquid plus thickening agent plus seasonings. Any chef can produce fine sauces by learning to do the following:

1 Make good stocks.
2 Use thickening agents properly to achieve the desired texture, flavor and appearance.
3 Use seasonings properly to achieve desired flavors.

In the following sections, we first discuss thickening and finishing techniques that work with a number of sauces. We then go on to describe classic leading and small sauces in more detail as well as introduce and discuss traditional sauces and contemporary sauces. We also include and discuss recipes for a variety of common sauces.

Thickening Agents for Sauces

One of the most traditional and commonly used methods for thickening sauces is the gelatinization of starches. As discussed in Chapter 10, Principles of Cooking, gelatinization is the process by which starch granules absorb moisture when placed in a liquid and heated. As the starch granules absorb moisture, the product thickens. Starches used to thicken sauces include flour, cornstarch and arrowroot. Gelatinization may sound easy, but it takes practice to produce a good sauce that:

- is lump-free
- has a good clean flavor that is not pasty or floury
- has a consistency that coats the back of a spoon (the French call this **_nappé_**)
- does not separate or break when the sauce is kept warm for service or reduced

nappé [nap-ay] the consistency of a liquid, usually a sauce, that will coat the back of a spoon; from the verb *naper* in French or *nap* in English, meaning to coat a food with sauce

Roux

Adding a roux [roo] is the principal way of thickening classic sauces. A roux is a combination of equal parts, by weight, of flour and fat, cooked together to form a paste. Cooking the flour in fat coats the starch granules with the fat and prevents them from lumping together or forming lumps when introduced into a liquid. In large production kitchens, large amounts of roux are prepared and held for use as needed. Smaller operations may make roux as required for each recipe.

There are three types of roux:

- **White roux** is cooked only briefly and should be removed from the heat as soon as it develops a frothy, bubbly appearance. It is used in white sauces, such as béchamel, or in dishes where little or no color is desired.

White roux

- **Blond roux** is cooked slightly longer than white roux and should begin to take on a little color as the flour caramelizes. It is used in ivory-colored sauces, such as velouté, or where a richer flavor is desired.

- **Brown roux** is cooked until it develops a darker color and a nutty aroma and flavor. Brown roux is used in brown sauces and dishes where a dark color is desired. It is important to remember that cooking a starch before adding a liquid breaks down the starch granules and prevents gelatinization. Therefore, because brown roux is cooked longer than white roux, more brown roux is required to thicken a given quantity of liquid.

Blond roux

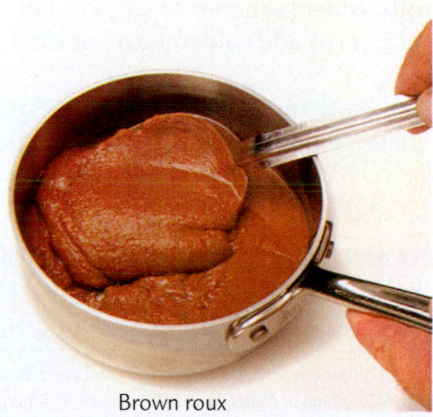

Brown roux

Procedure for Preparing Roux

Cooking the roux.

Whether it is white, blond or brown, the procedure for making a roux is the same:

1   Using a heavy saucepan to prevent scorching, heat the clarified butter or other fat.
2   Add all the flour and stir to form a paste. Although all-purpose flour can be used, it is better to use cake or pastry flour because they contain a higher percentage of starch. Do not use high-gluten flour because of its greatly reduced starch content. (Flours are discussed in Chapter 30, Principles of the Bakeshop.) A gluten-free roux can be made using rice flour in place of wheat flour. Sauces made using gluten-free roux may be somewhat grainy.
3   Cook the paste over medium heat until the desired color is achieved. Stir the roux often to avoid burning. Burnt roux will not thicken a liquid; it will simply add dark specks and an undesirable flavor.

The temperature and amount of roux being prepared determine the exact length of cooking time. Generally, however, a white roux needs to cook for only a few minutes, long enough to minimize the raw flour taste. Blond roux is cooked longer, until the paste begins to become a slightly darker color. Brown roux requires a much longer cooking time to develop its characteristic color and aroma. A good roux is stiff, not runny or pourable.

Incorporating Roux into a Liquid

There are two ways to incorporate roux into a liquid without causing lumps. See Figure 11.3:

1   Cold stock can be added to the hot roux while stirring vigorously with a whisk.
2   Room-temperature roux can be added to a hot stock while stirring vigorously with a whisk.

When the roux and the liquid are completely incorporated and the sauce begins to boil, the sauce must be cook for a time to remove any raw flour taste that may remain. Most chefs feel a minimum of 20 minutes is necessary.

Using Roux

General guidelines for making and using roux include the following:

- Do not use aluminum pots. The scraping action of the whisk turns light sauces gray and imparts a metallic flavor.
- Use sufficiently heavy pots to prevent sauces from scorching or burning during extended cooking times.
- Avoid extreme temperatures. Roux should be no colder than room temperature when used so that the fat is not fully solidified. Extremely hot roux is dangerous and can spatter when combined with a liquid. Stocks should not be ice cold when combined with roux; the roux will become very cold, and the solidified pieces may be difficult to work out with a whisk.
- Do not overthicken. See Table 11.2. Roux does not begin to thicken a sauce until the sauce is almost at the boiling point; the thickening action continues for several minutes while the sauce simmers. If a sauce is to cook for a long time, it will also thicken by reduction.

(a)

Cold stock

Hot roux

(b)

Hot stock

Cold roux

Figure 11.3 When thickening stock with roux, either (a) add cold stock to hot roux or (b) add cold roux to hot stock.

PROPORTIONS OF ROUX TO LIQUID								TABLE 11.2
FLOUR	+	BUTTER	=	ROUX	+	LIQUID	=	SAUCE
6 oz./180 g	+	6 oz./180 g	=	12 oz./360 g	+	1 gal./4 lt	=	light
8 oz./240 g	+	8 oz./240 g	=	1 lb./480 g	+	1 gal./4 lt	=	medium
12 oz./360 g	+	12 oz./360 g	=	24 oz./720 g	+	1 gal./4 lt	=	heavy

Variables: The starch content of a flour determines its thickening power. Cake flour, being lowest in protein and highest in starch, has more thickening power than bread flour, which is high in protein and low in starch. In addition, a dark roux has less thickening power than a lighter one, so more will be needed to thicken an equal amount of liquid.

Cornstarch

Cornstarch, a very fine white powder, is a pure starch derived from corn. It is used widely as a thickening agent for hot and cold sauces and is used extensively in Asian cuisines to thicken sauces and soups. Liquids thickened with cornstarch have a glossy sheen that may or may not be desirable.

One unit of cornstarch thickens about twice as much liquid as an equal unit of flour. Sauces thickened with cornstarch are less stable than those thickened with roux because cornstarch can break down and lose its thickening power after prolonged heating. Products thickened with cornstarch should not be reheated. Cornstarch can also break down when products thickened with it are frozen. Choose a different thickening method when making a sauce that will be frozen.

Cornstarch must be mixed with a cool liquid before it is introduced into a hot one. The cool liquid separates the grains of starch and allows them to begin absorbing liquid without lumping. A solution of a starch and a cool liquid is a **slurry**.

The starch slurry may be added to either a hot or cold liquid. If added to a hot liquid, it must be stirred continuously during incorporation. Unlike roux, cornstarch begins to thicken almost immediately if the liquid is hot. Sauces thickened with cornstarch must be cooked gently until the raw starch flavor disappears, usually about 5 minutes.

Whisking cornstarch slurry into simmering liquid.

slurry a mixture of raw starch and cold liquid used for thickening

Arrowroot

Arrowroot, derived from the roots of several tropical plants, is similar in texture, appearance and thickening power to cornstarch and is used in exactly the same manner. Arrowroot does not break down as quickly as cornstarch, and it produces a slightly clearer finished product although it is much more expensive than cornstarch.

Beurre Manié

Beurre manié [burr mahn-YAY] is a combination of equal amounts, by weight, of flour and soft whole butter. Beurre manié is used for quick thickening at the end of the cooking process. Beurre manié adds shine and flavor to the sauce as it melts.

Procedure for Using Beurre Manié

❶ Kneading flour and butter together until smooth.

❷ Forming the mixture into pea-sized balls, and whisking them gradually into a simmering sauce.

Liaison

Unlike the thickeners already described in this chapter, a liaison [lee-yeh-ZON] does not thicken a sauce through gelatinization. A liaison is a mixture of egg yolks and heavy cream; it adds richness and smoothness with minimal thickening. Special care must be taken to prevent the yolks from coagulating when they are added to a hot liquid because this could curdle the sauce.

Procedure for Using a Liaison

tempering gradually raising the temperature of a cold liquid such as eggs by slowly stirring in a hot liquid

1 Whisk together one part egg yolk and three parts whipping cream. Combining the yolk with cream raises the temperature at which the yolk's proteins coagulate, making it easier to incorporate them into a sauce without lumping or curdling.

2 **Temper** the egg yolk and cream mixture by slowly adding a small amount of the hot liquid while stirring continuously.

3 When enough of the hot liquid has been added to the liaison to warm it thoroughly, begin adding the warmed liaison to the remaining hot liquid. Be sure to stir the mixture carefully to prevent the yolk from overcooking or lumping. Plain egg yolks coagulate at temperatures between 149°F and 158°F (65°C and 70°C). Mixing them with cream raises the temperatures at which they coagulate to approximately 180°F–185°F (82°C–85°C). Temperatures over 185°F (85°C) will cause the yolks to curdle. Great care must be taken to hold the sauce above 135°F (57°C) for food safety and sanitation reasons, yet below 185°F (85°C) to prevent curdling.

❶ Adding hot liquid to the egg yolk and cream mixture.

❷ Adding the tempered egg yolk and cream liaison to the hot liquid.

Emulsification

emulsification the process by which generally unmixable liquids, such as oil and water, are forced into a uniform distribution

Sauces can also be thickened by the process of **emulsification**. Emulsification takes place when ingredients that are normally unmixable, such as fat and water, are forced into a creamy state through the action of beating, blending, shaking, stirring or whisking. The agitation breaks the fat into microscopic droplets that are dispersed in the water. Usually an emulsifying agent, such as the lecithin found in egg yolks, must be present to aid in the process.

In scientific terms, this is called a fat-in-water emulsion, where the fat (the dispersed phase) is dispersed into water (the continuous phase). Cream and milk are examples of fat-in-water emulsions created during the process of homogenization. Butter whisked into vinegar and egg yolks for hollandaise sauce is another example of a fat-in-water emulsion. The microscopic droplets of fat suspended in the liquid give the emulsion its creamy, cloudy appearance. See Figure 11.4.

The action of stirring or whisking a sauce to incorporate the ingredients produces one of three types of emulsion: **permanent**, **semipermanent** or **temporary**. A permanent emulsion, such as that formed when making mayonnaise, will last for several days. A semipermanent emulsion will last for a few hours. Hollandaise sauce, discussed on page 230, is an example of a semipermanent emulsion. A temporary emulsion lasts very briefly and usually does not contain an emulsifying agent. Instead, vigorous whisking aerates the mixture, causing the temporary suspension of liquids. When oil and vinegar are whisked together to make a simple salad dressing, the dressing is a temporary emulsion. Emulsified sauces are discussed in detail in Chapter 25, Salads and Salad Dressings.

Figure 11.4 Visualizing an emulsion: (left) Oil floats on the surface of water before blending, (center) stirring breaks up the oil into large droplets and (right) vigorous stirring disperses the oil throughout the water.

Finishing Techniques for Sauces

Several techniques can be used to finish sauces. Among these are reduction, straining and monter au beurre. Each of these techniques is briefly described in the following sections.

Reduction

As sauces cook, moisture is released in the form of steam. As steam escapes, the remaining ingredients concentrate, thickening the sauce and strengthening its flavors. This process, known as **reduction**, is commonly used to thicken sauces because no starches or other flavor-altering ingredients are needed. Sauces are often finished by allowing them to reduce until the desired consistency is reached.

Straining

Smoothness is important quality that contributes to the success of most sauces. To smooth a sauce, strain it through either a china cap lined with several layers of cheesecloth or a fine-mesh chinois. As discussed later, often vegetables, herbs, spices and other seasonings are added to a sauce for flavor. Straining removes these ingredients as well as any lumps of roux or thickener remaining in the sauce.

Monter au Beurre

Monter au beurre [mohn-TAY oh burr] is the process of swirling or whisking whole butter into a sauce to impart shine, flavor and richness. Compound or flavored butters, discussed later, can be used in place of whole butter to add specific flavors. Monter au beurre is widely used to enrich and finish small sauces.

CLASSIC SAUCE FAMILIES

In classic French cuisine, sauces that are served warm are divided into two groups: **leading sauces**, which are also sometime referred to as **grand** or **mother sauces** (Fr. *sauce mère*) and **small** or **compound sauces**. The five classic mother sauces are béchamel, velouté, espagnole (brown), tomato and hollandaise. Except for hollandaise, a leading sauce is rarely served as is; more often leading sauces are used to create the

reduction cooking a liquid such as a sauce until its quantity decreases through evaporation. To reduce by one-half means to reduce until one-half of the original amount remains. To reduce by three-fourths means that only one-fourth of the original amount remains. To reduce **au sec** means that the liquid is cooked until nearly dry.

Using a wire whisk to finish a sauce with whole butter.

Using a hand blender to finish a sauce with whole butter.

many small sauces. These five leading sauces are the foundation for the classic repertoire and can be seasoned and garnished to create a wide variety of small or compound sauces. These five leading sauces are distinguished principally by the liquids and thickeners used to create them. See Table 11.3.

Small or compound sauces are grouped into families based on their leading sauce. Some small sauces have a variety of uses; others are traditional accompaniments for specific foods. A small sauce may be named for its ingredients, place of origin or creator. Although there are many classic small sauces, we have included only a few of the more popular ones following each of the leading sauce recipes. Table 11.4 lists some popular uses for the classic sauces discussed in this section.

The Béchamel Family

Among the oldest sauces in the classic repertoire is béchamel. Béchamel [bay-shah-mel] is one of two sauces also known as white sauce. Traditionally béchamel was made by adding heavy cream to a thick veal velouté, which is the other sauce known as white sauce (and is discussed on page 222). Although some chefs still believe a béchamel should contain veal stock, today the sauce is almost always made by thickening scalded milk with a white roux and adding seasonings. Béchamel is often used for vegetable, egg and gratin dishes. Cheese sauce made from béchamel is indispensable when making macaroni and cheese. However béchamel has fallen into relative disfavor in recent decades because of its rich, heavy nature. It is nevertheless important to understand its production and its place in traditional sauce making.

A properly made béchamel is rich, creamy and absolutely smooth with no hint of graininess. The flavors of the onion and clove used to season it should be apparent but should not overwhelm the sauce's clean, milky taste. Béchamel sauce should be the color of heavy cream and have a deep luster. It should be thick enough to coat foods lightly but should not taste like the roux used to thicken it.

When making these cream sauces, it is important to simmer them gently and to stir to prevent the mixtures from overheating and sticking to the pan. Cream sauces such as béchamel are susceptible to scorching. **Scorching** takes place when egg or milk proteins are overheated then coagulate and stick to the pan before burning. Scorching changes the aroma, color and taste of the product. A scorched sauce must be discarded.

 Vegetarian

MISE EN PLACE

- Prepare the onion piqué.

Béchamel

YIELD 1 gal. (3.8 lt)

Onion piqué (page 168)	1	1
Milk	1 gal.	3.8 lt
Flour	8 oz.	240 g
Clarified butter	8 fl. oz.	240 ml
Salt and white pepper	TT	TT
Nutmeg, ground	TT	TT

1 Add the onion piqué to the milk in a heavy saucepan and simmer for 20 minutes.

2 In a separate pot, make a white roux with the flour and butter.

3 Remove the onion piqué from the milk. Gradually add the hot milk to the white roux while stirring constantly with a whisk to prevent lumps. Bring to a boil.

4 Reduce the sauce to a simmer, add the seasonings and continue cooking for 30 minutes.

5 Strain the sauce through a china cap lined with cheesecloth. Melted butter can be carefully ladled over the surface of the sauce to prevent a skin from forming (or cut a piece of parchment paper to fit the dimensions of the container and place it directly on top of the sauce to prevent the skin from forming). Hold for service or cool in a water bath.

Approximate values per 6-fl.-oz. (180-ml) serving: **Calories** 240, **Total fat** 15 g, **Saturated fat** 9 g, **Cholesterol** 50 mg, **Sodium** 180 mg, **Total carbohydrates** 18 g, **Protein** 7 g, **Vitamin A** 15%, **Calcium** 25%

CLASSIC SAUCE FAMILIES   TABLE 11.3

LEADING SAUCE	LIQUID	THICKENER
Béchamel	Milk	White roux

Velouté
   Veal velouté
   Chicken velouté
   Fish velouté
	White stock
	Veal stock
	Chicken stock
	Fish stock
		Blond roux

Espagnole (brown sauce)	Brown stock	Brown roux
Tomato sauce	Tomato	Blond roux (optional)
Hollandaise	Butter	Emulsification (egg yolks)

USING CLASSIC SAUCES   TABLE 11.4

SAUCE	QUALITIES	SMALL SAUCE OR FLAVORINGS	USE
Béchamel	Smooth, rich and creamy; no graininess; cream-colored with rich sheen	Cream Cheese Mornay Nantua Soubise	Vegetables, pasta, eggs, fish, shellfish Vegetables, pasta Fish, shellfish, poultry, vegetables Fish, shellfish Veal, pork, eggs

Velouté	Smooth and rich; ivory-colored; good flavor of the stock used; not pasty or heavy	Fish Velouté
		  Bercy
		  Cardinal
		  Normandy
		Allemande (veal or chicken)
		  Aurora
		  Horseradish
		  Mushroom
		  Poulette
		Suprême (chicken)
		  Albufera
		  Hungarian
		  Ivory
			
			Poached fish
			Lobster, white fish, crab, eggs
			Delicate white fish, oysters
			
			Eggs, chicken, sweetbreads
			Roast beef, corned beef, baked ham
			Sautéed poultry, white meats
			Vegetables, sweetbreads
			
			Braised poultry, sweetbreads
			Eggs, chicken, chops, sweetbreads
			Eggs, braised poultry

Espagnole	Smooth and rich; dark brown color; good meat flavor	Bordelaise Chasseur Châteaubriand Chevreuil Madeira/Port Marchand de vin Mushroom Périgueux/Périgourdine Piquant Poivrade Robert	Sautéed or grilled meats Sautéed or grilled meats and poultry Broiled meats Roasted meats and game Grilled or roasted meats and game, ham Grilled or roasted meats Sautéed or grilled meats and poultry Sautéed poultry, grilled meats and game, sweetbreads Pork Grilled or roasted meats, game Pork
Tomato	Thick and rich; slightly grainy; full-flavored	Tomato Creole Spanish Milanaise	Meats, poultry, vegetables, pasta and for making small sauces Fish, eggs, chicken Eggs, fish Pasta, grilled or sautéed poultry and white meats
Hollandaise	Smooth and rich; buttery flavor; light and slightly frothy; pale yellow color; no signs of separating	Béarnaise Choron Foyot Grimrod Maltaise Mousseline	Grilled or sautéed meats and fish Grilled meats and fish Grilled meats and fish Eggs, poached fish Poached fish Poached fish, eggs, vegetables

Small Béchamel Sauces

With a good béchamel, producing the small sauces in its family is quite straightforward. The quantities given in the follow recipes are appropriate to add to 1 quart (approximately 1 liter) of béchamel. The final step for each recipe is to season to taste with salt and pepper.

CHEESE Add to béchamel 8 ounces (240 grams) grated Cheddar or American cheese, a dash of Worcestershire sauce and 1 tablespoon (15 milliliters) dry mustard.

CREAM SAUCE Add to béchamel 8–12 fluid ounces (240–360 milliliters) scalded cream and a few drops of lemon juice.

MORNAY Add to béchamel 4 ounces (120 grams) grated Gruyère and 1 ounce (30 grams) grated Parmesan. Thin as desired with scalded cream. Remove the sauce from the heat and swirl in 2 ounces (60 grams) whole butter.

NANTUA Add to béchamel 4 fluid ounces (120 milliliters) heavy cream and 6 ounces (180 grams) crayfish butter (page 234). Add paprika to achieve the desired color. Garnish the finished sauce with diced crayfish meat.

SOUBISE (MODERN) Sweat 1 pound (480 grams) diced onions in 1 ounce (30 grams) whole butter without browning. Add béchamel and simmer until the onions are fully cooked. Strain through a fine chinois.

The Velouté Family

Velouté [veh-loo-TAY] sauces are made by thickening a white stock or fish stock with roux. The white stock can be made from veal or chicken bones. A properly made velouté should be rich, smooth and lump-free. If made from chicken or fish stock, it should taste of chicken or fish. A velouté made from veal stock should have a more neutral flavor. The sauce should be ivory-colored, with a deep luster. It should be thick enough to cling to foods without tasting like the roux used to thicken it.

A velouté sauce made from veal or chicken stock is usually used to make one of two intermediary sauces—allemande and suprême—from which many small sauces are derived. Table 11.5 is a guide to different types of velouté sauces

Velouté

YIELD 1 gal. (3.8 lt)

Clarified butter	8 fl. oz.	240 ml
Flour	8 oz.	240 g
Chicken, veal or fish stock	5 qt.	4.8 lt
Salt and white pepper	TT	TT

1 Heat the butter in a heavy saucepan. Add the flour and cook to make a blond roux.

2 Gradually add the stock to the blond roux, stirring constantly with a whisk to prevent lumps. Bring to a boil and reduce to a simmer. (Seasonings are optional; their use depends on the seasonings in the stock and the sauce's intended use.)

3 Simmer and reduce to 1 gallon (3.8 liters), approximately 30 minutes.

4 Strain through a china cap lined with cheesecloth.

5 Melted butter may be carefully ladled over the surface of the sauce to prevent a skin from forming. (Or cut a piece of parchment paper to fit the dimensions of the container then place it directly on top of the sauce to prevent a skin from forming.) Hold for service or cool in a water bath.

Approximate values per 1-fl.-oz. (30-ml) serving: **Calories** 25, **Total fat** 1.5 g, **Saturated fat** 1 g, **Cholesterol** 5 mg, **Sodium** 140 mg, **Total carbohydrates** 2 g, **Protein** 1 g

VELOUTÉ SAUCES

TABLE 11.5

STOCK		THICKENER		LEADING SAUCE		ADDITIONAL INGREDIENTS		SAUCE
Fish stock	+	Roux	=	Velouté				
Chicken stock	+	Roux	=	Velouté	+	Cream	=	Suprême
Chicken stock	+	Roux	=	Velouté	+	Liaison and lemon	=	Allemande
Veal stock	+	Roux	=	Velouté	+	Liaison and lemon	=	Allemande

Small Fish Velouté Sauces

A few small sauces can be made from fish velouté. The quantities given are appropriate to add to 1 quart (approximately 1 liter) fish velouté sauce. The final step for each recipe is to season to taste with salt and pepper.

BERCY Sauté 2 ounces (60 grams) finely diced shallots in butter. Then add 8 fluid ounces (240 milliliters) dry white wine and 8 fluid ounces (240 milliliters) fish stock. Reduce this mixture by one-third and add the fish velouté. Finish with butter and garnish with chopped parsley.

CARDINAL Add 8 fluid ounces (240 milliliters) fish stock to 1 quart (1 liter) fish velouté. Reduce this mixture by half and add 16 fluid ounces (480 milliliters) heavy cream and a dash of cayenne pepper. Bring to a boil and swirl in 1½ ounces (45 grams) lobster butter (page 234). Garnish with chopped lobster coral or roe at service time.

NORMANDY Add 4 ounces (120 grams) mushroom trimmings and 4 fluid ounces (120 milliliters) fish stock to 1 quart (960 milliliters) fish velouté. Reduce by one-third and finish with an egg yolk and cream liaison. Strain through a fine chinois.

Allemande Sauce

Allemande sauce is made by adding lemon juice and a liaison to either a veal or chicken velouté. (The stock used depends on the dish with which the sauce will be served.) See Table 11.5.

allemande [ah-leh-MAHND] an intermediary sauce made by adding lemon juice and a liaison to chicken or veal velouté

Allemande Sauce

YIELD 1 gal. (3.8 lt)

Veal or chicken velouté sauce	1 gal.	3.8 lt
Egg yolks	8	8
Heavy cream	24 fl. oz.	720 ml
Lemon juice	1 fl. oz.	30 ml
Salt and white pepper	TT	TT

1 Bring the velouté to a simmer.

2 In a stainless steel bowl, whisk the egg yolks with the cream to create a liaison. Ladle approximately one-third of the hot velouté sauce into this mixture, while whisking, to temper the yolk and cream mixture.

3 When one-third of the velouté has been incorporated into the now-warmed yolk-and-cream mixture, gradually add the liaison to the remaining velouté sauce while whisking continuously.

4 Reheat the sauce. Do not let it boil.

5 Add the lemon juice; season with salt and white pepper to taste.

6 Strain through a china cap lined with damp cheesecloth.

Approximate values per 1-fl.-oz. (30-ml) serving: **Calories** 40, **Total fat** 3.5 g, **Saturated fat** 2 g, **Cholesterol** 25 mg, **Sodium** 95 mg, **Total carbohydrates** 1 g, **Protein** 1 g, **Vitamin A** 4%

Small Allemande Sauces

Several small sauces are produced from an allemande sauce made with either a chicken or veal velouté. The quantities given are appropriate to add to 1 quart (approximately 1 liter) allemande. The final step for each recipe is to season to taste with salt and pepper.

AURORA Add to allemande 2 ounces (60 grams) tomato paste and finish with 1 ounce (30 grams) butter.

HORSERADISH Add to allemande 4 fluid ounces (120 milliliters) heavy cream and 1 teaspoon (5 milliliters) dry mustard. Just before service add 2 ounces (60 grams) freshly grated horseradish to the warm sauce. The horseradish should not be cooked with the sauce.

MUSHROOM Sauté 4 ounces (120 grams) sliced mushrooms in ½ ounce (15 grams) whole butter; add 2 teaspoons (10 milliliters) lemon juice. Add the allemande to the sautéed mushrooms. Do not strain.

POULETTE Sauté 8 ounces (240 grams) sliced mushrooms and ½ ounce (15 grams) diced shallot in 1 ounce (30 grams) whole butter. Add to the allemande; then add 2 fluid ounces (60 milliliters) heavy cream. Finish with lemon juice to taste and 1 tablespoon (15 milliliters) chopped parsley.

Suprême Sauce

suprême [soo-PREM] an intermediary sauce made by adding cream to chicken velouté

Suprême sauce is made by adding cream to a chicken velouté. See Table 11.5.

Suprême Sauce

YIELD   1 gal. (3.8 lt)

Chicken velouté sauce	1 gal.	3.8 lt
Mushroom stems and trimmings	8 oz.	240 g
Heavy cream	1 qt.	960 ml
Salt and white pepper	TT	TT

1 Simmer the velouté sauce with the mushroom trimmings until reduced by one-fourth.

2 Gradually whisk in the cream and return to a simmer.

3 Adjust the seasonings.

4 Strain through a china cap lined with damp cheesecloth.

Approximate values per 1-fl.-oz. (30-ml) serving: **Calories** 45, **Total fat** 4 g, **Saturated fat** 2.5 g, **Cholesterol** 15 mg, **Sodium** 95 mg, **Total carbohydrates** 1 g, **Protein** 1 g, **Vitamin A** 4%

Small Suprême Sauces

The following small sauces are made from a suprême sauce. The quantities given are appropriate to add to 1 quart (approximately 1 liter) suprême sauce. The final step for each recipe is to season to taste with salt and pepper.

ALBUFERA Add to suprême sauce 3 fluid ounces (90 milliliters) glace de volaille and 2 ounces (60 grams) red pepper butter (page 234).

HUNGARIAN Sweat 2 ounces (60 grams) diced onion in 1 tablespoon (15 milliliters) whole butter. Add 1 tablespoon (15 milliliters) paprika. Stir in suprême sauce. Cook for 2 to 3 minutes, strain and finish with whole butter.

IVORY Add to suprême sauce 3 fluid ounces (90 milliliters) glace de volaille.

The Espagnole Family

The mother sauce of the espagnole [ess-spah-NYOL] or brown sauce family is full-bodied and rich. It is made from a brown stock to which brown roux, mirepoix and tomato purée have been added although modern kitchens often prepare a modified version of this sauce made without roux. Most often this sauce is used to produce **demi-glace** [deh-mee glass]. Brown stock is also used to make **jus lié** [ZHOO lee-AY]. Demi-glace and jus lié are intermediary sauces used to create the small sauces of the espagnole family.

Espagnole (Brown Sauce)

YIELD 1 gal. (3.8 lt)

Mirepoix, medium dice	2 lb.	960 g
Clarified butter	8 fl. oz.	240 ml
Flour	8 oz.	240 g
Brown stock	5 qt.	4.8 lt
Tomato purée	8 oz.	240 g
Sachet:		
Bay leaf	1	1
Dried thyme	½ tsp.	2 ml
Peppercorns, crushed	¼ tsp.	1 ml
Parsley stems	8	8
Salt and pepper	TT	TT

MISE EN PLACE

- Peel and chop onions, carrots and celery for mirepoix.
- Prepare herb sachet.

1 Sauté the mirepoix in the butter until well caramelized.

2 Add the flour and cook to make a brown roux.

3 Add the stock and tomato purée to the roux. Stir to break up any lumps of roux. Bring to a boil; reduce to a simmer.

4 Add the sachet.

5 Simmer for approximately 1½ hours, allowing the sauce to reduce. Skim the surface as needed to remove impurities.

6 Strain the sauce through a china cap lined with several layers of cheesecloth. Adjust seasonings if the sauce will be used on its own and cool in a water bath or hold for service.

Approximate values per 1-fl.-oz. (30-ml) serving: **Calories** 35, **Total fat** 2 g, **Saturated fat** 1 g, **Cholesterol** 5 mg, **Sodium** 150 mg, **Total carbohydrates** 4 g, **Protein** 1 g, **Vitamin A** 6%, **Claims**—low fat; low calorie

Demi-Glace

Espagnole sauce can be made into demi-glace, which in turn is used to make the small sauces of the espagnole family. Demi-glace is half brown sauce, half brown stock, reduced by half. It is usually finished with a small amount of Madeira or sherry. Because demi-glace creates a richer, more flavorful base, it produces finer small sauces than those made directly from a brown sauce.

A properly made demi-glace is rich, smooth and lump-free. Its prominent roasted flavor comes from the bones used for the brown stock. There should be no taste of roux in demi-glace. The caramelized bones and mirepoix as well as the tomato product contribute to its glossy dark brown, almost chocolate, color. Demi-glace should be thick enough to cling to food without being pasty or heavy.

Demi-Glace

YIELD 1 qt. (960 ml)

Brown stock	1 qt.	960 ml
Brown sauce	1 qt.	960 ml

1 Combine the stock and sauce in a saucepan over medium heat.

2 Simmer until the mixture is reduced by half (a yield of 1 quart or 960 milliliters).

3 Strain and cool in a water bath.

Approximate values per 1-fl.-oz. (30-ml) serving: **Calories** 30, **Total fat** 1.5 g, **Saturated fat** 0.5 g, **Cholesterol** 5 mg, **Sodium** 200 mg, **Total carbohydrates** 4 g, **Protein** 1 g, **Vitamin A** 6%, **Claims**—low fat; low calorie

Jus Lié

Jus lié, also known as fond lié, is used like a demi-glace to produce small sauces. Jus lié is lighter and easier to make than a demi-glace, however, and it is more common in modern kitchens than demi-glace. A properly made jus lié is very rich and smooth. It shares many flavor characteristics with demi-glace. Its color should be dark brown and glossy from the concentrated gelatin content. Its consistency is somewhat lighter than demi-glace, but it should still cling lightly to foods.

Jus lié is made in one of two ways:

1 A rich brown stock is thickened with cornstarch or arrowroot and seasoned.
2 A rich brown stock is simmered and reduced so that it thickens naturally because of the concentrated amounts of gelatin and other proteins.

The starch-thickened method is a quick alternative to the long-simmering method. But because jus lié made with the starch-thickened method is simply a brown stock thickened with cornstarch or arrowroot, it is only as good as the stock with which it was begun. Sauces made from reduced stock usually have a better flavor but can be expensive to produce because of high ingredient costs and lengthy reduction time.

A vegetarian jus lié can be made from deeply-browned aromatic vegetables that give the sauce a rich flavor.

 Good Choice    Vegan

MISE EN PLACE

- Peel and chop carrots, celery, leeks and onions.
- Mince garlic.
- Chop thyme.

Vegetable Jus Lié

YIELD Approximately 1½ qt. (1.4 lt)

Carrots, chopped	8 oz.	240 g
Celery, chopped	8 oz.	240 g
Leeks, whites and greens, chopped	4 oz.	120 g
Onions, coarsely chopped	6 oz.	120 g
Olive oil	2 Tbsp.	30 ml
Tomato paste	4 oz.	120 g
Garlic cloves, minced	6	6
Red wine	12 fl. oz.	360 ml
Bay leaf	1	1
Vegetable Stock (page 212)	2 qt.	1.9 lt
Fresh thyme, chopped	1 tsp.	5 ml
Cornstarch or arrowroot	as needed	as needed

1 Sauté the vegetables in the oil until well browned, approximately 10–15 minutes. Stir in the tomato paste and garlic. Cook, stirring until the vegetables are well coated with the tomato paste.
2 Add 6 fluid ounces (180 milliliters) wine and reduce by half. Add the remaining wine and reduce by half.
3 Add the bay leaf, stock and thyme and cook until the liquid is reduced by half. Strain.
4 Adjust the thickness of the sauce by thickening it with a cornstarch or arrowroot slurry until the sauce coats a spoon. Cool and refrigerate.

Approximate values per 1-fl.-oz. (30-ml) serving: **Calories** 6, **Total fat** 0 g, **Saturated fat** 0 g, **Cholesterol** 0 mg, **Sodium** 0 mg, **Total carbohydrates** 0 g, **Protein** 0 g, **Claims**—fat free; low calorie

Small Brown Sauces

Demi-glace and jus lié are used to produce many small sauces. The quantities given are appropriate to add to 1 quart (approximately 1 liter) demi-glace or jus lié. The final step for each recipe is to season to taste with salt and pepper.

BORDELAISE Combine 16 fluid ounces (480 milliliters) dry red wine, 2 ounces (60 grams) chopped shallots, 1 bay leaf, 1 sprig thyme and 1 pinch black pepper in a saucepan. Reduce by three-fourths, then add demi-glace and simmer for 15 minutes. Strain through a fine chinois. Finish with 2 ounces (60 grams) whole butter and garnish with sliced, poached beef marrow.

CHASSEUR (HUNTER'S SAUCE) Sauté 4 ounces (120 grams) sliced mushrooms and ½ ounce (15 grams) diced shallots in whole butter. Add 8 fluid ounces (240 milliliters) white wine and reduce by three-fourths. Then add demi-glace and 6 ounces (180 grams) diced tomatoes; simmer for 5 minutes. Do not strain. Garnish with chopped parsley.

CHÂTEAUBRIAND Combine 16 fluid ounces (480 milliliters) dry white wine and 2 ounces (60 grams) diced shallots. Reduce the mixture by two-thirds. Add demi-glace and reduce by half. Season to taste with lemon juice and cayenne pepper. Do not strain. Swirl in 4 ounces (120 grams) whole butter to finish and garnish with chopped fresh tarragon.

CHEVREUIL Prepare a poivrade sauce (below) but add 6 ounces (180 grams) bacon or game trimmings to the mirepoix. Finish with 4 fluid ounces (120 milliliters) red wine and a dash of cayenne pepper.

MADEIRA OR PORT Bring demi-glace to a boil and reduce slightly. Add 4 fluid ounces (120 milliliters) Madeira wine or ruby port.

MARCHAND DE VIN Reduce 8 fluid ounces (240 milliliters) dry red wine and 2 ounces (60 grams) diced shallots by two-thirds. Add demi-glace, simmer and strain.

MUSHROOM Blanch 8 ounces (240 grams) mushroom caps in 8 fluid ounces (240 milliliters) boiling water seasoned with salt and lemon juice. Drain the mushrooms, saving the liquid. Reduce this liquid to 2 tablespoons (30 milliliters) and add it to the demi-glace. Just before service stir in 2 ounces (60 grams) whole butter and the mushroom caps.

PÉRIGUEUX Add finely diced truffles to Madeira sauce. **Périgourdine** sauce is the same as périgueux, except that in périgourdine the truffles are cut into relatively thick slices.

PIQUANT Combine 1 ounce (30 grams) shallots, 4 fluid ounces (120 milliliters) white wine and 4 fluid ounces (120 milliliters) white wine vinegar. Reduce the mixture by two-thirds. Then add demi-glace and simmer for 10 minutes. Add 2 ounces (60 grams) diced cornichons, 1 tablespoon (15 milliliters) fresh tarragon, 1 tablespoon (15 milliliters) fresh parsley and 1 tablespoon (15 milliliters) fresh chervil. Do not strain.

POIVRADE Sweat 12 ounces (360 grams) mirepoix in 2 tablespoons (30 milliliters) oil. Add 1 bay leaf, 1 sprig thyme and 4 parsley stems. Add 16 fluid ounces (480 milliliters) vinegar and 4 fluid ounces (120 milliliters) white wine. Reduce by half, add demi-glace and simmer for 40 minutes. Add 20 crushed peppercorns and simmer for 5 more minutes. Strain through a fine chinois and finish with up to 2 ounces (60 grams) whole butter.

ROBERT Sauté 8 ounces (240 grams) chopped onion in 1 ounce (30 grams) whole butter. Add 8 fluid ounces (240 milliliters) dry white wine and reduce by two-thirds. Add demi-glace and simmer for 10 minutes. Strain and then add 2 teaspoons (10 milliliters) prepared Dijon mustard and 1 tablespoon (15 milliliters) granulated sugar. If the finished Robert sauce is garnished with sliced sour pickles, preferably cornichons, it is known as **Charcutière**.

The Tomato Sauce Family

Classic tomato sauce is made from tomatoes, vegetables, seasonings and white stock and thickened with a blond or brown roux. In today's kitchens, however, most tomato sauces are not thickened with roux. Rather they are created from tomatoes, herbs, spices, vegetables and other flavoring ingredients simmered together and puréed. They are thickened by reduction not roux.

A **gastrique** is sometimes added to reduce the acidity of a tomato sauce. To prepare a gastrique, caramelize a small amount of sugar, then thin or deglaze with vinegar. This mixture is used to finish the tomato sauce.

gastrique [gas-STREEK] caramelized sugar deglazed with vinegar; used to flavor tomato or savory fruit sauces

A properly made tomato sauce is thick, rich and full-flavored. Its texture should be grainier than most other classic sauces, but it should still be smooth. The vegetables and other seasonings should add flavor, but none should be pronounced. Tomato sauce should not be bitter, acidic or overly sweet. It should be deep red and thick enough to cling to foods.

♥ Good Choice

Tomato Sauce

Unlike the other mother sauces, there are many variations of tomato sauce depending on the intended use. This contemporary tomato sauce retains the bright fresh taste of tomatoes, garlic and fresh basil. It is made without a mirepoix, which could be substituted for the onions in this recipe, giving the sauce a sweeter flavor. Simmering pork or ham bones with the tomatoes enriches the sauce, but it is optional.

MISE EN PLACE

- Peel and chop onions and garlic.
- Wash pork or ham bones.

YIELD   1 gal. (3.8 lt)

Olive oil	4 fl. oz.	120 ml
Onion, small dice	1 lb.	480 g
Garlic, chopped	3 Tbsp.	45 ml
Whole plum tomatoes, canned	7 lb.	3.4 kg
Tomato purée, canned	3 lb.	1.4 kg
Pork or ham bones, optional	2 lb.	960 g
Fresh basil	1 oz.	30 g
Salt and pepper	TT	TT

1 In a wide, heavy bottomed, nonreactive, saucepot or rondeau, heat the oil over medium heat and add the onion. Cook, stirring often, until the onion begins to brown slightly, approximately 10 minutes.

2 Add the garlic and cook until the garlic is soft and fragrant, for approximately 1 minute.

3 Add the tomatoes, tomato purée and bones, if using. Bring to a simmer and cook, stirring often, until the sauce reduces slightly and develops a sauce like consistency, approximately 1–1 ½ hours.

4 Remove the bones, if using. Stir in the fresh basil and season to taste with salt and pepper.

5 Use the sauce immediately, or for a smoother sauce, pass it through a food mill or process it in a food processor before using. Cool in a water bath and refrigerate.

Note To make the sauce with fresh tomatoes, substitute 12 pounds (5.8 kilograms) ripe plum tomatoes for the whole canned plum tomatoes and the tomato puree. Core and chop the fresh tomatoes before using. Pass the sauce through a food mill after cooking to remove the tomato seeds and skin.

Approximate values per 1-fl.-oz. (30-ml) serving: **Calories** 15, **Total fat** 1 g, **Saturated fat** 0.2 g, **Cholesterol** 0.7 mg, **Sodium** 50 mg, **Total carbohydrates** 2 g, **Protein** 2 g, **Claims**—low fat; low calorie

❶ Passing the tomato sauce through a food mill.

❷ The finished sauce.

Small Tomato Sauces

The following small sauces are made by adding the listed ingredients to 1 quart (1 liter) tomato sauce. The final step for each recipe is to season to taste with salt and pepper.

CREOLE Sauté 6 ounces (180 grams) finely diced onion, 4 ounces (120 grams) thinly sliced celery and 1 teaspoon (5 milliliters) garlic in 1 fluid ounce (30 milliliters) oil. Add tomato sauce, a bay leaf and 1 pinch thyme; simmer for 15 minutes. Add 4 ounces (120 grams) finely diced green pepper and a dash of hot pepper sauce; simmer for 15 minutes longer. Remove the bay leaf.

SPANISH Prepare creole sauce as directed, adding 4 ounces (120 grams) sliced mushrooms to the sautéed onions. Garnish with sliced black or green olives.

MILANAISE Sauté 5 ounces (150 grams) sliced mushrooms in ½ ounce (15 grams) whole butter. Add tomato sauce and then stir in 5 ounces (150 grams) cooked ham (julienne) and 5 ounces (150 grams) cooked tongue (julienne). Bring to a simmer.

The Hollandaise Family

Hollandaise and the small sauces derived from it are emulsified sauces. Egg yolks, which contain large amounts of lecithin, a natural emulsifier, are used to emulsify warm butter and a small amount of water, lemon juice or vinegar. When the egg yolks are vigorously whipped with the liquid while the warm butter is slowly added, the lecithin coats the individual fat droplets and holds them in suspension in the liquid.

A properly made hollandaise is smooth, buttery, pale lemon-yellow-colored and very rich. It is lump-free and does not exhibit any signs of separation. The buttery flavor dominates but does not mask the flavors of the egg, lemon and vinegar. Hollandaise sauce should be frothy and light, not heavy like a mayonnaise.

Temperatures and Sanitation Concerns

Temperature plays an important role in the proper production of a hollandaise sauce. As the egg yolks and liquid are whisked together, they are cooked over a bain marie until they thicken to the consistency of slightly whipped cream. Do not overheat this mixture, because even slightly cooked eggs lose their ability to emulsify. For this reason, the clarified butter used to make the sauce should be warm but not so hot as to further cook the egg yolks. Although hollandaise sauce can be made from whole butter, a more stable and consistent product is achieved by using clarified butter. (Clarification is described in Chapter 9, Mise en Place.)

Rescuing a Broken Hollandaise

Occasionally a hollandaise will break or separate and appear thin, grainy or even lumpy. A sauce breaks when the emulsion has not formed or the emulsified butter, eggs and liquid have separated. This may happen for several reasons: The temperature of the eggs or butter may have been too high or too low; the butter may have been added too quickly; the egg yolks may have been overcooked; too much butter may have been added or the sauce may not have been whipped vigorously enough.

To rescue and re-emulsify broken hollandaise you must first determine whether it is too hot or too cold. If it is too hot, allow the sauce to cool. If it is too cold, reheat the sauce over a double boiler before attempting to rescue it.

For 1 quart (approximately 1 liter) of broken sauce, place 1 tablespoon (15 milliliters) water in a clean stainless steel bowl and slowly beat in the broken sauce. If the problem seems to be that the eggs were overcooked or too much butter was added, add a yolk to the water before incorporating the broken sauce.

> ⚠ **Safety Alert**
>
> *Handling Emulsified Butter Sauces*
>
> Emulsified butter sauces must be held at the specific temperatures most conducive to bacterial growth: 41–135°F (5–57°C). If the sauce is heated above 150°F (65°C), the eggs will cook and the sauce will break and become grainy. If the sauce temperature falls below 45°F (7°C), the butter will solidify, making the sauce unusable. In order to minimize the risk of food-borne illnesses:
>
> - Always use clean, sanitized utensils.
> - Schedule sauce production as close to the time of service as possible. Never hold hollandaise-based sauces more than 1½ hours.
> - Make small batches of sauce.
> - Never mix an old batch of sauce with a new one.

Broken hollandaise separates, appearing thin and curdled.

Hollandaise

🌿 Vegetarian

MISE EN PLACE

- Crush white peppercorns.
- Warm clarified butter.

YIELD 1½ pt. (720 ml)

White peppercorns, crushed	½ tsp.	2 ml
White wine vinegar	3 fl. oz.	90 ml
Water	3 fl. oz.	90 ml
Egg yolks, pasteurized	6	6
Lemon juice	1½ fl. oz.	45 ml
Clarified butter, warm	1 pt.	480 ml
Salt and white pepper	TT	TT
Cayenne pepper	TT	TT

1 Combine the peppercorns, vinegar and water in a small saucepan and reduce by one-half.

2 Place the egg yolks in a stainless steel bowl. Strain the vinegar-and-pepper reduction through a chinois into the yolks. Use ½ fluid ounce (15 milliliters) of the acidic reduction for each egg yolk.

3 Place the bowl over a double boiler, whipping the mixture continuously with a wire whip. As the yolks cook, the mixture will thicken. When the mixture is thick enough to leave a trail across the surface when the whip is drawn away, remove the bowl from the double boiler. Do not overcook the egg yolks.

4 Whisk in 1 fluid ounce (30 milliliters) lemon juice to stop the yolks from cooking.

5 Begin to add the warm clarified butter to the egg yolk mixture a few drops at a time, while constantly whipping the mixture to form an emulsion. Once the emulsion is started, the butter may be added more quickly. Continue until all the butter is incorporated.

6 Whisk in the remaining lemon juice. Adjust the seasonings.

7 Strain the sauce through cheesecloth if necessary and hold for service in a warm (not simmering) bain marie. This sauce may be held for approximately 1 to 1½ hours.

Approximate values per 1-fl.-oz. (30-ml) serving: **Calories** 170, **Total fat** 18 g, **Saturated fat** 11 g, **Cholesterol** 90 mg, **Sodium** 180 mg, **Total carbohydrates** 0 g, **Protein** 1 g, **Vitamin A** 20%

❶ Combining the egg yolks with the vinegar and pepper reduction in a stainless steel bowl.

❷ Whipping the mixture over a double boiler until it is thick enough to leave a trail when the whip is removed.

❸ Using a kitchen towel and saucepot to firmly hold the bowl containing the yolks, add the butter slowly while whipping continuously.

❹ Hollandaise at the proper consistency, smooth, lump-free and frothy.

Small Hollandaise Sauces

The following small sauces are easily made by adding the listed ingredients to 1 quart (approximately 1 liter) hollandaise. The final step for each recipe is to season to taste with salt and pepper. Béarnaise is presented here as a small sauce although some chefs consider it a leading sauce.

BÉARNAISE [bair-NAYZ] Combine 2 ounces (60 grams) chopped shallots, 5 tablespoons (75 milliliters) chopped fresh tarragon, 3 tablespoons (45 milliliters) chopped fresh chervil and 1 teaspoon (5 milliliters) crushed peppercorns with 8 fluid ounces (240 milliliters) white wine vinegar. Reduce to 2 fluid ounces (60 milliliters). Add this reduction to the egg yolks and proceed with the hollandaise recipe. Strain the finished sauce and season to taste with salt and cayenne pepper. Garnish with additional chopped fresh tarragon.

CHORON Combine 2 ounces (60 grams) tomato paste and 2 fluid ounces (60 milliliters) heavy cream; add the mixture to a béarnaise.

FOYOT Add to béarnaise 3 fluid ounces (90 milliliters) melted glace de viande.

GRIMROD Infuse a hollandaise sauce with saffron.

MALTAISE Add to hollandaise 2 fluid ounces (60 milliliters) orange juice and 2 teaspoons (10 milliliters) finely grated orange zest. Blood oranges are traditionally used for this sauce.

MOUSSELINE (CHANTILLY SAUCE) Whip 8 fluid ounces (240 milliliters) heavy cream until stiff. Fold it into the hollandaise just before service. Mousseline sauce is also used as a **glaçage** coating.

glaçage [glah-SAHGE] browning or glazing a food, usually under a salamander or broiler

TRADITIONAL SAUCES

Not all sauces fall into classic French classifications. There are other sauces, which we refer to in this chapter as traditional sauces. For example, beurre blanc (French for "white butter") and beurre rouge ("red butter"), are based on an acidic reduction in which whole butter is incorporated. Other traditional sauces use purées of fruits or vegetables as their base; they are known as **coulis**. Pan gravy and other pan sauces are as common in American kitchens as they are in France. Table 11.6 lists popular uses for the traditional and contemporary sauces discussed in this section.

beurre fondu [burr fon-DOO] French for "melted butter"; often served over steamed vegetables such as asparagus or poached white fish

beurre noir [burr NWAR] French for "black butter"; whole butter cooked until dark brown (not black) sometimes flavored with vinegar or lemon juice, capers and parsley and served over fish, eggs and vegetables

Beurre Blanc and Beurre Rouge

Beurre blanc [burr blahnk] and **beurre rouge** [burr rooge] are emulsified butter sauces made without egg yolks. The small amounts of casein (the protein in milk), lecithin and other emulsifiers naturally found in butter form an oil-in-water emulsion. Although similar to hollandaise in concept, these emulsified butter sauces are not considered to be classic leading nor compound sauces. Beurre blanc and beurre rouge are thinner and lighter than hollandaise and béarnaise. They should be smooth and slightly thicker than heavy cream.

beurre noisette [burr nwah-ZEHT] French for "brown butter"; butter cooked until it is a light brown color that is flavored and used in much the same manner as beurre noir

USING TRADITIONAL AND CONTEMPORARY SAUCES			TABLE 11.6
SAUCE	QUALITIES	FLAVORINGS	USE
Beurre blanc and beurre rouge	Rich and buttery; thinner than hollandaise; light and airy; pale	A wide variety of seasonings and flavorings	Steamed, grilled or poached fish, chicken or vegetables
Compound butters	Flavor ingredients should be evenly distributed	A wide variety of seasonings and flavorings	Grilled meats, poultry, fish or vegetables; finishing sauces
Pan gravy (jus lié)	Smooth; deep rich color; meaty flavor	Pan drippings	Roasted meats and poultry
Coulis	Rich color; moderately thin, grainy texture; strongly flavored	A wide variety of vegetables or fruits	Vegetables, grilled or poached meats, poultry and fish
Salsa and relish	Chunky; bright colors; not watery	A wide variety of vegetables, fruits and seasonings	Meats, fish, vegetables and poultry; used as a sauce or condiment
Flavored oils	Smooth; bright colors; intense flavors	A variety of herbs, spices and seasonings	Used as a garnish
Foams	Smooth; light, aerated texture; delicate flavor	A variety of thickened stocks or juices	Meats, fish, vegetables and poultry; used as a sauce or condiment

Beurre blanc and beurre rouge are made from three main ingredients: shallots, white (Fr. *blanc*) wine or red (Fr. *rouge*) wine and whole butter (not clarified). The shallots and wine provide flavor, while the butter becomes base of the sauce. A good beurre blanc or beurre rouge is rich and buttery, with a neutral flavor that responds well to other seasonings and flavorings, thereby lending itself to the addition of herbs, spices and vegetable purées to complement the dish with which it is served. The pale color of beurre blanc or beurre rouge changes depending on the flavorings added. Beurre blanc or beurre rouge should be light and airy yet still liquid, while thick enough to cling to food.

Procedure for Preparing Beurre Blanc or Beurre Rouge

1   Use a nonaluminum pan to prevent discoloring the sauce. Do not use a thin-walled or non-stick pan, as heat is not evenly distributed in a thin-walled pan and a nonstick pan makes it difficult for an emulsion to set.

2   Over medium heat, reduce the wine, shallots and herbs or other seasonings, if used, until au sec (i.e., nearly dry). Some chefs add a small amount of heavy cream at this point and reduce the mixture. Although not necessary, the added cream helps stabilize the finished sauce.

3   Whisk in cold butter a small amount at a time. The butter should be well chilled, as this allows the butterfat, water and milk solids to be gradually incorporated into the sauce as the butter melts and the mixture is whisked.

4   When all the butter is incorporated, strain the sauce and hold in a bain marie.

There are some important temperature considerations to keep in mind when making beurre blanc or beurre rouge. Do not let the sauce become too hot. At 136°F (58°C) some of the emulsifying proteins begin to break down and release the butterfat they hold in emulsion. Extended periods at temperatures over 136°F (58°C) will cause the sauce to separate. If the sauce separates, it can be corrected by cooling to approximately 110–120°F (43–49°C) and whisking to reincorporate the butterfat.

If the sauce is allowed to cool below 85°F (30°C), the butterfat will solidify. If the sauce is reheated it will separate into butterfat and water; whisking will not re-emulsify it. Cold beurre blanc can be used as a soft, flavored butter, however. Whisk it at room temperature until it smooths out to the consistency of mayonnaise.

🌿 Vegetarian

MISE EN PLACE

- Peel and mince shallot.

Beurre Blanc

YIELD   1 qt. (960 ml)

White wine vinegar	1 fl. oz.	30 ml
White wine	4 fl. oz.	120 ml
Salt	1½ tsp.	7 ml
White pepper	½ tsp.	2 ml
Shallot, minced	1 oz.	30 g
Whole butter, chilled	2 lb.	960 g

1   Combine the white wine vinegar, white wine, salt, white pepper and shallot in a small saucepan. Reduce the mixture until approximately 2 tablespoons (30 milliliters) of liquid remain. If more than 2 tablespoons of liquid are allowed to remain, the resulting sauce will be too thin. For a thicker sauce, reduce the mixture au sec.

2   Cut the butter into pieces approximately 1 ounce (30 grams) in weight. Over low heat, whisk in the butter a few pieces at a time, using the chilled butter to keep the sauce between 100°F and 120°F (38°C and 49°C).

3   Once all the butter has been incorporated, remove the saucepan from the heat. Strain through a chinois and hold the sauce at a temperature between 100°F and 130°F (38°C and 54°C) for service.

Variations:

Beurre Rouge—Substitute a dry red wine for the white wine and red wine vinegar for the white wine vinegar.

Lemon-Dill—Heat 2 tablespoons (30 milliliters) lemon juice and whisk it into the beurre blanc. Stir in 4 tablespoons (60 milliliters) chopped fresh dill.

Herb Butter Sauce—Add 2 tablespoons (30 milliliters) of chopped fresh herbs such as basil, dill or tarragon to the finished sauce.

Approximate values per 1-fl.-oz. (30-ml) serving: **Calories** 210, **Total fat** 23 g, **Saturated fat** 14 g, **Cholesterol** 60 mg, **Sodium** 340 mg, **Total carbohydrates** 0 g, **Protein** 0 g, **Vitamin A** 20%

1 Reducing the shallots and wine au sec.

2 Whisking in the cold butter a little at a time.

3 Straining the beurre blanc sauce.

Compound Butters

A compound butter is made by incorporating various seasonings into softened whole butter. These butters, also known as *beurres composés*, give flavor and color to small sauces or may be served as sauces in their own right. For example, a slice of maître d'hôtel butter (parsley butter) is often placed on a grilled steak or piece of fish at the time of service. The butter quickly melts, creating a sauce for the beef or fish.

Butter and flavoring ingredients can be combined with a blender, food processor or mixer. Using parchment paper or plastic wrap, the butter is rolled into a cylinder, chilled and sliced as needed, or a compound butter can be piped into rosettes and refrigerated until firm. Most compound butters keep for 2–3 days in the refrigerator, or they can be frozen for longer storage.

1 To form compound butter into a cylinder, place it on plastic wrap or parchment paper.

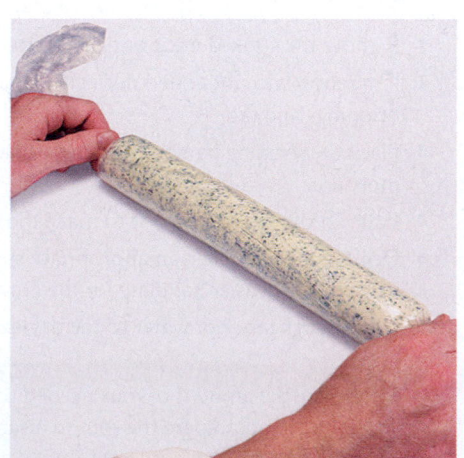

2 Roll the butter in the plastic wrap or parchment paper to form a cylinder.

Recipes for Compound Butters

For each of the following butters, add the listed ingredients to 1 pound (480 grams) of softened, unsalted butter. The compound butter should be seasoned with salt and pepper to taste.

BASIL BUTTER Mince 2 ounces (60 grams) fresh basil and 2 ounces (60 grams) shallots; add to the butter with 2 teaspoons (10 milliliters) lemon juice.

HERB BUTTER Add to the butter up to 1 cup (240 milliliters) mixed chopped fresh herbs such as parsley, dill, chives, tarragon or chervil.

CHILE LIME BUTTER Add to the butter 2 tablespoons (30 milliliters) minced red chile pepper, 2 teaspoons (10 milliliters) minced garlic, 1 teaspoon (5 milliliters) grated lime zest, 2 teaspoons (10 milliliters) lime juice and ½ teaspoon (2 milliliters) hot sauce.

LOBSTER OR CRAYFISH BUTTER Grind 8 ounces (240 grams) cooked lobster or crayfish meat, shells and/or coral with 1 pound (480 grams) butter. Place in a saucepan and clarify. Strain the butter through a fine chinois lined with cheesecloth. Refrigerate, then remove the butterfat when firm.

MAÎTRE D'HÔTEL BUTTER Mix into the butter 4 tablespoons (60 milliliters) finely chopped fresh parsley, 3 tablespoons (45 milliliters) lemon juice and a dash of white pepper.

RED PEPPER BUTTER Purée 8 ounces (240 grams) roasted, peeled red bell peppers until liquid, then add to the butter.

SHALLOT BUTTER Blanch 8 ounces (240 grams) peeled shallots in boiling water. Dry and finely dice them and mix with the butter.

Pan Gravy

gravy a sauce made from meat or poultry juices combined with a liquid and thickening agent; usually made in the pan in which the meat or poultry was cooked

Pan gravy is aptly named: It is made directly in the pan used to roast the poultry, beef, lamb or pork that the **gravy** will accompany. Pan gravy is actually a sauce; it is a liquid thickened with a roux. Pan gravy gains additional flavors from the drippings left in the roasting pan; a portion of the fat rendered during the roasting process is used to make the roux. This technique is used in the recipe for Roast Turkey with Chestnut Dressing and Giblet Gravy (page 432).

A properly made pan gravy should have all the characteristics of any brown sauce. However, pan gravy typically has a meatier flavor than simple brown sauce because pan gravy is made with pan drippings.

Procedure for Preparing Pan Gravy

1 Remove the cooked meat or poultry from the roasting pan.
2 If mirepoix was not added during the roasting process, add it to the pan containing the drippings and fat.
3 Place the roasting pan on the stove top and clarify the fat by cooking off any remaining moisture.
4 Pour off the fat, reserving it to make the roux.
5 Deglaze the pan using an appropriate stock. The deglazing liquid may be transferred to a saucepan for easier handling, or the gravy may be finished directly in the roasting pan.
6 Add enough stock or water to the deglazing liquid to yield the desired amount of finished gravy.
7 Determine the amount of roux needed to thicken the amount of liquid being used (see Table 11.2) and prepare the roux in a separate pan, using a portion of the reserved fat.
8 Add the roux to the liquid and bring the mixture to a simmer. Simmer until the mirepoix is well cooked, the flavor is extracted and the flour taste is cooked out.
9 Strain the gravy and adjust the seasonings.

① Deglazing the roasting pan.

② Thickening the gravy with a roux.

③ Straining the gravy.

Pan Sauces

Sauces served with sautéed meats, poultry or fish are often made directly in the sauté pan in which the dish was cooked. Once the food is sautéed, it is removed from the pan and kept warm while the sauce is prepared. Stock, jus lié or other liquid is added to deglaze the pan. Like pan gravy, these pan sauces gain flavor from the drippings left in the pan. Unlike pan gravy, pan sauces are usually thickened by reduction, not with a starch. Many chefs prefer the intense flavor that comes from reducing liquids in a pan sauce over sauces thickened with roux, and because there is no added fat and starch, pan sauces usually are lower in calories than other sauces. Pan sauces are discussed in Chapter 13, Principles of Meat Cookery.

Coulis

The term *coulis* most often refers to a sauce made from a purée of vegetables and/or fruit that is strained before serving. A vegetable coulis can be served as either a hot or a cold accompaniment to other vegetables, starches, meat, poultry, fish or shellfish. It is often made from a single vegetable base (popular examples include broccoli, tomatoes and sweet red peppers), cooked with flavoring ingredients such as onions, garlic, shallots, herbs and spices and then puréed. An appropriate liquid (stock, water or cream) may be added to thin the purée if necessary. Vegetable coulis are often prepared with very little fat and served as healthy alternatives to heavier, classic sauces.

Typically, both vegetable and fruit coulis have a texture similar to that of a thin tomato sauce, but their textures can range from slightly grainy to almost lumpy, depending on their intended use. The flavor and color of a coulis should be that of the main ingredient. The flavors of herbs, spices and other flavoring ingredients should complement, not dominate, the coulis.

coulis [koo-LEE] a sauce made from a purée of vegetables and/or fruit; may be served hot or cold

Procedure for Preparing a Vegetable Coulis

1 Cook the main ingredient and any additional flavoring ingredients with the liquid of your choice.
2 Purée the main ingredient and flavoring ingredients in a food mill, blender or food processor. (Some vegetables may be ready to strain and serve at this point.)
3 Combine the purée with additional liquid if the mixture seems too thick and simmer to blend the flavors.
4 Strain, then thin and season the coulis as desired.

Note Procedures for making fruit coulis are included as recipes in Chapter 35, Custards, Creams, Frozen Desserts and Dessert Sauces.

MISE EN PLACE

- Peel and chop garlic.
- Peel onion and chop into small dice.
- Wash red peppers and chop into medium dice.

Red Pepper Coulis

YIELD 1 qt. (960 ml)

Vegetable oil	1 fl. oz.	30 ml
Garlic, chopped	2 tsp.	10 ml
Onion, small dice	3 oz.	90 g
Red bell peppers, medium dice	3 lb.	1.4 kg
White wine	8 fl. oz.	240 ml
Chicken stock	1 pt.	480 ml
Salt and pepper	TT	TT

1 Heat the oil and sweat the garlic and onion until translucent, without browning.

2 Add the bell peppers and sweat until tender.

3 Deglaze the pan with the wine.

4 Add the stock, bring to a simmer and cook for 15 minutes. Season with salt and pepper.

5 Purée in a blender or food processor and strain through a china cap.

6 Adjust the consistency and seasonings and hold for service.

Approximate values per 1-fl.-oz. (30-ml) serving: **Calories** 20, **Total fat** 1 g, **Saturated fat** 0 g, **Cholesterol** 0 mg, **Sodium** 45 mg, **Total carbohydrates** 2 g, **Protein** 1 g, **Vitamin C** 50%, **Claims**—low fat; low sodium; low calorie

❶ Sweating the red peppers.

❷ Puréeing the cooked peppers.

❸ Straining the coulis.

CONTEMPORARY SAUCES

Flavored butters, **flavored oils**, **foams**, **salsas**, **relishes** and **pan gravy** are also used as sauces in food service operations. Chefs are currently relying less on traditional sauces and more on salsas, relishes, juices, broths, foams, essences and infused oils in their work. Unlike classic sauces, these accompaniments do not rely on meat-based stocks and starch thickeners, but rather on fresh vegetables, vegetable juices, aromatic broths and intensely flavored oils. The names for these sauces are not codified, as are those in the classic sauce repertoire. Chefs apply various terms freely, using whatever name best fits the dish and the overall menu. Most of these contemporary sauces can be prepared more quickly than their classic counterparts, and the use of fresh fruits and vegetables enhances the healthfulness of the dish. These so-called contemporary or modern sauces may have a lighter body and less fat than classic sauces, but they are still derived from classical culinary techniques and principles. The sauces should be appropriate in flavor, texture and appearance and should complement, not overwhelm, the food they accompany.

Salsa and Relish

Many people think of salsa (Spanish for "sauce") as a chunky mixture of raw vegetables and chiles eaten with corn chips or ladled over Mexican food. Similarly many people think of relish as a sweet green condiment spooned onto a hot dog. But salsas and relishes—generally, cold chunky mixtures of herbs, spices, fruits and/or vegetables—can be used as sauces for many meat, poultry, fish and shellfish items. They can include ingredients such as oranges, pineapple, papaya, black beans, jicama, tomatillos or an array of other vegetables.

Although not members of any classic sauce family, salsas, **chutneys**, and relishes are popular because of their intense fresh flavors, ease of preparation and low fat and calorie content. Salsas and relishes are often a riot of colors, textures and flavors, simultaneously cool and hot, spicy and sweet.

Nut-crusted halibut served with a fresh tomato salsa.

chutney a sweet-and-sour condiment made of fruits and/or vegetables cooked in vinegar with sugar and spices; some chutneys are reduced to a purée, whereas others retain recognizable pieces of their ingredients

Procedure for Preparing a Salsa or Relish

1 Cut or chop the ingredients.

2 Precook and chill items as directed in the recipe.

3 Toss all ingredients together and refrigerate, allowing the flavors to combine for at least 30 minutes before service.

Pico de Gallo (Tomato Salsa)

 Good Choice    Vegan

YIELD 1 qt. (960 ml)

Tomatoes, seeded, small dice	5	5
Green onions, sliced	1 bunch	1 bunch
Garlic cloves, minced	3	3
Fresh cilantro, chopped	½ bunch	½ bunch
Jalapeños, chopped fine	3	3
Fresh lemon or lime juice	2 fl. oz.	60 ml
Cumin, ground	½ tsp.	2 ml
Salt and pepper	TT	TT

1 Combine all ingredients and gently toss. Adjust seasonings and refrigerate.

Approximate values per 1-fl.-oz. (30-ml) serving: **Calories** 5, **Total fat** 0 g, **Saturated fat** 0 g, **Cholesterol** 0 mg, **Sodium** 30 mg, **Total carbohydrates** 1 g, **Protein** 0 g, **Claims**—fat free; very low sodium; low calorie

MISE EN PLACE

- Wash and peel vegetables if necessary.
- Chop tomatoes into small dice.
- Slice green onions.
- Mince garlic cloves.
- Chop cilantro leaves.
- Remove seeds from jalapeños and finely chop.

Vegetable Juice Sauces

Juice extractors make it possible to prepare juice from fresh, uncooked vegetables such as carrots, beets and spinach. Thinner and smoother than a purée, vegetable juice can be heated, reduced, flavored and enriched with butter or oil to create colorful, intensely flavored sauces. Cream or stock can be added to finish the sauce. A sauce made from vegetable juice is sometimes referred to as an **essence** or **tea** on menus.

Juice from a single type of vegetable provides the purest, most pronounced flavor, but two or more vegetables sometimes can be combined successfully. Be careful of mixing too many flavors and colors in the juice, however. Juiced vegetable sauces are particularly appropriate with pasta, fish, shellfish and poultry, and they can be useful in vegetarian cuisine or as a healthier alternative to classic sauces. A well-prepared juice sauce has the bright color and flavor of the vegetables from which it is made. It has body and does not separate.

Procedure for Preparing a Vegetable Juice Sauce

1 Wash and peel vegetables as needed.

2 Process the vegetables through a juice extractor.

3 Place the juice in a saucepan and add stock, lemon juice, herbs or other flavorings as desired.

4 Bring the sauce to a simmer and reduce as necessary.

5 Strain the sauce through a fine chinois if required.

6 Adjust the seasonings. Enrich the sauce by whisking in whole butter or other fat if desired.

🌿 Vegetarian   ♥ Good Choice

Carrot Juice Sauce

MISE EN PLACE

- Wash carrots and put through juice extractor.
- Chop fresh herbs.

YIELD 8 fl. oz. (240 ml)

Carrot juice	1 pt.	480 ml
Cinnamon, ground	pinch	pinch
Clove, ground	pinch	pinch
Nutmeg, ground	pinch	pinch
Salt and white pepper	TT	TT
Cayenne pepper	pinch	pinch
Lemon juice	1 Tbsp.	15 ml
Unsalted butter, diced	3 oz.	90 g
Fresh chervil, chives or tarragon, chopped	2 Tbsp.	30 ml

1 Combine the carrot juice, spices and lemon juice in a small sauce pan. Bring to a simmer and reduce the liquid by half.

2 Whisk the butter into the simmering sauce one or two pieces at a time until all the butter is incorporated.

3 Remove from the heat and stir in the herbs. Hold for service.

Approximate values per 1-fl.-oz. (30-ml) serving: **Calories** 100, **Total fat** 9 g, **Saturated fat** 5 g, **Cholesterol** 25 mg, **Sodium** 40 mg, **Total carbohydrates** 6 g, **Protein** 1 g, **Vitamin A** 230%, **Vitamin C** 10%

❶ Juicing the carrots.

❷ The finished carrot juice sauce has body, a rich color and smooth texture.

Broths

Broth, which also appears on menus as a tea, **au jus**, essence or nage, is a thin, flavorful liquid served in a pool beneath the main food. The broth should not be so abundant as to turn an entrée into a soup, but it should provide moisture and flavor. The essence, broth or nage is often made by simply reducing and straining the liquid in which the main food was cooked. Alternatively, a specifically flavored infusion or stock—tomato, for example—can be prepared, then clarified like consommé to create a broth or essence to accompany an appetizer or entrée.

au jus [oh ZHEW] roasted meats, poultry or game served with their natural, unthickened juices

Foams

Contemporary chefs also create light sauces using whipping siphons to **aerate** liquids and purées. These sauces offer unusual texture and flavors. Frequently the base for such sauces, called foams, is thickened with gums, stabilizers and other products more commonly found in industrial kitchens.

aerate to incorporate air into a mixture through sifting and mixing. Gas discharged from a whipping siphon will also aerate mixtures.

Aeration takes place when a gas, usually air, is incorporated into a mixture. This is what happens, for example, when heavy cream or egg whites are beaten with a wire whisk. Air becomes trapped in bubbles that form in the mixture, causing it to expand in volume and transform into a foam. In scientific terms, a foam is a gas-in-water emulsion, where the gas (the dispersed phase) is dispersed into water (the continuous phase). As with an oil-in-water emulsion discussed on page 218, a foam requires a stabilizing agent. For example, fat in heavy cream coats the air bubbles formed when cream is whipped. The fat helps stabilize the mixture into a semipermanent foam. When egg whites are whipped, egg proteins unfold into a network that traps the air into a semipermanent foam. Foams that are stable enough to serve on a plated dish require a liquid that will trap air bubbles without bursting.

A variety of modern thickeners such as **hydrocolloids** or gums alter the texture and **viscosity** of liquids and sauces. Such products, which bind water, help to stabilize sauce bases when whipped. The choice of which product to use depends on a number of factors including the intended use and serving temperature. **Xanthan gum** is widely available and among the more popular choices for stabilizing foam mixtures because it can be used in hot or cold liquids and is freezer stable. Follow manufacturer's directions when working with such thickeners. Because of their power, these ingredients are used in very small quantities.

hydrocolloid substance such as a gum or agar that bonds with water to form a gel

viscosity the measurement of a fluid's resistance to flow; in common terms, it is the thickness of a liquid. For example, water has a low viscosity while honey has a high viscosity

xanthan gum a stabilizer produced by fermenting the sugar in corn; used to thicken, stabilize and emulsify prepared sauces, dairy products, ice creams and baked goods

Light foams, which have a consistency like the froth on a cup of cappuccino, can be made by hand using a wire whisk or hand blender but they must be made to order and deflate quickly. Whipping siphons (see page 85) discharge CO_2 gas into a liquid. The foam made in a whipping siphon holds up well on the plate. The sauce base can be kept warm for service and discharged to order. The Wild Mushroom Foam recipe that follows calls for a whipping siphon to make a foam sauce. Other techniques for making foam sauce appear throughout this text.

Procedure for Preparing a Foam Sauce Using a Whipping Siphon

1 Prepare the stock or sauce that will be used to make the foam.
2 Strain the stock or sauce through a fine chinois and adjust the seasonings.
3 Thicken the mixture by combining the gum, stabilizer or other thickening agent as specified.
4 For service, fill a whipping siphon with the heated mixture. Discharge the gas cartridge into the mixture as close to service time as possible.
5 Hold the sauce in a warm bain marie until needed. Discharge the foam onto each plate as needed.

 Good Choice   Vegan

MISE EN PLACE

- Peel and julienne shallots and carrots.
- Chop celery and peeled carrots into medium dice.
- Stem and trim mushrooms.

⚠ Safety Alert

Handling Flavored Oils

Flavored oils must be stored under refrigeration. Raw garlic, fresh herbs or other fresh ingredients can become time and temperature control for safety (TCS) foods when added to oil. Serve them within 2 days of preparation.

decant to separate liquid from solids without disturbing the sediment by pouring off the liquid; vintage wines are often decanted to remove sediment

vinaigrette a temporary emulsion of oil and vinegar seasoned with salt and pepper

Wild Mushroom Foam

YIELD 1 pt. (480 ml)

Shallots, julienned	1 lb.	480 g
Celery, medium dice	8 oz.	240 g
Carrots, medium dice	8 oz.	240 g
Mushrooms, stem and trim	3 lb.	1.4 kg
Vegetable oil	2 fl. oz.	60 ml
White wine	24 fl. oz.	720 ml
Mushroom or vegetable stock	1 gal.	3.8 lt
Xanthan gum	1 tsp.	5 ml
Cayenne pepper	1 pinch	1 pinch

1 Sweat the shallots, celery, carrots and mushrooms in the oil in a large saucepan over medium high heat until soft, approximately 10 minutes. Deglaze with the white wine and reduce au sec.

2 Add the mushroom stock. Simmer until reduced to approximately 1 pint (480 milliliters).

3 Strain the mixture through a fine chinois and chill.

4 When ready to serve, bring the mushroom sauce to a simmer. Using an immersion blender, slowly add the xanthan gum to the warm liquid, blending continuously while adding the fine powder. Adjust the seasonings with cayenne pepper.

5 Pour the mixture into the canister of a 1-quart (1-liter) thermal whipping siphon. As close to service time as possible, charge the siphon with a gas cartridge. Shake well, then charge it with a second gas cartridge. Hold the sauce in a warm bain marie until service.

6 Direct the whipping siphon head toward a plate then discharge some Wild Mushroom Foam onto each serving.

Approximate values per 1-oz. (30-g) serving: **Calories** 60, **Total fat** 2.5 g, **Saturated fat** 0 g, **Cholesterol** 0 mg, **Sodium** 120 mg, **Total carbohydrates** 7 g, **Protein** 0 g, **Vitamin A** 20%

Flavored Oils

Small amounts of intensely flavored oils can dress or garnish a variety of dishes. Salads, soups, vegetable and starch dishes and entrées can be enhanced with a drizzle of colorful, appropriately flavored oil. Because such small quantities are used, these oils provide flavor and moisture without adding too many calories or much fat.

Unless the flavoring ingredient goes especially well with olive oil (e.g., basil), select a high-quality but neutral oil such as peanut, safflower or canola. Although flavoring ingredients can be simply steeped in oil for a time, a better way to flavor oil is to crush, purée or cook the flavoring ingredients first. Warming the oil before infusing it with dry herbs or spices is recommended, as is **decanting** the oil to remove solids before using. A well-prepared flavored oil is clear with the bright color and fresh flavor of the herbs, spices or seasonings used to make it.

Chefs also use **vinaigrettes**, a combination of oil and vinegar, citrus or other acidic liquid, as quick light sauces. Vinaigrettes give the illusion of lightness that many health-conscious customers are demanding, although the oil in vinaigrettes can add to fat and calorie content. Vinaigrettes are discussed in Chapter 25, Salads and Salad Dressings.

Procedure for Preparing a Flavored Oil

1 Purée or chop fresh herbs, fruits or vegetables if required. Sweat dry spices or seeds in a small amount of oil to form a paste.

2 Place the selected oil and the flavoring ingredients in a jar or other tightly lidded container.

3 Allow the mixture to stand at room temperature until sufficient flavor is extracted or warm the selected oil and flavoring ingredients gently over low heat then cool to room temperature. If a mixture is left at room temperature and not heated, it may take from

1 to 24 hours to extract the flavor. Shake the jar periodically. Do not allow the flavoring ingredients to remain in the oil indefinitely, as the flavor may become harsh or bitter.

4 Strain the oil through a chinois lined with a coffee filter, which will trap any sediment from the spices or seeds used to flavor the oil.

5 Store the flavored oil in a covered container in the refrigerator.

Basil Oil

 **Vegan**   **Good Choice**

YIELD 12 fl. oz. (360 ml)

Fresh basil (or other soft herb such as cilantro, chives, or tarragon)	6 oz.	180 g
Olive oil	1 pt.	480 ml

1 Blanch the basil leaves in boiling water for 10 seconds. Refresh in cold water and drain well. Squeeze out all excess water.

2 Place the blanched basil leaves in a blender. Add the oil and blend for approximately 15 seconds.

3 Transfer the basil oil to a small saucepan and heat over medium heat until the oil begins to bubble for approximately 5 minutes.

4 Remove from the heat and allow to cool to room temperature.

5 Strain the oil through a chinois lined with a coffee filter. Do not press or force the oil through the filter or the finished oil will become cloudy.

6 Place the flavored oil in a covered container and refrigerate until ready to use.

Approximate values per ½-fl.-oz. (15-ml) serving: **Calories** 120, **Total fat** 14 g, **Saturated fat** 2.5 g, **Cholesterol** 0 mg, **Sodium** 1 mg, **Total carbohydrates** 0 g, **Protein** 0 g, **Claims**—no cholesterol; no sodium

The finished basil oil is clear with a bright color and fresh flavor.

Sauces are used in many recipes in this text and in the professional kitchen. Table 11.7 is a troubleshooting chart to be used when problems arise with sauce preparation.

TROUBLESHOOTING CHART FOR SAUCES		TABLE 11.7
PROBLEM	**REASON**	**SOLUTION**
Lumpy	Roux undercooked Stock cold when roux added Cornstarch not properly dissolved	Increase cooking time for roux. Heat stock before adding roux; strain through chinois to remove lumps. Strain, make cornstarch slurry and cook until thickened, stirring constantly.
Pasty or floury taste	Sauce undercooked after starch was added	Increase cooking time.
Grainy texture	Starch or flour not properly gelatinized Eggs overheated in liaison	Increase cooking time. Pass through a fine mesh strainer. Discard sauce.
Thick consistency	Too much thickener Sauce reduced too much	Decrease thickener; add additional liquid. Decrease cooking time; add additional liquid.
Thin consistency	Not enough thickener Starch-thickened sauce overheated Insufficiently reduced	Add more roux or cornstarch slurry. Do not reheat sauces thickened with cornstarch. Continue cooking until sauce thickens.
Separates, breaks	Temporary emulsion failed Eggs overcooked	Whisk sauce again (vinaigrette); cool to 110°F–120°F (43°C–49°C), then whisk again to reincorporate fat (beurre blanc); reheat sauce over double boiler, then beat into water (hollandaise). Beat an egg yolk and water together, then beat into sauce (hollandaise); discard sauce if liaison was used and overheated.
Gray color or metallic taste	Aluminum pan used	Discard (cream sauce); use nonreactive pan to make cream sauce.

USING SAUCES

Sauces provide chefs with many ways to build upon the flavors in a dish. This enhances a dish's visual appeal and the diner's taste experience when eating it. As you will learn in your culinary career, many sauces are integral to classic dishes. You cannot make Eggs Benedict without hollandaise sauce, for example. Often, in addition to being called upon to make classic sauces for classic dishes, you may need to select sauces to accompany foods using your training and instinct.

Follow these guidelines to help you in this process:

- Select the appropriate sauce based on the cooking method used to prepare the dish.

    Grilled foods develop a crisp exterior flavored with smoke from the cooking fire. Select a sauce that stands up to the robust grilled flavor such as a chunky salsa with seared beef.

    When serving deep-fried foods such as chicken wings or onion rings, look for a sauce that will preserve the food's crisp crust.

    When serving finger foods to be dipped into a sauce, choose a sauce that is thick enough to cling to the food.

- Select the appropriate sauce based on the richness of the main ingredient.

    Lean cuts of meat, fish or poultry and many vegetable dishes are enhanced with sauces made with butter, cream or oil. Grilled chicken breasts, for example, are enhanced with maitre d'hôtel butter. The butter melts over the chicken adding moisture and richness to the poultry.

    Sauces with some acidity such as one made with capers, lemon juice or wine contrast with fatty cuts of beef, lamb or pork.

- Consider the flavor profile of the foods on the plate.

    Amplify the flavors in a dish by selecting the appropriate sauce. Use lamb stock in a brown sauce to accompany braised or roasted lamb for example.

    Use sauce to introduce a global flavor profile. White sauce, for example, takes on a Scandinavian flavor profile when fresh dill and white pepper are used to season it. When chile peppers, diced tomatoes and cumin are added instead, the white sauce takes on a Latin American flavor.

- Consider the visual appearance of the dish.

    Flavored oils made with fresh herbs such as basil or vegetable coulis made from red peppers add bright color and intense flavor to the foods they accompany. Wine reductions and pan sauces add a sheen to the plate.

    Consider using two or more sauces on the same plate to offer contrasting or complimentary flavors, but resist the urge to over embellish a dish.

    Create visual contrast when choosing a sauce such as a creamy velouté or beurre blanc over rosy-fleshed salmon. Consider the texture of a sauce as a source of visual contrast such as a chunky tomato sauce served over pan-fried fish.

QUESTIONS FOR DISCUSSION

1 Why are the bones of younger animals preferred for making stocks?

2 Why should a stock made from beef or veal bones cook longer than a stock made from fish bones? What is the result if a stock does not cook long enough?

3 What can cause a stock to become cloudy? How can you prevent this from happening?

4 List three differences in the production of a white stock and a brown stock.

5 List the five classic mother sauces and explain how they are used to prepare small sauces.

6 Why is demi-glace preferred when making brown sauces? Is jus lié different from classic demi-glace? Can they be used interchangeably?

7 Why is temperature important when making hollandaise sauce? What precautions must be taken when holding hollandaise for service?

8 Compare a beurre blanc and a hollandaise sauce. How are they similar? How are they different?

9 How are compound butters used in making sauces? What are the ingredients for a traditional maître d'hôtel butter?

10 What are the differences between a salsa, a chutney and a relish? Can these items be used in place of classic sauces? Explain your answer.

11 What are the differences between a vegetable juice sauce and a broth?

12 What can be done to stabilize a sauce so that the sauce can be used to make a foam?

Additional Stock and Sauce Recipes

❤ Vegan   ❤ Good Choice

Rich Brown Vegetable Stock

YIELD 1 gal. (3.8 lt)

Vegetable oil	2 fl. oz.	60 ml
Garlic cloves, chopped	10	10
Mirepoix, small dice	4 lb.	1.9 kg
Leeks, whites and greens, chopped	1 lb.	480 g
Turnip, diced	4 oz.	120 g
Tomato, diced	4 oz.	120 g
Red wine	1 pt.	480 ml
Tomato paste	2 oz.	60 g
Onion brûlé	1	1
Water	4 qt.	3.8 lt
Sachet:		
Bay leaf	1	1
Dried thyme	½ tsp.	2 ml
Peppercorns, crushed	¼ tsp.	1 ml
Parsley stems	8	8

1 Heat the oil. Add the garlic and vegetables and sweat for 10 minutes. Increase heat to medium-high and cook the vegetables until lightly caramelized, approximately 10 more minutes.

2 Add the wine, tomato paste, onion brûlé, water and sachet.

3 Bring the mixture to a boil, reduce to a simmer and cook for 1 hour 30 minutes.

4 Strain. Reduce to make a glace or cool and refrigerate.

Approximate values per 1-fl.-oz. (30-ml) serving: **Calories** 5, **Total fat** 0 g, **Saturated fat** 0 g, **Cholesterol** 0 mg, **Sodium** 0 mg, **Total carbohydrates** 0 g, **Protein** 0 g, **Claims**—fat free; low calorie

---

🌿 Vegetarian

Hollandaise, Blender Method

YIELD 1 qt. (1 lt)

Egg yolks	9	9
Water, warm	3 fl. oz.	90 ml
Lemon juice	1 fl. oz.	30 ml
Cayenne pepper	TT	TT
Salt	1 tsp.	5 ml
White pepper	¼ tsp.	1 ml
Tabasco sauce	TT	TT
Whole butter	24 oz.	750 g

1 Place the egg yolks, water, lemon juice, cayenne pepper, salt, white pepper and Tabasco sauce in the bowl of the blender. Cover and blend on high speed for approximately 5 seconds.

2 Heat the butter to approximately 175°F (80°C). This allows the butter to cook the yolks as it is added to them.

3 Turn the blender on and immediately begin to add the butter in a steady stream. Incorporate all the butter in 20–30 seconds. Adjust the seasonings.

4 If any lumps are present, strain the sauce through a mesh strainer. Transfer the sauce to a stainless steel container and adjust the seasonings. Hold for service in a bain marie, following the sanitation precautions discussed in the chapter.

Approximate values per 1-fl.-oz. (30-ml) serving: **Calories** 120, **Total fat** 12 g, **Saturated fat** 7 g, **Cholesterol** 70 mg, **Sodium** 170 mg, **Total carbohydrates** 0 g, **Protein** 1 g, **Vitamin A** 15%

Horseradish Cream Sauce

🌿 Vegetarian

Cornstarch	2 Tbsp.	30 ml
Cold water	1 fl. oz.	30 ml
Heavy cream	1 qt.	1 lt
Horseradish, grated	4 oz.	120 g
Sour cream	2 fl. oz.	60 ml
Salt	TT	TT

1 Stir the cornstarch and water together in a small bowl.

2 Bring the cream to a boil over moderate heat. Whisk in the cornstarch slurry and simmer until the cream thickens and the starchy taste is cooked out, approximately 3–5 minutes.

3 Remove the thickened cream from the heat and whisk in the horseradish and the sour cream. Season to taste with salt. Keep warm for service.

Approximate values per 1-fl.-oz. (30-ml) serving: **Calories** 110, **Total fat** 12 g, **Saturated fat** 7 g, **Cholesterol** 40 mg, **Sodium** 30 mg, **Total carbohydrates** 2 g, **Protein** 1 g

Duxelles Sauce

Duxelles is a coarse paste made of finely chopped mushrooms sautéed with shallots in butter. It is used in sauces and stuffing.

Mushrooms, chopped fine	8 oz.	240 g
Shallot, chopped fine	3 oz.	90 g
Clarified butter	1 fl. oz.	30 ml
Olive oil	1 fl. oz.	30 ml
Dry white wine	12 fl. oz.	360 ml
Demi-Glace (page 225)	24 fl. oz.	720 ml
Heavy cream	2 fl. oz.	60 ml
Salt and pepper	TT	TT
Fresh parsley, chopped fine	1 Tbsp.	15 ml

1 Sauté the mushrooms and shallot in the butter and oil. The mushrooms will release their liquid and darken. Cook until completely dry.

2 Deglaze with the wine and reduce by two-thirds.

3 Add the demi-glace. Bring to a boil, then simmer for 5 minutes.

4 Stir in the cream. Adjust the seasonings. Garnish with parsley.

Approximate values per 1-fl.-oz. (30-ml) serving: **Calories** 100, **Total fat** 10 g, **Saturated fat** 6 g, **Cholesterol** 30 mg, **Sodium** 40 g, **Total carbohydrates** 2 g, **Protein** 1 g, **Vitamin A** 15%

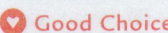 Good Choice   Vegan

Fresh Tomato Sauce for Pasta

YIELD 1 qt. (960 ml)

Onion, small dice	4 oz.	120 g
Carrot, small dice	2 oz.	60 g
Garlic, minced	2 tsp.	10 ml
Olive oil	2 fl. oz.	60 ml
Tomato **concassée**	3 lb.	1.4 kg
Fresh oregano	2 tsp.	10 ml
Fresh thyme	1 tsp.	5 ml
Salt	2 tsp.	10 ml
Pepper	½ tsp.	2 ml
Fresh basil, chopped	½ oz.	15 g

concassée peeled, seeded and diced tomato

1 Sweat the onion, carrot and garlic in the oil until tender.

2 Add the tomato concassée, oregano and thyme. Simmer for approximately 1 hour or until the desired consistency is reached.

3 Pass the sauce through a food mill if a smooth consistency is desired. Do not purée if a chunkier sauce is desired.

4 Adjust the seasonings and add the basil.

Approximate values per 1-fl.-oz. (30-ml) serving: **Calories** 20, **Total fat** 1 g, **Saturated fat** 0 g, **Cholesterol** 0 mg, **Sodium** 35 mg, **Total carbohydrates** 2 g, **Protein** 0 g, **Vitamin C** 15%, **Claims**—low fat; low sodium; low calorie

 Vegan

Fresh Tomato Vinaigrette for Pasta

Use this vinaigrette to season up to 4 pounds (approximately 2 kilograms) of any type of cooked pasta, adjusting the seasonings before serving warm or chilled. May also be served as a topping for sandwiches or cooked poultry or fish.

YIELD 1 qt. (960 ml)

White balsamic vinegar	6 fl. oz.	180 ml
Salt	1 Tbsp.	15 ml
Olive oil	10 fl. oz.	300 ml
Tomato concassée	1 lb.	480 g
Fresh basil, thyme or marjoram, chopped	1 oz.	30 g
Shallot, minced	4 Tbsp.	60 ml
Black pepper	1 tsp.	5 ml

1 Dissolve the salt in the vinegar in a small stainless steel bowl.

2 Whisk in the olive oil. Then stir in the tomato, fresh herbs and shallot. Season with pepper.

Approximate values per 3-fl.-oz. (90-ml) serving: **Calories** 270, **Total fat** 27 g, **Saturated fat** 3 g, **Cholesterol** 0 mg, **Sodium** 780 mg, **Total carbohydrates** 6 g, **Protein** 0 g

Mole

Mole ("mixture" in Spanish) is a harmonious blend of fresh and dried chiles, spices, seeds, nuts and chocolate. Poultry, especially turkey, and other meats are simmered in mole sauces. Variations of this savory sauce are found throughout Mexico, where mole recipes are revered and mole is served at festive occasions.

YIELD 1 qt. (960 ml)

Cinnamon stick	1	1
Allspice	½ tsp.	2 ml
Guajillo chiles	2	2
Pasilla chiles	2	2
Sesame seeds	4 oz.	120 g
Pumpkin seeds	6 oz.	180 g
Cumin seeds	1 tsp.	5 ml
Onion, small	1	1
Olive oil	as needed	as needed
Plum tomatoes	4	4
Garlic cloves	4	4
Fresh thyme	1 sprig	1 sprig
Dried oregano	1 tsp.	5 ml
Chicken stock	1 qt.	960 ml
Salt	TT	TT
Semisweet chocolate, chopped	2 oz.	60 g

1 Grind the cinnamon and allspice in a spice grinder.

2 Stem and seed the guajillo and pasilla chiles. Break them into small pieces and simmer them in water for 15 minutes. Drain well.

3 Combine the sesame seeds, pumpkin seeds and cumin seeds and fry them in a dry sauté pan until well toasted.

4 Slice the onion approximately ½ inch (1.2 centimeters) thick. Brush the slices with oil and grill until well colored.

5 Roast the tomatoes over the open flame of a gas burner until they are evenly charred and blistered. Remove the cores, peel the tomatoes and chop them coarsely.

6 Combine the cinnamon and allspice with the chiles, toasted seeds, onion, tomatoes, garlic, thyme, oregano and stock in a saucepan. Season with salt and bring to a boil. Reduce to a simmer and cook for 15 minutes. Remove from the heat, cool and remove the sprig of thyme.

7 Blend the mixture in a blender until smooth. Strain through a china cap and stir in the chocolate until melted. Adjust the seasonings.

8 Serve the mole over grilled chicken, turkey, duck, quail or a meat such as pork or rabbit, or reheat cooked turkey or chicken pieces in the sauce until hot and serve with a portion of the sauce.

Approximate values per 1-fl.-oz. (30-ml) serving: **Calories** 70, **Total fat** 5 g, **Saturated fat** 1 g, **Cholesterol** 0 mg, **Sodium** 90 mg, **Total carbohydrates** 4 g, **Protein** 2 g, **Iron** 10%

1 Roasting the tomatoes.

2 Combining ingredients in a sauce pan.

3 The finished sauce.

Bolognese Sauce

Bolognese sauce is named for the city of Bologna in Italy's culinary heartland. The mirepoix that gives this sauce its characteristic flavor is called soffritto *in Italian. The length of cooking time and the degree to which the mirepoix is cooked alters the taste and texture of the finished sauce. Serve this sauce over spaghetti, any wide noodle or large tubular pasta.*

YIELD 2 qt. (1.9 lt)

Clarified butter	2 fl. oz.	60 ml
Olive oil	2 fl. oz.	60 ml
Onion, small dice	12 oz.	360 g
Carrot, small dice	6 oz.	180 g
Celery, small dice	6 oz.	180 g
Pancetta or smoked bacon, small dice	4 oz.	120 g
Ground beef	1 lb.	480 g
Ground pork	1 lb.	480 g
Italian sausage	6 oz.	180 g
Chicken liver, chopped, optional	6 oz.	180 g
Dry white wine	8 fl. oz.	240 ml
Tomato paste	3 Tbsp.	45 ml
Chicken stock	24 fl. oz.	720 ml
Heavy cream	4 fl. oz.	120 ml
Salt and pepper	TT	TT
Whole butter, cubed	4 oz.	120 g

1 Heat the clarified butter and olive oil over medium heat. Add the onion, carrot, celery and pancetta. Cook until the vegetables are tender and the pancetta has rendered its fat, approximately 10 minutes.

2 Add the beef, pork, sausage and chicken livers (if using). Cook over high heat stirring to break the meat apart until the meat and chicken liver are fully cooked.

3 Add the white wine and reduce until nearly dry.

4 Add the tomato paste and stock to the pot. Bring the sauce to a simmer, cover, and cook for 1 hour to allow the flavors to develop.

5 Add the cream and cook uncovered until the sauce reduces and thickens slightly, approximately 15 minutes. Season with salt and pepper. Stir the butter into the sauce.

Approximate values per 2-fl.-oz. (60-ml) serving: **Calories** 190, **Total fat** 17 g, **Saturated fat** 7 g, **Cholesterol** 40 mg, **Sodium** 105 mg, **Total carbohydrates** 2 g, **Protein** 7 g, **Vitamin A** 25%

 Vegan

Orange Gastrique

YIELD 12 fl. oz. (360 ml)

Oranges	3	3
Granulated sugar	8 oz.	240 g
Water	2 fl. oz.	60 ml

1 Remove the zest and squeeze the juice from the oranges.

2 Combine the sugar and water in a small stainless steel sauce pan and cook over medium heat until the sugar is lightly caramelized, approximately 10 minutes.

3 When the sugar is a golden color, add the juice to the pot. The mixture will spatter and boil violently for a moment.

4 Stir the zest into the sauce and simmer, stirring occasionally, until the sugar dissolves and the sauce is smooth, approximately 5 minutes. Strain the sauce.

5 Serve the sauce warm or at room temperature or cover and refrigerate for later use.

Variations:

Citrus Gastrique—Substitute 12 fluid ounces (360 milliliters) lemon, grapefruit or blood orange juice for juice from 3 oranges. Omit the zest.

Orange Butter Sauce—Add 8 fluid ounces (240 milliliters) of rich chicken, duck or pork demi-glace along with the citrus zest in Step 4. Monté au beurre with 1 tablespoon (15 milliliters) butter then strain. Serve with grilled or roasted chicken, duck, pork or quail.

Approximate values per 1-fl.-oz. (30-ml) serving: **Calories** 90, **Total fat** 0 g, **Saturated fat** 0 g, **Cholesterol** 0 mg, **Sodium** 0 mg, **Total carbohydrates** 22 g, **Protein** 0 g, **Vitamin C** 25%

Basil Pesto Sauce

🍃 Vegetarian

Taken from the word that means "paste" in Italian, pesto is traditionally made using basil and pine nuts pounded by hand with a heavy pestle in a mortar. The nuts bind with the herbs and oil and act as a thickener in the sauce. Other herbs and nuts can be substituted; blanched almonds or walnuts work well, as does cilantro, mint or parsley.

YIELD   1 qt. (960 ml)

Olive oil	1 pt.	480 ml
Pine nuts	3 oz.	90 g
Fresh basil leaves	8 oz.	240 g
Garlic, chopped	1 Tbsp.	15 ml
Parmesan, grated	4 oz.	120 g
Romano, grated	4 oz.	120 g
Salt and pepper	TT	TT

1 Place one-third of the oil in a blender or food processor and add all the remaining ingredients.

2 Blend or process until smooth. Add the remaining oil and blend a few seconds to incorporate.

Variations:

Walnut Pesto—Substitute walnuts for pine nuts.

Sun-Dried Tomato Pesto—Add 1 ounce (30 grams) sun-dried tomatoes that have been softened in oil or water. Add oil as necessary.

Arugula and Pecan Pesto—Substitute pecans for pine nuts. Reduce the amount of basil to 4 ounces (120 grams) and add 4 ounces (120 grams) arugula leaves.

Approximate values per 1-fl.-oz. (30-ml) serving: **Calories** 170, **Total fat** 17 g, **Saturated fat** 4 g, **Cholesterol** 5 mg, **Sodium** 120 mg, **Total carbohydrates** 1 g, **Protein** 3 g

❶ Combining the pesto ingredients.

❷ The finished pesto sauce.

 Vegetarian

Citrus Beurre Blanc

This version of beurre blanc is easier to master than a traditional beurre blanc. The cream in this recipe helps stabilize the sauce and prevent it from breaking.

YIELD	1 qt. (960 ml)	
Shallots, minced	3 oz.	90 g
Dry white wine	6 fl. oz.	180 ml
Orange or lemon juice	4 fl. oz.	120 ml
Heavy cream	6 fl. oz.	180 ml
Whole butter, unsalted, chilled	24 oz.	680 g
Salt	TT	TT
White pepper	TT	TT
Orange or lemon zest, grated	2 Tbsp.	30 ml
Chives, chopped	as needed for garnish	

1 Combine the shallots, white wine and juice in a small sauce pan. Bring to a boil and reduce until 2 tablespoons (30 milliliters) of liquid remain. The remaining liquid should begin to thicken slightly.

2 Add the heavy cream and reduce until 3–4 fluid ounces (90–120 milliliters) of liquid remain.

3 Cut the butter into pieces approximately 1 ounce (30 grams) in weight. Over low heat, whisk in the butter a few pieces at a time, using the chilled butter to keep the sauce between 100°F and 120°F (38°C and 49°C). Continue until all of the butter has been incorporated.

4 Remove the sauce from the heat and season it with salt and white pepper. Add the zest. Allow the sauce to stand for 5 minutes. Strain the sauce if desired, or add chopped chives before serving if desired.

5 Hold the sauce in a warm place for service.

Approximate values per 1-fl.-oz. (30-ml) serving: **Calories** 180, **Total fat** 18 g, **Saturated fat** 12 g, **Cholesterol** 53 mg, **Sodium** 5 mg, **Total carbohydrates** 1 g, **Protein** 1 g, **Vitamin A** 12%

♥ Good Choice

Barbecue Sauce

YIELD	1 qt. (960 lt)	
Ketchup	1 qt.	960 ml
Water	8 fl. oz.	240 ml
Apple cider vinegar	8 fl. oz.	240 ml
Worcestershire sauce	4 fl. oz.	120 ml
Molasses	2 oz.	60 g
Brown sugar	3 oz.	90 g
Yellow mustard	4 oz.	120 g
Garlic powder	2 Tbsp.	30 ml
Onion, grated	1 oz.	30 g
Black pepper	½ tsp.	2.5 ml
Cayenne pepper	¼ tsp.	1 ml

1 Combine all ingredients in a heavy 4-quart (4-liter) sauce pot. Bring to a simmer over medium heat, stirring often. Simmer until the sauce is reduced by half, 20–30 minutes.

2 Brush the sauce over grilled foods during the last 15 or 20 minutes of cooking.

Approximate values per 1-fl.-oz. (30-ml) serving: **Calories** 25, **Total fat** 1 g, **Saturated fat** 0 g, **Cholesterol** 0 mg, **Sodium** 80 mg, **Total carbohydrates** 4 g, **Protein** 0 g, **Claims**—low fat; low sodium; low calorie

Southeast Asian-Style Peanut Sauce

In Thailand, Vietnam and other Southeast Asian countries, peanut sauce is served with skewered and grilled foods, such as chicken or pork, and as an accompaniment to rice crackers. The peanut butter binds with the coconut milk and stock to thicken and flavor the sauce.

YIELD 1 qt. (960 ml)

Garlic, chopped	1 tsp.	5 ml
Onion, small dice	6 oz.	180 g
Red pepper flakes, crushed	1 tsp.	5 ml
Fragrant lime leaves, optional	4	4
Curry powder	2 tsp.	10 ml
Lemongrass, minced	1 oz.	30 g
Vegetable oil	1 fl. oz.	30 ml
Coconut milk	8 fl. oz.	240 ml
Cinnamon sticks	2	2
Bay leaves	4	4
Lime juice	1 fl. oz.	30 ml
Rice wine vinegar	4 fl. oz.	120 ml
Chicken stock	12 fl. oz.	360 ml
Peanut butter	12 oz.	360 g

1 Sauté the garlic, onion, red pepper flakes, lime leaves, curry powder and lemongrass in the oil for 5 minutes.

2 Add the remaining ingredients and simmer for 15 minutes. Stir often, as the sauce can burn easily. Remove the cinnamon and bay leaves and serve warm.

Variation:

Vegetarian Peanut Sauce—Substitute vegetable stock or water for the chicken stock.

Approximate values per 1-fl.-oz. (30-ml) serving: **Calories** 90, **Total fat** 8 g, **Saturated fat** 2.5 g, **Cholesterol** 0 mg, **Sodium** 50 mg, **Total carbohydrates** 4 g, **Protein** 3 g

Coconut Sauce

YIELD 1 qt. (960 ml)

Coconut milk, unsweetened	1 pt.	480 ml
Fish sauce	4 fl. oz.	120 m
Sugar	4 oz.	120 g
Lemon juice	2 fl. oz.	60 ml
Lime juice	2 fl. oz.	60 ml
Asian chile sauce such as Sriracha	2 fl. oz.	60 ml
Garlic, minced	½ oz.	15 g

1 Stir together all of the ingredients into a smooth sauce. Use as a marinade or sauce to serve with grilled chicken, fish or pork.

Approximate values per 1-fl.-oz. (30-ml) serving: **Calories** 90, **Total fat** 3 g, **Saturated fat** 3 g, **Cholesterol** 0 mg, **Sodium** 570 mg, **Total carbohydrates** 15 g, **Protein** 1 g

coconut milk a coconut-flavored liquid made by pouring boiling water over shredded coconut; may be sweetened or unsweetened

♥ Good Choice   Ⓥ Vegan

Tomatillo Salsa

YIELD   1 qt. (960 ml)

Tomatillos	2 lb 8 oz.	1.2 kg
Water	4 fl. oz.	120 ml
Jalapeños	2	2
Salt	2 tsp.	10 ml
Black pepper	¼ tsp	2 ml
Garlic, chopped	1 Tbsp.	15 ml
Onion, chopped	2 oz.	60 g
Fresh cilantro, chopped	1 oz.	30 g

1 Remove the husks from the tomatillos.

2 Combine the tomatillos with the water, jalapeños, salt, pepper, garlic and onion in a small sauce-pan. Bring to a boil and simmer until tender, approximately 20 minutes.

3 Chop the mixture in a food processor or purée in a blender for a smoother sauce.

4 Add the cilantro and adjust the seasonings. The sauce may be served warm or cold.

Approximate values per 1-fl.-oz. (30-ml) serving: **Calories** 15, **Total fat** 0 g, **Saturated fat** 0 g, **Cholesterol** 0 mg, **Sodium** 150 mg, **Total carbohydrates** 2 g, **Protein** 0 g, **Claims**—fat free; low sodium; low calorie

Ⓥ Vegan

pimentón Spanish paprika produced from one of several varieties of *Capsicum annuum* peppers; in Extremadura, these peppers are dried over an oak fire, giving the region's Pimentón de la Vera a subtle smoky flavor

Spanish Romesco Sauce

Romesco sauce is based on key ingredients found in the Catalonian region of Spain, where red peppers, garlic, onions, tomatoes and nuts are abundant. The sauce is finished with oil and emulsified like mayonnaise. **Pimentón,** *if available, gives this sauce an authentic flavor. Serve Romesco Sauce with grilled foods or with toasted bread as a dip or spread.*

YIELD   1 qt. (960 ml)

Red bell peppers, whole	1 lb.	480 g
Tomatoes, whole	1 lb.	480 g
Blanched almonds	4 oz.	120 g
Rustic white bread, toasted, cubed	3 oz.	90 g
Garlic cloves	2	2
Smoked paprika or pimentón	2 tsp.	10 ml
Cayenne	TT	TT
Sherry vinegar	2 fl. oz.	60 ml
Salt	2 tsp.	10 ml
Black pepper	TT	TT
Extra virgin olive oil	4 fl. oz.	120 ml

1 Roast the bell peppers and tomatoes over an open flame of a gas burner until the skins are well charred. Remove from the heat and allow to cool. Core, peel and seed the vegetables. Cut them into large dice.

2 Toast the almonds in a dry sauté pan over medium heat until they darken slightly and become fragrant. When they are the proper color, immediately remove them from the sauté pan to prevent further browning and allow to cool.

3 Put the cubed bread in the bowl of a food processor. Add the toasted almonds and garlic. Process until they are the consistency of fine bread crumbs.

4 Add the tomatoes, peppers, smoked paprika, cayenne, sherry vinegar, salt and pepper. Process into a smooth paste, scraping down the sides of the bowl periodically, approximately 1 minute.

5 With the processor running, add the oil in a slow stream to emulsify the sauce. Season to taste.

Approximate values per 1-fl.-oz. (30-ml) serving: **Calories** 70, **Total fat** 5 g, **Saturated fat** 0.5 g, **Cholesterol** 0 mg, **Sodium** 150 mg, **Total carbohydrates** 4 g, **Protein** 1 g, **Vitamin A** 10%, **Vitamin C** 30%

Mignonette Sauce

This piquant vinegar sauce is traditionally served with raw shellfish such as oysters or clams on the half shell.

YIELD 1 pt. (480 ml)

Coarse ground black pepper	2 tsp.	10 ml
Red wine vinegar	1 pt.	480 ml
Shallot, minced	4 oz.	120 g
Salt	TT	TT

1 Combine all ingredients.

Approximate values per 1-fl.-oz. (30-ml) serving: **Calories** 5, **Total fat** 0 g, **Saturated fat** 0 g, **Cholesterol** 0 mg, **Sodium** 0.8 mg, **Total carbohydrates** 1 g, **Protein** 0 g, **Claims**—fat free; very low sodium; low calorie

Nuoc Cham
(Vietnamese Dipping Sauce)

Vietnam's national condiment, nuoc cham, combines the pungency of fish sauce with sweetness, heat and acidity. Ideal as a dipping sauce for spring rolls or grilled foods, it is also used to dress cucumber and green salads. Grated carrots can be added for color and texture.

YIELD 1 pt. (480 ml)

Granulated sugar	4 oz.	120 g
Water	2 fl. oz.	60 ml
Fish sauce (nuoc mam)	4 fl. oz.	120 ml
Fresh lemon or lime juice	6 fl. oz.	180 ml
Garlic clove, minced	2	2
Thai chile, seeded and minced	2	2
Shallot, minced	4 oz.	120 g

1 Whisk all the ingredients together in a small nonreactive bowl and allow to stand for at least 30 minutes at room temperature before serving.

Approximate values per 1-fl.-oz. (30-ml) serving: **Calories** 40, **Total fat** 0 g, **Saturated fat** 0 g, **Cholesterol** 0 mg, **Sodium** 710 mg, **Total carbohydrates** 10 g, **Protein** 1 g **Claims**—no calories; fat free

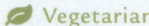

Persillade

Although not a liquid sauce, persillade [payr-see-yade] is a classic parsley topping used to finish a dish in much the same way as sauces are used. Persillade adds flavor and texture to grilled or roasted meats, especially beef and lamb, or vegetables.

YIELD 1 lb. (480 g)

Garlic, minced	1 oz.	30 g
Fresh parsley, chopped	3 oz.	90 g
Fresh bread crumbs	6 oz.	180 g
Whole butter, melted	6 oz.	180 g

1 Combine the garlic, parsley and bread crumbs. Drizzle the butter over the mixture and toss to blend.

2 Sprinkle the persillade over cooked meats or vegetables as a topping, then place the dish under a broiler until lightly browned.

Approximate values per ½-oz. (15-g) serving: **Calories** 50, **Total fat** 4.5 g, **Saturated fat** 3 g, **Cholesterol** 10 mg, **Sodium** 30 mg, **Total carbohydrates** 3 g, **Protein** 1 g

Soups 12

After studying this chapter, you will be able to:

▶ describe the different classifications of soup

▶ prepare a variety of clear broths and consommés

▶ prepare thick cream and purée soups

▶ prepare cold soups

▶ garnish and serve soups appropriately

The variety of ingredients, seasonings and garnishes you can use for soups is virtually endless, provided you understand the basic procedures for making different kinds of soup. Great soups can be made from the finest and most expensive ingredients or from leftovers from the previous evening's dinner service and trimmings from the day's production. Soups are universally recognized as comfort foods in which seasonal ingredients can shine. Although fresh ingredients are preferable, the wise use of leftovers means a daily soup special can be an economical, practical menu item.

This chapter applies to soups the skills and knowledge learned in Chapter 11, Stocks and Sauces. In Chapter 11, we discussed making stocks, thickening liquids, using a liaison and skimming impurities, techniques that apply to soup making as well. Here we discuss techniques such as clarifying consommés and thickening soups with vegetable purées. This chapter also covers guidelines for preparing, garnishing and serving a variety of soups.

CHARACTERISTICS OF SOUP

Most soups can be classified by cooking technique and appearance as either clear or thick. **Clear soups** include **broths** (Fr. *bouillon*) made from meat, poultry, game, fish or vegetables as well as **consommés**, which are broths clarified to remove impurities.

Thick soups include cream soups and purée soups. The most common **cream soups** are those made from vegetables cooked in a liquid that is thickened with a starch and puréed; cream is then incorporated to add richness and flavor. **Purée soups** are generally made from starchy vegetables or legumes. After the main ingredient is simmered in a liquid, the mixture—or a portion of it—is puréed.

Some soups discussed in this chapter (notably **bisques** and **chowders** as well as **cold soups** such as gazpacho and fruit soup) are neither clear nor thick soups. Rather they are the result of special preparation methods or a combination of the methods mentioned before.

A soup's quality is determined by its flavor, appearance and texture. A good soup should be full-flavored, with no off or sour tastes. Flavors from each of the soup's ingredients should blend and complement, with no one flavor overpowering another. Consommés should be crystal clear. The vegetables in vegetable soups should be brightly colored, not gray. Ingredients added to enhance the soup's appearance and flavor should be attractive and uniform in size and shape. The soup's texture should be very precise. If it is supposed to be smooth, then it should be very smooth and lump-free. If the soft and crisp textures of certain ingredients are supposed to contrast, the soup should not be overcooked, as this causes all the ingredients to become mushy and soft.

Garnishing is an important consideration when preparing soups. When applied to soups, the word *garnish* has two meanings. The first is the one more typically associated with the word. It refers to foods added to the soup as decoration—for example, a broccoli floret floated on a bowl of cream of broccoli soup. The second refers to foods that may serve not only as decorations but also as critical components of the final product—for example, noodles in a bowl of chicken noodle soup. In this context, the noodles are not ingredients because they are not used to make the chicken soup. Rather they are added to chicken soup to create a different dish. These additional items are still referred to as garnishes, however.

CLEAR SOUPS

All clear soups start as stock or broth. Broths may be served as finished items, used as the base for other soups or refined (clarified) into consommés.

Broths

The techniques for making stocks discussed in Chapter 11 are identical to those used for making broths. Like stocks, broths are prepared by simmering flavoring ingredients in a liquid for a long time. Broths and stocks differ, however, in two ways. First, broths are made with meat instead of just bones. Second, broths (often with a garnish) can be served as finished dishes, whereas stocks are generally used to prepare other items.

Broths are made from meat, poultry, fish or vegetables cooked in a liquid. An especially full-flavored broth results when a stock and not just water is used as the liquid. Cuts of meat from the shank, neck or shoulder result in more flavorful broths, as does the flesh of mature poultry. Proper temperature, skimming and straining help produce well-flavored, clear broths.

Procedure for Preparing Broths

1 Truss or cut the main ingredient.
2 Brown (caramelize) the meat; brown (caramelize) or sweat the mirepoix or vegetables as necessary.
3 Place the main ingredient and mirepoix or vegetables in an appropriate stockpot and add enough cold water or stock to cover. Add a bouquet garni or sachet d'épices if desired.
4 Bring the liquid slowly to a boil; reduce to a simmer and cook, skimming occasionally, until the main ingredient is tender and the flavor is fully developed.
5 Carefully strain the broth through a china cap lined with damp cheesecloth; try to disturb the flavoring ingredients as little as possible in order to preserve the broth's clarity.
6 Cool and store following the procedures for cooling stocks discussed in Chapter 11, or bring to a boil, garnish as desired and hold for service.

Noodle Bowls

In Asian cuisines many hearty noodle soups serve as stand-alone meals. A well-prepared broth and the type of noodle distinguish the best of these one-pot meals. Diners are encouraged to season these broths with such condiments as chiles, citrus juice, green onions, chopped nori and soy or fish sauce. Japanese noodle soups may brim with a cornucopia of vegetables garnished with thin soba noodles made from buckwheat flour or thick udon noodles made from wheat flour. Tempura-fried shrimp or vegetables are a welcome addition. In Vietnam, noodle soups are simply called *phô* [fuh], a word that refers to a soup made with beef and rice noodles as well as to the noodles themselves. The broth, usually flavored with star anise, may be spiked by the diner with lime juice, hot chili paste and fresh cilantro. Korean *kalguksu* presents fresh knife-cut wheat noodles in a rich broth often made from dried fish or other seafood. Chinese or Mongolian hot pot is an interactive meal centered on a simmering pot of water or light broth. Diners plunge pieces of beef, seafood, mushrooms, tofu and vegetables into the pot, eating them when they are cooked to their taste. Any of a variety of Asian noodles may be added at the end to make a hearty soup richly flavored with any leftover bits of food, sliced scallions and condiments.

♥ Good Choice

Beef Broth

MISE EN PLACE

- Cut beef shank into pieces.
- Peel and chop onions, carrots and celery for mirepoix.
- Wash and peel turnips and leeks and chop into medium dice.
- Wash, peel, seed and dice tomatoes.
- Prepare herb sachet.

YIELD	2 gal. (7.6 lt), 42 Servings, 6 fl. oz. (180 ml) each	METHOD	Broth
Beef shank, neck or shoulder cut in 2-in.- (5-cm-) thick pieces		12 lb.	5.7 kg
Vegetable oil		8 fl. oz.	240 ml
Beef stock or water, cold		2 gal.	7.6 lt
Mirepoix		2 lb.	960 g
Turnips, medium dice		8 oz.	240 g
Leeks, medium dice		8 oz.	240 g
Tomatoes, seeded and diced		8 oz.	240 g
Sachet:			
Bay leaf		1	1
Dried thyme		½ 1 tsp.	5 ml
Peppercorns, crushed		½ 1 tsp.	5 ml
Parsley stems		8	8
Garlic cloves, crushed		2	2
Salt		TT	TT

1 Brown the meat in 4 fluid ounces (120 milliliters) oil, then place it in a stockpot. Add the stock or water and bring to a simmer. Simmer gently for 2 hours, skimming the surface as necessary.

2 Caramelize the mirepoix in the remaining oil and add it to the liquid after the meat has simmered for 2 hours. Add the turnips, leeks, tomatoes and sachet.

3 Simmer until full flavor has developed, approximately 1 hour. Skim the surface as necessary.

4 Carefully strain the broth through cheesecloth and season to taste. Cool and refrigerate.

Approximate values per 6-fl.-oz. (180-ml) serving: **Calories** 30, **Total fat** 1 g, **Saturated fat** 0 g, **Cholesterol** 0 mg, **Sodium** 55 mg, **Total carbohydrates** 1 g, **Protein** 4 g

❶ Browning the meat.

❷ Adding mirepoix to the broth.

❸ Straining the broth.

Broth-Based Soups

Broths are often used as bases for familiar soups such as vegetable, chicken noodle and beef barley. Transforming a broth into a broth-based vegetable soup, for example, is quite simple. Although a broth may be served with a vegetable (or meat) garnish, a broth-based vegetable soup is a soup in which the vegetables (and meats) are cooked directly in the broth, adding flavor, body and texture to the finished product. Any number of vegetables can be used to make a vegetable soup; it could be a single vegetable as in onion soup or a dozen different vegetables in a hearty minestrone.

When making broth-based vegetable soups, each ingredient must be added at the proper time so that all ingredients are cooked when the soup is finished. The ingredients must cook long enough to add their flavors and soften sufficiently but not so long that they lose their identity and become too soft or mushy. Soups that simmer too long can reduce in volume, concentrating seasonings, especially salt. Add additional plain broth to adjust the seasonings. A raw diced potato or carrot can also be added to a salty broth and simmered to absorb some of the excess saltiness.

Broth-based vegetable soups made by simmering ingredients directly in the broth are generally not as clear as plain broths. But appearance is still important. When cutting ingredients for the soup, pay particular attention so that the pieces are uniform and visually appealing. Small dice, julienne, bâtonnet or paysanne cuts are recommended. Broth and broth-based soups are naturally low in calories and fat, so they often make ideal healthy menu options.

Procedure for Preparing Broth-Based Vegetable Soups

1 Sweat long-cooking vegetables in butter or fat.
2 Add the appropriate stock or broth and bring to a simmer.
3 Add seasonings, such as bay leaves, dried thyme, crushed peppercorns, parsley stems and garlic, in a bouquet garni or sachet, allowing enough time for the seasonings to fully flavor the soup.
4 Add additional ingredients according to their cooking times.
5 Simmer the soup to blend all the flavors.
6 If the soup is not going to be served immediately, cool and refrigerate it.
7 Just before service, add any garnishes that were prepared separately or that do not require cooking.

♥ Good Choice

MISE EN PLACE

- Peel onions, carrots and celery and chop into small dice for mirepoix.
- Wash and peel turnip and chop into fine dice.
- Peel and chop garlic.
- Cut beef into fine dice.
- Prepare herb sachet.
- Cut green beans.
- While broth is simmering, wash, peel, seed and dice tomato for concassée.
- Chop oregano and thyme.

❶ Sweating the vegetables.

❷ The finished soup.

Hearty Vegetable Beef Soup

YIELD	1 gal. (3.8 lt), 21 Servings, 6 fl. oz. (180 ml) each		METHOD	Broth

Butter or beef fat		4 oz.	120 g
Mirepoix, small dice		2 lb.	960 kg
Turnip, small dice		6 oz.	180 g
Garlic cloves, chopped		4	4
Beef broth or stock		3 qt.	2.8 lt
Beef, small dice		1 lb.	480 g
Sachet:			
Bay leaf		2	2
Dried thyme		½ tsp.	2 ml
Peppercorns, crushed		½ tsp.	2 ml
Parsley stems		8	8
Green beans, fresh or frozen, cut ½ in. (1.2 cm) in length, optional		6 oz.	180 g
Tomato concassée		6 oz.	180 g
Corn kernels, fresh, frozen or canned		6 oz.	180 g
Fresh oregano, chopped		1 tsp.	5 ml
Fresh thyme, chopped		1 tsp.	5 ml
Salt and pepper		TT	TT

1 In a soup pot, sweat the mirepoix and turnip in the butter or fat until tender.

2 Add the garlic and sauté lightly.

3 Add the broth or stock and the diced beef; bring to a simmer. Add the sachet. Skim or degrease as necessary.

4 Simmer until the beef and vegetables are tender, approximately 1 hour.

5 Add the green beans, tomato concassée, corn, oregano and thyme. Season with salt and pepper; simmer for 15 minutes. Season to taste with salt and pepper.

6 Serve the soup in warm bowls.

Variations:

A wide variety of vegetables can be added or substituted in this recipe. If leeks, rutabagas, parsnips or cabbage are used, they should be sweated to bring out their flavors before the liquid is added. Potatoes, fresh beans, summer squash and other vegetables that cook more quickly should be added according to their cooking times. Seasonal leafy greens such as turnip tops, dandelion greens or arugula can be shredded and stirred in near the end of cooking. Rice, barley and pasta garnishes should be cooked separately and added just before service.

To make a vegan version of this soup, use vegetable stock in place of the beef stock and substitute a mixture of diced sautéed mushrooms and other vegetables for the diced beef.

Approximate values per 6-fl.-oz. (180-ml) serving: **Calories** 100, **Total fat** 6 g, **Saturated fat** 3 g, **Cholesterol** 25 mg, **Sodium** 590 mg, **Total carbohydrates** 7 g, **Protein** 7 g, **Vitamin A** 45%

Consommés

A consommé is a stock or broth that has been clarified to remove impurities so that it is crystal clear. Traditionally all clear broths were referred to as consommés. A clear broth further refined, using the process we describe in the following material, was referred to as a double consommé. The term *double consommé* is still used occasionally to describe any strongly flavored consommé.

Well-prepared consommés should be rich in the flavor of the main ingredient. Beef and game consommés should be dark in color; consommés made from poultry should have a golden to light amber color. All consommés should have substantial body as a result of their high gelatin content and should be perfectly clear with no trace of fat. Because a consommé is a refined broth, it is absolutely essential that the broth or stock used be of the highest quality. Although the clarification process adds some flavor to the consommé, the finished consommé will be only as good as the stock or broth from which it was made.

The Clarification Process

To make a consommé, you clarify a stock or broth. The stock or broth to be clarified must be cold and grease-free. During clarification, the cold degreased stock or broth is combined with a mixture known as a **clearmeat** or clarification. A clearmeat is a mixture of egg whites; ground meat, poultry or fish; mirepoix, herbs and spices; and an acidic product, usually tomatoes, lemon juice or wine. (An onion brûlé, also known as an oignon brûlé, is also often added to help flavor and color the consommé. See Chapter 9, Mise en Place.)

In the next step of clarification, the stock or broth and clearmeat are slowly brought to a simmer. As the albumen in the egg whites and meat begins to coagulate at 120°F (48°C), it traps impurities suspended in the liquid. As coagulation continues, the albumen-containing items combine with the other clearmeat ingredients and rise to the liquid's surface, forming a **raft**. As the mixture simmers, the raft ingredients release their flavors, further enriching the consommé.

After simmering, the consommé is carefully strained through several layers of damp cheesecloth to remove any trace of impurities. It is then completely degreased, either by cooling and refrigerating, then removing the solidified fat, or by carefully ladling the fat from the surface. The result is a rich, flavorful, crystal-clear consommé.

raft a crust formed during the process of clarifying consommé; it is composed of the clearmeat and impurities from the stock, which rise to the top of the simmering stock and release additional flavors

Procedure for Preparing Consommés

1 Prepare the clearmeat. Whip the egg whites until frothy. In a suitable stockpot (if available, one with a spigot makes it much easier to strain the consommé when it is finished), combine the ground meat, lightly whipped egg whites and other clearmeat ingredients.

2 Add the cold stock or broth and stir to combine with the clearmeat ingredients, onion brûlé and sachet d'épices.

3 Over medium heat, slowly bring the mixture to a simmer, stirring occasionally. Stop stirring once the raft begins to form.

4 As the raft forms, make a hole in its center so that the liquid can bubble through. This will allow the raft to cook completely and will extract as much flavor as possible from the raft ingredients.

5 Simmer the consommé until full flavor develops, approximately 1 to 1½ hours.

6 Carefully strain the consommé through several layers of damp cheesecloth and degrease completely.

7 If the consommé will not be used immediately, it should be cooled and refrigerated, following the procedures for cooling stocks discussed in Chapter 11, Stocks and Sauces. When the consommé is completely cold, remove any remaining fat that solidifies on its surface.

8 If, after reheating the consommé, small dots of fat appear on the surface, remove them by blotting with a small piece of paper towel.

Classic Consommés

Many classic consommés are known by their garnishes. A few are listed here with their characteristic garnishes:

Consommé brunoise: Blanched or sautéed brunoise of turnip, leek, celery and onion

Consommé julienne: Blanched or sautéed julienne of carrot, turnip, leek, celery, cabbage and onion

Consommé paysanne: Blanched or sautéed paysanne of leek, turnip, carrot, celery and potato

Consommé bouquetière: Assorted blanched vegetables

Consommé madrilène: Tomatoes or tomato juice; served hot or cold

Consommé royale: Cooked custard cut into tiny shapes

Angel hair consommé: Cooked angel hair (vermicelli) pasta

Consommé with profiteroles: Tiny profiteroles (pâte à choux rounds) stuffed with foie gras

💙 Good Choice

Beef Consommé

MISE EN PLACE

- Peel and chop onions, carrots and celery for mirepoix.
- Seed and dice tomato.
- Prepare onions brûlés and herb sachet.

YIELD 1 gal. (3.8 lt), 21 Servings, 6 fl. oz. (180 ml) each		METHOD Consommé
Egg whites	10	10
Ground beef, lean, preferably shank, neck or shoulder	2 lb.	960 g
Mirepoix	1 lb.	480 g
Tomatoes, seeded and diced	12 oz.	360 g
Beef broth or stock, cold	5 qt.	4.8 lt
Onions brûlés	2	2
Sachet:		
Bay leaves	2	2
Dried thyme	½ tsp.	2 ml
Peppercorns, crushed	½ tsp.	2 ml
Parsley stems	8	8
Cloves, whole	2	2
Salt	TT	TT

1 Whip the egg whites until slightly frothy.

2 Combine the egg whites, beef, mirepoix and tomatoes in an appropriate stockpot.

3 Add the broth or stock; mix well and add the onions brûlés and sachet.

4 Bring the mixture to a simmer over medium heat, stirring occasionally. Stop stirring when the raft begins to form.

5 Break a hole in the center of the raft to allow the consommé to bubble through.

6 Simmer until full flavor develops, approximately 1½ hours.

7 Strain through several layers of moist cheesecloth, degrease and adjust the seasonings. Cool and refrigerate or hold for service.

Note Guidelines for garnishing consommés as well as some classic garnishes are listed on page 274.

Approximate values per 6-fl.-oz. (180-ml) serving: **Calories** 20, **Total fat** 0 g, **Saturated fat** 0 g, **Cholesterol** 0 mg, **Sodium** 500 mg, **Total carbohydrates** 1 g, **Protein** 4 g, **Claims**—low fat; low calorie

❶ Combining the ingredients for the clearmeat.

❷ Making a hole in the raft to allow the liquid to bubble through.

❸ Degreasing the consommé with a paper towel.

❹ The finished consommé is clear with no trace of fat.

Correcting a Poorly Clarified Consommé

A clarification may fail for a variety of reasons. For example, if the consommé is allowed to boil or if it is stirred after the raft has formed, a cloudy consommé can result. If the consommé is insufficiently clear, a second clarification can be performed using the following procedure. This second clarification should be performed only once, however, and only if absolutely necessary, because the eggs remove not only impurities but also some of the consommé's flavor and richness.

1   Thoroughly chill and degrease the consommé.
2   Lightly beat together four egg whites for each gallon (approximately 4 liters) of consommé. Stir the whites into the cold degreased consommé.
3   Slowly bring the consommé to a simmer, stirring occasionally. Stop stirring when the egg whites begin to coagulate.
4   When the egg whites are completely coagulated, carefully strain the consommé through moist cheesecloth.

THICK SOUPS

There are two kinds of thick soups: cream soups and purée soups. In general, cream soups are thickened with a roux or other starch, whereas purée soups rely on a purée of the main ingredient for thickening. But in certain ways the two soups are very similar; some purée soups are finished with cream or partially thickened with a roux or other starch. See Tables 12.1 and 12.2.

Cream Soups

Most cream soups are made by simmering the main flavoring ingredient (e.g., broccoli for cream of broccoli soup) in a white stock or thin **velouté** sauce to which seasonings have been added. The mixture is then puréed and strained. After the consistency has been adjusted, the soup is finished by adding cream. In classic cuisine, thin **béchamel** sauce is often used as the base for cream soups and can be substituted for velouté in many cream soup recipes if desired. Properly made cream soups should have a silken texture and the thickness of heavy cream. The flavor of the soups' main ingredient should be pronounced.

Both hard vegetables (e.g., carrots, celery and squash) and soft or leafy vegetables (e.g., spinach, corn, broccoli, mushrooms and asparagus) are used in cream soups. Hard vegetables are generally sweated in butter without browning before the liquid is added. Soft and leafy vegetables are generally added to the soup after the liquid is brought to a boil. Because cream soups are puréed, it is important to cook the flavoring ingredients until they are soft and can be passed through a food mill easily.

SOUPS, THEIR THICKENING AGENTS AND FINISHES			TABLE 12.1
CATEGORY	TYPE	THICKENING AGENT OR METHOD	FINISH
Clear soups	Broths	None	Assorted garnishes
	Consommés	None	Assorted garnishes
Thick soups	Cream soups	Roux and/or puréeing	Assorted garnishes, cream or béchamel sauce
	Purée soups	Puréeing	Assorted garnishes; cream is optional
Other soups	Bisques	Roux or rice and puréeing	Garnish of main ingredient, cream and/or butter
	Chowders	Roux	Cream
Cold soups	Cooked cold soups	Roux, arrowroot, cornstarch, puréeing, sour cream, yogurt	Assorted garnishes, cream, crème fraîche, sour cream or yogurt
	Uncooked cold soups	Puréeing	Assorted garnishes, cream, crème fraîche, sour cream or yogurt

CREAM AND PURÉE SOUPS		TABLE 12.2
	CREAM SOUPS	PURÉE SOUPS
Technique	Cook principal ingredient in stock or velouté sauce	Cook principal ingredient in stock or water
Thickener	Roux or roux-thickened sauce	Purée of starchy ingredients
Texture	Strained; very smooth and rich	Not strained; slightly coarse and grainy

All cream soups are finished with milk or cream. Milk thins the soup while adding richness; the same amount of cream adds much more richness without the same thinning effect. Cold milk and cream curdle easily if added directly to a hot or acidic soup.

To prevent curdling:

1 Never add cold milk or cream to hot soup. Bring the milk or cream to a simmer before adding it to the soup, or temper the milk or cream by gradually adding some hot soup to it and then incorporating the warmed mixture into the rest of the soup.

2 Add the milk or cream to the soup just before service, if possible.

3 Do not boil the soup after the milk or cream has been added.

cream sauce a sauce made by adding cream to a béchamel sauce

4 Use béchamel or **cream sauce** instead of milk or cream to finish cream soups; the roux or other starch helps prevent curdling.

Procedure for Preparing Cream Soups

1 In a soup pot, sweat hard vegetables, such as squash, onions, carrots and celery, in oil or butter without browning.

2 In order to thicken the soup:
   a. add flour to the vegetables and cook to make a blond roux, then add the stock or other liquid as required, or
   b. add the stock to the vegetables, bring the stock to a simmer and add a blond roux that was prepared separately, or
   c. add a thin velouté or béchamel sauce (which contain roux) to the vegetables and then add the stock.

3 Bring to a boil and reduce to a simmer.

4 Add any soft vegetables such as broccoli or asparagus, and a sachet or bouquet garni as desired.

5 Simmer the soup, skimming occasionally, until the vegetables are very tender.

6 Purée the soup by passing it through a food mill or by using a blender, food processor or vertical cutter/mixer (VCM). Strain through a china cap if desired. If the soup is too thick, adjust the consistency by adding hot white stock.

7 Finish the soup by adding hot milk or cream or a thin béchamel or cream sauce. Adjust the seasonings and serve.

Cream of Broccoli Soup

YIELD	1 gal. (3.8 lt), 21 Servings, 6 fl. oz. (180 ml) each	METHOD	Cream

Whole butter	4 oz.	120 g
Onions, medium dice	8 oz.	240 g
Celery, medium dice	4 oz.	120 g
Broccoli, chopped	2 lb.	960 g
Chicken velouté sauce, hot	3 qt.	2.8 lt
Chicken stock, hot	1 pt.	480 ml
Heavy cream, hot	1 pt.	480 ml
Salt and white pepper	TT	TT
Broccoli florets	as needed for garnish	
Croutons, sautéed in butter	as needed for garnish	

MISE EN PLACE

- Peel onions. Chop onions and celery into medium dice.
- Chop broccoli.
- Prepare velouté sauce and keep warm.
- While the soup is simmering, blanch broccoli florets and prepare the croutons.

1 Sweat the onions and celery in the butter, without browning, until they are nearly tender, approximately 2 minutes. Add the broccoli and sweat until tender, approximately 10 minutes.

2 Add the velouté sauce. Bring to a simmer and cook until the vegetables are tender, approximately 15 minutes. Skim the surface periodically.

3 Purée the soup by passing it through a food mill or by using a blender, food processor or vertical cutter/mixer (VCM). If a smoother product is desired, strain it through a china cap.

4 Return the soup to the stove and thin it to the desired consistency with some of the stock.

5 Bring the soup to a simmer and add the cream. Season to taste.

6 Serve the soup in warm bowls garnished with blanched broccoli florets and croutons just before service.

Variations:

To make cream of asparagus, cauliflower, corn, pea or spinach soup, substitute an equal amount of the chosen vegetable for the broccoli. If using fresh spinach, precook the leaves slightly before proceeding with the recipe.

Approximate values per 6-fl.-oz. (180-ml) serving: **Calories** 250, **Total fat** 20 g, **Saturated fat** 13 g, **Cholesterol** 60 mg, **Sodium** 1010 mg, **Total carbohydrates** 13 g, **Protein** 7 g, **Vitamin A** 35%, **Vitamin C** 70%

❶ Adding the velouté sauce.

❷ Puréeing the soup by passing it through a food mill.

❸ The finished soup has a silken texture and the thickness of heavy cream.

Purée Soups

Purée soups are hearty soups made by cooking starchy vegetables or legumes in a stock or broth, then puréeing all or a portion of them to thicken the soup. Purée soups are similar to cream soups in that they both consist of a main ingredient that is first cooked in a liquid, then puréed. The primary difference is that unlike cream soups, which are thickened with starch, purée soups generally do not use additional starch for thickening. Rather, purée soups depend on the starch content of the main ingredient for thickening. Also purée soups are generally coarser than cream soups and are typically not strained after puréeing. See Table 12.2. When finishing purée soups with cream, follow the guidelines discussed for adding cream to cream soups.

Purée soups can be made with dried or fresh beans such as peas, lentils and navy beans, or with any number of vegetables, including cauliflower, celery root, turnips and potatoes. Diced potato or rice is often used to help thicken vegetable purée soups. Purée pea, bean or vegetable soups, when not enriched with fat and cream, are good sources of dietary fiber and considered healthy alternatives to cream soups.

Procedure for Preparing Purée Soups

1 Sweat the mirepoix in butter or other fat without browning.
2 Add the cooking liquid.
3 Add the main ingredients and a sachet or bouquet garni.
4 Bring to a boil, reduce to a simmer and cook until all the ingredients are soft enough to purée easily. Remove and discard the sachet or bouquet garni.
5 Reserve a portion of the liquid, if available, to adjust the soup's consistency. Purée the rest of the soup by passing it through a food mill or by using a blender, food processor or VCM.
6 Add enough of the reserved liquid or hot stock to bring the soup to the desired consistency.
7 Return the soup to a simmer and adjust the seasonings.
8 Add hot cream to the soup if desired.

Purée of Split Pea Soup

YIELD 1 gal. (3.8 lt), 21 Servings, 6 fl. oz. (180 ml) each		**METHOD** Purée	
Bacon, diced	3 oz.	90 g	
Mirepoix, medium dice	1 lb.	480 g	
Garlic cloves, chopped	2	2	
Chicken stock	3 qt.	2.8 lt	
Split peas, washed and sorted	1 lb.	480 g	
Ham hocks or meaty ham bones	1½ lb.	720 g	
Sachet:			
Bay leaves	2	2	
Dried thyme	½ tsp.	2 ml	
Peppercorns, crushed	½ tsp.	2 ml	
Salt and pepper	TT	TT	
Croutons, sautéed in butter	as needed for garnish		

MISE EN PLACE

- Dice bacon.
- Peel onions, carrots and celery and chop into medium dice for mirepoix.
- Peel and chop garlic.
- Wash and sort split peas.
- Prepare herb sachet.
- While the soup is simmering, prepare the croutons.

render to melt and clarify fat

1 In a stockpot, **render** the bacon by cooking it slowly and allowing it to release its fat; sweat the mirepoix and garlic in the fat without browning them.
2 Add the stock, peas, ham hocks or bones and sachet. Bring to a boil, reduce to a simmer and cook until the peas are soft, approximately 1–1½ hours.
3 Remove the sachet and ham hocks or bones. Purée the soup by passing it through a food mill or by using a blender, food processor or vertical cutter/mixer (VCM). Return the soup to the stockpot.

4 Remove the meat from the hocks or bones. Cut the meat into medium dice and add it to the soup.

5 Bring the soup to a simmer and, if necessary, adjust the consistency by adding hot chicken stock. Adjust the seasonings and serve, garnished with croutons.

Variations:

White beans, yellow peas and other dried beans can be soaked overnight in water and used instead of split peas.

Approximate values per 6-fl.-oz. (180-ml) serving: **Calories** 110, **Total fat** 4 g, **Saturated fat** 1.5 g, **Cholesterol** 20 mg, **Sodium** 870 mg, **Total carbohydrates** 6 g, **Protein** 11 g

❶ Adding peas to the stockpot.   ❷ Puréeing the split pea soup.   ❸ Garnishing the finished soup with croutons.

Adjusting the Consistency of Thick Soups

Cream and purée soups tend to thicken when made in advance and refrigerated. To dilute a portion being reheated, add hot stock, broth, water or milk to the hot soup as needed.

If the soup is too thin, additional roux, beurre manié or cornstarch mixed with cool stock can be used to thicken it. If additional starch is added to thicken the soup, it should be used sparingly and the soup should be simmered a few minutes to cook out the starchy flavor. A liaison of egg yolks and heavy cream can be used to thicken cream soups when added richness is also desired. Remember, the soup must not boil after the liaison is added or it may curdle.

OTHER SOUPS

Several popular types of soup do not fit the descriptions of, or follow the procedures for, either clear or thick soups. Soups such as bisques and chowders as well as many cold soups use special methods or a combination of the methods used for clear and thick soups.

Bisques

Traditional bisques are shellfish soups thickened with cooked rice. Today bisques are prepared using a combination of cream and purée soup procedures. They are generally made from shrimp, lobster or crayfish and are thickened with a roux instead of rice for better stability and consistency.

Much of a bisque's flavor comes from crustacean shells, which are simmered in the cooking liquid, puréed (along with the mirepoix), returned to the cooking liquid and strained after further cooking. Puréeing the shells and returning them to the soup also adds the thickness and grainy texture associated with bisques.

Bisques are enriched with cream, following the procedures for cream soups, and can be finished with butter for additional richness. The garnish should be diced flesh from the appropriate shellfish.

Procedure for Preparing Bisques

1 Caramelize the mirepoix and main flavoring ingredient in fat.
2 Add a tomato product. Flavor with brandy if desired and deglaze with wine.
3 Add the cooking liquid (stock or velouté sauce).
4 Incorporate roux if needed.
5 Simmer, skimming as needed.
6 Strain the soup, reserving the solids and liquid if desired. (If called for, purée the solids in a food mill, blender or food processor and return them to the liquid.) Return to a simmer.
7 Strain the soup through a fine chinois or a china cap lined with cheesecloth.
8 Return the soup to a simmer and finish with hot cream.

To add even more richness to the bisque, monté au beurre with whole butter or a compound butter such as shrimp or lobster butter just before the soup is served. Also, if desired, add 3 ounces (90 milliliters) sherry to each gallon (approximately 4 liters) of soup just before service.

Shrimp Bisque

MISE EN PLACE

- Peel onions, carrots and celery and chop fine for mirepoix.
- Peel and chop garlic.
- Prepare fish velouté with shrimp stock.
- Prepare herb sachet.
- Peel and devein shrimp.
- While the bisque is simmering, wash and chop basil in chiffonade.

YIELD 1 gal. (3.8 lt), 32 Servings, 4 fl. oz. (120 ml) each		METHOD Bisque	
Clarified butter		3 fl. oz.	90 ml
Mirepoix, chopped fine		1 lb.	480 g
Shrimp shells and/or lobster or crayfish shells and bodies		2 lb.	960 g
Garlic cloves, chopped		2	2
Tomato paste		2 oz.	60 g
Brandy		4 fl. oz.	120 ml
White wine		12 fl. oz.	360 ml
Fish velouté (made with shrimp stock)		1 gal.	3.8 lt
Sachet:			
Bay leaf		1	1
Dried thyme		½ tsp.	2 ml
Peppercorns, crushed		½ tsp.	2 ml
Parsley stems		8	8
Heavy cream, hot		1 pt.	480 ml
Salt and white pepper		TT	TT
Cayenne pepper		TT	TT
Dry or cream sherry wine, optional		4 fl. oz.	120 ml
Shrimp, peeled and deveined		1 lb.	480 g
Fresh basil, chiffonade		as needed for garnish	

1 Caramelize the mirepoix and shrimp shells in the butter.

2 Add the garlic and tomato paste and sauté lightly.

3 Add the brandy and flambé.

4 Add the wine. Deglaze and reduce the liquid by half.

5 Add the velouté and sachet and simmer for approximately 1 hour, skimming occasionally.

6 Strain, discarding the sachet and reserving the liquid and solids. Purée the solids and return them to the liquid. Return to a simmer and cook for 10 minutes.

7 Strain the bisque through a fine chinois or china cap lined with cheesecloth.

8 Return the bisque to a simmer and add the cream.

9 Season to taste with salt, white pepper and cayenne pepper. Add sherry, if using.

10 Cook the shrimp and slice or dice them as desired. Garnish each portion of soup with cooked shrimp and the basil chiffonade.

Approximate values per 4-fl.-oz. (120-ml) serving: **Calories** 110, **Total fat** 10 g, **Saturated fat** 6 g, **Cholesterol** 60 mg, **Sodium** 160 mg, **Total carbohydrates** 2 g, **Protein** 4 g, **Vitamin A** 10%

Chowders

Although chowders are usually associated with the eastern United States where fish and clams are plentiful, they are of French origin. Undoubtedly the word chowder is derived from the Breton phrase *faire chaudière*, which means to make a fish stew in a caldron. The procedure was probably brought to Nova Scotia by French settlers and later introduced to New England.

Chowders are hearty soups with chunks of the main ingredients (including, virtually always, diced potatoes) and garnishes. With some exceptions (notably Manhattan clam chowder), chowders contain milk or cream. Although there are thin chowders, most chowders are thickened with roux. The procedures for making chowders are similar to those for making cream soups except chowders are not puréed and strained before the cream is added.

Seasonings for Soups

The addition of herbs and spices ensures memorable soups. Tender, mild fresh herbs such as chervil, chives, cilantro, dill and parsley add a bright, clean taste to broth, starch and vegetable combinations, especially when added just before serving. Many thick purée soups, when made without milk or cream, benefit from a splash of citrus juice or vinegar immediately before serving. The piney flavors of fresh basil or mint work well in hearty vegetable or bean soups such as minestrone. Pungent herbs such as rosemary and thyme or strong spices should be used judiciously if at all in soups, although a delicate grating of nutmeg complements most cream soups.

Procedure for Preparing Chowders

1 Prepare the broth or stock for the chowder.
2 Render finely diced salt pork over medium heat.
3 Sweat mirepoix or other aromatic vegetables in the rendered pork.
4 Add flour to make a roux.
5 Add the liquid.
6 Add the seasoning and flavoring ingredients according to their cooking times.
7 Simmer, skimming as needed.
8 Add milk or cream.

New England–Style Clam Chowder

MISE EN PLACE

- Peel and dice potatoes.
- Dice the salt pork.
- Peel and dice onions and celery.
- While the chowder is simmering, peel and julienne carrot garnish and prepare the croutons.

The finished chowder has a creamy, silken texture with the rich flavor of clams.

YIELD 1 gal. (3.8 lt), 21 Servings, 6 fl. oz. (180 ml) each		METHOD Cream
Canned clams with juice	2 qt.	1.9 lt
Water or fish stock	approx. 1 qt.	approx. 960 lt
Potatoes, small dice	1 lb.	480 g
Salt pork, small dice	8 oz.	240 g
Whole butter	2 oz.	60 g
Onions, small dice	1 lb.	480 g
Celery, small dice	8 oz.	240 g
Flour	4 oz.	120 g
Milk	1 qt.	960 ml
Heavy cream	8 fl. oz.	240 ml
Salt and pepper	TT	TT
Tabasco sauce	TT	TT
Worcestershire sauce	TT	TT
Fresh thyme	TT	TT
Fresh herbs	as needed for garnish	
Croutons, sautéed in oil	as needed for garnish	
Slab bacon, julienne, cooked	as needed for garnish	

1 Drain the clams, reserving both the clams and their liquid. Add enough water or stock so that the total liquid equals 1½ quarts (1.4 liters).

2 Simmer the potatoes in the clam liquid until nearly cooked through. Strain and reserve the potatoes and the liquid.

3 Render the salt pork with the butter. Add the onions and celery to the rendered fat and sweat until tender but not brown.

4 Add the flour and cook to make a blond roux.

5 Add the clam liquid to the roux, whisking away any lumps.

6 Bring to a simmer and cook for 30 minutes, skimming as necessary.

7 Bring the milk and cream to a boil and add to the soup.

8 Add the clams and potatoes, and season to taste with salt, pepper, Tabasco sauce, Worcestershire sauce and thyme. Return to a simmer.

9 Garnish each serving with fresh herbs, croutons and cooked bacon.

Note If using fresh clams for the chowder, wash and steam ½ bushel (15 liters) chowder clams in a small amount of water to yield 1¼ quarts (1.2 liters) clam meat. Chop the clams. Strain the liquid through cheesecloth to remove any sand that may be present. Add enough water or stock so that the total liquid is 1½ quarts (1.4 liters). Continue with the recipe, starting at Step 2.

Approximate values per 6-fl.-oz. (180-ml) serving: **Calories** 260, **Total fat** 17 g, **Saturated fat** 8 g, **Cholesterol** 50 mg, **Sodium** 790 mg, **Total carbohydrates** 15 g, **Protein** 11 g, **Vitamin A** 10%, **Calcium** 10%

Cold Soups

Cold soups can be as simple as a chilled version of a cream soup or as creative as a cold fruit soup blended with yogurt. Cold fruit soups have become popular on contemporary dessert menus. Other than the fact that they are cold, cold soups are difficult to classify because many of them use unique or combination preparation methods. Regardless they are divided here into two categories: cold soups that require cooking and those that do not.

Cooked Cold Soups

Many cold soups are simply a chilled version of a hot soup. For example, consommé madrilène and consommé portugaise are prepared hot and served cold. Vichyssoise is a cold version of puréed potato-leek soup. When serving a hot soup cold, there are several considerations:

- If the soup is to be creamed, add the cream at the last minute. Although curdling is not as much of a problem as it is with hot soups, adding the cream at the last minute helps extend the soup's shelf life.
- Cold soups should have a thinner consistency than hot soups. To achieve the proper consistency, use less starch if starch is used as the thickener, or use a higher ratio of liquid to main ingredient if the soup is thickened by puréeing. Consistency should be checked and adjusted at service time.
- Cold dulls the sense of taste, so cold soups require more seasoning than hot ones. Taste the soup just before service and adjust the seasonings as needed.
- Always serve cold soups as cold as possible, using chilled bowls.

⚠ Safety Alert

Cooked Cold Soup

Cooked cold soups, especially those made with potatoes, beans, dairy products or other high-protein foods, require time and temperature control for safety (TCS). They must be chilled quickly and held at or below 41°F (5°C). Because these soups will not be reheated for service, cross-contamination is also a concern. Keep the soup covered and store it above any raw meat, poultry or seafood in the cooler.

Vichyssoise (Cold Potato-Leek Soup)

YIELD 1 gal. (3.8 lt), 21 Servings, 6 fl. oz. (180 ml) each

METHOD Purée

Leeks, white part only	2 lb.	960 g
Whole butter	8 oz.	240 g
Russet potatoes, large dice	2 lb.	960 g
Chicken stock	3½ qt.	3.3 lt
Salt and white pepper	TT	TT
Heavy cream	24 fl. oz.	720 ml
Chives, snipped	as needed for garnish	
Leek slices, cooked	as needed for garnish	
Slab bacon, julienne, cooked	as needed for garnish	

MISE EN PLACE

- Wash and trim leeks.
- Peel and dice potatoes.
- While the soup is chilling, snip chives, cook sliced leeks and prepare bacon garnish.

1 Split the leeks lengthwise and wash well to remove all sand and grit. Slice them thinly.

2 Sweat the leeks in the butter without browning them.

3 Add the diced potatoes and stock, season with salt and white pepper and bring to a simmer.

4 Simmer until the leeks and potatoes are very tender, approximately 45 minutes.

5 Purée the soup in a food processor, blender or food mill; strain through a fine sieve.

6 Chill the soup well.

7 At service time, incorporate the cream and adjust the seasonings. Serve in chilled bowls, garnished with snipped chives, cooked leek slices and bacon.

Approximate values per 6-fl.-oz. (180-ml) serving: **Calories** 300, **Total fat** 22 g, **Saturated fat** 13 g, **Cholesterol** 70 mg, **Sodium** 660 mg, **Total carbohydrates** 19 g, **Protein** 6 g, **Vitamin A** 20%, **Vitamin C** 20%

Many cooked cold soups use fruit juice (typically apple, grape or orange) as a base and are thickened with cornstarch or arrowroot as well as with puréed fruit. For additional flavor, wine is sometimes used in the place of a portion of the fruit juice. Cooked cold soups may be based on a cooked fruit that is puréed. Cinnamon, ginger and other spices that complement fruit are commonly added, as is lemon juice, lime juice or vinegar, which add acidity as well as flavor. Buttermilk, crème fraîche, yogurt or sour cream can be used as an ingredient or garnish to add richness.

Chilled Melon Soup

MISE EN PLACE

- Peel and chop onions and garlic.
- Wash, peel, seed and dice melon.
- Chop basil and prepare Crisp Prosciutto Chips while soup is chilling.

YIELD 1 gal. (3.8 lt), 21 Servings, 6 oz. (180 ml) each		**METHOD** Cooked Cold	
Olive oil	6 fl. oz.	180 ml
Almonds, sliced, blanched	4 oz.	120 g
Onion, chopped	12 oz.	360 g
Garlic, chopped	4 Tbsp.	60 ml
Cantaloupe, peeled, seeded, large dice	4 lbs.	1.2 kg
Honeydew, peeled, seeded, large dice	4 lbs.	1.2 kg
Agave nectar or honey	4 Tbsp.	60 ml
Buttermilk	1 qt.	1 lt
Basil leaves, chopped	4 Tbsp.	60 ml
Salt	TT	TT
Balsamic vinegar	1 fl. oz.	30 ml
Crisp Prosciutto Chips (recipe follows)	as needed	as needed
Micro greens	as needed	as needed

1 Heat a large sauce pot over medium heat. Add the olive oil to the pot. Add the almonds and cook until they are golden brown.

2 Add the onions and garlic and sweat until translucent.

3 Add the melons and cook for approximately 10 minutes or until the fruit softens and breaks down.

4 Add the agave nectar and buttermilk and return to a simmer and cook for approximately 15 minutes until the melon is completely soft and the flavors have blended.

5 Remove from the heat and cool for several minutes. Process the soup in a blender with the basil leaves until smooth. This can be done in several batches if necessary.

6 Season the soup with salt. Strain the soup through a coarse mesh strainer into a nonreactive container. Cool, cover and refrigerate.

7 Serve the soup in chilled soup bowls garnished with crumbled Crisp Prosciutto Chips and micro greens.

Crisp Prosciutto Chips

YIELD 1 oz. (30 g)		
Prosciutto ham, sliced thin	2 oz.	60 g

1 Line a sheet pan with a silicone baking pan liner. Place the slices of prosciutto on the pan and cover with another silicone baking pan liner.

2 Bake at 350°F (180°C) until the slices are uniformly crisp and firm like bacon, approximately 15 minutes.

3 Transfer the cooked prosciutto slices to a sheet pan lined with paper towels to drain any excess fat.

Approximate values per 6-fl.-oz. (180-ml) serving: **Calories** 180, **Total fat** 10 g, **Saturated fat** 1.5 g, **Cholesterol** 0 mg, **Sodium** 120 mg, **Total carbohydrates** 23 g, **Protein** 4 g, **Vitamin A** 60%, **Vitamin C** 80%

Uncooked Cold Soups

Some cold soups are not cooked at all. Rather they rely only on puréed fruits or vegetables for thickness, body and flavor. Cold stock is sometimes used to adjust the soup's consistency. Dairy products such as cream, sour cream and crème fraîche may also be added to enrich and flavor the soup.

Gazpacho

 Good Choice    Vegan

YIELD 1 gal. (3.8 lt), 21 Servings, 6 fl. oz. (180 ml) each	METHOD Uncooked Cold	
Tomatoes, peeled and diced	2 lb. 8 oz.	1.2 kg
Onions, medium dice	8 oz.	240 g
Green bell pepper, medium dice	1	1
Red bell pepper, medium dice	1	1
Cucumbers, peeled, seeded, medium dice	1 lb.	480 g
Garlic, minced	1 oz.	30 g
Red wine vinegar	2 fl. oz.	60 ml
Lemon juice	2 fl. oz.	60 ml
Olive oil	4 fl. oz.	120 ml
Salt and pepper	TT	TT
Cayenne pepper	TT	TT
Fresh bread crumbs, optional	3 oz.	90 g
Tomato juice	3 qt.	2.8 lt
Vegetable Stock (page 212)	as needed	as needed
Garnish:		
Tomatoes, peeled, seeded, small dice	8 oz.	240 g
Red bell pepper, small dice	4 oz.	120 g
Green bell pepper, small dice	4 oz.	120 g
Yellow bell pepper, small dice	4 oz.	120 g
Cucumber, peeled, seeded, small dice	3 oz.	90 g
Green onion, sliced fine	2 oz.	60 g
Green onion, julienne	as needed for garnish	

MISE EN PLACE

- Peel and dice tomatoes, onions and peppers.
- Peel, seed and dice cucumbers.
- Peel and mince garlic.
- Peel and slice green onions.

1 Combine and purée all ingredients except the tomato juice, stock and garnish in a VCM, food processor or blender.

2 Stir in tomato juice.

3 Adjust the consistency with stock.

4 Stir in the vegetable garnishes and adjust the seasonings.

5 Serve in chilled cups or bowls garnished with green onion julienne.

Variation:

A chunky gazpacho can be made by not puréeing all the ingredients completely. Less garnish will be required.

Approximate values per 6-fl.-oz. (180-ml) serving: **Calories** 70, **Total fat** 0.5 g, **Saturated fat** 0 g, **Cholesterol** 0 mg, **Sodium** 600 mg, **Total carbohydrates** 14 g, **Protein** 3 g, **Vitamin A** 15%, **Vitamin C** 70%, **Claims**—low fat; no cholesterol

---

⚠ Safety Alert

Uncooked Cold Soup

Because uncooked cold soups are never heated, enzymes and bacteria are not destroyed and the soup can spoil quickly. Many cold soups also contain dairy products, which makes them a time and temperature control for safety (TCS) food. When preparing uncooked cold soups, always prepare small batches as close to service time as possible. Keep the soup at or below 41°F (5°C) at all times. Cover and store leftovers properly.

GARNISHING SOUPS

Garnishes and toppings can range from a simple sprinkle of chopped parsley on a bowl of cream soup to tiny profiteroles stuffed with foie gras adorning a crystal-clear bowl of consommé. Some soups are so full of attractive, flavorful and colorful foods that are integral parts of the soup (e.g., vegetables and chicken in chicken vegetable soup) that no additional garnishes are necessary. In others, the garnish determines the type of soup. For example, a beef broth garnished with cooked barley and diced beef becomes beef barley soup.

Guidelines for Garnishing Soups

Although some soups (particularly consommés) have traditional garnishes, many soups depend on the chef's imagination and the kitchen's inventory for the finishing garnish. The only rules are as follows:

1   The garnish should be attractive.
2   The meats and vegetables used should be neatly cut into an appropriate and uniform shape and size. This is particularly important when garnishing a clear soup such as a consommé, as the consommé's clarity highlights the precise (or imprecise) cuts.
3   The garnish's texture and flavor should complement the soup.
4   Starches and vegetables used as garnishes should be cooked separately, reheated and placed in the soup bowl before the hot soup is added. If they are cooked in the soup, they may cloud or thicken the soup or alter its flavor, texture and seasoning.
5   Garnishes should be cooked just until done; meat and poultry should be tender but not falling apart, vegetables should be firm but not mushy, and pasta and rice should maintain their identity. These types of garnishes are usually held on the side and added to the hot soup at the last minute to prevent overcooking.

Garnishing Suggestions

Some garnishes are used to add texture, as well as flavor and visual interest, to soups. Items such as crunchy croutons or oyster crackers, crispy crumbled bacon on a cream soup or diced meat in a clear broth soup add a textural variety that makes the final product more appealing.

Clear soups: Any combination of julienne cuts of the same meat, poultry, fish or vegetable that provides the dominant flavor in the stock or broth; vegetables (cut uniformly into any shape), pasta (flat, small tortellini or tiny ravioli), gnocchi, quenelles, barley, spaetzle, white or wild rice, croutons, crepes, tortillas or won tons.

Cream soups, hot or cold: Toasted slivered almonds, sour cream or crème fraîche, croutons, grated cheese or baked puff pastry cut-outs; cream vegetable soups are usually garnished with slices or florets of the main ingredient.

Purée soups: Julienne cuts of poultry or ham, sliced sausage, croutons, grated cheese or bacon bits.

Any soup: Finely chopped fresh herbs, snipped chives, edible flowers, parsley or watercress.

SOUP SERVICE

Most soups can be made ahead of time, cooled down rapidly to ensure food safety and refrigerated until needed. To preserve freshness and quality, small batches of soup should be reheated as needed throughout the meal service.

Clear soups are quite easy to reheat because there is little danger of scorching. If garnishes are already added to a clear soup, care should be taken not to overcook the garnishes when reheating the soup. All traces of fat should be removed from a consommé's surface before reheating.

Thick soups present more of a challenge. To increase shelf life and reduce the risk of spoilage, cool and refrigerate a thick soup when it is still a base (i.e., before it is finished with milk or cream). Just before service, carefully reheat the soup base using a heavy-gauge pot over low heat. Stir often to prevent scorching. Then finish the soup (following the guidelines noted earlier in this chapter) with boiling milk or cream, a light béchamel sauce or a liaison and adjust the seasonings. Always taste the soup after reheating and adjust the seasonings as needed.

A cold cream soup served in small glasses as a passed hors d'oeuvre.

Temperatures

The rule is simple: Serve hot soup hot and cold soup cold. Hot clear soups should be served near boiling; 210°F (99°C) is ideal. Hot cream soups should be served at slightly lower temperatures; 190–200°F (88–93°C) is acceptable. Cold soups should be served at a temperature of 41°F (5°C) or below and can be presented in special serving pieces surrounded by ice.

Portion Sizes

Soup portion sizes will vary depending on the meal course. When offered as an hors d'oeuvre on trays passed by the service staff, 2–3 fluid ounces (60–90 milliliters) of soup may be adequate. Appetizer portions of soup are customarily 6–9 fluid ounces (180–270 milliliters), but this can vary. Rich bisque made from costly shellfish, for example, may be served in a smaller portion size. When serving soup as a main course, plan on 10–14 fluid ounces per portion, and accompany it with bread, breadsticks, crackers and the kind of garnish that will satisfy a hungry guest.

QUESTIONS FOR DISCUSSION

1 What are the differences between a stock and a broth?

2 What are the differences between a beef consommé and a beef-based broth? How are they similar?

3 What are the differences between a cream soup and a purée soup? How are they similar?

4 Create a recipe for veal consommé.

5 Create a cream soup recipe using seasonal ingredients available in your local market. Discuss the changes required when adapting the recipe on page 265 for your chosen ingredient.

6 Discuss ways to incorporate seasonal produce currently available in your area of the country into a soup that is served cold. Which produce items might be best in cooked cold soups rather than in uncooked cold soups?

7 Explain how and why soups are garnished. Describe several ways to garnish a broth style soup.

8 Discuss options for serving soup. What can be done to ensure that soups are served at the correct temperature?

Additional Soup Recipes

Chicken and Sausage Gumbo

Gumbo, a thick, spicy stew, is traditional fare in the delta region of the American South. Gumbo is usually made with poultry, fish, shellfish or sausage and is thickened with dark roux. Okra or filé powder (ground sassafras leaves) may also be added for thickening. Filé powder is also sometimes added at the time of service for additional flavor. Gumbo is traditionally served over white rice.

YIELD 1 gal. (3.8 lt), 16 Servings, 8 fl. oz. (240 ml) each   **METHOD** Broth

Cayenne pepper	2 tsp.	10 ml
Garlic powder	2 tsp.	10 ml
Salt	1 Tbsp.	15 ml
Black pepper	2 tsp.	10 ml
Flour	10 oz.	300 g
Chicken, boneless, skinless cut in 1-in. (2.5-cm) pieces	3 lb.	1.4 kg
Vegetable oil	12 fl. oz.	360 g
Onions, medium dice	1 lb.	480 g
Celery, medium dice	8 oz.	240 g
Green bell pepper, medium dice	8 oz.	240 g
Garlic, chopped	2 Tbsp.	30 ml
Filé powder	2 Tbsp.	30 ml
Chicken stock	2 qt.	1.9 lt
Bay leaves	4	4
Andouille sausage, sliced, cut in half circles	1 lb.	480 g
Cooked long grain white rice	4 lb.	1.4 kg
Green onion tops, sliced	6 oz.	180 g

1. Combine the cayenne pepper, garlic powder, salt, black pepper and flour in a small bowl. Place the chicken in a medium stainless steel bowl. Add half of the seasoned flour to the chicken and toss to coat.

2. Heat 4 fluid ounces (120 milliliters) of the oil over medium-high heat in a heavy, wide bottomed saucepan or rondeau. Pan-fry the chicken until well browned. Remove the chicken from the pan and reserve.

3. Add the remaining oil to the pan and stir in the remaining seasoned flour to make a roux. Cook the roux over medium heat, stirring constantly, until the roux becomes a red-brown color, approximately 10–15 minutes. When the roux reaches the desired color, immediately add the onions, celery, green bell peppers and chopped garlic to the pan and stir to stop the roux from browning further.

4. Cook the vegetables in the roux until tender, approximately 10 minutes. Whisk in the filé powder and chicken stock. Add the bay leaves, bring the stock to a simmer and cook for 45 minutes, skimming any fat from the surface as necessary.

5. Add the andouille sausage and simmer for 15 minutes. Add the browned chicken and drippings to the gumbo. Return the gumbo to a simmer and cook for 5 minutes. Adjust the seasonings with cayenne, salt and pepper.

6. Serve each portion of gumbo with white rice and garnish with sliced green onion tops.

Approximate values per 8-fl.-oz. (240-ml) serving: **Calories** 420, **Total fat** 21 g, **Saturated fat** 3 g, **Cholesterol** 60 mg, **Sodium** 590 mg, **Total carbohydrates** 34 g, **Protein** 22 g, **Vitamin C** 25%, **Iron** 15%

Chicken Soup with Matzo Balls

❤ Good Choice

YIELD	1 gal. (3.8 lt) 21 Servings, 6 fl. oz. (180 ml) each	METHOD	Broth	
Chicken, cut into pieces, dark and light meat		4–5 lb.	1.8–2.2 kg	
Chicken stock		6 qt.	5.8 lt	
Mirepoix		1 lb.	480 g	
Sachet:				
Bay leaf		1	1	
Dried thyme		½ tsp.	2 ml	
Peppercorns, crushed		½ tsp.	2 ml	
Parsley stems		10	10	
Salt and pepper		TT	TT	
Fresh parsley, chopped		as needed for garnish		
Matzo Balls (recipe follows)		as needed for garnish		

❶ Simmering the matzo balls.

1 Combine the chicken and stock in a stock pot. Bring to a simmer and cook for 2 hours, skimming as necessary.

2 Add the mirepoix and sachet. Simmer for another hour.

3 Strain and degrease the broth. Adjust seasonings. The soup is now ready to serve after matzo balls are added. Cool, cover and refrigerate for later use.

4 Bring to a boil at service time. Portion into heated bowls and garnish with chopped parsley and one or two matzo balls.

Matzo Balls

YIELD	24 Balls		
Eggs		4	4
Water		2 fl. oz.	60 ml
Chicken fat or butter, softened		2 oz.	60 g
Matzo meal		4 oz.	120 g
Salt and white pepper		TT	TT

❷ The finished chicken soup with matzo balls.

1 Beat the eggs with the water. Stir in the fat or butter.

2 Add matzo meal, salt and white pepper. The batter should be as thick as mashed potatoes.

3 Chill for at least 1 hour.

4 Bring 2 quarts (2 liters) water to a gentle boil. Using a #70 portion scoop, shape the batter into balls. Carefully drop each ball into the hot water. Cover and simmer until fully cooked, approximately 30 minutes. Remove the matzo balls from the water and serve in hot chicken soup.

Approximate values per 6-fl.-oz. (180-ml) serving with 2 matzo balls: **Calories** 120, **Total fat** 7 g, **Saturated fat** 2.5 g, **Cholesterol** 70 mg, **Sodium** 130 mg, **Total carbohydrates** 8 g, **Protein** 6 g, **Claims**—low fat

French Onion Soup

YIELD 1 gal. (3.8 lt), 21 Servings, 6 fl. oz. (180 ml) each		METHOD Broth	
Yellow onions, sliced thin	8 lb.	3.8 kg	
Clarified butter	8 fl. oz.	240 ml	
Beef stock	3 qt.	2.8 lt	
Chicken stock	2 qt.	1.9 lt	
Fresh thyme	½ oz.	15 g	
Salt and pepper	TT	TT	
Sherry	8 fl. oz.	240 ml	
Toasted French bread slices	as needed for garnish		
Gruyère cheese, grated	as needed for garnish		

1 Sauté the onions in the butter over low heat in a large, heavy saucepan stirring often. Carefully cook the onions until they caramelize thoroughly and soften without burning, approximately 1 hour.

2 Deglaze the pan with 8 fluid ounces (240 milliliters) beef stock. Stir, scraping the pan to release the browned onions. Cook au sec, approximately 5 minutes. Add more stock and repeat this process 4 to 6 times until the onions are a very dark, even brown.

3 Add the remaining beef stock, the chicken stock and thyme.

4 Bring to a simmer and cook 20 minutes to develop flavor. Adjust the seasonings and add the sherry.

5 Serve in warm bowls. Top each portion with a slice of toasted French bread and a thick layer of cheese. Place under the broiler or salamander until the cheese is melted and lightly browned.

Approximate values per 6-fl.-oz. (180-ml) serving: **Calories** 280, **Total fat** 12 g, **Saturated fat** 6 g, **Cholesterol** 25 mg, **Sodium** 1370 mg, **Total carbohydrates** 34 g, **Protein** 9 g, **Vitamin A** 25%, **Vitamin C** 20%

❶ Caramelizing the onions thoroughly.

❷ Sprinkling grated cheese on top of each serving of soup.

❸ The finished French onion soup.

Miso Soup

Miso soup is iconic in Japanese cuisine, where it is an essential part of the traditional breakfast. A simple broth of miso paste dissolved in **dashi***, miso soup is typically garnished with blanched mushrooms, seaweed and cubes of soft tofu. Do not boil the broth after adding the miso paste, as this can destroy its flavor and aroma. Stir miso paste gradually into any hot liquid, then heat only to a simmer.*

YIELD	1 gal. (3.8 lt), 16 Servings, 8 fl. oz. (240 ml) each	METHOD	Broth
Dried **wakame**		½ oz.	15 g
Nameko or shiitake mushrooms, sliced		2 pt.	960 ml
Dashi (page 214)		7 pt.	3.1 lt
Miso paste		1 pt.	480 ml
Silken tofu, firm, small dice		1 lb.	480 g
Green onions, sliced thinly on the bias		1 oz.	30 g

1 Cut away any stems from the wakame. Cut the leaves into small pieces and soak in hot water for 30 minutes. Drain and then blanch for 10 seconds in boiling water. Refresh the wakame in cold water for a few seconds and then drain it well. Place the blanched wakame in a double layer of rinsed cheesecloth and twist the cloth to extract excess water.

2 Blanch the sliced mushrooms in boiling water just until tender. Drain well.

3 In a large saucepot, bring the dashi to a simmer. Temper the miso with some hot dashi, then whisk the thinned miso into the pot of dashi. Bring the soup back to a simmer for service.

4 For each serving, place a portion of the tofu, wakame and mushrooms in soup bowls. Ladle the hot dashi over the ingredients and garnish with the sliced green onions.

Approximate values per 8-fl.-oz. (240-ml) serving: **Calories** 130, **Total fat** 1 g, **Saturated fat** 0 g, **Cholesterol** 0 mg, **Sodium** 870 mg, **Total carbohydrates** 27 g, **Protein** 3 g, **Vitamin A** 70%, **Vitamin C** 15%, **Claims**—low fat; no saturated fat; no cholesterol

wakame a seaweed or kelp cultivated in East Asia because of its popularity in soups and salads; known as *miyeok* (sea mustard) in Korea, *Undaria pinnatifida* is high in minerals and vitamins; it grows in long strands, which may be sold fresh or dried, and should be cut into small pieces before rehydrating or cooking

nameko a small, round-capped, golden-brown mushroom that grows on hardwoods; similar to shiitake, it is widely cultivated in Japan, China and Russia; nameko is traditionally used in miso soup because of its nutty flavor and gelatinous texture; known in the United States as butterscotch mushrooms

dashi Japanese stock or fish broth made with seaweed (kombu) and flakes of dried fish (bonito); used in soups, sauces and as a simmering liquid

miso paste a thick paste made by salting and fermenting soybeans and inoculating the mixture with yeast; used in Japanese and vegetarian cuisines as a favoring and thickener

Pouring the hot dashi over the soup garnishes.

Phô Bo (Hanoi Beef and Noodle Soup)

Phô is the ubiquitous Vietnamese soup; it is widely eaten for breakfast and appears at meals throughout the day and into the evening. Beef (bo) is the most typical version, especially in the north. Each vendor has his or her own methods for flavoring and enriching the broth, but all allow customers to season and garnish their own bowls to taste with an assortment of chiles, fish sauces, fresh herbs and condiments. Phô is a perfect example of the Vietnamese belief that diners should be participants in preparing their food. Such rituals reinforce respect for the food and the friends with whom it is shared.

YIELD 1 gal. (3.8 lt), 16 Servings, 8 fl. oz. (240 ml) broth and 4 oz. (120 g) vermicelli each		METHOD Broth	
Oxtails or beef bones		10 lb.	4.8 kg
Water or beef stock		6 qt.	5.8 lt
Ginger, 3-in. (7.5-cm) piece		3	3
Onions brûlés		3	3
Fish sauce		6 fl. oz.	180 ml
Sachet:			
Star anise, whole		8	8
Cloves		6	6
Cinnamon stick		2	2
Bay leaves		4	4
Whole coriander seeds		1 Tbsp.	15 ml
Salt		TT	TT
Garnishes:			
Onions, sliced thin		as needed	as needed
Mung beans		as needed	as needed
Fresh herbs: mint, cilantro, basil		as needed	as needed
Lime wedges		as needed	as needed
Fish sauce		as needed	as needed
Fresh chiles, minced		as needed	as needed
Chile sauce		as needed	as needed
Rice vermicelli, cooked		3 lb.	1.4 kg
Lean beef such as tenderloin, raw, sliced thin		1 ½ lb.	720 g

1 Place the oxtails in a stockpot and add enough water to cover them by approximately 4 inches (10 centimeters). Bring to a boil and then reduce to a simmer, skimming the surface as necessary.

2 Split the ginger lengthwise and char its surface. Add the onions brûlés, charred ginger, fish sauce and sachet to the stockpot. Toast the coriander seeds in a dry pan over medium heat until fragrant and brown, for 1 minute. Add them to the stockpot.

3 Simmer the broth for 4–5 hours. Remove the sachet and strain the broth through a chinois. Adjust the seasonings with salt and more fish sauce and maintain the broth at a simmer.

4 Put the garnishes in bowls or trays and place them on each table.

5 Reheat the vermicelli by dropping them into boiling water for a few seconds. Divide the reheated vermicelli noodles into six large warm bowls. Place several pieces of raw beef tenderloin on top of each portion of vermicelli. Pour boiling hot broth over the meat into each bowl.

6 Serve the hot broth to diners, allowing them to garnish their portions with onions, mung beans, herbs, lime wedges, fish sauce, chiles and chile sauce as desired. (The meat will cook when stirred into the hot broth.)

Approximate values per 8-fl.-oz. (240-ml) serving: **Calories** 140, **Total fat** 2.5 g, **Saturated fat** 1 g, **Cholesterol** 25 mg, **Sodium** 1270 mg, **Total carbohydrates** 16 g, **Protein** 12 g

Minestrone

Minestrone is a rich Italian vegetable soup. Northern Italian versions are made with beef stock, butter, rice and ribbon-shaped pasta. Southern Italian versions, such as the one in this recipe, contain tomatoes, garlic, olive oil and tube-shaped pasta. The vegetables should be fresh and varied. Substitute or change those listed as necessary to reflect the season.

YIELD 1 gal. (3.8 lt), 21 Servings,
6 fl. oz. (180 ml) each

METHOD Broth

Dry white beans	8 oz.	240 g
Olive oil	2 Tbsp.	30 ml
Onion, medium dice	6 oz.	180 g
Garlic cloves, minced	2	2
Celery, medium dice	8 oz.	240 g
Carrot, medium dice	6 oz.	180 g
Zucchini, medium dice	8 oz.	240 g
Green beans, cut in ½- inch (1.2-cm) pieces	6 oz.	180 g
Cabbage, diced	8 oz.	240 g
Vegetable Stock (page 212)	5 pt.	2.5 lt
Tomato concassée	8 oz.	240 g
Tomato paste	6 oz.	180 g
Fresh oregano, chopped	1 Tbsp.	15 ml
Fresh basil, chopped	2 Tbsp.	30 ml
Fresh parsley, chopped	1 Tbsp.	15 ml
Salt and pepper	TT	TT
Elbow macaroni, cooked	4 oz.	120 g
Cherry tomatoes	48	48
Basil Pesto Sauce (page 249)	as needed for garnish	
Parmesan, shaved	as needed for garnish	

1 Soak the beans in cold water overnight, then drain.

2 Cover the beans with water and simmer until tender, about 40 minutes. Reserve the beans.

3 Sauté the onions in the oil. Add the garlic, celery and carrots and cook for 3 minutes.

4 Add the zucchini, green beans and cabbage, one type at a time, cooking each briefly.

5 Add the stock, tomato concassée and tomato paste. Cover and simmer for 2½–3 hours.

6 Stir in the chopped herbs and season to taste with salt and pepper.

7 Add the drained beans, cooked macaroni and cherry tomatoes.

8 Bring the soup to a simmer and simmer for 15 minutes. Serve in warm bowls, garnished with Basil Pesto Sauce and Parmesan.

Approximate values per 6-fl.-oz. (180-ml) serving: **Calories** 100, **Total fat** 1.5 g, **Saturated fat** 0 g, **Cholesterol** 1 mg, **Sodium** 290 mg, **Total carbohydrates** 17 g, **Protein** 4 g, **Vitamin A** 40%, **Vitamin C** 20%, **Claims**—low fat, cholesterol-free, excellent source of vitamins A and C, good source of dietary fiber and iron

Posole

posole also known as hominy or samp; dried corn that has been soaked in hydrated lime or lye; posole (Sp. *pozole*) also refers to a stewlike soup made with pork and hominy served in Mexico and Central America; its name derives from the ancient Aztec *pozolli*, a corn beverage of the Aztecs and Mayans

YIELD 1 gal. (3.8 lt), 21 Servings,
6 fl. oz. (180 ml) each

METHOD Broth

Pork shoulder, trimmed, medium dice	2 lb.	960 g
Chicken stock	2 qt.	1.9 lt
Onions, medium dice	1 ½ lb.	720 g
Garlic, chopped	2 Tbsp.	30 ml
Fresh oregano, chopped	2 tsp.	10 ml
Salt	2 tsp.	10 ml
Black pepper	½ tsp.	2 ml
Cayenne pepper	½ tsp.	2 ml
Olive oil	as needed	as needed
Chicken meat, boneless, skinless, medium dice	2 lb.	960 g
Hominy, canned, drained	2 lb.	960 g
Fresh cilantro, chopped	1 oz.	30 g
Garnishes:		
Lime wedges	as needed	as needed
Corn tortillas cut into thin strips	as needed	as needed
Romaine lettuce, chiffonade	as needed	as needed
Onions, small dice	as needed	as needed

1 Place the diced pork and the stock in a heavy saucepot. Add more stock if necessary to just cover the meat. Bring to a simmer and cook for 2 minutes skimming the scum from the surface as necessary.

2 Add half of the onions, half of the garlic and the oregano, salt, black pepper and cayenne pepper. Simmer for 1 hour.

3 Sweat the remaining onions in a sauté pan in a little oil until soft. Add the remaining garlic and cook an additional 2 minutes. Add the raw chicken. Stir to break the meat apart and cook for a few minutes until it loses its raw look. Add the hominy and stir to break any clumps apart. Cook for 5 minutes. Add the chicken and hominy mixture to the pork mixture in the saucepot.

4 Bring the soup to a simmer. Adjust the consistency with more stock if necessary and continue to simmer for 10 minutes to allow the chicken to cook and the flavors to blend. Add the cilantro and adjust the seasonings.

5 For service, cut the tortillas in half, then cut them crosswise into thin strips and fry them in hot oil until crisp. Serve the soup in hot bowls accompanied by lime wedges, the fried corn tortilla strips, chiffonade lettuce and diced onions.

Approximate values per 6-fl.-oz. (180-ml) serving: **Calories** 210, **Total fat** 8 g, **Saturated fat** 2.5 g, **Cholesterol** 65 mg, **Sodium** 460 mg, **Total carbohydrates** 11 g, **Protein** 22 g

Cream of Tomato Soup

Kendall College School of Culinary Arts, Chicago, IL
Chef Mike Artlip, CEC, CCE, CHE

YIELD 1 gal. (3.8 lt) 21 Servings,
6 fl. oz. (180 ml) each

METHOD Cream

Mirepoix, chopped fine	1 lb. 4 oz.	600 g
Olive oil	1 fl. oz.	30 ml
Whole butter	1 oz.	30 g
Tomato juice, canned	1 pt.	480 ml
Water	3 pt.	1.4 lt
Tomatoes, crushed, #10 can	1	1
Salt	2 Tbsp.	30 ml
Black pepper	1 tsp.	5 ml
Sachet:		
Parsley stems	¼ oz.	8 g
Black peppercorns, crushed	5	5
Bay leaves	2	2
Fresh thyme	5 sprigs	5 sprigs
Worcestershire sauce	1 Tbsp.	15 ml
Fresh thyme, chopped	as needed	as needed
Heavy cream, scalded	12 fl. oz.	360 ml
Heavy cream	as needed for garnish	
Red and green bell peppers, diced	as needed for garnish	
Fresh basil	as needed for garnish	
French bread, sliced, grilled	as needed for garnish	

① Puréeing the soup with an immersion blender.

1 Sweat the mirepoix in the oil and butter in a heavy saucepan without caramelizing.

2 Deglaze the pan with the tomato juice. Add the water, crushed tomatoes, salt, pepper and sachet. Bring to a boil, reduce to a low simmer and cook for 30 minutes.

3 Stir in the Worcestershire sauce and thyme. Continue simmering for 15 minutes.

4 Remove the sachet and purée the soup with an immersion blender until smooth. Strain the scalded cream through a china cap and add it to the soup. Simmer for 5 minutes; adjust the seasonings.

5 Garnish each bowl with a swirl of heavy cream, the diced peppers and basil. Serve with slices of grilled French bread.

Approximate values per 6-fl.-oz. (180-ml) serving: **Calories** 140, **Total fat** 9 g, **Saturated fat** 5 g, **Cholesterol** 20 mg, **Sodium** 1010 mg, **Total carbohydrates** 14 g, **Protein** 3 g, **Vitamin A** 35%, **Vitamin C** 50%

② The finished soup.

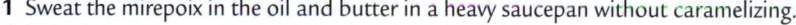

Cheddar and Leek Soup

YIELD	1 gal. (3.8 lt), 21 Servings, 6 fl. oz. (180 ml) each	METHOD	Cream

Clarified butter	6 fl. oz.	180 ml
Mirepoix, chopped fine	1 lb.	480 g
Leeks, chopped fine	1 lb.	480 g
Flour	4 oz.	120 g
Chicken stock	5 pt.	2.5 lt
Sachet:		
Bay leaves	3	3
Dried thyme	1 tsp.	5 ml
Peppercorns, crushed	1 tsp.	5 ml
Dry mustard	1 Tbsp.	15 ml
Heavy cream	12 fl. oz.	360 ml
Dry white wine or flat beer	12 fl. oz.	360 ml
Cheddar cheese, grated	3 lb.	1.4 kg
Worcestershire sauce	1 Tbsp.	15 ml
Salt	TT	TT
Cayenne pepper	TT	TT
Fresh parsley, chopped	as needed for garnish	
Croutons, sautéed in butter	as needed for garnish	

1 Sweat the mirepoix and leeks in the butter until tender.

2 Stir in the flour and cook to make a blond roux.

3 Stir in the stock. Bring to a boil, stirring frequently. Add the sachet. Reduce the heat and simmer for 30 minutes, stirring occasionally.

4 Strain the soup through a china cap into a clean pot. Bring it to a simmer.

5 Shortly before service, stir the dry mustard into the cream and add the cream, wine or beer, cheese and Worcestershire sauce to the soup. Stir until smooth.

6 Adjust seasonings with salt and cayenne pepper. Thin with additional warm stock if necessary.

7 Serve in warm bowls, garnished with parsley and croutons, or hold for service in a hot (not simmering) bain marie. This soup may be held for approximately 2–3 hours.

Approximate values per 6-fl.-oz. (180-ml) serving: **Calories** 440, **Total fat** 36 g, **Saturated fat** 21 g, **Cholesterol** 95 mg, **Sodium** 510 mg, **Total carbohydrates** 9 g, **Protein** 17 g, **Vitamin A** 45%, **Calcium** 50%

Mulligatawny Soup

Chef Ken Morlino, CEC

Mulligatawny is a complex and substantial soup that combines chicken or lamb, apples and curry spices in a rich broth. Its name comes from the Anglicized version of the word for "pepper water" in Tamil, a dialect of south India. This soup is familiar to Britons, as it was developed during the British occupation of India from a vegetable-based sauce to which meat was added. Later the dish traveled back to England and to other British colonies, including Australia and parts of Africa.

YIELD	1 gal. 21 Servings, 6 fl. oz. (180 ml) each	METHOD	Cream

Unsalted butter	4 oz.	120 g
Mirepoix, chopped fine	3 lb.	1.4 kg
Flour	3 oz.	90 g
Curry powder	2 Tbsp.	60 ml
Chicken stock	2 qt.	1.9 lt
Chicken meat, cooked, diced	1 lb.	480 g
Green apple, diced	4 oz.	120 g
Mushrooms, sliced	4 oz.	120 g
Half-and-half, warm	1 pt.	480 ml
Salt and white pepper	TT	TT
Fresh chives, snipped	as needed for garnish	

1 In a saucepot, heat the butter over medium heat; add the mirepoix and sauté for 10 minutes without coloring

2 Add the flour and curry powder and cook to form a blond roux.

3 Add the stock. Bring to a simmer and cook for 15 minutes.

4 Add the chicken, apple and mushrooms and cook for 15 more minutes.

5 Add the half-and-half and return to a simmer. Season with salt and white pepper. Serve in warmed bowls garnished with fresh chives.

Approximate values per 6-fl.-oz. (180-ml) serving: **Calories** 160, **Total fat** 8 g, **Saturated fat** 4.5 g, **Cholesterol** 35 mg, **Sodium** 130 mg, **Total carbohydrates** 12 g, **Protein** 9 g, **Vitamin A** 80%, **Vitamin C** 10%, **Iron** 10%

Potato Chowder with Hot Smoked Salmon

YIELD	1 gal. (3.8 lt), 21 Servings, 6 fl. oz. (180 ml) each		METHOD	Cream
Prosciutto ham, small dice		8 oz.	240 g	
Clarified butter		4 fl. oz.	120 ml	
Onion, small dice		8 oz.	240 g	
Flour		3 oz.	90 g	
Chicken stock		2 qt.	1.9 lt	
Yukon gold potatoes (or other waxy variety), medium dice		3 lb.	1.4 kg	
Dried dill		2 tsp.	10 ml	
Dried thyme		2 tsp.	10 ml	
Heavy cream		10 fl. oz.	300 ml	
Hot Smoked Salmon (page 854), diced		6 oz.	180 g	
Salt and pepper		TT	TT	
Fresh dill sprigs		as needed for garnish		

1 Place the prosciutto and butter in a heavy saucepot and cook over medium heat to render the fat. Add the onion and sauté until translucent.

2 Add the flour and cook for 5 minutes to make a blond roux. Whisk in the chicken stock, bring to a simmer. Add the potatoes, return to a simmer and cook until the potatoes are nearly tender.

3 Add the dill, thyme, cream and salmon. Stir gently to incorporate all of the flavors.

4 Simmer for 5 minutes. Adjust the seasonings and serve immediately in warmed bowls garnished with fresh dill sprigs.

Variation:

Nonfat, 1% or 2% milk may be substituted for the cream in the recipe to lower the fat content.

Approximate values per 6-fl.-oz. (180-ml) serving: **Calories** 270, **Total fat** 14 g, **Saturated fat** 8 g, **Cholesterol** 75 mg, **Sodium** 330 mg, **Total carbohydrates** 16 g, **Protein** 19 g, **Vitamin C** 10%

Sausage, White Bean and Kale Soup

| YIELD | 1 gal. (3.8 lt), 21 Servings,
6 fl. oz. (180 ml) each | | METHOD | Broth |

Italian pork sausage, cut into ½-inch pieces	1 lb.	480 g
Extra virgin olive oil	2 Tbsp.	30 ml
Onion, small dice	1 lb.	480 g
Garlic, minced	2 Tbsp.	30 ml
White wine	1 pt.	480 ml
Plum tomatoes, blanched, peeled, seeded and chopped	1 lb.	480 ml
Chicken stock	2 qt.	1.9 lt
Salt	2 Tbsp.	30 ml
Pepper	1 tsp.	5 ml
Kale, ribs removed, chiffonade	4 oz.	120 g
Cooked white beans, rinsed	1 ½ lb.	720 g
Crushed red pepper	as needed for garnish	
Parmesan, grated	as needed for garnish	
Garlic Croutons (page 753) made from French bread	as needed for garnish	

1 Sauté the sausage in the oil in a large saucepan, breaking it into small pieces, until cooked through. Remove from the pan, reserving the oil.

2 Sweat the onion and garlic in the oil. Add the wine, tomatoes and stock. Season with salt and pepper. Cover and simmer for 15 minutes.

3 Add the kale and white beans. Simmer until the kale wilts. Stir in the reserved sausage. Adjust the seasonings to taste.

4 Serve in warm bowls, garnished with crushed red pepper, Parmesan and Garlic Croutons.

Approximate values per 6-fl.-oz. (180-ml) serving: **Calories** 140, **Total fat** 5 g, **Saturated fat** 1.5 g, **Cholesterol** 5 mg, **Sodium** 780 mg, **Total carbohydrates** 14 g, **Protein** 8 g, **Vitamin A** 15%, **Vitamin C** 20%, **Iron** 10%

Callaloo with Crab

Newbury College, Brookline, MA
Senior Instructor Scott Doughty, Ret.

Callaloo is a soup made throughout the Caribbean. Its name comes from the type of greens used to make the soup: callaloo or dasheen, the large edible leaves of the taro plant. Spinach, kale, Swiss chard or other related varieties of greens can be used to give this soup its green color, which is intensified when part or all of the broth is puréed. Called "pepperpot" in Jamaica, this soup is heavily seasoned with pepper and chiles. Ham hocks or bacon can be added as well as okra, which thickens the soup.

YIELD 1 gal. (3.8 lt), 21 Servings,
6 fl. oz. (180 ml) each

METHOD Purée

Callaloo or spinach	1 lb. 8 oz.	720 g
Olive oil	2 fl. oz.	60 ml
Onions, small dice	1 lb. 8 oz.	720 g
Green onions, chopped fine	12 oz.	360 g
Garlic cloves, minced	4	4
Coconut milk	24 fl. oz.	720 ml
Milk	1 qt.	1 lt
Fresh pumpkin, peeled, seeded, small dice	1 lb. 8 oz.	720 g
Salt	2 Tbsp.	30 ml
Black pepper	2 tsp	10 ml
Crab meat	2 lb.	960 g

1 Wash the callaloo or spinach. Remove the stems and tough ribs and chop coarsely.

2 Heat the oil in a rondeau and sweat the diced onions. Add the green onions and garlic and sweat for 2 more minutes. Add the callaloo or spinach, coconut milk, milk, pumpkin, salt and pepper. Bring the soup to a boil and reduce to a simmer. Cook for 30 minutes.

3 Purée half of the soup in a blender, food processor or food mill. Return it to the pot with the remaining soup.

4 Pick over the crab meat to remove any bits of shell and add the meat to the soup. Adjust the seasonings and serve.

Approximate values per 6-fl.-oz. (180-ml) serving: **Calories** 190, **Total fat** 11 g, **Saturated fat** 7 g, **Cholesterol** 45 mg, **Sodium** 870 mg, **Total carbohydrates** 11 g, **Protein** 12 g, **Vitamin A** 80%, **Vitamin C** 40%, **Calcium** 20%, **Iron** 15%

Roasted Corn Chowder

YIELD	1 gal. (3.8 lt), 16 Servings, 8 fl. oz. (240 ml) each		METHOD	Purée

Corn, unshucked	8 ears	8 ears
Milk, warm	1 qt.	960 ml
Salt pork, small dice	8 oz.	240 g
Celery, small dice	10 oz.	300 g
Onions, small dice	12 oz.	360 g
Garlic cloves, minced	1 Tbsp.	15 ml
Flour	1 oz.	30 g
Chicken stock	1 qt.	960 ml
Potatoes, peeled, medium dice	1 lb.	480 g
Heavy cream, warm	8 fl. oz.	240 ml
Worcestershire sauce	1 Tbsp.	15 ml
Fresh thyme	1 tsp.	5 ml
Salt and white pepper	TT	TT

1 Roast the ears of corn, in their husks, in a 400°F (200°C) oven for 45 minutes. Cool, shuck the corn and cut off the kernels. Purée half the corn kernels in a blender, adding a small amount of milk if necessary.

2 Render the fat from the salt pork. Add the celery, onions and garlic and sauté lightly.

3 Stir in the flour and cook to make a blond roux.

4 Add the stock and remaining milk and bring to a simmer.

5 Add the potatoes, the puréed corn and the remaining corn kernels. Bring to a simmer and cook for 10 minutes.

6 Add the cream, Worcestershire sauce and thyme. Adjust the consistency with hot stock if necessary. Adjust the seasonings with salt and white pepper and simmer for 5 minutes.

7 Serve in warm bowls.

Approximate values per 8-fl.-oz. (240-ml) serving: **Calories** 220, **Total fat** 15 g, **Saturated fat** 7 g, **Cholesterol** 25 mg, **Sodium** 350 mg, **Total carbohydrates** 17 g, **Protein** 5 g, **Vitamin C** 10%

Borsch (Chilled Beet Soup)

YIELD 1 gal. (3.8 lt), 21 Servings, 6 fl. oz. (180 ml) each

METHOD Cooked Cold

Sour cream or crème fraîche	12 fl. oz.	360 ml
Onions, chopped fine	10 oz.	300 g
Carrots, chopped fine	6 oz.	180 g
Celery, chopped fine	6 oz.	180 g
Extra virgin olive oil	2 fl. oz.	60 ml
Red cabbage, sliced	1 lb.	480 g
Chicken or vegetable stock	3 qt.	2.8 lt
Sachet:		
Thyme sprig	8	8
Cinnamon stick	2	2
Cloves, whole	4	4
Black peppercorns	10	10
Red beets, large, roasted, grated	2 lb.	960 g
Red wine vinegar	6 fl. oz.	180 ml
Salt and pepper	TT	TT
Baby golden and red beets, cooked, halved	as needed for garnish	
Fresh chives or fennel fronds, chopped	4 Tbsp.	60 ml

1 Spread the sour cream out into a thin layer in a quarter hotel pan. Cover and freeze.

2 Sweat the onions, carrots and celery in the oil in a medium saucepan until tender. Add the cabbage, stock and sachet. Bring to a boil, then cover and simmer the mixture until the vegetables are tender, approximately 30 minutes.

3 Add the beets and vinegar. Bring to a boil, reduce heat and simmer 15 minutes.

4 Remove the sachet. Purée the soup using a blender or food processor.

5 When cooled to room temperature, season to taste with salt and pepper. If the soup is too thick, dilute it with additional chicken stock. Chill thoroughly.

6 Garnish with sliced gold and red beets and chives or fennel fronds. Scrape the frozen sour cream with the tines of a fork. Spoon this on top of each serving.

Approximate values per 6-fl.-oz. (180-ml) serving: **Calories** 90, **Total fat** 5 g, **Saturated fat** 2 g, **Cholesterol** 10 mg, **Sodium** 135 mg, **Total carbohydrates** 9 g, **Protein** 2 g, **Vitamin A** 35%, **Vitamin C** 25%, **Claims**—low calorie, low fat

 Good Choice   Vegetarian

Chilled Cucumber and Yogurt Soup

YIELD 2 qt. (1.9 lt), 10 Servings, 6 fl. oz. (180 ml) each		METHOD Uncooked Cold	
Cucumbers, peeled, seeded		1½ lb.	720 g
Plain yogurt		1 pt.	480 ml
Buttermilk		1 pt.	480 ml
Lemon juice		1 fl. oz.	30 ml
Garlic, minced		1 tsp.	5 ml
Salt and white pepper		TT	TT
Cucumbers, grated		12 oz.	360 g
Radishes, fine julienne		as needed for garnish	

1 Grate the seeded cucumbers over the large holes of a box grater into a bowl.

2 Combine the yogurt, buttermilk, lemon juice and garlic. Add the cucumbers. Adjust the seasonings. Purée the soup in a blender. If the soup is too thick, dilute it with some additional buttermilk. Stir in the additional grated cucumbers.

3 Chill thoroughly. Serve in chilled bowls garnished with radish julienne.

Approximate values per 6-fl.-oz. (180-ml) serving: **Calories** 70, **Total fat** 1.5 g, **Saturated fat** 1 g, **Cholesterol** 5 mg, **Sodium** 105 mg, **Total carbohydrates** 8 g, **Protein** 5 g, **Calcium** 20%, **Claims**—low fat, low cholesterol, good source of calcium

Principles of Meat Cookery 13

After studying this chapter, you will be able to:

▶ describe the structure and composition of meats

▶ explain meat inspection and grading practices

▶ purchase appropriate meats

▶ store meats properly

▶ prepare meats for cooking

▶ apply various dry-heat, moist-heat and combination cooking methods to meats

primal cuts the primary divisions of muscle, bone and connective tissue produced by the initial butchering of the carcass

subprimal cuts the basic cuts produced from each primal

fabricated cuts individual portions cut from a subprimal

shrinkage the loss of weight in a food due to evaporation of liquid or melting of fat during cooking

grain refers to the direction that bundles of muscle fibers run in a piece of meat. These fibers will appear as parallel lines within the meat. Cutting against the grain means to cut the meat perpendicular to the length of the lines of bundles, which makes the meat more tender by shortening the muscle fibers.

Meats—beef, veal, lamb and pork—often consume the largest portion of a food purchasing dollar. In this chapter, we discuss how to protect that investment. You will learn how to determine the quality of meat, how to purchase meat in the form that best suits your needs and how to store it. We also discuss several of the dry-heat, moist-heat and combination cooking methods, introduced in Chapter 10, Principles of Cooking, and how they can best be used so that a finished meat item is appealing to both the eye and palate. Although each of the cooking methods is illustrated with a single beef, veal, lamb or pork recipe, the analysis is intended to apply to all meats.

In Chapters 14–17, you will learn about the specific cuts of beef, veal, lamb and pork typically used in food service operations, as well as some basic butchering procedures. Recipes using these cuts and applying the various cooking methods are included at the end of each of those chapters.

MUSCLE COMPOSITION OF MEATS

The carcasses of cattle, sheep, hogs and furred game animals consist mainly of edible lean muscular tissue, fat, connective tissue and bones. Carcasses are divided into large cuts called **primals**. Primal cuts are rarely cooked. They are usually reduced to **subprimal cuts**, which are cooked as is or used to produce **fabricated cuts**. For example, the beef primal known as a short loin is divided into subprimals, including the strip loin. The strip loin can be fabricated into other cuts, including New York steaks. The primals, subprimals and fabricated cuts of beef, veal, lamb and pork are discussed in Chapters 14–17, respectively; game is discussed in Chapter 19, Game.

Muscle tissue gives meat its characteristic appearance; the amount of connective tissue determines the meat's tenderness. Muscle tissue is approximately 72 percent water, 20 percent protein, 7 percent fat and 1 percent minerals. Meat shrinks during cooking as water evaporates and fats melt. Proper cooking helps prevent excessive **shrinkage**, which can cause the loss of finished weight and irregularly shaped meats after cooking.

A single muscle is composed of many bundles of muscle cells or fibers held together by connective tissue. See Figures 13.1 and 13.2. The thickness of the muscle cells, the size of the cell bundles and the connective tissues holding them together form the **grain** of the meat and determine the meat's texture. If the fiber bundles are small, the meat will have a fine grain and texture. Grain also refers to the direction in which the muscle fibers travel.

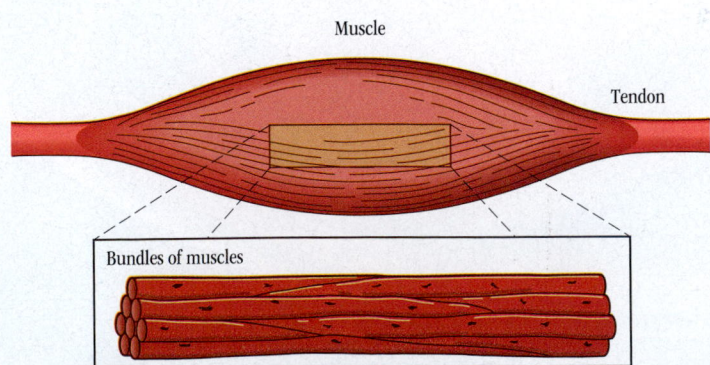

Figure 13.1 Muscle tissue.

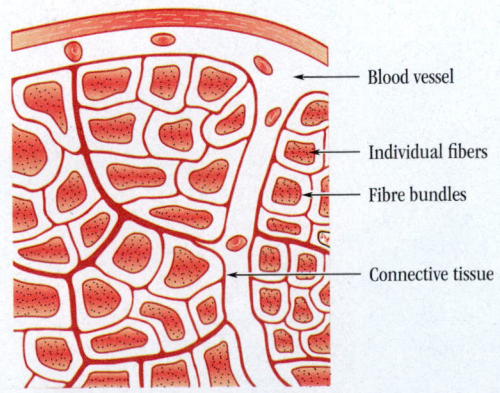

Figure 13.2 Enlarged crosscut of a bundle of muscle cells (fibers).

When an animal fattens, some of the water and proteins in the lean muscle tissue are replaced with fat, which appears as **marbling**. Marbling adds tenderness and flavor to meat and is a principal factor in determining meat quality.

Connective tissue forms the walls of the long muscle cells and binds them into bundles. It surrounds the muscle as a membrane and also appears as the tendons and ligaments that attach the muscles to the bone. Most connective tissue consists of either **collagen** or **elastin**. When cooked using moist heat, collagen contracts, then becomes more tender and breaks down into gelatin and water. Elastin, on the other hand, will not break down under normal cooking conditions. Because elastin remains stringy and tough, tendons and ligaments should be trimmed away before meat is cooked.

Connective tissue develops primarily in the frequently used muscles. Therefore cuts of meat from the shoulder (also known as the **chuck**), which the animal uses constantly, tend to be tougher than those from the back (also known as the **loin**), which are used less frequently. As an animal ages, the collagen present within the muscles becomes more resistant to breaking down through moist-heat cooking, so the meat of an older animal tends to be tougher than that of a younger one. Generally the tougher the meat, the more flavorful it is, however.

The way that meat is **fabricated** also affects its tenderness. Cutting raw meat against the grain, pounding thinly sliced raw meat or grinding raw meat before cooking tenderizes tougher cuts. Butchering techniques have evolved to maximize the usability of primal cuts.

INSPECTION AND GRADING OF MEATS

All meat produced for public consumption in the United States is subject to United States Department of Agriculture (USDA) **inspection**. Inspections ensure that products are processed under strict sanitary guidelines and are wholesome and fit for human consumption. Inspections do not indicate a meat's quality or tenderness, however. Whole carcasses of beef, pork, lamb and veal are labeled with a round stamp identifying the slaughterhouse. See Figure 13.3. The stamp shown in Figure 13.4 is used for fabricated or processed meats and is found on either the product or its packaging.

USDA **grading** provides a voluntary, uniform system by which producers, distributors and consumers can compare the quality and price of meats. There are two parts to the USDA grading system: quality grades and yield grades.

Quality grades, established in 1927, are a guide to the eating qualities of meat: its tenderness, juiciness and flavor. Based on an animal's age and the meat's color, texture and degree of marbling, the USDA quality grades, listed from highest quality to lowest, are as follows:

- *Beef:* USDA Prime, Choice, Select, Standard, Commercial, Utility, Cutter and Canner
- *Veal:* USDA Prime, Choice, Good, Standard, Utility
- *Lamb:* USDA Prime, Choice, Good, Utility
- *Pork:* USDA No. 1, No. 2, No. 3, Utility

marbling whitish streaks of inter- and intramuscular fat

subcutaneous fat also known as exterior fat; the fat layer between the hide and muscles

collagen a protein found in connective tissue; it is converted into gelatin when cooked with moisture

elastin a protein found in connective tissues, particularly ligaments and tendons; it often appears as the white or silver covering on meats known as silverskin

butcher to slaughter and/or dress or fabricate animals for consumption

dress to trim or otherwise prepare an animal carcass for consumption

fabricate to cut a larger portion of raw meat (e.g., a primal or subprimal), poultry or fish into smaller portions

carve to cut cooked meat or poultry into portions

Domestication of Animals

Early humans were hunter-gatherers, dependent on what their immediate environment offered for food. As "opportunistic" meat eaters, they ate meat when they could obtain it.

Anthropologists believe that the cultivation of grains and the birth of agriculture, which took place sometime around 9000 BCE, led directly to the domestication of animals. Wild sheep and goats were attracted to the fields of grain, and wild dogs and pigs to the garbage heaps of the new communities. Rather than allow these animals to interfere with food production, people tamed them, thus providing a steadier supply of meat. The first animals to be domesticated were most likely sheep, soon followed by goats. These animals—ruminants—can digest cellulose (humans cannot), so they could feed on stalks instead of valuable grains. Dogs and pigs, which prefer the same foods as humans, were tamed later, once there were more certain food supplies. Cattle were the most recently domesticated food animal, probably coming under control between 6100 and 5800 BCE.

Figure 13.3 USDA inspection stamp for whole carcasses.

Figure 13.4 USDA inspection stamp for fabricated or processed meats.

Figure 13.5 Quality grade stamp for USDA prime.

Figure 13.6 Quality grades of beef—no roll (top), Choice and Prime (bottom).

Figure 13.7 USDA yield grade stamp.

vacuum packaging a food preservation method in which fresh or cooked food is placed in an airtight container (usually plastic). Virtually all air is removed from the container through a vacuum process before it is sealed.

USDA Prime meats are produced in limited quantities for use in the finest restaurants, hotels and gourmet markets. They are well marbled and have thick coverings of firm fat. See Figure 13.5. USDA Choice meat is the most commonly used grade in quality food service operations and retail markets. Choice meat is well marbled (but with less fat than Prime) and produces a tender and juicy product.

Although lacking the flavor and tenderness of the higher grades, beef graded USDA Select or USDA Standard, and lamb and veal graded USDA Good, are also used in food service operations and retail outlets. The term "no roll" refers to beef that has not been grade-stamped (rolled) by a USDA inspector. Much of the beef sold in the United States, is no roll, but would have been USDA Select if graded. The lower grades of beef, lamb and veal are usually used for processed, ground or manufactured items such as meat patties or canned meat products. Figure 13.6 illustrates the three quality grades in a cut of beef. Note the moderately abundant marbling in the Prime New York strip shown on the bottom compared to only slight marbling in the Choice strip in the center.

Yield grades, established in 1965, measure the amount of usable meat (as opposed to fat and bones) on a carcass and provide a uniform method of identifying cutability differences among carcasses. Yield grades apply only to beef and lamb and appear in a shield similar to that used for the quality grade stamp. The shields are numbered from 1 to 5, with number 1 representing the greatest yield and number 5 the smallest. See Figure 13.7. Beef and lamb can be graded for quality or yield or both.

Grading is a voluntary program. Many processors, purveyors and retailers (especially pork and veal producers) develop and use their own labeling systems to indicate quality. These private systems do not necessarily apply the USDA's standards. In fact, some pork inspection programs apply more stringent quality standards.

AGING MEATS

When animals are slaughtered, their muscles are soft and flabby. Within 6–24 hours, rigor mortis sets in, causing the muscles to contract and stiffen. Rigor mortis begins to disappear within 48–72 hours under refrigerated conditions. All meats should be allowed to rest, or age, long enough for rigor mortis to disappear completely. Meats that have not been aged long enough for rigor mortis to dissipate, or that have been frozen during this period, are known as "green meats." They are very tough and flavorless when cooked.

Typically initial aging takes place while the meat is being transported from the slaughterhouse to the supplier or food service operation. As meat continues to rest, natural enzymes begin to break down the muscle into more tender meat. Beef and lamb are sometimes aged for longer periods to increase their tenderness and flavor characteristics. Pork is not aged further because its high fat content turns rancid easily. Veal is not aged as it does not have enough fat to protect it during an extended aging period.

Wet Aging

Most preportioned or precut meats are packaged and shipped in vacuum-sealed plastic packages (sometimes referred to generically by the manufacturer's trade name, Cryovac). Wet aging is the process of storing **vacuum-packaged** meats under refrigeration for up to 6 weeks. This allows the natural enzymes and microorganisms enough time to break down connective tissue, which tenderizes and flavors the meat. As this chemical process takes place, the meat develops an unpleasant odor that is released when the package is opened; the odor dissipates in a few minutes. If the order persists, rinse the meat, dry it with clean paper towels and let it rest, refrigerated. Discard if the meat is discolored and retains its odor after 30 minutes. Exercise great care when wet aging meats to prevent spoilage. Of all types of meat, beef can be wet aged for the longest period—6 weeks. Other meats must be consumed sooner. The shelf life for vacuum-sealed refrigerated pork is approximately 3 weeks.

Wet-aged New York strip

Dry Aging

Dry aging is the process of storing fresh meats in an environment of controlled temperature, humidity and air flow for up to 6 weeks. This allows enzymes and microorganisms to break down connective tissues. Dry aging is actually the beginning of the natural decomposition process. Dry-aged meats can lose from 5 to 20 percent of their weight through moisture evaporation. They can also develop mold, which adds flavor but must be trimmed off later. Moisture loss combined with the need for additional trimming can substantially increase the cost of serving dry-aged meats. Dry-aged meats are prized for their rich beefy flavor, however. They are generally available only through smaller distributors and specialty butchers.

Dry-aged beef short loin

PURCHASING AND STORING MEATS

Several factors determine the cuts of meat your food service operation should use:

- *Menu:* The menu identifies the types of cooking methods used. If meats are going to be broiled, grilled, roasted, sautéed or fried, more tender cuts should be used. If they are going to be stewed or braised, flavorful cuts with more connective tissue can be used.
- *Menu price:* Cost constraints may prevent an operation from using the best-quality meats available. Generally the more tender the meat, the more expensive it is. But the most expensive cuts are not always the best choice for a particular cooking method. For example, a beef tenderloin is one of the most expensive cuts of beef. Although excellent grilled, it does not necessarily produce a better braised dish than the tougher, fattier brisket.
- *Quality:* Often, several different cuts or grades of meat can be used for a specific dish. Each food service operation should develop its own quality specifications.

Purchasing Meats

Once you have identified the cuts of meat your operation needs, you must determine the forms in which these cuts will be bought. Meats are purchased in a variety of forms: as large as an entire carcass that must be further fabricated or as small as an individual cut (known as **portion control** or **P.C.**) ready to cook and serve. Consider the following when deciding how to purchase meats:

Employee skills: Do your employees have the skills necessary to reduce large pieces of meat to the desired cuts?

Menu: Can you use the variety of bones, meat and trimmings that result from fabricating large cuts into individual portions?

Storage: Do you have ample refrigeration and freezer space so that you can be flexible in the way you purchase your meats?

Cost: Considering labor costs and trim usage, is it more economical to buy larger cuts of meat or P.C. units?

IMPS/NAMP

The USDA publishes Institutional Meat Purchase Specifications (IMPS) describing products customarily purchased in the food service industry. IMPS identifications are illustrated and described in *The Meat Buyers Guide*, published by the National Association of Meat Purveyors (NAMP). The IMPS/NAMP system is a widely accepted and useful tool in preventing miscommunications between purchasers and purveyors. Meats are indexed by a numerical system: Beef cuts are designated by the 100 series, lamb by the 200 series, veal by the 300 series, pork by the 400 series, and portion cuts by the 1000 series. Commonly used cuts of beef, veal, lamb and pork and their IMPS numbers, as well as applicable cooking methods and serving suggestions, are discussed in Chapters 14–17.

Grass-Fed Meats

Most domestic cattle, sheep and hogs are fed grains while they are confined in large pens known as feedlots before slaughter. This practice results in meat that has a milder flavor and higher fat content than the meat of purely grass-fed animals. Meat from grass-fed ruminants, however, is high in the powerful antioxidant conjugated linoleic acid, which has been identified as a cancer preventative. Advocates for consuming grass-fed livestock also cite the greater environmental impact of animal farming in enclosed feedlots as a reason to choose grass-fed meat.

Most meat animals consume grains for some part of their lives. Even cattle that graze on grassland are finished on grains for 4–8 months in feedlots before slaughter. The Agricultural Marketing Service of the USDA has published voluntary standards for the labeling of purely grass-fed meat. The standards state that grass and forage shall be the only feed source consumed for the lifetime of the animal except for the milk consumed prior to weaning. *Free-range, range-fed, pastured* and *pasture-raised* are some of the terms used to describe meat raised without grain-based feeds, but none of these terms are regulated. Should you be interested in serving grass-fed meats, speak to your suppliers about the source of their livestock.

The meat from grass-fed animals tends to be leaner because the animals are allowed to wander over large grazing areas. Consequently meat from grass-fed animals requires less cooking time. When broiled or grilled, grass-fed beef is best served rare to medium rare because longer cooking toughens and dries out the meat. When cooking meat from grass-fed animals, brush it with oil to prevent it from sticking to the pan or grill. Marinating tenderizes leaner cuts before dry-heat cooking. Some grass-fed meats may be best suited to moist-heat cooking methods.

Storing Meats

Meat products are highly perishable and require time and temperature control for safety (TCS). Temperature control is the most important thing to remember when storing meats. Fresh meats should be stored at temperatures between 30°F and 35°F (–1°C and 2°C). Vacuum-packed meats should be left in their packaging until they are needed. Under proper refrigeration, vacuum-packed meats with unbroken seals have a shelf life of 3–4 weeks. If the seal is broken, shelf life is reduced to only a few days. Ground meats have a shorter shelf life than whole-muscle meats and should be consumed within 1 or 2 days. Meats that are not vacuum packed should be wrapped tightly in air-permeable paper. Do not wrap meats tightly in plastic wrap, as this creates a good breeding ground for bacteria and significantly shortens shelf life. Store meats on trays and away from other foods to prevent cross-contamination.

When freezing meats, the faster the better. Slow freezing produces large ice crystals that tend to rupture the muscle tissues, allowing water and nutrients to drip out when the meat is thawed. See Figure 13.8. Most commercially packaged meats are frozen by **blast freezing**, which quickly cools by blasting –40°F (–40°C) air across the meat. Most food service facilities, however, use a slower and more conventional method known as **still-air freezing**. Still-air freezing involves placing meat in a standard freezer at about 0°F (–18°C) until it is frozen.

The ideal temperature for maintaining frozen meat is –50°F (–45°C). Frozen meat should not be maintained at any temperature warmer than 0°F (–18°C). Moisture- and vaporproof packaging help prevent **freezer burn**. The length of frozen storage life varies with the species and type of meat. As a general rule, properly handled meats can be frozen for 6 months. Frozen meats should be thawed at refrigerator temperatures, not at room temperature or in warm water.

Fresh and frozen beef, lamb, pork, shellfish, poultry and other foods may be irradiated in order to control the presence of microorganisms, such as *E. coli* and *Salmonella*, which can cause food-borne illnesses. Although the permitted dose of ionizing radiation kills significant numbers of insects, pathogenic bacteria and organisms that can cause spoilage, it does not make food radioactive or compromise the food's nutritional values. Nor does radiation noticeably alter a food's flavor, texture or appearance. Radiation of foodstuffs is

freezer burn the surface dehydration and discoloration of food that results from moisture loss at below-freezing temperatures

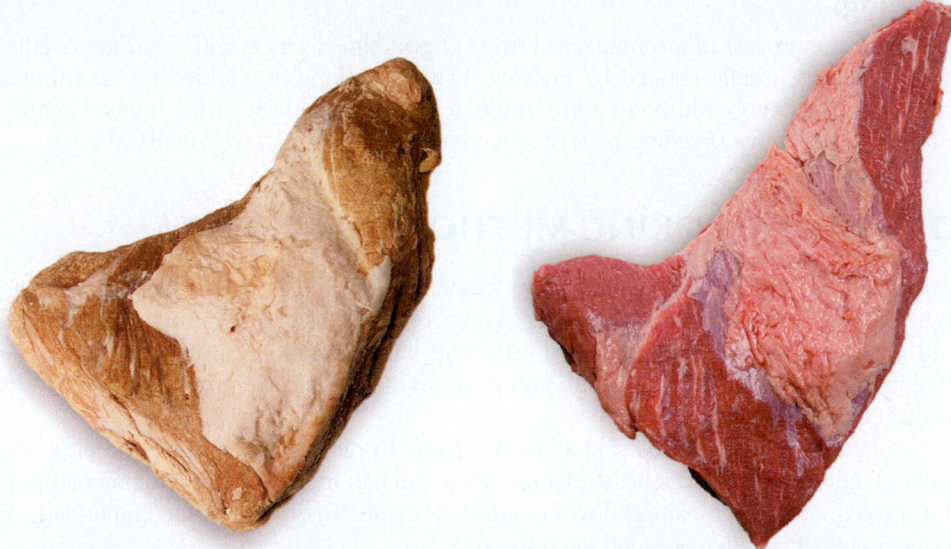

Figure 13.8 Meat damaged by freezer burn—freezer burned bottom sirloin butt tri tip (left) and fresh bottom sirloin butt tri tip (right).

Figure 13.9 Irradiation (Radura) symbol.

approved by the World Health Organization (WHO), the Centers for Disease Control and Prevention (CDC) and the National Aeronautics and Space Administration (NASA).

The FDA requires that any packaged food subjected to radiation for preservation be labeled "treated with radiation" or "treated by irradiation" and display the radura symbol shown in Figure 13.9. Note that irradiated food must still be handled and stored with care, as it can become contaminated after irradiation if basic food safely rules are not followed.

PREPARING MEATS

Certain procedures are often applied to meats before cooking to shape, to tenderize or to add flavor and/or moisture. These include brining, marinating and seasoning with rubs. Brines, marinades and rubs, which may contain acids and salts that break down cells walls and collagen, also help to tenderize meats before cooking. These methods are discussed in Chapter 9, Mise en Place. Trussing, barding and larding are described here.

Loin of veal tied for roasting.

Tying and Trussing

Some meats, especially roasts and whole birds, require tying or trussing before cooking. **Tying** larger roasts with butcher's twine holds loose pieces of meat together during cooking and ensures that the meat retains its shape. (Meat suppliers will sell large cuts of meat such as oven-ready rib roast wrapped in netting, which serves the same purpose as butcher's twine.) **Trussing** involves using butcher's twine to tie up the legs and wings of poultry. Poultry is often trussed to protect the more delicate white breast meat during cooking. Tying and trussing techniques are discussed along with specific cuts and types of meat in Chapters 14–18.

Barding

Barding is the process of covering the surface of meat or poultry with thin slices of pork **fatback** and tying them in place with butcher's twine. Barded meat or poultry is usually roasted. As the item cooks, the fatback continuously bastes it, adding flavor and moisture. A drawback to barding is that the fatback prevents the meat or poultry from developing the crusty exterior associated with roasting.

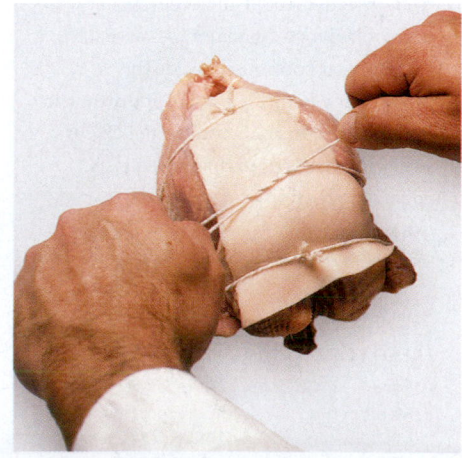

Barding a pheasant.

fatback fresh pork fat from the back of a pig, used for barding lean meats and poultry and for seasoning vegetables or other dishes

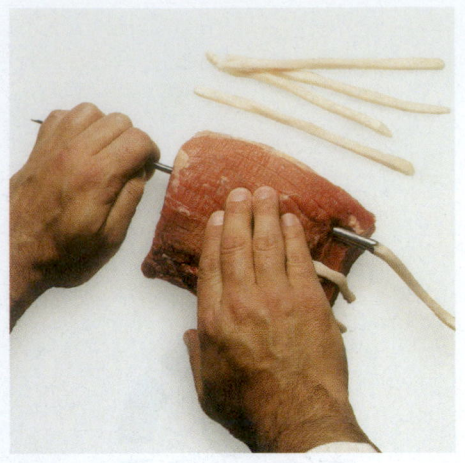

Larding meat.

Larding

Larding is the process of inserting small strips of pork fat into meat with a larding needle. Larded meat is usually cooked by braising. During cooking, the added fat contributes moisture and flavor. Although once popular, larding is rarely used today because advances in selective breeding now produce consistently tender, well-marbled meat.

DRY-HEAT COOKING METHODS FOR MEATS

In Chapter 10, Principles of Cooking, you learned the basic techniques for broiling, grilling, roasting, sautéing, pan-frying, deep-frying, poaching, simmering, braising, stewing and cooking *sous vide*. In Chapters 14–17, you will learn more about applying these cooking methods to beef, veal, lamb and pork. In this chapter we apply these methods to meat cookery in general.

Dry-heat cooking methods subject food directly to the heat of a flame (broiling and grilling), hot air (roasting) or heated fat (sautéing and pan-frying). These cooking methods firm proteins without breaking down connective tissue. They are not recommended for tougher cuts or cuts that are high in connective tissue.

Broiling and Grilling

The broiling or grilling process adds flavor; additional flavors are derived from the seasonings. The broiler or grill should brown the exterior of the meat, keeping the interior juicy. The grill should leave appetizing crosshatch marks on the meat's surface. To serve a good-quality broiled or grilled product, start with good-quality meat.

Selecting Meats to Broil or Grill

Only the most tender cuts such as cuts from the loin or rib should be broiled or grilled because direct heat does not tenderize. Because fat adds flavor as the meat cooks, choose meat that is well marbled. Some external fat is also beneficial. Too much fat, however, will cause the broiler or grill to flare up, burning or discoloring the meat and adding objectionable flavors. Connective tissue toughens when meat is broiled or grilled, so trim away as much of it as possible.

Seasoning Meats to Broil or Grill

Meats that have not been marinated should be well seasoned with salt and pepper just before being placed on the broiler or grill. If they are preseasoned and allowed to rest, the salt will dissolve and draw out moisture, making it difficult to brown the meat properly. Some chefs feel so strongly about this that they season broiled or grilled meats only after they are cooked. Dry off any meat, especially those that have been marinated, with clean paper towels before broiling or grilling. Pork and veal, which have a tendency to dry out when cooked, should be basted with seasoned butter or oil during cooking to help keep them moist. (Some cuts of pork benefit from a light brining before cooking, discussed in Chapter 17, Pork.) Meats can be glazed or basted with barbecue sauce as they cook.

Cooking Temperatures for Broiled and Grilled Meats

Red meats should be cooked at sufficiently high temperatures to caramelize their surface, making them more attractive and flavorful. At the same time, the broiler or grill cannot be too hot, or the meat's exterior will burn before the interior is cooked.

Because veal and pork are normally cooked to higher internal temperatures than beef and lamb, they should be cooked at slightly lower temperatures so that their exteriors are not overcooked when their interiors are cooked properly. The exterior of white meats should be a deep golden color when properly broiled or grilled.

Doneness of Broiled and Grilled Meats

Consumers request and expect meats to be properly cooked to specific degrees of doneness. It is the chef's responsibility to understand and comply with these requests. Meats

---

> ### ⚠ Safety Alert
>
> *Serving Meat*
>
> The Food Safety and Inspection Service of the USDA recommends the following as safe internal temperatures for serving various meats. Note that these temperatures are approximately 10–15°F (5–8°C) higher than the temperatures generally preferred by chefs and diners. Most diners would find the USDA's recommended 160°F unacceptably overcooked for a "medium" steak. Each chef or meat cook must decide for themselves whether it is more important to their clientele to cook meat to the USDA's safety standards or to diners' requests.
>
> FRESH BEEF, VEAL AND LAMB
>
> | | |
> |---|---|
> | Rare | not recommended |
> | Medium rare | 145°F (63°C) |
> | Medium | 160°F (71°C) |
> | Well done | 170°F (77°C) |
>
> FRESH PORK
>
> | | |
> |---|---|
> | Rare | not recommended |
> | Medium rare | not recommended |
> | Medium | 160°F (71°C) |
> | Well done | 170°F (77°C) |
>
> GROUND MEAT AND MEAT MIXTURES
>
> | | |
> |---|---|
> | Beef, veal, lamb and pork | 160°F (71°C) or higher |

can be cooked very rare (or **bleu** or blue), rare, medium rare, medium, medium well or well done. Figure 13.10 shows the proper color for some of these degrees of doneness. Use this guide for red meats cooked by any method.

Larger cuts of meat, such as a châteaubriand or thick chops, are often started on the broiler or grill to develop color and flavor and then finished to temperature in the oven to ensure complete, even cooking. Broiled and grilled meats that are cooked well done tend to be dry. Finishing them in the oven may help preserve some of the meat's moisture.

Broiling or grilling meat to the proper degree of doneness is an art. Larger pieces of meat take longer to cook than smaller ones, but how quickly a piece of meat cooks is determined by many other factors: the temperature of the broiler or grill, the temperature of the piece of meat when placed on the broiler or grill, the type of meat and the thickness of the cut. Because of these variables, timing alone is not a useful tool in determining doneness. Grilling is further complicated because often grills may have some sections that are hotter than others. In order to master grilling techniques, it is best to gain experience cooking on different pieces of equipment.

The most reliable method of determining doneness of a small piece of meat is by pressing the piece of meat with a finger and gauging the amount of resistance it yields. Very rare (bleu) meat will offer almost no resistance and feel almost the same as raw meat. Meat cooked rare will feel spongy and offer slight resistance to pressure. Meat cooked medium will feel slightly firm and springy to the touch. Meat cooked well done will feel quite firm and spring back quickly when pressed. See Table 13.1. Allowing broiled and grilled meats to rest for 3–4 minutes before serving helps preserve juiciness. While resting, the surface of the meat cools and the muscle fibers shrink slightly allowing the juices to redistribute themselves.

Figure 13.10 Degrees of doneness: (from top to bottom) meat cooked rare, medium rare, medium and medium well.

Accompaniments to Broiled and Grilled Meats

A broiler or grill cannot be deglazed to form the base for a sauce. For this reason, compound butters, salsas, vinaigrettes or sauces such as béarnaise are often served with broiled or grilled meats. Brown sauces such as bordelaise, chasseur, périgueux or brown mushroom sauce also complement many broiled or grilled items. Additional sauce suggestions are found in Tables 11.4 and 11.6.

DETERMINING DONENESS OF BROILED AND GRILLED ITEMS			TABLE 13.1
DEGREES OF DONENESS	COLOR	DEGREE OF RESISTANCE	IDEAL TEMPERATURE
Very rare (bleu)	Very red and raw-looking center (the center is cool to the touch)	Almost no resistance	115–120°F 46–49°C
Rare	Large deep-red center	Spongy; very slight resistance	125–130°F 52–54°C
Medium rare	Bright red center	Some resistance, slightly springy	130–140°F 54–60°C
Medium	Rosy pink to red center	Slightly firm; springy	140–150°F 60–66°C
Medium well	Very little pink at the center; almost brown throughout	Firm; springy	155–165°F 68–74°C
Well done	No red	Quite firm; springs back quickly when pressed	Not recommended

⚠ Safety Alert

Grill Flare-Ups

Fat dripping onto a grill can cause flames to flare up and burn foods. Prevent flames by trimming excess fat from foods before cooking. Control the flame by moving the food to another section of the grill. The fat should burn off the coals within a few seconds. Should the flare-up become uncontrollable, suppress the flame with a lid or sheet tray.

Procedure for Broiling or Grilling Meats

1   Heat the overhead broiler, salamander or grill.

2   Use a wire brush to remove any charred or burnt particles that may be stuck to the broiler or grill grate. The grate can be wiped with a lightly oiled towel to remove any remaining particles and to help season it.

3   Prepare the item to be broiled or grilled by trimming off any excess fat and connective tissue and marinating or seasoning it as desired. The meat may be brushed lightly with oil to help protect it and prevent it from sticking to the grate.

4   Place the item in the broiler or on the grill presentation side down. Following the method introduced in Chapter 10, Principles of Cooking rotate the meat 90 degrees to produce the attractive crosshatch marks associated with grilling. Use a chef's fork or tongs to turn or flip the meat without piercing the surface (this prevents valuable juices from escaping).

5   Cook the meat to the desired doneness while developing the proper surface color. To do so, adjust the position of the meat on the broiler or grill, or adjust the distance between the grate and heat source. Allow the meat to rest 3–5 minutes before serving.

Grilled Lamb Chops with Herb Butter

YIELD 2 Servings, 6½ oz. (195 g) each		METHOD Grilling
Lamb chops, loin or rib, approx. 1 in. (2.5 cm) thick	6	6
Oil	as needed	as needed
Salt and pepper	TT	TT
Herb butter		6 thin slices or 6 small rosettes

1   Preheat the grill for 15 minutes.

2   Brush the lamb chops with oil; season with salt and pepper.

3   Place the lamb chops on the grill, rotating them as necessary to produce the proper crosshatching. Turn the chops over and cook them to the desired doneness.

4   Remove the lamb chops from the grill and place a slice or rosette of herb butter on each chop.

5   Let the meat rest in a warm place for 3–5 minutes as the herb butter melts. The plate can be placed under the broiler for a few seconds to help melt the herb butter.

Approximate values per 3-chop serving: **Calories** 623, **Total fat** 50 g, **Saturated fat** 27 g, **Cholesterol** 224 mg, **Sodium** 1186 mg, **Total carbohydrates** 0 g, **Protein** 42 g, **Vitamin A** 40%

❶ Brushing the lamb chops with oil.

❷ Placing the lamb chops on the grill.

❸ Rotating the lamb chops 90 degrees to create crosshatch marks.

❹ Turning the chops to finish them on the other side.

Roasting

Properly roasted meats should be tender, juicy and evenly cooked to the appropriate degree of doneness. They should have a pleasant appearance when whole as well as when sliced and plated.

Selecting Meats to Roast

Because roasting is a dry-heat cooking method and does not tenderize the finished product, meats that are to be roasted should be tender and well marbled. Good roasting options are cut from the rib, loin or leg sections.

Seasoning Meats to Roast

Seasonings are especially important with smaller roasts and roasts with little or no fat covering. With these roasts, some of the seasonings penetrate the meat while the remainder help create the highly seasoned crust associated with a good roast. A large roast with heavy fat covering (e.g., a steamship round or prime rib) does not benefit from being seasoned on the surface because the seasonings does not penetrate the fat layer, which is trimmed away before service.

When practical, excess fat should be trimmed from a roast. Leaving just a thin fat layer allows the roast to baste itself while cooking. A lean roast can be barded or larded before cooking to add richness and moisture. Lamb legs are sometimes studded with garlic cloves by piercing the meat with a paring knife and then pressing slivers of raw garlic into the holes.

A roast is sometimes cooked on a bed of mirepoix, or mirepoix is added to the roasting pan as the roast cooks. The mirepoix raises the roast off the bottom of the roasting pan, preventing the bottom from overcooking. This mirepoix, however, does not add any flavor to the roast. Rather it combines with the drippings to add flavor to the jus, sauce or gravy that is made with the drippings.

Cooking Temperatures for Roasted Meats

Small roasts such as a rack of lamb or a beef tenderloin should be cooked at high temperatures, 375–450°F (191–232°C) so that they develop good color during their short cooking times. Traditionally large roasts were started at high temperatures to sear the meat and seal in the juices; they were then finished at lower temperatures. Studies have shown, however, that searing does not seal in juices and that roasts cooked at constant, low temperatures provide a better yield with less shrinkage than roasts that have been seared. Temperatures between 275°F and 325°F (135°C and 163°C) are ideal for large roasts. These temperatures produce a large, evenly cooked pink center portion.

Doneness of Roasted Meats

The doneness of small roasts such as a rack of lamb is determined in much the same way as broiled or grilled meats. With experience, the chef develops a sense of timing as well as a feel for gauging the amount of resistance by touching the meat. These techniques, however, are not infallible, especially with large roasts.

Bear in mind that the shape, thickness and weight of a roast affect cooking time. A roast with a thinner shape cooks more quickly than a squat thick one even if both roasts weigh the same. A long thin 5-pound (2.2-kilogram) tenderloin of beef cooks more quickly than a square 5-pound (2.2-kilogram) sirloin roast. A bone-in roast cooks more quickly than a boneless roast because bones conduct heat quickly. Also the temperature of the meat before cooking affects cooking time. A piece of meat at room temperature before roasting cooks more quickly than a chilled one. Although timing is useful as a general guide for determining doneness, there are too many variables for it to be relied on exclusively. With this caution in mind, Table 13.2 lists general cooking times and the proper finished temperatures for roasted meats.

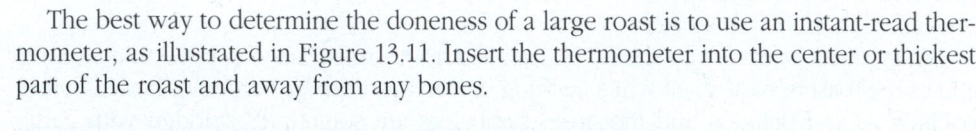

DETERMINING DONENESS OF ROASTS		TABLE 13.2
DEGREE OF DONENESS	IDEAL INTERNAL TEMPERATURE AFTER CARRYOVER	MINUTES PER POUND*
Very rare	125–130°F 52–54°C	12–15
Rare	130–140°F 54–60°C	15–18
Medium	140–150°F 60–66°C	18–20
Well done	150–165°F 66–74°C	20–25

*Assumes meat was at room temperature before roasting and cooked at a constant 325°F (163°C).

The best way to determine the doneness of a large roast is to use an instant-read thermometer, as illustrated in Figure 13.11. Insert the thermometer into the center or thickest part of the roast and away from any bones.

Carryover Cooking and Resting for Roasted Meats

Cooking does not stop the moment a roast is removed from the oven. Through conduction, the heat applied to the outside of the roast continues to penetrate, cooking the center for several more minutes. The internal temperature of a small roast can rise by as much as 5–10°F (3–6°C) after being removed from the oven. With a larger roast, such as a 50-pound steamship round, it can rise by as much as 25°F (14°C). Remove roasted meats before they reach the desired degree of doneness, and allow carryover cooking to complete the cooking process. Remove small (4–15-pound/1.8–6.8-kilo) roasts from the oven when their internal temperature has reached 10–15°F (6–8°C) below the desired final internal temperature. Remove large (16 or more pounds/7.25 or more kilo) roasts when their when their internal temperature has reached 15–25°F (8–14°C) below the desired final internal temperature. Table 13.2 lists final desired internal temperatures after **carryover cooking**.

As meat cooks, its juices flow toward the center. If the roast is carved immediately after it is removed from the oven, its juices will run from the meat, causing it to lose its color and become dry. Letting the meat rest, uncovered, before slicing allows carryover cooking to take place and allows the juices to redistribute themselves evenly throughout the roast so that the flesh retains more juices when carved. Small roasts, such as a rack of lamb, need to rest only 10–20 minutes; larger roasts such as a leg of lamb or a sirloin roast need to rest an hour and a steamship round of beef may require as much as 2 hours of resting time. The size, shape and weight of the roast determine the ideal resting time as does the temperature in the kitchen. As a rule of thumb, allow small 2-pound (1-kilo) roasts to rest a minimum of 10 minutes. For larger roasts, calculate 3–5 minutes of resting time per pound of meat.

Accompaniments to Roasted Meats

Roasts may be served with a sauce based on their natural juices (called *au jus*), as described in the following recipe for Roast Prime Rib of Beef au Jus or with a pan gravy made with drippings from the roast. Additional sauce suggestions are found in Tables 11.4 and 11.6.

Figure 13.11 Proper placement of an instant-read thermometer.

carryover cooking the cooking that occurs after a food is removed from a heat source; it is accomplished by the residual heat remaining in the food

Procedure for Roasting Meats

silverskin the tough connective tissue that surrounds certain muscles

1   Trim excess fat, tendons and **silverskin** from the meat. Leave only a thin fat covering, if possible, so that the roast bastes itself as it cooks.

2   Season the roast as appropriate and place it in a roasting pan. The roast may be placed on a bed of mirepoix or on a rack.

3 Roast the meat, uncovered, at the desired temperature (the larger the roast, the lower the temperature), usually 275–425°F (135–220°C).

4 If au jus or pan gravy is desired and a mirepoix was not added at the start of cooking, mirepoix may be added 30–45 minutes before the roast is done, thus allowing the vegetables to caramelize while the roast finishes cooking.

5 Cook to a temperature that will allow carryover cooking to raise the internal temperature to the desired final temperature.

6 Remove the roast from the oven, allowing carryover cooking to raise the internal temperature to the desired degree of doneness. Allow the roast to rest before slicing or carving it. As the roast rests, prepare the jus, sauce or pan gravy.

Roast Prime Rib of Beef au Jus

YIELD 18 Boneless Servings, 8 oz. (240 g) each	METHOD	Roasting
Oven-ready rib roast, IMPS #109, approx. 16 lb. (7.6 kg)	1	1
Salt and pepper	TT	TT
Garlic, chopped	4 oz.	120 g
Mirepoix	1 lb.	480 g
Brown Stock	2 qt.	1.9 lt

MISE EN PLACE

- Peel and chop garlic.
- Peel and chop onions, carrots and celery for mirepoix.

1 Pull back the netting, fold back the thick layer of surface fat or fat cap and season the roast well with the salt, pepper and garlic. Replace the fat cap and netting; place the roast in an appropriate-sized roasting pan. Roast at 300–325°F (150–160°C).

2 Add the mirepoix to the pan around the roast approximately 45 minutes before the roast is finished cooking. Continue cooking until the internal temperature reaches 125°F (52°C), approximately 3–4 hours. Carryover cooking will raise the internal temperature of the roast to approximately 138°F (59°C).

3 Remove the roast from the pan and allow it to rest in a warm place for 30 minutes.

4 Drain the excess fat from the roasting pan, reserving the mirepoix and any drippings in the roasting pan.

5 Caramelize the mirepoix on the stove top; allow the liquids to evaporate, leaving only brown drippings in the pan.

6 Deglaze the pan with the brown stock to create the jus. Stir to loosen all the drippings.

7 Simmer the jus, reducing it slightly and allowing the mirepoix to release its flavor; season with salt and pepper if necessary.

8 Strain the jus through a china cap lined with cheesecloth. Skim any remaining fat from the surface with a ladle.

9 Remove the netting from the roast. Trim and slice the roast as described on page 304 and serve with approximately 1–2 ounces (30–60 milliliters) jus per person.

Approximate values per 8-oz. (240-g) serving: **Calories** 951, **Total fat** 79 g, **Saturated fat** 32 g, **Cholesterol** 214 mg, **Sodium** 278 mg, **Total carbohydrates** 1 g, **Protein** 56 g, **Iron** 40%

❶ Draining the excess fat from the roasting pan.

❷ Caramelizing the mirepoix.

❸ Deglazing the pan with brown stock.

❹ Simmering the jus to reduce it slightly and allow the mirepoix to release its flavors.

❺ Straining the jus through a cheesecloth lined china cap.

Carving Roasts

All the efforts that went into selecting and cooking a perfect roast will be wasted if the roast is not carved properly. Roasts are always carved against the grain; carving with the grain produces long stringy, tough slices. Cutting across the muscle fibers produces a more attractive and tender portion. Portions may be cut in a single thick slice, as with Roast Prime Rib of Beef, or in many thin slices. The following procedures and photographs illustrate several different carving methods.

Carving pork tenderloin against the grain.

Procedure for Carving Prime Rib

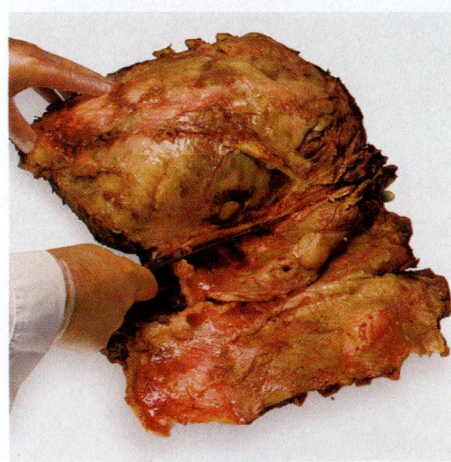

❶ Removing fat cap and **chine** bones.

chine the backbone or spine of an animal; a subprimal cut of beef, veal, lamb, pork or game carcass containing a portion of the backbone with some adjoining flesh.

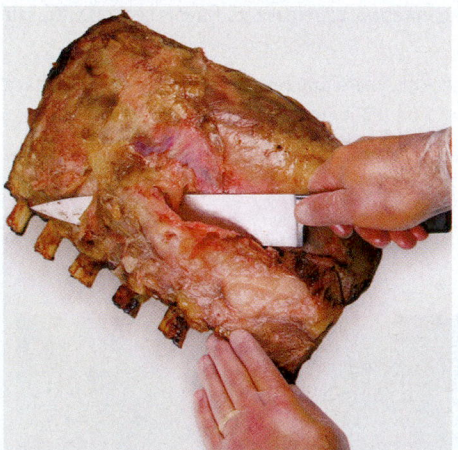

❷ Trimming the excess fat from the center or eye muscle portion of the prime rib of beef (**ribeye**).

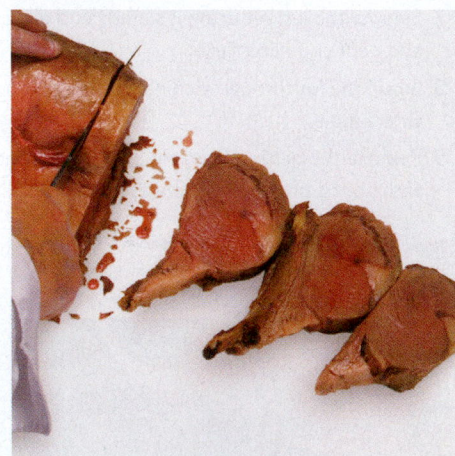

❸ Slicing the rib in long, smooth strokes, the first cut (**end cut**) without a rib bone, the second cut with a rib bone, the third without, and so on.

Procedure for Carving Prime Rib on the Slicer

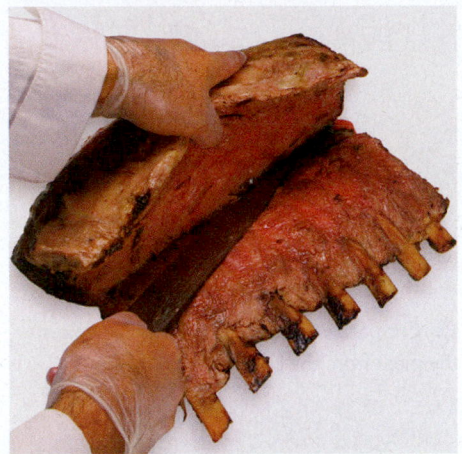

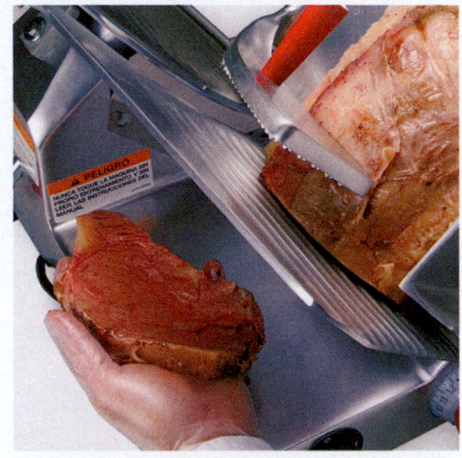

1 When producing large quantities of prime rib, it is often more practical to slice it on a slicing machine. Following the steps illustrated in the previous procedure, remove the netting, fat cap and chine bone; trim excess fat from the eye muscle. Use a long slicer and completely remove the ribeye from the rib bones, being careful to stay as close as possible to the bones to avoid wasting any meat.

2 Place the rib on the slicing machine and set the machine to the desired thickness. The blade will have to be adjusted often because a roast's thickness fluctuates.

Procedure for Carving a Steamship Round of Beef

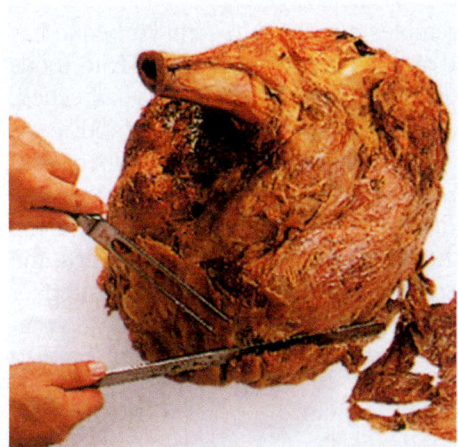

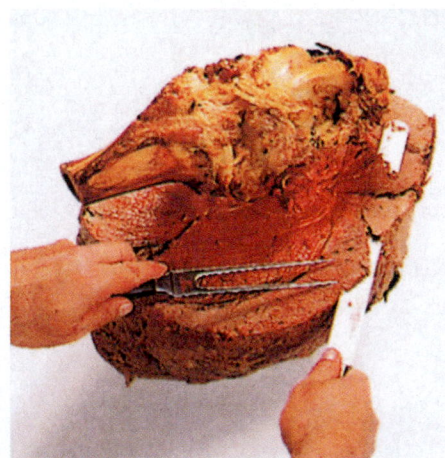

1 Place the roast on the cutting board with the exposed femur bone (large end of the roast) down and the tibia (**shank bone** or "**handle**") up. Trim the excess exterior fat to expose the lean meat.

2 Begin slicing with a horizontal cut toward the shank bone, then make vertical cuts to release the slices of beef.

3 Keeping the exposed surface as level as possible, continue carving, turning the roast as necessary to access all sides.

Procedure for Carving a Leg of Lamb

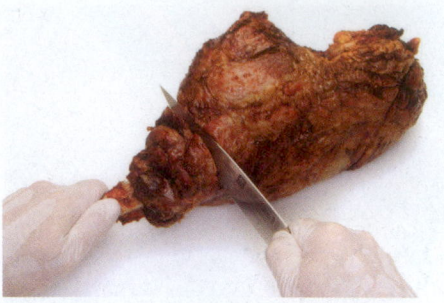

① Holding the shank bone firmly, cut toward the bone.

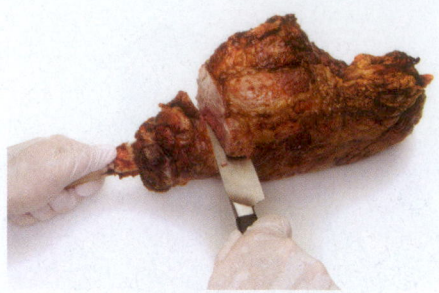

② Cut parallel to the shank bone to separate the meat from the bone.

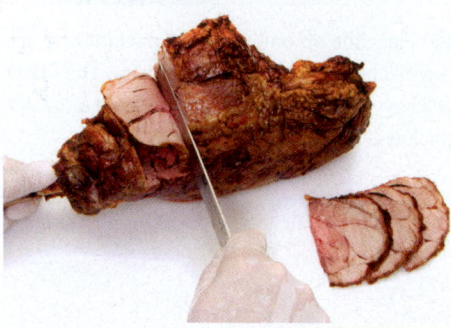

③ Make vertical cuts to release the slices of lamb.

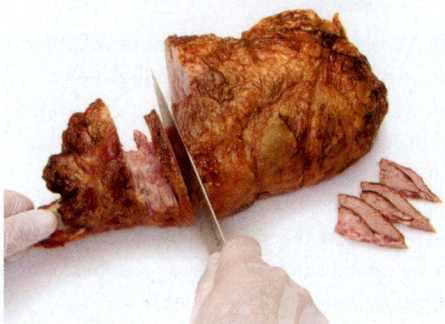

④ Rotate the leg as needed to access the meat on all sides.

Barbecue

Barbecue is a dry-heat cooking method that resembles roasting. The term barbeque has various meanings in different parts of the world and is generally used to refer to foods that are cooked slowly over a hardwood charcoal or wood fire. When food is barbecued, heat from the fire cooks through natural convection while smoke flavors the food.

In traditional barbecue, meats are cooked directly over the glowing embers of a wood fire in a partially covered **pit**. Other types of equipment such as **smoker ovens** may be used to prepare barbecue, however. Some smoker ovens contain two chambers, one for a wood fire and one for the meat. In these two-chambered smoker ovens, the meat cooks through indirect convection while smoke flavors it. Single-chamber smoker ovens heated with gas or electricity are common in restaurant kitchens. A small compartment with a heating element within the oven holds wood chips, which burn to release smoke.

Selecting Meats to Barbecue

Tougher cuts of well-marbled beef and pork are ideal for barbecue because the long slow cooking tenderizes their connective tissues. Well-marbled cuts with ample fat such as beef brisket, beef ribs, pork shoulder and pork ribs produce moist finished products. Poultry and sausages may also be barbecued. Smaller and more tender cuts of meat cook more quickly than large pieces.

Seasoning Meats to Barbecue

Seasoning is done in stages with wet or dry rubs, marinades, injections and mops. Often a spice mixture or **rub** is massaged into the meat, which then sits overnight before cooking. The mixture may be made from dry spices, seasonings and sugar (**dry rub**) or dry spices and seasonings blended with honey, chopped chiles, garlic and other ingredients into a wet paste (**wet rub**). Precise flavor combinations are often closely-guarded secrets of experienced barbecue cooks known as pitmasters. Meats may be marinated or injected with seasoning solutions or brine before smoking. During cooking, a vinegary basting liquid called a **mop** may be applied to enhance flavor. The liquid also helps smoke adhere to the surface of the meat as it cooks.

Cooking Temperatures for Barbecue

Cooking temperatures for barbecue depend on the meat and type of equipment. When cooking over the indirect heat of a wood fire, prepare the fire and allow the wood to burn until the flames subside and only glowing embers remain. Maintain embers by feeding the fire with wood to keep the cooking temperature between 200°F (93°C) and 325°F (162°C) depending on the wood and type of equipment being used and the meat being cooked. For cooking in a smoker oven, preheat to the desired temperature, which is usually between 225°F (107°C) and 250°F (120°C).

Doneness of Barbecued Meats

Doneness is not determined by internal temperature, although meats must reach safe food temperatures, but by tenderness and feel. The finished meat should have a uniform exterior color from the slow cooking, the smoke and the rub mixture. The meat should fall off the bone and be moist and tender enough to cut with a fork or to be torn and shredded. When cut, barbecued meats have a noticeable pink edge called a **smoke ring** that is caused by a reaction between meat proteins and chemicals in the smoke. Properly cooked barbecued meat should have a pronounced and pleasant smoke flavor.

Accompaniments to Barbecued Meats

Barbecued meats may be served plain. Or they may be served with any number of traditional barbecue sauces depending on the regional style of the barbecue. Tart, vinegary or sweet accompaniments such as coleslaw, pickles or pickled vegetables complement barbecue. Mashed white or sweet potatoes and white bread may be served to absorb the meat juices and sauce.

Procedure for Barbecuing Meats

1 Trim, shape and truss the meat for barbecue.

2 Prepare the seasoning or marinade to be used on the meat. This may be a dry or wet rub, a marinade, a brine solution or a mop.

3 Season, marinate or massage the rub into the meat. Cover and refrigerate the meat to absorb the seasoning for 12–24 hours.

4 Allow the meat to sit at room temperature for 30 minutes immediately before barbecuing.

5 Prepare the fire or barbecue equipment.

6 Place the meat on the racks of the barbecue or in the smoker oven leaving adequate space so that air flows freely around the meat on all sides.

7 Cook the meat, mopping it every hour, if desired, until it is **fork tender**, crusty and cooked through. Allow the meats to cook from 2 hours for smaller, tender cuts and poultry, up to 12 hours for large cuts.

8 If desired, brush the meat with barbecue sauce and return it to the smoker for another 30 minutes to create a final crust.

9 Allow larger pieces of meat to rest for 30 minutes to one hour before serving.

fork tender describes cooked food that is so tender it shows little resistance when pierced with a fork

Pulled Pork Sandwiches

MISE EN PLACE

- Prepare the Barbecue Sauce and Creamy Coleslaw while the pork cooks.

YIELD 2 lb. (960 kg)		METHOD Barbecuing	
Pork butts, bone in, 4 lb. (3.3 kg)		2	2
Dry rub:			
Paprika		2 Tbsp.	30 ml
Kosher salt		3 Tbsp.	90 ml
Granulated sugar		2 Tbsp.	30 ml
Brown sugar		2 Tbsp.	30 ml
Ground cumin		1 Tbsp.	15 ml
Black pepper		2 Tbsp.	30 ml
Cayenne		2 tsp.	10 ml
Barbecue Sauce (page 250), optional as needed			
Hamburger buns		as needed	as needed
Creamy Coleslaw (page 766)		as needed	as needed

1 Remove the skin from the pork butts if necessary. Trim the excess fat leaving a layer ½-inch (1.2-centimeters) thick or score the fat. Place the pork butts into a hotel pan.

2 Combine the ingredients for the dry rub and pour it over the pork butts. Rub the spice mixture into the pork butts coating all sides evenly.

3 Cover and refrigerate the seasoned pork butts for 24 hours.

4 Place the seasoned pork butts on the rack in a commercial smoker. Smoke the pork butts at 250°F (120°C) until the internal temperature reaches 195°F (90°C) and the meat is very tender, approximately 7–8 hours. When the meat is fully cooked, grip the blade bone with a kitchen towel. Twist firmly and pull to remove. If the blade bone does not come free, return the pork butt to the smoker and continue cooking, testing every 30 minutes, until the blade bone is easily removed.

5 Allow the pork butts to rest for 1 hour. Pull the meat apart with gloved hands removing excess fat and connective tissue.

6 Serve the pulled pork with Barbecue Sauce on hamburger buns accompanied by Creamy Coleslaw as desired.

Approximate values per 3-oz. (180-g) serving: **Calories** 540, **Total fat** 34 g, **Saturated fat** 12 g, **Cholesterol** 190 mg, **Sodium** 1000 mg, **Total carbohydrates** 6 g, **Protein** 44 g

❶ Placing the pork butt on the rack in the chamber of a smoker oven set to the proper temperature.

❷ The barbecued pork butt with the desired pink smoke ring caused by smoke combining with proteins and moisture during cooking.

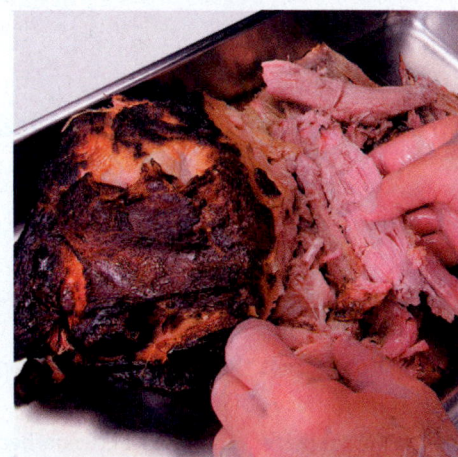

❸ The barbecued pork butt has a crusty dark surface, tender texture and pronounced smoke flavor.

Barbecue Basics

Barbecue is many techniques and many flavors; it is a noun, a verb and an adjective. It is entertainment, a party, a competition and fellowship. Barbecue (BBQ, Bar-B-Que or simply Que) is the history of a region and its people reflected on a plate.

The word springs from *barbacoa,* the Spanish term for cooking meat in a pit dug into the ground and filled with logs burned down to charcoal, a technique observed in the Caribbean islands by early explorers. Smoke served as both a preservative and a tenderizer. Along the U.S. Atlantic coast, early settlers cooked venison and turkey with this technique. Spanish explorers brought pigs to the New World and Native Americans introduced those pigs to the smoky pits.

Barbecue is not grilling, which is a high-temperature process, nor is it merely outdoor cooking. True barbecue is a slow process, requiring many hours of low temperature heat and smoke to tenderize tough cuts or whole carcasses. A world of nuances are created by regional preferences based on meat, wood and finishing

Meat: Pork and beef are the most common meats for barbecue, but mutton, goat and chicken are also used. The preferred meat depends on availability, so the deep South focuses on pigs while Texas prefers beef, especially the tougher cuts such as brisket. Sausage is part of barbecue tradition in locales settled by Germans and Eastern Europeans, where smoked sausages were common.

Wood: Barbecue requires smoke and smoke arises from wood. Real barbecue is never produced over gas or electric grills. Hardwood charcoal and embers are required for the long, slow burn necessary to tenderize and flavor tougher cuts of meat. The preferred wood again traditionally depends on availability—pecan in Mississippi, hickory in Tennessee, fruitwoods and oak throughout the Southeast, mesquite in the Southwest. Conifers (pine, fir, cedar) should never be used, nor should old lumber, moldy wood or green wood. Some pitmasters use whole logs, but this requires great skill as the logs burn at higher temperatures. More commonly, logs are preburned into embers that are added to the pit as needed to maintain the correct temperature.

Finishing: Four general styles of sauces are found in authentic barbecue. The oldest and simplest is vinegar and pepper. It is still popular in parts of the Carolinas, Virginia, Georgia and Kentucky, generally where Scots settled. Mustard-based sauces originated in South Carolina, developed by German immigrants of the early 1700s. This style is the most distinctly regional, known worldwide as South Carolina upcountry barbecue.

Light tomato sauce is a sweetened tomato ketchup–enhanced version of the vinegar-pepper sauce. It became popular in Tennessee (Memphis) and North Carolina beginning in the early 1900s. More recently, a heavy tomato sauce developed in western and Midwestern areas and has been widely promoted by commercial manufacturers. It is thick and sweet; even spicy-hot versions have an underlying sweetness. Unfortunately, commercially bottled tomato sauces now represent "barbecue" for those who know little about American barbecue traditions.

Other regional styles of sauce exist, such as the white sauce of northwest Alabama made with sour cream, and the spicy au jus–style mop sauce served with beef brisket in parts of Texas.

Sautéing

Sautéing is a dry-heat cooking method in which heat is conducted by a small amount of fat. Sautéed meats should be tender and of good color and have a good overall flavor. Tenderness is a reflection of the quality of the raw product and color is determined by proper cooking temperatures. Any accompanying sauce should be well seasoned and complement the meat without overpowering it.

Selecting Meats to Sauté

As with broiling, grilling and roasting, use tender meats of the highest quality in order to produce good results when sautéing. Cuts from the rib, loin and leg, slices that have been cut into cutlets or scallops and meat pounded thin for tenderness are preferred for sautéeing. The cuts should be uniform in size, shape and thickness in order to promote even cooking.

Seasoning Meats to Sauté

The sauces that almost always accompany sautéed meats provide much of the seasoning. Alternatively the meat can be marinated or simply seasoned with salt and pepper. If marinated, the meat must be patted dry before cooking to ensure proper browning. Some meats are dusted with flour before cooking to seal in juices and promote even browning.

Doneness of Sautéed Meats

As with broiled and grilled meats, the doneness of sautéed meats is determined by touch and timing. Red meats should be well browned with a crisp surface; veal and pork should be somewhat lighter.

Accompaniments to Sautéed Meats

fond (1) French for "stock" or "base"; (2) the concentrated juices, drippings and bits of food left in pans after foods are roasted or sautéed; it is used to flavor sauces made directly in the pans in which the foods were cooked

Sauces served with sautéed meats are usually made directly in the sauté pan, using the *fond*. They often incorporate a previously thickened sauce. Sauce suggestions for sautéed meats are found in Tables 11.4 and 11.6.

Procedure for Sautéing Meats

cutlet a relatively thick, boneless slice of meat

scallop (Fr. *escalope*; It. *scaloppa*, pl. *scaloppine*) a thin, boneless slice of meat

émincé [eh-man-SAY] a small, thin, boneless piece of meat

medallion a small, round, relatively thick slice of meat

mignonette [mean-yo-NETT] a medallion

noisette [nwah-ZETT] a small, usually round, portion of meat cut from the rib

paillard [pah-YAHR] a scallop of meat, usually chicken or veal, pounded until large and thin, usually grilled or sautéed

chop a cut of meat, including part of the rib

1 Cut the meat into **cutlets**, **scallops**, **émincés**, **medallions**, **mignonettes**, **noisettes**, **paillards**, **chops** or small even-sized pieces.

2 Heat a sauté pan and add enough oil or clarified butter to just cover the bottom. The pan should be large enough to hold the meat in a single layer. An overcrowded pan will cool quickly and cook slowly overcooking the meat before it browns. A pan that is too large may cause the fat or meat to burn.

3 Remove any excess surface moisture from the meat with clean paper towels. Season the meat and dredge in flour if desired. Add the meat to the sauté pan in a single layer. Do not crowd the pan.

4 Adjust the temperature so that the meat's exterior browns properly without burning and the interior cooks. The heat should be high enough to complete the cooking process before the meat begins to stew in its own juices.

5 Small items may be tossed using the sauté pan's sloped sides to flip them back on top of themselves. Do not toss the meat more than necessary, however. The pan should remain in contact with the heat source as much as possible to maintain proper temperatures. Larger items should be turned using tongs or a kitchen fork. Avoid burns by not splashing hot fat.

6 Larger items such as chops and thick steaks can be finished in an oven. Either place the sauté pan in the oven or transfer the meat to another pan to cook in the oven. The latter procedure allows a sauce to be made in the original pan as the meat continues to cook.

Procedure for Preparing a Sauce in the Sauté Pan

1 If a sauce is to be made in the pan, hold the meat on a warm platter in a warm spot while preparing the sauce. When the meat is removed from the pan, leave a small amount of fat as well as the *fond*. If there is excessive fat, degrease the pan, leaving just enough to cover its bottom. Add ingredients such as garlic, shallots and mushrooms as garnishes and sauce flavorings; sauté them.

2 Deglaze the pan with wine or stock. Scrape the pan, loosening the *fond* and allowing it to dissolve in the liquid. Reduce the deglazing liquid by approximately three-fourths.

3 Add additional jus lié or stock to the pan. Cook and reduce the sauce to the desired consistency.

4 Add any ingredients that do not require cooking to the sauce, such as herbs and spices. Adjust the seasonings with salt and pepper.

5 For service, the meat may be returned to the pan for a moment to reheat it and coat it with the finished sauce. The meat should remain in the sauce just long enough to reheat. Do not attempt to cook the meat in the sauce. It will lose its crisp surface and may overcook.

Sautéed Veal Scallops with White Wine Lemon Sauce

YIELD 6 Servings, 8 oz. (240 g) each	METHOD Sautéing	
Veal scallops, 3 oz. (90 g) each	12	12
Clarified butter	4 fl. oz.	120 ml
Flour	4 oz.	120 g
Salt and pepper	TT	TT
Shallots, chopped	2 Tbsp.	30 ml
White wine	6 fl. oz.	180 ml
Lemon juice	2 fl. oz.	60 ml
Brown veal stock	4 fl. oz.	120 ml
Unsalted butter	2 oz.	60 g
Lemon wedges	12	12

MISE EN PLACE
• Peel and chop shallots.

1 Pound the scallops to a uniform thickness, as described in Chapter 15, Veal.

2 Heat a sauté pan over high heat and add enough clarified butter to coat the bottom of the pan.

3 Dredge the scallops in flour seasoned with salt and pepper and add to the pan in a single layer. Sauté on each side for 1–2 minutes, adjusting the heat if necessary so that the meat browns without burning. As the first scallops are done, remove them to a warm platter and sauté the remaining scallops. This can be done in several batches, adding additional clarified butter as needed should the pan become dry.

4 After all the scallops are done and have been removed from the pan, add the chopped shallots to the pan and sauté until tender.

5 Deglaze the pan with the wine and lemon juice.

6 Add the stock and reduce by half.

7 Swirl in the butter (monté au beurre).

8 Adjust the seasonings with salt and pepper.

9 Serve two scallops per person with approximately 1 ounce (30 milliliters) sauce. Garnish with lemon wedges.

Approximate values per 8-oz. (240-g) serving: **Calories** 537, **Total fat** 28 g, **Saturated fat** 13 g, **Cholesterol** 208 mg, **Sodium** 325 mg, **Total carbohydrates** 17 g, **Protein** 47 g, **Vitamin A** 22%

❶ Adding the veal scallops to the pan. Note the relationship of scallops to pan size.

❷ Adding the chopped shallots to the pan and sautéing them.

❸ Deglazing the pan with white wine and lemon juice.

❹ Adding the brown veal stock before reducing by half.

❺ Swirling in the butter and adjusting the seasonings.

Pan-Frying

Pan-frying uses more fat than sautéing to conduct heat. Pan-fried meats should be tender and of good color and have a good overall flavor. As is the case with sautéing, tenderness in pan-fried meats is a reflection of the quality of the raw product and color is determined by proper cooking temperatures. Meats to be pan-fried are usually breaded. In addition to providing flavor, breading seals the meat. The breading should be free from breaks, thus preventing the fat from coming into direct contact with the meat or collecting in a pocket formed between the meat and the breading. Pan-fried items should be golden in color, and the breading should not be soggy.

Selecting Meats to Pan-Fry

As with other dry-heat cooking methods, tender meats of high quality should be pan-fried because the meat will not be tenderized by the cooking process. Meats that will be pan-fried are often cut into cutlets or scallops.

Seasoning Meats to Pan-Fry

Pan-fried meats are usually seasoned lightly with salt and pepper. Either apply salt and pepper directly to the meat or add them to the flour or bread crumbs used to bread the meat.

Doneness of Pan-Fried Meats

The most accurate way to determine the doneness of a pan-fried item is by timing. The touch method is difficult to use because of the large amounts of hot fat. The touch method is often not as accurate as it is with broiled or grilled meats because pan-fried meats are often quite thin. The thinness of the meat also means that thermometer readings may not be accurate.

Accompaniments to Pan-Fried Meats

Sauces served with pan-fried meats are usually made separately because no *fond* is created during the pan-frying process. Sauce suggestions are listed in Tables 11.4 and 11.6.

Procedure for Pan-Frying Meats

1 Slice and pound the meat into scallops, as described in Chapter 15, Veal. Season the scallops.
2 Bread the meat using the standard breading procedure detailed in Chapter 9, Mise en Place.
3 Heat a moderate amount of fat or oil in a heavy pan. There should be enough fat so that it comes one-third to halfway up the side of the meat. The temperature should be slightly lower than that used to sauté so that the breading will be nicely browned when the item is fully cooked.
4 Place the meat in the pan, being careful not to splash the hot fat. Fry until brown. Turn and brown the other side. Ideally pan-fried meats should be cut or pounded to a thickness so that they are fully cooked when they are well browned on both sides.
5 Remove the meat from the pan; drain it on absorbent paper before serving.

Breaded Veal Cutlets

MISE EN PLACE

• Set up containers with flour; eggs and milk; and bread crumbs for breading following standard breading procedure. See page 170.

YIELD 10 Servings, 5 oz. (150 g) each		METHOD Pan-Frying	
Veal cutlets, 4 oz. (120 g) each		10	10
Salt and pepper		TT	TT
Flour		as needed for breading	
Eggs		as needed for breading	
Milk		as needed for breading	
Bread crumbs		as needed for breading	
Vegetable oil		as needed	as needed
Whole butter		6 oz.	180 g
Lemon wedges		20	20

1 Using a mallet, pound the cutlets to an even thickness, approximately ¼ inch (6 millimeters).

2 Season the cutlets with salt and pepper.

3 Bread the cutlets using the standard breading procedure described in Chapter 9, Mise en Place.

4 Heat a heavy pan over medium heat; add approximately ⅛ inch (3 millimeters) oil.

5 Add the cutlets in a single layer. Do not crowd the pan. Brown on one side, then the other. Total cooking time should be approximately 4 minutes.

6 Remove the cutlets and drain on absorbent paper.

7 Melt the butter in a small pan until it foams.

8 Place one cutlet on each plate and pour approximately ½ fluid ounce (15 milliliters) butter over each portion. Garnish with lemon wedges.

Approximate values per 5-oz. (150-g) serving: **Calories** 501, **Total fat** 37 g, **Saturated fat** 17 g, **Cholesterol** 193 mg, **Sodium** 338 mg, **Total carbohydrates** 5 g, **Protein** 36 g, **Vitamin A** 17%

① Adding the breaded cutlets to the hot pan.

② Turning the cutlets to brown on the second side.

③ Melting the butter in a separate pan until it foams.

④ Pouring the butter over the cutlet.

Deep-Frying

Deep-frying quickly cooks foods submerged in hot fat. This cooking method does not have a tenderizing effect. As even the choicest cuts of meat can always benefit from some tenderizing, deep-frying is not usually used for beef, veal, lamb or pork. There are exceptions, however. For example, commercially available frozen breaded meat cutlets are often deep-fried, and some Asian dishes involve deep-frying small pieces of beef or pork before finishing the meat in a sauce.

MOIST-HEAT COOKING METHODS FOR MEAT

Moist-heat cooking methods subject food to heat and moisture. Moist heat is often, but not always, used to tenderize tougher cuts of meat through long, slow cooking. Simmering is the only moist-heat cooking method discussed here, as it is the only one frequently used with meat.

Simmering

Simmering is usually associated with specific tougher cuts of meat that need to be tenderized through long, slow, moist cooking. Quality simmered meats have good flavor and texture. The flavor is determined by the cooking liquid; the texture is a result of proper cooking temperatures and time.

Selecting Meats to Simmer

Meats such as fresh or corned beef brisket, fresh or cured hams and tongue are often simmered. Beef briskets and tongues, pork butts and hams are often simmered whole.

pickle (1) to preserve food in a brine or vinegar solution; (2) food that has been preserved in a seasoned brine or vinegar, especially cucumbers.

Seasoning Meats to Simmer

If the meat to be simmered was cured by either smoking (as with cured hams, ham hocks and smoked pork butt) or **pickling** (as with corned beef and pickled tongue), the cooking liquid will not be used to make a sauce and should not be seasoned. Simmering cured meats helps leach out some of the excess salt, making the finished dish more palatable.

Cooking Temperatures for Simmered Meats

Moist-heat cooking methods generally use lower temperatures than dry-heat cooking methods. Meats are normally simmered at temperatures between 185°F and 205°F (85°C and 96°C). In some food service operations, meats such as hams and corned beef are cooked at temperatures as low as 150°F (66°C) for up to 12 hours. Although lower cooking temperatures result in less shrinkage and a more tender finished product, the required cooking times may be increased to the point that very low cooking temperatures may not be practical.

Doneness of Simmered Meats

Simmered meats are always cooked well done, which is determined by tenderness. The size and quality of the raw product determines the cooking time. Undercooked meats will be tough and chewy. Overcooked meats will be stringy and may fall apart. When testing large cuts of meat for doneness, a kitchen fork should be easily inserted into the meat and the meat should slide off the fork. Smaller pieces of meat should be tender to the bite or easily cut with a fork.

Accompaniments to Simmered Meats

Simmered meats are often served with boiled or steamed vegetables, as in the case of corned beef and cabbage. Pickled meats are usually served with mustard or horseradish sauce on the side.

Procedure for Simmering Meats

1 Cut, trim or tie the meat according to the recipe.

2 Bring enough liquid to cover the meat completely to a boil. Too much liquid will leach off much of the meat's flavor; too little will leave a portion of the meat exposed, preventing it from cooking. Because the dish's final flavor is determined by the flavor of the liquid, add plenty of mirepoix, flavorings and seasonings to the liquid.

3 When simmering smoked or cured items, start them in cold water. This helps draw off some of the strong smoked or pickled flavors.

4 Add the meat to the liquid.

5 Reduce the heat to the desired temperature and cook until the meat is tender. Do not allow the cooking liquid to boil. Boiling results in a tough or overcooked and stringy product. If the simmered meat is to be served cold, a moister and juicier product can be achieved by removing the pot from the stove before the meat is fully cooked. The meat and the liquid can be cooled in a water bath (such as the one used for a stock, as described in Chapter 11, Stocks and Sauces). This allows the residual heat in the cooking liquid to finish cooking the meat.

New England Boiled Dinner

YIELD 12 Servings, 6 oz. (180 g) each	METHOD Simmering		MISE EN PLACE
Corned beef brisket, 8 lb. (3.8 kg)	1	1	• Prepare herb sachet.
White Stock	as needed	as needed	
Sachet:			
Bay leaves	2	2	
Dried thyme	½ tsp.	2 ml	
Peppercorns, cracked	½ tsp.	2 ml	
Parsley stems	10	10	
Mustard seeds	1 Tbsp.	15 ml	
Cinnamon sticks	2	2	
Allspice berries	4	4	
Baby red beets	24	24	
Baby turnips	24	24	
Baby carrots	24	24	
Brussels sprouts	24	24	
Pearl onions	24	24	
Cabbage wedges	12	12	

1 Place the beef in a pot and add enough stock to cover it. Add the sachet, bring to a boil and reduce to a simmer.

2 Simmer until the beef is tender, approximately 3 hours. Remove the beef and hold in a hotel pan in a small amount of the cooking liquid.

3 Peel or prepare the vegetables and potatoes as needed and cook separately in a portion of the cooking liquid.

4 Carve the beef and serve with two of each of the vegetables and Horseradish Cream Sauce (page 245).

Approximate values per 6-oz. (180-g) serving: **Calories** 1067, **Total fat** 58 g, **Saturated fat** 19 g, **Cholesterol** 296 mg, **Sodium** 3844 mg, **Total carbohydrates** 73 g, **Protein** 64 g, **Vitamin A** 27%, **Vitamin C** 200%, **Iron** 66%

❶ Placing the corned beef brisket and sachet in an appropriate pot and covering with stock.

❷ Presenting the carved beef with vegetable garnish.

COMBINATION COOKING METHODS FOR MEATS

Braising, stewing and *sous vide* cooking are referred to as combination cooking methods because both dry heat and moist heat are used to achieve the desired results.

Braising

Braised meats are first browned and then cooked in a liquid that becomes a sauce for the meat. A well-prepared braised dish has the rich flavor of the meat in the sauce and the moisture and flavor of the sauce in the meat. Braised meat should be fork tender but not falling apart. It should have an attractive color from the initial browning and final glazing.

Selecting Meats to Braise

Braising is often used with tougher cuts that are tenderized by the long, moist cooking process. Tough cuts from the chuck and shank are popular choices, as they are very flavorful and contain relatively large amounts of collagen, which adds richness to the finished product. Any meat to be braised should be well marbled with an ample fat content in order to produce a moist finished product. Large pieces of meat can be braised, then carved like a roast. Portion control cuts and diced meats can also be braised.

If tender cuts such as veal chops or pork chops are braised, the finished dish has a different flavor and texture than if the meats were cooked by a dry-heat method. Tender cuts require shorter cooking times because there is less connective tissue to break down.

Seasoning Meats to Braise

The seasoning and overall flavor of a braised dish is largely due to the quality of the cooking liquid and the mirepoix, vegetables, herbs, spices and other ingredients that season the meat as it cooks. Braised meats can also be marinated before cooking to tenderize them and add flavor. The marinade is then sometimes incorporated into the braising liquid. Salt and pepper may be added to the flour if the meat is dredged before it is browned, or the meat may be seasoned directly (although the salt may draw out moisture, wetting the surface of the meat and thereby inhibiting browning).

A standard herb sachet and a tomato product are usually added at the start of cooking. The tomato product adds flavor and color to the finished sauce as well as acid to tenderize the meat during the cooking process. Final seasoning should not take place until cooking is complete and the sauce will not be reduced further.

Cooking Temperatures for Braised Meats

Braised meats are always browned before simmering. As a general rule, smaller cuts are floured before browning; larger cuts are not. Flour seals the meat, promotes even browning and adds body to the sauce that accompanies the meat. Whether floured or not, the meat is browned in fat. After browning, white meats should be golden to amber in color; red meats should be dark brown. Do not brown the meat too quickly at too high a temperature because it is important to develop a well-caramelized surface. The caramelized surface adds color and flavor to the final product.

After the meat is browned, the braising liquid is added and brought to a boil over direct heat. The temperature is reduced to a simmer and the pot is covered. Cooking can be finished in the oven or on the stove top. The oven provides gentle, even heat without the risk of scorching. If braising is finished on the stove top, proper temperatures must be maintained throughout the cooking process, and care must be taken to prevent scorching or burning. Lower temperatures and longer cooking times result in more even cooking and absorption of the cooking liquid, providing a more flavorful final product.

Finishing Braised Meats

Near the end of the cooking process, the lid may be removed from oven-braised meats. Finishing braised meats without a cover makes it easier to baste the meat. Frequent basting produces an attractive glaze. As the basting liquid evaporates, the meat is browned

Properly browned meat to be braised or stewed is evenly well-caramelized.

and a strongly flavored glaze forms. Removing the lid also allows the cooking liquid to reduce, thickening it and concentrating its flavors for use as a sauce.

Doneness of Braised Meats

Braised meats are done when they are tender. A fork inserted into the meat should meet little resistance. Properly braised meats should remain intact and not fall apart when handled gently. Braised meats that fall apart or are stringy are overcooked. If the finished braised product is tough, it was probably undercooked or cooked at too high a temperature. If the entire dish lacks flavor, the meat may not have been properly browned or the cooking liquid may have been poorly seasoned.

Accompaniments to Braised Meats

Large braised items are often carved against the grain in thin slices and served with their sauce. Vegetables can be cooked with the braised meat, cooked separately and added when the main item has finished cooking or added at service. If the vegetables are cooked with the main item, they should be added to the pan at intervals based on their individual cooking times to prevent overcooking.

Procedure for Braising Meats

The liquid used for braising is usually thickened in one of three ways:

- With a roux added at the start of the cooking process; the roux thickens the sauce as the meat cooks.
- Prethickened before the meat is added by cooking the liquid with starch or roux until it coats the back of a spoon.
- Thickened after the meat is cooked either by puréeing the mirepoix or by using roux, arrowroot, cornstarch or other thickener.

The procedure for braising meats includes variations for whichever thickening method is selected.

1 Heat a small amount of oil in a heavy pan.
2 Dredge the meat to be braised in seasoned flour, if desired, and add meat to the oil.
3 Brown the meat well on all sides and remove from the pan.
4 Add a mirepoix or the appropriate vegetables to the pan and caramelize well. If using roux, it should be added at this time.
5 Add the appropriate stock or sauce so that when the meat is returned to the pan the liquid comes approximately one-third of the way up the side of the meat.
6 Add aromatics and seasonings.
7 Return the meat to the sauce. Tightly cover the pot and bring it to a simmer. Cook slowly either on the stove top or by placing the covered pot directly in an oven at 250–300°F (120–150°C).
8 Cook the item, basting or turning it often so that all sides of the meat benefit from the moisture and flavor of the sauce.
9 When the meat is tender, remove it from the pan and hold it in a warm place while the sauce is finished.
10 Degrease the sauce. The sauce may be reduced on the stove top to intensify its flavors. If the meat was braised in a stock, the stock may be thickened using a roux, arrowroot or cornstarch. Strain the sauce or, if desired, purée the mirepoix and other ingredients and return them to the sauce. Adjust the sauce's consistency and seasonings as desired.

MISE EN PLACE

- Peel onions and slice thinly.
- Peel and mince garlic.

1 Browning the brisket.

2 Sautéing the onions and garlic.

3 Basting the brisket. Note the proper amount of cooking liquid.

Aunt Ruthie's Pot Roast

YIELD 12 Servings, 6 oz. (180 g) meat and 4 oz. (120 g) sauce		METHOD Braising	
Vegetable oil		3 fl. oz.	90 ml
Beef brisket		6 lb.	2.8 kg
Onions, thinly sliced		3 lb.	1.4 kg
Garlic, minced		2 Tbsp.	30 ml
Brown veal stock		1 qt.	960 ml
Tomato sauce		1 pt.	480 ml
Brown sugar		4 oz.	120 g
Paprika		1 tsp.	5 ml
Dry mustard		2 tsp.	10 ml
Lemon juice		8 fl. oz.	240 ml
Ketchup		8 oz.	240 g
Red wine vinegar		8 fl. oz.	240 ml
Worcestershire sauce		2 fl. oz.	60 ml
Salt and pepper		TT	TT

1 Heat the oil in a large rondeau. Add the beef and brown thoroughly. Remove and reserve the brisket.

2 Add the onions and garlic to the pan and sauté.

3 Add the stock and tomato sauce to the pan.

4 Return the brisket to the pan, cover tightly and bring to a boil. Braise at 325°F (160°C) for ½ hours, basting or turning the brisket often.

5 Combine the remaining ingredients and add to the pan.

6 Continue cooking and basting the brisket until tender, approximately 1 hour. Add additional stock or water as needed during braising.

7 Remove the pan from the oven and remove the brisket, degrease the sauce and adjust its consistency and seasonings. Do not strain the sauce.

8 Slice the brisket against the grain and serve with the sauce.

Approximate values per serving: **Calories** 803, **Total fat** 52 g, **Saturated fat** 16 g, **Cholesterol** 224 mg, **Sodium** 3290 mg, **Total carbohydrates** 40 g, **Protein** 46 g, **Vitamin A** 25%, **Vitamin C** 100%

Stewing

Stewing, like braising, is a combination cooking method. In many ways, the procedures for stewing are identical to those for braising, although stewing is usually associated with smaller or bite-sized pieces of meat. There are two main types of stews: brown stews and white stews.

When making **brown stews**, the meat is first browned in fat; then a cooking liquid is added. The initial browning adds flavor and color to the finished product. The same characteristics apply to a good brown stew that apply to a good braised dish: It should be fork tender and have an attractive color and a rich flavor.

There are two types of **white stews**: **fricassees**, in which the meat is first cooked in a small amount of fat without coloring, then combined with a cooking liquid; and **blanquettes**, in which the meat is first blanched, then rinsed and added to a cooking liquid. A white stew should have the same flavor and texture characteristics as a brown stew, but should be white or ivory in color.

Selecting Meats to Stew

Stewing uses moist heat to tenderize meat just as braising does; therefore many of the same cuts can be used for stewing and braising. Meats that are to be stewed should be trimmed of excess fat and connective tissue and cut into 1- to 2-inch (2.5- to 5-centimeter) cubes.

Seasoning Meats to Stew

Stews, like braised meats, derive much of their flavor from their cooking liquid. A stew's seasoning and overall flavor is a direct result of the quality of the cooking liquid and the vegetables, herbs, spices and other ingredients added during cooking.

Cooking Temperatures for Stewed Meats

Meats for brown stews are first cooked at high temperatures over direct heat until well browned. Meats for fricassees are first sautéed at low temperatures so that they do not develop color.

Once the cooking liquid has been added and the moist-heat cooking process has begun, do not allow the stew to boil. Stews benefit from low-temperature cooking. When oven space and time permits, stews can be covered and finished in the oven.

Doneness of Stewed Meats

Stewed meats are done when they are fork tender. Test by removing a piece of meat to a plate and cutting it with a fork. Any vegetables that are cooked with the meat should be added at the proper times so that they and the meat are completely cooked at the same time. Many firm vegetables such as carrots, potatoes and turnips will cook in fifteen minutes. String beans, tender greens and leafy vegetables may take as little as five minutes. See Chapter 22, Vegetables.

Accompaniments to Stewed Meats

Stews are often complete meals in themselves, containing meat, vegetables and potatoes in one dish. Stews that do not contain a starch are often served with pasta or rice.

Procedure for Stewing Meats—Brown Stews

Red meats, lamb and game are used in brown stews. The procedure for making a brown stew is very similar to braising.

1 Trim the meat of excess fat and silverskin and cut into 1- to 2-inch (2.5- to 5-centimeter) pieces.
2 Dredge the meat in flour, if desired. Heat an appropriate-sized pan and add enough oil to cover the bottom. Cook the meat in the oil, browning it well on all sides. Onions and garlic can be added at this time and browned.
3 Add flour to the meat and fat and cook to make a roux, if desired.
4 Gradually add the liquid to the roux, stirring to prevent lumps. Bring the stew to a boil and reduce to a simmer.
5 Add a tomato product and an herb sachet or a bouquet garni. Cover and place in the oven at 250–300°F (120–150°C) or continue to simmer on the stove top until the meat is tender. Add other ingredients such as vegetables or potatoes at the proper time so that they will be done when the meat is tender.
6 When the meat is tender, remove the sachet or bouquet garni. Degrease the sauce. The meat may be strained out and the sauce thickened with roux, cornstarch or arrowroot or reduced to concentrate its flavors.
7 If not added during the cooking process, vegetables and other garnishes may be cooked separately and added to the finished stew. (When cooked separately, vegetables and garnishes will retain their color, shape and texture.)

Stew Terminology

Ragoût: [ra-GOO] A general term that refers to white or brown stews in which the meat is cooked by dry heat before a liquid is added. In French, *ragoût* means "to bring back the appetite."

Fricassee: [FRIHK-uh-see] A white ragoût usually made from white meat or small game, seared without browning and garnished with small onions and mushrooms.

Navarin: [nah-veh-RAHNG] A brown ragoût generally made with turnips, other root vegetables, onions, peas and lamb.

Blanquette: [blahn-KEHT] A white stew in which the meat is first blanched, then added to a stock or sauce to complete the cooking and tenderizing process. Blanquettes are finished with a liaison of egg yolks and heavy cream.

Chili con carne: A ragoût of ground or diced meat cooked with onions, chile peppers, cumin and other spices. Despite the objections of purists, chili sometimes contains beans.

Goulash: A beef stew with Hungarian origins made with onions and paprika and garnished with potatoes.

Tagine: [tah-JEAN] A North African stew in which meat, poultry, fish or vegetables are flavored with onions, cilantro, spices and aromatics and then braised over a fire in a covered earthenware vessel of the same name.

Adobo: A stew of Spanish origin in which meats are simmered with onions and spices in a savory red chili sauce. In the Philippines, *adobo* refers to a stew in which ingredients such as meats, poultry or fish are pickled in vinegar, oil and spices before cooking.

Brown Beef Stew

MISE EN PLACE

- Cube trimmed beef.
- Peel and chop onions into small dice.
- Peel and chop garlic.
- Prepare herb sachet.

YIELD 8 Servings, 8 oz. (240 g) each		METHOD Stewing	
Oil		2 fl. oz.	60 ml
Beef chuck or shank, trimmed and cut into 1½-in. (3.5-cm) cubes		4 lb. 8 oz.	2.1 kg
Salt		2 tsp.	10 ml
Black pepper		½ tsp.	2 ml
Onions, small dice		10 oz.	300 g
Garlic, chopped		1 tsp.	5 ml
Flour		1½ oz.	45 g
Red wine		8 fl. oz.	240 ml
Brown stock		1 qt.	960 ml
Tomato purée		4 oz.	120 g
Sachet:			
Bay leaves		2	2
Dried thyme		½ tsp.	2 ml
Peppercorns, crushed		½ tsp.	2 ml
Parsley stems		10	10

1 Heat a heavy pot until very hot and add the oil.

2 Season the beef with salt and pepper and add it to the pot, browning it well on all sides. Do not overcrowd the pot. If necessary, cook the beef in several batches.

3 Add the onions and garlic and sauté until the onions are slightly browned.

4 Add the flour and stir to make a roux. Brown the roux lightly.

5 Add the wine and stock slowly, stirring to prevent lumps.

6 Add the tomato purée and the sachet.

7 Bring to a simmer and cook covered until the beef is tender, approximately 1½–2 hours.

8 If desired, remove the cooked beef from the sauce and strain the sauce. Return the beef to the sauce.

9 Degrease the stew by skimming off the fat.

Variation:

Vegetables such as turnips, carrots, celery and pearl onions can be cooked separately and added to the stew as garnish.

Approximate values per 8-oz. (240-g) serving: **Calories** 590, **Total fat** 32 g, **Saturated fat** 11 g, **Cholesterol** 185 mg, **Sodium** 710 mg, **Total carbohydrates** 15 g, **Protein** 58 g, **Vitamin A** 45%, **Iron** 40%

❶ Browning the beef.

❷ Sautéing the garlic and onions until slightly browned.

❸ Adding the flour to make a roux.

4 Adding the red wine.

5 Adding the tomato purée and sachet.

6 Degreasing the stew.

Procedure for Stewing Meats—Braised White Stews (Fricassees)

The procedure for making fricassees is similar to the procedure for brown stews. The primary difference is that the meat is sautéed but not allowed to brown. The braised white stew (fricassee) procedure outlined here is the basis for Veal Fricassee (page 370).

1 Trim the meat of excess fat and silverskin and cut into 1- to 2-inch (2.5- to 5-centimeter) pieces.

2 Heat a pan that is large enough to accommodate the meat without crowding, and add enough oil to cover the bottom. Add the meat (and often an onion) to the pan and cook without browning.

3 Sprinkle the meat (and onion) with flour and cook to make a blond roux.

4 Gradually add the liquid, stirring to prevent lumps. Bring the stew to a boil and reduce to a simmer.

5 Add a bouquet garni and seasonings. Cover the stew and place in the oven or continue to simmer on the stove top, being careful not to burn or scorch the stew.

6 Continue to cook until the meat is tender. If the sauce is too thin, remove the meat from the sauce and hold the meat in a warm place. Reduce the sauce to the proper consistency on the stove top or thicken it by adding a small amount of blond roux, cornstarch or arrowroot.

Procedure for Stewing Meats—Simmered White Stews (Blanquettes)

Unlike fricassees, blanquettes contain meat that is blanched, not sautéed. (Because the meat is cooked only by moist heat and never by dry heat, the blanquette cooking process is not a true combination cooking method; nevertheless, because of its striking similarities to stewing, it is included here.) The most common blanquette is made with veal and is known as blanquette de veau, but any white meat or lamb can be prepared in this manner using a variety of garnishes. The simmered white stew (blanquette) procedure outlined here is the basis for Blanquette of Lamb (page 384).

1 Trim the meat of excess fat and silverskin and cut into 1- to 2-inch (2.5- to 5-centimeter) pieces.

2 Blanch the cubed meat by placing the meat in an appropriate pot, covering with cool water, adding salt, and bringing it rapidly to a boil. Drain the water. Rinse the meat to remove any impurities.

3 Return the meat to the pot and add enough stock to cover. Add a bouquet garni, salt and pepper. Simmer until the meat is tender, approximately 1–1½ hours.

4 Strain the meat from the stock. Discard the bouquet garni. Bring the stock to a boil, thicken it with a blond roux and simmer for 15 minutes.

5 Return the meat to the thickened stock. Add a liaison of cream and egg yolks, as explained in Chapter 11, Stocks and Sauces, to enrich and thicken the stew. Heat the stew to a simmer. Do not boil or the egg yolks will curdle.

6 If any vegetables are to be added, they should be cooked separately and added to the thickened stock with the meat.

7 Adjust the seasonings with a few drops of lemon juice, nutmeg or salt and pepper as needed.

Cooking *Sous Vide*

Sous vide is a combination cooking method that involves cooking meats sealed in food grade plastic pouches at precise temperatures. Tough cuts of meat may be cooked *sous vide* to become tender while retaining flavor. Tender cuts of meat may be cooked evenly and to precise temperatures with little shrinkage. Browning the meat after *sous vide* cooking develops flavor and a surface texture.

Selecting Meats to Cook *Sous Vide*

Like braising, *sous vide* can be used to cook tougher cuts of meat such those from the chuck or shank. Because they are cooked in a sealed environment, these tough cuts retain more moisture and shrink less when cooked *sous vide* than when conventionally braised or stewed. As when braising or stewing, when cooking *sous vide* select cuts that are well-marbled to produce a tender finished product.

Tender cuts of meat suitable for broiling, grilling or sautéing such as cuts from the loin and rib or poultry may also be cooked *sous vide*. These cuts are cooked to precise temperatures that preserve their moistness without drying out. Tender cuts of meat cooked *sous vide* will cook evenly from the center to the edge.

Meat to be cooked *sous vide* should be trimmed of excess fat. It should be cut to a uniform size and thickness. To ensure that the meat reaches safe internal temperatures quickly, cut the meat into individual portions or small pieces. Package the meat in a single layer in each pouch.

Seasoning Meats to Cook *Sous Vide*

Adding aromatics, herbs and oil to the pouches before cooking meat *sous vide* enhances the flavor of the finished dish. When preparing tough cuts of meat that will be cooked for an extended period in the water bath, add salt *after* the meat is cooked. This prevents the meat from developing a tough cured texture.

Temperatures for Cooking *Sous Vide*

When cooking tougher cuts of meat *sous vide*, the optimal temperature range is between 148°F (64°C) and 185°F (90°C). When tough meats are cooked at the lower temperatures in this range, they retain a pink color unlike conventionally simmered or braised meats. But due to the long holding time at that temperature, from 8 to 48 hours, the collagen will soften and the meat will be tender. Small changes in the temperatures and cooking times affect the texture of the cooked meat.

For tender cuts of meat such as steaks, cook to the desired internal temperature corresponding to the degree of doneness—rare, medium rare, medium or well done—making certain that the meat is in the temperature danger zone (41–135°F/5–57°C) for less than 4 hours. (See Table 2.2.)

Doneness of Meat Cooked *Sous Vide*

The temperature of the water bath and the time in the water bath determine when the meat is done. Tougher cuts of meat cooked *sous vide* may be tender enough to cook with a fork or they may have a firmer texture depending on the temperature of the water bath and the time. Once the meat reaches the desired temperature, it can be held in the heated water bath for 2–3 hours.

⚠ Safety Alert

Sous Vide *Cooking Temperatures and Time*

Foods packaged in plastic pouches and cooked *sous vide* are highly susceptible to bacterial contamination. Although a range of cooking temperatures and times may be used to prepare foods *sous vide*, to ensure food safety, follow the temperatures and cooking times exactly as outlined in the recipes provided.

Tender cuts of meat cooked *sous vide* are done when they reach the desired internal temperature. To take the internal temperature of meat in a *sous vide* pouch, apply a piece of **closed cell foam tape** to the top of the pouch. Then pierce the tape with a **needle probe thermometer** designed for use with *sous vide* bags. The tape will seal itself after the probe is removed. Individual cuts of meat approximately 1-inch (2.5-centimeters) thick should be fully cooked in 1–2 hours. Meats cooked *sous vide* do not overcook because the internal temperature will not exceed the precise temperature of the water bath. (Although the meat will not overcook, it may soften and become mushy if left for too long.) To ensure that the meat stays out of the temperature danger zone, tender cuts of meats and poultry cooked *sous vide* should be finished and served immediately.

Finishing Meat Cooked *Sous Vide*

Because there is no Maillard browning when cooking *sous vide*, the meats should be quickly browned in a sauté pan, on a grill, under a broiler or salamander or with a propane torch before serving. This final browning adds the caramelized flavors and colors associated with many meat preparations.

Accompaniments to Meats Cooked *Sous Vide*

Cooking liquids collect in the *sous vide* pouch but rarely in sufficient quantity to properly garnish the meat. Generally any accompanying sauce is prepared separately. Many of the sauce suggestions found in Tables 11.4 and 11.6 are appropriate accompaniments.

> **⚠ Safety Alert**
>
> Sous Vide *Sanitation*
>
> Food safety is of utmost concern when using *sous vide* techniques because of the low cooking temperatures. To prevent the growth of microorganisms, any food to be cooked *sous vide* must be chilled below the temperature danger zone (41°F/5°C) before cooking. Keep all cutting boards, knives and food contact surfaces clean and sanitary and wear clean disposable gloves. Use only the freshest unblemished ingredients. Consult your local health department for regulations for preparing food *sous vide*. Special permission and a HACCP plan may be required.

Procedure for Preparing Foods Sous Vide

1. Assemble sanitizing equipment, single-use gloves and thermometer. Use a water oven or an immersion circulator to bring a water bath to the desired temperature.

2. Cut, trim or otherwise prepare meat to be cooked *sous vide*. Sear meat to add flavor to the meat as it cooks, if desired. (Quickly chill any seared meat in the refrigerator below the temperature danger zone [41°F/5°C] before proceeding.)

3. Wearing single-use gloves to prevent cross-contamination with microorganisms, place the meat in a single layer in plastic pouches. Add fat, seasonings and cooking liquids as desired.

4. Vacuum seal the pouches using a chamber vacuum machine.

5. Place the pouches in the heated water bath or water oven allowing enough space for the water to flow freely around them without overcrowding. Doneness is determined by temperature or texture of the food.

6. Season, sear and serve the meat immediately. Or, for later service, prepare an ice and water bath with salt. Transfer the pouches of cooked food to the ice and water bath. Leave them in the ice and water bath for at least 30 minutes. Pouches of cooked food must be chilled to below 41°F/5°C or lower in 2 hours or less. Label the pouches with the date, the time of production and the use-by date, then refrigerate.

7. To serve meat previously cooked and chilled, reheat the pouch in a water bath until the meat reaches the desired temperature. Remove the meat from the pouch then season and sear it quickly before serving.

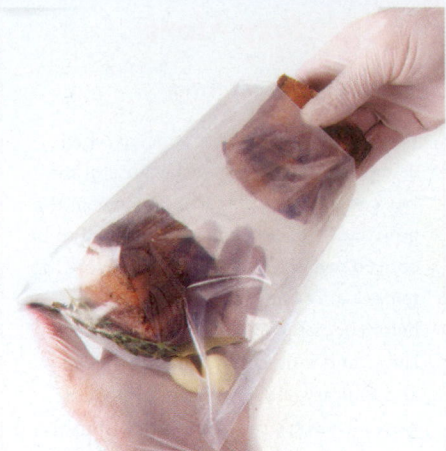

① Sliding the chilled, seared short ribs into a plastic pouch.

② The *sous vide* braised short ribs are pink in color and tender yet firm after 16 hours of cooking.

Sous Vide Short Ribs

YIELD 4 Servings	METHOD *Sous Vide* Braising	
Vegetable oil	2 fl. oz.	60 ml
Beef short ribs, 5 oz. each, chilled	4	4
Garlic cloves	2	2
Bay leaves	2	2
Sprigs of thyme	2	2
Salt and pepper	TT	TT
Mashed potatoes	as needed for garnish	
Carrots, green beans, broccoli or other vegetables, cooked	as needed for garnish	
Brown Sauce (page 225)	as needed for garnish	

1 Heat a water bath with a thermal circulator or a water oven to 158°F (70°C).

2 Heat oil in a large heavy sauté pan over medium high heat. Sear the short ribs on all sides.

3 Remove the short ribs from the pan. Quickly chill them below the temperature danger zone (41°F/5°C) in a single layer on a sheet pan in the refrigerator.

4 Prepare two plastic pouches for *sous vide* cooking. Place one garlic clove, a bay leaf and a sprig of thyme into each bag. Slide two chilled, seared short ribs into each bag. Vacuum seal the bags.

5 Cook the sealed bags of short ribs for 16–24 hours in the thermal circulator.

6 For service, remove the short ribs from the pouches. Season them with salt and pepper. Sear them briefly in a heated skillet until lightly browned. Serve them with mashed potatoes, vegetable garnishes and Brown Sauce as desired.

Approximate values per serving: **Calories** 440, **Total fat** 42 g, **Saturated fat** 13 g, **Cholesterol** 65 mg, **Sodium** 35 mg, **Total carbohydrates** 0 g, **Protein** 15 g

QUESTIONS FOR DISCUSSION

1 What is connective tissue composed of, and where is it found? What happens to connective tissue in meat at normal cooking temperatures?

2 Describe the difference between primals, subprimals and fabricated cuts of meat. Why is it important to be skilled in meat fabrication?

3 Discuss the government's role in regulating the marketing and sale of meat.

4 At what temperature should fresh meat be stored? At what temperature should frozen meat be stored?

5 Would it be better to grill or braise a piece of meat that contains a great deal of connective tissue? Explain your answer.

6 List three ways to optimize the taste and texture of lean meats. What cooking techniques can be used to compensate for the lack of fat?

7 List four ways that meat can be made more tender before cooking. Discuss the usefulness of each technique.

8 Compare and contrast sautéing and pan-frying meats.

9 Compare and contrast braising and stewing meats.

10 Compare and contrast conventional braising and *sous vide* braising of meats.

Beef 14

After studying this chapter, you will be able to:

- identify the primal, subprimal and fabricated cuts of beef
- describe and perform basic butchering procedures
- explain appropriate cooking methods for different cuts of beef
- apply appropriate cooking methods to several common cuts of beef

Beef is the meat of domesticated cattle. Most of the beef people in the United States eat comes from steers, which are male cattle castrated as calves and specifically raised for beef. Although U.S. diners are consuming less beef today than before, Americans still consume far more beef than any other meat. The beef in the U.S. is leaner than that of years past, thanks to advances in animal husbandry and closer trimming of exterior fat. Cattle ranchers and small regional farmers are rediscovering older breeds of livestock and new ways to fabricate beef, bringing excitement to the assortment of beef products available to chefs and consumers.

PRIMAL AND SUBPRIMAL CUTS OF BEEF

After the steer is slaughtered, the carcass is cut into four pieces (called **quarters**) for easy handling. This is done by first splitting the carcass down the backbone into two bilateral halves called **sides** of beef. Each half is divided into the **forequarter** (the front portion) and the **hindquarter** (the rear portion) by cutting along the natural curvature between the 12th and 13th ribs. The quartered carcass is then further reduced into the primal cuts and the subprimal and fabricated cuts.

The eight primal cuts of beef are the chuck, brisket and shank, rib, short plate, short loin, sirloin, flank and round. Figure 14.1 illustrates the relationship between a steer's bone structure and the eight primal cuts. It is important to know the location of bones when cutting or working with meats. This makes meat fabrication and carving easier and aids in identifying cuts. Figure 14.2 shows the primal cuts of beef and their location on the carcass. An entire beef carcass can range in weight from 500 to more than 800 pounds (240 to 380 kg).

FOREQUARTER PRIMAL CUTS OF BEEF

The forequarter consists of the four primal cuts, the chuck, the brisket and shank, the rib and the short plate. The forequarter represents approximately 55 percent of the carcass weight.

Chuck

The primal **chuck** is the animal's shoulder; it accounts for approximately 28 percent of carcass weight. It contains a portion of the backbone, five rib bones and portions of the blade and arm bones.

Because an animal constantly uses its shoulder muscles, chuck contains a high percentage of connective tissue and is quite tough. This tough cut of beef, however, is one of the most flavorful and least costly.

The primal chuck is used less frequently than other primal cuts in food service operations. If cooked whole, the chuck is difficult to cut or carve because of the large number of bones and relatively small muscle groups that travel in different directions. When fabricating their own meats, chefs often purchase beef chuck as **chuck square cut**, which is a two-piece cut. The smaller of the two pieces, both of which are shown here, is referred to as the shoulder or **shoulder clod**.

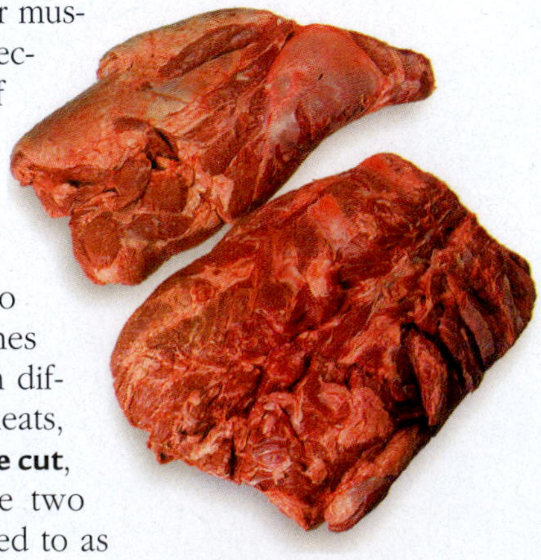

Chuck square cut (two pieces)

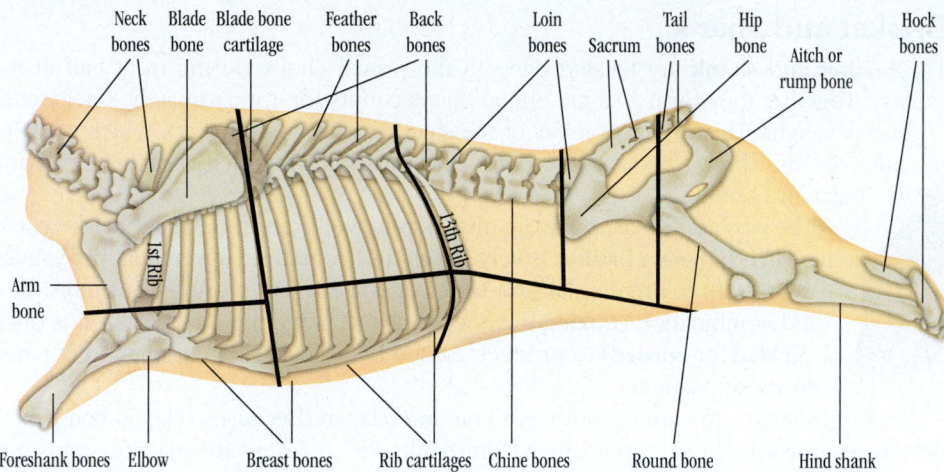

Figure 14.1 The skeletal structure of a steer.

Neck bones • Blade bone • Blade bone cartilage • Feather bones • Back bones • Loin bones • Sacrum • Tail bones • Hip bone • Aitch or rump bone • Hock bones

Arm bone • 1st Rib • 13th Rib

Foreshank bones • Elbow • Breast bones • Rib cartilages • Chine bones • Round bone • Hind shank

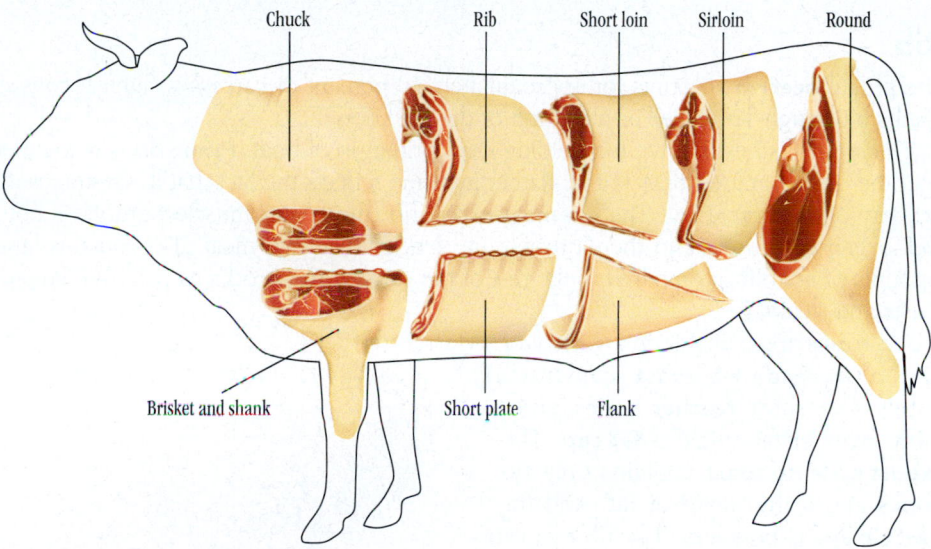

Figure 14.2 The eight primal cuts of beef.

Chuck • Rib • Short loin • Sirloin • Round

Brisket and shank • Short plate • Flank

A Cow by Any Other Name . . .

Cattle is the collective name for all domesticated oxen (genus *Bos*). Cattle are classified as follows:

Bulls: Male cattle, raised for breeding (usually not to be eaten).

Calves: Young heifers or bulls prized for their meat.

Cows: Female cattle after their first calving, raised in the United States principally for milk and calf production. In France, cows are used for beef when they are no longer needed for milk.

Heifers: Young female cattle that have not given birth (calved).

Stags: Male cattle castrated after maturity, principally used for dog food.

Steers: Male cattle castrated prior to maturity and principally raised for beef.

The primal chuck produces several fabricated cuts: cross rib pot roast, chuck short ribs, cubed or tenderized steaks, stew meat and ground chuck used to make hamburgers, meatloaf and related items. Because chuck meat is less tender, these fabricated cuts usually benefit from moist-heat cooking or combination cooking methods such as stewing and braising. There are exceptions, however. The beef industry is developing new products from affordable and underutilized cuts of meat. The **shoulder top blade**, cut from the shoulder clod of the chuck can be cut into **blade steaks (flat iron)**. This cut is gaining popularity as an alternative and less costly steak suitable for dry-heat cooking. The whole shoulder clod is a popular cut for traditional barbecue. The slow cooking of the barbeque method tenderizes the tough cut.

Shoulder top blade

Blade steak (flat iron)

boxed beef industry terminology for primal and subprimal cuts of beef that are vacuum sealed and packed into cardboard boxes for shipping from the packing plant to retailers and food service operations

Certified Angus Beef a brand created in 1978 to distinguish the highest-quality beef produced from descendants of the black, hornless Angus cattle of Scotland. The meat must meet American Angus Association standards for yield, marbling and age and be graded as high choice or prime

Brisket (boneless)

Brisket and Shank

The **brisket** and **shank** are located beneath the primal chuck on the front half of the carcass. Together they form a single primal that accounts for approximately 8 percent of carcass weight. This primal consists of the steer's breast (the brisket), which contains the ribs and breast bone, and its arm (the **foreshank**), which contains the shank meat and bone.

The ribs and breast bone are always removed from the brisket before cooking. The **boneless brisket** is very tough and contains a substantial percentage of fat, both intermuscular and subcutaneous. It is well suited for moist-heat and combination cooking methods such as simmering or braising. It is often **pickled** (or **corned**) to produce corned beef brisket, or cured and peppered to make pastrami.

Beef foreshanks are very flavorful and high in collagen. Because collagen converts to gelatin when cooked using moist heat, foreshanks are excellent for making soups and stocks. Ground shank meat is often used to help clarify and flavor consommés because of its rich flavor and high collagen content. **Marrow**, the soft tissue in the center of the foreshank and hindshank bones, is considered a delicacy when cooked and added to sauces or spread on toast. (The **hindshank** is the animal's leg; the term *shank* generally is used to refer to either the foreshank or the hindshank.)

Rib

The primal **beef rib** accounts for approximately 10 percent of carcass weight. It consists of ribs 6 through 12 as well as a portion of the backbone.

This primal is best known for yielding roast prime rib of beef. **Prime rib** is not named after the quality grade USDA Prime. Rather its name reflects the fact that it constitutes the majority of the primal cut. The **eye meat** of the rib (the center muscle portion) is not a well-exercised muscle and therefore is quite tender. The eye meat also contains large amounts of marbling compared to the rest of the carcass and produces rich, full-flavored roasts and steaks.

Oven-ready rib roast

Rib roasts are available in a variety of styles. The **oven-ready rib roast** contains rib bones, the short **feather bones** and a thick layer of fat called a **fat cap**. The **export style rib roast** contains only rib bones and a thin layer of fat. And the **beef rib eye** is boneless. The rib eye can be cut into boneless rib eye steaks (also called entrecôtes). The rib bones that are separated from the rib eye meat are quite meaty and flavorful and can be served as barbecued beef ribs. (The ends of the rib bones that are trimmed off the primal rib to produce the rib roast are known as beef short ribs. This is one of several sources for beef short ribs; beef short ribs are also cut from the primal short plate as discussed in the following section as well as from the primal chuck.)

Export style rib roast

Beef rib eye

Short Plate

The **short plate** is located directly below the primal rib; it accounts for approximately 9 percent of the overall weight of the carcass. The short plate contains rib bones and cartilage and is the source for short ribs and skirt steak. **Beef short ribs** are meaty, yet high in connective tissue, and are best when braised. **Skirt steak**, which is the animal's diaphragm muscle, is often marinated and grilled as fajitas. Other, less meaty portions of the short plate are trimmed and ground for hamburger and related uses.

Skirt steak

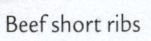

Beef short ribs

HINDQUARTER PRIMAL CUTS OF BEEF

The hindquarter consists of four primal cuts: the short loin, sirloin, flank and round. It represents approximately 45 percent of the carcass weight.

Short Loin

The primal **short loin** is the anterior (front) portion of the beef loin. The short loin is located just behind the rib and is the first primal cut of the hindquarter when the side of beef is divided into a forequarter and hindquarter. It accounts for approximately 8 percent of carcass weight.

T-bone steak   Porterhouse steak

The short loin contains a single rib, the 13th, and a portion of the backbone. With careful butchering, this small primal can yield several subprimal and fabricated cuts, which are among the most tender, popular and expensive cuts of beef.

The short loin eye muscle, a continuation of the rib eye muscle, runs along the top of the T-shaped bones that form the backbone. Beneath the loin eye muscle on the other side of the backbone is the **tenderloin**, the most tender beef cut of all.

When the short loin is cut in cross-sections with the bone in, it produces—starting with the rib end of the short loin—**club steaks** (which do not contain any tenderloin), **T-bone steaks** (which contain only a small portion of tenderloin) and **porterhouse** steaks (which are cut from the sirloin end of the short loin and contain a large portion of tenderloin).

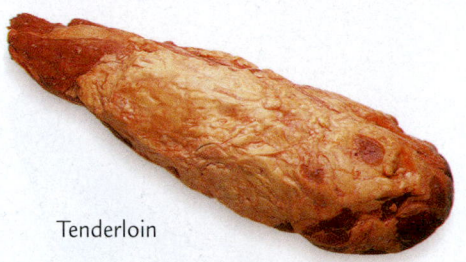

Tenderloin

The whole tenderloin can also be removed and cut into **châteaubriand**, **filet mignon** and **tournedos**. A portion of the tenderloin is located in the sirloin portion of the loin. When the entire beef loin is divided into the primal short loin and primal sirloin, the large end of the tenderloin (the butt tenderloin) is separated from the remainder of the tenderloin and remains in the sirloin; the smaller end of the tenderloin (the short tenderloin) remains in the short loin. If the tenderloin is to be kept whole, it must be removed before the short loin and sirloin are separated. The loin eye meat can be removed from the bones, producing a boneless **strip loin**, which is very tender and can be roasted or cut into boneless strip steaks.

Strip loin

Another cut is found between the flank and the plate near the kidneys. The **hanging tender** is close to the backbone between the 12th and 13th ribs. It is a pair of lean V-shaped muscles approximately 7 inches long. Each **hanger steak** weighs about 8–12 ounces (250–360 grams). Also known as bistro steaks or butcher's tenderloins, hanger steaks are highly flavorful and popular with chefs. The hanger steak benefits from being marinated and should be seared, grilled or broiled rare to medium rare, then sliced on the bias for service.

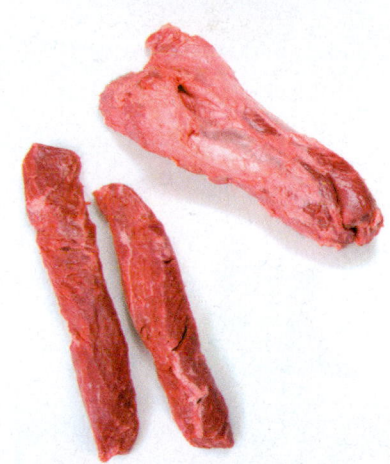

Hanging tender (top) and hanger steaks (bottom)

Sirloin

The primal **sirloin** is located in the hindquarter, between the short loin and the round. It accounts for approximately 7 percent of carcass weight and contains part of the backbone as well as a portion of the hip bone.

The sirloin produces bone-in or boneless roasts such as the **top sirloin butt** and the **bottom sirloin butt tri tip**, steaks that are flavorful and tender. With the exception of the tenderloin portion, however, the subprimals and fabricated cuts from the sirloin are not as tender as those from the strip loin. (A portion of the tenderloin called the butt tenderloin is located in the sirloin portion of the loin.)

Top sirloin butt

Cuts from the sirloin are cooked using dry-heat methods such as broiling, grilling or roasting.

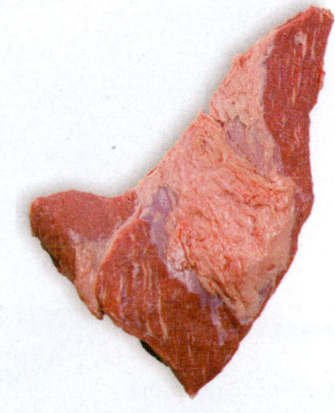

Bottom sirloin butt tri tip

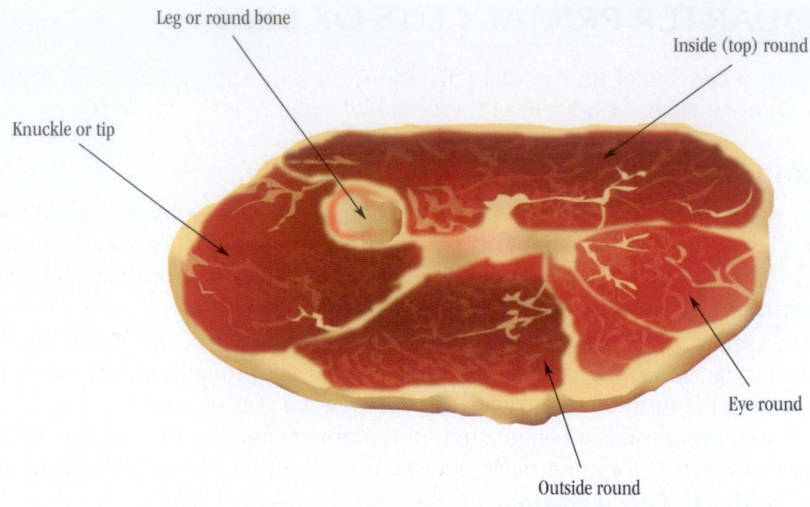

Figure 14.3 Cross cut of muscles in a whole primal round.

Flank steak

Flank

The **flank** is located directly beneath the loin, posterior to (behind) the short plate. The flank accounts for approximately 6 percent of carcass weight. It contains no bones.

Although quite flavorful, it is a less tender cut with a good deal of fat and connective tissue. Flank meat is usually trimmed and ground, with the exception of the **flank steak**, which is often marinated, broiled and sliced thinly to prepare a dish known as **London broil**.

Round

The **primal round** is very large, weighing as much as 100 pounds (45 kilos) and accounting for approximately 24 percent of carcass weight. It is the hind leg of the animal and contains the round bone, aitch bone, shank bone and tail bones.

Meat from the round is flavorful, fairly tender and reasonably priced. The round yields a wide variety of subprimal and fabricated cuts: the **inside (top) round**, **eye round**, **outside round** (the outside round and the eye round together are called the **bottom round**), knuckle and hindshank with the leg bone. See Figure 14.3. Steaks cut from the round are less tender, but because they have large muscles and limited intermuscular fat, the top round and knuckle make good roasts when cooked rare and sliced thin to preserve tenderness. The bottom round is best when braised. The **steamship round** is very large roast weighing as much as 70 pounds (30 kilos), comprising nearly the entire primal round. It is usually roasted whole and carved to order for special events or buffets.

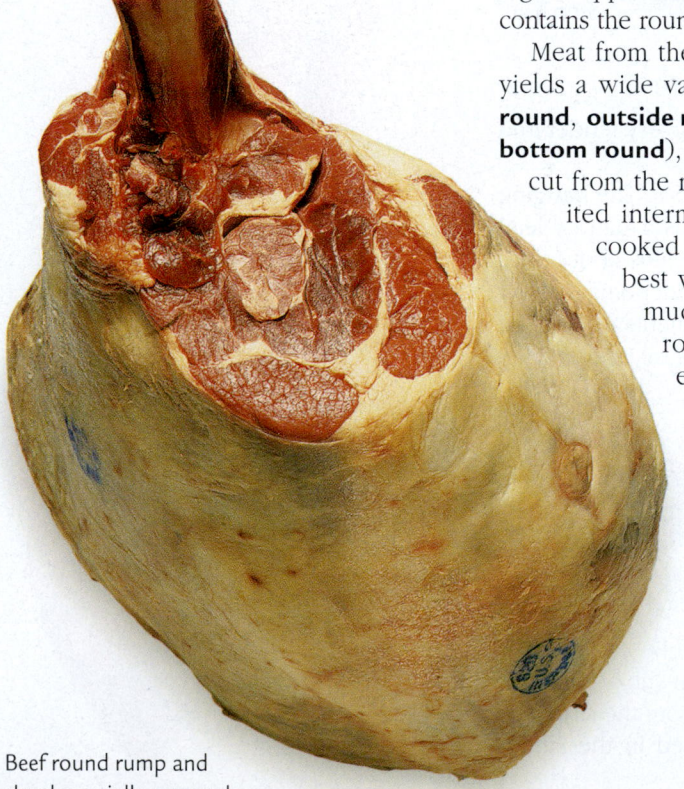

Beef round rump and shank partially removed (steamship round)

Top (or inside) round

BEEF ORGAN MEATS

Several organ meats are used in food service operations. This group of products is known as **offal**. It includes cuts that come from either a gland or a muscle. Glandular meats, which are tender with no connective tissue, are the brain, kidney and liver. They are best when cooked briefly using dry heat cooking methods although brains can be poached before pan frying. Muscle meats are the heart, tongue, tripe (stomach lining) and oxtails. With the exception of the heart, which can be grilled or sautéed, these muscle cuts benefit from moist-heat cooking and are often used in soup, stew or braised dishes. **Beef tongue** is a fatty meat that should be cooked gently by poaching. After cooking, the tough outer membrane of the tongue can be peeled away easily and the rich, flavorful flesh sliced for sandwiches, or paired with a sauce made from the poaching liquid.

Tripe is the lining of a cow's stomach. It is usually blanched then cut into strips and simmered in a highly seasoned liquid until tender. Despite the name, **oxtails** refers to any bovine tail. Oxtails are usually cut into short lengths for stewing.

Tongue

offal [OFF-uhl] also called variety meats; edible entrails (e.g., the heart, kidneys, liver, sweetbreads and tongue) and extremities (e.g., oxtail and pig's feet) of an animal.

Tripe

Oxtails

NUTRITION INFORMATION FOR BEEF

Beef is a major source of protein and the primary food source of zinc as well as B vitamins, trace minerals and other nutrients. Although well-marbled beef does contain a high percentage of saturated fat, lean cuts of beef such as eye round and top round roasts, top sirloin and shoulder pot roast have less fat than chicken thighs, a standard level of comparison. Excess fat should be trimmed as much as possible before cooking and serving.

BUTCHERING PROCEDURES FOR BEEF

Although many food service operations buy their beef previously cut and portioned, it is still important for a cook to be able to fabricate cuts of beef and perform basic butchering tasks. Performing some basic fabrication procedures in the kitchen saves money and allows chefs to cut the meat to their exact specifications. Given the growing interest in purchasing locally-grown ingredients, the ability to break down larger cuts of beef is even more essential because smaller producers usually sell beef split or quartered. (See Table 14.1 for a list of standard fabricated cuts.)

Classic Flavor Combinations for Beef

Antonin Carême once said that "beef is the soul of cooking." Beef's flavor stands up well to most any sauce and seasoning. From pungent basil pesto on grilled strip steak to the assertive flavors of chilli powder in a hearty stew, beef shines in robust preparations. Yet tender cuts, such as the loin, marry well with such subtle sauces as tarragon-scented hollandaise or red wine reductions.

Beef Sustainability

The increasing rate of global beef consumption concerns many people because of the land, water and feed required to raise animals for human consumption. Transporting meat to kitchens and storing it under refrigeration requires energy in the form of gas, oil and electricity. There is also the environmental impact of animal waste and gas emissions to consider. One step chefs can take to mitigate these issues is to choose suppliers committed to raising animals sustainably. Local farms may be a good alternative to national meat suppliers. Buying locally also reduces the energy used to deliver meat to your establishment.

A number of leaders in the food industry recommend that chefs also work to reduce the amount of beef and other animal products that diners consume because overconsumption of meat can lead to obesity and chronic diseases. Decreasing the amount of meat consumed each week, for example, may go a long way towards improving the environment and preserving our health.

Here are some additional steps you can take to reduce the amount of meat, particularly beef, you serve while still providing your customers with appealing menu options.

- Reduce the portion size of the meat served when possible. In many instances, the difference between a 7 and an 8-ounce steak may be imperceptible.

- Balance items served on each plate between beef, for example, and beans, whole grains, vegetables and greens.

- Use beef as a condiment in dishes where this is appropriate. The recipe for Beef Fajitas on page 342, for example, emphasizes a small portion of flavorful skirt steak accompanied by fresh bell peppers, guacamole and tomato salsa.

Procedure for Cutting a New York Steak from a Boneless Strip Loin

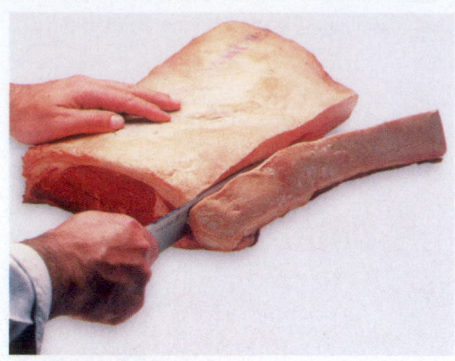

1 Square up the strip loin by trimming off the lip so it extends 1–2 inches (2.5–5 centimeters) from the eye muscle.

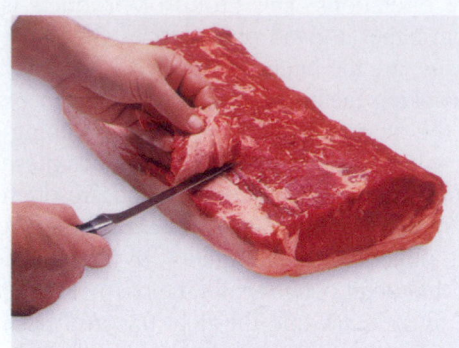

2 Turn the strip over and trim off any fat or connective tissue.

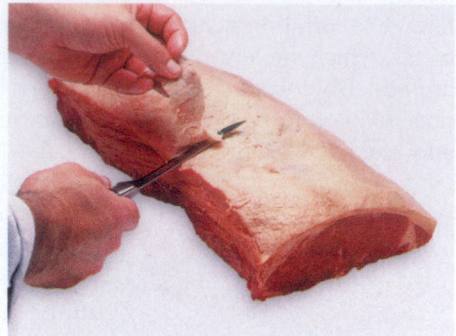

3 Turn the strip back over and trim the fat covering to a uniform thickness of ¼ inch (6 millimeters).

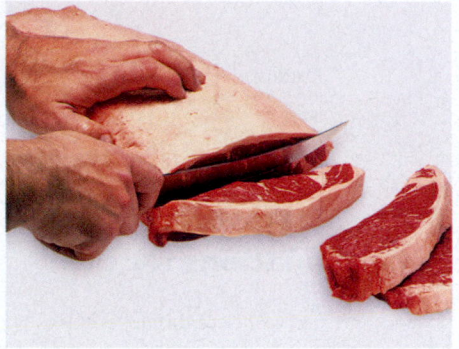

4 Cut the steaks to the thickness or weight desired.

5 The eye meat of steaks located on the sirloin end of the strip is divided by a strip of connective tissue. Steaks cut from this area are called **vein steaks** and are inferior to steaks cut from the rib end of the strip.

Procedure for Trimming a Full Beef Tenderloin and Cutting It into Châteaubriand, Filet Mignon and Tender Tips

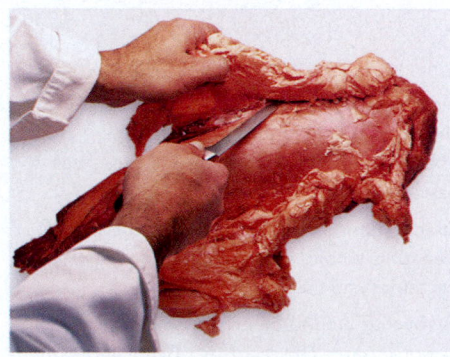

1 Cut and pull the excess fat from the entire tenderloin to expose the meat.

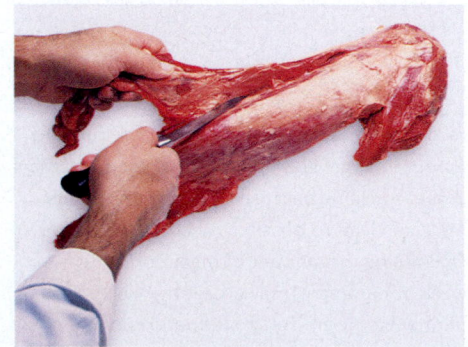

2 Remove the chain muscle from the side of the tenderloin. Although it contains much connective tissue, the chain muscle may be trimmed and the meat used in soups, stews or ground.

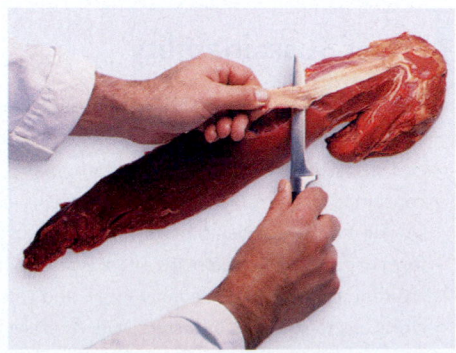

3 Trim away all of the fat and silverskin. Do so by loosening a small piece of silverskin; then, holding the loosened silverskin tightly with one hand, cut it away in long strips, angling the knife up toward the silverskin slightly so that only the silverskin is removed and no meat is wasted.

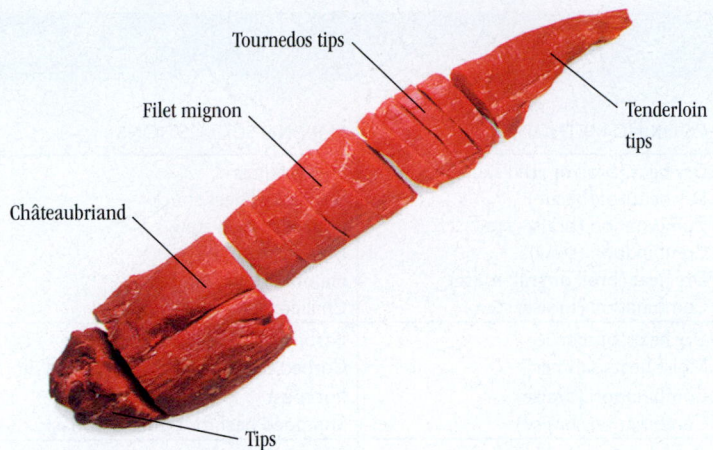

The completely portioned beef tenderloin producing (from left to right) tips, châteaubriand, filet mignon, tournedos tips and tenderloin tips.

Procedure for Butterflying Meats

Many cuts of boneless meats such as tenderloin steaks and boneless pork chops can be butterflied to create a thinner cut that has a greater surface area and cooks more quickly.

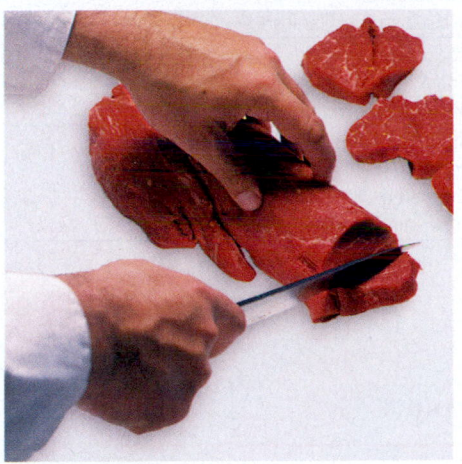

❶ Make the first cut nearly all the way through the meat, keeping it attached by leaving approximately ¼ inch (6 millimeters) uncut.

❷ Make a second cut, this time cutting all the way through, completely removing the steak from the tenderloin.

Kobe Beef

Kobe beef is an exclusive type of beef traditionally produced in Kobe, Japan, from specific Japanese breeds of cattle (Jp. *wagyu*). These animals are fed a special diet, which includes beer to stimulate the animal's appetite during summer months. The animals are massaged with sake to relieve stress and muscle stiffness in the belief that calm, contented cattle produce better-quality meat. This special treatment produces meat with generous and uniform marbling. It is extraordinarily tender and full-flavored, and extraordinarily expensive. Kobe Beef America introduced Wagyu cattle to the United States in 1976. KBA's cattle are raised without hormones and the meat is dry-aged for 21 days prior to sale.

USING COMMON CUTS OF BEEF

TABLE 14.1

PRIMAL	SUBPRIMAL OR FABRICATED CUT	IMPS	COOKING METHODS	SERVING SUGGESTIONS
Chuck	Top blade (flat iron)	114D	Dry heat (broil or grill; sauté)	Steak; fajitas
	Beef chuck, boneless	115	Dry heat (barbecue)	Barbecued beef chuck
			Combination (braise; stew)	Pot roast; beef stew
	Stew meat	135A	Combination (stew)	Beef stew
	Ground beef	136	Dry heat (broil or grill; roast)	Hamburger; meatloaf
			Combination (braise; stew)	Chili con carne; beef stew
Brisket and shank	Brisket	120	Dry heat (barbecue)	Barbecued brisket
			Moist heat (simmer)	Corned beef; New England boiled dinner
			Combination (braise)	Pot roast
	Shank	117	Combination (braise)	Shredded beef for tamales or hash
Rib	Oven-ready rib roast	109	Dry heat (roast)	Roast prime rib
	Rib eye	112A	Dry heat (roast)	Roast prime rib
	Rib eye steak	1112	Dry heat (broil or grill; sauté)	Steak; bone-in rib eye steak; Delmonico steak,
Short plate	Skirt steak	121D	Dry heat (broil or grill; sauté)	Steak; fajitas
	Short ribs	123A	Dry heat (barbecue)	Barbecued ribs
			Combination (braise)	Braised short ribs
Short loin	Porterhouse or T-bone steaks	1173, 1174	Dry heat (broil or grill; sauté)	Steaks
	Strip loin	180	Dry heat (broil or grill; roast; sauté)	New York steak; minute steak; entrecôte bordelaise
	Tenderloin	189B	Dry heat (broil or grill; roast; sauté)	Tournedos Rossini; beef Wellington
	Hanging tender steak	1140	Dry heat (broil or grill; sauté)	Steak
Sirloin	Top sirloin butt	184	Dry heat (broil or grill; roast)	Steak; roast beef
	Tri tip	185C	Dry heat (broil or grill; roast)	Steak; stir-fry; fajitas
Flank	Flank steak	193	Dry heat (broil or grill; sauté)	London broil
			Combination (braise)	Braised stuffed flank steak
Round	Steamship round	166B	Dry heat (roast)	Roast beef
	Top (inside) round	168	Dry heat (roast)	Roast beef
			Combination (braise)	Braised beef roulade
Organ meats	Liver	1724	Dry heat (broil or grill; sauté)	Broiled or sautéed liver with onions
	Oxtail	1791	Combination (braise; stew)	Soup; stew
	Tongue	1710	Combination (braise; stew)	Simmered; sliced sandwich meat
	Tripe	1739	Combination (braise; stew)	Stew; simmered with stock, tomatoes

QUESTIONS FOR DISCUSSION

1 List each beef primal cut and describe its location on the carcass. For each primal cut, identify two subprimal or fabricated cuts taken from it.

2 Would it be better to use the chuck for grilling or stewing? Explain your answer.

3 Which fabricated cuts contain a portion of the tenderloin? Explain which cooking methods are best suited for these cuts.

4 Most steaks are cut from the hindquarter. What popular steak is cut from the forequarter? Discuss why is it tender when other cuts from the forequarter are relatively tough?

5 Describe where organ meats come from on a cow and how to prepare them.

6 Visit the National Cattleman's Beef Association website to learn more. Does cooking method affect the fat and cholesterol content of a beef steak? How has consumer demand for beef products changed over the past year?

7 Learn about the breeds of cattle being raised for beef around the world. Describe how the breeds differ in terms of fat content and finished weight. Have other countries evolved different techniques for fabricating beef?

Beef Recipes

Flat Iron Steak with Coffee Beans

YIELD	6 Servings, 10 oz. (300 g) each	METHOD	Grilling
Flat iron steaks, 8 oz. (240 g) each		6	6
Kosher salt		2 tsp.	10 ml
Black pepper		1 tsp.	5 ml
Coffee beans, ground very fine		2 Tbsp.	30 ml
Cocoa powder		1 Tbsp.	15 ml
Cinnamon, ground		⅛ tsp.	0.5 ml
Olive oil		1 fl. oz.	30 ml
Pasilla chile broth:			
Whole butter		½ oz.	15 g
White onions, roughly chopped		8 oz.	240 g
Garlic cloves, whole, peeled		6	6
Pasilla chiles, stemmed, seeded, torn into large pieces		½ oz.	15 g
White corn tortilla, shredded		¾ oz.	22 g
Chicken stock		20 fl. oz.	600 ml
Heavy cream		2 fl. oz.	60 ml
Kosher salt		1 tsp.	5 ml
Brown sugar		1 tsp.	5 ml
Cooked chard or other vegetables		as needed for garnish	

1 Season the steaks with salt and pepper on both sides.

2 Grind the coffee, cocoa powder and cinnamon together. Brush the steaks with olive oil on all sides and rub them with the coffee mixture. Allow the steaks to marinate for approximately 30 minutes.

3 To prepare the pasilla chile broth, heat a medium saucepan over medium-high heat. Add the butter and sauté the onions and garlic until browned. Add the pasilla chiles and tortilla pieces and sauté until golden brown.

4 Add the stock to the pasilla chile broth and bring to a boil. Reduce to a simmer, cover loosely and cook for 10 minutes. Remove from the heat and cool. Purée the chile broth in a blender until smooth and strain through a china cap. Add the cream, salt and brown sugar and stir to combine. The chile broth should not be very thick; thin it with additional stock or water if necessary. Hold for service.

5 Grill the steaks to the desired doneness. Allow the steaks to rest for 2 minutes, then cut them across the grain and plate with a portion of the sauce and vegetables.

Approximate values per 10-oz. (300-g) serving: **Calories** 440, **Total fat** 25 g, **Saturated fat** 10 g, **Cholesterol** 155 mg, **Sodium** 730 mg, **Total carbohydrates** 11 g, **Protein** 44 g, **Vitamin A** 20%, **Iron** 30%

Marinated London Broil

YIELD	1 Flank Steak, 6 Servings, 5–8 oz. (150–240 g) each	METHOD	Grilling

Marinade:		
Olive oil	4 fl. oz.	120 ml
Balsamic vinegar	4 fl. oz.	120 ml
Fresh rosemary, chopped	2 Tbsp.	30 ml
Garlic, minced	2 oz.	60 g
Black pepper	1 tsp.	5 ml
Salt	1 Tbsp.	15 ml
Beef flank steak, 2–3 lb. (1–1½ kg)	1	1

1 Combine the marinade ingredients in a hotel pan.

2 Add the flank steak to the marinade and coat completely. Allow the meat to marinate for at least 4 hours.

3 Grill the steak rare to medium rare. If cooked further, the meat will become extremely tough.

4 Carve into ¼-inch- (6-millimeter-) thick slices, cutting diagonally across the grain.

Approximate values per 8-oz. (240-g) serving: **Calories** 310, **Total fat** 16 g, **Saturated fat** 5 g, **Cholesterol** 75 mg, **Sodium** 370 mg, **Total carbohydrates** 2 g, **Protein** 38 g, **Iron** 15%

Châteaubriand

French chefs of the late 19th century began referring to the classic filet de boeuf *(a very thick steak cut from the best part of the filet) as Châteaubriand in reference to the 19th-century statesman and author of the same name. As traditionally prepared by his chef, the dish is served with béarnaise sauce, a bouquetière of vegetables and château potatoes.*

YIELD	1 Tenderloin, 2–4 Servings	METHOD	Roasting

Beef filet, cut from the large (butt) end of the tenderloin, 16 oz. (480 g)	1	1
Salt and pepper	TT	TT
Clarified butter	as needed	as needed
Béarnaise sauce (page 231)	4 fl. oz.	120 ml

1 Tie the beef with butcher's twine and season with salt and pepper.

2 Sauté the beef in clarified butter until it is well browned.

3 Transfer the beef to a 450°F (230°C) oven and roast until done, approximately 10–12 minutes for rare (internal temperature of 125°F/52°C), or 15–18 minutes for medium (140°F/60°C).

4 Remove the beef from the oven and allow it to rest for at least 5 minutes before carving.

5 At service time, slice the beef evenly on a slight diagonal bias. Serve lightly coated (napped) with the béarnaise sauce. Or present the sliced beef with a bouquetière of vegetables such as roasted baby carrots, sautéed cherry tomatoes, roasted potatoes and steamed green cauliflower with the sauce on the side.

Approximate values per 10-oz. (300-g) serving: **Calories** 705, **Total fat** 40 g, **Saturated fat** 18 g, **Cholesterol** 270 mg, **Sodium** 1350 mg, **Total carbohydrates** 1 g, **Protein** 80 g, **Vitamin A** 13%, **Iron** 66%

Beef Wellington

YIELD	1 Tenderloin, 10 Servings	METHOD	Roasting
Beef tenderloin, trimmed, 4 lb.–4 lb. 8 oz. (1.9–2.1 kg)		1	1
Salt and pepper		TT	TT
Vegetable oil		as needed	as needed
Pâté de foie gras (page 419)		8 oz.	240 g
Truffle peelings, chopped fine		1 oz.	30 g
Puff Pastry (page 993)		2 lb.	960 g
Egg wash		as needed	as needed
Madeira sauce (page 227)		20 fl. oz.	600 ml

1. Trim 3–4 inches (7.5–10 centimeters) of the tail from the tenderloin. (The small tail portion can be used in a stir-fry or other preparation.) Season the tenderloin with salt and pepper and sear in a small amount of oil in a large rondeau. Remove from the pan and cool.

2. Spread the surface of the tenderloin with the pâté de foie gras. Sprinkle the truffles over the pâté.

3. Roll the puff pastry dough into a rectangle approximately ³⁄₁₆ inch (5 millimeters) thick and large enough to wrap around the entire tenderloin.

4. Turn the tenderloin over and place it lengthwise, pâté side down, in the center of the pastry. Fold the pastry ends over the meat and wrap the pastry around the tenderloin, sealing it with egg wash and trimming off any excess.

5. Transfer the Wellington to a baking sheet, placing the seam side down. Brush the surface with egg wash.

6. Bake the Wellington in a 350°F (180°C) oven until the center reaches 125–130°F (52–54°C), approximately 40 minutes. Do not overcook; the crust holds in steam and heat, thus enhancing the effects of carryover cooking.

7. Allow the meat to rest 5 minutes after baking. Carve the Wellington tableside or on a buffet with Madeira sauce served on the side.

Variation:

Individual Wellingtons can be made by cutting the tenderloin into 4- to 5-ounce (120- to 150-gram) filet mignons, using smaller pieces of puff pastry and reducing the cooking time to approximately 20 minutes.

Approximate values per ¹⁄₁₀-tenderloin serving: **Calories** 720, **Total fat** 44 g, **Saturated fat** 14 g, **Cholesterol** 160 mg, **Sodium** 700 mg, **Total carbohydrates** 29 g, **Protein** 48 g, **Vitamin A** 15%, **Iron** 40%

❶ Spreading the browned tenderloin with pâté de foie gras.

❷ Wrapping the pastry around the seared tenderloin.

❸ Slicing the cooked Beef Wellington.

Home-Style Meatloaf

YIELD 4 Loaves, 21 Servings, 6 oz. (180 g) each	METHOD Baking	
Onions, small dice	1 lb.	480 g
Celery, small dice	8 oz.	240 g
Garlic, chopped	2 Tbsp.	30 ml
Vegetable oil	2 fl. oz.	60 ml
Fresh bread crumbs	6 oz.	180 g
Tomato juice	1 pt.	480 ml
Beef chuck, ground	4 lb.	1.9 kg
Ground pork	4 lb.	1.9 kg
Eggs, beaten	4	4
Salt	4 tsp.	20 ml
Black pepper	1 Tbsp.	15 ml
Fresh parsley, chopped	4 Tbsp.	60 ml
Worcestershire sauce	1½ fl. oz.	45 ml
Ketchup	as needed	as needed

1 Sauté the onions, celery and garlic in the oil until tender. Remove from the heat and cool.

2 Combine all the ingredients except the ketchup and mix well.

3 Form into loaves of the desired size and place in loaf pans.

4 Brush the top of each loaf with ketchup as desired. Bake at 350°F (180°C) until the meatloaf reaches an internal temperature of 165°F (74°C), approximately 1 hour for a 9-inch × 5-inch (22-centimeter × 12-centimeter) loaf pan.

5 Allow the loaves to rest for 15 minutes before slicing. Cut slices of the desired thickness and serve with a tomato or mushroom sauce and a small salad if desired.

Approximate values per ⅓-loaf serving: **Calories** 490, **Total fat** 35 g, **Saturated fat** 12 g, **Cholesterol** 155 mg, **Sodium** 690 mg, **Total carbohydrates** 8 g, **Protein** 33 g, **Vitamin C** 35%, **Iron** 20%

Italian Country Meatballs

YIELD 30 Meatballs, 2 oz. (60 g) each	METHOD Roasting/Stewing	
Fresh bread crumbs	5 oz.	150 g
Whole milk	4 fl. oz.	120 ml
Ground pork	12 oz.	360 g
Beef chuck, ground	12 oz.	360 g
Italian sausage, ground	12 oz.	360 g
Prosciutto, small dice	2 oz.	60 g
Fresh flat-leaf parsley, chopped coarse	½ oz.	15 g
Kosher salt	1 Tbsp.	15 ml
Dried oregano	2 tsp.	10 ml
Fennel seeds	1½ tsp.	7 ml
Dried chile flakes	1 tsp.	5 ml
Fresh ricotta	6 oz.	180 g
Eggs, beaten	3	3
Italian plum tomatoes, canned with juice	28 oz.	840 g
Basil Pesto Sauce (page 249)	as needed for garnish	
Parmesan or grana padano cheese	as needed for garnish	

1   Soak the breadcrumbs in 2 fluid ounces (60 milliliters) of the milk until it is absorbed.

2   Combine the ground pork, beef, Italian sausage, prosciutto, bread crumbs, parsley, 2 teaspoons (10 milliliters) of the salt, oregano, fennel seeds and chile flakes. Mix lightly by hand.

3   In a separate bowl, whisk together the ricotta, eggs and remaining milk until the ricotta curds are broken up without whipping. Add the ricotta mixture to the ground meat mixture. Mix lightly until just incorporated.

4   Test the seasonings by cooking a small amount of the mixture in a sauté pan. Adjust the seasonings accordingly.

5   Using a #16 portion scoop, divide into 2-ounce (60-gram) meatballs and round evenly.

6   Place on olive-oil coated baking sheets and bake at 400°F (204°C) for 10 minutes. Rotate the baking sheets and continue cooking until the meatballs are browned, for a total of 15–20 minutes.

7   Arrange the meatballs in a single layer with sides touching in shallow hotel pans.

8   Pass the plum tomatoes through a food mill. Add the remaining 1 teaspoon of salt. Pour over the meatballs. Cover tightly. Braise at 325°F (162°C) until the meatballs are tender and have absorbed some of the sauce, approximately 40–50 minutes.

9   Serve the meatballs drizzled with Basil Pesto Sauce and garnished with slices of parmesan.

Approximate values per meatball: **Calories** 300, **Total fat** 26 g, **Saturated fat** 6 g, **Cholesterol** 45 mg, **Sodium** 420 mg, **Total carbohydrates** 6 g, **Protein** 11 g

---

Meatballs: A Blank Slate for Culinary Creativity

When making meatballs, the combination of meat used affects the final flavor; ground beef, lamb, pork and veal work well alone or in combination. Select meat that is 20% fat and 80% lean to ensure a juicy product. Dry bread crumbs give the meatball a firm texture; moist fresh bread crumbs yield a soft, tender meatball. Fresh herbs, such as cilantro, dill, mint, rosemary, sage and tarragon, and spices, such as curry powder and Cajun seasoning, provide the ethnic flavor profile desired. Form the meat mixture into miniature sizes for soups or larger sizes for main course portions. Then chill thoroughly before baking, pan-frying or simmering so that the meatballs hold their shape while cooking.

Minute Steak Dijonaise

YIELD 2 Servings, 7 oz. (210 g) each	METHOD Sautéing	
Sirloin steaks, trimmed, 6 oz. (180 g)	2	2
Dijon mustard	1 oz.	30 g
Onion, small dice	2 oz.	60 g
Clarified butter	1 fl. oz.	30 ml
Heavy cream	3 fl. oz.	90 ml
Whole butter	1 oz.	30 g
Salt and pepper	TT	TT

1   Pound the steaks to a ¼-inch (6-millimeter) thickness.

2   Cover one side of each steak first with 1½ teaspoons (8 milliliters) mustard and then half of the onion, pressing the onion firmly into the steak.

3   Sauté the steaks in the clarified butter, presentation (onion) side down first. Remove and hold in a warm place.

4   Degrease the pan. Add the cream and reduce by half. Add the rest of the mustard.

5   Monté au beurre. Adjust the seasonings. Serve each portion with some of the sauce.

Approximate values per 7-oz. (210-g) serving: **Calories** 671, **Total fat** 45 g, **Saturated fat** 23 g, **Cholesterol** 255 mg, **Sodium** 2050 mg, **Total carbohydrates** 6 g, **Protein** 60 g, **Vitamin A** 36%, **Iron** 44%

Beef Stroganoff

YIELD 8 Servings, 8 oz. (240 g) each	METHOD Sautéing	
Tenderloin tips, émincé	2 lb.	960 g
Clarified butter	1½ fl. oz.	45 ml
Onion, medium dice	4 oz.	120 g
Mushrooms, halved	1 lb.	480 g
Demi-Glace (page 225)	10 fl. oz.	300 ml
Heavy cream	10 fl. oz.	300 ml
Sour cream	8 oz.	240 g
Dijon mustard	1 Tbsp.	15 ml
Fresh dill, chopped	1 Tbsp.	15 ml
Fresh parsley, chopped	1 Tbsp.	15 ml
Salt and pepper	TT	TT
Egg noodles, cooked	24 oz.	720 g
Sour cream	as needed for garnish	

1 Sauté the tenderloin tips in the butter, searing on all sides. Remove the meat and set aside.

2 Add the onion to the pan and sauté lightly. Add the mushrooms and sauté until dry.

3 Add the demi-glace. Bring to a boil, reduce to a simmer and cook for 10 minutes.

4 Add the cream, sour cream, mustard and any meat juices that accumulated while holding the meat.

5 Return the meat to the sauce to reheat. Stir in the dill and parsley. Adjust the seasonings and serve over hot egg noodles. Garnish with sour cream if desired.

Approximate values per 8-oz. (240-g) serving: **Calories** 635, **Total fat** 39 g, **Saturated fat** 20 g, **Cholesterol** 201 mg, **Sodium** 510 mg, **Total carbohydrates** 32 g, **Protein** 40 g, **Vitamin A** 41%, **Iron** 46%, **Calcium** 11%

Entrecôtes Bordelaise

YIELD 4 Servings, 14 oz. (420 g) each	METHOD Sautéing	
Beef marrow	4 oz.	120 g
Entrecôtes (rib eye steaks), 14 oz. (400 g) each	2	2
Salt and pepper	TT	TT
Clarified butter	2 fl. oz.	60 ml
Shallots, chopped	2 Tbsp.	30 ml
Red wine	8 fl. oz.	240 ml
Demi-Glace (page 225)	12 fl. oz.	360 ml
Whole butter	1 oz.	30 g

1 Slice the marrow into rounds and poach in salted water for 3 minutes. Drain the marrow and set it aside.

2 Season the steaks and sauté them in the clarified butter to the desired doneness. Finish in the oven if desired. Remove to a platter and hold in a warm place.

3 Sauté the shallots in the same pan.

4 Deglaze the pan with the wine and reduce by half. Add the Demi-Glace; simmer for 5 minutes.

5 Monté au beurre.

6 Add the marrow to the sauce. Adjust the seasonings. Divide each steak into two portions and serve the steaks with the sauce.

Approximate values per 14-oz. (420-g) serving: **Calories** 610, **Total fat** 35 g, **Saturated fat** 17 g, **Cholesterol** 200 mg, **Sodium** 810 mg, **Total carbohydrates** 5 g, **Protein** 57 g, **Vitamin A** 21%, **Iron** 44%

Pepper Steak

YIELD 2 Servings, 8 oz. (240 g) each		METHOD Sautéing	
Boneless strip steaks, approx. 8 oz. (240 g) each	2	2	
Salt	TT	TT	
Peppercorns, cracked	3 Tbsp.	45 ml	
Clarified butter	1 fl. oz.	30 ml	
Cognac	2 fl. oz.	60 ml	
Heavy cream	4 fl. oz.	120 ml	
Whole butter	2 oz.	60 g	

1 Season the steaks with salt. Spread the peppercorns in a hotel pan and press the steaks into them, lightly coating each side.

2 Sauté the steaks in the clarified butter over high heat for 2–3 minutes on each side.

3 Remove the pan from the heat. Pour the cognac over the steaks, return the pan to the heat and flambé. When the flames subside, remove the steaks from the pan and keep them warm on a plate.

4 Add the cream to the pan. Bring to a boil and reduce for 2 minutes over high heat; monté au beurre. Pour this sauce over the steaks and serve immediately.

Approximate values per 8-oz. (240-g) serving: **Calories** 950, **Total fat** 73 g, **Saturated fat** 42 g, **Cholesterol** 300 mg, **Sodium** 1525 mg, **Total carbohydrates** 8 g, **Protein** 51 g, **Vitamin A** 72%, **Iron** 46%, **Calcium** 13%

⚠ Safety Alert

Cooking with Alcohol

When alcohol comes into contact with a flame, it can ignite. In order to avoid singed eyebrows and kitchen fires, observe care when adding wine, liqueurs or liquor to a dish near the stove. When a dish calls for flambéing, follow these procedures. Stand away from the pan being flamed. Tilt the pan away from you, allowing the fumes to be ignited by the open flame. Be careful, as the flames can leap from the pan.

❶ Pressing the steaks into the peppercorns.

❷ Flambéing the cognac on the steaks.

❸ Pouring the finished sauce over each steak.

Beef Fajitas

YIELD 6 Servings, 6 oz. (180 g) each	METHOD Grilling/Sautéing	
Marinade:		
Garlic cloves	4	4
Salt	1½ tsp.	8 ml
Black pepper, ground coarse	1½ tsp.	8 ml
Cumin, ground	1½ tsp.	8 ml
Onion powder	1½ tsp.	8 ml
Chilli powder	1½ tsp.	8 ml
Skirt steak	2 lb.	960 g
Vegetable oil	1 fl. oz.	30 ml
Bell peppers, mixed, red, yellow and green, sliced thin	3	3
Onion, sliced thin	1	1
Garlic cloves, chopped	2	2
Cilantro sprigs	as needed for garnish	
Flour or corn tortillas, warm	as needed for garnish	
Pico de Gallo (page 237)	as needed for garnish	
Sour cream	as needed for garnish	
Guacamole (page 888)	as needed for garnish	

1 Make the marinade by chopping and mashing the garlic into a paste. In a bowl, combine the garlic paste with the remaining marinade ingredients.

2 Trim the fat from the skirt steak. Cut the steak into two or three pieces if necessary. Add the steaks to the marinade, turning them several times to coat all sides. Cover the steak and marinate in the refrigerator for at least 1 hour or overnight.

3 Grill the steak on a hot grill to the desired doneness. Remove the steak from the grill and allow it to rest for 10 minutes.

4 Add the oil to a heavy sauté pan, heat the pan until very hot and sauté the bell peppers, onion and garlic just until they begin to soften.

5 Slice the steak against the grain into thin slices. Arrange the steak and the pepper mixture on very hot cast-iron platters and garnish with the cilantro. The platters should be sizzling as they are presented to the table.

6 Serve the fajitas accompanied by warm flour or corn tortillas, Pico de Gallo, sour cream, and Guacamole.

Approximate values per 6-oz. (180-g) serving: **Calories** 630, **Total fat** 24 g, **Saturated fat** 7 g, **Cholesterol** 80 mg, **Sodium** 700 mg, **Total carbohydrates** 61 g, **Protein** 41 g, **Vitamin A** 25%, **Vitamin C** 170%, **Iron** 35%, **Claims**—good source of fiber, vitamins A and C and iron

Thai Beef Salad

YIELD 4 Servings	METHOD *Sous Vide* Poaching/Sautéing	
New York strip steak, 12 oz. (360 g), 1-in. (2.5-cm) thick	1	1
Salt	TT	TT
White pepper	TT	TT
Olive oil	½ fl. oz.	15 ml
Garlic clove, crushed	1	1
Baby salad greens	10 oz.	300 g
Fresh cilantro leaves	½ cup	120 ml
Thai basil leaves	¼ cup	60 ml
Cucumber, sliced thin	4 oz.	120 g
Carrot, julienned	6 oz.	180 g
Nuoc Cham (page 253)	4 fl. oz.	120 ml
Peanut oil	2 fl. oz.	60 ml
Green onions, sliced	2 oz.	60 g

1 Heat a thermal circulator or a water oven to 129°F (54°C).

2 Wearing clean disposable gloves, season the steak with salt and white pepper. Place it into a plastic pouch for cooking *sous vide*. Add the olive oil and garlic. Vacuum seal the bag.

3 Cook the sealed pouch in the thermal circulator for 1 hour or until the internal temperature reaches 129°F (54°C).

4 Combine the salad greens, cilantro, Thai basil, cucumber and carrots. Cover and refrigerate.

5 For service, remove the steak from the pouch. Dry it on clean paper towels.

6 Sear the steak in a small amount of peanut oil in a hot frying pan until well browned on each side. Remove it from the pan and keep warm.

7 Toss the salad ingredients with the Nuoc Cham and peanut oil. Plate the dressed greens. Slice the steak against the grain and place a few slices on top of each salad. Sprinkle with green onions before serving.

Note At 129°F (54°C), the steak will be cooked rare. To cook the steak to a different degree of doneness, adjust the temperature of the water bath to 136°F (58°C) for medium or 154°F (68°C) for well done. Or sear the steak longer in Step 6.

Approximate values per 6-oz. (180-g) serving: **Calories** 360, **Total fat** 24 g, **Saturated fat** 6 g, **Cholesterol** 50 mg, **Sodium** 640 mg, **Total carbohydrates** 16 g, **Protein** 20 g, **Vitamin A** 270%, **Vitamin C** 45%, **Iron** 30%

 Safety Alert

Sous Vide *Sanitation*

Food safety is of utmost concern when using *sous vide* techniques because of the low cooking temperatures. To prevent the growth of microorganisms, any food to be cooked *sous vide* must be chilled below the temperature danger zone (41°F/5°C) before cooking. Keep all cutting boards, knives and food contact surfaces clean and sanitary and wear clean disposable gloves. Use only the freshest unblemished ingredients. Consult your local health department for regulations for preparing food *sous vide*. Special permission and a HACCP plan may be required.

Braised Oxtails and Barley Stew

YIELD 8 Servings, 8 oz. (240 g) each	METHOD Braising	
Oxtails	3 lbs.	1.4 kg
Onions, sliced thin	6 oz.	180 g
Beef or chicken stock	1½ qt.	1.4 lt
Bay leaves	2	2
Salt and pepper	TT	TT
Barley:		
Carrots, small dice	4 oz.	120 g
Onions, small dice	4 oz.	120 g
Celery, small dice	4 oz.	120 g
Parsnips, small dice	4 oz.	120 g
Olive oil	3 fl. oz.	90 ml
Barley, soaked	8 oz.	240 g
Baby beets, cooked	16	16
Spinach, stems removed	1 lb.	480 g
Horseradish	as needed	as needed

1 Place the oxtails in a roasting pan one layer deep and brown in a 375°F (190°C) oven. Turn the bones to brown them evenly.

2 Drain 3 tablespoons (45 milliliters) of the fat from the bones into a saucepot. Add the onions and sauté until softened and caramelized, approximately 10–15 minutes.

3 Add the browned oxtails to the saucepot. Deglaze the roasting pan with the stock. Add this liquid to the saucepot along with the bay leaves. Season with salt and pepper.

4 Bring to a boil, cover and simmer on low until the oxtails are tender, approximately 2–2½ hours.

5 Remove the oxtails from the broth and let cool. Cool and degrease the oxtail broth.

6 To prepare the barley, sauté the carrots, onions, celery and parsnips in the olive oil over medium heat until softened. Add the soaked barley, the reserved oxtail broth and enough water to make 1 quart (960 milliliters) of liquid. Bring to a boil, cover and simmer until the barley is tender, approximately 25–35 minutes. Season to taste.

7 Pick the meat from the oxtail bones, discarding any excess fat and gristle. Chop coarse. Combine the oxtail meat with the barley.

8 Swirl in the spinach and adjust the seasonings. Heat briefly until the spinach wilts. Serve garnished with cooked baby beets and horseradish.

Approximate values per 8-oz. (240 g) serving: **Calories** 520, **Total fat** 28 g, **Saturated fat** 9 g, **Cholesterol** 130 mg, **Sodium** 320 mg, **Total carbohydrates** 30 g, **Protein** 39 g, **Vitamin A** 50%, **Vitamin C** 10%, **Iron** 30%

① Testing the meat to see that it is tender.

② The Swiss Steak served with mashed potatoes, roasted tomatoes and green beans.

Swiss Steak

YIELD 10 Servings, 10 oz. (300 g) each		METHOD Braising
Beef bottom round steaks, 6 oz. (180 g) each	10	10
Flour	as needed for dredging	as needed for dredging
Salt and pepper	TT	TT
Oil	2 fl. oz.	60 ml
Onions, small dice	1 lb.	480 g
Garlic cloves, crushed	3	3
Celery, diced	8 oz.	240 g
Flour	4 oz.	120 g
Brown Stock (page 209)	5 pt.	2.4 lt
Tomato purée	6 oz.	180 g
Sachet:		
Bay leaves	2	2
Dried thyme	½ tsp.	2 ml
Peppercorns, crushed	½ tsp.	2 ml
Parsley stems	8	8
Mashed Potatoes (page 664)	as needed	as needed
Plum tomatoes, roasted	as needed	as needed
Green beans, steamed	as needed	as needed

1 Dredge the steaks in flour seasoned with salt and pepper.

2 Heat the oil in a roasting pan and brown the steaks well on both sides. Remove the steaks.

3 Add the onions, garlic and celery; sauté until tender.

4 Add the flour and cook to a brown roux.

5 Gradually add the stock, whisking until the sauce is thickened and smooth. Add the tomato purée and sachet.

6 Return the steaks to the braising pan, cover and cook in a 300°F (150°C) oven until tender, approximately 2 hours. Test the meat with a kitchen fork to ensure that it is tender.

7 Remove the steaks from the sauce. Discard the sachet. Strain the sauce and adjust the seasonings. Serve the steaks with mashed potatoes and the sauce. Garnish with roasted plum tomatoes and steamed green beans.

Approximate values per 10-oz. (300-g) serving: **Calories** 601, **Total fat** 26 g, **Saturated fat** 7 g, **Cholesterol** 170 mg, **Sodium** 390 mg, **Total carbohydrates** 30 g, **Protein** 61 g, **Vitamin A** 49%, **Vitamin C** 12%, **Iron** 52%

① Straining the sauce.

Braised Short Ribs of Beef

YIELD 8 Servings, 8 oz. (240 g) each		METHOD Braising
Flour	4 oz.	120 g
Salt	1 Tbsp.	15 ml
Black pepper	1 tsp.	5 ml
Dried rosemary	½ tsp.	2 ml
Short ribs of beef, cut into 2-in. (5-cm) portions	6 lb.	2.8 kg
Vegetable oil	1 fl. oz.	30 ml
Onion, chopped	6 oz.	180 g
Celery, chopped	4 oz.	120 g
Brown Beef Stock (page 209)	24 fl. oz.	720 ml
Roux	as needed	as needed
Salt and pepper	TT	TT
Mashed Potatoes (page 664)	as needed	as needed
Scallions, steamed	12	12
Cherry tomatoes	as needed	as needed

1 Combine the flour, salt, pepper and rosemary. Dredge the ribs in the seasoned flour.

2 Heat the oil in a heavy brazier and brown the ribs well. Remove and hold in a warm place.

3 Add the onion and celery to the brazier and sauté lightly.

4 Return the ribs to the pan, add the stock and cook in a 300°F (150°C) oven until done, approximately 2½ hours.

5 Remove the ribs from the liquid and skim off the excess fat.

6 Bring the liquid to a boil on the stove top; thicken it with roux to the desired consistency and simmer for 15 minutes. Strain the sauce and adjust the seasonings. Return the ribs to the sauce and simmer for 5 minutes.

7 Serve one or two ribs per serving with mashed potatoes garnished with the scallions, some cherry tomatoes and additional sauce.

Variations:

Orange-Scented Braised Short Ribs of Beef—Omit the rosemary. Add 4 tablespoons (60 milliliters) julienned orange zest and 8 fluid ounces (240 milliliters) orange juice in Step 4. Decrease the stock by 8 fluid ounces (240 milliliters).

Ginger Braised Short Ribs of Beef—Omit the rosemary. Sauté 3 ounces (90 grams) peeled and chopped fresh ginger with the onions and celery in Step 3. Substitute 2 fluid ounces (60 milliliters) soy sauce for an equal amount of the beef stock and add 1 tablespoon (15 milliliters) ground ginger to the ribs before braising in Step 4.

Approximate values per 8-oz. (240-g) serving: **Calories** 1150, **Total fat** 70 g, **Saturated fat** 27 g, **Cholesterol** 320 mg, **Sodium** 1154 mg, **Total carbohydrates** 18 g, **Protein** 110 g, **Vitamin A** 18%, **Iron** 85%

2 The finished Braised Short Ribs of Beef.

Hungarian Goulash

YIELD	9 Servings, 12 oz. (360 g) each	METHOD	Stewing
Onions, medium dice		2 lb.	960 g
Lard or vegetable oil		2 fl. oz.	60 ml
Hungarian paprika		4 Tbsp.	60 ml
Garlic, chopped		1 Tbsp.	15 ml
Caraway seeds		½ tsp.	2 ml
Salt		TT	TT
Black pepper		½ tsp.	2 ml
White Stock (page 207)		1 qt.	1 lt
Tomato paste		4 oz.	120 g
Beef stew meat, cut in 1½-in. (4-cm) cubes		5 lb.	2.4 kg

1 Sauté the onions in the lard or oil, browning lightly.

2 Add the paprika, garlic, caraway seeds, salt and pepper; mix well.

3 Add the stock and tomato paste. Bring to a boil, then reduce to a simmer.

4 Add the meat and continue simmering until the meat is very tender, approximately 1½ hours. Adjust the seasonings and serve with buttered egg noodles or mashed potatoes as desired.

Approximate values per 12-oz. (360-g) serving: **Calories** 645, **Total fat** 32 g, **Saturated fat** 12 g, **Cholesterol** 235 mg, **Sodium** 910 mg, **Total carbohydrates** 13 g, **Protein** 73 g, **Vitamin A** 28%, **Vitamin C** 20%, **Iron** 63%

Beef Bourguignon

YIELD 10 Servings, 8 oz. (240 g) each	METHOD Stewing	
Marinade:		
Garlic cloves, crushed	3	3
Onions, sliced	3	3
Carrots, sliced	2	2
Parsley stems	10	10
Bouquet garni:		
Carrot stick, 4 in. (10 cm)	1	1
Leek, split, 4-in. (10-cm) piece	1	1
Fresh thyme	1 sprig	1 sprig
Bay leaf	1	1
Peppercorns, crushed	10	10
Salt	TT	TT
Dry red wine, preferably Burgundy	26 fl. oz.	780 ml
Beef chuck, cut into 2-in. (5-cm) cubes	4 lb.	1.9 kg
Vegetable oil	2 fl. oz.	60 ml
Flour	2 Tbsp.	30 ml
Tomato paste	1 Tbsp.	15 ml
Tomatoes, quartered	4	4
Brown Stock (page 209)	1 pt.	480 ml
Mushrooms, quartered	1 lb.	480 g
Unsalted butter	1½ oz.	45 g
Pearl onions, boiled and peeled	30	30
Salt and pepper	TT	TT

1 Combine the garlic, onions, carrots, parsley, bouquet garni, peppercorns, salt and wine to make a marinade.

2 Marinate the meat for several hours under refrigeration.

3 Remove and drain the meat. Reserve the marinade.

4 Dry the beef and sauté it in the oil in a large rondeau until well browned. Do this in several batches if necessary.

5 Return all the meat to the rondeau. Sprinkle with flour and cook to make a blond roux.

6 Stir in the tomato paste and cook for 5 minutes.

7 Add the reserved marinade, tomatoes and stock. Cook in a 350°F (180°C) oven until the meat is tender, approximately 2½ hours.

8 Remove the meat from the sauce. Strain the sauce through a china cap, pressing to extract all the liquid. Discard the solids. Return the liquid and the beef to the pot.

9 Sauté the mushrooms in the butter and add them to the meat and sauce. Add the pearl onions and adjust the seasonings. Simmer for 10 minutes to blend the flavors.

Approximate values per 8-oz. (240-g) serving: **Calories** 315, **Total fat** 15 g, **Saturated fat** 6.5 g, **Cholesterol** 97 mg, **Sodium** 640 mg, **Total carbohydrates** 8 g, **Protein** 30 g, **Vitamin A** 27%, **Vitamin C** 13%, **Iron** 26%

Chili Con Carne

Serve chili with cornbread, corn chips or soft rolls garnished with sour cream, shredded Monterey Jack cheese and chopped scallions. Chili can also be spooned over baked potatoes or served in a hollowed-out round of crusty bread.

YIELD	4 qt. (3.8 lt), 10 Servings, 12 fl. oz. (360 ml) each	METHOD	Stewing
Coarse ground beef		4 lb.	1.8 k
Vegetable oil		3 fl. oz.	120 ml
Onions, medium dice		1 lb.	480 g
Garlic, chopped		1 oz.	30 g
Jalapeño peppers		4 oz.	120 g
Ancho chili powder		5 Tbsp.	75 ml
Dried oregano		2 tsp.	10 ml
Cumin, ground		2 Tbsp.	30 ml
Coriander, ground		1 tsp.	5 ml
Cornmeal		3 oz.	90 g
Cocoa powder		2 tsp.	10 ml
Salt and pepper		TT	TT
Brown stock		3 pt.	1.4 lt
Dark beer or Brown Stock (page 209)		24 fl. oz.	720 ml
Crushed tomatoes		24 fl. oz.	720 ml
Cheddar or Monterey Jack cheese, shredded		as needed	as needed
Cilantro, chopped		as needed	as needed

1 Brown the beef in the vegetable oil in a large rondeau.

2 Add the onions, garlic and jalapeños to the browned beef. Cook until tender. Drain off the excess fat.

3 Stir in the spices, cornmeal and cocoa powder. Season with salt and pepper.

4 Deglaze the pan with the Brown Stock. Add dark beer (or additional stock) and tomatoes. Bring to a simmer. Cover and cook for 1 hour, skimming the fat as it cooks. Adjust the seasonings.

5 Serve the chili with shredded cheese and chopped cilantro.

Variations:

Chili with Beans—Add 1 quart (1 liter) of cooked pinto, black or kidney beans to the chili during the last 15 minutes of cooking.

Venison Chili—Substitute ground venison round and 2 ounces (60 grams) diced bacon for the beef in Step 1.

Chili-Stuffed Baked Sweet Potatoes—Lightly oil then pierce 8 large sweet potatoes. Bake at 350°F (180°C) until cooked through yet still firm. Slice each potato in half lengthwise. Remove the flesh and cube. Combine the sweet potato cubes with the warm chili. Fill the sweet potato skins with the chili mixture. Place the potatoes on a sheet pan. Cover with 10 ounces (300 grams) shredded Monterey Jack cheese. Bake the potatoes at 375°F (190°C) until hot, approximately 20 minutes.

Chili-Stuffed Bread Bowl—For each serving, slice the top third from a 6-ounce (180-gram) round French or Italian loaf. Hollow out the bowl leaving a ¼-inch- (6-millimeter-) thick shell. Fill the bread with 7 fluid ounces (210 milliliters) of the chili. Top each serving with shredded Monterey Jack cheese and diced onions as desired.

Chili-Stuffed Bread Bowl

Approximate values per 12-fl.-oz.-(360-ml) serving: **Calories** 620, **Total fat** 40 g, **Saturated fat** 11 g, **Cholesterol** 125 mg, **Sodium** 460 mg, **Total carbohydrates** 25 g, **Protein** 39 g, **Vitamin A** 30%, **Vitamin C** 40%, **Calcium** 10%, **Iron** 40%

Carpaccio

Carpaccio is paper-thin slices of raw beef often served drizzled with olive oil and garnished with shaved Parmesan cheese. The dish takes its name from that of the Italian Renaissance artist Vittore Carpaccio, known for his lavish use of rich red colors in his paintings. A salad of pungent greens such as arugula or watercress is a traditional accompaniment.

YIELD	8 Servings, 4 oz. (120 g) each		
Beef tenderloin, trimmed of all silverskin and fat		1 lb.	480 g
Fresh mayonnaise		8 oz.	240 g
Dijon mustard		1 Tbsp.	15 ml
Salt and pepper		TT	TT
Capers, chopped		4 tsp.	20 ml
Black pepper, ground coarse		TT	TT
Onion, sliced thin		4 oz.	120 g
Olive oil		1½ fl. oz.	45 ml

1 Place the tenderloin in the freezer until nearly frozen, approximately 45 minutes to 1 hour.

2 Combine the mayonnaise with the mustard. Season with salt and pepper.

3 Slice the nearly frozen tenderloin on an electric slicer very thin, almost transparent. On eight very cold plates, arrange one slightly overlapping layer of thin slices of beef.

4 Sprinkle each plate of beef with ½ teaspoon (2.5 milliliters) capers, a generous amount of coarse ground black pepper, salt and ½ ounce (15 grams) sliced onions. Drizzle with 1 teaspoon (5 milliliters) oil and spoon ½ ounce (15 grams) mayonnaise mustard mixture in the center of each plate. Serve very cold.

Approximate values per 4-oz. (120-g) serving: **Calories** 360, **Total fat** 33 g, **Saturated fat** 7 g, **Cholesterol** 70 mg, **Sodium** 250 mg, **Total carbohydrates** 1 g, **Protein** 16 g

⚠ Safety Alert

Serving Raw Beef

Although culturally appropriate in the cuisines of many countries, raw beef is a potentially hazardous food that requires time and temperature controls for safety (TCS). It may carry harmful bacteria including *Salmonella*, *Listeria*, *Campylobacter* and *E. coli*. According to the 2013 Food Code of the FDA, uncooked meat may be served as long as a consumer advisory is printed on the menu. (It may not be offered on menus serving at-risk communities such as children or the elderly.) Observe the strictest sanitary standards when preparing raw meat dishes to prevent cross-contamination. Serve only fresh beef from the most reliable suppliers. Keep it chilled below 41°F (5°C). Always wear clean disposable gloves when preparing meat that is to be consumed without cooking. Check local regulations for the most accurate information for your area.

Veal is the meat of young, usually male, calves that are by-products of the dairy industry. Dairy cows must calve before they begin to give milk. Calves that aren't used in the dairy herds are used in today's veal industry. Although veal may come from any calf under the age of 9 months, most comes from calves slaughtered when they are 8–16 weeks old. Veal is lighter in color than beef, has a more delicate flavor and is generally more tender. Young veal has a firm texture, light pink color and very little fat. As soon as a calf starts eating solid food, the iron in the food begins to turn the young animal's meat red. Meat from calves slaughtered between 5 and 9 months of age is called **calf**. It tends to be a deeper red, with some marbling and external fat.

Veal's mild flavor and low fat content makes it a popular meat, especially among Europeans and those looking for an alternative to beef. Its delicate flavor is complemented by both classic and modern sauces.

PRIMAL AND SUBPRIMAL CUTS OF VEAL

After slaughter, a calf carcass can be split down the backbone into two bilateral halves or, more typically, cut along the natural curvature between the eleventh and twelfth ribs into a foresaddle (front portion) and a hindsaddle (rear portion). The veal carcass yields five primal cuts: three from the foresaddle (the shoulder, foreshank and breast and rib) and two from the hindsaddle (the loin and leg). The veal shoulder, rib and loin primals contain both bilateral portions; that is, a veal loin contains both sides of the animal's loin.

Figure 15.1 illustrates the relationship between the calf's bone structure and the primal cuts. Knowing the location of bones when cutting or working with veal (as well as all other types of meats) makes fabrication and carving easier and aids in identifying cuts. Figure 15.2 shows the primal cuts of veal and their location. A veal carcass weighs in a range of 60–245 pounds (27–110 kg).

FORESADDLE PRIMAL CUTS OF VEAL

The **foresaddle** of veal consists of the shoulder, foreshank and breast and rib. It may be purchased whole or divided into the primal or subprimal cuts.

Veal Shoulder

Similar to the beef shoulder or chuck, the **veal shoulder** accounts for 21 percent of the carcass weight. It contains four rib bones (as opposed to five in the beef chuck) and portions of the backbone, blade and arm bones.

In veal, the backbone, blade and arm bones are sometimes removed and the meat roasted or stuffed and roasted. Although **veal shoulder chops** and steaks can be fabricated, they are inferior to the chops cut from more tender areas such as the loin or rib. Often the shoulder and neck meat is ground or cubed for stew. Because of the relatively large amount of connective tissue it contains, meat from the shoulder is relatively tough and best braised or stewed.

Veal Foreshank and Breast

The **veal foreshank** and **veal breast** are located beneath the shoulder and rib sections on the front half of the carcass. They are considered one primal cut. Combined, they account

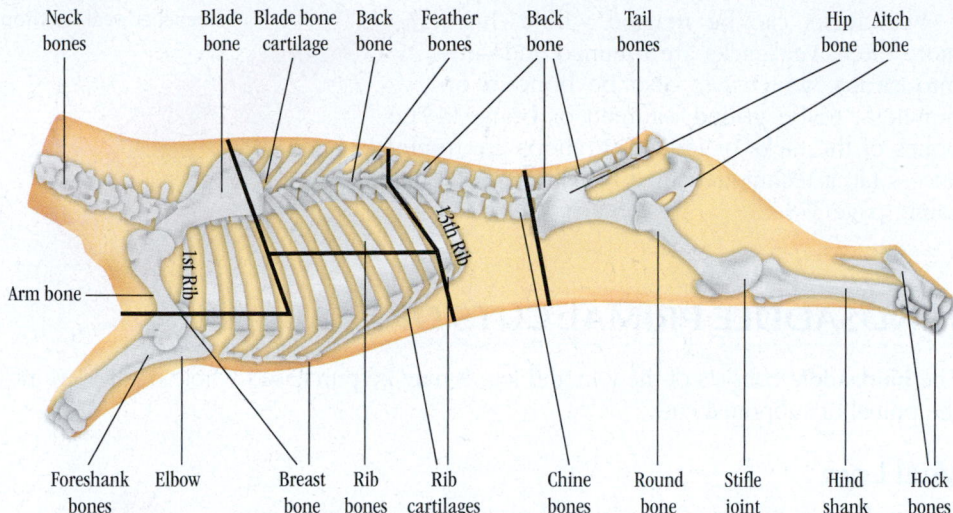

Figure 15.1 The skeletal structure of a calf.

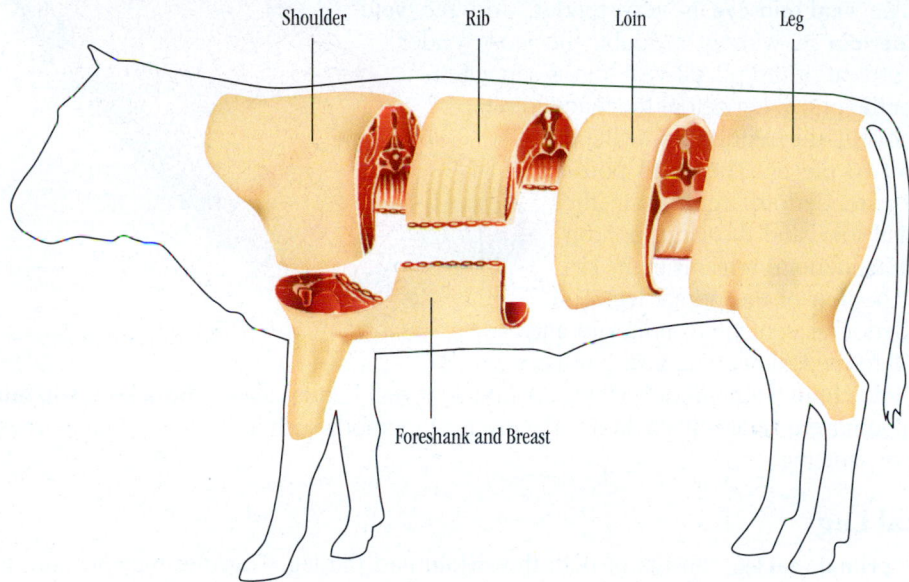

Figure 15.2 The five primal cuts of veal.

for approximately 16 percent of the carcass weight. This primal contains rib bones and rib cartilage, breast bones and shank bones. Because the calf is slaughtered young, many of the breast bones are cartilaginous rather than bony.

This cartilage, as well as the ample fat and connective tissue present in the breast, breaks down during long moist cooking, thus making the flavorful breast a good choice for braising. Veal breast can also be cubed for stews such as veal fricassee and veal blanquette, rolled and stuffed or trimmed and ground.

The foreshank is also very flavorful but tough. It can be braised whole or sliced perpendicular to the shank bone and braised to produce **osso buco**.

Veal Rib

The **veal double rib**, also known as a **veal hotel rack**, is a very tender, relatively small primal cut accounting for approximately 9 percent of the carcass weight. It is very popular and very expensive. The double rack consists of two **racks**, each with seven rib bones and a portion of the backbone.

Veal hotel rack, split

rack a set of connected rib bones that may be cooked and served in one piece

frenching a method of trimming racks or individual chops of meat, especially lamb, in which the excess fat is cut away, leaving the eye muscle intact; all meat and connective tissue are removed from the rib bone

Veal racks can be roasted whole, but more often, veal racks are trimmed and cut into chops, which can also be bone-in or boneless, to be grilled, sautéed or braised. The bones of the racks or individual chops are trimmed of excess fat, a technique called **frenching**. See Chapter 16, Lamb, page 378.

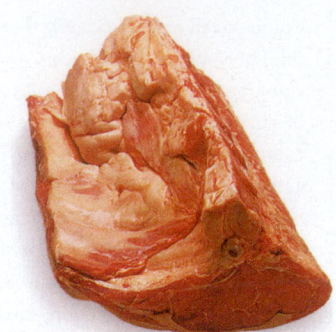

Veal loin

HINDSADDLE PRIMAL CUTS OF VEAL

The **hindsaddle** consists of the loin and leg. It may be purchased whole or divided into the primal or subprimal cuts.

Veal Loin

The **veal loin** is posterior to the primal rib, contains two ribs (numbers 12 and 13) and accounts for approximately 10 percent of the carcass weight. The loin consists of the loin eye muscle on top of the rib bones and the tenderloin under them.

The **veal loin eye** is very tender, and the **veal tenderloin** is, without a doubt, the most tender cut of veal. If the primal veal loin is separated from the primal leg before the tenderloin is removed, the tenderloin will be cut into two pieces. The small portion (short tenderloin) remains in the primal loin, and the large portion (butt tenderloin) remains in the sirloin portion of the primal leg. The tenderloin is sometimes removed and cut into medallions. The veal loin is often cut into **chops**, bone-in or boneless. A boneless veal loin is called a **boneless strip loin**. Veal loin meat is usually cooked using dry-heat methods such as broiling, grilling, roasting or sautéing.

Frenched veal rib chop

Veal loin chops

Boneless strip loin of veal

Veal top round

Veal Leg

The **primal veal leg** consists of both the **sirloin** and the leg. Together they account for approximately 42 percent of the carcass weight. The primal leg is separated from the loin by a cut perpendicular to the backbone immediately anterior to the hip bone. The leg contains portions of the backbone, tail bone, hip bone, aitch bone, round bone and hindshank.

Although it is tender enough to be roasted whole, the veal leg is typically fabricated into **cutlets** and **scallops** for scallopine or schnitzel. As shown on pages 354–356, to fabricate these cuts, the veal leg is first broken down into its major muscles: the **top round**, **eye round**, knuckle, sirloin, **bottom round** (which includes the sirloin) and butt tenderloin. Each of these muscles can be reduced to scallops by trimming all fat and visible connective tissue and slicing against the grain to the desired thickness. The scallops then should be pounded carefully to tenderize them further and to prevent them from curling when cooked.

The **veal hindshank** is somewhat meatier than the foreshank, but both are prepared and cooked in the same manner.

Veal leg

Hindshank cut for osso buco

VEAL ORGAN MEATS

Several veal organ meats (offal) are used in food service operations. Calf organ meats are more tender with a milder flavor than those from beef.

Sweetbreads

Sweetbreads are the thymus glands of veal (Fr. *ris de veau*) and lamb (Fr. *ris d'agneau*). As an animal ages, its thymus gland shrinks; therefore sweetbreads are not available from older cattle or sheep. Veal sweetbreads are much more popular than lamb sweetbreads in the United States. Good-quality sweetbreads should be plump and firm, with the exterior membrane intact. Delicately flavored and tender, they are usually blanched before being sautéed or pan-fried, although sweetbreads can be prepared by almost any cooking method.

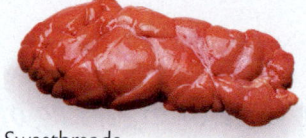

Sweetbreads

Calves' Liver

Calves' liver is much more popular than beef liver because of its tenderness and mild flavor. Good-quality calves' liver should be firm and moist, with a shiny appearance and without any off-odor. It is most often sliced and sautéed or broiled and served with a sauce.

Veal Kidneys

Veal kidneys are more popular in other parts of the world than in the United States. Good-quality kidneys should be plump, firm and encased in a shiny membrane. Properly prepared kidneys have a rich flavor and firm texture; they are best prepared by moist-heat cooking methods and are sometimes used in stew or kidney pie. The hard, flavorful fat (**suet**) that collects on veal kidneys can be used in forcemeats, for barding and, when rendered, for deep-frying.

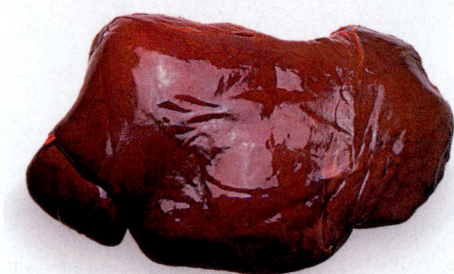

Calves' liver

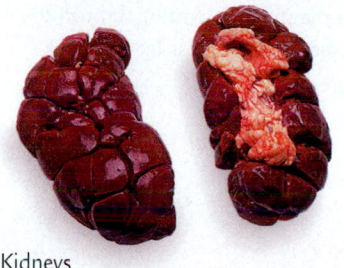

Kidneys

PURCHASING VEAL

Veal quality varies greatly among purveyors. Purchase veal only from reputable companies to be sure of receiving a consistently high-quality product. Veal meat should be moist and fresh looking with a pale color. A large quantity of outside fat, marbling and fat that is yellow in color indicates that the calf was too old when slaughtered. The meat may be tough.

Because the veal carcass is small enough to be handled easily, it is sometimes purchased in forms larger than the primal cuts described in this chapter. Depending on employee skill, available equipment, storage space and ability to utilize fully all the cuts and trimmings that fabricating meat produces, a chef may want to purchase veal in one of the following forms:

- *Foresaddle:* The anterior (front) portion of the carcass after it is severed from the hindsaddle by a cut following the natural curvature between the eleventh and twelfth ribs. The foresaddle contains the primal shoulder, foreshank and breast and rib.
- *Hindsaddle:* The posterior portion of the carcass after it is severed from the foresaddle. The hindsaddle contains the primal loin and leg.
- *Back:* The trimmed rib and loin sections in one piece. The back is particularly useful when producing large quantities of veal chops.
- *Veal side:* A single bilateral half of the carcass, produced by cutting lengthwise through the backbone.

NUTRITION INFORMATION FOR VEAL

Like beef, veal is a major source of protein as well as niacin, zinc and B vitamins. Veal has less marbling than beef. When trimmed of any visible fat, veal is lower in fat and calories than comparable beef cuts. And it is leaner than many cuts of pork and poultry.

BUTCHERING PROCEDURES FOR VEAL

As noted earlier, because veal carcasses are relatively small, they are sometimes purchased as primal or other large cuts and fabricated in-house to the operation's own specifications. See Table 15.1 for a list of standard fabricated veal cuts. A chef should master several important veal fabrication and butchering techniques.

Procedure for Boning a Leg of Veal

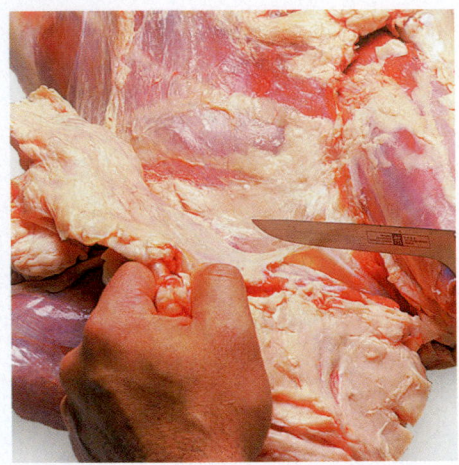

1 Remove the shank by cutting through the knee joint. Remove the excess fat and flank meat.

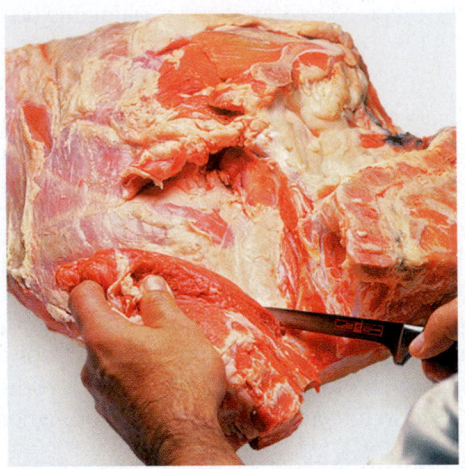

2 Remove the butt tenderloin from the inside of the pelvic bone.

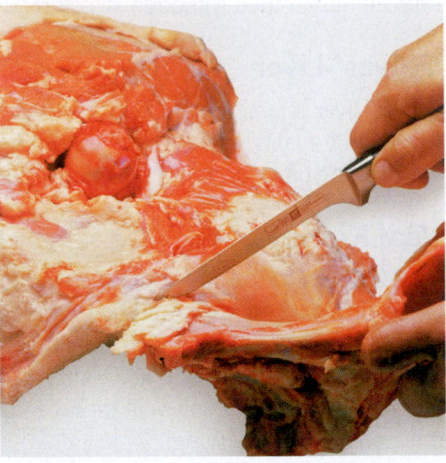

3 Remove the pelvic bone by carefully cutting around the bone, separating it from the meat. Continue until the bone is completely freed from the meat.

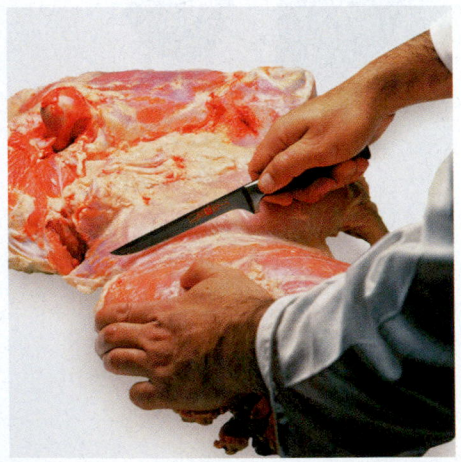

4 With the inside of the leg up, remove the top round by cutting along the natural seam.

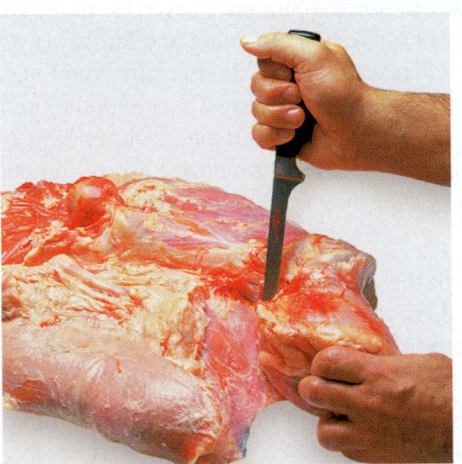

5 Remove the shank meat. (It is the round piece of meat lying between the eye round and the bone, on the shank end of the leg.)

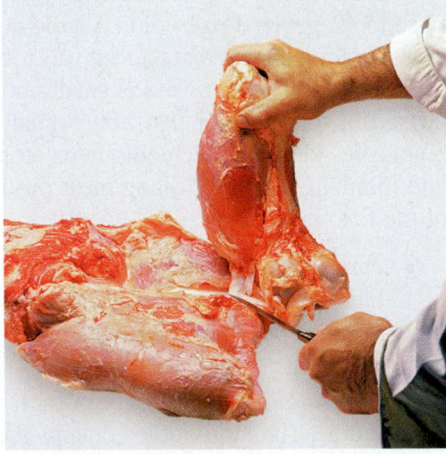

6 Remove the round bone and the knuckle together by cutting around the bone and through the natural seams separating the knuckle from the other muscles. Separate the knuckle meat from the bone.

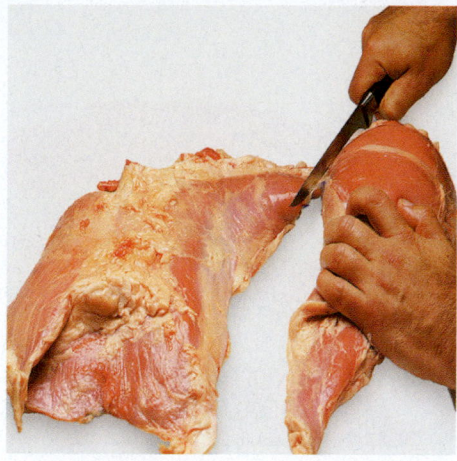

7 Remove the sirloin.

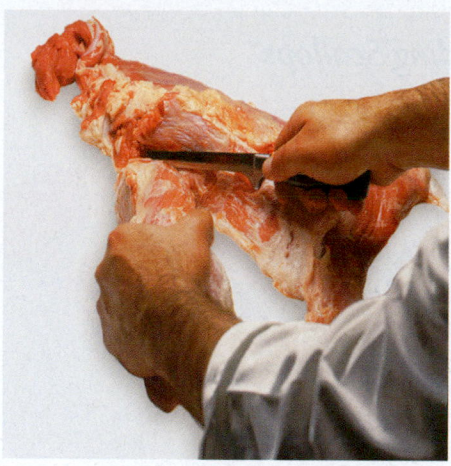

8 Remove the eye round from the bottom round.

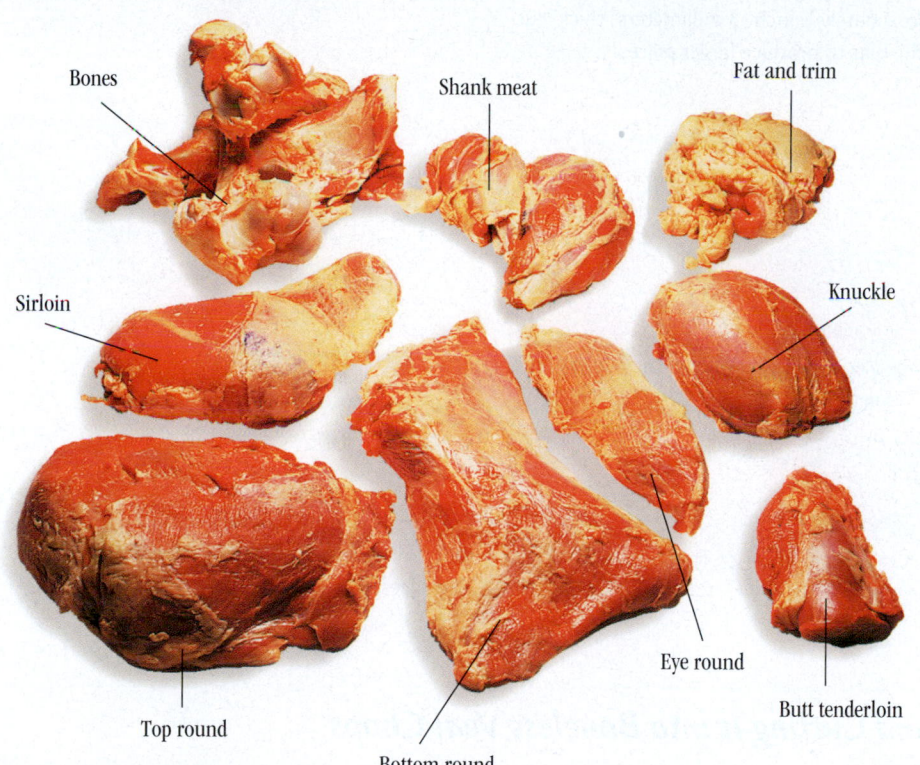

The completely boned-out veal leg produces a top round, eye round, knuckle, shank meat, butt tenderloin, sirloin, bottom round, bones and trimmings.

Formula-Fed Veal versus Free-Range Veal

Most veal produced today is **formula-fed veal**. Formula-fed calves are fed only nutrient-rich liquids and they are tethered in pens only slightly larger than their bodies in order to restrict their movements. Preventing the calves from eating grasses and other foods containing iron keeps their flesh white; restricting movement keeps their muscles from toughening. In recent years, controversy and allegations of cruelty have arisen concerning these methods, which has led some farmers to raise their calves in open pens with access to the outdoors. **Free-range veal** is produced from calves that are allowed to roam freely and eat grasses and other natural foods. Because they consume feed containing iron, their flesh is a reddish pink and has a substantially different flavor than meat from formula-fed calves of the same age.

Opinions differ on which type of veal has the better flavor. Some chefs prefer the consistently mild, sweet taste of formula-fed veal. Others prefer the more substantial flavor of free-range veal. The two are interchangeable in recipes. Cost, however, may be the ultimate deciding factor when determining which to use. Free-range veal is more expensive than formula-fed veal because of its limited production.

Procedure for Cutting and Pounding Scallops

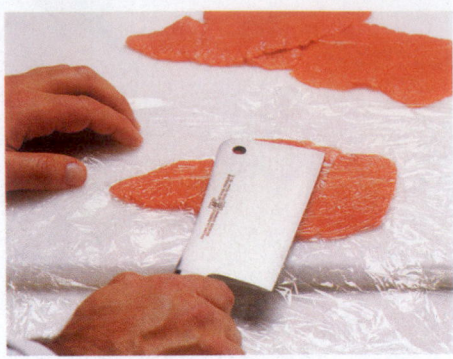

① Veal scallops are cut from relatively large pieces of veal (in these photos, we begin with a portion of the top round). Trim all fat and silverskin. Going against the grain, cut slices approximately ¼ inch (3 millimeters) thick; cut on the bias to produce larger pieces.

② Place the scallops between two pieces of plastic wrap and pound lightly with a spreading motion to flatten and tenderize the meat. Be careful not to tear or pound holes in the meat.

Procedure for Cutting Émincé

Émincé is cut from relatively small, lean pieces of meat. Here veal is cut across the grain into small, thin slices.

Procedure for Boning a Veal Loin and Cutting It into Boneless Veal Chops

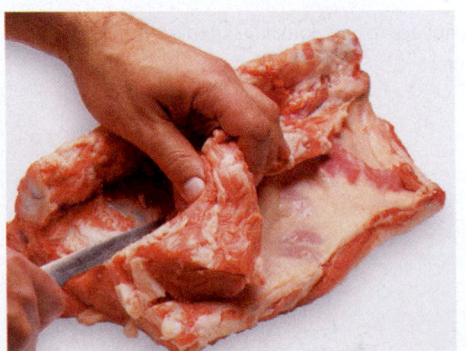

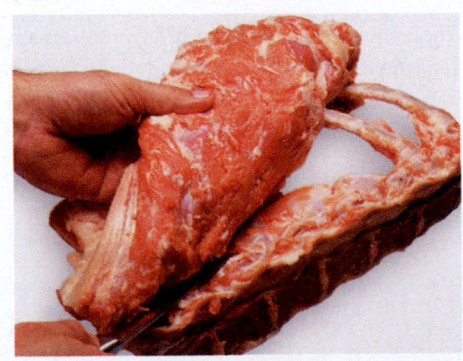

① Remove the tenderloin in a single piece from the inside of the loin by following the vertebrae and cutting completely around the tenderloin.

② From the backbone side, cut along the natural curve of the backbone, separating the loin meat from the backbone.

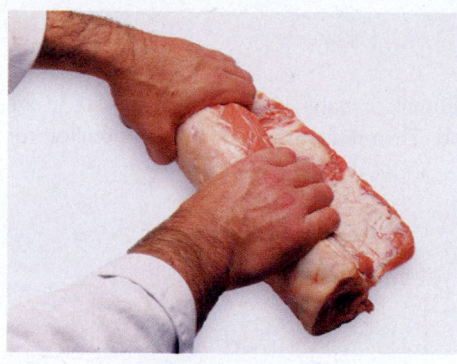

❸ Trim any excess fat from the loin, and trim the flank to create a 3-inch (7.5-centimeter) lip. Tightly roll up the loin with the flank on the outside.

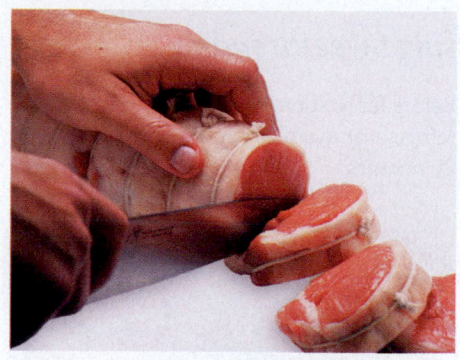

❹ Tie the loin, using the procedure described next, at 1-inch (2.5-centimeter) intervals. Cut between the pieces of twine for individual boneless loin chops.

Procedure for Tying Meats

Here we apply the tying procedure to a boneless veal loin; the same procedure can be used on any type of meat.

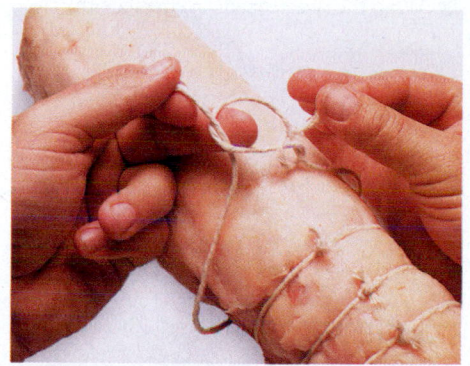

❶ Cut a piece of string long enough to wrap completely around the loin. Holding one end between the thumb and forefinger, pass the other end around it and across the strings. Loop the loose end of the string around your finger.

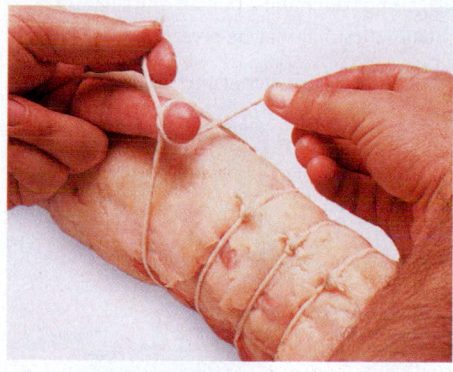

❷ Wrap the string around itself and pass the loose end back through the hole.

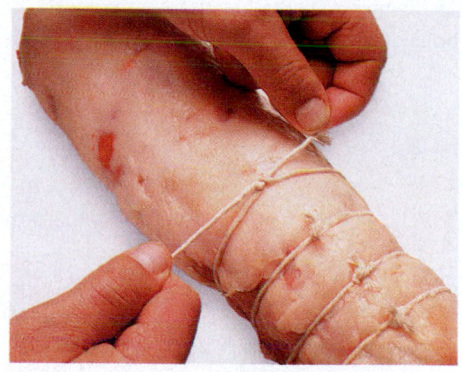

❸ Pull to tighten the knot. Adjust the string so it is snug against the meat.

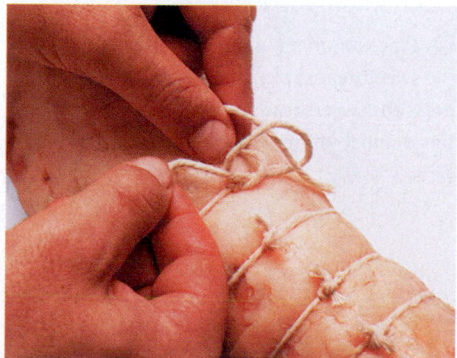

❹ Loop one end of the string around your thumb and forefinger. Reach through with your thumb and forefinger and pull the other string back through the loop. Pull both strings to tighten the knot, thus preventing the first knot from loosening. Trim the ends of the strings.

❺ Continue in this fashion until the entire loin is tied. The strings should be tied at even intervals, just snug enough to hold the shape of the loin; they should not dig into or cut the meat.

Procedure for Cleaning and Pressing Sweetbreads

Before fabrication, submerge the sweetbreads in cold milk or water, cover them and place in the refrigerator overnight in order to soak out any blood. Then poach them in a court bouillon for 20 minutes.

1 Remove the sweetbreads from the court bouillon and allow them to cool.

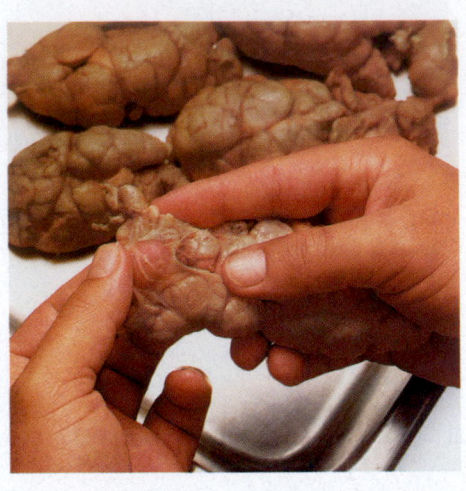

2 Using your hands, pull off any sinew or membranes that may be present on the surface of the sweetbreads.

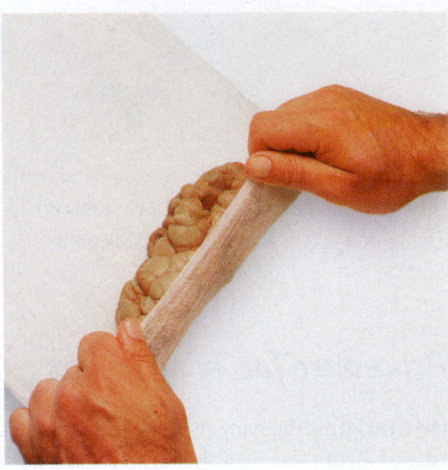

3 Wrap the sweetbreads in cheesecloth.

4 Tie the ends with butcher's twine.

5 Place the wrapped sweetbreads in a half-size hotel pan or similar container.

6 Place another half-size hotel pan on top of the sweetbreads; place a weight in the pan to press the sweetbreads. Pressing sweetbreads in this manner improves their texture.

Procedure for Cleaning Calves' Liver

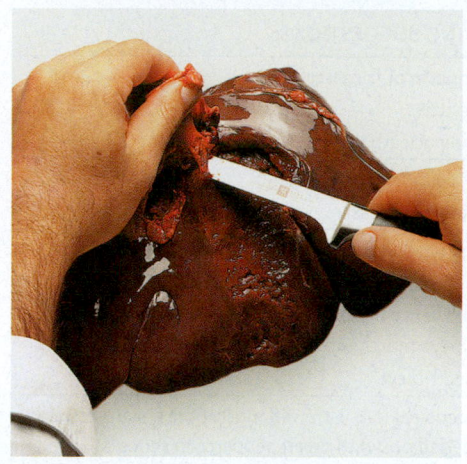

1 Trim the large sinew and outer membrane from the bottom of the liver.

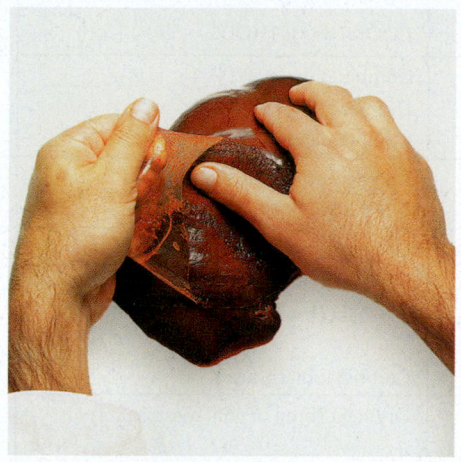

2 Turn the liver over and peel the membrane off with your hands.

3 The liver can be cut into thick or thin slices as needed.

Procedure for Cleaning Veal Kidneys

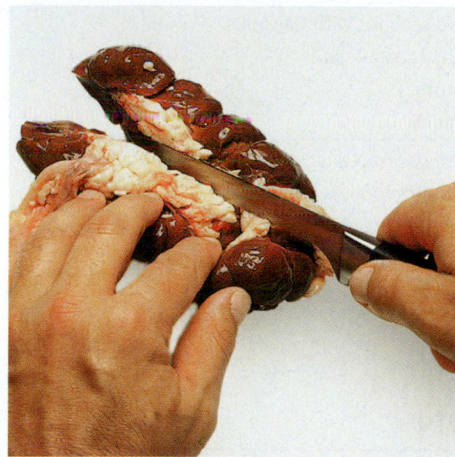

1 Split the kidneys lengthwise, exposing the fat and sinew.

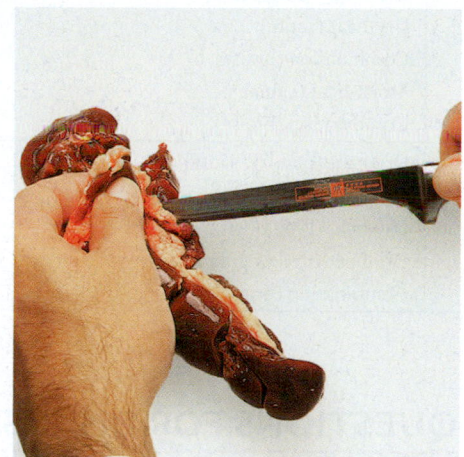

2 With a sharp knife, trim away the fat; the kidney is now ready for cooking.

USING COMMON CUTS OF VEAL   TABLE 15.1

PRIMAL	SUBPRIMAL OR FABRICATED CUT	IMPS	COOKING METHODS	SERVING SUGGESTIONS
Shoulder	Veal for stewing	395	Combination (stew)	Blanquette or fricassee
	Ground veal	396	Dry-heat (broil or grill)	Veal patties
			Combination (braise)	Stuffing; meatballs
Foreshank and breast	Foreshank	312	Combination (braise)	Osso buco
	Breast	313	Combination (braise)	Stuffed veal breast
Rib	Rib chops	1306	Dry-heat (broil or grill)	Grilled veal chop
			Combination (braise)	Braised veal chop with risotto
	Rib eye	307	Dry-heat (broil or grill; roast)	Broiled veal rib eye with chipotle sauce; roasted veal rib eye marchand de vin
			Combination (braise)	Braised rib eye
Loin	Veal loin	348	Dry-heat (broil or grill; roast; sauté)	Roasted veal loin with wild mushrooms; sautéed veal medallions with green peppercorn sauce
	Loin chops	1332	Dry-heat (broil or grill; sauté)	Broiled or sautéed veal chops with mushroom sauce
			Combination (braise)	Braised veal chops lyonnaise
	Boneless strip loin	344	Dry-heat (broil or grill; roast; sauté)	Roasted veal loin sauce poulette
	Veal tenderloin	348	Dry-heat (broil or grill; roast; sauté)	Grilled tenderloin; roasted tenderloin; sautéed tenderloin with garlic and herbs
Leg	Leg	334	Dry-heat (roast; sauté)	Veal scallopini
			Combination (stew)	Blanquette
	Top round	349A	Dry-heat (roast; sauté)	Veal marsala; schnitzel
	Bottom (outside)	350A	Dry-heat (sauté)	Sautéed scallops with Calvados
			Combination (braise)	Stuffed veal scallops
	Hindshank	337	Moist-heat (simmer)	Veal broth
			Combination (braise)	Osso buco
Organ meats (offal)	Sweetbreads	3722	Dry-heat (pan-fry; sauté)	Sautéed sweetbreads beurre noisette
			Combination (braise)	Braised sweetbreads Madeira
	Calves' liver	3724	Dry-heat (broil or grill; sauté)	Broiled or sautéed calves' liver with onion and bacon
	Kidneys	3728	Dry-heat (broil or grill; sauté)	Broiled or sautéed kidneys with mustard
			Combination (braise)	Kidney pie

QUESTIONS FOR DISCUSSION

1   Compare the appearance and flavor of beef and veal.

2   What are the differences between formula-fed veal and free-range veal?

3   Describe two differences between a beef carcass and a veal carcass. What characteristics are desirable when selecting veal for purchase?

4   List each veal primal and describe its location on the carcass. For each primal, identify two subprimals or fabricated cuts taken from it.

5   Would it be better to use a veal loin for grilling or braising? Explain your answer.

6   What are veal sweetbreads? Describe how sweetbreads should be prepared for cooking.

7   Certain groups oppose the use of formula-fed veal, saying that the animals are treated in an inhumane manner. Use the Internet to research this issue. What are these organizations? Are their arguments valid? What are the alternatives?

Veal Recipes

Wood-Grilled Veal Chops with Basil Butter

YIELD	8 Servings, 6 oz. (180 g) each	METHOD	Grilling
Veal rib chops, frenched, 8 oz. (240 g) ea.		2	2
Garlic clove, split		1	1
Fresh thyme leaves, chopped		1 Tbsp.	15 ml
Olive oil		1 fl. oz.	30 ml
Black pepper		½ tsp.	2 ml
Basil Butter (page 234)		3 oz.	90 g
Micro greens		as needed for garnish	

1 Trim the chops so that only ¼-inch layer of fat remains. Rub the bone and surface of each veal chop with the cut side of the garlic clove.

2 Combine the thyme and olive oil in a shallow pan. Add the veal chops, turning them over in the marinade to cover evenly. Marinate the chops in the refrigerator for 2–4 hours.

3 Grill the chops over a hot grill to the desired doneness, from 4 to 5 minutes per side depending on the thickness of the meat. Allow the meat to rest for 5 minutes after grilling.

4 Serve each chop on a heated plate topped with 1½ ounces (45 grams) of Basil Butter. Garnish with micro greens and additional accompaniments as desired.

Approximate values per 6-oz. (180-g) serving: **Calories** 550, **Total fat** 48 g, **Saturated fat** 22 g, **Cholesterol** 180 mg, **Sodium** 105 mg, **Total carbohydrates** 2 g, **Protein** 28 g, **Vitamin A** 20%

Weisswurst with Braised Red Cabbage and Rösti Potatoes

YIELD	6 Servings, 5 oz. (150 g) each	METHOD	Sautéing
Weisswurst sausage, 4 oz. each		6	6
Vegetable oil		2 fl. oz.	60 ml
Braised Cabbage with Red Apples (page 650)		1½ lb.	720 g
Rösti Potatoes (page 688), 10-inches, cut into 6 wedges		1	1

1 Heat the oil in a 12-inch skillet over medium high heat. Add the veal sausage and cook, turning until each side is browned and heated through.

2 Serve the sausage with a portion of Braised Cabbage with Red Apples and a wedge of Rösti Potatoes.

Approximate values per 5-oz. (150-g) serving: **Calories** 960, **Total fat** 73 g, **Saturated fat** 29 g, **Cholesterol** 125 mg, **Sodium** 1980 mg, **Total carbohydrates** 53 g, **Protein** 26 g, **Vitamin C** 80%

Sautéed Veal Scallops with Calvados

YIELD	6 Servings, 11 oz. (330 g) each	METHOD	Sautéing
Mushrooms, sliced		12 oz.	360 g
Clarified butter		4 fl. oz.	120 ml
Golden Delicious apples		3	3
Veal scallops, pounded, 6 oz. (180 g) each		6	6
Salt and pepper		TT	TT
Shallots, minced		2	2
Calvados		2 fl. oz.	60 ml
Crème fraîche		8 fl. oz.	240 ml
Fresh parsley, chopped		1 Tbsp.	15 ml

1 Sauté the mushrooms in a portion of the clarified butter until dry. Remove and reserve.

2 Peel and core the apples. Cut each into 12 wedges.

3 Sauté the apple wedges in a portion of the clarified butter until slightly browned and tender. Remove and reserve.

4 Season the veal scallops with salt and pepper. Sauté in the remaining clarified butter. (This may be done in two or three batches.) Remove and reserve.

5 Add the shallots to the pan and sauté without browning.

6 Deglaze with the Calvados. Flambé the Calvados.

7 Add the sautéed mushrooms and crème fraîche to the pan. Bring to a boil and reduce the sauce until it thickens slightly.

8 Return the scallops to the pan to reheat. Serve each scallop with sauce, garnished with six apple slices and chopped parsley.

Approximate values per 11-oz. (330-g) serving: **Calories** 650, **Total fat** 41 g, **Saturated fat** 21 g, **Cholesterol** 295 mg, **Sodium** 710 mg, **Total carbohydrates** 14 g, **Protein** 56 g, **Vitamin A** 30%

Veal Marsala

YIELD 6 servings, 7 oz. (210 g) each	METHOD Sautéing	
Veal scallops, pounded, 3 oz. (90 g) each	12	12
Salt and pepper	TT	TT
Flour	as needed for dredging	
Clarified butter	2 fl. oz.	60 ml
Olive oil	2 fl. oz.	60 ml
Dry Marsala wine	6 fl. oz.	180 ml
Brown veal stock	4 fl. oz.	120 ml
Whole butter	1½ oz.	45 g

1. Season the scallops with salt and pepper. Dredge the scallops in flour and sauté them in a mixture of the clarified butter and oil, a few at a time, until all are cooked.

2. Remove the scallops and set aside. Degrease the pan and deglaze with the wine. Add the stock and reduce until it begins to thicken.

3. Return the scallops to the sauce to reheat. Remove the scallops to plates or a serving platter.

4. Reduce the sauce until it becomes syrupy; adjust the seasonings. Monté au beurre and spoon the sauce over the veal.

5. Serve the veal with mashed potatoes and cooked baby carrots or other garnishes.

Variation:

Wild Mushroom Veal Marsala—Slice or quarter 12 ounces (360 grams) assorted wild mushrooms. Sauté the mushrooms in 2 ounces (60 grams) butter. Prepare the veal and sauce. Divide the mushrooms evenly between the plates. Garnish with some of the sauce.

Approximate values per 7-oz. (210-g) serving: **Calories** 430, **Total fat** 28 g, **Saturated fat** 12 g, **Cholesterol** 165 mg, **Sodium** 650 mg, **Total carbohydrates** 9 g, **Protein** 36 g, **Vitamin A** 15%

Wild Mushroom Veal Marsala

Veal Cordon Bleu

YIELD 4 Servings, 6 oz. (180 g) each	METHOD Deep-frying	
Veal cutlets, 4 oz. (120 g) each	4	4
Salt and white pepper	TT	TT
Parsley, chopped	4 tsp.	20 ml
Ham slices, 1 oz. (30 g) each	4	4
Swiss cheese slices, 1 oz. (30 g) each	4	4
Flour	as needed for breading	
Egg wash	as needed for breading	
Bread crumbs	as needed for breading	
Lemon wedges	as needed for garnish	

1 Place the veal cutlets on a film-covered cutting board and cover them with a layer of plastic wrap. Using a meat mallet, gently pound the cutlets to an even thickness of approximately ¼ inch (6 millimeters). Remove the plastic wrap.

2 Season the cutlets with salt and white pepper and sprinkle them with the parsley.

3 Place one slice of ham and one slice of cheese on each cutlet. If the slices are larger than the cutlet, cut the slices in half and layer them on the cutlet.

4 Begin rolling the veal cutlet. Fold the ends toward the center to close the ends of the roll and finish rolling. Refrigerate the veal rolls for 15 minutes.

5 Bread the veal rolls using the standard breading procedure described in Chapter 9, Mise en Place, and refrigerate for an additional 15 minutes.

6 Using the basket method, deep-fry the veal rolls at 325°F (160°C) until fully cooked, approximately 8 minutes. Serve with lemon wedges. Flavored hollandaise or béarnaise sauce may also be served with this dish.

Variation:

Turkey Cordon Bleu—Substitute 4-ounce (120-gram) turkey breast cutlets for the veal.

Approximate values per 6-oz. (180-g) serving: **Calories** 470, **Total fat** 34 g, **Saturated fat** 13 g, **Cholesterol** 140 g, **Sodium** 500 mg, **Total carbohydrates** 1 g, **Protein** 40 g, **Calcium** 30%

❶ Pounding the veal cutlets to an even thickness.

❷ Rolling the veal cutlets.

Veal Pojarski

YIELD 6 Servings, 8 oz. (240 g) each	METHOD Pan-frying	
Dried porcini mushrooms	½ oz.	15 g
Butter, melted	1 fl. oz.	30 ml
Shallots, minced	1 fl. oz.	30 ml
Garlic cloves, chopped	2	2
Ground veal	2 lb.	960 g
Nutmeg, ground	¼ tsp.	1 ml
Salt	1 tsp.	5 ml
Black pepper	¼ tsp.	1 ml
Heavy cream, cold	16 fl. oz.	480 ml
Fresh breadcrumbs	9½ oz.	285 g
Lamb or veal rib bones,	6	6
cleaned and roasted, optional		
Clarified butter	as needed	as needed
Baby fennel, braised	6	6
Large wild mushroom	6	6
such as Blue Foot, sautéed		
Chasseur sauce (page 227)	as needed	as needed

1 Soak the porcini mushrooms in hot water until soft, for approximately 30 minutes. Drain then rinse them under cold running water to remove any sand.

2 Heat a small sauté pan over medium heat and add the butter, mushrooms, shallots and garlic. Sauté until the shallots are translucent and the mushrooms are tender, for approximately 5 minutes. Set aside to cool then chill in the refrigerator.

3 Place the veal to a well-chilled bowl. Add the nutmeg, salt and pepper. Gradually stir the heavy cream into the veal mixture until it is all incorporated. Fold in 4 ounces (120 grams) of the bread crumbs and the chilled mushroom mixture.

4 Divide the mixture into six portions approximately 8 ounces (240 grams) each. Shape them into patties approximately 1 inch (2.5 centimeters) thick. If desired, insert a roasted rib bone in each of the patties so that it resembles a veal chop. Carefully roll the patties in the remaining bread crumbs; chill until ready to cook.

5 Heat two large sauté pans over medium heat. Add enough clarified butter to cover the bottom of the pans. Place three patties in each of the pans and pan fry until they are golden brown, approximately 5 minutes. Carefully turn them over and continue cooking until fully cooked, approximately 5 more minutes. Or remove the patties from the pan and bake them at 350°F (180°C) until the meat reaches an internal temperature of 165°F (74°C).

6 Serve with braised baby fennel, sautéed mushrooms and Chasseur sauce.

Approximate values per 8-oz. (240-g) serving: **Calories** 780, **Total fat** 54 g, **Saturated fat** 29 g, **Cholesterol** 175 mg, **Sodium** 830 mg, **Total carbohydrates** 34 g, **Protein** 38 g, **Vitamin A** 40%, **Vitamin C** 20%, **Calcium** 20%, **Iron** 30%

1 Adding the cream to the veal mixture.

2 Pan-frying the Veal Pojarski patties.

Sweetbreads Grenoble

YIELD 8 Servings, 5 oz. (150 g) each	METHOD Sautéing	
Sweetbreads, blanched and pressed	8	8
Salt and pepper	TT	TT
Flour	as needed for dredging	
Clarified butter	2 fl. oz.	60 ml
Dry white wine	2 fl. oz.	60 ml
Whole butter	4 oz.	120 g
Capers	3 oz.	90 g
Lemons, cut into segments, membranes removed	3	3
Veal demi-glace	2 fl. oz.	60 ml

1 Slice the sweetbreads and season with salt and pepper. Dust each piece lightly with flour.

2 Heat the clarified butter in a large sauté pan; add the sweetbreads and cook on each side for 1 to 2 minutes, until golden brown. Transfer the sweetbreads to a roasting pan and bake in a 375°F (190°C) oven for 5 minutes.

3 Deglaze the sauté pan with the wine. Add the whole butter, capers and lemon segments and cook over high heat for 1–2 minutes. Add the demi-glace and cook until thoroughly heated, approximately 1 more minute.

4 Arrange the sweetbreads on plates and top with the sauce.

Approximate values per 5-oz. (150-g) serving: **Calories** 345, **Total fat** 22 g, **Saturated fat** 13 g, **Cholesterol** 512 mg, **Sodium** 461 mg, **Total carbohydrates** 4 g, **Protein** 33 g, **Vitamin A** 14%, **Vitamin C** 51%

Sautéed Calves' Liver with Onions

YIELD 10 Servings, 6 oz. (180 g) each	METHOD Sautéing	
Onions, julienne	1 lb. 8 oz.	720 g
Clarified butter	3 fl. oz.	90 ml
Salt and pepper	TT	TT
White wine	8 fl. oz.	240 ml
Fresh parsley, chopped	1 Tbsp.	15 ml
Calves' liver, 3-oz. (90-g) slices	20	20
Flour	as needed for dredging	

1 Sauté the onions in 1 fluid ounce (30 milliliters) clarified butter until golden brown. Season with salt and pepper.

2 Add the wine, cover and braise until the onions are tender, approximately 10 minutes. Stir in the parsley.

3 Dredge the liver in flour seasoned with salt and pepper.

4 In a separate pan, sauté the liver in the remaining clarified butter until done. The liver should be slightly pink in the middle.

5 Serve the liver with a portion of the onions and their cooking liquid.

Approximate values per 6-oz. (180-g) serving: **Calories** 270, **Total fat** 9 g, **Saturated fat** 3 g, **Cholesterol** 535 mg, **Sodium** 520 mg, **Total carbohydrates** 16 g, **Protein** 30 g, **Vitamin A** 1190%, **Vitamin C** 50%

Veal Marengo

YIELD 6 Servings, 10 oz. (300 g) each	METHOD Stewing	
Lean boneless veal, cut in 2-in. (5-cm) cubes	2 lb. 8 oz.	1.2 kg
Salt and pepper	TT	TT
Flour	as needed for dredging	
Vegetable oil	1½ fl. oz.	45 ml
Clarified butter	3 fl. oz.	90 ml
Onions, medium dice	12 oz.	360 g
Carrots, medium diced	10 oz.	300 g
Garlic cloves, crushed	2	2
Tomato paste	1 oz.	30 g
Flour	2 Tbsp.	30 ml
Dry white wine	6 fl. oz.	180 ml
Brown veal stock	1 pt.	480 ml
Bouquet garni:		
Carrot stick, 4 in. (10 cm)	1	1
Leek, split, 4-in. (10-cm) piece	1	1
Fresh thyme	1 sprig	1 sprig
Bay leaf	1	1
Mushrooms, washed and quartered	8 oz.	240 g
Tomatoes, diced	1 lb.	480 g
Pearl onions, boiled and peeled	24	24

1 Season the veal cubes with salt and pepper and dredge in flour.

2 Heat a heavy-bottomed 8-quart (8-liter) sauce pan over medium heat. Add 1 fluid ounce (30 milliliters) oil and 1 fluid ounce (30 milliliters) clarified butter to the pan. Add the veal and cook, browning well on all sides. Remove and set aside.

3 Add 1½ fluid ounces (45 milliliters) clarified butter and sauté the onions, carrots and garlic without coloring. Stir in the tomato paste and return the veal to the pan. Sprinkle with 2 tablespoons (30 milliliters) flour and cook to make a roux.

4 Add the wine, stock and bouquet garni to the pan; bring to a boil. Cover and simmer until the meat is tender, approximately 1½ hours.

5 Sauté the mushrooms until dry in the remaining oil and butter without browning. Add the tomatoes to the pan and sauté over high heat for 3 minutes. Season with salt and pepper. Remove from the heat and reserve.

6 When the veal is tender, remove it from the pan with a slotted spoon and set aside. Strain the sauce. Return the sauce to the pan and bring it to a boil. The sauce should be the consistency of a light cream sauce. Adjust the consistency of the sauce by reducing it on the stove top or by adding additional brown veal stock.

7 Return the veal to the sauce along with the mushrooms, tomatoes and pearl onions. Bring to a boil and simmer for 5 minutes. Adjust the seasonings before serving.

Approximate values per 10-oz. (300-g) serving: **Calories** 340, **Total fat** 16 g, **Saturated fat** 6 g, **Cholesterol** 125 mg, **Sodium** 490 mg, **Total carbohydrates** 15 g, **Protein** 32 g, **Vitamin A** 70%, **Vitamin C** 25%

Osso Buco

YIELD 4 Servings, 15 oz. (450 g) each	METHOD Braising	
Veal shank, cut in 2-in. (2.5-cm) thick pieces	4–6 pieces	4–6 pieces
Salt and pepper	TT	TT
Flour	as needed for dredging	
Olive oil	as needed	as needed
Garlic clove, minced	2	2
Carrot, diced	6 oz.	180 g
Lemon zest, grated	1 Tbsp.	15 ml
White wine	8 fl. oz.	240 ml
Brown veal stock	1 qt.	960 ml
Tomato purée	2 Tbsp.	30 ml
Gremolada:		
Garlic clove, chopped fine	1	1
Lemon zest	1 Tbsp.	15 ml
Fresh Italian parsley, chopped	1 Tbsp.	15 ml
Risotto Milanese (page 673)	1½ lb.	720 g

1 Season the veal with salt and pepper and dredge the pieces in flour. Sauté them in oil until brown on both sides.

2 Add the garlic and carrot and sauté briefly.

3 Add the lemon zest, wine, stock and tomato purée. Bring to a boil and reduce to a simmer. Braise on the stove top or in a 325°F (160°C) oven until the meat is tender but not falling from the bone, 1 to 1½ hours.

4 Remove the cover and reduce the sauce until thick. Adjust the seasonings.

5 Combine the Gremolada ingredients in a small bowl.

6 At service time, place one or two pieces of veal shank on each plate with some of the Risotto Milanese and sauce. Sprinkle the Gremolada over the meat and sauce.

Approximate values per 15-oz. (450-g) serving: **Calories** 400, **Total fat** 15 g, **Saturated fat** 7 g, **Cholesterol** 65 mg, **Sodium** 930 mg, **Total carbohydrates** 24 g, **Protein** 30 g, **Vitamin A** 150%, **Vitamin C** 15%, **Iron** 15%

Veal Fricassee

YIELD 8 Servings, 8 oz. (240 g) each	METHOD Stewing	
Veal stew meat, cut in 2-in. (5-cm) cubes	4 lb.	1.9 kg
Salt and white pepper	TT	TT
Whole butter	3 oz.	90 g
Onions, small dice	6 oz.	180 g
Garlic, chopped	½ tsp.	2 ml
Flour	3 oz.	90 g
White wine	2 fl. oz.	60 ml
White stock	1½ qt.	1.4 lt
Bouquet garni:		
Carrot stick, 4 in. (10 cm)	1	1
Leek, split, 4-in. (10-cm) piece	1	1
Fresh thyme	1 sprig	1 sprig
Bay leaf	1	1
Heavy cream, hot	8 fl. oz.	240 ml
Classic Rice Pilaf (page 674)	as needed	as needed

1 Season the veal with salt and white pepper and sauté in the butter without browning, approximately 2 minutes.

2 Add the onions and garlic and sauté without coloring, approximately 2 minutes.

3 Add the flour and cook to make a blond roux, approximately 3 minutes.

4 Add the wine and stock, stir well to remove any lumps of roux and bring to a boil. Add the bouquet garni, cover and simmer until the veal is tender, approximately 30 minutes.

5 Remove the veal from the sauce and reserve. Strain the sauce through a fine chinois and return it to the pan. Degrease the sauce.

6 Add the cream to the sauce. Reduce slightly to thicken if necessary. Return the veal to the sauce and adjust the seasonings.

7 Serve the fricassee with Classic Rice Pilaf.

Approximate values per 8-oz. (240-g) serving: **Calories** 340, **Total fat** 18 g, **Saturated fat** 8 g, **Cholesterol** 165 mg, **Sodium** 540 mg, **Total carbohydrates** 6 g, **Protein** 40 g, **Vitamin A** 10%

❶ Adding flour to the veal, onions and garlic.

❷ Adding the cream to the sauce.

Lamb 16

L amb is the meat of sheep slaughtered when they are less than one year old. Both the meat and the animal, whether male or female, are referred to as lamb. Meat from sheep slaughtered after 12 months of age is generally called *mutton,* although in some regions of Asia mutton refers to goat meat.

Even though lamb accounts for a small percentage of the meat consumed in the United States, many people who do not prepare lamb at home will order it in a restaurant. Because of its age, lamb meat is tender and can be prepared by almost any cooking method. Its strong, distinctive flavor allows chefs to offer bold, robust sauces and accompaniments that might mask the flavors of other meats.

PRIMAL AND SUBPRIMAL CUTS OF LAMB

After the young sheep is slaughtered, it is usually reduced to the five primal cuts: shoulder, breast, rack, loin and leg. Like some veal primals, lamb primals are crosscut sections and contain both bilateral halves (e.g., the primal leg contains both hind legs).

Figure 16.1 illustrates the relationship between the lamb's bone structure and the primal cuts. Knowing the location of bones when cutting or working with lamb (as well as all other types of meats) makes fabrication and carving easier and aids in identifying cuts. Figure 16.2 shows the primal cuts of lamb and their location on the carcass. A lamb carcass generally weighs between 41 and 75 pounds (20 and 35 kg).

Lamb Shoulder

The primal **lamb shoulder** is a relatively large cut accounting for 36 percent of the carcass weight. The lamb shoulder contains the first four rib bones and the arm, blade and neck bones as well as many small, tough muscles whose grains travel in different directions.

All these bones and muscle groups make it nearly impossible to cook and carve a whole lamb shoulder. Although lamb shoulder may be cut into chops or boned and then roasted or braised, with or without stuffing, it is more commonly diced for stew or ground for patties.

Lamb shoulder

Lamb Breast

The primal lamb breast contains the **lamb breast** and **lamb foreshank** portions of the carcass. Together they account for approximately 17 percent of the carcass weight and contain the rib, breast and shank bones. The primal lamb breast is located beneath the primal rack and contains the rib tips, which are cut off to produce the rack. When separated from the rest of the breast, these small ribs are called **Denver ribs** and can be substituted for pork ribs when desired. Although the breast is not used extensively in food service operations, it can be stuffed and braised, either bone-in or boneless. Lamb foreshanks are quite meaty and may be braised and served as an entrée, used for broths or ground.

Lamb Rack

The primal **lamb rack** is also known as the **hotel rack**. It is located between the primal shoulder and loin. Containing eight bilateral ribs (ribs 5–12) and portions of the backbone, it accounts for approximately 8 percent of the carcass weight.

The lamb rack is valued for its tender rib eye muscle. The hotel rack is usually split in half and trimmed before cooking so that each set of ribs can be easily cut into chops. The split racks can then be grilled, broiled or roasted as racks or cut into single or

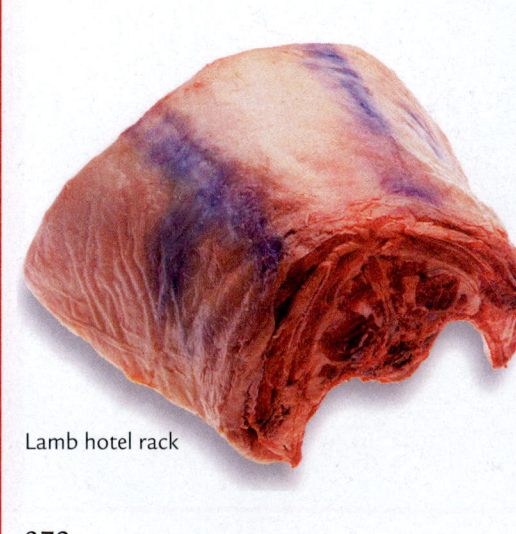
Lamb hotel rack

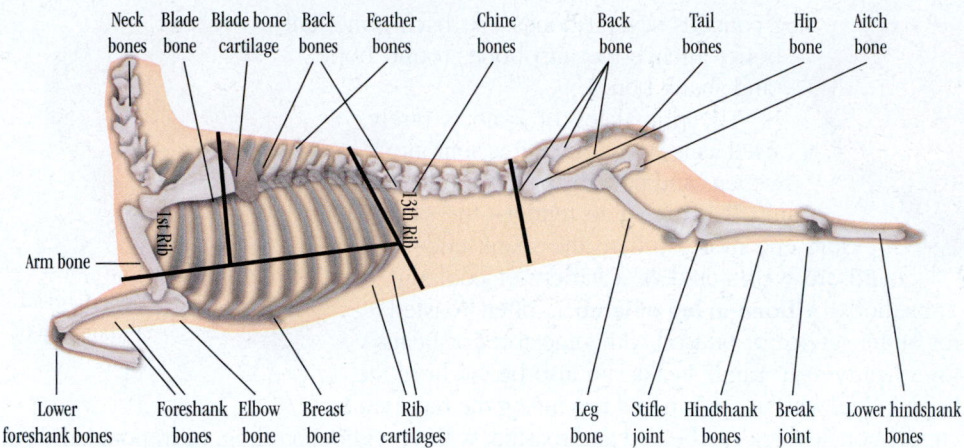

Neck bones | Blade bone | Blade bone cartilage | Back bones | Feather bones | Chine bones | Back bone | Tail bones | Hip bone | Aitch bone

Arm bone

1st Rib

13th Rib

Lower foreshank bones | Foreshank bones | Elbow bone | Breast bone | Rib cartilages | Leg bone | Stifle joint | Hindshank bones | Break joint | Lower hindshank bones

Figure 16.1 The skeletal structure of a lamb.

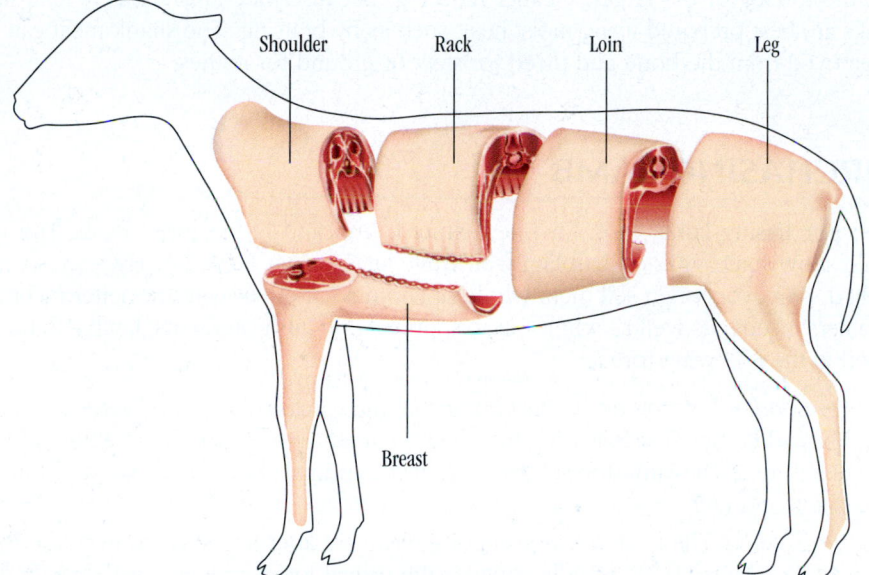

Shoulder | Rack | Loin | Leg

Breast

Figure 16.2 The five primal cuts of lamb.

Classic Lamb Flavors

Lamb and its fat have a pronounced flavor, which lends itself to pairing with garlic and resinous herbs such as mint, oregano and rosemary. Many world cuisines incorporate some acid in their lamb preparations to balance fattiness; vinegar is the basic ingredient in mint sauce served with roasted lamb in Australia, Great Britain and New Zealand. Citrus juice, wine and yogurt are also used to brighten the flavor in lamb stews and sauces served with lamb. In North African tagine, Indian curry and classic French lamb navarin, the sweetness of dried fruits and root vegetables balances the fattiness of lamb.

double rib chops before cooking. Often the bones of the racks or individual chops are trimmed of excess fat, a technique called **frenching**.

Lamb Loin

The **lamb loin** is located between the primal rib and leg. It contains rib number 13 and portions of the backbone as well as the loin eye muscle, tenderloin and flank. It accounts for approximately 13 percent of the carcass weight.

Except for the flank, lamb loin meat is very tender and is invariably cooked using a dry-heat method such as broiling, grilling or roasting. The loin may be boned to produce boneless roasts or chops or cut into chops with the bone in. The loin eye may be removed and cut into lamb medallions or noisettes, which may be prepared in the same manner as filet mignon and tenderloin of beef.

Lamb Leg

The primal **lamb leg** is a large section accounting for approximately 34 percent of the carcass weight. It is the posterior portion of the carcass, separated from the loin by a straight cut anterior to the hip bone cartilage. The primal includes both of an animal's hind legs. As with veal, the cut of meat that would be the sirloin on a beef carcass is separated from the lamb loin by this cut and becomes part of the primal leg. The lamb

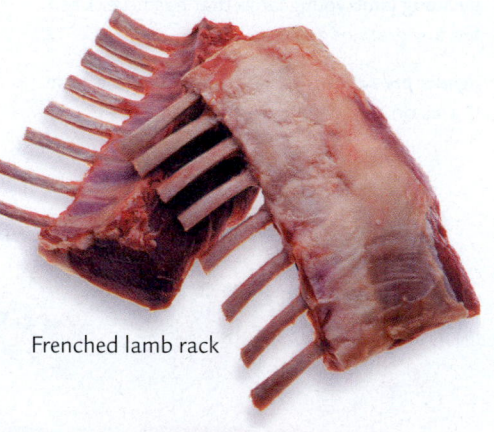

Frenched lamb rack

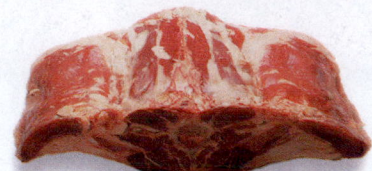

Lamb loin trimmed

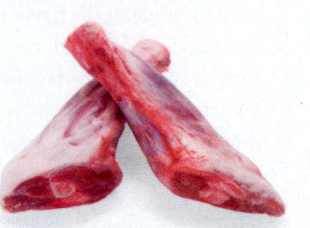

Bone-in lamb leg

Lamb shanks

leg contains several bones: the back bone, tail bone, aitch bone, hip bone, round bone and shank bones.

The primal leg of lamb is rarely used as is. More often, it is split into two legs and partially or fully boned. Lamb legs are quite tender—the sirloin end more so than the shank end—and are well suited to a variety of cooking methods. A **bone-in leg of lamb** is often roasted for buffet service or braised with vegetables or beans for a hearty dish. Lamb steaks can also be cut from the bone-in leg, with the sirloin end producing the most tender cuts. A boneless leg can be tied and roasted, with or without stuffing, or trimmed and cut into scallops. The shank end can be cut crosswise into sections containing a portion of bone, with its marrow, and the muscles alongside the bone. **Lamb shanks** may be cut from the foreleg or the larger, meatier hind leg. Because they are relatively lean, lamb shanks are best prepared using moist heat, such as by braising. The shank meat can also be removed from the bone and diced for stew or ground for patties.

Boned, rolled and tied leg of lamb

PURCHASING LAMB

When purchasing lamb, look for fine textured, firm and red colored flesh. The meat should show some signs of marbling with white fat. Because lamb carcasses are so easily handled, purveyors often sell them whole or cut in a variety of ways to better meet their customers' needs. As well as whole-carcass, primal and fabricated cuts, lamb can be purchased in the following forms:

- *Foresaddle:* The anterior (front) portion of the carcass after it is severed from the hindsaddle by a cut following the natural curvature between the twelfth and thirteenth ribs. The lamb foresaddle contains the primal shoulder, breast and foreshank and rack.
- *Hindsaddle:* The posterior portion of the carcass after it is severed from the foresaddle. The lamb hindsaddle contains the primal loin and legs together with the kidneys.
- *Back:* The trimmed rack and loin sections in one piece. The back is particularly useful when producing large quantities of lamb chops.
- *Bracelet:* The primal hotel rack with the connecting breast sections.

spring lamb young lamb born in the early spring and slaughtered when 3 to 5 months old; spring lamb is often served roasted whole

suckling lamb young lamb that has never been fed any grass or grains

agneau pre-salé distinctively flavored lamb that grazes on salt marshes in France

Domestic vs. Imported Lamb

Technologies that increase shelf life have made imported fresh lamb commonplace. Lamb imported from New Zealand and Australia accounts for nearly 50 percent of the lamb meat sold in the United States. Domestic lamb differs from imported lamb in a few ways. Domestic lamb is primarily grain fed and has a milder flavor than its grass-fed imported counterparts. And domestic lamb is raised to approximately 135 pounds, larger than imported lamb, resulting in larger cut sizes. Be aware that the cooking time may take twice as long for **domestic rack of lamb** as when cooking Australian or New Zealand rack of lamb.

Goat

Closely related to lamb is **goat**, the meat of the species *Capra hircus*. This ruminant thrives in rocky mountainous terrains, preferring scrub and bark to grass. Tender young goat under one year of

Domestic (left) and New Zealand lamb chops

age is called **kid**. Most goats are bred for milk and cheese production although goat meat is consumed in 75 percent of the world. In Mediterranean countries as well as in the West Indies, kid or goat is served whole and spit-roasted or in stews and curries. Commercially-available kid and goat carcasses weigh between 15 and 75 pounds (6.8 and 34 kilograms). Goat is available whole and in fabricated cuts. All goat meat sold in the United States is USDA inspected, but it is not graded for quality or yield.

Young kid or goat may be cooked using dry- or moist-heat cooking methods. Mature goat is best when prepared using moist-heat methods such as braising and stewing.

Goat shank

NUTRITION INFORMATION FOR LAMB

Lamb, especially when purchased in subprimal cuts to be fabricated on-site, is an economical source of high-quality protein. Lean and lower in cholesterol than other red meat proteins, lamb is a good source of iron as compared with chicken, fish or poultry. Lamb has less marbling than other red meats. Its excess fat appears on the outside of many cuts and can easily be trimmed before cooking. Grass-fed lamb, like meat from other grass-fed ruminants, is high in the powerful antioxidant conjugated linoleic acid, identified as a cancer preventative. Goat meat is paler in color than lamb with little marbling. It has a nutritional profile comparable to chicken.

BUTCHERING PROCEDURES FOR LAMB

Lamb is unique among the common meat animals in that it is small enough to be handled easily in its carcass form. Thus food service operations sometimes purchase lamb whole and fabricate the desired cuts themselves. This is practical if the operation has the necessary employee skills, equipment and storage space as well as a need for all the various cuts and trimmings that butchering a whole carcass produces. Table 16.1 on page 379 lists some cuts of lamb commonly available, and a few important lamb fabrication and butchering techniques follow.

Procedure for Cutting Lamb Noisettes from a Loin

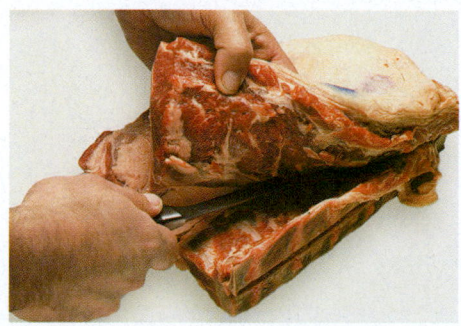

❶ Remove the loin eye muscle by cutting down along the backbone and along the vertebrae. Trim the eye muscle, leaving a thin layer of fat, which may be desirable if the meat will be grilled.

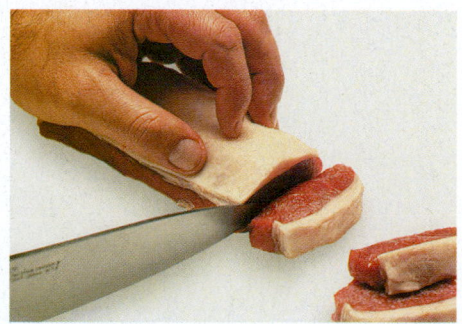

❷ Cut the eye meat into noisettes of the desired thickness.

Procedure for Trimming and Boning a Lamb Leg for Roasting or Grilling

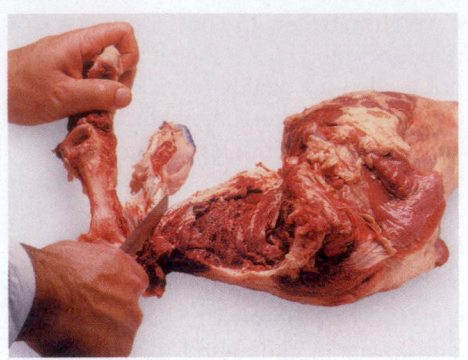

1 With the tip of the knife, trim around the pelvic bone; stay close to the bone to avoid wasting any meat. Cut the sinew inside the socket and remove the bone.

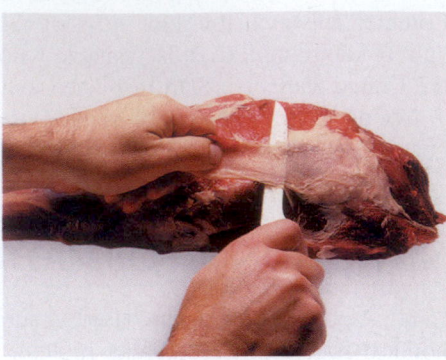

2 Trim away most of the exterior fat.

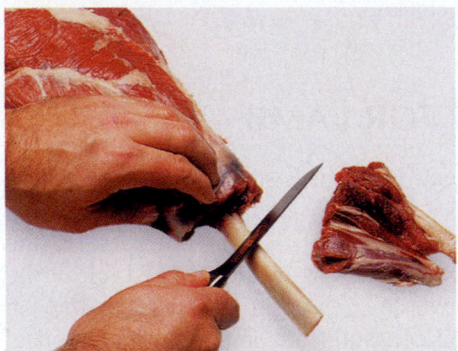

3 Cut off the meat from the shank portion and scrape the bone clean with the back of a knife. This makes a handle to hold while carving the lamb.

4 Fold the flap of the sirloin over on top of the ball of the leg bone and tie with butcher's twine. This helps the leg cook evenly.

Procedure for Boning a Lamb Loin for Roasting

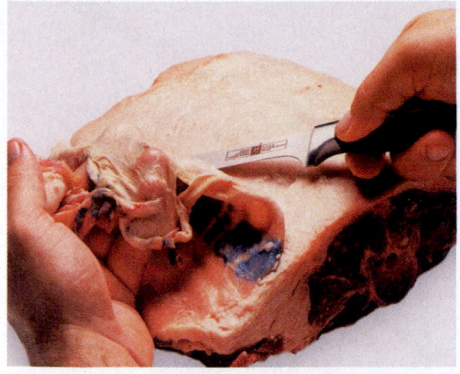

1 Start with a trimmed lamb loin (double). With the skin side up, trim the thin layer of connective tissue called the **fell** from the loin's surface.

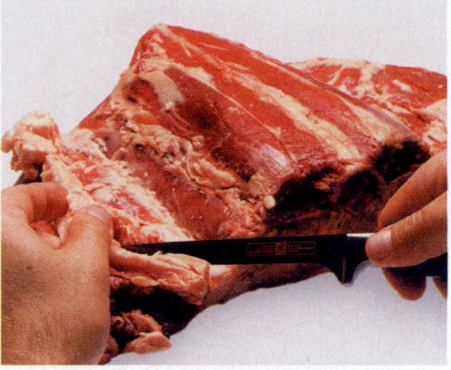

2 Turn the loin over and trim the fat from around the tenderloins.

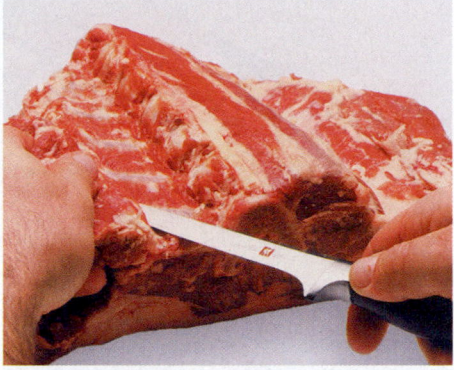

3 Starting in the middle of the backbone, cut between the tenderloin and the vertebrae, separating the tenderloin from the vertebrae but leaving the tenderloin attached to the flank. Continue until you reach the end of the vertebrae. Repeat on the other side.

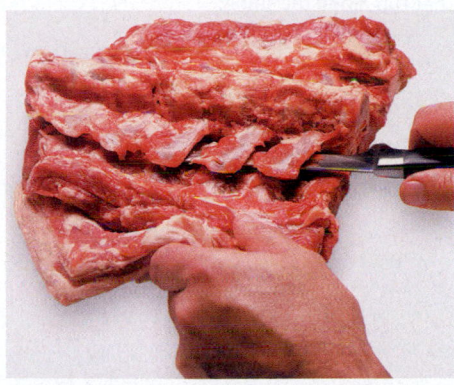

4 Slide the knife under the vertebrae and the rib and cut back all the way to the backbone, separating the eye muscle from the vertebrae.

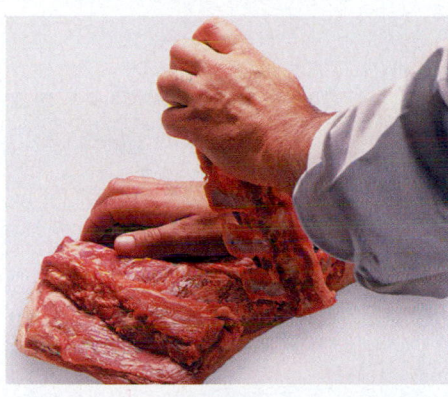

5 Pull the backbone out with your hands, keeping the loins intact.

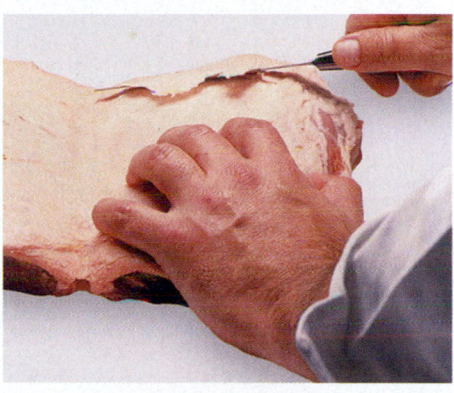

6 Turn the loins over and trim the surface fat to ¼ inch (6 millimeters).

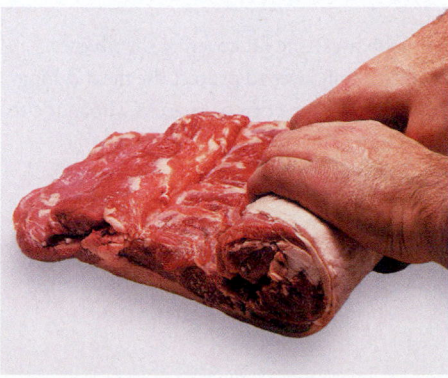

7 Roll the flank flaps under from each side.

8 Tie the roast with butcher's twine at even intervals.

Procedure for Frenching a Rack of Lamb

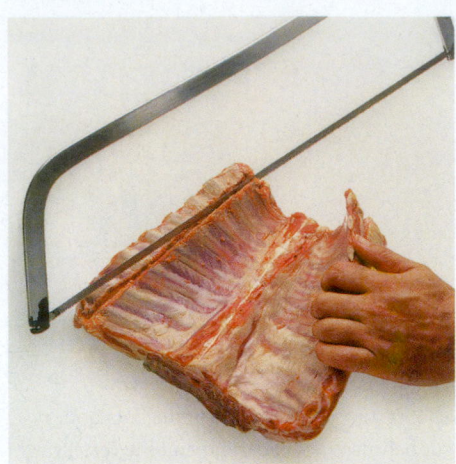

① With a meat saw, trim the ribs to approximately 3 inches (7.5 centimeters), measuring from the rib eye on each side of the rack.

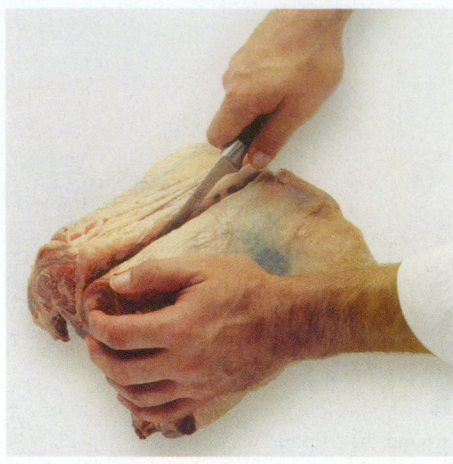

② Turn the rack over and cut down both sides of the feather bones, completely separating the meat from the bone.

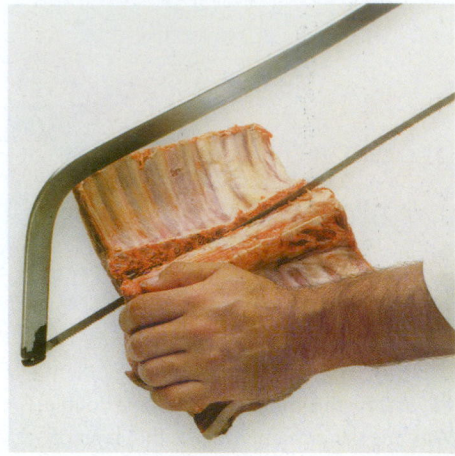

③ Turn the rack back over. Using a meat saw, cut between the ribs and the chine bone (backbone or spine) at a 45-degree angle, exposing the lean meat between the ribs and the bones that run along the spine.

④ By pulling and cutting along the natural seam, remove the thick layers of fat and the meat between the fat layers from the rack's surface leaving an even layer of fat on the eye muscle.

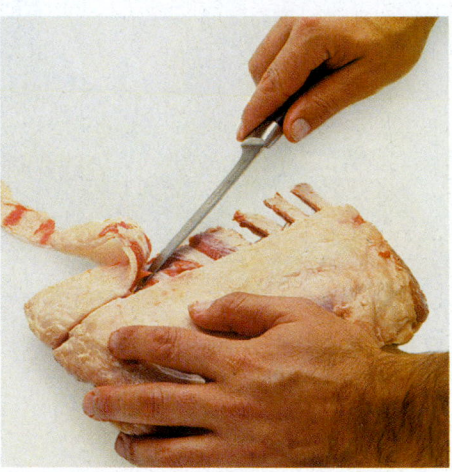

⑤ Make an even cut through the fat, perpendicular to the ribs, 1 inch (2.5 centimeters) from the rib eye. Trim away all meat and fat from the rib ends. The ribs should be completely clean.

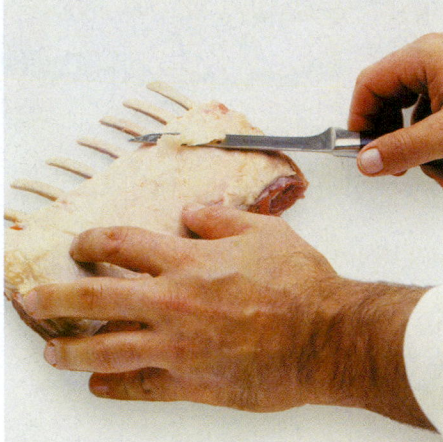

⑥ Trim away the fat covering the rib eye leaving a thin layer to protect the meat during cooking. The rack can be roasted whole or cut into chops.

USING COMMON CUTS OF LAMB

TABLE 16.1

PRIMAL	SUBPRIMAL OR FABRICATED CUT	IMPS	COOKING METHODS	SERVING SUGGESTIONS
Shoulder	Shoulder lamb chop	1207	Dry heat (broil or grill)	Broiled or grilled lamb chops
	Lamb for stewing	295	Combination (stew)	Lamb stew; lamb curry
	Ground lamb	296	Dry heat (broil or grill; sauté)	Patties
Breast	Breast	209	Combination (braise)	Lamb breast stuffed with mushrooms
	Foreshank	210	Combination (braise)	Lamb shank braised with vegetables and white beans
Hotel rack	Lamb rack	204	Dry heat (broil or grill; roast; sauté)	Roast rack of lamb with garlic and rosemary
	Frenched lamb rack	204C	Dry heat (broil or grill; roast; sauté)	Broiled lamb with mustard and hazelnut crust
Loin	Lamb loin, trimmed	232	Dry heat (broil or grill; roast; sauté)	Noisettes of lamb with roasted garlic sauce
	Loin chops	1232A	Dry heat (broil or grill; sauté)	Broiled loin chops with herb butter
Leg	Lamb leg	233A	Dry heat (broil or grill; roast)	Kebabs; roast leg of lamb
	Boned, rolled, tied leg of lamb	234	Dry heat (roast)	Roast leg of lamb

QUESTIONS FOR DISCUSSION

1 Describe the basic differences between a lamb carcass and a beef carcass.

2 List each lamb primal and describe its location on the carcass. Identify two subprimals or fabricated cuts taken from each primal.

3 Which cooking methods are most appropriate for a breast of lamb? Explain your answer.

4 Describe the procedure for preparing a frenched rack of lamb from a primal hotel rack.

5 What is the best way for a food service operation that cuts its own meat and uses large quantities of lamb chops to purchase lamb? Explain your answer.

6 Visit the website of the Agricultural Marketing Service of the USDA to learn more about grading standards for lamb. What are the characteristics of lamb and mutton according to their grading system? What is the difference between yearling mutton and mutton? How would you prepare the different grades of lamb?

7 Lamb was one of the first animals domesticated for human consumption. Research the historical ways in which lamb was served. Discuss how the ways of preparing lamb have changed over the centuries.

Lamb Recipes

Turkish Spicy Lamb Kebabs

YIELD 24 Servings, approximately 3 oz. (90 g) each	**METHOD** Grilling	
Ground lamb	4 lb.	1.9 kg
Garlic, minced	1 oz.	30 g
Onions, minced	6 oz.	120 g
Paprika	1 tsp.	5 ml
Allspice, ground	½ tsp.	2 ml
Coriander, ground	½ tsp.	2 ml
Cinnamon, ground	½ tsp.	2 ml
Cumin, ground	2 tsp.	10 ml
Red pepper flakes	1 tsp.	5 ml
Salt and black pepper	TT	TT
Vegetable oil	4 fl. oz.	120 ml
Spanish Romesco Sauce (page 252)	as needed	as needed
Flatbread	as needed	as needed

1 Place the lamb in a bowl and mix in the garlic, onions, paprika, allspice, coriander, cinnamon, cumin and red pepper flakes. Add salt and pepper to taste. Form the mixture into 3-ounce (90-gram) portions.

2 Flatten each portion of seasoned ground lamb. Wrap each portion around long metal or bamboo skewers. Season with salt. Brush lightly with oil, then grill to taste. Serve with Spanish Romesco Sauce, and flatbread.

Approximate values per 3-oz. (90-g) serving: **Calories** 150, **Total fat** 10 g, **Saturated fat** 4 g, **Cholesterol** 50 mg, **Sodium** 45 mg, **Total carbohydrates** 1 g, **Protein** 13 g

Chimichurri Sauce

This vibrant sauce from Argentina is served with grilled lamb, beef or poultry. For a rustic appearance, whisk the ingredients together and serve the sauce without blending.

YIELD 24 fl. oz. (720 ml)		
Coarse salt	1 Tbsp.	15 ml
Water, boiling	8 fl. oz.	240 ml
Garlic cloves, chopped	8	8
Italian parsley, chopped	1 oz.	30 g
Fresh oregano, chopped	1 oz.	30 g
Red pepper flakes, crushed	1 tsp.	5 ml
Red wine vinegar	2 fl. oz.	60 ml
Extra virgin olive oil	4 fl. oz.	120 ml

1 Dissolve the salt in the boiling water. Cool.

2 Add the remaining ingredients. Blend the mixture until smooth using an immersion blender or food processor.

Approximate values per 1-fl.-oz. (30-ml) serving: **Calories** 45, **Total fat** 4.5 g, **Saturated fat** 0.5 g, **Cholesterol** 0 mg, **Sodium** 140 mg, **Total carbohydrates** 2 g, **Protein** 0 g

Shish Kebab

YIELD	10 Servings, 7½ oz. (225 g) each	METHOD	Grilling or Broiling

Marinade:		
Onions, small dice	12 oz.	360 g
Garlic, chopped	1 oz.	30 g
Lemon juice	4 fl. oz.	120 ml
Salt	2 tsp.	10 ml
Black pepper	1 tsp.	5 ml
Fresh oregano, chopped	2 tsp.	10 ml
Olive oil	8 fl. oz.	240 ml
Cumin, ground	2 tsp.	10 ml
Coriander, ground	1 Tbsp.	15 ml
Fresh mint, chopped	2 tsp.	10 ml
Lamb leg or shoulder, boneless, trimmed and cut in 2-in. (5-cm) cubes	5 lb.	2.4 kg

1 Combine the marinade ingredients and add the lamb. Marinate under refrigeration for 2 hours.

2 Place three or four cubes of lamb on each of 10 skewers. Grill or broil to the desired doneness.

Approximate values per 7½-oz. (225-g) serving: **Calories** 410, **Total fat** 17 g, **Saturated fat** 6 g, **Cholesterol** 205 mg, **Sodium** 170 mg, **Total carbohydrates** 0 g, **Protein** 64 g, **Iron** 30%

Rack of Lamb with Mustard and Hazelnuts

YIELD	2 Racks, 4 Servings, 3 chops each	METHOD	Roasting
Lamb racks, domestic, frenched, 2 lb.–2 lb. 8 oz. (0.9–1.2 kg) each	2	2	
Salt and pepper	TT	TT	
Olive oil	2 fl. oz.	60 ml	
Dijon mustard	2 oz.	60 g	
Fresh bread crumbs	1 oz.	30 g	
Hazelnuts, chopped fine	2 oz.	60 g	
Molasses	1 fl. oz.	30 ml	

1 Season the racks with salt and pepper and brown well in the oil.

2 Spread the mustard over the surface of the racks.

3 Combine the bread crumbs, hazelnuts and molasses and press this mixture into the mustard to form a crust.

4 Roast the racks at 375°F (190°C) until medium rare, approximately 30 minutes.

5 Allow the racks to rest 15 minutes. Carve into chops and serve with a marchand de vin sauce made with lamb jus lié.

Variation:

Rack of Lamb Persillé—In Step 3, sauté 2 teaspoons (10 milliliters) chopped garlic in 2 tablespoons (30 milliliters) olive oil and 2 tablespoons (30 milliliters) butter until soft. Add 1 cup (250 milliliters) fresh bread crumbs and 2 tablespoons (30 milliliters) chopped parsley to the garlic mixture. Season with salt and pepper and toss to combine. Press this mixture into the mustard to form a crust. Proceed with Steps 4 and 5 as in original recipe.

Approximate values per 3-chop serving: **Calories** 700, **Total fat** 43 g, **Saturated fat** 10 g, **Cholesterol** 195 mg, **Sodium** 880 mg, **Total carbohydrates** 14 g, **Protein** 64 g, **Iron** 35%

The finished rack of lamb Persillé variation, served with risotto and pea shoots.

❶ Spreading mustard over the rack.

❷ Pressing the bread crumb mixture into the mustard.

❸ Slicing the cooked rack into chops.

Rack of Spring Lamb with Mint Pesto

YIELD 8 Racks, 18 Servings, 3 chops each	METHOD Grilling	
Fresh mint leaves	2 oz.	60 g
Pine nuts, toasted	1 oz.	30 g
Garlic cloves, chopped	2	2
Parmesan cheese, grated	1 oz.	30 g
Red pepper flakes	½ tsp.	2 ml
Salt	½ tsp.	2 ml
Black pepper	½ tsp.	2 ml
Olive oil	4 fl. oz.	120 ml
Spring lamb racks, frenched, 1 lb.–1 lb. 4 oz. (0.45–0.56 kg) each	8	8
Beets, red and yellow, diced, cooked	as needed for garnish	

1 To prepare the mint pesto, combine all ingredients except the lamb in the bowl of a blender or food processor and blend to a coarse paste.

2 Spread approximately 1 tablespoon (15 milliliters) mint pesto on each lamb rack. Allow the lamb to marinate under refrigeration for at least 1 hour or preferably overnight.

3 Grill the lamb on a hot grill, browning the meat well for approximately 10 minutes while being careful not to burn the rib bones. Wrap the rib bones in aluminum foil to help prevent them from burning if desired.

4 Remove the lamb from the grill and brush each rack with an additional 1 tablespoon (15 milliliters) pesto. Place the lamb racks on a sheet pan and finish cooking them in a 350°F (180°C) oven to the desired doneness, approximately 15 minutes for medium rare.

5 Carve the lamb into chops and plate them with some of the pesto and cooked diced beets.

Approximate values per 3-chop serving: **Calories** 700, **Total fat** 43 g, **Saturated fat** 10 g, **Cholesterol** 195 mg, **Sodium** 880 mg, **Total carbohydrates** 14 g, **Protein** 64 g, **Iron** 35%

Honey Mustard Denver Ribs

YIELD 14 Servings, 12 oz. (360 g) each	METHOD Roasting	
Denver lamb racks, trimmed	20 lb.	9.6 kg
Salt	4 oz.	120 g
Black pepper	2 oz.	60 g
Honey	2 lb.	960 g
Dijon mustard	1 lb. 8 oz.	720 g
Lemon juice	8 fl. oz.	240 ml

1 Rub the ribs with salt and pepper.

2 Place the ribs on a rack and roast at 375°F (190°C) for 30 minutes.

3 Combine the honey, mustard and lemon juice.

4 Baste the ribs generously with the honey mustard mixture. Roast an additional 30 minutes, basting every 10 minutes.

Approximate values per 12-oz. serving: **Calories** 1020, **Total fat** 47 g, **Saturated fat** 16 g, **Cholesterol** 285 mg, **Sodium** 2110 mg, **Total carbohydrates** 61 g, **Protein** 88 g, **Vitamin C** 15%, **Iron** 35%

Stuffed Leg of Lamb

YIELD 1 Leg, 12 Servings, 5–6 oz. (150–180 g) each		METHOD Roasting	
Bacon, fine dice	3 oz.	90 g	
Fennel bulb, fine dice	1	1	
Garlic cloves, chopped fine	2	2	
Wild mushrooms such as shiitake, chanterelles or porcini, chopped	12 oz.	360 g	
Fresh parsley, chopped	2 Tbsp.	30 ml	
Fresh thyme	½ tsp.	2 ml	
Fresh rosemary	½ tsp.	2 ml	
Salt and pepper	TT	TT	
Dry white wine	8 fl. oz.	240 ml	
Fresh bread crumbs	3 oz.	90 g	
Leg of lamb, 6–8 lb. (2.7–3.6 kg)	1	1	
Mirepoix	1 lb.	480 g	

1 To make the stuffing, sauté the bacon until crisp. Add the fennel and sauté lightly.

2 Add the garlic and sauté. Add the mushrooms, parsley, thyme, rosemary, salt and pepper and sauté for an additional 2 minutes.

3 Deglaze with the wine and reduce by three-fourths. Remove from the heat.

4 Stir in the bread crumbs.

5 Completely bone out the leg, following the natural seams in the meat. Cut off the shank meat for use in another recipe. Fill the cavity where the bone was with stuffing.

6 Season the lamb with salt and pepper. Close the leg around the stuffing and seal the opening by tying with butcher's twine.

7 Place the stuffed leg in a roasting pan on a bed of mirepoix.

8 Roast at 375°F (190°C) until medium rare, approximately 1 hour. Serve au jus or with a pan gravy.

Approximate values per 6-oz. (180-g) serving: **Calories** 540, **Total fat** 20 g, **Saturated fat** 7 g, **Cholesterol** 230 mg, **Sodium** 630 mg, **Total carbohydrates** 12 g, **Protein** 78 g, **Iron** 35%

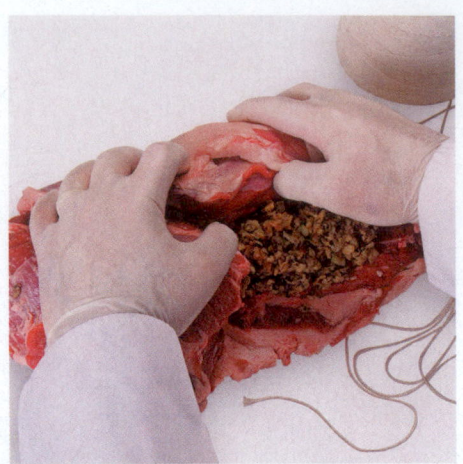

Closing the leg of lamb around the stuffing before tying it with butcher's twine.

Stuffing

Many flavors of stuffing would work for a leg of lamb. Avoid raw meat, however, because it would not cook completely in the time it takes to roast the lamb to medium rare. For a more traditional flavor profile, use a simple mirepoix, or use fresh mint, oregano and lemon zest for a Greek version. A stuffing seasoned with Spanish paprika and diced cooked chorizo offers an Iberian flavor.

Blanquette of Lamb

YIELD 10 Servings, 10 oz. (300 g) each		METHOD Stewing	
White beans, dried	1 lb.	480 g	
Onion piqué	2	2	
Carrot stick, 4 in. (10 cm)	2	2	
Leek, split, 4-in. (10-cm) piece	2	2	
Fresh thyme	2 sprigs	2 sprigs	
Bay leaf	2	2	
Lamb leg or shoulder, cut in 1½-inch (4-cm) cubes	4 lb.	1.9 kg	
White stock	2 qt.	1.4 lt	
Sachet:			
Bay leaf	1	1	
Dried thyme	½ tsp.	2 ml	
Peppercorns, crushed	½ tsp.	2 ml	
Parsley stems	10	10	
Garlic cloves, crushed	4	4	
Salt	TT	TT	
Blond roux	2 oz.	60 g	
Heavy cream	8 fl. oz.	240 ml	
Dijon mustard	2 Tbsp.	30 ml	
Egg yolks	4	4	

1 Soak the beans covered in cold water for 12 hours. Drain, then add enough fresh water to cover the beans by 2–4 inches (5–10 centimeters).

2 Make two bouquet garni using the carrots, leeks, thyme and bay leaves. Add one onion piqué and one bouquet garni to the beans and cook until they are tender, approximately 1½ hours. Remove and discard the onion piqué and bouquet garni.

3 Blanch the lamb cubes in boiling salted water.

4 Place the blanched lamb in an 8-quart (8-liter) saucepot. Add the stock and the second onion piqué, the second bouquet garni, the sachet and salt. Cover and simmer until the meat is tender, approximately 1½ hours.

5 Strain the meat from the liquid, reserving the meat and the liquid. Discard the onion piqué, bouquet garni and sachet. Return the cooking liquid to the saucepot and reduce to 1 quart (approximately 1 liter). Whisk the roux into the liquid and simmer for 10 minutes.

6 Combine the cream, mustard and egg yolks in a nonreactive bowl. Whisk half of the hot sauce into the cream mixture to temper and then add the combined tempered sauce and cream to the reduced stock as a liaison.

7 Return the lamb to the sauce and adjust the seasonings. Heat the sauce and meat thoroughly but do not allow it to boil. Serve the blanquette with the cooked beans.

Approximate values per 10-oz. (300-g) serving: **Calories** 600, **Total fat** 24 g, **Saturated fat** 11 g, **Cholesterol** 240 mg, **Sodium** 530 mg, **Total carbohydrates** 40 g, **Protein** 54 g, **Iron** 40%

① Simmering the lamb.

② Whisking the roux into the reduced cooking liquid.

③ Whisking the liaison into the sauce.

④ Returning the lamb to the sauce.

Saffron and Spice Braised Lamb Shanks

YIELD 4 Servings, 1 shank each		METHOD Braising	
Salt		1½ tsp.	7 ml
Pepper		1 tsp.	5 ml
Cinnamon, ground		1 tsp.	5 ml
Nutmeg		1 tsp.	5 ml
Turmeric		1 tsp.	5 ml
Lamb shanks, approx. 1 lb. (480 g) each		4	4
Saffron		½ tsp.	3 ml
Lamb or chicken stock, hot		3 pt.	1.4 lt
Vegetable oil		2 fl. oz.	60 ml
Onion, medium dice		8 oz.	240 g
Limes, juice and zest		2	2
Orange, juice and zest		1	1
Fresh thyme sprigs		4	4
Bay leaves		2	2
Farro Risotto (page 673)		as needed for garnish	
Plain yogurt		as needed for garnish	
Mint chiffonade and sprigs		as needed for garnish	

1 Combine the salt, pepper, cinnamon, nutmeg and turmeric. Pat the lamb shanks dry and rub them with the spice mixture. Cover and refrigerate for at least 1 hour or overnight.

2 Stir the saffron into the hot stock immediately before cooking the lamb shanks.

3 Heat the oil in a rondeau over medium heat. Sear the lamb shanks. Remove the shanks from the rondeau and keep warm.

4 Add the onions and cook until soft, approximately 5 minutes. Add the lime and orange juice and zest, thyme, bay leaves and saffron stock mixture. Return the lamb shanks to the rondeau. Cover and place in a 350°F (180°C) oven. Cook until the meat is very tender, approximately 2 hours.

5 Remove the shanks from the pan and keep warm. Strain the braising liquid and skim the fat. Cook over medium heat until the braising liquid is reduced by half and has thickened to a thin sauce consistency. Season to taste with salt and pepper.

6 Serve each lamb shank on a bed of Farro Risotto with some of the sauce, yogurt and chiffonade and sprigs of fresh mint.

Approximate values per 1-shank serving: **Calories** 510, **Total fat** 25 g, **Saturated fat** 5 g, **Cholesterol** 160 mg, **Sodium** 1160 mg, **Total carbohydrates** 15 g, **Protein** 57 g, **Vitamin C** 35%, **Iron** 25%

Irish Lamb Stew

YIELD 12 Servings, 8 oz. (240 g) each	METHOD Stewing	
Lamb shoulder, 1½-in. (4-cm) cubes	4 lb.	1.9 kg
White stock	3 pt.	1.4 lt
Sachet:		
Bay leaf	1	1
Dried thyme	½ tsp.	2 ml
Peppercorns, crushed	½ tsp.	2 ml
Parsley stems	10	10
Garlic cloves, crushed	4	4
Onions, sliced	1 lb.	480 g
Leeks, sliced	8 oz.	240 g
Potatoes, peeled, large dice	1 lb. 8 oz.	720 g
Salt and white pepper	TT	TT
Carrots, tournée or bâtonnet	24	24
Turnips, tournée or bâtonnet	24	24
Potatoes, tournée or bâtonnet	24	24
Pearl onions, peeled	24	24
Fresh parsley, chopped	1 Tbsp.	15 ml

1 Combine the lamb, stock, sachet, onions, leeks and diced potatoes in a rondeau. Season with salt and white pepper. Bring to a simmer and skim the surface. Simmer the stew on the stove top or cover and cook in the oven at 350°F (180°C) until the lamb is tender, approximately 1 hour.

2 Degrease the stew; remove and discard the sachet.

3 Remove the pieces of diced potato and purée them in a food mill or ricer. Use the potato purée to thicken the stew to the desired consistency.

4 Simmer the stew for 10 minutes to blend the flavors.

5 Cook the tournée or bâtonnet carrots, turnips and potatoes and the pearl onions separately in salted water. At service, heat the vegetable garnishes and add to each portion of stew.

6 Garnish with chopped parsley and serve.

Approximate values per 8-oz. (240-g) serving: **Calories** 560, **Total fat** 26 g, **Saturated fat** 10 g, **Cholesterol** 175 mg, **Sodium** 840 mg, **Total carbohydrates** 26 g, **Protein** 54 g, **Vitamin A** 80%, **Iron** 30%

❶ Skimming the surface to degrease the stew.

❷ Thickening the stew with the puréed potatoes.

Lamb in Indian-Style Coconut Curry Sauce

pappadam [PAH-pah-dahm] a thin, crisp East Indian flatbread made with chickpea, lentil or rice flour; may be flavored with black pepper, garlic or other seasonings; generally fried or toasted and served before or during meals

YIELD 9 Servings, 5 oz. (150 g) each		METHOD Stewing	
Salt		1 Tbsp.	15 ml
Cumin, ground		2 Tbsp.	30 ml
Coriander, ground		2 Tbsp.	30 ml
Turmeric, ground		2 Tbsp.	30 ml
Cayenne pepper		1 tsp.	5 ml
Garam masala		2½ Tbsp.	40 ml
Black pepper		1 tsp.	5 ml
Lamb leg, 3 lb. (1.4 kg)		1	1
Ginger, 4-in. (10-cm) piece		1	1
Garlic cloves		8	8
Water		8 fl. oz.	240 ml
Vegetable oil		3 fl. oz.	90 ml
Onion, chopped fine		4 oz.	120 g
Tomatoes, peeled and chopped fine		8 oz.	240 g
Coconut milk		24 fl. oz.	720 ml
Steamed rice		as needed for garnish	
Naan (page 966) or **pappadam** bread		as needed for garnish	
Chutney		as needed for garnish	
Raisins		as needed for garnish	
Almonds, toasted chopped		as needed for garnish	

1 Combine the salt, cumin, coriander, turmeric, cayenne pepper, garam masala and black pepper.

2 Trim the lamb leg and then cut it into 1-inch (2.5-centimeter) pieces. Place the lamb in a stainless steel bowl and season it with approximately half of the spice mix. Marinate, refrigerated, for at least 1 hour or overnight.

3 Chop the ginger to a paste, place the paste in a double layer of cheesecloth and squeeze out as much juice as possible. Reserve the ginger juice and discard the pulp.

4 Purée the garlic in a blender or food processor with the water and ginger juice until fairly smooth.

5 Heat the oil in a heavy-bottomed pot and add the lamb. Brown the lamb on all sides and then remove it from the pot.

6 Sauté the onion in the same pot until lightly caramelized and then add the garlic-ginger purée. Cook until all of the liquid has evaporated and only oil remains. Add the remaining spice mix and cook for approximately 20 seconds.

7 Add the tomatoes, reduce the heat and continue cooking for 3–4 minutes. Add the coconut milk a little at a time, incorporating it into the sauce each time before adding more. Return the lamb to the pan and simmer for 30 minutes or until the lamb is tender. Serve with steamed rice and Naan or pappadam bread. Accompany the curry with chutney, raisins, almonds or other condiments.

Variation:

Goat in Indian-Style Coconut Curry Sauce—Substitute 3 pounds (1.4 kilograms) of goat leg or shoulder meat for the lamb in this recipe. In Step 7, check the goat for doneness after 20 minutes.

Approximate values per 5-oz. (150-g) serving: **Calories** 440, **Total fat** 36 g, **Saturated fat** 19 g, **Cholesterol** 75 mg, **Sodium** 660 mg, **Total carbohydrates** 7 g, **Protein** 23 g, **Vitamin C** 10%, **Iron** 30%

Moroccan-Style Lamb Tagine with Preserved Lemon

YIELD 6 Servings, 10 oz. (300 g) each	METHOD Stewing	
Lamb shoulder, boned, cut into 2-inch cubes	3 lb.	1.4 kg
Marinade:		
Olive oil	1 fl. oz.	30 ml
Cumin, ground	1 tsp.	5 ml
Ginger, ground	1 tsp.	5 ml
Cinnamon, ground	¼ tsp.	1 ml
Turmeric	½ tsp.	2 ml
Paprika	1 tsp.	5 ml
Olive oil	2 fl. oz.	60 ml
Onion, minced	6 oz.	180 g
Garlic, minced	1½ Tbsp.	45 ml
Saffron	¼ tsp.	1 ml
Lamb or beef stock	1 pt.	480 ml
Moroccan-Style Preserved Lemons, (recipe follows), cut into strips	1	1
Green or Kalamata olives	6 oz.	180 g
Cilantro, chopped	1 oz.	30 g

1 Combine the lamb with the marinade ingredients. Cover and refrigerate for 8–14 hours.

2 Brown the lamb in the olive oil in a clay tagine or heavy saucepan. Stir in the onion, garlic and saffron. Add the stock and bring to a boil. Reduce heat to a low simmer. Cover and cook until the lamb is tender, approximately 1½–2 hours.

3 Remove the lamb from the pot. Increase the heat and cook for 10 minutes to reduce the liquid slightly.

4 Stir in the lamb, Moroccan-Style Preserved Lemons, olives and cilantro. Simmer for 15 minutes. Adjust the seasonings to taste. Serve with flatbread or steamed couscous.

Approximate values per 10-oz. (300-g) serving: **Calories** 690, **Total fat** 52 g, **Saturated fat** 17 g, **Cholesterol** 170 mg, **Sodium** 1500 mg, **Total carbohydrates** 8 g, **Protein** 45 g, **Vitamin C** 20%, **Iron** 25%

Moroccan-Style Preserved Lemons

 Vegan

YIELD 6 Lemons, 18 pieces		
Lemons, organic	6	6
Coarse sea salt	2½ oz.	75 g
Lemon juice, fresh	8 fl. oz.	240 ml

1 Trim the ends of the lemons, then cut each one into six wedges.

2 Toss the lemon wedges and salt in a quarter hotel pan. Spread the lemon wedges out in one layer. Top with the lemon juice. Cover and bake at 200°F (90°C) for 3 hours, stirring occasionally.

3 Cool, and then transfer the lemons and their cooking liquid to a storage container. Will keep for 1 month under refrigeration.

Lamb Navarin

YIELD 10 Servings, 10 oz. (300 g) each		METHOD Stewing	
Olive oil	3 Tbsp.	45 ml	
Lean lamb shoulder, large dice	3 lb.	1.4 kg	
Sugar, optional	1 Tbsp.	15 ml	
Salt and pepper	TT	TT	
Flour	3 Tbsp.	45 ml	
White stock	1 qt.	960 ml	
White wine	4 fl. oz.	120 ml	
Tomato concassée	8 oz.	240 g	
Bouquet garni:			
Carrot stick, 4 in. (10 cm)	1	1	
Leek, split, 4-in. (10-cm) piece	1	1	
Fresh thyme	1 sprig	1 sprig	
Bay leaf	1	1	
Potatoes, peeled, medium dice	1 lb. 8 oz.	720 g	
Carrots, medium dice	1 lb.	480 g	
White turnips, peeled, medium dice	1 lb.	480 g	
Pearl onions, peeled	12	12	
Fresh green peas	6 oz.	180 g	

1 In a braiser, brown the meat in the oil. This can be done in several batches so that the meat browns properly.

2 Return all of the lamb to the braiser. Sprinkle the meat with the sugar (if used) and season with salt and pepper.

3 Add the flour and cook to make a blond roux.

4 Add the stock and wine. Add the tomato concassée and bouquet garni; bring to a boil. Cover and cook in the oven at 375°F (190°C) until the meat is almost tender, approximately 1–1½ hours.

5 Remove the meat and hold it in a warm place. Strain the sauce and skim off any excess fat.

6 Combine the sauce, meat, potatoes, carrots, turnips and onions. Cover and cook until the vegetables are almost tender, approximately 25 minutes.

7 Add the peas and cook for 10 minutes more. Adjust the seasonings before serving.

Approximate values per 10-oz. (300-g) serving: **Calories** 480, **Total fat** 24 g, **Saturated fat** 9 g, **Cholesterol** 100 mg, **Sodium** 280 mg, **Total carbohydrates** 32 g, **Protein** 31 g, **Vitamin A** 160%, **Vitamin C** 45%, **Iron** 20%

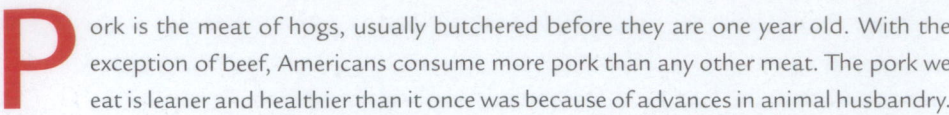

- identify the primal, subprimal and fabricated cuts of pork

- purchase pork appropriate for your needs

- describe and perform basic pork butchering procedures

- explain and apply appropriate cooking methods to several common cuts of pork

cure to preserve eggs, fish, game, meat or poultry with brine, dry air, salt, smoke or a combination of these methods.

P ork is the meat of hogs, usually butchered before they are one year old. With the exception of beef, Americans consume more pork than any other meat. The pork we eat is leaner and healthier than it once was because of advances in animal husbandry.

Because hogs are butchered at a young age, their meat is generally very tender with a delicate flavor. Pork can be enjoyed cured, processed or fresh. The mild flavor of fresh pork blends well with many different seasonings, making it a popular menu item. Pork is naturally tender and can be prepared by almost any dry-heat, moist-heat or combination cooking method. More than two-thirds of the pork marketed in the United States is **cured** (preserved) to produce products such as smoked hams and smoked bacon. Cured pork products are discussed in Chapter 28, Charcuterie.

PRIMAL AND SUBPRIMAL CUTS OF PORK

After a hog is slaughtered, it is generally split down the backbone. This divides the carcass into bilateral halves. Like the beef carcass, each side of the hog carcass is then further broken down into the primal cuts: shoulder, Boston butt, belly, loin and fresh ham.

Hogs are bred specifically to produce long loins. The loin contains the highest-quality meat and is the most expensive cut of pork. Pork is unique among meats in that the ribs and loin are considered a single primal. They are not separated into two different primals, as are the ribs and loin of beef, veal and lamb.

Figure 17.1 illustrates the relationship between the hog's bone structure and the primal cuts. Knowing the location of bones when cutting or working with pork (as well as all other types of meats) makes fabrication and carving easier and aids in identifying cuts. Figure 17.2 shows the primal cuts of pork and their location on the carcass. A hog carcass generally weighs between 120 and 210 pounds (55 and 110 kilograms).

Pork Shoulder

The primal pork **shoulder** is the lower portion of the hog's foreleg; it accounts for approximately 20 percent of the carcass weight. The shoulder contains the arm and shank bones and has a relatively high ratio of bone to lean meat.

Because all pork comes from hogs slaughtered at a young age, the shoulder is tender enough to be cooked by any method. It is, however, one of the least tender cuts of pork with a high percentage of connective tissue that requires long cooking. Pork shoulder is available smoked or fresh. The shoulder is fairly inexpensive and, when purchased fresh, it can be cut into shoulder butt steaks or boned and cut into smaller pieces for sautéing or stewing. Whole pork shoulder is the cut preferred by many barbecue pit masters throughout the American South.

The pork foreshank is called the shoulder hock and is almost always smoked. Shoulder hocks are often simmered for long periods in soups, stews and braised dishes to add flavor and richness. When a pork shoulder includes the foreshank it is referred to as a **picnic shoulder** or **picnic ham**.

Boston Butt

The primal **Boston butt** is a square cut located just above the primal pork shoulder. It accounts for approximately 7 percent of the carcass weight.

The Boston butt is very meaty and tender, with a good percentage of fat to lean meat. Containing only a small portion of the blade bone, the Boston butt is a good choice when a recipe calls for a solid piece of lean pork. The fresh Boston butt is sometimes cut into steaks or chops to be broiled or sautéed. When the Boston butt is smoked, it is usually boneless and called a cottage **ham**.

Boston butt

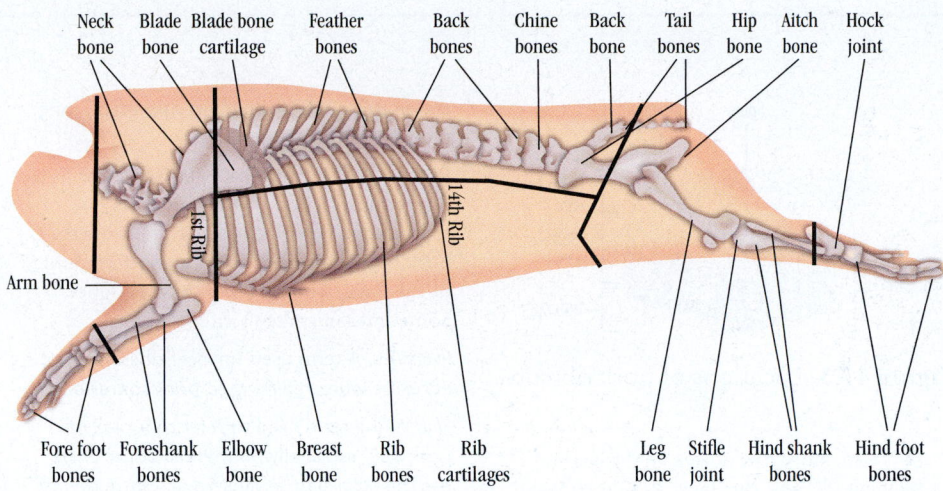

Neck bone · Blade bone · Blade bone cartilage · Feather bones · Back bones · Chine bones · Back bone · Tail bones · Hip bone · Aitch bone · Hock joint

1st Rib · 14th Rib · Arm bone

Fore foot bones · Foreshank bones · Elbow bone · Breast bone · Rib bones · Rib cartilages · Leg bone · Stifle joint · Hind shank bones · Hind foot bones

Figure 17.1 The skeletal structure of a hog.

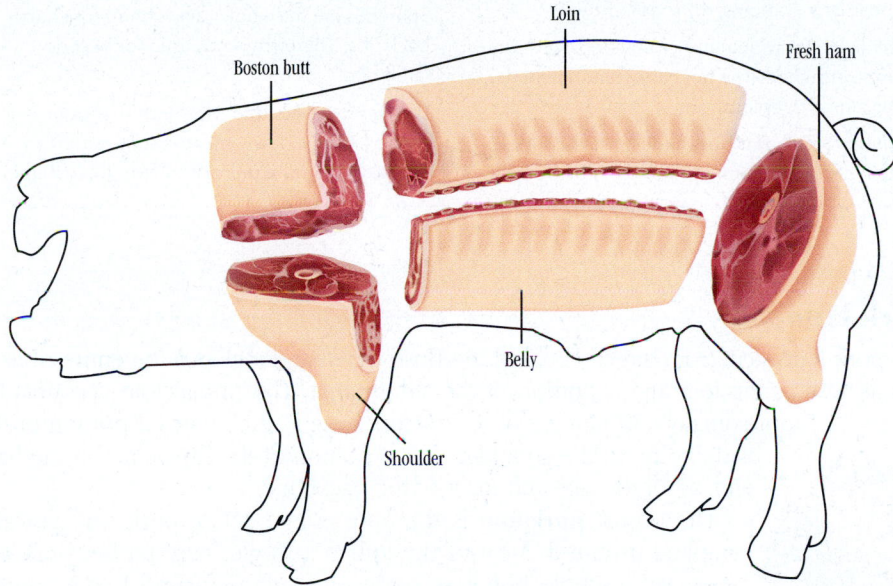

Boston butt · Loin · Fresh ham · Belly · Shoulder

Figure 17.2 The six primal cuts of pork.

Classic Pork Flavors

With a heavy layer of fat and many well-marbled cuts, pork benefits from robust seasonings that penetrate into the meat. Pork shoulder and fresh leg roasts can be studded with garlic and strong herbs such as marjoram, oregano, rosemary or thyme before slow roasting. These cuts also lend themselves to the flavors of American barbecue (smoke, whiskey, sugar and salt curing) as well as spices used in Asian-style grilling (lemongrass, star anise, ginger, sesame oil and soy sauce.) Lean cuts such as pork loin pair well with mild cream sauces flavored with mustard or herbs such as tarragon, as well as richer brown sauces and caramelized apples, fresh or dried stone fruits or mushrooms.

Pork Belly

The primal **pork belly** is located below the loin. Accounting for approximately 16 percent of the carcass weight, it is very fatty with only streaks of lean meat. It contains the spareribs, which are always separated from the rest of the belly before cooking. **Pork spareribs** usually are sold fresh but can also be smoked. Containing less meat than back ribs from the loin, discussed later, and a generous amount of fat, which makes them tender, spareribs are simmered and then grilled or baked while being basted with a spicy barbecue sauce. The remainder of the **boneless pork belly** is nearly always cured and smoked to produce **bacon**.

Boneless pork belly

Pork spareribs

Pork Rib Identification

Consumers and chefs might be better informed about meat if the names used for various cuts were the same from one animal to another, and from one region or country to another. Ribs are an especially confusing cut, which can come from either the primal pork loin or the primal pork belly. The following definitions can be helpful in identifying pork ribs:

Baby back ribs: Lean, tender pork ribs cut from the top (spine) end of the ribs closest to, and often including a portion of, the loin meat. The word *baby* is used because they are small, only 3 to 6 inches (7.5 to 15 centimeters) long.

Back ribs: Another name for baby back ribs or loin ribs.

Country-style ribs: Meaty cuts from the loin near the shoulder; available either boneless or with a portion of the blade bone attached. These are not actual ribs.

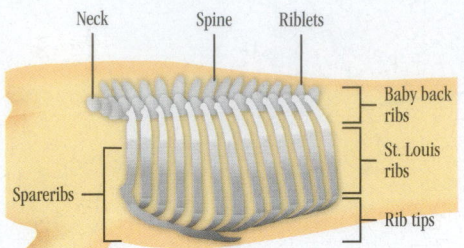

Figure 17.3 Locations of pork rib cuts.

Rack: An entire row of ribs held together by meat, fat and cartilage; should contain at least 10 of the animal's 13 rib bones. A rack of lamb ribs also includes loin meat and is the same cut as a pork rib roast or a standing rib roast of beef.

Rib chops: Individual pork loin chops with the bone attached. The bone is often frenched for a nicer presentation.

Riblets: Small, flat ribs made by cutting a full rack of pork or lamb ribs so that the bones

are only about 2 inches (5 centimeters) long; often served as an appetizer.

Rib tips: A narrow strip (1- to 3-inch [2.5- to 7.5-centimeter]) cut from the lower end of the rib cage when producing St. Louis-style pork ribs. Rib tips contain a good amount of cartilage, which makes them tougher. Sometimes mistakenly called riblets.

Short ribs: A term used for beef ribs only; not accurate when referring to pork spareribs.

Slab: Slang term used to refer to a rack of pork ribs, especially on menus. Some chefs use the term slab to refer to an entire row of untrimmed ribs.

Spareribs: A large portion of a rack of pork ribs including the St. Louis ribs and the rib tips, Spareribs are the whole rack without the baby back ribs. This term is not used for beef or lamb ribs.

St. Louis-style ribs: Spareribs with the tougher rib tips removed; the meat is squared off so the rack is a more uniform rectangular shape.

Pork Loin

The pork loin is cut from directly behind the Boston butt and includes the entire rib section as well as the loin and a portion of the sirloin area. The primal loin accounts for approximately 20 percent of the carcass weight. It contains a portion of the blade bone on the shoulder end, a portion of the hip bone on the ham end, all of the ribs and most of the backbone.

The primal **pork loin** is the only primal cut of pork not typically smoked or cured. Most of the loin is a single, very tender **pork eye muscle**. A whole boneless pork loin weighs from 8 to 10 pounds (3.6 to 4.5 kilograms) and is covered on one side by a solid layer of fat, which can be trimmed away. Boneless pork loin is quite lean but contains enough intramuscular and subcutaneous fat to make it an excellent choice for a moist-heat cooking method such as braising, or it can be prepared with dry-heat cooking methods such as roasting or sautéing.

The most popular cut from the loin is the **pork loin chop**. Chops can be cut from the entire loin. The choicest chops are **center-cut chops**, which are cut from the primal loin after the blade bone and sirloin portions at the front and rear of the loin are removed. **Double rib chops** have the thickness of two ribs and may include two rib bones. The pork loin can be purchased boneless or boned and tied as a roast. A **boneless pork loin** is smoked to produce **Canadian bacon**. The rib bones, when trimmed from the loin, can be served as barbecued **pork back ribs**. Although smaller than spareribs, pork back ribs are meatier.

The loin also contains the pork tenderloin, located on the inside of the rib bones on

Pork loin

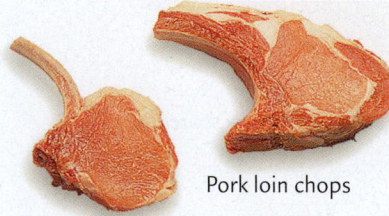

Pork loin chops

Pork back ribs

the sirloin end of the loin. The pork **tenderloin** is rather small, weighing only 1–1½ pounds (450–680 grams). It is the most tender cut of pork with a mild flavor. The tenderloin is very versatile and can be trimmed, cut into medallions and sautéed, or the whole tenderloin can be roasted or braised.

Although not actually part of the primal loin, **fatback** is the thick layer of pork fat—sometimes more than an inch (2.5 centimeters) thick—between the skin and the lean eye muscle. It has a variety of uses in the kitchen, especially in the preparation of charcuterie items.

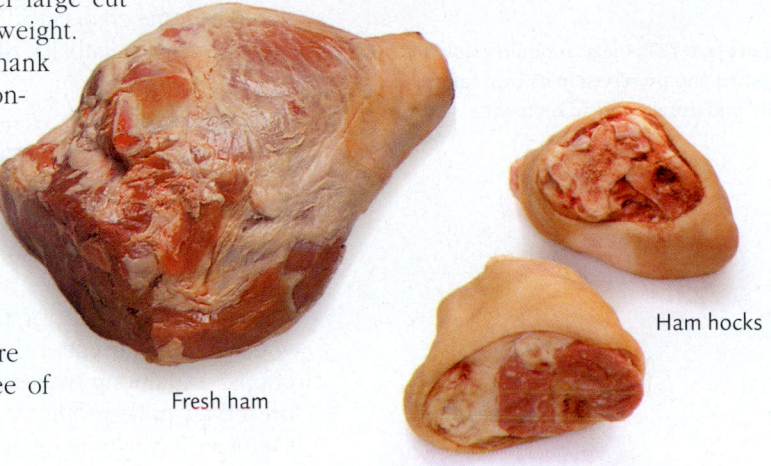

Pork tenderloin

Fresh Ham

The primal **fresh ham** is the hog's hind leg. It is a rather large cut accounting for approximately 24 percent of the carcass weight. The ham contains the aitch bone, leg bone and hindshank bones. Fresh ham, like the legs of other meat animals, contains large muscles with relatively small amounts of connective tissue. Like many other cuts of pork, hams are often cured and smoked. But fresh hams also produce great roasts and can be prepared using almost any cooking method. When cured and smoked, hams are available in a variety of styles; they can be purchased bone-in, shankless or boneless and partially or fully cooked. Fully cooked hams are also available canned. There is a specific ham for nearly every use and desired degree of convenience.

Ham hocks

Fresh ham

Hocks and Trotters

Fresh ham hocks and pig's feet (trotters) are not primal portions, but are inexpensive, flavorful cuts that are gaining popularity among chefs. **Ham hocks** are round crosscuts from the lower end of the rear leg (the ham) just above the foot. Cuts from the hog's front legs may also be referred to as hocks, although they have less meat than those from the hind legs. Bone-in hocks are available fresh or cured and smoked for added flavor and a longer shelf life. Smoked hocks are used as a seasoning for stews and braised dishes.

Trotters are **pig's feet** or hooves, made up of bone, connective tissue and a thick skin. Trotters are generally used to make gelatinous pork stock or added to dishes to flavor slow-cooked beans or vegetables, then removed and discarded. Trotters may also be cooked, then pickled in brine and eaten as a snack. The meaty bits from hocks and trotters are used in Pennsylvania Dutch scrapple and rich, rustic terrines and potted meats.

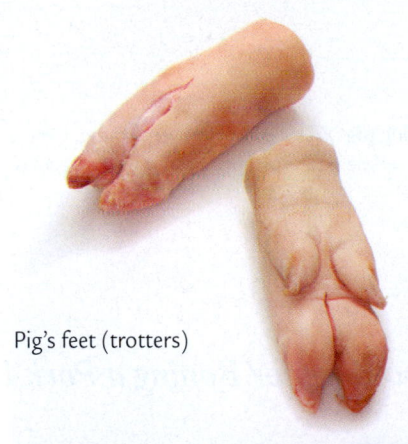

Pig's feet (trotters)

PURCHASING PORK

When purchasing pork, look for firm, bright pink colored flesh. It should appear moist but not watery. Pale or gray coloration indicates lack of freshness. Meat from pork shoulders and legs will be reddish pink in color and should display even fat marbling.

Heritage or **heirloom breeds** of pork are gaining in popularity. These breeds vary considerably in flavor and fat content. For example, Berkshire hogs produce pork that is well marbled, moist and tender. Durocs have a bright pink flesh that is tender with a higher pH, and Red Wattles yield a moist but very lean flesh. The once obscure Mangalitsa is a wooly pig developed in Hungary for lard. Chefs describe the fat and well-marbled meat of Mangalitsas as melting on the tongue. Other rare breeds produced primarily for their fat include the Mulefoot and Guinea Hog. Because of their high fat content, such hogs are desirable for charcuterie products.

Scarcity and the longer time required for many of these heritage breeds to mature makes such hogs costly. Producers of **niche pork**, a term used to refer to these specialty

heritage or **heirloom breed** a loosely defined term that refers to breeds of pork, meat or poultry less commonly raised in modern agricultural systems; many believe that protecting a genetically diverse population of livestock by raising and consuming such animals is important culturally and scientifically and will help ensure human survival.

niche pork industry term for alternative or specialty pork products; meat from specific breeds such as Duroc or Tamworth hogs, or meat raised using a particular practice such as free-range feeding or antibiotic- and hormone-free, are considered niche products.

organic farming a method of farming that does not rely on synthetic pesticides, fungicides, herbicides or fertilizers; organic practices require that animals have access to outdoors, sunlight and clean water and that they are raised without antibiotics and hormones on organically grown feed.

breeds, generally use sustainable and **organic farming** practices. They often raise their hogs on free-roaming farms and feed them vegetarian diets. Although the quantity sold is less than 1 percent of total U.S. production, specialty hog products have found a market with chefs and consumers who care more about taste and quality than cost.

The farm-to-table movement has spawned an interest in chefs purchasing whole animals from local farms. Relatively small in size, thus easy to break down, pigs lend themselves to many uses on a restaurant's menu. The challenge chefs face comes once the popular cuts—the loin, the shoulder roasts and ribs—have been served. Here some culinary ingenuity and experience is helpful. Pork trotters may be brined or pickled. Gelatin-rich trotters and pigs' head enrich stocks. Fatty sections of pig skin when rendered become crisp cracklings used as a garnish. And trim from any cut of pork may be used to make meatballs, **rillettes** and terrines.

rillette [ree-YET] meat or poultry slowly cooked, mashed and preserved in its own fat; served cold and usually spread on toast

NUTRITION INFORMATION FOR PORK

Like other meats, pork is a good source of protein, B vitamins, iron and other essential nutrients, but it is also high in fat, especially saturated fats. Through new breeding and feeding techniques, the fat content of pork has been lowered in recent years. (Pork from specialty or heritage breeds may have a higher fat content than more widely available cuts.) Cuts from the loin, such as the tenderloin and boneless loin chops, are among the leaner cuts of meat available. Sodium content of smoked and preserved pork products, such as bacon, ham and sausage, which are discussed in Chapter 28, Charcuterie, is high, but reduced-sodium preserved and smoked products are increasingly available.

BUTCHERING PROCEDURES FOR PORK

suckling pig (Fr. *cochon de lait*) very young, very small whole pigs typically roasted or barbecued whole

Other than **suckling pigs** and heritage breeds of pork produced on small scale farms, pork products generally are not purchased in forms larger than the primal cuts described earlier. Table 17.1 lists some cuts of pork commonly available. Chefs should master a few important pork fabrication and butchering techniques, however.

Procedure for Boning a Pork Loin

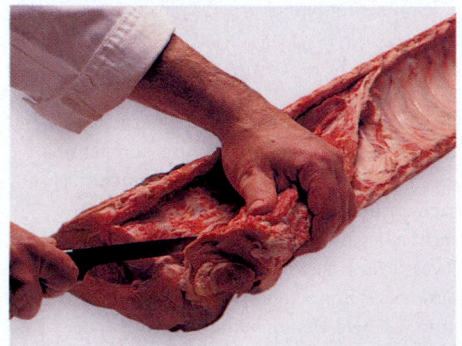

1 Starting on the sirloin end of a full pork loin, remove the tenderloin in one piece by making smooth cuts against the inside of the rib bones. Pull gently on the tenderloin as you cut.

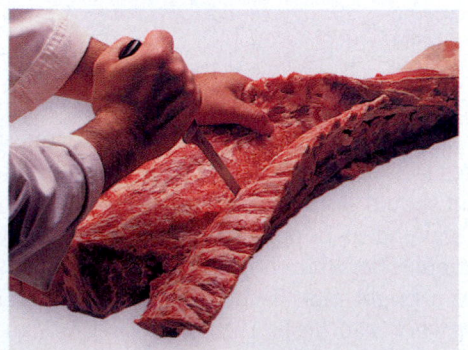

2 Turn the loin over and cut between the ribs and the eye meat. Continue separating the meat from the bones, following the contours of the bones, until the loin is completely separated from the bones.

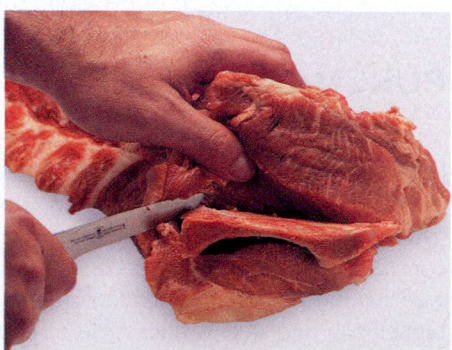

3 Trim around the blade bone on the shoulder end of the loin and remove it.

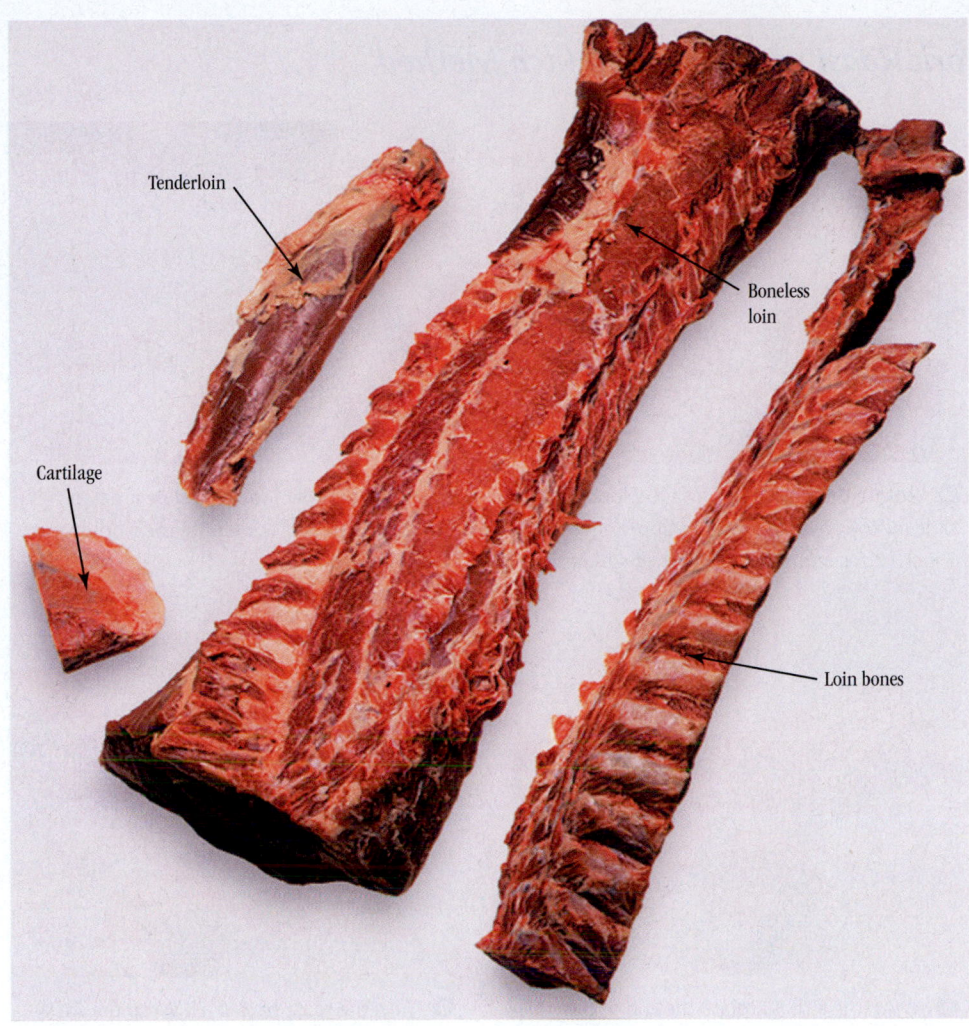

The fully boned loin consists of (from left to right) cartilage, the tenderloin, boneless loin and loin bones.

Procedure for Tying a Boneless Pork Roast with the Half-Hitch Method

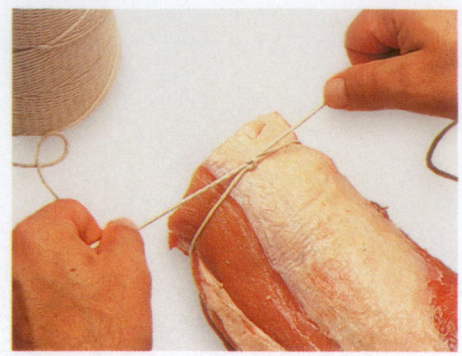

1 Wrap the loose end of the string around the pork loin and tie it with a double knot.

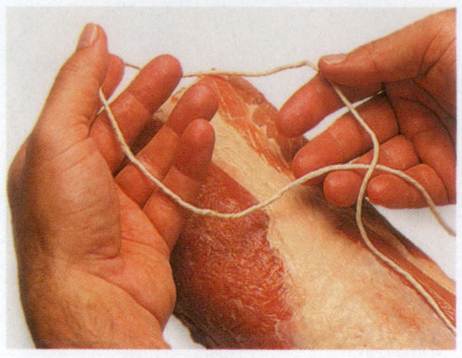

2 Rotate the roast 180°. Make a loop and slide it down over the roast to approximately 1 inch (2.5 centimeters) from the first knot.

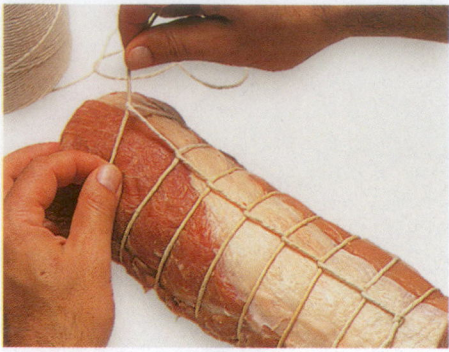

3 Make another loop and slide it down. Continue in this fashion until the whole roast has been tied.

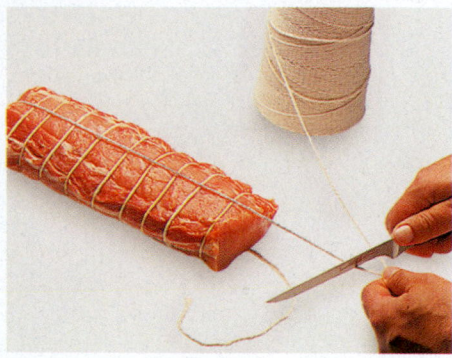

4 Turn the roast over and cut the string, leaving enough to wrap lengthwise around the roast to the original knot.

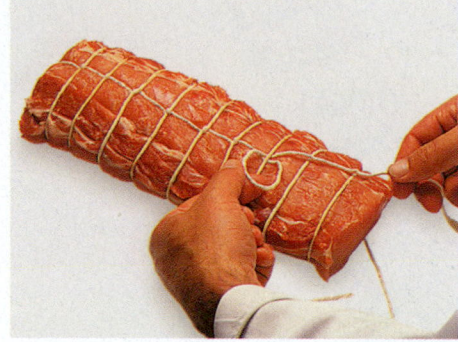

5 Wrap the string around the end of the roast, then around the string that formed the last loop. Continue in this fashion for the length of the roast, pulling the string tight after wrapping it around each loop.

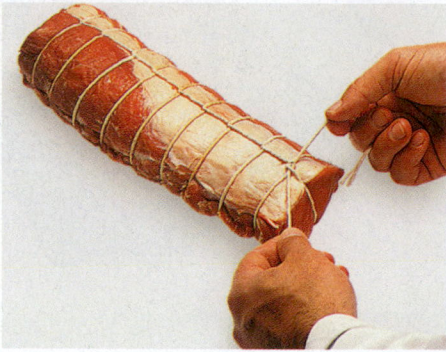

6 Turn the roast back over. Wrap the string around the front end of the roast and secure it to the first loop at the point where you tied the first knot.

7 The tied roast. Note the even intervals at which the strings are tied. They should be just snug enough to hold the shape of the roast; they should not dig in or cut the meat.

Procedure for Cutting a Center-Cut Pork Chop

A center-cut pork chop can be cut from the center portion of a bone-in pork loin without the aid of a saw by using a boning knife and a heavy cleaver. Trim the excess fat from the loin, leaving a ¼-inch (6-millimeter) layer to protect the meat during cooking.

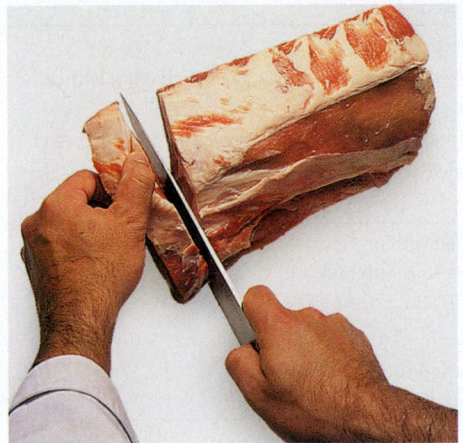

❶ Cut through the meat with the knife.

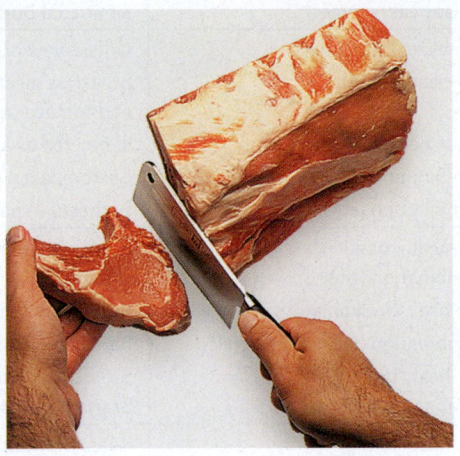

❷ Use the cleaver to chop through the chine bone.

❸ To produce a cleaner chop, trim the meat from the end of the rib bone. Then with the boning knife, separate the loin meat from the chine bones and separate the chine bone from the rib with the cleaver.

Procedure for Cutting a Pocket in a Pork Chop

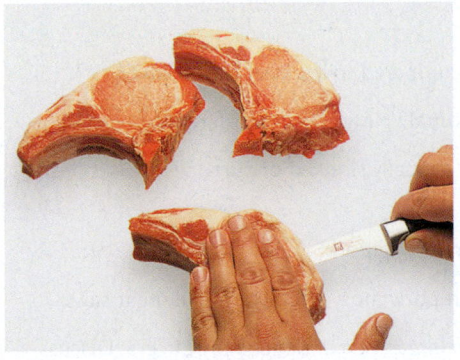

To make a pocket in a pork chop for stuffing, start with a thick chop or a double rib chop. Use the tip of a boning knife to cut a pocket. Cut the pocket deep enough to hold ample stuffing, but be careful not to puncture either surface of the chop.

Procedure for Trimming a Pork Tenderloin

Trim the fat and silverskin from the tenderloin following the procedures outlined in Chapter 14, Beef, for trimming a beef tenderloin. Use a boning knife to remove the silverskin from a pork tenderloin.

USING COMMON CUTS OF PORK

TABLE 17.1

PRIMAL	SUBPRIMAL OR FABRICATED CUT	IMPS	COOKING METHODS	SERVING SUGGESTIONS
Shoulder	Picnic shoulder	405	Dry-heat (roast or bake)	Roasted whole with rosemary and garlic, smoked picnic shoulder
Boston butt	Boston butt	406	Dry-heat (broil or grill; sauté)	Broiled Boston butt steaks
			Moist-heat (simmer)	Simmered Boston butt and beans
Belly	Belly	409	Dry-heat (sauté; roast)	Grilled for Korean barbecue
	Bacon	539	Dry-heat (sauté)	Breakfast meat; cooked and crumbled as a garnish; bacon, lettuce and tomato sandwich
			Moist-heat (simmer)	Simmered as a flavoring in bean soup, beef stew and cooked greens
			Combination (braise)	Boston baked beans with bacon
	Spareribs	416A	Combination (steam, then grill)	Barbecued spareribs
Loin	Pork loin	410	Dry-heat (roast)	Roast pork loin stuffed with prunes
			Combination (braise)	Braised boneless pork loin with milk and sage
	Pork tenderloin	415	Dry-heat (broil or grill; sauté; roast)	Roast pork tenderloin
	Pork back ribs	422	Combination (steam, then grill)	Barbecued back ribs
	Pork loin chops	1410	Dry-heat (broil or grill)	Broiled loin chop with mushroom sauce
			Combination (braise)	Braised loin chop with leeks and fennel
Fresh ham	Fresh ham	401A	Dry-heat (roast)	Roast pork with apricots and almonds

QUESTIONS FOR DISCUSSION

1 List each pork primal and describe its location on the carcass. Identify two subprimals or fabricated cuts taken from each primal.

2 Discuss the characteristics of pork shoulder and explain why it is the preferred cut for American barbecue.

3 What is unique about the primal pork loin as compared to the beef or veal loin?

4 Are fatback and bacon taken from the same primal? How are they different?

5 What is the only primal cut of pork that is not typically smoked or cured? How is it best cooked? Explain your answer.

6 Describe the indications of freshness when purchasing pork.

7 Describe the procedure used to cut a center cut pork chop without using a meat saw.

8 Research various breeds of pork available from large-scale and niche producers. Discuss how to best prepare loin and shoulder cuts from the different available products. Explain your answers.

Pork Recipes

Carolina Barbecued Ribs

YIELD	6 Servings, approx. 4 ribs each	METHOD	Roasting
Salt and pepper		TT	TT
Crushed red pepper flakes		1 Tbsp.	15 ml
Pork back ribs, 3–4 lb. (1.4–1.9 kg) rack		2	2
White vinegar		1 pt.	480 ml
Sauce:			
Onion, chopped coarse		5 oz.	150 g
Garlic cloves		3	3
Green bell pepper, chopped coarse		4 oz.	120 g
Plum tomatoes, canned		1 pt.	480 ml
Red Devil hot sauce		8 fl. oz.	240 ml
Brown sugar		10 oz.	300 g
Lemon juice		2 fl. oz.	60 ml

1 Combine the salt, pepper and red pepper flakes. Remove the tough membrane from the bone (concave) side of the rack of ribs. Rub this mixture over both sides of the ribs, coating them well.

2 Place the ribs in a nonreactive pan and add the vinegar. Cover and refrigerate several hours or overnight.

3 Uncover the ribs, turn them presentation side down and bake in a 375°F (190°C) oven for 1½ hours.

4 Remove the ribs from the liquid and place on a clean sheet pan, turning them so that the presentation side is up. Increase the oven temperature to 400°F (200°C) and bake for an additional 30 minutes.

5 Prepare the sauce by puréeing the onion, garlic, bell pepper and tomatoes in a food processor or blender. Pour this mixture into a nonreactive saucepan and add the remaining sauce ingredients.

6 Simmer the sauce over low heat until it thickens, approximately 15–20 minutes.

7 Brush the ribs with the sauce and serve additional sauce on the side. Serve with Creamy Coleslaw (page 766) and Baked Beans (page 639).

Approximate values per 4-rib serving: **Calories** 1410, **Total fat** 68 g, **Saturated fat** 23 g, **Cholesterol** 315 mg, **Sodium** 1280 mg, **Total carbohydrates** 65 g, **Protein** 134 g, **Vitamin A** 20%, **Vitamin C** 120%, **Iron** 35%

Beer-Marinated Pork Tenderloin

YIELD	6 Servings, 6 oz. (180 g) each	METHOD	Grilling
Pork tenderloins, approx. 14 oz. (420 g) each		3	3
Marinade:			
Light soy sauce		4 fl. oz.	120 ml
Light ale or beer, room temperature		12 fl. oz.	360 ml
Light brown sugar		2 oz.	60 g
Fresh ginger, grated		1½ Tbsp.	22 ml

1 Clean the tenderloins, removing all visible fat and silverskin.

2 Combine the marinade ingredients, stirring until the sugar dissolves.

3 Place the tenderloins in a hotel pan and cover with the marinade. Cover the pan and refrigerate for 2 to 6 hours.

4 Remove the tenderloins from the marinade and grill over medium-hot coals, turning as needed.

5 Allow the cooked tenderloins to rest for 5 minutes, then slice thinly on the bias. Serve the tenderloins with Mango Chutney (page 806), salsa or other sauce.

Approximate values per 6-oz. (180-g) serving: **Calories** 592, **Total fat** 42 g, **Saturated fat** 16 g, **Cholesterol** 143 mg, **Sodium** 762 mg, **Total carbohydrates** 13 g, **Protein** 35 g, **Iron** 13%

Kebab

The term *kebab* (also known as *kabob*, *shish kabab*, *shashlik* and *brochette*) refers to grilling small pieces of meat on a skewer. Historians reason that in urban centers in the Middle East and Persia, where this style of cooking is thought to originate, fuel was in short supply. Therefore smaller cuts of meats were preferred because they could be cooked more easily over portable charcoal-fired grills or braziers. Threading the meat on skewers made turning the meat to cook it evenly feasible. Meat, poultry, fish and vegetables all lend themselves to this style of cooking. Because of the short cooking time, tender cuts should be used for kebabs. Marinating preserves moisture and adds flavor. When using bamboo skewers, soak them in water first to keep them from burning on the grill.

Pork Chimichurri Kabobs

Chimichurri is a thick, fresh herb sauce from Argentina, where it is traditionally served as an accompaniment to grilled meats. In this recipe, it is used as both a marinade and a sauce.

YIELD	8 Servings of pork, 4 oz. (120 g) each, 1 pt. (480 ml) sauce	METHOD	Grilling
Pork loin, boneless, trimmed		2 lb.	1.9 kg
Chimichurri Sauce (page 380)		1 pt.	480 ml
Black beans, cooked		as needed	as needed
Rice, cooked		as needed	as needed

1 Cut the pork into 1-inch (2.5-centimeter) cubes and place them in a nonreactive pan. Add approximately three-fourths of the Chimichurri Sauce and stir thoroughly. Cover and refrigerate for 4 to 6 hours. Reserve the remaining sauce to serve with the kabobs.

2 Remove the pork from the marinade, discarding any marinade left in the pan. Arrange the pork on eight skewers. Cook on a hot grill, turning as necessary to cook thoroughly and brown evenly. Serve with black beans and rice and the reserved Chimichurri Sauce.

Variations:

Use boneless, skinless chicken or cubes of lamb shoulder meat in place of the pork.

Approximate values per 4-oz.- (120-g-)serving with ½ Tbsp. (7 ml) sauce: **Calories** 200, **Total fat** 11 g, **Saturated fat** 3.5 g, **Cholesterol** 70 mg, **Sodium** 85 mg, **Total carbohydrates** 1 g, **Protein** 25 g

Fresh Roasted Ham

YIELD 1 Ham, 25–30 Servings, 5 oz. (150 g) each	METHOD	Roasting
Fresh ham, approx. 22 lb. (10.5 kg)	1	1
Garlic cloves, slivered	15	15
Fresh rosemary sprigs	1 oz.	30 g
Salt and pepper	TT	TT

1 Trim the skin from the entire surface of the fresh ham leaving a thin even layer of fat. Score the fat at 1½-inch (3.8-centimeter) intervals in parallel diagonal lines cutting only deep enough to score the fat without cutting the flesh. Using a skewer or meat fork, poke holes approximately 1–2 inches (2.5–5 centimeters) deep where the lines intersect.

2 Insert slivers of garlic and some of the fresh rosemary into the holes in the surface of the fresh pork. Season the ham with salt and pepper.

3 Place the ham on a rack in a roasting pan. Roast at 325°F (160°C) until the center reaches 155°F (68°C), approximately 4 hours.

4 Allow the ham to rest for 30 minutes before carving.

Approximate values per 5-oz. (150-g) serving: **Calories** 350, **Total fat** 21 g, **Saturated fat** 7 g, **Cholesterol** 135 mg, **Sodium** 115 mg, **Total carbohydrates** 0 g, **Protein** 39 g, **Iron** 15%

Chinese-Style Barbecued Spareribs

YIELD 2 Racks, 10–12 Servings, 4 ribs each	METHOD	Roasting
Sparerib racks, 2 lb. 8 oz. (1.2 kg) each	2	2
Garlic cloves, crushed	2	2
Tomato ketchup	1 fl. oz.	30 ml
Soy sauce	1 fl. oz.	30 ml
Hoisin sauce	1 fl. oz.	30 ml
Red wine	1 fl. oz.	30 ml
Fresh ginger, grated	1 Tbsp.	15 ml
Honey	1 Tbsp.	15 ml

1 Cut the sparerib racks into individual ribs and arrange them on a rack in a baking pan. Roast for 45 minutes at 300°F (150°C).

2 Combine the remaining ingredients into a sauce. Brush the spareribs lightly with the sauce. Roast for 30 minutes more.

3 Turn the spareribs and brush with more sauce. Roast until the ribs are well browned, approximately 30 minutes.

Approximate values per 4-rib serving: **Calories** 724, **Total fat** 44 g, **Saturated fat** 16 g, **Cholesterol** 196 mg, **Sodium** 472 mg, **Total carbohydrates** 4 g, **Protein** 64 g

Pork Loin with Prunes

YIELD 6 Servings, 6 oz. (180 g) each		METHOD Roasting
Boneless pork loin roast, 3 lb. (1.4 kg)	1	1
Salt and pepper	TT	TT
Prunes, pitted*	1 lb.	480 g
Vegetable oil	1 Tbsp.	15 ml
Clarified butter	1 Tbsp.	15 ml
Carrot, chopped coarse	3 oz.	90 g
Onion, chopped coarse	6 oz.	180 g
Fresh rosemary	1 tsp.	5 ml
Fresh thyme	1 tsp.	5 ml
Bay leaf, crushed	1	1
Garlic cloves	2	2
Apple juice	4 fl. oz.	120 ml
White stock	4 fl. oz.	120 ml
Sugar	2 oz.	60 g
Vinegar	2 fl. oz.	60 ml
Pan Roasted Brussels Sprouts (page 623)	as needed	as needed

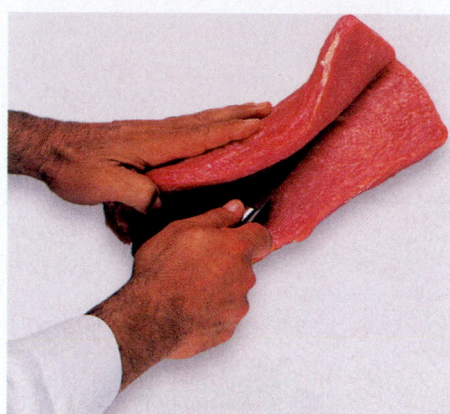

❶ Butterflying the pork loin.

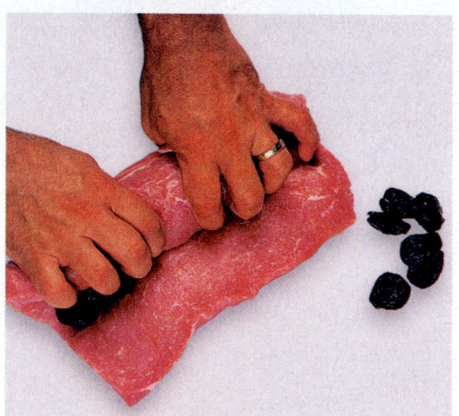

❷ Rolling the pork loin around the filling.

1 Trim and butterfly the pork loin; reserve the trimmings. (To butterfly the loin, slice it partway through the center and open it like a book, then flatten it into a rectangular shape.) Season with salt and pepper.

2 Arrange the prunes along the length of the loin. Roll up the loin around the filling and tie with butcher's twine.

3 Brown the pork roll in a small rondeau in the oil and butter. Remove the pork loin from the pan. Add the pork trimmings, carrot and onion and cook until they brown. Add the herbs and garlic and cook for one minute.

4 Place the pork loin, and cooking juices that have collected on the bed of trimmings and vegetables. Roast the pork loin at 350°F (180°C), basting frequently with the fat that accumulates in the pan, until done, approximately 45–60 minutes.

5 Remove the roast from the pan and keep it warm. Deglaze the pan with the apple juice and the stock. Simmer on top of the stove for 15 minutes, then strain.

6 Combine the sugar and vinegar in a saucepan. Bring to a boil and cook without stirring until the mixture turns a caramel color. Immediately remove from the heat and add the strained cooking juices. The sauce will sputter and bubble actively for a few moments. When the sputtering stops, return the pan to the heat and simmer until the sugar is completely dissolved. Skim any fat from the surface; keep the sauce warm over low heat.

7 Remove the twine from the roast. Slice and serve the meat with the sauce and Pan Roasted Brussels Sprouts.

* Dried apricots can be substituted for the prunes in this recipe.

Approximate values per 6-oz. (180-g) serving: **Calories** 850, **Total fat** 16 g, **Saturated fat** 5 g, **Cholesterol** 185 mg, **Sodium** 530 mg, **Total carbohydrates** 110 g, **Protein** 66 g, **Vitamin A** 45%, **Vitamin C** 15%, **Iron** 30%

Sous Vide Rosemary Garlic Pork Tenderloin

YIELD 4 Servings, 4.5 oz. (120 g) each		METHOD *Sous Vide* Poaching/Sautéing	
Pork tenderloin, trimmed		1 lb. 6 oz.	720 g
Salt and freshly ground black pepper		TT	TT
Sliced garlic		¼ oz.	7 g
Fresh rosemary sprigs		2	2
Unsalted butter		2 oz.	60 g
Beef or chicken stock		2 fl. oz	60 ml
Olive oil		3 fl. oz.	90 ml
Duxelles Sauce (page 245)		as needed for garnish	
Swiss chard, julienne, sautéed		as needed for garnish	

1 Cut the pork tenderloin into four uniform pieces. Season the pieces with salt and pepper.

2 Wearing clean disposable gloves, prepare two plastic pouches for *sous vide* cooking. Arrange two pieces of pork tenderloin in each pouch in a single layer without touching.

3 Divide the sliced garlic, rosemary sprigs, butter and stock evenly between the two bags. Add 1 fluid ounce (30 milliliters) of the olive oil to each bag. Vacuum seal the bags.

4 Cook the pork tenderloin in a thermal circulator heated to 142°F (61°C) for 1–1½ hours, until the core temperature of the pork reaches 142°F (61°C) when checked with a digital probe thermometer. (Reseal the bag before returning it to the circulator if necessary.)

5 Remove each portion of the pork tenderloin from the bag. Drain on clean paper towels.

6 Heat the remaining olive oil in a large heavy frying pan over high heat. Sear the pork tenderloin on all sides until crisp and brown, approximately 2 minutes per side.

7 Slice the tenderloin thinly on the bias. Serve with Duxelles Sauce and sautéed Swiss chard or other vegetable.

Approximate values per 4.5-oz. (120-g) serving: **Calories** 450, **Total fat** 36 g, **Saturated fat** 11 g, **Cholesterol** 115 mg, **Sodium** 75 mg, **Total carbohydrates** 1 g, **Protein** 31 g

> ## ⚠ Safety Alert
>
> Sous Vide *Sanitation*
>
> Food safety is of utmost concern when using *sous vide* techniques because of the low cooking temperatures. To prevent the growth of microorganisms, any food to be cooked *sous vide* must be chilled below the temperature danger zone (41°F/5°C) before cooking. Keep all cutting boards, knives and food contact surfaces clean and sanitary and wear clean disposable gloves. Use only the freshest unblemished ingredients. Consult your local health department for regulations for preparing food *sous vide*. Special permission and a HACCP plan may be required.

Escalope De Porc à la Normande (Pork Scallops with Apples)

Joliet Junior College, Joliet, IL
Chef Keith G. Vonhoff, Ret.

YIELD 2 Servings, 7 oz. (210 g) each		METHOD Sautéing	
Pork scallops, 3 oz. (90 g) each, pounded thin		4	4
Flour		as needed for dredging	
Clarified butter		1 fl. oz.	60 g
Apple, peeled, sliced		3 oz.	90 g
Veal stock		2 fl. oz.	60 ml
Apple juice		2 fl. oz.	60 ml
Heavy cream		3 fl. oz.	90 ml
Nutmeg, freshly ground		TT	TT
Salt and pepper		TT	TT
Lyonnaise Potatoes (page 660)		as needed	as needed
Green beans, steamed		as needed	as needed

1 Dredge the pork scallops in flour and shake off the excess.

2 Heat the butter in a medium sauté pan over medium-high heat. Add the pork scallops to the pan without overcrowding.

3 Lightly brown the pork scallops on one side. Turn and brown on the other side. Remove the pork scallops from the pan and keep warm.

4 Add the apple and sauté until tender without browning.

5 Add the stock and juice and reduce au sec.

6 Add the cream and nutmeg. Reduce until the sauce reaches nappé consistency. Adjust the seasonings.

7 Return the pork scallops to the pan along with any accumulated juices. Warm the pork scallops in the sauce for a few seconds.

8 Serve two pork scallops per portion, garnished with the sauce, Lyonnaise Potatoes and steamed green beans.

Approximate values per 7-oz. (210-g) serving: **Calories** 530, **Total fat** 40 g, **Saturated fat** 22 g, **Cholesterol** 190 mg, **Sodium** 160 mg, **Total carbohydrates** 7 g, **Protein** 35 g, **Vitamin A** 20%

Nataing
(Cambodian-Style Red Pork)

YIELD	4 Servings, 6 oz. (180 g) each		METHOD	Sautéing
Vegetable oil			1 fl. oz.	30 ml
Ground pork			8 oz.	240 g
New Mexico chile, ground			2 Tbsp.	30 ml
Cayenne pepper			½ tsp.	2 ml
Garlic cloves, sliced very thin			6	6
Fresh ginger, minced			2 tsp.	10 ml
Shallot, sliced very thin			1	1
Granulated sugar			2 Tbsp.	30 ml
Coconut milk, unsweetened			8 fl. oz.	240 ml
Fish sauce			1 Tbsp.	15 ml
Peanuts, raw, chopped			2 oz.	60 g
Cilantro sprigs			as needed for garnish	
Rice, cooked			as needed for garnish	

1   In a sauté pan, heat the oil and sauté the pork with the chile and cayenne pepper until the meat is browned.

2   Add the garlic, ginger and shallot and sauté until soft.

3   Add the sugar, coconut milk and fish sauce. Cook for approximately 10 minutes or until the pork is fully cooked and the flavors are well blended. Add the peanuts.

4   Garnish with the cilantro sprigs and serve warm with plain or jasmine rice.

Variation:

Cambodian-Style Red Vegetarian Stir-Fry—Substitute tofu or seitan for the ground pork. Use an additional 2 tablespoons (30 milliliters) vegetable oil when sautéing and cook until browned. Substitute light soy sauce for the fish sauce.

Approximate values per 6-oz. (180-g) serving: **Calories** 450, **Total fat** 39 g, **Saturated fat** 17 g, **Cholesterol** 40 mg, **Sodium** 430 mg, **Total carbohydrates** 15 g, **Protein** 15 g, **Vitamin A** 25%, **Iron** 20%

Pan-Fried Herb-Brined Pork Chops with Black Pepper Cream Gravy

YIELD 2 Servings, 5 oz. (150 g) each		METHOD Pan-Frying
Brine:		
Water	10 fl. oz.	300 ml
Kosher salt	1 oz.	30 g
Fresh sage leaves or thyme	¼ oz.	7.5 g
Dark brown sugar	½ oz.	15 g
Whole garlic cloves, peeled and crushed	1 oz.	30 g
Cracked black pepper	1 Tbsp.	15 ml
Crushed ice	10 oz.	300 ml
Pork loin chops, 6 oz. (180 g) each, cut ½- to ¾-inch thick	2	2
Seasoned flour	as needed for dredging	
Vegetable oil	as needed for frying	
All-purpose flour	2 Tbsp.	30 ml
Chicken stock	4 fl. oz.	120 ml
Light cream	2 fl. oz.	60 ml
Salt and freshly ground black pepper	TT	TT
Carrots, peeled and roasted	as needed for garnish	

1 Bring the water and salt to boil in a saucepan for the brine. Stir to dissolve the salt. Remove from the heat and add the sage, brown sugar, garlic cloves and pepper. Stir in the crushed ice. Cool to 35°F (1°C).

2 Pour the brine into a quarter hotel pan or resealable food storage bag. Add the pork chops to the brine making certain the chops are covered in the liquid. Refrigerate for 6–8 hours.

3 Remove the pork chops from the brine. Dry them with clean paper towels.

4 Dredge the chops in seasoned flour.

5 Heat a sauté pan over medium heat and add ¼-inch (6 millimeter) of oil. When the oil is hot, pan-fry the pork chops until golden brown, approximately 4 minutes. Turn and cook until golden brown on the other side, approximately 4 more minutes. Remove the pork chops from the pan and drain them on clean paper towels. Keep warm.

6 Degrease the pan, leaving 1 tablespoon (15 milliliters) of fat. Add the flour and whisk over medium heat to make a blond roux. Add the stock and cream whisking constantly until the gravy thickens. Season with salt and black pepper.

7 Serve the pork chops with some of the cream gravy and roasted carrots or cooked greens.

Approximate values per 5-oz. (150-g) serving: **Calories** 340, **Total fat** 21 g, **Saturated fat** 6 g, **Cholesterol** 85 mg, **Sodium** 670 mg, **Total carbohydrates** 8 g, **Protein** 28 g

Stuffed Pork Chops

YIELD 10 Servings, 10 oz. (300 g) each	METHOD Braising	
Thick-cut pork chops, approx. 8 oz. (240 g) each	10	10
Celery, small dice	4 oz.	120 g
Onion, small dice	6 oz.	180 g
Whole butter, melted	6 oz.	180 g
Fresh bread cubes, ½ in. (1.2 cm)	8 oz.	240 g
Parsley, chopped	1 Tbsp.	15 ml
Salt and pepper	TT	TT
White stock	approx. 8 fl. oz.	approx. 240 ml
Olive oil	2 fl. oz.	60 ml
Demi-glace	1 qt.	960 ml

1 Cut pockets in the chops.

2 Sauté the celery and onion in 2 ounces (60 grams) butter until tender.

3 Combine the celery, onion and remaining butter with the bread cubes, parsley, salt and pepper. Add enough stock to moisten the dressing.

4 Stuff the mixture into each of the pork chops. Seal the pockets with toothpicks and tie with butcher's twine.

5 Heat the olive oil in a braiser; brown the stuffed chops well on each side.

6 Add the demi-glace. Bring to a simmer, cover and place in a 325°F (160°C) oven. Cook until tender, approximately 45 minutes.

7 Remove the chops from the pan. Degrease the sauce and reduce to the desired consistency. Strain the sauce and adjust the seasonings. Serve the stuffed chops with some of the sauce and Sautéed Broccoli Rabe (page 643), Braised Red Cabbage with Apples (page 650) or other vegetables.

Approximate values per 10-oz. (300-g) serving: **Calories** 650, **Total fat** 38 g, **Saturated fat** 16 g, **Cholesterol** 225 mg, **Sodium** 390 mg, **Total carbohydrates** 5 g, **Protein** 70 g, **Vitamin A** 15%, **Iron** 15%

❶ Stuffing the pork chops.

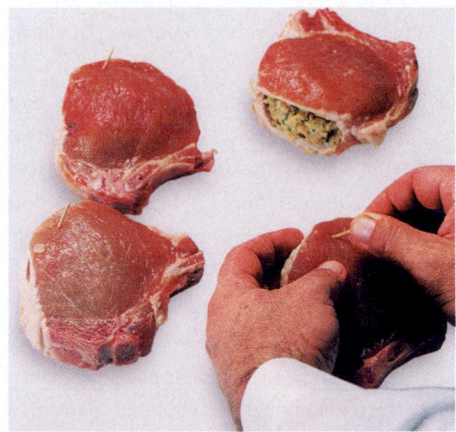

❷ Sealing the stuffed chops with toothpicks.

❸ The finished Stuffed Pork Chops.

Carnitas Tostada
(Mexican Pulled Pork and Corn Tortillas)

panela a soft fresh Mexican cheese made from pasteurized cow's milk that holds its shape when heated

farmer's cheese a soft, creamy fresh cheese made from cow's, goat's or cheep's milk

YIELD 10 Servings, 10 oz. (300 g) each	**METHOD** Braising	
Carnitas:		
Pork butt, boneless	4 lb.	1.8 kg
Lard	1 lb.	480 g
Water	8 fl. oz.	240 ml
Oranges	2	2
Garlic cloves, peeled	6	6
Onion, chopped coarse	8 oz.	240 g
Cinnamon sticks	2	2
Bay leaves	4	4
Kosher salt	2 Tbsp.	30 ml
Mexican oregano	1 tsp.	5 ml
Dried thyme	1 tsp.	5 ml
Milk	8 fl. oz.	240 ml
Chicken stock	4 fl. oz.	120 ml
Refried Beans (page 649), hot	1 lb. 14 oz.	900 g
Corn tortillas, deep-fried	10	10
Iceberg lettuce, chiffonade	10 oz.	300 g
Panela or **farmer's cheese**, shredded	10 oz.	300 g
Tomato, medium dice	5 oz.	150 g
Green onion, sliced	5 oz.	150 g
Cilantro, chopped	1 oz.	30 g
Red onion rings, thinly sliced	20	20
Pico de Gallo (Tomato Salsa), (page 237)	as needed for garnish	

1 Cut the pork butt into 3-inch (7.5-centimeter) pieces. In a heavy bottomed, 6-quart (5.8-liter) saucepot, combine the lard and water. Bring to a low boil and add the pork.

2 Halve and juice the oranges. Add the juice and the squeezed orange halves to the pork. Return the pork to a low boil and cook, uncovered, for 1 hour stirring occasionally to prevent the meat from sticking. As the water evaporates, the lard will become clear and the pork will begin to brown slightly.

3 Stir in the garlic, onion, cinnamon sticks, bay leaves, salt, oregano, thyme, milk and stock. Continue cooking, uncovered, at a low boil for 1 more hour stirring often and scraping the meat from the bottom of the pan. The pork will be very tender and begin to fall apart when it is done.

4 Remove the pan from the heat. Using a slotted spoon, remove the meat from the fat and drain it well. When it is cool enough to handle, pull it apart with gloved hands or chop it coarsely with a knife. Hold the meat warm for service.

5 To build the tostadas, spread 3 ounces (90 grams) of the refried beans on each corn tortilla.

6 Top with 1 ounce (30 grams) iceberg lettuce, 4 ounces (120 grams) of the cooked pork, 1 ounce (30 grams) cheese, 1 tablespoon (15 milliliters) diced tomatoes, ½ ounce (15 grams) green onions, two red onion rings and chopped cilantro. Serve the tostadas with Pico de Gallo.

Approximate values per 10-oz. (300-g) serving: **Calories** 740, **Total fat** 46 g, **Saturated fat** 18 g, **Cholesterol** 175 mg, **Sodium** 1400 mg, **Total carbohydrates** 28 g, **Protein** 50 g, **Vitamin A** 20%, **Vitamin C** 25%, **Calcium** 20%, **Iron** 15%

Jambalaya

A centerpiece of Louisiana Creole cooking, jambalaya is a rich stew of crab, shrimp, duck, chicken, pork, beef and vegetables in myriad combinations. Some historians claim that its name derives from the word jamón, *Spanish for "ham," because ham and rice are the two key ingredients that are found in all such stews. Tasso ham is a heavily smoked ham made from lean pork and flavored with seasonings characteristic of Louisiana cooking. Use Canadian bacon or smoked ham if tasso ham is unavailable.*

YIELD 6 Servings, 10 oz. (300 g) each **METHOD** Stewing

Andouille or smoked sausage, sliced	10 oz.	300 g
Tasso ham, medium dice, optional	6 oz.	180 g
Garlic, chopped	1 oz.	30 g
Onions, medium dice	6 oz.	180 g
Green bell peppers, medium dice	3 oz.	90 g
Red bell pepper, medium dice	1 oz.	30 g
Celery, medium dice	3 oz.	90 g
Green onions, chopped	2 oz.	60 g
Cajun Spice Mix (recipe follows)	TT	TT
Olive oil	as needed	as needed
Long-grain white rice	6 oz.	180 g
Tomatoes, diced, canned, with liquid	1 lb.	480 g
Chicken stock	6 oz.	180 g
Shrimp, peeled and deveined	10 oz.	300 g
Salt and pepper	TT	TT
Shrimp, head-on, tails peeled, optional	24	24
Green onions, sliced	as needed for garnish	

1 In a large rondeau, sauté the andouille and tasso (if using) to render their fat. Add the garlic, onions, bell peppers, celery and green onions to the pan and season with 1 teaspoon (5 milliliters) of Cajun Spice Mix. Sauté until the vegetables are tender, approximately 2 minutes. Add a small amount of olive oil if more fat is needed.

2 Add the rice and toss until it is coated with the fat.

3 Stir in the tomatoes and their liquid, the stock and the peeled shrimp. Bring to a simmer. Adjust the seasoning with more Cajun Spice Mix, salt and pepper as necessary.

4 Cover and cook at a low simmer for 10 minutes. Add the head-on shrimp (if using) and cook until the rice and shrimp are done, approximately 5–10 more minutes.

5 Serve the jambalaya mounded on a plate garnished with the head-on shrimp and sliced green onions.

Approximate values per 10-oz. (300-g) serving: **Calories** 280, **Total fat** 7 g, **Saturated fat** 3 g, **Cholesterol** 85 mg, **Sodium** 720 mg, **Total carbohydrates** 35 g, **Protein** 19 g, **Vitamin A** 15%, **Vitamin C** 50%, **Iron** 15%

Cajun Spice Mix

YIELD 6 oz. (180 g)

Salt	1 oz.	30 g
Garlic powder	1 oz.	30 g
White pepper	½ oz.	15 g
Dried oregano, ground	½ oz.	15 g
Onion powder	1 oz.	30 g
Black pepper	½ oz.	15 g
Cayenne pepper	¼ oz.	7 g
Dried thyme, ground	½ oz.	15 g
Paprika	1 oz.	30 g

1 Combine all ingredients and mix well.

Approximate values per ½-oz. (15-g) serving: **Calories** 35, **Total fat** 0.5 g, **Saturated fat** 0 g, **Cholesterol** 0 mg, **Sodium** 920 mg, **Total carbohydrates** 8 g, **Protein** 1 g, **Vitamin A** 35%, **Iron** 15%

Thai-Style Tea-Smoked Ribs

YIELD 6 Servings, 4 ribs each	METHOD Simmering/Smoking	
Pork ribs, St. Louis style,	2	2
3–4 lb. (1.4–1.9 kg) rack		
Simmering liquid:		
Water	3 qt.	3 lt
Sugar	2 oz.	60 ml
Soy sauce	3 fl. oz.	90 g
Sherry or dry white wine	2 fl. oz.	60 ml
Green onions, chopped	2 oz.	60 g
Coriander seeds	2 Tbsp.	30 ml
Fresh ginger, sliced thin	1 oz.	30 g
Garlic cloves, smashed	1 oz.	30 g
Star anise	4	4
Five spice powder	½ tsp.	2 ml
Smoke:		
Rice	2 oz.	60 g
Black tea leaves	1 oz.	30 g
Marinade:		
Dark soy sauce	2 fl. oz.	60 ml
Mushroom soy sauce	2 fl. oz.	60 ml
Fresh ginger, minced	1 oz.	30 g
Garlic, minced	1 oz.	30 g
Green onions, minced	3 oz.	90 g
Brown sugar	1 oz.	30 g
Dry Rub:		
Brown sugar	1½ oz.	45 g
Black pepper	1½ tsp.	7 ml
Sichuan peppercorns	½ tsp.	2 ml
Black sesame seeds, ground	1 Tbsp.	15 ml
Coriander, ground	1½ tsp.	7 ml
Sichuan peppercorns	as needed for garnish	
Green onions, sliced	as needed for garnish	

❶ Smoking the ribs in a wok.

❷ The finished Thai-Style Tea-Smoked Ribs.

1 Cut the racks of ribs into four sections of 4 or 5 ribs each. Blanch the ribs in boiling water for 4 minutes. Rinse under cold water and dry.

2 Combine all of the simmering liquid ingredients in a large rondeau and bring to a boil. Add the ribs, return the liquid to a simmer and cook the ribs for 2 hours, turning them occasionally. Drain the ribs on a rack and refrigerate until chilled.

3 To smoke the ribs, place the rice and tea leaves in the smoking tray of a commercial smoker. Place the ribs in the smoker and smoke at low heat for 15 minutes. Alternatively, place the smoking ingredients in the bottom of a stove-top or wok-style smoker. Place a rack in the stove-top smoker or wok and arrange the ribs on the rack. Place the smoker or wok over medium high heat. When the mixture in the pan starts to smoke, cover, reduce the heat and smoke the ribs for 10–15 minutes. Remove the ribs from the smoker.

4 Combine the marinade ingredients. Toss the smoked ribs in the marinade ingredients, coating them evenly. Marinate the ribs in the refrigerator for at least 1 hour or overnight.

5 Combine the dry rub ingredients. For service, roast the ribs at 400°F (200°C) until heated through, approximately 10–15 minutes. Sprinkle the presentation side of the ribs with the dry rub mixture and finish them under a broiler or salamander until lightly crisp. Plate the ribs and garnish with Sichuan peppercorns and sliced green onions.

Approximate values per 4-rib serving: **Calories** 880, **Total fat** 64 g, **Saturated fat** 23 g, **Cholesterol** 250 mg, **Sodium** 690 mg, **Total carbohydrates** 12 g, **Protein** 61 g, **Calcium** 15%, **Iron** 25%

Poultry 18

Poultry is the collective term for domesticated birds bred for eating, including chickens, ducks, geese, guineas, pigeons and turkeys. (Game birds such as pheasant, quail and partridge are described in Chapter 19, Game; farm-raised ratites—ostrich, emu and rhea—are discussed here.) The renowned French gastronome and author Jean-Anthelme Brillat-Savarin (1755–1826) once observed that "poultry is for the cook what canvas is for the painter." Poultry can be cooked by almost any method, and its mild flavor goes well with a wide variety of sauces and accompaniments. Poultry is generally the least expensive and most versatile of all center-of-the-plate meats.

In this chapter we discuss the different kinds and classes of poultry and how to choose those that best suit your needs. In addition we discuss how to store poultry properly to prevent food-borne illnesses and spoilage, how to butcher birds to produce specific cuts and how to apply a variety of cooking methods properly.

Many of the cooking methods discussed here have been applied previously to red meats. Although there are similarities with these methods, there are also many distinct differences. As you study this chapter, review the corresponding cooking methods for meats and note the similarities and differences.

MUSCLE COMPOSITION OF POULTRY

The muscle tissue of poultry is similar to that of mammals in that it contains approximately 72 percent water, 20 percent protein, 7 percent fat and 1 percent minerals and it consists of bundles of muscle cells or fibers held together by connective tissue. Unlike red meat, poultry does not contain the intramuscular fat known as marbling. Instead, a bird stores fat in its skin, its abdominal cavity and the fat pad near its tail. Poultry fat is softer and has a lower melting point than other animal fats. It is easily rendered during cooking.

As with red meats, poultry muscles that are used more often tend to be tougher than those used less frequently. Also the muscles of an older bird tend to be tougher than those of a younger one. Because the majority of poultry is marketed at a young age, however, it is generally very tender.

The breast and wing flesh of chickens and turkeys is lighter in color than the flesh of their thighs and legs. For this reason, it is often referred to as "white meat." This color difference is due to a higher concentration of the protein **myoglobin** in the thigh and leg muscles. Myoglobin is the protein that stores oxygen for the muscle tissues to use. More-active muscles require more myoglobin and tend to be darker than less-active ones. Because chickens and turkeys generally do not fly, their breast and wing muscles contain little myoglobin and are therefore a light color. Birds that do fly have only dark meat. Dark meat also contains more fat and connective tissue than light meat and it takes longer to cook.

Skin color may vary from white to golden yellow, depending on what the bird was fed and the temperature during processing. Such color differences are not an indication of overall quality. Figure 18.1 illustrates the skeletal structure of a chicken. Figure 18.2 shows the relationship between the whole chicken and the parts cut from it.

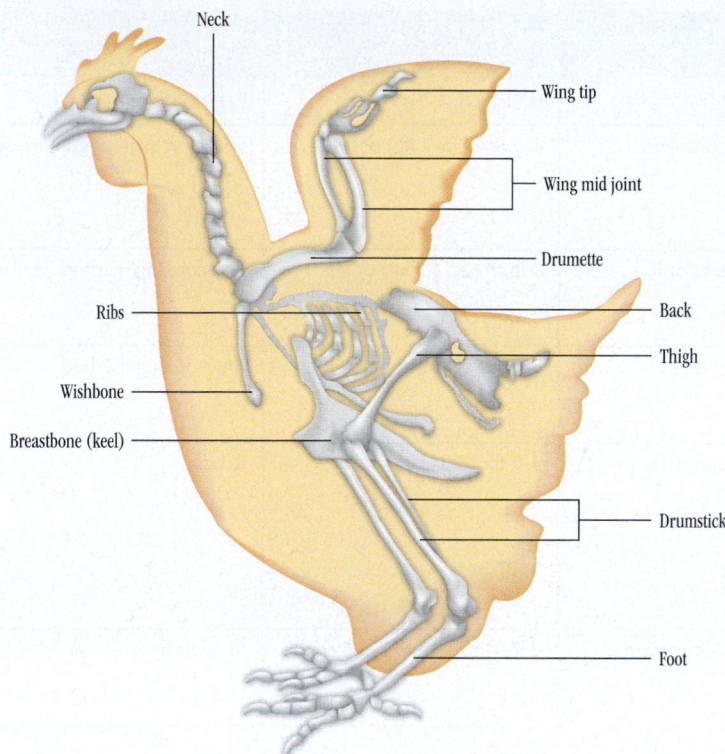

Figure 18.1 The skeletal structure of a chicken.

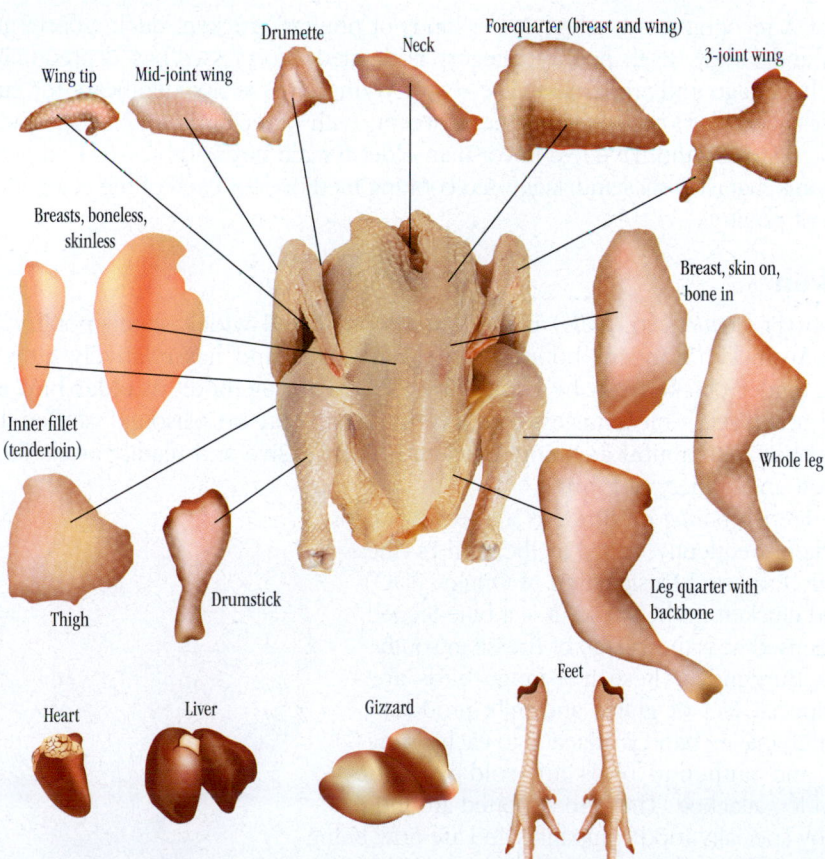

Figure 18.2 The parts of a chicken. (Smaller cuts to the left are fabricated from the larger cuts to the right.)

USDA CHICKEN CLASSES				TABLE 18.1
CLASS	DESCRIPTION	AGE	WEIGHT	COOKING METHOD
Game hen	Young or immature progeny of Cornish chickens or of a Cornish chicken and a White Rock chicken; very flavorful	5 weeks or less	1–2 lb. (0.5–1 kg) or less	Split and broil or grill; roast
Broiler/fryer	Young with soft, smooth-textured skin; relatively lean; flexible breastbone	10 weeks or less	3 lb. 8 oz. (1.5 kg) or less	Any cooking method; very versatile
Roaster	Young with tender meat and smooth-textured skin; breastbone is less flexible than broiler's	8–12 weeks	5 lb. (2 kg) or more	Any cooking method
Capon	Surgically castrated male; tender meat with soft, smooth-textured skin; bred for well-flavored meat; contains a high proportion of light to dark meat and a relatively high fat content	4–8 months	4–7 lb. (1.8–3 kg)	Roast
Hen/stewing	Mature female; flavorful but less tender meat; nonflexible breastbone	Over 10 months	2 lb. 4 oz.–8 lb. (1–3.5 kg)	Stew or braise

Rock Cornish game hen

Chicken broiler/fryer

poussin a French term for a small, immature chicken; in the United States, *poussin* is another name for a small chicken such as a Rock Cornish game hen

IDENTIFYING POULTRY

The USDA recognizes six categories or kinds of poultry: chicken, duck, goose, guinea, pigeon and turkey. Each poultry category is divided into classes based predominantly on the bird's age and tenderness. The sex of young birds is not significant for culinary purposes. The bird's sex does matter, however, with older birds; older male birds are tough and stringy and have less flavor than older female birds. Tables 18.1 and 18.2 list identifying characteristics and suggested cooking methods for each of the categories and classes of poultry.

Chicken

Chicken (Fr. *poulet*; Sp. *pollo*) is the most popular and widely eaten poultry in the world. A chicken contains both light and dark meat and has relatively little fat. A young, tender chicken can be cooked by almost any method; an older bird is best stewed or braised. Chicken is extremely versatile and may be seasoned, stuffed, basted or garnished with almost anything. Chicken is inexpensive and readily available, fresh or frozen, in a variety of forms.

The French *poulet de Bresse* is a special category of chicken, frequently touted as the world's finest. The only Protected Designation of Origin (PDO)-certified chicken in the world, it is a blue-legged variety raised near the village of Bresse in southeastern Burgundy. These free-range birds are fed a special diet of grains and milk products. An identifying leg band is attached to each young chick, and authentic birds are sold with the banded leg attached. They are exported around the world by specialty food companies and are now being grown in the United States on small farms and marketed as American Bresse.

Capon

USDA DUCK, GOOSE, GUINEA, PIGEON AND TURKEY CLASSES   TABLE 18.2

USDA Duck Classes

CLASS	DESCRIPTION	AGE	WEIGHT	COOKING METHOD
Broiler/fryer	Young bird with tender meat; a soft bill and windpipe	8 weeks or less	3 lb. 8 oz.–4 lb. (1.5–1.8 kg)	Roast at high temperature
Roaster	Young bird with tender meat; rich flavor; easily dented windpipe	16 weeks or less	4–6 lb. (1.8–2.5 kg)	Roast
Mature	Old bird with tough flesh; hard bill and windpipe	6 months or older	4–6 lb. (1.8–2.5 kg)	Braise

USDA Goose Classes

CLASS	DESCRIPTION	AGE	WEIGHT	COOKING METHOD
Young	Rich, tender dark meat with large amounts of fat; easily dented windpipe	6 months or less	6–12 lb. (2.5–5.5 kg)	Roast at high temperature, accompany with acidic sauces
Mature	Tough flesh and hard windpipe	Over 6 months	10–16 lb. (4.5–7 kg)	Braise or stew

USDA Guinea Classes

CLASS	DESCRIPTION	AGE	WEIGHT	COOKING METHOD
Young	Tender meat; flexible breastbone	3 months or less	12 oz.–1 lb. 8 oz. (0.3–0.7 kg)	Bard and roast; sauté
Mature	Tough flesh; hard breastbone	Over 3 months	1–2 lb. (0.5–1 kg)	Braise or stew

USDA Pigeon Classes

CLASS	DESCRIPTION	AGE	WEIGHT	COOKING METHOD
Squab	Immature pigeon; very tender, dark flesh and a small amount of fat	4 weeks or less	12 oz.–1 lb. 8 oz. (0.3–0.7 kg)	Broil, roast or sauté
Pigeon	Mature bird; coarse skin and tough flesh	Over 4 weeks	1–2 lb. (0.5–1 kg)	Braise or stew

USDA Turkey Classes

CLASS	DESCRIPTION	AGE	WEIGHT	COOKING METHOD
Fryer/roaster	Immature bird of either sex (males are called *toms*); tender meat with smooth skin; flexible breastbone	16 weeks or less	4–9 lb. (2–4 kg)	Roast or cut into scallops and sauté or pan-fry
Young	Tender meat with smooth skin; less-flexible breastbone	8 months or less	8–22 lb. (3.5–10 kg)	Roast or stew
Yearling	Fully mature bird; reasonably tender meat and slightly coarse skin	15 months or less	10–30 lb. (4.5–13 kg)	Roast or stew
Mature	Older bird with coarse skin and tough flesh	15 months or older	10–30 lb. (4.5–13 kg)	Stew; ground or used in processed products

roaster duckling a duck of either sex slaughtered before it is sixteen weeks old. Fryer and broiler ducklings are slaughtered before eight weeks of age and still retain their soft bill and windpipe

magret [may-gray] a breast from the moulard duck, traditionally taken from the ducks that produce foie gras; magret is usually served boneless but with the skin intact

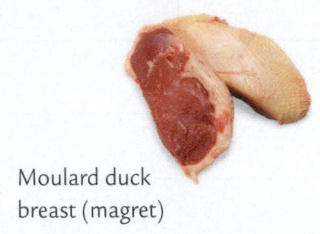

Moulard duck
breast (magret)

Young
guinea fowl

Young pigeon
or squab

Duck

The **ducks** (Fr. *canard*) used most often in commercial food service operations are **roaster ducklings** of the Pekin or Long Island breed. This duck contains only dark meat and large amounts of fat. In order to make the fatty skin palatable, it is important to render as much fat as possible. Duck has a high percentage of bone and fat to meat; for example, a 4-pound duck serves only two people, whereas a 4-pound roasting chicken serves four to six people.

For a larger duck breast with a richer, meatier flavor, chefs prefer the **Moulard**, also known as Mullard, a hybrid of the Pekin and Muscovy breeds. (The Muscovy is a lean, thin-skinned South American breed with a strong, musky flavor.) The Moulard's large breast, called a **magret**, has a rich flavor and a texture similar to beef. The magret is often aged for several days and may be smoked whole or cooked by grilling, roasting or pan-searing. Moulards are also the source for foie gras [fwah grah] (see page 419).

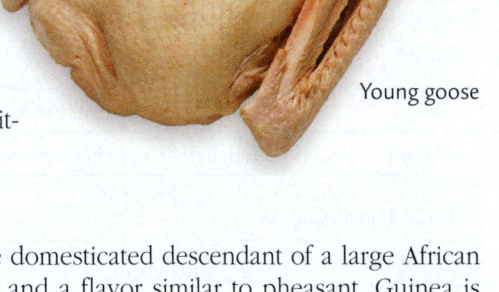

Roaster duckling

Goose

A **goose** (Fr. *oie*) contains only dark meat and has very fatty skin. It is usually roasted at high temperatures to render the fat. Roasted goose is popular at holidays and is often served with an acidic fruit-based sauce to offset the fattiness.

Young goose

Guinea Fowl

A **guinea** or **guinea fowl** (Fr. *pintade*) is the domesticated descendant of a large African game bird. It has both light and dark meat and a flavor similar to pheasant. Guinea is tender enough to sauté. Because it contains little fat, a guinea is usually barded (covered with thin slices of pork fatback) before roasting. Guinea, which is relatively expensive, is not as popular in the United States as it is in Europe.

Pigeon

The **young pigeon** (Fr. *pigeon*) used in commercial food service operations is referred to as **squab**. Its meat is dark, tender and well suited for broiling, sautéing or roasting. Squab has very little fat and benefits from barding.

Turkey

Turkey (Fr. *dinde*) is the second most popular category of poultry in the United States. It has both light and dark meat and a relatively small amount of fat. Younger turkey is an economical option and can be prepared in almost any manner.

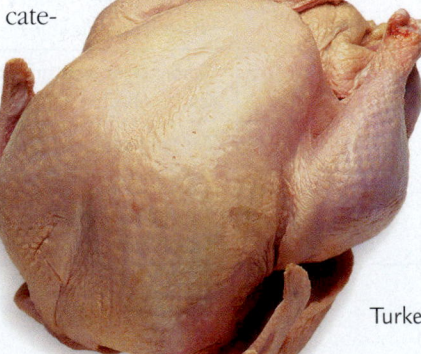

Turkey

Ratites

Ratites are a family of flightless birds with small wings and flat breastbones. They include the **ostrich** (which is native to Africa), the **emu** (native to Australia) and the **rhea** (native to South America). Ratite meat, which is classified as red meat even though it is poultry flesh, is a dark, cherry-red color with a flavor similar to beef; it is a little sweeter and has a soft texture. Ratite meat is low in fat and calories. Most ratite meat is from birds slaughtered at 10–13 months of age. It is generally cut from the back (which contains the very tender tenderloin), the thigh (also known as the **fan**) and the leg, and is available as steaks, filets, medallions, roasts, cubes or ground.

Ratite meat is often prepared like veal. The more tender cuts, such as those from the back or thigh, can be marinated and then cooked by dry-heat cooking methods, especially broiling, grilling, roasting and pan-frying. Because it has little fat, care must be taken to avoid overcooking, and these products are usually served medium rare to medium. Allowing these products to rest after cooking helps ensure tenderness. Tougher cuts, such as those from the leg, are best ground or prepared with combination cooking methods.

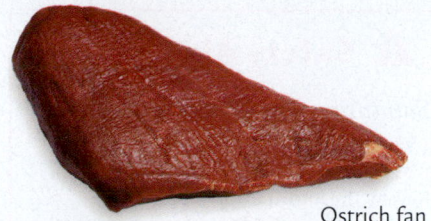

Ostrich fan

Livers, Gizzards, Hearts and Necks

Poultry livers, gizzards, hearts and necks are commonly referred to as **giblets** and can be used in a variety of ways. **Gizzards** (a bird's second stomach), hearts and necks are often used to make giblet gravy. Gizzards are sometimes trimmed and deep-fried; hearts are sometimes served sautéed and creamed. Necks are very flavorful and can be added to stocks for flavor and richness. In contrast, livers, hearts and gizzards are not added to stocks because of their strong flavors. Chicken livers are often made into pâtés or sautéed or broiled with onions and served as an entrée.

Chicken giblets

Foie Gras

Foie gras is the enlarged liver of a duck or goose. Considered a delicacy since Roman times, it is now produced in many parts of the world, including the United States. Foie gras is produced by methodically fattening the birds by force-feeding them specially prepared corn while limiting their activity. Fresh foie gras consists of two lobes that must be separated, split and deveined. Good foie gras is smooth, round and putty-colored. It should not be yellow or grainy. Goose foie gras is lighter in color and more delicate in flavor than that of duck. Duck foie gras has a deeper, winy flavor and is more common than goose foie gras. Fresh foie gras can be grilled, roasted, sautéed or made into pâtés or terrines. No matter which cooking method is used, care must be taken not to overcook the liver. Foie gras is so high in fat that overcooking results in the liver actually melting away. Most foie gras is pasteurized or canned and may consist of solid liver or small pieces of liver compacted to form a block. Canned foie gras mousse is also available, often packaged with truffles, which are a natural accompaniment.

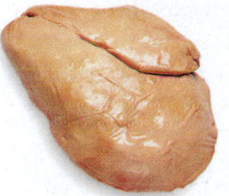

Duck foie gras

NUTRITION INFORMATION FOR POULTRY

Poultry is an economical source of high-quality protein. Poultry's nutritional values are similar to those of other meats, except that chicken and turkey breast meat is lower in fat and higher in niacin than other lean meats. Generally dark meat contains more niacin and riboflavin than white meat. Much of the fat in poultry is found in the skin, which can be easily removed before cooking for a leaner dish.

Figure 18.3 USDA inspection stamp for poultry.

INSPECTION AND GRADING OF POULTRY

All poultry produced for public consumption in the United States is subject to USDA inspection. Inspections ensure that products are processed under strict sanitary guidelines and are wholesome and fit for human consumption. Inspections do not indicate a product's quality or tenderness. The round inspection stamp illustrated in Figure 18.3 is found either on a tag attached to the wing or on the package label.

Grading poultry is voluntary but virtually universal. Birds are graded according to their overall quality, with the grade (USDA A, B or C) shown on a shield-shaped tag affixed to the bird or on a processed product's packaging. See Figure 18.4.

Grade Mark

Figure 18.4 Grade stamp for USDA Grade A poultry.

According to the USDA, Grade A poultry is free from deformities, with thick flesh and a well-developed fat layer; free of pinfeathers, cuts or tears and broken bones; free from discoloration and, if it is frozen, free from defects that can occur during handling or storage of frozen foods. Nearly all poultry used in wholesale and retail outlets is Grade A. Grade B and C birds are used primarily for processed poultry products.

Quality grades have no bearing on the product's tenderness or flavor. A bird's tenderness is usually indicated by its class (e.g., a young turkey is younger and more tender than a yearling). The grades (USDA A, B or C) within each class are determined by overall quality.

PURCHASING POULTRY

Poultry can be purchased in many forms: fresh or frozen, whole or cut up, bone-in or boneless, skin-on or skinless, portion controlled (P.C.), individually quick-frozen (IQF) or ground. Chickens and turkeys are also widely used in prepared and convenience items and are available fully cooked and vacuum-wrapped or boned and canned. Although purchasing poultry in a ready-to-use form is convenient, it is not always necessary; poultry products are easy to fabricate and portion. Whole poultry is also less expensive than precut fresh or frozen products. You should consider your menu, labor costs, storage facilities and employee skills when deciding whether to purchase whole poultry or some other form.

In addition to economics, other considerations when purchasing poultry include the variety and how the birds are raised and processed, as discussed here.

Free-Range Poultry

Chicken has become increasingly popular in recent years, in part because it is inexpensive, versatile and considered healthier than red meat. Indeed U.S. per capita consumption is at an all-time high of more than 108 pounds annually. To meet an ever-increasing demand, chickens are raised indoors in huge chicken houses that may contain as many as 20,000 birds. They are fed a specially formulated mixture composed primarily of corn and soybean meal. Animal protein, vitamins, minerals and small amounts of antibiotics are added to produce quick-growing, healthy birds.

Many consumers feel that the flavor of chickens and other poultry raised this way is not as good as the flavor of poultry that is allowed to move freely and forage for food. In addition some consumers are concerned about the residual effects of the vitamins, minerals and antibiotics added to the chicken feed. To meet the demand for chickens and poultry raised the old-fashioned way, some farmers raise (and many fine establishments serve) free-range and pasture-raised chickens, duck, geese, turkey and other birds.

Although the USDA has not standardized regulations for **free-range poultry**, generally birds that are allowed access to an area outside the chicken house can be labeled for sale as "free-range." In some cases this means simply that they were raised without cages with limited access to the out of doors. The term **pasture-raised** generally refers to birds that have been raised out-of-doors with access to fresh vegetation, although this term is not standardized. Some poultry farms go beyond government requirements and raise birds without antibiotics, feeding them a vegetarian diet (no animal fat or by-products), allowing them to forage for food, employing more humane growing methods, and processing them without preservatives. True free-range chickens are marketed at 9–10 weeks old and weigh 4½–5 pounds (2–2½ kilograms), which is considerably more mature and heavier than conventional broilers. They may be sold with heads and feet intact and are more expensive than conventionally raised chickens.

Free-range chickens roosting outside of their chicken house.

Heritage Breed Poultry

Chicken breeders and farmers are making an effort to bring back breeds of poultry that fell out of favor when meaty, quick-growing hybrids that are suitable to mass production were introduced. Rhode Island Red, Wyandotte and Jersey Giant Chicken are among the American heritage breeds regaining popularity. To bring attention to these varieties, the American Livestock Breeds Association has defined **heritage poultry** as breeds with the following traits: The breeds must have been on the American Poultry Association's list prior to 1950; they must mate naturally; they must be slow-growing (taking as long as 16–18 weeks to mature); and they must have a long, productive outdoor life.

The main reason for cooking with heritage breeds is their flavor, which is rich and intense. These breeds generally have thicker skin and darker meat than commercial chickens. Many breeds yield very lean meat that is not suitable for every cooking method. When deciding how to best serve heritage chicken, purchase and prepare a few to test which cooking method is suitable. Moist-heat cooking methods such as braising may be preferable to grilling. When roasting a heritage chicken consider barding the bird with fat or bacon and trussing the bird to compensate for its leanness.

Air-Chilled Poultry

After poultry is slaughtered, it must be cleaned then chilled. To do so, the carcasses are typically submerged in a series of iced water baths to reduce the core temperature to safe temperatures below 40°F (4°C) within 4 hours of death. During processing, the poultry absorbs moisture, particularly in its skin. An alternative method, called **air chilling**, employs cold purified air to reduce the core temperature of the birds in lieu of water. The poultry carcasses are suspended in chambers where circulating cold air rapidly cools them. Proponents of air chilling, which is more costly and time consuming than water chilling, praise the flavor and crisp skin of poultry processed using this method. Because air chilling reduces water consumed and reduces the risk of cross contamination during poultry processing, it is attracting industry attention and may lead to a shift in practices although there may be a higher risk of airborne contaminants passing from one bird to another using this method.

STORING POULTRY

Poultry requires time and temperature control for safety (TCS). It is highly perishable and particularly susceptible to contamination by salmonella bacteria. It is critical that poultry be stored at the correct temperatures. Fresh chickens and other small birds can be stored on ice or at 32–34°F (0–2°C) for up to 2 days; larger birds can be stored up to 4 days at these temperatures. Frozen poultry should be kept at 0°F (–18°C) or below (the colder the better) and can be held for up to 6 months. It should be thawed gradually under refrigeration, allowing 2 days for chickens and as long as 4 days for larger birds. Never attempt to cook poultry that is still partially frozen; it will be impossible to cook the product evenly, and the areas that were still frozen may not reach the temperatures necessary to destroy harmful bacteria. Never partially cook poultry one day and finish cooking it later; bacteria are more likely to grow under such conditions.

BUTCHERING PROCEDURES FOR POULTRY

Poultry is easier to butcher than meats and is often processed on-site. You should be able to perform the following commonly encountered procedures. Because the different kinds of poultry are similar in structure, these procedures apply to a variety of birds.

Procedure for Cutting a Bird in Half

Often the first step in preparing poultry is to cut the bird in half. Broiler and fryer chickens are split to make two portions. This procedure removes the backbone and breastbone (also known as the **keel** bone) for a neat finished product.

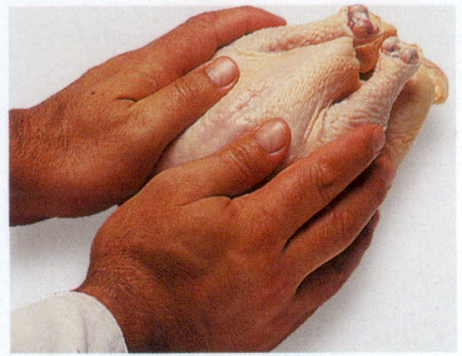

1 Square up the bird by placing it on its back and pressing on the legs and breast to create a more uniform appearance.

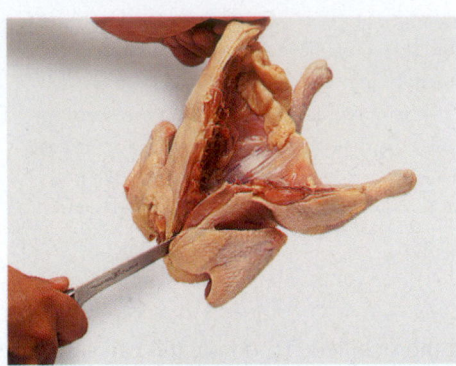

2 Place the bird on its breast and hold the tail tightly with the thumb and forefinger of one hand. Using a rigid boning knife and in a single swift movement, cut along the backbone from the bird's tail to the head.

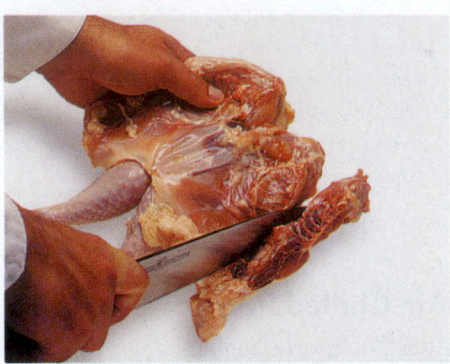

3 Lay the bird flat on the cutting board and remove the backbone by cutting through the ribs connecting it to the breast using a chef's knife.

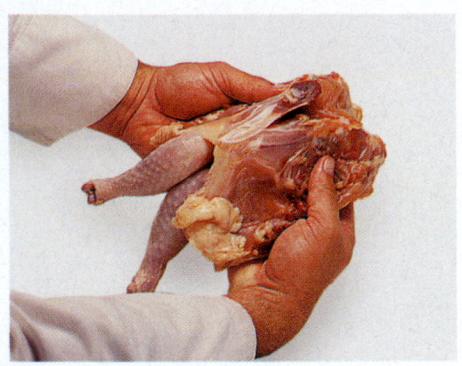

4 Bend the bird back, breaking the breast-bone free.

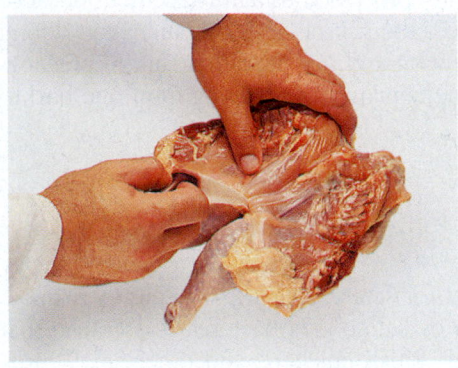

5 Run your fingers along the breastbone to separate the breast meat from the bone; pull the bone free. Be sure to remove the flexible cartilage completely.

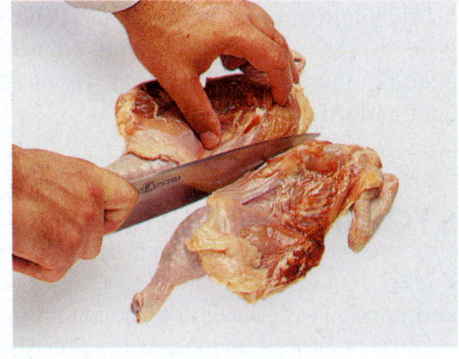

6 Cut through the skin to separate the bird into two halves. The halves are ready to be cooked; for a more attractive presentation, follow Steps 7 and 8.

7 Trim off the wing tips and the ends of the leg bone.

8 Make a slit in the skin below the leg and tuck the leg bone into the slit.

Procedure for Cutting a Bird into Pieces

Cutting a bird into pieces is one of the most common butchering procedures. Reviewing the bird's structure illustrated in Figures 18.1 and 18.2 will help you find each joint and simplify the process of cutting poultry.

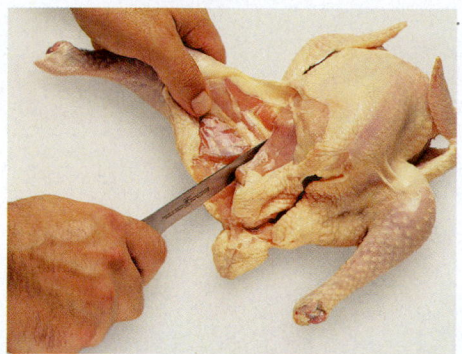

1 Remove the leg by pulling the leg and thigh away from the breast and cutting through the skin and flesh toward the thigh joint using a rigid boning knife.

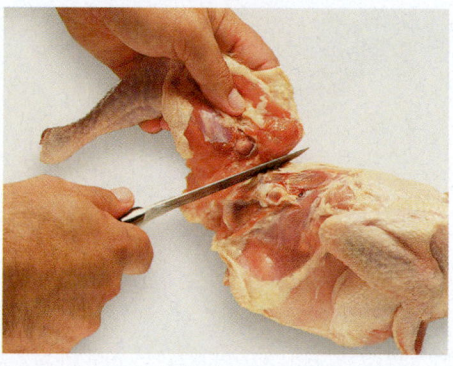

2 Cut down to the thigh joint, twist the leg to break the joint and cut the thigh and leg from the carcass. Be careful to trim around the **oyster meat** (the tender morsel of meat located next to the backbone); leave it attached to the thigh. Repeat with the other leg.

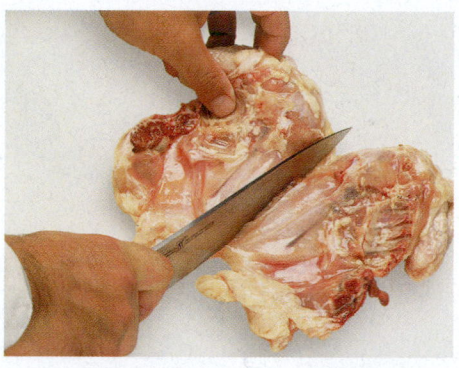

3 To split the breast, follow Steps 2 through 6 in the procedure for cutting a bird in half. Cut the breast into two halves.

4 The bird is now cut into four quarters.

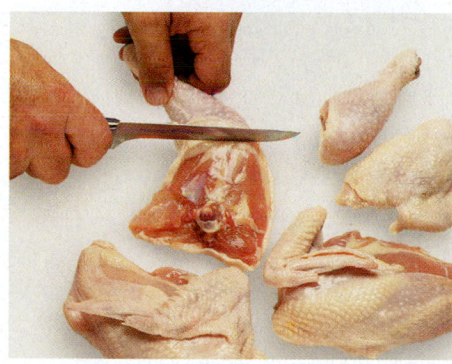

5 To cut the bird into six pieces, separate the thigh from the leg by making a cut along the line of fat on the inside of the thigh and leg.

6 To cut the bird into eight pieces, separate the wing from the breast by cutting the joint, or split the breast, leaving a portion of the breast meat attached to the wing.

Procedure for Preparing a Suprême or Airline Breast

A **chicken suprême** or **airline breast** is half of a boneless chicken breast with the first wing bone attached. The tip of the wing bone is removed, yielding a neat and attractive portion that can be prepared by a variety of cooking methods. The skin can be left on or removed.

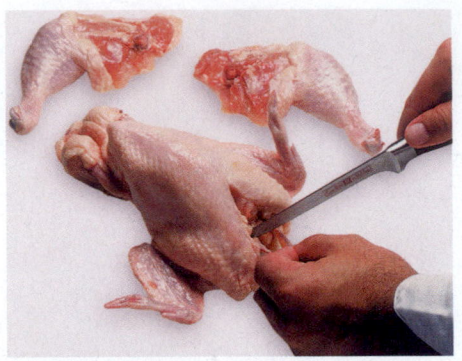

1 Remove the legs following Steps 1 and 2 in the procedure for cutting a bird into pieces. Place the chicken on its back. Locate the wishbone, trim around it and remove it.

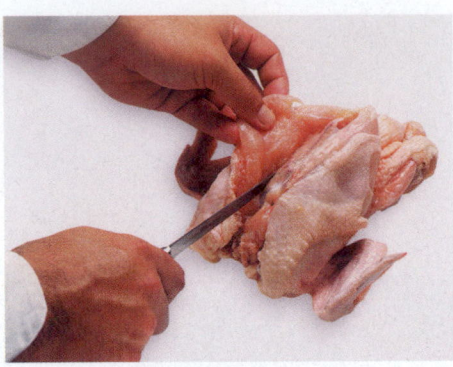

2 Cut along one side of the breastbone, separating the meat from the bone.

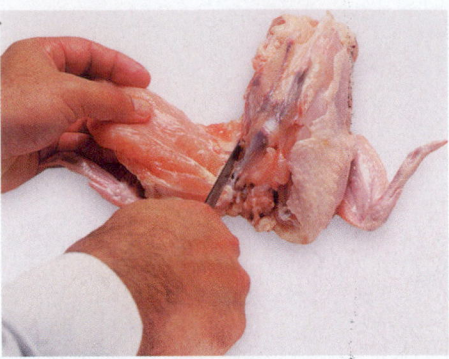

3 Following the natural curvature of the ribs, continue cutting to remove the meat from the bones.

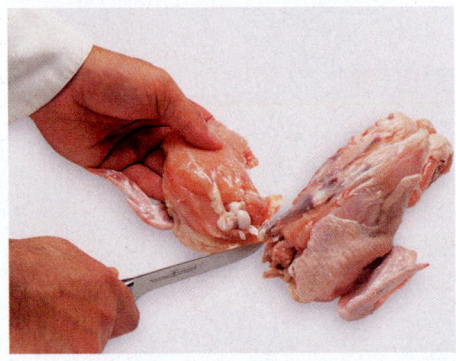

4 When you reach the wing joint, cut through the joint, keeping the wing attached to the breast portion. Cut the breast free from the carcass.

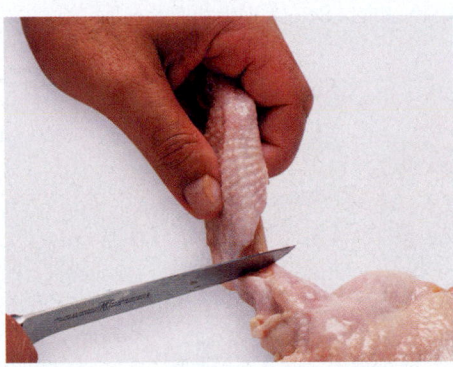

5 Make a cut on the back of the joint between the first and second wing bones.

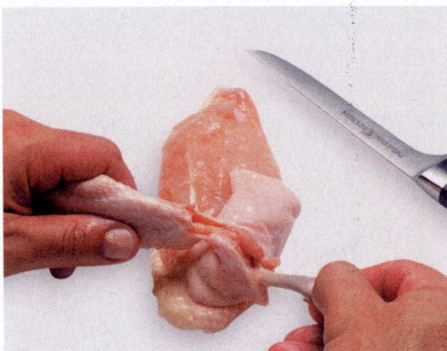

6 Break the joint and pull the meat and skin back to expose a clean bone. Trim the wing bone.

7 The suprême can be prepared skin-on or skinless.

Procedure for Preparing a Boneless Breast

A boneless chicken breast is one of the most versatile and popular poultry cuts. It can be broiled, grilled, baked, sautéed, pan-fried or poached. Boneless turkey breast can be roasted or sliced and sautéed as a substitute for veal. The skin can be removed or left intact. The breast can be left in one piece, known as a **double breast**, or cut into two pieces.

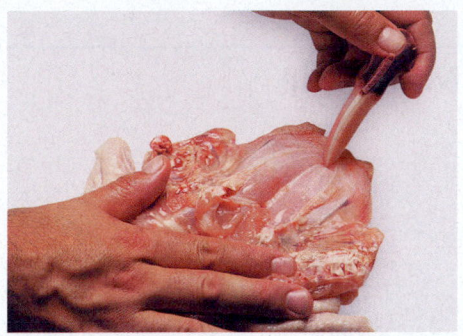

1 Place the chicken on its back. Remove the legs and the backbone following Steps 1, 2 and 3 in the procedure for cutting a bird into pieces. Remove the keel bone from the bone-in breast, following Steps 4 and 5 in the procedure for cutting a bird in half.

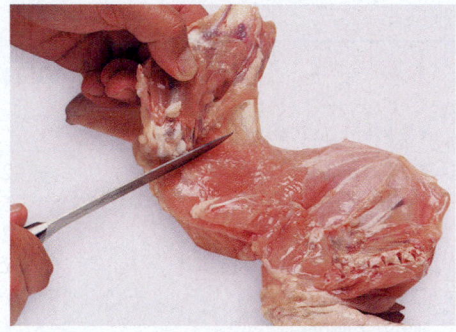

2 With the chicken breast lying skin side down, separate the rib bones, wing and wishbone from the breast. Leave the two tender pieces of meat known as the **tenderloins** attached to the breast. Repeat the procedure on the other side, being sure to remove the small wishbone pieces from the front of the breast.

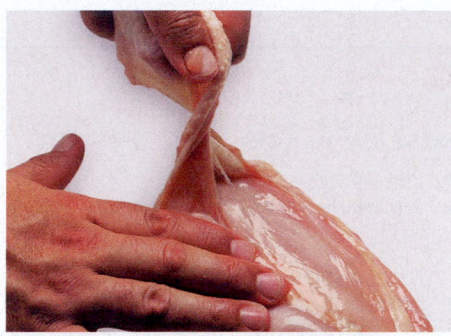

3 Cut through the meat and skin to separate the chicken breast into two pieces. The skin may be left intact or removed to produce a skinless boneless breast.

Procedure for Boning a Chicken Leg and Thigh

Chicken breasts are usually more popular than legs and thighs. There are, however, uses for boneless, skinless leg and thigh meat; they can be stuffed or used for **ballotines**, for example.

ballotine [bahl-lo-TEEN]; classic French preparation made by stuffing a deboned poultry leg with forcemeat; it is poached or braised and served hot; similar to a galantine, which is served cold

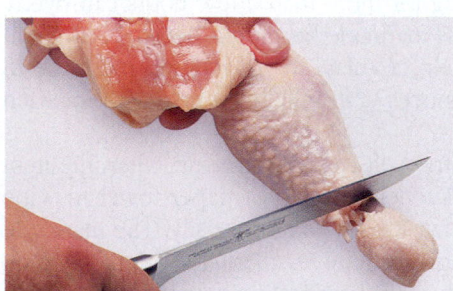

1 Carefully cut through the skin, meat and tendons at the base of the leg. Be sure to cut through to the bone.

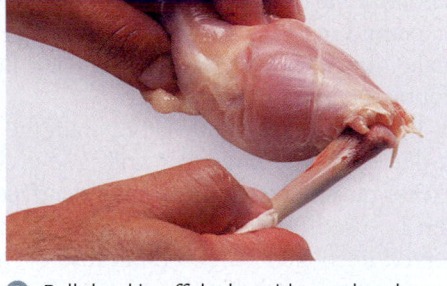

2 Pull the skin off the leg with your hands, then break the joint between the leg and thigh. Twist and pull out the leg bone.

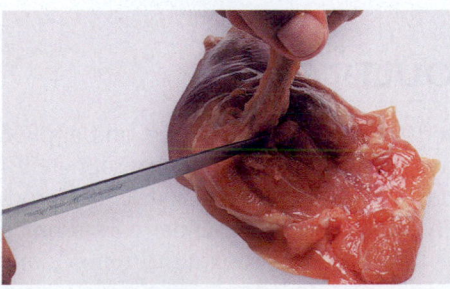

3 Working from the inside of the thigh bone, separate the bone from the meat.

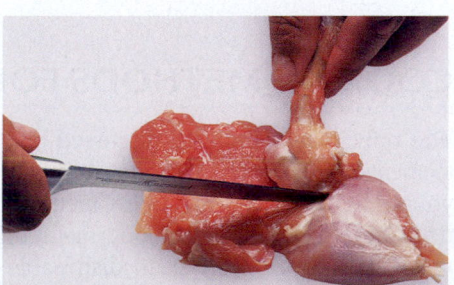

4 Cut around the cartilage at the joint between the leg and thigh and remove the thigh bone and cartilage.

MARINATING POULTRY

Most poultry is quite mild in flavor. A marinade or spice rub adds flavor and moisture, especially to poultry that will be broiled or grilled. Barbecued chicken is a simple and popular example of marinated poultry. Other poultry marinades can be a mixture of white wine or lemon juice, oil, salt, pepper, herbs and spices such as the ones in the following recipe.

♥ Good Choice

MISE EN PLACE
- Peel and mince garlic.
- Peel and chop onions into small dice.

Marinating chicken breasts.

White Wine Marinade

YIELD 1 qt. (960 ml)

Garlic, minced	2 tsp.	10 ml
Onion, small dice	5 oz.	150 g
Dry white wine	24 fl. oz.	720 ml
Bay leaves	2	2
Dried thyme	2 tsp.	10 ml
White pepper	1 tsp.	5 ml
Salt	1 Tbsp.	15 ml
Lemon juice	1 fl. oz.	30 ml
Vegetable oil	4 fl. oz.	120 ml

1 Combine all ingredients. Use approximately 8 fluid ounces (240 milliliters) marinade for each double breast of chicken. Marinate the poultry under refrigeration.

Approximate values per fluid ounce (30 ml): **Calories** 35, **Total fat** 3.5 g, **Saturated fat** 0 g, **Cholesterol** 0 mg, **Sodium** 220 mg, **Total carbohydrates** 1 g, **Protein** 0 g, **Claims**—no saturated fat; no cholesterol; no sugar; low calorie

Poultry absorbs flavors quickly, so if pieces are left too long in an acidic marinade, they may take on undesirable flavors. Two hours is often sufficient. Smaller pieces require less time in the marinade than larger ones. The texture of the protein will be affected by the acid in the marinade; marinating for more than a few hours can overly tenderize meats and poultry. Avoid using excess marinade because it becomes contaminated and must be discarded after using. To help calculate the quantity of marinade to make, figure on using approximately 8 fluid ounces (240 milliliters) marinade for each double breast of chicken.

If the marinade contains oil, drain the poultry well to avoid flare-up when the item is placed on the broiler or grill. Use a clean kitchen towel or a paper towel to wipe excess moisture from the poultry's surface so that it browns more easily. The marinade can be used to baste the item during cooking, but leftover marinade should not be served uncooked or reused because of the danger of bacterial contamination from the raw poultry.

As discussed in Chapter 9, Mise en Place, poultry, especially whole chickens, can be lightly brined before cooking.

COOKING METHODS FOR POULTRY

The principles of cooking discussed in Chapter 10, Principles of Cooking, and applied to meats in earlier chapters also apply to poultry. Dry-heat methods are appropriate for young, tender birds. Moist-heat methods should be used with older, less tender products. Regardless of the cooking method, poultry should be rinsed under cold running water, then dried with clean disposable paper towels before cooking to remove any collected juices.

DRY-HEAT COOKING METHODS FOR POULTRY

Cooking poultry with dry-heat methods—broiling, grilling, roasting, sautéing, pan-frying and deep-frying—presents some unique challenges. Large birds such as turkeys benefit from low-heat cooking but are better when served with the crispy skin gained through higher temperatures. Duck and goose skins contain a great deal of fat that must be rendered during the cooking process. Small birds such as squab must be cooked at sufficiently high temperatures to crisp their skins but can be easily over-cooked. Boneless chicken breasts, particularly flavorful and popular when broiled or grilled, are easily overcooked and become dry because they are lean and do not contain bones to help retain moisture during cooking. Chicken legs, although fattier than breast meat, require longer cooking time to tenderize them. Proper application of the dry-heat cooking methods described in this chapter will help meet these challenges and ensure a good-quality finished product.

Broiling and Grilling Poultry

Broiled and grilled poultry should have a well-browned surface and can show cross-hatched grill marks. It should be moist, tender and juicy throughout. It may be seasoned to enhance its natural flavors or marinated or basted with any number of flavored butters or sauces.

Selecting Poultry to Broil or Grill

Smaller birds such as Cornish hens, chickens and squab are especially well suited for broiling or grilling. Whole birds should be split or cut into smaller pieces before cooking; their joints may be broken so that they lie flat. Quail and other small birds can be skewered before being broiled to help them cook evenly and retain their shape. Be especially careful when cooking breast portions or boneless pieces; the direct heat of the broiler or grill can overcook items very quickly.

Seasoning Poultry to Broil or Grill

Poultry is fairly neutral in flavor and responds well to marinating. Poultry may also be basted periodically during the cooking process with flavored butter, oil or barbecue sauce. At the very least, broiled or grilled poultry should be well seasoned with salt and pepper just before cooking.

Determining Doneness of Broiled and Grilled Poultry

With the exception of duck breasts and squab, which are sometimes left pink, broiled or grilled poultry is cooked well done. This makes the poultry particularly susceptible to becoming dry and tough because it contains little fat and is cooked at very high temperatures. Particular care must be taken to ensure that items do not become overcooked.

Four methods are used to determine the doneness of broiled or grilled poultry:

- *Touch:* When poultry is done, it will have a firm texture, resist pressure and spring back quickly when pressed with a finger.
- *Temperature:* Use an instant-read thermometer to determine the item's internal temperature. This may be difficult because of the item's size and the heat from the broiler or grill. Insert the thermometer in the thickest part of the item away from any bones. It should read 165–170°F (74–77°C) at the coolest point.
- *Looseness of the joints:* When bone-in poultry is done, the leg moves freely in its socket.
- *Color of the juices:* Poultry is done when its juices run clear or show just a trace of pink. This degree of doneness is known in French as **à point**.

Classic Poultry Flavors

Ever versatile, chicken can be flavored with delicate herbs or robust, fiery spices. When roasted, chicken benefits from a simple grating of salt and pepper. Light sauces made from pan juices or velouté accented with tender herbs, lemon and white or black pepper are typical accompaniments that enhance the pure flavor of the poultry. But skin-on chicken pieces withstand marinating in wet or dry spice mixtures before grilling, roasting or stewing. Spice blends from adobo to garam masala can be used with any type of poultry. The versatility of poultry may account for its popularity. Dark meat from turkey legs can substitute for lamb or pork in kebabs or stews. And boneless skinless chicken or turkey breast, when sliced thinly and pounded, makes excellent cutlets.

à point [ah PWEN] (1) French term for cooking to the ideal degree of doneness; (2) when applied to meat, refers to cooking it medium rare

Accompaniments to Broiled and Grilled Poultry

If the item was basted with an herb butter, it can be served with additional butter; if the item was basted with barbecue sauce, it should be served with the same sauce. Be careful, however, that any marinade or sauce that came in contact with the raw poultry is not served unless it is cooked thoroughly to destroy harmful bacteria. Sauce suggestions are listed in Table 11.6.

Broiled or grilled poultry is very versatile and goes well with almost any side dish. Seasoned and grilled vegetables are a natural accompaniment, and deep-fried potatoes are commonly served.

Procedure for Broiling or Grilling Poultry

Like red meats, broiled or grilled poultry can be prepared by placing items directly on the grate. Poultry is also often broiled using a rotisserie.

1 Heat the broiler or grill.

2 Use a wire brush to remove any charred or burnt particles that may be stuck to the broiler or grill grate. The grate can be wiped with a lightly oiled towel to remove any remaining particles and help season it.

3 Prepare the item to be broiled or grilled by marinating or seasoning as desired; it may be brushed lightly with oil to keep it from sticking to the grate.

4 Place the item on the grate, presentation side (skin side) down. Following the example in Chapter 10, Principles of Cooking, turn the item to produce the attractive crosshatch marks associated with grilling. Baste the item often. Use tongs to turn or flip the item without piercing the surface so that juices do not escape.

5 Develop the proper surface color while cooking the item until it is done *à point*. To do so, adjust the position of the item on the broiler or grill, or adjust the distance between the grate and heat source. Large pieces and bone-in pieces that are difficult to cook completely on the broiler or grill can be finished in the oven.

A commonly used procedure to cook a large volume of poultry is to place the seasoned items in a broiler pan or other shallow pan and place the pan directly under the broiler. Baste the items periodically, turning them once when they are halfway done. Items begun this way can be easily finished by transferring the entire pan to the oven.

Grilled Chicken Breast with Red Pepper Butter

MISE EN PLACE

- Bone and skin chicken breasts.
- Peel and chop garlic.
- Prepare the Red Pepper Butter.

YIELD 4 Servings, 5 oz. (150 g) each	METHOD	Grilling
Whole chicken breasts, boneless, skinless, from 2 chickens	2	2
Salt and pepper	TT	TT
Garlic, chopped	1 tsp.	5 ml
Vegetable oil	1 Tbsp.	15 ml
Red Pepper Butter (page 234)	2 oz.	60 g

1 Trim any excess fat from the breasts. Split each breast into two pieces by removing the small piece of cartilage that joins the halves.

2 Season the breasts with the salt, pepper and garlic. Coat the breasts on all sides with the vegetable oil.

3 Heat and prepare the grill.

4 Grill the chicken breasts until done, turning them 90 degrees to produce attractive crosshatch markings.

5 Remove the chicken from the grill and place on a plate for service. Place a ½-ounce (15-gram) slice of Red Pepper Butter on top of each breast. If necessary, place the plate under a broiler or salamander for a few seconds so that the butter begins to melt.

① Seasoning the chicken breasts.

② Placing the chicken on the grill at a 45-degree angle to the grates.

③ Using tongs to turn the chicken and cook the other side.

Variation:

   Grilled Marinated Chicken Breasts—Omit the garlic. Marinate the chicken breasts in 8 fluid ounces (240 milliliters) White Wine Marinade (page 426) for up to 1 hour. Blot excess marinade from the chicken with a paper towel before grilling.

Approximate values per 5-oz. (150-g) serving: **Calories** 240, **Total fat** 14 g, **Saturated fat** 6 g, **Cholesterol** 95 mg, **Sodium** 60 mg, **Total carbohydrates** 1 g, **Protein** 28 g, **Vitamin A** 10%, **Vitamin C** 15%

Roasting Poultry

Properly roasted (or baked) poultry is attractively browned on the surface and tender and juicy throughout. Proper cooking temperatures ensure a crisp exterior and juicy interior. Most roasted poultry is cooked until the juices run clear. Squab and duck breasts are exceptions; they are often served medium rare or pink.

Selecting Poultry to Roast

Almost every kind of poultry is suitable for roasting, but younger birds produce a more tender finished product. Because of variations in fat content, different kinds of poultry require different roasting temperatures and procedures.

Seasoning Poultry to Roast

Although the mild flavor of most poultry is enhanced by a wide variety of herbs and spices, roasted poultry is often only lightly seasoned with salt and pepper. Whole birds may be soaked in light brine for 2–8 hours before roasting to retain moisture and tenderize the meat. See Chapter 9, Mise en Place. Poultry that is roasted at high temperatures should never be seasoned with herbs on its surface because the high cooking temperatures will burn them. If herbs or additional spices are used, they should be stuffed into the cavity. A mirepoix or a bouquet garni may also be added to the cavity for additional flavor. The cavities of dark-meated birds such as ducks and geese are often stuffed with fresh or dried fruits.

Chicken Wisdom

"To know how to cook is to understand a recipe so that it can be expressed in different terms, at changing levels of sophistication for different occasions," writes Chef Jacques Pépin of preparing roast chicken. When served with a plain green salad, he calls a roast chicken *cuisine bourgeoise*, home-style cooking. Garnished with a sauce made from its pan juices, the chicken is casual dinner fare. When the roasting pan is deglazed with cognac and sautéed mushrooms and cream are added, the bird is transformed into *haute cuisine*, for more formal occasions. "This ability to extend or vary a basic dish is essential to the work of good cooks and enables them to change the cost of a meal or alter the calorie count at will," he writes. What does not vary is the skill needed to properly roast a chicken, a technique by which chefs are often judged.

Procedure for Trussing Poultry

Trussing is tying a bird into a more compact shape with thread or butcher's twine. Trussing allows the bird to cook more evenly, helps the bird retain moisture and improves the appearance of the finished product. When a bird is trussed before roasting, the lean breast meat is kept from drying out in the time it takes the darker leg meat to cook. There are many methods for trussing poultry, some of which require a special tool called a trussing needle. Here we show a simple method using butcher's twine.

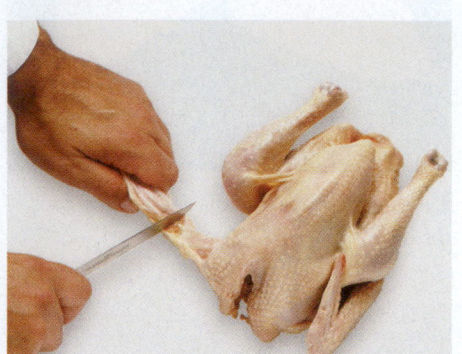

1 Square up the bird by pressing it firmly with both hands. Tuck the first joint of the wing behind the back or trim off the first and second joints as shown.

2 Cut a piece of butcher's twine approximately three times the bird's length. With the breast up and the neck toward you, pass the twine under the bird approximately 1 inch (2.5 centimeters) in front of the tail.

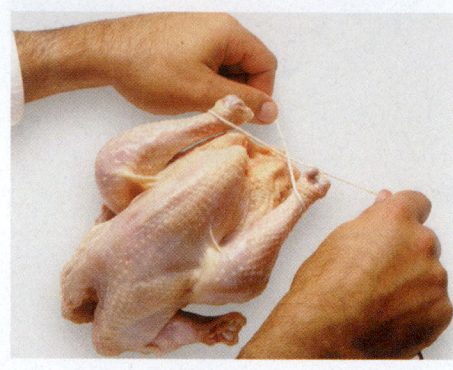

3 Bring the twine up around the legs and cross the ends, creating an X between the legs. Pass the ends of the twine below the legs.

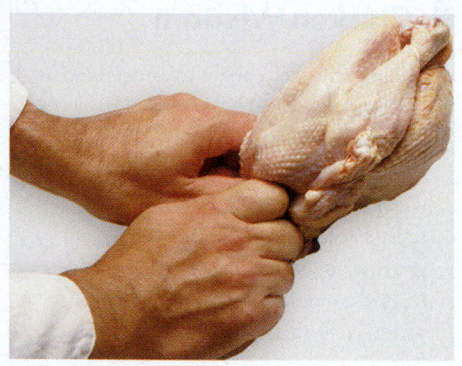

4 Pull the ends of the twine tightly across the leg and thigh joints and across the wings if the first and second joints are trimmed off, or just above the wings if they are intact.

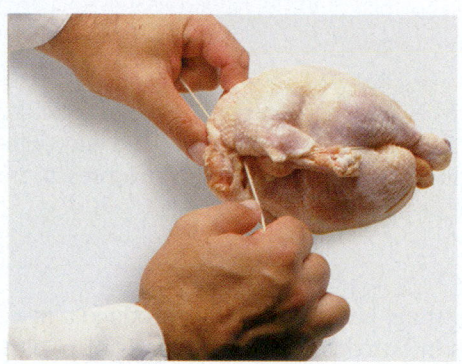

5 Pull the string tight and tie it securely just above the neck.

6 Two examples of properly trussed birds: one with the wings intact (top) and one with the first and second wing joints removed (bottom).

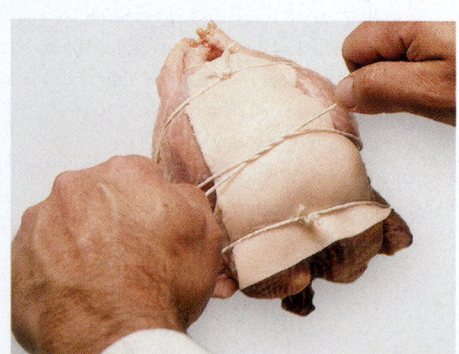

Barding a pheasant.

Barding Poultry to Roast

Guineas, squabs or any skinless birds without an adequate fat covering to protect them from drying out during roasting can be barded. Bard the bird by covering its entire surface with thin slices of fatback, securing them with butcher's twine.

Cooking Temperatures for Roasted Poultry

Small birds such as squab and Cornish game hens should be roasted at the relatively high temperatures of 375–400°F (190–200°C). These temperatures produce crisp, well-colored skins without overcooking the flesh. Chickens are best roasted between 350°F and 375°F (180°C and 190°C). This temperature range allows the skin to crisp and the flesh to cook without causing the bird to stew in its own juices. (Some chefs prefer to roast small unstuffed squab, Cornish game hens or chickens at higher temperatures, between 450°F and 500°F (230 and 260°C). These temperatures crisp the skin and cook the meat quickly before the lean meat dries out, but finishing the cooking at a lower temperature may be necessary.)

Large birds such as capons and turkeys are started at high temperatures of 400–425°F (200–220°C) to brown the skin, then finished at lower temperatures of 275–325°F (135–160°C) to promote even cooking and produce a moister product. Ducks and geese, which are very high in fat, must be roasted at the high temperatures of 375–425°F (190–220°C) to render as much fat from the skin as possible. Duck and goose skins are often pricked before roasting so that the rendered fat can escape; this helps create a crispy skin.

Basting Roasted Poultry

With the exception of fatty birds such as ducks and geese, all poultry items should be basted while they roast in order to help retain moisture. To baste a bird, spoon or ladle the fat that collects in the bottom of the roasting pan over the bird at 15-to-20-minute intervals. Lean birds that are not barded will not produce enough fat for basting and may be brushed with butter or oil.

Determining Doneness of Roasted Poultry

Four methods are used to determine the doneness of roasted poultry. It is best to use a combination of these methods.

- *Temperature:* Test the internal temperature of the bird with an instant-read thermometer. The thermometer should be inserted in the bird's thigh, which is the last part to be fully cooked. The thermometer should not touch the bone and should read 165–170°F (74–77°C). This method works best with large birds such as capons and turkeys. Large birds are subject to some degree of carryover cooking. This is not as much of a concern with poultry as it is with red meat because large birds are always cooked well done.
- *Looseness of the joints:* The thigh and leg begin to move freely in their sockets when the bird is done.
- *Color of juices:* This method is used with birds that are not stuffed. Use a kitchen fork to tilt the bird, allowing some of the juices that have collected in the cavity to run out. Clear juices indicate that the bird is done. If the juices are cloudy or pink, the bird is undercooked.
- *Time:* Because there are so many variables, timing alone is less reliable than other methods. It is useful, however, for planning production when large quantities are roasted and as a general guideline when used with other methods. Table 18.3 lists general timing guidelines for roasting several kinds of poultry.

Accompaniments to Roasted Poultry

The most common accompaniments to roasted poultry are bread stuffing or **dressing** and gravy. Large birds, such as capons and turkeys, produce adequate drippings for sauce or pan gravy. Small birds, such as squab and Cornish game hens, are often stuffed with wild rice or other ingredients and served with a sauce that is made separately.

Ducks and geese are complemented by stuffings containing rice, fruits, berries and nuts. These birds are very fatty, and if stuffed, they should be roasted on a rack or mirepoix bed to ensure that the fat that collects in the pan during roasting does not penetrate the cavity, making the stuffing greasy. Duck and goose are often served with a citrus- or fruit-based sauce. Its high acid content complements these rich, fatty birds.

dressing another name for a bread stuffing used with poultry

ROASTING TEMPERATURES AND TIMES			TABLE 18.3
POULTRY KIND OR CLASS	COOKING TEMPERATURES		MINUTES PER LB. (450 G)
Capons	350–375°F	180–190°C	18–20 min.
Chickens	375–400°F	190–200°C	15–18 min.
Ducks and geese	375–425°F	190–220°C	12–15 min.
Game hens	375–400°F	190–200°C	45–60 min. total
Guineas	375–400°F	190–200°C	18–20 min.
Squab	400°F	200°C	30–40 min. total
Turkeys (large)	325°F	160°C	12–15 min.

Procedure for Stuffing Poultry

> ### ⚠ Safety Alert
>
> #### Handling Stuffed Poultry
>
> Stuffing requires time and temperature control for safety (TCS). All ingredients used to make stuffing must be cold and stay below 45°F (7°C) when mixing and stuffing into poultry. Stuff a bird as close to cooking time as possible to keep it out of the temperature danger zone. Observe proper cooking temperatures and roast until the bird reaches an internal temperature of 165°F (74°C) as indicated by an instant-read thermometer placed deep into the stuffing. Remove all stuffing from the bird's cavity promptly. If left in the cavity, stuffing will not cool and will become a potential breeding ground for bacteria.

Small birds such as Cornish game hens, small chickens and squab can be stuffed successfully. Stuffing larger birds, especially for volume production, is impractical and can be dangerous for the following reasons:

- Stuffing is a bacterial breeding ground, and because it is difficult to control temperatures inside a stuffed bird, there is a risk of food-borne illness.
- Stuffing poultry is labor intensive.
- Stuffed poultry must be cooked longer to cook the stuffing properly; this may cause the meat to be overcooked, becoming dry and tough.

When stuffing any bird, use the following guidelines:

1 Always be aware of temperatures when mixing the raw ingredients. All ingredients should be cold when they are mixed together, and the mixture's temperature should never be allowed to rise above 45°F (7°C).
2 Stuff the raw bird as close to roasting time as possible.
3 The neck and main body cavities should be loosely stuffed. The stuffing will expand during cooking.
4 After the cavities are filled, their openings should be secured with skewers and butcher's twine or by trussing.
5 After cooking, remove the stuffing from the bird and store separately.

Procedure for Roasting Poultry

1 Season, bard, stuff and/or truss the bird as desired.
2 Place the bird in a roasting pan. It may be placed on a rack or a bed of mirepoix in order to prevent scorching and promote even cooking.
3 Roast uncovered, basting every 15 minutes.
4 Allow the bird to rest before carving to allow even distribution of juices. As the bird rests, prepare the pan gravy or sauce.

Roast Turkey with Chestnut Dressing and Giblet Gravy

MISE EN PLACE

- Peel and chop onions, carrots and celery for mirepoix.
- While turkey is roasting peel and chop onion and celery into small dice for dressing.
- Beat eggs.
- Chop parsley.
- Cook, peel and coarsely chop chestnuts for dressing.

YIELD 16 Servings, 4 oz. (120 g) turkey, 3 oz. (90 g) dressing and 4 fl. oz. (120 ml) gravy each

METHOD Roasting

Young turkey, 12–15 lb. (5.5–6.5 kg) with giblets	1	1
Chicken stock	4 qt.	4 lt
Salt and pepper	TT	TT
Mirepoix, medium dice	20 oz.	600 g
Onions, small dice	8 oz.	240 g
Celery, small dice	6 oz.	180 g
Whole butter	4 oz.	120 g
Dried bread cubes	1¼ lb.	600 g
Eggs, beaten	1	1
Fresh parsley, chopped	1 Tbsp.	15 ml
Chestnuts, cooked and peeled, chopped coarse	8 oz.	240 g
All-purpose flour	3 oz.	90 g

1 Remove the giblets (neck, heat and gizzard) from the turkey's cavity. While preparing the turkey, simmer them in 2 quarts (2 liters) stock until tender and the liquid is reduced by half, approximately 1½ hours. Cool and refrigerate promptly.

2 Season the turkey inside and out with salt and pepper. Truss the turkey.

3 Place the turkey in a roasting pan. Roast at 400°F (200°C) for 30 minutes. Reduce the temperature to 325°F (160°C) and continue cooking the turkey to an internal temperature of 165°F (74°C), approximately 2½ to 3 hours. Baste the turkey often during cooking. Approximately 45 minutes before the turkey is done, add the mirepoix to the roasting pan. If the turkey begins to overbrown, cover it loosely with aluminum foil.

4 To make the dressing, sauté the onions and celery in the butter until tender.

5 In a large bowl, toss together the bread cubes, salt, pepper, eggs, parsley, sautéed onions and celery, 24 fluid ounces (720 milliliters) stock and the chestnuts.

6 Place the dressing in a buttered hotel pan and cover with aluminum foil or buttered parchment paper. Bake at 350°F (180°C) until done, approximately 45 minutes.

7 When the turkey is done, remove it from the roasting pan and set it aside to rest. Degrease the roasting pan, reserving 3 fluid ounces (90 milliliters) of the fat to make a roux.

8 Place the roasting pan on the stove top and brown the mirepoix.

9 Deglaze the pan with a small amount of stock. Transfer the mirepoix and stock to a saucepot and add the remaining stock and the broth from the giblets. Bring to a simmer and degrease.

10 Make a blond roux with the reserved fat and the flour. Add the roux to the liquid, whisking well to prevent lumps. Simmer 15 minutes. Strain the gravy through a china cap lined with cheesecloth.

11 Remove the meat from the turkey neck. Trim the gizzard. Finely chop the neck meat, heart and gizzard and add to the gravy. Adjust the seasonings.

12 Carve the turkey and serve with a portion of chestnut dressing and giblet gravy.

Approximate values per serving: **Calories** 720, **Total fat** 23 g, **Saturated fat** 9 g, **Cholesterol** 250 mg, **Sodium** 700 mg, **Total carbohydrates** 41 g, **Protein** 87 g, **Vitamin A** 6%, **Iron** 40%

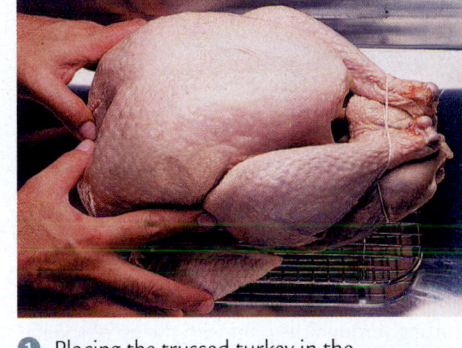

❶ Placing the trussed turkey in the roasting pan.

❷ Adding the mirepoix to the roasting pan.

❸ Tossing the dressing ingredients together.

❹ Browning the mirepoix.

❺ Deglazing the roasting pan.

❻ Transferring the mirepoix and stock to a saucepan.

❼ Straining the gravy through a china cap and cheesecloth.

Carving Roasted Poultry

Poultry can be carved in the kitchen, at tableside or on a buffet in a variety of manners. The carving methods described next produce slices of both light and dark meat.

Procedure for Carving a Turkey, Capon or Other Large Bird

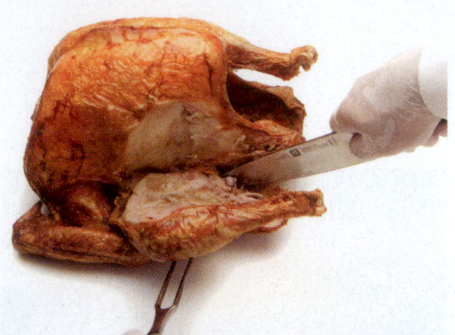

1 After roasting, allow the turkey to stand for 20 minutes so that the juices can redistribute themselves. Holding the turkey firmly with a carving fork, pry a leg outward and locate the joint. Remove the leg and thigh in one piece by cutting through the joint with the tip of a knife.

2 Repeat the procedure on the other side. Once both legs and thighs have been removed, slice the meat from the thigh by holding the leg firmly with one hand and slicing parallel to the bone.

3 Separate the thigh from the leg bone by cutting through the joint. Slice the meat from the leg by cutting parallel to the bone.

4 Cut along the backbone, following the natural curvature of the bones separating the breast meat from the ribs.

5 Remove an entire half breast and slice it on the cutting board. Cut on an angle to produce larger slices.

6 Alternatively, the breast can be carved on the bird. Make a horizontal cut just above the wing in toward the rib bones.

7 Slice the breast meat.

Procedure for Portioning Turkey and Dressing for Buffet Service

1 For buffet service, portion the dressing into hotel pans using a No. 6 scoop.

2 Layer portions of dark meat on the dressing.

3 Cover the dark meat and the dressing with white meat.

Procedure for Carving a Chicken or Other Small Bird

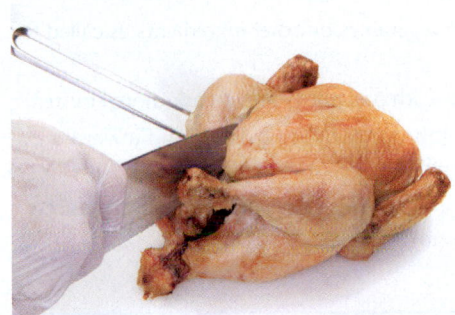

1 After allowing the roasted chicken to rest for 15 minutes so that the juices can redistribute themselves, cut through the skin between the leg and breast.

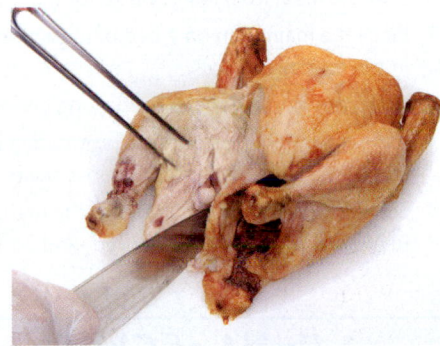

2 Use a kitchen fork to pry the leg and thigh away from the breast. Locate the thigh's ball joint and cut through it with the knife tip, separating it completely from the rest of the chicken.

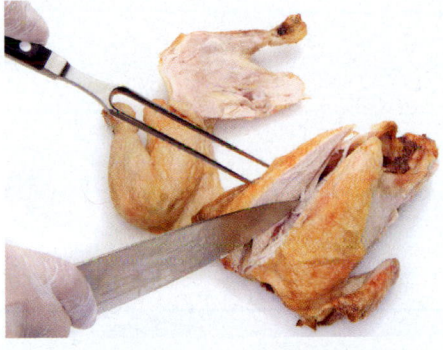

3 With the knife tip, cut through the skin and meat on one side of the breastbone. Cut and pull the meat away from the bones with the knife.

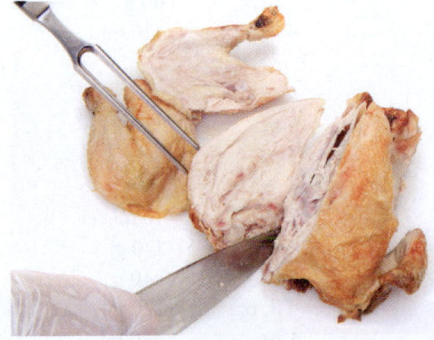

4 Cut through the wing joint, separating the breast meat and wing from the carcass. Repeat this procedure on the other side of the bird.

5 The chicken is now quartered.

6 To cut it into eight pieces, separate the wings from the breasts and the thighs from the legs.

Poêléing Poultry

Poêléing [pwah-LAY-ing] is a cooking method similar to roasting and braising. The item is cooked in the oven in a covered pot so that it cooks in its own juices and steam. Although this is a moist-heat cooking technique (because the item steams in its own juices), it is used only for tender cuts, not those that need long, slow braising. The cooking time is usually less than that needed for dry roasting.

The item to be poêléed can first be browned in hot fat and then laid on a bed of matignon, covered and cooked in the oven. (Recall from Chapter 11, Stock and Sauces, that a matignon is a standard mirepoix plus diced smoked bacon or smoked ham and, depending on the dish, mushrooms and herbs. A matignon is usually cut more uniformly than a standard mirepoix and left in the finished dish as a garnish.) If the item was not first browned in hot fat, it can later be browned by removing the lid toward the end of cooking. Doneness is determined using the techniques for determining the doneness of roasted poultry.

Vegetables to be served with the dish can be added to the poêlé as it cooks or cooked separately and plated with the finished item.

The sauce for a poêlé is made from the flavorful cooking juices left in the pan. They are mixed with a liquid (stock, jus lié or demi-glace) and finished using the same techniques as those for a braised dish. The matignon can be left in the finished sauce or strained out.

Procedure for Poêléing Poultry

1 Sear the main item in hot butter or oil, if desired.

2 Place the main item on a bed of matignon. Add vegetables or other ingredients as called for in the recipe.

3 Cover and cook in the oven, basting periodically with pan juices or with additional butter.

4 If the main item was not first browned in hot fat, brown it by removing the lid toward the end of the cooking period. Remove the poultry when done.

5 To make a sauce, add a liquid to the matignon and cooking juices in the pan and reduce. Remove the matignon, if desired, and add flavorings as directed in the recipe.

Poêlé of Chicken with Pearl Onions and Mushrooms

MISE EN PLACE

- Dice bacon and peel and chop onions, celery, carrots and garlic for matignon.
- Blanch and peel pearl onions.
- Stem mushrooms.
- Wash, peel and chop tomato for concassée.
- Chop fresh herbs.

YIELD	2 Chickens, 4 Servings	METHOD	Poêléing
Chickens, 2 lb. 8 oz.–3 lb. (1.2–1.4 kg) each		2	2
Salt and pepper		TT	TT
Fresh herbs, assorted stems and sprigs		2 oz.	60 g
Clarified butter		4 fl. oz.	120 ml
Matignon:			
Slab bacon or smoked ham, small dice		3 oz.	90 g
Onions, small dice		6 oz.	180 g
Celery, small dice		3 oz.	90 g
Carrots, small dice		3 oz.	90 g
Garlic, chopped		2 tsp.	10 ml
Pearl onions, blanched and peeled		4 oz.	120 g
Button mushrooms, stemmed		8 oz.	240 g
White wine		4 fl. oz.	120 ml
Demi-Glace (page 225)		1 qt.	960 ml
Tomato concassée		4 oz.	120 g
Fresh herbs, assorted, chopped		2 tsp.	10 ml

1   Season the chicken cavities with salt and pepper and stuff them with the herb stems and sprigs. Truss the birds and season the outside with salt and pepper.

2   Heat half the butter in a roasting pan that is just large enough to hold the birds without crowding. Sear the chicken, if desired. Remove it from the pan. Sauté the bacon until most of the fat is rendered. Add the diced onions, celery and carrots and sauté until they begin to brown. Add the garlic and cook for 1 more minute.

3   Place the trussed chickens on top of the matignon. Baste them with the remaining butter. Cover the roasting pan with its lid and place in a 325°F (160°C) oven until done, approximately 1½ hours, basting the chickens with fat from the pan every 20 minutes. Remove the lid for the last 30 minutes of cooking to allow the chickens to brown lightly.

4   Remove the chickens from the pan and allow them to rest in a warm place. Place the roasting pan on the stove top. Remove a small amount of the accumulated fat from the roasting pan to a sauté pan and sauté the pearl onions and mushrooms in the sauté pan until nearly tender.

5   Bring the liquid in the roasting pan to a boil; remove any excess fat or scum with a ladle. Add the wine and reduce by half. Add the Demi-Glace and bring to a simmer. Adjust the thickness of the sauce. If desired, strain the sauce. Add the pearl onions, mushrooms, tomato concassée and chopped herbs to the sauce. Bring to a simmer and adjust the seasonings.

6   Carve the chickens and serve them with a portion of the sauce and vegetables.

Approximate values per ½-chicken serving: **Calories** 1670, **Total fat** 106 g, **Saturated fat** 39 g, **Cholesterol** 475 mg, **Sodium** 2110 mg, **Total carbohydrates** 48 g, **Protein** 129 g, **Vitamin A** 170%, **Vitamin C** 50%, **Calcium** 10%, **Iron** 45%

❶ Placing the chicken on the matignon.

❷ Basting the chicken with fat from the pan during cooking.

❸ Carefully removing the cooked chicken from the pan.

Sautéing Poultry

Sautéed poultry should be tender and juicy, its flavor developed by proper browning. Additional flavors come from a sauce made by deglazing the pan, usually with wine, and adding garnishes, seasonings and liquids. Stir-frying is a popular method of sautéing poultry; boneless pieces are cut into strips and quickly cooked with assorted vegetables and seasonings.

Selecting Poultry to Sauté

Most poultry is quite tender and well suited for sautéing. Although small birds such as squab can be sautéed bone-in, large pieces and bone-in cuts from larger birds should not be sautéed. Boneless breasts, suprêmes, scallops and cutlets are the most common and practical cuts for sautéing. Because they are high in fat, boneless duck breasts can be sautéed without additional fat.

Seasoning Poultry to Sauté

Poultry has a delicate flavor that is enhanced by a wide variety of herbs, spices, condiments and marinades. Flavor combinations are limited only by your imagination. When poultry items are dusted with flour before sautéing, seasonings may first be added to the flour.

Cooking Temperatures for Sautéed Poultry

The sauté pan and the cooking fat must be hot before the poultry is added. The temperature at which the poultry is then sautéed is determined by its thickness and the desired color of the finished product. A thin, boneless slice requires relatively high temperatures so that its surface is browned before the center is overcooked. A thicker cut such as a suprême requires lower temperatures so that neither its surface nor the fond are burned before the item is fully cooked. Adjust the temperature throughout the cooking process in order to achieve the desired results, never letting the pan become too cool. If the pan is overcrowded or otherwise allowed to cool, the poultry will cook in its own juices and absorb oil from the pan, resulting in a poor-quality product.

Determining Doneness of Sautéed Poultry

Thin cuts of poultry cook very quickly and, with them, timing is a useful tool. Timing is less useful with thicker cuts. Experienced cooks can tell the doneness of an item by judging the temperature of the sauté pan and the color of the item being cooked.

A more practical method is to press the item with your finger and judge the resistance. Very undercooked poultry will offer little resistance and feel mushy. Slightly underdone poultry will feel spongy and will not spring back when your finger is removed. Properly cooked poultry will feel firm to the touch and will spring back when your finger is removed. Overcooked poultry will feel very firm, almost hard, and will spring back quickly when your finger is removed.

Accompaniments to Sautéed Poultry

Sautéed poultry is usually served with a sauce made directly in the pan in which the item was cooked. The sauce uses the fond for added flavor. A wide variety of ingredients, including garlic, onions, shallots, mushrooms and tomatoes, are commonly added to the pan as well as wine and stock. Table 11.6 suggests several sauces for sautéed poultry. Sautéed poultry items are often served with a starch such as pasta, rice, cooked grains or potatoes.

Procedure for Sautéing Poultry

1 Heat a sauté pan and add enough fat or oil to just cover the bottom.
2 Add the poultry item, presentation side down, and cook until browned.
3 Turn the item, with a chef's fork or tongs or by tossing the item back on itself using the pan's sloped sides.
4 Larger items can be finished in an oven. Either place the sauté pan in the oven or transfer the poultry to another pan. The latter procedure allows a sauce to be made in the original pan while the poultry cooks in the oven. Hold smaller pieces that are thoroughly cooked in a warm place so that the pan can be used for making the sauce.

Procedure for Preparing a Sauce in the Sauté Pan

1 Pour off any excess fat or oil from the sauté pan, leaving enough to sauté the sauce ingredients.
2 Add and sauté ingredients such as garlic, shallots and mushrooms that will be used as garnishes and sauce flavorings.
3 Deglaze the pan with wine, stock or other liquids. Scrape the pan, loosening the fond and allowing it to dissolve in the liquid. Reduce the liquid.
4 Add any ingredients that do not require long cooking times such as herbs and spices. Adjust the sauce's consistency and seasonings.
5 For service, the poultry can be returned to the pan for a moment to reheat it and to coat it with the sauce. The poultry should remain in the sauce just long enough to reheat. Do not attempt to cook the poultry in the sauce.
6 Serve the poultry with the accompanying sauce.

Chicken Sauté with Onions, Garlic and Basil

YIELD 6 Servings, 5 oz. (150 g) each	METHOD Sautéing	
Whole chicken breasts, boneless, skinless, approximately 10 oz. (300 g) each	3	3
Salt and pepper	TT	TT
Flour	as needed for dredging	
Clarified butter	1 fl. oz.	30 ml
Onion, small dice	2 oz.	60 g
Garlic cloves, chopped	6	6
Dry white wine	4 fl. oz.	120 ml
Lemon juice	1 Tbsp.	15 ml
Tomato concassée	6 oz.	180 g
Chicken stock	4 fl. oz.	120 ml
Fresh basil leaves, chiffonade	6	6

MISE EN PLACE

- Bone and skin chicken breasts.
- Peel and chop onion and garlic into fine dice.
- Wash, peel and chop tomato for concassée.
- Slice basil in chiffonade.

1 Trim any excess fat from the breasts. Split each breast into two pieces by removing the keel bone, the small piece of cartilage that joins the halves.

2 Season the chicken with salt and pepper; dredge in flour.

3 Sauté the breasts in the butter, browning them and cooking *à point*. Hold in a warm place.

4 Add the onion and garlic to the fond and butter in the pan; sauté until the onion is translucent.

5 Deglaze the pan with the wine and lemon juice.

6 Add the tomato concassée and stock. Sauté to combine the flavors; reduce the sauce to the desired consistency.

7 Add the basil to the sauce and return the chicken breasts for reheating. Adjust the seasonings and serve one half breast per portion with a portion of the sauce.

Approximate values per 5-oz. (150-g) serving: **Calories** 230, **Total fat** 8 g, **Saturated fat** 3.5 g, **Cholesterol** 90 mg, **Sodium** 580 mg, **Total carbohydrates** 9 g, **Protein** 30 g, **Vitamin C** 10%, **Iron** 10%

❶ Sautéing the breasts in butter.

❷ The fond left in the pan after sautéing the chicken.

❸ Sautéing the onions and garlic.

❹ Deglazing the pan with white wine and lemon juice.

❺ Adding tomato concassée and stock and sautéing to combine flavors.

❻ Returning the chicken to the pan to reheat.

Pan-Basting Poultry

Pan-basting is a variation of pan-frying and sautéing. Lean cuts of poultry that cook quickly, such as a boneless breast, are well suited to this method. The poultry is seared in a generous amount of butter, oil or a combination. Fresh herbs, flavorings and spices such as thyme and lemon may be added to the melted fat for flavor. Once the poultry is seared, hot butter from the pan is spooned over it to enhance the appearance, flavor and surface texture of the meat.

Pan-Frying Poultry

Pan-fried poultry should be juicy. Its coating or batter should be crispy, golden brown, not excessively oily and free from any breaks that allow fat to penetrate. Both the poultry and the coating should be well seasoned.

Selecting Poultry to Pan-Fry

The most common pan-fried poultry is fried chicken. Young tender birds cut into small pieces produce the best results. Other cuts commonly pan-fried are boneless portions such as chicken breasts and turkey scallops.

Seasoning Poultry to Pan-Fry

Pan-fried poultry is usually floured, breaded or battered before cooking. (Breadings and batters are discussed in Chapter 9, Mise en Place.) Typically the seasonings are added to the flour, breading or batter before the poultry is coated. Seasonings can be a blend of any number of dried herbs and spices. Sometimes only salt and pepper are required because the poultry will be served with a sauce or other accompaniments for additional flavors.

Cooking Temperatures for Pan-Fried Poultry

The fat should be hot before the poultry is added. The temperature at which poultry is cooked is determined by the length of time required to cook it thoroughly. Pan-frying generally requires slightly lower temperatures than those used for sautéing. Within this range, thinner items require higher temperatures to produce good color in a relatively short time. Thicker items and those containing bones require lower cooking temperatures and longer cooking times.

Determining Doneness of Pan-Fried Poultry

Even the largest pan-fried items may be too small to be accurately tested with an instant-read thermometer, and using the touch method can be difficult and dangerous because of the amount of fat used in pan-frying. So timing and experience are the best tools to determine doneness. Thin scallops cook very quickly, so it is relatively easy to judge their doneness. On the other hand, fried chicken can take as long as 30–45 minutes to cook, requiring skill and experience to determine doneness.

Accompaniments to Pan-Fried Poultry

Because pan-frying does not produce fond or drippings that can be used to make a sauce, pan-fried poultry is usually served with lemon wedges, a vegetable garnish or a separately made sauce. Fried chicken is an exception; it is sometimes served with a country gravy made by degreasing the pan, making a roux with a portion of the fat and adding milk or stock and seasonings.

Procedure for Pan-Frying Poultry

1 Heat enough fat in a heavy sauté pan to cover the item to be cooked one-fourth to halfway up its side. The fat should be at approximately 325°F (160°C).

2 Add the floured, breaded or battered item to the hot fat, being careful not to splash. The fat must be hot enough to sizzle and bubble when the item is added.

3 Turn the item when the first side is the proper color; it should be half cooked at this point. Larger items may need to be turned more than once to brown them properly on all sides.

4 Remove the browned poultry from the pan and drain it on absorbent paper.

Pan-Fried Chicken with Pan Gravy

YIELD 8 Servings, 6–7 oz. (180–210 g) each	METHOD	Pan-Frying
Frying chickens, 2 lb. 8 oz.–3 lb. (1.2–1.4 kg) each, cut into 8 pieces	2	2
Salt and pepper	TT	TT
Garlic powder	2 tsp.	10 ml
Onion powder	2 tsp.	10 ml
Dried oregano	1 tsp.	5 ml
Dried basil	1 tsp.	5 ml
Flour	9½ oz.	285 g
Buttermilk	8 fl. oz.	240 ml
Oil	as needed	as needed
Onion, small dice	4 oz.	120 g
Half-and-half or chicken stock	1½ pt.	720 ml
Collard Greens (page 648)	as needed	as needed

Collard Greens (page 648)

MISE EN PLACE
- Cut chicken into eight pieces.
- Peel and chop onion into small dice.

1 Season the chicken with salt and pepper.

2 Add the herbs and spices to 8 ounces (240 grams) of the flour.

3 Dip the chicken pieces in the buttermilk.

4 Dredge the chicken in the flour seasoned with salt and pepper.

5 Pan-fry the chicken in oil until done, approximately 40 minutes, turning so that it cooks evenly. Reduce the heat as necessary to prevent the chicken from becoming too dark. Or remove the chicken when well browned, drain it and finish cooking it in the oven.

6 To make the pan gravy, pour off all but 3 tablespoons (45 milliliters) oil from the pan, carefully reserving the fond.

7 Add the diced onion and sauté until translucent.

8 Add 1½ ounces (45 grams) flour and cook to make a blond roux.

9 Whisk in the half-and-half or stock and simmer approximately 15 minutes.

10 Strain through cheesecloth and adjust the seasonings.

11 Serve two pieces of chicken per person with 4 fluid ounces (120 milliliters) gravy and Collard Greens.

Approximate values per 2-piece serving (6–7 oz.), before frying: **Calories** 650, **Total fat** 31 g, **Saturated fat** 12 g, **Cholesterol** 190 mg, **Sodium** 190 mg, **Total carbohydrates** 32 g, **Protein** 57 g, **Vitamin A** 15%, **Vitamin C** 4%, **Calcium** 15%, **Iron** 20%

1 Dipping the chicken pieces in the buttermilk.

2 Dredging the chicken in the flour.

3 Adding the chicken to the oil. The bubbling fat indicates the proper cooking temperature.

4 Turning the chicken so that it cooks evenly.

5 Sautéing the diced onions until translucent.

6 Adding the liquid to the roux.

Deep-Frying Poultry

Young, tender poultry is an excellent and popular choice for deep-frying. The pieces should be golden brown on the outside and moist and tender on the inside. They should be neither greasy nor tough. Chopped cooked poultry can also be mixed with a heavy béchamel or velouté sauce and seasonings, breaded and deep-fried as **croquettes**, which are discussed in Chapter 20, Fish and Shellfish.

Portioned chickens and whole small birds, such as Rock Cornish game hen, are best for deep-frying. Although they can be marinated or seasoned directly, it is more common to season the batter or breading that will coat them. Additional flavors come from the sauces and accompaniments served with the deep-fried poultry. Lemon wedges, sweet and sour sauce and tangy barbecue sauces are popular accompaniments to deep-fried poultry.

croquette [crow-KEHT] a food that has been puréed or bound with a thick sauce (usually béchamel or velouté), made into small shapes and then breaded and deep-fried

Procedure for Deep-Frying Poultry

1 Cut, trim or otherwise prepare the poultry to be deep-fried. Season and bread or batter it, as desired.

2 Heat the fat to the desired temperature, usually around 350°F (177°C). Breaded or battered poultry cooks quickly, and the fat must be cool enough to cook the food's interior without burning its surface.

3 Carefully place the poultry in the hot fat using the basket method.

4 Deep-fry the food until done. It should have a crispy, golden brown surface.

5 Remove the deep-fried poultry from the fat and hold it over the fat, allowing the excess fat to drain. Transfer the food to a hotel pan either lined with absorbent paper or fitted with a rack. Season with salt, if desired.

6 If the deep-fried poultry is to be held for later service, place it under a heat lamp.

Spicy Fried Chicken Tenders with Herb Buttermilk Dressing

MISE EN PLACE

- Remove tendons from chicken tenderloins.
- Prepare the Herb Buttermilk Dressing.

YIELD 6 Servings, 4 oz. (120 g) each		METHOD Deep-Frying	
Chicken tenderloins (tenders), tendons removed		24	24
Seasoned flour:			
Flour		8 oz.	240 g
Chilli powder		3 Tbsp.	45 ml
Paprika		3 Tbsp.	45 ml
Granulated garlic		2 Tbsp.	30 ml
Black pepper		2 tsp.	10 ml
Cayenne pepper		1 Tbsp.	15 ml
Dried thyme		1 Tbsp.	15 ml
Dried oregano		1 Tbsp.	15 ml
Salt		3 Tbsp.	45 ml
Egg wash:			
Eggs		4	4
Milk		4 Tbsp.	120 ml
Bread crumbs		as needed	as needed
Herb Buttermilk Dressing (page 757)		8 fl. oz.	240 ml

1 Lightly pound the chicken pieces to an even thickness.

2 Combine the ingredients for the seasoned flour.

3 Beat the eggs and milk together.

4 Bread the chicken tenders using the standard breading procedure described in Chapter 9, Mise en Place, placing each fully breaded piece in a single layer on a parchment-lined sheet pan. Refrigerate until ready to cook.

5 Using the basket method, deep-fry the chicken pieces at 325°F (160°C) until done, approximately 4 minutes. Drain and serve with the Herb Buttermilk Dressing.

Approximate values per 4-oz. (120-g) serving: **Calories** 380, **Total fat** 12 g, **Saturated fat** 2.5 g, **Cholesterol** 160 mg, **Sodium** 2680 mg, **Total carbohydrates** 33 g, **Protein** 34 g, **Vitamin A** 60%, **Vitamin C** 15%, **Iron** 25%

MOIST-HEAT AND COMBINATION COOKING METHODS FOR POULTRY

The moist-heat cooking methods most often used with poultry are poaching and simmering. Poaching is appropriate for cooking tender birds for short periods. Simmering is appropriate for cooking older, tougher birds for longer periods in order to tenderize them. Poaching and simmering are similar procedures, the principal differences being the temperature of the cooking liquid and the cooking time. Combination cooking methods for poultry employ dry heat cooking techniques such as sautéing to brown poultry before it is simmered.

Moist-Heat Cooking Methods: Poaching and Simmering Poultry

Poached or simmered poultry should be moist, tender and delicately flavored. Although the poultry is cooked in water, overcooking will cause it to become dry and tough. During cooking, some of the poultry's flavor is transferred to the cooking liquid, which can be used to make a sauce for the finished product. Poultry may be packaged under vacuum in plastic pouches and cooked *sous vide* in a temperature controlled water bath. See Chapter 10, Principles of Cooking. Poultry prepared using this technique is moist and retains more juices than poultry that is poached directly in a liquid.

Selecting Poultry to Poach or Simmer

Young birds are best for poaching; boneless chicken breast pieces are the most commonly used parts. Older, tougher birds are usually simmered. Duck and geese are rarely poached or simmered because of their high fat content. (Dry heat cooking methods such as grilling and roasting are preferred to render their fat.)

Seasoning Poultry to Poach or Simmer

When poaching poultry, use a well-seasoned and highly flavored liquid in order to infuse as much flavor as possible into the item being cooked. Either strong stock with a sachet or a mixture of stock or water and white wine with a bouquet garni or onion piqué produces good results. The poultry should be completely covered with liquid so that it cooks evenly. However, if too much liquid is used and it is not strongly flavored, flavors may leach out of the poultry, resulting in a bland finished product.

Poultry is often simmered in water instead of stock. A sachet and a generous mirepoix should be added to help flavor the water. Typically simmering birds creates a strong broth that may be used to complete the recipe or reserved for other uses, such as in sauces or soup.

Cooking Temperatures for Poached or Simmered Poultry

For best results, poultry should be poached in liquids at low temperatures, between 160°F and 175°F (71°C and 79°C). Cooking poultry to the proper doneness at these temperatures produces a moist and tender product.

Simmering is done at slightly higher temperatures, between 185°F (85°C) and the boiling point of the chosen simmering liquid. When simmering, do not allow the liquid to boil, as this may result in a dry, tough and stringy finished product.

Determining Doneness of Poached or Simmered Poultry

Poached poultry, whether whole or boneless, is cooked just until done. An instant-read thermometer inserted in the thigh or thicker part of the bird should read 165°F (74°C). Any juices that run from the bird should be clear or show only a trace of pink.

Simmered poultry is usually cooked for longer periods to allow the moist heat to tenderize the meat. A chicken that weighs 3 pounds 8 ounces (1.5 kilograms), for example, may take 2½ hours to cook.

Accompaniments to Poached or Simmered Poultry

Poached or simmered poultry can be served hot or cold. The meat from these birds can be served cold in salads, served hot in casseroles or used in any dish that calls for cooked poultry.

Poached items are typically served with a flavored mayonnaise or a sauce made from the reduced poaching liquid, such as Sauce Suprême (page 224). Poultry is also often poached as a means of producing a low-calorie dish. If so, a vegetable coulis makes a good sauce, or the poultry can be served with a portion of its cooking liquid and a vegetable garnish.

Simmered poultry to be served cold will be moister and more flavorful if it is cooled in its cooking liquid. To do so, remove the pot containing the bird and the cooking liquid from the heat when the bird is still slightly undercooked. Cool the meat and broth in a water bath following the procedure in Chapter 11, Stocks and Sauces. Once cooled, remove the meat and wipe off any congealed broth before proceeding with the recipe.

Procedure for Poaching or Simmering Poultry

1. Cut or truss the item to be cooked as directed in the recipe.
2. Prepare the cooking liquid and bring it to a simmer. Submerge the poultry in the cooking liquid, or arrange the items to be poached in an appropriate pan and add the poaching liquid to the pan.
3. Poach or simmer the item to the desired doneness in the oven or on the stove top. Maintain the proper cooking temperature throughout the process.
4. Remove the poultry and hold it for service in a portion of the cooking liquid or, using an ice bath, cool the item in its cooking liquid.
5. The cooking liquid may be used to prepare an accompanying sauce or reserved for use in other dishes.

Poached Breast of Chicken with Tarragon Sauce

MISE EN PLACE

- Bone and skin the chicken breasts.

YIELD 8 Servings, 4 oz. (120 g) each		METHOD Poaching	
Whole chicken breasts, boneless, skinless, approximately 10 oz. (300 g) each	4	4	
Whole butter	1½ oz.	45 g	
Salt and white pepper	TT	TT	
White wine	4 fl. oz.	120 ml	
Chicken stock	1 pt.	480 ml	
Bay leaf	1	1	
Dried thyme	¼ tsp.	1 ml	
Dried tarragon	1 tsp.	5 ml	
Flour	1 oz.	30 g	
Heavy cream	4 fl. oz.	120 ml	
Fresh tarragon sprigs	as needed for garnish		

1. Trim any rib meat and fat from the breasts. Cut the breasts into two pieces, removing the keel bone, the strip of cartilage that joins the halves.
2. Select a pan that will just hold the breasts when they are placed close together. Rub the pan with approximately ½ ounce (15 grams) butter.
3. Season the chicken breasts with salt and white pepper and arrange them in the buttered pan, presentation side up.
4. Add the wine, stock, bay leaf, thyme and dried tarragon.
5. Cut and butter a piece of parchment paper and cover the chicken breasts.
6. Bring the liquid to a simmer and reduce the temperature to poach the chicken.

7 Make a blond roux with 1 ounce (30 grams) butter and the flour; set aside to cool.

8 When the breasts are done, remove them from the liquid. Thicken the liquid with the roux. Add the cream. Simmer and reduce to the desired consistency.

9 Strain the sauce through cheesecloth and adjust the seasonings.

10 Serve each half breast napped (lightly coated) with approximately 2 fluid ounces (60 milliliters) sauce; garnish each portion with a sprig of fresh tarragon.

Approximate values per 4-oz. (120-g) serving: **Calories** 250, **Total fat** 13 g, **Saturated fat** 7 g, **Cholesterol** 105 mg, **Sodium** 590 mg, **Total carbohydrates** 4 g, **Protein** 29 g, **Vitamin A** 10%

❶ Arranging the breasts in an appropriate pan.

❷ Adding the white wine, chicken stock and seasonings to the pan.

❸ Covering the breasts with a piece of buttered parchment paper.

❹ Adding the cream to the thickened sauce.

❺ Plating the poached chicken breast.

Combination Cooking Methods: Braising and Stewing Poultry

Braising and stewing use both dry and moist heat to produce a moist, flavorful product. The principal difference between braising and stewing is the size of the cut being cooked: Large cuts are braised; smaller ones are stewed. Because most poultry is relatively small, this distinction does not readily apply in poultry cookery; therefore the two cooking methods are discussed together here.

Braised or stewed poultry should be moist and fork tender. The poultry is always served with the liquid in which it was cooked. Ducks and geese are braised or stewed in much the same way as red meats. Chicken cacciatore, Coq au Vin (page 457) and Chicken Fricassee (page 447) are examples of braised or stewed chicken dishes.

Selecting Poultry to Braise or Stew

Braising and stewing, which involve slow, moist cooking processes, are often thought of as methods to tenderize tough red meats. Although they can be used to tenderize older, tougher birds, these cooking methods are more often selected as a means of adding moisture and flavor to poultry that is inherently tender, such as young ducks and chickens. Typically the birds are disjointed and cooked bone-in, just until done, so that they retain their juiciness.

Seasoning Poultry to Braise or Stew

Braised or stewed items obtain much of their flavor from the cooking liquid and other ingredients added during the cooking process. The main item and the cooking liquid should be well seasoned. If additional seasonings such as an onion piqué, sachet, bouquet garni or dried herbs and spices are required, they should be added at the beginning of the cooking process rather than at the end. This allows the flavors to blend and penetrate the larger pieces of poultry. If the poultry is dredged in flour before browning, seasonings may be added directly to the flour. The finished dish should have the flavor of the poultry in the sauce and the moisture and flavor of the sauce in the poultry.

Cooking Temperatures for Braised or Stewed Poultry

Some recipes, such as chicken cacciatore and Coq au Vin (page 457), require the main item to be thoroughly browned during the initial stages; others, such as Chicken Fricassee (page 447), do not. In either case, after the liquid is added, it is important to maintain a slow simmer rather than a rapid boil. This can be done on the stove top or in the oven. Low temperatures control the cooking and produce a tender, juicy finished product.

Determining Doneness of Braised or Stewed Poultry

Tenderness is the key to determining doneness. It can be determined by inserting a kitchen fork into the poultry. There should be little resistance, and the poultry should freely fall off the fork. The pieces should retain their shape, however; if they fall apart, they are overdone. Small boneless pieces can be tested by cutting into them with a fork.

Accompaniments to Braised or Stewed Poultry

All braises and stews are cooked in a liquid that results in a sauce or broth served as part of the finished dish. Rice, pasta, cooked grains and boiled potatoes are natural accompaniments to almost any braised or stewed dish, as are boiled vegetables.

Procedure for Braising or Stewing Poultry

1 Sear the main item in butter or oil, developing color as desired.
2 Add vegetables and other ingredients as called for in the recipe and sauté.
3 Add flour or roux if used.
4 Add the appropriate liquid.
5 Cover and simmer on the stove top or in the oven until done.
6 Add seasonings and garnishes at the appropriate times during the cooking process.
7 Finish the dish by adding cream or a liaison to the sauce or by adjusting its consistency. Adjust the seasonings.
8 Serve a portion of the poultry with the sauce and appropriate garnish.

Chicken Fricassee

YIELD 8 Servings, 8 oz. (240 g) each	METHOD	Braising
Frying chickens, 2 lb. 8 oz.–3 lb. (1.2–1.4 kg) each, cut into 8 pieces	2	2
Salt and white pepper	TT	TT
Clarified butter	3 fl. oz.	90 ml
Onions, medium dice	10 oz.	300 g
Flour	3 oz.	90 g
Dry white wine	8 fl. oz.	240 ml
Chicken stock	1 qt.	960 ml
Sachet:		
Bay leaf	1	1
Dried thyme	½ tsp.	2 ml
Peppercorns, cracked	½ tsp.	2 ml
Parsley stems	8	8
Garlic clove, crushed	1	1
Heavy cream	8 fl. oz.	240 ml
Nutmeg, ground	TT	TT

MISE EN PLACE
- Cut chickens into eight pieces.
- Peel and chop onions into medium dice.
- Prepare herb sachet.

1 Season the chicken with salt and white pepper.

2 Sauté the chicken in the butter without browning. Add the onions and continue to sauté until they are translucent.

3 Sprinkle the flour over the chicken and onions and stir to make a roux. Cook the roux for 2 minutes without browning.

4 Deglaze the pan with the wine. Add the stock and sachet; season with salt. Cover and simmer until done, approximately 30–45 minutes.

5 Remove the chicken from the pan and hold in a warm place. Strain the sauce through damp cheesecloth and return it to a clean pan.

6 Add the cream and bring the sauce to a simmer. Add the nutmeg and adjust the seasonings. Return the chicken to the sauce to reheat it for service.

Approximate values per 8-oz. (240-g) serving: **Calories** 700, **Total fat** 20 g, **Saturated fat** 12 g, **Cholesterol** 60 mg, **Sodium** 795 mg, **Total carbohydrates** 113 g, **Protein** 15 g, **Vitamin A** 20%

1 Sautéing the chicken and onions in butter.

2 Sprinkling the flour over the chicken.

3 Deglazing the pan with wine.

4 Removing the chicken from the pan.

5 Straining the sauce through damp cheesecloth.

6 Returning the chicken to the sauce to reheat it for service.

QUESTIONS FOR DISCUSSION

1 List the six categories of poultry recognized by the USDA. How are these categories then divided into classes?

2 How is inspection of poultry different from grading of poultry? Which government agencies oversee these procedures?

3 How should fresh poultry be stored? Discuss several procedures that should be followed carefully when working with poultry to prevent cross-contamination.

4 What are the typical eight cuts that can be made from any poultry item? Why do some parts of a bird's carcass have dark meat, while other parts have white meat?

5 List the steps for cutting a chicken into eight pieces before cooking.

6 What is a suprême? Describe the step-by-step procedure for preparing a chicken suprême.

7 What is trussing? Why is this technique used with poultry?

8 Which poultry items are best suited for broiling or grilling? Explain your answer.

9 Describe the characteristics of properly roasted poultry. Which classes of poultry are recommended for roasting?

10 Contact a local poultry supplier or farmer. Research the types of poultry available. Explain the cooking methods and preparations suitable for their products.

Additional Poultry Recipes

Jamaican-Style Jerk Chicken

YIELD	12 Servings, 10 oz. (300 g) each	METHOD	Grilling
Scotch bonnet or habañero chiles		2 oz. (8–9 chiles)	4 oz. (8–9 chiles)
Allspice, whole		2 Tbsp.	30 ml
Black peppercorns, whole		2 Tbsp.	30 ml
Cinnamon, ground		1 tsp.	5 ml
Nutmeg, ground		½ tsp.	2 ml
Green onions, green and white parts, chopped coarse		8 oz.	240 g
Fresh ginger, grated		1½ oz.	45 g
Garlic cloves		1 oz.	30 g
Soy sauce		1 fl. oz.	30 ml
Lime juice		4 fl. oz.	120 ml
Brown sugar		1 oz.	30 g
Chicken leg and thigh quarters, split		12	12

1 Wearing gloves, seed the chiles following the procedure on page 592.

2 Grind the allspice and peppercorns in a spice mill. Combine them with the cinnamon, nutmeg, green onions, seeded chiles, ginger, garlic, soy sauce, lime juice and brown sugar in the bowl of a food processor or blender. Blend into a coarse paste.

3 Pour the paste over the chicken in a half hotel pan. Rub the chicken pieces with the paste, making sure to cover them evenly with the mixture. Cover the pan and refrigerate the chicken at least 6 hours, or up to 18 hours.

4 Heat the grill to a medium heat, between 275°F (135°C) and 325°F (160°C). Sear the chicken on the grill on both sides then move it to a cool section of the grill. Cover and allow the chicken to cook slowly, basting it from time to time with any of the marinade that is left in the pan. Cook until the chicken is cooked through, tender and crisp, approximately 45 minutes.

5 Serve the jerk chicken with rice simmered with coconut milk, rice and peas or mashed sweet potatoes.

Approximate values per 10-oz. (300-g) serving: **Calories** 510, **Total fat** 23 g, **Saturated fat** 6 g, **Cholesterol** 330 mg, **Sodium** 410 mg, **Total carbohydrates** 8 g, **Protein** 63 g, **Vitamin C** 25%, **Iron** 20%

Grilling the chicken.

Chicken Yakitori

Yakitori is a popular Japanese dish traditionally made with small pieces of chicken threaded on wooden skewers and grilled over aromatic hardwood charcoal. Yakitori stands and restaurants are ubiquitous in Japan, where quality is judged by the sauce in which the chicken is dipped before grilling.

YIELD 8 Servings, 6 oz. (180 g) each	METHOD Grilling	
Dark soy sauce	8 fl. oz.	240 ml
Sake	8 fl. oz.	240 ml
Granulated sugar	2 oz.	60 g
Chicken breast halves, boneless, skinless, approximately 5 oz. (150 g) each	8	8
Cornstarch	1 Tbsp.	15 ml
Sesame seeds	1 Tbsp.	15 ml

1 Combine the soy sauce, sake and sugar. Set aside 8 fluid ounces (240 milliliters) of the mixture for making the sauce in Step 3.

2 Brush the chicken with the remaining soy sauce mixture and grill over hot charcoal until done, basting regularly.

3 To make the sauce, combine 2 fluid ounces (60 milliliters) of the soy sauce mixture set aside for this purpose with the cornstarch. Bring the remainder to a boil in a small saucepan and stir in the cornstarch slurry. Stirring constantly, continue boiling until the sauce thickens. Simmer 1 minute.

4 Serve each breast sliced and fanned with a small amount of the sauce accompanied with short-grain white rice. Garnish with sesame seeds and fresh chives, if desired.

Approximate values per 6-oz. (180-g) serving: **Calories** 240, **Total fat** 4.5 g, **Saturated fat** 1 g, **Cholesterol** 95 mg, **Sodium** 1700 mg, **Total carbohydrates** 12 g, **Protein** 37 g

Grilled Cornish Game Hens with Basil Butter

YIELD 4 Game Hens, 4 Servings, 10 oz. (300 g) each	METHOD Grilling	
Rock Cornish game hens, whole	4	4
Fresh basil leaves	16	16
White Wine Marinade (page 426)	1 pt.	480 ml
Basil butter (page 234)	6 oz.	180 g

1 Remove the backbone and breastbone from each game hen. The birds will lie flat and remain in one piece.

2 Make a slit below each leg and tuck the leg bone into the slit.

3 Carefully slide two basil leaves under the skin over each breast to cover the meat.

4 Marinate the game hens in the White Wine Marinade for 1–2 hours.

5 Heat and prepare the grill.

6 Remove the game hens from the marinade and pat dry.

7 Melt approximately 4 ounces (120 grams) basil butter, leaving enough for eight thin slices to be served with the finished dish.

8 Brush the game hens with the melted butter and place them on the grill, skin side down. Grill the game hens, turning once and basting periodically with the melted basil butter. Finish in the oven until the hens reach an internal temperature of 165°F (74°C), if necessary.

9 Serve the game hens with a slice of basil butter melting over each breast.

Approximate values per 10-oz. (300-g) serving: **Calories** 690, **Total fat** 50 g, **Saturated fat** 26 g, **Cholesterol** 260 mg, **Sodium** 1070 mg, **Total carbohydrates** 0 g, **Protein** 60 g, **Vitamin A** 40%

❶ Marinating the game hens.

❷ Drying the game hens.

③ Brushing the game hens with melted basil butter.

④ Grilling the game hens.

⑤ Serving the game hens with basil butter.

Roast Cornish Game Hen with Wild Rice Stuffing

YIELD	4 Game Hens, 4 Servings, 14 oz. (420 g) each	METHOD	Roasting

Stuffing:		
Onion, fine dice	2 oz.	90 g
Mushrooms, chopped	4 oz.	120 g
Whole butter, melted	4 oz.	120 g
Wild rice, cooked	8 oz.	360 g
Dried thyme, crushed	½ tsp.	2 ml
Dried marjoram, crushed	¼ tsp.	1 ml
Salt and pepper	TT	TT
Rock Cornish game hens	4	4

1 Sauté the onion and mushrooms in 1 ounce (30 grams) of the melted butter until tender. Cool.

2 Stir in the rice and herbs and season to taste with salt and pepper. Stuffing can be made up to 2 days ahead and refrigerated before using.

3 Stuff the cavity of each hen loosely with the rice mixture. Truss and place in a roasting pan.

4 Brush the hens with the remaining butter and season with salt and pepper. Roast at 400°F (200°C) for 15 minutes.

5 Reduce the oven temperature to 300°F (150°C) and roast until the internal temperature reaches 165°F (74°C), approximately 30 minutes. Baste two or three times with melted butter.

6 Serve the hens with a pan gravy or a sauce made separately, such as mushroom sauce.

Approximate values per 14-oz. (420-g) serving: **Calories** 970, **Total fat** 65 g, **Saturated fat** 26 g, **Cholesterol** 330 mg, **Sodium** 1580 mg, **Total carbohydrates** 12 g, **Protein** 86 g, **Vitamin A** 35%, **Iron** 25%

① Stuffing each hen loosely with some of the wild rice mixture.

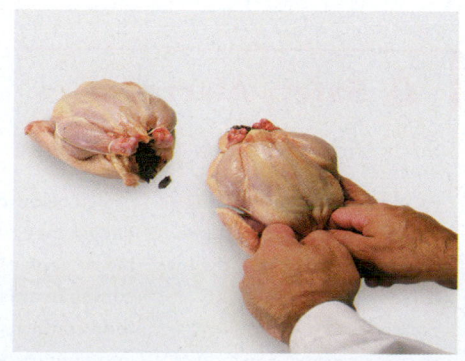

② Trussing the hens.

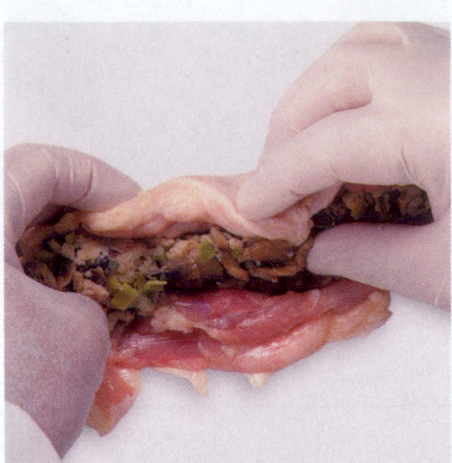

① Closing the chicken leg around the stuffing.

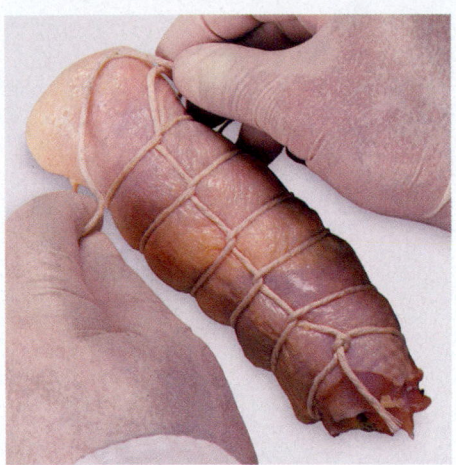

② Tying the chicken leg with butcher's twine.

③ The sliced Chicken Leg Stuffed with Mushrooms and Prosciutto.

Chicken Leg Stuffed with Mushrooms and Prosciutto

YIELD 6 Servings, 2 pieces each		METHOD Roasting	
Chicken leg and thigh quarters, whole	6	6
Whole butter	1 oz.	30 g
Green onions, sliced	3	3
Prosciutto, small dice	4 oz.	120 g
Mushrooms, chanterelles, morels or other varieties as desired, sliced	6 oz.	180 g
Leek, small dice	2 oz.	60 g
Heavy cream	6 fl. oz.	180 ml
Bread crumbs, fresh	4 oz.	120 g
Salt and pepper	TT	TT
Whole butter, melted	1 oz.	30 g
Bordelaise (page 226)	12 fl. oz.	360 ml
Sautéed vegetables	as needed for garnish	

1 Bone the chicken legs and thighs as described on page 425, leaving the skin attached.

2 Heat the butter in a large sauté pan. Add the onions and prosciutto and sauté for 30 seconds. Add the mushrooms and leek and sauté for 2 minutes or until the mushrooms are tender.

3 Add the cream and reduce by half. Remove the pan from the heat. Add the bread crumbs and toss to combine all ingredients. Season the stuffing with salt and pepper.

4 Divide the stuffing into six portions. Open the chicken legs on a cutting board with the flesh side up. Season the legs with salt and pepper. Stuff each leg with a portion of the stuffing. Close the chicken legs around the stuffing. Tie the stuffed legs with butcher's twine at close intervals so the legs retain their shape during cooking.

5 Place the legs in a roasting pan and brush with melted butter. Roast the legs at 375°F (190°C) until the internal temperature reaches 165°F (74°C), approximately 30 minutes.

6 Remove the legs from the oven and remove the twine. Slice the chicken into ½-inch- (12-millimeter-) thick slices. Lightly coat each plate with Bordelaise and fan the slices of stuffed chicken on the sauce. Serve with an appropriate accompaniment such as sautéed vegetables.

Variation:

Sous Vide Chicken Legs Stuffed with Mushrooms and Prosciutto—Chill the stuffed chicken legs thoroughly in Step 4. Wearing clean disposable gloves, slide each stuffed chicken leg into a plastic pouch for *sous vide* cooking. Vacuum seal the bags. Cook in a thermal circulator heated to 167°F (75°C) for 1–1½ hours until the core temperature of the chicken reaches 167°F (75°C) when checked with a digital probe thermometer. The stuffed chicken legs may be held for service in the circulator for up to 2 hours. For service, remove a chicken leg from the bag. Drain on clean paper towels. Heat ½ ounce (15 milliliters) clarified butter in a heavy frying pan over medium high heat. Sear the chicken leg on all sides until crisp and brown, approximately 2 minutes per side.

Approximate values per 2-piece serving: **Calories** 540, **Total fat** 37 g, **Saturated fat** 17 g, **Cholesterol** 185 mg, **Sodium** 610 mg, **Total carbohydrates** 13 g, **Protein** 38 g, **Vitamin A** 20%

⚠ Safety Alert

Sous Vide *Sanitation*

Food safety is of utmost concern when using *sous vide* techniques because of the low cooking temperatures. To prevent the growth of microorganisms, any food to be cooked *sous vide* must be chilled below the temperature danger zone (41°F/5°C) before cooking. Keep all cutting boards, knives and food contact surfaces clean and sanitary and wear clean disposable gloves. Use only the freshest unblemished ingredients. Consult your local health department for regulations for preparing food *sous vide*. Special permission and a HACCP plan may be required.

Roast Chicken with Mashed Potatoes and Natural Pan Gravy

YIELD 1 Chicken, 4 Servings, 2 pieces each	METHOD Roasting	
Chicken, 3–4 lb. (1.4–1.9 kg)	1	1
Salt and pepper	TT	TT
Whole butter, room temperature	2 oz.	60 g
Lemon, halved	1	1
Chicken stock	1 pt.	480 ml
All-purpose flour	1 Tbsp.	15 ml
Garlic Mashed Potatoes (page 664)	1 lb.	480 g
Asparagus, steamed, hot	16 spears	16 spears

1 Remove the neck, giblets and liver from the chicken's cavity. Reserve for another use. Season the chicken inside and out with salt and pepper. Loosen the skin above the breast. Slide the butter evenly under the chicken skin without tearing. Place the lemon halves inside the chicken cavity. Truss the chicken.

2 Place the chicken on a rack in a roasting pan. Roast at 400°F (200°C) for 15 minutes. Baste the chicken with the fat and pan juices. Continue to roast the chicken for 30 additional minutes basting it at least two additional times. Reduce the temperature to 325°F (160°C) and continue cooking the chicken to an internal temperature of 165°F (74°C), approximately 15–30 additional minutes.

3 When the chicken is done, remove it from the roasting pan and set it aside to rest. Degrease the roasting pan, reserving 1 tablespoon (15 milliliters) of the fat to make a roux.

4 Deglaze the pan with a small amount of stock.

5 Make a blond roux with the reserved fat and the flour. Add the roux to the deglazing liquid and remaining stock, whisking well to prevent lumps. Simmer 15 minutes. Adjust the seasonings.

6 Carve the chicken into eight pieces. Plate each serving with the mashed potatoes, asparagus spears and pan gravy.

Approximate values per 2-piece serving: **Calories** 780, **Total fat** 45 g, **Saturated fat** 19 g, **Cholesterol** 255 mg, **Sodium** 530 mg, **Total carbohydrates** 33 g, **Protein** 59 g, **Vitamin A** 45%, **Vitamin C** 30%, **Iron** 25%

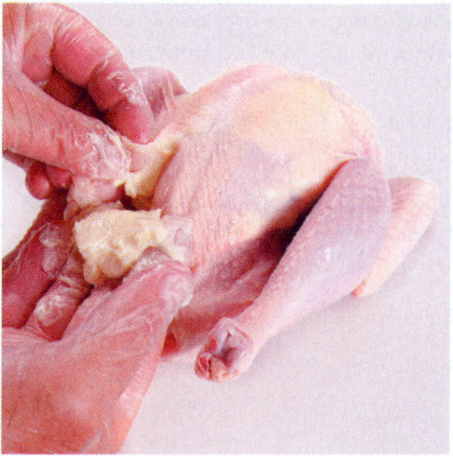

❶ Sliding the butter under the skin.

❷ Basting the chicken.

Chicken Stuffed with Spinach and Ricotta Cheese in Saffron Sauce

YIELD 4 Servings, 17 oz. (510 g) each		METHOD *Sous Vide* Poaching/Sautéing	
Spinach, stemmed		1 lb.	480 g
Ricotta		4 oz.	120 g
Egg whites, lightly beaten		2	2
Salt and pepper		TT	TT
Airline chicken breasts, skin on, 9 oz. (270 g) each		4	4
White wine		1 pt.	480 ml
Saffron		1 pinch	1 pinch
Chicken Velouté (page 222)		8 fl. oz.	240 ml
Heavy cream, hot		2 fl. oz.	60 ml
Clarified butter		1 fl. oz.	30 ml

1 Blanch, refresh and drain the spinach. Squeeze it tightly to remove as much moisture as possible, then chop it finely.

2 To make the stuffing, combine the ricotta, egg whites and spinach in a mixing bowl; season to taste.

3 Place the chicken breasts on a cutting board, skin side down. Using a boning knife, carefully make a pocket that runs the length of each breast.

4 Put the stuffing in a pastry bag and pipe the stuffing into each pocket. Do not overfill the chicken breasts; the stuffing will expand as it cooks.

5 Chill the stuffed chicken breasts thoroughly. Wearing clean disposable gloves, wrap each stuffed chicken breast in plastic wrap then slide each one into a plastic pouch for *sous vide* cooking. Vacuum seal the bags.

6 Cook in a thermal circulator heated to 167°F (75°C) for 1–1 ½ hours until the core temperature of the chicken reaches 167°F (75°C) when checked with a digital probe thermometer. The stuffed chicken breasts may be held for service in the circulator for up to 2 hours.

7 Make the sauce while the chicken cooks. Bring the white wine and saffron to a boil. Reduce by half. Add the velouté and the cream. Adjust the seasonings and consistency; strain.

8 For service, remove each portion from the bags. Drain them on clean paper towels. Sauté the chicken in the butter until well browned. Heat the clarified butter in a large heavy frying pan over medium high heat. Sauté the chicken breasts skin-side down until crisp and browned, for approximately one to two minutes.

9 Ladle the sauce onto four warm plates. Slice the chicken and arrange it in the sauce; serve with appropriate accompaniment such as cooked broccoli and roasted vegetables.

Approximate values per 17-oz. (510-g) serving: **Calories** 700, **Total fat** 33 g, **Saturated fat** 16 g, **Cholesterol** 215 mg, **Sodium** 560 mg, **Total carbohydrates** 13 g, **Protein** 65 g, **Vitamin A** 230%, **Vitamin C** 50%, **Iron** 30%

⚠ Safety Alert

Sous Vide *Sanitation*

Food safety is of utmost concern when using *sous vide* techniques because of the low cooking temperatures. To prevent the growth of microorganisms, any food to be cooked *sous vide* must be chilled below the temperature danger zone (41°F/5°C) before cooking. Keep all cutting boards, knives and food contact surfaces clean and sanitary and wear clean disposable gloves. Use only the freshest unblemished ingredients. Consult your local health department for regulations for preparing food *sous vide*. Special permission and a HACCP plan may be required.

Lemongrass Chicken Lettuce Wrap

YIELD	8 Servings, 1 wrap each		METHOD	Stir-Frying

Chicken marinade:		
Sugar	1 Tbsp.	15 ml
Fish sauce	1 fl. oz.	30 ml
Garlic, minced	½ oz.	15 g
Shallot, minced	1 oz.	30 g
Lemongrass, minced	1 oz.	30 g
Vegetable oil	1 fl. oz.	30 ml
Black pepper	½ tsp.	2 ml
Asian chile sauce (Sriracha)	1 fl. oz.	30 ml
Chicken, boneless, skinless, small dice	2 lb.	960 g
Pickled carrot and daikon:		
Carrot, julienne	4 oz.	120 g
Daikon radish, julienne	4 oz.	120 g
Lemon juice	1½ fl. oz.	45 ml
Sugar	3 Tbsp.	45 ml
Fish sauce	1 fl. oz.	30 ml
Vegetable oil	4 fl. oz.	120 ml
Dried shiitake mushrooms, rehydrated, small dice	8 oz.	240 g
Green onions, thinly sliced	8 Tbsp.	120 ml
Iceberg lettuce leaves, trimmed into cups	24	24
Fresh mint	as needed	as needed
Fresh cilantro	as needed	as needed
Fresh Thai sweet basil	as needed	as needed
Coconut Sauce (page 251)	12 fl. oz.	360 ml

1 Combine all the marinade ingredients. Stir in the chicken. Refrigerate for at least 4 hours or overnight.

2 Place the julienne carrot and daikon in separate small bowls. Stir the lemon juice, sugar and fish sauce together and pour half of the mixture over each bowl of vegetables and toss gently. Refrigerate for 30 minutes before serving.

3 Heat a wok over high heat until very hot. Add the vegetable oil and stir fry the marinated chicken, mushrooms and green onions until the chicken is cooked, approximately 4 minutes. (For restaurant service, stir fry one portion of the chicken at a time.)

4 Portion the chicken onto eight plates. Garnish each plate with 3 lettuce leaf cups, pickled carrots, pickled daikon, fresh herbs and a small dish of Coconut Sauce.

Approximate values per wrap: **Calories** 510, **Total fat** 25 g, **Saturated fat** 7 g, **Cholesterol** 60 mg, **Sodium** 900 mg, **Total carbohydrates** 53 g, **Protein** 24 g, **Vitamin A** 50%, **Vitamin C** 20%

Chicken and Mushroom Crêpes with Sauce Mornay

YIELD 6 Servings, 2 crêpes each	METHOD Poaching	
Chicken, light and dark meat, boneless, skinless, poached	1 lb.	480 g
Shallots, chopped	1 Tbsp.	15 ml
Mushrooms, sliced	6 oz.	180 g
Clarified butter	1 Tbsp.	15 ml
White wine	2 fl. oz.	60 ml
Lemon juice	1 Tbsp.	15 ml
Fresh thyme	1 tsp.	5 ml
Gruyère cheese, shredded	2 oz.	60 g
Parmesan cheese, grated	1 oz.	30 g
Chicken Velouté (page 222)	8 fl. oz.	240 ml
Black pepper	TT	TT
Savory Crêpes (page 567), 8 in. (20 cm) each	8	8
Mornay sauce (page 222)	1 pt.	480 ml
Fresh chives	as needed for garnish	

1 Cut the chicken into julienne strips.

2 Sauté the shallots and mushrooms in the butter until the mushrooms are tender. Deglaze the pan with white wine. Add the lemon juice and thyme and cook just until the liquid has evaporated. Add the poached chicken strips.

3 Add the cheeses and velouté to the chicken. Stir to combine, adjust the seasonings with salt and pepper, and cook over medium heat until the mixture is hot.

4 Spoon 2 ounces (60 grams) of the filling into each crêpe. Roll the crêpes around the filling. For each portion, place two crêpes, seam side down, on a heat resistant plate. Ladle 2½ fluid ounces (75 milliliters) of Mornay sauce over each portion of crêpes leaving the ends of the crepes exposed.

5 Brown the sauce lightly under a broiler or salamander for a few seconds. Or lightly brown the sauce with a handheld propane torch. Garnish with sliced chives.

Approximate values per 2-crêpe serving: **Calories** 520, **Total fat** 30 g, **Saturated fat** 16 g, **Cholesterol** 205 mg, **Sodium** 260 mg, **Total carbohydrates** 32 g, **Protein** 31 g, **Calcium** 25%

Chicken Curry

YIELD 4 Servings, 8 oz. (240 g) each	METHOD Simmering	
Wet masala:		
Fresh ginger, fine dice	2 oz.	60 g
Turmeric, ground	1½ tsp.	8 ml
Coriander seeds, ground	1½ tsp.	8 ml
Cumin seeds, ground	1 tsp.	5 ml
Cayenne pepper	1 tsp.	5 ml
Fenugreek, ground	½ tsp.	2 ml
Coconut milk, unsweetened	18 fl. oz.	540 ml
Onions, small dice	8 oz.	240 g
Garlic, crushed	2 tsp.	10 ml
Ghee or clarified butter	1 fl. oz.	30 ml
Roasting chicken, 3 lb. (1.4 kg), cut in 8 pieces	1	1
Salt	1 tsp.	5 ml
Green chiles, split lengthwise	3	3
Lemon juice	1 fl. oz.	30 ml

1 To make the wet masala, mix the ginger, turmeric, coriander seeds, cumin seeds, cayenne pepper and fenugreek; add just enough of the coconut milk to form a paste.

2 Stir-fry the onions and garlic in the ghee until the onions are golden brown.

3 Add the wet masala to the onions and stir-fry for 8 minutes.

4 Add the chicken pieces and cook, turning them frequently, for 6–8 minutes.

5 Add the remaining coconut milk, salt and chiles. Bring to a boil, cover and reduce to a simmer. Cook until the chicken is done, approximately 45 minutes.

6 Just before service, stir in the lemon juice and adjust the seasonings. Serve with steamed rice and a chutney.

Approximate values per 8-oz. (240-g) serving: **Calories** 680, **Total fat** 51 g, **Saturated fat** 33 g, **Cholesterol** 135 mg, **Sodium** 710 mg, **Total carbohydrates** 17 g, **Protein** 44 g, **Vitamin A** 20%, **Vitamin C** 150%, **Iron** 40%

Coq au Vin

YIELD 8 Servings, 12 oz. (360 g) each	METHOD Braising	
Chickens, 3 lb. (1.4 kg) each, cut in 8 pieces	2	2
Flour	as needed for dredging	
Salt and pepper	TT	TT
Clarified butter	2 fl. oz.	60 ml
Brandy	4 fl. oz.	120 ml
Bouquet garni:		
Carrot stick, 4 in. (10 cm)	1	1
Leek, split, 4-in. (10-cm) piece	1	1
Fresh thyme	1 sprig	1 sprig
Bay leaf	1	1
Garlic cloves, peeled and crushed	6	6
Red wine	24 fl. oz.	720 ml
Chicken stock	1 pt.	480 ml
Bacon **lardons**, diced	4 oz.	120 g
Pearl onions, peeled	18	18
Mushrooms, medium, quartered	10	10
Beurre manié	as needed	as needed

1 Dredge the chicken pieces in flour seasoned with salt and pepper.

2 Heat the clarified butter in a 12-inch (30-centimeter) braiser; brown the chicken in two or three batches.

3 Add the brandy and ignite. When the flame dies, add the bouquet garni, garlic, wine and stock. Bring to a boil, then reduce to a simmer.

4 Cover the pan and simmer until the chicken is tender, approximately 40 minutes.

5 In a separate pan, sauté the bacon until the fat begins to render. Add the onions and sauté until they begin to brown. Cook the bacon and onions covered, over low heat, until the onions are tender. Add the mushrooms and cook them until tender.

6 Remove the chicken from the pan and adjust the sauce's consistency with the beurre manié. Strain the sauce through a china cap and adjust the seasonings.

7 Spoon the bacon, onions and mushrooms onto a serving platter, place the chicken over them and ladle the sauce over the finished dish.

Approximate values per 12-oz. (360-g) serving: **Calories** 860, **Total fat** 51 g, **Saturated fat** 17 g, **Cholesterol** 330 mg, **Sodium** 910 mg, **Total carbohydrates** 17 g, **Protein** 83 g, **Vitamin A** 60%, **Iron** 35%

Individual Chicken Pot Pie

Chicken Pot Pie

YIELD 16 Servings, 8 oz. (240 g) each

Whole butter	1 oz.	30 g
White mushrooms, quartered	8 oz.	240 g
Salt and pepper	TT	TT
Red potatoes, medium dice	6 oz.	180 g
Carrots, medium dice	6 oz.	180 g
Pearl onions	6 oz.	180 g
Peas	6 oz.	180 g
Corn kernels	6 oz.	180 g
Chicken Velouté (page 222)	3 pt.	1.4 lt
Heavy cream	8 fl. oz.	240 ml
Chicken, light and dark meat, cooked, large dice	2 lb. 8 oz.	1.2 kg
Biscuit dough, cut into small discs	as needed	as needed
Egg wash	as needed	as needed

1 Heat the butter in a small sauté pan and sauté the mushrooms. Season with salt and pepper.

2 Blanch or steam the potatoes, carrots, onions, peas and corn separately until tender.

3 Bring the velouté to a simmer. Add the cream and simmer for 5 minutes.

4 Add the chicken, potatoes and vegetables to the sauce, season with salt and pepper and ladle into a shallow half-size hotel or other pan.

5 Cover the pan with the biscuit dough. Egg-wash the top of the dough. Bake at 400°F (200°C) until the top is well browned, approximately 15 minutes.

Variations:

Replace the biscuits with a sheet of flaky pie dough or puff pastry. Brush the edges of the pan with egg wash, then cover the pan with the dough. Brush with egg wash and vent before baking.

Individual Chicken Pot Pies—Portion the chicken mixture into small ramekins or bowls. Cover each one with flaky pie dough, brush with egg wash and vent before baking.

Turkey Pot Pie—Substitute an equal amount of turkey for the chicken.

Approximate values per 8-oz. (240-g) serving, without crust: **Calories** 330, **Total fat** 18 g, **Saturated fat** 9 g, **Cholesterol** 110 mg, **Sodium** 530 mg, **Total carbohydrates** 16 g, **Protein** 27 g, **Vitamin A** 70%

Lavender and Spice-Crusted Duck Breast with Apricot Compote

YIELD 2 Servings, 9 oz. (270 g) each	METHOD	Sautéing
Moulard duck breast half, boneless, approximately 14 ounces (420 grams)	1	1
Lavender buds, dried	¼ tsp.	1 ml
Coriander, ground	¼ tsp.	1 ml
Fennel seeds, ground	¼ tsp.	1 ml
Lemon zest, grated	½ tsp.	2 ml
Black pepper	¼ tsp.	1 ml
Onion, chopped	3 oz.	90 g
Dried apricots, diced, conditioned in boiling water	3 oz.	90 g
White vermouth	2 fl. oz.	60 ml
Duck or chicken stock	2 fl. oz.	60 ml
Sherry vinegar	1 tsp.	5 ml
Salt and pepper	TT	TT
Gratin Dauphinoise (page 659) cut into discs (page 1098)	2	2

1 Trim any excess fat from the duck breast. Score the skin in parallel diagonal lines cutting only deep enough to score the skin without cutting the flesh.

2 Combine the lavender, coriander, fennel, lemon zest and pepper. Rub the duck breast with this mixture. Refrigerate and allow to marinate for at least 2 hours.

3 Sauté the duck breast skin side down over medium heat until the skin is crisp and most of the fat has rendered out, approximately 6–8 minutes. Cook on the other side until medium rare 135–140°F (57–60°C), approximately 3 more minutes.

4 Remove the breasts from the pan and keep warm.

5 Pour out all but 2 tablespoons (30 milliliters) of the fat. Add the onion and cook until it is softened and rich brown. Add the apricots, vermouth and stock. Simmer until reduced by half. Add the vinegar. Season to taste.

6 Slice the duck breast skin side down on the diagonal. Fan the slices on the plates around the Gratin Dauphinoise and garnish with some of the sauce.

Approximate values per 9-oz. (270-g) serving: **Calories** 560, **Total fat** 17 g, **Saturated fat** 7 g, **Cholesterol** 205 mg, **Sodium** 310 mg, **Total carbohydrates** 47 g, **Protein** 48 g, **Vitamin A** 35%, **Vitamin C** 40%, **Iron** 60%

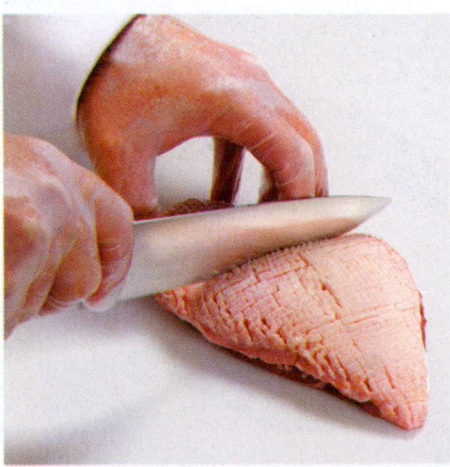

❶ Scoring the duck breast skin on the diagonal.

❷ Turning the duck breast after cooking the skin side.

Duck Confit

YIELD 1 Duck, 4 Servings

Duck, 4 lb. (1.9 kg), cut in 4 pieces	1	1
Kosher salt	2 Tbsp.	30 ml
Black pepper, cracked	1 tsp.	5 ml
Bay leaves, crumbled	4	4
Fresh thyme	6 sprigs	6 sprigs
Garlic cloves, crushed	6	6
Duck or goose fat, melted	2 lb.	960 g
Frisée salad greens	as needed	as needed
Cherry tomatoes	as needed	as needed
Artichoke hearts, cooked	as needed	as needed
Herb Vinaigrette Dressing (page 740)	as needed	as needed
Roasted Fingerling Potatoes (page 686)	as needed	as needed

1 Rub the duck with the salt. Place it skin side down in a roasting pan just large enough to hold the pieces in one layer; season with the pepper, bay leaves, thyme and garlic. Cover and refrigerate overnight.

2 Dry the duck with clean paper towels. Place it, skin side up, in a clean roasting pan, just large enough to hold the pieces in one layer. Bake the duck at 325°F (160°C) until brown, approximately 15–20 minutes. Add enough melted duck or goose fat to cover the pieces completely.

3 Cover the pan and cook in a 300°F (150°C) oven until the duck is very tender, approximately 2 hours.

confit [kohn-FEE] meat or poultry (often lightly salt-cured) slowly cooked and preserved in its own fat and served hot

4 Remove the duck from the fat and place in a deep hotel pan. Ladle enough of the cooking fat over the pieces to cover them completely. Be careful not to add any of the cooking juices.

5 Cover the pan and refrigerate for 2 days to allow the flavors to mellow.

6 To serve, remove the duck from the fat and scrape off the excess fat. Bake at 350°F (180°C) until the skin is crisp and the meat is hot, approximately 30 minutes.

7 Serve the heated duck leg with frisée salad greens, cherry tomatoes and cooked artichoke hearts dressed with Herb Vinaigrette Dressing accompanied by Roasted Fingerling Potatoes, if desired.

Approximate values per ¼-duck serving: **Calories** 670, **Total fat** 16 g, **Saturated fat** 4.5 g, **Cholesterol** 700 mg, **Sodium** 3960 mg, **Total carbohydrates** 6 g, **Protein** 125 g, **Vitamin C** 25%, **Iron** 130%

❶ Seasoning the duck.

❷ Covering the duck with melted fat after it browns.

❸ Removing the duck from the congealed fat and scraping off the excess fat.

Roast Duckling

YIELD 4 Servings, 28 oz. (840 g) each	METHOD Roasting	
Duckling, 5–6 lb. (2.4–2.8 kg)	1	1
Salt and pepper	TT	TT
Duck or chicken stock	8 fl. oz.	240 ml
Orange Gastrique (page 248)	12 fl. oz.	360 ml
White wine vinegar	1 fl. oz.	30 ml
Whole butter	1 tsp.	5 ml
Dried Fruit Compote (page 799)	12 oz.	360 g

1 Prick the duck skin with a fork and season well with salt and pepper.

2 Roast the duck at 400°F (200°C) for 15 minutes. Reduce the heat to 350°F (180°C) and cook until the internal temperature reaches 165°F (74°C) and the meat is tender, approximately 45–60 minutes. Remove the duck from the roasting pan and hold in a warm place.

3 Degrease the roasting pan. Place the pan on the stove top and deglaze with the stock.

4 Add the Orange Gastrique and vinegar. Reduce until the sauce is slightly thickened, approximately 10–15 minutes. Strain the sauce.

5 Monté au beurre.

6 Cut the duck into four pieces. Serve one piece of the duck with a portion of the sauce garnished with Dried Fruit Compote and appropriate garnish.

Approximate values per 28-oz. (840-g) serving: **Calories** 1810, **Total fat** 147 g, **Saturated fat** 54 g, **Cholesterol** 475 mg, **Sodium** 1050 mg, **Total carbohydrates** 30 g, **Protein** 91 g, **Vitamin A** 60%, **Vitamin C** 190%, **Iron** 50%

Turkey Meatloaf

YIELD 1 Meatloaf, 8 Servings, 7 oz. (210 g) each		METHOD Baking	
Onions, small dice		8 oz.	240 g
Celery, small dice		3 oz.	90 g
Olive oil		1 fl. oz.	30 ml
Garlic cloves, minced		3	3
Dried thyme		2 tsp.	10 ml
Dried sage		1 tsp.	5 ml
Salt		1 tsp.	5 ml
Black pepper, freshly ground		½ tsp.	2 ml
Ground turkey		2½ lb.	1.2 kg
Wheat bran		2 oz.	60 g
Ketchup		2 oz.	60 g
Worcestershire sauce		1 Tbsp.	15 ml
Italian parsley, chopped fine		1 Tbsp.	15 ml
Egg whites, beaten		2	2
Mashed butternut squash		as needed	as needed
Fresh Cranberry Orange Relish (page 805)		as needed	as needed
Jus lié or gravy		as needed for garnish	

1 Sauté the onions and celery in oil until translucent but not brown. Add the garlic, herbs, salt and pepper and sauté for 2 minutes. Remove from the pan and cool.

2 Place the turkey in a bowl and add the bran, ketchup, Worcestershire sauce, parsley and egg whites and mix well. Stir in the cooled onion mixture and adjust the seasonings.

3 Spray a 9-inch × 5-inch × 3-inch (22.5-centimeter × 12.5-centimeter × 7.5-centimeter) loaf pan with nonstick cooking spray and fill the pan with the turkey mixture.

4 Bake the loaf at 350°F (180°C) to an internal temperature of 165°F (74°C), approximately 1 hour 20 minutes.

5 Allow the meatloaf to cool in the pan for 15 minutes. Remove from the pan, slice and serve with mashed butternut squash, Fresh Cranberry Orange Relish and jus lié.

Variation:

The turkey meatloaf mixture can be formed into meatballs of the desired size, browned in a sauté pan, finished in the oven and used in place of traditional meatballs in any recipe.

Approximate values per ⅛-loaf serving: **Calories** 290, **Total fat** 16 g, **Saturated fat** 3.5 g, **Cholesterol** 110 mg, **Sodium** 560 mg, **Total carbohydrates** 11 g, **Protein** 27 g, **Vitamin C** 15%, **Iron** 20%

Turkey Scallopine with Capers and Lemon

YIELD 4 Servings, 6 oz. (180 g) each	METHOD Sautéing	
Turkey breast, cut in ⅛-in. (3-mm) scallops, 3 oz. (90 g) each	8	8
Salt and white pepper	TT	TT
Flour	as needed for dredging	
Clarified butter	2 fl. oz.	60 ml
Dry white wine	4 fl. oz.	120 ml
Fresh lemon juice	2 fl. oz.	60 ml
Capers	3 Tbsp.	45 ml
Cooked rice	as needed	as needed
Cooked broccoli, carrots or other vegetables	as needed	as needed

1 Gently pound each turkey slice with a meat mallet. Season with salt and white pepper and dredge in flour.

2 Sauté the turkey in the butter until golden brown. Remove and hold in a warm place.

3 Deglaze the pan with the wine, then add the lemon juice and capers. Return the turkey to the pan to coat with the sauce and reheat.

4 Serve two slices with a portion of the sauce accompanied with cooked rice and vegetables.

Approximate values per 6-oz. (180-g) serving: **Calories** 390, **Total fat** 13 g, **Saturated fat** 8 g, **Cholesterol** 180 mg, **Sodium** 910 mg, **Total carbohydrates** 13 g, **Protein** 56 g, **Vitamin A** 10%

Sautéed Chicken Livers

YIELD 8 Appetizer Servings, 8 oz. (240 g) each	METHOD Sautéing	
Chicken livers, trimmed	1 lb.	480 g
Salt and pepper	TT	TT
Flour	as needed for dredging	
Vegetable oil	2 Tbsp.	30 ml
Shallots, minced	2 Tbsp.	30 ml
Raspberry vinegar	4 fl. oz.	120 ml
Raspberry jam	2 Tbsp.	30 ml
Potato Pancakes (page 688)	8	8
Braised greens	8 oz.	240 g
Red Beet Purée (page 647)	4 fl. oz.	120 ml

1 Rinse the livers and pat dry. Season with salt and pepper and dredge in flour.

2 Sauté the livers in the oil until just barely pink in the center, approximately 3–4 minutes. Remove the livers from the pan and hold in a warm place.

3 In the fat remaining in the pan, sauté the shallots until tender. Deglaze with the vinegar.

4 Add the jam. Simmer until thickened. Return the livers to the pan and toss to coat with the sauce.

5 For each serving, top one hot Potato Pancake with 1 ounce (30 grams) of hot braised greens. Carefully place 2 ounces (60 grams) of livers on top of the greens and spoon a little of the raspberry sauce over each serving. Garnish each plate with the Red Beet Purée.

Approximate values per 8-oz. (240-g) serving: **Calories** 350, **Total fat** 20 g, **Saturated fat** 4 g, **Cholesterol** 260 mg, **Sodium** 210 mg, **Total carbohydrates** 26 g, **Protein** 17 g, **Vitamin A** 140%, **Vitamin C** 45%, **Calcium** 15%, **Iron** 35%

Spiced Ostrich Tenderloin

YIELD 2 Servings, 4 oz. (120 g) each			METHOD Broiling	
Cumin seeds	1 Tbsp.	15 ml		
Fennel seeds	1 Tbsp.	15 ml		
Black peppercorns	2 tsp.	10 ml		
White peppercorns	2 tsp.	10 ml		
Garlic cloves, minced	2	2		
Ostrich tenderloins, 4 oz. (120 g) each	2	2		
Olive oil	1 Tbsp.	15 ml		
Salt	TT	TT		

1 Grind the cumin, fennel and peppercorns together in a spice grinder. Combine the ground spices with the garlic.

2 Brush the tenderloins with the oil, coat with the spice mixture and season lightly with salt.

3 Cook the ostrich under a broiler to an internal temperature of at least 155°F (68°C).

4 Remove from the broiler, allow the meat to rest for 5 minutes then slice against the grain for service.

Approximate values per 4-oz. (120-g) serving: **Calories** 169, **Total fat** 5 g, **Saturated fat** 1 g, **Cholesterol** 91 mg, **Sodium** 106 mg, **Total carbohydrates** 5 g, **Protein** 27 g, **Iron** 46%

Bangkok-Style Deep-Fried Chicken Wings

YIELD	7 Servings, 6 pieces each		METHOD	Deep-Frying

Marinade:		
Fish sauce	4 fl. oz.	120 ml
Granulated sugar	4 fl. oz.	120 ml
Garlic, minced	1 oz.	15 g
Chicken wings, 1st and 2nd joints	3 lb.	1.5 kg
Caramel sauce:		
Granulated sugar	7 oz.	210 g
Water	1 fl. oz.	30 ml
Fish sauce	4 fl. oz.	120 ml
Black pepper	1 tsp.	5 ml
Shallots, minced	1 oz.	30 g
Whole butter	1 Tbsp.	15 ml
Sherry vinegar	1 Tbsp.	15 ml
Thai chile, seeded, minced	3	3
Asian chile sauce	2 tsp.	10 ml
Cornstarch	2 oz.	60 g
All-purpose flour	2 Tbsp.	30 ml
Baking soda	1 tsp.	5 ml
Milk	6 fl. oz.	180 ml
Green onions, sliced	as needed for garnish	
Asian-Style Chile Dipping Sauce,	5 fl. oz.	150 ml
optional, recipe follows		

1 In a nonreactive pan, combine the fish sauce, sugar, garlic and chicken wings. Cover and refrigerate for at least 2 hours or overnight.

2 To make the caramel sauce, combine the sugar and water in a heavy bottomed sauce pan. Cook over medium heat until the sugar caramelizes to a deep golden brown. Immediately whisk in the fish sauce to stop the caramelization process, then whisk in the black pepper, shallots, butter, vinegar, chiles and chile sauce. Set aside or refrigerate until service.

3 In a stainless steel bowl, combine the cornstarch, flour, baking soda and milk. Whisk together to make a light batter.

4 Drain the marinated chicken wings well. Pass them through the batter. Using the basket method, deep-fry the chicken wings at 300°F (148°C) until cooked through and lightly golden brown, approximately 4–5 minutes. Remove from the oil and drain. Hold the cooked chicken wings in a single layer on a baking sheet or hotel pan. Refrigerate until service.

5 For service, deep-fry the chicken wings a second time at 350°F (177°C) until deep golden in color, approximately 5 minutes.

6 If the caramel sauce was refrigerated, warm it gently over low heat or in a microwave. In a stainless steel bowl, toss the cooked chicken wings in the warm caramel sauce. Plate the wings and drizzle with the remaining caramel sauce from the bowl. Garnish with sliced green onions and serve with Asian-Style Chile Dipping Sauce, if desired.

Approximate values per 6-piece serving: **Calories** 550, **Total fat** 31 g, **Saturated fat** 7 g, **Cholesterol** 70 mg, **Sodium** 1970 mg, **Total carbohydrates** 46 g, **Protein** 22 g

gochujang a fermented Korean chile paste made from cooked rice or barley, powdered soybeans, salt and chiles. Its spicy pungent flavor is used to season stews, fried foods, rice dishes and grilled meats.

Asian-Style Chile Dipping Sauce

YIELD 5 fl. oz. (150 ml)

Gochujang or Asian chile sauce	2 fl. oz.	60 ml
Honey	1 Tbsp.	15 ml
Sherry	1 tsp.	5 ml
Soy sauce	1 fl. oz.	30 ml
Sesame oil, toasted	1 tsp.	5 ml
Orange juice	1 fl. oz.	30 ml
Fresh ginger, grated	1 tsp.	5 ml
Cilantro, chopped	1 Tbsp.	15 ml
Green onion, sliced	1 Tbsp.	15 ml

1 Stir ingredients together in a nonreactive bowl. Store in the refrigerator.

Approximate values per ½-fl.-oz. (15-ml) serving: **Calories** 30, **Total fat** 0 g, **Saturated fat** 0 g, **Cholesterol** 0 mg, **Sodium** 330 mg, **Total carbohydrates** 6 g

---

Sautéed Foie Gras on Wild Mushroom Duxelles with Toasted Brioche

Sinplicity Catering, Falls Church, VA
Chef Leland Atkinson

YIELD 4 Servings, 4 oz. (120 g) each		**METHOD** Sautéing	
Fresh foie gras, A grade	1 lb.	480 g	
Wild mushrooms	1 lb.	480 g	
Shallots, chopped	2 Tbsp.	30 ml	
Garlic, chopped	1 tsp.	5 ml	
Whole butter	1 Tbsp.	15 ml	
Tomato paste	1 tsp.	5 ml	
Brandy	1 Tbsp.	15 ml	
Fresh thyme	1 tsp.	5 ml	
Salt and pepper	TT	TT	
Madeira sauce (page 227)	8 fl. oz.	240 ml	
Brioche (page 968)	8 slices	8 slices	

1 Allow the foie gras to come to near room temperature. With a sharp knife, scrape the thin membrane from the outside of the liver. Gently pull the pieces apart and pull out any visible veins. Slice the liver on a slight bias into slices approximately 1 inch (2.5 centimeters) thick. Cover and chill until service.

2 To make the duxelles, clean and chop the mushrooms.

3 Sauté the shallots and garlic in the butter.

4 Add the mushrooms and cook until they first release their moisture and then begin to dry, approximately 5 minutes.

5 Add the tomato paste and brandy and cook until dry, stirring often.

6 Add the thyme and adjust the seasonings with salt and pepper. Remove the duxelles from the heat.

7 Quickly sauté the foie gras in a hot dry pan until it is browned on both sides but still bright pink in the middle, approximately 2 minutes.

8 Portion the duxelles onto four warm serving plates. Ladle the Madeira sauce around the duxelles. Blot the foie gras on a dry towel and arrange it over the top of the duxelles. Serve with toasted brioche.

Approximate values per 4-oz. (120-g) serving: **Calories** 790, **Total fat** 69 g, **Saturated fat** 25 g, **Cholesterol** 535 mg, **Sodium** 1280 mg, **Total carbohydrates** 37 g, **Protein** 22 g, **Vitamin A** 1100%, **Iron** 50%

Game **19**

After studying this chapter, you will be able to:

- identify a variety of game
- purchase game appropriate for your needs
- store game properly
- prepare game for cooking
- explain appropriate cooking methods for different types and cuts of game
- apply cooking methods to game

Game (Fr. *gibier*) are animals hunted for sport or food. Traditionally game supplies depended on the season and the hunter's success. But game's popularity in food service operations has led to farm-raising and animal husbandry techniques. As a result, pheasant, quail, deer, rabbit and other animals, although still considered game, are now farm- or ranch-raised and commercially available throughout the year.

The life of game creatures is reflected in their flesh's appearance, aroma, flavor and texture. Generally game flesh has a dark color and a strong but not unpleasant aroma. It has a robust flavor and less fat than other meats or poultry and is more compact. The flesh becomes quite tough in older animals.

The best cooking methods for game depends on the animal's age and the particular cut of flesh. Younger animals are more tender than older ones. Flesh from the loin or less-used muscles is tender and therefore can be prepared with dry-heat cooking methods. Flesh from much-used muscles, such as the leg and shoulder, is tougher and should be prepared with combination cooking methods. Less-tender cuts can also be used in sausages, pâtés and forcemeats, as discussed in Chapter 28, Charcuterie.

Game appeals to consumers who seek leaner, healthier meats. Only farm-raised game can be used in food service operations. Luckily many popular game items are now farm-raised, government-inspected and readily available. Table 19.1 lists some common cuts of game discussed in this chapter.

FURRED OR GROUND GAME

Furred game includes large animals such as deer, moose, bear, wild boar and elk as well as the small ground game animals such as rabbit, squirrel, raccoon and opossum. Although these animals (and many others) are hunted for sport and food, only a few species are widely available to U.S. food service operations.

Although consuming venison, boar and elk may seem unusual to many Americans, even rarer meats are available to the daring diner. Zebra, bear, wildebeest and other "big game" animals are sometimes available through exotic game purveyors. Most often these meats are grilled, roasted or stewed. Reptiles, particularly rattlesnake and alligator, are now also being raised on farms to meet increased demand. Reptiles are usually braised or sliced and deep-fried. They have a mild flavor with a texture similar to lobster.

Large game animals are rarely sold whole or in primal portions. Instead the meat is marketed precut in subprimals or portions. Therefore the only butchering technique included in this chapter is for rabbit.

Antelope

The blackbuck **antelope**, about half the size of a large deer, is ranch-raised in the United States. Although it has almost no body fat, antelope meat retains a high amount of moisture. The meat is fine-grained, with a flavor that is only slightly stronger than that of deer meat. Antelope should be butchered and cooked in a manner similar to other venison animals.

Bison (American Buffalo)

Once found in huge herds roaming the plains states, **bison** or buffalo were hunted into near-extinction during the 19th century. Buffalo now live on reservations or ranches, where they are raised like beef cattle. Their meat is juicy and flavorful and may be prepared in the same manner as lean beef. **Beefalo** is a cross between a bison and a

Game Flavors

The tart sweetness of fruit such as apricots, blueberries, cranberries, peaches, pears, plums or raspberries balances the assertive flavor of furred game. Spiced fruit compotes, discussed in Chapter 26, Fruits, are a great foil for game preparations. Some acidity in the form of citrus juice or rind, other acidic fruit juices, vinegar or wine tames the flavor of most furred game, whether used in the marinade, sauce or accompaniment.

Buffalo steak

468

domestic beef animal that looks and tastes much like modern beef. Because bison and beefalo have a low fat content, they are lower in cholesterol and calories than beef and poultry. The fine-grained meat cooks in one-third to one-half the time of beef and is best when prepared rare to medium rare.

Deer

The deer family includes elk, moose, reindeer, red-tailed deer, white-tailed deer (Fr. *chevreuil*) and mule deer. Meat from any of these animals is known as **venison** (Fr. *venaisan*). Farm-raised venison, particularly from the Scottish red deer, which is bred in New Zealand and the United States, is commercially available all year. Axis deer, a species originally from India and Nepal, provides some of the finest-quality venison. Like cattle, axis deer graze on grass, so their meat is especially mild and tender. Venison is typically dark red with a mild aroma. It is leaner than other meats, having almost no intramuscular fat or marbling.

The most popular commercial venison cuts are the loin, leg and rack. The loin is tender enough to roast, sauté or grill to medium rare. It is often barded with bacon before roasting. It can be left attached along the backbone to form a cut known as the **saddle**. The leg is often marinated in red wine and prepared with combination cooking methods. Other cuts can also be stewed or braised or used in sausages and pâtés. Butchering procedures for venison are similar to those for lamb, discussed in Chapter 16.

venison flesh from any member of the deer family, including antelope, elk, moose, reindeer, red-tailed deer, white-tailed deer, mule deer and axis deer

Venison saddle

Rabbit

Rabbits (Fr. *lapin*) are small burrowing animals with mild, lean and relatively tender flesh that have long been raised for food. The flavor and texture of rabbit are similar to chicken. Ranch-raised rabbit is available all year, either whole (full carcass) or cut, fresh or frozen. The average weight of a whole dressed rabbit is 2 pounds 8 ounces to 3 pounds (1.2 to 1.4 kilograms). **Hare** (Fr. *lièvre*) are a species of larger rabbits weighing up to 14 pounds with lean, dark and strongly flavored meat. Although hare have not been domesticated, they are available from importers of wild game. Young rabbit can be roasted, pan-fried, stewed or braised and is popular in rustic "country-style" dishes, especially casseroles and pâtés. Hare are usually marinated with vinegar or wine before stewing with aromatics and spices. Squirrel and other small ground game animals are not available for food service use in the United States, but they can be fabricated in the same manner as rabbit.

USING FURRED AND GROUND GAME			TABLE 19.1
ANIMAL	COMMONLY PURCHASED CUTS	COOKING METHODS	SUGGESTED USE
Antelope	Purchased and prepared in the same manner as deer		
Bison	Purchased and prepared in the same manner as lean beef		
Deer	Loin	Dry-heat (roast; sauté; grill)	Sautéed medallions; whole roast loin; grilled steaks
	Leg	Combination (braise; stew)	Marinate and braise; pot roast with cranberries; chili; sausage; forcemeat
	Rack	Dry-heat (roast; grill)	Grilled chops
Rabbit	Full carcass	Dry-heat (sauté; pan-fry; roast; grill)	Pan-fried
		Combination (braise; stew)	Braised
Wild boar	Loin, saddle	Dry-heat (roast)	Roast loin
	Chops	Combination (braise)	Marinate and braise; stew with red wine and sour cream; sausage; forcemeat
	Ribs	Dry-heat and smoking	Barbecue ribs

Procedure for Butchering a Rabbit

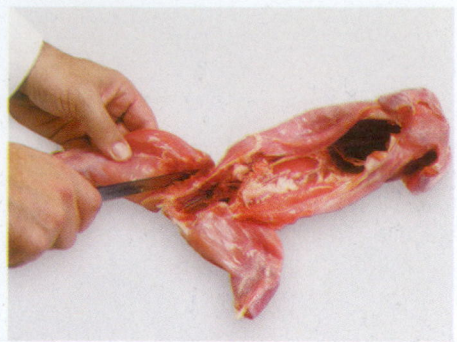

1 Place the rabbit on its back. Remove the hind legs by cutting close to the backbone and through the joint on each side. Each thigh and leg can be separated by cutting through the joint.

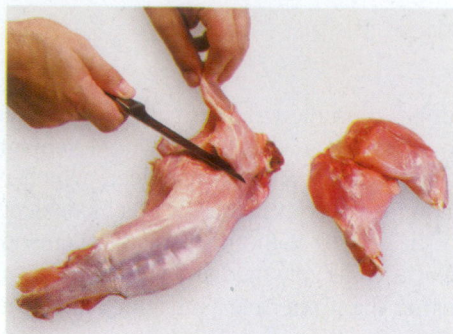

2 Remove the forelegs by cutting beneath the shoulder blades.

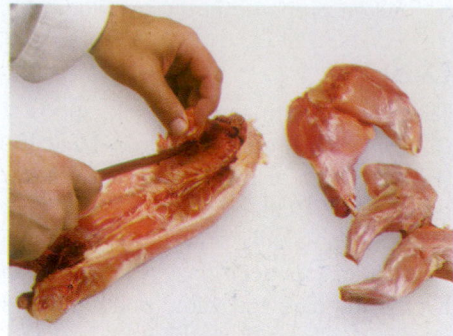

3 Cut through the breast bone and spread open the rib cage. Using a boning knife, separate the flesh from the rib bones and remove the bones.

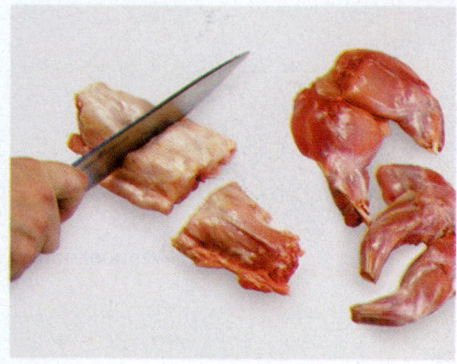

4 Cut through the backbone to divide the loin into the desired number of pieces.

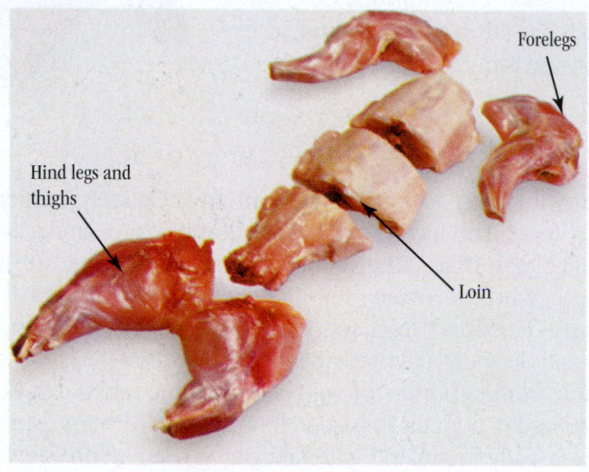

The butchered rabbit: hind legs, thighs, loin in three pieces, forelegs.

Wild boar loin saddle

upland birds bird species that do not swim and do not need to live near water (rivers, marshes, lakes) in order to breed and raise chicks (e.g., pheasant, quail, dove, grouse)

waterfowl bird species that swim; waterfowl breed and raise chicks near or on bodies of water, including marshes, lakes and rivers (e.g., duck, swans, geese)

Wild Boar

A close relative of the domesticated hog, **wild boar** (Fr. *sanglier*) is leaner, with a dark red color and a stronger flavor. Wild boars are plentiful throughout Europe and parts of North Africa, Asia and the Americas, where they are considered an invasive species. A good supply of farm- or ranch-raised wild boar is available from specialty purveyors for food service use in the United States.

Tender baby boar (under 6 months old) is considered a delicacy, but mature animals (1–2 years old) have the best flavor. Wild boar meat is most often roasted and may be used in sausages or terrines. The bones in a **boar loin saddle** protect the lean meat from drying out during roasting. Boar can often be substituted in recipes for venison or pork but in this case larding may be helpful because wild boar meat contains less marbling than domestic pork.

FEATHERED OR WINGED GAME

Feathered game includes **upland birds**, such as wild turkeys, pheasants, quails, doves and woodcocks; songbirds, such as larks; and **waterfowl**, such as wild geese and ducks. Wild birds cannot be sold for food service use in the United States. These birds are farm-raised to meet consumer demand, however.

Game birds are available whole or precut into pieces, fresh or frozen. Butchering techniques are not shown in this chapter, as they are the same as those for domesticated poultry, discussed in Chapter 18. Because game birds tend to have less fat than other poultry, they are often barded with fat and cooked to medium rare. If cooked well done, game birds become dry and stringy.

Partridge

Two types of game partridges, the **Hungarian** or **gray partridge** and the **chukar partridge** (Fr. *perdrix*), were introduced into the United States and Canada from Europe during the 19th century. Now found principally in the prairie and western mountain states, partridges are widely raised on game preserves and farms, producing a good commercial supply. The flavor of both breeds of partridge is less delicate than that of pheasant, and the meat tends to be tougher. During the autumn hunting season, wild red legged partridge are imported from Europe for use in food service and domestic kitchens. They have a richer flavor than the farmed breeds. Partridge may be roasted or cut into pieces and sautéed or braised. Each bird weighs about 1 pound (450 grams) dressed.

Chukar partridge

Pheasant

The most popular of game birds, the **pheasant** (Fr. *faisan*) was introduced into Europe from Asia during the Middle Ages. The mild flavor of pheasant makes it excellent for roasting, stewing or braising. The hen is smaller and more tender than the cock. Both have less flesh than a chicken of comparable weight. Stock made from the carcass is often used for consommé or sauce. Farm-raised birds are available fresh or frozen. A dressed bird weighs about 1 pound 8 ounces to 2 pounds 4 ounces (680 grams to 1 kilogram) and serves two people.

Pheasant

Quail

The **quail** (Fr. *caille*) is a migratory game bird related to the pheasant. The more popular European and Californian species are farm-raised and available all year.

Quail are very small, with only about 1–2 ounces (30–60 grams) of breast meat each. Quail may be grilled (especially on skewers), roasted, broiled or sautéed and are often boned and served whole with a stuffing of forcemeat or rice. Because they are so lean, roasted quail benefit from barding.

Quail

NUTRITION INFORMATION FOR GAME

Although they are more protected and managed than wild game, ranch-raised game animals live in the wild and are generally active and must forage for food. This lifestyle produces animals whose meat has less fat than that of domesticated livestock. The meat of large game animals is also lower in cholesterol, especially saturated fats, and has approximately one-third fewer calories than beef. Game is also generally high in good-quality protein and minerals such as iron and zinc.

PURCHASING AND STORING GAME

The USDA and most states restrict the sale of wild game. As noted earlier in the chapter, only farm-raised game can be served in food service operations. Truly wild game can be served only by those who hunt and share their kill without charge.

Unlike meat and poultry from domesticated animals, game is not graded for quality. Farm- or ranch-raised game is subject only to voluntary inspections for wholesomeness. Generally, however, game is processed under the same federal inspection requirements as domesticated meats and poultry. State regulations vary and are constantly being expanded and improved in response to consumer demands.

Game may be imported from other countries. Only USDA-approved countries are permitted to export game to the United States. On arrival in this country, game shipments are subject to USDA spot inspections. Game birds and furred game meats are available fresh or frozen. Use the same criteria to determine the freshness of game as you would any other meat or poultry: The flesh should be firm, without slime or an off-odor. Commercially available game is generally fully aged and ready to use when sold. It does not need, nor will it benefit from, additional aging.

As with any fresh or frozen meat, game should be well wrapped and stored under refrigeration at temperatures below 41°F (5°C). Because the flesh is generally dry and lean, frozen game should be used within 4 months. Thaw frozen game slowly under refrigeration to prevent moisture loss.

MARINATING FURRED GAME

Traditionally game, particularly furred game, is marinated in strong mixtures of red wine, herbs and spices. Commercially-raised game does not have to be marinated. Modern animal husbandry techniques used at game ranches assure that the meat is from young, tender animals. Farm-raised game animals also have a naturally milder flavor than their truly wild cousins.

The following Red Wine Marinade is suitable for most game, such as antelope, elk, rabbit, deer or wild boar. After the meat is removed, the marinade may be added to the cooking liquid or reduced and used in a sauce. Do not serve uncooked marinade.

♥ Good Choice

MISE EN PLACE

- Peel and finely chop carrot and onion.
- Peel and mince garlic.

Red Wine Marinade

YIELD   1½ qt. (1.4 lt)

Carrot, chopped fine	2 oz.	60 g
Onion, chopped fine	2 oz.	60 g
Garlic, minced	1 Tbsp.	15 ml
Dried thyme	1 tsp.	5 ml
Bay leaves	2	2
Juniper berries, whole	2 tsp.	10 ml
Peppercorns, whole	1 Tbsp.	15 ml
Sage, ground	½ tsp.	2 ml
Red wine	1 qt.	960 ml
Red wine vinegar	4 fl. oz.	120 ml

1 Combine all ingredients.

2 Place the meat in the marinade. Marinate under refrigeration for the desired time. Tender, farm-raised game may need only 30 minutes; older, wild animals may need 1–2 days.

Approximate values per fluid ounce (30 ml): **Calories** 5, **Total fat** 0 g, **Saturated fat** 0 g, **Cholesterol** 0 mg, **Sodium** 0 mg, **Total carbohydrates** 1 g, **Protein** 0 g, **Vitamin A** 6%, **Claims**—fat free; no saturated fat; no cholesterol; no sodium; low calorie

Creepy Crawley Cuisine

Entomophagy, the consumption of insects as food, has been practiced for millennia, especially in Asia, South and Central America and Africa. From Ancient Greece to modern-day Mexico, various bugs, larvae and worms have been regularly consumed, sometimes raw, other times fried, steamed, boiled or baked. The practice has never been as popular in western Europe or North America, primarily because of the "ick" factor associated with eating a whole creature--head, eyes, legs and all. Nevertheless a 2013 report from the United Nations Food and Agriculture Organization (FAO) notes that some 2 billion people around the world regularly engage in entomophagy and at least 1900 species of insects are edible by humans.

According to the FAO and entomophagy proponents, insects are high in protein, minerals and fiber, yet low in fat and calories. They do not emit greenhouse gases and are easily farmed in small spaces. Insects are also good recyclers, living on animal manure and food waste, without consuming additional water. In addition, ground or powdered insect meal or worm meal can be used to feed livestock, lowering the cost of beef, lamb or chicken, while simultaneously making more land available for cultivating food crops.

As many diners also know, some bugs taste great. Grasshoppers, the most widely consumed insects, have a neutral flavor that blends well

Fried crickets

with sauces and seasonings. They are often fried (Sp. *chapulines*) as a crunchy snack or added to tacos. Waxworms taste like bacon and beetle larvae have a flavor similar to shrimp. Other insects can only be described as tasting like nothing else you've ever tasted, yet good. Cricket meal is already used to add protein and a nutty crunch to chips and protein bars marketed in the Unites States.

One chef leading the research into insect cuisine is René Redzepi, famous for his restaurant, Noma. His non-profit culinary research institute, the Nordic Food Lab in Copenhagen seeks to help people eat well by employing a wider variety of under-used ingredients. The lab intends to expand food choice and encourage people to embrace all the edible resources in their environment. The researchers know that eating bugs will not be a

cure-all for meeting global food needs, but it is one way to diversify our sources of nutrition.

The environmental benefits derived from insect cuisine may be moot if they are farmed in large industrial operations and fed traditional grains, however. And according to a 2015 study published by the University of California, Davis, the protein conversion rate for crickets varies widely depending on what they are fed. Insects that are fed high-quality grains grow the best and produced the most usable protein. Crickets fed solely on organic waste and by-products show very little potential to supplement the global need for dietary protein. In other words, for crickets (and presumably other bugs) to convert the protein they ingest into protein that humans can ingest, they must be fed a diet very similar to that given commercially raised chickens, creating an increased need for feed grains.

Even producing insect meal as food for livestock will not completely replace current agricultural stock feeding methods. While insect farms can be smaller in size than animal farms, they require more energy than it takes to produce the fish and soy meal currently used in livestock feed. Current European Union (EU) policies ban using waste products to feed "farmed animals," including insects. The EU also bans feeding livestock "processed animal proteins" such as insect meal. So, for now at least, these potential uses are off limits in Europe.

QUESTIONS FOR DISCUSSION

1 Explain the differences between truly wild game and ranch-raised game.

2 Describe the differences between wild boar and domestic pork. What technique is recommended when roasting wild boar?

3 Which cuts of furred game are best suited to dry-heat cooking methods? Which are best for combination cooking methods?

4 Can game birds be purchased whole? How are they fabricated?

5 Which degree of doneness is the best option for game birds? Explain your answer.

6 Which preservation and storage techniques should be used for furred game? Which for feathered game? Does the lean nature of game affect how it should be stored?

Additional Game Recipes

Grilled Rosemary Quail

YIELD 2 Servings, 2 quail each	METHOD	Grilling
Orange rind, cut into ½-in. (1.2-cm) strips	6	6
Olive oil	1 fl. oz.	30 ml
Garlic, chopped	1 tsp.	5 ml
Fresh rosemary, minced	1 Tbsp.	15 ml
Salt and pepper	TT	TT
Quail, whole, boned	4	4
Fresh figs, quartered or sliced	4	4
Sugar	2 tsp.	10 ml
Vegetable oil	1 Tbsp.	15 ml
Fennel Gratin (page 638)	as needed for garnish	
Orange Gastrique (page 248)	6 fl. oz.	180 ml

1 In a bowl large enough to hold the quail, combine the orange rind, olive oil, garlic, rosemary, salt and pepper. Marinate the quail in the mixture for 3–8 hours under refrigeration.

2 Bring the quail to room temperature.

3 Place the quail on a preheated grill, breast side down. Grill the quail, turning once, for approximately 5 minutes per side. If necessary, finish in the oven until the quail reach an internal temperature of 165°F (74°C).

4 While the quail cooks, toss the quartered figs with the sugar and oil. Bake the figs at 450°F (230°C) until tender and lightly browned, approximately 8–10 minutes.

5 Serve two quail on each plate with the Fennel Gratin. Nap the plates with the Orange Gastrique and garnish with the warm figs.

Approximate values per 10-oz. (300-g) serving: **Calories** 910, **Total fat** 39 g, **Saturated fat** 10 g, **Cholesterol** 170 mg, **Sodium** 830 mg, **Total carbohydrates** 91 g, **Protein** 51 g, **Vitamin A** 15%, **Vitamin C** 80%, **Iron** 60%

Venison Medallions Grand Veneur

YIELD 2 Servings, 6 oz. (180 g)	METHOD	Sautéing
Venison medallions, 3 oz. (90 g) each	4	4
Salt and pepper	TT	TT
Clarified butter	1 fl. oz.	30 ml
White wine	1 fl. oz.	30 ml
Poivrade sauce (page 227)	6 fl. oz.	180 ml
Red currant jelly	2 tsp.	10 ml
Heavy cream	1 fl. oz.	30 ml
Roasted carrots, potatoes and baby zucchini	as needed for garnish	
Fried gaufrette potatoes (page 106)	as needed for garnish	

1 Season the medallions with salt and pepper and sauté in the butter to the desired doneness. Remove and reserve.

2 Degrease the pan and deglaze with the wine.

3 Add the Poivrade sauce and bring to a simmer. Stir in the jelly, add the cream and adjust the seasonings.

4 Return the medallions to the sauce to reheat. Serve two medallions per person with a portion of the sauce. Garnish with the roasted vegetables served with fried gaufrette potatoes.

Approximate values per 6-oz. (180-g) serving: **Calories** 410, **Total fat** 21 g, **Saturated fat** 12 g, **Cholesterol** 195 mg, **Sodium** 1250 mg, **Total carbohydrates** 15 g, **Protein** 39 g, **Vitamin A** 15%

Braised Rabbit with Orecchiette Pasta

YIELD 4 Servings, 12 oz. (360 g) each	METHOD	Braising
Rabbit, 3 lb. (1.4 kg), cut into quarters	1	1
Salt and pepper	TT	TT
Olive oil	2 fl. oz.	60 ml
Carrot, small dice	2½ oz.	75 g
Celery, small dice	2½ oz.	75 g
Onion, small dice	5 oz.	180 g
Garlic, minced	1 Tbsp.	15 ml
Tomato paste	1 oz.	30 g
Fresh oregano, minced	½ tsp.	2 ml
Fresh sage, minced	½ tsp.	2 ml
Rabbit or chicken stock	1 qt.	960 ml
Pasta:		
Olive oil	1 Tbsp.	15 ml
Shallots, minced	1 Tbsp.	15 ml
Garlic, minced	1½ tsp.	7 ml
Fresh thyme leaves	½ tsp.	2 ml
Pea shoots or spinach	¾ oz.	4 ml
Lemon zest, grated	1 Tbsp.	15 ml
Orecchiette, cooked, hot	1 lb.	480 g
White wine	2 fl. oz.	60 ml
Lemon juice	1 Tbsp.	15 ml
Heavy cream	2 fl. oz.	60 ml
Butter	1 Tbsp.	15 ml

1 Season the rabbit pieces with salt and pepper.

2 In a large heavy sautoir, heat the oil and quickly brown the rabbit in several batches if necessary. Remove and reserve.

3 Add the carrot, celery and onion to the pan. Sauté until very lightly browned.

4 Return the rabbit to the pan and add the garlic, tomato paste, oregano, sage and stock. Cover and simmer until the rabbit is tender and begins to pull away from the bones, approximately 45–50 minutes.

5 Remove the rabbit and keep warm.

6 Bring the sauce to a boil and cook over high heat to reduce and thicken slightly, approximately 8–10 minutes. Purée the sauce with an immersion blender. Keep warm.

7 To prepare the pasta, sweat the shallots, garlic and thyme in the olive oil. Add the pea shoots, lemon zest, orecchiette, white wine and lemon juice. Sauté until most of the liquid is absorbed. Monté with the cream and butter. Adjust the seasonings to taste.

8 Place the pasta and sauce in warm serving bowls with one rabbit quarter on each serving.

Approximate values per 12-oz. (360-g) serving: **Calories** 850, **Total fat** 42 g, **Saturated fat** 12 g, **Cholesterol** 160 mg, **Sodium** 440 mg, **Total carbohydrates** 54 g, **Protein** 59 g, **Vitamin A** 70%, **Vitamin C** 20%, **Iron** 35%

Braised Rabbit with Chorizo

Chef Jim Fitzgerald, PhD

YIELD	4 Servings, 11 oz. (330 g) each	METHOD	Braising
Rabbit, 2–3 lb. (1–1.4 kg)		1	1
Salt and pepper		TT	TT
Oil or clarified butter		8 fl. oz.	240 ml
Yellow onion, medium dice		1	1
Garlic clove, minced		1	1
Celery stalks, medium dice		2	2
Carrot, grated		1 oz.	30 g
Cloves, ground		⅛ tsp.	1 ml
Cayenne pepper		⅛ tsp.	1 ml
Port wine		4 fl. oz.	120 ml
Chorizo sausages, sliced		4 oz.	120 g
Unsweetened chocolate, chopped		1 oz.	30 g
All-purpose flour		2 oz.	60 g
Veal or chicken stock		2 pt.	960 ml

1 Cut the rabbit into seven pieces and season with salt and pepper. In a rondeau, brown the rabbit in the oil or butter. Remove from the pan and reserve.

2 In the same pan, brown the onion and then add the garlic and cook for 1 minute. Add the celery, carrot, cloves and cayenne pepper and cook for 2 more minutes.

3 Deglaze the pan with the wine and reduce au sec. Add the chorizo and chocolate, stirring well to prevent the chocolate from scorching.

4 Sprinkle the flour into the pan and cook to make a roux.

5 Whisk in 1 pint (480 milliliters) stock and cook until it thickens.

6 Add the remaining stock and the rabbit and bring to a simmer. Cover and place in a 325°F (160°C) oven and braise, basting the rabbit pieces with the braising liquid as needed, until fork tender, approximately 45 minutes. Adjust the seasonings to taste with salt and pepper.

Approximate values per 11-oz. (330-g) serving: **Calories** 610, **Total fat** 46 g, **Saturated fat** 9 g, **Cholesterol** 85 mg, **Sodium** 560 mg, **Total carbohydrates** 14 g, **Protein** 31 g, **Vitamin A** 25%, **Iron** 15%

Roast Pheasant with Cognac and Apples

YIELD 1 Pheasant, 2 Servings	**METHOD** Roasting	
Pheasant	1	1
Salt and pepper	TT	TT
Fatback	as needed	as needed
Mirepoix	12 oz.	360 g
Tart apples	2	2
Whole butter	1 oz.	30 g
Cognac	3 fl. oz.	90 ml
Crème fraîche	4 fl. oz.	120 ml

1 Season the pheasant with salt and pepper. Bard the body with the fatback.

2 Roast on a bed of mirepoix at 350°F (180°C) until done, approximately 1½ hours.

3 Peel and core each apple and slice into eight pieces. Sauté the apples in the butter just until tender.

4 When the pheasant is done, remove it from the pan and reserve in a warm place. Deglaze the pan with the cognac, add the crème fraîche and bring to a simmer. Strain the sauce and adjust the seasonings.

5 Serve one half pheasant per person, accompanied by the sliced apples and sauce.

Approximate values per ½-pheasant serving: **Calories** 630, **Total fat** 40 g, **Saturated fat** 23 g, **Cholesterol** 220 mg, **Sodium** 1360 mg, **Total carbohydrates** 21 g, **Protein** 46 g, **Vitamin A** 45%

Venison and Black Bean Chili

YIELD 4 qt. (4 lt)		METHOD Braising
Dried black beans	1 lb.	450 g
Water	2 qt.	2 lt
Venison round, trimmed, medium dice	3 lb.	1.3 kg
Peanut oil	3 fl. oz.	90 ml
Garlic cloves, minced	6	6
Onions, small dice	1 lb. 8 oz.	680 g
Jalapeño peppers, seeded and chopped fine	3	3
Masa harina (corn flour)	2 oz.	60 g
Chilli powder	1 oz.	30 g
Cayenne pepper	1 tsp.	5 ml
Cumin, ground	3 Tbsp.	45 ml
Peeled tomatoes, canned	1 lb. 8 oz.	680 g
Beef or veal stock	1 qt.	1 lt
Salt and pepper	TT	TT
Tabasco sauce	TT	TT
Monterey Jack or cheddar cheese, grated	as needed for garnish	
Green onion, chopped	as needed for garnish	
Cilantro, chopped	as needed for garnish	

1 Soak the beans in water overnight. Drain and simmer in 2 quarts (2 liters) of water until tender, approximately 30–40 minutes.

2 Sauté the venison in the oil until browned. Remove the venison from the pan and set aside. Add the garlic, onions and jalapeños and sauté until tender. Add the masa harina, chilli powder, cayenne and cumin. Cook for 5 minutes.

3 Add the tomatoes, stock and reserved venison. Cover and braise on the stove top or in a 325°F (160°C) oven for 30–40 minutes.

4 Drain the beans if necessary. Add them to the venison and cook for an additional 15 minutes. Season to taste with salt, pepper and Tabasco sauce. Thin with additional stock if necessary. Serve with grated Monterey Jack or cheddar cheese, chopped green onions and cilantro.

Approximate values per 8-fl.-oz. (240-ml) serving: **Calories** 320, **Total fat** 9 g, **Saturated fat** 2 g, **Cholesterol** 70 mg, **Sodium** 510 mg, **Total carbohydrates** 31 g, **Protein** 28 g, **Vitamin A** 15%, **Iron** 30%

Fish and Shellfish 20

species a group of organisms that share common characteristics and are capable of breeding

shellfish aquatic invertebrates with shells or carapaces

Fish are aquatic vertebrates with fins for swimming and gills for breathing. Of the more than 30,000 **species** of fish known, most live in the seas and oceans; freshwater species are far less numerous. **Shellfish** are aquatic invertebrates with shells or carapaces. They are found in both fresh and salt water.

Always an important food source, fish and shellfish have become increasingly popular in recent years, due in part to demand from health-conscious consumers. Because of increased demand and improved preservation and transportation techniques, good-quality fish and shellfish, once found only along seacoasts and lakes, are now readily available to almost every food service operation.

Many fish and shellfish species are very expensive; all are highly perishable. Because fish and shellfish cooking times are generally shorter and their flavors more delicate than meat or poultry, special attention must be given to prevent spoilage and to produce high-quality finished products.

In this chapter, you will learn how to identify a large assortment of fish and shellfish as well as how to properly purchase and store them, fabricate or prepare them for cooking and cook them by a variety of dry-heat and moist-heat cooking methods. This chapter presents many of the cooking methods applied to meats and poultry in the previous chapters. Review the corresponding procedures for meats and poultry, and note the similarities and differences.

STRUCTURE AND MUSCLE COMPOSITION OF FISH AND SHELLFISH

The fish and shellfish used in food service operations can be divided into three categories: fish, mollusks and crustaceans.

Fish (Fr. *poisson*) include both fresh- and saltwater varieties. Fish have fins and an internal skeleton of bone and cartilage. Based on shape and skeletal structure, they can be divided into two groups: round fish and flatfish. **Round fish** swim in a vertical position and have eyes on both sides of their heads. See Figure 20.1. Their bodies may be truly round, oval or compressed. **Flatfish** have asymmetrical, compressed bodies, swim in a horizontal position and have both eyes on top of their heads. See Figure 20.2. Flatfish are bottom dwellers and begin life in coastal saltwater areas. They move to deeper water as adults, which is where most commercial fishing occurs. The skin on top of their bodies is dark, to camouflage flatfish from predators, and can sometimes change color according to their surroundings. Flatfish have small scales and their dorsal and anal fins run the length of their bodies. **Mollusks** (Fr. *mollusque*) are shellfish characterized by soft, unsegmented bodies with no internal skeleton. Most mollusks have hard outer shells. Single-shelled mollusks, such as abalone, are known as **univalves**. Those with two shells, such as clams, oysters and mussels, are known as **bivalves**. Unlike mollusks, squid and octopus, which are known as **cephalopods**, do not have a hard outer shell. Rather cephalopods have a single thin internal shell called a *pen* or *cuttlebone*.

Crustaceans (Fr. *crustacés*) are also shellfish. They have hard outer skeletons or shells and jointed appendages. Crustaceans include lobsters, crabs and shrimp.

The flesh of fish and shellfish consists primarily of water, protein, fat and minerals. Fish flesh is composed of short muscle fibers, pleated in shape and separated by delicate sheets of connective tissue. See Figure 20.3. Unlike the connective tissue in meat, the connective tissue in fish is weak and does not require long cooking to break it down. Fish, as well as most shellfish, are naturally tender, so the purpose of cooking is to firm proteins and enhance flavor. The absence of the oxygen-carrying protein myoglobin makes fish flesh very light or white in color. (The orange color of salmon and some trout comes from pigments found in their food.)

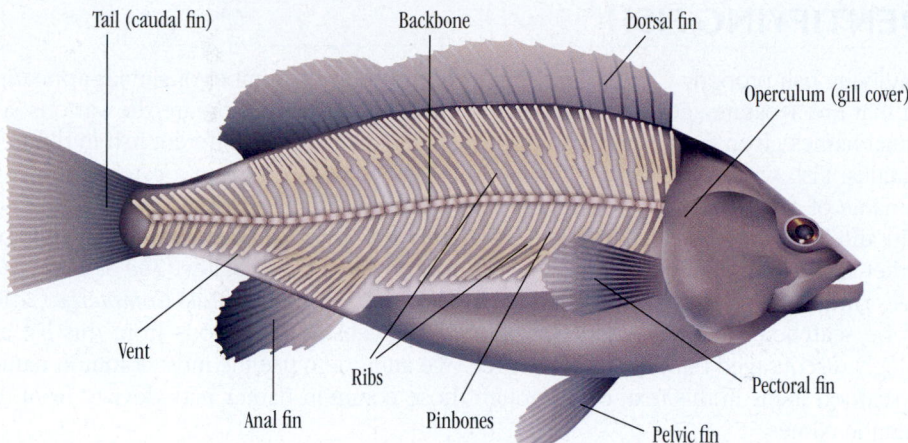

Figure 20.1 Bone structure of a round fish.

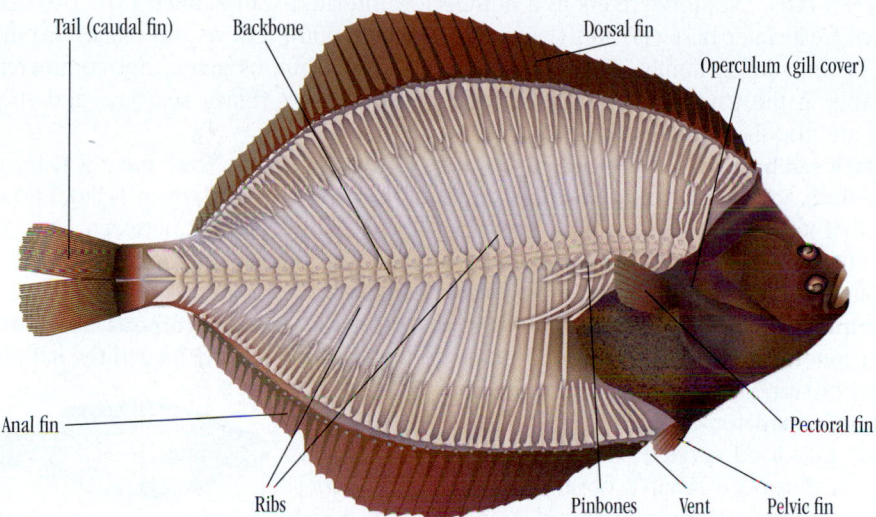

Figure 20.2 Bone structure of a flatfish.

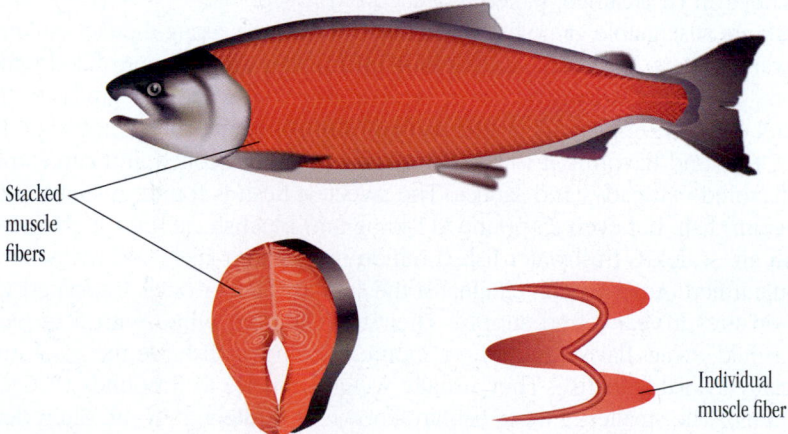

Figure 20.3 Muscle fibers in a round fish.

Compared to meats, fish do not contain large amounts of intermuscular fat. But the amount of fat a fish does contain affects the way it responds to cooking. Fish containing a relatively large amount of fat, such as salmon and mackerel, are known as fatty or oily fish. Fish containing very little fat, such as cod and haddock, are referred to as lean fish. Shellfish are also very lean.

IDENTIFYING FISH

Identifying fish properly can be difficult because of the vast number of similar-appearing fish that are separate species within each family. Adding confusion are the various colloquial names given to the same fish or the same name used for different fish in different localities. Fish with an unappealing name may also have been given a catchier name or the name of a similar but more popular item for marketing purposes.

In an effort to avoid confusion and fraud, the U.S. FDA maintains a list of acceptable market names for many fish and shellfish sold in the United States. *The Seafood List: FDA's Guide to Acceptable Market Names for Seafood Sold in Interstate Commerce* (2016) can be searched or downloaded from the FDA's website. Deviations from this list are strongly discouraged but difficult to enforce. We attempt to use the most common names for seafood items in this text, even though those common names may deviate from the scientific names.

Round Fish

Bass (Fr. *bar*) commonly refers to a number of unrelated spiny-finned fish. The better-known freshwater bass varieties (largemouth, smallmouth, redeye and black) are members of the sunfish family. They are lean and delicate but, as game, not commercially available in the United States. The saltwater bass varieties (black sea bass and striped bass) are popular commercial items.

Black sea bass are sometimes referred to as rock sea bass. They have a lean, firm white flesh with a mild flavor and flaky texture. They usually weigh from 1½ to 3 pounds (720 to 1360 grams) and are most prevalent in the Atlantic Ocean between New York and North Carolina. Black sea bass can be prepared by almost any cooking method and are often served whole in Chinese and Italian cuisines.

Striped bass, often erroneously referred to as rockfish, are **anadromous**. True striped bass cannot be marketed because pollution and overfishing have damaged the supply. A hybrid of striped bass and either white bass or white perch is **aquafarmed** for commercial use, however. It is this hybrid that food service operations receive as striped bass. (A European relative of striped bass called *branzino* in Italian and *loup de mer* in French is also widely available to chefs in the United States.) Whole fish weigh from 1 to 5 pounds (450 grams to 2.2 kilograms). Striped bass have a rich, sweet flavor and firm texture. They can be steamed, baked, poached or broiled.

Bluefish are sustainable game fish that migrate in schools along the U.S. Atlantic coast seeking warm waters. They have a long blue-green body and a mouth filled with razor-sharp teeth. Their fatty flesh is brown or blueish grey when raw and similar to the flesh of mackerel. It can be unpleasant tasting and oily if not extremely fresh, however. Because bluefish is firm and flavorful, it is good smoked, grilled or broiled and can stand up to strongly-flavored marinades and sauces. The sweetest flesh is found in small 2–4-pound (1–2-kilogram) fish, but even 25-pound (11-kilogram) bluefish can be caught in season.

Catfish are scaleless freshwater fish common in southern lakes and rivers and extensively aquafarmed. Aquafarming eliminates the "muddy" flavor once associated with catfish and ensures a year-round supply. Their flesh is pure white with a moderate fat content; a mild, sweet flavor; and a firm texture. Channel catfish are the most important commercially available catfish. They usually weigh from 1½ to 5 pounds (720 grams to 2.2 kilograms). The smaller of these fish are known as **fiddlers**; they are often deep-fried and served whole. Catfish may be prepared by almost any cooking method but are especially well suited to frying. Note that other species are often imported to the United States under the generic name *catfish*. Only products labeled "U.S. Farm-Raised Catfish" provide the consistent high quality and flavor that consumers have come to expect, however.

The **cod** (Fr. *cabillaud*) family includes Atlantic and Pacific cod as well as pollock, haddock, whiting and hake. Cod have a mild, delicate flavor and lean, firm white flesh that flakes apart easily. Cod can be prepared by most cooking methods, although grilling is not recommended because the flesh is too flaky.

Black sea bass

anadromous describes a fish that migrates from a saltwater habitat to spawn in fresh water

aquaculture, also known as **aquafarming** the business, science and practice of raising large quantities of fish and shellfish in tanks, ponds or ocean pens

Bluefish

Catfish

Striped bass

Sustainable Seafood

In the past 50 years, the supply of seafood has declined precipitously due to damaged habitat, overfishing, specific fishing practices and increased demand. Certain fish, especially slow-growing species, face extinction. There are choices, however, that may help ensure future supplies, including sourcing farmed fish, preparing specific types of fish or catching fish in certain ways.

Sustainable fish farming operations protect the habitat and the spread of disease. Regulations and management practices vary widely, affecting the sustainability of different aquaculture farms. More than 55% of the shrimp sold is farmed, yet there are few places where the farming practices are considered sustainable. Gulf Coast and West Coast wild shrimp are among the better choices

when looking for sustainably harvested products, for example.

Before writing a menu, chefs should learn about the species they use. Bluefin tuna, shark, orange roughy and freshwater eel (unagi) are among the fish species to avoid. Bluefin tuna and orange roughy are seriously overfished, threatening these species' ability to restore their numbers. The fishing methods used to catch bluefin tuna result in excessive by-catch of other species, including endangered sea turtles, sharks and sea birds. Orange roughy are caught using bottom trawling, which destroys coral and the seabed. Freshwater eels, although raised in farms, put pressure on the wild fish population because juvenile eels are taken from the wild to stock the farms.

Suggestions to consider when purchasing seafood include:

- Work with suppliers committed to sustainable practices. Ask suppliers where seafood is from, how it is caught and/or farmed.
- Find species of fish that replicate the texture of an endangered fish such as shark.
- Serve lesser-known species of fish, which may offer a new flavor profile to your customer.
- Learn about sustainable species and production methods for fish and shellfish. Consult the websites of organizations such as The Safina Center, the Chefs Collaborative, the National Oceanic and Atmospheric Administration's FishWatch and the Monterey Bay Aquarium Seafood Watch Program to inform your seafood purchasing decisions.

Atlantic cod are available fresh or frozen, whole or **drawn** or cut into fillets or steaks. Smoked cod and dried salt cod (Sp. *bacalao*) are also available. Most of the cod marketed today comes from the North Atlantic, especially Iceland, as U.S. and Canadian cod has been overfished, almost to the point of extinction. Although individual cod may reach 200 pounds (90 kilograms), most market cod weigh 10 pounds (4.4 kilograms) or less. **Scrod** is a marketing term for cod or haddock that weighs less than 2½ pounds (1.1 kilograms) or measures less than 20 inches (50 centimeters) in length.

Haddock look like thin, small Atlantic cod and weigh about 2–5 pounds (900 grams to 2.3 kilograms). They have a stronger flavor and more delicate texture than Atlantic cod.

Pacific cod, also known as gray cod, are found in the northern Pacific Ocean. Weighing from 5 to 10 pounds (2.3 to 4.6 kilograms) on average, they are most often available frozen. Pacific cod should be distinguished from rock cod and black cod, which are unrelated.

Atlantic cod

Pollock, also known as Boston bluefish or blue cod, are found in the northern Atlantic and Pacific Oceans. Their flesh is gray-pink when raw, turning white when cooked. Pollock, which weigh from 1 to 2 pounds (450 to 900 grams), are often frozen at sea, then reprocessed into **surimi**. They can also be salted or smoked.

Pollock

Cobia is a quick-growing sustainable fish found in warm waters of the Atlantic Ocean, in the Caribbean and off the coast of Australia. Although popular with sport fishermen, cobia also easily adapts to open-ocean

Cobia

farming, and is often imported from farms in Panama and Taiwan. Also known as black salmon, ling or black bonito, the cobia has an elongated silver body and a protruding lower jaw. Market weight is typically 3–4 pounds (6–8 kilograms). The flesh is lean, firm and pinkish-white with a sweet, nutty flavor. You may grill, bake, smoke or sauté cobia fillets; frying can hide its natural flavor. Cobia is also used in sushi and sashimi.

drawn a market form for fish in which the viscera (internal organs) is removed

Surimi

Surimi is made from a highly processed fish paste colored, flavored and shaped to resemble shrimp, lobster, crab or other shellfish. Most surimi is based on Alaskan pollock, but some blends include varying amounts of real crab, shrimp or other items. Available chilled or frozen, surimi is already fully cooked and ready to add to salads, pasta, sauces or other dishes. Surimi is very low in fat and relatively high in protein. Because of processing techniques, however, it has more sodium and fewer vitamins and minerals than the actual fish or shellfish it replaces. Americans now consume more than 100 million pounds of surimi each year, and its popularity continues to grow. The FDA no longer requires that all surimi products be labeled "imitation."

Eel

Grouper

Sardines

John Dory

Mackerel

Eels (Fr. *anguilles*) are long, snakelike freshwater fish with dorsal and anal fins running the length of their bodies. (The conger eel, used in Japanese cooking, is from a different family.) American and European eels are available live, whole, gutted or as fillets. Although wild stocks have been severely depleted in recent years, farmed eels are plentiful. Eels have a high fat content and firm flesh; they are sweet and mildly flavored. They are marketed in a variety of sizes and ages, from babies the size of linguine to giants the size of a beef tenderloin. The tough skin of larger mature eels should be removed before cooking. Eels may be steamed, baked, fried or used in stews. Baby eels are a springtime delicacy, especially in Spain, where they are pan-fried in olive oil and garlic with hot red peppers. Smoked eels are also available.

The **grouper** family includes almost four hundred varieties found in temperate waters worldwide. The more common Atlantic Ocean varieties are the yellowfin grouper, black grouper, red grouper and gag. The Pacific Ocean varieties are the sea bass, also known as jewfish and different from the black sea bass, and spotted cabrilla. Although some species can reach 800 pounds or more, most commercial varieties are sold in the 5- to 20-pound (2.2- to 8.8-kilogram) range. Grouper have lean white flesh with a mild to sweet flavor and very firm texture. Their skin, which is tough and strongly flavored, is generally removed before cooking. Grouper fillets may be baked, deep-fried, broiled or grilled.

Herring (Fr. *hareng*) are long, silvery-blue fish found in both the northern Atlantic and Pacific Oceans. Their strongly flavored flesh has a moderate to high fat content. Whole herring weigh up to 8 ounces (225 grams). Fresh herring may be butterflied or filleted and roasted, broiled or grilled. But because herring are very soft and tend to spoil quickly, they are rarely available fresh in the United States. More often they are smoked (and known as kippers) or cured in brine.

Very young, small herring, weighing from 5 to 6 ounces (140 to 170 grams) on average, are known as **sardines** (Fr. *sardine*). They have fatty, oily flesh with a flaky texture. Small sardines are usually sold canned, whole or as skinned and boned fillets, or fried or smoked and packed in oil or sauce. Canned sardines are used primarily for sandwiches and salads.

John Dory (Fr. *St. Pierre*), also known as St. Peter's fish, is a wild ocean fish especially popular in Europe and Australia. They have a distinctive round, black spot with a yellow halo on each side of the body. Generally marketed between ½ to 2½ pounds (450 grams to 2.5 kilograms), their flesh is lean, white, firm and finely flaked. Dory may be filleted and prepared by deep frying, baking or steaming and is a classic ingredient in bouillabaisse.

Mackerel (Fr. *maquereau*) of culinary importance include king and Spanish mackerel which are sustainably managed wild-caught varieties found along the Atlantic coast and in the Gulf of Mexico. Typical market size is from 1 to 3 pounds (500 gram to 1.5 kilograms), although they commonly reach as much as 12 pounds (5.5 kilograms). (The species known as Atlantic and Pacific mackerel are not generally used for food because of their small size and high fat content.) Mackerel flesh has a high fat content that is rich in Omega-3 fatty acids. The flesh is gray to pink colored, becoming off-white when cooked. Mackerel flavor ranges from mild to strong and rich. Mackerel is best broiled, grilled, smoked or baked.

Mahi-mahi

Mahi-mahi is the more commonly used name for dolphin or dolphinfish. The Hawaiian name mahi-mahi is used to distinguish them from the marine mammal of the same name. (Dolphins and porpoises are marine mammals.) Also known by their Spanish name, *dorado*, mahi-mahi are brilliantly colored fish found in tropical seas. Mahi-mahi weigh about 15 pounds (6.6 kilograms) and are sold whole or as fillets. Their flesh is off-white to pink, lean and firm with a sweet flavor. Dolphinfish can be broiled, grilled or baked. The meat may become dry when cooked, however, so a sauce or marinade is recommended.

Monkfish tail

Monkfish are also known as angler fish, goosefish, rape and lotte. These extraordinarily ugly fish are rarely seen whole, for the large head is usually discarded before reaching market. Only the tail is edible; it is available whole or in fillets and steaks, fresh or frozen. The scaleless skin must be removed. The flesh is lean, pearly white, very firm and not flaky. Its texture and flavor have earned monkfish the nickname of "poor man's lobster." Monkfish absorb flavors easily and are baked, steamed, fried, grilled or broiled. They are also used in stews and soups.

Red snapper is also known as the American or northern red snapper. Although there are many members of the snapper family, only one is the true red snapper, most of which is found in the Gulf of Mexico. Once severely overfished, wild populations of red snapper are growing, but harvest quantities are still limited. Red-skinned rockfish are often mislabeled as the more popular red snapper or Pacific snapper, a practice that is currently legal only in California. True red snapper have red skin and eyes and lean, pink flesh that becomes white when cooked and is sweet-flavored and flaky. Red snapper are sold whole or as fillets with the skin left on for identification. A fish may reach 35 pounds, but most are marketed at only 4–6 pounds (1.8–2.7 kilograms) or as 1- to 3-pound (450-gram to 1.3-kilogram) fillets. Red snapper can be prepared using almost any cooking method. The head and bones are excellent for stock.

Red snapper

Salmon (Fr. *saumon*) live in both the northern Atlantic and Pacific Oceans, returning to the freshwater rivers and streams of their birth to spawn. Salmon flesh gets its distinctive pink-red color from fat-soluble carotenoids found in the crustaceans on which they feed.

Atlantic salmon is the most important commercially, accounting for one-fourth of all salmon produced worldwide. Extensive aquafarms in Chile, Norway, Canada and Scotland produce a steady supply of Atlantic salmon, although the farming methods have been associated with environmental problems. For marketing purposes, the salmon's point of origin is often added to the name (e.g., Norwegian, Scottish or Shetland Atlantic salmon). Atlantic salmon have a rich, pink color and moist, fatty flesh. Their average weight is from 4 to 12 pounds (1.8 to 5.4 kilograms). Fishing for wild Atlantic salmon is prohibited in U.S. waters.

Atlantic salmon

Chinook or **king salmon** from the Pacific are also highly desirable. They average from 5 to 30 pounds (2.2 to 13.2 kilograms) and have red-orange flesh with a high fat content and rich, buttery flavor. Like other salmon, their flesh separates into large flakes when cooked. Chinooks are often marketed by the name of the river from which they are harvested (e.g., Columbia, Yukon or Copper Chinook salmon). They are distinguished by the black interior of their mouth.

Coho or **silver salmon** have a fatty, reddish-orange flesh and are available fresh or frozen, wild or from aquafarms. Wild coho average from 3 to 12 pounds (1.3 to 5.4 kilograms), whereas aquafarmed coho are much smaller, usually less than 1 pound (450 grams).

Chinook or king salmon

Other varieties, such as chum, sockeye, red, blueback and pink salmon, are usually canned but may be available fresh or frozen.

Salmon can be prepared by many cooking methods: broiling, grilling, poaching, steaming or baking. Frying is not recommended, however, because of their high fat content. Salmon fillets are often cured or smoked. **Gravlax** is salmon that has been cured for one to three days with salt, sugar and dill. **Lox** is salmon that has been cured in a salted brine and then, typically, cold-smoked. The term **nova** is used in the eastern United States to refer to a less-salty, cold-smoked salmon.

Coho salmon

Sea bream is the name of a large family of fish found in the Mediterranean (gilthead bream), the Caribbean (porgy), the Atlantic (black sea bream) and the Indo-Pacific (emperor and snapper). Because the marketing term *bream* is applied to so many different fish, it is difficult to generalize about their characteristics. Some bream have very few bones, others have quite a few; some have a rich flavor, others are very mild; some weigh up to 20 pounds (9.6 kilograms), others rarely exceed 5 pounds (2.2 kilograms). Black sea bream, for example, is a good pan fish, reaching only 35 centimeters in length and weighing less than 6 pounds (2.9 kilograms). Their flesh is firm, mild and lean. Also marketed as Thai snapper, they are good for baking, grilling or frying.

Black sea bream

Swordfish wheel

Rainbow trout

Arctic char

Tilapia

Swordfish take their name from the long, swordlike bill extending from their upper jaw. These popular fish average about 250 pounds (112.5 kilograms). Their flesh is sweet with a very firm, meatlike texture; it may be gray, pink or off-white when raw, becoming white when cooked. Swordfish from the North Atlantic have a moderate fat content; those from the Pacific are fattier. Swordfish are most often available cut into cross sections called wheels or portioned into steaks perfect for grilling or broiling.

Tilapia is the name given to several species of freshwater, aquafarm-raised fish bred worldwide. They grow quickly in warm water and are marketed at about 3 pounds (1.4 kilograms). Tilapia is widely available whole or filleted, fresh or frozen. The lean flesh is similar to catfish—white and sweet, with a firm texture that can be used in almost any culinary preparation. Tilapia are sometimes marketed as cherry snapper or sunshine snapper, even though they are not members of the snapper family.

Trout (Fr. *truite*) are members of the salmon family. Most of the freshwater trout commercially available are aquafarm-raised **rainbow trout**, although brown trout and brook trout are also being aquafarmed. Some trout species spend part of their lives at sea, returning to fresh water to spawn. On the West Coast, these are called salmon trout or steelhead. Trout have a low to moderate fat content, a flaky texture and a delicate flavor that can be easily overwhelmed by strong sauces. The flesh may be white, orange or pink. Trout are usually marketed at 8–10 ounces (225–280 grams) each, just right for an individual portion. Lake trout resemble trout and salmon. They are fresh or saltwater fish and are widely aquafarmed. Trout and char can be baked, pan-fried, smoked or steamed.

Wild red mountain trout

Arctic char (Fr. *alose*), also known as alpine trout, is a member of the salmon family, with similarly pink-colored flesh and silvery skin. Market weight averages from 2 to 8 pounds (1 to 4 kilograms), although much larger fish can be found in the wild. Char are anadromous and are found throughout the Arctic Ocean and in the rivers and lakes of Northern Canada, Russia and Europe. Commercial fisheries operate in both rivers and ocean tidal areas, but line-caught free-running char are considered to have the finest flavor and texture. Arctic char is currently considered a good choice for sustainability with a low environmental impact. Like salmon, char is high in fat but with a thinner, tender skin. Char is best prepared by baking, grilling or smoking and is also used in sushi.

Tuna (Fr. *thon*) varieties include the bluefin, yellowfin, bonito, bigeye and blackfin. Ahi is the popular market name for either yellowfin or bigeye tuna. All are members of the mackerel family and are found in tropical and subtropical waters around the world. Tuna are large fish, weighing up to several hundred pounds each. Bluefin, with its fatty belly flesh (Jp: *o-toro*), which is highly desirable for sashimi, is seriously endangered because of overfishing. Most canned tuna is prepared from yellowfin or skipjack; canned white tuna is prepared from albacore, also known as longfin tuna. Any of these species may be found fresh or frozen. Tuna are usually cut into four boneless loins for market. The loins are then cut into steaks, cubes or chunks. The flesh has a low to moderate fat content (a higher fat content is preferred for sashimi) and a deep red color. The dark, reddish-brown muscle that runs along the lateral line is very fatty and can be removed. Tuna flesh turns light gray when cooked and is very firm, with a mild flavor. Tuna work well for grilling or broiling and may be marinated or brushed with seasoned oil during cooking. Tuna are often prepared medium rare to prevent dryness.

Wahoo, also known as *ono*, are found throughout tropical and subtropical waters but are particularly associated with Hawaii (*ono* means "good to eat" in Hawaiian). They are actually a type of mackerel with a leaner pink to grey flesh. Wahoo are a popular game fish, generally marketed between 8 to 30 pounds (17 to 66 kilograms) in weight. Prepare wahoo using any technique suitable for lean fish.

Yellowfin tuna

Wahoo

Whitefish species inhabit the freshwater lakes and streams of North America. Lake whitefish, the most important commercially, are related to salmon. They are marketed at 7 pounds (3.2 kilograms) or less and are available whole or filleted. The flesh is firm and white, with a moderate amount of fat and a sweet flavor. Whitefish may be baked, broiled, grilled or smoked and are often used in processed fish products such as breaded fish fillets or sticks.

Whitefish

Flatfish

Flounder (Fr. *flet*) have lean, firm flesh that is pearly or pinkish-white with a sweet, mild flavor. Flounder can grow to more than 30 inches (76 centimeters) in length and weigh more than 20 pounds (9 kilograms), but 1 to 3 pound (450 gram to 1.3 kilogram) fish are more typical. Although they are easily boned, most flounder are deheaded and gutted at sea and sold as fresh or frozen fillets. These fillets are very thin and can dry out or spoil easily, so extra care should be taken in handling, preparing and storing them. Recipes that preserve moisture work best with flounder; poaching, steaming and frying are recommended. Many types of flounder are marketed as sole, perhaps in an attempt to cash in on the popularity of true sole. The FDA permits this practice. See Table 20.1. Some common types of flounder, often labeled as sole, are discussed in the material that follows.

English sole are actually flounder caught off the West Coast of the United States. They are usually marketed simply as "fillet of sole" and are of fair to average quality.

Yellowfin sole, another type of flounder that is harvested off the coast of Alaska, are one of the most abundant flatfish species. The smallest of the Pacific soles, they have a delicate texture and thin fillets.

Petrale sole, another West Coast flounder, are generally considered the finest of the domestic "soles." They are most often available as fillets, which tend to be thicker and firmer than other sole fillets.

Domestic Dover sole is Pacific flounder, not a true sole. They are not as delicate or flavorful as other species. Moreover, they are often afflicted with a parasite that causes their flesh to have a slimy, gelatinous texture. Domestic Dover sole are not recommended if other sole or flounder are available.

English sole

Petrale sole

Lemon sole are among the most popular East Coast flounder. They are also known as blackback or winter flounder (during the winter, they migrate close to shore from the deeper, colder waters). They average 2 pounds (900 grams) in weight.

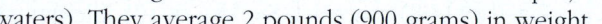

Lemon sole

FLOUNDER (AKA SOLE)	TABLE 20.1

Note that the FDA allows many flatfish to be called "sole" for marketing purposes. No true sole is commercially harvested in U.S. waters, however. Any flatfish harvested in U.S. waters and marketed as sole is actually in the flounder family.

ATLANTIC OCEAN	PACIFIC OCEAN
Lemon sole/blackback/winter flounder	Arrowtooth
Fluke/summer flounder	Sand dab
Starry flounder	Petrale sole
Yellowtail flounder	Rex sole
Windowpane flounder	English sole
Gray sole/witch flounder	Rock sole
American plaice	Yellowfin sole
	Domestic Dover sole/Pacific flounder
	Butter sole

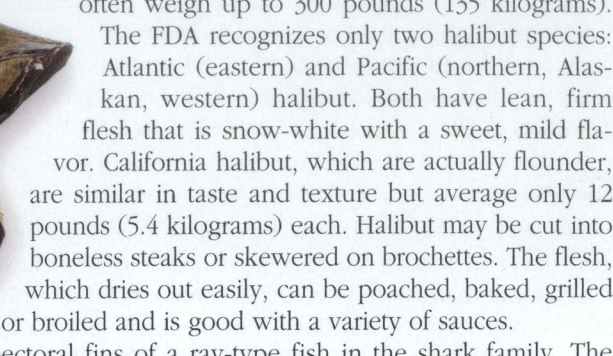

Halibut are among the largest flatfish; a halibut can often weigh up to 300 pounds (135 kilograms). The FDA recognizes only two halibut species: Atlantic (eastern) and Pacific (northern, Alaskan, western) halibut. Both have lean, firm flesh that is snow-white with a sweet, mild flavor. California halibut, which are actually flounder, are similar in taste and texture but average only 12 pounds (5.4 kilograms) each. Halibut may be cut into boneless steaks or skewered on brochettes. The flesh, which dries out easily, can be poached, baked, grilled or broiled and is good with a variety of sauces.

Halibut

Skate wings are the large pectoral fins of a ray-type fish in the shark family. The wings are usually sold in triangles weighing from 1 to 2 pounds (450 to 960 grams), with each fish yielding four such triangles. There are no bones in skate wings, but the rough skin must be peeled off and the fillets separated from a central plate of cartilage before cooking. The flesh is sweet and tender but gelatinous with deep corrugated grooves. Skate wings are often pan-fried and served with a sauce containing capers, lemon or another acidic element to create a balance of flavors. Poaching and baking are also suitable cooking techniques. Look for skate from New England or the U.S. West Coast; avoid purchasing products from British Columbia for environmental reasons.

Sole (Fr. *sole*) are probably the most flavorful and finely textured flatfish. Indeed because of the connotations of quality associated with the name, "sole" is widely used for many species that are not members of the *Soleidae* family. Even though the FDA allows many species of flatfish to be called "sole" for marketing purposes, no true sole is commercially harvested in U.S. waters. Any flatfish harvested in U.S. waters and marketed as sole is actually flounder.

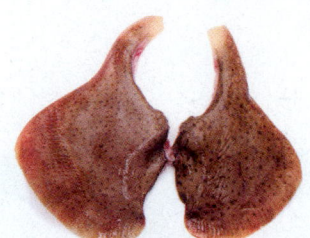

Skate wings

True **Dover sole**, a staple of classic cuisine, is a lean fish with firm, pearly-white flesh and a delicate flavor that can stand up to a variety of sauces and seasonings. They are a member of the *Soleidae* family and come only from the waters off the coasts of England, Africa and Europe. They are imported into the United States as fresh whole fish weighing from 1 to 2½ pounds (450 to 1200 grams), or fresh or frozen fillets. Skin Dover sole after it is filleted.

True Dover sole

In North America, **Turbot** are a Pacific flatfish of no great culinary distinction. In Europe, however, the species known as turbot (Fr. *turbot*) are large diamond-shaped fish highly prized for their delicate flavor and lean, firm, white flesh. European turbot (sometimes marketed as brill) can reach 55 pounds (25 kilograms) and 40 inches (1 meter) in length. Their bodies are scaleless but covered with small bumps (tubercles). Turbot are traditionally roasted whole in specially-shaped pans, but fillets are also prepared by poaching, pan-frying and grilling.

Turbot

IDENTIFYING SHELLFISH: MOLLUSKS

Mollusks are invertebrate shellfish with soft bodies covered by a shell of one or more pieces. They live in both fresh water and salt water habitats and many varieties are now farmed around the world. As noted earlier, mollusks are further classified as univalves, bivalves or cephalopods. Univalves are mollusks with a single shell in which the soft-bodied animal resides. They are actually marine snails with a single foot, used to attach the creature to fixed objects such as rocks. Various species of univalves are found worldwide; the most common in culinary use are abalone, conch and sea snails, such as periwinkles and whelks. Univalves are most popular in their native locales where they are available fresh. Univalves must be prepared with care to prevent the flesh from becoming tough or rubbery.

Bivalves are mollusks with two shells attached by a central hinge, including numerous varieties of clams, mussels, oysters and scallops. Cephalopods are marine mollusks with distinct heads, well-developed eyes, a number of arms that attach to the head near the mouth and a saclike, fin-bearing mantle. They do not have an outer shell; instead there is a thin internal shell called a **pen** or **cuttlebone**. Octopus and squid are cephalopods.

Bivalves

Clams (Fr. *palourdes*) are harvested along both the U.S. East and West Coasts, with Atlantic clams being more significant commercially. Atlantic Coast clams include hard-shell, soft-shell and surf clams. Fresh clams are available all year, either live in the shell or fresh-shucked (meat removed from the shell). Canned clams, whether minced, chopped or whole, are also available.

Atlantic hard-shell clams, also known as **quahogs**, have hard, blue-gray shells. Their chewy meat is not as sweet as other clam meat and has a briny, mild flavor. Quahogs have different names, depending on their size. **Littlenecks** are generally under 2 inches (5 centimeters) across the shell and usually are served raw on the half shell or steamed. They are the most expensive clams. **Topnecks** are generally under 3 inches (7.5 centimeters) across the shell and are sometimes eaten raw but are more often cooked.

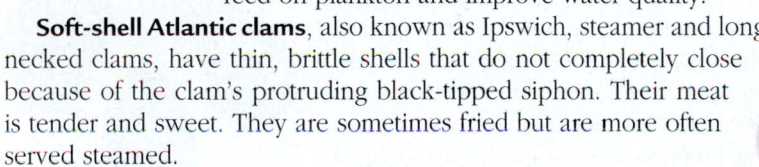

Littlenecks

Cherrystones average 3–3½ inches (7.5–9 centimeters) across and are usually cooked. Cherrystones are often used for stuffed clams. **Chowders**, the largest quahogs, are always cooked, usually minced, for chowder or soup. Quahogs are farm-raised in tidal areas along the east coast of the United States where they feed on plankton and improve water quality.

Cherrystones

Soft-shell Atlantic clams, also known as Ipswich, steamer and long-necked clams, have thin, brittle shells that do not completely close because of the clam's protruding black-tipped siphon. Their meat is tender and sweet. They are sometimes fried but are more often served steamed.

Soft-shell Atlantic clams

Surf clams are deep-water clams from the Atlantic that reach sizes of 8 inches (20 centimeters) across. They are most often cut into strips for frying or are minced, chopped, processed and canned. The flesh is sweet and yellow to orange colored. The United States is the only source of wild-harvested Atlantic surf clams.

The most common **Pacific clam** is the **Manila clam**, which was introduced along the Pacific coast during the 1930s. Resembling a quahog, but with a ridged shell, Manila clams can be served steamed or raw on the half shell. **Geoducks** are the largest Pacific clam, sometimes weighing up to 10 pounds (4.5 kilograms) each. They look like huge soft-shell clams with a large, protruding siphon. Their tender, rich bodies and briny flavor are popular in Asian cuisines.

Manila clams

Razor clams, also known as hamaguri, are a long, narrow variety farmed worldwide or harvested along the Pacific Ocean shoreline from California to Alaska. They are typically 3–6 inches (8–15 centimeters) in length. The meat is firm and white with a delicate, sweet flavor. Generally prepared by steaming or grilling in the shell, the meat can also be pan-fried or used in chowders.

Mussels (Fr. *moules*) are found in waters worldwide. They are excellent steamed in wine or seasoned broth and can be fried or used in soups or pasta dishes.

Blue mussels are the most common edible mussel. They are found in the wild along the Atlantic Coast and are aquafarmed on both U.S. coasts. Their meat is plump and sweet with a firm, muscular texture. The orangish-yellow meat of cultivated mussels tends to be much larger than that of wild mussels and therefore worth the added cost. Blue mussels are sold live in the shell and average from 10 to 20 per pound. Although available all year, the best-quality blue mussels are harvested during the winter months.

Land Snails

Although snails (more politely known by their French name, *escargots*) are univalve land animals, they share many characteristics with their marine cousins. They can be poached in court bouillon or removed from their shells and boiled or baked briefly with a seasoned butter or sauce. They should be firm but tender; overcooking makes snails tough and chewy. The most popular varieties are the large white Burgundy snail and the small garden variety called *petit gris*. Fresh snails are available from snail ranches through specialty suppliers. The great majority of snails, however, are purchased canned; most canned snails are produced in France or Taiwan.

Snail (left) and snail shell (right)

QUAHOG SIZES	WIDTH	NUMBER PER POUND (PER 450 G)
Littlenecks	1–2 in. (2.5–5 cm)	7–10
Topnecks	2–3 in. (5–7.5 cm)	6–10
Cherrystones	3–3½ in. (7.5–9 cm)	Varies; avg. = 4
Chowders	>3½ in. (>9 cm)	2–3

Razor clams

Blue mussels

Greenshell mussels

Olympia oysters

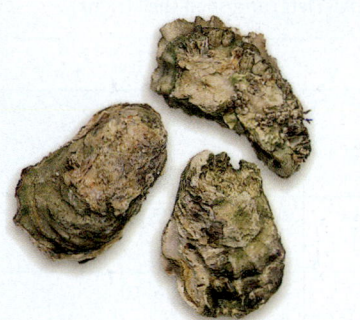

Hamma-Hamma oysters

Sea scallops

Greenshell (or greenlip) mussels from New Zealand and Thailand are much larger than blue mussels, averaging 8–12 mussels per pound. Their shells are paler gray, with a distinctive bright-green edge.

Oysters (Fr. *huitres*) have a rough gray shell. Their soft, gray, briny flesh can be eaten raw directly from the shell. They can also be steamed or baked in the shell, shucked and fried, sautéed or added to stews or chowders. Most oysters available in the United States are commercially farmed and sold either live in the shell or shucked. There are four main domestic species.

Atlantic oysters, also called American or Eastern oysters, have darker, flatter shells than other oysters.

European flat oysters are often incorrectly called Belon (true Belon oysters live only in the Belon river of France); they are very round and flat and look like giant brownish-green Olympias.

Olympias are native to Washington state's Pacific Coast, which is the only place they are currently produced. Olympias are so tiny (about the size of a half dollar) that a pint of meat requires approximately 250 of these sweet, intensely-flavored clams.

Pacific oysters, also called Japanese oysters, are farmed along the Pacific Coasts of Canada, Australia, Korea, Japan and the United States. They have curly, thick striated shells and silvery-gray to gold to almost-white meat.

Although it may seem as though there are hundreds of oyster species on the market, only two are commercially significant: the Atlantic oyster and the Pacific oyster. These two species yield dozens of different varieties, however, depending on their origin. For example, Atlantic oysters may be referred to as bluepoints, Chesapeake Bay, Florida Gulf, Long Island and so on, whereas Pacific oysters include Penn Cove Select, Westcott Bay, Hamma-Hamma, Kumamoto and Portuguese, among others. An oyster's flavor reflects the minerals, nutrients and salts in its water and mud bed, so a Bristol from Maine and an Apalachicola from Florida will taste very different, even though they are the same Atlantic species.

Scallops (Fr. *coquilles Saint Jacques*) contain an edible white adductor muscle that holds together the fan-shaped shells. Because they die quickly, they are almost always shucked and cleaned on board the ship. The sea scallop and the bay scallop, both cold-water varieties, and the calico scallop, a warm-water variety, are the most important commercially. Sea scallops are the largest, with an average count of 20–30 per pound. Larger sea scallops are also available. Bay scallops average 70–90 per pound; calico scallops average 70–110 per pound. Fresh or frozen shucked, cleaned scallops are the most common market form, but live scallops in the shell and shucked scallops with roe attached (very popular in Europe) are also available. Scallops are sweet, with a tender texture. Raw scallops should be a translucent ivory color, asymmetrically round and feel springy. They can be steamed, broiled, grilled, fried, sautéed or baked. When overcooked, scallops quickly become chewy and dry. Only extremely fresh scallops should be eaten raw.

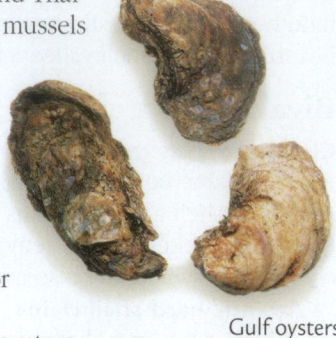

Gulf oysters

European flat oysters

Bluepoint oysters

Octopus

Cephalopods

Octopus is a saltwater dweller with a rounded head and eight tentacles. It is found in tropical and subtropical waters worldwide, but commercial farming is not yet practical. Most octopus available in the United States is imported, though fresh octopus are found on the East Coast during the winter. Octopus is marketed live, fresh or frozen, in sizes ranging from 8 ounces to 60 pounds (250 grams to 27 kilograms). With larger species, the meat is generally quite tough and requires mechanical tenderization or long, moist-heat cooking. Octopus skin is gray when raw, turning purple when cooked. The interior flesh is white, lean, firm and flavorful.

Squid, also known by their Italian name, *calamari*, have elongated bodies, each with two tentacles and eight arms. They are harvested along both U.S. coasts and elsewhere around the world. They range in size from an average of 8–10 per pound to the giant South American squid, which is sold as tenderized steaks. Most market squid are less than 10 inches (25 centimeters) in length. The squid's tentacles, mantle (body tube) and fins as well as their briny ink sacs are edible. Squid meat is white to ivory in color, turning darker with age. It is moderately lean, slightly sweet, firm and tender, but it toughens quickly if overcooked. Squid are available either fresh or cleaned, cut-up and frozen.

Squid

IDENTIFYING SHELLFISH: CRUSTACEANS

Crustaceans are found in both fresh and salt water. They have a hard outer shell and jointed appendages, and they breathe through gills.

Crayfish (Fr. *écrevisses*), generally called *crayfish* in the Northern United States and *crawfish* or *crawdad* in the Southern United States, are freshwater creatures that look like miniature lobsters. They are harvested from the wild or aquafarmed in Louisiana and the Pacific Northwest. They are from 3½ to 7 inches (8 to 17.5 centimeters) in length when marketed and may be purchased live or precooked and frozen. The lean meat, found mostly in the tail, is sweet and tender. Crayfish can be boiled whole and served hot or cold. The tail meat can be deep-fried or used in soups, bisque or sauces. Crayfish are a staple of Cajun cuisine, often used in gumbo, étouffée and jambalaya. Whole crayfish turn brilliant red when cooked and have been used as a luxurious garnish since the days of French *grande cuisine*.

Crayfish

Crabs (Fr. *crabes*) are found along both North American coasts in great numbers and are shipped throughout the world in fresh, frozen and canned forms. Crab meat varies in flavor and texture and can be used in a range of prepared dishes, from chowders to curries to casseroles. Crabs purchased live should stay alive up to five days with proper storage; dead crabs should not be used.

King crabs are the largest crabs, usually around 10 pounds (4.5 kilograms). They are caught in the very cold waters of the northern Pacific and are synonymous with Alaska. Their meat is sweet and snow-white. King crabs are generally sold frozen, quickly steamed or grilled and served in the shell, either hot or cold. In-shell forms include sections or clusters, legs and claws or split legs. The meat is also available in "fancy" packs of whole leg and body meat, or shredded and minced pieces that can be used in salads or other preparations.

King crab legs

Dungeness crabs are only found in the Pacific Ocean along the West Coast of the United States and Canada. They weigh 1½–4 pounds (680 grams to 1.8 kilograms) and have delicate, sweet meat. They are sold live, precooked and frozen, or as picked meat, usually in 5-pound (2.2-kilogram) vacuum-packed cans. Dungeness crab is often used in crab cakes, sauces and prepared dishes or served whole after being quickly steamed.

Blue crabs are found along the entire eastern seaboard and account for approximately 50 percent of the total weight of all crab species harvested in the United States. Their meat is rich and sweet. Blue crabs are available as hard-shell or soft-shell. Hard-shell crabs are sold live, precooked and frozen, or as picked meat.

Dungeness crab

Soft-shell crabs

Blue crab

Soft-shell crabs are those harvested within 6 hours after shedding their shells (molting) and are available live or frozen. They are often steamed and served whole. Soft-shells can be sautéed, fried, broiled or added to soups or stews. Blue crabs are sold by size, with an average diameter of 4–7 inches (10–18 centimeters).

The **Jonah crab** has become increasingly popular in recent years as a less-expensive alternative to other crab species. They are harvested year-round along the Atlantic coast from Florida to Newfoundland. Although related to the Pacific Dungeness crab, Atlantic Jonah crabs are slightly larger, averaging 7 inches (17.5 centimeters) in width, with larger claws. Their mild, white flesh can be used in virtually any crab recipe, and their claws can be substituted for stone crab claws.

Snow or **queen crabs**, also known as opie, are an abundant species, most often used as a substitute for the scarcer and more expensive king crab. They are harvested from Alaskan waters and along the eastern coast of Canada. Whole snow crabs are marketed at 1.5–2.5 pounds (720–1200 grams). Snow crab is usually sold precooked, canned or frozen. The delicate, flaky meat can be used in soups, salads, omelets or other prepared dishes.

Stone crabs live in the Atlantic Ocean from Connecticut to the Caribbean and in the Gulf of Mexico; however, over 95 percent of those commercially harvested in the United States come from Florida. Stone crabs are generally available only as cooked claws, either fresh or frozen (the claws cannot be frozen raw because the meat sticks to the shell). In stone crab fishery, only the claw is harvested. After the claw is removed, the crab is returned to the water, where in approximately 18 months it regenerates a new claw. Claws average 2½–5½ ounces (75–155 grams) each. The meat is firm, with a sweet flavor similar to lobster. Cracked claws are served hot or cold, usually with cocktail sauce or lemon butter.

Lobsters have brown to blue-black outer shells and firm, white meat with a rich, sweet flavor. Lobster shells turn red when cooked. They are usually poached, steamed, simmered, baked or grilled and can be served hot or cold. Picked meat can be used in prepared dishes, soups or sautés. Lobsters must be kept alive until just before cooking. Dead lobsters should not be eaten. The Maine, also known as American or clawed lobster, and the spiny lobster are the most commonly marketed species.

Maine lobsters have edible meat in both their tails and claws. Considered superior in flavor to all other lobsters. They come from the cold waters along the northeast coast of the United States and are most often sold live. Maine lobsters may be purchased by weight (e.g., 1¼ pounds [525 grams], 1½ pounds [650 grams] or 2 pounds [900 grams] each), or as chix (weighing less than 1 pound [450 grams]). They are available frozen or as cooked, picked meat. Maine lobsters may also be purchased as culls (lobsters with only one claw) or bullets (lobsters with no claws).

Figure 20.4 shows a cross-section of a Maine lobster and identifies the stomach, **tomalley** (the olive-green liver) and **coral** (the roe or fish egg sacs). The stomach is not eaten; the tomalley and coral are very flavorful and are often used in the preparation of sauces and other items.

Spiny lobsters, harvested in many parts of the world, have very small claws and are valuable only for their meaty tails. Nearly all spiny lobsters marketed in the United States are sold as frozen tails weighing 1–5 pounds (450 grams to 2.4 kilograms), often identified as **rock lobster**. Those found off Florida and Brazil and in the Caribbean are

Snow crab legs

Stone crab claws

Maine lobster

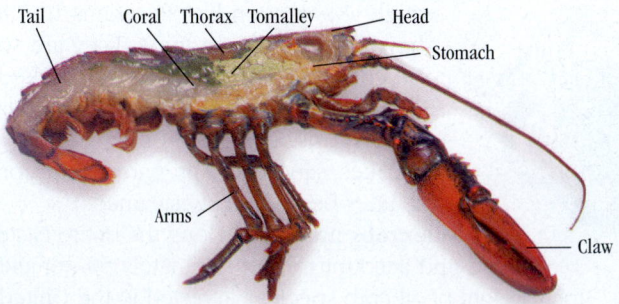

Figure 20.4 Parts of a Maine lobster.

marketed as warm-water tails; those found off South Africa, Australia and New Zealand are called cold-water tails. Cold-water spiny tails are considered superior in flavor and texture to their warm-water cousins.

Shrimp

Tiger shrimp

Shrimp (Fr. *crevettes*) are found worldwide and are widely popular. Gulf whites, pinks, browns and black tigers are just a few of the dozens of shrimp varieties used in food service operations. Although fresh, head-on shrimp are available, the most commonly sold form is raw, head-off (also called green head-less) shrimp with the shell on. Most shrimp are deheaded and frozen at sea. Shrimp are available in many forms: raw, peeled and deveined; cooked, peeled and deveined; and individually quick-frozen, as well as in a variety of processed, breaded or canned products.

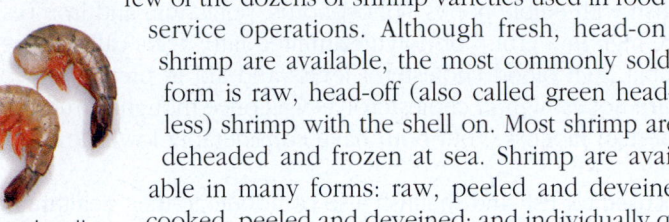

Green headless shrimp

Shrimp are graded by size, which can range from 400 per pound (titi) to 8 per pound (extra-colossal), and are sold in counts per pound. For example, shrimp marketed as "21–26 count" means that there is an average of 21–26 shrimp per pound; shrimp marketed as "U-10" means that there are fewer than 10 shrimp per pound.

Prawn is often used interchangeably with the word *shrimp* in English-speaking countries. Although it is perhaps more accurate to refer to freshwater species as prawns and saltwater species as shrimp, in commercial practice, prawn refers to any large shrimp. Equally confusing, *scampi* is the Italian name for the Dublin Bay prawn (which is actually a species of miniature lobster), but in the United States *scampi* refers to a dish of shrimp sautéed in garlic butter.

Prawn

Ocean Invaders

An invasive species refers to any living organism—fish, plant, amphibian, bacteria, insect, mammal—that is not indigenous (native) to an area in which it is now causing damage. Invasive species are usually brought into the new area by humans, intentionally or unintentionally. In its native environment, the organism may be a well-controlled part of the food chain, but unleashed in a new environment, it can reproduce rapidly without natural predators and will overwhelm native plants and animals by eating them or competing with them for food and habitat. An invasive species can destroy diversity, change soil and water chemistry and clog lakes, streams and sewage pipes, causing long term financial and environmental damage. Eradication efforts are generally unsuccessful, meaning that humans must learn to control or prevent the spread of an invasion as best they can.

Varieties of invasive fish and crustaceans making new homes for themselves in North American waterways include several species of Asian carp, zebra mussels, green crabs and sea squirts. One of the most well-known recent invaders is the tropical lionfish with its beautiful but toxic fins. Lionfish were unintentionally transplanted from their native western Pacific waters to the Caribbean, Gulf of Mexico and

Lionfish

Atlantic when they were dumped into waterways from home aquariums. Because lionfish reproduce rapidly, grow quickly and have no natural predators in these oceans, they quickly became a multi-billion-dollar problem. Lionfish eat small crustaceans and the young of commercially important fish, especially grouper and snapper. The huge appetite of the lionfish is destroying reef habitats. When other options failed, scientists turned to chefs for help.

Lionfish fins have venomous spikes that serve as protection against predators, but the toxin does not affect its flesh or internal organs. The venom is also destroyed by the heat of cooking. Lionfish must be caught by spearfishing divers, but once brought ashore they are cleaned and

prepped like any other fish, yielding small, firm, white fillets with a mild flavor. Chefs throughout the Caribbean and eastern Latin America initially offered wild-caught lionfish as a local delicacy for tourists. Because the fish works well with a wide range of cooking techniques, from deep-frying to ceviche and sashimi, it can be used in different cuisines and with different flavor profiles.

It turns out that lionfish are also healthy; they are high in Omega-3 fatty acids, low in saturated fat and heavy metals. Wild-caught lionfish are listed as a "Best Choice" sustainable fish by the Monterey Bay Aquarium. Restaurants and grocery chains in affected areas of the United States now sell fresh lionfish fillets. Scientists hope that the culinary interest will spread, helping to reduce the lionfish population to manageable levels.

Lionfish is not the only invasive species that might be controlled by human predators. Tiny Asian shore crabs, several varieties of Asian carp, sea squirts, cannibalistic tiger shrimp and other aquatic creatures that are foodstuffs in their native regions, could be delicious menu additions. All chefs need is an increase in consumer demand. Scientists hope that food writers and chefs working to educate consumers about these unusual, but tasty, invaders may generate the demand necessary to reduce their environmental impact.

NUTRITION INFORMATION FOR FISH AND SHELLFISH

Fish and shellfish are low in calories, fat and sodium and are high in protein and vitamins A, B and D. Fish and shellfish are also high in minerals, especially calcium (particularly in canned fish with edible bones), phosphorus, potassium and iron (especially mollusks). Fish are high in a group of polyunsaturated fatty acids called Omega-3, which may help combat high blood cholesterol levels and aid in preventing some heart disease. Shellfish are not as high in cholesterol as was once thought. Crustaceans are higher in cholesterol than mollusks, but both have considerably lower levels than red meat or eggs.

The cooking methods used for fish and shellfish also contribute to their healthfulness. The most commonly used cooking methods—broiling, grilling, poaching and steaming—add little or no fat.

Figure 20.5 PUFI mark and statements.

INSPECTION AND GRADING OF FISH AND SHELLFISH

Unlike mandatory meat and poultry inspections, fish and shellfish inspections are voluntary. They are performed in a fee-for-service program supervised by the United States Department of Commerce (USDC).

Type 1 inspection services cover plant, product and processing methods from the raw material to the final product. The "Processed under Federal Inspection" (PUFI) mark or statement shown in Figure 20.5 can be used only on product labels processed under Type 1 inspection services. It signifies that the product is safe and wholesome, is properly labeled, has reasonably good flavor and odor and was produced under inspection in an approved establishment.

Type 2 inspection services are usually performed in a warehouse, processing plant or cold storage facility on specific product lots. See Figure 20.6. A lot inspection determines whether the product complies with purchase agreement criteria (usually defined in a spec sheet) such as condition, weight, labeling and packaging integrity.

Type 3 inspection services are for sanitation only. Fishing vessels or plants that meet the requirements are recognized as official establishments and are included in the *USDC Approved List* of the NOAA seafood inspection program. The list is useful for purchasing agents and seafood buyers. Updated copies of the list are published online.

Only fish processed under Type 1 inspection services are eligible for grading. Each type of fish has its own grading criteria, but because of the great variety of fish and shellfish, the USDC has been able to set grading criteria for only the most common types.

The grades assigned to fish are A, B or C. Grade A products are top quality and must have good flavor and odor and be practically free of physical blemishes or defects. The great majority of fresh and frozen fish and shellfish consumed in restaurants is Grade A. See Figure 20.7. Grade B indicates good quality; Grade C indicates fairly good quality. Grade B and C products are most often canned or processed.

Figure 20.6 Product lot inspection stamp.

Figure 20.7 Grade A stamp.

PURCHASING AND STORING FISH AND SHELLFISH

High-quality fish and shellfish are some of the most expensive, and most perishable, food items on a restaurant's menu. It is extremely important to purchase these products at the peak of freshness and to ensure that frozen items were not mishandled during shipping or storage. You must be able to judge the freshness of fish and shellfish for yourself and determine which market form is best for the needs of your operation. Once received, proper storage is essential to the shelf life of the product and to the health and safety of your customers.

Determining Freshness of Fish and Shellfish

Because fish and shellfish are highly perishable, an inspection stamp does not necessarily ensure top quality or freshness. A few hours at the wrong temperature or a couple of days in the refrigerator can turn high-quality inspected fish or shellfish into garbage. Freshness should be checked before purchasing and again just before cooking.

Determine freshness with the following criteria:

Smell: This is by far the easiest way to determine freshness. Fresh fish should have a slight sea smell or no odor at all. Any off-odors or ammonia odors are a sure sign of aged or improperly handled fish.

Eyes: The eyes should be clear and full. Sunken eyes mean that the fish is drying out and is probably not fresh.

Gills: The gills should be intact and bright red. Brown gills are a sign of age.

Texture: Generally the flesh of fresh fish should be firm. Mushy flesh or flesh that does not spring back when pressed with a finger is a sign of poor quality or age.

Fins and scales: Fins and scales should be moist and full without excessive drying on the outer edges. Dry fins or scales are a sign of age; damaged fins or scales may be a sign of mishandling.

Moistness: Fish cuts should be moist and glistening, without bruises or dark spots. Edges should not be brown or dry.

Movement: Shellfish should be purchased live and should show movement. Lobsters and other crustaceans should be active. Clams, mussels and oysters that are partially opened should snap shut when tapped with a finger. (Exceptions are geoduck, razor and steamer clams whose siphons protrude, preventing the shell from closing completely.) Ones that do not close are dead and should not be used. Avoid mollusks with broken shells or heavy shells that may be filled with mud or sand.

How Fresh Is Frozen Fish?

Fresh: The item is not and has never been frozen.

Chilled: Now used by some in the industry to replace the more ambiguous "fresh"; indicates that the item was refrigerated, that is, held at 30–34°F (−1–1°C).

Flash-frozen: The item was rapidly flash frozen at extreme low temperatures on board the ship or at a processing plant within hours of being caught.

Fresh-frozen: The item was **quick-frozen** while still fresh but not as quickly as flash-frozen.

Frozen: The item was subjected to temperatures of 0°F (−18°C) or lower to preserve its inherent quality.

Glazed: A frozen product dipped in water; the ice forms a glaze that protects the item from freezer burn.

Fancy: Marketing term used to indicate the product was previously frozen.

Fish fillets, whole fish and shellfish, such as shrimp, may be coated with water or glazed during the freezing process to help protect them from dehydrating. The addition of water-retaining agents and antioxidants to help preserve the fish is permitted.

Farming the Seas

Aquaculture or fish farming has been practiced in Asia for thousands of years. As wild fish and shellfish have been depleted by overfishing, aquaculture has grown into a major industry in the United States and many other non-Asian countries. More than 90 percent of the seafood consumed in the United States today is imported, and more than half of this imported seafood is farm-raised.

Aquaculture can take place in closed environments, where water is constantly circulated through tanks and ponds. Net pens or cages employed offshore can also hold vast numbers of fish. Mollusks (clams, oysters and mussels) are farmed in near-shore beds or, sometimes in the case of mussels, on long lines or even on the bases of offshore oil rigs. Catfish and trout have long been farm-raised in the United States, but now salmon, tilapia, hybrid striped bass, abalone, crayfish, freshwater prawns, shrimp and sturgeon are also farmed. Constant experimentation is taking place with different varieties: Norwegian scientists are working to raise halibut in aquafarms, and in California, sturgeon are being raised for their caviar with the help of Russian experts.

For the food service industry, aquaculture can mean that many fish are no longer seasonal; there is a constant supply, less price fluctuation and more standardized quality. As with all industries involved in food production, aquaculture is subject to federal and state regulation for both domestic and imported products. Fish farming is not without its critics, however, as environmental damage can result from poor management practices. Concerns have been raised regarding the use of chemicals and antibiotics. The food given to aquafarmed species also raises concerns. The feed may contain genetically modified ingredients or excessive amounts of soy and corn, and requires large quantities of other fish. In response to such concerns, an organic movement is growing (although still unregulated) within the industry.

Purchasing Fish and Shellfish

Fish are available from wholesalers in a variety of market forms:

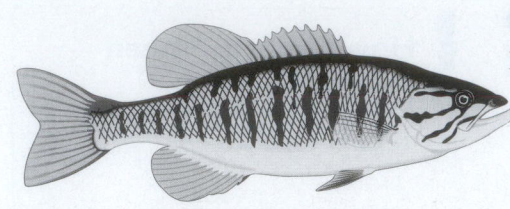

Whole or round

- **Whole** or **round**: As caught, intact.

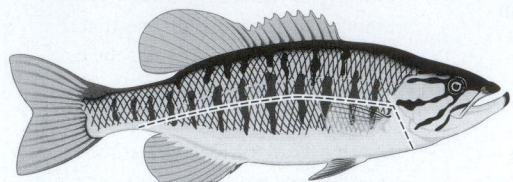

Drawn

- **Drawn:** Viscera (internal organs) are removed; most whole fish are purchased this way.

Dressed or pan-dressed

- **Dressed:** Viscera, gills, fins and scales are removed.
- **Pan-dressed:** Viscera and gills are removed; fish is scaled and fins and tail are trimmed. The head is usually removed, although small fish, such as trout, may be pan-dressed with the head still attached. Pan-dressed fish are ready to be pan-fried.

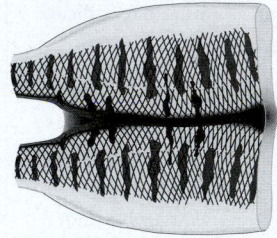

Butterflied fillet

- **Butterflied:** A pan-dressed fish or fillet, boned and opened flat like a book. The two sides remain attached by the back or belly skin.

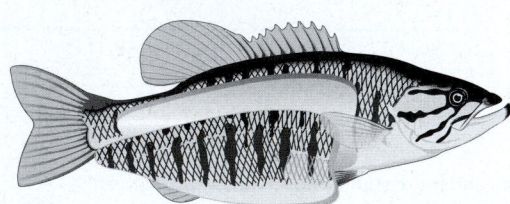

Fillet

- **Fillet:** The side of a fish removed intact, boneless or semiboneless, with or without skin.

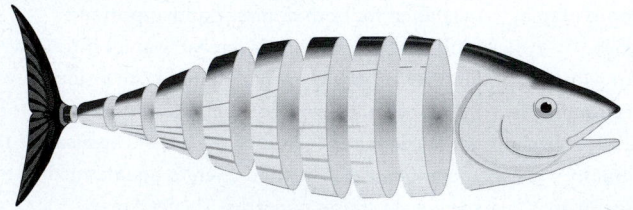

Steaks

- **Steak:** A cross-section slice, with a small section of backbone attached known as *darne* in French; usually prepared from large round fish such as salmon, swordfish or tuna.

Wheel or center-cut

- **Wheel or center-cut:** Used for swordfish and sharks, which are cut into large boneless pieces from which steaks are then cut.

Chefs purchase fish in the market forms most practical for each operation. Although fish fabrication is a relatively simple chore requiring little specialized equipment, before deciding to cut fish on premises, consider the following:

- The food service operation's ability to utilize the bones and trim that cutting whole fish produces; yield after fabrication can vary depending on a chef's skill
- Employees' ability to fabricate fillets, steaks or portions as needed
- Storage facilities
- The product's intended use

Most shellfish can be purchased live in the shell, shucked (the meat removed from the shell) or processed. Both live and shucked shellfish are usually purchased by counts (i.e., the number per volume). For example, standard live Eastern oysters are packed 200–250 (the count) per bushel (the unit of volume); standard Eastern shucked oyster meats are packed 350 per gallon. Crustaceans are sometimes packed by size based on the number of pieces per pound; for example, crab legs or shrimp are often sold in counts per pound. Crustaceans are also sold either by grades based on size (whole crabs) or by weight (lobsters).

Storing Fish and Shellfish

The most important concern when storing fish and shellfish is temperature. All fresh fish should be stored at temperatures between 30°F and 34°F (–1°C and 1°C). Fish stored in a refrigerator at 41°F (5°C) will have approximately half the shelf life of fish stored at 32°F (0°C).

Whole fish properly stored in a perforated pan and covered with crushed ice

Most fish are shipped on ice and should be stored on ice in the refrigerator as soon as possible after receipt. Whole fish should be layered directly in crushed or shaved ice in a perforated pan so that the melted ice water drains away. If crushed or shaved ice is not available, cubed ice may be used provided it is put in plastic bags and gently placed on top of the fish to prevent bruising and denting. Fabricated and portioned fish may be wrapped in moisture-proof packaging before icing to prevent the ice and water from damaging the exposed flesh. Fish stored on ice should be drained and re-iced daily.

Fresh scallops, fish fillets that are purchased in plastic trays and oyster and clam meats should be set on or packed in ice. Do not let scallops, fillets or meats come into direct contact with the ice.

Clams, mussels and oysters should be stored at 41°F (5°C), at high humidity and left in the boxes or net bags in which they were shipped. Under ideal conditions, shellfish can be kept alive for up to 1 week. Never store live shellfish in plastic bags, and do not ice them.

If a saltwater tank is not available, live lobsters, crabs and other crustaceans should be kept in boxes with seaweed or damp newspaper to keep them moist. Most crustaceans circulate salt water over their gills; icing them or placing them in fresh water will kill them. Lobsters and crabs will live for several days after purchase under ideal conditions.

Like most frozen foods, frozen fish should be kept at temperatures of 0°F (–18°C) or colder. Colder temperatures greatly increase shelf life. Frozen fish should be thawed in the refrigerator; once thawed, they should be treated like fresh fish.

FABRICATING PROCEDURES FOR FISH AND SHELLFISH

As discussed, fish and shellfish can be purchased in many forms. Here we present several procedures for cutting, cleaning and otherwise fabricating or preparing fish and shellfish for cooking and serving.

Procedure for Scaling Fish

This procedure is used to remove the scales from fish that will be cooked with the skin on.

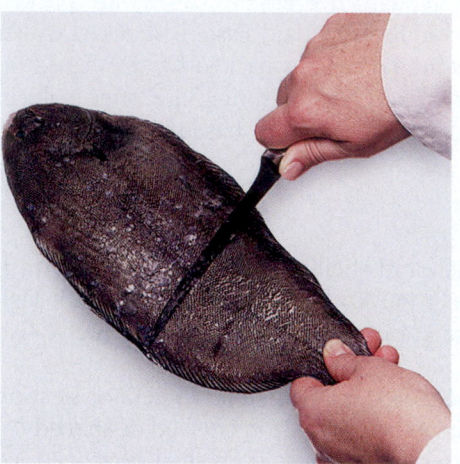

Place the fish on a work surface or in a large sink. Grip the fish by the tail and, working from the tail toward the head, scrape the scales off with a fish scaler or the back of a knife. Be careful not to damage the flesh by pushing too hard. Turn the fish over and remove the scales from the other side. Rinse the fish under cool water.

Procedure for Pan-Dressing Flatfish

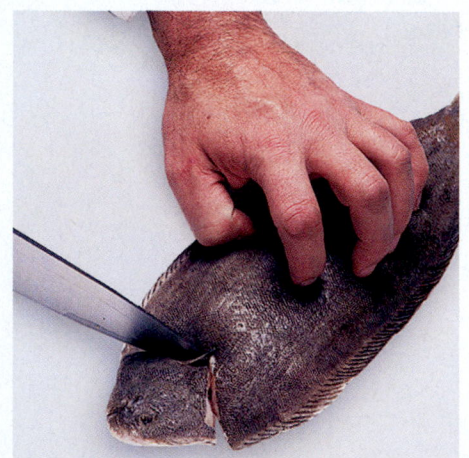

❶ Place the scaled fish on a cutting board and remove the head by making a V-shaped cut around it with a chef's knife. Pull the head away and remove the viscera.

❷ Rinse the fish under cold water, removing all traces of blood and viscera from the cavity.

❸ Using a pair of kitchen shears, trim off the tail and all of the fins.

Procedure for Filleting Round Fish

Round fish produce two fillets, one from either side.

❷ Turn the knife toward the tail; using smooth strokes, cut from head to tail, parallel to the backbone. The knife should bump against the backbone so that no flesh is wasted; you will feel the knife cutting through the small pin bones. Cut the fillet completely free from the bones. Repeat on the other side.

❶ Using a chef's knife, cut down to the backbone just behind the gills. Do not remove the head.

❸ Trim the rib bones from the fillet with a flexible boning knife.

❹ The finished fillet.

Procedure for Filleting Flatfish

Flatfish produce four fillets: two large bilateral fillets from the top and two smaller bilateral fillets from the bottom. If the fish fillets are going to be cooked with the skin on, the fish should be scaled before cooking (it is easier to scale the fish before it is filleted). If the skin is going to be removed before cooking, it is not necessary to scale the fish.

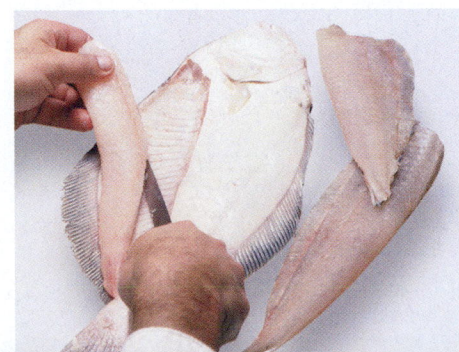

❶ With the dark side of the fish facing up, cut along the backbone from head to tail with the tip of a flexible boning knife.

❷ Turn the knife and, using smooth strokes, cut between the flesh and the rib bones, keeping the flexible blade against the bone. Cut the fillet completely free from the fish. Remove the second fillet, following the same procedure.

❸ Turn the fish over and remove the fillets from the bottom half of the fish, following the same procedure.

Procedure for Skinning Fish Fillets

We use a salmon fillet in the photos to demonstrate the procedure for skinning fish fillets. Use the same procedure to skin all types of fish fillets.

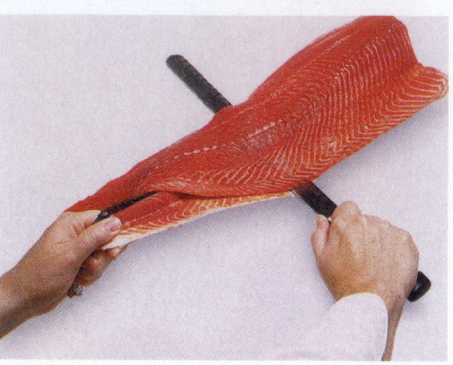

Place the fillet on a cutting board with the skin side down. Starting at the tail, use a meat slicer or a chef's knife to cut between the flesh and skin. Angle the knife down toward the skin, grip the skin tightly with one hand and use a smooth sawing motion to cut the skin cleanly away from the flesh.

Procedure for Pulling Pin Bones from Salmon Fillets

Round fish fillets contain a row of intramuscular bones running the length of the fillet. Known as pin bones, they are usually cut out with a knife to produce boneless fillets. In the case of salmon, they can be removed with salmon tweezers or small needle-nose pliers.

Place the fillet (either skinless or not) on the cutting board, skin side down. Starting at the front or head end of the fillet, use your fingertips to locate the bones and use the pliers to pull them out one by one.

Procedure for Cutting Tranches

A **tranche** is a slice cut from fillets of large flat or round fish. Usually cut on an angle, tranches look large and increase plate coverage.

Place the fillet on the cutting board, skin side down. Using a slicer or chef's knife, cut slices of the desired weight. The tranche can be cut to the desired size by adjusting the angle of the knife. The greater the angle, the larger the surface area of the tranche.

Procedure for Cutting Steaks from Salmon and Similarly Sized Round Fish

Steaks are produced from salmon and similarly sized round fish by making crosscuts of the whole fish. First scale, gut and remove the fins from the fish. Then:

Using a chef's knife, cut through the fish, slicing steaks of the desired thickness. The steaks will contain some bones that are not necessarily removed.

Procedure for Cleaning Squid

1 Pull the tentacles (left) and mantle or body (right) apart.

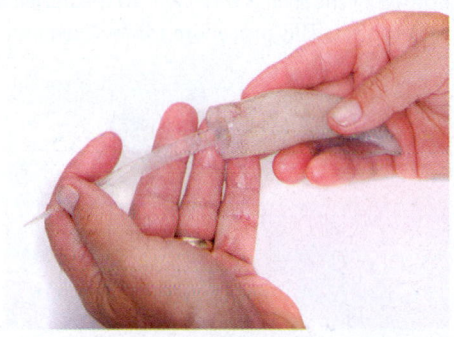

2 Pull the transparent quill (left) from the mantle and discard.

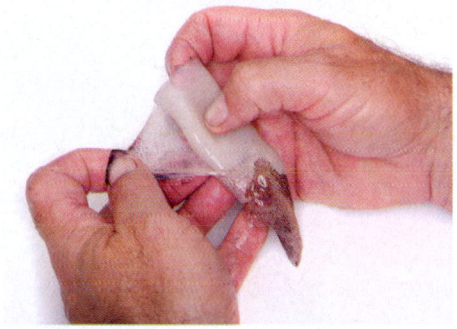

3 Peel off the brown skin and discard.

4 Cut the tentacles from the head, inserting the knife just below the eyes. Reserve the ink sac if desired and discard the remaining organs.

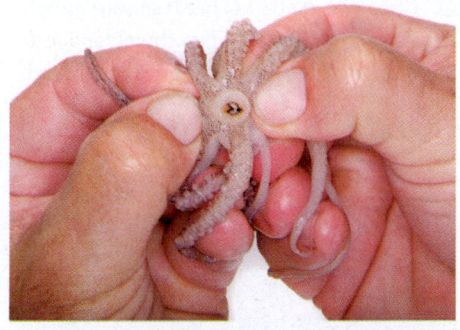

5 Open the tentacles to expose the beak. Pull the beak out and discard.

6 Rinse the squid in cold water. If desired the squid may be cut into strips for cooking.

Procedure for Cleaning Soft-Shell Crab

1 Using kitchen shears, cut off the front of the crab about ½ inch (1.2 centimeters) behind the eyes and mouth. Squeeze out the contents of the sac located behind the crab face.

2 Lift one of the pointed ends of the shell and remove the gills and discard them. Repeat on the other side.

3 Turn the crab over and snip off the flap (known as the apron). Rinse the crab in cold water and pat dry.

Procedure for Peeling and Deveining Shrimp

Peeling and deveining shrimp is a simple procedure done in most commercial kitchens. The tail portion of the shell is often left on the peeled shrimp to give it an attractive appearance or make it easier to eat. This procedure can be used on both cooked and uncooked shrimp.

1 Grip the shrimp's tail between your thumb and forefinger. Use your other thumb and forefinger to grip the legs and the edge of the shell.

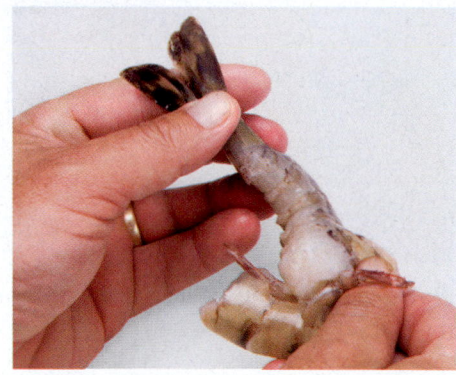

2 Pull the legs and shell away from the flesh, leaving the tail and first joint of the shell in place if desired.

3 Place the shrimp on a cutting board and use a paring knife to make a shallow cut down the back of the shrimp, exposing the digestive tract or "vein."

4 Pull out the vein while rinsing the shrimp under cold water.

Procedure for Butterflying Shrimp

Butterflying raw shrimp improves their appearance and increases their surface area for even cooking. To butterfly shrimp, first peel them using the procedure just outlined. Then:

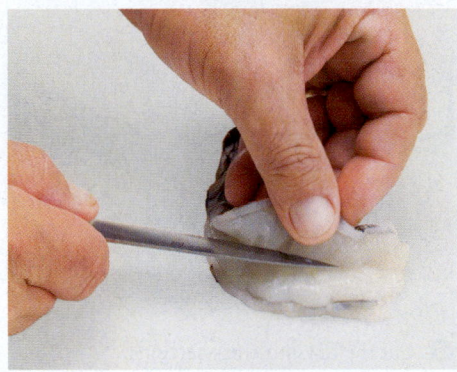

Instead of making a shallow cut to expose the vein, make a deeper cut that nearly slices the shrimp into two bilateral halves. Pull out the vein while rinsing the shrimp under cold water.

Procedure for Preparing Live Lobsters for Broiling

A whole lobster can be cooked by plunging it into boiling water or court bouillon. If the lobster is to be broiled, it must be split lengthwise before cooking.

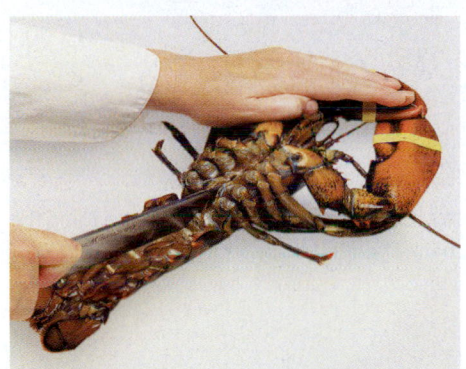

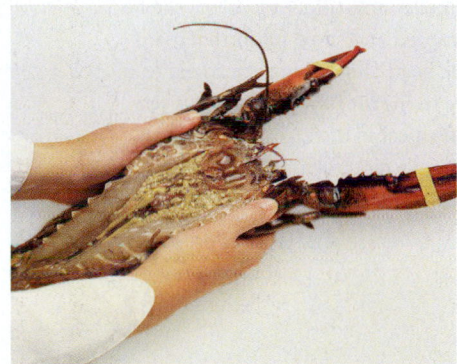

➊ Place the live lobster on its back on a cutting board and pierce its head with the point of a chef's knife. Then, in one smooth stroke, bring the knife down and cut through the body and tail without splitting it completely in half.

➋ Use your hands to crack the lobster's back so that it lies flat. Crack the claws with the back of a chef's knife.

➌ Cut through the tail and curl each half of the tail to the side. Remove and discard the stomach. The tomalley (the olive-green liver) and if present the coral (the roe) can be removed and saved for a sauce or other preparation.

Procedure for Preparing Live Lobsters for Sautéing

A whole live lobster may also be cut into smaller pieces for sautéing or other preparations.

1 Using the point of a chef's knife, pierce the lobster's head.

2 Cut off the claws and arms.

3 Cut the tail into cross-sections.

4 Split the head and thorax in half. The tomalley and coral (if present) can be removed and saved for further use. The head and legs may be added to the recipe for flavor, but there is very little meat in them and they are typically discarded.

5 Crack the claws with a firm blow, using the back of a chef's knife.

Procedure for Removing Cooked Lobster Meat from the Shell

Many recipes call for cooked lobster meat. Cook the live lobster by plunging it into a boiling court bouillon and simmering for 6–8 minutes per pound. Remove the lobster and allow it to cool until it can be easily handled. Then:

1 Pull the claws and large legs away from the body. Break the claw away from the leg. Split the legs with a chef's knife and remove the meat, using your fingers or a pick.

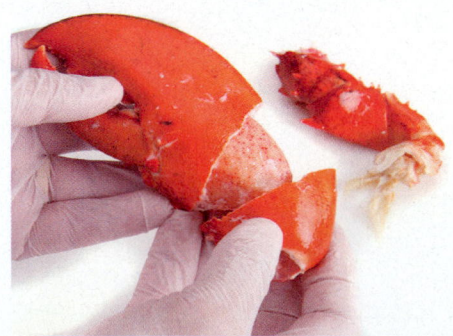

2 Carefully crack the claw with a mallet or the back of a chef's knife without damaging the meat. Pull out the claw meat in one piece.

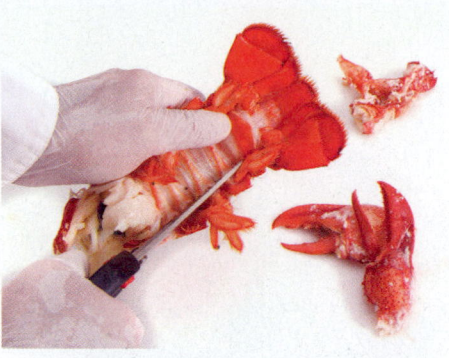

3 Pull the lobster's tail away from its body and use kitchen shears to trim away the soft membrane on the underside of the tail.

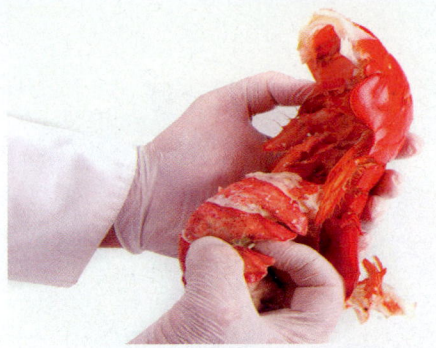

4 Pull the meat out of the shell in one piece.

Procedure for Opening Clams

Opening raw clams efficiently requires practice. Like all mollusks, clams should be cleaned under cold running water with a brush to remove all mud, silt and sand that may be stuck to their shells. A knife is more easily inserted into a clam if the clam is washed and allowed to relax in the refrigerator for at least 1 hour.

1 Wearing a mesh safety glove, hold the cleaned clam in the palm of your hand; the notch in the edge of the shell should be toward your thumb. With the fingers of the same hand, squeeze and pull the blade of the clam knife between the clamshells. Do not push on the knife handle with your other hand; you will not be able to control the knife if it slips and you can cut yourself.

2 Wearing a mesh safety glove, pull the knife between the shells until it cuts the muscle. Twist the knife to pry the shells apart. Slide the knife tip along the top shell and cut through the muscle. Twist the top shell, breaking it free at the hinge; discard it.

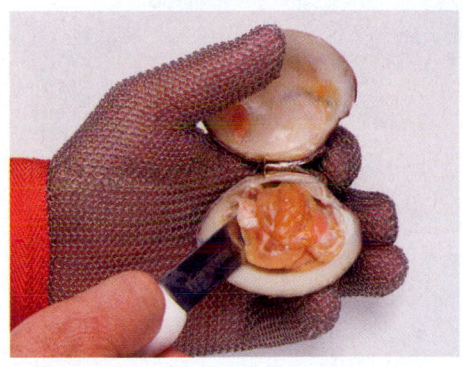

3 Use the knife tip to release the clam from the bottom shell.

Procedure for Opening Oysters

1 Clean the oyster by brushing it under running water.

2 Wearing a mesh safety glove, hold the cleaned oyster firmly in the palm of your hand. Insert the tip of an oyster knife in the hinge and use a twisting motion to pop the hinge apart. Do not put too much forward pressure on the knife; it can slip and you could stab yourself.

3 Slide the knife along the top of the shell to release the oyster from the shell. Discard the top shell.

4 Use the knife tip to release the oyster from the bottom shell.

5 Fresh raw oysters on the half shell with seaweed garnish.

Procedure for Cleaning and Debearding Mussels

Mussels are not normally eaten raw. Before cooking, a clump of dark threads called the **beard** must be removed. Because this could kill the mussel, cleaning and debearding must be done as close to cooking time as possible.

1 Clean the mussel with a brush under cold running water to remove sand and grit.

2 Pull the beard away from the mussel with your fingers or a small pair of pliers.

COOKING FISH AND SHELLFISH

Fish and shellfish can be prepared by the dry-heat cooking methods of broiling and grilling, roasting (baking), sautéing, pan-frying and deep-frying as well as the moist-heat cooking methods of steaming, poaching and simmering.

Substituting Fish

When selecting fish for a particular recipe, consult Table 20.2 to find the appropriate fish substitute. Any of the fish in the five lefthand column categories can serve as substitutes for each other.

FISH SUBSTITUTIONS FOR CULINARY PURPOSES*		TABLE 20.2
FISH	**CHARACTERISTICS**	**COOKING METHODS**
Cod, Atlantic Dover sole Haddock Lake whitefish Pacific sand dab Halibut Pacific sole Spotted cabrilla Tilapia	White flesh with very light, delicate flavor and flaky, tender, delicate texture; lean	Bake, roast, sauté, poach, steam, *en papillote*
Sea bream Lionfish American plaice John Dory Arrowtooth and starry flounder Butter, English, and rock sole Cobia Sea trout	White flesh with a moderate flavor and flaky, tender to firm texture; lean to moderately fatty	Bake, broil, poach, sauté, steam, deep-fry, *en papillote*
Alaskan pollock Brook and rainbow trout Catfish Grouper Mahi-mahi Pacific ocean perch Red snapper Skate White sea bass Wahoo/Ono	Light flesh, moderate flavor and moderately firm texture; moderately fatty	Bake, roast, grill, broil, poach, sauté, pan-fry, deep-fry
Atlantic, coho and king (Chinook) salmon European Turbot Eel Pacific cod Lake Chub Herring Lake sturgeon Arctic char (lake trout) Monkfish Pollock Striped bass Swordfish Vermillion snapper	Darker flesh, moderate flavor and moderately firm texture; fatty	Bake, grill, broil, sauté, steam, poach, *en papillote*, smoke
Black sea bass Bluefish King mackerel Tuna (all varieties) Spanish mackerel	Dark flesh, moderate to strong flavor and firm texture; fatty	Grill, broil, sauté, poach, steam, pickle, stew, smoke

* The fish listed here are not endangered and are mentioned in this text.

Determining Doneness

Unlike most meats and poultry, nearly all fish and shellfish are inherently tender and should be cooked just until done. Overcooking is the most common mistake made when preparing fish and shellfish. The Canadian Department of Fisheries recommends that all fish be cooked 10 minutes for every inch (2.5 centimeters) of thickness, regardless of cooking method. Although this may be a good general policy, variables such as the type and the form of fish and the exact cooking method used suggest that one or more of the following methods of determining doneness are more appropriate for professional food service operations:

- *Translucent flesh becomes opaque:* The raw flesh of most fish and shellfish appears somewhat translucent. As the proteins coagulate during cooking, the flesh becomes opaque.
- *Flesh becomes firm:* The flesh of most fish and shellfish firms as it cooks. Doneness can be tested by judging the resistance of the flesh when pressed with a finger. Raw or undercooked fish or shellfish are mushy and soft. As it cooks, the flesh offers more resistance and springs back quickly.
- *Flesh separates from the bones easily:* The flesh of raw fish remains firmly attached to the bones. As the fish cooks, the flesh and bones separate easily.
- *Flesh begins to flake:* Fish flesh consists of short muscle fibers separated by thin connective tissue. As the fish cooks, the connective tissue breaks down and the groups of muscle fibers begin to flake, that is, separate from one another. Fish is done when the flesh begins to flake. If the flesh flakes easily, the fish will be overdone and dry.

Like other foods, fish and shellfish are subject to carryover cooking. Because they cook quickly and at low temperatures, it is better to undercook fish and shellfish and allow carryover cooking or residual heat to finish the cooking process.

DRY-HEAT COOKING METHODS FOR FISH AND SHELLFISH

Dry-heat cooking methods are those that do not require additional moisture at any time during the cooking process. The dry-heat cooking methods used with fish and shellfish are broiling and grilling, roasting (usually referred to as baking when used with fish and shellfish), sautéing, pan-frying and deep-frying.

Broiling and Grilling

After brushing with oil or butter, fish can be grilled directly on the grate or placed on a heated platter under the broiler. Broiled or grilled fish should have a lightly charred surface and a slightly smoky flavor as a result of the intense radiant heat of the broiler or grill. The interior should be moist and juicy. Broiled or grilled shellfish meat should be moist and tender with only slight coloration from the grill or broiler.

Selecting Fish and Shellfish to Broil or Grill

Nearly all types of fish and shellfish can be successfully broiled or grilled. Salmon, trout, swordfish and other oily fish are especially well suited to grilling. Lean fish such as bass and snapper are as well. Fillets of lean flatfish with delicate textures, such as flounder and sole, are better broiled. The fillets should be placed on a preheated broiling (sizzler) platter before being placed under the broiler.

Oysters and clams are often broiled on the half shell with flavored butters, bread crumbs or other garnishes and served sizzling hot. Squid can be stuffed, secured with a toothpick and broiled or grilled. Split lobsters, king crabs and snow crabs are often broiled or grilled after being brushed with butter. Whole lobsters can be split and broiled or grilled, or their tails can be removed, split and cooked separately. Large crab legs can also be split and broiled or grilled. Shrimp and scallops are often broiled in flavored butters or grilled on skewers for easy handling.

Seasoning Fish and Shellfish to Broil or Grill

All fish should be brushed lightly with butter or oil before being placed on the grill or under the broiler. The butter or oil prevents sticking and helps leaner fish retain moisture. For most fish, a simple seasoning of salt and pepper suffices. But some fish respond well to marinades, especially marinades made with white wine and lemon juice. Delicately flavored fish should be marinated for only a brief time. (Even marinated fish should be brushed with butter or oil before cooking.) Herbs should be avoided because they will burn from the intense heat of the broiler or grill, although the smoke from herbs such as fennel, lavender or thyme can impart flavor to the outside of fish when it is grilled whole.

Clams, oysters and other shellfish that are stuffed or cooked with butters, vegetables, bacon or other accompaniments or garnishes gain flavor from these ingredients. Be careful, however, not to overpower the delicate flavors of the shellfish by adding too many strong flavorings.

Accompaniments to Broiled and Grilled Fish and Shellfish

Lemon wedges are the traditional accompaniment to broiled or grilled fish and shellfish. Lemon wedges can be served as the only accompaniments or with sauces made separately. Butter sauces such as Beurre Blanc (page 232) are popular, as their richness complements the lean fish. Vegetable coulis are a good choice for a healthier, lower-fat accompaniment. Additional sauce suggestions are found in Tables 11.4 and 11.6. If an item is cooked on a broiler platter with a seasoned butter, it is often served with that butter.

Almost any side dish goes well with broiled or grilled fish or shellfish. Fried or boiled potatoes, pasta and rice are all good choices. Grilled vegetables are a natural choice.

Procedure for Broiling or Grilling Fish and Shellfish

Fish is delicate and must be carefully handled to achieve an attractive finished product. When broiling whole fish or fillets with their skin still on, score the skin by making several diagonal slashes approximately ¼ inch (6 millimeters) deep at even intervals. This prevents the fish from curling during cooking, promotes even cooking and creates a more attractive finished product. Pat the skin dry because moisture will prevent it from browning. Be especially careful not to overcook the item. It should be served as hot as possible as soon as it is removed from the broiler or grill.

1 Heat the broiler or grill.

2 Use a wire brush to remove any charred or burnt particles that may be stuck to the broiler or grill grate. Wipe the grate with a lightly oiled towel to remove any remaining particles and help season it.

3 Prepare the item to be broiled or grilled. For example, cut the fish into steaks or tranches of even thickness; split the lobster; peel and/or skewer the shrimp. Season or marinate the item as desired. Brush the item with oil or butter.

4 Place the item on a grill, presentation side down. If using a broiler, place the item directly on the grate or on a preheated broiler platter. Tender fish are usually broiled presentation side up on a broiler platter.

5 If practical, turn the item to produce the attractive crosshatch marks associated with grilling that are discussed in Chapter 10, Principles of Cooking. Items less than ½ inch (1.2 centimeters) thick cooked on a preheated broiler platter do not have to be turned.

6 Cook the item to the desired doneness and serve immediately.

Broiled Black Sea Bass with Herb Butter and Sautéed Leeks

MISE EN PLACE

- Melt butter and keep warm.
- Wash, clean and julienne the leek.
- Prepare the Herb Butter.

YIELD 1 Serving, 9 oz. (270 g)		METHOD Broiling	
Black sea bass or any type of bass fillet, skin on, approx. 8 oz. (240 g)	1	1	
Salt and pepper	TT	TT	
Whole butter, melted	as needed	as needed	
Leek, julienne	1	1	
Lemon juice	2 tsp.	10 ml	
Herb Butter (page 234)	2 slices	2 slices	

1 Score the skin of the fillet with three diagonal cuts approximately ¼ inch (6 millimeters) deep.

2 Season the fillet with salt and pepper and brush with melted butter.

3 Place the fillet on a preheated broiler platter, skin side up, and place under the broiler.

4 Blanch the leek in boiling water until nearly tender.

5 Drain the leek and sauté in 1 tablespoon (15 milliliters) whole butter until tender. Add the lemon juice; season with salt and pepper.

6 Remove the fish from the broiler when done. Top with the Herb Butter and serve on a bed of sautéed leeks.

Approximate values per 9-oz. (270-g) serving: **Calories** 260, **Total fat** 15 g, **Saturated fat** 8 g, **Cholesterol** 80 mg, **Sodium** 790 mg, **Total carbohydrates** 11 g, **Protein** 21 g, **Vitamin A** 15%, **Vitamin C** 15%

❶ Scoring the fish skin.

❷ Placing the fish on a broiler platter, under the broiler.

❸ Serving the fish on a bed of sautéed leeks.

Baking

The terms *baking* and *roasting* are used interchangeably when applied to fish and shellfish. One disadvantage of baking fish is that the short baking time does not allow the surface of the fish to caramelize. To help address this concern, fish can be browned in a sauté pan with a small amount of oil to achieve the added flavor and appearance of a browned surface and then finished in an oven.

Selecting Fish and Shellfish to Bake

Fatty fish produce the best baked fish. Fish fillets and steaks are the best market forms to bake, as they cook quickly and evenly and are easily portioned. Although lean fish can be baked, it tends to become dry and must be basted often.

Seasoning Fish and Shellfish to Bake

The most popular seasonings for baked fish are lemon, butter, salt and pepper. Fish can also be marinated before baking for added flavor. But baked fish usually depend on the accompanying sauce for much of their flavor.

Shellfish are often stuffed or mixed with other ingredients before baking. For example, raw oysters on the half shell can be topped with spinach, watercress and Pernod

(Oysters Rockefeller, page 538) and baked. Shrimp are often butterflied, stuffed and baked; lobsters are split, stuffed and baked. Many food service operations remove clams from their shells; mix them with bread crumbs, seasonings or other ingredients; refill the shells and bake the mixture.

Accompaniments to Baked Fish and Shellfish

Baked fish is often served with a flavorful sauce such as a Creole sauce (page 229) or Beurre Blanc (page 232). Additional sauce suggestions are found in Tables 11.4 and 11.6. Almost any type of rice, pasta or potato is a good accompaniment, as is any variety of sautéed vegetable.

Procedure for Baking Fish and Shellfish

1. Portion the fish or shellfish and arrange on a well-oiled or buttered pan, presentation side up.
2. Season as desired and brush the surface of the fish or shellfish generously with melted butter; add garnishes or flavorings as desired or directed in the recipe.
3. Place the pan in a preheated oven at approximately 400°F (200°C).
4. Baste periodically during the cooking process (more often if the fish is lean). Remove from the oven when the fish is slightly underdone.

Baked Tilapia

YIELD 4 Servings, 9 oz. (270 g) each	METHOD Baking		MISE EN PLACE
Tilapia fillets, 8 oz. (240 g) each	4	4	• Melt whole butter and keep warm.
Salt and white pepper	TT	TT	• Wash and chop mint leaves.
Whole butter, melted	2 oz.	60 g	• Peel and mince garlic.
Fresh mint leaves, chopped	1 Tbsp.	15 ml	
Garlic, minced	1 tsp.	5 ml	
Tomato concassée	4 oz.	120 g	
White wine	2 fl. oz.	60 ml	
Lemon juice	2 fl. oz.	60 ml	

1. Place the fillets on a buttered baking pan. Season with salt and white pepper; brush with butter.
2. Combine the mint, garlic and tomato concassée, and spoon on top of each fillet of the fish.
3. Add the wine and lemon juice to the pan.
4. Bake at 400°F (200°C), basting once halfway through the cooking process, until done, approximately 15 minutes.

Note Ling or red rock cod or other firm flesh white fish may be used in place of tilapia in this recipe.

Approximate values per 9-oz. (270-g) serving: **Calories** 600, **Total fat** 16 g, **Saturated fat** 8 g, **Cholesterol** 140 mg, **Sodium** 850 mg, **Total carbohydrates** 55 g, **Protein** 60 g, **Vitamin A** 25%, **Vitamin C** 35%

❶ Brushing the fillets with butter.

❷ Spooning the mint and tomato concassée onto each portion.

❸ The finished baked tilapia.

Sautéing

Sautéing is a very popular cooking method for fish and shellfish that lightly caramelizes the food's surface, giving it additional flavor. Typically other ingredients such as garlic, onions, vegetables, wine and lemon juice are added to the fond to make a sauce.

Selecting Fish and Shellfish to Sauté

Both fatty and lean fish may be sautéed. Flatfish are sometimes dressed and sautéed whole, as are small round fish such as trout. To sauté larger fish such as salmon, choose steaks, fillets or tranches. The portions should be relatively uniform in size and thickness and fairly thin to promote even cooking. Although clams, mussels and oysters are not often sautéed, scallops and crustaceans are popular sauté items.

Seasoning Fish and Shellfish to Sauté

Many types of fish—especially sole, flounder and other delicate, lean fish fillets—are often dredged in plain or seasoned flour before sautéing. Seasoned butter is used to sauté some items, such as scampi-style shrimp. These items derive their flavor from the butter; additional seasonings should not be necessary.

Cooking Temperatures for Sautéing

The sauté pan and cooking fat must be hot before the fish or shellfish are added. Do not add too much fish or shellfish to the pan at one time, or the pan and fat will cool. This will allow the foods to simmer in their own juices and cook the fish before it browns. See Figure 20.8. Thin slices and small pieces of fish and shellfish require a short cooking time; use high temperatures in order to caramelize their surfaces without overcooking. Slightly lower cooking temperatures may be better for large, thick pieces of fish or shellfish being cooked in the shell. This ensures that they are cooked without overbrowning their surfaces.

Accompaniments to Sautéed Fish and Shellfish

Sautéed fish and shellfish are nearly always served with a sauce made directly in the sauté pan. This sauce may be as simple as browned butter (*beurre noisette*) or a complicated sauce flavored with the fond. In some cases, seasoned butter is used to sauté the fish or shellfish and the butter is then served with the main item. See Tables 11.4 and 11.6 for additional sauce suggestions. Mildly flavored rice and pasta are good choices to serve with sautéed fish or shellfish.

Figure 20.8 A properly sautéed fish fillet (left) is lightly brown and holds its shape without sticking to the pan. An improperly sautéed fish fillet (right) is pale, falls apart and sticks to the pan.

Procedure for Sautéing Fish and Shellfish

1 Cut or portion the fish or shellfish.
2 Season the fish or shellfish and dredge in seasoned flour if desired.
3 Heat a suitable sauté pan over medium heat; add enough oil or clarified butter to cover the bottom to a depth of about ⅛ inch (3 millimeters).
4 Add the fish or shellfish to the pan (fish should be placed presentation side down); cook until done, turning once halfway through the cooking process. Add other items as called for in the recipe.
5 Remove the fish or shellfish. If a sauce is to be made in the sauté pan, follow the procedures discussed in Chapter 18, Poultry, on page 438.

Sautéed Halibut with Three-Color Peppers and Spanish Olives

YIELD 4 Servings, 10 oz. (300 g) each	METHOD	Sautéing
Halibut, fluke or swordfish fillets, 6 oz. (180 g) each	4	4
Salt and pepper	TT	TT
Olive oil	2 fl. oz.	60 ml
Onion, sliced	3 oz.	90 g
Garlic, minced	2 tsp.	10 ml
Green bell pepper, julienne	3 oz.	90 g
Red bell pepper, julienne	3 oz.	90 g
Yellow bell pepper, julienne	3 oz.	90 g
Tomato concassée	8 oz.	240 g
Spanish olives, pitted and quartered	2 oz.	60 g
Fresh thyme, chopped	2 tsp.	10 ml
Lemon juice	2 fl. oz.	60 ml
Fish stock	2 fl. oz.	60 ml

MISE EN PLACE

- Peel and slice onions.
- Peel and mince garlic.
- Wash, seed and julienne bell peppers.
- Pit and quarter olives.
- Wash and chop thyme.

1 Season the fillets with salt and pepper.
2 Heat a sauté pan large enough to hold the fillets without crowding and add the oil.
3 Sauté the fillets, turning once. Remove fish and reserve in a warm place.
4 Add the onion and garlic to the same pan and sauté for approximately 1 minute. Add the bell peppers and sauté for 1–2 minutes more.
5 Add the tomato concassée, olives and thyme; sauté briefly.
6 Add the lemon juice and deglaze the pan. Add the stock, simmer for 2 minutes to blend the flavors and adjust the seasonings.
7 Return the fish to the pan to reheat. Serve each fish fillet on a bed of vegetables with sauce and an appropriate garnish.

Approximate values per 10-oz. (300-g) serving: **Calories** 420, **Total fat** 21 g, **Saturated fat** 3 g, **Cholesterol** 70 mg, **Sodium** 870 mg, **Total carbohydrates** 10 g, **Protein** 47 g, **Vitamin A** 15%, **Vitamin C** 110%

❶ Sautéing the fillets.

❷ Sautéing the onions, garlic and peppers.

❸ Adding the fish stock.

❹ Returning the fish to the pan to reheat.

Pan-Frying

Pan-frying is very similar to sautéing, but more fat is used to cook the main item when pan-frying. Pan-fried fish is always coated with flour, batter or breading to help seal the surface and prevent the flesh from coming into direct contact with the cooking fat. Properly prepared pan-fried fish and shellfish should be moist and tender with a crisp surface. If fish is battered or breaded, the coating should be intact with no breaks.

Selecting Fish and Shellfish to Pan-Fry

Both fatty and lean fish may be pan-fried. Trout and other small fish are ideal for pan-frying, as are portioned fillets of lean fish such as halibut. Fish and shellfish for pan-frying should be uniform in size and relatively thin so that they cook quickly and evenly.

Seasoning Fish and Shellfish to Pan-Fry

Although fish and shellfish can be marinated or seasoned directly, it is more common to season the flour, batter or breading that will coat them. Batters, for example, can contain cheese, and breadings can contain nuts and other ingredients to add various flavors to the fish or shellfish. Review the battering and breading procedures discussed in Chapter 9, Mise en Place. Additional seasonings are provided by sauces and other accompaniments served with the pan-fried fish or shellfish.

Cooking Temperatures for Pan-Frying

The fat should always be hot before the fish or shellfish are added. Breaded or battered fish fillets cook very quickly, and the fat should be hot enough to brown the coating without overcooking the interior. Whole pan-fried fish take longer to cook and therefore require a slightly lower cooking temperature so that the surface does not become too dark before the interior is cooked.

Accompaniments to Pan-Fried Fish and Shellfish

Lemon wedges are the classic accompaniment to pan-fried fish and shellfish. Sauces that accompany pan-fried items are made separately. Mayonnaise-based sauces such as Tartar Sauce (page 758) and Rémoulade Sauce (page 759) are especially popular; rich, wine-based sauces should be avoided. Vegetable coulis, such as tomato, also complement many pan-fried items. Additional sauce suggestions are found in Tables 11.4 and 11.6.

Procedure for Pan-Frying Fish and Shellfish

1 Heat enough clarified butter or oil in a heavy sauté pan so that it is one-third to halfway up the side of the item. The fat should be at a temperature between 325°F and 350°F (163°C and 177°C).

2 Add the floured, breaded or battered item to the pan, being careful not to splash the hot fat. Cook until done, turning once halfway through the cooking process.

3 Remove the fish or shellfish and drain on absorbent paper.

4 Serve promptly with an appropriate sauce.

Pan-Fried Trout

YIELD 2 Servings, 5 oz. (150 g)	METHOD Pan-Frying	
Trout fillets, skin-on, 5 oz. (300 g)	2	2
Salt and pepper	TT	TT
Flour	as needed for dredging	
Clarified butter	2 fl. oz.	60 ml
Whole butter	½ oz.	15 g
Lemon juice	2 fl. oz.	60 ml
Fresh parsley, chopped	1 tsp.	4 ml

MISE EN PLACE
- Chop parsley.

1 Season the trout fillets with salt and pepper; dredge in flour.

2 Heat a sauté pan over medium heat and add enough clarified butter to cover the bottom approximately ¼ inch (6 millimeters) deep.

3 Carefully place the trout fillets in the pan, presentation side down, and cook until done. Turn once when the first side is nicely browned.

4 Remove the fillets from the pan. Drain them on absorbent paper and place them on heated plates.

5 Degrease the pan, add the whole butter and cook until it begins to brown.

6 Add the lemon juice and parsley and swirl to combine with the butter.

7 Top the fillets with the butter sauce and serve.

Approximate values per 5-oz. (150-g) serving: **Calories** 260, **Total fat** 22 g, **Saturated fat** 11 g, **Cholesterol** 70 mg, **Sodium** 32 mg, **Total carbohydrates** 1 g, **Protein** 15 g

❶ Dredging the trout fillets in flour.

❷ Placing the trout fillets into the pan, presentation side down.

❸ Turning the trout fillets when browned.

Deep-Frying

Deep-frying is the process of cooking foods by submerging them in hot fat. Typically fish or shellfish are breaded or battered before deep-frying. Alternatively they can be formed into croquettes or fritters. Properly deep-fried fish and shellfish should be moist and tender, not greasy or tough. Their coating should be crispy and golden brown.

Selecting Fish and Shellfish to Deep-Fry

Whole small fish and fillets of lean fish such as catfish or halibut are excellent for deep-frying. The fillets should be of uniform size and relatively thin so that they cook quickly and evenly. Fatty fish, such as salmon, are ideal for croquettes. Peeled shrimp and shucked mollusks, especially clams and oysters, can be breaded, battered or formed into fritters and deep-fried. Deep-fried breaded or battered sliced squid or octopus served with a dipping sauce makes excellent hors d'oeuvre.

Seasoning Fish and Shellfish to Deep-Fry

Typically seasonings used for deep-fried fish or shellfish are added to the breading or batter. In contrast, salt and pepper should be added after frying. Additional flavors come from sauces or accompaniments.

Accompaniments to Deep-Fried Fish and Shellfish

As with pan-fried fish and shellfish, lemon wedges and mayonnaise-based sauces such as Tartar Sauce (page 758) and Creole Rémoulade Sauce (page 759) are popular accompaniments to deep-fried fish and shellfish. Spicy tomato- or soy-based dipping sauces are also excellent choices. Traditional English fish and chips is served with malt vinegar.

Procedure for Deep-Frying Fish and Shellfish

1 Shuck, peel, cut, trim or otherwise prepare the fish or shellfish to be deep-fried. Season, bread or batter it as desired.
2 Heat the fat to the desired temperature, usually around 350°F (177°C). Breaded or battered fish or shellfish cook quickly and the fat must be hot enough to cook the food's interior without burning its surface.
3 Carefully place the food in the hot fat using either the basket method or the swimming method.
4 Deep-fry the fish or shellfish until done. Determine doneness by color, timing or sampling.
5 Remove the deep-fried food from the fat and hold it over the fryer, allowing the excess fat to drain off. Transfer the food to a hotel pan either lined with absorbent paper or fitted with a rack. Season with salt if desired.
6 If the deep-fried fish or shellfish is to be held for later service, place it under a heat lamp.

MISE EN PLACE

- Cut fish into uniform-sized pieces.
- Heat deep-fat fryer.

Deep-Fried Catfish Fillets with Tartar Sauce

YIELD 8 Servings, 8 oz. (240 g) each	METHOD Deep-Frying	
Catfish or tilapia fillets, cut into uniform-sized pieces	3 lb.	1.4 kg
Salt and pepper	TT	TT
Flour	as needed for breading	
Egg wash	as needed for breading	
Cornmeal	as needed for breading	
Tartar Sauce (page 758)	12 fl. oz.	360 ml

1 Season the fillets with salt and pepper.
2 Bread the fillets using the standard breading procedure described in Chapter 9, Mise en Place.
3 Using the basket method, deep-fry the fillets until done. Drain well and serve with the Tartar Sauce.

Approximate values per 8-oz. (240-g) serving: **Calories** 600, **Total fat** 46 g, **Saturated fat** 10 g, **Cholesterol** 160 mg, **Sodium** 910 mg, **Total carbohydrates** 16 g, **Protein** 31 g, **Iron** 15%

❶ Flouring the seasoned fish fillets.

❷ Passing the floured fillets through the egg wash.

❸ Coating the fillets with cornmeal.

MOIST-HEAT COOKING METHODS FOR FISH AND SHELLFISH

Fish and shellfish lend themselves well to moist-heat cooking methods, especially steaming, poaching and simmering. Steaming best preserves the food's natural flavors and cooks without adding fat. Poaching is also popular, especially for fish. Poached fish can be served hot or cold, whole or as steaks, fillets or portions. Boiling, which is actually simmering, is most often associated with crustaceans.

Steaming

Steaming is a way to cook fish and shellfish without adding fats. Fish are steamed by suspending them over a small amount of boiling liquid in a covered pan. The steam trapped in the pan gently cooks the food while preserving natural flavors and most nutrients. The liquid used to steam fish and shellfish can be water or a court bouillon with herbs, spices, aromatics or wine added to infuse the item with additional flavors. Mussels and clams can be steamed by placing them directly in a pan, adding a small amount of wine or other liquid and covering them. Their shells will hold them above the liquid as they cook. Fish and shellfish can also be steamed by wrapping them in parchment paper together with herbs, vegetables, butters or sauces as accompaniments and baking them in a hot oven. This method of steaming is called **_en papillote_**.

Properly steamed fish and shellfish should be moist and tender with clean and delicate flavors. Any accompaniments or sauces should complement the main item without masking its flavor. Fish and shellfish cooked _en papillote_ should be served piping hot so that the aromatic steam trapped by the paper escapes as the paper is cut open tableside.

en papillote [awn pa-pee-YOTE] a cooking method in which food is wrapped in paper or foil and heated so that the food steams in its own moisture

Selecting Fish and Shellfish to Steam

Mollusks (e.g., clams and mussels), fatty fish (e.g., salmon and sea bass) and lean fish (e.g., sole) all produce good results when steamed. Portions should be of uniform thickness and no more than 1 inch (2.5 centimeters) thick to promote even cooking.

Seasoning Fish and Shellfish to Steam

The natural flavors of steamed fish and shellfish are highlighted by this cooking method and often require very little seasoning. Nevertheless salt, pepper, herbs and spices can be applied directly to the raw food before steaming. Clams and mussels, however, often do not require additional salt, as the liquid released when they open during cooking is sufficiently salty. Flavored liquids used to steam fish and shellfish also contribute additional flavors. If the steaming liquid is to be served as a broth or used to make a sauce to accompany the item, it is especially important that the liquid be well seasoned. Lemons, limes and other fruits or vegetables can also be cooked with the fish or shellfish to add flavors.

Accompaniments to Steamed Fish and Shellfish

Steamed fish and shellfish are popular partly because they are low in fat. A low or nonfat sauce or a simple squeeze of lemon and steamed fresh vegetables are good accompaniments. If fat is not a concern, then an emulsified butter sauce, such as Beurre Blanc (page 232) or Hollandaise (page 230), may be a good choice. Tables 11.4 and 11.6 list several sauce suggestions.

Classic New England steamed clams are served with a portion of the steaming liquid; steamed mussels are served with a sauce that is created from the wine and other ingredients used to steam them.

Procedure for Steaming Fish or Shellfish

1 Portion the fish to an appropriate size or clean the shellfish.
2 Prepare the cooking liquid. Add seasoning and flavoring ingredients as desired and bring to a boil.
3 Place the fish or shellfish in the steamer on a rack or in a perforated pan and cover tightly.
4 Steam the fish or shellfish until done.
5 Serve the fish or shellfish immediately with the steaming liquid or an appropriate sauce.

Steamed Salmon with Lemon and Olive Oil

MISE EN PLACE

- Blanch lemon zest.
- Wash, peel and chop leek.
- Crush peppercorns.

YIELD 1 Serving, 9 oz. (270 g)   **METHOD** Steaming

Dressing:		
Lemon zest, blanched	1 Tbsp.	15 ml
Lemon juice	2 Tbsp.	30 ml
Salt and pepper	TT	TT
Extra virgin olive oil	2 Tbsp.	30 ml
White wine	8 fl. oz.	240 ml
Bay leaf	1	1
Leek, chopped	2 oz.	60 g
Fresh thyme	1 sprig	1 sprig
Peppercorns, crushed	1 tsp.	5 ml
Salmon tranche or steak,	1	1
approx. 6 oz. (180 g)		

1 To make the dressing, combine the lemon zest, lemon juice, salt and pepper. Whisk in the oil.
2 Combine the wine, bay leaf, leek, thyme and peppercorns in the bottom of a steamer.
3 Season the salmon with salt and pepper and place it in the steamer basket.
4 Cover the steamer and bring the liquid to a boil. Cook the fish until done, approximately 4–6 minutes.
5 Plate the salmon and spoon the dressing over it.

Note Arctic char, striped bass or other firm fleshed white fish may be used in place of salmon in this recipe.

Approximate values per 9-oz. (270-g) serving: **Calories** 620, **Total fat** 40 g, **Saturated fat** 6 g, **Cholesterol** 95 mg, **Sodium** 700 mg, **Total carbohydrates** 16 g, **Protein** 48 g, **Vitamin C** 50%

❶ Placing the fish in the steamer basket.

❷ Spooning the dressing over the fish.

Red Snapper *en Papillote*

YIELD	6 Servings, 9 oz. (270 g) each	METHOD	Steaming
Clarified butter		as needed	as needed
Leek, julienne		3 oz.	90 g
Fennel bulb, julienne		4 oz.	120 g
Carrot, julienne		3 oz.	90 g
Celery, julienne		3 oz.	90 g
Red bell pepper, julienne		3 oz.	90 g
Red snapper fillets, skin on, 6 oz. (180 g) each		6	6
Salt and pepper		TT	TT
Basil Butter (page 234)		9 oz.	270 g

MISE EN PLACE

- Wash, clean and julienne leek.
- Wash, peel if necessary, and julienne fennel bulb, carrot and celery.
- Wash, seed and julienne bell pepper.
- Prepare Basil Butter.
- Cut parchment paper for papillote.

1. Cut six heart-shaped pieces of parchment paper large enough to each contain one portion of the fish and vegetables when folded in half.
2. Brush each piece of parchment paper with clarified butter.
3. Toss the vegetables together. Place one-sixth of the vegetables on half of each piece of the buttered parchment paper.
4. Place one portion of red snapper on each portion of vegetables, skin side up; season with salt and pepper.
5. Top each portion of fish with 1½ ounces (45 grams) Basil Butter.
6. Fold each piece of paper over and crimp the edges to seal it and form envelopes (papillotes).
7. Place the envelopes on sheet pans and bake in a preheated oven at 450°F (230°C) for 8–10 minutes.
8. When baked, the parchment paper should puff up and brown. Remove from the oven and serve immediately. The envelope should be carefully cut open tableside to allow the aromatic steam to escape.

Note Ling or red rock cod, halibut or tilapia may be used in place of snapper in this recipe.

Approximate values per 9-oz. (270-g) serving: **Calories** 380, **Total fat** 19 g, **Saturated fat** 11 g, **Cholesterol** 125 mg, **Sodium** 680 mg, **Total carbohydrates** 6 g, **Protein** 46 g, **Vitamin A** 50%, **Vitamin C** 30%

① Cutting heart-shaped pieces of parchment paper.

② Placing the vegetables, red snapper and compound butter on the buttered parchment paper.

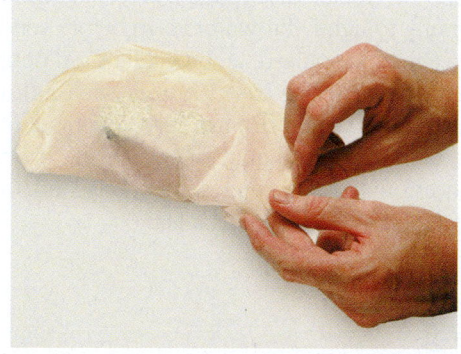

③ Crimping the edge of the parchment paper to seal.

④ The finished papillotes.

Poaching

Poaching is a versatile and popular method for cooking fish. Shellfish are rarely poached, however. The exception is squid, which can be quickly poached and chilled for use in salads and other preparations.

There are two distinct poaching methods. The first is the **submersion method**, in which the fish is completely covered with a liquid, usually a court bouillon, fish stock or fish fumet. It is cooked until just done and has an internal temperature of 145°F (63°C).

The poached fish is then served (either hot or cold) with a sauce sometimes made from a portion of the cooking liquid but more often made separately. Whole fish (wrapped in cheesecloth to preserve its shape during cooking), tranches and steaks can all be cooked by submersion poaching.

Shallow poaching, the second method, combines poaching and steaming to achieve the desired results. The main item, usually a fillet, tranche or steak, is placed on a bed of aromatic vegetables in enough liquid to come approximately halfway up its sides. The liquid, called a **cuisson**, is brought to a simmer on the stove top. The pan is then covered with a piece of buttered parchment paper or a lid, and cooking is completed either on the stove top or in the oven. Shallow-poached fish is usually served with a sauce made with the reduced cooking liquid. (Sometimes the main item is sautéed lightly before the cooking liquid is added. If so, the cooking method is more accurately described as braising, as both dry- and moist-heat cooking methods are used.)

Selecting Fish to Poach

Lean white fish, such as turbot, bass and sole, are excellent for poaching. Some fatty fish, such as salmon and trout, are also excellent choices.

Seasoning Fish to Poach

Fish poached by either submersion or shallow poaching gain all of their seasonings from the liquid in which they are cooked and the sauce with which they are served. Therefore it is very important to use a properly prepared court bouillon, fish fumet or good-quality fish stock well seasoned with vegetables such as shallots, onions or carrots as well as herbs, spices and other seasonings. Citrus, especially lemon, is a popular seasoning; lemon juice or zest may be added to the poaching liquid, the sauce or the finished dish. Many poached fish recipes call for wine. When using wine in either the cooking liquid or the sauce, be sure to choose a high-quality wine. Most fish are very delicately flavored, and poor-quality wine may ruin an otherwise excellent dish.

Accompaniments to Poached Fish

Poached fish cooked by submersion go well with rich sauces such as Beurre Blanc (page 232) or Hollandaise (page 230). Once coated with either sauce, the fish may be broiled briefly to lightly brown or glaze before serving. If fat is a concern, a better choice may be a vegetable coulis (e.g., broccoli or red pepper). Cold poached fish are commonly served with mayonnaise-based sauces such as sauce verte or Rémoulade Sauce (page 759). Shallow-poached fish are served with sauces such as a white wine sauce made from a reduction of the liquids in which the fish were poached. See Tables 11.4 and 11.6 for additional sauce suggestions. Poached fish are often served with rice or pasta and steamed or boiled vegetables.

Procedure for Submersion Poaching

1 Prepare the cooking liquid. Whole fish should be started in a cold liquid; gradually increasing the liquid's temperature helps preserve the appearance of the fish. Portioned fish should be started in a simmering liquid to preserve their flavor and more accurately estimate cooking time.

2 Use a rack to lower the fish into the cooking liquid. Be sure the fish is completely submerged.

3 Poach the fish at 175–185°F (79–85°C) until done.

4 Remove the fish from the poaching liquid, moisten with a portion of the liquid and hold in a warm place for service. Or remove the fish from the poaching liquid, cover it to prevent drying and allow it to cool, then refrigerate.

5 Serve the poached fish with an appropriate sauce.

Whole Poached Salmon

YIELD	1 Salmon, 10–14 servings, 4 oz. (120 g) each	METHOD	Submersion Poaching

MISE EN PLACE
- Scale and gut whole salmon.
- Prepare Court Bouillon.

Salmon, drawn, 4–5 lb. (1.9–2.4 kg)		1	1
Court Bouillon (page 212), unstrained		as needed	as needed

1 Place the fish on a lightly oiled rack or screen and secure it to the rack with butcher's twine.

2 Place the rack or screen in a fish poacher, tilting kettle or large pot and cover with cold Court Bouillon.

3 Bring the Court Bouillon to a simmer over medium heat. Reduce the heat and poach the fish at 175–180°F (79–85°C) until it reaches an internal temperature of 145°F (63°C), approximately 30–45 minutes.

4 If the fish is to be served hot, remove it from the Court Bouillon, draining well, and serve immediately with an appropriate garnish. If it is to be served cold, remove it from the Court Bouillon, draining well, cool and refrigerate up to several hours before decorating and garnishing as desired.

Approximate values per 4-oz. (120-g) serving: **Calories** 114, **Total fat** 3 g, **Saturated fat** 1 g, **Cholesterol** 29 mg, **Sodium** 80 mg, **Total carbohydrates** 0 g, **Protein** 22 g, **Calcium** 6%

❶ The Court Bouillon.

❷ Securing the whole fish to a rack.

❸ Removing and draining the fish.

Procedure for Shallow Poaching

1 Butter a sauteuse and add aromatic vegetables as directed in the recipe.

2 Add the fish to the pan.

3 Add the cooking liquid to the pan.

4 Cover the pan with buttered parchment paper or a lid.

5 Bring the liquid to a simmer and cook the fish on the stove top or in the oven until done.

6 Remove the fish from the pan, moisten with a portion of the liquid and hold in a warm place for service.

7 Reduce the cuisson (the liquid used for shallow poaching) and finish the sauce as directed in the recipe.

8 Serve the poached fish with the sauce.

Fillets of Sole Bonne Femme

MISE EN PLACE

- Peel and mince shallots.
- Wash and slice mushrooms.
- Wash, dry and chop parsley.

YIELD 2 Servings, 9 oz. (270 g) each		METHOD Shallow Poaching	
Sole fillets, approx. 2½ oz. (75 g) each	4	4	
Salt and pepper	TT	TT	
Whole butter	1 oz.	30 g	
Shallots, minced	1 tsp.	5 ml	
Mushrooms, sliced	4 oz.	120 g	
White wine	3 fl. oz.	90 ml	
Fish stock	4 fl. oz.	120 ml	
Fish velouté	4 fl. oz.	120 ml	
Lemon juice	TT	TT	
Fresh parsley, chopped	1 tsp.	5 ml	

1 Season the fillets with salt and pepper.

2 Melt the butter in a sauté pan. Add the shallots and mushrooms. To ensure even cooking, fold the tail portion of each fillet under the fillet. Then arrange the fillets over the shallots and mushrooms in the pan. Add the wine and stock.

3 Bring the liquid to a simmer. Cover the fish with buttered parchment paper and cook on the stove top or in a 350°F (180°C) oven until done, approximately 5–8 minutes.

4 Remove the fish and reserve in a warm place.

5 Reduce the cuisson until approximately 1 fluid ounce (30 milliliters) remains. Add the velouté. Add lemon juice to taste and adjust the seasonings. Serve the fish with the sauce, sprinkled with chopped parsley.

Note Ling or red rock cod or tilapia may be used in place of sole in this recipe.

Approximate values per 9-oz. (270-g) serving: **Calories** 440, **Total fat** 14 g, **Saturated fat** 5 g, **Cholesterol** 120 mg, **Sodium** 375 mg, **Total carbohydrates** 27 g, **Protein** 42 g

❶ Arranging the fillets on the bed of shallots and mushrooms.

❷ Covering the fish with buttered parchment paper after the liquid is added.

❸ Adding the velouté to the cuisson.

Simmering

"Boiled" lobster, crab and shrimp are not actually boiled; rather, they are cooked whole in their shells by simmering. Although they are not as delicate as some fish, these crustaceans can become tough and are easily overcooked if the cooking liquid is allowed to boil.

Selecting Shellfish to Simmer

Lobsters, crabs and shrimp are commonly cooked by simmering. Their hard shells protect their delicate flesh during the cooking process.

Seasoning Shellfish to Simmer

The shellfish being simmered are not seasoned. Rather they gain flavor by being cooked in a seasoned or flavored liquid, typically salted water or court bouillon. A sachet of pickling spice or Old Bay seasoning is sometimes used for additional flavor.

Doneness of Simmered Shellfish

Timing is the best method for determining the doneness of simmered shellfish. This varies depending on the size of the shellfish and how quickly the liquid returns to a simmer after the shellfish is added. Shrimp cook in as little as 3–5 minutes; crabs cook in 5–10 minutes; and it can take as little as 6–8 minutes for a 1-pound (450-gram) lobster to cook and 15–20 minutes for a 2½-pound (1.1-kilogram) lobster.

Accompaniments to Simmered Shellfish

The standard accompaniments to simmered shellfish are lemon wedges and melted butter. If the shellfish will be eaten cold, the traditional sauce is a tomato-based cocktail sauce. Nearly any type of vegetable or starch goes well with simmered shellfish, the most common being fresh corn on the cob and boiled potatoes.

Procedure for Simmering or Boiling Shellfish

1 Bring court bouillon or water to a boil.
2 Add the shellfish to the liquid. Bring the liquid back to a boil and reduce to a simmer. (Whenever an item is added to boiling water, it lowers the water's temperature. The greater the amount of water, however, the faster it will return to a boil. To accelerate the time within which the water returns to a boil after the shellfish is added, use as much water as possible.)
3 Cook until done.
4 Remove the shellfish from the liquid and serve immediately, or cool shellfish by dropping into ice water if they are to be eaten cold.

Boiled Lobster

To accommodate their growth, Atlantic lobsters lose their shells once a year, usually in the summer. After molting, the lobsters emerge in soft new shells, which are easy to crack. But these lobsters yield less meat than their hard-shell cousins.

YIELD 1 Serving		METHOD Boiling
Lobster, live, 1 lb. 8 oz. (720 g)	1	1
Boiling salted water	4 gal.	15 lt
Lemon wedges	4	4
Whole butter, melted	2 oz.	60 g

MISE EN PLACE
- Melt butter while the lobster is boiling.

1 Drop the lobster into the boiling water. Bring the water back to a boil, reduce to a simmer and cook the lobster until done, approximately 12 minutes.
2 Remove the lobster from the pot, drain and serve immediately with lemon wedges and melted butter on the side.
3 If the lobster is to be eaten cold, place it in a sink of ice water to stop the cooking process. When cool enough to handle, remove the meat from the shell following the procedures discussed in this chapter.

Approximate values per 1-lb. (480-g) serving: **Calories** 650, **Total fat** 26 g, **Saturated fat** 15 g, **Cholesterol** 390 mg, **Sodium** 1960 mg, **Total carbohydrates** 11 g, **Protein** 93 g, **Vitamin A** 035%, **Vitamin C** 45%

COMBINATION COOKING METHODS FOR FISH AND SHELLFISH

Combination methods are used to cook meats, game and poultry in part to tenderize them. Because fish and shellfish are inherently tender, they do not necessarily benefit from such procedures. As noted in the section on shallow poaching, fish can, on occasion, be lightly sautéed or browned and then poached. Although this procedure is a combination cooking method, it is used to enhance flavors and not to tenderize the product. Some fish or shellfish recipes include the word *braised* or *stew* in the title. Note, however, that these recipes rarely follow the traditional combination cooking methods discussed in this text.

Fish and shellfish may be packaged under vacuum in plastic pouches and cooked *sous vide* in a temperature controlled water bath. See Chapter 10, Principles of Cooking. Using this *sous vide* technique, which resembles poaching, produces soft and moist fish and shellfish that is cooked through but not overcooked. For service, *sous vide* fish and shellfish may be seared to give it an attractive browned appearance and surface texture.

When cooking fish using this *sous vide* combination cooking method, select species with relatively firm flesh. The *sous vide* cooking temperatures and times are much shorter for fish than for tough cuts of meat or poultry. Shellfish such as clams, shrimp or lobster, cook more quickly than fin fish and may benefit from the addition of oil in the cooking pouch.

Procedure for Preparing Fish and Shellfish Sous Vide

1 Assemble the safety equipment—single-use gloves, digital probe thermometer with pointed tip, ice and water bath with salt and sanitizing solution—for preparing food *sous vide*.

2 Wearing clean single-use gloves, place the fish and seasonings in a single layer into plastic pouches.

3 Vacuum seal the pouches of food in a chamber vacuum machine.

4 Place sealed pouches in a pre-heated thermal bath with a circulator. Cook until fish reaches the desired internal temperature.

5 Unless the fish is being served immediately, use an ice bath to quickly chill pouches below the temperature danger zone.

6 For service, open *sous vide* pouches and drain the fish on paper towels. Sear the fish in a pre-heated pan until crisp. Serve with the appropriate garnishes.

Arctic Char with Orange Beurre Blanc

MISE EN PLACE

- Prepare Red Rice Pilaf.
- Prepare Citrus Beurre Blanc.
- Segment orange.
- Cut chives.

	YIELD 4 Servings, 8 oz. (240 g) each		METHOD *Sous Vide* Poaching/ Sautéing
Arctic char fillets, skinless, 4 oz. (120 g) each		4	4
Salt and pepper		TT	TT
Olive oil		2 fl. oz.	60 ml
Red Rice Pilaf (page 675)		12 oz.	360 g
Citrus Beurre Blanc (page 250) made with orange juice		4 fl. oz.	120 ml
Orange segments		as needed	as needed
Chives, cut into 1-in. (2.5-cm) segments		as needed for garnish	

1 Season the fillets with salt and pepper.

2 Wearing clean disposable gloves, prepare four plastic pouches for *sous vide* cooking. For each portion, add 1 teaspoon (5 milliliters) of olive oil to the pouch. Slide a portion of fish into each bag. Vacuum seal the pouches. Once sealed, the portioned fish can be held in the refrigerator for up to 48 hours before serving.

3 For service, *sous vide* the fish in a thermal circulator heated to 122°F (50°C) until the core temperature of the fish reaches 122°F (50°C) when checked with a digital probe thermometer, approximately 30 minutes. (Reseal bags before returning it to the circulator if necessary.) The fish may be held for up to one hour in the thermal circulator until ready to serve.

4 Remove each portion of fish from the bags. Drain fish on clean paper towels.

5 Heat a medium size sauté pan over medium high heat. Add the olive oil then place the fish, presentation side down, in the pan leaving some space between fillets so that they will cook properly. Cook the fish undisturbed until lightly browned and crisp, for approximately 1 minute.

6 Remove the fish from the pan. Drain any excess oil from the fish on a paper towel. Serve each portion of fish on 3 ounces (90 grams) of Red Rice Pilaf accompanied by Citrus Beurre Blanc, orange segments and cut chives.

Note Salmon or steelhead trout may be used in place of the char in this recipe.

Approximate values per 8-oz. (240-g) serving: **Calories** 570, **Total fat** 40 g, **Saturated fat** 17 g, **Cholesterol** 110 mg, **Sodium** 25 mg, **Total carbohydrates** 26 g, **Protein** 27 g, **Vitamin A** 15%

SERVING RAW FISH AND SHELLFISH

For centuries, people have consumed uncooked fresh fish and shellfish. The coastal cuisines of Japan, Sicily and South America include numerous raw fish dishes, for example. And clams and shellfish served raw on the half shell figure prominently in the classical culinary traditions in Europe and the United States. Now that chefs worldwide are exploring lighter preparations and the cuisines of Asia, serving raw fish and shellfish is common. Raw fish requires time and temperature control for safety (TCS). Check local health department regulations for recommendations on properly serving raw fish. Sourcing the freshest products from licensed suppliers is essential. The products must be kept very cold from the moment they arrive until the moment they are prepared. Wear clean disposable gloves and observe stringent sanitary conditions when handling raw fish and shellfish.

Raw Fish and Shellfish Dishes

Raw fish and shellfish dishes are about texture as much as flavor. Citrus, especially lemon and lime, fresh delicate herbs and oils are popular additions to raw fish dishes. Raw fish dishes often include crisp accompaniments such as raw vegetables for textural contrast. The recipes for Seviche (page 549) and Fin Fish Carpaccio with Lemon Thyme Vinaigrette (page 549) are examples of raw fish preparations.

Sushi and Sashimi

Generally **sushi** refers to cooked or raw fish and shellfish rolled in or served on seasoned rice. **Sashimi** is raw fish eaten without rice. In Japan, the word sushi (or **zushi**) refers only to the flavored rice. Each combination of rice and another ingredient or ingredients has a specific name. These include *nigiri zushi* (rice with raw fish), *norimaki zushi* (rice rolled in seaweed), *fukusa zushi* (rice wrapped in omelet), *inari zushi* (rice in fried bean curd) and *chirashi zushi* (rice with fish, shellfish and vegetables). Although a Japanese sushi master spends years perfecting style and technique, many types of sushi can be produced in any professional kitchen with very little specialized equipment.

Fish for Sushi and Sashimi

The key to good sushi and sashimi is the freshness of the fish. All fish must be of the highest quality and absolutely fresh, preferably no more than one day out of the water. Ahi and yellowfin tuna, salmon, flounder and sea bass are typically used for sushi. Cooked shrimp and eel are also popular.

⚠ Safety Alert

Sous Vide Sanitation

Food safety is of utmost concern when using *sous vide* techniques because of the low cooking temperatures. To prevent the growth of microorganisms, any food to be cooked *sous vide* must be chilled below the temperature danger zone (41°F/5°C) before cooking. Keep all cutting boards, knives and food contact surfaces clean and sanitary and wear clean disposable gloves. Use only the freshest unblemished ingredients. Consult your local health department for regulations for preparing food *sous vide*. Special permission and a HACCP plan may be required.

⚠ Safety Alert

Raw Fish

Raw fish requires time and temperature control for safety (TCS). Many health departments enforce strict regulations to ensure that raw fish, shellfish and sashimi are properly prepared and served. Many species of fin fish carry parasites that are harmless to the fish but can cause illness in humans. To destroy these parasites, such fish should be frozen before service according to procedures outlined in The 2013 Food Code of the U.S. Food and Drug Administration (FDA), July 2015 supplement. Observe the strictest sanitation standards when preparing raw fish dishes to prevent cross-contamination. Check local regulations for the most accurate information for your area.

mirin a Japanese rice wine; low in alcohol and naturally sweet, mirin is used as a condiment

Rice for Sushi

Sushi rice is prepared by adding seasonings such as vinegar, sugar, salt and rice wine (sake or **mirin**) to steamed short-grain rice. The consistency of the rice is very important. It must be sticky enough to stay together when formed into finger-shaped oblongs, but not too soft.

Seasonings for Sushi and Sashimi

Seasonings for sushi and sashimi include the following:

Shoyu: Japanese soy sauce, which is lighter and more delicate than the Chinese variety.
Wasabi: A strong aromatic root, purchased as a green powder. It is sometimes called green horseradish, although it is not actually related to common horseradish.
Pickled ginger: Fresh ginger pickled in vinegar, which gives it a pink color.
Nori: A dried seaweed purchased in sheets; nori adds flavor and is sometimes used to contain rolled rice and other ingredients.

The procedure for making sushi and sashimi is illustrated by the recipe for Nigiri Sushi.

❤ Good Choice

MISE EN PLACE

- Prepare and chill Sushi Rice.

Nigiri Sushi

YIELD 24 Pieces

Sushi-quality fish fillets such as ahi, salmon, flounder or sea bass	1 lb.	480 g
Wasabi powder	1 oz.	30 g
Water	1 fl. oz.	30 ml
Sushi Rice (recipe follows)	2 lb.	960 g
Sliced pickled ginger	2 oz.	60 g
Shoyu	3 fl. oz.	90 ml

1 Trim the fish fillets of any skin, bone, imperfections or blemishes. Cut the fillets into 24 thin slices, approximately 2 inches by 1 inch (5 centimeters by 2.5 centimeters).

2 Mix the wasabi powder and water to form a firm paste.

3 With your hands, form a 1½-ounce (50-gram) portion of rice into a finger-shaped mound.

4 Rub a small amount of wasabi paste on one side of a slice of fish.

5 Holding the rice mound in one hand, press the fish, wasabi side down, onto the rice with the fingers of the other hand.

6 Serve with additional wasabi, pickled ginger and shoyu.

Approximate values per piece: **Calories** 80, **Total fat** 2 g, **Saturated fat** 0 g, **Cholesterol** 10 mg, **Sodium** 310 mg, **Total carbohydrates** 11 g, **Protein** 5 g, **Claims**—low fat; low cholesterol; no sugar

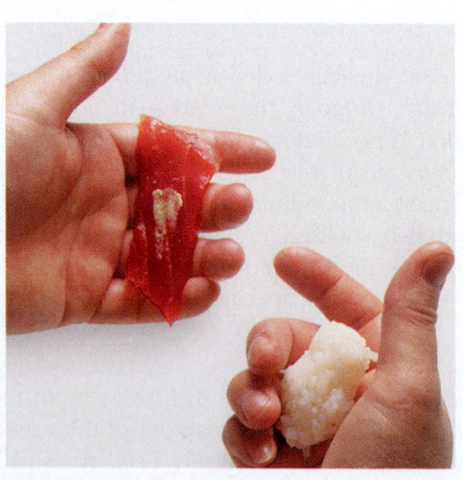

❶ Cutting the fish for sushi.

❷ Forming a finger-shaped rice mound.

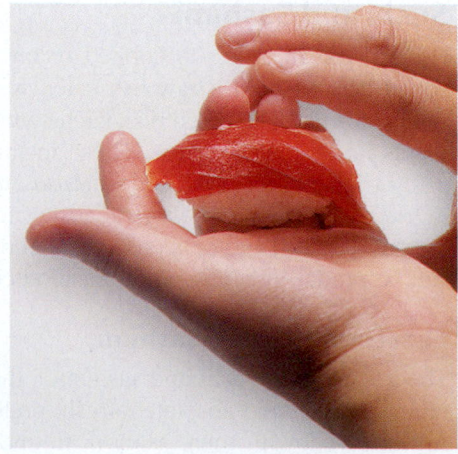

❸ Pressing the fish onto the rice.

Zushi
(Sushi Rice)

 **Vegan**   **Good Choice**

YIELD   2 lb. (1 kg)

Short-grain rice	1 lb.	480 g
Water	20 fl. oz.	600 ml
Rice vinegar	2 fl. oz.	60 ml
Granulated sugar	3 Tbsp.	45 ml
Salt	2½ tsp.	12 ml
Mirin	1 fl. oz.	30 ml

1 Wash the rice and allow it to drain for 30 minutes.

2 Combine the rice and water in a saucepan. Bring to a boil, lower to a simmer, cover and steam for 20 minutes.

3 Combine the rice vinegar, sugar, salt and mirin and add to the rice. Mix well and cool to room temperature.

Approximate values per 1-oz. (30-g) serving: **Calories** 60, **Total fat** 0 g, **Saturated fat** 0 g, **Cholesterol** 0 mg, **Sodium** 140 mg, **Total carbohydrates** 13 g, **Protein** 1 g, **Claims**—fat free

Adding the seasonings to the cooked rice.

QUESTIONS FOR DISCUSSION

1 What are the physical differences between a flatfish and a round fish? How do fabrication techniques vary for these fish?

2 List four market forms for fish and discuss several factors that may determine the form most appropriate for an operation to purchase.

3 List the three categories of mollusks and give an example of a commonly used food from each category.

4 Discuss six techniques for determining the freshness of fish and shellfish.

5 Explain the importance of avoiding the use of endangered species of seafood. How is sustainable production of seafood relevant to a chef's purchasing decisions?

6 Describe the proper storage methods for shellfish that is still alive when purchased. Why is this different from the proper techniques for storing fish?

7 Discuss four methods for determining the doneness of fish or shellfish. Why is it important not to overcook fish and shellfish?

8 Compare and contrast shallow poaching and submersion poaching. Why is poaching a commonly used method for preparing fish and shellfish?

9 Describe the proper techniques for sautéing fish fillet. Explain how each step ensures that the fish will be crisp and browned without falling apart.

10 Why are combination cooking methods rarely used with fish and shellfish? Why are "boiled" shellfish preparation not literally boiled?

11 Describe the key considerations when preparing raw fish or shellfish dishes for service.

12 Research international fish recipes and discuss the types of fish that can be substituted when regional or sustainable varieties are not available.

⚠ **Safety Alert**

Sushi Rice

Cooked sushi rice should be kept chilled at 41°F (5°C) or lower. Observe the strictest sanitation standards when preparing sushi rice to prevent cross-contamination. Many health departments enforce strict regulations to ensure that sushi and sashimi are properly prepared and served. Check local regulations for the most accurate information for your area.

Additional Fish and Shellfish Recipes

Roasted Monkfish with Bacon and Garlic

YIELD 4 Servings, 8 oz. (240 g) each	METHOD Roasting	
Garlic cloves, peeled	24	24
Monkfish fillets, 6-oz. (180-g) portions	4	4
Salt and pepper	TT	TT
Flour	as needed for dredging	
Olive oil	1½ fl. oz.	45 ml
Slab bacon, julienne	4 oz.	120 g
Shallots, minced	1 Tbsp.	15 ml
Sherry wine vinegar	1 Tbsp.	15 ml
Crème fraîche	4 fl. oz.	120 ml
Chicken stock	4 fl. oz.	120 ml
Whole butter	1 oz.	30 g

1 Blanch the garlic cloves for 5–10 minutes to soften. Drain and reserve the garlic.

2 Season the monkfish with salt and pepper and dredge in the flour. Heat a sauté pan and add the oil. Sauté the monkfish for 4–6 minutes, browning it well on all sides.

3 Add the garlic and bacon to the pan and coat with the oil. Place the pan in a preheated 400°F (200°C) oven for 8–10 minutes or until the monkfish is cooked and the bacon and garlic cloves are browned.

4 Remove the pan from the oven. Remove the monkfish, bacon and garlic from the pan and hold in a warm place while preparing the sauce.

5 Degrease the pan, leaving 1 tablespoon (15 milliliters) of fat. Add the shallots and sauté 1 minute without coloring. Deglaze the pan with the vinegar. Add the crème fraîche and the stock. Bring to a boil and reduce the sauce to nappé consistency. Adjust the seasonings with salt and pepper. Monté au beurre.

6 Slice the monkfish portions and plate with an appropriate accompaniment such as sautéed spinach. Spoon the sauce over the fish and sprinkle with garlic cloves and bacon.

Note Halibut, mahi-mahi, sea bass or snapper may be substituted for the monkfish in this recipe.

Approximate values per 8-oz. (240-g) serving: **Calories** 440, **Total fat** 29 g, **Saturated fat** 11 g, **Cholesterol** 80 mg, **Sodium** 280 mg, **Total carbohydrates** 14 g, **Protein** 32 g, **Vitamin A** 10%, **Vitamin C** 15%

Teriyaki Salmon

YIELD 4 Servings, 4 oz. (120 g) each	METHOD Grilling	
Marinade:		
Soy sauce	8 fl. oz.	240 ml
Mirin	8 fl. oz.	240 ml
Garlic, crushed	1 tsp.	5 ml
Ginger, minced	1 tsp.	5 ml
Brown sugar	2 oz.	60 g
Sake	4 fl. oz.	120 ml
Salmon, tranches, 4 oz. (120 g) each	4	4
Vegetable oil	as needed	as needed
Sticky rice, steamed, hot	as needed	as needed
Green onion, julienne	as needed for garnish	

1 To make the marinade, combine the soy sauce, mirin, garlic, ginger, brown sugar and sake.

2 Marinate the salmon in the marinade for 15 minutes.

3 Remove the salmon from the marinade and pat dry. Brush the tranches with oil and broil or grill until done.

4 Serve the salmon on a bed of hot sticky rice garnished with green onions.

Note Halibut, tilapia or other firm white fish may be substituted for salmon in this recipe.

Approximate values per 4-oz. (120-g) serving: **Calories** 330, **Total fat** 9 g, **Saturated fat** 2 g, **Cholesterol** 65 mg, **Sodium** 3770 mg, **Total carbohydrates** 28 g, **Protein** 35 g, **Vitamin C** 60%

Oven-Fried Pecan Catfish

YIELD 12 Servings, 8 oz. (240 g) each	METHOD Baking	
Dijon mustard	8 fl. oz.	240 ml
Milk	6 fl. oz.	180 ml
Pecans, ground	14 oz.	420 g
U.S. farm-raised catfish fillets, 5–6 oz. (150–180 g) each	12	12
Creole Rémoulade Sauce (page 759)	18 fl. oz.	540 ml
Country Biscuits (page 930)	12	12

1 Mix the mustard and milk in a shallow dish. Spread the pecans out on a piece of parchment paper.

2 Dip each fillet into the mustard mixture. Scrape off any excess mustard, then carefully roll each fillet in the ground pecans. Coat each fillet thoroughly, shaking off any excess. Place the fillets on a lightly oiled baking sheet.

3 Bake at 450°F (230°C) until the catfish flakes easily when tested with a fork, approximately 10–12 minutes.

4 Serve the catfish with Creole Rémoulade, a Country Biscuit and vegetables.

Note Tilapia may be substituted for catfish in this recipe.

Variation:

Tropical Oven-Fried Catfish—Combine 4 fluid ounces (120 milliliters) low-fat buttermilk with 1 teaspoon (5 milliliters) each of black pepper, salt and ginger and ⅛ teaspoon (1 milliliter) ground cinnamon. Crush 9 ounces (270 grams) cornflakes into crumbs. Bread 12 catfish fillets using the standard breading procedure described in Chapter 9, Mise en Place. Cover and refrigerate for at least 30 minutes to set the coating, and then bake as directed in Step 3.

Approximate values per 8-oz. (240-g) serving: **Calories** 410, **Total fat** 31 g, **Saturated fat** 4.5 g, **Cholesterol** 75 mg, **Sodium** 600 mg, **Total carbohydrates** 6 g, **Protein** 29 g, **Iron** 10%

Cha Ca
(Hanoi-Style Fish with Dill)

Although it is prepared by frying, cha ca means "braised fish" in Vietnamese; the marinade adds some moisture to the fish as it cooks. This dish is so popular in Hanoi that a street has been named in its honor.

YIELD 4 Servings, 7 oz. (210 g) each		METHOD Sautéing/Stir-Frying
Marinade:		
Fresh ginger, 1-in. (2.5-cm) piece, peeled and chopped	1 oz.	30 g
Fresh Thai or serrano chiles	2	2
Granulated sugar	1 Tbsp.	15 ml
Nuoc mam (fish sauce)	1 fl. oz.	30 ml
Turmeric, ground	1 Tbsp.	15 ml
Yogurt	2 fl. oz.	60 ml
Fresh lemon juice	1 fl. oz.	30 ml
Catfish fillets	1 lb.	480 g
Fresh dill	6 oz.	180 g
Vegetable oil	1 ½ fl. oz.	45 ml
Shallot, thinly sliced	1 oz.	30 g
Garlic cloves, thinly sliced	2	2
Green onions, cut in 1 in. (2.5 cm) pieces	4	4
Fish stock	4 fl. oz.	120 ml
Rice vermicelli, cooked	as needed	as needed
Peanuts, roasted, chopped	4 Tbsp.	60 ml
Nuoc Cham (page 253)	as needed	as needed

1 Prepare the marinade by grinding the ginger, chiles and sugar in the bowl of a food processor into a paste. Add the remaining marinade ingredients and stir until dissolved.

2 Cut the catfish into 1-inch × 2-inch (2.5-centimeter × 5-centimeter) pieces. Toss the catfish in the marinade. Cover and refrigerate for 1 hour.

3 Trim the coarse stems from the dill and cut the leaves into 1½-inch (3.75-centimeter) pieces.

4 Heat a sauté pan or wok and add the oil. Sauté the shallot and garlic until translucent, but not brown. Add the fish and any remaining marinade to the hot pan and cook, stirring carefully until the fish is almost done, approximately 2 minutes.

5 Add half of the dill, half of the green onions and the fish stock to the fish and cook until the dill wilts. Arrange the remaining dill and green onions on a warm serving platter. Pour the fish and wilted herbs on top.

6 Reheat the vermicelli in boiling water for a few seconds. Drain well.

7 Serve the sautéed fish and herbs with individual bowls of rice vermicelli. At the table, each diner places some of the herbs and fish on top of the noodles, adds a sprinkle of chopped peanuts and drizzles with Nuoc Cham.

Note Ling cod, tilapia, mahi-mahi or other firm white fish may be used in place of catfish in this recipe.

Approximate values per 7-oz. (210-g) serving: **Calories** 320, **Total fat** 23 g, **Saturated fat** 4 g, **Cholesterol** 55 mg, **Sodium** 770 mg, **Total carbohydrates** 6 g, **Protein** 19 g, **Vitamin A** 30%, **Vitamin C** 60%, **Iron** 10%

Macadamia Nut–Crusted Halibut with Red Onion, Tomato and Balsamic Salsa

Newbury College, Brookline, MA
Senior Instructor Scott Doughty, Ret.

YIELD	4 Servings, 8 oz. (240 g) fish and 2 fl. oz. (60 ml) salsa each	METHOD	Sautéing
Macadamia nuts		4 oz.	120 g
Flour		8 oz.	240 g
Halibut fillet		2 lb.	960 g
Salt and pepper		TT	TT
Egg, slightly beaten		1	1
Olive oil		as needed	as needed
Red Onion, Tomato and Balsamic Salsa (recipe follows)		2 fl. oz.	240 ml
Herb sprigs		as needed for garnish	

1 Place the nuts on a half-sheet pan and toast them lightly in the oven. Combine the toasted nuts with 4 ounces (120 grams) of the flour in a food processor. Process until the nuts are chopped finely but not pulverized.

2 Cut the halibut into four portion-sized fillets.

3 Season the fillets with salt and pepper and then bread them using the remaining flour and egg, following the standard breading procedure described in Chapter 9, Mise en Place. The nut–flour mixture is the final coating.

4 Heat a sautoir and add a thin film of oil. Place the breaded fillets in the oil, leaving some space between each fillet so that they will cook properly. Sauté the fillets until they are a deep golden brown and crusty, then turn them over and cook until the fish is medium rare to medium. Remove the fillets from the pan. Residual heat will complete the cooking.

5 Spoon some of the Red Onion, Tomato and Balsamic Salsa onto a serving platter and place the fillets on top. Spoon a small dollop on each fillet and place a small herb sprig next to it. Serve the remaining Red Onion, Tomato and Balsamic Salsa on the side.

Approximate values per 8-oz. (240-g) serving: **Calories** 740, **Total fat** 42 g, **Saturated fat** 6 g, **Cholesterol** 125 mg, **Sodium** 300 mg, **Total carbohydrates** 36 g, **Protein** 55 g, **Vitamin A** 25%, **Vitamin C** 40%, **Calcium** 15%, **Iron** 30%

Red Onion, Tomato and Balsamic Salsa

 Vegan

YIELD	4 Servings, 2 fl. oz. (60 ml) each		
Red onion, small dice		1	1
Tomato concassée, medium dice		8 oz.	240 g
Balsamic vinegar		2 fl. oz.	60 ml
Olive oil		2 fl. oz.	60 ml
Salt		½ tsp.	2 ml
Cayenne pepper		⅛ tsp.	1 ml

1 Combine all of the ingredients in a bowl. Cover and chill until ready to serve.

Approximate values per 2-fl.-oz. (60-ml) serving: **Calories** 100, **Total fat** 7 g, **Saturated fat** 1 g, **Cholesterol** 0 mg, **Sodium** 160 mg, **Total carbohydrates** 8 g, **Protein** 1 g, **Vitamin A** 15%, **Vitamin C** 40%

Blue Crab Cakes

YIELD 15 Cakes, 2 oz. (60 g) each		METHOD Pan-Frying	
Blue crab meat	1 lb.	480 g
Heavy cream	6 fl. oz.	180 ml
Red bell pepper, small dice	2 oz.	60 g
Green bell pepper, small dice	2 oz.	60 g
Clarified butter	as needed	as needed
Green onions, sliced	1 bunch	1 bunch
Fresh bread crumbs	6 oz.	180 g
Salt and pepper	TT	TT
Dijon mustard	1 Tbsp.	15 ml
Worcestershire sauce	TT	TT
Tabasco sauce	TT	TT
Egg, slightly beaten	1	1

1 Carefully pick through the crab meat, removing any pieces of shell. Keep the lumps of crab meat as large as possible.

2 Place the cream in a saucepan and bring to a boil. Reduce by approximately one-half. Chill the cream well.

3 Sauté the bell peppers in a small amount of clarified butter until tender.

4 Combine the crab meat, reduced cream, bell peppers, green onions and approximately 3 ounces (90 grams) bread crumbs along with the salt, pepper, Dijon mustard, Worcestershire sauce, Tabasco sauce and egg. Mix to combine all ingredients, trying to keep the lumps of crab meat intact.

5 Using a 2-ounce (60-gram) mold, form the crab mixture into cakes.

6 Place the remaining bread crumbs in an appropriately sized hotel pan. Place the crab cakes, a few at a time, in the hotel pan and cover with the bread crumbs. To help crumbs adhere, press the crumbs lightly into the cakes.

7 Heat a sauté pan over medium heat and add enough clarified butter to cover the bottom approximately ¼ inch (6 millimeters) deep.

8 Add the crab cakes to the pan and pan-fry until done, turning once when the first side is nicely browned. Remove and drain on absorbent paper.

Approximate values per 2-oz. (60-g) cake serving: **Calories** 130, **Total fat** 6 g, **Saturated fat** 3.5 g, **Cholesterol** 60 mg, **Sodium** 650 mg, **Total carbohydrates** 9 g, **Protein** 10 g, **Vitamin C** 15%

❶ Mixing to combine ingredients for the crab cakes.

❷ Forming the crab cakes.

❸ Pan-frying the crab cakes.

Miso-Glazed Broiled Black Cod

YIELD 6 Servings, 6 oz. (180 g) each		METHOD Broiling	
Sake		2 fl. oz.	60 ml
Mirin		2 fl. oz.	60 ml
White miso paste		4 fl. oz.	120 ml
Granulated sugar		2½ oz.	75 g
Black cod, sablefish or Atlantic sea bass fillets, skin on approx. 6 oz. (180 g) each		6	6
English cucumber, seedless, peeled		1	1
Pickled ginger, sliced		as needed for garnish	

1 Boil the sake and mirin in a small saucepan. Stir in the miso and sugar. Simmer until the sugar dissolves. Transfer the marinade to a quarter-size hotel pan and allow it to cool.

2 Place the fish fillets in the marinade. Turn them over then cover the pan and refrigerate for 6–24 hours.

3 Slice the cucumber thinly on a mandolin. Line each plate with overlapping slices of cucumber. Refrigerate plates while cooking the fish.

4 Place the fish fillets on a preheated broiler platter, skin side down, and place under the broiler.

5 Remove the fish from the broiler when done. Serve on the prepared plates garnished with pickled ginger.

Approximate values per 6-oz. (180-g) serving: **Calories** 160, **Total fat** 1.5 g, **Saturated fat** 0 g, **Cholesterol** 65 mg, **Sodium** 310 mg, **Total carbohydrates** 6 g, **Protein** 28 g, Claims—low fat, no cholesterol

Salmon Croquettes

Croquettes are made from cooked meats, poultry, vegetables, fish, shellfish or potatoes, usually bound with a heavy béchamel or velouté sauce and seasoned. The mixture is shaped into cones or patties, then breaded and deep-fried.

YIELD 14 Croquettes		METHOD Deep-Frying	
Onion, small dice		2 oz.	60 g
Whole butter		2 oz.	60 g
Flour		2 oz.	60 g
Milk		5 fl. oz.	150 ml
Salmon, poached and flaked		1 lb.	480 g
Fresh dill, chopped		2 tsp.	10 ml
Salt and pepper		TT	TT
Lemon juice		4 tsp.	20 ml
Flour, seasoned with salt and pepper		as needed for breading	
Egg wash		as needed for breading	
Fine bread crumbs		as needed for breading	

1 Sauté the onion in the butter until translucent.

2 Add the flour and cook to make a white roux.

3 Add the milk to make a heavy béchamel sauce. Cook the sauce until very thick, approximately 5 minutes.

4 Remove the sauce from the heat and transfer it to a mixing bowl. Add the flaked salmon. Season with dill, salt, pepper and lemon juice and mix well.

5 Spread the mixture in a hotel pan, cover and refrigerate until cold.

6 Portion the mixture using a #20 portion scoop. Form each portion into a cone shape. Bread the croquettes using the standard breading procedure described in Chapter 9, Mise en Place.

7 Using the basket method, deep-fry the breaded croquettes until done.

Approximate values per croquette: **Calories** 140, **Total fat** 9 g, **Saturated fat** 4.5 g, **Cholesterol** 40 mg, **Sodium** 470 mg, **Total carbohydrates** 7 g, **Protein** 9 g, **Vitamin A** 8%, **Calcium** 10%

1 Portioning the croquette mixture.

2 Forming the mixture into cone shapes.

3 Deep-frying the breaded Salmon Croquettes using the basket method.

Poached Halibut with Chanterelles, Fiddlehead Ferns and Wild Mushroom Foam

YIELD 6 Servings, 7 oz. (210 g) each			METHOD Shallow Poaching	
Chanterelle mushrooms	6 oz.	180 g		
Whole butter	5 oz.	150 g		
Salt and pepper	TT	TT		
Halibut fillets, 5 oz. (150 g) ea.	6	6		
Fish Stock (page 210)	1 qt.	1 lt		
Fresh peas, cooked	6 oz.	180 g		
Fiddleheads or asparagus tips, trimmed, cooked	8 oz.	240 g		
Roasted Fingerling Potatoes (page 686)	1 lb.	480 g		
Wild Mushroom Foam (page 240)	as needed	as needed		

fiddleheads the young unfurled tips of several species of fern plants, which are harvested in early spring

1 Sauté the mushrooms in 1 ounce (30 grams) of the butter until tender. Season with salt and pepper and set aside.

2 Melt 1 ounce (30 grams) of butter in each of two sauté pans. Season the halibut with salt and pepper. Sauté three fillets in each pan for approximately 20 seconds without browning.

3 Add half of the fish stock, mushrooms, peas and fiddleheads to each pan of halibut and bring to a simmer. Place the pans of halibut and other ingredients in a 300°F (150°C) oven, uncovered, and bake until done, approximately 8–10 minutes. Remove from the oven and return to the stove.

4 Position the halibut onto six heated plates. Garnish with the vegetables and Roasted Fingerling Potatoes. Direct the whipping siphon head toward a plate then discharge some Wild Mushroom Foam onto each serving.

Approximate values per 7-oz. (210-g) serving: **Calories** 500, **Total fat** 25 g, **Saturated fat** 13 g, **Cholesterol** 170 mg, **Sodium** 550 mg, **Total carbohydrates** 17 g, **Protein** 52 g, **Vitamin A** 20%, **Vitamin C** 10%, **Calcium** 15%, **Iron** 15%

Garnishing the plate with the foamed sauce.

Paupiettes of Sole with Mousseline of Shrimp

paupiette a thin slice of meat or fish that is rolled around a filling of finely ground meat or vegetables, then fried, baked or braised in wine or stock

YIELD 6 Servings		METHOD Poaching
Mousseline:		
Raw shrimp meat	12 oz.	360 g
Egg white	1	1
Heavy cream	6 fl. oz.	180 ml
Salt and white pepper	TT	TT
Lemon sole or flounder fillets, skinless, 4 oz. (120 g) each	12	12
Whole butter	as needed	as needed
Shallot, chopped	2 oz.	60 g
Parsley stems, chopped	6	6
White vermouth	6 fl. oz.	180 ml
Shrimp stock	12 fl. oz.	360 ml
Beurre manié (page 217)	approx. 1½ oz.	approx. 45 g

1 To make the mousseline, purée the shrimp meat in a food processor. Add the egg white and pulse to incorporate. Slowly add 2 fluid ounces (60 milliliters) cream to the shrimp while pulsing the processor. Season the mousseline with salt and white pepper.

2 Place the fillets, skin side up, on a cutting board. Pat them dry and cover them with plastic wrap. Then flatten the fillets slightly with a mallet.

3 Spread each fillet with a portion of the mousseline. Roll up the fillets, starting with the thickest part and finishing with the tail portion.

4 Butter a sauteuse and sprinkle with the shallot and parsley stems. Place the paupiettes in the sauteuse and add the vermouth and stock. Bring the liquid to a boil, cover with a piece of buttered parchment paper and place in a 350°F (180°C) oven. Poach until nearly done.

5 Remove the paupiettes from the sauteuse and reserve in a warm place.

6 Return the sauteuse to the heat and reduce the cuisson slightly. Thicken the cuisson to the desired consistency with the beurre manié. Add the remaining cream, bring the sauce to a boil and strain through a fine chinois. Adjust the seasonings.

7 Serve two paupiettes per portion on a pool of sauce.

Approximate values per serving: **Calories** 450, **Total fat** 18 g, **Saturated fat** 9 g, **Cholesterol** 310 mg, **Sodium** 970 mg, **Total carbohydrates** 4 g, **Protein** 69 g, **Vitamin A** 35%

❶ Using a mallet to flatten a fillet slightly.

❷ Spreading the fillet with the mousseline.

❸ Rolling the fillets to make the paupiettes.

Clams Casino

YIELD	6 Servings, 6 clams each	METHOD	Baking
Bacon slices, diced		4	4
Onion, minced		1 oz.	30 g
Red bell pepper, minced		1 oz.	30 g
Green bell pepper, minced		1 oz.	30 g
Whole butter		6 oz.	180 g
Lemon juice		1 Tbsp.	15 ml
Worcestershire sauce		2 tsp.	10 ml
Tabasco sauce		TT	TT
Littleneck clams, scrubbed		36	36
Fresh bread crumbs		2 oz.	60 g
Asian chile sauce such as Sriracha		as needed for garnish	
Baby lettuce		as needed for garnish	

1 Fry the bacon until well done. Drain the fat, reserving 2 tablespoons (30 milliliters).

2 Sauté the onion and bell peppers in the bacon fat until tender; remove from the heat and cool.

3 Combine 4 ounces (120 grams) of the butter with the lemon juice, Worcestershire sauce, Tabasco sauce, bacon pieces and sautéed vegetables and chill.

4 Open the clams, leaving the meat in the bottom shell. Top each clam with 1 teaspoon (5 milliliters) of the seasoned butter.

5 Melt 2 ounces (60 grams) of butter in a sauté pan and toss the bread crumbs in the butter. Top each clam with a portion of the bread crumbs.

6 Bake at 400°F (200°C) until light brown and bubbling, approximately 10 minutes. Serve immediately. Garnish each plate with chile sauce and baby lettuce if desired.

Approximate values per 6-clam serving: **Calories** 390, **Total fat** 31 g, **Saturated fat** 17 g, **Cholesterol** 110 mg, **Sodium** 890 mg, **Total carbohydrates** 9 g, **Protein** 18 g, **Vitamin A** 25%, **Vitamin C** 40%

Oysters Rockefeller

Food historians credit Antoine's Restaurant in New Orleans, in operation since the 1840s, with the invention of this classic American dish. Chef Jules Alciatore, son of the restaurant's founder, was seeking a replacement for European snails in a popular dish. He experimented using cooked oysters, until then more commonly served raw on the half shell. Alciatore named the resulting dish Oysters Rockefeller, the richness of the sauce reflected in its name.

YIELD 36 Oysters		METHOD Baking
Unsalted butter	8 oz.	240 g
Fresh parsley, chopped	1 oz.	30 g
Celery, chopped	2 oz.	60 g
Fennel bulb, chopped	2 oz.	60 g
Shallots, chopped	2 oz.	60 g
Garlic, chopped	1 tsp.	5 ml
Watercress, chopped	4 oz.	120 g
Pernod	2 fl. oz.	60 ml
Fresh bread crumbs	2½ oz.	75 g
Salt and pepper	TT	TT
Oysters, on the half shell	36	36
Rock salt	as needed	as needed

1 Heat the butter in a sauté pan. Add the parsley, celery, fennel, shallots and garlic and cook for 5 minutes.

2 Add the watercress and cook for 1 minute.

3 Add the Pernod and bread crumbs; season with salt and pepper.

4 Transfer the mixture to a food processor and purée.

5 Top each oyster with approximately 2 teaspoons (10 milliliters) of the vegetable mixture; it should coat the oyster's entire surface.

6 Bake the oysters on a bed of rock salt at 450°F (230°C) until the topping bubbles, approximately 6–7 minutes.

Approximate values per oyster: **Calories** 170, **Total fat** 9 g, **Saturated fat** 4.5 g, **Cholesterol** 105 mg, **Sodium** 450 mg, **Total carbohydrates** 9 g, **Protein** 13 g, **Vitamin A** 15%, **Iron** 60%

Pan-Seared Diver Scallops with Squash Three Ways

YIELD 4 Servings, 6 oz. (180 g) each	METHOD Sautéing	
Raw squash garnish:		
Kabocha, butternut or acorn, squash, unpeeled, washed	as needed	as needed
Sherry vinegar	1 fl. oz.	30 ml
Extra virgin olive oil	1 fl. oz.	30 ml
Kabocha, butternut or acorn, squash, paper thin slices, unpeeled	12	12
Fresh sage leaves	8	8
Diver scallops, large	12	12
Kosher salt	TT	TT
Black pepper	TT	TT
Olive oil	1 fl. oz.	30 ml
Kabocha Squash Purée, warm (recipe follows)	8 oz.	240 g
Whole butter	2 oz.	60 g
Pepitas, toasted, chopped	2 tsp.	10 ml

Kabocha squash a Japanese variety of winter squash with an orange or green knobby rind and firm, brightly-hued flesh, which resembles sweet potatoes when cooked

diver scallops scallops that are harvested from the ocean by divers who hand-pick each one; diver scallops tend to be less gritty than those harvested by dragging, and hand-harvesting is more ecologically friendly

1 To make the raw Kabocha squash garnish, cut the squash into quarters. Scrape out the seeds. Using an electric slicer, slice 8 paper-thin slices from the squash and lay the slices out in a small hotel pan. Brush the slices with the sherry vinegar and olive oil. Set aside.

2 Deep-fry the 12 unpeeled squash slices at 375°F (190°C) until golden brown. Drain and set aside. Deep-fry the sage leaves at 375°F (190°C) until crisp. Drain and set aside.

3 Heat a sauté pan over high heat until very hot. Season each scallop with salt and pepper on both sides. Add the olive oil to the sauté pan. Carefully place one scallop at a time in the pan. Without moving the scallops, sear them over high heat until a dark crust forms, approximately 1–2 minutes. Turn the scallops and cook for 10 more seconds. Remove the scallops from the pan and hold in a warm place.

4 Place a portion of the Kabocha Squash Purée in the center of each plate. Arrange 3 scallops on top of the squash purée, seared side up. Roll the seasoned, raw squash garnish slices (see Step 1) into tubes and arrange them on the plate.

5 In a small sauté pan, heat the butter until it begins to brown. Immediately drizzle the brown butter over the scallops on each plate.

6 Garnish the plates with the deep-fried squash slices (see Step 2), sage leaves and toasted pepitas. Other steamed vegetables may be added as garnish.

Approximate values per 6-oz. (180-g) serving: **Calories** 410, **Total fat** 28 g, **Saturated fat** 12 g, **Cholesterol** 80 mg, **Sodium** 890 mg, **Total carbohydrates** 22 g, **Protein** 20 g, **Vitamin A** 190%, **Vitamin C** 30%

Kabocha Squash Purée

Kabocha squash

YIELD 4 Servings, 6 oz. (180 g) each		
Kabocha, butternut or acorn squash, quartered and seeded	1 lb. 8 oz.	720 g
Extra virgin olive oil	1 fl. oz.	30 ml
Butter	1 Tbsp.	15 ml
Heavy cream	2 fl. oz.	60 ml
Nutmeg	TT	TT
Kosher salt	1 tsp.	5 ml
Shallot, peeled, sliced	2 oz.	60 ml

1 Toss the ingredients together in a large stainless steel bowl. Transfer to a half-size hotel pan and cover tightly with aluminum foil. Bake at 350°F (180°C) for 1 hour until tender. Remove from the oven, cool and refrigerate for 1 hour.

2 Remove the skin from the squash and pass all the ingredients through a food mill. Adjust the seasonings. Refrigerate until needed for service.

Approximate values per 6-oz. (180-g) serving: **Calories** 200, **Total fat** 16 g, **Saturated fat** 6 g, **Cholesterol** 30 mg, **Sodium** 590 mg, **Total carbohydrates** 16 g, **Protein** 2 g, **Vitamin A** 160%

Bouillabaisse (Provençal Fish Stew)

YIELD 8 Servings	METHOD	Simmering
Olive oil	2 fl. oz.	60 ml
Leek, trimmed, julienne	4 oz.	120 g
Onion, chopped fine	4 oz.	120 g
Fennel bulb, julienne	1	1
Garlic, chopped	1 Tbsp.	15 ml
Salt and pepper	TT	TT
Orange zest	2 tsp.	10 ml
Fennel seeds	¼ tsp.	1 ml
Dry white wine	4 fl. oz.	120 ml
Tomatoes, crushed	1 lb.	480 g
Fish stock or clam juice	8 fl. oz.	240 ml
Saffron, soaked in 1 oz. (30 ml) hot water	¼ tsp.	1 ml
Pernod or other anise liqueur	2 fl. oz.	60 ml
Assorted flat fish, mackerel, bass, perch, pike, whole or filleted, cut into 2 inch- (5-cm-) thick chunks	3 lbs.	1.4 kg
Lobsters, 1 lb. 4 oz. (600 g) each, cut into pieces	2	2
Clams	8	8
Shrimp, 21–25 count, peeled and deveined	16	16
Mussels	16	16
Garlic croutons	8	8
Rouille (recipe follows)	as needed	

1 Heat the olive oil in a large rondeau over medium heat. Add the leek, onion, fennel and garlic. Cook until the vegetables soften, approximately 5 minutes. Season to taste. Add the orange zest, fennel seeds, wine, tomatoes, stock, saffron and Pernod. Bring to a boil, then simmer to combine the flavors, approximately 10 minutes. Broth may be prepared up to 2 days ahead to this point.

2 To make the bouillabaisse, place the firmest flatfish, lobster and clams in the bottom of the rondeau with the broth. Cook over high heat for 5 minutes, then add the remaining fish, shrimp and mussels. Cover and boil rapidly until all of the clams are opened and the fish is well cooked, approximately 10–15 minutes.

3 Divide the fish and shellfish evenly among eight serving bowls. Adjust the seasoning of the broth, then ladle it into each bowl and top with a toasted garlic crouton with Rouille on top.

Approximate values per serving: **Calories** 1030, **Total fat** 71 g, **Saturated fat** 14 g, **Cholesterol** 350 mg, **Sodium** 1960 mg, **Total carbohydrates** 29 g, **Protein** 71 g, **Vitamin A** 20%, **Vitamin C** 70%, **Calcium** 20%, **Iron** 30%

Rouille

V Vegan   **🍃** Vegetarian

YIELD 8 Servings, 1 fl. oz. (30 ml) each

White bread	1 slice	1 slice
Garlic, chopped	2 tsp.	10 ml
Cayenne pepper	¼ tsp.	1 ml
Olive oil	8 fl. oz.	240 ml
Salt	TT	TT

1 Tear the bread and place in the bowl of a food processor. Process for 40 seconds to make fresh bread crumbs.

2 Add the garlic and cayenne pepper and process to blend.

3 Slowly drizzle in the oil until the mixture resembles mayonnaise. Add a small amount of warm water if necessary to thin the sauce and make it creamier.

4 Adjust the seasoning with salt.

Approximate values per 1-fl.-oz. (30-ml) serving: **Calories** 470, **Total fat** 35 g, **Saturated fat** 5 g, **Cholesterol** 0 mg, **Sodium** 770 mg, **Total carbohydrates** 20 g, **Protein** 7 g

Fried Oysters with Rémoulade Sauce

YIELD 6 Appetizer Servings, 4 oysters each		**METHOD** Deep-Frying	
Leeks, julienne	3	3
Oysters, scrubbed	24	24
Flour	4 oz.	120 g
Eggs	2	2
Egg yolks	2	2
Fresh bread crumbs	8 oz.	240 g
Rémoulade Sauce (page 759) or Aïoli (Garlic Mayonnaise) (page 742)	6 fl. oz.	180 ml

1 Deep-fry the leeks at 280°F (138°C) until golden brown. Drain and set aside.

2 Open the oysters. Strain and reserve the liquor.

3 Poach the oysters in the liquor for 30 seconds. Drain, reserving the liquid. Cool the liquid and oysters separately.

4 Bread the oysters using the standard breading procedure described in Chapter 9, Mise en Place.

5 Deep-fry the oysters at 375°F (190°C) until browned, approximately 1 minute.

6 Serve the oysters on a nest of leeks with sauce.

Approximate values per 4-oyster serving: **Calories** 1220, **Total fat** 44 g, **Saturated fat** 17 g, **Cholesterol** 785 mg, **Sodium** 2870 mg, **Total carbohydrates** 118 g, **Protein** 89 g, **Vitamin A** 50%, **Vitamin C** 70%, **Iron** 380%

Fried Calamari with Lemon, Olive and Pepper Relish

YIELD 4 Servings, 6½ oz. (195 g) each	METHOD Deep-Frying	
Red bell pepper, fine dice	4 oz.	120 g
Serrano chiles, seeded, fine dice	2	2
Kalamata olives, chopped	10	10
Chives, minced	2 Tbsp.	30 ml
Lemon zest	2 Tbsp.	30 ml
Squid, bodies and tentacles, cleaned	1 lb.	480 g
Flour	8 oz.	240 g
Salt	¾ tsp.	4 ml
White pepper	½ tsp.	2 ml
Lemon slices or wedges	as needed for garnish	

1   Combine the red bell pepper, chiles, olives, chives and lemon zest.

2   Slice the squid bodies into rings approximately ¼–½ inch (6–12 millimeters) thick.

3   Combine the flour, salt and pepper. Toss the squid in the seasoned flour. Shake off the excess flour. Deep-fry the squid at 350°F (177°C) until crispy and golden brown.

4   Drain and toss the cooked squid with the pepper mixture. Serve the squid with lemon slices and wedges as desired.

Approximate values per 6½-oz. (195-g) serving: **Calories** 310, **Total fat** 11 g, **Saturated fat** 1.5 g, **Cholesterol** 265 mg, **Sodium** 420 mg, **Total carbohydrates** 29 g, **Protein** 21 g, **Vitamin A** 20%, **Vitamin C** 80%, **Iron** 15%

Maryland-Style Steamed Blue Crabs

Blue crabs are found along the Atlantic Coast from Canada to South America. These hard-shell crustaceans, usually steamed whole and coated with a boldly flavored seasoning mixture, are a specialty of the Chesapeake Bay area of Maryland. The Maryland blue crab season lasts from April through December, but those harvested in the fall contain the most meat.

YIELD 2 Servings, 6 crabs each	METHOD Steaming	
Beer	12 fl. oz.	360 ml
Cider vinegar	6 fl. oz.	180 ml
Blue crabs, live or Rock crab claws	12	12
Old Bay Seasoning or other seafood seasoning mixture	4 oz.	120 g

1   Place a steamer insert into the bottom of a large stock pot. Add the beer and vinegar. Layer four live crabs in the steamer. Sprinkle with one third of the seasoning mixture. Cover with four more crabs and one third of the seasoning mixture. Place the remaining crabs on top and sprinkle with the remaining seasoning mixture.

2   Cover and bring the liquid to a boil. Reduce the heat and steam the crabs until they are cooked through and turn a uniform bright orange color, approximately 20–30 minutes depending upon the size of the crabs.

3   To serve, pile the hot crabs on a large platter or clean newspaper.

4   To eat the crabs, twist the legs to separate them from the body. Crack the legs and claws with a knife or scissors. Remove the cartilage in the claw meat before eating. Turn the crab over, remove and discard the apron. Use fingers or small forks to pry out the back meat. Avoid eating the gills and lungs. Break the crab in half vertically to expose the lump crab meat. If desired, eat the green tomalley on crackers or toasted bread.

Approximate values per 6-crab serving: **Calories** 140, **Total fat** 10 g, **Saturated fat** 1 g, **Cholesterol** 100 mg, **Sodium** 1860 mg, **Total carbohydrates** 0 g, **Protein** 22 g

Steamed Mussels with Leeks and Carrots

YIELD	2 Servings	METHOD	Steaming
Dry white wine		8 fl. oz.	240 ml
Garlic, chopped		1 oz.	30 g
Black pepper		½ tsp.	2 ml
Fresh thyme		4 sprigs	4 sprigs
Leek, julienne		2 oz.	60 g
Carrot, julienne		2 oz.	60 g
Mussels, debearded and scrubbed		2 lb.	960 g
Whole butter		4 oz.	120 g
Fresh parsley, chopped		1 Tbsp.	15 ml
Croutons, sauteed in butter		as needed for garnish	

1 Combine the wine, garlic, pepper, thyme, leek and carrot in a large sautoir.

2 Cover the pan and bring to a boil. Add the mussels. Cover and steam until their shells open.

3 Remove the opened mussels and arrange them in two large soup plates.

4 Reduce the cooking liquid by half, monté au beurre and pour the sauce over the mussels. The carrot and leek should remain on top of the mussels as garnish.

5 Sprinkle with chopped parsley and serve with croutons.

Approximate values per serving: **Calories** 1220, **Total fat** 67 g, **Saturated fat** 33 g, **Cholesterol** 375 mg, **Sodium** 2170 mg, **Total carbohydrates** 44 g, **Protein** 110 g, **Vitamin A** 140%, **Vitamin C** 120%, **Iron** 200%

Paella

Paella [pah-AY-lyah] is one of the classic dishes of Spain. The word paella refers to both a shallow, black steel pan and the dish made in it; paella is a combination of poultry, meats, shellfish, game, chorizo, vegetables and short-grain rice with saffron. Traditionally this dish is cooked over an open wood fire. The most well-known paella is from Valencia and consists of a colorful mixture of shellfish, poultry and saffron rice.

YIELD 4 Servings		METHOD Steaming	
Chicken thighs	4	4	
Salt and pepper	TT	TT	
Olive oil	1 fl. oz.	30 ml	
Onion, medium dice	2 oz.	60 g	
Garlic, chopped	1 Tbsp.	15 ml	
Long-grain rice	6 oz.	180 g	
Saffron	1 pinch	1 pinch	
Chicken stock, well seasoned, hot	14 fl. oz.	420 ml	
Chorizo, cooked, chopped fine	2 oz.	30 g	
Littleneck clams, scrubbed	6	6	
Shrimp, 16–20 count	4	4	
Mussels, debearded and scrubbed	6	6	
Peas, fresh or frozen and thawed	2 oz.	60 g	

1 Season the chicken with salt and pepper. Pan-fry it in the oil, browning it well. Cook until done, approximately 20 minutes. Remove the chicken and reserve.

2 Add the onion and garlic to the pan and sauté until tender.

3 Add the rice and sauté until it turns translucent.

4 Add the saffron to the chicken stock. Stir the chicken stock into the rice and bring to a boil.

5 Add the chorizo and clams to the pan. Cover and place in a 375°F (190°C) oven for 10 minutes.

6 Add the shrimp and cooked chicken to the pan. Cover and cook for an additional 15 minutes.

7 Add the mussels and peas to the pan and cook until the shrimp are done, the chicken is hot and all the shellfish are opened, approximately 5 minutes.

Approximate values per serving: **Calories** 550, **Total fat** 24 g, **Saturated fat** 6 g, **Cholesterol** 155 mg, **Sodium** 670 mg, **Total carbohydrates** 44 g, **Protein** 36 g, **Vitamin C** 20%, **Iron** 25%

Crawfish Étouffée

YIELD 4 Servings		METHOD Simmering
Corn oil	4 fl. oz.	120 ml
Flour	4 oz.	120 g
Onion, large, chopped fine	1	1
Celery stalk, chopped fine	1	1
Green bell pepper, chopped	½	½
Garlic cloves, minced	2	2
Shrimp broth or clam juice	1¼ pt.	600 ml
Lemon juice	1 Tbsp.	15 ml
Crawfish fat, optional	2 oz.	60 g
Salt	1 tsp.	5 ml
Black pepper	½ tsp.	2 ml
Cayenne pepper	½ tsp.	2 ml
Dried thyme	½ tsp.	2 ml
Bay leaf	1	1
Louisiana hot sauce	1 Tbsp.	15 ml
Crawfish tails, frozen	1 lb.	480 g
Green onions, sliced	2	2
White rice, cooked	1 qt.	1 lt

1 Heat the oil in a large sauté pan. Whisk in the flour and cook, stirring constantly, to make a medium-dark roux.

2 Add the onion, celery, bell pepper and garlic and sauté over medium-low heat until the vegetables are tender, approximately 10 minutes.

3 Slowly add the broth or clam juice and bring to a boil. Reduce the heat to a simmer and add the lemon juice; crawfish fat, if using; salt; black pepper; cayenne pepper and herbs. Simmer for 15 minutes to thicken.

4 Add the hot sauce and the crawfish tails and simmer for approximately 10 minutes. Add the green onions and adjust the seasonings. Serve over cooked rice.

Approximate values per serving: **Calories** 880, **Total fat** 32 g, **Saturated fat** 4 g, **Cholesterol** 130 mg, **Sodium** 1190 mg, **Total carbohydrates** 107 g, **Protein** 40 g, **Vitamin A** 300%, **Vitamin C** 480%, **Calcium** 45%, **Iron** 90%

Soft-Poached Salmon with Root Vegetables and Pernod Beurre Blanc

Present Company, Simsbury, CT
Chef Jeffrey Lizotte

Sous vide *oil poaching produces meltingly tender salmon. Here layers of fresh and smoked salmon and sheets of seaweed are formed into a terrine, which is compressed under vacuum to hold its shape. For service, individual portions are vacuum sealed then cooked to order in a thermal circulator. To enhance its appearance and to ensure that the* sous vide *fish remains hot, each portion is seared on one side immediately before plating.*

transglutaminase natural enzyme derived from bacterial fermentation that binds proteins into a solid mass. It is widely used commercially for making sausages and surimi; chefs use it to join pieces of meat, fish or poultry into a single cut

---

⚠ Safety Alert

Sous Vide *Sanitation*

Food safety is of utmost concern when using *sous vide* techniques because of the low cooking temperatures. To prevent the growth of microorganisms, any food to be cooked *sous vide* must be chilled below the temperature danger zone (41°F/5°C) before cooking. Keep all cutting boards, knives and food contact surfaces clean and sanitary and wear clean disposable gloves. Use only the freshest unblemished ingredients. Consult your local health department for regulations for preparing food *sous vide*. Special permission and a HACCP plan may be required.

YIELD 10 Servings, 5–6 oz. (150–180 g) each   **METHOD** *Sous Vide* Poaching

Terrine:		
Salmon fillet, skinned, 3½–4 lb. (1.6–1.9 kg)	1 side	1 side
Transglutaminase, optional	½ oz.	15 grams
Salt and pepper	TT	TT
Nori	8 sheets	8 sheets
Smoked salmon, 1-oz. (30-g) slices	10 slices	10 slices
Olive oil	10 fl. oz.	300 ml
Baby carrots, cooked, hot	30	30
Beurre Blanc (page 232)	10 fl. oz.	300 ml
Pernod	1 fl. oz.	30 ml
Fresh chervil	as needed for garnish	

1 To make the terrine, line a 6⅜ × 10⅞ × 2½-inch (16 × 27 × 6-centimeter) quarter-size hotel pan with plastic wrap. Cut a cardboard cake board or a piece of heavy plastic to make a template the same size as the interior of the hotel pan.

2 Trim the salmon fillet of any skin, bone, imperfections or blemishes. Cut the fillet in half, then trim each piece the same length as the quarter-size hotel pan. (Reserve trim for other uses.)

3 Trim two pieces of the salmon to fit into the bottom of the hotel pan. Lay one piece of salmon in the bottom of the pan. Evenly sprinkle some of the transglutaminase, if using, over the edge of the fish. Place another piece of the salmon with its thinnest edge overlapping the salmon in the pan. Evenly sprinkle the seam where the pieces of salmon overlap with more transglutaminase. Season to taste with salt and pepper.

4 Cover the salmon with four sheets of the nori. Lay out the slices of smoked salmon overlapping in one even layer to cover the nori. Cover the smoked salmon with another layer of nori. Then cover the nori with the remaining pieces of salmon fillet.

5 Evenly sprinkle the seam where the pieces of salmon overlap with the remaining transglutaminase. Season to taste.

6 Fold the plastic wrap over the salmon. Place the template on top of the terrine. Slide the pan into a large vacuum bag. Vacuum seal on high to help the terrine keep its shape. Once sealed, the terrine can be held in the refrigerator for up to 36 hours before preparing for service.

7 Remove the terrine from the bag and unmold it onto a cutting board. Slice it lengthwise into two 3 × 10-inch (7.5 × 22-centimeter) strips. Cut each strip into five uniform portions.

8 For each portion, add 1 tablespoon (15 milliliters) of the olive oil to a vacuum bag. Slide a portion of salmon into each bag. Vacuum seal. Once sealed, the portioned salmon can be held in the refrigerator for up to 48 hours before serving.

9 For service, cook the salmon in a thermal circulator heated to 122.5°F (50°C) until the core temperature of the fish reaches 122.5°F (50°C) when checked with a digital probe thermometer, approximately 12 minutes. (Reseal the bag before returning it to the circulator if necessary.) The salmon may be held in the thermal circulator until ready to serve.

10 Whip the Pernod into the Beurre Blanc. Keep warm.

11 Remove the portions of salmon from the bags. Drain on clean paper towels.

12 Heat the remaining olive oil in a sauté pan over high heat. Sear the salmon, presentation side down, until crisp.

13 Cut each portion of the salmon in half. Place the portions on warmed plates with some of the cooked baby carrots and Beurre Blanc. Garnish with chervil.

Approximate values per 5–6 oz. (150–180 g) serving: **Calories** 660, **Total fat** 52 g, **Saturated fat** 18 g, **Cholesterol** 150 mg, **Sodium** 660 mg, **Total carbohydrates** 4 g, **Protein** 40 g, **Vitamin A** 150%

1 Sprinkling the salmon in the hotel pan with transglutaminase.

2 Covering the salmon with sheets of nori.

3 Laying out slices of smoked salmon over the nori.

4 Placing the terrine into the chamber vacuum machine and vacuum-sealing which will help it hold its shape.

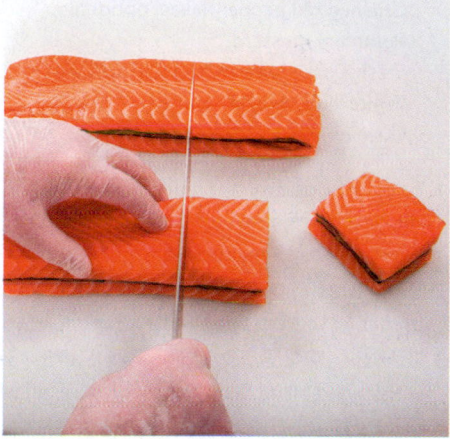

5 Cutting the salmon terrine into portions.

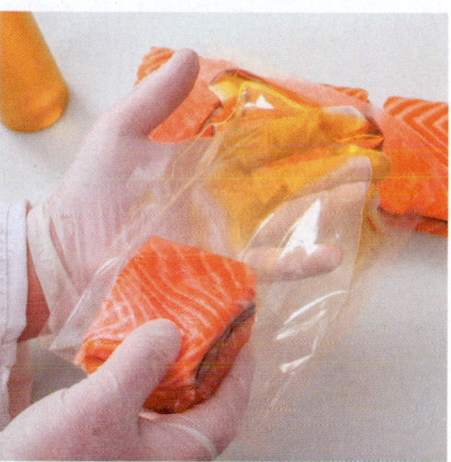

6 Sliding a portion of salmon terrine into a plastic vacuum bag with the olive oil.

7 Vacuum sealing two portions of salmon.

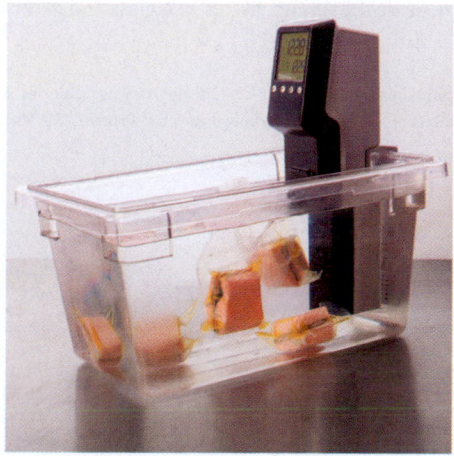

8 Cooking the vacuum-sealed bags of salmon in the thermal circulator.

9 Draining a cooked portion of salmon before searing.

Pickled Shrimp

YIELD 2¼ lb. (1 kg), 6 Servings, 6 oz. (180 g) each	**METHOD** Poaching	
Water	1½ pt.	720 ml
Lemon, quartered	1	1
Cajun seasoning	1 oz. (4 Tbsp.)	30 g
Large shrimp, peeled and deveined	2¼ lb.	1 kg
Garlic, sliced thin	1 oz.	30 g
Lemon, sliced thin	1	1
Onion, sliced thin	3 oz.	90 g
Bay leaves	6	6
Dressing:		
Celery seed	1 tsp.	5 ml
Black pepper	½ tsp.	2 ml
Salt	2 tsp.	10 ml
Creole seasoning	1 Tbsp.	15 ml
Louisiana hot sauce	1 tsp.	5 ml
Crushed red pepper flakes, optional	½ tsp.	2 ml
Pommery mustard	1 Tbsp.	15 ml
Fresh lemon juice	2 fl. oz.	60 ml
White wine vinegar	6 fl. oz.	180 ml
Olive oil	8 fl. oz.	240 ml

1 Bring the water, quartered lemon and Cajun seasoning to a boil in a medium sauce pan. Reduce the heat and simmer for 5 minutes. Add the shrimp to the simmering water and cook until pink, approximately 3 minutes.

2 Drain the shrimp, discarding the cooking liquid and the pieces of lemon. Set aside to cool while preparing the dressing.

3 To make the dressing, combine all of the seasonings, lemon juice and vinegar in a small bowl, whisking to blend. Slowly add the olive oil, whisking to form a temporary emulsion.

4 Place a layer of the cooked shrimp in a glass or plastic container with a tightly fitting lid. Top with about one-third of the thinly sliced lemon, garlic, onion and 2 bay leaves. Add another layer of the shrimp and repeat the layers two more times.

5 Pour the dressing over the shrimp and seal the container. Refrigerate for 12–24 hours, tossing the container gently once or twice to redistribute the dressing.

6 Serve the shrimp layered in a glass and garnished as desired as an appetizer or use on a green salad with arugula.

Approximate values per 6-oz. (180-g) serving: **Calories** 310, **Total fat** 25 g, **Saturated fat** 3.5 g, **Cholesterol** 145 mg, **Sodium** 1410 mg, **Total carbohydrates** 5 g, **Protein** 16 g, **Vitamin C** 15%

Seviche

In a seviche, the fish and shellfish are "cooked" by the acids in the citrus juice. Although a variety of fish or shellfish may be used, it is extremely important that the products be absolutely fresh. Use a nonreactive container such as stainless steel or plastic for mixing and storing seviche. Aluminum and other metals may react with the acids in the lime juice, giving the food a metallic flavor.

YIELD 3 lb. (1.4 kg), 12 Servings, 4 oz. (120 g) each

Raw scallops and/or shrimp	1 lb.	480 g
Raw firm white fish	1 lb.	480 g
Fresh lime juice	8 fl. oz.	240 ml
Serrano chiles, minced	4	4
Red onion, fine dice	6 oz.	180 g
Fresh cilantro, minced	4 Tbsp.	60 ml
Olive oil	1 fl. oz.	30 ml
Tomato concassée	8 oz.	240 g
Garlic, chopped	2 tsp.	10 ml
Salt and pepper	TT	TT

1 Chop the scallops, shrimp and fish coarsely but evenly into ¾-inch (1.9-centimeter) pieces. Place in a nonreactive container and add the lime juice. Cover and marinate in the refrigerator for 4 hours. The fish should turn opaque and become firm.

2 Toss in the remaining ingredients and season to taste with salt and pepper. Chill thoroughly and serve as a salad or with tortilla chips.

3 If the seviche is going to be held for more than 2 hours, drain the liquid and refrigerate separately. The reserved liquid can then be tossed with the other ingredients at service time.

Approximate values per 4-oz. (120-g) serving: **Calories** 120, **Total fat** 4.5 g, **Saturated fat** 0.5 g, **Cholesterol** 30 mg, **Sodium** 250 mg, **Total carbohydrates** 5 g, **Protein** 13 g, **Vitamin A** 10%, **Vitamin C** 20%, **Claims**—low saturated fat

Fin Fish Carpaccio with Lemon Thyme Vinaigrette

YIELD 4 Servings, 3 oz. (90 g) each

Sushi-grade fish fillets such as tuna, salmon or snapper	8 oz.	240 g
Fresh lemon juice	2 fl. oz.	60 ml
Fresh thyme leaves	½ tsp.	2 ml
Salt and pepper	TT	TT
Extra virgin olive oil	4 fl. oz.	120 ml
Saffron threads	1 tsp.	5 ml

1 Slice the tuna into four equal portions. (If using salmon or snapper, slice into thin tranches.) Place the fish between sheets of heavy waxed paper or plastic wrap.

2 Lightly pound the fish with the side of a cleaver until paper thin. Remove the top sheet of paper, then carefully flip each piece onto a chilled serving plate. Cover with plastic wrap. Refrigerate until ready to serve.

3 Combine the lemon juice, thyme leaves, salt and pepper. Whisk in olive oil.

4 For service, season each portion of fish with salt and pepper. Whisk the vinaigrette together and drizzle it over the fish. Sprinkle with the saffron threads and serve immediately with crusty bread.

Approximate values per 3-oz. (90-g) serving: **Calories** 310, **Total fat** 27 g, **Saturated fat** 4 g, **Cholesterol** 20 mg, **Sodium** 25 mg, **Total carbohydrates** 1 g, **Protein** 14 g

Norimaki Zushi

YIELD 36 Pieces

Dried shiitake mushrooms	4	4
Water, hot	8 fl. oz.	240 ml
Shoyu	4 fl. oz.	120 ml
Brown sugar	1 Tbsp.	15 ml
Cucumber	12	12
Sushi-quality fish fillets such as ahi, salmon, flounder or sea bass	5 oz.	150 g
Nori	3 sheets	3 sheets
Sushi rice	18 oz.	540 g
Wasabi paste	4 Tbsp.	60 ml
Pickled ginger	2 oz.	60 g

1 Soak the mushrooms in hot water for 20 minutes. Remove the mushrooms and reserve 4 ounces (120 grams) of the liquid. Trim off the mushroom stems.

2 Julienne the mushroom caps. Combine the reserved mushroom soaking liquid with 2 tablespoons (30 milliliters) of the shoyu and the sugar. Simmer the caps in this liquid and reduce au sec. Remove from the heat and refrigerate.

3 Peel and seed the cucumber; cut it into strips the size of pencils, approximately 6 inches (15 centimeters) long.

4 Trim the fish fillets of any skin, bone, imperfections or blemishes. Cut the fillets into strips the same size as the cucumbers.

5 Cut the sheets of nori in half and place one half sheet on a napkin or bamboo rolling mat. Divide the rice into six equal portions; spread one portion over each half sheet of nori, leaving a ½-inch (1.2-centimeter) border of nori exposed.

6 Spread 1 teaspoon (5 milliliters) wasabi paste evenly on the rice.

7 Lay one-sixth of the mushrooms, cucumber and fish strips in a row down the middle of the rice.

8 Use the napkin or bamboo mat to roll the nori tightly around the rice, mushrooms, cucumber and fish.

9 Slice each roll into six pieces and serve with the remaining shoyu, wasabi and pickled ginger.

Approximate values per piece: **Calories** 40, **Total fat** 0 g, **Saturated fat** 0 g, **Cholesterol** 5 mg, **Sodium** 220 mg, **Total carbohydrates** 6 g, **Protein** 2 g, **Vitamin C** 15%, **Claims**—fat free; low cholesterol; low calorie

1 Cutting the fillets into strips.

2 Spreading the rice over the nori.

3 Laying the cucumber and fish strips in a row down the middle of the rice.

4 Using the bamboo mat to roll the nori around the rice, mushrooms, cucumber and fish.

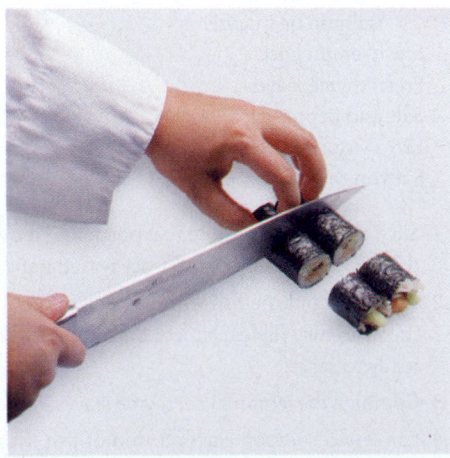

5 Slicing the Norimaki Zushi roll into six pieces.

Eggs and Breakfast 21

After studying this chapter, you will be able to:

▶ describe the composition of eggs

▶ purchase and store eggs properly

▶ apply various cooking methods to eggs

▶ prepare pancakes and other griddlecakes

▶ plan breakfast menus to provide a variety of food options for customers

▶ prepare breakfast coffee and tea beverages

Eggs are the food source for developing chicks. Eggs, particularly chicken eggs, are also an excellent food for humans because of their high protein content, low cost and ready availability. They are extremely versatile and are used throughout the kitchen, either served alone or as ingredients in a prepared dish. Cooked eggs and egg dishes are most often associated with breakfast and brunch. In addition to eggs, food service operations must offer a variety of other breakfast options to appeal to a wide range of consumers.

Breakfast cookery is often one of the first line positions a new cook will be offered. This important duty requires speed, timing and precision and can help an apprentice or beginning cook develop organized, efficient work habits.

This chapter discusses cooking methods for eggs as well as breakfast meats, griddlecakes, crêpes, cereals and the beverages coffee and tea. Other foods typically served at breakfast, such as quick breads, fruit, fruit beverages and cheese, are discussed elsewhere in this text.

EGGS

Eggs provide *texture, flavor, structure, moisture* and *nutrition* to a variety of foods, from soups and sauces to breads and pastries. Eggs *leaven* and *thicken* bakery items, and *bind ingredients* such as crumbs on breaded foods, or ingredients in a dough or sauce. Eggs *enrich* and *tenderize* breads and *extend the shelf life* of some baked goods.

Chicken eggs are most common, but quail, duck, goose and other poultry eggs are also suitable for culinary use. Unless otherwise stated, all of the recipes in this text use large chicken eggs, and information is based on chicken eggs only.

The primary parts of an egg are the shell, yolk and albumen. See Figure 21.1.

The **shell**, composed of calcium carbonate, is the outermost covering of the egg. It prevents microbes from entering and moisture from escaping, and also protects the egg during handling and transport. The breed of the hen determines shell color; for chickens, it can range from bright white to brown. Shell color has no effect on quality, flavor or nutrition.

The **yolk** is the yellow portion of the egg. It constitutes just over one-third of the egg and contains three-fourths of the calories, most of the minerals and vitamins and all the fat. The yolk also contains lecithin, the compound responsible for emulsification in products such as hollandaise sauce and mayonnaise. Egg yolk solidifies (coagulates) at temperatures between 149°F and 158°F (65°C and 70°C). Although the color of a yolk may vary depending on the hen's feed, color does not affect quality or nutritional content.

Function of Ingredients

Eggs

■ provide texture, flavor, structure, moisture and nutrition

■ leaven and thicken items such as custards, pie fillings and sauces

■ bind ingredients such as crumbs on breaded items or ingredients in dough or sauce

■ enrich and tenderize breads and cakes

■ extend the shelf life of some baked goods

Average Weight of Large Egg, Without Shells

Whole 1.6 ounces (50 grams)

White 1 ounce (30 grams)

Yolk 0.6 ounce (20 grams)

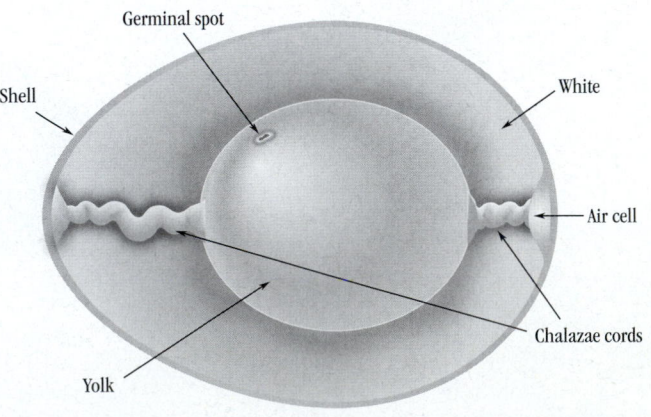

Figure 21.1 An egg.

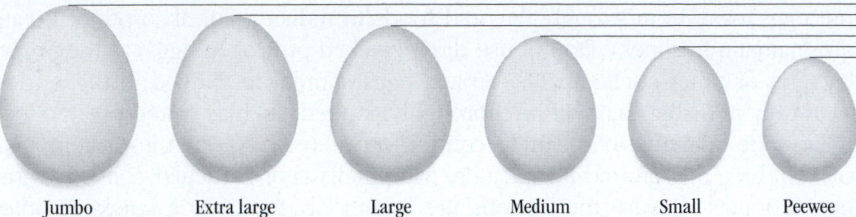

Jumbo   Extra large   Large   Medium   Small   Peewee

Figure 21.2 Egg sizes.

The **albumen**, often referred to as the **egg white**, is the clear portion of the egg. It constitutes about two-thirds of the egg and contains more than half of the protein and riboflavin. Egg white coagulates, becoming firm and opaque, at temperatures between 144°F and 149°F (62°C and 65°C).

An often-misunderstood portion of the egg are the **chalazae cords**. These thick, twisted strands of egg white called chalaza, anchor the yolk in place. They are neither imperfections nor embryos. The more prominent the chalazae cords, the fresher the egg. Chalazae cords do not interfere with cooking or with whipping egg whites.

Eggs are sold in Jumbo, Extra Large, Large, Medium, Small and Peewee sizes, as determined by weight per dozen. See Figure 21.2. Food service operations generally use Large eggs, which weigh 24 ounces per dozen. Other sizes are based on plus or minus 3 ounces per dozen; Medium eggs weigh 21 ounces per dozen, whereas Extra Large eggs weigh 27 ounces per dozen.

Eggs are graded by the USDA or a state agency following USDA guidelines. The grade AA, A or B is given to an egg based on interior and exterior quality, not size. Table 21.1 describes the qualities for each grade. Grade has no effect on nutritional values.

Egg Storage and Sanitation

Improper handling quickly diminishes egg quality. Eggs should be stored at temperatures below 45°F (7°C) and at a relative humidity of 70–80 percent. Eggs age more during 1 day at room temperature than they do during 1 week under proper refrigeration. As eggs age, the white becomes thinner and the yolk becomes flatter. This changes the appearance of poached or fried eggs, making it important to use very fresh eggs for these cooking techniques. Older eggs, however, should be used for hard-cooking, as their shells will be easier to remove.

Cartons of fresh, uncooked eggs will keep for at least 4–5 weeks beyond the pack date if kept refrigerated at 36°F (2°C). Hard-cooked eggs left in their shells and refrigerated should be used within 1 week.

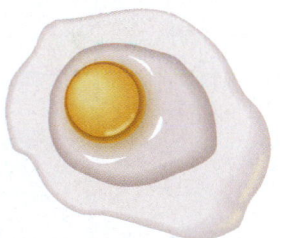

Grade AA

Grade A

EGG GRADES			TABLE 21.1
	GRADE AA	**GRADE A**	**GRADE B**
Spread*	Remains compact	Spreads slightly	Spreads over wide area
Albumen	Clear, thick and firm; prominent chalazae cords	Clear and reasonably firm; prominent chalazae cords	Clear; weak or watery
Yolk	Firm; centered; stands round and high; free from defects	Firm; stands fairly high; practically free from defects	Enlarged and flattened; may show slight defects
Shell	Clean; of normal shape; unbroken	Clean; of normal shape; unbroken	Slight stains permissible; abnormal shape; unbroken
Use	Any use, especially frying and poaching	Any use, especially frying, poaching and cooking in shell	Baking; scrambling, used in bulk egg products

Grade B

*Spread refers to the appearance of the egg when first broken onto a flat surface.

pasteurization the process of heating something to a certain temperature for a specific period in order to destroy pathogenic bacteria

Store eggs away from strongly flavored foods to reduce odor absorption. Rotate egg stock to maintain freshness. Do not use dirty, cracked or broken eggs, as they may contain bacteria or other contaminants. Frozen eggs should be thawed in the refrigerator and used only in dishes that will be thoroughly cooked, such as baked products.

Eggs require time and temperature control for safety (TCS). Rich in protein, eggs are an excellent breeding ground for bacteria. Salmonella is of particular concern with eggs and egg products because the bacteria are commonly found in a chicken's intestinal tract. Although egg shells are cleaned at packinghouses, some bacteria may remain. Therefore, to prevent contamination, it is best to avoid mixing a shell with the liquid egg.

Inadequately cooking or improperly storing eggs may lead to food-borne illnesses. Hold egg dishes below 41°F (5°C) or above 135°F (57°C). Never leave an egg dish at room temperature for more than 1 hour, including preparation and service time. Never reuse a container after it has held raw eggs without thoroughly cleaning and sanitizing it.

Pasteurized eggs are required to safely prepare mayonnaise, mousse or other dishes that will not be cooked. USDA guidelines state that **pasteurization** is achieved and harmful bacteria such as *Salmonella enteritidis* are destroyed when the whole egg stays at a temperature of 140°F (60°C) for 3½ minutes. (By law, all liquid eggs sold without their shells and dried egg products must be pasteurized before sale as discussed in the following text.) To pasteurize eggs in their shells, place fresh room temperature eggs in a saucepan. Cover them with cool water. Slowly heat the water to 140°F (60°C). Maintain the water at this temperature, monitoring it with an instant read thermometer for 3–5 minutes. Immediately chill the eggs in an ice and water bath. Refrigerate them for up to four days before using.

Pasteurized eggs with their shells on are also available for purchase. While these cost more than unpasteurized eggs, the convenience of using eggs without risking salmonella may outweigh the increased cost for some operations. Pasteurized eggs are a good option for environments where sanitation is a particular concern, such as schools or hospitals.

Egg Products

Food service operations often want the convenience of buying eggs out of the shell in the exact form needed: whole eggs, yolks only or whites only. These processed items are called *egg products* and are subject to strict pasteurization standards and USDA inspections. Egg products are available refrigerated, frozen or dried. Frozen egg products are useful when making batters for French toast, omelets or scrambled eggs as well as in baking. Dried egg products are often used in baking but are not recommended for breakfast cookery.

Concerns about the cholesterol content of eggs have increased the popularity of **egg substitutes**. There are two general types of substitutes. The first is a complete substitute made from soy or milk proteins. It should not be used in recipes in which eggs are required for thickening. The second substitute contains real albumen, but the egg yolk has been replaced with vegetable or milk products. Check the ingredients listed on the label; unless lecithin is added, an egg substitute cannot be used for emulsifying or thickening. Powdered egg substitutes are useful in baked goods but will not work for scrambled eggs. Generally the higher the ratio of eggs in a recipe or formula, the less likely that any egg substitute will be an acceptable substitute and perform adequately. The flavor of egg substitutes is different from real eggs, but they can still be useful for people on a restricted diet.

For anyone with an egg allergy, **egg replacements** are the best option. Replacements do not contain any egg product and are usually available as a powder that can be used for thickening.

NUTRITION INFORMATION FOR EGGS

Eggs contain vitamins A, D, E and K and the B-complex vitamins. They are rich in minerals and contain less cholesterol now than previously thought. Research indicates that the cholesterol in whole eggs does not impact serum cholesterol as much as was once feared. In fact, the American Heart Association no longer sets specific limits on the number of egg yolks one should consume per week as part of a balanced diet. Egg whites do not contain cholesterol and are often added to egg dishes such as omelets to reduce total fat content.

Roaming Poultry

Free range refers to chickens that are allowed to roam freely in the farmyard as opposed to living in cages. *Free-range eggs* are produced from such chickens. The USDA requires that producers demonstrate that the chickens have access to the outdoors, but the amount and quality of that access is not defined. Some producers may add the term *cage-free*, which indicates that the birds were not confined to cages but were kept indoors, usually in large barns. Although this term is regulated (companies must apply to the Food Safety and Inspection Service of the USDA for permission to use this term), egg laying operations are not actually inspected.

WHIPPED EGG WHITES

Egg whites are often whipped into a foam that is then incorporated into cakes, custards, **soufflés**, pancakes and other products. The air beaten into the egg foam gives products lightness and assists with leavening. For the best volume, allow egg whites to come to room temperature before whipping and make sure that no trace of egg yolk (or any other fat) is present. Adding an acid ingredient, such as cream of tartar or lemon juice, helps stabilize the egg foam. For every 8 ounces (240 milliliters) of egg whites from shell eggs, add 1 teaspoon (5 milliliters) cream of tartar or lemon juice. (If using pasteurized fresh egg whites, reduce the amount of cream of tartar or lemon juice by half.) Add the acid when the egg whites begin to foam. The proper addition of sugar also acts as a foam stabilizer, but sugar is not used in savory dishes. Add salt, which disrupts the egg whites ability to foam, only after the egg whites have begun to foam.

soufflé [soo-FLAY] a sweet or savory fluffy dish made with a custard base lightened with whipped egg whites and then baked; the whipped egg whites cause the dish to puff when baked

Procedure for Whipping Egg Whites

1 Use fresh egg whites that are completely free of egg yolk and other impurities. Warm the egg whites to room temperature before whipping; this helps to form a better foam.

2 Use a clean bowl and whisk. Even a tiny amount of fat can prevent the egg whites from foaming properly.

3 Whip the whites until very foamy, then add cream of tartar, lemon juice or other acid as directed.

4 Continue whipping until soft peaks form, then gradually add granulated sugar and/or salt as directed.

5 Whip until stiff peaks form. Properly whipped egg whites should be moist and shiny; over whipped egg whites appear dry and spongy or curdled.

6 Use the whipped egg whites immediately. If liquid begins to separate from the whipped egg whites, discard them; they cannot be rewhipped successfully.

1 Egg whites whipped to soft peaks.

COOKING METHODS FOR EGGS

No other food is as popular for breakfast in the United States or as versatile, as the egg. Eggs can be cooked by almost any method and served with a wide array of seasonings, accompaniments and garnishes. Whatever cooking method is selected, be sure to prepare the eggs carefully: Overcooked eggs and those cooked at too high a temperature will be tough and rubbery. Undercooked eggs may transmit pathogenic bacteria and pose a risk of food-borne illness.

The cooking methods discussed in this chapter are those most used for eggs and egg-based dishes. They include dry-heat cooking methods (baking, sautéing and pan-frying) and moist-heat cooking methods (in-shell cooking and poaching).

2 Egg whites whipped to stiff peaks.

DRY-HEAT COOKING METHODS FOR EGGS

As with other protein foods, dry-heat cooking methods are used to apply heat to eggs by surrounding them with hot air (oven) or hot fat (sautéing and pan-frying). Some foods that are prepared using eggs for binding ingredients or breading may be deep-fried, but eggs themselves are not cooked by deep-frying. Because egg proteins coagulate at relatively low temperatures, dry-heat cooking methods are usually completed quickly to avoid overcooking or making eggs rubbery.

Baking

Eggs are baked together with other ingredients in egg-based dishes, such as shirred eggs and quiche. Eggs are also essential to baked items, such as soufflés and custards. The procedure for making these types of baked egg dishes is described in Chapter 35, Custards, Creams, Frozen Desserts and Dessert Sauces. A recipe for a Cheese Soufflé suitable for breakfast or brunch appears in this chapter on page 581.

3 Spongy, over whipped egg whites.

Shirred Eggs

Baked eggs, also referred to as **shirred eggs**, are normally prepared in individual rame-kins or baking dishes. The ramekins can be lined or partially filled with ingredients such as bread, ham, creamed spinach or artichokes. The eggs are often topped with grated cheese, fresh herbs or a sauce. When properly cooked, the egg whites of baked eggs should be set while the yolks are soft and creamy.

Procedure for Preparing Shirred Eggs

1 Coat each ramekin with melted butter. Add flavoring ingredients as desired.

2 Break one or two eggs into each ramekin. Do not break the yolks. Season with salt and pepper.

3 Bake the eggs until the white is firm, approximately 12–15 minutes. Approximately 3–5 minutes before the eggs are done, add cream or top the eggs with grated cheese, diced ham, fresh herbs or other ingredients as desired.

Shirred Eggs with Ham

MISE EN PLACE

- Melt butter.
- Slice ham.
- Heat cream.
- Grate cheese.

YIELD 1 Serving		METHOD Baking
Whole butter, melted	as needed	as needed
Baked ham, sliced thin	½ oz.	15 g
Eggs	2	2
Salt and pepper	TT	TT
Heavy cream, hot	1 Tbsp.	15 ml
Swiss cheese, grated	1 Tbsp.	15 ml

1 Brush the interior of a 6-fluid-ounce (180-milliliter) ramekin with melted butter. Line the ramekin with the ham.

2 Break the eggs into a cup and pour them carefully into the ramekin on top of the ham. Season with salt and pepper.

3 Bake at 325°F (160°C) until the eggs begin to set, approximately 8–10 minutes. Remove from the oven, then add the cream and cheese. Return to the oven until the eggs are cooked and the cheese is melted. Serve immediately.

Approximate values per serving: **Calories** 280, **Total fat** 22 g, **Saturated fat** 10 g, **Cholesterol** 470 mg, **Sodium** 300 mg, **Total carbohydrates** 2 g, **Protein** 17 g, **Vitamin A** 30%

1 Pouring the eggs into the ramekin on top of the ham.

2 The finished shirred eggs with ham.

Quiche

Quiche is a classic breakfast and brunch entrée. It consists of an egg custard (eggs, cream or milk and seasonings) and fillings baked in a crust. The filling usually includes at least one type of cheese and can also include any number of other ingredients, such as cooked, diced meats or blanched vegetables. The flavor and texture of these ingredients should complement one another without overpowering the delicate egg custard. Quiche is a good way of using leftovers, but ingredients must still be fresh and of good quality. A recipe for quiche dough is given on page 1004.

Procedure for Preparing Quiche

1 Prepare and bake a pie shell.

2 Prepare the garnishes and flavoring ingredients and add them to the pie shell.

3 Prepare a custard and add it to the pie shell. Ratios of eggs to milk or heavy cream vary depending on the specific recipe, but 6 to 8 eggs to 1 quart (1 liter) of liquid is usually sufficient to bind the custard.

4 Bake the quiche until set and it reaches 160°F (71°C) on an instant-read thermometer; allow it to cool slightly before cutting.

Quiche Lorraine

YIELD 1 Quiche, 10 in. (25 cm)	METHOD Baking	
Bacon, diced and cooked	4 oz.	120 g
Swiss or Gruyère cheese, shredded	2 oz.	60 g
Pie shell, 10-in. (25-cm) diameter, baked	1	1
Eggs	4	4
Milk	1 pt.	480 ml
Heavy cream	4 fl. oz.	120 ml
Salt and pepper	TT	TT
Nutmeg, ground	TT	TT

1 Place the bacon and cheese in the pie shell.

2 To make the custard, combine the eggs, milk and cream, and season with salt, pepper and nutmeg.

3 Pour the custard over the bacon and cheese and bake at 350°F (180°C) until the custard is set and it reaches an internal temperature of 160°F (71°C), approximately 1 hour.

Approximate values per ⅛-quiche serving: **Calories** 330, **Total fat** 25 g, **Saturated fat** 11 g, **Cholesterol** 105 mg, **Sodium** 420 mg, **Total carbohydrates** 14 g, **Protein** 12 g, **Vitamin A** 10%, **Calcium** 15%

MISE EN PLACE

- Dice, cook and drain the bacon.
- Shred cheese.
- Bake pie shell.

Sautéing

Eggs may be sautéed in a small amount of fat in a slope-sided sauté pan or on a flat top griddle (as explained on page 562). Sautéing is also the basic cooking method used when making omelets and frittatas. Egg proteins coagulate at relatively low temperatures, so care must be used to avoid overcooking or making the eggs rubbery.

Scrambled Eggs

Scrambled eggs are lightly beaten to break up the egg yolk, whisked with seasonings and then sautéed. They are stirred nearly constantly during cooking. The finished eggs should be light and fluffy with a tender, creamy texture. A small amount of milk or cream may be added to the eggs before cooking to provide a more delicate finished product. Overcooking or cooking at too high a temperature causes the eggs to become tough and rubbery.

Scrambled eggs are often flavored by sautéing other foods (e.g., onions, mushrooms or diced ham) in the pan before adding the eggs or by adding other foods (e.g., grated cheeses or herbs) to the eggs just before cooking is complete.

Scrambled eggs can also be prepared using only egg whites. Because all of an egg's fat is stored in the yolk, scrambled egg white dishes are lower in fat, cholesterol and calories. Water or nonfat milk can be used in place of whole milk or cream to further reduce the fat and calorie content of the finished dish. Remember that egg whites coagulate at a lower temperature than yolks, so adjust the cooking time and temperature accordingly.

The Versatile Egg

For versatility, the egg has few rivals. Poached eggs work in breakfast and brunch dishes but also complement tender green salads. When stuffed, hard-boiled eggs become simple hors d'oeuvre. Finely chopped and bound with mayonnaise, hard-boiled eggs fill sandwiches and canapés. An omelet, frittata, quiche or scrambled egg can be flavored and enhanced with countless additions, including finely diced bell peppers, onions, mushrooms, zucchini or tomatoes; cottage cheese, creamy goat cheese or any variety of shredded firm cheese; crumbled bacon or pancetta; diced ham, turkey or beef; bits of smoked salmon, cooked shrimp or cooked sausage and fresh herbs.

Procedure for Preparing Scrambled Eggs

1 Break the eggs into a mixing bowl. Season lightly with salt and pepper. Add 1 scant tablespoon (12 milliliters) milk or cream per egg and whisk everything together.

2 Heat a sauté pan, add clarified butter or oil and heat until the fat begins to sizzle.

3 Sauté any additional ingredients in the hot fat.

4 Pour the eggs into the pan all at once. As the eggs begin to set, slowly stir the mixture with a spatula. Lift cooked portions to allow uncooked egg to flow underneath.

5 Sprinkle on additional ingredients such as cheese or herbs.

6 Cook just until the eggs are set, but still shiny and moist. Remove from the pan and serve immediately.

 Vegetarian

Scrambled Eggs

YIELD	6 Servings, 4 oz. (120 g) each	METHOD	Sautéing
Eggs, lightly beaten		12	12
Heavy cream		2 fl. oz.	60 ml
Salt and pepper		TT	TT
Clarified butter		2 fl. oz.	60 ml

1 Combine the eggs, cream, salt and pepper in a mixing bowl. Whisk until well blended.

2 Heat the butter in a sauté pan.

3 Pour the egg mixture into the hot pan and cook, stirring frequently, until set, approximately 2 minutes. The eggs should be set, but still shiny and moist.

Approximate values per 4-oz. (120-g) serving: **Calories** 250, **Total fat** 21 g, **Saturated fat** 10 g, **Cholesterol** 460 mg, **Sodium** 210 mg, **Total carbohydrates** 1 g, **Protein** 13 g, **Vitamin A** 30%

❶ Stirring the cooking eggs.

❷ The properly cooked eggs.

Omelets

Omelets are usually prepared as individual servings using two or three whole eggs. They begin as scrambled eggs and are either folded around or filled with a warm savory mixture. The filling may contain vegetables, cheeses and/or meats. Any filling ingredient that needs cooking should be cooked before being added to the omelet. A shallow, well-seasoned or nonstick pan with gently sloping sides is used for cooking omelets. Should an omelet stick to the pan, run a spatula under the omelet to loosen it.

Procedure for Preparing Folded Omelets

1 Fully cook any meats and blanch or otherwise cook any vegetables that will be incorporated into the omelet.

2 Heat an omelet pan over moderately high heat, then add clarified butter.

3 Whisk the eggs together in a small bowl. Season with salt and pepper if desired.

4 Pour the eggs into the pan and stir until they begin to set, approximately 10 seconds.

5 Pull cooked egg from the sides of the pan toward the center, allowing raw egg to run underneath. Continue doing so for 20–30 seconds.

6 Spoon any fillings on top of the eggs or add any other garnishes.

7 When cooked as desired, flip one side of the omelet toward the center with a spatula or a shake of the pan. Slide the omelet onto the serving plate so that it lands folded in thirds with the seam underneath.

8 Spoon any sauce or additional filling on top, garnish as desired and serve immediately.

Shrimp and Avocado Omelet

YIELD 1 Serving			METHOD Sautéing
Shrimp, peeled, deveined and cut into pieces	3 oz.	90 g	
Green onion, sliced	1 Tbsp.	15 ml	
Clarified butter	2 Tbsp.	30 ml	
Eggs	3	3	
Salt and pepper	TT	TT	
Avocado, peeled and diced	¼	¼	
Fresh cilantro, chopped	2 tsp.	10 ml	

MISE EN PLACE
- Peel, devein and cut shrimp.
- Wash and slice green onions.
- Peel and dice avocado.
- Rinse and chop cilantro.

1 Sauté the shrimp and onion in half of the butter until the shrimp is firm and the onion is translucent, approximately 2 minutes. Remove from the heat and set aside.

2 Heat an omelet pan and add the remaining butter.

3 Whisk the eggs together in a small bowl, season with salt and pepper and pour into the omelet pan.

4 Stir the eggs as they cook. Stop when they begin to set. Lift the edges as the omelet cooks to allow the raw eggs to run underneath.

5 When the eggs are nearly set, add the shrimp filling, avocado and cilantro. Fold the front of the eggs and roll the omelet onto a plate.

Approximate values per serving: **Calories** 590, **Total fat** 47 g, **Saturated fat** 19 g, **Cholesterol** 865 mg, **Sodium** 620 mg, **Total carbohydrates** 4 g, **Protein** 39 g, **Vitamin A** 60%, **Vitamin C** 20%, **Iron** 30%

1 Lifting the edge of the eggs to allow them to cook evenly.

2 Adding the filling to the omelet.

3 Folding the eggs.

4 Rolling the omelet onto the plate.

To reduce fat, omelets can also be made using egg whites only. Use three egg whites per serving. Before cooking, whisk the egg whites until foamy. This helps to reduce their tendency to toughen during cooking. To prevent egg whites from sticking, use a well-seasoned pan. To enhance the bland flavor of the egg whites, season the omelet with minced fresh herbs, such as chives or parsley, or aged cheese, such as Parmesan.

French-style omelets are similar to the omelets in the procedure for folded omelets, but the eggs are cooked while constantly shaking the pan to keep them light and fluffy. French omelets are tightly rolled onto a plate for service. For an elegant presentation, the filling may be added after cooking. A cut is made into the finished omelet and the filling is spooned in.

Procedure for Preparing French-Style Omelets

1 Heat an omelet pan over moderately high heat and add clarified butter.

2 Whisk the eggs together in a small bowl. Season with salt and pepper if desired.

3 Pour the eggs into the pan. Stir the eggs while shaking the pan, pulling cooked eggs from the sides of the pan toward the center, allowing raw egg to run underneath. Continue doing so for 30–40 seconds.

4 When cooked as desired, flip one side of the omelet toward the center with a spatula or a shake of the pan. Roll the omelet onto the serving plate so that it lands with the seam underneath.

5 For a filled French-style omelet, cut a slit in the center with a paring knife, then spoon in the filling.

1 Stirring the eggs while shaking the pan.

2 Rolling the omelet onto the serving plate.

3 Using a paring knife to cut into the center of the omelet.

4 Spooning in the filling.

Frittatas

Frittatas are essentially open-faced omelets of Spanish-Italian heritage. They may be cooked in small pans as individual portions or in large pans, then cut into wedges for service. A relatively large amount of hearty ingredients is mixed directly into the eggs. The eggs are first cooked on the stove top, then the pan is transferred to an oven or placed under a salamander or broiler to finish cooking.

Procedure for Preparing Frittatas

1 Fully cook any meats and blanch or otherwise prepare any vegetables that will be incorporated into the frittata.

2 Heat a sauté pan and add clarified butter.

3 Whisk the eggs, flavorings and any other ingredients together; pour into the pan.

4 Stir gently until the eggs begin to set. Gently lift cooked egg at the edge of the frittata so that raw egg can run underneath. Continue cooking until the eggs are almost set.

5 Place the pan in a hot oven or underneath a salamander or broiler to finish cooking and lightly brown the top.

6 Slide the finished frittata out of the pan onto a serving platter.

Asparagus Frittata with Goat Cheese and Parsley Radish Salad

 Vegetarian

YIELD 2 Servings, 10 oz. (300 g) each	METHOD Pan-Frying	
Asparagus, ends peeled, cut into 2-in. (5-cm) pieces	8 oz.	240 g
Clarified butter	1½ fl. oz.	45 ml
Salt and pepper	TT	TT
Eggs, lightly beaten	3	3
Parmesan cheese, grated	1 oz.	30 g
Chives, fresh, chopped	2 tsp.	10 ml
Goat cheese, soft	4 oz.	120 g
Fresh flat leaf parsley	½ cup	120 ml
Radishes, sliced thin	2	2
Capers	½ tsp.	2 ml
Basic Vinaigrette Dressing (page 740)	1 fl. oz.	30 ml

MISE EN PLACE

- Peel and cut the asparagus.
- Beat the eggs.
- Grate the Parmesan.
- Chop the chives and slice the radishes.
- Make Basic Vinaigrette Dressing.

1 Sauté the asparagus in the butter in a 9-inch (22-centimeter) pan over medium heat. Season with salt and pepper and cook until tender and lightly browned.

2 Beat together the eggs, Parmesan and chives.

3 Add the egg mixture to the pan of asparagus. Dot the surface of the eggs with the goat cheese. Cook the mixture, stirring and lifting the eggs to help them cook evenly, until they begin to set. Slide the pan into a 400°F (200°C) oven to finish cooking, approximately 4 minutes.

4 Slide the frittata onto a cutting board and cut into two portions.

5 Garnish with the parsley, radishes and capers tossed with the Basic Vinaigrette Dressing.

Approximate values per 10-oz. (300-g) serving: **Calories** 600, **Total fat** 52 g, **Saturated fat** 26 g, **Cholesterol** 365 mg, **Sodium** 590 mg, **Total carbohydrates** 7 g, **Protein** 28 g, **Vitamin A** 80%, **Vitamin C** 50%, **Calcium** 35%, **Iron** 25%

Pan-Frying

Pan-fried eggs are commonly referred to as sunny side up or over easy, over medium or over hard. These are visibly different products produced with proper timing and technique. Very fresh eggs are best for pan-frying, as the yolk holds its shape better and the white spreads less.

Sunny-side-up eggs are not turned during cooking; their yellow yolks remain visible. They should be cooked over medium-low heat long enough to firm the whites and partially firm the yolks: approximately 4 minutes if cooked on a 250°F (120°C) cooking surface. The edges should not be brown or crisp.

Sunny-side-up eggs

For "over" eggs, the egg is partially cooked on one side, then gently flipped and cooked on the other side until done. The egg white should be firm, and its edges should not be brown. The yolk should never be broken regardless of the degree of doneness. Not only is a broken yolk unattractive, but the spilled yolk will coagulate on contact with the hot pan, making it difficult to serve.

For **over-easy eggs**, the yolk should remain very runny; on a 250°F (120°C) cooking surface, the egg should cook for about 3 minutes on the first side and 2 minutes on the other. **Over-medium eggs** should be cooked slightly longer, until the yolk is partially set. For **over-hard eggs**, the yolk should be completely cooked.

Procedure for Pan-Frying Eggs

1. Select a sauté pan just large enough to accommodate the number of eggs being cooked. (An 8-inch- [20-centimeter-] diameter pan is appropriate for up to three eggs.)
2. Add a small amount of clarified butter and heat until the fat just begins to sizzle.
3. Carefully break the eggs into a bowl. Use the bowl to carefully slide the eggs into the pan.
4. Cook over medium-low heat until the eggs reach the appropriate degree of firmness. Sunny-side-up eggs are not flipped during cooking; "over" eggs are flipped once during cooking.
5. When done, gently flip the "over" eggs once again so that the first side is up. Lift the pan by its handle so that the eggs slide to the opposite side. Using a swift forward motion, gently flip the eggs up and over. Then gently slide the cooked eggs out of the pan onto the serving plate. Serve immediately.

1 Sliding the eggs from a bowl into the sauté pan.

2 Flipping the eggs.

3 Sliding the over eggs onto a plate for service.

Basted eggs are a variation of sunny-side-up eggs. Basted eggs are cooked over low heat with the hot butter from the pan spooned over them as they cook. Another version of basted eggs is made by adding 1–2 teaspoons (5–10 milliliters) water to the sauté pan and then covering the pan. The steam cooks the top of the eggs.

Griddling

Griddling resembles pan-frying or sautéing without the confinement of a pan. Instead, food is cooked directly on the heated surface of a flat top griddle. The heating elements in a griddle are usually set with warmer and cooler zones to allow various foods to be cooked or held warm at the same time. Meats such as bacon, sausage and hamburgers, breads such as pancakes and buns and vegetables are frequently prepared on a flat top griddle in quick service restaurants. Scrambled and fried eggs can also be cooked on a griddle, making the griddle an extremely versatile piece of kitchen equipment

When cooking fried eggs on a flat top, the griddle should be heated to 250°F (120°C) and the procedures for turning eggs at the correct time, as described above, should be followed.

Adding a beaten egg to vegetables cooking on a griddle.

MOIST-HEAT COOKING METHODS FOR EGGS

Moist heat cooking methods are used to apply heat to food by submerging it directly into a hot liquid. When cooking eggs, the liquid is water because you are not using the cooking liquid to flavor the eggs. In-shell eggs are cooked by simmering; unshelled eggs are cooked by poaching. In both methods, it is essential that the water not be too hot and that the eggs not be overcooked.

In-Shell Cooking (Simmering)

The difference between **soft-cooked eggs** (also called **soft-boiled**) and **hard-cooked eggs** (also called **hard-boiled**) is time. Both styles refer to eggs cooked in their shells in hot water. Despite the word *boiled* in their names, an egg cooked in the shell should never be boiled. Boiling toughens eggs and causes a green discoloration, which results from sulfur in the whites reacting with iron in the yolks. See Figure 21.3.

Instead of boiling, the eggs should be simmered. Soft-cooked eggs are usually simmered for 4–6 minutes; hard-cooked eggs may be simmered for as long as 12–15 minutes. In either case, running the eggs under water immediately after simmering helps stop carryover cooking.

Sometimes it is difficult to remove the shell from very fresh eggs. Eggs that are a few days old are better for cooking in the shell.

Figure 21.3 Properly hard-boiled eggs (top) are uniformly cooked through and gold colored. A green discoloration covers the yolk when in-shell eggs are overcooked (bottom).

Procedure for Preparing Soft-Cooked Eggs

1 Fill a saucepan or stockpot with sufficient water to cover the eggs. Bring the water to a simmer.

2 Gently stir the water in a circular motion. Carefully lower each egg into the simmering water. Simmer uncovered for 3–5 minutes, depending on the firmness desired.

3 Lift each egg out of the water with a slotted spoon or spider. Crack the large end of the shell carefully and serve immediately.

Procedure for Preparing Hard-Cooked Eggs

1 Repeat Steps 1 and 2 for soft-cooked eggs but simmer the eggs for 12–15 minutes.

2 Lift each egg out of the water with a slotted spoon or spider and place in an ice bath. When the eggs are cool enough to handle, peel them and use as desired or cover and refrigerate for up to 5 days.

Poaching

Eggs that are to be poached should always be very fresh. They should also be kept very cold until used, as a cold egg white will hold its shape better when dropped into hot water. The water for poaching eggs is held at approximately 200°F (90°C), a gentle simmer. Properly poached eggs are soft and moist; the whites should be firm enough to encase the yolk completely, but the yolk should still be runny.

Some chefs add salt to the poaching water for flavor; others believe that the salt causes the egg whites to separate. To help the egg whites cling together, add 2 tablespoons (30 milliliters) white vinegar per quart (liter) of water.

Procedure for Poaching Eggs

1 Fill a saucepan or stockpot with at least 3 inches (7.5 centimeters) water. Add salt and vinegar if desired. Bring the water to a simmer and hold at a temperature of approximately 200°F (90°C).

2 One at a time, crack the eggs into a small ramekin or cup. If a piece of shell falls into the egg, it should be removed; if the yolk breaks, set aside the egg for some other use.

3 Gently slide each egg into the simmering water and cook for 3–5 minutes.

4 Lift the poached egg out of the water with a slotted spoon. Trim any ragged edges with a paring knife. Serve immediately.

For quantity service, eggs can be poached in advance and held for up to 1 day. To do so, cook the eggs as described. As each egg is removed from the hot water, set it in a hotel pan filled with ice water to stop the cooking process. The eggs can then be stored in the ice water until needed. For banquet-style service, all the eggs can be reheated at once by placing the entire pan on the stove top. Or the eggs can be reheated one or two at a time by placing them in a pan of barely simmering water until they are hot.

 ♥ Good Choice 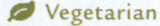 🌿 Vegetarian

❶ Adding an egg to simmering water.

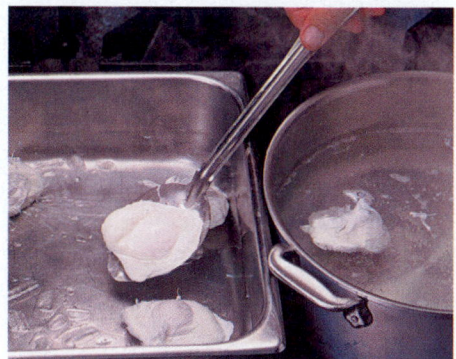

❷ Lowering eggs into ice water to cool them for future use.

Poached Eggs

YIELD 1 Serving		METHOD Poaching
Water	as needed	as needed
Salt	1 tsp.	5 ml
Vinegar	1 fl. oz.	30 ml
Eggs	2	2

1 Bring the water to a simmer; add the salt and vinegar.

2 Crack one egg into a cup and carefully add it to the water. Repeat with the second egg.

3 Cook the eggs to the desired doneness, approximately 3–5 minutes. Remove eggs from the water with a slotted spoon and serve as desired or carefully lower them into ice water and refrigerate for later use.

Approximate values per 3½-oz. (105-g) serving: **Calories** 140, **Total fat** 10 g, **Saturated fat** 3 g, **Cholesterol** 425 mg, **Sodium** 280 mg, **Total carbohydrates** 1 g, **Protein** 12 g, **Vitamin A** 20%

BREAKFAST AND BRUNCH

Breakfast is often an on-the-go, rushed experience; hence the popularity of breakfast sandwiches, jumbo muffins and disposable coffee cups. Brunch, on the other hand, is a leisurely experience, combining breakfast and lunch into a social occasion. Brunch menus include traditional breakfast foods along with almost anything else. Unlike breakfast, brunch may be accompanied by champagne or other alcoholic beverages and concludes with a pastry or dessert.

Food service operations must offer a variety of breakfast options to appeal to a wide range of consumers. Hotels and resorts may offer a continental-style breakfast of coffee, juice and sweet rolls; a full-service à la carte dining room; a room service menu and a casual snack bar. The grand hotel Sunday and holiday brunch buffet is an American institution for celebrations and special occasions.

The foods served at breakfast include most of the foods served at other times during the day. A diner's perceptions of a proper breakfast depends on his or her cultural, ethnic, economic and geographic background as well as sleep patterns and work schedule.

Breakfast menus typically include the following items:

- Coffee, tea or other hot beverages
- Fruits and fruit juices
- Eggs
- Breads, including sweet breads
- Cereals and grains
- Potatoes
- Pancakes, waffles and French toast
- Meats and fish
- Dairy products, including milk, cheese and yogurt

Although few people could sit down to a breakfast including all of these components even occasionally, most food service operations find it necessary to offer some items from each category in order to meet customer expectations.

Breakfast Meats

At other meals, meat is typically the principal food, but at breakfast it is usually an accompaniment. Breakfast meats tend to be spicy or highly flavored. A hearty breakfast menu may include a small beef steak (usually sirloin and often pan-fried) or pork chop. Corned beef, roast beef or roast turkey can be diced or shredded, then sautéed with potatoes and other ingredients for a breakfast hash. Fish, particularly smoked products, are also served at breakfast.

But the most popular breakfast meats are bacon (including Canadian-style bacon), ham and sausages. They are all discussed in Chapter 28, Charcuterie. Bacon can be cooked on a flat griddle or in a heavy skillet or baked on a sheet pan. Regardless of the method used, the cooked bacon should be drained on absorbent paper towels to remove excess fat. Canadian-style bacon is very lean and requires little cooking, although slices are usually sautéed briefly before serving. The round slices may be served like ham and are essential for Eggs Benedict. A ham steak is simply a thick slice ideal for breakfast. Fully cooked ham needs to be heated only briefly on a griddle or in a sauté pan before service. The most popular breakfast sausages are made from uncured, uncooked meats. They can be mild to spicy, slightly sweet or strongly seasoned with sage. Recipes for country-style and other sausages are at the end of Chapter 28, Charcuterie. Breakfast sausage is available in bulk, links or preformed patties. Link sausage is often partially cooked by steam, then browned by sautéing at service time. It should be drained on absorbent paper towels to remove excess fat before service.

Griddlecakes

Pancakes and **waffles** are types of griddlecakes or griddle breads, which refers to any batter or dough baked on a heated flat metal surface or griddle. They are usually leavened with baking soda or baking powder and are quickly cooked on a hot griddle heated to 350°F (175°C) or in a waffle iron with very little fat. These griddlecakes should be more than just a vehicle for butter and maple syrup, however; they should have a rich flavor and a light, tender, moist interior.

Pancake and waffle batters may be flavored with tangy buckwheat flour, fruits, whole grains or nuts. Both pancakes and waffles are usually served with plain or flavored butter and fruit compote or syrup. Waffles must be cooked in a special waffle iron, which gives the cakes a distinctive gridlike pattern and a crisp texture. Electric waffle irons are available with square, round and even heart-shaped grids. The grids should be seasoned well, then never washed. (Follow the manufacturer's directions for seasoning.) **Belgian waffles** are especially light and crisp because of the incorporation of whipped egg whites and/or yeast. They are often made in a waffle iron with extra deep grids and are served for breakfast or for dessert, topped with fresh fruit, whipped cream or ice cream.

Procedure for Making Pancakes

1 Prepare the batter.

2 Heat a flat griddle or large sauté pan over moderately high heat, approximately 350°F (175°C). Add clarified butter.

3 Portion the pancake batter onto the hot griddle using a portion scoop, ladle or adjustable batter dispenser. Pour the portioned batter in one spot; it should spread into an even circle. Pour the batter so that no two pancakes will touch after the batter spreads.

4 Cook until bubbles appear on the surface, and the bottom of the cake is set and golden brown. Flip the pancake using an offset spatula.

5 Cook the pancake until the second side is golden brown. Avoid flipping the pancake more than once, as this causes it to deflate.

 Vegetarian

MISE EN PLACE

- Melt butter.
- Beat eggs.

Buttermilk Pancakes

YIELD 24 Pancakes, 4-in. (10-cm) each	METHOD Griddling	
Flour	1 lb.	480 g
Granulated sugar	2 Tbsp.	30 ml
Baking powder	1 Tbsp.	15 ml
Salt	1½ tsp.	7 ml
Buttermilk	1½ pt.	720 ml
Unsalted butter, melted	2 oz.	60 g
Eggs, beaten	3	3
Clarified butter	as needed	as needed

1 Sift the flour, sugar, baking powder and salt together.

2 Combine the buttermilk, melted butter and eggs and add them to the dry ingredients. Mix until the ingredients are just combined.

3 If the griddle is not well seasoned, coat it lightly with clarified butter. Once the griddle temperature reaches 375°F (190°C), pour the batter onto it in 2-fluid-ounce (60-milliliter) portions using a ladle, portion scoop or batter portioner.

4 When bubbles appear on the pancake's surface and the bottom is browned, flip the pancake to finish cooking.

Variations:

Blueberry Pancakes—Gently stir 1 pint (480 milliliters) fresh or frozen blueberries into the batter. If using frozen berries, drain them thoroughly, then pat dry with paper towels before adding them to the batter. Serve with blueberry syrup or compote.

Apple-Pecan Pancakes—Gently fold 4 ounces (120 grams) chopped cooked apples, ¼ teaspoon (2 milliliters) cinnamon and 1 ounce (30 grams) finely chopped pecans into the batter.

Approximate values per 4-in. (10-cm) pancake: **Calories** 120, **Total fat** 4 g, **Saturated fat** 2.5 g, **Cholesterol** 35 mg, **Sodium** 250 mg, **Total carbohydrates** 17 g, **Protein** 4 g

Crêpes

Crêpes are thin, delicate, unleavened pancakes. They are made with a very liquid egg batter cooked in a small, very hot sauté pan or crêpe pan. Crêpe batter can be flavored with buckwheat flour, cornmeal or other grains. Refrigerating crêpe batter after mixing is recommended to allow the moisture to evenly distribute through the mixture. Crêpes are not eaten plain, but are usually filled and garnished with sautéed fruits, scrambled eggs, cheese or vegetables. Crêpes can be prepared in advance, then filled and reheated in the oven. **Blintzes** are crêpes that are cooked on only one side, then filled with cheese, browned in butter and served with sour cream, fruit compote or preserves.

Procedure for Preparing Crêpes

1 Prepare the batter at least 1 hour before using and keep refrigerated.

2 Heat a well-seasoned crêpe pan or small sauté pan over moderately high heat. Add a small amount of clarified butter.

3 Ladle a small amount of batter into the pan. Tilt the pan so that the batter spreads and coats the bottom evenly.

4 Cook until the crêpe is set and the bottom begins to brown, approximately 1 minute. Flip the crêpe over with a quick flick of the wrist or by lifting it carefully with a spatula.

5 Cook the crêpe for an additional 30 seconds. Slide the finished crêpe from the pan. Crêpes can be stacked between layers of parchment paper for storage.

Crêpes

🌿 Vegetarian

YIELD 30 Crêpes, 6 in. (15 cm) each

Whole eggs	6	6
Egg yolks	6	6
Water	12 fl. oz.	360 ml
Milk	18 fl. oz.	540 ml
Granulated sugar	6 oz.	180 g
Salt	1 tsp.	5 ml
Flour	14 oz.	420 g
Unsalted butter, melted	5 oz.	150 g
Clarified butter	as needed	as needed

MISE EN PLACE

- Prepare batter at least 1 hour before needed.
- Melt butter.

❶ Coating the bottom of the pan evenly with the batter.

1 Whisk together the eggs, egg yolks, water and milk. Add the sugar, salt and flour; whisk together. Stir in the melted butter. Cover and set aside to rest for at least 1 hour before cooking.

2 Heat a small sauté or crêpe pan; brush lightly with clarified butter. Pour in 1½–2 fluid ounces (45–60 milliliters) of batter; swirl to coat the bottom of the pan evenly.

3 Cook each crêpe until set and light brown, approximately 30 seconds. Flip it over and cook a few seconds longer. Remove from the pan. Repeat this process until all the batter is used.

4 Cooked crêpes may be used immediately or covered and held briefly in a warm oven. Crêpes can also be wrapped well in plastic wrap and refrigerated for 2–3 days or frozen for several weeks.

❷ Flipping the crêpe. Notice the proper light brown color.

Variations:

Cheese Blintz—Prepare sweet crêpes. To make the filling, drain 12 ounces (360 grams) ricotta through a mesh strainer, discarding the liquid. Blend in 1 egg, 1 teaspoon (5 milliliters) lemon juice and 1 teaspoon (5 milliliters) vanilla extract. Place 1 ounce (30 grams) of the filling in the center of each crepe. Fold the opposite ends in and then roll up to form a small package. Sauté each blintz in butter over medium-low heat until hot. Serve with sour cream or fruit compote.

Savory Crêpes—Reduce the sugar to 1 tablespoon (15 milliliters). Substitute up to 5 ounces (150 grams) buckwheat flour or whole-wheat flour for an equal amount of the all-purpose flour if desired.

Savory Crêpes Florentine—Fill Savory Crêpes with creamed spinach topped with Mornay sauce (page 222).

Approximate values per 2-oz. (60-g) crêpe: **Calories** 140, **Total fat** 7 g, **Saturated fat** 3.5 g, **Cholesterol** 95 mg, **Sodium** 100 mg, **Total carbohydrates** 17 g, **Protein** 4 g

Cheese blintz

Cereals and Grains

Oats, rice, corn and wheat are perhaps the most widely eaten breakfast foods. Processed breakfast cereals are ready-to-eat products made from these grains. Most U.S. consumers now think of breakfast cereal as a cold food, but not so long ago only hot grains were

Oatmeal garnished with fresh blueberries

muesli [MYOOS-lee] a breakfast cereal made from raw or toasted cereal grains, dried fruits, nuts and dried milk solids and usually eaten with milk or yogurt; sometimes known as granola

breakfast staples. **Oatmeal** served as a hot porridge is popular, especially with health-conscious diners. Oatmeal is often topped with cream, brown sugar, nuts, fresh or dried fruit or fruit preserves for a more appealing presentation. **Grits**, made from ground hominy corn, are another grain product served hot at breakfast. Grits may be topped with butter and presented as a starch side dish or served in a bowl as a porridge with cream and brown sugar. Oats and oatmeal, grits and other grains are discussed in Chapter 23, Potatoes, Grains and Pasta.

Ready-to-eat (cold) cereal is usually topped with milk or light cream and sugar. Creative cooks can avoid overly sweet, artificially flavored commercial products by making their own ready-to-eat breakfast cereals such as **muesli** or **granola**, a toasted blend of whole grains, nuts and dried fruits. The results are less expensive, more nutritious and far more interesting.

Contemporary tastes are influencing what constitutes breakfast. **Breakfast bowls** and breakfast salads offer the chef an opportunity to incorporate several elements in one dish. (See the recipe for Avocado, Bacon and Red Rice Breakfast Salad on page 579.) Breakfast bowls consist of a base such as cooked oatmeal, rice or grains or cold cereal or granola garnished with sliced avocadoes, berries, citrus fruit, nuts, and seeds. The flavor profile may be savory or sweet with complimenting garnishes. A poached or fried egg can be added to many fresh green salads or stewed vegetables to create a breakfast or brunch item, and the traditional Asian breakfast of seasoned rice topped with a fried egg is popular among some western diners, too. The vegan Chia Pudding on page 730 and the Mango, Pineapple and Strawberry Salad with Coconut Cream on page 801 are suitable for breakfast.

Ⓥ Vegan

① Tossing the granola.

② Granola topping berries and yogurt.

Crunchy Granola

YIELD 3 qt. (3 lt)

Brown sugar	8 oz.	240 g
Water, hot	4 fl. oz.	120 ml
Canola oil	6 fl. oz.	180 ml
Old-fashioned rolled oats	18 oz.	540 g
Wheat germ	4 oz.	120 g
Coconut, unsweetened, shredded	2½ oz.	75 g
Salt, optional	1 Tbsp.	15 ml
Whole-wheat flour	2 oz.	60 g
Amaranth flour	2 oz.	60 g
Unbleached all-purpose flour	2 oz.	60 g
Yellow cornmeal	2 oz.	60 g
Pecans, chopped	4 oz.	120 g

1 Dissolve the brown sugar in the hot water. Add the oil.

2 Combine the dry ingredients in a large bowl. Mix thoroughly by hand.

3 Add the brown-sugar-and-oil mixture to the dry ingredients; toss to combine.

4 Spread out the granola in a thin layer on a sheet pan. Bake at 200°F (90°C) until crisp, approximately 1½–2 hours. Toss lightly with a metal spatula every 30 minutes.

5 Cool granola completely at room temperature, then store in an airtight container. Chopped dried fruits, additional nuts or fresh fruits can be added at service time. Serve plain or as a topping on fresh berries and yogurt.

Approximate values per 1-oz. (30-g) serving: **Calories** 140, **Total fat** 7 g, **Saturated fat** 1 g, **Cholesterol** 0 mg, **Sodium** 5 mg, **Total carbohydrates** 17 g, **Protein** 3 g

From Health Food to Sugar Snack

The multibillion-dollar-a-year American breakfast cereal industry, unlike any other in the world, is rooted in health foods. During the 1890s, Dr. John Harvey Kellogg directed a sanitarium in Battle Creek, Michigan. Among the healthful foods prescribed for his patients was his special mixture of whole grains called "granula." John, along with his brother Will, next created and began marketing wheat flakes as a nutritious breakfast food. They were not an immediate success, however; initially people found a cold breakfast unappealing. Undeterred, Will continued toying with cold cereals, eventually creating flakes made from toasted corn and malt. Thanks to a massive advertising campaign, the American public finally embraced corn flakes and a financial empire was born.

Charles W. Post was a patient of Dr. Kellogg's Battle Creek Sanitarium in 1891. He adopted the principles of healthful eating espoused by the Kellogg brothers and soon opened his own spa, complete with a factory producing his "Post Toasties" and "Grape-Nuts." He promoted them as a cure for appendicitis, consumption and malaria.

Soon Battle Creek became a boomtown, home to more than 40 breakfast cereal companies. Unfortunately for the consumer, not all manufacturers—then and now—were as concerned about health as John, Will and C. W. The addition of sugar, sometimes totaling more than half the cereal's weight, makes some of today's breakfast products more sugary than candy bars. Even some of the granola cereals touted as healthier alternatives to other breakfast cereals and snacks contain 20 percent sugar or more. But at least they no longer claim to cure malaria.

COFFEE

Most restaurant beverage menus feature coffee. Despite its relatively low cost to produce, a good cup of coffee can be extremely valuable to customers and important to their impression of the entire food service operation. Coffee is often either the very first or the very last item consumed during a restaurant meal, so it is important to learn to prepare and serve it properly.

Coffee (Fr. *café*) begins as the fruit of a small tree grown in tropical and subtropical regions throughout the world. The fruit, referred to as a cherry, is bright red with translucent flesh surrounding two flat-sided seeds. These seeds are the **coffee beans**. When ripe, the cherries are harvested by hand, cleaned, fermented and hulled, leaving the green coffee beans. The beans are then roasted, blended, ground and brewed. Note that any coffee bean can be roasted to any degree of darkness, ground to any degree of fineness and brewed by any number of methods.

Two species of coffee bean are the most widely used: **arabica** and **robusta**. Arabica beans are the most important commercially and the ones from which the finest coffees are produced. Robusta beans do not produce as flavorful a drink as arabica. Nevertheless robusta beans are significant commercially because robusta trees are heartier and produce more fruit than arabica trees. Coffee takes much of its flavor and character from the soil, sunlight and air, so the beans' origin is critical to quality. Each valley and mountain produces coffee distinct from all others, so geographic names are used to identify the beans. Thus purveyors offer beans known as Colombian Supremo, Ethiopian Yirgacheffe, Yemen Mocha, Tanzanian Kilimanjaro, Jamaican Blue Mountain, Indonesian Java and Sumatra or Hawaiian Kona to name just a few.

Coffee tree with ripe berries

Roasting Coffee

Roasting releases and enhances the flavors in coffee beans. It also darkens the beans and brings natural oils to the surface. In general, roasts fall into categories based on color as follows:

City roast: Also called American or brown roast, city roast is medium brown in color. It produces a beverage that may lack brilliance or be a bit flat, yet it is the roast most often used in mass-market blends.

Brazilian: Somewhat darker than a city roast, Brazilian roast begin to show a hint of dark-roast flavor. The beans show a trace of oil.

Viennese: Also called medium-dark roast, Viennese roast generally falls somewhere between a standard city roast and French roast.

Green unroasted coffee beans

City-roast beans

French-roast beans

French roast: French roast, also called New Orleans or dark roast, approaches espresso in flavor without sacrificing smoothness. French roasted beans are the color of semisweet chocolate, with apparent oiliness on the surface.

Espresso roast: Espresso roast, also called Italian roast, is the darkest of all. The beans are black with a shiny, oily surface.

Grinding Coffee

Unlike roasting, which is best left to the experts, the grinding of coffee beans is best left to the consumer or food service operation. Whole coffee beans stay fresh longer than ground coffee. Ground coffee kept in an airtight container away from heat and light will stay fresh for 3 or 4 days. Whole beans stay fresh for a few weeks, even longer if they are vacuum sealed.

The fineness of the grind depends entirely on the type of coffee maker being used. The grind determines the length of time it takes to achieve the best flavor extraction from the beans. The proper grind is whichever grind allows this to happen in the time it takes a specific coffee maker to complete its brewing cycle. As a general rule, finer grinds are used for espresso, coarser grinds are used for drip or filter brewing. Follow the directions for your coffee maker or ask your specialty coffee purveyor for guidance.

Brewing Coffee

Coffee is brewed by one of two methods: decoction or infusion. **Decoction** is boiling a substance until its flavor is removed. Boiling is the oldest method of making coffee, but is no longer used except in preparing extremely strong Turkish coffee. Percolating is undesirable, as the continuous boiling ruins the coffee's flavor. **Infusion** involves the extraction of flavors at temperatures below boiling. Infusion techniques include steeping (mixing hot water with ground coffee), filtering (slowly pouring hot water over ground coffee held in a disposable cloth or paper filter) and dripping (pouring hot water over ground coffee and allowing the liquid to run through a strainer). Another coffee brewing process is a version of infusion called Dutch process, in which ice water slowly drips through ground coffee. The process takes 3–5 hours and produces only small quantities. Commercially made "cold-brew" coffee is similarly prepared, but cold-brew coffee is made by seeping grounds in room temperature water for up to 24 hours, and then straining out the grounds. The use of cool water is said to prevent bitterness and create a strong, smooth coffee perfect for iced beverages.

The secrets to brewing a good cup of coffee are knowing the exact proportion of coffee to water as well as the length of time to maintain contact between the two. This varies depending on the type of coffee brewing equipment being used.

Drip Brewing

Drip coffee is most commonly made from a machine that operates on the principle of gravity. Water is placed in a reservoir, heated and released slowly over the coffee grounds, which are held in a filter.

For drip coffee, the best results are achieved by using 2 level tablespoons (30 milliliters) of ground coffee per ¾ cup (6 fluid ounces; 180 milliliters) water. (A standard cup of coffee is three-fourths the size of a standard measuring cup; 1 pound (454 grams) of coffee yields approximately 80 level tablespoons or enough for 40 "cups" of coffee.) Premeasured packages of ground coffee are generally used with commercial brewing equipment. These packages are available in a range of sizes for making single pots or large urns of coffee. If stronger coffee is desired, use more coffee per cup of water, not a longer brewing time. For weaker coffee, prepare regular-strength coffee and dilute it with hot water. Never reuse coffee grounds.

Drip or filtered coffee is the most common style served in the United States. It is simple, unsweetened and black (without milk or cream). The customer adds the desired amount of sweetener and milk.

Drip coffee maker

Café au lait: The French version of the Italian caffè latte is made with strong drip coffee instead of espresso and hot, not steamed, milk. It is traditionally served in a handleless bowl.

Dutch coffee: A cold drip method that uses a long extraction time (3–5 hours) and ice water to produce a strong, well-rounded and intensely flavored beverage that is consumed cold. The glass towers used for brewing also add visual appeal to coffee shops and cafés. Despite its name, this contemporary technique originated in Japan, not the Netherlands.

Iced coffee: Strong drip coffee served over ice. Iced coffee can also be served with milk or cream. In Australia, a dollop of vanilla ice cream is often added. In Vietnam, it is made with a small Vietnamese filter pot using condensed milk as a sweetener. Cold leftover coffee should not be used to make iced coffee.

Espresso

Espresso Brewing

Espresso refers to a brewing method in which hot water is forced through finely ground and packed coffee under high pressure. Properly made espresso is strong, rich and smooth, not bitter or acidic. As the coffee drains into the cup, it is golden brown, forming a *crema* or foam that lies on top of the black coffee. Espresso is often used in making iced and flavored coffee beverages, but plain espresso is not served iced. An espresso machine also has a steaming rod to heat and froth milk for espresso-based beverages.

Coffee beans used in making espresso should be finely ground immediately before brewing; however, premeasured packets, or pods, that enable a consistent level of quality are available. A single serving of espresso uses about ¼ ounce (7 grams) of ground beans to 1½ fluid ounces (45 milliliters) water. Americans tend to prefer a larger portion, known as *espresso lungo*, made with 2–3 fluid ounces (60–90 milliliters) water. It is important that the espresso be made quickly: If the machine pumps water through the coffee for too long, too much water is added to the cup and the intense espresso flavor is lost.

Cappuccino

Espresso is used in the following popular drinks:

Espresso: A single or double shot served black in a small warm cup

Espresso macchiato: Espresso "marked" with a tiny portion of **steamed milk**

Cappuccino: One-third espresso, one-third steamed milk and one-third **foamed milk**

Caffè latte: One-third espresso and two-thirds steamed milk without foam; usually served in a tall glass; also served iced without steaming the milk

Caffè mocha: One-third espresso and two-thirds steamed milk, flavored with chocolate syrup; usually topped with whipped cream and chocolate shavings or cocoa

Americano: Espresso diluted with water to the strength of drip coffee; can be served hot or iced

Caffè latte

steamed milk milk that is heated with steam generated by an espresso machine; it should be approximately 150–170°F (66–77°C)

foamed milk milk that is heated and frothed with air and steam generated by an espresso machine; it will be slightly cooler than steamed milk

barista Italian for "bartender"; used to describe someone who has been professionally trained in the art of preparing espresso and espresso-based beverages

Any type of milk can be used to make cappuccino and other espresso beverages. Whole, skim, almond and soy milk are commonly offered. A higher fat content milk produces a creamier tasting beverage but is more difficult to froth with steam. To foam milk, pour it into a metal pitcher and position it under the steam spout of the espresso machine. Activate the steam control only when the head of the spout is under the surface of the milk. Moving the pitcher around while keeping the spout just under the surface of the milk creates foam. Leftover foamed milk can be refrigerated and reheated for the next serving, although many baristas prefer not to re-foam milk.

Conditions That Affect the Quality of Brewed Coffee

Several less obvious factors affect the quality of coffee beverages. For example, water quality can alter flavors and cause mineral deposits to build-up in a machine. Therefore many commercial

Espresso machine

establishments install in-line water filters or purifiers for their coffee machines. Oils from coffee beans form an invisible film on the inside of the maker and pots, imparting a rancid or stale flavor to later batches. Brew pots and carafes should be cleaned well with hot water between each use; coffee makers should be periodically disassembled and cleaned according to the manufacturer's directions.

Finally coffee should be served as soon as it is brewed. Oxidation takes a toll on the aroma and flavor, which soon becomes flat and eventually bitter. Drip coffee may be held for a short time on the coffee maker's hot plate at temperatures of 185–190°F (85–88°C). A better holding method, however, is to use a thermal carafe or air pot. Never attempt to reheat cold coffee, as drastic temperature changes can destroy flavor.

Tasting Coffee

cupping testing coffee or tea for taste and quality, often performed by a professional taster trained to identify key coffee or tea characteristics and test for problems or faults

Coffee is judged on four characteristics: aroma, acidity, body and flavor. **Cupping** is a traditional method used worldwide by professional coffee buyers and merchants to evaluate these characteristics. It is also used to create and produce consistent blends from various beans.

Aroma refers to the way a coffee smells during grinding and brewing. Hundreds of aromatic compounds are found in coffee and aroma is the most important element for judging coffee quality.

Acidity, also called *wininess*, refers to the tartness of the coffee. Acidity is a desirable characteristic that indicates snap, life or thinness.

Body refers to the feeling of heaviness or thickness that coffee provides on the palate. *Aftertaste* or *finish* is one aspect of body.

Flavor, of course, is the most ambiguous as well as the most important characteristic. Terms such as *mellow*, *harsh*, *grassy* and *earthy* are used to describe the rather subjective characteristics of flavor.

Flavored Coffees

Dried, ground chicory root has long been added to coffee, particularly by the French, who enjoy its bitter flavor. Toasted barley and spices have also been traditionally used with coffee in various cultures. Coffees flavored with vanilla, chocolate, liqueurs, spices and nuts are widely popular. These flavors are added to roasted coffee beans by tumbling the beans with flavoring oils. The results are strongly aromatic flavors such as vanilla hazelnut, chocolate raspberry or maple walnut. Coffee beverages, such as caffè latte, are also flavored with sweet syrups available in dozens of flavors, from vanilla to pumpkin spice and salted caramel. These syrups are blended with coffee, steamed milk and other ingredients to create seasonal or trendy flavor profiles.

A Cup of Coffee History

A hot beverage made from berries of the tropical coffee tree (*coffea*) may first have been consumed sometime during the ninth century C.E. in Persia. Made by a decoction of ripe beans, the drink was probably very thick and acrid. Nevertheless, by the year 1000, the elite of the Arab world were regularly drinking a decoction of dried coffee beans and enjoying the effects of caffeine. The beans were harvested in Abyssinia (Ethiopia) and brought to market by Egyptian merchants. Within a century or so, *kahwa* became immensely popular with members of all strata of Arab society. Coffeehouses opened throughout the Eastern Mediterranean, catering to

customers who sipped the thick, brown brew while discussing affairs of heart and state.

Coffee did not become popular in Europe until the 17th century, its popularity due in great part to Suleiman Aga, the Grand Panjandrum of the Ottoman Empire. In 1669 he arrived at the court of King Louis XIV of France as ambassador, bringing with him many exotic treasures, including coffee. Served at opulent parties, coffee soon became the drink of choice for the French aristocracy.

Coffee became popular in Vienna as a fortune of war. By 1683 the Turks were at the gates of Vienna. A decisive battle was fought and the Turks fled, leaving behind stores of

gold, equipment, supplies and a barely known provision—green coffee beans. One of the victorious leaders, Franz George Kolschitzky, recognized the treasure, took it as his own and soon opened the first coffeehouse in Vienna, The Blue Bottle.

Coffee was exorbitantly expensive, in part the result of the sultan's monopoly on coffee beans. But the monopoly was not to survive. By the end of the 17th century, the Dutch had stolen coffee plants from Arabia and began cultivating them in Java. By the early 18th century, the French had transported seedlings to the West Indies; from there coffee plantations spread throughout South and Central America and the Caribbean islands.

Decaffeinated Coffee

Caffeine is a water-soluble alkaloid found in coffee beans (as well as in tea leaves and cocoa beans). It is a stimulant that can improve alertness or reduce fatigue. In excess, however, caffeine can cause some people to suffer palpitations or insomnia. Regular filtered coffee contains 85–100 milligrams of caffeine per cup. Robusta beans contain more caffeine than arabica beans. To remove the caffeine, green unroasted coffee beans are treated with water and liquid carbon dioxide, activated charcoal or certain chemicals. The resulting beans (with 97–99 percent of their caffeine removed) are roasted and processed like any other beans.

TEA AND TISANES

Tea and tisanes are beverages made from dried leaves, herbs, spices, flowers or fruits that are prepared by infusion, which are steeped in fresh boiling water. **Tea** (Fr. *thé*) is the name given to the leaves of *Camellia sinensis*, a tree or shrub that grows at high altitudes in damp tropical regions. Drinks made from tea leaves contain caffeine and are consumed by more than half the world's population, both hot and cold. **Tisanes** are herbal infusions, which do not contain any true tea leaves. Tisanes have long been popular in Asia for their perceived health benefits and healing properties. As customers have become familiar with the endless varieties of caffeine-free herbal teas, worldwide consumption of tisanes has increased.

Variety of cups of brewed tea (from left): Chinese tea, Japanese tea, Moroccan mint tea and black tea with milk

Tea Varieties

Although tea comes from only one species of plant, there are three general types of tea: black, green and oolong. The differences among the three are the result of the manner in which the leaves are fermented after harvest.

Black tea is amber-brown and strongly flavored. Its color and flavor result from fermenting the leaves. Black tea leaves are named or graded by leaf size. Because larger leaves brew more slowly than smaller ones, teas are sorted by leaf size for efficient brewing. *Souchong* denotes large leaves, *pekoe* denotes medium-sized leaves and *orange pekoe* denotes the smallest whole leaves. (Note that orange pekoe does not refer to any type of orange flavor.) Broken tea is smaller, resulting in a darker, stronger brew and is most often used in tea bags. Black teas may be served hot or iced and are usually accompanied by lemon or milk and sweeteners, depending on preference. Eighty-five percent of the tea consumed in the United States is iced, a uniquely American preference.

Green tea is yellowish-green in color with a grassy, earthy flavor and a slight bitterness. The leaves used are not fermented or oxidized. Green tea is considered to be especially healthy due to its high antioxidant content. Japanese green tea, known as *sencha*, is steamed rather than roasted and is prized for its green color, low tannin content and umami flavor. Green tea is also made into a high-quality powder known as *matcha*, which is used in traditional tea ceremonies. Lesser grades of green tea powder are used to flavor and color foods from ice cream to bread. Green teas should be brewed at lower temperatures than black teas, (160–170°F [70–80°C]) and are often served cool, rather than hot. **White tea** is a variation of green tea that is produced in China, Eastern Nepal and Northern Thailand. There are no international standards for marketing a tea as "white," although white tea is generally made with young leaves that are air dried without any further processing. Green and white teas are rarely served with milk, lemon or sweeteners.

Oolong tea is partially fermented to combine the characteristics of black and green teas. Oolong is popular in China and Japan, often flavored with jasmine flowers. Oolong tea is most often served hot, usually without milk or lemon.

As with coffee, tea takes much of its flavor from the geographic conditions in which it is grown. Teas are named for their place of origin—for example, Darjeeling, Ceylon (now Sri Lanka) or Assam. Many commercially available teas are actually blends of leaves from various sources. Blended and unblended teas may also be flavored with essential oils, dried fruit, spices, flowers or herbs; they are then referred to as **flavored teas**. Bright herbs such as mint and citrus rind or oil, especially bergamot, which gives Earl Grey tea

Tea Bags

The invention of the tea bag was apparently inadvertent. According to the Tea Association of America, in 1904 Thomas Sullivan, a New York tea merchant, sent potential customers samples of tea in small muslin or silk bags. Finding that they could make tea by simply pouring boiling water over the bags, Sullivan's new customers clamored for more.

flavored tea tea to which flavorings such as essential oils, dried fruit, spices, flowers or herbs have been added

its flavor, add complexity to brewed teas. **Chai** is a black tea and milk beverage that is sweetened and flavored with cinnamon, cardamom, vanilla or other spices. It may be served hot or iced and takes its name from the Chinese word for tea.

Tasting Tea

Tea is described according to three key characteristics: astringency or briskness, body and aroma. *Astringency* is not bitterness, which is undesirable, but rather a sharp, dry feeling on the tongue that contributes to the refreshing taste of a tea. *Body* refers to the feeling of thickness on the tongue. Teas range from light to full bodied. *Aroma* is the smell of the brewed tea.

The following descriptions apply to some of the most common teas. The same flavor of tea from different blenders or distributors may taste different, however. Certain flavors are more or less appropriate for different times of the day as noted.

Black Teas

Assam: A rich black tea from northeastern India with a reddish color. It is valued by connoisseurs, especially for breakfast.

Ceylon: A full-flavored black tea with a golden color and delicate fragrance. Ideal for serving iced, it does not become cloudy when cold.

Darjeeling: The champagne of teas, grown in the foothills of the Himalayas in northeastern India. It is a full-bodied, black tea with a muscat flavor.

Earl Grey: A blend of black teas, usually including Darjeeling, flavored with oil of bergamot. A popular choice for afternoon tea.

English Breakfast: An English blend of Indian and Sri Lankan black teas. It is full-bodied and robust, with a rich color.

Lapsang Souchong: A large-leafed (souchong) tea from the Lapsang district of China. It has a distinctive tarry, smoky flavor and aroma, appropriate for afternoon tea or dinner.

Green Teas

Gunpowder: A green Chinese tea with a tightly curled leaf and gray-green color. It has a pungent flavor and a light straw color. It is often served after the evening meal.

Sencha (common): A delicate Japanese green tea that has a light color with a pronounced aroma and a bright, grassy taste.

White tea: A delicate green tea with a subtle flavor made from young buds picked before they open. Allowed to wither so that moisture evaporates naturally, these leaves are lightly dried to a pale silvery color.

Oolong Teas

Formosa Oolong: An expensive large-leafed oolong tea with the flavor of ripe peaches. It is appropriate for breakfast or afternoon tea.

Monkey Picked Oolong: Legend has it that Chinese Buddhist monks trained monkeys to pick the tiny new leaves from wild tea bushes, which were then lightly fermented and reserved for the Imperial court. Regardless of its true history, the orchid aroma makes this the highest grade of oolong in the world.

Tisanes (Herbal Teas)

Tisanes are herbal infusions that do not contain any "real" tea. They are commonly made from fresh or dried flowers, fruits, herbs, seeds or roots; chamomile, mint, ginseng, ginger and hibiscus are among the more popular herbal teas. Many flavors and varieties are marketed as prepackaged blends ready for brewing. In Europe and Asia, a tisane may be served after meals to aid digestion or taken before bed as a sleep aid. (Herbal teas usually contain no caffeine.) Modern restaurants and coffee shops typically offer herbal teas as an option for customers who prefer to avoid stimulants.

Fruit tea

Gunpowder

Darjeeling

Southern Sweet Tea

Sweet tea is an iced beverage traditionally offered in the American South. It is now making its way into many bottled tea drinks, fast-food menus and even vodka flavorings and cocktails. Sweet tea is not merely iced tea plus sugar. To achieve the desired flavor, which most closely resembles a tea-flavored soft drink, a large quantity of granulated sugar is dissolved in strong, hot, black tea—typically 1½–2 cups of sugar per gallon of tea. The tea must be brewed very strong to compensate for the dilution caused by melting ice. Adding sugar to chilled tea will not produce the famed "sweet tea" flavor.

Brewing Tea

Hot tea may be brewed by the cup or the pot. In either case, it is important to use the following procedure:

1 Always begin with clean equipment and fresh cold water. Water that has been sitting in a kettle or hot water tank contains less air and will taste flat or stale.

2 Warm the teapot by rinsing its interior with hot water. This will help relax the tea leaves and ensure that the water will stay hot when it comes in contact with the tea.

3 Place 1 teaspoon (5 milliliters) loose tea or one tea bag per ¾ cup (6 fluid ounces/180 milliliters) of water capacity in the warmed teapot.

4 As soon as the water comes to a boil, pour the appropriate amount over the tea. Do not allow the water to continue boiling before pouring as this removes the oxygen, leaving a flat taste. The water should be at a full boil when it comes in contact with the tea so that the tea leaves will uncurl and release their flavor.

5 Replace the lid of the teapot and allow the tea to infuse for 3–5 minutes. Time the brew. Color is not a reliable indication of brewing time; tea leaves release color before flavor, and different types of tea will be different colors when properly brewed.

6 Remove the tea bags or loose tea from the water when brewing is complete. This can be accomplished easily if the teapot is fitted with a removable leaf basket or if a tea bag or a perforated tea ball is used. Otherwise decant the tea through a strainer into a second warmed teapot.

7 Serve immediately, accompanied with sugar, lemon, milk (not cream, which may curdle) and honey as desired. Dilute the tea with hot water if necessary.

8 Do not reuse tea leaves. One pound of tea yields 200 cups, making it the most inexpensive beverage after tap water.

For iced tea, prepare regular brewed tea using 50 percent more tea. Then pour the tea into a pitcher or glass filled with ice. The stronger brew will hold its flavor better as the ice melts. For clarity and flavor, freshly brewed tea is best, but if iced tea will not be used immediately, it can be brewed slowly at room temperature or in a refrigerator for several hours to prevent cloudiness.

A Cup of Tea History

Legend holds that the Chinese emperor Shen Nung discovered tea drinking in 2737 B.C.E. Supposedly he was boiling his drinking water beneath a tree when some leaves fell into the pot. Enchanted with the drink, he began to cultivate the plant. Whether this is myth or truth, it is known that a hot drink made from powdered dried tea leaves whipped into hot water was being regularly consumed in China beginning sometime after the fourth century. But it was not until the Ming dynasty (1368–1644) that infusions of tea leaves became commonplace.

By the ninth century, tea drinking had spread to Japan. In both Chinese and Japanese cultures, tea drinking developed into a ritual. For the Chinese, a cup of tea became the mirror of the soul. For the Japanese, it was the drink of immortality.

Tea was first transported from China to Europe by Dutch merchants during the early 1600s. By midcentury it was introduced into England. In 1669 the British East India Company was granted a charter by Queen Elizabeth I to import tea, a monopoly it held until 1833. To ensure a steady supply, the English surreptitiously procured plants from China and started plantations throughout the Indian subcontinent, as did the Dutch.

Tea drinking became fashionable in England, at least in court circles, through Charles II (raised in exile at The Hague in Holland, he reigned from 1660 to 1685) and his Portuguese wife, Catherine of Braganza. Queen Anne of England (who reigned from 1702 to 1714) introduced several concepts that eventually became part of the English tea custom. For example, she substituted tea for ale at breakfast and began using large silver pots instead of tiny china pots.

The social custom of afternoon tea began in the late 1700s, thanks to Anna, Duchess of Bedford. Historians attribute to her the late-afternoon ritual of snacking on sandwiches and pastries accompanied by tea. She began the practice in order to quell her hunger pangs between breakfast and dinner.

Eventually two distinct types of teatime evolved. Low tea was aristocratic in origin and consisted of a snack of pastries and sandwiches, with tea, served in the late afternoon as a prelude to the evening meal. High tea was bourgeois in origin, consisting of leftovers from the typically large middle-class lunch, such as cold meats, bread and cheeses. High tea became a substitute for the evening meal.

QUESTIONS FOR DISCUSSION

1 When is the use of pasteurized eggs recommended? How can eggs be pasteurized for use?

2 List and describe the four parts of a hen egg. Where is the fat located in an egg?

3 Describe three or four ways in which uncooked eggs and egg products can be purchased. Why are fresh eggs kept refrigerated?

4 Explain the difference between an omelet and a frittata.

5 Describe four different types of pan-fried eggs, and explain how each is prepared.

6 What is the difference between a soft-cooked egg and a hard-cooked egg? Why are eggs simmered instead of boiled?

7 Explain the differences between a typical breakfast and a typical brunch. Create a sample menu for each of these meals.

8 List three types of griddlecakes and explain how they are prepared.

9 Describe the difference between drip coffee and espresso coffee.

10 Name and describe the three principal varieties of tea.

11 Research egg dishes from several different countries. Describe the different preparations and compare them with traditional American egg dishes. Discuss the primary ingredients used and when these dishes are served.

Additional Egg and Breakfast Recipes

Shakshuka Eggs

🌿 Vegetarian

This breakfast dish is popular in North Africa, the Middle East and Israel where it may be garnished with preserved lemon, fresh feta and other cheeses.

YIELD 5 Servings, 5 oz. (150 g) each	METHOD Baking	
Olive oil	1½ fl. oz.	45 ml
Red, yellow and orange bell pepper, julienne	14 oz.	420 g
Onion, peeled and thinly sliced	8 oz.	240 g
Tomato sauce	8 fl. oz.	240 ml
Water	2 fl. oz.	60 ml
Ground cumin	½ tsp.	3 ml
Chopped cilantro	1 Tbsp.	15 ml
Chopped flat-leaf parsley	1 Tbsp.	15 ml
Aleppo pepper or sweet paprika	¼ tsp.	1 ml
Salt and pepper	TT	TT
Eggs	5	5
Flat leaf parsley	as needed for garnish	

1 Heat the oil on medium heat in a wide sauté pan. Add the bell peppers and sliced onion. Sauté until tender, approximately 10–15 minutes. Add the tomato sauce and water. Cook for a few minutes to blend the ingredients.

2 Sprinkle in the cumin, chopped herbs and chili pepper. Season with salt and pepper.

3 Divide the mixture between 5 small sauté pans. Crack an egg into the center of each pan. Cover and bake at 350°F (170°C) until the eggs are done yet still soft, approximately 5–8 minutes. Or cook covered on top of the stove over low heat.

4 Season with black pepper and garnish with parsley sprigs. Serve hot.

Approximate values per 5-oz. (150-g) serving: **Calories** 200, **Total fat** 13g, **Saturated fat** 3 g, **Cholesterol** 185 mg, **Sodium** 290 mg, **Total carbohydrates** 12 g, **Protein** 8 g, **Vitamin A** 60%, **Vitamin C** 180%, **Iron** 10%

Eggs Benedict

Few dishes inspire as many variations as Eggs Benedict. Crisp bacon, Serrano ham, sautéed mushrooms, crab cakes, shrimp or smoked trout may replace the Canadian bacon. And anything from a brioche bun to hash browns works in place of the muffin. As long as the dish includes expertly prepared poached eggs, hollandaise sauce and companionable ingredients, consider naming it benedict.

YIELD 1 Serving	METHOD	Poaching
English muffin, split	1	1
Canadian bacon slices, ¼ in. (6 mm) thick	2	2
Salt	TT	TT
Vinegar	1 fl. oz.	30 ml
Eggs	2	2
Hollandaise (page 230)	4 fl. oz.	120 ml
Truffle slices or black olive halves	2	2

1 Toast the English muffin.

2 Sauté or griddle the bacon slices until hot.

3 Bring 1 quart (1 liter) water to a boil and add the salt and vinegar.

4 Reduce the heat to a strong simmer. Add the eggs and poach until done.

5 Place the muffins on a plate and top with the bacon slices. Place an egg on each slice of bacon and cover with the Hollandaise.

6 Garnish each egg with a truffle slice or black olive half and serve.

Variations:

Poached Eggs Florentine—Serve poached eggs on an English muffin or pastry shell over creamed spinach with hollandaise or béchamel sauce.

Poached Eggs Norwegian Style—Serve poached eggs on an English muffin with smoked salmon and hollandaise sauce.

Poached Eggs Princess Style—Serve poached eggs on an English muffin with asparagus tips and hollandaise sauce.

Poached Eggs Sardou—Serve poached eggs and creamed spinach on an artichoke bottom with hollandaise sauce.

Approximate values per serving: **Calories** 970, **Total fat** 69 g, **Saturated fat** 33 g, **Cholesterol** 610 mg, **Sodium** 2480 mg, **Total carbohydrates** 53 g, **Protein** 33 g, **Vitamin A** 80%, **Iron** 25%

Avocado, Bacon and Red Rice Breakfast Salad

YIELD 6 Servings	METHOD Poaching	
Grape tomatoes	8 oz.	240 g
Olive oil	3 Tbsp.	45 ml
Salt and pepper	TT	TT
Red rice, cooked	12 oz.	360 g
Baby salad greens	6 oz.	180 g
Bacon, thick sliced, cooked	6 slices	6 slices
Avocados, sliced into large pieces	2	2
Micro greens	as needed for garnish	
Eggs	6	6
Basic Vinaigrette Dressing (page 740)	12 fl. oz.	360 ml

1 Toss the grape tomatoes with 2 tablespoons (30 milliliters) of olive oil. Season with salt and pepper. Spread the tomatoes out on a half sheet pan and bake them at 225° F (110° C) for 30 minutes.

2 Place the cooked red rice in a stainless steel bowl. Drizzle with 1 tablespoon (15 milliliters) of olive oil and season with salt and pepper and toss gently.

3 For each salad, arrange 1 ounce (30 grams) baby greens on a chilled plate with a portion of grape tomatoes, 2 half slices of bacon, 2 ounces (60 grams) of red rice, a portion of the avocado pieces and a sprinkling of micro greens.

4 Poach the eggs in gently simmering water until the whites are cooked but the yolks are still runny. Place one poached egg on top of each salad. Serve immediately with the dressing on the side.

Approximate values per serving: **Calories** 610, **Total fat** 51 g, **Saturated fat** 9 g, **Cholesterol** 190 mg, **Sodium** 400 mg, **Total carbohydrates** 29 g, **Protein** 14 g, **Vitamin A** 50%, **Vitamin C** 40%

Fried Egg BLT Sandwich

YIELD 1 Sandwich	METHOD Pan-Frying	
Rustic white bread	2 slices	2 slices
Mayonnaise	1 Tbsp.	15 ml
Butter lettuce	2 leaves	2 leaves
Bacon slices, cooked crisp, warm	3	3
Tomato slices	3	3
Cheddar cheese	2 slices	2 slices
Unsalted butter	1 tsp.	5 ml
Egg	1	1
Salt and pepper	TT	TT

1 Toast the bread slices and lay them out on a cutting board. Spread one slice with the mayonnaise. Position the lettuce on the bread and top with the bacon and the tomato slices. Place the Cheddar cheese on the other slice.

2 Heat a small nonstick sauté pan over medium heat. Melt the butter in the pan. Crack the egg into the pan, season with salt and pepper and cook, turning once, until the white is cooked but the yolk is still runny. Place the egg on top of the tomatoes.

3 Close the sandwich and serve immediately.

Approximate values per sandwich: **Calories** 710, **Total fat** 41 g, **Saturated fat** 15 g, **Cholesterol** 285 mg, **Sodium** 1440 mg, **Total carbohydrates** 52 g, **Protein** 33 g, **Vitamin A** 35%, **Calcium** 30%, **Iron** 30%

Scotch Eggs

A popular snack or picnic food in Great Britain, Scotch eggs consist of hard-cooked eggs wrapped in breakfast sausage, then deep-fried. They make an excellent breakfast buffet or brunch item because they can be served hot or cold and are easy to hold for extended service. Use Peewee (see Figure 21.2) or quail eggs for a more refined presentation.

YIELD 4 Eggs	METHOD Hard-Cooking	
Breakfast sausage, bulk	8 oz.	240 g
Fresh sage, chopped	½ tsp.	2 ml
Fresh thyme, chopped	½ tsp.	2 ml
Worcestershire sauce	½ tsp.	2 ml
Salt and pepper	TT	TT
All-purpose flour	as needed	as needed
Eggs, hard cooked, peeled	4	4
Egg, beaten	1	1
Bread crumbs, dry	as needed	as needed

1 Combine the breakfast sausage, herbs, Worcestershire sauce, salt and pepper in a small bowl.

2 With lightly floured hands, divide the sausage mixture into four equal portions. Flatten each portion into a thin patty. Dust the eggs with flour and wrap each egg in a portion of the sausage meat. Be sure the meat is of even thickness and there are no cracks.

3 Bread the sausage-covered eggs using the standard breading procedure described in Chapter 9, Mise en Place.

4 Deep-fry the eggs approximately 7–8 minutes at 350°F (180°C) or until the sausage meat is fully cooked. The eggs may be finished in the oven if they begin to get too dark in the fryer.

5 Serve the eggs halved or quartered lengthwise, hot or cold.

Approximate values per egg: **Calories** 200, **Total fat** 130 g, **Saturated fat** 5 g, **Cholesterol** 280 mg, **Sodium** 440 mg, **Total carbohydrates** 2 g, **Protein** 13 g

Corned Beef Hash

YIELD 12 Servings, 6 oz. (180 g) each	METHOD Pan-Frying	
Potatoes, waxy	1 lb. 8 oz.	720 g
Onions, large dice	8 oz.	240 g
Carrots, medium dice	2 oz.	60 g
Parsnips, peeled, medium dice	4 oz.	120 g
Vegetable oil or bacon fat	2 fl. oz.	60 ml
Corned beef, cooked, large dice	2 lb.	960 g
Eggs, beaten	2	2
Salt and pepper	TT	TT

1 Peel and quarter the potatoes. Simmer them in a saucepan of salted water until tender. Drain the potatoes, allow them to cool completely then coarsely chop them.

2 Sauté the onions, carrots and parsnips in 1 ounce (30 milliliters) oil over medium heat until tender. Remove the vegetables from the pan and let them cool.

3 Combine the cubed potatoes, sautéed vegetables and corned beef and grind through the medium die of a meat grinder.

4 Combine the ground mixture with the eggs. Season with salt and pepper. (The hash may be prepared to this point and refrigerated until needed.)

5 Form the mixture into 6-ounce (180-gram) patties or divide the mixture between 12 greased ring molds.

6 Heat the remaining oil in a large sauté pan over medium heat. Add the hash patties or the ring molds of hash. Cook until heated through, turning once when well browned on the first side. (Slide off the ring molds, if using, before serving.) Serve with fried or poached eggs.

Approximate values per 6-oz. (180-g) serving: **Calories** 300, **Total fat** 20 g, **Saturated fat** 5 g, **Cholesterol** 110 mg, **Sodium** 880 mg, **Total carbohydrates** 13 g, **Protein** 16 g

Tortilla Española (Spanish Egg and Onion Omelet)

YIELD 1 Tortilla, 8 Servings	METHOD Sautéing	
Olive oil	4 fl. oz.	120 ml
Onion, chopped	6 oz.	180 g
Eggs	6	6
Garlic, minced	2 tsp.	10 ml
Fresh parsley, chopped	3 Tbsp.	15 ml
Serrano ham, chopped	3 oz.	90 g
Sweet smoked paprika	½ tsp.	3 ml
Salt	TT	TT
Potatoes, peeled ½-inch dice, cooked	22 oz.	660 g

1 Heat 2 fluid ounces (60 milliliters) of the olive oil in a well-seasoned 10-inch (25-centimeter) sauté pan. Sweat the onions in the oil until soft and translucent.

2 Beat together the eggs, garlic, parsley, ham, paprika and salt in a large bowl. Add the cooked onions and potatoes.

3 Add the remaining oil to the sauté pan. Heat over medium high heat, then pour in the egg mixture. Flatten the mixture with a spatula.

4 Cook, shaking the pan from time to time to keep the tortilla from sticking. Lift the edges of the tortilla. If browning too quickly, reduce the temperature.

5 When the eggs have set, invert the firm tortilla onto a flat platter. Then slide it back into the pan to finish cooking.

6 Serve the tortilla cut in wedges hot or at room temperature.

Approximate values per ⅛-tortilla serving: **Calories** 270, **Total fat** 18 g, **Saturated fat** 3.5 g, **Cholesterol** 125 mg, **Sodium** 180 mg, **Total carbohydrates** 18 g, **Protein** 8 g

---

Cheese Soufflé

 Vegetarian

YIELD 6 Servings	METHOD Baking	
Butter	2 oz.	60 g
All-purpose flour	3 oz.	90 g
Milk	12 fl. oz.	360 ml
Salt	½ tsp.	2 ml
Cayenne pepper	¼ tsp.	1 ml
Eggs, separated	6	6
Gruyère cheese, grated	8 oz.	240 g
Cream of tartar	⅛ tsp.	0.5 g
Parmesan, grated	4 Tbsp.	60 ml

1 Make a blond roux with the butter and flour. Cook 1 minute, then whisk in the milk. Cook, stirring constantly, until thickened, approximately 2 minutes. Whisk in the salt, cayenne and egg yolks. Let the mixture, which is the soufflé base, cool slightly.

2 Stir the Gruyère into the soufflé base. Scrape the base and cheese mixture into a large bowl.

3 Whip the egg whites until foamy, then add the cream of tartar to help stabilize the egg foam. Whip until stiff but not dry. Fold the whites into the soufflé base and cheese mixture in three additions.

4 To bake the soufflés, brush 6 individual-serving-sized ramekins lightly with melted butter and sprinkle with 2 tablespoons (30 milliliters) Parmesan. Pipe the egg white and soufflé mixture into the prepared ramekins to within ¼ inch (6 millimeters) of the rim. Sprinkle with the remaining Parmesan.

5 Bake immediately at 400°F (200°C) until well puffed and lightly browned, approximately 20–25 minutes. Do not touch the soufflés to test doneness as this may cause them to fall.

Approximate values per serving: **Calories** 400, **Total fat** 28 g, **Saturated fat** 6 g, **Cholesterol** 280 mg, **Sodium** 470 mg, **Total carbohydrates** 14 g, **Protein** 22 g, **Vitamin A** 20%, **Calcium** 50%

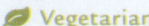 Vegetarian

Waffles

YIELD 20 Waffles, 2½ oz. (75 g) each

All-purpose flour	18 oz.	540 g
Salt	2 tsp.	10 ml
Baking powder	2 Tbsp.	30 ml
Granulated sugar	2 oz.	60 g
Eggs	4	4
Milk, warm	24 fl. oz.	720 ml
Unsalted butter, melted	5 oz.	150 g
Vanilla extract	2 tsp.	10 ml

1 Mix the dry ingredients together in a large bowl.

2 Whisk the eggs together in a separate bowl; add the milk, butter and vanilla extract. Stir to combine.

3 Pour the liquid mixture into the dry ingredients, stirring to blend. Keep refrigerated until ready to use. Batter may be made up to 1 day in advance.

4 Cook batter in a preheated waffle iron according to the manufacturer's directions. Serve waffles immediately with your choice of toppings.

Variation:

Pecan Waffles—Sprinkle 1 tablespoon (15 milliliters) chopped pecans over the batter as soon as it is poured onto the waffle iron. Substitute 1 teaspoon (5 milliliters) pecan flavoring for the vanilla extract if desired.

Approximate values per 2½-oz. (75-g) waffle: **Calories** 190, **Total fat** 8 g, **Saturated fat** 4.5 g, **Cholesterol** 65 mg, **Sodium** 480 mg, **Total carbohydrates** 25 g, **Protein** 5 g, **Calcium** 20%

Cinnamon French Toast

French toast begins with slices of day-old bread. (It is known in France as pain perdu, *meaning "lost bread," probably because it provided a way to use bread that would otherwise have been discarded.) French bread, sourdough bread, raisin bread, challah, whole-wheat bread and even stale croissants can be used. The bread is dipped into a batter of eggs, sugar, milk or cream and flavorings, then sautéed in butter and served very hot. It may be topped with powdered sugar, fresh fruit, fruit compote or maple syrup as desired.*

YIELD 6 Servings, 5 oz. (150 g) each	METHOD Griddling	
Eggs, beaten	10	10
Heavy cream	4 fl. oz.	120 ml
Salt	TT	TT
Cinnamon, ground	TT	TT
Thick-sliced bread such as sourdough, cinnamon, banana or brioche	12 slices	12 slices
Unsalted butter	as needed	as needed
Powdered sugar	as needed	as needed

1 Whisk together the eggs, cream, salt and cinnamon.

2 Place the egg mixture in a shallow pan. Place the slices of bread in the egg mixture and let soak for 2–3 minutes, turning them over after the first minute or so.

3 Cook the soaked slices of French toast in a lightly buttered, preheated sauté pan or griddle set at 350°F (180°C) until well browned. Turn the slices and cook on the second side until done.

4 Cut each slice of French toast into two triangles.

5 Arrange four triangles on each plate and top with butter and powdered sugar.

Variation:

Baked Banana Praline French Toast—Prepare the batter as above. Cut slices of bread in half diagonally and arrange in rows in a well-buttered half-sized hotel pan. Slice 2 large bananas and scatter the bananas over the bread. Sprinkle 6 ounces (180 grams) of dark brown sugar evenly over the bananas and bread. Pour the batter over the bread, pressing down on the bread to make sure it is covered with the egg mixture. Cover and allow to rest for at least 1 hour. Uncover and bake at 325° F (160° C) until set and lightly browned.

Approximate values per 5-oz. (150-g) serving: **Calories** 320, **Total fat** 17 g, **Saturated fat** 7 g, **Cholesterol** 380 mg, **Sodium** 420 mg, **Total carbohydrates** 28 g, **Protein** 15 g, **Vitamin A** 25%, **Iron** 15%

Popovers

Popovers are crisp hollow muffins made from a rich egg batter. The steam released from the eggs and milk as the popovers bake is trapped in the gluten web of the batter, causing it to rise. Popovers and other products that rely on steam for leavening are baked at a high temperature so that the steam forms quickly before the gluten bond sets. These muffins resemble products baked from éclair paste discussed on page 995. Yorkshire pudding, a popular accompaniment to roasted rib of beef, is made from this same batter. Yorkshire pudding is baked in beef fat in a shallow pan and then served cut into squares.

YIELD 20 Popovers, approximately 2 oz. (60 g) each

Beef fat or vegetable oil	10 fl. oz.	300 ml
All-purpose flour	8 oz.	240 g
Salt	1 tsp.	5 ml
Eggs	6	6
Whole milk	1 pt.	480 ml
Whole butter, melted	3 oz.	90 g

1 Place twenty 4-ounce (120-milliliter) greased ramekins or popover tins on a sheet pan and put 1 tablespoon (15 milliliters) of beef fat or vegetable oil in the bottom of each ramekin. Place the ramekins in a 425°F (220°C) oven until the fat smokes.

2 Sift the flour and salt together into a large bowl. In a separate bowl, whisk together the eggs, milk and butter. Pour the liquid ingredients into the dry ingredients and whip until smooth to create popover batter.

3 Remove the ramekins from the oven and fill each approximately two-thirds full with batter. Bake at 425°F (220°C) for 20 minutes without opening the oven door. After 20 minutes, lower the heat to 375°F (190°C) and bake until the popovers dry out inside, approximately 10 more minutes.

4 Remove the popovers from the oven, unmold and serve.

5 For crisper popovers, slit the sides of the unmolded popovers to allow the steam to escape. Place on a sheet pan and return them to the oven until the tops are firm, crisp and brown, approximately 10 minutes.

Variation:

Onion Popovers—Sauté 2 ounces (60 grams) finely chopped onion in 1 tablespoon (15 grams) butter until tender. Sprinkle the onions over the batter just before baking.

Approximate values per 2-oz. (60-g) popover: **Calories** 250, **Total fat** 21 g, **Saturated fat** 11 g, **Cholesterol** 95 mg, **Sodium** 150 mg, **Total carbohydrates** 10 g, **Protein** 4 g

Vegetables 22

- identify a variety of vegetables
- purchase vegetables appropriate for your needs
- store vegetables properly
- explain various ways of preserving vegetables
- prepare vegetables prior to cooking and service
- apply various cooking methods to vegetables

fiber also known as dietary fiber; indigestible carbohydrates found in grains, fruits and vegetables; fiber aids digestion

cruciferous plants from the cabbage family including broccoli, cauliflower, cabbage, kale, rutabaga and turnip, also called brassicas

Fresh, properly prepared vegetables can add flavor, color and variety to almost any dish. By reducing the use of animal products and shifting the focus onto vegetable preparations, contemporary chefs are making plant-based dishes the center of attention. Vegetables are no longer an afterthought or merely added to a plate for color. Chefs and consumers now understand the important role plant-centered meals play in personal health and the health of our planet. Many restaurants routinely offer vegetarian entrées, an extensive selection of vegetable side dishes or an entire vegetarian menu. This reflects the demands of knowledgeable and health-conscious consumers as well as the increased availability of high-quality fresh produce. (Cooking with vegetables and other ingredients in meatless diets is discussed in Chapter 24, Healthy Cooking and Special Diets.)

In this chapter, we identify many vegetables typically used in food service operations. (Potatoes are discussed in Chapter 23, Potatoes, Grains and Pasta; greens and ingredients for salads are discussed in Chapter 25, Salads and Salad Dressings.) We also discuss how to purchase, store and prepare fresh and preserved vegetables for service or cooking and how to apply many of the cooking methods introduced in Chapter 10, Principles of Cooking, to vegetables.

The term **vegetable** refers to any herbaceous plant that can be partially or wholly eaten. An herbaceous plant is one with little or no woody tissue. The portions of these plants humans consume may include the leaves, stems, roots, tubers, seeds and flowers. Vegetables contain more starch and less sugar than fruits. Therefore vegetables tend to be savory, not sweet. Also in contrast to fruits, vegetables are often eaten cooked, not raw. Because they are generally high in dietary **fiber** and complex carbohydrates, low in fat or fat-free and good sources of vitamins, minerals and phytochemicals, vegetables are considered a vital part of a balanced diet. Refer to the discussion of essential nutrients in Chapter 3, Nutrition, for more detailed information on the healthful properties of vegetables.

IDENTIFYING VEGETABLES

This book presents fruits and vegetables according to the ways most people view them and use them, rather than by rigid botanical classifications. Although produce such as tomatoes, peppers and eggplants are botanically fruits, they are prepared and served like vegetables so we include them here under the category "fruit vegetables." Potatoes, although botanically vegetables, are discussed with other starches in Chapter 23, Potatoes, Grains and Pasta.

We sort vegetables into nine categories based on either botanical relationship or edible part: cabbages, fruit vegetables, gourds and squashes, greens, mushrooms and truffles, onions, pods and seeds, roots and tubers, and stalk vegetables. Some vegetables have several names that vary from region to region or on a purveyor's whim. The names used here follow generally accepted custom and usage.

Cabbages

The *Brassica* or cabbage family includes a wide range of vegetables used for their heads, flowers or leaves. They are part of a group of vegetables referred to as **cruciferous**, widely recognized for their health-promoting properties. Brassicas are high in vitamins C and K, folate, potassium and other minerals as well as phytochemicals that constitute important components of a healthy diet. Brassicas also contain sulfur compounds that give these vegetables a strong aroma and bitter flavor when overcooked.

Members of this family are generally quick-growing, cool-weather crops. Many are ancient plants with unknown origins. Cabbages are inexpensive, readily available and easy to prepare.

Bok Choy

Bok Choy is a white-stemmed variety of southern Chinese cabbage. The relatively tightly packed leaves are dark green, with long white ribs attached at a bulbous stem. The stems are crisp and mild with a flavor similar to romaine lettuce. Although Bok Choy may be eaten raw, it is most often stir-fried or used in soups. Choose heads of Bok Choy with bright white stems and dark green leaves; avoid those with brown, moist spots.

Bok Choy

Broccoli

Broccoli

Broccoli has a thick central stalk with grayish-green leaves topped with heads of green florets. Broccoli is eaten raw or steamed, microwaved or sautéed and served warm or cold. Broccoli stalks are extremely firm and benefit from blanching. Stems are often slow-cooked for soups. Generally broccoli leaves are not eaten. Choose broccoli with firm stalks and compact clusters of tightly closed dark green florets. Avoid stalks with yellow florets.

Procedure for Cutting Broccoli Spears

Cut off the thick, woody portion of the stalk, then cut the florets and stems into spears. Peel the stems if using.

Broccoli Rabe

Broccoli rabe, also known as raab [rob] and rapini [rah-PEE-nee] (It. *broccoli di rape, cime di rapa*) is a leafy green with small florets that look similar to broccoli florets. The entire plant is eaten, although some prefer to separate the spiky leaves and green florets from the more bitter stems. Broccoli rabe may be boiled, steamed, roasted or sautéed, and its peppery, bitter flavor is a popular ingredient in both Chinese and Mediterranean, especially Italian, cuisine. Select rabe with bright green leaves and unopened buds; avoid plants with wilted or yellow leaves.

Broccoli rabe

Brussels Sprouts

Brussels sprouts (Fr. *choux de Bruxelles*) consist of numerous small heads arranged in neat rows along a thick stalk. The tender young sprouts look like baby cabbages and are usually steamed or roasted. Brussels sprouts have a strong, nutty flavor that blends well with game, ham, duck or rich meats. Choose small, firm sprouts that are compact and heavy. The best size is ¾–1½ inches (2–4 centimeters) in diameter. They should be bright green and free of blemishes. Brussels sprouts last longer when purchased on the stem. The flavor of Brussels sprouts intensifies with longer storage.

Brussels sprouts

Cauliflower

Cauliflower

Cauliflower (Fr. *chou-fleur*) like broccoli grows on a thick stalk. Each stalk produces one flower, called a head, surrounded by large green leaves. The head, composed of creamy white florets, can be cooked whole or cut into separate florets for roasting, steaming, blanching or stir-frying. Choose firm, compact cauliflower heads. Any attached leaves should be bright green and crisp. A yellow color or spreading florets indicate that the vegetable is overly mature.

Procedure for Cutting Cauliflower Florets

1 Cut off the stem and leaves.

2 Cut the florets off the core.

Green and red cabbages

Head Cabbages (Green and Red)

Cabbage (Fr. *chou*) has been a staple of northern European cuisine for centuries. The familiar green cabbage has a large, firm, round head with tightly packed pale green leaves. Flat and cone-shaped heads are also available. Red (or purple) cabbage is a different strain and may be tougher than green cabbage. Cabbage can be eaten raw (as in coleslaw) or used in soups or stews; it can be braised, steamed or stir-fried. The large, waxy leaves can also be steamed until soft, then wrapped around a filling of seasoned meat. Choose firm cabbage heads without dried cores.

Kale

Kale has large ruffled, curly or bumpy leaves. Its rather bitter flavor goes well with beans and rich meats such as game, pork or ham. Kale is typically boiled, stuffed or used in soups. Tender baby kale suitable for eating raw is also popular in salads. Ornamental or flowering kale, sometimes marketed as "savoy," is edible but bitter and tough; its pink, purple, yellow or white-and-green variegated leaves are best used for decoration and garnish. Choose leaves that are crisp, with a grayish-green color.

Baby kale

Kale

Kohlrabi

Although it looks rather like a round root, kohlrabi is actually a bulbous stem vegetable created by crossbreeding cabbages and turnips. Both the leaves (which are attached directly to the bulbous stem) and the roots are generally removed before sale. Depending on the variety, kohlrabi skin may be light green, purple or green with a hint of red. The interior flesh is white, with a sweet flavor similar to that of turnips. (Kohlrabi can be substituted for turnip in many recipes.) Younger plants are milder and more tender than large, mature ones. The outer skin must be removed from mature stems; young stems only need to be well scrubbed before cooking. Kohlrabi can be eaten raw, or it can be cooked (whole, sliced or diced) with moist-heat cooking methods such as boiling and steaming. Kohlrabi may also be hollowed out and stuffed with meat or vegetable mixtures. Choose small, tender kohlrabi with fresh, green leaves.

Kohlrabi

Napa Cabbage

Napa cabbage, also known as Chinese cabbage, is widely used in Asian cuisines. It has a stout, elongated head with relatively tightly packed, firm, pale green leaves. It is moister and more tender than common green and red cabbages, with a milder, more delicate flavor. Napa cabbage may be eaten raw but is particularly well suited for stir-frying or steaming. Choose Napa cabbage heads with crisp leaves that are free of blemishes.

Napa cabbage

Savoy Cabbage

Savoy cabbage has curly or ruffled leaves, often in variegated shades of green and purple. Savoy cabbage tends to be milder and more tender than regular cabbages and can be substituted for them, cooked or uncooked. Savoy leaves also make an attractive garnish. Savoy cabbage heads can be loose or tight, depending on the variety. Choose heads with tender, unblemished leaves.

Fruit Vegetables

Botanists classify avocados, eggplants, peppers and tomatoes as fruits because they develop from the ovary of flowering plants and contain one or more seeds. Chefs, however, prepare and serve them like vegetables; therefore they are discussed here.

Savoy cabbage

Avocados

Avocados include several varieties of pear-shaped fruits with rich, high-fat flesh. This light golden-green flesh surrounds a large, inedible, oval-shaped seed (pit). Some avocado varieties have smooth, green skin; others have pebbly, almost black skin. Avocados should be used at their peak of ripeness, a condition that lasts only briefly. Firm avocados lack the desired flavor and creamy texture. Ripe avocados are soft to the touch but not mushy. Firm avocados can be left at room temperature to ripen and refrigerated for 1 or 2 days once they are ripe. Avocados are used raw to garnish salads, mashed or puréed for sauces, sliced for sandwiches or diced for omelets. Avocado halves are popular containers for chilled meat, fish, shellfish or poultry salads. Because avocado flesh turns brown very quickly once cut, dip avocado halves or slices in lemon juice and keep unused portions tightly covered with plastic wrap. Choose avocados that are free of blemishes or moist spots. The flesh should be free of dark spots or streaks. Avocados are available all year.

Hass avocados

Procedure for Cutting and Pitting Avocados

1 Cut the avocado in half lengthwise. Separate the two halves with a twisting motion.

2 Insert a chef's knife into the pit and twist to remove.

3 Scoop the flesh out of the skin with a large spoon.

Eggplants

Two types of eggplants (Fr. *aubergine*) are commonly available: Asian and western. Asian varieties, such as the **Japanese eggplant** and the tiny round **Indian** or Thai eggplants, are either small spheres or long and thin, with skin colors ranging from creamy white to deep purple. Western, also known as Italian eggplants, tend to be shaped like a plump pear with a shiny lavender to purple-black skin.

Both types have a dense, khaki-colored flesh with a rather bland flavor that absorbs other flavors well during cooking. Eggplants can be grilled, baked, steamed, fried or sautéed. They are commonly used in Mediterranean. Thai and Indian cuisines, especially in vegetarian dishes. The skin may be left intact or removed before or after cooking as desired. Sliced eggplants may be salted and left to drain for 30 minutes to remove moisture and bitterness before cooking. (They will also absorb less oil when fried.) Choose plump, heavy eggplants with a smooth, shiny skin that is not blemished or wrinkled. Asian varieties tend to be softer than western.

Japanese eggplants

Indian eggplants

Western eggplants

Peppers

Members of the *Capsicum* family are native to the New World. When "discovered" by Christopher Columbus, he called them "peppers" because of their sometimes fiery flavor. These peppers, which include sweet peppers and hot peppers (chiles), are unrelated to peppercorns, the Asian spice for which Columbus was searching. Interestingly, New World peppers were readily accepted in Indian and Asian cuisines, in which they are now considered staples.

Fresh peppers are found in a wide range of colors—green, red, yellow, orange, purple and white—as well as shapes, from tiny teardrops to cones to spheres. They have dense flesh and a hollow central cavity. Pepper flesh is lined with placental ribs (the white internal veins), to which tiny yellowish-white seeds are attached. A core of seeds is also attached to the stem end of each pepper.

Chile peppers get their heat from capsaicin, which is found not in the flesh or seeds, but in the placental ribs. A pepper's heat can be greatly reduced by carefully removing the ribs and attached seeds. Generally the smaller the chile, the hotter it is. The searing heat of a Scotch bonnet or habañero can burn. Wearing gloves is recommended when working with these hot peppers. The amount of heat varies from variety to variety, however, and even from one pepper to another depending on growing conditions. Hot, dry conditions result in hotter peppers than do cool, moist conditions. Choose peppers that are plump and brilliantly colored with smooth, unblemished skins. Avoid wrinkled, pitted or blistered peppers. A bright green stem indicates freshness.

Green bell peppers

Sweet Peppers

Common sweet peppers, known as bell peppers, are thick-walled fruits available in green, red, yellow, purple, orange and other colors. They are heart-shaped or boxy, with a short stem and crisp flesh. Their flavor is warm, sweet (red peppers tend to be the sweetest) and relatively mild. Raw bell peppers may be sliced or diced and used in salads or sandwiches. Bell peppers can also be stuffed and baked, grilled, fried, sautéed or puréed for soups, sauces or condiments.

Red and yellow bell peppers

Procedure for Cutting Peppers Julienne

❶ Trim off the ends of the pepper; cut away the seeds and core.

❷ Cut away the pale ribs, trimming the flesh to the desired thickness.

❸ Slice the flesh in julienne.

Hot Peppers

Hot peppers, also known as chiles, are also members of the *Capsicum* family. Although a chile's most characteristic attribute is its pungency, each chile actually has a distinctive flavor, from mild and rich to spicy and sweet to fiery hot. (And some such as the padrón and **shishito** can be either mild or hot depending on growing conditions.) Plant breeders continue to develop chile pepper varieties with increasingly punishing heat.

Chiles are commonly used in Asian, Indian, Mexican and Latin American cuisines. The larger (and milder) of the hot peppers, such as Anaheim and poblano, can be stuffed and baked or sautéed as a side dish. Most chiles, however, are used to add flavor and seasoning to sauces and other dishes. Chiles are available fresh and are also available canned in a variety of processed forms such as whole or diced, roasted, pickled or marinated.

Clockwise from bottom left: red and green serrano, green and red jalapeño, yellow hot, poblano and Anaheim chiles

Shishito chiles

Habañero chiles

Chile Pepper Pungency

A pepper's heat can be measured by Scoville heat units, a subjective rating created to measure the perception of capsaicin when tasting chile peppers. The higher the Scoville rating, the larger the concentration of capsaicin and the hotter the pepper will taste. Some of the ranges of heat of common chile peppers as measured in this system are listed here.

PEPPER	PUNGENCY (SCOVILLE)
Bell, sweet Italian	0
New Mexico, pimento	500–1000
Anaheim, ancho, pasilla, poblano	1000–1500
Chipotle, jalapeño	2500–10,000
Serrano	5000–23,000
De árbol	15,000–30,000
Aji, cayenne, piquin, tabasco	30,000–50,000
Habañero, Scotch bonnet	80,000–300,000
Bhut jolokia (ghost chile), Trinidad moruga scorpion	1,000,000– 1,200,000
Pure capsaicin	16,000,000

Procedure for Coring Jalapeños

Cut the jalapeño in half lengthwise. Push the core and seeds out with your thumb. You can avoid burning your fingers by wearing rubber gloves when working with hot chiles.

Dried chiles (top to bottom): California, ancho and de árbol

Dried chiles are widely used in East Asian, Mexican, Central American and southwestern U.S. cuisines. They can be ground and used in a powdered spice blend called *chilli*, or soaked in a liquid and then puréed for sauces or condiments. Drying radically alters the flavor of chiles, making them stronger and more pungent. Just as one type of fresh chile cannot be substituted for another without altering a dish's flavor, dried chiles cannot be substituted without flavor changes. Choose dried chiles that are clean and unbroken, with some flexibility. Avoid any with white spots or a stale aroma.

Procedure for Roasting Peppers

A Pepper by Any Other Name

The popularity of southwestern cuisine, hot condiments and salsas has brought with it a new appreciation and respect for chiles. Diners and chefs may find the names given to the various chiles confusing, however. Most chiles can be used either fresh or dried; drying changes not only the pepper's flavor, but also its name. Regional variations in chile names also add to the confusion. Several of the more frequently encountered chiles are listed here according to the names most commonly used for both their fresh and dried forms.

FRESH (FRESCO)	DRIED (SECO)
Anaheim	Mild red or California
Ancho	Ancho or pastilla
Chilaca	Pastilla or negro
Jalapeño	Chipotle (smoked)
Mirasol	Guajillo
New Mexico green	New Mexico red
New Mexico red	Chile Colorado
Pimento	Paprika
Poblano	Mulato

❶ Roast the pepper over an open flame until completely charred and then place the pepper in a plastic bag to sweat for a few minutes.

❷ Remove the burnt skin and rinse under running water.

Tomatillos

Tomatillos, also known as Mexican or husk tomatoes, grow on small, weedy bushes. They are bright green, about the size of a small tomato and covered with a thin, papery husk. Tomatillos have a tart, lemony flavor and crisp, moist flesh. Although they are an important ingredient in southwestern and northern Mexican cuisines, tomatillos may not be readily available in other areas. Tomatillos can be used raw in salads, puréed for salsa or cooked in soups, stews or vegetable dishes. Choose tomatillos with husks that are split but still look fresh. The skin should be plump, shiny and slightly sticky.

Tomatillos

Tomatoes

Tomatoes (Fr. *tomate* or *pomme d'amour*; It. *pomodoro*) are available in a wide variety of colors and shapes. They vary from green (unripe) to golden yellow to ruby red; from tiny spheres (currant tomatoes) to huge, squat ovals (beefsteak). Some, such as the plum tomato, have lots of meaty flesh with only a few seeds; others, such as the slicing tomato, have lots of seeds and juice, but only a few meaty membranes. Heirloom varieties, such as Brandywine, German Green and Golden Queen, are irregularly shaped and may be prone to cracking. All tomatoes have a similar flavor, but the levels of sweetness and acidity vary depending on the species, growing conditions and ripeness at harvest. Ripe tomatoes are a natural source of glutamate and add umami flavor to foods.

Heirloom tomato varieties

Because tomatoes are highly perishable, they are usually harvested when mature but still green (unripe), then shipped to wholesalers who ripen them in temperature- and humidity-controlled rooms. The effect on flavor and texture is unfortunate. Tomatoes should be stored at room temperature to preserve their flavor and texture.

Tomatoes are used widely in salads, soups, sauces and baked dishes. They are most often eaten raw but can be grilled, pickled, pan-fried, roasted or sautéed as a side dish. Choose fresh tomatoes that are plump with a smooth, shiny skin. The color should be uniform and true for the variety. Many canned tomato products are also available (e.g., purée, paste, sauce or stewed whole). Sun-dried and air-dried tomatoes are available in crumbs, pieces, slivers or halves, dry or packed in oil. The dry-pack version can be soaked in oil or steeped in hot water to soften before use.

Sun-dried tomatoes

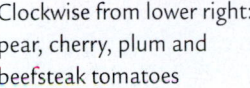

Clockwise from lower right: pear, cherry, plum and beefsteak tomatoes

Three Treasures of the New World

In lieu of many spices, golden treasures and precious gems, early Spanish explorers returned to Spain with items of much greater significance: tomatoes, potatoes and corn.

The Spanish and the Italians hailed the tomato (whose name comes from the Aztec name *tomatl*) as an aphrodisiac—perhaps because of its resemblance to the human heart—when it arrived from the New World during the 16th century. But even though tomatoes soon became part of Spanish and Italian cuisines, other Europeans, New World colonists and, later, Americans considered tomatoes poisonous. (There is some truth to this notion: tomato vines and leaves contain tomatine, an alkaloid that can cause health problems.) Thus for many years in many societies, only the adventurous ate tomatoes.

The potato, first delivered to Europe from its native Peru by Francisco Pizarro in the 16th century, did not win wide acceptance in haute cuisine until Antoine-Augustin Parmentier (1737–1813), a French army pharmacist, induced King Louis XVI of France (who reigned from 1775 to 1793) to try one. The king and his courtiers liked them so much they even began wearing potato blossom boutonnières. Parmentier was ultimately honored for his starchy contribution to French cuisine by having several potato dishes named for him, including *potage Parmentier* (potato soup). Not only did Parmentier lobby for the acceptance of the potato as a food fit for a king, he also prophesied that the potato would make starvation impossible. Potatoes ultimately did become a staple of many diets. But, sadly, Parmentier's prophecy was proven untrue during the Irish potato famine of 1846–1848, when a terrible blight destroyed the Irish potato crop. Nearly 1.5 million people died, and an equal number emigrated to the United States. They brought with them a cuisine that incorporated potatoes and an appreciation of the common potato was reintroduced to its native land.

When returning from his second voyage to the New World, Columbus took corn with him. Called *mahiz* or *maize* by West Indian natives, corn had been a staple of Central American diets for at least 5000 years. Although Europeans did not actively shun corn as they did tomatoes and potatoes, corn never really caught on in most of Europe. Grown for human consumption mostly in Italy, Spain and southwestern France, most corn was and still is usually eaten ground and boiled as polenta. Despite the unenthusiastic European reception, corn's popularity quickly spread: Within 50 years of Columbus's journey, corn was being cultivated in lands as distant from the New World as China, India and sub-Saharan Africa.

Procedure for Preparing Tomato Concassée

❶ With a paring knife, cut an X on the bottom of the tomatoes just deep enough to penetrate the skin.

❷ Blanch the tomatoes in boiling water for 20 seconds; refresh in ice water.

❸ Cut out the cores and peel the tomatoes using a paring knife.

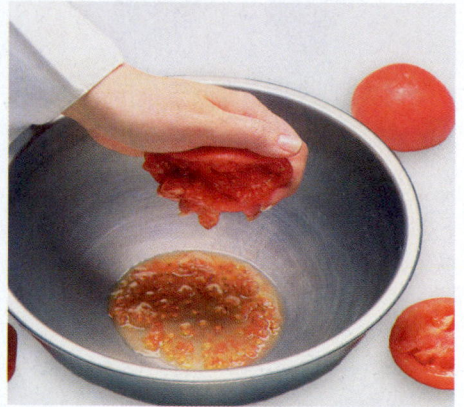

❹ Cut the tomatoes in half horizontally and squeeze out the seeds and juice.

❺ Chop or dice the tomatoes as desired for the recipe.

Gourds and Squashes

The *Cucurbitaceae* or gourd family includes almost 750 species; its members are found in warm regions worldwide. Gourds are characterized by large, complex root systems with quick-growing, trailing vines and large leaves. Their flowers are often attractive and edible. Although some members of the gourd family originated in Africa, most squashes are native to the Americas.

Cucumbers

Cucumbers can be divided into two categories: pickling and slicing. The two types are not interchangeable. Cucumbers are valued for their refreshing cool taste and astringency. Slicing cucumbers are usually served raw, in salads or mixed with yogurt and dill or mint as a side dish, especially for spicy dishes. Pickling cucumbers are generally served pickled, with no further processing. Pickling cucumbers include the cornichon, Kirby and gherkin. They are recognizable by their sharp black or white spines and are quite bitter when raw. Slicing cucumbers include the burpless, the seedless English (or hothouse), the seedless **Persian cucumber** (which is

Counterclockwise from top left: kirby for pickling, green and English hothouse cucumbers

Persian cucumbers

small and smooth-skinned), the lemon (which is round and yellow) and the common green market cucumber. Most cucumber varieties have relatively thin skins and may be marketed with a wax coating to prevent moisture loss and improve appearance. Waxed skins should be peeled unless the cucumbers will be pickled. Choose cucumbers that are firm but not hard. Avoid those that are limp or yellowed or have soft spots.

Procedure for Seeding a Cucumber

Remove the seeds from a cucumber by slicing it in half lengthwise, then scrape out the seeds with a spoon or melon ball cutter.

Procedure for Making Decorative Cucumber Slices

Use a zester or fork to score the rind of a cucumber before slicing.

Squashes

Squashes are the fleshy fruits of a large number of plants in the gourd family. Many varieties are available in a range of colors, shapes and sizes. Squashes are classified as winter or summer based on their peak season and skin type. All squashes have a center cavity filled with many seeds, although in winter varieties the cavity is more pronounced. Squash blossoms are also edible; blossoms may be added to salads raw, dipped in batter and deep-fried or filled with cheese or meat and baked. Choose squashes with unbroken skins and good color for the variety. Avoid any with soft, moist spots.

Acorn squashes

Spaghetti squash

Butternut squashes

Procedure for Peeling Hard Squashes

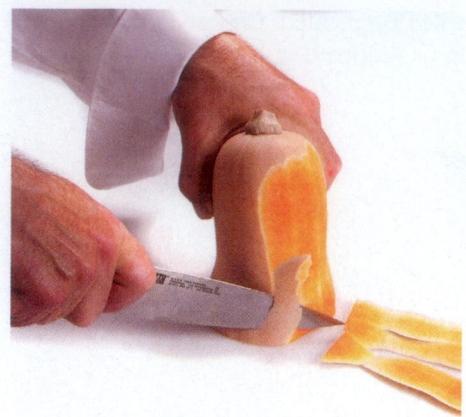

Trim the bottom of the squash to create a flat side to stabilize it. Hold the squash in one hand and cut down with a sharp knife to remove the peel.

Pumpkins

Yellow crookneck squashes

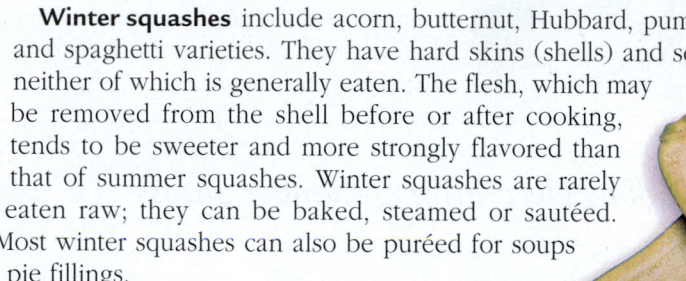

Zucchini

Winter squashes include acorn, butternut, Hubbard, pumpkin and spaghetti varieties. They have hard skins (shells) and seeds, neither of which is generally eaten. The flesh, which may be removed from the shell before or after cooking, tends to be sweeter and more strongly flavored than that of summer squashes. Winter squashes are rarely eaten raw; they can be baked, steamed or sautéed. Most winter squashes can also be puréed for soups or pie fillings.

Summer squashes include pattypan, yellow crookneck and zucchini varieties. They have soft, edible skins and seeds that are generally not removed before cooking. Most summer squashes may be eaten raw but are also suitable for grilling, sautéing, steaming or baking.

Greens

The term *greens* refers to a variety of leafy green vegetables that may be served raw, but are usually cooked. Greens have long been used in the cuisines of India, Asia and the Mediterranean and are an important part of regional cuisine in the southern United States. Most greens have strong, spicy flavors. Milder varieties are almost always eaten raw and include the lettuces discussed in Chapter 25, Salads and Salad Dressings.

Greens have an extremely high water content, which means that cooking causes drastic shrinkage. As a general rule, allow 8 ounces (240 grams) per portion before cooking. Choose young, tender greens that have good color and are not limp. Avoid greens with dry-looking stems or yellow leaves.

Collard Greens

Collard greens, often simply referred to as collards, are a type of wild cabbage with loose, leafy heads of bright green leaves. Collards have a sharp, tangy flavor and look like a cross between mustard greens and kale. Considered a staple ingredient in cooking of the American South, collards are typically slow-simmered with ham hocks or bacon until very tender, then served with their cooking liquid. Collards are high in iron and vitamins A and C and are best if picked young or after the first frost of autumn.

Collard greens

Mustard Greens

Mustard, a member of the cabbage family, was brought to America by early European immigrants. Mustard has large, dark green leaves with frilly edges and is known for its assertive, bitter flavor. Mustard greens can be served raw in salads or used as garnish. They can also be cooked, often with white wine, vinegar and herbs. Choose crisp, bright green leaves without discoloration.

Mustard greens

Sorrel

Sorrel is a wild member of the buckwheat family. Its tartness and sour flavor are used in soups and sauces and to accent other vegetables. It is particularly good with fatty fish or rich meats. Sorrel leaves naturally become the texture of a purée after only a few minutes of moist-heat cooking. Choose sorrel leaves that are fully formed, with no yellow blemishes.

Sorrel

Spinach

Spinach (Fr. *épinard*) is a versatile green that grows rapidly in cool climates. It has smooth, bright green leaves attached to thin stems. Spinach may be eaten raw in salads, cooked by almost any moist-heat method, microwaved or sautéed. It can be used in stuffings, baked or creamed dishes, soups or stews. Spinach grows in sandy soil and must be rinsed repeatedly in cold water to remove all traces of grit from the leaves. It bruises easily and should be handled gently during washing. Stems and large midribs should be removed. Choose bunches with crisp, tender, deep green leaves; avoid yellow leaves or those with blemishes.

Spinach

Procedure for Preparing Spinach

To remove the stem and the tough midrib, fold the leaf in half in one hand. Grasp the stem and pull.

Swiss Chard

Chard—the reference to "Swiss" is inexplicable—is a type of beet that does not produce a tuberous root. The wide, flat, dark green leaves are consumed. (Golden-, orange- and pink-stemmed varieties are also available.) Chard can be steamed, sautéed or used in soups. Chard's tart, spinachlike flavor blends well with sweet ingredients such as fruit. Choose chard leaves that are crisp, with some curliness. Ribs should be unblemished and uniform in color.

Pink, golden and orange chard

Swiss chard

Turnip greens

Portabella mushrooms

Morel mushrooms

Hen of the woods mushrooms

Turnip Greens

The leaves of the turnip root have a pleasantly bitter flavor, similar to peppery mustard greens. The dark green turnip leaves are long, slender and deeply indented. Turnip greens are best eaten steamed, sautéed, baked or microwaved.

Mushrooms and Truffles

Mushrooms and truffles are fungi, which have no seeds, stems or flowers; they reproduce through microscopic spores. Cultivated mushrooms are grown above ground on a moist substrate of wood, wood chips, straw or sawdust. In the wild, mushrooms are often found growing around trees or on decaying fallen trees and limbs, where the fungal spores sprout from the soil. Mushrooms do not need light; they grow best in dark, cool, humid conditions. Mushrooms are valuable for the nutrition they offer; they are high in certain vitamins, low in calories and contain no fat. Some varieties of mushrooms have a meaty texture that makes them popular in vegetarian dishes or as a meat substitute.

Truffles are a variety of fungus that grows like a tuber attached to tree roots just below ground. Truffles have a strong preference for the chalky soil around oak, hazelnut and beech trees. They can only be cultivated by planting groves of such trees and waiting, sometimes for many years. Once a grove becomes productive, truffles will appear annually but to be harvested they must be located and rooted out by animals (originally pigs, but trained dogs are now preferred) that are attracted to the fungus' distinctive aroma.

Oyster mushrooms

Mushrooms

Mushrooms (Fr. *champignons*; It. *funghi*) have a stalk with an umbrellalike top. Although not actually a vegetable, mushrooms are used and served in much the same manner as vegetables.

Several types of cultivated mushroom are available. They include the common (or white), shiitake, cremini (also known as the Italian brown), beech, straw, enokidake (also called enoki), king oyster, blue foot and cloud ear (also known as wood ear or Chinese black). Button mushrooms are the smallest, most immature form of the common mushroom. The largest cultivated mushroom is the portabella, which is an overgrown cremini; portabellas can be up to 6 inches (15 centimeters) in diameter.

Many wild mushrooms are gathered and sold by specialty purveyors. Because wild mushroom spores are spread around the world by air currents, the same item may be found in several areas, each with a different common name. Wild mushrooms have a stronger earthy or nutty flavor than cultivated mushrooms and should be cooked before eating.

Mushrooms, whether cultivated or gathered from the wild, are available fresh, canned or dried. Because mushrooms are composed of up to 80 percent water, dried products are often the most economical, even though they may cost hundreds of dollars per pound. Dried mushrooms can be stored in a cool, dry place for months. When needed, they are rehydrated by soaking in warm water until soft, approximately 10–20 minutes.

Enokidake (enoki) mushrooms

Porcini (cèpe or cep) mushrooms

Black trumpet mushrooms

Shiitake mushrooms

White (button) mushrooms

> ### ⚠ Safety Alert
>
> *Mushroom Safety*
>
> Some mushrooms are deadly; others can cause severe illness. Picking edible mushrooms in the wild is not simply a process of comparing specimens with photographs or illustrations in a guidebook. Do not gather mushrooms from the wild unless you are accompanied by a well-trained, experienced mycologist or guide. Always purchase wild mushrooms from reputable purveyors.

Choose fresh mushrooms that are clean, without soft or moist spots or blemishes. Cultivated mushrooms with exposed gills (the ridges on the underside of the umbrellalike top) are old and should be avoided. Fresh mushrooms can be refrigerated in an open container for up to 5 days. Normally it is not necessary to peel mushrooms; if they are dirty, they should be quickly rinsed (not soaked) in cool water just before use. Peel mushrooms when the skin is discolored or when a more uniform color is desired.

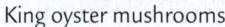

King oyster mushrooms

Blue foot mushrooms

Procedure for Fluting Mushrooms

Use the sharp edge of a straight paring knife to cut thin curves into the mushroom cap. Fluted mushrooms may be baked or poached, then used as garnish.

Truffles

Two principal varieties of European truffles are the Périgord (black) and the Piedmontese (white). Fresh truffles are gathered in the fall and should be used promptly. Truffles, especially white ones, have a strong aroma and flavor, requiring only a small amount to add their special flavor to soups, sauces, pasta and other items. Black truffles are often used as a garnish or to flavor pâtés, terrines or egg dishes. Because fresh truffles can cost hundreds of dollars per pound, most kitchens purchase truffles canned, dried or processed. Avoid imitation truffles originating from Asia or Africa as the flavor and aroma is inferior. True truffles are never inexpensive.

Black truffles

Onions

Onions are strongly flavored, aromatic members of the lily family. Most have edible grasslike or tubular leaves. Almost every culture incorporates onions into its cuisine as a vegetable and for flavoring.

Bulb Onions

Common or bulb onions (Fr. *oignons*) may be white, yellow (Bermuda or Spanish) or red (purple). Medium-sized yellow and white onions are the most strongly flavored. Larger onions tend to be sweeter and milder. Onions are indispensable in mirepoix. Onions are also prepared as side dishes by deep-frying, roasting, grilling, steaming or boiling.

Pearl onions are small, about ½ inch (1.25 centimeters) in diameter, with yellow or white skins. These small bulb onions have a mild flavor and can be grilled, boiled, roasted or sautéed whole as a side dish, or used in soups or stews. Cipollini, Italian for

Red onion

Yellow onion

Shallots

Pearl onions

Walla Walla sweet onions   White onions

small onions, are a small, slightly flat, mild bulb onion variety that can be pickled, roasted or stewed.

Sweet onion varieties include the Vidalia, Maui, Walla Walla, Texas 1015 SuperSweet and Oso Sweet. Sweet bulb onions have a higher water content, more sugar and less sulfuric compounds than other onions. They are best for eating raw, making them good choices for sandwiches, salads, hamburgers and the like. Cooking destroys much of the perceived sweetness and special flavor. All sweet onions have a very short shelf life and should not be stored more than a few weeks.

Choose onions that are firm and dry and feel heavy. The outer skins should be dry and brittle. Avoid onions that have begun to sprout. Store onions in a cool, dry, well-ventilated area. Do not refrigerate onions until they are cut.

Garlic

Garlic

Like onions, garlic (Fr. *ail*; It. *aglio*; Sp. *ajo*) is used in almost all the world's cuisines. A head or bulb of garlic is composed of many small cloves. The entire head is encased in several thin layers of papery husk; each **clove** is wrapped in a thin husk or peel. Of the 300 or so types of garlic known, only three are commercially significant. The most common is pure white, with a sharp flavor. A Mexican variety is pale pink and more strongly flavored. Elephant garlic is apple-sized and particularly mild. Black garlic is not a variety, but the result of a detailed heating and aging process applied to common white garlic. Used in Northeast Asia for its purported health benefits, black garlic is chewy, with a mild, sweet, molasses-like flavor. Although whole heads of garlic can be baked or roasted, garlic is most often separated into cloves, peeled, sliced, minced or crushed and used to flavor a wide variety of dishes. When using garlic, remember that the more finely the cloves are crushed, the stronger the flavor is. Cooking reduces garlic's pungency; the longer garlic is cooked, the milder it becomes. Choose firm, dry garlic bulbs with tightly closed cloves and smooth skins. Avoid bulbs with green sprouts. Store fresh garlic in a cool, well-ventilated place; do not refrigerate. Jars of processed and pickled garlic products are also available.

Leeks

Leeks

Leeks (Fr. *poireaux*) look like large, overgrown scallions with a fat white tip and wide green leaves. Their flavor is sweeter and stronger than scallions but milder than common bulb onions. Leeks must be carefully washed to remove the sandy soil that gets between the leaves. Leeks can be baked, braised or grilled as a side dish, or used to season stocks, soups or sauces. Choose leeks that are firm, with stiff roots and stems. Avoid those with dry leaves, soft spots or browning.

Procedure for Cleaning Leeks

❶ Trim the root end from the leek.

❷ Cut away the dark green top and slice the white portion in half lengthwise.

❸ Rinse the cut leek thoroughly under running water to remove soil.

The Olive

Olives (*Olea europaea*) are the fruit of a tree native to the Mediterranean area. Green olives are harvested unripened; black olives are fully ripened. The fruit is inedibly bitter and must be washed, soaked and cured or pickled before eating. Green olives should have a smooth, tight skin. Ripe olives are glossy but softer, with a slightly wrinkled skin. Many varieties and flavors of olives are available, from the tiny black French Niçoise to the large purplish Greek Kalamata. Black olives are packaged in a range of seven sizes, from small to supercolossal. Green olives are available in 11 sizes, from subpetite to supercolossal. Both black and green olives are available whole (with the pit), pitted, sliced, halved or in pieces. Pitted green olives are often stuffed with strips of pimento, jalapeño pepper, almonds or other foods for flavor and appearance.

Olives are served as a finger food for snacks or hors d'oeuvre, or added to salads, pastas, breads, soups, sauces, stews and casseroles. A paste made of minced ripe olives, known as **tapenade**, is used as a dip or condiment.

Jumbo Spanish olives

Ripe California olives

Kalamata olives

Niçoise olives

Scallions

Scallions, also known as green onions or bunch onions, are the immature green stalks of bulb onions. The leaves are bright green with either a long and slender or slightly bulbous white base. Green onions are used in stir-fries and as a flavoring in other dishes. The green tops can also be sliced in small rings and used as a garnish. Choose scallions with bright green tops and clean white bulbs. Avoid those with limp or slimy leaves.

Shallots

Shallots (Fr. *échalotes*) are shaped like small bulb onions with one flat side. When peeled, a shallot separates into multiple cloves, similar to garlic. Shallots have a mild, yet rich and complex flavor. Shallots are the basis of many classic sauces and meat preparations; they can also be sautéed or baked as a side dish. Choose shallots that are plump, symmetrical and heavy for their size. Avoid those that appear dry or have sprouted. Store shallots in a cool, dry, unrefrigerated place.

Pods and Seeds

Pod and seed vegetables include corn, legumes and okra. We group them together here because the parts consumed are the seeds of their respective plants. In some cases only the seeds are eaten; in others the pod containing the seeds is eaten as well. Seeds are generally higher in protein and carbohydrates (starch and dietary fiber) than other vegetables.

Corn

Sweet corn (Fr. *maïs*; Sp. *maíz*) is a grain, a type of grass. Corn kernels, like peas, are plant seeds. (Dried corn products are discussed in Chapter 23, Potatoes, Grains and Pasta.) Corn kernels, which may be white or yellow, are attached to a woody, inedible cob. The cob is encased by strands of hairlike fibers called silks and covered in layers of thin leaves called husks. Shuck the ears (remove the silks and husks) before cooking; the husks may be left on for roasting or grilling, however. Shucked corn on the cob can be grilled, boiled, microwaved or steamed. The kernels can be cut off the cob before or after cooking. Corn on the cob is available fresh or frozen; corn kernels are available canned or frozen. Choose freshly picked ears with firm, small kernels. Avoid those with mold or decay at the tip of the cob or brownish silks. Seek out the freshest corn on the cob and serve it promptly because its sugar turns to starch once it is picked.

Scallions

Shallots

Yellow and white corn

Procedure for Cutting Kernels Off Ears of Corn

Hold the cob upright and use a chef's knife to slice off the kernels.

Legumes

Beans (Fr. *haricots*; It. *fagioli*) and peas (Fr. *pois*) are members of the legume family, a large group of vegetables with double-seamed pods containing a single row of seeds. Of the hundreds of known varieties of beans, some are used for their edible pods, others for shelling (removing from the pod) fresh and some only for their dried seeds. Dried beans are seeds or peas left in the pod until mature, then shelled and dried.

Fresh Beans

Beans with edible pods, commonly referred to as green beans, string beans, runner beans or snap beans, are picked when immature. Except for the stem, the entire pod can be eaten. This category includes the American green bean, the yellow wax bean, the broad bean and the French haricot vert, a long, slender pod with an intense flavor and tender texture. Any strings along the pod's seams should be pulled off before cooking. Beans may be left whole, cut lengthwise into thin slivers (referred to as French cut) or cut crosswise on the diagonal.

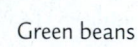
Green beans

Shelling beans are grown primarily for the edible seeds inside the pod. Common examples are flageolets, lima beans and fava (broad) beans. Their tough pods are not usually eaten.

All fresh beans can be prepared by steaming, microwaving or sautéing. They can be added to soups or stews, and they blend well with a variety of flavors, from coconut milk to garlic and olive oil. Cooked beans can be chilled and served as a salad or crudité. Choose fresh beans that have a bright color without brown or soft spots. Large pods may be tough or bitter. Most fresh bean varieties are available frozen or canned, including pickled and seasoned products.

Fava (broad) beans

Haricots verts

Dried Beans

For thousands of years, cultures around the world have preserved certain legumes by drying. Common dried beans include kidney beans, pinto beans, chickpeas, lentils, black beans, black-eyed peas and split green peas. Shape is the clearest distinction among these products: Beans are oval or kidney-shaped; lentils are small, flat disks; peas are round.

Beans and peas destined for drying are left on the vine until they are fully matured and just beginning to dry. They are then harvested, shelled and quickly dried with warm air currents. Some dried legumes are sold split, which means the skin is removed, causing the seed's two halves to separate.

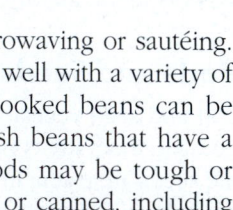

Black beans

Red kidney beans

Pinto beans

Most dried beans need to be soaked in water before cooking. Soaking softens and rehydrates the beans, thus reducing cooking time. Lentils and split peas generally do not require soaking, however, and cook faster than dried beans. After soaking, dried beans are most often simmered or baked in a liquid until soft and tender. Most types of dried beans may be substituted for one another in most recipes, although variations in color, starch content and flavor should be considered.

Lentils

Great Northern beans

Black-eyed peas

Dried beans and peas are available in bulk or in 1-pound (450-gram) poly bags. They should be stored in a cool, dry place, but not refrigerated. Many types of dried beans are also available fully cooked, then canned or frozen. Some dried beans are fermented or processed into flour, oil, bean curd or sauce.

Procedure for Soaking Dried Beans

1 Pick through the dried beans and remove any grit, pebbles or debris.
2 Place the beans in a bowl and cover with cold water; remove any skins or other items that float to the surface.
3 Drain the beans in a colander, then rinse under cold running water.
4 Return the beans to a bowl and cover with fresh cold water. Allow approximately 3 cups (750 milliliters) water for each cup of beans.
5 Soak the beans in the cold water for the time specified in the recipe, usually several hours or overnight. Drain through a colander, discarding the water.

Procedure for Quick-Soaking Dried Beans

The soaking procedure can be accelerated by the following technique:

1 Rinse and pick through the beans.
2 Place the beans in a saucepan and add enough cool water to cover them by 2 inches (5 centimeters).
3 Bring to a boil and simmer for 2 minutes.
4 Remove from the heat, cover and soak for 1 hour.
5 Drain and discard the soaking liquid. Proceed with the recipe.

Fresh Shelling Peas

Of the shelling peas that are prepared fresh, the most common are green garden peas (English peas) and the French petit pois. Because they lose flavor rapidly after harvest, most shelling peas are sold frozen or canned. Shelling peas have a delicate, sweet flavor best presented by simply steaming until tender but still al dente. Peas may also be braised with rich meats such as ham or used in soups. Cooked peas are attractive in salads or as garnish. Choose small fresh pea pods that are plump and moist.

Fresh shelling peas

Fresh soybeans

Fresh green **soybeans (soya)** (Ja. *edamame*) are a type of shelling pea picked before maturity. Fresh soybeans have a light green, fuzzy pod and a tender, sweet pea. They are steamed in the pod, then popped open and eaten out of hand as a snack and are often served this way in sushi restaurants. When allowed to mature and then prepared like other dried beans, however, soybeans become extremely tough, hard to digest and bitter. Mature soybeans are best used for processing into oil, tofu, soy sauce and other foodstuffs.

Snow peas

Edible Pea Pods

Snow peas, also known as Chinese pea pods, are a common variety of edible pea pod. They are flat with only a few very small green peas. Snow peas have a string along their seams that can be removed by holding the leafy stem and pulling from end to end. Edible pea pods can be served raw, lightly blanched or steamed, or stir-fried.

Procedure for Preparing Snow Peas

Use a paring knife to grab the leafy stem and then pull the string from snow peas.

Pea shoots

Another variety of edible pea pod is the sugar snap pea, a cross between the garden pea and snow pea. Sugar snap peas are plump, juicy pods filled with small, tender peas. The entire pod is eaten; do not shell the peas before cooking. Choose pea pods that are firm, bright green and crisp. Avoid those with brown spots or a shriveled appearance.

Pea shoots are the delicate tendrils that form before the plant bears pods. In Chinese cuisine, the shoots are harvested and stir-fried like spinach or other leafy greens. Tendrils are also used raw as a garnish.

Okra

Okra, a common ingredient in African and Arab cuisines, was brought to the United States by slaves and French settlers. It is now integral to Creole, Cajun, southern and southwestern cuisines. Its mild flavor is similar to asparagus. Okra is not eaten raw; it is best pickled, boiled, steamed or deep-fried. Okra develops a gelatinous texture when cooked for long periods, so it is used to thicken gumbos and stews. To avoid the slimy texture that some people find objectionable, do not wash okra until ready to cook, then trim the stem end only. Cook okra in stainless steel because other metals cause discoloration. Choose small to medium pods (1½–2 inches/3.75–5 centimeters) that are deep green, without soft spots. Pale spears with stiff tips tend to be tough. Frozen okra is widely available.

Okra

Roots and Tubers

Taproots (more commonly referred to as roots) are single roots that extend deep into the soil to supply the plant with nutrients. Tubers are fat underground stems. Most roots and tubers can be used interchangeably. All store well at cool temperatures, without refrigeration. Potatoes, the most popular tuber, are discussed in Chapter 23, Potatoes, Grains and Pasta.

Beets

Beets

Although history suggests that they were first eaten in ancient Greece, beets are associated with cold northern climates, where they grow most of the year. Both the beet root and the green leaves are eaten. Common beets have a deep reddish-purple flesh and are cooked by boiling, steaming or roasting, then peeled and used in soups, salads or as a side dish. Pickling is a traditional preservation method still used for beets. Golden beets have orange, yellow or variegated flesh and are prepared in the same manner. Beet leaves, called greens, are high in vitamins, potassium and iron. Beet greens can be cooked by boiling, sautéing or slow simmering. Choose medium sized beets that are firm, with smooth skins. Avoid beets with hairy root tips, as they may be tough. Small and baby-sized beets are often used for garnish or in salads.

Golden beets

Carrots

Carrots (Fr. *carottes*), among the most versatile of vegetables, are large taproots. Although several kinds of carrots exist, the Imperator is the most common. It is long and pointed, with a medium to dark orange color and a mild, sweet flavor. Carrots can be cut into a variety of shapes and eaten raw, used in mirepoix or prepared by moist-heat cooking methods, grilling, microwaving or roasting. They are also grated raw and used in baked goods, particularly cakes and muffins. Choose firm carrots that are smooth and well-shaped, with a bright orange color. If the tops are still attached, they should be fresh-looking and bright green.

Carrots

Celery Root

Celery root, also known as celeriac, is a large, round root, long popular in northern European cuisines. It is a different plant from stalk celery, and its stalks and leaves are not eaten. Celery root has a knobby brown exterior; a creamy white, crunchy flesh; and a mild, celerylike flavor. Its thick outer skin must be peeled off; the flesh is then cut as desired. Often eaten raw, celery root can also be baked, steamed or boiled. It is used in soups, stews or salads and goes well with game and rich meats. Place raw celery root in acidulated water to prevent browning. Choose small to medium-sized celery roots that are firm and relatively clean, with a pungent smell.

Celery root

Jerusalem Artichoke

Despite their name, Jerusalem artichokes are actually tubers from a variety of sunflower unrelated to artichokes. Consequently growers are now marketing these vegetables as **sunchokes**. Their lumpy brown skin is usually peeled off (even though the skin is edible) to reveal a crisp, white interior with a slightly nutty flavor. Although they may be eaten raw, cooking them before serving makes them easier to digest. Jerusalem artichokes are eaten chopped or grated into salads, or boiled or steamed for a side dish or soup.

Jerusalem artichokes (sunchokes)

Jicama

Jicama is a legume that grows underground as a tuber. Jicama is popular because of its sweet, moist flavor; crisp texture; low calorie content and long shelf life. After its thick brown skin is peeled off, the crisp, moist white flesh can be cut as desired. Jicama is often eaten raw in salads, with salsa or as a crudité. It is also used in stir-fried dishes. Choose firm, well-shaped jicamas that are free of blemishes. Size is not an indication of quality or maturity.

Jicama

Parsnips

Parsnips (Fr. *panais*) are taproots that look and taste like white carrots and have the texture of sweet potatoes. Parsnips should be 5–10 inches (12.5–25 centimeters) in length, with smooth skins and tapering tips. Parsnips, peeled like carrots, can be eaten raw or cooked by almost any method. When steamed until very soft, they can be mashed like potatoes. Choose small to medium-sized parsnips that are firm, smooth and well-shaped; avoid large, woody ones.

Parsnips

Radishes

Radishes (Fr. *radis*) have a peppery flavor and crisp texture. Radishes are available in many colors, including white, black and all shades of red; most have a creamy to pure white interior. Asian radishes, known as **daikons**, produce roots 2–4 inches (5–10 centimeters) in diameter and 6–20 inches (15–20 centimeters) long. Radishes can be braised, steamed or stir-fried, but most often are eaten raw or in salads or used as garnish. Radish leaves can be used in salads or cooked as greens. Choose radishes that are firm, not limp. Their interior should not be dry or hollow.

Daikon

Red radishes

Procedure for Making Radish Rosettes

With a straight paring knife, make parallel horizontal and vertical cuts three quarters of the way through the root end of a cleaned radish.

Rutabagas

Rutabagas

Rutabagas are a root vegetable and a member of the cabbage family. The skin is purple to yellow, and the flesh is yellow with a distinctive starchy, cabbage-like flavor. Rutabagas and turnips are similar in flavor and texture when cooked and may be used interchangeably. Rutabaga leaves are not eaten. Rutabagas should be peeled with a vegetable peeler or chef's knife, and then cut into quarters, slices or cubes. They are often baked, boiled and then puréed, or sliced and sautéed. Rutabagas are especially flavorful when seasoned with caraway seeds, dill or lemon juice. Choose small to medium-sized rutabagas that are smooth and firm and feel heavy.

Turnips

Also a root vegetable from the cabbage family, turnips have white skin with a rosy-red or purple blush and a white interior. Their flavor, similar to that of a radish, can be rather hot. Turnips should be peeled, then diced, sliced or julienned for cooking. They may be baked or cooked with moist-heat cooking methods, and are often puréed like potatoes. Choose small to medium-sized turnips that have smooth skin and feel heavy. They should be firm, not rubbery or limp. Any attached leaves should be bright green and tender.

Water Chestnuts

Water chestnuts are the tuber of an Asian plant that thrives in water. The brownish-black skin is peeled away to reveal a moist, crisp, white interior, which can be eaten raw or cooked. When cooked, water chestnuts retain their crunchy texture, making them a popular addition to stir-fried dishes. They are also used in salads and casseroles or wrapped in bacon for hors d'oeuvre.

Stalk Vegetables

Stalk vegetables are plant stems with a high percentage of **cellulose**, a type of insoluble dietary fiber. These vegetables should be picked while still young and tender and any tough outer layers or peel should be removed or trimmed before cooking.

Artichokes

Artichokes (Fr. *artichauts*) are the immature flowers of a thistle plant introduced to America by Italian and Spanish settlers. Young, tender artichokes can be cooked whole, but more mature plants need to have the fuzzy center (known as the choke) removed first. Whole artichokes can be simmered, steamed or microwaved; they are often served with lemon juice, garlic butter or hollandaise sauce. The heart may be cooked separately, then served in salads, puréed as a filling or served as a side dish. Place raw trimmed artichokes in acidulated water to prevent browning. Choose fresh artichokes with tight, compact heads that feel heavy. Their color should be solid green to gray-green. Brown spots on the surface caused by frost are harmless. Artichoke hearts and leafless artichoke bottoms are both available canned.

Turnips

Water chestnuts

cellulose fiber found in the cell wall of plants; it is edible but indigestible by humans

Artichokes

Procedure for Preparing Fresh Artichokes

❶ With a pair of kitchen shears or scissors, trim the barbs from the large outer leaves of the artichoke.

❷ With a chef's knife, cut away the stem and the top of the artichoke. Steam or boil the artichoke as desired.

Procedure for Cleaning Artichoke Hearts

❶ Cut off the stem and the outer leaves from the artichoke.

❷ Trim the inner stem from the base with a chef's knife.

❸ Using a paring knife, trim the edges into a neat cup with no tough leaves remaining.

❹ Scoop out the fuzzy choke with a melon ball cutter.

❺ The cleaned artichoke bottoms are ready to cook.

Asparagus

Asparagus (Fr. *aspèrges*), a member of the lily family, has bright green spears with a ruffle of tiny leaves at the tip. Larger spears tend to be tough and woody but can be used in soups or for purée. Asparagus is eaten raw or steamed briefly, stir-fried, microwaved or grilled. Fresh spring asparagus is excellent with nothing more than lemon juice or clarified butter; asparagus with hollandaise sauce is a classic preparation.

Choose firm, plump spears with tightly closed tips and a bright green color running the full length of the spear. Asparagus should be stored refrigerated at 40°F (4°C), upright in ½ inch (1.25 centimeters) of water or with the ends wrapped in moist paper towels. The stalks should not be washed until just before use. Canned and frozen asparagus are also available.

A European variety of white asparagus is sometimes available fresh or readily available canned. White asparagus has a milder flavor and soft, tender texture. It is produced by covering the asparagus stalks with soil as they grow; this prevents sunlight from reaching the plant and retards the development of chlorophyll, the green-colored natural chemical that plants produce.

Asparagus

Procedure for Peeling Asparagus

Remove the tough outer skin from large asparagus spears with a vegetable peeler.

Bamboo Shoots

Stripped of their tough brown outer skins, the tender young shoots of certain varieties of bamboo are edible. Bamboo shoots make excellent additions to stir-fried dishes or they can be served like asparagus. Although fresh shoots are available in Asia, canned peeled shoots packed in brine or water are more common in the United States. Canned shoots should be rinsed well before use.

Fresh bamboo shoots

Celery

Once a medicinal herb, stalk celery (Fr. *céleri*) is now a common sight in kitchens worldwide. Stalk celery is pale green with stringy curved stalks. Often eaten raw in salads or as a snack, celery can be braised or steamed as a side dish. Celery is also a mirepoix component. Choose stalks that are crisp, without any sign of dryness.

Celery

Procedure for Peeling Celery

Use a paring knife to grasp strings from the outside of a piece of celery, and then gently pull them away.

Fennel

Chioggia beets

Fennel

Fennel (Fr. *fenouil*, It. *finocchio*) is a Mediterranean favorite used for thousands of years as a vegetable (the bulb), an herb (the leaves) and a spice (the seeds). The fennel bulb (often incorrectly referred to as sweet anise) has short, tight, overlapping celerylike stalks with feathery leaves. The flavor is similar to that of anise or licorice, becoming milder when cooked.

Fennel bulbs may be eaten raw or grilled, steamed, sautéed, baked or microwaved. Choose a fairly large, bright white bulb on which the cut edges appear fresh, without dryness or browning. The bulb should be compact, not spreading.

Baby Vegetables

Many fine restaurants serve baby vegetables: tiny turnips, finger-length squashes, miniature carrots and petite heads of cauliflower. Baby vegetables include both hybrids bred to be true miniatures as well as regular varieties picked before maturity. Baby vegetables are often marketed with blossoms or greens still attached. They tend to be easily bruised and are highly perishable. Many baby vegetables can be eaten raw, but they are usually left whole, then steamed or lightly sautéed and attractively presented as an accompaniment to meat, fish or poultry entrées.

Baby globe carrots

Baby zucchini with blossoms

Baby yellow squashes with blossoms

NUTRITION INFORMATION FOR VEGETABLES

Most vegetables are more than 80 percent water; the remaining portions consist of carbohydrates (primarily starches) and small amounts of protein and fat. The relative lack of protein and fat makes most vegetables especially low in calories.

Much of a vegetable's physical structure is provided by generally indigestible substances, specifically two types of dietary fiber, cellulose and **lignin**. The dietary fiber in vegetables produces the characteristic stringy, crisp or fibrous textures associated with vegetables.

Vegetables are also a good source of vitamins and minerals. They are important dietary sources of vitamins A, C and the B group, folate and potassium. Brassicas and legumes are good sources of Omega-3, a fatty acid tied to reduced risk of heart disease. Care must be taken during preparation to preserve the nutritional content of vegetables, however. Once peeled or cut, vegetables lose nutrients to the air or to any liquid in which they are allowed to soak. Water-soluble vitamins and folate are sensitive to air and heat. Prepare vegetable by steaming and reserve their cooking liquid when possible. Many vitamins are concentrated just under the skin, so peel vegetables thinly, if at all.

lignin organic substance that binds together the cells in wood and woody vegetables

PURCHASING AND STORING FRESH VEGETABLES

Fresh vegetables should be selected according to seasonal availability. Using a vegetable at the peak of its season has several advantages: Price is at its lowest, selection is at its greatest and the vegetable's color, flavor and texture are at their best. The prime growing seasons for each vegetable depends on the region of the country where it is grown. Consult Appendix II, Fresh, Locally-Grown Produce Availability Chart, and speak to your produce supplier and local farmers to learn what is available seasonally in your location.

Grading Vegetables

The USDA has a voluntary grading system for fresh vegetables traded on wholesale markets. The system is based on appearance, condition and other factors affecting waste or eating quality. Grades for all vegetables include, in descending order of quality, U.S. Extra Fancy, U.S. Fancy, U.S. Extra No. 1 and U.S. No. 1. There are also grades that apply only to specific vegetables (e.g., U.S. No. 1 Boilers for onions).

Consumer or retail grading is currently required only for a few products, such as potatoes, carrots and onions. This grading system uses alphabetical listings, with Grade A being the finest.

Purchasing Vegetables

Fresh vegetables are sold by weight or count. They are packed in cartons referred to as cases, lugs, bushels, flats or crates. The weight or count packed in each of these containers varies depending on the size and type of vegetable as well as the packer. For example, celery is packed in 55-pound cartons containing 18–48 heads, depending on the size of each head.

Some of the more common fresh vegetables (e.g., onions, carrots, celery and lettuces) can be purchased from wholesalers trimmed, cleaned and cut according to your specifications. Although the unit price will be higher for diced onions than for whole onions, for example, the savings in time, labor, yield loss and storage space can be substantial. Processed vegetables may suffer a loss of nutrients, moisture and flavor, however.

Ripening Vegetables

Although vegetables do not ripen in the same manner as fruits, they do continue to breathe (respire) after harvesting. The faster the respiration rate, the faster the produce ages or decays. This decay results in wilted leaves and dry, tough or woody stems and stalks. Respiration rates vary according to the vegetable variety, its maturity at harvest and its storage conditions after harvest.

Ripening proceeds more rapidly in the presence of ethylene gas. Ethylene gas is emitted naturally by fruits and vegetables and can be used to encourage further ripening in some produce, especially fruit vegetables such as tomatoes. Items harvested and shipped when mature but green (unripe) can be exposed to ethylene gas to induce color development (ripening) just before sale.

Storing Vegetables

When storing fresh vegetables, always ensure there is good airflow and the proper temperature to prevent spoilage. Some fresh vegetables are best stored at cool temperatures, between 50°F and 60°F (10°C and 16°C), ideally in a separate produce refrigerator. These include winter squashes, potatoes, onions, shallots and garlic. If a produce refrigerator is not available, store these vegetables at room temperature in a dry area with good ventilation. Do not store them in a refrigerator set at conventional temperatures. Colder temperatures convert the starches in these vegetables to sugars, changing their texture and flavor.

Most other vegetables benefit from cold storage at temperatures between 34°F and 40°F (2°C and 4°C) with relatively high levels of humidity. Greens and other delicate vegetables should be stored away from apples, tomatoes, bananas and melons, as the latter give off a great deal of ethylene gas. Avocadoes and tomatoes continue to ripen when stored at room temperature. Tomato cells break down in colder temperatures

altering their texture. Tomatoes should be stored at room temperature and used quickly. When buying root vegetables with the greens attached, remove the greens, which can leech moisture from the root, before refrigerating. (Use the greens as soon as possible.) As noted earlier, Brussels sprouts last longer on the stem, but their flavor intensifies with age.

Clean produce immediately before use. Moisture from washing may cause bacterial growth and spoilage.

PURCHASING AND STORING PRESERVED VEGETABLES

Preservation techniques, including irradiation, canning, freezing and drying, extend the shelf life of vegetables. Except for drying, these techniques do not substantially change the vegetable's texture or flavor. Canning and freezing can also be used to preserve cooked vegetables.

Irradiated Vegetables

The irradiation process uses ionizing radiation (usually gamma rays of cobalt 60 or cesium 137) to sterilize foods. When foods are subjected to radiation, parasites, insects and bacteria are destroyed, ripening is slowed and sprouting is prevented. Irradiation works without a noticeable increase in temperature; consequently the flavor and texture of fresh foods are not affected. Some nutrients, however, may be destroyed. Irradiated vegetables do not need to be sprayed with post-harvest pesticides, and they have an extended shelf life.

The FDA classifies irradiation as a food additive. Although irradiation is not yet approved for all foods, grains, fruits and vegetables may be treated with low-dose radiation. Irradiated foods must be labeled "Treated with radiation" or "Treated by irradiation." The symbol shown in Figure 22.1 may also be used. Irradiated produce is purchased, stored and used like fresh produce.

Canned Vegetables

Canned vegetables are the backbone of menu planning for many food service operations. In commercial canning, raw vegetables are cleaned and placed in a sealed container, then subjected to high temperatures for a specific period. Heating destroys the microorganisms that cause spoilage, and the sealed environment created by the can eliminates oxidation and retards decomposition. But the heat required by the canning process also softens the texture of most vegetables and alters their nutritional content; many vitamins and minerals may be lost through the canning process. Green vegetables may also suffer color loss, becoming a drab olive color.

Canned vegetables are graded by the USDA as U.S. Grade A or Fancy, U.S. Grade B or Extra-Select, and U.S. Grade C or Standard. U.S. Grade A vegetables must be top quality, tender and free of blemishes. U.S. Grade C vegetables may lack uniformity or flavor, but can be used in casseroles or soups when cost is a concern.

Combinations of vegetables as well as vegetables with seasonings and sauces are available canned. For example, corn kernels are available canned in water, in seasonings and sauces, combined with other vegetables or creamed. Canned vegetables are easy to serve because they are essentially fully cooked during the canning process.

Canned vegetables are purchased in cases of standard-sized cans. See "Canned Good Sizes" in Appendix I, Measurement and Conversion Charts. They may also be packaged in vacuum-sealed foil packages. Canned vegetables can be stored almost indefinitely at room temperature. Once a can is opened, any unused contents should be transferred to an appropriate storage container and refrigerated. Cans with bulges–a sign of the growth of harmful toxins–should be discarded immediately, without opening.

Figure 22.1 Irradiation symbol.

Hydroponics: Working Water

Hydroponics is the science of growing plants in water without soil in an inert medium such as gravel, peat, sand or other sterile material. Nutrients are distributed in water that is circulated over the plant's roots. In a hydroponic farm temperature and light are controlled to maximize production. Because hydroponic farms are indoors, plants can be grown in any climate; both Canada and Holland are major producers of hydroponically grown vegetables.

Lettuce growing hydroponically

Frozen Vegetables

Frozen vegetables are almost as convenient to use as canned. However they often require some cooking as well as expensive freezer space. Regardless, freezing is a highly effective method for preserving vegetables. It severely inhibits the growth of microorganisms that cause spoilage without destroying many nutrients. Generally frozen green vegetables retain their color, although the appearance and texture of most frozen vegetables is somewhat altered by freezing. Because of the high water content in vegetables, ice crystals form from the water in the cells and burst the cells' walls during the freezing process.

Some vegetables are available **individually quick frozen (IQF)**. This method employs blasts of cold air, refrigerated plates, liquid nitrogen, liquid air or other techniques to chill the vegetables quickly. Speeding the freezing process can greatly reduce the formation of ice crystals.

Combinations of vegetables as well as vegetables with seasonings and sauces are available frozen. Vegetable may be chopped or sliced before freezing. Some frozen vegetables are raw when frozen; others are blanched before freezing so that final cooking time is reduced and color is preserved. Others are fully cooked before freezing and only need to be thawed or heated for service. Frozen vegetables generally do not need to be thawed before being heated. Once thawed or cooked, frozen vegetables should be stored in the refrigerator and reheated in the same manner as fresh vegetables. Do not refreeze previously frozen vegetables.

Frozen vegetables are graded in the same manner as canned vegetables. They are usually packed in cases containing 1- to 2-pound (450- to 900-gram) boxes or bags. All frozen vegetables should be sealed in moisture-proof wrapping and kept at a constant temperature of 0°F (–18°C) or below. Temperature fluctuations can draw moisture from the vegetables, causing poor texture and flavor loss. Adequate packaging also prevents **freezer burn**, which results in an irreversible change in the color, texture and flavor of frozen foods.

Dried Vegetables

Except for beans, peas, peppers, mushrooms and tomatoes, few vegetables are commonly preserved by drying. Unlike other preservation methods, drying dramatically alters flavor, texture and appearance. The loss of moisture concentrates flavors and sugars and greatly extends shelf life. Sun-drying is an ancient but time-consuming technique dependent on the weather. Alternatively vegetables can now be dried quickly with warm, dry circulating air. Professional kitchens are often equipped with small dehydrators for preparing dried vegetable garnishes or for preserving vegetables for later use.

COOKING METHODS FOR VEGETABLES

Vegetables are cooked in order to break down their cellulose and gelatinize their starches. Cooking gives vegetables a pleasant flavor; creates a softer, more tender texture; and makes them easier to digest. Ideally most vegetables should be cooked as briefly as possible to preserve their flavor, nutrients and texture. Unfortunately sometimes you must choose between emphasizing appearance and maintaining nutrition because cooking methods that preserve color and texture often remove nutrients.

Fiber Content and Vegetable Cookery

Although fiber in the diet is beneficial, we need to tenderize it to make some vegetables palatable. The best choice of cooking method and the length of cooking time is determined by the fiber content of the vegetable. Cooking affects the structure of vegetables by breaking down plant fiber, such as cellulose and **pectin**.

⚠ Safety Alert

Proper Washing of Vegetables

Surface contaminants from soil, water and handling must be removed from all vegetables to avoid the spread of food-borne illnesses. First remove all labels, tags and ties. Wash whole produce under cold, running water. Water temperature should be only slightly warmer than the produce being washed; cold water causes the surface of the vegetable to contract, creating a vacuum that can draw contaminated water into the plant. Soaking is not recommended because it can extract nutrients, nor is the use of soap or detergents. Potatoes, turnips and other root vegetables may be scrubbed with a clean brush to remove dirt. Refrigerate clean vegetables promptly and prevent cross-contamination during storage.

freezer burn surface dehydration and discoloration of food that results from moisture loss at below-freezing temperatures

pectin a water-soluble fiber found primarily in fruits, also a major component in some vegetables, such as carrots, fresh peas, parsnips, potatoes and green beans

Water-soluble pectin can be broken down by moist-heat cooking methods such as steaming or boiling, while vegetables containing a higher amount of cellulose (e.g., cabbage, turnips and legumes) retain their shape even when cooked with moist heat. The amount of fiber varies by type of vegetable and age. Brassicas and stalk vegetables contain a high percentage of cellulose fiber; they should be picked when young and prepared in ways to reduce the fiber. Asparagus stems are peeled, for example, so that the tender tips cook in the same amount of time as the stems, which can be woody and tough. Older vegetables are more fibrous than younger ones. Older vegetables may require a longer cooking time and will cook more quickly if cut or diced first. Vegetables that are low in fiber, such as mushrooms and spinach, cook quickly regardless of their age.

Acid/Alkali Reactions and Vegetable Cookery

The acid or alkali content of the cooking liquid affects the texture and color of many vegetables such as asparagus, broccoli, green beans and red cabbage. Discoloration of vegetables during cooking is of greater concern with moist-heat cooking methods, but it is also a consideration with dry-heat cooking methods, as they often call for blanched or parboiled vegetables.

Texture

The acidity or alkalinity of the vegetable's cooking liquid influences the finished product's texture. If an acid such as lemon juice, vinegar or wine is added to the liquid for flavoring, the vegetable will resist softening and will require a longer cooking time. On the other hand, an alkaline cooking medium, such as water with baking soda added, will quickly soften the vegetable's texture and may cause it to become mushy. Alkalinity also causes nutrient (especially thiamin) loss and may impart a bitter flavor. Alkalinity can be caused by tap water, detergent residue on utensils or the addition of baking soda (a base) to the cooking liquid. (For example, adding ⅛ teaspoon/0.6 milliliter baking soda per cup/225 milliliters of dried beans speeds softening.)

Color

The acidity or alkalinity of cooking liquid can also affect the plant's pigments, causing both desirable and undesirable color changes. There are three principal pigment categories in plants: chlorophyll, carotenoid and flavonoid. A plant's unique color is the result of a combination of these pigments. **Chlorophyll** pigments predominate in green vegetables such as spinach, green beans and broccoli. **Carotenoid** pigments predominate in orange and yellow vegetables such as carrots, tomatoes, red peppers and winter squashes. **Flavonoid** pigments predominate in red, purple and white vegetables such as red cabbage, beets and cauliflower.

Initially, as vegetables are cooked, their original colors intensify. Exposure to heat makes pigments, especially chlorophyll, appear brighter. Exposure to acids and bases affects both chlorophyll and flavonoid pigments. Acids gradually turn green vegetables an olive-drab color, whereas a slight alkalinity promotes chlorophyll retention. The opposite occurs with vegetables containing flavonoids: They retain desirable colors in a slightly acidic environment but lose colors in an alkaline one. (Carotenoids are not affected by either acidity or alkalinity.) Color changes alone do not affect flavor, but the altered appearance can make the product visually unappealing. See Table 22.1.

Colors also change as the naturally occurring acids in vegetables are released during cooking. If the cooking pan is kept covered, the acids can concentrate, creating richer flavonoid pigments but destroying chlorophyll pigments.

Therefore if color is the only concern, vegetables with a high amount of chlorophyll such as spinach should be cooked in an alkaline liquid, and vegetables with a high amount of flavonoids such as red cabbage should be cooked in an acidic liquid. But remember, the improvement in color usually comes at the expense of texture and nutrients.

ACID/ALKALI REACTIONS   TABLE 22.1

VEGETABLE	PIGMENT FAMILY	EFFECT OF ACID ON		EFFECT OF ALKALI ON*		COOK COVERED?
		COLOR	TEXTURE	COLOR	TEXTURE	
Spinach, broccoli	chlorophyll	olive-drab green	firm	bright green	mushy	no
Carrots, rutabagas	carotenoid	no change	firm	no change	mushy	no difference
Cauliflower	flavonoid	white	firm	yellow	mushy	yes
Red cabbage	flavonoid	red	firm	blue	mushy	yes

*Alkalinity always causes a loss of thiamin and other nutrients.

❶ Spinach cooked with an alkali (left) and an acid (right).

❷ Cauliflower cooked with an alkali (left) and an acid (right).

❸ Red cabbage cooked with an alkali (left) and an acid (right).

Guidelines for Vegetable Cookery

The following general guidelines for vegetable cookery should be considered regardless of the cooking method used:

- Carefully cut vegetables into uniform shapes and sizes to promote even cooking and provide an attractive finished product.
- Peel the tough outer skin on vegetables such as squashes and turnips, and trim any tough leaves or woody stems as needed to ensure tenderness after cooking.
- Cook vegetables for as short a time as possible to preserve texture, color and nutrients.
- Cook vegetables as close to service time as possible so that they retain nutrients and look appetizing. Pre-cooked vegetables held in a steam table or sauté pan near the stovetop soon become overcooked.
- When necessary, vegetables may be blanched in advance, refreshed in ice water and refrigerated. They can then be reheated as needed.
- To help retain their color, cook white and red vegetables (those with flavonoid pigments) with a small amount of acid such as lemon juice, vinegar or white wine.
- When preparing an assortment of vegetables, cook each type separately, then combine them. If cooked together, some vegetables become overcooked in the time required to properly cook others.

Determining Doneness of Vegetables

Chefs find vegetables exciting to prepare because of the variety of colors, flavors and textures they provide. Because there are so many types of vegetables, with such varied responses to cooking, no one standard for doneness is appropriate. Generally most cooked vegetables are done when they are just tender when pierced with a fork or the tip of a paring knife. Starchy vegetables should hold their shape but yield to a fork. Green vegetables should be tender yet retain their color. Leafy vegetables should be wilted but still have a bright color and be tender with no stringiness.

Avoid overcooking vegetables by remembering that some carryover cooking will occur through the residual heat contained in the foods. Always rely on subjective tests—sight, feel, taste and aroma—rather than the clock.

Preserving Nutritional Qualities in Vegetables

Just as cooking alters the physical properties of vegetables, it also affects vitamin, mineral and antioxidant properties. Raw vegetables have more vitamins and minerals than cooked vegetables. The fiber content of raw vegetables enhances the feeling of fullness after eating them, a help for those looking to reduce calorie consumption. In order to preserve the nutrients in vegetables, pay attention to the cooking time, the temperature and the cooking method used.

To retain vitamins when preparing vegetable consider the following guidelines:

- Cook vegetables only as long as required to alter their texture.
- Dry-heat cooking methods generally preserve vitamins better than moist-heat cooking methods.
- Steaming vegetables reduces the amount of vitamin and mineral loss compared to boiling.
- When boiling vegetables, reserve cooking liquid, which is rich in vitamins, for another use, such as for stocks or soups.

Conversely cooking also can make some nutrients more digestible. Lycopene, the cancer-fighting antioxidant found in tomatoes and red peppers, is released when plant cell walls are broken down during cooking. Beta-carotene, a pigment associated with eye and skin health, gives carrots and pumpkins their orange color. Cooking makes beta-carotene in vegetables easier to absorb. Serve vegetables prepared in a variety of ways, both raw and cooked, to ensure that diners benefit from all their nutrients.

DRY-HEAT COOKING METHODS FOR VEGETABLES

Dry-heat cooking methods used to cook vegetables include broiling, grilling, roasting, baking, sautéing, stir-frying, pan-frying, pan-roasting and deep-frying. These techniques concentrate flavors and bring out the natural sugars present in most vegetables. Because vegetables contain very little, if any, fat, butter, oil or another fat is added when using dry-heat cooking methods.

Broiling and Grilling

Broiling and grilling use high heat to cook vegetables quickly. This preserves nutritional content and natural flavors. The radiant heat of the broiler or grill caramelizes vegetables, creating a pleasant flavor that is not generally achieved when vegetables are cooked by other methods.

Selecting and Preparing Vegetables to Broil or Grill

Broiling is often used to cook soft vegetables such as tomatoes or items that might not rest easily on a grill rack. Broiling is also used to warm and brown items just before service. If necessary the vegetables can be basted to prevent them from drying out under the broiler's direct heat. Sometimes a cooked vegetable is napped with sauce or clarified butter and placed briefly under the broiler as a finishing touch at service time.

A large range of vegetables can be grilled. Carrots, peppers, squashes, eggplants and similar vegetables should be cut into broad, thin slices. They can then be placed on the grill in the same manner as a portion of meat or fish to create attractive crosshatchings.

Root-to-Stem Cooking

As much as 40 percent of the food grown in the United States is wasted each year. The EPA estimates that discarded food from farms, food manufacturers, restaurants and home kitchens constitutes the largest percentage of waste in landfills and trash incinerators. Chefs and their guests have good reason to be concerned.

Chefs concerned with sustainability can also use their skills and ingenuity to find more uses for the foods they purchase. One of the most effective ways to reduce food waste is to prevent it from happening in the first place. A good place to start is by purchasing produce wisely, anticipating your needs for just two or three days at a time. This ensures freshness and therefore allows all parts of a vegetable or fruit to be used. For example, some chefs assert that broccoli stems taste like asparagus and are well suited to roasting whole or slicing and

Cutting fresh carrot tops for pesto sauce.

sautéing. Fresh young carrot, fennel and radish tops and stems of soft herbs such as cilantro and parsley can be chopped or puréed with other herbs to use as seasonings, in spreads such as pesto, or in vinaigrettes. Clean potato, sweet potato or turnip peels can be tossed in oil and baked into crisp garnishes or chips for

dips and spreads. Scraps from non-cruciferous vegetables such as green beans can be used to make vegetable stock and soup base.

Another way to prevent waste is to use less-than-perfect produce. Add it to purées and soups. Instead of tossing out an entire head of wilted and blemished greens or lettuce, remove discolored or wilted leaves and sauté with garlic and onions to use as a side dish, or cook and purée for a sauce. Mushroom stems and the dark green tops from leeks often land in the compost. Egg dishes such as frittatas and quiche can be enhanced with these cooked scraps. Remove and discard soft spots from firm vegetables such as zucchini instead of discarding the entire vegetable. Use the rest of the vegetable in a stew or other preparation where the appearance is less important.

(See Chapter 10, Principles of Cooking.) Thread smaller vegetables such as mushrooms, cherry tomatoes and pearl onions onto skewers for easy handling. (Bamboo or wooden skewers should be soaked in cold water for 15 minutes before using to help prevent them from burning on the grill.)

Seasoning Vegetables to Broil or Grill

Vegetables contain little fat and therefore benefit greatly from added fat when being broiled or grilled. The added fat can be clarified butter or a marinade such as one made from olive oil and herbs. Some vegetables may be brushed with butter and coated with bread crumbs or Parmesan before broiling.

Techniques used to season and prepare meat for grilling may also be used to prepare vegetables. Brining works well on firm vegetables such as beets, carrots and radishes that may otherwise burn under the broiler or on the grill before they soften. Brine adds flavor and allows the vegetables to be kept on the grill longer. (See Chapter 9, Mise en Place.) Salting achieves similar results and is one way to prepare firm cabbage leaves for grilling. Dry rubs such as those used to season steak amp up the flavor of vegetables such as grilled mushrooms. Oil the vegetables first so that the rub adheres and the vegetable don't stick to the grill. Slices of eggplant, squash and zucchini as well as leafy greens benefit from marinating before broiling or grilling. After the vegetables absorb some of the marinade, brush with oil before cooking.

Procedure for Broiling or Grilling Vegetables

1 Heat the grill or broiler.
2 Use a wire brush to remove any charred or burnt particles that may be stuck to the broiler or grill grate. The grate may be wiped with a lightly oiled towel to remove any remaining particles and help season it.
3 Prepare the vegetables to be broiled or grilled by cutting them into appropriate shapes and sizes, then seasoning, marinating or otherwise preparing them as desired or directed in the recipe.
4 Place the vegetables on the broiler grate, broiler platter or grill grate and cook to the desired doneness while developing the proper surface color.

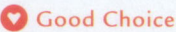 Good Choice   Vegan

MISE EN PLACE

- Peel and chop garlic.
- Wash broccoli and cauliflower and cut into large florets.
- Peel and dice onion.
- Wash and seed bell pepper and cut into large dice.
- Wash mushroom caps.

Grilling skewers of marinated vegetables.

Grilled sliced vegetables as an accompaniment to an entrée plate.

Grilled Vegetable Skewers

		YIELD 12 Skewers		METHOD Grilling
Marinade:				
Rice wine vinegar		4 fl. oz.		120 ml
Vegetable oil		8 fl. oz.		240 ml
Garlic, chopped		1 oz.		30 g
Dried thyme		2 tsp.		10 ml
Salt		1 Tbsp.		15 ml
Black pepper		½ tsp.		2 ml
Zucchini		6 oz.		180 g
Yellow squash		6 oz.		180 g
Broccoli florets, large		12		12
Cauliflower florets, large		12		12
Onion, large dice		24 pieces		24 pieces
Red bell pepper, large dice		12 pieces		12 pieces
Mushroom caps, medium		12		12

1 Combine all the marinade ingredients and set aside.

2 Cut the zucchini and yellow squash into ½-inch- (1.2-centimeter-) thick semicircles.

3 Blanch and refresh the zucchini, yellow squash, broccoli florets, cauliflower florets, onion and bell pepper as discussed in Moist-Heat Cooking Methods for Vegetables on page 625.

4 Drain the blanched vegetables well and combine them with the marinade. Add the mushroom caps. Marinate the vegetables for 30–45 minutes, remove and drain well.

5 Skewer the vegetables by alternating them on 6-inch (15-centimeter) bamboo skewers.

6 Place the vegetable skewers on a hot grill and cook until done, turning as needed. The vegetables should brown and char lightly during cooking. Serve hot.

Variation:

Grilled Sliced Vegetables—Slice the zucchini, yellow squash, onion and bell pepper into large pieces. Marinate and then grill these vegetables along with the broccoli, cauliflower and mushroom caps without skewering.

Approximate values per skewer: **Calories** 60, **Total fat** 2.5 g, **Saturated fat** 0 g, **Cholesterol** 0 mg, **Sodium** 610 mg, **Total carbohydrates** 8 g, **Protein** 2 g, **Vitamin C** 90%, **Claims**—low fat; no cholesterol; good source of fiber

Roasting and Baking

The terms *roasting* and *baking* are used interchangeably when referring to vegetables. Roasting or baking brings out the natural sweetness of many vegetables while preserving their nutritional values. The procedures are basically the same as those for roasting meats.

Selecting and Preparing Vegetables to Roast or Bake

Hearty vegetables such as winter squashes and eggplant are especially well suited for roasting or baking. Vegetables such as onions, carrots and turnips are sometimes cooked alongside roasting meats or poultry. The vegetables add flavor to the finished roast and accompanying sauce, and the fats and juices released from the cooking roast add flavor to the vegetables. Vegetables can be baked whole or cut into uniform-sized pieces. Squash, for example, is usually cut into large pieces. Vegetables may be peeled or left unpeeled, depending on the desired finished product.

Seasoning Vegetables to Roast or Bake

Vegetables may be seasoned with salt and pepper and rubbed with butter or oil before baking, or they may be seasoned afterward with a wide variety of herbs and spices. Oiling the vegetables helps them brown and crisp in the hot oven. Some vegetables, such as winter squashes and sweet potatoes, may be seasoned with brown sugar or honey as well.

Procedure for Roasting or Baking Vegetables

1 Wash the vegetables. Peel, cut and prepare them as desired or directed in the recipe.

2 Season the vegetables and rub or toss with oil or butter if desired.

3 Place the vegetables in a baking dish and bake in a preheated oven until done.

Baked Butternut Squash, Cumin Yogurt and Pumpkin Seeds

♥ Good Choice   🌿 Vegetarian

YIELD 8 Servings, 4 oz. (120 g) each	METHOD Baking	
Butternut squash, peeled	1 lb.	480 g
Olive or vegetable oil	1 fl. oz.	30 ml
Salt and pepper	TT	TT
Sauce:		
Yogurt, plain	1 pt.	480 ml
Cumin, ground	1 tsp.	5 ml
Salt	½ tsp.	2 ml
Fresh cilantro	as needed for garnish	
Aleppo pepper or Spanish paprika	as needed for garnish	
Pumpkin seeds, toasted	as needed for garnish	

1 Cut the peeled squash into ½-inch- (1.2-centimeter-) thick slices. Toss the slices in the oil. Place them in a single layer on a half-sheet pan. Season with salt and pepper.

2 Bake, uncovered, in a 350°F (180°C) oven until tender, approximately 40 minutes.

3 While the squash bakes, prepare the sauce. Stir together the yogurt, cumin and salt.

4 Drizzle with the sauce and garnish with cilantro, Aleppo pepper and pumpkin seeds. Serve as a first course or side dish.

Approximate values per 4-oz. (120-g) serving: **Calories** 90, **Total fat** 5 g, **Saturated fat** 1 g, **Cholesterol** 3 mg, **Sodium** 190 mg, **Total carbohydrates** 10 g, **Protein** 3 g, **Vitamin A** 100%, **Vitamin C** 15%, **Calcium** 15%, **Claims**—low calorie; low fat; excellent source of vitamin A, vitamin C and calcium

MISE EN PLACE

- Wash and peel butternut squash.
- Toast pumpkin seeds.

1 Baking peeled slices of butternut squash.

2 Baked butternut squash garnished with yogurt sauce, pumpkin seeds and cilantro.

Sautéing

Sautéed vegetables should be brightly colored and slightly crisp when done and show little moisture loss. When sautéing vegetables, complete all preparation before cooking begins as timing is important and cooking progresses rapidly. Have all vegetables, herbs, spices, seasonings and sauces ready in advance.

Selecting and Preparing Vegetables to Sauté

A wide variety of vegetables can be sautéed. Whatever vegetables are used, they should be cut into uniform-sized pieces to ensure even cooking.

Quick-cooking vegetables such as summer squashes, onions, greens, stalks, fruit vegetables and mushrooms can be sautéed without any preparation except washing and cutting. Other vegetables such as Brussels sprouts, green beans, winter squashes, broccoli, cauliflower and most root vegetables are typically first blanched or otherwise partially cooked by baking, steaming or simmering. They are then sautéed to reheat and finish. Carrots, squashes and other vegetables are sometimes finished by sautéing in butter and adding a small amount of honey or maple syrup to glaze them. Some cooked vegetables are reheated by simply sautéing them in a small amount of stock or sauce.

Seasoning Vegetables to Sauté

Sautéed vegetables can be seasoned with a great variety of herbs and spices. Seasonings should be added toward the end of the cooking process after all other ingredients have been incorporated in order to accurately evaluate the flavor of the finished dish.

Because sautéing vegetables is done at slightly lower temperatures than sautéing meats and poultry, usually whole butter can be used instead of clarified butter. For additional flavors, fats such as bacon fat, olive oil, nut oils or sesame oil can be used in place of butter.

Procedure for Sautéing Vegetables

1　Wash the vegetables and cut into uniform shapes and sizes.

2　Heat a sauté pan and add enough fat to just cover the bottom. The pan should be large enough to hold the vegetables without overcrowding.

3　When preparing an assortment of vegetables, add the ingredients according to their cooking times (first add the vegetables that take the longest to cook). Plan carefully so that all vegetables will be done at the same time. Do not overcrowd the pan; maintain high enough heat so that the vegetables do not cook in their own juices.

4　Toss the vegetables using the sloped sides of the sauté pan to flip them back on top of themselves. Do not toss more than necessary. The pan should remain in contact with the heat source as much as possible to maintain proper temperatures.

5　Add any sauces or vegetables with high water content, such as tomatoes, last.

6　Season the vegetables as desired with herbs or spices, or add ingredients for a glaze.

🌿 Vegetarian

MISE EN PLACE

- Peel mushrooms.
- Chop thyme.

Sautéed mushrooms served on a crouton.

Sautéed Mushrooms with Garlic and Thyme

YIELD 6 Servings, 2 oz. (60 g) each		METHOD Sautéing	
Mushrooms, brown or button		8 oz.	240 g
Beech or other small mushrooms		8 oz.	240 g
Vegetable oil		1 fl. oz.	30 ml
Whole butter		1 oz.	30 g
Garlic, minced		1 tsp.	5 ml
Fresh thyme, chopped		¼ tsp.	1 ml
Salt and pepper		TT	TT

❶ Adding the mushrooms to the heated pan.

❷ Sautéing the mushrooms.

1 Wipe the mushrooms with a moist clean paper towel, or rinse lightly as needed, then slice or quarter them into uniformly-sized pieces.

2 Heat the oil and butter in a sauté pan over medium high heat. Add the garlic and sauté for 1 minute.

3 Add the mushrooms and thyme. Sauté, stirring and tossing frequently until the mushrooms have released their liquid, browned and cooked through, approximately 8–10 minutes.

4 Season with salt and pepper.

Approximate values per 2-oz. (60-g) serving: **Calories** 60, **Total fat** 6 g, **Saturated fat** 2 g, **Cholesterol** 10 mg, **Sodium** 0 mg, **Total carbohydrates** 1 g, **Protein** 1 g

Stir-Frying

Stir-frying is a form of sautéing that uses a wok or deeply curved sauté pan and high heat. Vegetables are cut into uniformly sized small pieces to ensure even cooking. They are then tossed with a moderate amount of fat over high heat. Although often associated with Chinese dishes, stir-frying can be used with many other flavor profiles and types of cuisine. The procedure for stir-frying is illustrated with the recipe for Stir-Fried Asparagus with Shiitake Mushrooms.

Stir-Fried Asparagus with Shiitake Mushrooms

YIELD 4 Servings, 4 oz. (120 g) each		METHOD Stir-Frying	
Asparagus		1 lb.	480 g
Fresh shiitake mushrooms		6 oz.	180 g
Vegetable oil		1 Tbsp.	15 ml
Sesame oil		1 Tbsp.	15 ml
Garlic, chopped		2 tsp.	10 ml
Oyster sauce		4 fl. oz.	120 ml
Crushed red chiles, optional		TT	TT

MISE EN PLACE
● Peel and chop garlic.

1 Wash the asparagus, trim the ends and slice on the bias into 1- to 2-inch (2.5- to 5-centimeter) pieces.

2 Wash the mushrooms, trim off the stems and slice the caps into ½-inch- (1.2-centimeter-) thick slices.

3 Heat the oils in a wok over high heat.

4 Add the garlic and stir-fry for a few seconds.

5 Add the asparagus and mushrooms and stir-fry for 1 minute.

6 Add the oyster sauce and crushed red chiles, if using, and continue to stir-fry until the asparagus is nearly tender, approximately 3 minutes.

Approximate values per 4-oz. (120-g) serving: **Calories** 140, **Total fat** 8 g, **Saturated fat** 1 g, **Cholesterol** 10 mg, **Sodium** 1130 mg, **Total carbohydrates** 13 g, **Protein** 5 g, **Vitamin C** 50%

Pan-Frying

Pan-fried vegetables are cooked in a generous amount of fat in a frying pan or on a hot griddle. Vegetables to be pan-fried are usually sliced uniformly then seasoned and floured. Green tomatoes, eggplants and zucchini are examples of popular vegetables to pan-fry. When pan-frying vegetables, follow the procedures outlined in Chapter 10, Principles of Cooking. Maintaining the proper temperature so that the vegetables cook through without burning is essential when pan-frying. The recipe for Fried Green Tomatoes with Shrimp and Creole Rémoulade illustrates the techniques for pan-frying vegetables.

♥ Good Choice

Fried Green Tomatoes with Shrimp and Creole Rémoulade

YIELD 2 Servings, 10 oz. (300 g) each	METHOD Pan-Frying	
Cornmeal	3 oz.	90 g
Salt and pepper	TT	TT
Buttermilk	6 fl. oz.	180 ml
Green tomato, large, sliced ½-inch (1.25-cm) thick	1	1
Vegetable oil	as needed	as needed
Creole Rémoulade (page 759)	4 fl. oz.	120 ml
Shrimp, 21–25 count, peeled, cooked	4	4
Micro greens	as needed for garnish	
Cherry tomatoes, red or green	as needed for garnish	

1 Season the cornmeal with salt and pepper. Using the buttermilk and cornmeal, bread the tomato slices using the standard breading procedure described in Chapter 9, Mise en Place (finishing with the cornmeal). Arrange breaded slices in a single layer on a half-sheet pan.

2 Heat a sautoir and add a ¼-inch (6-millimeter) layer of oil. When the oil is hot, pan-fry the tomato slices until golden brown, then turn and cook until tender. Remove and drain slices on clean paper towels or a rack. Repeat until all the tomatoes are cooked, adding more oil as necessary.

3 Pool some Creole Rémoulade on each plate. Arrange two tomato slices on each plate and garnish with the shrimp, micro greens and cherry tomatoes.

Approximate values per 10-oz. (300-g) serving: **Calories** 780, **Total fat** 60 g, **Saturated fat** 5 g, **Cholesterol** 160 mg, **Sodium** 700 mg, **Total carbohydrates** 45 g, **Protein** 17 g, **Vitamin A** 30%, **Vitamin C** 30%, **Iron** 15%

❶ Frying the green tomato slices.

❷ The fried green tomatoes with shrimp and remoulade.

Pan-Roasting

Pan-roasting is a dry-heat cooking method that combines sautéing and roasting techniques. Pan-roasted vegetables are first sautéed in a pan then finished in the oven. Sautéing browns the vegetables and begins the cooking process that is finished in the oven. Pan-roasted vegetables should be evenly browned and cooked through when done. Almost any vegetable is suitable for pan-roasting except for greens and watery vegetables such as cucumbers. When pan-roasting vegetables, cut them uniformly to ensure they cook thoroughly. Finish pan-roasted vegetables with chopped fresh herbs, seasoned butter or oil, rich stock or a splash of an acidic liquid such as lemon juice. The recipe for Pan-Roasted Brussels Sprouts illustrates the techniques for pan-roasting vegetables.

Pan-Roasted Brussels Sprouts

 Good Choice   Vegan

YIELD	6 Servings, approximately 3 oz. (90 g) each	METHOD	Pan-Roasting	
Brussels sprouts			1 lb.	480 g
Olive oil			2 fl. oz	60 ml
Kosher salt			TT	TT
Salt and pepper			TT	TT
Fresh lemon juice or balsamic vinegar			2 fl. oz.	60 ml

1 Wash and cut each Brussels sprout in half vertically through the stem.

2 Heat the oil in a large, heavy frying pan over medium heat. Sprinkle the Brussels sprouts with some kosher salt. Place the Brussels sprouts, cut side down, in one layer in the pan.

3 Cook without stirring until the Brussels sprouts develop a dark golden color, approximately 5–8 minutes. Turn over the Brussels sprouts, adding more oil if needed.

4 Put the frying pan of sprouts in an oven pre-heated to 350°F (180°C). Roast until the sprouts are fork tender and browned, approximately 8–10 additional minutes.

5 Season with salt, pepper and the lemon juice before serving.

Approximate values per 3-oz. (90-gram) serving: **Calories** 110, **Total fat** 9 g, **Saturated fat** 1.5 g, **Cholesterol** 0 mg, **Sodium** 20 mg, **Total carbohydrates** 7 g, **Protein** 3 g, **Vitamin** C 110%, **Claims**—no cholesterol; good source of fiber; excellent source of vitamin C

❶ Placing the Brussels sprouts, cut side down, in the pan.

❷ Turning over the Brussels sprouts before roasting them in the oven.

Deep-Frying

Deep-frying is a popular method of preparing vegetables such as potatoes, squashes and mushrooms. Deep-fried vegetables can be served as hors d'oeuvre, appetizers or accompaniments to a main dish. Vegetables can also be grated or chopped and incorporated into fritters or croquettes and deep-fried. Any deep-fried item should have a crisp, golden exterior with a tender, nongreasy center.

Except for potatoes (which are discussed in Chapter 23, Potatoes, Grains and Pasta), most vegetables are breaded, battered or floured before deep-frying. Slow-cooking vegetables such as broccoli and cauliflower should be blanched in boiling water before breading or battering. Blanching speeds cooking and allows the interior to cook completely before the surface burns. Cutting firm vegetables, such as beets, carrots and squashes, into thin slices or strips helps speed their cooking.

Although vegetables that will be deep-fried can be marinated or seasoned directly, it is more common to season the batter, flour or breading that will coat them. Additional flavors are provided by the sauces and accompaniments served with the deep-fried vegetables. Creamy herb dressings or spicy tomato or soy-based dipping sauces are popular accompaniments.

Procedure for Deep-Frying Vegetables

1 Slice, trim or otherwise prepare the vegetables to be deep-fried. Cut into uniform shapes and sizes to ensure even frying. Blanch if necessary. Season and bread or batter vegetables as desired.

2 Heat the fat to the desired temperature, usually between 325°F and 350°F (160°C and 180°C). Breaded, battered or floured vegetables cook quickly and the fat must be hot enough to cook the food's interior without burning its surface.

3 Carefully place the vegetables in the hot fat using either the basket method or swimming method as appropriate.

4 Deep-fry the vegetables until done. They should have a crispy, golden brown surface.

5 Remove the deep-fried vegetables from the fat and hold them over the fryer, allowing the excess fat to drain off. Transfer the food to a hotel pan either lined with absorbent paper or fitted with a rack. Season with salt if desired.

6 If the deep-fried vegetables are to be held for later service, place them under a heat lamp.

Beer-Battered Onion Rings

YIELD Approximately 1 qt. (1 lt) Batter, enough for approximately 4 lb. (1.9 kg) rings

METHOD Deep-Frying

Batter:		
Flour	10 oz.	300 g
Baking powder	2 tsp.	10 ml
Salt	2 tsp.	10 ml
White pepper	¼ tsp.	1 ml
Egg	1	1
Beer	1 pt.	480 ml
Onions, whole	4 lb.	1.9 kg
Flour	as needed for dredging	

1 Sift together the dry ingredients.

2 Beat the egg in a separate bowl. Add the beer to the beaten egg.

3 Add the egg-and-beer mixture to the dry ingredients; mix until smooth.

4 Peel the onions and cut in ½-inch- (1.2-centimeter-) thick slices.

5 Break the slices into rings and dredge in flour.

6 Dip the rings in the batter a few at a time. Using the swimming method, deep-fry at 375°F (191°C) until done. Drain on absorbent paper, season with additional salt and white pepper and serve hot.

Approximate values per 3-oz. (90-g) serving: **Calories** 180, **Total fat** 10 g, **Saturated fat** 1 g, **Cholesterol** 10 mg, **Sodium** 280 mg, **Total carbohydrates** 19 g, **Protein** 3 g

① Dredging the onion slices in flour.

② Dipping the floured slices in batter.

③ Frying the onion rings using the swimming method.

MOIST-HEAT COOKING METHODS FOR VEGETABLES

Moist-heat cooking methods, especially boiling and steaming, work well with most vegetables. Fiber and starches in the vegetables break down more easily with moist heat, which makes those foods softer and their nutrients more accessible. Steaming makes green vegetables brighter by making chlorophyll more visible. Overcooking, however, turns green vegetables a dull, unappealing grey-green.

Blanching and Parboiling

Blanching and parboiling are variations on boiling; the difference between them is the length of cooking time. Blanched or parboiled vegetables are often finished by other cooking methods such as sautéing.

Blanching is the partial cooking of foods in a large amount of boiling water for a very short time, usually only a few seconds. Besides preparing vegetables for further cooking, blanching is used to remove strong or bitter flavors, soften firm foods, set colors or loosen skins for peeling. Kale, chard, snow peas and tomatoes are examples of vegetables that are sometimes blanched for purposes other than preparation for further cooking.

Parboiling is the same as blanching, but the cooking time is longer, usually several minutes. Parboiling is used to soften vegetables and shorten final cooking times. Parboiling is commonly used for preparing root vegetables, cauliflower, broccoli and winter squashes.

Boiling

Vegetables are often boiled. Boiled vegetables can be served or they can be further prepared by quickly sautéing with other ingredients, puréeing or mashing. Boiled vegetables can also be chilled, and then used in salads.

Starchy root vegetables are generally not boiled but rather simmered slowly so that the heat penetrates to their interiors and cooks them evenly. Green vegetables should be boiled quickly in a large amount of salted water in order to retain their color and flavor.

Refreshing

Unless boiled, blanched or parboiled vegetables will be eaten immediately, they must be quickly chilled in ice water after they are removed from the cooking liquid. This prevents further cooking and preserves (sets) their colors. This process is known as **refreshing** or **shocking** the vegetables. The vegetables are removed from the ice water as soon as they are cold. Never soak or hold the vegetables in the water longer than necessary, or valuable nutrients and flavor will be leached away.

refreshing submerging a food in cold water to quickly cool it and prevent further cooking, also known as shocking

Procedure for Refreshing Vegetables

❶ Blanch, parboil or boil the vegetables to the desired doneness.

❷ Remove the vegetables from the cooking liquid and submerge them in ice water just until they are cold.

Selecting and Preparing Vegetables to Boil

Nearly any type of vegetable can be boiled. Carrots, cabbages, green beans, turnips and red beets are just a few of the most common ones. Vegetables should be uniform in size to ensure even cooking. Some vegetables are cooked whole and require only washing before boiling. Others must be washed, peeled and trimmed or cut into smaller or more manageable sizes. Cruciferous vegetables such as broccoli, Brussels sprouts and turnips release off odors when boiled for too long.

Seasoning Vegetables to Boil

Often vegetables are boiled in nothing more than salted water. There should be enough water so that the vegetables float freely. If too densely packed, green vegetable may take longer to cook and will discolor. Lemon juice, citrus zest, wine and other acidic ingredients are sometimes added to white and red vegetables; if so, they should be added to the liquid before the vegetables. Herbs and spices in a sachet or a bouquet garni add flavor to boiled vegetables and should be added according to the recipe. After boiling, vegetables are sometimes finished with herbs, spices, butter, cream or sauces.

Procedure for Boiling Vegetables

1 Wash, peel and trim the vegetables and cut into uniform shapes and sizes.

2 Bring an adequate amount of water, stock, court bouillon or other liquid to a boil. The liquid should cover the vegetables, which should be able to move around freely without overcrowding.

3 Add seasonings if desired or directed in the recipe.

4 Add the vegetables to the boiling liquid. If more than one vegetable is to be cooked and they have different cooking times, they should be cooked separately to ensure that all are cooked to the proper doneness. The pot may be covered if cooking white, red or yellow vegetables. Do not cover the pot when boiling green vegetables.

5 Cook the vegetables to the desired doneness. Vegetables to be reheated before serving should be slightly undercooked and firm.

6 Remove the vegetables from the water with a slotted spoon or a spider or drain through a colander.

7 Refresh the vegetables in ice water, drain and refrigerate until needed or finish the hot boiled vegetables as desired and serve immediately.

 Good Choice    Vegan

MISE EN PLACE

- Prepare the Herb Vinaigrette.
- Mince shallots.
- Toast and chop hazelnuts.

Green Beans with Herbed Vinaigrette and Toasted Hazelnuts

YIELD 6 Servings, 4 oz. (120 g) each		METHOD Boiling
Green beans, trimmed	1 lb.	480 g
Herb Vinaigrette (page 740)	6 fl. oz.	180 ml
Shallots, minced	1 oz.	30 g
Salt and pepper	TT	TT
Hazelnuts, toasted and chopped	4 oz.	120 g

1 Boil the green beans in salted water until tender, approximately 8 minutes.

2 Drain and refresh the green beans in an ice and water bath.

3 Remove the green beans from the water bath and drain them thoroughly.

4 Whisk together the Herb Vinaigrette and the shallots in a large bowl. Add the green beans and toss to blend flavors. Adjust the seasonings and serve garnished with the hazelnuts.

Approximate values per 4-oz. (120-g) serving: **Calories** 320, **Total fat** 30 g, **Saturated fat** 2.5 g, **Cholesterol** 0 mg, **Sodium** 75 mg, **Total carbohydrates** 10 g, **Protein** 4 g, **Vitamin C** 15%, **Claims**—no cholesterol; good source of fiber and vitamins A and C

❶ Refreshing the green beans in an ice and water bath.

❷ The cooked green beans with Herb Vinaigrette and toasted hazelnuts.

Procedure for Cooking Dried Beans

Dried beans require a two-step moist-heat cooking technique. They are best rehydrated by soaking, as discussed earlier on page 603, and then cooking in a boiling (actually simmering) liquid. After rehydration and cooking, the beans can be served or further cooked in baked, sautéed or puréed dishes.

1 After soaking, place the drained beans in a heavy saucepan and cover with cold water or stock. Allow approximately three times as much liquid as there are beans. Add flavoring ingredients as directed in the recipe, but do not add acids or salt until the beans have reached the desired tenderness. Acids and salt cause the exterior of beans to toughen and resist any further efforts at tenderizing.

2 Slowly bring the liquid to a boil. Boil uncovered for 10 minutes or as directed in the recipe. Use a ladle to remove any scum that rises to the surface.

3 Cover and reduce the heat. Simmer until the beans are tender. Whole beans generally require 1–2½ hours, lentils 20–35 minutes and split peas 30–60 minutes. Add additional hot liquid if necessary to keep the beans adequately covered. Do not stir the beans during cooking.

4 Drain the cooked beans through a colander.

♥ Good Choice   🌿 Vegetarian

White Bean Salad

MISE EN PLACE

- Make an onion piqué.
- Juice the fresh lemon.
- Grate lemon zest.
- Crumble cheese.
- Pit and halve olives.
- Halve the cherry tomatoes and slice the kale in chiffonade.

YIELD 3 pt. (1.4 lt), 12 Servings, 4 oz. (120 g) each

White beans	12 oz.	360 g
Water	as needed	as needed
Onion piqué (page 168)	1	1
Dressing:		
Fresh lemon juice	2 fl. oz.	60 ml
Lemon zest, grated	1 Tbsp.	15 ml
Olive oil	6 fl. oz.	180 ml
Salt and pepper	TT	TT
Feta, crumbled	4 oz.	120 g
Black olives, pitted, halved	3 oz.	90 g
Cherry tomatoes, halved	9 oz.	270 g
Kale, chiffonade	2 oz.	60 g

1 Pick through the beans to remove any grit, pebbles or debris. Place the beans in a bowl of water and remove any skins or other items that float to the top. Drain and rinse the beans. Place the beans in a clean bowl and soak them for at least several hours or overnight.

2 Drain the beans and place them in a saucepot with 1½ quarts (1.4 liters) water and the onion piqué. Bring to a boil, reduce to a simmer and cook until the beans are tender, approximately 1 hour. Drain the beans, spread on a sheet pan, cool and refrigerate.

3 To make the dressing, combine the lemon juice and zest. Whisk in the oil a little bit at a time. Season with salt and pepper.

4 Toss the beans with the feta, olives, cherry tomatoes and kale. Add the dressing and toss together. Adjust the seasonings and serve chilled with flatbread.

Approximate values per 4-fl.-oz. (120-ml) serving: **Calories** 300, **Total fat** 25 g, **Saturated fat** 2g, **Cholesterol** 15 mg, **Sodium** 240 mg, **Total carbohydrates** 15 g, **Protein** 7 g, **Vitamin A** 20%, **Vitamin C** 30%, **Claims**—good source of fiber

❶ Simmering the soaked beans.

❷ Draining the beans.

❸ Tossing the salad ingredients together.

Steaming

Vegetables can be steamed in a convection steamer or by placing them in a basket or on a rack and suspending them over boiling liquid in a wok, saucepan or hotel pan. Vegetables can also be pan-steamed by cooking them in a covered pan with a small amount of liquid; most of the cooking is done by steam because only a small portion of the food is submerged in the liquid. Steamed vegetables can be eaten plain, partially cooked and sautéed lightly to finish, incorporated into casseroles or puréed. If they are not served immediately, refresh and refrigerate until used.

Properly steamed vegetables should be moist and tender. They generally retain their shape better than boiled vegetables. Vegetables cook very rapidly in steam, and overcooking is a common mistake.

Selecting and Preparing Vegetables to Steam

Nearly any vegetable that can be boiled can also be steamed successfully. All vegetables should be washed, peeled and trimmed if appropriate and cut into uniform-sized pieces. Pan-steaming is appropriate for vegetables that are small or cut into fairly small pieces such as peas and beans or broccoli and cauliflower florets.

Seasoning Vegetables to Steam

Steaming produces vegetables with clean, natural flavors. Foods cooked in convection steamers can be seasoned with herbs and spices; convection steamers use plain water to produce steam, so the foods being cooked do not gain flavor from the cooking liquid. Vegetables steamed over liquids or pan-steamed in small amounts of liquids can be flavored by using stocks or court bouillon as the cooking liquid. Add herbs, spices and aromatic vegetables to any liquid for additional flavor.

Procedure for Steaming Vegetables

1. Wash, peel and trim the vegetables and cut into uniform shapes and sizes.
2. If a convection steamer is not being used, prepare a steaming liquid and bring it to a boil in a covered pan or double boiler.
3. Place the vegetables in a perforated pan in a single layer; do not crowd the pan. Place the pan over the boiling liquid or add the vegetables to the liquid.
4. Cover the pan and cook to the desired doneness.
5. Remove the vegetables from the steamer and serve, or refresh and refrigerate until needed.

🍃 Vegetarian

MISE EN PLACE

● Peel and mince garlic.

❶ Placing the broccoli spears in a perforated pan.

❷ Drizzling the browned almonds and butter over the broccoli.

Broccoli Amandine

YIELD 6 Servings, 6 oz. (180 g) each	METHOD Steaming	
Fresh broccoli	2 lb.	960 g
Salt and pepper	TT	TT
Whole butter	2 oz.	60 g
Almonds, sliced	1 oz.	30 g
Garlic clove, minced	1	1
Lemon juice	2 fl. oz.	60 ml

1 Cut the broccoli into uniform spears. Rinse and sprinkle lightly with salt and pepper.

2 Place the broccoli in a single layer in a perforated hotel pan and cook in a convection steamer until tender but slightly crisp, approximately 3 minutes.

3 Melt the butter in a sauté pan. Add the almonds and garlic and cook just until the nuts are lightly browned.

4 Arrange the broccoli on plates for service and sprinkle with the lemon juice. Drizzle the almonds and butter over the broccoli and serve immediately.

Approximate values per 6-oz. (180-g) serving: **Calories** 160, **Total fat** 10 g, **Saturated fat** 5 g, **Cholesterol** 20 mg, **Sodium** 500 g, **Total carbohydrates** 10 g, **Protein** 6 g, **Vitamin A** 35%, **Vitamin C** 110%

Microwaving

Fresh vegetables are among the few foods that can be consistently well prepared in a microwave oven. Often microwave cooking can be accomplished without any additional liquid, thus preserving nutrients. With microwaving, colors and flavors stay true, and textures remain crisp.

Microwave cooking is actually a form of steaming. As explained in Chapter 10, Principles of Cooking, microwaves agitate water molecules, thus creating steam. The water may be the moisture found naturally in the food or may be added specifically to create the steam. Cooking time depends on the type of microwave oven as well as on the freshness, moisture content, maturity and quantity of vegetables being prepared.

Selecting and Preparing Vegetables to Microwave

Any vegetable that can be steamed successfully can be microwaved with good results. Because typical microwave ovens are relatively small, they are impractical for producing large quantities of food. They are most useful for reheating small portions of vegetables that have been blanched or partially cooked using another cooking method.

Seasoning Vegetables to Microwave

Microwaving, like steaming, brings out the natural flavors of food. Herbs and spices can be added to the vegetables before they are microwaved. Or after microwaving, the vegetables can be tossed with butter, herbs and spices or combined with a sauce.

Procedure for Microwaving Vegetables

1 Wash, peel and trim the vegetables and cut into uniform shapes and sizes.

2 Place the vegetables in a steamer designed for microwave use or arrange the vegetables in a microwavable dish. Cover the vegetables with a lid or plastic wrap. If using plastic wrap, puncture it to allow some steam to escape during cooking.

3 Cook the vegetables to the desired doneness, allowing for some carryover cooking, or reheat previously cooked vegetables until hot. Stir or turn the vegetables as necessary to promote even cooking.

4 Serve the vegetables or refresh and refrigerate until needed.

Combination Cooking Methods: Braising and Stewing Vegetables

Classic combination cooking methods of braising and stewing can be used with vegetables to soften fibers and create a flavorful sauce in which the main ingredient will be served. In contrast to the tougher cuts of meat or poultry generally associated with combination cooking methods, vegetables are braised or stewed at lower temperatures for shorter times, and less cooking liquid is usually added. The braising liquid, including any given off by the vegetables, is reduced to a light sauce, becoming part of the finished product. Generally a braised dish is prepared with only one vegetable; a stew is a mixture of several vegetables. The main ingredients are sometimes browned in fat before the liquid is added in order to enhance flavor and color.

Both braises and stews can be exceptionally flavorful because they are served with all of their cooking liquid. (Boiled vegetables, in contrast, lose some of their flavor to the cooking liquid.) Braised and stewed vegetables generally can be held hot for service longer than vegetables prepared by other cooking methods. Vegetables may be braised using the *sous vide* method described in Chapter 10, Principles of Cooking. The flavor of *sous vide* vegetables is intensified because the juices are retained when cooking in the plastic pouch. (See the recipe for Butter-Braised Honey Carrots page 650.)

Selecting and Preparing Vegetables to Braise or Stew

Various lettuces, especially romaine and Boston, are often braised. Cabbages, Belgian endive, leeks and many other vegetables are also commonly braised. Stews may contain a wide variety of vegetables such as summer or winter squashes, eggplant, onions, peppers, tomatoes, carrots, celery and garlic. Leafy green vegetables are less commonly braised or stewed.

The vegetables should be washed and peeled or trimmed if appropriate. Vegetables to be braised may be left whole, cut into uniform pieces or shredded as desired. Heads of lettuce are usually cut into halves or quarters; cabbage is often shredded. Strongly flavored vegetables such as celery root and turnips are usually parboiled first in order to mute their influence.

Seasoning Vegetables to Braise or Stew

Both braises and stews may include flavoring ingredients such as garlic, herbs, bacon or mirepoix. The liquid can be water, wine, stock or tomato juice. Vegetables can even be braised in butter and sugar or honey to create a glazed dish.

Both braises and stews can be seasoned with a variety of herbs and spices. Add the seasonings before covering the pot to finish the cooking process.

Procedure for Braising and Stewing Vegetables

1 Wash, peel, trim and cut the vegetables.

2 Sauté or sweat the flavoring ingredients in fat to release their flavors. Or sauté or sweat the main ingredients in fat.

3 For a braise, add the main ingredient in a single layer. For a stew, add the ingredients according to their cooking times or as directed in the recipe.

4 Add the cooking liquid; it should partially cover the vegetables. Bring the liquid to a boil, reduce to a simmer, cover and cook in the oven or on the stove top until done.

5 If desired, remove the main ingredients from the pan and reduce the sauce or thicken it with beurre manié, cornstarch or arrowroot. Then return the main ingredients to the sauce.

Braised Celery with Basil

- Peel onions and cut into small dice.
- Peel and mince garlic.
- Slice basil in chiffonade.

YIELD 12 Servings, 3 oz. (90 g) each		METHOD Braising
Celery heads	3	3
Onions, small dice	8 oz.	240 g
Garlic, minced	2 tsp.	10 ml
Whole butter	2 oz.	60 g
Olive oil	1 fl. oz.	30 ml
Fresh thyme	1 tsp.	5 ml
Fresh basil leaves, chiffonade	20	20
Dry white wine	8 fl. oz.	240 ml
Chicken stock	1 pt.	480 ml
Salt and pepper	TT	TT

❶ Trimming the celery.

1 Trim the outer ribs from the celery heads, leaving only the tender hearts. Trim the heads to 6-inch (15-centimeter) lengths. Trim the root slightly, leaving each head together. Cut each head lengthwise into quarters.

2 Sauté the onions and garlic in the butter and oil, without coloring, until tender. Add the celery quarters to the pan and sauté, turning occasionally.

3 Add the thyme, basil, wine and stock. Bring to a boil, reduce to a simmer, cover and braise in the oven at 350°F (180°C) until tender, approximately 1 hour.

4 Remove the celery and reserve. Reduce the cooking liquid on the stove top until it thickens. Adjust the liquid's seasonings and return the celery to the pan to reheat. Serve the celery with a portion of the sauce.

Approximate values per 3-oz. (90-g) serving: **Calories** 60, **Total fat** 4.5 g, **Saturated fat** 1.5 g, **Cholesterol** 5 mg, **Sodium** 170 mg, **Total carbohydrates** 2 g, **Protein** 1 g

❷ Adding the thyme, basil, wine and stock to the celery.

Puréeing Vegetables

Vegetables may be puréed into a smooth paste after being fully cooked. Cooked vegetable purées can be served as is, or they can be used as an ingredient in other preparations such as pumpkin pie, mashed potatoes or vegetable soufflés. Purées can also be bound with eggs, seasoned and used to make vegetable timbales and terrines. Modernist culinary presentations may employ smears, drops or splashes of intensely flavored vegetable purées to add color and contrast to plated dishes.

Puréed vegetables are generally first cooked by baking, boiling, steaming or microwaving. White, red and yellow vegetables should be cooked until quite soft. They are more easily puréed when hot or warm; this also helps ensure a smooth finished purée. For most preparations, green vegetables must be refreshed after cooking and puréed while cold, or they will overcook and become discolored.

❸ Reducing the cooking liquid to make sauce.

Seasoning Vegetables to Purée

Vegetables for purées can be seasoned before they are puréed following the guidelines for the cooking procedure used. They can also be seasoned after they are puréed with a wide variety of ingredients such as herbs, spices, alcoholic spirits, cheese, honey or brown sugar.

Finishing Puréed Vegetables

Purées can be finished with stocks, sauces, butter or cream to add richness and flavor. First purée the main ingredient, then add additional liquids to obtain the desired consistency.

Procedure for Puréeing Vegetables

1 Cook the vegetables. White, red and yellow vegetables should be cooked until very soft. Green vegetables should be cooked until tender but not overcooked to the point of being discolored. If cooking the vegetables in a liquid, drain them well.

2 Purée the vegetables in a vertical cutter/mixer (VCM), food processor or blender or by passing them through a food mill.

3 Season or finish the puréed vegetables as desired or directed in the recipe, or use them in another recipe.

Parsnip Purée

🌿 Vegetarian

YIELD 2 qt. (1.9 lt), 16 Servings, 4 fl. oz. (120 ml) each   **METHOD** Boiling/Puréeing

Parsnips	4 lb.	1.9 kg
Russet potatoes	1 lb. 8 oz.	720 g
Heavy cream, hot	8 fl. oz.	240 ml
Whole butter, melted	4 oz.	120 g
Salt and white pepper	TT	TT

MISE EN PLACE

• Heat the cream and melt the butter while the parsnips and potatoes are cooking.

1 Peel the parsnips and potatoes and cut into large pieces of approximately the same size.

2 Boil the vegetables separately in salted water until tender.

3 Drain the vegetables well. Purée them through a food mill.

4 Add the cream and butter and mix to combine. Adjust the consistency by adding cream as desired. Season the mixture with salt and white pepper and serve hot.

Variations:

Turnip or Sunchoke Purée—Substitute turnips or sunchokes for the parsnips.

Winter Squash Purée—Select approximately 6½ pounds (3 kilograms) winter squash (such as acorn, butternut, pumpkin) and cut them in halves or quarters. Scoop out the seeds and then roast the squash, cut side down, in a 375°F (190°C) oven until tender. Scoop the flesh from the shells and substitute it for the parsnips.

Approximate values per 4-fl.-oz. (120-ml) serving: **Calories** 240, **Total fat** 12 g, **Saturated fat** 7 g, **Cholesterol** 35 mg, **Sodium** 220 mg, **Total carbohydrates** 31 g, **Protein** 3 g, **Vitamin A** 10%, **Vitamin C** 35%

❶ Passing the parsnips and potatoes through a food mill.

❷ The finished purée.

Fermented and pickled vegetables (from left): kosher dill pickles, sauerkraut and kimchee

PRESERVING VEGETABLES

For millennia people have preserved vegetables in times of plenty in order to have food available in times of need. Modern preservation techniques of canning and freezing aim to maintain vegetables in a state as close to fresh as possible. Ancient preservation techniques, such as drying, fermenting and pickling, alter the flavor and texture of vegetables dramatically, and are used today to add complex flavors to vegetables as well as to preserve them. Drying, also known as dehydration, uses air and gentle heat to remove moisture from foods, so that bacteria can no longer cause spoilage or decay. Foods such as dried mushrooms and sun-dried tomatoes are rehydrated in water or a flavorful liquid before use. Drying intensifies the glutamate content of mushrooms and tomatoes making them a good source of umami taste.

Fermenting involves aging foods with a dry salt or brine to draw out water and sugar while simultaneously reducing the food's contact with oxygen. Traditionally fruits and vegetables were fermented in tightly sealed jars stored underground to maintain the desired temperature. It is the appropriate combination of salt and temperature, plus the effect of desirable microorganisms that determines the final flavor and texture of the fermented foodstuffs. Examples include kimchee and sauerkraut, both of which are made with cabbage, as well as olives, Moroccan-Style Preserved Lemons (page 389) and the preserved plums, radishes and fruits common in Japan. The procedure for fermenting vegetables is illustrated by the recipe for Baechu-Kimchee (Korean Spicy Cabbage) on page 652.

Pickling refers to the direct addition of an acid, usually vinegar, to destroy microorganisms and prevent the bacterial process of deterioration. Herbs, spices, salt and sugar are added to a hot vinegar solution, in which the pickled items are submerged. Pickling is faster than fermentation and the final flavors are less deep or complex. Popular examples include a wide variety of pickled cucumbers and other fruits and vegetables, such as okra, watermelon rind, green beans, peaches and carrots. For longer storage, the jars of pickled vegetable may be canned or processed in a water bath. (Consult your local health department for regulations about preparing and serving restaurant-canned products in your area.) Fresh vegetables may be cured in brine or a pickling solution before grilling as discussed on page 169.

Procedure for Pickling Vegetables

1 Prepare the brine or pickling mixture. Bring the liquid to a boil and cool if necessary.
2 Wash, trim and cut vegetables as desired. Blanch vegetables if necessary. Drain and dry them.
3 Place vegetables in sterilized non-reactive containers.
4 Cover the vegetables with the brine or pickling mixture.
5 Cover the containers, refrigerate and let the vegetables cure in the brine for the length of time specified.

Giardiniera (Pickled Vegetables)

 Good Choice   **Vegan**

A combination of vegetables is used in the Italian-American vegetable giardiniera [jar-dih-NEEAIR-ah], composed of celery, carrot, cauliflower, onion, red bell pepper, plus spicier peppers for hot versions, all steeped in vinegar seasoned with salt and peppercorns. Giardiniera is served with salads, meat sandwiches and antipasti.

YIELD 40 Servings, 2 oz. (60 g) each   **METHOD** Pickling

Pickling liquid:		
Distilled white vinegar	24 fl. oz.	600 ml
Water	24 fl. oz.	600 ml
Granulated sugar	4 oz.	120 g
Kosher salt	5 Tbsp.	75 ml
Yellow mustard seeds	1 tsp.	5 ml
Hot pepper flakes	½ tsp.	2 ml
Cauliflower, trimmed, cut into 2-inch florets	2 lb.	960 g
Red bell pepper, cut into ½-inch strips	1	1
Yellow bell pepper, cut into ½-inch strips	1	1
Carrots, baby, peeled and trimmed	20	20
Celery ribs, cut diagonally 1-inch thick	12 oz.	360 g
Fiddlehead ferns, if available	4 oz.	120 g
Green olives, brine cured	6 oz.	180 g

MISE EN PLACE
- Wash, trim and cut cauliflower and celery.
- Wash, seed and cut peppers.
- Wash, peel and trim carrots.

1 Bring pickling-liquid ingredients to a boil in a 3-quart nonreactive saucepan over moderate heat, stirring until the sugar is dissolved. Transfer to a 4-quart nonreactive bowl and cool about 30 minutes.

2 Blanch the cauliflower in boiling salted water until tender crisp, approximately 4–5 minutes. Refresh the cauliflower in an ice bath. Blanch the remaining vegetables in the same manner, adjusting the cooking time for each type of vegetable.

3 Once all of the vegetables have been cooked then refreshed, drain them thoroughly in a colander. Set the vegetables on paper towel-lined sheet trays to drain completely.

4 Add the cooked vegetables and olives to the cooled pickling liquid. Place a plate on top of the vegetables, cover with plastic wrap and refrigerate. The vegetable will be ready to eat in 18–24 hours.

Approximate values per 2-oz. (120-g) serving: **Calories** 20, **Total fat** 1 g, **Saturated fat** 0 g, **Cholesterol** 0 mg, **Sodium** 300 mg, **Total carbohydrates** 3 g, **Protein** 1 g, **Vitamin C** 40%, **Claims**—low fat; no cholesterol; excellent source of vitamin C

QUESTIONS FOR DISCUSSION

1 Explain how the season affects the price, quality and availability of vegetables.

2 List and describe three processing techniques commonly used to extend the shelf life of vegetables.

3 What special concerns exist regarding the storage of fresh vegetables? Explain why some vegetables should not be refrigerated.

4 Discuss proper ways to wash vegetables before using them and why these methods are important.

5 Why is it important to cut vegetables into a uniform size before cooking?

6 Discuss several techniques used for determining the doneness of vegetables. Is carryover cooking a concern when preparing vegetables? Explain your answer.

7 Discuss the role of acid in a cooking liquid used for preparing vegetables. Which vegetables, if any, benefit from an acidic cooking environment?

8 Describe the necessary mise en place and procedure for refreshing vegetables.

9 List and describe two ways to prepare and preserve vegetables for extended storage.

10 Locate information on farmer's markets in your area. What are the advantages and disadvantages of purchasing vegetables from a local grower?

Additional Vegetable Recipes

Grilled Portabella Mushrooms

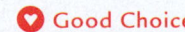

YIELD 3 Servings, 4 oz. (120 g) each	METHOD Grilling	
Portabella mushroom caps	1 lb.	480 g
Olive oil	1½ fl. oz.	45 ml
Garlic, chopped	1 tsp.	5 ml
Salt and pepper	TT	TT
Fresh thyme	1 tsp.	5 ml

1 Wipe the mushroom caps clean with a damp towel. Scrape the gills from the underside of the mushroom caps, if desired.

2 Combine the oil and garlic and brush the mixture on the mushroom caps.

3 Season the mushrooms with salt, pepper and thyme.

4 Grill or broil the mushrooms until tender, approximately 8 minutes, depending on the size of the caps.

Approximate values per 4-oz. (120-g) serving: **Calories** 140, **Total fat** 10 g, **Saturated fat** 1.5 g, **Cholesterol** 0 mg, **Sodium** 790 mg, **Total carbohydrates** 8 g, **Protein** 6 g, **Claims**—no cholesterol; high fiber

Turning over mushroom caps to grill on the other side

Garlic Timbales

YIELD 8 Timbales, 2 fl. oz. (60 ml) each	METHOD Baking	
Garlic cloves, peeled	10	10
Milk	3 fl. oz.	90 ml
Heavy cream	8 fl. oz.	240 ml
Eggs	2	2
Dried thyme	1 tsp.	5 ml
Salt and pepper	TT	TT

1 Butter eight small ramekins or timbales.

2 Place the garlic in a small saucepan, add enough water to cover and bring to a boil. Drain. Repeat this blanching procedure two more times.

3 Place the garlic in a blender with the milk and blend. Add the cream, eggs and thyme; blend until smooth. Season with salt and pepper.

4 Divide the custard among the timbales and place in a water bath. Bake for 30–45 minutes at 325°F (160°C).

5 Run a paring knife around the rim and unmold onto the serving plate. Serve the timbales as a side dish or garnish with baby lettuce or cooked greens as an appetizer.

Variation:

Broccoli or Cauliflower Timbales—Place 1 ounce (30 grams) blanched broccoli or cauliflower in each buttered timbale before adding the garlic custard mixture.

Approximate values per timbale: **Calories** 130, **Total fat** 12 g, **Saturated fat** 7 g, **Cholesterol** 95 mg, **Sodium** 320 mg, **Total carbohydrates** 3 g, **Protein** 3 g, **Vitamin A** 15%

 Good Choice   Vegan

Oven-Roasted Garlic

YIELD	9 Servings		METHOD	Baking
Garlic, whole heads		9	9	
Olive oil		3 fl. oz.	90 ml	
Salt and pepper		TT	TT	

1 Cut the top from each head of garlic and discard. Place the garlic, cut side up, in a half-size hotel pan. Brush the tops of the garlic with oil, then season generously with salt and pepper.

2 Cover the pan and bake at 300°F (150°C) until the garlic softens, approximately 1 hour. Remove the cover and continue baking until any moisture has evaporated and the garlic develops a deep golden color, approximately 15 minutes.

3 Serve the garlic heads whole as a garnish with roasted meats, poultry or vegetables or squeeze out the softened pulp to use in sauces and purées.

Approximate values per serving: **Calories** 120, **Total fat** 0 g, **Saturated fat** 0 g, **Cholesterol** 0 mg, **Sodium** 490 mg, **Total carbohydrates** 26 g, **Protein** 4 g, **Vitamin C** 15%, **Claims**—fat free; good source of fiber

1 Seasoning the heads of garlic.   2 The finished Oven-Roasted Garlic.

Vegetarian

Fennel Gratin

YIELD	1 Half-Size Hotel Pan, 10 Servings, 4 oz. (120 g) each		METHOD	Blanching/Baking
Cream or half and half		8 fl. oz.	240 ml	
Milk		4 fl. oz.	120 ml	
Kosher salt		½ tsp.	2 ml	
Garlic, chopped		1 Tbsp.	15 ml	
Black pepper		TT	TT	
All-purpose flour		1 Tbsp.	15 ml	
Fennel bulbs, tops removed		2 lbs.	960 g	
Gruyère, shredded		4 oz.	120 g	

1 Combine the cream, milk, salt and garlic in a small saucepan. Simmer for 5 minutes. Season to taste with black pepper. Stir in the flour. Set aside.

2 Slice the fennel vertically into ¼ -inch- (6-millimeter-) thick slices. Blanch the fennel in boiling salted water for 5 minutes to soften.

3 Drain the fennel, and then arrange it in a buttered, 2½-inch- (6-centimeter-) deep, half-size hotel pan. Top it with the cream mixture. Adjust the seasoning. Sprinkle with the Gruyère cheese.

4 Bake at 350°F (180°C) until the fennel is tender and the crust is golden, approximately 25–30 minutes.

Approximate values per 4-oz. (120-g) serving: **Calories** 170, **Total fat** 13 g, **Saturated fat** 8 g, **Cholesterol** 45 mg, **Sodium** 160 mg, **Total carbohydrates** 9 g, **Protein** 6 g, **Vitamin C** 10%, **Calcium** 20%

Baked Beans

♥ Good Choice

YIELD 1½ qt. (1.4 lt), 16 Servings, 3 fl. oz. (90 ml) each	METHOD Baking	
Great Northern beans, soaked	1 lb.	480 g
Onion, small dice	4 oz.	120 g
Anaheim chile, small dice	1 oz.	30 g
Molasses	3 oz.	90 g
Brown sugar	3 oz.	90 g
Ketchup	8 oz.	240 g
Prepared mustard	1 oz.	30 g
Cider vinegar	1 Tbsp.	15 ml
Worcestershire sauce (omit for vegetarians)	1 fl. oz.	30 ml
Tabasco sauce	TT	TT
Salt and pepper	TT	TT

1 Simmer the beans in water until almost tender, approximately 45 minutes. Drain well.

2 Combine the remaining ingredients, blending well.

3 Add the sauce to the beans, tossing to coat thoroughly. Adjust the seasonings.

4 Place the beans in a hotel pan or a 2-quart (2-liter) baking dish. Cover and bake in a 350°F (180°C) oven until the beans are completely tender, approximately 30–40 minutes.

Variation:

Boston-Style Baked Beans—Omit the chile and Tabasco sauce. Arrange 12 slices of bacon over the beans in Step 4 before baking.

Approximate values per 3-fl.-oz. (90-ml) serving: **Calories** 120, **Total fat** 0 g, **Saturated fat** 0 g, **Cholesterol** 0 mg, **Sodium** 490 mg, **Total carbohydrates** 26 g, **Protein** 4 g, **Vitamin C** 15%, **Claims**—fat free; good source of fiber

 Vegetarian

Mushroom and Leek Tart

YIELD 8 Tarts			METHOD Sautéing/Baking	
Clarified butter	2 fl. oz.	60 ml		
Leeks, white part only, sliced thin	24 oz.	720 g		
Garlic, chopped	1 tsp.	5 ml		
White mushrooms, trimmed and sliced	1 lb.	480 g		
Shiitake mushrooms, trimmed and sliced	1 lb.	480 g		
Salt	1 Tbsp.	15 ml		
Pepper	½ tsp.	2 ml		
Havarti, shredded	6 oz.	180 g		
Fresh thyme, chopped	1 Tbsp.	15 ml		
Dried basil	½ tsp.	2 ml		
Heavy cream	8 fl. oz.	240 ml		
Puff pastry	4 lb.	1.9 kg		
Egg wash	as needed	as needed		
Parmesan, grated	8 oz.	240 g		

1 Heat the butter in a large sauté pan. Add the leeks, garlic and mushrooms and sauté until tender.

2 Add the salt, pepper, Havarti, herbs and cream, bring to a boil and reduce until the mixture is thick. Adjust the seasonings. Remove from the heat and cool.

3 Roll the puff pastry approximately ¼ inch (6 millimeters) thick and cut eight circles approximately 9 inches (22 centimeters) in diameter from the pastry to make each tart shell. Brush a 1-inch (6-millimeter) band of egg wash around the edge of each circle. Fold the edge of the pastry in toward the center to form a 1-inch (6-millimeter) rim and crimp.

4 Fill each tart shell with 6 ounces (180 grams) of the leek-and-mushroom filling. Spread the filling to the edge of the tart and sprinkle the top with Parmesan. Brush the edge of each tart with egg wash and bake in a 400°F (200°C) convection oven until the pastry is well browned, approximately 10–12 minutes.

Variation:

Any type of mushroom or mixture of mushrooms can be used in place of the white and shiitake mushrooms and any variety of cheese that melts well can be substituted for the Havarti. The tarts can also be formed into other shapes or sizes as desired.

Approximate values per tart: **Calories** 1710, **Total fat** 119 g, **Saturated fat** 42 g, **Cholesterol** 100 mg, **Sodium** 213 mg, **Total carbohydrates** 123 g, **Protein** 38 g, **Vitamin A** 25%, **Vitamin C** 20%, **Calcium** 60%, **Iron** 50%

Maple-Glazed Carrots

🌿 Vegetarian

YIELD	16 Servings, 4 oz. (120 g) each	METHOD	Sautéing
Carrots, full-size or baby		4 lb.	1.9 kg
Whole butter		4 oz.	120 g
Salt and pepper		TT	TT
Maple syrup		4 fl. oz.	120 ml
Fresh parsley, chopped		2 Tbsp.	30 ml

1 If using full-size carrots, peel them and cut into a shape such as oblique, tournée or rondelle. If using baby carrots, wash, trim and cut them as necessary or desired.

2 Parboil the carrots in salt water and refresh. The carrots should be very firm.

3 Sauté the carrots in the butter until nearly tender.

4 Season the carrots with salt and pepper and add the maple syrup. Cook briefly, tossing the carrots so that they are coated with the maple syrup. Garnish with the parsley.

Approximate values per 4-oz. (120-g) serving: **Calories** 120, **Total fat** 6 g, **Saturated fat** 3.5 g, **Cholesterol** 15 mg, **Sodium** 260 mg, **Total carbohydrates** 16 g, **Protein** 1 g, **Vitamin A** 220%, **Vitamin C** 15%

Duxelles

❤ Good Choice   🌿 Vegetarian

duxelles a coarse paste made of finely chopped mushrooms sautéed with shallots in butter used in sauces and stuffing

YIELD	12 oz. (360 g)	METHOD	Sautéing
Mushrooms		1 lb.	480 g
Shallots, minced		2 Tbsp.	30 ml
Garlic, chopped		1 tsp.	5 ml
Whole butter		½ oz.	15 g
Salt and pepper		TT	TT
Fresh parsley, chopped		1 Tbsp.	15 ml

1 Chop the mushrooms very finely.

2 Sauté the shallots and garlic in the butter until tender. Add the mushrooms and sauté until dry.

3 Season with salt and pepper and add the parsley. Cool and then use the duxelles as a stuffing for vegetables or as a flavoring ingredient in other recipes.

Approximate values per 1-oz. (30-g) serving: **Calories** 20, **Total fat** 1 g, **Saturated fat** 0.5 g, **Cholesterol** 5 mg, **Sodium** 210 mg, **Total carbohydrates** 2 g, **Protein** 1 g, **Claims**—low fat; low cholesterol; low calorie

① Sautéing the mushrooms and shallots.

② The finished Duxelles.

Good Choice   Vegan

Ratatouille

YIELD 16 Servings, 4 oz. (120 g) each		METHOD Sautéing	
Onions, medium dice		12 oz.	360 g
Garlic, chopped		1 Tbsp.	15 ml
Olive oil		4 fl. oz.	120 ml
Green bell pepper, medium dice		6 oz.	180 g
Red bell pepper, medium dice		6 oz.	180 g
Eggplant, medium dice		12 oz.	360 g
Zucchini, medium dice		8 oz.	240 g
Tomato concassée		24 oz.	720 g
Fresh basil leaves, chiffonade		1 oz.	30 g
Salt		1 oz.	30 g
Black pepper		TT	TT

1 Sauté the onion and garlic in the oil.

2 Add the bell peppers, eggplant and zucchini and sauté until tender, approximately 10 minutes.

3 Add the tomato concassée, basil and seasonings. Sauté for 5 minutes. Adjust the seasonings. Serve as a side dish with grilled, sautéed or roasted foods or as a hot or cold appetizer.

Approximate values per 4-oz. (120-g) serving: **Calories** 90, **Total fat** 7 g, **Saturated fat** 1 g, **Cholesterol** 0 mg, **Sodium** 690 mg, **Total carbohydrates** 6 g, **Protein** 1 g, **Vitamin C** 35%, **Claims**—low saturated fat; no cholesterol

❶ Sautéing the onions and garlic.

❷ Adding the peppers, eggplant and zucchini.

Beet and Corn Salad

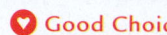 Good Choice    Vegetarian

YIELD 8 Servings, 6 oz. (180 g) each	METHOD Boiling	
Beets, small, red	1 lb.	480 g
Salt	TT	TT
Ears of corn, husk and silk removed	6	6
Fresh goat cheese such as Montrachet	4 oz.	120 g
Green onion, minced	1	1
Fresh cilantro leaves, chopped	¼ c.	60 ml
Sherry Walnut Vinaigrette (page 759)	10 fl. oz.	300 ml
Black pepper	TT	TT
Candy striped or gold beets, cooked, sliced	as needed for garnish	
Fresh thyme sprigs	as needed for garnish	

1 Boil the beets in salted water until tender, approximately 15 minutes. Drain, cool, peel, dice and reserve.

2 Boil the ears of corn in salted water until tender, approximately 3 minutes. Drain, cool, cut the kernels from the cobs and reserve.

3 Roll the goat cheese into small balls.

4 In a stainless steel bowl, mix together the corn, green onion and cilantro. Toss with half of the Sherry Walnut Vinaigrette and adjust the seasoning with salt and pepper. Toss the diced red beets with the remaining Sherry Walnut Vinaigrette. Divide the beet mixture evenly between eight ring molds on eight plates. Top with the corn mixture.

5 Remove the ring molds. Garnish with the balls of goat cheese, the sliced beets and fresh thyme.

Approximate values per 6-oz. (180-g) serving: **Calories** 370, **Total fat** 31 g, **Saturated fat** 6 g, **Cholesterol** 10 mg, **Sodium** 400 mg, **Total carbohydrates** 20 g, **Protein** 7 g, **Vitamin C** 15%, **Claims**—good source of fiber and vitamin C

Sautéed Broccoli Rabe

 Good Choice    Vegetarian

Turnip, beet, escarole, arugula or other tender greens can be cooked using this same method.

YIELD 4 Servings, 6 oz. (180 g) each	METHOD Sautéing	
Broccoli rabe	1¼ lbs.	600 g
Olive oil	2 fl. oz.	60 ml
Garlic cloves, sliced thin	2	2
Red pepper flakes	¼ tsp.	1 ml
Vegetable stock	8 fl. oz.	240 ml
Salt and pepper	TT	TT

1 Wash the broccoli rabe and cut off the stems. Leave on any excess water.

2 In a large sauté pan over medium heat, heat the oil, garlic and red pepper flakes. Sauté until the garlic softens without browning. Add the broccoli rabe and sauté for 5 minutes. Add the vegetable stock, cover and cook until tender and cooked through, approximately 6–8 more minutes.

3 Season with salt and pepper before serving.

Approximate values per 6-oz. (180-g) serving: **Calories** 170, **Total fat** 15 g, **Saturated fat** 2 g, **Cholesterol** 0 mg, **Sodium** 125 mg, **Total carbohydrates** 6 g, **Protein** 5 g, **Vitamin A** 60%, **Vitamin C** 40%, **Claims**—good source of fiber and vitamins A and C

 Good Choice    Vegetarian

Pan-Fried Eggplant with Tomato Sauce

YIELD 4 Servings, 10 oz. (300 g) each	METHOD Pan-Frying	
Eggplant, large	1	1
Tomato sauce	12 fl. oz.	360 ml
Flour	4 oz.	120 g
Salt	TT	TT
White pepper	1 tsp.	5 ml
Egg wash	4 fl. oz.	120 ml
Fresh bread crumbs, crustless	6 oz.	120 g
Vegetable oil	as needed	as needed
Ricotta	2 oz.	60 g
Mozzarella, sliced	8 slices	8 slices
Basil sprigs	4	4
Basil Oil (page 241)	as needed for garnish	

1 Trim the ends from the eggplant. Remove strips of peel, lengthwise, with a chef's knife, leaving narrow strips of peel between the cuts. Cut into 12 round slices ¼ inch (6 millimeters) thick.

2 Warm the tomato sauce.

3 Season the flour with salt and add the white pepper. Bread the eggplant slices using the standard breading procedure described in Chapter 9, Mise en Place (finishing with the bread crumbs), and arrange them in a single layer on a sheet pan. Separate the layers with parchment.

4 Heat two sautoirs and add a ¼-inch (6-millimeter) layer of oil in each. When the oil is hot, pan-fry the eggplant slices until golden brown, then turn and cook until tender. Remove and drain on clean paper towels or a rack. Keep warm. Repeat until all the slices are cooked, adding more oil as necessary.

5 To serve, place a slice of fried eggplant on each plate. Add ½ ounce (15 grams) of the ricotta and some tomato sauce then top with a second slice of fried eggplant. Place a slice of mozzarella and some tomato sauce on top then a third slice of fried eggplant. Garnish each stack with a slice of mozzarella and a sprig of basil. Dot each plate with some Basil Oil.

Approximate values per 10-oz. (300-g) serving: **Calories** 700, **Total fat** 38 g, **Saturated fat** 12 g, **Cholesterol** 165 mg, **Sodium** 1070 mg, **Total carbohydrates** 63 g, **Protein** 28 g, **Vitamin A** 50%, **Vitamin C** 40%, **Calcium** 45%, **Iron** 25%, **Claims**—excellent source of fiber, vitamins A and C, calcium and iron

 Good Choice    Vegan

Stir-Fried Snow Peas

YIELD 6 Servings, 3 oz. (90 g) each	METHOD Stir-Frying	
Snow peas	1 lb.	500 g
Garlic, chopped	2 tsp.	10 ml
Vegetable oil	2 fl. oz.	60 ml
Sesame oil	1 tsp.	5 ml
Water chestnuts, sliced	4 oz.	120 g
Salt	TT	TT

1 Snap the snow peas and remove the strings.

2 Blanch the snow peas and refresh.

3 Stir-fry the garlic in the vegetable and sesame oils for 10 seconds. Add the water chestnuts.

4 Add the snow peas and stir-fry until tender, approximately 1 minute. Season to taste with salt.

Approximate values per 3-oz. (90-g) serving: **Calories** 130, **Total fat** 10 g, **Saturated fat** 1.5 g, **Cholesterol** 0 mg, **Sodium** 0 mg, **Total carbohydrates** 8 g, **Protein** 2 g, **Vitamin C** 80%, **Claims**—no cholesterol; no sodium

Tempura Vegetables with Dipping Sauce

🌿 Vegetarian

YIELD Approximately 1 qt. (1 lt) Batter,
enough for 4 lb. (1.9 kg) vegetables

METHOD Deep-Frying

Dipping sauce:		
Mirin	2 fl. oz.	60 ml
Soy sauce	4 fl. oz.	120 ml
Rice wine vinegar	2 fl. oz.	60 ml
Lemon juice	1 Tbsp.	15 ml
Wasabi powder	1 tsp.	5 ml
Tempura batter:		
Eggs	2	2
Sparkling water, cold	1 pt.	480 ml
Flour	10 oz.	300 g
Sweet potato, approximately 8 oz. (240 g)	1	1
Broccoli florets	8 oz.	240 g
Mushrooms, small, whole	1 lb.	480 g
Zucchini, bâtonnet	8 oz.	240 g

1 Combine all of the dipping sauce ingredients. Set aside.

2 To prepare the batter, beat the eggs and add the cold water.

3 Add the flour to the egg-and-water mixture and mix until the flour is incorporated. There should still be small lumps in the batter. Overmixing develops gluten, which is undesirable.

4 Peel the sweet potato and cut it into ¼-inch- (6-millimeter-) thick slices. If the potato is large, cut each slice in half to make semicircles.

5 Blanch the broccoli florets briefly in boiling water. Drain and pat dry with paper towels.

6 Drop the vegetables in the batter a few at a time. Remove them from the batter one at a time and drop them into the deep-fryer using the swimming method. Cook until done. Remove and drain.

7 Arrange the tempura vegetables on a serving platter. Serve the dipping sauce on the side.

Variations:

Panko Crust Tempura—Dip the batter-coated vegetables into **panko** crumbs in Step 6 before deep-frying.

Shrimp Tempura—Substitute peeled and deveined shrimp for some of the vegetables.

panko light, crisp Japanese-style breadcrumbs; traditionally made from crust less white yeast bread that is dried then ground into sliver shaped crumbs

Approximate values per 4-oz. (120-g) serving: **Calories** 240, **Total fat** 15 g, **Saturated fat** 2.5 g, **Cholesterol** 25 mg, **Sodium** 530 mg, **Total carbohydrates** 22 g, **Protein** 5 g, **Vitamin A** 50%, **Vitamin C** 30%, **Iron** 10%

❶ Mixing the tempura batter.

❷ Battering the vegetables.

❸ Deep-frying the vegetables using the swimming method.

 Vegan

Deep-Fried Carrots or Leeks for Garnishing

Root vegetables, soft herbs and even vegetable trimmings make appealing garnishes for salads and main dishes when deep-fried. Use a mandolin or slicer to cut thin, uniform pieces that will cook evenly. Although such garnishes taste best when freshly prepared, they may be prepared a day ahead. When stored airtight, they retain their crispness.

YIELD Varies		METHOD Deep-Frying	
Carrots, peeled	as needed	as needed	
Leeks, washed, trimmed	as needed	as needed	
Corn or soybean oil, hot	as needed	as needed	
Salt and pepper	TT	TT	

1 Cut the peeled carrots into julienne strips or curls using a mandolin or special slicer as shown in Chapter 6, Knife Skills.

2 Cut the leeks in half. Trim the root and the tough green tops. Cut the leeks into 4-inch (10-centimeter)-long pieces, then julienne.

3 Using the basket method, deep-fry the carrots and leeks separately in 350°F (180°C) fat until golden and done. Drain them well. Season to taste with salt and pepper.

Approximate values per ½-oz. (15-g) serving: **Calories** 35, **Total fat** 3 g, **Saturated fat** 0 g, **Cholesterol** 0 mg, **Sodium** 5 mg, **Total carbohydrates** 2 g, **Protein** 0 g, **Vitamin A** 30%

Crispy deep-fried carrot curls and julienned leeks

 Vegetarian

Glazed Pearl Onions

YIELD 1 lb. (480 g), 8 Servings, 2 oz. (60 g) each		METHOD Boiling	
Pearl or cipollini onions, peeled	1 lb.	480 g	
Whole butter	1½ oz.	45 g	
Granulated sugar	1 Tbsp.	15 ml	
Salt and pepper	TT	TT	

1 Place the onions, butter and sugar in a sauté pan and add enough water to barely cover.

2 Boil the onions, allowing the water to evaporate. As the water evaporates, the butter-and-sugar mixture will begin to coat the onions. When the water is nearly gone, test the doneness of the onions. If they are still firm, add a small amount of water and continue to boil until the onions are tender.

3 Sauté the onions in the butter-and-sugar mixture until they are glazed. Season to taste. Serve the glazed onions as an accompaniment to roasted meats, fish and vegetables or as a garnish with cured and smoked meats.

1 Boiling the onions.

2 Sautéing the onions in butter-and-sugar mixture until they are glazed.

Variations:

Vegetables such as carrots, turnips, zucchini and other squashes can also be glazed with this procedure. They should be cut into appropriate shapes such as a tournée and be large enough so that they glaze properly without overcooking. When preparing a mix of glazed vegetables, cook each type separately because each has a different cooking time. Water, stock, orange juice or other mild liquid can be used to add flavor to vegetables prepared using this technique.

Approximate values per 2-oz. (60-g) serving: **Calories** 70, **Total fat** 4.5 g, **Saturated fat** 2.5 g, **Cholesterol** 10 mg, **Sodium** 340 mg, **Total carbohydrates** 8 g, **Protein** 1 g

---

Red Beet Purée

YIELD 6 Servings, 4 oz. (120 g) each	METHOD Boiling/Puréeing	
Red beets, peeled, large dice	1 lb.	480 g
Chicken stock	1 qt.	960 ml
Shallots, peeled, chopped	8 oz.	240 g
Fresh thyme sprig	1	1
Butter, cold, cubed	4 oz.	120 g
Horseradish, ground	2 tsp.	10 ml
Salt and white pepper	TT	TT

1 Bring the red beets, chicken stock, shallots and thyme to a boil in a small saucepot. Simmer until the beets are very tender, approximately 45 minutes.

2 Remove the thyme sprig and purée the beets in a blender until very smooth.

3 Return the beet purée to a clean saucepot. Dilute the purée to the desired consistency depending on the application by stirring in a small amount of water or chicken stock.

4 Warm the beet purée over medium heat. Stir in the cubes of butter a few pieces at a time until they are completely melted. Stir in the horseradish and season to taste with salt and white pepper. Serve the beet purée with grilled or sautéed meats and poultry such as Sautéed Chicken Livers (page 463) or as the base for grilled or roasted vegetables.

Variation:

Carrot Ginger Purée—Substitute 1 pound (480 grams) peeled diced carrots for the beets. Cook the carrots in the stock with 1 ounce (30 grams) chopped fresh ginger until tender in Step 2. Drain and purée the carrots and ginger. Omit the horseradish. Season with salt, white pepper and dried ginger.

Approximate values per 4-oz. (120-g) serving: **Calories** 50, **Total fat** 4 g, **Saturated fat** 2.5 g, **Cholesterol** 10 mg, **Sodium** 25 mg, **Total carbohydrates** 3 g, **Protein** 3 g, **Vitamin A** 40%, **Vitamin C** 25%, **Iron** 15%

♥ Good Choice

Collard Greens with fried chicken

Collard Greens

YIELD 6 Servings, 3 oz. (90 g) each	METHOD Simmering	
Ham hocks, smoked, 1 lb. (480 g)	1 hock	1 hock
Chile flakes	½ tsp.	2 ml
Water	as needed	as needed
Collard greens, washed and trimmed	1½ lb.	1.9 kg
Green onions, small dice	2	2
Cider vinegar	1 fl. oz.	30 ml
Salt and pepper	TT	TT

1 In a medium saucepot, combine the ham hock and chile flakes. Cover with 1 inch (2.5 centimeters) water, bring to a boil, reduce to a simmer and cook until the hock is tender, approximately 1 hour. Remove the hock from the pot, reserving the cooking liquid, which is also known as **pot liquor**.

2 Cut the collard greens into 2-inch (centimeter) strips. Add them to the pot liquor and simmer until tender, approximately 45 minutes to 1 hour.

3 Add the green onions and vinegar to the greens. Bring to a simmer and reduce the liquid until it coats the collard greens. Season to taste with salt and pepper.

4 Remove the meat from the ham hock and cut into medium dice. Stir the diced ham into the greens and serve. Collard greens are the traditional accompaniment to fried chicken and Southern-style pork dishes.

Approximate values per 3-oz. (90-g) serving: **Calories** 130, **Total fat** 9 g, **Saturated fat** 2.5 g, **Cholesterol** 35 mg, **Sodium** 460 mg, **Total carbohydrates** 5 g, **Protein** 11 g, **Vitamin A** 70%, **Vitamin C** 40%, **Calcium** 15%, **Claims**—good source of fiber and calcium; excellent source vitamins A and C

♥ Good Choice   ♥ Vegan

Warm Zucchini, Red Pepper and Chickpea Salad

YIELD 10 Servings, 5 oz. (150 g) each	METHOD Steaming/Sautéing	
Zucchini, sliced into ¼-in. (6 ml) rounds	1¼ lb.	300 g
Olive oil	1½ fl. oz.	45 ml
White onion, peeled, chopped fine	8 oz.	240 g
Garlic, minced	1 Tbsp.	15 ml
Sweet paprika	2 tsp.	20 ml
Cumin, ground	1½ tsp.	7 ml
Cayenne pepper	¼ tsp.	1 ml
Roasted red pepper, coarsely chopped	8 oz.	240 g
Tomato, seeded, chopped coarse	6 oz.	120 g
Salt and pepper	TT	TT
Chickpeas, cooked	10 oz.	300 g
Lemon juice	as needed	as needed

1 Steam the zucchini until tender, approximately 6 minutes. Drain and let cool slightly.

2 Heat the olive oil over medium high heat in a large frying pan. Sauté the onions and garlic in the oil until softened, approximately 3 minutes.

3 Add the paprika, cumin, cayenne, roasted red pepper and tomato. Season with salt and pepper and cook for about 5 minutes.

4 Stir in the chickpeas and drained zucchini Cook for 5 more minutes to blend the seasonings. Season with salt, pepper and lemon juice. Serve salad warm or at room temperature.

Approximate values per 5-oz. (130-g) serving: **Calories** 100, **Total fat** 5 g, **Saturated fat** 0.5 g, **Cholesterol** 0 mg, **Sodium** 10 mg, **Total carbohydrates** 14 g, **Protein** 4 g, **Vitamin C** 35%, **Claims**—no cholesterol; good source of vitamin A, iron and fiber; excellent source of vitamin C

Red Beans and Rice with Andouille

YIELD 10 Servings, 8 oz. (240 g) each	METHOD Simmering	
Red kidney beans, dry	1 lb.	480 g
Water	as needed	as needed
Spice mix:		
Bay leaves	5	5
Dried thyme	2 tsp.	10 ml
Dried oregano	2 tsp.	10 ml
Cayenne pepper	½ tsp.	2 ml
Black pepper	½ tsp.	2 ml
Water	1 gal.	3.8 lt
Smoked ham hocks	2	2
Celery, small dice	8 oz.	240 g
Onions, small dice	13 oz.	390 g
Green bell pepper, small dice	5 oz.	150 g
Garlic cloves	1 oz.	30 g
Andouille, sliced on the bias	1 lb.	480 g
¼ in. (6 mm) thick		
Salt and pepper	TT	TT
Simmered Rice (page 672)	2 pt.	960 ml

1 Soak the beans in water overnight and drain.

2 Combine the spice mix ingredients and reserve.

3 In a heavy-bottomed saucepot, combine 1 gallon (3.8 liters) water with the ham hocks, beans, celery, onions, bell pepper, garlic and spice mix. Bring to a boil, reduce to a simmer and cook for 1 hour.

4 Remove the ham hocks from the pot. Separate the meat from the bones and discard the skin, bones and cartilage. Cut the meat into medium dice. Add the meat and the andouille slices to the beans and simmer, stirring often, until the beans are very tender and begin to break up, approximately 30 minutes. Add more water if necessary to prevent the beans from burning. Remove the bay leaves and adjust the seasonings.

5 To serve, mound a portion of the Simmered Rice on a soup plate and ladle the bean mixture around it.

Approximate values per 8-oz. (240-g) serving: **Calories** 430, **Total fat** 17 g, **Saturated fat** 6 g, **Cholesterol** 45 mg, **Sodium** 460 mg, **Total carbohydrates** 48 g, **Protein** 21 g, **Vitamin C** 30%, **Calcium** 10%, **Iron** 30%

Refried Beans

 ♥ Good Choice

YIELD 16 Servings, 4 oz. (120 g) each	METHOD Simmering/Sautéing	
Onion, chopped coarse	4 oz.	120 g
Bell pepper, seeded, chopped coarse	1	1
Garlic, chopped	1 oz.	30 g
Dry pinto beans, rinsed	1 lb.	480 g
Salt pork, diced	5 oz.	150 g
Water	3 qt.	2.8 lt
Lard	6 oz.	180 g
Kosher salt	TT	TT

1 Bring the onion, bell pepper, garlic, beans and salt pork to a boil in a large sauce pot. Simmer uncovered stirring occasionally and adding boiling water if needed to keep the beans submerged. Simmer until beans are tender, approximately 2–2½ hours.

2 Heat a large frying pan over medium high heat. Add 3 ounces (120 grams) of the lard and half of the cooked beans and their cooking liquid. Carefully fry the beans until most of the liquid has evaporated, approximately 10 minutes. Crush the beans with a wooden spoon or potato masher until the mixture is thick with a few visible chunks of beans left. Season to taste with salt.

3 Transfer to a large bowl. Repeat the cooking process with remaining beans and lard.

4 Serve the beans as a side dish with rice and cooked meat, or use as a filling or topping for burritos, enchiladas or tostadas.

Approximate values per 4-oz. (120-g) serving: **Calories** 270, **Total fat** 18 g, **Saturated fat** 7 g, **Cholesterol** 20 mg, **Sodium** 680 mg, **Total carbohydrates** 19 g, **Protein** 7 g, **Vitamin C** 15%, **Claims**—excellent source of fiber

Braised Red Cabbage with Apples

YIELD 16 Servings, 4 oz. (120 g) each	METHOD Braising	
Red cabbage	3 lb.	1.4 kg
Bacon, medium dice	12 oz.	360 g
Onions, medium dice	8 oz.	240 g
Salt and pepper	TT	TT
Red wine	8 fl. oz.	240 ml
White stock	8 fl. oz.	240 ml
Cinnamon sticks	2	2
Apples, tart, cored and diced	12 oz.	360 g
Brown sugar	1 oz.	30 g
Cider vinegar	2 fl. oz.	60 ml

1 Shred the cabbage.

2 Render the bacon. Add the onions and sweat in the bacon fat until tender.

3 Add the cabbage and sauté for 5 minutes. Season with salt and pepper. Add the wine, stock and cinnamon sticks. Cover and braise until the cabbage is almost tender, approximately 20 minutes.

4 Add the apples, sugar and vinegar and mix well.

5 Cover and braise until the apples are tender, approximately 5 minutes. Remove the cinnamon sticks before service. Serve the braised cabbage with roasted poultry, pork or pork sausages.

Approximate values per 4-oz. (120-g) serving: **Calories** 170, **Total fat** 11 g, **Saturated fat** 4 g, **Cholesterol** 20 mg, **Sodium** 540 mg, **Total carbohydrates** 11 g, **Protein** 8 g, **Vitamin C** 50%

❤ Good Choice    Vegetarian

Butter-Braised Honey Carrots

YIELD 4 Servings, 3 oz. (90 g) each	METHOD *Sous Vide* Poaching	
Baby carrots, yellow and orange, 12 oz. (360 g)	12	12
Butter	2 oz.	60 g
Honey or maple syrup	2 tsp.	10 ml
Vegetable Stock (page 212)	2 fl. oz.	60 ml
Salt and pepper	TT	TT
Watercress microgreens	as needed for garnish	

1 Peel and trim the tops from the carrots.

2 Wearing clean disposable gloves, prepare four plastic pouches for *sous vide* cooking. Arrange three carrots in each pouch in a single layer without touching.

3 Divide the butter, honey and stock evenly between the four bags. Season with salt and pepper. Vacuum seal the pouches.

4 Cook the carrots in a thermal circulator heated to 180°F (82°C) until tender to the touch, approximately 20 minutes.

5 Remove the carrots from each bag as needed for service. Garnish with watercress microgreens.

Approximate values per 3-oz. (120-g) serving: **Calories** 120, **Total fat** 12 g, **Saturated fat** 7 g, **Cholesterol** 30 mg, **Sodium** 55 mg, **Total carbohydrates** 5 g, **Protein** 0 g, **Vitamin A** 90%, **Claims**—excellent source of vitamin A

⚠ Safety Alert

Sous Vide *Sanitation*

Food safety is of utmost concern when using *sous vide* techniques because of the low cooking temperatures. To prevent the growth of microorganisms, any food to be cooked *sous vide* must be chilled below the temperature danger zone (41°F/5°C) before cooking. Keep all cutting boards, knives and food contact surfaces clean and sanitary and wear clean disposable gloves. Use only the freshest unblemished ingredients. Consult your local health department for regulations for preparing food *sous vide*. Special permission and a HACCP plan may be required.

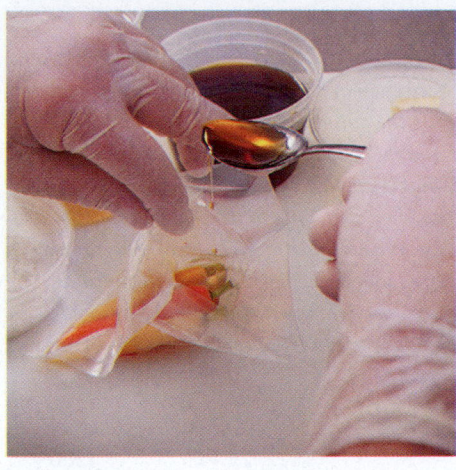

1 Adding stock to the carrots.

2 The cooked carrots with salmon.

Artichokes Hollandaise

❤ **Good Choice**

YIELD 8 Servings, 1 artichoke and
3 fl. oz. (90 ml) sauce each

METHOD Simmering

Artichokes	8	8
Lemon juice	2 fl. oz	60 ml
Salt	1 Tbsp.	15 ml
Hollandaise (page 230)	24 fl. oz.	720 ml

1 Peel the stems and remove any tough outer leaves from the artichokes. Trim the barbs from the tops of the remaining leaves. Keep the trimmed artichokes in water acidulated with the lemon juice until ready to cook them.

2 Bring a gallon of water to boil in a large stock pot. Add the salt and the trimmed artichokes. Bring the water back to a simmer. Invert a heavy lid and place it on top of the artichokes to keep them submerged in the water. Cover the pot and simmer the artichokes until tender and leaves come out easily, approximately 40–45 minutes.

3 Drain the artichokes in a colander. Gently press down on the sides of each artichoke to remove any excess water.

4 Serve each artichoke with a ramekin of Hollandaise on the side and a small bowl for the discarded leaves.

Variation:

Serve the cooked artichokes with Aïoli (Garlic Mayonnaise) (page 742) or Dijon Vinaigrette (page 740) in place of the Hollandaise.

Approximate values per serving: **Calories** 610, **Total fat** 60 g, **Saturated fat** 35 g, **Cholesterol** 230 mg, **Sodium** 80 mg, **Total carbohydrates** 15 g, **Protein** 6 g, **Vitamin A** 40%, **Vitamin C** 20%, **Claims**—rich in fiber; high in vitamins A and C

♥ Good Choice

Baechu-Kimchee (Korean Spicy Cabbage)

Although there are close to 200 recognized varieties of Kimchee in Korea, the most common and popular version is made from large Napa cabbages. During the autumn kimjang season families gather to preserve enough cabbages to last through the winter. The cabbages are soaked in brine, and then coated with a pungent paste of blended seasonings that is applied by hand. The seasonings vary by region and family tradition. The seasoned cabbage is stored in a cool place to ferment and is eaten daily over the next few months. Spicy baechu kimchee *appears as a side dish at every meal, but it is also incorporated into stews and soups, sautéed with rice, stuffed into dumplings and fried in pancakes. When fermenting cabbage, always wear gloves to prevent cross-contamination. Store the finished cabbage in plastic or ceramic containers with tight-fitting lids. Leave a bit of space at the top of any storage container to allow the fermenting vegetables to breathe.*

YIELD 18 Servings, approximately 3 oz. (90 g) each	METHOD Fermenting	
Napa cabbage, 1 large head	2½ lb.	1200 g
Spring water	as needed	as needed
Sea salt or kosher salt	as needed	as needed
Seasoning paste:		
Sweet (glutinous) rice flour*	1 Tbsp.	15 ml
Fresh spring water	4 fl. oz.	120 ml
Green onion, cleaned	1 oz.	30 g
Garlic chives or Korean chives	2 oz.	60 g
Daikon radish, fine julienne	8 oz.	240 g
Asian pear, peeled and grated	1 oz.	30 g
Coarse Korean red chile powder	2–3 oz.	60–90 g
Anchovy sauce or Korean fish sauce	1 fl. oz.	30 ml
Salted shrimp	1 oz.	30 g
Garlic, minced	1 oz.	30 g
Fresh ginger, minced	¼ oz.	7 g
Corn or rice syrup	½ oz.	15 g

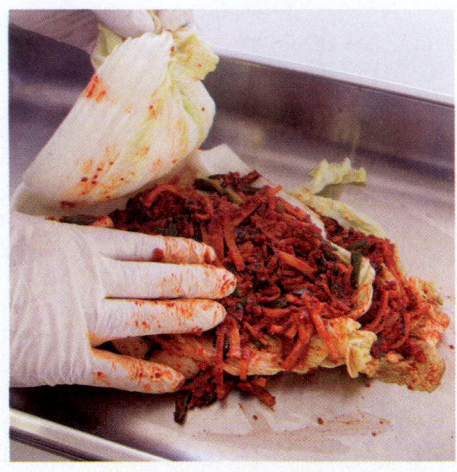

❶ Spreading the seasoning paste onto each leaf of cabbage.

❷ A portion of the fermented kimchee.

1 Remove the tough outer leaves from the cabbage and trim the root, leaving enough root to hold the head together. Rinse the cabbage, and cut it in half lengthwise. Rinse the halves again and drain.

2 Place the cabbage halves in a large non-reactive bowl, cut side up. Add enough water to cover the cabbage. Sprinkle a generous amount of salt over the cabbage and stir the salt into the water. Add enough salt to create a 10-percent salt solution. Soak at room temperature for approximately 5 hours, turning the cabbage once halfway through.

3 Remove the cabbage from the brine when it is softened, but still crisp. Do not discard the brine. Rinse the cabbage carefully under cool running water and place it, cut side down, on a cooling rack or in a large colander to drain.

4 To prepare the seasoning paste, moisten the rice flour with 2 fluid ounces (60 milliliters) of the fresh water. In a small saucepan, combine the wet rice flour and remaining 2 fluid ounces (60 milliliters) of fresh water; bring to a boil. Reduce the heat to a simmer and cook, stirring constantly, until a thick paste is formed. Remove from the heat and pour into a bowl to cool.

5 Slice the green onions and the chives into 1-inch (2.5-centimeter) pieces and combine with the rice flour paste and the remaining seasoning ingredients. Adjust the amount of chile powder used depending on the flavor desired.

6 Wearing gloves, lay each portion of cabbage on a work surface, cut side up. Starting with the outer leaves and working in, spread some of the seasoning mixture between each leaf, being careful not to break the leaves off from the root. The outer leaves will be very soft, and can be wrapped tightly around the cabbage to hold it together during aging.

7 Place the cabbage in an airtight plastic or glass container. Pour about 2 cups of the brine water into the bowl that held the seasoning paste. Stir the water to mix in all the remaining seasoning from the bowl, and then pour this seasoning and brine mixture over the cabbage. Cover and leave at room temperature for 24 hours, then refrigerate. The kimchee will keep for up to 5 months, but will become more strongly flavored due to fermentation as it ages.

* You may grind short-grain rice by hand with a mortar and pestle to make the flour.

Approximate values per 3-oz. (90-g) serving: **Calories** 35, **Total fat** 1 g, **Saturated fat** 0 g, **Cholesterol** 0 mg, **Sodium** 330 mg, **Total carbohydrates** 6 g, **Protein** 2 g, **Vitamin A** 35%, **Vitamin C** 20%, **Claims**—low calorie; no cholesterol; good source of fiber; excellent source of vitamins A and C

Potatoes, Grains and Pasta 23

After studying this chapter, you will be able to:

▶ identify a variety of potatoes

▶ apply various cooking methods to potatoes

▶ identify a variety of grains

▶ apply various cooking methods to grains

▶ identify and cook pasta products

▶ make and cook fresh pasta

farinaceous a food made from flour or meal, or having a starchy, mealy texture; from the Latin *farina* meaning a flour made from cereal grains or nuts; refers to food that is high in starch, especially pasta, noodles, rice and polenta

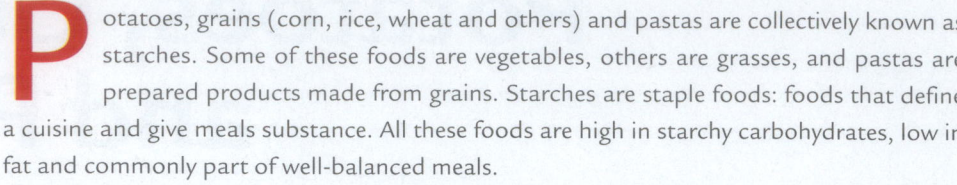

Potatoes, grains (corn, rice, wheat and others) and pastas are collectively known as starches. Some of these foods are vegetables, others are grasses, and pastas are prepared products made from grains. Starches are staple foods: foods that define a cuisine and give meals substance. All these foods are high in starchy carbohydrates, low in fat and commonly part of well-balanced meals.

Today's chefs are rediscovering traditional and ethnic dishes that rely on grains seldom used in typical American food service operations. Pasta and other **farinaceous** dishes made from a world of grains now regularly appear on menus in addition to the ubiquitous potato.

POTATOES

Potatoes (Fr. *pommes de terre*) are one of the few vegetables native to the New World, probably originating in the South American Andes. Botanically, potatoes are succulent, nonwoody annual plants. The portion consumed is the tuber, the swollen fleshy part of the underground stem. Potatoes are hardy and easy to grow, making them inexpensive and widely available. The average person in the United States eats nearly 35 pounds of fresh potatoes and 50 pounds of frozen potatoes annually, making potatoes one of the top five vegetable crops in the United States and the fourth-most consumed crop in the world, after rice, wheat and corn.

Identifying Potatoes

In this chapter we discuss some of the more commonly used types of potatoes. Other potato varieties are regularly being developed or rediscovered and tested in the market place.

Choose potatoes that are heavy and very firm with clean skin and few eyes. Avoid those with many eyes, sprouts, green streaks, soft spots, cracks or cut edges. Most varieties are available all year. When ordering potatoes, note that size A is larger than size B. Size B must be between 1½ and 2¼ inches (3.75 and 5.5 centimeters) in diameter. Size C potatoes, or **creamers**, are the smallest, measuring ¾–1⅛ inches (2–4 centimeters) in diameter.

New potatoes are small, immature potatoes (of any variety) that are harvested before their starches develop. Although red potatoes can be "new," not all new potatoes are necessarily red-skinned. Conversely, not all red-skinned potatoes are new. True new potatoes are waxy with a high moisture content and a thin, delicate skin.

Fingerlings

Fingerling potatoes are typically heirloom varieties, related to the original potato varieties from the Andes. They are generally small, long and oblong with good flavor. The Russian Banana looks like a small banana and has a firm texture and rich, buttery flavor. The red-streaked French Fingerling has a nutty flavor; the red Ruby Crescent has a strong, earthy flavor. Fingerling varieties tend to be low in starch and are good for roasting and in potato salads.

Purple Potatoes

Purple (or blue) potatoes have a deep purple skin. The flesh is bright purple, becoming lighter when cooked. They are mealy, with a flavor and texture similar to russets. The most common varieties are All Blue and Caribe, which were also quite popular in the mid-19th century.

Fingerlings

Purple potatoes

Red Potatoes

Red potatoes have a thin, red skin and crisp, white, waxy flesh, that is best suited to boiling or steaming. They do not have the dry, mealy texture that successful baking requires. Red potatoes are round, instead of long or oblong; popular varieties are Red Bliss, Red Pontiac and Norland.

Red potatoes

Russet Potatoes

Russet potatoes, commonly referred to as Idaho potatoes, are the standard baking potato. They are long with rough, reddish-brown skin and mealy flesh. Russets are excellent baked and are the best potatoes for frying. They tend to fall apart when boiled. There are over a dozen varieties of russet potato, the most widely planted is the Burbank (named for its developer, the agriculture scientist Luther Burbank). They are marketed in several size categories. Select those in the size most appropriate for their intended use.

Russet potatoes

White Potatoes

White potatoes are available in round or long varieties. They have a thin, tender skin with a tender, waxy yellow or white flesh. Round white potatoes are also referred to as chef or all-purpose potatoes. White potatoes are usually cooked with moist heat or used for sautéing. White Rose and Finnish Yellow (or Yellow Finn) are popular varieties.

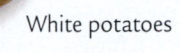

White potatoes

Another variety of white potato known as the **Yukon Gold** is a medium-sized, slightly flattened, oval potato. Yukon Golds have a delicate pale yellow skin with shallow pink eyes. Their pale yellow flesh has a creamy texture and rich, buttery, nutty flavor. They are suitable for most cooking methods and will retain their yellow color when baked, boiled or fried. First bred by botanists in Canada, Yukon Golds are now grown throughout the United States. Other lesser-known, gold-fleshed white potato varieties include Michigold, Donna, Delta Gold, Banana and Saginaw Gold.

Yukon Gold potatoes

Sweet Potatoes

Sweet potatoes are from a different botanical family than other potatoes, although they are also tubers that originated in the New World. Two types of sweet potatoes are commonly available. One has yellow flesh and a dry, mealy texture; it is known as a boniato, white or Cuban sweet potato. The other has a darker orange, moister flesh and is high in sugar; it is known as a red sweet potato. Both types have thick skins ranging in color from light tan to brownish red. (Sometimes dark-skinned sweet potatoes are erroneously labeled yams.) Sweet potatoes, which have a high moisture content, should be chosen according to the desired degree of sweetness. They are best suited for boiling, baking and puréeing, although the less sweet varieties can also be deep-fried. The cooked flesh can be used in breads, pies and puddings. Sweet potatoes are available canned, often in a spiced or sugary sauce.

Sweet potatoes

Yams

Yams are a third type of tuber that is botanically different from other potatoes. Yams are less sweet than sweet potatoes, but yams and sweet potatoes can be used interchangeably. The flesh of yams ranges from creamy white to deep red. Yams are Asian in origin and are now found in Africa, South America and the southern United States.

Nutrition of Potatoes

Potatoes contain a high percentage of easily digested complex carbohydrates and little or no fat. They are a good source for minerals and vitamins, especially vitamin B_6, vitamin C and potassium, although much of the vitamin C can be destroyed when potatoes are cooked in liquid.

Red yams

COMPARISON OF MEALY AND WAXY POTATOES   TABLE 23.1

		CONTENT OF			BEST TO			
		STARCH	MOISTURE	SUGAR	BAKE	BOIL	SAUTÉ	DEEP-FRY
Russet, white (White Rose), purple	*mealy*	high	low	low	✓			✓
Yukon Gold, purple	*all-purpose*	medium	medium	medium	✓	✓		✓
Red, new (immature), white (Finnish Yellow), Fingerlings	*waxy*	low	high	high		✓	✓	

Purchasing and Storing Potatoes

One of the most important considerations in selecting potatoes is choosing between the mealy (starchy) and waxy varieties. It is important to understand the differences and purchase the type of potatoes best suited to the type of dish being prepared. A comparison of mealy and waxy potatoes and their uses is presented in Table 23.1.

Mealy potatoes (also known as starchy potatoes) have a high starch content and thick skin. They are best for baking and are often referred to simply as "bakers" when ordered from suppliers. The low sugar content of mealy potatoes allows them to be deep-fried long enough to fully cook the interior without burning the exterior. Mealy potatoes tend to fall apart when boiled, making them a good choice for whipped or puréed potatoes.

All-purpose potatoes have a medium starch content somewhere between mealy and waxy potatoes, which makes them suitable for most cooking methods, although they may fall apart when boiled.

Waxy potatoes have a low starch content and thin skin. They are best for boiling and will hold their shape better when used in soups or potato salad. They do not develop the desired fluffy texture when baked. Waxy potatoes tend to become limp and soggy when deep-fried because of their high moisture content.

Grading

Like other vegetables, potatoes are subject to the voluntary USDA grading system. Select U.S. No. 1 potatoes, the top grade, when perfect appearance is required. U.S. Commercial or U.S. No. 2 potatoes work in applications involving peeling and cutting.

Purchasing

Potatoes are usually packed in 50-pound cartons. Counts vary depending on average potato size. For example, in a 100-count carton, each potato weighs an average of 8 ounces. Eighty-, 90- and 100-count cartons are the most common. Generally larger-sized potatoes (that is, smaller counts) are more expensive. But their higher price does not reflect higher quality, however, so select the size according to their intended use.

Storing

Temperatures between 50°F and 65°F (10°C and 18°C) are best for storing potatoes. Do not store raw potatoes in the refrigerator. At temperatures below 40°F (4°C), potato starch turns to sugar, making the prepared product too sweet and increasing the risk that the potato will develop gray-colored streaks when cooked. Potatoes with a high sugar content also burn more easily when fried.

Potatoes should be stored in a dark room, as light promotes chlorophyll production, turning the potatoes green and bitter. A green patch indicates the possible presence of **solanine**, a toxin harmful if eaten in large amounts. Any green patches should be peeled away. Solanine is also present in the eyes and sprouts, and they, too, should be removed and discarded before cooking.

Under proper conditions, fresh baking or general-purpose potatoes should last for 2 months; new potatoes will keep for several weeks. Do not wash potatoes until ready to use, as washing promotes spoilage. Once peeled, potatoes should be stored covered in water and refrigerated to prevent enzymatic browning.

Cooking Methods for Potatoes

Potatoes have a relatively neutral flavor, making them a perfect accompaniment to many savory dishes. They can be prepared with almost any dry- or moist-heat cooking method: baking, sautéing, pan-frying, deep-frying, boiling or steaming. They can be combined with other ingredients in braises and stews. Potatoes are used in soups (vichyssoise), dumplings (gnocchi), breads, pancakes (latkes), puddings, salads and even vodka.

Many potato dishes, both classic and modern, employ more than one cooking method. For example, lorette potatoes require boiling and deep-frying; hash browns require par-boiling, then sautéing. Even French fries are best when first blanched in hot oil before final deep frying.

Determining Doneness

Most potatoes are considered done when they are soft and tender or offer little resistance when pierced with a knife tip. Fried potatoes should have a crisp, golden-brown surface; the interior should be moist and tender.

Roasting and Baking

Potatoes are often roasted with meat or poultry. As they roast, they become coated with the fat and drippings released from the meat as it cooks. Either mealy or waxy potatoes, peeled or unpeeled, can be roasted successfully.

Mealy potatoes such as russets are ideal for baking. The skin is left intact, although it may be pierced with a fork to allow steam to escape. A true baked potato should not be wrapped in foil or cooked in a microwave; this changes the cooking method to steaming and prevents a crisp skin from forming. A properly baked potato should be white and fluffy, not yellowish or soggy. Once baked, potatoes can be eaten plain (or with butter, sour cream and other garnishes) or used in other recipes.

> **⚠ Safety Alert**
>
> *Cooked Potatoes*
>
> Cooked potato dishes, especially those with cream, butter or custard, require time and temperature control for safety (TCS). They must be held for service at 135°F (57°C) or higher. Be sure to reheat potato dishes to 165°F (74°C) or higher before serving.

Procedure for Baking Potatoes

1 Scrub the potatoes well.
2 Using a fork, pierce potato skins if desired.
3 Rub the potatoes with oil and salt if desired. Do not wrap them in foil.
4 Bake the potatoes until done. A paring knife should penetrate them easily.

Baked Potatoes

YIELD 8 Servings		METHOD Baking
Russet potatoes	8	8
Vegetable oil	1½ fl. oz.	45 ml
Kosher salt	3 Tbsp.	45 ml

1   Scrub the potatoes well, but do not peel them. Pierce the skin of each potato to allow steam to escape.

2   Rub the potatoes with oil, then sprinkle with salt.

3   Place the potatoes on a rack over a sheet pan. Bake in a 400°F (200°C) oven until done, approximately 1 hour. The potatoes should yield to gentle pressure and a paring knife inserted in the thickest part should meet little resistance.

4   Hold uncovered in a warm spot and serve within 1 hour.

Variation:

Twice-Baked Potatoes—(Yield: 16 Servings) Cut baked potatoes in half lengthwise. Carefully scoop out the flesh, leaving the skins intact. Whip the potato flesh with 8 ounces (240 grams) sour cream, 2 ounces (60 grams) butter and 2 ounces (60 grams) cooked, crumbled bacon and then add salt and pepper to taste. Thin with hot milk if necessary. The mixture should be light and fluffy, not lumpy. Pile the filling back into the skins, mounding the tops. Brush the mounded potatoes with clarified butter and sprinkle with Parmesan. Arrange on a sheet pan and bake at 425°F (220°C) until thoroughly reheated and lightly browned.

Approximate values per 7.5-oz. (225-g) potato: **Calories** 270, **Total fat** 5 g, **Saturated fat** 0.5 g, **Cholesterol** 0 mg, **Sodium** 2630 mg, **Total carbohydrates** 51 g, **Protein** 5 g, **Vitamin C** 45%, **Claims**—low saturated fat; no cholesterol; good source of fiber

❶ Piercing the potato skins.

❷ Seasoning the potatoes with salt.

Many classic potato dishes require baking either raw or parboiled potatoes with sauce, cheese, meat or other seasonings in a baking dish or casserole. Well-known examples include scalloped potatoes, which are baked in béchamel sauce, and potatoes au gratin, which are topped with cheese and baked. These dishes usually develop a crisp, brown crust, which is part of their appeal.

The casserole should hold its shape when cut; the potatoes should be tender, and the sauce should be smooth, not grainy.

Potato casseroles can be fully baked, then held loosely covered in a steam table for service. Portions can be reheated or browned briefly under a broiler or salamander at service time.

Procedure for Baking Potatoes en Casserole

1 Prepare the potatoes by washing, peeling, slicing or partially cooking as desired or as directed in the recipe.

2 Add the potatoes to the baking pan in layers, alternating with the sauce, cream, cheese or other ingredients. Or combine the potatoes with the other ingredients and place in a buttered baking pan.

3 Bake the potatoes until done.

Gratin Dauphinois

🍃 Vegetarian

Although this dish is customarily made with potatoes, celery root, fennel, sweet potatoes and other firm tubers or squash may be prepared in this manner as well.

YIELD 1 Full-Size Hotel Pan, 4–5 lb. (1.9–2.4 kg), 24 Servings

METHOD Baking en Casserole

MISE EN PLACE
- Grate Gruyère cheese.

Russet potatoes	3 lb.	1.4 kg
Whole butter	as needed	as needed
Salt and white pepper	TT	TT
Nutmeg, ground	¼ tsp.	2 ml
Gruyère, grated	8 oz.	240 g
Half-and-half	24 fl. oz.	720 ml
Egg yolks	3	3

1 Peel the potatoes and cut into ¼-inch- (centimeter-) thick slices.

2 Place a single layer of potatoes in a well-buttered, full-size hotel pan.

3 Season with salt, white pepper and a small amount of nutmeg. Sprinkle on a thin layer of cheese.

4 Add another layer of potatoes, seasonings and cheese and repeat until all the potatoes and about three-fourths of the cheese are used.

5 Heat the half-and-half to a simmer. Whisk the egg yolks together in a bowl, then gradually add the hot half-and-half.

6 Pour the half-and-half and egg mixture over the potatoes. Top with the remaining cheese.

7 Bake uncovered at 350°F (180°C) until the potatoes are tender and golden brown, approximately 50–60 minutes.

Variation:

Potato and Celery Root Gratin—Substitute 1½ pounds (720 grams) peeled celery root for half of the potatoes. Alternate layers of sliced potatoes with layers of sliced celery root.

Approximate values per 4-oz. (120-g) serving: **Calories** 160, **Total fat** 8 g, **Saturated fat** 5 g, **Cholesterol** 55 mg, **Sodium** 160 mg, **Total carbohydrates** 15 g, **Protein** 6 g, **Vitamin C** 15%, **Calcium** 15%

❶ Layering gratin potatoes.

❷ Serving the finished gratin potatoes.

Sautéing and Pan-Frying

Waxy potatoes, such as red- and white-skinned varieties, are best for sautéing or pan-frying. Often they are first parboiled or even fully cooked. This is a convenient way to use leftover boiled potatoes. They are then cooked in fat following the general procedures for sautéing and pan-frying discussed in Chapter 10, Principles of Cooking.

The fat can be clarified butter, oil, bacon fat or lard, depending on the desired flavor of the finished dish. The fat must be hot before the potatoes are added so that the potatoes will develop a crust without absorbing too much fat. Sautéed potatoes should have a crisp, well-browned crust and tender interior. They should be neither soggy nor greasy.

Potatoes can be sautéed or pan-fried by two methods: tossing and still-frying. The **tossing method** is used to cook relatively small pieces of potatoes in a small amount of fat. The potatoes are tossed using the pan's sloped sides so that they brown evenly on all sides. The **still-frying method** creates a disc-shaped potato product. Shredded or sliced potatoes are added to the pan, usually covering the pan's bottom, and allowed to cook without stirring or flipping until they are well browned on the first side. The entire mass is then turned and cooked on the second side. When the potatoes are done, they can be cut into wedges for service.

Procedure for Sautéing and Pan-Frying Potatoes

1 Wash, trim, peel, cut and/or cook the potatoes as desired or as directed in the recipe.

2 Heat the pan, add the fat and heat the fat. Add the potatoes to the hot fat. Do not overcrowd the pan. Use enough fat to prevent the potatoes from sticking to the pan. Depending on the recipe, use either the tossing method or the still-frying method.

3 Add garnishes, seasonings and other ingredients as desired or as directed in the recipe.

4 Cook the potatoes until done.

🌿 Vegetarian

MISE EN PLACE

• Peel and julienne onions.

Lyonnaise Potatoes

YIELD 8 Servings, 4 oz. (120 g) each		METHOD Sautéing
Potatoes, waxy	2 lb.	960 g
Onions, sliced thin	8 oz.	240 g
Clarified butter	4 fl. oz.	120 ml
Salt and pepper	TT	TT

1 Partially cook the potatoes by baking, boiling or steaming until they are barely tender to the touch. Drain off any water and allow the potatoes to cool.

2 Peel the potatoes and cut into ¼-inch- (½-centimeter-) thick slices.

3 Sauté the onions in half of the butter until tender but not brown. Remove the onions from the pan with a slotted spoon and set aside.

4 Add the remaining butter to the pan. Add the potatoes and sauté, tossing as needed, until well browned on all sides.

5 Return the onions to the pan and sauté to combine the flavors. Season to taste with salt and pepper.

Approximate values per 4-oz. (120-g) serving: **Calories** 170, **Total fat** 12 g, **Saturated fat** 7 g, **Cholesterol** 30 mg, **Sodium** 650 mg, **Total carbohydrates** 16 g, **Protein** 1 g, **Vitamin A** 10%

Deep-Frying

Potato chips and French fries (Fr. *pommes frites*) are extremely popular in a variety of shapes, sizes and seasonings. Although a wide range of shapes, sizes and preseasoned frozen products are available, fresh fried potatoes can be a delicious, economical menu item.

Top-quality russet potatoes are recommended for deep-frying. The peel may be removed or left attached. If peeled, the potatoes should be soaked in clear, cold water until ready to cut and cook. This keeps them crisp and white by leaching some of the starch that might otherwise make the potatoes gummy or cause smaller cuts to stick together when cooked. The soaked potatoes must be drained and dried thoroughly with clean towels before deep-frying.

Deep-fried potatoes are usually blanched in oil ranging in temperature from 300–325°F (150–170°C) until tender and translucent. They are then drained and held for service, at which time they are finished in hotter oil, usually at a temperature between 350°F and 375°F (180°C and 190°C) until they are uniformly golden brown.

Deep-frying is also used to finish cooking several classic potato dishes such as croquettes and dauphine, in which fully cooked potatoes are puréed, seasoned, shaped and fried. Deep-fried potatoes should be drained on absorbent paper briefly and served immediately. See Table 23.2 for solutions to common problems when deep-frying potatoes.

Procedure for Deep-Frying Potatoes

1 Wash, peel or trim the potatoes as desired.
2 Cut the potatoes into uniform-sized pieces. Rinse, drain and dry the cut potatoes.
3 Using the basket method, blanch the potatoes in deep fat at 300°F (150°C) for 2–3 minutes, depending on the size of the pieces.
4 Drain the potatoes and spread them out in a single layer on a baking sheet or in a hotel pan.
5 Just before service, submerge the potatoes in deep fat at 350–375°F (177–191°C), using the basket method, shaking the basket occasionally while the potatoes cook.
6 Cook until golden brown. Remove from the fat, drain, salt to taste and serve immediately.

Deep-Fried Potatoes

 Vegan

MISE EN PLACE

- Wash and chop parsley.

YIELD Varies		METHOD Deep-Frying
Mealy potatoes, such as Idaho 70 count	as needed	as needed
Corn or soybean oil, hot	as needed	as needed
Salt and pepper	TT	TT
Parsley, chopped	as needed for garnish	

1 Peel if necessary, then cut each potato into the desired shape; for example:
   Cottage fries—Circles ¼ inch (6 millimeters) thick
   Shoestring potatoes—Long juliennes (allumettes)
   French fries—Sticks ⅜ inch × ⅜ inch × 3 inches (1 centimeter × 1 centimeter × 7 centimeters)
   Steak fries—Cut each potato into four large wedges

2 Using the basket method, deep-fry the potatoes in 300–325°F (150–170°C) fat until blanched and lightly browned, approximately 3–4 minutes depending on the size of the potatoes. Remove and drain. Hold the partially cooked potatoes in a single layer on a baking sheet or in a hotel pan.

3 For service, deep-fry the partially cooked potatoes in 350–375°F (180–191°C) fat until golden in color and done. Season to taste with salt and pepper.

4 Garnish with parsley if desired.

Approximate values per 1-oz. (30-g) serving: **Calories** 90, **Total fat** 4.5 g, **Saturated fat** 1.5 g, **Cholesterol** 0 mg, **Sodium** 60 mg, **Total carbohydrates** 11 g, **Protein** 1 g

Cottage fries

Shoestring potatoes

French fries

Steak fries

Blanched fried potatoes are soft and pale in color.

When properly fried, the potatoes are evenly golden brown and crisp.

Overcooked fried potatoes are dark and bitter tasting.

TROUBLESHOOTING CHART FOR DEEP-FRIED POTATOES		TABLE 23.2
PROBLEM	CAUSE	SOLUTION
Color too dark	Cooked too long Dirty oil Oil too hot Excessive sugar in potato	Reduce fry time Change oil Check thermostat; reduce temperature Fry longer at a lower temperature
Color too light	Oil too cold New oil Slow recovery time	Check thermostat; increase temperature Oil will darken with use Fry smaller batch
Excessive color variation	Fried twice Excessive sugar in potatoes Potatoes not completely submerged in fat	Fry only once Fry longer at a lower temperature Place fewer items in basket; add more oil
Potatoes stick together	Basket overfilled	Place fewer items in basket; shake while frying
Too greasy	Potatoes moist Dirty or old oil Oil too cold Basket overfilled	Dry potatoes completely before frying Change oil Check thermostat; increase temperature Place fewer items in basket

Boiling

Waxy potatoes are best for all moist-heat cooking methods because they hold their shape. Boiled potatoes (which are actually simmered) may be served as is or used in purées, salads, soups and baked casseroles. Potatoes are usually boiled in water, although stock may be used or milk added for flavor. Always begin cooking potatoes in cold liquid to ensure even cooking. Unlike other vegetables, potatoes should not be refreshed in cold water after boiling; it makes them soggy.

Procedure for Boiling Potatoes

1. Wash, peel or trim the potatoes as desired.
2. Cut the potatoes into uniform-sized pieces to promote even cooking. The pieces should not be too small, or they will absorb a large amount of water as they cook, making the final product soggy.
3. Add the potatoes to enough cool liquid to cover them by several inches. Bring to a boil, reduce to a simmer and cook until done. If a slightly firm finished product is desired, remove and drain the potatoes when they are slightly underdone and allow carryover cooking to finish cooking them.
4. Drain the potatoes in a colander and serve or use for further preparation.
5. When making mashed or puréed potatoes, the potatoes should be spread out on sheet pans and oven-dried at 250°F (120°C) immediately after draining.

🌿 Vegetarian

Mashed Potatoes

MISE EN PLACE

● Melt butter and heat milk while potatoes are cooking.

YIELD 4 lb. (1.9 kg), 16 Servings, 4 oz. (120 g) each			METHOD Boiling
Potatoes, mealy	5 lb.	2.4 kg	
Salt	1 Tbsp.	15 ml	
Whole butter, melted, hot	4 oz.	120 g	
Milk, hot	8 fl. oz.	240 ml	
Salt	2 tsp.	10 ml	
White pepper	¼ tsp.	2 ml	

1 Wash and peel the potatoes. Cut each potato into four to six uniform-sized pieces.

2 Place the potatoes in a pot, cover them with water and add 1 tablespoon (15 milliliters) salt to the water. Bring the water to a boil, reduce to a simmer and cook until the potatoes are tender. Do not overcook the potatoes.

3 When the potatoes are cooked, drain them well in a colander. The potatoes must be very dry before mashing. Transfer them to the bowl of an electric mixer. Using the whip attachment, whip the potatoes for 30–45 seconds. Scrape the sides and bottom of the bowl and whip for another 15 seconds or until the potatoes are smooth and free of lumps. The potatoes must be smooth before adding any liquids or they will remain lumpy.

4 Add the butter, milk and seasonings. Whip on low speed to incorporate all of the ingredients. Scrape the sides and bottom of the bowl and whip again for several seconds. Adjust consistency and seasoning.

Variations:

Garlic Mashed Potatoes—Sweat 1 ounce (30 grams) chopped garlic in the melted butter for 5–10 minutes without browning. Strain the butter if desired. Add the hot garlic butter in place of the melted butter in the recipe.

Horseradish Mashed Potatoes—Add 1 ounce (30 grams) freshly grated horseradish to the potatoes with the seasonings.

Mashed Sweet Potatoes or Rutabagas—Substitute sweet potatoes or rutabagas for the mealy potatoes. Add 1 fluid ounce (30 milliliters) maple syrup to the potatoes with the seasonings if desired.

Approximate values per 4-oz. (120-g) serving: **Calories** 190, **Total fat** 7 g, **Saturated fat** 4.5 g, **Cholesterol** 20 mg, **Sodium** 350 mg, **Total carbohydrates** 29 g, **Protein** 3 g, **Vitamin C** 20%

Potato Classics

Anna—Thin potato slices are arranged in several circular layers in a round pan coated with clarified butter; additional butter is brushed on, and the potatoes are baked until crisp, then cut into wedges for service.

Boulangère—Onions and potatoes are sautéed in butter, then transferred to a baking pan or added to a partially cooked roast in a roasting pan; stock is added, and the potatoes are cooked uncovered.

Château—Tournéed potatoes are sautéed in clarified butter until golden and tender.

Parisienne—Small spheres are cut from raw, peeled potatoes with a Parisienne scoop; they are seasoned and sautéed in clarified butter, then tossed with a meat glaze and garnished with chopped parsley.

Rösti—Potatoes are shredded, seasoned and pan-fried in the shape of a pie and cut into wedges for service.

❶ Adding water to cover the uniformly cut potatoes.

❷ Checking the consistency of the mashed potatoes.

GRAINS

Botanically, grains are grasses that bear edible seeds. Corn, rice and wheat are the most significant grasses in our diets. The fruit (i.e., the seed or kernel) and the plant of these common grasses are both referred to as a grain.

Most grain kernels are protected by a **hull** or husk. All kernels are composed of three distinct parts: the bran, endosperm and germ. See Figure 23.1. The **bran** is the tough outer layer covering the endosperm. Bran is a good source of fiber and B-complex vitamins. The **endosperm** is the largest part of the kernel and is a source of protein and carbohydrates (starch). It is the part used primarily in products such as flour. The **germ** is the smallest portion of the grain and is the only part that contains fat. The germ is also rich in thiamin. The bran, endosperm and germ can be separated by milling. If parts of the grains have not been separated or removed that product is known as whole or unrefined grain.

Milling is the process of modifying a grain from its natural state to make it more palatable and useful for humans to consume. Milling is a repetitive process of grinding and sifting grains to separate the bran, endosperm and germ. Commercial grinding is generally done with large stainless steel rollers. Some grain products, however, are also available in traditional **stone-ground** form. This means that the grains are ground with a stone mill rather than by the steel rollers typically used. Stone grinders are gentler and more precise, so they are less likely to overgrind the grain. Stone-ground products are always labeled as such and are usually more expensive than steel-ground ones.

The milling stages known as **cracking**, **hulling**, **grinding** and **pearling** create different products with different uses and different cooking requirements.

Identifying Grains

This section presents information on corn, rice and wheat as well as several minor grains that are nutritionally significant and gaining in culinary popularity.

cracking a milling process in which grains are broken open and cut into smaller pieces

hulling a milling process in which the hull or husk is removed from grains

grinding a milling process in which grains are reduced to powder; the powder can be of differing degrees of fineness or coarseness

pearling a milling process in which all or part of the hull, bran and germ are removed from grains

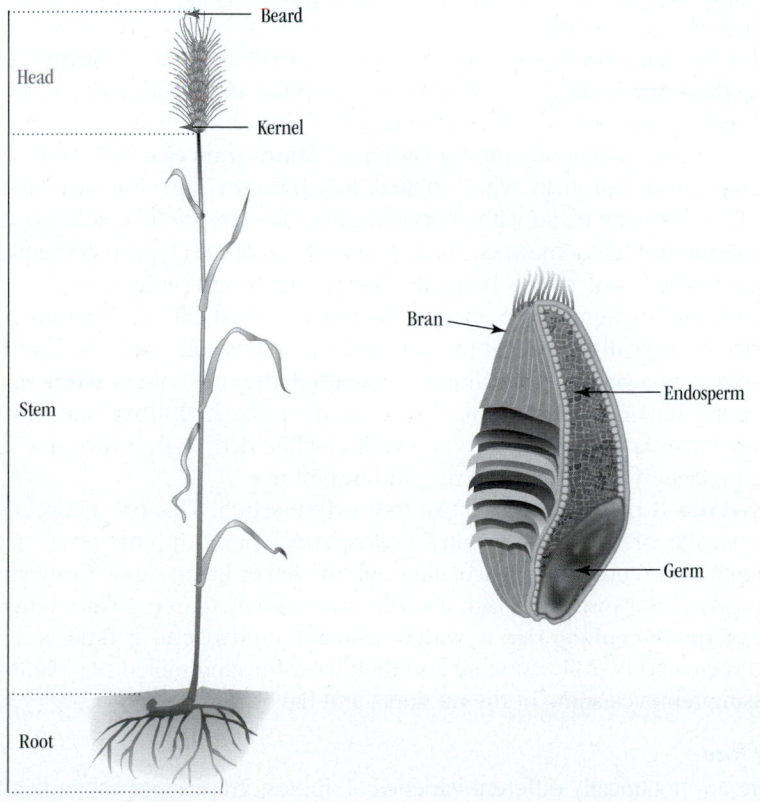

A wheat plant.   A kernel of wheat.

Figure 23.1 Wheat.

Cornmeal

Hominy

Grits

Long-grain brown rice

Converted rice

Corn

Corn (Sp. *maíz*; It. *granturco*) is the only grain that is also eaten fresh as a vegetable. (Fresh corn is discussed in Chapter 22, Vegetables.) The use of corn as a dried grain dates back several thousand years in Central America, long preceding its consumption as a vegetable.

Cornmeal is made by drying and grinding a special type of corn known as **dent**, which may be yellow, white or blue. Cornmeal is used in breads, as a coating for fried foods or cooked as polenta or mush. Products made with cornmeal have a gritty texture and a sweet but starchy flavor.

Hominy, also known as posole or samp, is dried corn that has been soaked in hydrated lime or lye. This preparation causes the kernels to swell, loosening the hulls. The hulls and germs are removed and the kernels dried. These white or yellow kernels resemble popcorn, but they have a soft, chewy texture and smoky-sour flavor. Hominy is available dried or cooked and canned. It may be served as a side dish or used in stews or soups. **Masa harina**, a finely ground flour made from dried hominy, is used to make breads, tortillas, tamales and other Mexican and southwestern dishes.

Like masa harina, **grits** are traditionally made by grinding dried hominy. These small white granules may be used in baked dishes but are most often served as a hot breakfast cereal, usually topped with butter or cheese. Quick-cooking and instant grits are available.

Rice

Rice (Fr. *riz*; It. *riso*; Sp. *arroz*) is the starchy seed of a semiaquatic grass. Probably originating on the Indian subcontinent or in Southeast Asia, rice is a dietary staple for more than half the world's population.

Rice can be incorporated into almost any cuisine, from Asian to Spanish to classic French. Its flavor adapts to the foods and seasonings with which the rice is cooked or served. Its texture adds an appealing chewiness to meat and poultry dishes, salads, breads and puddings. Rice is not limited to side dishes and may be used in stews or curries; for stuffing vegetables or game birds; and in puddings, salads, beverages (such as Mexican horchata) and breads.

Rice is divided into three types based on seed size: long-grain, medium-grain and short-grain. **Long-grain rice** is the most versatile and popular worldwide. The grains remain firm, fluffy and separate when cooked. (Long-grain rice can, however, become sticky if overcooked or stirred frequently during cooking.) **Short-grain rice** has more starch and becomes quite tender and sticky when cooked. Italian risotto, Japanese sushi and Spanish paella are all traditionally made with short-grain rice. The appearance and starch content of **medium-grain rice** falls somewhere in between the other two types. Medium-grain rice becomes sticky when cool, so it is best eaten freshly made and piping hot.

Long-grain, medium-grain and short-grain rice are available in different processed forms. All rice is originally brown. If the grains can be left whole, with the bran attached, the rice is sold as **brown rice**. If the grains are **pearled**, they are sold as **white rice**. Brown rice has a nutty flavor and chewy texture caused by the high-fiber bran. Brown rice absorbs more water and takes longer to cook than white rice. Both brown rice and white rice can be processed into converted rice and instant rice.

Converted rice is parboiled to remove the surface starch. This procedure also forces nutrients from the bran into the grain's endosperm. Therefore converted rice retains more nutrients than regular white rice, although the flavor is the same. Converted rice is neither precooked nor instant; in fact, it cooks more slowly than regular white rice.

Instant or **quick-cooking rice** is widely available and useful if time is a concern. Instant rice is created by fully cooking and then flash-freezing milled rice. Unfortunately this processing removes some of the nutrients and flavor.

Varieties of Rice

Just as there are botanically different varieties of apples, grapes and cabbage and different breeds of beef cattle, many different varieties of rice are grown throughout the world. Flavor, texture and color differences among rice varieties are obvious, and cooking time or preparation procedures may also vary according to the type of rice.

Arborio rice is a variety of rice with round, short grains. It is used primarily in Italian dishes such as risotto. It is very starchy or sticky, with a white color and mild flavor.

Basmati rice is one of the finest long-grain rices in the world. It grows in the Himalayan foothills and is preferred in Indian cuisine. It is highly aromatic, with a sweet, delicate flavor and a creamy yellow color. Basmati rice is usually aged at least 12 months to dry the grains so they stay separate and less sticky when cooked. Imported basmati rice should be washed well before cooking to remove surface starch and talc that might be used in processing. **Jasmine rice** is another aromatic long-grain rice. Similar to basmati, it is grown in Thailand and used throughout Southeast Asia.

Arborio rice

Basmati rice

Bhutanese red rice, native to the Himalayan region of Bhutan, is a medium grain rice with the outer deep-red bran still attached. This variety of rice has a bold, earthy flavor; it cooks more quickly than brown rice and should be served very moist. Its intense color works well in rice blends or it can be cooked alone in desserts and puddings and with meats such as duck or lamb where its flavor does not overpower the other ingredients. A traditional Bhutanese preparation mixes red rice with hot chiles and wild mushrooms. Although other varieties of red rice are widely available, this special grain from Bhutan is still quite rare in the United States.

Bhutanese red rice

Black rice refers to a number of varieties of rice high in the antioxidant anthocyanin, which gives it a striking black color. (The same antioxidant gives blueberries and eggplants their purple skins.) There are long grain, short grain and glutinous varieties of black rice, which is grown in China, India, Indonesia and Thailand. An Italian hybrid called *venere* cooks like Arborio. Also known as "forbidden rice" or emperor's rice, black rice has a distinctive chewy texture.

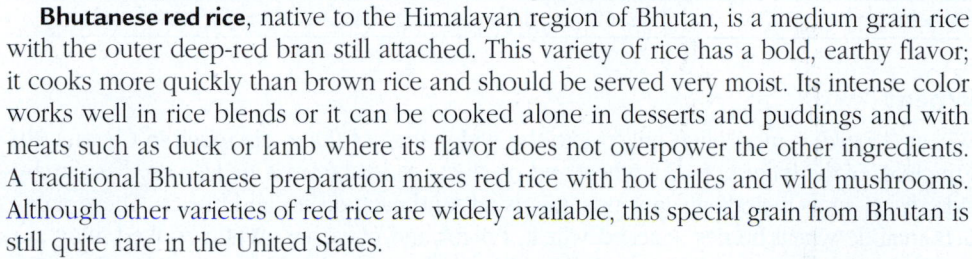

Black rice

Sticky rice is a short-grain rice used in many Asian cuisines. The short grains are fat and round with a high starch (amylopectin) content, which makes them sticky, and a pearly white color. When cooked, the grains tend to clump together, forming a sticky mass. Sticky rice must be soaked for several hours before being cooked. Also known as glutinous rice or sweet rice, sticky rice can be ground into flour and used for dumplings and pastries. Japanese sake and mirin and Chinese shaoxing are made from fermented sticky rice, as is rice vinegar.

Purple sticky rice

Wild rice is prepared in the same manner as traditional rice, although wild rice is actually the seed of a reedlike aquatic plant that is botanically unrelated to traditional rice. Wild rice has long, slender grains with a dark brown to black color. It has a nuttier flavor and chewier texture than traditional rice. Three grades of wild rice are available: giant (the best quality, with very long grains), fancy (a medium-sized grain, suitable for most purposes) and select (a short grain, suitable for soups, pancakes or baked goods). Cultivated in California, Idaho and Washington, it is generally served with game, used as a stuffing for poultry or combined with regular rice for a side dish. Wild rice is expensive, but small quantities are usually sufficient.

Wild rice

Guidelines for Cooking Rice

Rice may be rinsed before cooking to remove dirt and debris, but doing so also removes some of its nutrients. It is not necessary to rinse most American-grown rice, which is generally clean and free of insects. Rice may also be soaked before cooking. Soaking softens the grains, removes some starch and speeds cooking.

The standard ratio for cooking rice is two parts liquid to one part rice. The actual ratio varies, however, depending on the type of rice. Guidelines for cooking rice are found in Table 23.3.

> ## ⚠ Safety Alert
>
> *Cooked Rice*
>
> Once cooked, rice is highly perishable. Because of its neutral pH and high protein content, cooked rice requires time and temperature control for safety (TCS). To avoid the risk of food-borne illnesses, be sure to hold hot rice at 135°F (57°C) or higher. Leftover rice must be quickly cooled and stored at 41°F (5°C) or below. Leftover rice must be reheated to 165°F (74°C) or higher.

GUIDELINES FOR COOKING RICE				TABLE 23.3
TYPE OF RICE	RATIO OF RICE TO WATER (BY VOLUME)	PREPARATION	COOKING TIME (SIMMERING)	YIELD FROM 1 CUP (240 ML) RAW RICE
Arborio	1:3–4	Do not rinse or soak	15–20 min.	2½–3 cups (600–720 ml)
Basmati, sticky, glutinous	1:1.75	Rinse well; soak	15 min.	3 cups (720 ml)
Black rice	1:4	Rinse well in cold water	30–40 min.	2 cups (480 ml)
Brown, long-grain	1:2.5	Do not rinse; may soak	45–50 min.	3–4 cups (720–960 ml)
Converted, red	1:2.5	Do not rinse	20–25 min.	3–4 cups (720–960 ml)
White, long-grain, milled	1:2	Do not rinse	15 min.	3 cups (720 ml)
Wild	1:3	Rinse	35–60 min., depending on grade	3–4 cups (720–960 ml)

Wheat

Wheat (Fr. *blé*) is most often milled into the wide range of flours discussed in Chapter 30, Principles of the Bakeshop. But wheat and products derived from it are also used as starchy side dishes or as ingredients in soups, salads, ground meat dishes and breads. These products include wheat berries, cracked wheat, bulgur and couscous. When cooked, they are slightly chewy with a mild flavor. All should be fluffy; none should be soggy or sticky.

Wheat germ and **wheat bran** are highly touted for their nutritional values. Bran and germ are not generally used plain, but may be added to bread or other cooked dishes.

Wheat berries are the whole wheat kernels. The berries are high in starch, fiber and vitamins but require soaking followed by long cooking, usually by boiling, before they are tender enough to eat in side dishes and salads. **Cracked wheat** is the whole wheat kernel broken into varying degrees of coarseness. The kernels' white interiors should be visible in cracked wheat. The bran and germ are still intact, so cracked wheat has a great deal of fiber but a short shelf life because the bran is perishable. Cracked wheat must be soaked for several hours before it can be fully cooked by long, gentle simmering. Neither wheat berries nor cracked wheat are precooked.

Bulgur is wheat berries that have had their bran removed and are then steam-cooked, dried and ground into varying degrees of coarseness. Bulgur has a nutlike flavor and texture; it is a uniform golden-brown color (uncooked cracked wheat is not) and cooks more quickly than cracked wheat. Generally cracked wheat and bulgur cannot be substituted for one another in recipes.

Bulgur can be mixed with boiling hot water, covered and left to soak for 10–15 minutes, then drained for use in salads. Bulgur can be briefly cooked when used in stews or pilafs. Bulgur is good as an accompaniment to grilled meats and as an alternative to rice in stuffings and other dishes. The fine grind is most often used in packaged products such as those for tabouli; the medium grind is most often available in bulk.

Couscous is made from coarsely ground semolina flour from hard **durum wheat** berries. The semolina is moistened and rolled until small pellets form, then dried. Couscous is available in varying degrees of coarseness and is prepared by steaming over water or stock in a pot called a couscousière. Couscous, traditionally served with North African stews, can be used or served like rice.

Israeli couscous, more accurately known as ptitim, is a toasted wheat pasta usually shaped as small spheres or large grains of rice. It was developed under the direction of the Israeli government during the 1950s as a substitute for rice, which was scarce. Today's ptitim is available in various colors and extruded into shapes such as stars, rings or hearts. The individual pieces are relatively large and cooked by boiling until **al dente**, rather than the steaming method used for North African couscous. Ptitim is often sautéed in butter or olive oil, then boiled in water or stock and seasoned with herbs as a side dish, or used in cold vegetable salads.

Bulgur

Couscous

durum wheat a species of very hard wheat with a particularly high amount of protein; it is used to make couscous or milled into semolina flour, which is used for making pasta

al dente [al DEN-tay] Italian for "to the tooth"; used to describe a food, usually pasta, that is cooked only until it gives a slight resistance when one bites into it

Israeli couscous (ptitim)

Other Grains

Many types of grain are consumed throughout the world. Although some grains such as barley and oats are commonly prepared in the United States, others such as amaranth and teff are just beginning to gain popularity for the flavor, texture and nutritional value they add to dishes.

Amaranth is the tiny oval seeds of a type of annual plant native to South America. These high-protein seeds are consumed as a cooked grain and flour. When cooked, amaranth remains pleasantly crunchy. Because of its high starch content, amaranth should be cooked in a generous amount of water then rinsed before using. Amaranth may also be popped like kernel corn.

Barley is one of the oldest culinary grains, eaten by humans since prehistoric times. Barley is extremely hardy and is cultivated in climates from the tropics to the near-Arctic. Although much of the barley crop is used to make beer or feed animals, some does find its way into soups, stews and stuffings. The most common type is pearled to produce a small, round white nugget of endosperm. Barley has a sweet, earthy flavor similar to oats and goes well with onions, garlic and strong herbs. Barley's texture ranges from chewy to soft, depending on the amount of water in which it is cooked. Its starchiness can be used to thicken soups or stews.

Buckwheat is not a type of wheat; it is not even a grain. Rather it is the fruit of a plant distantly related to rhubarb. We include buckwheat here, however, because it is prepared and served in the same manner as grains.

The whole buckwheat kernel is known as a **groat**. The product most often sold as buckwheat is actually **kasha**, which is hulled, roasted buckwheat groats. Kasha is reddish brown with a strong, nutty, almost scorched flavor. It is available whole or ground to varying degrees of coarseness. Whole kasha remains in separate grains after cooking; the finer grinds become rather sticky. Kasha can be served as a side dish, usually combined with pasta or vegetables, or it can be chilled and used in salads.

Raw buckwheat groats are ground into flour used in pasta, blini and other pancakes. Buckwheat flour contains no gluten-forming proteins, and it tends to remain grainy, with a sandy texture. Therefore it should not be substituted for all the wheat flour in breads or baked goods.

Flax is a grain plant also known as linseed. When flax hulls and seeds are crushed into a meal or flour, they release beneficial compounds, such as Omega-3 fatty acids, a compound also found in oily fish, purported to promote heart and arterial health. Flax seeds can be incorporated in bread products to add flavor, crunchiness and nutrition. Because of their high fat content, flax seeds are generally stored under refrigeration.

Millet is a high-protein cereal grain with a bland, slightly nutty flavor and a white color. Used principally as animal fodder in the United States, millet can be cooked and eaten like rice or toasted like buckwheat and cooked like kasha. It can also be ground for flour (when used for baking, it is best combined with wheat flour). Millet is usually sold hulled, as the husk is extremely hard.

After rice, **oats** are probably the most widely accepted whole-grain product in the American diet, with per capita annual consumption of 4½ pounds (2 kilograms). Oats are consumed daily as a hot breakfast cereal (oatmeal) and are used in breads, muffins, cookies and other baked goods.

An oat groat is the whole oat kernel with only the husk removed. It contains both the bran and germ. **Steel-cut oats**, sometimes known as Irish oats, are groats that are toasted and then cut into small pieces with steel blades. **Rolled oats**, marketed as "old-fashioned oats," are groats that have been steamed, then rolled into flat flakes. **Quick-cooking oats** are rolled oats cut into smaller pieces to reduce cooking time. **Instant oats** are partially cooked and dried before rolling so that they need only to be rehydrated in boiling water. Rolled oats and quick-cooking oats can be used interchangeably, but instant oats should not be substituted for them in most recipes.

Oat bran is the outer covering of a hulled oat. It is available as a separate product, although rolled and cut oats do contain some oat bran.

The processed groats known as **oatmeal** are a gray-white color with a starchy texture and sweet flavor. They cook into the soft, thick porridge with a robust flavor also called oatmeal.

Amaranth

Barley

Buckwheat/kasha

Flax seeds

Millet

Oats

Quinoa

Teff flour

Ancient Grains for Modern Times

As an awareness of the nutritional benefits of eating whole grains grows, long-neglected grains are regaining popularity with chefs and consumers. **Farro** (*Triticum dicoccum*) is one of the oldest forms of wheat. Also known as emmer, it was a staple in the diet of ancient Roman armies. Farro is still eaten cooked as a whole grain in Tuscany, where it is prized for its chewy, nutty flavor. **Spelt** (*Triticum aestivum* var. *spelta*), a related subspecies of common wheat, is also prized for its taste and consistency. In general spelt must be soaked like beans before cooking, whereas farro may be cooked without soaking. (Milled or pearled versions are available and will cook more quickly.) Treat these grains like barley. Use them to add texture to soups or cook them to add a meaty texture to salads and vegetable dishes.

Farro

Quinoa [KEEN-wa] is native to the South American Andes and was a common food of the Incas, who referred to it as the "mother grain." Although not botanically a true grain, quinoa's tiny seeds can be prepared like a grain. The grains (seeds) are small, flattened spheres, approximately 1/16 inch (1.5 millimeters) in diameter, ringed with the germ. They become translucent when cooked and have a slightly smoky or sesamelike flavor. Several varieties of quinoa are available, ranging in color from dark brown to almost white. The larger, whiter varieties are most common and are considered superior.

Quinoa seeds have a natural, bitter-tasting coating, which protects them from birds and insects. Consequently they should be placed in a fine-meshed colander and rinsed well with cool water for several minutes before use. Quinoa can then be cooked like rice, and will absorb about twice its volume of water. For a nuttier taste, toast the grain in a hot dry pan for about 5 minutes before adding the liquid. Quinoa can also be eaten as a hot breakfast cereal, served in lieu of rice, used as a thickener for soups or stews and in salads, casseroles, breads and desserts.

Quinoa is marketed as the world's "supergrain" because the seeds form a complete protein (with all of the essential amino acids) and contain important vitamins and minerals as well as carbohydrates and fat. Quinoa should be kept in the refrigerator or freezer for long-term storage. The leaves of the quinoa plant are similar to spinach and can be eaten as a vegetable. Quinoa flour, ground from whole seeds, has a delicate nutty flavor. A gluten-free product, it is suitable for anyone bothered by wheat allergies.

Teff is the seed of a species of grass native to North Africa. Teff is a staple in the traditional Eritrean and Ethiopian cultures. The feather-light grains resemble poppy seeds. When ground into flour, teff is used to make the sourdough flatbread call *injera* served with Ethiopian stews. Featuring a distinctive nutty flavor, teff is high in calcium, iron and protein.

Nutrition of Grains

Grains are an excellent source of vitamins, minerals, proteins and fiber. The amount of milling or refining and the method of preparation affect their nutritional values, however. Unrefined or whole grains are excellent sources of dietary fiber, because the bran is still attached. Rice is also quite nutritious: It is low in sodium and calories and contains all the essential amino acids. Some grains, especially white rice and oats, are usually enriched with calcium, iron and B-complex vitamins.

Purchasing and Storing Grains

When buying grains, look for fresh, plump kernels with a bright, even color. Fresh grains should not be shriveled or crumbly; there should be no sour or musty odors.

Grains are sold by weight. They come in bags or boxes ranging from 1 to 100 pounds. Ten-, 25- and 50-pound units are usually available.

All grains should be stored in airtight containers placed in a dark, cool, dry place. Airtight containers prevent dust and insects from entering. Airtight containers and darkness also reduce nutrient loss caused by oxidation or light. Coolness inhibits insect infestation; dryness prevents mold.

Grains in vacuum-sealed packages will last for extended periods. Whole grains, which contain the oily germ, can be refrigerated to prevent rancidity.

Cooking Methods for Grains

Three basic cooking methods are used to prepare grains: **simmering**, **risotto** and **pilaf**. Unlike simmered grains, those cooked by either the risotto or pilaf method are first coated with hot fat. The primary distinction between the pilaf and risotto methods is the manner in which the liquid is then added to the grains. See Figure 23.2. When grains are used in puddings, breads, stuffings and baked casseroles, they are almost always first fully cooked by one of these methods.

Determining Doneness

Most grains should be cooked until tender, although a chewier product is preferred for some dishes. Doneness can usually be determined by cooking time and the amount of liquid remaining in the pan. Some grains, such as wild rice, are fully cooked when they puff open.

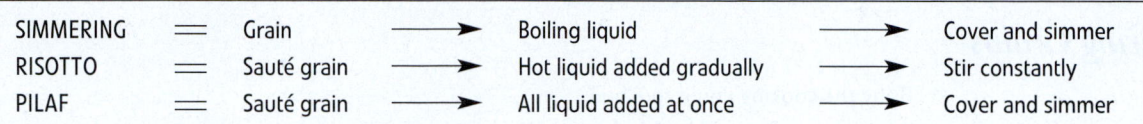

SIMMERING	=	Grain →	Boiling liquid →	Cover and simmer
RISOTTO	=	Sauté grain →	Hot liquid added gradually →	Stir constantly
PILAF	=	Sauté grain →	All liquid added at once →	Cover and simmer

Figure 23.2 Cooking methods for grains.

In general grains are fully cooked when almost all the cooking liquid has been absorbed. This is indicated by the appearance of tunnel-like holes between the grains. Grains can be cooked until almost all of the liquid is absorbed, then removed from the heat and left to stand, covered, for 5–10 minutes. This allows the cooked grains to absorb the remaining moisture without burning. Consult Table 23.4 for guidelines on cooking grains. Yields from cooked rice and grains differ because grains absorb different quantities of liquid. Most grain serving sizes in recipes in this text are calculated based on ¾ cup (180 milliliter) servings. In the case of rice and many other cooked grains, a ¾-cup (180-milliliter) serving weighs 4 ounces (120 grams).

Simmering

The most common method for preparing grains is simmering in water on the stove top. The grains can be flavored by using stock as the cooking liquid. Herbs and spices can also be added during simmering. Simmering is used to prepare grains such as rice served as a side dish. Simmering is also the method used to cook grains such as oatmeal or other porridge served for breakfast. (The procedure for simmering grains for porridge or breakfast is illustrated with the recipe for Oatmeal with Bananas and Cinnamon on page 693.)

GUIDELINES FOR COOKING AND USING GRAINS						TABLE 23.4
TYPE OF GRAIN	RATIO GRAIN TO WATER (BY VOLUME)	MISE EN PLACE	COOKING TIME (SIMMERING)	YIELD FROM 1 CUP (240 ML) RAW GRAIN	FLAVOR AND TEXTURE	SUBSTITUTES
Amaranth	1:5	Do not rinse or soak; drain and rinse after cooking	20 min.	2–2½ c. (480–600 ml)	Light nutty, peppery flavor; crunchy	Millet, quinoa
Barley, hulled	1:3.5	Soak overnight	1 hr.	3½ c. (840 ml)	Sweet, earthy; soft to chewy	Farro, rice, wheat berries
Bulgur	1:2	Do not rinse	12–15 min.	2 c. (480 ml)	Nut-like flavor and texture	Rice; do not substitute for cracked wheat products
Buckwheat, kasha, hulled roasted	1:2	Do not rinse or soak	15–20 min.	3 c. (720 ml)	Nutty almost scorched flavor; chewy	Barley, rice; do not substitute for bulgur
Farro	1:2–3	May soak overnight	30–45 min.	2½ c. (600 ml)	Nutty; chewy	Spelt, barley
Millet	1:3	Do not rinse or soak	25–30 min.	3 c. (720 ml)	Bland, slightly sweet; creamy or fluffy	Oats, rice
Quinoa	1:2	Do not rinse or soak	15 min.	3 c. (720 ml)	Sesame-like, mild smokiness; crunchy	Barley, rice
Oats, steel-cut	1:4	Do not rinse or soak	20 min.	4 c. (960 ml)	Bland; chewy or creamy	Quick-cooking oats, millet, buckwheat groats
Spelt	1:3	Soak overnight	1 hr.	2½–3 c. (600–720 ml)	Nutty; chewy	Farro, barley
Teff	1:4	Do not rinse or soak; toast in dry pan	20 min.	3¾ c. (900 ml)	Strong nutty flavor; slightly chewy	Quinoa, millet
Wheat Berries	1:4	Soak overnight	1½–2 hr.	4 c. (960 ml)	Mild, nutty flavor; fluffy, slightly chewy	Barley, rice, farro

Yields and cooking times are approximate. Pearled and cracked grains may take less time.

Procedure for Simmering Grains

1 Bring the cooking liquid to a boil.

2 Stir in the grains. Add herbs or spices as desired or as directed in the recipe.

3 Return the mixture to a boil, cover and reduce to a simmer.

4 Simmer the grains without stirring until tender and most of the liquid is absorbed.

5 Remove the grains from the heat.

6 Drain if appropriate or keep covered and allow the excess moisture to evaporate, approximately 5 minutes. Fluff with a fork to separate the grains before service.

 Good Choice  Vegan

Simmered Rice

YIELD 5 Servings, 4 oz. (120 g) each	METHOD Simmering	
Water	1 pt.	480 ml
Salt	½ tsp.	2 ml
Long-grain white rice	8 oz.	240 ml

1 Bring the water and salt to a boil in a heavy saucepan. Slowly add the rice.

2 Cover the pan and reduce the heat so that the liquid simmers gently. Cook until the rice is tender and the water is absorbed, approximately 15–20 minutes.

3 Remove from the heat and transfer to a hotel pan. Do not cover. Allow any excess moisture to evaporate for approximately 5 minutes.

4 Fluff the rice with a fork to separate the grains and serve, or refrigerate for use in another recipe.

Approximate values per 4-oz. (120-g) serving: **Calories** 240, **Total fat** 0 g, **Saturated fat** 0 g, **Cholesterol** 0 mg, **Sodium** 240 mg, **Total carbohydrates** 39 g, **Protein** 1 g **Claims**—fat free; no sugar

Risotto Method

Risotto is a classic northern Italian rice dish in which the grains remain firm but merge with the cooking liquid to become a creamy, almost pudding-like dish. True risotto is made with a short-grain starchy rice such as Arborio, but the risotto method can also be used to cook other grains such as barley and oats.

The grains are not rinsed before cooking, as this removes the starches needed to achieve the desired consistency. The grains are coated, but not cooked, in a hot fat such as butter or oil. A hot liquid is gradually added to the grains so that the mixture is kept at a constant simmer. The cooking liquid should be a rich, flavorful stock. Unlike simmering and the pilaf method, the risotto method requires frequent, sometimes constant, stirring.

When finished, the grains should be creamy and tender, but still al dente (firm but tender) in the center. Grated cheese, heavy cream, cooked meat, poultry, fish, shellfish, herbs and vegetables can be added to create a flavorful side dish or a complete meal.

Procedure for Preparing Grains by the Risotto Method

1 Bring the cooking liquid (usually a stock) to a simmer.

2 Heat the fat in a heavy saucepan over medium heat. Add any onions, garlic or other flavoring ingredients and sauté for 1–2 minutes without browning.

3 Add the grains to the saucepan. Stir well to make sure the grains are well coated with fat. Do not allow the grains to brown.

4 Add any wine and cook until it is fully absorbed.

5 Begin to add the simmering stock, 4 fluid ounces (120 milliliters) at a time, stirring frequently. Wait until each portion of cooking liquid is almost fully absorbed before adding the next.

6 Test for doneness after the grains have cooked for approximately 18–20 minutes.

7 Remove from heat and stir in butter, grated cheese, herbs or other flavoring ingredients as directed. Garnish and serve immediately.

Risotto Milanese

In Italy, risotto and pasta dishes are usually served as a separate course (primo piatto) *preceding the main dish* (secondo piatto) *and following the appetizer* (antipasto). *Like pasta, risotto is a vehicle for many flavors; it can be made with lemon juice or red wine and include bitter greens, seafood or wild mushrooms. This saffron-flavored risotto is often paired with Osso Buco (page 369), rich stewed veal shank.*

MISE EN PLACE
- Heat water.
- Peel and mince onions.
- Grate cheese.

YIELD	12 Servings, 4 oz. (120 g) each	METHOD	Risotto
Chicken stock		2 qt.	1.9 lt
Saffron threads, crushed		½ tsp.	2 ml
Water, hot		2 fl. oz.	60 ml
Whole butter		6 oz.	360 g
Onions, minced		5 oz.	150 g
Arborio rice		1 lb. 8 oz.	720 g
Dry white wine		8 fl. oz.	240 ml
Parmesan, grated		4 oz.	120 g

1. Bring the stock to a simmer. Soak the saffron threads in the hot water.

2. Heat 3 ounces (90 grams) butter in a large, heavy saucepan. Add the onions and sauté until translucent.

3. Add the rice to the onions and butter. Stir well to coat the grains with butter, but do not allow the rice to brown. Add the wine and stir until it is completely absorbed.

4. Add the saffron and soaking liquid. Add the simmering stock, 4 fluid ounces (120 milliliters) at a time, stirring frequently. Wait until the stock is absorbed before adding the next 4-fluid-ounce (120-milliliter) portion.

5. After approximately 18–20 minutes, all the stock should be incorporated and the rice should be tender. Remove from the heat and stir in the remaining 1 ounce (30 grams) butter and the grated cheese. Serve immediately.

Variations:

Risotto with Radicchio (al Radicchio)—Omit the saffron and Parmesan. Just before the risotto is fully cooked, stir in 4 fluid ounces (120 milliliters) heavy cream and 3 ounces (90 grams) finely chopped radicchio.

Risotto with Four Cheeses (al Quattro Formaggi)—Omit the saffron. When the risotto is fully cooked, remove from the heat and stir in 2 ounces (60 grams) each grated Parmesan, Gorgonzola, Fontina and mozzarella. Garnish with toasted pine nuts and chopped parsley.

Farro Risotto—Soak 1 pound 5 ounces (630 grams) farro overnight covered in cold water. Drain and use it in place of the Arborio rice. Sauté 1 pound (480 grams) thinly sliced wild mushrooms with the onions and butter in Step 3. Omit the saffron. Cook 30 minutes, adding additional stock in Step 5 if necessary.

Approximate values per 4-oz. (120-g) serving: **Calories** 370, **Total fat** 15 g, **Saturated fat** 9 g, **Cholesterol** 40 mg, **Sodium** 270 mg, **Total carbohydrates** 49 g, **Protein** 8 g

❶ Sautéing the rice and onions in butter.

❷ Adding the stock gradually while stirring frequently.

❸ Stirring in the butter and grated cheese.

Pilaf Method

For the pilaf method, raw grains are lightly sautéed in oil or butter, usually with onions or seasonings for additional flavor. A measured amount of hot liquid, often a stock, is then added. The pan is covered and the mixture is left to simmer until the liquid is absorbed.

Procedure for Preparing Grains by the Pilaf Method

1 Bring the cooking liquid (either water or stock) to a boil.

2 Heat the fat in a heavy saucepan over medium heat. Add any onions, garlic or other flavorings and sauté for 1–2 minutes without browning.

3 Add the grains to the saucepan. Stir well to make sure the grains are well coated with fat. Do not allow the grains to brown.

4 All at once, add the hot cooking liquid to the sautéed grains.

5 Return the liquid to a boil, reduce to a simmer and cover.

6 Allow the mixture to simmer, either in the oven or on the stove top, until the liquid is absorbed.

Classic Rice Pilaf

MISE EN PLACE

- Peel onion and chop into fine dice.
- Heat chicken stock.

YIELD 10 Servings, 4 oz. (120 g) each		METHOD Pilaf	
Clarified butter		1 fl. oz.	30 ml
Olive oil		1 fl. oz.	30 ml
Onion, fine dice		3 oz.	90 g
Bay leaf		1	1
Long-grain rice		1 lb.	480 g
Chicken stock, boiling		1 qt.	960 ml
Salt		TT	TT

1 Heat the butter and oil in a heavy sautoir or saucepot.

2 Add the onion and bay leaf and sauté until the onion is tender, but not brown.

3 Add the rice and stir to coat it completely with the hot fat. Do not allow the rice to brown.

4 Pour in the boiling stock and season with salt.

5 Cover the pot tightly and place it in a 350°F (180°C) oven. Bake until the liquid is absorbed and the rice is fluffy and tender, approximately 18–20 minutes.

6 Transfer the cooked rice to a hotel pan and fluff the rice with a fork. Remove the bay leaf and keep the rice hot for service.

❶ Coating the rice in butter.

❷ Adding the hot stock to the rice.

❸ Fluffing the finished rice.

Variations:

Spanish Rice—Substitute 2 ounces (60 grams) bacon fat for the butter. Add three chopped garlic cloves and 1 tablespoon (15 milliliters) pure ground chile powder with the diced onion. In Step 3, sauté the rice until it browns slightly. In place of the chicken stock, use half chicken stock and half chopped canned tomatoes with juice. Add 1 tablespoon (15 milliliters) chopped cilantro when adding the liquids.

Red Rice Pilaf—Add an additional 8 fluid ounces (240 milliliters) of boiling stock in Step 2. Add 2 tablespoons (30 milliliters) chopped dried porcini mushrooms when adding the liquid. Cook 25–30 minutes in Step 5.

Bulgur Pilaf—Substitute 10 ounces (300 grams) bulgur for the rice.

Barley Pilaf—Substitute 14 ounces (420 grams) pearled barley for the rice. Increase the chicken stock to 40 fluid ounces (1200 milliliters). Cooking time may increase by 10 to 15 minutes.

Approximate values per 6-oz. (180-g) serving: **Calories** 130, **Total fat** 7 g, **Saturated fat** 3 g, **Cholesterol** 7.5 mg, **Sodium** 440 g, **Total carbohydrates** 12 g, **Protein** 4 g

PASTA

Pasta is made from an unleavened dough of flour mixed with a liquid. The liquid is usually egg and/or water. The flour can be from almost any grain: wheat, buckwheat, rice or a combination of grains. The dough can be colored and flavored with puréed vegetables, herbs or other ingredients, and it can be rolled and cut or **extruded** into a wide variety of shapes and sizes.

Pasta can be cooked fresh while the dough is still moist and pliable, or the dough can be allowed to dry completely before cooking. Pasta can be filled or sauced in an endless variety of ways. It can stand alone or be used in salads, desserts, soups or casseroles.

Pasta is common in the cuisines of Asia, North America and Europe. In Italy, pasta dishes are usually served as a separate course, often referred to as the *minestra* or *primo piatto* (first course). In other European countries, Asia and the United States, pasta dishes are served as appetizers, entrées or side dishes.

extrusion the process of forcing pasta dough through perforated plates to create various shapes; pasta dough that is not extruded is rolled flat and then cut

Identifying Pasta

The pastas that are most familiar are prepared based on the Italian tradition of kneading wheat flour with water and eggs to form a smooth, resilient dough. This dough is rolled very thin and cut into various shapes before being boiled in water or dried for longer storage.

Commercially prepared dried pasta products are usually made with **semolina flour**. Semolina flour, ground from hard durum wheat and available from specialty purveyors, has a rich cream color and produces a very smooth, durable dough. Semolina dough requires a great deal of kneading, however, and bread flour is an acceptable substitute when preparing fresh pasta by hand.

Asian pasta, generally known as noodles, is made from wheat, rice, bean or buckwheat flour. It is available fresh or dried from commercial purveyors and at specialty markets.

Semolina

Italian-Style Pasta

The finest Italian-style pastas made commercially are those made with pure semolina flour, which gives the dough a rich, yellow color. Pasta dough that is gray or streaked probably was made from softer flours. Dried pasta should be very hard and break with a clean snap. The surface should be lightly pitted or dull. (A smooth or glossy surface will not hold or absorb sauces as well.)

Dried pasta, both domestic and imported, is available in a wide range of flavors and shapes. In addition to the traditional white (plain), green (spinach) and red (tomato) pastas, manufacturers also offer flavor combinations such as lemon-peppercorn, whole wheat–basil and carrot-ginger. Small pieces of herbs or other flavorings are often visible in these products.

The Macaroni Myth

The popular myth holds that noodles were first invented in China and discovered there by the Venetian explorer Marco Polo during the 13th century. He introduced noodles to Italy and from there the rest of Europe. Although there is little doubt that the Chinese were making noodles by the first century C.E., it is now equally clear that they were not alone.

Middle Eastern and Italian cooks were preparing macaroni long before Marco Polo's adventures. A clear reference to boiled noodles appears in the *Jerusalem Talmud* of the fifth century B.C.E. There rabbis debated whether noodles violated Jewish dietary laws (they do, but only during Passover). Tenth-century Arabic writings refer to dried noodles purchased from vendors. Literary references establish that dishes called *lasagna*, *macaroni* and *ravioli* were all well known (and costly) in Italy by the mid-13th century.

Pasta's more recent popularity dates from the 18th century, when mass production by machine began in Naples, Italy. English gentlemen on their "grand tours" of the European continent developed a fondness for pasta; so much so that the word *macaroni* became a synonym for a dandy or a vain young man. Macaroni arrived in America with English colonists, who preferred it with cream sauce and cheese or in a sweet custard. Domestic factories soon opened in the United States, and by the Civil War (1861–1865), macaroni was available to the working class. Pasta became a staple of the American middle-class diet in the wake of the wave of Italian immigrants in the late 19th century.

During the 1980s pasta became ubiquitous. Restaurants began serving it in ways previously unimagined. Corner grocery stores and local supermarkets began offering at least a dozen different shapes, often fresh and sometimes flavored. Dedicated cooks began to make pasta from scratch, though they sometimes tossed it with bottled sauce. Many also became interested in Asian noodles. Chinese, Japanese, Korean and Thai restaurants expanded their menu offerings to include traditional noodle dishes. Pasta's popularity continues to grow as chefs continue to explore the versatility of this inexpensive, nutritious food.

There are hundreds of recognized shapes of pasta. When experimenting with unusual flavors and shapes, be sure to consider the taste and appearance of the final dish after the sauce and any garnishes are added.

Italian-style pasta can be divided into three groups based on the shape of the final product: ribbons, tubes and shapes. There is no consistent English nomenclature for these pastas; the Italian names are recognized and applied virtually worldwide. (A specific shape or size may be given different names in different regions of Italy, however. These distinctions are beyond the scope of this text.)

Pasta dough can be rolled very thin and cut into strips or **ribbons** of various widths. All ribbon shapes work well with tomato, fish and shellfish sauces. Wider ribbons, such as **fettuccine**, are preferred with cream or cheese sauces.

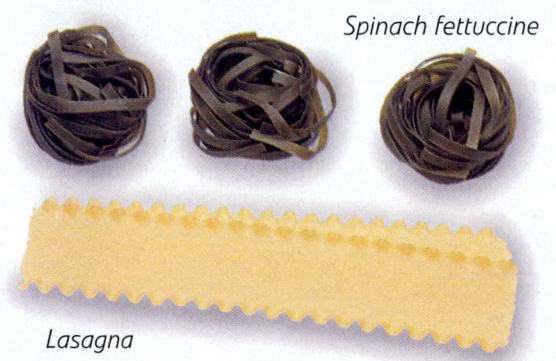

Spinach fettuccine

Lasagna

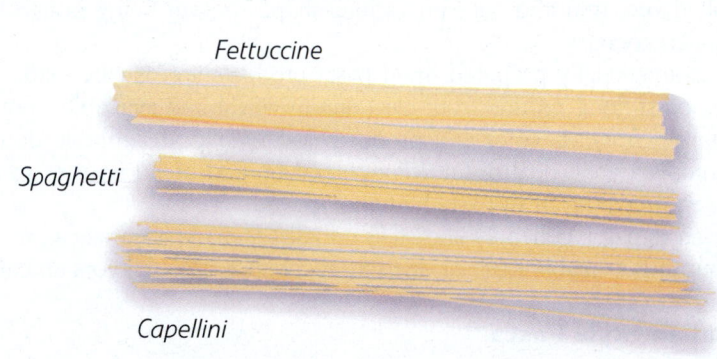

Fettuccine

Spaghetti

Capellini

Cylindrical forms or **tubes** of pasta are made by extrusion. The hollow tubes can be curved or straight, fluted or smooth. Tubes are preferred for meat and vegetable sauces and are often used in baked casseroles.

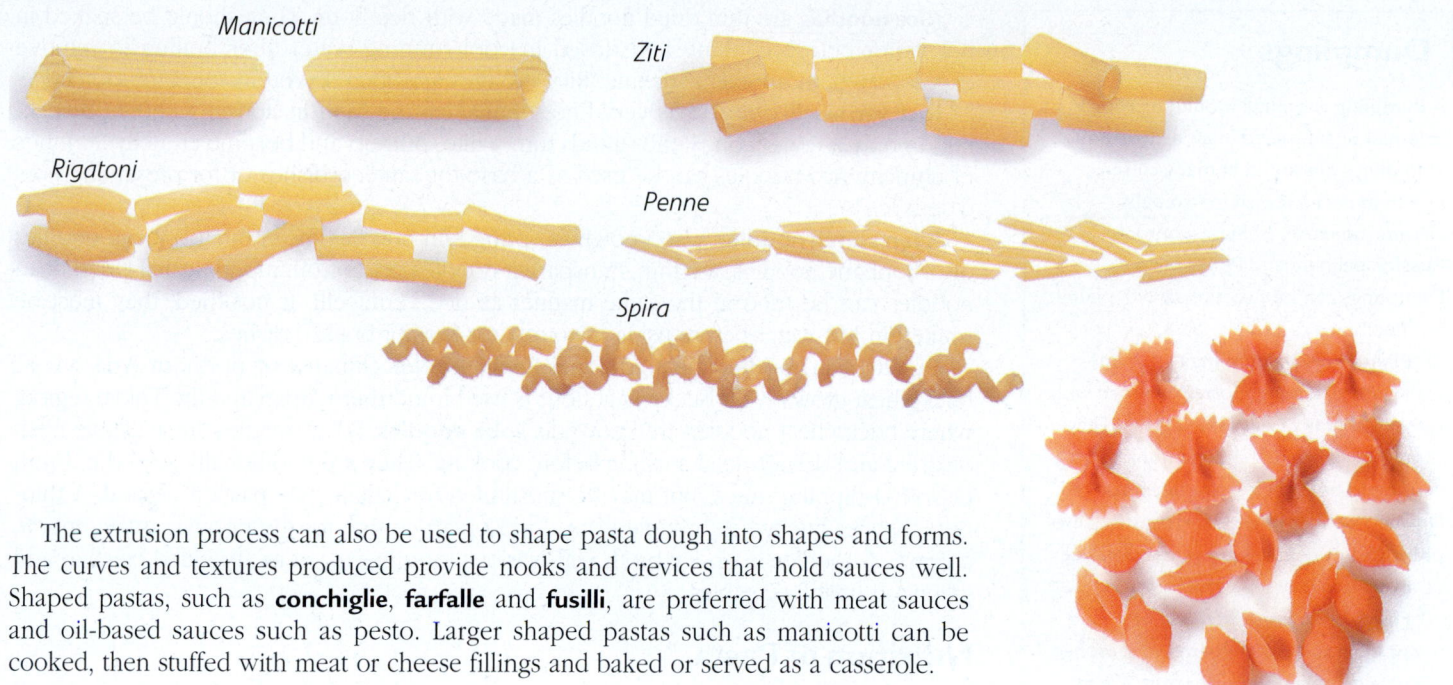

Manicotti

Ziti

Rigatoni

Penne

Spira

The extrusion process can also be used to shape pasta dough into shapes and forms. The curves and textures produced provide nooks and crevices that hold sauces well. Shaped pastas, such as **conchiglie**, **farfalle** and **fusilli**, are preferred with meat sauces and oil-based sauces such as pesto. Larger shaped pastas such as manicotti can be cooked, then stuffed with meat or cheese fillings and baked or served as a casserole.

Whole wheat bow tie and shell pasta

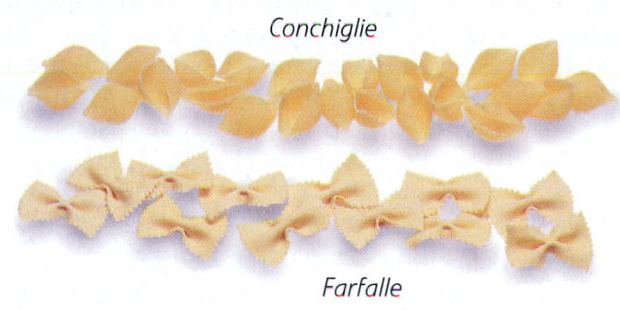

Conchiglie

Farfalle

Fusilli

Rotelle

Orzo

Asian Noodles

Asian noodles are not cut into the same variety of shapes and sizes as Italian-style pasta, nor are they flavored or colored with vegetable purées, herbs or other ingredients.

Virtually all Asian noodles are ribbons—some thin, some thick—folded into bundles and packaged. Differences arise because of the flours used for the dough.

Most dried Asian noodles benefit by soaking in hot water for several minutes before further preparation. The water softens the noodle strands; the bundles separate and the noodles cook more evenly.

Wheat noodles, also known as egg noodles, are the most popular and most widely available of the Asian-style noodles. They are thin, flat noodles with a springy texture; they are available fresh or dried. Dried egg noodles can be deep-fried after boiling to create crisp golden noodles (chow mein) used primarily as a garnish. Japanese wheat noodles, known as **somen** (if thin) and **udon** (if thick), may be round, square or flat. They are eaten in broth or with a dipping sauce.

Flour Stick Wheat Noodles (without egg)

Fresh Wheat and Egg Noodles

Rice Vermicelli

Cellophane Noodles

Japanese Wheat Somen

Dumplings

A **dumpling** is a small mound of dough steamed or simmered in a flavorful liquid. Dumplings are found in many cuisines: Italian gnocchi, Jewish matzo balls, German spaetzle, Chinese wontons, Russian pelmeni and Polish pierogi. Dumplings can be sweet or savory, plain or filled.

Plain or **drop dumplings** are made with breadlike dough, often leavened with yeast or chemical leavening agents. They should be light and tender, but firm enough to hold their shape when cooked. Drop dumplings may be served with stews or broths, or coated with butter or sauce as an appetizer or side dish.

Filled dumplings are made by wrapping noodle dough around seasoned meat, vegetables, cheese or fruit. These parcels are then steamed, fried or baked and served as a snack food, appetizer or side dish. A recipe for deep-fried wontons is included in Chapter 29, Hors d'Oeuvre.

Stuffed Wontons with Apricot Sauce

Rice noodles are thin dried noodles made with rice flour. They should be soaked in hot water before cooking and rinsed in cool running water after boiling to remove excess starch and prevent sticking. Rice noodles are often served in soups or sautéed.

Rice vermicelli, which has very fine strands, can be fried in hot oil without presoaking. In only a few seconds, the strands turn white, puff up and become crunchy. Mounds of crunchy rice noodles can be used as a base for sautéed dishes or for presenting hors d'oeuvre.

Bean starch noodles, also known as spring rain noodles, bean threads, bean noodles or cellophane noodles, are thin, transparent noodles made from mung beans. Dried bean noodles can be fried in the same manner as rice vermicelli. If not fried, they must be soaked in hot water before using in soups, stir-fries or braised dishes.

Buckwheat noodles are traditional in the cooler climates of northern Asia where buckwheat grows well. Buckwheat flour is used in northern Japan and the Tokyo region, where buckwheat noodles are known as **soba noodles**. Soba noodles are available fresh or dried and do not need soaking before cooking. They are traditionally served in broth or with a dipping sauce, but may be substituted for Italian-style pasta if desired. A thinner, chewier buckwheat noodle is used in Korean cuisine for the popular *naengmyeon*, a bowl of noodles in an icy broth with various toppings, such as shredded chicken and julienned fresh vegetables.

Nutrition of Pasta

Pastas are a healthy choice in a balanced diet because they are very low in sodium and fat (and cholesterol free if made without eggs). Wheat pasta is a good source of B vitamins, minerals, proteins and carbohydrates. Purchased pastas and noodles are sometimes enriched with additional nutrients, such as folate and vitamin D. In addition to the wheat flour-based pastas discussed in this text, manufacturers now offer Italian-style pastas made from other flours such as rice, potato, bean or lentil flour. These alternatives may be gluten free and suitable for those with a wheat protein allergy and can provide other nutritional benefits.

Purchasing and Storing Pasta

Pasta products are purchased by weight, either fresh or dried. Tubes and shapes are not generally available fresh. Dried products, by far the most common, are available in boxes or bags, usually in 1-, 10- and 20-pound units. They can be stored in a cool, dry place for several months. Fresh pasta can be stored in an airtight wrapping in the refrigerator for a few days or in the freezer for a few weeks.

Making Fresh Pasta

Fresh pasta is easy to make, requiring almost no special equipment and only a few staples. The dough can be mixed by hand for small batches or in a mixer. Mixing by hand allows the chef to get a feel for the dough, adjusting the amount of flour added as needed.

Procedure for Mixing Pasta Dough by Hand

1 Mound the flour on a workbench. Make a well in the center. Place the eggs in the well and whip them with a fork.

2 Use your fingers to stir the eggs, gradually bringing more flour into the center.

3 Use a dough scraper, to add more flour to the egg mixture, stirring constantly until a firm dough is formed.

4 Knead the dough until smooth.

🌿 Vegetarian

Basic Pasta Dough

YIELD 4 lb. (1.9 kg)

Eggs	15	15
Olive oil	1 fl. oz.	30 ml
Salt	1 Tbsp.	15 ml
Bread flour*	2 lb. 8 oz.	1.2 kg

1 Place the eggs, oil and salt in a large mixer bowl. Use the paddle attachment to combine.

2 Add one-third of the flour and stir until the mixture begins to form a soft dough. Remove the paddle attachment and attach the dough hook.

3 Gradually add more flour until the dough is dry and cannot absorb any more flour.

4 Remove the finished dough from the mixer, wrap it well with plastic wrap and set it aside at room temperature for 20–30 minutes.

5 After the dough has rested, roll it into flat sheets by hand or with a pasta machine. Work with only a small portion at a time, keeping the remainder well covered to prevent it from drying out.

6 While the sheets of dough are pliable, cut them into the desired width with a chef's knife or pasta machine. Sheets can also be used for making ravioli, as illustrated next.

*Semolina flour can be substituted for all or part of the bread flour in this recipe, although it makes a stronger dough that is more difficult to work with by hand.

Variations:

Garlic-Herb Pasta Dough—Roast one head of garlic. Peel and purée the cloves and add to the eggs. Add up to 2 ounces (60 grams) finely chopped assorted fresh herbs just before mixing is complete.

Spinach Pasta Dough—Add 8 ounces (240 grams) cooked, puréed and well-drained spinach to the eggs. Increase the amount of flour slightly if necessary.

Tomato Pasta Dough—Add 4 ounces (120 grams) tomato paste to the eggs; omit the salt. Increase the amount of flour slightly if necessary.

Approximate values per 1-oz. (30-g) serving: **Calories** 80, **Total fat** 2 g, **Saturated fat** 0.5 g, **Cholesterol** 50 mg, **Sodium** 125 mg, **Total carbohydrates** 13 g, **Protein** 3 g

1 Adding the flour to the mixing bowl and using the paddle until the mixture forms a firm dough.

2 Removing the finished dough from the mixer.

The basic form for pasta dough is the sfoglia, a thin, flat sheet of dough that is cut into ribbons, circles or squares. Sheets of fresh pasta dough can be filled and shaped to create ravioli, cappelletti and tortellini. Filled pasta is usually served with a light cream or tomato sauce that complements the filling's flavors.

Although pasta dough can be kneaded by hand, stretched and rolled with a rolling pin and cut with a chef's knife, pasta machines make these tasks easier. Pasta machines are either electric or manual. Some electric models mix and knead the dough, then extrude it through a cutting disk. These electric extrusion machines are most practical in a food service operation that regularly serves large quantities of pasta. The pasta machine more often encountered is operated manually with a hand crank. It has two rollers that knead, press and push the dough into a thin, uniform sheet. Adjacent cutting rollers slice the thin dough into various widths for fettuccine, spaghetti, capellini and the like.

Procedure for Rolling and Cutting Pasta Dough

1 Work with a small portion of the dough. Leave the rest covered with plastic wrap to prevent it from drying out.

2 Flatten the dough with the heel of your hand.

3 Set the pasta machine rollers to their widest setting. Insert the dough and turn the handle with one hand while supporting the dough with the other hand. Pass the entire piece of dough through the rollers.

4 Dust the dough with flour, fold it in thirds and pass it through the pasta machine again.

5 Repeat the folding and rolling procedure until the dough is smooth. This may require four to six passes.

6 Tighten the rollers one or two marks, then pass the dough through the machine. Without folding it in thirds, pass the dough through the machine repeatedly, tightening the rollers one or two marks each time.

7 When the dough is thin enough to see your hand through it, but not so thin that it begins to tear, it is ready to use or cut into ribbons. This sheet is the sfoglia.

8 To cut the sfoglia into ribbons, gently feed a manageable length of dough through the desired cutting blades.

9 Lay out the pasta in a single layer on a sheet pan dusted with flour to dry. Layers of pasta ribbons can be separated with parchment paper.

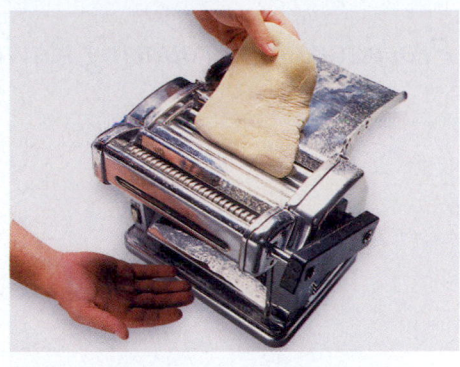

❶ Pass the entire piece of dough through the pasta machine.

❷ Fold the dough in thirds.

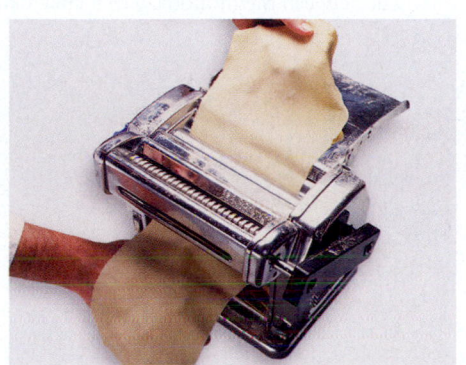

❸ Pass the dough through the pasta machine to achieve the desired thickness.

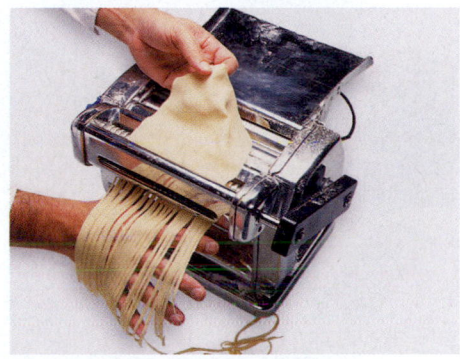

❹ Use the pasta machine to cut the dough to the desired width.

Filling Pasta

Sheets of raw pasta dough can be filled or folded to create **ravioli** (circles or squares), **tortellini** (round "hats" with a brim of dough), **lunettes** (circles of dough folded into half-moons), **agnolotti** (squares of dough folded into rectangles), **cappelletti** (squares of dough folded and shaped into rings) and other shapes. The filled pieces of dough are cooked in boiling water using the procedure for cooking pasta ribbons discussed later. The filling can include almost anything—cheese, herbs, vegetables, fish, shellfish, meat or poultry. It can be uncooked or precooked. Any meat filling should be fully cooked before the pasta is assembled, as the time it takes for the dough to cook may not be sufficient to cook the filling.

Cannelloni is a different type of filled pasta: A large square of cooked dough is wrapped around a meat or cheese filling and baked. **Lasagna** are wide, flat sheets of pasta that are cooked and then layered with cheese, tomato sauce and meat or vegetables as desired. The finished casserole is baked and cut into portions.

Some of the larger, commercially prepared pasta shapes such as large shells (**conchiglioni** or **rigate**) or large tubes (**manicotti**) can be partially cooked in boiling water, then filled, sauced and baked as a casserole.

Asian noodle dough is also made into filled items such as dumplings, **wontons**, **egg rolls** (made with egg noodle dough) and **spring rolls** (made with rice paper). These items are usually steamed, pan-fried or deep-fried. When making filled pasta, consider the flavors and textures of the filling, dough and sauce. Each should complement the others.

Procedure for Preparing Ravioli

1 Prepare a basic pasta dough.

2 Prepare and chill the desired filling.

3 Roll out two thin sheets of dough between the rollers of a pasta machine. Gently lay the dough flat on the work surface.

4 Using a piping bag or a small portion scoop, place small mounds of filling on one of the dough pieces. Space the filling evenly, allowing approximately 2 inches (5 centimeters) between each mound.

5 Brush the exposed areas of dough with water.

6 Gently place the second sheet of dough over the mounds and press firmly around each mound to remove air pockets and seal the dough.

7 Cut between the mounds with a chef's knife, pastry wheel or circular cutter.

1 Piping the filling onto the dough.

2 Pressing around the mounds of filling to seal the dough and remove any air pockets.

3 Cutting around the mounds with a circular cutter.

Cooking Method for Pasta

Italian-style pastas are properly cooked when they are al dente, firm but tender. Cooking times vary depending on the shape and quantity of pasta, the amount of water used, the hardness of the water and even the altitude. Fresh pasta cooks rapidly, sometimes in seconds. Noodles and dried pasta may require several minutes to cook. Unlike Italian pasta, Asian noodles are not served al dente. Rather, they are either boiled until very soft or stir-fried until very crisp.

Determining Doneness

Although package or recipe directions offer some guidance, the only way to accurately test doneness is to bite into a piece. When the pasta is slightly firmer than desired, remove it from the stove and drain. It will continue to cook through residual heat.

Boiling

All Italian-style pasta and most Asian noodles are cooked by boiling. The secret to boiling pasta successfully is to use ample water. Allow 1 gallon (4 liters) of water for each pound (450 grams) of pasta.

Use a saucepan or stockpot large enough to allow the pasta to move freely in the boiling water; otherwise the starch released by the dough makes the pasta gummy and sticky. Bring water to a rapid boil, add salt, then add all the pasta at once. Salt should be added to the water. Pasta absorbs water and salt during cooking. Adding salt to the pasta after it is cooked will not provide the same seasoning effect.

Chefs disagree on whether to add oil to the cooking water. Purists argue against adding oil, on the theory that it makes the dough absorb water unevenly. Others think oil should be added to reduce surface foam. Another theory is that oil keeps the pasta from sticking, although this works only when added to cooked, drained pasta.

Asian noodles may be prepared by boiling until fully cooked, or they may be parboiled and then stir-fried with other ingredients to finish cooking.

Procedure for Cooking Pasta to Order

1 Bring the appropriate amount of water to a boil over high heat.
2 Add oil to the water if desired.
3 Add the pasta and salt to the rapidly boiling water.
4 Stir the pasta to prevent it from sticking together. Bring the water back to a boil and cook until the pasta is done.
5 When the pasta is properly cooked, immediately drain it through a colander. A small amount of oil may be gently tossed into the pasta if desired to prevent it from sticking together.
6 Serve hot pasta immediately, or refresh it in cold water for later use in salads or other dishes. (Do not rinse pasta that is to be served hot.)

Procedure for Cooking Dried Pasta in Advance

Fresh pasta is so delicate and cooks so rapidly (sometimes in as little as 15 seconds) that it should be cooked to order. Dried pasta, however, can be cooked in advance for quantity service.

1 Follow the preceding directions for cooking pasta, but stop the cooking process when the pasta is about two-thirds done.
2 Drain the pasta, rinse it lightly and toss it in a small amount of oil.
3 Divide the pasta into appropriate-sized portions. Individual portions can be wrapped in plastic or laid on a sheet pan and covered. Refrigerate until needed.
4 When needed, place a portion in a china cap and immerse in boiling water to reheat. Drain, add sauce and serve immediately.

Accompaniments to Pasta

Pasta is popular with diners and easily incorporated in a variety of cuisines—from Italian and Chinese to Eastern European. It can be served in broths; as a bed for stews, fish, shellfish, poultry or meat; or tossed with sauce. Creative chefs are constantly developing nontraditional but delicious ways of serving pasta.

Cooked pasta is best eaten with some form of sauce or liquid accompaniment. There are hundreds of traditional Italian pasta sauces as well as modern sauces for Italian-style pasta, but most can be divided into six categories: ragus, seafood sauces, vegetable sauces, cream sauces, garlic-oil sauces and uncooked sauces. Recipes for a selection of pasta sauces are included in Chapter 11, Stocks and Sauces.

Small pasta shapes can be cooked in a broth with which they will be served, or the pasta can be cooked separately, then added to the hot broth at service time. Soups such as *cappelletti in brodo* and chicken noodle are examples.

Although there are no firm rules governing the combinations of sauces and pasta, Table 23.5 offers some of the more common combinations.

COMBINING SAUCES, PASTA AND GARNISHES			TABLE 23.5
SAUCE	DESCRIPTION	PASTA SHAPE	GARNISH
Ragu	Braised dishes used as sauce; flavorings, meat or poultry are browned, then a tomato product and stock, wine, water, milk or cream are added	Ribbons, tubes, shapes, filled	Grated cheese
Seafood	White seafood sauces are flavored with herbs and made with white wine or stock; red seafood sauces are tomato-based	Ribbons (fettuccine and capellini)	Fish or shellfish
Vegetable	Includes both traditional sauces made with tomatoes and stock, flavored with garlic and red pepper, and modern sauces such as primavera	Ribbons, tubes, filled	Meatballs, sausage, grated cheese
Cream	Milk- or cream-based and sometimes include roux; usually cheese is added	Thick ribbons (spaghetti and fettuccine), filled	Ham, peas, sausage, mushrooms, smoked salmon, nuts, grated cheese
Garlic-oil	(It. *aglio-olio*) Olive oil flavored with garlic and herbs, usually parsley; can be hot or cold, cooked or uncooked (pesto is an uncooked, cold sauce)	Ribbons, shapes, filled	Grated cheese (if uncooked or cold), herbs
Uncooked	A variety of dressings and garnishes such as fresh tomatoes, basil and olive oil; or olive oil, lemon juice, parsley, basil and hot red pepper flakes; capers, anchovies, olives, fresh herbs, fresh vegetables, flavored oils and cubed cheeses can also be used	Ribbons, shapes	Cubed or grated cheese, fresh vegetables, herbs

QUESTIONS FOR DISCUSSION

1   Explain the differences between mealy and waxy potatoes. Give two examples of each.

2   Describe the two methods of sautéing or pan-frying potatoes.

3   Discuss the steps required to prepare deep-fried potatoes and some of the techniques to use to ensure the best results.

4   All grains are composed of three parts. Name and describe each of these parts.

5   Describe and compare the three general cooking methods used to prepare grains.

6   Name two ancient types of grains and offer suggestions for serving them in modern preparations.

7   What type of rice is preferred for making risotto? Explain the reason for this choice.

8   Name the three categories of Italian-style pasta shapes and give an example of each.

9   Why is it necessary to use ample water when cooking pasta? Should pasta be cooked in salted water? Should oil be added to the cooking water? Explain your answers.

10   Discuss the differences between cooking fresh pasta and cooking dried, factory-produced pasta.

11   Different names are given to Italian pasta shapes from one region of Italy to another. Research the various regional Italian cuisines to determine other names for some of the pastas shown on pages 676–677.

12   Each of the types of sauce listed in Table 23.5 comes from a specific region of Italy. Research which region is most closely associated with each type of sauce.

Additional Potato, Grain and Pasta Recipes

Château Potatoes

YIELD 10 Servings, 5 oz. (150 g) each	METHOD Boiling/Sautéing	
Potatoes, waxy	5 lb.	2.4 kg
Salt	TT	TT
Clarified butter	6 fl. oz.	180 ml
White pepper	TT	TT
Whole butter	2 oz.	60 g

1 Peel the potatoes if desired. Cut the potatoes into 2-inch (5-centimeter) lengths and tournée.

2 Place the potatoes in a pan of salted water. Bring to a simmer and parcook the potatoes for approximately 5 minutes. They should still be raw in the middle.

3 Remove the potatoes from the water and spread on a hotel pan so that the steam is released and the potatoes dry completely.

4 Heat an appropriately sized sauté pan over medium heat. Add enough clarified butter to cover the bottom of the pan approximately ¼ inch (6 millimeters) deep. Sauté the potatoes in batches, adding more butter as necessary and turning them often until all sides are golden brown. If the potatoes are properly browned but not yet fully cooked, place them in a 350°F (180°C) oven for a few minutes until tender.

5 Season the potatoes with salt and white pepper and toss in a small amount of whole butter at service time.

Variation:

Parisienne Potatoes and Noisette Potatoes—Parisienne and noisette potatoes are prepared in the same manner as château potatoes but for these variations, the potatoes are cut into balls with a Parisienne scoop or melon ball cutter. Parisienne potatoes are generally larger than 1 inch (2.5 centimeters) and noisette potatoes are generally smaller than 1 inch (2.5 centimeters). Parcooking time is greatly reduced because of the smaller size. The potatoes can also be cooked from the raw state without parcooking.

Approximate values per 5-oz. (150-g) serving: **Calories** 280, **Total fat** 20 g, **Saturated fat** 12 g, **Cholesterol** 50 mg, **Sodium** 5 mg, **Total carbohydrates** 23 g, **Vitamin C** 25%, **Claim**—high in vitamin C

❶ Tournéeing the potatoes.

❷ Parcooking the potatoes.

❸ Sautéing the potatoes.

Good Choice   Vegan

Roasted Fingerling Potatoes

YIELD	4 Servings, 4 oz. (120 g) each	METHOD	Roasting
Fingerling potatoes, assorted		1 lb.	480 g
Fresh lemon juice		from 2 lemons	from 2 lemons
Italian herb blend		1 Tbsp.	15 ml
Salt		1 tsp.	5 ml
Black pepper		⅛ tsp.	1 ml
Olive oil		1½ fl. oz.	45 ml

1 Cut the potatoes in halves or quarters and place in a bowl. Add the lemon juice, seasonings and oil and toss to coat the potatoes thoroughly.

2 Place the seasoned potatoes in a shallow baking pan and roast at 425°F (220°C). Stir or turn the potatoes two or three times during cooking to promote even browning. Cook until the potatoes are tender, approximately 30 minutes.

Approximate values per 4-oz. (120-g) serving: **Calories** 200, **Total fat** 10 g, **Saturated fat** 1.5 g, **Cholesterol** 0 mg, **Sodium** 590 mg, **Total carbohydrates** 27 g, **Protein** 2 g, **Vitamin C** 45%, **Iron** 10%, **Claim**—good source of fiber, vitamin C and iron

Vegetarian

Scalloped Potatoes

YIELD	1 Half-Size Hotel Pan, 24 Servings	METHOD	Baking
Potatoes, mealy russet		5 lb.	2.4 kg
Béchamel (page 220)		36 fl. oz.	1 lt
Salt and white pepper		TT	TT
Nutmeg, ground		TT	TT
Whole butter		as needed	as needed

1 Peel the potatoes and hold them in water to prevent browning. Pour the Béchamel into a stainless steel bowl. Slice the potatoes thinly (a mandoline works well for this purpose) directly into the Béchamel. Stir occasionally so that the sauce coats the potatoes.

2 Season as desired with the salt, white pepper and nutmeg.

3 Layer the potatoes and sauce in a buttered half-size hotel pan. Pour any remaining sauce over the top of the potatoes.

4 Bake covered at 350°F (180°C) for approximately 30 minutes. Uncover and bake until the potatoes are cooked and brown on top, approximately 20–30 minutes.

Approximate values per 4-oz. (120-g) serving: **Calories** 110, **Total fat** 3.5 g, **Saturated fat** 2 g, **Cholesterol** 10 mg, **Sodium** 25 mg, **Total carbohydrates** 18 g, **Protein** 3 g

❶ Layering the potatoes and sauce in a hotel pan.

❷ Pouring the remaining Béchamel over the potatoes.

❸ Plating the finished Scalloped Potatoes for service.

Delmonico Potatoes

🌿 Vegetarian

YIELD	1 Full-Size Hotel Pan, 36–40 Servings	METHOD	Steaming/Baking

Potatoes, mealy, peeled, medium dice	6 lb.	2.8 kg
Green bell peppers, small dice	4	4
Pimentos, small dice	12 oz.	360 g
Béchamel (page 220)	3 pt.	1.4 lt
Salt and pepper	TT	TT
Nutmeg, ground	TT	TT

1 Steam the potatoes until cooked through but firm, approximately 7 minutes. Spread them on sheet pans and refrigerate.

2 Blanch and chill the bell peppers.

3 Combine all ingredients in a large bowl. Mix carefully so as not to break up the potatoes.

4 Place the potatoes in a shallow full-size hotel pan, cover and bake at 350°F (180°C) until the internal temperature reaches at least 165°F (74°C).

Approximate values per 4-oz. (120-g) serving: **Calories** 100, **Total fat** 4 g, **Saturated fat** 2 g, **Cholesterol** 10 mg, **Sodium** 340 mg, **Total carbohydrates** 15 g, **Protein** 2 g, **Vitamin C** 35%

German-Style Potato Salad

YIELD	16 Servings, 4 oz. (120 g) each	METHOD	Boiling or Steaming

Bacon, cut in lardons	4 oz.	120 g
Onions, small dice	4 oz.	120 g
Flour	1 oz.	30 g
Granulated sugar	½ oz.	15 g
Cider vinegar	3 fl. oz.	90 ml
Chicken stock	8 fl. oz.	240 ml
Russet potatoes, boiled, peeled, sliced ¼ in. (6 mm) thick	2 ½ lb.	1.2 kg
Eggs, hard cooked, peeled, sliced	3	3
Green onions, sliced thin	1 oz.	30 g
Salt and pepper	TT	TT

1 In a heavy saucepan large enough to hold all of the ingredients, cook the bacon, rendering the fat without browning the bacon. Remove the bacon and set aside.

2 Add the onions to the pan of bacon fat and cook until tender without browning, approximately 2 minutes.

3 Stir in the flour to make a blonde roux. Whisk in the sugar, vinegar and stock. Bring to a boil and reduce heat to a simmer.

4 Carefully fold in the potatoes, eggs, green onions and cooked bacon. Season to taste with salt and pepper. Serve warm.

Approximate values per 4-oz. (120-g) serving: **Calories** 110, **Total fat** 2 g, **Saturated fat** 0.5 g, **Cholesterol** 40 mg, **Sodium** 95 mg, **Total carbohydrates** 19 g, **Protein** 4 g, **Vitamin C** 15%

Potato Pancakes

YIELD 12 Pancakes, 2½ oz. (75 g) each		METHOD Pan-Frying	
Potatoes, all-purpose, mealy		2 lb.	960 g
Eggs, beaten		3	3
Onion, minced		4 oz.	120 g
Flour		2 oz.	60 g
Baking powder		1 Tbsp.	15 ml
Nutmeg, ground		TT	TT
Salt and pepper		TT	TT
Vegetable oil		4 fl. oz.	120 ml
Applesauce		as needed	as needed

1 Peel and coarsely grate the potatoes.

2 Transfer the grated potatoes to a bowl and add the eggs, onion, flour and baking powder. Season with nutmeg, salt and pepper. Blend well.

3 Heat the oil. Form the potato mixture into 12 uniform-sized pancakes and pan-fry pancakes until tender, turning once when well browned on the first side. Remove from the pan and drain well. Serve hot with applesauce if desired.

Approximate values per 2½-oz. (75-g) pancake: **Calories** 140, **Total fat** 6 g, **Saturated fat** 1 g, **Cholesterol** 55 mg, **Sodium** 140 mg, **Total carbohydrates** 18 g, **Protein** 3 g, **Vitamin C** 10%

Rösti Potatoes

Rösti, a rich potato cake, is a mainstay of the hearty alpine cuisine of Switzerland. On menus in restaurants that cater to mountaineers and skiers, rösti frequently appears with various garnishes such as mit spiegeleier *(with fried eggs),* mit speck *(with bacon) or* mit schinken *(with ham).*

YIELD 6 Servings, 4 oz. (120 g) each		METHOD Pan-Frying	
Potatoes, all-purpose, mealy, large		4	4
Bacon fat		2 oz.	60 g
Butter		2 oz.	60 g
Kosher salt and pepper		TT	TT
Whole butter		1 oz.	30 g

1 Partially cook the potatoes in salted water until almost done. Drain and cool the potatoes, then peel and coarsely grate them.

2 Heat the bacon fat and butter in a heavy, shallow 10-inch (25-centimeter) skillet with sloping sides until quite hot. Spread half the potatoes over the bottom of the pan; sprinkle with salt and pepper. Cover with the remaining potatoes and cook over medium-high heat until the bottom turns brown and crusty, approximately 10 minutes.

3 Turn the potatoes in one piece. This is easiest to do by placing a large plate over the pan and turning both together so that the potatoes fall onto the plate. Slip the turned-over potatoes off the plate back into the pan, browned side up. Cook until the bottom is browned.

4 Before serving, smooth the edges of the potatoes with a spatula. Sprinkle with salt and brush the edge of the pan with whole butter. It will melt and run into the potatoes.

Variation:

Cheddar Cheese Rösti Potatoes—Make two thin cakes from the coarsely grated potatoes. Top one with a layer of 7 ounces (210 grams) sour cream, 2 ounces (60 grams) cubed sharp Cheddar cheese and 2 tablespoons (30 milliliters) chopped chives. Top with the other cake. Dot with 1 tablespoon (15 milliliters) whole butter and bake at 400°F (200°C) for 15 minutes.

Approximate values per 4-oz. (120-g) serving: **Calories** 290, **Total fat** 23 g, **Saturated fat** 10 g, **Cholesterol** 30 mg, **Sodium** 430 mg, **Total carbohydrates** 19 g, **Protein** 2 g, **Vitamin C** 20%

Duchesse Potatoes

🌿 Vegetarian

YIELD 10 Servings, 3 oz. (90 g) each	METHOD Boiling	
Potatoes, mealy	2 lb.	1 kg
Whole butter	1 oz.	30 g
Nutmeg, ground	⅛ tsp.	½ ml
Salt and pepper	TT	TT
Eggs	1	1
Egg yolks	2	2
Clarified butter	as needed	as needed

1 Peel and quarter the potatoes. Boil in salted water until tender. Drain and immediately turn them out onto a sheet pan to allow the moisture to evaporate.

2 While still warm, press the potatoes through a food mill, or grind through a grinder's medium die. Blend in the butter and season to taste with nutmeg, salt and pepper.

3 Mix in the eggs and egg yolks, blending well.

4 Transfer the mixture to a piping bag fitted with a large star tip. Pipe single portion-sized spirals onto a parchment-lined sheet pan. Brush with clarified butter and bake at 375°F (190°C) until the edges are golden brown, approximately 8–10 minutes. Serve immediately.

Note The duchesse potatoes mixture is used to decorate platters used for buffets or tableside preparations or to present châteaubriand. To create borders and garnishes, the standard mixture for duchesse potatoes is forced through a piping bag while still very hot and relatively soft.

Variation:

Potato Croquettes—Shape the duchesse mixture into short cylinders resembling fat corks. Coat the cylinders with bread crumbs using the standard breading procedure described in Chapter 9, Mise en Place. Using the basket method, deep-fry at 360°F (182°C) until golden brown.

Approximate values per 3-oz. (90-g) serving: **Calories** 120, **Total fat** 3.5 g, **Saturated fat** 2 g, **Cholesterol** 65 mg, **Sodium** 250 mg, **Total carbohydrates** 18 g, **Protein** 3 g, **Vitamin C** 20%

More than a French Fry

Thanks to the genius of Carême, Escoffier and others, few vegetables have as extensive a classic repertoire as potatoes. Some of these dishes begin with the **duchesse** [duh-SHEES] potatoes mixture; in this regard, duchesse potatoes can be considered the mother of many classic potato preparations. For example:

Duchesse + Tomato concassée = *Marquis*

Duchesse + Chopped truffles + Almond coating + Deep-frying = *Berny*

Duchesse + Shaping + Breading + Deep-frying = *Croquettes*

Duchesse + Pâte à choux = *Dauphine*

Dauphine + Grated Parmesan + Piped shape + Deep-frying = *Lorette*

❶ Pressing the boiled potatoes through a food mill.

❷ Piping the potatoes.

❸ The finished Duchesse Potatoes.

Dauphine Potatoes

YIELD 3 lb. (1.4 kg), 12 Servings, 4 oz. (120 g) each			METHOD Deep-Frying
Duchesse Potatoes (page 689)	2 lb.	960 g	
Éclair Paste (page 996)	20 oz.	600 g	

1 Combine the Duchesse Potatoes with the Éclair Paste while both mixtures are still warm.

2 Pipe the mixture into the desired shapes onto strips of parchment paper. Chill until ready to cook. At service, deep-fry using the swimming method by carefully sliding the pieces of paper into the fryer; remove the paper with tongs when the potatoes float loose. Cook until golden brown.

Variation:

Lorette Potatoes—Add 4 ounces (120 grams) grated Parmesan in Step 2. Pipe the mixture into small crescents on pieces of parchment paper. Deep-fry by carefully sliding the pieces of paper into the fryer; remove the paper with tongs when the potatoes float loose.

Approximate values per 4-oz. (120-g) serving: **Calories** 270, **Total fat** 18 g, **Saturated fat** 8 g, **Cholesterol** 140 mg, **Sodium** 470 mg, **Total carbohydrates** 23 g, **Protein** 5 g, **Vitamin C** 15%

❶ Deep-frying the potatoes using the swimming method.

❷ The finished Dauphine Potatoes.

Potato Gnocchi

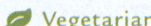
♥ Good Choice   🌿 Vegetarian

As an alternative to broiling the gnocchi with a cheese topping, they can be sautéed and served with a brown butter sauce or with traditional pasta sauces such as cream sauce, tomato sauce or pesto sauce. Hold and reheat gnocchi as you would any stuffed pasta such as tortellini or ravioli.

YIELD 5 lb. (2.4 kg); 10 Servings, 8 oz. (240 g) each	METHOD Boiling	
Potatoes, mealy, peeled	4 lb.	1.9 kg
Salt	2 tsp.	10 ml
Egg, beaten	1	1
Egg yolks, beaten	3	3
Salt	1 tsp.	5 ml
Pepper	½ tsp.	2 ml
Clarified butter	2 fl. oz.	60 ml
Nutmeg, ground	TT	TT
Flour	1 lb.	480 g
Whole butter	as needed	as needed
Parmesan, grated	4 oz.	120 g
Fontina, sliced	6 oz.	180 g

Potato gnocchi

1 Cut the potatoes into uniform-sized pieces. Cover with water. Add the salt and simmer the potatoes until tender. Drain the potatoes well and spread on a sheet pan. Place the pan in a 300°F (150°C) oven for 5 minutes to dry the potatoes well. Remove the potatoes from the oven and immediately pass them through a ricer or food mill into a stainless steel bowl.

2 Add the beaten egg and yolks, salt, pepper, clarified butter and nutmeg to the potatoes and mix until incorporated. Add half the flour to the bowl and mix well.

3 Spread a portion of the remaining flour on a work surface. Place the dough on the work surface and knead additional flour into the dough until it is firm and workable. Divide the dough into eight equal pieces. Roll each piece into a cylinder approximately 2 feet (60 centimeters) long. With a dough knife, cut the dough into ¼- to ½-ounce (7- to 15-gram) pieces. Round each piece into a ball. Flour the tines of a dinner fork and draw the fork firmly across each ball to form ridges around the surface of the gnocchi and create an indentation on one side. Place the formed gnocchi on a floured sheet pan. Cover and refrigerate until service.

4 Boil the gnocchi in salted water for 2–3 minutes. A few seconds after they begin to float, remove the gnocchi from the water with a spider or slotted spoon and drain well.

5 Sauté the gnocchi in small batches in whole butter, browning them slightly. Portion them into serving dishes, top with grated Parmesan and Fontina slices and place under the broiler for 1–2 minutes to melt the cheese. Serve immediately.

Approximate values per 8-oz. (240-g) serving: **Calories** 560, **Total fat** 22 g, **Saturated fat** 13 g, **Cholesterol** 145 mg, **Sodium** 560 mg, **Total carbohydrates** 72 g, **Protein** 18 g, **Vitamin A** 15%, **Vitamin C** 40%, **Calcium** 25%, **Iron** 15%, **Claims**—good source of vitamin A and iron; high in fiber, vitamin C and calcium

 Vegetarian

Polenta

YIELD 1 lb. 12 oz. (840 g), 7 Servings, 4 oz. (120 g) each		METHOD Simmering	
Shallots, chopped	2 tsp.	10 ml	
Whole butter	as needed	as needed	
Milk, white stock or water	1 qt.	960 ml	
Cornmeal, yellow or white	6 oz.	180 g	
Salt and pepper	TT	TT	

1 Sauté the shallots in 1 tablespoon (15 milliliters) butter for 30 seconds. Add the milk, stock or water and bring to a boil.

2 Slowly add the cornmeal while stirring constantly to prevent lumps, then simmer for 30 minutes. Season with salt and pepper.

3 Scrape the polenta into a buttered nonaluminum dish; spread to an even thickness with a spatula that has been dipped in water. Refrigerate the polenta until well chilled.

4 To serve, unmold the polenta and cut into shapes. Sauté or grill the polenta for service, or sprinkle with grated Parmesan and heat under a broiler or salamander.

Approximate values per 4-oz. (120-g) serving: **Calories** 190, **Total fat** 7 g, **Saturated fat** 3.5 g, **Cholesterol** 20 mg, **Sodium** 55 mg, **Total carbohydrates** 25 g, **Protein** 6 g, **Calcium** 15%

❶ Spreading the cooked polenta into a stainless steel pan.

❷ Cutting the polenta into shapes.

❸ Grilling the polenta for service.

Polenta vs. Grits

Polenta and grits are both types of cornmeal mush, made by stirring the ground grain into a hot liquid and cooking on the stovetop. Both require almost constant stirring to prevent lumps and both can be chilled into a firm mass, then cut into portions and sautéed or grilled. Both began as peasant foods; grits shares its history with the American South, while polenta developed in northern Italy. There are some differences with the way the corn is milled for the two products, however. Grits are coarser and generally made from white corn, while polenta is made with a smoother meal ground from yellow corn.

The wide availability of coarse-ground whole grain cornmeal blurs these lines nowadays. Shrimp and grits and similar entrées may be made with the finer polenta cornmeal, while grits can be cooked into a mush and referred to as polenta. It's now a matter of "chef's choice" based on taste and texture preferences.

Creamy Polenta with Wild Mushrooms

YIELD 8 Servings, 8 oz. (240 g) each		METHOD Simmering	
Yellow onions, chopped fine		12 oz.	340 g
Garlic, chopped fine		2 Tbsp.	30 ml
Olive oil		5 fl. oz.	150 ml
Chicken or vegetable stock		2 qt.	1.9 lt
Coarse polenta		12 oz.	360 g
Salt and pepper		TT	TT
Heavy cream		1 pt.	480 ml
Aged Asiago or Fontina, grated fine		4 oz.	120 g
Fresh wild mushrooms		8–10	8–10
Fresh thyme sprigs		as needed for garnish	

1 Sauté the onions and garlic in 4 fluid ounces (120 milliliters) oil until lightly colored. Add the stock; bring to a boil.

2 Slowly stir in the polenta. Simmer for 10 minutes, stirring regularly. The polenta should be thick and creamy. Add more stock if necessary. Adjust the seasonings and keep warm.

3 Just before serving, add the cream and cheese to the polenta and stir vigorously.

4 Sauté the fresh wild mushrooms in the remaining oil until tender. Spoon the polenta onto warm plates and garnish with the wild mushrooms and a sprig of fresh thyme.

Approximate values per 8-oz. (240-g) serving: **Calories** 550, **Total fat** 46 g, **Saturated fat** 19 g, **Cholesterol** 95 mg, **Sodium** 1090 mg, **Total carbohydrates** 21 g, **Protein** 13 g, **Vitamin A** 35%, **Vitamin C** 15%, **Calcium** 20%, **Iron** 15%

Oatmeal with Bananas and Cinnamon

 ♥ Good Choice 🌿 Vegetarian

YIELD 4 Servings, 8 oz. (240 g) each		METHOD Simmering	
Milk or water		24 fl. oz.	720 ml
Rolled oats		4½ oz.	135 g
Salt		pinch	pinch
Brown sugar		1½ Tbsp.	45 ml
Honey		4 tsp.	20 ml
Bananas, sliced thick		4 oz.	120 g
Cinnamon, ground		1 tsp.	5 ml

1 Heat the milk until simmering. Add the salt and slowly stir in the oats. Cook over medium heat, stirring just until the oats start to thicken. Continue cooking, uncovered, until the oats soften and the liquid is absorbed, approximately 6–8 minutes.

2 Remove from the heat. Cover and let stand until the oatmeal thickens, approximately 5 minutes.

3 To hold for service, cover to prevent the oatmeal from drying out. To serve, spoon the oatmeal into warm bowls. Top with the honey, banana slices and cinnamon.

Approximate values per 8-oz. (240-g) serving: **Calories** 300, **Total fat** 4 g, **Saturated fat** 4 g, **Cholesterol** 20 mg, **Sodium** 115 mg, **Total carbohydrates** 46 g, **Protein** 12 g, **Calcium** 25%, **Iron** 10%, **Claims**—good source of dietary fiber and iron, excellent source of calcium

Vegetarian

Grits and Cheddar Soufflé

YIELD 8 Servings, 4 oz. (120 g) each		METHOD Simmering/Baking	
Grits		8 oz.	240 g
Water		1½ pt.	720 ml
Milk		1½ pt.	720 ml
Unsalted butter		4 oz.	120 g
Salt		TT	TT
Tabasco sauce		½ tsp.	2 ml
Sharp Cheddar cheese, grated		8 oz.	240 g
Eggs, separated		6	6
Granulated sugar		2 tsp.	10 ml

1 Combine the grits, water, milk, butter and salt in a heavy saucepan. Bring to a simmer and cook, stirring constantly, until thick, approximately 5–10 minutes.

2 Remove from the heat and stir in the Tabasco sauce and 6 ounces (180 grams) cheese.

3 Whisk the egg yolks together, then stir them into the grits mixture.

4 Whip the egg whites to soft peaks, add the sugar and whip to stiff peaks. Fold the egg whites into the grits mixture.

5 Pour the soufflé into a well-buttered 2-quart (2-liter) casserole or soufflé dish. Top with the remaining 2 ounces (60 grams) cheese. Bake at 350°F (180°C) until set and browned, approximately 30 minutes. Serve immediately.

Approximate values per 4-oz. (120-g) serving: **Calories** 410, **Total fat** 25 g, **Saturated fat** 9 g, **Cholesterol** 215 mg, **Sodium** 640 mg, **Total carbohydrates** 32 g, **Protein** 16 g, **Vitamin A** 40%, **Calcium** 30%

Saffron Rice

🌿 Vegetarian

YIELD 10 Servings, 4 oz. (120 g) each	METHOD	Pilaf
Basmati rice	1 lb.	480 g
Saffron threads	1 tsp.	5 ml
Boiling water	1 qt.	1 lt
Ghee or clarified butter	3 fl. oz.	90 ml
Cinnamon stick, 2 in. (5 cm) long	1	1
Cloves, whole	4	4
Onions, fine dice	5 oz.	150 g
Dark brown sugar	1 Tbsp.	15 ml
Salt	2 tsp.	10 ml
Cardamom seeds	¼ tsp.	2 ml

1 Wash the rice and drain thoroughly.

2 Steep the saffron in 2 fluid ounces (60 milliliters) boiling water.

3 In a saucepan, heat the ghee, then add the cinnamon and cloves. Add the onions and stir-fry until the onions are soft and slightly brown.

4 Add the rice and stir until it is well coated with the ghee and the grains are a light golden color.

5 Stirring constantly, add the remaining boiling water, sugar, salt and cardamom. Bring to a boil and reduce to a simmer.

6 Gently stir in the steeped saffron and its water, cover and simmer until the rice has absorbed all the liquid.

7 Fluff with a fork and serve at once.

Variation:

Pilau (Indian-Style Rice Pilaf)—Add 4 teaspoons (20 milliliters) minced fresh ginger, 2 teaspoons (10 milliliters) ground cumin, 1 teaspoon (5 milliliters) ground coriander, 1 teaspoon (5 milliliters) ground turmeric and ¼ teaspoon (1 milliliter) crushed red pepper flakes to the saucepan in Step 3. Add 6 ounces (180 grams) raisins, 6 ounces (180 grams) frozen peas, thawed and 2 ounces (60 grams) slivered almonds or cashews in Step 7. Let stand 5 minutes before serving.

Approximate values per 4-oz. (120-g) serving: **Calories** 370, **Total fat** 16 g, **Saturated fat** 9 g, **Cholesterol** 35 mg, **Sodium** 780 mg, **Total carbohydrates** 51 g, **Protein** 4 g

Pilau (Indian-Style Rice Pilaf)

Thai-Style Fried Rice

YIELD 16 Servings, 4 oz. (120 g) each	METHOD Stir-Frying	
Vegetable oil	4 fl. oz.	120 ml
Fresh ginger, grated	1 Tbsp.	15 ml
Garlic, mashed	3 Tbsp.	45 ml
Assorted vegetables such as carrots, peppers, mushrooms, medium dice	1½ pt.	720 ml
Long-grain white rice, cooked and thoroughly chilled	17 oz.	510 g
Eggs, slightly beaten	6	6
Tomato concassée	1 pt.	480 ml
Hot chile paste	1 oz.	30 g
Fish sauce	3 fl. oz.	90 ml
Fresh lime juice	1 Tbsp.	15 ml
Fresh cilantro, chopped	as needed	as needed

1 Heat the oil in a wok or rondeau. Add the ginger and garlic and stir-fry until lightly browned. Remove from the pan.

2 Stir-fry the vegetables and remove them from the pan.

3 Stir-fry the rice until warmed through.

4 Make a well in the center of the rice and pour in the eggs. Cook the eggs until almost set before mixing them into the rice.

5 Add the tomato concassée, garlic, ginger and vegetables. Mix in the chile paste, fish sauce and lime juice. Stir-fry to an internal temperature of 165°F (74°C). Garnish with chopped cilantro.

Variations:

Chinese-Style Fried Rice—Omit the hot chile paste, fish sauce, and lime juice. Add ½ cup (120 ml) chopped green onions to the assorted vegetables. Season with 1 tablespoon (15 milliliters) sesame oil and 4–6 tablespoons (120–180 milliliters) soy sauce. Omit the cilantro garnish.

Forbidden Fried Rice—Prepare Chinese-Style Fried Rice, using black rice and adding 4 ounces (120 grams) diced, cooked pork; 2 ounces (60 grams) thinly sliced, cooked chicken and 2 ounces (60 grams) cooked shrimp in Step 5.

Note Prepare the rice a day ahead and cool thoroughly. This separates the grains and keeps the fried rice from becoming sticky during cooking.

Approximate values per 4-oz. (120-g) serving: **Calories** 310, **Total fat** 18 g, **Saturated fat** 3.5 g, **Cholesterol** 160 mg, **Sodium** 1100 mg, **Total carbohydrates** 30 g, **Protein** 9 g, **Vitamin A** 110%, **Vitamin C** 35%

Wild Rice and Cranberry Stuffing

YIELD	5 pt. (2.5 lt), 20 Servings, 4 oz. (120 g) each	METHOD	Simmering

Dried morels	1 oz.	30 g
Wild rice	12 oz.	360 g
Onions, minced	8 oz.	240 g
Butter or chicken fat	2 oz.	60 g
Chicken stock, hot	approx. 1 qt.	approx. 1 lt
Dried cranberries	6 oz.	180 g
Salt and pepper	TT	TT
Fresh parsley, chopped fine	4 Tbsp.	60 ml

1 Cover the dried morels in lightly salted water. Soak them overnight. Drain, reserving the soaking liquid. Rinse well, drain again and chop coarsely.

2 Rinse the wild rice well in cold water.

3 Sauté the onions in the butter or chicken fat until tender. Add the mushrooms and wild rice.

4 Strain the reserved liquid from the mushrooms through several layers of cheesecloth to remove all sand and grit. Add enough chicken stock so that the liquid totals 3 pints (1.5 liters). Add the stock mixture and cranberries to the rice. Cover and simmer until the rice is dry and fluffy, approximately 45 minutes.

5 Season to taste with salt and pepper and stir in the parsley. This rice may be served as a side dish or used for stuffing duck or game hens.

Approximate values per 4-oz. (120-g) serving: **Calories** 190, **Total fat** 6 g, **Saturated fat** 3 g, **Cholesterol** 10 mg, **Sodium** 380 mg, **Total carbohydrates** 28 g, **Protein** 7 g

Hoppin' John

♥ Good Choice

This dish from the American South, a combination of black-eyed peas and rice, is traditionally served on New Year's Day to bring good luck and prosperity in the coming year.

YIELD	12 Servings, 7 oz. (210 g) each	METHOD	Simmering

Dried black-eyed or field peas	1 lb.	480 g
Bacon slices, chopped	3	3
Onions, chopped	8 oz.	240 g
Chicken stock	as needed	as needed
Long-grain rice	1 lb.	480 g
Salt and pepper	TT	TT

1 Rinse, sort and soak the peas. Cook until tender, following the procedure for cooking dried beans on page 627. Drain the peas, reserving the cooking liquid.

2 Fry the bacon in a large sauté pan. Add the onions and cook until tender. Add 28 fluid ounces (840 milliliters) of the reserved cooking liquid from the peas. If there is not enough cooking liquid reserved, add stock as necessary.

3 Stir in the rice and the cooked peas. Bring to a boil, reduce the heat, cover and simmer without stirring until the rice is cooked and the liquid is absorbed, approximately 20 minutes.

4 Season to taste with salt and pepper. Stir well before serving.

Approximate values per 7-oz. (210-g) serving: **Calories** 270, **Total fat** 3 g, **Saturated fat** 1 g, **Cholesterol** 5 mg, **Sodium** 80 mg, **Total carbohydrates** 48 g, **Protein** 11 g, **Iron** 20%, **Claims**—low fat; low saturated fat; low cholesterol; good source of fiber and iron

🌿 Vegetarian

Quinoa, Beet, Squash and Spinach Salad

YIELD 12 Servings, 3½ oz. (105 g) each

Butternut squash, peeled and cut into large dice	8 oz.	240 g
Olive oil	2 fl. oz.	60 ml
Quinoa	6 oz.	180 g
Vegetable stock or water	1 pt.	480 ml
Baby spinach, stems removed	2½ oz.	75 g
Lemon juice	2 fl. oz.	60 ml
Salt	1 tsp.	5 ml
Beets, roasted, peeled and cut into wedges	8 oz.	240 g
Feta or goat cheese, crumbled, optional	3 oz.	90 g
Chives, minced	3 Tbsp.	45 ml
Salt and black pepper	TT	TT

1. Toss the squash in 1 teaspoon of the olive oil. Spread it out in a single layer onto a half-sheet pan. Roast at 400°F (200°C) until tender and lightly browned, approximately 20–25 minutes.

2. Bring quinoa and vegetable stock to a boil in a saucepan over high heat. Reduce the heat to medium-low, cover, and simmer until the quinoa is tender and the liquid is absorbed, approximately 10–15 minutes. Remove from the heat. Stir lightly with a fork and let sit, covered, for 5 minutes.

3. Stir the spinach into the warm quinoa.

4. Whisk together the lemon juice, salt and remaining olive oil. Fold it into the quinoa.

5. Adjust the seasonings with salt and pepper; serve warm or at room temperature garnished with the beets, squash, feta (if using) and chives.

Approximate values per 3½-oz. (105-g) serving: **Calories** 110, **Total fat** 5 g, **Saturated fat** 240 g, **Cholesterol** 0 mg, **Sodium** 240 mg, **Total carbohydrates** 14 g, **Protein** 3 g, **Iron** 20%, **Vitamin A** 50%, **Vitamin C** 15%

🌿 Vegetarian

Fettuccine Alfredo

YIELD 4 Servings, 6 oz. (180 g) each

Fresh fettuccine	8 oz.	240 g
Whole butter	2 oz.	60 g
Heavy cream	12 fl. oz.	360 ml
Parmesan, grated	2 oz.	60 g
Salt and white pepper	TT	TT

1. Boil the pasta, keeping it slightly undercooked. Refresh and drain.

2. To make the sauce, combine the butter, cream and Parmesan in a sauté pan. Bring to a boil and reduce slightly.

3. Add the pasta to the pan and boil the sauce and pasta until the sauce is thick and the pasta is cooked. Adjust the seasonings and serve.

Approximate values per 6-oz. (180-g) serving: **Calories** 630, **Total fat** 49 g, **Saturated fat** 29 g, **Cholesterol** 170 mg, **Sodium** 1000 mg, **Total carbohydrates** 33 g, **Protein** 14 g, **Vitamin A** 50%, **Calcium** 25%

Fettuccine Carbonara

Carbonara is a popular pasta dish in Rome usually made with spaghetti; visitors often call it "spaghetti and egg pasta." The heat of the hot pasta and pancetta set the eggs, creating a creamy sauce. Traditionally this dish is rather salty; blanch the chopped pancetta before cooking to reduce the salty taste if desired.

YIELD 4 Servings, 7 oz. (210 g) each

Eggs, pasteurized	2	2
Parmesan, grated	3 oz.	90 g
Whole butter	1 oz.	30 g
Olive oil	1½ fl. oz.	45 ml
Pancetta or salt pork, lardons	3 oz.	90 g
Garlic cloves, minced	2	2
Fettuccine	9 oz.	270 g
Freshly ground black pepper	TT	TT
Salt	TT	TT
Red pepper flakes, optional	as needed	as needed

1 Beat the eggs and Parmesan together. Set aside.

2 Heat the butter and oil in a sauté pan large enough to hold the cooked pasta. Add the pancetta and garlic. Cook gently for 8–10 minutes until the pancetta is lightly browned and the fat is rendered. Remove from the heat and set aside.

3 Boil the fettuccine in salted water until almost done.

4 Drain the pasta and add it to the oil and pancetta. Toss over low heat, then add the egg mixture, tossing to coat the pasta evenly and gently cook the eggs without scrambling. Add freshly ground black pepper and adjust the seasonings with salt and red pepper flakes, if using. Serve immediately.

Approximate values per 7-oz. (210-g) serving: **Calories** 680, **Total fat** 49 g, **Saturated fat** 28 g, **Cholesterol** 300 mg, **Sodium** 770 mg, **Total carbohydrates** 35 g, **Protein** 26 g, **Vitamin A** 35%, **Calcium** 45%, **Iron** 15%

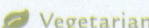 Vegetarian

Macaroni and Cheese

YIELD   18 Servings, 5 oz. (150 g) each

Macaroni	1 lb.	480 g
Béchamel (page 220)	2½ pt.	1.2 lt
Salt	1 tsp.	5 ml
White pepper	¼ tsp.	2 ml
Dry mustard	1 tsp.	5 ml
Hot sauce	TT	TT
Milk, warm, optional	as needed	as needed
Cheddar cheese, shredded	1 lb.	480 g

1 Cook the macaroni in salted water, drain and transfer it to a bowl.

2 Heat the Béchamel in a large saucepan over low heat. Season it with the salt, white pepper, dry mustard and hot sauce. Add hot milk if necessary to thin the sauce.

3 Stir the Cheddar cheese into the sauce. Continue stirring until the cheese is completely melted and the sauce is smooth.

4 Stir the sauce into the macaroni. Transfer the macaroni and cheese to a half hotel pan and hold for service.

Variations:

Baked Macaroni and Cheese—Pour the macaroni and cheese into a buttered hotel pan. Toss 1 pint (480 milliliters) of fresh bread crumbs with 4 fluid ounces (120 milliliters) melted butter. Top the macaroni with the breadcrumbs. Bake at 375°F (190°C) for 15 minutes or until browned.

Macaroni and Cheese with Ham and Tomato—Stir 2 pounds (1 kilogram) each of diced cooked ham and tomato concassée into the macaroni and cheese before pouring it into the hotel pan.

Approximate values per 5-oz. (300-g) serving: **Calories** 280, **Total fat** 14 g, **Saturated fat** 8 g, **Cholesterol** 45 mg, **Sodium** 360 mg, **Total carbohydrates** 26 g, **Protein** 12 g, **Calcium** 20%

Baked Ziti with Fresh Tomato Sauce

YIELD 1 Full-Size Hotel Pan,
30 Servings, 5 oz. (150 g) each

Eggs	3	3
Ricotta	2 lb.	960 g
Fresh thyme, chopped	1 Tbsp.	15 ml
Fresh oregano, chopped	1 Tbsp.	15 ml
Fresh basil, chopped	1 Tbsp.	15 ml
Salt and pepper	TT	TT
Italian sausage links	2 lb. 8 oz.	1.2 kg
Ziti, cooked, refreshed and drained	3 lb.	1.4 kg
Parmesan, grated	4 oz.	120 g
Fresh Tomato Sauce for Pasta (page 246)	2 qt.	1.9 lt
Mozzarella, shredded	1 lb.	480 g

1 Combine the eggs, ricotta, thyme, oregano, basil, salt and pepper. Mix well and refrigerate.

2 Place the sausage links in a 2-inch- (5-centimeter-) deep full-size hotel pan; cook in a 350°F (180°C) oven for 20 minutes. Remove and drain the sausage. Slice the links into rounds and reserve.

3 Pour off the sausage fat, then place the ziti in the hotel pan. Top pasta and sausage with an even coating of the cheese mixture, sausage slices and Parmesan.

4 Pour the Fresh Tomato Sauce for Pasta over the top layer and stir slightly to distribute the sauce.

5 Bake at 375°F (190°C) for 1 hour. Sprinkle the mozzarella evenly over the pasta and return to the oven for 10 minutes. Serve.

Note Ziti may also be prepared in individual casseroles. Decrease baking time as necessary.

Approximate values per 5-oz. (30-g) serving: **Calories** 450, **Total fat** 23 g, **Saturated fat** 10 g, **Cholesterol** 130 mg, **Sodium** 1290 mg, **Total carbohydrates** 27 g, **Protein** 35 g, **Vitamin A** 40%, **Calcium** 70%, **Iron** 15%, **Claims**—good source of fiber, vitamin C and iron; high in vitamin A and calcium

Vegetable Lasagna

YIELD 1 Half-Size Hotel Pan,
9 Servings, 10 oz. (300 g) each

Olive oil	4 fl. oz.	120 ml
Onion, diced	2 oz.	60 g
Garlic, chopped	1 tsp.	5 ml
Arugula	4 oz.	120 g
Salt and pepper	TT	TT
Mushrooms, sliced	8 oz.	240 g
Eggplant, washed, trimmed and sliced ⅛-in. (3-mm) thick	8 oz.	240 g
Carrot, washed, trimmed, peeled and sliced ⅛-in. (3-mm) thick	8 oz.	240 g
Yellow squash, washed, trimmed and sliced ⅛-in. (3-mm) thick	8 oz.	240 g
Zucchini, washed, trimmed and sliced ⅛-in. (3-mm) thick.	8 oz.	240 g
Ricotta cheese	12 oz.	360 g
Egg, beaten	1	1
Parmesan cheese, grated	2 oz.	60 g
Fresh basil, chopped	1 oz.	30 g
Fresh Tomato Sauce for Pasta (page 246)	2½ pt.	1.2 lt
Fresh pasta sheets, 8½ in. × 11 in. (22 cm × 28 cm)	4	4
Mozzarella cheese, shredded	1 lb.	480 g

1 Heat 2 tablespoons (30 milliliters) of the olive oil in a sauté pan over medium heat. Sauté the onions and garlic in the oil for 1 minute. Add the arugula and sauté just until it wilts. Season with salt and pepper, remove from the pan and cool.

2 Add 2 more tablespoons (30 milliliters) of the olive oil to the pan. Sauté the mushrooms in the pan until dry. Season with salt and pepper. Remove from the pan and cool.

3 Toss the eggplant, carrot, yellow squash and zucchini separately with some of the olive oil. Season the vegetables with salt and pepper. Spread each type of vegetable out onto separate sheet pans. Bake them at 350°F (180°C) until tender but not brown, approximately 10 minutes. Cool the vegetables.

4 Combine the ricotta, egg, Parmesan and fresh basil. Season with salt and pepper.

5 Set aside 1 pint (480 milliliters) of the tomato sauce for plating. Ladle 6 fluid ounces (180 milliliters) of the tomato sauce into the bottom of a half-size hotel pan. Cover the sauce with a layer of cooked pasta. Add the eggplant slices in a single, even layer. Layer the carrots on top of the eggplant. Spread half of the cheese mixture and one quarter of the mozzarella on the carrots.

6 Place a sheet of pasta on top of the cheese. Spread 6 fluid ounces (180 milliliters) of the tomato sauce over the pasta. Layer the mushrooms on top of the sauce. Spread the remaining cheese mixture on top of the mushrooms and sprinkle on one quarter of the mozzarella cheese.

7 Add another layer of pasta, 6 fluid ounces (180 milliliters) of the tomato sauce, the yellow squash in an even layer and the zucchini slices on top. Sprinkle with one quarter of the mozzarella. Place the arugula on top of the cheese. Top with the remaining sheet of pasta. Spread a layer of sauce over the pasta and top with the remaining mozzarella cheese.

8 Cover with foil. Bake at 325°F (160°C) for 1 hour. Uncover and bake an additional 15 minutes until lightly browned. Allow the lasagna to rest for 15 minutes before cutting.

9 Cut the lasagna into nine portions and plate each on a pool of the reserved tomato sauce.

Approximate values per 10-oz. (300-g) serving: **Calories** 270, **Total fat** 38 g, **Saturated fat** 14 g, **Cholesterol** 100 mg, **Sodium** 910 mg, **Total carbohydrates** 70 g, **Protein** 31 g, **Vitamin A** 140%, **Vitamin C** 50%, **Calcium** 50%

Soba Noodles with Chicken and Green Onions

YIELD 1 qt. (960 ml),
4 Servings, 12 oz. (360 g) each

White chicken stock (page 207)	1 qt.	1 lt
Sachet:		
Peppercorns, crushed	¼ tsp.	2 ml
Cilantro stems	8	8
Fresh ginger, chopped coarse	2 Tbsp.	30 ml
Shiitake mushroom stems	3 Tbsp.	45 ml
Thai chile peppers, chopped	2	2
Soy sauce	TT	TT
Salt and black pepper	TT	TT
Chicken breast halves, boneless, skinless, approx. 6 oz. (180 g) each	2	2
Soba noodles	8 oz.	240 g
Sesame oil	1 tsp.	5 ml
Green onions, chopped	4 oz.	120 g

1 Bring the stock and sachet to a simmer. Season to taste with soy sauce, salt and pepper. Poach the chicken in the stock until cooked through. Remove the chicken from the broth and set aside.

2 Strain the broth into a saucepan. Bring to a simmer over moderate heat. Add the soba noodles and the sesame oil and cook until the noodles are tender.

3 Cut the chicken into large pieces and add them to the broth. Simmer until the chicken is heated through.

4 Serve in heated bowls. Top each serving with a generous portion of the chopped green onions.

Variation:

Chopped bok choy, julienned snow peas and carrots and sautéed sliced shiitake mushrooms can be cooked in the stock and added to the soup for service.

Approximate values per 12-oz. (360-g) serving: **Calories** 320, **Total fat** 4 g, **Saturated fat** 0.5 g, **Cholesterol** 60 mg, **Sodium** 630 mg, **Total carbohydrates** 45 g, **Protein** 29 g, **Iron** 15%, **Claims**—Good source of iron

Spaetzle

In Austria, Germany and Switzerland, spaetzle is a traditional accompaniment to roasted meats and game stews.

YIELD 30 Servings, 3 oz. (90 g) each

Eggs	12	12
Water	1 qt.	960 ml
Flour	3 lb.	1.4 kg
Salt	2 tsp.	10 ml
Nutmeg, ground	½ tsp.	2 ml
Whole butter	8 oz.	240 g
Salt and white pepper	TT	TT
Fresh parsley, chopped	as needed for garnish	

1 Whisk the eggs to blend. Add the water, flour, salt and nutmeg. Mix by hand until well blended; the batter should be a smooth, gooey paste. Cover and refrigerate the batter.

2 Place the batter in a spaetzle maker, perforated steam table pan or colander suspended over a large pot of boiling water. Work the batter through the holes using a plastic bowl scraper or rubber spatula; the batter should drop into the boiling water. Lower the water temperature to a simmer.

3 Cook the spaetzle in the simmering water until they float to the surface, approximately 3–4 minutes. Remove them with a skimmer and refresh in a bowl of ice water.

4 For service, sauté the spaetzle in butter to heat through. Season with salt and white pepper; garnish with chopped parsley.

Approximate values per 3-oz. (90-g) serving: **Calories** 250, **Total fat** 9 g, **Saturated fat** 4.5 g, **Cholesterol** 100 mg, **Sodium** 250 mg, **Total carbohydrates** 35 g, **Protein** 7 g, **Vitamin A** 10%, **Iron** 15%

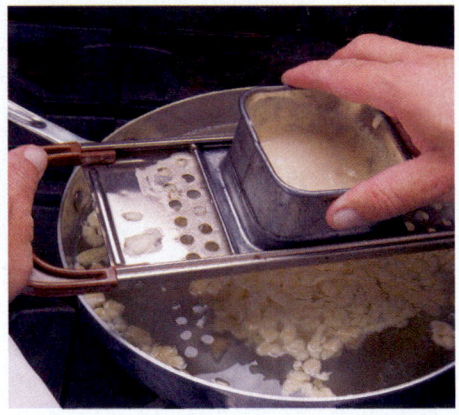

❶ Pushing the batter into the boiling water through the holes in a spaetzle maker.

❷ Forcing the batter through a perforated hotel pan.

❸ Sautéing the spaetzle in butter.

Healthy Cooking 24
and Special Diets

After studying this chapter, you will be able to:

▶ create nutritious menus for health-conscious adults

▶ use alternative ingredients and substitutes to develop recipes that provide guests with healthy foods and foods that meet special dietary needs

▶ identify and use techniques to modify recipes for special diets

▶ describe the range of vegetarian diets and employ a variety of ingredients as alternatives to meat, poultry, fish or dairy

R estaurant guests may follow a special diet to control allergies, for other health-related reasons or simply because of personal preference. Whatever the reason, today's chef must understand the importance of properly preparing foods for someone requiring a special diet and should be able to accommodate these needs. Building on the information in Chapter 3, Nutrition, this chapter offers a framework for understanding ingredient substitutions and alternatives. Guidelines for chefs seeking to incorporate healthy dishes into their menus are included along with procedures for preparing dishes suitable for gluten-free, vegan, vegetarian and other special diets. Vegetarian eating patterns and ingredients are discussed in detail and a selection of healthy, special diet and vegetarian recipes concludes this chapter.

PRINCIPLES OF HEALTHY COOKING

Healthy cooking is based on sound culinary techniques that adhere to dietary guidelines established through nutritional research. The ingredients chefs offer their guests, the cooking techniques used and the amount of food served all impact customers' health. Here we explore the ways you can adapt your thinking about portion size and ingredients to incorporate healthful eating into your menu.

Portion Size

Portion size refers to the amount of food served at a single occasion, such as a meal or a snack. Portion size should not be confused with serving size, which refers to a unit of measure of food, such as the amount recommended by the Dietary Guidelines for Americans. A serving size is the amount recommended for consumption while a portion size refers to what is actually consumed. A person may eat the entire contents of a package of snacks or cookies, for example, even though the recommended serving size on the package indicates that it includes two servings. When the amount consumed is double the recommended serving size, the portion the consumer has eaten contains twice as many calories, fat, sodium and other nutrients as intended.

The portions of food served in restaurants have gradually increased over the past 40 years. Since the 1980s, calorie counts in popular items such as a fast-food portion of French fries or a turkey sandwich have nearly tripled. The weight of bagels, hamburgers, muffins and many other common foods has increased exponentially. According to a study by the National Heart, Lung and Blood Institute, the average portion of spaghetti and meatballs served in restaurants has increased from 8 ounces (240 grams) to 16 ounces (480 grams) in the past 20 years.

As a chef, you should be aware of the amount of food you are serving. Consider the comparison of the calories and nutrients in the three portions of chicken salad in Figure 24.1. Although the 2-ounce portion on the left may seem insufficient for a luncheon plate, it may be suitable when served with a green or grain salad and sliced vegetables or a cup of hearty vegetable soup. Side dishes made from whole unrefined grains or vegetables provide satisfaction with the least amount of added calories and fat. The 6-ounce portion to the right is triple its size and may well provide too many calories and other nutrients for the average diner.

As a chef, you should weigh or measure portions for consistency, but you will also benefit from learning to visually recognize an appropriate portion size. Portion size impacts food costs, another reason to pay attention to the quantity on the plate.

Figure 24.1 Comparison of portions of chicken salad—2 ounces (60 grams), 4 ounces (120 grams) and 6 ounces (180 grams)

Rethinking the Center of the Plate

The center of the plate refers to the dominant foodstuff or the focal point of a dish. For too long, the first thing a chef or a diner considered was the meat or protein component on the plate. Vegetables, salads, grains and fruits were seen as mere accompaniments, included for appearance or as a token nod to a balanced meal. By refocusing the center of the plate toward vegetables and healthier foods and away from high-fat meats, chefs are creating dishes that are better for customers' health and the health and sustainability of our planet.

It is not just portion size that impacts the healthfulness of what's served but all the ingredients a chef places on the plate. It's not just what is removed—less fat to control overall calories—but what delicious ingredients the chef can add to increase the healthfulness of a dish. As discussed in Chapter 3, Nutrition, there are many steps to follow when creating healthy menu items. As you read this chapter, you may want to revisit the guidelines for preparing healthy meals and menus on page 51).

As a general rule use only whole, minimally processed foods free from **additives**. Select foods that are available fresh from local producers. Think about seasonality and seek to incorporate foods that are in season and use cooking techniques appropriate to the season, such as braising during colder months and grilling during warmer ones. You can go a long way toward preparing more healthful dishes by first focusing on fruits, vegetables, grains and greens. Then you can consider how to incorporate smaller quantities of high fat meat, poultry, game, dairy products and sugar. As guests seek to reduce their consumption of animal products, they appreciate seeing other foods as the focal point on their plates including nuts, grains and beans, all of which are high in beneficial fats, protein and other nutrients.

Because they often work in hot, sweaty environments, cooks may unintentionally add too much salt when seasoning foods. Try to add salt only when necessary. Customers can add more salt to their food at the table. And remember to apply cooking techniques that intensify flavors without relying on excess salt, fat and sugar.

Creating a new menu item that conforms to government health standards (discussed in Chapter 3, Nutrition) can challenge a chef's creativity. You need an understanding of ingredients, flavor dynamics, cooking techniques and nutrition, not to mention a healthy dose of imagination. When creating new inherently healthful menu items, find inspiration in familiar dishes and menu items.

The three chicken dishes shown in Figure 24.2 illustrate approaches a chef might use to adapt a recipe to produce a more healthful dish. Few meals are as satisfying and appealing as roast chicken served with puréed potatoes, asparagus and pan gravy shown below. The 10 ounce (300 gram) portion on the left features a skin-on chicken

additives substances added to many foods to prevent spoilage or improve appearance, texture, flavor or nutritional value; they may be synthetic materials copied from nature (e.g., sugar substitutes) or naturally occurring substances (e.g., lecithin); some food additives may cause allergic reactions in sensitive people.

Roast chicken with mashed potatoes and natural pan gravy

Pan-seared chicken, potato purée, beets and carrots and pan gravy

Gingered chicken broth, chicken, bitter greens, star anise, squash and chile oil

Figure 24.2 Chicken three ways

leg and thigh as well as a slice of the breast meat. The calories, fat and cholesterol in the dish are high according to the Daily Calorie Requirements discussed on page 48. Nutritional information for this dish is as follows: **Calories** 780, **Total fat** 45 g, **Saturated fat** 19 g, **Cholesterol** 255 mg.

Some of the flavors of roast chicken are captured by the dish shown in the center photo. Here the bone-in chicken has been replaced by a boneless skinless airline breast, which was sautéed to develop a golden color. The portion size was reduced to 6 ounces (180 grams), and the skin was removed to reduce fat and cholesterol. Skillful browning of the boneless breast develops rich umami flavors and approximates the color of the roast chicken. Serving the chicken with puréed potatoes and root vegetables replicates the satisfying, traditional flavors associated with roasted poultry. Nutritional information for this dish is as follows: **Calories** 240, **Total fat** 14 g, **Saturated fat** 6 g, **Cholesterol** 95 mg.

The chicken preparation shown on the right in Figure 24.2 captures the rich flavors of roast chicken in a radically different dish. This gingered chicken broth still features chicken in a hot and aromatic preparation. In this version, however, only 4 ounces (120 grams) of boneless, skinless chicken breast is poached in a flavorful broth that is defatted and seasoned with fresh ginger. It is filling without the calories, starchiness and fat of puréed potatoes. The cooking method and leaner cut of poultry lowers the calories and saturated fat in the dish. Colorful, lightly cooked greens and steamed squash improve the dish's nutrient content and appearance. Nutritional information for this dish is as follows: **Calories** 210, **Total fat** 1.4 g, **Saturated fat** 0.4 g, **Cholesterol** 90 mg.

RECIPE MODIFICATION

To prepare healthy foods and cook for special diets, chefs must adapt recipes or create new ones that reduce, replace or eliminate specific ingredients. This "reduce, replace or eliminate" process is referred to as recipe modification. When adapting and modifying dishes, chefs must review and test their recipes, giving thoughtful consideration to the ingredients, cooking techniques, flavors and presentation.

Reduce, Replace or Eliminate

When modifying a recipe, first identify the ingredient(s) or cooking method(s) that may need to be changed. Then use the following principles to make a dish more healthful or acceptable to the customer on a special diet:

- *Reduce* the amounts of the ingredient(s) that need to be changed if doing so will not alter the structure, taste or appearance of the dish and make it unrecognizable to the original. In many recipes reducing the amount of oil, butter or other fat does not dramatically alter the dish. Note that this is not the case with baking formulas.
- *Replace* the problematic ingredient(s) with a substitute that will result in the least change to the flavor profile and appearance of the dish.
- *Eliminate* the ingredient(s) if doing so will not destroy the integrity of the dish. It may be necessary to compromise a dish's integrity when serving a customer who is allergic to an ingredient for which there is no suitable substitute. Whenever a customer is allergic to an ingredient, safety must come first and the allergen must be eliminated completely from the dish and not allowed to contact the equipment used to prepare that dish. Even a trace amount of the allergen could be fatal. (You may want to review the content on food allergies and intolerances in Chapter 2, Food Safety, for more information on this topic.)

In this chapter, we use the term **ingredient substitute** to mean replacing one ingredient with another that has presumably similar—although not necessarily identical—flavor, texture, appearance and other sensory characteristics. In some cases the substitute ingredient may be more nutritious than the ingredient or preparation technique it replaces. For example, instead of thickening a soup with a roux, the chef may add puréed potatoes as a thickener or purée cooked vegetables to thicken the soup. In either case the soup thickened with potatoes or puréed vegetables is more nutritious than one made with a roux. Similarly those seeking to prepare dishes with less fat can use reduced-fat or nonfat sour cream in place of regular sour cream when baking quick breads. The differences in flavor, texture, appearance and baking quality should be minimal.

We use the term **ingredient alternative** to mean replacing one ingredient with another that has a different flavor, texture, appearance or another characteristic. An alternative does not compromise—although it may change—the flavor of the dish. As with the ingredient substitute, the ingredient alternative may be more nutritious. Lemon juice and herbs, for instance, can be used in place of salt; a salsa of fresh vegetables can replace a cream-based sauce. The dishes will not taste the same but they will still taste good.

Many menu items can be modified to make them more healthful or to accommodate special diets. Care must be taken to ensure that taste is not compromised, however. Often ingredient substitutes and alternatives change the flavor, texture or appearance of a dish. Sometimes these changes are acceptable; sometimes they are not. Because some changes result in unsatisfactory flavors, textures or appearance, many recipes are not suitable for substitution or alteration. Use your judgment. Test your new recipes and evaluate whether the ingredient substitutions and cooking techniques used result in an appealing dish. Understanding the function of the ingredients in your recipe will help you to adapt the recipe to meet dietary needs. The quality of the final product must be as good as, if not better than, the original to meet the public's expectations. If your superb reduced-fat, sugar-free lemon cheesecake has an unexpected flavor or texture that might disappoint a traditional cheesecake fan, consider renaming it. A name such as Lemon Cheese Soufflé Cake may establish more realistic customers' expectations.

Steamed fresh soy beans (edamame) served with salt is a satisfying and healthful appetizer.

Modifying Recipes

As we noted previously, when beginning the recipe modification process, you should first identify recipe ingredients and menu items that are good candidates for alteration. When developing a recipe for a low-fat diet, for example, start with recipes that are moderate in fat and do not rely heavily on fat for the dish's flavor, moisture and structure. A fruit-based carrot or apple cake can tolerate the reduction of some of the fat from butter, oil or nuts. But a classic pound cake or shortbread that relies on butterfat for its characteristic taste and texture may not. Types of recipes that lend themselves to modification include bean and puréed soups; rice-based dishes, such as paella; creamy dressings and vinaigrettes; ground meat dishes, such as meat loaf or meatballs; or fruit and frozen desserts.

Carefully consider the flavors, textures and sensations of the original recipe when you are using substitute ingredients. You can replace fat-laden dairy products with low-fat counterparts. For example, use evaporated skim milk instead of heavy cream. Purée part-skim ricotta or cottage cheese to use as a substitute for full-fat cream cheese. Use lean meats in place of high-fat cuts or grades of beef.

Consider the wide array of cooking techniques available to you. Often it makes sense to apply alternative cooking techniques when modifying a recipe to make it more healthful or acceptable for a special diet. Use techniques that intensify flavor without adding fat, salt or ingredients that are unacceptable to your customer. Reductions, for example, intensify the flavor of sauces without adding caloric thickeners or fat. Toasting enhances the flavor of nuts and spices. The judicious use of herbs, spices, lemon juice, vinegar, onions, peppers and condiments can enhance flavor in place of salt. Oven-roast cut potatoes instead of deep-frying them. Review the discussion of cooking methods in Chapter 10, Principles of Cooking, to understand which preparation methods will achieve the color, flavor and texture you want in your dish. And always remember to moderate amounts of unnecessary fat, salt and sugar in any preparation. Use high-fat ingredients, such as whipped cream, in moderation or only as a garnish.

COMPARISON OF NUTRIENTS IN THREE VERSIONS OF STROGANOFF			TABLE 24.1
	BEEF STROGANOFF (PAGE 340)	MODIFIED BEEF STROGANOFF (PAGE 711)	VEGAN STROGANOFF (PAGE 723)
Calories	635	280	370
Total fat	39 g	11 g	5 g
Saturated fat	20 g	0 g	0 g
Cholesterol	201 mg	70 mg	0 mg
Sodium	510 mg	400 mg	610 mg
Total carbohydrates	32 g	17 g	52 g
Protein	40 g	29 g	27 g
Vitamin A	41%	30 %	50%
Iron	46%	15%	15%
Calcium	11%	20%	15%

In this chapter, we compare two recipe alternatives to the Beef Stroganoff recipe on page 340. Table 24.1 lists the nutritional profile of the three versions of the recipe featured in this text and will be referred to in this chapter. The recipe for Modified Beef Stroganoff illustrates the Procedure for Modifying Recipes. Recipe modifications on pages 711 and 723 are listed in red type in the margin and in the list of ingredients for the alternative recipes.

Procedure for Modifying Recipes

1 Identify the dish that needs to be modified, whether it is an hors d'oeuvre, appetizer, main course or dessert.

2 Identify the goal of the recipe modification: improve healthfulness, reduce fat, reduce sodium, reduce sugar and/or eliminate allergens.

3 Review the original recipe and note ingredients of concern. Consider the flavor profile. Identify which ingredients are critically important to the dish and which can be adjusted. Can whole grains, vegetables, fruits, lean meats, fish or naturally low-fat ingredients be substituted? Think about how to emulate the flavors, textures and sensations of the original recipe using substitute ingredients.

4 Decide on the ingredient substitutes or alternatives to use in the modified recipe.

5 Reduce the amount of high-fat, high-sodium ingredients and increase ingredients with high fiber or other suitable ingredients as appropriate.

6 Note cooking techniques that are essential to the texture, flavor, body, appearance and identity of the original dish. Consider and select alternative cooking techniques to intensify flavors. Build flavor using cooking methods such as roasting, grilling, baking, poaching or steaming.

7 Balance the flavor profile desired with additional condiments, sauces or other preparations that complement the finished recipe.

8 Calculate and adjust the portion size with healthfulness or the special diet in mind.

9 Consider the balance of color and textures and plate the dish in an appealing manner.

Modified Beef Stroganoff (Low-Calorie, Low-Fat)

 **Good Choice**

YIELD 8 Servings, 8 oz. (240 g) each	METHOD Sautéing	
Zucchini, ends removed	24 oz.	720 g
Tenderloin tips, emincé	2 lb.	960 g
Canola oil	1 Tbsp.	15 ml
Onion, medium diced	4 oz.	120 g
Mushrooms, halved	1 lb.	480 g
Jus lié	10 fl. oz.	300 ml
Evaporated skim milk	10 fl. oz.	300 ml
Arrowroot flour	1 Tbsp.	15 ml
Non-fat sour cream	8 oz.	240 g
Dijon-style mustard	1 Tbsp.	15 ml
Fresh dill, chopped	1 Tbsp.	15 ml
Fresh parsley, chopped	1 Tbsp.	15 ml
Salt	½ tsp.	2 ml
Black pepper	¼ tsp.	1 ml

MODIFICATIONS

- Reduce carbohydrates and calories: Replace egg noodles with zucchini.
- Reduce fat, cholesterol and calories: Replace butter with canola oil. Replace heavy cream with evaporated skim milk, arrowroot flour and non-fat sour cream.

1 Slice the zucchini lengthwise on a mandolin into long, thin ribbons. Steam the zucchini ribbons until tender. Keep warm.

2 Sauté the tenderloin tips in the oil, searing on all sides. Remove the meat and set aside.

3 Add the onion to the pan and sauté lightly. Add the mushrooms and sauté until dry.

4 Add the jus lié. Bring to a boil then simmer for 8–10 minutes.

5 Make a slurry with the evaporated skim milk and arrowroot. Whisk the slurry into the jus lié mixture. Bring to a boil and then simmer until thickened, approximately 3–4 minutes. Add the sour cream, mustard and any meat juices that accumulated while holding the meat.

6 Return the meat to the sauce to reheat. Stir in the dill and parsley. Adjust the seasonings and serve with the zucchini ribbons.

Approximate values per 8-oz. (240-g) serving: **Calories** 280, **Total fat** 11 g, **Saturated fat** 0 g, **Cholesterol** 70 mg, **Sodium** 400 mg, **Total carbohydrates** 17 g, **Protein** 29 g, **Vitamin** 30%, **Calcium** 20%, **Iron** 15%, **Claims**—low calorie, low fat

ACCOMMODATING SPECIAL DIETS

More and more diners are becoming health-conscious consumers. Many are trying to cut down on foods high in salt, fat, added sugar, starch and/or cholesterol. For others, specific physical conditions prevent them from enjoying traditional recipes. In this section we discuss ingredient substitutes and alternatives and the special requirements of a variety of special diets, such as gluten-free, low-fat, low-sugar, dairy-free, low-sodium and allergen-free.

Low-Sodium Diets

Chefs are sometimes taught to use salt liberally to enhance flavors. Excessive consumption of sodium, which is a major component of table salt (sodium chloride), is a dietary concern for many people, however. Excess sodium leads to the retention of fluids in the body. This can lead to hypertension (high blood pressure), heart failure, kidney diseases and strokes. Overconsumption of sodium is of special concern to older adults. The average American consumes 3000–7000 milligrams of sodium per day, far more than the recommended daily allowance of 2300 milligrams. A low-sodium diet contains no more than 2000 milligrams of sodium per day; less than 1500 milligrams of sodium per day is ideal.

Salt Substitutes and Alternatives

Salt substitutes look and measure like table salt and are readily available under various brand names. Most traditional salt substitutes (which are primarily composed of potassium chloride) do not enhance flavors like salt does and some people feel that they contribute an "off" metallic taste to food. Newer salt substitutes contain seaweed granules or potassium lactate, sometimes with other chemicals added for flavor.

Modifying Recipes for Low-Sodium Diets

To reduce the amount of salt in a dish, you can reduce the quantity of salt used, reduce the quantity of sodium-containing ingredients used and use lower-sodium alternatives whenever possible. Soy sauce is a good example; often the quantity can be reduced and excellent low-sodium soy products are also available.

Reduce the use of salt while focusing on developing the flavors in foods by using flavorful, low-sodium ingredients such as acids (vinegars, citrus, tomatoes), fresh herbs or spices, sweet and hot peppers or onions and garlic. Consider adding flavor with a low-sodium marinade or rub, infusion or reduction. Choose cooking methods that develop the flavor in foods such as grilling, roasting, smoking and poaching in a flavorful liquid.

Limit use of high-sodium condiments and ingredients. Brined, cured and smoked fish and meats are unsuitable for low-sodium diets as are canned vegetables or tomato juice (unless they are low-sodium versions). Commercially prepared baked goods and snacks foods (such as potato chips and pretzels) are usually higher in sodium than the same foods made in house. Reducing or eliminating salt is usually successful in baked goods but avoid recipes that use chemical leaveners, discussed on page 910, because these leaveners contain sodium. Use natural leaveners such as eggs or yeast instead.

Low-Sugar Diets

Overconsumption of sugar leads to obesity and cardiovascular disease. Added sugars in sweetened soft drinks, salad dressings and most processed foods are contributing to a global obesity epidemic that should be of concern to chefs. Consumption of excess calories and sugar can lead to type 2 diabetes, a chronic condition that impacts the way the body processes glucose (sugar). For those born with type 1 diabetes, a disease that interrupts the body's ability to produce the hormone insulin, consumption of sugar must be closely regulated if not totally avoided. Many people who are seeking to lose weight for health and cosmetic reasons also limit their consumption of sugars and may appreciate the low-sugar options in a restaurant or café.

Sugar Substitutes and Alternative Sweeteners

Sugar and other sweeteners add flavor and help promote browning and caramelization. In baked goods, sugar adds structure, texture and volume. Natural sweeteners, such as honey and agave, date or maple syrup, are suitable for those who prefer not to consume refined white sugar. The calorie content of these liquid sweeteners is just as high or even slightly higher than refined granulated sugar, however. Because natural sweeteners are usually in liquid form, appropriate adjustments should be made to recipes.

Several non-carbohydrate, low-calorie, artificial sweeteners suitable for those on a sugar-free diet are also readily available to consumers and foodservice operations. Sugar substitute **saccharin** (brand name Sweet'N Low, Sweet Twin or Necta Sweet), the oldest artificial sugar substitute, has been available for more than a century. It has no calories and tastes 200–700 times as sweet as table sugar. At one time, saccharin was linked to cancer in laboratory animals, but scientific evidence for safety in humans was convincing enough to permit the continued legal use of saccharin in food. Saccharin has a bitter aftertaste, however, and many people find it unpalatable.

Aspartame (brand name NutraSweet, Equal or Sugar Twin) is 180–200 times as sweet as table sugar. Unlike saccharin, aspartame does not have an aftertaste. Aspartame breaks down when heated, so it cannot be used in cooked foods. It is widely used in soft drinks,

Natural sweeteners such as maple syrup shown here are good alternatives to refined sugar.

frozen yogurts, fruit spreads, candies and similar products. According to the FDA, aspartame is a safe substitute for sugar, although it is a risk for those people with the rare disorder phenylketonuria (PKU), who cannot metabolize the phenylalanine in aspartame.

Sucralose (brand name Splenda) is 600 times as sweet as sugar and can be used like sugar in some baked goods. Sucralose, a derivative of table sugar, is virtually calorie-free because its sweetness is so intense that only tiny amounts are needed to replace the sweetness of sugar. Original Splenda cannot be used in baking but is appropriate in recipes that use sugar for sweetness. The granulated form is used measure for measure like regular table sugar. Splenda is also available blended with sugar in a product designed for baking.

Rebaudioside A is a sweet-tasting compound extracted from the stevia plant. Generally referred to as simply stevia, it is not metabolized by the body so it is non-caloric. It is used commercially as a sweetener for beverages in place of aspartame. PureVia and Truvia are two brands in wide distribution. Stevia can be heated or frozen without loss of flavor, but it will not replace the bulk provided by sugar in dessert products.

Modifying Recipes for Low-Sugar Diets

When your goal is reducing sugar in the foods you serve, consider ingredients that provide a natural source of sweetness. The following suggestions can also help you to create recipes that are lower in sugar or sugar-free:

- Ripe fresh fruits, berries, dates and dried fruits add natural sweetness to sauces, stews, salads, marinades and glazes.
- When cooking for those who prefer to avoid eating refined sugar, substitute sweeteners derived from natural sources such as agave or maple syrup or honey. Keep in mind, however, that these liquid sweeteners add their distinctive flavors to dishes, unlike refined sugar, which is simply sweet.
- You can eliminate or reduce the sugar in any recipe where sugar is not absolutely necessary. Recipes that may not require sugar include salad dressing and sauces for savory foods or marinades.
- Use fruit purées as sauces in place of sugar syrups.
- The sugar in many recipes for muffins and cookies can be reduced by 10–15% with no effect on the product.
- When cooking for people with type 2 diabetes who eat only sugar-free foods, consider the sugar substitutes discussed above. Use high-intensity sweeteners when a liquid sugar is called for in beverages, sauces or syrups. Note that liquid sugar substitutes are not suitable for baking without formula adjustments.

Naturally sweet mango purée

Low-Fat Diets

Consuming too much fat has been linked to an increased risk for cancer and heart disease. However more recent studies suggest that it is the type of fat, not the calories from fat, that are of concern. As discussed in Chapter 3, Nutrition, fats are nutrient-dense and caloric. Overconsumption of fat contributes to weight gain, which can lead to other physical problems and chronic illnesses.

Fat Substitutes and Alternatives

Low-fat or fat-free dairy substitutes are usually good alternatives to full-fat products in most applications. Low-fat milk, cream cheese, sour cream and yogurt can be substituted for the full-fat counterparts in most applications.

To find an appropriate substitute, first determine whether the dairy fat is necessary for the success of the product. If it is, try a low-fat or fat-free substitute combined with additional ingredients to substitute for some of the fat you are removing. If the formula calls for whole milk, cream, sour cream, cream cheese or other cheese, a low-fat dairy alternative will usually work. Table 24.2 lists lower-fat or fat-free alternatives to some common dairy products.

DAIRY SUBSTITUTES			TABLE 24.2
INSTEAD OF	IN THIS APPLICATION	USE	COMMENTS
Cream	Custards, hot soups or sauces; baking	Evaporated skim milk	May effect texture; will not whip
Cream cheese	Any	Light cream cheese (Neufchâtel)	
	Cold creams or spread	Light cream cheese or fat-free cream cheese; part-skim ricotta or cottage cheese	Purée ricotta or cottage cheese until creamy before using
Mascarpone	Any	Light cream cheese (Neufchâtel)	Thin with low-fat sour cream
Sour cream	Cold dressing and sauces	Fat-free, gelatin-free yogurt	Strain yogurt to thicken and remove excess water
	Custards, hot sauces and stews	Fat-free, gelatin-free yogurt	Stabilize with starch and heat gently to prevent separation
Whole milk	Any	Buttermilk, skim milk, reduced-fat milk or evaporated skim milk	Buttermilk and evaporated skim milk have distinct flavors

Modifying Recipes for Low-Fat Diets

When preparing foods for a low-fat diet, the simplest solution is to reduce the amount of fat used. The fat in most soups, stews, fried foods and roasted dishes can often be reduced by 20–30 percent without significant negative results. You can also use cooking methods that reduce the need for fat. For example, broiling, grilling, baking, poaching and steaming do not require the addition of fat. Use reduced or lower fat dairy ingredients as discussed in the previous section. Or substitute one type of dairy product for another.

Cholesterol is a component of meat, poultry, game, shellfish, eggs and milk products. Reducing the quantity of red meat in a dish, removing the skin on poultry, cooking with lean cuts of beef and pork are a few techniques that will reduce the quantity of fat in foods. Substituting monounsaturated fats, such as those found in canola oil, olive oil, sunflower oil and avocados, for saturated fats will improve the health profile of a recipe but will neither reduce the total fat nor the calories in the dish. Oils made from nuts including almonds, hazelnuts or walnuts will also add a unique flavor and can work well in some recipes although they may be allergens for some consumers.

Egg substitutes, discussed in Chapter 21, Eggs and Breakfast, can help those on a restricted diet enjoy breakfast foods, but egg substitutes have limited applications in baking and general cooking. Two ounces (60 grams) or two large egg whites can substitute for one whole egg in some recipes. For dishes using a large quantity of eggs, it is best, however, to include at least a small portion of egg yolks for both color and texture. Pastry items made with whipped egg-white meringues are often used to create fat-free and low-fat desserts.

Dairy-Free Diets

Lactose is a natural sugar found in milk and dairy products. People who are **lactose intolerant** do not have the enzyme necessary to digest this milk sugar. For people who are lactose-intolerant, consuming milk and dairy products can result in digestive problems and intestinal discomfort, but it is rarely life-threatening. In contrast, a serious allergy to **casein**, one of the proteins found in all types of milk, can cause life threatening reactions if dairy products are eaten. If a customer reports that they cannot consume dairy products be sure to remove any such items from their meal, no matter how small the portion.

Dairy Substitutes and Alternatives

For those intolerant to lactose (milk sugar), both true dairy products and plant sources of "milk" may be suitable. Commercially available lactose-free dairy products will work well in most culinary applications. Some lactose-reduced and lactose-free dairy products may taste a bit sweeter than milk, however.

Plant-based dairy-free milks made from oats, hazelnuts and almonds

Milk-like liquids made from tree nuts and soy beans are suitable dairy substitutes as they do not contain either lactose or casein. The many milk alternatives on the market have different flavors and perform differently in culinary applications. Research the best alternative for your specific recipe needs.

Modifying Recipes for Dairy-Free Diets

When preparing dairy-free foods, avoid using all milk products as well as foods made from milk such as butter, cream, cheese, ice cream and yogurt. Vegetable fats may be a suitable alternative for butter, depending on the application. Many soy-based products are now available to replace yogurt, ice cream, liquid milk and cheese. Vegetarian and vegan cheeses made without animal products can also be consumed by people on a dairy-free diet. Some lactose-intolerant customers may be able to eat cheese or other dairy products made from goat's or sheep's milk, but do not assume that this is the case for everyone.

Gluten-Free Diets

Celiac disease is an inherited autoimmune disease that causes damage to nutrient receptors (*villi*) in the small intestine when gluten is consumed. Gluten is composed of proteins found in wheat, rye, barley and products made from these grains such as malt and brewer's yeast. Gluten allergies and intolerances affect as many as 15 million people in the United States; approximately 3 million (1 percent of the population) have true celiac disease; 2 million have wheat and gluten allergies and the remainder are sensitive to wheat products.

Unlike most diseases, celiac disease is treated exclusively with diet. By removing all wheat, rye and barley from the diet, people with celiac disease can live a normal, healthy life. Consuming even small amounts of gluten can damage nutrient receptors in the small intestines, even without noticeable symptoms, however.

Gluten-Free Substitutes and Alternatives

Gluten-free substitutes for wheat flour include flours made from arrowroot, **buckwheat**, coconut, corn, potato, rice, tapioca, soy, **amaranth**, **beans** such as chickpeas, flax meal, **millet**, quinoa, **sorghum** and ground nuts. See Table 24.3. Teff and oats can be substituted safely if they are free from wheat cross-contamination. Commercially available gluten-free baking flours ease the preparation of suitable gluten-free products.

Millet and amaranth flours

buckwheat flour a dark, nutty-tasting gluten-free flour milled from the seeds of the buckwheat plant; used for centuries in Middle Eastern and Asian countries to make bread, cereals, noodles and baked goods

bean flour cooked beans including chickpeas, soybeans and white beans that are dried and ground into a fine powder; many bean flours, especially soy flour with a 50% protein content, are added to wheat flour mixtures to boost protein content.

sorghum grain harvested from a plant that resembles corn, used primarily for animal feed and food processing applications; also called milo. When ground, sorghum may be blended with other flours to make gluten-free preparations.

INGREDIENTS SAFE FOR GLUTEN-FREE DIETS		TABLE 24.3
INGREDIENTS	FORM	APPLICATIONS
Almond flour/meal	Flour	Batter, breading, dredging, some baking applications
Amaranth	Flour, grain	Batter, salads, texturizer in baked goods, some baking applications
Brown, white and wild rice	Grain, flour	Side dish, thickener, batter, breading, dredging, gluten-free flour blends
Buckwheat	Flour, grain	Batter, breading, dredging, gluten-free flour blends
Coconut flour	Flour	Batter, breading, dredging, some baking applications
Corn, cornstarch	Grain, meal, flour, powder	Batter, breading, thickener, breads, gluten-free flour blends
Guar gum, tapioca, xanthan gum	Thickener	Thickener, salad dressing, sauces, baked goods, breads, gluten-free flour blends
Millet	Flour, grain	Side dish, texturizer in baked goods, salads
Pea flour	Flour	Gluten-free flour blends
Potatoes, potato flour, potato starch	Vegetable, flour, powder	Side dish, thickener, gluten-free flour blends
Quinoa	Grain	Side dish, texturizer in baked goods, salads
Sorghum	Flour	Gluten-free flour blends
Soy flour	Flour	Gluten-free flour blends
Teff	Flour, grain	Side dish, texturizer in baked goods, salads

Keeping Halal

Many Muslims follow dietary laws based on the Qur'an (the revealed book), the Hadith (the sayings or traditions of the prophet Muhammad) and the collective wisdom of Muslim scholars. *Halal*, which means "allowed" or "lawful," refers to foods and beverages that can be consumed by observant Muslims. Foods and beverages that are *haram* are not allowed, and those that are of a questionable or suspect nature are referred to as *mushbooh*.

As all fruits and vegetables are halal, most Muslim dietary laws address permitted and prohibited meats. Cooked (not raw) beef, lamb and chicken are halal, provided the animals are slaughtered and butchered according to certain rituals and methods. Fish and shellfish are also halal. Pork, game, carnivorous animals, birds of prey, carrion (the meat of animals that died of natural causes), and blood are haram, as are products derived from them. Eggs and dairy products from permitted animals are halal, as are baked goods made with ingredients from permitted animals. Any halal food contaminated with blood, pork or other haram product is deemed haram and cannot be eaten. Alcohol, whether consumed as a beverage, used as a flavoring or even present in a cleaning solution for dishes, is haram. Gelatin, emulsifiers, animal-based fats and certain dairy products are considered *mushbooh* unless certified as halal. Halal certification is often denoted as a capital H inside a triangle.

In food service operations, it is best if equipment dedicated solely to halal cooking is used. If this is impractical and the same equipment is used to cook halal and haram foods, the equipment must be thoroughly sanitized before it can be used for halal products. Normally a careful visual inspection of the equipment suffices.

Preparing dishes that are truly gluten-free requires that you educate yourself about suitable foods and ingredients. Because gluten hides in many prepared foods, such as sauces, soups, candy, cold cuts, processed meats, frozen French fries, surimi and even oatmeal, be certain to purchase and use only commercial products labeled as "gluten-free." To be gluten-free, your dishes must not include products such as malt, brewer's yeast, panko bread crumbs, semolina, wheat varieties such as einkorn, farro and spelt and any product contaminated by these ingredients.

Modifying Recipes for Gluten-Free Diets

Finding gluten-free alternatives for basic ingredients is the best place to start when preparing gluten-free foods. Substituting rice flour noodles for pasta, thickening with arrowroot in place of roux, using almond flour, cornmeal or coconut flour when breading pan-fried foods, or substituting mashed root vegetables for pasta or rice are some of the easier solutions to common challenges when cooking for the celiac diner.

Cooking for the gluten-free customer is an opportunity for creativity. Most meats, poultry, fish, dairy products, fruits and vegetables are safe for those with celiac disease, so create new ways to serve these foods without adding ingredients that contain gluten. Offer potato pancakes with smoked fish instead of blinis, for example. Polenta makes an excellent crust for tartlets or pizza. (See Polenta Vegetable Tart on page 728.) Serve Southern-style cornbread made from 100% cornmeal. Use eggplant or ribbon-cut zucchini in place of pasta for lasagna. Because a gluten-free diet lacks the beneficial dietary fiber found in many whole grains, incorporate fiber from beans, rice, vegetables and gluten-free whole grains.

Some baked goods can be made gluten-free by substituting a variety of gluten-free flours and starches, such as rice, sorghum, buckwheat or millet, with the addition of at least 30 percent starch from corn, potatoes or tapioca. Gums help replace the elasticity of gluten in baked goods. Use 1 teaspoon (15 milliliters) of xanthan, guar or locust bean gum per cup of gluten-free flour blend when making pastries and 1½–2 teaspoons (22–30 milliliters) per cup (240 milliliters) of gluten-free flour blend when making bread. Additional eggs help build structure in gluten-free baked goods. Numerous gluten-free baking blends are available for making breads, pizza dough, cookies and other flour-based foods. Brands vary so be sure to follow each manufacturer's directions for the best results.

When cooking and baking for those with celiac disease, be especially mindful of cross contamination from tiny particles of wheat flour or gluten-containing foodstuffs. In addition to kitchen surfaces that come into contact with food, pasta cooking water and deep-fat fryer oil may harbor gluten. Segregate cooking vessels when preparing gluten-free foods.

Allergen-Free Diets

Allergies to wheat, dairy, nuts, eggs, soy and shellfish are widespread, affecting millions of consumers. The consumption or contact with any of these ingredients can cause a potentially fatal allergic reaction or severe discomfort for the allergy sufferer. Review the material in Chapter 2, Food Safety, for a better understanding of the procedures to follow when preparing dishes for allergy sufferers. For example, in the case of a peanut allergy, mise en place should be considered when removing peanuts from a given recipe. To avoid peanut oil or peanut oil–containing products, pans may need to be prepared with an alternative oil and utensils untouched by peanut products must be used.

Many consumers may be allergic to more than one ingredient. In some situations, you might accommodate their needs by making a few simple ingredient switches. For example, if a customer who has celiac disease and is also allergic to nuts orders pan-fried eggplant, select a gluten-free breading that does not contain any nut flour. Should no suitable alternative be available, suggest a different dish rather than attempt to adapt one for a customer's specific needs. If a customer who has celiac disease and is also lactose intolerant orders macaroni and cheese, for example, recommend another dish with a similar flavor and consistency. Focus on the ingredients that are safe for the person to eat when you craft alternatives. When planning your menu, anticipate customers with multiple allergies and intolerances. Include some items on your menu that are completely free from the most common allergens: milk, eggs, fish, shellfish, tree nuts, peanuts, wheat and soy.

Keeping Kosher

To one degree or another, many observant Jews keep kosher; that is, they adhere to dietary laws rooted in the Torah (the first five books of the Old Testament) and developed over the centuries by Jewish scholars. These laws (1) categorize foods and (2) define basic dietary principles.

Kosher foods: Only meat from animals that chew their cud and have split hooves can be eaten. These include cattle, goats, deer and other game; swine are not a kosher species. Poultry can be kosher, provided it is not from a bird of prey; thus chicken, duck, goose and turkey are allowed, but hawk and eagle are not. For fish to be kosher, it must have both scales and gills; this eliminates catfish and eel, and no shellfish can be kosher. For a meat to be kosher, the species must be kosher and the animal must be slaughtered and butchered according to religious rules. Dairy products are kosher if the species from which they come is kosher; for cheese to be kosher,

it must be made without rennet. Fresh fruits and vegetables are always kosher, as are baked goods that are not made with animal fats. Commercially prepared foods marked with U, K or a similar symbol (often in a circle) indicates that the food product is kosher, the producer has used appropriate ingredients and met certain standards and its facilities have been inspected and approved by a rabbi.

Kosher dietary principles: All foods are either (1) meat, (2) dairy or (3) pareve (parve). **Pareve** refers to neutral (neuter) foods such as fruits, vegetables, breads, fish, eggs and certain commercially prepared foods that can be eaten with either meat or dairy items. The principal dietary rule for keeping kosher is that meat and dairy foods cannot be cooked or eaten together. People who keep kosher have two sets of cooking utensils, dishes and even dishcloths, one used for meat, the other for dairy, so that there is

no accidental mixing. Particularly observant Jews wait for 1–6 hours after eating a meat dish before consuming a dairy dish.

Not all Jews keep strictly kosher. Those who do dine out only in restaurants that regularly observe the same religious laws that they do at home, or in one that has been specially inspected and approved by a rabbi for the occasion (an option often used by catering facilities to accommodate kosher weddings, bar mitzvahs, bat mitzvahs and other Jewish celebrations). Other Jews keep kosher by not eating any shellfish, meat, poultry or fish from nonkosher species or mixing dairy and meat, but they do not insist that separate meat and dairy cooking and eating utensils be used. The latter group will generally dine in nonkosher restaurants, provided that the menu (sometimes referred to as "kosher-style") offers appropriate selections from kosher species.

VEGETARIAN AND VEGAN DIETS

Approximately 8 million people in the United States are choosing to forgo some or all animal products in their diets. According to a 2016 Harris Poll of adults in the United States, 3.3 percent of men and 3.5 percent of women follow a vegetarian or vegan diet. The highest percentages are in northeastern states and in the 18–34 age group. Average percentages are essentially the same for Caucasian, African-American and Hispanic groups. About half of vegetarians identify as **vegan**.

The Dietary Guidelines for Americans 2015–2020, as well as recommendations from major health groups (including the American Cancer Society, the American Heart Association, and the American Dietetic Association), stress the importance of eating fruits, vegetables, legumes and whole grains, which are the foundation of a plant-based diet. Studies have shown that the incidence of chronic diseases such as obesity, cardiovascular disease, cancer and type 2 diabetes are lower for vegetarians than for nonvegetarians. It is important to note that other healthy lifestyle factors (including not smoking, regular exercise and moderate use or abstinence from alcohol), which some vegetarians follow may also be responsible for the lower disease rates.

The vegetarian diet has many variations. A person who follows a vegetarian diet can be any (or a combination) of the following:

A colorful vegetarian ribbon salad made with zucchini, carrots, green beans and cherry tomatoes

- **Vegan** [VEE-gun]: A person who eats no meat, fish or poultry or any products derived from animals such as milk, cheese, eggs, honey or gelatin; also referred to as a **strict** or **pure vegetarian**.
- **Raw foodist:** Typically a vegan who eats only raw or slightly warmed plant products (adherents believe that cooking foods to a temperature of 116°F/47°C or higher destroys enzymes and nutrients). A person on a raw foods diet, also referred to as a **living foodist**, may soak certain foods such as nuts and sprouts to soften them and increase nutrient absorption.
- **Fructarian** or **fruitarian:** A person who eats only fruits, nuts, seeds and other plant products that can be gathered without harming the plant. Some fructarians eat only plant matter that has already fallen off the plant.

- **Ovo-vegetarian:** A vegetarian who eats eggs but not dairy products.
- **Ovo-lacto-vegetarian** or **lacto-ovo-vegetarian:** A person who eats plant products as well as dairy products and eggs (although some may not eat cheeses made with animal-based enzymes such as rennet, or eggs produced by factory farms). This diet is one of the most typical vegetarian diets, and the terms *ovo-lacto-vegetarian* and *lacto-ovo-vegetarian* are often used interchangeably with the term *vegetarian*.
- **Lacto-vegetarian:** A vegetarian who eats dairy products but not eggs.

People following a vegetarian or vegan diet must consume the same types of nutrients, in the same quantities, as all consumers, adjusting for age, sex and any illness or physical condition. Legumes, whole grains, nuts, seeds and certain vegetables provide protein in vegetarian and vegan diets. Research shows that a well-balanced vegetarian or vegan diet supplies adequate amounts of protein and contains less saturated fat and cholesterol than diets including meats and other animal products. Vegetarian diets likely include more than the minimum daily recommendation for five servings of fruits and vegetables and more fiber, folic acid, antioxidants, vitamins and minerals. Note that a lack of balanced food sources or a reliance on processed foods, especially those high in sodium or sugar, is unhealthful even if the overall diet is vegetarian or vegan.

Ingredients for Vegetarian and Vegan Diets

You can prepare flavorful, visually stimulating vegetarian and vegan dishes with a traditional range of ingredients available in most restaurant kitchens. Potatoes, grains, starches, vegetables and fruits (discussed in Chapter 22, Vegetables; Chapter 23, Potatoes, Grains, and Pasta; Chapter 25, Salads and Salad Dressings; and Chapter 26, Fruits) form the foundation of vegetarian and vegan cooking. To help chefs in planning vegetarian and vegan dishes, Table 24.4 lists common ingredients and substitutes that are free of dairy, fish, meat and poultry.

Although the professional kitchen offers hundreds of foods appropriate for all vegetarian diets, you can use a number of ingredients to enhance the complexity of your own vegetarian and vegan menu items. Some foods that replace the protein found in animal products as well as other ingredients that may mimic more traditional animal-based foods are discussed in the material that follows.

Soybean-Based Ingredients

The versatile and protein-rich soybean forms the basis for a wide range of products used in vegetarian, vegan and traditional ethnic cuisines worldwide. Soy-based foods are one of the most important sources of protein in the vegetarian diet and have been favorites in Asian cuisines for centuries. Although there are brown, black and green varieties, most soybeans are yellow. According to the United Soybean Board, soy protein is the only plant protein that is equivalent to animal protein; it is a rich source of phytochemicals, making soy an ideal ingredient for vegetarian and vegan cooking. Soy beans can be made into a diverse range of foods, including flour, milk, cheese and oil.

Soy milk is made from dried soybeans that are soaked and then finely ground and pressed to extract a milky liquid. Soy milk comes in liquid or powdered form. Liquid soy milk resembles skim milk and has a slightly nutty flavor. Most liquid soy milk is sold in aseptic packaging and has a one-year shelf life if unopened. Like dairy milk, once opened, liquid soy milk requires refrigeration and lasts approximately 5–7 days. Powdered soy milk is shelf-stable and lasts for a year at room temperature. Soy cheese, soy yogurt and flavored soy beverages are dairy substitutes made from soy milk.

Use soy milk measure for measure in any recipe that calls for dairy milk. Manufacturing technologies have evolved to produce soy milk products with a richer texture and flavor, more suitable for enriching sauces. However at high temperatures soy milk can separate and brown; simmer foods with soy milk gently and add the soy milk near the end of the cooking time to prevent it from separating and scorching.

Tofu or bean curd (Fr. *fromage de soja*) is a staple of Japanese and Chinese cuisines that is appreciated internationally for its high nutritional value, low cost and flavor adaptability. Tofu is made by processing soybeans into soy milk that is coagulated and formed into a cake. The result is a soft, creamy-white substance similar to cheese. Tofu is easy to digest and is a good source of protein, low in fat and sodium with no cholesterol.

Tofu may be eaten fresh; added to soup, broth or noodle dishes; tossed in cold salads; grilled, deep-fried or sautéed; or puréed to make a creamy spread. Its flavor is bland, but it readily absorbs flavors from other ingredients. Two types of tofu are widely available: cotton (or traditional) and silken.

Cotton tofu is the most common type of tofu in the United States. It is solid, with an irregular surface caused by the weave of the cotton fabric in which it is wrapped for pressing. This traditional tofu comes in three styles—soft, firm and extra firm—each style being progressively drier and firmer. Select the style of tofu suited to the preparation. Firmer tofu is solid enough to be grilled or sautéed. It absorbs the flavors of rubs and marinades. Softer tofu may be scrambled like eggs or processed to form a smooth spread.

Silken tofu (Ja. *kinugoshi*) has a silky-smooth appearance and texture and a somewhat more delicate flavor than cotton tofu. Silken tofu is made in a process that is similar to the way yogurt is cultured. No curds are formed, nor is whey produced. This makes a tofu with a custard-like texture suitable for use as a base for dips or in spreads or smoothies. Because the water has not been pressed out of silken tofu, it should not be cooked at high temperatures or for a long time, as it falls apart easily. Silken tofu can also be drained to make a thicker spread with a consistency resembling that of mascarpone or cream cheese.

Fresh tofu is usually packaged in water. It should be refrigerated and kept in water until used. If the water is drained and changed daily, the tofu should last for 1 week. Tofu can be frozen for several months, though its texture will be drier after thawing. Weight down frozen tofu while it is thawing to create a denser, firmer product, suitable for grilling.

Miso [MEE-so] is a thick paste made by salting and fermenting soybeans and rice or barley. After soaking, the soybeans are steamed, then crushed. The mixture is blended with water. Rice or barley is added along with salt before the mixture is inoculated with a living culture (either koji or *Aspergillus* mold). After fermenting and aging, the paste is ready to use. In Japan, where the manufacture of miso is a fine art akin to cheese making, there are countless styles of miso ranging in color from pale to rust and in taste from sweet to salty. In the United States two types of miso are commonly available: **white (sweet) miso** and **red (dark) miso**. Creamy-colored white miso contains a high percentage of rice and has a mild, somewhat sweet flavor. Red or dark miso, which contains a higher percentage of soybeans, is aged longer and has a stronger, saltier flavor.

Miso can be used in cold and warm preparations but should never be boiled; it contains beneficial enzymes and bacteria that can be killed at high temperatures. Miso can be used to enhance the flavor in sauces, soups, stews and marinades where it will impart a rich full-bodied flavor to vegetarian and vegan foods. A pungent seasoning, miso should be used judiciously so as not to overpower a dish. As little as 1 teaspoon (5 milliliters) per portion can be adequate to flavor a simple broth. Due to its high salt content, miso will keep indefinitely under refrigeration.

Tempeh [TEHM-pay] is a type of bean cake made from fermented whole soybeans mixed with a grain such as rice or millet. The mixture is inoculated with *Rhizopus* mold, which binds the grains into a firm cake. A traditional food of Indonesia, tempeh has a chewy consistency and a yeasty, nutty flavor.

With its chunky texture, tempeh makes a pleasant meat substitute. It can be marinated for grilling or sautéing. When crumbled, tempeh can be added to soups or stews to replace ground beef, poultry or pork. A firm cake, tempeh is easily sliced or cut into cubes. Because of the type of live culture used to make it, tempeh should be cooked before eating. Proper cooking also tempers its pronounced flavor. Tempeh is sold both fresh and frozen. It lasts for approximately 1 week in the refrigerator or several months when frozen.

> ⚠️ **Safety Alert**
>
> *Fresh Tofu*
>
> Fresh unpasteurized tofu packed in water requires time and temperature control for safety (TCS). Exercise care when handling this product; use clean sanitized equipment and avoid cross-contamination when handling unpasteurized tofu. Store it below 41°F (5°C). When fresh unpasteurized tofu packed in water is served to at-risk populations, it should be precooked and held at 165°F (74°C) for 3 minutes before using.

Silken tofu

White miso

Red miso

Tempeh

Textured soy protein

Seitan

Textured vegetable protein (TVP), also known as textured soy protein (TSP), is made from soy flour and other dehydrated proteins that are compressed into granules or chunks or extruded into shapes. Food manufacturers use it as a meat extender and in commercially produced meat replacements. Granulated textured vegetable protein must be rehydrated before cooking, which causes it to take on a texture like that of meat and makes it easy to use as a substitute for ground beef or pork. Larger forms of TVP benefit from simmering after rehydration. Adding some vinegar or lemon juice to the simmering liquid helps speed rehydration. A shelf-stable dry product, TVP can be stored for up to a year when tightly sealed at room temperature. Once it has been rehydrated, it must be refrigerated and should be used within a few days.

Other Popular Ingredients in Vegetarian and Vegan Diets

Vegetarian and vegan diets can lack the umami-rich flavors found in meats and cheese. Marine vegetables such as kombu, a type of seaweed, provide natural salinity and glutamic acid, the main ingredient that provides umami taste. **Liquid amino acids**, a product made from soybeans and water, acts as a flavor enhancer and is a good substitute for soy sauce. A powdered form of deactivated yeast called **nutritional yeast** is another popular ingredient in vegetarian and vegan diets for the nutty, creamy flavor it provides.

Seitan [SAY-tan], often referred to as "wheat meat," is a form of wheat gluten, the insoluble protein in wheat. A staple in the diets of Buddhist monks for centuries, seitan has a firm, chewy texture and a bland flavor. Seitan is made by preparing a dough from wheat gluten or wheat flour and water. The dough is repeatedly rinsed to remove any remaining starch or bran. The spongy pieces of seitan are then simmered in a broth of soy sauce or tamari with ginger, garlic and kombu (seaweed). Cooking tenderizes seitan and imbues it with the flavors of the cooking liquid. Because it absorbs flavors readily, seitan can be flavored to mimic many foods. Using seasonings associated with poultry such as thyme and sage brings out a chicken-like flavor in the seitan, whereas using dark soy sauce and meaty mushrooms can give it a meaty flavor. Fully cooked fresh seitan is sold refrigerated in irregularly sized chunks. Seitan should be added to a dish near the end of cooking, as it is already fully cooked. Once opened, it should be consumed within a few days. Powdered seitan mix, which can be used to make seitan dough, is also available.

Grain and nut beverages that resemble dairy milk can be used in place of stock or dairy products when making vegetarian or vegan soups, sauces and custards. Almond, hazelnut, oat and rice milks are commercially available. These ingredients tend to be lower in fat but higher in carbohydrates than their dairy counterparts—and they are cholesterol-free.

Analogous Foods

Numerous products made from soy, wheat, grains or other plant materials are designed to mimic the appearance and texture of popular animal-based products. These commercially prepared analogous food products offer a texture and appearance like that of their animal-protein-based counterparts. Although their flavors are less successful in imitating the actual flavor of their fish, meat or poultry counterparts, many offer vegetarian and vegan consumers the pleasure of eating familiar foods in traditional dishes. Plant-based products are available in the form of "nuggets," "burgers," "sausage," "hot dogs," "ground meat," "bacon," "cold cuts" and even "pastrami." Soy protein extract and judicious use of appropriate seasonings, such as sage in a breakfast sausage analogue, mimic the flavor of their meat counterparts.

In most cases these analogous food products may be prepared in the same way as their meat, poultry or fish counterparts. Steaming, sautéing, simmering, grilling and baking work well. Follow the manufacturer's directions, keeping in mind that these products are usually fully cooked, requiring only crisping or heating, and may suffer if overcooked.

Vegetarian and Vegan Cuisine: Focusing on Plant-Based Ingredients

The principles of vegetarian and vegan cuisine are no different from those of the classic kitchen. When creating an appetizing and satisfying vegetarian or vegan dish, you should use the same professional judgment as when preparing a roast or steak. Flavors must be in balance. Ingredients must be thoughtfully selected and skillfully prepared. Only the ingredients themselves vary. Apply the basic principles of cooking and work with the textures and flavors offered by plant-based ingredients.

Chefs also need to understand the unique role played by animal products in specific recipes they are considering adapting for a vegetarian or vegan diner. As discussed in Chapter 13, Principles of Meat Cookery, the muscle fibers in different cuts of meat, poultry and game yield foods with a chewy texture not easily mimicked by vegetable or soy or analogous food products.

Well-marbled meat has fat throughout. When cooked, this fat melts, adding tenderness and flavor to the finished dish. It may be necessary to add fat to enhance flavor and add moisture to dishes cooked without meats. Replacing animal protein in a main dish with an equal amount of tofu, texturized soy protein, grain, bean purée or plant food may not result in a dish with the same appearance and depth of flavor as the original made with meat. Appropriate use of seasonings enhances the appeal of vegetarian and vegan dishes. Flavors of traditional foods such as barbecue can be applied to vegetarian dishes.

Chefs must carefully choose the ingredients they use in vegetarian and vegan dishes. Vegetables should be chosen for their flavor and texture. The mouthfeel each ingredient contributes to a finished dish should also be considered. Ripe avocados, for example, have a rich, creamy texture that can mimic the mouthfeel of a soft cream cheese. Replacing some fat with coconut oil can also contribute to a rich mouthfeel.

Baking without eggs poses many challenges because of the function eggs perform in many baked goods. Quick-bread formulas using chemical leavening may be better suited to adapting to vegetarian or vegan preparation than creaming-method cakes.

With these considerations in mind, the following are some suggestions on how to plan and prepare to add vegetarian and vegan dishes to a restaurant menu:

A vibrant plate of grilled vegetables on rich squash purée

- *Use or adapt items from the regular menu.* Many items on existing menus may be vegetarian or vegan or can easily be adapted for a vegetarian or vegan diner. Soups, salads, stir-fried vegetables and pasta dishes lend themselves to vegetarian and vegan ingredients.

- *Grains and beans add texture and satiation.* Think about these versatile starches as the center-of-the-plate offerings when planning a vegetarian or vegan menu. Chewy grains such as cooked bulgur, barley and millet offer a good textural appeal that can be lacking in plant-based cuisine. Ensuring that a customer feels sufficiently fed is another consideration, something that a plate of steamed vegetables may not ensure.

- *Feature meaty vegetables and soy products in a vegetarian dish.* Eggplant, mushrooms (especially portabellas), okra, sweet potatoes and parsnips have flavor and body that mimics that of meat. Pan-fried breaded eggplant slices or grilled whole portabella mushroom caps offer hearty vegetable alternatives to a slice of chicken or beef.

- *Compose dishes with an eye to balancing color.* We eat with our eyes as well as our taste buds. When combining grains and beans on a plate, consider using different colors, such as black beans and red rice or yellow lentils and black-eyed peas.

- *Balance textures on the same plate.* Look for complementary and contrasting textures in a vegetarian or vegan plate. When serving a creamy purée, such as mashed sweet potatoes, for example, balance the texture with something crunchy or crisp such as fried zucchini or a risotto cake. A crisp garnish such as crumbled nori or oven-dried onions adds texture and a burst of flavor.

- *Layer flavors for complexity of taste.* A dish prepared with few ingredients need not be bland or boring. Combine cooking methods in one dish to bring out a complex taste. Sun-dried tomatoes added to a fresh tomato sauce add a rich dimension of taste that might otherwise be lacking.
- *Create a pantry stocked with ingredients that help enhance plant-based cooking.* Without base flavor notes created from rich meat stocks, vegetarian and vegan dishes can lack depth of flavor. Varieties of fresh and dried mushrooms help enrich flavorful stocks, soups and stews. Dried seaweed such as kombu (sea kelp) adds a briny flavor mimicking seafood stock. Soy sauce, miso and nutritional yeast can give a vegetable broth a savory taste and appealing dark color, as can wine reductions. Richly flavored nut oils, such as sesame oil, hazelnut oil and walnut oil, can add complex tastes to dishes prepared without rich meat stocks or butter. Olives and dried fruit have intense flavors and pleasing textures that can add variety to a vegetarian dish. Toasted sesame and other seeds and nuts add bursts of flavor and a textural contrast to a dish.
- *Seek inspiration from ethnic cuisines in which vegetarian food is traditional.* Asian, Indian, Mexican, Middle Eastern and South American cuisines offer many exciting vegetarian and vegan options.

In this chapter, we compare two alternative recipes to the Beef Stroganoff recipe on page 340. Review Table 24.1 on page 710, which compares the nutritional profile of the three versions of this recipe. The recipe for Vegan Stroganoff illustrates the Procedure for Modifying a Recipes for Vegetarian and Vegan Diets. Recipe modifications are listed in red type in the margin and highlighted in the list of ingredients.

Procedure for Modifying a Recipe for Vegetarian and Vegan Diets

1. Review the original recipe and note all the ingredients that might not be acceptable for vegetarian or vegan diners.
2. Eliminate animal products. Remember that dairy and eggs are animal products. Keep in mind that many vegans also avoid honey. Be mindful of products that might contain animal ingredients, such as gelatin, fish sauce and Worcestershire sauce made with fish.
3. Consider what role each of those ingredients plays in the finished dish's texture, flavor and appearance.
4. Decide which ingredients can be used in a modified recipe. Consider satiety or fullness and diners' satisfaction and ensure that the plate offers a balance of carbohydrates, proteins, vegetables and fats. When selecting the vegetables, grains and starches, keep your diners' protein needs in mind.
5. Consider the cooking techniques that will be needed for all ingredients on the plate.
6. Ensure the dish is plated and garnished appropriately and with attention to eye appeal. Pay attention to contrasting textures and colors.

Vegan Stroganoff

 Good Choice   Vegan

YIELD 8 Servings, 8 oz. (240 g) each	METHOD Sautéing	
Vegetable oil	1 Tbsp.	15 ml
Onions, small dice	8 oz.	240 g
Garlic clove, chopped	1	1
Seitan, sliced	12 oz.	360 g
Carrot, small dice	4 oz.	120 g
Mushrooms, sliced	3 oz.	90 g
Shiitake mushrooms, trimmed, sliced	3 oz.	90 g
Miso	1 oz.	30 g
Soy sauce	1 fl. oz.	30 ml
Vegetable stock	4 fl. oz.	120 ml
Silken tofu	8 oz.	240 g
Lemon juice	1 Tbsp.	15 ml
Soy cream	4 fl. oz.	120 ml
Salt and pepper	TT	TT
Wide noodles, cooked	24 oz.	720 g
Fresh parsley, chopped	2 Tbsp.	60 ml

MODIFICATIONS

- Eliminate dairy: Replace butter with vegetable oil. Replace heavy cream with silken tofu. Replace sour cream with lemon juice and soy cream.
- Eliminate beef: Replace beef with seitan for texture and protein and with miso and soy sauce for umami. Replace demi-glace with rich vegetable stock.
- Enhance umami: Use two types of mushrooms.
- Eliminate eggs: Replace egg noodles with egg-free pasta noodles.

1. Heat the oil in a large sauté pan. Add the onions and garlic and sauté for 1 minute. Add the seitan, carrot and mushrooms and cook until the mushrooms release their liquid and the liquid is nearly evaporated.

2. Stir the miso and soy sauce into the vegetable stock and then add it to the cooked seitan mixture. Bring to a simmer and remove from the heat.

3. Combine the tofu, lemon juice and soy cream in the bowl of a food processor and process until smooth.

4. Stir the tofu mixture into the seitan mixture until smooth. Do not bring to a boil or the sauce will curdle. Season to taste with salt and pepper.

5. Serve over noodles and garnish with chopped parsley.

Note These modifications to the Beef Stroganoff recipe reduce the calories in the dish by 42 percent from the original. The fat is reduced by 87 percent and the cholesterol is eliminated.

Approximate values per 8-oz. (240-g) serving: **Calories** 370, **Total fat** 5 g, **Saturated fat** 0 g, **Cholesterol** 0 mg, **Sodium** 610 mg, **Total carbohydrates** 52 g, **Protein** 27 g, **Vitamin A** 50%, **Iron** 15%, **Calcium** 15%, **Claims**—no cholesterol; good source of fiber and iron; excellent source of vitamin A

The recipes at the end of this chapter are suitable for most vegetarian diets and most do not include animal proteins or eggs. Many are suitable for vegan diets. Vegetarian dishes appear throughout this book, indicated with the symbol shown in Figure 24.3. These recipes do not contain any meat, fish, shellfish or poultry but may contain dairy products and/or eggs. Vegetarian dishes are not necessarily low in calories, fat or sodium, nor are they automatically good sources of vitamins, protein, fiber or calcium, as defined by government standards. Vegan dishes appear throughout this book, indicated with the symbol shown in Figure 24.4.

Figure 24.3 Symbol for a vegetarian recipe.

Figure 24.4 Symbol for a vegan recipe.

VEGETARIAN INGREDIENT SUBSTITUTES			TABLE 24.4
INSTEAD OF	IN THIS APPLICATION	USE	COMMENTS
Butter	Sautéing	Coconut oil, vegetable oil or vegetable oil spray	
	Flavoring	Nut oil: hazelnut, pecan or walnut; nut butter: almond, cashew, peanut or sesame butter	Additional oil or liquid may be needed; thin nut butters with oil, fruit juices or nut, rice or soy milks
	Spreading	Ground nut spread: almond, cashew, peanut or sesame butter; vegetable purées: bean, roasted eggplant, red pepper	
	Baking	Purées made from dried fruit or cooked vegetables	Quick breads, cookies and general baking; substitutions may affect color, taste and texture
Cream	Hot soups, sauces	Coconut, soy or rice milk; puréed silken tofu	Add at last moment, heating gently to prevent separation
	Cold creams or spreads	Coconut cream, enriched soy milk	Oil may be needed to improve mouthfeel
Sour cream, yogurt	Beverage or custard	Soy coffee creamer	
	Cold creams or spreads	Puréed silken tofu	
Eggs	Leavening	Chemical leavening	Consider loss of color from lack of egg yolk; texture will be denser than products containing eggs
	Emulsifier in sauces such as mayonnaise	Form a temporary emulsion; form an emulsion using ground nuts or soaked bread	
Beef, fish or poultry stock	Sauces, soups, stews	Vegetable stock; broth made from miso or seaweed	
Demi-glace	Sauces, stews	Rich vegetable stock made with a larger proportion of vegetables, reduced and thickened with starch	
Gelatin	Thickening, gelling	Agar	Gels more firmly than gelatin
Prepared sauces made with fish, such as nuoc mam, oyster or Worcestershire	Flavoring	Soy sauce, balsamic or red wine vinegar	

QUESTIONS FOR DISCUSSION

1 Explain the difference between serving sizes and portion sizes. Why do chefs pay attention to the amount of food they serve?

2 Describe the ways you might improve the healthfulness of a hamburger or fried chicken sandwich.

3 List several ingredient substitutes you might use to thicken a stock for a guest following a low-fat diet.

4 What procedures should a restaurant use when serving customers with food allergies? What menu substitutions should be available for diners who have more than one allergy, for example, someone who is allergic to both nuts and dairy products?

5 Identify three popular recipes that use meat, fish or poultry. Discuss how you would adapt these recipes for the vegetarian customer.

6 Vegetarian and vegan restaurants and restaurants that offer vegetarian and vegan menu options exist worldwide. Schools, corporations, airlines and hospitals also offer vegetarian and vegan menu options. Use the Internet to research vegetarian and vegan menus. Analyze two or three such menus and discuss how they address the concerns of their customers.

Additional Healthy, Special Diet and Vegetarian Recipes

Southwestern Black Bean Soup
(Gluten-Free, Vegan)

 ♥ Good Choice Ⓥ Vegan

YIELD Approximately 3 qt. (2.8 lt),
16 Servings, 6 fl. oz. (180 ml) each

METHOD Purée

Dried black beans, soaked	1 lb.	480 g
Vegetable stock	4 qt.	3.8 lt
Sachet:		
Bay leaves	2	2
Dried thyme	½ tsp.	2 ml
Peppercorns, cracked	10	10
Canola oil	1 Tbsp.	15 ml
Onion, diced	4 oz.	120 g
Garlic cloves, minced	2	2
Anaheim pepper, diced	1 oz.	30 g
Jalapeño or serrano pepper, minced	1 Tbsp.	15 ml
Cumin, ground	1 tsp.	5 ml
Coriander, ground	1 tsp.	5 ml
Dried oregano	1 tsp.	5 ml
Salt and pepper	TT	TT
Lime wedges	as needed for garnish	
Fresh cilantro, chopped	as needed for garnish	

1 Combine the beans and stock or water in a medium stockpot and bring to a simmer. Add the sachet.

2 Sauté the onion, garlic and peppers in the oil. Add to the stockpot.

3 Stir in the cumin, coriander and oregano.

4 Simmer the soup, uncovered, approximately 2½–3½ hours. The beans should be very soft, just beginning to fall apart. Add additional stock if necessary during cooking.

5 Purée about half of the soup. Stir the puréed portion back into the remaining soup. Season to taste with salt and pepper.

6 Serve in warmed bowls garnished with lime wedges and chopped cilantro.

Approximate values per 6-fl.-oz. (180-ml) serving: **Calories** 70, **Total fat** 2 g, **Saturated fat** 0 g, **Cholesterol** 0 mg, **Sodium** 1010 mg, **Total carbohydrates** 9 g, **Protein** 4 g, **Claims**—low fat; no saturated fat; no cholesterol

♥ Good Choice   🌿 Vegetarian

Falafel
(Vegetarian)

YIELD 12 Sandwiches

Chickpeas, dried	1 lb.	480 g
Garlic cloves, minced	6	6
Fresh parsley, chopped	½ oz.	15 g
Chives, minced	½ oz.	15 g
Cumin, ground	1 Tbsp.	15 ml
Coriander, ground	2 tsp.	10 ml
Cayenne pepper	TT	TT
Eggs	3	3
Salt	TT	TT
Flour	5 oz.	150 g
Silken tofu, puréed	6 oz.	180 g
Lemon juice	2 fl. oz.	60 ml
Pita bread	12 pieces	12 pieces
Iceberg lettuce, shredded	6 oz.	180 g
Tomatoes, diced	6 oz.	180 g

1 To make the falafel, soak the chickpeas following the procedures for soaking dried beans in Chapter 22, Vegetables. Drain the chickpeas, place them in a pot and cover with cool water. Simmer until tender, approximately 2–3 hours; remove from the heat and drain well.

2 Process the chickpeas in a food processor or a food chopper until coarsely chopped. Add the garlic, parsley, chives, cumin, coriander and cayenne pepper and process for a few seconds.

3 Add the eggs, salt and flour and process briefly. Remove the falafel from the machine and chill in the refrigerator for 1 hour.

4 Combine the tofu and lemon juice and mix well to make a sauce. Set aside.

5 Portion the falafel using a #50 scoop (there should be approximately 60 balls) and deep-fry the balls using the swimming method at 375°F (190°C) until crisp and hot. Drain well and keep warm.

6 To assemble each sandwich, cut a pita bread in half or open it to form a pocket and stuff with several balls of falafel and ½ ounce (15 grams) each of the shredded lettuce and diced tomatoes. Dress with the tofu sauce. Serve hot. Or plate the falafel and serve with the sauce, pita bread and garnishes.

Approximate values per sandwich: **Calories** 290, **Total fat** 3 g, **Saturated fat** 0.5 g, **Cholesterol** 55 mg, **Sodium** 470 mg, **Total carbohydrates** 55 g, **Protein** 12 g, **Claims**—low fat; low saturated fat; good source of fiber

♥ Good Choice   Ⓥ Vegan

Tofu and Walnut Tabouli
(Gluten-Free, Vegan)

YIELD 6 Servings, 4 oz. (120 g) each

Firm tofu	8 oz.	240 g
Fresh parsley, stems removed	8 oz.	240 g
Fresh mint leaves, stems removed	3 oz.	90 g
Green onions	2 oz.	60 g
Cherry tomatoes, cut in half	12	12
Olive oil	1½ fl. oz.	45 ml
Red onion, minced	4 oz.	120 g
Walnuts, chopped	4 oz.	120 g
Lemon	1	1
Salt and pepper	TT	TT

1 Freeze the tofu. Thaw it and drain it well. This will cause it to become quite dry. Crumble the thawed, drained tofu with your hands into small pieces.

2 Chop the parsley, mint and green onions coarsely and combine with the tofu in a stainless steel bowl.

3 Add the tomatoes to the chopped parsley mixture. Stir in the oil, red onion and walnuts.

4 Zest the lemon and chop the zest finely. Squeeze the juice from the lemon. Add the zest and juice to the mixture. Season with salt and pepper.

5 Allow the tabouli to rest for 1 hour to blend the flavors before serving.

Approximate values per 4-oz. (120-g) serving: **Calories** 150, **Total fat** 11 g, **Saturated fat** 1.5 g, **Cholesterol** 0 mg, **Sodium** 35 mg, **Total carbohydrates** 9 g, **Protein** 8 g, **Vitamin A** 80%, **Vitamin C** 110%, **Calcium** 35%, **Iron** 20%, **Claims**—no cholesterol; good source of fiber; high in calcium, iron and vitamins A and C

Mushroom Bolognese (Vegan)

 Good Choice   Vegan

YIELD 3 pt. (1.4 lt), 12 Servings, 9 oz. (270 g) each

White mushrooms	1½ lb.	720 g
Lobster, portabella, cremini or other mushrooms	1½ lb.	720 g
Onion, small dice	8 oz.	240 g
Garlic, chopped	1 oz.	30 g
Carrot, small dice	4 oz.	120 g
Olive oil	6 fl. oz.	180 ml
Burgundy wine	6 fl. oz.	180 ml
Whole peeled plum tomatoes, canned, chopped coarse	2 lb.	960 g
Oregano	1 tsp.	5 ml
Chile flakes	1 tsp.	5 ml
Salt	2 tsp.	10 ml
Pepper	1 tsp.	5 ml
Sherry wine vinegar	2 Tbsp.	30 ml
Cavatelli or penne pasta	1½ lb.	720 g
Roasted mushrooms	as needed for garnish	

MODIFICATIONS

- Eliminate beef: Use assorted mushrooms for texture, color and umami.
- Eliminate butter: Use olive oil.
- Balance flavors without using animal products: Use sherry wine vinegar.

1 Trim and clean the mushrooms. Chop and reserve.

2 Sweat the onion, garlic and carrot in the olive oil over medium heat for 2 minutes.

3 Add the chopped mushrooms and cook over high heat until dry, approximately 30 minutes.

4 Add the wine and cook until dry, approximately 10 minutes.

5 Add the chopped tomatoes, oregano, chile flakes, salt and pepper. Simmer until thickened and the tomatoes break down, approximately 30 minutes.

6 Stir in the sherry wine vinegar. Adjust the seasoning with salt and pepper and additional sherry wine vinegar if additional acidity is desired. Hold warm until service.

7 Boil the pasta in salted water until done.

8 Drain the pasta then toss it with the warm sauce. Garnish with roasted mushrooms and fresh herbs.

Approximate values per 9-oz. (270-g) serving: **Calories** 400, **Total fat** 15 g, **Saturated fat** 2 g, **Cholesterol** 0 mg, **Sodium** 490 mg, **Total carbohydrates** 53 g, **Protein** 13 g, **Vitamin A** 40%, **Vitamin C** 25%, **Iron** 15%, **Claims**—no cholesterol; excellent source of dietary fiber and vitamins A and C; good source of iron

♥ Good Choice   Ⓥ Vegan

Polenta Vegetable Tart
(Vegan)

YIELD 6 Servings, 4½-in.
(11-cm) each

Vegetable stock	20 fl. oz.	600 ml
Salt	TT	TT
Yellow cornmeal	5 oz.	150 g
Extra virgin olive oil	2 fl. oz.	60 ml
Mirepoix, small dice	8 oz.	240 g
Tomato concassé	4 oz.	120 g
Ground cumin	1 tsp.	5 ml
Dried oregano	1 tsp.	5 ml
Pepper	TT	TT
Fresh Tomato Sauce for Pasta (page 246)	12 fl. oz.	360 ml
Yellow squash, sliced into ⅛ in. (3 mm) rounds	6 oz.	180 g
Zucchini, sliced into ⅛ in. (3 mm) rounds	6 oz.	180 g
Roma tomatoes, sliced into ⅛ in. (3 mm) rounds	6 oz.	180 g
Basil Oil (page 241)	as needed for garnish	

① Pressing a cup into the warm polenta to form the shell.

② The finished polenta tarts are garnished with basil oil.

1 Bring the vegetable stock to a boil. Season the stock with salt then slowly whisk in the cornmeal to prevent lumps. Simmer the polenta for 20 minutes until very think.

2 Brush 6 individual shallow 4½-inch (11-centimeter) diameter ramekins generously with olive oil. Scoop 3 ounces (90 grams) of cooked polenta into each ramekin. Press a cup with a base that is slightly smaller than the ramekin into the warm polenta to form the polenta into shells. Allow the shells to cool then carefully remove them from the ramekins.

3 Heat the olive oil in a small sauté pan over medium heat. Sauté the mirepoix, tomato concassé, cumin and oregano in the oil until softened. Remove from the heat and reserve.

4 Spread 1 tablespoon (15 milliliters) of the Fresh Tomato Sauce in the bottom of each polenta shell. Mound 3 tablespoons (45 milliliters) of the sautéed mirepoix mixture in the center of each shell. Layer alternating slices of yellow squash, zucchini and tomatoes around the edge of the tarts leaning the slices on the mound of the sautéed mirepoix mixture. Top each tart with a spoonful of the sautéed mirepoix mixture.

5 Brush the vegetables and the polenta shells gently with olive oil. Season with salt and pepper.

6 Bake the tarts at 350°F (180°C) until the vegetables are tender and begin to brown, approximately 15 minutes.

7 For service, evenly divide the remaining fresh tomato sauce between 6 serving plates. Place a tart in the center of each plate. Garnish with the Basil Oil.

Approximate values per serving: **Calories** 260, **Total fat** 13 g, **Saturated fat** 2 g, **Cholesterol** 0 mg, **Sodium** 550 mg, **Total carbohydrates** 32 g, **Protein** 4 g, **Vitamin A** 80%, **Vitamin C** 50%, **Iron** 20%, **Claims**—no cholesterol; good source of dietary fiber and iron; excellent source of vitamins A and C

Dal Bhat
(Indian-Style Lentil Stew with Rice)
(Gluten-Free, Vegan)

 Good Choice Vegan

YIELD 3½ qt., 18 Servings,
¾ c. (180 ml) each

Red or yellow lentils (dal)	12 oz.	360 g
Yellow peas	12 oz.	360 g
Water	2 qt.	1.9 lt
Yukon Gold potatoes, peeled, large dice	12 oz.	360 g
Fresh ginger, 1-in. (2.5-cm) piece, chopped fine	1 oz.	30 g
Turmeric, ground	2 tsp.	10 ml
Garam masala	1 tsp.	5 ml
Cardamom pods	4	4
Cinnamon stick	1	1
Salt	TT	TT
Onion, peeled, chopped	9 oz.	270 g
Garlic cloves, chopped	4	4
Green chile, seeded	1½ oz.	45 g
Tomato seeded and chopped	14 oz.	420 g
Coconut oil or butter	6 oz.	180 g
Cumin seeds	1 Tbsp.	15 ml
Black mustard seeds	2 Tbsp.	30 ml
Fresh lemon juice	2 fl. oz.	60 ml
Basmati rice, cooked	as needed for garnish	

1 Bring the lentils, peas, water, potatoes, ginger, turmeric, garam masala, cardamom, cinnamon stick and salt to a boil. Skim the surface. Cover and simmer until the lentils are tender and the water is absorbed, approximately 1 hour.

2 Combine the onion, garlic, chile and tomato in a food processor and blend into a coarse purée.

3 In a large sauté pan, melt the coconut oil and add the cumin and mustard seeds. Cook until the seeds sizzle. Add the reserved tomato purée. Sauté the mixture for a few minutes until it thickens slightly.

4 Combine the tomato mixture with the cooked lentils and peas.

5 Transfer to a large mixing bowl and mash the tomato mixture, peas, potatoes and lentils into a chunky sauce with a wooden spoon. Season with salt and pepper and stir in the lemon juice. Hold warm for service. Serve with rice.

Approximate values per serving: **Calories** 250, **Total fat** 10 g, **Saturated fat** 8 g, **Cholesterol** 0 mg, **Sodium** 10 mg, **Total carbohydrates** 31 g, **Protein** 10 g, **Vitamin C** 25%, **Iron** 15%, **Claims**—no cholesterol; excellent source of fiber and vitamin C; good source of iron

Vegan

Pan-Seared Tofu Provençal (Gluten-Free, Vegan)

YIELD 4 Servings		METHOD Sautéing
Extra-firm tofu, drained	24 oz.	720 g
Canola oil	1 fl. oz.	30 ml
Extra virgin olive oil	1½ fl. oz.	45 ml
Red onions, sliced into rings	6 oz.	180 g
Garlic, chopped	2 tsp.	10 ml
White wine	8 fl. oz.	240 ml
Lemon juice	1 fl. oz.	30 ml
Kalamata olives, pitted	4 oz.	120 g
Capers	1 Tbsp.	15 ml
Red cherry tomatoes, halved	6 oz.	180 g
Yellow cherry tomatoes, halved	6 oz.	180 g
Fresh basil, chopped	4 Tbsp.	120 ml
Fresh oregano, chopped	1 Tbsp.	15 ml
Salt and pepper	TT	TT

1 Cut the tofu into eight 3-ounce (90-gram) triangles and pat dry on paper towels. Heat the canola oil in a large sauté pan. Sear the tofu on both sides until brown. Remove the tofu to a platter and keep warm.

2 Add the olive oil to the pan. Add the onions and garlic to the pan and sauté for 3–4 minutes. Deglaze the pan with the wine and lemon juice.

3 Add the olives and capers to the pan and simmer in the wine sauce until it begins to thicken slightly.

4 Add the tomatoes to the pan and reduce the sauce to the desired consistency. Stir in the basil and oregano. Return the tofu to the sauce to reheat. Adjust the seasonings. Serve the tofu with some of the sauce spooned over it.

Approximate values per serving: **Calories** 460, **Total fat** 35 g, **Saturated fat** 3.5 g, **Cholesterol** 0 mg, **Sodium** 550 mg, **Total carbohydrates** 15 g, **Protein** 19 g, **Vitamin A** 15%, **Vitamin C** 30%, **Calcium** 35%, **Iron** 20%, **Claims**—no cholesterol

---

 Good Choice   Vegan

Chia Pudding (Gluten-Free, Vegan)

YIELD 8 Servings, 4 oz. (120 g) each		
Coconut milk	24 fl. oz.	720 ml
Agave syrup	2 Tbsp.	30 ml
Vanilla extract	1 tsp.	5 ml
Chia seeds	½ cup	120 ml
Fresh lemon juice	2 Tbsp.	30 ml
Lemon zest, chopped	2 Tbsp.	30 ml
Pomegranate seeds	1 cup	240 ml
Mango, small dice	1 cup	240 ml
Strawberries, small dice	1 cup	240 ml
Raspberries and blackberries	as needed	as needed
Fresh mint	as needed	as needed

1 In a small bowl, stir together the coconut milk, agave syrup and vanilla extract. Stir in the chia seeds, lemon juice and zest. Allow the mixture to rest, refrigerated, for 4 hours or overnight.

2 To serve, layer the chia pudding, pomegranate seeds and diced fruit attractively in 8 glasses.

3 Garnish with raspberries, blackberries and fresh mint as desired. Serve cold.

Approximate values per 4-oz. (120-g) serving: **Calories** 270, **Total fat** 22 g, **Saturated fat** 16 g, **Cholesterol** 0 mg, **Sodium** 15 mg, **Total carbohydrates** 20 g, **Protein** 4 g, **Vitamin C** 45%, **Calcium** 10%, **Iron** 15%, **Claims**—no cholesterol; excellent source of dietary fiber, vitamin C and iron; good source of calcium

Salads and Salad Dressings 25

After studying this chapter, you will be able to:

▶ identify a variety of salad greens

▶ prepare a variety of salad dressings

▶ explain the procedures for preparing tossed, bound and composed salads

▶ prepare a variety of salads using leafy greens as well as fruits, grains, potatoes and vegetables

▶ present salads attractively

This chapter discusses all types of salads including the small plate of crisp iceberg lettuce with tomato wedges, cucumber slices and ranch dressing; the dinner plate of sautéed duck breast fanned across bright red grilled radicchio and toothy green arugula, sprayed with a vinaigrette dressing; the scoop of shredded chicken, mango chutney and seasonings, bound with mayonnaise; and the bowl of cooked grains, green beans and mushrooms marinated in olive oil and lemon juice.

Each of these dishes fits the definition of a **salad**: a single food or a mix of different foods accompanied or bound by a dressing. A salad can contain meat, grains, fruits, vegetables, nuts or cheese and absolutely no lettuce. It can be an appetizer, a second course served after the appetizer, an entrée (especially at lunch), a course following the entrée in the European manner or even a dessert.

Harmony is critical to a salad's success—no matter what type of salad is being prepared. The color, texture and flavor of each salad ingredient should complement those of the others, and the dressing should complement all the ingredients.

This chapter opens with sections about identifying and preparing greens commonly used in salads. A discussion of salad dressings follows. Finally techniques for making green salads (both tossed and composed), bound salads, vegetable salads, fruit salads and gelatin salads are discussed.

IDENTIFYING SALAD GREENS

Salad greens are not necessarily green: Some are red, yellow, white or brown. They are all, however, leafy vegetables. Many are members of the lettuce or chicory family.

Lettuce

Lettuce (Fr. *laitue*; It. *lattuga*) has been consumed for nearly as long as people have kept records of their dining habits. Archaeologists found that Persian royalty were served lettuce at their banquets more than 2500 years ago. Grown and served worldwide, lettuces are members of the genus *Lactuca*. The most common types of lettuce are butterhead, crisp head, leaf and romaine.

Boston

Boston and bibb are two of the most popular butterhead lettuces. Their soft, pliable, pale green leaves have a buttery texture and flavor. Boston is larger and paler than bibb. Both Boston and bibb lettuce leaves form cups when separated from the heads; these cups make convenient bases for holding other foods on cold plates.

Iceberg

Iceberg lettuce is the most common of all lettuce varieties in the United States; it outsells all other varieties combined, although its appeal is declining now that other types of greens are widely available. Iceberg's tightly packed spherical head is composed of crisp, pale green leaves that have a very mild flavor. Iceberg lettuce remains crisp for a relatively long time after being cut or prepared. Select heads that are firm but not hard and leaves that are free of burnt or rusty tips.

Boston

Iceberg

Leaf

Leaf lettuce grows in bunches. It has separate, ruffle-edged leaves branching from a stalk. Because it does not grow into a firm head, it is easily damaged when handled. Both red and green leaf lettuce have mild flavors and tender leaves. Good-quality leaf lettuce should have nicely shaped leaves free of bruises, breaks or brown spots.

Romaine

Romaine lettuce, also known as **cos**, is a loosely packed head lettuce with elongated leaves and thick midribs. Its outer leaves are dark green and although they look coarse, they are crisp, tender and tasty without being bitter. The core leaves are paler and more tender but still crisp. Romaine has enough flavor to stand up to strongly flavored dressings such as the garlic and Parmesan cheese used in a Caesar salad. Small heads can be grilled. A good-quality head of romaine has dark green outer leaves that are free of blemishes or yellowing.

Red and green leaf

Baby Lettuces

Baby greens have similar but more subtle flavors than their mature versions. They are often less bitter and are always more tender and delicate. Because of their size and variety, baby lettuces are perfect for composed salads and as delicate garnish on light entrées. **Mesclun** is a mixture of several kinds of baby lettuces.

Romaine

Brune d'Hiver

Lola Rosa

Red Sails

Baby Green Bibb

Baby Red Oak Leaf

Pirate

Baby Red Bibb

Baby Red Romaine

Micro greens are even smaller than baby lettuces. They are the first true leaves of virtually any edible greens, such as lettuce, spinach, kale and so on. Micro greens are very fragile and must be handpicked and carefully packaged for shipping. Chefs use them as garnish, especially on entrée and appetizer plates.

Micro greens

Chicory

Chicories come in a variety of colors, shapes and sizes; most are slightly bitter. Chicories are quite hearty and can also be cooked, usually grilled or braised.

Belgian Endive

Belgian endive grows in small, tight heads with pointed leaves. It is actually the shoot of a chicory root. The small sturdy leaves are white at the base with yellow fringes and tips. (A purple-tipped variety is sometimes available.) Whole Belgian endive leaves can be

Belgian endive

Curly endive

Escarole

Radicchio

Arugula

Dandelion

separated, trimmed and filled with soft butters, cheeses or spreads and served as an hors d'oeuvre, or they can be used for composed salads. The leaves, cut or whole, can also be added to cold salads. Heads of Belgian endive are often braised or grilled and served with meat or poultry.

Curly Endive

In the United States, curly endive is often called by its family name, chicory, or its French name, frisée [free-ZAY]. The dark green outer leaves are pointed, sturdy and slightly bitter. The yellow inner leaves are more tender and less bitter. Curly endive has a strong flavor that goes well with strong cheeses, game and citrus. It is mixed with other greens to add texture and flavor.

Escarole

Escarole [es-kah-ROLE], sometimes called broadleaf endive, has thick leaves and a slightly bitter flavor. It has green outer leaves and pale green or yellow center leaves. Escarole is very sturdy and is mixed with other salad greens for added texture. Its strong flavor stands up to full-flavored dressings and is a good accompaniment to grilled meats and poultry. Escarole leaves may also be cooked in soups and pasta dishes, or lightly sautéed as a side dish.

Radicchio

Radicchio [rah-DEE-kee-oh] resembles a small red cabbage. It retains its bright reddish color when cooked and is popular braised or grilled and served as a vegetable side dish. Because of its attractive color, radicchio is popular in cold salads, but it has a very bitter flavor and should be used sparingly and mixed with other greens in tossed salads. Radicchio leaves form cups when separated and can be used to hold other ingredients when preparing composed salads.

Other Salad Greens and Ingredients

Leafy vegetables besides lettuce and chicory as well as other ingredients are used to add texture, flavor and color to salads. A partial list follows.

Arugula

Arugula [ah-ROO-guh-lah], also known as rocket, is a member of the cabbage family. Arugula leaves are somewhat similar to broad dandelion leaves in size and shape. They are best when 2–4 inches (5–10 centimeters) long. Arugula has a very strong, spicy, peppery flavor. It is used to add zip to salads by combining it with other greens and as a fresh topping on cheesy pizza.

Dandelion

Dandelion grows as a weed throughout most of the United States. It has long, thin, toothed leaves with a prominent midrib. When purchasing dandelion for salads, look for small leaves; they are more tender and less bitter. Older, tougher leaves can be cooked and served as a vegetable.

Mâche

Mâche [mahsh] or lamb's lettuce is very tender and very delicately flavored. Its small, curved, pale to dark green leaves have a slightly nutty flavor. Because its flavor is so delicate, mâche should be combined only with other delicately flavored greens such as Boston or bibb lettuce and dressed sparingly with a light vinaigrette dressing.

Mâche

Sorrel

Sorrel, sometimes called sourgrass, has leaves similar to spinach in color and shape. Sorrel has a very tart, lemony flavor that goes well with fish and shellfish. It should be used sparingly and combined with other greens in salads. Sorrel can also be made into soups, sauces and purées.

Spinach

Like sorrel, spinach can be cooked or used as a salad green. As a salad green, it is traditionally served tossed with hot bacon dressing. Spinach is deep green with a rich flavor and tender texture. Good-quality spinach should be fairly crisp. Avoid wilted or yellowed bunches.

Sorrel

Spinach

Sprouts

Sprouts are not salad greens but are often used as such in salads and sandwiches. Sprouts are very young alfalfa, daikon or mustard plants. Alfalfa sprouts are very mild and sweet. Daikon and mustard sprouts are quite peppery.

Sprouts

Watercress

Watercress has tiny, dime-sized leaves and substantial stems. It has a peppery flavor and adds spice to salads. Good-quality fresh watercress is dark green with no yellowing. To preserve its freshness, watercress must be kept very cold and moist. It is often packed topped with ice. Individual leaves are plucked from the stems and rinsed just before service.

Watercress

Edible Flowers

Many specialty produce growers offer edible, pesticide-free blossoms. They are used for salads and as garnishes wherever a splash of color is appreciated. Some flowers such as nasturtiums, calendulas and pansies are grown and picked specifically for eating. Others, such as yellow cucumber flowers and squash blossoms, are by-products of the vegetable industry.

Squash blossoms and other very large flowers should be cut in julienne strips before being added to salads. Pick petals from large and medium-sized flowers. Smaller, whole flowers can be tossed in a salad or used as a garnish. Very small flowers or petals should be sprinkled on top of a salad so that they are not hidden by the greens.

Nasturtiums

Fresh Herbs

Basil, thyme, tarragon, oregano, dill, cilantro, marjoram, mint, sage, savory and even rosemary are used to add interesting flavors to salads. Because many herbs have strong flavors, use them sparingly so that the delicate flavors of the greens are not overpowered. Leafy herbs such as basil and sage can be cut chiffonade. Other herbs can be picked from their stems and added directly to salads or chopped before being tossed with the salad greens. Flowering herbs such as chive blossoms are used like other edible flowers to add color, flavor and aroma. Refer to Chapter 7, Flavors and Flavorings, for more information on herbs.

Pansies

Calendulas

⚠ Safety Alert

Flowers

Many flowers and blossoms are toxic, especially those grown from bulbs. Even flowers that would otherwise be edible may contain pesticides that can be harmful if ingested. Use only flowers grown specifically for use as food; purchase edible flowers only from reputable purveyors.

Nutrition of Salads

Salad greens are an especially healthful food. Greens contain virtually no fat and few calories and are high in vitamins A, K and C, folate, iron and dietary fiber. Darker, loose-leaf greens, such as spinach, kale and romaine, contain more nutrients and antioxidants than lighter colored head lettuces. But if greens are served in salads garnished with too much meat and cheese and tossed with dressing (many of which are oil based), fat and calories quickly add up. In an attempt to maintain the health benefits of salads, low-fat or fat-free dressings should be made available to customers. House-prepared salad dressings prepared with fruit juice, spices (e.g., ginger, cardamom, cracked pepper), herbs (e.g., basil, lavender, thyme) and oils high in monounsaturated fats (e.g., olive, peanut, canola) are healthy, flavorful and distinctive options.

The nutritional value of fresh salads can be enhanced by adding dried or fresh fruit, seeds or nuts, cooked grains, legumes or a variety of fresh or blanched vegetables. Lean proteins, such as grilled fish or chicken breast, cooked egg whites, water-packed canned tuna and tofu, also improve the nutritional value and boost the feeling of fullness provided by salads. Reduce or avoid the use of high-fat meats and cheeses, buttery croutons, fried tortillas or refined wheat pastas in salads.

Purchasing and Storing Salad Greens

Lettuces are grown in nearly every part of the United States; nearly all types are available year-round. Other important salad greens such as spinach are available all year; many of the specialty greens are seasonal. Consult Appendix II, Fresh Locally-Grown Produce Availability Chart for more information about greens available in your area.

Lettuce is generally packed in cases of 24 heads with varying weights. Other salad greens are packed in trays or boxes of various sizes and weights.

Because salad greens are simply washed and eaten, it is extremely important that they be as fresh and blemish-free as possible. Try to purchase salad greens daily. All greens should be fresh looking, with no yellowing. Heads should be heavy, with little or no damage to the outer leaves. Do not wash greens until needed as excess water causes them to deteriorate quickly.

Many types of salad greens are available precut and prewashed. These greens are often packed with nitrogen to increase shelf life, although delicate greens are sometimes loosely packaged in 5- to 10-pound (2- to 5-kilogram) boxes. Precut and prewashed greens are relatively expensive but can reduce labor costs dramatically. Although it is important to visually inspect and remove wilted leaves, do not rinse or wash packaged greens that are labeled "ready to eat" or "pre-washed." These products are treated with food-safe levels of hydrogen peroxide or chlorine and are truly ready to serve. Handling the greens creates an opportunity for cross-contamination from hands, sinks, cutting boards and other sources. Furthermore a standard kitchen rinse-and-dry will not remove or destroy pathogenic bacteria that survived commercial sanitation procedures.

Although some types of salad greens are hearty enough to keep for a week or more under proper conditions, all salad greens are highly perishable. Generally softer-leaved varieties such as Boston and bibb tend to perish more quickly than the crisper-leaved varieties such as iceberg and romaine. Frequently greens that have wilted slightly can be revived by soaking them in chilled water for up to an hour. The greens should then be drained and refrigerated until crisp. Although not useable raw in salads, wilted greens can be cleaned and used in cooked dishes such as gratins, purées and soups.

Greens should be stored in their original protective cartons in a specifically designated refrigerator at temperatures between 34°F and 38°F (1°C and 3°C). (Most other vegetables should be stored at warmer temperatures of 40–50°F [4–10°C].) Greens should not be stored with tomatoes, apples or other fruits that emit ethylene gas, which causes greens to wilt and accelerates spoilage.

PREPARING SALAD GREENS

Salad greens that are not pre-rinsed with sanitizing solution need to be prepared before service. Preparation principally involves tearing, cutting, washing and drying.

Tearing and Cutting Salad Greens

Some chefs want all salad greens torn by hand. Delicate greens such as butterhead and baby lettuces look nicer, and it is less likely that they will be bruised if hand-torn. But often it is not practical to hand-tear all greens. It is perfectly acceptable to cut hardy greens with a knife. And it can be more practical to snip small lettuce leaves and fresh herbs with kitchen scissors than to tear them by hand.

> ### ⚠ Safety Alert
>
> *Handling Salad Greens*
>
> Because salads are not cooked, it is especially important to be careful about proper hand washing when preparing them. Most health departments prohibit bare hand contact with foods that are ready to eat (i.e., food that will not be heated again before service). Bare hand contact can be avoided by proper use of gloves, deli tissues, napkins, tongs, spatulas or other utensils.

Remove wilted leaves and trim discolorations on lettuce before using.

Trimmed head of romaine lettuce ready for tearing or cutting.

Procedure for Cutting Romaine Lettuce

1 To cut romaine lettuce, trim the outer leaves and damaged tips with a chef's knife and split the head lengthwise.

2 Make one or two cuts along the length of the head, leaving the root intact, then cut across the width of the head.

3 Alternative method: Trim the outer leaves and damaged tips with a chef's knife. Pull the leaves from the core and cut the rib out of each leaf. The leaf can then be cut to the desired size.

Procedure for Coring Iceberg Lettuce

1 Loosen the core by gripping the head and smacking the core on the cutting board. (Do not use too much force or you may bruise the lettuce.)

2 Remove the core and cut the lettuce as desired.

Washing Salad Greens

All lettuces and other salad greens that are not pre-rinsed with sanitizing solution should be washed before use. Even when they look clean, greens may harbor hidden insects, sand, soil and pesticides. Pay special attention to greens sourced from local farms, which may not have facilities to preclean their produce. All greens should be washed after they are torn or cut. Although whole heads can be washed by repeatedly dipping them in cold water and allowing them to drain, washing whole heads is not recommended. It will not remove anything trapped near the head's center, and water trapped in the leaves can accelerate spoilage.

Procedure for Washing Salad Greens

❶ Clean and sanitize a sink, then fill it with cold water that is slightly warmer than the temperature of the greens. Place cut or torn greens in the water.

❷ Gently stir the water and greens with your hands and remove the greens. Do not allow the greens to soak. Using fresh water each time, repeat the procedure until no grit can be detected on the bottom of the sink after the greens are removed.

Drying Salad Greens

Salad greens should be dried after washing. Wet greens do not stay as crisp as thoroughly dried ones. Also wet greens tend to repel oil-based dressings and dilute the flavors of the dressing. Greens may be dried by draining them well in a colander and blotting them with absorbent cloth or paper towels, or, preferably, they can be dried in a salad spinner, which uses centrifugal force to remove the water. Sanitize the spinner before each use; wash, rinse, sanitize and air dry it after use.

Procedure for Drying Greens

Place washed greens in the basket of a salad spinner and spin for approximately 30 seconds.

SALAD DRESSINGS

A dressing is a sauce for a salad. Just as sauces for hot foods should complement rather than mask the flavor of the principal food, dressing for salads should complement rather than mask the flavors of the other ingredients. Although a great many ingredients can be used to make salad dressings, most dressings are based on either a mixture of oil and vinegar, called a **vinaigrette**, or a mayonnaise or other emulsified product. Vinaigrette-style dressings can be made without oil; creamy dressings similar to mayonnaise-based dressings can be made with sour cream, yogurt or buttermilk instead of mayonnaise. Nevertheless, for all practical purposes, these dressings are still prepared like vinaigrettes and mayonnaise-based dressings, and they are treated that way here. Review the material on oils and vinegars in Chapter 7, Flavors and Flavorings, for more information on specific ingredients.

Vinaigrette Dressings

The simple vinaigrette, also known as basic **French dressing**, is a temporary emulsion of oil and vinegar seasoned with salt and pepper. The standard vinaigrette ratio is three parts oil to one part vinegar. The ratio can vary, however, depending upon the flavor and quality of these key ingredients. When using strongly flavored oils, less than three parts oil generally suffices. In some recipes, all or part of the vinegar is replaced with citrus juice, in which case it may take more than one part vinegar and citrus juice to achieve the proper acidity level. Mild or sweet vinegars, such as balsamic, may require less oil to balance the flavors in the dressing. The best way to determine the correct ratio of oil to vinegar is to taste the oil and vinegar before preparing the dressing and make adjustments to the ratio of oil and vinegar accordingly.

Oils and vinegars have unique flavors that can be mixed and matched to achieve the correct balance for a particular salad. Extra virgin olive oil goes well with red wine vinegar; nut oils go well with white wine or sherry vinegars. Neutral-flavored oils such as canola, corn or safflower can be mixed with a flavored vinegar. Consult Table 25.1 for general guidelines for preparing vinaigrettes.

Oil and vinegar repel each other and separate almost immediately when mixed. For this reason, they must be whisked together immediately before use.

Oils

Many types of oil can be used to make salad dressings. Light, neutral-flavored vegetable oils such as canola, corn, cottonseed, soybean and safflower are relatively low priced and used extensively for dressings. Other oils can be used to add flavor. Olive oil is very popular; both mild-flavored pure olive oil and full-flavored extra virgin olive oil are used. Nut oils such as hazelnut and walnut are expensive, but they add unique and interesting flavors to dressings. Oils infused with herbs, garlic or spices adds additional layers of flavor to vinaigrette dressing. See page 130.

French dressing classically, a vinaigrette dressing made from oil, vinegar, salt and pepper; in the United States, the term also refers to a commercially prepared dressing that is creamy, tartly sweet and red-orange in color

Not Just for Salads

With its light taste and texture, vinaigrette dressing makes an appealing sauce where a delicate touch is desired. It is quick to make and versatile; changing the taste of a vinaigrette is only a matter of switching the type of oil and vinegar used. Its balanced acidity makes vinaigrette a good foil for fish dishes, as shown in Fin Fish Carpaccio with Lemon Thyme Vinaigrette (page 549).

RATIOS AND INGREDIENTS FOR VINAIGRETTE DRESSING			TABLE 25.1
TYPE OF VINAIGRETTE	RATIO OF OIL TO VINEGAR	TYPE OF OIL	TYPE OF VINEGAR
Lower-fat vinaigrette dressing	2:1	Full-flavored oils, such as extra virgin olive, toasted almond, hazelnut, peanut or walnut	Mild or sweet vinegars, such as balsamic, fig, rice wine or sherry; orange or other mild citrus juice
Standard vinaigrette dressing	3:1	Light neutral-flavored oils, such as canola, corn, cottonseed, olive, safflower or soybean; herb, garlic or spice-infused oils	Mild champagne vinegar, red or white wine vinegars; fruit vinegars
Higher-fat vinaigrette dressing	4:1	Light neutral-flavored oils, such as canola, corn, cottonseed, olive, safflower or soybean; herb, garlic or spice-infused oils	Strong white or red wine vinegars; cider vinegar

acetic acid organic compound produced during fermentation; acetic acid bacteria consume glucose in a liquid and convert it to ethanol (alcohol) then acetic acid; vinegar consists of acetic acid diluted to 3–20 percent.

Convenience Products

A great many prepared and dry-mix salad dressings are available. Although they vary greatly in quality, they can be very economical; they offer consistency, reduced labor costs and, sometimes, reduced food costs. Some of these products use stabilizers, artificial flavorings and colors; nearly all contain preservatives. When considering the advantages of prepared or dry-mix salad dressings, always keep quality in mind.

Vinegars

Many different vinegars can be used in salad dressings. Red wine vinegar is the most common, because it is inexpensive and its flavor blends well with many foods. But other vinegars such as cider, balsamic, sherry and white wine are also used as well as vinegars made from varietal wines such as cabernet or zinfandel. The acidity of vinegars varies by type of vinegar and manufacturer; it is usually in the range of 4–8 percent **acetic acid**. In general wine vinegars are required by law to have at least 6 percent acetic acid. Rice vinegar, made from fermented rice wine, has a mild acidity (4 percent acetic acid) and is popular when making Asian-inspired salad dressings. Malt vinegar made from fermented barley has a sweeter and more complex flavor than white wine vinegar. Fruit-flavored vinegars, such as fig or lemon, are popular and widely available, as are herb- and garlic-flavored ones.

Flavored vinegars are easy to make. Fruit, herbs or garlic are added to a wine vinegar (either red or white) and left for several days for the flavors to blend. The vinegar is then strained and used as desired.

Juices from acidic fruit, such as lemon, orange and lime, are sometimes substituted for all or part of the vinegar in a salad dressing.

Other Flavoring Ingredients

Herbs, spices, shallots, garlic, mustard and sugar are only a few of the many flavoring ingredients used to enhance vinaigrette dressings. These flavoring ingredients should be considered accents that help balance the acidity of the vinegar and the bitterness (sweetness) of the salad greens. Items such as herbs, shallots and garlic should be minced or chopped before they are added to the dressing. If dried herbs are used, add them to the vinegar before adding the oil then let the dressing rest for at least 1 hour to allow the flavors to develop. Other ingredients such as grated cheese, olives and conditioned dried fruits may be added at any time.

Procedure for Preparing a Vinaigrette

1 Choose an oil and vinegar that complement each other as well as the foods they will dress.
2 Combine the vinegar, seasonings and any other flavorings in a bowl.
3 Whisk in the oil gradually.
4 Allow the finished dressing to rest a few hours at room temperature before using so that the flavors can blend.
5 Rewhisk immediately before use.

 Good Choice Vegan

Basic Vinaigrette Dressing

YIELD Approximately 1 qt. (1 lt)

Wine vinegar	8 fl. oz.	240 ml
Salt	2 tsp.	10 ml
Pepper	TT	TT
Vegetable oil	24 fl. oz.	720 ml

1 Combine the vinegar, salt and pepper and mix well. Whisk in the oil gradually. Store at room temperature.

Variations:

Dijon Vinaigrette—Add 4 ounces (120 grams) Dijon-style mustard to the vinegar and proceed with the recipe.

Herb Vinaigrette—Add 2 tablespoons (30 milliliters) fresh herbs or 1 tablespoon (15 milliliters) dried herbs such as basil, tarragon, thyme, marjoram and chives to the vinaigrette.

Approximate values per 1-fl.-oz. (30-ml) serving: **Calories** 190, **Total fat** 22 g, **Saturated fat** 3 g, **Cholesterol** 0 mg, **Sodium** 75 mg, **Total carbohydrates** 0 g, **Protein** 0 g, **Claims**—no cholesterol; low sodium; no sugar

Whisking the vinaigrette dressing.

Mayonnaise-Based Dressings

Mayonnaise-based salad dressings use mayonnaise as a base with other ingredients added for flavor, color and texture. Other ingredients include dairy products (especially buttermilk and sour cream), vinegar, fruit juice, vegetables (puréed or minced), tomato paste, garlic, onions, herbs, spices, condiments, capers, anchovies and boiled eggs. Recipes for several mayonnaise-based salad dressings appear at the end of this chapter.

Preparing Mayonnaise

Although most food service operations buy commercially prepared mayonnaise, every chef should know how mayonnaise is made to more fully understand how to use it and why it reacts the way it does when used. Knowing how to make mayonnaise also allows the chef to create a mayonnaise with the exact flavor desired.

Mayonnaise is an **emulsion**. Recall that an emulsion, or emulsified sauce, is formed when two liquids that would not ordinarily form a stable mixture are forced together and held in suspension, as discussed in Chapter 11, Stocks and Sauces. To make mayonnaise, oil is whisked together with a very small amount of vinegar. (It is the water in the vinegar that does not normally mix with oil.) As the oil and vinegar are whisked together, the oil breaks into microscopic droplets that are separated from each other by a thin barrier of vinegar. If left alone, the droplets would quickly regroup, forming a large puddle of oil and a small puddle of vinegar. To prevent the oil droplets from regrouping, an emulsifier is added. For mayonnaise, the emulsifier is lecithin, a protein in egg yolks. (The acid in the vinegar also helps form the emulsion.) Lecithin has the unique ability to combine with both oil and water. It surrounds the oil droplets, preventing them from coming in contact with each other and regrouping.

The balance of vinegar, oil, lecithin and agitation (whipping) is crucial to achieve a proper emulsion. The higher the proportion of oil to vinegar, the thicker the sauce will be. The higher the proportion of vinegar to oil, the thinner the sauce will be. Some chefs add ½ fluid ounce (15 milliliters) boiling water to each 7 fluid ounces (210 milliliters) finished mayonnaise to help maintain the emulsion.

Mayonnaise Ingredients

A neutral-flavored vegetable oil is most often used for a standard mayonnaise. Other oils are used to contribute their special flavors. For example, olive oil is used to make a strong garlic mayonnaise called *aïoli*.

Wine vinegar is used for a standard mayonnaise. Flavored vinegars, such as tarragon vinegar, can be used to create unique flavors. Seasonings vary according to the intended use but typically include dry mustard, salt, pepper and lemon juice.

Procedure for Preparing Mayonnaise

1 Gather all ingredients and allow the eggs to come to room temperature for 30 minutes. Room-temperature ingredients emulsify more easily than cold ones.

2 By hand or in an electric mixer or food processor, whip the egg yolks on high speed until frothy.

3 Add the seasonings to the yolks and whip to combine. Salt and other seasonings will dissolve or blend more easily when added at this point rather than to the finished mayonnaise.

4 Add a small amount of the liquid (e.g., vinegar) from the recipe and whip to combine.

5 With the mixer on high or whisking vigorously by hand, begin to add the oil very slowly until an emulsion forms.

6 After the emulsion forms, the oil can be added a little more quickly but still in a slow, steady stream. The mayonnaise can now be whipped at a slightly slower speed.

7 The mayonnaise will become very thick as more oil is added. A small amount of liquid can be added if it becomes too thick. Alternate between adding oil and liquid two or three times until all the oil is added and the correct consistency is reached. Note that a large egg yolk can emulsify up to 7 fluid ounces (210 milliliters) of oil; adding more oil may cause the mayonnaise to break.

8 Adjust the seasonings and refrigerate immediately.

Mayonnaise vs. Salad Dressing

Commercially prepared salad dressing is often used as a substitute for "real" mayonnaise. Although it may look, smell and spread like the real thing, salad dressing tends to be sweeter than mayonnaise. Salad dressing costs less than real mayonnaise because it is made without egg yolks, relying instead on chemical thickening agents. The cost is reduced further because the FDA requires salad dressing to contain only 30 percent oil, whereas mayonnaise must contain at least 65 percent oil.

emulsion a uniform mixture of two unmixable liquids; it is often temporary (e.g., oil in water)

aïoli mayonnaise made with olive oil and flavored with garlic

⚠ Safety Alert

Mayonnaise

The raw eggs in freshly prepared mayonnaise make it a time and temperature control for safety (TCS) food. Use pasteurized eggs if possible, and keep the finished mayonnaise at 41°F (5°C) or below. Freshly prepared mayonnaise will keep for 2–4 days, if properly refrigerated. Commercially prepared mayonnaise may be stored at room temperature before opening, but should also be refrigerated at 41°F (5°C) or below after the package is opened. If held at the proper temperature, commercial mayonnaise will last 2–3 months after opening.

TROUBLESHOOTING MAYONNAISE

TABLE 25.2

PROBLEM	CAUSE	SOLUTION
Too thin	Not enough oil Too much lemon juice or vinegar	Continue adding oil until mixture thickens Adjust formula
Too thick	Too much oil for the amount of yolks Insufficient vinegar	Adjust formula Add more vinegar
Sauce breaks or curdles	Inadequate emulsification when mixing	Whisk vigorously, adding oil slowly; use electric mixer to make a more stable emulsion; attempt repairing the mayonnaise
	Oil too cold	Use room-temperature oil; attempt repairing the mayonnaise
	Oil added too quickly	Attempt repairing the mayonnaise
	Too much oil	Adjust formula using additional egg yolks or less oil; attempt repairing the mayonnaise

🌿 Vegetarian

Mayonnaise

YIELD 1 qt. (1 lt)

Egg yolks, pasteurized	4	4
Salt	1 tsp.	5 ml
White pepper	TT	TT
Dry mustard	1 tsp.	5 ml
Wine vinegar	1½ fl. oz.	45 ml
Vegetable oil	28 fl. oz.	840 ml
Lemon juice	TT	TT

1 Place the egg yolks in the bowl of a mixer and whip on high speed until thick and lemon-colored.

2 Add the dry ingredients and half the vinegar to the yolks; whisk to combine.

3 Begin to add the oil a drop at a time until the mixture begins to thicken and an emulsion begins to form.

4 Add the remaining oil in a slow steady stream, thinning the mayonnaise occasionally by adding a little vinegar. Continue until all the oil and vinegar have been incorporated.

5 Adjust the seasonings and add lemon juice to taste.

6 Refrigerate until needed, up to 2–4 days.

Variation:

Aïoli (Garlic Mayonnaise)—Mash 4 garlic cloves into a paste. Add to the egg yolks in Step 1. Omit the mustard. Replace the wine vinegar with lemon juice and the salad oil with olive oil.

Approximate values per 1-fl.-oz. (30-ml) serving: **Calories** 230, **Total fat** 26 g, **Saturated fat** 3.5 g, **Cholesterol** 25 mg, **Sodium** 75 mg, **Total carbohydrates** 0 g, **Protein** 0 g

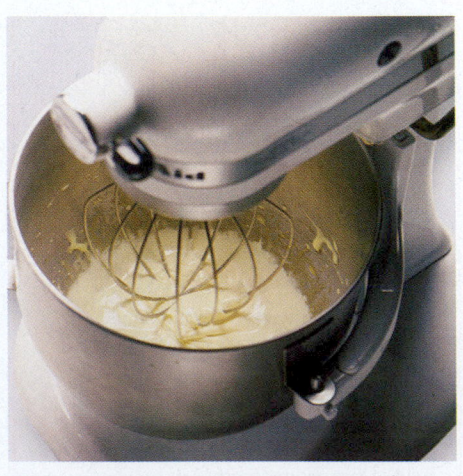

❶ Whipping the egg yolks until thick and lemon colored.

❷ Adding the oil very slowly, allowing the emulsion to form.

❸ The finished mayonnaise.

Repairing Broken Mayonnaise

There is a limit to how much oil each egg yolk can emulsify. One yolk contains enough lecithin to emulsify approximately 7 fluid ounces (210 milliliters) of oil. If more than that amount of oil per egg yolk is added, the sauce may break; that is, the oil and vinegar will separate, and the mayonnaise will become very thin. Often mayonnaise that has broken can be repaired by beating the broken mayonnaise into additional egg yolks or prepared mayonnaise until the emulsion re-forms. To repair a broken mayonnaise, slowly beat 7 fluid ounces (210 milliliters) broken mayonnaise into one egg yolk or 4 fluid ounces (120 milliliters) prepared mayonnaise. Adjust the amount of egg yolk or prepared mayonnaise to be used according to the size of the batch that has broken. Table 25.2 lists common problems that can occur when making mayonnaise and some solutions.

Broken mayonnaise is thin and separated or curdled.

Emulsified Vinaigrette Dressings

An emulsified vinaigrette is a standard vinaigrette dressing emulsified with whole eggs. An emulsified vinaigrette dressing is thinner and lighter than a mayonnaise-based dressing and heavier than a basic vinaigrette. The flavor of an emulsified vinaigrette is similar to a basic vinaigrette, but an emulsified vinaigrette will not separate and it clings to greens quite easily.

Procedure for Preparing an Emulsified Vinaigrette Dressing

1 Gather all ingredients and hold at room temperature. Room-temperature ingredients emulsify more easily than cold ones.

2 Whip the eggs until frothy.

3 Add the dry ingredients and any flavorings such as garlic, shallots and herbs.

4 Add a small amount of the liquid called for in the recipe and whip to incorporate the ingredients.

5 With the mixer on high or whisking vigorously by hand or with an immersion blender, begin adding the oil very slowly until the emulsion forms.

6 After the emulsion is formed, add the oil a little more quickly, but still in a slow, steady stream.

7 Alternate between oil and liquid two or three times until all the oil is added. The dressing should be much thinner than mayonnaise. If it is too thick, it can be thinned with a little water, vinegar or lemon juice. Determine which to add by first tasting the dressing.

Caesar Dressing

MISE EN PLACE
- Chop garlic.
- Grate Parmesan.

YIELD 1 qt. (1 lt)	METHOD Emulsion	
Eggs, pasteurized	2	2
Garlic, chopped	1 Tbsp.	15 ml
Parmesan, grated	4 oz.	120 g
White balsamic vinegar	2 fl. oz.	60 ml
Whole-grain mustard	1 Tbsp.	15 ml
Dijon-style mustard	1 Tbsp.	15 ml
Anchovy fillets	1 oz.	30 g
Salt	1 Tbsp.	15 ml
Black pepper	1 tsp.	5 ml
Vegetable oil	12 fl. oz.	360 ml
Olive oil	12 fl. oz.	360 ml
Red wine vinegar	2 fl. oz.	60 ml

1 Place the eggs in a stainless steel bowl. Using an immersion blender, whip until frothy, approximately 10 seconds. Add the garlic, Parmesan, balsamic vinegar, mustards, anchovies, salt and pepper to the bowl and blend until smooth, approximately 20 seconds.

2 Combine the vegetable oil with the olive oil. With the blender at high speed, slowly begin adding the oils to the egg mixture to form an emulsion.

3 Once an emulsion is formed, alternate between adding the oil mixture and the red wine vinegar two or three times until all the oil and vinegar is incorporated.

Approximate values per 1-fl.-oz. (30-ml) serving: **Calories** 180, **Total fat** 19 g, **Saturated fat** 3 g, **Cholesterol** 15 mg, **Sodium** 290 mg, **Total carbohydrates** 1 g, **Protein** 2 g

1 Blending the eggs and seasonings until frothy.

2 The finished emulsified dressing.

SALAD PREPARATION METHODS

There are two types of **green salads**: tossed and composed. The more informal **tossed salad** is prepared by placing the greens, garnishes and dressing in a large bowl and tossing to combine. A **composed salad** usually has a more elegant look. It is prepared by arranging each of the ingredients on plates in an attractive fashion.

Other types of salads include **bound salads**, which are cooked meats, poultry, fish, shellfish, pasta or potatoes bound with a dressing; bean and grain salads; **vegetable salads**; **fruit salads** and **gelatin salads**.

MATCHING DRESSINGS AND SALAD GREENS	TABLE 25.3
DRESSING	**GREENS**
Vinaigrette dressing made with vegetable oil and red wine vinegar	Iceberg, romaine, leaf lettuce, butterhead lettuce, escarole, curly endive, Belgian endive, radicchio, baby lettuces, sorrel, arugula, dandelion, micro greens
Vinaigrette dressing made with nut oil and white wine or sherry vinegar	Delicate greens: Butterhead lettuce, bibb lettuce, Belgian endive, baby lettuces, mâche, watercress, micro greens
Vinaigrette dressing made with vegetable oil and balsamic vinegar	Romaine, leaf lettuce, radicchio, arugula
Emulsified vinaigrette dressing	Romaine, leaf lettuce, butterhead lettuce, escarole, curly endive, Belgian endive, radicchio, baby lettuces, sorrel, arugula, watercress
Mayonnaise-based dressing, such as blue cheese or Thousand Island	Hardy greens: iceberg, romaine, leaf lettuce, escarole, curly endive, sorrel, dandelion

Tossed Green Salads

Tossed salads are made from leafy vegetables such as lettuce, spinach, watercress, arugula or dandelion greens. They may consist only of greens and dressing, or they can be garnished with fruits, vegetables, nuts or cheese. They can be dressed with a variety of dressings, from light oil and vinegar to hearty hot bacon. It is important that salad dressings be added at the last possible moment before service. Acidic dressings cause most greens to wilt and become soggy. Salting greens lightly before dressing with vinaigrette helps keep them crisp.

Matching Dressings and Salad Greens

There is a simple rule to follow when choosing dressings for salads: The more delicate the texture and flavor of the greens or other ingredients, the lighter and more subtle the dressing should be. Vinaigrette-based dressings are much lighter than mayonnaise-based or similar dressings and should be paired with butterhead lettuces, mâche or other delicate greens. Crisp head lettuce such as iceberg and hardy lettuce such as romaine can stand up to heavier, mayonnaise-based or similar dressings. Vinaigrette dressings coat greens evenly, whereas thicker dressings tend to clump. When making a tossed salad, begin with a portion of the dressing, adding additional dressing only as needed, in order to prevent the greens from wilting. Table 25.3 lists some successful greens and dressing combinations.

Garnishing Salads

The following is a partial list of the garnishes that can be combined with salad greens for a tossed salad:

- *Vegetables:* Nearly any vegetable (raw, blanched or fully cooked) cut into appropriate sizes and uniform shapes
- *Fruits:* Citrus segments, apples or pears; dried fruits such as raisins, currants or apricots
- *Eggs, meats, poultry, fish and shellfish:* Poached or hard-boiled eggs; cooked meats and poultry sliced or diced neatly and uniformly; poached, grilled or cured fish, diced or flaked; small, whole cooked shellfish such as shrimp and scallops; lobster or crab sliced, diced or chopped
- *Cheeses:* Grated hard cheeses such as Parmesan, Romano or Asiago; semihard cheeses such as Cheddar or Swiss, cut julienne or shredded
- *Nuts:* Nearly any are appropriate, roasted, candied or smoked
- *Grains and legumes:* Cooked barley, farro or wheat berries; cooked beans, chickpeas, lentils or soybeans
- *Fresh herbs or flowers:* Small sprigs of mild fresh herbs, fresh flower petals or small flowers can be used to add color or flavor
- *Croutons:* Assorted breads, seasoned in various ways and toasted

Croutons

A crouton is simply a piece of bread that is toasted, sautéed or dried. Two types are often used.

The more familiar ones are small seasoned cubes of bread that are baked or toasted and sprinkled over soups or salads.

A more classic variety is made by sautéing slices of bread in clarified butter or olive oil until brown and crisp. The bread may be rough slices from a baguette, or shapes (such as hearts, diamonds or circles) cut from larger slices. Sautéed croutons have two advantages over the toasted variety: They stay crisp longer after coming in contact with moist foods and they gain flavor from the butter or olive oil in which they are cooked. Sautéed croutons can be used to decorate the border of a serving dish, as a base for canapés, as a garnish for soups, as an accompaniment to spreads or caviar or as a base under some meat and game dishes.

Procedure for Making Tossed Green Salads

1 Select greens with various colors, textures and flavors.
2 Carefully cut or tear, wash and dry the greens.
3 Prepare the garnishes as directed or desired.
4 Prepare the dressing.
5 Combine the greens, garnishes and dressing by tossing them together, or toss the greens and garnishes and, using a spray bottle, spray the greens with the dressing.
6 Serve the salads on chilled plates.

 Vegetarian

Mesclun Salad with Raspberry Vinaigrette

YIELD 6 Servings		METHOD Tossed
Baby lettuces, assorted	approx. 8 heads	approx. 8 heads
Mâche	4 oz.	120 g
Fresh herbs	2 Tbsp.	30 ml
Edible flowers	approx. 12	approx. 12
Raspberry Vinaigrette (page 754)	4 fl. oz.	120 ml

1 Trim, wash and dry the baby lettuces and mâche.
2 Pick the fresh herbs from their stems. Leafy herbs such as basil may be cut chiffonade or left as whole leaves.
3 If desired, pick the petals from the edible flowers. Small flowers may be left whole.
4 Place the lettuces and mâche in a bowl and add the herbs. Ladle the Raspberry Vinaigrette over them and toss gently, using two spoons.
5 Transfer the salad to six cold plates. Some of the larger leaves may be used as liners if desired.
6 Garnish each salad with flowers or flower petals.

Approximate values per serving: **Calories** 150, **Total fat** 9 g, **Saturated fat** 1 g, **Cholesterol** 0 mg, **Sodium** 180 mg, **Total carbohydrates** 14 g, **Protein** 4 g, **Vitamin A** 35%, **Vitamin C** 120%

Transferring composed salads to chilled plates for service.

Composed Green Salads

In composed green salads, a green is usually the base. The salads are built by attractively arranging other ingredients on the plate. There are usually four components: the base, body, garnish and dressing.

The **base** is typically a layer of salad greens that line the plate on which the salad will be served. Depending on the desired effect, the leaves can be cup-shaped or flat.

The **body** is the main ingredient. It can be lettuce or other greens, or another salad made from cooked or blended ingredients, such as chicken salad or fruit.

The **garnish** is added to the salad for color, texture and flavor. It can be as substantial as a grilled, sliced duck breast or as simple as a sprinkling of chopped herbs. Garnishes can be warm or cold. The choice is unlimited, but whatever is used should always complement and balance the flavor of the body.

The **dressing** should complement rather than mask the other flavors in the salad. If the body already contains a dressing, as a bound salad does, additional dressing may not be necessary.

Composed green salads are usually dressed by ladling the dressing over the salad after it is plated. Alternatively the individual ingredients can be dressed before they are arranged on the plate. A third method that may be limited by the intricacy of the salad but will save precious time during a busy period is to prepare individual salads on a sheet pan. Just before service, mist them with dressing using a spray bottle designated for this purpose; then transfer them to chilled plates using a spatula.

Procedure for Making Composed Salads

1. Gather all ingredients for the salad and wash, trim, cut, cook, chill or otherwise prepare them as necessary or as called for in the recipe.
2. Arrange all ingredients attractively on the plates, dressing each ingredient as desired or as directed in the recipe.
3. At service time, heat or cook any items that are being served hot and add them to the salad.

Salad Niçoise

YIELD 6 Servings, 12 oz. (360 g) each	METHOD Composed	
Red wine vinegar	2 fl. oz.	60 ml
Salt and pepper	TT	TT
Virgin olive oil	6 fl. oz.	180 ml
Fresh basil leaves, chiffonade	12	12
English cucumber	1 lb.	480 g
Green beans	12 oz.	360 g
Eggs, hard-boiled, chilled	3	3
Red bell pepper	1	1
Artichokes	3	3
Romaine lettuce, large leaves, washed	12	12
Mixed baby lettuce, leaves, washed	18	18
Fingerling potatoes, boiled, peeled, sliced, chilled	12 oz.	360 g
Cherry tomatoes	24	24
Red onion, sliced thin	3 oz.	90 g
Tuna, packed in oil, drained	1 lb.	480 g
Niçoise olives	4 oz.	120 g

1. Make a vinaigrette dressing using the red wine vinegar, salt, pepper, olive oil and basil.
2. Cut the cucumber in half, then into thin slices.
3. Trim the green beans and cook al dente.
4. Peel the eggs and cut into wedges.
5. Remove the stem and seeds from the red pepper and slice it into thin rings.
6. Cook the artichokes. Trim the outer leaves from each artichoke, leaving only the heart. Remove the choke from the heart and cut each heart into quarters.
7. Line each cold plate with two romaine lettuce leaves and three mixed lettuce leaves. Arrange the remaining ingredients attractively. Use the contrasting shapes, colors and textures to create an attractive presentation.
8. At service time, whisk the dressing to combine the ingredients and pour approximately 2 fluid ounces (60 milliliters) over each salad.

Approximate values per 12-oz. (360-g) serving: **Calories** 560, **Total fat** 38 g, **Saturated fat** 6 g, **Cholesterol** 105 mg, **Sodium** 460 mg, **Total carbohydrates** 26 g, **Protein** 30 g, **Vitamin A** 100%, **Vitamin C** 100%, **Iron** 20%

MISE EN PLACE

- Wash and slice basil in chiffonade.
- Hard-boil eggs and chill.
- Wash pepper, lettuce and cherry tomatoes.
- Boil, peel, slice and chill the potatoes.
- Slice red onion.
- Drain the tuna.

1 Lining a cold salad plate with a base of lettuce leaves.

2 The composed salad ready to serve.

Bound Salads

The creative chef can prepare a wide variety of salads by combining cooked meats, poultry, fish, shellfish, potatoes, pasta, grains and/or legumes with a dressing and garnishes. Although the combinations vary greatly in these types of salads, they are grouped here because their ingredients are all bound together. That is, each salad consists of one or more ingredients held together in a cohesive mass. The binding agent is either a vinaigrette or a mayonnaise-based or similar dressing. The ingredients should be evenly distributed throughout. The degree of cohesiveness can range from tightly packed to flaky and easily separated.

The foods that can be used to produce bound salads are so varied that it is impossible to list them all. Generalizing preparation techniques is also difficult. There are as many ways to prepare a bound salad as there are ingredients, dressings and garnishes.

Bound salads can be used as the body of a composed salad (e.g., a serving of egg salad on a bed of greens). Some bound salads (e.g., tuna or chicken salad) are used in sandwiches, but they are not ordinarily served as side dishes. Other bound salads (e.g., coleslaw and potato or pasta salad) are served as side dishes but not in sandwiches. Follow specific recipes and traditional uses for each salad to build confidence. Then use these skills and imagination to create enticing new salad combinations.

General guidelines for making bound salads include the following:

- Preparing a salad from cooked foods is a good opportunity to use leftovers, but be sure they are fresh and of good quality. The finished salad can be only as good as each of its ingredients.
- When making a bound salad, choose ingredients whose flavors blend well and complement each other.
- Choose ingredients for color; a few colorful ingredients turn a plain salad into a spectacular one.
- To improve appearance, cut all ingredients the same size.
- All ingredients should be cut into pieces that are small enough to be eaten easily with a fork.
- Be sure all meats, poultry, fish and shellfish are properly cooked before using them. Improperly cooked foods can cause food-borne illness and spoilage.
- Always chill cooked ingredients well before using them. Warm ingredients promote bacterial growth, especially in mayonnaise-based salads.
- Use dressings sparingly. They should enhance the flavors of the other salad ingredients, not mask them.

Chutney Chicken Salad

MISE EN PLACE

- Cook chicken and chill.
- Wash and peel celery and chop into small dice.
- Wash and slice green onions.
- Wash the grapes.

YIELD 5 lb. (2.2 kg)		METHOD Bound
Chicken meat, cooked	3 lb.	1.4 kg
Celery, small dice	6 oz.	180 g
Green onions, sliced	2 oz.	60 g
Mango chutney	8 oz.	240 g
Mayonnaise	12 fl. oz.	360 ml
Seedless grapes	6 oz.	180 g

1 Remove any bones, skin and fat from the chicken and cut the meat into large dice.

2 Combine the chicken meat, celery, green onions, mango chutney and mayonnaise in a bowl; mix well.

3 Cut the grapes in half. Add them to the chicken mixture and toss gently to combine.

Approximate values per 4-oz. (120-g) serving: **Calories** 250, **Total fat** 15 g, **Saturated fat** 2.5 g, **Cholesterol** 65 mg, **Sodium** 310 mg, **Total carbohydrates** 2 g, **Protein** 22 g

Cooked beans and grains are popular main ingredients for bound salads. They are flavorful and filling and can be prepared without any animal products for people who prefer not to eat meat. Beans and grains may be served alone as in White Bean Salad (page 628) or combined to highlight a range of tastes and textures. The texture of cooked beans and grains, from soft and tender to crunchy and chewy, add to the salad's appeal. Most bean or grain salads are bound with vinaigrette then combined with such ingredients as cooked meats, fish, vegetables and greens, nuts, cheese and dried or fresh fruits.

The dressing for a bean or grain salad should enhance the flavor of the main ingredient without overwhelming it. Cooked wheat berries can stand up to the pungent flavor

GUIDELINES FOR BEAN AND GRAIN SALADS				TABLE 25.4
	COMBINE WITH			
BEANS AND GRAINS	**FRUIT, DICED OR SLICED**	**PROTEIN**	**VEGETABLES, RAW OR COOKED; DICED, SLICED OR SHREDDED**	**GARNISHES**
Barley, buckwheat, bulgur, farro, quinoa, spelt, wheat berries	Apples, apricots, pears; avocado, citrus suprêmes, dried cranberries, grapes, mangoes	Chicken, chickpeas, cooked shellfish, lentils, lamb, legumes, pulled pork, sliced beef, smoked meats, poultry, fish or cheese, tofu	Carrots, cauliflower, raw or roasted chiles, corn, cucumber, dark leafy greens, onions, parsnips, tomatoes, peppers, winter squash	Dressing Cheese; fresh herbs, such as chives, dill, tarragon; nuts; pomegranate seeds; dried currants or raisins; spices

of blue cheese dressing that would overwhelm the delicate taste of quinoa, for example. A light citrus vinaigrette may be more appropriate for a quinoa salad. Add visual interest to these salads by combining cooked beans or grains with brightly-colored raw or cooked fruits, vegetables or greens such as arugula, kale or spinach. Strongly-flavored garnishes such as cubes of cheese, diced onions or pomegranate seeds add bursts of flavor that contribute to the pleasure of eating bean and grain salads. Table 25.4 lists general guidelines for creating bean and grain salads.

Cooked beans and grains are highly perishable TCS foods. Bound salads made from them should be kept well chilled and served promptly. Because beans and grains take time to cook, make large batches, then chill and freeze them for use when needed.

Vegetable Salads

Vegetable salads are made from cooked or raw vegetables or a combination of both. They can be served on buffets, as an appetizer or as a salad course. Like other salads, a successful vegetable salad combines color, texture and flavor. Some vegetable salads, such as coleslaw and carrot raisin salad, are made with mayonnaise. Most vegetable salads, however, are made by either marinating the vegetables or combining them with a vinaigrette dressing.

Almost any vegetable can be successfully marinated. The amount of time depends on the vegetable and the marinade, but several hours to overnight is usually sufficient for flavors to blend. Soft vegetables, such as mushrooms, zucchini and cucumbers, can be added directly to a cold marinade. Hard vegetables, such as carrots and cauliflower, should be blanched in salted water, refreshed, drained and then added to a cold marinade. Carrots, artichokes, mushrooms, cauliflower, zucchini, pearl onions and the like are sometimes simmered quickly in a marinade flavored with lemon juice and olive oil and served cold. This style is called **à la grecque**.

Many marinated salads last several days under proper refrigeration. As the salads age in the marinade, they change in appearance and texture. This may or may not be desirable. For example, mushrooms and artichokes become more flavorful, whereas green vegetables become discolored by the acids in the marinade. If marinated salads are prepared in advance, check their appearance as well as their seasonings carefully at service time.

à la grecque [ah la GREHK] a preparation style in which vegetables are marinated in olive oil, lemon juice and herbs, then served cold

Procedure for Preparing Vegetable Salads

1 Gather and wash all vegetables.

2 Trim, cut, shred or otherwise prepare the vegetables as desired or as directed in the recipe.

3 Blanch or cook the vegetables if necessary.

4 Combine the vegetables with the marinade or dressing. Adjust the seasonings.

 Vegetarian

Tomato and Asparagus Salad with Fresh Mozzarella

MISE EN PLACE

- Blanch the asparagus.
- Prepare the dressing.
- Slice lemon zest into strips.

YIELD 6 Servings, 8 oz. (240 g) each		METHOD Composed	
Asparagus, blanched	2 lb.	960 g
Basic Vinaigrette Dressing (page 740)	8 fl. oz.	240 ml
Cherry tomatoes, orange, red and yellow, rinsed	18	18
Bibb lettuce	1 head	1 head
Fresh mozzarella, bocconcini or diced	10 oz.	300 g
Black pepper	TT	TT
Lemon zest, sliced	1 Tbsp.	15 ml

1 Trim the asparagus and marinate in 6 fluid ounces (180 milliliters) Basic Vinaigrette Dressing for approximately 15 minutes.

2 Halve, quarter or slice the cherry tomatoes as desired.

3 Clean the lettuce and separate the leaves.

4 Toss the mozzarella with some of the cherry tomatoes. Season with pepper.

5 Arrange the tomatoes, cheese and asparagus on six plates, using the lettuce as a base. Pour on the remaining dressing and garnish the cheese with the lemon zest.

Approximate values per 8-oz. (240-g) serving: **Calories** 390, **Total fat** 35 g, **Saturated fat** 9 g, **Cholesterol** 35 mg, **Sodium** 115 mg, **Total carbohydrates** 8 g, **Protein** 11 g, **Vitamin A** 40%, **Vitamin C** 25%

Fruit Salads

There are so many different fruits with beautiful bright colors and sweet delicious flavors that preparing fruit salads is easy work. Fruit salads are a refreshing addition to buffets and can be served as the first course of a lunch or dinner. A more elaborate fruit salad can be served as a light lunch.

Always prepare fruit salads as close to service time as possible. The flesh of many types of fruit becomes soft and translucent if cut too long before service. Other fruits, such as apples, bananas and peaches, turn brown in a matter of minutes after cutting. Refer to Chapter 26, Fruits, for more information on this browning reaction and for information on specific fruits. (Sliced apples and pears, for example, can be tossed with lemon juice to prevent enzymatic browning.)

If a fruit salad is dressed at all, the dressing is usually sweet and made with honey or yogurt mixed with fruit juices or purées. Alternatively Grand Marnier, créme de menthe or other liqueurs sprinkled over the salad can serve as a dressing. Fruit salads can be tossed or composed and should offer the diner a pleasing blend of colors, shapes, sizes, flavors and textures.

Gelatin Salads

Gelatin salads are made from diced or sliced fresh fruits, drained canned fruits, cooked vegetables, cooked meat, poultry or fish, dried fruits or nuts coated with a flavorful liquid into which gelatin has been dissolved. Gelatin binds these ingredients into a firm yet tender mixture that melts in the mouth when eaten. Gelatin salads are closely related to aspic jelly, discussed in Chapter 28, Charcuterie. These cool, refreshing salads are served as a first course or accompaniment to main dishes. Gelatin salads, also known as congealed salads, are often prepared in decorative molds then unmolded for service. Before beginning to make such dishes, familiarize yourself with gelatin, which is discussed in Chapter 30, Principles of the Bakeshop.

The ingredients added to gelatin salads must be chopped, diced, grated or sliced into uniform pieces so that each bite contains a taste of each ingredient in the salad. Almost any type of fresh fruit is suitable for gelatin salad, however, certain enzymes in raw figs, kiwi, mango, guava, pineapple and papaya interfere with gelatin's ability to set. These fruits should not be used unless they are cooked or canned, as the heating process destroys this enzyme. Canned fruits or vegetables must be well drained before using.

The quantity of gelatin required to set a liquid varies depending on the ingredients used. One ounce (30 grams) of unflavored granulated gelatin sets 2 quarts (1.9 liters) of liquid into a firm mixture that is still tender and will melt in the mouth when eaten. But the addition of acids in the form of lemon juice, vinegar and acidic fruit juice will require more gelatin for the mixture to set. As much as 3 total ounces (90 grams) of gelatin may be needed to set the same quantity of an acidic liquid. Granulated gelatin must first be softened (bloomed) in cold liquid. The amount of liquid should be approximately four times the weight of the granulated gelatin (e.g., 2 tablespoons cold liquid to ¼ ounce granulated gelatin). Note that one envelope of granulated gelatin is ¼ ounce (7 grams).

Allow the gelatin mixture to set and thicken to the consistency of unwhipped egg whites in the refrigerator before adding the main ingredients. This step ensures that the pieces of food are evenly distributed in the gelatin. Always prepare gelatin salads in advance to ensure that the ingredients set properly in time for service. To speed the setting of gelatin, dissolve the gelatin in half of the heated liquid called for in the recipe. After the hot liquid is added, incorporate chilled liquid or crushed ice cubes equal to the remaining volume of cold liquid. As the ice melts, it chills the gelatin mixture so that it sets more quickly.

Flavored gelatin, which contains sugar and flavoring agents, is also a popular and convenient medium used to make gelatin salads. Commercially available in 5-pound (2.2-kilo) bags, flavored gelatin is suitable for sweet fruit-based salads.

Gelatin salads are often accompanied by an emulsified dressing or savory cream sauce. Sweetened gelatin salads with fruits may be accompanied by sour cream, whipped cream or yogurt.

Procedure for Making Gelatin Salad

1 Prepare the ingredients for the gelatin salad. Peel, chop dice and prepare all fruits and vegetables as required. Cook and thoroughly chill any ingredients such as meats, poultry, fish and vegetables.

2 Measure the quantity of gelatin.

3 Soften the gelatin in cold water for 5 minutes. Make sure that the granulated gelatin is completely softened at this stage.

4 Combine the softened gelatin with the hot liquid, stirring to ensure that the gelatin is completely dissolved.

5 For a layered salad, pour enough gelatin in the mold to anchor the first layer of ingredients.

6 For a blended salad, cool the gelatin until it is as thick as unwhipped egg whites before adding any prepared fruits, vegetables, nuts or other ingredients. Fold in additional ingredients then pour into one large mold or portion into timbales, decorative glasses or bowls for service.

7 Chill until set.

♥ Good Choice

MISE EN PLACE

- Chop the garlic.
- Wash, peel and dice the tomatoes, cucumber and green pepper.
- Slice the green onions.
- Prepare Guacamole.

Molded Gazpacho Salad

YIELD 1 Mold, 12 Servings, 3½ oz. (105 g) each			METHOD Gelatin	
Granulated gelatin	2 Tbsp.	30 ml		
Water, cold	2 fl. oz.	45 ml		
Tomato juice, seasoned	14 fl. oz.	420 ml		
Sherry vinegar	1 Tbsp.	15 ml		
Garlic, chopped	1 tsp.	5 ml		
Salt and pepper	TT	TT		
Tomatoes, peeled, seeded, fine dice	14 oz.	420 g		
Cucumber, peeled, seeded, fine dice	6 oz.	180 g		
Green pepper, peeled, seeded, fine dice	4 oz.	120 g		
Green onions, sliced	2 Tbsp.	60 ml		
Guacamole (page 888)	12 fl. oz.	360 ml		
Watercress	as needed for garnish			

1 Soften the gelatin in the cold water.

2 Bring the tomato juice to a boil. Add the softened gelatin stirring until it dissolves. Stir in the vinegar, garlic and salt. Season to taste with pepper.

3 Cool then refrigerate the juice mixture until slightly set and syrupy, approximately 30 minutes.

4 Stir in the tomatoes, cucumber, green pepper and green onions. Pour into a 1½-quart (1.4-liter) mold and refrigerate until set.

5 For service, dip the mold in a hot water bath for a few seconds. Dry the bottom of the mold then invert it onto a sheet tray or serving platter. Remove the mold.

6 Cut congealed salad into portions and serve each portion garnished with Guacamole and fresh watercress.

Variation:

Molded Gazpacho Salad with Shrimp—Add 4 ounces (120 grams) 51-count cooked shrimp in Step 4.

Approximate values per 3½-oz. (105-g) serving: **Calories** 20, **Total fat** 0 g, **Saturated fat** 0 g, **Cholesterol** 0 mg, **Sodium** 290 mg, **Total carbohydrates** 4 g, **Protein** 2 g, **Vitamin A** 10%, **Vitamin C** 70%, **Claims**—good source of vitamin A; excellent source of vitamin C

QUESTIONS FOR DISCUSSION

1 Name several factors that cause salad greens to wilt or deteriorate.

2 Describe the proper procedure for washing and drying lettuce.

3 Raw salad greens have been the source of salmonella and *E. coli* outbreaks. Locate information on a recent recall of salad greens and discuss why the outbreak occurred and what could have been done to prevent it from happening.

4 Explain the difference between a vinaigrette and an emulsified vinaigrette dressing.

5 Describe the procedure for making mayonnaise. How can the flavor of a mayonnaise be altered?

6 Describe the ingredients used and the basic steps in preparing a bound salad. How does a bound salad differ from a dressed salad?

7 List five ways salads can be presented or offered on a menu.

8 In France and other parts of Europe, salad is traditionally served after the main course. Research the types of salads served after meals and the reason they are served at that time.

Additional Salad and Salad Dressing Recipes

Garlic Croutons

YIELD 1 lb. 14 oz. (900 g)

Whole butter	6 oz.	180 g
Garlic, chopped	1 Tbsp.	15 ml
French or sourdough bread cubes	1 lb. 8 oz.	720 g
Parmesan, grated	1 oz.	30 g
Dried basil	2 tsp.	10 ml
Dried oregano	2 tsp.	10 ml

1 Melt the butter in a small saucepan and add the garlic. Cook the garlic in the butter over low heat for 5 minutes.

2 Place the bread cubes in a bowl; add the Parmesan and herbs.

3 Pour the garlic butter over the bread cubes and immediately toss to combine.

4 Spread the bread cubes on a sheet pan in a single layer and bake at 350°F (180°C). Stir the croutons occasionally and cook until dry and lightly browned, approximately 15 minutes.

Approximate values per 1-oz. (30-g) serving: **Calories** 200, **Total fat** 9 g, **Saturated fat** 5 g, **Cholesterol** 20 mg, **Sodium** 390 mg, **Total carbohydrates** 25 g, **Protein** 5 g, **Iron** 10%, **Calcium** 10%

Carrot Ginger Miso Dressing

YIELD 1 qt. (960 ml)	METHOD Temporary Emulsion	
Carrots, grated fine	10 oz.	300 g
Fresh ginger, peeled, minced	2 oz.	60 g
White miso paste	4 oz.	120 g
Rice wine vinegar	10 fl. oz.	300 ml
Black pepper	TT	TT
Water, as needed	8 fl. oz.	240 ml

1 Combine half of the carrots, the ginger, miso, vinegar and pepper in the bowl of a food processor or blender. Mix until well blended. Stir in the remaining grated carrots and the water to achieve a thick yet pourable consistency.

Approximate values per 1-fl.-oz. (30-ml) serving: **Calories** 15, **Total fat** 0 g, **Saturated fat** 0 g, **Cholesterol** 0 mg, **Sodium** 120 mg, **Total carbohydrates** 3 g, **Protein** 0 g, **Vitamin A** 30%, **Claims**—no cholesterol; fat free; excellent source of vitamin A

🌿 Vegetarian

Raspberry Vinaigrette

YIELD	1 qt. (960 ml)		METHOD	Temporary Emulsion
Red wine vinegar	4 fl. oz.	120 ml		
Rice wine vinegar	4 fl. oz.	120 ml		
Lemon juice	1 fl. oz.	30 ml		
Dried thyme	2 tsp.	10 ml		
Salt	2 tsp.	10 ml		
Black pepper	1 tsp.	5 ml		
Garlic, minced	2 tsp.	10 ml		
Honey	2 oz.	60 g		
Raspberry preserves, without seeds	4 oz.	120 g		
Olive oil	8 fl. oz.	240 ml		
Vegetable oil	8 fl. oz.	240 ml		

1 Whisk together the vinegars, lemon juice, thyme, salt, pepper and garlic.

2 Whisk in the honey and raspberry preserves.

3 Slowly whisk in the oils, emulsifying the dressing.

Approximate values per 1-fl.-oz. (30-ml) serving: **Calories** 140, **Total fat** 14 g, **Saturated fat** 1.5 g, **Cholesterol** 0 mg, **Sodium** 150 mg, **Total carbohydrates** 4 g, **Protein** 0 g

❤ Good Choice

Fat-Free Vinaigrette

YIELD	1 qt. (960 ml)		METHOD	Temporary Emulsion
Shallots	12 oz.	360 g		
White wine vinegar	6 fl. oz.	180 ml		
Dijon-style mustard	2 oz.	60 g		
Fresh herbs, assorted, chopped	4 fl. oz.	120 ml		
Rich chicken or vegetable stock	12 fl. oz.	360 ml		
Salt	1 tsp.	5 ml		
Pepper	½ tsp.	3 ml		

1 Place the shallots in a small pan. Cover with a lid and roast in a 375°F (190°C) oven for 45 minutes or until very tender. Remove from the oven and cool to room temperature. Chop the shallots coarsely.

2 Place all of the ingredients in the bowl of a blender and blend until smooth.

Approximate values per 1-fl.-oz. (30-ml) serving: **Calories** 20, **Total fat** 0 g, **Saturated fat** 0 g, **Cholesterol** 0 mg, **Sodium** 85 mg, **Total carbohydrates** 3 g, **Protein** 1 g, **Vitamin A** 15%, **Vitamin C** 25%, **Claims**—low calorie; fat free; high in vitamin C; source of vitamin A

Blue Cheese Vinaigrette

🌿 Vegetarian

YIELD 1 qt. (960 ml)		METHOD Temporary Emulsion
Blue cheese	12 oz.	360 g
Salt	2 tsp.	10 ml
Garlic, chopped	2 tsp.	10 ml
White wine vinegar	6 fl. oz.	180 ml
Pepper	½ tsp.	3 ml
Olive oil	8 fl. oz.	240 ml
Vegetable oil	8 fl. oz.	240 ml

1 Set aside 2 ounces (60 grams) of the blue cheese for garnish. Place the remaining cheese in the bowl of a food processor and add the salt, garlic, vinegar and pepper.

2 Combine the olive oil and vegetable oil. Turn on the processor and add the oils in a steady stream. Process until the dressing is smooth. Remove the dressing from the machine. Chop or crumble the reserved blue cheese and stir it into the dressing.

Approximate values per 1-fl.-oz. (30-ml) serving: **Calories** 190, **Total fat** 19 g, **Saturated fat** 4.5 g, **Cholesterol** 10 mg, **Sodium** 270 mg, **Total carbohydrates** 1 g, **Protein** 2 g

Poppy Seed Dressing

🌿 Vegetarian

YIELD 1 qt. (960 ml)		METHOD Temporary Emulsion
Cider vinegar	12 fl. oz.	360 ml
Honey	8 oz.	240 g
Salt	2 tsp.	10 ml
Dry mustard	1 Tbsp.	15 ml
Vegetable oil	6 fl. oz.	180 ml
Olive oil	6 fl. oz.	180 ml
Poppy seeds	3 Tbsp.	45 ml
Green onion, minced	2 oz.	60 g

1 In the bowl of a food processor, combine the vinegar, honey, salt and mustard.

2 Combine the vegetable oil and olive oil. With the processor running, add the oil very slowly then in a steady stream.

3 When all of the oil has been incorporated, stir in the poppy seeds and green onions.

Approximate values per 1-fl.-oz. (30-ml) serving: **Calories** 140, **Total fat** 11 g, **Saturated fat** 1 g, **Cholesterol** 0 mg, **Sodium** 90 mg, **Total carbohydrates** 11 g, **Protein** 0 g

Sauce Gribiche

Gribiche is a cold mayonnaise-type sauce made with hard-cooked egg yolks instead of raw egg yolks. It is traditionally flavored with capers and herbs and served with fish or vegetables.

YIELD	1 qt. (960 ml)	METHOD	Emulsion
Hard-cooked egg yolks		4	4
Salt and pepper		TT	TT
Dijon-style mustard		1 Tbsp.	15 ml
Olive oil		1½ pt.	720 ml
White wine vinegar		3 fl. oz.	90 ml
Cornichons, chopped		1 oz.	30 g
Capers, chopped		1 Tbsp.	15 ml
Fresh mixed herbs such as parsley, chervil, tarragon or chives, chopped		1 oz.	30 g

1 Blend the egg yolks with the salt, pepper and mustard.

2 Very slowly, as for mayonnaise, whisk in the oil. Occasionally add a few drops of vinegar to thin the sauce.

3 Add the cornichons, capers and herbs; mix well. Adjust the seasonings and acidity with the remaining vinegar.

Approximate values per 1-fl.-oz. (30-ml) serving: **Calories** 190, **Total fat** 21 g, **Saturated fat** 3 g, **Cholesterol** 25 mg, **Sodium** 95 mg, **Total carbohydrates** 0 g, **Protein** 1 g

Thousand Island Dressing

YIELD	1 qt. (960 ml)	METHOD	Mayonnaise-Based
Red wine vinegar		2 Tbsp.	30 ml
Granulated sugar		1 Tbsp.	15 ml
Mayonnaise		12 oz.	360 g
Ketchup		6 oz.	180 g
Sweet pickle relish		4 oz.	120 g
Hard-cooked eggs, chopped		4	4
Fresh parsley, chopped		2 Tbsp.	30 ml
Green onions, chopped		2 oz.	60 g
Salt and pepper		TT	TT
Soy or Worcestershire sauce		TT	TT

1 Combine the vinegar and sugar; stir to dissolve the sugar.

2 Add the remaining ingredients and mix well.

3 Adjust the seasonings with the salt, pepper and soy sauce.

Approximate values per 1-fl.-oz. (30-ml) serving: **Calories** 90, **Total fat** 9 g, **Saturated fat** 1.5 g, **Cholesterol** 30 mg, **Sodium** 230 mg, **Total carbohydrates** 3 g, **Protein** 1 g

Herb Buttermilk Dressing

YIELD 1 qt. (960 ml)		METHOD Temporary Emulsion
Green onions, white part only, cut into fine rings	2 oz.	60 g
Oven Roasted Garlic (page 638), pulp	3 oz.	90 g
Buttermilk	6 fl. oz.	180 ml
Lemon juice	1 fl. oz.	30 ml
Egg yolks, pasteurized	3	3
Vegetable oil	1 pt.	480 ml
Chives, minced	1 oz.	30 g
Fresh thyme, chopped	1 Tbsp.	15 ml
Fresh parsley, chopped	1 oz.	30 g
Black pepper	2 tsp.	10 ml
Salt	2 tsp.	10 ml
Dijon-style mustard	1 Tbsp.	15 ml
Louisiana Hot Sauce	TT	TT

1 Combine the green onions, garlic pulp, buttermilk, lemon juice and egg yolks in a blender for 1 minute. With the machine running, slowly add the oil to form an emulsion.

2 Remove dressing from the blender and fold in the remaining ingredients. Adjust seasoning to taste.

Note: This dressing appears in the photo on page 442.

Approximate values per 1-fl.-oz. (30-ml) serving: **Calories** 140, **Total fat** 15 g, **Saturated fat** 1.5 g, **Cholesterol** 30 mg, **Sodium** 230 mg, **Total carbohydrates** 3 g, **Protein** 1 g

Roquefort Dressing

YIELD 1 qt. (960 ml)		METHOD Mayonnaise-Based
Mayonnaise	8 fl. oz.	240 ml
Red wine vinegar	1 fl. oz.	30 ml
Sour cream	8 fl. oz.	240 ml
Buttermilk	4 fl. oz.	120 ml
Garlic, chopped	1 tsp.	5 ml
Worcestershire sauce	1 tsp.	5 ml
Tabasco sauce	TT	TT
White pepper	TT	TT
Roquefort, crumbled	12 oz.	360 g

1 Combine all the ingredients except the Roquefort and mix well.

2 Add the crumbled Roquefort and combine. Thin with additional buttermilk if desired.

Approximate values per 1-fl.-oz. (30-ml) serving: **Calories** 110, **Total fat** 10 g, **Saturated fat** 4 g, **Cholesterol** 20 mg, **Sodium** 240 mg, **Total carbohydrates** 1 g, **Protein** 3 g

Low-Fat Blue Cheese Dressing

YIELD 1 qt. (960 ml)		METHOD Temporary Emulsion
Nonfat yogurt	20 oz.	600 g
Low-fat buttermilk	6 fl. oz.	180 ml
Blue cheese, crumbled	4 oz.	120 g
White pepper	¼ tsp.	1 ml
Granulated sugar	3 Tbsp.	30 ml
Soy or Worcestershire sauce	TT	TT
Dry mustard	1 tsp.	5 ml
Tabasco sauce	TT	TT

1 Combine all the ingredients in the bowl of a mixer or food processor and process until smooth.

Approximate values per 1-fl.-oz. (30-ml) serving: **Calories** 30, **Total fat** 1 g, **Saturated fat** 0.5 g, **Cholesterol** 5 mg, **Sodium** 70 mg, **Total carbohydrates** 3 g, **Protein** 2 g, **Claims**—low fat; low cholesterol; low sodium; low calorie

Tartar Sauce

YIELD Approximately 1 pt. (480 ml)		METHOD Mayonnaise-Based
Mayonnaise	1 pt.	480 ml
Capers, chopped	2 oz.	60 g
Sweet pickle relish	3 oz.	90 g
Onion, minced	2 Tbsp.	30 ml
Fresh parsley, minced	2 Tbsp.	30 ml
Lemon juice	1 Tbsp.	15 ml
Salt	TT	TT
Soy or Worcestershire sauce	TT	TT
Tabasco sauce	TT	TT

1 Stir all the ingredients together until well blended. Chill thoroughly before serving.

Approximate values per 1-fl.-oz. (30-ml) serving: **Calories** 220, **Total fat** 23 g, **Saturated fat** 4 g, **Cholesterol** 20 mg, **Sodium** 420 mg, **Total carbohydrates** 2 g, **Protein** 0 g

Rémoulade Sauce

YIELD 1 pt. (480 ml)	METHOD	Emulsion
Egg yolks, pasteurized	3	3
Lemon juice	2 Tbsp.	30 ml
Dijon-style mustard	2 tsp.	10 ml
Vegetable oil	10 fl. oz.	300 ml
Capers, drained and chopped	2 oz.	60 g
Cornichons, chopped	2 oz.	60 g
Fresh chives, sliced	2 Tbsp.	30 ml
Anchovy fillets, chopped	3	3
Worcestershire sauce	½ tsp.	2 ml
Salt and white pepper	TT	TT
Tabasco sauce	TT	TT

1 Combine the egg yolks, lemon juice and Dijon-style mustard in the bowl of a food processor. While processing, add the oil in drops to form an emulsion. As the emulsion forms and the mixture thickens, the oil may be added in a slow stream. Process only until all of the oil is incorporated.

2 Transfer the sauce to a mixing bowl and stir in the capers, cornichons, chives, anchovy fillets and Worcestershire sauce.

3 Adjust the seasoning with salt, white pepper and Tabasco. If the sauce is too thick, thin it with a few drops of lemon juice or red wine vinegar.

Variation:

Creole Rémoulade—Omit the capers, cornichons and chives. In Step 3, add ½ cup (120 milliliters) finely chopped yellow onion, 1 ounce (30 grams) ketchup, 2 tablespoons (30 milliliters) minced garlic, 1 fluid ounce (30 milliliters) lemon juice, ¼ teaspoon (1 milliliter) cayenne pepper and ⅓ cup (85 milliliters) finely chopped fresh parsley.

Approximate values per 1-fl.-oz. (30-ml) serving: **Calories** 220, **Total fat** 24 g, **Saturated fat** 2 g, **Cholesterol** 45 mg, **Sodium** 210 mg, **Total carbohydrates** 1 g, **Protein** 1 g

Sherry Walnut Vinaigrette

 Vegan

YIELD 1 qt. (960 ml)	METHOD	Temporary Emulsion
Sherry wine vinegar	8 fl. oz.	240 ml
Shallots, minced	2 oz.	60 g
Salt	1 Tbsp.	15 ml
Black pepper	2 tsp.	10 ml
Walnut oil	24 fl. oz.	720 ml

1 Whisk together the vinegar, shallots, salt and pepper.

2 Slowly whisk in the walnut oil, emulsifying the dressing.

Approximate values per 1-fl.-oz. (30-ml) serving: **Calories** 180, **Total fat** 20 g, **Saturated fat** 2 g, **Cholesterol** 0 mg, **Sodium** 230 mg, **Total carbohydrates** 0 g, **Protein** 0 g

 Good Choice  Vegetarian

Khira Raita
(Cucumber-Yogurt Salad)

Raita [RA-tah] are yogurt and vegetable salads typically served as condiments in Indian cuisine. Raita may be made with many types of vegetables, including eggplants, cooked potatoes, tomatoes and even bananas, and are meant as a cooling counterpoint to the spiciness of other dishes.

YIELD 1 lb. (480 g), 6 Servings, 2½ oz. (75 g) each	METHOD Bound	
Plain yogurt	8 fl. oz.	240 ml
Cucumber, peeled and grated	6 oz.	180 g
Cumin	½ tsp.	2 ml
Salt and pepper	TT	TT
Granulated sugar	2 tsp.	10 ml
Lime juice	2 tsp.	10 ml
Fresh cilantro, chopped	1 Tbsp.	15 ml
Jalapeño pepper, minced	½ tsp.	2 ml
Paprika, optional	as needed	as needed

1 Stir together all the ingredients except the paprika. Chill for several hours before service.

2 At service time, dust the top lightly with paprika, if using.

Approximate values per 2½-oz. (75-g) serving: **Calories** 35, **Total fat** 1.5 g, **Saturated fat** 1 g, **Cholesterol** 5 mg, **Sodium** 20 mg, **Total carbohydrates** 4 g, **Protein** 2 g, **Claims**—low calorie

---

 Good Choice  Vegetarian

Carrot Salad

YIELD 3 lb. (1.4 kg), 12 Servings, 4 oz. (120 g) each	METHOD Bound	
Carrots, peeled, finely shredded	2 lb.	960 g
Dried currants	4 oz.	120 g
Almonds, toasted, chopped fine	4 oz.	120 g
Mayonnaise	8 fl. oz.	240 ml
Cumin, ground	¾ tsp.	3 ml
Dry mustard	1 tsp.	5 ml
Salt	½ tsp.	2 ml
Black pepper	½ tsp.	2 ml
Honey	3 oz.	90 g

1 Place the carrots, currants and almonds in a stainless steel bowl.

2 In a separate bowl, whisk together the mayonnaise, cumin, dry mustard, salt, pepper and honey.

3 Pour the honey mixture over the carrot mixture and stir to combine. Adjust the seasonings if necessary.

Approximate values per 4-oz. (120-g) serving: **Calories** 260, **Total fat** 19 g, **Saturated fat** 2.5 g, **Cholesterol** 10 mg, **Sodium** 270 mg, **Total carbohydrates** 23 g, **Protein** 3 g, **Vitamin A** 250%, **Claims**—good source of fiber; excellent source of vitamin A

Spinach and Edamame Salad

Good Choice   Vegetarian

YIELD 6 Servings	METHOD Tossed	
Baby spinach leaves, cleaned	12 oz.	360 g
Edamame, cooked and shelled	12 oz.	360 g
Cherry tomatoes, assorted, halved	12 oz.	360 g
Red grapes, halved	12 oz.	360 g
Salt and pepper	TT	TT
Herb Vinaigrette (page 740)	6 fl. oz.	180 ml
Walnut halves, toasted	6 oz.	180 g
Goat cheese, crumbled	6 oz.	180 g

1 Place the spinach, edamame, cherry tomatoes and grapes in a large bowl. Season with salt and pepper. Add enough dressing to moisten the salad and toss to coat the ingredients evenly.

2 Arrange the dressed salad in bowls and top with walnuts and goat cheese.

3 Alternatively arrange all of the ingredients in serving bowls and serve the salad dressing on the side.

Approximate values per serving: **Calories** 590, **Total fat** 49 g, **Saturated fat** 9 g, **Cholesterol** 20 mg, **Sodium** 240 g, **Total carbohydrates** 23 g, **Protein** 20 g, **Vitamin A** 130%, **Vitamin C** 50%, **Calcium** 20%, **Iron** 20%, **Claims**—excellent source of fiber, vitamins A and C, calcium and iron

Ribbon Salad of Zucchini, Carrots, Green Beans and Tomatoes

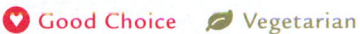
Good Choice   Vegetarian

YIELD 6 Servings	METHOD Tossed	
Zucchini, trimmed	1 lb.	480 g
Carrots, peeled and trimmed	1 lb.	480 g
Green beans, trimmed	8 oz.	240 g
Salt	½ tsp.	2 ml
Cherry tomatoes, heirloom red and green varieties, halved	1 pt.	480 ml
Edamame or fresh peas, cooked	3 oz.	90 g
Lemon juice	1½ fl. oz.	45 ml
Virgin olive oil	4 fl. oz.	120 ml
Salt and pepper	TT	TT
Asiago cheese, optional	2 oz.	60 g
Basil leaves	⅓ cup	80 g

1 Slice the zucchini, carrots and green beans lengthwise on a mandolin into long, thin ribbons. Toss the vegetables with the salt in a large bowl.

2 Add the cherry tomatoes and the edamame to the sliced vegetables.

3 Combine the lemon juice and olive oil in a small bowl. Season with salt and pepper. Toss the vegetables with the dressing.

4 Arrange the salad ingredients attractively on serving plates. Use a chef's fork to lift up the ribbons of vegetables and create an attractive presentation. Shave the cheese over each salad and garnish with the basil leaves.

Approximate values per 1½-c. (360-ml) serving: **Calories** 240, **Total fat** 19 g, **Saturated fat** 2.5 g, **Cholesterol** 0 mg, **Sodium** 260 mg, **Total carbohydrates** 15 g, **Protein** 4 g, **Vitamin A** 250%, **Vitamin C** 60%, **Claims**—good source of fiber; high in vitamins A and C

Wilted Spinach Salad
with Warm Bacon Dressing

YIELD 2 Servings, 12 oz. (360 g) each	METHOD Tossed	
Spinach	1 lb.	480 g
Eggs, hard-cooked, chilled	2	2
Bacon slices, cut into ½-in. (1.25-cm) pieces	2	2
Red wine vinegar	2 fl. oz.	60 ml
Heavy cream	1 fl. oz.	30 ml
Salt and pepper	TT	TT
Mushrooms, sliced thin	2 oz.	60 g
Red onion, sliced thin	2 oz.	60 g

1 Stem, wash and dry the spinach. Put the spinach into a large bowl.

2 Peel and quarter the eggs.

3 Cook the bacon until crisp. Remove the bacon from the pan. Drain off the fat, reserving 2 teaspoons (10 milliliters) of the fat in the pan. Deglaze the pan with the vinegar. Add the cream. Boil until the mixture is thickened and hot. Season to taste with salt and pepper.

4 Pour the hot dressing over the spinach, holding the hot pan over the bowl to wilt the greens slightly. Toss with a pair of metal tongs to coat and wilt the leaves.

5 Garnish the salad with the eggs, mushrooms, red onions and crisp bacon.

Approximate values per 12-oz. (360-g) serving: **Calories** 250, **Total fat** 15 g, **Saturated fat** 6 g, **Cholesterol** 215 mg, **Sodium** 390 mg, **Total carbohydrates** 13 g, **Protein** 17 g, **Vitamin A** 440%, **Vitamin C** 110%, **Calcium** 25%, **Iron** 40%

1 Pouring hot dressing over greens.

2 The plated spinach salad ready for service.

Curly Endive, Apple and Gorgonzola Salad

 ♥ Good Choice   🍃 Vegetarian

YIELD 6 Servings	METHOD Composed	
Belgian endive	2 heads	2 heads
Curly endive	1 head	1 head
Granny Smith apple	1	1
Red Delicious apple	1	1
Heavy cream	4 fl. oz.	120 ml
Red wine vinegar	2 fl. oz.	60 ml
Gorgonzola, crumbled	3 oz.	90 g
Salt and pepper	TT	TT
Walnuts, toasted	1 oz.	30 g

1 Separate the leaves of the Belgian endive. Tear the curly endive into small pieces. Wash and thoroughly dry the leaves.

2 Core the apples and cut them into thin wedges.

3 Combine the cream, vinegar and Gorgonzola and season to taste with salt and pepper. Add the apple wedges to the cream mixture.

4 Divide the Belgian endive spears among six plates, forming a flower pattern. Place a portion of the curly endive in the center of each plate on top of the Belgian endive.

5 Spoon a portion of the apple mixture onto each plate, arranging the apple wedges attractively. Garnish with toasted walnuts.

Approximate values per serving: **Calories** 240, **Total fat** 17 g, **Saturated fat** 8 g, **Cholesterol** 40 mg, **Sodium** 260 mg, **Total carbohydrates** 17 g, **Protein** 8 g, **Vitamin A** 120%, **Vitamin C** 30%, **Calcium** 25%, **Iron** 15%, **Claims**—good source of iron; high in fiber, vitamins A and C and calcium

Caprese Salad

 ♥ Good Choice    🍃 Vegetarian

YIELD 6 Servings	METHOD Composed	
Tomato slices	18	18
Fresh mozzarella slices, approximately 1½ oz. (45 g) each	18	18
Fresh basil leaves	36	36
Kosher or other coarse salt	TT	TT
Fresh ground pepper	TT	TT
Extra virgin olive oil	2 Tbsp.	30 ml
Basil oil	3 fl. oz.	90 ml
Red and yellow cherry tomatoes, halved	as needed for garnish	

1 Arrange 3 tomato slices, 3 mozzarella cheese slices and 6 basil leaves attractively on 6 chilled plates.

2 Season each salad generously with salt and pepper.

3 Drizzle each salad with 1 teaspoon (5 milliliters) of extra virgin olive oil.

4 Using a small spoon, garnish each salad with 1 tablespoon (15 milliliters) of basil oil and cherry tomatoes.

Approximate values per serving: **Calories** 410, **Total fat** 39 g, **Saturated fat** 15 g, **Cholesterol** 20 mg, **Sodium** 50 mg, **Total carbohydrates** 2 g, **Protein** 16 g, **Vitamin C** 25%, **Vitamin** C 15%, **Calcium** 30%, **Claims**—excellent source vitamin A and calcium; good source of vitamin C

♥ Good Choice

Cobb Salad

YIELD 6 Main Course Servings	METHOD Composed	
Romaine lettuce	6 oz.	180 g
Green leaf lettuce	4 oz.	120 g
Watercress	2 oz.	60 g
Quail eggs	18	18
Avocados	3	3
Bacon slices	12	12
Roquefort, crumbled	6 oz.	180 g
Turkey breast, roasted, julienne	12 oz.	360 g
Cherry tomatoes, halved	18	18
Dijon Vinaigrette (page 740)	12 fl. oz.	360 ml

1 Tear, wash and dry the lettuces. Pick over and wash the watercress.

2 Hard-cook the quail eggs, then peel and halve them.

3 Pit and peel the avocados and cut into slices.

4 Cook the bacon slices on a sheet pan in the oven until crisp. Remove and drain well.

5 Toss the salad greens together and attractively arrange the eggs, avocado, bacon, cheese, turkey and tomatoes on top of the greens. Serve the Dijon Vinaigrette on the side.

Approximate values per serving: **Calories** 840, **Total fat** 75 g, **Saturated fat** 14 g, **Cholesterol** 305 mg, **Sodium** 870 mg, **Total carbohydrates** 11 g, **Protein** 32 g, **Vitamin A** 80%, **Vitamin C** 35%, **Calcium** 25%, **Iron** 15%, **Claims**—good source of iron; rich in fiber, vitamins A and C and calcium

♥ Good Choice   🌿 Vegetarian

Greek Salad

YIELD 6 Servings, 6 oz. (180 g) each	METHOD Tossed/Composed	
Extra virgin olive oil	4 fl. oz.	120 ml
Lemon juice	1 fl. oz.	30 ml
Red wine vinegar	2 fl. oz.	60 ml
Garlic, minced	1 tsp.	5 ml
Fresh oregano, chopped	1 Tbsp.	15 ml
Cucumbers	1 lb.	480 g
Feta	6 oz.	180 g
Olives, Kalamata or other Greek variety	12 oz.	360 g
Fresh parsley, chopped	4 Tbsp.	60 ml
Green onions, sliced	2 oz.	60 g
Pepper	TT	TT
Bibb lettuce	as needed	as needed
Tomatoes, cut into 6 wedges	4	4

1 To make the dressing, whisk together the oil, lemon juice, vinegar, garlic and oregano.

2 Peel the cucumbers and slice in half lengthwise. Remove the seeds and slice thinly.

3 Dice or crumble the feta into small pieces.

4 Combine the olives, cucumbers, parsley and green onions in a bowl and add the dressing. Toss to combine and season to taste with pepper.

5 Line plates or a platter with the bibb lettuce leaves. Add the olive-cucumber mixture and sprinkle on the feta cheese. Garnish as desired with the tomato wedges.

Approximate values per 6-oz. (180-g) serving: **Calories** 310, **Total fat** 24 g, **Saturated fat** 6 g, **Cholesterol** 25 mg, **Sodium** 1510 mg, **Total carbohydrates** 8 g, **Protein** 5 g, **Vitamin A** 25%, **Vitamin C** 25%, **Calcium** 15%, **Claims**—rich in vitamins A and C; good source of calcium

New Potato Salad with Mustard and Dill

Vegetarian

YIELD 5 lb. (2.2 kg)	METHOD Bound	
New potatoes	4 lb.	1.9 kg
Mayonnaise	4 fl. oz.	120 ml
Sour cream	4 oz.	120 g
Garlic, chopped	1½ tsp.	7 ml
Salt	TT	TT
Black pepper	1½ tsp.	7 ml
Fresh dill, chopped	2 Tbsp.	30 ml
Dijon-style mustard	1 fl. oz.	30 ml
Green bell pepper, julienne	1	1
Red bell pepper, julienne	1	1
Red onion, julienne	6 oz.	180 g
Celery, julienne	4 oz.	120 g

1 Boil the potatoes in salted water until thoroughly cooked but still firm. Chill well and cut into quarters.

2 Combine the mayonnaise, sour cream, garlic, salt, pepper, dill and mustard; mix well.

3 Combine all the ingredients and adjust the seasonings with salt and pepper.

Approximate values per 4-oz. (120-g) serving: **Calories** 110, **Total fat** 6 g, **Saturated fat** 1.5 g, **Cholesterol** 5 mg, **Sodium** 360 mg, **Total carbohydrates** 12 g, **Protein** 1 g, **Vitamin C** 25%

Potato Salad

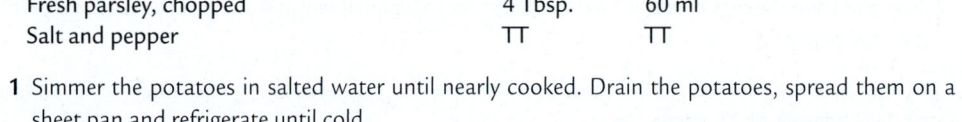

Vegetarian

YIELD 5 lb. (2.2 kg)	METHOD Bound	
Potatoes, chef	3 lb.	1.4 kg
Eggs, hard-cooked, chilled	6	6
Celery, medium dice	10 oz.	300 g
Green onions, sliced	2 oz.	60 g
Radishes, chopped coarse	4 oz.	120 g
Mayonnaise	12 fl. oz.	360 ml
Dijon-style mustard	1 oz.	30 g
Fresh parsley, chopped	4 Tbsp.	60 ml
Salt and pepper	TT	TT

1 Simmer the potatoes in salted water until nearly cooked. Drain the potatoes, spread them on a sheet pan and refrigerate until cold.

2 Peel the cold potatoes and cut into large dice.

3 Peel and chop the eggs.

4 Combine all the ingredients and adjust the seasonings with salt and pepper.

Approximate values per 4-oz. (120-g) serving: **Calories** 190, **Total fat** 14 g, **Saturated fat** 2.5 g, **Cholesterol** 65 mg, **Sodium** 410 mg, **Total carbohydrates** 13 g, **Protein** 3 g, **Vitamin C** 15%, **Claims**—good source of vitamin C

Creamy Coleslaw

YIELD 5 lb. (2.2 kg)		METHOD Bound
Mayonnaise	1 pt.	480 ml
Sour cream or crème fraîche	8 oz.	240 g
Granulated sugar	3 oz.	60 g
Cider vinegar	2 fl. oz.	60 ml
Garlic clove, minced	2	2
Green cabbage, shredded	2 lb.	960 g
Red cabbage, shredded	10 oz.	300 g
Carrot, shredded	6 oz.	180 g
Salt and white pepper	TT	TT

1 Combine the mayonnaise, sour cream or crème fraîche, sugar, vinegar and garlic in a bowl; whisk together.

2 Add the shredded cabbages and carrot to the dressing and mix well. Season to taste with salt and white pepper.

Approximate values per 4-oz. (120-g) serving: **Calories** 200, **Total fat** 19 g, **Saturated fat** 4.5 g, **Cholesterol** 20 mg, **Sodium** 340 mg, **Total carbohydrates** 8 g, **Protein** 1 g, **Vitamin A** 20%, **Vitamin C** 50%

Egg Salad

YIELD 5 lb. (2.2 kg)		METHOD Bound
Mayonnaise	12 oz.	360 g
Lemon juice	2 fl. oz.	60 ml
Yellow mustard	2 oz.	60 g
Salt	2 tsp.	10 ml
Pepper	TT	TT
Green onions, sliced, optional	2 oz.	60 g
Dill pickle, chopped, optional	4 oz.	120 g
Eggs, hard cooked, cold	40	40
Salt and pepper	TT	TT

1 Combine the mayonnaise, lemon juice, mustard, salt, pepper, green onions and pickles, if using, in a large bowl.

2 Peel and chop the eggs coarsely. Fold them into the mayonnaise mixture. Adjust the seasoning with salt and pepper.

Approximate values per 4-oz. (120-g) serving: **Calories** 270, **Total fat** 23 g, **Saturated fat** 5 g, **Cholesterol** 380 mg, **Sodium** 500 mg, **Total carbohydrates** 2 g, **Protein** 13 g

Tuna Salad

YIELD 5 lb. (2.2 kg)	METHOD Bound	
Canned tuna, water packed, chilled, drained	48 oz.	1.4 kg
Fresh parsley, chopped	2 Tbsp.	30 ml
Celery, small dice	8 oz.	240 g
Onion, small dice	4 oz.	120 g
Mayonnaise	20 oz.	600 g
Lemon juice	2 fl. oz.	60 ml
Salt	2 tsp.	10 ml
White pepper	TT	TT
Green onions, sliced, optional	1 oz.	30 g

1 Combine the ingredients in a stainless steel bowl. Stir gently until well mixed. Refrigerate immediately.

Approximate values per 4-oz. (120-g) serving: **Calories** 250, **Total fat** 22 g, **Saturated fat** 3.5 g, **Cholesterol** 35 mg, **Sodium** 580 mg, **Total carbohydrates** 1 g, **Protein** 13 g

Farro, White Bean and Cucumber Salad with Spiced Dressing

 ♥ Good Choice 🌿 Vegetarian

YIELD 6 Servings, 6 oz. (180 g) each	METHOD Bound	
Dressing:		
Garlic, minced	1 tsp.	5 ml
Fresh ginger, chopped	1 tsp.	5 ml
Pommery mustard	2 Tbsp.	30 ml
Sherry vinegar	2 fl. oz.	60 ml
Honey*	2 fl. oz.	60 ml
Cumin, ground	½ tsp.	3 ml
Cinnamon, ground	¼ tsp.	2 ml
Powdered sumac	1 Tbsp.	15 ml
Vegetable oil	4 fl. oz.	120 ml
Olive oil	4 fl. oz.	120 ml
Salt and pepper	TT	TT
Farro, cooked	12 oz.	360 g
Great Northern beans, cooked	8 oz.	240 g
Cherry tomatoes, halved	12	12
Cucumber, quartered, cut into ¼-in. (6-ml) slices	12 oz.	360 g
Chopped fresh herbs	1 Tbsp.	15 ml
Salt and pepper	TT	TT
Micro greens	as needed	as needed

1 Blend the dressing ingredients in the bowl of a blender.

2 Toss together the farro, beans, cherry tomatoes, cucumbers and chopped fresh herbs in a mixing bowl. Gently stir in approximately 4 fluid ounces (120 milliliters) of the dressing, adding more as necessary to moisten and bind the farro and vegetables. Adjust seasoning with salt and pepper as needed.

3 Arrange approximately 6 ounces (180 grams) of the salad on each plate with a sprinkling of micro greens, 1 tablespoon (15 milliliters) of reserved dressing and a garnish of powdered sumac.

*For a vegan dish, replace the honey with agave syrup.

Approximate values per 6-oz. (180-g) serving: **Calories** 500, **Total fat** 37 g, **Saturated fat** 4 g, **Cholesterol** 0 mg, **Sodium** 140 mg, **Total carbohydrates** 38 g, **Protein** 7 g, **Vitamin A** 15%, **Vitamin C** 10%, **Iron** 20%, **Claims**—no cholesterol; excellent source of dietary fiber; good source of vitamins A and C and iron

Couscous Salad

YIELD 3 lb. (1.4 kg)	METHOD Bound	
Couscous, pearl or Israeli	6 oz.	180 g
Red bell pepper, medium dice	1	1
Green bell pepper, medium dice	1	1
Cucumbers, peeled, seeded, medium dice	6 oz.	180 g
Black olives, pitted, sliced	4 oz.	120 g
Red onion, diced	6 oz.	180 g
Feta cheese, diced	2 oz.	60 g
Dressing:		
Lemon juice	3 fl. oz.	90 ml
Lemon zest, grated	2 tsp.	10 ml
Dijon-style mustard	1 Tbsp.	15 ml
Honey	1 fl. oz.	30 ml
Garlic, chopped	1 fl. oz.	30 ml
Smoked paprika	2 tsp.	10 ml
Salt	1 tsp.	5 ml
Black pepper	2 tsp.	2 ml
Vegetable oil	6 fl. oz.	180 ml

1 Steam the couscous until tender; set aside to cool.

2 Combine the couscous with the vegetables, olives and cheese.

3 Whisk together all the dressing ingredients.

4 Combine the salad ingredients with as much of the dressing as needed to moisten and flavor the couscous. Chill thoroughly before serving. Check the seasonings after chilling, adding more dressing if needed.

Approximate values per 3-oz. (30-g) serving: **Calories** 170, **Total fat** 12 g, **Saturated fat** 1.5 g, **Cholesterol** 5 mg, **Sodium** 250 mg, **Total carbohydrates** 15 g, **Protein** 2 g, **Vitamin A** 10%, **Vitamin C** 35%, **Claims**—good source of vitamin A; rich in vitamin C

Tabouli

Tabouli is one of many small plate appetizers served throughout the Middle East with drinks before dinner. It also accompanies grilled fish, meat or vegetables.

YIELD 6 Servings, 4 oz. (120 g) each	METHOD Bound	
Bulgur	4 oz.	120 g
Green onions, finely chopped	4 oz.	120 g
Fresh parsley, chopped	2 oz.	60 g
Fresh mint, chopped	1 oz.	30 g
Lemon juice	3 fl. oz.	90 ml
Salt	TT	TT
Olive oil	3 fl. oz.	90 ml
Tomatoes, seeded, medium dice	4 oz.	120 g
Pepper	TT	TT
Black olives, pitted	2 oz.	60 g
Pita bread	as needed	as needed
Butterhead lettuce, washed	as needed	as needed

1 Place the bulgur in a bowl and cover with cold water. Soak the bulgur until tender, approximately 2–4 hours. (Timing varies depending on freshness.)

2 Drain the bulgur and squeeze out all the excess water.

3 Add the green onions, parsley and mint. Season the lemon juice with salt. Beat in the olive oil, then mix into the bulgur.

4 Fold in the tomatoes. Adjust the seasoning with salt and pepper.

5 Garnish with the olives and serve with pita bread or lettuce leaves.

Approximate values per 4-oz. (120-g) serving: **Calories** 280, **Total fat** 21 g, **Saturated fat** 3 g, **Cholesterol** 0 mg, **Sodium** 280 mg, **Total carbohydrates** 17 g, **Protein** 5 g, **Vitamin A** 30%, **Vitamin C** 60%, **Iron** 70%, **Claims**—no cholesterol; good source of fiber

Good Choice   Vegan

Raw Kale and Avocado Salad with Carrots, Raisins and Lemon Dressing

YIELD 6 Servings, 8 fl. oz. (240 ml) each   **METHOD** Tossed

Kale, stems removed, chiffonade	8 oz.	240 g
Olive oil	1 fl. oz.	30 ml
Salt and pepper	TT	TT
Avocado, ripe, peeled and diced	6 oz.	180 g
Garlic, minced	1½ tsp.	7 ml
Carrots, julienned	4 oz.	120 g
Raisins	2 oz.	60 g
Lemon juice	1 fl. oz.	30 ml
Cashews, chopped coarse, or sunflower seeds	2 oz.	60 g
Lavash or flatbread	as needed for garnish	

1 Combine the kale and olive oil in a large bowl. Toss together until the kale is evenly coated with the oil. Season with salt and pepper. Stir the diced avocado and garlic into the kale, mashing and stirring until the greens are coated with the avocado.

2 Add the carrots, raisins and lemon juice. Adjust the seasonings. Garnish each serving with the cashews or sunflower seeds and lavash.

Approximate values per 8-fl.-oz. (240-ml) serving: **Calories** 200, **Total fat** 13 g, **Saturated fat** 2 g, **Cholesterol** 0 mg, **Sodium** 30 mg, **Total carbohydrates** 19 g, **Protein** 4 g, **Vitamin A** 140%, **Vitamin C** 90%, **Claims**—low sodium; good source of fiber; high in vitamins A and C

Panzanella
(Italian Bread Salad)

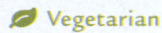 Vegetarian

YIELD 6 Servings, 6 oz. (180 g) each	METHOD Tossed	
Crusty bread, cut into 1-in. (2.5-cm) cubes	1 lb.	480 g
Olive oil	4 fl. oz.	120 ml
Mushrooms, sliced	4 oz.	120 g
Green onions, sliced	2 oz.	60 g
Garlic, chopped	2 tsp.	10 ml
Tomatoes, diced	12 oz.	360 g
Fresh basil, chopped	1 oz.	30 g
Fresh parsley, chopped	½ oz.	15 g
Capers	1 oz.	30 g
Golden raisins	2 oz.	60 g
Dressing:		
Red wine vinegar	3 fl. oz.	90 ml
Salt and black pepper	TT	TT
Garlic, chopped	1 tsp.	5 ml
Olive oil	3 fl. oz.	90 ml
Fresh parsley, chopped	as needed for garnish	
Fresh basil leaves	as needed for garnish	
Parmesan, grated	as needed for garnish	

1 Toss the bread cubes with 2 fluid ounces (60 milliliters) of olive oil. Spread the bread cubes out onto a full-sheet pan and bake at 400°F (200°C) for 10 minutes. Stir the bread cubes then return them to the oven. Bake until lightly browned.

2 Transfer the bread cubes to a large bowl.

3 Sauté the mushrooms, green onions and garlic in the remaining oil until softened. Toss them with the toasted bread cubes.

4 Stir in the tomatoes, basil, parsley, capers and raisins.

5 Whisk together the ingredients for the dressing.

6 Add the dressing to the bread cubes. Toss the salad to coat the ingredients thoroughly with the dressing. Adjust the seasonings with salt and pepper. Allow the salad to rest for at least 30 minutes before serving to allow the bread cubes to absorb the dressing and soften slightly.

7 Serve at room temperature, garnished with chopped parsley, basil leaves and grated Parmesan.

Approximate values per 6-oz. (180-g) serving: **Calories** 240, **Total fat** 16 g, **Saturated fat** 2.5 g, **Cholesterol** 0 mg, **Sodium** 260 mg, **Total carbohydrates** 22 g, **Protein** 4 g, **Vitamin A** 20%, **Vitamin C** 25%

Cranberry Orange Gelatin Salad

YIELD 1 Mold, 25 Servings,
3 oz. (90 g) each

METHOD Gelatin

Raspberry flavored gelatin	6 oz.	180 g
Water, boiling	1 qt.	960 ml
Fresh cranberries	1 lb.	480 g
Sugar	7 oz.	210 g
Celery, fine dice	4 oz.	120 g
Grated orange zest	2 Tbsp.	30 ml
Seedless red grapes, halved	8 oz.	240 g
Chopped pecans	2 oz.	60 g

1 Dissolve the flavored gelatin in the boiling water in a large bowl.

2 Chill the mixture in the refrigerator until slightly set, for 30 minutes.

3 Grind the cranberries and the sugar in the bowl of a food processor until fine.

4 Stir the cranberry mixture and remaining ingredients into the gelatin. Pour into a 2-quart (2-liter) tube pan or other mold.

5 Refrigerate until firm, for at least 3 hours.

6 For service, dip the mold in a hot water bath for a few seconds. Dry the bottom of the mold and invert it onto a sheet tray or serving platter. Lift the mold from the salad. Chill the unmolded salad briefly, then slice or decorate as desired for service.

Approximate values per 3-oz. (90-ml) serving: **Calories** 90, **Total fat** 15 g, **Saturated fat** g, **Cholesterol** 0 mg, **Sodium** 30 mg, **Total carbohydrates** 18 g, **Protein** 1 g

- ▶ identify a variety of fruits
- ▶ purchase appropriate fruits for various needs
- ▶ store fruits properly
- ▶ describe how fruits are preserved
- ▶ prepare fruits for cooking or service
- ▶ apply various cooking methods to fruits

Botanically, a fruit is an organ that develops from the ovary of a flowering plant and contains one or more seeds. Culinarily, a fruit is the perfect snack food, the basis of a dessert, colorful sauce or soup or an accompaniment to meat, fish, shellfish or poultry. No food group offers a greater variety of colors, flavors and textures than fruit.

This chapter identifies many of the fruits typically used by food service operations. It then addresses general considerations in purchasing fresh and preserved fruits. A discussion follows about some of the cooking methods presented in Chapter 10, Principles of Cooking, as they apply to fruits. Recipes in which fruit is the primary ingredient are presented at the chapter's end.

IDENTIFYING FRUITS

This book presents fruits according to the ways most people view them and use them, rather than by rigid botanical classifications. Fruits are divided here into eight categories: berries, citrus, exotics, grapes, melons, pomes, stone fruits and tropicals, according to either their shape, seed structure or natural habitat. Botanically, tomatoes, beans, eggplant, capsicum peppers and other produce are fruits. But in ordinary thinking, they are not; they are vegetables and are discussed in Chapter 22, Vegetables.

A fruit may have several names, varying from region to region or on a purveyor's whim. Botanists are also constantly reclassifying items to fit new findings. The names we use in this chapter follow generally accepted custom and usage.

Berries

Berries are small, juicy fruits that grow on vines and bushes worldwide. Berries are characterized by thin skins and many tiny seeds that are often so small they go unnoticed. Some of the fruits discussed in this section do not fit the botanical definition (e.g., raspberries and strawberries) of berries and we cover some fruits that are classified as berries botanically (e.g., bananas and grapes) elsewhere in the chapter.

Berries may be eaten plain or used in everything from beer to bread, soup to sorbet. They make especially fine jams and compotes. Berries must be fully **ripened** on the vine, as they will not ripen further after harvesting. Select berries that are plump and fully colored. Avoid juice-stained containers and berries with whitish-gray or black spots of mold. All berries should be refrigerated and used promptly. Do not wash berries until just before they are needed, as washing removes some of their aroma and softens them.

ripe fully grown and developed; a ripe fruit's flavor, texture and appearance are at their peak, and the fruit is ready to use as food

Blackberries

Blackberries are similar to raspberries, but are larger and shinier, with a deep purple to black color. Thorny blackberry vines are readily found in the wild; commercial production is limited. Loganberries, marionberries, olallieberries and boysenberries are blackberry hybrids.

Blueberries

Blueberries (Fr. *myrtilles*) are small and firm, with a true blue to almost black skin and a juicy, light gray-blue interior. Cultivated berries (high-bush varieties) tend to be larger than wild (low-bush) ones. Blueberries are native to North America and are grown commercially from Maine to Oregon and along the Atlantic seaboard.

Cranberries

Cranberries, another native North American food, are tart, firm fruit with a mottled red skin. They grow on low vines in cultivated bogs (swamps) throughout Massachusetts,

Blackberries

Blueberries

Oregon, Washington State, Wisconsin and New Jersey. Rarely eaten raw, they are made into sauce or relish or are used in breads, pies or pastries. Cranberries are available frozen or made into a jelly-type sauce and canned. Color does not indicate ripeness. Cranberries should be picked over before cooking and those that are soft or bruised should be discarded.

Cranberries

Currants

Currants are tiny, tart fruits that grow on shrubs in grapelike clusters. The most common currants are a beautiful, almost translucent red, but black and golden (or white) varieties also exist. All varieties are used for jams, jellies and sauces, and black currants are made into a liqueur, crème de cassis. Although rarely grown in the United States, currants are very popular and widely available in Europe, with a peak season during the late summer. (The dried fruits called currants are not produced from these berries; they are a special variety of dried grapes.)

White currants

Red currants

Raspberries

Raspberries (Fr. *framboises*) are perhaps the most delicate of all fruits. They have a tart flavor and velvety texture. Red raspberries are the most common, although black, purple and golden berries are available in some markets. When ripe, the berry pulls away easily from its white core, leaving the characteristic hollow center. Because they can be easily crushed and are susceptible to mold, most of the raspberries grown are marketed frozen. Raspberries grow on thorny vines in cool climates from Washington State to western New York and are imported from New Zealand and South America.

Raspberries

Strawberries

Strawberries (Fr. *fraises*) are brilliant red, heart-shaped fruits that grow on vines. The strawberry plant is actually a perennial herb; the berry's flesh is covered by tiny black seeds called achenes, which are the plant's true fruits. Select berries with a good red color and intact green leafy hull. (The hulls can be easily removed with a paring knife.) Avoid berries with soft or brown spots. Huge berries may be lovely to look at, but they often have hollow centers and little flavor or juice.

The tiny wild or Alpine strawberries, known by their French name, *fraises des bois*, have a particularly intense flavor and aroma. They are not widely available in the United States.

Strawberries

Procedure for Fanning Strawberries

Cut thin parallel slices into the base of the strawberry without cutting through the stem. Press lightly to fan out the strawberry, exposing the cut slices.

Citrus

Citrus fruits include lemons, limes, grapefruits, tangerines, kumquats, oranges and several hybrids. They are characterized by a thick rind, most of which is a bitter white pith (albedo) with a thin exterior layer of colored skin known as the **zest**. Their flesh is segmented and juicy. Citrus fruits are acidic, with a strong aroma; their flavors vary from bitter to tart to sweet.

Citrus fruits grow on trees and shrubs in tropical and subtropical climates worldwide. All citrus fruits are fully ripened on the tree and will not ripen further after harvesting. They should be refrigerated for longest storage.

Select fruits that feel heavy and have thin, smooth skins. Avoid those with large blemishes or moist spots.

zest the colored outer portion of the rind of citrus fruit; contains the oil that provides flavor and aroma

White grapefruits

Grapefruits

Grapefruits (Fr. *pamplemousses*) are large and round with a yellow skin, thick rind and tart flesh. They are an 18th-century hybrid of the orange and pummelo (a large, coarse fruit used mostly in Middle and Far Eastern cuisines). Two varieties of grapefruit are widely available all year: white-fleshed and pink- or ruby-fleshed. White grapefruits produce the finest juice, although pink grapefruits are sweeter. Fresh grapefruits are best eaten raw or topped with brown sugar and lightly broiled.

Red grapefruits

Kumquats

Kumquats are very small, oval-shaped, orange-colored fruits with a soft, sweet skin and slightly bitter flesh. They are eaten whole, either raw or preserved in syrup or jam.

Kumquats

Lemons

The most commonly used citrus fruits, lemons (Fr. *citrons*), are oval-shaped, bright yellow fruits with a strongly acidic flavor that makes them unpleasant to eat raw but perfect for flavoring desserts and confections. Lemon juice is also widely used in sauces, especially for fish, shellfish and poultry. Lemon zest is candied or used as garnish. The round, smooth-skinned and juicy Meyer lemon has a sweet, less acidic flavor and strong aroma. It may be used in place of common lemons, especially in desserts and sauces where lemon is the dominant flavor.

Lemons

Limes

Limes (Fr. *limons*) are small fruits with thin skins ranging from yellow-green to dark green. Limes are too tart to eat raw and are often substituted for lemons in prepared dishes. They are also juiced or used in cocktails, curries or desserts. Lime zest can be grated and used to give color and flavor to a variety of dishes. The **key lime** is a small tart lime variety native to South Florida used to make key lime pie.

Key limes

Limes

Oranges

Oranges (Sp. *naranjas*) are round fruits with a juicy, orange-colored flesh and a thin, orange skin. They can be either sweet or bitter.

Valencia oranges and **navel oranges** (a seedless variety) are the most popular sweet oranges. They can be juiced for beverages or sauces, and the flesh may be eaten raw, added to salads, cooked in desserts or used as a garnish. Orange zest may be grated or julienned for sauces or garnish.

Blood oranges are also sweet but are small, with a rough, reddish skin. Their flesh is streaked with a blood-red color. Blood oranges are available primarily during the

Valencia oranges

Navel oranges

winter months and are eaten raw, juiced or used in salads or sauces. When selecting sweet oranges, look for fruits that feel plump and heavy, with unblemished skin. The color of the skin depends on weather conditions; a green rind does not affect the flavor of the flesh.

Bitter oranges include the **Seville** and **bergamot**. They are used primarily for the essential oils found in their zest. Oil of bergamot gives Earl Grey tea its distinctive flavor; oil of Seville is essential to curaçao, Grand Marnier and orange flower water. Seville oranges are also used in marmalades and sauces for meats and poultry.

Blood oranges

Mandarin Oranges

Mandarin oranges are a group of small citrus characterized by their thin loose peels, intense flavor and perishability. Clementines, satsuma mandarins and **tangerines** are among the most popular mandarin varieties available. They are small with dark orange to red-orange skin. Their rind is loose and easily removed to reveal sweet, juicy, aromatic segments, which may or may not contain seeds. Mandarin oranges are most often eaten fresh in-hand and uncooked, but are available canned.

Tangerines

Tangelos are a hybrid of tangerines and grapefruits. They are the size of a medium orange; they have a bulbous stem end and few to no seeds.

Procedure for Segmenting Citrus Fruits

Citrus segments, known as **supremes**, are made by first carefully cutting off the entire peel (including the bitter white pith) in even slices.

Individual segments are then removed by gently cutting alongside each membrane.

Hybrids and Varieties

A number of fruits are extremely responsive to selective breeding and crossbreeding and have been experimented with by botanists and growers since at least the time of ancient Rome. Two distinct products are recognized: hybrids and varieties. **Hybrids** result from crossbreeding fruits from different species that are genetically unalike. The result is a unique product. Citrus is particularly responsive to hybridization; for example, **tangelos** result from a cross between tangerines and grapefruits. **Varieties** result from breeding fruits of the same species that have different qualities or characteristics. Breeding two varieties of peaches, for instance, produces a third variety with the best qualities of both parents. **Nectarines** are a peach variety with smooth skin that are easier to eat than fuzzy peach varieties.

Procedure for Zesting Citrus Fruits

A five-hole zester, left, or a rasp grater, right, are used to remove paper-thin strips of the colored rind.

Procedure for Cutting Citrus Peels

Large strips of citrus zest may be used as a garnish or to flavor soups or sauces.

Exotic Fruits

Improved transportation has led to the increasing availability (although sporadic in some areas) of exotic or unusual fresh fruits such as figs, persimmons, pomegranates, rhubarb and star fruits. Other exotic fruits, such as breadfruit, durian, feijoa, loquat and prickly pear are still available only on a limited basis from specialty purveyors and are not discussed here.

Figs

Calimyrna figs

Figs (Fr. *figues*) are the fruit of ficus trees. They are small, soft, pear-shaped fruits with an intensely sweet flavor and rich, moist texture made crunchy by a multitude of tiny seeds. Fresh figs can be sliced and served in salads or with cured meats such as prosciutto. Figs can also be baked, poached or used in jams, preserves or compotes.

Dark-skinned figs, known as Mission figs, are a variety originally planted at Pacific Coast missions during the 18th century. They have a thin skin and small seeds and are available fresh, canned or dried. White-skinned figs grown commercially include the White Adriatic, used principally for drying and baking, and the all-purpose Kadota. The most important domestic fig variety, however, is the **Calimyrna fig**. These large figs have a rich yellow color and large nutty seeds. Fresh Calimyrna figs are the finest for eating out of hand; they are also available dried. For the best flavor, figs should be fully ripened on the tree. Unfortunately fully ripened figs are very delicate and difficult to transport.

Gooseberries

Cape gooseberries

Several varieties of gooseberry (Fr. *groseille maquereau*) are cultivated for culinary purposes. One well-known variety is the European gooseberry, a member of the currant family that grows on spiny bushes in cool, moist regions of the Northern Hemisphere. Its berries can be relatively large, like small plums, but are usually less than 1 inch (2.5 centimeters) in diameter. The skin, which is firm and smooth or only slightly hairy, can be green, white (actually gray-green), yellow or red. The tart berries contain many tiny seeds. They are eaten fresh or used for jellies, preserves, tarts and other desserts or as a traditional accompaniment to rich or fatty dishes, such as goose and mackerel. North American gooseberry varieties are smaller, perfectly round, and pink to deep red at maturity. Although more prolific, these varietals lack flavor and are generally considered inferior to European gooseberries.

Cape gooseberries, also known as physalis, ground cherries or poha, are unrelated to European and American gooseberries. Native to Peru, cape gooseberries became popular during the 19th century along the African Cape of Good Hope, for which they are named. Australia and New Zealand are currently the largest producers. Cape gooseberries are covered with a paper-thin husk or calyx. About the size of cherries, they have a waxy, bright orange skin and many tiny seeds. Their flavor is similar to coconut and oranges, but tarter. Cape gooseberries may be eaten raw, made into jam or used in desserts. Fresh, they are an especially striking garnish, especially when dipped in chocolate.

Guava

Guava [GWAH-vah] are small, oval or pear-shaped fruits with a strong fragrance and a mild, slightly grainy flesh. They are excellent in jams and preserves, and guava juice is available plain or blended with other tropical fruit juices. Guava paste, a thick, sliceable gel, is a popular treat throughout Central America and the Caribbean. Guava, which will ripen if stored at room temperature, is best when slightly soft and fully ripened.

Guava

Lychees

The lychee [LEE-chee], also spelled *litchi* or *leechee*, is the fruit of a large tree native to southern China and Southeast Asia. The fruit, which grows in clusters, is oval to round, red and about 1 inch (2.5 centimeters) in diameter. The tough outer skin encloses juicy, white, almost translucent flesh and one large seed. Neither the skin nor the seed is edible. The fruit travels well and is now cultivated in Florida and Hawaii, so supplies are relatively stable. Lychees are eaten fresh out of hand or juiced and are widely available canned or dried. Fresh lychees are mild but sweet with a pleasant perfume.

Lychees

Mangosteens

The mangosteen, another native of Southeast Asia, is cultivated in Java, Sumatra and the Philippines. Mangosteens (no relation to mangos) are the size of small oranges and have flattened ends. They have a thick, hard, deep reddish-purple rind with hard white petal-shaped protrusions at the stem end. The interior flesh is snow-white and segmented, looking something like a mandarin orange. The texture is juicy and delicate with a slightly astringent flavor. Because the fruit must ripen on the tree and keeps only a short time, it is rarely found fresh except in outdoor local markets. Mangosteens are usually eaten fresh, although canned fruit and juice is available.

Mangosteens

Persimmons

Persimmons, sometimes referred to as kaki or Sharon fruits, are a bright orange, acorn-shaped fruit, roughly the same size as apples, with glossy skin and large papery blossoms. The flesh is bright orange and jellylike, with a mild but rich flavor similar to honey and plums. Persimmons should be peeled before use; any seeds should be discarded. Select bright orange fruits and refrigerate only after they are completely ripe. When ripe, persimmons are very soft and the skin has an almost translucent appearance.

Ripe persimmons are delicious eaten raw; halved and topped with cream or soft cheese; or peeled, sliced and added to fruit salads. Persimmon bread, muffins, cakes and pies are also popular. Underripe persimmons are almost inedible, however. They are strongly tannic with a chalky or cottony texture. Persimmons are tree fruits grown in subtropical areas worldwide, although the Asian varieties—now grown in California—are the most common.

Persimmons

Pomegranates

An ancient fruit native to Persia (now Iran), pomegranates [POM-uh-gran-uhtz] have long been a subject of poetry and a symbol of fertility. Pomegranates are round, about the size of large oranges, with pronounced calyx. The skin forms a hard shell with a pinkish-red color. The interior is filled with hundreds of small, red seeds (which are, botanically, the actual fruits) surrounded by juicy, red pulp. An inedible yellow membrane separates the seeds into compartments. Pomegranates are sweet-sour, and the seeds are pleasantly crunchy. The bright-red seeds make an attractive garnish. Pomegranate juice is a popular beverage in Mediterranean cuisines, and grenadine syrup is made from concentrated pomegranate juice.

Select heavy fruits that are not rock-hard, cracked or heavily bruised. Whole pomegranates can be refrigerated for several weeks.

Pomegranates

Dragon fruit

Rhubarb

Star fruits

Dragon Fruit

Dragon fruit are any of several species of the *Cactaceae* family native to South America now widely grown in tropical climates. About the size of eggplants with a flavor that resembles a kiwi or melon, the fruit is eaten raw and made into a refreshing juice. Dragon fruit are easily peeled with a paring knife before serving.

Rambutans

Rambutans [ram-BOOT-enz], the fruit of a tree in the soapberry family, are closely related to lychees. Native to Malaysia, they are now cultivated throughout Southeast Asia. The bright-red, oval fruit is about the size of a small hen's egg and is covered with long, soft spines. The interior has a white, lightly acidic pulp. Rambutans darken with age, so select brightly colored fruit with soft, fleshy spines. Rambutans are eaten fresh and used in preserves and ice cream; they are also available canned.

Rambutans

Rhubarb

Although botanically a vegetable, rhubarb [ROO-barb] is most often prepared as a fruit. It is a perennial plant that grows well in temperate and cold climates. Only the pinkish-red stems are edible; the leaves contain high amounts of oxalic acid, which is toxic.

Rhubarb stems are extremely acidic, requiring the addition of large amounts of sugar to create the desired sweet-sour taste. Cinnamon, ginger, orange and strawberry are particularly compatible with rhubarb. It is excellent for pies, cobblers, preserves or stewing. Young, tender stalks of rhubarb do not need to be peeled. When cooked, rhubarb becomes very soft and turns a beautiful light-pink color.

Fresh rhubarb is sold as whole stalks, with the leaves removed. Select crisp, unblemished stalks. Frozen rhubarb pieces are readily available and work well for pies, tarts or jams.

Star Fruits

Star fruits, also known as carambola, are oval, up to 5 inches (12.5 centimeters) long, with five prominent ribs or wings running their length. A cross-section cut is shaped like a star. The edible skin is a waxy orange-yellow; it covers a dry, paler yellow flesh. The flavor is similar to that of plums, sweet but bland. Star fruits do not need to be peeled or seeded. They are most often sliced unpeeled and added to fruit salad or used as a garnish. Unripe fruits can be cooked in stews or chutneys.

Color and aroma are the best indicators of ripeness. Star fruits should be a deep golden-yellow, and there should be brown along the edge of the ribs. The aroma should be full and floral. Green fruits can be kept at room temperature to ripen, then refrigerated for up to 2 weeks. Star fruits are cultivated in Hawaii, Florida and California, though some are still imported from the Caribbean.

Yuzu

Yuzu [YOO-zoo] is a sour citrus fruit from Japan. Its aromatic rind is used as a garnish and flavor enhancer. Tart yuzu juice is used by pastry chefs in confections and creams. Although the fresh fruit is rarely available in the United States, both the bottled juice and dried rind are available from specialty producers.

Grapes

Grapes (Fr. *raisins*; Sp. *uvas*) are the single largest fruit crop in the world, due to their use in wine making. This section, however, discusses only table grapes, those grown for eating. Grapes are berries that grow on vines in large clusters. California is among the world's larger producers, with more than a dozen varieties grown for table use. Grapes are classified by color as white (which are actually green) or black (which are actually red). White grapes are generally blander than black ones, with a thinner skin and firmer flesh.

The grape's color and most of its flavor are found in the skin. Grapes are usually eaten raw, either alone or in fruit salads. They are also used as a garnish or accompaniment to desserts and cheeses. Dried grapes are known as **raisins** (Fr. *raisins sec*; dried Thompson Seedless or muscat grapes), **currants** (dried Black Corinth grapes and labeled Zante currants) or **sultanas** (dried sultana grapes).

Grapes are available all year because the many varieties have different harvesting schedules. Look for firm, unblemished fruits that are firmly attached to the stem. A surface bloom or dusty appearance is caused by yeasts and indicates recent harvesting. Wrinkled grapes or those with brown spots around the stem are past their prime. All grapes should be rinsed and drained before use.

Red Flame Grapes

Red Flame grapes are seedless California hybrid grapes. They are large and round with a slightly tart flavor and variegated red color.

Red Flame grapes

Thompson Seedless Grapes

The most commercially important table grapes are a variety known as Thompson Seedless, which are pale green with a crisp texture and sweet flavor. Many are dried in the hot desert sun of California's San Joaquin Valley to produce dark raisins. For golden raisins, Thompson Seedless grapes are treated with sulfur dioxide to prevent browning, then dried mechanically.

Other Table Grapes

Of the table grapes containing seeds, the most important varieties are the Concord, Ribier and Emperor. These varieties range from light red to deep black. **Concord grapes**, one of the few grape varieties native to the New World, are especially important for making juices and jellies.

Virtually all the fine wine made in the world comes from varieties of a single grape species, *Vitis vinifera*. It is grown in the United States, Europe, South Africa, South America, the Middle East, Australia and wherever fine wine is made. The variety of grapes used in any given wine determines the wine's character, which is discussed in Chapter 7, Flavor and Flavorings.

Thompson Seedless grapes

Melons

Like pumpkins and cucumbers, melons are members of the gourd family (*Cucurbitaceae*). The dozens of melon varieties can be divided into two general types: sweet (or dessert) melons and watermelons. Sweet melons have a tan, green or yellow netted or furrowed rind and dense, fragrant flesh. Watermelon has a thick, dark green rind surrounding crisp, watery flesh.

Melons are almost 90 percent water, so cooking destroys their texture, quickly turning the flesh to mush. Most melons are served simply sliced, perhaps with a bit of lemon or lime juice. Melons also blend well in fruit salads or with rich, cured meats such as prosciutto. Melons may be puréed and made into sorbet or chilled, uncooked soup.

Although they will continue to soften once picked, melons do not develop additional sweetness after harvest and should be vine-ripened. A ripe melon should have a strong aroma and yield slightly and spring back when pressed at the blossom end (opposite the stem). Avoid melons that are very soft or feel damp at the stem end. Ripe melons may be stored in the refrigerator, although the flavor is better at room temperature. Slightly underripe melons can be stored at room temperature to allow flavor and aroma to develop.

Concord grapes

Cantaloupes

Cantaloupes

American cantaloupes, which are actually muskmelons, have a thick, yellow-green netted rind; a sweet, moist, orange flesh and a strong aroma. (European cantaloupes are more craggy and furrowed in appearance.) As with all sweet melons, the many small seeds are found in a central cavity. Cantaloupes are excellent for eating alone and are especially good with ham or rich meats.

Avoid cantaloupes with the pronounced yellow color or moldy aroma that indicates overripeness.

Casaba Melons

The casaba melon is a teardrop-shaped sweet melon, used like a cantaloupe. It has a coarse, yellow skin and a thick, ridged rind; its flesh is creamy-white to yellow. Casaba melons do not have an aroma. Look for an intense golden skin color and the absence of dark or moist patches.

Casaba melons

Crenshaw melons

Crenshaw Melons

Crenshaw (or cranshaw) melons have a mottled, green-yellow, ridged rind and orange-pink flesh. They are large, pear-shaped, sweet melons with a strong aroma. The flesh has a rich, spicy flavor and may be used like cantaloupe.

Honeydew Melons

Honeydew melons are large, oval, sweet melons with a smooth rind that ranges from white to pale green. Although honeydew flesh is generally pale green, with a mild, sweet flavor, pink- or gold-fleshed honeydews are also available. Like casaba melons, honeydew melons have little to no aroma.

Green honeydews

Gold honeydews

Watermelons

Watermelons are large (up to 30 pounds or 13.5 kilograms) round or oval-shaped melons with a thick rind. The skin may be solid green, green-striped or mottled with white. The flesh is crisp and extremely juicy with small, hard, black seeds throughout. Seedless hybrids are available. Most watermelons have pink to red flesh, although golden-fleshed varieties are becoming more common. Watermelons are of a different genus from the sweet melons described earlier. They are native to tropical Africa and are now grown commercially in Texas and several southern states.

Watermelon

Gold watermelons

Pomes

Pomes are tree fruits with thin skin and firm flesh surrounding a central core containing many small seeds called **pips** or carpels. Pomes include apples, pears and quince.

Apples

Apples (Fr. *pommes*), perhaps the most common and commonly appreciated of all fruits, grow on trees in temperate zones worldwide. They are popular because of their convenience, flavor, variety and availability. Apples can be eaten raw out of hand, or they can be used in a wide variety of cooked or baked dishes. They can be incorporated in breads, desserts or vegetable dishes and go well with game, pork and poultry. Classic dishes prepared with apples are often referred to as *à la Normande*. Apple juice (cider) can be made into alcoholic and nonalcoholic beverages and cider vinegar.

Of the hundreds of known apple varieties, only 20 or so are commercially significant in the United States. Several varieties and their characteristics are noted in Table 26.1. Most apples have a moist, creamy-white flesh with a thin skin of yellow, green or red. They range in flavor from very sweet to very tart, with an equally broad range of textures, from firm and crisp to soft and mealy.

In Europe apples are divided into distinct cooking and eating varieties. Cooking varieties are those that disintegrate to a purée when cooked. American varieties are less rigidly classified. Nevertheless not all apples are appropriate for all types of cooking. Firm apples that retain their shape better during cooking are the best choices when slices or appearance are important. Apple varieties with a higher **malic acid** content break down easily, making them more appropriate for applesauce or juicing. Any type of apples may be eaten out of hand, depending on personal preference.

Although not native to North America, apples are now grown commercially in 32 states, with Washington, New York and Michigan leading in production. Apples are harvested when still slightly underripe, then stored in a controlled atmosphere (in which temperature and oxygen are greatly reduced) for extended periods until ready for sale.

When selecting apples, look for smooth, unbroken skins and firm fruits, without soft spots or bruises. Badly bruised or rotting apples should be discarded immediately because they emit ethylene gas that speeds spoilage of nearby fruits. (Remember the saying that "one bad apple spoils the barrel.") Store apples chilled for up to 6 weeks. Apple peels (the skin) may be eaten or removed as desired, but all peeled and unpeeled apples should be washed just before use to remove pesticides and any wax that was applied to improve appearance. Apple slices can be frozen (often with sugar or citric acid added to slow spoilage) or dried.

Rome   Red Delicious

Granny Smith   Golden Delicious

McIntosh

Gala

APPLE VARIETIES				TABLE 26.1
VARIETY	SKIN COLOR	FLAVOR	TEXTURE	USE
Fiji	Yellow-green with red highlights	Sweet-spicy	Crisp	Out of hand, salads
Gala	Yellow-orange with red stripes	Sweet	Crisp	Out of hand, salads, sauce
Golden Delicious	Glossy, greenish-gold	Sweet	Semifirm	Tarts, with cheese, salads
Granny Smith	Bright green	Tart	Firm and crisp	Out of hand, tarts
Honeycrisp	Bright red and green mottled	Sweet-tart	Firm and crisp	Out of hand, all-purpose
Jonathan	Deep red	Tart to acidic	Tender	Out of hand, all-purpose
McIntosh	Red with green background	Tart to acidic	Soft	Applesauce, closed pies
Pippin (Newton)	Greenish-yellow	Tart	Semifirm	Out of hand, pies, baking
Red Delicious	Deep red	Sweet but bland	Soft to mealy	Out of hand
Rome	Red	Sweet-tart	Firm	Baking, pies, sauces
Winesap	Dark red with streaks	Tangy	Crisp	Baking, cider, all-purpose

Procedure for Coring Apples

❶ Remove the core from a whole apple with an apple corer by inserting the corer from the stem end and pushing out the cylinder containing the core and seeds.

❷ Alternatively cut an apple into quarters, then use a paring knife to cut away the core and seeds.

Pears

Pears (Fr. *poires*) are an ancient tree fruit grown in temperate areas throughout the world. Most of the pears marketed in the United States are grown in California, Washington and Oregon. Although thousands of pear varieties have been identified, only a dozen or so are commercially significant. Several varieties and their characteristics are noted in Table 26.2. Pear varieties vary widely in size, color and flavor. They are most often eaten out of hand but can be baked or poached. Pears are delicious with cheese, especially blue cheeses, and can be used in fruit salads, compotes or preserves.

Asian pears, also known as Chinese pears or apple-pears, are a different species than common pears. They have the moist, sweet flavor of a pear and the round shape and crisp texture of an apple. They are becoming increasingly popular in the United States, particularly the Twentieth Century or Nijisseiki varieties.

When selecting pears, look for fruits with smooth, unbroken skin and intact stems. Pears do not ripen properly on the tree, so they are picked while still firm and should be allowed to soften before use. Underripe pears may be left at room temperature to ripen. A properly ripened pear has a good fragrance and yields to gentle pressure at the stem end. Pears can be prepared or stored in the same ways as apples.

Anjou

Asian pears

Red d'Anjou

Bosc

Bartlett

PEAR VARIETIES				TABLE 26.2
VARIETY	APPEARANCE	FLAVOR	TEXTURE	USE
Anjou (Beurre d'Anjou)	Greenish-yellow skin; egg-shaped with short neck; red variety also available	Sweet, juicy	Firm, keep well	Out of hand, poaching
Bartlett (Williams)	Thin, yellow skin; bell-shaped; red variety also available	Very sweet, buttery, juicy	Tender	Out of hand, canning, salads
Bosc	Golden-brown skin; long, tapered neck	Buttery	Dry, hold shape well	Poaching, baking
Comice	Yellow-green skin; large; chubby	Sweet, juicy	Smooth	Out of hand
Sekel	Brown to yellow skin; tiny	Spicy	Very firm, grainy	Poaching, pickling

Quince

Common quince [kwince; Fr. *coing*] resemble large, lumpy, yellow pears. Their flesh is hard, with many pips or seeds, and they have a wonderful fragrance. Too astringent to eat raw, quince develop a sweet flavor and pink color when cooked with sugar. Quince are used in meat stews, jellies, marmalades and pies. They have a high **pectin** content and may be added to other fruit jams or preserves to encourage gelling.

Quince

pectin a gelatin-like carbohydrate obtained from certain fruits; used to thicken jams and jellies

Select firm fruits with a uniform yellow color. Small blemishes may be cut away before cooking. Quince will keep for up to a month under refrigeration.

Stone Fruits

Stone fruits, also known as **drupes**, include apricots, cherries, nectarines, peaches and plums. They are characterized by a thin skin, soft flesh and single, woody stones or pits. Although most originated in China, the shrubs and trees that produce stone fruits are now grown in temperate climates worldwide.

The domestic varieties of stone fruits are in season from late spring through summer. They tend to be fragile fruits, are easily bruised and difficult to transport, and have a short shelf life. Do not wash stone fruits until ready to use, as moisture can cause deterioration. Stone fruits are excellent dried and are often used to make liqueurs and brandies. (The kernel inside the pits of many stone fruits contains amygdalin, a compound that has a bitter almond flavor. Eating the raw kernel can cause digestive discomfort or more serious side effects and should be avoided. When cooked it is harmless and can add flavor to jams and creams.)

Apricots

Apricots (Fr. *abricots*) are small, round stone fruits with velvety skin. They vary in color from deep yellow to vivid orange. The juicy, orange flesh of apricots surrounds a dark, almond-shaped pit. Apricots can be eaten out of hand, poached, stewed, baked or candied. They are often used in fruit compotes or savory sauces for meat or poultry and are also popular in quick breads and fruit tarts or puréed for dessert sauces, jams, custards or mousses.

Apricots

Apricots have a short season and do not travel well. Select apricots that are well shaped, plump and fairly firm. Avoid greenish-yellow or mushy fruit. Fresh apricots last for several days under refrigeration, but their flavor is best at room temperature. If fresh fruits are unavailable, canned apricots are usually an acceptable substitute. Dried apricots and apricot juice (known as nectar) are readily available.

Cherries

From the northern states, particularly Washington, Oregon, Michigan and New York, come the two most important types of cherry: the sweet cherry and the sour (or tart) cherry.

Rainier cherries

Sweet cherries (Fr. *cerises*) are round to heart-shaped, about 1 inch (2.5 centimeters) in diameter, with skin that ranges from yellow to deep red to nearly black. The flesh, which is sweet and juicy, may vary from yellow to dark red. The most common and popular sweet cherries are the dark-red **Bing cherries**. Yellow-red Royal Ann and **Rainier cherries** are also available in some areas.

Sweet cherries are marketed fresh, made into maraschino cherries or candied for use in baked goods. Cherries do not ripen further after harvesting. Select fruits that are firm and plump with a green stem still attached. There should not be any brown spots around the stem. A dry or brown stem indicates that the cherry is less than fresh. Once the stem is removed, the cherry will deteriorate rapidly. Store fresh cherries in the refrigerator and do not wash them until ready to use.

Sour cherries are light to dark red and are so acidic they are rarely eaten uncooked. The most common sour cherries are the Montmorency and Morello. Most sour cherries are canned or frozen, or cooked with sugar and starch (usually cornstarch or tapioca) and sold as prepared pastry and pie fillings. Both sweet and sour cherries are available dried.

Bing cherries

Procedure for Pitting Cherries

Remove the stem and place the cherry in the pitter with the indentation facing up. Squeeze the handles together to force out the pit.

Peaches and Nectarines

Peaches (Fr. *pêches*) are round fruits with a juicy, sweet flesh. Nectarines are a variety of peach. The main difference between peaches and nectarines are their skins. Peaches have a thin skin covered with fuzz, whereas nectarines have a thin, smooth skin. The flesh of either fruit ranges from white to pale orange. Although their flavors are somewhat different, they may be substituted for each other in most recipes.

Peaches and nectarines are excellent for eating out of hand or in dessert tarts or pastries. They are also used in jams, chutneys, preserves and savory relishes, having a particular affinity for Asian and Indian dishes. Although the skin is edible, peaches are generally peeled before being used. (Peaches are easily peeled if blanched first.)

Peaches and nectarines are either **freestones** or **clingstones**. In freestones, the flesh separates easily from the stone; freestone fruits are commonly eaten out of hand. The flesh of clingstones adheres firmly to the stone; they hold their shape better when cooked and are the type most often canned.

Select fruits with a good aroma; an overall creamy, yellow or yellow-orange color; and unwrinkled skin free of blemishes. Red patches are not an indication of ripeness; a green skin indicates that the fruit was picked too early and it will not ripen further. Peaches and nectarines soften but do not become sweeter after they are harvested.

California is the largest producer of peaches and nectarines in the United States. Canned and frozen peaches are readily available.

Plums

Plums (Fr. *prunes*) are round to oval-shaped fruits that grow on trees or bushes. Dozens of plum varieties are known, although only a few are commercially significant. Plums vary in size from very small to 3 inches (7.5 centimeters) in diameter. Their thin skins can be green, red, yellow or various shades of blue-purple.

Plums are excellent for eating out of hand. Plums can also be baked, poached or used in pies, cobblers or tarts; they are often used in jams or preserves, and fresh slices can be used in salads or compotes.

When selecting plums, look for plump, smooth fruits with unblemished skin. Generally they should yield to gentle pressure, although the green and yellow varieties remain quite firm. Avoid plums with moist, brown spots near the stem. Plums may be left at room temperature to ripen, then stored in the refrigerator. Prunes, discussed later, are produced by drying special plum varieties, usually the French Agen.

Tropical Fruits

Tropical fruits are native to the world's hot, tropical or subtropical regions. Most are readily available throughout the United States thanks to rapid transportation and distribution

Peaches

Nectarines

Santa Rosa plums

Damson plums

Heirloom Varieties and Genetic Diversity

David Mas Masumoto, a third-generation Japanese American peach farmer, writes eloquently of an old variety of peaches grown in his orchards. The Sun Crest peach, he claims, melts in the mouth with "the message of summer" in every bite. Because it doesn't keep well when picked fully ripe, this variety is less suited to the demands of commercial agriculture. In his book *Epitaph for a Peach*, Masumoto writes of the challenges faced by a small family farmer and trying to find a market for these unique peaches.

Many chefs and home gardeners seek out older or *heirloom* varieties like those that Masumoto grows. Despite the fact that they may bruise easily or be irregular in size and appearance, heirloom fruits and vegetables are appealing because of their unique flavor and suitability to specific growing conditions. According to botanists and farmers, these neglected varieties are also essential to ensuring a continued food supply. The intensive agriculture on which the world's

David Mas Masumoto harvesting a peach in his orchard.

food supply increasingly depends means less genetic diversity. With less diversity, crops become more vulnerable to insect and environmental stress. Recognizing the need to protect all species, the USDA has organized the National Plant Germplasm System (NPGS), a collection of state, federal and private farms where genetically diverse assortments of plants are grown and distributed. More than 30 such repositories or farms exist across the country. There, countless species of stone fruits, berries, legumes, nuts and all manner of plants are grown to enhance breeding for future fruit and vegetable crops. Seeds of wild species are stored for future propagation.

Organizations such as Chefs Collaborative and Slow Food USA are good resources for more information about fruits, vegetables and other food products for which cultivation is in jeopardy. Slow Food's Ark of Taste is a catalog of more than 4500 cherished and delicious foods in danger of extinction, including the Blenheim apricot, the Hatcher mango and Masumoto's beloved Sun Crest peach.

---

methods. All can be eaten fresh, without cooking. The flavors of tropical fruits complement each other and go well with rich or spicy meat, fish and poultry dishes.

Bananas

Common yellow bananas (Fr. *bananes*) are actually the berries of a large tropical herb. Grown in bunches called hands, bananas are about 7–9 inches (17.5–22.5 centimeters) long, with a sticky, soft, sweet flesh. Their inedible yellow skin is easily removed. Small "baby" bananas (Niño, Lady Finger or finger bananas) each measure 4–5 inches long (10–12.5 centimeters) and have yellow or red skin. Their flesh is denser and sweeter than most larger banana varieties, and their diminutive size makes them ideal for many dessert applications.

Properly ripened bananas are excellent eaten out of hand or in salads. Lightly bruised or overripe fruits are best for breads or muffins. Bananas blend well with other tropical fruits and citrus. Their unique flavor is also complemented by curry, cinnamon, ginger, honey and chocolate.

Fresh bananas are available all year. Bananas are always harvested when still green, because the texture and flavor is adversely affected if the fruits are allowed to turn yellow on the tree. Unripe bananas are hard, dry and starchy. Because bananas ripen after harvesting, it is acceptable to purchase green bananas if there is sufficient time for final ripening before use. Bananas should be left at room temperature to ripen. A properly ripened banana has a yellow peel with brown flecks. The tip of a ripe banana should not have any remaining green coloring. As bananas continue to age, the peel darkens and the starches turn to sugar, giving the fruits a sweeter flavor. Avoid bananas that have large brown bruises or a gray cast (a sign of cold damage).

Plantains, also referred to as cooking bananas, are larger than, but not as sweet as common bananas. They are frequently cooked as a starchy vegetable in tropical cuisines.

Common yellow bananas

Plantains

Medjool dates

Dates

Dates (Fr. *dattes*) are the fruits of the date palm tree, which has been cultivated since ancient times. Dates are about 1–2 inches (2.5–5 centimeters) long, with a paper-thin skin and single grooved seeds. Most dates are golden to dark brown when ripe.

Although dates appear to be dried, they are actually fresh fruits. They have a sticky-sweet, almost candied texture and rich flavor. Dates provide flavor and moisture to breads, muffins, cookies and tarts. They can also be served with fresh or dried fruits, or stuffed with meat or cheese as an appetizer.

Pitted dates are available in several packaged forms: whole, chopped or extruded (for use in baking). Whole unpitted dates are available in bulk. Date juice is also available for use as a beverage and date syrup is a natural sweetener used in baked goods. When selecting dates, look for those that are plump, glossy and moist.

Kiwis

Kiwis

Kiwis, sometimes known as kiwifruits or Chinese gooseberries, are small oval fruits, about the size of large eggs, with thin, fuzzy, brown skin. The flesh is bright green or golden yellow with a white core surrounded by hundreds of tiny black seeds.

Kiwis are sweet, but somewhat bland. They are best used raw, peeled and eaten out of hand or sliced for fruit salads or garnish. Although kiwis are not recommended for cooking because heat causes them to fall apart, they are a perfect addition to glazed fruit tarts and can be puréed for sorbets, sauces or mousses. Kiwis contain an enzyme similar to that in fresh pineapple and papaya, which has a tenderizing effect on meat and prevents gelling. They should not be used in salads bound with gelatin.

Mangoes

Mangoes

Mangoes (Fr. *mangues*) are oval or kidney-shaped fruits that normally weigh between 6 ounces and 1 pound (180 and 480 grams) each. Their skin is smooth and thin but tough, varying from yellow to orange-red, with patches of green, red or purple. As mangoes ripen, the green disappears. The juicy, bright-orange flesh clings to a large, flat pit.

A mango's unique flavor is spicy-sweet, with an acidic tang. Mangoes can be puréed for use in drinks or sauces, or the flesh can be sliced or cubed for use in salads, pickles, chutneys or desserts. Mangoes go well with spicy foods such as curry and with barbecued meats.

Although Florida produces some mangoes, most of those available in the United States are from Mexico and Central America. Select fruits with good color that are firm and free of blemishes. Ripe mangoes should have a good aroma and should not be too soft or shriveled. Allow mangoes to ripen completely at room temperature, then refrigerate for up to 1 week.

Procedure for Pitting and Cutting Mangoes

1 Cut along each side of the pit to remove two sections.

2 Cube each section using the "hedgehog" technique: Make crosswise cuts through the flesh, just to the skin; press up on the skin side of the section, exposing the cubes.

3 Serve the mango "hedgehog" whole or cut off the cubes to use in salads or other dishes.

Papayas

The papaya [puh-PIE-yuh] is a greenish-yellow fruit shaped rather like a large pear and weighing 1–2 pounds (500–1000 grams). When halved, a papaya resembles a melon. The flesh is golden to reddish-pink; its center cavity is filled with round, silver-black seeds resembling caviar. Ripe papayas can be eaten raw, with only a squirt of lemon or lime juice. They can also be puréed for sweet or spicy sauces, chilled soups or sorbets.

Papayas contain **papain**, which breaks down proteins, and therefore papayas are an excellent meat tenderizer. Meats can be marinated with papaya juice or slices before cooking. The papain in fresh papayas, however, makes them unsuitable for use in gelatins because it inhibits gelling. Unripe (green) papayas are often used in pickles or chutneys and can be baked or stewed with meat or poultry.

Papaya seeds are edible, with a peppery flavor and slight crunch. They are occasionally used to garnish fruit salads or add flavor to fruit salsas and compotes.

Papayas are grown in tropical and subtropical areas worldwide. Select papayas that are plump, with a smooth, unblemished skin. Color is a better determinant of ripeness than is softness: The greater the proportion of yellow to green skin color, the riper the fruit. Papayas may be held at room temperature until completely ripe, then refrigerated for up to 1 week.

Red papayas

papain an enzyme found in papayas that breaks down proteins; used as the primary ingredient in many commercial meat tenderizers

Papayas

Passion Fruits

Passion fruits (Fr. *fruits de la passion*) have a firm, almost shell-like purple skin with orange-yellow pulp surrounding large, black, edible seeds. They are about the size and shape of large hen eggs, with a sweet, rich and unmistakable citrusy flavor. The pulp is used in custards, sauces and ice creams.

Select heavy fruits with dark, shriveled skin and a strong aroma. Allow them to ripen at room temperature if necessary, then refrigerate. Passion fruits are grown in New Zealand, Hawaii and California. Bottles or frozen packs of purée are readily available and provide a strong, true flavor.

Passion fruits

Pineapples

Pineapples (Fr. *ananas*) are the fruits of a shrub with sharp, spear-shaped leaves. Each fruit is covered with rough, brown eyes, giving it the appearance of a pine cone. The pale-yellow flesh, which is sweet and very juicy, surrounds a cylindrical, woody core that is edible but too tough for most uses. Most pineapples weigh approximately 2 pounds (1 kilogram), but dwarf varieties are also available.

Pineapples are excellent eaten raw, alone or in salads. Slices can be baked or grilled to accompany pork or ham. The cuisines of Southeast Asia incorporate pineapple into various curries, soups and stews. Pineapple juice is a popular beverage, often used in punch or cocktails. Canned or cooked pineapple can be added to gelatin mixtures, but avoid using fresh pineapple; an enzyme (bromelin) found in fresh pineapple breaks down gelatin.

Pineapples do not ripen after harvesting although they will continue to soften once picked. They must be left on the stem until completely ripe, at which time they are extremely perishable. Most pineapples come from Central America, Southeast Asia and Brazil. Select heavy fruits with a strong, sweet aroma and rich color. Avoid those with dried leaves or soft spots. Pineapples should be used as soon as possible after purchase. Pineapples are also available canned in slices, cubes or crushed, dried or candied.

Pineapples

Procedure for Trimming and Slicing Pineapples

① Slice off the leaves and stem end. Stand the fruit upright and cut the peel off in vertical strips.

② Cut the peeled fruit in quarters, then cut away the woody core.

③ Cut the flesh as desired.

NUTRITION OF FRUITS

Most fruits are quite nutritious. They have a high water content (usually 75–95 percent) and low protein and fat contents, all of which makes them low in calories. They are also an excellent sources of dietary fiber, much of which is found in the edible peels of such fruit as apples, mangoes and pears. The sugar content of ripe fruits is a good source of energy. Some fruits, such as citrus, melons and strawberries, contain large amounts of vitamin C (which may be destroyed, however, by cooking or processing). Deep yellow and green fruits, such as apricots, mangoes and kiwis, are high in vitamin A; bananas, raisins and figs are a good source of potassium.

PURCHASING FRESH FRUITS

Fresh fruits have not been subjected to any processing (e.g., canning, freezing or drying). Fresh fruits may be ripe or unripe, depending on their condition when harvested or the conditions under which they have been stored. In order to use fresh fruits to their best advantage, it is important to make careful purchasing decisions. Pay attention to the size of each piece of fruit, its grade or quality, its ripeness on delivery and its storage in order to serve fruit in an appropriate and cost-effective manner. The prime growing seasons for each fruit depends on the region of the country where it is grown. Consult Appendix II, Fresh, Locally Grown Produce Availability Chart, and speak to your produce supplier and local farmers to learn what is available seasonally in your location.

Grading

Fresh fruits may be graded under the USDA's voluntary program. The grades, based on size and uniformity of shape, color and texture as well as the absence of defects, are U.S. Fancy, U.S. No. 1, U.S. No. 2 and U.S. No. 3. Most fruits purchased for food service operations are U.S. Fancy. Fruits with lower grades are suitable for processing into sauces, jams, jellies or preserves.

Ripening

Several important changes take place in a fruit as it ripens. The fruit reaches its full size; its pulp or flesh becomes soft and tender; its color changes. In addition, the fruit's acid content declines, making it less tart, and its starch content converts into the sugars fructose and glucose, which provide sweetness, flavor and aroma.

Unfortunately these changes do not stop when the fruit reaches its peak of ripeness. Rather they continue, deteriorating the fruit's texture and flavor and eventually causing spoilage.

Depending on the species, fresh fruits can be purchased either fully ripened or unripened. See Table 26.3. Figs and pineapples, for example, ripen only on the plant and are harvested at or just before their peak of ripeness, then rushed to market. These fruits should not be purchased unripened as they will never attain full flavor or texture after harvesting. On the other hand, some fruits, including bananas and pears, continue to ripen after harvesting and can be purchased unripened.

With most harvested fruits, the ripening time as well as the time during which the fruits remain at their peak of ripeness can be manipulated. For instance, ripening can be delayed by chilling. Chilling slows the fruit's **respiration rate** (fruits, like animals, consume oxygen and expel carbon dioxide). The slower the respiration rate, the slower the conversion of starch to sugar. For quicker ripening, fruit can be stored at room temperature.

Ripening is also affected by **ethylene gas**, a colorless, odorless hydrocarbon gas. Ethylene gas is naturally emitted by ripening fruits and can be used to encourage further ripening in most fruits. Apples, tomatoes, melons and bananas give off the most ethylene and should be stored away from delicate fruits and vegetables, especially greens. Fruits that are picked and shipped unripened can be exposed to ethylene gas to induce ripening just before sale. Conversely to extend the life of ripe fruits a day or two, isolate them from other fruits and keep them well chilled.

Fresh fruits will not ripen further once they are cooked or processed. The cooking or processing method applied, however, may soften the fruits or add flavor.

Purchasing

Fresh fruits are sold by weight or by count. They are packed in containers referred to as crates, bushels, cartons, cases, lugs or flats. The weight or count packed in each of these containers varies depending on the type of fruit, the purveyor and the state in which the fruits were packed. For instance, Texas citrus is packed in cartons equal to $7/10$ of a bushel; Florida citrus is packed in cartons equal to $4/5$ of a bushel. Sometimes fruit size must be specified when ordering. A 30-pound case of lemons, for example, may contain 96, 112 or 144 individual lemons, depending on the size of the fruit.

Some fresh fruits, especially melons, pineapples, peaches and berries, are available trimmed, cleaned, peeled or cut. Sugar and preservatives are sometimes added. They are sold in bulk containers, sometimes packed in water. These items offer a consistent product with a significant reduction in labor costs. However the purchase price may be greater than that of fresh fruits, and flavor, freshness and nutritional qualities may suffer somewhat from the processing.

Storing

Like vegetables, fruit must be stored in a way that ensures airflow at the proper temperatures to prevent spoilage. Fresh fruit should be stored at 34–40°F (2–4°C) with relatively high levels of humidity. Citrus fruit, melons, papayas and pineapples benefit from slightly warmer storage temperatures of 40–50°F (4–10°C). Store bananas and unripe mangoes in a dry area with good ventilation at 56–60°F (13–15°C). When refrigerated, bananas discolor. Although unsuitable for eating out of hand, brown bananas may still be used in baked goods. Pay particular attention to the storage conditions for ripe berries, which are especially perishable. They require good ventilation and cold conditions. If you purchase more than needed, immediately wash the berries, dry them and freeze them for use in baked goods, fillings and sauces.

FRUITS THAT RIPEN AFTER HARVEST	TABLE 26.3

The following fruits will soften, change color and texture and develop sweetness, flavor and aromas after picking.

Apples

Apricots

Bananas

Kiwi

Mangoes

Papayas

Passion fruit

Pears

Persimmons

Plums

Quince

Star fruits

respiration rate the speed with which the cells of a fruit use oxygen and produce carbon dioxide during ripening

ethylene gas a colorless, odorless hydrocarbon gas naturally emitted from fruits and fruit-vegetables that encourages ripening

Figure 26.1 Irradiation symbol.

PRESERVING FRUITS

Preservation techniques are designed to extend the shelf life of fruits. These methods include irradiation, acidulation, canning, freezing and drying. Except for drying, these techniques do not substantially change the fruits' texture or flavor. Canning and freezing can also be used to preserve cooked fruits.

Fruit preserves, such as jellies and jams, are cooked products and are discussed later in this chapter.

Irradiation

As described in Chapter 22, Vegetables, some fruits can be subjected to ionizing radiation to destroy parasites, insects and bacteria. The treatment also slows ripening without a noticeable effect on the fruits' flavor and texture. Irradiated fruits must be labeled "treated with radiation," "treated by irradiation" or with the symbol shown in Figure 26.1.

Acidulation

Apples, pears, bananas, peaches and other fruits turn brown when cut. Although this browning is commonly attributed to exposure to oxygen, it is actually caused by the reaction of enzymes. Enzymatic browning can be retarded by immersing cut fruits in an acidic solution such as lemon or orange juice. This simple technique is referred to as **acidulation**. Soaking fruits in water or lemon juice and water (called acidulated water) is not recommended. Unless a sufficient amount of salt or sugar is added to the water, the fruits become mushy and if enough salt or sugar is added to retain texture, the flavor is affected.

Canning

Almost any type of fruit can be canned successfully; pineapple and peaches are the most popular types of canned fruit. In commercial canning, raw fruits are cleaned and placed in a sealed container, then subjected to high temperatures for a specific amount of time. Heating destroys the microorganisms that cause spoilage, and the sealed environment created by the can eliminates oxidation and retards decomposition. But the heat required by the canning process also softens the texture of most fruits. Canning has little or no effect on vitamins A, B, C and D. Canning also has no practical effect on proteins, fats or carbohydrates.

In solid-pack cans, little or no water is added. The only liquid is from the fruits' natural moisture. Water-pack cans have water or fruit juice added, which must be taken into account when determining costs. Syrup-pack cans have a sugar syrup—light, medium or heavy—added. The syrup should also be taken into account when determining food costs, and the additional sweetness should be considered when using syrup-packed fruits. Cooked fruit products such as pie fillings are also available canned.

Canned fruits are purchased in cases of standard-sized cans (see Appendix I, Canned Good Sizes). Once a can is opened, any unused contents should be transferred to an appropriate storage container and refrigerated. Cans with bulges should be discarded immediately, without opening.

Freezing

Freezing is a highly effective method for preserving fruits. It severely inhibits the growth of microorganisms that cause fruits to spoil. Freezing does not destroy nutrients, although the appearance or texture of most fruits can be affected because of their high water content. This occurs when ice crystals formed from the water in the cells burst the cells' walls.

Many fruits, especially berries and apple and pear slices, are now **individually quick frozen (IQF)**. This method employs blasts of cold air, refrigerated plates, liquid nitrogen, liquid air or other techniques to chill the produce quickly. Speeding the freezing process greatly reduces the formation of ice crystals.

Fruits can be trimmed and sliced before freezing and are also available frozen in sugar syrup, which adds flavor and prevents browning. Berries are frozen whole, whereas stone fruits are usually peeled, pitted and sliced. Fruit purées are also available frozen.

Frozen fruits are graded as U.S. Grade A (Fancy), U.S. Grade B (Choice or Extra Standard), or U.S. Grade C (Standard). The "U.S." indicates that a government inspector has graded the product, but packers may use grade names without an actual inspection if the contents meet the standards of the grade indicated.

IQF fruits can be purchased in bulk by the case. All frozen fruits should be sealed in moisture-proof wrapping and kept at a constant temperature of 0°F (−18°C) or below. Temperature fluctuations can cause freezer burn. Frozen berries such as blueberries and blackberries should not be thawed before adding to batters because their juice can easily discolor the batter.

Drying

Drying is the oldest known technique for preserving fruits, having been used for more than 5000 years. When ripe fruits are dried, they lose most of their moisture. This concentrates their flavors and sugars and dramatically extends shelf life. Although most fruits can be dried, plums (prunes), grapes (raisins, sultanas and currants), apricots and figs are the most commonly dried fruits. The drying method can be as simple as leaving ripe fruits in the sun to dry naturally or the more cost-efficient technique of passing fruits through a compartment of hot, dry air to quickly extract moisture.

Dried apricots

Dried fruits actually retain from 16 to 26 percent residual moisture, which leaves them moist and soft. They are often treated with sulfur dioxide to prevent browning (oxidation) and to extend shelf life. Dried fruits may be eaten out of hand; added to cereals or salads; baked in muffins, breads, pies or tarts; stewed for chutneys or compotes; or used as a stuffing for roasted meats or poultry. Before use, dried fruits may be softened by steeping them for a short time in a hot liquid such as water, wine, rum, brandy or other liquor. Some dried fruits should be simmered in a small amount of water before use.

Store dried fruits in airtight containers to prevent further moisture loss; keep in a dry, cool area away from sunlight. Dried fruits may mold if exposed to both air and high humidity.

Dried pears

JUICING FRUITS

Fruit juice is consumed as a beverage, alone or mixed with other ingredients. Fruit juice also serves as the liquid ingredient in other preparations. **Juice** can be extracted from fruits (and some vegetables) in two ways: pressure and blending.

Pressure is used to extract juice from fruits such as citrus that have a high water content. Pressure is applied by hand-squeezing or with a manual or electric reamer. All reamers work on the same principle: A ribbed cone is pressed against the fruit to break down its flesh and release the juice. Always strain juices to remove seeds, pulp or fibrous pieces.

A blender or an electric juice extractor can liquefy less-juicy fruits and vegetables such as apples, carrots, tomatoes, beets and cabbage. The extractor pulverizes the fruit or vegetable, then separates and strains the liquid from the pulp with centrifugal force.

Interesting and delicious beverages can be made by combining the juices of one or more fruits or vegetables: pineapple with orange, apple with cranberry, strawberry with tangerine and papaya with orange. Color should be considered when creating mixed-juice beverages, however. Although yellow and orange juices are not a problem, those containing red and blue flavonoid pigments (such as Concord grapes, cherries, strawberries, raspberries and blueberries) can create unappetizing colors. Adding an acid such as lemon juice helps retain the correct red and blue hues.

Golden raisins

Currants

Dried persimmons

Dried apples

juice the liquid extracted from any fruit or vegetable

nectar the diluted, sweetened juice of peaches, apricots, guavas, black currants or other fruits, the juice of which would be too thick or too tart to drink straight

cider mildly fermented apple juice; nonalcoholic apple juice may also be labeled cider

compote whole or cut pieces of fruit stewed in sugar syrup

COOKING METHODS FOR FRUITS

Although most fruits are edible raw and typically served that way, some fruits can also be cooked. Commonly used cooking methods are broiling and grilling, baking, sautéing, deep-frying, poaching, simmering and preserving.

When cooking fruits, proper care and attention are critical. Even minimal cooking can render fruits overly soft or mushy. To combat this irreversible process, sugar can be added. When fruits are cooked with sugar, the sugar is absorbed slowly into the cells, firming the fruits. Acids (notably lemon juice) also help fruits retain their structure. (Alkalis, such as baking soda, cause the cells to break down more quickly, reducing the fruits to mush.)

Determining Doneness

There are so many different fruits with such varied responses to cooking that no one standard for doneness is appropriate. Each item should be evaluated on a recipe-by-recipe basis. As a general rule, however, most cooked fruits are done when they are just tender when pierced with a fork or the tip of a paring knife. Simmered fruits, such as **compotes**, should be softer, cooked just to the point of disintegration. To avoid over-cooking fruits, remember that some carryover cooking will occur through the residual heat contained in the foods. Always rely on subjective tests—sight, feel, taste and aroma—rather than the clock.

Dry-Heat Cooking Methods for Fruits

Using dry-heat cooking methods to prepare fruit, concentrates their flavors by reducing moisture, which may be significant. Select the dry-heat cooking method suitable for the fruit being used. Small delicate fruits such as berries, for example, may not be suitable for grilling. although they can be sautéed to release their juices and extract flavor.

Broiling and Grilling

Fruits are usually broiled or grilled just long enough to caramelize sugars; cooking must be done quickly in order to avoid breaking down the fruits' structure. Good fruits to broil or grill are pineapples, apples, grapefruits, bananas, persimmons and peaches. The fruits may be cut into slices, chunks or halves as appropriate. Sugar, honey or liqueur add flavor, as do lemon juice, cinnamon and ginger.

When broiling fruits, use an oiled sheet pan or broiling platter. When grilling fruits, place on a clean grill grate or thread the pieces onto skewers. Only thick fruit slices need to be turned or rotated to heat fully. Broiled or grilled fruits can be served alone, as an accompaniment to meat, fish or poultry or as topping for ice creams or custards.

Procedure for Broiling or Grilling Fruits

1 Select ripe fruits and peel, core or slice as necessary. Cut fruit into pieces that are large enough so that they do not fall through the grill grate.

2 Top with sugar or honey to add flavor and aid caramelization.

3 Place the fruits on the broiler platter, sheet pan or grill grate.

4 Broil or grill at high temperatures, turning as necessary to heat the fruits thoroughly but quickly.

Broiled Grapefruit

YIELD 8 Servings	METHOD Broiling	
Ruby grapefruits	4	4
Sweet sherry	1 fl. oz.	30 ml
Brown sugar	4 Tbsp.	60 ml

1 Cut each grapefruit in half (perpendicular to the segments), then section with a sharp knife, removing any visible seeds.

2 Sprinkle the grapefruit halves with the sherry and sugar.

3 Arrange on a baking sheet and place under a preheated broiler. Cook briefly, for 4–5 minutes just until well heated and the sugar caramelizes. Serve immediately.

Approximate values per serving: **Calories** 70, **Total fat** 0 g, **Saturated fat** 0 g, **Cholesterol** 0 mg, **Sodium** 0 mg, **Total carbohydrates** 16 g, **Protein** 1 g, **Vitamin C** 80%, **Claims**—fat free; no sodium

Baking

After washing, peeling, coring or pitting, most pomes, stone fruits and tropicals can be baked. Baked fruits are hot, flavorful desserts. Fruits with sturdy skins, particularly apples and pears, are excellent for baking alone, as their skins (peels) hold in moisture and flavor. To use them as edible containers, fill the cavity left by coring with a variety of sweet or savory mixtures.

Combinations of fruits can also be baked successfully; try mixing fruits for a balance of sweetness and tartness (e.g., strawberries with rhubarb or apples with plums).

Several baked desserts are simply fruits (fresh, frozen or canned) topped with a crust or biscuit dough (cobbler), streusel (crumple or crisp) or batter (buckle). Fruits, sometimes poached first, can also be baked in a wrapper of puff pastry, flaky dough or phyllo dough to produce an elegant dessert.

Procedure for Baking Fruits

1 Select ripe but firm fruits. Peel, core, pit or slice as necessary.

2 Add sugar or any flavorings.

3 Wrap the fruits in pastry dough if desired or directed in the recipe.

4 Place the fruits in a baking dish and bake uncovered in a moderate oven until tender or appropriately browned.

Warm Baked Peaches or Nectarines

YIELD 8 Servings	METHOD Baking	
Freestone peaches or nectarines	4	4
Vanilla bean	1	1
Granulated sugar	2 oz.	60 g
Lemon juice	1 fl. oz.	30 ml
Unsalted butter	2 oz.	60 g
Pastry Cream (page 1069) or ice cream	as needed	as needed

1 Cut the peaches or nectarines in half. Remove the pits. Place fruit, cut side up, in a well-buttered half-size hotel pan or ovenproof dish.

2 Split the vanilla bean and scrape the seeds into the sugar. Sprinkle the fruit with the sugar and lemon juice.

3 Place a small piece of butter in the center of each fruit half and bake at 350°F (180°C) until tender and lightly browned, approximately 20 minutes. Serve warm with Pastry Cream or ice cream.

Approximate values per serving: **Calories** 100, **Total fat** 6 g, **Saturated fat** 3.5 g, **Cholesterol** 15 mg, **Sodium** 0 mg, **Total carbohydrates** 13 g, **Protein** 0 g, **Vitamin A** 10%, **Vitamin C** 10%, **Claims**—low calorie; no sodium

Sautéing

Fruits develop a rich, syrupy flavor when sautéed briefly in butter, sugar and, if desired, spices or liqueur. Cherries, bananas, apples, pears and pineapples are good choices. Peel, core and seed as necessary and cut into uniform-size pieces before sautéing.

For dessert, sauté fruits with sugar to create a caramelized glaze or syrup. The fruits and syrup can be used to fill crêpes or top spongecakes or ice creams. Liquor may be added and the mixture flamed (flambéed) in front of diners. For savory mixtures, onions, shallots or garlic are often added.

In both sweet and savory fruit sautés, the fat used should be the most appropriate for the finished product. Butter and bacon fat are typical choices.

Procedure for Sautéing Fruits

1 Peel, pit and core the fruits as necessary and cut into uniform-size pieces.
2 Melt the fat in a hot sauté pan.
3 Add the fruit pieces and any flavoring ingredients. Do not crowd the pan, as this will cause the fruit to stew in its own juices.
4 Cook quickly over high heat.

♥ Good Choice

MISE EN PLACE

- Wash and peel onions and cut into fine dice.
- Chop apricots.

Savory Fruit Compote

YIELD Approximately 2 lb. (1 kg)		METHOD Sautéing	
Onions, fine dice	6 oz.		180 g
Whole butter or bacon fat	1 oz.		30 g
Apples (tart) or pears	3		3
Apricots, chopped coarse	3		3
Granulated sugar	4 oz.		120 g
Hot paprika	TT		TT
Salt and white pepper	TT		TT

1 Sweat the onions in the butter or bacon fat without browning.
2 Slice the apples or pears into thin, even pieces. Add the sliced fruit and apricots to the onions and sauté for 1–2 minutes.
3 Sprinkle the sugar over the fruit and cook, uncovered, over medium heat until tender. Season with paprika, salt and white pepper.
4 Serve warm as a savory accompaniment to grilled or roasted pork, game or other meat.

Approximate values per 1-oz. (30-g) serving: **Calories** 60, **Total fat** 1.5 g, **Saturated fat** 1 g, **Cholesterol** 5 mg, **Sodium** 50 mg, **Total carbohydrates** 12 g, **Protein** 0 g, **Vitamin A** 4%, **Claims**—low fat; low cholesterol; low sodium

Deep-Frying

Only a few fruits are suitable for deep-frying. Apples, bananas, pears, pineapples and firm peaches mixed in or coated with batter, however, produce fine results. These fruits should be peeled, cored, seeded and cut into evenly sized slices or chunks. They may also need to be dried with paper towels so that the batter or coating can adhere.

Fruit fritters are also popular snacks or dessert items. **Fritters** contain diced or chopped fish, shellfish, vegetables or fruits bound together with a thick batter and deep-fried. Because frying time is very short, the main ingredient is usually precooked. Fritters are spooned or dropped directly into the hot fat; they form a crust as they cook. Popular examples are clam fritters, corn fritters, artichoke fritters and apple fritters.

Procedure for Deep-Frying Fritters

1 Cut, chop and otherwise prepare the food to be made into fritters.
2 Precook any ingredients if necessary.
3 Prepare the batter as directed.
4 Scoop the fritters into deep fat at 350°F (180°C), using the swimming method.
5 Cook until done. The fritters should be golden brown on the outside and moist but set on the inside.
6 Remove the fritters from the fat and hold them over the fryer, allowing the excess fat to drain off. Transfer the food to a hotel pan either lined with absorbent paper or fitted with a rack. Serve hot.
7 If the fritters are to be held for later service, place them under a heat lamp.

Apple Fritters

🌿 Vegetarian

YIELD 100 Fritters, 2 in. (5 cm) each	METHOD	Deep-Frying
Eggs, separated	6	6
Milk	1 pt.	480 ml
Flour	1 lb.	480 g
Baking powder	1 Tbsp.	15 ml
Salt	1 tsp.	5 ml
Granulated sugar	2 oz.	60 g
Cinnamon, ground	½ tsp.	2 ml
Apples, peeled, cored, medium dice	1 lb. 8 oz.	720 g
Powdered sugar	as needed	as needed

MISE EN PLACE
- Separate eggs.
- Peel and core apples and cut into medium dice.

1 Combine the egg yolks and milk.
2 Sift together the flour, baking powder, salt, sugar and cinnamon. Add the dry ingredients to the milk-and-egg mixture; whisk until smooth.
3 Allow the batter to rest 1 hour.
4 Stir the apples into the batter.
5 Just before the fritters are to be cooked, whip the egg whites to soft peaks and fold into the batter.
6 Scoop the fritters into deep fat at 350°F (180°C), using the swimming method. Cook until uniformly browned, approximately 5 minutes.
7 Dust with powdered sugar and serve hot.

Variation:

Banana Fritters—Omit the cinnamon and apples. Add 3 tablespoons (45 milliliters) finely grated orange zest, 4 fluid ounces (120 milliliters) orange juice and 2 large bananas, peeled and diced (not puréed).

Approximate values per fritter: **Calories** 60, **Total fat** 4 g, **Saturated fat** 1 g, **Cholesterol** 15 mg, **Sodium** 5 mg, **Total carbohydrates** 6 g, **Protein** 1 g

① Adding the dry ingredients to the milk-and-egg mixture.

② Folding the whipped egg whites into the batter.

③ Scooping the fritters into the deep fat.

④ Dusting the fritters with powdered sugar.

Moist-Heat Cooking Methods for Fruits

Moist heat cooking methods are used to soften, tenderize and flavor fruits by submerging them directly into a hot liquid. Whether poaching a whole fruit such as a peeled pear or simmering a mixture of cut fruit for a compote, the liquid used should enhance the flavor of the fruit.

Poaching

A popular cooking method for preparing fruits is poaching. Poaching softens and tenderizes fruits and infuses them with additional flavors such as spices or wine. Poached fruits can be served hot or cold and used in tarts or pastries or as an accompaniment to meat or poultry dishes.

The poaching liquid can be water, wine, liquor or sugar syrup. (As noted earlier, sugar helps fruits keep their shape, although it takes longer to tenderize fruits poached in sugar syrup.) The low poaching temperature (185°F/85°C) allows fruits to soften gradually. The agitation created at higher temperatures would damage them.

Cooked fruits should be allowed to cool in the flavored poaching liquid or syrup. Most poaching liquids can be used repeatedly. If they contain sufficient sugar, they can be reduced to a sauce or glaze to accompany the poached fruits.

Procedure for Poaching Fruits

1 Peel, core and slice the fruits as necessary.

2 In a sufficiently deep, nonreactive saucepan, combine the poaching liquid (usually water or wine) with sugar, spices, citrus zest and other ingredients as desired or as directed in the recipe.

3 Submerge the fruits in the liquid. Place a circle of parchment paper over the fruits to help them stay submerged.

4 Place the saucepan on the stove top over a medium-high flame; bring to a boil.

5 As soon as the liquid boils, reduce the temperature. Simmer gently.

6 Poach until the fruits are tender enough for the tip of a small knife to be easily inserted. Cooking time depends on the type and variety of fruit used, its ripeness and the cooking liquid.

7 Remove the saucepan from the stove top and allow the liquid and fruits to cool.

8 Remove the fruits from the liquid and then refrigerate. The liquid can be returned to the stove top and reduced until thick enough to use as a sauce or glaze or refrigerated for further use.

♥ Good Choice   🌿 Vegetarian

Pears Poached in Red Wine

MISE EN PLACE

- Chop basil.
- Toast and chop pistachios.

YIELD 8 Servings		METHOD Poaching
Ripe pears, Anjou or Bartlett	8	8
Zinfandel wine	52 fl. oz.	1.5 l
Whole peppercorns	8–10	8–10
Vanilla bean	1	1
Granulated sugar	12 oz.	360 g
Fresh basil, chopped	1 oz.	30 g
Orange zest	from 1 orange	from 1 orange
Pistachios, toasted, chopped	as needed for garnish	
Vanilla Custard Sauce (page 1068)	as needed for garnish	

1 Peel and core the pears, leaving the stems intact.

2 Combine the remaining ingredients in a large nonreactive saucepan. Arrange the pears in the liquid in a single layer.

3 Place the pears on the stove top over a medium-high flame. Bring to just below a boil, then immediately reduce the heat and allow the liquid to simmer gently. Cover with a round of parchment paper if necessary to keep the pears submerged.

4 Continue poaching the pears until tender, approximately 1–1½ hours. Remove the saucepan from the stove and allow the pears to cool in the liquid.

5 Remove the pears from the poaching liquid and return the liquid to the stove top. Reduce until the liquid is thick enough to coat the back of a spoon, then strain.

6 Serve the pears chilled or at room temperature in a pool of the reduced wine syrup garnished with chopped toasted pistachios and Vanilla Custard Sauce if desired.

Approximate values per 7-oz. (210-g) serving: **Calories** 410, **Total fat** 1.5 g, **Saturated fat** 0 g, **Cholesterol** 0 mg, **Sodium** 35 mg, **Total carbohydrates** 91 g, **Protein** 6 g, **Vitamin A** 40%, **Calcium** 90%, **Iron** 110%, **Claims**—low fat; no cholesterol; low sodium; high fiber

Simmering

Simmering techniques are used to make stewed fruits and compotes. Fresh, frozen, canned and dried fruits can be simmered or stewed. As with any moist-heat cooking method, simmering softens and tenderizes fruits. The liquid used can be water, wine or the juices naturally found in the fruits. Sugar, honey and spices may be added as desired. Stewed or simmered fruits can be served hot or cold, as a first course, a dessert or an accompaniment to meat or poultry dishes.

Procedure for Simmering Fruits

1 Peel, core, pit and slice the fruits as necessary.

2 Bring the fruits and cooking liquid, if used, to a simmer. Cook until the fruit is tender.

3 Add sugar or other sweeteners as desired or as directed in the recipe.

Dried Fruit Compote

 Good Choice  Vegan

YIELD	3 lb. (1.4 kg)	METHOD	Simmering
Dried apricots		5 oz.	150 g
Prunes, pitted		5 oz.	150 g
Dried pears or apples		5 oz.	150 g
Dried peaches		5 oz.	150 g
Water, hot		24 fl. oz.	720 ml
Cinnamon stick		1	1
Light corn syrup		12 fl. oz.	360 ml
Cointreau		2 fl. oz.	60 ml

MISE EN PLACE

● Pit the prunes.

Dried Fruit Compote served with grilled pork tenderloin.

1 Coarsely chop the fruits. Place the pieces in a nonreactive saucepan and add the water and cinnamon stick.

2 Bring the mixture to a simmer, cover and cook until tender, approximately 12–15 minutes.

3 Add the corn syrup and Cointreau. Simmer uncovered until thoroughly heated. Remove the cinnamon stick. Serve warm or refrigerate for longer storage.

Approximate values per 1-oz. (30-g) serving: **Calories** 60, **Total fat** 0 g, **Saturated fat** 0 g, **Cholesterol** 0 mg, **Sodium** 15 mg, **Total carbohydrates** 15 g, **Protein** 0 g, **Claims**—fat free; very low sodium

concentrate also known as a fruit paste or compound; a reduced fruit purée, without a gel structure, used as a flavoring

jam a fruit gel made from fruit pulp and sugar

jelly a fruit gel made from fruit juice and sugar

marmalade a citrus jelly that also contains unpeeled slices of citrus fruit

preserve a fruit gel that contains large pieces or whole fruits

Making Fruit Preserves

Fresh fruits can be preserved with sugar if the fruit-and-sugar mixture is concentrated by evaporation to the point that microbial spoilage cannot occur. The added sugar also retards the growth of, but does not destroy, microorganisms.

Pectin, a substance present in varying amounts in all fruits, can cause cooked fruits to form a semisolid mass known as a gel. Fruits that are visually unattractive but otherwise of high quality can be made into gels, which are more commonly known as **jams**, **jellies**, **marmalades** and **preserves**.

The essential ingredients of a fruit gel are fruit, pectin, acid (usually lemon juice) and sugar. These ingredients must be carefully combined in the correct ratio for the gel to form. For fruits with a low pectin content (such as strawberries) to form a gel, pectin must be added, either by adding a fruit with a high pectin content (e.g., apples or quinces) or by adding packaged pectin.

Apple jelly   Apricot jam   Orange marmalade

QUESTIONS FOR DISCUSSION

1 Define ripeness and explain why ripe fruits are most desirable. How does the ripening process affect the availability of some fruits?

2 Describe the proper storage conditions for most fruits. Which fruits emit ethylene gas, and why is this a consideration when storing fruits?

3 Explain why some apple varieties are preferred for cooking, whereas other varieties are preferred for eating. Which varieties are generally preferred for making applesauce?

4 Which types of fruits are best for dry-heat cooking methods? Explain your answer. Why is sugar usually added when cooking fruit?

5 List and describe three preservation techniques used to prepare fruits for extended storage.

6 Research a tropical or exotic fruit that is not available in your local area. Where is this fruit originally from? How is it eaten or used in cooking? What challenges face producers and importers in bringing this fruit to market in the United States?

7 What fruits are native to your region of the country? Consult with the Cooperative State Research, Education, and Extension Service or Farm Service Agency in your state and report on one fruit grown where you live. Discuss the season when it is harvested, the number and location of farms growing the fruit and the uses for the fruit.

Additional Fruit Recipes

Mango, Pineapple and Strawberry Salad with Coconut Cream

YIELD   8 Servings, 6 oz. (180 g) each

Sauce:		
Coconut milk, chilled	8 fl. oz.	240 ml
Lime juice	1 fl. oz.	30 ml
Honey	4 Tbsp.	60 ml
Mango, sliced thinly	8 oz.	240 g
Pineapple, cut into 1-inch pieces	8 oz.	240 g
Strawberries, sliced	8 oz.	240 g
Green apple, peeled and cut into large pieces	8 oz.	240 g
Coconut, large flake	2 oz.	30 g
Passion fruit, cut in half	4	4
Edible flowers	8	8
Dragon fruit and star fruit, slices	as needed for garnish	

1   Whisk together the sauce ingredients.

2   Fold together the mango, pineapple, strawberry, apple and coconut flakes in a bowl. Divide the fruit mixture evenly between eight serving glasses.

3   Spoon some of the coconut cream over the fruit. Garnish each glass with half a passion fruit, an edible flower and slices of dragon fruit and star fruit.

Approximate values per 6-oz. (180-g) serving: **Calories** 190, **Total fat** 9 g, **Saturated fat** 8 g, **Cholesterol** 0 mg, **Sodium** 25 mg, **Total carbohydrates** 29 g, **Protein** 2 g, **Vitamin A** 10%, **Vitamin C** 70%, **Claims**—excellent source of vitamin C; good source of dietary fiber and vitamin A

Pineapple Papaya Salsa

YIELD   2 qt. (2 lt)

Tomatoes	3	3
Fresh pineapple, approx. 2 lb. (960 g)	1	1
Fresh papaya, approx. 1 lb. (480 g)	1	1
Green onions, sliced	5	5
Fresh cilantro, chopped	3 oz.	90 g
Jalapeño peppers, seeded, minced	2	2
Lemon juice	1½ fl. oz.	45 ml
Garlic, chopped	1 tsp.	5 ml
Salt	2 tsp.	10 ml

1   Core and dice the tomatoes.

2   Peel and dice the pineapple.

3   Peel, seed and dice the papaya.

4   Combine all the ingredients and chill well.

Approximate values per 2-fl.-oz. (60-ml) serving: **Calories** 50, **Total fat** 0 g, **Saturated fat** 0 g, **Cholesterol** 0 mg, **Sodium** 660 mg, **Total carbohydrates** 10 g, **Protein** 0 g, **Vitamin C** 20%, **Claims**—fat free; low calorie

Good Choice   Vegan

Watermelon and Cherry Salad with Fresh Mint Syrup

YIELD 5 lb. 14 oz. (2.8 kg)

Water	8 fl. oz.	240 ml
Fresh mint leaves	3 oz.	90 g
Granulated sugar	3 oz.	90 g
Watermelon	3 lb.	1.4 kg
Cherries, fresh, pitted	2 lb.	960 g
Fresh mint sprigs	as needed for garnish	

1 Bring the water to a boil in a small saucepan. Blanch the mint leaves in the water for 20 seconds. Remove the leaves and refresh them in cold water. Reserve the blanching water.

2 Add the sugar to the blanching water, bring to a boil and cook for 2 minutes.

3 Drain the mint leaves. Squeeze all of the water out of them and chop them finely. Add the chopped mint to the sugar syrup. Refrigerate the syrup until cold.

4 Dice the watermelon or scoop balls from it with a melon ball cutter. Combine the watermelon with the pitted cherries in a stainless steel bowl. Pour the mint syrup over the fruit and toss gently.

5 Serve garnished with sprigs of fresh mint.

Approximate values per 9-oz. (240-g) serving: **Calories** 140, **Total fat** 0 g, **Saturated fat** 0 g, **Cholesterol** 0 mg, **Sodium** 0 mg, **Total carbohydrates** 35 g, **Protein** 2 g, **Vitamin A** 25%, **Vitamin C** 35%, **Claims**—fat free; no saturated fat; no cholesterol; no sodium; good source of fiber; high in vitamins A and C

 Good Choice    Vegan

Baked Apples

YIELD 8 Apples		**METHOD** Baking
Apples, Red or Golden Delicious	8	8
Raisins	6 oz.	180 g
Orange zest	1½ Tbsp.	23 ml
Brown sugar	4 oz.	120 g

1 Rinse and core each apple. Scored or partially remove the peels to allow the pulp to expand without bursting the skin during baking.

2 Plump the raisins by soaking them in boiling water for 10 minutes. Drain the raisins thoroughly.

3 Combine the raisins, zest and sugar. Fill the cavity of each apple with this mixture.

4 Stand the apples in a shallow baking dish. Add enough water to measure about ½ inch (1.2 centimeters) deep.

5 Bake the apples at 375°F (190°C) for 15 minutes. Reduce the temperature to 300°F (150°C) and continue baking until the apples are tender but still hold their shape, approximately 1 hour. Baste the apples with liquid from the baking dish occasionally.

Approximate values per apple: **Calories** 220, **Total fat** 0.5 g, **Saturated fat** 0 g, **Cholesterol** 0 mg, **Sodium** 10 mg, **Total carbohydrates** 52 g, **Protein** 1 g, **Vitamin C** 15%, **Claims**—low fat; no cholesterol; very low sodium; good source of fiber

Grilled Fruit Kebabs

 Good Choice Vegan

YIELD 8 Skewers	METHOD Grilling	
Cantaloupe	½ melon	½ melon
Honeydew	¼ melon	¼ melon
Pineapple	½ pineapple	½ pineapple
Strawberries	8	8
Brown sugar	2 oz.	60 g
Lime juice	4 fl. oz.	120 ml
Cinnamon, ground	¼ tsp.	1 ml

1 Remove the rind and cut the melons and pineapple into 1-inch (2.5-centimeter) cubes. Hull the strawberries and leave whole.

2 To make the sugar glaze, combine the sugar, lime juice and cinnamon, stirring until the sugar dissolves.

3 Heat the grill and clean the grate thoroughly.

4 Thread the fruits onto bamboo skewers, alternating colors for an attractive appearance.

5 Brush the fruits with the sugar glaze. Grill, rotating the skewers frequently to develop an evenly light brown surface.

6 Serve immediately as an appetizer, a garnish for ice cream or an accompaniment to rich meats such as pork or lamb.

Approximate values per skewer: **Calories** 70, **Total fat** 0 g, **Saturated fat** 0 g, **Cholesterol** 0 mg, **Sodium** 10 mg, **Total carbohydrates** 16 g, **Protein** 1 g, **Vitamin C** 50%, **Claims**—fat free; very low sodium

Cherry Confit

 Good Choice  Vegetarian

YIELD 1 lb. (480 g)	METHOD Sautéing	
Red onion, small dice	4 oz.	120 g
Whole butter	3 oz.	90 g
Dried cherries	12 oz.	360 g
Brandy	2 fl. oz.	60 ml
Port wine	2 fl. oz.	60 ml
Sherry vinegar	2 tsp.	10 ml

1 Sauté the onion in the butter without coloring.

2 Add the cherries. Add the brandy and flambé.

3 Add the wine and vinegar; cook until almost dry. Serve warm or at room temperature with charcuterie items or grilled or roasted meats.

Approximate values per 1-oz. (30-g) serving: **Calories** 35, **Total fat** 2 g, **Saturated fat** 1 g, **Cholesterol** 5 mg, **Sodium** 20 mg, **Total carbohydrates** 3 g, **Protein** 0 g, **Claims**—low fat; very low sodium; low calorie

Cherry Confit served with roasted veal.

⚠ Safety Alert

Cooking with Alcohol

When alcohol comes into contact with a flame, it can ignite. In order to avoid singed eyebrows and kitchen fires, observe care when adding wine, liqueurs or liquor to a dish near the stove. When a dish calls for flambéing, follow these procedures. Stand away from the pan being flamed. Tilt the pan away from you, allowing the fumes to be ignited by the open flame. Be careful, as the flames can leap from the pan.

♥ Good Choice   🌿 Vegetarian

Braised Rhubarb

YIELD 5 lb. (2.4 kg)		METHOD Braising
Tart green apples, peeled and cubed	1 lb. 4 oz.	600 g
Rhubarb, IQF pieces	3 lb. 8 oz.	1.6 kg
Unsalted butter	2 oz.	60 g
Sweet white wine	4 fl. oz.	120 ml
Brown sugar	7 oz.	210 g
Vanilla extract	1 tsp.	5 ml
Cinnamon, ground	2 tsp.	10 ml
Nutmeg, ground	pinch	pinch
Orange juice	1 fl. oz.	30 ml
Salt	¼ tsp.	1 ml

1 Sauté the apples and rhubarb in the butter until they begin to soften.

2 Add the wine and reduce by half. Add the remaining ingredients. Simmer until the rhubarb is very tender.

3 Serve at room temperature in prebaked pastry cups, topped with Crème Chantilly or crème fraîche and fennel greens, or serve warm over ice cream.

Approximate values per 1-oz. (30-g) serving: **Calories** 60, **Total fat** 2 g, **Saturated fat** 0.5 g, **Cholesterol** 0 mg, **Sodium** 25 mg, **Total carbohydrates** 11 g, **Protein** 0 g, **Claims**—low fat; no cholesterol; very low sodium

♥ Good Choice   🌿 Vegetarian

Berry Compote

YIELD 4 Servings, 4 fl. oz. (120 ml) each		METHOD Simmering
Berries, fresh or frozen	1 pt.	480 ml
Granulated sugar	4 oz.	120 g
Oranges	2	2
Honey	3 fl. oz.	90 ml
Cinnamon stick	1	1
Brandy	1½ fl. oz.	45 ml
Ice cream	as needed for garnish	

1 Select an assortment of fresh or frozen berries—strawberries, blueberries, raspberries, blackberries and cherries can be used, depending on availability.

2 Place the fruits and sugar in a nonreactive saucepan. Finely grate the zest from one orange and set aside. Add the juice from the two oranges to the saucepan. Bring to a simmer over low heat; cook until the fruits are soft but still intact.

3 Strain the mixture, saving both the fruits and the liquid. Return the liquid to the saucepan. Add the finely grated zest from one orange and the honey, cinnamon and brandy.

4 Bring to a boil and reduce until the mixture thickens enough to coat the back of a spoon. Remove from the heat and cool to room temperature.

5 Remove the cinnamon stick. Gently stir the reserved fruits into the sauce, cover and chill. Serve with ice cream or poundcake.

Approximate values per 4-fl.-oz. (120-ml) serving: **Calories** 190, **Total fat** 0 g, **Saturated fat** 0 g, **Cholesterol** 0 mg, **Sodium** 0 mg, **Total carbohydrates** 41 g, **Protein** 1 g, **Vitamin C** 80%, **Claims**—fat free; no sodium; good source of fiber; excellent source of vitamin C

Applesauce

YIELD	Approximately 1 qt. (1 lt)	METHOD	Simmering
McIntosh apples	4 lb.	1.9 g	
Cinnamon sticks	2	2	
Granulated sugar	5 oz.	150 g	
Lemon juice	1 Tbsp.	15 ml	

1 Peel, core and quarter the apples. Place in a saucepan with just enough cold water to cover the bottom of the pan. Add the cinnamon sticks.

2 Bring to a simmer, cover and cook until the apples are tender, approximately 15 minutes.

3 Add the sugar and lemon juice. Simmer for 10 minutes.

4 Remove the cinnamon sticks and press the apples through a food mill.

Approximate values per 1-oz. (30-g) serving: **Calories** 50, **Total fat** 0 g, **Saturated fat** 0 g, **Cholesterol** 0 mg, **Sodium** 0 mg, **Total carbohydrates** 13 g, **Protein** 0 g, **Claims**—fat free; no sodium

❶ Pressing the apples through a food mill.

❷ The finished applesauce.

Fresh Cranberry-Orange Relish

YIELD	3 qt. (3 lt)	METHOD	Simmering
Granulated sugar	1 lb.	480 g	
Orange juice	4 fl. oz.	120 ml	
Water	4 fl. oz.	120 ml	
Fresh or frozen cranberries	1 lb. 8 oz.	720 g	
Cinnamon stick	1	1	
Golden raisins, optional	6 oz.	180 g	
Orange liqueur	2 fl. oz.	60 ml	
Orange zest, finely grated	2 Tbsp.	30 ml	
Orange segments	20	20	

1 Combine the sugar, orange juice and water in a nonreactive rondeau or saucepan; bring to a boil.

2 Add the cranberries and cinnamon stick and simmer uncovered until the berries begin to burst, approximately 15 minutes. Skim off any foam that rises to the surface.

3 Add the golden raisins, if using, orange liqueur and zest and simmer for another 15–20 minutes.

4 Remove from the heat and remove the cinnamon stick. Add the orange segments. Cool and refrigerate. Serve with roasted game, poultry or charcuterie items.

Variation:

Jalapeño-Cranberry Relish—Omit the golden raisins, if using, orange liqueur, zest and segments. Add 1 fresh jalapeño pepper, minced, and ½ cup (120 milliliters) hot pepper jelly.

Approximate values per 1-fl.-oz. (30-ml) serving: **Calories** 25, **Total fat** 0 g, **Saturated fat** 0 g, **Cholesterol** 0 mg, **Sodium** 0 mg, **Total carbohydrates** 6 g, **Protein** 0 g, **Claims**—fat free; no sodium; low calorie

 Good Choice   ♥ Vegan

Mango Chutney

YIELD 1½ qt. (1.4 lt)		METHOD Simmering
Mangoes, peeled and diced	2 lb.	960 g
Onion, fine dice	4 oz.	120 g
Garlic cloves, minced	2	2
Cider vinegar	8 fl. oz.	240 ml
Dark brown sugar	8 oz.	240 g
Golden or dark raisins	2½ oz.	75 g
Crystallized ginger	4 oz.	120 g
Salt	½ tsp.	2 ml
Cinnamon sticks	2	2
Crushed red pepper flakes	½ tsp.	2 ml
Mustard seeds	½ tsp.	2 ml
Fresh ginger, minced	1 tsp.	5 ml
Lime juice	1 fl. oz.	30 ml

1 Combine the mangoes, onion, garlic, vinegar and sugar in a large, heavy saucepan. Cook until the sugar dissolves.

2 Stir in the raisins, crystallized ginger, salt and spices. Simmer until the onion and raisins are very soft, approximately 45 minutes. Skim foam from the surface as necessary.

3 Stir in the lime juice and adjust the seasonings.

4 Remove from the heat and cool uncovered. The chutney will thicken somewhat as it cools but should be thinner than fruit preserves.

Approximate values per 1-fl.-oz. (30-ml) serving: **Calories** 50, **Total fat** 0 g, **Saturated fat** 0 g, **Cholesterol** 0 mg, **Sodium** 30 mg, **Total carbohydrates** 12 g, **Protein** 0 g, **Vitamin C** 10%, **Claims**—fat free; very low sodium

Candied Citrus Rind

 Vegan

YIELD	50–100 Candied Strips	METHOD	Preserving

Citrus fruit, organic, washed	5–10 fruits	5–10 fruits
Water	1 qt.	960 ml
Salt	½ tsp.	2 ml
Granulated sugar	1 lb.	480 g
Corn syrup	7 oz.	210 g
Granulated sugar	as needed for storage	

1 With a sharp knife, cut large, thin pieces of the peel from the citrus fruits. Remove as much of the white pith as possible.

2 Cut the peel into long, thin strips, about ¼ inch (6 millimeters) wide.

3 Bring 1 pint (480 milliliters) water and the salt to boil in a saucepan large enough to hold the citrus rind. Add the rind and simmer for 2 minutes. Drain.

4 Bring the remaining water, sugar and corn syrup to a boil. Add the blanched citrus rind and reduce the heat to a low simmer. Cook the rinds for about 15–20 minutes until they are translucent and tender. Store the rind in the syrup in the refrigerator. Or drain the rind on a screen until cool. Sprinkle the drained rind with granulated sugar and store in an airtight container.

Note Orange, lemon, grapefruit, mandarins, or tangerines may be used.

Approximate values per strip: **Calories** 35, **Total fat** 0 g, **Saturated fat** 0 g, **Cholesterol** 0 mg, **Sodium** 20 mg, **Total carbohydrates** 9 g, **Protein** 0 g

Compressed Fresh Watermelon

Slices of fruit can be compressed using the same chamber vacuum machines employed in sous vide *cooking. Compression renders juicy fruits, such as pineapple or watermelon, firm and intensely flavorful. Liquid seasonings such as fruit juice or vinaigrette dressing may be added to the vacuum bag before compression, as the fruit will absorb any seasoning or liquid sealed in the bag. Serve compressed fruit as garnishes or in salads and dessert preparations.*

YIELD 4 Servings, 6 oz. (180 g) each

Seedless watermelon slices, 1½ inches (3.8 centimeters) thick	2	2
Apple or lemon juice or other flavoring	2 fl. oz.	60 ml

1 Trim the rind from the watermelon slices. Cut the slices into even 5-inch (12-centimeter) lengths.

2 For each portion, fold back the top of a plastic vacuum bag 1 inch (2.5 centimeters). Add 1 table-spoon (15 milliliters) of the apple juice to each bag. Slide a piece of watermelon into each bag. Vacuum seal using as much pressure as possible so that the bag shrinks tightly around the fruit.

3 Serve the compressed watermelon in fruit salads or alone garnished with toasted nuts.

Approximate values per 6-oz. (180-g) serving: **Calories** 50, **Total fat** 0 g, **Saturated fat** 0 g, **Cholesterol** 0 mg, **Sodium** 0 mg, **Total carbohydrates** 13 g, **Protein** 1 g, **Vitamin A** 15%, **Vitamin C** 20%

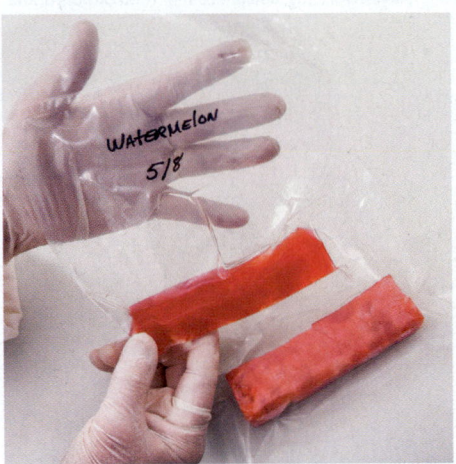

Comparing compressed watermelon (left) with watermelon before compression (right).

Compressed watermelon (top) shrinks and darkens in color. Uncompressed watermelon (bottom) is larger and lighter in color.

Sandwiches 27

▶ identify and describe key sandwich
  components

▶ choose and maintain high-quality
  sandwich ingredients

▶ identify different types and styles of
  sandwiches

▶ prepare a variety of hot and cold
  sandwiches to order

A sandwich is often the first meal a person learns to prepare. Even those who claim that they cannot cook often make delicious hot and cold sandwiches without considering it cooking. Mastering a grilled cheese or assembling the quintessential BLT may not require a degree in the culinary arts, but it does require the ability to select and use ingredients wisely.

Sandwiches, which are usually quick and easy to assemble, lend themselves well to a chef's creativity. Imaginative sandwiches can become sensational menu additions in even the most formal restaurants, and amazing sandwiches can keep lunch customers visiting regularly. They may be the focal point of a menu, or a smaller part of the pantry cook's responsibilities. Sandwiches offer larger food service operations economical opportunities for using leftovers, and they offer customers less expensive, quickly prepared meal options. Thus the ability to correctly prepare hot and cold sandwiches to order is a fundamental skill in many food service operations.

INGREDIENTS FOR SANDWICHES

Sandwiches are constructed from bread, a spread and one or more fillings. These components should be selected and combined carefully so that the finished sandwich is flavorful and visually appealing. Sandwiches may be served hot, cold or with a combination of hot and cold fillings. An understanding of proper timing, efficient assembly skills and correct holding temperatures is essential for successful sandwich service.

Sandwich Breads

Bread holds or contains the spread and fillings and gives the sandwich its shape. Bread also adds flavor, texture, nutrition and color, and often determines the appearance of the finished product. Virtually any bread can be used in sandwich making. Rectangular sandwich or **Pullman** loaves are used to make classic club sandwiches and tea sandwiches but rolls, biscuits, bagels, croissants, fruit and nut breads, whole-grain breads and savory breads as well as flatbreads such as naan, **lavash** and tortillas; pocket breads such as pitas; and flavorful breads such as focaccia and Swedish limpa are all good choices.

Whatever bread is used and whether its flavor is mild or intense, the bread should complement the fillings and not overpower them. Breads with dried fruit, nuts or seeds give a sandwich added flavor and textures. Boldly flavored dark breads such as dark rye and pumpernickel can be used with fillings having pronounced flavors, such as cured or smoked meat or fish. Any sandwich bread should be fresh (although day-old bread is easier to slice and is excellent toasted). Texture should also be considered when choosing bread for a sandwich. A coarse, open-grained loaf is unsuitable for moist, loose fillings such as a bound chicken salad. A bread's texture should be able to withstand moisture from the spread and fillings without becoming soggy or pasty. An overly hard or crusty bread, however, may make a sandwich difficult to eat.

Sandwich Spreads

A spread adds flavor, moisture and richness to the sandwich, and sometimes helps to hold or bind the bread and fillings together. Some spreads, especially plain or flavored butters, also act as barriers to prevent the moisture in the filling from soaking into the bread.

There are three principal types of spreads: butter and soft cheese, mayonnaise and vegetable and bean purées. Generally only one spread is used on a sandwich, although other condiments such as mustard, ketchup, or hot pepper sauce should be available to accommodate customers' requests.

A fine-grained sliced Pullman loaf is suitable for club and tea sandwiches.

Challah, whole grain and crusty loaves and rolls are good options for sandwiches.

Pullman a long rectangular loaf of bread for slicing; also, the lidded pan in which this bread is baked

lavash a thin flatbread made from wheat baked in a tandoor oven; commonly served in Afghanistan, Iran, Turkey and Eurasian countries

Butter and Soft Cheeses

One of the most common spreads, plain butter adds flavor and richness; it is also an effective moisture barrier. Flavored or compound butters, discussed in Chapter 11, Stocks and Sauces, make excellent sandwich spreads, adding flavor dimensions to the finished product. For example, try caper butter on a Cajun-style blackened beef sandwich or a red chile honey butter on a smoked turkey sandwich. Any butter spread should be softened or whipped so that it spreads easily without tearing the bread.

Like butter, cream cheese and soft cheese spreads such as flavored ricotta or the Herb Cheese Spread on page 150, add richness and serve as a moisture barrier. Cream cheese can be flavored with herbs, condiments or minced vegetables to represent many international flavor profiles, while still serving as a classic sandwich spread.

Mayonnaise

Mayonnaise, perhaps the most popular sandwich spread, adds moisture, richness and flavor and complements most meat, poultry, fish, shellfish, vegetable, egg and cheese fillings. Like butter, mayonnaise can be enlivened by adding flavoring ingredients. Condiments (e.g., coarse-grained mustard or grated horseradish), herbs, spices and spice blends (e.g., curry or chilli powder) and other ingredients such as garlic and pesto sauce can be stirred into fresh or commercially prepared mayonnaise. Fresh mayonnaise can also be prepared with flavorful oils, such as olive oil, walnut oil or chile oil. See Chapter 25, Salads and Salad Dressings, for recipes and additional information on mayonnaise.

Vegetable and Bean Purées

Puréed vegetables or beans make healthy, flavorful sandwich spreads. Options include roasted red pepper purée for a sandwich of Italian meats and cheeses, or a well-seasoned chickpea purée or guacamole for a vegetarian sandwich. Unlike butter, vegetable and bean purées usually do not provide a moisture barrier between the bread and the fillings, although roasted nut butters and peanut butter prevent bread from becoming soggy.

Sandwich Fillings

The filling is the body of the sandwich, providing most of its flavor. A sandwich often contains more than one filling. For example, the filling in a Reuben sandwich is corned beef, cheese and sauerkraut, whereas in a BLT it is bacon, lettuce and tomato. Fillings for cold sandwiches must be precooked and properly chilled. Some hot sandwich fillings may be cooked or reheated to order.

When choosing fillings, be sure that the flavors complement each other. Their textures may be similar or contrasting. If an ingredient, such as lettuce, is supposed to be crisp, it should be very crisp, not limp. If an ingredient is supposed to be tender and moist, make sure it is tender and moist. Improperly prepared, poor-quality or mishandled filling ingredients can ruin an otherwise wonderful sandwich. The following material discusses popular sandwich fillings in more detail.

Meats and Poultry

Almost any type of meat or poultry can be used as a sandwich filling. The only limitation is the creativity of the chef. Although the classic hot beef sandwich is the hamburger, other hot or cold beef products are also commonly used. For example, hot or cold small steaks, slices of larger steak cuts such as the tenderloin, thin slices of roast beef and so on make excellent fillings. Also popular are sliced hot or cold cured beef products, including corned beef, pastrami and smoked tongue as well as beef sausages such as salami, bologna and hot dogs. Lamb and pork are equally popular sandwich fillings whether the meat is ground and cooked like a hamburger patty or sliced from a well-seasoned roast. Lamb or pork loin and tenderloin are leaner meats that adapt well to various flavor combinations and cooking methods.

History of Sandwiches

The term *sandwich* came into use approximately 200 years ago. The fourth Earl of Sandwich, John Montagu (1718–1792), is credited with popularizing the concept of eating meats and cheeses between two slices of bread. Apparently the earl, not wanting to leave the gaming tables that he loved so much, would demand that his servants bring him meat and bread. He combined the two and ate them with one hand, allowing him a free hand to continue playing at the tables. Some historians argue that a more likely scenario is that, as the head of defense, the earl was kept busy planning British strategy for the Revolutionary War underway in the American colonies. Whichever the case, the name stuck.

Cured meats, especially various ham and bacon products, served either hot or cold, are perennially popular sandwich fillings. Barbecued pork, pork sausages and pork hot dogs work well in sandwiches. Sliced turkey breast, either roasted or smoked, and processed turkey as well crispy fried chicken breasts and chicken or turkey patties are commonly served in hot and cold sandwiches. Turkey bologna, turkey pastrami, turkey hot dogs and turkey ham may be chosen by customers because they generally have a lower fat content than the beef or pork options. Boneless chicken breast, either sliced or whole, can be prepared by a variety of methods and complements a broad range of sandwich flavors. A cold chicken or turkey salad bound with mayonnaise and incorporating fruit, nuts, celery, pickles or seasonings is another old-fashioned, but still beloved, option.

Fish and Shellfish

Fried and grilled fish fillets are sandwich standards, and the fried oyster, shrimp and crawfish po'boys of New Orleans have evolved from the working man's lunch to gourmet entrées. Canned fish products, particularly tuna and salmon, are also widely used as is smoked fish. Often fish and shellfish, especially tuna, shrimp, lobster or crab, serve as the foundation for mayonnaise-based bound salads. Sardines, anchovies and pickled herring are sometimes mixed into bound salads or arranged artistically on open-faced sandwiches.

Vegetables

Vegetables add texture, moisture, flavor and nutrition to sandwiches. Lettuce, onions and tomatoes are commonly used in combination with meat, cheese and other fillings. Celery or bell peppers add a nice crunchy texture to cheese or mayonnaise-based bound salad fillings. Vegetables can also stand on their own as sandwich fillings. Marinated, grilled or roasted vegetables can be featured in hot or cold sandwiches, and a combination of sliced, fresh vegetables and a flavorful dressing wrapped in soft pita bread, lavash or a tortilla becomes a portable salad.

Eggs

Hard-cooked eggs often appear as an ingredient in mayonnaise-based salads, where they are chopped and combined with seasonings. Hard-cooked eggs can also be sliced thin and used as an attractive garnish on open-faced sandwiches. Fried or scrambled eggs can be layered between pieces of bread or rolled in a tortilla for a breakfast sandwich or burrito. Fried eggs also top hamburgers or other meat and cheese sandwiches in regional specialties.

Cheeses

Cheese is available in such a variety of textures, flavors, colors and styles that it is a welcome addition to nearly any sandwich. Sliced cheese can fill hot or cold sandwiches, and melted cheese or a cheese sauce makes an excellent topping for hot open-faced sandwiches. Flavored cream cheese is a popular filling, particularly with bagels and fruit or nut breads. Semi-soft and firm cheese can be sliced, while rind-ripened cheese such as brie can be incorporated like a spread.

Bound Salads

Protein salads—such as chicken, tuna, egg and ham salads—bound with mayonnaise or salad dressing work well alone in sandwiches as well as in combination with other ingredients. Thin slices of fruit pair well with curried chicken or tuna salads. Smoked fish complements egg salad. And thin sliced pickled vegetables are always a welcome addition to bound salad sandwiches. Bound bean and grain salads are often the main element in a vegetarian sandwich. Bound salads are discussed in Chapter 25, Salads and Salad Dressings.

TYPES OF SANDWICHES

Sandwiches can be hot or cold, closed or open-faced, depending on the way in which the ingredients are assembled and presented.

Hot Sandwiches

Hot closed sandwiches include those in which the filling ingredients are served hot, such as a hamburger or hot dog, and those where the entire sandwich is heated for service, such as a grilled cheese or Monte Cristo. Hot closed sandwiches can be categorized as basic, grilled or deep-fried.

Basic hot closed sandwiches are generally those in which the principal filling is served hot between two pieces of bread. These sandwiches may also include fillings that are not hot, such as tomato slices and lettuce leaves. Variations of the basic hot closed sandwich include tacos, quesadillas, burritos (or burros) and wraps, in which the fillings are folded or wrapped in a tortilla or other supple flatbread. See the procedure on page 815.

Sliders are versions of basic hot closed hamburger sandwiches prepared on small buns. These small two-bite portions are said to slide down easily, hence their name. Popular fillings for sliders are miniature hamburger patties, grilled sausages, meatballs, miniature crab cakes, fried oysters or smaller quantities of spreads or other fillings.

Grilled sandwiches are those in which the filling is placed between two pieces of bread, which are buttered on the outside and then browned on a griddle or in a sauté pan. In grilled sandwiches, the fillings are warmed during this procedure but do not cook. Therefore fillings such as bacon or sliced meat should be fully cooked before the sandwich is assembled and grilled. Avoid overfilling the bread for grilled sandwiches.

Pulled pork sliders

Procedure for Preparing Grilled Sandwiches

1 Butter bread for grilled sandwich. Precook ingredients as required. Assemble sandwich.
2 Place the closed sandwich into a pre-heated buttered pan over medium heat.
3 When the bread is evenly browned, flip the sandwich over and brown on the other side.

When preparing grilled cheese sandwiches for production, for each sandwich place two slices of buttered bread on a hot griddle. Position the cheese so that when it melts, it covers the bread evenly. When the cheese has melted and the bread has browned, close the sandwich.

Flip the grilled sandwich over to brown on the other side.

Close the grilled sandwich prepared on a hot griddle when the cheese has melted and the bread has browned.

A sandwich grill, also known as a **panini grill**, with a heated hinged lid, makes quick work of grilling sandwiches because it allows them to be toasted on both sides without flipping. The weight of the heated lid presses on the sandwich flattening it slightly and leaving decorative grill marks. When a hinged grill is not available, a weight may be placed on top of a sandwich to flatten it during cooking. The procedure for preparing sandwiches on a panini grill is illustrated in the recipe for an Arugula, Capicola Ham and Provolone Panino on page 824.

Procedure for Preparing Sandwiches on a Panini Grill

1 Place filled sandwiches on a preheated panini grill, then close the lid.

2 Remove sandwiches when heated through and visibly browned.

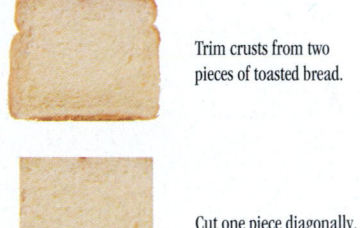

Trim crusts from two pieces of toasted bread.

Cut one piece diagonally.

Arrange trimmed, cut toast on plate.

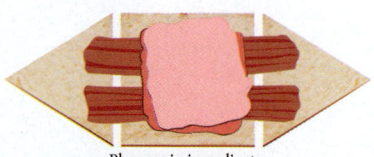

Place main ingredient – e.g., bacon, roast beef, sliced turkey – on toast.

Cover with cheese or sauce and heat.

Figure 27.1 Arranging hot open-faced sandwiches.

Deep-fried sandwiches are made by dipping a closed sandwich in egg batter or bread crumbs and then deep-frying it. The most common example is the **Monte Cristo**, which is white bread filled with sliced ham, Swiss cheese and Dijon mustard.

Not all sandwiches must be eaten by hand, as the hot open-faced turkey or steak sandwich proved long ago. In the typical **hot open-faced sandwich**, bread (grilled, toasted or fresh) is placed on a serving plate, covered with hot meat or other filling and topped with an appropriate gravy, sauce or cheese. The completed dish is often browned under a broiler immediately before service. Condiments and garnishes are usually served on the side. Figure 27.1 illustrates one method for preparing a hot open-faced sandwich.

Cold Sandwiches

Cold sandwiches are made with raw ingredients that are not intended to be cooked, such as vegetables and cheese, or with meat, poultry, fish or shellfish that is precooked and chilled before use as a filling. Cold sandwiches may be closed or open-faced.

Cold closed sandwiches contain two or more pieces of bread with one or more fillings and one or more spreads. Cold closed sandwiches are usually eaten with the hands and come in three basic styles: basic, multidecker and tea.

Basic cold sandwiches are made with two pieces of bread (or one split roll), one spread and one or more fillings. A tuna salad sandwich and an Italian-style submarine are examples of basic cold closed sandwiches. A variation of the basic cold sandwich is a wrap with cold fillings—for example, an herb-flavored tortilla spread with peanut sauce wrapped around spinach leaves, diced grilled chicken and cold cooked rice. (See Grilled Chicken, Avocado and Vegetable Wrap on page 825.)

Multidecker cold sandwiches are made with three or more pieces of bread, one or more spreads and two or more fillings. The **club sandwich**, in which sliced turkey, bacon, lettuce and tomato are layered with three slices of toasted bread, is a classic example of a multidecker sandwich (see Club Sandwich on page 820).

Procedure for Preparing Wrap Sandwiches

1 Top the flatbread or tortilla with a spread or dressing.

2 Mound the vegetables and meat, fish or poultry items across the flatbread or tortilla.

3 Roll the flatbread or tortilla tightly around the filling.

Procedure for Preparing Cold Multidecker Sandwiches

1 Spread the first slice of toasted bread with butter or mayonnaise, then top with meat and vegetables.

2 Add the second slice of bread and spread with mayonnaise.

3 Add a second layer of vegetables and meat.

4 Cut the finished sandwich into quarters for service.

Tea sandwiches are small, fancy constructions made with light, soft, trimmed breads and delicate fillings and spreads. The name derives from their service at afternoon tea. They are usually cut or rolled into shapes such as diamonds, circles or pinwheels and served as a finger food at parties and receptions; on these occasions they may also be called finger sandwiches.

Smørbrød featuring smoked salmon (top), roast beef and shrimp (bottom) are attractively garnished with items that complement the principal ingredient.

smørbrød [SMURR-brur] Norwegian cold open-faced sandwiches; the related Swedish term *smörgåsbord* [SMORE-guhs-bohrd] refers to a buffet table of bread and butter, salads, open-faced sandwiches, pickled or marinated fish, sliced meats and cheeses

tartine fresh or toasted bread spread with butter, jam or savory spreads and toppings

Cold open-faced sandwiches are larger versions of canapés, which are discussed in Chapter 29, Hors d'Oeuvre. Popular styles are the open-faced Norwegian sandwich known as **smørbrød** and the French open-faced sandwich known as **tartine**. As with canapés, much emphasis is placed on visual appeal. A single slice of bread is coated with a spread, then covered with thin slices of meat, poultry or fish, or a thin layer of a bound salad. Carefully cut and arranged garnishes, such as hard-cooked eggs, fresh herbs, grilled vegetables, pickles, onions and radishes, are used to complete the presentation. A simple version of an open-faced cold sandwich is a delicatessen classic—a bagel with lox and cream cheese.

SANDWICH MISE EN PLACE

Sandwiches are generally prepared to order, and their preparation usually requires a great deal of handwork. The goal is to assemble all ingredients and equipment within easy reach to minimize movement and ensure efficiency at the time of final assembly. Because each menu and food service operation has its own requirements, there is no one correct station setup, but there are a few basic guidelines.

A cook prepares a sandwich at a well-stocked refrigerated sandwich bar.

- *Prepare ingredients.* All sandwich ingredients should be cooked, mixed, sliced and prepared ahead of service to facilitate quick, efficient assembly at service time. Before service, slice the meats, cheeses and vegetables; clean and dry lettuce and other fresh vegetable ingredients; blend the flavored spreads; mix the bound salads; and so on.

- *Arrange and store ingredients.* Arrange all sandwich ingredients within easy reach of the work area. Cold items must be properly refrigerated at all times. A sandwich bar (pictured in the nearby photo) similar to a steam table but with refrigerated compartments, is frequently used for this purpose. Under-counter refrigeration can be used for backup supplies and less frequently used ingredients. Sliced meats, cheeses and vegetables must be well covered to prevent dehydration or contamination. Many ingredients can be pre-portioned, either by weight or count and wrapped in individual portions for storage.

- *Select and arrange equipment.* The heavy equipment needed for making sandwiches can include preparation equipment such as meat slicers, griddles, grills, fryers and broilers as well as storage equipment such as refrigerated sandwich bars for cold ingredients and steam tables for hot ingredients. Even the simplest sandwich menu requires the use of basic hand tools such as spatulas, spreaders, portion scoops, knives and cutting boards. Be sure that the supply of such items is adequate to permit quick handwork and to avoid delays or cross-contamination.

PRESENTING AND GARNISHING SANDWICHES

Sandwiches, especially cold closed sandwiches, are usually cut into halves, thirds or quarters for service. Cutting makes a sandwich easier to handle and eat and allows for a more attractive presentation; the sandwich wedges can be arranged to add height to the plate and to expose the fillings' colors and textures. For sit-down service, hot closed sandwiches such as hamburgers are often presented open-faced. Condiments, such as mustard and mayonnaise, and garnishes, such as sliced tomatoes, onions, pickles and lettuce leaves, are served on the side or on one of the open bun halves. This attractive presentation allows the customer to assemble and add ingredients to the sandwich as desired.

Although a sandwich can be a meal unto itself, it may be served with a salad or starch accompaniment. These accompaniments can serve as functional garnishes that are more than decorative and enhance the foods on the plate. Potato chips or French-fried potatoes are standard fare, perhaps because they are also finger foods and they provide a crunchy texture. Bound salads, such as potato and macaroni, are also common starch accompaniments. Plated sandwiches have long been served with coleslaw, fruit salad or a small mixed green salad as side dishes. The standard soup-and-sandwich combo—half a sandwich with a cup of soup—remains a popular lunch selection.

Greatest Hits from the Sandwich Counter

Writing in *Le Guide culinaire* in 1903, Auguste Escoffier describes just two types of sandwiches: those "with two slices of buttered bread . . . covering a slice of ham or tongue, etc." and "the kind served at elaborate functions," which are much smaller, and in which the "sandwiched product (whatever this be)" is diced. Among his list of common sandwich ingredients are ham, beef, chicken, foie gras, caviar and watercress.

Today's cook must recognize a somewhat wider variety of sandwiches, however. And, as the following list shows, often a sandwich's popular name bears no connection to its ingredients.

Bao: Chinese steamed yeast bun traditionally filled with braised pork. Such buns are now filled with everything from spicy fried chicken to kimchee and roast duck.

Croque Monsieur: Ham and cheese sandwich dipped in beaten egg and grilled; made popular by bars and bistros throughout Paris.

Fluffernutter: Peanut butter and marshmallow fluff spread on—what else?—white bread; popular during the 1960s.

French Dip: Thin slices of roast beef in a crusty French-bread roll served au jus.

Gyro: Well-seasoned rotisserie-roasted lamb, thinly sliced and served wrapped in pita bread with onions and cucumber-yogurt dressing. A Greek-American creation, the gyro [(YEAR-o] became popular at Greek lunch counters in New York City during the 1970s.

Panino: A crusty roll layered with cold cuts and cheese such as salami, ham, prosciutto and fontina; usually grilled and served warm. The plural form, *panini*, is often used when referring to this Italian specialty.

Patty Melt: Thin hamburger patty on rye bread with cheddar or Swiss or Emmenthaler cheese and sautéed onions griddled in butter. Many claim the sandwich originated in the 1950s in Hollywood at Tiny Naylor's Drive-In.

Pimento Cheese: Cheddar, mayonnaise and pimento cheese spread on sliced white bread. Popular in the Southeastern United States, the sandwich may be embellished with jalapeños, ham or sliced pickles.

Po' Boy: French bread loaf split and filled with various ingredients, especially fried oysters or shrimp and rémoulade sauce. Created during the 1920s, it is New Orleans' version of a submarine sandwich.

Reuben: Corned beef, Swiss or Emmenthaler cheese, sauerkraut and mustard or Thousand Island dressing grilled between two slices of rye bread. The Reuben was probably created during the early 1900s by Arnold Reuben, owner of New York City's Reuben's Restaurant.

Taco al Pastor: Chile-marinated rotisserie pork shoulder and pineapple, similar to the gyro. The meat and fruit are shaved onto warm corn tortillas, served with salsa and onions in a dish that migrated from taco trucks into the dining room.

QUESTIONS FOR DISCUSSION

1   List examples for each of the three primary sandwich components.

2   Explain the differences between a hot open-faced and a hot closed sandwich.

3   List hand tools used in sandwich production, and explain the need for an ample supply of these tools.

4   Why is cross-contamination a concern when preparing sandwiches? What simple steps can be taken to avoid the spread of pathogenic microorganisms?

5   Create three sandwich concepts for a college town café. Describe the types of bread, the fillings and the accompaniments for each one. Discuss the preparation required in order to produce these sandwiches quickly during a busy lunchtime rush.

6   Sandwiches have become nearly universal, consumed in countries around the world. Use the Internet to research popular sandwiches served in three or four different regions of the world. Discuss and compare the different sandwich components and preparation methods used for each one.

Sandwich Recipes

Grilled Vegetable Sandwich

🍃 Vegetarian

YIELD 6 Sandwiches

Eggplant, cut into ¼-inch thick slices	1	1
Salt	1 tsp.	5 ml
Zucchini, cut lengthwise into ¼-inch- (6-millimeters-) thick slices	1	1
Yellow squash, cut lengthwise into ¼-inch- (6-millimeters-) thick slices	1	1
Red onion, cut into ¼-inch- (6-millimeters-) thick slices	1	1
Olive oil	3 fl. oz.	90 ml
Garlic, minced	2 Tbsp.	30 ml
Herbes de Provence	¾ tsp.	4 ml
Black pepper	as needed	as needed
Sandwich rolls, multigrain	6	6
Herb Cheese Spread (page 150)	4 oz.	120 g
Lettuce	6 leaves	6 leaves
Red bell peppers, roasted, cut into strips	6 oz.	180 g

1 Sprinkle the eggplant with salt and set aside in a colander for 10 minutes.

2 Dry the sliced zucchini, squash and eggplant with paper towels. Place them on a sheet pan with the onion slices. Brush the vegetables with the oil and sprinkle with the garlic and herbes de Provence. Season with salt and pepper.

3 Place the sliced vegetables on a hot grill without crowding. Grill until lightly charred and tender, approximately 4–5 minutes on each side. (The vegetables may be prepared ahead of serving. Refrigerate until needed.)

4 Split each roll in half. Spread the Herb Cheese Spread generously on the top half of each roll. Arrange one-sixth of the lettuce, onion, bell peppers, squash and eggplant in layers on each roll. Place the tops on the sandwiches and serve immediately.

Approximate values per sandwich: **Calories** 480, **Total fat** 24 g, **Saturated fat** 7 g, **Cholesterol** 25 mg, **Sodium** 970 mg, **Total carbohydrates** 59 g, **Protein** 11 g, **Vitamin A** 45%, **Vitamin C** 80%, **Calcium** 15%, **Iron** 20%

Club Sandwich

YIELD 1 Sandwich

Sliced bread, toasted	3 slices	3 slices
Mayonnaise	as needed	as needed
Lettuce leaves	2	2
Tomato slices	3	3
Bacon slices, cooked crisp	3	3
Salt and pepper	TT	TT
Cooked turkey breast, sliced thin	3 oz.	90 g
Deep-Fried Potatoes (page 662) or chips	as needed	as needed
Ketchup, optional	as needed for garnish	
Chopped parsley, optional	as needed for garnish	

1 Spread one side of each slice of bread with mayonnaise.

2 Arrange the lettuce, tomato and bacon on one slice of toast. Season with salt and pepper.

3 Place another slice of toast on top of the bacon.

4 Arrange the turkey breast on top of the second slice of toast.

5 Place the third slice of toast on top of the turkey breast, mayonnaise side down.

6 Place 4 frilled toothpicks in the sandwich, one on each side, approximately 1 inch (2.5 centimeters) in from the edge. Cut the sandwich diagonally into quarters and arrange as desired for service. Garnish with fried potatoes, ketchup and chopped parsley, if using.

Approximate values per sandwich: **Calories** 530, **Total fat** 24 g, **Saturated fat** 6 g, **Cholesterol** 95 mg, **Sodium** 830 mg, **Total carbohydrates** 38 g, **Protein** 39 g, **Vitamin A** 4%, **Vitamin C** 10%

Mahi-Mahi Fish Taco

YIELD 8 Servings, 2 tacos each

Marinade:		
Cilantro	2 oz.	60 g
Garlic clove	1	1
Red onion, chopped	1 oz.	30 g
Ground coriander	2 tsp.	10 ml
Ground cumin	2 tsp.	10 ml
Salt	1 Tbsp.	15 ml
Vegetable oil	4 fl. oz.	120 ml
Mahi-Mahi or tilapia fillets, ½ in. (1.2 cm) thick, 3 oz. (90 g) each	16	16
Relish:		
Tomatillos, small dice	8 oz.	240 g
Roma tomatoes, seeded, small dice	8 oz.	240 g
Cilantro, chopped	2 Tbsp.	30 ml
Red onion, small dice	1 oz.	30 g
Serrano chile, seeded, minced	1 Tbsp.	15 ml
Lime juice	2 tsp.	10 ml
Extra virgin olive oil	2 tsp.	10 ml
Mexican oregano	pinch	pinch
Salt and pepper	TT	TT
Corn tortillas, 6 in. (15 cm)	32	32
Creamy Coleslaw (page 766)	1 lb.	480 g
Avocados, peeled, sliced	4	4
Cotija cheese, crumbled	4 oz.	120 g
Red Beans and Rice with Andouille, prepared without the rice (page 649), optional	as needed	as needed

1 Destem the cilantro leaves and place in the bowl of a blender. Add the remaining marinade ingredients and blend until smooth, approximately 15 seconds.

2 Place the fish fillets in a nonreactive pan and pour the marinade over them. Mix gently so that the fish is evenly coated. Refrigerate until service or overnight.

3 In a stainless steel bowl, combine the ingredients for the tomatillo relish and stir gently to combine. Refrigerate until service.

4 At service, place the fish fillets on a hot grill. Grill turning once until done. Remove and keep warm for service.

5 Heat the corn tortillas by toasting them on the grill for a few seconds on each side. When they begin to brown, remove from the grill and stack them on a clean towel.

6 Place two stacks of two tortillas each on each plate. Place one piece of fish on each stack of tortillas. Top each piece of fish with 1 ounce (30 grams) of Creamy Coleslaw, several slices of avocado, 2 tablespoons (30 milliliters) of the tomatillo relish and crumbled cotija cheese.

7 Serve with a ramekin of Red Beans with Andouille if desired.

Approximate values per 2-taco serving: **Calories** 730, **Total fat** 36 g, **Saturated fat** 7 g, **Cholesterol** 140 mg, **Sodium** 630 mg, **Total carbohydrates** 65 g, **Protein** 42 g, **Vitamin A** 25%, **Vitamin C** 50%, **Calcium** 30%, **Iron** 25%

Hamburger

YIELD 1 Sandwich

Beef, ground round	4–6 oz.	120–180 g
Salt and pepper	TT	TT
Hamburger bun or other appropriate bread	1	1
Garnishes	as desired	as desired

1 Form the ground round into a patty, handling the beef as little as possible.

2 Season the patty with salt and pepper and broil or grill to the desired doneness, turning once. While the patty is cooking, toast the bun or bread if desired.

3 Remove the patty from the broiler or grill, place on half of the bun or one slice of bread and garnish the other with a lettuce leaf, a slice of onion, a slice of tomato and/or pickles. Serve with condiments such as ketchup and mustard.

Approximate values per sandwich: **Calories** 580, **Total fat** 32 g, **Saturated fat** 9 g, **Cholesterol** 99 mg, **Sodium** 355 mg, **Total carbohydrates** 40 g, **Protein** 29 g

Variations:

Cheeseburger—Place one or two slices of American, Cheddar, Swiss or other cheese on the cooking patty approximately 1 minute before it is done.

Approximate values per sandwich: **Calories** 680, **Total fat** 42 g, **Saturated fat** 15 g, **Cholesterol** 130 mg, **Sodium** 520 mg, **Total carbohydrates** 42 g, **Protein** 36 g, **Calcium** 20%

Bacon Blue Cheeseburger—Place approximately 1 tablespoon (15 milliliters) crumbled blue cheese and two slices of crisp bacon on top of the cooking patty approximately 1 minute before it is done.

Approximate values per sandwich: **Calories** 650, **Total fat** 39 g, **Saturated fat** 12 g, **Cholesterol** 110 mg, **Sodium** 560 mg, **Total carbohydrates** 41 g, **Protein** 33 g

Mushroom Burger—Sauté 2 ounces (60 grams) sliced mushrooms in 1–2 teaspoons (5–10 milliliters) butter or olive oil. Top the cooked hamburger or cheeseburger with the cooked mushrooms.

Approximate values per sandwich, without cheese: **Calories** 660, **Total fat** 37 g, **Saturated fat** 12 g, **Cholesterol** 110 mg, **Sodium** 400 mg, **Total carbohydrates** 48 g, **Protein** 33 g

California Burger—Prepare a hamburger or cheeseburger and serve on a whole-wheat bun accompanied by 2 ounces (60 grams) guacamole, 1 ounce (30 grams) alfalfa sprouts, two slices of ripe tomato and one thin slice of red onion.

Approximate values per sandwich, without cheese: **Calories** 690, **Total fat** 40 g, **Saturated fat** 9 g, **Cholesterol** 100 mg, **Sodium** 770 mg, **Total carbohydrates** 50 g, **Protein** 33 g, **Vitamin C** 20%

Blended Mushroom Burger—Sauté 3 ounces (90 grams) chopped mushrooms in 2 teaspoons (10 milliliters) olive oil. Chill. Substitute the cooked mushrooms for 2 ounces (60 grams) of the raw ground beef in Step 1.

Approximate values per sandwich: **Calories** 450, **Total fat** 29 g, **Saturated fat** 8 g, **Cholesterol** 60 mg, **Sodium** 260 mg, **Total carbohydrates** 25 g, **Protein** 22 g, **Calcium** 10%, **Iron** 20%, **Claims**—good source of calcium; excellent source of iron

Hamburger Boom

Recognizing the undisputed popularity of the hamburger, chefs are responding with burgers from humble to *haute*. Smothered with pulled pork or studded with foie gras, hamburgers lend themselves to customization. Consider the following to inspire your creativity. Combine different cuts of beef to enhance flavor. Make burgers from ground chicken, chorizo sausage, lamb, salmon, tuna or grilled vegetables. Incorporate flavors from diverse cuisines such as German (sauerkraut), Korean (gochujang sauce and kimchee) or Peruvian (aji chile mayonnaise). Add texture by layering julienne vegetables or fries under the bun. Explore the world of fine cheese when choosing a topping. And reconsider the bun. Use portabella mushroom caps, rosti potato cakes or miniature waffles in place of a standard bread product.

Turkey Burger

YIELD 4 Sandwiches

Fresh ginger, minced	2 tsp.	10 ml
Garlic, chopped	1 tsp.	5 ml
Sesame oil	1 tsp.	5 ml
White mushrooms, chopped	4 oz.	120 g
Green onion, chopped fine	1	1
Ground turkey	20 oz.	600 g
Salt	½ tsp.	2 ml
Black pepper	¼ tsp.	1 ml
Glaze:		
Soy sauce	4 tsp.	20 ml
Sesame oil	2 tsp.	10 ml
Fresh ginger, minced	½ tsp.	2 ml
Garlic, chopped	1 tsp.	5 ml
Brioche bun, flatbread or other bread as desired	4 buns	4 buns
Herb Cheese Spread (page 150)	4 Tbsp.	60 ml
Baby spinach and red onions	as needed for garnish	
Deep-fried sweet potatoes	as needed for garnish	

1 Sauté the ginger and garlic in the sesame oil for 1 minute. Add the mushrooms and onion and sauté approximately 1 minute longer. Do not fully cook the mushrooms; allow them to retain most of their liquid in order to add moisture to the finished burgers. Remove the mushroom mixture from the heat, spread on a sheet pan and refrigerate until cold.

2 Combine the cold mushroom mixture with the ground turkey, salt and pepper and mix well. Form the mixture into four patties.

3 Stir the glaze ingredients together.

4 Oil the grate of a hot grill. Brush the burgers with the glaze and grill to an internal temperature of 165°F (74°C), basting occasionally with the glaze.

5 Serve each burger on a toasted bun or warm flatbread coated with Herb Cheese Spread. Serve accompanied by baby spinach leaves, red onion slices and deep-fried sweet potatoes or other garnishes as desired.

Approximate values per sandwich: **Calories** 370, **Total fat** 17 g, **Saturated fat** 4 g, **Cholesterol** 110 mg, **Sodium** 960 mg, **Total carbohydrates** 22 g, **Protein** 30 g, **Iron** 20%

Arugula, Capicola Ham and Provolone Panino

YIELD 1 Sandwich

Ciabatta or hard roll, 4 in. × 2½ in. (10 cm × 6 cm)	1	1
Mayonnaise	1 fl. oz.	30 ml
Basil Pesto Sauce (page 249)	2 tsp.	10 ml
Arugula	½ oz.	15 g
Capicola, prosciutto or ham, sliced thin	2 oz.	60 g
Provolone, sliced thin	1 oz.	30 g
Oven-dried tomato wedges	1 oz.	30 g
Black pepper	TT	TT
Olives	as needed for garnish	
Tomatoes, quartered	as needed for garnish	

1 Cut the roll in half horizontally. Spread the cut sides of the roll with the mayonnaise and Basil Pesto Sauce.

2 Arrange the arugula, capicola, provolone and tomatoes in layers on the bottom portion of the roll. Season the layers with pepper as desired. Cover with the top half of the roll.

3 Place the sandwich on a preheated panini grill or on a griddle. Cook until heated through and browned, approximately 3–5 minutes. (If using a griddle, place a weight on the sandwich as it cooks, then flip it halfway through to brown on both sides.)

4 Cut on the diagonal and serve immediately garnished with olives and fresh tomato wedges on the side.

Approximate values per sandwich: **Calories** 670, **Total fat** 57 g, **Saturated fat** 14 g, **Cholesterol** 60 mg, **Sodium** 2200 mg, **Total carbohydrates** 16 g, **Protein** 24 g, **Vitamin C** 80%, **Calcium** 30%

capicola Italian dry-cured salami made from pork shoulder that is seasoned with garlic, hot pepper, spices and wine, then smoked and cured

Cubano (Cuban Grilled Ham and Pork Sandwich)

YIELD 1 Sandwich

Sub roll, 6 in. (15 cm)	1	1
Dijon mustard	1 fl. oz.	30 ml
Ham, shaved thin	2 oz.	60 g
Pork loin, roasted, shaved thin	2 oz.	60 g
Swiss or Emmenthaler cheese	2 slices	2 slices
Dill pickle, thinly sliced lengthwise	1	1

1 Split the sub roll in half lengthwise. Spread the cut sides of the roll with mustard.

2 Arrange the ham, pork loin and cheese in layers on the roll, finishing with the pickle slices.

3 Place the sandwich in a preheated and lightly greased panini grill or on a griddle. Press down to compress the sandwich. Cook until heated through and browned, approximately 2–4 minutes. (If using a griddle, place a weight on the sandwich as it cooks and flip it halfway through to brown on both sides.)

4 Cut on the diagonal and serve immediately, garnished with potato or vegetable chips if desired.

Approximate values per sandwich: **Calories** 650, **Total fat** 23 g, **Saturated fat** 9 g, **Cholesterol** 105 mg, **Sodium** 2320 mg, **Total carbohydrates** 65 g, **Protein** 42 g, **Calcium** 35%, **Iron** 20%

Grilled Chicken, Avocado and Vegetable Wrap

YIELD 8 Servings, 1 half-wrap each

Chicken breast, boneless, skinless, grilled	12 oz.	360 g
Lavash bread or tortillas, 14 in. (35 cm)	4	4
Hummus (page 875)	1 pt.	480 ml
Baby spinach	4 oz.	120 g
Red bell pepper, julienne	4 oz.	120 g
Cucumber, sliced thin	4 oz.	120 g
Red onion, sliced thin	2 oz.	60 g
Black olives, sliced	4 oz.	120 g
Feta cheese, crumbled	4 oz.	120 g
Fresh mint, chopped	4 Tbsp.	60 ml
Salt and pepper	TT	TT

1 Dice the chicken.

2 To make each wrap, place one lavash bread on a cutting board and spread with approximately 4 ounces (120 grams) hummus.

3 Sprinkle one-fourth of the spinach, bell pepper, chicken, cucumber, onion, olives, cheese and mint over the Hummus. Season to taste with salt and pepper.

4 Fold in each end of the lavash. Then roll the bread around the ingredients tightly enough so that the sandwich will hold its shape. Cut each wrap in half for service.

Approximate values per half-wrap serving: **Calories** 500, **Total fat** 18 g, **Saturated fat** 5 g, **Cholesterol** 50 mg, **Sodium** 920 mg, **Total carbohydrates** 57 g, **Protein** 28 g, **Vitamin A** 40%, **Vitamin C** 40%, **Calcium** 15%, **Iron** 35%

Grilled Cheese with Arugula, Sun-Dried Tomatoes and Bacon

YIELD 1 Sandwich

Sliced bread	2 slices	2 slices
Whole butter, softened	1 oz.	30 g
Gruyère, provolone or cheddar cheese, sliced	2 oz.	60 g
Sautéed onions	½ oz.	15 g
Sun dried tomatoes, chopped coarse	1 oz.	30 g
Baby arugula	½ oz.	15 g
Bacon slices, cooked	2	2

1 Spread one side of each slice of bread with butter. Place one slice of bread, butter side down, in a sauté pan over medium low heat. Place half of the sliced cheese on the bread. Top the cheese with the sautéed onions, sun-dried tomatoes, baby arugula and the bacon. Place the remaining sliced cheese on top of the bacon

2 Place the other slice of bread on top of the cheese, butter side up.

3 Cook over medium low heat until the bread is evenly browned, approximately 3–4 minutes. Carefully turn the sandwich over with a spatula and cook the second side until the bread is browned, the sandwich is hot, the cheese is melted and the arugula is wilted, approximately 2 minutes.

Approximate values per sandwich: **Calories** 810, **Total fat** 54 g, **Saturated fat** 29 g, **Cholesterol** 145 mg, **Sodium** 1120 mg, **Total carbohydrates** 51 g, **Protein** 35 g, **Calcium** 35%, **Vitamin A** 35%, **Vitamin C** 25%, **Calcium** 70%, **Iron** 30%

Reuben Sandwich

YIELD 1 Sandwich

Dark or light rye bread	2 slices	2 slices
Thousand Island Dressing (page 756)	1 fl. oz.	30 ml
Cooked corned beef, hot, sliced very thin	4 oz.	120 g
Sauerkraut, hot, drained well	2 oz.	60 g
Swiss or Emmenthaler cheese	2 slices	2 slices
Whole butter, softened	as needed	as needed

1 Spread each slice of bread with approximately 1 tablespoon (15 milliliters) Thousand Island Dressing.

2 Place the corned beef, sauerkraut and cheese on one slice of bread. Top with the second slice of bread, dressing side in the sandwich.

3 Butter the top slice of bread and place the sandwich on a hot griddle, butter side down. Carefully butter the second slice of bread.

4 Griddle the sandwich, turning once when the first side is well browned. The sandwich is done when both sides are well browned, the fillings are very hot and the cheese is melted.

5 Cut the sandwich in half diagonally and arrange as desired for service.

Approximate values per sandwich: **Calories** 560, **Total fat** 27 g, **Saturated fat** 10 g, **Cholesterol** 85 mg, **Sodium** 2150 mg, **Total carbohydrates** 39 g, **Protein** 40 g, **Vitamin A** 10%, **Vitamin C** 30%

Monte Cristo Sandwich

YIELD 1 Sandwich

White bread	2 slices	2 slices
Whole butter, softened	as needed	as needed
Cooked turkey breast, sliced thin	1 oz.	30 g
Ham, sliced thin	1 oz.	30 g
Swiss or Emmenthaler cheese	2 slices	2 slices
Egg	1	1
Milk	1 fl. oz.	30 ml
Powdered sugar, optional	as needed for garnish	
Cranberry sauce	as needed for garnish	

1 Spread one side of each slice of bread with butter.

2 Arrange the turkey breast, ham and cheese on top of the butter on one slice of bread.

3 Place the other slice of bread on top of the cheese, butter side against the cheese.

4 Beat the egg and milk together. Dip the sandwich in the egg batter and allow the batter to soak into the bread for approximately 4–5 minutes.

5 Using the swimming method, deep-fry the sandwich in oil at 375°F (190°C) until it is evenly browned. Remove from the oil and drain well. Cut the sandwich into two or four pieces and arrange as desired. Dust with powdered sugar, if using, and serve with cranberry sauce.

Approximate values per sandwich: **Calories** 630, **Total fat** 42 g, **Saturated fat** 24 g, **Cholesterol** 345 mg, **Sodium** 1050 mg, **Total carbohydrates** 27 g, **Protein** 35 g, **Vitamin A** 40%

Kentucky Hot Brown Sandwich

YIELD 6 Sandwiches

Ingredient	US	Metric
Heavy cream, hot	6 fl. oz.	180 ml
Romano, grated	6 oz.	180 g
Velouté, hot (page 222)	1 qt.	960 ml
Dry sherry	1 fl. oz.	30 ml
White toast, crust removed	12 slices	12 slices
Turkey breast, cooked, sliced	1 lb. 8 oz.	720 g
Parmesan, grated	2 oz.	60 g
Tomato wedges	12	12
Bacon slices, lean, cooked crisp	12	12

1 To make the sauce, add the cream and the Romano to the Velouté and bring to a simmer. Simmer for 1 minute, then strain the sauce through a china cap. Stir in the sherry. Hold in a warm place for service.

2 Cut the toast diagonally into triangles.

3 To assemble each sandwich, arrange four toast triangles in a gratin dish and top with 4 ounces (120 grams) turkey and 4 fluid ounces (120 milliliters) sauce. Bake at 350°F (180°C) until brown, approximately 15 minutes.

4 Top each sandwich with Parmesan, two tomato wedges and two strips of bacon and serve very hot.

Approximate values per sandwich: **Calories** 720, **Total fat** 34 g, **Saturated fat** 17 g, **Cholesterol** 185 mg, **Sodium** 2180 mg, **Total carbohydrates** 45 g, **Protein** 59 g, **Vitamin A** 20%, **Calcium** 50%

Muffuletta Sandwich

YIELD 4 Servings, ¼ sandwich each

Olive salad:		
Red bell pepper, roasted, chopped	8 oz.	240 g
Niçoise or Gaeta olives, pitted, chopped	4 oz.	120 g
Olives, green, pitted, chopped	4 oz.	120 g
Olive oil	4 fl. oz.	120 ml
Fresh Italian parsley, chopped	2 Tbsp.	30 ml
Anchovy fillets, mashed	2	2
Dried oregano	1 tsp.	5 ml
Lemon juice	1 Tbsp.	15 ml
Round Italian bread, 8-in. (18-cm) diameter	1	1
Arugula or curly endive, chiffonade	1½ oz.	45 g
Tomato concassée	6 oz.	180 g
Mortadella, sliced thin	6 oz.	180 g
Soppressata, sliced thin	4 oz.	120 g
Provolone or Fontina, sliced thin	4 oz.	120 g
Black pepper	TT	TT

1 To make the olive salad, combine the bell pepper, olives, oil, parsley, anchovies, oregano and lemon juice and marinate in the refrigerator for several hours.

2 Cut the loaf of bread in half horizontally. Remove some of the soft interior of the bread to create a slight hollow area.

3 Drain the olive salad, reserving the oil. Brush the interior of the bread with the reserved oil, using it all.

4 Arrange the olive salad, greens, tomato concassée, mortadella, soppressata and cheese in layers on the bottom portion of the loaf of bread, finishing with a thick layer of olive salad. Season the layers with pepper as desired.

5 Place the top on the sandwich and wrap tightly with plastic wrap. Refrigerate the sandwich for several hours so that the layers will remain in place when the sandwich is cut.

6 Cut the sandwich into four to six wedges and arrange as desired for service.

Approximate values per ¼-sandwich serving: **Calories** 970, **Total fat** 69 g, **Saturated fat** 19 g, **Cholesterol** 65 mg, **Sodium** 2750 mg, **Total carbohydrates** 56 g, **Protein** 30 g, **Vitamin A** 30%, **Vitamin C** 40%, **Calcium** 40%, **Iron** 30%

Pan Bagnat
(Provençal Tuna Sandwich)

Pan bagnat *means "bathed bread" in French. The juices from the tuna and vegetables soak into the crusty bread, which is already "swimming" with garlicky oil. This popular sandwich from southern France keeps well and should be made at least 30 minutes in advance of service.*

YIELD 1 Loaf, 4 Servings

French bread, 12-in. (30-cm) loaf	1	1
Garlic, chopped	1 Tbsp.	15 ml
Salt	½ tsp.	2 ml
Olive oil	2 fl. oz.	60 ml
Tomato	1	1
Red bell pepper, roasted, seeded	6 oz.	180 g
Green bell pepper, roasted, seeded	6 oz.	180 g
Tuna, canned, water-packed, undrained	12 oz.	360 g
Capers, drained	2 Tbsp.	30 ml
Green onions, minced	2	2
Red onion, sliced thin	4 oz.	120 g
Anchovy fillets, optional	4	4

1 Cut the French bread almost in half, keeping the top and bottom attached. Combine the garlic, salt and oil and brush the inside of the loaf with this mixture. Heat the loaf in a 350°F (180°C) oven until the crust is crisp, approximately 5–6 minutes.

2 Cut the tomato into thin slices. Cut the bell peppers into four pieces each. Combine the tuna, capers and green onions.

3 Spread the tuna mixture evenly on the loaf. Cover the tuna with the tomato, bell peppers and red onion slices. Top with anchovy fillets, if using. Press down on loaf. Secure it in four places with toothpicks, then cut into four uniform portions. Alternatively wrap the loaf securely in parchment paper. Press down and cut into uniform portions.

Approximate values per ¼-loaf serving: **Calories** 340, **Total fat** 9 g, **Saturated fat** 1.5 g, **Cholesterol** 20 mg, **Sodium** 1010 mg, **Total carbohydrates** 38 g, **Protein** 25 g, **Vitamin A** 30%, **Vitamin C** 150%, **Iron** 20%

Three tartines: Saucisson Tartine (bottom), Radish and Butter Tartine (upper left) and Grilled Asparagus Tartine (upper right).

 Vegetarian

 Vegetarian

Saucisson Tartine

YIELD   1 Open-faced sandwich

Sliced rye bread	1 slice	1 slice
Pommery mustard	1 tsp.	5 ml
Dry-cured French or Italian sausage, sliced thin	4 slices	4 slices
Cornichon, sliced thin	1	1
Rosemary leaves	as needed for garnish	

1 Toast the bread on a heated panini grill.

2 Spread one side of the bread with the mustard. Arrange the sausage on top of the mustard-coated bread. Garnish with the sliced cornichon and rosemary.

Approximate values per sandwich: **Calories** 140, **Total fat** 45 g, **Saturated fat** 1.5 g, **Cholesterol** 15 mg, **Sodium** 540 mg, **Total carbohydrates** 16 g, **Protein** 8 g

Radish and Butter Tartine

YIELD   1 Open-faced sandwich

Sliced sourdough bread	1 slice	1 slice
Unsalted butter, softened	1½ Tbsp.	22 ml
Radishes, sliced thin	2	2
Chives or thyme, cut fine	as needed for garnish	
Sea salt,	as needed for garnish	

1 Toast the bread on a heated panini grill.

2 Spread one side of the bread with the butter. Arrange the sliced radishes on top. Garnish with herbs and salt.

Approximate values per sandwich: **Calories** 250, **Total fat** 18 g, **Saturated fat** 11 g, **Cholesterol** 45 mg, **Sodium** 210 mg, **Total carbohydrates** 18 g, **Protein** 4 g

Grilled Asparagus Tartine

YIELD   1 Open-faced sandwich

Sliced multigrain bread	1 slice	1 slice
Ricotta cheese	1½ Tbsp.	22 ml
Asparagus spears, trimmed, grilled	3	3
Sliced green onions	1 tsp.	5 ml
Salt and pepper	TT	TT
Olive oil	as needed	as needed

1 Toast the bread on a heated panini grill.

2 Spread one side of the bread with the ricotta. Arrange the grilled asparagus on top. Garnish with the green onions and season with salt, pepper and olive oil.

Approximate values per sandwich: **Calories** 120, **Total fat** 40 g, **Saturated fat** 2 g, **Cholesterol** 10 mg, **Sodium** 120 mg, **Total carbohydrates** 14 g, **Protein** 7 g, **Vitamin A** 10%, **Claims**— good source of fiber

Charcuterie 28

Charcuterie [shar-COO-tuhr-ree] is the classic art of preparing meat products—especially pork—into pâtés, galantines, sausages and hams. Over the years, however, the term has also come to refer to similar products made with game, poultry, fish, shellfish and vegetables. Charcuterie also encompasses food preservation by curing and smoking, as well as the fine art of elegant food presentation using decorative coatings. It has regained popularity as chefs look to prevent food waste and use every cut of meat, poultry or fish in flavorful and economical ways.

Charcuterie is an art and science in itself, an important set of skills of the chef garde manger. This chapter is not intended to be a complete guide to the charcutier's art. Instead this chapter focuses on procedures for making common charcuterie items that can be prepared easily in most kitchens. We discuss sausage preparation and curing methods, including salt curing, brining and both cold and hot smoking, after forcemeats are introduced and described. The chapter ends with information about several cured pork products.

FORCEMEATS

A forcemeat is a preparation made from uncooked ground meat, poultry, fish or shellfish that is seasoned and then emulsified with fat. Forcemeats are the primary ingredient in pâtés, terrines, galantines and sausages.

The word *forcemeat* is derived from the French word *farce*, meaning "stuffing." Depending on the preparation method, a forcemeat can be very smooth and velvety, well-textured and coarse, or anything in between. Regardless of its intended use, forcemeat has a glossy appearance when raw and slices cleanly when cooked. A properly emulsified forcemeat provides a rich flavor and a comforting texture on the palate.

Forcemeats are emulsified products. Emulsification is the process of binding two ingredients that ordinarily do not combine. (Emulsified sauces are discussed in Chapter 11, Stocks and Sauces; emulsified salad dressings are discussed in Chapter 25, Salads and Salad Dressings.) Proteins present in meat, poultry, fish and shellfish combine easily with both fat and liquids. In forcemeats, these proteins act as a stabilizer that allows the fat and liquids, which ordinarily would not combine, to bind. When improperly emulsified forcemeats are cooked, they lose their fat, shrink and become dry and grainy. To ensure proper emulsification of a forcemeat:

- the ratio of fat to other ingredients must be precise
- the temperature must be maintained below 41°F (5°C)
- the ingredients must be mixed properly

EQUIPMENT FOR PREPARING FORCEMEAT

To properly prepare forcemeats, a foodservice operation needs certain equipment. A food chopper or food processor and a heavy-duty drum sieve with a metal band are essential for forcemeat preparation. A standard meat grinder or meat-grinding attachment with various-sized grinding dies is also useful especially when preparing meats for coarse pâtés and sausage. The meat-grinding attachment is affixed to the front hub of a stand mixer or may be a stand-alone unit.

To use a meat-grinder, push cubes of cold meat and fat through the feed tube of the grinder's hopper. See Figure 28.1. Provided that the meat is properly chilled, it is fed by the screw (worm feed) to the blade. The sharp-edged X-blade cuts the meat while forcing it through the holes in the die (grinding plate). The size of the holes in the die determines the texture of the grind. The cover (ring) holds the die and X-blade in place.

An X-blade and assorted dies for a standard meat grinder

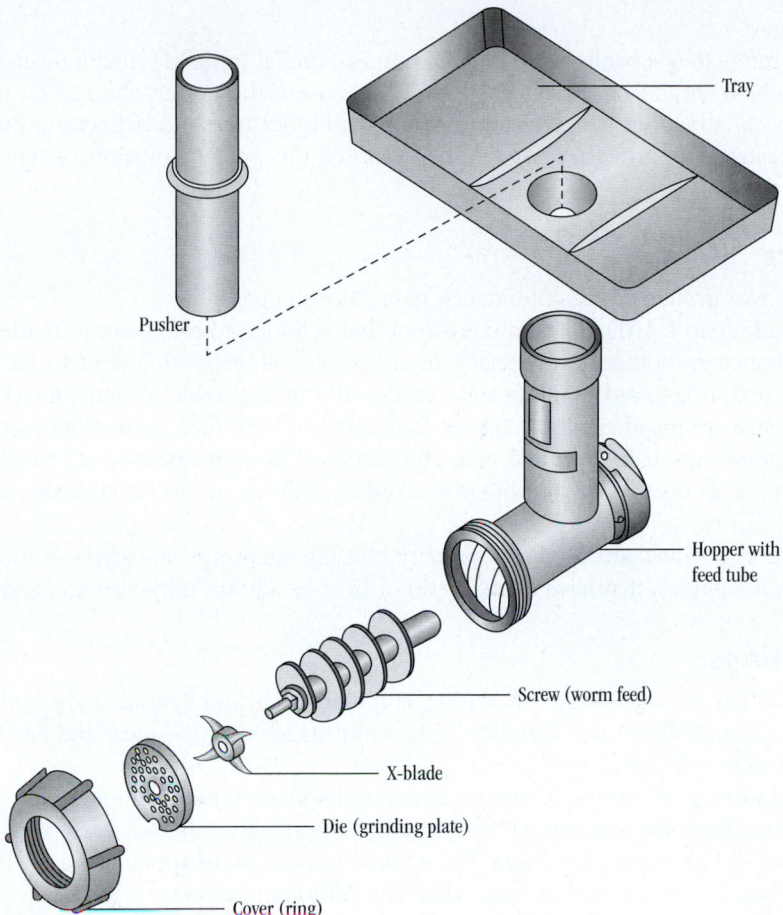

Figure 28.1 Parts of a meat grinder.

FORCEMEAT INGREDIENTS

Forcemeats are meat, poultry, fish or shellfish combined with binders, seasonings and sometimes garnishes. Chefs use selections from each of these basic protein and flavoring categories to prepare a wide array of forcemeats. All ingredients should be of the finest quality and added in just the right proportions.

Meats

The **dominant meat** is the meat, poultry, fish or shellfish that gives the forcemeat its name and essential flavor. When preparing meats, poultry or fish for forcemeat, it is important to trim all silverskin, gristle and small bones so that the meat can be more easily ground and produces a smoother finished product.

Many forcemeats contain some pork. Pork adds moisture and smoothness to the forcemeat. Without it, poultry-based forcemeats tend to be rubbery and venison and other game-based forcemeats tend to be dry. The traditional ratio is one part pork to two parts dominant meat.

Many forcemeats also contain some liver. Pork liver is commonly used, as is chicken liver. Liver contributes flavor as well as binding to the forcemeat. For a finer texture, grind the livers and force them through a drum sieve before incorporating them into the forcemeat.

Fats

Here, fat refers to a separate added ingredient, not the fat in the dominant meat or pork, both of which should be quite lean in order to ensure the correct ratio of fat to meat. Usually pork fatback or heavy cream is used to add moisture and richness to the forcemeat. Because fat carries flavor, it also promotes the proper infusion of flavors and smoke.

Binders

There are two principal types of binders: panadas and eggs.

A **panada** [pah-NAHD-ah] is an ingredient that is added to a forcemeat in addition to fat to enhance smoothness (especially in fish mousselines, which tend to be slightly grainy in texture), to aid emulsification (especially in vegetable terrines, in which the protein levels are insufficient to bind on their own) or both (e.g., in liver mousses). The panada should not make up more than 20 percent of the forcemeat's total weight. Usually a panada is crustless white bread soaked in milk or, more traditionally, a heavy béchamel or rice.

Eggs or egg whites are used as a primary binding agent in some styles of forcemeat. If used in forcemeats that have a large ratio of liver or liquids, eggs also add texture.

Seasonings

Forcemeats are seasoned with salt, curing salt, marinades and various herbs and spices. Salt not only adds flavor but also aids in the emulsification of the meat and fat. A forcemeat that lacks salt will taste flat.

Curing salt (Fr. *sel rose*) is a mixture of salt and sodium nitrite. Sodium nitrite controls spoilage by inhibiting bacterial growth. Equally important, curing salt preserves the rosy pink colors of forcemeats that might otherwise oxidize to an unappetizing gray. It is usually tinted pink to distinguish it from table salt. Although currently regarded as substantially safer than the previously used potassium nitrate (saltpeter), some studies suggest that sodium nitrite is a carcinogen. For a typical consumer, however, the tiny amount of sodium nitrite consumed from cured meats should not pose a substantial health threat.

Traditionally ingredients for forcemeats were marinated for long periods, sometimes days, before grinding. The trend today is for a shorter marinating time so that the true flavors of the main ingredients shine through. Both classic and contemporary marinades include herbs, citrus zest, spices and liquors, all of which lend flavor, character and nuance to the forcemeat.

Pâté spice is a mixture of spices and dried herbs that can be premixed and used as needed.

Pâté Spice

YIELD   7⅔ oz. (220 g)

Cloves	1 oz.	30 g
Dried ginger	1 oz.	30 g
Nutmeg	1 oz.	30 g
Paprika	1 oz.	30 g
Dried basil	⅔ oz.	20 g
Black pepper	⅔ oz.	20 g
White pepper	⅔ oz.	20 g
Bay leaf	⅓ oz.	10 g
Dried thyme	1 oz.	30 g
Dried marjoram	⅓ oz.	10 g

1 Grind all the ingredients in a spice grinder.

2 Pass the mixture through a sieve to remove any large pieces.

Variation:

This mixture can be used as is, or mix 1 ounce (30 grams) (or any amount desired) with 1 pound (480 grams) salt. The salt-and-spice mixture can then be used to season forcemeats; ⅓ ounce (10 grams) per pound of forcemeat usually suffices for most pâtés.

Approximate values per 1-oz. (30-g) serving: **Calories** 20, **Total fat** 1 g, **Saturated fat** 0 g, **Cholesterol** 0 mg, **Sodium** 0 mg, **Total carbohydrates** 3 g, **Protein** 1 g, **Vitamin A** 6%

Garnishes

Forcemeat garnishes are limited quantities of meats, fat, vegetables or other foods added to provide contrasting flavors and textures and to improve appearance. The garnishes are usually diced, chopped or more coarsely ground than the dominant meat. Common garnishes include pistachio nuts, diced fatback, truffles or truffle peelings and diced ham or tongue.

PREPARING FORCEMEATS

The three common forcemeat preparations are **country-style**, **basic** and **mousseline**. Each can be produced easily in a typical food service operation. Other types of forcemeat preparations such as the emulsified mixture used to make hot dogs and bratwurst are not commonly encountered in food service operations and are not discussed here.

When preparing any forcemeat, it is important to follow these guidelines:

- Forcemeat preparations include raw meats, liver, eggs and dairy products. If improperly handled, these time and temperature control for safety (TCS) foods create a good environment for the growth of microorganisms. To avoid the risk of food-borne illness, temperatures must be carefully controlled, and all cutting boards and food contact surfaces must be as sanitary as possible at all times.

- To ensure a proper emulsification, the forcemeat must be kept cold—below 41°F (5°C)—at all times. Refrigerate all moist ingredients, and keep forcemeats in progress in an ice bath. Chilling or freezing metal grinder and food processor parts helps keep the ingredients as cold as possible.

- Cut all foods into convenient sizes that fit easily into grinder openings. Do not overstuff grinders or overfill food processors. When grinding items twice, always begin with a larger die, followed by a medium or small die. For exceptional smoothness, press the forcemeat through a sieve after grinding to remove any lumps or pieces of membrane.

To test a forcemeat's seasoning and texture, cook a small portion before the entire forcemeat is cooked. (Unlike sauces, stews and other dishes, a forcemeat cannot be tasted during the cooking process to adjust the seasonings.) A small portion of a hearty forcemeat can be sautéed; a small portion of a more delicate forcemeat should be poached for 3–5 minutes. When cooked, the forcemeat should hold its shape and be slightly firm but not rubbery. If it is too firm, add a little cream. Adjust the seasonings appropriately; keep in mind that foods served cold may require additional salt and seasonings.

Country-Style Forcemeats

A traditional country-style forcemeat is heavily seasoned with onions, garlic, pepper, juniper berries and bay leaves. It is the simplest of the forcemeats to prepare and yields the heartiest and most distinctive pâtés and sausages.

The dominant meat for a country-style forcemeat is usually ground once through the grinder's large die, then ground again through the medium die. This produces the characteristic coarse, country-style texture. As with most forcemeats, the dominant meat for a country-style forcemeat is usually marinated and seasoned before grinding and then mixed with some liver.

Procedure for Preparing a Country-Style Forcemeat

1 Chill all ingredients and equipment thoroughly. Throughout preparation, ingredients and equipment should remain at temperatures below 41°F (5°C).

2 Cut all meats into an appropriate size for grinding.

3 Marinate, under refrigeration, the dominant meat and pork with the desired herbs, spices and liquors.

4 If using liver, grind it and force it through a sieve.

5 Cut the fatback into an appropriate size and freeze.

6 Prepare an ice bath for the forcemeat. Then grind the dominant meat, pork and fat as directed in the recipe, usually once through the grinder's largest die and a second time through the medium die.

7 If using liver, eggs, panada or garnishes, fold them in by hand, keeping the forcemeat over an ice bath at all times.

8 Cook a small portion of the forcemeat; adjust the seasonings and texture as appropriate.

9 Refrigerate the forcemeat until needed.

Country-Style Forcemeat

MISE EN PLACE

- Chill the equipment.
- Prepare Pâté Spice.
- Dice pork and fatback.
- Clean and dice pork liver.
- Peel onion and cut into small dice.
- Peel and mince garlic.
- Wash and chop fresh parsley.

YIELD 4 lb. 8 oz. (2.1 kg)

Lean pork, diced	2 lb.	960 g
Pâté Spice (page 834)	2 Tbsp.	30 ml
Salt	1 Tbsp.	15 ml
Black pepper	TT	TT
Brandy	2 fl. oz.	60 ml
Pork liver, cleaned and diced	1 lb.	480 g
Fatback, diced	1 lb.	480 g
Onion, small dice	3 oz.	90 g
Garlic, minced	1 Tbsp.	15 ml
Fresh parsley, chopped	3 Tbsp.	45 ml
Eggs	6	6

❶ Marinating the meat, spices and brandy before refrigerating with the diced fatback.

❷ Forcing the ground liver through a drum sieve.

❸ Grinding half of the pork and fatback a second time.

1 Combine the diced pork with the Pâté Spice, salt, pepper and brandy; marinate under refrigeration for several hours.

2 Grind the liver or purée it in a blender, then force it through a drum sieve. Reserve.

3 Grind the marinated pork and fatback through the chilled grinder's large die.

4 Grind half of the pork and fatback a second time through the medium die along with the onion, garlic and parsley.

5 Working over an ice bath, combine the coarse and medium ground pork with the liver and eggs.

6 Cook and taste a small portion of the forcemeat and adjust the seasonings as necessary. The forcemeat is now ready to use as desired in the preparation of pâtés, terrines, galantines and sausages.

Approximate values per 1-oz. (30-g) serving: **Calories** 90, **Total fat** 8 g, **Saturated fat** 3 g, **Cholesterol** 50 mg, **Sodium** 105 mg, **Total carbohydrates** 1 g, **Protein** 5 g, **Vitamin A** 30%

Basic Forcemeats

Smoother and more refined than a country-style forcemeat, a basic forcemeat is probably the most versatile forcemeat of all. It should be well seasoned, but the seasonings should not mask the dominant meat's flavor. Examples of basic forcemeats are those used in most game pâtés and terrines as well as traditional pâtés en croûte.

A basic forcemeat is made by grinding the meat and fat separately—the meat twice and the fat once. The fat is then worked into the meat, either by hand or in a food processor or chopper. A quicker method involves grinding the fat and meat together and then blending them in a food processor. Whichever method is used, some recipes call for the incorporation of crushed ice to minimize friction, reduce temperature and add moisture.

④ Combining the liver and eggs into the coarse and medium ground pork mixture over an ice bath to keep the forcemeat cold.

Procedure for Preparing a Basic Forcemeat

1 Chill all ingredients and equipment thoroughly. Throughout preparation, ingredients and equipment should remain at temperatures below 41°F (5°C).

2 Cut all meats into an appropriate size for grinding.

3 Marinate, under refrigeration, the dominant meat and pork with the desired herbs, spices and liquors.

4 If using liver, grind it and force it through a sieve.

5 Cut the fatback into an appropriate size and freeze.

6 Grind the meats twice, once through the grinder's large die and then through the medium die; hold over an ice bath.

7 Grind the chilled or frozen fat once through the medium die and add it to the meat mixture.

8 Work the fat into the meat over an ice bath or in a well-chilled food processor or chopping machine.

9 Over an ice bath, add any required eggs, panada and/or garnishes and work them into the mixture. Be careful not to overmix the forcemeat ingredients as this can cause air bubbles to appear in the finished product.

10 Cook a small portion of the forcemeat in stock or water; adjust the seasonings and texture as appropriate.

11 Refrigerate the forcemeat until needed.

An alternative method for preparing a basic forcemeat replaces Steps 6–9 with the following procedures:

ALT 6 Grind the meats and fats together twice.

ALT 7 Place them in a food processor or chopper and blend until smooth.

ALT 8 Add any required eggs or panada while the machine is running and blend them in with the meat and fat.

ALT 9 Remove the forcemeat from the machine and, working over an ice bath, fold in any garnishes by hand.

Whichever method is used, a particularly warm kitchen or a lengthy running time in the food processor or chopping machine may necessitate the addition of small quantities of crushed ice to properly emulsify the forcemeat. Add the ice bit by bit while the machine is running.

Basic Forcemeat

MISE EN PLACE

- Chill the equipment.
- Dice veal, lean pork and fatback.
- Prepare Pâté Spice.
- Cut ham into medium dice.
- Chop black olives coarsely.

YIELD　4 lb. 8 oz. (2.1 kg)

Veal, diced	1 lb. 8 oz.	720 g
Lean pork, diced	1 lb. 8 oz.	720 g
Brandy	2 fl. oz.	60 ml
Pâté Spice (page 834)	2 tsp.	10 ml
Salt	1½ tsp.	7 ml
White pepper	TT	TT
Fatback, diced	1 lb. 8 oz.	720 g
Eggs	4	4
Ham, medium dice	4 oz.	120 g
Pistachio nuts	2 oz.	60 g
Black olives, chopped coarse	2 oz.	60 g

1 Combine the veal and pork with the brandy, Pâté Spice, salt and white pepper; marinate under refrigeration for several hours.

2 Grind the meats through the chilled grinder's large die and again through the small die.

3 Grind the fatback through the chilled grinder's small die.

4 Combine the meat and fat in the bowl of a food processor and blend until they are emulsified.

5 Work in the eggs until the forcemeat is smooth and well emulsified. To avoid incorporating air and overheating the forcemeat, do not overprocess it. Stop mixing as soon as the mixture is smooth and emulsified.

6 Fold in the ham, pistachio nuts and olives.

7 Cook a small portion of the forcemeat by poaching or sautéing it. Taste and adjust the seasonings as necessary. The forcemeat is now ready to use as desired in the preparation of pâtés, terrines, galantines and sausages.

Approximate values per 1-oz. (30-g) serving: **Calories** 140, **Total fat** 12 g, **Saturated fat** 4.5 g, **Cholesterol** 45 mg, **Sodium** 80 mg, **Total carbohydrates** 1 g, **Protein** 7 g

❶ Grinding the meat through the chilled grinder.

❷ Combining the fat and the meat in the food processor.

❸ Working the eggs into the meat.

❹ Folding the garnishes into the forcemeat.

Mousseline Forcemeats

A properly made mousseline [moos-uh-LEEN] forcemeat is light, airy and delicately fla-vored. It is most often made with fish or shellfish but sometimes with veal, pork, feath-ered game or poultry. (A mousseline forcemeat is not the same as a mousse, which usually contains gelatin and is discussed later.)

A mousseline forcemeat is prepared by processing ground meats and cream in a food processor; often egg whites are added to lighten and enrich the mixture. The proportion of fish or dominant meat to eggs and cream is very important: too many egg whites, and the mousseline will be rubbery; too few, and it may not bind together. If too much cream is added, the mousseline will be too soft or will fall apart during cooking.

A mousseline forcemeat can be served hot or cold. It can be used to make fish sau-sages and a variety of timbales and terrines, or it can be used to make quenelles, which are discussed later. A shrimp mousseline is used with paupiettes of sole or flounder (page 536).

Procedure for Preparing a Mousseline Forcemeat

1. Chill all ingredients and equipment thoroughly. Throughout preparation, ingredients and equipment should remain at temperatures below 41°F (5°C).
2. Cut all meats into an appropriate size for processing.
3. Grind the meat in a cold food processor until smooth. To avoid incorporating air and over-heating the forcemeat, do not overprocess it.
4. Add eggs and pulse until just blended.
5. Add cream and seasonings in a steady stream while the machine is running. Stop the machine and scrape down the sides of the bowl once or twice during the processing. Do not run the machine any longer than necessary to achieve a smooth forcemeat.
6. If desired, pass the forcemeat through a drum sieve to remove any sinew or bits of bone.
7. Over an ice bath, fold in any garnishes by hand.
8. Poach a small amount of the mousseline in stock or water. Taste and adjust the seasonings and texture as necessary.
9. Refrigerate until needed.

MISE EN PLACE

- Chill the equipment.

Mousseline Forcemeat

Fish, scallops, skinless chicken breast or lean veal	2 lb.	960 g
Egg whites	4	4
Salt	1 Tbsp.	15 ml
White pepper	TT	TT
Nutmeg, ground	TT	TT
Cayenne pepper	TT	TT
Heavy cream	up to 1 qt.	up to 960 ml

1 Grind the dominant meat through a large die.

2 Process the meat in a food processor until smooth.

3 Add the egg whites one at a time, pulsing the processor until each egg is incorporated.

4 Scrape down the sides of the processor's bowl and add the spices.

5 With the machine running, add the cream in a slow, steady stream. Check the consistency, adding only enough cream to make a firm but smooth forcemeat.

6 Scrape down the bowl again and process the mousseline until it is smooth and well mixed. To avoid incorporating air and overheating the forcemeat, do not overprocess it.

7 Remove the mousseline from the machine and hold in an ice bath. If additional smoothness is desired, force the mousseline through a drum sieve in small batches using a plastic scraper or rubber spatula.

8 Cook a small portion of the forcemeat by poaching it. Taste and adjust the seasonings and texture as necessary. The forcemeat is now ready to cook as quenelles or use as desired in the preparation of pâtés, terrines, galantines and sausages.

Notes: Forcemeat made only from fish requires the least amount of cream of any forcemeat. Meat that is very cold, near 32°F (0°C) or colder absorbs less cream than meat that is merely chilled.

Approximate values per 1-oz. (30-g) serving: **Calories** 80, **Total fat** 7 g, **Saturated fat** 4 g, **Cholesterol** 30 mg, **Sodium** 25 mg, **Total carbohydrates** 1 g, **Protein** 4 g, **Vitamin A** 8%

1 Processing the ground meat in the chilled food processor just until smooth.

2 Adding the egg whites and pulsing until blended.

3 Adding the cream in a slow steady stream while the machine runs.

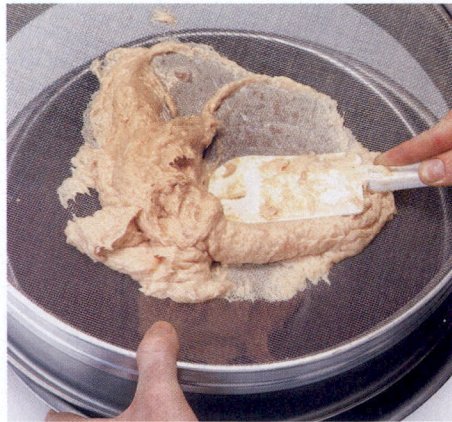

4 Passing the forcemeat through a drum sieve to ensure a smooth finished product.

Quenelles

Quenelles [kuh-NEHL] are small dumpling-shaped portions of a mousseline forcemeat poached in an appropriately flavored stock. The technique used to make and poach quenelles is the same technique used to test the seasoning and consistency of mousseline forcemeat.

Procedure for Preparing Quenelles

1 Prepare a mousseline forcemeat.

2 Bring an appropriately flavored poaching liquid to a simmer.

3 Use two spoons to form the forcemeat into oblong-shaped dumplings. For small quenelles, use small spoons; for larger quenelles, use larger spoons.

4 Poach the quenelles until done. Test by breaking one in half to check the center's doneness.

5 Small soup-garnish-sized quenelles can be chilled in ice water, drained and held for service. Reheat them in a small amount of stock before garnishing the soup.

Form the quenelles using two spoons and poach until done.

USING FORCEMEATS

Forcemeats are basic components in the preparation of terrines, pâtés, galantines and sausages. Aspic jelly is also an important component of these products.

Traditionally a **pâté** [pah-TAY] was a fine savory meat filling wrapped in pastry, baked and served hot or cold. A **terrine** was considered more basic, consisting of coarsely ground and highly seasoned meats baked in an earthenware mold and always served cold. (The mold is also called a terrine, derived from the French word *terre*, meaning "earth.") Today many types of pâtés are baked in loaf-type pans without a crust, which according to tradition would make them terrines, whereas pâtés baked in pastry are called **pâtés en croûte** [pah-TAY awn croot]. Thus the terms *pâté* and *terrine* are now used almost interchangeably. **Galantines** [gal-uhn-TEEN] are forcemeats of poultry, game or suckling pig that are wrapped in the skin of the bird or animal and poached in an appropriate stock. They are usually served cold. **Ballotines** [bahl-lo-TEEN] are similar but are generally made of deboned poultry legs and are served hot.

Terrines, pâtés and galantines are often made with forcemeats layered with garnishes to produce a decorative or mosaic effect when sliced. A wide variety of foods can be used as garnishes, including strips of ham, fatback or tongue; mushrooms or other vegetables; truffles and pistachio nuts. Garnishes should always be cooked before they are added to the pâté, terrine or galantine, or they shrink during cooking, creating air pockets.

Pâté pans, molds and terrines come in a variety of shapes and sizes. Pâtés that are not baked in a crust can be prepared in standard metal loaf pans of any shape, although rectangular ones make portioning the cooked pâté much easier. For pâtés en croûte, the best pans are collapsible or hinged, made of thin metal with a nonstick surface. They make it easier to remove the pâté after baking. Collapsible and hinged pans come in various shapes and sizes, from small plain rectangles to large intricately fluted ovals. Traditional earthenware molds and terrines as well as ones made from enameled cast iron, metal, glass or even plastic are available. Most terrines are rectangular or oval in shape. See Chapter 5, Tools and Equipment.

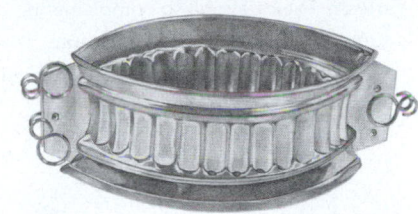

Pâté en croûte mold

Aspic Jelly

Aspic jelly is a versatile ingredient used in the finishing and presentation of terrines, pâtés and galantines as well as other foods. (It is also used extensively to enhance the presentation of foods for buffets and in culinary competitions.) Because of its range of applications when preparing and serving forcemeats, we introduce it here in the content of using forcemeats. Procedures for using aspic jelly are discussed later in the chapter on page 845.

Aspic jelly is a savory jelly produced by increasing the gelatin content of a strong stock and then clarifying the stock following the process for preparing consommé discussed in Chapter 12, Soups.

Although gelatin is a natural ingredient present in all good meat or poultry stocks, additional gelatin is usually added to the stock in order to assist gelling (setting). One

GELATIN CONCENTRATIONS		TABLE 28.1
TYPE OF GEL	AMOUNT OF GELATIN PER GALLON (4 LITERS) WATER	TYPICAL USE
Soft	2 oz. (60 g)	Cubed aspic jelly for edible garnishes
Firm	4 oz. (120 g)	Brushing slices of pâté or galantine; glazing edible centerpieces; molding terrines, aspics and brawns that will be sliced
Very firm	8 oz. or more (240 g or more)	Nonedible purposes such as coating nonedible centerpieces or trays for presentations

Garnishing Sliced Terrines and Pâtés

Cornichons, a petite sour pickle flavored with tarragon, can be sliced into decorative fans as an attractive garnish. Their flavor also complements country terrines and pâtés en croûte.

way is to produce a stock with an extremely high gelatin content by using gelatinous meats and bones such as calves' feet, pigs' ears and pork skin; another is to add plain gelatin to a finished stock. An easier method of preparing aspic jelly is to add gelatin directly to a flavorful finished consommé.

Aspic jelly is used to bind savory mousses, glaze slices of pâté and coat molded mousses. Aspic jelly is funneled into cooked pâtés en croûte to fill the gaps created when the forcemeat shrinks during the cooking process. Aspic jelly is also the basis of aspic molds or terrines (often simply called aspics), in which layers of cooked meats or vegetables are bound together and held in place by the aspic jelly. In addition to adding flavor and shine, a coating of aspic jelly prevents displayed foods from drying out and inhibits the oxidation of sliced red meats. Aspic jelly is often lightly flavored with a liquor such as Madeira and cut into decorative garnishes for both plated presentations and buffet displays. Decorative platters on which pâtés are displayed may be coated with aspic jelly. (Closely related to aspic jelly is sauce chaud-froid discussed on page 856.)

The gelatin content of aspic jelly varies depending on its intended use. Table 28.1 lists guidelines for quantities of gelatin to use in various applications. Aspic jelly to be used only on a display can have a very high gelatin content for easier handling. Aspic jelly to be eaten should be fairly firm when cold. At room temperature it should be gelled but tender enough to melt quickly in the mouth when eaten. To test the gelatin content of a liquid, pour a teaspoon (5 milliliters) onto a plate and refrigerate the plate for a few minutes. If the liquid does not gel firmly, soften additional gelatin in a small amount of cool liquid and add it to the hot liquid.

Terrines

Terrines are forcemeats baked in a mold without a crust. The mold can be a traditional earthenware dish or some other appropriate metal, enameled cast iron or glass mold. Any type of forcemeat can be used to make a terrine. A terrine can be as simple as a baking dish filled with a forcemeat and baked until done. A more attractive terrine can be constructed by layering the forcemeat with garnishes to create a mosaic effect when sliced. A terrine can even be layered with different forcemeats—for example, a pink salmon mousseline layered with a white pike mousseline.

A thin layer of fat is used to line the terrine mold. The fat helps keep the forcemeat moist during cooking. Sliced fatback and **caul fat** are most commonly used for this purpose. Caul fat (Fr. *crepine*) is a web-like fatty membrane that surrounds the stomach and intestines of cattle, sheep and pigs. Caul fat is used to wrap terrines, sausages and pâtés as well as other forcemeat products such as **crépinettes**. The membrane holds the meat together, and during cooking the melting fat bastes the meat, adding moisture and flavor. Pork caul fat is generally preferred for these purposes. Using fatback or caul fat is essentially a form of barding (see page 297) that does not require any tying, twine or toothpicks.

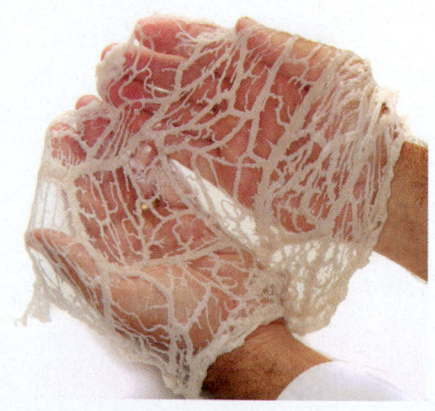

Caul fat

crépinettes a small flat disc of forcemeat wrapped in caul fat, cooked and served as a fresh sausage

Procedure for Preparing Terrines

1 Prepare the desired forcemeat and garnishes and refrigerate until needed.

2 Line a mold with thin slices of fatback, blanched leafy vegetables or other appropriate liner. (Some chefs claim that the fatback keeps the terrine moist during cooking; most modern chefs do not agree but nevertheless use it for aesthetic purposes.) The lining should overlap slightly, completely covering the inside of the mold and extending over the edge of the mold by approximately 1 inch (2.5 centimeters). Alternatively line the mold with plastic wrap.

3 Fill the terrine with the forcemeat and garnishes, being careful not to leave air pockets. Tap the mold several times on a solid work surface to remove any air pockets.

4 Fold the liner or plastic wrap over the forcemeat and, if necessary, use additional pieces to completely cover its surface.

5 If desired, garnish the top of the terrine with the herbs used in the preparation of the forcemeat.

6 Cover the terrine with its lid or aluminum foil and bake in a water bath in a 350°F (180°C) oven. Regulate the oven temperature so that the water stays between 170°F and 180°F (77°C and 82°C).

7 Cook the terrine to an internal temperature of 140°F (60°C) for fish-based forcemeats, 150°F (66°C) for meat-based forcemeats or 160°F (71°C) for poultry-based forcemeats. Carryover cooking will bring the temperature to 145°F (63°C), 155°F (68°C) or 165°F (74°C) respectively, as required for food safety.

8 Remove the terrine from the oven and allow it to cool slightly. If desired, pour off any fat and liquid from around the terrine and cover it with cool liquid aspic jelly.

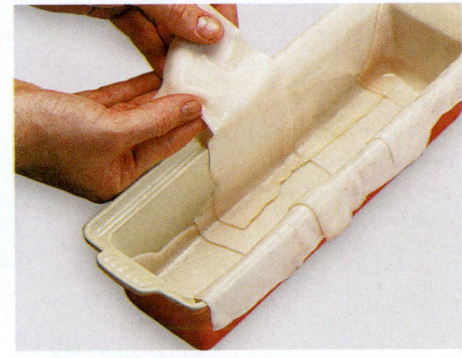

❶ Line a mold with thin slices of fatback.

❷ Fill the terrine with the forcemeat and garnish.

❸ Place the herb-garnished terrine in a water bath.

❹ Slice the finished terrine.

Types of Terrines

Several types of terrines are not made from traditional forcemeats; many others are not made from forcemeats at all. But all are nonetheless called terrines because they are molded or cooked in the earthenware mold called a terrine. Terrines include liver (and foie gras) terrines, vegetable terrines, brawns or aspic terrines, mousses, rillettes and confits. In the following material, we describe each of these in detail.

Liver terrines are popular and easy to make. Puréed poultry, pork or veal livers are mixed with eggs and a panada of cream and flour, then baked in a fatback-lined terrine. Although most livers purée easily in a food processor, a smoother finished product is achieved by forcing livers through a drum sieve after or in lieu of puréeing them in the processor.

Foie gras terrines are made with the fattened goose or duck livers called foie gras. Foie gras is unique, even among other poultry livers, in that it consists almost entirely of fat. (See Chapter 18, Poultry.) Foie gras requires special attention during cooking; if it is cooked improperly or too long, it turns into a puddle of very expensive fat.

Foie gras terrine with toast

headcheese (Fr. *fromage de tête*) a gelled loaf or sausage made from calf or hog head that had been simmered in a gelatinous broth, molded into a loaf and served sliced with pickles and mustard

Vegetable terrines have a relatively low fat content and stunning eye appeal. Beautiful vegetable terrines are made by lining a terrine with a blanched leafy vegetable such as spinach, then alternating layers of two or three separately prepared vegetable fillings to create contrasting colors and flavors. A different style of vegetable terrine is made by suspending brightly colored vegetables in a mousseline forcemeat to create a mosaic pattern when sliced.

Brawns or **aspic terrines** are made by simmering gelatinous cuts of meat (most notably, pigs' feet and head, including the tongue) in a rich stock with wine and flavorings. The stock is enriched with the gelatin and flavor from the meat, creating an unclarified aspic jelly. The meat is pulled from the bone, diced and packed into the terrine mold. The stock is reduced to concentrate its gelatin content, strained through cheesecloth and poured over the meat in the terrine. After the terrine has set, it is removed from the mold and sliced for service. The finished product is a rustic and flavorful dish. **Headcheese** is a popular example of an aspic terrine.

A more elegant-appearing brawn is made by lining a terrine mold with aspic jelly, arranging a layer of garnish (e.g., sliced meats, vegetables or low-acid fruits) along the mold's bottom, adding aspic jelly to cover the garnish and repeating the procedure until the mold is full.

A **mousse** can be sweet or savory. Sweet mousses are described in Chapter 35, Custards, Creams, Frozen Desserts and Dessert Sauces. A savory mousse—which is not a mousseline forcemeat—is made from fully cooked meats, poultry, game, fish, shellfish or vegetables that are puréed and combined with a béchamel or other appropriate sauce, bound with gelatin and lightened with whipped cream. A mousse can be molded in a decorated, aspic-jelly-coated mold such as the one described in the procedure that follows, or it can be formed in a mold lined with plastic wrap, which is peeled off after the mousse is unmolded. A small mousse can be served as an individual portion; a larger molded mousse can be displayed on a buffet. (See Roasted Red Pepper Mousse on page 865 and Salmon Mousse on page 865.)

Rillettes and confits are actually preserved meats. **Rillettes** [ree-YEHT] are prepared by seasoning and slow-cooking pork or fatty poultry such as duck or goose in generous amounts of their own fat until the meat falls off the bone. The warm meat is mashed and combined with a portion of the cooking fat. The mixture is then packed into a crock or terrine, and rendered fat is strained over the top to seal it. Rillettes are eaten cold as a spread accompanied by bread or toast. (See Pork Rillettes on page 861.)

Confit [kohn-FEE] is prepared in a similar manner as rillettes except that before cooking, the meat or poultry is often lightly salt-cured to draw out some moisture. The confit is then cooked until very tender but not falling apart. (See Duck Confit on page 460.) Confits are generally served hot. Like rillettes, confits can be preserved by sealing them with a layer of strained rendered fat. Properly prepared and sealed rillettes and confits will keep for several weeks under refrigeration.

Although it is sometimes incorrectly called chicken liver pâté, **chopped chicken liver** is prepared in a similar fashion to a rillette. Chopped chicken liver, however, does not have the keeping qualities of traditional rillettes or confits because it is not normally sealed in a crock or terrine with rendered fat. It should be eaten within a day or two of its preparation. (See Chopped Chicken Liver on page 866.)

Preparing Molds When Making Terrines

When making a terrine, a mold can be lined with aspic jelly, then decorated and filled with cold mousse. The aspic-jelly-coated mousse is unmolded for an attractive presentation.

Procedure for Preparing Aspic-Jelly-Coated Chilled Mousses

1 Set a metal mold in ice water and fill with cool liquid aspic jelly. Swirl the mold so the aspic jelly adheres to all sides. Pour out the excess. Repeat as needed to achieve the desired thickness; ¼ inch (6 millimeters) or less is usually sufficient.

2 Garnish the mold by dipping pieces of vegetable or other foods in the liquid aspic jelly and placing them carefully inside the aspic-jelly-coated mold. The mold can now be filled with a cold filling such as a mousse.

3 Refrigerate the mold until it is well chilled. Unmold the aspic by dipping the mold in warm water, then inverting and tapping the mold on a plate.

Procedure for Glazing Pâté Slices with Aspic Jelly

Slices of chilled terrines, pâtés en croûte or galantines may be garnished and coated with aspic to preserve their color, prevent drying and create a more attractive presentation.

1 Cool the clarified aspic jelly by slowly stirring it over an ice bath.

2 Brush or spoon the aspic jelly over slices of chilled pâté arranged on a cooling rack. Repeat until the coating reaches the desired thickness.

Pâtés en Croûte

Considered by some to be the pinnacle of the charcutier's art, pâtés en croûte are forcemeats baked in a crust. The forcemeat can be country-style, basic or mousseline, but a basic forcemeat is most commonly used. Although pâtés en croûte can be baked without using a mold, a mold helps produce a more attractive finished product.

Making Pâté Dough

The crust surrounding a baking forcemeat must be durable enough to withstand the long baking process and hold in the juices produced as the pâté bakes. Unfortunately some of the more durable crusts are tough and unpleasant to eat.

   The goal when making pâté dough (Fr. *pâte au pâté*) is to achieve a balance so that the crust will hold the juices of the baking pâté and still be tender enough to be pleasing to the palate. Some pâtés, especially more delicate ones such as fish mousselines, can be wrapped in Brioche dough (page 968).

Pâté Dough

YIELD 1 lb. 8 oz. (720 g)

All-purpose flour	1 lb.	480 g
Shortening	7 oz.	210 g
Salt	1½ tsp.	7 ml
Water	5 fl. oz.	150 ml
Egg	1	1

1 Place the flour in the bowl of a mixer. Add the shortening and mix on low speed until smooth.

2 Combine the salt, water and egg; add them to the flour and shortening mixture.

3 Knead until smooth and refrigerate. The dough will be easier to work with if allowed to rest for at least 1 hour.

Approximate values per 1-oz. (30-g) serving: **Calories** 150, **Total fat** 9 g, **Saturated fat** 2 g, **Cholesterol** 10 mg, **Sodium** 100 mg, **Total carbohydrates** 15 g, **Protein** 2 g

Assembling, Baking and Glazing Pâté

After preparing a forcemeat and pastry dough, all that remains is to assemble and bake the pâté en croûte. The amount of pastry dough and forcemeat needed is determined by the size of the mold or pan chosen. Once the pâté is baked and cooled, aspic jelly is poured into holes in the dough to fill the space created when the pâté shrank during cooking. Slices of pâté can also be glazed with aspic for a more formal presentation.

Procedure for Assembling and Baking Pâtés en Croûte

1 Prepare the pâté dough and the forcemeat, keeping the forcemeat refrigerated until needed.

2 Roll out the dough into a rectangular shape ⅛ inch (3 millimeters) thick.

3 Using the pâté mold as a pattern, determine how much dough is needed to line its inside; allow enough dough along each side of the mold's length to cover the top when folded over. Mark the dough. Cut the dough slightly larger than the marked lines. Cut a second rectangular piece of dough that is slightly larger than the top of the mold; it will be used as a lid.

4 Lightly butter the inside of the mold.

5 Lightly dust the large rectangle of dough with flour, fold it over and transfer it to the mold.

6 Use your thumbs and a dough ball made from dough trimmings to form the dough neatly into the corners of the mold. This helps push the dough against the mold without tearing. Continue until the dough is of even thickness on all sides and in the corners.

7 Trim the dough, leaving ¾ inch (2 centimeters) on the ends and enough dough to cover the top along the sides.

8 Place thin slices of fatback or ham inside the dough-lined mold, allowing ¾ inch (2 centimeters) extra around the top of the mold, or as directed in the recipe. This layer helps protect the dough from coming in contact with the moist forcemeat, which would make it soggy.

9 Fill the lined mold with the forcemeat to ½ inch (1.2 centimeters) below the top of the mold, pressing it well into the corners to avoid air pockets. Layer and garnish as appropriate.

10 Fold the fatback or ham over the top of the forcemeat, using additional pieces if necessary to cover its entire surface. Fold the dough over the fatback-covered forcemeat.

11 Brush the exposed surface of the dough with egg wash; carefully cap with the top piece of dough. Press any overlapping dough down inside the sides of the mold with a small spatula.

12 Using round cutters, cut one or two holes in the top to allow steam to escape during cooking. Egg-wash the surface. Place a doughnut-shaped piece of dough around each of the holes. Egg-wash any decorations.

13 Bake the pâté in a preheated 450°F (230°C) oven for 15 minutes. Then cover the surface of the pâté with aluminum foil. Reduce the heat to 350°F (180°C) and continue baking until the internal temperature reaches 140°F (60°C) for fish-based forcemeats, 150°F

1 Cut the dough into a large rectangle.

2 Press the dough into the mold with a floured dough ball made from trimmings.

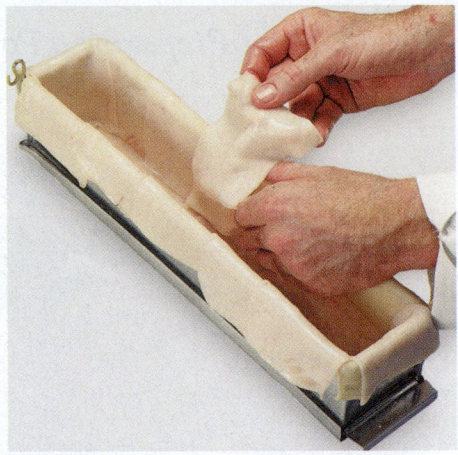

3 Place thin slices of fatback inside the dough-lined mold.

4 Fill the lined mold with the forcemeat and garnish.

5 Cap with the top piece of dough.

6 Pour cool aspic jelly into the holes of the baked pâté through an aluminum foil chimney.

(66°C) for meat-based forcemeats or 160°F (71°C) for poultry-based forcemeats. Carryover cooking will bring the temperature to 145°F (63°C), 155°F (68°C) or 165°F (74°C), respectively, as required for food safety.

14 Allow the pâté to cool for at least 1 hour or overnight. Using a funnel, pour cool liquid aspic jelly through the holes to fill the space created when the pâté shrank during cooking. Allow the pâté en croûte to cool overnight before slicing.

Galantines

A classic galantine is a boned chicken stuffed with a chicken-based forcemeat so that it resembles its original shape after it is poached. Today galantines are still prepared from whole ducks or chickens, but they can also be made from game, veal, fish or shellfish. When appropriate the forcemeat is stuffed in the bird's skin, which has been removed in one piece, sometimes with flesh still attached. When the bird's skin is not available, or in the case of fish and shellfish where there is no skin, the galantine is made by forming the forcemeat into a cylindrical shape and wrapping it in cheesecloth, or plastic wrap and foil, before poaching. Galantines are always served cold and are often displayed on buffets, sliced and glazed with aspic jelly.

A ballotine is similar to a galantine. It is made by removing the bones from a poultry leg, filling the cavity with an appropriate forcemeat and poaching or braising the leg with vegetables. Ballotines are often served hot with a sauce made from the cooking liquid.

7 Slices of the cooled pâté en croûte.

Procedure for Preparing a Poultry Galantine

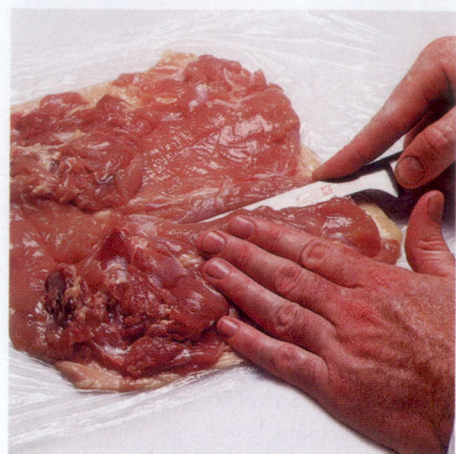

❶ Butterfly the breasts and tenderloins and cover the skin with a thin layer of meat.

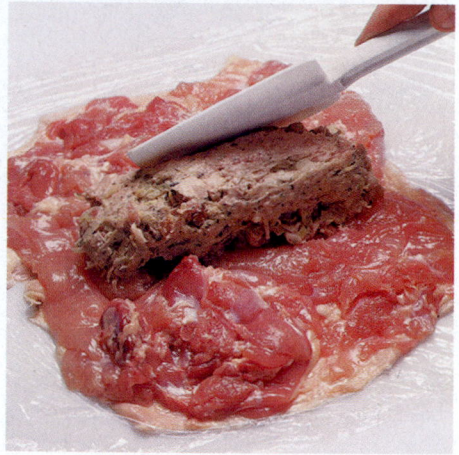

❷ Arrange the forcemeat and garnishes in a cylindrical shape across the center of the skin.

1 Bone the chicken by cutting through the skin along the length of the backbone and then following the natural curvature of the carcass. Keep all the meat attached to the skin. Remove the legs and wings by cutting through the joints when you reach them; leave the legs and wings attached to the skin. Then cut off the wings. Bone the thighs and legs, leaving the skin and meat attached to the rest of the bird. Trim the skin to form a large rectangle.

2 Prepare a forcemeat using the meat from the skinned bird or any other appropriate meat. Reserve a portion of the meat as garnish if desired. Prepare any other garnishes. Refrigerate the forcemeat and garnishes until needed.

3 Spread out the skin and meat on a cutting board with the skin side down and the flesh up. Trim it into a uniform rectangle. Transfer the trimmed skin onto a sheet of plastic wrap or several layers of cheesecloth with the skin side down and the flesh up.

4 Remove the chicken tenderloins and pull the tendon out of each. Butterfly the breasts and tenderloins and cover the entire skin with a thin layer of meat.

5 Arrange the forcemeat and garnishes in a cylindrical shape across the center of the skin.

6 Using the plastic or cheesecloth to assist the process, tightly roll the skin around the forcemeat and garnishes to form a tight cylinder.

7 Tie the ends of the cheesecloth with butcher's twine and secure the galantine at even intervals using strips of cheesecloth. If plastic wrap was used, wrap the galantine with heavy-duty aluminum foil.

8 Poach the galantine in water (or a full-flavored stock if wrapped in cheesecloth) to an internal temperature of 160°F (71°C). Carryover cooking will bring the temperature to 165°F (74°C), as required for food safety.

9 Cool the galantine in its cooking liquid until it can be handled. Remove the cheesecloth or plastic wrap and aluminum foil and rewrap the galantine in clean cheesecloth or plastic wrap. Refrigerate overnight before decorating or slicing.

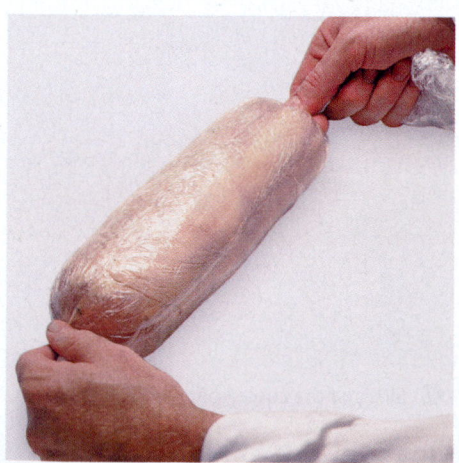

❸ Use plastic wrap to tightly roll the galantine and form a tight cylinder.

❹ Wrap the galantine with heavy-duty aluminum foil.

❺ Slice the finished product.

Sausages

Sausages are forcemeats stuffed into casings. For centuries sausages consisted of ground meat, usually pork, and seasonings. Today sausages are made not only from pork, but also from game, beef, veal, poultry, fish, shellfish and even vegetables.

There are three main types of sausages:

1 **Fresh sausages** include breakfast sausage links and Italian sausages. They are made with fresh ingredients that have not been cured or smoked.

2 **Smoked** and **cooked sausages** are made with raw meat products treated with chemicals, usually the preservative sodium nitrite. Examples are kielbasa, bologna and hot dogs.

3 **Dried** or **hard sausages** are made with cured meats, then air-dried under controlled conditions. Dried sausages may or may not be smoked or cooked. Dried or hard sausages include salami, **pepperoni** and **soppressata**.

Smoked and cooked sausages and dried or hard sausages are rarely prepared in typical food service operations, although chefs are increasingly interested in preparing these artisanal foods. Rather they are produced by specialty shops in facilities where sanitation is ensured. (For the proper fermentation and preserving of dry-cured products, controlled temperatures under sanitary conditions are essential. A HACCP plan and a health code variance may be required in order to prepare dry-cured foods on site.) Here we discuss the ingredients and procedures for preparing a variety of fresh sausages and the fundamentals of sausage-making that can be carried out in almost any kitchen.

Sausage Meats

Sausage meats are forcemeats with particular characteristics and flavorings. Both coarse Italian and lamb sausages, for example, are simply country-style forcemeats without liver and with different seasonings, stuffed into casings and formed into links. Hot dogs, bratwurst and other fine-textured sausages are also variations of basic forcemeats stuffed into casings and formed into links.

Sausage Casings

Although sausage mixtures can be cooked without casings, most sausages are stuffed into casings before cooking. Two types of sausage casings are commonly used in food service operations:

1 **Natural casings** are portions of hog, sheep or cattle intestines sold by the bundle (also called a **hank**). The diameters of casings are measured in millimeters, and they come in several sizes depending on the animal or portion of the intestine used. Sheep casings are considered the finest-quality small casings. Both hog and sheep casings are used to make hot dogs and many types of pork sausage. Beef casings are quite large and are used to make sausages such as ring bologna and Polish sausage. Most natural casings are purchased in salt packs. In order to rid them of salt and impurities, the casings must be carefully rinsed in warm water and allowed to soak in cool water for at least 1 hour or overnight before use.

2 **Collagen casings** are manufactured from collagen extracted from cattle hides. They are generally inferior to natural casings in taste and texture, but they do have advantages: Collagen casings do not require any washing or soaking before use, they have a long shelf life and they are uniform in size. Because of their texture, collagen casings are often used for smoked sausages and snack sticks.

Slices of Rosette de Lyon, a dry-cured French sausage, also known as saucisson sec

andouille [an-DOO-ee] a very spicy smoked pork sausage, popular in Cajun cuisine

mortadella [mohr-tah-DEH-lah] an Italian smoked sausage made with ground beef, pork and pork fat, flavored with coriander and white wine; it is air-dried and has a delicate flavor; also a large American bologna-type pork sausage studded with pork fat and garlic

pepperoni [peh-peh-ROH-nee] a hard, thin, air-dried sausage seasoned with red and black pepper

saucisson sec [soh-see-SOHN seck] a hard, air-dried French sausage seasoned with garlic and black pepper

soppressata [soh-preh-SAH-tah] a hard, aged Italian salami, sometimes coated with cracked peppercorns or herbs

Before using, wash natural sausage casings in cold water.

Sausage nozzles

Equipment for Making Sausages

Sausage-stuffing machines are a good idea for those who engage in large-scale sausage production. For smaller operations, all that is needed is a grinder with a **sausage nozzle**. Nozzles are available in several sizes to accommodate various casing sizes.

Procedure for Preparing Sausages

1 Prepare a forcemeat.

2 Thoroughly chill all parts of the sausage stuffer that will come in contact with the forcemeat.

3 Rinse and soak the casings if using natural ones. Cut the casings into 4- to 6-foot (1.2- to 1.8-meter) lengths.

4 Put the sausage in the sausage stuffer.

5 Slide the entire casing over the nozzle of the sausage stuffer. Tie the end in a knot and pierce with a skewer to prevent air pockets.

6 Support and guide the casing off the end of the nozzle as the sausage is extruded from the nozzle into the casing.

7 After all the sausage has been stuffed into the casing, twist or tie the sausage into uniform links of the desired size.

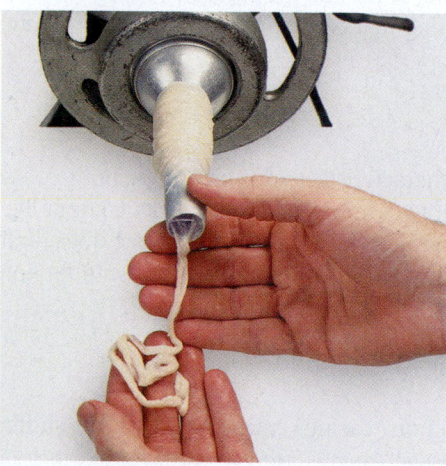

❶ Slide the casing over the nozzle of the sausage stuffer.

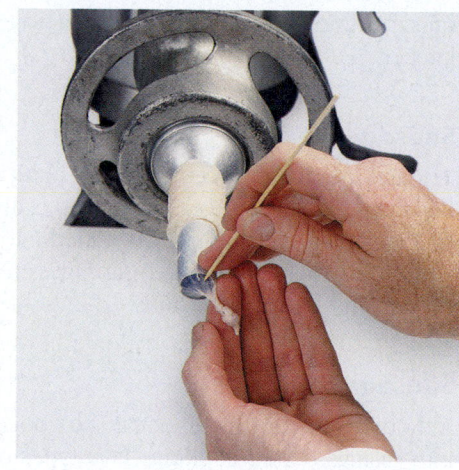

❷ Knot and pierce the casing with a skewer.

❸ Support and guide the casing off the end of the nozzle as the sausage is extruded from the machine into the casing.

❹ Twist the sausage into uniform links.

SALT CURING, BRINING AND SMOKING

Curing, brining and smoking are ancient techniques for preserving food. Today foods such as hams, corned beef and smoked salmon are salt-cured, brined or smoked for flavor and to extend their shelf life. Cured meats have a characteristic pink color caused by the reaction between the curing salts, which are added during processing, and the naturally occurring myoglobin protein in the meat.

Salt Curing

Salt curing is the process of surrounding a food with salt or a mixture of salt, sugar, nitrite-based curing salt, herbs and spices. Salt curing dehydrates the food by drawing out moisture, inhibits bacterial growth and adds flavor. It is most often used with pork products and fish. Salt curing as a preservation method is not a quick procedure—and the time involved adds money to production costs. For example, country-style hams are salt-cured. Proper curing requires approximately one and a half days per pound of ham, which means three weeks for the average ham.

Some salt-cured hams such as Smithfield and prosciutto are not actually cooked. The curing process preserves the meat and makes it safe to consume raw. Gravlax (page 868) is a well-known salmon dish prepared by salt-curing salmon fillets with a mixture of salt, sugar, pepper and dill.

Brining

A **brine** is actually a very salty marinade. Most brines have approximately 20 percent salinity, which is equivalent to 1 pound (480 grams) of salt per gallon (4 liters) of water. (See Chapter 9, Mise en Place.) Like dry-salt cures, brines can also contain sugar, nitrites, herbs and spices. Brining is sometimes called **pickling**.

Today most cured meats are prepared in large production facilities where the brine is injected into the meat for rapid and uniform distribution. Commercially brined corned beef is cured by this process, as are most common hams. After brining, hams are further processed by smoking.

Smoking

Smoking preserves flavors and protects foods for longer storage. There are two types of smoking, cold and hot. **Cold smoking** dries and flavors foods at low temperatures between 40°F and 85°F (4°C and 85°C). Cold smoked foods usually require additional cooking before they can be eaten. **Hot smoking** cooks foods at higher temperatures than cold smoking, usually between 160°F and 185°F (71°C and 85°C), in an enclosed oven for a long period of time. Hot smoked foods are fully cooked by the hot smoking process and do not require additional cooking before eating.

Cold smoking is the process of exposing foods to smoke at temperatures between 40°F and 85°F (4°C and 29°C). Cold smoking at the lowest temperature of 40°F (4°C) promotes food safety because it is below the temperature danger zone. Meat, poultry, game, fish, shellfish, cheese, nuts and even vegetables can be cold-smoked successfully. Cold-smoked foods are actually still raw. Some, such as smoked salmon (lox), are eaten without further cooking. Most, such as bacon and hams, must be cooked before eating.

Hot smoking is the process of exposing foods to smoke at temperatures between 160°F and 185°F (71°C and 85°C). As with cold smoking, a great variety of foods can be prepared by hot smoking including meats, poultry, game, fish and shellfish. Although most hot-smoked foods are fully cooked when removed from the smoker, some such as bacon are used in other recipes that call for further cooking.

Select fresh, unblemished food of the highest quality to smoke. If frozen products are being smoked, properly thaw them under refrigeration before smoking. All foods to be smoked should be salt cured or brined first under refrigeration. Salt curing and brining adds flavor, allows the nitrites (which give the ham, bacon and other smoked meats their distinctive pink color) to penetrate the flesh and, most important, extracts moisture from the food, allowing the smoke to penetrate more easily. Before smoking, wash the food to remove its cure or brine. Allow the food to dry until its surface develops a sticky skin called a **pellicle**. The pellicle protects the food from drying out during smoking. Compounds in the smoke stick to the skin, flavoring and coloring it.

pellicle (Fr. *pellicule*) a thin, sticky membrane or skin that forms on the surface of cured fish, meat or poultry exposed to air. It seals in moisture and helps smoke adhere to the product's surface

Smoking Temperatures

Smoke protects the surface of foods from bacteria or mold and gives foods a deep color. Properly smoked foods have a sweet, delicate smoke flavor from the properly combusted burning wood. Accurate temperature controls ensure food safety when smoking foods. For hot smoking, the temperature of the smoking chamber must be maintained in the proper range to ensure food safety. The temperature at which a food is smoked may be increased gradually to ensure that the food is well flavored and properly pasteurized. Sausages, for example, may be smoked for an initial period at a lower temperature (125°F/51°C) to set the proteins in the meat then at higher temperature (160°F/71°C) to cook the meat.

Temperatures above 185°F (85°C) are not recommended for hot smoking because higher heat causes foods to shrink and dry out. (Barbecue, a dry heat cooking method that resembles hot smoking, is an exception to this general rule. It employs higher temperatures to smoke and cook foods. See Chapter 13, Principles of Meat Cookery.) The food items must reach safe internal temperatures during hot smoking. For cold smoking, the temperature of the smoking chamber is maintained between 40°F (4°C) and 85°F (29°C). Foods are held at this temperature just long enough to absorb the desired smoky flavor. Recall that cold-smoked foods are cooked after smoking before they are served.

Smoking Equipment

Both cold and hot smoking occur in a **smoker** specifically designed for this purpose. Smokers can be wood-burning, gas or electric. Smokers vary greatly in size and operation, but they have several things in common: All smokers consist of a chamber that holds the food being smoked, a means of burning wood to produce smoke and a heating element.

Although smoking large quantities of foods requires specialized equipment, three affordable options exist for imparting a smoked flavor to small-batch food preparation. A **stove top smoker**, which resembles a hotel pan with a tight-fitting lid, can be used to hot smoke small cuts of meat, fish, poultry or vegetables. Wood chips are scattered inside the bottom of the pan. Foods to be smoked sit on top of a mesh rack inside the box. The heat of the stove top ignites the wood chips, surrounding the food with flavorful smoke.

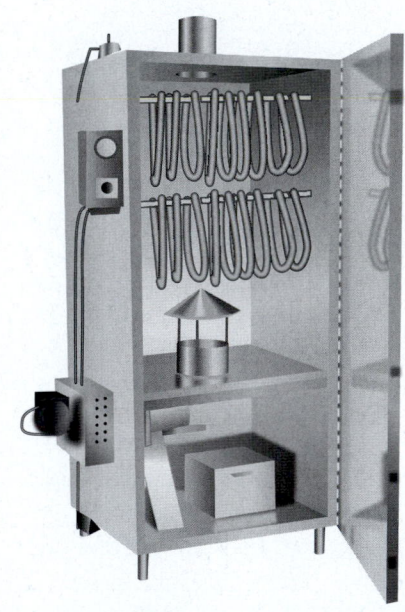

Commercial smoker

The second option is to use a small electric **smoke box** placed inside a traditional oven. The box holds an electric heating coil surrounded by wood chips. The box lid has holes that can be adjusted to control the amount of smoke released into the oven chamber. Foods being flavored with a smoke box can be cooked simultaneously by heat from the traditional oven. Foods smoked with either a stove top smoker or a smoke box must reach proper internal temperatures to be served without additional cooking.

A final option for imparting a smoky taste to foods is **liquid smoke**, a flavoring made from smoke, condensed from the burning of wood chips. When used judiciously, liquid smoke can impart a pleasant smoky taste to barbecue sauces and marinades.

Different types of wood can be used to smoke food. Specific woods are selected to impart specific flavors. Hickory is often used for pork products; alder is excellent for smoked salmon. Maple, chestnut, juniper, mesquite and many other woods are also used. Avoid resinous woods such as pine that give food a bitter flavor.

Procedure for Smoking Foods

1. Cut, trim and prepare the food for smoking. Trim excess surface fat from large cuts of meat. Tie up poultry into uniform shapes. Bone and trim fins from fish.

2. Brine or cure the item before smoking. For brine, immerse the food in a salt water brine flavored with herbs, spices and other seasonings. For curing, coat the food with a dry mixture of salt and seasonings and refrigerate for the time required.

3. Rinse off any brine or cure.

4. Dry the item before smoking using clean disposable towels. Place the item on a stainless steel rack and refrigerate uncovered until a pellicle forms. Larger items may be hung from racks that allow them to air dry and form a pellicle.

5. Heat a smoker to the desired temperature. Smoke the item using hot or cold smoke. For hot smoking, bring the food gradually to temperatures between 160°F and 185°F (71°C and 85°C). Smoke the food until it reaches the desired internal temperature. For cold smoking, bring the food gradually to temperatures between 40°F and 85°F (4°C and 29°C). Doneness is determined by internal temperature or time and smoked flavor of the food.

6. Cool the food prior to storing under refrigeration.

Hot Smoked Trout

YIELD 8 Fillets, approximately 6 oz. (180 g) each;
16 servings, 3 oz. (90 g) each

Trout fillets, skin on, 7–8 oz. (210–240 g) each	8	8
Dry Cure:		
Kosher salt	4 oz.	120 g
Granulated sugar	4 oz.	120 g
Coriander, ground	2 tsp.	10 ml
Black pepper	2 tsp.	10 ml
Cayenne pepper	¼ tsp.	1 ml
Allspice, ground	1 tsp.	5 ml
Lemon zest, grated	1 Tbsp.	5 ml

1 Trim any fins and rough edges from the trout fillets.

2 To make the dry cure, combine the salt, sugar, coriander, black and cayenne peppers and allspice in a small bowl.

3 Coat the trout fillets with the dry cure and lemon zest. Place the fillets on a paper-lined sheet pan and refrigerate uncovered. Allow the fish to cure until it is noticeably firm to the touch with some spring, approximately 2½–4 hours depending on the thickness of the fillets.

4 Rinse and dry each fillet well. Place the fillets on a lightly oiled rack set over a sheet tray. Refrigerate the fillets, uncovered, and allow them to air dry until the pellicle forms, approximately 8 hours or overnight.

5 Soak approximately 1 cup (240 milliliters) of wood chips in water for 15 minutes. Prepare a stovetop smoker or select a hotel pan with a tight-fitting lid. Place the smoker over two burners set on low heat. Scatter the wood chips in the bottom of the pan. (If using a hotel pan, place a perforated insert into the pan.) Place the rack of trout fillets in the smoker. As soon as smoke appears, cover tightly.

6 Hot smoke the trout at 185°F (85°C) until the flesh is firm and an internal temperature of 145°F (63°C) is reached, approximately 8–14 minutes. Hold the trout in the smoker for a total of 30 minutes.

7 Chill the trout before serving.

Variation:

Hot Smoked Salmon—Substitute one 3 pound (1.4 kilograms) salmon fillet, with skin attached. Cure the salmon for 4–8 hours in Step 3.

Approximate values per 3-oz. (90-g) serving: **Calories** 160, **Total fat** 7 g, **Saturated fat** 1 g, **Cholesterol** 60 mg, **Sodium** 410 mg, **Total carbohydrates** 1 g, **Protein** 22 g

❶ Placing a perforated insert over the soaked wood chips.

❷ Covering the rack of trout fillets as soon as smoke appears.

❸ The Hot Smoked Trout, ready to chill and serve.

Cured Pork Products

Preparing hams and curing and smoking pork products are traditional parts of charcuterie. In the following section we describe some of the more common cured pork products available to chefs.

Sliced bacon

Common bacon is produced by brining and cold-smoking trimmed pork belly. This fatty cut of pork absorbs flavors well during the smoking process. Bacon is sold in slab or sliced form. Sliced bacon is sold by count (number of slices) per pound; thick-sliced bacon runs 10–14 slices per pound, whereas thin-sliced bacon may contain as many as 28–32 slices per pound.

Canadian bacon is produced from a boneless pork loin, trimmed so that only a thin layer of fat remains on its surface. It is then brined and smoked.

Canadian bacon

Pancetta [pan-CHEH-tuh] is an Italian pork-belly bacon that is not smoked. It is salt-cured, peppered and often rolled into a cylinder shape. It can be sliced into rounds and fried; it is diced, rendered and combined with sauce to make pasta carbonara.

Pancetta

A **fresh ham** is a hog's hind leg; it is a primal cut. Many processed products produced from the primal fresh ham are also called ham.

Ham, in the United States, describes a variety of processed pork products, most of which come from the primal fresh ham. **Boneless hams**, which are also called **formed hams**, are produced by separating a primal ham into its basic muscles, defatting the meat, curing it, stuffing the meat into casings of various sizes and shapes and cooking it. Boneless or formed hams either are smoked or have chemical smoke flavoring added during the curing process. The quality of boneless or formed hams varies greatly. The best hams are formed from only one or two large muscles and have low fat content and no added water other than that used during the curing process. Hams of lesser quality are formed from many small pieces of muscle and have a higher fat and water content. Many boneless or formed hams are listed in *The Meat Buyer's Guide* and are indexed by the IMPS system. Bone-in and boneless hams are also sliced horizontally into individual **ham steaks** that can be sautéed or pan-fried.

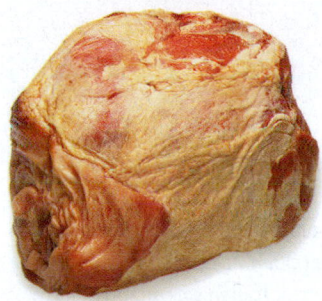

IMPS No. 510, ham, boneless, skinless, cured and smoked, fully cooked

Country ham is a specialty of the southeastern United States. Country hams are dry-cured, smoked and hung to air-dry for a period ranging from several weeks to more than a year. During drying, a mold develops on the ham rind that must be scrubbed off before the ham is cooked. A country ham is best cooked by first soaking, then slow simmering. The most famous country hams are Virginia hams; those from Smithfield, Virginia, are considered the finest. Only hams produced in rural areas can be called country hams; others must be labeled country-style ham.

IMPS No. 501, ham short shank, cured and smoked

Prosciutto [proh-SHOO-toe] is the Italian word for ham. What we call prosciutto in the United States is called **Parma** in Italy. Parma ham, produced near that Italian city, is made from hogs fed on the whey of cheese processed nearby. The meat is salt-cured and air-dried but not smoked. The curing process makes it safe to consume raw. Several domestic varieties of prosciutto are produced in the United States, varying widely in quality. Imported prosciuttos are much larger than the domestic varieties because Italian hogs are larger when butchered.

Ham steak (cured and smoked)

Prosciutto

Jamón [AH-mohn] is the Spanish word for ham. Jamón Serrano (mountain ham) is salt-cured and air-dried but not smoked. Jamón Iberico is a salted, dry-cured ham from specific breeds of hogs, a Spanish delicacy prized since Roman times. The most esteemed Jamón Iberico is that made from the Bellota breed that feed on foraged acorns. Like prosciutto, these hams are served raw, thinly sliced.

Westphalian ham is dry-cured, brined and then smoked with beechwood. Authentic Westphalian hams are produced in the Westphalia region of Germany and are quite similar to prosciutto. They are sold bone-in or boneless. Their characteristic flavor is derived from the juniper berries used in the curing process and the beechwood used for smoking.

Bresaola, dried beef from the Lombardy region of Italy

A charcuterie plate composed of cured meats with garnishes (clockwise starting from the left); pork rillettes, Italian salami, prosciutto, cured, cooked bacon and French saucisson sec in the foreground

Other Cured Meat Products

Although pork is the most common meat in classic charcuterie, other meats and poultry lend themselves to preservation. Beef is used to make **pastrami**, pickled beef brisket that is spiced and then air-dried. Pastrami is steamed, then sliced for sandwiches. **Bresaola**, a specialty of the Lombardy region of Italy, is salted, spiced and dry-aged beef, served raw and thinly sliced. It is made from the eye round of beef and has a subtle flavor of juniper berries. The similar specialty of the Swiss Alps is known as **bunderfleisch**. Smoked chicken, duck and turkey are delicious alternatives to ham in sandwiches and on salads. Few cured lamb products exist, possibly because of the strong flavor of lamb fat when aged.

SAUCE CHAUD-FROID

Sauce chaud-froid [shoh-FRAWH] (French for "hot-cold") is a decorative coating used in the presentation of cold cooked foods. It derives its name from its method of preparation; the sauce is prepared hot but served cold. Knowing how to prepare and use sauce chaud-froid is an essential skill of the garde manger chef and considered part of the craft of charcuterie.

Traditionally used to coat meats, poultry or fish that were eaten cold, sauce chaud-froid is now more typically used to coat a whole poached salmon or a whole roasted poultry item, which is then further decorated and used as a centerpiece. Like aspic jelly, chaud-froid that is to be eaten should be fairly firm when cold, gelled at room temperature but tender enough to melt quickly in the mouth. Chaud-froid used only for decorative purposes should have a heavier gelatin content and be quite firm, which makes it easier to work with.

A classic sauce chaud-froid is a mixture of one part cream and two parts stock (veal, chicken and/or fish) strengthened with gelatin. Depending on the stock used, it ranges in color from cream to beige. A more modern sauce chaud-froid (also known as a mayonnaise chaud-froid or mayonnaise collée) is made from mayonnaise; it is easier to make than the classic sauce and provides a whiter product, which is more desirable when used for centerpieces.

Mayonnaise Chaud-Froid

YIELD 2 qt. (1.9 lt)

Aspic jelly (firm to very firm)	1 qt.	960 ml
Mayonnaise (commercially made)	1 lb.	480 g
Sour cream	1 lb.	480 g

1 Melt the aspic jelly.

2 In a stainless steel bowl, combine the mayonnaise with the sour cream and mix until smooth.

3 Stir the aspic jelly into the mayonnaise and sour cream mixture until smooth.

4 Warm the sauce over a double boiler, stirring gently with a spoon until smooth and all the air bubbles disappear.

Procedure for Coating Foods with Sauce Chaud-Froid

1   Cook (usually by poaching or roasting), trim and otherwise prepare the item to be decorated.

2   Place the item on a cooling rack over a clean sheet pan and refrigerate until ready to decorate. (Sauce that drips into the clean pan can be reused.)

3   Warm an ample amount of sauce chaud-froid in a stainless steel bowl over a double boiler until it is completely melted. Stir the sauce gently with a spoon rather than a whisk in order to prevent air bubbles from forming.

4   When the sauce is warm and smooth, remove the bowl from the double boiler and place it in an ice bath.

5   Using the back of a large ladle, stir the sauce by spinning the bowl and holding the ladle stationary. This should be done almost continuously while the sauce cools. Do not scrape the solidified chaud-froid from the sides of the bowl as lumps will form.

6   When the sauce has cooled to room temperature, remove the item to be decorated from the refrigerator and place it on the worktable.

7   Coat the item with the sauce in a single, smooth motion. Use a ladle if the item is small; if the item is large, pour the sauce directly from the bowl. The sauce should adhere to the cold food, and the coating should be free of bubbles or runs.

8   Repeat as necessary, reusing the sauce that drips onto the sheet pan, until the desired thickness is achieved.

9   Using a paring knife, carefully cut away any sauce from areas that are to be left uncoated.

10 Decorate the item as desired with vegetable flowers or other garnishes. If desired, finish the item by coating the vegetable garnishes with a layer of clear aspic jelly, using the same procedure.

❶ Coating a fish with sauce chaud-froid.

❷ A finished salmon coated with chaud-froid sauce.

QUESTIONS FOR DISCUSSION

1 Explain why the art of charcuterie is relevant to the training of modern chefs.

2 Compare the three styles of forcemeat preparation.

3 In what way is a terrine different from a pâté? How does a pâté differ from a pâté en croûte?

4 Explain the differences and similarities between a ballotine and a galantine.

5 Describe the typical procedure for making sausages. Why is the selection of casings important?

6 Explain the difference between hot smoking and cold smoking. Describe a food typically prepared by each of these methods.

7 List the types of cured products that may be consumed without further cooking. What makes these products safe to eat?

8 Describe the differences and the similarities between aspic jelly and sauce chaud-froid. How are aspic jelly and sauce chaud-froid used?

9 Research the types of salts and curing agents used to make cold cuts, pâtés and forcemeats commercially. Explain when and why they are used. Discuss potential health hazards associated with consuming such ingredients and list some alternatives.

Additional Charcuterie Recipes

Basic Game Forcemeat

YIELD 4 lb. 8 oz. (2.1 kg)

Venison, cubed	1 lb. 8 oz.	720 g
Veal, cubed	1 lb. 8 oz.	720 g
Brandy	4 fl. oz.	120 ml
Salt	2 tsp.	10 ml
Pepper	½ tsp.	2 ml
Dried thyme	1 tsp.	5 ml
Pork fatback, cubed	1 lb.	480 g
Eggs	3	3
Game stock, cold	1 pt.	480 ml
Fresh parsley, chopped	1 oz.	30 g
Green peppercorns	½ oz.	15 g

1 Combine the venison and veal with the brandy, salt, pepper and thyme; marinate for several hours or overnight.

2 Grind the marinated meat and marinade ingredients in a chilled meat grinder once through a large die and then once through a small die; refrigerate.

3 Grind the fatback once through the small die.

4 Emulsify the fat with the ground meats in the bowl of a cold food processor. This can be done in several batches. Place the forcemeat in a stainless steel bowl over an ice bath.

5 Add the eggs, stock, parsley and peppercorns to the forcemeat in several batches; fold them in by hand.

6 Additional garnishes such as diced cured pork, beef tongue, fatback, dried fruit, or nuts may be added as desired. The forcemeat can be used to make a variety of pâtés or terrines.

Approximate values per 1-oz. (30-g) serving: **Calories** 100, **Total fat** 7 g, **Saturated fat** 3 g, **Cholesterol** 40 mg, **Sodium** 110 mg, **Total carbohydrates** 1 g, **Protein** 7 g

1 Emulsifying the fat with the ground meats.

2 Folding in the eggs, stock, parsley and peppercorns.

3 Filling a terrine with the forcemeat.

Liver Terrine

YIELD 1 Terrine, 12 × 4 × 3 in.
(30 × 10 × 7.5 cm), 20 Servings

Onions, diced	6 oz.	180 g
Vegetable oil	½ fl. oz.	15 ml
Pork liver	1 lb. 4 oz.	600 g
Fatback, diced	12 oz.	360 g
Eggs	2	2
Salt	1 Tbsp.	15 ml
Green peppercorns	½ tsp.	2 ml
Allspice, ground	½ tsp.	2 ml
Cloves, ground	¼ tsp.	1 ml
Ginger, ground	¼ tsp.	1 ml
Cream sauce	8 fl. oz.	240 ml
Brown veal stock	6 fl. oz.	180 ml
Fatback, sliced	as needed	as needed

1 In a small sauté pan, sweat the onions in the vegetable oil until tender without coloring. Refrigerate the onions until cold.

2 Trim and dice the liver.

3 Grind the liver and diced fatback through a grinder with a fine die. Add the onions and pass the liver and fatback through the grinder again.

4 Gently beat the eggs together by hand and add the salt, green peppercorns, allspice, cloves and ginger.

5 Combine the cream sauce and brown veal stock, add the egg mixture and mix well.

6 Add the ground liver mixture and beat until smooth.

7 Line a terrine with slices of fatback. Fill the mold with the forcemeat and cover with the overhanging slices of fatback.

8 Cover the terrine with its lid or aluminum foil and bake in a water bath at 350°F (180°C) to an internal temperature of 165°F (74°C), approximately 1½ hours.

9 Allow the terrine to cool for 1 hour, then refrigerate the terrine until cold. Unmold, slice and serve with toasted French bread accompanied by condiments such as coarse mustard, cornichons, pickled onions or Cherry Confit (page 803).

Approximate values per ½0-loaf serving: **Calories** 490, **Total fat** 46 g, **Saturated fat** 20 g, **Cholesterol** 265 mg, **Sodium** 800 mg, **Total carbohydrates** 5 g, **Protein** 14 g, **Vitamin A** 250%, **Iron** 45%

1 Filling the mold with forcemeat.

2 Slicing the Liver Terrine.

Pork Rillettes

YIELD 5 lb. (2.4 kg)

Lard or pork fat	1 lb.	480 g
Onions, thinly sliced	14 oz.	420 g
Garlic	¾ oz.	22 g
Thyme sprigs	4	4
Bay leaves	2	2
White wine or meat stock	1 pt.	480 ml
Pork shoulder, fatty, boneless	3 lb.	1.4 kg
Bacon, diced	12 oz.	360 g
Salt and pepper	TT	TT
Pâté Spice (page 834) or other seasoning blend	as needed	as needed

1 Place the lard or pork fat, onions, garlic, thyme, bay leaves and white wine in a heavy saucepan large enough to hold all the ingredients. Heat over low heat until the fat melts and the liquid reduces in half, approximately 30 minutes.

2 Cut the pork shoulder into long strips approximately ½-inch (1.2-centimeters) thick.

3 Add the pork to the fat and seasonings. Cook over low heat, stirring occasionally until the meat is soft and breaks up easily, 3½–4 hours. Cover after 2 hours if the meat is getting dry.

4 Transfer the cooked mixture into a large bowl and shred it into small pieces using two forks. Alternately place the cooked pork mixture into the bowl of a food processor and pulse just until the meat is shredded.

5 Adjust the seasonings with salt, pepper and Pâté Spice or other seasoning mixture. Pack the pork rillettes into several terrines or individual serving crocks and spoon some of the cooking liquid and fat over the top. Cover and refrigerate. Serve with toasted French bread accompanied by condiments such as coarse mustard, cornichons, pickled onions or Fresh Cranberry Orange Relish (page 805).

Approximate values per 3-oz. (90-g) serving: **Calories** 367, **Total fat** 35 g, **Saturated fat** 15 g, **Cholesterol** 198 mg, **Sodium** 650 mg, **Total carbohydrates** 10 g, **Protein** 14 g

Salmon and Sea Bass Terrine with Spinach and Basil

YIELD   1 Terrine, 12 × 4 × 3 in.
(30 × 10 × 7.5 cm), 20 Servings

Salmon fillet, boneless, skinless	1 lb. 8 oz.	720 g
Egg whites	3	3
Salt and white pepper	TT	TT
Cayenne pepper	TT	TT
Heavy cream	24 fl. oz.	720 ml
Fresh basil leaves	12	12
Truffles, brunoise, optional	¾ oz.	22 g
Spinach leaves, cleaned	6 oz.	180 g
Sea bass fillet	12 oz.	360 g
Mayonnaise (page 856), optional	as needed	as needed
Fresh dill, chopped fine, optional	as needed	as needed

1   Grind the salmon through the large die of a well-chilled meat grinder.

2   Place the salmon in the bowl of a food processor and process until smooth.

3   Add the egg whites, one at a time, pulsing the processor to incorporate. Scrape down the bowl and season with salt, white pepper and cayenne pepper.

4   With the machine running, add the cream in a steady stream. Scrape down the bowl again and process the mousseline until it is smooth and well mixed.

5   Blanch the basil leaves and refresh. Chop them finely.

6   Remove the mousseline from the bowl of the processor. Fold in the basil leaves and truffles, if using, and refrigerate.

7   Blanch and refresh the spinach leaves.

8   Spread the spinach leaves on a piece of plastic wrap, completely covering a rectangle approximately the length and width of the terrine mold.

9   Cut the sea bass fillet into strips approximately 1 inch (2.5 centimeters) wide and place end to end on the spinach leaves. Season with salt and white pepper.

10   Use the plastic wrap to wrap the spinach leaves tightly around the fish fillets.

11   Grease a terrine and line it with plastic wrap.

12   Half-fill the lined terrine with the salmon mousseline.

13   Carefully unwrap the spinach and sea bass fillets and place them down the center of the terrine. Fill the terrine with the remaining mousseline.

14   Tap the terrine mold firmly to remove any air pockets, then fold the plastic wrap over the top.

15   Cover and bake the terrine in a water bath at 300°F (150°C) to an internal temperature of 155°F (68°C), approximately 1½ hours.

16   Cool the terrine well, unmold, slice or decorate and serve with dill-flavored mayonnaise if desired.

Approximate values per ½₀-loaf serving: **Calories** 210, **Total fat** 16 g, **Saturated fat** 8 g, **Cholesterol** 75 mg, **Sodium** 180 mg, **Total carbohydrates** 1 g, **Protein** 15 g, **Vitamin A** 25%

Vegetable Terrine

YIELD 1 Terrine, 8 × 4 × 3 in.
(20 × 10 × 7.5 cm), 10 Servings

Carrots, diced	10 oz.	300 g
Cauliflower florets	20 oz.	600 g
Broccoli florets	10 oz.	300 g
Cream cheese	3 oz.	90 g
Eggs, separated	3	3
Almonds, ground	2 Tbsp.	30 ml
Salt and pepper	TT	TT
Nutmeg, grated	¼ tsp.	1 ml
Lemon juice	1 tsp.	5 ml
Fresh mint, chopped	1 Tbsp.	15 ml

1 Cook each vegetable separately in a steamer until tender, but not mushy.

2 Purée each vegetable separately in a food processor with 1 ounce (30 grams) cream cheese and 1 egg yolk.

3 Add the ground almonds to the carrot purée and season with salt and pepper.

4 Add the nutmeg and lemon juice to the cauliflower purée and season with salt and pepper.

5 Add the mint to the broccoli purée and season with salt and pepper.

6 Whip the egg whites to stiff peaks. Fold one-third of the whipped egg whites into each of the vegetable purées.

7 Layer the three purées in a terrine mold. Place the terrine in a water bath and bake at 325°F (160°C) until firm, approximately 45 minutes. Chill for service.

Approximate values per ⅒-loaf serving: **Calories** 114, **Total fat** 7 g, **Saturated fat** 3 g, **Cholesterol** 91 mg, **Sodium** 87 mg, **Total carbohydrates** 8.5 g, **Protein** 6 g, **Vitamin A** 171%, **Vitamin C** 87%

Vegetable Terrine in Brioche

Sinplicity Catering, Falls Church, VA
Chef Leland Atkinson

YIELD 1 Terrine, 12 × 4 × 3 in.
(30 × 10 × 7.5 cm), 16 Servings

Chicken breast meat, lean	2 lb.	960 g
Egg whites	3	3
Heavy cream	4 fl. oz.	120 ml
Brandy	2 fl. oz.	60 ml
Nutmeg, ground	TT	TT
Salt and pepper	TT	TT
Carrot, medium dice	3 oz.	90 g
Broccoli florets	8 oz.	240 g
Shiitake mushrooms, trimmed	12–18	12–18
Olive oil	1 fl. oz.	30 ml
Red bell pepper, medium dice	2 oz.	60 g
Leek, white part only, medium dice	2 oz.	60 g
Fresh chives, basil and parsley, chopped	4 Tbsp.	60 ml
Brioche dough (page 968)	1 lb.	480 g
Egg yolks, beaten	2	2
Eggs	2	2
Water	1 fl. oz.	30 ml
Madeira aspic	as needed	as needed

1 Dice or grind the chicken and place it in the bowl of a cold food processor and process.

2 Add the egg whites followed by the cream and brandy in a steady stream while the motor is running.

3 Season the mousseline with nutmeg, salt and pepper and poach a small amount to test for texture and seasonings.

4 Adjust the seasonings and transfer to a metal mixing bowl in an ice bath.

5 Separately blanch the carrot and broccoli; drain and blot dry on a paper towel.

6 Sauté the mushrooms in oil. Drain and chill. In the same pan, sauté the bell pepper and leek. Remove from the stove and add the herbs. Fold the carrot, bell pepper, leek and herbs into the mousseline.

7 Roll the Brioche dough out to approximately ⅛ inch (3 millimeters) thick and refrigerate until well chilled.

8 Line a buttered pâté mold with the chilled Brioche dough, reserving the excess for the top and garnish.

9 Fill the mold one-fourth full with the mousseline. Layer the mushrooms over the mousseline and cover them with another layer of mousseline, followed by the broccoli. Repeat this process until the mold is filled, finishing with a layer of mousseline.

10 Fold the ends of the Brioche dough over the filling and brush with the beaten egg yolks.

11 Make a top from the remaining Brioche dough and place it over the mold; cut a vent and insert a foil funnel into the vent.

12 Beat the eggs with the water to make an egg wash. Brush the exposed Brioche dough with the egg wash and bake at 425°F (220°C) until the internal temperature reaches 125°F (52°C), approximately 35–40 minutes.

13 When cold, fill the pâté with Madeira aspic, if needed.

Approximate values per ¹⁄₁₆-loaf serving: **Calories** 450, **Total fat** 20 g, **Saturated fat** 6 g, **Cholesterol** 185 mg, **Sodium** 520 mg, **Total carbohydrates** 35 g, **Protein** 34 g, **Vitamin A** 45%, **Vitamin C** 150%, **Claims**—high fiber

Roasted Red Pepper Mousse

YIELD   6 Timbales, 3 fl. oz. (90 ml) each

Onion, small dice	3 oz.	90 g
Garlic, chopped	1 tsp.	5 ml
Olive oil	1 fl. oz.	30 ml
Red bell peppers, roasted and peeled, small dice	10 oz.	300 g
Salt and pepper	TT	TT
Chicken stock	8 fl. oz.	240 ml
Granulated gelatin	1 Tbsp.	15 ml
Dry white wine	2 fl. oz.	60 ml
Heavy cream, whipped	6 fl. oz.	180 ml

1 Sauté the onion and garlic in the oil until tender, approximately 2 minutes.

2 Add the bell peppers, salt, pepper and stock. Bring to a boil, lower to a simmer and cook for 5 minutes.

3 Soften the gelatin in the wine and add it to the bell pepper mixture. Purée the bell pepper mixture in a blender or food processor. Strain it through a china cap.

4 Place the bell pepper purée over an ice bath. Stir until cool but do not allow the gelatin to set. Fold in the whipped cream. Pour the mousse into six 3-ounce (90-milliliter) aspic-lined or well-oiled timbales or molds and refrigerate several hours or overnight.

5 Unmold the mousse and serve as desired.

Variation:

Broccoli Mousse—Substitute 8 ounces (240 grams) blanched, chopped broccoli for the red bell peppers.

Approximate values per 3-fl.-oz. (90-ml) serving: **Calories** 180, **Total fat** 16 g, **Saturated fat** 8 g, **Cholesterol** 40 mg, **Sodium** 25 mg, **Total carbohydrates** 5 g, **Protein** 3 g, **Vitamin C** 25%

Salmon Mousse

YIELD   12 Timbales 3 fl. oz. (90 ml) each

Salmon, boneless, skinless	12 oz.	360 g
Fish velouté, warm	8 fl. oz.	240 ml
Heavy cream	8 fl. oz.	240 ml
Granulated gelatin	1½ Tbsp.	23 ml
White wine	4 fl. oz.	120 ml
Salt and white pepper	TT	TT
Cayenne pepper	TT	TT

1 Steam the salmon and transfer it to a food processor while still warm. Add the warm velouté in a steady stream while the machine is running.

2 Whip the cream to soft peaks and reserve.

3 Add the gelatin to the wine and allow it to rest for 5 minutes. Heat the gelatin mixture to a simmer.

4 Transfer the salmon and velouté to a mixing bowl and stir in the gelatin mixture. Season with salt, white pepper and cayenne pepper.

5 When the mixture has cooled to near room temperature, use a rubber spatula to fold in the whipped cream until just mixed. Pour the mousse into twelve 3-ounce (90-milliliter) aspic-lined or well-oiled timbales or molds and refrigerate several hours or overnight.

Salmon Mousse with green onions garnished with smoked salmon and dill

Approximate values per 3-fl.-oz. (90-ml) serving: **Calories** 160, **Total fat** 12 g, **Saturated fat** 6 g, **Cholesterol** 45 mg, **Sodium** 120 mg, **Total carbohydrates** 2 g, **Protein** 8 g

Chopped Chicken Liver

YIELD 20 oz. (600 g)

Chicken livers, trimmed	1 lb.	480 g
Chicken fat or butter	2 oz.	60 g
Eggs, hard-cooked	2	2
Onions, small dice	6 oz.	180 g
Kosher salt and pepper	TT	TT

1 Sauté the livers in the chicken fat or butter until lightly browned with a slightly pink interior.

2 Chop the livers with a chef's knife, blending in the eggs and onions. Season to taste with salt and pepper.

3 The final product should be slightly coarse and peppery. Blend in additional chicken fat or butter if necessary to make the mixture hold together.

4 Cover well and chill for 24 hours. Serve with crackers, toast or matzos and sliced red onions or radishes.

Approximate values per 1-oz. (30-g) serving: **Calories** 60, **Total fat** 4 g, **Saturated fat** 1 g, **Cholesterol** 105 mg, **Sodium** 240 mg, **Total carbohydrates** 1 g, **Protein** 4 g, **Vitamin A** 70%

1 Sautéing the chicken livers.

2 Chopping the cooked livers, eggs and onions.

Breakfast Sausage Patties

YIELD 5 lb. 8 oz. (2.6 kg), 44 Servings, 2 oz. (60 g) each

Salt	¾ oz.	22 g
Ground white pepper	¼ oz.	7 g
Sage	⅓ oz.	10 g
Crushed red pepper flakes	⅛ oz.	3 g
Pork butt, 70% lean, 30% fat, cubed	5 lb.	2.4 kg
Water, ice cold	8 fl. oz.	240 ml

1 Combine the seasonings in a small bowl.

2 In a large stainless steel bowl, toss the pork butt with the seasonings.

3 Grind the pork and seasonings through the medium plate of a cold meat grinder into a large stainless steel bowl placed over an ice bath.

4 Place the ground pork and seasonings in the chilled bowl of a mixer and mix on low speed for approximately 1 minute while gradually adding the cold water. Continue to mix until the mixture becomes sticky to the touch, approximately 5–10 more seconds.

5 Cook a small portion of the sausage to test the flavor and texture. Adjust the seasonings if necessary.

6 Form the sausage into patties or fill casings as desired. Pan-fry, broil, bake or grill as desired until done.

Approximate values per 2-oz. (60-g) serving: **Calories** 70, **Total fat** 3 g, **Saturated fat** 1 g, **Cholesterol** 30 mg, **Sodium** 250 mg, **Total carbohydrates** 0 g, **Protein** 10 g

Spicy Italian Sausage

YIELD 5 lb. (2.4 kg), 20 Sausages, 4 oz. (120 g) each

Pork butt	5 lb.	2.4 kg
Salt	1½ Tbsp.	23 ml
Black pepper	1½ tsp.	7 ml
Fennel seeds	1½ tsp.	7 ml
Paprika	1 Tbsp.	15 ml
Crushed red pepper flakes	1½ tsp.	7 ml
Coriander, ground	¾ tsp.	4 ml
Water, cold	5 fl. oz.	150 ml

1 Cut the pork into 2-inch (5-centimeter) cubes.

2 Combine the pork with the remaining ingredients except the water.

3 Grind the meat once through the coarse die of a well-chilled grinder.

4 Add the water and mix well.

5 Stuff the sausage into casings.

Variations:

Mild Italian Sausage—Omit the crushed red pepper flakes. Add 2 tablespoons (30 milliliters) fresh basil chiffonade, 1 tablespoon (15 milliliters) minced garlic and 2 ounces (60 grams) grated Parmesan cheese in Step 2. Substitute 2 fluid ounces (60 milliliters) red wine for 2 fluid ounces (60 milliliters) of water in Step 4.

Maple Sage Sausage—Omit the fennel seeds, paprika and the crushed red pepper flakes. Add 1 ounce (30 grams) minced fresh parsley, 4 tablespoons (60 milliliters) minced fresh sage and a pinch of ground nutmeg in Step 2. Substitute 5 fluid ounces (150 milliliters) pure maple syrup for the water in Step 4.

Thai Basil and Ginger Sausage—Omit the fennel seeds, paprika, crushed red pepper flakes and coriander. Add 2 ounces (60 grams) Thai basil chiffonade, 3 tablespoons (45 milliliters) seeded and minced Thai chiles, 2 tablespoons (30 milliliters) minced garlic, 2 tablespoons (30 milliliters) grated fresh ginger and 1 tablespoon (30 milligrams) ground ginger in Step 2. Substitute 2 fluid ounces (60 milliliters) lime juice for 2 fluid ounces (60 milliliters) of water in Step 4.

Approximate values per 4-oz. (120-g) serving: **Calories** 220, **Total fat** 9 g, **Saturated fat** 3 g, **Cholesterol** 80 mg, **Sodium** 260 mg, **Total carbohydrates** 0 g, **Protein** 36 g

Chorizo

YIELD 7 lb. 8 oz. (3.4 kg)

Pork, lean	5 lb.	2.4 kg
Fatback	2 lb. 8 oz.	1.2 kg
Crushed red pepper flakes	1 tsp.	5 ml
Garlic, chopped	1 oz.	30 g
Cumin, ground	3 Tbsp.	45 ml
Cayenne pepper	2 Tbsp.	30 ml
Salt	4 tsp.	20 ml
Paprika	5 Tbsp.	75 ml
Red wine vinegar	3 fl. oz.	90 ml

1 Cut the pork and fatback in 1-inch (2.5-centimeter) pieces. Grind the pork once using a medium die. Grind half of the pork a second time together with the fatback through a fine die.

2 Combine all the ingredients in the bowl of a mixer fitted with a paddle. Use the sausage in bulk or form into links as desired.

chorizo [chor-EE-zoh] a coarse, spicy pork sausage flavored with ground chiles; the Mexican version, which may be made without a casing, must be cooked before serving while the Spanish version is dried and cured

Approximate values per 3-oz. (90-g) serving: **Calories** 160, **Total fat** 12 g, **Saturated fat** 6 g, **Cholesterol** 45 mg, **Sodium** 120 mg, **Total carbohydrates** 2 g, **Protein** 8 g

Gravlax

Gravlax is a centuries-old Scandinavian method for preserving fresh salmon. The modern technique consists of rubbing a salt-and-sugar mixture into the cut fillets of salmon. The rub extracts moisture from the fish, which firms the flesh and extends its keeping properties. As liquid is extracted, the gentle flavors of white pepper and dill permeate the fish. (Although white pepper and dill are the classic seasonings for gravlax, other herbs and spices can be used. Adding grated lemon rind to the rub imparts a citrus note, for example.) Paper-thin slices of gravlax are usually served with a slightly sweet mayonnaise flavored with mustard and dill.

YIELD Approximately 5 lb. (2.42 kg)

Salmon, drawn, 10–12 lb. (4.8–5.5 kg)	1	1
Dry cure:		
Kosher salt	8 oz.	240 g
White peppercorns, cracked	1 oz.	30 g
Fresh dill, chopped	2 bunches	2 bunches
Granulated sugar	8 oz.	240 g

1 Fillet the salmon, removing the pin bones but leaving the skin attached.

2 To make the salt cure, combine the salt, peppercorns, dill and sugar.

3 Coat the salmon fillets with the salt cure and wrap each fillet separately in plastic wrap.

4 Place the fillets in a hotel pan and place another hotel pan on top. Place two #10 cans in the top hotel pan to weigh it down and press the fish.

5 Refrigerate the salmon for 2–3 days.

6 Unwrap the gravlax, scrape off the salt cure and slice the gravlax very thin.

Approximate values per 1-oz. (30-g) serving: **Calories** 110, **Total fat** 4.5 g, **Saturated fat** 1 g, **Cholesterol** 30 mg, **Sodium** 1130 mg, **Total carbohydrates** 3 g, **Protein** 16 g, **Claims**—low saturated fat

❶ Coating the salmon fillet with the salt cure.

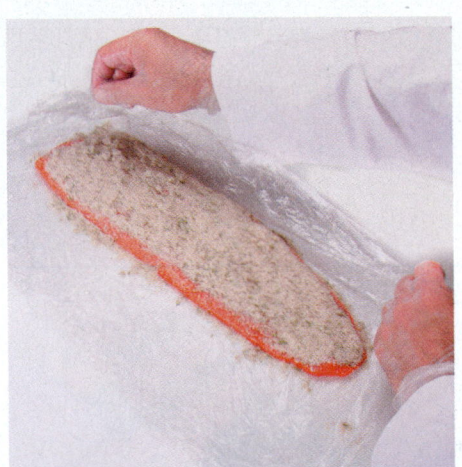

❷ Wrapping the fillets in plastic wrap.

❸ Weighting down a pan placed on top of the wrapped fish.

❹ Thinly slicing the cured gravlax.

Hors d'Oeuvre 29

▶ prepare and serve a variety of cold and hot hors d'oeuvre

▶ identify and describe international hors d'oeuvre

▶ choose hors d'oeuvre that are appropriate for the meal or event

hors d'oeuvre [ohr durv] very small portions of hot or cold foods served before the meal to stimulate the appetite

appetizers also known as first courses, usually small portions of hot or cold foods intended to whet the appetite in anticipation of the more substantial courses to follow

Salami cornet canapés

canapé [KAN-ah-pay] a tiny open-faced sandwich served as an hors d'oeuvre; usually composed of a small piece of bread or toast topped with a savory spread and garnish

crouton [KROO-tawn] a bread or pastry garnish, usually toasted or sautéed until crisp

Hors d'oeuvre are very small portions of foods served to whet the appetite before a meal. Hors d'oeuvre, whether hot or cold, are usually passed by waiters or displayed on buffets and should be no larger than one or two bites each. Elegant and flavorful, hors d'oeuvre are meant to delight and set the tone for the meal to come. The term *hors d'oeuvre* is often used interchangeably with the term **appetizers**, which can lead to some confusion. Appetizers, also referred to as starters, are generally the first course or introduction to a seated meal; they are more typically served with dinner than with lunch. Appetizers are listed on printed menus in most full service restaurants.

In this chapter we discuss the preparation of many types of hot and cold hors d'oeuvre and international finger foods and how to present and serve them. Appetizers are discussed throughout this book. A section on small plates that are often served before a meal or as a collective meal in themselves appears in Chapter 36, Plate Presentation.

The French term *hors d'oeuvre* translates as "outside the work." This usage made sense under the classic kitchen brigade system, for it was the service staff's responsibility to prepare small tidbits for guests to enjoy while the kitchen prepared the meal. Today, however, the kitchen staff prepares the hors d'oeuvre as well as the meals. Cold hors d'oeuvre are usually prepared by the garde manger; hot ones are prepared in the main kitchen.

Preparing hors d'oeuvre involves a wide arsenal of skills. Because they can consist of meat, poultry, fish, shellfish, vegetables, potatoes, grains, pasta, fruits, baked goods or sauces, hors d'oeuvre preparation requires a detailed knowledge of almost every work station. There are really only two limitations on the type of food and manner of preparation that can be used for hors d'oeuvre: the chef's imagination and the available foods. There are, however, a few guidelines.

General guidelines for hors d'oeuvre ideas and preparation include the following:

- They should be small, only one to two bites each.
- They should be flavorful and well seasoned without being overpowering.
- They should be visually attractive.
- They should complement whatever foods may follow without duplicating their flavors.

COLD HORS D'OEUVRE

In this chapter, we divide cold hors d'oeuvre into four broad categories based on preparation method, principal ingredient or presentation style. Those four categories are canapés, crudités, dips and caviar. These categories may vary somewhat from classical teachings, but they are completely appropriate for modern menus and food service operations.

Canapés

Classic canapés are tiny open-faced sandwiches, ideally no more than 1–2 inches (2.5–5 centimeters) in diameter. They are constructed from a base, a spread and one or more garnishes. Many modern interpretations exist, such as those in which toasted, sautéed, or dried French bread slices, also called **croutons**, contain the garnish.

The most common **canapé base** is a thin slice of bread cut into an interesting shape and toasted. Almost any variety of bread can be used; however, spiced, herbed or otherwise flavored breads may be inappropriate for some spreads or garnishes. Melba toasts, plain and seeded crackers and slices of firm vegetables, such as cucumbers or zucchini, are also popular canapé bases. Whatever item is used, the base must be strong enough to support the weight of the spread and garnish without falling apart when handled.

A SELECTION OF CANAPÉ SPREADS AND SUGGESTED GARNISHES	TABLE 29.1
SPREAD	**SUGGESTED GARNISHES**
Aïoli	Asparagus, roast beef, lamb, salmon, shrimp, cucumber slice, grilled peppers, green onion
Anchovy butter	Hard-cooked eggs, capers, green or black olive slices
Blue cheese	Grape half, walnuts, roast beef roulade, pear slice, currants, watercress
Fromage blanc or ricotta	Roasted beets, fava beans, radish slices, chives
Horseradish butter	Smoked salmon, roast beef, smoked trout, marinated herring, capers, parsley
Lemon butter	Shrimp, crab, caviar, salmon gravlax, chives, dill, parsley, capers
Liver pâté	Truffle slice, apple slice, cornichon
Mustard butter	Smoked meats, pâté, dry salami coronet, pickled onions
Pimento cream cheese	Smoked oyster, sardine, pimento, parsley, green olive slices
Pesto sauce	Cooked mushrooms, dry salami, prosciutto, tomato, Parmesan slices
Shrimp butter	Poached bay scallops, shrimp, caviar, parsley
Tuna salad	Capers, cornichons, radish slices
Wasabi mayonnaise	Grilled tuna, smoked fish, daikon slices, sprouts

The **canapé spread** provides much of the canapé's flavor. Spreads are usually flavored butters, cream cheese or a combination of the two. Table 29.1 lists several examples of spreads. Each spread is made by adding the desired amount of the main ingredient (chopped or puréed as appropriate) and seasonings to softened butter or cream cheese and mixing until combined. Quantities and proportions vary according to individual tastes. Other canapé spreads include bound salads (e.g., tuna or egg), finely chopped shrimp or liver mousse, ricotta cheese or flavored mayonnaise. Any of a number of ingredients can be combined for spreads.

General guidelines for preparing canapé spreads include the following:

- The spread's texture should be smooth enough to produce attractive designs when piped through a pastry bag fitted with a decorative tip.
- The spread's consistency should be firm enough so that the spread holds its shape when piped onto the base, yet soft enough to stick to the base and hold the garnishes in place.
- The spread's flavor should complement the garnishes and be flavorful enough to stimulate the appetite without being overpowering.

A spread may be a substantial portion of the canapé as well as its distinguishing characteristic. Or a spread can be applied sparingly and used more as a means of gluing the garnish to the base than as a principal ingredient. In the latter case, a smooth texture is not essential.

Canapés with bread bases tend to become soggy quickly from both the moisture in the spread and the moisture in the refrigerator where they are stored. A spread made with butter keeps the bread bases crisper, as does buttering the base with a thin coat of softened plain butter before piping on the spread. However the best way to ensure a crisp base is to make the canapés as close to service time as possible.

A canapé garnish can dominate or complement the spread, or it can be a simple sprig of parsley intended to provide visual appeal but little flavor. Although several ingredients can be used to garnish the same canapé, remember the limitations imposed by the canapé's size and purpose. Also consider the time involved in preparing and garnishing them. Traditional garnishes can be made by shaping thinly sliced smoked salmon into rosettes, or thin slices of salami or cucumber into cornets, into which additional spread can be piped. The natural shape of a boiled, peeled shrimp also makes an attractive canapé garnish.

Shrimp and caviar canapés

Salmon rosette canapés

An assortment of canapés (clockwise starting from top left): pimento cheese canapés, pea and prosciutto canapé and sautéed mushroom canapé

Procedure for Preparing Canapés

This procedure can be adapted and used with a variety of ingredients to produce a variety of canapés. If the canapé base is a bread crouton, begin with Step 1. If some other product is used as the base, prepare that base and begin with Step 4.

1 Trim the crust from an unsliced loaf of bread. Slice the bread lengthwise approximately ⅓ inch (8 millimeters) thick.

2 Cut the bread slices into the desired shapes using a serrated bread knife or canapé cutter. See Figure 29.1.

3 Brush the bread shapes with melted butter or olive oil and bake in a 350°F (180°C) oven until they are toasted and dry. Remove and cool. Alternatively the entire bread slice can be buttered and toasted, then cut into shapes.

4 If desired, spread each base with a thin layer of softened plain butter.

5 Apply the spread to the base. If a thin layer is desired, use a palette knife. If a thicker or more decorative layer is desired, pipe the spread onto the base using a pastry bag and decorative tip. Alternatively the entire bread slice can be buttered, toasted, cooled, covered with a spread and then cut into the desired shapes.

6 Garnish the canapé as desired.

7 If desired, glaze each canapé with a thin coating of aspic jelly. The aspic jelly can be applied with a small spoon or a spray bottle designated for that purpose.

❶ Cut bread slices into the desired shapes.

❷ Apply the spread to the base with a palette knife.

❸ Pipe the spread onto the base.

❹ Alternatively cover the entire slice of toasted bread with a spread before cutting it into canapés.

❺ Garnish the canapés.

❻ If desired, spray the finished canapés with aspic.

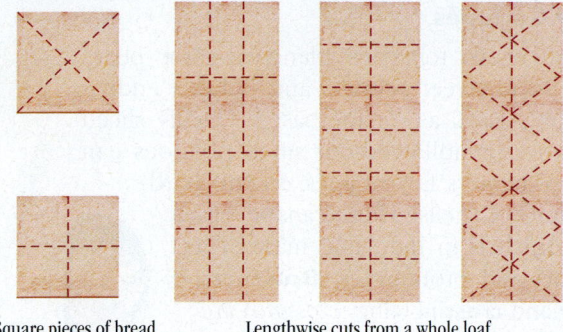

Square pieces of bread   Lengthwise cuts from a whole loaf

Figure 29.1 Bread can be cut into several basic shapes to avoid waste.

Barquettes, Tartlets and Profiteroles

Barquettes, tartlets and profiteroles are all adaptations of the basic canapé. A barquette is a tiny boat-shaped shell made from a savory dough such as pâte brisée. A tartlet is a round version of a barquette. A profiterole is a small puff made from Éclair Paste (Pâte à Choux); page 996. Prepare barquettes, tartlets and profiteroles like canapés by filling them with flavored spreads and garnishing as desired.

Procedure for Preparing Barquettes

❶ Roll out the pastry dough.

❷ Press the dough into the barquette pan.

❸ Prick the dough with a fork to allow steam to escape during baking.

❹ Place a second barquette pan on top of the dough to prevent it from rising as it bakes.

Amuse-Bouche

Amuse-bouche, "mouth pleaser" in French, are small samples of food served in restaurants before a meal. Many chefs create these one-bite dishes as a gesture of hospitality and an expression of their creativity. Unlike appetizers, these hors d'oeuvre are chosen by the chef and offered free of charge. *Amuse-bouche* may be simple or elaborate, made from luxury ingredients, such as caviar, or seasonal ingredients in limited supply.

Stuffed egg canapés

Other Types of Canapés

Vegetables such as cherry tomatoes, blanched snow peas, mushroom caps, small sweet peppers and Belgian endive leaves are sometimes used as canapé bases. Thickly sliced rounds of cucumber or hollowed-out small potatoes can also be used as containers for canapés, as can hard-cooked eggs or mussel shells. These canapé bases are filled and garnished in the same manner as barquettes, tartlets and profiteroles. **Bruschette** (sing. *bruschetta*) and **crostini** (sing. *crostino*) are slices of country bread that are grilled, brushed with garlic and olive oil and then garnished with diced tomatoes or other toppings. These Italian-style canapés are versatile and easy to prepare. Because they are hearty and rustic in appearance, bruschette and crostini are well suited to informal settings and occasions.

An assortment of canapés (clockwise from left): steamed mussel, cream-cheese-filled endive and pico de gallo tartlet

Crudités

Crudité, a French word meaning "raw thing," generally refers to raw or slightly blanched vegetables served as an hors d'oeuvre. Although almost any vegetable can be a crudité, the most common are broccoli, cauliflower, carrots, celery, asparagus and green beans, all of which are typically blanched, and cucumbers, zucchini, yellow squash, radishes, green onions, cherry tomatoes, Belgian endive leaves, snow peas, mushrooms, peppers and jicama, which are served raw.

When preparing crudités, use only the freshest and best-looking produce available. Because they are displayed and eaten raw, vegetables must be free from blemishes and imperfections. Vegetables, both blanched and raw, should be cut into attractive shapes. Crudités are usually served with one or more dips in a large display or in individual serving glasses.

Crudités and dip in individual serving glasses

Dips

Dips are a type of thick sauce served with crudités, crackers, chips, toasts, breads or other foods. Dips, which may be cold or hot, must be viscous (thick and sticky) enough to cling to foods dipped in them.

Cold dips often use mayonnaise, sour cream or cream cheese as a base. These dips are prepared using the methods for preparing mayonnaise-based salad dressings discussed in Chapter 25, Salads and Salad Dressings. The principal difference between dressings and dips is that dips are normally thicker. Soft spreadable cheese such as cream cheese and fromage blanc make flavorful dips. To use spreadable cheese as a base, first soften it by mixing it in an electric mixer fitted with a paddle. Then add the flavoring ingredients such as chopped cooked vegetables, chopped cooked fish or shellfish, herbs, spices, garlic or onions. Adjust the consistency of the dip by adding milk, buttermilk, cream, sour cream, lemon juice or other appropriate liquid.

Some cold dips such as Guacamole (page 888), Hummus (page 875) and Spanish Romesco Sauce (page 252) use purées of fruits, vegetables, beans or nuts as the base. Hot dips often use a béchamel, cream sauce or cheese sauce as a base and usually contain a dominant flavoring ingredient such as chopped spinach or shellfish.

Dips can be served in small bowls or hollowed-out cabbages, squash, pumpkins or other vegetables. Hot dips are often served in chafing dishes. The combinations of ingredients and seasonings that can be used to make dips as well as the foods that are dipped in them are limited only by the chef's imagination.

Artful array of crudités and dip

Hummus

YIELD 1 qt. (960 ml)

Chickpeas, cooked	1 lb.	480 g
Tahini	8 oz.	240 g
Garlic, chopped	2 tsp.	10 ml
Cumin, ground, optional	½ tsp.	2 ml
Lemon juice	4 fl. oz.	120 ml
Water or vegetable stock	4 fl. oz.	120 ml
Salt	1 tsp.	5 ml
Cayenne pepper	½ tsp.	2 ml
Olive oil	2 fl. oz.	60 ml
Fresh parsley, chopped	2 tsp.	10 ml

MISE EN PLACE

- Cook chickpeas.
- Chop garlic.
- Chop parsley.

1 Combine the chickpeas, tahini, garlic, cumin, if using, and lemon juice in a food processor; process until smooth. If necessary, with the food processor running, add as much water or stock as needed to make the mixture the consistency of firm mayonnaise. Season with salt and the cayenne pepper.

2 Spoon the hummus onto a serving platter and smooth the surface. Drizzle the oil over the hummus and garnish with the chopped parsley. Serve with warm pita bread that has been cut into quarters.

Note If using canned chickpeas, drain and reserve the liquid. Use it in place of the water or stock if needed to adjust the consistency of the mixture in Step 1.

Approximate values per 2-fl.-oz. (60-ml) serving: **Calories** 210, **Total fat** 16 g, **Saturated fat** 1 g, **Cholesterol** 0 mg, **Sodium** 250 mg, **Total carbohydrates** 10 g, **Protein** 7 g, **Iron** 8%

tahini [tah-HEE-nee] a thick, oily paste made from crushed sesame seeds

Caviar

Caviar, the salted **roe** (eggs) of the sturgeon fish, is a classic hors d'oeuvre and a universal symbol of refined dining. Caviar is served alone with toast or as an elegant garnish on canapés and other foods.

In the United States, only sturgeon roe can be labeled simply "caviar." Roe from other fish must be identified as such on the label (e.g., salmon roe or lumpfish caviar). Much of the world's caviar once came from sturgeon harvested in the Caspian Sea and imported from Russia and Iran. True caviar is classified according to the sturgeon species (such as beluga, osetra or sevruga) and roe size and color. **Beluga** is the most expensive caviar and comes from the largest species (these sturgeon can weigh up to 1750 pounds/800 kilograms). Beluga's dark gray eggs are the largest and most fragile variety of caviar. Because of severe depletion of the species of Caspian sturgeon that produces beluga caviar, its sale is banned in the United States. **Osetra** eggs are medium-sized, golden yellow to brown and quite oily. **Sevruga** caviar is harvested from small sturgeon; the eggs are small and light to dark gray.

Beluga caviar

Osetra caviar

Sevruga caviar

Most of the caviar consumed in the United States comes from domestic sturgeon or another fish, as identified on the label. Roe from **American sturgeon**, harvested in the coastal waters of the American Northwest and the Tennessee River as well as from fish farms in California, is becoming increasingly popular as its quality is comparable to Caspian sea varieties. **Golden whitefish caviar** is a small and very crisp roe; it is a natural golden color and comes from whitefish in the northern Great Lakes. **American paddlefish caviar** is large steel-grey roe from the paddlefish or spoonbill. Its flavor is similar to sevruga—earthy, buttery and rich with a soft texture. **Lumpfish caviar** is widely available and inexpensive. The eggs are small and very crisp and are dyed black, red or gold. This food coloring is not stable, however, and the coloring tends to bleed. **Salmon caviar**, the eggs of the chum and silver salmon, is a popular garnish. The eggs are large with a good flavor and natural orange color.

American paddlefish caviar

American salmon roe

blini a small yeast-raised pancake of Russian origin made with buckwheat flour, traditionally served with caviar, smoked fish and other delicacies

Purchasing and Storing Caviar

Although all caviar is processed with salt, some caviar is labeled **malassol**, which means "little salt." (At one time this term distinguished highly salted inferior caviar from superior lightly salted caviar, although this is no longer the case.) Caviar should smell fresh, with no off-odors. The eggs should be whole, not broken, and they should be crisp and pop when eaten. Excessive oiliness may be caused by broken eggs. The best way to test caviar's quality is to taste it.

Most caviar can be purchased fresh or pasteurized in tins or jars ranging from 1 ounce (28 grams) to more than 4 pounds (1.8 kilograms). Some caviars are also available frozen, but these are only suitable for use as a garnish. In order to ensure the freshest possible product, purchase caviar frequently in small quantities based on the needs of the restaurant.

Store fresh caviar at 32°F (0°C). Because most refrigerators are warmer than that, place the caviar on ice in the coldest part of the refrigerator and change the ice often. If properly handled, fresh caviar will last 1–2 weeks before opening and several days after opening. Pasteurized caviar does not require refrigeration until it is opened and will last several days in the refrigerator after opening.

Serving Caviar

Fine caviar should be served in its original container or a nonmetal bowl on a bed of crushed ice, accompanied only by lightly buttered toasts or **blinis** and sour cream. Always use nonmetal utensils for service; metal reacts with the caviar, producing off-flavors.

Lesser-quality caviars may be served on ice, accompanied by minced onion, chopped hard-cooked egg whites and yolks, lemon wedges, sour cream and buttered toasts from which guests build their own canapés. One serving is approximately ½ teaspoon (3 milliliters); a 2 ounce jar (60 gram) provides enough for canapés to serve 8 people. Lumpfish and other nonsturgeon caviars are rarely served by themselves. Rather they are used as ingredients in or garnishes for other dishes. Caviar can be mixed into softened butter or cream cheese for a spread, or scrambled into eggs and is an appropriate garnish for many fish or shellfish presentations. Even a tiny amount of roe used as a carefully placed garnish can increase a dish's perceived value.

Other Cold Hors d'Oeuvre

Salted nuts, cured olives, cornichons or other pickled vegetables are often served as cold hors d'oeuvre. These savory tidbits enhance other items such as platters of cubed cheese, sliced cured or preserved meats and grilled vegetables. Due to the popularity of sushi and sashimi, raw fish dishes are common on hors d'oeuvre menus. Preparations such as ceviche discussed in Chapter 20, Fish, can be made ahead and served in small glasses or serving spoons.

HOT HORS D'OEUVRE

To provide a comprehensive list of hot hors d'oeuvre would be virtually impossible. Therefore in this chapter, we discuss just a few of the more commonly encountered ones that can be easily made in almost any kitchen.

Filled Pastry Shells

Because savory (unsweetened) barquettes and tartlets, éclair puffs and bouchées can hold a small amount of liquid, they are often baked and then filled with warm meat, poultry or fish purées or ragoûts, garnished and served hot. They become soggy quickly, however, and must be prepared at the last possible minute before service.

Skewers

Small skewers of meat, poultry, game, fish, shellfish or vegetables make ideal hot hors d'oeuvre. The foods are typically marinated, then baked, grilled or broiled, and served with a dipping sauce. These skewers, also called **brochettes**, can hold small pieces of boneless chicken breast marinated in white wine and grilled, beef cubes glazed with teriyaki sauce, alternating strips of red and green peppers or lamb or chicken satay (saté) with peanut sauce.

In order to increase visual appeal, the main ingredients should be carefully cut and consistent in size and shape. The ingredients are normally diced, but strips of meat, poultry and vegetables can also be threaded onto the skewers.

As hors d'oeuvre, the skewers should be very small, slightly larger than a toothpick. When assembling, leave enough exposed skewer so that diners can pick them up easily. Bamboo and wooden skewers have a tendency to burn during cooking. Soaking them in water before assembling helps reduce the risk of burning.

Lamb Satay

YIELD 16 Skewers

Lamb leg meat, boned, trimmed	2 lb.	960 g
Marinade:		
Vegetable oil	2 fl. oz.	60 ml
Lemongrass, chopped	2 Tbsp.	30 ml
Garlic, chopped	1 Tbsp.	15 ml
Crushed red pepper flakes	1 tsp.	5 ml
Curry powder	1 Tbsp.	15 ml
Honey	1 Tbsp.	15 ml
Fish sauce	1 Tbsp.	15 ml
Southeast Asian-Style	as needed	as needed
Peanut Sauce (page 251)		
Cilantro	as needed for garnish	
Lime, cut into wedges	as needed for garnish	

MISE EN PLACE
- Trim and bone lamb.
- Prepare the Peanut Sauce.
- Cut lime wedges.
- Soak skewers in water.

1 Cut the lamb into 2-ounce (60-gram) strips approximately 4 inches (10 centimeters) long. Lightly pound the strips with a mallet. Thread the strips onto 6-inch (15-centimeter) bamboo skewers that have been soaked in water.

2 To make the marinade, combine the marinade ingredients in the bowl of a food processor and purée until smooth.

3 Brush the meat with the marinade and allow to marinate for 1 hour.

4 Grill the skewers until done, approximately 2 minutes. Serve with Southeast Asian-Style Peanut Sauce garnished with cilantro and lime wedges.

Variation:

Beef or chicken satay can be made by substituting well-trimmed beef or boneless, skinless chicken meat for the lamb.

Approximate values per skewer: **Calories** 118, **Total fat** 7 g, **Saturated fat** 2 g, **Cholesterol** 37 mg, **Sodium** 40 mg, **Total carbohydrates** 2 g, **Protein** 12 g

Meatballs

Meatballs made from ground beef, veal, pork or poultry and served in a sauce buffet style are a popular hot hors d'oeuvre. Any meatball recipe is suitable for use as an hors d'oeuvre as long as the meatballs are sized to be eaten in one bite. (See Italian Country Meatballs, page 338.) One of the best known is the Swedish meatball, made from ground beef, veal and pork bound with eggs and bread crumbs and served in a velouté or cream sauce seasoned with dill. Other sauces that can go well with meatballs include mushroom sauce, red wine sauce or any style of tomato sauce.

MISE EN PLACE

- Peel onions and chop into fine dice.
- Grind fresh bread for bread crumbs.
- Heat demi-glace and cream and chop dill while the meatballs are baking.

Swedish Meatballs

YIELD 4 lb. 8 oz. (2.1 kg); 48 Meatballs, 1½ oz. (45 g) each

Onions, small dice	8 oz.	240 g
Whole butter	2 oz.	60 g
Ground beef	2 lb.	960 g
Ground pork	2 lb.	960 kg
Bread crumbs, fresh	4 oz.	120 g
Eggs	3	3
Salt	1 Tbsp.	15 ml
Black pepper	TT	TT
Nutmeg, ground	TT	TT
Allspice, ground	TT	TT
Lemon zest, grated	1 tsp.	5 ml
Demi-glace, hot	1 qt.	1 lt
Heavy cream, hot	8 fl. oz.	240 ml
Fresh dill, chopped	2 Tbsp.	30 ml

1 Sauté the onions in the butter without coloring. Remove and cool.

2 Combine the cooled onions with all of the ingredients except the demi-glace, cream and dill. Mix well.

3 Portion the meat with a #20 scoop; form into balls with your hands and place on a sheet pan.

4 Bake the meatballs at 400°F (200°C) until firm, approximately 15 minutes. Remove the meatballs from the pan with a slotted spoon, draining well, and place in a hotel pan.

5 Combine the demi-glace, cream and dill; pour over the meatballs.

6 Cover the meatballs and bake at 350°F (180°C) until done, approximately 20 minutes. Skim the grease from the surface and serve.

Approximate values per 2-meatball serving: **Calories** 250, **Total fat** 16 g, **Saturated fat** 7 g, **Cholesterol** 105 mg, **Sodium** 420 mg, **Total carbohydrates** 7 g, **Protein** 20 g, **Calcium** 30%

Hors d'Oeuvre Wrapped in Cheese, Meat or Vegetables

A slice of cheese, savory meat or roasted pepper wrapped around a complementary or contrasting slice of fruit or vegetable makes a flavorful hot hors d'oeuvre. Shrimp wrapped in bacon, asparagus spears in prosciutto or a cube of mozzarella in a slice of roasted red pepper are popular options. Choose a flavorful slice of meat, such as cured ham, bacon or salami, or cheese, such as fontina or gouda, as the wrapping. The hors d'oeuvre known as rumaki is a good example of an appealing flavor combination and technique. Traditionally rumaki were made by wrapping chicken livers in bacon and broiling or baking them. Now many other foods prepared in the same fashion are also called rumaki. For example, blanched bacon can be wrapped around olives, pickled watermelon rind, water chestnuts, pineapple, dates or scallops. These morsels are then broiled, baked or fried and served piping hot.

Rumaki

YIELD 60 Pieces

Chicken livers	1 lb.	480 g
Marinade:		
Brown sugar	1 Tbsp.	15 ml
Water, hot	1 Tbsp.	15 ml
Dark soy sauce	1 Tbsp.	15 ml
Garlic, minced	1 Tbsp.	15 ml
Bacon, thin sliced	30 slices	30 slices
Water chestnuts, sliced	60 slices	60 slices

1 Trim the livers and cut into 60 equal-sized pieces. Place the livers in a stainless steel bowl.

2 Combine the marinade ingredients. Pour the marinade over the livers and refrigerate for 1 hour.

3 Cut the bacon slices in half, spread them on a sheet pan and parcook at 375°F (190°C) for approximately 5 minutes. Pour off and discard the excess fat.

4 Drain the livers. To assemble the rumaki, roll one piece of liver and one water chestnut slice in one piece of bacon and secure with a toothpick. Repeat with the remaining ingredients. Place on a baking rack over a sheet pan with the seam side down.

5 Bake the rumaki in a 400°F (200°C) convection oven until the bacon is crisp and the liver is cooked, approximately 10 minutes. Do not overcook or the rumaki will be dry. Serve hot.

Approximate values per piece: **Calories** 60, **Total fat** 5 g, **Saturated fat** 1.5 g, **Cholesterol** 30 mg, **Sodium** 170 mg, **Total carbohydrates** 1 g, **Protein** 4 g, **Vitamin A** 10%

Hors d'Oeuvre Wrapped in Dough

Any number of doughs including savory pie dough or Puff Pastry (page 993) can serve as the base of numerous hot hors d'oeuvre. These doughs can be stuffed with a wide variety of pork, chicken, fish or vegetable stuffings before baking or deep-frying. Prepared doughs such as phyllo dough or wonton skins simplify the preparation of filled hors d'oeuvre.

Phyllo Dough

Phyllo [FEE-low], also spelled *filo* or *fillo,* is from the Greek *phyllon,* meaning "thin sheet or leaf." Although its name is Greek, the dough's origin is unknown. Indians, Turks, Syrians, Yugoslavs and Austrians all claim it as their own. Blandly flavored phyllo sheets are brushed with melted butter or oil, stacked and then used in Mediterranean, Middle Eastern and Central Asian dishes as a tart crust or a wrapper for various sweet or savory fillings. Phyllo dough is now also used for strudels and various hors d'oeuvre. Shredded phyllo dough, called **kataifi**, is also used in some Mediterranean and Middle Eastern specialties.

Phyllo dough is made from flour, water, a bit of oil and eggs. The dough is stretched tissue-paper thin, using techniques that can take years to master. Fortunately excellent commercially prepared phyllo dough is available in frozen sheets. Sheets of phyllo dough can stick together if thawed too quickly, so thaw frozen dough slowly for a day or so in the refrigerator. Then temper the package of dough at room temperature for at least 1 hour before opening. (Unused phyllo dough should not be refrozen; it will keep for several days in the refrigerator if tightly wrapped.)

When the phyllo dough is ready to use, open the package and unfold the stack of sheets. Place them flat on a sheet pan or work surface and cover with a piece of plastic wrap topped with a damp towel. Remove one sheet at a time from the stack, keeping the remainder well covered to prevent them from drying out. Brush melted butter or oil over the sheet's entire surface. Chopped nuts, sugar, cocoa powder or bread crumbs can be dusted over the butter or oil for additional flavor. Repeat with additional sheets until the desired number of layers have been prepared and stacked. The number of layers depends on the thickness of the sheets and their use. Cut the stacked phyllo sheets with scissors or a very sharp knife and use as directed in the recipe.

- Mince garlic.
- Slice water chestnuts while liver is marinating in Step 2.

❶ Rolling the liver and the water chestnut in the bacon.

❷ Removing the finished rumaki from the baking rack.

♥ Good Choice   🍃 Vegetarian

MISE EN PLACE

- Dice onion.
- Melt butter.
- Cook and cool spinach. Thaw frozen spinach before if using.
- Chop mint.
- Crumble feta.
- Beat eggs.

Spanakopita

YIELD 90 Pieces

Onion, small dice	4 oz.	120 g
Unsalted butter, melted	6 oz.	180 g
Fresh spinach, cooked and cooled, or frozen spinach, thawed	24 oz.	720 g
Fresh mint, chopped	1 Tbsp.	15 ml
Feta, crumbled	1 lb.	480 g
Eggs, beaten	3	3
Salt and pepper	TT	TT
Phyllo dough	1 lb.	480 g

1 Sauté the onion in 1 tablespoon (15 milliliters) butter until tender. Remove and cool.

2 Combine the cooled onion, spinach, mint, feta and eggs. Season with salt and pepper and mix well.

3 Spread one sheet of phyllo dough on the work surface; brush with melted butter. Place another sheet of phyllo dough on top of the first; brush it with butter. Stack a third sheet of phyllo dough on top of the second and brush it with butter as well.

4 Cut the stack of phyllo dough sheets into 2-inch- (5-centimeter-) wide strips.

5 Place 1 tablespoon (15 milliliters) of the spinach mixture on the end of each strip of phyllo dough sheets.

6 Starting with the end of the phyllo dough strip with the spinach mixture, fold one corner of the phyllo dough over the spinach mixture to the opposite side of the strip to form a triangle. Continue folding the phyllo dough, as you would fold a flag, keeping it in a triangular shape.

7 Place the phyllo dough triangles on a sheet pan and brush with melted butter. Bake at 375°F (190°C) until brown and crisp, approximately 20 minutes.

Approximate values per piece: **Calories** 45, **Total fat** 3 g, **Saturated fat** 2 g, **Cholesterol** 15 mg, **Sodium** 105 mg, **Total carbohydrates** 3 g, **Protein** 2 g, **Vitamin A** 8%, **Claims**—low fat; low cholesterol; no sugar

① Stacking the sheets of buttered phyllo dough.

② Placing the filling on the stack of phyllo dough sheets.

③ Folding the phyllo dough and spinach mixture into triangles.

Wonton Skins

Wonton skins are an Asian noodle filled to produce egg rolls and dumplings (wontons) that are fried or served in broths. The dough is made from wheat flour bound with eggs and water and then rolled paper-thin. Wonton skins are ideal for making a wide variety of hors d'oeuvre, such as a miniature egg roll or a puff filled with a mixture of seasoned cream cheese and crab. The skins, which are commercially available in rounds or squares, can be stuffed with a wide variety of fillings before cooking. As hors d'oeuvre, stuffed wonton skins can be steamed, but they are more often pan-fried or deep-fried. (Wonton skins can also be baked and used as a canapé base, as shown in the recipe for Baked Wonton Crisps, page 885.)

Stuffed Wontons with Apricot Sauce

YIELD 24 Pieces

Cream cheese	8 oz.	240 g
Crab meat	8 oz.	240 g
Garlic, chopped	1 tsp.	5 ml
Green onions, sliced	1 oz.	30 g
Salt and pepper	TT	TT
Worcestershire sauce	TT	TT
Sesame oil	TT	TT
Wonton skins, 3½-in. (9-cm) squares	24	24
Apricot Sauce (recipe follows)	as needed	as needed

1 Place the cream cheese in the bowl of a mixer and mix until soft.

2 Add the crab meat, garlic and green onions. Season with salt and pepper, Worcestershire sauce and a drop or two of sesame oil.

3 Place several wonton skins on a work surface. Brush the edges with water. Place 1 tablespoon (15 milliliters) of the cream cheese mixture in the center of each skin. Fold the wonton skin in half to form a triangle; seal the edges.

4 Using the swimming method, deep-fry the wontons at 350°F (180°C) for 10 seconds. Remove the wontons, drain well and refrigerate.

5 At service time, deep-fry the wontons at 350°F (180°C) until crisp, approximately 1 minute. Serve with Apricot Sauce.

Approximate values per piece, with sauce: **Calories** 130, **Total fat** 8 g, **Saturated fat** 2.5 g, **Cholesterol** 20 mg, **Sodium** 105 mg, **Total carbohydrates** 11 g, **Protein** 4 g

❶ Brushing the edges of the wonton skins with water.

❷ Folding the wontons and sealing the edges.

 Good Choice    Vegan

Apricot Sauce

YIELD 8 oz. (240 g)

Apricot preserves	8 oz.	240 g
Fresh ginger, grated	1 Tbsp.	15 ml
Dry mustard	1 tsp.	5 ml
Red wine vinegar	½ fl. oz.	15 ml

1 Combine all ingredients in a small saucepan.

2 Heat, stirring occasionally, until the preserves melt and the flavors blend.

Approximate values per 1-oz. (30-g) serving: **Calories** 70, **Total fat** 0 g, **Saturated fat** 0 g, **Cholesterol** 0 mg, **Sodium** 10 mg, **Total carbohydrates** 19 g, **Protein** 0 g, **Claims**—fat free

Other Hot Hors d'Oeuvre

Other types of hot hors d'oeuvre include tiny red potatoes filled with sour cream and caviar or Roquefort cheese and walnuts; scaled-down taco shells filled with chili; sliders or miniature hamburgers; or chicken wings that are seasoned or marinated, baked, fried, broiled or grilled and served with a cool and soothing or outrageously spicy sauce. The aroma and crisp texture of fried foods such as Salmon Croquettes (page 534) and Arancini (page 895) make them appealing hot hors d'oeuvre.

The secret is to use creativity, to keep the ingredients harmonious and, if the hors d'oeuvre are to precede a meal, not to allow them to duplicate or overpower the foods to be served. Mainstays of the menu are, however, another source for interesting hors d'oeuvre. Miniature versions of main dishes such as a rich beef stew in a barquette, a cooked ravioli in tomato sauce or miniature crab cakes can add variety to an hors d'oeuvre assortment without taxing the kitchen staff.

ANTIPASTI, MEZZE, TAPAS AND ZAKUSKI

Many cultures have a tradition of serving finger foods and small dishes before a main meal. Antipasti, mezze, tapas and zakuski represent four such traditions.

In Italy, small bites of food served before a meal are called **antipasti** (sing. *antipasto*), an Italian word which means "before the pasta course." These savory salty foods are chosen to whet the appetite for the main meal rather than to sate hunger. An assortment of antipasti may include olives, salted anchovies, slices of dry-cured sausage and cured meats, Italian cheeses or pickled vegetables such as Giardiniera (page 635) served to the guests from a platter or in small bowls.

Mezze are small plates of assorted salads such as Hummus (page 875) and Baba Ghanoush (page 887) that are served with alcoholic or nonalcoholic drinks to allow guests to linger and relax before the main meal. Mezze (also spelled *meze* and *mezedes*) are part of the dining tradition in countries from North Africa, Greece and Turkey to the Middle East. Mezze may be accompanied by the flatbread typical of the country (see Naan, page 966) and are often served to seated guests as appetizers before their main meal.

Spaniards observe a similar custom when they prepare and consume **tapas**. These are small portions of hot or cold savory foods such as sliced chorizo, shrimp in garlic sauce or deep-fried olives, which are served in bars at any time. These little bites serve two purposes: They stimulate the appetite and keep patrons drinking. Often tapas are eaten by patrons standing in a lively and crowded bar. Modern tapas bars may feature small plates of sophisticated foods garnished with truffles or a foam whereas a classic tapa might be a humble dish of *pan con tomate* (toasted bread smeared with ripe tomato) or a cube of egg and potato omelet. (See Tortilla Española, page 581.)

Zakuski is the Russian word meaning "small morsels" and the name given to snacks and small dishes offered before a meal. Caviar, smoked fish, bracing vinegar-pickled vegetables, radishes in sour cream, pork in aspic, pirogi dumplings and mayonnaise-bound salads are typical zakuski offerings. Chilled vodka, said to cleanse the palate, is the preferred accompaniment.

As North American chefs explore global cuisines, they are discovering more hors d'oeuvre recipes and inspiration for new ways to serve hors d'oeuvre.

SERVING HORS D'OEUVRE

Hors d'oeuvre are not served only as a precursor to a seated dinner. At many events, the only foods served may be hors d'oeuvre. They may be passed to the guest or served from an hors d'oeuvre buffet or a combination of the two. Whether the hors d'oeuvre are served before dinner or as dinner, passed to the guests or buffet style, they must always be attractively prepared and displayed.

Trio of salads served as mezze

All events have themes and varying degrees of formality. Long buffets with overflowing baskets of crudités and sweet potato chips with dips presented in hollowed squashes and cabbages may be appropriate for one event, whereas elegant silver trays of carefully prepared canapés served to guests by white-gloved, tuxedoed staff (also referred to as *butler service*) may be appropriate for another. When preparing and serving hors d'oeuvre, always keep the event's theme in mind and plan accordingly.

When choosing hors d'oeuvre, select an assortment with contrasting flavors, textures and styles. There are no limits to the variety of hors d'oeuvre that can be served, but three to four cold and three to four hot selections are sufficient for most occasions. The following is a sample selection of hot and cold hors d'oeuvre that offers the recommended contrasts.

Cold

- Canapés of smoked salmon or trout on brioche
- Barquettes filled with Gorgonzola cheese and garnished with grapes and toasted almonds
- Tiny tortilla cups filled with grilled ginger chicken and spicy mango salsa
- Serving spoons filled with ratatouille and black olives

Hot

- Deep-fried vegetables or turnovers with an appropriate sauce
- Stuffed mushroom caps
- Shrimp grilled with fresh rosemary
- Small cheese tarts

Seared scallops in hors d'oeuvre spoons

Butler Service

Butler service, "butlered," or "passed" hors d'oeuvre, are presented to guests on trays by the service staff. The hors d'oeuvre can be hot or cold and should be very small to make it easier for the guests to eat them without the aid of a knife or fork. (Custom utensils such as hors d'oeuvre forks and spoons allow guests to sample one-bite appetizers while standing up.) Soups can be portioned into small cups or glasses so no spoon is needed when passed as hors d'oeuvre.

Hot and cold hors d'oeuvre should be passed separately so that they can be kept at the correct temperatures. For hot hors d'oeuvre, serving plates and trays should be heated to keep the food warm during service. Plates and trays on which hot or cold hors d'oeuvre are served must be kept meticulously clean and decorated with attractive and appropriate garnishes. For a one-hour cocktail reception before a dinner, three to five hors d'oeuvre per person is usually sufficient. If hors d'oeuvre are the only food being served, however, four to five pieces per person per hour may be more appropriate.

Small portions of soup served as passed hors d'oeuvre

Buffet Service

An hors d'oeuvre buffet should be beautiful and appetizing. It may consist of a single table to serve a small group of people or several huge multilevel displays designed to feed thousands. Take colors, flavors and textures into account when planning the menu.

Both hot and cold hors d'oeuvre may be served on buffets. Hot hors d'oeuvre are often kept hot by holding them in chafing dishes. Alternatively hot hors d'oeuvre can be displayed on trays or platters; the trays and platters, however, must be replaced frequently to ensure that the food stays hot. Cold hors d'oeuvre can be displayed on trays, mirrors, platters, baskets, leaves, papers or other serving pieces. Individual portions of shrimp cocktail or other appetizers, such as beef tenderloin and puréed potatoes, can work well on buffets, especially when seating is available for guests.

Individual servings of beef tenderloin and puréed potatoes for an hors d'oeuvre buffet

Cold canapé presentation

Buffet Platters

When displaying hors d'oeuvre and other foods on trays or platters, the foods should be displayed in a pattern that is pleasing to the eye and flows toward the guest or from one side to the other. An easy and attractive method for accomplishing this is to arrange the items on a tray with or without an attractive centerpiece. The food can be placed in parallel diagonal lines, alternating the various styles and shapes as shown in the accompanying photograph. Be careful not to make the tray too fussy or cluttered, however; often the best approach is to keep it simple. A variety of levels and heights also adds to the visual excitement when displaying hors d'oeuvre platters.

QUESTIONS FOR DISCUSSION

1 Discuss four guidelines for preparing hors d'oeuvre.

2 Identify and describe the three parts of a canapé.

3 Compare and contrast authentic beluga, osetra and sevruga caviars, and explain how these differ from varieties produced in the United States.

4 Select several recipes for sauces and fillings from other chapters in this book that would be suitable to use in the preparation of hors d'oeuvre. Describe the techniques and other ingredients you would use to adapt these recipes.

5 Create an hors d'oeuvre menu for a small cocktail party. Include three hot and three cold items and explain your choices.

6 Use the Internet to research what is being done to protect future sturgeon fish supplies from the Caspian Sea. Discuss how these initiatives will ensure the world wide supply of caviar.

7 Research the mezze tradition of the Middle East or North Africa. Create a menu of mezze dishes suitable for a large buffet. List five dishes and describe the way they would be served.

Additional Hors d'Oeuvre Recipes

Buckwheat Blini

🌿 Vegetarian

Blini may be used as a canapé base and are frequently topped with crème fraîche and garnished with caviar.

24 fl. oz. (720 ml) Batter, 24 Blini, 1 oz. (30 g) each

Granulated sugar	2 tsp.	10 ml
Active dry yeast	¼ oz.	7 g
Milk, lukewarm	14 fl. oz.	420 ml
Buckwheat flour	4 oz.	120 g
All-purpose flour	3 oz.	90 g
Salt	½ tsp.	2 ml
Unsalted butter, melted	1½ fl. oz.	45 ml
Vegetable oil	1 fl. oz.	30 ml
Egg yolks	3	3
Egg whites	2	2

1 Stir the sugar and yeast into the milk and let stand until foamy, approximately 5 minutes.

2 Whisk in the flours, salt, butter, oil and egg yolks. Beat until smooth.

3 Cover the batter and allow it to rise in a warm place until doubled, approximately 1 hour.

4 Beat the egg whites to stiff peaks, then fold them into the risen batter.

5 Lightly oil and preheat a large sauté pan. Drop 2 tablespoons (30 milliliters) of batter into the sauté pan, spacing the blini at least 1 inch (2.5 centimeters) apart. Cook until the bottom of each blini is golden, approximately 1 minute. Turn the blini and cook an additional 30 seconds. Remove from the pan and keep warm for service.

Approximate values per 1-oz. (30-g) blini: **Calories** 70, **Total fat** 4 g, **Saturated fat** 1.5 g, **Cholesterol** 35 mg, **Sodium** 60 mg, **Total carbohydrates** 7 g, **Protein** 2 g

Baked Wonton Crisps

🅥 Vegan

YIELD 64 Crisps

Wonton skins, 7-in. (17-cm) squares	16	16
Vegetable oil	6 fl. oz.	180 ml
Black sesame seeds	2 oz.	60 g
Salt and black pepper	TT	TT
Cayenne pepper	TT	TT

1 Cut the wonton skins on the diagonal to make four triangles from each sheet.

2 Brush a sheet pan with 3 fluid ounces (90 milliliters) of the oil. Position the triangles on the oiled sheet pan. Brush the wontons with the remaining oil.

3 Sprinkle the triangles evenly with the sesame seeds, salt, black pepper and cayenne pepper. Bake at 400°F (200°C) until evenly golden and crisp, approximately 8–10 minutes. Serve with spreads and dips such as Hummus (page 875), Tapenade (page 888) or Baba Ghanoush (page 887) or topped with bound salads as a canapé. Store in an airtight container for up to 1 week.

Approximate values per crisp: **Calories** 40, **Total fat** 4 g, **Saturated fat** 0 g, **Cholesterol** 0 mg, **Sodium** 60 mg, **Total carbohydrates** 7 g, **Protein** 0 g

Tortilla Cups with Grilled Chicken Pico de Gallo

YIELD 36 Pieces

Corn tortillas, 14 in. (35 cm)	9	9
Chicken breast, boneless, skinless	10 oz.	300 g
Salt and pepper	TT	TT
Garlic, chopped	1 tsp.	5 ml
Ground cumin	1 tsp.	5 ml
Ground New Mexican chile	1 tsp.	5 ml
Pico de Gallo (page 237)	1 pt.	480 ml
Fresh cilantro	as needed	as needed

1 Cut the tortillas into 2½-inch (6.2-centimeter) circles.

2 Press the tortilla cut-outs into small muffin cups. Fill the tortilla cut-outs with dried beans or baking weights. Bake at 350°F (180°C) for 10–15 minutes or until the tortilla cut-outs are crisp. Cool, then remove the tortilla cups from the muffin cups. Remove the dried beans.

3 Season the chicken breast with salt and pepper and the garlic, cumin and chile.

4 Grill the chicken until done. Cool and refrigerate until cold. Cut the chicken into a small dice.

5 Stir the diced chicken together with the Pico de Gallo and adjust the seasoning with salt and pepper.

6 Fill each baked tortilla cup with approximately 1 tablespoon (15 milliliters) of the chicken mixture. Garnish each cup with a small cilantro leaf and serve.

Approximate values per piece: **Calories** 35, **Total fat** 0 g, **Saturated fat** 0.5 g, **Cholesterol** 5 mg, **Sodium** 25 mg, **Total carbohydrates** 6 g, **Protein** 2 g, **Claims**—low fat; very low sodium; low calorie

❶ Filling the tortilla cut-outs with beans before baking.

❷ Serving the finished tortilla cups filled with cooked chicken and Pico de Gallo.

Pimento Cheese

YIELD   1 qt. (960 ml)

Mild cheddar cheese, finely grated	1 lb.	480 g
Cream cheese, softened	3 oz.	90 g
Canned pimento chiles, diced	5 oz.	150 g
Mayonnaise, commercially prepared	6 oz.	180 g
Hot paprika	1½ tsp.	7 ml
Dijon mustard, optional	1 tsp.	5 ml
Louisiana-style hot sauce	½ tsp.	2 ml

1 Combine ingredients in a large bowl and blend with a spatula until uniformly combined and spreadable.

2 Refrigerate for at least two hours before serving. Pimento cheese keeps for 1 week when covered under refrigeration.

Variation:

Pimento Cheese and Olive Crostini—Spread 1 tablespoon (30 milliliters) of the pimento cheese on each toasted crouton. Garnish with slices of pimento-stuffed green olives and julienned green onions or chives.

Approximate values per 1-oz. (30-g) serving: **Calories** 120, **Total fat** 10 g, **Saturated fat** 4 g, **Cholesterol** 20 mg, **Sodium** 140 mg, **Total carbohydrates** 4 g, **Protein** 4 g, **Vitamin A** 30%, **Claims**—excellent source of vitamin A

Pimento Cheese and Olive Crostini

Baba Ghanoush

 Vegan

YIELD   1 qt. (960 ml)

Eggplants	3 lb.	1.4 kg
Virgin olive oil	4 fl. oz.	120 ml
Salt, black pepper and cayenne pepper	TT	TT
Fresh lemon juice	4 fl. oz.	120 ml
Garlic cloves	1 Tbsp.	15 ml
Tahini	6 oz.	180 g

1 Cut the eggplants in half and score the cut surface of each half from edge to edge in a crosshatch pattern approximately ½ inch (1.2 centimeters) deep.

2 Brush the cut surfaces with 2 fluid ounces (60 milliliters) of the oil, season with salt and black pepper and cayenne pepper and place cut side down on a sheet pan. Roast in a 350°F (180°C) oven until very soft, approximately 45 minutes.

3 Cool the roasted eggplants and scoop out the flesh. Purée the flesh in a food processor with the lemon juice, garlic, tahini, salt and pepper. Add the remaining oil and blend in. Adjust the seasonings. Serve in a bowl, drizzled with additional oil, if desired, and accompanied by pita bread or crudités.

Approximate values per 1-fl.-oz. (30-ml) serving: **Calories** 60, **Total fat** 5 g, **Saturated fat** 0.5 g, **Cholesterol** 0 mg, **Sodium** 0 mg, **Total carbohydrates** 3 g, **Protein** 1 g

Tapenade

YIELD 1 qt. (960 ml)

Ingredient	US	Metric
Garlic cloves	2 Tbsp.	30 ml
Kalamata olives, pitted	1 lb. 4 oz.	600 g
Anchovies	2 oz.	60 g
Capers	4 Tbsp.	60 ml
Fresh thyme	1 Tbsp.	15 ml
Fresh rosemary	1 Tbsp.	15 ml
Fresh oregano	1 Tbsp.	15 ml
Fresh lemon juice	4 fl. oz.	120 ml
Extra virgin olive oil	6 fl. oz.	180 ml

1 Place the garlic, olives, anchovies and capers in the bowl of a food processor and pulse or process until the mixture forms a coarse paste.

2 Scrape down the sides of the bowl. Add the remaining ingredients and process until the mixture is smooth. Refrigerate.

Approximate values per tablespoon (15 ml): **Calories** 35, **Total fat** 3.5 g, **Saturated fat** 0 g, **Cholesterol** 0 mg, **Sodium** 160 mg, **Total carbohydrates** 1 g, **Protein** 0 g

 Good Choice   Vegan

Guacamole

YIELD Approximately 1 qt. (960 ml)

Ingredient	US	Metric
Haas avocados, ripe	6	6
Lemon juice	2½ fl. oz.	75 ml
Green onions, sliced	4 Tbsp.	60 ml
Fresh cilantro, chopped	3 Tbsp.	45 ml
Tomato, seeded, diced	3 Tbsp.	45 ml
Garlic, chopped	1 tsp.	5 ml
Dried oregano	½ tsp.	2 ml
Jalapeño, seeded, chopped	1	1
Salt	TT	TT
Cilantro	as needed for garnish	
Tomato concassée	as needed for garnish	

1 Cut each avocado in half. Remove the seed and scoop out the pulp.

2 Add the lemon juice to the avocado pulp and mix well, mashing the avocado pulp.

3 Add the remaining ingredients except the tomato concassée. Season with salt and mix well. Garnish with cilantro and tomato concassée and serve with assorted corn chips.

Approximate values per 2-fl.-oz. (60-ml) serving: **Calories** 120, **Total fat** 12 g, **Saturated fat** 0 g, **Cholesterol** 0 mg, **Sodium** 25 mg, **Total carbohydrates** 1 g, **Protein** 2 g, **Vitamin C** 15%, **Claims**—no saturated fat; no cholesterol; no sugar; high fiber

Spinach and Artichoke Dip

YIELD 4 lb. 6 oz. (2.1 kg)

Onion, medium dice	3 oz.	90 g
Garlic, chopped	2 tsp.	10 ml
Clarified butter	1 fl. oz.	30 ml
Frozen chopped spinach, thawed, drained	1 lb. 8 oz.	720 g
Artichoke hearts, canned, chopped coarse	1 lb.	480 g
Cream sauce (page 222)	1 qt.	960 ml
Worcestershire sauce	2 tsp.	10 ml
Parmesan, grated	6 oz.	180 g
Salt and pepper	TT	TT
Tabasco sauce	TT	TT

1 Sauté the onion and garlic in the butter until tender without coloring.

2 Add the spinach and sauté until hot.

3 Add the artichoke hearts, cream sauce, Worcestershire sauce and 4 ounces (120 grams) Parmesan. Mix well.

4 Season with salt, pepper and Tabasco sauce.

5 Transfer the dip to a half-size hotel pan. Top with the remaining Parmesan and bake at 350°F (180°C) until hot and browned on top, approximately 20 minutes.

Approximate values per 2-oz. (60-g) serving: **Calories** 110, **Total fat** 6 g, **Saturated fat** 3.5 g, **Cholesterol** 15 mg, **Sodium** 250 mg, **Total carbohydrates** 8 g, **Protein** 5 g, **Vitamin A** 20%

1 Sautéing the onion, garlic and spinach.

2 Serving the hot dip in a chafing dish.

Brandade de Morue
(French Salt Cod Spread)

YIELD 3 lb. (1.4 kg); 12 Servings,
4 oz. (120 g) each

Dried salt cod	1 lb.	480 g
Bay leaf	1	1
Fresh thyme sprig	1	1
Garlic cloves	3	3
Russet potatoes	1 lb.	480 g
Pepper	TT	TT
Olive oil	2 fl. oz.	60 ml
Milk	4 fl. oz.	120 ml
Black olives, oil-cured	3 oz.	90 g
Sautéed Garlic Croutons	as needed	as needed
(recipe follows)		

1 Rinse the dried salt cod under cold running water to remove the surface salt. Place the cod in a bowl of cold water and soak under refrigeration for 24 hours, changing the water at least once.

2 Drain the soaked cod. Place in a saucepan and cover with cold water. Bring to a boil, drain and cover with cold water again. Add the bay leaf and thyme and bring to a simmer. Simmer the cod for 10 minutes or until it flakes easily. Drain the cod. Flake the cod into the bowl of a food processor, removing any bones or dark flesh. Add the garlic and process until the cod is a shaggy paste.

3 While the cod is cooking, simmer the potatoes until done. Peel them while still warm and pass them through a food mill or ricer.

4 In a mixing bowl, combine the cod and potatoes. Season with pepper and stir in the oil and milk. The brandade mixture should resemble soft mashed potatoes. The mixture may be used immediately or refrigerated and held for up to 1 week.

5 To serve, spread the brandade mixture into a shallow casserole. Lightly score the surface in a cross-hatch pattern. Bake uncovered at 375°F (190°C) for 15–20 minutes or until lightly browned on top and hot. Serve garnished with black olives and Sautéed Garlic Croutons.

Approximate values per 4-oz. (120-g) serving: **Calories** 220, **Total fat** 9 g, **Saturated fat** 1 g, **Cholesterol** 60 mg, **Sodium** 380 mg, **Total carbohydrates** 9 g, **Protein** 25 g

 Vegan

Sautéed Garlic Croutons

YIELD 16 Croutons

Olive oil	1 fl. oz.	30 ml
Garlic cloves	2	2
Country bread slices, crusts removed,	4	4
cut into 4 triangles		

1 Heat a sauté pan and add the oil. Flatten the garlic cloves with the back of a knife and add to the oil. Cook the garlic until brown. Remove the garlic and discard.

2 Add the bread triangles to the pan and quickly toss to coat evenly with the oil.

3 Cook the croutons, browning evenly on both sides, adding a little more oil if necessary.

Approximate values per crouton: **Calories** 30, **Total fat** 2 g, **Saturated fat** 0 g, **Cholesterol** 0 mg, **Sodium** 30 mg, **Total carbohydrates** 3 g, **Protein** 0 g

Date and Chorizo Rumaki

32 Pieces

Bacon, sliced thin	16 slices	16 slices
Chorizo (page 867)	8 oz.	240 g
Cream cheese	4 oz.	120 g
Whole dates, pitted	32	32

1 Partially cook the bacon on a sheet pan in a 350°F (180°C) oven for approximately 5 minutes.

2 Sauté the chorizo over medium heat to render the excess fat. If the chorizo is in links, remove the meat from the casings before cooking.

3 Remove the cooked chorizo from the pan and drain in a mesh strainer or china cap to remove excess fat. Then blend the cream cheese into the meat. Cool completely.

4 Cut the dates open, butterfly style. Stuff each date with a portion of the chorizo cream cheese mixture.

5 Wrap each date with a half slice of bacon, securing with a toothpick.

6 Arrange the prepared dates on a rack placed over a sheet pan. Bake at 350°F (180°C) until the bacon is crisp and the rumaki are hot, approximately 15–20 minutes.

Approximate values per piece: **Calories** 90, **Total fat** 5 g, **Saturated fat** 2.5 g, **Cholesterol** 15 mg, **Sodium** 150 mg, **Total carbohydrates** 7 g, **Protein** 3 g

Stuffed Figs with Taleggio and Orange Basil Glaze

12 Pieces

Glaze:		
Oranges	2	2
Honey	1 fl. oz.	30 ml
White balsamic vinegar	1 fl. oz.	30 ml
Basil leaves, fresh	3	3
Salt and black pepper	TT	TT
Prosciutto, thin slices	3	3
Taleggio cheese	2 oz.	60 g
Mission figs, washed, trimmed and quartered	3	3
Pistachios, toasted, finely chopped	½ oz.	15 g

1 To make the orange basil glaze, zest and juice the oranges. Combine the zest, juice, honey, white balsamic vinegar and basil leaves in a small nonreactive sauce pan. Season with a pinch of salt and black pepper. Reduce the mixture over medium heat until it forms a thin glaze and a yield of approximately 2 fluid ounces (30 milliliters). Remove from the heat, strain and reserve at room temperature.

2 Cut each slice of prosciutto in half lengthwise and in half again crosswise to make 12 pieces approximately 3 inches (8 centimeters) in length.

3 Cut the cheese into 12 equal rectangles approximately 1 inch (2.5 centimeters) long.

4 Position a wedge of fig on each piece of prosciutto, cut side up and place a piece of cheese on top of the fig. Roll to make a neat packet.

5 Arrange the wrapped figs on a plate or serving platter. Drizzle with orange basil glaze and sprinkle with chopped pistachios. Serve immediately.

Approximate values per piece: **Calories** 60, **Total fat** 2.5 g, **Saturated fat** 1 g, **Cholesterol** 10 mg, **Sodium** 135 mg, **Total carbohydrates** 8 g, **Protein** 3 g, **Vitamin C** 15%

Stuffed Mushroom Caps

YIELD 48 Pieces

White mushrooms, medium	60	60
Clarified butter	2 fl. oz.	60 ml
Onion, minced	4 oz.	120 g
All-purpose flour	1 Tbsp.	15 ml
Heavy cream	4 fl. oz.	120 ml
Ham, cooked, chopped	4 oz.	120 g
Fresh parsley, chopped	2 Tbsp.	30 ml
Salt and pepper	TT	TT
Swiss cheese, shredded	2 oz.	60 g

1 Wash the mushrooms. Separate stems from the caps and chop the stems and 12 of the caps.

2 Sauté the whole mushroom caps in 1 ounce (30 grams) clarified butter until partially cooked but still firm. Remove from the pan and reserve.

3 Add the remaining butter to the pan. Sauté the onion and chopped mushroom stems and caps until dry.

4 Add the flour and cook for 1 minute. Add the cream; bring to a simmer and cook for 2 minutes.

5 Add the ham and parsley and season to taste with salt and pepper; stir to combine. Remove from the pan and cool slightly.

6 Stuff the mushroom caps with the ham mixture and sprinkle with shredded Swiss cheese.

7 Bake the stuffed mushrooms at 350°F (180°C) until hot, approximately 10–15 minutes.

Approximate values per piece: **Calories** 30, **Total fat** 2.5 g, **Saturated fat** 1.5 g, **Cholesterol** 10 mg, **Sodium** 35 mg, **Total carbohydrates** 1 g, **Protein** 1 g, **Claims**—low fat; low cholesterol; low sodium; low calorie; no sugar

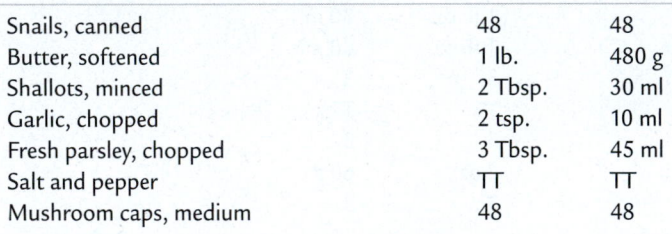

Escargots in Garlic Butter

YIELD 48 Pieces

Snails, canned	48	48
Butter, softened	1 lb.	480 g
Shallots, minced	2 Tbsp.	30 ml
Garlic, chopped	2 tsp.	10 ml
Fresh parsley, chopped	3 Tbsp.	45 ml
Salt and pepper	TT	TT
Mushroom caps, medium	48	48

1 Drain and rinse the snails.

2 Combine the butter, shallots, garlic, parsley, salt and pepper in a mixer or food processor and mix or process until well blended.

3 Sauté the mushroom caps in a small amount of the garlic butter until cooked but still firm. Remove from the heat.

4 Place a snail in each mushroom cap and top with a generous amount of the garlic butter. Alternatively place the snails in clean shells and top each one with the garlic butter.

5 Bake the mushrooms and snails at 450°F (230°C) for 5–7 minutes and serve hot.

Variation:

Prepare 48 small bouchées from puff pastry. Sauté the snails in a generous amount of the garlic butter and place one snail in each bouchée. Drizzle the snails with the garlic butter and serve.

Approximate values per piece: **Calories** 63, **Total fat** 6 g, **Saturated fat** 4 g, **Cholesterol** 19 mg, **Sodium** 64 mg, **Total carbohydrates** 0.5 g, **Protein** 1 g, **Vitamin A** 6%

escargot [ays-skahr-GO] French for "snail"; those used for culinary purposes are land snails (genus *Helix*); the most popular are the large Burgundy snails and the smaller but more flavorful common or garden snail known as *petit gris*

Rosemary and Garlic Grilled Shrimp

YIELD 32 Shrimp

Shrimp, 16–20 count, peeled and deveined	32	32
Salt and black pepper	TT	TT
Red pepper flakes	¼ tsp.	1 ml
Fresh rosemary sprigs, 6 in. (15 cm) each	2 sprigs	2 sprigs
Garlic, chopped	1 tsp.	5 ml
Olive oil	as needed	as needed

1 Season the shrimp with salt and pepper as desired. Sprinkle the shrimp with the red pepper flakes.

2 Strip the rosemary leaves from the stems and chop the leaves.

3 Toss the shrimp with the rosemary, chopped garlic and a small amount of oil until lightly and evenly coated. Marinate the shrimp for 10–15 minutes.

4 Arrange the shrimp on a preheated grill. Cook until the shrimp are cooked one-third of the way through and have attractive grill marks, approximately 1–2 minutes. Turn them and repeat. Remove the shrimp from the grill when they are still slightly underdone in the middle; allow carryover cooking to finish cooking them.

Approximate values per 1-shrimp serving: **Calories** 50, **Total fat** 2 g, **Saturated fat** 0 g, **Cholesterol** 80 mg, **Sodium** 55 mg, **Total carbohydrates** 0 g, **Protein** 8 g

🌿 Vegetarian

Chèvre Tarts

YIELD 12 Tarts

Tomato concassée	4 oz.	120 g
Black pepper	TT	TT
Parmesan, grated	3 oz.	90 g
Puff pastry	8 oz.	240 g
Olive oil	as needed	as needed
Basil Pesto Sauce (page 249)	2 fl. oz.	60 ml
Goat cheese (chèvre), Montrachet style	4 oz.	120 g
Zucchini, shredded	4 oz.	120 g

1 Season the tomato concassée with the pepper and sprinkle with 2 tablespoons (30 milliliters) Parmesan.

2 Roll out the puff pastry until it is approximately ¼ inch (6 millimeters) thick. Cut puff pastry into 12 circles, approximately 2½ inches (6.2 centimeters) in diameter.

3 Brush mini-muffin tins with oil and line each with a puff pastry circle.

4 Add 1 teaspoon (5 milliliters) Basil Pesto Sauce to each tart.

5 Add ⅓ ounce (10 grams) goat cheese to each tart.

6 Add enough shredded zucchini to each tart to nearly fill it.

7 Top each tart with the tomato concassée and sprinkle with the remaining Parmesan.

8 Bake at 375°F (190°C) until the tarts are brown on top and the dough is cooked, approximately 15–20 minutes.

Approximate values per tart: **Calories** 210, **Total fat** 15 g, **Saturated fat** 4.5 g, **Cholesterol** 15 mg, **Sodium** 270 mg, **Total carbohydrates** 11 g, **Protein** 7 g, **Vitamin A** 20%

Flavor Profiles

The flavor profile of many hors d'oeuvre can be adjusted to accommodate various themes or international cuisines by adjusting a few seasonings or ingredients. For example, if you use hot salsa in place of the Basil Pesto Sauce and queso fresco in place of the French-style goat cheese, your Chèvre Tarts become suitable for a Mexican- or Southwestern-themed event. Adding minced Iberico ham and replacing the goat cheese with manchego produces a Spanish-flavored option. Other recipes from this text can be adapted in a similar fashion. Try using an unflavored risotto stuffed with chopped kimchee in the Arancini (Deep-Fried Rice Balls) for a Korean-inspired appetizer. Stuffed mushrooms can be filled with many different ingredients and seasonings. If a recipe works successfully, do not be afraid to experiment with flavors and seasonings as long as the foundation ingredients and fundamental techniques remain unchanged.

❶ Lining mini-muffin tins with puff pastry circles.

❷ Filling the tarts.

Arancini (Deep-Fried Rice Balls)

YIELD 52 Rice Balls

Risotto Milanese (page 673)	3 lb.	1440 g
Fontina cheese	6 oz.	180 g
All-purpose flour	6 oz.	180 g
Salt and pepper	TT	TT
Egg wash	10 oz.	300 g
Dried bread crumbs	10 oz.	300 g

1 Spread the cooked risotto out in a half-sheet pan. Chill until firm.

2 Cube the Fontina cheese into 52 pieces. Using a #30 portion scoop, gather up a portion of the risotto. Press a cube of cheese into the center, then form the risotto into a ball around the cheese.

3 Season the flour with salt and pepper. Bread the risotto balls using the standard breading procedure described in Chapter 9, Mise en Place (finishing with the bread crumbs), and arrange them in a single layer on a sheet pan. Chill.

4 Deep-fry the risotto balls in 335°F (168°C) oil until golden and heated through, approximately 7–9 minutes.

Approximate values per rice ball: **Calories** 370, **Total fat** 15 g, **Saturated fat** 9 g, **Cholesterol** 40 mg, **Sodium** 270 mg, **Total carbohydrates** 49 g, **Protein** 8 g

Tuna Tartar

♥ Good Choice

YIELD 24 Servings, ½ oz. (15 g) each

Sushi-quality ahi tuna fillet	8 oz.	240 g
Egg, hard cooked	1	1
Chives	6	6
Extra virgin olive oil	2 fl. oz.	60 ml
Cornichons, minced	1½ oz.	45 g
Red onion, minced	1 oz.	30 g
Black salt	¼ tsp.	1 ml
Black pepper	¼ tsp.	1 ml

1 Trim the tuna fillets of any skin, bone, imperfections or blemishes. Cut the tuna into fine ⅛-inch- (3-millimeter-) dice. Hold over ice while preparing the remaining ingredients.

2 Separate the egg yolk from the white. Press the yolk through a fine mesh sieve. Finely chop the egg white.

3 Cut the chives into thin slices.

4 Portion the tuna into 24 chilled hors d'oeuvre spoons or other bite-sized containers.

5 Drizzle a small amount of extra virgin olive oil over each portion of tuna.

6 Sprinkle the tuna with the cornichons, red onion, egg whites, egg yolks, chives, salt and pepper. Serve immediately.

Approximate values per ½-oz. (15-g) serving: **Calories** 50, **Total fat** 3.55 g, **Saturated fat** 0.5 g, **Cholesterol** 20 mg, **Sodium** 60 mg, **Total carbohydrates** 0 g, **Protein** 4 g, **Claims**—low calorie; low fat

Samosas (Deep-Fried Indian Turnovers)

YIELD 30 Samosas

Pastry:

All-purpose flour	9 oz.	270 g
Salt	1 tsp.	5 ml
Garam masala	1 tsp.	5 ml
Peppercorns, cracked	1 tsp.	5 ml
Turmeric	1 tsp.	5 ml
Vegetable oil	1½ Tbsp.	23 ml
Water, warm	7 fl. oz.	210 ml

Filling:

Potatoes, peeled, small dice	4 oz.	120 g
Fresh ginger	1 oz.	30 g
Clarified butter or ghee	1 Tbsp.	15 ml
Ground lamb, lean	12 oz.	360 g
Garlic, minced	1 tsp.	5 ml
Onion, small dice	2 oz.	60 g
Garam masala	2 tsp.	10 ml
Chilli powder	1 tsp.	5 ml
Turmeric	1 tsp.	5 ml
Salt	1 tsp.	5 ml
Green peas	3 oz.	90 g
Fresh lemon juice	1 Tbsp.	15 ml
Fresh cilantro, chopped	2 Tbsp.	30 ml

1 In the bowl of an electric mixer fitted with a dough hook, combine the flour, salt, garam masala, peppercorns and turmeric and mix thoroughly. With the mixer at medium speed, add the oil, then add enough of the warm water to make a stiff dough. Knead the dough in the mixer until it is completely smooth and pliable. Cover the dough with a damp cloth and allow it to rest for 20 minutes.

2 Blanch the potatoes in salted water until nearly tender. Remove, refresh and reserve the potatoes.

3 Grate the fresh ginger into a cheesecloth-lined strainer set over a small bowl. Gather the edges of the cheesecloth and squeeze the ginger juice into the bowl.

4 Heat the clarified butter in a sauté pan and sauté the lamb until it begins to brown. Add the ginger juice, garlic and onion and sauté for approximately 5 minutes. Add the spices, salt, potatoes and peas and gently cook until the potatoes and peas are tender, approximately 5 minutes. Stir in the lemon juice and cook until the liquid evaporates. Stir in the cilantro. Transfer the filling to a sheet pan to cool completely.

5 Roll the dough into a rope and cut into 15 evenly sized pieces. Roll each piece out to a round approximately 5 inches (12 centimeters) in diameter, then cut each round in half. Place a spoonful of the filling toward one half of each piece of pastry. Run a wet finger around the edge and fold over to make a triangular pastry with one curved side. Pinch the edges together, then press the edges with the tines of a fork to seal them.

6 Using the basket method, deep-fry the turnovers at 350°F (180°C) until done, approximately 3 minutes. Drain and serve hot with chutney.

Variation:

Vegetarian Samosas—Omit the lamb. Add 2 ounces (60 grams) chopped unsalted peanuts and 6 ounces (180 grams) chopped mushrooms in Step 3. Increase the amount of onion to 4 ounces (120 grams).

Approximate values per samosa: **Calories** 60, **Total fat** 2 g, **Saturated fat** 0.5 g, **Cholesterol** 10 mg, **Sodium** 160 mg, **Total carbohydrates** 8 g, **Protein** 3 g

Cha Gio (Deep-Fried Vietnamese Spring Rolls)

YIELD 1 lb. (480 g) Filling; approximately 32 Rolls

Cellophane noodles	2 oz.	60 g
Vegetable oil	1 fl. oz.	30 ml
Garlic cloves, minced	1 Tbsp.	15 ml
Shrimp, raw, peeled, deveined and chopped	4 oz.	120 g
Pork, minced	4 oz.	120 g
Carrot, grated	1	1
Green onions, sliced	3	3
Mung bean sprouts	1 oz.	30 g
Fish sauce	2 tsp.	10 ml
Vietnamese chile sauce	1 Tbsp.	15 ml
Cornstarch	2 tsp.	10 ml
Water, cold	2 tsp.	10 ml
Spring roll wrappers	32	32

1 Soak the cellophane noodles in boiling water for 5 minutes. Drain and cut into 1- to 2-inch (2.5- to 5-centimeter) pieces.

2 Heat a wok or sauté pan and add the oil. Stir-fry the garlic for a few seconds. Add the shrimp and pork and stir-fry, breaking up any large lumps. Add the carrot, green onions, bean sprouts, fish sauce, chile sauce and drained noodles. Cook until the carrots are slightly softened. Remove from the heat and cool completely.

3 Mix the cornstarch and water together in a small bowl. Moisten the spring roll wrappers with water and cover with a clean damp towel to prevent them from drying out.

4 Place approximately 1 tablespoon (30 milliliters) filling in the center of a spring roll wrapper. Fold the sides toward the middle and roll up into a cigar shape. Paint the edge of the wrapper with the water-and-cornstarch mixture to seal. Roll the wrapper into a tight cylinder.

5 Using the swimming method, deep-fry the spring rolls at 325°F (160°C) until hot and crisp, approximately 45 seconds. Drain on absorbent paper and serve with Nuoc Cham (page 253).

Approximate values per roll: **Calories** 60, **Total fat** 2 g, **Saturated fat** 0 g, **Cholesterol** 10 mg, **Sodium** 70 mg, **Total carbohydrates** 7 g, **Protein** 2 g, **Vitamin A** 15%

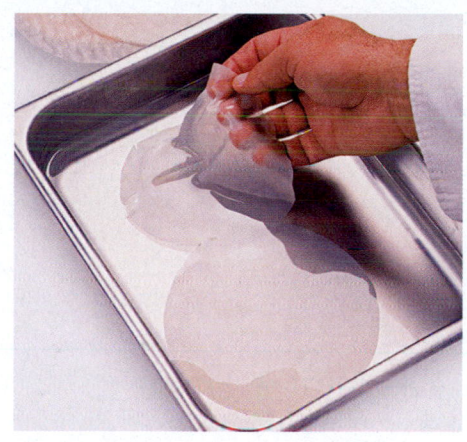

❶ Moistening the spring roll wrappers.

❷ Placing the filling in the spring roll wrappers.

❸ Folding the spring roll wrapper around the filling.

❹ Painting the edge of the wrapper with the water-and-cornstarch mixture, then rolling the spring roll into a tight cylinder.

🌿 Vegetarian

Stuffed Cherry Tomato Bites

YIELD Approximately 60 Pieces

Cherry and miniature heirloom tomatoes	3–3½ lb.	1.4–1.6 kg
Salt and pepper	TT	TT
Tapenade (page 888)	12 fl. oz.	360 ml
Hummus (page 875)	1 lb.	480 g
Tabouli (page 769)	1 lb.	480 g

1 Cut a very small slice from the bottom of each tomato so that it sits flat.

2 Remove any stem then cut off the top of each tomato. Cut any larger tomatoes in half. Scoop out the seeds with a Parisienne scoop. Place the tomatoes, cut side down on paper-towel-lined sheet pans to drain.

3 Season the tomatoes with salt and pepper. Using a pastry bag and plain tip, fill one-third of the tomatoes with the Tapenade. Fill half of the remaining tomatoes with the Hummus. Using a small spoon, fill the remaining tomatoes with the Tabouli.

Approximate values per piece: **Calories** 60, **Total fat** 4.5 g, **Saturated fat** 0 g, **Cholesterol** 0 mg, **Sodium** 95 mg, **Total carbohydrates** 4 g, **Protein** 0 g

Principles of the Bakeshop 30

▶ identify the specialized tools and equipment used in the bakeshop

▶ identify and select ingredients including flours, sugars, fats and flavorings used in the bakeshop

▶ control the development of gluten

▶ cook sugar correctly

▶ use chemical leavening agents properly

▶ describe and explain the baking process

formula the standard term used throughout the industry for a bakeshop recipe; formulas rely on weighing to ensure accurate measuring of ingredients

pâtisserie [pah-tees-air-EE] (1) bakery or bakeshop where pastry is sold; (2) French pastries, cakes and cookies

Bakeshop Mise en Place

Proper planning helps the baker avoid mishaps. The baker or pastry chef should make special note of these important elements in every formula:

Exact ingredients in precise amounts

Components in a formula that need advance preparation

Temperature of ingredients

Special equipment required

Equipment preparation

Refrigeration time required

Oven temperatures required

Flour, sugar, eggs, milk, butter, flavorings—with this simple list of ingredients a seemingly endless variety of sweet goods, from breads to sauces to pastries, can be made. But to produce consistently good brioche, Bavarians, biscuits or the like, careful attention must be paid to the character and quantity of each ingredient, the way the ingredients are combined and how heat is applied to them. Unlike, for example, a cut of meat that can be grilled, roasted, sautéed or braised and still be the same cut of meat, bakeshop products depend on careful, precise preparation for their very identity.

Accurate measurements are critical in the bakeshop. It is equally important to follow bakeshop **formulas** carefully and completely. Unlike mistakes in other types of cooking, baking mistakes often are not discovered until the product is finished, by which time it is too late to correct them. For example, if salt is left out when preparing a stew, the mistake can be corrected by adding salt at service time. If salt is left out of a batch of bread dough, its texture and flavor may be ruined and the mistake cannot be corrected after the bread has baked. For this reason, it may be more important to follow a written formula, measure ingredients precisely and combine them accurately in the bakeshop than anywhere else in the kitchen.

In order to provide a thorough introduction to the skills needed in a bakeshop, this text focuses on preparing the types of breads and desserts usually found in a small retail shop or restaurant. Because this text is not designed for large wholesale or commercial bakeries, mixes, stabilizers and mechanical preparation and shaping skills are not included.

BAKESHOP TOOLS AND EQUIPMENT

Beginning cooks may find the tools of the bakeshop a bit complex. Indeed, the tools required for a professional **pâtisserie** are quite specialized. A chef who is educated and accomplished need not be concerned with possessing every gadget available, but should recognize and be familiar with most of the items shown in Figure 30.1. Although many of these hand tools make a task easier, most can be improvised by a creative chef. Several of the items shown, such as the springform pans, tartlet pans and petit four molds, are for shaping or holding batters and doughs. The various spatulas are for spreading icings or fillings. The piping tools and cake comb are for decorating and finishing baked goods. When purchasing tools and equipment for the bakeshop, look for quality and durability.

Bakeshop ovens may be conventional, convection or steam injection models. The baking instructions in the following chapters are based on the use of a conventional oven. If a convection oven is used instead, the temperature and baking time may need to be reduced. Convection ovens can reduce cooking time, but the air currents may damage delicate products such as spongecake or puff pastry. Steam injection ovens use conventional heat flow, but allow the baker to automatically add steam to the cooking chamber as needed to produce crisp-crusted breads. Although expensive, steam injection ovens are a necessity for commercial bakeries and most larger restaurant and hotel bakeshops.

Figure 30.1 Bakeshop tools (clockwise from center back): cake turntable, cake pans, flan ring, tartlet pans, cannoli form, cake comb, offset spatulas, flat cake spatula, blade for scoring breads, flower nail, rectangular tartlet pans, piping bag and tips, metal spatula, dough cutter, rolling pin, springform pan, copper sugar pot (on cooling rack), nest of round cutters.

BAKESHOP INGREDIENTS

Although substituting ingredients may have little or no effect on some dishes (carrots can be substituted for turnips in a stew, for instance), this is not the case with baked goods. Different flours, fats, liquids and sweeteners function differently. Bread flour and cake flour are not identical, nor are oil and butter. If one ingredient is substituted for another, the results will be different.

Understanding ingredients, why they function the way they do and how to adjust for their differences makes the baking experience more successful and consistent. This chapter discusses flours, sugar and other sweeteners, fats, thickeners and flavorings such as chocolate, vanilla and nuts. Flavorings such as herbs, spices and liquors are discussed in Chapter 7, Flavors and Flavorings. Dairy products, also common in baked goods, are discussed in Chapter 8, Dairy Products. Eggs, coffee and tea are discussed in Chapter 21, Eggs and Breakfast. Table 30.4 on page 919, describes the functions of these ingredients in bakeshop preparations and is a useful reference.

Flours

Flour *provides bulk and structure* to baked goods. Flours can be *used to thicken liquids* in items such as custards and pie fillings, or to *prevent foods from sticking during preparation and baking.* Flour is produced when grain kernels are milled or ground into a powder. Grains are grasses that bear edible seeds. Corn, rice and wheat are the most

Function of Ingredients

Flours

■ provide bulk and structure
■ thicken liquids in items such as custards and pie fillings
■ prevent foods from sticking

significant grains in the human diet, but the most frequently used—and therefore the most important—ingredient in the bakeshop is wheat flour.

Wheat Flour

Wheat flour (Fr. *farine*) is produced by milling wheat kernels (berries). Recall from Chapter 23, Potatoes, Grains and Pasta, that a wheat kernel has an outer covering called bran. The bran is composed of several layers that protect the endosperm, which contains starches and proteins. The innermost part of the kernel is the germ, which contains fat and serves as the wheat seed. See Figure 23.1. During milling, the kernels first pass through metal rollers to crack them. The bran and germ are then removed through repeated stages of sifting and separation. The remaining endosperm is ground into flour. Flour made from the portion of the endosperm closest to the germ (also known as patent flour) is finer; flour made from the portion of the endosperm nearer the bran (clear flour) is coarser and darker.

Composition of Flour

Flour consists primarily of five nutrients: fat, minerals, moisture, starches and proteins. Fat and minerals each generally account for less than 1 percent of flour's content. The moisture content of flour is also relatively low—when packaged, it cannot exceed 14 percent under U.S. government standards. But actual moisture content varies depending on climatic conditions and storage. In humid climates or in damp areas of the kitchen, flour absorbs moisture from the atmosphere. This additional moisture may affect other ingredients in the formula or the final product made from the flour.

Starches constitute 63–77 percent of flour and are necessary for the absorption of moisture during baking. This process of absorbing moisture, known as gelatinization, occurs primarily at temperatures above 150°F (65°C). Starches also provide food for yeast during fermentation.

Protein constitutes a relatively low percentage (6–15 percent) of the nutrients in wheat flour, but it is an extremely important component. The type of wheat used determines its protein content and therefore the characteristics of the flour. Wheat is classified as soft or hard depending on the kernel's hardness. The harder the wheat kernel, the higher its protein content. Soft wheat yields a soft flour with a low protein content. **Soft flour**, also called **weak flour**, is best for tender products such as cakes. Hard wheat yields a **hard flour** with a high protein content. Hard flour, also known as **strong flour**, is used for bagels, buns, rolls, crusty yeast breads, flatbreads and sandwich breads.

Various types of flour are created by mixing or blending flours from different varieties of wheat. **Cake flour** is a fine, white flour with a low protein content. Ground from deep within the endosperm, cake flour is treated with bleaching agents to produce its pure color. The bleaching also contributes to the properties of cake flour, which absorbs moisture but develops a weak gluten network. High-ratio cakes, which contain a high percentage of liquid and sugar, require cake flour in order to rise properly. **Pastry flour** is a low-protein flour usually milled from soft red winter wheat and not usually bleached. **All-purpose flour**, a blend of hard and soft flours, is designed for use in a wide range of foods. It is often labeled *Hotel and Restaurant* flour. Sold both bleached and unbleached, all-purpose is referred to throughout this text because it is readily available in quantities appropriate for small food service operations. Large bakeshops rarely use all-purpose flour; instead, they choose flours specifically milled and blended for specific characteristics. **Bread flour,** milled from hard red spring or hard red winter wheat, has the higher protein content necessary to produce baked goods with a chewy crumb and crisp crust. **High-gluten flour**, as its name implies, is a blend of the highest-protein-content flour and is used to make bagels and hard rolls.

Flour proteins are extremely important because of their gluten-forming potential. **Gluten** is the tough, rubbery substance created when wheat flour is mixed with water. Gluten strands are both plastic (they change shape under pressure) and elastic (they resume their original shape when that pressure is removed). Gluten is responsible for the volume, texture and appearance of baked goods. It provides structure and enables dough to expand in volume and rise or **leaven**. The gluten structure helps the dough

Cake flour

Squeezing soft, low-protein pastry flour (left) between one's fingers results in clumping. Higher-protein bread flour (right) does not clump when squeezed.

gluten an elastic network of proteins created when wheat flour is moistened and manipulated

leaven an ingredient or process that produces or incorporates gases in a baked product in order to increase volume, provide structure and give texture

retain the gases given off by leavening agents, such as baking powder and baking soda, discussed later in this chapter, and yeast discussed in Chapter 32, Yeast Breads. Without gluten, producing raised breads is challenging. The gases created by yeast fermentation or chemical leaveners simply escape if there is no network of gluten strands to trap them in the dough.

The proteins in flour responsible for gluten formation are *glutenin* and *gliadin*. Flour does not contain gluten; only a dough or batter can contain gluten. Gluten is produced when glutenin and gliadin are moistened and manipulated (e.g., when they are stirred or kneaded). In general, the higher a flour's protein content, the greater that flour's gluten-forming potential. In some instances, however, this is not the case. For example, flour with 13% protein may perform better than one with 14% protein because the proteins in the former flour are of superior quality. In order to make a chewy product, such as a crusty French loaf, flour with a high protein content must be used. Lower-protein flours are used for tender or soft products, such as cakes or muffins.

Table 30.1 lists the protein content and uses for several common flours. Substituting one type of flour for another may be acceptable in some formulas as long as the ratio of fats, moisteners and other ingredients is adjusted accordingly. In most cases, however, substituting one type of flour for another results in a changed and probably less desirable product.

Gluten development is affected by a number of factors, including mixing time and the presence of fat. Generally the longer a substance is mixed, the more gluten develops. Extreme overmixing in industrial equipment can break down the gluten structure, however. The type and balance of ingredients in a formula also affects gluten development. Fats coat the protein in the flour, inhibiting the formation of the gluten network. Flour needs to absorb liquid in order for the proteins to form gluten strands. Firm bread dough that can be kneaded and shaped before baking requires a high-protein flour. When this dough is made with water it bakes into a product with a solid structure. When whole milk is used in the same formula, the product is more tender because the milkfat weakens the gluten bond.

Aging and Bleaching of Flours

Any flour develops better baking qualities if allowed to rest for several weeks after milling. Freshly milled flour produces sticky doughs and products with less volume than those made with aged flour. During aging, flour turns white through a natural oxidation process that is referred to as bleaching.

Natural aging and bleaching are somewhat unpredictable, time-consuming processes, however, so some flour mills use chemicals to control and speed aging and bleaching. Chlorine dioxide and other chemicals remove yellow pigments and produce a uniform white color. Bleaching destroys small amounts of the flour's naturally occurring vitamin E. Potassium bromate helps rapidly age flour. It strengthens the gluten structure in bread dough and helps make bread rise faster–important considerations when making bread in an industrial or commercial setting. Once a popular additive, potassium bromate has

PROTEIN CONTENT OF FLOURS   TABLE 30.1

TYPE OF FLOUR	TYPE OF WHEAT	PERCENT PROTEIN	USES
Cake flour	Soft wheat	6–8	Tender cakes
Pastry flour	Soft wheat	7–9.5	Biscuits, pie crusts
All-purpose flour	Blend of hard and soft wheat	9.5–12	General baking
Bread flour	Hard wheat	12.5–14	Yeast breads
Whole-wheat flour	Hard wheat	13–14	Breads
High-gluten flour	Hard wheat	13.5–14.5	Bagels; used to increase protein content of weaker flour such as rye, whole-grain or specialty flours

been identified as a possible carcinogen. Its use is banned in Canada, the E.U. and China, as well as in some states in America. Flour millers are moving away from using potassium bromate and substituting other additives such as ascorbic acid combined with enzymes. Many bakers use unbleached and unbromated flours exclusively.

Specialty Flours

Whole-wheat flour is made by milling the entire wheat kernel, including the bran and nutritious germ. Whole-wheat flour has a nutty, sweet flavor and brown, flecked color. Products made with whole-wheat flour are denser, with less volume than those made with white flour. Bran particles cut through the gluten strands in whole-wheat dough, giving the bread a denser **crumb**, or internal structure. Whole-wheat flour has a reduced shelf life because fats in the germ can become rancid during storage. The granulation size of whole-wheat flour varies from fine to coarse, depending on the manufacturer. A finer grind absorbs more water; therefore, it is important to adjust formulas according to the type of whole-wheat flour used. A strain of white wheat produces a lighter-colored whole-wheat flour with the nutritional benefits of whole wheat. Whole-wheat pastry and high-gluten flours are available. **Graham flour** is a type of coarse whole-wheat flour used to add texture to crackers and baked goods.

Though not a flour, **wheat germ** is often used in place of some wheat flour for flavor and fiber. Wheat germ can be used in place of up to one-third of the wheat flour in a dough formula. The finished product will have a denser texture, however.

Vital wheat gluten (gluten flour) is the pure protein extracted from wheat flour. With an average protein content of 75 percent, it is used to boost the protein content of weaker flours such as rye and whole-wheat flour. Vital wheat gluten must be blended with other ingredients to form a dough or batter.

Self-rising flour is an all-purpose flour to which salt and a chemical leavener, usually baking powder, have been added. It is not recommended for professional use. Chemicals lose their leavening ability over time and may cause inconsistent results. Furthermore, different formulas call for different ratios of salt and leaveners; no commercial blend is appropriate for all purposes.

Nonwheat flours, also referred to as **composite flours**, are made from grains, seeds or beans. Corn, soybeans, rice, oats, buckwheat, potatoes and other items provide flours, but none of them contain the gluten-forming proteins of wheat flour. Composite flours are generally blended with a high-protein wheat flour for baking. Substituting composite flour for wheat flour changes the flavor and texture of the finished product.

Rye flour is commonly used in bread baking. It is milled from the rye berry in the same way that wheat flour is milled from the wheat berry. Rye flour comes in four grades or colors: white, medium, dark and rye meal. White rye flour is made from only the center of the rye berry. Medium and dark rye flours are made from the whole rye berry after the bran is removed and have the most intense rye flavor. Rye meal is the entire rye berry milled into a flour of different granulations, most often a coarse-textured flour. Some mills refer to their rye meal as pumpernickel flour. Others use the term *pumpernickel* to describe dark rye flour. All rye flours have a warm, pungent flavor similar to caraway and a gray-brown color. Although rye flour contains proteins, they will not form gluten, so bread made with 100% rye flour is dense and flat. Therefore rye flour is usually blended with a high-protein wheat flour to produce a more acceptable product.

Nutrition of Flours

Flours are generally high in carbohydrates and low in fat. The grains from which they are milled are often rich in vitamins and minerals. Some of these nutrients, however, are lost during milling. In enriched flours, thiamin, riboflavin, niacin and iron are added at levels set by the government.

Purchasing and Storing Flours

Food service operations often purchase flour in 25- or 50-pound bags. These bags should be stored in a lit, ventilated room at temperatures no higher than 80°F (27°C). Flour can

Whole-wheat flour

crumb the texture, appearance and general structure of the interior of baked bread and cake; may be elastic, aerated, fine grained or coarse grained

Wheat germ

Rye flour

be stored in a refrigerator or freezer if necessary to prevent the onset of rancidity. Refrigeration may cause the flour to absorb moisture, however, which will limit the flour's ability to absorb additional moisture during use. An open bag of flour should be transferred to a closed container to prevent contamination. Even unopened bags of flour should not be stored near items with strong smells, as flour readily absorbs odors. Whole grains should be stored in airtight containers in cool, dry, dark conditions. Coolness inhibits insect infestations; dryness prevents mold. Using airtight containers stored in darkness helps prevent nutrient loss.

Sugar and Sweeteners

Sugar (Fr. *sucre*) and other sweeteners serve several purposes in the bakeshop. They provide *flavor and color; tenderize products by weakening gluten strands; provide food for yeasts; serve as preservatives* and *act as creaming or foaming agents to assist with leavening.*

Sugar

Sugars are simple carbohydrates. They are classified as either (1) single or simple sugars (monosaccharides), such as glucose and fructose, which occur naturally in honey and fruits, or (2) double or complex sugars (disaccharides), which occur both naturally, for example as lactose in milk, as well as in refined sugars.

The sugar most often used in the kitchen is **sucrose**, a refined sugar obtained from both the large tropical grass called sugarcane (*Saccharum officinarum*) and the root of the sugar beet (*Beta vulgaris*). Sucrose is a disaccharide, composed of one molecule each of glucose and fructose. The chemical composition of beet and cane sugars is identical. The two products taste, look, smell and react the same. Sucrose is available in many forms: white granulated, light or dark brown granulated, molasses and powdered.

Sugar Manufacturing

Common refined or table sugar is produced from sugarcane or sugar beets. The first step in sugar production is to crush the cane or beet to extract the juice. This juice contains tannins, pigments, proteins and other undesirable components that must be removed through refinement. Refinement begins by dissolving the juice in water, then boiling it in large steam evaporators. The solution is crystallized in heated vacuum pans. The uncrystallized liquid by-product, known as molasses, is separated out in a centrifuge. The remaining crystallized product, known as **raw sugar**, contains many impurities; the USDA considers it unfit for direct use in food.

Raw sugar is washed with steam to remove some of the impurities. This yields a product known as turbinado sugar. Refining continues as the turbinado is heated, liquefied, centrifuged and filtered. Chemicals may be used to bleach and purify the liquid sugar. Finally the clear liquid sugar is recrystallized in vacuum pans as granulated white sugar.

Pure sucrose is sold in granulated and powdered forms and is available in several grades. Because there are no government standards regulating grade labels, various manufacturers' products may differ slightly.

Types of Sugar

Turbinado sugar, sometimes called Demerara sugar, is the closest consumable product to raw sugar. It is partially refined and light brown in color, with coarse crystals and a caramel flavor. It is sometimes used in beverages and certain baked goods. Because of its high and variable moisture content, turbinado sugar is not recommended as a substitute for granulated or brown sugar.

Sanding sugar has a large, coarse crystal structure that prevents it from dissolving easily. It is used almost exclusively for decorating cookies and pastries.

Granulated sugar is the all-purpose sugar used throughout the kitchen. The crystals are a fine, uniform size suitable for a variety of purposes. **Sugar cubes** are formed by pressing moistened granulated sugar into molds and allowing it to dry. Cubes are typically used for beverage service.

Brown sugar is regular refined cane sugar with some of the molasses returned to it. Light brown sugar contains approximately 3.5% molasses; dark brown sugar contains

sucrose the chemical name for common refined sugar; it is a disaccharide, composed of one molecule each of glucose and fructose

Clockwise from top left: Demerara sugar cubes, light brown sugar, powdered sugar, sugar cubes, brown sugar crystals, granulated sugar

about 6.5%. Molasses adds moisture and a distinctive flavor. Brown sugar can be substituted for refined sugar, measure for measure, in any formula where its flavor is desired. Because of the added moisture, brown sugar tends to lump, trapping air into pockets making it difficult to measure accurately by volume. (Should you need to measure by volume, pack the brown sugar tightly into the measuring cup and press lightly to remove any air pockets.) Always store brown sugar in an airtight container to prevent it from drying and hardening.

Superfine or **castor sugar** is granulated sugar with a smaller-sized crystal. It can be produced by processing regular granulated sugar in a food processor for a few moments. Superfine sugar dissolves quickly in liquids and produces light and tender cakes.

Powdered sugar (Fr. *sucre en poudre*) is also called confectioner's sugar. It is made by grinding granulated sugar crystals through varying degrees of fine screens. Powdered sugar cannot be made in a food processor. It is widely available in various degrees of fineness: 10X is the finest and most common; 6X and 4X are progressively coarser. Because of powdered sugar's tendency to lump, 3% cornstarch is added by the manufacturer to absorb moisture and to prevent lumping. Powdered sugar is used in icings and glazes and for decorating baked products.

Liquid Sweeteners

Although they do not act as creaming or foaming agents to assist with leavening, liquid sweeteners can be used to achieve the same benefits as sugar in baked goods. Most of these liquids have a distinctive flavor as well as sweetness. Some liquid sweeteners are made from sugarcane; others are derived from other plants, grains or bees.

Corn syrup is produced by extracting starch from corn kernels and treating it with acid or an enzyme to develop a sweet syrup. The syrup is extremely thick or viscous and less sweet tasting than honey or refined sugar. Its viscosity gives foods a thick, chewy texture. It stabilizes products made with sugar, preventing them from recrystallization. Corn syrup is available in light and dark forms, which can be used interchangeably. Dark syrup has caramel coloring and molasses added for flavor. Corn syrup is a **hygroscopic** (water-attracting) sweetener, which means it will attract water from the air on humid days and lose water through evaporation more slowly than granulated sugar. Thus it keeps products moister and fresher longer.

Honey (Fr. *miel*) is a strong sweetener consisting of fructose and glucose. It is created by honeybees from nectar collected from flowers. Its flavor and color vary depending on the season, the type of flower the nectar came from and the honey's age. Commercial honey is often a blend, prepared to be relatively neutral and consistent. Like corn syrup, honey is highly hygroscopic. Its distinctive flavor is found in several international foods such as baklava and halvah.

Maple syrup is made from the sap of sugar maple trees. Sap is collected during the spring, then boiled to evaporate its water content, yielding a sweet brown syrup. One sugar maple tree produces about 12 gallons of sap each season; 30–40 gallons of sap will produce 1 gallon of syrup. Pure maple syrup must weigh not less than 11 pounds per gallon; it is graded according to color, flavor and sugar content. The more desirable products, Grades AA and A, have a light amber color and delicate flavor. Pure maple syrup is expensive, but it does add a distinct flavor to baked goods, frostings and, of course, pancakes and waffles. Maple-flavored syrups, often served with pancakes, are usually corn syrups with artificial colorings and flavorings added.

As mentioned earlier, **molasses** (Fr. *mélasse*) is the liquid by-product of sugar refining. Only molasses derived from cane sugar is edible, as beet molasses has an unpleasant odor and bitter flavor. Sulfured molasses contains some of the sulfur dioxide used in secondary sugar processing. It is dark and has a strong, bitter flavor. Most of today's unsulfured molasses is not a true by-product of sugar making. It is now intentionally produced from pure cane syrup and is preferred to sulfured molasses because of its lighter color and milder flavor.

The final stage of sucrose refinement yields blackstrap molasses, which is somewhat popular in the American South. Blackstrap molasses is very dark and thick, with a strong, unique flavor.

hygroscopic describes a food that readily absorbs moisture from the air

Honey

Molasses

Sorghum molasses is produced by cooking down the sweet sap of a brown corn plant known as sorghum, which is grown for animal feed. The flavor and appearance of sorghum molasses are almost identical to that of unsulfured sugarcane molasses.

Nutrition of Sugars and Sweeteners

Sweeteners are carbohydrates. They are high in calories and contain no fiber, protein, fat, vitamin A or vitamin C. They contain only trace amounts of thiamin, riboflavin and niacin.

Cooking Sugar

Sugar can be incorporated into a prepared item in its dry form or first liquefied into a syrup. **Sugar syrups** (not to be confused with liquid sweeteners such as molasses) take two forms: **simple syrups**, which are mixtures of sugar and water, and **cooked syrups**, which are made of melted sugar cooked until it reaches a specific temperature.

Simple Sugar Syrups

Simple syrups are solutions of sugar and water. They are used to moisten cakes and to make sauces, sorbets and beverages.

A syrup's **density** or concentration is dictated by its intended purpose. Cold water will dissolve up to double its weight in sugar; heating the solution forms denser, more concentrated syrups. A **hydrometer**, which measures specific gravity and shows degrees of concentration on the Baumé scale, is the most accurate guide to density. The higher the number, the greater the density of the solution. A syrup with a higher density has more sugar dissolved in it.

Simple syrups can be prepared without the aid of a hydrometer, however. To make a simple sugar syrup, combine specific amounts of water and sugar in a saucepan and bring them to a boil. Once the solution boils, it is important not to stir, as this may cause recrystallization or lumping. For successful simple sugar syrups, the following formulas must be followed precisely:

Light syrup: Boil 2 parts water with 1 part sugar for 1 minute. This concentration measures 17–20° on the Baumé scale. A light syrup can be used for making sorbet or moistening spongecake.

Medium syrup: Boil 1½ parts water with 1 part sugar for 1 minute. This concentration measures 21–24° on the Baumé scale. A medium syrup can be used for candying citrus peel.

Heavy syrup: Boil equal parts water and sugar for 1 minute. This concentration measures 28–30° on the Baumé scale, and the solution should be at 220°F (104°C). Heavy syrup is a basic, all-purpose syrup kept on hand in many bakeshops to moisten cakes and adjust the consistency of icings and dessert sauces.

Cooked Sugars

Caramel sauce, meringue, buttercream, candy and other confections often need liquid sugar that is firm when cool or has a cooked caramel flavor. For these purposes, sugar is cooked to temperatures far higher than for simple syrups. A small amount of water is generally added at the beginning to help the sugar dissolve evenly. As the mixture boils, the water evaporates, the solution's temperature rises and its density increases. The syrup's concentration depends on the amount of water remaining in the final solution: the less water, the harder the cooked syrup will be when it cools.

The sugar's temperature indicates its concentration. If a great deal of water is present, the temperature will not rise much above 212°F (100°C). As water evaporates, however, the temperature will rise until it reaches 320°F (160°C), the point at which all water is evaporated. At temperatures above 320°F (160°C), the pure sugar begins to brown or caramelize. As sugar caramelizes, its sweetening power decreases dramatically. At approximately 375°F (191°C), sugar will burn, developing a bitter flavor. If allowed to continue cooking, sugar will ignite.

density the relationship between the mass and volume of a substance ($D = m/v$). For example, as more and more sugar is dissolved in a liquid, the heavier or denser the liquid will become. Sugar density is measured on the Baumé scale using a hydrometer or saccharometer.

> **⚠ Safety Alert**
>
> *Hot Sugar*
>
> Be extremely careful when working with hot sugar syrups. Because sugar can be heated to very high temperatures, these syrups can cause severe burns. Do not touch liquefied or caramelized sugar with your bare hand until it has cooled completely.

Preparing cooked sugar syrups and caramel.

Brushing sugar crystals from the side of the pan.

Sugar solutions are unstable because of their molecular structure. They can recrystallize because of agitation or uneven heat distribution. To prevent recrystallization:

1 Always use a heavy, clean saucepan, preferably copper.

2 Stir the solution to make sure all sugar crystals dissolve before it reaches a boil. Do not stir the solution after it begins boiling, however.

3 An **interferent** may be added when the solution begins to boil. Cream of tartar, vinegar, glucose (a monosaccharide) and lemon juice are known as interferents because they interfere with the formation of sugar crystals. Some formulas specify which interferent to use, although most interferents are used in such small quantities that their flavor cannot be detected.

4 Brush down the sides of the pan with cold water to wash off crystals that may be deposited there. These sugar crystals may seed the solution, causing more crystals (lumps) to form if not removed. Instead of using a brush to wash away crystals, the pan can be covered for a few moments as soon as the solution comes to a boil. Steam will condense on the cover and run down the sides of the pan, washing away the crystals.

The concentration of sugar syrup should be determined with a candy thermometer that measures very high temperatures. If a thermometer is not available, use the traditional but less accurate ice-water test: Spoon a few drops of the hot sugar into a bowl of very cold water. Check the hardness of the cooled sugar with your fingertips. Each stage of cooked sugar is named according to its firmness when cool (e.g., soft ball or hard crack). Table 30.2 lists the various stages of cooked sugar and the temperature for each. Each stage is also identified by the ice-water test result. Note that even a few degrees make a difference in the syrup's concentration.

Soft ball stage

Hard ball stage

Hard crack stage

STAGES OF COOKED SUGAR		TABLE 30.2
STAGE	TEMPERATURE	ICE-WATER TEST—ONE DROP
Thread	236°F (113°C)	Spins a 2-in. (5-cm) thread when dropped
Soft ball	240°F (116°C)	Forms a soft ball
Firm ball	246°F (119°C)	Forms a firm ball
Hard ball	260°F (127°C)	Forms a hard, compact ball
Soft crack	270°F (132°C)	Separates into a hard, but not brittle, thread
Hard crack	300°F (149°C)	Separates into a hard, brittle sheet
Caramel	338°F (170°C)	Liquid turns dark brown in the pan

Fats

Fat is the general term for butter, margarine, lard, shortening and oil. Fats *provide flavor and color, add moisture and richness, assist with leavening, extend shelf life* and *shorten gluten strands*, producing tender baked goods.

The flavor and texture of a baked good depends on the type of fat used and the manner in which it is incorporated with other ingredients. In pastry doughs, solid fat shortens (tenderizes) the gluten strands; in bread doughs, fat increases loaf volume and lightness; in cake batters, fat incorporates air bubbles and helps leaven the mixture. Fats should be selected based on their flavor, melting point and ability to form emulsions. See Table 30.3.

Most bakeshop ingredients combine completely with liquids; fats do not. Fats will not dissolve but will break down into smaller and smaller particles through mixing. With proper mixing, these fat particles are distributed, more or less evenly, throughout the other ingredients, causing fat and liquid to blend or emulsify.

Butter and Margarine

Butter is prized for its flavor; however, it melts at a relatively low temperature of approximately 93°F (33°C) and burns easily. Unsalted butter is preferred for baking because it tends to be fresher and additional salt might interfere with product formulas. Margarine melts at a slightly higher temperature than butter, making it useful for some rolled-in doughs such as puff pastry or Danish. Because they require higher temperatures to melt, margarine and other vegetable-based shortenings can leave a greasy taste on the tongue. Butter and margarine are discussed in Chapter 8, Dairy Products.

Lard

Lard (Fr. *saindoux*) is rendered pork fat. It is a solid white product of almost 100% pure fat; it contains only a small amount of water. Lard yields flaky, flavorful pastries, such as pie crusts, but is rarely used commercially because it turns rancid quickly.

Shortening

Any fat is a **shortening** in baking because fat shortens gluten strands and tenderizes the product. The fat that is specifically referred to as shortening, however, is a type of solid, white, generally flavorless fat, specially formulated for baking. Shortenings are made from animal fats and/or vegetable oils that are solidified through hydrogenation. These products are 100% fat with a relatively high melting point. Solid all-purpose shortening is ideal for greasing baking pans because it is flavorless and odorless. When substituting shortening in a formula calling for butter, additional liquid must be added to compensate for the lack of moisture in the shortening.

Lard

<table>
<tr><td colspan="2">MELTING POINT OF FATS*   TABLE 30.3</td></tr>
<tr><td>Butter, whole</td><td>92–98°F (33–36°C)</td></tr>
<tr><td>Butter, clarified</td><td>92–98°F (33–36°C)</td></tr>
<tr><td>Cocoa butter</td><td>88–93°F (31–34°C)</td></tr>
<tr><td>Lard</td><td>89–98°F (32–36°C)</td></tr>
<tr><td>Margarine, solid</td><td>94–98°F (34–36°C)</td></tr>
<tr><td>Shortening, all-purpose vegetable</td><td>120°F (49°C)</td></tr>
<tr><td>Shortening, emulsified vegetable</td><td>115°F (46°C)</td></tr>
<tr><td>Shortening, heavy-duty fryer</td><td>97–107°F (36–42°C)</td></tr>
</table>

*The melting point of any fat depends on its specific ratio of fatty acids, its intended use and its manufacturer. Natural products such as butter and lard will vary more from one lot to the next than will manufactured products such as margarine or shortening. (This information was obtained from a variety of manufacturers and assumes that the fat is pure and previously unused.)

Function of Ingredients

Fats

- provide flavor and color
- add moisture and richness
- assist with leavening
- help extend shelf life
- tenderize by shortening gluten strands

Emulsifiers may be added to regular shortening to assist with moisture absorption and retention as well as leavening. **Emulsified shortenings**, also known as high-ratio shortenings, are used in the commercial production of cakes and frostings when the formula contains a large amount of sugar. If a formula calls for an emulsified shortening, use it. If you substitute any other fat, the product's texture suffers.

Oil

Unlike butter and other fats, oil blends thoroughly throughout a mixture. It therefore coats more of the proteins, and the gluten strands produced are much shorter, a desirable result in fine-textured products such as muffins or chiffon cakes. For baking, select a neutral-flavored oil unless the distinctive taste of olive oil is desired, as in some breads. Never substitute oil in a formula requiring a solid shortening. For detailed information on oil, see Chapter 7, Flavors and Flavorings.

Chemical Leavening Agents

The shape, texture and crumb of a baked product is partly the result of gases such as air and carbon dioxide (CO_2) trapped in the batter or dough before and during baking. Air is incorporated by the baker during mixing, as described later in this chapter. Carbon dioxide, however, is produced by chemical leavening agents or the life process of **yeast** (a living organism). The proper use of yeast for leavening is discussed in Chapter 32, Yeast Breads.

Chemical leavening agents release gases (primarily carbon dioxide) through reactions between **acids** and **bases**. The gases form bubbles (air pockets) throughout the dough or batter. As the product bakes, the gases expand, causing the product to increase in volume and rise. The proteins in the dough or batter set around these air pockets, giving cakes, cookies and quick breads their shape and texture.

Baking Soda

Sodium bicarbonate ($NaHCO_3$) is more commonly known as household baking soda. Baking soda is an alkaline compound (a base), which releases carbon dioxide gas if both an acid and moisture are present. Heat is not necessary for this reaction to occur. Because the reaction can start before heat is applied, products made with baking soda must be baked at once, before the carbon dioxide has a chance to escape from the batter or dough.

Acids commonly used with baking soda are buttermilk, sour cream, lemon juice, honey, molasses or fruits high in acid such as citrus. Generally the amount of baking soda used in a formula is only the amount necessary to neutralize the acids present. If more leavening action is needed, baking powder, not more baking soda, should be used. Too much baking soda causes a product to taste soapy or bitter; it may also cause a yellow color and brown spots to develop.

Baking Powder

Baking powder is a mixture of sodium bicarbonate and one or more acids, generally cream of tartar ($KHC_4H_4O_6$) and/or sodium aluminum sulfate ($Na_2SO_4 \cdot Al_2[SO_4]_3$). Baking powder also contains a starch to prevent lumping and to balance the chemical reactions. Because baking powder contains both the acid and the base necessary for the desired chemical reaction, a formula that includes baking powder does not need to include any additional acid. Only moisture is necessary to release the gases.

There are two types of baking powder: single-acting and double-acting. An excess of either type produces undesirable flavors, textures and colors in baked products.

Single-acting baking powder requires only the presence of moisture to begin releasing gas. The eggs, milk, water or other liquids in a formula supply this moisture. Like products made with baking soda, products using single-acting baking powder must be baked immediately.

Double-acting baking powder is more popular than single-acting. With double-acting baking powder, there is a small release of gas on contact with moisture and a second,

---

Function of Ingredients

Chemical Leaveners

- produce carbon dioxide to leaven batters and doughs
- tenderize baked goods
- contribute to the characteristic texture of some quick breads

acid a substance that neutralizes a base (alkaline) in a liquid solution; foods such as citrus, juice, vinegar and wine that have a sour or sharp flavor (most foods are slightly acidic); acids have a pH of less than 7

base a substance that neutralizes an acid in a liquid solution; ingredients such as sodium bicarbonate (baking soda) that have an alkaline or bitter flavor; bases have a pH of more than 7

Modern Science

The practice of mixing an acid and an alkali to leaven bread began during the Industrial Revolution, a period of rapid development in scientific thought and technological ability. The first commercial leaveners were marketed in 1850. Sodium bicarbonate was first marketed as baking soda in 1867 under the brand name Arm & Hammer. The first double-acting baking powder became available in 1889 under the brand name Calumet.

stronger release of gas when heat is applied. Products made with double-acting baking powder do not need to be baked immediately. They can sit for a short time without loss of leavening ability. All formulas in this text call for double-acting baking powder.

Baking soda and baking powder are sometimes both included in a formula. This is because baking soda can release CO_2 only to the extent that there is also an acid present. If the soda/acid reaction alone is insufficient to leaven the product, baking powder is required for additional leavening.

Baking Ammonia

Baking ammonia (ammonia bicarbonate [CH_5NO_3] or ammonia carbonate [$(NH_4)_2CO_3$]) is a leavening agent that adds crispness to some baked goods, primarily cookies and crackers. Baking ammonia releases ammonia and carbon dioxide very rapidly when heated. The strong odor it releases as it bakes dissipates once the product is cooked above 140°F (60°C). Baking ammonia is suitable for low-moisture products with large surface areas that are baked at high temperatures, such as crackers and biscotti. It should not be used in thicker quick breads, such as muffins, loaves or scones as the ammonia smell and flavor will remain.

Purchasing and Storing Chemical Leavening Agents

Purchase chemical leaveners in the smallest unit appropriate for the style of the operation. Although a large can of baking powder may cost less than several small ones, if not used promptly the contents of a larger container can deteriorate, resulting in unusable baked goods and waste.

Chemical leavening agents should always be kept tightly covered. Not only is there a risk of contamination if left open, but chemical leavening agents can also absorb moisture from the air and lose their effectiveness. They should be stored in a cool place, as heat deteriorates them. A properly stored and unopened container has a shelf life of several years.

Thickening Agents

Thickening agents perform several functions in the bakeshop. Starches *absorb moisture to thicken liquids*. Gelatin *traps liquids in a protein structure* to solidify and thicken.

Starch

Starches are often used as thickening agents in the bakeshop. Cornstarch, arrowroot and flour are used to thicken pastry creams, sauces, custards and fruit fillings. **Cornstarch** is a grain-based starch. It must be dissolved in cold water, then added to the mixture to be thickened and then heated. Once it reaches just below the boiling point, it must be cooked until it thickens into an opaque gel. Products thickened with cornstarch should not be vigorously stirred once cooled or they can break down. Products thickened with cornstarch tend to separate when thawed after freezing.

Arrowroot is dissolved in cold water and added to a liquid to thicken it. Used primarily to thicken hot sauces, arrowroot can break down if overcooked, making it most appropriate for thickening sauces that will be served immediately.

Although less commonly encountered in professional bakeshops, tapioca can be used to thicken a variety of pastry products. **Tapioca** is a starch produced from the root of the tropical cassava (manioc) plant. It is available as a flour or as balls, referred to as pearls. Tapioca flour can be used in the same manner as cornstarch to thicken sauces and fruit mixtures. Pearl tapioca is used to thicken milk for tapioca pudding or to thicken fruit pie fillings. Most pearl tapioca must be soaked in a cold liquid for several hours before cooking. Instant tapioca, which is smaller than pearls, needs to soak for only 20–30 minutes before cooking.

Gelatin

One of the most commonly used thickeners in the bakeshop is **gelatin**, a natural product derived from collagen, an animal protein. It is available in two forms: granulated gelatin

Function of Ingredients

Thickeners

- absorb moisture to thicken liquids, (starch, pectin or vegetable gums)
- trap liquids in a protein structure to thicken liquids, (gelatin)

Pearl tapioca

bloom to soften granulated gelatin in a cold liquid before dissolving and using

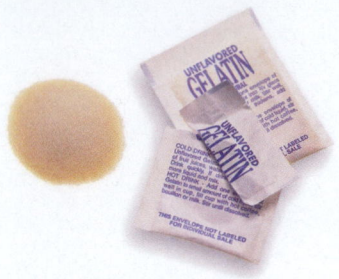

Granulated gelatin

and sheet (also called leaf) gelatin. A two-step process is necessary to use either form. The gelatin must first be softened in a cold liquid—a process referred to as **blooming**—then dissolved in a hot liquid.

Granulated gelatin is available in bulk or in ¼-ounce (7-gram) envelopes (slightly less than 1 tablespoon). One envelope is enough to set 1 pint (480 milliliters) of liquid into a firm gel or 3 cups (720 milliliters) of liquid into a softer mousse consistency. Granulated gelatin should be softened in four times its weight of cold liquid for at least 5 minutes, then heated gently to dissolve. The initial softening in a cold liquid is necessary to separate the gelatin molecules so that they do not lump together when the hot liquid is added. Melting over a double boiler prevents scorching.

Sheet or **leaf gelatin** is available in 1-kilogram boxes, sometimes further packaged in envelopes containing five or six sheets. The sheets are produced in varying thicknesses and weights; the average weighs about ⅒ ounce (3 grams) per sheet. They must be separated and soaked in ice water until very soft, at least 15 minutes. They are then removed from the water, squeezed to remove excess moisture and stirred into a hot liquid until completely dissolved. When sheet gelatin is added to a hot liquid, it is not necessary to melt it first.

Procedure for Using Sheet Gelatin

❶ Gelatin sheets are submerged in ice water for several minutes to soften.

❷ Softened gelatin sheets are then removed from the ice water and incorporated into a hot liquid.

Substituting Granulated for Sheet Gelatin

Unflavored granulated and sheet gelatin can be substituted for each other in formulas, but granulated gelatin must be softened (bloomed) in a cold liquid before it is dissolved in order to prevent lumps. When sheet gelatin is specified in this text, the number of sheets is listed. The weight of granulated gelatin to be used is also listed. To calculate the amount of additional water or liquid required when substituting granulated for sheet gelatin, multiply the weight of sheet gelatin called for in the formula by 6. Then soften the granulated gelatin in this amount of an appropriate cold liquid—water, stock or liquor, for example—before dissolving it in the hot mixture as instructed in the formula.

Granulated and sheet gelatin can be used interchangeably in any formula. Sheet gelatin, though more expensive, is preferred for its lack of flavor and color. It also tends to dissolve more readily and evenly and has a longer shelf life than granulated gelatin. Once incorporated into a product such as a Bavarian, gelatin can be frozen, or melted and reset once or twice, without a loss of thickening ability. Because it scorches easily, gelatin and mixtures containing gelatin should not be allowed to boil. Boiling also destroys gelatin's ability to thicken. Products thickened with gelatin, such as mousse or custard, can become rubbery after a few days in the refrigerator.

Flavorings

Many flavoring ingredients are used in the bakeshop. Practically any herb, spice, beverage or extract can be used to *impart their characteristic flavors to baked goods, creams and confections.* As with all baking ingredients, select flavoring components for overall quality and freshness, and combine flavorings carefully to achieve a balanced, good-tasting finished product. Recommendations for using herbs and spices in the bakeshop are found in Chapter 7, Flavors and Flavorings.

Function of Ingredients

Flavorings

- give characteristic flavors to baked goods, creams and confections

Emulsions and Extracts

Emulsions and extracts are liquid flavoring agents derived from various flavoring oils (**essential oils**) extracted from fruits, beans, spices or seeds.

Emulsions are flavoring oils mixed into water with the aid of emulsifiers. Lemon and orange are the most common emulsions. Emulsions are much stronger than extracts and should be used carefully and sparingly. **Extracts** are mixtures of flavoring oils or essential oils and ethyl alcohol. Vanilla, almond and lemon are frequently used extracts. An extract may be made with pure flavoring oils or with artificial flavors and colors. Emulsions and extract contents are regulated by the FDA, and package labels must indicate any artificial ingredients. Emulsions and extracts are highly volatile. They should be stored in sealed containers in a cool area away from direct light.

essential oils pure oils extracted from the skins, peels and other parts of plants used to give their aroma and taste to flavoring agents in foods, cosmetics and other products

Vanilla

Vanilla (Fr. *vanille*) is the most frequently used flavoring in the bakeshop. It comes from the pod fruit, called a bean, of a vine in the orchid family. Vanilla beans are purchased whole, individually or by the pound. They should be soft and pliable, with a rich brown color and good aroma. The finest vanilla comes from Tahiti and Madagascar.

In lieu of beans, pure vanilla extract is an easy and less expensive way to give bakeshop products a true vanilla flavor. Vanilla extract is dark brown and aromatic, and it comes in several strengths, referred to as folds. The higher the number of folds, the stronger the flavor of the extract. By law, any product labeled "vanilla extract" must not contain artificial flavorings and must be at least 35% alcohol by volume. Vanilla extract should be stored at room temperature in a closed, opaque container. It should not be frozen.

To use a vanilla bean, cut it open lengthwise with a paring knife. Scrape out the moist seeds with the knife's tip and stir them into the mixture being flavored. The seeds do not dissolve and will remain visible as small black or brown flecks. After all the seeds have been removed, the bean can be placed in a covered container with sugar to create vanilla sugar. Because the intensity of vanilla extract varies, it is difficult to recommend an equivalent in vanilla beans. Generally, ½ fluid ounce (15 milligrams) vanilla extract can be substituted for 1 vanilla bean; however, taste should be the ultimate guide.

Vanilla beans should be stored in an airtight container in a cool, dark place. During storage, the beans may develop a white coating. This is not mold, but rather crystals of vanilla flavor known as **vanillin**. Vanillin should not be removed.

Artificial or imitation vanilla flavoring is made with synthetic vanillin. Artificial flavoring is available in a clear form, which is useful for white buttercreams in which the dark brown color of pure vanilla extract is undesirable. Although inexpensive, artificial vanilla is, at best, weaker and less aromatic than pure extract. It can also impart a chemical or bitter taste to foods.

Scraping the seeds from the interior of a vanilla bean.

Chocolate

Chocolate is one of the most popular flavorings—perhaps the most popular—for candies, cookies, cakes and pastries. Chocolate is also served as a beverage and is an ingredient in traditional spicy Mexican mole sauce. Chocolate is available in a variety of forms and degrees of sweetness.

Chocolate Manufacturing

Chocolate (Fr. *chocolat*) begins as yellow fruit pods dangling from the trunk and main branches of the tropical cacao tree. A native species of the Amazon rainforest, the cacao tree is found in the Caribbean, parts of Africa, Asia and Latin America. Each pod contains about 40 almond-sized cocoa beans. After the pods ripen, the beans are placed in the sun for several days to dry and ferment. Although time-consuming, this process helps develop the aroma and essential oils in the beans. The beans are then cleaned, dried a second time, cured and roasted to develop flavor and reduce bitterness. Next the beans are crushed to remove their shells, yielding the prized chocolate **nib**. Like coffee beans, chocolate beans are blended to the specifications of the chocolate manufacturer—a closely guarded trade secret—to obtain the desired flavor and aroma in the end product.

Cocoa beans

Melting Chocolate

For use in baked goods, solid bars or blocks of chocolate usually must be portioned and melted. Using improper melting techniques can quickly ruin costly chocolate. If working from a large block of solid chocolate, cut off small pieces, weighing them until the necessary amount of chocolate is portioned. The smaller the pieces of chocolate, the quicker they will melt. Chocolate may be melted in a microwave oven or over a bain marie.

If using a microwave, place the pieces of chocolate in a microwave-safe bowl. Heat at low power in 60-second intervals, stirring frequently. When most of the chocolate is melted, remove the bowl from the oven and stir gently until completely melted.

If using a bain marie, place the pieces of chocolate in a metal bowl that fits suspended over a pan of water. Heat the water only to a simmer and ensure that no steam or water gets into the chocolate itself, as this will cause lumping or seizing.

Chocolate has a very sharp melting point, which means that it will appear solid one moment and then almost instantly, when the correct temperature is reached, it will liquefy. Stirring is necessary to even out the temperature and prevent overheating. Never allow the temperature of high-quality dark chocolate to exceed 120°F (49°C) as this can affect its flavor and texture. The solid portion of chocolate can seize into dry lumps and develop a bitter, scorched flavor at relatively low temperatures. When this happens it is best to discard it and start over.

In summary:

- Cut chocolate into small pieces or purchase pistoles (discs) for melting.
- Do not allow water or steam to touch the chocolate; make sure bowls and spatulas are completely dry before use.
- Keep the temperature low; do not exceed 120°F (49°C) for dark chocolate, 115°F (46°C) for milk or white chocolate.
- Stir frequently to blend.

conching stirring melted chocolate with large stone or metal rollers to create a smooth texture in the finished chocolate

Bean-to-Bar Chocolate

Chocolatiers, who make chocolate candies and decorations professionally, have become extremely interested in the source of their chocolates. Some chocolatiers have become chocolate makers themselves, manufacturing their own chocolates from beans they purchase directly from growers around the world. By controlling the source, the roasting and the blending of their cacao beans, these chocolatiers can produce uniquely flavored products and specialized flavor profiles. The term *bean-to-bar chocolate* is used to refer to chocolate bars or candies made by such companies, whether small batch or industrial scale.

Nibs are shipped to manufacturers worldwide where they can be further roasted. They are crushed into a thick (nonalcoholic) paste known as **chocolate liquor** or **chocolate mass**. Chocolate mass contains about 53% fat, known as cocoa butter. The chocolate mass is further refined depending on the desired product. To produce cocoa powder, virtually all the cocoa butter is removed. Adding more cocoa butter, sugar, milk solids and flavorings to the chocolate mass creates a variety of other products. Most manufacturers of fine chocolates use the Swiss technique of **conching** to increase smoothness. Conching involves stirring large vats of blended chocolate with a heavy granite roller or paddle to smooth out sugar crystals and mellow the flavor, a process that may last from 12 hours to 3 days.

Tasting Chocolates

There are three types of cocoa beans: a very hardy, abundant African variety used as a base bean and two flavorful, aromatic varieties used for flavor. Most chocolates are blends, created by their manufacturer to be unique yet consistent. Varietal chocolates, those made from one type of bean grown in one specific area, have become trendy, though expensive, for both chocolate bars and baking chocolates. In contrast to wine or coffee, it is difficult to taste processed chocolate and tell which beans were used.

Roasting greatly affects the final flavor of chocolate. Generally German and Spanish manufacturers use a high (or strong) roast; Swiss and American makers use a low (or mild) roast. Refining is also a matter of national taste. Swiss and German chocolate are the smoothest, followed by English chocolates. American chocolate is noticeably grainier.

Chocolate quality is actually the product of several factors in addition to flavor. All of the following factors should be evaluated when selecting chocolate:

1 *Appearance:* Color should be even and glossy, without any discoloration
2 *Smell:* Should smell chocolatey with no off-odors or staleness
3 *Break:* Should snap cleanly without crumbling
4 *Texture:* Should melt quickly and evenly on the tongue

Types of Chocolate

Unsweetened chocolate is pure hardened chocolate liquor without any added sugar or milk solids. It is frequently used in baking and is sometimes referred to as baking chocolate. Unsweetened chocolate is approximately 53% cocoa butter and 47% cocoa solids. Its flavor is pure and chocolatey, but the absence of sugar makes it virtually inedible as is.

Both **bittersweet** and **semisweet chocolates** contain at least 35% chocolate liquor plus additional cocoa butter, sugar, flavorings and sometimes emulsifiers. Generally semisweet chocolate is sweeter than bittersweet chocolate, but there are no precise definitions, so flavor and sweetness vary from brand to brand. Both bittersweet and semisweet chocolates are excellent eating chocolates and can usually be substituted measure for measure in any formula.

Couverture [koo-vehr-TYOOR] refers to high-quality chocolate containing at least 32% cocoa butter. Professional chocolatiers generally prefer couverture chocolate, which has a higher fluidity than other chocolates when melted. It is available in a range of flavors, such as bittersweet, semisweet and milk chocolate. Couverture has a glossy appearance and can be used to create a thin, smooth coating on confections and pastries.

U.S. government standards require that **sweet chocolate** contain not less than 15% chocolate liquor and varying amounts of sugar, milk solids, flavorings and emulsifiers. As the name implies, sweet chocolate is sweeter, and thus less chocolatey, than semisweet chocolate.

Clockwise from lower left: semisweet chips, disks of chocolate liquor, block of bittersweet chocolate, block of milk chocolate, disks of white chocolate, alkalized cocoa powder

Milk chocolate is the favorite eating chocolate in the United States. It contains sugar, vanilla, perhaps other flavorings and milk solids. The milk solids that make the chocolate milder and sweeter than other chocolates also make it less suitable for baking purposes. Do not substitute milk chocolate for dark chocolate in any product that must be baked, as the milk solids tend to burn. If melted slowly and carefully, milk chocolate can be used in glazes, mousses or candies.

Chocolate chips are drops of chocolate available in count sizes from 14 to 160 per ounce (average chips are 800–1000 per pound). Their form makes them easy to add to cookies, muffins and cakes. Like the larger **chocolate chunks**, chips are available in many flavors including white chocolate, butterscotch, peanut butter and fruit flavors. **Pistoles** or **calets** are small round pieces or discs of chocolate, often the finest couverture, designed to eliminate the need for chopping chocolate in the bakeshop—especially useful when tempering.

Cocoa powder is the brown powder left after the fat (cocoa butter) is removed from cocoa beans. It does not contain any sweeteners or flavorings and is used primarily in baked goods. Alkalized or Dutch-processed cocoa powder has been treated with an alkaline solution, such as potassium carbonate, to raise the powder's pH from 5.5 to 7 or 8. Alkalized powder is darker and milder than non-alkalized powder and has a reduced tendency to lump. Either type of powder can be used in baked goods, depending on your flavor preference or cost concerns.

Chocolate pistoles

Cocoa Butter

Chocolate liquor is approximately 53% fat, known as **cocoa butter**. Cocoa butter has long been prized for its resistance to rancidity and its use as a cosmetic. Cocoa butter has a very precise melting point, just below body temperature. Fine chocolatiers use high percentages of cocoa butter to give their chocolates melt-in-the-mouth quality.

cocoa butter fat found in cocoa beans and used in fine chocolates; it is white, solid at room temperature and tasteless

White Chocolate

This ivory-colored substance is not the product of an albino cocoa bean. It is actually a confectionery product that does not contain any chocolate solids or liquor. (Thus it is usually labeled *white confectionery* or *coating* in the United States.) The finest white chocolate couverture contains a minimum of 31% cocoa butter, a maximum of 55% sugar, 20% milk solids and vanilla or other flavors. Lower quality white chocolate products replace all or part of the cocoa butter with vegetable oils. These confectionery products are less expensive than those containing pure cocoa butter, but their flavor and texture is noticeably inferior. White chocolate melts at a lower temperature than dark chocolate and burns easily. It is excellent for mousses, sauces and candy making but is less often used in baked products.

Dutch-processed cocoa powder (left) and American-style non-alkalized cocoa powder

Tempering Chocolate

In order to create chocolate candies with a high gloss and a crisp, sharp snap when eaten, chocolate must be **tempered**. When chocolate is not tempered correctly, it will be crumbly and develop gray streaks known as bloom when dry. Untempered chocolate takes a long time to set and sticks to candy molds.

Tempering chocolate is a controlled process of melting, cooling and reheating chocolate within specific temperature ranges. The ideal temperature depends on the type of chocolate and the percent of cocoa butter that it contains.

There are several tempering methods, such as seeding, tabling, microwave oven and cocoa butter methods. Each method relies on melting chocolate and heating it to a certain temperature, then cooling and rewarming it. Great care must be taken when tempering chocolate. The chocolate must be chopped into small, uniform pieces so that it melts evenly. If overheated, the chocolate needs to be cooled then reheated before resuming the tempering process. Equally important, steam or water must not enter the chocolate because

this would cause it to seize. When stirring chocolate during tempering, if excess air is incorporated into the mass of chocolate, it will become thick and unmanageable. Reheating and retempering will restore the chocolate's fluidity. Consult a specialized text and information provided by chocolate manufacturers for precise instructions on how to temper chocolate.

The welcome news is that, for general use, chocolate melted for mousses, creams, ganache and baking does not need to be tempered.

Imitation Chocolate or Chocolate-Flavored Coating

A less-expensive product substituted for chocolate in many prepared foods, imitation chocolate is made with hydrogenated vegetable oils instead of cocoa butter, as little as 8% defatted cocoa powder and as much as 55% sugar, plus emulsifiers, flavorings and perhaps milk solids. The resulting product melts at a higher temperature and requires no tempering. Imitation chocolates have an inferior taste and leave a waxy feel in the mouth. When quality is no concern, imitation chocolate may be used in place of real chocolate, but customers should be informed that the item is only "chocolate flavored."

Nutrition of Chocolate

Chocolate is high in calories and fat. It contains minimal amounts of vitamin A and trace amounts of other vitamins as well as some sodium, phosphorus, potassium and other minerals. Cocoa powder as well as dark chocolate with a high cocoa content and a minimal amount of sugar contain antioxidants called flavanols, which studies suggest may promote heart and vascular health.

Storing Chocolate

All chocolates should be stored at a cool, consistent temperature, away from strong odors and moisture. Chocolate should never be stored under refrigeration. Dark chocolate, white chocolate and cocoa powder can be kept for up to 1 year without loss of flavor. Milk chocolate will not keep as well because it contains milk solids.

Chocolate may develop grayish-white spots during storage referred to as **bloom**. Two types of bloom can develop on chocolate. **Fat bloom** occurs when cocoa butter crystals rise and crystallize on the chocolate's surface. Chocolate stored above 70°F (21°C) will develop fat bloom over time. Because fat bloom has no effect on taste, tempering the product will remedy the problem. **Sugar bloom** occurs when moisture collects on the surface of the chocolate and blends with the sugar in the chocolate, leaving a white sugar film. The result is a gritty chocolate that cannot be improved by tempering.

Nuts

Nuts (Fr. *noix*) provide texture and flavor to baked goods and are often substituted for all or part of the wheat flour in a pastry such as Gluten-Free Orange Chiffon Cake (page 1036) or a dacquoise (page 1013). A true nut, according to the botanical definition, is the edible single-seed kernel of a fruit surrounded by a hard shell. A hazelnut is an example of a true nut. The term *nut* is used more generally, however, to refer to any seed or fruit with an edible kernel in a hard shell. Walnuts and peanuts are examples of non-nut "nuts" (peanuts are legumes that grow underground; walnuts have two kernels). Nuts are high in fat, making them especially susceptible to rancidity and odor absorption. Nuts should be stored in nonmetal, airtight containers in a cool, dark place. Most nuts may be kept frozen for up to 1 year.

Nuts are often roasted in a low (325°F/162°C) oven in order to heighten their flavor. (See Chapter 9, Mise en Place.) Some nuts such as hazelnuts, pistachios, almonds, peanuts and cashews are ground into nut butters used to flavor pastries. Allowing roasted nuts to cool to room temperature before grinding prevents them from releasing too much oil. When sweetened, nut butter is referred to as a paste and is used to flavor chocolates, ice creams and other baked items.

Almonds

Almonds (Fr. *amandes*) are the seeds of a plumlike fruit native to western India that was first cultivated by the ancient Greeks. It is now a major commercial crop in California. Almonds are available whole, sliced, slivered or ground. Blanched almonds have had their brown, textured skins removed; natural almonds retain their skins. Unless the brown color of natural almond skin is undesirable, the two types can be used interchangeably in recipes. Almonds are frequently used in pastries and candies and are the main ingredient in almond paste and marzipan.

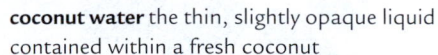

Almond paste

Cashews

Cashews (Fr. *noix de caju*), native to the Amazon, are actually the seeds of a plant related to poison ivy. Because of toxins in the shell, cashews are always sold shelled. Cashews are expensive and have a pronounced flavor. They make a wonderful addition to cookies and candies.

Chestnuts (Fr. *marrons*) are true nuts that must be cooked before using. Available steamed, dried, boiled or roasted, they are often sold as a canned purée, with or without added sugar. Candied or glazed chestnuts are also available. Most chestnuts are grown in Europe, primarily Italy, but new varieties are beginning to flourish in North America. The distinctive flavor of chestnuts is found in many sweet dishes and pastries.

Chestnuts

Coconuts

Coconuts (Fr. *noix de coco*) are the seeds from one of the largest of all fruits. They grow on the tropical coconut palm tree. The nut is a dark brown oval, covered with coarse fibers. The shell is thick and hard; inside is a layer of white, moist flesh. The interior also contains a clear liquid known as **coconut water**. (This is not the same as **coconut milk** or **coconut cream**, both of which are prepared from coconut flesh.) Coconut has a mild aroma, a sweet, nutty flavor and a crunchy, chewy texture. Fresh coconuts are readily available but require some effort to use. A good fresh coconut should feel heavy; you should be able to hear the coconut water sloshing around inside. Avoid cracked, moist or moldy coconuts. Coconut flesh is available shredded or flaked, with or without added sugar. Commercially prepared coconut purée is available for use in beverages, frozen desserts and pastries.

Coconut is used in pastries and candies and is also an important ingredient in Indian, Southeast Asian and Caribbean cuisines.

Hazelnuts (Fr. *noisettes*) are true nuts that grow wild in the northwestern and upper midwestern U.S. states. The cultivated form, known as a filbert, is native to temperate regions throughout the Northern Hemisphere. A bit larger than the hazelnut, the filbert has a weaker flavor than its wild cousin. Both nuts look like smooth brown marbles. Filberts are more abundant, so they are generally less expensive. Their distinctive flavor goes well with chocolate and coffee.

Hazelnuts

coconut water the thin, slightly opaque liquid contained within a fresh coconut

coconut milk a coconut-flavored liquid made by pouring boiling water over shredded coconut; may be sweetened or unsweetened; do not substitute cream of coconut for coconut milk

coconut cream (1) a coconut-flavored liquid made like coconut milk but with less water; it is creamier and thicker than coconut milk; (2) the thick fatty portion that separates and rises to the top of canned or frozen coconut milk; do not substitute cream of coconut for true coconut cream

cream of coconut a canned commercial product consisting of thick, sweetened coconut-flavored liquid; used for baking and in beverages

To remove hazelnut skin, roast whole nuts in a 275°F (135°C) oven for 12–15 minutes. They should give off a good aroma and just begin to darken. While still hot, rub the nuts in a dry towel or against a mesh sifter to remove the skin.

Hazelnut paste (Fr. *praline*) is a smooth composition made from finely ground roasted hazelnuts and sugar. It is used to flavor creams, chocolates and icings. Gianduja [zhahn-DOO-yah] refers to chocolate blended with hazelnut paste that is used as a filling or in candies.

Macadamia nuts are small, round, creamy white nuts with a sweet, rich flavor and high fat content, native to Australia. The shell is extremely hard and must be removed by machine, so the macadamia is always sold out of the shell. Its flavor blends well with fruit, coconut and white and dark chocolate.

Peanuts (Fr. *arichides*) are actually legumes that grow underground. The peanut is native to South America; it made its way into North America via Africa and the slave trade, however. Peanuts may be eaten raw or roasted and are available shelled or unshelled, with or without their thin red skins. Peanuts are ubiquitous ground with a bit of oil into peanut butter.

Pecans (Fr. *noix pacane*), native to the Mississippi River Valley, are perhaps the most popular nuts in America. Their flavor is rich and mapley and appears most often in breads, sweets and pastries. They are available whole in the shell or in various standard sizes and grades of pieces.

Pine nuts (Fr. *pignons*), also known as piñon nuts and pignole, are the seeds of several species of pine tree. The small, creamy white, teardrop-shaped nuts are commonly used in pastries from Spain, Italy and the American Southwest. They are rarely chopped or ground because of their small size and need roasting only if used in a dish that will not receive further cooking.

Pistachios (Fr. *pistaches*) are native to central Asia, where they have been cultivated for more than 3000 years. California now produces most of the pistachios marketed in the United States. Pistachios are unique for the green color of their meat. When ripe, the shell opens naturally at one end, aptly referred to as "smiling," which makes shelling the nuts quite easy. Red pistachios are dyed, not natural. Pistachios are sold whole, shelled or unshelled and are used in pastries and confections.

Walnuts (Fr. *noix*), relatives of the pecan, are native to Asia, Europe and North America. The black walnut, native to Appalachia, has a dark brown meat and a strong flavor. The English walnut, now grown primarily in California, has a milder flavor, is easier to shell and is less expensive. Walnuts are more popular than pecans outside the United States. They are used in baked goods and pressed for oil.

Hazelnut paste

Macadamia nuts

Peanuts

Pecans

Pistachios

Pine nuts

English walnuts

FUNCTIONS OF INGREDIENTS IN THE BAKESHOP	TABLE 30.4
INGREDIENT	**FUNCTION**
Chemical leaveners	Produce carbon dioxide to leaven batters and doughs Tenderize baked goods Contribute to the characteristic texture of some quick breads
Eggs	Flavor, leaven and thicken items Enrich and tenderize yeast breads Extend shelf life of some baked goods (Whites) firm and leaven baked goods, custards and creams
Fats	Provide flavor and color Add moisture and richness Assist with leavening Extend shelf life Shorten gluten strands to produce tender baked goods
Flavorings	Give characteristic flavors to baked goods, creams and confections
Flour	Provide bulk and structure to baked goods Thicken liquids in items such as custards and pie fillings Prevent foods from sticking to pans
Fruits	Add flavor, moisture and texture Add nutritional value Enhance appearance Garnish foods for visual appeal (Juice) contribute acids that support chemical reactions with baking soda
Liquids	Dissolve ingredients such as salt in a batter or dough Activate compounds such as yeast or chemical leavening Moisten ingredients Adjust the temperature of ingredients
Milk and dairy products	Provide texture, flavor, volume, color and nutritional value to baked goods Contribute to browning as well as softness in the crust and structure of a baked item
Salt	Enhance flavors of other foods Suppress bitterness and heighten contrasting tastes Slow yeast fermentation Strengthen gluten structure
Sugar and other sweeteners	Provide flavor, sweetness and color Tenderize products by weakening gluten strands Provide food for yeasts Serve as preservatives by retaining moisture Act as creaming or foaming agents to assist with leavening
Thickeners	Absorb moisture to thicken liquids (starch, pectin or vegetable gums) Trap liquids in a protein structure to solidify and thicken liquids (gelatin)

MEASURING INGREDIENTS IN THE BAKESHOP

Precise, accurate measurement of ingredients is extremely important for bakeshop products. As a result, baking formulas often list weights, even for liquid ingredients. (The term to **scale up** (or **scale down**) refers to increasing (or decreasing) a formula's yield.) Measuring ingredients by weight is more accurate, and, once the basic procedures are mastered, it is faster than measuring by volume. It is also important to remember that most foods do not weigh their volume. In other words, 1 cup of flour equals 8 fluid ounces of flour (a measure of volume) but it does not contain 8 ounces of flour by weight. For best results, use the measurement specified in each formula.

Because accurate weights are so important, balance scales are commonly employed in the bakeshop. Procedures for using these scales are included here. Electronic scales calibrated in both grams and fractions of an ounce are also used in bakeshops but must be handled with care. Good quality electronic scales are expensive and can be damaged if loaded beyond their maximum weight. Even airborne flour particles or spilled ingredients can ruin an electronic scale. Be sure to calibrate and maintain scales frequently according to the manufacturer's recommendations.

Procedure for Using a Balance Scale

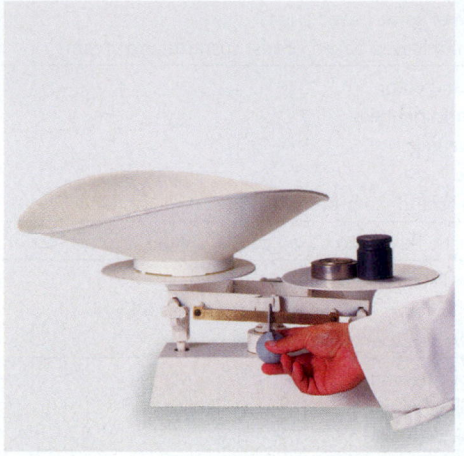

① To use a balance scale to weigh an ingredient, place an empty container on the left. Next set a counterbalance to that container on the right. Use weights and the sliding beam weight to add an amount equal to the amount of the ingredient needed.

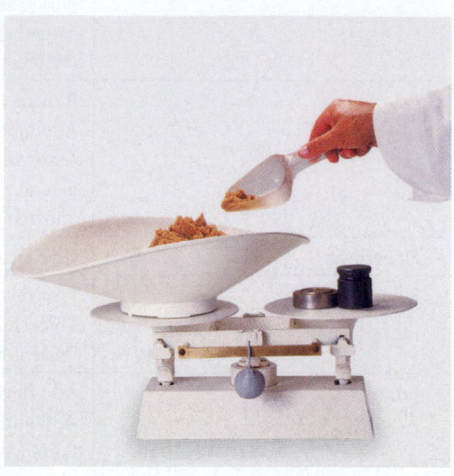

② Place the ingredient on the left side of the scale until the two platforms are balanced.

Baker's Percentage

Many formulas for baked goods, especially those for cookies, cakes and breads, list ingredients as a percentage in addition to, or in place of, a specific weight or volume measurement. Percentages make accurate formula conversions possible and are a convenient type of shorthand. Simply by considering the percentages in formulas, bakers who are familiar with the function of ingredients can tell at a glance how rich, moist or crisp a finished product will be. For example, a cookie dough with a high percentage (ratio) of fat in relation to flour will bake into a more crumbly pastry than cookie dough containing a lower percentage of fat. When formulas list ingredients in proportion to other ingredients, the experienced baker can select formulas with the proper ratios for the product desired.

The percentage formula most commonly used in the bakeshop is the **baker's percentage**. When using baker's percentage, the quantity of each ingredient is expressed as *a percentage of the total amount of flour* used in the formula. The weights of all the ingredients must be in the same unit of measure, such as ounces, grams, pounds or kilos. (The examples in this chapter use ounces, but baker's percentage is used for metric weights as well.) The flour in the formula is always 100%. If a formula calls for two or more types of flour, the total of all the flours must equal 100%. A formula that does not contain flour, such as a custard or cake frosting, is not given in baker's percentages.

Baker's percentage is included in bakeshop formulas in Chapter 31, Quick Breads, through Chapter 35, Custards, Creams, Frozen Desserts and Sauces, only when flour is a primary ingredient. In formulas in which baker's percentage is used, the percentages are what dictate the quantity of ingredients in either the U.S. or metric column. The metric ingredient measurements are not always exact equivalents of the U.S. ingredient measurement. Quantities may be rounded to the nearest whole number to make the formulas usable. An exception is made for significant ingredients when their weight is less than 5% of the weight of flour.

baker's percentage a system for measuring ingredients in a formula by expressing ingredient weights as a percentage of the total flour weight

Calculating Baker's Percentage

To calculate the baker's percentage in a formula:

Step 1 Identify the weight of the flour in the formula. This weight is 100%.

Step 2 Assure that the weights of all ingredients are given in the same unit of measure.

Step 3 Divide the weight of each of the other ingredients in the formula by the weight of the flour.

$$\text{Weight of Ingredient} \div \text{Weight of Flour}$$

Step 4 Multiply the number obtained by 100% to calculate the baker's percentage for each ingredient.

$$\text{Weight of Ingredient} \div \text{Weight of Flour} \times 100\% = \text{Baker's Percentage of Ingredient}$$

$$\frac{\text{Weight of Ingredient}}{\text{Weight of Flour}} \times 100 = \text{B.P.}$$

EXAMPLE 30.1 Converting a Formula to Baker's Percentage

You need to convert the Sugar Cookie Dough formula in Figure 30.2 to baker's percentage so that it can be scaled up. Follow these steps to convert the formula:

Step 1 Determine the weight of the flour, which is 100%.

$$1 \text{ pound (16 ounces) of flour} = 100\%$$

Step 2 Divide the weight of the sugar by the weight of the flour.

$$6 \text{ ounces} \div 16 \text{ ounces} = 0.375$$

Step 3 Multiply the number obtained by 100 to obtain the baker's percentage for the sugar.

$$0.375 \times 100 = 37.5\%$$

Step 4 Calculate the baker's percentage for each of the remaining ingredients in the formula as outlined in Steps 1, 2 and 3.

$$\text{Butter: } 7 \div 16 = 0.437 \times 100 = 43.7\%$$

$$\text{Vanilla extract: } 1 \div 16 = 0.062 \times 100 = 6.2\%$$

Comparing Formulas Using Baker's Percentage

An experienced baker can tell at a glance that this sugar cookie with 43.7% butter will be more tender and crumbly than one made from a formula with just 20% butter. With 37.5% sugar, this cookie will be sweet and somewhat crisp but not as sweet and brittle as a similar cookie with 60% sugar. Baker's percentage makes it easy to compare formulas. Compare the Spritz Cookies on page 1022 and the Sugar Cookie Dough in Figure 30.2. Simply by reading the formula, you can tell that the Spritz Cookies with 80% butter are richer and more buttery than the Sugar Cookies with 43.7% butter.

Customizing a Formula Using Baker's Percentage

You can also more readily customize a formula by using percentages. Seeing that the vanilla extract in the Sugar Cookie Dough is 6.2%, we can see that adding 6% of another flavoring, ground nuts or chocolate chips will transform this cookie without significantly altering the texture of the finished product.

Sample Baker's Percentage Formula

This is an example of a formula written in baker's percentage. The column to the right indicates the relationship of all ingredients in this formula to the quantity of total flour in the formula. The total batch weight and baker's percentage can be used to scale a formula up or down.

SUGAR COOKIE DOUGH

Yield: 20 Cookies, 1½ oz. each

INGREDIENT	QUANTITY	BAKER'S PERCENTAGE
Flour	1 lb. (16 oz.)	100%
Granulated sugar	6 oz.	37.5%
Butter	7 oz.	43.7%
Vanilla extract	1 fl. oz.	6.2%
Total:	1 lb. 14 oz. (30 oz.)	187.4%

Figure 30.2 Sample baker's percentage formula.

Increasing (or Decreasing) a Formula's Yield Using Baker's Percentage

In a formula that is in baker's percentage, the relationship or ratio of ingredients remains constant, making it very easy to scale the formula up or down. To increase (or decrease) a formula's yield using baker's percentage, first determine the new formula yield. Then divide the total baker's percentage for the original formula by 100 to obtain a baker's percentage conversion factor. Multiply the new formula yield by the conversion factor to determine the quantity of flour needed for the new scaled formula. Once you determine the total amount of flour, it is straightforward to calculate the quantities of other ingredients in the formula. Determine the remaining ingredient quantities by multiplying the new flour weight by the baker's percentage for each ingredient.

To scale a formula:

Step 1   Determine the new formula yield required. Converting the total yield from pounds (kilograms) to ounces (grams) ensures accuracy.

Step 2   Divide the total baker's percentage for the original formula by 100 to obtain the baker's percentage (B.P.) conversion factor for the formula.

$$\text{Total Baker's Percentage} \div 100 = \text{B.P. Conversion Factor}$$

Step 3   Divide the new formula yield by the B.P conversion factor.

$$\text{New Formula Yield} \div \text{B.P. Conversion Factor} = \text{Quantity of Flour for New Formula}$$

Step 4   Calculate the quantity of other ingredients required by multiplying the baker's percentage for each ingredient by the new flour weight.

$$\frac{\text{Total Baker's Percentage}}{100} = \text{B.P. Conversion Factor}$$

$$\frac{\text{New Formula Yield}}{\text{B.P.C.F}} = \text{New Flour Quantity}$$

EXAMPLE 30.2 Increasing (or Decreasing) a Formula's Yield Using Baker's Percentage

The formula for Sugar Cookie Dough yields 20 cookies at 1.5 ounces each (20 cookies × 1.5 ounces = 30 ounces of dough). You need 48 cookies weighing 1.5 ounces each (48 cookies × 1.5 ounces = 72 ounces of dough). See Figure 30.3.

Increasing (or Decreasing) Formula Yield Using Baker's Percentage
SUGAR COOKIE DOUGH

Yield: _20 Cookies, 1½ oz. each_   New Yield: _48 Cookies, 1½ oz. each_

INGREDIENT	ORIGINAL QUANTITY	BAKER'S PERCENTAGE	NEW QUANTITY	ROUNDED
Flour	1 pound (16 oz.)	100%	38.4 oz.	39 oz.
Granulated sugar	6 oz.	37.5%	14.4 oz.	14 oz.
Butter	7 oz.	43.7%	16.8 oz.	17 oz.
Vanilla extract	1 fl. oz.	6.2%	2.3 fl. oz.	2 fl. oz.
Total:	1 lb. 14 oz. (30 oz.)	187.4%	71.9 oz. 72 oz.	72 oz. (4 lb. 8 oz.)

Figure 30.3 Increasing (or decreasing) formula yield using baker's percentage. Note that the weight of ingredients may be rounded to make scaling more efficient.

Follow these steps to convert the formula:

Step 1   Calculate the new formula yield.

$$4.5 \text{ lb.} \times 16 \text{ oz./lb.} = 72 \text{ oz.}$$

Step 2   Divide the total baker's percentage for the original formula by 100 to obtain the baker's percentage conversion factor for the formula.

$$187.4 \div 100 = 1.874$$

Step 3   Divide the new formula yield by the B.P. conversion factor.

$$72 \text{ oz.} \div 1.874 = 38.42 \text{ oz. flour}$$

Step 4   Calculate the quantity of other ingredients required by multiplying the new flour weight by the baker's percentage for each ingredient.

$$\text{Sugar: } 38.42 \text{ oz.} \times 37.5\% = 14.4 \text{ oz.}$$
$$\text{Butter: } 38.42 \text{ oz.} \times 43.7\% = 16.8 \text{ oz.}$$
$$\text{Vanilla extract: } 38.42 \text{ oz.} \times 6.2\% = 2.3 \text{ fl. oz.}$$

Note that you may round the weight of ingredients to make scaling more efficient.

MIXING METHODS

A critical step in the production of all baked goods is mixing the ingredients. The techniques used to mix or combine ingredients affect the baked good's final volume, appearance and texture. Mixing distributes ingredients evenly. Mixing activates the proteins in wheat flour, causing the formation of gluten. Mixing incorporates air into (**aerates**) a mixture to help it rise and develop a light texture when baked. Different mixing methods ensure that ingredients are combined in the proper order to achieve the desired results.

There are several mixing methods—**beating**, **blending**, **creaming**, **cutting**, **folding**, **kneading**, **sifting**, **stirring** and **whipping**. See Table 30.5. Learn the differences among these mixing methods, then use the designated method with the appropriate equipment or tool to ensure a good-quality finished product.

Baked goods are made from doughs and batters. A **dough** has a low water content. The water-protein structure known as gluten forms the continuous medium into which other ingredients are embedded in a dough. A dough is usually prepared by beating, blending, cutting or kneading and is often stiff enough to cut into various shapes.

MIXING METHODS		TABLE 30.5
METHOD	PURPOSE	EQUIPMENT
Beating	Vigorously agitating foods to incorporate air or develop gluten	Spoon or electric mixer fitted with a paddle
Blending	Mixing two or more ingredients until evenly distributed	Spoon, rubber spatula, whisk or electric mixer fitted with a paddle
Creaming	Vigorously combining fat and sugar while incorporating air	Electric mixer fitted with a paddle on medium speed
Cutting	Incorporating solid fat into dry ingredients only until lumps of the desired size remain	Pastry cutters, fingers or electric mixer fitted with a paddle
Folding	Very gently incorporating ingredients such as whipped cream or whipped eggs with dry ingredients, a batter or cream	Rubber spatula or balloon whisk
Kneading	Working a dough to develop gluten	Hands or electric mixer fitted with a dough hook; if done by hand, the dough must be vigorously and repeatedly folded and turned in a rhythmic pattern
Sifting	Passing one or more dry ingredients through a wire mesh to remove lumps and combine and aerate	Rotary or drum sifter or mesh strainer
Stirring	Gently mixing ingredients by hand until evenly distributed and blended	Spoon, whisk or rubber spatula
Whipping	Beating vigorously to incorporate air	Whisk or electric mixer fitted with a whip; whipping siphon

A **batter** generally contains more liquids, fat, and sugar than a dough. Gluten development is minimized and liquid forms the continuous medium in which other ingredients are dispersed. A batter bakes into softer, moister products. A batter is usually prepared by blending, creaming, stirring or whipping and is generally thin enough to pour.

THE BAKING PROCESS

Many changes occur in a dough or batter as it bakes. A pourable liquid solidifies into a tender, light cake; a sticky mass becomes chewy cookies; a soft, elastic dough becomes firm, crusty French bread. These physical changes are the result of the ingredients used, the mixing methods employed and the effect of heat during the baking process. During baking, gases form and are trapped within the dough or batter; starches, proteins and sugars cook; fats melt; moisture evaporates and staling begins.

By learning to control these changes, the student baker also learns to control the final product. Control can be exerted in the selection of ingredients and the methods by which those ingredients are combined as well as the baking temperature and duration. Batters and dough pass through nine stages during and after the baking process. Each step is described and discussed in the following sections.

Gases Form

A baked good's final texture is determined by the amount of leavening or rise that occurs both before and during baking. This rise is caused by the gases present in the dough or batter. These gases are carbon dioxide, air and steam. See Table 30.6. Air and carbon dioxide are present in doughs and batters before they are heated. (Air may be incorporated during the mixing process. Carbon dioxide is released as a by-product of leaveners used in the mixture.) Other gases form when heat is applied. For example, steam is created as the moisture in a dough is heated and yeast and baking powder release additional carbon dioxide in a hot oven. These gases expand and leaven the product.

Gases Are Trapped

The stretchable network of proteins, either egg proteins or gluten, created in a batter or dough traps gases in the product. Without an appropriate network of proteins, the gases would just escape without causing the dough or batter to rise.

Starches Gelatinize

Starches are complex carbohydrates present in plants and grains such as potatoes, wheat, rice and corn. Flour made from these and other grains is the primary ingredient in most baked goods. When starch granules in a batter or dough reach a temperature of approximately 150°F (65°C), they absorb additional moisture—up to 10 times their own weight—and expand. This contributes to the baked good's structure. (See Figure 10.3.)

Proteins Coagulate

Gluten and dairy and egg proteins begin to coagulate (solidify) when the dough or batter reaches a temperature of 140°F (60°C). This process provides most of the baked good's structure. (See Figure 10.2.)

GASES THAT LEAVEN BAKED GOODS	TABLE 30.6
GAS	**PRESENT IN**
Air	All products, especially those containing whipped eggs or creamed fat
Steam	All products when liquids evaporate or fats melt
Carbon dioxide	Products containing baking soda, baking powder, baking ammonia or yeast

Proper baking temperatures are important for controlling the point at which proteins coagulate. If the temperature is too high, proteins will solidify before the gases in the product have expanded fully, resulting in a product with poor texture and volume. If the temperature is too low, gases will escape before the proteins coagulate, resulting in a product that may collapse.

Fats Melt

As fats melt, steam is released and fat droplets are dispersed throughout the product. These fat droplets coat the starch (flour) granules, thus moistening and tenderizing the product by keeping the gluten strands short. Shortenings melt at different temperatures. It is important to select a fat with the proper melting point for the product being prepared.

Water Evaporates

Throughout the baking process, the water contained in the liquid ingredients turns to steam and evaporates. This steam is a useful leavener. As steam is released, the dough or batter dries out starting from the outside, and the result is the formation of a crust.

Sugars Caramelize

As sugars are heated above 250°F (121°C) they begin to brown. At 320°F (160°C), they caramelize, adding flavor and causing the product to darken. Caramelization of sugars is responsible for most of the flavors associated with baked goods. Because high temperatures are required for caramelization, most foods brown only on the outside and only through the application of dry heat. (See Chapter 10, Principles of Cooking.)

Carryover Baking

The physical changes in a baked good do not stop when it is removed from the oven. The residual heat contained in the hot baking pan and within the product itself continues the baking process as the product cools. This is why a crisp-style cookie or biscuit may be soft and seem a bit underbaked when removed from the oven; it will finish baking as it cools.

As a baked product cools, other noticeable changes take place. At first, these changes yield pleasing characteristics. Fats resolidify, causing the product to firm. Sugars recrystallize, giving a pleasant crunchiness to the crust of a cookie, for example. When these changes become unpleasantly noticeable, a product is considered stale.

Staling

Staling is a change in a baked good's texture and aroma caused by both moisture loss and changes in the structure of the starch granules. Stale products have lost their fresh aroma and are firmer, drier and more crumbly than fresh goods.

Staling is not just a general loss of moisture into the atmosphere; it is also a change in the location and distribution of water molecules within the product. This process, known as **starch retrogradation**, occurs as starch molecules cool, becoming more dense and expelling moisture.

In breads, this moisture migrates from the interior to the drier crust, causing the crust to become tough and leathery. If the product is not well wrapped, moisture will escape completely into the surrounding air. In humid conditions, unwrapped bread crusts absorb moisture from the atmosphere, resulting in the same loss of crispness. The flavor and texture of breads can be revived by reheating them to approximately 140°F (60°C), the temperature at which starch gelatinization occurs. Usually products can be reheated only once without causing additional quality loss.

The retrogradation process is temperature dependent. It occurs most rapidly at temperatures of approximately 40°F (4°C). Therefore baked products should not be refrigerated unless they contain perishable components such as cream fillings. It is better to store products frozen or at room temperature, as long as food safety is not of concern.

Products containing fats and sugars, which retain moisture, tend to stay fresh longer. Commercial bakeries usually add chemical emulsifiers, modified shortening or special sweeteners to retard staling, but these additives are not as practical for small-scale production.

starch retrogradation the process whereby starch molecules in a batter or dough lose moisture after baking; the result is baked goods that are dry or stale

QUESTIONS FOR DISCUSSION

1. What is the importance of protein in flour for bread making? Name the general types of flours and their uses in the bakeshop.

2. What is gluten? How is it created and how can you, as the baker, control proper gluten formation?

3. Discuss the four functions of sugar and sweeteners in baked goods.

4. What precautions should be taken when cooking sugar syrups or caramelizing sugar?

5. Many varieties of fat and shortening are available to today's baker and pastry chef. Discuss which fats are preferred for various bakeshop applications.

6. Name two chemical leavening agents and explain how they cause batters and doughs to rise. Describe the role of leavening agents in baked goods. Explain why baking soda is used with an acid in baked goods.

7. Use the Internet to locate a U.S. producer of European-style pastry ingredients. What type of flavorings and nut products do they produce and market?

8. Discuss the various mixing methods and the tools used for each method.

9. List and describe the nine stages in the baking process.

10. Explain the process that causes staling. List ways to minimize staling of breads and cakes.

11. List and describe one piece of heavy equipment and two smallware items that are commonly used in bakeries but not in culinary kitchens.

Quick Breads 31

crumb the interior of bread or cake; may be elastic, aerated, fine grained or coarse grained

---

Biscuits and Scones: A Genealogy

Biscuit is a French word used to describe any dry, flat cake, whether sweet or savory. It was, perhaps, originally coined to describe twice-baked cakes (*bis* = twice, *cuit* = cooked). Crusader chronicles, for example, mention soldiers eating a "bread called 'bequis' because it is cooked twice" and still today a French product called Reims biscuit is returned to the oven for further baking after it is removed from its tin.

Over the centuries, the French began to use the term *biscuit* generically and appended modifiers to identify the particular type of dry, flat cake. For example, a *biscuit de guerre* was the very hard, barely risen product of flour and water used from the time of the Crusades to the era of Louis XIV as an army ration (*guerre* is French for "war"); *biscuit de Savoie* is a savory spongecake; *biscuit de pâtisserie* is a sweet biscuit.

To the British, a biscuit is what Americans call a cracker or cookie. There appears to be no British quick bread quite comparable to the American biscuit—the closest relative would be the scone. Because a scone contains eggs and butter, it is much richer than a biscuit, however.

Buttermilk biscuits, blueberry muffins, banana nut bread and currant scones are all quick breads. They are called quick breads because they are quick to make and quick to bake. With only a few basic ingredients almost any food service operation can provide its customers with fresh muffins, biscuits, scones and loaf breads. The variety of ingredients for quick breads is virtually limitless: Cornmeal, whole wheat, fruits, nuts, spices and vegetables all yield popular products. And the appeal of these products is not limited to breakfast service—quick breads are equally appropriate for lunch, snacks and buffets.

Quick breads are made with chemical leavening agents, especially baking soda and baking powder, which are explained in Chapter 30, Principles of the Bakeshop. This sets quick breads apart from breads that are made with yeast and require additional time for fermentation and proofing. Review the material on chemical leavening agents in Chapter 30, as understanding how these ingredients work is essential to successfully producing quick breads.

MIXING METHODS FOR QUICK BREADS

Quick breads are tender products, sometimes a bit flaky, but always with a soft **crumb** created by minimizing gluten development. This is possible because quick bread formulas generally contain some type of fat, which shortens gluten strands, and any wheat flour is mixed in swiftly and gently. Three mixing methods are used for preparing quick breads. These methods are also used for making other bakery items, such as pie crusts, high-fat cakes and brownies. Mastering these basic mixing techniques now will make your other baking experiences easier and more successful.

Quick breads are typically mixed by the **biscuit method**, the **muffin method** or the **creaming method**. The mixing method employed is directly related to the type and consistency of fat used in the recipe. Cold solid fats, such as butter, lard or vegetable shortening, are used in the biscuit method to produce flaky products. Liquid fats, such as oil or melted butter, are used in the muffin method to produce moist, tender products. Fats that are soft but not liquid are used in the high-fat creaming method. See Table 31.1.

QUICK BREAD MIXING TECHNIQUES		TABLE 31.1
MIXING TECHNIQUE	FAT	RESULT
Biscuit method	Solid (chilled)	Flaky dough
Muffin method	Liquid (oil or melted butter)	Soft, tender, cakelike texture
Creaming method	Softened (room temperature)	Rich, tender, cakelike texture

Biscuit Method

The biscuit method is used for biscuits, shortcakes and scones and is very similar to the technique used to make flaky pie doughs. The goal is to create a baked good that is light, flaky and tender. Flakiness is created by coating small pieces of fat with the dry ingredients in a process referred to as "cutting in" the fat. Similarly, the fat may be broken up into small pieces then incorporated into the flour by rubbing the fat between your fingertips. As these small flour-coated pieces of fat melt and release steam during baking, flaky layers are created.

Procedure for Preparing Products with the Biscuit Method

1   Preheat the oven. Measure all ingredients.

2   Sift the dry ingredients together.

3   Cut or rub in the fat, which should be in a solid form.

4   Combine the liquid ingredients, including any eggs.

5   Add the liquid ingredients to the dry ingredients. Mix just until the ingredients are combined. Do not overmix, as this causes toughness and inhibits the product's rise.

6   Place the dough on the workbench and knead it lightly 5 or 6 times (approximately 20–30 seconds). The dough should be soft and slightly elastic, but not sticky. Too much kneading toughens the biscuits. Use a slow speed and a short mixing time when kneading biscuit dough in a mixer.

7   The dough is now ready for **make-up** and baking.

make-up the cutting, shaping and forming of dough products before baking

Procedure for Make-Up of Biscuit-Method Products

1   Roll out the dough on a floured surface to a thickness of ½–¾ inch (1.2–1.8 centimeters). Be careful to roll the dough evenly. Biscuits should double in height during baking.

2   Cut dough into the desired shapes using a sharp knife or shaped cutters. Press straight down; do not twist the cutters, as this inhibits rise. Space cuts as close together as possible to minimize scraps.

3   Position the biscuits on a lightly greased or paper-lined sheet pan. If placed with sides nearly touching, the biscuits will rise higher and have softer sides. Place farther apart for crusty sides.

4   Reworking and rerolling the dough may result in tough, misshapen biscuits. Nevertheless it may be possible to reroll scraps once by pressing the dough together gently without kneading.

5   Brush tops with egg wash before baking or with melted butter after baking. Bake immediately in a hot oven.

6   Cool the finished products on a wire rack.

Country Biscuits

YIELD 36 Biscuits, 2¼ oz. (66 g) each		METHOD Biscuit	
All-purpose flour	2 lb. 8 oz.	1.2 kg	100%
Salt	0.75 oz.	24 g	2%
Granulated sugar	2 oz.	60 g	5%
Baking powder	2 oz.	60 g	5%
Unsalted butter, cold	14 oz.	420 g	35%
Milk	24 fl. oz.	720 ml	60%
Total dough weight:	5 lb. 2 oz.	2484 g	207%

1 Sift together the dry ingredients (flour, salt, sugar and baking powder)

2 Cut in the butter. The mixture should look mealy; do not overmix.

3 Add the milk and stir, combining only until the mixture holds together.

4 Transfer the dough to a lightly floured work surface; knead until it forms one mass, approximately five or six kneadings.

5 Roll out the dough to a thickness of ½ inch (1.2 centimeters). Cut biscuits with a floured cutter and place them on a paper-lined sheet pan.

6 Bake at 425°F (220°C) until biscuit tops are light brown, the sides almost white and the interiors still moist, approximately 10–12 minutes. Internal heat will continue to cook the biscuits after they are removed from the oven.

7 Remove the biscuits to a wire rack to cool.

Approximate values per 2¼-oz. (66-g) biscuit: **Calories** 210, **Total fat** 10 g, **Saturated fat** 6 g, **Cholesterol** 25 mg, **Sodium** 240 mg, **Total carbohydrates** 27 g, **Protein** 4 g, **Vitamin A** 10%

1 Sifting the dry ingredients together.

2 Cutting in the fat.

3 Kneading the dough.

4 Cutting the biscuits.

Figure 31.1 Properly mixed corn muffins (left) rise evenly and show no signs of tunneling. Improperly mixed corn muffins (right) rise unevenly and have large irregular holes.

Muffin Method

Muffins are any small, cakelike baked good made in a muffin tin (pan). Batters are prepared using either the muffin method or the creaming method, described below. These batters can be used for any size muffin, from bite-sized miniatures to jumbo muffins. The same batters are also used for loaf breads. For example, banana muffin batter may be baked in a loaf pan to produce banana bread, provided the baking time is altered. A pourable, more liquid muffin method batter is used to prepare waffles, pancakes and crêpes, variations on quick breads that are discussed in Chapter 21, Eggs and Breakfast.

When preparing baked goods by the muffin method, the goal is to produce a tender product with an even shape and an even distribution of fruits, nuts or other ingredients. The most frequent problem encountered with muffin-method products is overmixing. This causes toughness and may cause holes to form inside the baked product, a condition known as **tunneling**, illustrated in Figure 31.1.

tunneling large tubular holes in muffins and cakes, a defect caused by improper mixing

Procedure for Preparing Products with the Muffin Method

1 Preheat the oven. Measure all ingredients.
2 Sift the dry ingredients together.
3 Combine the liquid ingredients, including melted fat or oil. Melted butter or shortening may resolidify when combined with the other liquids; this is not a cause for concern.
4 Add the liquid ingredients to the dry ingredients and stir just until combined. Do not overmix. The batter will be lumpy.
5 The batter is now ready for make-up and baking.

Procedure for Make-Up of Muffin-Method Products

1 Grease muffin pans or loaf pans with butter, shortening or commercial pan grease. Paper liners may be used instead of greasing and will prevent sticking if the batter contains fruits or vegetables.
2 A portion scoop is a useful tool for ensuring uniform-sized muffins. Be careful not to drip or spill batter onto the edge of the muffin tins; it will burn and cause sticking.
3 Allow muffins and loaf breads to cool for several minutes before attempting to remove them from the pan.
4 Cool the finished products on a wire rack.

Blueberry Muffins

MISE EN PLACE

- Preheat oven to 350°F (180°C).
- Melt butter.
- Zest lemon.
- Grease or line muffin tins.

The batter used for these blueberry muffins is versatile and can be used to create many varieties of muffins. Substitute blackberries, diced apples, diced bananas, diced pears, raspberries or sliced strawberries for the blueberries in this batter. Omit the blueberries and stir in 3 ounces (90 grams) chocolate chips or diced nuts or 2 ounces (60 grams) diced dried fruit. Use buttermilk or coconut milk in place of the milk. After baking, the muffins can be cooled then glazed or dipped in cinnamon sugar. For richer, more tender muffins, increase the butter in the batter to 4 ounces (120 grams) if desired. The additional butter is recommended when baking this batter in a loaf pan.

YIELD 12 Muffins, 2½ oz. (75 g) each		METHOD Muffin		
All-purpose flour	8 oz.		240 g	100%
Granulated sugar	5 oz.		150 g	62.5%
Baking powder	0.35 oz. (2½ tsp.)		10 ml	4.3%
Salt	0.05 oz. (¼ tsp.)		1.5 g	0.6%
Eggs	3.3 oz. (2 eggs)		98 g	41%
Milk	8 fl. oz.		240 ml	100%
Unsalted butter, melted	2 oz.		60 g	25%
Vanilla extract	0.15 fl. oz. (1 tsp.)		5 ml	1.8%
Blueberries	5 oz.		150 g	62.5%
Lemon zest, grated	0.2 oz. (1 Tbsp.)		6 g	2.5%
Total batter weight:	2 lb.		960 g	400.2%

1 Sift together the dry ingredients (flour, sugar, baking powder, salt).

2 Stir together the liquid ingredients (eggs, milk, melted butter, vanilla extract).

3 Stir the liquid mixture into the dry ingredients. Do not overmix. The batter should be lumpy.

4 Gently fold in the blueberries and lemon zest.

5 Portion into greased or paper-lined muffin tins and bake at 350°F (180°C) until light brown and set in the center, approximately 18 minutes.

6 Cool the muffins in the pan for several minutes before removing.

Variations:

Cranberry Orange Muffins—Substitute fresh orange zest for the lemon zest and 4 ounces (120 grams/50%) dried cranberries for the blueberries.

Pecan Spice Muffins—Omit the blueberries and lemon zest. Add 4 ounces (120 grams/50%) chopped pecans, 0.04 oz. (½ teaspoon/1 gram/0.5%) cinnamon and 0.02 oz. (¼ teaspoon/0.5 gram/0.2%) each nutmeg and ground ginger to the batter.

❶ Combining the liquid ingredients.

❷ Folding in the blueberries.

❸ Portioning the batter.

Cinnamon Sugar Muffins—Omit the blueberries and lemon zest. Add 0.04 oz. (½ teaspoon/ 1 gram/0.5%) cinnamon and 0.02 oz. (¼ teaspoon/0.5 gram/0.2%) ground nutmeg to the batter. While the muffins bake, combine 10 ounces (300 grams) granulated sugar and 0.6 ounces (3 tablespoons/36 grams) ground cinnamon. Melt 8 ounces (240 grams) butter. Dip the tops of the baked, cooled muffins in the melted butter then into the cinnamon sugar.

Approximate values per 2½-oz. (75-g) muffin: **Calories** 180, **Total fat** 6 g, **Saturated fat** 3 g, **Cholesterol** 50 mg, **Sodium** 150 mg, **Total carbohydrates** 29 g, **Protein** 4 g

Creaming Method

The creaming method is comparable to the mixing method used for many butter cakes. In fact, many butter cake recipes may be baked in muffin pans and served as muffins or cupcakes. The softened fat (butter, margarine or vegetable shortening) and granulated sugar should be properly creamed to incorporate air, which helps leaven the product as it bakes. The final product is cakelike, with a fine texture. There is less danger of over-mixing with this method because the higher fat content shortens gluten strands and tenderizes the batter.

Procedure for Preparing Products with the Creaming Method

1 Preheat the oven. Measure all ingredients.

2 Sift the dry ingredients together.

3 Combine the softened fat and sugar in a mixer bowl. Cream on low speed until the color lightens and the mixture fluffs.

4 Add eggs gradually, mixing well.

5 Add the dry and liquid ingredients to the creamed fat alternately. In other words, a portion of the flour is added to the fat and incorporated, then a portion of the liquid is added and incorporated. Repeat these steps until all the liquid and dry ingredients are incorporated. By adding the liquid and dry ingredients alternately, you avoid overmixing the batter and prevent the butter and sugar mixture from curdling.

6 The batter is now ready for make-up and baking. Panning and baking procedures are the same as those for quick breads prepared with the muffin method.

Sour Cream Muffins

MISE EN PLACE

- Allow butter and eggs to come to room temperature.
- Preheat oven to 350°F (180°C).
- Grease or line muffin tins.

YIELD 12 Muffins, 3¼ oz. (100 g) each   **METHOD** Creaming

All-purpose flour	10 oz.	300 g	100%
Baking powder	0.14 oz. (1 tsp.)	4 g	1.4%
Baking soda	0.14 oz. (1 tsp.)	4 g	1.4%
Salt	0.2 oz. (1 tsp.)	4 g	2%
Unsalted butter, room temperature	8 oz.	240 g	80%
Granulated sugar	8 oz.	240 g	80%
Eggs, lightly beaten	3.3 oz. (2 eggs)	100 g	33%
Sour cream	10 oz.	300 g	100%
Vanilla extract	0.15 fl. oz. (1 tsp.)	5 ml	1.5%
Total batter weight:	2 lb. 7 oz.	1199 g	399%

1 Sift together the dry ingredients (flour, baking powder, baking soda and salt).

2 Cream the butter and sugar until light and fluffy. Stir the eggs in one at a time.

3 Stir the dry ingredients and sour cream, alternately, into the butter mixture in three additions. Stir in the vanilla extract.

4 Portion the batter into greased muffin tins and bake at 350°F (180°C) until light brown and set, approximately 20 minutes.

5 Allow the muffins to cool briefly in the pan before removing.

Variations:

streusel a crumbly mixture of fat, flour, sugar and sometimes nuts and spices, used to top baked goods

Sour cream muffins can be topped with **streusel** or flavored with a wide variety of fruits or nuts by adding approximately 4–6 ounces (1 cup/120–180 grams/40–60%) fresh or frozen drained fruit to the batter. Blueberries, dried cherries, candied fruits, pecans and diced pears yield popular products. To make basic spice muffins, add 0.04 ounces (½ teaspoon/1 gram/0.3%) each of ground cinnamon and nutmeg.

Approximate values per 3¼-oz. (100-g) muffin: **Calories** 290, **Total fat** 17 g, **Saturated fat** 10 g, **Cholesterol** 70 mg, **Sodium** 260 mg, **Total carbohydrates** 31 g, **Protein** 4 g, **Vitamin A** 15%

❶ Creaming the butter and sugar.

❷ Adding the sour cream.

❸ Topping the muffins with the streusel.

Streusel Topping

YIELD 4 lb. 11 oz. (2.25 kg)

All-purpose flour	2 lb.	960 g	100%
Cinnamon, ground	0.14 oz. (2 tsp.)	4 g	0.4%
Salt	0.4 oz. (2 tsp.)	12 g	1.25%
Brown sugar	11 oz.	336 g	35%
Granulated sugar	8 oz.	240 g	25%
Unsalted butter, cold	1 lb. 8 oz.	720 g	75%
Total weight:	4 lb. 11 oz.	2272 g	236%

1 Combine the dry ingredients (flour, cinnamon, salt and sugars). Cut in the butter until the mixture is coarse and crumbly.

2 Sprinkle on top of muffins or quick breads before baking. Streusel topping will keep for several weeks under refrigeration and may be frozen for longer storage. There is no need to thaw before use.

Approximate values per 1-oz. (30-g) serving: **Calories** 190, **Total fat** 8 g, **Saturated fat** 5 g, **Cholesterol** 20 mg, **Sodium** 45 mg, **Total carbohydrates** 29 g, **Protein** 2 g

QUALITIES OF QUICK BREADS

Quick breads are distinguished by their light and tender texture. Biscuits should have a crisp and level crust. They should rise evenly and have a light golden brown surface. Muffins and loaf breads made from muffin batter should be tender without visible tunneling. They should rise evenly to a uniform height and be slightly domed. The outer surface of loaf breads should have a thin crust that remains tender. Burned edges or a hard crust are signs of overbaking or baking at too high of a temperature. Quick breads can be frozen for up to three months if well wrapped. The best results will be achieved by quickly freezing quick breads in a single layer using a blast chiller. Frozen products can then be thawed at room temperature while still wrapped. Refer to Table 31.2 below to troubleshoot quick bread mixing and baking.

TROUBLESHOOTING CHART FOR QUICK BREADS		TABLE 31.2
PROBLEM	CAUSE	SOLUTION
Soapy or bitter flavor	Chemical leaveners not properly mixed into batter Too much baking soda	Sift chemicals with dry ingredients Adjust recipe
Elongated holes (tunneling)	Overmixing	Do not mix until smooth; mix only until moistened
Crust too thick	Too much sugar Oven temperature too low	Adjust recipe Adjust oven temperature
Flat top with only a small peak in center	Oven temperature too low	Adjust oven temperature
Cracked, uneven top	Oven temperature too high	Adjust oven temperature
No rise; dense product	Old batter Damaged leavening agents Overmixing	Bake promptly Store new chemicals properly Do not mix until smooth; mix only until moistened
Berries, nuts or other additions settle to the bottom of the pan	Not folded in properly	Stir into dry ingredients to coat with flour before adding liquids

QUESTIONS FOR DISCUSSION

1 List three common methods used for mixing quick breads. What is the significance of the type of fat used for each of these mixing methods?

2 What is the most likely explanation for discolored and bitter-tasting biscuits? What is the solution?

3 Explain what happens when muffin batter has been overmixed.

4 Visit the websites for King Arthur Flour and White Lily Foods to learn more about the varieties of flours and flavoring ingredients that are available for use in biscuits and muffins. What are each of these companies famous for? How do the products of these two regional flour manufacturers differ?

Additional Quick Bread Formulas

Chocolate Cherry Scones

Houston Community College, Houston, TX

Pastry Chef Eddy Van Damme

YIELD 24 Scones, approx. 4¼ oz. (130 g) each	METHOD Biscuit		
Unsalted butter, cold	14 oz.	420 g	44%
Granulated sugar	4 oz.	120 g	12.5%
Buttermilk	8 fl. oz.	240 ml	25%
Sour cream	1 lb.	480 g	50%
Salt	0.6 oz. (1 Tbsp.)	18 g	2%
Vanilla extract	0.5 fl. oz. (1 Tbsp.)	15 ml	1.5%
All-purpose or pastry flour	2 lb.	960 g	100%
Baking powder	2 oz.	60 g	6%
Dried cherries	1 lb.	480 g	50%
Chocolate chunks	9 oz.	270 g	28%
Powdered sugar	as needed	as needed	
Total dough weight:	6 lb. 6 oz.	3063 g	319%

1 Chill a mixer bowl and paddle attachment in the freezer for at least 15 minutes before mixing.

2 Cut the butter into 1-inch (6-millimeter) cubes. Set aside in the refrigerator.

3 Whisk together the sugar, buttermilk, sour cream, salt and vanilla extract in a bowl until smooth. Set aside in the refrigerator.

4 Put the flour and baking powder in the chilled mixer bowl. Place the butter on top. Mix on low speed using the paddle attachment until the mixture resembles coarse meal.

5 Add the buttermilk mixture to the dry ingredients and mix very briefly, until just combined. Mix in the cherries and chocolate until just combined.

6 Scale the dough into three uniform pieces. On a lightly floured surface, press each piece of dough out into an 8-inch (20.5-centimeter) disk using a metal torte ring or other form as a guide.

7 Cut each disk of dough into eight wedges. Position the wedges of dough spaced 2 inches (5 centimeters) apart on parchment-lined baking sheets. Bake at 375°F (190°C) until light golden brown, approximately 18–24 minutes. When cool, dust with powdered sugar if desired.

Variation:

Cinnamon Orange Scones—Omit the sun-dried cherries and chocolate chunks. Add 0.5 ounce (2 tablespoons/15 grams/1.5%) ground cinnamon and 0.2 ounce (1 tablespoon/6 grams/0.6%) grated orange zest in Step 3. Yield is reduced to 4 pounds 15 ounces (2313 grams).

Approximate values per 4¼-oz. (130-g) scone: **Calories** 430, **Total fat** 21 g, **Saturated fat** 13 g, **Cholesterol** 45 mg, **Sodium** 550 mg, **Total carbohydrates** 58 g, **Protein** 6 g, **Vitamin A** 25%, **Calcium** 20%, **Iron** 15%

❶ Mixing in the chilled butter.

❷ Adding the chilled buttermilk mixture.

❸ Placing the portioned dough on baking sheets.

Cream Scones

YIELD 24 Scones, 1½ oz. (45 g) each		METHOD Biscuit	
All-purpose flour	1 lb.	480 g	100%
Granulated sugar	1.5 oz.	43 g	9%
Baking powder	0.4 oz. (1 Tbsp.)	12 g	2.5%
Baking soda	0.14 g (1 tsp.)	4 g	0.9%
Salt	0.2 oz. (1 tsp.)	5 g	1%
Unsalted butter, cold	4 oz.	120 g	25%
Egg yolks	1.3 oz. (2 yolks)	40 g (2 yolks)	8%
Half-and-half	11 fl. oz.	330 ml	69%
Total dough weight:	2 lb. 2 oz.	1034 g	214%

1 Combine all ingredients using the biscuit method.

2 Roll out the dough to a thickness of approximately ½ inch (1.2 centimeters). Cut as desired.

3 Bake at 400°F (200°C) for approximately 10 minutes.

4 Brush the tops with butter while hot.

Variations:

Add 3 ounces (90 grams/0.18%) raisins, sultanas or currants to the dry ingredients.

Approximate values per 1½-oz. (45-g) scone: **Calories** 130, **Total fat** 6 g, **Saturated fat** 3.5 g, **Cholesterol** 35 mg, **Sodium** 160 mg, **Total carbohydrates** 17 g, **Protein** 3 g

♥ Good Choice

Morning Glory Muffins

YIELD 18 Large Muffins, 5 oz. (150 g) each		METHOD Muffin	
All-purpose flour	1 lb.	480 g	100%
Granulated sugar	18 oz.	540 g	112%
Baking soda	0.56 oz. (4 tsp.)	17 g	3.5%
Salt	0.6 oz. (1 Tbsp.)	18 g	3.7%
Cinnamon, ground	0.6 oz. (4 tsp.)	18 g	3.7%
Carrots, grated	14 oz.	420 g	87.5%
Raisins	6 oz.	180 g	37.5%
Pecan pieces	4 oz.	120 g	25%
Coconut, shredded	4 oz.	120 g	25%
Apple, unpeeled, grated	6 oz.	180 g	37.5%
Eggs	10 oz. (6 eggs)	300 g	62.5%
Corn oil	10.5 fl. oz.	315 ml	65.6%
Vanilla extract	0.6 fl. oz. (4 tsp.)	18 ml	3.7%
Total dough weight:	5 lb. 10 oz.	2726 g	567.2%

1 Sift the dry ingredients together and set aside.

2 Combine the carrots, raisins, pecans, coconut and apple.

3 Whisk together the eggs, oil and vanilla extract.

4 Toss the carrot mixture into the dry ingredients. Then add the liquid ingredients, stirring just until combined.

5 Bake in well-greased muffin tins at 350°F (180°C) until done, approximately 25 minutes.

Approximate values per 5-oz. (150-g) muffin: **Calories** 520, **Total fat** 27 g, **Saturated fat** 5 g, **Cholesterol** 70 mg, **Sodium** 310 mg, **Total carbohydrates** 63 g, **Protein** 6 g, **Vitamin A** 45%, **Claims**—good source of fiber

Basic Bran Muffins

♥ Good Choice

YIELD 24 Muffins, 2 oz. (60 g) each   **METHOD** Muffin

Wheat bran	6 oz.	180 g	50%
All-purpose flour	12 oz.	360 g	100%
Granulated sugar	4 oz.	120 g	30%
Baking powder	0.6 oz. (4 tsp.)	18 g	5%
Salt	0.2 oz. (1 tsp.)	6 g	1.6%
Milk	12 fl. oz.	360 ml	100%
Honey	3 oz.	90 g	25%
Molasses	3 oz.	90 g	25%
Eggs	3.3 oz. (2 eggs)	99 g	27.5%
Vanilla extract	0.15 fl. oz. (1 tsp.)	5 ml	1.2%
Unsalted butter, melted	4 oz.	120 g	30%
Total dough weight:	3 lb.	1450 g	395.3%

1 Combine all ingredients using the muffin method. Allow the batter to rest at least 30 minutes or up to 36 hours in the refrigerator so that all of the moisture is absorbed by the bran and the flour.

2 Scoop into greased or paper-lined muffin tins. Bake at 350°F (180°C) until lightly brown and firm, approximately 20 minutes.

Variations:

Up to 6 ounces (180 grams/50%) raisins or chopped nuts may be added to the batter if desired.

Approximate values per 2-oz. (60-g) muffin: **Calories** 170, **Total fat** 5 g, **Saturated fat** 2.5 g, **Cholesterol** 30 mg, **Sodium** 110 mg, **Total carbohydrates** 26 g, **Protein** 4 g, **Claims**—low sodium; good source of fiber

Lemon Poppy Seed Muffins

YIELD 48 Muffins, 2¾ oz. (83 g) each   **METHOD** Creaming

Pastry flour	2 lb.	960 g	80%
Bread flour	8 oz.	240 g	20%
Baking soda	0.14 oz. (1 tsp.)	4 g	0.3%
Baking powder	0.4 oz. (1 Tbsp.)	12 g	1%
Poppy seeds	3 oz.	90 g	7.5%
Unsalted butter, room temperature	1 lb.	480 g	40%
Granulated sugar	1 lb. 10 oz.	780 g	65%
Glucose or honey	4 fl. oz.	120 g	10%
Olive oil	4 fl. oz.	120 ml	10%
Eggs	20 oz. (12 eggs)	600 g	50%
Salt	0.4 oz. (2 tsp.)	12 g	1%
Vanilla extract	1 fl. oz.	30 ml	2.5%
Lemon zest, grated	0.5 oz. (1 Tbsp.)	15 g	1.25%
Sour cream	1 lb.	480 g	40%
Powdered sugar	as needed	as needed	
Total batter weight:	8 lb. 3 oz.	3935%	328%

1 Sift together the flours, baking soda and baking powder. Stir in the poppy seeds and set aside.

2 Using a mixer fitted with the paddle attachment, cream the butter until lump-free and fluffy. Add the sugar, glucose or honey and oil and blend until light.

3 Gradually add the eggs followed by the salt, vanilla extract, lemon zest and sour cream. Then stir in the sifted dry ingredients.

4 Portion the batter into 5-ounce (150-gram) portions using a scale or #6 scoop and place in greased or paper-lined muffin tins.

5 Bake at 425°F (220°C) until the centers of the muffins bounce back when lightly pressed, approximately 15–18 minutes. When cool, dust muffins with powdered sugar.

Approximate values per 2¾-oz. (83-g) muffin: **Calories** 580, **Total fat** 29 g, **Saturated fat** 14 g, **Cholesterol** 155 mg, **Sodium** 310 mg, **Total carbohydrates** 72 g, **Protein** 9 g, **Vitamin A** 15%, **Vitamin C** 15%

Irish Soda Bread

YIELD 1 Round Loaf, 8 in. (20 cm)		METHOD Muffin		
Currants	2 oz.	60 g	16.7%
Irish whiskey	1.5 fl. oz.	45 ml	12.5%
All-purpose flour, sifted	12 oz.	360 g	100%
Salt	0.2 oz. (1 tsp.)	6 g	1.6%
Baking powder	0.2 oz. (1½ tsp.)	6 g	1.6%
Baking soda	0.14 oz. (1 tsp.)	4 g	1.1%
Brown sugar	0.5 oz. (1 Tbsp.)	14 g	4.1%
Low-fat buttermilk	1 lb.	480 g	133%
Total batter weight:	2 lb.	975 g	270.5%

1 Soak the currants in the whiskey until plump, at least 1 hour.

2 Sift the dry ingredients together. Stir in the currants and whiskey.

3 Stir in the buttermilk, making a stiff batter.

4 Spread the batter in a greased 8-inch (20-centimeter) round cake pan. Bake at 350°F (180°C) until well browned and firm, approximately 30 minutes.

Approximate values per ⅒-loaf serving: **Calories** 150, **Total fat** 1 g, **Saturated fat** 0 g, **Cholesterol** 0 mg, **Sodium** 480 mg, **Total carbohydrates** 31 g, **Protein** 5 g, **Calcium** 10%, **Claims**—low fat; no cholesterol; no saturated fat

Basic Corn Muffins

YIELD 20 Muffins, 3¾ oz. (112 g) each		METHOD Muffin		
Yellow cornmeal	12 oz.	360 g	50%
All-purpose flour	12 oz.	360 g	50%
Granulated sugar	10 oz.	300 g	42%
Baking powder	0.4 oz. (1 Tbsp.)	12 g	1.6%
Baking soda	0.14 oz. (1 tsp.)	4 g	0.6%
Salt	0.15 oz. (¾ tsp.)	4 g	0.6%
Buttermilk	24 oz.	720 g	100%
Eggs	10 oz. (6 eggs)	300 g	42%
Unsalted butter, melted	6 oz.	180 g	25%
Total batter weight:	4 lb. 10 oz.	2244 g	311%

1 Combine all the ingredients using the muffin method.

2 Portion into greased muffin tins, filling two-thirds full.

3 Bake at 375°F (190°C) until done, approximately 20–25 minutes.

Variations:

Southern-Style Cornbread—Omit the sugar. Pour the batter into cast-iron skillets or molds that are preheated and well greased with shortening or bacon fat. Bake at 425°F (220°C) until golden.

Tijuana Cornbread—Add 0.2 oz. (1 tablespoon/6 g/0.8%) chilli powder and 0.07 oz. (1 teaspoon/2 grams/0.3%) ground cumin to the dry ingredients. Add 6 ounces (180 grams/25%) roasted Anaheim chiles and 6 ounces (180 grams/25%) shredded Cheddar cheese to the recipe when adding the liquid ingredients.

Approximate values per 3¾-oz. (112-g) muffin: **Calories** 180, **Total fat** 6 g, **Saturated fat** 3.5 g, **Cholesterol** 55 mg, **Sodium** 140 mg, **Total carbohydrates** 28 g, **Protein** 4 g

Flavorful Cornbread

Corn muffin batter is extremely versatile. Replace some of the cornmeal with blue or white varieties. Fold in cooked meats, diced fresh corn, other vegetables or shredded basil and herbs. Any type of grated cheese is a welcome addition. Bake the bread in timbale molds or loaf pans instead of traditional muffin tins. Adjust baking time if needed.

Zucchini Bread

YIELD 2 Loaves, 9 in. × 5 in. (24 cm × 12 cm) each	**METHOD** Muffin		
Eggs	5 oz. (3 eggs)	150 g	35.7%
Corn oil	8 fl. oz.	240 ml	57.2%
Granulated sugar	9 oz.	270 g	64.3%
Brown sugar	9 oz.	270 g	64.3%
Vanilla extract	0.15 fl. oz. (1 tsp.)	4 ml	1 %
Cinnamon, ground	0.14 oz. (2 tsp.)	4 g	1%
Salt	0.2 oz. (1 tsp.)	6 g	1.4%
Baking soda	0.07 oz. (½ tsp.)	2 g	0.5%
Baking powder	0.14 g (1 tsp.)	4 g	1%
All-purpose flour	14 oz.	420 g	100%
Zucchini, coarsely grated	11 oz.	330 g	78.6%
Pecans, chopped	4 oz.	120 g	28.6%
Total batter weight:	3 lb. 12 oz.	1820 g	433.6%

1 Combine all ingredients using the muffin method.

2 Bake in two greased loaf pans at 350°F (180°C), approximately 1 hour.

Approximate values per ½-loaf serving: **Calories** 270, **Total fat** 13 g, **Saturated fat** 1.5 g, **Cholesterol** 25 mg, **Sodium** 160 mg, **Total carbohydrates** 35 g, **Protein** 3 g

Hush Puppies (Deep-Fried Cornbread)

YIELD 60 Pieces, 2 in. (5 cm) each	**METHOD** Muffin		
Yellow cornmeal	1 lb.	480 g	66%
All-purpose flour	8 oz.	240 g	34%
Baking powder	0.4 oz. (1 Tbsp.)	12 g	1.6%
Salt	0.6 oz. (1 Tbsp.)	18 g	2.5%
Black pepper	0.2 oz. (1 Tbsp.)	6 g	0.8%
Granulated sugar	2 oz.	60 g	8%
Onions, minced	8 oz.	240 g	34%
Eggs	6.75 oz. (4 eggs)	200 g	28%
Milk	1 lb.	480 g	66%
Total batter weight:	3 lb. 10 oz.	1736 g	241%

1 Scooping the hush puppy batter into the deep-fat fryer.

1 Combine all ingredients using the muffin method.

2 Drop small scoops (using a #60 or #70 portion scoop) into deep fat at 375°F (190°C). Using the swimming method, deep-fry until golden brown.

3 Remove from the fat and drain. Serve immediately.

Approximate values per piece: **Calories** 70, **Total fat** 3 g, **Saturated fat** 1 g, **Cholesterol** 5 mg, **Sodium** 120 mg, **Total carbohydrates** 10 g, **Protein** 1 g

2 Draining the cooked Hush Puppies.

Sour Cream Coffeecake

YIELD 1 Tube Cake, 10 in. (25 cm)   **METHOD** Creaming

Filling:			
All-purpose flour	0.4 oz. (1½ Tbsp.)	12 g	5.7%
Cinnamon, ground	0.2 oz. (1 Tbsp.)	6 g	2.8%
Brown sugar	6 oz.	180 g	86%
Pecans, chopped	4 oz.	120 g	57%
Unsalted butter, melted	1 oz.	30 g	14%
Cake:			
Unsalted butter	4 oz.	120 g	57%
Granulated sugar	8 oz.	240 g	114%
Eggs	3.3 oz. (2 eggs)	100 g	47%
Sour cream	8 oz.	240 g	114%
Cake flour, sifted	7 oz.	210 g	100%
Salt	0.05 oz. (¼ tsp.)	1 g	0.7%
Baking powder	0.14 oz. (1 tsp.)	4 g	2%
Baking soda	0.14 oz. (1 tsp.)	4 g	2%
Vanilla extract	0.15 fl. oz. (1 tsp.)	5 ml	2.1%
Total batter weight:	2 lb. 10 oz.	1272 g	604%

1 To make the filling, blend all the filling ingredients together in a small bowl. Set aside.

2 To make the cake batter, cream the butter and sugar. Add the eggs one at a time, beating well after each addition. Add the sour cream. Stir until smooth.

3 Sift the sifted flour, salt, baking powder and baking soda together twice. Stir into the batter. Stir in the vanilla extract.

4 Spoon half of the batter into a greased 10-inch (25-centimeter) tube pan. Top with half of the filling. Cover the filling with the remaining batter and top with the remaining filling. Bake at 350°F (180°C) for approximately 35 minutes.

Approximate values per ¹⁄₁₆-cake serving: **Calories** 240, **Total fat** 13 g, **Saturated fat** 6 g, **Cholesterol** 40 mg, **Sodium** 130 mg, **Total carbohydrates** 29 g, **Protein** 2 g

Yeast Breads 32

After studying this chapter, you will be able to:

- select appropriate types of yeast and use yeast properly

- perform the 10 steps involved in yeast bread production

- mix yeast doughs using the straight dough method and the sponge method

- describe and use basic shaping techniques

- prepare rolled-in yeast doughs for making sweet or savory products

- bake a variety of breads from lean, rich and rolled-in yeast doughs

artisan a person who works in a skilled craft or trade; one who works with his or her hands; applied to bread bakers, cheese makers, confectioners, charcutiers and other craftspeople who prepare foods using traditional methods

leavener an ingredient or process that produces or incorporates gases in a baked product in order to increase volume, provide structure and give texture

fermentation the process by which yeast converts sugar into alcohol and carbon dioxide; the term also refers to the time that yeast dough is left to rise—that is, the time it takes for carbon dioxide gas cells to form and become trapped in the gluten network

Bread making is an art that dates back to ancient times. Over the centuries, bakers have learned to manipulate the basic ingredients—flour, water, salt and leavening—to produce a vast variety of breads. Thin-crusted baguettes, tender Parker House rolls, crisp flatbreads and chewy bagels derive from careful selection and handling of the same key ingredients. Chefs' and customers' interest in the traditional craft of baking has led to many **artisan** bread bakeries opening in recent years. Customers are demanding and more restaurants are serving exciting bread assortments to their guests with each meal.

Yeast breads can be divided into two major categories: lean doughs and rich doughs. **Lean doughs**, such as those used for crusty French and Italian breads, contain little or no sugar or fat. Traditional sourdough and rye breads are lean doughs that require special handling to bring out their unique flavor. **Enriched doughs**, such as brioche and challah, contain significantly more sugar and fat than lean doughs. **Laminated** or **rolled-in doughs**, so called because the fat is rolled into the dough in layers, are a type of rich dough used for baked goods such as croissants and sweetened Danish pastries.

This chapter covers the basic production techniques for making lean, sourdough and other yeast-raised products. It may help you to review the discussion of the functions of ingredients found in Chapter 30, Principles of the Bakeshop, before beginning this chapter.

YEAST

Yeast breads are made from dough prepared with yeast. Under the right conditions, yeast acts as a **leavener** in dough, causing the dough to rise and become less dense. Yeast is a living organism: a one-celled fungus. Various strains of yeast are naturally present everywhere and are an essential component to life on Earth. Yeast cells are in the air and soil, even in deep seas; in animal intestines and on the skin of berries and peaches; in every part of the world, including arctic glaciers and the Gobi desert. Yeast feeds on carbohydrates present in the starches and sugars in bread dough, converting these carbohydrates into carbon dioxide and ethyl alcohol, in an organic process known as **fermentation**:

$$\text{Yeast} + \text{Carbohydrates} = \text{Ethyl Alcohol} + \text{Carbon Dioxide}$$

When yeast releases carbon dioxide gas during bread making, the gas becomes trapped in the dough's gluten network. (See Chapter 30, Principles of the Bakeshop.) The trapped gas leavens the bread, providing the desired rise and texture. The small amount of alcohol produced by fermentation evaporates during baking.

Like most living things, yeast is very sensitive to temperature and moisture. It prefers temperatures between 75°F and 95°F (24°C and 35°C). At temperatures below 34°F (2°C), yeast becomes dormant; above 138°F (59°C), it dies. Table 32.1 lists the temperatures for yeast development. Moisture activates the yeast cells, helping the yeast convert carbohydrates in the dough into food.

Salt is used in bread making because salt conditions gluten, making it stronger and more elastic. Salt also affects yeast fermentation. Because salt inhibits the growth of yeast, it helps control the dough's rise. Too little salt and not only will the bread taste bland, it will rise too rapidly. Too much salt, however, and the yeast will be destroyed. By controlling the amount of food for the yeast, the salt in the dough and the temperatures of fermentation, bakers control the texture and flavor of yeast-leavened products.

Types of Yeast

Baker's yeast (*Saccharomyces cerevisiae*) is available in three forms: compressed, active dry and instant. (Do not be confused by a product called brewer's yeast; it is a nutritional supplement with no leavening ability.) Although some bakers claim their bread tastes

TEMPERATURES FOR YEAST DEVELOPMENT		TABLE 32.1
TEMPERATURE		YEAST DEVELOPMENT
34°F	(2°C)	Inactive
60–70°F	(16–21°C)	Slow action
75–95°F	(21–32°C)	Best temperature for yeast activity
85–100°F	(29–38°C)	Best water temperature for hydrating instant yeast
100–110°F	(38–43°C)	Best water temperature for hydrating active dry yeast
138°F	(59°C)	Yeast dies

better when made with fresh yeast, the choice of which type of yeast to use is entirely up to the baker.

Compressed Yeast

Compressed yeast is a mixture of yeast and starch with a moisture content of approximately 70 percent. Also referred to as **fresh yeast**, compressed yeast must be kept refrigerated. It should be creamy white and crumbly with a fresh, yeasty smell. Do not use compressed yeast that has a sour odor, brown color or slimy film. Before being added to bread dough, compressed yeast is typically softened in twice its weight of lukewarm water at 90°F (32°C). Some bakers add compressed yeast directly to the dry mix, however.

Compressed yeast is available in 1-pound (450-gram) blocks. Under proper storage conditions, compressed yeast has a shelf life of 2–3 weeks or it may be frozen for 1 month. Compressed yeast that has been frozen will lose about 5 percent of its leavening ability, however, so quantities may need to be adjusted accordingly.

Compressed (fresh) yeast

Active Dry Yeast

Active dry yeast differs from compressed yeast in that virtually all the moisture has been removed from the active dry yeast by hot air. The absence of moisture renders the organisms dormant and allows the yeast to be stored without refrigeration for several months. Dry yeast is generally rehydrated in a warm (approximately 110°F [43°C]) liquid before being added to the other ingredients, when preparing doughs.

Dry yeast is available in ¼-ounce (7-gram) packages and 1- or 2.2-pound (500-gram or 1-kilogram) vacuum-sealed bags. It should be stored in a cool, dry place and refrigerated after opening.

Dry yeast

Instant Dry Yeast

Instant dry yeast is popular because of its ease of use; it is added directly to the dry ingredients in a bread formula without rehydrating. The water in the formula activates it. Like all yeasts, instant dry yeast is a living organism and dies at temperatures above 138°F (59°C). (See Table 32.1.) Although instant yeast can be added to flour without hydration, some bakers still prefer to hydrate instant yeast before using it in certain types of formulas. When doughs are mixed briefly or are very firm, such as bagel or croissant dough, instant dry yeast may not fully dissolve during mixing. In such cases the yeast is moistened in four to five times its weight of water before it is added to the dough. Deduct this amount of water from the total water called for in the formula.

Substituting Yeasts

The flavors of dry and compressed yeasts are virtually indistinguishable, but dry yeasts are at least twice as strong as compressed yeasts. Because too much yeast can ruin bread, always remember to use less than the specified weight of compressed yeast in a formula when substituting compressed yeast for dry yeast or active dry yeast. Likewise, if a formula specifies dry or active dry yeast, increase the quantity specified when substituting compressed yeast.

The Rise of Yeast Breads

How and when the first yeast-leavened breads came into being, no one knows. Perhaps some wild yeasts—the world is full of them—drifted into a dough as it awaited baking. Perhaps some ancient baker substituted fermenting beer for water one day. In any case, the resulting yeast-leavened bread was lighter and more appetizing.

Based on models, images and writings found in excavated tombs, historians are fairly certain that the ancient Egyptians saved a bit of fermented dough from one day's baking to add to the next day's. This use of **sourdough starter** continues today, enjoying widespread popularity.

Other cultures developed their own leavening methods. The Greeks and Romans prepared a wheat porridge with wine to ferment their doughs. The Gauls and Iberians added the foamy head from ale to doughs. Both methods resulted in lighter breads that retained their fresh textures longer.

Since ancient times bread baking has been one of the first household tasks readily turned over to professionals. The first cooks to work outside homes during the Greek and Roman Empires were bakers. The bakery trade flourished during the Middle Ages, and a wide variety of breads were produced. Yeast-leavened breads remained the exception, not the norm,

until well into the 17th century, however. The first real collection of bread recipes is found in Nicolas de Bonnefons's *Les Délices de la campagne*, published in 1654. Bonnefons's instructions, meant for those dissatisfied with commercial products of the time, included beer yeast. By the end of the 17th century, published works included recipes for breads leavened with sourdough starter and the yeasts used in breweries.

Louis Pasteur finally identified yeast as a living organism in 1857. Soon after, a process for distilling or manufacturing baker's yeast was developed. By 1868 commercial baking yeast was available in stores.

Starter activity at three stages: just mixed (lower right), 3 hours after mixing (left) and 12 hours later (upper right).

Any type of yeast may be used in the formulas in this book. Use the formulas in Table 32.2 to convert one type of yeast to another. Multiply the weight of the original type of yeast called for in the formula by the conversion factor (C.F.) listed in Table 32.2 to obtain the quantity of the new type of yeast.

Original Type of Yeast Quantity × Conversion Factor (C.F.) = New Yeast Quantity

Old Quantity × C.F. = New Yeast Quantity

For example, if the formula calls for 2 ounces compressed (fresh) yeast and you would like to use active dry yeast, multiply 2 ounces compressed (fresh) yeast times .05, the conversion factor from Table 32.2, to obtain the new quantity of 1 ounce active dry yeast.

Natural Yeast Leaveners: Sourdough Starter

Before commercial yeast production, bakers relied on **natural yeast leaveners**, also called **starters**, to make bread rise. Early starters were simple mixtures of flour and a liquid (water, potato broth, milk) left out in the open air to capture wild yeasts and beneficial acid-producing bacteria from the environment. Once the mixture fermented, it was used to leaven bread and contribute a distinctive flavor, from mild and buttery to sharp and tangy, to the finished product. Only a portion of the starter was used at a time. The rest was kept for later use, replenished or fed periodically with additional flour and liquid so that the yeast activity could continue. Over time and in different regions, bakers

YEAST SUBSTITUTIONS				TABLE 32.2
Use these formulas to convert from one type of yeast to another:				
ORIGINAL TYPE OF YEAST		**CONVERSION FACTOR (C.F.)**		**NEW TYPE OF YEAST**
Compressed (fresh) yeast	×	0.5	=	Active dry yeast
Compressed (fresh) yeast	×	0.33	=	Instant yeast
Active dry yeast	×	2	=	Compressed (fresh) yeast
Active dry yeast	×	0.75	=	Instant yeast
Instant yeast	×	3	=	Compressed (fresh) yeast
Instant yeast	×	1.33	=	Active dry yeast

developed numerous strategies for using natural yeast starters to create different flavors and textures in bread.

The making of a natural starter begins by combining equal parts flour and water into a wet mixture. A small amount of grapes, apple peels or orange rinds may be added to seed the mixture with the natural yeast spores living on these items. Alternatively a small amount of prepared yeast (dry or compressed) may be used to seed the mixture. After several hours, bubbles should appear on the surface, indicating that yeast activity has begun. Within 12–24 hours, yeast activity should be noticeable and the mixture should double or triple in volume. Over time the starter develops a mellow flavor with some noticeable acidity. The flavor and acidity is what gives sourdough breads their desirable aroma, taste and texture.

To maintain a natural starter, you must frequently replenish (feed) it with more flour and water so that the yeast continues to reproduce and create carbon dioxide. When making bread in a production bakery, feed the starter as often as every 8 hours to keep the yeast active. The amount of flour and water necessary to feed a starter varies, but never add so much flour and water that you double the mixture at one time. Yeast is more active in a wet starter than a dry one; add more flour when the starter will not be used for an extended period of time. More water can be added to make the yeast in the starter more lively and active on the day when it will be used.

Simple Sourdough Starter

YIELD 3 lb. 12 oz. (1805 g)

Active dry yeast	0.15 oz. (1 tsp.)	5 g	0.5%
Water, warm (110°F/43°C)	4 fl. oz.	120 ml	12.5%
Water, room temperature (70°F/21°C)	24 fl. oz.	720 ml	75%
All-purpose flour	2 lb.	960 g	100%
Total weight:	3 lb. 12 oz.	1805 g	188%

1 Combine the yeast and warm water. Let stand until foamy, approximately 10 minutes.

2 Stir in the room-temperature water, then add the flour, 2 ounces (60 grams) at a time.

3 Blend by hand or with a mixer fitted with the paddle attachment on low speed for 2 minutes.

4 Place the starter in a warmed bowl and cover with plastic wrap. Let stand at room temperature for 8–12 hours. The starter should triple in volume but still be wet and sticky. Refrigerate until ready to use.

5 Each time a portion of the starter is used, it must be replenished. Remove the starter from the refrigerator several hours before using. Replenish the starter to activate the yeast cells. Once there is visible yeast activity in the form of large bubbles on its surface, use it. To replenish the starter, stir in equal amounts by volume of flour and warm water. Allow the mixture to ferment at room temperature for several hours or overnight before using again or refrigerating.

Note If liquid rises to the top of the starter, it can be drained off or stirred back into the mixture. If the starter develops a pink or yellow film, it has been contaminated and must be discarded.

Approximate values per ounce (30 g): **Calories** 100, **Total fat** 0 g, **Saturated fat** 0 g, **Cholesterol** 0 mg, **Sodium** 0 mg, **Total carbohydrates** 22 g, **Protein** 3 g

ARTISAN BREAD

The term *artisan bread* is used to describe many kinds of bread but the term is not easily defined because it has been adopted by small-scale independent bakers as well as industrial producers. Some generally recognized characteristics of artisan bread are that they are handcrafted and made with high-quality, traditional ingredients without additives or preservatives. Unbleached, unbromated and organic flours are employed to make doughs that contain natural starters. Artisan bread may be mixed and baked in small batches. Mixers may be used to prepare the dough, but rounding and forming is usually done by hand. The bread dough is allowed to rise for a long period at cool temperatures to develop its flavor. And artisan breads are often baked without pans, directly on the heated stone deck of what is called a **hearth oven**. (Such ovens have floors made from stone or masonry on which bread or pizzas are baked directly.) Many of the formulas in this book produce artisan bread when made with care by those attentive to the craft of bread making.

PRODUCTION STEPS FOR YEAST BREADS

The production of yeast breads can be divided into 10 steps:

1   Scaling the ingredients
2   Mixing and kneading the dough
3   Fermenting the dough
4   Punching down the dough
5   Portioning the dough
6   Rounding the portions
7   Make-up: Shaping the portions
8   Proofing the products
9   Baking the products
10   Cooling and storing the finished products

Step 1: Scaling the Ingredients

absorption the ability of flour to absorb moisture when mixed into a dough; varies according to protein content, growing conditions and storage conditions of the flour

As with any other bakeshop product, it is important to scale or measure ingredients accurately and to have all ingredients at the proper temperature when making a yeast bread. Liquids such as water, milk and eggs can all be weighed to ensure accuracy in a formula. When a minute quantity of an ingredient is required, such as for salt and spices, a volume measurement is useful.

The amount of flour required in yeast bread varies depending on the humidity level, storage conditions of the flour and the accuracy with which other ingredients are measured. Flour from different mills or from different batch lots may **absorb** more or less water depending on the type of wheat used. Flour with a higher protein content absorbs more liquid than one with a lower protein content. Even switching flour batches affects the amount of water needed in a formula. The amount of flour stated in most formulas is to be used as a guide. Have additional flour available before mixing. Experience will help you to learn when more or less flour is actually needed.

Different types of flours absorb different amounts of water. Dough made with all-purpose flour and water (left) will be softer and stickier than dough made with the same amount of whole-wheat flour and water (right).

Step 2: Mixing and Kneading the Dough

The way ingredients are combined affects the outcome of the bread. Yeast dough must be mixed and kneaded properly in order to combine the ingredients uniformly, distribute the yeast and develop the gluten. If dough is not mixed properly, the bread's texture and shape suffer. There are two common ways to mix yeast breads: the **straight dough method** (direct method) or the **sponge method**. Another method used for rich, flaky doughs is discussed later in the section on rolled-in doughs.

Once the ingredients are combined, the dough must be kneaded to develop gluten, the network of proteins that gives bread its shape and texture. Kneading achieves certain key results. It helps the protein hydrate, ensuring development of the gluten web in the bread dough, and it warms the dough to a temperature conducive to keeping the yeast active. Kneading can be done by hand or with a mixer fitted with a dough hook.

① To knead dough, first bring a portion of the dough toward you.

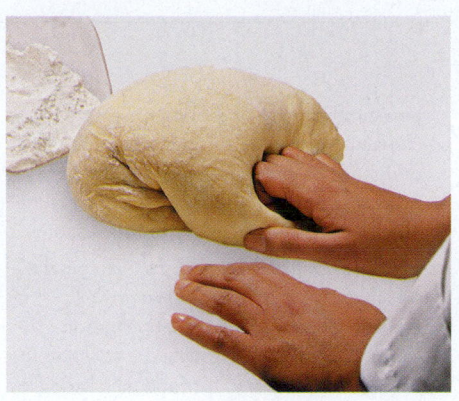

② Then push the dough away with your fist.

③ Repeat until the dough is properly kneaded and is smooth and elastic.

In a mixer, knead with a dough hook on medium speed for approximately 5–10 minutes until the dough looks smooth. In many cases, the dough will clear away from the machine bowl toward the end of the kneading process. Kneading by hand may require more time, depending of the quantity and type of dough and the skill of the baker. The goal with either method is to create a dough that is smooth and moderately elastic.

Straight Dough Method for Mixing Yeast Bread Dough

The simplest and most common method for mixing yeast dough is the straight dough method. With this method, all ingredients are simply combined and mixed. Once the ingredients are combined, the dough is kneaded until it is smooth and elastic. Kneading time varies according to the kneading method used and the type of dough being produced. The straight dough method is illustrated by the recipe for Soft Yeast Dinner Rolls (page 954).

Sponge Method for Mixing Yeast Bread Dough

The sponge method of mixing yeast dough has two stages. During the first stage the yeast, the liquid and approximately half the flour are combined to make a thick batter known as a **sponge**. The sponge is allowed to rise until bubbly and doubled in size. During the second stage, the remaining ingredients are added to the sponge. The dough is kneaded and allowed to rise again. These two fermentations give sponge method breads a somewhat different flavor and a lighter texture than breads made with the straight dough method.

Do not confuse sponge method breads with sourdough starters. The sponge method is often used to improve the texture of heavy doughs such as rye and some yeast doughs enriched with butter and sugar. Unlike a sourdough starter, a first-stage sponge is prepared only for use in the specific formula and is not reserved for later use. The sponge method is illustrated by the recipe for Light Rye Bread (page 956).

sponge a thick flour, water and yeast batter used to improve the flavor and texture of breads

Step 3: Fermenting the Dough

As mentioned earlier, fermentation is the natural process by which yeast converts sugar into alcohol and carbon dioxide. Fermentation begins the moment the dough is finished mixing and continues until the dough is baked and reaches a temperature high enough to kill the yeast cells, 138°F (59°C).

Fermentation also refers to the period when yeast dough is left to rise—that is, the time it takes for carbon dioxide gas to form and become trapped in the gluten network. Fermentation is divided into two stages: **Bulk fermentation** refers to the time the entire mass of yeast dough ferments and rises before the dough is shaped; **proofing** refers to the time shaped yeast products ferment and rise just before baking.

Controlling Fermentation

The ingredients in the formula, the dough temperature and the temperature of the environment in which the dough ferments affect the total fermentation time. Bakers use different strategies to regulate fermentation time to achieve desired results.

Ingredients: Dough with more yeast and more yeast food such as sugar ferments more quickly. Increasing the yeast in a formula increases the rate of fermentation, thus speeding production time. Adding sugar, honey or other carbohydrates speeds

fermentation also, although too much sugar can actually slow yeast's activity; enriched dough formulas, those prepared with a high percentage of fats and sugars, often include a higher percentage of yeast for this reason.

Dough temperature: Using warmer water in the dough and fermenting it in a warm environment speeds up the fermentation process. Conversely kneading the dough to the proper dough temperature and then letting it ferment in a cool environment slows down this process. When mixing yeast dough, keep in

mind that during wintertime baking in colder climates, you may need very warm water to initiate yeast activity. During summertime baking in hot climates, you may need to use very cool water to prevent bread dough from fermenting too quickly.

Room temperature: Bakeries often extend the fermentation time of certain doughs in a specially designed refrigerator called a **retarder**. The cool temperature slows down yeast activity, giving the dough the maximum opportunity to develop its flavor.

Dough develops characteristics during fermentation that enhance the taste and texture of the finished bread. As it feeds on the sugars and starches in the dough, the yeast converts them to flavorful enzymes and bacteria. The gluten strengthens during fermentation, ensuring that the bread holds its structure when baked. For fermentation, place the kneaded dough into a container large enough to allow the dough to expand, or scrape the dough onto a floured workbench. The surface of the dough may be oiled to prevent drying. Cover the dough loosely with plastic, a clean towel or other covering and place it in a draft-free place at a temperature between 75°F and 85°F (24°C and 29°C).

Fermentation is complete when the dough has approximately doubled in size and no longer springs back when pressed gently with two fingers. The time necessary varies depending on the type of dough, the temperature of the room and the temperature of the dough.

Step 4: Punching Down the Dough

After fermentation, the dough is gently folded down to expel and redistribute the gas pockets with a technique known as **punching down**. The procedure reactivates the yeast cells, encouraging more yeast activity. Punching down dough also helps even out the dough's temperature and relaxes the gluten.

Step 5: Portioning the Dough

The dough is now ready to be divided into portions. For loaves, the dough is scaled (weighed) to the desired weight. For individual rolls, the dough can be rolled into an even log from which portions are cut off with a chef's knife or dough cutter. Weighing the cut dough pieces on a scale ensures even-sized portions. When portioning, work quickly and keep the dough covered to prevent it from drying out.

Step 6: Rounding the Portions

The portions of dough must be shaped into smooth, round balls in a technique known as **rounding**. Rounding stretches the outside layer of gluten into a smooth coating. This helps hold in gases and makes it easier to shape the dough. Unrounded rolls rise unevenly and have a rough, lumpy surface.

Step 7: Make-Up: Shaping the Portions

Lean doughs and some rich doughs can be shaped into a variety of forms: large loaves, small loaves, free-form or country-style rounds or individual dinner rolls. Table 32.3 identifies common pan sizes and the approximate weight of the dough used to fill these pans. Free-form loaves are often placed between the floured folds of heavy linen canvas (**couche**) to hold their shape while proofing. Alternatively these loaves

Rounding bread dough.

couche [coo-SH] heavy linen canvas that is floured and folded to hold yeast dough while it rises before baking

PAN SIZE		TABLE 32.3
PAN	APPROXIMATE SIZE	WEIGHT OF DOUGH*
Sandwich loaf	16 in. × 4 in. × 4½ in. (40 cm × 10 cm × 11.2 cm)	4 lb. (1920 g)
Pullman	13 in. × 4 in. × 3 in. (32.5 cm × 10 cm × 7.5 cm)	3 lb. (1440 g)
Large	9 in. × 5 in. × 3 in. (22.5 cm × 12.5 cm × 7.5 cm)	2 lb. (960 g)
Medium	8 in. × 4 in. × 2 in. (20 cm × 10 cm × 5 cm)	1 lb. 8 oz. (720 g)
Small	7 in. × 3 in. × 2 in. (17.5 cm × 7.5 cm × 5 cm)	1 lb. (480 g)
Miniature	5 in. × 3 in. × 2 in. (12.5 cm × 7.5 cm × 5 cm)	8 oz. (240 g)

* Weights given are approximate; variations may occur based on the type of dough used as well as the temperature and length of proofing.

may be placed in linen-lined baskets (**bannetons**) or coiled willow or plastic baskets (**brotform**). These baskets hold the loaves' shape and leave a distinctive imprint on the loaves when they are removed from them before baking. Some shaping techniques are shown in the following procedures. Other doughs, particularly brioche, croissant and Danish, are shaped in very specific ways. Those techniques are discussed and illustrated with their specific formulas.

bagel a dense, donut-shaped yeast roll; it is cooked in boiling water, then baked, which gives it a shiny glaze and chewy texture

bun any of a variety of small, round yeast rolls; can be sweet or savory

club roll a small oval-shaped roll made of crusty French bread

Kaiser roll a large round yeast roll with a crisp crust and a curved pattern stamped on the top; used primarily for sandwiches

banneton [ban-a-TON] a traditional willow basket, often lined with canvas, in which yeast bread is placed to rise before baking

brotform [BROT-form] a traditional woven basket in which yeast bread is placed to rise before baking. The basket leaves marks in the dough's surface. Heavy plastic versions are available for commercial food service use

Loaves in a brotform.

Bread dough being placed in a canvas couche before being proofed.

Procedure for Forming a Twisted Knot Roll or Loaf

1 Roll a portion of dough into a long rope. Form a loop by attaching the left end to the middle of the rope. Pinch to seal the dough.
2 Pass the right end of the rope through the loop.
3 Fold down the top of the loop and twist slightly.
4 Thread the loose end of the loaf through the loop.

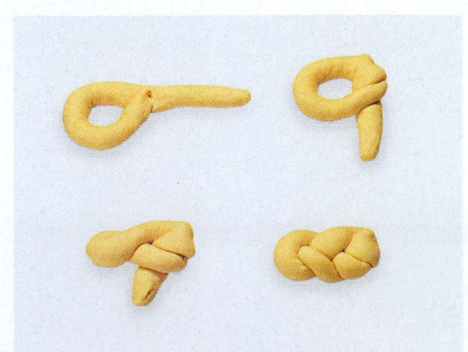

Forming a twisted knot loaf.

Procedure for Rolling a Long Loaf or Baguette

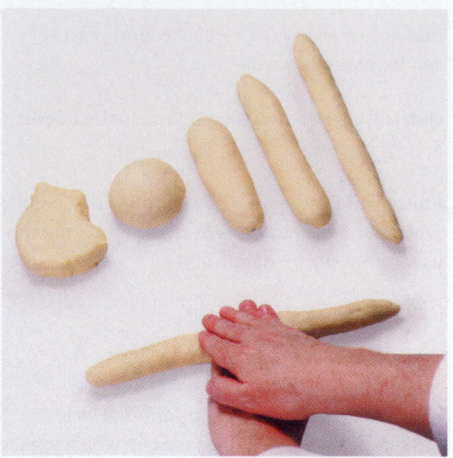

Forming and then rolling a long loaf or baguette.

oven spring the rapid rise of yeast goods in a hot oven, resulting from the production and expansion of trapped gases

1 Round a portion of dough into a ball by rolling it under cupped hands across the surface of the lightly floured workbench.
2 Roll the ball of dough out into a short cylinder.
3 With both hands together, roll the dough until it gradually begins to lengthen.
4 Roll to the desired length.

Step 8: Proofing the Products

Proofing is the final rise of shaped or panned yeast products before baking. For most bread, the temperature should be between 80°F and 115°F (27°C and 46°C), slightly higher than the temperature for fermentation. Some humidity is also desirable to prevent the dough from drying or forming a crust during proofing. Temperature and humidity can be controlled with a special cabinet known as a **proof box**.

Most products are proofed until the dough doubles in size and springs back slowly when lightly touched. Underproofing results in poor volume and texture. Overproofing results in a sour flavor, poor volume and a paler color after baking. Some doughs made with low-protein flours such as rye or multigrains and some enriched yeast doughs should be proofed less, until they have expanded only 50–70 percent in volume. The weaker gluten structure and the heavy weight of the fats in the dough make them fragile. Proofing these doughs until doubled in volume can result in loaves that collapse in the oven.

Step 9: Baking the Products

As yeast breads bake, a variety of chemical and physical changes turn the dough into an edible product. These changes are discussed in Chapter 30, Principles of the Bakeshop. Because of the expansion of gases, yeast products experience a sudden rise, referred to as **oven spring**, when first placed in a hot oven. As the dough's temperature increases, the yeast dies, the gluten fibers become firm, the starches gelatinize, the moisture evaporates and, finally, the crust forms and turns brown. To assist the rise during baking and to improve their appearance when baked, loaves may be washed and/or scored before baking.

Washes

The appearance of yeast breads can be altered by applying a glaze or **wash** to the dough before baking. The crust is made shiny or matte, hard or soft, darker or lighter by the proper use of washes. See Table 32.4. Washes are also used to attach seeds, wheat germ, oats or other toppings to the dough's surface.

The most commonly used wash is an egg wash, composed of whole egg and water—usually 1 part water to 3 parts egg. Yeast products can also be topped with plain water,

WASHES FOR YEAST PRODUCTS	TABLE 32.4
WASH	USE
Whole egg and water	Shine and color
Whole egg and milk	Shine and color with soft crust
Egg white and water	Shine with a firm crust
Egg yolk and cream or milk	Shine and color with soft crust
Milk or cream	Color with a soft crust
Water	Crisp crust
Flour	Texture and contrast
Starch wash	Shine and color

a mixture of egg and milk, plain milk or richer glazes containing sugar and flavorings. Even a light dusting of white flour can be used to top dough. (This is commonly seen with potato rolls.) Rye breads are often coated with a starch wash made from cornstarch cooked in water, which produces a dark shiny crust.

Washes may be applied before or after proofing. If applied after proofing, be extremely careful not to deflate the product. Avoid using too much wash, as it can burn or cause the product to stick to the pan. Puddles or streaks of egg wash on the dough cause uneven browning.

Occasionally a formula will specify that melted butter or oil be brushed on the product after baking. Do not, however, apply egg washes to already baked products, as the egg will remain raw and the desired effect will not be achieved.

Scoring and Docking

The shape and appearance of some breads can be improved by cutting their tops with a sharp knife or razor (**lame**) just before baking. This is referred to as **scoring** or **slashing**. Hard-crusted breads are usually scored to allow for continued rising and the escape of gases after the crust has formed. Breads that are not properly scored will burst or break along the sides. Scoring can also be used to make an attractive design on the product's surface. Some flatbreads such as pizza and crackers may be **docked** or pricked with small holes to prevent the formation of irregular air bubbles in the finished product.

Steam in the Oven

The crisp crust desired for certain breads and rolls is achieved by introducing moisture into the oven during baking. Steam revitalizes the yeast in the dough and keeps the surface of the dough soft so that it can rise fully in the oven. Steam is introduced into the oven in the early baking stages only. Excessive steam produces a crust that is pale and thick. Professional bakers' ovens have built-in steam injection jets to provide moisture as needed. Steam must not be present during the final stages of baking so the bread can brown.

To create steam in any oven, spray or mist the bread with water several times during baking, or place a pan on the oven's lowest rack to receive hot water. Pour ½–¾ cup (120–180 milliliters) hot water into the pan just before placing the bread in the oven. This creates a burst of steam and a moist oven during the first few minutes of baking. Rich doughs, which do not form crisp crusts, are usually baked without steam.

Determining Doneness

Baking time is determined by a variety of factors: the product's size, the oven thermostat's accuracy and the desired crust color. Larger items require a longer baking time than smaller ones. Lean dough products bake faster and at higher temperatures than enriched dough products.

Bread loaves are commonly tested for doneness by tapping them on the bottom and listening for a hollow sound. This indicates that air, not moisture, is present inside the loaf. If the bottom is damp or heavy, the loaf probably needs more baking time. The texture and color of the crust are also a good indication of doneness, particularly with individual rolls. Browning (caramelization) on the outside of bread flavors the entire loaf. A pale loaf has less flavor than a well-browned one. Yeast breads should have a uniform, richly burnished gold to brown colored crust. The baking times indicated in these recipes are estimates only and may vary depending on the equipment used. Experience will teach how to determine doneness without strict adherence to elapsed time.

Step 10: Cooling and Storing the Finished Products

The quality of even the finest yeast breads suffers if they are cooled or stored improperly. Yeast products should be cooled on racks at room temperature and away from drafts. Yeast breads and rolls should be removed from their pans for cooling unless indicated otherwise. Allow loaves to cool completely before slicing. This allows the internal structure to settle and evaporates any excess moisture remaining after baking.

Guidelines for Determining Bread Doneness

- Uniform, rich, burnished gold to brown crust color
- Hollow sound when bottom of loaf is tapped
- The internal temperature can be gauged with great accuracy using an instant-read thermometer.

  Lean dough: Internal temperature of 190–210°F (88–99°C).

  Rich dough: Internal temperature of 180–190°F (82–88°C).

Once cool, yeast products should be stored at room temperature or frozen for longer storage. Do not refrigerate baked goods, as refrigeration promotes staling. Do not wrap crisp-crusted breads, such as Italian or French loaves, as this causes the crust to soften.

Procedure for Preparing Yeast Bread

Straight Dough Method

1 Scale the ingredients. Adjust the water to the proper temperature and rehydrate the yeast if necessary.

2 Combine all ingredients in a mixer fitted with a dough hook on low speed to moisten.

3 Adjust the mixture with more water or flour if needed to correct dough consistency as described in the formula.

4 Knead the dough on medium speed to properly develop the gluten, approximately 5–10 minutes.

5 Ferment the dough until double in bulk, then punch it down to release gases.

6 Scrape the dough onto the workbench, divide and portion into uniform pieces. Round each piece into a smooth ball, then rest before rolling into desired shapes. Make up the formed dough as desired.

7 Proof the dough. Apply egg wash and score the dough if necessary; bake.

♥ **Good Choice**

MISE EN PLACE

- Adjust water temperature.
- Soften butter.
- Prepare the egg wash.
- Line sheet pans with parchment while the dough ferments.

Soft Yeast Dinner Rolls

YIELD	64 Rolls, approximately 1¼ oz. (38 g) each	**METHOD**	Straight Dough	
Water, warm (110°F/43°C)		24 fl. oz.	720 ml	54.5%
Active dry yeast		2 oz.	60 g	4.5%
Bread flour		2 lb. 12 oz.	1320 g	100%
Salt		1 oz.	30 g	2.3%
Granulated sugar		4 oz.	120 g	9%
Nonfat dry milk powder		2 oz.	60 g	4.5%
Shortening		2 oz.	60 g	4.5%
Unsalted butter, softened		2 oz.	60 g	4.5%
Eggs		3.3 oz. (2 eggs)	100 g	7.5%
Egg wash		as needed	as needed	
Total dough weight:		5 lb. 4 oz.	2530 g	191.3%

1 Combine the water and yeast in a small bowl. Combine the remaining ingredients (except the egg wash) in the bowl of a mixer.

2 Add the water-and-yeast mixture to the remaining ingredients; stir to combine.

3 Knead with a dough hook on medium speed for 10 minutes.

4 Transfer the dough to a lightly greased bowl, cover with plastic and place in a warm spot. Ferment until doubled, approximately 1 hour.

5 Punch down the dough. Let it rest a few minutes to allow the gluten to relax.

6 Divide the dough then scale (weigh) it into 1¼-ounce (38-gram) portions and round. Shape as desired and arrange on paper-lined sheet pans. Proof until doubled in size.

7 Carefully brush the proofed rolls with egg wash. Bake at 400°F (200°C) until medium brown, approximately 12–15 minutes.

Approximate values per 1¼-oz. (38-g) roll: **Calories** 90, **Total fat** 1.5 g, **Saturated fat** 0.5 g, **Cholesterol** 10 mg, **Sodium** 160 mg, **Total carbohydrates** 15 g, **Protein** 3 g, **Claims**—low fat; low saturated fat; low cholesterol

1 Mixing the soft yeast dough:
(a) Combining the ingredients in the bowl of a mixer fitted with a dough hook.

(b) Adding the yeast-and-water mixture.

2 Kneading the dough.

3 The dough before fermenting.

4 Punching down the risen dough:
(a) Pressing down on the center of the dough with your fist.

(b) Folding the edges of the dough in toward the center and pressing to deflate the dough.

5 Dividing the dough into uniform pieces then scaling it to obtain a uniform weight.

6 Rounding the rolls.

7 Egg-washing the rolls.

Procedure for Preparing Yeast Bread

Sponge Method

1 Scale the ingredients. Adjust the water to the proper temperature and rehydrate the yeast if necessary.

2 Mix the sponge using a portion of the flour, the water and the yeast. Usually half the total flour weight is used in the sponge.

3 Ferment the sponge until bubbly and about double in size, approximately 1 hour.

4 Add the remaining ingredients, knead the dough on medium speed until properly developed, approximately 5–10 minutes.

5 Ferment the dough until double in bulk; punch it down to release gases.

6 The dough is ready for scaling, shaping, proofing and baking.

♥ Good Choice

MISE EN PLACE

- Adjust water temperature.
- Crush caraway seeds.
- Melt butter.
- Prepare the egg wash.
- Dust sheet pan with cornmeal while the dough ferments.

Light Rye Bread

YIELD 2 Large Loaves, approximately 1½ lb. (720 g) each		METHOD Sponge	
Unbleached wheat flour	1 lb.	480 g	66%
Medium rye flour	8 oz.	240 g	34%
Dark molasses	3 oz.	90 g	12.5%
Water, warm (110°F/43°C)	14 fl. oz.	420 ml	58%
Active dry yeast	0.5 oz.	15 g	2%
Nonfat dry milk powder	1.5 oz.	45 g	6%
Caraway seeds, crushed	0.6 oz.	20 g	3%
Kosher salt	0.5 oz.	15 g	2%
Unsalted butter, melted	0.5 oz.	15 g	2%
Egg wash	as needed	as needed	
Total dough weight:	2 lb. 12 oz.	1340 g	185.5%

1 Stir the flours together and set aside.

2 To make the sponge, combine the molasses, water and yeast. Add 8 ounces (240 grams) of the flour mixture. Stir vigorously for 3 minutes. Cover the bowl and set the sponge aside to rise until doubled and very bubbly, approximately 1 hour.

3 Stir the milk powder, caraway seeds, salt and butter into the sponge.

4 Transfer the sponge to a mixer fitted with a dough hook.

5 Gradually add the remaining flour to the sponge. Mix on low speed and continue adding flour until the dough is stiff but slightly tacky. Knead for 5 minutes on low speed.

6 Transfer the dough to a lightly greased bowl, cover and place in a warm place until doubled, approximately 45–60 minutes.

7 Punch down the dough and divide into two pieces. Shape each piece into a round loaf and place on a sheet pan that has been dusted with cornmeal or lightly oiled. Brush the loaves with egg wash and let rise until doubled, approximately 45 minutes.

8 Score the tops with a razor or knife. Bake at 375°F (190°C) until golden brown and crusty, approximately 25 minutes.

Approximate values per ¹⁄₁₀-loaf slice: **Calories** 160, **Total fat** 1.5 g, **Saturated fat** 0 g, **Cholesterol** 15 mg, **Sodium** 370 mg, **Total carbohydrates** 31 g, **Protein** 6 g, **Claims**—low fat; no saturated fat; low cholesterol

1 Rye bread sponge.

2 Mixing the rye dough.

3 Shaping the rye loaves.

ROLLED-IN DOUGHS

Baked goods made with rolled-in (laminated) doughs include croissants, Danish pastries and non-yeast-leavened puff pastry. (Puff pastry is discussed in Chapter 33, Pies, Pastries and Cookies.) The dough is so named because the fat is incorporated through a detailed process of rolling and folding. Products made with a rolled-in dough have a distinctive flaky texture created by the repeated layering of fat and dough. As the dough bakes, moisture is released from the fat in the form of steam. The steam is then trapped between the layers of dough, causing them to rise and separate.

Rolled-in doughs are made following most of the 10 production steps discussed earlier. The principal differences are (1) the butter is incorporated through a turning process after the dough base is fermented and punched down, (2) rolled-in doughs are portioned somewhat differently from other yeast doughs and (3) the portions are shaped without rounding.

Butter is often used for rolled-in products because of its flavor. Unfortunately butter is hard to work with because it cracks and breaks when cold and becomes too soft to roll at room temperature. Margarine, shortening or specially formulated high-moisture fats, however, can be used—sometimes in combination with butter—in order to reduce costs or to make working with the dough easier. Take care when proofing rolled-in dough products that the temperature does not become too hot. If the fat melts during proofing, flakiness will be ruined and the products will fry in their own fat in the oven.

The dough base should not be kneaded too much, as gluten continues to develop during the rolling and folding process. An **electric dough sheeter** can be used to mechanically roll dough out quickly to a uniform thickness. This time-saving device consists of a cloth conveyor belt that moves beneath a stationary rolling pin. The height of the pin is adjusted to change the thickness of the product.

Procedure for Preparing Yeast-Raised Rolled-In Doughs

1 Mix the dough and allow it to rise.

2 Prepare the butter or shortening. The butter may be formed into a rectangle to be enclosed in the dough or it may be softened and spread on the dough.

3 Roll out the dough evenly, then top it with the butter.

4 Fold the dough around the butter, enclosing it completely.

5 Roll out the dough into a rectangle, about ¼–½ inch (0.6–1.2 centimeters) thick. Always be sure to roll at right angles; do not roll haphazardly or in a circle as you would pastry doughs.

6 Fold the dough in thirds. Be sure to brush off any excess flour from between the folds. This completes the first **turn**. Chill the dough for 20–30 minutes.

7 Roll out the dough and fold it in the same manner a second and third time, allowing the dough to rest, chilled, for between 20 and 30 minutes between each turn. After completing the third turn, wrap the dough carefully in plastic wrap and allow it to rest, refrigerated, for several hours or overnight before shaping and baking. (Additional turns may be given to this dough; three or four are common.)

Parisian Croissants

YIELD 60 Rolls, 1½ oz. (45 g) each		METHOD Rolled-In Dough		
Bread flour	2 lb. 4 oz.	1080 g	100%
Salt	1 oz.	30 g	3%
Granulated sugar	6 oz.	180 g	17%
Milk	21 fl. oz.	625 ml	58%
Active dry yeast	1 oz.	30 g	3%
Unsalted butter, softened	1 lb. 8 oz.	720 g	67%
Egg wash	as needed	as needed	
Total dough weight:	5 lb. 9 oz.	2665 g	248%

1 Stir the flour, salt and sugar together in the bowl of a mixer fitted with a dough hook.

2 Warm the milk to approximately 90°F (32°C). Stir in the yeast.

3 Add the milk-and-yeast mixture to the dry ingredients. Stir until combined, then knead on medium speed for 10 minutes.

4 Place the dough in a large floured bowl, cover and let rise until doubled in size, approximately 1 hour.

5 Prepare the butter while the dough is rising. Place the butter in an even layer between two large pieces of plastic wrap and roll into a flat rectangle, approximately 8 inches × 11 inches (20 centimeters × 27.5 centimeters) and chill.

6 After the dough has risen, punch it down. Roll out the dough into a large rectangle, approximately ½ inch (1.2 centimeters) thick and large enough to enclose the rectangle of butter. Place the unwrapped butter in the center of the dough and fold the dough around the butter, enclosing it completely.

7 Roll out the block of dough into a long rectangle, approximately 1 inch (2.5 centimeters) thick. Fold the dough in thirds, brushing off excess flour from between the folds. This single book fold completes the first turn. Wrap the dough in plastic and chill for approximately 20–30 minutes.

8 Repeat the rolling and folding process two more times, chilling the dough between each turn. When finished, wrap the dough well and chill it overnight before shaping and baking.

9 To shape the dough into croissant rolls, cut off one-fourth of the block at a time, wrapping the rest and returning it to the refrigerator. Roll each section of dough into a large rectangle, about ¼ inch (6 millimeters) thick.

10 Cut the dough into uniform triangles. Starting with the large end, roll each triangle and shape it into a crescent and place on a paper-lined sheet pan.

11 Brush lightly with egg wash. Proof until doubled, but do not allow the dough to become so warm that the butter melts.

12 Bake at 375°F (190°C) until golden brown, approximately 12–15 minutes.

Approximate values per 1½-oz. (45-g) roll: **Calories** 200, **Total fat** 12 g, **Saturated fat** 7 g, **Cholesterol** 40 mg, **Sodium** 230 mg, **Total carbohydrates** 19 g, **Protein** 3 g, **Vitamin A** 10%

1 Rolling the butter into a flat rectangle between two sheets of plastic wrap.

2 Folding the dough around the butter, which has been placed in the center.

3 Brushing the excess flour from the rolled-out dough.

4 Folding the dough in thirds.

5 The finished croissant dough.

6 Cutting the dough into triangles.

QUALITIES OF BREAD

Bread is judged by its external and internal appearance, flavor, aroma and shelf life. Well-crafted bread has a pleasing uniform brown surface color. The crust is neither too thick nor too thin, depending on the type of formula. The crust is crisp or tender without being leathery and excessively thick. With the exception of long-fermented sourdough, which may have an irregular surface dotted with bubbles, the crust should be uniform and free from surface blisters. The interior (**crumb**) of a tender crusted bread or enriched dough product should be even and moist without being sticky. A long-fermented country bread or sourdough may contain an irregular cell structure and large holes characteristic of this type of bread. Well-crafted bread has good keeping properties; improperly made bread will stale in a matter of hours. Table 32.5 identifies common problems when making yeast breads and possible solutions.

TROUBLESHOOTING CHART FOR YEAST BREAD   TABLE 32.5

PROBLEM	CAUSE	SOLUTION
Dense leaden dough	Too much flour forced into the dough	Gradually add water to dough; adjust formula
Crust too pale	Oven temperature too low Dough overproofed	Adjust oven Proof only until almost doubled, then bake immediately
Crust too dark	Too much steam in oven Oven too hot Too much sugar in the dough	Reduce amount of steam or moisture in oven Adjust oven temperature Measure sugar carefully; adjust formula if necessary
Top crust separates from loaf	Dough improperly shaped Crust not scored properly Dough dried out during proofing	Shape dough carefully Score dough to a depth of ½ in. (1.2 cm) Cover dough during proofing; increase humidity in proof box
Sides of loaf are cracked	Bread expanded after crust formed in oven Bread underproofed	Score top of loaf before baking Proof until loaf almost doubled
Dense texture	Not enough yeast Not enough fermentation time Bread underproofed Improper molding technique Too much salt	Adjust formula or measure yeast carefully Let dough rise until doubled or as directed Proof until loaf almost doubled Handle dough gently Adjust formula or measure salt carefully
Ropes of undercooked dough running through product	Insufficient kneading Insufficient rising time Oven too hot	Knead dough until it is smooth and elastic or as directed Allow adequate time for proofing Adjust oven
Free-form loaf spreads and flattens	Dough too soft	Adjust formula or measure carefully
Large holes in bread	Too much yeast Overkneaded Inadequate punch-down	Measure yeast carefully; adjust formula if necessary Knead only as directed Punch down properly to knead out excess air before shaping
Blisters on crust	Too much liquid Improper shaping Too much steam in oven	Measure ingredients carefully; adjust formula if necessary Knead out excess air before shaping Reduce amount of steam or moisture in oven

QUESTIONS FOR DISCUSSION

1   Describe the characteristics of lean and rich doughs and give an example of each.

2   Compare and contrast active dry yeast, instant dry yeast and compressed yeast. Describe the correct procedures for working with these yeasts.

3   Explain the differences between a sponge and a sourdough starter. How is each of these items used?

4   Describe the straight dough mixing method and give two examples of products made with this procedure.

5   List the 10 production steps for yeast breads. Which of these steps also apply to quick-bread production? Explain your answer.

6   Discuss strategies for fermenting yeast dough during the summer months when the kitchen temperature can be very hot. Which procedures might be handled differently under those conditions? How would these procedures be different in the colder winter months?

7   Briefly describe the procedure for making a rolled-in dough and give two examples of products made from rolled-in doughs.

8   What can happen when croissant dough is proofed at high temperatures or for too long?

9   Locate a professional organization for bread bakers. What services are available to its members?

Additional Yeast Bread Formulas

White Sandwich Bread

YIELD	2 Large Loaves, approximately 1 lb. 5 oz. (645 g) each	METHOD	Straight Dough	

Water, warm (110°F/43°C)	12 fl. oz.	360 ml	50%
Nonfat dry milk powder	1.25 oz.	35 g	5%
Granulated sugar	1 oz.	30 g	4%
Salt	0.5 oz.	15 g	2%
Active dry yeast	0.5 oz.	15 g	2%
Bread flour	1 lb. 8 oz.	720 g	100%
Unsalted butter, softened	1 oz.	30 g	4%
Eggs	3.3 oz. (2 eggs)	100 g	14%
Egg wash	as needed	as needed	
Total dough weight:	2 lb. 11 oz.	1305 g	181%

1 Combine the water, milk powder, sugar, salt, yeast and 12 ounces (340 grams) flour in the bowl of a mixer fitted with a paddle. Blend well. Add the butter and eggs and beat for 2 minutes.

2 Stir in the remaining flour, 2 ounces (60 grams) at a time. Knead until the dough is smooth and elastic, approximately 8 minutes.

3 Place the dough in a lightly greased bowl, cover and let it ferment at room temperature until doubled, approximately 1–1½ hours.

4 Shape into loaves, pan and proof until doubled.

5 Brush the dough with egg wash. Bake at 375°F (190°C) until brown and hollow sounding, approximately 50 minutes.

Variations:

Whole-Wheat Sandwich Bread—Substitute up to 12 ounces (360 grams/50%) whole-wheat flour for an equal amount of the bread flour.

Cloverleaf Rolls—Divide the dough into 1-ounce (30-gram) pieces. Roll each piece of dough into a tight ball. Place three balls of dough into each greased muffin tin. Proof, egg wash and bake at 375°F (190°C) until lightly browned and cooked through, approximately 20–25 minutes.

Panning the dough for Cloverleaf Rolls.

Approximate values per ¹⁄₁₆-loaf serving: **Calories** 150, **Total fat** 2 g, **Saturated fat** 1 g, **Cholesterol** 25 mg, **Sodium** 250 mg, **Total carbohydrates** 28 g, **Protein** 6 g, **Vitamin A** 4%, **Claims**—low fat

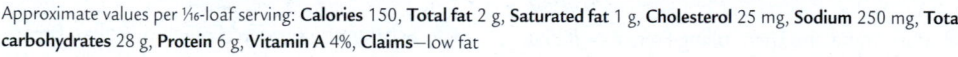

♥ Good Choice

French or Italian Bread

YIELD 4 Loaves, 1 lb. 9 oz. (750 g) each	METHOD Straight Dough		
Water, lukewarm (90°F/32°C)	39 fl. oz.	1170 ml	65%
Active dry yeast	1 oz.	30 g	1.7%
Bread flour	3 lb. 12 oz.	1800 g	100%
Salt	1.25 oz.	36 g	2%
Total dough weight:	6 lb. 5 oz.	3036 g	168.7%

1 Combine the water and yeast in a mixer bowl. Add the remaining ingredients and mix on low speed with a dough hook until all the flour is incorporated.

2 Increase to medium speed and knead the dough until it is smooth and elastic.

3 Let the dough ferment until doubled. Punch down, then scale the dough into 1 pound 9 ounces (750 gram) pieces. Round the dough then shape into baguettes or as desired. Proof the loaves until doubled.

4 Score the loaves. Bake at 400°F (200°C) with steam during the first few minutes of baking, until the crust is well developed and golden brown and the bread is baked through, approximately 12 minutes for rolls and 20 minutes for small loaves.

Approximate values per ¼-loaf serving: **Calories** 80, **Total fat** 0 g, **Saturated fat** 0 g, **Cholesterol** 0 mg, **Sodium** 135 mg, **Total carbohydrates** 16 g, **Protein** 3 g, **Claims**—fat free; low sodium; no sugar

❶ Portioning and then rolling French or Italian Bread dough into baguettes in two stages.

❷ Scoring the proofed French or Italian Bread loaves to allow steam to escape.

♥ Good Choice

Whole-Wheat Bread

YIELD 2 Large Loaves, approximately 24 oz. (735 g) each or 35 Dinner Rolls, 1¼ oz. (45 g) each	METHOD Straight Dough		
Salt	0.4 oz. (2 tsp.)	12 g	1.5%
Nonfat dry milk powder	1.25 oz.	4 g	0.5%
Whole-wheat flour	1 lb. 10 oz.	780 g	100%
Water, warm (110°F/43°C)	17 fl. oz.	510 ml	65%
Active dry yeast	0.5 oz.	15 g	2%
Honey	3 oz.	90 g	11.5%
Unsalted butter, softened	1 oz.	30 g	3.8%
Whole butter, melted	as needed	as needed	
Total dough weight:	3 lb. 1 oz.	1441 g	184.3%

1 Combine the salt and milk powder with 12 ounces (360 grams) flour in a large mixer bowl.

2 Stir in the water, yeast, honey and softened butter. Beat until combined into a thick, batterlike dough.

3 Add the remaining flour 2 ounces (60 grams) at a time. Knead on medium speed approximately 8 minutes until the dough is smooth and elastic.

4 Place the dough in a lightly greased bowl and cover. Let the dough ferment in a warm place until doubled.

5 Punch down, then scale the dough into pieces. Shape into round loaves.

6 Let the shaped dough proof until doubled. Bake at 375°F (190°C) until firm and dark brown, approximately 1 hour for loaves and 20 minutes for rolls. Brush the top of the loaves or rolls with melted butter after baking.

Approximate values per 1⁄16-loaf serving: **Calories** 170, **Total fat** 2 g, **Saturated fat** 1 g, **Cholesterol** 5 mg, **Sodium** 250 mg, **Total carbohydrates** 32 g, **Protein** 6 g, **Claims**—low fat; low saturated fat; low cholesterol; good source of fiber

---

San Francisco-Style Sourdough Bread

 **Good Choice**

Ercolino Consulting, Newberg, OR
Chef Ercolino Crugnale

YIELD 1 Loaf, 2 lb. (960 g)	METHOD Straight Dough		
Active dry yeast	0.5 oz.	15 g	3%
Water, warm (110°F/43°C)	8 fl. oz.	240 ml	50%
Sourdough starter	6 oz.	180 g	37.5%
Bread flour	1 lb.	480 g	100%
Kosher salt	0.5 oz.	15 g	3%
Cornmeal	as needed	as needed	
Egg white, beaten	1 oz. (1 white)	30 g	6%
Total dough weight:	2 lb.	960 g	199.5%

1 Sprinkle the dry yeast over 2 fluid ounces (60 milliliters) warm water and set aside until dissolved and foamy.

2 In the bowl of a mixer fitted with a dough hook, combine the starter and the remaining warm water. Add 6 ounces (180 grams) bread flour.

3 Stir until a dough forms, then add the yeast mixture. Knead 5 minutes on medium speed.

4 Add the remaining flour and the salt. Knead until the dough is smooth and elastic, approximately 10 minutes.

5 Place the dough in a lightly greased bowl and cover with a damp cloth. Ferment the dough in a warm place, approximately 80–90°F (27–32°C), until doubled.

6 Punch down the dough and shape it into a round loaf. Place the loaf on a greased and cornmeal-dusted sheet pan.

7 Proof the dough in a warm place, covered with a damp cloth, until it has risen to 2½ times its original size.

8 Brush the risen loaf with the beaten egg white and score the top of the loaf with a sharp knife.

9 Bake at 450°F (230°C), with steam in the oven during the first 5 minutes of baking.

10 Reduce the oven temperature to 375°F (190°C), remove the water and continue baking until the loaf is well browned, approximately 35–45 minutes.

Approximate values per 1⁄12-loaf serving: **Calories** 135, **Total fat** 0.5 g, **Saturated fat** 0 g, **Cholesterol** 0 mg, **Sodium** 355 mg, **Total carbohydrates** 27 g, **Protein** 4 g, **Claims**—low fat; no saturated fat; no cholesterol

Focaccia (Roman Flatbread)

YIELD 1 Half-Sheet Pan, 36 pieces, 1 oz. (30 g) each		METHOD Straight Dough		
Granulated sugar	0.4 oz. (1 Tbsp.)	11 g	2%
Active dry yeast	0.4 oz. (1 Tbsp.)	11 g	2%
Water, warm (110°F/43°C)	12 fl. oz.	350 ml	66%
All-purpose flour	1 lb. 2 oz.	540 g	100%
Kosher salt	0.3 oz. (2 tsp.)	10 g	1.7%
Onion, chopped fine	3 oz.	90 g	17%
Olive oil	2 fl. oz.	60 ml	11%
Fresh rosemary, crushed	0.2 oz. (2 Tbsp.)	5 g	1%
Total dough weight:	2 lb. 4 oz.	1077 g	200%

1 Dimpling the surface of the dough.

1 Combine the sugar, yeast and water. Stir to dissolve the yeast. Stir in the flour 4 ounces (120 grams) at a time.

2 Stir in 1½ teaspoons (7 milliliters) salt and the onion. Mix well, then knead on a lightly floured board or in the bowl of a mixer fitted with a dough hook until smooth.

3 Place the dough in an oiled bowl, cover and ferment until doubled.

4 Punch down the dough, then flatten it onto an oiled half-sized sheet pan. It should measure between ½ and 1 inch (1.2 and 2.5 centimeters) thick and will fill the pan completely. Brush the top of the dough with 1 fluid ounce (30 milliliters) of the olive oil. Let the dough proof until doubled, approximately 15 minutes.

5 Dimple the surface of the dough with your fingers. Brush the remaining 1 fluid ounce (30 milliliters) of olive oil over the dough. Sprinkle it with the rosemary and remaining ½ teaspoon (2 milliliters) salt. Bake at 400°F (200°C) until lightly browned, approximately 20 minutes.

Approximate values per 1-oz. (30-g) serving: **Calories** 100, **Total fat** 0.5 g, **Saturated fat** 0 g, **Cholesterol** 0 mg, **Sodium** 230 mg, **Total carbohydrates** 21 g, **Protein** 3 g, **Claims**—low fat; no saturated fat; no cholesterol

2 The Focaccia cut into pieces for serving.

Pizza Dough

YIELD 1 Large or 8 Individual Pizzas		METHOD Straight Dough		
Active dry yeast	0.4 oz. (1 Tbsp.)	12 g	3%
Water, warm (110°F/43°C)	2 fl. oz.	60 ml	14%
Bread flour	14 oz.	420 g	100%
Water, cool	6 fl. oz.	180 ml	43%
Salt	0.2 oz. (1 tsp.)	6 g	1.4%
Olive oil	1 fl. oz.	30 ml	7%
Honey	0.75 oz.	20 g	5%
Total dough weight:	1 lb. 8 oz.	728 g	173%

1 Stir the yeast into the warm water to dissolve. Add the flour.

2 Stir the remaining ingredients into the flour mixture. Knead with a dough hook or by hand until smooth and elastic, approximately 5 minutes.

3 Place the dough in a lightly greased bowl and cover. Allow the dough to ferment in a warm place for 30 minutes. Punch down the dough and divide into portions. The dough may be wrapped and refrigerated for up to 2 days.

4 On a lightly floured surface, roll the dough into very thin rounds and top as desired. Bake at 400°F (200°C) until crisp and golden brown, approximately 8–12 minutes.

Approximate values per 2-oz. (60-g) serving: **Calories** 220, **Total fat** 4 g, **Saturated fat** 0.5 g, **Cholesterol** 0 mg, **Sodium** 290 mg, **Total carbohydrates** 41 g, **Protein** 6 g, **Claims**—low saturated fat; no cholesterol

Swiss Chard and Ricotta Calzone

YIELD   8 Servings, 10 oz. (300 g) each

Pizza Dough (page 964)	1 lb. 8 oz.	720 g
Filling:		
Olive oil	3 fl. oz.	60 ml
Onion, small dice	1	1
Garlic, minced	0.5 oz.	15 g
Swiss chard, chopped	24 oz.	675 g
Fresh thyme, minced	1 tsp.	5 ml
Ricotta	8 oz.	240 g
Mozzarella, shredded	8 oz.	240 g
Salt	0.2 oz. (1 tsp.)	6 g
Black pepper, ground	0.08 oz. (1 tsp.)	2 g
Salami, diced	4 oz.	120 g
Parmesan cheese, grated	2 oz.	60 g
Egg wash	as needed	as needed
Fresh Tomato Sauce for Pasta (page 246)	as needed	as needed

1   Heat the olive oil in a sauce pan. Add the onion and garlic. Sauté lightly, then add the Swiss chard. Cook until the chard is wilted and tender.

2   Transfer the mixture to a bowl. Stir in the thyme, ricotta, mozzarella, salt and pepper. Refrigerate the mixture on a sheet pan until completely cool.

3   To make up the calzones, divide the dough into 8 equal pieces. Roll out each piece of dough into an 8-inch (20-centimeter) round. Place 4–5 ounces (120–150 grams) of the Swiss chard mixture in the middle of each round. Sprinkle each round with some of the salami and parmesan. Brush the edges of the dough with egg wash. Fold the dough in half around the filling, forming a half circle. Seal the edges with the tines of a fork. Place the calzones on a parchment-lined sheet pan.

4   Brush the calzones with egg wash and bake at 425°F (220°C) until the crust is evenly browned and the filling is hot, approximately 7–10 minutes. Serve the calzones hot, with tomato sauce on the side if desired.

Approximate values per 10-oz. (300-g) serving: **Calories** 670, **Total fat** 34g, **Saturated fat** 11g, **Cholesterol** 55 mg, **Sodium** 1490 mg, **Total carbohydrates** 68 g, **Protein** 26 g, **Vitamin A** 110%, **Vitamin C** 45%, **Calcium** 35%

♥ Good Choice

Naan (Indian Flatbread)

YIELD	6 Loaves, approximately 10 oz. (300 g) each		METHOD	Sponge	
Active dry yeast	0.15 oz. (1 tsp.)		4 g		0.4%
Water	17 fl. oz.		510 ml		47%
Bread flour	24 oz.		720 g		67%
Whole-wheat flour	12 oz.		360 g		33%
Yogurt	10 oz.		300 g		28%
Olive oil	1 fl. oz.		30 ml		3%
Baking powder	0.07 oz. (½ tsp.)		2 g		0.2%
Baking soda	0.07 oz. (½ tsp.)		2 g		0.2%
Salt	0.7 oz. (3½ tsp.)		20 g		2%
Vegetable or olive oil	as needed		as needed		
Black sesame seeds	as needed		as needed		
Total dough weight:	4 lb. 1 oz.		1948 g		180.8%

1 To prepare the sponge, dissolve 0.04 ounce (½ teaspoon/1 gram/0.1%) yeast in 6 fluid ounces (180 milliliters) water in the bowl of a mixer fitted with a dough hook. Add 8 ounces (240 grams) bread flour and mix until well incorporated. Cover and set aside. Ferment at room temperature until cracks appear on the surface of the starter, approximately 3 hours.

2 Place the sponge and the remaining 16 ounces (480 grams) bread flour, 11 fluid ounces (330 milliliters) water, whole-wheat flour, yogurt, olive oil, baking powder and baking soda in the bowl of a mixer fitted with a dough hook. Mix on low speed for 3 minutes. Stop the mixer and scrape down the bowl. Add the remaining yeast and mix on high speed for an additional 3 minutes. Add the salt, then mix until the dough is smooth and elastic, approximately 5 minutes more.

3 Cover the dough and let it ferment for 3 hours.

4 Punch down the dough and divide it into 6 uniform pieces. Round the portioned dough. Cover and let rest for 30 minutes.

5 Stretch each piece of dough out until it measures 12 inches (30 centimeters) long. Place the dough on flour-dusted sheet pans and proof until doubled, approximately 50 minutes.

6 Dimple the surface of the dough with your fingertips. Brush the dough with oil and sprinkle it with black sesame seeds. Place the dough directly on the heated surface of a hearth oven at 485°F (252°C) or place the sheet pan of dough on a rack in the oven. Bake until the breads are well browned and crisp, approximately 10–12 minutes. To prevent a soggy crust, open the oven door or vent during the last two minutes of baking to remove any excess steam that may build up in the oven. Cool the loaves on cooling racks, then serve immediately.

Variation:

Garlic Naan—Add 0.5 ounces (15 grams/1.3%) minced garlic to the dough with the salt in Step 2. After baking, brush the tops of the hot naan with melted butter before serving.

Approximate values per ⅙-loaf serving: **Calories** 100, **Total fat** 1 g, **Saturated fat** 0 g, **Cholesterol** 0 mg, **Sodium** 230 mg, **Total carbohydrates** 19 g, **Protein** 4 g, **Claims**—low fat; no saturated fat; no cholesterol

Challah

Challah [HAH-la] is the traditional bread for Jewish Sabbath and holiday celebrations. It is rich with eggs and flavored with honey; time-honored tradition dictates that challah be braided or formed into a turban-shaped loaf and topped with poppy or sesame seeds. Challah is excellent for toast or sandwiches.

YIELD	2 Large Loaves, 1 lb. 8 oz. (720 g) each		METHOD	Straight Dough	
Active dry yeast	0.5 oz.	15 g	1.8%		
Water, warm (110°F/43°C)	7 fl. oz.	210 ml	25%		
Honey	3 fl. oz.	92 ml	11%		
Unsalted butter, melted	4 oz.	120 g	14%		
Eggs	6.6 oz. (4 eggs)	200 g	24%		
Bread flour	1 lb. 12 oz.	840 g	100%		
Salt	0.6 oz.	18 g	2.1%		
Egg wash	as needed	as needed			
Sesame or poppy seeds	as needed	as needed			
Total dough weight:	3 lb. 1 oz.	1495 g	178%		

1 Dissolve the yeast in the warm water in a small bowl. Stir in the honey.

2 Place the remaining water, butter, eggs, 8 ounces (240 grams) flour and the salt in a mixer bowl. Add the yeast mixture. Stir until smooth.

3 Add the remaining flour. Using a dough hook, knead the dough on medium speed until smooth and elastic, approximately 5 minutes.

4 Place the dough in a lightly greased bowl, cover and ferment until doubled, approximately 1 to 1½ hours.

5 Punch down the dough and divide into six equal portions. Roll each portion into a long strip, about 1 inch (2.5 centimeters) in diameter and 12 inches (30 centimeters) long. Lay three strips side by side and braid. Pinch the ends together, then roll the ends of the braid together to seal. Tuck the ends under the loaf. Place the loaf on a paper-lined sheet pan. Braid the three remaining pieces of dough in the same manner.

6 Brush the loaves with egg wash and sprinkle with sesame or poppy seeds. Proof until doubled, approximately 45 minutes.

7 Bake at 350°F (170°C) until the loaves are golden brown and sound hollow when thumped, approximately 40 minutes.

Approximate values per ½-loaf serving: **Calories** 156, **Total fat** 4 g, **Saturated fat** 2 g, **Cholesterol** 44 mg, **Sodium** 145 mg, **Total carbohydrates** 25 g, **Protein** 6 g

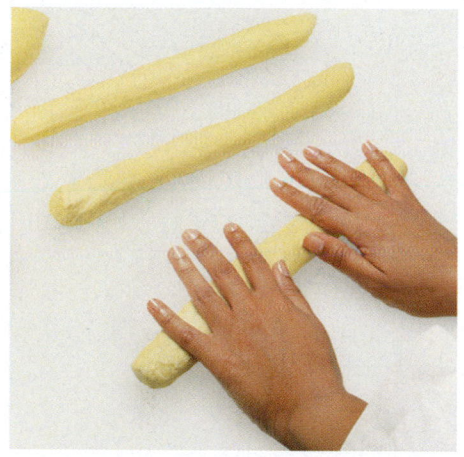

❶ Rolling challah dough into strips.

❷ Pressing three strips together.

❸ Crossing the strips one over the other to make the braid.

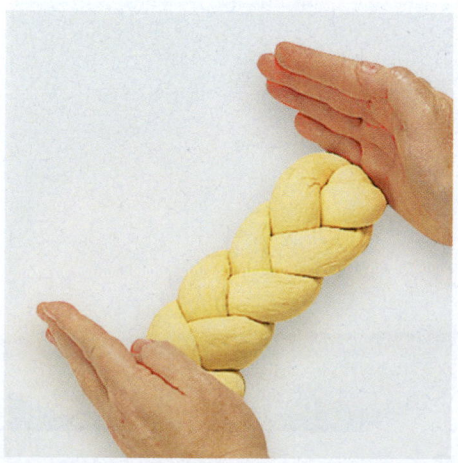

❹ Rolling the ends together to seal the braid.

Brioche

Brioche [bree-OHSH] is a rich, tender bread made with a generous amount of eggs and butter. The high ratio of fat makes this dough difficult to work with, but the flavor is well worth the extra effort. The molded dough is washed with beaten egg or egg yolks and milk or cream before and after proofing. It is important to keep the wash from touching the sides of the pan, where it could coagulate and prevent the dough from rising when baked. Brioche is traditionally baked in fluted pans and has a cap or topknot of dough; this shape is known as brioche à tête. *The dough may also be baked in a loaf pan, making it perfect for toast or canapés.*

YIELD 7 Large Loaves, 1 lb. 8 oz. (720 g) each or 60 Rolls, 2¾ oz. (82 g) each		**METHOD** Straight Dough	
All-purpose flour	4 lb. 7 oz.	2130 g	100%
Eggs	2 lb. 6 oz. (24 eggs)	1130 g	53%
Salt	1.75 oz.	50 g	2.4%
Granulated sugar	7 oz.	210 g	10%
Active dry yeast	1.75 oz.	50 g	2.4%
Water, warm (110°F/43°C)	7 fl. oz.	210 ml	10%
Unsalted butter, room temperature	3 lb.	1430 g	67%
Egg wash	as needed	as needed	
Total dough weight:	10 lb. 14 oz.	5210 g	244.8%

1 Place the flour, eggs, salt and sugar into the bowl of a mixer fitted with a dough hook. Stir the ingredients together.

2 Combine the yeast and water and add to the other ingredients.

3 Knead approximately 20 minutes on medium speed. The dough will be smooth, shiny and moist. It should not form a ball.

4 Slowly add the butter, in pieces, to the dough. Knead only until all the butter is incorporated. Remove the dough from the mixer and place it into a bowl dusted with flour. Cover and let the dough ferment at room temperature until doubled.

5 Punch down the dough, cover tightly with plastic wrap and refrigerate overnight.

6 Portion and shape the chilled dough as desired. Place the shaped dough in well-greased pans and proof at room temperature until doubled.

7 Gently brush the dough with egg wash. Bake at 375°F (190°C) until the brioche is a dark golden brown and sounds hollow. Baking time will vary depending on the temperature of the dough and the size of the rolls or loaves being baked.

1 Combining the ingredients for brioche.

2 Adding the yeast-and-water mixture to the other ingredients.

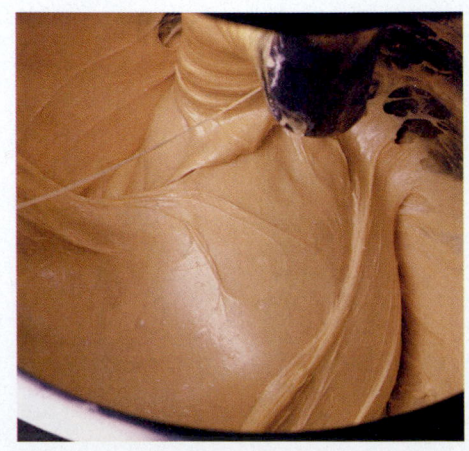

3 Brioche dough after kneading for 20 minutes.

④ Adding the butter to the brioche dough.

⑤ The finished brioche dough ready for fermentation.

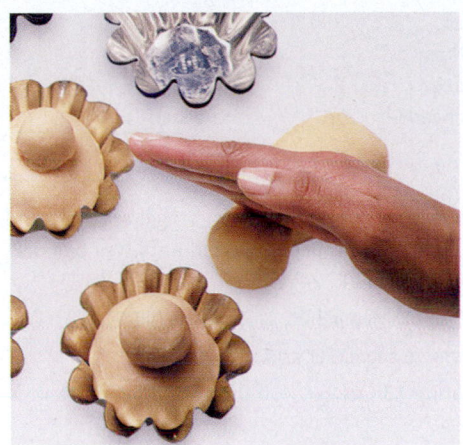

⑥ Shaping a small Brioche à Tête.

⑦ Panning small Brioche à Tête rolls.

Variations:

Large Brioche à Tête—Divide the dough into four ¾-ounce (142-gram) pieces and round. Generously butter seven large brioche pans. Fill each brioche pan with five rounded pieces of dough. First position four rounded pieces of dough in the bottom of each pan and then taper one side of the fifth piece of dough and place it in the center on top of the other four pieces, tapered end down.

Raisin Brioche—Gently warm 3 fluid ounces (90 milliliters) rum with 6 ounces (180 grams) raisins. Set aside until the raisins are plumped. Drain off the remaining rum and add the raisins to the dough after the butter is incorporated.

Brioche for Sandwiches—Reduce the sugar to 3 ounces (90 grams). Ferment the dough, then retard it overnight. Mold in a rectangular loaf pan for slicing.

Savory Cheese and Herb Brioche—Reduce the sugar to 3 ounces (90 grams). Add 4 ounces (120 grams) grated Parmesan, 4 ounces (120 grams) grated Gruyère cheese, ¼ teaspoon (1 milliliter) black pepper and ¼ teaspoon (1 milliliter) dried thyme to the dough with the flour. Mold in rectangular or conical pans. Serve sliced thin with smoked salmon, pâté or other savory spreads.

A finished large Brioche à Tête and slices.

Approximate values per 2¾-oz. (82-g) serving: **Calories** 475, **Total fat** 30 g, **Saturated fat** 17 g, **Cholesterol** 192 mg, **Sodium** 138 mg, **Total carbohydrates** 43 g, **Protein** 9 g, **Vitamin A** 30%, **Iron** 16%

Jumbo Cinnamon Buns

YIELD 24 Large Rolls, 3 oz. (90 g) each

METHOD Straight Dough

Dough:			
Buttermilk	12 fl. oz.	360 ml	37.5%
Active dry yeast	1 oz.	30 g	3%
Egg	1.6 oz. (1 egg)	48 g	5%
Egg yolks	2 oz. (3 yolks)	60 g	6%
Vanilla extract	0.15 fl. oz. (1 tsp.)	5 ml	0.5%
All-purpose flour	2 lb.	960 g	100%
Granulated sugar	5 oz.	150 g	16%
Salt	0.75 oz.	22.5 g	2.3%
Unsalted butter, softened	1 lb. 2 oz.	540 g	56%
Total dough weight:	4 lb. 8 oz.	2175 g	226%
Filling:			
Unsalted butter, melted	6 oz.	180 g	
Cinnamon, ground	0.5 oz.	15 g	
Brown sugar	6 oz.	180 g	
Pecans, chopped	12 oz.	360 g	
Raisins, optional	12 oz.	360 g	
Powdered Sugar Glaze (recipe follows)	as needed	as needed	

1 In the bowl of a mixer fitted with a dough hook, combine the buttermilk, yeast, egg, egg yolks and vanilla. Add the flour, sugar, salt and softened butter. Mix on medium speed until well blended, smooth and elastic and the dough reaches approximately 75°F (24°C).

2 Ferment the dough until doubled, approximately 1 hour. Meanwhile, prepare the filling.

3 Whisk together the melted butter, cinnamon and brown sugar. Set aside.

4 Roll the fermented dough into a rectangle measuring 18 inches × 30 inches (45 centimeters × 75 centimeters).

5 Spread the filling evenly over the entire surface of the dough. Sprinkle with the pecans and raisins (if using).

6 Starting with the longer side, roll the dough into a spiral. Cut into 24 pieces, each approximately 1½ inches (3.7 centimeters) thick. Place the rolls close together, cut side up, on a paper-lined sheet pan and allow them to rise until the rolls have increased 70 percent in volume.

7 Bake at 350°F (180°C) until golden brown, approximately 20–25 minutes.

8 Cool slightly, then top with Powdered Sugar Glaze.

Approximate values per 3-oz. (90-g) roll: **Calories** 510, **Total fat** 35 g, **Saturated fat** 16 g, **Cholesterol** 100 mg, **Sodium** 370 mg, **Total carbohydrates** 45 g, **Protein** 8 g, **Vitamin A** 15%, **Iron** 15%

Powdered Sugar Glaze

YIELD 18 fl. oz. (530 ml)

Powdered sugar, sifted	1 lb.	480 g
Vanilla extract	0.3 fl. oz. (2 tsp.)	10 ml
Lemon juice	0.3 fl. oz. (2 tsp.)	10 ml
Water, warm	2 fl. oz.	60 ml

1 Combine all the ingredients in a small bowl. Stir to blend thoroughly and dissolve any lumps. Cover and store at room temperature.

Approximate values per 1-fl.-oz. (30-ml) serving: **Calories** 160, **Total fat** 0 g, **Saturated fat** 0 g, **Cholesterol** 0 mg, **Sodium** 0 mg, **Total carbohydrates** 41 g, **Protein** 0 g

Pecan Sticky Buns

YIELD 12–15 Buns, 2–2½ oz. (60–75 g) each		**METHOD** Straight Dough	

Dough:			
Active dry yeast	1 oz.	30 g	6.2%
Granulated sugar	2 oz.	60 g	12.5%
Milk	0.5 fl. oz.	15 ml	3%
Buttermilk	5.5 fl. oz.	163 ml	34%
Salt	0.4 oz. (2 tsp.)	12 g	2.5%
Vanilla extract	0.15 fl. oz. (1 tsp.)	5 ml	1%
Lemon zest, grated	0.2 oz. (1 Tbsp.)	6 g	1.2%
Lemon juice	0.15 fl. oz. (1 tsp.)	5 ml	1%
Egg yolks	1.2 oz. (2 eggs)	36 g	7.5%
All-purpose flour	1 lb.	480 g	100%
Unsalted butter, very soft	8 oz.	240 g	50%
Total dough weight:	2 lb. 3 oz.	1052 g	219%
Topping:			
Honey	3 fl. oz.	90 ml	
Brown sugar	3 oz.	90 g	
Pecans, chopped	2 oz.	60 g	
Filling:			
Cinnamon, ground	0.07 oz. (1 tsp.)	2 g	
Pecans, chopped	3 oz.	90 g	
Brown sugar	4 oz.	120 g	
Unsalted butter, melted	3 oz.	90 g	

1 To make the dough, stir the yeast, sugar and milk together in a small bowl. Set aside.

2 Stir the buttermilk, salt, vanilla extract, lemon zest and lemon juice together and add to the yeast mixture.

3 Add the egg yolks, flour and softened butter to the liquid mixture. Knead until the butter is evenly distributed and the dough is smooth and elastic, approximately 6 minutes. Cover and ferment until doubled.

4 Prepare the topping and filling mixtures while the dough is fermenting. To make the topping, cream the honey and sugar together. Stir in the pecans. This mixture will be very stiff. To make the filling, stir the cinnamon, pecans and sugar together.

5 Lightly grease muffin cups, then distribute the topping mixture evenly, about 1 tablespoon (15 milliliters) per muffin cup. Set the pans aside at room temperature.

6 Punch down the dough and let it rest 10 minutes. Roll out the dough into a rectangle about ½ inch (1.2 centimeters) thick. Brush with melted butter and top evenly with the filling.

7 Starting with either long edge, roll up the filling in the dough. Cut into slices about ¾ to 1 inch (1.8 to 2.5 centimeters) thick. Place a slice in each muffin cup over the topping.

8 Let the buns proof until doubled, approximately 20 minutes. Bake at 325°F (160°C) until very brown, approximately 25 minutes. Immediately invert the muffin pans onto paper-lined sheet pans to let the buns and their topping slide out.

Approximate values per 2-oz. (60-g) bun: **Calories** 480, **Total fat** 26 g, **Saturated fat** 11 g, **Cholesterol** 75 mg, **Sodium** 100 mg, **Total carbohydrates** 55 g, **Protein** 5 g, **Vitamin A** 15%, **Iron** 15%

❶ Brushing melted butter over the sticky bun dough.

❷ Rolling up the filling in the sticky bun dough.

❸ Cutting and placing the sticky bun dough into the pan.

Danish Pastries

According to baking lore, Danish pastry was actually created by a French baker more than 350 years ago. He forgot to knead butter into his bread dough and attempted to cover the mistake by folding in softened butter. This rich, flaky pastry is now popular worldwide for breakfasts, desserts and snacks. The dough may be shaped in a variety of ways and is usually filled with jam, fruit, cream or marzipan. Applying a sugar syrup wash to the pastries when they are hot from the oven adds sheen and flavor.

YIELD 36 Pastries, approximately 1½ oz. (45 g) each	METHOD Rolled-In Dough		
Active dry yeast	0.5 oz.	15 g	2.5%
All-purpose flour	1 lb. 4 oz.	600 g	100%
Granulated sugar	4 oz.	120 g	20%
Water, lukewarm (90°F/32°C)	4 fl. oz.	120 ml	20%
Milk, lukewarm (90°F/32°C)	4 fl. oz.	120 ml	20%
Eggs, room temperature	3.3 oz. (2 eggs)	100 g	17%
Salt	0.2 oz. (1 tsp.)	6 g	1%
Vanilla extract	0.15 fl. oz. (1 tsp.)	4 ml	0.7%
Cinnamon, ground	0.04 oz. (1 tsp.)	1 g	0.2%
Unsalted butter, melted	1.5 oz.	45 g	7.5%
Unsalted butter, cold	1 lb.	480 g	80%
Egg wash	as needed	as needed	
Total dough weight:	3 lb. 5 oz.	1611 g	268%

1 In a large bowl, stir together the yeast and 12 ounces (360 grams) flour. Add the sugar, water, milk, eggs, salt, vanilla, cinnamon and melted butter. Stir until well combined.

2 Add the remaining flour gradually, kneading the dough by hand or with a mixer fitted with a dough hook. Knead until the dough is smooth and only slightly tacky to the touch, approximately 2–3 minutes.

3 Place the dough in a bowl that has been lightly dusted with flour. Cover and refrigerate for 1 to 1½ hours.

4 Prepare the remaining butter while the dough is chilling. Start by sprinkling flour over the work surface and placing the cold butter on the flour. Then pound the butter with a rolling pin until the butter softens. Using a pastry scraper or the heel of your hand, knead the butter and flour until the mixture is spreadable. The butter should still be cold. If the butter begins to melt, refrigerate it until firm. Keep the butter chilled until the dough is ready.

5 On a lightly floured surface, roll out the dough into a large rectangle, about ½ inch (1.2 centimeters) thick. Brush away any excess flour.

6 Spread the chilled butter evenly over two-thirds of the dough. Fold the unbuttered third over the center, then fold the buttered third over the top. Press the edges together to seal in the butter.

7 Roll the dough into a rectangle about 12 inches × 18 inches (30 centimeters × 45 centimeters). Fold the dough in thirds as before. This rolling and folding must be done a total of six times. Each time you roll and fold the dough is referred to as a turn. Chill the dough between turns as necessary. After the final turn, wrap the dough well and retard for at least 4 hours or overnight.

8 Cut, shape and fill the Danish dough as desired (see accompanying photos of snail and pinwheels). Filling recipes follow. Place the shaped pastries on a paper-lined baking sheet and proof for approximately 15–20 minutes.

9 Brush the pastries with egg wash and sprinkle lightly with sugar if desired. Bake at 400°F (200°C) for 5 minutes. Decrease the oven temperature to 350°F (180°C) and bake until light brown, approximately 12–15 minutes.

Approximate values per 1½-oz. (45-g) pastry, without filling: **Calories** 85, **Total fat** 1.5 g, **Saturated fat** 0 g, **Cholesterol** 15 mg, **Sodium** 65 mg, **Total carbohydrates** 15.5 g, **Protein** 2 g

① Kneading the cold butter with the flour using a pastry scraper and the heel of the hand.

② Spreading the chilled butter over two-thirds of the rolled-out dough.

③ Folding the dough in thirds to cover the butter.

④ Rolling out the dough with the butter sealed inside.

⑤ Folding the dough in thirds to complete a turn.

⑥ Cutting rectangles of Danish dough.

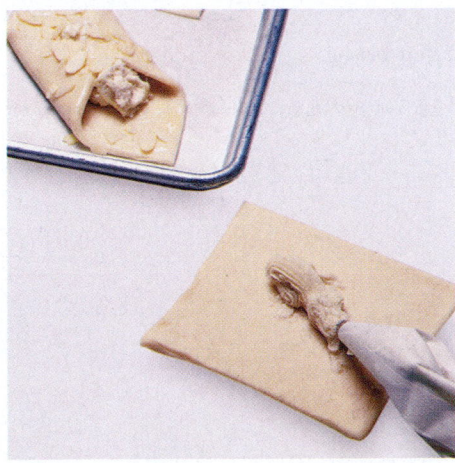

⑦ Piping Cream Cheese Filling onto Danish dough.

⑧ Shaping snails from Danish dough.

Procedure for Shaping Pinwheels or Windmills

Roll out the Danish dough approximately ⅛–½ inch (3–6 millimeters) thick and cut it into even 4-inch (10-centimeter) squares (upper left). Starting at each corner, make four diagonal cuts 1 inch (2.5 centimeters) long in the dough without cutting the dough in half (upper right). Fold one point in each triangular section of dough down toward the center to form the pinwheel shape (lower left and right).

Fillings for Danish Pastries

Cream Cheese Filling

YIELD 2 lb. 4 oz. (1091 g)

Cream cheese	1 lb. 8 oz.	720 g
Granulated sugar	4 oz.	120 g
Eggs	5 oz. (3 eggs)	150 g
Lemon zest, grated fine	0.07 oz. (1 tsp.)	5 ml
Vanilla extract	0.5 fl. oz.	15 ml
All-purpose or pastry flour	3 oz.	90 g

1 In the bowl of a mixer fitted with the paddle attachment, blend the cream cheese and sugar on low speed until smooth. Scrape down the bowl and gradually add the eggs.

2 Stir in the lemon zest and vanilla. Fold in the flour.

3 Pipe or spread this mixture over the pastry dough before baking.

Approximate values per 1-oz. (30-g) serving: **Calories** 100, **Total fat** 6 g, **Saturated fat** 4 g, **Cholesterol** 25 mg, **Sodium** 75 mg, **Total carbohydrates** 10 g, **Protein** 1 g

Apricot Filling

YIELD 2 lb. (961 g)

Dried apricots	8 oz.	240 g
Orange juice	1 pt.	480 ml
Granulated sugar	6 oz.	180 g
Salt	0.05 oz. (¼ tsp.)	1 g
Unsalted butter	2 oz.	60 g

1 Place the apricots and orange juice in a small saucepan. Cover and simmer until the apricots are very tender, approximately 25 minutes. Stir in the sugar and salt. When the sugar is dissolved, add the butter and remove from the heat.

2 Purée the mixture in a blender until smooth. Cool completely before using.

Approximate values per 1-oz. (30-g) serving: **Calories** 60, **Total fat** 1.5 g, **Saturated fat** 1 g, **Cholesterol** 5 mg, **Sodium** 20 mg, **Total carbohydrates** 13 g, **Protein** 0 g, **Vitamin A** 20%, **Vitamin C** 15%, **Claims**—low fat; low sodium; good source of vitamins A and C

Ricotta Filling

YIELD 2 lb. 14 oz. (1395 g)

Cream cheese	1 lb. 8 oz.	720 g
Ricotta	10 oz.	300 g
Granulated sugar	5 oz.	150 g
Eggs	3.3 oz. (2 eggs)	100 g
Vanilla extract	0.15 fl. oz. (1 tsp.)	5 ml
Pastry flour	4 oz.	120 g

1 In the bowl of a mixer fitted with a paddle, combine the cream cheese and ricotta on low speed until no lumps remain.

2 Add the sugar; gradually add the eggs and scrape down the bowl between additions.

3 Add the vanilla extract and then the flour and combine well.

Approximate values 1-oz. (30-g) serving: **Calories** 90, **Total fat** 6 g, **Saturated fat** 4 g, **Cholesterol** 25 mg, **Sodium** 50 mg, **Total carbohydrates** 6 g, **Protein** 2 g

Almond Paste Filling

YIELD 2 lb. (973 g)

Almond paste, room temperature	20 oz.	600 g
Unsalted butter, softened	8 oz.	240 g
Salt	0.1 oz. (½ tsp.)	3 g
Vanilla extract	0.3 fl. oz. (2 tsp.)	10 ml
Egg whites	3 oz. (3 whites)	90 g

1 Blend the almond paste until smooth in the bowl of a mixer fitted with the paddle attachment. Add in the butter in four increments, waiting for the butter to be fully incorporated before adding more. Add the salt and vanilla, and then the egg whites. Blend well.

2 Fill pastries with this mixture before baking.

Approximate values per 1-oz. (30-g) serving: **Calories** 130, **Total fat** 11 g, **Saturated fat** 4 g, **Cholesterol** 15 mg, **Sodium** 45 mg, **Total carbohydrates** 9 g, **Protein** 2 g

Kugelhopf

This brioche-styled bread, rich with raisins, is a specialty of Alsace, France, and regions to the east of Alsace. Its name refers to both the bread and the mold in which it is baked. Traditional turban-shaped kugelhopf molds are made from terra cotta, copper or tin. Kugelhopf is served with coffee as a breakfast bread or afternoon snack.

YIELD 4 Loaves, approximately   1 lb. 9 oz. (750 g) each

METHOD Straight Dough

Milk, lukewarm (90°F/32°C)	10 fl. oz.	300 ml	29.4%
Active dry yeast	1.5 oz.	45 g	4.4%
Eggs	1 lb. (10 eggs)	480 g	47%
Vanilla extract	0.15 fl. oz. (1 tsp.)	5 ml	0.4%
Bread flour	2 lb. 2 oz.	1020 g	100%
Granulated sugar	5 oz.	150 g	15%
Salt	0.75 oz.	22 g	2.2%
Unsalted butter, softened	18 oz.	540 g	53%
Raisins	1 lb.	480 g	47%
Total dough weight:	6 lb. 5 oz.	3042 g	298%

1 In the bowl of a mixer fitted with the paddle, combine the milk and the yeast. Stir to moisten the yeast then add the eggs and vanilla. Add the bread flour, sugar and salt. Mix on medium speed until well blended.

2 Switch to the dough hook. Knead until the ingredients are thoroughly mixed and the dough is soft and smooth. Gradually add the butter, kneading until the dough is smooth. Add the raisins and gently mix them into the dough.

3 Ferment the dough, covered, until doubled, approximately 1–1½ hours. Punch down the dough and let it bench rest for 15 minutes, covered.

4 Divide the dough into four equal pieces. Round the dough and place each piece into a buttered kugelhopf mold. Proof until the loaves have gained 70 percent in volume, approximately 1 hour.

5 Bake at 350°F (175°C) for approximately 45 minutes. If the loaves brown too quickly, cover them with lightly buttered aluminum foil.

6 Cool the loaves in the pans for approximately 30 minutes before unmolding to prevent collapsing.

Approximate values per ½-loaf serving: **Calories** 100, **Total fat** 5 g, **Saturated fat** 3 g, **Cholesterol** 30 mg, **Sodium** 90 mg, **Total carbohydrates** 12 g, **Protein** 2 g

Pies, Pastries and Cookies 33

Mention pastries to diners and most conjure up images of buttery dough baked to crisp flaky perfection and filled or layered with rich cream, ripe fruit or smooth custard. Mention pastries to novice chefs and most conjure up images of sophisticated, complex and intimidating work. Although the diners are correct, the novice chefs are not. Pastry making is the art of creating containers for various fillings. Taken one step at a time, most pastries are nothing more than building blocks assembled in a variety of ways to create traditional or unique desserts.

Perhaps the most important (and versatile) building block is the pastry dough. Pastries can be made with flaky dough, mealy dough, sweet dough, puff pastry, éclair dough, meringue or phyllo. See Table 33.1. Because pies, tarts and cookies are constructed from some of these same doughs (principally pie dough and sweet dough), we discuss them, as well as pie fillings, in this chapter in the section on pies and tarts. We discuss puff pastry, éclair paste and baked meringue in the section on classic pastries. Cakes and frostings are covered in Chapter 34, Cakes and Frostings. The cream, custard and mousse fillings used in some of the recipes at the end of this chapter are discussed in Chapter 35, Custards, Creams, Frozen Desserts and Dessert Sauces.

PIES AND TARTS

A **pie** is composed of a sweet or savory filling in a baked crust. It can be open-faced (without a top crust) or, more typically, topped with a full or lattice crust. A pie is generally made in a round, slope-sided pan and cut into wedges for service. A **tart** is similar to a pie except it is made in a shallow, straight-sided pan, often with fluted edges. A tart can be almost any shape. Round, square, rectangular and petal shapes are the most common tart shapes. Tarts are usually open-faced and derive much of their beauty from an attractive arrangement of glazed fruit, piped cream or chocolate decorations.

Crusts

Pie crusts and tart shells can be made from several types of dough or crumbs. Flaky dough, mealy dough and crumbs are best for pie crusts; sweet dough is usually used for tart shells. A pie crust or tart shell can be shaped and completely baked before filling (known as baked blind) or filled and baked simultaneously with the filling.

CLASSIFICATION OF PASTRY DOUGHS			TABLE 33.1
DOUGH	FRENCH NAME	CHARACTERISTICS AFTER BAKING	USE
Flaky dough	Pâte brisée	Very flaky; not sweet	Prebaked pie shells; pie top crusts
Mealy dough	Pâte brisée	Moderately flaky; not sweet	Custard, cream or fruit pie crusts; quiche crusts
Sweet dough	Pâte sucrée	Very rich; crisp; not flaky	Tart and tartlet shells
Éclair paste	Pâte à choux	Hollow with crisp exterior	Cream puffs; éclairs; savory products
Puff pastry	Pâte feuilletée	Rich but not sweet; hundreds of light, flaky layers	Tart and pastry cases; cookies; layered pastries; savory products
Meringue	Meringue	Sweet; light; crisp or soft depending on preparation	Topping or icing; baked as a shell or component for layered desserts; cookies
Phyllo	Phyllo	Very thin, crisp, flaky layers; bland	Middle Eastern pastries and savory dishes, especially hors d'oeuvre; baklava

Flaky and Mealy Doughs

Dough for pie and tart crust may be made with or without sugar. Because of its low moisture and high fat content, dough for pie crust is usually made with low-protein flour, which ensures a tender product after baking. Most pies are made using an unsweetened pie dough that may be flaky or mealy depending on how it is mixed.

Flaky pie dough takes its name from its final baked texture. It is best for pie top crusts and lattice coverings and may be used for prebaked shells that will be filled with a cooled filling shortly before service. **Mealy pie dough** takes its name from its raw texture. It is used whenever a soggy crust would be a problem (e.g., as the bottom crust of a custard or fruit pie) because it is sturdier and resists sogginess better than flaky dough. Both flaky and mealy doughs are sometimes known as **pâte brisée** [paht bree-ZAY], although the French version may contain eggs. See page 1004. They are best for pies as they are too delicate for tarts that will be removed from the pan for service. Sweet dough, described later, is better for these types of tarts.

Flaky and mealy doughs contain little or no sugar and can be prepared from the same formula with only a slight variation in mixing method. For both flaky and mealy dough, a cold fat, such as butter or shortening, is cut into the flour. The amount of flakiness in the baked crust depends on the size of the fat particles in the dough. The larger the pieces of fat, the flakier the crust will be. This is because the flakes are actually the sides of fat pockets created during baking by the melting fat and steam. In flaky dough, the fat is left in larger pieces, about the size of peas or peanuts. In mealy dough, the fat is blended in more thoroughly, until the mixture resembles coarse cornmeal. Because the resulting fat pockets are smaller, the mealy dough crust is less flaky.

The type of fat used affects dough flavor and flakiness. Butter contributes a delicious flavor but does not produce as flaky a crust as other fats. Butter is also more difficult to work with than other fats because of its lower melting point and its tendency to become brittle when chilled. Hydrogenated vegetable shortening produces a flaky crust but contributes nothing to its flavor. The flakiest pastry is made with lard. Because some people dislike lard's flavor in sweet pies or do not eat pork products, lard is more often used for pâté en croûte or other savory preparations. Some chefs prefer to use a combination of butter and either shortening or lard. Oil is not an appropriate substitute as it disperses too thoroughly throughout the dough; when baked, a crust made with oil is extremely fragile but without any flakiness.

After the fat is cut into the flour, water or milk is added to form a soft dough. Less water is needed for mealy dough because more flour is already in contact with the fat in the dough, reducing its ability to absorb liquid. Cold water is normally used for both flaky and mealy doughs. The water should be well chilled with ice to prevent softening the fat. Milk may be used to increase richness and nutritional value. Milk will produce a darker, less crisp crust, however. If dry milk powder is used for convenience, the powder should be dissolved in water first.

Hand mixing is best for small to moderate quantities of flaky or mealy pie dough. The chef retains better control over the procedure when he or she can feel the fat being incorporated. It is very difficult to make flaky dough with an electric mixer or food processor, as machines tend to cut the fat in too thoroughly. (If a food processor is used, the mixing time should be brief.) Overmixing develops too much gluten, making the dough elastic and difficult to use. If an electric mixer must be used for large quantities of flaky or mealy pie dough, use the paddle at the lowest speed and be sure the fat is well chilled, even frozen. Refrigerating pie dough after mixing is recommended to allow the moisture to evenly distribute through the mixture and to firm the fat for ease of handling. The recipe for Basic Pie Dough on page 980 and the recipe for Quiche Dough (Pâte Brisée) on page 1004 may be mixed using the following procedure.

Procedure for Preparing Flaky and Mealy Doughs

1 Sift flour, salt and sugar (if used) together in a large bowl.

2 Cut or rub the fat into the flour as described on page 929. For flaky dough, blend coarsely and leave the fat in large pieces the size of peas or peanuts. For mealy dough, blend finely until the mixture resembles coarse cornmeal.

3 Gradually add a cold liquid, mixing gently until the dough holds together. Do not overmix.

4 Cover the dough with plastic wrap and chill thoroughly before using.

5 Remember that rerolled scraps will be tough and elastic.

Basic Pie Dough

YIELD 2 lb. 10 oz. (1267 g) Dough,
approximately 3 Shells, 9 in. (22 cm) each

Unsalted butter, chilled	1 lb.	475 g	76%
Pastry flour	1 lb. 5 oz.	630 g	100%
Buttermilk or water	4 fl. oz.	120 ml	19%
Salt	0.4 oz. (2 tsp.)	12 g	1.9%
Granulated sugar, optional	0.5 oz. (1 Tbsp.)	15 g	2.4%
Vanilla extract, optional	0.5 fl. oz. (1 Tbsp.)	15 ml	2.4%
Total dough weight:	2 lb. 10 oz.	1267 g	201%

1 Cut butter into medium dice ⅜ inch (9 millimeters) square. Sift the flour onto a work surface or into a large bowl.

2 Cut the butter into the flour mixture until the desired consistency (flaky or mealy) is reached.

3 Combine the buttermilk, salt, sugar and vanilla extract (if using) in a bowl with a whisk. Gradually add the liquid to the flour-butter mixture. Mix gently until the dough holds together. Do not overmix or add too much liquid.

4 Cover the dough with plastic wrap and chill thoroughly before using.

Approximate values per 1-oz. (30-g) serving: **Calories** 130 **Total fat** 9 g, **Saturated fat** 6 g, **Cholesterol** 25 mg, **Sodium** 110 mg, **Total carbohydrates** 11 g, **Protein** 2 g

❶ Cutting the fat into the flour coarsely for flaky dough.

❷ Cutting the fat into the flour finely for mealy dough.

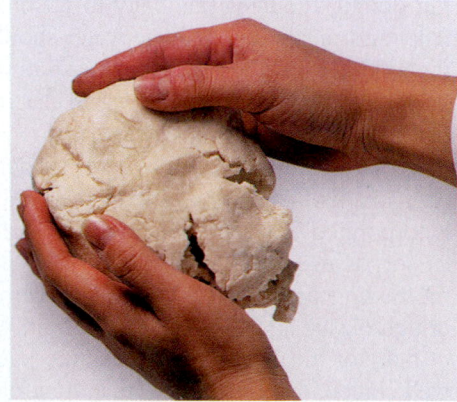

❸ The finished dough.

Sweet Dough

Sweet dough or **pâte sucrée** [paht soo-KRAY] is a rich, nonflaky dough used for sweet tart shells. It is sturdier than flaky or mealy dough because it contains egg yolks and the fat is blended in thoroughly. Because more fat coats the flour, less gluten is formed, making for a tender dough when baked. Sweet dough scraps may be rerolled once or twice without toughening unlike flaky or mealy doughs. Sweet dough is more cookie-like than classic pie dough and has the rich flavor of butter. It creates a crisp but tender crust and is excellent for tartlets as well as for straight-sided tarts that will be removed from their pans before service. Raw sweet dough may be kept refrigerated for up to 2 weeks or frozen for up to 3 months.

Procedure for Preparing Sweet Dough

1 Cream softened butter. Add sugar and beat until the mixture is light and fluffy.
2 Slowly add eggs, blending well.
3 Slowly add flour, mixing only until incorporated. Overmixing toughens the dough.
4 Cover the dough with plastic wrap and chill thoroughly before using.
5 Scraps may be rerolled once or twice, provided the dough is still cool, nongreasy and pliable. If too much gluten develops, the crust will shrink and toughen.

Sweet Dough

YIELD 3 lb. 12 oz. (1788 g) Dough;
approximately 5 Shells, 9 in. (22 cm) each

Unsalted butter, softened	12 oz.	360 g	43%
Powdered sugar	10 oz.	300 g	36%
Egg yolks	8 oz. (13 yolks)	240 g	29%
Eggs	1.6 oz. (1 egg)	48 g	5.7%
All-purpose flour	1 lb. 12 oz.	840 g	100%
Total dough weight:	3 lb. 11 oz.	1788 g	213%

1 Cream the butter and powdered sugar in the large bowl of a mixer fitted with the paddle attachment.
2 Combine the egg yolks and whole eggs. Slowly add the eggs to the creamed butter. Mix until smooth and free of lumps, scraping down the bowl as needed.
3 With the mixer on low speed, slowly add the flour to the butter-and-egg mixture. Mix only until incorporated; do not overmix. The dough should be firm, smooth and not sticky.
4 Dust a half-sheet pan with flour. Pack the dough into the pan evenly. Wrap well in plastic wrap and chill until firm.
5 Work with a small portion of the chilled dough when shaping tart shells or other products.

Approximate values per 1-oz. (30-g) serving: **Calories** 120, **Total fat** 5 g, **Saturated fat** 3 g, **Cholesterol** 15 mg, **Sodium** 0 mg, **Total carbohydrates** 16 g, **Protein** 2 g, **Vitamin A** 4%

Shaping Crusts

To shape crusts, roll out the dough to fit into a pie pan or tart shell (mold) or to sit on top of fillings. Mealy, flaky and sweet doughs are all easier to roll out and work with if well chilled, as chilling keeps the fat firm and prevents stickiness. When rolling and shaping the dough, work on a clean, flat surface (wood or marble is best). Lightly dust the work surface, rolling pin and dough with pastry flour before starting to roll the dough to prevent sticking. Roll the dough to a thickness of ⅛–¼ inch (3–6 millimeters.) Work only with a manageable amount at a time: usually one crust's worth for a pie or standard-sized tart or enough for 10–12 tartlet shells.

Roll out the dough from the center, working toward the edges. Periodically lift the dough gently and rotate it. This keeps the dough from sticking and helps produce an even thickness. If the dough sticks to the rolling pin or work surface, sprinkle on a bit more flour. Too much flour, however, makes the crust dry and crumbly and causes gray streaks.

MISE EN PLACE
• Soften butter.

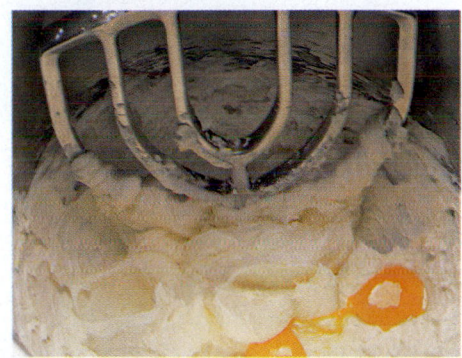
① Mixing sweet dough.

② Packing the finished sweet dough into the pan.

Procedure for Rolling and Shaping Pie Dough

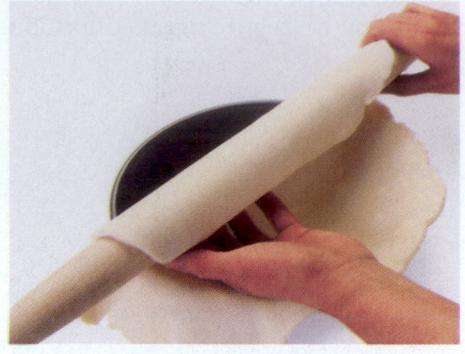

① Dough for a typical pie crust or tart shell should be rolled to a thickness of approximately ⅛ inch (3 millimeters); it should be at least 2 inches (5 centimeters) larger in diameter than the baking pan.

② When you have rolled the dough to the desired thickness, carefully roll the dough up onto a rolling pin. Position the pin over the pie pan or tart shell and unroll the dough, easing it into the pan or shell.

③ Press the dough into the pan. For a single crust pie, trim the edge. Use the index finger and thumb on one hand and the index finger on the other to create a scalloped edge. Bake or fill as desired.

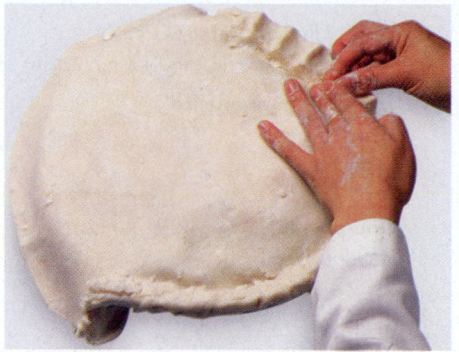

④ To make a double crust pie, roll the dough out as before, making the circle large. Press the dough into the pan and trim the edges as needed.

⑤ Roll out the remaining dough, making the circle large enough to hang over the pan's edge. The dough may be lifted into place by rolling it onto the rolling pin, as with the bottom crust.

⑥ Seal the top crust to the bottom crust with egg wash or water. Pinch the top and bottom crust together between your fingertips or crimp as desired. Slits or designs should be cut from the top crust to allow steam to escape.

Procedure for Rolling and Shaping Dough for Lattice Crusts

1 Roll the dough out and line the pan as specified in the previous procedure. Using a ruler as a guide, cut even strips of the desired width, typically ½ inch (1.2 centimeters).

2 Spoon or pour the filling into the dough-lined-pan. Using an over-under-over pattern, weave the strips together on top of the filling. Be sure the strips are evenly spaced for an attractive result. Crimp the lattice strips to the bottom crust to seal.

Of Tarts and Tortes

The names given to desserts can be rather confusing. One country or region calls an item a torte while another region calls the same item a gâteau. The following definitions are based on classic French terms. You will, no doubt, encounter variations depending on your location and the training of those with whom you work.

Cake: In the United States and Great Britain, *cake* refers to a broad range of pastries, including layer cakes, coffee cakes and gâteaux. *Cake* may refer to almost everything that is baked, tender, sweet and sometimes frosted. But to the French, *le cake* is a loaf-shaped butter cake with fruit, similar to an American poundcake with the addition of fruit, nuts and rum.

Gâteau (pl. *gâteaux*): To the French, *gâteau* refers to various pastry items made with puff pastry, éclair paste, pie dough or sweet dough. In America, *gâteau* often refers to any cake-type dessert.

Pastry: *Pastry* refers to a group of doughs made primarily with flour, water and fat. *Pastry* can also refer to foods made with these doughs or to a large variety of fancy baked goods.

Tart: A tart is a pastry shell filled with sweet or savory ingredients. Tarts have straight, shallow sides and are usually prepared open-face. In France and Britain, the term *flan* is sometimes used to refer to the same items. (In Spain and France, *flan* also refers to an egg custard.) A tartlet is a small, individual-sized tart.

Torte: In Central and Eastern European countries, a torte (pl. *torten*) is a rich cake in which all or part of the flour is replaced with finely chopped nuts or bread crumbs. Other cultures refer to any round sweet cake as a torte.

Procedure for Rolling and Shaping Dough for Tartlet Shells

1. A typical crust for tartlets should be approximately ⅛ inch (3 millimeters) thick. It is usually made from sweet dough.
2. Roll the dough out as described earlier. Then roll the dough up onto the rolling pin.

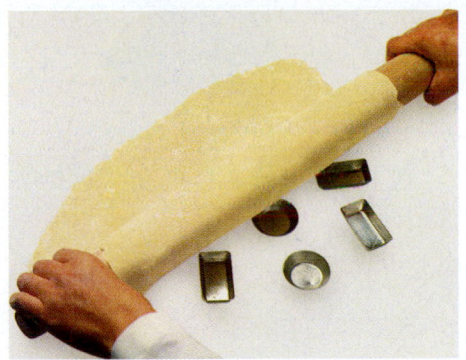

3. Lay out a single layer of tartlet pans. Unroll the dough over the shells, pressing the dough gently into each one.

4. Roll the rolling pin over the top of the pans. The edge of the pans will cut the dough. Be sure the dough is pressed against the sides of each pan. Bake or fill as desired.

Baking Crusts

Pie crusts can be filled and then baked, or baked and then filled. To retain their shape, pie crusts are **baked blind**—lined with parchment or buttered foil, then filled with baking (or pie) weights or dry rice or beans and baked without the filling. Unfilled baked crusts can be stored at room temperature for 2–3 days or wrapped in plastic wrap and frozen for as long as 3 months.

baked blind describes a pie shell or tart shell that is baked unfilled, using baking weights or beans to support the crust as it bakes

Procedure for Rolling and Baking Unfilled (Baked Blind) Crusts

1 Roll the dough out to the desired thickness.

2 Place a tart ring on a paper-lined sheet pan. Carefully roll the dough up onto a rolling pin. Position the pin over the tart ring and unroll the dough.

3 Ease the dough into the tart ring, pressing to make a smooth edge.

4 Run a rolling pin over the edge of the tart ring to remove excess dough and produce a level edge to the tart. **Dock** the tart dough with a fork.

dock to prick small holes in an unbaked dough or crust to allow steam to escape and to prevent the dough from rising when baked

5 Cover the dough with heat-resistant plastic, parchment paper or greased aluminum foil (greased side down). Press the plastic, paper or foil against the walls of the shell, allowing a portion of it to extend above the pan. Fill the pan with baking weights or dry rice or beans.

6 Bake the weighted crust at 350°F (180°C) for 10–15 minutes. Remove the weights and paper.

7 Brush the baked crust with egg wash, then return the crust to the oven. Bake until golden brown and fully cooked, approximately 10–15 minutes. Allow to cool, then fill as desired.

Crumb Crusts

A quick and tasty bottom crust can be made from finely ground cookie crumbs moistened with melted butter. Crumb crusts can be used for unbaked pies such as those with cream or chiffon fillings, or they can be baked with their fillings, as with cheesecakes. Chocolate cookies, graham crackers, gingersnaps, vanilla wafers and macaroons are popular choices for crumb crusts. Some breakfast cereals such as corn flakes or bran flakes are also used. Ground nuts and spices can be added for flavor. If packaged crumbs are unavailable, use a food processor, blender or rolling pin to grind crumbs. Make sure to grind cookies or any other ingredients you use to a fine, even crumb.

The typical ratio for a crumb crust is 1 part melted butter, 2 parts sugar and 4 parts crumbs. For example, 8 ounces (240 grams) graham crackers mixed with 4 ounces (120 grams) sugar and 2 ounces (60 grams) melted butter produces enough crust to line one 9- or 10-inch (22- or 25-centimeter) pan. The amount of sugar may need to be adjusted depending on the type of crumbs. For example, chocolate sandwich cookies need less sugar than graham crackers. If the mixture is too dry to stick together, gradually add more melted butter. Press the mixture into the bottom of the pan and chill or bake it before filling.

Making a crumb crust.

Fillings

Fillings make pies and tarts distinctive and flavorful. The role of starch in pie filling and four types of fillings are discussed here: cream, fruit, custard and chiffon. There is no one correct presentation or filling-and-crust combination. The apples in an apple pie, for example, may be sliced, seasoned and topped with streusel; caramelized, puréed and blended with cream; chopped and covered with a flaky dough lattice; or poached, arranged over pastry cream and brushed with a shiny glaze. An understanding of the fundamental techniques for making fillings—and some imagination—ensures success.

Starches for Pies

A variety of pie fillings rely on starches for stability and thickening. Even custard fillings, which include eggs for thickening and flavor, may contain starch to keep the filling from separating. The type of starch depends on the desired results.

Although flour is somewhat unreliable as a thickener, it can be used in traditional baked fruit pies in which the fruit is not excessively juicy, such as Pippin apples or Bosc pears. Cornstarch is preferred for custard and fruit fillings because it sets up into a somewhat firm, clear gel. However, cornstarch loses its potency when combined with sugar or an acid such as lemon juice, and when a pie is to be frozen, cornstarch is not recommended as a thickener. The gel formed by cornstarch when cooking breaks down during freezing. Use tapioca or tapioca starch instead. Tapioca is a good choice for fruit fillings because it thickens at a lower temperature than cornstarch, withstands freezing and cooks into a clear gel. Instant tapioca can be measured and ground into a powder before using. Grinding makes the tapioca disperse more readily. **Modified starch** made from corn, also known as **waxy maize**, can also be used for pies that must be frozen.

Cream Fillings

A cream filling is a flavored pastry cream—a type of starch-thickened egg custard discussed in Chapter 35, Custards, Creams, Frozen Desserts and Dessert Sauces. When used as a pie filling, pastry cream should be thickened with cornstarch so that it is firm enough to hold its shape when the pie is sliced. The cornstarch must be cooked long enough so that the starch fully gelatinizes and thickens before using. Popular cream filling flavors are chocolate, banana, coconut and lemon.

A cream filling is fully cooked on the stove top, so a prebaked or crumb crust is needed. The prebaked or crumb crust can be filled while the cream filling is still warm, or the filling can be chilled and piped into the crust later. A cream pie is often topped with meringue, which is then browned quickly in an oven or under a broiler.

MISE EN PLACE

- Prepare and bake pie shells.

1 Filling a baked pie shell with chocolate custard according to the Chocolate Cream Pie variation of the recipe.

2 Topping with Crème Chantilly.

Basic Cream Pie

YIELD 3 Pies, 9 in. (22 cm) each		METHOD Cream Filling
Filling:		
Granulated sugar	14 oz.	420 g
Milk	44 fl. oz.	1.3 lt
Heavy cream	20 fl. oz.	600 ml
Egg yolks, pasteurized	4.8 oz. (8 yolks)	144 g
Cornstarch	4.5 oz.	135 g
Unsalted butter	4 oz.	120 g
Vanilla extract	1 fl. oz.	30 ml
Flaky pie dough shells, baked	3 shells	3 shells
Crème Chantilly (page 1075) or meringue	as needed	as needed

1 In a heavy saucepan, dissolve 8 ounces (240 grams) sugar in the milk. Add the heavy cream and bring to a boil.

2 Meanwhile, whisk the egg yolks and the remaining sugar together in a small bowl. Add the cornstarch and whisk until smooth.

3 Temper the egg mixture with approximately half of the hot milk. Stir the warmed egg mixture back into the remaining milk and return it to a boil, whisking constantly.

4 Whisking constantly and vigorously, allow the cream to boil until thick, approximately 2 minutes. Remove from the heat and stir in the butter and vanilla extract. Stir until the butter is melted and incorporated.

5 Pour the cream into the pie shells. Chill the pies.

6 The pies can be topped with Crème Chantilly once the filling is very cold or with meringue (see page 997) while the filling is still warm. The meringue is then lightly browned in a 425°F (210°C) oven.

7 Chill the pies for service.

Variations:

Chocolate Cream Pie—Melt 12 ounces (340 grams) bittersweet chocolate. Fold the melted chocolate into the hot cream after adding the butter and vanilla extract.

Banana Cream Pie—Layer 12 ounces (340 grams) sliced bananas (about 3 medium bananas) into the baked shell with the warm cream. Do not purée the bananas, as this will make the filling runny.

Coconut Cream Pie I—Substitute 12 fluid ounces (340 milliliters) cream of coconut for 12 fluid ounces (340 milliliters) milk and 4 ounces (120 grams) sugar. Top the pie with meringue and shredded coconut.

Coconut Cream Pie II—Stir 8 ounces (250 grams) toasted coconut into the warm cream.

Approximate values per ⅛-pie serving: **Calories** 220, **Total fat** 9 g, **Saturated fat** 5 g, **Cholesterol** 130 mg, **Sodium** 55 mg, **Total carbohydrates** 29 g, **Protein** 5 g, **Vitamin A** 10%

Fruit Fillings

A fruit filling is a mixture of fruit, fruit juice, spices and sugar thickened with a starch. Apple, cherry, blueberry and peach are traditional favorites. The fruit can be fresh, frozen or canned. (See Chapter 26, Fruits, for more information about selecting the best fruits for fillings.) The starch can be flour, cornstarch, tapioca or a packaged commercial instant or pregelatinized starch. Streusel topping is used for some pies, particularly fruit pies. A standard streusel recipe is given in Chapter 31, Quick Breads.

The ingredients for a fruit filling are most often combined using one of three methods: **cooked fruit**, **cooked juice** or **baked**.

Cooked Fruit Fillings

Cooked fruit filling is often appropriate when the desired fruit needs to be softened by cooking (e.g., apples or rhubarb) or is naturally rather dry such as dried apricots or raisins. Canned fruits should not be used in cooked fruit fillings as they have already been cooked and would break down in the process. Combine a cooked fruit filling with a prebaked or crumb crust.

Procedure for Preparing Cooked Fruit Fillings

1 Combine the fruit, sugar and juice or liquid in a heavy, nonreactive saucepan and bring to a boil.
2 Dissolve the starch (usually cornstarch) in a cold liquid, then add to the boiling fruit.
3 Stirring constantly, cook the fruit-and-starch mixture until the starch is clear and the mixture is thickened.
4 Add any other flavorings and any acidic ingredients such as lemon juice. Stir to blend.
5 Remove from the heat and cool before filling a prebaked pie or crumb crust.

Apple-Cranberry Pie

YIELD 1 Pie, 9 in. (22 cm)	METHOD	Cooked Fruit Filling
Filling:		
Fresh tart apples such as Granny Smiths, peeled, cored and cut in 1-in. (2.5-cm) cubes	1 lb.	480 g
Brown sugar	4 oz.	120 g
Granulated sugar	4 oz.	120 g
Orange zest, grated fine	0.2 oz. (1 Tbsp.)	6 g
Cinnamon, ground	0.07 oz. (1 tsp.)	2 g
Salt	0.05 oz. (¼ tsp.)	1.5 g
Cornstarch	0.18 oz. (2 tsp.)	6 g
Orange juice	3 fl. oz.	90 ml
Fresh cranberries, rinsed	8 oz.	240 g
Mealy dough pie shell, partially baked	1 shell	1 shell
Streusel Topping (page 935)	7 oz.	210 g

MISE EN PLACE
- Peel, core and cut apples.
- Grate orange zest.
- Prepare and par-bake pie shell.

1 Combine the apples, brown sugar, granulated sugar, orange zest, cinnamon and salt in a large, nonreactive saucepan.
2 Dissolve the cornstarch in the orange juice and add it to the apples.
3 Cover and simmer until the apples begin to soften, stirring occasionally. Add the cranberries, cover and continue simmering until the cranberries begin to soften, approximately 2 minutes.
4 Place the apple-cranberry mixture in the pie shell and cover with the prepared Streusel Topping. Bake at 400°F (200°C) until the filling is bubbling hot and the topping is lightly browned, approximately 20 minutes.

Variation:

Apple-Rhubarb Pie—Substitute cleaned rhubarb, cut into 1-inch (2.5-centimeter) chunks, for the cranberries. Add 0.01 ounce (⅛ teaspoon/0.3 grams) nutmeg.

Approximate values per ⅛-pie serving: **Calories** 300, **Total fat** 10 g, **Saturated fat** 4 g, **Cholesterol** 5 mg, **Sodium** 254 mg, **Total carbohydrates** 63 g, **Protein** 3 g, **Vitamin C** 15%, **Claims**—good source of fiber

Cooked Juice Fillings

The cooked juice filling method works with juicy fruits such as berries, especially when they are canned or frozen. This method is also recommended for delicate fruits that cannot withstand cooking, such as strawberries, pineapple and blueberries. Only the juice is cooked in this process, so the fruit retains its shape, color and flavor better. Use a cooked juice filling to fill a prebaked or crumb crust.

Procedure for Preparing Cooked Juice Fillings

1   Drain the juice from the fruit. Measure the juice and add water if necessary to create the desired volume.

2   Combine the liquid with sugar in a nonreactive saucepan and bring to a boil.

3   Dissolve the starch in cold water, then add it to the boiling liquid while whisking to prevent lumps from forming. Cook until the starch is clear and the juice is thickened, about 3 minutes.

4   Add any other flavoring ingredients.

5   Pour the thickened juice over the fruit and stir gently.

6   Cool the filling before placing it in a prebaked pie shell.

♥ **Good Choice**

MISE EN PLACE

• Grate lemon zest.

Blueberry Pie Filling

YIELD 8 lb. (3.8 kg), Filling for 4–5 Pies		METHOD Cooked Juice Filling	
Canned blueberries, #10 can, unsweetened	1 can	1 can
Granulated sugar	1 lb. 12 oz.	840 g
Cornstarch	4.5 oz.	135 g
Water	8 fl. oz.	240 ml
Cinnamon, ground	0.04 oz. (½ tsp.)	1 g
Lemon juice	1 fl. oz.	30 ml
Lemon zest, grated fine	0.2 oz. (1 Tbsp.)	6 g

1   Drain the juice from the canned blueberries, reserving both the fruit and the juice.

2   Measure the juice and, if necessary, add enough water to provide 1 quart (1 liter) of liquid. Bring to a boil, add the sugar and stir until dissolved.

3   Dissolve the cornstarch in 8 fluid ounces (240 milliliters) water.

4   Add the cornstarch to the boiling juice and return to a boil. Cook until the mixture thickens and clears. Remove from the heat.

5   Add the cinnamon, lemon juice, lemon zest and reserved blueberries. Stir gently to coat the fruit with the cooked juice.

6   Allow the filling to cool to room temperature, then use it to fill prebaked pie shells or tarts.

Approximate values per 1-oz. (30-g) serving: **Calories** 40, **Total fat** 0 g, **Saturated fat** 0 g, **Cholesterol** 0 mg, **Sodium** 0 mg, **Total carbohydrates** 10 g, **Protein** 0 g, **Claims**—fat free; no cholesterol; no sodium; low calorie

Baked Fruit Fillings

The baked fruit filling method is a traditional technique in which the fruit, sugar, flavorings and starch are combined in an unbaked shell. The dough and filling are then baked simultaneously. Results are not always consistent with this technique, however, as thickening is difficult to control.

Procedure for Preparing Baked Fruit Fillings

1 Combine the starch, spices and sugar.
2 Peel, core, cut and drain the fruit as desired or as directed in the recipe.
3 Toss the fruit with the starch mixture, coating well.
4 Add a portion of juice to moisten the fruit. Small lumps of butter are also often added.
5 Fill an unbaked shell with the fruit mixture to just below the rim. Cover with a top crust, lattice or streusel and bake.

Cherry Pie

YIELD 2 Pies, 9 in. (22 cm) each	METHOD Baked Fruit Filling	
Tapioca, instant	1.5 oz.	45 g
Salt	0.12 oz. (1 pinch)	1 g
Granulated sugar	1 lb.	480 g
Almond extract	0.08 fl. oz. (½ tsp.)	2 ml
Canned pitted cherries, drained, liquid reserved	3 lb.	1.4 kg
Mealy dough pie shells, unbaked	2 shells	2 shells
Unsalted butter	1 oz.	30 g
Egg wash	as needed	as needed
Sanding sugar	as needed	as needed

MISE EN PLACE

- Drain cherries, reserving the liquid.
- Prepare and shape pie shells.
- Make the egg wash.
- Preheat the oven and sheet pan to 400°F (200°C) while filling rests.

1 Stir the tapioca, salt and granulated sugar together. Add the almond extract and cherries.
2 Stir in up to 8 fluid ounces (240 milliliters) of the liquid drained from the cherries, adding enough liquid to moisten the mixture thoroughly.
3 Allow the filling to stand for 30 minutes. Then stir gently and place the filling in the unbaked pie shells.
4 Cut the butter into small pieces. Dot the filling with the butter.
5 Place a top crust or a lattice crust over the filling; seal and flute the edges. If using a full top crust, cut several slits in the dough to allow steam to escape. Brush the top crust or lattice with egg wash and sprinkle with sanding sugar.
6 Place on a preheated sheet pan and bake at 400°F (200°C) for 50–60 minutes.

Approximate values per ⅛-pie serving: **Calories** 340, **Total fat** 9 g, **Saturated fat** 3 g, **Cholesterol** 5 mg, **Sodium** 170 mg, **Total carbohydrates** 63 g, **Protein** 2 g

Custard Fillings

A **custard pie** has a soft filling that bakes along with the crust. Popular examples include pumpkin, egg custard and pecan pies. As explained in Chapter 35, Custards, Creams, Frozen Desserts and Dessert Sauces, custards are liquids thickened by coagulated egg proteins. To make a custard pie, an uncooked liquid containing eggs is poured into a pie shell. When baked, the egg proteins coagulate, firming and setting the filling.

The procedure for making custard pies is straightforward: Combine the ingredients and bake. However, it can be a challenge to bake the bottom crust completely without overcooking the filling. For the best results, start baking the pie near the bottom of a hot oven at 400°F (200°C). After 10 minutes, lower the heat to 325–350°F (160–180°C) to finish cooking the filling slowly.

To determine the doneness of a custard pie:

1 Shake the pie gently. It is done if it is no longer liquid. The center should show only a slight movement.
2 Insert a thin knife about 1 inch (2.5 centimeters) from the center. The filling is done if the knife comes out clean.

Pumpkin Pie

- Beat eggs.
- Prepare and shape pie shells.
- Preheat the oven and sheet pan to 400°F (200°C) while the filling rests.

YIELD 2 Pies, 9 in. (22 cm) each   **METHOD** Custard Filling

Filling:		
Eggs, beaten slightly	6.75 oz. (4 eggs)	200 g
Pumpkin purée	2 lb.	960 g
Granulated sugar	12 oz.	360 g
Salt	0.2 oz. (1 tsp.)	6 g
Nutmeg, ground	0.04 oz. (½ tsp.)	1 g
Cloves, ground	0.04 oz. (½ tsp.)	1 g
Cinnamon, ground	0.14 oz. (2 tsp.)	4 g
Ginger, ground	0.07 oz. (1 tsp.)	2 g
Evaporated milk	24 fl. oz.	720 ml
Flaky dough pie shells, unbaked	2 shells	2 shells

1 Using a whisk, combine the eggs and pumpkin. Blend in the sugar.

2 Add the salt and spices, and then the evaporated milk. Whisk until completely blended and smooth.

3 Allow the filling to rest for 15–20 minutes before filling the pie shells. This allows the starch in the pumpkin to begin absorbing liquid, making it less likely to separate (weep) after baking.

4 Pour the filling into the unbaked pie shells. Place in the oven on a preheated sheet pan at 400°F (200°C). Bake for 15 minutes. Lower the oven temperature to 350°F (180°C) and bake until a knife inserted near the center comes out clean, approximately 40–50 minutes.

Approximate values per ⅛-pie serving: **Calories** 210, **Total fat** 10 g, **Saturated fat** 2.5 g, **Cholesterol** 30 mg, **Sodium** 230 mg, **Total carbohydrates** 25 g, **Protein** 4 g, **Vitamin A** 6%

TROUBLESHOOTING CHART FOR PIES		TABLE 33.2
PROBLEM	**CAUSE**	**SOLUTION**
Crust shrinks	Overmixing	Adjust mixing technique, reduce mixing time and speed
	Overworking dough	Handle dough gently; avoid rerolling scraps
	Not enough fat	Increase fat in the formula
	Did not let dough rest after mixing; dough was stretched or rolled incorrectly	Refrigerate dough after mixing; improve handling technique
Soggy crust	Wrong dough used	Use mealier dough, cutting in the fat until it resembles coarse cornmeal
	Oven temperature too low	Increase oven temperature
	Not baked long enough	Bake longer
	Filling too moist	Reduce liquid in filling; use more thickener
Crumbly crust	Not enough liquid	Increase liquids
	Not enough fat	Increase fat in the formula
	Improper mixing	Increase mixing time
Tough crust	Not enough fat	Increase fat in the formula
	Overmixing	Reduce mixing speed and time
Runny filling	Insufficient starch	Increase starch in formula
	Starch insufficiently cooked	Cook longer
Lumpy cream filling	Starch not incorporated properly	Blend starch with sugar before adding liquid; stir filling while cooking
	Filling overcooked	Reduce oven temperature or cooking time
Custard filling separates (weeps)	Too many eggs	Reduce egg content or add starch to the filling
	Eggs overcooked	Reduce oven temperature or baking time

SUGGESTIONS FOR ASSEMBLING PIES AND TARTS			TABLE 33.3
FILLING	**CRUST**	**TOPPING**	**GARNISH**
Vanilla or lemon cream	Prebaked flaky dough or crumb	None, meringue or whipped cream	Crumbs from the crust
Chocolate cream	Prebaked flaky dough or crumb	None, meringue or whipped cream	Crumbs from the crust or shaved chocolate
Banana cream	Prebaked flaky dough	Meringue or whipped cream	Dried banana chips
Coconut cream	Prebaked flaky dough	Meringue or whipped cream	Shredded coconut
Fresh fruit	Unbaked mealy dough, or sweet dough if shallow tart	Lattice, full crust or streusel	Sanding sugar or cut-out designs if lattice or top crust is used
Canned or frozen fruit	Unbaked mealy dough	Lattice, full crust or streusel	Sanding sugar or cut-out designs if lattice or top crust is used
Chiffon or mousse	Crumb or prebaked, sweetened flaky dough	None or whipped cream	Crumbs, fruit or shaved chocolate
Custard	Unbaked mealy dough	None	Whipped cream, cinnamon
Vanilla pastry cream	Prebaked sweet dough	Fresh fruit	Glaze
Lemon or citrus curd	Prebaked sweet dough	Fresh fruit, berries	Glaze, Italian meringue

Chiffon Fillings

A chiffon filling is created by adding gelatin to a stirred custard or a fruit purée. Whipped egg whites are then folded into the mixture. The filling is placed in a prebaked crust and chilled until firm. These preparations are the same as those for chiffons, mousses and Bavarians discussed in Chapter 35, Custards, Creams, Frozen Desserts and Dessert Sauces.

Assembling Pies and Tarts

The various types of pie fillings can be used to fill almost any crust or shell, provided the crust is prebaked as necessary. The filling can then be topped with meringue or whipped cream as desired. Garnishes such as toasted coconut, cookie crumbs and chocolate curls are often added for appearance and flavor. Table 33.2 is a troubleshooting chart to be used when problems arise with pie making. Table 33.3 lists some popular combinations to use when making pies and tarts.

Arranging fresh fruit decoratively over a filled tart shell.

Storing Pies and Tarts

Pies and tarts filled with cream or custard must be refrigerated to retard bacterial growth. Unbaked fruit pies or pie shells may be frozen for up to 2 months. Freezing baked fruit pies is not recommended, but they may be stored for 2–3 days at room temperature or in the refrigerator. Custard, cream and meringue-topped pies should be stored in the refrigerator for no more than 2–3 days. They should not be frozen, as the eggs will separate, making the product runny.

CLASSIC PASTRIES

Puff pastry, éclair paste and meringue are classic components of French pastries used to create a wide variety of dessert and pastry items. Many combinations are traditional. Once you master the skills necessary to produce these products, however, you will be free to experiment with other flavors and assembly techniques.

Puff Pastry

Puff pastry is one of the bakeshop's most elegant and sophisticated products. Also known as **pâte feuilletée** [paht fuh-yuh-TAY], puff pastry is a rich, buttery dough that bakes into hundreds of light, crisp layers. Puff pastry is used for both sweet and savory preparations. It can be baked and then filled, or filled first and then baked. Puff pastry may be used to wrap beef (for Beef Wellington, page 337), pâté (for pâté en croûte, page 845) or Almond Cream (for an apple tart, page 1008). It can be shaped into shells or cases known as vol-au-vents or bouchées and filled with shellfish in a cream sauce or berries in a pastry cream. Puff pastry is essential for palmiers, page 1010, napoleons page 1009 and other French pastries.

Like croissant and Danish dough (discussed in Chapter 32, Yeast Breads), puff pastry is a rolled-in dough. But unlike those doughs, puff pastry does not contain any yeast or chemical leavening agents. Fat is rolled into the dough in horizontal layers; when baked, the fat melts, separating the dough into layers. The fat's moisture turns into steam, which causes the dough to rise and the layers to further separate.

Butter is the preferred fat for puff pastry because of its flavor and melt-in-the-mouth quality. But butter is rather difficult to work with because it becomes brittle when cold and melts at a relatively low temperature. Therefore, in some instances, specially formulated puff pastry shortenings are used to compensate for butter's shortcomings. They do not, however, provide the true flavor of butter.

Making Puff Pastry

The procedure described here for making and folding puff pastry dough is just one of several acceptable methods. All successful methods depend on the proper layering of fat and dough through a series of turns to give the pastry its characteristic flakiness and rise.

Some chefs prefer to prepare a dough called **blitz** or **quick puff pastry**. It does not require the extensive rolling and folding procedure used for true puff pastry. Blitz puff pastry is less delicate and flaky but may be perfectly acceptable for rustic tarts and galettes.

Procedure for Preparing Puff Pastry

1. Prepare the dough base, which is referred to as **détrempe**, by combining the flour, water, salt and a small amount of fat. Do not overmix. Overmixing results in gluten formation, and too much gluten can make the pastry undesirably tough.
2. Wrap the détrempe in plastic wrap and chill for several hours or overnight. This allows the gluten to relax and the flour to absorb the liquid.
3. Shape the butter into a rectangle of even thickness; wrap and chill until ready to use.
4. Allow the détrempe and butter to sit at room temperature until slightly softened and of the same consistency.
5. Roll out the détrempe into a rectangle of even thickness large enough to completely cover the butter rectangle. Uneven layers of dough will create irregular layers in the puff pastry after baking.
6. Position the butter in the center of the dough. Fold each edge of the dough around the butter, enclosing it completely so that none of the butter is exposed.
7. Roll out the block of dough and butter into a long, even rectangle. Roll only at right angles so that the layered structure is not destroyed.
8. Use a dry pastry brush to brush away any flour from the dough's surface. Loose flour can cause gray streaks and can prevent the puff pastry from rising properly when baked. Fold the dough like a business letter: Fold the bottom third up toward the center so that it covers the center third, then fold the top third down over the bottom and middle thirds. This is the **single book fold**. This completes the first **turn**.
9. Rotate the block of dough one quarter turn (90 degrees) on the work surface. Roll out again into a long, even rectangle.
10. Fold the dough in thirds again, like a business letter. This completes the second turn. Wrap the dough and chill for approximately 30 minutes. The resting period allows the gluten to relax; the chilling prevents the butter from becoming too soft.
11. Repeat the rolling and folding process, chilling for at least 30 minutes between every one or two turns, until the dough has been turned a total of five times.
12. Wrap well and chill overnight. Raw dough may be refrigerated for a few days or frozen for 2–3 months.
13. Shape and bake as needed. Baked, unfilled puff pastry can be stored at room temperature for 2–3 days.

Perennial Favorites

Year in, year out, certain combinations top the lists of dessert favorites. Pastry chefs and restaurant consultants are in agreement that these dessert flavor profiles are always popular. Build your dessert menu with an offering from each category.

- Fruit desserts from the humble pie to a berry-topped tart appeal to a wide range of consumers. Layer berries or sliced stone fruits in a glass with Crème Chantilly and sorbet and serve with crisp tuile cookies for a contemporary dessert.

- Cheesecake continues to wow customers. It can be a traditional wedge or a lighter version made in an individual mold. Blend in a small amount of locally made farmer's cheese to give it an artisan flavor.

- Lemon desserts such as lemon meringue and key lime pie, lemon mousse or lemon cake strike the right note. For a refreshing twist, use exotic citrus such as blood oranges or yuzu in a sorbet, curd or sauce.

- Caramel flavors, whether in the form of a hot fudge sundae with hot caramel sauce or a wedge of cake with caramel icing, appear on top restaurant dessert lists. Caramel pairs well with toasted nuts, creams and cheesecakes.

- And no dessert menu would be complete without chocolate—chocolate cream filled tarts, white and dark chocolate chips in cookies or a reinvented brownie sundae. There's always room for chocolate.

détrempe a paste made with flour and water during the first stage of preparing a pastry dough, especially rolled-in doughs

Puff Pastry

YIELD 2 lb. 1 oz. (999 g)	**METHOD** Rolled-In Dough		
All-purpose flour	13 oz.	390 g	100%
Salt	0.3 oz. (1½ tsp.)	9 g	2.3%
Unsalted butter, cold	3 oz.	90 g	23%
Water, cold	7 fl. oz.	210 ml	54%
Unsalted butter, softened	10 oz.	300 g	77%
Total dough weight:	2 lb. 1 oz.	999 g	256%

1 To form the détrempe, sift the flour and salt together in a large bowl. Cut the cold butter into small pieces and cut the pieces into the flour until the mixture resembles coarse cornmeal.

2 Make a well in the center of the mixture and add all the water at once. Using a rubber spatula or your fingers, gradually draw the flour into the water. Mix until all the flour is incorporated. Do not knead. The détrempe should be sticky and shaggy-looking.

3 Turn the détrempe out onto a lightly floured surface. Knead the dough a few times by hand, rounding it into a ball. Make several shallow cuts in the dough. Wrap the dough tightly in plastic and chill overnight.

4 To roll in the butter, first prepare the softened butter by placing it between two sheets of plastic wrap. Use a rolling pin to roll the softened butter into a rectangle, approximately 5 inches × 8 inches (12.5 centimeters × 20 centimeters). It is important that the détrempe and butter be of almost equal consistency. If necessary, allow the détrempe to sit at room temperature to soften or chill the butter briefly to harden.

5 On a lightly floured board, roll the détrempe into a rectangle approximately 12 inches × 15 inches (30 centimeters × 37.5 centimeters). Lift and rotate the dough as necessary to prevent sticking.

6 Use a dry pastry brush to brush away any flour from the dough's surface. Loose flour can cause gray streaks and can prevent the puff pastry from rising properly when baked.

7 Peel one piece of plastic wrap from the butter. Position the butter in the center of the rectangle and remove the remaining plastic. Fold the four edges of the détrempe over the butter, enclosing it completely. Stretch the dough if necessary; it is important that none of the butter be exposed.

8 With the folded side facing up, press the dough several times with a rolling pin. Use a rocking motion to create ridges in the dough. Place the rolling pin in each ridge and slowly roll back and forth to widen the ridge. Repeat until all the ridges are doubled in size.

9 Using the ridges as a starting point, roll the dough out into a smooth, even rectangle approximately 8 inches × 24 inches (20 centimeters × 60 centimeters). Be careful to keep the corners of the dough at right angles.

10 Use a dry pastry brush to remove any loose flour from the dough's surface. Fold the dough in thirds, like a business letter. If one end is damaged or in worse condition, fold it in first; otherwise, start at the bottom. This completes the first turn.

11 Rotate the block of dough 90 degrees so that the folded edge is on your left and the dough faces you like a book. Roll out the dough again, repeating the ridging technique. Once again, the dough should be in a smooth, even rectangle of approximately 8 inches × 24 inches (20 centimeters × 60 centimeters).

12 Fold the dough in thirds again, completing the second turn. Cover the dough with plastic wrap and chill for at least 30 minutes.

13 Repeat the rolling and folding technique until the dough has had a total of five turns. Do not perform more than two turns without a resting and chilling period. Cover the dough completely and chill overnight before shaping and baking.

Note The détrempe can be made in a food processor. To do so, combine the flour, salt and pieces of cold butter in the bowl of a food processor fitted with a metal blade. Process until a coarse meal is formed. With the processor running, slowly add the water. Turn the machine off as soon as the dough comes together to form a ball. Proceed with the remainder of the formula.

Approximate values per 1-oz. (30-g) serving: **Calories** 120, **Total fat** 9 g, **Saturated fat** 6 g, **Cholesterol** 25 mg, **Sodium** 110 mg, **Total carbohydrates** 9 g, **Protein** 1 g, **Vitamin A** 8%

❶ Détrempe (left) and butter for puff pastry.

❷ Folding the dough around the butter.

❸ Rolling out the dough, using a rocking motion to create ridges in the dough.

❹ Folding the dough in thirds.

Shaping Puff Pastry

Once puff pastry dough is prepared, it can be shaped by cutting it into various sizes and shapes. **Bouchées** are small puff pastry shells often used for hors d'oeuvre or appetizers. **Vol-au-vents** are larger, deeper shells, often filled with savory mixtures for a main course. Although vol-au-vent cutters may be simply round or square, special vol-au-vent cutters are available in the shape of fish, hearts or petals. **Feuilletées** are square, rectangular or diamond-shaped puff pastry boxes. They can be filled with a sweet or savory mixture.

It is not necessary to work with the entire block of dough when making bouchées, cookies and the like. You can cut the block into thirds or quarters and work with one portion at a time. When making straight cuts in puff pastry, press the tip of your knife into the dough and cut by pressing down on the handle. Do not drag the knife through the dough or you will crush the layers and prevent the dough from rising properly.

Procedure for Shaping Vol-au-Vents and Bouchées

1 Roll out the puff pastry dough to a thickness of approximately ¼ inch (6 millimeters).

2 Cut the desired shape and size using a vol-au-vent cutter or dough rings.

3 Place the vol-au-vent or bouchée on a paper-lined sheet pan. If you used dough rings, place the base on the paper-lined sheet pan, brush lightly with water, then top it with the dough ring; score the edge with the back of a paring knife. Chill for 20–30 minutes to allow the dough to relax before baking.

4 Brush with egg wash if desired and dock the center with a fork.

❶ A vol-au-vent cutter looks like a double cookie cutter with one cutter about 1 inch (2.5 centimeters) smaller than the other. To cut the pastry, position the cutter and press down.

❷ To shape with rings, use two rings, one approximately 1 inch (2.5 centimeters) smaller in diameter than the other. Use the larger ring to cut two rounds. One round will be the base and is set aside. Use the smaller ring to cut an interior circle from the second round, leaving a border ring of dough that is placed on top of the base round. (Save the dough ring's center to reroll for tart shells or turnovers.)

Procedure for Shaping Feuilletées

1 Roll out the puff pastry dough into an even rectangle, approximately ⅛ to ¼ inch (3 to 6 millimeters) thick. Square off the edges of the dough using a pastry cutter and a straightedge, reserving the scraps for other uses.

2 Using a sharp paring knife or chef's knife, cut squares that are about 2 inches (5 centimeters) larger than the desired interior of the finished feuilletée.

3 Fold each square in half diagonally. Cut through two sides of the dough, about ½ inch (1.2 centimeters) from the edge. Cut a V, being careful not to cut through the corners at the center fold.

4 Open the square and lay it flat. Brush water on the edges to seal the dough. Lift opposite sides of the cut border at the cut corners and cross them.

5 Place the feuilletées on a paper-lined sheet pan.

6 Score the edges with the back of a paring knife. Chill for 20–30 minutes to allow the dough to relax before baking.

7 Brush with egg wash if desired and dock the center with a fork.

Puff pastry scraps cannot be rerolled and used for products needing a high rise. The additional rolling destroys the layers. Scraps (known as **rognures**), however, can be used for cookies such as Palmiers (page 1010), turnovers, decorative crescents (fleurons), tart shells, napoleons or any item for which rise is less important than flavor and flakiness. Most puff pastry products bake best in a hot oven, about 400–425°F (200–220°C).

Éclair Paste

Éclair paste, also known as **pâte à choux** [paht ah SHOO], bakes up into golden brown, crisp pastries. Inside these light pastries are mostly air pockets with a bit of moist dough. They can be filled with sweet cream, custard, fruit or even savory mixtures. The dough is most often piped into rounds for **cream puffs**, fingers for **éclairs** or rings for **Paris-Brest**. Éclair paste may also be piped or spooned into specific shapes and deep-fried for doughnut-type products known as **beignets**, **churros** and **crullers**. This dough may also be flavored with cheese and sometimes herbs and spices and made into savory puffs known as **gougères**.

Éclair paste is unique among doughs because it is cooked before baking. The cooking occurs when the flour is added to a boiling mixture of water, milk and butter. This process breaks down the starches in the flour, allowing them to absorb the liquid, speeding gelatinization. Eggs are added to the flour mixture for leavening. The dough produced is batterlike with a smooth, firm texture; it does not have the dry, crumbly texture of other doughs. This technique makes the dough puff up and develop the desired large interior air pockets when baked.

cream puffs baked rounds of éclair paste cut in half and filled with pastry cream, whipped cream, fruit or other filling

éclairs baked fingers of éclair paste filled with pastry cream; the top is then coated with chocolate glaze or fondant

Paris-Brest rings of baked éclair paste cut in half horizontally and filled with light pastry cream and/or whipped cream; the top is dusted with powdered sugar or drizzled with chocolate glaze

beignets squares or strips of éclair paste deep-fried and dusted with powdered sugar

churros a Spanish and Mexican pastry in which sticks of éclair paste flavored with cinnamon are deep-fried and rolled in sugar while still hot

crullers a Dutch pastry in which a loop or strip of twisted éclair paste is deep-fried

gougère [goo-JAIR] éclair pastry flavored with cheese baked and served as a savory hors d'oeuvre

croquembouche [kroh-kum-BOOSH] a pyramid of small puffs, each filled with pastry cream; a French tradition for Christmas and weddings, it is held together with caramelized sugar and decorated with spun sugar or marzipan flowers

profiteroles [proh-fee-teh-ROLE] small baked rounds of éclair paste filled with ice cream and topped with chocolate sauce or filled with savory mixtures

Cream puff filled with pastry cream and whipped cream

Procedure for Preparing Éclair Paste

1 Combine the liquid ingredients and butter cut into small cubes. Bring to a boil.

2 As soon as the water-and-butter mixture comes to a boil, add all the flour to the saucepan. If the liquid is allowed to boil, evaporation occurs; this can create an imbalance in the liquid-to-flour ratio.

3 Stir vigorously until the liquid is absorbed. Continue cooking the dough until it forms a ball that comes away from the sides of the pan, leaving only a thin film of dough on the sides of the pan.

4 Transfer the dough to a mixing bowl. Allow it to cool to below 140°F (60°C), then add the eggs one at a time, beating well after each addition. (This may be done in a mixer fitted with the paddle attachment or by hand.) The number of eggs used varies depending on the size of each egg and the moisture content of the flour mixture. Stop adding eggs when the dough just begins to fall away from the beaters.

5 The finished dough should be smooth and pliable enough to pipe through a pastry bag; it should not be runny.

6 Pipe the dough as desired and bake immediately. A high oven temperature is necessary at the start of baking; it is then lowered gradually to finish baking and drying the product. Do not open the oven door during the first half of the baking period.

7 Allow the dough to bake until completely dry. If the products are removed from the oven too soon, they collapse. Test doneness by breaking open one pastry. If the interior is moist and eggy, continue baking.

8 Baked éclair paste can be stored, unfilled, for several days at room temperature or frozen for several weeks. Once filled, the pastry should be served within 2 or 3 hours, as it quickly becomes soggy.

Éclair Paste (Pâte à Choux)

MISE EN PLACE

- Preheat oven to 400°F (200°C).
- Line sheet pans with parchment paper.

YIELD   2–2½ lb. (1.2–1.3 kg) Dough

Ingredient			
Milk*	8 fl. oz.	240 ml	80%
Water	8 fl. oz.	240 ml	80%
Salt	0.3 oz. (1½ tsp.)	9 g	3%
Granulated sugar	0.3 oz. (2 tsp.)	9 g	3%
Unsalted butter	7 oz.	210 g	70%
All-purpose flour	10 oz.	300 g	100%
Eggs	14–16 oz. (9–10 eggs)	432–480 g	144–160%
Total dough weight:	3 lb.–3 lb. 1 oz.	1440–1488 g	480–496%

1 Preheat the oven to 400°F (200°C). Have a pastry bag with a large plain tip ready.

2 Place the milk, water, salt, sugar and butter in a saucepan. Bring to a boil. Make sure the butter is fully melted.

3 Remove the mixture from the heat and immediately add all the flour. Vigorously beat the dough by hand. Put the pan back on the heat and continue beating the dough until it comes away from the sides of the pan. The dough should look relatively dry and should just begin to leave a film on the saucepan.

4 Transfer the dough to the bowl of a mixer fitted with the paddle attachment and beat it for a few seconds at medium speed. Then beat in the eggs one at a time.

5 Continue to add the eggs one by one until the mixture is shiny but firm. It may not be necessary to use all of the eggs. The dough should pull away from the sides of the bowl in thick threads; it will not clear the bowl.

*For a crisper product, replace the milk with water.

6 Put a workable amount of dough into the pastry bag and pipe onto the parchment-lined sheet pans in the desired shapes at once.

7 Bake immediately, beginning at 425°F (220°C) for 10 minutes, then lowering the heat to 350°F (180°C). Continue baking until the shapes are brown and dry inside, approximately 25 more minutes. Open the oven door as little as possible to prevent rapid changes in the oven's temperature.

8 Cool baked shapes completely, then fill as desired. Leftovers can be frozen or stored at room temperature.

Approximate values per 1-oz. (30-g) serving: **Calories** 90, **Total fat** 7 g, **Saturated fat** 4 g, **Cholesterol** 60 mg, **Sodium** 180 mg, **Total carbohydrates** 6 g, **Protein** 2 g, **Vitamin A** 8%

1 Heating the milk, water, salt, sugar and butter.

2 Adding the flour to the hot liquid.

3 Vigorously beating the dough to dry it.

4 The finished batter after the eggs are incorporated.

5 Piping éclairs.

Meringue

Meringue refers to both a basic mixture of egg whites whipped with sugar and a confection or cake baked from this preparation. Meringue texture—hard or soft—depends on the ratio of sugar to egg whites.

Hard meringue is made with 2 parts sugar or more, by weight, to 1 part egg whites. Hard meringue can be incorporated into a buttercream, page 1041, or pastry cream, page 1069, or used to top a pie or baked Alaska. Meringue toppings are usually placed briefly under a broiler to caramelize the sugar, creating an attractive brown surface.

With twice as much sugar, by weight, as egg whites, hard meringue can be piped into cookies, disks or other shapes and baked in an oven. A low oven temperature evaporates

Versatile Meringue

Naturally low in fat, soft meringue is an ideal reduced-calorie substitute for topping pies and filling cakes. Italian meringue can be substituted for some of the whipped cream in a mousse to reduce the fat content. When flavored with vanilla or other extracts, cocoa powder, ground nuts or coconut, hard meringue bakes into a light, gluten-free cookie or pie shell. You can also use baked disks of hard meringue in place of biscuits when making fruit shortcakes.

the eggs' moisture, leaving a crisp, sugary, honeycomb-like structure. Disks of baked meringue made in this way can be used as layers in a torte or cake. Cups or shells of baked meringue can be filled with cream, mousse, ice cream or fruit. Often baked meringues also contain ground nuts (and are then known as **dacquoise**), cocoa powder or other flavorings. A recipe for hard meringue is on page 1012.

Soft meringue is made with 1 part sugar or less, by weight, to 1 part egg whites. The lower percentage of sugar than the mixture used to make hard meringues creates a softer texture. Soft meringue can be folded into a mousse or Bavarian to lighten it, or used in a spongecake or soufflé. Meringues with only a small amount of sugar are always soft; they do not become crisp no matter how they are used.

There are three methods for making meringue: **common (French)**, **Swiss** and **Italian**. See Table 33.4. Regardless of which preparation method is used, the final product should be smooth, glossy and moist. See Table 33.5. A meringue should never be dry or sponge-like. Review the procedure for whipping egg whites given in Chapter 21, Eggs and Breakfast. Remember to use a clean bowl and whisk. Even a tiny amount of fat can prevent the egg whites from foaming properly.

Common (French) Meringue

Common (French) meringue is made by first beating egg whites to a soft foam (soft peaks). Granulated sugar is then slowly beaten or folded into the egg whites. The final product may be hard or soft depending on the ratio of sugar to egg whites.

Swiss Meringue

Swiss meringue is made by combining unwhipped egg whites with sugar and warming the mixture over a bain marie to a temperature of approximately 100°F (38°C) until the sugar is dissolved. The syrupy solution is then whipped until cool and stiff. The final product may be hard or soft, depending on the ratio of sugar to egg whites. Swiss meringue is extremely stable once finished but rather difficult to prepare. If the mixture gets too hot, it will not whip properly; the result will be syrupy and runny. Swiss meringue is often used as a topping or in buttercream.

Italian Meringue

Italian meringue is made by slowly pouring a hot sugar syrup into whipped egg whites. The heat from the syrup cooks the egg whites, adding stability. Be sure that the sugar syrup reaches the correct temperature and that it is added to the egg whites in a slow, steady stream. Italian meringue is used in buttercream (see Chapter 34, Cakes and Frostings) or folded into pastry cream to produce crème Chiboust. Italian meringue may also be flavored and used as a cake filling and frosting, which is called boiled icing.

TYPES OF MERINGUE			TABLE 33.4
TYPE	RATIO OF SUGAR TO EGG WHITES BY WEIGHT	PREPARATION	USE
Common (French)—hard	2 parts sugar (or more) to 1 part egg whites	Whip or fold sugar into whipped egg whites	Baked into cookies, decorations or dessert shells
Common (French)—soft	1 part sugar (or less) to 1 part egg whites	Whip or fold sugar into whipped egg whites	Pie topping; soufflé; cake ingredient
Swiss	Varies	Warm egg whites with sugar to 100°F (38°C), then whip	Buttercream; pie topping; baked into cookies, decorations or dessert shells
Italian	Varies	Pour hot sugar syrup into whipped egg whites	Buttercream; frosting; crème Chiboust, mousse, baked into cookies, decorations or dessert shells

TROUBLESHOOTING CHART FOR MERINGUE		TABLE 33.5
PROBLEM	CAUSE	SOLUTION
Weeps or beads of sugar syrup are released	Old eggs	Use fresher eggs or add starch or stabilizer
	Egg whites overwhipped	Whip only until stiff peaks form
	Not enough sugar	Increase sugar
	Not baked long enough	Increase baking time
	Moisture in the air	Avoid preparing in humid conditions
Browning too rapidly	Too much sugar; oven too hot	Do not dust with sugar before baking; reduce oven temperature
Fails to attain any volume or stiffness	Fat present	Start over with clean bowls and utensils
	Sugar added too soon	Allow egg whites to reach soft peaks before adding sugar
Lumps	Not enough sugar	Add additional sugar gradually or start over
	Overwhipping	Whip only until stiff peaks form
Not shiny	Not enough sugar	Add additional sugar gradually or start over
	Overwhipping	Whip only until stiff peaks form

Italian Meringue

♥ Good Choice

YIELD 1 lb. 7 oz. (690 g), 14 Servings,
1¾ oz. (52 g) each

Granulated sugar	13 oz.	390 g
Corn syrup	2 oz.	60 g
Water	3 fl. oz.	90 ml
Egg whites, pasteurized, room temperature	8 oz.	240 g

1 Place 12 ounces (360 grams) sugar in a heavy saucepan with the corn syrup and water. Attach a candy thermometer to the pan and bring the sugar to a boil over high heat.

2 Place the egg whites in the bowl of an electric mixer fitted with the whip attachment. As the temperature of the boiling sugar approaches 220°F (104°C), begin whipping the egg whites. When the whites form soft peaks, gradually add the remaining 1 ounce (30 grams) sugar. Lower the mixer speed and continue whipping.

3 When the sugar reaches the soft ball stage (240°F/116°C), remove it from the heat. (See Table 30.2 on page 908.) Pour the sugar into the whites, with the mixer running at high speed. Pour in a steady stream between the side of the bowl and the beater. Once all the sugar is incorporated, whip 1 more minute at high speed, then reduce to medium speed and whip until the meringue is cool.

Approximate values per 1¾-cup (52-g) servings: **Calories** 130, **Total fat** 0 g, **Saturated fat** 0 g, **Cholesterol** 0 mg, **Sodium** 30 mg, **Total carbohydrates** 32 g, **Protein** 1 g, **Claims**—fat free; no cholesterol; low sodium

COOKIES

Cookies are small, flat pastries usually eaten alone (although not singularly) as a snack or with coffee at the end of a meal. They are one of America's best-loved foods, enjoyed frequently because of their versatility. Cookies may be eaten as a midmorning coffee break or as the elegant end to a formal dinner. Cookies also provide the finishing touch to a serving of ice cream, custard or fruit. Flavors are limited only by the baker's imagination; chocolate, oatmeal, cornmeal, fresh and dried fruit and nuts all find their way into several types of cookies. Several cookie formulas are given at the end of this chapter.

Mixing Methods for Cookie Dough

Most cookies are made from a rich dough that is mixed by the **creaming method** used for quick breads and cake batters. (See Chapter 31, Quick Breads, and Chapter 34, Cakes

The Story of the Chip

History was made in 1930 when Ruth Wakefield, innkeeper of the Toll House Inn in Whitman, Massachusetts, cut up a semisweet chocolate bar and added the pieces to her cookie dough. When she took the cookies out of the oven, however, she was disappointed that the pieces kept their shape when baked—until her first bite, that is.

Mrs. Wakefield contacted Nestlé Foods Corporation, which published her cookie recipe on the wrapper of their semisweet chocolate bars. The recipe's popularity led Nestlé to create and begin selling chocolate chips in 1939.

Today's cookie maker can now choose from milk, white, dark, semisweet or bittersweet chocolate chips, along with mint, butterscotch, peanut butter, cinnamon and other flavor chips, offered in several sizes from a variety of manufacturers.

Drop cookie dough

Icebox cookie dough

and Frostings.) However, because cookie dough contains less liquid than these batters, the liquid and flour need not be added alternately. Cookies can be leavened with baking soda, baking powder or just air and steam. Most cookies are high in fat, which contributes flavor and tenderness and extends shelf life. In cookies made with formulas that have a high percentage of fat and low moisture content, overdevelopment of gluten is usually not a problem. However, careless mixing can still produce tough and dense cookies. When there are eggs or liquid in cookie dough, the flour is blended in gently to minimize gluten development. Add-ins such as chopped nuts, chocolate and pieces of fruit are folded or stirred gently into the dough for this same reason.

Procedure for Mixing Cookie Doughs

1 Cream the fat and sugar together to make a lump-free mixture, to incorporate air and to blend the ingredients completely.
2 Add the eggs gradually, scraping down the bowl frequently as needed.
3 Stir in the liquid ingredients.
4 Stir in the flour, salt, spices and leaveners.
5 Fold in any nuts, chocolate chips or chunky ingredients by hand.

Make-Up Methods for Cookies

Cookie varieties are usually classified by the way in which the individual cookies are prepared. This section describes eight preparation or make-up techniques: drop, icebox, bar, sheet, cut-out, piped, rolled or molded and wafer. Some doughs can be made up by more than one method. For example, chocolate chip cookie dough can be (1) baked in sheets and cut into squares, (2) dropped in mounds or (3) rolled into logs, chilled and sliced like icebox cookies. Regardless of the make-up method used, uniformity of size and shape is important for appearance and baking time. Cookies should also be evenly spaced on sheet pans for proper air circulation and crust formation.

Drop Cookies

Drop cookies are made from soft dough that is spooned or scooped into mounds for baking. Doughs with chunks of flavoring ingredients such as Chocolate Chip Cookies (page 1017) and Oatmeal Raisin Cookies (page 1016) are common examples. Although a uniform appearance is not as important for drop cookies as for other types, uniform size and placement results in uniform baking time. Space the dough to allow room for spread, which is common with drop cookies. A portion scoop is recommended for portioning the dough. Drop cookies tend to be thick with a soft or chewy texture.

Icebox Cookies

Icebox cookies are made from dough that is shaped into logs or rectangles, chilled thoroughly, then sliced into individual pieces and baked as needed. Icebox cookies can be as simple as a log of chocolate chip dough or as sophisticated as elegant pinwheel and checkerboard cookies assembled with two colors of short dough. The icebox make-up method usually produces uniform, waferlike cookies with a crisp texture.

Bar Cookies

Bar cookies are made from a stiff dough that is rolled into a log, then baked. The bars are then cut into thick slices. Biscotti (page 1018) are bar cookies that are baked a second time after the log has been baked. This produces a dry cookie with a long shelf life.

Sheet Cookies

Sheet cookies are made from a dough or batter that is pressed, poured or layered in shallow pans and cut into portions after baking, usually squares or rectangles to avoid

Bar cookies

Sheet cookies

waste or scraps. This category contains a wide variety of layered or fruit-filled cookies. Often a short dough such as that used for a fruit tart or shortbread cookie forms the base of the bar cookies, and then a topping is layered on the cookie before or after baking. See the formula for Lemon or Lime Bars (page 1019). Brownies, sometimes considered a sheet cookie, have more in common with cakes and are discussed in Chapter 34, Cakes and Frostings.

Cut-Out Cookies

Cut-out cookies are made from a firm dough that is rolled out into a sheet and then cut into various shapes before baking. A seemingly infinite selection of cookie cutters is available, or you can use a paring knife or pastry wheel to cut the dough into desired shapes. Always start cutting cookies from the edge of the dough, working inward. Cut the cookies as close to each other as possible to avoid scraps. Cut-out cookies are usually baked on an ungreased pan to prevent the dough from spreading.

Sliced nuts, coarse granulated sugar or other garnishes can be pressed into the cookie dough before baking. Doing this as soon as the cookies are rolled helps ensure that the ingredients adhere to the surface. After baking, cut-out cookies are sometimes decorated with sugar glaze or colored frostings, an especially popular bakery offering during holiday seasons. See Sugar Cookies and Decorative Cookie Icing (page 1020). Ice cookies only after they have cooled completely. Decorative icing should not be applied to cookies that will be frozen; it is best to ice those closer to service.

Piped Cookies

Also referred to as bagged or **spritz cookies**, piped cookies are made with a soft dough that is forced through a pastry tip or **cookie press**. Piped cookies are usually small, with a distinct, decorative shape. The task of piping out dozens of identical cookies may seem daunting, but the skill can be mastered with practice and an understanding of doughs. Doughs for piped cookies often use eggs as their only liquid. Eggs, which firm and thicken, contribute body and help the cookies retain their shape. Using too much fat or flour that is too soft (i.e., one low in protein) can cause the cookies to spread and lose their shape.

Rolled or Molded Cookies

Rolled or molded cookies are made from stiff dough that is hand-shaped into spheres, crescents or other traditional shapes. Most drop cookies can also be rolled or molded. Often shortbread cookie dough is pressed into decorative carved molds before baking. Dough for molding is firm and dry so that it holds its shape and keeps the impression intact during baking. Traditional European gingerbread cookies and Scandinavian springerle cookies are molded cookies.

Cut-out or rolled cookie dough

Piped cookie dough

cookie press also known as a cookie gun, a hollow tube fitted with a plunger and an interchangeable decorative tip or plate; soft cookie dough is pressed through the tip to create shapes or patterns

Wafer cookie dough

Wafer Cookies

Wafer cookies are extremely thin and delicate. They are made with a thin batter that is poured or spread onto a baking sheet and baked. While still hot, the wafer is molded into a variety of shapes. The most popular shapes are the tightly rolled cigarette, the curved tuile and the cup-shaped tulipe. Wafer batter, also known as **stencil batter**, is sweet and buttery and may be flavored with citrus zest, herbs, ground pepper or ground nuts.

The textures associated with cookies—crispness, softness, chewiness or spread—are affected by various factors, including the ratio of ingredients in the dough, the oven's temperature and the pan's coating. Understanding these factors allows you to adjust formulas or techniques to achieve the desired results described in Table 33.6.

Storing Cookies

Most cookies can be stored for up to 1 week in an airtight container. Do not store crisp cookies and soft cookies in the same container, however. The crisp cookies will absorb moisture from the soft cookies, ruining the texture of both. Do not store strongly flavored cookies, such as spice, with those that are milder, such as shortbread.

Most cookies freeze well if wrapped airtight to prevent moisture loss or freezer burn. Raw dough can also be frozen, either in bulk or shaped into individual portions.

COOKIE TEXTURES						TABLE 33.6
DESIRED TEXTURE	FAT	SUGAR	LIQUID	FLOUR	SIZE OR SHAPE	BAKING
Crispness	High	High; use granulated sugar	Low	Strong	Thin dough	Well done; cool on baking sheet
Softness	Low	Low; use hygroscopic sugars (see page 906)	High	Weak	Thick dough	Use parchment-lined pan; under bake
Chewiness	High	High; use hygroscopic sugars (see page 906)	High	Strong	Not relevant; chilled dough	Under bake; cool on rack
Spread	High	High; use coarse granulated sugar	High; especially from eggs	Weak	Not relevant; room-temperature dough	Use greased pan; low temperature

QUESTIONS FOR DISCUSSION

1 How does the type of pie filling influence the selection of a pie crust? What type of crust would be most appropriate for a pie made with fresh, uncooked fruit? Explain your answer.

2 How does rolling fat into a dough in layers (as with puff pastry) produce a flaky product? Why isn't sweet dough (which contains a high ratio of butter) flaky?

3 Explain the difference between a cream pie filling and a custard pie filling. Give two examples of each type of filling.

4 List and describe three ways of preparing fruit fillings for pies.

5 Why is it said that éclair paste is the only dough that is cooked before it is baked? Why is this step necessary? List three ways of using éclair paste in making classic desserts.

6 Compare and contrast common, Swiss and Italian meringues.

7 List and describe four make-up methods for cookie doughs.

Additional Pie, Pastry and Cookie Formulas

Several of the formulas in the following pages are combinations of the pastry items presented in this chapter and the creams, custards and other dessert products covered in other chapters. For example, the Strawberry Napoleon is made with the puff pastry discussed in this chapter, the Pastry Cream and Crème Chantilly discussed in Chapter 35, Custards, Creams, Frozen Desserts and Dessert Sauces, and the Basic Sugar Glaze discussed in Chapter 34, Cakes and Frostings. As a student, you should first learn to prepare a variety of pastry components. You can then combine and assemble them appropriately into both classic and modern desserts.

Shortbread Tart Dough (Pâte Sablée)

Houston Community College, Houston, TX
Pastry Chef Eddy Van Damme

YIELD 4 lb. 7 oz. (2139 g) Dough; approximately
7 Tart Shells, 8 in. (20 cm) each,
or 46 Tartlet Shells, 2½ in. (7.5 cm) each

Egg yolks, hard-boiled	5 oz. (8 yolks)	150 g	19%
Unsalted butter, softened	1 lb. 8 oz.	720 g	92%
Powdered sugar	11 oz.	330 g	42%
Vanilla extract	0.5 fl. oz. (1 Tbsp.)	15 ml	2%
Salt	0.3 oz. (2 tsp.)	9 g	1.2%
Almond or hazelnut flour	4.5 oz.	135 g	17%
Pastry or all-purpose flour	1 lb. 10 oz.	780 g	100%
Total dough weight:	4 lb. 7 oz.	2139 g	273%

1. Press the egg yolks through a sieve using a plastic pastry scraper to prevent lumps from forming in the dough. Set aside.

2. Using a mixer fitted with the paddle attachment, cream the butter. Add the sugar, combining well.

3. Add the vanilla extract, salt and almond or hazelnut flour, then the sieved egg yolks, and mix until combined.

4. Add all of the pastry flour and mix on low speed just until combined. Do not overmix.

5. Wrap the dough in plastic and chill for several hours or overnight.

6. When ready to use, roll out the chilled dough on a lightly floured board. The dough may be crumbly and difficult to work with, which is normal. Simply press the dough back together with your fingertips.

Approximate values per 2-oz. (60-g) serving: **Calories** 227, **Total fat** 19 g, **Saturated fat** 10 g, **Cholesterol** 93 mg, **Sodium** 103 mg, **Total carbohydrates** 25 g, **Protein** 4 g

Quiche Dough (Pâte Brisée)

Quiche Lorraine (page 557)

YIELD 7 lb. 5 oz. (3830 g),
9 Shells, 10 in. (25 cm) each

All-purpose flour	4 lb. 7 oz.	2130 g	100%
Salt	1.5 oz.	45 g	2%
Unsalted butter, cold	2 lb. 4 oz.	1080 g	51%
Eggs	1 lb. 4 oz. (12 eggs)	600 g	28%
Total dough weight:	8 lb.	3855 g	181%

1 Combine the flour and salt in the bowl of a mixer fitted with the paddle attachment. Cut in the butter until the mixture looks like coarse cornmeal.

2 Whisk the eggs together to blend, then add them slowly to the dry ingredients. Blend only until the dough comes together in a ball.

3 Remove from the mixer, cover and chill until ready to use.

Approximate values per 1-oz. (30-g) serving: **Calories** 120, **Total fat** 7 g, **Saturated fat** 4 g, **Cholesterol** 35 mg, **Sodium** 140 mg, **Total carbohydrates** 12 g, **Protein** 2 g

Lemon Meringue Pie

Topping the pie with meringue.

YIELD 2 Pies, 9 in. (22 cm) each   **METHOD** Cream Filling

Filling:		
Granulated sugar	1 lb. 4 oz.	600 g
Cornstarch	3 oz.	90 g
Salt	1 pinch	1 pinch
Water, cold	24 fl. oz.	720 ml
Egg yolks	6 oz. (10 yolks)	180 g
Lemon juice, fresh	8 fl. oz.	240 ml
Lemon zest, grated	0.4 oz. (2 Tbsp.)	60 ml
Unsalted butter	1 oz.	60 g
Flaky dough pie shells, baked	2 shells	2 shells
Egg whites, pasteurized	8 oz. (8 whites)	240 g
Granulated sugar	8 oz.	240 g

1 To make the filling, combine 1 pound 4 ounces (600 grams) sugar and the cornstarch, salt and water in a heavy saucepan. Cook over medium-high heat, stirring constantly, until the mixture becomes thick and almost clear.

2 Remove from the heat and slowly whisk in the egg yolks. Stir until completely blended. Return to the heat and cook, stirring constantly, until thick and smooth.

3 Stir in the lemon juice and zest. When the liquid is completely incorporated, remove the filling from the heat. Add the butter and stir until melted.

4 Set the filling aside to cool briefly. Fill the pie shells with the lemon filling.

5 To prepare the meringue, whip the egg whites until soft peaks form. Slowly add 8 ounces (240 grams) sugar while whisking constantly. The meringue should be stiff and glossy, not dry or spongy-looking.

6 Mound the meringue over the filling, creating decorative patterns with a spatula. Be sure to spread the meringue to the edge of the crust so that all of the filling is covered.

7 Place the pies in a 400°F (200°C) oven until the meringue is golden brown, approximately 5–8 minutes. Let cool at room temperature, then refrigerate. Serve the same day.

Approximate values per ⅛-pie serving: **Calories** 400, **Total fat** 12 g, **Saturated fat** 4 g, **Cholesterol** 135 mg, **Sodium** 310 mg, **Total carbohydrates** 67 g, **Protein** 5 g, **Vitamin C** 10%

Fresh Strawberry Pie

YIELD 2 Pies, 9 in. (22 cm) each		METHOD Cooked Juice Filling	
Filling:			
Granulated sugar		1 lb. 7 oz.	710 g
Water		8 fl. oz.	240 ml
Cornstarch		2.5 oz.	75 g
Water, cold		12 fl. oz.	360 ml
Salt		0.1 oz. (½ tsp.)	2 g
Lemon juice		2 fl. oz.	60 ml
Natural red food coloring		as needed	as needed
Fresh strawberries, rinsed and sliced in half		2 qt.	2 lt
Flaky dough pie shells, baked		2 shells	2 shells

1 Bring the sugar and 8 fluid ounces (240 milliliters) water to a boil.

2 Dissolve the cornstarch in the cold water and add to the boiling liquid. Cook over low heat until clear, approximately 5 minutes.

3 Stir in the salt, lemon juice and enough red food coloring to produce a bright red color.

4 Pour this glaze over the strawberries and toss gently to coat them. Spoon the filling into the prepared pie shells. Chill thoroughly before serving.

Approximate values per ⅛-pie serving: **Calories** 330, **Total fat** 8 g, **Saturated fat** 2 g, **Cholesterol** 0 mg, **Sodium** 200 mg, **Total carbohydrates** 63 g, **Protein** 2 g, **Vitamin C** 80%

Freeform Apple Pies

Chef Jamie Roraback, Hartford, CT

YIELD 4 Pies, 6 in. (15 cm) each		METHOD Baked Fruit Filling		
Dough:				
Unsalted butter	8 oz.	240 g	100%	
All-purpose flour	8 oz.	240 g	100%	
Salt	0.2 oz. (1 tsp.)	6 g	2.5%	
Water, ice cold	3 fl. oz.	90 ml	37.5%	
Total dough weight:	1 lb. 3 oz.	576 g	240%	
Filling:				
Apples, peeled, cored, large dice	1 lb.	480 g		
Unsalted butter	1 oz.	30 g		
Granulated sugar	2 oz.	60 g		
Cinnamon, ground	0.02 oz. (¼ tsp.)	0.5 g		
Vanilla extract	0.5 fl. oz. (1 Tbsp.)	15 ml		
Apple brandy	2 fl. oz.	60 ml		
Egg wash	as needed	as needed		
Sanding sugar	as needed for garnish			
Ice cream and Caramel Sauce (page 1084)	as needed for garnish			

1 To prepare the dough, cut the butter into medium dice and place it in the freezer for 5 minutes. Sift the flour with the salt. Toss the butter with the flour and salt and place the mixture in the bowl of a food processor. Pulse until the butter chunks are the size of very small peas. Drizzle in the ice water and pulse just until the dough barely comes together. Do not overmix.

2 Turn the dough out onto a work surface. Press it together gently and quickly, then divide the dough into four rounds. Place the rounds on a sheet pan, cover them with plastic wrap and refrigerate for approximately 20 minutes before rolling out.

3 To prepare the filling, heat a sauté pan over high heat, add the apples and let them brown slightly. Add the butter and let it melt so that it loosens and frees the apples from the bottom of the pan. Then cook for approximately 1 minute, add the sugar and let it brown, stirring occasionally. Add the cinnamon and vanilla extract. Add the apple brandy and flambé. Cool the filling before assembling the pies.

4 On a floured surface, roll out each round of dough into a circle approximately 8 inches (20 centimeters) in diameter. Place an appropriate-size plate or other circular object on top of the rolled-out dough and cut out a circle.

5 Place one-quarter of the apple filling in the center of each dough round, leaving 1½ inches (3.7 centimeters) of dough exposed along the edges. Brush the dough with egg wash and then fold the border over the filling in approximately five or six folds, each fold slightly overlapping the previous one. Place the pies on a sheet pan and brush additional egg wash over the surface. Sprinkle with sanding sugar.

6 Place the pies in the freezer until frozen. (Freezing will help prevent the butter running from the crust during baking.)

7 Preheat the oven to 400°F (200°C). Bake the frozen pies, rotating them occasionally. Bake until the apples are tender and the crust is evenly browned, approximately 20 minutes. Serve warm or at room temperature, dusted with powdered sugar and accompanied by whipped cream or ice cream and Caramel Sauce.

Approximate values per ½-pie serving: **Calories** 420, **Total fat** 27 g, **Saturated fat** 16 g, **Cholesterol** 95 mg, **Sodium** 300 mg, **Total carbohydrates** 36 g, **Protein** 4 g, **Vitamin A** 20%

⚠ Safety Alert

Cooking with Alcohol

When alcohol comes into contact with a flame, it can ignite. In order to avoid singed eyebrows and kitchen fires, be careful when adding wine, brandy, liqueurs or liquor to a dish on or near the stove. Often a dish will require flaming or flambéing, which means igniting the brandy, rum or other liquor so that the alcohol burns off and the flavor of the liquor is retained. When a dish calls for flambéing, stand away from the pan being flamed and tilt the pan away from you before putting a match to the liquid, as the flames can leap from the pan, igniting anything they contact.

Blackberry Crumble

A crumble is homestyle baked fruit dessert, usually covered with a crumbly mixture of flour, sugar and butter, which merges to form a piecrust-like topping. The finished product will be slightly runny and is often served warm in a bowl or rimmed dish, accompanied by whipped cream or ice cream. Closely related is a cobbler—fruit topped with biscuit dough.

YIELD	1 Half-Size Hotel Pan, 10 Servings, 6 oz. (180 g) each	METHOD	Baked Fruit Filling
Blackberries, IQF, thawed and drained		2 qt.	2 lt
Granulated sugar		8 oz.	240 g
Tapioca, instant		2 oz.	60 g
Water		10 fl. oz.	300 ml
Unsalted butter, cut in small pieces		2 oz.	60 g
Lemon zest, grated		0.2 oz. (1 Tbsp.)	6 g
Streusel Topping (page 935)		16 oz.	480 g

1 Combine the berries, sugar, tapioca, water, butter and lemon zest, tossing the berries gently until well coated with the other ingredients.

2 Transfer to a lightly buttered half-size hotel pan, then set aside for at least 30 minutes before baking.

3 Cover the top of the crumble with an even layer of the Streusel Topping. It can also be topped with Basic Pie Dough (page 980) or the dough for Country Biscuits (page 930) before baking.

4 Bake at 350°F (180°C) until the berry mixture bubbles and the topping is appropriately browned, approximately 40–50 minutes.

Approximate values per 6-oz. (180-g) serving: **Calories** 210, **Total fat** 5 g, **Saturated fat** 3 g, **Cholesterol** 20 mg, **Sodium** 10 mg, **Total carbohydrates** 39 g, **Protein** 1 g, **Vitamin C** 45%

Fresh Berry Tart

YIELD	1 Tart, 9 in. (22 cm)		
Sweet Dough (page 981) tart shell, 9 in. (22 cm), fully baked		1	1
Pastry Cream (page 1069)		1 pt.	480 ml
Fresh berries such as strawberries, blackberries, blueberries or raspberries		3 pt.	1.5 lt
Apricot glaze		as needed	as needed

1 Fill the cool tart shell with Pastry Cream.

2 Arrange the berries over the Pastry Cream in an even layer. Be sure to place the berries so that the Pastry Cream is covered.

3 Heat the apricot glaze and brush over the fruit to form a smooth coating.

Approximate values per ⅛-tart serving: **Calories** 135, **Total fat** 3 g, **Saturated fat** 1 g, **Cholesterol** 2 mg, **Sodium** 62 mg, **Total carbohydrates** 26 g, **Protein** 2 g

French Apple Tart

This procedure can be used for individual tartlets or large round, rectangular or daisy-shaped tart pans. The amount of each ingredient, the yield and the baking time depends on the capacity and number of tart molds used.

YIELD 1 Tart, 12 in. (30 cm)

Sweet Dough (page 981)	20 oz.	600 g
Almond Cream (recipe follows)	1½ pt.	720 ml
Tart apples, peeled, cored and sliced thin	5–6	5–6
Unsalted butter, melted	2 fl. oz.	60 ml
Granulated sugar	as needed	as needed
Apricot glaze, melted	as needed	as needed

1 Line the tart pan with Sweet Dough. Do not dock the dough.

2 Pipe in an even layer of Almond Cream over the tart shell.

3 Arrange the apples in overlapping rows, covering the Almond Cream completely.

4 Brush the top of the apples with the melted butter and sprinkle lightly with granulated sugar.

5 Bake at 375°F (190°C) until the crust is done and the apples are light brown.

6 Allow the tart to cool to room temperature. Brush the top with apricot glaze.

Approximate values per ⅒-tart serving: **Calories** 395, **Total fat** 17 g, **Saturated fat** 7 g, **Cholesterol** 234 mg, **Sodium** 98 mg, **Total carbohydrates** 56 g, **Protein** 7 g, **Vitamin A** 12%

Almond Cream

YIELD 3 lb. (1.4 kg)

Unsalted butter, softened	8 oz.	240 g
Granulated sugar	1 lb.	480 g
Eggs	8 oz. (5 eggs)	240 g
All-purpose flour	5 oz.	150 g
Almonds, ground	12 oz.	360 g

1 Cream the butter and sugar. Slowly add the eggs, scraping down the bowl as necessary.

2 Stir the flour and almonds together, then add to the butter mixture. Blend until no lumps remain.

3 Almond cream may be stored under refrigeration for up to 3 weeks.

Approximate values per 1-oz. (30-g) serving: **Calories** 140, **Total fat** 8 g, **Saturated fat** 3 g, **Cholesterol** 30 mg, **Sodium** 5 mg, **Total carbohydrates** 13 g, **Protein** 2 g

Rustic Vegetable Galettes

YIELD 6 Individual Tarts, 5 in. (15 cm) each

Onion, sliced thin	8 oz.	240 g
Chopped garlic	0.1 oz. (1 Tbsp.)	3 g
Olive oil	2 fl. oz.	60 ml
Puff Pastry (page 993)	1 lb. 3 oz.	576 g
Zucchini, small, sliced ¼-in. (6-mm) thick	12 oz.	360 g
Tomato, small, sliced ¼-in. (6-mm) thick	8 oz.	240 g
Fresh thyme, chopped fine	0.05 oz. (1½ tsp.)	1.5 g
Salt and pepper	TT	TT

1 Sauté the onions and garlic in 1 fluid ounce (30 milliliters) of the oil with the salt for 2 minutes. Reduce the heat to medium, cover and let the onions soften for 6–8 minutes. Uncover and cook until the moisture evaporates. Set aside.

2 Roll the dough ⅛-inch (3-millimeters) thick and cut six rounds approximately 7 inches (17 centimeters) in diameter from the dough. Place the dough rounds onto a parchment-lined sheet pan.

3 Place one-sixth of the onion mixture in the center of each dough round leaving ¾-inch (centimeters) of dough exposed along the edges. Arrange the zucchini and tomato slices in overlapping rows on top of the onion mixture.

4 Fold the dough border over the filling in several folds. Lightly press down on the dough rounds with cupped hands to maintain their shape. Season with salt and pepper. Drizzle with the remaining olive oil.

5 Bake at 400°F (200°C) until golden brown and the vegetables are cooked, approximately 40–50 minutes.

Approximate values per 5-in. (12-cm) tart: **Calories** 470, **Total fat** 35 g, **Saturated fat** 20 g, **Cholesterol** 80 mg, **Sodium** 390 mg, **Total carbohydrates** 36 g, **Protein** 6 g, **Vitamin A** 25%, **Vitamin C** 30%

Strawberry Napoleon

YIELD 10 Servings, 1½ in. × 4 in.
     (3.8 cm × 10 cm) each

Puff Pastry (page 993), 4-in. × 15-in. (10-cm × 37-cm) strips, docked and baked	3	3
Pastry Cream (page 1069)	1 pt.	480 ml
Fresh strawberries, sliced	1 qt.	1 lt
Crème Chantilly (page 1075)	1 pt.	480 ml
Basic Sugar Glaze (page 1046)	as needed	as needed
Dark chocolate, melted	1 oz.	30 g

1 Allow the puff pastry to cool completely before assembling.

2 Place a strip of puff pastry on a cake cardboard for support. Pipe on a layer of Pastry Cream, leaving a clean margin of almost ½ inch (1.2 centimeters) on all four sides.

3 Top the cream with a layer of berries.

4 Spread on a thin layer of Crème Chantilly and top with a second layer of puff pastry. Repeat the procedure for cream and berries on the second layer of puff pastry and chill.

5 Prepare the Basic Sugar Glaze. Place the melted chocolate in a piping cone. When ready to glaze, place the third strip of puff pastry on an icing rack, flat side up. Pour the Basic Sugar Glaze down the length of the pastry and spread evenly with a metal cake spatula. Allow the excess to drip over the sides.

6 Immediately pipe thin lines of chocolate across the glaze. Drag a toothpick through the piped chocolate to make a decorative pattern in the glaze. Chill to set the glaze, then place the top in position on the napoleon.

Approximate values per 1/10-pastry serving: **Calories** 320, **Total fat** 20 g, **Saturated fat** 9 g, **Cholesterol** 115 mg, **Sodium** 65 mg, **Total carbohydrates** 29 g, **Protein** 4 g, **Vitamin A** 15%, **Vitamin C** 60%

Palmiers

Puff pastry	as needed	as needed
Granulated sugar	as needed	as needed

1 Roll out the puff pastry into a very thin rectangle. The length is not important, but the width should be at least 7 inches (17.5 centimeters).

2 Using a rolling pin, gently press the sugar into the dough on both sides.

3 Make a 1-inch (2.5-centimeter) fold along the long edges of the dough toward the center. Sprinkle on additional sugar.

4 Make another 1-inch (2.5-centimeter) fold along the long edges of the dough toward the center. The two folds should almost meet in the center. Sprinkle on additional sugar.

5 Fold one side on top of the other. Press down gently with a rolling pin or your fingers so that the dough adheres. Chill for 1 hour.

6 Cut the log of dough in thin slices. Place the cookies on a paper-lined sheet pan and bake at 400°F (200°C) until the edges are brown, approximately 8–12 minutes.

Approximate values per 1-oz. (30-g) serving: **Calories** 130, **Total fat** 5 g, **Saturated fat** 1 g, **Cholesterol** 0 mg, **Sodium** 35 mg, **Total carbohydrates** 19 g, **Protein** 1 g

1 Folding the puff pastry dough for Palmiers toward the center from both edges.

2 Slicing the log of Palmier dough into individual cookies.

Chocolate Éclairs

YIELD 20 Éclairs, 4-in. (10 cm) each

Baked éclair shells, 4 in. (10 cm) long, made from Éclair Paste (page 996)	20	20
Vanilla Pastry Cream (page 1069)	1 qt.	960 ml
Chocolate glaze:		
Unsweetened chocolate	4 oz.	120 g
Semisweet chocolate	4 oz.	120 g
Unsalted butter	4 oz.	120 g
Light corn syrup	2.75 oz. (4 tsp.)	82 g
White chocolate, melted, optional	as needed	as needed

1 Use a paring knife or skewer to cut a small hole into the end of each baked, cooled éclair shell.

2 Pipe the Vanilla Pastry Cream into each shell using a piping bag fitted with a small plain tip. Be sure that the cream fills the full length of each shell. Refrigerate the filled éclairs.

3 To prepare the chocolate glaze, melt all the ingredients together over a bain marie. Remove from the heat and allow to cool until slightly thickened, stirring occasionally.

4 In a single, smooth stroke, drag the top of each filled éclair through the glaze. Only the very top of each pastry should be coated with chocolate.

5 Melted white chocolate may be piped onto the wet glaze, then pulled into patterns using a tooth-pick. Keep the finished éclairs refrigerated and serve within 8–12 hours.

Approximate values per éclair: **Calories** 410, **Total fat** 31 g, **Saturated fat** 17 g, **Cholesterol** 110 mg, **Sodium** 230 mg, **Total carbohydrates** 27 g, **Protein** 5 g, **Vitamin A** 20%

❶ Using a piping bag to fill the éclairs with pastry cream.

❷ Dipping the éclairs in chocolate glaze.

Baked Meringue

YIELD   1 lb. 8 oz. (795 g) Meringue,
12 Disks, 4 in. (10 cm) each

Egg whites	8 oz. (8 whites)	240 g
Granulated sugar	1 lb.	480 g
Coffee extract, optional	2.5 fl. oz.	75 ml

1 Whip the egg whites to soft peaks. With the mixer running at medium speed, slowly add the sugar and continue whipping until very stiff and glossy.

2 If desired, whip in the coffee extract.

3 Spread or pipe the meringue into the desired shapes on parchment-lined sheet pans.

4 Bake at 200°F (90°C) for 5 hours or overnight in a nonconvection oven; circulating air causes the meringue to bake unevenly. The baked meringues should be firm and crisp but not browned.

5 Use in assembling dessert or pastry items.

Approximate values per disk: **Calories** 160, **Total fat** 0 g, **Saturated fat** 0 g, **Cholesterol** 0 mg, **Sodium** 30 mg, **Total carbohydrates** 38 g, **Protein** 2 g, **Claims**—no fat; no saturated fat; no cholesterol; low sodium

Chocolate Délice

YIELD   1 Cake, 8 in. (20 cm)

Ganache (page 1048)	8 oz.	240 g
Classic Dacquoise (recipe follows), 8-in. (20-cm) disks	3	3
Crème Chantilly (page 1075)	2 qt.	2 lt
Candied Almonds (recipe follows)	as needed	as needed

1 Spread an even layer of Ganache over two of the Classic Dacquoise disks.

2 Top one disk with approximately ¾ cup (170 milliliters) Crème Chantilly. Place the second disk on top, chocolate side up. Top with another ¾ cup (170 milliliters) Crème Chantilly. Position the third disk on top, flat side up.

3 Spread the remaining Crème Chantilly over the top and sides.

4 Sprinkle Candied Almonds over the top and sides of the cake.

5 Freeze to firm the cream, approximately 1 hour. Remove from freezer and refrigerate for service.

Approximate values per ⅛-cake serving: **Calories** 490, **Total fat** 32.5 g, **Saturated fat** 13 g, **Cholesterol** 50 mg, **Sodium** 35 mg, **Total carbohydrates** 39 g, **Protein** 10 g, **Vitamin A** 16%

❶ Piping out the dacquoise meringue disks.

❷ Layering the ganache-covered dacquoise.

❸ Frosting the Chocolate Délice.

Classic Dacquoise

YIELD   3 Disks, 8 in. (20 cm) each

Blanched almonds	2 oz.	60 g
Granulated sugar	6 oz.	180 g
Egg whites	3 oz. (3 whites)	90 g

1 Preheat oven to 225°F (110°C). Line a baking sheet with parchment. Draw three 8-inch (20-centimeter) circles on the parchment.

2 Grind the almonds in a food processor. They should be the consistency of cornmeal and as dry as possible. Combine with 2 ounces (60 grams) sugar and set aside.

3 Whip the egg whites on medium speed until foamy. Increase the speed and gradually add 1 ounce (30 grams) sugar.

4 Continue whipping until the egg whites form soft peaks. Gradually add the remaining sugar.

5 Continue whipping until smooth and glossy, approximately 2 minutes.

6 Sprinkle the almond-sugar mixture over the meringue and fold together by hand.

7 Using a pastry bag with a plain tip, pipe the meringue onto the circles you have drawn on the parchment paper to form three 8-inch (20-centimeter) rounds.

8 Bake until firm and crisp but not brown, approximately 60–75 minutes. Cool completely.

Approximate values per 1-oz. (30-g) serving: **Calories** 100, **Total fat** 2.5 g, **Saturated fat** 0 g, **Cholesterol** 0 mg, **Sodium** 15 mg, **Total carbohydrates** 16 g, **Protein** 2 g, **Claims**—low fat; low saturated fat; no cholesterol; very low sodium

Candied Almonds

YIELD   10 oz. (300 g)

Egg whites	2 oz. (2 whites)	60 g
Granulated sugar	2 oz.	60 g
Sliced almonds	8 oz.	240 g

1 Preheat oven to 325°F (160°C).

2 Whisk the egg whites and sugar together. Add the almonds. Toss with a rubber spatula to coat the nuts completely.

3 Spread the nuts in a thin layer on a lightly greased baking sheet. Bake until lightly toasted and dry, approximately 15–20 minutes. Watch closely to prevent burning.

4 Stir the nuts with a metal spatula every 5–7 minutes during baking.

5 Cool completely. Store in an airtight container for up to 10 days.

Approximate values per 1-oz. (30-g) serving: **Calories** 160, **Total fat** 10 g, **Saturated fat** 1 g, **Cholesterol** 0 mg, **Sodium** 10 mg, **Total carbohydrates** 10 g, **Protein** 6 g, **Claims**—no saturated fat; no cholesterol; very low sodium

Apple Strudel

YIELD 2 Rolls, 12 in. (30 cm) each

Apples, peeled, cored and slivered	1 lb. 8 oz.	720 g
Lemon juice	0.5 fl. oz. (1 Tbsp.)	15 ml
Granulated sugar	8 oz.	240 g
Raisins	2 oz.	60 g
Orange zest, grated	0.2 oz. (1 Tbsp.)	6 g
Cinnamon, ground	0.07 oz. (1 tsp.)	2 g
Phyllo dough	12 sheets	12 sheets
Clarified butter, melted	4 fl. oz.	120 ml
Almonds, ground	0.5 oz.	15 g

1 Toss the apples with the lemon juice and half of the sugar in a medium bowl. Let stand for 30 minutes, then drain off the liquid that forms.

2 Gently combine the drained apples with the raisins, orange zest, cinnamon and remaining sugar.

3 Prepare the phyllo dough by laying one sheet out on a piece of parchment paper. Brush lightly with butter and top with a second sheet of phyllo. Brush this sheet lightly with butter and sprinkle with about 1 teaspoon (5 milliliters) ground almonds. Top with a third sheet of dough, more butter and nuts and repeat until six sheets of phyllo are stacked.

4 Place half of the apple mixture along the long edge of the assembled dough. Using the paper to assist with rolling the dough, roll the phyllo around the filling tightly. Repeat Steps 3 and 4 with the remaining phyllo sheets and filling.

5 Place the strudels, seam side down, on a parchment-lined baking sheet. Brush the surface lightly with melted butter. Bake at 375°F (190°C) until golden brown and crisp, approximately 18 minutes.

Approximate values per ⅛-roll serving: **Calories** 260, **Total fat** 10 g, **Saturated fat** 6 g, **Cholesterol** 20 mg, **Sodium** 0 mg, **Total carbohydrates** 42 g, **Protein** 2 g

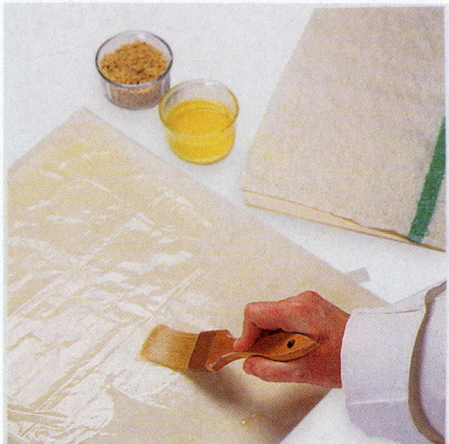

❶ Brushing a sheet of phyllo with clarified butter.

❷ Sprinkling a sheet of phyllo with chopped nuts before adding another layer of phyllo.

❸ Topping a stack of phyllo sheets with the apples.

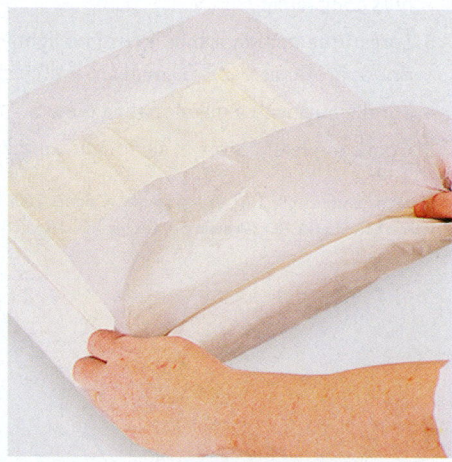

❹ Rolling up the strudel.

Chocolate-Mint Crinkle Cookies

YIELD	6 Dozen Cookies, approximately ½ oz. (15 g) each	METHOD	Drop Cookies		

Dark chocolate, chopped	12 oz.	360 g	400%
Unsalted butter	2 oz.	60 g	66.6%
Eggs	5 oz. (3 eggs)	150 g	166%
Granulated sugar	4 oz.	120 g	133%
Peppermint schnapps	3 fl. oz.	90 ml	100%
Blanched almonds, finely ground	3.5 oz.	105 g	116%
All-purpose flour	3 oz.	90 g	100%
Baking powder	0.1 oz. (¾ tsp.)	3 g	3.3%
Total dough weight:	2 lb.	978 g	1085%
Coating:			
Granulated sugar	6 oz.	180 g	
Powdered sugar	4 oz.	120 g	

1 Melt chocolate and butter together over barely simmering water. Remove from the heat and let stand until ready to use.

2 In a mixer fitted with a whisk attachment, whip the eggs and sugar together until thick and pale, approximately 5 minutes.

3 Whisk the schnapps into the melted chocolate, and then whisk the chocolate mixture into the egg mixture, blending well.

4 Stir the ground almonds, flour and baking powder together in a bowl, then whisk the flour mixture into the chocolate. Chill until firm, at least 4 hours.

5 Scoop the chilled dough into 1-inch (2.5-centimeter) balls and place on a sheet pan. Refrigerate until firm, approximately 10 minutes.

6 Place the granulated sugar and the powdered sugar in separate small bowls. Roll each ball of dough in the granulated sugar first and then in the powdered sugar, making sure to coat the surface thoroughly with powdered sugar. Place the cookies on a parchment-lined sheet pan and bake at 325°F (160°C) until they are firm enough to be lifted off the sheet pan, approximately 12–15 minutes.

Approximate values per ½-oz. (15-g) cookie: **Calories** 70, **Total fat** 3 g, **Saturated fat** 1.5 g, **Cholesterol** 10 mg, **Sodium** 10 mg, **Total carbohydrates** 10 g, **Protein** 1 g

Oatmeal Raisin Cookies

YIELD 32 Cookies, 2 oz. (60 g) each		METHOD Drop Cookies	
All-purpose or pastry flour	10.5 oz.	315 g	100%
Baking soda	0.14 oz. (1 tsp.)	4 g	1.3%
Cinnamon, ground	0.2 oz. (1 Tbsp.)	6 g	2%
Quick-cooking oats	9 oz.	270 g	86%
Unsalted butter	9 oz.	270 g	86%
Granulated sugar	9 oz.	270 g	86%
Brown sugar	9 oz.	270 g	86%
Eggs	3.3 oz. (2 eggs)	97 g	31%
Orange juice concentrate	1.5 fl. oz.	45 ml	14%
Vanilla extract	0.5 fl. oz.	15 ml	4.7%
Salt	0.2 oz. (1 tsp.)	6 g	2%
Raisins	12 oz.	360 g	114%
Total dough weight:	4 lb.	1928 g	613%

1 Sift together the flour, baking soda and cinnamon. Stir in the oats. Set aside. Cream the butter until light and fluffy. Add the sugars and continue creaming until the mixture is lightened. Add the eggs one at a time, scraping down the bowl frequently and mixing well after each addition. Add the orange juice concentrate, vanilla extract and salt.

2 Fold in the dry ingredients and the raisins.

3 Portion the dough onto paper-lined sheet pans and bake at 375°F (191°C) until golden, approximately 10–12 minutes.

Approximate values per 2-oz. (60-g) cookie: **Calories** 150, **Total fat** 5 g, **Saturated fat** 1.5 g, **Cholesterol** 10 mg, **Sodium** 105 mg, **Total carbohydrates** 24 g, **Protein** 2 g, **Claims**—low cholesterol; low sodium

Peanut Butter Sandies

YIELD 4½ Dozen Cookies, 1⅓ oz. (40 g) each		METHOD Drop Cookies	
Pastry flour	1 lb. 4 oz.	720 g	100%
Baking soda	0.14 oz. (1 tsp.)	4 g	0.6 %
Baking powder	0.14 oz. (1 tsp.)	4 g	0.6%
Unsalted butter, softened	1 lb.	475 g	66%
Granulated sugar	1 lb.	475 g	66%
Eggs	3.3 oz. (2 eggs)	100 g	14%
Peanut butter	10 oz.	300 g	42%
Salt	0.4 oz. (2 tsp.)	12 g	1.7%
Peanut halves, optional	2 oz.	60 g	8%
Total dough weight:	4 lb. 8 oz.	2150 g	299%

1 Sift together the flour, baking soda and baking powder. Set aside. Cream the butter. Add the sugar and continue creaming. Gradually add the eggs, followed by the peanut butter and salt.

2 Add the dry ingredients to the butter mixture and mix to make a firm dough.

3 Scale the dough into 1-pound (480-gram) pieces. Roll the dough into 12-inch (36-centimeter) logs. Cut into 1-inch (3-centimeter) pieces.

4 Roll each cookie into a ball and place on a sheet pan. Using the bottom of a measuring cup, press each ball down to slightly less than ½ inch (1 centimeter). The edges of the cookies will develop some cracks, which is a desired look.

5 Using a fork, press crisscross markings on the surface of each cookie. Lightly brush the cookies with water. Sprinkle lightly with granulated sugar and press one peanut half, if using, into each cookie.

6 Bake at 400°F (200°F) until golden brown, approximately 12 minutes.

Approximate values per 1⅓-oz. (40-g) cookie: **Calories** 190, **Total fat** 12 g, **Saturated fat** 5 g, **Cholesterol** 20 mg, **Sodium** 160 mg, **Total carbohydrates** 22 g, **Protein** 3 g

Chocolate Chip Cookies

YIELD 4 Dozen Cookies, 2 oz. (60 g) each   **METHOD** Drop Cookies

Unsalted butter, softened	1 lb.	480 g	80%
Granulated sugar	8 oz.	240 g	40%
Brown sugar	12 oz.	360 g	60%
Eggs	5 oz. (3 eggs)	150 g	25%
Vanilla extract	0.3 fl. oz. (2 tsp.)	9 ml	1.5%
Salt	0.4 oz. (2 tsp.)	12 g	2%
Pastry flour	1 lb. 4 oz.	600 g	100%
Baking soda	0.14 oz. (1 tsp.)	4 g	0.7%
Pecans or walnut pieces, chopped	8 oz.	240 g	40%
Chocolate chips or chunks	2 lb.	960 g	160%
Total dough weight:	6 lb. 5 oz.	3055 g	509.5%

1 Cream the butter and the sugars in the bowl of a mixer fitted with the paddle attachment. Beat until light, approximately 5 minutes at medium speed.

2 Add the eggs to the creamed mixture one at a time. Add the vanilla extract.

3 Stir the salt, flour and baking soda together and add to the creamed mixture.

4 Stir in the pecans and chocolate chips.

5 Portion the dough using a #20 scoop onto a paper-lined sheet pan and bake at 350°F (180°C) until the cookies are golden brown and cooked through, approximately 10–12 minutes.

Approximate values per 2-oz. (60-g) cookie: **Calories** 310, **Total fat** 20 g, **Saturated fat** 7 g, **Cholesterol** 20 mg, **Sodium** 160 mg, **Total carbohydrates** 35 g, **Protein** 3 g

Biscotti

Italian in origin, biscotti are twice-baked cookies served with coffee, wine or other beverages. The dough is mixed and shaped into a log. The log of dough is baked, then cut on a diagonal into individual cookies, which are returned to the oven to bake further. This twice-baked process ensures that the cookies have a long-lasting firm, crisp texture.

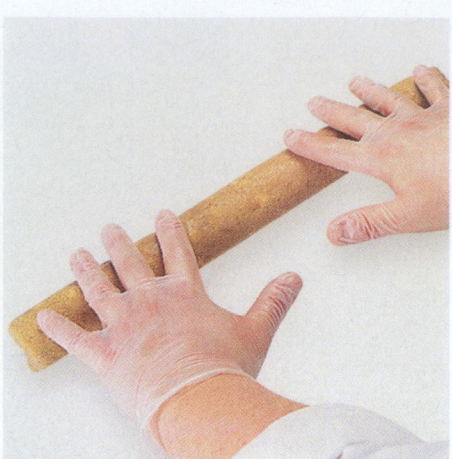

❶ Biscotti dough rolled into a log before the first baking.

YIELD 3 Dozen Biscotti, 2 oz. (60 g) each		METHOD Bar Cookies		
Cinnamon, ground	0.2 oz. (1 Tbsp.)	4 g	1%
Ammonium carbonate or baking powder	0.3 oz. (2 tsp.)	9 g	2%
Hazelnut flour	10 oz.	300 g	62%
Almond flour	3 oz.	90 g	19%
Pastry flour	1 lb.	480 g	100%
Eggs	8.5 oz. (5 eggs)	250 g	52%
Granulated sugar	1 lb.	480 g	100%
Unsalted butter, melted	8 oz.	240 g	50%
Whole hazelnuts	10 oz.	300 g	62%
Total dough weight:	4 lb. 8 oz.	2153 g	448%
Chocolate, melted and tempered, optional	as needed	as needed	

1. Sift together the cinnamon and ammonium carbonate or baking powder. Stir in the hazelnut, almond and pastry flours. Set aside.

2. In a large bowl, whisk together the eggs and sugar to the ribbon stage, approximately 3 minutes. Add the butter. Stir in the flour mixture with a rubber spatula, then stir in the whole hazelnuts.

3. Divide the dough into three even pieces. Refrigerate until cold.

4. Roll each piece of dough into a 12-inch (30-centimeter) log. Place on a paper-lined sheet pan, leaving at least 3 inches (7.5 centimeters) of space between each log.

5. Bake at 350°F (180°C) until golden in color, approximately 20 minutes. Cool the logs, then slice them into 1-inch- (3-centimeter-) thick slices.

6. Place the sliced cookies upright on paper-lined sheet pans.

7. Double-tray the pans. Reduce heat to 325°F (160°C) and bake until the biscotti are thoroughly crisp, approximately 40 minutes.

8. Once cool, the biscotti may be dipped in tempered chocolate.

❷ Slicing biscotti before the second baking.

Variations:

Orange Biscotti—Add 0.5 ounces (1 Tablespoon/15 grams/3%) grated orange zest to the flour mixture.

Anise Biscotti—Add 0.25 ounce (1 teaspoon/7 grams/1.5%) chopped anise seeds to the flour mixture.

Chocolate Biscotti—Replace 5 ounces (150 grams/31%) pastry flour with cocoa powder. Add 0.3 fluid ounces (½ teaspoon/2 milliliters/2%) coffee extract and 0.3 ounce (½ teaspoon/9 grams/2%) cinnamon to the flour mixture.

Approximate values per 2-oz. (60-g) cookie: **Calories** 260, **Total fat** 17 g, **Saturated fat** 4 g, **Cholesterol** 45 mg, **Sodium** 30 mg, **Total carbohydrates** 26 g, **Protein** 5 g

Lemon or Lime Bars

YIELD	1 Half-Sheet Pan, 3 Dozen Bars, 2 in. × 3 in. (5 cm × 7.5 cm) each	METHOD	Sheet Cookies

Sweet Dough (page 981), chilled	2 lb. 8 oz.	1200 g
Egg wash	as needed	as needed
Filling:		
Granulated sugar	1 lb. 6 oz.	640 g
Eggs	13.2 oz. (8 eggs)	400 g
Pastry flour	2 oz.	60 g
Lemon or lime juice	11 fl. oz.	330 ml
Milk	5 fl. oz.	150 ml
Salt	0.1 oz. (½ tsp.)	3 g
Powdered sugar for garnish	4 oz.	120 g

1 Roll the chilled Sweet Dough out on parchment paper cut to fit the sides and bottom of a half-sheet pan. Flip the parchment-covered dough onto a half-sheet pan. Remove the parchment. Trim uneven edges and reserve dough scraps. Prick the surface of the dough with a fork and bake at 350°F (180°C) until the dough is light golden, approximately 15 minutes. If cracks develop during the baking process, patch with the leftover dough and return briefly to the oven.

2 Brush the baked dough with egg wash and return to the oven for 3 minutes or until the egg wash has set.

3 To prepare the filling, whip the sugar and the eggs just until smooth. Whisk in the pastry flour until well combined, then add the lemon juice, milk and salt.

4 Pour the lemon filling into the prebaked shell.

5 Bake at 325°F (160°C) until set, approximately 25 minutes.

6 Cool, then cut into 2 inch × 3 inch (5 centimeter × 7.5 centimeter) bars. Dust liberally with powdered sugar.

Approximate values per bar: **Calories** 140, **Total fat** 6 g, **Saturated fat** 3 g, **Cholesterol** 40 mg, **Sodium** 80 mg, **Total carbohydrates** 21 g, **Protein** 2 g

Linzer Cookies

YIELD	4 Dozen Cookies, 2½ in. (6 cm) each	METHOD	Cut-out Cookies

Shortbread Tart Dough (page 1003), made with hazelnuts, chilled	4 lb. 7 oz.	2130 g
Raspberry jam	1 lb.	480 g

1 On a well-floured surface, roll the chilled hazelnut shortbread dough ¼ inch (6 millimeters) thick.

2 Cut the dough with a floured cutter into 2½-inch (6-centimeter) circles or ovals. Place the dough cutouts on paper-lined sheet pans.

3 Using a slightly smaller cookie cutter, remove the center from half of the dough cutouts. These will be the cookie tops for the sandwich cookies. (Save these dough scraps for more cookies.)

4 Bake at 375°F (190°C) until pale blond in color, approximately 8–10 minutes. Cool the cookies completely.

5 Melt 3 ounces (120 grams) of the raspberry jam. Brush the solid cookies with the melted jam. Place the remaining cookie tops on the jam-coated cookies. Using a pastry bag fitted with a small plain tip, fill the center of each cookie with raspberry jam.

Approximate values per cookie: **Calories** 200, **Total fat** 15 g, **Saturated fat** 7 g, **Cholesterol** 65 mg, **Sodium** 75 mg, **Total carbohydrates** 24 g, **Protein** 4 g

Piping icing on top of each cookie.

Sugar Cookies

YIELD	2 Dozen Cookies, 1 oz. (30 g) each		METHOD	Cut-Out Cookies

All-purpose flour	12 oz.	360 g	100%
Baking powder	0.3 oz. (2 tsp.)	9 g	2.5%
Mace, ground	0.02 oz. (¼ tsp.)	0.5 g	0.1%
Unsalted butter, softened	4 oz.	120 g	33.3%
Granulated sugar	8 oz.	240 g	66.6%
Vanilla extract	0.15 fl. oz. (1 tsp.)	4.5 ml	1.2%
Egg	1.6 oz. (1 egg)	49 g	13.7%
Total dough weight:	1 lb. 10 oz.	783 g	217%
Decorative Cookie Icing (recipe follows)	as needed	as needed	

1 Stir together the flour, baking powder and mace. Set aside.

2 Cream the butter and sugar until light and fluffy. Blend in the vanilla extract. Add the egg and beat again until fluffy. Gradually add the flour mixture, beating just until well combined.

3 Wrap the dough in plastic wrap and refrigerate until firm, approximately 1–2 hours.

4 Work with half of the dough at a time, keeping the remainder refrigerated. On a lightly floured board, roll out the dough to a thickness of approximately ⅛ inch (3 millimeters). Cut as desired with cookie cutters about 3 inches (7.5 centimeters) wide. Carefully transfer the cookies to parchment-lined baking sheets.

5 Bake at 325°F (160°C) until golden brown, approximately 10–12 minutes. Let stand for 1 minute, then transfer to wire racks to cool.

6 To decorate the cookies, use a pastry bag fitted with a small plain tip to pipe a fine outline of Decorative Cookie Icing around the edge of each cookie. Allow the icing to set for 5 minutes. Thin the remaining icing with water until it has the texture of thick cream. Fill in the top of each cookie with additional icing.

Approximate values per 1-oz. (30-g) cookie: **Calories** 90, **Total fat** 3 g, **Saturated fat** 1.5 g, **Cholesterol** 15 mg, **Sodium** 0 mg, **Total carbohydrates** 14 g, **Protein** 1 g, **Claims**—low fat; low cholesterol; no sodium

Decorative Cookie Icing

YIELD	1 lb. 6 oz. (665 g)	

Powdered sugar	1 lb.	480 g
Lemon juice or water	4 fl. oz.	120 ml
Corn syrup	2 fl. oz.	60 ml
Vanilla extract	0.15 fl. oz. (1 tsp.)	5 ml
Food coloring	as needed	as needed

1 Combine the powdered sugar, lemon juice, corn syrup and vanilla extract in the bowl of a mixer fitted with the paddle attachment. Blend on low speed until the sugar dissolves and the mixture is smooth. Adjust the consistency of the icing if necessary by adding more water if it is too thick to pipe or spread. Color as needed.

2 Apply the icing to cookies and let them air dry until the icing hardens. Cover leftover icing and store it in the refrigerator, where it will keep for about 3 weeks.

Approximate values per ¾-oz. (20-g) serving: **Calories** 60, **Total fat** 0 g, **Saturated fat** 0 g, **Cholesterol** 0 mg, **Sodium** 0 mg, **Total carbohydrates** 16 g, **Protein** 0 g

Gingerbread Cookies

YIELD 1 Dozen Cookies, 2⅓ oz. (70 g) each	METHOD Cut-Out Cookies		
Unsalted butter, softened	4 oz.	120 g	33%
Brown sugar	4 oz.	120 g	33%
Molasses	6 fl. oz.	180 ml	50%
Egg	1.6 oz. (1 egg)	50 g	13.7%
All-purpose flour	12 oz.	360 g	100%
Baking soda	0.14 oz. (1 tsp.)	4 g	1%
Salt	0.1 oz. (½ tsp.)	3 g	0.8%
Ginger, ground	0.14 oz. (2 tsp.)	4 g	1%
Cinnamon, ground	0.07 oz. (1 tsp.)	2 g	0.6 %
Nutmeg, ground	0.03 oz. (½ tsp.)	1 g	0.2%
Cloves, ground	0.03 oz. (½ tsp.)	1 g	0.2%
Total dough weight:	1 lb. 12 oz.	845 g	233%

1 Cream the butter and sugar until light and fluffy. Add the molasses and egg and beat to blend well; set aside.

2 Stir together the remaining ingredients. Gradually add the flour mixture to the butter mixture, beating until just blended. Gather the dough into a ball and wrap in plastic wrap; refrigerate for at least 1 hour.

3 On a lightly floured board, roll out the gingerbread to a thickness of ¼ inch (6 millimeters). Cut out the cookies with a floured cutter and transfer to greased baking sheets.

4 Bake at 325°F (160°C) until the cookies are lightly browned around the edges and feel barely firm when touched, approximately 10 minutes. Transfer to wire racks to cool. Decorate as desired with Royal Icing (page 1047), Decorative Cookie Icing (page 1020) or melted chocolate.

Approximate values per 2⅓-oz. (70-g) cookie: **Calories** 260, **Total fat** 8 g, **Saturated fat** 5 g, **Cholesterol** 40 mg, **Sodium** 220 mg, **Total carbohydrates** 41 g, **Protein** 4 g, **Vitamin A** 8%

Spritz Cookies

YIELD 4 Dozen Cookies, ½ oz. (15 g) each		METHOD Piped Cookies		
Unsalted butter, softened	8 oz.	240 g	80%
Granulated sugar	4 oz.	120 g	40%
Salt	0.05 oz. (¼ tsp.)	1.5 g	0.5 %
Vanilla extract	0.15 fl. oz. (1 tsp.)	5 ml	1.5%
Egg	1.6 oz. (1 egg)	50 g	16%
Cake flour, sifted	10 oz.	300 g	100%
Raspberry jam	as needed	as needed	
Total dough weight:	1 lb. 7 oz.	716 g	238%

1 Cream the butter and sugar until light and fluffy. Add the salt, vanilla extract and egg; beat well.

2 Gradually add the flour, beating until just blended. The dough should be firm but neither sticky nor stiff.

3 Pipe the dough onto an ungreased sheet pan using a cookie press or a piping bag fitted with a large star tip.

4 Bake at 350°F (180°C) until lightly browned around the edges, approximately 10 minutes. Transfer to wire racks to cool.

5 Pipe raspberry jam onto each cookie once cooled, if desired.

Approximate values per ½-oz. (15-g) cookie: **Calories** 40, **Total fat** 2.5 g, **Saturated fat** 1.5 g, **Cholesterol** 10 mg, **Sodium** 10 mg, **Total carbohydrates** 4 g, **Protein** 0 g, **Claims**—low fat; low cholesterol; very low sodium; low calorie

Lacy Pecan Cookies

YIELD 4 Dozen Cookies, 3 in. (7.5 cm) each	METHOD Wafer Cookies		
Brown sugar	6 oz.	180 g	100%
Unsalted butter	5 oz.	150 g	83%
Dark corn syrup	7.5 oz.	225 g	125%
Vanilla extract	0.15 fl. oz. (1 tsp.)	4.5 ml	2.5%
Salt	0.15 oz. (¾ tsp.)	4.5 g	2.5%
All-purpose flour	6 oz.	180 g	100%
Pecans, finely chopped	5 oz.	150 g	83%
Total dough weight:	1 lb. 13 oz.	894g	496%

1 Combine the sugar, butter, corn syrup and vanilla extract in a large, heavy saucepan. Bring to a boil.

2 Mix the salt, flour and nuts together.

3 As soon as the sugar mixture comes to a boil, start timing it. Let it boil for 1 minute. Remove from the heat and stir in the flour-nut mixture. Pour into a hotel pan and cool completely.

4 Use a small portion scoop to make equal-sized balls of dough. Flatten out the balls of dough and place on a silicone baking mat or paper-lined sheet pans.

5 Bake at 325°F (160°C) until very dark brown and no longer moist in center, approximately 15–18 minutes. Remove from oven and shape as desired.

Approximate values per cookie: **Calories** 80, **Total fat** 4.5 g, **Saturated fat** 1.5 g, **Cholesterol** 5 mg, **Sodium** 45 mg, **Total carbohydrates** 10 g, **Protein** 1 g

❶ Portioning the pecan cookie dough on a sheet pan lined with a silicone mat.

❷ Shaping the baked Lacy Pecan Cookies over a rolling pin while still hot.

Tulipe Cookies

YIELD 3 Dozen Cookies, approximately 6 in. (15 cm) each		METHOD Wafer Cookies		
Unsalted butter		1 lb.	480 g	100%
Powdered sugar		1 lb.	480 g	100%
All-purpose flour		1 lb.	480 g	100%
Egg whites		1 lb.	480 ml	100%
Butter, melted		as needed	as needed	
Total batter weight:		4 lb.	1920 g	400%

1 Melt the unsalted butter and place in the bowl of a mixer fitted with the paddle attachment. Add the sugar and blend until almost smooth.

2 Add the flour and blend until smooth. With the mixer running, add the egg whites very slowly. Beat until blended, but do not incorporate air into the batter.

3 Strain the batter through a china cap and set aside to cool completely.

4 Coat several sheet pans with melted butter or line with silicone mats. Spread the batter into 6-inch (15-centimeter) circles on the pans. Bake at 400°F (200°C) until the edges are brown and the dough is dry, approximately 12–18 minutes.

5 To shape into cups, lift the hot cookies off the sheet pan one at a time with an offset spatula. Immediately place over an inverted glass and top with a ramekin or small bowl. The cookies cool very quickly, becoming firm and crisp. The cookie cups can be used for serving ice cream, crème brûlée, fruit or other items.

Approximate values per 2½-oz. (75-g) cookie: **Calories** 240, **Total fat** 12 g, **Saturated fat** 8 g, **Cholesterol** 35 mg, **Sodium** 40 mg, **Total carbohydrates** 37 g, **Protein** 4 g, **Vitamin A** 10%

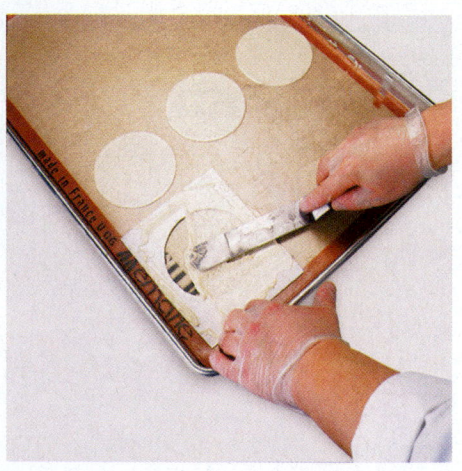

❶ Spreading the Tulipe Cookie batter into circles on a sheet pan lined with a silicone mat.

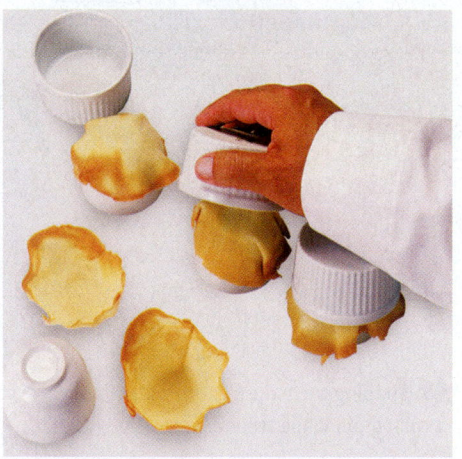

❷ Shaping the baked Tulipe Cookies into cups while still hot.

❸ Serving lemon sorbet and fresh berries in a Tulipe Cookie cup.

Cakes and Frostings 34

- describe the function of ingredients used to make cakes
- prepare a variety of cakes using the creamed fat and whipped-egg mixing methods
- prepare a variety of frostings
- explain basic cake finishing techniques
- assemble a variety of cakes

Cakes are popular in most bakeshops because a wide variety of finished products can be created from only a few basic cake, filling and frosting formulas. Many of these components can even be made in advance and assembled into finished desserts as needed. Cakes are also popular because of their versatility. Cake can be served from unadorned sheets in a high-volume cafeteria or as the elaborate centerpiece of a wedding buffet.

Cake making need not be difficult or intimidating, but it does require an understanding of ingredients and mixing methods. This chapter begins by explaining how typical cake ingredients interact. Each of the traditional mixing methods is then explained and illustrated with a formula. Information on panning batters, baking temperatures, determining doneness and cooling methods follows. The second portion of this chapter presents mixing methods and formulas for a variety of frostings and icings. The third section covers cake assembly and presents some simple and commonly used cake-decorating techniques. A selection of popular cake formulas concludes the chapter.

CAKE INGREDIENTS

Most cakes are created from liquid batters with high fat and sugar contents. The baker's job is to combine all the ingredients to create a structure that will support these rich ingredients yet keep the cake as light and delicate as possible. As with other baked goods, it is impossible to taste a cake until it is fully cooked and too late to alter the formula. Therefore it is extremely important to study any formula before beginning and to follow it with particular care and attention to detail.

Good cakes begin with high-quality ingredients (see Chapter 30, Principles of the Bakeshop); however, even the finest ingredients must be combined in the proper balance. Too much flour and the cake may be dry; too much egg and the cake may be tough and hard. Changing one ingredient may necessitate a change in one or more of the other ingredients. Cake ingredients should be at room temperature, approximately 70°F (21°C), before mixing begins. If one ingredient is too cold or too warm, it may affect the batter's ability to trap and hold the gases necessary for the cake to rise.

Each cake ingredient performs a specific function and has a specific effect on the final product. Cake ingredients can be classified by function as **tougheners**, **tenderizers**, **moisteners**, **driers**, **leaveners** and **flavorings**. In the following list, we explain the role of each of these classes of ingredients. Some ingredients fulfill more than one of these functions. For example, eggs contain water, so they are moisteners, and they contain protein, so they are tougheners. Understanding the function of various ingredients can help you understand why cakes are made in particular ways and why a preparation sometimes fails. With additional experience you will be able to recognize and correct flawed formulas, which is the first step toward developing your own cake formulas.

Tougheners: Flour, milk and eggs contain protein. Protein provides structure and strengthens the cake once it is baked. Too little protein and the cake may collapse; too much protein and the cake may be tough and coarse-textured.

Tenderizers: Sugar, fats and egg yolks interfere with the development of the gluten structure when the cake is mixed. They shorten the gluten strands, making the cake tender and soft. These tenderizing ingredients also improve the cake's keeping qualities.

Moisteners: Liquids such as water, milk, juice and eggs add moisture to the mixture. Moisture is necessary for gluten formation and starch gelatinization, as well as for improving the cake's keeping qualities.

Driers: Flour, starches and milk solids absorb moisture, giving body and structure to the cake.

Leaveners: The cake rises because gases in the batter expand when heated. Cakes are leavened by air that is trapped when fat and sugar are creamed together, by carbon dioxide released from baking powder and baking soda and by air trapped in beaten eggs. All cakes rely on natural leaveners—steam and air—to create the proper texture and rise.

Flavorings: Flavorings such as extracts, cocoa, chocolate, spices, salt, sugar and butter provide the cake with flavor. Acidic flavoring ingredients such as sour cream, chocolate and fruit also provide the acid necessary to activate baking soda.

MIXING METHODS FOR CAKES

Even the finest ingredients cannot make a good cake if the cake batter is not mixed correctly. When mixing any cake batter, the goals are to combine the ingredients uniformly, incorporate air cells and develop the proper texture.

All mixing methods can be divided into two categories: *high fat*, those that create a structure that relies primarily on **creamed fat**, and *egg foam*, those that create a structure that relies primarily on **whipped eggs**. These broad categories include several mixing methods or types of cakes. Creamed-fat cakes include **butter cakes** (also known as **creaming method cakes**) and **high-ratio cakes**. Whipped-egg cakes include **genoise**, **spongecakes**, **angel food cakes** and **chiffon** cakes. See Table 34.1. Although certain general procedures are used to prepare each cake type, there are numerous variations. (Certain European-style cake formulas include both creaming and egg foam mixing techniques. Sacher Torte (page 1059), for example, is made from a creamed-fat batter into which whipped egg whites are folded before baking.) Follow specific formula instructions precisely.

Creamed-Fat Cakes

Creamed-fat/high-fat cakes include most of the popular American-style cakes: poundcakes, layer cakes, coffeecakes and even brownies. All of these are based on high-fat formulas, most containing chemical leaveners. A good high-fat cake has a fine grain, cells of uniform size and a crumb that is moist rather than crumbly. Crusts should be thin and tender. Creamed-fat/high-fat cakes can be divided into two classes: butter cakes and high-ratio cakes.

Butter Cakes

Butter cakes, also known as creaming method cakes, begin with softened butter or shortening **creamed** to incorporate air cells. Proper creaming ensures a fine even crumb and uniform rise, although because of their high fat content, these cakes usually also need the assistance of a chemical leavener to achieve the proper rise.

Modern-day butter cakes—the classic American layer cakes, popular for birthdays and special occasions—are made with the creaming method. These cakes are tender yet sturdy enough to handle rich buttercreams or fillings. High-fat cakes are too soft and delicate, however, to use for roll cakes or to slice into extremely thin layers.

Creaming fat mechanically leavens the cake and creates a mixture in which fats and liquid are suspended. Air cells are trapped in the fat, lightening the mixture. As eggs are mixed into the creamed fat, the mixture emulsifies. In an emulsion, fats and liquids, which normally do not blend, are held in suspension. This emulsification ensures that the batter will hold the additional liquids and flour necessary to produce the desirable cake texture.

Poundcakes

Poundcakes are the original high-fat, creaming method cake. They are called poundcakes because early formulas specified one pound each of butter, eggs, flour and sugar. Poundcakes should have a close grain and compact texture but still be very tender. They should be neither heavy nor soggy.

As bakers experimented with poundcake formulas, they reduced the amount of eggs and fat, substituting milk instead. These changes led to the development of the modern butter cake, which has a lighter texture that is more suitable for layering, filling and coating with buttercream icing or fondant.

The two containers hold equal weights of butter. The volume of the butter increases when creamed thoroughly (right) but expands very little when creamed insufficiently (left).

CAKES			TABLE 34.1
CATEGORY	TYPE OF CAKE/MIXING METHOD	KEY FORMULA CHARACTERISTICS	TEXTURE
Creamed fat (high fat)	Butter (creaming method)	High-fat formula; chemical leavener used	Fine grain; air cells of uniform size; moist crumb; thin and tender crust
	High-ratio (two-stage)	Emulsified shortening; two-part mixing method	Very fine grain; moist crumb; relatively high rise
Whipped egg (egg foam)	Genoise	Whole eggs are whipped with sugar; no chemical leaveners	Dry and spongy
	Sponge	Egg yolks are mixed with other ingredients, then whipped egg whites are folded in	Moister and more tender than genoise
	Angel food	No fat; large quantity of whipped egg whites; high percentage of sugar	Tall, light and spongy
	Chiffon	Vegetable oil used; egg yolks mixed with other ingredients, then whipped egg whites folded in; baking powder may be added	Tall, light and fluffy; moister and richer than angel food

Procedure for Preparing Butter Cakes (Creaming Method)

1 Preheat the oven and prepare the pans. Have ingredients at room temperature, 70°F (21°C), for effective creaming

2 Sift the dry ingredients together and set aside.

3 Cream the butter or shortening on low speed until it is light and fluffy. Add the sugar and cream until the mixture is fluffy and smooth. Scrape down the bowl frequently to make certain the entire mixture is well creamed.

4 Add the eggs slowly, beating well after each addition. Scrape down the bowl after each addition.

5 Add the dry and liquid ingredients alternately to prevent development of gluten and to preserve the emulsion.

6 Divide the batter into prepared pans and bake immediately.

American Poundcake

MISE EN PLACE

- Soften butter.
- Grease pans.
- Preheat oven to 325°F (160°C).

YIELD 3 lb. 10 oz. (1750 g) Batter, 2 Loaves, 8 in. × 4 in. (20 cm × 10 cm) each

METHOD Creaming

Cake flour	1 lb.	480 g	100%
Baking powder	0.3 oz. (2 tsp.)	8 g	1.8%
Salt	0.1 oz. (½ tsp.)	3 g	0.6%
Unsalted butter, softened	1 lb.	480 g	100%
Granulated sugar	12 oz.	360 g	75%
Eggs	14.8 oz. (9 eggs)	437 g	91.2%
Vanilla extract	0.15 fl. oz. (1 tsp.)	5 ml	1%
Lemon extract	0.15 fl. oz. (1 tsp.)	5 ml	1 %
Total batter weight:	3 lb. 11 oz.	1778 g	370.6%

1 Sift the flour, baking powder and salt together. Set aside.

2 Cream the butter until light and lump-free. Add the sugar and cream until light and fluffy. Add the eggs one at a time, scraping down the bowl frequently and mixing well after each addition. Stir in the extracts.

3 Fold in the dry ingredients by hand in three stages. Divide the batter into two 8-inch × 4-inch (20-centimeter × 10-centimeter) greased loaf pans. Spread evenly with a spatula.

4 Bake at 325°F (160°C) until golden brown and springy to the touch, approximately 1 hour and 10 minutes.

① Creaming the butter.

② Folding in the dry ingredients by hand.

③ Panning the batter.

Variation:

French-Style Fruitcake—Add 6 ounces (180 grams/37.5%) finely diced nuts, raisins and candied fruit to the batter. Substitute vanilla extract for the lemon extract and add 1.5 fluid ounces (45 milliliters/1%) rum to the batter. After baking, brush the warm cake with additional rum.

Approximate values per ⅒-loaf serving: **Calories** 340, **Total fat** 21 g, **Saturated fat** 12 g, **Cholesterol** 130 mg, **Sodium** 140 mg, **Total carbohydrates** 35 g, **Protein** 5 g

High-Ratio Cakes

Commercial bakeries often use a special two-stage mixing method to prepare large quantities of a very liquid cake batter with high sugar content. These formulas require special **emulsified shortenings** to help give the cake its structure. They are known as **two-stage cakes** because the liquids are added in two stages or portions. If emulsified shortenings are not available, do not substitute all-purpose shortening or butter, as those fats cannot absorb the large amounts of sugar and liquid in the formula.

Because they contain a high ratio (percentage) of sugar and liquid to flour, these cakes are often known as high-ratio cakes. They have a very fine, moist crumb and relatively high rise. High-ratio cakes can be used interchangeably with modern butter cakes and are most common in high-volume bakeries.

emulsified shortening a vegetable-oil based shortening made with additional emulsifiers (mono- and diglycerides), used to make cake batters containing higher than normal amounts of water and sugar; also referred to as icing shortening, cake shortening or high ratio shortening

Procedure for Preparing High-Ratio Cakes

1 Preheat the oven and prepare the pans.
2 Place all of the dry ingredients and emulsified shortening into a mixer bowl. Blend on low speed for several minutes.
3 Add approximately half of the liquid ingredients and blend.
4 Scrape down the bowl and add the remaining liquid ingredients. Blend into a smooth batter, scraping down the bowl as necessary.
5 Pour the batter into prepared pans, using liquid measurements to ensure uniform division.

High-Ratio Yellow Cake

MISE EN PLACE

- Grease pans.
- Preheat oven to 340°F (170°C).
- Allow shortening and eggs to come to room temperature.

YIELD 1½ to 2 Full-Sheet Pans **METHOD** Two-Stage

Cake flour	2 lb. 8 oz.	1200 g	100%
Granulated sugar	2 lb. 10 oz.	1260 g	105%
Emulsified shortening, room temperature	1 lb. 4 oz.	600 g	50%
Salt	1 oz.	30 g	2.5%
Baking powder	2 oz.	60 g	5%
Dry milk powder	4 oz.	120 g	10%
Light corn syrup	6 oz.	180 g	15%
Water, cold	36 fl. oz.	1080 ml	90%
Eggs, room temperature	1 lb. 4 oz.	600 g	50%
Lemon extract	0.5 fl. oz.	15 ml	1.2%
Total batter weight:	10 lb. 11 oz.	5145 g	428.7%

1. Combine the flour, sugar, shortening, salt, baking powder, milk powder, corn syrup and 1 pint (480 milliliters) cold water in a large bowl of a mixer fitted with the paddle attachment. Beat for 5 minutes on low speed, scraping down the bowl halfway through the mixing.

2. Combine the eggs, the remaining water and the lemon extract in a separate bowl. Add these liquid ingredients to the flour and fat mixture in three additions. Scrape down the bowl after each portion of liquid is added.

3. Beat for 2 minutes on low speed.

4. Divide the batter into greased and floured pans. Pans should be filled only halfway. One gallon of batter is sufficient for an 18-inch × 24-inch × 2-inch (45-centimeter × 60-centimeter × 5-centimeter) sheet pan. Bake at 340°F (170°C) until a cake tester comes out clean and the cake springs back when lightly touched, approximately 12–18 minutes.

Approximate values per 3-oz. (90-g) serving: **Calories** 390, **Total fat** 16 g, **Saturated fat** 5 g, **Cholesterol** 60 mg, **Sodium** 320 mg, **Total carbohydrates** 57 g, **Protein** 5 g, **Calcium** 10%

Whipped-Egg Cakes

Cakes based on whipped-egg foams include European-style genoise as well as sponge-cakes, angel food cakes and chiffon cakes. Some whipped-egg cake formulas contain chemical leaveners, but the air whipped into the eggs (whether whole or separated) is the primary leavening agent. Egg-foam cakes contain little or no fat. Genoise and sponge-cake are pliable; moisture in the eggs develops the protein in the flour, making these cakes springy and elastic. These cakes are well suited for rolling, as for a Swiss Jelly Roll (page 1033) or for cutting into thin layers or using to line a torte ring.

Genoise

Genoise is the classic European-style cake. It is based on whole eggs whipped with sugar until very light and fluffy. Chemical leaveners are not used. Slightly warming the egg mixture helps improve the volume of the egg foam. For flavor and moisture, a small amount of oil or melted butter is sometimes added to the batter after mixing. Genoise to which fat is added after mixing bakes into a cake that is more tender than a plain genoise because the fat helps shorten gluten strands. Often genoise is baked in a thin sheet and layered with buttercream, puréed fruit, jam or chocolate filling to create multilayered specialty desserts, sometimes known as **torten**. Because genoise is rather dry, it is usually soaked with a flavored sugar syrup (see Chapter 30, Principles of the Bakeshop) or liqueur for additional flavor and moisture. A basic genoise recipe is included here.

Procedure for Preparing Genoise

1. Preheat the oven and prepare the pans.
2. Sift the flour with any additional dry ingredients.
3. Combine the whole eggs and sugar in a large bowl and warm over a double boiler to a temperature of 100°F (38°C).
4. Whip the egg-and-sugar mixture to the **ribbon stage**, that is, until they fall from the beater in thick ribbons that slowly disappear into the surface. The batter will be very light and tripled in volume
5. Fold the sifted flour into the whipped eggs carefully but quickly.
6. Fold in oil or melted butter if desired.
7. Divide into pans and bake immediately.

ribbon stage a term used to describe the consistency of a batter or mixture, especially a mixture of beaten egg and sugar; when the beater or whisk is lifted, the mixture will fall back slowly onto its surface in a ribbonlike pattern

---

Classic Genoise

YIELD 1 Full-Sheet Pan or 2 Rounds, 8 in. (20 cm) each

METHOD Egg Foam

Eggs	1 lb. (10 eggs)	480 g	178%
Granulated sugar	8 oz.	240 g	89%
Vanilla extract	0.3 fl. oz. (2 tsp.)	9 ml	3%
Cake flour, sifted	9 oz.	270 g	100%
Unsalted butter, melted, optional	1.5 oz.	45 g	17%
Total batter weight:	2 lb. 2 oz.	1044 g	387%

MISE EN PLACE
- Melt butter, if using.
- Line pan with parchment paper.
- Sift flour.
- Preheat the oven to 425°F (220°C).

1. Whisk the eggs and sugar together in a large mixer bowl. Place the bowl over a bain marie and whisk the mixture continuously to warm the eggs to approximately 105–113°F (40–45°C).
2. When the eggs are warm, remove the bowl from the bain marie and attach it to a mixer fitted with the whip attachment. Whip the egg-and-sugar mixture at medium speed until the mixture is cool, very light and tripled in volume and forms thick ribbons, approximately 12–15 minutes.
3. Using a rubber spatula or balloon whisk, delicately fold the flour into the genoise batter by hand. Carefully fold in the melted butter, if using.
4. Spread the batter immediately onto a paper-lined sheet pan. Bake at 425°F (220°C) until light brown and springy to the touch, approximately 10 minutes.

Variation:

Chocolate Genoise—Reduce the cake flour to 7 ounces (210 grams/78%). Sift 2 ounces (60 grams/22%) cocoa powder with the flour.

Approximate values per 2-oz. (60-g) serving: **Calories** 140, **Total fat** 4 g, **Saturated fat** 2 g, **Cholesterol** 110 mg, **Sodium** 30 mg, **Total carbohydrates** 21 g, **Protein** 4 g, **Vitamin A** 6%

① Whipped eggs.

② Folding in the flour.

③ Adding the melted butter, if used.

④ Spreading the batter into the paper-lined pan.

Spongecakes

Spongecakes (Fr. *biscuits*) are made with separated eggs. A batter is prepared with egg yolks and other ingredients, and then egg whites are whipped with a portion of the sugar to firm but not dry peaks and folded into the batter. Spongecakes are leavened primarily with air, but baking powder may be included in the formula. As with genoise, oil or melted butter may be folded in, if desired, to add flavor and moisture.

Spongecakes are extremely versatile. They can be soaked with sugar syrup or a liqueur and assembled with buttercream as a traditional layer cake. Or they can be sliced thinly and layered, like genoise, with a jam, custard, chocolate or cream filling.

Procedure for Preparing Spongecakes

1 Preheat the oven and prepare the pans.
2 Sift the dry ingredients together with a portion of the sugar.
3 Separate the eggs. Whip the egg yolks to the ribbon stage. Whip in any flavorings.
4 In a separate bowl with a clean whip, whip the egg whites with a portion of the sugar, then carefully fold the whipped yolks and whipped whites together with the remaining sugar.
5 Gently fold the sifted dry ingredients into the egg foam in two or three additions.
6 Pour the batter into the pans and bake immediately.

♥ Good Choice

MISE EN PLACE

- Sift flour.
- Preheat the oven to 375°F (190°C).

Swiss Jelly Roll made from Classic Spongecake batter

Classic Spongecake

YIELD 2 Rounds, 9 in. (22 cm) each		METHOD Egg Foam	
Cake flour, sifted	6 oz.	180 g	100%
Granulated sugar	11 oz.	330 g	183%
Eggs	1 lb. (10 eggs)	480 g	266%
Vanilla extract	0.3 fl. oz. (2 tsp.)	9 ml	5%
Cream of tartar	0.2 oz. (1½ tsp.)	7 ml	3.3%
Total batter weight:	2 lb. 1 oz.	1006 g	557%

1 Line the bottom of two springform pans with parchment. Do not grease the sides of the pans.
2 Sift the flour and 6 ounces (180 grams) sugar together and set aside.
3 Separate the eggs, placing the yolks and the whites in separate mixing bowls. Whip the yolks on high speed until thick, pale and at least doubled in volume, approximately 3–5 minutes. Whip in the vanilla. The yolks should be whipped to the ribbon stage.
4 Place the bowl of egg whites on the mixer and, using a clean whip, beat until foamy. Add the cream of tartar and 1 ounce (30 grams) sugar. Whip at medium speed until the whites are glossy and stiff but not dry.
5 Remove the bowl from the mixer. Pour the egg yolks onto the whipped whites. Quickly fold the two mixtures together by hand. Sprinkle the remaining sugar over the mixture and fold in lightly.
6 Sprinkle one-third of the sifted flour-sugar mixture over the batter and fold in. Repeat the procedure until all the flour is incorporated. Do not overmix; fold just until incorporated.
7 Pour the batter into the prepared pans, smoothing the surface as needed. Bake immediately at 375°F (190°C) until the cake is golden brown and spongy, approximately 30 minutes. A toothpick inserted in the center will be completely clean when removed.
8 Allow the cakes to rest in their pans until completely cool, approximately 2 hours.
9 To remove the cakes from their pans, run a thin metal spatula around the edge of each pan. When the cake is completely cool, it can be frosted or wrapped in plastic wrap and frozen for 2–3 months.

① The eggs whipped to the ribbon stage.

② Folding the flour into the batter.

③ Panning the batter.

Variations:

Swiss Jelly Roll—Spread the cake batter onto a paper-lined half-sheet pan. Bake at 375°F (190°C) until the cake is golden brown and spongy, approximately 20 minutes. Cool the cake for 10 minutes. Invert the warm cake onto a piece of parchment dusted with powdered sugar. Carefully remove the paper on which the cake baked. Spread the warm cake with 8 ounces (240 grams) seedless raspberry or other jam. Roll the cake tightly. Trim the ends and dust with more sugar before serving.

Chocolate Spongecake—Reduce the cake flour to 5 ounces (150 grams/83%) and sift it with 1.5 ounces (45 grams/25%) cocoa powder.

Approximate values per 2-oz. (60-g) serving: **Calories** 130, **Total fat** 2.5 g, **Saturated fat** 1 g, **Cholesterol** 105 mg, **Sodium** 30 mg, **Total carbohydrates** 23 g, **Protein** 4 g, **Claims**—low fat; low saturated fat; very low sodium

Angel Food Cakes

Angel food cakes are tall, light cakes made without fat and leavened with a large quantity of whipped egg whites. Care must be taken when whipping egg whites because egg whites will not foam properly if grease or egg yolk is present in the mixing bowl. Angel food cakes are traditionally baked in ungreased tube pans, but large loaf pans can also be used. The pans are left ungreased so that the batter can cling to the sides as it rises. The cakes should be inverted as soon as they are removed from the oven and left in the pan to cool. This technique allows gravity to keep the cakes from collapsing or sinking as they cool.

Although they contain no fat, angel food cakes are not low in calories, as they contain a high percentage of sugar. The classic angel food cake is pure white, but flavorings, ground nuts or cocoa powder may be added for variety. Although angel food cakes are usually not frosted, they may be topped with a fruit-flavored or chocolate glaze. They are often served with fresh fruit, fruit compote or whipped cream.

Procedure for Preparing Angel Food Cakes

1 Preheat the oven.

2 Combine the dry ingredients, including a portion of the sugar, in a bowl and set aside.

3 Whip the egg whites with a portion of the sugar until glossy and stiff but not dry.

4 Gently fold the dry ingredients into the egg whites.

5 Spoon the batter into an ungreased pan and bake immediately.

6 Allow the cake to cool inverted in its pan.

♥ **Good Choice**

MISE EN PLACE

• Sift flour.
• Preheat the oven to 350°F (180°C).

Chocolate Angel Food Cake

YIELD 1 Tube Cake, 10 in. (25 cm)   **METHOD** Egg Foam

			Sugar at 100%
Cocoa powder, alkalized	1 oz.	30 g	8%
Water, warm	2 fl. oz.	60 ml	16%
Vanilla extract	0.5 fl. oz. (1 Tbsp.)	15 ml	4%
Granulated sugar	12 oz.	360 g	100%
Cake flour, sifted	3.5 oz.	105 g	29%
Salt	0.05 oz. (¼ tsp.)	1.5 g	0.4%
Egg whites	1 lb. (10 whites)	480 g	133%
Cream of tartar	0.3 oz. (2 tsp.)	9 g	2.5%
Powdered sugar	as needed	as needed	
Total batter weight:	2 lb. 3 oz.	1060 g	293%

1 Combine the cocoa powder and water in a bowl. Add the vanilla and set aside.

2 In another bowl, stir together 5 ounces (150 grams) of the granulated sugar, the flour and the salt.

3 Whip the egg whites until foamy, add the cream of tartar and beat to soft peaks. Gradually beat in the remaining granulated sugar. Continue beating until the egg whites are stiff but not dry.

4 Whisk a very large spoonful of the whipped egg whites into the cocoa mixture. Fold this into the remaining egg whites with a rubber spatula or balloon whisk.

5 Sift the dry ingredients over the whites and fold in quickly but gently.

6 Pour the batter into an ungreased tube pan and smooth the top with a spatula. Bake immediately at 350°F (180°C) until the cake springs back when lightly touched and a cake tester comes out clean, approximately 40–50 minutes. The cake's surface will have deep cracks.

7 Remove the cake from the oven and immediately invert the pan onto the neck of a bottle. Allow the cake to rest upside down until completely cool.

8 To remove the cake from the pan, run a thin knife or spatula around the edge of the pan and the edge of the interior tube. If a two-piece tube pan was used, lift the cake and tube portion out of the pan. Use a knife or spatula to loosen the bottom of the cake, then invert it onto a cardboard circle or serving platter. Dust with powdered sugar before serving. This cake may also be frosted with Basic Sugar Glaze (page 1046).

① Folding the egg-white-and-cocoa mixture into the whipped egg whites.

② Cooling the cake upside down in its pan.

③ Removing the cake from the pan.

Variations:

Vanilla Angel Food Cake—Omit the cocoa powder and warm water. Increase the vanilla extract to 1 fluid ounce (2 tablespoons/30 milliliters/8%) and fold it in at the end of Step 5.

Lemon Angel Food Cake—Omit the cocoa powder and warm water. Add 0.14 oz. (2 teaspoons/ 4 grams/1.1%) fresh lemon zest to the sugar-and-flour mixture. Add 0.15 fluid ounces (1 teaspoon/5 milliliters/1.2%) lemon extract, folding it and the vanilla extract in at the end of Step 5.

Approximate values per ⅒-cake serving: **Calories** 210, **Total fat** 0.5 g, **Saturated fat** 0 g, **Cholesterol** 0 mg, **Sodium** 150 mg, **Total carbohydrates** 44 g, **Protein** 7 g, **Claims**—low fat; no saturated fat; no cholesterol

Chiffon Cakes

Although chiffon cakes are similar to angel food cakes in appearance and texture, the addition of egg yolks and vegetable oil makes them moister and richer. Chiffon cakes are usually leavened with whipped egg whites but may contain baking powder as well. Like angel food cakes, chiffon cakes are baked in an ungreased pan to allow the batter to cling to the pan as it rises. Chiffon cakes can be frosted with a light buttercream or whipped cream or topped with a glaze. Lemon and orange chiffon cakes are the most traditional, but formulas containing chocolate, nuts or other flavorings are also common.

A Hollywood Classic

Chiffon cake is one of the few desserts whose history can be traced with absolute certainty. According to Gerry Schremp in her book *Kitchen Culture: Fifty Years of Food Fads*, a new type of cake was invented by Henry Baker, a California insurance salesman, in 1927. Dubbed chiffon, it was as light as angel food and as rich as poundcake. For years he kept the formula a secret, earning fame and fortune by selling his cakes to Hollywood restaurants. The cake's secret ingredient—vegetable oil—became public knowledge in 1947 when Baker sold the formula to General Mills, which promoted it on packages of cake flour. Chiffon cakes, in a variety of flavors, became extremely popular nationwide.

Procedure for Preparing Chiffon Cakes

1 Preheat the oven.
2 Sift the dry ingredients together. Add the liquid ingredients, including oil.
3 Whip the egg whites with a portion of the sugar until almost stiff.
4 Fold the whipped egg whites into the batter.
5 Spoon the batter into an ungreased pan and bake immediately.
6 Allow the cake to cool inverted in its pan.

MISE EN PLACE

- Sift flour.
- Preheat oven to 325°F (160°C).

❶ Folding the whipped egg whites into the cake batter.

❷ The glazed orange chiffon cake.

Orange Chiffon Cake

YIELD 1 Tube Cake, 10 in. (25 cm)		**METHOD** Egg Foam	
Cake:			
Cake flour, sifted	8 oz.	240 g	100%
Granulated sugar	12 oz.	360 g	150%
Baking powder	0.4 oz. (1 Tbsp.)	12 g	5%
Salt	0.2 oz. (1 tsp.)	6 g	2.5%
Vegetable oil	4 fl. oz.	120 ml	50%
Egg yolks	4 oz. (6 yolks)	120 g	50%
Water, cool	2 fl. oz.	60 ml	25%
Orange juice	4 fl. oz.	120 ml	50%
Orange zest, grated	0.2 oz. (1 Tbsp.)	6 g	2.5%
Vanilla extract	0.5 fl. oz. (1 Tbsp.)	15 ml	6%
Egg whites	8 oz. (8 whites)	240 g	100%
Total batter weight:	2 lb. 11 oz.	1299 g	541%
Glaze:			
Powdered sugar, sifted	3 oz.	90 g	
Orange juice	1 fl. oz.	30 ml	
Orange zest, grated	0.14 oz. (2 tsp.)	4 g	

1 Sift together the flour, 6 ounces (180 grams) granulated sugar and the baking powder and salt.

2 In a separate bowl, mix the oil, yolks, water, orange juice, orange zest and vanilla. Add the liquid mixture to the dry ingredients.

3 In a clean bowl, beat the egg whites until foamy. Slowly beat in the remaining 6 ounces (180 grams) granulated sugar. Continue beating until the egg whites are stiff but not dry.

4 Stir one-third of the egg whites into the batter to lighten it. Fold in the remaining egg whites.

5 Pour the batter into an ungreased 10-inch (25-centimeter) tube pan. Bake at 325°F (160°C) until a toothpick comes out clean, approximately 1 hour.

6 Immediately invert the pan over the neck of a bottle. Allow the cake to hang upside down until completely cool, then remove from the pan.

7 Stir the glaze ingredients together in a small bowl and drizzle over the top of the cooled cake.

Variations:

Lemon Chiffon Cake—Substitute 2 fluid ounces (60 milliliters/25%) fresh lemon juice and 2 fluid ounces (60 milliliters/2%) water for the orange juice. Substitute grated lemon zest for the orange zest. Top with Basic Sugar Glaze (page 1046).

Gluten-Free Orange Chiffon Cake—Substitute 6 ounces (180 grams/75%) blanched almond flour and 3.5 ounces (105 grams/43.7%) potato starch for the cake flour in the batter. Omit the water. Reduce the sugar to 7 ounces (210 grams/87.5%).

Approximate values per 1/10-cake serving: **Calories** 370, **Total fat** 15 g, **Saturated fat** 2.5 g, **Cholesterol** 130 mg, **Sodium** 280 mg, **Total carbohydrates** 54 g, **Protein** 6 g, **Vitamin C** 10%

PANNING, BAKING AND COOLING CAKES

Proper panning, baking and cooling cake batters ensures a quality final product. Pans must be prepared to prevent cakes from sticking during baking. When pans are filled with the correct amount of batter, they rise evenly without spilling over the edges. Baking temperatures depend upon the type of batter used as well as the altitude. Cakes may crack or shrink after baking, a problem avoided when they are cooled correctly. Methods for panning, baking and cooling cakes are described here.

PAN PREPARATIONS	TABLE 34.2
PAN PREPARATION	USED FOR
Ungreased	Angel food and chiffon cakes
Ungreased sides; paper on bottom	Genoise layers
Greased	High-fat cakes, poundcakes
Greased and papered	High-fat cakes, egg foam sheet cakes, dark chocolate cakes
Greased and coated with flour	High-fat cakes, anything in a Bundt or shaped pan
Greased, floured and lined with paper	Cakes containing chunks of chocolate or fruit or fruit and vegetable purées

Preparing Cake Pans

In order to prevent cakes from sticking, most baking pans are coated with fat or fat plus a light dusting of flour or nonstick baking parchment. Pans should be prepared before the batter is mixed so that they may be filled and the cakes baked as soon as the batter is finished. If the batter stands while the pans are prepared, air cells within the batter will deflate and volume may be lost.

Solid shortening is better than butter for coating pans because it does not contain any water; butter and margarine contain water and this may cause the cake to stick in places. Solid shortening is also less expensive, tasteless and odorless. Finally solid shortening does not burn as easily as butter, and it holds a dusting of flour better.

Pan release sprays are useful but must be applied carefully and completely. Although relatively expensive, sprays save time and are particularly effective when used with parchment pan liners.

In kitchens where a great deal of baking is done, quantities of pan coating are kept available for use as needed. **Pan coating** is a mixture of equal parts oil, shortening and flour that can be applied to cake pans with a pastry brush. It is used whenever pans need to be greased and floured. Pan coating will not leave a white residue on the cake's crust, as a dusting of flour often does. Apply pan coating sparingly, because a thick coating may leave a discernible taste. Pan coating is not appropriate for all cakes, however. Angel food and chiffon cakes are baked in ungreased, unlined pans because these fragile cakes need to cling to the sides of the pan as they rise. Table 34.2 lists various pan preparations.

Pan Coating

YIELD 3 lb. (1440 g)

Vegetable oil	1 lb.	480 g
All-purpose shortening	1 lb.	480 g
Bread flour	1 lb.	480 g

1 Place all the ingredients in the bowl of a mixer fitted with the paddle attachment. Blend on low speed for 5 minutes or until smooth.

2 Store in an opaque airtight container at room temperature for up to 1 month. Apply to baking pans in a thin, even layer using a pastry brush.

Filling Cake Pans

Pans should be filled no more than one-half to two-thirds full. This allows the batter to rise during baking without spilling over the edges. If batter is divided between pans, the pans should be filled to uniform depths. High-fat and egg-foam cake batters can be ladled into pans according to weight. High-ratio cake batter is so liquid that it can be measured by volume and poured. Filling the pans uniformly prevents both uneven layers

CAKE PAN SIZES TABLE 34.3

PAN SHAPE AND SIZE	VOLUME OF BATTER	WEIGHT FOR BUTTER/ HIGH-FAT	WEIGHT FOR EGG-FOAM	SERVINGS PER TWO-LAYER CAKE
Round, 2 in. (5 cm) Deep				
6 in. (15 cm)	1 pt.	8–10 oz.	5–6 oz.	6
8 in. (20 cm)	3 c.	12–16 oz.	8–10 oz.	12
9 in. (22 cm)	5½ c.	18–20 oz.	12–14 oz.	16
10 in. (25 cm)	1½ qt.	24–32 oz.	16–18 oz.	20
12 in. (30 cm)	1 qt. + 3½ c.	32–36 oz.	18–22 oz.	30
14 in. (35 cm)	2½ qt.	40–48 oz.	24–30 oz.	40
Square, 2 in. (5 cm) Deep				
8 in. (20 cm)	1 qt.	16–18 oz.	10–12 oz.	16
10 in. (25 cm)	1½ qt.	24–30 oz.	16–18 oz.	20
12 in. (30 cm)	2½ qt.	40–48 oz.	26–30 oz.	36
14 in. (35 cm)	3 qt. + 1½ c.	48–52 oz.	32–40 oz.	48
Rectangular, 2 in. (5 cm) Deep				
6 in. × 8 in. (15 cm × 20 cm)	2½ c.	10–12 oz.	6–8 oz.	12
9 in. × 13 in. (22 cm × 34 cm)	2 qt.	32–36 oz.	20–24 oz.	24
Half sheet, 12 in. × 18 in. (30 cm × 45 cm)	2 qt. + 3 c.	56–64 oz.	28–32 oz.	48
Full sheet, 18 in. × 24 in. (45 cm × 60 cm)	5 qt.	6–8 lb.	40–48 oz.	96
Cupcakes, 2 in. (5 cm) Deep	¼–⅓ c.	1 ½–2 oz.	¾–1 oz.	

*Quantities given are approximate and are based on filling the pans two-thirds full of batter. The weight of cake batter needed to properly fill a pan varies depending on the type of batter, additional flavor ingredients and the amount of air incorporated during mixing.

and over- or underfilled pans. If when baking three layers to be stacked for one presentation, the amount of batter is different in each pan, the baking times will vary and the final product will be uneven. Table 34.3 lists average quantities of batter needed to fill standard-sized baking pans.

Cake batter should always be spread evenly in the pan. Use an offset spatula. Do not work the batter too much, however, as this destroys air cells and prevents the cake from rising properly.

Baking Temperatures

Most butter cakes are baked at temperatures between 325°F and 375°F (160°C and 190°C). The temperature must be high enough to create steam within the batter and cause that steam and other gases in the batter to expand and rise quickly. If the temperature is too high, however, the cake may rise unevenly and the crust may burn before the interior is completely baked. The temperature must also be low enough so that the batter can set or firm completely and evenly without drying out. If the temperature is too low, however, the cake will not rise sufficiently and may dry out before baking completely. Delicate egg-foam cakes and spongecakes may be baked at slightly higher temperatures than butter cakes when panned in thin layers. Always preheat the oven before preparing the batter. If the finished batter must wait while the oven reaches the correct temperature, valuable leavening will be lost and the cake will not rise properly.

If no temperature is given in a formula or the dimensions of the baking pans being used are different from those specified, use common sense in setting the oven temperature. In general the larger the surface area, the higher the temperature. Tall cakes, such as Bundt or tube cakes, should be baked at a lower temperature than thin layer or sheet cakes. Tube or loaf cakes take longer to bake than thin sheet cakes. Butter cakes, because they contain more liquid, take longer to bake than genoise or spongecake.

Altitude Adjustments for Baking

As discussed in Chapter 10, Principles of Cooking, altitude affects the temperatures at which foods cook. The decreased atmospheric pressure at altitudes above 3000 feet affects the creation of steam and the expansion of hot air in dough and cake batters. These factors must be considered when making cakes. Because gases expand more easily at higher altitudes, cakes and breads may rise so much that their structure cannot support the increased volume and the bread or cake collapses.

Therefore the amount of leavening should be decreased at higher altitudes. Chemical leaveners should usually be reduced by one-third at 3500 feet and by two-thirds at altitudes over 5000 feet. Eggs should be underwhipped to avoid incorporating too much air, which would also create too much rise. In general, oven temperatures should also be increased by 25°F (14°C) at altitudes over 3500 feet to help set the product's structure rapidly.

Because the boiling point decreases at higher altitudes, more moisture evaporates from baked goods in the oven. This may cause dryness and an excessive proportion of sugar, which shows up as white spots on a cake's surface. Correct this by reducing every 8 ounces (240 grams) sugar by ½ ounce (15 grams) at 3000 feet and by 1½ ounces (45 grams) at 7000 feet.

Attempting to adjust typical (i.e., sea-level) formulas for high altitudes is somewhat risky, especially in a commercial operation. Furthermore different types of baked goods will need different adjustment techniques. Try to find and use formulas developed especially for the area where the baking is taking place, or contact the local offices of the region's state department of agriculture or the agricultural extension service for detailed assistance.

Determining Doneness of Cakes

In addition to following the baking time suggested in a formula, several simple tests can be used to determine doneness. Whichever tests are used, avoid opening the oven door to check the cake's progress. Cold air or a drop in oven temperature can cause the cake to fall. Use a timer to note the minimum suggested baking time. Then, and only then, should the following tests be used to evaluate the cake's doneness:

Appearance: The cake's surface should be a light to golden brown. Unless noted otherwise in the formula, the edges should just begin to pull away from the pan. The cake should not jiggle or move beneath its surface.

Touch: When you touch the cake lightly with your finger, it should spring back quickly without feeling soggy or leaving an indentation.

Cake tester: If appearance and touch indicate that the cake is done, test the interior by inserting a toothpick, bamboo skewer or metal cake tester into the cake's center. With most cakes, the tester should come out clean. If wet crumbs cling to the tester, the cake probably needs to bake a bit longer.

If a formula provides particular doneness guidelines, they should be followed. For example, some flourless cakes are fully baked even though a cake tester does not come out clean.

Cooling Cakes

Generally a cake is allowed to cool in its pan set on a cooling rack for 10–15 minutes after taking it out of the oven. This helps prevent the cake from cracking or breaking when it is removed from its pan.

To remove the partially cooled cake from its pan, run a thin knife or spatula blade between the pan and the cake to loosen it. Place a wire rack, piece of clean cardboard or sheet pan over the cake and invert. Then remove the pan. The cake can be left upside down to cool completely or inverted again to cool top side up. Wire racks are preferred for cooling cakes because they allow air to circulate, speeding the cooling process and preventing steam from making the cake soggy.

Angel food and chiffon cakes should be turned upside down in their pans immediately after they are removed from the oven. They are left to cool completely in their pans to prevent the cake from collapsing or shrinking. The top of the pan should not touch the countertop, so that air can circulate under the inverted pan.

Brownies

Where do you draw the line between cakes and brownies? The decision must be a matter of texture and personal preference, for the preparation methods are nearly identical. Brownies are generally chewy and fudgy, sweeter and denser than even the richest of butter cakes. Brownies are a relatively inexpensive and an easy way for a food service operation to offer its customers a fresh-baked dessert. Although not as sophisticated as an elaborate gâteau, a well-made brownie can always be served with pride (and a scoop of ice cream).

Brownies are prepared using the same procedures used for high-fat cakes. Eggs and air incorporated during the mixing process are usually the only leaveners in a traditional brownie formula. Good brownies are achieved with a proper balance of ingredients: A high ratio of butter to flour and not too many eggs produces a dense, fudgy brownie. The fat coats the flour, preventing the protein from developing into gluten. Less butter produces a more cakelike brownie. Increasing the eggs produces a brownie with a crumb structure that more closely resembles a true cake. Likewise the higher the ratio of sugar to flour, the gooier the finished brownie will be. In some brownie formulas the fat is creamed to incorporate air, as with butter cakes. In others the fat is first melted and combined with other liquid ingredients. Brownies are rarely made with whipped egg whites, however, as this makes their texture too light and cakelike.

Each customer and cook has his or her own idea of the quintessential brownie. Some brownies are cloyingly sweet, with a creamy texture and an abundance of chocolate; others are bitter and crisp. Some are frosted; others need only a dusting of powdered sugar. Baked brownies can be frozen for 2–3 months if well wrapped.

TROUBLESHOOTING CHART FOR CAKES   TABLE 34.4

PROBLEM	CAUSE	SOLUTION
Butter curdles during mixing	Ingredients too warm or too cold Incorrect fat is used Fat inadequately creamed before liquid was added	Eggs must be at room temperature and added slowly Use correct ingredients Add a portion of the flour, then continue adding the liquid
Cake lacks volume	Flour too strong Old chemical leavener Egg foam underwhipped Oven too hot	Use a weaker flour Replace with fresh leavener Use correct mixing method; do not deflate eggs during folding Adjust oven temperature
Crust burst or cracked	Too much flour or too little liquid Oven too hot	Adjust formula; scale accurately Adjust oven temperature
Cake shrinks after baking	Weak internal structure Too much sugar or fat for the batter to support Cake not fully cooked	Adjust formula Adjust formula Test for doneness before removing from oven
Texture is dense or heavy	Too little leavening Too much fat or liquid Improper leavening Oven too cool	Adjust formula Adjust formula Cream fat or whip eggs properly Adjust oven temperature
Texture is coarse with an open grain	Overmixing Oven too cool	Alter mixing method Adjust oven temperature
Poor flavor	Poor ingredients Unclean pans	Check flavor and aroma of all ingredients Do not grease pans with rancid fats
Uneven shape	Butter not incorporated evenly Batter spread unevenly Oven rack not level Uneven oven temperature	Incorporate fats completely Spread batter evenly Adjust oven racks Rotate pans during baking; professionally recalibrate oven

All cakes should be left to cool away from drafts or air currents that may cause them to collapse. Cakes should not be refrigerated to speed the cooling process, as rapid cooling can cause cracking. Prolonged refrigeration also causes cakes to dry out.

FROSTINGS

Frosting, also known as **icing**, is a sweet decorative coating used as a filling between the layers or as a coating over the top and sides of a cake. It is used to add flavor and to improve a cake's appearance. Frosting can also extend a cake's shelf life by forming a protective coating.

There are seven general types of frosting: buttercream, foam, fudge, fondant, glaze, royal icing and ganache. See Table 34.5. Each type can be produced with a number of formulas and in a range of flavorings.

FROSTINGS   TABLE 34.5

FROSTING	PREPARATION	TEXTURE/FLAVOR
Simple buttercream	Mixture of sugar and fat (usually butter); can contain egg yolks or egg whites	Rich but light; smooth; fluffy
Foam	Meringue made with hot sugar syrup	Light, fluffy; very sweet
Fudge	Cooked mixture of sugar, butter and water or milk; applied warm	Heavy; rich and candylike
Fondant	Cooked mixture of sugar and water; applied warm	Thick, opaque; sweet
Glaze	Powdered sugar with liquid	Thin; sweet
Royal icing	Uncooked mixture of powdered sugar and egg whites	Hard and brittle when dry; chalky
Ganache	Blend of melted chocolate and cream; may be poured or whipped	Rich, smooth; intense chocolate flavor

Because frosting is integral to the flavor and appearance of many cakes, it should be made carefully using high-quality ingredients and natural flavors and colors. A good frosting is smooth; it is never grainy or lumpy. It should complement the flavor and texture of the cake without overpowering it.

Buttercream

A **buttercream** is a light, smooth, fluffy mixture of sugar and fat (butter, margarine or shortening). It may also contain egg yolks for richness or whipped egg whites for lightness. Pasteurized eggs must always be used in buttercreams to ensure food safety. A good buttercream will be sweet, but not cloying; buttery, but not greasy.

Buttercreams are popular and suitable for most types of cakes and may be flavored or colored as desired. They may be stored, covered, in the refrigerator for several days but must be softened before use.

The three most popular styles of buttercream, which are discussed here, are **simple**, **Italian** and **French**.

Simple Buttercream

Simple buttercream, sometimes known as **American-style buttercream**, is made by creaming butter and powdered sugar together until the mixture is light and smooth. Cream, pasteurized eggs and flavorings may be added as desired. Simple buttercream requires no cooking and is quick and easy to prepare.

If cost is a consideration, hydrogenated all-purpose shortening can be substituted for a portion of the butter, but the flavor and mouth feel will be different. Buttercream made with shortening tends to feel greasier and heavier because shortening does not melt on the tongue like butter. It will be more stable than pure butter buttercream, however, and is necessary when a pure white frosting is desired.

Procedure for Preparing Simple Buttercreams

1 Cream softened butter or shortening until the mixture is light and fluffy.
2 Beat in pasteurized egg if desired.
3 Beat in sifted powdered sugar, scraping down the sides of the bowl as needed.
4 Beat in the flavoring ingredients.

Simple Buttercream

YIELD   Approximately 3 lb. (1.5 kg)

Lightly salted butter, softened	1 lb.	480 g
Pasteurized egg, optional	2 oz.	60 g
Powdered sugar, sifted	2 lb.	960 g
Vanilla extract	0.3 fl. oz. (2 tsp.)	10 ml

MISE EN PLACE
- Soften butter.
- Sift powdered sugar.

1 Using a mixer fitted with the paddle attachment, cream the butter until light and fluffy.
2 Beat in the egg, if using. Gradually add the sugar, frequently scraping down the bowl.
3 Add the vanilla and continue beating until the frosting is smooth and light.

Variations:

Light Chocolate Buttercream—Dissolve 1 ounce (30 grams) sifted cocoa powder in 2 fluid ounces (60 milliliters) cool water. Add to the buttercream along with the vanilla.

Lemon Buttercream—Decrease the vanilla extract to 0.15 fluid ounce (1 teaspoon/5 milliliters). Add 0.15 fluid ounce (1 teaspoon/5 milliliters) lemon extract and the finely grated zest of one lemon.

Approximate values per 1-oz. (30-g) serving: **Calories** 170, **Total fat** 6 g, **Saturated fat** 4 g, **Cholesterol** 25 mg, **Sodium** 70 mg, **Total carbohydrates** 28 g, **Protein** 0 g, **Vitamin A** 10%

Italian Buttercream

Italian buttercream, also known as **meringue buttercream**, is based on an Italian meringue, which is whipped egg whites cooked with hot sugar syrup. (See Chapter 33, Pies, Pastries and Cookies.) Softened butter is then whipped into the cooled meringue, and the mixture is flavored as desired. This type of buttercream is extremely soft and light. It can be used on most types of cakes and is particularly popular for multilayered genoise and spongecakes.

Procedure for Preparing Italian Buttercreams

1 Whip the egg whites until soft peaks form.

2 Beat granulated sugar into the egg whites and whip until firm and glossy.

3 Meanwhile, combine additional sugar with water and cook to the soft ball stage (240°F/116°C), brushing down the sides of the pan with clean water to prevent the sugar from crystallizing.

4 With the mixer on medium speed, pour the sugar syrup into the whipped egg whites. Pour slowly and carefully to avoid splatters.

5 Continue whipping the egg-white-and-sugar mixture until completely cool.

6 Whip softened, but not melted, butter into the cooled egg-white-and-sugar mixture.

7 Add flavoring ingredients as desired.

MISE EN PLACE

- Soften butter.

Italian Buttercream

YIELD Approximately 5 lb. 5 oz. (2.5 kg)

Egg whites, pasteurized	14 oz. (14 whites)	420 g
Granulated sugar	1 lb. 11 oz.	810 g
Water	as needed	as needed
Lightly salted butter, softened but not melted	2 lb. 12 oz.	1320 g

1 All ingredients should be at room temperature before beginning.

2 Place the egg whites in a mixer bowl. Have 9 ounces (270 grams) sugar nearby.

3 Place 1 pound 2 ounces (540 grams) sugar in a heavy saucepan with enough water to moisten. Bring to a boil over high heat, brushing down the sides of the pan with clean water to prevent the sugar from crystallizing.

4 As the sugar syrup's temperature approaches soft ball stage (240°F/116°C), begin whipping the egg whites. Watch the sugar closely so that the temperature does not exceed 240°F (116°C).

5 When soft peaks form in the egg whites, gradually add 9 ounces (270 grams) sugar to them. Reduce the mixer speed to medium and continue whipping the egg whites to stiff peaks.

6 When the sugar syrup reaches soft ball stage, immediately pour it into the whites while the mixer is running. Pour the syrup in a steady stream between the side of the bowl and the beater. If the syrup hits the beater, it will splatter and cause lumps. Continue beating at medium speed until the egg whites are completely cool. At this point, the product is known as Italian meringue.

7 Gradually add the softened butter to the Italian meringue. When all the butter is incorporated, add flavoring ingredients as desired.

① Adding the sugar syrup to the whipped egg whites.

② Adding the softened butter to the cooled Italian meringue.

Variations:

Chocolate Italian Buttercream—Add 0.5 fluid ounces (1 tablespoon/15 milliliters) vanilla extract to the buttercream, then stir in 10 ounces (300 grams) melted and cooled bittersweet chocolate.

Coffee Italian Buttercream—Add 2 fluid ounces (60 milliliters) coffee extract or strong coffee to the buttercream.

Approximate values per 1-oz. (30-g) serving: **Calories** 175, **Total fat** 13 g, **Saturated fat** 8 g, **Cholesterol** 34 mg, **Sodium** 140 mg, **Total carbohydrates** 16 g, **Protein** 1 g, **Vitamin A** 10%

French Buttercream

French buttercream, also known as **mousseline buttercream**, is similar to Italian buttercream except that the hot sugar syrup is whipped into beaten egg yolks (not egg whites). Softened butter and flavorings are added when the sweetened egg yolks are fluffy and cool. An Italian meringue such as the one created in the preceding formula is sometimes folded in for additional body and lightness. French buttercream is perhaps the most difficult type of buttercream to master, but it has the richest flavor and smoothest texture. Like a meringue buttercream, mousseline buttercream may be used on almost any type of cake.

Procedure for Preparing French Buttercreams

1 Prepare a sugar syrup and cook to soft ball stage (240°F/116°C), brushing down the sides of the pan with clean water to prevent the sugar from crystallizing.

2 Beat egg yolks to a thin ribbon.

3 Slowly beat the sugar syrup into the egg yolks.

4 Continue beating until the yolks are pale, stiff and completely cool.

5 Gradually add softened butter to the cooled yolks.

6 Fold in Italian meringue.

7 Stir in flavoring ingredients.

French Mousseline Buttercream

MISE EN PLACE

● Soften butter.

YIELD 6 lb. (3 kg)

Granulated sugar	1 lb. 10 oz.	780 g
Water	8 fl. oz.	240 ml
Egg yolks	9.6 oz. (16 yolks)	288 g
Lightly salted butter, softened but not melted	3 lb.	1440 g
Italian Meringue (page 999)	1 lb.	480 g
Vanilla, coffee, lemon or other flavoring extracts	2 fl. oz.	60 ml

1 Combine the sugar and water in a small saucepan and bring to a boil. Continue boiling until the syrup reaches 240°F (116°C), brushing down the sides of the pan with clean water to prevent the sugar from crystallizing.

2 Meanwhile beat the egg yolks in the bowl of a mixer fitted with the whisk attachment on low speed. When the sugar syrup reaches 240°F (116°C), pour it slowly into the egg yolks, gradually increasing the speed at which they are whipped. Continue beating at medium-high speed until the mixture is very pale, stiff and cool, approximately 10 minutes.

3 Gradually add the softened butter to the egg mixture, frequently scraping down the bowl.

4 Fold in the Italian Meringue with a spatula. Fold in flavoring extracts just until well distributed throughout the buttercream.

Variation:

Chocolate Mousseline Buttercream—Add 2 fluid ounces (60 milliliters) vanilla extract to the buttercream, then stir in 10 ounces (300 grams) melted and cooled bittersweet chocolate.

Approximate values per 1-oz. (30-g) serving: **Calories** 230, **Total fat** 20 g, **Saturated fat** 12 g, **Cholesterol** 105 mg, **Sodium** 190 mg, **Total carbohydrates** 12 g, **Protein** 1 g, **Vitamin A** 20%

Flavor Combinations for Cakes

Citrus, coffee, maple, peanut butter and vanilla are popular flavorings for buttercream icings but the possible cake and filling combinations are limitless. Chocolate cakes can be filled with almond, citrus, coffee, hazelnut and red fruit-flavored icings. Dense chocolate ganache paired with apricot, cherry, raspberry or other jam works well in plain or chocolate butter cakes. Tropical fruit flavors, such as kiwi, key lime and pineapple, complement butter and sponge cakes as do rich custards and flavored creams.

Foam Frosting

Foam or **boiled frosting** is simply an Italian meringue (made with hot sugar syrup). Foam frosting is light and fluffy but very sweet. It may be flavored with extract, liqueur or melted chocolate. It is frequently used to ice layer cakes and complements a cake with lemon, coconut or chocolate flavor.

Foam frosting is rather unstable. It should be used immediately and served the day it is prepared. Refrigeration often makes the foam weep beads of sugar. Freezing causes it to separate or melt.

An easy foam frosting can be made by following the formula for Italian Meringue (page 999). As soon as the meringue has cooled to room temperature, it can be flavored as desired with an extract or emulsion.

Fudge Frosting

A **fudge frosting** is a warmed mixture of sugar, butter and water or milk. It is heavy, rich and candylike. It is also stable and holds up well. A fudge frosting should be applied warm and allowed to dry on the cake or pastry. When dry, it will have a thin crust and a moist interior. A fudge frosting can be vanilla- or chocolate-based and is suitable for cupcakes, layer cakes and sheet cakes.

Procedure for Preparing Fudge Frostings

1 Place sifted powdered sugar in the bowl of a mixer fitted with the paddle attachment.
2 Heat the butter or shortening, corn syrup and water.
3 Blend the hot liquids into the sugar. Add extracts or flavorings.
4 Use fudge frosting while still warm.

Basic Fudge Frosting

YIELD 2 lb. 11 oz. (1.3 kg)

Powdered sugar, sifted	2 lb.	960 g
Unsalted butter	3 oz.	90 g
Shortening	2 oz.	60 g
Corn syrup	2 oz.	60 g
Water	4 fl. oz.	120 ml
Salt	0.03 oz. (⅛ tsp.)	1 g
Vanilla extract	0.15 fl. oz. (1 tsp.)	5 ml

1 Place the powdered sugar in the bowl of a mixer fitted with the whisk attachment.
2 Bring the butter, shortening, corn syrup, water and salt to a boil in a saucepan over medium high heat. Remove the pan from heat.
3 With the machine running, pour the hot mixture over the powdered sugar. Whip until the mixture is smooth and fluffy. Stir in the vanilla.
4 The icing can be used immediately.

Variation:

Cocoa Fudge Frosting—Sift 3 ounces (90 grams) cocoa powder with the powdered sugar. Add 2 ounces (60 grams) melted unsalted butter with the shortening.

Approximate values per 1-oz. (30-g) serving: **Calories** 140, **Total fat** 2.5 g, **Saturated fat** 0.5 g, **Cholesterol** 0 mg, **Sodium** 15 mg, **Total carbohydrates** 30 g, **Protein** 0 g, **Claims**—low fat; low saturated fat; very low sodium

MISE EN PLACE

● Sift powdered sugar.

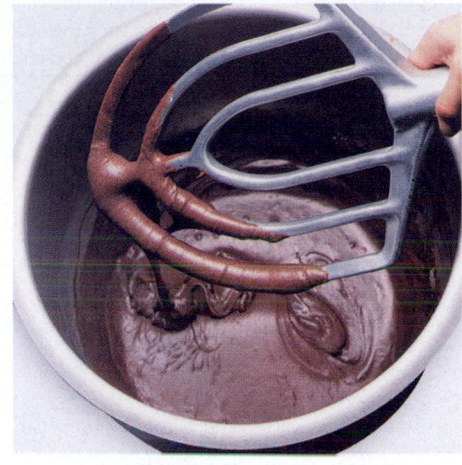

Cocoa fudge frosting

Fondant

Fondant is a thick, opaque sugar paste commonly used for glazing Napoleons, petits fours and other pastries as well as some cakes. It is a cooked mixture of sugar and water, with **glucose** or corn syrup added to encourage the correct type of sugar crystallization. Poured over a surface, fondant quickly dries to a shiny, nonsticky coating. It is naturally pure white and can be tinted with food coloring. Fondant can also be flavored with melted chocolate.

Fondant is rather tricky to make, so it is usually purchased prepared either as a ready-to-use paste or a powder to which water is added. To use **prepared fondant**, thin it with water or simple syrup and carefully warm to 100°F (38°C). Watch the temperature; when overheated, the fondant will lose its opacity and will dry with an uneven appearance. Commercially prepared fondant will keep for several months at room temperature in an airtight container. The surface of the fondant should be coated with simple syrup, however, to prevent a crust from forming.

Rolled fondant is a very stiff doughlike type of fondant that is used for covering cakes and for making flowers and other decorations. As the name implies, it is rolled out to the desired thickness, then draped over a cake or torte to create a very smooth, flat coating. Rolled fondant is available in a ready-to-use form. It can be flavored or colored if desired. Be sure to keep the rolled fondant tightly wrapped in plastic and stored in an airtight container to prevent it from drying out and cracking.

glucose a thick, sweet syrup made from cornstarch, composed primarily of dextrose; light corn syrup can usually be substituted for it in baked goods or candy making

Celebration cake covered with rolled fondant

TROUBLESHOOTING CHART FOR FROSTINGS

TABLE 34.6

PROBLEM	CAUSE	SOLUTION
Frosting breaks or curdles	Fat added too slowly or eggs too hot when fat was added Butter too cold when added	Add shortening or sifted powdered sugar Soften butter before adding
Frosting is lumpy	Powdered sugar not sifted Ingredients not blended Sugar syrup lumps in frosting	Sift dry ingredients Use softened fats Add sugar syrups carefully
Frosting is too stiff	Not enough liquid Too cold	Adjust formula; add small amount of water or milk to thin the frosting Bring frosting to room temperature; heat gently over simmering water
Frosting will not adhere to cake	Cake too hot Frosting too thin Frosting too stiff Frosting too cold	Cool cake completely Adjust frosting formula Adjust frosting formula Soften frosting at room temperature before using

Glaze

A **glaze** is a thin coating meant to be poured or drizzled onto a cake or pastry. A glaze is usually too thin to apply with a knife or spatula. It is used to add moisture and flavor to cakes (e.g., a chiffon or angel food cake) on which a heavy frosting would be undesirable. Glazes are often tinted with food coloring.

Flat frosting or water frosting is a specific type of glaze used on Danish pastries and coffeecakes. It is pure white and dries to a firm gloss. A glaze made from fondant is also used for this purpose. The glucose in fondant prevents it from crystallizing.

Procedure for Preparing Sugar Glazes

1 Blend sifted powdered sugar with a small amount of liquid and flavorings.
2 Use immediately.

Basic Sugar Glaze

MISE EN PLACE

- Sift powdered sugar.
- Melt butter.

YIELD Approximately 12 oz. (360 g)

Powdered sugar, sifted	9.5 oz.	285 g
Light cream or milk	2 fl. oz.	60 ml
Unsalted butter, melted	1 oz.	30 g
Vanilla, lemon or almond extract	0.3 fl. oz. (2 tsp.)	10 ml

1 Stir the ingredients together in a small bowl until smooth.

2 Adjust the consistency by adding more cream or milk to thin the glaze if necessary.

3 Adjust the flavor as necessary.

4 Use immediately, before the glaze begins to dry.

Variation:

Flavored Sugar Glaze—Stir 0.04 fluid ounces (¼ teaspoon/1 milliliter) lemon or orange oil into the glaze. Fruit juice and other flavorings may be substituted for the vanilla extract.

Approximate values per 1-oz. (30-g) serving: **Calories** 110, **Total fat** 2 g, **Saturated fat** 1.5 g, **Cholesterol** 5 mg, **Sodium** 0 mg, **Total carbohydrates** 23 g, **Protein** 0 g, **Claims**—low fat; low cholesterol; no sodium

Royal Icing

Royal icing, also known as **decorator's icing**, is similar to flat frosting except it is much stiffer and becomes hard and brittle when dry. It is an uncooked mixture of powdered sugar and pasteurized egg whites and can be dyed with food coloring pastes.

Royal icing is used for making decorations, particularly intricate flowers or lace patterns. Prepare royal icing in small quantities, and always keep any unused portion well covered with a damp towel and plastic wrap to prevent hardening.

Procedure for Preparing Royal Icing

1 Combine pasteurized egg white and lemon juice, if using.
2 Beat in sifted powdered sugar until the correct consistency is reached.
3 Beat until very smooth and firm enough to hold a stiff peak.
4 Color as desired with paste food colorings.
5 Store covered with a damp cloth and plastic wrap.

Royal Icing

YIELD Approximately 7 oz. (210 g)

Powdered sugar	6 oz.	180 g
Egg white, pasteurized, room temperature	1 oz. (1 white)	30 g
Lemon juice	0.04 fl. oz. (¼ tsp.)	1 ml

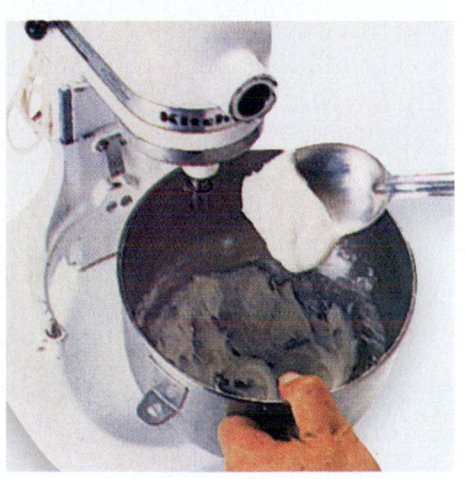

1 Sift the sugar and set aside.
2 Place the egg white and lemon juice in a stainless steel bowl.
3 Add 4 ounces (120 grams) sugar and beat with an electric mixer or metal spoon until blended. The mixture should fall from a spoon in heavy globs. If it pours, it is too thin and will need the remaining 2 ounces (60 grams) sugar.
4 Once the consistency is correct, continue beating for 3–4 minutes. The icing should be white, smooth and thick enough to hold a stiff peak. Food coloring paste can be added at this time if desired.
5 Cover the icing with a damp towel and plastic wrap to prevent it from hardening. Royal icing will keep refrigerated for 1–2 days.

Approximate values per 1-oz. (30-g) serving: **Calories** 120, **Total fat** 0 g, **Saturated fat** 0 g, **Cholesterol** 0 mg, **Sodium** 10 mg, **Total carbohydrates** 28 g, **Protein** 1 g, **Claims**—fat free; no saturated fat; no cholesterol; very low sodium

Ganache

Ganache is a sublime blending of pure chocolate and cream. It can also include butter, liqueur or other flavorings. Any bittersweet, semisweet or dark chocolate may be used to make ganache; the choice depends on personal preference and cost considerations.

Depending on its consistency, ganache may be used as a candy or as a filling, frosting or glaze-type coating on cakes or pastries. The ratio of chocolate to cream determines how thick the cooled ganache will be. Equal parts by weight of chocolate and cream generally are best for frostings and fillings. Increasing the percentage of chocolate produces a thicker ganache. Warm ganache can be poured over a cake or pastry and allowed to harden as a thin glaze, or it can be cooled and whipped to create a rich, smooth frosting. If it becomes too firm, ganache can be remelted over a bain marie.

Procedure for Preparing Ganache

1 Melt finely chopped chocolate with cream in a double boiler. Alternatively bring cream just to a boil; then pour it over finely chopped chocolate and allow the cream's heat to gently melt the chocolate. Do not attempt to melt chocolate and then add cool cream. This will cause the chocolate to resolidify and lump.

2 Stir the ganache with a rubber spatula to emulsify the cream and chocolate. (Whisking the ganache using a whip may be quicker, but the ganache will be grainy and less creamy.)

3 Whichever method is used, cool the cream and chocolate mixture over an ice bath.

Chocolate Ganache

YIELD 2 lb. (960 g)

Bittersweet chocolate	1 lb.	480 g
Heavy cream	1 pt.	480 ml
Almond or coffee liqueur	1 fl. oz.	30 ml

1 Chop the chocolate into small pieces and place in a large metal bowl.

2 Bring the cream just to a boil, then immediately pour it over the chocolate, stirring with a rubber spatula to blend. Stir gently until all the chocolate has melted.

3 Stir in the liqueur.

4 Allow to cool, stirring frequently with a rubber spatula until the desired consistency is achieved.

Approximate values per 1-oz. (30-g) serving: **Calories** 130, **Total fat** 10 g, **Saturated fat** 6 g, **Cholesterol** 20 mg, **Sodium** 5 mg, **Total carbohydrates** 8 g, **Protein** 1 g, **Vitamin A** 6%

❶ Pouring the hot cream over the chopped chocolate.

❷ Cool, firm ganache.

Ganache is also the foundation of one of the world's most sophisticated candies, the chocolate truffle. Truffles take their name from the rough, black, highly prized fungus they resemble, but there the similarity ends. Chocolate truffles should have a rich, creamy ganache center with a well-balanced, refined flavor.

To prepare chocolate truffles, a firm ganache is flavored as desired, then piped or allowed to harden. Once firm, the ganache is rolled in cocoa powder, confectioner's sugar or melted chocolate. The classic French truffle is a small, irregularly shaped ball of bittersweet chocolate dusted with cocoa powder. Americans, however, seem to prefer larger candies, coated with melted chocolate and decorated with nuts or additional chocolate, toasted sliced almonds, chocolate shavings, or candied citrus peel. The following recipe can be prepared in either style.

Dark Chocolate Truffles

YIELD 4 lb. 4 oz. (2 kg), 150 Medium-Sized
Truffles, ½ oz. (15 g) each

Dark chocolate	2 lb.	1 kg
Unsalted butter	1 lb.	480 g
Heavy cream	1 pt.	480 ml
Brandy, bourbon or liqueur	4 fl. oz.	120 ml

1 Chop the chocolate and butter into small pieces and place in a large metal bowl.

2 Bring the cream to a boil. Immediately pour the hot cream over the chocolate and butter. Stir until the chocolate and butter are completely melted.

3 Stir in the brandy. Pour the ganache into a flat, shallow, ungreased pan and chill until firm.

4 Shape the ganache into rough balls using a melon ball cutter. Immediately drop each ball into a pan of sifted cocoa powder or confectioner's sugar, rolling it around to coat completely.

5 Truffles can be stored in the refrigerator for 7–10 days. Allow them to soften slightly at room temperature before serving.

Approximate values per ½-oz. (15-g) truffle: **Calories** 70, **Total fat** 6 g, **Saturated fat** 3.5 g, **Cholesterol** 10 mg, **Sodium** 0 mg, **Total carbohydrates** 4 g, **Protein** 0 g

① Shaping chocolate truffles with a melon ball scoop and coating with cocoa powder.

② Alternatively, using a dipping spoon, dip chocolate truffles into tempered chocolate.

③ After dipping in tempered chocolate, truffles may also be coated with chopped toasted nuts.

ASSEMBLING AND DECORATING CAKES

Much of the initial appeal of cakes lie in their appearance. This is true whether the finished cake is a simple sheet cake topped with swirls of buttercream or an elaborate wedding cake with intricate garlands and bouquets of marzipan roses. Any cake assembled and decorated with care and attention to detail is preferable to a carelessly assembled or garishly overdecorated one.

Thousands of decorating styles or designs are possible, of course. This section describes a few simple options that beginning pastry cooks can prepare using a minimum of specialized tools. In planning a cake's design, consider the flavor, texture and color of the components used as well as the number of guests or portions that must be served. Consider who will be cutting and eating the cake and how long the dessert must stand before service.

Assembling Cakes

Before a cake can be decorated, it must be assembled and coated with frosting. First the cake is placed on a **cake cardboard** of the appropriate size. Most cakes can be assembled in a variety of shapes and sizes; sheet cakes, round layer cakes and rectangular layer cakes are the most common. When assembling any cake, the goal is to fill and stack the cake layers evenly and to apply an even coating of frosting that is smooth and free of crumbs. (A thin underlayer of frosting called a **crumb coat** may be spread on an assembled cake to seal loose surface crumbs before a final decorative layer of frosting is applied.)

Most of the photographs used in this section show the assembly and decoration of a celebration cake shown in the photograph to the left.

❶ Split the cake horizontally into thin layers if desired. Use cake cardboards to support each layer as it is removed. Brush away any loose crumbs with a dry pastry brush or your hand.

❷ Position the bottom layer on a cake board. Place the layer on a revolving cake stand, if available. Pipe a border of buttercream around the cake, then top the layer with a mound of filling. Use a cake spatula to spread it evenly.

❸ Position the next cake layer over the filling and continue layering and filling the cake as desired.

❹ Place a mound of frosting in the center of the cake top. Push it to the edge of the cake with a cake spatula. Do not drag the frosting back and forth or lift the spatula off the frosting, as these actions tend to pick up crumbs.

❺ Smooth a thin layer of frosting (the crumb coat) over the top of the cake. Cover the sides with excess frosting from the top. Chill the cake.

❻ Place another mound of frosting in the center of the cake top. Frost the cake with a second layer of icing. Hold the spatula upright against the side of the cake and, pressing gently, turn the cake stand slowly. This smooths and evens the sides. When the sides and top are smooth, the cake is ready to be decorated as desired.

Simple Decorating Techniques

An extremely simple yet effective way to decorate an iced cake is with a garnish of chopped nuts, fruit, toasted coconut, shaved chocolate or other foods arranged in patterns or sprinkled over the cake. Be sure to use a garnish that complements the cake and frosting flavors or reflects one of the cake's ingredients. For example, finely chopped pecans are an appropriate garnish for a carrot cake that contains pecans;

cake cardboard precut rounds, squares or rectangles of clean, thin, disposable cardboard used to support the layers of a cake for service or display; especially useful for retail purchases; generally coated with a water and fat resistant substance, which is often colored gold or white

shaved chocolate is not. A chocolate torte might be decorated with fresh raspberries even when it does not contain raspberries because chocolate and berries are compatible flavors.

Side masking is the technique of coating only the sides of a cake with garnish. Be sure to apply the garnish while the frosting is still moist enough for it to adhere. The top may be left plain or decorated with frosting designs or a message.

Stencils can be used to apply patterns of finely chopped garnishes, powdered sugar or cocoa powder to the top of a cake. A design can be cut from cardboard, or thin plastic stencil forms can be purchased. Even simple strips of parchment paper can be used to create an attractive pattern. If using a stencil on an iced cake, allow the frosting to set somewhat before placing the stencil on top of it. After the garnishes have been sprinkled over the stencil, carefully lift the stencil to avoid spilling the excess garnish and messing up the pattern.

A **cake** or **baker's comb** or a serrated knife can be used to create patterns on a cake iced with buttercream, fudge or ganache. Hold the comb against the side of an iced cake and rotate the cake turntable slowly and steadily to create horizontal lines in the frosting.

Side masking: Coating the sides of a carrot cake with chopped pistachios.

Stencils: Creating a design with confectioner's sugar and strips of parchment paper.

Cake comb: Creating a pattern on a frosted cake.

Piping Techniques

More elaborate and difficult decorations can be produced with the aid of a piping bag and an assortment of pastry tips. With these tools, buttercream or royal icing can be used to create borders, flowers and messages. Before applying any decorations, plan a design or pattern that is appropriate for the size and shape of the item being decorated.

When used properly, colored frostings can bring cake decorations to life. Buttercream, royal icing and fondant are easily tinted using paste food coloring. Liquid food colorings are not recommended as they may thin the frosting too much. Always add coloring gradually with a toothpick. Frosting colors tend to darken as they sit. It is easy to add more later to darken the color if necessary, but it is difficult to lighten the color if too much is added.

Piping bags made from plastic, nylon or plastic-coated canvas are available in a range of sizes. A disposable **piping cone** can also be made from parchment paper.

Most decorations and designs are made by using a piping bag fitted with a pastry tip. **Pastry tips** are available with dozens of different openings and are referred to by standardized numbers. Some commonly used tips are shown in the nearby photo. A variety of borders and designs can be produced by changing the pressure, the angle of the bag and the distance between the tip and the cake surface. The size of the piping bag and tip used depends on the task at hand. The larger the bag the less often it needs to be refilled. Smaller bags are easier to handle, however, especially when making small designs or piping handwriting.

Pastry tip patterns

Procedure for Making a Parchment-Paper Cone

① Begin with an equilateral triangle of uncreased parchment paper. Shape it into a cone as shown.

② Fold the top edges together to hold the shape.

③ Cut the tip of the filled parchment cone.

A plain piping tip may be used to apply a simple swirl of frosting to decorate a cupcake.

Procedure for Filling a Piping Bag

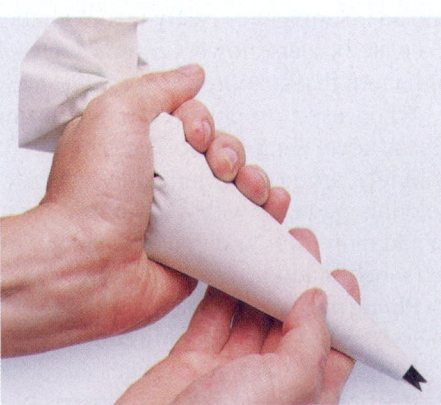

① Select the proper size piping bag for your task. Insert the desired tip.

② Fold down the top of the bag, then fill approximately half full with frosting. Do not overfill the bag.

③ Be sure to close the open end tightly before you start piping. Hold the bag firmly in your palm and squeeze from the top. Do not squeeze from the bottom or you may force the contents out the wrong end. Use the fingers of your other hand to guide the bag as you work.

Instead of leaving the sides of a frosted cake smooth or coating them with chopped nuts or crumbs, many designs can be piped on in artful patterns. Some simple but elegant designs are the vine border and basket weave shown here. Normally a border pattern is piped around the base of the cake and along the top edge. Borders should be piped on after nuts or any other garnishes are applied.

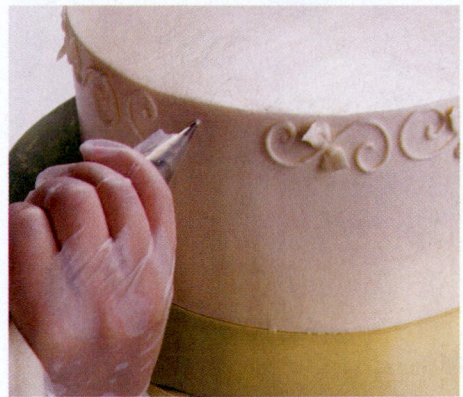

Applying a vine and leaf border onto a celebration cake.

Applying a bead border onto a celebration cake.

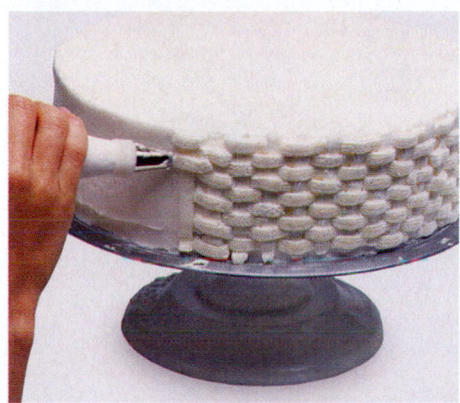

Applying a basket weave pattern to the sides of a celebration cake.

Applying a shell border to a celebration cake.

Each slice or serving of cake can be marked with its own decoration. For example, a rosette of frosting or a whole nut or piece of fruit could be used to indicate portions. This makes it easier to cut the cake evenly.

Delicate flowers such as roses can be piped onto parchment paper, allowed to harden, then placed on the cake in attractive arrangements. Royal icing is particularly useful for making decorations in advance because it dries very hard and lasts indefinitely.

The key to success with a piping bag is practice, practice, practice. Pipe plain all-purpose shortening on to parchment paper to practice and experiment with piping techniques. Once you are comfortable using a piping bag, try applying these newfound skills directly to cakes and pastries.

Placing raspberries onto a cake to mark the portions.

Procedure for Piping Buttercream Roses

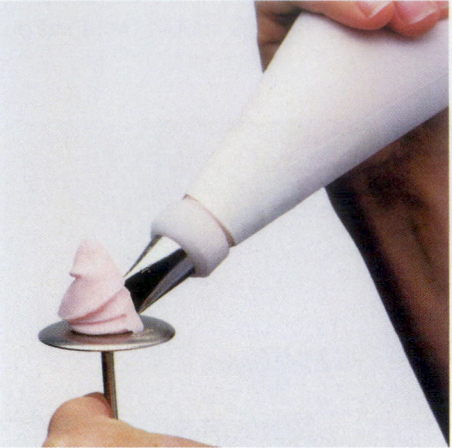

① Using a #104 tip, pipe a mound of frosting onto a rose nail.

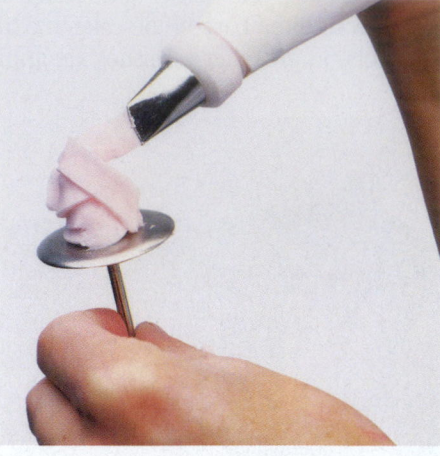

② Pipe a curve of frosting around the mound to create the center of the rose.

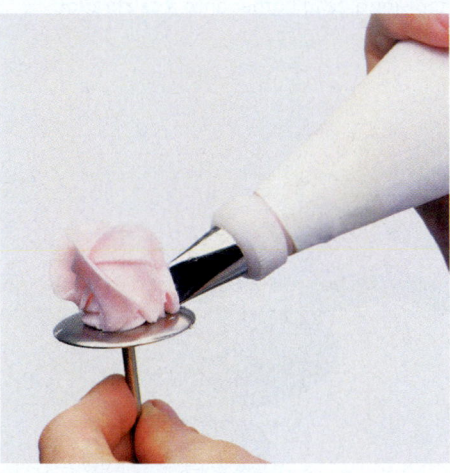

③ Pipe three overlapping petals around the center.

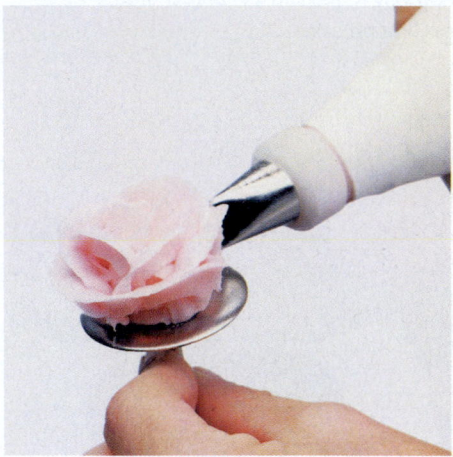

④ Pipe five more overlapping petals around the first three petals.

Advanced Pâtisserie

Sugar can be used to create a number of doughs, pastes and syrups used for artistic and decorative work. Mastering even some of these products takes years of experience and practice. Although formulas and preparation methods are beyond the scope of this book, it is important that all pastry cooks be able to recognize and identify certain decorative sugar products.

Blown sugar: A boiled mixture of sucrose, glucose and tartaric acid that is colored and shaped (in a manner very similar to glass blowing) using an air pump. It is used for making pieces of fruit and containers such as bowls and vases.

Gum paste: A smooth dough made of sugar and gelatin; it dries relatively slowly,

becoming very firm and hard. The paste can be colored and rolled out, cut and shaped, or molded. It is used for making flowers, leaves and small figures.

Marzipan: A mixture of almond paste and sugar that may be colored and used like modeling clay for sculpting small fruits, flowers or other objects. Marzipan can also be rolled out and cut into various shapes or used to cover cakes or pastries.

Nougat: A candy made of caramelized sugar and almonds that can be molded into shapes or containers. Unlike other sugar decorations, nougat remains deliciously edible.

Pastillage: A paste made with sugar, cornstarch and gelatin. Pastillage can be

rolled into sheets, then cut into shapes. It dries in a very firm and sturdy form, like plaster. Naturally pure white, it can be painted with cocoa or food colorings. Pastillage is used for showpieces and large decorative items.

Pulled sugar: A doughlike mixture of sucrose, glucose and tartaric acid that is colored, then shaped by hand. Pulled sugar is used for making birds, flowers, leaves, bows and other items.

Spun sugar: Long, fine, hairlike threads of sugar made by flicking caramelized sugar rapidly across dowels. Mounds or wreaths of these threads are used to decorate ice cream desserts, croquembouche and gâteaux.

STORING CAKES

Plain cake layers or sheets can be stored at room temperature for 2 or 3 days if well covered, although they may be easier to handle when chilled. Iced or filled cakes are usually refrigerated to prevent spoilage. Simple buttercreams or sugar glazes made without eggs or dairy products, however, can be left at room temperature for 1 or 2 days. Any cake containing custard filling, mousse or whipped cream must be refrigerated. Cakes made with foam-type frosting should be eaten the day they are prepared.

Cakes can usually be frozen with great success; this makes them ideal for baking in advance. Unfrosted layers or sheets should be well covered with plastic wrap and frozen at 0°F (–18°C) or lower. High-fat cakes will keep in a freezer for up to 6 months; egg-foam cakes begin to deteriorate after 2 or 3 months.

Frostings and fillings do not freeze particularly well, often losing flavor or changing texture when frozen. Buttercreams made with egg whites or sugar syrups tend to develop crystals and graininess. Foam frostings weep, expelling beads of sugar and becoming sticky. If a filled or a frosted cake must be frozen, it is best to freeze it unwrapped first, until the frosting is firm. The cake can then be covered with plastic wrap without damaging the frosting design. Leave a frozen cake wrapped until completely thawed. It is best to thaw cakes in the refrigerator; do not refreeze a thawed cake.

QUESTIONS FOR DISCUSSION

1 Cake ingredients can be classified into six categories according to the function they perform. List them and give an example of each.

2 What is the primary leavening agent in cakes made with the egg foam method? How is this similar to or different from cakes made with the creaming method?

3 What is the difference between a spongecake and a classic genoise?

4 Discuss for which types of cakes would a glaze be suitable. Why would buttercream be unsuitable for such a cake?

5 List the steps employed in assembling and frosting a three-layer cake.

6 Wedding cakes vary greatly from one region or culture to another. Investigate the various types or styles of cakes traditionally served at weddings in three or four different cultures. Discuss which recipes in this book would be appropriate for a wedding cake.

Additional Cake and Frosting Formulas

Carrot Cake with Cream Cheese Frosting

YIELD 5 Half-Sheet Cakes or 6 Rounds, 10 in. (25 cm) each   **METHOD** Creaming

Cake:

Vegetable oil	1 lb. 12 oz.	840 g	75.6%
Granulated sugar	1 lb. 14 oz.	900 g	81%
Eggs	14.8 oz. (9 eggs)	444 g	40%
Carrots, shredded	2 lb. 4 oz.	1076 g	97%
Canned crushed pineapple, with juice	1 lb. 9 oz.	750 g	67.5%
Baking soda	0.75 oz.	22 g	2%
Cinnamon, ground	1 oz.	33 g	3%
Pumpkin pie spice	0.75 oz.	22 g	2%
Salt	0.75 oz.	22 g	2%
Baking powder	0.6 oz. (1½ Tbsp.)	18 g	1.6%
Cake flour	2 lb. 5 oz.	1110 g	100%
Coconut, shredded	8 oz.	245 g	22%
Walnut pieces	10 oz.	300 g	27%
Total batter weight:	12 lb.	5782 g	521%
Cream Cheese Frosting (recipe follows)	as needed	as needed	

1 Blend the oil and sugar in the large bowl of a mixer fitted with the paddle attachment. Add the eggs, beating to incorporate.

2 Blend in the carrots and pineapple.

3 Sift the baking soda, cinnamon, pumpkin pie spice, salt, baking powder and flour together, and then add them to the batter. Stir in the coconut and walnuts.

4 Divide the batter into greased and floured pans.

5 Bake at 340°F (170°C) until springy to the touch and a cake tester comes out almost clean, approximately 30–40 minutes.

6 Allow the cakes to cool, then fill and frost as desired with Cream Cheese Frosting.

Approximate values per 5-oz. (150-g) serving: **Calories** 390, **Total fat** 22 g, **Saturated fat** 4 g, **Cholesterol** 40 mg, **Sodium** 490 mg, **Total carbohydrates** 44 g, **Protein** 5 g, **Vitamin A** 100%

Cream Cheese Frosting

YIELD 5 lb. 4 oz. (2.5 kg)

Unsalted butter, softened	6 oz.	180 g
Cream cheese, softened	1 lb. 8 oz.	720 g
Margarine	6 oz.	180 g
Vanilla extract	0.5 fl. oz. (1 Tbsp.)	15 ml
Powdered sugar, sifted	3 lb.	1440 g

1 Slowly cream the butter and cream cheese until smooth. Add the margarine and beat well.

2 Beat in the vanilla. Slowly add the sugar, scraping down the bowl frequently. Beat until smooth.

Approximate values per 1-oz. (30-g) serving: **Calories** 130, **Total fat** 6 g, **Saturated fat** 3 g, **Cholesterol** 15 mg, **Sodium** 45 mg, **Total carbohydrates** 17 g, **Protein** 1 g, **Vitamin A** 6%

Marble Cake

YIELD 1 Full-Sheet Cake, 4 Dozen Squares, approximately 3 in. (7 cm) each

METHOD Creaming

Cake:			
Cake flour, sifted	1 lb. 11 oz.	810 g	100%
Baking powder	1 oz. (2½ Tbsp.)	30 g	3.7%
Salt	0.5 oz.	15 g	1.8%
Unsalted butter	12 oz.	356 g	44%
Granulated sugar	1 lb. 11 oz.	810 g	100%
Milk	24 fl. oz.	720 ml	89%
Vanilla extract	0.15 fl. oz. (1 tsp.)	4 ml	0.5%
Dark chocolate, melted	4.5 oz.	130 g	16%
Baking soda	0.04 oz. (¼ tsp.)	1 g	0.1%
Coffee extract*	0.3 fl. oz. (2 tsp.)	8 ml	1%
Egg whites	12 oz. (12 whites)	360 g	44%
Total batter weight:	6 lb. 12 oz.	3238 g	400%
Cocoa Fudge Frosting (page 1045)	as needed	as needed	

1 Sift the flour, baking powder and salt together. Set aside.

2 Using an electric mixer fitted with the paddle attachment, cream the butter and sugar until light and fluffy.

3 Combine the milk and vanilla.

4 Add the dry ingredients to the creamed butter alternately with the milk. Stir the batter only until smooth.

5 Separate the batter into two equal portions. Add the melted chocolate, baking soda and coffee extract to one portion to create a chocolate batter; the other portion is the vanilla batter.

6 Using a clean mixer bowl, whip the egg whites until stiff but not dry. Fold half of the whites into the vanilla batter and half into the chocolate batter.

7 Spoon the batters onto a greased sheet pan, lined with a pan extender, alternating the two flavors. Pull a paring knife through the batter to swirl the colors together.

8 Bake at 350°F (180°C) until a tester comes out clean, approximately 25 minutes.

9 Allow the cake to cool, and then cover the top with Cocoa Fudge Frosting.

*The coffee extract is added to round out the chocolate flavor, not to impart a "coffee" flavor.

Variation:

Marble Cupcakes—Grease or line 36 muffin cups with paper liners. Pipe 1½ ounces (45 grams) of the chocolate and 1½ ounces (45 grams) of the plain batter into each cup. Bake until a tester comes out clean, approximately 20 minutes. Cover the top with Simple Buttercream (page 1041).

Approximate values per 5-oz. (150-g) serving: **Calories** 480, **Total fat** 17 g, **Saturated fat** 11 g, **Cholesterol** 40 mg, **Sodium** 250 mg, **Total carbohydrates** 75 g, **Protein** 7 g, **Vitamin A** 15%, **Calcium** 15%

Marble cupcakes

German Chocolate Cake

YIELD 1 Layer Cake, 9 in. (22 cm)   **METHOD** Creaming

Cake:

Sweet baking chocolate	8 oz.	240 g	80%
Water, boiling	4 fl. oz.	120 ml	40%
Unsalted butter	8 oz.	240 g	80%
Granulated sugar	1 lb.	480 g	160%
Egg yolks	2.4 oz. (4 yolks)	72 g	24%
Vanilla extract	0.15 fl. oz. (1 tsp.)	4.5 ml	1.5%
Cake flour	10 oz.	300 g	100%
Baking soda	0.1 oz. (¾ tsp.)	3 g	1%
Salt	0.1 oz. (½ tsp.)	3 g	1%
Buttermilk	8 fl. oz.	240 ml	80%
Egg whites	4 oz. (4 whites)	120 g	40%
Pecan halves	as needed for garnish		
Total batter weight:	3 lb. 12 oz.	1822 g	607.5%
Coconut Pecan Frosting (recipe follows)	1 lb. 13 oz.	870 g	

1 Chop the chocolate and melt it with the boiling water over a bain marie.

2 In the bowl of a mixer fitted with the paddle attachment, cream together the butter and sugar until light and fluffy.

3 Add the egg yolks, one at a time, to the butter, then stir in the vanilla and the melted chocolate.

4 Sift the dry ingredients together and add them alternately with the buttermilk, beating well after each addition.

5 Whip the egg whites to stiff peaks and fold into the batter.

6 Divide the batter into three 9-inch (22-centimeter) layer pans that have been greased and lined with parchment paper.

7 Bake at 350°F (180°C) until set and just beginning to pull away from the sides, approximately 30–40 minutes. When the cake has cooled completely, spread the Coconut Pecan Frosting between each layer and on top. The sides of this cake are traditionally left plain.

Approximate values per ½-cake serving: **Calories** 840, **Total fat** 47 g, **Saturated fat** 24 g, **Cholesterol** 210 mg, **Sodium** 240 mg, **Total carbohydrates** 101 g, **Protein** 10 g, **Vitamin A** 25%, **Calcium** 15%, **Iron** 20%

Coconut Pecan Frosting

YIELD 1 lb. 13 oz. (870 g), enough for
         1 three-layer cake

Evaporated milk	8 fl. oz.	240 ml
Granulated sugar	8 oz.	240 g
Egg yolks	1.8 oz. (3 yolks)	54 g
Unsalted butter	4 oz.	120 g
Vanilla extract	0.15 fl. oz. (1 tsp.)	5 ml
Coconut, flaked	4 oz.	120 g
Pecans, chopped	4 oz.	120 g

1 Combine the milk, sugar, egg yolks and butter in a saucepan over medium heat. Cook, stirring constantly, until the mixture thickens, approximately 12 minutes.

2 Remove from the heat and add the vanilla, coconut and pecans. Beat until cool and spreadable.

Approximate values per 1-oz. (30-g) serving: **Calories** 140, **Total fat** 11 g, **Saturated fat** 7 g, **Cholesterol** 25 mg, **Sodium** 10 mg, **Total carbohydrates** 10 g, **Protein** 1 g, **Vitamin A** 8%

Sacher Torte

YIELD	2 Layer Cakes, 8 in. (20 cm) each	METHOD	Creaming		

Cake:				
All-purpose flour	15 oz.		450 g	100%
Cocoa powder, alkalized	4.5 oz.		135 g	30%
Unsalted butter	18.75 oz.		562 g	125%
Granulated sugar	1 lb. 11 oz.		810 g	180%
Egg yolks	12 oz. (20 yolks)		360 g	80%
Hazelnuts, toasted and ground	4.5 oz.		135 g	30%
Egg whites	1 lb. 4 oz. (20 whites)		630 g	133%
Total batter weight:	6 lb. 5 oz.		3052 g	678%
Apricot jam	1 lb. 12 oz.		540 g	
Apricot glaze	as needed		as needed	
Dark Chocolate Glaze (recipe follows)	as needed		as needed	

1 Grease three 8-inch (20-centimeter) springform pans lightly with shortening and line with parchment paper.

2 Sift the flour and cocoa powder together twice. Set aside.

3 Cream the butter and 10 ounces (300 grams) of the sugar together until light and fluffy. Gradually add the egg yolks and beat well.

4 Fold in the sifted flour and cocoa and the hazelnuts by hand.

5 Whip the egg whites to soft peaks, then gradually add the remaining sugar and continue whipping until stiff, glossy peaks form.

6 Lighten the batter with approximately one-fourth of the egg whites, then fold in the remaining whites.

7 Pour the batter into the prepared pans and bake at 350°F (180°C) until the cakes are set, approximately 35–45 minutes.

8 Cool the cakes for 5 minutes before removing from the pans.

9 Cool completely, then cut each cake horizontally into two layers. Spread apricot jam on each layer and restack them, creating two three-layer cakes.

10 Heat the apricot glaze until spreadable. Pour it over the top and sides of each cake.

11 Allow the apricot glaze to cool completely, and then pour the Dark Chocolate Glaze over the top and sides of each cake to create a smooth, glossy coating.

Approximate values per 1/10-cake serving: **Calories** 450, **Total fat** 21 g, **Saturated fat** 10 g, **Cholesterol** 185 mg, **Sodium** 60 mg, **Total carbohydrates** 56 g, **Protein** 7 g, **Vitamin A** 20%

Dark Chocolate Glaze

YIELD	4 lb. (1.9 kg)		

Evaporated milk	14 oz.		420 g
Corn syrup	3 oz.		90 g
Simple syrup	14 oz.		420 g
Dark chocolate chips	17 oz.		510 g
Extra-bittersweet couverture, chopped fine	17 oz.		510 g

1 Bring the milk, corn syrup and simple syrup to a boil, stirring carefully. Do not whisk vigorously or you will incorporate too much air.

2 In a bowl, combine the dark chocolate chips and the extra-bittersweet couverture chocolate.

3 Slowly pour the cream mixture onto the chocolate. Let it sit for approximately a minute. Using a whisk, stir the mixture slowly to incorporate the chocolate and cream.

4 Keep the mixture refrigerated. When ready to use, warm it over a water bath to 100°F (38°C). If the temperature gets any hotter, the glaze will not be as shiny.

Approximate values per 1-oz. (30-g) serving: **Calories** 90, **Total fat** 6 g, **Saturated fat** 3 g, **Cholesterol** 0 mg, **Sodium** 10 mg, **Total carbohydrates** 12 g, **Protein** 1 g

Tres Leches Cake

YIELD 2 Cakes, 8 in. (20 cm) each	METHOD Spongecake		
Cake:			
Pastry flour	5 oz.	150 g	100%
Baking powder	0.5 oz.	15 g	10%
Egg yolks	5.2 oz. (8 yolks)	156 g	104%
Granulated sugar	5 oz.	150 g	100%
Egg whites	8 oz. (8 whites)	240 g	160%
Cream of tartar	0.04 oz. (⅛ tsp.)	1.2 g	0.8%
Total batter weight:	1 lb. 8 oz.	723 g	482%
Syrup:			
Media crema*	15 fl. oz.	420 ml	
Sweetened condensed milk	28 fl. oz.	790 ml	
Evaporated milk	24 fl. oz.	700 ml	
Vanilla extract	0.3 fl. oz.	9 ml	
Rum, dark	4 fl. oz.	120 ml	

1   Sift the flour and the baking powder together and set aside.

2   Whip the egg yolks with half of the sugar on high speed until they reach the ribbon stage, approximately 2 minutes.

3   In a separate bowl, use a clean whip to beat the egg whites until foamy. Add the cream of tartar and the remaining sugar. Whip on medium speed until the whites are glossy and stiff but not dry.

4   Fold one-third of the egg whites into the whipped yolks, then fold in the remaining whites.

5   Sprinkle one-third of the sifted flour over the batter and fold in. Repeat until all the flour is incorporated.

6   Divide the batter between greased and floured pans. Bake at 350°F (180°C) until the cake is golden brown and spongy, approximately 30 minutes.

7   Stir the syrup ingredients together in a bowl. Invert the hot cakes onto serving platters. Remove the parchment paper. Ladle the milk mixture over the hot cakes. (If necessary, poke holes in the cakes with a toothpick to allow the cakes to absorb more of the milk syrup.) Let the cakes soak at least 3 hours before serving.

*For this classic Latin American dish, *media crema* is often used in the syrup that moistens the cake. It is a canned milk available in the ethnic food section of many markets and can be used in place of some or all of the evaporated milk called for in a recipe.

Approximate values per ⅒-cake serving: **Calories** 370, **Total fat** 14 g, **Saturated fat** 8 g, **Cholesterol** 130 mg, **Sodium** 220 mg, **Total carbohydrates** 47 g, **Protein** 11 g, **Calcium** 35%

Flourless Chocolate Cake

| YIELD 1 Cake, 9 in. (22 cm) | METHOD Egg Foam | | |

Cake:			Sugar at 100%
Almonds, finely ground	1 oz. (¼ cup)	30 g	12.5%
Unsalted butter	12 oz.	360 g	150%
Bittersweet chocolate, chopped	12 oz.	360 g	150%
Granulated sugar	8 oz.	240 g	100%
Espresso, brewed	5 fl. oz.	150 g	62.5%
Eggs, lightly beaten	10 oz. (6 eggs)	300 g	125%
Cocoa powder	as needed for garnish		
Total batter weight:	3 lb.	1440 g	600%
Crème Chantilly (page 1075), optional	as needed	as needed	

1 Line one 9-inch (22 centimeter) round pan with aluminum foil allowing it to overhand the edge by 1 inch (2.5 centimeters). Grease the pan. Sprinkle the pan with the ground almonds.

2 Melt the butter and chocolate over a bain marie. Stir in the sugar and coffee.

3 Whisk the mixture in the bowl of a mixer fitted with the whip until well blended, approximately 5 minutes.

4 Reduce the speed to low and beat in the eggs a small amount at a time.

5 Pour the batter into the prepared pan.

6 Preheat the oven to 325°F (200°C). Place the batter-filled pan in a hotel pan and set the hotel pan in the preheated oven. Pour in enough water to come halfway up the sides of the pan. Bake until a cake tester comes out almost clean, approximately 50–55 minutes.

7 Cool the cake in the pan on a wire rack, then refrigerate overnight. Remove the cake from the pan.

8 Dust with cocoa powder. Serve with Crème Chantilly, if desired.

Approximate values per ½-cake serving: **Calories** 520, **Total fat** 40 g, **Saturated fat** 14 g, **Cholesterol** 155 mg, **Sodium** 35 mg, **Total carbohydrates** 24 g, **Protein** 6 g, **Vitamin A** 20%

Fudge Brownies

YIELD	1 Half-Sheet Pan, 4 Dozen Brownies,	METHOD	Egg Foam
	2 in. (5 cm) each		

Unsweetened chocolate	1 lb.	480 g	100%
Unsalted butter	1 lb. 2 oz.	540 g	112%
Eggs	1 lb. (10 eggs)	480 g	100%
Granulated sugar	2 lb. 8 oz.	1200g	250%
Salt	0.2 oz. (1 tsp.)	6 g	1.2%
Vanilla extract	1 fl. oz.	30 ml	6.2%
All-purpose flour	1 lb.	480 g	100%
Pecan pieces	8 oz.	240 g	50%
Total batter weight:	7 lb. 3 oz.	3456 g	719%
Powdered sugar, optional	as needed for garnish		

1 Melt the chocolate with the butter over a double boiler.

2 While the chocolate is melting, whip the eggs, granulated sugar and salt in the large bowl of a mixer fitted with the paddle attachment for 10 minutes.

3 Scrape down the bowl and add the melted chocolate and vanilla to the eggs. Stir to blend completely. Stir in the flour and nuts.

4 Spread the batter evenly onto a parchment-lined and buttered half-sheet pan. The pan will be very full. Bake at 325°F (160°C) until the center is set, approximately 40 minutes.

5 Allow to cool completely before cutting. Dust the brownies with powdered sugar, if using.

Approximate values per brownie: **Calories** 343, **Total fat** 18 g, **Saturated fat** 9 g, **Cholesterol** 70 mg, **Sodium** 16 mg, **Total carbohydrates** 41 g, **Protein** 4 g

German Chocolate Layered Brownies

YIELD 1 Full-Sheet Pan, 8 Dozen Brownies, 2 in. (5 cm) each

METHOD Egg Foam

Semi-sweet chocolate	1 lb.	480 g	114%
Unsalted butter	1 lb. 4 oz.	600 g	143%
Vanilla extract	0.5 fl. oz. (1 Tbsp.)	15 ml	3.5%
Eggs	1 lb. 4 oz. (12 eggs)	600 g	143%
Salt	0.1 oz. (½ tsp.)	3 g	0.7%
Granulated sugar	2 lb.	960 g	228%
Cocoa powder	2 oz.	60 g	14%
All purpose flour	14 oz.	420 g	100%
Pecans, chopped	1 lb.	480 g	114%
Topping:			
Unsalted butter	12 oz.	360 g	86%
Shredded coconut	12 oz.	360 g	86%
Coconut flavoring	0.6 fl. oz. (4 tsp.)	18 ml	4.3%
Vanilla extract	0.6 fl. oz. (4 tsp.)	18 ml	4.3%
Powdered sugar	1 lb. 4 oz.	600 g	143%
Cream cheese, softened	1 lb. 8 oz.	720 g	171%
Total weight:	11 lb. 13 oz.	5694 g	1355%

1 Melt chocolate and butter together and set aside. Stir in the vanilla extract.

2 Beat eggs, salt and sugar together in another bowl.

3 In a large bowl, stir together the cocoa powder, flour and pecans. Add the egg mixture to the flour, then stir in the melted chocolate.

4 Pour into a greased and floured sheet pan, spreading evenly.

5 To make the coconut topping, melt the butter in a large saucepan and then stir in the remaining ingredients except for the cream cheese. Cook over low heat until the sugar has dissolved and the mixture is creamy.

6 Cream the cream cheese in a mixer or food processor. Add the hot butter-and-sugar mixture and blend until no lumps of cheese remain in the coconut topping.

7 Immediately place the coconut topping over the unbaked chocolate brownie batter. Spread the topping into a thin layer using an offset spatula.

8 Bake at 300°F (149°C) until the center has set and the surface is golden brown, approximately 1 hour. Cool, then wrap and chill completely overnight before cutting into 2-×-2-inch (5-×-5-centimeter) squares.

Approximate values per brownie: **Calories** 220, **Total fat** 15 g, **Saturated fat** 8 g, **Cholesterol** 50 mg, **Sodium** 45 mg, **Total carbohydrates** 22 g, **Protein** 2 g

❶ Placing coconut topping over brownie batter in the sheet pan.

❷ Spreading topping over brownie batter before baking.

Banana Bars with Brown Butter Icing

YIELD 1 Half-Sheet Pan, 4 Dozen Bars, approximately 2 in. (5 cm) each

Bars:			
Granulated sugar	15 oz.	448 g	115%
Unsalted butter, softened	5 oz.	148 g	38%
Eggs	3.3 oz. (2 eggs)	97 g	25%
Sour cream	10 fl. oz.	304 ml	78%
Ripe bananas, peeled and chopped	14 oz. (4 bananas)	417 g	107%
Vanilla extract	0.5 fl. oz. (1 Tbsp.)	15 ml	4%
All-purpose flour	13 oz.	390 g	100%
Baking soda	0.17 oz. (1¼ tsp.)	5 g	1.3%
Cinnamon, ground	0.07 oz. (1 tsp.)	2 g	0.5%
Salt	0.2 oz. (1 tsp.)	6 g	1.5%
Walnuts, chopped, optional	3 oz.	90 g	23%
Total batter weight:	4 lb. 2 oz.	1922 g	492%
Icing:			
Unsalted butter	6 oz.	180 g	
Milk	2.5 fl. oz.	75 ml	
Vanilla extract	0.3 fl. oz. (2 tsp.)	10 ml	
Powdered sugar, sifted	1 lb. 8 oz.	720 g	

1 Cream the sugar and butter until smooth. Beat in the eggs, sour cream, bananas and vanilla.

2 In a separate bowl, sift together the flour, baking soda, cinnamon and salt. Stir the dry ingredients into the liquid mixture, stirring only until everything is combined.

3 Spread the batter evenly in a well-greased half-sheet pan. Bake at 375°F (190°C) until golden brown and a pick inserted near the center comes out clean, about 20 minutes.

4 Prepare the icing as soon as the cake is removed from the oven. Place the butter in a large saucepan over medium-high heat and bring to a simmer. Cook just until the butter turns a nutty brown, then remove from the heat.

5 Whisk the milk and vanilla into the butter. Add the powdered sugar gradually, whisking after each addition until the icing resembles a thick glaze. (If necessary, add a small amount of milk and whisk over low heat to thin it to the correct consistency.)

6 Immediately spread the hot icing over the hot cake. Cool completely at room temperature before cutting into portions. Store at room temperature.

Variation:

Chocolate Banana Bars—Add 6 ounces (180 grams/46%) of chocolate chips to the banana batter. When making the icing, whisk 1 ounce (30 grams) of unsweetened cocoa powder into the browned butter, and then reduce the amount of powdered sugar to 20 ounces (600 grams).

Approximate values per bar: **Calories** 252, **Total fat** 9g, **Saturated fat** 5g, **Cholesterol** 32 mg, **Sodium** 120 mg, **Total carbohydrates** 42 g, **Protein** 2 g

Custards, Creams, Frozen Desserts and Dessert Sauces

35

- prepare a variety of custards and creams
- prepare a variety of ice creams, sorbets and frozen dessert items
- prepare a variety of dessert sauces
- use these products in preparing and serving other pastry and dessert items

The bakeshop is responsible for more than just quick breads, yeast breads, pies, pastries, cookies and cakes. It also produces many delightfully sweet concoctions that are not baked and often not even cooked. These include sweet custards, creams, frozen desserts and dessert sauces. Sweet custards are cooked mixtures of eggs, sugar and milk; flour or cornstarch may be added. Sweet custards can be flavored in a variety of ways and eaten hot or cold. Some are served alone as a dessert or used as a filling, topping or accompaniment for pies, pastries or cakes. Creams include whipped cream and mixtures lightened with whipped cream such as Bavarians, chiffons and mousses. Frozen desserts include ice cream and sorbet as well as the still-frozen mousses called semifreddi.

Sauces for these desserts, including fruit purées, caramel sauces and chocolate syrup, are also made in the bakeshop and are discussed in this chapter. Indeed many of the items presented in this chapter are components, meant to be combined with pastries (Chapter 33) or cakes (Chapter 34) to form complete desserts. Guidelines for assembling desserts are given at this chapter's end.

CUSTARDS

A **custard** is any liquid thickened by the coagulation of egg proteins. A custard's consistency depends on the ratio of eggs to liquid, whether whole eggs or just yolks are used, and the type of liquid used. The more eggs used, the thicker and richer the final product will be. The richer the liquid (e.g., cream versus milk), the thicker the final product. Most custards, with the notable exception of pastry creams, are not thickened by starch. A custard can be stirred or baked. A **stirred custard** tends to be soft, rich and creamy. A **baked custard**, typically prepared in a bain marie, is usually firm enough to unmold and slice.

Stirred Custards

A stirred custard is cooked on the stove top either directly in a saucepan or over a double boiler. It must be stirred throughout the cooking process to prevent **curdling** (overcooking).

A stirred custard can be used as a dessert sauce, incorporated into a complex dessert or eaten alone. The stirred custards most commonly used in food service operations are vanilla custard sauce and pastry cream. Other popular stirred custards are lemon curd and sabayon.

Vanilla Custard Sauce

Vanilla custard sauce (Fr. *crème anglaise*) is made with egg yolks, sugar and milk or half-and-half. Usually flavored with vanilla bean or pure vanilla extract, a custard sauce can also be flavored with liqueur, chocolate, ground nuts or extracts. A custard sauce can be served with cakes, pastries, fruits and soufflés and is often used for decorating dessert plates. It may be served hot or cold. Custard sauce is also used as the base for many ice creams.

Custard sauce is prepared on the stovetop over direct heat in a nonreactive saucepan in order to prevent discoloration. (If a nonreactive pan is unavailable, cook the custard in a stainless steel bowl set over a bain marie of simmering water.) When making a custard sauce, be extremely careful to stir the mixture continually and do not allow it to boil, or it will curdle. Do not allow the temperature to exceed 190°F (88°C) or the custard will break. Use a thermometer to monitor the custard as it cooks and remove the sauce from the heat when it reaches 185°F (85°C). A properly made custard sauce should be smooth and thick enough to coat the back of a spoon. It should not contain any noticeable bits of cooked egg.

Pastry Cream

Pastry cream (Fr. *crème pâtissière*) is a stirred custard made with egg yolks, sugar and milk and thickened with starch (flour, cornstarch or a combination of the two). Because the starch protects the egg yolks from curdling, pastry cream must be boiled to fully gelatinize the starch and eliminate the taste of raw starch.

Pastry cream can be flavored with chocolate, liquors, extracts or fruits. (Pudding is simply flavored pastry cream.) Pastry cream is used for filling éclairs, cream puffs, napoleons, fruit tarts and other pastries. Pastry cream thickened with cornstarch is also the filling for cream pies (see Chapter 33, Pies, Pastries and Cookies). Pastry cream is thick enough to hold its shape without making pastry doughs soggy.

Pastry cream can be rather heavy. It can be lightened by folding in whipped cream or whipped eggs to produce a **mousseline**, or Italian meringue can be folded in to produce a **crème Chiboust**.

mousseline [moos-uh-LEEN] a cream or sauce lightened by folding in whipped cream, whipped eggs or meringue

crème Chiboust [krehm chee-BOOS] a vanilla pastry cream lightened by folding in Italian meringue; traditionally used in a gâteau St. Honoré

Procedure for Preparing Vanilla Custard Sauce and Pastry Cream

1 Place milk and/or cream in a heavy, nonreactive saucepan; add vanilla bean to **steep** in the cream if desired.

2 In a mixing bowl, whisk together the egg yolks, sugar and starch (if using). Do not use an electric mixer, as it incorporates too much air.

3 Bring the liquid just to a boil. **Temper** the egg mixture with approximately one-third of the hot liquid.

4 Pour the tempered eggs into the remaining hot liquid and return the mixture to the heat. When determining how hot to set your stove, keep in mind this guideline: The lower the temperature, the longer the custard will take to thicken; the higher the temperature, the greater the risk of curdling.

5 Cook, stirring constantly, until thickened. Custard sauce should reach a temperature of 185°F (85°C). Pastry cream should come to a true boil, begin to thicken slightly, then be allowed to boil for up to 2 minutes to thicken.

6 Immediately remove the cooked custard from the hot saucepan to avoid overcooking. Pour it through a fine mesh strainer. Butter, used to enrich pastry cream, should be added to the pastry cream at this time. Other flavorings can be added at this time also.

7 Cool in an ice bath. Store in a clean, shallow container. Cover to prevent pastry cream from developing a thick skin and refrigerate.

steep to soak food in a hot liquid in order to either extract its flavor or soften its texture

temper to heat gently and gradually; refers to the process of slowly adding a hot liquid to eggs or other foods to raise their temperature without causing them to curdle

Procedure for Salvaging Curdled Vanilla Custard Sauce

1 Strain the curdled sauce into a bowl. Place the bowl over an ice bath and whisk vigorously.

2 If this does not smooth out the overcooked sauce, place the sauce in a blender and process for a few moments.

Although these steps may reincorporate the curdled eggs, the resulting sauce will be thin and less creamy than a properly prepared vanilla custard sauce.

Vanilla Custard Sauce

MISE EN PLACE

- Split vanilla bean in half.
- Set up an ice bath and strainer.

YIELD 36 fl. oz. (1.2 lt)		METHOD Stirred Custard	
Half-and-half	1 qt.		960 ml
Vanilla bean, split	1		1
Egg yolks, pasteurized	7.2 oz. (12 yolks)		216 g
Granulated sugar	10 oz.		300 g

1 In a heavy nonreactive saucepan, bring the half-and-half and vanilla bean just to a boil.

2 Whisk the egg yolks and sugar together by hand in a mixing bowl. Temper the egg mixture with approximately one-third of the hot half-and-half, then return the entire mixture to the saucepan with the remaining half-and-half.

3 Cook the sauce over medium heat, stirring constantly, until it is thick enough to lightly coat the back of a spoon. Do not allow the sauce to exceed 185°F (85°C) or the mixture will curdle.

4 As soon as the sauce thickens, remove it from the heat and pour it through a fine mesh strainer into a clean bowl. Chill the sauce in an ice bath, then cover and keep refrigerated. The sauce should last 3–4 days.

Variations:

Chocolate Custard Sauce—Stir 6 ounces (180 grams) finely chopped dark chocolate into the strained custard while it is still warm. The heat of the custard will melt the chocolate.

Coffee Custard Sauce—Add 1–1½ fluid ounces (30–45 milliliters) coffee (café) extract or compound to the warm custard.

Hazelnut Custard Sauce—Omit the vanilla bean. Stir in ½ teaspoon (2 milliliters) vanilla extract and 2–3 tablespoons (30–45 milliliters) hazelnut liqueur, to taste.

Ginger Custard Sauce—Omit the vanilla bean. Steep 3 ounces (90 grams) chopped fresh ginger for 10 minutes in the half-and-half. Reheat and continue preparing the sauce as directed. The chopped ginger will be strained out in Step 4.

Pistachio Custard Sauce—Omit the vanilla bean. Place 4 ounces (120 grams) finely chopped pistachio nuts in the saucepan with the barely boiling half-and-half. Remove from the heat, cover and steep for up to 1 hour. Uncover the mixture, reheat and continue preparing the sauce as directed. The ground nuts will be strained out in Step 4.

Approximate values per 1-fl.-oz. (30-ml) serving: **Calories** 80, **Total fat** 4.5 g, **Saturated fat** 2.5 g, **Cholesterol** 75 mg, **Sodium** 15 mg, **Total carbohydrates** 8 g, **Protein** 2 g, **Vitamin A** 6%

❶ Mise en place for vanilla sauce.

❷ Tempering the eggs.

❸ The properly cooked sauce thickens slightly.

❹ Straining the sauce into a bowl.

Pastry Cream

YIELD Approximately 1½ qt. (720 ml)		METHOD Stirred Custard	
Milk		1 qt.	960 ml
Granulated sugar		7.5 oz.	225 g
Egg yolks		6 oz. (10 yolks)	180 g
Cornstarch		2.5 oz.	75 g
Unsalted butter		2 oz.	60 g

MISE EN PLACE
- Split vanilla bean in half.
- Set up an ice bath.

1 Boil the milk and 3 ounces (120 grams) sugar in a large nonreactive saucepan.

2 Whisk the egg yolks in a mixing bowl and gradually add the remaining sugar. Whisk in the cornstarch to combine.

3 Temper the egg yolk mixture with one-quarter of the boiling milk. Return the egg mixture to the pan and cook, whisking vigorously until the cream boils and is well thickened. Allow the pastry cream to boil approximately 1 minute, stirring constantly.

4 Remove the pastry cream from the heat and immediately pour it into a clean mixing bowl.

5 Fold in the butter until melted. Do not overmix, as this will thin the custard.

6 Cover by placing plastic wrap on the surface of the custard. Chill over an ice bath. Remove the vanilla bean just before using the pastry cream.

Variations:

Chocolate Pastry Cream—Stir 4 ounces (120 grams) finely chopped dark chocolate into the strained custard while it is still warm. The heat of the custard will melt the chocolate.

Coconut Pastry Cream—Replace 16 fluid ounces (480 milliliters) of the milk with an equal amount of unsweetened canned coconut milk.

Coffee Pastry Cream—Add 1 fluid ounce (30 milliliters) coffee extract or compound to the warm custard.

Mousseline Pastry Cream—Whip 12 fluid ounces (360 milliliters) heavy cream to stiff peaks. Fold into the chilled Pastry Cream filling.

Approximate values per 1-fl.-oz. (30-ml) serving: **Calories** 50, **Total fat** 2.5 g, **Saturated fat** 1.5 g, **Cholesterol** 55 mg, **Sodium** 10 mg, **Total carbohydrates** 6 g, **Protein** 1 g

❶ Whisking pastry cream as it comes to a boil.

❷ Folding butter into the cooked pastry cream.

ladyfingers small cakes or cookies made from spongecake batter piped into finger-length strips; used to line molds for desserts or layered with fillings

Sabayon

Sabayon [sah-bay-own; It. *Zabaglione*] is a foamy, stirred custard sauce made by whisking eggs, sugar and wine over low heat. The egg proteins coagulate, thickening the mixture, while the whisking incorporates air to make it light and fluffy. Usually a sweet wine is used; marsala and champagne are the most popular choices. As the flavor of the sabayon depends on the quality of the wine from which it is made, use the best quality available.

The mixture can be served warm, or it can be chilled and lightened with whipped cream or whipped egg whites. Sabayon may be served alone or as a sauce or topping with fruit or pastries such as spongecake or **ladyfingers**.

Procedure for Preparing Sabayon

1 Combine egg yolks, sugar and wine in the top of a double boiler.
2 Place the double boiler over low heat and whisk constantly until the sauce is foamy and thick enough to form a ribbon when the whisk is lifted.
3 Remove from the heat and serve immediately, or whisk over an ice bath until cool. If allowed to sit, the hot mixture may separate.
4 Whipped egg whites or whipped cream may be folded into the cooled sabayon.

Champagne Sabayon

YIELD Approximately 1 qt. (1 lt)	METHOD Stirred Custard	
Egg yolks	4.8 oz. (8 yolks)	240 g
Granulated sugar	4 oz.	120 g
Salt	0.05 oz. (¼ tsp.)	1.5 g
Marsala wine	2 fl. oz.	60 ml
Dry champagne	6 fl. oz.	180 ml

1 Combine the egg yolks, sugar and salt in a stainless steel bowl.
2 Add the marsala and champagne to the egg mixture.
3 Place the bowl over a pan of barely simmering water. Whisk vigorously until the sauce is thick and pale yellow, approximately 10 minutes. Serve immediately.

Variation:

Sabayon Mousseline—Place the bowl of finished sabayon in an ice bath and continue whisking until completely cold. In a separate bowl, whip 8 fluid ounces (240 milliliters) heavy cream to soft peaks then fold the whipped cream into the cold sabayon.

Approximate values per 1-fl.-oz. (30-ml) serving: **Calories** 50, **Total fat** 4 g, **Saturated fat** 2 g, **Cholesterol** 60 mg, **Sodium** 25 mg, **Total carbohydrates** 4 g, **Protein** 1 g, **Vitamin A** 6%

Baked Custards

Baked custard is based on the same principle as stirred custard: A liquid thickens by the coagulation of egg proteins. However, with a baked custard, the thickening occurs in an oven. The container of custard is usually placed in a water bath (bain marie) to help the custard cook evenly and protect the eggs from curdling. Even though the water bath's temperature will not exceed 212°F (100°C), care must be taken not to bake the custards for too long or at too high a temperature. An overbaked custard is watery or curdled; a properly baked custard is smooth-textured and firm enough to slice.

The family of baked custard includes simple mixtures of whole eggs or egg yolks with sugar and milk. If this mixture is baked over a layer of caramelized sugar it is called a crème caramel or a flan in Spain and Mexico. Baked custards also include egg mixtures in which other ingredients are suspended (e.g., cheesecake, rice pudding, bread pudding and quiche). The foundation for all of these products is a liquid thickened by the coagulation of egg proteins. Baked custards, like custard sauce and pastry cream, can be flavored with chocolate, liquors, extracts, herbs, fruits and spices.

Crème Caramel

Crème caramel, **crème renversée** and **flan** all refer to an egg custard baked over a layer of caramelized sugar and inverted for service. The caramelized sugar produces a golden-brown surface on the inverted custard and a thin caramel sauce.

Toffee Caramel Flan

YIELD 10 Ramekins, 6 fl. oz. (180 ml) each	METHOD Baked Custard	
Granulated sugar	1 lb. 4 oz.	600 g
Water	8 fl. oz.	240 ml
Milk	24 fl. oz.	720 ml
Heavy cream	24 fl. oz.	720 ml
Cinnamon sticks	2	2
Vanilla bean, split	1	1
Eggs	13.2 oz. (8 eggs)	396 g
Egg yolks	2.4 oz. (4 yolks)	72 g
Brown sugar	6 oz.	180 g
Molasses	0.75 oz. (1 Tbsp.)	20 g
Amaretto liqueur	1 fl. oz.	30 ml

MISE EN PLACE

- Gather the ramekins and hotel pan.
- Preheat the oven to 325°F (160°C).
- Split vanilla bean in half.

1 Combine the granulated sugar with the water in a small heavy saucepan; bring to a boil. Cook until the sugar caramelizes and turns a deep golden brown. Immediately pour about 2 tablespoons (30 milliliters) caramelized sugar into each ramekin. Tilt each ramekin to spread the caramel evenly along the bottom. Arrange the ramekins in a 2-inch- (5-centimeter-) deep hotel pan and set aside.

2 Combine the milk, cream, cinnamon sticks and vanilla bean in a large saucepan. Bring just to a boil, cover and remove from the heat. Allow this mixture to steep for about 30 minutes.

3 Whisk the eggs, egg yolks, brown sugar, molasses and amaretto together in a large bowl.

4 Uncover the milk mixture and return it to the stove top. Bring just to a boil. Temper the egg-and-sugar mixture with approximately one-third of the hot milk. Whisk in the remaining hot milk.

5 Strain the custard through a fine mesh strainer. Pour into the caramel-lined ramekins, filling to just below the rim.

6 Pour enough warm water into the hotel pan to reach halfway up the sides of the ramekins. Bake at 325°F (160°C) for approximately 30–40 minutes. The custards should be almost set, but still slightly soft in the center.

7 Completely chill the baked custards before serving. To unmold, run a small knife around the edge of the custard, invert onto the serving plate and give the ramekin a firm sideways shake. Garnish with fresh fruit or caramelized almonds.

Approximate values per 6-fl.-oz. (180-ml) serving: **Calories** 670, **Total fat** 33 g, **Saturated fat** 19 g, **Cholesterol** 355 mg, **Sodium** 120 mg, **Total carbohydrates** 82 g, **Protein** 10 g, **Vitamin A** 40%, **Calcium** 20%

> **⚠ Safety Alert**
>
> *Hot Sugar Syrups*
>
> Be extremely careful when working with hot sugar syrups. Because sugar can be heated to very high temperatures, these syrups can cause severe burns. Do not touch liquefied or caramelized sugar with your bare hand until it has cooled completely.

Crème Brûlée

Crème brûlée is a thick version of custard sauce with a consistency more like a **pudding** than a sauce. This custard is often served over fruit in a small ramekin or other container and then topped with caramelized sugar from which it gets its name; **crème brûlée** means "burnt cream" in French.

Crème brûlée can be made as either a stirred or a baked custard. Neither version should be considered superior, however; they are simply different. The stirred or stove top method is quicker, but requires constant attention and a practiced feel for the custard's consistency. The finished stirred version is heavier, creamier and softer than its baked counterpart. The baked version is served in the ramekin or bowl in which it was baked.

pudding a thick, spoonable dessert custard, usually made with eggs, milk, sugar and flavorings and thickened with flour or another starch

crème brûlée [krehm broo-LAY] French for "burnt cream"; used to describe a rich dessert custard topped with a crust of caramelized sugar

Unlike crème caramel or flan, baked crème brûlée is not inverted or removed from its baking dish for service. A formula for the baked version follows; a stirred version appears on page 1087.

Gentle heat is important for both methods. Overcooked stirred custard will curdle, turning into scrambled eggs. Overcooked baked custard will become watery, its texture marred with small bubbles.

Additional flavors and textures can be added to crème brûlée custard in several ways:

- Placing a layer of fresh berries or fruit compote under the custard
- Incorporating fruit, nuts or liqueurs directly into the custard
- Adding flavoring compounds and extracts to the custard
- Infusing the heavy cream with nuts, herbs, spices, tea or other flavorings before making the custard

If fruit purées or other liquids are used, the quantity of cream will have to be adjusted so the custard is not too watery or unable to set properly.

MISE EN PLACE

- Split vanilla bean in half.
- Preheat the oven to 325°F (160°C).

Baked Crème Brûlée

YIELD 10 Servings, 4 fl. oz. (120 ml) each	METHOD Baked Custard	
Heavy cream	1 qt.	1 lt
Vanilla bean, split	½	½
Granulated sugar	4 oz.	120 g
Egg yolks	6 oz. (10 yolks)	180 g
Granulated sugar	as needed	as needed

1 Heat the cream and the vanilla bean in a medium saucepan over medium-high heat until bubbles appear along the sides of the pan.

2 In a separate bowl, quickly whisk the sugar into the egg yolks.

3 When the cream is hot, slowly pour it into the sugar and yolk mixture. Whisk until well combined.

4 Strain through a fine sieve into a pitcher or large measuring cup. Scrape the vanilla bean with the tip of a paring knife to remove the remaining seeds; stir the seeds into the custard.

5 Preheat the oven to 325°F (160°C). Arrange 10 ramekins in a 2-inch- (5-centimeter-) deep hotel pan or baking dish. Pour the custard into the ramekins. Set the pan of ramekins inside the preheated oven, then carefully pour enough water into the pan to come two-thirds of the way up the sides of the ramekins. Bake until just set, approximately 45–50 minutes. Start checking the custards early; baking time will depend on the thickness and depth of your ramekins. The custard should be set, not soupy, with only a small area of jiggle in the center.

6 When the custards are done, carefully remove the baking dish from the oven and allow the ramekins to cool in the water bath. When the ramekins are cool enough to handle, remove them from the pan, cover with plastic wrap, and refrigerate for at least 4 hours or up to 2 days before service.

7 At service, sprinkle the top of each custard with granulated sugar, then immediately caramelize the sugar with a propane torch or under a broiler.

Approximate values per 4-fl.-oz. (120-ml) serving: **Calories** 430, **Total fat** 40 g, **Saturated fat** 24 g, **Cholesterol** 345 mg, **Sodium** 45 mg, **Total carbohydrates** 14 g, **Protein** 5 g, **Vitamin A** 35%

Cheesecake

Cheesecakes have undergone many changes and variations since the ancient Greeks devised the first known recipe. Americans revolutionized the dessert with the development of cream cheese in 1872.

Cheesecake is a baked custard that contains a smooth cheese, usually a soft, fresh cheese such as cream, ricotta, cottage or farmer cheese. A cheesecake may be prepared without a crust, or it may have a base or sides of short dough, cookie crumbs, ground nuts or spongecake. The filling can be dense and rich (New York style) or light and fluffy (Italian style). Fruit, nuts and flavorings may also be included in the filling. Cheesecakes are often topped with fruit or sour cream glaze. A recipe for New York Cheesecake (page 1088) appears at the end of this chapter. Some cheesecakes are unbaked and rely on gelatin for thickening; others are frozen. These are not really custards, however, but are more similar to the chiffons or mousses discussed later.

Cheesecakes should be cut when cold and firm. Use a knife dipped in hot water and wipe it clean after cutting each slice.

Bread Pudding

Bread pudding is a home-style dessert in which chunks of bread, flavorings and raisins or other fruit are mixed with an egg custard and baked. The result is somewhat of a cross between a cake and a pudding. Bread pudding is often served with custard sauce, ice cream, whipped cream or a whiskey-flavored butter sauce. Bread pudding is a delicious way to use stale or leftover bread or overripe fruit. A recipe for Bread Pudding with Bourbon Sauce appears on page 1089.

Soufflés

A **soufflé** is made with a custard base that is often thickened with a starch. The base is lightened with whipped egg whites and then baked. When heated, the air in the egg whites expands to create a light, fluffy texture and tall rise. During baking, the egg proteins set, giving some structure to the finished soufflé. A soufflé is not as stable as a cake or other pastry item, however, and will collapse as it cools.

Soufflés can be prepared in a wide variety of sweet and savory flavors. The flavorings can be incorporated into the custard, as in the following recipe. Alternatively, an unflavored pastry cream can be used as the base. In this case, liqueur, fruit or chocolate is added to each portion separately.

When making a soufflé, the custard base and egg whites should be at room temperature. There are two reasons for this. First, the egg whites will whip to a better volume; second, if the base is approximately the same temperature as the egg whites, the two mixtures can be more easily incorporated. The egg whites are whipped to stiff peaks with a portion of the sugar for stability. The whipped egg whites are then gently folded into the base immediately before baking.

A soufflé is baked in a straight-sided mold or in individual ramekins. The finished soufflé should be puffy with a lightly browned top. It should rise well above the rim of the baking dish. A soufflé must be served immediately, before it collapses. A warm custard sauce (crème anglaise) is often served as an accompaniment to a sweet soufflé.

A frozen soufflé is not a true soufflé. Rather it is a creamy custard mixture thickened with gelatin, lightened with whipped egg whites or whipped cream and placed in a soufflé dish wrapped with a paper or acetate collar. When the collar is removed, the mixture looks as if it has risen above the mold like a hot soufflé.

Procedure for Preparing Baked Soufflés

1 Butter the mold or ramekins and dust with granulated sugar. Preheat the oven to approximately 425°F (220°C).
2 Prepare the custard base. Add flavorings as desired. Keep warm or reheat before using.
3 Whip the egg whites and sugar to stiff peaks. Fold the whipped egg whites into the base.
4 Pour the mixture into the prepared mold or ramekins and bake immediately.

Chocolate Soufflés

YIELD 8 Servings, approximately 5½ oz. (165 g) each

Orange juice	1 pt.	480 ml
Eggs, separated	13.2 oz. (8 eggs)	396 g
Granulated sugar	4 oz.	120 g
All-purpose flour	3 oz.	90 g
Bittersweet chocolate, chopped fine	8 oz.	240 g
Orange liqueur	2 fl. oz.	60 ml
Unsalted butter, melted	as needed	as needed
Granulated sugar	as needed	as needed

1 To prepare the base, heat the orange juice to lukewarm in a heavy saucepan.

2 Whisk the egg yolks with 3 ounces (90 grams) sugar in a large mixing bowl. Whisk in the flour and warm orange juice, then return the mixture to the saucepan.

3 Cook over medium-low heat, stirring constantly, until the custard is thick enough to coat a spatula. Do not allow it to boil. Remove from the heat.

4 Stir in the chocolate until completely melted. Stir in the liqueur. Cover this base mixture with plastic wrap to prevent a skin from forming. Hold for use at room temperature. (Unused base can be kept overnight in the refrigerator; bring to room temperature before mixing with the egg whites.)

5 To prepare the soufflés, brush 4-fluid-ounce (120-milliliter) ramekins with melted butter and dust with granulated sugar.

6 Preheat the oven to 425°F (220°C). Place a sheet pan in the oven, onto which you will place the soufflés for baking. (This makes it easier to remove the hot soufflé cups from the oven.)

7 Whip the egg whites to stiff peaks with the remaining 1 ounce (30 grams) sugar. Fold the whites into the chocolate base and spoon the mixture into the prepared ramekins. The ramekins should be filled to within ¼ inch (6 millimeters) of the rim. Smooth the top of each soufflé with a spatula and bake immediately.

8 The soufflés are done when well risen, brown on top and the edges appear dry, approximately 12 minutes. Do not touch a soufflé to test doneness, as this may cause it to collapse.

9 Sprinkle the soufflés with powdered sugar if desired and serve immediately.

Approximate values per 5 ½-oz. (165-g) serving: **Calories** 350, **Total fat** 15 g, **Saturated fat** 8 g, **Cholesterol** 210 mg, **Sodium** 65 mg, **Total carbohydrates** 48 g, **Protein** 10 g, **Vitamin A** 10%, **Vitamin C** 50%

❶ Folding the whipped egg whites into the chocolate base.

❷ Filling the ramekins.

CREAMS

Creams (Fr. *crèmes*) include light, fluffy or creamy-textured dessert items made with whipped egg whites or whipped cream. Some, such as Bavarian creams and chiffons, are thickened with gelatin. Others, such as mousses and crèmes Chantilly, are softer and lighter. See Table 35.1. The success of all creams, however, depends on properly whipping and incorporating egg whites or heavy cream.

Review the material on whipping cream found in Chapter 8, Dairy Products. When preparing any whipped cream, be sure that the cream, the mixing bowl and all utensils are well chilled and clean. Recall that whipping cream has a butterfat content of 30–36 percent. A warm bowl can melt the butterfat, destroying the texture of the cream. Properly whipped cream should increase two to three times in volume.

Crème Chantilly

Crème Chantilly is simply heavy cream whipped to soft peaks and lightly flavored with sugar and vanilla. It can be used for garnishing pastry or dessert items, or it can be folded into cooled custard or pastry cream and used as a component in a pastry.

When making crème Chantilly, the vanilla extract and sugar should be added after the cream begins to thicken. Either granulated or powdered sugar may be used; there are advantages and disadvantages to both. Granulated sugar assists in forming a better foam than powdered sugar, but it may make the cream gritty. Powdered sugar dissolves more quickly and completely than granulated sugar but does nothing to assist with foaming. Whichever sugar is used, add it just before the whipping is complete to avoid interfering with the cream's volume and stability.

Overwhipped cream loses volume, curdles and separates.

Crème Chantilly (Chantilly Cream)

YIELD 2–2½ qt. (2–2.5 lt)

Heavy cream, chilled	1 qt.	1 lt
Powdered sugar	3 oz.	90 g
Vanilla extract	0.3 fl. oz. (2 tsp.)	10 ml

MISE EN PLACE
- Chill cream, mixing bowl and whisk.

1 Place the cream in a chilled mixing bowl. Using a balloon whisk, whisk the cream until slightly thickened.

2 Add the sugar and vanilla extract and continue whisking to the desired consistency. The cream should be smooth and light, not grainy. Do not overwhip.

3 Crème Chantilly may be stored in the refrigerator for several hours. If the cream begins to soften, gently rewhip as necessary.

Variations:

Stabilized Whipped Cream—Soften ¼ ounce (7 grams/2¾ teaspoons) granulated gelatin in 2 fluid ounces (60 milliliters) cold water. Melt the gelatin. Add to the cream just as it begins to form soft peaks. Whip to the desired consistency. Use to fill cakes or pastries. It will keep for 24 hours without deflating.

Chocolate Chantilly—Melt 1 pound 2 ounces (540 grams) bittersweet chocolate to 120°F (49°C) and remove from heat. Whip the cream to medium peaks. Whisk one-fourth of the whipped cream into the chocolate vigorously. Gently fold in the remaining cream. This mixture will have the texture of velvety ganache.

Approximate values per 1-fl.-oz. (30-ml) serving: **Calories** 60, **Total fat** 6 g, **Saturated fat** 3.5 g, **Cholesterol** 20 mg, **Sodium** 5 mg, **Total carbohydrates** 2 g, **Protein** 0 g

Properly whipped Crème Chantilly.

CREAM (CRÈME) COMPONENTS			TABLE 35.1
FOR A	BEGIN WITH A BASE OF	THICKEN WITH	THEN FOLD IN
Bavarian	Custard	Gelatin	Whipped cream
Chiffon	Custard or starch-thickened fruit	Gelatin	Whipped egg whites
Mousse	Melted chocolate, puréed fruit or custard	Nothing or gelatin	Whipped cream, whipped egg whites or both

Bavarian Cream

A **Bavarian cream** (Fr. *bavarois*) is prepared by first thickening custard sauce with gelatin, then folding in whipped cream. The final product is poured into a mold and chilled until firm enough to unmold and slice. Although a Bavarian cream can be molded into individual servings, it is traditionally poured into a round mold lined with spongecake or ladyfingers to create the classic dessert known as a **charlotte**.

Bavarians can be flavored by adding chocolate, puréed fruit, chopped nuts, extracts or liquors to the custard sauce base. Layers of fruit or liquor-soaked spongecake can also be added for flavor and texture.

When thickening a dessert cream with gelatin, it is important to use the correct amount of gelatin. If not enough gelatin is used or it is not incorporated completely, the cream will not become firm enough to unmold. If too much gelatin is used, the cream will be tough and rubbery. The recipe given here uses sheet gelatin, although an equal amount by weight of granulated gelatin can be substituted. Refer to Chapter 30, Principles of the Bakeshop, for information on using gelatin.

Procedure for Preparing Bavarian Creams

1 Prepare a custard sauce of the desired flavor.
2 While the custard sauce is still quite warm, stir in softened gelatin. Make sure the gelatin is completely incorporated.
3 Chill the custard until almost thickened, then fold in the whipped cream.
4 Pour the Bavarian into a mold or charlotte form. Chill until set.

Bavarian Cream

MISE EN PLACE

- Split vanilla bean in half.
- Soften gelatin in ice water.
- Prepare an ice bath.

Charlotte Bavarian

YIELD Approximately 2 qt. (2 lt)

Milk	14 fl. oz.	420 ml
Heavy cream	14 fl. oz.	420 ml
Granulated sugar	6 oz.	180 g
Vanilla bean, split in half	1	1
Egg yolks	4.8 oz. (8 eggs)	138 g
Sheet gelatin, softened	8 sheets (0.5 oz.)	15 g
Heavy cream, whipped to soft peaks	1 qt.	960 ml

1 To prepare the custard sauce, combine the milk, cream, 2 ounces (60 grams) sugar and the vanilla bean in a heavy saucepan. Bring to a boil.
2 Whisk the egg yolks and remaining 4 ounces (120 grams) sugar together to the ribbon stage. Temper the yolk mixture with one-quarter of the heated milk, whisking constantly.
3 Pour the egg mixture into the saucepan with the rest of the milk. Stir constantly with a rubber spatula until the custard reaches 185°F (85°C).
4 Remove the custard from the heat and pour it through a fine mesh strainer into a clean bowl.
5 Add the softened gelatin to the hot custard. Chill until thick in an ice bath, stirring regularly to prevent lumps from forming, until the custard reaches 75°F (24°C) or slightly cooler. Fold in the whipped cream.
6 Pour the Bavarian cream immediately into serving dishes or a cake-lined mold. Chill completely before serving.

Note Gelatin may separate in the freezer, so quick chilling is not recommended. Products made with gelatin keep well for 1–2 days but stiffen with age.

1 Adding softened gelatin to the hot custard base.

2 Folding in the whipped cream.

Variations:

Charlotte Bavarian—Line a 2–2½-quart (2–2.5-liter) charlotte mold with spongecake cut into strips or ladyfingers. Fill with alternating layers of fruit and Bavarian cream. Chill completely, then invert onto a serving platter when firm and garnish with whipped cream.

White Chocolate Hazelnut Bavarian—Omit the milk, sugar and egg yolks. Increase the cream to 1 quart (960 milliliters). Melt 2 pounds (960 grams) chopped white chocolate in the heavy cream. Remove from the heat and stir in 10 fluid ounces (300 milliliters) hazelnut liqueur. Add the softened gelatin. Chill as in Step 5 then fold in the whipped cream. Portion into individual serving dishes. Garnish with chopped hazelnuts and shaved chocolate.

Approximate values per 3.5-fl.-oz. (105-ml) serving: **Calories** 230, **Total fat** 15 g, **Saturated fat** 9 g, **Cholesterol** 135 mg, **Sodium** 30 mg, **Total carbohydrates** 19 g, **Protein** 3 g, **Vitamin A** 20%

White Chocolate Hazelnut Bavarian

Chiffon

A **chiffon** is similar to a Bavarian except that whipped egg whites instead of whipped cream are folded into the thickened base. The base may be a custard or a fruit mixture thickened with cornstarch. Although a chiffon may be molded like a Bavarian, it is most often used as a pie or tart filling.

Procedure for Preparing Chiffons

1 Prepare the base, which is usually a custard or a fruit mixture thickened with cornstarch.
2 Add gelatin to the warm base.
3 Fold in whipped egg whites.
4 Pour into a mold or pie shell and chill.

♥ Good Choice

Lime Chiffon

MISE EN PLACE

- Zest and juice limes.

YIELD 8 Servings, approximately 3 oz. (90 g) each

Granulated gelatin	0.25 oz. (¼ oz.)	7 g
Water	5 fl. oz.	150 ml
Granulated sugar	7 oz.	210 g
Fresh lime juice	5 fl. oz.	150 ml
Lime zest, grated fine	0.2 oz. (1 Tbsp.)	6 g
Egg yolks, pasteurized	2.4 oz. (4 yolks)	72 g
Egg whites, pasteurized	4 oz. (4 yolks)	120 g
Crumb or other pie crust, baked, optional	1 shell	1 shell

1 Soften the gelatin in 1 fluid ounce (30 milliliters) water.

2 Combine 4 ounces (120 grams) sugar with the remaining water, lime juice, lime zest and egg yolks in a bowl over a pan of simmering water.

3 Whisk the egg-and-lime mixture together vigorously until it begins to thicken. Add the softened gelatin and continue whipping until very thick and foamy.

4 Remove from the heat, cover and refrigerate until cool and as thick as whipping cream.

5 Meanwhile whip the egg whites to soft peaks. Whip in the remaining sugar and continue whipping until stiff but not dry.

6 Fold the whipped egg whites into the egg-and-lime mixture. Pour into serving dishes or a prepared pie crust and chill for several hours, until firm.

Variations:

Lemon Chiffon—Substitute lemon juice and lemon zest for the lime juice and zest.

Orange Chiffon—Substitute orange juice for the lime juice and for 4 fluid ounces (120 milliliters) water. Substitute orange zest for the lime zest. Reduce the amount of sugar in the egg yolk mixture to 1 ounce (30 grams).

Approximate values per 3-oz. (90-g) serving: **Calories** 140, **Total fat** 2.5 g, **Saturated fat** 1 g, **Cholesterol** 105 mg, **Sodium** 35 mg, **Total carbohydrates** 26 g, **Protein** 4 g, **Claims**—low fat; low saturated fat; low sodium

⚠ Safety Alert

Egg Products in Uncooked Mousses

Pasteurized egg products are recommended for most mousse formulas, because mousses require no further cooking. Pasteurized eggs are heated and held at the proper temperatures for sufficient time to kill harmful bacteria such as *Salmonella enteritidis*. One exception is Italian meringue; the hot sugar syrup cooks the egg whites to a temperature that makes them safe for consumption.

Mousse

The term *mousse* applies to an assortment of dessert creams not easily classified elsewhere. A **mousse** is similar to a Bavarian or chiffon in that it is lightened with whipped cream, whipped egg whites or both. A mousse is generally softer than these other products, however, and only occasionally contains a small amount of gelatin. A mousse is generally too soft to mold. A mousse may be served alone as a dessert or used as a filling in cakes or pastry items. Plan on serving 4–6 fluid ounces (120–360 milliliters) of mousse per serving as a stand-alone dessert. Sweet mousses can be based on a custard sauce, melted chocolate or puréed fruit. Savory mousses are discussed in Chapter 28, Charcuterie.

Procedure for Preparing Mousses

1 Prepare the base, which is usually a custard sauce, melted chocolate or puréed fruit.

2 If gelatin is used, it is softened first, then dissolved in the warm base.

3 Fold in whipped pasteurized egg whites (if using). If the base is slightly warm when the egg whites are added, their proteins will coagulate, making the mousse firmer and more stable.

4 Allow the mixture to cool completely, then fold in whipped cream (if using). Note that the egg whites are folded in before any whipped cream. Although the egg whites may deflate somewhat during folding, if the cream is added first it may become overwhipped when the egg whites are added, creating a grainy or coarse product.

Classic Chocolate Mousse

YIELD 1½–2 qt. (1.5–2 lt), 16 Servings, 3 fl. oz. (90 ml) each

Bittersweet chocolate	15 oz.	450 g
Unsalted butter	9 oz.	270 g
Egg yolks, pasteurized	4.2 oz. (7 yolks)	126 g
Egg whites, pasteurized	11 oz. (11 whites)	330 g
Granulated sugar	2.5 oz.	75 g
Heavy cream	8 fl. oz.	240 ml

1 Melt the chocolate and butter in a double boiler over low heat. Stir until no lumps remain.

2 Allow the mixture to cool slightly to 120°F (48°C), then whisk in the egg yolks one at a time.

3 Beat the egg whites until soft peaks form. Slowly beat in the sugar and continue beating until stiff peaks form. Whisk one-fourth of the whipped egg whites into the chocolate mixture to lighten, then fold in the remaining whites.

4 Whip the cream to soft peaks. Allow the mousse to cool to 90–95°F (32–35°C), then fold in the whipped cream. Make sure no streaks of egg white or cream remain.

5 Spoon the mousse into serving bowls and garnish with whipped cream, fresh berries, shaved chocolate or mint. Or chill the mousse completely, then pipe it into bowls or baked tartlet shells. The mousse may also be used as a cake or pastry filling.

Approximate values per 3-fl.-oz. (90-ml) serving: **Calories** 370, **Total fat** 31 g, **Saturated fat** 18 g, **Cholesterol** 215 mg, **Sodium** 50 mg, **Total carbohydrates** 16 g, **Protein** 7 g, **Vitamin A** 25%

① Folding in the whipped egg whites.

② Folding in the whipped cream.

FROZEN DESSERTS

Frozen desserts include ice cream and gelato and desserts assembled with ice cream, such as baked Alaska, bombes and parfaits. Frozen fruit purées, known as sorbets and sherbets, are also included in this category. Still-frozen desserts, known as **semifreddi**, are made from custards or mousses that are frozen without churning.

When making any frozen mixture, remember that cold dulls flavors. Even if something tastes perfect at room temperature, flavors seem weaker when a mixture is cold. Thus it may be necessary to oversweeten or overflavor creams or custards that will be frozen for service.

Although liquors and liqueurs are common flavoring ingredients, alcohol drastically lowers a liquid mixture's freezing point. Too much alcohol prevents the mixture from freezing, so any liqueurs or liquors must be used in moderation.

Ice creams and sorbets are usually served by the scoop, often in cookie cones. Or they can be served as sundaes. More formal presentations include **baked Alaska**, **bombes**, **coupes** and **parfaits**.

baked Alaska ice cream set on a layer of spongecake and encased in meringue, then baked until the meringue is warm and golden

bombe two or more flavors of ice cream, or ice cream and sherbet, shaped in a spherical mold; each flavor is a separate layer that forms the shell for the next flavor

coupe another name for an ice cream sundae, especially one served with a fruit topping

parfait ice cream served in a long, slender glass with alternating layers of topping or sauce; also the name of the mousse-like preparation that forms the basis for some still-frozen desserts

⚠ **Safety Alert**

Ice Cream

It is important to exercise extra care when preparing ice cream products because ice cream contains several foods that may require time and temperature control for safety (TCS), such as cream, milk and eggs. Properly cooking ice cream bases and using pasteurized egg products helps ensure a safe product. Ice cream makers have many grooves and crevices where bacteria can hide and grow. Always break down and clean an ice cream maker after each use, and sanitize all pieces according to the manufacturer's directions. Never store frozen ice cream products in a container that held raw or unprocessed custard without first cleaning and sanitizing the container. And, of course, wash your hands thoroughly and wear gloves when working with ice cream products.

overrun a measure of the air churned into an ice cream; expressed as a percentage, which reflects the increase in volume of the ice cream greater than the amount of the base used to produce the product

Ice Cream and Gelato

Ice cream and gelato are custards that are churned during freezing. They can be flavored with an endless variety of fruits, nuts, liqueurs, cookies and candies. Contemporary chefs and boutique ice cream producers also offer products made with vegetables, herbs and savory flavorings such as bacon. The USDA has established standards for the labeling of frozen products. They require that products labeled **ice cream** contain at least 10 percent milkfat and 20 percent milk solids and have no more than 50 percent **overrun**. French-style ice creams (**frozen custards**) contain a higher percentage of egg yolks and cream than standard ice cream. **Gelato** is an Italian-style ice cream made primarily with milk. Although it has a low milkfat content—from 4 to 9 percent—gelato is denser than American-style products because less air is incorporated during churning. **Ice milk** refers to products that do not meet the standards for ice cream. Low-fat products made without cream or egg yolks are also available for the calorie-conscious. **Frozen yogurt** uses yogurt as its base. Although touted as a nutritious substitute for ice cream, frozen yogurt may have whole milk or cream added for richness and smoothness.

One hallmark of good ice cream and gelato is smoothness. The ice crystals that would normally form during freezing can be avoided by incorporating air through constant stirring or churning. The air causes the mixture to expand. Gelato is denser than ice cream because it has less incorporated air. Good-quality ice creams have enough air to make them light; inferior products often contain excessive overrun and are therefore too light. The difference becomes obvious when equal volumes are weighed.

Many food service operations use ice cream makers that have internal freezing units to chill the mixture while churning it. Most commercial machines are suitable for churning either ice cream or sorbet. Follow the manufacturer's directions for using and cleaning any ice cream maker.

Ice Cream through History

Early ancestors of today's ice creams were flavored water ices, which have been popular in China since prehistoric times. They have also been popular in the Mediterranean and Middle East since the Golden Age of Greece. In fact, Alexander the Great had a penchant for wine-flavored ices, made with ice brought down from the mountains by runners. The Roman emperor Nero served his guests mixtures of fruit crushed with snow and honey. The Saracens brought their knowledge of making flavored ices with them when they migrated to Sicily in the ninth century. And 12th-century crusaders returned to Western Europe with memories of Middle Eastern sherbets.

The Italians are said to have developed gelato from a recipe brought back from China by Marco Polo in the 13th century. Somehow the dish spread to England by the 15th century, where it was recorded that King Henry V served it at his coronation banquet. Catherine de Medici brought the recipe with her when she married the future king of France in 1533. A different flavor was served during each of the 34 days of their marriage festivities.

Ice cream was first sold to the public in Paris during the late 17th century. It was available at fashionable cafés serving another new treat: coffee. French chefs quickly developed many elaborate desserts using ice creams, including bombes, coupes and parfaits.

Many of America's founders—Thomas Jefferson, Alexander Hamilton and James and Dolley Madison—were confirmed ice cream addicts. George Washington spent more than $200, a very princely sum, for ice cream during the summer of 1790.

The mechanized ice cream freezer was invented in 1846, setting the stage for mass production and wide availability. By the late 19th century, ice cream parlors were popular gathering places.

Despite the disappearance of most ice cream wagons, soda fountains and lunch counters, all of which were popular ice cream purveyors for much of the 20th century, ice cream sales remain steady. The United States leads the world in consumption, at 23 pounds per person per year, more than 80 percent of which is sold in supermarkets or convenience stores. The public's demand for high-fat, homemade-style, "super-premium" ice creams with rich and often-elaborate flavor combinations shows no sign of declining.

Procedure for Preparing Ice Creams

1 Place the milk and/or cream in a heavy saucepan. If a vanilla bean is being used, it may be added at this time.

2 Whisk the egg yolks and sugar together in a mixing bowl.

3 Bring the liquid just to a boil. Temper the egg mixture with approximately one-third of the hot liquid.

4 Pour the tempered eggs into the remaining hot liquid and return the mixture to the heat.

5 Cook, stirring constantly, until the custard reaches 180–185°F (82–85°C) and is slightly thickened.

6 Remove the ice cream base from the hot saucepan immediately. If left in the hot saucepan, it will overcook. Flavorings may be added at this time.

7 Cool the cooked ice cream base over an ice bath. Store covered and refrigerated at 36°F (2°C) 24 hours to mature the ice cream base before using.

8 Process according to the machine manufacturer's directions.

Ice Cream Base

YIELD 2½ qt. (2.5 lt)

Whole milk	1½ qt.	1.5 lt
Heavy cream	1 pt.	480 ml
Vanilla bean, split, optional	1	1
Egg yolks	9.6 oz. (16 yolks)	288 g
Granulated sugar	1 lb. 4 oz.	600 g

1 Combine the milk and cream in a heavy saucepan and bring to a boil. Add the vanilla bean (if using).

2 Whisk the egg yolks and sugar together in a mixing bowl.

3 Temper the eggs with one-third of the hot milk. Return the egg mixture to the saucepan.

4 Cook over medium heat, stirring constantly, until the custard reaches 180–185°F (82–85°C). Pour through a fine mesh strainer into a clean bowl.

5 Chill the cooked ice cream base in an ice bath, then refrigerate overnight before processing.

Variations:

Chocolate Ice Cream—Add approximately 9 ounces (270 grams) finely chopped bittersweet chocolate per quart (liter) of ice cream base. Add the chocolate to the hot mixture after it has been strained. Stir until completely melted.

Cappuccino Ice Cream—Steep the hot milk and cream with the vanilla bean and 2 or 3 cinnamon sticks. After the ice cream base is made, stir in 1–1½ fluid ounces (30–45 milliliters) coffee extract.

Brandied Cherry Ice Cream—Drain the liquid from one 16-ounce (500-gram) can of tart, pitted cherries. Soak the cherries in 1½ fluid ounces (45 milliliters) brandy. Reduce the sugar to 16 ounces (480 grams), omit the vanilla bean and prepare the ice cream base as directed. Add the brandy-soaked cherries to the cooled custard before processing.

Approximate values per 6-fl.-oz. (180-ml) serving: **Calories** 370, **Total fat** 20 g, **Saturated fat** 11 g, **Cholesterol** 270 mg, **Sodium** 65 mg, **Total carbohydrates** 41 g, **Protein** 7 g, **Vitamin A** 25%

MISE EN PLACE

- Set up an ice bath.
- Split vanilla bean in half (if using).

Mise en place for ice cream base

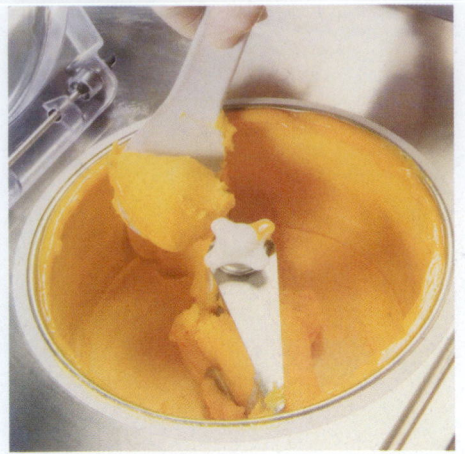

Scraping Mango Sorbet from a batch ice cream machine.

Sorbet and Sherbet

Sorbet is a churned mixture of sugar, water and fruit juice, wine, liqueurs or other flavorings. (Herb and vegetable flavorings are especially suitable for sorbet.) It is served as a first course, a palate refresher between courses or a dessert.

Sorbet may be made with fresh, frozen or canned fruit. A wide variety of quality, all-natural frozen purées are also available for sorbet making. Granulated sugar or sugar syrup is added for flavor and body. Pasteurized egg whites may also be added during churning for improved texture; the protein in the whites coats the water crystals as the sorbet freezes. Often an invert sugar such as corn syrup or glucose replaces some of the granulated sugar to prevent graininess. *Sherbet* is an Americanization of the French word *sorbet*, which has taken on a slightly different meaning on this side of the Atlantic. When it contains fruit juice and sugar, **sherbet** is identical to sorbet. But milk is often added to the mixture before churning, making it somewhat richer than sorbet and more appropriate to serve at the end of a meal than as a first course or palette refresher.

The ratio of sugar to fruit purée or juice depends to some extent on the natural sweetness of the specific fruit as well as personal preference. If too much sugar is used, however, the mixture will be soft and syrupy. If too little sugar is used, the sorbet will be very hard and grainy. Following the formula carefully helps avoid this problem.

♥ Good Choice   Ⓥ Vegan

Grapefruit Sorbet

YIELD 1½ qt. (1.5 lt)

Fresh grapefruit juice	1 qt.	1 lt
Granulated sugar	8 oz.	240 g

1 Combine the juice and sugar.

2 Process mixture in an ice cream maker according to the manufacturer's directions.

3 Pack into a clean container and freeze until firm.

Variations:

Lemon Sorbet—Substitute fresh lemon juice for the grapefruit juice in the recipe.

Mango Sorbet—Combine 2.2 pounds (1 kilogram) mango purée with 8 fluid ounces (240 milliliters) medium sugar syrup.

Raspberry Sorbet—Combine 2.2 pounds (1 kilogram) puréed, strained raspberries with 1 pound (500 grams) granulated sugar and 1 fluid ounce (30 milliliters) lemon juice.

Approximate values per 3-fl.-oz. (90-ml) serving: **Calories** 94, **Total fat** 0 g, **Saturated fat** 0 g, **Cholesterol** 0 mg, **Sodium** 1 mg, **Total carbohydrates** 23 g, **Protein** 0.5 g, **Vitamin C** 36%, **Claims**—no fat; no cholesterol; very low sodium; low calorie

Still-Frozen Desserts

Still-frozen desserts (It. *semifreddi*) are made with frozen mousse, custard or cream. Layers of spongecake and/or fruit may be added for flavor and texture. Because these mixtures are frozen without churning, air must be incorporated by folding in relatively large amounts of whipped cream or meringue. The air helps keep the mixture smooth and prevents it from becoming too hard.

Still-frozen products include frozen soufflés, **marquise**, mousses and **neapolitans**. The Chocolate Hazelnut Marquise recipe at the end of this chapter (page 1093) is an example of a still-frozen dessert.

marquise *a frozen mousse-like dessert, usually chocolate*

neapolitan *a three-layered loaf or cake of ice cream; each layer is a different flavor and different color, a typical combination is chocolate, vanilla and strawberry*

DESSERT SAUCES

Pastries and desserts are often accompanied by sweet sauces. Dessert sauces provide moisture, flavor and texture and enhance plate presentation. Sauces may be based on milk and cream, such as Vanilla Custard Sauce (page 1068), the principal dessert sauce. Like any master sauce, custard sauce can be flavored and colored with chocolate, coffee extract, liquor or fruit compound as desired. Other dessert sauces include fruit purées, caramel sauce and chocolate syrup. Sauces should be selected to contrast or complement the dessert or pastry with which they are served. For example, a raspberry soufflé can be complemented by an intense raspberry purée or contrasted with a rich chocolate sauce.

Sundae or coupe with raspberry coulis, Crème Chantilly and nuts

Fruit Purées

Many types of fruit can be puréed for dessert sauces; strawberries, raspberries, blackberries, apricots, mangoes and papayas are popular choices. They produce thick sauces with strong flavors and colors. Fresh ripe fruit or individually quick-frozen (IQF) fruit are recommended. Several commercial brands of prepared fruit purées are available. The best use only natural fruits and are excellent for making sauces and sorbets. They provide consistent flavor and color, reduce preparation time, and make out-of-season or hard-to-obtain tropical fruits available at a reasonable price.

coulis [coo-lee] a sauce made from a purée of fruits or vegetables

    Puréed fruit sauces, also known as **coulis**, can be cooked or uncooked. Cooking thickens the sauces by reduction and allows any starch thickener to gelatinize. They can also be sweetened with granulated sugar or sugar syrup. The amount of sweetener will vary depending on the fruit's natural sweetness and personal preference.

Procedure for Preparing a Fruit Coulis

1 Wash, peel and chop the fruit if necessary. Thaw frozen fruit before using.

2 Purée the fruit in a food mill, blender or food processor. Strain to remove seeds.

3 Combine the purée with flavorings and sweeteners (if using).

Raspberry Sauce

 Vegan    Good Choice

YIELD 1 qt. (1 lt)

Raspberries, fresh or frozen	2 lb.	1 kg
Granulated sugar	1 lb.	500 g
Lemon juice	1 fl. oz.	30 ml

1 Purée the berries and strain through a fine chinois.

2 Stir in the sugar and lemon juice. Adjust the flavor with additional sugar if necessary.

Approximate values per 1-fl.-oz. (30-ml) serving: **Calories** 70, **Total fat** 0 g, **Saturated fat** 0 g, **Cholesterol** 0 mg, **Sodium** 0 mg, **Total carbohydrates** 17 g, **Protein** 0 g, **Claims**—fat free; no saturated fat; no cholesterol; no sodium

MISE EN PLACE

• Thaw raspberries if necessary.

Caramel Sauce

Caramel sauce is a mixture of caramelized sugar and heavy cream. A liqueur or citrus juice may be used for added flavor. Review the material on caramelizing sugar in Chapter 30, Principles of the Bakeshop, before making caramel sauce.

Caramel Sauce

MISE EN PLACE

- Bring cream to room temperature.
- Cut butter into pieces.

YIELD 1 qt. (1 lt)

Granulated sugar	1 lb. 2 oz.	540 g
Water	4 fl. oz.	120 ml
Lemon juice	0.5 fl. oz.	15 ml
Heavy cream, room temperature	8 fl. oz.	240 ml
Unsalted butter, cut into pieces	1 oz.	30 g

1 Combine the sugar and water in a heavy saucepan. Stir to moisten the sugar completely. Place the saucepan on the stove top over high heat and bring to a boil. Brush down the sides of the pan with a pastry brush dipped in water to remove any sugar granules.

2 When the sugar comes to a boil, add the lemon juice. Do not stir the sugar, as this may cause lumping. Continue boiling until the sugar caramelizes at approximately 338°F (170°C). It will turn a dark golden brown and produce a rich aroma.

3 Remove the saucepan from the heat. Gradually add the cream. Be extremely careful, as the hot caramel may splatter. Whisk in the cream to blend.

4 Add the pieces of butter. Stir until the butter melts completely. If necessary, return the sauce to the stove to reheat enough to melt the butter.

5 Strain the sauce and cool completely at room temperature. The sauce may be stored for several weeks under refrigeration. Stir before using.

Approximate values per 1-fl.-oz. (30-ml) serving: **Calories** 130, **Total fat** 7 g, **Saturated fat** 4 g, **Cholesterol** 25 mg, **Sodium** 5 mg, **Total carbohydrates** 16 g, **Protein** 0 g, **Vitamin A** 8%

Chocolate Syrup

Chocolate syrup or sauce can be prepared by adding finely chopped chocolate to warm vanilla custard sauce. A darker syrup can be made with unsweetened chocolate or cocoa powder. Fudge-type sauces, like the Chocolate Fudge Sauce (page 1094) at the end of this chapter are variations on Chocolate Ganache (page 1048), discussed in Chapter 34, Cakes and Frostings.

Dark Chocolate Syrup

YIELD 1 qt. (1 lt)

Cocoa powder	4 oz.	120 g
Water	24 fl. oz.	720 ml
Granulated sugar	1 lb.	480 g
Unsalted butter	6 oz.	180 g
Heavy cream	2 fl. oz.	60 ml

1 Mix the cocoa powder with just enough of the water to make a smooth paste.

2 Bring the sugar and remaining water to a boil in a small, heavy saucepan. Immediately add the cocoa paste, whisking until smooth.

3 Simmer for 15 minutes, stirring constantly, then remove from the heat.

4 Stir the butter and cream into the warm cocoa mixture. Serve warm or at room temperature.

Approximate values per 1-fl.-oz. (30-ml) serving: **Calories** 120, **Total fat** 6 g, **Saturated fat** 3 g, **Cholesterol** 15 mg, **Sodium** 0 mg, **Total carbohydrates** 16 g, **Protein** 1 g, **Vitamin A** 6%

ASSEMBLING DESSERTS

As noted previously, many pastries and other desserts are assembled from the baked doughs discussed in Chapter 33, Pies, Pastries and Cookies; the cakes, icings and glazes discussed in Chapter 34, Cakes and Frostings; and the creams, custards and other products discussed in this chapter. Many of these desserts are classic presentations requiring the precise arrangement of specific components. With a basic mastery of the skills presented in this book, student chefs can use creativity, taste and judgment to combine these components into a wide selection of unique and tempting desserts.

Assembled pastries and other desserts generally consist of three principal components: the base, the filling and the garnish. The **base** is the dough, crust or cake product that provides structure and forms the foundation for the final product. The **filling** refers to whatever is used to add flavor, texture and body to the final product. The **garnish** is any glaze, fruit, sauce or accompaniment used to complete the dish.

The following are important guidelines for assembling desserts:

- There should be a proper blend of complementary and contrasting flavors. For example, pears, red wine and blue cheese go well together, as do chocolate and raspberries. Do not combine flavors simply for the sake of originality, however.
- There should be a proper blend of complementary and contrasting textures. For example, crisp puff pastry, soft pastry cream and tender strawberries are combined for a Strawberry Napoleon.
- There should be a proper blend of complementary and contrasting colors. For example, a garnish of red raspberries and green mint adds life to a brown-on-brown chocolate torte.
- Garnishes should not be overwhelming or garish.
- The base should be strong enough to hold the filling and garnish without collapsing, yet thin or tender enough to cut easily with a fork.
- The filling or garnish may cause the base to become soft or even soggy. This may or may not be desirable. If you want a crisp base, assemble the product very close to service. If you want this softening to occur, assemble the product in advance of service.
- Consider the various storage and keeping qualities of the individual components. It may be best to assemble or finish some products at service time.
- The final construction should not be so elaborate or fragile that it cannot be portioned or served easily or attractively.
- Consider whether the product would be better prepared as individual portions or as one large item. This may depend on the desired plate presentation and the ease and speed with which a large product can be cut and portioned for service.

Today's restaurant desserts are a far cry from a humble slice of apple pie and scoop of ice cream, although a well-crafted pie using ripe fruit in season cannot be beat. With the popularity of plated desserts, pastry chefs have more opportunity to develop their style. Plated desserts may include several sweets on one visually stunning plate: a main item served hot accompanied by a cold garnish and something acidic or crunchy as a contrast. Concepts for presenting desserts are covered in more detail in Chapter 36, Plate Presentation. A balance among contrasting tastes, textures and temperatures allows a dessert plate to appeal to all the senses.

Cheesecake baked in an individual mold, pineapple kebab and mango sorbet garnished with fresh fruit and chopped nuts

QUESTIONS FOR DISCUSSION

1 Eggs and dairy products are susceptible to bacterial contamination. What precautions should be taken to avoid food-borne illnesses when preparing custards?

2 Explain why pastry cream is boiled and why custard sauce is not.

3 Identify and describe three desserts that are based on a baked custard.

4 Compare a classically prepared Bavarian, chiffon, mousse and soufflé. How are they similar? How are they different? Describe how each might be used in making or serving a more complex pastry or dessert item.

5 Describe the procedure for making a typical still-frozen dessert. What is the purpose of including whipped cream or whipped egg whites?

6 Explain three ways to use sweet sauces when preparing or presenting a dessert.

7 Locate the websites of three manufacturers or distributors of prepared dessert sauces. How do these products compare with sauces that you could make from scratch? What additional information—not available on the Internet—would you need in order to make a decision about using these sauces?

Additional Custard, Cream, Frozen Dessert and Dessert Sauce Formulas

Crème Brûlée

Vincent on Camelback, Phoenix, AZ
Chef Vincent Guerithault

YIELD 11 Servings, 5 fl. oz. (150 ml) each	METHOD Stirred Custard	
Heavy cream	1 qt.	1 lt
Vanilla bean, split	1	1
Egg yolks	15 oz. (25 yolks)	450 g
Granulated sugar	10 oz.	300 g
Fresh berries	as needed	as needed
Tulipe Cookie cups (page 1024)	as needed	as needed
Granulated sugar	as needed	as needed

1 Place the cream and the vanilla bean in a large, heavy saucepan. Heat just to a boil.

2 Whisk the egg yolks and sugar together until smooth and well blended.

3 Temper the egg mixture with one-third of the hot cream. Return the egg mixture to the saucepan and cook, stirring constantly, until very thick. Do not allow the custard to boil.

4 Remove from the heat and strain into a clean bowl. Cool over an ice bath, stirring occasionally.

5 To serve, place fresh berries in the bottom of each Tulipe Cookie cup. Top with several spoonfuls of custard.

6 Sprinkle granulated sugar over the top of the custard and caramelize with a propane torch. Serve immediately.

Variation:

Passion Fruit Crème Brûlée—Replace 8 fluid ounces (240 milliliters) cream with 8 fluid ounces (240 milliliters) frozen, thawed passion fruit purée.

Approximate values per 5-fl.-oz. (150-ml) serving: **Calories** 460, **Total fat** 36 g, **Saturated fat** 20 g, **Cholesterol** 480 mg, **Sodium** 135 mg, **Total carbohydrates** 26 g, **Protein** 7 g, **Vitamin A** 50%

Chocolate Pots de Crème

YIELD 8 Servings, 4 fl. oz. (120 ml) each	METHOD Baked Custard	
Milk	1 pt.	480 ml
Bittersweet chocolate	8 oz.	240 g
Granulated sugar	7 oz.	210 g
Vanilla extract	0.15 fl. oz. (1 tsp.)	5 ml
Coffee liqueur	1 fl. oz.	30 ml
Egg yolks	4.2 oz. (7 eggs)	126 g

1 Heat the milk just to a simmer. Add the chocolate and sugar. Stir constantly until the chocolate melts; do not allow the mixture to boil. Remove from the heat and add the vanilla extract and liqueur.

2 Whisk the egg yolks together, then slowly whisk them into the chocolate mixture.

3 Pour the custard into ramekins. Place the ramekins in a hotel pan and add enough hot water to reach halfway up the sides of the ramekins.

4 Bake at 325°F (160°C) until the custards are almost set in the center, approximately 30 minutes. Remove from the water bath and refrigerate until thoroughly chilled. Serve garnished with whipped cream and chocolate shavings.

Approximate values per 4-fl.-oz. (120-ml) serving: **Calories** 360, **Total fat** 16 g, **Saturated fat** 9 g, **Cholesterol** 195 mg, **Sodium** 40 mg, **Total carbohydrates** 46 g, **Protein** 6 g, **Vitamin A** 10%, **Calcium** 10%

New York Cheesecake

YIELD 2 Cakes, 8 in. (20 cm) each	METHOD Baked Custard	
Crust:		
Graham crackers, crushed	1 lb.	480 g
Butter, melted	6 oz.	180 g
Batter:		
Cream cheese, room temperature	3 lb. 6 oz.	1620 g
Granulated sugar	14 oz.	420 g
Eggs	13.2 oz. (8 eggs)	396 g
Cake flour or cornstarch	2 oz.	60 g
Vanilla extract	0.5 fl. oz. (1 Tbsp.)	15 ml
Lemon zest, grated fine	0.1 oz. (1½ tsp.)	3 g
Heavy cream	14 fl. oz.	420 ml

1 Combine the graham cracker crumbs with the melted butter. Press the mixture into the bottom of two 8-inch (20-centimeter) round springform pans. Bake for 12–15 minutes at 375°F (180°C) until the crust is dry to the touch. Set aside.

2 Blend the cream cheese and sugar on low speed in the bowl of a mixer fitted with the paddle attachment until no lumps remain. Scrape down the bowl often.

3 Add the eggs one at a time, waiting for each egg to be fully incorporated before adding more. Scrape down the bowl and paddle between each addition.

4 Add the flour and mix until combined. Add the remaining ingredients and mix to blend.

5 Divide the cheesecake batter evenly between the two pans. Wrap the bottom and sides of each pan in several layers of aluminum foil.

6 Preheat the oven to 300°F (150°C). Place the batter-filled pans in a hotel pan and set the hotel pan in the preheated oven. Pour in enough water to come halfway up the sides of the pans. Bake until the batter is set and no longer trembles, approximately 75–90 minutes.

7 Cool the cakes on a wire rack in their pans, then refrigerate them overnight. Remove the cakes from their pans.

Approximate values per ⅛-cake serving: **Calories** 770, **Total fat** 57 g, **Saturated fat** 34 g, **Cholesterol** 265 mg, **Sodium** 500 mg, **Total carbohydrates** 53 g, **Protein** 13 g, **Vitamin A** 40%, **Iron** 15%

Bread Pudding with Bourbon Sauce

YIELD 1 Full-Size Hotel Pan, 25 Servings,
5¾-oz. (172-g) each

METHOD Baked Custard

Raisins	8 oz.	240 g
Brandy	4 fl. oz.	120 ml
Unsalted butter, melted	2 oz.	60 g
White bread, day-old	1 lb. 8 oz.	720 g
Heavy cream	1 qt.	1 lt
Eggs	10 oz. (6 eggs)	300 g
Granulated sugar	1 lb. 10 oz.	780 g
Vanilla extract	1 fl. oz.	30 ml
Milk	1 qt.	1 lt
Bourbon Sauce (recipe follows)	as needed	as needed

1 Combine the raisins and brandy in a small saucepan. Heat just to a simmer, cover and set aside.

2 Use a portion of the butter to thoroughly coat a 2-inch- (5-centimeter-) deep full-size hotel pan. Reserve the remaining butter.

3 Tear the bread into chunks and place in a large bowl. Pour the cream over the bread and set aside until soft.

4 Beat the eggs and sugar until smooth and thick. Add the vanilla extract and milk. Stir in the remaining melted butter and the raisins and brandy.

5 Toss the egg mixture with the bread gently to blend. Pour into the hotel pan and bake at 350°F (180°C) until browned and almost set, approximately 45 minutes.

6 Serve warm with 1–1½ fluid ounces (30–45 milliliters) Bourbon Sauce.

Variation:

Chocolate Bread Pudding—Omit the brandy, raisins and butter. Melt 6 ounces (180 grams) unsalted butter and 12 ounces (360 grams) bittersweet chocolate together. Add the chocolate and butter to the egg mixture in Step 4. Serve with Vanilla Custard Sauce (page 1068).

Approximate values per 5 ¾-oz. (172-g) serving: **Calories** 700, **Total fat** 44 g, **Saturated fat** 26 g, **Cholesterol** 270 mg, **Sodium** 260 mg, **Total carbohydrates** 67 g, **Protein** 9 g, **Vitamin A** 50%, **Calcium** 10%, **Iron** 10%

Bourbon Sauce

YIELD 1 qt. (960 ml)

Unsalted butter	8 oz.	240 g
Granulated sugar	1 lb.	480 g
Eggs	3.3 oz. (2 eggs)	99 g
Bourbon	8 fl. oz.	240 ml

1 Melt the butter; stir in the sugar and eggs and simmer to thicken.

2 Add the bourbon and hold in a warm place for service.

Approximate values per 1-fl.-oz. (30-ml) serving: **Calories** 150, **Total fat** 8 g, **Saturated fat** 5 g, **Cholesterol** 40 mg, **Sodium** 50 mg, **Total carbohydrates** 19 g, **Protein** 1 g, **Vitamin A** 8%

Cherry Clafouti

Clafouti is a country-style dessert from the Loire region of France and is similar to a quiche. Stone fruits, such as cherries, peaches or plums, are baked in an egg custard and served piping hot or at room temperature.

YIELD 1 Cake, 10 in. (25 cm)	METHOD Baked Custard	
Dark cherries, fresh or canned, pitted	1 lb.	480 g
Eggs	6.6 oz. (4 eggs)	198 g
Milk	12 fl. oz.	360 ml
Granulated sugar	2 oz.	60 g
Vanilla extract	0.15 fl. oz. (1 tsp.)	5 ml
All-purpose flour	2 oz.	60 g
Powdered sugar	as needed	as needed

1 Drain the cherries and pat them completely dry with paper towels. Arrange them evenly on the bottom of a buttered 10-inch (25-centimeter) pan. Do not use a springform pan or removable-bottom tartlet pan.

2 Make the custard by whisking the eggs and milk together. Add the granulated sugar, vanilla extract and flour and continue whisking until all the lumps are removed.

3 Pour the custard over the cherries and bake at 325°F (160°C) for 1–1½ hours. The custard should be lightly browned and firm to the touch when done.

4 Dust the clafouti with powdered sugar and serve while still warm.

Approximate values per ⅒-cake serving: **Calories** 170, **Total fat** 3.5 g, **Saturated fat** 1.5 g, **Cholesterol** 90 mg, **Sodium** 4.5 mg, **Total carbohydrates** 30 g, **Protein** 5 g, **Vitamin A** 6%

Lemon Curd

A curd, which is usually flavored with citrus fruit or tropical flavors such as mango and fresh ginger, is a stirred custard prepared on the stovetop. Curd is used to top or fill a cake, cookie or pastry, to fill tartlets, as a topping on cheesecake, served with scones, lightened with whipped cream and served as a pudding, or stirred into freshly churned ice cream.

YIELD 1½ qt. (1.4 lt)	METHOD Stirred Custard	
Eggs	19.8 oz. (12 eggs)	594 g
Egg yolks	2.6 oz. (4 yolks)	72 g
Granulated sugar	2 lb.	960 g
Unsalted butter, cubed	1 lb.	480 g
Lemon zest	1 oz.	30 g
Fresh lemon juice	12 fl. oz.	360 ml

1 Whisk everything together in a large metal bowl.

2 Place the bowl over a pan of simmering water and cook, stirring frequently, until very thick, approximately 20–25 minutes.

3 Strain, cover and chill completely. Serve with scones or use as a filling for tartlets or layer cakes.

Variation:

Lime Curd—Substitute lime juice and zest for the lemon juice.

Approximate values per 1-fl.-oz. (30-ml) serving: **Calories** 170, **Total fat** 9 g, **Saturated fat** 5 g, **Cholesterol** 90 mg, **Sodium** 20 mg, **Total carbohydrates** 20 g, **Protein** 2 g, **Vitamin A** 10%

Buttermilk Panna Cotta

YIELD 8 Ramekins, 4 oz. (120 ml) each

Milk	8 fl. oz.	240 ml
Heavy cream	8 fl. oz.	240 ml
Vanilla bean, split	½	½
Granulated sugar	6 oz.	180 g
Sheet gelatin, softened	¼ oz.	7 g
Buttermilk	1 pt.	480 ml
Fresh berries and mint	as needed for garnish	

1 Bring the milk, cream, vanilla bean and sugar to a boil in a heavy nonreactive saucepan.

2 Remove the pan from the heat, then add the softened gelatin. Stir until the gelatin dissolves.

3 Slowly whisk the milk mixture into the buttermilk. Pour into 4-ounce (120 milliliter) ramekins, filling to just below the rim.

4 Cover and chill until completely set, approximately 8 hours.

5 Unmold onto individual serving plates and garnish with fresh berries and mint.

Variation:

Caramel Buttermilk Panna Cotta—Combine 10 ounces (300 grams) granulated sugar and 5 fluid ounces (150 milliliters) water in a small heavy saucepan; bring to a boil. Cook until the sugar reaches a deep golden brown. Immediately divide the caramel between eight 4-ounce (120-milliliter) ramekins, then proceed with the recipe. Unmold the chilled custards before serving.

Approximate values per 4-oz. serving: **Calories** 230, **Total fat** 110 g, **Saturated fat** 13 g, **Cholesterol** 45 mg, **Sodium** 90 mg, **Total carbohydrates** 26 g, **Protein** 4 g, **Calcium** 15%

Raspberry Mousse

YIELD 10 Servings, 3 fl. oz. (90 ml) each

Raspberries, puréed	12 oz.	360 g
Granulated sugar	3 oz.	90 g
Raspberry brandy	1 fl. oz.	30 ml
Sheet gelatin, softened	0.37 oz. (6 sheets)	12 g
Heavy cream	8 fl. oz.	240 ml

1 Place the raspberry purée, sugar and brandy in a nonreactive saucepan and warm to 115°F (46°C) to dissolve the sugar. Remove from the heat and strain through a fine chinois.

2 Add the softened sheet gelatin, stirring until it is dissolved. Chill the mixture until thick but not set.

3 Whip the cream to soft peaks and fold it into the raspberry mixture.

Approximate values per 3-fl.-oz. (90-ml) serving: **Calories** 180, **Total fat** 11 g, **Saturated fat** 7 g, **Cholesterol** 40 mg, **Sodium** 15 mg, **Total carbohydrates** 16 g, **Protein** 5 g, **Vitamin A** 10%

❶ Adding the softened gelatin sheets to the warm raspberry purée.

❷ Folding the softly whipped cream into the chilled raspberry mixture.

❤ Good Choice   ♥ Vegan

Coffee Granita

Granita (Fr. granité) is made with fruit or other flavorings but with less sugar than sorbet. This produces a mixture that will freeze harder than sorbet. Instead of being churned, the granita mixture is still-frozen in a shallow stainless steel container, then scraped with a fork or spoon to obtain grainy flakes. Or, as the mixture freezes and ice crystals form, the mixture is periodically stirred until granulation is complete.

YIELD 6 Servings, 4 fl. oz. (120 ml) each

Water	20 fl. oz.	600 ml
Granulated sugar	5 oz.	150 g
Coffee, ground	0.75 oz.	22 g

1 Bring 4 fluid ounces (120 milliliters) water and the sugar to a boil. Stir to dissolve the sugar. Remove the syrup from the heat and let cool.

2 Bring the remaining 16 fluid ounces (480 milliliters) water to a boil. Add the coffee and steep for 5 minutes. Strain the mixture and set aside to cool.

3 Combine the sugar syrup with the coffee liquid.

4 Pour into a shallow stainless steel pan and freeze until the granita begins to harden, approximately 3 hours.

5 Scrape the surface of the granita with a metal fork or spoon to break up the ice crystals. Return the granita to the freezer until firm.

6 Scrape the surface of the frozen granita to loosen the ice crystals. Scoop into serving dishes and serve immediately.

Approximate values per 4-fl.-oz. (120-ml) serving: **Calories** 100, **Total fat** 0 g, **Saturated fat** 0 g, **Cholesterol** 0 mg, **Sodium** 0 mg, **Total carbohydrates** 26 g, **Protein** 0 g, **Vitamin C** 15%. **Claims**—no fat; no cholesterol; very low sodium

❶ Scraping the ice crystals as they form in the granita.

❷ Spooning the finished Coffee Granita into a serving dish.

Chocolate Hazelnut Marquise with Hazelnut Sauce

YIELD 12 Servings, 3 oz. (120 g) each

Melted butter	as needed	as needed
Dark chocolate	1 lb.	480 g
Unsalted butter	4 oz.	120 g
Hazelnuts, roasted, skinned and chopped coarse	4 oz.	120 g
Egg yolks, pasteurized	3.6 oz. (6 yolks)	108 g
Hazelnut liqueur	2 fl. oz.	60 ml
Egg whites, pasteurized	6 oz. (6 whites)	180 g
Salt	1 pinch	1 pinch
Hazelnut Custard Sauce (page 1068)	as needed	as needed
Hazelnuts, roasted and chopped coarse	as needed for garnish	

1 Line a 12- × 4- × 3-in. (30- × 10- × 7.5-cm) terrine mold with melted butter and parchment paper.

2 Melt the chocolate and unsalted butter over a bain marie. Remove from the heat and stir in the nuts, egg yolks and hazelnut liqueur. Set aside to cool to room temperature. Do not use an ice bath, as the chocolate will solidify.

3 Whip the egg whites with the salt until stiff but not dry. Fold the whipped whites into the chocolate mixture.

4 Pour the mixture into the terrine mold and freeze overnight.

5 Remove the marquise from the mold and peel off the paper. (Work quickly because this melts quickly.) While the loaf is still frozen, use a hot knife to slice it into ⅓-inch- (8-millimeter-) thick slices. Return the marquise to the freezer until just before service.

6 Serve one or two slices of marquise on a pool of Hazelnut Custard Sauce. Garnish with coarsely chopped hazelnuts.

Approximate values per ½-loaf serving: **Calories** 380, **Total fat** 28 g, **Saturated fat** 14 g, **Cholesterol** 125 mg, **Sodium** 35 mg, **Total carbohydrates** 25 g, **Protein** 6 g, **Vitamin A** 10%

Fruit Coulis

 Vegan    Good Choice

YIELD Approximately 2 qt. (2 lt)

Fruit purée, strained	52 fl. oz.	1560 ml
Granulated sugar	8 oz.	240 g
Glucose or corn syrup	3 oz.	90 g
Lemon juice	2 fl. oz.	60 ml

1 Combine the strained fruit purée with the sugar and glucose or corn syrup. Add as much lemon juice as needed to balance the flavor of the sauce.

2 Serve warm or cold with fresh fruit, as a topping for ice cream or cake, or use as a sauce for plating.

Approximate values per 1-fl.-oz. (30 ml) serving: **Calories** 35, **Total fat** 0 g, **Saturated fat** 0 g, **Cholesterol** 0 mg, **Sodium** 5 mg, **Total carbohydrates** 8 g, **Protein** 0 g, **Claims**—low fat; no cholesterol; low sodium

Butterscotch Sauce

YIELD Approximately 2 qt. (2 lt)

Granulated sugar	1 lb. 8 oz.	720 g
Light corn syrup	2 lb. 4 oz.	1 kg
Unsalted butter	4 oz.	120 g
Heavy cream	10 fl. oz.	300 ml
Scotch whisky	4 fl. oz.	120 ml

1 Cook the sugar to a dark brown caramel. Add the corn syrup.

2 Remove the sugar from the heat and slowly add the butter and cream, stirring until the butter is completely melted.

3 Stir in the Scotch and cool. The sauce can be served warm or at room temperature as a topping for ice cream or cake, or used as a sauce for plating.

Approximate values per 1-fl.-oz. (30-ml) serving: **Calories** 120, **Total fat** 3 g, **Saturated fat** 2 g, **Cholesterol** 23 mg, **Sodium** 20 mg, **Total carbohydrates** 23 g, **Protein** 0 g, **Vitamin A** 4%, **Claims**—low fat; very low sodium

Chocolate Fudge Sauce

YIELD Approximately 2 qt. (2 lt)

Heavy cream	1 qt.	960 ml
Light corn syrup	3 fl. oz.	90 ml
Granulated sugar	4 oz.	120 g
Bittersweet chocolate	2 lb.	960 ml

1 Combine the cream, corn syrup and sugar in a saucepan and bring just to a boil, stirring frequently.

2 Chop the chocolate and place in a large bowl.

3 Pour the hot cream over the chocolate and stir until completely melted.

4 Store covered and refrigerated. Gently rewarm over a bain marie if desired. Use as a plating sauce, or a topping for ice cream or pastries such as baked meringues and profiteroles.

Approximate values per 1-fl.-oz. (30-ml) serving: **Calories** 130, **Total fat** 9 g, **Saturated fat** 6 g, **Cholesterol** 20 mg, **Sodium** 10 mg, **Total carbohydrates** 10 g, **Protein** 1 g, **Vitamin A** 6%

Plate Presentation

composition a completed plate's structure of colors, shapes and arrangements

Finally the real test has come. It is time to put down the spatula and set the whisk aside. The food is ready to be served. Although food preparation is very much a science, food presentation is an art. Good plate presentation results from careful attention to the colors, shapes, textures and arrangements of the foods. Great plate presentation requires experience and style.

This chapter describes several methods of presenting foods. For every guideline suggested, there are exceptions. Note that these examples are not meant to take the place of more traditional techniques. They are intended only to spark the imagination. With experience your personal style as a chef will evolve. The final step in food preparation is to justify the hours of hard work spent cooking the food by serving and presenting it properly. It is important that the creativity and skill that goes into cooking, baking or otherwise preparing the foods are not wasted because of a sloppy presentation or an unattractive garnish.

Service is the process of delivering the selected foods to diners in the proper fashion. Hot foods should be served very hot and on heated plates; cold foods should be served very cold and on chilled plates. Foods should be cooked to the proper degree of doneness: A roast rack of lamb ordered medium rare should be medium rare—not medium, not rare. Pasta should be served al dente—slightly chewy, not mushy. Bread should be fresh, not stale. Portion sizes should be appropriate. First courses and appetizers should be small enough so that the diner can still appreciate the courses that follow.

Presentation is the process of offering the selected foods to diners in a fashion that is visually pleasing. When presenting foods, always bear in mind that diners consume first with their eyes and then with their mouths. The foods must be pleasantly and appropriately colored, cut or molded. The colors, textures, shapes and arrangements of all foods must work together to form a pleasing **composition** on the plate. Any decorative touches such as the manipulation of sauces or the addition of garnishes should be done thoughtfully and well. Most important, plates should be neat and clean. Inspect all plates before they leave the kitchen; wipe fingerprints, drops of sauce or specks of food from their rims with a clean towel.

Presentation techniques are divided in this chapter into two broad categories: techniques applied to specific foods and techniques applied to the plate as a whole. Most of the techniques and concepts described here are illustrated with foods or recipes that appear elsewhere in the text. A brief discussion on small plates concludes the chapter.

PRESENTATION TECHNIQUES FOR FOOD

The most attractive foods are always the ones that are properly prepared, but some food can be made even more attractive by cutting or molding it into various shapes. Both techniques—cutting and molding—preserve the integrity of the food. In other words neither technique changes the food itself, but only changes the presentation of the food.

Preparing Foods Properly

Foods look best when properly prepared. A sirloin steak grilled medium rare should be pink inside; its surface should glisten and be branded with well-defined and neatly executed crosshatch marks. When serving asparagus with hollandaise, the stalks should be bright green and crisp looking; the hollandaise sauce should be smooth and shiny, not grainy and dingy. A lemon meringue pie should be attractively browned on top; the filling should be a true lemony yellow and the crust golden brown and without cracks.

Whether a recipe calls for browning foods under a salamander before service, poaching a galantine of chicken wrapped in cheesecloth to maintain its shape or adding vinegar when braising red cabbage, proper cooking procedures can enhance the texture, shape and color of many cooked foods. Throughout this text we have discussed the proper cooking procedures for many, many foods. By using these procedures you can properly prepare food and ensure that it will be attractive to diners.

Cutting Foods

The careful cutting of foods often increases visual appeal and reflects the chef's attention to detail. Here we distinguish between cutting food items used to decorate the plate and cutting the foods that are consumed. Decorative garnishes, such as tomato and radish roses, scallion brushes, carved melons and the like, fall within the former category. Cutting foods into beautiful garnishes is an art unto itself, requiring skill and practice. Although beyond the scope of this text, books on creating food garnishes are listed in the bibliography.

The latter category—foods that are consumed—includes the meats, poultry, fish, shellfish, vegetables and starches that form the meal. Each should be carefully cut. Vegetables can be cut into uniform shapes and sizes such as julienne, bâtonnet or tournée, discussed in Chapter 7, Knife Skills. Firm vegetables, such as beets, carrots, leeks, parsnips, potatoes, scallions and turnips, can be sliced or julienned and deep-fried to add color, flavor and texture to a plated dish. Stalk and firm vegetables, such as asparagus, pictured in the photograph to the right, can be transformed by shaving them into thin slices.

Seared diver scallops with shaved asparagus and beet purée

If serving sliced meats or poultry, the slices should be even and of a consistent thickness. Fish can be cut into tranches as discussed in Chapter 20, Fish and Shellfish. Individual stew ingredients and soup or salad garnishes should be of uniform sizes. All these techniques are simple, fundamental and effective.

Some foods take the shape of the pan in which they are cooked. Polenta and gratin or escalloped potatoes, for example, can be presented attractively when baked in and removed from individual casseroles, or they can be baked in a hotel pan and cut into various shapes according to the procedures that follow.

Procedure for Cutting Polenta

1 Cook the polenta according to the recipe. When it is done, pour the polenta onto a well-oiled half-sheet pan. Chill until firm.

2 Once the polenta is firm, flip the pan over onto a worktable. Lift off the pan; the polenta will come out easily. Using a chef's knife or circular cutters, cut the polenta into the desired shape. The polenta can be sautéed or grilled for service.

Cutting polenta into various shapes.

Procedure for Cutting Gratin or Escalloped Vegetables

Cutting potatoes with a circular cutter.

1 Select a recipe that produces a firm finished product so that the finished dish holds its shape after cutting.

2 Bake the sliced vegetables (often potatoes) in a well-greased pan and refrigerate until cold and firm. Cut chilled food into various shapes with a chef's knife or circular cutters and remove them to a clean pan with a spatula.

3 For service, reheat the cut pieces in a 325°F (160°C) oven until hot.

Molding Foods

Some foods, particularly cooked vegetables bound by sauces, grains or bound salads, can be molded into attractive shapes by using metal rings, circular cutters, ramekins, timbale molds or other forms. These molded forms create height and keep the plate neat and clean. For example, molded Ratatouille (page 642) forms the base for a crisp portion of seared sea bass shown in the photograph below. For a reinterpretation of ratatouille, a mold was used to hold slices of cooked vegetables upright before unmolding.

Molded ratatouille serves as the base for a seared fillet of sea bass.

Slices of eggplant, squash, tomato and zucchini are molded in a ring, then plated on a bed of red pepper purée.

Procedure for Molding Vegetables

❶ Position a ring mold on the plate and fill it with the cooked vegetables. Press the foods into the ring to help them hold the shape. Level the top.

❷ Carefully lift off the ring.

Procedure for Molding Grains

1   Fill a timbale mold, soup cup or other mold of the appropriate size and shape with the hot grains, firmly pressing them together.

2   For à la carte service immediately unmold the grains onto the serving plate by placing the mold upside down on the plate and tapping its sides and bottom.

3   For banquet service place the filled molds in a hotel pan and refrigerate until needed. Shortly before service fill the hotel pan with hot water to a point about two-thirds up the side of the molds. Be careful not to splash any water onto the grains. Cover the pan with foil and place in the oven. Heat until the grains are hot, then unmold and plate as desired.

Unmolding a timbale of rice.

Many soft and creamy foods can be molded into small ovals. One example is the dumpling-shaped quenelle discussed in Chapter 28, Charcuterie. Purées and mousses, such as mashed potatoes, risotto and salmon mousseline, as well as ice creams, custards and sorbets can be attractively shaped into quenelles as shown below using two large spoons.

Forming grapefruit sorbet into a quenelle shape using two spoons.

PRESENTATION TECHNIQUES FOR THE PLATE

The goal of plate presentation is a balanced, harmonious composition. Great care should be taken when placing foods on the plates. Properly cook and portion foods before positioning them carefully.

Garnishes, crumbs and sauces can further enhance the plate composition. Some techniques, such as decorating a dessert plate with powdered sugar, do not substantially affect the flavors of the foods; they only make the completed presentation more attractive. Other techniques (e.g., garnishing a dessert with finely chopped nuts or painting a plate with sauces) add flavor and texture to the finished dish.

Choosing Plates

Restaurant china designed to withstand the rigors of repeated use is available in many different shapes, sizes, colors and styles. It is often the chef's responsibility to choose the china appropriate for the food being served. Frequently specific plates will be used for specific dishes, such as a white, oven-proof pottery ramekin for Crème Brûlée (page 1072).

Plate Sizes and Shapes

Plates come in all shapes and sizes; round plates are classic, but oval plates (also referred to as platters) and rectangular, square and triangular plates are also popular. Plates are available in a variety of sizes from a small 4-inch (10-centimeter) bread plate

Salmon mousse with smoked salmon garnish

to a large 14-inch (35-centimeter) charger or base plate. Plates are typically concave; their depths vary within a limited range of about 1 inch (2.5 centimeters). Plates may have rims of varying widths or be rimless. Soup bowls can also be rimmed or rimless. Soup plates are usually larger and shallower than soup bowls and have wide rims. Soup cups are also available. There are also dozens of plate designs intended for a specific purpose, such as plates with small indentations for holding escargots, or long, rectangular plates with grooves for holding asparagus.

Choose plates large enough to hold the food comfortably without overcrowding or spilling. Oversized, rimmed soup plates are popular for serving any food with a sauce. Be careful when using oversized plates, however, as the food may look sparse, creating poor value perception.

Whether a round, oval or less conventionally shaped plate is used, be sure to choose one with a size and shape that best highlights the food and supports the composition. For example, in the photograph on page 1099, the asymmetrical pentagon-shaped bowl with graceful curved edges and raised rim accentuates the geometrically simple yet effective composition of the oval salmon timbale draped with a slice of smoked salmon.

Plate Colors and Patterns

Although styles of plates change from year to year, white and cream are by far the most common colors for restaurant china. Almost any food looks good on these neutral colors. Colored and patterned plates can be used quite effectively to accent food, however. The obvious choice is to contrast dark plates with bright- or light-colored foods and light plates with dark-colored foods. The food should always be the focal point of any plate. The colors and shapes in the plate pattern should blend well and harmonize with the foods served. The intense plum color on the plate shown to the left, for example, contrasts effectively with the green fava bean purée and uniform beige spheres of deep-fried risotto.

Arranging Foods on Plates

Compose plates to make the food appetizing to the customer. Strive for a well-balanced plate composition. A good composition is achieved by carefully considering the shapes, colors, textures and arrangement of foods on the plate.

Shapes

For visual interest and pure drama, combine a variety of shapes on the plate. The plated venison entrée shown to the left is an excellent example of simple shapes artfully combined: round venison medallions with oval fingerling potatoes and long spears of carrots and baby zucchini. The three complementary shapes lend harmony and character to the dish.

Colors

Foods come in a rainbow of colors. When appropriate, foods of different colors should be presented together. Generally the colors should provide balance and contrast. But no matter how well prepared or planned, some dishes simply have dull, boring or similar colors. When this is the case, try adding another ingredient or garnish for a splash of color. Complementary colors, those directly opposite each other on the color wheel such as red and green or yellow and purple, look good together in plating designs. A sauce with chopped herbs, a vegetable medley combining peas and carrots or well-browned foods contrast well with solid colors. The flecks of crisp green chives shown here work well with the flavors in the dish and add striking color notes to a plated lobster entrée that would otherwise be monochromatic. The artful placement of the curved lobster claws also adds to the visual appeal.

Deep-fried risotto with fava bean purée

Venison medallions with black currant sauce

Lobster à l'Americaine

Textures

Texture refers to the sensation perceived when eating a food as well as the appearance of the surface of the food. A food's texture may be crisp, crumbly, grainy, flaky, smooth or creamy. Mashed potatoes and carrot purée both look smooth and soft. Salmon mousseline and spinach soufflé both have slightly grainy surfaces. Rösti potatoes and meatloaf both appear coarse. The flavors of each food in these pairs differ; their visual textures do not.

Typically foods with similar textures look boring together; foods with different textures look more exciting when paired. Serve carrots cut into julienne with the mashed potatoes to achieve a balance of hard and soft textures. Plate steamed leaf spinach with the salmon mousseline for a combination of smooth and grainy textures. Offer a baked potato with the meatloaf so fluffy and coarse textures are paired in your presentation. These pairings maintain the same range of flavors as the pairs mentioned in the previous paragraph but provide different visual textures.

Using various cooking techniques helps add texture to the plate. Crisp fried and crusty baked foods contrast with smooth and soft ones such as fried chicken with mashed potatoes or poached salmon with roasted asparagus. Achieving a balance of texture on a plate can be as simple as adding a crisp garnish such as the fried julienned vegetables shown here served with a rack of lamb. This plate harmoniously combines several textures in one dish: the pebbly rice, the slices of smooth lamb and the coarse fried vegetables.

Another reason to vary the cooking techniques on a plate is for kitchen efficiency. A plate consisting of only sautéed items, such as sautéed fillet of sole with a pan sauce served with sautéed spinach, for example, would put pressure on the sauté station. Each component of such a dish would need to be cooked at the last moment by the sauté cook and plated at once. Serving the sautéed fillet of sole with a sauce that can be prepared ahead and held for service reduces pressure on the sauté cook as does offering a baked or broiled side dish. Consider elements that can be prepared by different cooking stations and prepared ahead to simplify plating.

Rack of lamb on a bed of rice, garnished with fried julienned vegetables

Composition

Having decided on the colors, textures and shapes of the foods that will go on the plate, the next choice is where to place each individual item to achieve a balanced and unified composition. A well-balanced composition is achieved with careful consideration of the arrangement of featured or main items on the plate as well as the negative space—sections of the plate that will not be covered with food. During recipe development, chefs often use a plate diagram to visualize the final composition. Like an artist who sketches a rough outline before completing a canvas, a chef sketches out where the featured food item(s) and garnishes are placed on the plate. For example, the featured item may be placed in a triangular, a bull's-eye or an asymmetrical layout as shown in Figures 36.1, 36.2 and 36.3. These are just a few of the countless layouts you can use to inspire your culinary artistry.

Once you have decided on the plate layout for the featured food items, consider these general guidelines when selecting complementary foods and arranging them on a plate:

- Strike a balance between overcrowding the plate and leaving large gaps of space. Foods should not hang over the plate rim nor be confined to the very center of the plate. As a rule of thumb, leave a small margin of space, ½–1 inch (1–2.5 centimeters) between the food on the plate and the edge of the plate or rim.
- Consider the number of elements of food on the plate such as pieces of meat or garnishes. In visual design, odd numbers create a desirable tension and even numbers can be unstimulating.
- Choose a focal point for the plate—that is, a point to which the eye is drawn. This may be the highest point on the plate. Or it may be the center of a linear arrangement that flows across the plate symmetrically.
- Design the plate with the highest point to the rear or center. Avoid placing foods of equal heights around the edge of the plate, leaving a hole in the center—the eye will naturally be drawn to that gap. See Figure 36.2.

Triangular placement of the featured item, the three shrimp, is balanced by a swirl of fettucine garnish in the center of the plate.

Two seared scallops rest on a bed of squash purée centered on a round plate. The cascade of cooked cauliflower, fried sage leaves and translucent sauce encircles the featured items in a bull's-eye layout.

This asymmetrical plating features seared Arctic char paired with a curve of vegetables. Colorful smoked salmon, peas and herb garnishes sit in a thick pea purée. The white space between the salmon and sauce creates a design element.

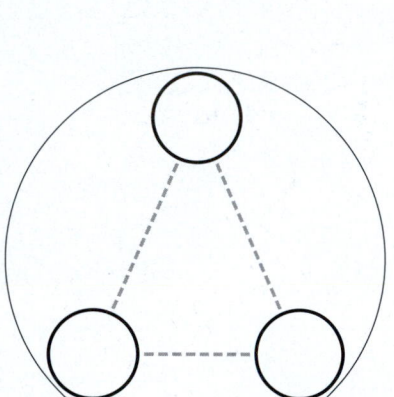

Figure 36.1 Triangular layout.

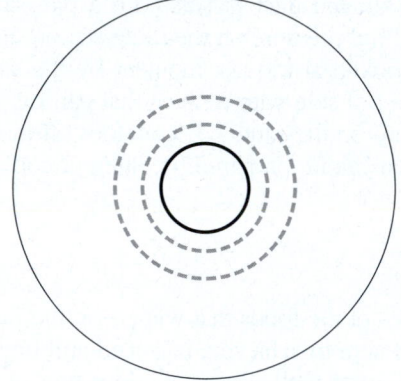

Figure 36.2 Bull's-eye layout.

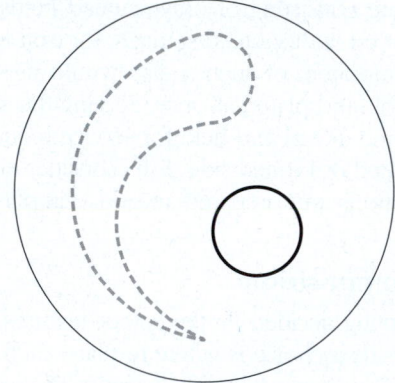

Figure 36.3 Asymmetrical layout.

- The plate's composition should flow naturally. As noted, it makes sense to establish the highest point at the back of the plate (12 o'clock from the customer's viewpoint) and have the rest of the food become gradually shorter toward the front of the plate. Fanning slices of food can attract the eye and help establish flow.
- Select garnishes and sauces for color as well as flavor. Orange and green are both secondary colors that work well together on the plate in Figure 36.3.

The seared scallops in Figure 36.2 elegantly illustrate these principles. Height is established by a structure composed of the squash purée, seared scallops and squash garnishes. The structure sits toward the back of the plate. Its height, placement and striking appearance make it the focal point. The cascade of cooked cauliflower, fried sage leaves and translucent sauce is in front of this focal point, drawing the viewer into the plate.

When planning the arrangement of foods and the accompanying garnishes on a plate, you must also keep the level of service and menu pricing in mind. In a casual diner or intimate café with a small kitchen staff and modest prices, a simple approach is appropriate. The featured item accompanied by a vegetable, a starch and some sauce may suffice. Designing a plate with several garnishes requires more time and staff to prepare and execute than a simpler plate. In a formal restaurant that offers a tasting menu, elaborate plating is expected by guests. Such restaurants have the staff required to execute such plates and charge for this accordingly.

The photographs shown here illustrate three ways to plate a pan-roasted boneless skinless airline chicken breast.

A traditional plating features a simple presentation of pan-roasted airline chicken breast on a bed of puréed potatoes. Sliced beets and whole cooked carrots are placed around the chicken, which is garnished with a small pool of pan gravy.

An alternative presentation of pan-roasted airline chicken breast employs an oversize oval plate and a flowing linear composition. The chicken is sliced then fanned out on a bed of puréed potatoes. The carrots and beets are cut asymmetrically and placed on the plate with dabs of pan gravy. Note that because the breast is sliced in this presentation, the same portion of chicken appears larger than in the traditional composition shown in the photograph on the left.

This plating of a pan-roasted airline chicken breast features baby carrots and candy cane beets. Visual interest is created by cutting the chicken breast in half and stacking it at an angle. The artfully-arranged carrot tops create a gentle arc punctuated with dabs of pan gravy and beet purée.

Deconstructed plating reinterprets traditional dishes and presents foods in unexpected ways. A chef may take the elements in a traditional preparation such as spaghetti and meatballs or lemon meringue pie and separate them into their component parts. The photograph below shows a Black Forest cherry cake reinterpreted into a plated dessert with the flavors and components of the classic cake presented in a fresh new way. The cake is transformed into a bar of dark chocolate, the cake's traditional creamy filling becomes a vanilla mousse and the cherry notes in the original are expressed in the quenelle of cherry sorbet and fresh cherry garnish. Deconstructed plates arrange the main item and garnishes artistically on the plate. Such plates encourage diners to sample a combination of flavors in each bite, as with the deconstructed beet salad shown below.

A quenelle of cherry sorbet garnishes this interpretation of a Black Forest cake.

The traditional flavors of Eastern Europe—beet salad, smoked fish mousse, pickled eggs and herring—are plated in a deconstructed style.

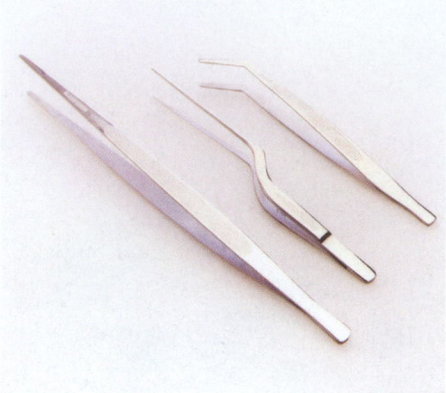

Plating tweezers

Decorating Plates

The colors, textures, shapes and arrangements of foods on a plate can be improved or highlighted by decorating a plate with herbs, greens, spices and other garnishes or sauces. If any of these are to be applied after the principal food is placed on the plate, be prepared to do so quickly so that the food is served at its proper temperature. Plates, bowls or other serving pieces must be chilled or heated before service. An attractive plate of properly prepared food will disappoint if it arrives cold (or melted) because of the time spent assembling it. Have the proper tools available to help staff plate food precisely. Spoons, forks, small spatulas, **plating tweezers**, pastry bags, squeeze bottles and clean towels ease the work of assembling and decorating plates.

Garnishing Plates with Herbs and Greens

Using fresh herbs and greens is one of the easiest ways to add color, texture and flow to a plate. Whether the herbs or greens are an ingredient in the dish (a functional garnish) or merely a decoration, they should always complement the foods and be consistent with their seasonings. A sprig of fresh rosemary garnishing a beautifully roasted rack of lamb or tiny leaves of chervil garnishing delicately poached fillets of sole are natural combinations. Microgreens add a delicate-tasting, light and lacy garnish to many dishes. Sprigs of fresh green mint (often with a fresh berry or two) can be the perfect decoration for a dessert plate.

Provided they complement the food, very finely chopped nuts can also be used to decorate plates for sweet or savory foods. Plates for savory foods may be decorated by sprinkling them with finely chopped herbs, such as thyme, or minced vegetables, such as a combination of brightly colored peppers.

To save time, herbs, microgreens, edible flowers, cut or sliced fruit or vegetables and other perishable garnishes may be prepared before service. Stretch a piece of plastic wrap tightly over a half-sheet tray or small plate. Wash, slice, trim and prepare the garnishes then lay them out on the plastic wrap leaving space between each garnish. Keep these garnishes refrigerated. Use plating tweezers or a small spatula to remove them from the plastic wrap and place them on the food as needed.

Garnishing a plate with chopped fresh parsley.

Garlic timbale garnished with microgreens

Decorating Plates with Sauces

The sauce is an integral part of most any dish. Sauce adds flavor and moisture; it also adds color, texture and flow to the plate. A rich, glossy bordelaise or Madeira sauce pooled beneath sautéed tournedos of beef is a classic example. Sauces are also used in other, less traditional ways to add visual appeal. For example, cream sauces and light mousses can be foamed and applied as a garnish using a whipping siphon. This technique is illustrated in the photograph below of risotto garnished with shrimp and corn mousse. Or if a dish calls for a generous amount of sauce, the service staff can pour the sauce tableside after the dish is presented, as illustrated in the photograph below of a fish and asparagus presentation. Tableside service adds drama to the presentation and ensures that the sauce is warm for service.

Adding a foamed sauce to a risotto appetizer plate.

Pouring sauce over a fish and asparagus plate tableside.

One or more colored sauces can be used to garnish plates. One technique is simply to drizzle or spoon the sauce onto the plate. In this photograph of plated venison, a rich game fond is boldly spooned onto the plate in an abstract swirl echoed in the curved shape of the venison chop. Such technique requires a deft hand.

Marinated loin of venison roasted with mustard

Alternatively, one or more colored sauces can be applied to a plate using squirt bottles. A tomato syrup is added to a plate of seared scallops with tomatillo sauce using a small squirt bottle in the photograph below. Squirt bottles can also be used to create abstract patterns or representational designs. For example, salad dressings or reduced sauces can be artfully squirted in lines or dots over some or all of a plate to create interest and eye appeal as shown in the photographs below.

Seared diver scallops with tomatillo sauce, avocado relish and tomato syrup

Baked fish fillets served with dots of lime vinaigrette

Ladles, pastry brushes, spatulas, spoons and other simple kitchen tools help when applying sauces, as shown in the following photographs.

Spooning basil oil onto a plate of Caprese Salad (page 763).

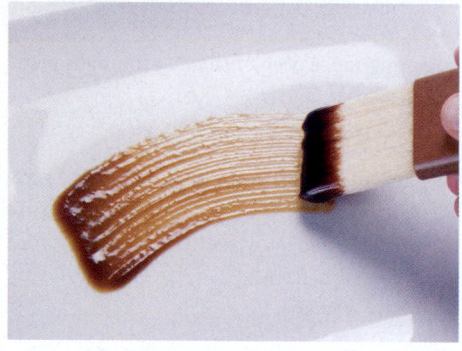

Painting balsamic reduction onto a plate with a pastry brush.

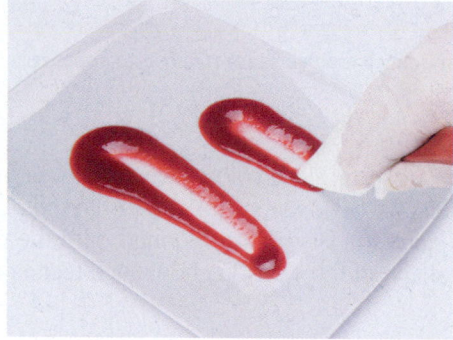

Running a spatula through a line of fruit coulis to create a shadow effect.

Two plates of New York Cheesecake are properly portioned and uniformly garnished with berry sauce.

Whichever style of saucing you choose, strive for consistency and neatness. This is always important but especially so when plating for a large group of people or at a banquet where many people are being served the same plated dish. The slices of New York Cheesecake (page 1088) in this photograph illustrate skilled plating and saucing. The cut edges are clean and crisp. A consistent quantity of berry sauce is poured neatly over one side of each slice.

SMALL PLATES

Diminutive dishes once reserved for the start of a meal have taken hold as an eating style all its own, referred to as small-plate dining. For consumers seeking variety, eating three or more small plates is an appealing alternative to ordering a traditional appetizer and entrée. Each dish on a small-plate menu is usually reduced in size and price, often reducing the cost of dining out. Exposure to chef tasting menus, where numerous dishes are served in dainty portions, may be one reason why more people are comfortable with this style of dining. Or perhaps ethnic dining styles such as Spanish tapas, Chinese dim sum and Middle Eastern mezze have whetted consumer appetites for eclectic eating. Studies suggest that consumers view eating a variety of small plates as a less formal, more relaxed way of dining. Small plates allow customers to experiment and try new dishes, offering an alternative to larger portions of protein-dominated entrées at a lower cost.

The principles for composing a small plate are the same as for preparing and presenting any dish. Choose shapes, colors and textures of food to enhance each item on the plate. Arrange foods to appeal to the eye. Visual appeal is an essential component in ensuring guests' satisfaction. Although composition on each plate is important, balance in the selections of dishes offered on a small-plate menu is of prime consideration because guests often order three or more dishes to create a meal.

While there are no specific rules to follow when creating small plates, the following are some useful guidelines.

- *Reduce the portion size of a conventional entrée.* From stews to sautés, any entrée can be adapted by reducing the portion size. A single crab cake, grilled sausage or large diver scallop makes an appealing small plate. As this photograph illustrates, a 2- to 3-ounce portion of seared salmon accompanied by braised cabbage and sauce makes an appealing yet satisfying miniature dish.

An assortment of small plates creates a full meal.

Small portion of grilled salmon on a bed of braised cabbage and sauce makes an appealing small plate.

■ *Use an unexpected garnish with a traditional protein.* Pairing a dish with a salad or vegetable instead of a heavier starch garnish lightens a conventional entrée. In this photograph, frisée greens, endive and tomatoes dressed with herb vinaigrette accompany a duck leg confit, which might be more commonly served with scalloped potatoes or wild rice.

Duck confit with friseé, endive and tomato salad

■ *Present entrée items in a new format.* Grilled brochettes or skewers of fish, game, meat or poultry served without garnishes are candidates for small-plate menus, as are miniature versions of items such as the hamburger sliders shown here.

Veal kebabs

Hamburger sliders

■ *Offer an assortment of starch dishes.* Small potato or grain dishes complement a variety of other foods. Perfectly crisp French fries or a more unexpected plate of roasted butternut squash with yogurt sauce make excellent accompaniments. Do not overlook the appeal of pasta or risotto served in small portions, too. By offering optional side dishes, guests are free to compose their own meal by combining a few small plates with their choice of starch items.

Roasted butternut squash, garnished with cumin-yogurt sauce and cilantro

- *Highlight vegetables as center of the plate items.* Fresh seasonal vegetables shine on small-plate menus. An assortment of cruciferous vegetables, such as the grilled broccoli and colorful cauliflower shown below, make compelling small plates. Salads presented in a novel manner such as a molded beet and corn salad satisfy the need for variety on small-plate menus.

Grilled broccoli, purple and white cauliflower on a bed of squash purée

Beet, corn and goat cheese salad

- *Look to the breakfast, lunch and appetizer menu for inspiration.* Crêpes, quiche and egg dishes make inviting small plates. Scotch eggs, hard-boiled eggs with assorted fillings, individual cheese soufflés, mini quiches or crêpes stuffed with mushrooms can be used on small-plate menus. Cheese and charcuterie platters that feature terrines, salami and condiments entice diners to share a plate before or with their meal. Also bear in mind the diminutive size of many appetizers, which naturally work well in the lineup of smaller dishes.

Creative plating of a simple Scotch egg elevates the dish to an appetizer or small plate option.

Mushroom crêpes and green salad

A trio of open-face sandwiches

- *Simplify the plating to compensate for the increased number of dishes needed.* When portions are small, customers order more dishes, which means more plates to send out from the kitchen. Consider the time and labor needed to compose each plate when designing small-plate menus. Streamline the presentation accordingly.

QUESTIONS FOR DISCUSSION

1   Explain why proper service and presentation are important in food service operations.

2   Distinguish between cutting and molding foods for visual appeal and creating garnishes out of foods.

3   How can the selection of service ware, such as bowls and platters, affect the visual appeal of the foods served?

4   List and describe four techniques for garnishing plates.

5   Describe how color, texture, shape and arrangement can be used to create a well-balanced plate composition.

6   Select one main course recipe and one dessert from this text. Explain how to use a plate diagram to design a plate composition for each one.

7   Restaurant menus composed entirely of small dishes are popular nowadays. Use the Internet to research small-plate menus. Analyze two or three menus and discuss how many items are offered and how customers can create a complete meal from the list of offerings.

Buffet Presentation 37

- identify opportunities for serving food and beverages in a buffet format

- explain the basic principles of buffet planning and set up

- communicate event plans with a banquet event order (BEO)

- address food safety issues when presenting foods for buffet service

- use a variety of specialized equipment to design and create appealing buffets

- use a variety of techniques to service and maintain appealing buffets

banquet a formal dinner, often with speakers or entertainment; a lavish celebration meal for a business group, a wedding party or academic gathering; the food at a banquet is sometimes served buffet style

venue location or site where an event, such as a banquet, wedding or other party, is held

This soup and salad station has plates stored below the counter and a live plant as a centerpiece.

A buffet offers diners all the dishes from a selected menu simultaneously, displayed in an attractive setting. Customers enjoy the benefit of being able to see the food offerings and serve themselves as much, or as little, as they wish of any item on display. A buffet offers food service professionals the opportunity to exercise their creativity by identifying themes and creating menus, displays and decorations to coordinate with these themes.

In this chapter, we use the word **buffet** to describe both the event at which all the dishes from a planned menu are displayed and served as well as the tables on which these foods are arranged and from which diners serve themselves or are served by wait staff. Buffet foods include virtually any of those found in this book. Another type of event you will encounter is a **banquet**. A banquet refers to a formal meal, often for a special event with entertainment or a speaker. The food at a banquet may be served buffet style, but buffets are not always banquets.

BUFFETS

Buffets are carefully designed to provide foods in an attractive fashion to an anticipated number of people within a specified time. Hotels, restaurants, caterers and cruise ships pride themselves on well-designed and presented buffets. Doing this well requires a collaborative effort among the chef, the catering sales staff and the dining room manager, banquet manager and senior front-of-the-house staff. Together they identify the theme for the event, select a location or venue and choose the menu. If the event is designed for a specific client, the client should participate in the planning. As soon as planning begins, decisions about every aspect of the buffet, or any other catered event, should be recorded in a banquet event order (BEO). See Figure 37.1 for a sample BEO form.

Planning the Buffet

The **theme** sets the tone of the event. The theme may be an elegant Sunday brunch, a showcase for new chefs, a culinary tour of Asian markets for a convention or a New England clambake birthday party. Regardless of the purpose for the event—a wedding, bar mitzvah, business luncheon, charity ball or college reunion—the theme defines the menu, decorations, props, linens and dinnerware; it should also determine the music, lighting and other details.

The **venue** further defines and determines details of the event. Buffets are often prepared and served by specialized catering companies who use their own building or premises for events. For on-premise events, the planner is extremely familiar with the site, the equipment needed and how the space can best be used to ensure guest comfort and maximize efficiency. Off-premise catering occurs when the caterer, restaurant or hotel transports food and equipment to a different event location. The off-premise location can be virtually anywhere: a customer's office building, a private home, an outdoor public park or a museum filled with priceless art. The event staff must be well-organized but flexible and creative in order to provide guests with a memorable culinary experience, regardless of the challenges posed by an unfamiliar venue.

Once the theme and venue are identified, a menu is designed. Essentially a lunch or dinner buffet offers the full range of items found on a restaurant à la carte menu (see Chapter 4, Menus and Recipes). The primary differences are that at a buffet the foods are presented all at once and the diners generally serve themselves or are served by wait staff stationed at the buffet table. Like an à la carte menu, the buffet menu should contain selections of first courses (soups and/or salads), entrées (hot and/or cold meat, poultry, fish and/or shellfish dishes), accompaniments (vegetables, starches and breads), desserts and beverages.

Breakfast buffets are especially popular in hotels. Some may only offer self-serve continental-style items; others may have elaborate displays, chef stations where omelets are prepared to order and servers available to assist guests.

Single-course buffets can be used as part of plated meals for banquets or in restaurants. In a single-course buffet, most of the meal is served to seated guests but one course is presented buffet style. For example, first-course or last-course buffets add action during a sit-down dinner, visual interest to the room and reduce staff costs by having guests serve themselves at their own pace. An appetizer or salad bar, a fruit and cheese display or a dessert and candies buffet can accompany a traditional meal service.

A hotel's breakfast buffet offers guests the traditional components of a continental breakfast in an attractive, easily accessible display.

Depending on the event the menu may need to accommodate particular dietary or religious concerns, such as the need for vegetarian entrées or kosher selections. Although costs are a consideration, the principal factors limiting a menu are the client's desires and the chef's imagination. It is also important to consider visual appeal and avoid repetition.

The following guidelines can help in planning buffet menus:

- *Offer dishes featuring different ingredients.* This avoids repetition and offers diners a wider array of choices. So if the buffet features two entrées, make one beef and the other poultry; if there is a third, use fish or shellfish. If there are two starch dishes, make one a pasta and the other a potato dish. Also avoid repeating ingredients in different dishes; for example, if the entrée is a stir-fry of beef and broccoli, do not offer steamed broccoli as a vegetable side dish.

- *Offer foods cooked by different methods.* For example, a balanced menu might include beef Bourguignon (a hot braised meat dish), roast turkey (a hot or cold roasted poultry dish) and salmon with dill sauce (a cold poached fish dish).

A dessert buffet ends a wedding banquet by offering guests a variety of colorful choices.

- *Offer foods with different colors.* Fettuccine Alfredo and poached sole in a béarnaise sauce may both taste good, but they look boring next to each other. Offer a salsa verde or basil pesto instead of the béarnaise sauce, or a penne with asparagus and tomatoes in place of the Alfredo. This variety will increase the buffet's visual appeal.

- *Offer foods with different textures.* If two or more soups are served, make one a clear soup and the other a cream or purée soup; use a variety of tossed and bound salads, each with different principal ingredients.

- *Offer seasonally appropriate foods.* Buffet menus may be planned months in advance. Consider the availability of the foods needed for the menu being offered. A fresh tomato, basil and mozzarella salad is ideal for a summer buffet but a poor choice in the winter months. Likewise a rich lamb stew may be easy to prepare and may hold well in a chafing dish, but it is not appropriate at a summer luncheon. Offer sliced grilled leg of lamb as a lighter option in warmer months.

When defining the theme and creating the menu, costs must be considered. It is then the responsibility of the chef, sales staff and/or dining room manager to create an attractive and satisfying buffet that stays within the client's budget while providing a reasonable profit to the food service operation. One typical method of meeting these sometimes-conflicting needs is to plan a menu that balances both high-end and less expensive items. When working within a budget, it is important to remember that some clients consider the food offered to be less important than the décor, venue or other aspects of an event. The client's preferences should always lead the planning and budgeting process.

Communicating the Plan

The best menu and event plan is meaningless if it is not recorded and communicated in a timely fashion to the staff responsible for preparing and executing the event. The industry standard for communicating event information is a form known as a **banquet event order (BEO)**. The sample BEO shown in Figure 37.1 includes the key details of an hypothetical business meeting and luncheon. Additional details may be included in an actual BEO; the format will vary from business to business, however.

A BEO form includes detailed information on more than just the menu. Date, time and place are important details for the kitchen and service staff, so are set-up instructions, from the placement of tables, to the color of linens, the type of table decorations and any audio-visual, entertainment or logistics needed. Everyone preparing for or working at a banquet or catered event must know what the customer expects, how the venue will be set up and any unusual or special request that must be accommodated.

banquet event order (BEO) the written record of the plans and arrangements for a specific catered event, buffet or banquet

---

EVENT DAY/DATE: Wednesday
                  9/19/2018

MAJESTIC HOTEL

123 Main Street
Anytown, USA
Tel: 555-123-4567 Fax: 555-890-1234

BEO #: 18072
Page: 1 of 1
Version:

BANQUET EVENT ORDER

Event:	Coffee Break & Lunch	Food Contact:	Chef John Doe
Function:	Annual Sales Meeting	Event Mgr:	Chantal
Account:	Pearson Publishing	Booked by:	Outside Sales Office

Date	Time	Function	Venue	GTD	Prep
Wednesday, 19 Sep	9:30 AM - 9:45 AM	Morning Coffee Break	Ballroom Lobby	120	130
Wednesday, 19 Sep	10:00 AM - 12:30 PM	*Setup*	Café Majestic	40	45
Wednesday, 19 Sep	1:00 PM - 2:00 PM	Luncheon	Café Majestic	40	45

Menu	Setup	Staffing
Wednesday, 19 Sep - Morning Coffee Break	**Buffet Style - 3 Stations**	Service Leader: **Mina**
Room: Ballroom Lobby　　　Ready: 9:15 AM	Tea water in urn	2 waiters
Assorted Morning Pastries:	Fruit tea in dispenser	
Cheese Croissants, Danish, Muffins (All **Hotel** Size)	Paper cups & condiments	
Brewed Coffee, Hot Tea Bags, Cold Milk, Fruit Tea	Paper plates & napkins	
Bottled Water, Still Water	Straws & moist towelettes	Kitchen Crew: **Chef Bennet, Chef Alvarez**
	Trash bins	
Wednesday, 19 Sep - Luncheon	**Family Style on Table**	
Room: Café Majestic　　　Ready: 12:45 PM	Plate, cutlery roll	Service Leader: **Troy**
Light Bistro Lunch - Family Style:	White wine glass	3 waiters
Vegetarian Soup of the Day (Served Individually)	Drinks pre-set before arrival	
Chicken Caesar Salad; Vegetarian Salad	Soup served individually (small portion)	
Assorted Artisan Sandwiches (Incl. Veg. Option)	Salad in family-style bowls	
Assorted French Pastries (Petit-Four Size)	Sandwiches on platters	
Still & Sparkling Water on Table (Large Bottles)	Tea in round dispenser	Kitchen Crew: **Chef Bennet, Chef Alvarez**
Homemade Lemon Ice Tea		
Espresso (Pass on Tray)		
Audio/Visual		**Décor**
None Needed		Host will bring floral centerpieces for lunch tables

Special Needs:	Lactose/Dairy-Free	2
	Gluten-Free	3
	Allergy: Shellfish	1

APPROVAL:_____

DATE:_____

Figure 37.1 Sample Banquet Event Order.

Event information is often arranged on a BEO in blocks or sections covering, for example, menu, floorplan, bar and beverage service, audio-visual needs and decorations. While the price agreed to by the customer is an important part of the event contract, prices are often omitted from the BEOs that circulate among the staff for privacy and competitive reasons.

Part of a BEO covers food and beverage arrangements. The event planner and the host should ensure that the following information is covered in the menu section:

- A complete menu, listing every item on the buffet
- Information about how each buffet station will be arranged and staffed
- Special dietary needs, such as vegetarian or gluten-free options
- Service and setup times
- Beverage service details, such as water on each table or wine served by waiters
- The guaranteed number of guests and the number to actually prepare for (usually an overage of 5 percent is included). The guarantee is the number of guests the customer contracts to pay for, even if fewer actually attend. In the BEO in Figure 37.1, these are indicated under the headings GTD (for guaranteed) and PREP (for the number to actually prepare for).

Staffing needs should also be listed, including managers by name and the number of each type of staff who will be needed during the event. This helps managers plan employee schedules well in advance and recruit temporary (or on-call) staff if necessary.

DESIGNING THE BUFFET

After the theme is established and agreed upon, members of the planning group should study the room, garden, patio or other venue where the event will be held. Space must be allocated for the buffet table(s) and the dining tables. Depending on the event, there may also need to be space for one or more bars, a dance floor, a stage for musicians, a podium for speakers, audiovisual equipment for presentations and so on. When allocating space, use common sense: The buffet should be in an area with easy access to both the kitchen and the dining tables—neither the wait staff nor the diners should have to cross a dance floor or walk in front of a podium to get to the buffet. Similarly a stage or podium should be within good sightlines of the dining tables. All of these plans and arrangements should also be included with the BEO.

Arranging the Tables

Once the room's layout is determined, the chef and/or banquet or dining room manager decides on the shape of the buffet table. A buffet table is usually composed of one or more standard-sized tables grouped together in a functional and attractive shape. Standard table shapes and sizes are listed and described in Table 37.1; ideas for table arrangements are shown in the procedures that follow. Buffet tables can be draped with a floor-length linen tablecloth, or a shorter tablecloth with a detachable skirt. An alternative to using standard-sized tables shrouded in linen is to use unique pieces of furniture such as cabinets, sideboards, armoires, garden benches, wagons, wine barrels or other firm, level surfaces, draped with linens or not, as appropriate for the theme. Some catering facilities and hotel buffet restaurants are equipped with permanent, temperature-controlled buffets. These are practical and convenient when the same style of buffet is set up for each meal every day.

An elegant cold salad and seafood buffet is positioned against a wall.

STANDARD BUFFET TABLE SIZES		TABLE 37.1
SHAPE	TABLE SIZE	SIZES FOR TABLECLOTHS OR SKIRTING
Rectangle	6 feet × 30 inches 8 feet × 30 inches	90 × 128 inches (floor length) 60 × 125 inches (lap length) or 90 × 153 inches (floor length)
Round	24-inch diameter 36-inch diameter 48-inch diameter 60-inch diameter 72-inch diameter	80-inch diameter (floor length) 96-inch diameter (floor length) 80-inch diameter (lap) or 108-inch diameter (floor) 96-inch diameter (lap) or 120-inch diameter (floor) 108-inch diameter (lap) or 132-inch diameter (floor)
Half-round	30-inch radius at 180-degree angle (i.e., half of a 60-inch diameter round)	160 inches of skirting
Quarter-round (wedge)	30-inch radius at 90-degree angle (i.e., one-quarter of a 60-inch-diameter round)	110 inches of skirting
Serpentine	Outside curve measures 8 feet, inside curve measures 4 feet, ends measure 30 inches (i.e., one-quarter of a circle's circumference)	Specialty cloths needed

The number of diners is a critical consideration when determining the size, arrangement and placement of the buffet table(s). As a general rule, a single-sided buffet can comfortably serve 50–75 people. See Figure 37.2. If more than 100 guests are expected, the buffet should be designed with at least two service lines. A good rule of thumb is to plan for one additional line for every 50 additional guests.

Several techniques make serving large groups more efficient. One option is to use a double-sided buffet line. On a double-sided buffet, the same foods are served from both sides of the table. All diners approach the table from the same direction and at the start of the buffet, the line is split, with half of the diners diverted to either side. Or a single-sided buffet can be divided into two or more zones, each of which offers the identical foods. Either option requires that the buffet provide the diners with appropriate visual cues to recognize that the two sides of the table or two ends of the table are offering identical foods.

Another option for serving larger crowds is to divide the menu among various stations that are scattered throughout the venue. One station can be devoted to cold salads or to an elaborate display of cold fish and shellfish surrounding an ice sculpture. Another can be devoted to pasta prepared to order by a cook assigned to the station. Equipped with a portable induction burner, the chef can finish precooked pasta in the diner's choice of sauce. Other stations can offer roasted meats and poultry kept warm by an infrared heat lamp and carved to order by another chef. Hotels and restaurants often assign culinary interns and new cooks to staff such buffet stations. The person assigned to the station should be able to not only handle a carving knife or cook eggs in public, but also be able to chat with guests while doing so.

Bowls, plates and utensils are placed at the beginning of a breakfast buffet adjacent to the fruit salads.

DÉCOR

Linens: buffet and dining tables draped with floor-length colored linens, buffet table with a contrasting overlay; linen napkins in the same colors as the table-cloths and overlay.

Centerpieces: fresh flowers (tulips, mums, lilies and greenery).

Serviceware: polished stainless steel or brass trays and chafing dishes; ceramic bowls.

Dinnerware: white or ivory china, stainless flatware and plain stemware.

Music: none

Wait staff uniforms: bistro attire (white button-down shirts, long tie, black pants and long aprons).

KEY FOR THE BUFFET TABLE

a. Rectangular table, 8 feet x 30 inches
1. Basket of flatware rolled in linen napkins
2. Dinner plates
3. Sunset Salad
4. Raspberry Vinaigrette
5. Caesar Salad
6. Chafing dish of Vegetable Medley
7. Centerpiece
8. Chafing dish of Dauphine Potatoes
9. Sweet and Flavored Butters
10. Baskets of Rolls
11. Chafing dish of Chicken with Wild Mushroom Sauce
12. Chafing dish of Salmon Fillets
13. Dessert plates
14. Cheesecake
15. Fruit Platter
16. Sacher Torte
17. Caramel Sauce for the Cheesecake
18. Raspberry Sauce for the Sacher Torte

Note: Beverages will be in pitchers on the table and replenished by the wait staff; coffee will be offered by circulating wait staff.

Menu

Sunset Salad of Mixed Greens, Citrus Wedges and Crispy Beet Frizzles with a Raspberry Vinaigrette

Caesar Salad with Herbed Croutons and Shredded Parmesan

Oven-Roasted Breast of Chicken with Wild Mushroom Sauce

Grilled Salmon Fillet on a Bed of Sautéed Leeks and Greens

Dauphine Potatoes

Medley of Zucchini, Yellow Squash and Carrots

Assorted Rolls with Sweet and Flavored Butters

Pistachio Citrus Cheesecake with Caramel Sauce

Fresh Fruit Platter

Sacher Torte with Raspberry Sauce

Iced Tea, Lemonade and Sparkling Water French Roast Coffee

A SINGLE-SIDED BUFFET TO FEED 50 PEOPLE

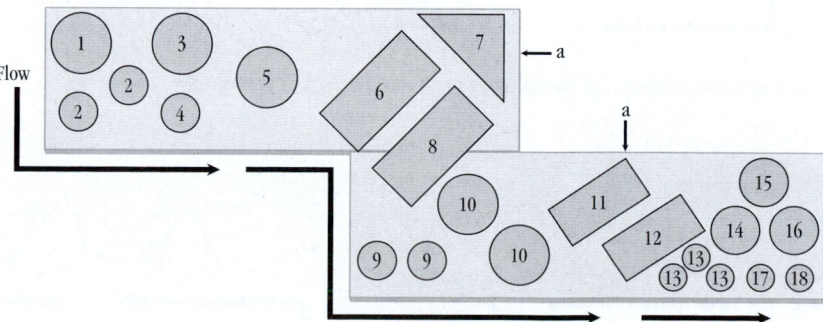

Figure 37.2 Business luncheon buffet plan.

Procedure for Arranging Buffet Tables

Double-sided buffet to feed 125 people

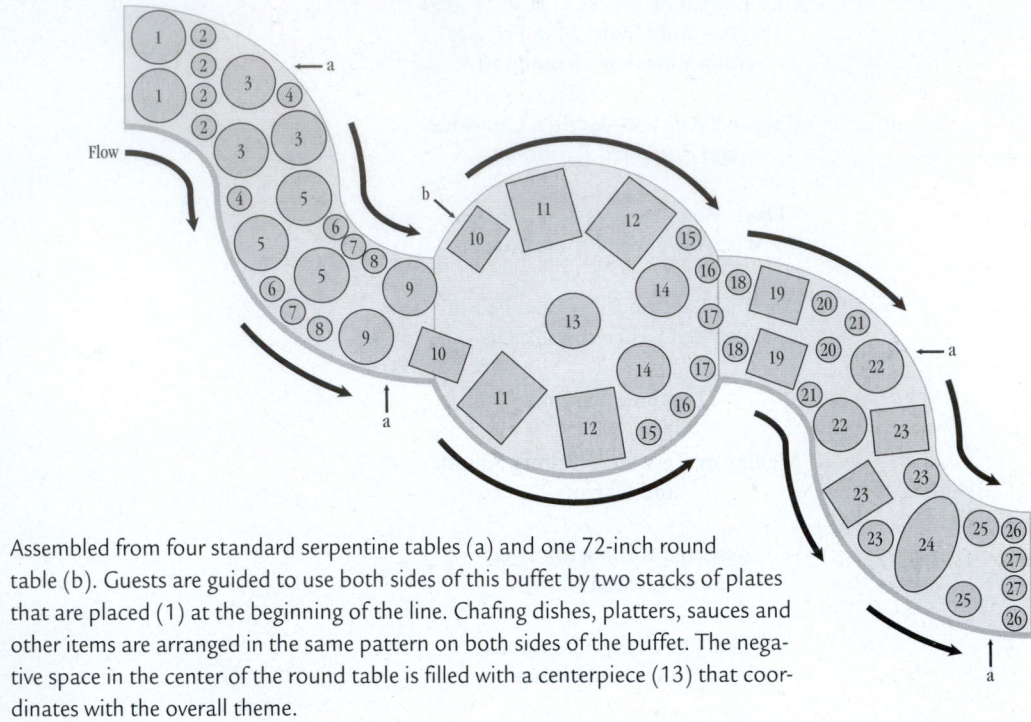

Assembled from four standard serpentine tables (a) and one 72-inch round table (b). Guests are guided to use both sides of this buffet by two stacks of plates that are placed (1) at the beginning of the line. Chafing dishes, platters, sauces and other items are arranged in the same pattern on both sides of the buffet. The negative space in the center of the round table is filled with a centerpiece (13) that coordinates with the overall theme.

Chef station

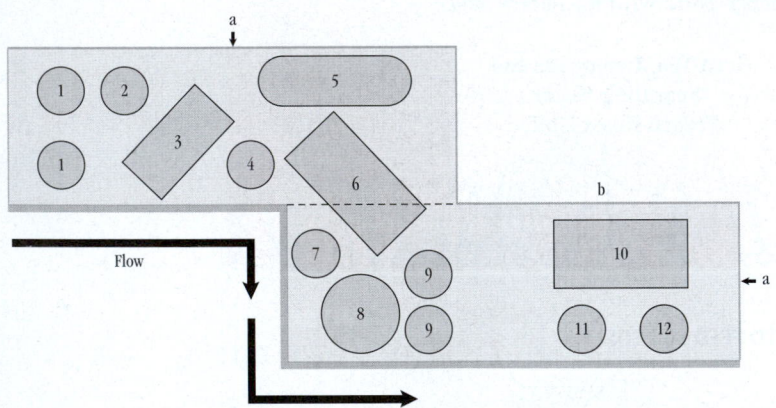

Assembled from two 6-foot rectangular tables. Plates (1) mark the entry point for guests. An induction burner or carving station (10) provides an action area where a chef might cook pasta, omelets or dessert crepes, or carve meats. Other platters, chafing dishes and containers of complimentary foods lead to the action area. The back of table (a) can be placed against a wall to save space and protect the chef's work area from guests.

Buffet divided into two zones to feed 125 people

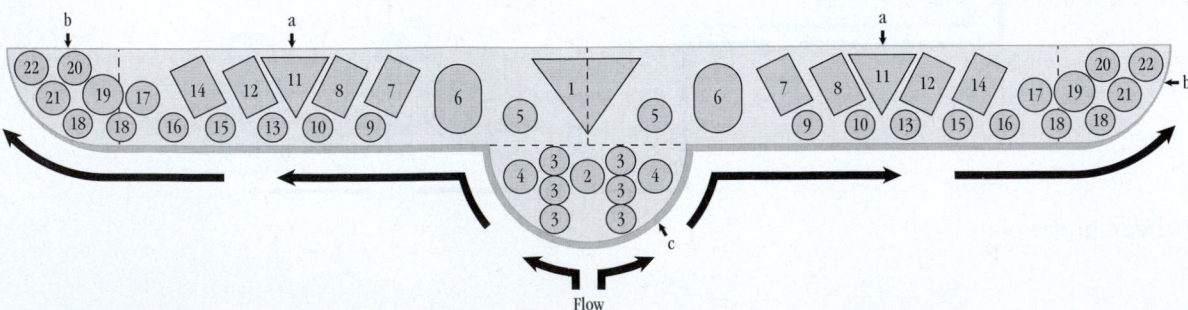

Assembled from two 8-foot tables (a), two 30-inch radius quarter-round tables (b) and one 30-inch half round table (c). The large centerpiece in the center (1) and additional decorations on the half round (2) indicate the starting point to guests. Plates (3) stacked on both sides of the decorations lead guests to mirror image arrangements of chafing dishes, platters and other items. The back of the table can be placed against the wall to save space.

The attractiveness of a well-designed buffet table depends principally on two factors: (1) the arrangement of the foods on their individual serving pieces and (2) the arrangement of the serving pieces and decorations on the buffet table.

Arranging Food on Serving Pieces

The chef is responsible for determining how to arrange the foods on their serving pieces. Most hot foods are presented in chafing dishes, whereas cold or room-temperature foods are usually served on trays, platters, bowls or mirrors. **Chafing dishes** are metal dishes, usually rectangular or round, with a heat source (flame or electric) located beneath, which are used to keep the foods warm. Foods are placed in a hotel pan or other receptacle that sits inside the chafing dish above a pan of hot water.

Trays, platters and mirrors for presenting foods are available in many sizes and shapes. They come in a wide variety of materials, including metal (silver, copper, tin and steel), ceramics (china and earthenware), glass, mirrors (glass and acrylic), plastic, wood or stone (especially slate and marble). The choice depends on the theme. Silver and mirror trays create a more formal feel at an event; ceramic and wood lend a more casual look.

Once the tray, platter, bowl or mirror is chosen, the chef must artfully arrange the food on it. When designing the presentation, the chef should consider the following:

- *Height:* The eye is naturally drawn toward the highest point on a platter or tray; typically, this will be the focal point. It can be an edible garnish or a **grosse piece**. Although the highest point is sometimes in the center of the tray, it is more often located toward the rear, either in the middle or off to one side. Foods placed at a level higher than the tray's centerpiece usually distract from the overall appearance.

- *Pattern:* Whenever possible, foods should be arranged in an interesting pattern. Three different types of canapés, each chosen for contrasting shapes, colors and textures, can march across a mirrored surface in alternating lines. Crudités can flow from baskets, bowls or hollowed squashes. Spirals of different pâtés can swirl around one another. Foods should generally flow toward the diner. Stack foods higher in the center or rear of the tray so that they cascade toward the front or edges. (Trays that are higher around all the edges than in the center tend to draw the eye into the hole in the center.)

- *Color:* The colors of the principal foods should complement or contrast with each other. If they cannot (e.g., a tray of pâtés or cheeses), they should be garnished with attractively contrasting colored foods such as fruits, vegetables and herbs.

- *Texture and shape:* Try to incorporate a variety of shapes and textures on displays. For example, avoid building trays with circular slices of galantine garnished with circular liver mousse molds and round tartlets of a vegetable purée. As all of these have the same shape and very similar textures, the presentation is not compelling. Instead consider molding the mousse or tartlets into different shapes or preparing a vegetable salad rather than a purée for the tartlets.

- *Negative space:* This refers to the areas left unused. Negative space is important in tray composition because empty space enhances the appeal of the object it surrounds and unused space prevents overcrowding. Try leaving an empty border around a tray or some space in between clusters of food on a platter.

Shell-shaped silver chafing dishes hold hot foods for service.

grosse piece on a tray, platter, or mirror, a large piece of the principal food that serves as a centerpiece for that dish; for example, a large wheel of cheese with slices of the cheese cascading around it

A small luncheon buffet of salads and charcuterie items attractively displayed on identical black platters. The meats and cheeses are arranged to feature various textures, shapes and colors. Note the elevated sheet of glass raising the salad ingredients and dressings for easier access.

Arranging Items on the Buffet Table

When designing the shape of the buffet table, the chef and/or banquet or dining room manager must first consider proper guest flow. The design should also consider how the various foods, centerpieces and props will be laid out on the table to incorporate color, height, shape and texture attractively. Later, as the buffet is built prior to the event, the staff might use the following guidelines:

1   *Flow:* Place foods in a logical order that affords guests the chance to construct a meal in a familiar order. This is important whether a single buffet table, a main buffet table with one or more stations or only stations are used. The start of the buffet line should be obvious and accessible; usually it is best located near the entrance to the room.

Typically on a single- or double-sided buffet table, the first items offered are plates. (Flatware and napkins can be located at the start or the end of the buffet or on the dining tables.) The first foods to be offered should be soups and salads. Follow these with appetizers such as cold sliced meats, pâtés and shellfish. Entrées should be next, along with vegetable and starch accompaniments. Desserts should be the last items on the buffet. Beverages can be available on a buffet table, at a separate bar, on the dining tables or offered by circulating wait staff.

Multiple stations offer greater flexibility. They also help minimize the line that usually forms at a single buffet table and allow diners to go in various directions, although this can sometimes cause traffic problems. Like a single buffet table, each station can be designed so that it offers diners sufficient selections to create a complete meal. The stations can also be arranged around a room in a sequence: soups and salads on the first station diners would approach, appetizers on the next, and so on. A third option is to arrange the stations so that the one with the most spectacular display of centerpiece, foods and decorations or the one featuring a chef making foods to order is the center of attention. Other stations are then situated around the room. Regardless of how they are arranged, each station should be self-contained with service ware and accompaniments for the main items as shown in the nearby photo.

One station at a larger buffet, which holds plates, forks and everything needed for the foods served here.

2   *Spacing:* Allow approximately 1 linear foot for each item on the buffet. In other words, if 16 items are to be placed on the table, including plates, a centerpiece and large props, then the buffet table should be approximately 16 feet long. If extremely large centerpieces are used or if food is presented on oversized platters, this will affect the total table space needed.

3   *Reach:* Try to place all foods within easy reach of the diners. Avoid stacking one item behind another. If items must be placed farther back on the table, set them on **risers** or on pedestals to add height to the platter. This extra height not only adds visual interest, it allows the diner to reach over the dish in front without disturbing its arrangement. Place foods that will not drip or splatter behind ones that will; that way, sauce from the back dish will not drip into the front dish on its way to the diner's plate. Trays with foods that will not shift can be propped at a slight angle to make the contents more accessible and attractive.

risers boxes, racks or pedestals, sometimes covered with linens, paper or other decorative items, used on a buffet table as a base to elevate platters, trays or displays

4   *Accompaniments:* Place the appropriate condiments, sauces or other accompaniments near their principal foods. Also place a small plate or napkin near each chafing dish or platter for serving utensils.

5   *Centerpieces:* A table centerpiece brings focus to the buffet, and its height or dominance increases the visual appeal of the overall table design. The buffet centerpiece can be a floral arrangement or a sculpture made of ice, tallow, pastillage, chocolate, blown or pulled sugar or other material. The centerpiece can also be a grosse piece such as a whole roast turkey or whole poached salmon decorated with sauce chaud-froid. See Chapter 28, Charcuterie.

6 *Decorations:* In addition to the buffet centerpiece, other nonedible objects or props may grace the table. Sometimes these are nothing more than smaller or modified versions of the centerpiece, such as flowers or leaves from a floral centerpiece. Anything from a wine barrel to a silver candelabra can be used, depending on the buffet's theme. Whatever items are chosen, they should be clean and arranged artfully but not in a manner that interferes with a diner's ability to see and reach the food. Props can also be used to mark divisions in the meal; for example, grouping all salads between one set of props divides salads from entrées. Sometimes unusable or dead space is inevitable due to the room or food layout. Try filling this empty space with props or other decorations.

7 *Labels:* Unlike a restaurant with a printed menu and an attentive wait staff, an unattended buffet may not give the diner an opportunity to ask questions about the food. This can be remedied by placing attractively printed cards bearing the name of the dish in front of each item. Labels are also a good way to guide guests to vegan, vegetarian, gluten-free or other specialty items.

Appetizer platters displayed on risers

PRESENTING AND MAINTAINING THE BUFFET

The way in which foods are portioned and presented on a buffet can affect the quantity of food that guests consume. The goal for any hotel, restaurant or caterer is for guests to have enough to eat and drink, given the time and type of event. But it is equally important to avoid leftovers or waste as this can negatively impact the profitability of the event. The size of each portion, the total quantity of food on display and the use of servers can help moderate the amount of food that guests consume and avoid waste.

Controlling Costs

Buffet menus can cost more per person than a plated restaurant meal because there is usually a larger variety of food available to guests at buffets. There is no magic formula to determine which foods or how much food each guest will eat during a buffet. There are, however, several ways to control costs when preparing food for buffets.

A common problem when planning a buffet is overproduction. Many novice chefs want to make enough of each menu item to serve the entire group. But this is unnecessary. Most people tend to sample a little from many dishes, so the more variety available, the smaller each portion will be. Experience will guide the chef to know which items are especially popular or guest favorites and need to be more plentiful. The total amount of food consumed depends on factors such as the general composition of the group (a luncheon buffet for female executives may require less food than one for male soccer players), the number of items offered, whether it will be convenient for people to return to the buffet for second helpings and whether diners serve themselves or are served by wait staff or chefs at the buffet.

Some chefs use a simple, although far from foolproof, formula of 1 pound (450 grams) of food per person as a starting point and adjust this amount. To determine how much food to prepare for a group, estimate how many ounces or grams of each menu item each guest will eat. Multiply this number by the total number of guests attending the event to determine the total weight of that item to prepare (e.g., for a group of 100 people, 1 ounce/30 grams of green salad per person = 100 ounces/3000 grams or 6.25 pounds/3 kilograms of green salad). Perform this same calculation for each item on the menu excluding side sauces, condiments, bread and butter and other miscellaneous items. Add the weights together to determine the total weight of the food you plan to produce for the group.

Buffet Cost Control

To control costs when preparing foods for a buffet:

- Create menus that include a variety of interesting foods. Remember that the more items on a buffet, the more food that will have to be prepared to ensure that you do not run out of an item.

- Create menus that offset expensive foods with items that are less expensive.

- Arrange the buffet so that the more expensive foods are at the end of the buffet line.

- Reduce the size of individually portioned items, allowing guests to have a sample of two or more items without wasting food.

FOOD QUANTITY GUIDELINES		TABLE 37.2
FOOD ITEM	PORTIONS PER PERSON	COMMENTS
Hors d'oeuvre with meal to follow	3 pieces per person	Per hour of service
Hors d'oeuvre as a meal	5–6 pieces per person per hour	Fewer after second hour of service
Leafy green salad	1 ounce (30 grams) per person	
Chilled bound salads	3–4 ounces (90–120 grams) per person	Divide total among number of salads offered
Cooked vegetables	3 ounces (90 grams) per person	Divide total among number of vegetables offered
Hot side dishes	3–4 ounces (90–120 grams) per person	Less if multiple side dishes served
Pasta as an entrée	6–8 ounces (180–240 grams) per person	Less if side dishes also served
Pasta as a side dish	3–4 ounces (90–120 grams) per person	
Lunch entrée	4–6 ounces (120–180 grams) per person	Divide total among the number of entrées offered
Dinner entrée	6–8 ounces (180–240 grams) per person	Divide total among the number of entrées offered

⚠ Safety Alert

Buffets

A properly maintained buffet is important for visual and culinary reasons. It is also important for food safety reasons. Because the public has direct access to food, cross-contamination is a potential problem. In addition to keeping foods at the proper temperatures, the following rules are critical:

- Do not add new food to old food in a serving dish or chafing dish.

- Do not use a chafing dish to heat food; make sure food is at the proper internal temperature before transferring it to a chafing dish or putting it under a heat lamp.

- Check food temperatures with instant-read thermometers at established time intervals to ensure that the food is being held at safe serving temperatures.

- Be careful of steam when changing pans in a chafing dish; do not leave the pan of hot water uncovered, exposing staff and guests to potential injury.

- Provide clean serving utensils for each dish and replace serving utensils often.

- Provide an ample supply of clean plates, so that diners do not reuse plates from which they have eaten.

Generally pre-cut portions should be small, especially if more than one item is served in a food category. For example, if grilled salmon fillet is served as a restaurant entrée, a typical serving might be 6 ounces (180 grams). If the same salmon fillet is served as one of three entrées at a dinner buffet for 100 people, portions can be smaller. The total of available fish should be 2–3 ounces (60–90 grams) per portion multiplied by 100 portions. Similarly if a plated dessert tart at a restaurant has a 4-inch (10-centimeter) diameter, the version offered on a dessert buffet should have a 2-inch (5-centimeter) diameter. For additional information on quantities to prepare see Table 37.2.

Most diners tend to serve themselves larger portions of foods found at the start of the buffet than at its middle. Thus if boiled shrimp and crab legs are being served, it may make economic sense to place them away from the start of the buffet. Less expensive items and those that occupy more space on the plate are often placed at the beginning of a buffet line. If guests fill their plate with salad greens, assorted toppings and bread near the beginning of a buffet line, they will have less room on the plate for more costly meats and entrées presented further down the line.

The additional food cost that is incurred when preparing food for a buffet is offset by several factors. Kitchen labor is lower when preparing food for buffets compared to preparing food for plated banquets or à la carte service. Buffet food is generally prepared in advance by a small kitchen team and finished just before the buffet opens. This differs from plated meals where the cooks must assemble each plate to order and the entire kitchen team must stand ready as orders come in throughout the meal period. Front of the house labor is also lower when food is served buffet style. As a rule, one server is needed for every 20 guests during buffet service in contrast to plated banquet service, which requires one server for every 10 guests.

Keeping Hot Foods Hot

Keeping hot foods hot on a buffet is a particular challenge, and an important one, for both food safety and presentation concerns. If possible, hot foods should be served in relatively small quantities on warm platters that are exchanged frequently. This is not always possible, however. More often, hot foods are maintained in chafing dishes or under heat lamps.

To maintain the quality of foods kept in a chafing dish, use the following guidelines:

- Choose foods that hold well. Rare meats and delicate pastas do not hold well in chafing dishes; they become overcooked and unattractive quickly. Instead try braised meats (which may actually benefit from the extended cooking) or hearty pastas such as tortellini or penne. This guideline also applies to garnishes: Delicate herbs such as basil do not do well in chafing dishes; instead try sprigs of rosemary or thyme.

- Cook and offer small amounts of delicate foods and change the insert pan in a chafing dish often. This prevents foods from sitting too long.

- Ladle a small amount of sauce in the bottom of the pan before placing sliced meats in the pan, or serve sliced meats, poultry or fish on a bed of vegetables. The sauce or the vegetable bed helps to absorb the heat from the chafing dish, insulating the more delicate items and providing a bit of steam to help keep the foods moist.

- Keep the chafing dish closed whenever possible. This holds in the steam, which helps keep the food moist. However a closed chafing dish can distract from a buffet's appeal and slow down the flow of diners through the buffet line.

- Heat lamps are generally used for keeping large cuts of meats or poultry warm during carving. These foods, however, become dry rapidly and should be replaced periodically.

- Always follow time and temperature principles of food safety.

Keeping Cold Foods Cold

Keeping cold foods cold on a buffet table is a little less of a challenge than keeping hot food at the proper temperature. As with hot foods, it is best if cold foods are served in relatively small quantities on cold platters that are exchanged frequently. Alternatively the items can be set on a bed of ice—usually a large bowl filled with ice into which a smaller bowl containing the food is placed.

Cold beverages may be arranged for self-service in thermal insulated pitchers or dispensers with ice inserts. Clean, polished glassware should be placed near the cold beverage station with extra glasses available for those who want to try multiple flavors or return for more.

Replenishing Foods

Dishes should be removed from the buffet table when they are approximately two-thirds empty or have deteriorated in some fashion (e.g., when the aspic on pâtés has softened, cut fruits begin to brown or a hot food has crusted over). As the used dish is removed, its fresh replacement should be placed on the buffet immediately, and the new dish should be as carefully arranged and garnished as the original. If items from the used dish are to be combined with a replacement dish, this should be done in the kitchen and not at the buffet table. New and previously prepared batches of time and temperature controlled for safety foods should not be combined.

Using two half-size hotel pans of different foods in a full-size chafing dish conserves space and allows smaller amounts of hot items to be displayed attractively.

A buffet display of chilled seafood is arranged on a bed of crushed ice.

For butler service, a waiter circulates in a crowd with trays of individual hors d'oeuvre for the guests.

Individual hors d'oeuvre can be presented on a buffet alongside beverages.

Serving the Guests

The responsibility for supervising an actual event usually falls to the **event captain**. The captain directs the crew of waiters and stewards assigned to set up the room, arrange tables and chairs, position flatware, china and glassware and set up chafing dishes or cooking stations as needed.

The captain also supervises the wait staff. One of the front waiters' principal responsibilities is to maintain the appearance of the buffet and to replenish items as needed. Depending on the function, service staff can be stationed behind the buffet table to serve diners, circulate in the crowd with trays of hors d'oeuvre or drinks (passing foods in this fashion is called **butler service**) or serve beverages to diners seated at the dining tables. Back waiters generally police (clean) the room and clear tables. Waiters should be particularly vigilant in removing used plates from dining tables whenever a guest goes back to the buffet for more food. The used plate should be removed before the guest returns with a new plate.

Typically servers or chefs are placed at stations where foods are prepared or carved to order. This helps control portioning. It also provides a greater opportunity for staff to police the buffet and ensure that the table and the individual items remain neat, attractive and fresh. Finally placing wait staff or kitchen staff at the buffet allows diners to ask questions about the foods being served.

A Block of Ice, a Chain Saw, a Chisel and a Little Caution and Creativity

Ice carvings have long been popular buffet centerpieces; they add elegance and sophistication to the setting and occasion. As with other arts, it may take years to master ice carving. Nevertheless, with some practice and care, chefs can usually create acceptable ice sculptures after only a few tries.

Blocks of carving ice are specially prepared to remove air bubbles. These large blocks (20 × 10 × 46 inches [50 × 25 × 115 centimeters]) weigh approximately 300 pounds (135 kilograms), and special ice tongs and caution are required when handling them.

At 0°F (−18°C), ice is very brittle and difficult to carve without breaking. Therefore, carving ice must be tempered before carving. To temper the ice, remove it from the freezer

and allow it to rest at room temperature for approximately 1 hour. When the surface is clear of frost, carving can begin.

A single carving can take from one to several hours to complete. Although chisels and specially designed saws for ice carving work quite well, chain saws are commonly used to speed up the process. Because most carving is done indoors, electric saws are used; unlike gas saws, they do not leave a greasy residue on the ice's surface. Be very careful when using any chain saw, particularly an electric one, around melting ice and pools of water.

To begin, trace the outline of the figure you want to carve on the surface of all four sides of the block of ice. There are several excellent ice carving books, some of which provide stencils

for this purpose. Then start removing the ice using a large saw or a chainsaw. As the figure begins to take shape, use smaller chisels and specialized tools to create the desired effect. Some carvers use chain saws for the entire process, however. After some practice, you will develop your own style and preferences.

When the carving is complete, carefully return the ice to the freezer until needed. When setting it on a buffet, use a pan designed to hold an ice carving and provide drainage. Avoid placing ice sculptures under hot air vents. At room temperature and average humidity, ice melts at the rate of approximately ½ inch (1.2 centimeters) per hour from all sides. Keep this in mind when carving thin pieces or small details into the surface.

The Buffet: An Ancient Extravaganza

The origin of the buffet is obscure, but it is possible that the idea evolved from Italian banquets of the early Renaissance. Gathering together to eat and drink on festive occasions was not new; one only has to think of banqueting scenes on ancient Egyptian or Roman frescoes. But the word *banchetto* was new and referred not only to the event but to the long table or bench at which the many guests were seated.

As the influence of Italian art and manners spread throughout Europe, the French adopted the *banquet*. Not only was it an occasion for eating and drinking prodigious amounts, but the resplendent display of food was often accompanied by an equally resplendent display of ornate gold and silver on dining room buffets or sideboards. And it was the chefs who were responsible for these imaginative displays. Paintings from the period of Louis XIV depict the unbridled creativity that went into these tableaux.

From France to England to America, the idea of the buffet migrated across time. There is *rijsttafel* in the Netherlands and *smorgasbord* in Scandinavia. In America the Chinese restaurant buffet began around the time of the 1849 gold rush, perhaps the first instance of the "all you can eat" experience. The typical cost for these buffets was $1.00 per person. The "midnight chuck wagon" buffet at the El Rancho in 1940s Las Vegas popularized the "all you can eat" buffet; it cost $1.50.

Whatever the case, the buffet has come a long way from the 16th-century Medici banquet that featured a ram poached in water, reinserted into its skin (horns and all) and set lifelike into a gold basin.

QUESTIONS FOR DISCUSSION

1 Describe how a buffet differs from a banquet. List four types of events where a buffet might be appropriate.

2 Explain the function of a BEO and describe some of the categories of information included on a typical BEO.

3 What food safety and sanitation factors must be considered when planning a buffet? Explain your answer.

4 Describe three things that can be done to keep hot foods attractive and fresh when using a chafing dish.

5 Describe two things that can be done to keep cold foods cold on a buffet.

6 What is a grosse piece? How is it different from a table centerpiece?

7 List three different stations for serving hot foods at a buffet and the equipment necessary for each station.

8 Identify three sources of information on current trends and styles of buffet arrangements. List two resources that are available to assist caterers in managing their business.

Appendix I

Measurement and Conversion Charts

FORMULAS FOR EXACT MEASURES			
	WHEN YOU KNOW:	MULTIPLY BY:	TO FIND:
Mass (weight)	ounces	28.35	grams
	pounds	0.45	kilograms
	grams	0.035	ounces
	kilograms	2.2	pounds
Volume (capacity)	teaspoons	5.0	milliliters
	tablespoons	15.0	milliliters
	fluid ounces	29.57	milliliters
	cups	0.24	liters
	pints	0.47	liters
	quarts	0.95	liters
	gallons	3.785	liters
	milliliters	0.034	fluid ounces
Temperature	Fahrenheit	$\frac{5}{9}$ (after subtracting 32)	Celsius
	Celsius	$\frac{9}{5}$ (then add 32) Fahrenheit	

ROUNDED MEASURES FOR QUICK REFERENCE		
MEASURE	U.S. CUSTOMARY SYSTEM	METRIC
1 oz.		= 30 g
4 oz.		= 120 g
8 oz.		= 240 g
16 oz.	= 1 lb.	= 480 g
32 oz.	= 2 lb.	= 960 g
36 oz.	= 2¼ lb.	= 1000 g (1 kg)
¼ tsp.	= ¹⁄₂₄ fl. oz.	= 1 ml
½ tsp.	= ¹⁄₁₂ fl. oz.	= 2 ml
1 tsp.	= ⅙ fl. oz.	= 5 ml
1 Tbsp.	= ½ fl. oz.	= 15 ml
1 c.	= 8 fl. oz.	= 240 ml
2 c. (1 pt.)	= 16 fl. oz.	= 480 ml
4 c. (1 qt.)	= 32 fl. oz.	= 960 ml
4 qt. (1 gal.)	= 128 fl. oz.	= 3.8 lt
32°F		= 0°C
122°F		= 50°C
212°F		= 100°C

CONVERSION GUIDELINES

1 gallon	=	4 quarts 8 pints 16 cups (8 fluid ounces) 128 fluid ounces
1 fifth bottle	=	approximately 1½ pints or exactly 26.5 fluid ounces
1 measuring cup	=	8 fluid ounces (a coffee cup generally holds 6 fluid ounces)
1 large egg white	=	1 ounce (average)
1 lemon	=	1 to 1¼ fluid ounces juice
1 orange	=	3 to 3½ fluid ounces juice

SCOOP SIZES

SCOOP NUMBER	LEVEL MEASURE
6	⅔ cup
8	½ cup
10	⅖ cup
12	⅓ cup
16	¼ cup
20	3⅕ tablespoons
24	2⅔ tablespoons
30	2⅕ tablespoons
40	1⅗ tablespoons

The number of the scoop determines the number of servings in each quart of a mixture: For example, with a No. 16 scoop, one quart of mixture will yield 16 2-ounce servings. (No. 16 scoop = 2 fluid ounces. One quart/32 fluid ounces divided by 2 = 16 servings.)

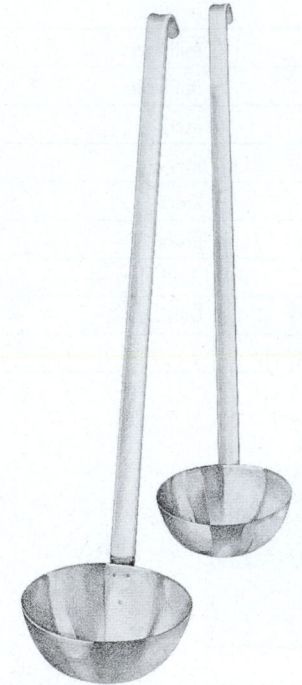

LADLE SIZES

SIZE	PORTION OF A CUP	NUMBER PER QUART	NUMBER PER LITER
1 fl. oz.	⅛	32	34
2 fl. oz.	¼	16	17
2⅔ fl. oz.	⅓	12	13
4 fl. oz.	½	8	8.6
6 fl. oz.	¾	5⅓	5.7

Various standard cans: (left to right, front row) No. ½ flat, No. ¼; (middle row) No. 300, No. 1 tall, No. ½; (back row) No. 10, No. 3 cylinder, No. 5

CANNED GOOD SIZES

SIZE	NO. OF CANS PER CASE	AVERAGE WEIGHT	AVERAGE NO. CUPS PER CAN
No. ¼	1 and 2 doz.	4 oz.	½
No. ½	8	8 oz.	1
No. 300	1 and 2 doz.	14 oz.	1¾
No. 1 tall (also known as 303)	2 and 4 doz.	16 oz.	2
No. 2	2 doz.	20 oz.	2½
No. 2½	2 doz.	28 oz.	3½
No. 3 vacuum	2 doz.	24 oz.	3
No. 3 cylinder	1 doz.	52 oz.	6½
No. 5	1 doz.	3 lb. 8 oz.	5½
No. 10	6	6 lb. 10 oz.	13

Appendix II

Fresh, Locally Grown Produce Availability Chart

The availability of fresh, locally grown produce depends on local climate and growing conditions. Gardeners in central Arizona may be enjoying vine-ripened tomatoes in March, while gardeners in Michigan or New England may still be buried under snow. Just by looking at what's available in the produce department of your local supermarket, you may not be able to tell whether it is July or January. That's because consumers have become accustomed to having the same foods available all year. Modern transportation and storage methods allow us to have out-of-season foods anytime, anywhere. But though we depend on and enjoy this convenience, it contributes to hidden costs that are not usually considered. For example, costly natural resources used to fuel vehicles and preserve produce are consumed in the movement of these foods over long distances.

Locally grown, in-season products appeal to restaurant patrons and demonstrate your concern for both food quality and the viability of local farmers and foragers. Chefs across the country are shopping for fruits and vegetables at local farmer's markets and working with local farmers who grow products especially for their kitchens. Although good produce wholesalers or even supermarkets carry out-of-season, imported produce, the taste is inferior and the cost is much higher. Sourcing locally grown produce reduces the food miles required to bring food into your establishment.

Chefs can also work with local farmers before planting begins to determine which specialty items grow well in the area and to encourage farmers to grow products that the restaurant agrees to purchase at harvest. Many states now have programs to assist and encourage chefs and farmers to work together. It's a shift from demand-driven (chef) to supply-driven (farm) choices.

Currently two percent of the U.S. population is farming the land and few Americans give a second thought to the sources of their food. Many of us may have lost our connection to agriculture, but we are still very dependent on that connection. What happens to farmers remains crucial to our nation's well-being. Even if we never set foot on a farm, our connection to the farmer and the land is there every time we buy a loaf of bread, munch an apple, plan a daily special or design a restaurant's menu. By creating markets for local agriculture, we can ensure that farmland remains active and viable.

The following chart is intended as only a general guide to the best availability of freshly harvested produce items grown in the continental United States. State departments of agriculture can provide charts of local produce availability and information on local farmer's markets and sustainable agriculture programs. The websites of the USDA and other public and private organizations also provide lists of seasonally available produce organized by state.

FRESH FRUIT AND VEGETABLE AVAILABILITY CHART

PRODUCT	JAN.	FEB.	MAR.	APR.	MAY	JUNE	JULY	AUG.	SEPT.	OCT.	NOV.	DEC.
	WINTER DEC 21–MAR 19		SPRING MAR 20–JUN 20			SUMMER JUN 21–SEP 21			AUTUMN SEP 22–DEC 20			
Apples*								X	X	X	X	
Apricots						X	X					
Artichokes			X	X	X	X			X	X	X	X
Asparagus				X	X	X						
Avocados, Hass			X	X	X	X	X	X	X	X		
Beans, green			X	X	X	X	X	X	X	X	X	X
Beets*			X	X	X	X	X	X	X			
Blueberries					X	X	X	X				
Bok choy*	X	X										X
Broccoli			X	X	X				X	X	X	X
Broccoli rabe*				X	X	X				X	X	X
Brussels sprouts	X	X	X						X	X	X	X
Cabbage, head *	X	X	X	X	X				X	X	X	X
Cabbage, Napa*									X	X	X	X
Carrots*							X	X	X	X	X	X
Cantaloupes						X	X	X	X			
Cauliflower *	X	X	X	X	X				X	X	X	X
Celery*		X	X	X	X	X	X	X	X	X	X	X
Celery root	X	X	X	X						X	X	X
Cherries					X	X	X	X				
Chestnuts									X	X	X	X
Citrus	X	X	X	X	X	X			X	X	X	X
Collards				X	X	X	X	X	X	X	X	
Corn						X	X	X				
Cranberries									X	X	X	X
Cucumbers*					X	X	X	X	X			
Dates	X									X	X	X
Eggplants						X	X	X	X			
Fennel					X	X	X	X	X			
Figs						X	X	X	X	X		
Garlic*							X	X	X	X		
Grapes						X	X	X	X	X	X	
Jicama*										X	X	X
Kale*	X	X	X									
Kohlrabi						X	X	X	X			
Leeks*	X	X	X							X	X	X
Lettuce*			X	X	X	X	X	X	X			
Lychees						X	X					
Mangoes					X	X	X	X				
Mushrooms, cultivated*	X	X	X	X	X	X	X	X	X	X	X	X
Mushrooms, morels			X	X	X							
Mushrooms, truffles	X	X								X	X	X

FRESH FRUIT AND VEGETABLE AVAILABILITY CHART

PRODUCT	JAN.	FEB.	MAR.	APR.	MAY	JUNE	JULY	AUG.	SEPT.	OCT.	NOV.	DEC.
	WINTER DEC 21–MAR 19		SPRING MAR 20–JUN 20			SUMMER JUN 21–SEP 21			AUTUMN SEP 22–DEC 20			
Mushrooms, wild					X	X	X	X	X	X	X	
Okra						X	X	X	X			
Onions*						X	X	X	X			
Onions, sweet				X	X	X						
Papayas			X	X	X	X						
Parsnips*	X	X	X									X
Peaches					X	X	X	X				
Pears	X	X	X	X						X	X	X
Peas, English				X	X	X						
Peas, field							X	X				
Peas, snow*			X	X								
Pecans											X	X
Peppers, bell*						X	X	X	X			
Peppers, chile										X	X	X
Persimmons										X	X	X
Pineapples			X	X	X	X	X	X				
Plums						X	X	X	X			
Pomegranates									X	X	X	X
Potatoes, russet*							X	X	X			
Potatoes, sweet							X	X	X	X	X	X
Pumpkins									X	X	X	X
Raspberries						X	X	X	X			
Radishes*				X	X	X			X	X	X	
Rhubarb		X	X	X	X							
Rutabagas	X	X	X						X	X	X	X
Scallions*						X	X	X				
Shallots*			X	X	X	X	X	X				
Spinach	X	X	X	X	X					X	X	X
Squash, summer*				X	X	X	X	X	X			
Squash, winter	X	X	X							X	X	X
Strawberries		X	X	X	X	X						
Tomatoes*						X	X	X	X			
Tomatillos*							X	X	X	X	X	X
Turnips				X	X	X				X	X	
Watermelons					X	X	X	X	X			

* Available all year. X indicates peak seasons for this vegetable.

Glossary

A

à la—[ah lah] French for "in the manner or style of"; used in relation to a food, it designates a style of preparation or presentation

à la carte—[ah lah kart] (1) a menu on which each food and beverage is listed and priced separately; (2) foods cooked to order as opposed to foods cooked in advance and held for later service

à la grecque—[ah lah GREHK] a preparation style in which vegetables are marinated in olive oil, lemon juice and herbs, then served cold

à point—[ah PWAN] (1) French term for cooking to the ideal degree of doneness; (2) when applied to meat, refers to cooking it medium rare

absorption—the ability of flour to absorb moisture when mixed into a dough; varies according to protein content, growing conditions and storage conditions of the flour

acetic acid—organic compound produced during fermentation; acetic acid bacteria consume glucose in a liquid and convert it to ethanol (alcohol) then acetic acid; vinegar consists of acetic acid diluted to 3–20 percent

acid—a substance that neutralizes a base (alkaline) in a liquid solution; foods such as citrus juice, vinegar and wine that have a sour or sharp flavor (most foods are slightly acidic); acids have a pH of less than 7

acidulation—the browning of cut fruit caused by the reaction of an enzyme (polyphenoloxidase) with the phenolic compounds present in these fruits; this browning is often mistakenly attributed to exposure to oxygen

additives—substances added to many foods to prevent spoilage or improve appearance, texture, flavor or nutritional value; they may be synthetic materials copied from nature (e.g., sugar substitutes) or naturally occurring substances (e.g., lecithin); some food additives may cause allergic reactions in sensitive people

aerate—to incorporate air into a mixture through sifting and mixing; gas discharged from a whipping siphon is also used to aerate mixtures

aerobic bacteria—bacteria that thrive on oxygen

aging—(1) the period during which freshly killed meat is allowed to rest so that the effects of rigor mortis dissipate; (2) the period during which freshly milled flour is allowed to rest so that it will whiten and produce less sticky doughs; the aging of flour can be chemically accelerated

aïoli—mayonnaise made with olive oil and flavored with garlic

airline breast—a boneless chicken breast with the first wing bone attached

al dente—[al DEN-tay] Italian for "to the tooth"; used to describe a food, usually pasta, that is cooked only until it gives a slight resistance when one bites into it

albumen—the principal protein found in egg whites; another name for egg whites

alkali—any substance with a pH higher than 7; baking soda is one of the few alkaline foods; also known as a base

allemande—[ah-leh-MAHND] an intermediary sauce made by adding lemon juice and a liaison to chicken or veal velouté

allergens—substances that may cause allergic reactions in some people

allumette—[al-yoo-MEHT] (1) a matchstick cut of ⅛ inch × ⅛ inch × 2 inches (3 millimeters × 3 millimeters × 5 centimeters) usually used for potatoes; (2) a strip of puff pastry with a sweet or savory filling

amino acid—the basic molecular component of proteins; each of the approximately two dozen amino acids contains oxygen, hydrogen, carbon and nitrogen atoms

amuse bouche—[ah-muze booch] French term meaning "entertains (the) mouth"; refers to a bite-sized appetizer, usually complimentary, served by a chef to welcome guests

anadromous—describes a fish that migrates from a saltwater habitat to spawn in fresh water

anaerobic bacteria—bacteria that are able to live and grow without the presence of oxygen

andouille—[an-DOO-ee] a very spicy smoked pork sausage, popular in Cajun cuisine

angus beef, certified—a brand created in 1978 to distinguish the highest-quality beef produced from descendants of the black, hornless Angus cattle of Scotland; the meat must meet American Angus Association standards for yield, marbling and age and be graded as high choice or prime

anterior—at or toward the front of an object or place; opposite of posterior

appetizers—also known as first courses, usually small portions of hot or cold foods intended to whet the appetite in anticipation of the more substantial courses to follow

aquaculture—the business, science and practice of raising large quantities of fish and shellfish in tanks, ponds or the ocean; also known as aquafarming

aroma—the sensations we detect when a substance comes in contact with certain receptors in the nose

aromatic—(1) having a characteristic and pleasant odor or smell; (2) a food added to enhance the natural aromas of another food; aromatics include most flavorings, such as herbs and spices, as well as some vegetables, especially celery, carrots and onions

artisan—a person who works in a skilled craft or trade; one who works with his or her hands; applied to bread bakers, cheese makers, confectioners, charcutiers and other craftspeople who prepare foods using traditional methods

as purchased (A.P.)—the condition or cost of an item when it is purchased or received from the supplier

aspic or **aspic jelly**—a clear jelly usually made from a clarified stock thickened with gelatin; used to coat foods, especially charcuterie items, and for garnish

aspic terrine—a dish in which layers of meats and/or vegetables are bound together and held in place with aspic jelly

au gratin—[oh GRAH-tan] foods with a browned or crusted top; often made by browning a food with a bread-crumb, cheese and/or sauce topping under a broiler or salamander

au jus—[oh ZHEW] roasted meats, poultry or game served with their natural, unthickened juices

au sec—[oh sek] a liquid reduced by evaporation until nearly dry

B

bacteria—single-celled microorganisms; pathogenic bacteria can cause food-borne illnesses

bagel—a dense, donut-shaped yeast roll; it is cooked in boiling water, then baked, which gives it a shiny glaze and chewy texture

bain marie—[bane mah-ree] (1) a hot-water bath used to gently cook food or keep cooked food hot; (2) a container for holding food in a hot-water bath

baked Alaska—ice cream set on a layer of spongecake and encased in meringue, then baked until the meringue is warm and golden

baked blind—describes a pie shell or tart shell that is baked unfilled, using baking weights or beans to support the crust as it bakes

baker's percentage—a system for measuring ingredients in a formula by expressing ingredient weights as a percentage of the total flour weight

baking—a dry-heat cooking method in which foods are surrounded by hot, dry air in a closed environment; the same as roasting, the term baking is usually applied to breads, pastries, vegetables and fish

baking powder—a mixture of sodium bicarbonate and one or more acids, generally cream of tartar and/or sodium aluminum sulfate, used to leaven baked goods; it releases carbon dioxide gas if moisture is present in a formula; single-acting baking powder releases carbon dioxide gas in the presence of moisture only in contrast to double-acting baking powder, which releases some carbon dioxide gas upon contact with moisture and more gas when heat is applied

baking soda—sodium bicarbonate, an alkaline compound that releases carbon dioxide gas when combined with an acid and moisture; used to leaven baked goods

ballotine—[bahl-lo-TEEN] classic French preparation made by stuffing a deboned poultry leg with forcemeat; it is poached or braised and served hot; similar to a galantine, which is served cold

banneton—[ban-eh-TON] a traditional willow basket, often lined with canvas, in which yeast bread is placed to rise before baking

banquet—a formal dinner, often with speakers or entertainment; a celebration meal for a business group, a wedding party or academic gathering; the food at a banquet is sometimes served buffet style

banquet event order (BEO)—the written record of the plans and arrangements for a specific catered event, buffet or banquet

barbecue—(1) to cook foods over dry heat created by the burning of hardwood or hardwood charcoals; (2) a tangy tomato- or vinegar-based sauce used for grilled foods; (3) foods cooked by this method and/or with this sauce

barding—tying thin slices of fat, such as bacon or pork fatback, over meats or poultry that have little to no natural fat covering in order to protect and moisten them during roasting

barista—Italian for "bartender"; used to describe someone who has been professionally trained in the art of preparing espresso and espresso-based beverages

base—a substance that neutralizes an acid in a liquid solution; ingredients such as sodium bicarbonate (baking soda) that have an alkaline

or bitter flavor; bases have a pH of more than 7; also known as an alkali

baste—to moisten foods during cooking (usually grilling, broiling or roasting) with melted fat, pan drippings, a sauce or other liquids to prevent drying and to add flavor

bâtonnet—[bah-toh-NAY] foods cut into matchstick shapes of ¼ inch × ¼ inch × 2 inches (6 millimeters × 6 millimeters × 5 centimeters)

batter—(1) a semiliquid mixture containing flour or other starch used to make cakes and breads; the gluten development is minimized and the liquid forms the continuous medium in which other ingredients are disbursed; generally contains more fat, sugar and liquids than a dough; (2) a semiliquid mixture of liquid and starch used to coat foods for deep-frying

Baumé scale—[boh-may] a hydrometer scale used to measure the specific gravity of liquids such as sugar solutions; syrup with a higher density contains more dissolved sugar

Bavarian cream—a sweet dessert mixture made by thickening custard sauce with gelatin and then folding in whipped cream; the final product is poured into a mold and chilled until firm

bean flour—cooked beans including chickpeas, soybeans and white beans that are dried, then ground into a fine powder; bean flours, especially soy flour with a 50% protein content, are added to wheat flour mixtures to boost protein content

beard—a clump of dark threads found on a mussel

béarnaise—[bare-NAYZ] a compound sauce made from hollandaise flavored with a reduction of vinegar, shallots, tarragon and peppercorns

beating—a mixing method in which foods are vigorously agitated to incorporate air or develop gluten; a spoon or electric mixer with its paddle attachment is used

béchamel—[bay-shah-mell] a leading sauce made by thickening milk with a white roux and adding seasonings

beefalo—the product of crossbreeding a bison (American buffalo) and a domestic beef animal

beer—an alcoholic beverage made from water, hops and malted barley, fermented by yeast; beer's alcohol content is 3–12 percent

beignets—squares or strips of éclair paste deep-fried and dusted with powdered sugar

berry—(1) the kernel of certain grains such as wheat; (2) small, juicy fruits that grow on vines and bushes

beurre blanc—[burr BLANHK] French for "white butter"; an emulsified butter sauce made from shallots, white wine and whole butter

beurre composé—[burr kom-poh-ZAY] see **compound butter**

beurre fondu—[burr fon-DOO] French for "melted butter"; often served over steamed vegetables such as asparagus or poached white fish

beurre manié—[burr man-YAY] a combination of equal amounts by weight of flour and soft, whole butter; it is whisked into a simmering sauce at the end of the cooking process for quick thickening and added sheen and flavor

beurre noir—[burr NWAR] French for "black butter"; whole butter cooked until dark brown (not black) sometimes flavored with vinegar or lemon juice, capers and parsley and served over fish, eggs and vegetables

beurre noisette—[burr nwah-ZEHT] French for "brown butter"; whole butter cooked until it is a light brown color; it is flavored and used in much the same manner as beurre noir

beurre rouge—[burr ROOGE] French for "red butter"; an emulsified butter sauce made from shallots, red wine and whole butter

biological hazard—a danger to the safety of food caused by disease-causing microorganisms such as bacteria, molds, yeasts, viruses or fungi

biscotti—twice-baked cookies with a long-lasting, firm, crisp texture; Italian in origin, they are usually served with coffee, wine or tea

biscuit method—a mixing method used to make biscuits, scones and flaky doughs; it involves cutting cold fat into the flour and other dry ingredients before any liquid is added

bisque—[bisk] a soup made from shellfish; classic versions are thickened with rice

bivalves—mollusks, such as clams, oysters and mussels, that have two bilateral shells attached at a central hinge

blanching—very briefly and partially cooking a food in boiling water or hot fat; used to assist preparation, as part of a combination cooking method or to remove undesirable flavors

blanquette—[blahn-KEHT] a white stew made of a white sauce and meat or poultry that is simmered without first browning

blast freezer—a commercial refrigeration unit that will quickly and uniformly reduce the temperature of foods below 40°F (4°C) by circulating cold air at high speeds; also known as a blast chiller

blending—a mixing method in which two or more ingredients are combined just until they are evenly distributed

blini—a small yeast-raised pancake of Russian origin made with buckwheat flour; traditionally served with caviar, smoked fish and other delicacies

bloom—(1) a white, powdery layer that sometimes appears on chocolate if the cocoa butter separates; (2) a measure of gelatin's strength; (3) to soften granulated gelatin in a cold liquid before dissolving and using

blue cheese—(1) a generic term for any cheese containing visible blue-green molds that contribute a characteristic tart, sharp flavor and aroma; also known as a blue-veined cheese or bleu; (2) a group of Roquefort-style cheeses made in the United States and Canada from cow's or goat's milk rather than ewe's milk and injected with molds that form blue-green veins; also known as blue mold cheese or blue-veined cheese

boiling—a moist-heat cooking method that uses convection to transfer heat from a hot (approximately 212°F/100°C) liquid to the food submerged in it; the turbulent waters and higher temperatures cook foods more quickly than do poaching or simmering

bombe—two or more flavors of ice cream, or ice cream and sherbet, shaped in a spherical mold; each flavor is a separate layer that forms the shell for the next flavor

bonito—thin flakes of dried fermented bonito fish, used in many Japanese dishes as a seasoning or topping; also known as *katsuobushi*

bouchées—[boo-SHAY] small puff pastry shells filled and served as bite-size hors d'oeuvre or petit fours

bound salad—a salad composed of cooked meats, poultry, fish, shellfish, pasta or potatoes combined with a dressing

bouquet garni—[boo-KAY gar-NEE] fresh herbs and vegetables tied into a bundle with twine and used to flavor stocks, sauces, soups and stews

bouquetière—[boo-kuh-TYEHR] a garnish (bouquet) of carefully cut and arranged fresh vegetables

boxed beef—industry terminology for primal and subprimal cuts of beef that are vacuum sealed and packed into cardboard boxes for shipping from the packing plant to retailers and food service operations

braising—a combination cooking method in which foods are first browned in hot fat, then covered and slowly cooked in a small amount of liquid over low heat; braising uses a combination of simmering and steaming to transfer heat from the liquid (conduction) and the air (convection) to the foods

bran—the tough outer layer of a cereal grain and the part highest in fiber

brandy—an alcoholic beverage made by distilling wine or the fermented mash of grapes or other fruits; brandy's alcohol content is 35–60 percent

brawn—also called an aspic terrine, made from simmered meats packed into a terrine and covered with aspic

brazier or **brasier**—a pan designed for braising; usually round with two handles and a tight-fitting lid

breading—(1) a coating of bread or cracker crumbs, cornmeal or other dry meal applied to foods that will typically be deep-fried or pan-fried; (2) the process of applying this coating

brigade—a system of staffing a kitchen so that each worker is assigned a set of specific tasks; these tasks are often related by cooking method, equipment or the types of foods being produced

brine—a mixture of salt, water and seasonings used to preserve and flavor foods

brioche—[bree-OHSH] a rich yeast bread containing large amounts of eggs and butter

brochettes—[bro-SHETTS] skewers, either small hors d'oeuvre or large entrée size, threaded with meat, poultry, fish, shellfish and/or vegetables and grilled, broiled or baked; sometimes served with a dipping sauce

broiling—a dry-heat cooking method in which foods are cooked by heat radiating from an overhead source

brotform—[BROT-form] a traditional woven basket in which yeast bread is placed to rise before baking; the basket leaves marks in the dough's surface; heavy plastic versions are available for commercial food service use

broth—a flavorful liquid obtained from the long simmering of meats and/or vegetables

brown stew—a stew in which the meat is first browned in hot fat

brown stock—a richly colored stock made of chicken, veal, beef or game bones and vegetables, all of which are caramelized before they are simmered in water with seasonings

brunch—a late morning to early afternoon meal that takes the place of both breakfast and lunch; a brunch menu generally offers both traditional breakfast and lunch items

brunoise—[BROO-nwaz] (1) foods cut into cubes of ⅛ inch × ⅛ inch × ⅛ inch (3 millimeters × 3 millimeters × 3 millimeters); a ¹⁄₁₆-inch (1.5-millimeter) cube is referred to as a fine brunoise; (2) foods garnished with vegetables cut in this manner

buckwheat flour—a dark, nutty-tasting gluten-free flour milled from the seeds of the buckwheat plant; used for centuries in Middle Eastern and Asian countries to make bread, cereals, noodles and baked goods

buffet—the tables or furniture on which food is arranged and from which diners serve themselves or are served by waitstaff

buffet service—restaurant service in which diners serve themselves from a counter or table or are served by workers assigned to specific areas of the buffet; usually buffet-service-style restaurants charge by the meal; restaurants offering buffet service that charge by the dish are known as cafeterias

bun—any of a variety of small, round yeast rolls; can be sweet or savory

butcher—(1) to slaughter and/or dress or fabricate animals for consumption; (2) a person who fabricates, prepares or sells meat

butler service—restaurant service in which servers pass foods (typically hors d'oeuvre) or drinks arranged on trays

buttercream—a light, smooth, fluffy frosting of sugar, fat and flavorings; egg yolks or whipped egg whites are sometimes added; there are three principal kinds: simple, Italian and French

butterfly—to slice boneless meat, poultry or fish nearly in half lengthwise so that it spreads open like a book

C

caffeine—an alkaloid found in coffee beans, tea leaves and cocoa beans that acts as a stimulant

cake—in U.S. usage, refers to a broad range of pastries, including layer cakes, coffee cakes and gâteaux; can refer to almost any food that is baked, tender, sweet and sometimes frosted

cake cardboard—precut rounds, squares or rectangles of clean, thin, disposable cardboard used to support the layers of a cake for service or display; especially useful for retail purchases; generally coated with a water and fat resistant substance, which is often colored gold or white

calf—(1) a young cow or bull; (2) the meat of calves slaughtered when they are older than five months

California or **New American cuisine**—a late 20th-century movement that first became popular in California and spread across the United States; it stresses the use of fresh, locally grown, seasonal produce and high-quality ingredients simply prepared in a fashion that preserves and emphasizes natural flavors

calorie—the unit of energy measured by the amount of heat required to raise 1000 grams of water one degree Celsius; also written as kilocalorie or kcal

canapé—[KAN-ah-pay] a tiny open-faced sandwich served as an hors d'oeuvre; usually composed of a small piece of bread or toast topped with a savory spread and garnish

capicola—Italian dry-cured salami made from pork shoulder that is seasoned with garlic, hot pepper, spices and wine, then smoked and cured

capon—[kay-pahn] the class of surgically castrated male chickens; they have well-flavored meat and soft, smooth skin

capsaicin—[kap-SAY-ee-zin] an alkaloid found in a chile pepper's placental ribs that provides the pepper's heat

caramelization—the process of cooking sugars; the browning of sugar enhances the flavor and appearance of foods

carbohydrates—a group of compounds composed of oxygen, hydrogen and carbon that supply the body with energy (4 calories per gram); carbohydrates are classified as simple (including certain sugars) and complex (including starches and fiber)

carotenoid—a naturally occurring pigment that predominates in red and yellow vegetables, such as carrots and red peppers

carryover cooking—the cooking that continues to occur after a food is removed from a heat source; caused by the residual heat remaining in the food

cartilage—also known as gristle; a tough, elastic, whitish connective tissue that helps give structure to an animal's body

carve—to cut cooked meat or poultry into portions

casein—a protein found in all types of milk

casings—membranes used to hold forcemeat for sausages; they can be natural animal intestines or manufactured from collagen extracted from cattle hides

casserole—(1) a heavy dish, usually ceramic, for baking foods; (2) foods baked in a casserole dish

caul fat—a fatty membrane from pig or sheep intestines; it resembles fine netting and is used to bard roasts and pâtés and to encase forcemeat for sausages

caviar—traditionally, the salted roe (eggs) of sturgeon fish; imported sturgeon caviar is classified by species, size and color as beluga, osetra, or sevruga

celiac disease—an inherited autoimmune disease that causes damage to nutrient receptors (*villi*) in the small intestine when gluten is consumed

cellulose—fiber found in the cell wall of plants; it is edible but indigestible by humans

cephalopods—mollusks with a single, thin internal shell called a pen or cuttlebone, well-developed eyes, a number of arms that attach to the head and a saclike fin-bearing mantle, such as squid and octopus

chafing dish—a metal dish with a heating unit (flame or electric) used to keep foods warm at tableside or during buffet service

chalazae cords—thick, twisted strands of egg white that anchor the yolk in place

challah—[HAH-la] a yeast bread enriched with eggs and flavored with honey; loaves are traditionally braided and topped with sesame or poppy seeds

charcuterie—[shahr-COO-tuhr-ree] the production of pâtés, terrines, galantines, sausages and similar foods

chaud-froid—[shoh-FRAWH] French for "hot-cold"; refers to a white sauce made with either mayonnaise or cream and stock thickened with gelatin; used to coat foods such as whole fish or poultry for decorative purposes

cheesecloth—a light, fine mesh gauze used to strain liquids and make sachets

chef de cuisine—[chef duh qui-zine] also known simply as chef; the person responsible for all kitchen operations, developing menu items and setting the kitchen's tone and tempo

chef de partie—also known as station chef; produces the menu items under the direct supervision of the chef or sous chef

chef's knife—an all-purpose knife used for chopping, slicing and mincing; its tapering blade is 8–14 inches (20–35 centimeters) long

chemical hazard—a danger to the safety of food caused by chemical substances, especially cleaning agents, pesticides or toxic metals

chèvre—[SHEHV-ruh] French for "goat"; generally refers to a cheese made from goat's milk

chiffon—(1) a cake leavened with whipped egg whites and enriched with egg yolks and oil, usually flavored with citrus and baked in a tube pan; (2) a pie filling or dessert preparation lightened with whipped egg whites and thickened with gelatin

chiffonade—[chef-fon-NAHD] to finely slice or shred leafy vegetables or herbs

chile—a member of the *Capsicum* family; may be used fresh or dried or dried and ground into a powder that is used as a spice

chili—a stew-like dish containing chiles

chilli—a commercial spice powder containing a blend of seasonings

china cap—a cone-shaped strainer made of perforated metal

chine—the backbone or spine of an animal; a subprimal cut of beef, veal, lamb, pork or game carcass containing a portion of the backbone with some adjoining flesh

chinois—[sheen-WAH] a conical strainer made of fine mesh, used for straining and puréeing foods

chlorophyll—a naturally occurring pigment that predominates in green vegetables, such as cabbage

cholesterol—a fatty substance found in foods derived from animal products and in the human body; it has been linked to heart disease

chop—(1) a cut of meat, including part of the rib; (2) to cut into pieces when uniformity of size and shape is not important

chorizo—[chor-EE-zoh] a coarse, spicy pork sausage flavored with ground chiles used in Mexican and Spanish cuisines

choux pastry—[shoo] see **éclair paste**

chowder—a hearty soup made from fish, shellfish and/or vegetables, usually containing milk and potatoes and often thickened with roux

churros—a Spanish and Mexican pastry in which sticks of éclair paste flavored with cinnamon are deep-fried and rolled in sugar while still hot

chutney—a sweet-and-sour condiment made of fruits and/or vegetables cooked in vinegar with sugar and spices; some chutneys are reduced to a purée, while others retain recognizable pieces of their ingredients

cider—mildly fermented apple juice; nonalcoholic apple juice may also be labeled cider

citrus—fruits characterized by a thick rind, most of which is a bitter white pith (albedo) with a thin exterior layer of colored skin (zest); their flesh is segmented and juicy and varies from bitter to tart to sweet

clarification—(1) the process of transforming a broth into a clear consommé by trapping impurities with a clearmeat consisting of the egg white protein albumen, ground meat, an acidic product, mirepoix and other ingredients; (2) the clearmeat used to clarify a broth

clarified butter—purified butterfat; the butter is melted and the water and milk solids are removed

classic cuisine—a late 19th- and early 20th-century refinement and simplification of French *grande cuisine*; classic (or classical) cuisine relies on the thorough exploration of culinary principles and techniques, and emphasizes the refined preparation and presentation of superb ingredients

clean—to remove visible dirt and soil

clear soups—unthickened soups, including broths, consommés and broth-based soups

clearmeat—see **clarification**

club roll—a small oval-shaped roll made of crusty French bread

coagulation—the irreversible transformation of proteins from a liquid or semiliquid state to a solid state

cocoa butter—fat found in cocoa beans and used in fine chocolates; it is white, solid at room temperature and tasteless

coconut cream—(1) a coconut-flavored liquid made like coconut milk but with less water; it is creamier and thicker than coconut milk; (2) the thick fatty portion that separates and rises to the top of canned or frozen coconut milk; do not substitute cream of coconut for true coconut cream

coconut milk—a coconut-flavored liquid made by pouring boiling water over shredded coconut; may be sweetened or unsweetened; do not substitute cream of coconut for coconut milk

coconut water—the thin, slightly opaque liquid contained within a fresh coconut

collagen—a protein found in connective tissue; it is converted into gelatin when cooked with moisture

composed salad—a salad prepared by arranging each of the ingredients (the base, body, garnish and dressing) on individual plates in an artistic fashion

composition—a completed plate's structure of colors, shapes and arrangements

compote—whole or cut pieces of fruit stewed in sugar syrup

compound butter—also known as a beurre composé, a mixture of softened whole butter and flavorings used as a sauce or to flavor and color other sauces

compound sauces—see **small sauces**

concassée—peeled, seeded and diced tomato

concentrate—also known as a fruit paste or compound; a reduced fruit purée, without a gel structure, used as a flavoring

conching—stirring melted chocolate with large stone or metal rollers to create a smooth texture in the finished chocolate

condiment—traditionally, any item added to a dish for flavor, including herbs, spices and vinegars; now also refers to cooked or prepared flavorings, such as prepared mustards, relishes, bottled sauces and pickles

conduction—the transfer of heat (energy) from one item to another through direct contact

confit—[kohn-FEE] meat or poultry (often lightly salt-cured) slowly cooked and preserved in its own fat and served hot

connective tissue—tissue found throughout an animal's body that binds together and supports other tissues such as muscles

consommé—a rich stock or broth that has been clarified with clearmeat to remove impurities

contaminants—biological, chemical or physical substances that can be harmful when consumed in sufficient quantities

contamination—the presence, generally unintentional, of harmful organisms or substances

convection—the transfer of heat (energy) through a fluid (such as water or air) by natural or mechanical circulation

conversion factor (C.F.)—a number used to increase or decrease ingredient quantities and recipe yields

cookery—the art, practice or work of cooking

cookie press—also known as a cookie gun, a hollow tube fitted with a plunger and an interchangeable decorative tip or plate; soft cookie dough is pressed through the tip to create shapes or patterns

cookies—small, sweet, flat pastries; usually classified by preparation or makeup techniques as drop, icebox, bar, sheet, cut-out, piped, rolled or molded and wafer

cooking—(1) the transfer of energy from a heat source to a food; this energy alters the food's molecular structure, changing its texture, flavor, aroma and appearance; (2) the preparation of food for consumption

cooking medium—the air, fat, water or steam in which a food is cooked

coring—the process of removing the seeds or pit from a fruit or fruit-vegetable

cost of goods sold—the total cost of food items sold during a given period; calculated as beginning inventory plus purchases minus ending inventory

cost per portion—the amount of the total recipe cost divided by the number of portions produced from that recipe; the cost of one serving

couche—[coo-SH] heavy linen canvas that is floured and folded to hold yeast dough while it rises before baking

coulibiac—a creamy mixture of salmon fillet, rice, hard-cooked eggs, mushrooms, shallots and dill enclosed in a pastry envelope usually made of brioche dough

coulis—[koo-LEE] a sauce made from a purée of vegetables or fruit; may be served hot or cold

count—the number of individual items in a given measure of weight or volume

coupe—another name for an ice cream sundae, especially one served with a fruit topping

court bouillon—a liquid in which fish or vegetables are poached; made by simmering vegetables and seasonings in water and an acidic liquid, such as vinegar or wine

couverture—[coo-vehr-TYOOR] high quality chocolate containing at least 32 percent cocoa butter

cracking—a milling process in which grains are broken open and cut into smaller pieces

cream of coconut—a canned commercial product consisting of thick, sweetened coconut-flavored liquid; used for baking and in beverages

cream puffs—baked rounds of éclair paste cut in half and filled with pastry cream, whipped cream, fruit or other filling

cream sauce—a sauce made by adding cream to a béchamel sauce

cream soup—a soup made of vegetables cooked in a liquid that is thickened with a starch and puréed; cream is incorporated to add richness and flavor

creaming or **creaming method**—a mixing method in which softened fat and sugar are vigorously combined to incorporate air

creams—also known as crèmes; include light, fluffy or creamy-textured dessert foods made with whipped cream or whipped egg whites, such as Bavarian creams, chiffons, mousses and crème Chantilly

crème anglaise—[khrem ahn-GLEHZ] also known as crème à l'anglaise; see **vanilla custard sauce**

crème brûlée—[krehm broo-LAY] French for "burnt cream"; used to describe a rich dessert custard topped with a crust of caramelized sugar

crème caramel—[khrem kair-ah-MEHL] like crème renversée [rehn-vehr-SAY] and flan, a custard baked over a layer of caramelized sugar that is inverted for service

crème Chantilly—[khrem shan-TEE] heavy cream whipped to soft peaks and flavored with sugar and vanilla; used to garnish pastries or desserts or folded into cooled custard or pastry cream for fillings

crème Chiboust—[krehm chee-BOOS] a vanilla pastry cream lightened by folding in Italian meringue; traditionally used in a gâteau St. Honoré

crème pâtissière—[khrem pah-tees-SYEHR] see **pastry cream**

crêpe—[krayp] a thin, delicate unleavened griddlecake made with a very thin egg batter cooked in a very hot sauté pan; used in sweet and savory preparations

crépinettes—a small flat disc of forcemeat wrapped in caul fat, cooked and served as a fresh sausage

critical control point (CCP)—a point, step or procedure at which control can be applied and a food safety hazard can be prevented, eliminated or reduced to an acceptable level

croquembouche—[kroh-kum-BOOSH] a pyramid of small puffs, each filled with pastry cream; a French tradition for Christmas and weddings, it is held together with caramelized sugar and decorated with spun sugar or marzipan flowers

croquette—[crow-KEHT] a food that has been puréed or bound with a thick sauce (usually béchamel or velouté), made into small shapes and then breaded and deep-fried

cross-contamination—the transfer of bacteria or other contaminants from one food, work surface or piece of equipment to another

crouton—[KROO-tawn] a bread or pastry garnish, usually toasted or sautéed until crisp

cruciferous—plants from the cabbage family including broccoli, cauliflower, cabbage, kale, rutabaga and turnip, also called brassicas

crudités—[croo-dee-TAYS] generally refers to raw or blanched vegetables served as an hors d'oeuvre and often accompanied by a dip

crullers—a Dutch pastry in which a loop or strip of twisted éclair paste is deep-fried

crumb—the texture, appearance and general structure of the interior of baked bread and cake; may be elastic, aerated, fine grained or coarse grained

crustaceans—shellfish characterized by a hard outer skeleton or shell and jointed appendages, such as lobsters, crabs and shrimp

cuisine—the ingredients, seasonings, cooking procedures and styles attributable to a particular group of people; the group can be defined by geography, history, ethnicity, politics, culture or religion

cuisson—[kwee-sohn] the liquid used for shallow poaching

culinarian—someone who is skilled in preparing food, generally a professional cook or chef

cupping—testing coffee or tea for taste and quality, often performed by a professional taster trained to identify key coffee or tea characteristics and test for problems or faults

curd—(1) the solid portion of milk when it separates, which becomes cheese; (2) a stirred custard made from eggs, sugar, butter and fruit juice, usually citrus

curdling—the separation of milk or egg mixtures into solid and liquid components; caused by overcooking, high heat or the presence of acids

cure—(1) to preserve eggs, fish, game, meat or poultry with brine, dry air, salt, smoke or a combination of these methods; (2) a brine or salt mixture used to prepare a food item for preservation or use

curing salt—a mixture of salt and sodium nitrite that inhibits bacterial growth; used as a preservative, often for charcuterie items

custard—any liquid thickened by the coagulation of egg proteins; its consistency depends on the ratio of eggs to liquid and the type of liquid used; can be baked in the oven or cooked in a bain marie or on the stove top

cutlet—a relatively thick, boneless slice of meat

cutting—(1) reducing a food to smaller pieces; (2) a mixing method in which solid fat is incorporated into dry ingredients until only lumps of the desired size remain

cutting loss—the unavoidable and unrecoverable loss of food during fabrication; the loss is usually the result of food particles sticking to the cutting board or the evaporation of liquids

cuttlebone—also known as the pen, the single, thin internal shell of cephalopods

D

dairy products—include cow's milk and foods produced from cow's milk such as butter, yogurt, sour cream and cheese; sometimes other milks and products made from them are included (e.g., goat's milk cheese)

dashi—Japanese stock or fish broth made with seaweed (kombu) and flakes of dried fish (bonito); used in soups, sauces and as a simmering liquid

decant—to separate liquid from solids without disturbing the sediment by pouring off the liquid; vintage wines are often decanted to remove sediment

decoction—(1) boiling a food until its flavor is removed; (2) a procedure used for brewing coffee

deep-frying—a dry-heat cooking method that uses convection to transfer heat to a food submerged in hot fat; foods to be deep-fried are usually first coated in batter or breading

deglaze—to swirl or stir a liquid (usually wine or stock) in a pan to dissolve cooked food particles remaining on the bottom; the resulting mixture often becomes the base for a sauce

degrease—to remove fat from the surface of a liquid such as a stock or sauce by skimming, scraping or lifting congealed fat

demi-glace—[deh-me glass] French for "half-glaze"; a mixture of half brown stock and half brown sauce reduced by half

density—the relationship between the mass and volume of a substance ($D = m/v$); for example, as more and more sugar is dissolved in a liquid, the heavier or denser the liquid will become; sugar density is measured on the Baumé scale using a hydrometer or saccharometer

détrempe—a paste made with flour and water during the first stage of preparing a pastry dough, especially rolled-in doughs

deveining—the process of removing a shrimp's digestive tract

deviled—describes meat, poultry or other food seasoned with mustard, vinegar and other spicy seasonings

diagonals—oval-shaped slices

dice—to cut into cubes with six equal-sized sides

dip—a thick, creamy sauce, served hot or cold, to accompany crudités, crackers, chips or other foods, especially as an hors d'oeuvre; dips are often based on sour cream, mayonnaise or cream cheese

direct contamination—the contamination of raw foods in their natural setting or habitat

distillation—the separation of alcohol from a liquid (or, during the production of alcoholic beverages, from a fermented mash); it is accomplished by heating the liquid or mash creating a gas that contains alcohol vapors; this vapor is then condensed into the desired alcoholic liquid (beverage)

diver scallops—scallops that are harvested from the ocean by divers who hand-pick each one; diver scallops tend to be less gritty than those harvested by dragging, and hand-harvesting is more ecologically friendly

dock—to prick small holes in an unbaked dough or crust to allow steam to escape and to prevent the dough from rising when baked

dough—a mixture of flour and other ingredients used in baking; has a low moisture content, and gluten forms the continuous medium into which other ingredients are embedded; it is often stiff enough to cut into shapes

drawn—a market form for fish in which the viscera (internal organs) are removed

dredging—coating a food with flour or finely ground crumbs; usually done prior to sautéing or frying or as the first step of the standard breading procedure

dress—to trim or otherwise prepare an animal carcass for consumption

dressed—a market form for fish in which the viscera, gills, fins and scales are removed

dressing—another name for a bread stuffing used with poultry

dry-heat cooking methods—cooking methods, principally broiling, grilling, roasting and baking, sautéing, pan-frying and deep-frying, that use air or fat to transfer heat through conduction and convection; dry-heat cooking methods allow surface sugars to caramelize

drying—a preservation method in which the food's moisture content is dramatically reduced; drying changes the food's texture, flavor and appearance

duchesse potatoes—[duh-shees] a purée of cooked potatoes, butter and egg yolks, seasoned with salt, pepper and nutmeg; can be eaten as is or used to prepare several classic potato dishes

duckling—a duck slaughtered before it is eight weeks old

dumpling—any of a variety of small starchy products made from doughs or batters that are simmered or steamed; can be plain or filled

durum wheat—a species of very hard wheat with a particularly high amount of protein; it is used to make couscous or milled into semolina flour, which is used for making pasta

duxelles—a coarse paste made of finely chopped mushrooms sautéed with shallots in butter; used in sauces and stuffing

E

éclair paste—[ay-clahr] a soft dough that produces hollow baked products with crisp exteriors; used for making éclairs, cream puffs and savory products; also known as pâte à choux

éclairs—baked fingers of éclair paste filled with pastry cream; the top is then coated with chocolate glaze or fondant

edible portion (E.P.)—the amount of a food item available for consumption or use after trimming or fabrication; a smaller, more convenient portion of a larger or bulk unit

egg wash—a mixture of beaten eggs (whole eggs, yolks or whites) and a liquid, usually milk or water, used to coat doughs before baking to add sheen

elastin—a protein found in connective tissues, particularly ligaments and tendons; it often appears as the white or silver covering on meats known as silverskin

émincé—[eh-man-SAY] a small, thin, boneless piece of meat

emulsification—the process by which generally unmixable liquids, such as oil and water, are forced into a uniform distribution

emulsified shortening—a vegetable-oil based shortening made with additional emulsifiers (mono- and diglycerides), used to make cake batters containing higher than normal amounts of water and sugar; also referred to as icing shortening, cake shortening or high ratio shortening

emulsifier—a substance (natural or manufactured) added to a mixture to assist in the binding of unmixable liquids such as oil and water; manufactured chemicals may be used as emulsifiers, but naturally-occurring soy and egg lecithin are commonly used in processed foods

emulsion—a uniform mixture of two unmixable liquids; it is often temporary (e.g., oil in water)

en croûte—[awn KROOT] describes a food encased in a bread or pastry crust

en papillote—[awn pa-pee-YOTE] a cooking method in which food is wrapped in paper or foil and heated so that the food steams in its own moisture

endosperm—the largest part of a cereal grain and a source of protein and carbohydrates (starch); used in milled products

entrée—the main dish of a meal in the United States and Canada, usually meat, poultry, fish or shellfish accompanied by a vegetable and starch; in France, the term entrée refers to the first course, served before the fish and meat courses

escargot—[ays-skahr-GO] French for "snail"; those used for culinary purposes are land snails (genus *Helix*); the most popular are the large Burgundy snails and the smaller but more flavorful common or garden snail known as *petit gris*

espagnole—[ess-spah-nyol] a leading sauce made of brown stock, mirepoix and tomatoes thickened with brown roux; often used to produce demi-glace; also known as brown sauce

espresso—a method for brewing coffee in which hot water is forced through finely ground and packed coffee under high pressure, the coffee beans used are traditionally roasted very dark before grinding; espresso coffee is the base for many drinks, such as cappuccino and caffé latte, to which steamed and/or foamed milk are added

essence—a sauce made from a concentrated vegetable juice

essential nutrients—nutrients that must be provided by food because the body cannot or does not produce them in sufficient quantities

essential oils—pure oils extracted from the skins, peels and other parts of plants used to give their aroma and taste to flavoring agents in foods, cosmetics and other products

ethnic cuisine—the cuisine of a group of people having a common cultural heritage, as opposed to the cuisine of a group of people bound together by geography or political factors

ethylene gas—a colorless, odorless hydrocarbon gas naturally emitted from fruits and fruit-vegetables that encourages ripening

evaporation—the process by which heated water molecules move faster and faster until the water turns to a gas (steam) and vaporizes; evaporation is responsible for the drying of foods during cooking

ewe's milk—produced by a female sheep; it has approximately 7.9% milkfat, 11.4% milk solids and 80.7% water

extracts—concentrated mixtures of ethyl alcohol and flavoring oils such as vanilla, almond and lemon

extrusion—the process of forcing pasta dough through perforated plates to create various shapes; pasta dough that is not extruded must be rolled and cut

F

fabricate—to cut a larger portion of raw meat (e.g., a primal or subprimal), poultry or fish into smaller portions

fabricated cuts—individual portions cut from a subprimal of raw meat, poultry or fish

facultative bacteria—bacteria that can adapt and will survive with or without oxygen

fair trade—a global social movement that helps commodity producers in developing countries obtain a fair deal for their export goods (e.g., fruit, coffee beans and cacao beans), supports sustainable farming practices and discourages the use of certain pesticides and bans child labor

fancy—(1) fish that has been previously frozen; (2) a quality grade for fruits, especially canned or frozen

farinaceous—a food made from flour or meal, or having a starchy, mealy texture; from the Latin *farina* meaning a flour made from cereal grains or nuts; refers to food that is high in starch, especially pasta, noodles, rice and polenta

farmer's cheese—a soft, creamy fresh cheese made from cow's, goat's or sheep's milk

farm-to-table movement—an awareness of the source of ingredients with an emphasis on serving locally grown and minimally processed foods in season

fatback—fresh pork fat from the back of a pig, used for barding lean meats and poultry and for seasoning vegetables or other dishes

fats—(1) a group of compounds composed of oxygen, hydrogen and carbon atoms that supply the body with energy (9 calories per gram); fats are classified as saturated, monounsaturated or polyunsaturated; (2) the general term for butter, lard, shortening, oil and margarine used as cooking media or ingredients

fermentation—the metabolic process by which certain bacteria and yeasts (fungi) convert carbohydrates into enzymes, carbon dioxide and ethyl alcohol; (2) the time that yeast dough is left to rise—that is, the time it takes for carbon dioxide gas cells to form and become trapped in the gluten network

feuilletées—[fuh-yuh-TAY] square, rectangular or diamond-shaped puff pastry boxes; filled with sweet or savory mixtures

fiber—also known as dietary fiber; indigestible carbohydrates found in grains, fruits and vegetables; fiber aids digestion

fiddleheads—the young unfurled tips of several species of fern plants, which are harvested in early spring

FIFO (first in, first out)—a system of rotating inventory, particularly perishable and semiperishable goods, in which items are used in the order in which they are received

filet, fillet—[fee-lay] (1) filet: a boneless tenderloin of meat; (2) fillet: the side of a fish removed intact, boneless or semiboneless, with or without skin; (3) to cut such a piece

fish velouté—a velouté sauce made from fish stock

flambé—[flahm-BAY] food served flaming; produced by igniting brandy, rum or other liquor

flan—a firm savory or sweet egg custard; dessert variety is baked over a layer of caramelized sugar and inverted for service

flash-frozen—describes food that has been frozen very rapidly using metal plates, extremely low temperatures or chemical solutions

flash point—the temperature at which a fat ignites and small flames appear on the surface of the fat

flatfish—fish with asymmetrical, compressed bodies that swim in a horizontal position and have both eyes on the top of the head such as sole, flounder and halibut

flavonoids—plant pigments that dissolve readily in water; they are found in red, purple and white vegetables such as blueberries, red cabbage, onions and tea

flavor—an identifiable or distinctive quality of a food, drink or other substance perceived with the combined senses of taste, touch and smell

flavored tea—tea to which flavorings such as essential oils, dried fruit, spices, flowers and herbs have been added

flavoring—an item that adds a new taste to a food and alters its natural flavors; flavorings include herbs, spices, vinegars and condiments; the terms *seasoning* and *flavoring* are often used interchangeably

flax—a grain plant also known as linseed; rich in omega-3 fatty acids, a compound beneficial for promoting heart and arterial health; flax hulls and seeds are crushed into a meal or flour

fleuron—[fluh-rawng] a crescent-shaped piece of puff pastry used as a garnish

flour—a powdery substance of varying degrees of fineness made by milling grains such as wheat, corn or rye

foamed milk—milk that is heated and frothed with air and steam generated by an espresso machine; it will be slightly cooler than steamed milk

foams—light sauces made by thickening a liquid base with gums or stabilizers, then aerating it in a whipping siphon; the final texture is similar to whipped egg whites, but with an intense flavor

foie gras—[fwah grah] liver of specially fattened geese or ducks

fold—(1) a mixing method; (2) a measurement of the strength of vanilla extract

folding—a mixing method in which light, airy ingredients are incorporated into heavier ingredients by gently moving them from the bottom of the bowl up over the top in a circular motion, usually with a rubber spatula

fond—(1) French for "stock" or "base"; (2) the concentrated juices, drippings and bits of food left in pans after foods are roasted or sautéed; *fond* is used to flavor sauces made directly in the pans in which foods were cooked

fond lié—[fahn lee-ay] see **jus lié**

fondant—[FAHN-dant] a sweet, thick opaque sugar paste commonly used for glazing pastries such as napoleons or making candies

fondue—a Swiss specialty made with melted cheese, wine and flavorings; diners dip pieces of bread into the hot mixture with long forks

food allergy—an immune system response to a substance in food; the response may be digestive discomfort, breathing difficulties, rashes and other physical reactions, some of which may be fatal

Food and Drug Administration (FDA)—U.S. agency that protects the nation's health against impure and unsafe foods as well as drugs and cosmetics; develops and administers programs addressing food safety

food cost—the cost of the materials that go directly into the production of menu items

food cost percentage—the ratio of the cost of foods used to the total food sales during a set period; calculated by dividing the cost of food used by the total sales in a restaurant

food intolerance—an abnormal response to a food or additive; it occurs when the body is unable to digest a certain component of a food

forcemeat—a preparation made from uncooked ground meats, poultry, fish or shellfish, seasoned, and emulsified with fat; commonly prepared as country-style, basic and mousseline and used for charcuterie items

fork tender—describes cooked food that is so tender it shows little resistance when pierced with a fork

formula—the standard term used throughout the industry for a bakeshop recipe; formulas rely on weighing to ensure accurate measuring of ingredients

frangipane—[fran-juh-pahn] a sweet almond and egg filling cooked inside pastry

free-range poultry—poultry allowed to move freely and forage for food; as opposed to those raised in coops; also known as pasture-raised

free-range veal—the meat of calves that are allowed to roam freely and eat grasses and other natural foods; meat is pinker and more strongly flavored than that of milk-fed calves

freezer burn—surface dehydration and discoloration of food that results from moisture loss at below-freezing temperatures

French dressing—classically, a vinaigrette dressing made from oil, vinegar, salt and pepper; in the United States, the term also refers to a commercially prepared dressing that is creamy, tartly sweet and red-orange in color

frenching—a method of trimming racks or individual chops of meat, especially lamb, in which the excess fat is cut away, leaving the eye muscle intact; all meat and connective tissue are removed from the rib bone

fricassee—[FRIHK-uh-see] a white stew in which the meat is cooked in fat without browning before the liquid is added

frittata—[free-TAH-ta] an open-faced omelet of Spanish-Italian origin

fritters—deep-fried sweet or savory cakes or spheres often made with chopped fruits or vegetables coated in batter

frosting—also known as icing, a sweet decorative coating used as a filling between the layers or as a coating over the top and sides of a cake

fruit—the edible organ that develops from the ovary of a flowering plant and contains one or more seeds (pips or pits)

frying—a dry-heat cooking method in which foods are cooked in hot fat; includes sautéing, stir-frying, pan-frying and deep-frying

fumet—[foo-may] a stock made from fish bones or shellfish shells and vegetables simmered in a liquid with flavorings

fungi—a large group of organisms ranging from single-celled organisms to giant mushrooms; the most common are molds and yeasts

fusion cuisine—the blending or use of ingredients and/or preparation methods from various ethnic, regional or national cuisines in the same dish; also known as transnational cuisine

G

galantine—[GAL-uhn-teen] similar to a ballotine; a charcuterie item made from a forcemeat of poultry, game or suckling pig usually wrapped in the skin of the bird or animal and poached in an appropriate stock; often served cold, usually in aspic

game—birds and animals hunted for sport or food; many game birds and animals are now ranch-raised and commercially available

game hen—the class of young or immature progeny of Cornish chickens or of a Cornish chicken and White Rock chicken; they are small and very flavorful

ganache—[ga-NAHSH] a rich blend of chocolate and heavy cream and, optionally, flavorings, used as a pastry or candy filling or frosting

garde-manger—[gar mawn-zhay] (1) also known as the pantry chef, the cook in charge of cold food production, including salads and salad dressings, charcuterie items, cold appetizers and buffet items; (2) the work area where these foods are prepared

garnish—(1) food used as an attractive decoration; (2) a subsidiary food used to add flavor or character to the main ingredient in a dish (e.g., noodles in chicken noodle soup)

gastrique—[gas-STREEK] caramelized sugar deglazed with vinegar; used to flavor tomato or savory fruit sauces

gastronomy—the art and science of eating well

gâteau—[gah-toe] (1) in U.S. usage, refers to any cake-type dessert; (2) in French usage, refers to various pastry items made with puff pastry, éclair paste, short dough or sweet dough

gaufrette—[goh-FREHT] a thin lattice or waffle-textured slice of vegetable cut on a mandoline

gauge—the thickness of a material such as aluminum; the lower the gauge number, the thicker the material

gelatin—a tasteless and odorless mixture of proteins (especially collagen) extracted from boiling bones, connective tissue and other animal parts; when dissolved in a hot liquid and then cooled, it forms a jellylike substance used as a thickener and stabilizer

gelatinization—the process by which starch granules are cooked; they absorb moisture when placed in a liquid and heated; as the moisture is absorbed, the product swells, softens and clarifies slightly

gelato—[jah-laht-toe] an Italian-style ice cream that is denser, softer and often more intensely flavored than American-style ice cream

genetically modified organism (GMO)—a plant, microorganism or animal in which genetic material (segments of DNA) have been modified or engineered in a laboratory in order to change inheritable characteristics, such as resistance to insects or herbicides

genoise—[zhen-waahz] (1) a form of whipped-egg cake that uses whole eggs whipped with sugar; (2) a French spongecake

germ—the smallest portion of a cereal grain and the only part that contains fat

ghee—a form of clarified butter in which the milk solids remain with the fat and are allowed to brown; originating in India and now used worldwide as an ingredient and cooking medium, it has a long shelf life, a high smoke point and a nutty, caramel-like flavor

gianduja—[zhahn-DOO-yah] chocolate blended with hazelnut paste

giblets—the collective term for edible poultry viscera, including gizzards, hearts, livers and necks

glaçage—[glah-SAHGE] browning or glazing a food, usually under a salamander or broiler

glace de poisson—[glahss duh pwah-sawng] a syrupy glaze made by reducing a fish stock

glace de viande—[glahss duh vee-awnd] a dark, syrupy meat glaze made by reducing a brown stock

glace de volaille—[glahss duh vo-lahy] a light brown, syrupy glaze made by reducing a chicken stock

glaze—(1) any shiny coating applied to food or created by browning; (2) the dramatic reduction and concentration of a stock; (3) a thin, flavored coating poured or dripped onto a cake or pastry

global cuisine—foods (often commercially produced items) or preparation methods that have become ubiquitous throughout the world; for example, curries and French-fried potatoes

glucose—(1) energy source for the body, also known as blood sugar; (2) a thick, sweet syrup made from cornstarch, composed primarily of dextrose; light corn syrup can usually be substituted for it in baked goods or candy making

gluten—an elastic network of proteins created when wheat flour is moistened and manipulated

goat's milk—milk produced by a female goat; it has approximately 4.1% milkfat, 8.9% milk solids and 87% water

gochujang—a fermented Korean chile paste made from cooked rice or barley, powdered soybeans, salt and chiles; its spicy, pungent flavor is used to season stews, fried foods, rice dishes and grilled meats

gougère—[goo-JAIR] éclair pastry flavored with cheese baked and served as a savory hors d'oeuvre

gourmand—a connoisseur of fine food and drink, often to excess

gourmet—a connoisseur of fine food and drink

gourmet foods—foods of the highest quality, perfectly prepared and beautifully presented

grading—a series of voluntary programs offered by the U.S. Department of Agriculture to designate a food's overall quality

grain—refers to the direction that bundles of muscle fibers run in a piece of meat; these fibers appear as parallel lines within the meat; cutting against the grain means to cut the meat perpendicular to the length of the lines of bundles, which makes the meat more tender by shortening the muscle fibers

grains—(1) grasses that bear edible seeds, including corn, rice and wheat; (2) the fruit (i.e., the seed or kernel) of such grasses

gram—the basic unit of weight in the metric system; equal to approximately 1/30 of an ounce; one ounce weighs 28.35 grams

grande cuisine—the rich, intricate and elaborate cuisine of the 18th- and 19th-century French aristocracy and upper classes based on the rational identification, development and adoption of strict culinary principles; by emphasizing the how and why of cooking, grande cuisine was the first to distinguish itself from regional cuisines, which tend to emphasize the tradition of cooking

grate—to cut a food into small, thin shreds by rubbing it against a serrated metal plate known as a grater

gravy—a sauce made from meat or poultry juices combined with a liquid and thickening agent; usually made in the pan in which the meat or poultry was cooked

gremolata—[greh-moa-LAH-tah] an aromatic garnish of chopped parsley, garlic and lemon zest used for osso buco

grilling—a dry-heat cooking method in which foods are cooked by heat radiating from a source located below the cooking surface; the heat can be generated by electricity or by burning gas, hardwood or hardwood charcoals

grind—to pulverize or reduce food to small particles using a mechanical grinder or food processor

grinding—a milling process in which grains are reduced to powder; the powder can be of differing degrees of fineness or coarseness

grosse piece—on a tray, platter, or mirror, a large piece of the principal food that serves as a centerpiece for that dish; for example, a large wheel of cheese with slices of the cheese cascading around it

gum paste—a smooth dough of sugar and gelatin that can be colored and used to make decorations, especially for pastries

H

HACCP—see **Hazard Analysis Critical Control Points**

halal—describes food prepared in accordance with Muslim dietary laws

Hazard Analysis Critical Control Points (HACCP)—a rigorous system of self-inspection used to manage and maintain sanitary conditions in all types of food service operations; it focuses on the flow of food through the food service facility to identify any point or step in preparation (known as a critical control point) where some action must be taken to prevent or minimize a risk or hazard

headcheese (Fr. *fromage de tête*)—a gelled loaf or sausage made from calf or hog head that has been simmered in a gelatinous broth, molded into a loaf and served sliced with pickles and mustard

herb—any of a large group of aromatic plants whose leaves, stems or flowers are used as a flavoring; used either dried or fresh

heritage or **heirloom breed**—refers to traditional breeds of pork, meat or poultry less commonly raised in modern agricultural systems; many believe that protecting a genetically diverse population of livestock by raising and consuming such animals is important culturally and scientifically and will help ensure human survival

high-ratio cake—a form of creamed-fat cake that uses emulsified shortening and a two-stage mixing method

hollandaise—[ohll-uhn-daze] an emulsified sauce made of butter, egg yolks and flavorings (especially lemon juice); one of the classic leading sauces

homogenization—the process by which milk fat is prevented from separating out of milk products

hors d'oeuvre—[ohr durv] very small portions of hot or cold foods served before the meal to stimulate the appetite

hotel pan—a rectangular, stainless steel pan with a lip allowing it to rest in a storage shelf or steam table; available in several standard sizes

hull—also known as the husk, the outer covering of a fruit, seed or grain

hulling—a milling process in which the hull or husk is removed from grains

hybrid—the result of crossbreeding different species that are genetically unalike; often a unique product

hydrocolloid—substance such as a gum or agar that bonds with water to form a gel

hydrogenated fat—unsaturated, liquid fats that are chemically altered to remain solid at room temperature, such as solid shortening or margarine

hydrogenation—the process used to harden oils; hydrogen atoms are added to unsaturated fat molecules, making them partially or completely saturated and thus solid at room temperature

hydrometer—a device used to measure specific gravity and show degrees of concentration on the Baumé scale; the higher the number, the greater the density of a solution, such as a sugar syrup

hygroscopic—describes a food that readily absorbs moisture from the air

I

IMPS—the Institutional Meat Purchasing Specifications (IMPS) published by the U.S. Department of Agriculture; the IMPS are illustrated and described in The Meat Buyer's Guide published by the North American Meat Institute (NAMI)

induction cooking—a cooking method that uses a special coil placed below the stove top's surface in combination with specially designed cookware to generate heat rapidly with an alternating magnetic field

infection—in the food safety context, a disease caused by the ingestion of live pathogenic bacteria that continue their life processes in the consumer's intestinal tract

infrared cooking—a heating method that uses an electric or ceramic element heated to such a high temperature that it gives off waves of radiant heat that cook the food

infuse—to flavor a liquid by steeping it with ingredients such as tea, coffee, herbs or spices

infusion—(1) the extraction of flavors from a food at a temperature below boiling; (2) a group of coffee brewing techniques, including steeping, filtering and dripping; (3) the liquid resulting from this process

instant-read thermometer—a thermometer used to measure the internal temperature of foods; the stem is inserted in the food, producing an instant temperature readout

intoxication—in the food safety context, a disease caused by the toxins that bacteria produce during their life processes

inventory—the listing and counting of all foods in the kitchen, storerooms and refrigerators

IQF (individually quick frozen)—describes the technique of rapidly freezing individual items of food such as slices of fruit, berries or pieces of fish before packaging; IQF foods are not packaged with syrup or sauce

irradiation—a preservation method used for certain fruits, vegetables, grains, spices, meat and poultry in which ionizing radiation sterilizes the food, slows ripening and prevents sprouting

J

jam—a fruit gel made from fruit pulp and sugar

jelly—a fruit gel made from fruit juice and sugar

juice—the liquid extracted from any fruit or vegetable

julienne—[ju-lee-EN] (1) to cut foods into stick-shaped pieces, approximately ⅛ inch × ⅛ inch × 2 inches (3 millimeters × 3 millimeters × 5 centimeters); a fine julienne has dimensions of 1⁄16 inch × 1⁄16 inch × 2 inches (1.5 millimeters × 1.5 millimeters × 5 centimeters); (2) stick-shaped pieces of food cut in this manner

jus lié—[zhoo lee-ay] a sauce made by thickening brown stock with cornstarch or similar starch; often used like a demi-glace, especially to produce small sauces; also known as fond lié

K

Kabocha squash—a Japanese variety of winter squash with an orange or green knobby rind and firm, brightly-hued flesh that resembles sweet potatoes when cooked

Kaiser roll—a large round yeast roll with a crisp crust and a curved pattern stamped on the top; used primarily for sandwiches

katsuobushi—see **bonito**

kneading—working a dough to develop gluten

Kobe beef—an exclusive type of beef traditionally produced in Kobe, Japan

kombu—an edible kelp or seaweed, usually the species *Laminaria japonica*, which grows wild in East Asian oceans; kombu's long, thin strips can be eaten raw, but are generally preferred frozen, pickled or dried

kosher—describes food prepared in accordance with Jewish dietary laws

L

lactose—a disaccharide that occurs naturally in mammalian milk; milk sugar

ladyfingers—small cakes or cookies made from spongecake batter piped into finger-length strips; used to line molds for desserts or layered with fillings

lamb—the meat of sheep slaughtered under the age of one year

lard—the rendered fat of hogs

larding—inserting thin slices of fat, such as pork fatback, into low-fat meats in order to add moisture

lardons—diced, blanched, fried bacon

lavash—a thin flatbread made from wheat and baked in a tandoor oven, commonly served in Afghanistan, Iran, Turkey and Eurasian countries

leading sauces—also known as mother sauces, the foundation for the entire classic repertoire of hot sauces; the five leading sauces (béchamel, velouté, espagnole, tomato and hollandaise) are distinguished by the liquids and thickeners used to make them; they can be seasoned and garnished to create a wide variety of small or compound sauces

leaven—to expand in volume and rise

leavener—an ingredient or process that produces or incorporates gases in a baked product in order to increase volume, provide structure and give texture; also known as leavening agent

lecithin—a natural emulsifier found in egg yolks

legumes—[lay-gyooms] (1) French for "vegetables"; (2) a large group of vegetables with double-seamed seed pods; depending upon the variety, the seeds, pod and seeds together, or the dried seeds are eaten

liaison—[lee-yeh-zon] a mixture of egg yolks and heavy cream used to thicken and enrich sauces

lignin—organic substance that binds together the cells in wood and woody vegetables

liqueur—a strong, sweet, syrupy alcoholic beverage made by mixing or redistilling neutral spirits with fruits, flowers, herbs, spices or other flavorings; also known as a cordial; liqueur's alcohol content is 15–30 percent

liquor—an alcoholic beverage made by distilling grains, fruits, vegetables or other foods; includes rum, whiskey and vodka; most distilled spirits' alcohol content is 40–60 percent

liter—the basic unit of volume in the metric system, equal to 1000 milliliters, slightly more than one quart

locavore—someone who eats foods grown locally whenever possible; the ideal is to avoid using foods that are transported long distances

lozenges—diamond-shaped pieces, usually of firm vegetables

M

macaroni—any dried pasta made with wheat flour and water; only in the United States does the term refer to elbow-shaped tubes

macerate—to soak foods in a liquid, usually alcoholic, to soften them

macronutrients—the nutrients needed in large quantities: carbohydrates, proteins, fats and water

Madeira—[muh-DEH-rah] a Portuguese fortified wine heated during aging to give it a distinctive flavor and brown color

magret—[may-gray] a breast from a moulard duck, traditionally taken from the ducks that produce foie gras; magret is usually served boneless but with the skin intact

maître d'hotel (maître d')—[may-tr doh-tel] (1) the leader of the dining room brigade, also known as the dining room manager; oversees the dining room or "front of the house" staff; (2) a compound butter flavored with chopped parsley and lemon juice

Maillard reaction—the process whereby sugar breaks down in the presence of protein

make-up—the cutting, shaping and forming of dough products before baking

malting—steeping barley or other grain until it germinates then drying it with warm air to develop its color and flavor

mandolin—a manually operated slicer with adjustable blades; has a narrow, rectangular body holding a blade and sits at a 45-degree angle; food is passed over and pressed against the blade to obtain uniform slices, matchstick shapes or waffle cuts

marbling—whitish streaks of inter- and intra-muscular fat

marinade—a liquid used to marinate foods that generally contains herbs, spices and other flavoring ingredients as well as an acidic product such as wine, vinegar or lemon juice

marinate—to soak a food in a seasoned liquid in order to tenderize the food and add flavor to it

marmalade—a citrus jelly that also contains unpeeled slices of citrus fruit

marquise—a frozen mousse-like dessert, usually chocolate

marrow—soft tissue in the center of animal bones, especially leg bones

Marsala—[mar-SAH-lah] a flavorful fortified sweet-to-semidry Sicilian wine

marzipan—[MAHR-sih-pan] a paste of ground almonds, sugar and egg whites used to fill and decorate pastries

masa harina—Spanish for "dough flour;" finely ground flour made from dried hominy, it is used to make tamales and tortillas

matignon—a standard mirepoix plus diced smoked bacon or smoked ham and, depending on the dish, mushrooms and herbs; sometimes called an edible mirepoix, it is usually cut more uniformly than a standard mirepoix and left in the finished dish as a garnish

mayonnaise—a thick, creamy sauce consisting of oil and vinegar emulsified with egg yolks; used as a salad dressing or sandwich spread

meal—(1) the coarsely ground seeds of any edible grain such as corn or oats; (2) any dried, ground substance, such as cracker meal or almond meal; (3) the food prepared for eating at one time, such as lunch or breakfast

mealy potatoes—also known as starchy potatoes; those with a high starch content and thick skin; they are best prepared by baking

medallion—a small, round, relatively thick slice of meat

melting—the process by which certain foods, especially those high in fat, gradually soften and then liquefy when heated

menu—a list of foods and beverages available for purchase

meringue—[muh-reng] a foam made of beaten egg whites and sugar

metabolism—all the chemical reactions and physical processes that occur continuously in living cells and organisms

meter—the basic unit of length in the metric system, equal to slightly more than 1 yard

micronutrients—nutrients that are needed only in small amounts; vitamins and minerals

microorganisms—single-celled organisms and tiny plants and animals that can be seen only through a microscope

microwave cooking—a heating method that uses radiation generated by a special oven to agitate water molecules, creating friction and heat; this energy spreads throughout the food and cooks it

mignonette—[mean-yo-NETT] (1) a medallion; (2) a vinegar sauce with shallots

milk-fed veal—also known as formula-fed veal; the meat of calves fed only a nutrient-rich liquid and kept tethered in pens; this meat is whiter and more mildly flavored than that of free-range calves

milling—the process by which grain is ground into flour or meal

mince—to cut into very small pieces when uniformity of shape is not important

minerals—inorganic micronutrients necessary for regulating body functions and proper bone and tooth structures

mirepoix—[meer-pwa] a mixture of coarsely chopped onions, carrots and celery used to flavor stocks, stews and other foods; generally, a mixture of 50 percent onions, 25 percent carrots and 25 percent celery, by weight, is used

mirin—a Japanese rice wine; low in alcohol and naturally sweet, mirin is used as a condiment

mise en place—(meez on plahs) French for "putting in place"; refers to the preparation and assembly of all necessary ingredients and equipment

miso paste—a thick paste made by salting and fermenting soybeans and inoculating the mixture with yeast; used in Japanese and vegetarian cuisines as a favoring and thickener

mix—to combine ingredients in such a way that they are evenly dispersed throughout the mixture

modernist cuisine—a term that refers to science-inspired techniques for food preparation; an avant-garde approach to food preparation, sanitation and health concerns based on science-inspired techniques

moist-heat cooking methods—cooking methods, principally simmering, poaching, boiling and steaming, that use water or steam to transfer heat through convection; moist-heat cooking methods are used to emphasize the natural flavors of foods

molding—the process of shaping foods, particularly grains and vegetables bound by sauces, into attractive, hard-edged shapes by using metal rings, circular cutters or other forms

molds—(1) algae-like fungi that form long filaments or strands; for the most part, molds affect only food appearance and flavor; (2) containers used for shaping foods

molecular gastronomy—a contemporary scientific movement that investigates the chemistry and physics of food preparation

mollusks—shellfish characterized by a soft, unsegmented body, no internal skeleton and a hard outer shell

monounsaturated fats—see **unsaturated fats**

monter au beurre—[mohn-tay ah burr] to finish a sauce by swirling or whisking in butter (raw or compound) until it is melted; used to give sauces shine, flavor and richness

mortadella—[mohr-tah-DEH-lah] an Italian smoked sausage made with ground beef, pork and pork fat, flavored with coriander and white wine; it is air-dried and has a delicate flavor; also a large American bologna-type pork sausage studded with pork fat and garlic

mortar and pestle—a hard bowl (the mortar) in which foods such as spices are ground or pounded into a powder with a club-shaped tool (the pestle)

mother sauces—(Fr. *sauces mères*) see **leading sauces**

mousse—[moose] a soft, creamy food, either sweet or savory, lightened by adding whipped cream, beaten egg whites or both

mousseline—[moos-uh-LEEN] a cream or sauce lightened by folding in whipped cream, whipped eggs or meringue

mouthfeel—the sensation created in the mouth by a combination of a food's taste, smell, texture and temperature

muesli—[MYOOS-lee] a breakfast cereal made from raw or toasted cereal grains, dried fruits, nuts and dried milk solids and usually eaten with milk or yogurt; sometimes known as granola

muffin method—a mixing method used to make quick-bread batters; it involves combining liquid fat with other liquid ingredients before adding them to the dry ingredients

muscles—animal tissues consisting of bundles of cells or fibers that contract and expand; the portions of a carcass usually consumed

mushrooms—members of a broad category of plants known as fungi; they are often used and served like vegetables

mutton—the meat of sheep slaughtered after they reach the age of one year

MyPlate—an educational tool developed by the USDA as a visual guide to help people implement the healthy eating guidelines from the *2010 Healthy Eating Guidelines for Americans*

N

nameko—a small, round-capped, golden-brown mushroom that grows on hardwoods; similar to shiitake, it is widely cultivated in Japan, China and Russia; nameko is traditionally used in miso soup because of its nutty flavor and gelatinous texture; known in the United States as butterscotch mushrooms

nappé—(nap-ay) the consistency of a liquid, usually a sauce, that will coat the back of a spoon; from the verb *naper* in French or *nap* in English, meaning to coat a food with sauce

national cuisine—the characteristic cuisine of a nation

navarin—[nah-veh-rahng] a brown ragoût generally made with turnips, other root vegetables, onions, peas and lamb

neapolitan—a three-layered loaf or cake of ice cream; each layer is a different flavor and a different color, a typical combination being chocolate, vanilla and strawberry

nectar—the diluted, sweetened juice of peaches, apricots, guavas, black currants or other fruits, the juice of which would be too thick or too tart to drink straight

neutral spirits or grain spirits—pure alcohol (ethanol or ethyl alcohol); they are odorless, tasteless and a very potent 190 proof (95 percent alcohol)

New American cuisine—a late-20th-century movement that began in California and spread across the United States; it stresses the use of fresh, locally grown, seasonal produce and high-quality ingredients simply prepared in a fashion that preserves and emphasizes natural flavors

niche pork—industry term for alternative or specialty pork products; meat from a specific breed such as Duroc or Tamworth hogs, or meat raised using a particular practice such as free-range feeding or antibiotic- and hormone-free, are considered niche products

noisette—[nwah-ZETT] a small, usually round, portion of meat cut from the rib

noodles—flat strips of pasta-type dough made with eggs; may be fresh or dried

nouvelle cuisine—French for "new cooking"; a mid-20th-century movement away from many classic cuisine principles toward a lighter cuisine based on natural flavors, shortened cooking times and innovative combinations

nut—(1) the edible single-seed kernel of a fruit surrounded by a hard shell; (2) generally any seed or fruit with an edible kernel in a hard shell

nutrients—the chemical substances found in food that nourish the body by promoting growth, facilitating body functions and providing energy; there are six categories of nutrients: proteins, carbohydrates, fats, water, minerals and vitamins

nutrition—the science that studies nutrients

O

oblique cuts—[oh-BLEEK] small pieces with two angle-cut sides; also known as roll cuts

offal—[OFF-uhl] also called variety meats; edible entrails (e.g., the heart, kidneys, liver, sweetbreads or tongue) and extremities (e.g., oxtail or pig's feet) of an animal

oignon brûlé—[ohn-neang brew-LAY] French for "burnt onion"; made by charring onion halves; used to flavor and color stocks and sauces; also written onion brûlé

oignon piqué—[ohn-neang pee-KAY] French for "pricked onion"; a bay leaf tacked with a clove to a peeled onion; used to flavor sauces and soups; also written onion piqué

oil—a type of fat that remains liquid at room temperature

organic farming—a method of farming that does not rely on synthetic pesticides, fungicides, herbicides or fertilizers; organic practices require that animals have access to outdoors, sunlight and clean water and that they are raised without antibiotics and hormones on organically grown feed

oven spring—the rapid rise of yeast goods in a hot oven, resulting from the production and expansion of trapped gases

overhead costs—expenses related to operating a business, including but not limited to costs for advertising, equipment leasing, insurance, property rent, supplies and utilities

overrun—a measure of the air churned into an ice cream; expressed as a percentage, which reflects the increase in volume of the ice cream greater than the amount of the base used to produce the product

P

paillard—[pah-YAHR] a scallop of meat, usually chicken or veal, pounded until large and thin, usually grilled or sautéed

palate—(1) the complex of smell, taste and touch receptors that contribute to a person's ability to recognize and appreciate flavors; (2) the range of an individual's recognition and appreciation of flavors

pan gravy—a sauce made by deglazing pan drippings from roast meat or poultry and combining them with a roux or other starch and stock

panada; panade—[pah-nahd] (1) something other than fat added to a forcemeat to enhance smoothness, aid emulsification or both such as béchamel, rice or crustless white bread soaked in milk; (2) a mixture for binding stuffings and dumplings, notably quenelles; often choux pastry, bread crumbs, frangipane, puréed potatoes or rice

pan-dressed—a market form for fish in which the viscera, gills and scales are removed and the fins and tail are trimmed

pan-frying—a dry-heat cooking method in which food is placed in a moderate amount of hot fat

panino—a type of sandwich in which the assembled product is placed on an electric griddle with ridged plates known as a panini press; when closed, the press heats the sandwich from the top and bottom simultaneously leaving distinctive grill marks

panko—light, crisp Japanese-style breadcrumbs; traditionally made from crustless white yeast bread ground into sliver shaped crumb

papain—an enzyme found in papayas that breaks down proteins; used as the primary ingredient in many commercial meat tenderizers

pappadam—[PAH-pah-dahm] a thin, crisp East Indian flatbread made with chickpea, lentil or rice flour; may be flavored with black pepper, garlic or other seasonings; generally fried or toasted and served before or during meals

parboiling—partially cooking a food in boiling or simmering liquid; similar to blanching but the cooking time is longer

parchment (paper)—heat-resistant paper used for tasks such as lining baking pans, wrapping foods to be cooked en papillote and covering foods during shallow poaching

parcooking—partially cooking a food by any cooking method

parfait—ice cream served in a long, slender glass with alternating layers of topping or sauce; also the name of the mousselike preparation that forms the basis for some still-frozen desserts

paring knife—a short knife used for detail work, especially cutting fruits and vegetables; it has a rigid blade approximately 2–4 inches (5–10 centimeters) long

Paris-Brest—rings of baked éclair paste cut in half horizontally and filled with light pastry cream and/or whipped cream; the top is dusted with powdered sugar or drizzled with chocolate glaze

Parisiennes—[pah-ree-zee-EN] spheres of fruits or vegetables cut with a small melon ball cutter

parstock (par)—the amount of stock necessary to cover operating needs between deliveries

pasta—(1) an unleavened paste or dough made from wheat flour (often semolina), water and eggs; the dough can be colored and flavored with herbs, spices or other ingredients and cut or extruded into a wide variety of shapes and sizes; it can be fresh or dried and is boiled for service; (2) general term for any macaroni product or egg noodle

pasteurization—the process of heating something to a certain temperature for a specific period in order to destroy pathogenic bacteria

pastillage—[pahst-tee-azh] a paste made of sugar, cornstarch and gelatin; it may be cut or molded into decorative shapes

pastry cream—a stirred custard made with egg yolks, sugar and milk and thickened with starch; used for pastry and pie fillings; also known as crème pâtissière

pâte—[paht] French for dough

pâté—[pah-TAY] traditionally a fine savory meat filling wrapped in pastry, baked and served hot or cold; as opposed to a terrine, which was a coarsely ground and highly seasoned meat mixture baked in an earthenware mold and served cold; today the words *pâté* and *terrine* are generally used interchangeably

pâte à choux—[paht ah SHOO] also known as pâte à choux; see **éclair paste**

pâte au pâté—[paht oh pah-TAY] a specially formulated pastry dough used for wrapping pâté when making pâté en croûte

pâte brisée—[paht bree-ZAY] a dough that produces a very flaky baked product containing little or no sugar; flaky dough is used for prebaked pie shells or crusts

pâté en croûte—[pah-tay awn croot] a pâté baked in pastry dough such as pâte au pâté

pâte feuilletée—[paht fuh-yuh-tay] also known as puff pastry; a rolled-in dough used for pastries, cookies and savory products; it produces a rich and buttery but not sweet baked product with hundreds of light, flaky layers

pâte sucrée—[paht soo-KRAY] a dough containing sugar that produces a very rich, crisp (not flaky) baked product; also known as sweet dough, it is used for tart shells

pathogens—organisms that cause disease; usually refers to bacteria; undetectable by smell, sight or taste, pathogens are responsible for as many as 95 percent of all food-borne illnesses

pâtisserie—[pah-tees-air-EE] (1) bakery or bake-shop where pastry is sold; (2) French pastries, cakes and cookies

pâtissier—[pah-tees-see-yay] a pastry chef; the person responsible for baked items, including breads, pastries and desserts

paupiette—a thin slice of meat or fish that is rolled around a filling of finely ground meat or vegetables, then fried, baked or braised in wine or stock

paysanne—[pay-ZAHN] foods cut into flat square, round or triangular items with dimensions of ½ inch × ½ inch × ⅛ inch (1.2 centimeters × 1.2 centimeters × 3 millimeters)

pearling—a milling process in which all or part of the hull, bran and germ are removed from grains

pectin—(1) a water-soluble fiber found primarily in fruits, also a major component in some vegetables, such as carrots, fresh peas, parsnips, potatoes and green beans; (2) a gelatin-like carbohydrate obtained from certain fruits; used to thicken jams and jellies

pellicle—(Fr. *pellicule*) a thin, sticky membrane or skin that forms on the surface of cured fish, meat or poultry exposed to air; it seals in moisture and helps smoke adhere to the product's surface

pepperoni—[peh-peh-ROH-nee] a hard, thin, air-dried sausage seasoned with red and black pepper

persillade—[payr-see-yad] (1) a food served with or containing parsley; (2) a mixture of bread crumbs, parsley and garlic used to coat meats, especially lamb

petit four—any type of pastry small enough to be consumed in one to two bites; often served between or after meals

pH—a measurement of the acid or alkali content of a solution, expressed on a scale of 0 to 14.0. A pH of 7.0 is considered neutral or balanced; the lower the pH value, the more acidic the substance; the higher the pH value, the more alkaline the substance

PHF foods—see **TCS foods**

physical hazard—a danger to the safety of food caused by particles such as glass chips, metal shavings, bits of wood or other foreign matter

pickle—(1) to preserve food in a brine or vinegar solution; (2) food that has been preserved in a seasoned brine or vinegar, especially cucumbers

pie—food item composed of a sweet or savory filling in a baked crust, generally prepared in a round, slope-sided pan

pigment—a substance that gives color to an item

pilaf—a cooking method for grains in which the grains are lightly sautéed in hot fat and then a hot liquid is added; the mixture is simmered without stirring until the liquid is absorbed

pimentón—Spanish paprika produced from one of several varieties of *Capsicum annuum* peppers; in Extremadura, these peppers are dried over an oak fire, giving the region's *Pimentón de la Vera* a subtle smoky flavor

poaching—a moist-heat cooking method that uses convection to transfer heat from a hot (approximately 160–180°F/71–82°C) liquid to the food submerged in it

poêléing—[pwah-lay] moist heat cooking method used for tender cuts of meat or poultry; the food is cooked in an oven in a covered pot and is often browned in hot fat first

polyunsaturated fats—see **unsaturated fats**

pomes—members of the *Rosaceae* family such as apples, pears and quince; tree fruits with a thin skin and firm flesh surrounding a central core containing many small seeds (called pips or carpels)

popovers—crisp hollow muffin-shaped breads made from a rich egg batter and leavened with steam

pork—the meat of hogs, usually slaughtered under the age of one year

posole—also known as hominy or samp; dried corn that has been soaked in hydrated lime or lye; posole (Sp. *pozole*) also refers to a stew-like soup made with pork and hominy served in Mexico and Central America; its name derives from the ancient Aztec *pozolli*, a corn beverage of the Aztecs and Mayans

posterior—at or toward the rear of an object or place; opposite of anterior

poultry—the collective term for domesticated birds bred for eating including chickens, ducks, geese, guineas, pigeons and turkeys

poussin—a French term for a small, immature chicken; in the United States, *poussin* is another name for a small chicken, such as a Rock Cornish game hen

preserve—(1) to prepare foods for longer storage by drying, dehydrating, salting, smoking or cooking with sugar; (2) a fruit gel that contains large pieces or whole fruits

primal cuts—the primary divisions of muscle, bone and connective tissue produced by the initial butchering of the carcass

prix fixe—[pree feeks] French for "fixed price"; refers to a menu offering a complete meal for a set price; also known as table d'hôte

professional cooking—a system of cooking based on a knowledge of and appreciation for ingredients and procedures

profiteroles—[proh-fee-teh-ROLE] small baked rounds of éclair paste filled with ice cream and topped with chocolate sauce or filled with savory mixtures

proofing—the rise given shaped yeast products just prior to baking

proteins—a group of compounds composed of oxygen, hydrogen, carbon and nitrogen atoms necessary for manufacturing, maintaining and repairing body tissues and as an alternative source of energy (4 calories per gram); protein chains are constructed of various combinations of amino acids

pudding—a thick, spoonable dessert custard, usually made with eggs, milk, sugar and flavorings and thickened with flour or another starch

puff pastry—see **pâte feuilletée**

pulled sugar—a doughlike mixture of sucrose, glucose and tartaric acid that can be colored and shaped by hand into decorative items

Pullman—a long rectangular loaf of bread for slicing; also, the lidded pan in which this bread is baked

pumpernickel—(1) coarsely ground rye flour; (2) bread made with this flour

purée—[pur-ray] (1) to process food to achieve a smooth pulp; (2) food that is processed by mashing, straining or fine chopping to achieve a smooth pulp

purée soup—a soup usually made from starchy vegetables or legumes; after the main ingredient is simmered in a liquid, the mixture, or a portion of it, is puréed

putrefactives—bacteria that spoil food without rendering it unfit for human consumption

Q

quality grades—a guide to the qualities of meat—tenderness, juiciness and flavor—based on an animal's age and the meat's color, texture and degree of marbling

quenelle—[kuh-nehl] a small, dumpling-shaped portion of a mousseline forcemeat poached in an appropriately flavored stock; it is shaped by using two spoons

quiche—a savory tart or pie consisting of a custard baked in a pastry shell with a variety of flavorings and garnishes

quick bread—a bread, including loaves and muffins, leavened by chemical leaveners or steam rather than yeast

R

rack—(1) strips of metal or wire fashioned into a frame for holding foods during cooking, cooling or transporting; (2) a set of connected beef, lamb, pork or venison rib bones that may be cooked and served in one piece

radiation—the transfer of heat (energy) by electromagnetic waves of energy or light spreading out from a central source, such as a ceramic toaster element or a magnetron in a microwave oven

raft—a crust formed during the process of clarifying consommé; it is composed of the clearmeat and impurities from the stock, which rise to the top of the simmering stock and release additional flavors

ragoût—[rah-goo] (1) traditionally a well-seasoned, rich stew containing meat, vegetables and wine; (2) any stewed mixture

ramekin—a small, ovenproof dish, usually ceramic

rancidity—the decomposition of fats by exposure to oxygen, resulting in off-flavors and destruction of nutritive components

recipe—a set of written instructions for producing a specific food or beverage; also known as a formula

recovery time—the length of time it takes a cooking medium such as fat or water to return to the desired cooking temperature after food is submerged in it

reduction—cooking a liquid such as a sauce until its quantity decreases through evaporation. To reduce by one-half means that one-half of the original amount remains; to reduce by three-fourths means that only one-fourth of the original amount remains; to reduce *au sec* means that the liquid is cooked until nearly dry

refreshing—submerging a food in cold water to quickly cool it and prevent further cooking, also known as shocking

regional cuisine—a set of recipes based on local ingredients, traditions and practices; within a larger geographical, political, cultural or social unit, regional cuisines are often variations of one another that blend together to create a national cuisine

relish—a cooked or pickled sauce usually made with vegetables or fruits and often used as a condiment; can be smooth or chunky, sweet or savory and hot or mild

remouillage—[rhur-moo-yahj] French for "rewetting"; a stock produced by reusing the bones left from making another stock; a remouillage will not be as clear or as flavorful as the original stock, however; often used to make glazes or in place of water when making stocks

render—(1) to melt and clarify fat; (2) to cook meat in order to remove the fat

rennet—an enzyme found in calves' stomachs used to coagulate milk proteins

respiration rate—the speed with which the cells of a fruit use oxygen and produce carbon dioxide during ripening

restaurateur—a person who owns or operates an establishment serving food, such as a restaurant

ribbon stage—a term used to describe the consistency of a batter or mixture, especially a mixture of beaten egg and sugar; when the beater or whisk is lifted, the mixture will fall back slowly onto its surface in a ribbon-like pattern

rillette—[ree-YET] meat or poultry slowly cooked, mashed and preserved in its own fat; served cold and usually spread on toast

ripe—fully grown and developed; a ripe fruit's flavor, texture and appearance are at their peak, and the fruit is ready to use as food

ripen—become or make ripe; aging process, which determines the texture, color and flavor of the final product, applied to a cheese under controlled conditions

risers—boxes, racks or pedestals, sometimes covered with linens, paper or other decorative items, used on a buffet table as a base to elevate platters, trays or displays

risotto—[re-zot-toe] (1) a cooking method in which grains are lightly sautéed in butter and a liquid is gradually added; the mixture is simmered with near-constant stirring until the still-firm grains merge with the cooking liquid; (2) a Northern Italian rice dish prepared this way

roaster duckling—a duck of either sex slaughtered before it is sixteen weeks old; fryer and broiler ducklings are slaughtered before eight weeks of age and still retain their soft bill and windpipe

roasting—a dry-heat cooking method in which food is surrounded with hot, dry air in a closed environment or on a spit over an open fire; the same as baking, the term roasting is usually applied to meats, poultry, game and vegetables

roe—[roh] fish eggs; see **caviar**

roll cuts—see **oblique cuts**

rolled fondant—a cooked mixture of sugar, glucose and water formulated to drape over cakes

rolled-in dough—a dough in which a fat is incorporated in many layers by using a rolling and folding procedure; used for flaky baked goods such as croissants, puff pastry and Danish pastry

rondeau—[ron-doe] a shallow, wide, straight-sided pot with two loop handles

rondelles—[ron-DELLZ] disk-shaped slices

rotate stock—when receiving new deliveries all perishable and semiperishable goods, whether fresh, frozen, canned or dry, should be used in the order in which they were received; known as the first in, first out (FIFO) principle

rotisserie—cooking equipment that slowly rotates meat or other foods in front of a heating element

roulade—[roo-lahd] (1) a slice of meat, poultry or fish rolled around a stuffing; (2) a filled and rolled spongecake

round fish—fish with round, oval or compressed bodies that swim in a vertical position and have eyes on both sides of their heads such as, salmon, swordfish and cod

rounding—the process of shaping dough into smooth, round balls; used to stretch the outside layer of gluten into a smooth coating

roux—[roo] a cooked mixture of equal parts flour and fat, by weight, used as a thickener for sauces and other dishes; cooking the flour in fat coats the starch granules with the fat and prevents them from lumping together or forming lumps when introduced into a liquid

royal icing—a decorative icing made with confectioners' sugar, egg whites and lemon juice; it is pure white and very hard when dry

rub—a mixture of fresh or dried herbs and spices ground together and applied to food before it is cooked; used dry or mixed with a little oil, lemon juice, prepared mustard or ground fresh garlic or ginger to make a wet rub

S

sabayon—[sa-by-on] a foamy, stirred custard sauce made by whisking eggs, sugar and wine over low heat; also known as zabaglione

sachet d'épices; sachet—[sah-shay day-peace] French for "bag of spices"; aromatic ingredients tied in a cheesecloth bag used to flavor stocks and other foods; a standard sachet contains parsley stems, cracked peppercorns, dried thyme, bay leaf, cloves and, optionally, garlic

salad—a single food or a mix of different foods accompanied or bound by a dressing

salad dressing—a sauce for a salad; most are based on a vinaigrette, mayonnaise or other emulsified product

salad greens—a variety of leafy vegetables usually eaten raw

salamander—a small broiler used primarily for browning or glazing the top of foods

salsa—[sahl-sah] Spanish for "sauce"; generally a chunky mixture of fresh herbs, spices, fruits and/or vegetables used as a cold sauce for meat, poultry, fish or shellfish

salt-curing—surrounding a food with salt or a mixture of salt, sugar, nitrite-based curing salt, herbs and spices; salt-curing dehydrates the food, inhibits bacterial growth and adds flavor

sanding sugar—granulated sugar with a large, coarse crystal structure that prevents it from dissolving easily; used for decorating cookies and pastries

sanitation—the creation and maintenance of conditions that prevent food contamination or food-borne illness

sanitize—to reduce pathogenic organisms on clean surfaces to safe levels

sansho—dried berries of the prickly ash tree, ground into a powder that is also known as Szechuan pepper, fagara and Chinese pepper; generally used in Japanese cooking to season fatty foods

sashimi—[sah-shee-mee] raw fish eaten without rice; usually served as the first course of a Japanese meal

saturated fats—fats found mainly in animal products, such as milk, butter, cheese, eggs and meat, as well as in tropical oils, such as coconut and palm; usually solid at room temperature

sauce—generally a thickened liquid used to flavor and enhance other foods

saucisson sec—[soh-see-SOHN seck] a hard, air-dried French sausage seasoned with garlic and black pepper

sausage—a seasoned forcemeat usually stuffed into a casing; a sausage can be fresh, smoked and cooked, dried or hard

sautéing—[saw-tay-ing] a dry-heat cooking method that uses conduction to transfer heat from a hot pan to food with the aid of a small amount of hot fat; cooking is usually done quickly over high temperatures

sauteuse—[saw-toose] a sauté pan with sloping sides and a single long handle

sautoir—[saw-twahr] a sauté pan with straight sides and a single long handle

savory—a food that is not sweet

scald—to heat a liquid, usually milk, to just below the boiling point

scallop—(1) (Fr. *escalope*, It. *scaloppa*, pl. *scaloppine*) a thin, boneless slice of meat; (2) (Fr. *coquilles Saint Jacques*) a bivalve shellfish with an edible white muscle and fan-shaped shells

scorch—to burn the surface of a food, changing its color and/or flavor

score—to cut shallow gashes across the surface of a food before cooking

Scoville heat units—a subjective rating for measuring a chile's heat; the sweet bell pepper usually rates 0 units, the tabasco pepper rates from 30,000 to 50,000 units and the habanero pepper rates from 100,000 to 300,000 units

seafood—an inconsistently used term encompassing some or all of the following: saltwater fish, freshwater fish, saltwater shellfish, freshwater shellfish and other edible marine life

sear—to brown food quickly over high heat; usually done as a preparatory step for combination cooking methods

season—(1) traditionally to enhance flavor by adding salt; (2) more commonly to enhance flavor by adding salt and/or pepper as well as herbs and spices; (3) to mature and bring a food (usually beef or game) to a proper condition by aging or special preparation; (4) to prepare a pot, pan or other cooking surface to prevent sticking

seasoning—an item added to enhance the natural flavors of a food without dramatically changing its taste; salt is the most common seasoning

seitan—[SAY-tan] a form of wheat gluten with a firm, chewy texture and a bland flavor; traditionally simmered in a broth of soy sauce or tamari with ginger, garlic and kombu (seaweed)

semifreddi—[seh-mee-frayd-dee] also known as still-frozen desserts such as frozen soufflés, marquise, mousses and neapolitans; made with frozen mousse, custard or cream into which large amounts of whipped cream or meringue are folded in order to incorporate air; layers of spongecake and/or fruits may be added for flavor and texture

semolina—a grainy yellow flour ground from durum or another hard wheat with a high protein content and gluten-forming potential; used principally for pasta dough

sfoglia—[sfo-lee-ah] a thin, flat sheet of pasta dough that can be cut into ribbons, circles, squares or other shapes

shallow poaching—a moist-heat cooking method that combines poaching and steaming; the food (usually fish) is placed on a vegetable bed and partially covered with a liquid (cuisson) and simmered

shank—the leg of beef, veal, pork or lamb (foreshanks are the front legs, hindshanks are the rear legs); although flavorful, the meat is filled with connective tissue and should be cooked with moist heat

shellfish—aquatic invertebrates with shells or carapaces

sherbet—a frozen mixture of fruit juice or fruit purée that contains milk and/or eggs for creaminess

shocking—also called refreshing; the technique of quickly chilling blanched or parcooked foods in ice water to prevent further cooking and set colors

shortening—(1) a white, flavorless, solid fat formulated for baking or deep-frying; (2) any fat used in baking to tenderize doughs by shortening protein strands (gluten)

shred—to cut into thin but irregular strips

shrinkage—the loss of weight in a food due to evaporation of liquid or melting of fat during cooking

shuck—(1) a shell, pod or husk; (2) to remove the edible portion of a food (e.g., clam meat, peas or an ear of corn) from its shell, pod or husk

sifting—shaking one or more dry substances through a sieve or sifter to remove lumps, incorporate air or combine

silverskin—the tough connective tissue that surrounds certain muscles; see **elastin**

simmering—(1) a moist-heat cooking method that uses convection to transfer heat from a hot (approximately 185–205°F/85–96°C) liquid to the food submerged in it; (2) maintaining the temperature of a liquid just below the boiling point

skim—to remove fat and impurities from the surface of a liquid during cooking

slice—to cut an item into relatively broad, thin pieces

slurry—a mixture of raw starch and cold liquid used for thickening

small sauces—also known as compound sauces; made by adding one or more ingredients to a leading sauce; they are grouped together into families based on their leading sauce; some small sauces have a variety of uses, while others are traditional accompaniments for specific foods

smoke point—the temperature at which a fat begins to break down and smoke

smoking—any of several methods for preserving and flavoring foods by exposing them to smoke; includes cold smoking (in which the foods are not fully cooked) and hot smoking (in which the foods are cooked)

smørbrød—[SMURR-brur] Norwegian cold open-faced sandwiches; the related Swedish term *smörgåsbord* [SMORE-guhs-bohrd] refers to a buffet table of bread and butter, salads, open-faced sandwiches, pickled or marinated fish, sliced meats and cheeses

solid pack—canned fruits or vegetables with little or no water added

soppressata—[soh-preh-SAH-tah] a hard, aged Italian salami, sometimes coated with cracked peppercorns or herbs

sorbet—[sore-bay] a frozen mixture of fruit juice or fruit purée; similar to sherbet but does not contain milk products

sorghum—grain harvested from a plant that resembles corn, used primarily for animal feed and food processing applications; also called milo. When ground, sorghum may be blended with other flours to make gluten-free preparations

soufflé—[soo-FLAY] a sweet or savory fluffy dish made with a custard base lightened with whipped egg whites and then baked; the whipped egg whites cause the dish to puff when baked

sourdough—a fermented mixture of flour and water added to dough for leavening and flavor

sous-chef—[soo-shef] a cook who supervises food production and who reports to the executive chef; second in command of a kitchen

sous-vide—a cooking technique that uses low temperature, moist-heat cooking methods similar to braising or poaching; the food item may be seared or browned before service to add color and flavor from caramelization

species—a group of organisms that share common characteristics and are capable of breeding

specifications; specs—standard requirements to be followed in procuring items from suppliers

spice—any of a large group of aromatic plants whose bark, roots, seeds, buds or berries are used as a flavoring; usually used in dried form, either whole or ground

sponge—a thick flour, water and yeast batter used to improve the flavor and texture of breads

spring lamb—young lamb born in the early spring and slaughtered when 3–5 months old; spring lamb is often served roasted whole

springform pan—a circular baking pan with a separate bottom and a side wall that is held together with a clamp, which can be released to free the baked product

spun sugar—a decoration made by rapidly flicking dark caramelized sugar to create long, fine, hairlike threads

squab—the class of young pigeon used in food service operations

stage—[stahzh] a brief, unpaid internship or training session in a professional kitchen; from the French *stagiaire*, meaning apprentice or intern

staling—also known as starch retrogradation; a change in the distribution and location of water molecules within baked products; stale products are firmer, drier and more crumbly than fresh baked goods

standard breading procedure—the procedure for coating foods with crumbs or meal by passing the food through flour, then an egg wash and then the crumbs; it gives deep-fried or pan-fried foods a relatively thick, crisp coating

standardized recipe—a recipe producing a known quality and quantity of food for a specific operation

staples—(1) certain foods regularly used throughout the kitchen; (2) certain foods, usually starches, that help form the basis for a regional or national cuisine and are principal components in the diet

starch—(1) complex carbohydrates from plants that are edible and either digestible or indigestible (fiber); (2) a rice, grain, pasta or potato accompaniment to a meal

starch retrogradation—the process whereby starch molecules in a batter or dough lose moisture after baking; the result is baked goods that are dry or stale

starchy potatoes—see **mealy potatoes**

station chef—the cook in charge of a particular department in a kitchen

steak—(1) a cross-section slice of a round fish with a small section of the bone attached; (2) a cut of meat, either with or without the bone

steamed milk—milk that is heated with steam generated by an espresso machine; it should be approximately 150–170°F (66–77°C)

steamer—(1) a set of stacked pots with perforations in the bottom of each pot; they fit over a larger pot filled with boiling or simmering water and are used to steam foods; (2) a perforated insert made of metal or bamboo placed in a pot and used to steam foods; (3) a type of soft-shell clam from the U.S. East Coast; (4) a piece of gas or electric equipment in which foods are steamed in a sealed chamber

steaming—a moist-heat cooking method in which heat is transferred from steam to the food being cooked by direct contact; the food to be steamed is placed in a basket or rack above a boiling liquid in a covered pan

steel—a tool, usually made of steel, used to hone or straighten knife blades

steep—to soak food in a hot liquid in order to either extract its flavor or soften its texture

sterilize—to destroy all living microorganisms

stewing—a combination cooking method similar to braising but generally involving smaller pieces of meat that are first blanched or browned, then cooked in a small amount of liquid that is served as a sauce

stir-frying—a dry-heat cooking method similar to sautéing in which foods are cooked over very high heat using little fat and are stirred constantly and briskly; often done in a wok

stirring—a mixing method in which ingredients are gently mixed by hand until blended, usually with a spoon, whisk or rubber spatula

stock—(Fr. *fond*) a clear, unthickened liquid flavored by soluble substances extracted from meat, poultry or fish bones as well as from a mirepoix, other vegetables and seasonings

stone fruits—members of the genus *Prunus*, also known as drupes; tree or shrub fruits with a thin skin, soft flesh and one woody stone or pit such as apricots, cherries, nectarines, peaches and plums

straight dough method—a mixing method for yeast breads in which all ingredients are simply combined and mixed

strain—to pour foods through a sieve, mesh strainer or cheesecloth to separate or remove the liquid component

streusel—a crumbly mixture of fat, flour, sugar and sometimes nuts and spices, used to top baked goods

strudel—a sweet or savory pastry made with a filling, such as sautéed apples or creamed mushrooms, that is rolled in many layers of a very thin dough, then baked until crisp and brown

subcutaneous fat—also known as exterior fat; the fat layer between the hide and muscles

submersion poaching—a poaching method in which the food is completely covered with the poaching liquid

subprimal cuts—the basic cuts produced from each primal

suckling lamb—young lamb that has never been fed any grass or grains

suckling pig—(Fr. *cochon de lait*) very young, very small pigs typically roasted or barbecued whole

sucrose—the chemical name for common refined sugar; it is a disaccharide, composed of one molecule each of glucose and fructose

sugar—a carbohydrate that provides the body with energy and gives a sweet taste to foods

sugar syrups—either simple syrups (thin mixtures of sugar and water) or cooked syrups (melted sugar cooked until it reaches a specific temperature)

supreme—[soo-PREEM] an intact segment of citrus fruit with all membrane removed

suprême—[soo-PREM] an intermediary sauce made by adding cream to chicken velouté

sushi—[szu-she] cooked or raw fish or shellfish rolled in or served on seasoned rice

sustainability—refers to the practices used to minimize human impact on the environment and protect natural resources; energy and water consumption, land use, building construction and waste disposal all impact sustainability

sweat—to cook a food in a pan (usually covered), without browning, over low heat until the item softens and releases moisture; sweating allows the food to release its flavor more quickly when cooked with other foods

sweetbreads—the thymus gland of a calf, lamb or young hog; has a mild, delicate flavor and texture

syrup—sugar that is dissolved in liquid, usually water, and often flavored with spices or citrus zest

syrup pack—canned fruits with a light, medium or heavy sugar syrup added

T

tahini—[tah-HEE-nee] a thick, oily paste made from crushed sesame seeds

tamale—a Mexican steamed dish consisting of seasoned meats, poultry and/or vegetables wrapped in a corn husk spread with masa dough

tang—the portion of a knife's blade that extends inside the handle

tapioca—starch produced from the root of the cassava (manioc) plant, sometimes used for thickening sauces or fruit mixtures

tare weight—the weight of a container or packaging without its contents

tart—a sweet or savory filling in a baked crust made in a shallow, straight-sided pan, usually without a top crust

tartine—fresh or toasted bread spread with butter, jam or savory spreads and toppings

tartlet—a small, single-serving tart

taste—the sensations we detect when food, drink or other substances come in contact with our taste buds; the basic tastes include sweet, sour, salt, bitter and umami

TCS foods—an abbreviation for "time and temperature controlled for safety"; foods on which bacteria can thrive, they are generally high in protein and include animal-based products, cooked grains and some raw and cooked vegetables; formerly known as potentially hazardous foods (PHF)

tempeh—[TEHM-pay] fermented whole soybeans mixed with a grain such as rice or millet; it has a chewy consistency and a yeasty, nutty flavor

temper—to heat gently and gradually; refers to the process of slowly adding a hot liquid to eggs or other foods to raise their temperature without causing them to curdle

temperature danger zone—the broad range of temperatures between 41°F and 135°F (5°C and 57°C) at which bacteria multiply rapidly

tempering—(1) a process for melting chocolate during which the temperature of the cocoa butter is carefully stabilized; this keeps the chocolate smooth and glossy; (2) gradually raising the temperature of a cold liquid, such as eggs, by slowly stirring in a hot liquid

terrine—[teh-reen] (1) traditionally a loaf of coarse forcemeat cooked in a covered earthenware mold without a crust; today, the word is used interchangeably with pâté; (2) the mold used to cook such items, usually a ceramic rectangle or oval shape

thickening agents—ingredients used to thicken sauces; include starches (flour, cornstarch and arrowroot), gelatin and liaisons

timbale—[tim-bahl] (1) a small pail-shaped mold used to shape foods; (2) a preparation made in such a mold

time and temperature control for safety—see **TCS foods**

tisanes—[tee-ZAHNS] beverages made from herbal infusions that do not contain any tea

tofu—also known as bean curd; created from soymilk using a method similar to the way animal milk is separated into curds and whey in the production of cheese

tomato sauce—a leading sauce made from tomatoes, vegetables, seasonings and white stock; it may or may not be thickened with roux

toque—[toke] the tall white hat worn by chefs

torchon—[TOR-shahn] French for a cloth or towel, such as a dishcloth; the term is sometimes used to refer to dishes in which the item has been shaped into a cylinder by being wrapped in a cloth or towel

torte—in Central and Eastern European usage, refers to a rich cake in which all or part of the flour is replaced with finely chopped nuts or bread crumbs

tossed salad—a salad prepared by placing the greens, garnishes and salad dressing in a large bowl and tossing to combine

total recipe cost—the total cost of ingredients for a particular recipe; total recipe cost does not reflect overhead, labor, fixed expenses or profit

tourner—[toor-NAY] to cut into football-shaped pieces with seven equal sides and blunt ends

toxins—by-products of living bacteria that can cause illness if consumed in sufficient quantities

tranche—[tranch] an angled slice cut from fish fillets

trans fats—a type of fat created when vegetable oils are solidified through hydrogenation

transglutaminase—natural enzyme derived from bacterial fermentation that binds proteins into a solid mass, widely used commercially for making sausages and surimi; chefs use it to join pieces of meat, fish or poultry into a single cut

tripe—the edible lining of a cow's stomach

truffles—(1) flavorful tubers that grow near the roots of oak or beech trees; (2) rich chocolate candies made with ganache

truss—to tie poultry with butcher's twine into a compact shape for cooking

tube pan—a deep round baking pan with a hollow tube in the center

tuber—the fleshy root, stem or rhizome of a plant from which a new plant will grow; some, such as potatoes, are eaten as vegetables

tunneling—large tubular holes in muffins and cakes, a defect caused by improper mixing

U

umami—the taste sensation caused by the naturally occurring amino acid glutamate; gives food a savory richness or meatiness; found primarily in fermented foods and those to which monosodium glutamate has been added

unit cost—the price paid to acquire one of the specified units

United States Department of Agriculture (USDA)—federal government agency that ensures food items are safe, wholesome and accurately labeled; manages inspections and grading of foodstuffs

univalves—single-shelled mollusks with a single muscular foot, such as abalone

unsaturated fats—fats with one (mono) or more (poly) double bonds, which eliminate hydrogen atoms from the molecule; found in plants and plant foods such as avocados, corn, cottonseed, olives, rapeseed (canola), safflower and sunflower, as well as fatty fish; liquid at room temperature

upland birds—bird species that do not swim and do not need to live near water (rivers, marshes, lakes) in order to breed and raise chicks (e.g., pheasant, quail, dove, grouse)

V

vacuum packaging—a food preservation method in which fresh or cooked food is placed in an airtight container (usually plastic); virtually all air is removed from the container through a vacuum process before it is sealed

vanilla custard sauce—a stirred custard made with egg yolks, sugar and milk or half-and-half and flavored with vanilla; served with or used in dessert preparations; also known as crème anglaise

variety—the result of breeding plants of the same species that have different qualities or characteristics; the new plant often combines features from both parents

variety meats—see **offal**

veal—the meat of calves under the age of nine months

vegan—[VEE-gun] a vegetarian who does not eat dairy products, eggs, honey or any other animal product; vegans usually also avoid wearing and using animal products such as fur, leather or wool

vegetable—any herbaceous plant (one with little or no woody tissue) that can be partially or wholly eaten

vegetarian—a person who does not eat any meat, poultry, game, fish, shellfish or animal by-products such as gelatin or animal fats; may also exclude dairy products or eggs from the diet

velouté—[veh-loo-tay] a leading sauce made by thickening a white stock (fish, veal or chicken) with roux

venison—flesh from any member of the deer family, including antelope, elk, moose, reindeer, red-tailed deer, white-tailed deer, mule deer and axis deer

vent—(1) to allow the circulation or escape of a liquid or gas; (2) to cool a pot of hot liquid by setting the pot on blocks in a cold water bath and allowing cold water to circulate around it

venue—location or site where an event, such as a banquet, wedding or other party, is held

vinaigrette—a temporary emulsion of oil and vinegar seasoned with salt and pepper

vinegar—a thin, acidic liquid used as a preservative, cooking ingredient and cleaning solution

viniculture—the art and science of making wine from grapes

vintner—a winemaker

viruses—the smallest known form of life; they invade the living cells of a host and take over those cells' genetic material, causing the cells to produce more viruses; some viruses can enter a host through the ingestion of contaminated food

viscera—internal organs

viscosity—the measurement of a fluid's resistance to flow; in common terms, it is the thickness of a liquid; for example, water has a low viscosity while honey has a high viscosity

vitamins—essential micronutrients present in foods; they do not provide calories (energy) but are essential for regulating many bodily functions

vol-au-vents—[vole-o-VOHN] deep, individual portion-sized puff pastry shells, often shaped as hearts, fish or fluted circles; filled with a savory mixture and served as an appetizer or main course

volume—the space occupied by a substance; calculated as length × width × height, volume measurements are expressed as liters, teaspoons, tablespoons, cups, pints and gallons

W

wakame—a seaweed or kelp cultivated in East Asia because of its popularity in soups and salads and known as *miyeok* (sea mustard) in Korea; high in minerals and vitamins. It grows in long strands, which may be sold fresh or dried, and should be cut into small pieces before rehydrating or cooking

wash—a glaze applied to dough before baking; a commonly used wash is made with whole egg and water

water bath—see **bain marie**

water buffalo's milk—milk produced by a female water buffalo; it has approximately 7.5% milkfat, 10.3% milk solids and 82.2% water

water pack—canned fruits with water or fruit juice added

waterfowl—bird species that swim; waterfowl breed and raise chicks near or on bodies of water, including marshes, lakes and rivers (e.g., duck, swans, geese)

waxy potatoes—those with a low starch content and thin skin; best used in boiled preparations

weight—the heaviness of a substance; commonly expressed as grams, ounces and pounds

whetstone—a dense, grained stone used to sharpen or hone a knife blade

whey—the watery liquid remaining after milk proteins coagulate into curds during the cheese making process; contains vitamins, minerals, proteins and trace amounts of fat and is used in making whey cheese, such as ricotta, and as a substitute for non-fat milk

whipping—a mixing method in which foods are vigorously beaten in order to incorporate air; a whisk or an electric mixer with its whip attachment is used

white stew—see **blanquette** and **fricassee**

white stock—a light-colored stock made from chicken, veal, beef or fish bones simmered in water with vegetables and seasonings

whitewash—a thin mixture or slurry of flour and cold water used like cornstarch for thickening

whole butter—butter that is not clarified, whipped or reduced-fat

wine—an alcoholic beverage made from the fermented juice of grapes or other fruits; may be sparkling (effervescent) or still (non-effervescent) or fortified with additional alcohol; wine's alcohol content is 10–15 percent

work station—a work area in the kitchen dedicated to a particular task, such as broiling or salad making; work stations using the same or similar equipment for related tasks are grouped together into work sections

X

xanthan gum—a stabilizer produced by fermenting the sugar in corn; used to thicken, stabilize and emulsify prepared sauces, dairy products, ice creams and baked goods

Y

yeasts—microscopic fungi whose metabolic processes are responsible for fermentation; they are used for leavening bread and in cheese, beer and wine making

yield—the total amount of a product made from a specific recipe; also, the amount of a food item remaining after cleaning or processing

yield grades—ratings awarded by a USDA grading program for meat that estimates the amount of usable meat on a carcass

yield percentage—the ratio of the usable weight of an ingredient after cleaning and trimming to the quantity purchased; calculated by dividing the trimmed weight by the as-purchased weight of the ingredient

yield test—measuring and weighing an ingredient before and after trimming to determine the usable portion; used to determine the quantity of an ingredient to purchase as well as actual ingredient cost

Z

zabaglione—see **sabayon**

zest—the colored outer portion of the rind of citrus fruit; contains the oil that provides flavor and aroma

zushi—[zhoo-she] the seasoned rice used for sushi

Bibliography and Recommended Reading

GENERAL INTEREST

Barber, Dan. *The Third Plate: Field Notes on the Future of Food*. New York: Little, Brown Book Group, 2014.

Bennion, Marion, and Barbara Scheule. *Introductory Foods*. 14th ed. Upper Saddle River, NJ: Prentice Hall, 2014.

Davidson, Alan. *The Oxford Companion to Food*. 2nd ed. Oxford: Oxford University Press, 2006.

Dornenburg, Andrew, and Karen Page. *Becoming a Chef*. New York: Wiley, 2003.

———. *Culinary Artistry*. New York: Wiley, 1996.

Escoffier, Auguste. *The Escoffier Cook Book and Guide to the Fine Art of Cookery for Connoisseurs, Chefs, Epicures*. New York: Crown, 1969. Originally published as *Le Guide culinaire*. Bibliotheque Professionnelle, Paris: 1903.

Herbst, Ron, and Sharon Tyler Herbst. *The New Food Lover's Companion*. 5th ed. Hauppauge, NY: Barron's Educational Series, 2013.

Hesterman, Oran B. *Fair Food: Growing a Healthy, Sustainable Food System for All*. New York: PublicAffairs™/Perseus Books, 2011.

Labensky, Steven, Gaye G. Ingram, and Sarah R. Labensky. *Webster's New World Dictionary of Culinary Arts*. 2nd ed. Upper Saddle River, NJ: Prentice Hall, 2000.

Larousse Gastronomique. English ed. Translated by Frank Kulla and Patricia Shannon Kulla. New York: Clarkson Potter, 2001.

Molt, Mary. *Food for Fifty*. 14th ed. Upper Saddle River, NJ: Pearson, 2017.

Pépin, Jacques. *The Art of Cooking*. New York: Knopf, 1987.

———. *La Technique*. New York: Pocket Books, 1987.

Point, Fernand. *Fernand Point: Ma Gastronomie*. English ed. Wilton, CT: Lyceum Books, 1974.

Saulnier, Louis. *Le Répertoire de la Cuisine*. rev. ed. New York: Barron's Educational Series, 1977. First published 1914.

FOOD HISTORY

Freedman, Paul. *Food: The History of Taste*. Davis: University of California Press, 2008.

Fussell, Betty. *The Story of Corn*. New York: Knopf, 1992.

Goldstein, Joyce. *Inside the California Food Revolution: Thirty Years That Changed Our Culinary Consciousness*. Berkeley: University of California Press, 2013.

Laudan, Rachel. *Cuisine and Empire: Cooking in World History*. Berkeley: University of California Press, 2013.

Lovegren, Sylvia. *Fashionable Food: Seven Decades of Food Fads*. New York: Macmillan General Reference, 1995.

Mintz, Sidney W. *Sweetness and Power: The Place of Sugar in Modern History*. New York: Viking Press, 1995.

Pollan, Michael. *Cooked: A Natural History of Transformation*. New York: Penguin Press, 2013.

Shapiro, Laura. *Perfection Salad: Women and Cooking at the Turn of the Century*. New York: Farrar, Straus & Giroux, 1986.

Spring, Justin. *The Gourmand's Way: Six Americans in Paris and the Birth of a New Gastronomy*. New York: Farrar, Straus & Giroux, 2017.

Smith, Andrew F. *Eating History: Thirty Turning Points in the Making of American Cuisine*. New York: Columbia University Press, 2011.

Toussaint-Samat, Maguelonne. *A History of Food*, 2nd ed. Cambridge, MA: Wiley-Blackwell, 2009.

Willan, Anne. *Great Cooks and Their Recipes: From Taillevent to Escoffier*. Boston: Little, Brown, 1992.

SANITATION AND SAFETY

Knechtges, Paul. *Food Safety: Theory and Practice*. Boston: Jones and Bartlett Learning, 2011.

McSwane, David, Richard Linton, Rue, Nancy R., and Williams, Anna Graf. *Food Safety Fundamentals*. 2nd ed. Edited by Lawrence R. Kohl. Arlington, VA: Food Marketing Institute, 2010.

National Restaurant Association Educational Foundation. *ServSafe CourseBook*. 7th ed. Upper Saddle River, NJ: Pearson, 2018.

NUTRITION

Baskette, Michael, and Eleanor Mainella. *The Art of Nutritional Cooking*. 3rd ed. Upper Saddle River, NJ: Prentice Hall, 2008.

Drummond, Karen E., and Lisa M. Brefere. *Nutrition for Foodservice and Culinary Professionals*. 9th ed. New York: Wiley, 2016.

Nestle, Marion, and Michael Pollan. *Food Politics: How the Food Industry Influences Nutrition and Health*. rev. ed. Berkeley: University of California Press, 2013.

Polenz, Katherine, and Culinary Institute of America. *Cooking for Special Diets*. New York: Wiley, 2015.

Powers, Catharine, and Mary Abbott Hess. *Essentials of Nutrition for Chefs*. 2nd ed. Medina, OH: Culinary Nutrition Publishing, 2013.

Winter, Ruth. *A Consumer's Dictionary of Food Additives*. 7th ed. New York: Harmony, 2009.

FOOD COSTING AND BUSINESS SKILLS

Drysdale, John, and Jennifer A. Galipeau. *Profitable Menu Planning*. 4th ed. Upper Saddle River, NJ: Prentice Hall, 2008.

Labensky, Sarah R. *Applied Math for Food Service*. Upper Saddle River, NJ: Prentice Hall, 1998.

Lynch, Francis T. *The Book of Yields*. 8th ed. New York: Wiley, 2010.

Traster, Daniel. *Foundations of Menu Planning*. 2nd ed. Upper Saddle River, NJ: Pearson, 2017.

TOOLS

Hiromitsu, Nozaki, Kate Klippensteen, and Yasuo Konishi. *Japanese Kitchen Knives: Essential Techniques and Recipes.* Tokyo: Kodansha International, 2009.

Ward, Chad. *An Edge in the Kitchen: The Ultimate Guide to Kitchen Knives.* New York: William Morrow, 2008.

Weinstein, Norman. *Mastering Knife Skills: The Essential Guide to the Most Important Tools in Your Kitchen.* New York: Stewart, Tabori & Chang, 2008.

FLAVORING INGREDIENTS AND FOOD SCIENCE

Bitterman, Mark. *Salted: A Manifesto on the World's Most Essential Mineral, with Recipes.* Berkeley: Ten Speed Press, 2010.

Coates, Clive. *An Encyclopedia of the Wines and Domaines of France.* Davis: University of California Press, 2001.

Cost, Bruce. *Asian Ingredients: A Guide to Foodstuffs of China, Japan, Korea, Thailand and Vietnam.* New York: Quill HarperCollins, 2000.

Delwiche, Jeannine. "You Eat with Your Eyes First." *Physiology & Behavior* 107 (November 2015): 502–504.

Goldstein, Darra, ed. *The Oxford Companion to Sugar and Sweets.* New York: Oxford University Press, 2015.

Katz, Sandor Felix. *The Art of Fermentation.* White River Junction, VT: Chelsea Green Publishing, 2012.

MacNeil, Karen. *The Wine Bible.* 2nd ed. New York: Workman, 2015.

McGee, Harold. *On Food and Cooking.* rev. ed. New York: Scribner, 2007.

McWilliams, Margaret. *Foods: Experimental Perspectives.* 8th ed. Upper Saddle River, NJ: Pearson, 2017.

Myhrvold, Nathan, Chris Young, and Maxime Bilet. *Modernist Cuisine: The Art and Science of Cooking.* Bellevue, WA: The Cooking Lab, 2011.

Norman, Jill. *The Complete Book of Spices.* American ed. New York: Viking Studio Books, 1991.

Page, Karen, and Andrew Dornenburg. *The Flavor Bible: The Essential Guide to Culinary Creativity, Based on the Wisdom of America's Most Imaginative Chefs.* New York: Little, Brown, 2008.

Patterson, Daniel and Mandy Aftel. *The Art of Flavor: Practices and Principles for Creating Delicious Food.* New York: Riverhead Books, 2017.

Robinson, Jancis, and Julia Harding, eds. *The Oxford Companion to Wine.* 4th ed. Oxford: Oxford University Press, 2015.

Sercarz, Lior Lev. *The Spice Companion: A Guide to the World of Spices.* New York: Clarkson Potter, 2016.

Stevens, Mark C. *Cooking with Spices: 100 Recipes for Blends, Marinades, and Sauces from Around the World.* Berkeley: Rockridge Press, 2017.

This, Hervé. *Building a Meal: From Molecular Gastronomy to Culinary Constructivism.* New York: Columbia University Press, 2008.

———. *Molecular Gastronomy: Exploring the Science of Flavor.* New York: Columbia University Press, 2008.

DAIRY AND CHEESE

Fletcher, Janet. *The Cheese Course.* San Francisco: Chronicle Books, 2002.

Harbutt, Juliet. *The World Encyclopedia of Cheese: The Definitive Illustrated Guide to the Cheeses of the World.* repr., London: Southwater, 2017.

Jenkins, Steven. *Steven Jenkins' Cheese Primer.* New York: Workman, 1996.

Mendelson, Anne. *Milk. The Surprising Story of Milk through the Ages.* New York: Random House, 2008.

STOCKS, SAUCES AND SOUPS

America's Test Kitchen, ed. *Soups, Stews & Chilis.* Brookline, MA.: Cook's Illustrated, 2010.

Clayton, Bernard. *The Complete Book of Soups and Stews.* New York: Simon & Schuster, 1987.

Larousse, David Paul. *The Sauce Bible: Guide to the Saucier's Craft.* New York: Wiley, 1993.

Peterson, James. *Sauces: Classical and Contemporary Sauce Making.* 4th ed. New York: Wiley, 2017.

Sokolov, Raymond A. *The Saucier's Apprentice.* New York: Knopf, 1976.

MEAT AND GAME

Aidells, Bruce, and Denis Kelly. *The Complete Meat Cookbook.* New York: Houghton Mifflin, 1998.

Henderson, Fergus. *The Whole Beast: Nose to Tail Eating.* New York: Ecco Press, 2004.

Jamison, Cheryl Alters, and Bill Jamison. *Smoke and Spice.* rev. upd. ed. Boston: Harvard Common Press, 2014.

Keller, Thomas. *Under Pressure: Cooking Sous Vide.* New York: Artisan, 2008.

LaFrieda, Pat. *Meat: Everything You Need to Know.* New York: Atria Books, 2014.

North American Meat Institute. *The Meat Buyer's Guide.* 8th ed. Washington, DC: NAMI, 2014.

Peterson, James. *Meat: A Kitchen Education.* Berkeley: Ten Speed Press, 2011.

Raichlen, Steven. *Project Smoke: Seven Steps to Smoked Food Nirvana.* New York: Workman, 2016.

Griffiths, Jesse. *A Chef's Guide to Preparing and Cooking Wild Game and Fish.* New York: Welcome Books, 2012.

Webster, Harold W., Jr. *The Complete Venison Cookbook.* Brandon, MS: Quail Ridge Press, 1996.

Wipfli, John. *Venison: The Slay to Gourmet Field to Kitchen Cookbook.* Minneapolis: Voyageur Press, 2017.

FISH AND SHELLFISH

Barber, Kimiko, and Hiroki Takemura. *Sushi: Taste and Techniques.* Upper Saddle River, NJ: Prentice Hall, 2008.

Green, Aliza. *Field Guide to Seafood.* Philadelphia: Quirk Productions, 2007.

Kurlansky, Mark. *The Last Fish Tale.* New York: Riverhead Books, 2009.

Peterson, James. *Fish and Shellfish.* New York: Morrow, 1998.

The Seafood Handbook: The Comprehensive Guide to Sourcing, Buying and Preparation. 2nd ed. Rockland, ME: Seafood Business Magazine, 2009.

The Seafood List: FDA's Guide to Acceptable Market Names for Seafood Sold in Interstate Commerce. Washington, D.C.: Center for Food Safety and Applied Nutrition, 2012.

Seaver, Barton. *American Seafood: Heritage, Culture and Cookery from Sea to Shining Sea.* New York: Sterling Epicure, 2017.

Thompson, Jennifer Trainer. *Fresh Fish: A Fearless Guide to Grilling, Shucking, Searing, Poaching and Roasting Seafood.* North Adams, MA: Storey Publishing, 2016.

Urner Barry. *The Commercial Guide to Fish and Shellfish.* 3rd ed. Toms River, NJ: Urner Barry, 2016.

EGGS AND BREAKFAST COOKERY

Eggcyclopedia. 5th ed. American Egg Board. Accessed August 21, 2017. https://www.incredibleegg.org/eggcyclopedia/.

Khong, Rachel and the Editors of Lucky Peach. *All about Eggs: Everything We Know about the World's Most Important Food.* New York: Clarkson Potter, 2017.

Pendergrast, Mark. *Uncommon Grounds: The History of Coffee and How It Transformed Our World.* rev. ed. New York: Basic Books, 2010.

Pettigrew, Jane. *The Tea Companion.* Jackson, TN: Running Press, 2004.

Ruhlman, Michael. *Egg: A Culinary Exploration of the World's Most Versatile Ingredient.* New York: Little, Brown and Company, 2014.

VEGETABLES AND FRUITS

America's Test Kitchen, ed. *Vegan for Everybody.* Brookline, MA: America's Test Kitchen, 2017.

Follas, Mat. *Vegetable Perfection.* London: Ryland Peters & Small, 2014.

Kafka, Barbara. *Vegetable Love.* New York: Artisan, 2005.

Keith, Lierre. *The Vegetarian Myth: Food, Justice, and Sustainability.* Crescent City, CA: Flashpoint Press, 2009.

Liano, Jodi, Tasha DeSerio, and Jennifer Maiser. *Cooking from the Farmers' Market.* San Francisco: Weldon Owen, 2012.

Madison, Deborah. *Local Flavors: Cooking and Eating from America's Farmer's Markets.* New York: Broadway Books, 2002.

Masumota, David Mas. *Epitaph for a Peach: Four Seasons on My Family Farm.* New York: HarperOne, 1996.

———. *Wisdom of the Last Farmer: Harvesting Legacies from the Land.* New York: Free Press, 2009.

Miller, Mark, with John Harrisson. *The Great Chile Book.* Berkeley: Ten Speed Press, 1991.

Morgan, Laura. *Roots: The Definitive Compendium with More Than 225 Recipes.* San Francisco: Chronicle Books, 2012.

Peterson, James, and Justin Schwartz. *Vegetables.* rev. ed. Berkeley: Ten Speed Press, 2012.

Presilla, Maricel E. *Peppers of the Americas.* Berkeley: Ten Speed Press, 2017.

Schneider, Elizabeth. *Vegetables from Amaranth to Zucchini: The Essential Reference.* New York: Morrow, 2001.

GRAINS AND PASTA

Bugialli, Giuliano. *On Pasta.* New York: Simon & Schuster, 1988.

Kummer, Corby. "Pasta." *The Atlantic* 258, no. 1 (July 1986): 35–47.

Sass, Lorna. *Whole Grains Every Day, Every Way.* New York: Clarkson Potter, 2006.

Speck, Maria. *Ancient Grains for Modern Meals.* Berkeley: Ten Speed Press, 2011.

COOKING FOR VEGETARIAN AND SPECIAL DIETS

Bergeron, Ken. *Professional Vegetarian Cooking.* New York: Wiley, 1999.

Case, Shelly. *Gluten Free: The Definitive Resource Guide.* 5th ed. Boston: Case Nutrition Consulting, 2016.

Hagler, Louise. *Tofu Cookery.* 25th Anniversary ed. Summertown, TN: Book Publishing Co., 2008.

Landau, Rich, and Kate Jacoby. *Vedge: 100 Plates Large and Small That Redefine Vegetable Cooking.* New York: The Experiment, LLC, 2013.

Mangini, Cara. *The Vegetable Butcher: How to Select, Prep, Slice, Dice, and Masterfully Cook Vegetables from Artichokes to Zucchini.* New York: Workman, 2016.

Madison, Deborah. *The New Vegetarian Cooking for Everyone.* rev. ed. Berkeley: Ten Speed Press, 2014.

Medrich, Alice. *Gluten-Free Flavor Flours: A New Way to Bake with Non-Wheat Flours, Including Rice, Nut, Coconut, Teff, Buckwheat, and Sorghum Flours.* New York: Artisan, 2017.

Moskowitz, Isa Chandra and Terry Hope Romero. *Veganomicon.* 10th Anniversary ed. New York: Hachette Book Group, 2017.

Page, Karen. *The Vegetarian Flavor Bible.* New York: Little, Brown, 2014.

SANDWICHES

Colicchio, Tom, and Sisha Ortuzar. *'wichcraft: Craft a Sandwich into a Meal—and a Meal into a Sandwich.* New York: Crown, 2009.

Russo, Susan. *The Encyclopedia of Sandwiches: Recipes, History and Trivia for Everything between Sliced Bread.* Philadelphia: Quirk Books, 2010.

Silverton, Nancy. *Nancy Silverton's Sandwiches.* repr., New York: Knopf, 2005.

CHARCUTERIE

Boetticher, Taylor, and Toponia Miller. *In the Charcuterie.* Berkeley: Ten Speed Press, 2013.

Ehlert, Friedrich W., Edouard Lonque, Michael Raffael, and Frank Wesel. *Pâtés and Terrines.* London: Hearst Books, 1984.

Rhulman, Michael, and Brian Polcyn. *Charcuterie.* rev. ed. New York: Norton, 2013.

HORS D'OEUVRE AND BUFFETS

Aloni, Nicole. *Secrets from a Caterer's Kitchen.* Tucson, AZ: HP Books, 2001.

Blashford-Snell, Victoria. *Hors d'Oeuvres.* repr., New York: DK Adult, 2017.

Clark, Pamela. *Tapas: Tantalizing Small Plates from the Mediterranean.* repr., New York: Sterling, 2013.

Clyne, Carol Murphy and Vincent Clyne. *Modern Buffet Presentation.* New York: Wiley, 2014.

Shiring, Stephen B. *Professional Catering.* Independence, KY: Cengage Learning, 2012.

Taylor, Milli. *Party Perfect Bites: Delicious Recipes for Canapes, Finger Foods and Party Snacks.* London: Ryland Peters & Small, 2014.

BREADS

Clayton, Bernard. *Bernard Clayton's New Complete Book of Breads.* rev. ed. New York: Fireside Books, 1995.

David, Elizabeth. *English Bread and Yeast Cookery.* With notes by Karen Hess. American ed. New York: Viking Press, 1980.

Forkish, Ken. *Flour Water Salt Yeast: The Fundamentals of Artisan Bread and Pizza.* Berkeley: Ten Speed Press, 2012.

Gibson, Heidi. *Muffins and Biscuits.* San Francisco: Chronicle Books, 2017.

Glezer, Maggie. *Artisan Baking across America.* New York: Artisan, 2000.

Hamelman, Jeffrey. *Bread: A Baker's Book of Techniques and Recipes.* New York: Wiley, 2004.

Leader, Daniel, and Lauren Chattman. *Local Breads: Sourdough and Whole-Grain Recipes from Europe's Best Artisan Bakers.* New York: Norton, 2008.

Suas, Michael. *Advanced Bread and Pastry.* Clifton Parks, NY: Delmar Cengage, 2009.

PASTRIES AND DESSERTS

Braker, Flo. *The Simple Art of Perfect Baking.* Shelburne, VT: Chapters, 1992.

Ecole Grand Chocolat Valrhona. *Chocolate Master Class: Essential Recipes and Techniques.* Edited by Frédéric Bau. Paris: Flammarion, 2014.

Healy, Bruce, and Paul Bugat. *Mastering the Art of French Pastry.* Woodbury, NY: Barron's Educational Series, 1984.

Heatter, Maida. *Maida Heatter's Book of Great Desserts.* Kansas City, MO: Andrews McMeel, 1999.

Kayser, Eric. *Maison Kayser's French Pastry Workshop.* New York: Black Dog & Leventhal Publishers, 2017.

Labensky, Sarah, Priscilla Martel, and Eddy Van Damme. *On Baking: A Textbook of Baking and Pastry Fundamentals.* 3rd ed. Update. Upper Saddle River, NJ: Prentice Hall, 2016.

Lenotre, Gaston, *The Best of Gaston Lenotre's Desserts.* Translated by Philip Hyman and Mary Hyman. Woodbury, NY: Barron's Educational Series, 1983.

Madison, Deborah. *Seasonal Fruit Desserts: From Orchard, Farm, and Market.* New York: Clarkson Potter, 2010.

Schreiber, Cory, and Julie Richardson. *Rustic Fruit Desserts: Crumbles, Buckles, Cobblers, Pandowdies, and More.* Berkeley Ten Speed Press, 2009.

Silverton, Nancy. *Desserts by Nancy Silverton.* New York: Harper & Row, 1986.

GARNISHING AND PRESENTATION

Budgen, June. *The Book of Garnishes.* Los Angeles: HP Books, 1986.

de Costa, Narahenapitage Sumith Premalal. *Edible Art: Tricks and Tools for Master Centerpieces.* Atglen, PA: Schiffer Publishing, 2006.

Hobday, Cara, and Jo Denbury. *Food Presentation Secrets: Styling Techniques of Professionals.* Ontario: Firefly Books, 2010.

Hongwiwat, Nidda, ed. *Complete Step by Step Vegetable and Fruit Carving.* 3rd ed. Bangkok: Sangdad, 2005.

INTERNATIONAL CUISINES

Adrià, Ferran, Julie Soler, and Albert Adrià. *A Day at el Bulli.* London: Phaidon Press, 2008.

Alford, Jeffrey. *Hot Sour Salty Sweet: A Culinary Journey through Southeast Asia.* New York: Artisan, 2000.

Andoh, Elizabeth. *Washoku: Recipes from the Japanese Home Kitchen.* San Francisco: Ten Speed Press, 2005.

Bayless, Rick. *Authentic Mexican: Regional Cooking from the Heart of Mexico.* With Deann Groen Bayless. New York: Morrow, 1987.

Bugialli, Giuliano. *The Fine Art of Italian Cooking.* New York: Random House, 1990.

Garces, Jose. *Latin Evolution.* New York: Lake Isle Press, 2008.

Harris, Jessica. *The Africa Cookbook: Tastes of a Continent.* New York: Simon & Schuster, 1998.

Hazan, Marcella. *Essentials of Classic Italian Cooking.* New York: Knopf, 1993.

Jaffrey, Madhur. *An Invitation to Indian Cooking.* New York: Ecco Press, 1999.

Kennedy, Diana. *The Cuisines of Mexico.* rev. ed. New York: Harper & Row, 1986.

Korean Food Foundation. *The Korean Kitchen: 75 Healthy, Delicious and Easy Recipes.* Seoul: KFF, 2014.

Lo, Kenneth. *The Encyclopedia of Chinese Cooking.* New York: Bristol Books, 1997.

Morimoto, Masaharu. *Morimoto: The New Art of Japanese Cooking.* New York: Dorling Kindersley, 2008.

Pham, Mai. *Pleasures of the Vietnamese Table.* New York: HarperCollins, 2001.

Presilla, Maricel E. *Gran Cocina Latina.* New York: Norton, 2012.

Roden, Claudia. *The New Book of Middle Eastern Food.* New York: Knopf, 2000.

Rose, Evelyn. *The New Complete International Jewish Cookbook.* New York: Carroll & Graf, 1992.

Rozin, Elisabeth. *Ethnic Cuisine: How to Create the Authentic Flavors of 30 International Cuisines.* repr., New York: Penguin, 1992.

Solomon, Charmaine. *The Complete Asian Cookbook.* rev. ed. Boston: Tuttle, 2002.

Von Bremzen, Anya, and John Welchman. *Please to the Table: The Russian Cookbook.* New York: Workman, 1990.

Young, Grace, and Alan Richardson. *The Breath of a Wok: Unlocking the Spirit of Chinese Wok Cooking through Recipes and Lore.* New York: Simon & Schuster, 2004.

Index

W

Credits

All photos courtesy of Richard Embery/Pearson Education except the following:

CHAPTER OPENER PHOTOS

p. 1: Paul Poplis/Photolibrary/Getty Images
p. 17: Eric Futran—Chefshots/Photolibrary/Getty Images
p. 39: Richard Embery/Pearson Education, Inc.
p. 53: Ginasanders/123RF.com
p. 71: Luca Pescucci/123RF.com
p. 93: Debby Wolvos/Pearson Education, Inc.
p. 107: Foodandmore/123RF.com
p. 143: Richard Embery/Pearson Education, Inc.
p. 161: Richard Embery/Pearson Education, Inc.
p. 173: Richard Embery/Pearson Education, Inc.
p. 201: Richard Embery/Pearson Education, Inc.
p. 255: Richard Embery/Pearson Education, Inc.
p. 291: Richard Embery/Pearson Education, Inc.
p. 325: Richard Embery/Pearson Education, Inc.
p. 349: Richard Embery/Pearson Education, Inc.
p. 371: Richard Embery/Pearson Education, Inc.
p. 391: Richard Embery/Pearson Education, Inc.
p. 413: Richard Embery/Pearson Education, Inc.
p. 467: Richard Embery/Pearson Education, Inc.
p. 479: Richard Embery/Pearson Education, Inc.
p. 551: Richard Embery/Pearson Education, Inc.
p. 585: Richard Embery/Pearson Education, Inc.
p. 653: Richard Embery/Pearson Education, Inc.
p. 705: Richard Embery/Pearson Education, Inc.
p. 731: Richard Embery/Pearson Education, Inc.
p. 773: Debby Wolvos/Pearson Education, Inc.
p. 809: Debby Wolvos/Pearson Education, Inc.
p. 831: Richard Embery/Pearson Education, Inc.
p. 869: Richard Embery/Pearson Education, Inc.
p. 899: Claudio Ventrella/123RF.com
p. 927: Richard Embery/Pearson Education, Inc.
p. 943: Richard Embery/Pearson Education, Inc.
p. 977: Richard Embery/Pearson Education, Inc.
p. 1025: Richard Embery/Pearson Education, Inc.
p. 1065: Debby Wolvos/Pearson Education, Inc.
p. 1095: Debby Wolvos/Pearson Education, Inc.
p. 1111: Maksim Shebeko/123RF.com

INTERIOR PHOTOS AND RECIPES

p. 3: (Marie-Antoine Carême) Bridgeman Images
p. 4: (Auguste Escoffier) Musée Escoffier de l'Art Culinaire
p. 5: MICKE Sebastien/Paris Match/Getty Images
p. 6: (Olive oil poached turnip) Sally Ryan/ZUMA Press, Inc./Alamy Stock Photo; (Sauce spooned over a dish . . .) Rob Kim/Getty Images; (Roast foie gras . . .) Adam James/Alamy Stock Photo
p. 7: (Chef Ferran Adria) ALBERT GEA/REUTERS/Alamy Stock Photo; (Liquid olives . . .) Lucas Vallecillos/Alamy Stock Photo
p. 9: Andrew Fox/Alamy Stock Photo
p. 10: (The farm at Fäviken, . . .) Leisa Tyler/LightRocket/Getty Images
p. 11: Spencer Weiner/Los Angeles Times/Getty Images
p. 14: RIEGER Bertrand/hemis.fr/Alamy Stock Photo
p. 31: (Figure 2.6) Apple pie, Denise Kappa/Shutterstock; fresh salad, Nrt/Shutterstock; smoked meat, MaraZe/Shutterstock;

Dorado fish, Africa Studio/Shutterstock; salmon steak, Alex Staroseltsev/Shutterstock; egg carton, Nito/Shutterstock; prime rib, Hannamariah/Shutterstock; pork chops, Rj lerich/Shutterstock; minced beef, E.G. Pors/Shutterstock; raw whole chicken, Elena Schweitzer/Shutterstock; raw chicken leg, Bergamont/Shutterstock
p. 41: (Figure 3.2) Robynmac/123RF.com
p. 42: (Figure 3.3) Tina Rencelj/Shutterstock
p. 43: (Figure 3.5) JPC-PROD/Shutterstock; (Figure 3.6) Belchonock/123RF.com
p. 48: (Figure 3.10) United States Department of Agriculture; (Quote) Qualified Health Claims: Letter of Enforcement Discretion—Nuts and Coronary Heart Disease, U.S. Food and Drug Administration
p. 49: (Figure 3.11) Denis Pepin/Shutterstock
p. 51: (Figure 3.13) Africa Studio/Shutterstock
p. 52: (Figure 3.14) Dave Gandy/Font Awesome
p. 72: (Figure 5.1) NSF International
p. 89: (Chamber vacuum) Jim Smith/Pearson Education, Inc.
p. 110: Text reprinted by permission of Jeannine Delwiche
p. 134: (White, rosé and red wine) Shebeko/Shutterstock
p. 135: (Corkscrew) Andy Crawford/Dorling Kindersley
p. 137: (Ale) Valentyn Volkov/Shutterstock; (Irish stout) Kitkana/123RF.com
p. 138: (Pilsner) Johnfoto18/Shutterstock; (Hops flowers) Steve Gorton/Dorling Kindersley
p. 149: Reprinted by permission of Paula Lambert
p. 166: (Weighing dark powder . . .) Ron Kloberdanz/Shutterstock
p. 185: (Safety Alert: Flambéing: Cooking with alcohol) Stockyimages/Shutterstock
p. 199: (Procedure for preparing foods *sous vide,* Steps 1–3) Jim Smith/Pearson Education, Inc.
p. 276: Recipe reprinted by permission of Donald Link
p. 282: Recipe reprinted by permission of Assistant Professor Scott H. Doughty
p. 283: Recipe reprinted by permission of Michael Artlip
p. 284: (Mulligatawny soup) Recipe reprinted by permission of Kenneth P. Morlino, former professor at Nashville State Community College
p. 285: (Potato chowder with hot smoked salmon) Recipe reprinted by permission of William Wiklendt
p. 287: Recipe reprinted by permission of Assistant Professor Scott H. Doughty
p. 293: (Figures 13.3 and 13.4) United States Department of Agriculture (USDA)
p. 294: (Figures 13.5 and 13.7) United States Department of Agriculture (USDA)
p. 297: (Figure 13.9) United States Department of Agriculture (USDA)
p. 333: (Kobe beef) Hungryworks/Shutterstock
p. 375: (Goat shank) Edward Westmacott/Shutterstock
p. 419: (Figures 18.3 and 18.4) United States Department of Agriculture (USDA)
p. 466: (Sautéed foie gras . . .) Recipe reprinted by permission from Leland Atkinson
p. 473: (Fried crickets) R. Thanuthattaphong/123RF.com
p. 493: (Lionfish) Nicram Sabod/Shutterstock

THE CAMBRIDGE ENCYCLOPEDIA OF SPACE

CAMBRIDGE UNIVERSITY PRESS

CAMBRIDGE · NEW YORK · PORT CHESTER · MELBOURNE · SYDNEY

THE
CAMBRIDGE
ENCYCLOPEDIA
OF
SPACE

The right of the
University of Cambridge
to print and sell
all manner of books
was granted by
Henry VIII in 1534.
The University has printed
and published continuously
since 1584.

This English language edition published by the
Press Syndicate of the University of Cambridge,
The Pitt Building, Trumpington Street, Cambridge CB2 1RP
40 West 20th Street, New York, NY 10011, USA
10 Stamford Road, Oakleigh, Melbourne 3166, Australia

Original edition
Le Grand Atlas de l'Espace
© Encyclopaedia Universalis 1987, 1989

English Language Edition
© Cambridge University Press 1990

First published 1990

Printed in France

British Library cataloguing in publication data
The Cambridge encyclopedia of space
1. Space sciences
I. Rycroft, M. J. (Michael John) 1938–
II. Le grand atlas de l'espace. English
500.5

Library of Congress cataloguing in publication data
[Espace. English]
The Cambridge encyclopedia of space
Rev. ed of: Espace: le grand atlas de l'espace
Includes bibliographical references and index
1. Astronautics – Encyclopedias
2. Rocketry – Encyclopedias
I. Rycroft, Michael J.   II. Title
TL788.E7713   1990   629.4   90–2444

ISBN 0 521 36426 4 hardback

For Encyclopaedia Universalis

Editors   Jean Claude Falque
             Annie Humbert-Droz Swezey
Production   Hans Schweizer

For Cambridge University Press

Development editor   Peter Richards
Text editor   Susan Bowring
Index   Emanuele Wijsenbeck

The Cambridge Encyclopedia of Space

Editor   Michael Rycroft

Translator   Alison Bullough

Authors   Frédéric d'Allest

Jean Arets

Phillip J. Baker

Georges Balmino

Hans Barth

Alexander Bazilevsky

Robert H. Benson

Jean-Pierre Bibring

Michel Bignier

Philippe Binet

Amy K. Bodnar

Pierre M. Boudreau

Jean-Claude Bouillot

Gérard Brachet

Robert W. Breithaupt

Richard E. Butler

Nathalie Cabrol

Marie-Claude Canivet

Claude Carlier

Jean-Pierre Carrou

Eric Chassefière

Chen Gengtao

Mikhail Chernichov

Phillip S. Clark

Henry J. Clarks

Jean Clavel

Lawrence Colin

Pierre Contensou

Marie-Rose Cukierman

Alexandre Dauguet

Geneviève Debouzy

Mario De Leo

James A. Dunne

Alain Dupas

Margaret B. Edwards

Bernhard F. Fabis

Terence T. Finn

Thomas L. Fischetti

Pierre M. Gallois

Chantal M. Gauthier

Roger Gendrin

Michel Giroux

Jacques Goimard

Olivier de Goursac

Gottfried Greger

Jerry Grey

James M. Grimwood

Claude Honvault

Rainer Jansen

Nandasiri Jasentuliyana

Ola M. Johannessen

Nicholas L. Johnson

Nikolai Kardachev

Akira Kikuchi

Francis Klefstad-Sillonville

Andrei A. Kokochine

Ivan S. Korochentsev

Yves Langevin

Christian Lardier

André Lebeau

Chester M. Lee

John C. Leeming

Philippe Lemaire

Joel I. Leonard

Jeffrey Maclure

Bethene E. McNealy

Philippe Masson

Masafumi Miyazawa

Robert Mory

Larissa Moskaleva

Linda Neuman-Ezell

Olof Nordling

Charles D. Odorizzi

William A. Oran

Frederick I. Ordway III

Fumio Otsuki

Daniel Pichoud

Théo Pirard

Marcel Pouliquen

Boris V. Rauchenbakh

Hugh M. Reekie

Noah Rifkin

Andrés Ripoll

Josette Runavot

Olivier de Saint-Lager

Yuri Semionov

David Shapland

Mitchell R. Sharpe

Michiyoshi Shiraishi

Jerome Simonoff

Jürgen Stegemann

Brian Stockwell

Hermann A. Strub

Brian G. Taylor

Pierre Thomas

US National Commission on Space

Guy Valentiny

Alexei A. Vassiliev

Evgeni P. Velikhov

Jacques Villain

Jean-Michel Villetorte

Adelin Villevieille

Ronald J. White

Contents

Exploring the Universe 146

Living with space 228

Preface

This *Encyclopedia of Space*, which covers the entire field of space science and technology, could equally well have been entitled *The Cambridge Encyclopedia of the Future* but for the crucial fact that, to borrow a famous phrase, the future has already begun.

Whether one's personal reaction to the events of the last thirty years encompasses elation or disappointment, the era has unquestionably gone in which the human exploration of space was purely visionary, confined to the imaginary flights of artists and philosophers whose dreams stretched to the great beyond. Today, even the launch into orbit of the Sputnik satellite in 1957 seems to belong more in the realm of history than science. From then on reality seemed stranger than fiction; even science-fiction had been surpassed.

It is this ever more complex reality, as much a part of the future as the present, that our *Encyclopedia of Space* sets out to explore. After the hasty predictions and sensational coverage that have sometimes plagued the subject in the past, the time seems ripe to appraise objectively not only the knowledge already gained and that likely to be acquired in the future, but also the practical applications and ideas that have been generated by that most remarkable of ventures, humankind's conquest of space.

Planned by Encyclopaedia Universalis under the guidance of Jean Claude Falque and Annie Humbert-Droz Swezey and adapted for English speaking readers by Professor Michael Rycroft and a team at Cambridge University Press, this vast survey of space research has been structured along straightforward thematic and chronological lines. An introductory section charts precisely how the dream of exploring space has in this century been transformed into reality; there then follow three major divisions of the book, in turn describing 'going into space', 'exploring the universe' and 'living with space' to give a unified view of the whole enormous enterprise.

Most importantly, throughout the encyclopedia the human aspects of space exploration are given as much weight as the purely scientific. In this way, taken together with our *Grand atlas de l'astronomie* (published in English as *The Cambridge Atlas of Astronomy*), this *Encyclopedia of Space* brings the human odyssey of space exploration right up to date. While its companion charted planets, stars and galaxies from the closest to the most far-flung, the present volume explores the methods and the means employed. Above all, you will find it a celebration of the courage, human ingenuity and indomitable spirit called upon ceaselessly on our path to becoming, in the words of Descartes, 'the masters and possessors of nature'.

Jacques Bersani

Editor-in-chief
Encyclopaedia Universalis, Paris

Introduction

The Cambridge Encyclopedia of Space is the most complete and up-to-date account of the conquest of space ever published in a single volume. Created for a general readership by a team of 100 experts from a dozen different countries, it brings together the history, the science, the technology – and the adventure – of space research in a way that will appeal to anyone curious about the exploration of this, our final frontier.

The Encyclopedia opens with a vivid history of space exploration – from the work of rocket pioneers like Robert H. Goddard and Wernher von Braun, and the Gagarin and Glenn missions of 1961 to 1962 – and takes the story through to the occupation of the Mir space station, Voyager 2's triumphant fly-past of Neptune, and the 1990 launch of the Hubble Space Telescope. There are in addition comprehensive, thematic sections on all aspects of space technology and space science, the exploration of the solar system, living in space, and the uses – both present and future – of Earth orbiting satellites and space stations.

At once readable and packed with information, the Encyclopedia charts in detail the progress of the world's space programmes. Fully international in scope, it gives due weight to the Soviet and European, as well as the Chinese, Japanese, and Indian contributions to space exploration without in the least detracting from the massive achievements of the United States. It also provides invaluable summary descriptions of individual missions and their results, not just in the text but through extensive tables and an impressive array of action photographs and specially prepared diagrams.

The excitement of space research, as well as the challenges and opportunities that it presents, shine through the pages that follow. *The Cambridge Encyclopedia of Space* throws a powerful spotlight on to the greatest scientific and technological challenge to face the human race at the dawn of the third millennium.

Michael Rycroft

The dream. In Britain in 1638, Francis Godwin, Bishop of Hereford, published a work entitled *The Man in the Moone: or a Discourse of a Voyage Thither*, under the pseudonym of Domingo Gonsales, 'the Speedy Messenger.' He described a journey to the Moon using imaginary geese called 'gansas'. The voyage took eleven days (Trustees of the British Library).

The reality. On 16 July 1969, the Saturn V rocket carrying Apollo 11 blasted off from Cape Kennedy in Florida. Four days later, the lunar module, Eagle, carrying Neil Armstrong and Edwin Aldrin, landed on the Moon (NASA/Colorific).

From dream to reality

The rocket – from East to West

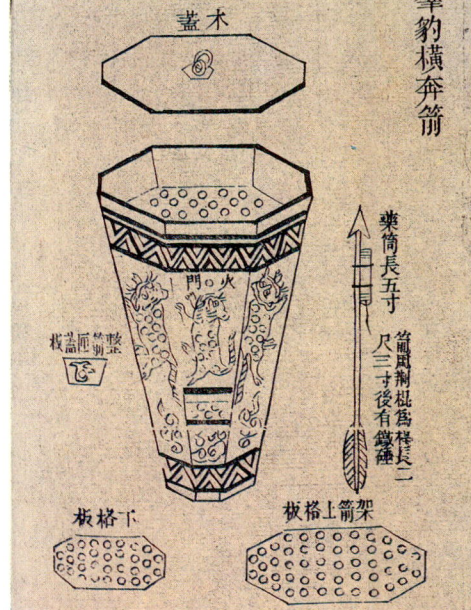

The discovery of the reaction principle was the key to space travel and represents one of the great milestones in the history of scientific thought. Not only did it solve a problem that had intrigued man for ages, but it literally opened the door to his exploration of the Universe.

An intellectual breakthrough, brilliant though it may be, does not automatically ensure that the transition is made from theory to practice. Despite the fact that rockets had been used sporadically for several hundred years, they remained a relatively minor artefact of civilisation until the twentieth century. Prodigious efforts, accelerated during two world wars, were required before the technology of primitive rocketry could be translated into the reality of sophisticated astronautics.

It is strange that the rocket was generally ignored by writers of fiction to transport their heroes to mysterious realms beyond the Earth, despite the fact that it was commonly used in firework displays from the Far East to Great Britain. The reason is that nobody associated the reaction principle with the idea of travelling through space to a neighbouring world. Until the very close of the nineteenth century, writers looked to geese, bottles of dew, spirits, demons, chariots strapped on wings, antigravity materials, and cannons to escape from the Earth's gravity into space.

A simple analogy can help us to understand how a rocket operates. It is much like a machine gun mounted on the rear of a boat. In reaction to the backward discharge of bullets, the gun, and hence the boat, move forwards. A rocket motor's 'bullets' are minute, high speed particles produced by burning propellants in a suitable chamber. The reaction to the ejection of these small particles causes the rocket to move forwards.

There is evidence that the reaction principle was applied practically well before the rocket was invented. In his *Noctes Atticae* or 'Attican nights', Aulus Gellius (*c* 130 to 180) describes the pigeon of Archytas, an invention dating back to about 360 BC. Made of wood and hanging from a string, it was moved to and fro by steam blowing out from small exhaust ports. The reaction to the discharging steam provided the bird with motive power.

The invention of rockets is linked inextricably to the invention of 'black powder'. Most historians of technology credit the Chinese with its discovery. They base their belief on studies of Chinese writings or of the notebooks of early Europeans who settled in, or made long visits to, China to study its history and civilisation. It is probable that, sometime in the tenth century, black powder was first compounded from its basic ingredients of saltpetre, charcoal and sulphur. But this does not mean that it was immediately used to propel rockets.

The French sinologists Joseph Toussaint Reinaud and Idelphonse Fave, in their *Histoire de l'artillerie: du feu grégeois, des feux de guerre, et des origines de la poudre à canon* (History of artillery: Greek fire, weapons of war and the origins of gunpowder, 1845), write 'unfortunately, no Chinese treatise on fireworks written before the thirteenth century has come down to us.' They point out that French

Actioni contrariam semper & æqualem esse reactionem : sive corporum duorum actiones in se muno semper esse æquales & in partes contrarias dirigi.

Quicquid premit vel trahit alterum, tantundem ab eo premitur vel trahitur. Siquis lapidem digito premit, premitur & hujus digitus a lapide. Si equus lapidem funi allegatum trahit, retrahetur etiam & equus æqualiter in lapidem: nam funis utrinqʒ distentus eodem relaxandi se conatu urgebit Equum versus lapidem, ac lapidem versus equum, tantumqʒ impediet progressum unius quantum promovet progressum alterius. Si corpus aliquod in corpus aliud impingens, motum ejus vi sua quomodocunqʒ mutaverit, idem quoque vicissim in motu proprio eandem mutationem in partem contrariam vi alterius (ob æqualitatem pressionis mutuæ) subibit. His actionibus æquales fiunt mutationes non velocitatum sed motuum, (scilicet in corporibus non aliunde impeditis :) Mutationes enim velocitatum, in contrarias itidem partes factæ, quia motus æqualiter mutantur, sunt corporibus reciproce proportionales.

Newton's third law of motion, the key to space travel. The *Philosphiae naturalis principia mathematica* opened with *Definitions* and then *Axioms*, or laws of movement, of which there were three. In the 1687 edition the third law appeared as follows:

'For every action there is always an equal and opposite reaction, or, the reciprocal actions that two bodies exert on each other are always equal and directed towards the other body. Anything which presses against or pulls something is also pressed against and pulled by the other thing. ... If a horse pulls a rope attached to a rock, then the rock also pulls the horse, but in the opposite direction. The rope between the two pulls the horse towards the rock and also the rock towards the horse; it opposes the horse's forward movement and causes the rock to move forwards. If one body strikes another body and by its force causes the other body to change its movement, then it is itself subjected to a change in its motion which is equal and opposite to that of the other body (due to the equality of action and reaction). The changes caused by the actions are not equal in speed, but in movement [actually the 'momentum', the product of mass and velocity]. By exerting itself in the same way on both bodies, because the movements are modified by an equal amount, then the charges in the velocities are reciprocally (or inversely) proportional to the mass of the bodies.'

Newton's third law is the principle upon which reaction engines and thus rockets operate. How does a rocket produce its propulsive force? The best analogy is to consider a machine gun which is fired from a small boat. When the gun is fired from the back of the boat, there is an almost continuous flow of bullets, and the reaction is that the boat begins to move forwards. Applying Newton's third law, the change of momentum of the bullets is equal to the change of momentum of the boat. In a rocket, the bullets are replaced by high velocity gas molecules produced by burning the fuel. As the gas is ejected through the nozzle of the rocket, the rocket is forced to move forwards (Bibliothèque nationale, Paris).

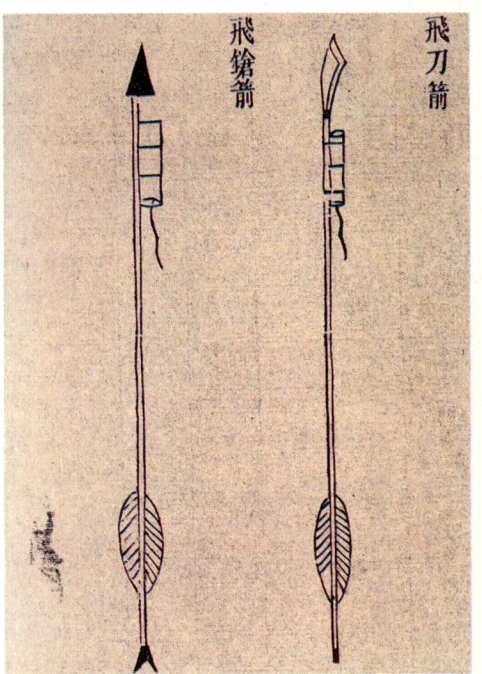

The pyrotechnic engines of the *Wubei zhi*. This military treatise, written at the beginning of the seventeenth century by Mao Yuanyi, ran to 80 volumes and 240 chapters. It was presented to the Emperor Shun-zhi in 1628, at the beginning of his reign. The *Wubei zhi* (Treatise on preparations for war) contained the formulae and methods for building a gunpowder cannon as well as numerous instructions and illustrations on how to make rockets and other pyrotechnic devices.

The uppermost drawing shows a launching device called 'arrows like flying leopards'. The characters below the leopard mean 'carrier of fire'. The arrows in the basket are nearly 0·7 metres long, and each has a 13 centimetres long tube of gunpowder attached near its point. They can all be fired at the same time, and have a range of 400 paces.

The basket only weighed a few kilograms and could be easily carried by a soldier. The second illustration, 'arrows shot from a fire basket', shows two soldiers in combat.

The 'arrow as a flying lance' and the 'arrow as a flying sabre' (third illustration) could also be fired from crossbows; the rocket was designed to increase the range. A small iron weight was attached to the bamboo shaft, just below the feathers, to increase the arrow's stability by moving the centre of gravity to a position below the rocket.

'The deposit of gold where one scatters fire' was a launch device mounted on a rudimentary carriage. It contained the arrows and rockets which 'flew out like a hundred tigers' (bibliothèque de l'Institut des hautes études chinoises, Collège de France, J.-L. Princelle).

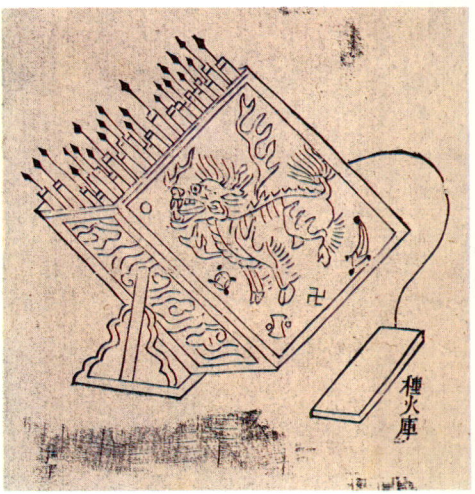

From dream to reality

Some weapons of *Kitāb al-Furūsīya wal-manāsib al-harbīya* (The book of horsemanship and the offices of war) from the end of the thirteenth century. The lefthand drawing shows the 'egg which moves and burns', which was rocket propelled. It may have been used against the troops of Saint Louis during the seventh crusade. In his *Histoire de Saint-Louis*, Joinville describes how the Arabs launched a projectile from one bank of the Nile to the other. This 'was as big as a wine cask, and the tail of fire which stretched out behind it seemed as big as a two bladed sword. It made such a noise as it came that it was like a thunderbolt from the Heavens; it seemed as if a dragon flew through the air.' This 'egg' was apparently full of gunpowder, stabilised by a tail, and propelled and guided by two rockets.

The drawing on the right shows a fire lance propelled by two rockets attached to two guiders, near the iron head (Bibliothèque nationale, Paris).

 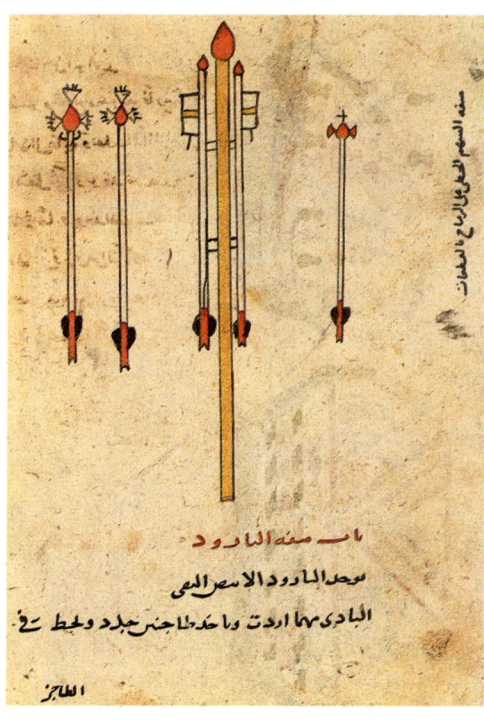

A miniature from *Bellifortis* (1395 to 1405). This page of Konrad Kyeser von Eichstädt's manuscript is illustrated with a picture of a pyro-technician standing next to a rudimentary launch ramp; at the edge of the page is a flying rocket. The text states that a guider is necessary. However, the artist did not understand rocket theory – he placed it on the end of a rope where it could not stabilise the rocket.

Konrad Kyeser von Eichstädt understood that the rocket was propelled by hot gases escaping from it. He recommended that the combustion should take place in a channel, rather than at one end of the gunpowder. This increased the combustion surface and the flow of gases and therefore also the thrust. This idea has been adopted in most modern rocket engines.

The use of such rockets was undoubtedly military, because he makes a reference to carrying incendiary devices, or explosives, separately from the fuel (Deutsches Museum, Munich).

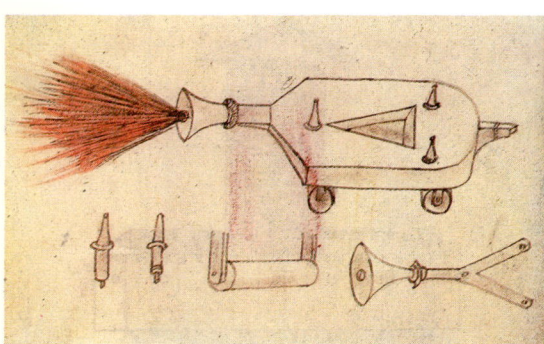

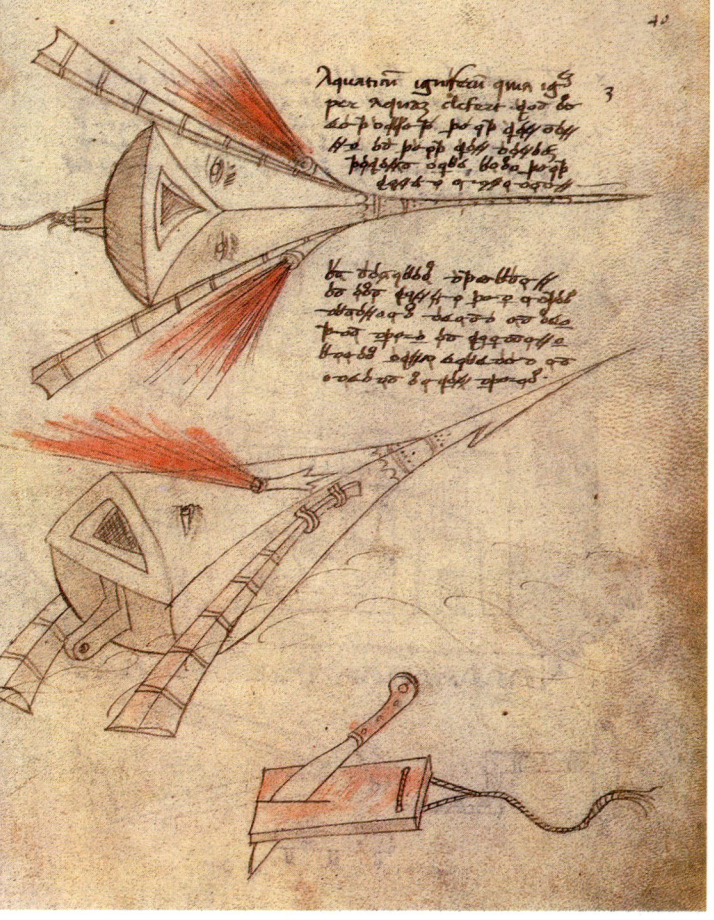

Giovanni da Fontana's design for a battering ram and a torpedo. In his *Bellicorum instrumentorum liber* (Book of instruments of war) (1420), the Venetian engineer Giovanni da Fontana described a number of pyrotechnic engines for air, sea and ground. These include the battering ram (above), driven by a single rocket, and the torpedo (right) which moved across the water, driven by two rockets. It was designed to ram boats; the cutlass was designed to act as a keel. We have no knowledge as to whether or not these machines ever existed (Bayerische Staatsbibliothek, Munich).

and other missionaries established in China had access to many documents. Another French scholar, Père Joseph Marie Amiot, describes in his *Mémoire concernant l'histoire, les sciences, les arts, etc. des Chinois* (Memoir on Chinese history, science and arts), Volume VIII, what was termed a *ny-fung-yo*: 'the "powder which goes against the wind" ... is probably a "flying" compound, and the smoke advances against the wind at the same time as the rocket.

By the thirteenth century, powder propelled fire arrows had become rather common. The Song dynasty, under continuous pressure from the North, relied on such technological developments as incendiary projectiles of many types, explosive grenades and, possibly, cannons. They also made good use of rocket fire arrows at the battle of Kaifeng (then called Bianjing) in 1232. A good description of the battle appears in Père Antoine Gaubil's *Histoire de Gentchiscan et de toute la dynastie de Mongous, ses successeurs, conquérants de la Chine* (History of Genghis Khan and the Mongol dynasty, conquerors of China, 1739).

Five years after the death of Genghis Khan in 1227, the town of Kaifeng, south of the Yellow River, was heavily besieged by Mongol hordes. The town's governor, Jiangjin planned his defensive strategy from the palace, Long-dedong. This strategy enabled the defenders to resist the onslaught of at least thirty thousand invaders for many months. Against Jiangjin's defences, the Mongols could do little, so they withdrew, regrouped and changed generals. The Chinese unleashed a new fire weapon that had a strong effect on the Mongols. Père Gaubil wrote, 'when it was lit, it made a noise like thunder and could be heard at a distance of about one hundred li (about five leagues). The place where it fell was burnt and the fire extended over two thousand feet.' Another priest, Père Joseph Anne-Marie Moriac de Maillac, in his *Histoire générale de la Chine* (General history of China, 1777 to 1784), Volume 9, wrote 'moreover the besiegers had fire arrows (*fei-ho-tsiang*) at their disposal.' When lit, they would take off rapidly, fly along a straight trajectory and, on landing, spread fire over a distance of ten paces.

The late sixteenth century *Wu Pei Chih* by Mao Yuan-i contains much historical information and many illustrations pertaining to these early rocket devices. One such was a launcher whose fire arrows 'rush out on a solid front like 100 tigers'. It weighed about 2 or 3 kilograms, and was small enough for a soldier to carry.

Already in the late thirteenth century, the Mongols had introduced rockets to the borders of their empire – the Arabs seem to have learned about them following the Mongol capture of Baghdad in 1258. At the same time in Western Europe, Marchus Graecus describes in his *Liber ignium ad comburendos hostes* (Book of fire to destroy the enemy) devices that sound like rockets. He talks of *tunica ad volandum* ('casings destined to fly') and *ignis volatilis in aere* ('flying fire').

In Giovanni da Fontana's 1420 sketchbook *Bellicorum instrumentorum liber* (Book of instruments of war), military rockets are suggested. An anonymous French work, *Livre de cannonerie et artifice de feu* (Book of cannons and rockets, 1561), tells how to make a metre long rocket. Important, later works include *De la pyrotechnie* (Pyrotechnics, 1630) by Hanzelet Lorrain, using the pseudonym, Jean Appier, and Nathaneal Nye's *The Art of Gunnery* (1649).

The Italians were the first Europeans to advance seriously the art of firework making. In a 1572 work on artillery, Vanochio gives credit to the Florentines and Siennese as the first to place fireworks on wooden pedestals. Great firework displays were held regularly in many parts of Italy which, until the end of the seventeenth century, reigned supreme in pyrotechnic displays. Meanwhile, under the influence of Louis XIV and Louis XV, France began to take

Rockets for fun and rockets for war. These engravings are taken from '*Recueil de plusiers machines militaires, et feux artificiels pour la guerre, et la récréation*' (A collection of several military machines and rockets for war and recreation) by Hanzelet Lorrain (Jean Appier) and François Thybourel (1620).

The upper drawing shows a practical use for rockets. A rocket drives the dragon along the rope between two buildings. The other rope has a double line rocket. The rockets are placed head to toe, so that, when one of them has burnt out, it ignites the other rocket and the device moves in the opposite direction.

The lower engraving shows a castle under attack from rockets launched from a wooden ramp (Bibliothèque nationale, Paris).

'Die Raketenschiesser'. This is one of 402 water colours by Johann l'Ancien, Count of Nassau, and is dated 1610. It shows two rocket launchers (*Raketenschiesser*). The rockets are fitted with stabilisers (Staatsbibliothek Preussischer Kulturbesitz, Berlin).

Two rockets of Conrad Haas. Conrad Haas was the chief of the arsenal of Sibiu (now part of Romania), from 1529 to 1569. He left a manuscript containing the first designs of a rocket with control surfaces (ailerons) and a rocket with several stages. A particular example is the rocket shown in the lefthand drawing. The envelope of the first stage burnt slowly, causing the rocket to become progressively lighter, and finally igniting the second stage (Smithsonian Institution).

The righthand drawing shows the cylindrical housing at the top of a rocket. It is a naïve drawing of an orbiting space station (Dr David Baker).

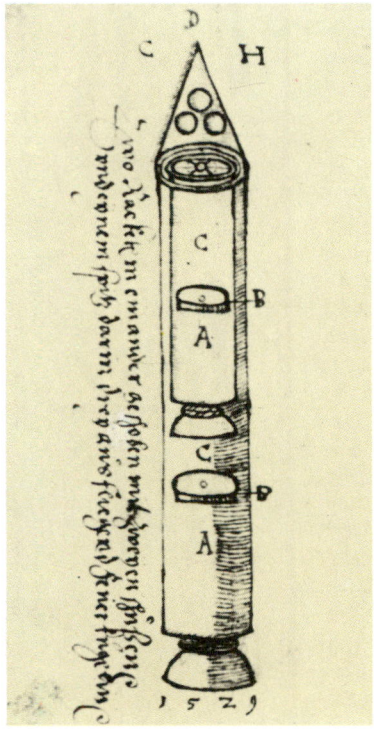

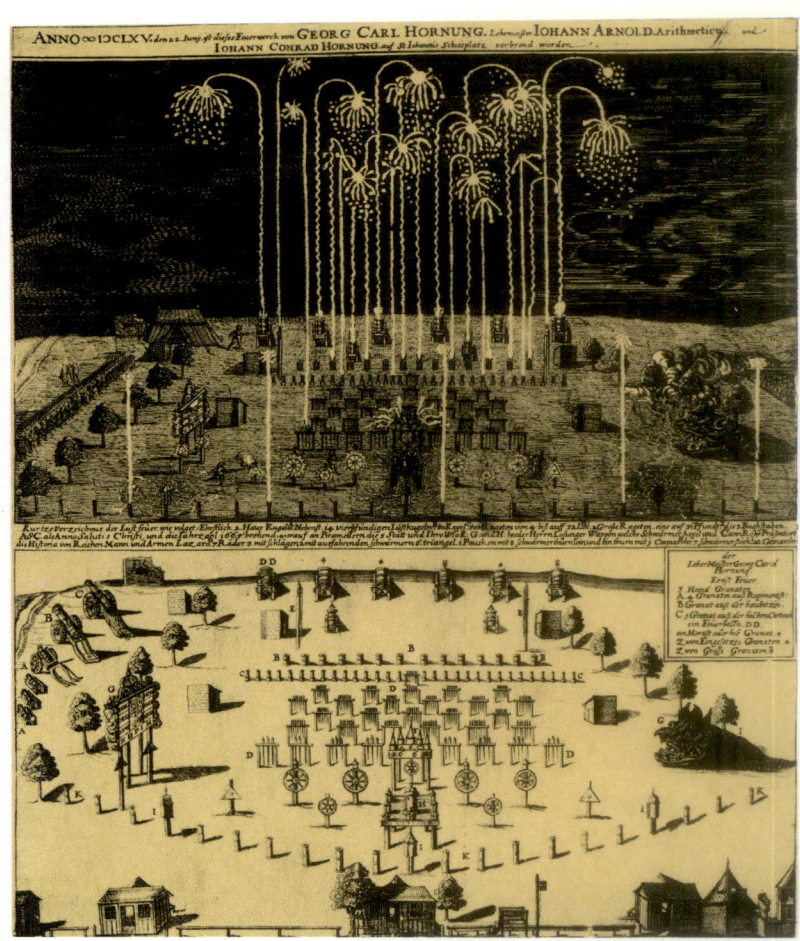

over the leadership, with such pyrotechnists as Morel Torré and the brothers Ruggieri making outstanding contributions. Firework displays with rockets were routinely used at major celebrations in France and throughout much of Europe.

It was not until the eighteenth century that Europe became seriously interested in the possibilities of using the rocket as a weapon of war. The incentive came not from within the European continent but from far away India where Hyder Ali of Mysore had built up a corps of rocketeers which, by 1788, numbered twelve hundred men. Subsequently, his son Tippoo Sultan increased the corps to five thousand, using rockets successfully against the British during the battles of Seringapatam in 1792 and 1799.

According to Captain Moritz Meyer, writing on pyrotechnics in a book published in 1836, it was these developments in India that led directly to intense British and European interest in the rocket as a weapon of war. He described the Indian rocket as being 'an iron envelope about 8 inches [200 millimetres] long and 1½ inches [40 millimetres] in diameter, with sharp points at the top', and three metre long bamboo guiding sticks. The rockets were launched by hand.

Roderick Mackenzie, a Lieutenant in the British Army, reports on operations in the region of Coimbatore in June 1791 in his *A Sketch of the War with Tippoo Sultan* (1799). He wrote that the Indian army was equipped with, among other things, 'four camels loaded with rockets'. The besieged British were bombarded with incendiary rockets, also receiving a 'smart cannonade'. But, 'as all the straw roofs and other combustible erections had been pulled down, little damage ensued'. He added that, later on, a discharge of 'cannon, musketry and rockets was kept up without intermission'.

Alexander Diron, in *A Narrative of the Campaign in India, which Terminated the War with Tippoo Sultan* (1793), described Indian rockets as 'consisting of an iron tube about a foot [300 millimetres] long, and an inch [25 millimetres] in diameter, fixed to a bamboo rod of ten or twelve feet [up to four metres] long. The tube, filled with combustible material, is lit and, directed by the hand, flies like an arrow, to the distance of upwards of a thousand yards [one kilometre]. Some of the rockets have a chamber, and burst like a shell; others, called the ground rockets, have a serpentine motion, and on striking the ground, rise again, and bound along till their force be spent. The rockets make a great noise, and exceedingly annoy the native cavalry in India, who move in great bodies; but are easily avoided, or seldom take the effect against our [British as opposed to Indian units attached to the British] troops, who are formed in lines of great extent, and no great depth'.

The pleasures of the enchanted isle. The festival of pleasures of the enchanted isle was the magical inauguration of Versailles. Organised by Molière, Lully and Carlo Vigarani, it lasted from 7 to 13 May 1664. The evening of 9 May culminated in a firework display which caused the fire at the palace of Alcine built on an island in the Grand Rondeau. Molière wrote that 'the height and number of flying rockets coming from the shore or the water, where they had been hidden, made a spectacle so great and magnificent that there could be no better way to end the enchantments' (Bibliothèque nationale, Paris).

Fireworks became widespread throughout Europe. This engraving shows a firework display held, in 1665, in a German town. The arrangement of the different pieces is clearly seen. Mortars and cannons were also fired as part of the celebrations (Bibliothèque nationale, Paris).

Parts of fireworks and launch devices. The engraving on the left was taken from *Traité des feux d'artifice pour le spectacle* (Fireworks for displays, 1747), by François Frézier. It shows a rocket guided by a weight suspended on a cord, and not by the usual rod (31), a three piece rocket (36 and 32), a rocket stabilised by ailerons (33), and its hand held launching device (34). It also depicts a two stage rocket (35), the rockets in the head being ignited after the first stage had burnt out, a rocket fitted with a star (37), a large rocket which jettisoned smaller rockets as it climbed (38), and a cutaway view of these rockets showing how they were ignited (39). In a three stage rocket (40), the first two stages were stabilised by rods and the third stage by a delta wing. A cutaway view is shown of a rocket called

'Fury', because 'its effects were sometimes considerable and sometimes moderate' (41).

The righthand plate was taken from *Essay sur les feux d'artifice pour le spectacle et pour la guerre* (Fireworks for displays and war, 1750) by Perrinet d'Orval. In the launching device (1), the guiding rods are placed in the grooves of the lower cross piece, and the rockets rest against the upper cross piece. The launch device (3) allows the rockets to be launched at any angle. A two stage rocket is also shown (2). The smaller drawings show what can be carried, a '*saucisson*' (sausage, 4) and '*pots-à-feu*' (hotpots, 5 and 6) (collection of F. I. Ordway III).

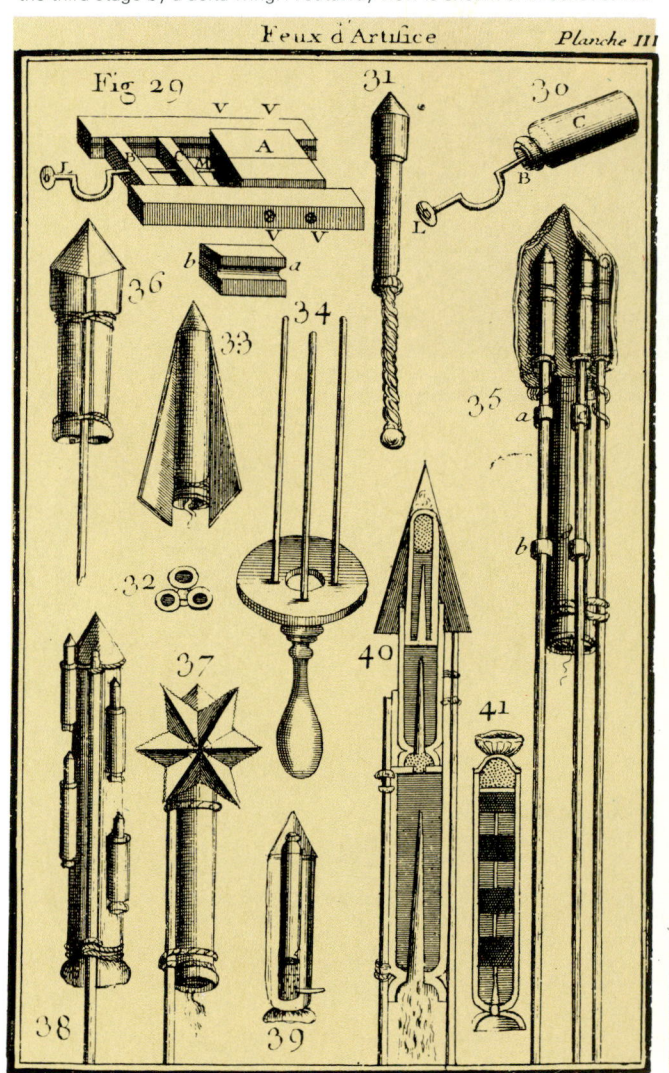

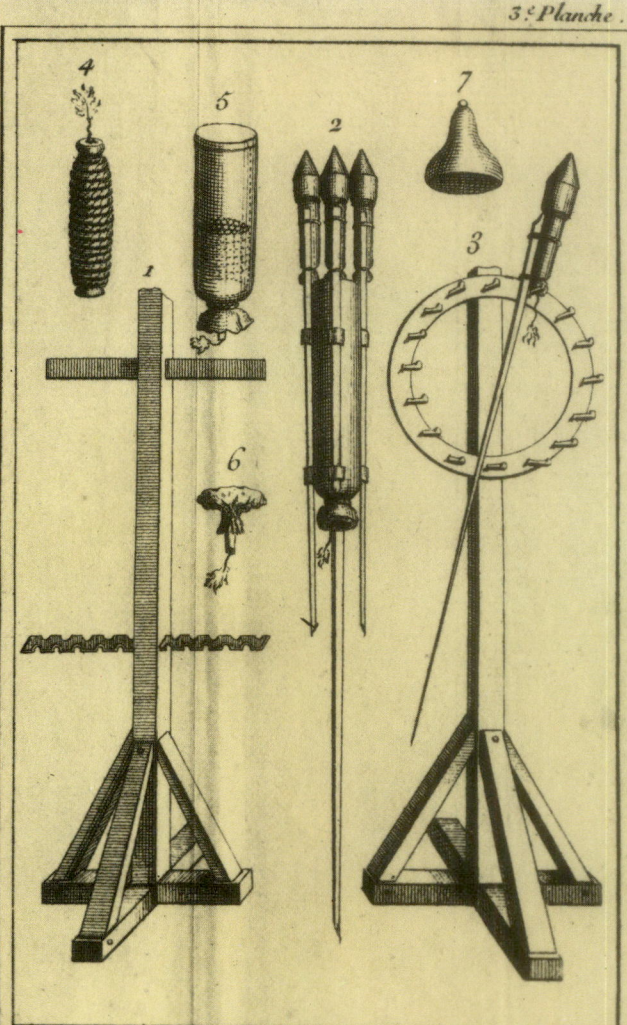

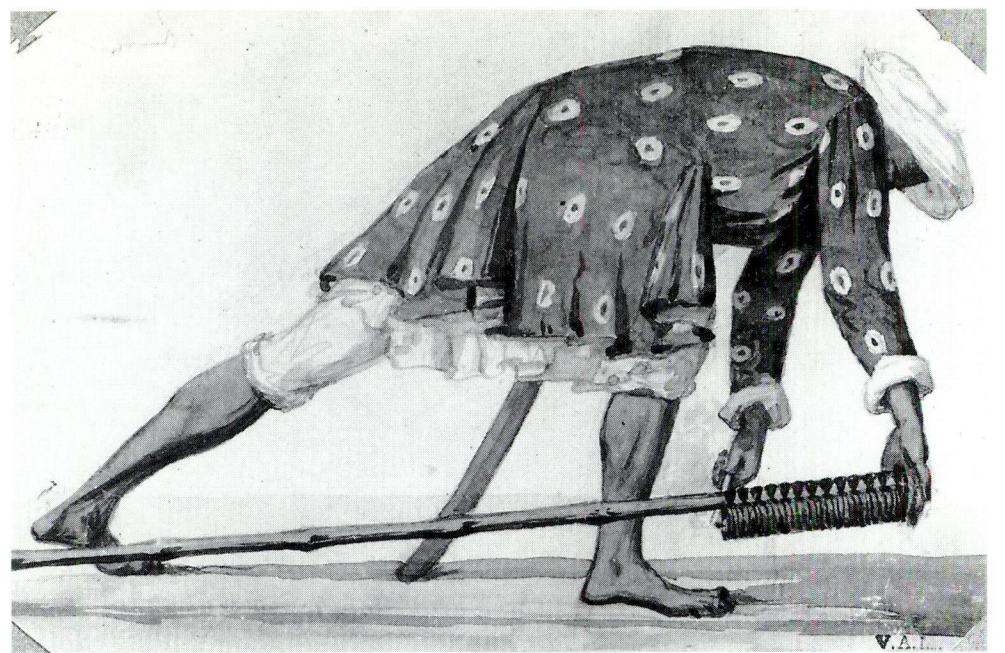

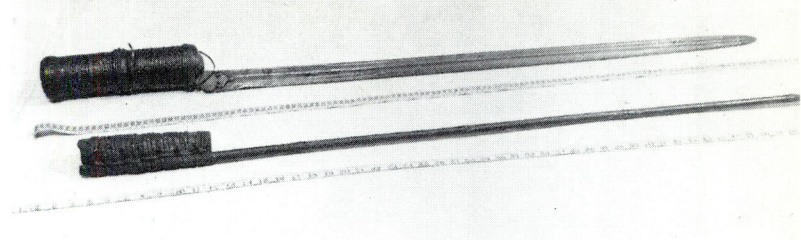

Indian rockets. The photograph above shows two Indian rockets dating from the end of the eighteenth century, on display at the Museum of Artillery, at Woolwich in London. The lower rocket is 200 millimetres long and 38 millimetres in diameter. The bamboo guider is 1·9 metres long and attached by leather strips. The upper rocket is 250 millimetres long and 60 millimetres in diameter; the guider is a sword blade, 1 metre long. During its flight, this vicious weapon could cut down soldiers both in the infantry and cavalry (rights reserved).

The drawing (left) is taken from an *Album of Sketches Including Classical and Renaissance* by Robert Home, in the Victoria and Albert Museum, London. It shows an Indian rocket launcher (collection of F. I. Ordway III).

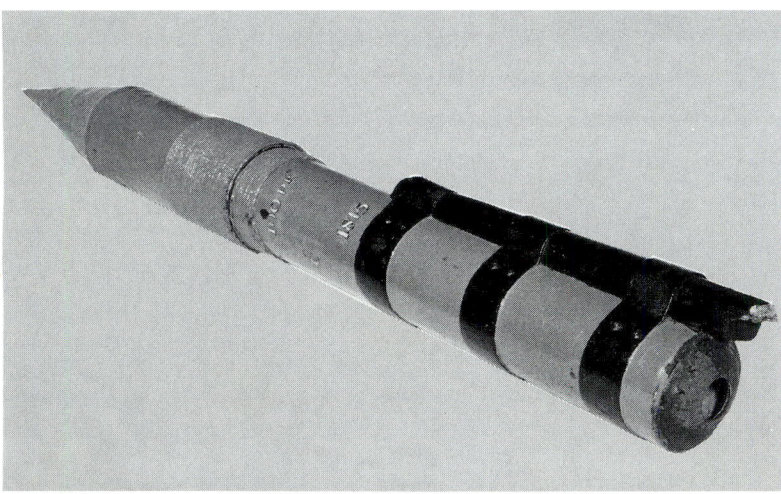

A Congreve rocket. The Congreve rocket system included fifteen types of rocket devices with incendiary charges, explosives or grapeshot. The smallest weighed just over a kilogram and the largest, an experimental rocket never used in combat, 140 kilograms. The 45 kilogram rocket shown has fixing rings for the guider, which is broken, attached along its side. After 1815, the guider was attached through the centre of the rocket and the gases escaped through five holes around it. This made the rocket both more stable and more accurate (collection of F. I. Ordway III).

Transporting and preparing to use Congreve rockets. This engraving, taken from *The Details of the Rocket System ...* (1814), by Congreve, shows (above) soldiers carrying a launching device and the projectiles — 10 or 15 kilogram rockets — and (below) erecting the launching device. This consisted of a 3 metre ramp, which rested on a two legged structure, to which the rocket was fixed with crampons.

A hundred soldiers could transport and use three hundred rockets and ten launch ramps. The maximum rate of firing was four launches per minute per ramp. A 15 kilogram rocket, with a range of 2·7 kilometres, could knock holes in walls (collection of F. I. Ordway III).

The bombardment of Copenhagen (1807). About 2000 Congreve rockets were fired at Boulogne by the British on 8 and 9 October 1806, without much effect. However, between 2 and 5 September 1807, Copenhagen was bombarded by the British navy, and three quarters of it was destroyed by the fire caused by the rockets.

Christoph Wilhelm Eckersberg painted this picture in the same year, showing the sky lit up by rockets. It was thought that between 20 000 and 40 000 rockets were launched; however, Frank H. Winter of the National Air and Space Museum in Washington believes a more realistic number to be 300 (Museum of Natural History, Frederiksberg Castle).

The attack on Fort Washington. Congreve rockets were frequently used by the British during the American fighting of 1812 to 1814.

This water colour by John Bevan shows the bombardment of Fort Washington, on the Potomac, on the evening of 27 August 1814. The British fleet consisted of seven ships, including the *Erebus*, a sloop, whose twenty cannons had been replaced by twenty rocket launch tubes for 15 kilogram rockets. This bombardment caused the explosion of the powder magazine, and the fort was taken on 28 August.

On the night of 13 to 14 September 1814, the *Erebus* also participated in the bombardment of Fort McHenry, one of the forts which defended Baltimore. The rockets caused little damage, but the sight of the American flag lit up by 'the rockets' red glare' inspired the young American lawyer, Francis Scott Key, to write a poem called *The Star Spangled Banner*. This he published anonymously on 20 September in the *Baltimore Patriot*, under the title of the *Defence of Fort M'Henry*. This poem was set to the music of an English drinking song and became so popular that, in 1931, the US Congress made it the national anthem (The Mariners' Museum, Newport Mews, Virginia).

British rocket launch boats at the beginning of the nineteenth century. This engraving from Congreve's work *The Details of the Rocket System ...* (1814) shows two launches fitted with rocket launchers. The forward mast acts as part of the two legged stand, and the angle of elevation of the ramp could be altered using hoists (Explorer Archives).

British rocket launchers in the Bengali army in 1817. In this picture, taken from *A Route across India, through Egypt, to England (1817–1818)*, published in 1819 by Lieutenant Colonel G. Fitz-Clarence, are seen the guider rods of rockets carried by camels (The British Library).

The battle of Waterloo. This 1817 British water colour shows Congreve rockets being used during the battle of Waterloo, on 18 June 1815. A company of rocket launchers, led by Captain Whinyates, succeeded in breaking through a unit of the Imperial Guard.

During the Napoleonic wars, the British used rockets on the Isle of Aix, in the estuary of the Escaut, against the Spanish fleet at Callao (1809), at Cadiz (1810), at the battle of Leipzig (1813) and at the siege of Danzig (1813) amongst others (Bibliothèque nationale, Paris).

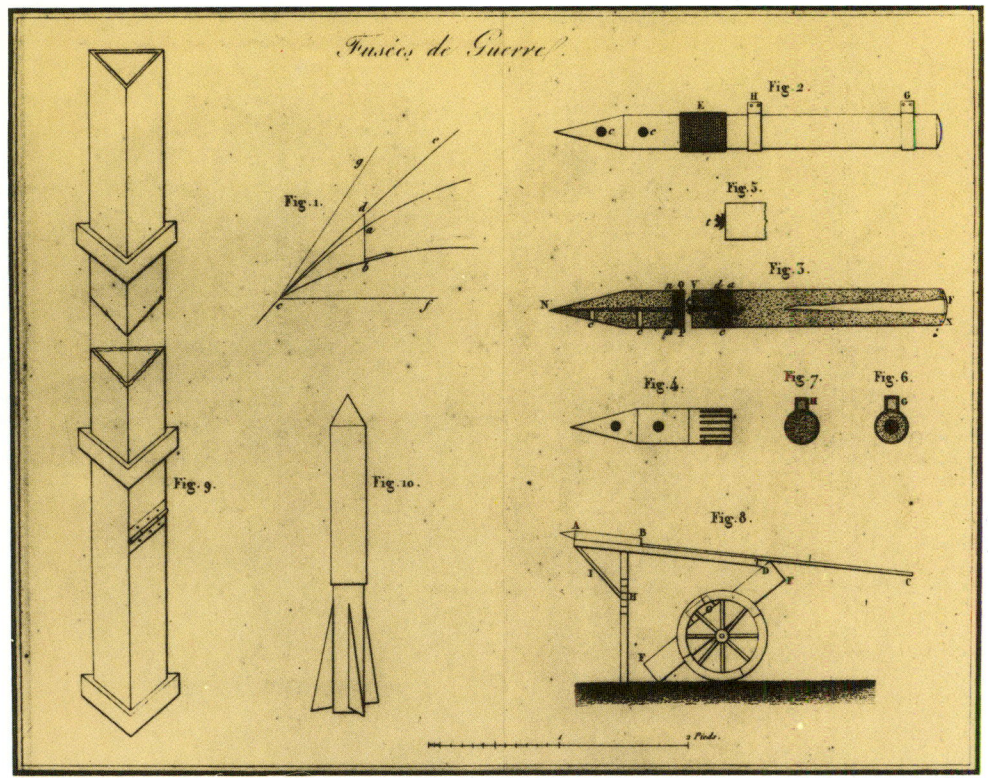

French war rockets. This engraving is taken from an article by Merignon de Mongéry, called *Traité des fusées de guerre ...* (A treatise on war rockets), published in 1825 in the *Journal des sciences militaires des armées de terre et de mer* (Journal of military science of the army and navy). The plate shows various types of rockets and a launch ramp mounted on a chariot (collection of F. I. Ordway III).

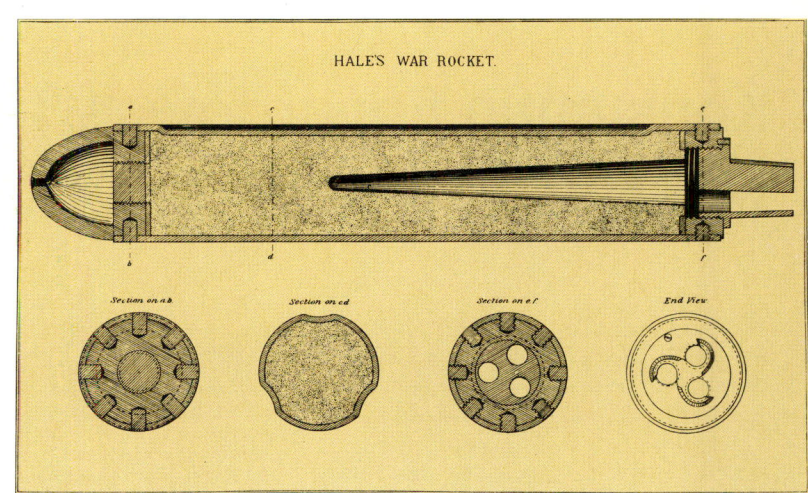

A Hale rocket. In 1844, an Englishman, William Hale, took out a patent on a rocket which was stabilised by spinning about its axis.

Initially, rotation was obtained by passing exhaust gases through holes in the side of the rocket casing; however, this technique reduced the thrust. Hale then placed a series of deflectors next to the gas jet. This arrangement can be seen on this 11 kilogram rocket, which had a range of about 5·3 kilometres when launched at an elevation of 37 degrees. Combustion lasted for only 5 to 10 seconds (Smithsonian Institution).

A nineteenth century American rocket launcher. Congreve and Hale rockets were used by the Americans during the war against Mexico (1846 to 1848) and during the American Civil War (1861 to 1865), on both sides, especially during the battles of Gaines Mill (1862) and Franklin (1862), in Virginia, during the siege of Charleston (1862) and at Cole's Island (1864) in South Carolina.

Brigadier General George D. Ramsay, a Unionist, wrote on 15 July 1864: 'The experience of rocket batteries which we have acquired during this war is not at all favourable to their use ... These rockets have only a limited range and accuracy, they often explode prematurely, and their behaviour in flight is sometimes very eccentric'. This rocket launcher is displayed at the West Point Military Academy (collection of F. I. Ordway III).

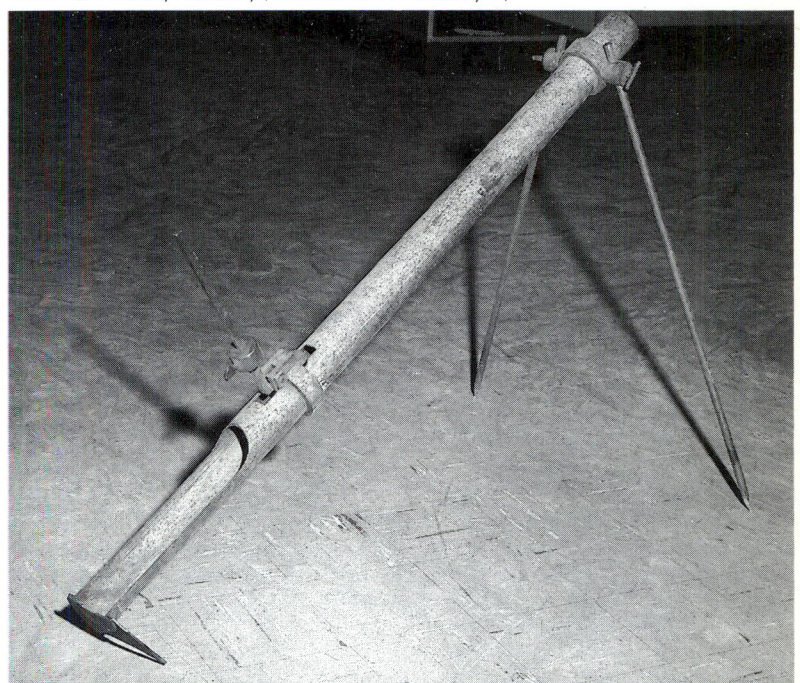

Word of the Indian rockets quickly reached Europe. The nineteenth century had hardly started when Colonel William Congreve (later General and Sir William Congreve) began to experiment with incendiary barrage rockets at the Royal Laboratory of Britain's Woolwich Arsenal. In discussing Indian operations, Congreve cites Colonel Gerrard, 'the late adjutant general of the Indian army, who served in all the campaigns of Lord Cornwallis, in the Mysore, and in Lord Lake's campaigns'. The 'largest Indian war rocket is not more than one fourth that of the [British] 32-pounder [15 kilogram] rocket, and its range not more than one half ...'. Yet they were very effective. Colonel Gerrard recalls that 'he once saw three men killed and four desperately wounded by the same rocket'. In the trenches in front of Seringapatam, the British 'suffered more from them than from the shells or any other weapon used by the enemy'.

Congreve carefully recorded his many activities for posterity, in the *Memoir on the Possibility, The Means, and the Importance, of the Destruction of the Boulogne Flotilla, in the Present Crisis* (1806) and in *A Concise Account on the Origin and Progress of the Rocket System* (1817).

The idea of using rockets against French military targets developed in Congreve's mind. He wrote 'in the year 1804 it first occurred to me that, as the projectile force of the rocket is exerted without any reaction upon the point from which it is discharged, it might be successfully applied, both afloat and ashore, as a military engine ... I knew that rockets were used for military purposes in India; but that their magnitude was inconsiderable, and their range not exceeding 1000 yards [one kilometre].' He then designed and built a rocket with a range of 2 kilometres, which he proposed be used in combat, as part of a 'plan for the annoyance of Boulogne'.

Congreve described his rocket clearly. Its 'carcass is the largest of the kind that has hitherto been constructed for use; it is completely cased in a stout, iron cylinder, terminating in a conical head; it is 3 feet 6 inches [around one metre] in length, 4 inches [100 millimetres] in diameter, and weighs, when complete, 32 pounds [15 kilograms] ... . The stick is 15 feet [almost five metres] long, and 1½ inches [40 millimetres] in diameter and is so constructed, that it may be firmly attached to the body of the rocket, by a simple and quick operation, at any required time'. He reported that thirteen thousand rockets had been manufactured up to August 1806.

Congreve rockets were used quite extensively during the nineteenth century. First Britain and later Austria, Russia, France, Italy, Sweden, Denmark and other nations introduced them into their inventories of weapons. Colonial powers used them in Asia, Africa and the Americas. Improvements to the Congreve rocket were made, particularly by William Hale, who introduced the idea of spin stabilisation, by the Austrian Vincenz Augustin, and also by the Russian Konstantin Ivanovich Konstantinov.

In France, the rocket did not assume the importance that it did in Britain, Austria and Russia. Although there were exceptions among individual military officers, most French artillery generals and ordnance planners had only a moderate interest in rockets. This was due in part to the fact that no great innovator appeared on the scene to 'sell' rocketry to the military, in part because of the swiftly changing military and political climate, and in part because of the nature of the wars conducted by French troops. Nevertheless, France accomplished a considerable amount of research and development on rockets, propellants, warheads and launchers between about 1810 and the early 1860s.

A non-military use of rockets. During the nineteenth century rockets were used by whalers to power harpoons. Their efficiency is hard to judge. This advertisement appeared in the *Whaleman's Shipping List and Merchants' Transcript* (collection of F. I. Ordway III).

Konstantin Edvardovich Tsiolkovsky (1857 to 1935)

Челокиссиносне не остангетя вочно на землю, но, въ топоть за сектомъ и пространствомъ, сначала робко прониквеъ за предълы атмосферы, а затъмъ завоюетъ сеть все около солнечное пространство

К. Уфинкоский

Facsimile of one of Tsiolkovsky's letters, dated 12 August 1911, to the engineer Boris Vorobiev. 'Mankind will not remain on the Earth forever, but in the pursuit of light and space, we will, timidly at first, overcome the limits of the atmosphere and then conquer all the area around the Sun' (APN).

Konstantin Edvardovich Tsiolkovsky was born on 17 September 1857, at Izhevskoye, a small village in the Spassky district, governed from Ryazan. He came from a poor family, his father being a forest warden. At the age of two, he contracted scarlet fever, which left him almost completely deaf. He was unable to attend the local school, so his mother, Maria Ivanovna, taught him to read when he was about seven or eight. He became a passionate reader, and from the age of fourteen decided to study only mathematics and physics. One of the books which influenced him most was by the French teacher, Ganaud, *Le Cours complet de physique avec bref exposé des phénomènes météorologiques* (A complete physics course including a small section on meteorological phenomena). He began his first experiments, and later wrote in his autobiography: 'I was passionate about air balloons. I even collected enough data to calculate the necessary volume of a "montgolfière" [hot air balloon], made out of metal sheets of a certain width, and capable of flying with men on board ... From that day I have been obsessed by the idea of a metal air balloon'. Faced with this inventive spirit, his father sent him to Moscow in 1873, to enrol at the renowned Technical College. Unfortunately, Tsiolkovsky was not sufficiently prepared for the entrance exams, and he failed them. However, he remained in Moscow, and continued to teach himself.

For three years, Tsiolkovsky frequented the public libraries, studying analytical geometry, spherical trigonometry, algebra, differential and integral calculus and mechanics. He became familiar with the work of the French astronomer and physicist, François Arago. He turned his attention to a variety of scientific and technical problems, spending the money that his father sent him on books and equipment for his experiments. In 1876, his father asked him to return home. He went to live at Vyatka and earned his living as a private tutor. He remained a voracious reader and became very interested in works on the theory of mechanics by Brachman, and by Weissbach. He also began to study Newton's laws of motion.

Tsiolkovsky spent his free time building all sorts of machines, and he even constructed a workshop at his home. In the autumn of 1879, he entered himself as an independent candidate for the teaching examinations, and obtained a teaching post at Borovsk, near Kaluga. It was here that he published his first scientific works: *The Theory of Gases*, in which he expounded the basic elements of the kinetic theory of gases, and *The Mechanics of an Animal Organism*, which was very well received by the eminent Russian physiologist, Ivan Sechenov. In 1884, Tsiolkovsky was elected a member of the Physical and Chemical Society at Saint Petersburg. He again turned his attention to the problems which had fascinated him since his youth – the metallic airship with a variable volume, the aeroplane, vehicles travelling on a cushion of air and rockets, which he considered to be the prerequisites of space conquest.

In *Empty Space* (1883), he put forward the hypothesis of the principle of propulsion by reaction, for movements in the cosmic vacuum. In *The Exploration of Cosmic Space by means of Reaction Devices*, published in 1903, and reprinted with additions in 1911, 1912, 1914 and 1926, he explained his theory of rockets and liquid fuel engines.

Tsiolkovsky's work on rockets helped him to solve several problems concerning the motion of bodies with variable mass, for example landing on a celestial body without an atmosphere. He calculated the speeds necessary to put a vehicle into orbit and for it to break free from the Earth's attractive force of gravity. He elaborated the theory of multistage rockets, and calculated the amount of fuel a rocket would require to overcome gravity. He was the first person to realise that artificial satellites and space stations orbiting around the Earth were actually possible. He also addressed himself to medical questions, of the effects of long periods in zero gravity. During his work on the theory of spaceflight, he designed control rudders for guiding the rocket, and he suggested using liquid fuel to cool the walls of the combustion chamber and the engine exhaust. He even proposed using liquid hydrogen and oxygen as fuels.

During his free time, Tsiolkovsky wrote several science fiction books. In *Beyond the Earth*, published in 1918, he put forward the necessity of international cooperation when exploring space. He described the construction of large cities in space. He produced more than six hundred publications, of which four hundred were written after the 1917 October Revolution. His subjects of study included aeronautics and astronautics, as well as astronomy, biology, psychology, philosophy and sociology.

Tsiolkovsky died on 19 September 1935, at Kaluga. In 1936, his house became a museum. The Russian Academy of Sciences created a medal in his honour, which is awarded to authors of outstanding works in the field of interplanetary travel.

Ivan S. Korochentsev

One of Tsiolkovsky's passions was metallic airships. In 1885, Tsiolkovsky began work on a metallic airship, which had a variable sized metallic envelope which kept the rising force constant whatever the atmospheric temperature or altitude. This idea originally came to him during his youth.

This photograph shows Tsiolkovsky in 1913, with several scale models of his airships. The envelopes of corrugated metal are made of tinplate or brass, and an internal system of pulleys distorts the shape and changes the volume. Tsiolkovsky also envisaged heating the hydrogen by hot gases circulating in pipes inside the envelope (Tass).

Tsiolkovsky's interplanetary spacecraft. This mock-up, on display at the National Air and Space Museum, Washington DC, was constructed by the Tsiolkovsky museum, at Kaluga, USSR. It is based on sketches and written descriptions by the Russian pioneer. It represents a spacecraft designed to explore the cosmos. The real version would be about 50 metres long and carry a team of three men.

The reservoir of liquid hydrogen and the reservoir of combustible liquid fuel surround a conical exhaust, like those shown in the 1903 and 1915 drawings. The fuel supply pumps and the inlet valves are situated above the reservoirs. A second compartment contains 'bath tubs'. Tsiolkovsky believed that human beings would be better able to withstand accelerations if they were immersed in a liquid with the same density as themselves. Next is a command room, which contains an airlock. Above that there is a glass greenhouse, where there would be plants to regenerate the oxygen by photosynthesis under the action of the Sun's radiation.

Tsiolkovsky's manuscript which is reproduced on the screen behind the spacecraft describes an aerodynamic wind tunnel (Smithsonian Institution).

Tsiolkovsky's rockets. Tsiolkovsky was the first person to advocate using liquids as rocket fuel. The upper drawing is taken from the 1903 edition of *The Exploration of Cosmic Space by means of Reaction Devices*. It is the oldest known drawing of a liquid fuel rocket. On the left are two reservoirs, of liquid hydrogen (upper) and liquid oxygen (lower). These react in A, and the hot gases which are produced are released into the conical tube and ejected at B. A jet rudder, used to steer the rocket is just visible on the extreme left. On the right in the cockpit is the word 'man'.

The middle drawing is from the cover of the same book, but from the 1911 edition. It shows the hot gases circulating in two perpendicular rings; the gyroscopic effect of this circulation was supposed to stabilise the rocket. A passenger is stretched out along the length of the cabin, to help him withstand the effects of acceleration.

The bottom drawing was made in 1915, and appeared in the 1935 book, *Dreams of Earth and Sky*. Here, c and d represent the inlet valves for the liquid hydrogen and oxygen (rights reserved).

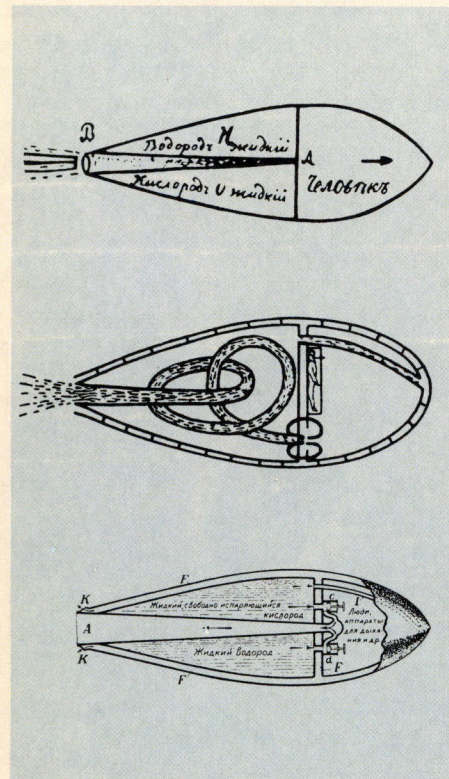

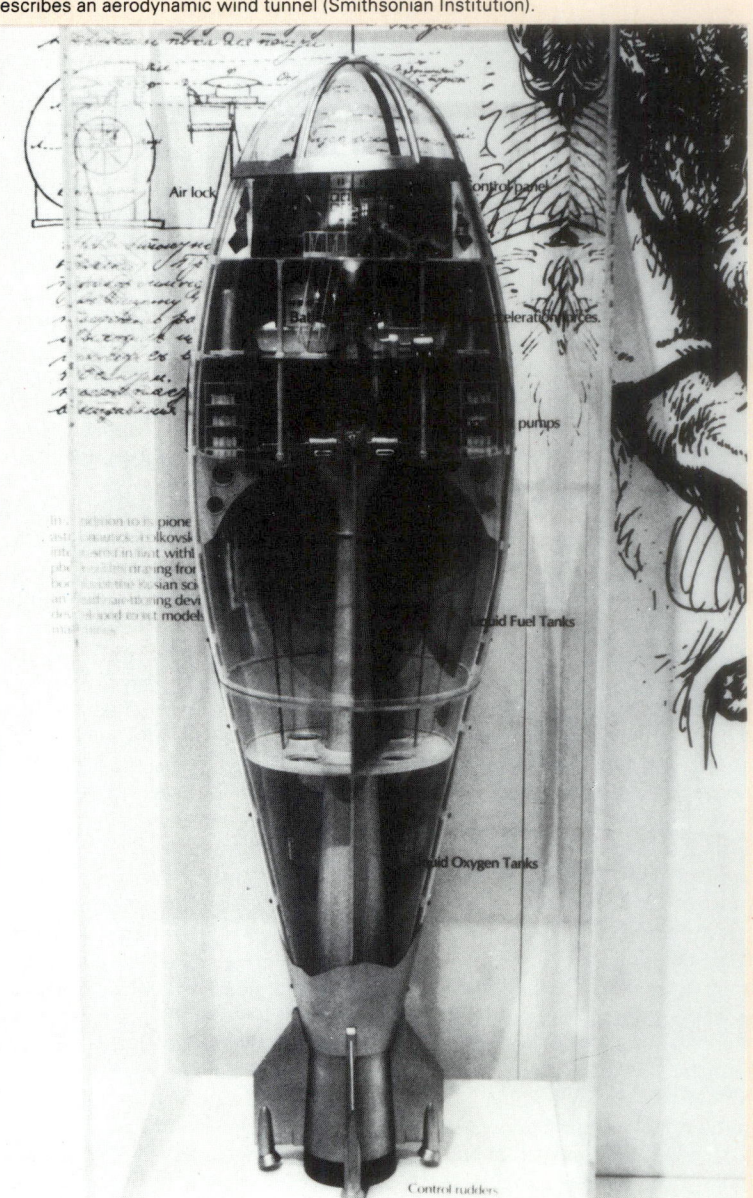

Rockets during the Crimean War. This picture shows an English boat with a rocket launcher, and a raft equipped with a cannon, during the bombardment of Taganrog, on the Azov Sea, on 29 May 1855.

The Crimean War was the last nineteenth century war where rockets played an important role. The English fired 382 rockets at Sebastopol and an even greater number against Eupatoria (collection of F. I. Ordway III).

Kibalchich, a Russian forerunner. Tsar Alexander II was killed by a bomb at Saint Petersburg, on 1 March 1881. The attack was carried out by the secret society 'Narodnaya Volya' (The People's Will), a member of which, Nikolai Kibalchich, constructed the bomb.

Kibalchich was arrested and condemned to death. Whilst in prison, shortly before his death, he drafted a scheme for a reaction engine. This is a reproduction of a sheet of his manuscript which explains the principle. 'Here is a schematic diagram of my machine. A gunpowder candle K is fixed inside a cylinder A, which has an opening at the base C (these candles are compacted tubes of gunpowder). The cylinder A is fixed to the centre of a platform P by means of the supports N and N₁, where the pilot is positioned ...

The gunpowder 'candles' were to be continuously introduced into the cylinder which would act as a combustion chamber. The hot gases escaping through the exhaust hole would lift the platform. By rotating the cylinder about its horizontal axis through the tops of the supports, the pilot would be able to alter its trajectory.

The manuscript was only discovered and published in 1918; therefore, Tsiolkovsky could not have been influenced by it. However, it represents the first project for a rocket powered flying machine ever planned by a Russian (APN).

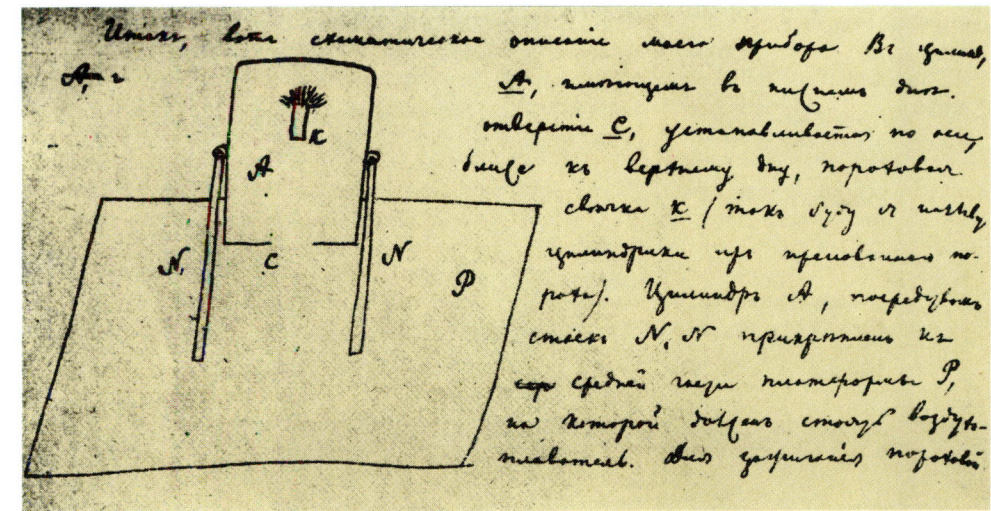

The rockets return to battle. This historic photograph shows ten 'Le Prieur' rockets mounted on a French Farman 40 biplane, during the First World War. The lower photograph shows an aeroplane, possibly a Newport, firing a cluster of these rockets at a German observation balloon (Musée de l'Air et de l'Espace, Le Bourget).

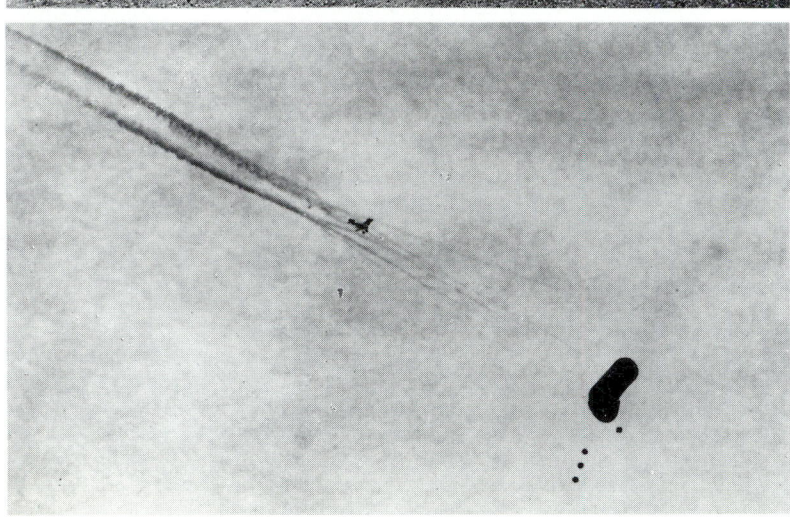

Unexploded Congreve rockets came to the attention of Jean Pierre Joseph d'Arcet, who conducted a thorough investigation at Vincennes and reported on the results in the Bulletin of the Société d'encouragement pour l'industrie nationale. In 1812, a commission was established to assess rockets in terms of French military needs. In 1824, an Ecole de Pyrotechnie was founded in Metz, but lack of funds made it impossible for progress to be made. Mérignon de Mongéry, a naval captain intensely interested in rocketry, complained in 1826 that only three major countries remained completely indifferent to the rocket – Spain, Turkey and France.

Around the time Mongéry was expressing his pessimism, the Englishman Robert Bedford proposed, in December 1826, that the French contract with him to build up military rocket production and deployment. Baron Charles Dupin had then just returned from Britain, where he had made a study of military and naval progress, and he helped to persuade his government to accept Bedford's overtures. Agreement came in May 1827, and Bedford moved to Metz where he remained until 1845. By 1834 four basic rockets had been developed under Bedford's supervision, with calibres of between 50 and 90 millimetres.

While rockets were never fully accepted by the French artillery service, they saw action in a number of engagements. They were used sporadically in Algeria during the 1850s, in the Crimean War (1853 to 1856), at Solferino (1859), Morocco (1859) and in China (1858 to 1865). After that, rockets were only used occasionally, for example against the Annamese along the East coast of Indo-China, and at Vera Cruz in Mexico.

After half a century of often exaggerated reputation, the war rocket had come to be all but abandoned. It could no longer compete with modern artillery – rifled barrels, breech loading and other techniques had become greatly improved. Yet, during the First World War (1914 to 1918), the rocket made a modest comeback. Rockets were used by both sides for signalling, for illuminating enemy positions, and for laying smoke screens. They also were useful in ground to air and air to air roles. Lieutenant Commander Yves Le Prieur developed versions that could be fired from the ground or, more commonly, from aircraft against German Zeppelins and observation balloons.

At the dawn of the twentieth century space travel remained a dream. However, a handful of men had begun to lay the foundations of the science of astronautics. For a thousand years rocketry had scarcely progressed but then, within a few decades, the technical obstacles were overcome. Tsiolkovsky, Goddard, Oberth and Esnault-Pelterie were all at work, and the era of the pioneers had begun.

Frederick I. Ordway III

Early flights of fancy

Space travel is not only the fruit of technological progress, but also the fulfilment of a long awaited dream. Man has always wanted to fly, to reach the sky, to touch the Moon. Even our earliest ancestors dreamt of being birds.

Long before it was the object of scientific and technical research, space inspired myths, legends and stories. For different reasons, throughout history, wise people have encouraged this type of literature, now called science fiction.

The Greeks recount the story of the ingenious Daedalus who worked in the service of King Minos. Daedalus built a labyrinth for the king from which no one could escape. One day, the king's daughter, Ariadne, fell in love with the handsome Theseus. Daedalus helped them to escape from the labyrinth, and flee. King Minos was furious with Daedalus, and imprisoned both him and his son, Icarus, in the labyrinth. Daedalus then constructed a pair of wings for himself and for his son. He instructed Icarus not to fly either too high or too low and they set out to escape. But the wings were attached to their backs with wax and, in a moment of pride, Icarus flew up to see how close he could get to the Sun. The wax melted and the wings fell away. Icarus fell to earth and was killed.

The simple myth powerfully illustrates the differences between science and science fiction.

Daedalus represents science, always seeking to extend the boundaries of knowledge without ever being unrealistic. Icarus is science fiction, imagining the fantastic, often with disastrous results. Whilst fiction has never caused actual death, there have unquestionably been examples of real life Icarus characters, who have put their faith in modern feathers, soared high for a brief instant and then crash landed.

The earliest example of literature concerning spaceflight is that of Lucian of Samosata (*c* 117 to 180). His story *Icaromenippus* owes a lot to the Daedalus story. Menippus, fed up with the sterile arguments of philosophers, obtains a pair of wings, one from an eagle and one from a vulture. He flies up 'above the clouds'. On reaching the Moon, he stops for a while to contemplate the follies of man, which distance has made very clear. Then he carries on with his flight and arrives at Olympus, where Zeus, tired of being petitioned by the absurd and contradictory prayers of men, decides to strike down all philosophers.

Lucian is an ironical writer, who here used a fantastic story as an allegory. He comes closer to science fiction in *True History*. In this book, he recounts how, driven by 'the desire for something new' and for knowledge, he sailed through the Pillars of Hercules (the Straits of Gibraltar), headed for the west and ... reached the Moon. He had perhaps never heard of the

discoveries of Aristarchus and Eratosthenes, some four centuries before, which had since been shrouded in disagreement. He believed that the Earth floated on the Ocean which was joined to the Sky at the horizon.

The essential thing, however, to Lucian was not the journey itself. It was the discovery of new lands where everything – the scenery, the inhabitants, the buildings and the clothes – was extraordinary. He extended the Hellenic tradition of stories of journeys through strange lands, such as India, Ethiopia and even as far as the pole, in which the geography is left to the imagination. He allowed his readers the pleasure of dreaming, whilst mocking those who claimed their fancies as realities. He warned them 'I write of things I have never seen', adding the rider 'if someone does not want to believe me, then, when he has been there, he will believe me'. This type of story is already recognisable science fiction, something springing from the imagination which is not necessarily untrue.

True History was translated into Latin in 1475, and almost certainly inspired Ariosto who, in *Orlando Furioso*, recounts how Astolphe, mounted in a chariot driven by Saint John the Evangelist reached the Moon. 'There was everything which interested us on Earth, except folly which we are never free of'. According to medical opinion of the time, good sense was a

The Icarus myth, turned into a picture story. At the top left of the picture, the Sun is riding across the sky in a chariot. At the top right, Icarus has just started to fall to Earth, and one of his wings has become detached. The damaged area in the centre originally portrayed Daedalus, though all that is left is the very tips of his wings. On the right, below the damaged area, are two boats, possibly carrying Ariadne and Theseus. In the lower lefthand corner is Greece, and two women are pointing at Icarus. Yet it is too late. Icarus has plummeted to the shore, and a man is running towards him. This Roman fresco of the first century AD was found in the house of Sacerdos Amandus, at Pompei (1·25 by 0·89 metres, courtesy éditions Payot, Lausanne).

Gulliver's travels. Swift's hero is abandoned in a canoe. He lands on an islet, where he sees the flying city of Laputa. On the horizon is the terrestrial capital of the floating kingdom. The Laputians notice Gulliver when he waves at them with his hat and handkerchief, and they come down to collect him. Laputa ascends, descends and moves using an enormous magnet. The floating city represents utopia – an aspect of literature about journeys in space not dealt with in this book (Bibliothèque nationale, Paris).

Victorin's flight. In *La Découverte australe* (The Southern Discovery, 1781), Restif de La Bretonne recounts the story of a young Dauphinois who, in his native Alps, invents a solo flying machine. He sets off to reach the top of an inaccessible mountain. He discovers a hidden kingdom, and then uses his flying contraption to explore the southern continent. Flying machines of this type are usually made by eccentric individuals, and the consequences are usually fatal (Viollet collection).

The tripod invasion. The Martians in *The War of the Worlds* were the first in a long list of extraterrestrial invaders. Their fighting machines appeared in the nightmares of several generations of readers. The illustration below, from the late 1920s, is faithful to the model drawn in most of the first editions of the book. It is proof, if that were needed, that the space invader is a very powerful image (illustration by Frank R. Paul, on the cover of *Amazing Stories*, August 1927, for *The War of the Worlds* by H. G. Wells (© 1927 Experimenter Publishing Company).

The scene from *The Other World*, where Cyrano de Bergerac flies for the first time (left). 'I attached to my body a number of phials containing dew and the Sun's heat, which lifted me so high that eventually I was flying above the highest clouds. But this attraction made me rise too fast ... and several of my phials broke. Eventually the upwards attraction decreased enough to overcome the force of gravity, and I drifted back towards the Earth. My experience was in no way imagined, because I repeated it several times after' (illustration by Bernard Buffet, for *Fantastic Journeys*, 1967, ADAGP).

The launch of the Columbiad (right). This is the crucial instant when the giant cannon, operated by the Gun Club, fired its unique shell. Jules Verne's scientific errors have been well documented; the first readers of *From the Earth to the Moon* did that. This criticism did not only apply to Jules Verne, but he was the first person to give the impression that interplanetary voyages were technically possible. He was worth denouncing because people took him seriously (Bibliothèque nationale, Paris).

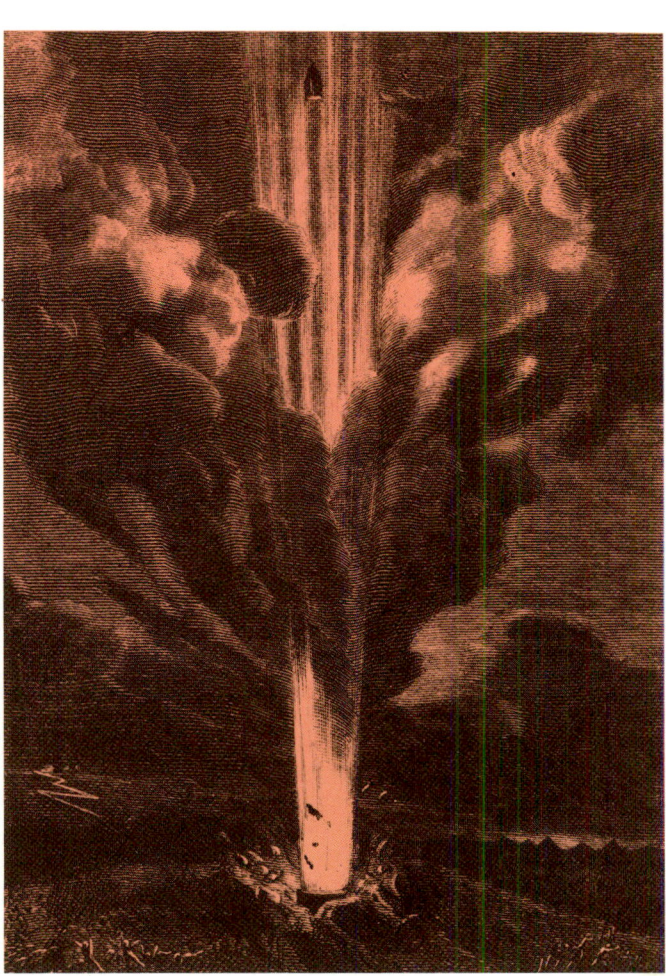

LE VOYAGE DANS LA LUNE.
(LE CLAIR DE TERRE) 10ᵉ TABLEAU

G. MÉLIÈS.

'Earthlight', one of Méliès' original drawings, illustrating the tenth tableau of Voyage to the Moon (1902). The shell is similar to the Gun Club's in the book. Jules Verne, who was still living, considered a lawsuit. Méliès did not attempt to be realistic: the stars in the sky represented a beautiful fantasy which had always inspired him. Educated in the school of conjuring and fairies, Méliès knew that his public loved to be filled with wonder. He was wise enough to realise that it is not the science which matters, but the entertainment value.

It should also be noted that, while the artist's drawings are simple, he produced some very strong images. The contrast between the blacks and the bright tints appears, to modern people, not comic but expressionistic. There is a technical reason for this. The film was coloured image by image by hand, and the black flat tints compensate for the shortcomings of the overlay. *Voyage to the Moon* was a colour film, which was technically ahead of its time (© Méliès by Spadem).

vapour, and Ariosto imagined that it evaporated to the Moon, where it was collected in phials. Astolphe brought back to Earth the phial containing Orlando's good sense, and thus delivered him of his madness. Orlando then took up the struggle against the Saracens.

Lucian's influence is even more noticeable in *The Man in the Moone: or a Discourse of a Voyage Thither by Domingo Gonsales, the Speedy Messenger* (1638), by Francis Godwin. In this story, the voyager travels to the Moon in a machine pulled by wild geese. Some of the situations in the book were inspired by the laws of gravity, such as the region between the Moon and the Earth, where there is weightlessness. The 'Moonpeople' have to be careful not to jump too high or else they will not come down again.

The best example of this type of book during the seventeenth century, was *L'Autre Monde* (The other world, 1657 to 1662) by Cyrano de Bergerac. It is remarkable for its foresight, because the flying machine is fitted with a battery of rockets, and for its fantasy, which owes nothing to Lucian. This book, like others, was written at a time when people were fascinated by science and philosophy. The ideas in the book are very bold, but at the same time the author is careful to disguise his beliefs (in Cyrano's case, his atheism), under the guise of a fairy story. This type of book with a message is still found today in Soviet science fiction.

Up to this date, the most visible astronomical objects (the Moon and, to a lesser extent, the Sun), monopolised such stories. The narrative was based on an unproved assumption that the stars were not inhabited. This changed with Bernard Fontenelle and his *A Plurality of Worlds* (1686). He reasoned, by analogy, that the processes which had led to life on Earth could be reproduced on other planets, and that the advances made in transport systems offered hopes that were not merely fanciful: 'The art of flying has just been born; it will improve until one day we will go to the Moon'.

In the nineteenth century, much progress was made in astronomy. The press kept the public informed, and also misinformed. On 21 August 1835, the *New York Sun* began publishing articles about the discoveries made by Sir John Herschel, using his giant telescope installed at the Cape of Good Hope. John Herschel observed vegetation, animals and winged men on the Moon. This hoax was later published under the title of *The Moon Hoax*.

Three weeks before this, Edgar Allan Poe published *The Unparalleled Adventure of One Hans Pfaall*. There he recounted the story of Hans' voyage to the Moon in an air balloon – but this time the hoax was established as such at the end of the story. These hoaxes were the first in a long line which ended with the celebrated radio broadcast of *The War of the Worlds* by Orson Welles in 1938.

The hoax is convincing because it does not leave any detail to chance. During the latter half of the nineteenth century, science fiction moved away from the atmosphere of fairy tales, and encompassed the wealth of scientific and technical notions which were being developed. Jules Verne appeared on the literary space scene with his books, *From the Earth to the Moon* (1865) and *Trip Around the Moon* (1870). His travellers were in a shell fired from a giant cannon, which became stuck in an orbit around the Moon by accident. Following the publication of these two books, people took great delight in drawing up lists of the many scientific errors.

By now, the curiosity of the general public was awakened and at the end of the century popular astronomy flourished. Camille Flammarion demonstrated his knowledge in a series of popular semi-fictional books, such as *Lumen* (1887). It became known that the surface of the Moon was deserted, and so science fiction authors came up with 'Moon people' who lived below the surface in caves, or on the dark side of the Moon, or who had once lived there before the disappearance of the Moon's atmosphere. The first hypothesis belonged to Fontenelle, and was picked up by H. G. Wells in *The First Men in the Moon* (1901). Here the voyage was made using an anti-gravity substance called cavorite, a famous ploy used by science fiction writers to overcome the difficulties of gravity.

This was the era when Giovanni Schiaparelli discovered the 'canals' on Mars (1877). These led Percival Lowell to describe the planet as a dry Earth which probably supported life, notably in his books, *Mars* (1895), *Mars and its Canals* (1906) and *Mars as the Abode of Life* (1908). Science fiction authors seized upon another theme. The 'Martians' were an older civilisation than ours and therefore more advanced. When they ran short of water, they had the means to come looking for it on Earth. This was the subject of H. G. Wells' book, *The War of the Worlds*, in 1898, which spawned many memorable stories of extraterrestrial invasions. Edgar Rice Burroughs wrote *Under the Moons of Mars* (1912), where the hero from Earth goes to live on the dying planet of Mars, and has adventures packed with princesses, monsters and sword fights. Mars replaced the Moon as the setting for imaginary epics.

Burroughs' books were, however, only read by a minority of the population. In the same era, the cinema was born, and began developing a universal appeal. In 1898, one of the pioneers, Georges Méliès, made a film about the moon in which an astronomer had a very powerful telescope. This made the Moon appear enormous – it opened its mouth and swallowed the observer. The same spirit of derision lay behind a version of Jules Verne's *Voyage to the Moon* (1902), where the story was retold in 'music hall' style.

As transport technology improved, the representations in film and fiction of spacecraft and rockets began to resemble something we would recognise today. Konstantin Tsiolkovsky (1857 to 1935) was well ahead of his time. His descriptions of spacecraft were very similar to how they actually are. Although a scientist, he did not balk at resorting to fiction when he thought it appropriate. In *On the Moon* (1887) he described a dream voyage to the Moon, making use of Kepler's discoveries. His greatest foresight was shown in 1903, when in *The Exploration of Cosmic Space by means of Reaction Devices* he described how the rocket was the ideal vehicle for space travel. In the story *Beyond the Earth* (1920), he described how this type of journey was made by an international team. Tsiolkovsky went on to describe the colonisation of the solar system. The age of science fiction had begun, even before the space age.

Jacques Goimard

The pioneers

All real progress in the field of knowledge, as in that of action, requires the perseverance of one or more intelligent men.

Henri Bergson
(*The two sources of morality and religion*, 1932)

The pioneers and science fiction

The main preoccupation of the young people who survived the First World War was living. In the following years, dreams became a refuge from the realities of recovering from the hardships that it had caused. Fuelled by an abundance of science fiction stories and the cinema, people dreamt of escaping far away, on interplanetary voyages. This general cultural phenomenon and the growing fame of such astronautical pioneers as Konstantin Tsiolkovsky, Hermann Oberth, Robert H. Goddard and Robert Esnault-Pelterie affected a whole generation in Europe and the USA. It was this generation that lived through the spectacular development of rockets at the end of the 1930s which opened the way for man to conquer space.

Only five years after the end of the First World War, Hermann Oberth wrote a fundamental book on interplanetary journeys, *Die Rakete zu den Planetenräumen* (The rocket into interplanetary space, 1923), and Aleksei Tolstoy wrote *Aelita*, one of the first Soviet science fiction stories. This was turned into a silent film by Yakov Protazanov the following year. In 1926, Willy Ley published his *Die Fahrt ins Weltall* (A voyage through the Universe). The French writer, J.-H. Rosny, invented the word astronautics on 26 December 1927, while Robert Esnault-Pelterie and his friend André-Louis Hirsch founded the REP-Hirsch prize to promote space travel. In 1929, the film maker, Fritz Lang, produced *Frau im Mond* (The woman in the Moon), which had Hermann Oberth as the scientific adviser. Between 1928 and 1932, Nikolai Rynin wrote his monumental encyclopedia *Interplanetary Communications,* while in 1932 Robert Esnault-Pelterie published a major work called simply *Astronautics*. The first American astronautics book, *The Conquest of Space* by David Lasser, appeared in 1931.

Even if the writings of the interwar period carry the clear imprint of science fiction, Tsiolkovsky, Oberth, Goddard and Esnault-Pelterie all included accurate predictions about rockets and their components. Moreover, with the exception of Tsiolkovsky, they verified their theories by experimentation.

However, the man who can truly be called the father of the modern rocket is Robert H. Goddard. From July 1914, he obtained patents on rockets consisting of several stages, the engine fuel supply systems, the exhausts and the combustion chambers. At Worcester, Massachusetts, he carried out rocket trials. Between 1915 and 1916, he tested powder rockets, the only ones of their type which existed at this period. In 1919, he published his most important work, *A Method of Reaching Extreme Altitudes*, in which he announced his ambition to leave the Earth and fly to the Moon. However, it was not until 1925 that Goddard really began work on the project closest to his heart – a liquid fuel rocket. On 16 March 1926, all his work came to fruition when he launched the first liquid fuel rocket in the world. It was based on a liquid oxygen and petrol (gasoline) engine, and flew to a height of

The father of modern rockets. Robert H. Goddard founded the subject of astronautics when he launched the first liquid fuel rocket on 16 March 1926.

From the beginning of the twentieth century to the 1940s, Goddard worked to develop rocket technology. Despite many problems, he developed a number of propulsion, guidance and piloting systems. Unfortunately, during most of his working life, Goddard pursued his studies alone.

Goddard had been fascinated by the conquest of space since his youth, and in 1912 he began mathematical studies on rockets. In 1915, he was the first person to demonstrate that rockets could move through a vacuum. He very quickly realised that liquid fuels were the only sort of fuel that was capable of taking a rocket beyond the Earth's gravitational field, and that solid (powder) fuels were not powerful enough. At the beginning of the 1920s, he decided to use a mixture of liquid oxygen and petrol (gasoline). A number of problems had to be resolved, the most difficult one being how to supply the fuel to the rocket motor. Goddard began by working on a two pump system, one for each type of fuel. In 1925, after two years of work on a piston pump fuel supply system, he began to develop a double pump system.

This photograph, taken in November 1925, shows Goddard standing next to a rocket fitted with the double pump in his workshop in Worcester, Massachusetts. The fuel reservoirs are at the base of the structure, and the rocket motor at the top. This model was too heavy to fly. In order to reduce the weight, Goddard therefore adopted a pressurised fuel supply system. Static trials began on 5 December 1925, and the rocket was successfully launched on 16 March 1926. (© Esther C. Goddard/NASA/collection F. I. Ordway III).

Two historical publications. In 1923, Hermann Oberth published his first work, *Die Rakete zu den Planetenräumen* (The rocket into interplanetary space). A small book of about 92 pages, it explained how to put satellites into Earth orbit. In 1929, his completed theories were published in a second book *Wege zur Raumschiffahrt* (Ways to spaceflight).

The *Verein für Raumschiffahrt* (The Society for Space Travel), created in 1927, carried out thorough studies on the theory of rockets and also experimental tests. Oberth edited the first world magazine devoted to astronautics, *Die Rakete* (The rocket). This was produced by Johannes Winkler, and extended the reputation of the group beyond Germany. Its first edition was dated 15 July 1927 and had, on the cover, a diagram of a combustion chamber, surrounded by cooling pipes (left, all rights reserved; right, Deutsches Museum, Munich).

The Verein für Raumschiffahrt. This group of very talented people, all of them fascinated by rockets, rapidly became notorious. One of the most prestigious members was Wernher von Braun, shown in this photograph of about 1932, aged nineteen or twenty. He is with Rudolf Nebel, on the Raketenflugplatz (the rocket launch site), at Berlin carrying models of the streamlined Repulsor rockets.

Von Braun was employed by the German land army in 1932 to carry out work on military missiles and he was behind nearly all the large projects in this field until 1944. His most famous creation was the V2 rocket, which he produced at Peenemünde. After the Second World War, this rocket led to the spectacular development of ballistic missiles and space launchers (Smithsonian Institution).

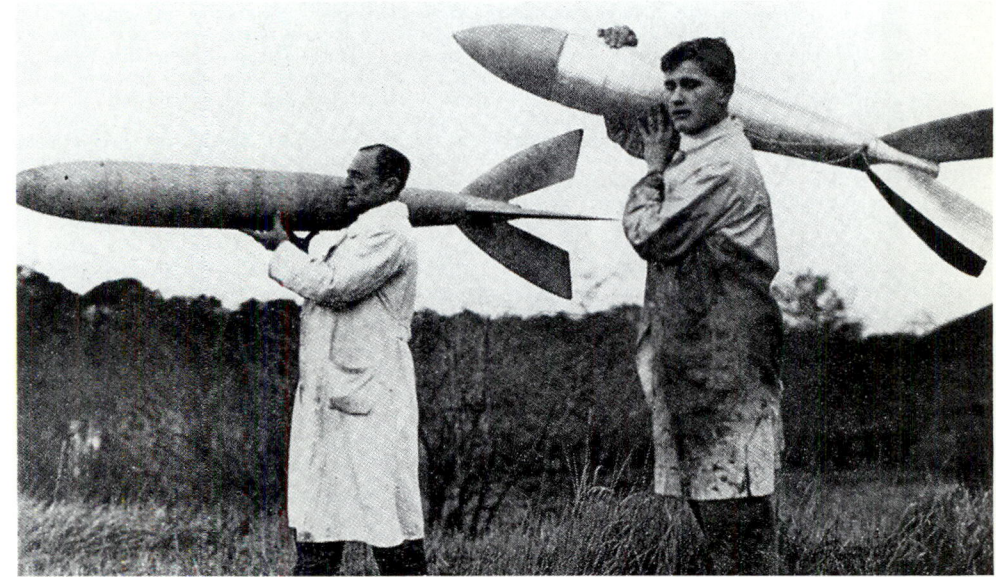

Robert Hutchings Goddard (1882 to 1945)

When he was but 17 years old, Robert Hutchings Goddard, born on 5 October 1882 at Worcester, Massachusetts, began to wonder what it would be like to travel to Mars. Ten years later, he realised that the only way to reach that – or any other – world in space would be to use a rocket. It was then that he resolved to dedicate himself to its development.

During an extraordinary and at times lonely career, Goddard combined theory and practice to an extent that eventually would earn him the title 'father of modern rocketry'. Like Russia's Konstantin Tsiolkovsky before him and France's Robert Esnault-Pelterie and Germany's Hermann Oberth after him, he would demonstrate to a sceptical public that the entire subject of astronautics was based upon the rocket propulsion system.

As a boy, Goddard showed an aptitude for science and engineering, and was particularly adept at physics and mathematics. At the same time, he also found time to read such science fiction classics as H. G. Wells' *The War of the Worlds* and Jules Verne's *From the Earth to the Moon*. Like many spaceflight enthusiasts both before and since, Goddard was inspired. In an autobiographical article written in 1927 but unpublished for more than three decades, he acknowledged his debt to such writers by recalling that they '... gripped my imagination tremendously. Wells' wonderful true psychology made the thing very vivid, and possible ways and means of accomplishing the physical marvels set forth kept me busy thinking'.

During his life, Goddard was little known by the public at large. Yet his efforts had a profound influence on the evolution of rocketry and spaceflight. Only after his death did his genius reveal itself to his country and the world. In 1902, while a student at Worcester's South High School, he submitted to *Popular Science Monthly* an article entitled 'The navigation of space'. It was not published. In a second article, he developed the scheme of multistage space vehicles. This article ended with the statement: 'we may safely infer that space navigation is an impossibility at the present time. Yet it is difficult to predict the achievements of science in this direction in the distant future'.

Cautious notes like this were to characterise Goddard's writings and statements all his life. He had no doubt that the reaction principle underlying rocket motion eventually would permit man to explore the solar system. 'I began to realize that there might be something after all to Newton's Laws,' he wrote. '[The Third Law] made me realise that if a way to navigate space were to be discovered or invented, it would be as the result of knowledge of physics and mathematics ...'. But he was reluctant, as Tsiolkovsky and later European spaceflight pioneers were not, to apply his full energies to the task of promoting spaceflight.

After graduating in 1908 from Worcester Polytechnic Institute, Goddard went on to Clark University in the same city. He received his doctorate in 1911 and subsequently became professor of physics. While there, he calculated that liquid hydrogen and liquid oxygen would be ideal rocket propellants. During a year at Princeton (1912 to 1913), he further convinced himself that he was following a path that would one day reach into space. Goddard kept detailed diaries of his activities, so that it is possible to follow closely the development of his work. A combination of experiments and theoretical investigations resulted in a succession of patents, most of which are basic to the operation of a modern rocket engine. For example, during July 1914, he was granted patents covering combustion chambers, nozzles, propellant feed systems and multistage rockets.

With the approach of World War I, Goddard became involved in flight testing simple powder rockets near Worcester, some of which attained altitudes of about 150 metres. These tests soon suggested more elaborate experiments, ones that would remain out of the question unless he could find suitable financial support. One potential source was the Smithsonian Institution in Washington, DC. In September 1916, Goddard approached that august body. His proposal was studied carefully, his mathematics checked and his approach assessed. To his great delight, the Smithsonian exhibited interest and enquired how much money he would need to proceed. He answered that ten thousand dollars should be adequate to develop a rocket capable of making scientific measurements high in the atmosphere. The Smithsonian thought the sum high and, on 5 January 1917, offered him a grant of five thousand dollars, enough to allow him to begin in earnest.

During World War I Goddard went to California to work on military devices, one of which was a forerunner of the World War II bazooka, a shoulder launched device. In September 1918, he showed two US Army Signal Corps officers several rockets that were ready for production. One of them could be fired by a soldier in the trenches; the largest could carry a 3·6 kilogram payload about 1·2 kilometres. Goddard's rockets were demonstrated at an Army proving ground in Aberdeen, Maryland, on 7 November 1918, just a few days before the Armistice.

The end of the war meant an end to military interest in rockets, with the result that Goddard returned to Clark University and his work on scientific applications. One of his first tasks was to write a report on work conducted to date, the state of the art of rocketry, and the rocket's future potential. Essentially this was the report that he had submitted to justify his request for the Smithsonian grant. He did this in 1919 and, in January 1920, it appeared (with a 1919 date) as *Smithsonian Miscellaneous Collections*, Volume 71, Number 2, Publication No. 2540.

Goddard introduced the report with the following observation. 'A search for methods of raising recording apparatus beyond the range for sounding balloons (about 20 miles [32 kilometres]) led the writer to develop a theory of rocket action, in general, taking into account air resistance and gravity. The problem was to determine the minimum initial mass of an ideal rocket necessary in order that, on continuous loss of mass, a final mass of one pound [0·45 kilograms] would remain at any desired altitude.' The report carried such section titles as 'Reduction of equation to the simplest forms', 'Efficiency of ordinary rocket', 'Calculations based on theory and experiment', and 'Calculation of minimum mass to raise one pound to various altitudes in the atmosphere'. It would have doubtless gone unnoticed by all but a tiny segment of the academic community were it not for the inclusion, at the end of the report, of the section: 'Calculation of minimum mass required to raise one pound to an "infinite" altitude'. This term attracted attention for it seemed to mean flight into the depths of space. He broached the subject obliquely, first noting that it would be interesting 'to speculate upon the possibility of proving that such extreme altitudes had been reached even if they actually were attained'. He realised that it would be 'a difficult matter', to establish 'even if a mass of flash powder were ignited at the peak of the trajectory', for 'it would be difficult to foretell, even approximately, the direction in which it would be most likely to appear'.

Then he came to his point. 'The only reliable procedure would be to send the smallest mass of flash powder possible to the dark surface of the moon when in conjunction [that is, the 'new moon], in such a way that it would be ignited on impact. The light would then be visible in a powerful telescope.' He went on to calculate the amount of flash powder needed to be 'just visible' and 'strikingly visible' to a 300 millimetre aperture tele-

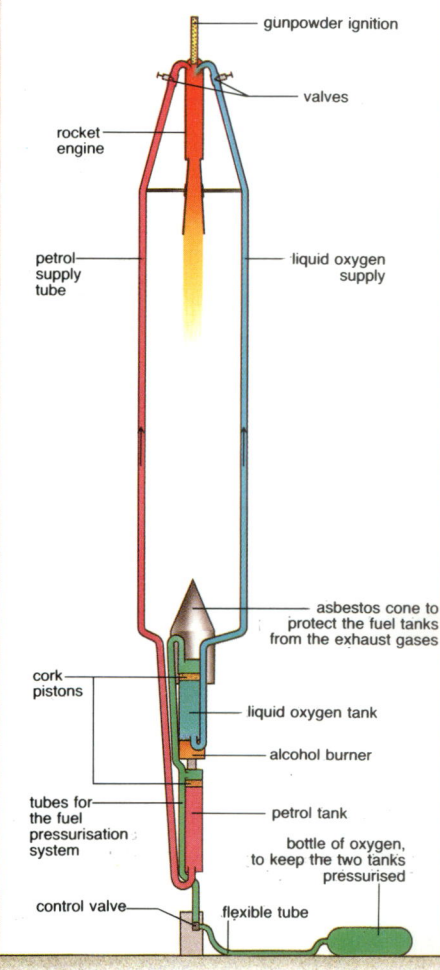

gunpowder ignition
valves
rocket engine
petrol supply tube
liquid oxygen supply
asbestos cone to protect the fuel tanks from the exhaust gases
cork pistons
liquid oxygen tank
alcohol burner
tubes for the fuel pressurisation system
petrol tank
bottle of oxygen, to keep the two tanks pressurised
control valve
flexible tube

Roswell: the early years. In *Liquid-Propellant Rocket Development* Goddard describes how, in September 1930, a modest workshop was built at Roswell, New Mexico, behind the ranch. The photograph on the left shows the first rocket to be launched at Roswell in the launch tower. This 3·3 metres long rocket, weighing 15 kilograms when empty, was launched on 30 December 1930. It reached a height of 600 metres and a speed of 800 kilometres per hour. The engine was situated at the base of the rocket, underneath the oxygen and petrol tanks and the pressurised gas container.

The photograph on the right was taken in November 1935, prior to a static test firing of a K series rocket. In the foreground is Albert W. Kisk, Goddard's brother in law. In the tower is Nils J. Ljungquist, the mechanic, and Charles Mansur, the welder, is on the ladder. Goddard, wearing a cap, is watching Mansur. A thrust of 2770 newtons was achieved on 12 February 1936 (left: © Esther C. Goddard/NASA; right: © Esther C. Goddard/collection of F. I. Ordway III).

scope and to work out the total initial mass of the launching rocket. Characteristically, he closed his report with words of caution. 'This plan of sending a mass of flash powder to the surface of the moon, although a matter of much general interest, is not of obvious scientific importance. There are, however, *developments of the general method under discussion, which involve a number of important features not herein mentioned*, which could lead to results of much scientific interest. These developments involve many experimental difficulties, to be sure; but they depend upon nothing that is really impossible.'

What happened next caught Goddard unprepared. Newspaper editors seized on these statements and sensationalised them, turning the quiet Massachusetts professor into the 'moon man'. Goddard, who had sought only the attention of fellow scientists, was profoundly irritated by the wave of publicity, some of which made him a butt for jokes. An editorial writer in the *New York Times* (12 January 1920) went so far as to suggest that he '... does not know the relation of action to reaction, and of the need to have something better than a vacuum against which to react ... . Of course he only seems to lack the knowledge ladled out daily in high schools'. Goddard finally decided that all he could do was wait until the newspapers lost interest, which they inevitably did. But he did answer the *New York Times* on 19 January 1920 by stating 'too much attention has been concentrated on the proposed flash powder experiment, and too little on the exploration of the atmosphere'.

Goddard's first grant from the Smithsonian was used up by the summer of 1920. Fortunately, his request for continued support brought the promise of another three thousand five hundred dollars. At about the same time, arrangements were made for him to work for the US Navy's Bureau of Ordnance's Indian Head Powder Factory in Maryland. He remained there from 1920 to 1923 working on rocket depth charges and rocket boosted, armour piercing projectiles.

Upon return to Worcester, he began a series of static tests of liquid propellant rockets. On 21 June 1924, he married Esther Christine Kisk of Worcester, his secretary at Clark University. Throughout their married life she attended his rocket tests and photographed the results. Goddard continued working with liquid fuels during 1924 and 1925. On 16 March 1926, in nearby Auburn on the farm of his Aunt Effie Ward, he successfully fired the world's first liquid propellant rocket. It was strange looking indeed, with tube-like fuel tanks placed one behind the other, the combustion chamber and exhaust nozzle above supported by 'spidery arms which also carried the fuel lines'.

Other tests followed, one of which (on 17 July 1929) was quite noisy and attracted considerable attention. Publicity was inevitable, and Goddard felt it necessary to issue a statement explaining that 'the test this afternoon was one of a long series of experiments with rockets using entirely new propellants. There was no attempt to reach the Moon or anything of such a spectacular nature... . The test was thoroughly satisfactory; nothing exploded in the air, and there was no damage except incident to landing'. The combustion chamber was located at the rear of the rocket which, observed Goddard, was 'the best location, inasmuch as no part of the rocket is in the high velocity stream of ejected gases, and none of the gases are directed at an angle with the rocket axis'.

Subsequently, Goddard was invited by the War Department to conduct his tests at an abandoned farm near the Camp Devens artillery range, 40 miles north of Worcester. The first static test there was conducted in early December 1929.

Meanwhile, the press continued to watch Goddard with some fascination. On 13 October 1929, the *New York Times* did a piece on him, and about the same time *Popular Science Monthly* editorialised 'while others have talked of shooting rockets to the Moon, Professor Goddard's success thus far proves him the most successful of the lot'.

Reports of Goddard's research reached the attention of Colonel Charles A. Lindbergh, then at the peak of his popularity. One Sunday afternoon in late November, he spent a couple of hours learning at first hand of Goddard's experiments and plans for the future. Subsequently, Lindbergh arranged for fifty thousand dollars to be granted to the rocket pioneer from the Daniel Guggenheim Fund for the Promotion of Aeronautics, to be paid through Clark University. A smaller grant from the Carnegie Institution was earmarked for test facilities, with additional funding coming from Clark University.

Realising that Massachusetts was too crowded for him to conduct the type of flights this level of funding now made possible, Goddard went West to search for a suitable location. He found one at the Mescalero Ranch near Roswell, New Mexico, where he, his wife, and four assistants set up in 1930. From then until 1941, except for a break from 1932 to 1934 when he returned to Worcester, Goddard undertook one of the most amazing private development programmes in the history of technology. Goddard described the opening years of his work in his second Smithsonian report, '*Liquid-Propellant Rocket Development*', *Smithsonian Miscellaneous Collections*, Volume 95, Number 3, Publication No. 3381, 16 March 1936. He subsequently described the testing conducted from December 1929 at Fort Devens to 10 October 1941 in New Mexico in the book *Rocket Development: Liquid-Fuel Rocket Research 1929–1941*.

In a letter to his colleague C. N. Hickman on 14 February 1937, Goddard emphasised how different working with liquid oxygen and petrol (gasoline) propellants was from the old 'multiple charge [solid propellant] days'. He wrote that his 'present rockets weigh between 90 and 100 lbs [40 and 45 kilograms], have about 50 lbs [20 kilograms] of propellant, and fire steadily for 20 to 30 seconds'. Whilst working in New Mexico, Goddard became the first person to develop and fire a liquid fuel rocket faster than the velocity of sound, the first to develop gyro steering for rockets, vanes in the exhaust for steering and pumps suitable for liquid propellants in flight.

Goddard's funds ran out in the spring of 1932 as the Great Depression deepened, so in June he returned to Clark University. Renewed Guggenheim support made it possible for him to return to New Mexico in the late summer of 1934. There, until the eve of America's entry into the Second World War, he continued his testing.

In June 1940, Goddard received a letter from C. N. Hickman in which he requested Goddard's permission 'to call the attention of our government to the possibilities of your rocket for defensive purposes'. Goddard promptly replied 'go ahead, and God bless you', explaining that on a 'recent trip East' he and Harry F. Guggenheim had met with a joint committee of Army and Navy officials on 28 May. There, Goddard had presented information on both solid and liquid fuel rockets. The Army was 'unsympathetic towards any long range projectile', while the Navy had several ideas for applications of liquid rockets. 'Frankly', Goddard wrote, 'I have been filled with disgust at the fact that no intensive fundamental work appears possible, and I suspect I have been hard to live with since my return. I am, however, endeavoring to make a few more attacks to see if it is not possible to carry on the work on the liquid fuel rockets, at least, on an intensive scale'.

After that, Goddard and Guggenheim met with Brigadier General George H. Brett, of the Army Air Corps Material Division. This session resulted in a proposal by Goddard on 27 July to investigate the problem of assisted takeoff for bombers and other airplanes. On 26 September, General Brett wrote that, while the Air Corps was 'deeply interested in the research work being carried out by your organisation under the auspices of the Guggenheim

Worcester (1928–29) 3 April 1926	Flight of the second liquid fuel rocket. Duration, 4.2 seconds. Landed 15 metres from the launch ramp.
26 December 1928	Flight of third liquid fuel rocket. Duration, 3.2 seconds. Landed 62 metres from the launch tower. Maximum speed greater than 95 kilometres per second.
17 July 1929	Fourth liquid fuel rocket flight. Landed 52 metres from the launch tower.
Camp Devens (December 1929 to June 1930)	Sixteen static tests, with a view to improving liquid fuel rockets. No launches.
Roswell (1930–32) 30 December 1930	First launch at Roswell.
27 October 1931	Flight of rocket fitted with new valve for the petrol. Duration, 8.6 seconds. Altitude greater than 400 metres. Landed 280 metres from the launch tower.
Worcester (1932–34) 1932–33	Laboratory work on materials, soldering light metals, gyroscopes, pumps (for pistons and centrifuges) and combustion chambers.
Roswell (1934–41) September 1934 to October 1935	Testing the A series rockets. Fuels supplied under pressure from the reservoirs. Stabilised by gyroscope controlled jet deflectors.
8 March 1935	An A series rocket reaches a velocity greater than 1130 kilometres per hour (perhaps supersonic).
28 March 1935	An A series rocket reaches an altitude greater than 1460 metres and lands nearly 4 kilometres from the launch tower. The rocket, 4.51 metres long and 35.6 kilograms when empty, had an improved gyroscopic stabilisation system which worked perfectly during the 20 second flight with an average speed of 880 kilometres per hour.
November 1935 to February 1936	Static tests on the K series, with a view to increasing the thrust.
May 1936 to August 1938	Flight test on the L series, using nitrogen to pressurise the fuel tanks. The combustion chambers were 250 millimetres in diameter.
26 March 1937	The L 13 rocket, with adjustable fins, reached an altitude of between 2.4 and 2.7 kilometres.
20 April 1938	A rocket carrying a barograph reached an altitude of 1.26 kilometres. Duration of propulsion phase, 25.3 seconds.
October 1938 to February 1939	Development of fuel supply pumps. Goddard quickly produced a small chamber which could generate oxygen gas for driving the turbines.
March 1939 to August 1939	Static test on gas generators.
November 1939 to October 1941	Static and flight tests on rockets fitted with turbopumps.
9 August 1940	The first flight of a rocket fitted with turbopumps reached a maximum height of 90 metres.
8 May 1941	Second flight of a rocket fitted with turbopumps reached an altitude of 75 metres.

Landmarks in the work and launches carried out by Robert H. Goddard after the first flight of a liquid fuel rocket

Summary of the tests performed at Roswell

	Static tests	Flight tests
First series (1930–32)	21	8 (5)*
Series A (September 1934 to October 1935)	1	14 (7)*
Series K (November 1935 to February 1936)	10	0
Series L (May 1936 to August 1938)	13	17 (17)*
Pump tests (October 1938 to February 1939)	more than 24	0
Gas generator tests (March to August 1939)	19	0
Turbopump tests (November 1939 to October 1941)	15	9 (2)*

(*) The number in parentheses is the number of rockets which at least cleared the top of the launch tower.

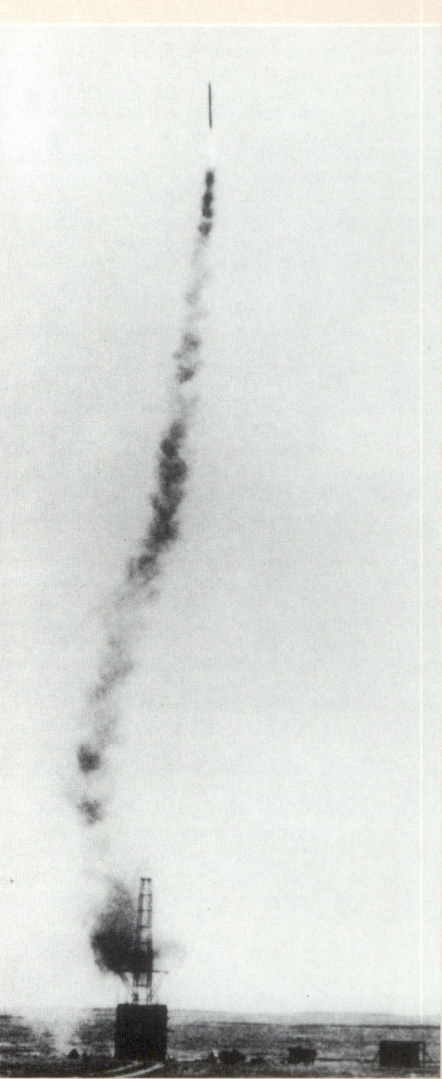

Foundation, it does not, at this time, feel justified in obligating further funds for basic jet propulsion research and experimentation'. He added that when Goddard's experiments had 'reached a point which indicates the probability of successful reduction to practice of a device, capable of being incorporated in or attached to an airplane to assist in accelerating takeoff and upon which an evaluation can be made in order to determine the feasibility and practicability of military application, the Air Corps will then entertain further proposals involving the actual construction, installation, and test of such device'.

Goddard went on to produce such a device on his own – only then did the Air Corps become interested. Later he commented that 'after trying to do a good piece of work over a period of years and actually getting flights before anyone else, it is discouraging to have the implication made that nothing of value had been accomplished.'

The following year the government's mood changed. Beginning in September 1941, Goddard began to work under contracts with the Navy's Bureau of Aeronautics and with the previously uninterested Army Air Corps. In July 1942, personnel and equipment were moved to the Naval Engineering Experiment Station at Annapolis, Maryland, where work continued until July 1945. During this period, a liquid fuel, jet assisted take-off unit for flying boats led to the development of variable thrust rocket motors.

After his death in Baltimore on 10 August 1945, Goddard was honoured by the United States Congress and received the first Louis W. Hill Space Transportation Award of the Institute of Aeronautical Sciences. One of the National Aeronautics and Space Administration's major facilities, the Goddard Space Flight Center, was named after him on 1 May 1959. In 1960, the Smithsonian Institution bestowed on him the coveted Langley Medal. Also in 1960, the United States government awarded the Guggenheim Foundation and Mrs Goddard one million dollars in settlement for government use of more than two hundred of the pioneer's patents.

On 16 March 1970, the Committee on Aeronautical and Space Sciences of the United States Senate took testimony to provide recognition of the Goddard Rocket and Space Museum at Roswell, New Mexico, near where Goddard had worked for so many years. Werner von Braun stated that 'in the history of rocketry, Dr Robert H. Goddard has no peers. He was first. He was ahead of everyone in the design, construction, and launching of liquid fuel rockets which eventually paved the way into space. When Dr Goddard did his greatest work, all of us who were to come later in the rocket and space business were still in kneepants'.

Frederick I. Ordway III

The launch of L 17. Launched on 26 August 1937, this rocket was 5·62 metres long, 230 millimetres in diameter and had a mass of 73 kilograms when empty. Its launch was assisted by a catapult, and the rocket reached an altitude of more than 600 metres.

The shape of the smoke trail bears witness to the efficiency of the gyroscope stabilisation system which acted at the base of the rocket (© Esther C. Goddard/collection of F. I. Ordway III).

The L 13 rocket. On 26 March 1937, the L 13 rocket reached an altitude of between 2·4 and 2·7 kilometres in 22·3 seconds. The rocket had an empty mass of 45 kilograms, and had gyroscope controlled, movable fins. This system worked perfectly, correcting the trajectory throughout the propulsion phase (collection of F. I. Ordway III).

A rocket with turbopumps. This photograph was taken in 1940, when Goddard and his assistants were working on a rocket with turbopumps. From left to right are Goddard, Nils J. Ljungquist, Albert W. Kisk, and Charles Mansur.

On the left of the photograph, the engine is visible and the petrol and oxygen tanks are on the right. The turbopumps are in the centre of the rocket. In this rocket, the combustion chamber was cooled by the petrol, which flowed around it in copper tubes before being injected into the rocket engine (B. Anthony Stewart, © National Geographic Society/NASA/collection of F. I. Ordway III).

12·5 metres at a speed of 27 metres per second; the flight lasted 2·5 seconds and marked a historic step in the history of spaceflight.

During the years that followed, Goddard improved his rockets, and incorporated new components including valves, guidance systems, gyroscopic stabilisation, a recovery system using a parachute, and nitrogen to pressurise the reservoirs. By 1931, he was carrying out an average of one static trial or one rocket launch every nineteen days. In 1941, one of his motors produced a thrust of just over 4 kilonewtons for 43·5 seconds. This was greater than any thrust he had ever recorded.

At first Goddard worked alone, with little interest being shown by the American government. However, as soon as the Americans entered the Second World War, their attitude changed. Goddard was given contracts by the US Navy and Army to study liquid fuel rocket motors to assist the take-off of seaplanes, and to produce different sized rockets. The American government had finally expressed an interest in space technology.

Born in Romania of German speaking parents, Hermann Oberth played a comparable role in rocket development in Germany. He was, however, more of a theoretician than an experimenter. In 1917, he approached the German War Minister about studying a long range, liquid fuel ballistic missile. This was probably the first time that a government had been approached with a project of this type. Because the German military were convinced that the maximum range would be 7 kilometres, they declined the offer. Oberth's plan was rejected again in 1922. He then decided to devote his studies to rockets capable of making interplanetary journeys. In the following year, he published his book *Die Rakete zu den Planetenraümen*. He described rockets which had one reservoir for the fuel and one for the oxidant. He also discussed a two stage rocket, the first stage using liquid oxygen and alcohol and the second liquid hydrogen and liquid oxygen. He also suggested the use of gyroscopes in the inertial guidance system, and accelerometers.

Oberth's suggestions for the propulsion, guidance and definition of rockets were so accurate that they formed the basis of the German V2 rocket some twenty years later. The V2 rocket was the first operational ballistic missile in history.

Oberth performed only a little experimental work, but it was all original. In 1928, he was the scientific adviser on Fritz Lang's film, *Frau im Mond*. He had the idea of launching a rocket when the film was released, but he was not given enough time to prepare for that and the project fell through. However, he was able to produce a small rocket motor, the Kegeldüse. The tests of this took place on 23 July 1930. It flew upwards for 96·4 seconds, delivering a maximum thrust of 70 newtons.

Astronautical societies

During the 1920s, especially during the latter half of the decade, a great passion for astronautics developed. Many groups and societies devoted to various aspects of space travel and rockets were set up. The basic aim soon became apparent, to build rockets.

Rocket fever was strongest in Germany. The most famous society was the *Verein für Raumschiffahrt* (The Society for Space Travel), or VfR, created on 5 July 1927 at Breslau. Amongst the founder members were Johannes Winkler, Max Valier and Willy Ley. Although the VfR did not have large funds, it soon became very active, producing and distributing a magazine called *Die Rakete* (The rocket).

In 1929, when Oberth became president, the society had 870 members and many other Europeans were associated with it through their work. In 1930, the VfR moved its headquarters from Breslau to Berlin. Its members by then included men who went on to become famous,

The first European liquid fuel rockets. In August 1930, the Mirak I rocket was the first rocket to be built and flight tested at the Raketenflugplatz (rocket launch site), by the team from the Verein für Raumschiffahrt. It was nearly 1·3 metres long (of which the tail was about 1 metre), and used liquid oxygen and petrol (gasoline). Its motor was constructed out of copper and was based on the Kegeldüse motor made by Hermann Oberth during the same period. Mirak I's rocket tests were not very successful. The reason for this was the inadequate cooling system around the combustion chamber, which also caused test failures in the Mirak II series in 1931. The drawing on the right represents the Mirak I rocket.

The photograph shows Johannes Winkler in about 1931 with his HW I, the first successful European liquid fuel rocket. The motor was situated at the tip; two of the three supporting pipes contained liquid oxygen, and the other contained the fuel, which was liquid methane (Smithsonian Institution).

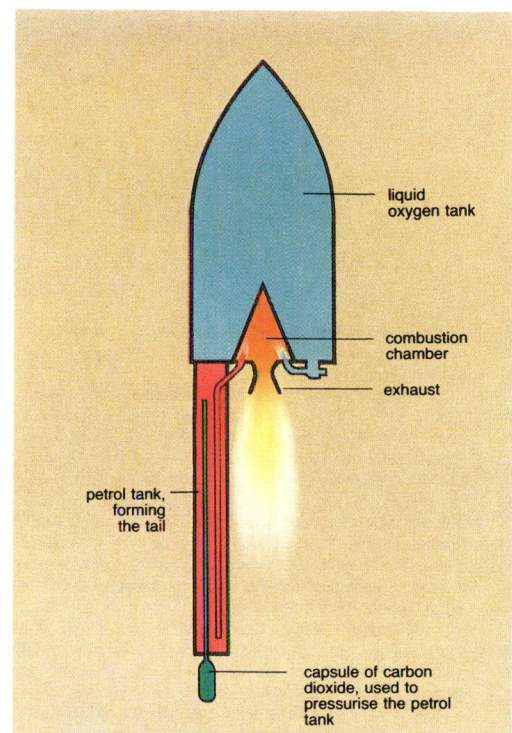

liquid oxygen tank

combustion chamber

exhaust

petrol tank, forming the tail

capsule of carbon dioxide, used to pressurise the petrol tank

Klaus Riedel and his Zweistab Repulsor II rocket. On 23 May 1931, Klaus Riedel's Zweistab Repulsor II rocket attained a height of 61 metres, and landed 600 metres from the launch pad. Like Winkler's HW I rocket, the motor is situated at the top of the structure, and the liquid oxygen and petrol fuels are in the two pipes down the sides (*Zweistab* means two sticks). The petrol reservoir is pressurised by a capsule of nitrogen.

The influence of science fiction on science can be seen here: *Repulsor* is the name of the spacecraft in Kurt Lasswitz's story *Auf zwei Planeten* (On two planets), published in 1897. It was suggested to Riedel by Willy Ley (Smithsonian Institution).

Johannes Winkler and his Hückel Winkler II rocket. The HW II rocket was constructed in 1932. It contained a number of improvements on the earlier model, in particular a stabilising system. Unfortunately, the rocket had to be launched from the island of Frische Nehrung in the Baltic Sea, and the marine air corroded the fuel inlet valves. No one had noticed this and, on 6 October 1932, the rocket caught fire just after take off and exploded at an altitude of about fifteen metres.

The photograph on the near right shows this rocket. It was 1·9 metres high and 0·4 metres in diameter on its launch pad; the white triangles are not fins, but part of the launch pad. Two manometers are visible through the two holes pierced in the shell. The photograph on the far right was taken inside Winkler's workshop, and shows the same rocket with part of the casing removed. The key is as follows:
1 liquid oxygen reservoir
2 manometers
3 liquid methane reservoir
4 combustion chamber/exhaust
(Deutsches Museum, Munich).

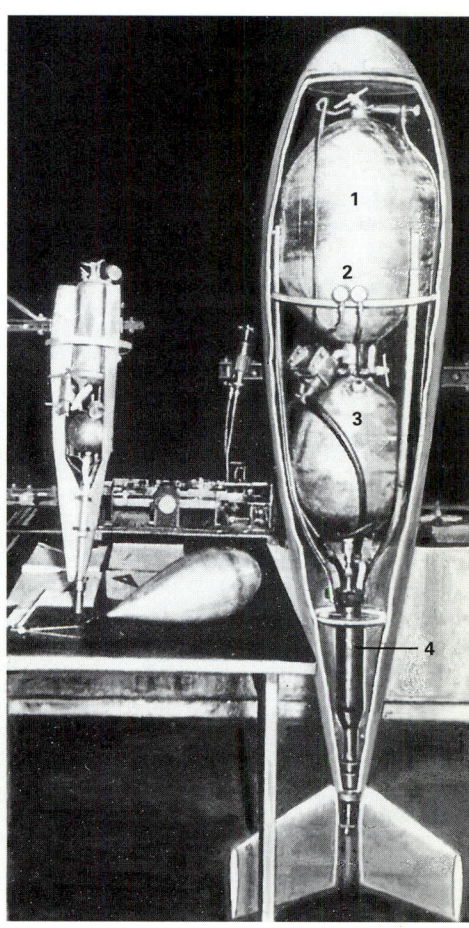

Hermann Oberth (1894 to 1989)

Hermann Oberth was born on 25 June 1894 in Hermannstadt, a town in Transylvania, which was then part of the Austro-Hungarian Empire, and is now Sibiu in Romania.

At the age of twelve he read *From the Earth to the Moon* and *Around the Moon* by Jules Verne. He was fascinated by these books, and began thinking about space travel. In 1913, he went to Munich to study medicine, but his studies were interrupted by the outbreak of the First World War.

From 1919, Oberth studied physics at Klausenburg (now called Cluj, in Romania), Munich, Göttingen and Heidelberg. He read all about fundamental research into rockets and space navigation. In 1922, he submitted a thesis to the University of Heidelberg entitled *Die Rakete zu den Planetenräumen* (The rocket into interplanetary space). The thesis was turned down for being too improbable, although the possibility of spaceflight had already been demonstrated, using rigorously tested scientific data. However, in 1923, Oberth published the text, the first time the subject of astronautics had been tackled in a book.

Between 1924 and 1938, Oberth worked as a teacher of mathematics and physics at a school in Medias, Transylvania. During this period, he remained interested in the fundamental problems

at Reinickendorf, in the Berlin suburbs, at the end of 1930. Later that year, Oberth returned to his native Transylvania.

In 1938, Oberth went to the Technische Hochschule in Vienna, where he was given a research post. In 1941, he was transferred to the Technische Hochschule at Dresden, and then in July he was sent to Peenemünde, where he stayed until September 1943. During his time at Peenemünde, Oberth did not take part in any of the development work that was being carried out, even though it was his theoretical work, his inventions, his discoveries and his experiments which led to the construction of the Aggregat 4, also known as the V2 rocket. In 1941, he completed some fundamental work on the optimisation of multistage rockets. This formed part of a technical document which he sent to America after the collapse of the Third Reich.

After the end of the war, Oberth stayed in Germany. In 1948 he went to Switzerland for two years, where he acted as an adviser whilst continuing to write. Between 1950 and 1953, in Italy, he developed a rocket fuelled by a powder based on ammonium nitrate. In 1954, he published his third book on spaceflight, *Menschen im Weltraum* (Men in space), which was subsequently translated into eight languages.

Hermann Oberth in 1930. This photograph, taken on 5 August 1930, shows Oberth and several members of the Verein für Raumschiffahrt presenting the rocket which they had built for the launch of the film, *Frau im Mond*. From left to right they are Rudolf Nebel; Franz Ritter, the director of Chemisch-Technischen Reichsanstalt, where the Kegeldüse rocket had been tested two weeks previously; Hans Bermüller; Kurt Heinisch; an unknown person; Klaus Riedel, who was involved in constructing Mirak I; Wernher von Braun, aged eighteen; and another unknown.

The demonstration rocket was 2·1 metres tall and contained 7·6 litres of liquid oxygen and petrol. It was never launched. This work, however, led to the construction of the Kegeldüse rocket (Smithsonian Institution).

Kegeldüse motor-rocket. On 23 July 1930, the Kegeldüse (conical exhaust) functioned perfectly for 96·4 seconds, in the presence of Franz Ritter, who certified that the thrust produced was 70 newtons during the first 50·8 seconds and 60 newtons during the rest of the trajectory. The exhaust gas speed reached 756 metres per second, and 6·6 kilograms of liquid oxygen and 1 kilogram of petrol were consumed. The motor, with the exhaust pointing upwards, was immersed in water, to keep it cool.

This photograph of the Kegeldüse, which is now on display at the Hermann Oberth museum, shows the conical shape of the combustion chamber, which is bolted onto the exhaust, and the two fuel supply tubes.

The Kegeldüse was probably the first liquid fuel rocket engine to be constructed by the Verein für Raumschiffahrt. Many rockets of the same series were built (Smithsonian Institution).

of space travel and rockets. He became involved with all the pioneers of astronautics, including Tsiolkovsky, Goddard, Esnault-Pelterie, Hermann Ganswindt, Walter Hohmann, Max Valier, Franz Oskar von Hoefft and Gustave A. Crocco. Between 1925 and 1928, at Medias, Oberth wrote his major book, *Wege zur Raumschiffahrt* (Ways to spaceflight), which was published in Munich in 1929. Esnault-Pelterie called this book the 'bible of scientific astronautics', and nominated Oberth for the REP–Hirsch prize, presented by the Astronautics Society of France, which Esnault-Pelterie had cofounded that year. Because Oberth's work was so important, the prize money, initially 5000 francs, was doubled.

In 1927, Oberth became a member of the Verein für Raumschiffahrt (The Society for Space Travel) which had just been formed. He published several articles in the society's magazine, *Die Rakete* (The rocket). In Berlin, in 1928 and 1929, Oberth was also the scientific adviser for the first film about space travel, *Frau im Mond* (The Woman in the Moon), produced by Fritz Lang. Lang provided Oberth with the opportunity to study an experimental rocket using liquid fuels. This rocket was never finished. However, on 23 July 1930, a committee of experts officially confirmed that his Kegeldüse rocket worked successfully. Several technicians and German students had helped Oberth in his work, including Rudolf Nebel, Klaus Riedel and Wernher von Braun, who went on to found the first German centre for rocket launches – the Raketenflugplatz –

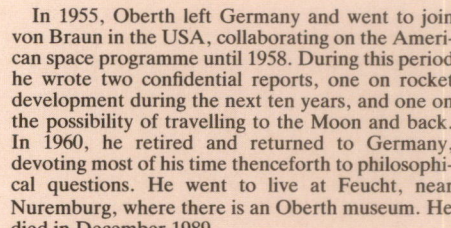

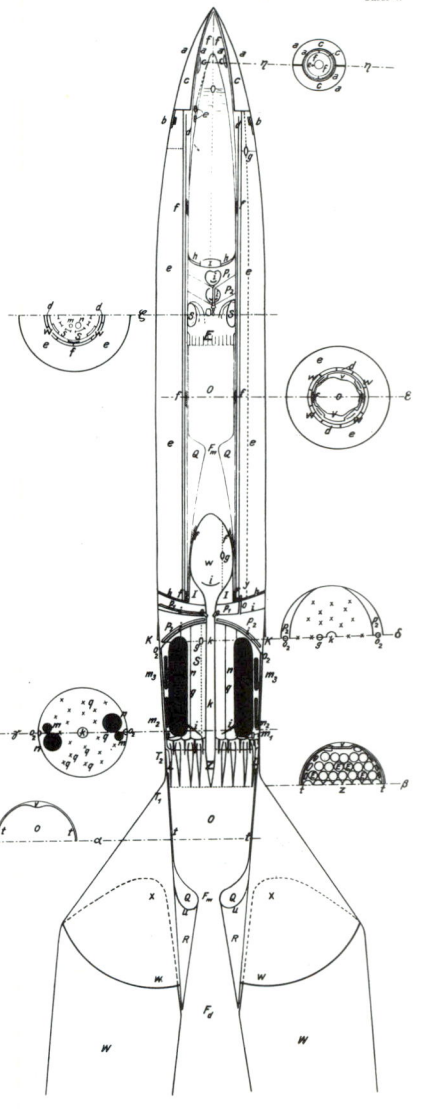

The Model B rocket. In 1923, in *Die Rakete zu den Planetenräumen*, Oberth published a diagram of a two stage liquid fuel rocket probe, to be used for geophysical research in the high atmosphere. This rocket was never built, but it was the inspiration behind some other German rockets. The second stage, drawn in grey, is situated inside the fuel tank of the first.

The first stage uses liquid oxygen and a mixture of alcohol and water as the fuel. This also cools the combustion chamber and the neck of the exhaust. The fuel for the second is liquid hydrogen and liquid oxygen (Bayerische Staatsbibliothek, Munich).

In 1955, Oberth left Germany and went to join von Braun in the USA, collaborating on the American space programme until 1958. During this period he wrote two confidential reports, one on rocket development during the next ten years, and one on the possibility of travelling to the Moon and back. In 1960, he retired and returned to Germany, devoting most of his time thenceforth to philosophical questions. He went to live at Feucht, near Nuremburg, where there is an Oberth museum. He died in December 1989.

Oberth made a considerable contribution to astronautics. Firstly, he established the theoretical relations which explain the connections between the consumption of fuel, the exhaust gas speed, the speed of the rocket, the effect of gravity during the launch phase, the duration of the flight, the distance travelled and so on. From these relations, he was able to derive the fundamental laws governing the design of rockets. This was after Goddard announced in 1920 that it was impossible to present all these relations and laws analytically. He was responsible for the Oberth trajectory, that is the optimal trajectory for a rocket, established from energy considerations. These relate speed, fuel consumption, acceleration and aerodynamic resistance as a function of the cross section of the rocket. Oberth's formulae and methods of graphical representation still enable scientists to establish the optimum number of rocket stages and the relationship between the optimal mass of the different stages. The first mathematical and physical studies on an electric propulsion unit, operating in space, can also be credited to him.

Thus astronautics is indebted to Oberth for more than two hundred relations and laws on mathematical, physical and technical principles. Aggregat 4 used ninety-five of Oberth's inventions and technical solutions in its construction, and was the first operational rocket in the modern sense of the word. Von Braun said of Oberth that he had been the first 'who, starting from thoughts on the possibility of spaceflight, got out his slide rule and turned the propositions of studies and concepts into mathematical calculations'. Oberth also discovered two other physical phenomena. One was called the Oberth effect by Esnault-Pelterie, while the other related to the behaviour of fuel droplets during combustion.

In one of Oberth's early books, *Wege zur Raumschiffahrt*, he outlined a project to build a space shuttle, the Pendelrakete or shuttle-rocket. Oberth also suggested a large number of uses for technical satellites. These included telecommunications, geographic and geological observational satellites; rockets and satellites for meteorological and climatic research, and for astronomical and astrophysical observations; and satellites for navigation and positioning, and for treating materials in the microgravity conditions of space. He suggested using solar energy captured by gigantic mirrors in space, geological exploitation of the planets, the Moon and the asteroids, biological, medical and parapsychology experiments.

The initial development of astronautics owes much to this pioneer. More of a theoretician than an experimentalist, he influenced a whole generation of young engineers.

Hans Barth

in particular Wernher von Braun, Klaus Riedel and Rudolf Nebel.

In June 1930, Riedel, Nebel and Kurt Heinisch built their first rocket which they called Mirak I (i.e. the *Minimum-rakete*, or Minimum rocket). It weighed 3 kilograms and had a small motor based on the Kegeldüse. Rocket trials were carried out during the summer of 1930 on land belonging to Riedal's grandparents farm, at Bernstadt.

Unfortunately one explosion followed another and all the rocket tests failed. On April 1931, the improved performance Mirak II rockets were tested, with no more success. It turned out to be the rocket motor design which was at fault. A new model, built in aluminium, whose walls were cooled by circulating water was soon constructed. It attained a thrust of 310 newtons. This motor was installed on the Mirak III version. On its first flight, on 10 May 1931, it attained a height of 18 metres. It was recovered, repaired and renamed Repulsor I. Its first official flight took place four days later.

From September 1930, VfR rocket tests were carried out in the Berlin suburbs, at Reinickendorf, on land which had been abandoned by the German army. Covering an area of 1·2 square kilometres, it possessed strong blockhouses which the experimenters used. Because there was no other equivalent centre, the VfR gave it the name Raketenflugplatz (rocket launch site); it was here that the rocket enthusiasts spent several years working on the technology which has formed the basis of all modern missiles and launchers.

The first flight by a liquid fuel rocket built by the VfR took place on 14 May 1931. It was not, however, the first of its type in the world. Five years previously, the American scientist Robert H. Goddard had accomplished this feat. In Europe, it seems that the Austrian Friedrich Sander had even achieved a similar flight, in secret, on 10 April 1929, with a liquid fuel rocket of his own design. More importantly Johannes Winkler, one of the founders of the VfR, who had severed his links with the group in order to work with the aeroplane company Junkers, had constructed a rocket which he tested on 21 February 1931. As the rocket only attained a height of 3 metres, the test was only a partial success. It was not until 14 March 1931 that another of his oxygen and liquid methane rockets reached a height of 60 metres.

The rivalry between liquid and solid fuel rockets continued. On the evening of the same day that Winkler launched his 'first' European liquid fuel rocket, Karl Poggensee's solid fuel rocket attained a height of 450 metres over Berlin's suburbs. In the following month, Reinhold Tiling, a German, launched six black powder rockets; one of these attained a record height of 9·5 kilometres. And in July 1931, an Austrian, Friedrich Schmiedl, carried out flight tests on a rocket designed to carry messages.

The performance of the VfR rockets improved. By 1932, rockets from the Repulsor IV series were attaining altitudes of 1·5 kilometres and had a range of 5 kilometres. A new fuel mixture was used – liquid oxygen and alcohol. This mixture was used to achieve forces exceeding 600 newtons, and the speed of the exhaust gas was about 1·7 kilometres per second. The reputation of VfR increased considerably, and its work programme intensified. With rockets weighing anything between 3 and 250 kilograms, 87 flight tests, 270 rocket motor and non-flight tests, 23 demonstrations for clubs and societies, and 9 public displays were performed at the Raketenflugplatz from September 1930 to May 1932.

The VfR work soon took on an international flavour when it signed an agreement with the American Interplanetary Society (AIS) on 12 April 1931. (The AIS changed its name, in 1934, to become the American Rocket Society.) From this union, throughout the 1930s, static tests on rocket motors were carried out, though there were no notable successes.

In the USA, other space oriented societies

The popularisers. By the end of the 1920s, propulsion by powdered solid fuel rocket had been tested on cars, rail vehicles, sledges and gliders. Max Valier was responsible for most of these demonstrations, because he wanted to popularise the work of the Verein für Raumschiffahrt. At the beginning of 1928, he joined forces with the automobile industrialist, Fritz von Opel, in the quest for publicity. On 23 May 1928, an Opel-Sander car, the Rak 2, equipped with twenty-four powder rockets by Friedrich Sander and driven by Fritz von Opel himself, reached a speed of 170 kilometres per hour on the Berlin racing track, Avus.

On 22 January 1929, a sledge piloted by Max Valier, called the Rak Bob 1, went at more than 100 kilometres per hour on the frozen Eibsee, in the Bavarian Alps (Deutsches Museum, Munich).

Max Valier at the wheel of his own rocket car, Rak 6. Paul Heylandt, the owner of a liquid gas factory, helped Max Valier to build liquid fuel rocket motors for cars at the beginning of the 1930s. His first motor using liquid oxygen and ethanol was fitted to the Rak 6 car. Subsequently modified and renamed Rak 7, this vehicle was demonstrated to the public on 19 April 1930, at the Berlin airport, Tempelhof. Valier died a month later in a rocket motor explosion during tests in the Heylandt workshops (Deutsches Museum, Munich).

The Opel-Sander Rak I rocket glider. On 30 September 1929, Fritz von Opel flew a Hatry Glider, from Rebstock, near Frankfurt. The glider had 16 Friedrich Sander powder rockets, which produced a thrust greater than 3·5 kilonewtons. The rocket glider was 5·4 metres long, with a wingspan of 11 metres. It flew more than 1·5 kilometres during the 75 seconds of powered flight, and reached a speed of 150 kilometres per hour.

The first rocket plane in history only made its first flight on 11 made its first flight on 11 June June 1928, on the rocky slopes of the Wasserkuppe (Deutsches Museum, Munich).

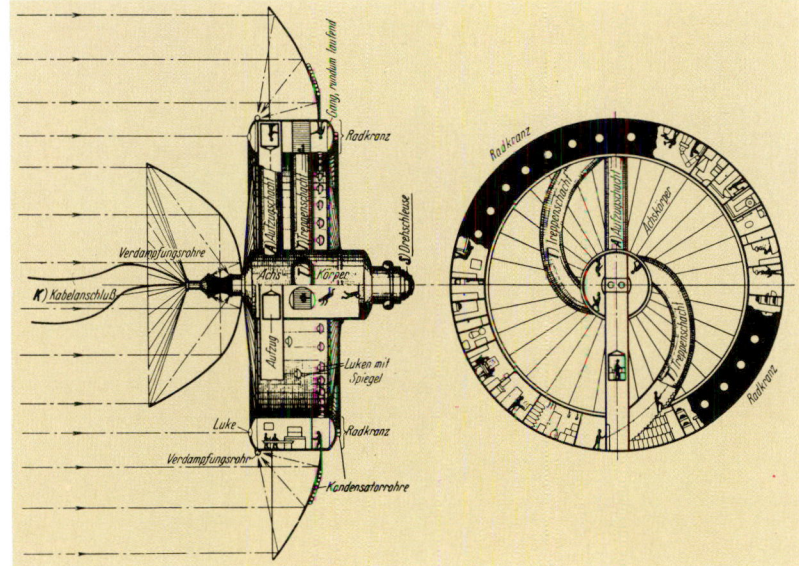

Hermann Noordung's 'Inhabitable Wheel'. In 1929, an Austrian called Hermann Potocnik published a book under the pseudonym of 'Noordung'. The book was *Das Problem der Befahrung des Weltraums* (The problem of space navigation). It was the first book to devote most of its pages to space stations. Noordung proposed the *Wohnrad* (inhabitable wheel) design. This strongly influenced the work of technicians and researchers, as well as of science fiction authors. It inspired many space station designs during the 1950s, even the one appearing in *2001 – A Space Odyssey*.

The *Wohnrad* had an outer diameter of 50 metres, and rotated about its axis in order to create artificial gravity in the inhabitable outer ring (*Radkranz*). This contained the cabins, laboratories, workshops, kitchen, and bathroom. There was also a circular gallery (*Gang, rundum laufend*). There were portholes (*Luken*) used for observing the Earth and the stars. There was also a lift shaft and two staircases leading to the 'hub' (*Achskörper*), with a rotating airlock (*Drehschleuse*). The station's energy would be provided by two large concave mirrors to focus solar radiation onto heat pipes (*Verdampfungsrohre*) containing a liquid which would vapourise and operate turbines to produce a continuous electrical current. The vapour would then condense in other pipes (*Kondensatorrohre*) shaded from the Sun (Deutsches Museum, Munich).

Robert Esnault-Pelterie (1881 to 1957)

Among the pioneers in the conquest of space, Robert Esnault-Pelterie is perhaps most famous for his contribution to the development of aeronautics. He was born into a wealthy industrial family, and therefore always had a certain financial independence. His early studies were oriented towards natural history and then, at the beginning of the twentieth century, like many of his generation, he caught 'flying fever'.

He was the fourth person to be issued with a pilot's licence by the Aéro-Club de France. However, his name is not mentioned in any list of achievements of the early pilots, because from the beginning his aim was to demonstrate the possibilities of flying. He thus sacrificed performance for the quality and reliability of his equipment. In the circuit of Europe race in 1911, for example, he came fifth, but he was the only person to finish without having to change his engine.

Esnault-Pelterie considered aviation to be a small step along the path to conquering space and abandoned a promising career in aviation to devote his time to astronautics.

In 1912, he presented a paper to the Société française de physique (French Physics Society). He published it under the unassuming title of *Considérations sur les résultats d'un allègement indéfini des moteurs* (Discussion of the effect of the continuous loss of mass experienced by an engine). The title referred to the mass loss which a rocket experiences as it burns its fuel reserves. The paper itself considered the possibilities of interplanetary travel offered by the principle of the rocket. The Moon was the first objective. Esnault-Pelterie calculated the mass ratios necessary if rockets were to be fuelled by conventional substances, and he found results which seemed to be untenable. He concluded that such voyages would only be possible when 'the internal energy of the atom' had been mastered, an extremely pessimistic conclusion due to the fact that he performed his calculations for a single stage, fully recoverable space plane. This is still a dream, even at the end of the twentieth century.

He subsequently learnt of the patent registered in 1911 by the Belgian scientist, André Bing, on the principle of a multistage rocket. He commented that this would open 'the possibility of attaining almost any altitude, using a series of rocket stages which could be jettisoned once all the fuel had been used up'.

Following the First World War, Esnault-Pelterie made contact with other like-minded people in different countries. These included Robert H. Goddard, in the USA, who had already launched rockets based on Bing's principle, and the Germans, Hermann Oberth and Walter Hohmann. Esnault-Pelterie was anxious to promote international collaboration, and so he founded an annual astronautics prize with his friend the banker André Hirsch. The original prize money was 5000 francs, and the first recipient, in 1929, was Hermann Oberth.

By 1930, Esnault-Pelterie had developed his ideas enough to publish a major work called simply *L'Astronautique* (Astronautics). It contained a short history of all the work which had been carried out in the field in which he tried to discuss the merits of each. A study based on the thermodynamics of propulsion led him to not only confirm but also be slightly optimistic about the performance that Oberth had predicted for a mixture of hydrogen and oxygen. After a detailed study of the mechanics of such a project, he finally agreed with Oberth that a return voyage to the Moon was possible. This optimism was justified because the Earth's atmosphere could be used to slow a space vehicle down on the return journey. This type of braking was originally proposed by Hohmann; Esnault-Pelterie argued that it was crucial to calculate the optimum angle of reentry into the atmosphere.

The book's most original and farsighted contribution to astronautics was, however, in the field of navigation. The author demonstrated the possibility of what is now known as inertial navigation. This system, installed on a moving vehicle, provides the position coordinates without referring to an external frame of reference. It achieves this by carrying out a double integration of the acceleration measurements, the first deriving the three components of the velocity vector and the second the position coordinates. Esnault-Pelterie proposed design criteria for an accelerometer integrator. The accelerometers should be placed on a platform, stabilised by gyroscopes and keeping its orientation with respect to the external frame of reference. The accelerometers could also maintain the attitude of the spacecraft. Finally, he realised that the part of the acceleration due to gravity was not measured by

A pioneer of aviation. Esnault-Pelterie, who was known affectionately as REP, his initials, designed monoplanes. These consisted of a basic metal structure with wings mounted using pneumatic shock absorbers. They were much more the forerunners of modern planes than the 'hen houses' of his contemporaries. These planes had a metal propeller driven by a radial engine, the basic design used until the turbojet was developed. Esnault-Pelterie designed, built and developed theories of the propeller which are still in use today. He devised the static resistance test on the ability of the wing structure to support the weight of the engine. He also invented the joystick, which has two degrees of freedom to control the longitudinal and lateral level of an aeroplane in flight. This photograph was taken in about 1908 (Musée de l'Air et de l'Espace, France).

Publicising space travel. Although Esnault-Pelterie's contribution to space travel may have been less than those of Goddard and Oberth, he did much to publicise astronautics. His fame spread as far as the USA, as shown by this invitation to a lecture. The film in question was *Frau im Mond* by Fritz Lang, for which Oberth was scientific adviser (G. Edward Pendray Papers, Seeley Mudd Manuscript Library, Princeton University).

THE AMERICAN INTERPLANETARY SOCIETY

cordially invites you to attend an address by

ROBERT ESNAULT-PELTERIE
the distinguished French scientist and engineer

"BY ROCKET TO THE MOON"

in the Main Auditorium
The American Museum of Natural History
77th Street and Central Park West

on the evening of January 27th, 1931, at 8:30 o'clock

A motion picture, prepared under the direction of Professor Hermann Oberth of Germany, showing the actual flight to the moon of an imaginary but scientifically possible rocket, will accompany the address.

There will be no charge for admission

DAVID LASSER,
President

Two seats will be reserved for you until 8:30
Please present this card at the door

Predicting combustion reactions. This diagram, published in *Astronautics*, shows the ejection speed of a rocket engine fuelled by hydrogen and oxygen as a function of the composition of the mixture and for various pressures of injection into the combustion chamber. The composition is described by the parameter a which represents the proportion of excess hydrogen with respect to the amount corresponding to the chemical reaction $H_2 + \frac{1}{2}O_2 \rightarrow H_2O$. The dotted lines represent the ejection speeds which were calculated ignoring the energy required for vaporisation and for the initial heating of the chemicals.

This graph illustrates the phenomenon of disassociation, which causes the combustion reaction to remain incomplete. To appreciate the value of these calculations, consider the example of the modern, third stage engine of the Ariane launcher. This uses a combustion chamber pressure of 35 atmospheres and a coefficient a of 1·11. On the diagram, this corresponds to an ejection speed of 4820 metres per second, which is just 10% greater than the ejection speed of 4350 metres per second obtained by this engine (Bibliothèque nationale, Paris).

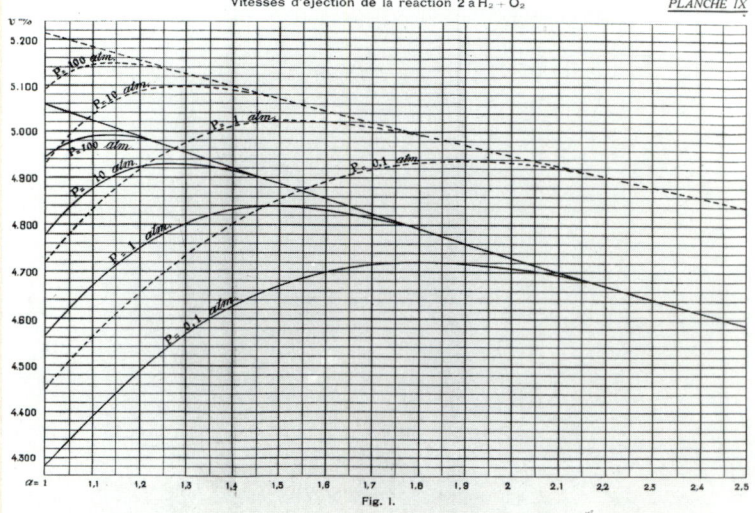

the accelerometers, and that it was therefore necessary to add this at each instant that the acceleration was measured. If the space vehicle is moving through a known gravitational field, then this can be calculated as a function of position.

When *L'Astronautique* appeared in 1930, Esnault-Pelterie's ideas were far in advance of the available technology and it was not until the advent of the computer that his designs were successfully developed. Today, his three principles governing accelerometer integrators and the two application modes of the inertial navigation system are all in wide use.

In spite of all the other problems, such as designing a habitable cabin for man in space and the need to adapt to weightlessness, Esnault-Pelterie was convinced that the major problem in astronautics was the right choice of fuel. Between 1930 and 1940, he spent his time searching for the ideal fuel. He was given only a tiny grant by the government which did not believe rockets had any real military use. First of all, Esnault-Pelterie attempted to develop tetranitromethane, in the process losing three fingers of his left hand in an accident. He then began work on a mixture of liquid oxygen and petrol (gasoline). He succeeded in constructing an engine capable of producing a thrust of one kilonewton for more than a minute. The weak point in this engine was the cooling system, which used tap water – not available in flight. Despite the possibilities offered by using liquid oxygen as a cooling agent, Esnault-Pelterie concentrated his attention on designing a non-cooled system using refractory materials. He spent a lot of time working on this problem, but there were many difficulties to overcome and he had not had any success when the invasion of France in 1940 put an end to his work.

Esnault-Pelterie was elected a member of the French Academy of Sciences in 1936. After the Second World War, he followed the progress of rocket propulsion and the earliest stages of the conquest of space. Although he spoke at conferences on the subject, he did not carry out any more personal work because he felt uneasy with some of the possible applications of space research.

He had the satisfaction of being involved in putting the first artificial satellite into orbit around the Earth. Unfortunately, however, he did not live long enough to witness his lifelong dream come true when the first man travelled to the Moon and back. He would have been delighted to know that his hopes had become a reality and his theoretical analyses had been proved correct.

Pierre Contensou

were formed, such as the Cleveland Rocket Society. Between 1936 and 1939, Robert C. Truax, a midshipman at the US Naval Academy, built and tested small liquid fuel rocket motors, while the artillery department of the US Army studied rockets from 1932 onwards.

In Great Britain, the British Interplanetary Society was formed in 1933. Its activities remained purely theoretical, due to a clause in the 1875 Explosives Act which prohibited rocket tests. Other societies, similar to the British one, were formed in Japan, the Netherlands and Argentina.

In France, in 1928, following theoretical work, Robert Esnault-Pelterie put before the French military a proposal to construct ballistic missiles. During the 1930s he obtained several contracts to build liquid fuel engines and solid fuel propellants to be used to launch bombs. And in Boulogne, at the beginning of the 1930s, he constructed what was a very high performance engine for the era. It had a thrust of one kilonewton for more than a minute.

Around the same time in Austria, in Vienna, Eugen Sänger constructed rockets which used oxygen gas and heavy oil. These operated for between 20 and 30 minutes, obtaining a thrust of the order of 200 newtons.

In the years leading up to the Second World War, the Soviet Union, like other countries, became involved in the new field of astronautics. Under both state and military control, units were created to study various aspects of the subject. In May 1929, Valentin Glushko founded the Gas Dynamics Laboratory (GDL), at Leningrad. In 1931, preliminary tests on the ORM 1 engine were very successful. It produced a thrust of 200 newtons using a fuel of nitrogen peroxide. Following this, a series of engines fuelled by either nitric acid or paraffin oil (kerosene) were developed. During tests in 1933, the ORM 52 engine produced a thrust of 3 kilonewtons.

A research organisation was set up in 1932 to study liquid fuel ballistic missiles, to develop testbeds for ramjets and fluid dynamic tests, and to study jet aircraft and interplanetary spacecraft carrying sails using solar radiation pressure. The first liquid fuel rocket designed and built in the USSR was launched on 17 August 1933. It reached an altitude of 400 metres, a performance which was comparable with that of Goddard's rockets between 1930 and 1932.

In September 1933, the Institute for Scientific Research into Rocket Propulsion (RNII) was established. Between 1933 and 1938, as part of this institute, Glushko developed the ORM 52 to ORM 102 rockets which were fuelled by either nitric acid or paraffin. Tsiolkovsky built several rockets in conjunction with the RNII until his death in 1935.

Immediately before the Second World War, the RNII's activity turned more towards aerodynamic missiles and rocket planes than to ballistic missiles. The most famous success of this period was the development of the rocket glider, RP 318-1, which performed its maiden flight on 28 February 1940.

Kummersdorf and the farsightedness of the German military

A colonel in the German army, Karl Becker, who had collaborated with the well known ballistics expert Carl Cranz, decided in 1929 to evaluate the military possibilities of rockets. The study was put under the control of Captain Walter Dornberger, who had just taken up duties at Heereswaffenamt, the army's arms system service. It was decided to concentrate on a light and economical solid fuel rocket weighing between 5 and 9 kilograms, whilst at the same time carrying out theoretical studies on a liquid fuel rocket.

In fact, this decision by the German army was as much due to operational considerations as to

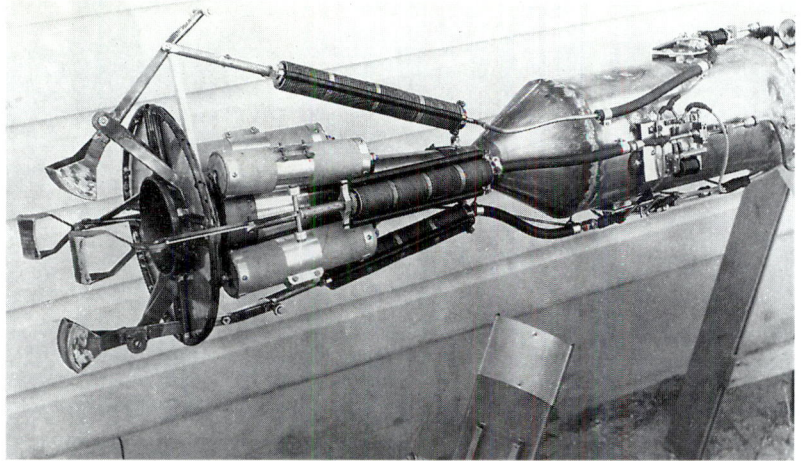

One of Goddard's rockets stabilised by adding adjustable flaps over the exhaust jet. Between September 1934 and October 1935, Robert H. Goddard performed trials on his A series of rockets, at Roswell in New Mexico. These rockets were the first to be stabilised by a gyroscopic system which controlled rods to move adjustable flaps. Clearly visible on this photograph taken in 1935, one of the rods has been extended to its maximum and the flap is pushed right over the exhaust jet (© Esther C. Goddard/NASA/collection F. I. Ordway III).

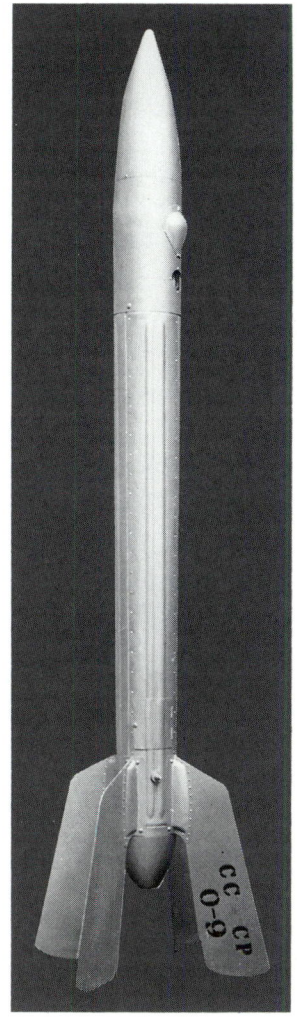

The Soviet rocket GIRD 09. The Russians began studying the possibility of constructing rockets at the end of the 1920s. On 17 August 1933, in the Forest of Nakhibino, near Moscow, the first Soviet liquid fuel rocket, the GIRD 09, was launched to a height of 400 metres. This was during the time when Sergei Korolev was director. The GIRD X, with two liquid fuels, was successfully launched three months later (on 25 November) by the same group.

The GIRD 09 rocket, constructed under Mikhail Tikhonravov, was 2·4 metres high and 18 centimetres in diameter. It weighed 19 kilograms before take-off and carried 5 kilograms of fuel. This used liquid oxygen, driven by its own vapour pressure to the combustion chamber, which was lined with petroleum jelly. The rocket produced a thrust of from 245 to 320 newtons (V. Cheredintsev, Tass).

The first rocket to be constructed by the American Interplanetary Society. On 12 November 1932, at Stockton, New Jersey, G. Edward Pendray put the finishing touches to the ARS 1 rocket. In this photograph, he is accompanied by his wife and Hugh F. Pierce, one of the rocket's designers. The rocket was 2 metres high and weighed 6·8 kilograms. It was based on the Repulsor 2 design, with two fuel pipes running down the sides. Its engine was fuelled by liquid oxygen and petrol and delivered a thrust of 270 newtons. The ARS 1 was never launched, although the testbed trials were more than satisfactory. ARS 2 was built using the fuel tanks and the engine from ARS 1. On 14 May 1933, it reached an altitude of 76 metres (Smithsonian Institution).

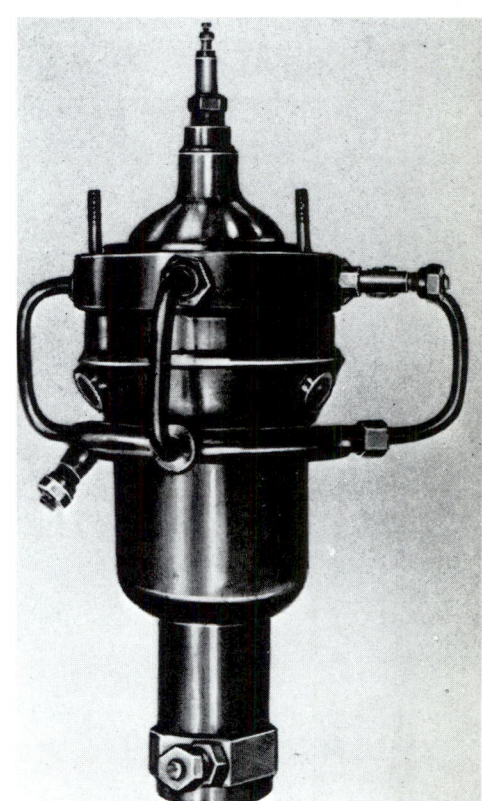

The Soviet ORM rocket engines. During the 1930s, Valentin Glushko built a series of liquid fuel rocket motors called ORM (the initials standing for Opytnyj Raketnyj Motor, or Experimental Rocket Motor). ORM 1 to 52 were built between 1930 and 1933. They produced thrusts of between 200 and 3000 newtons. After 1933, ORM 53 to 102 produced thrusts of between 800 and 6000 newtons.

The ORM 65, shown in this photograph, was capable of delivering a variable thrust of between 480 and 1720 newtons. This type of engine was mounted on Korolev's 212 rocket, and a recast version powered the RP 318-1 rocket glider (rights reserved).

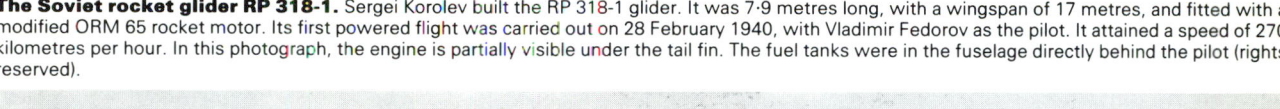

The Soviet rocket glider RP 318-1. Sergei Korolev built the RP 318-1 glider. It was 7·9 metres long, with a wingspan of 17 metres, and fitted with a modified ORM 65 rocket motor. Its first powered flight was carried out on 28 February 1940, with Vladimir Fedorov as the pilot. It attained a speed of 270 kilometres per hour. In this photograph, the engine is partially visible under the tail fin. The fuel tanks were in the fuselage directly behind the pilot (rights reserved).

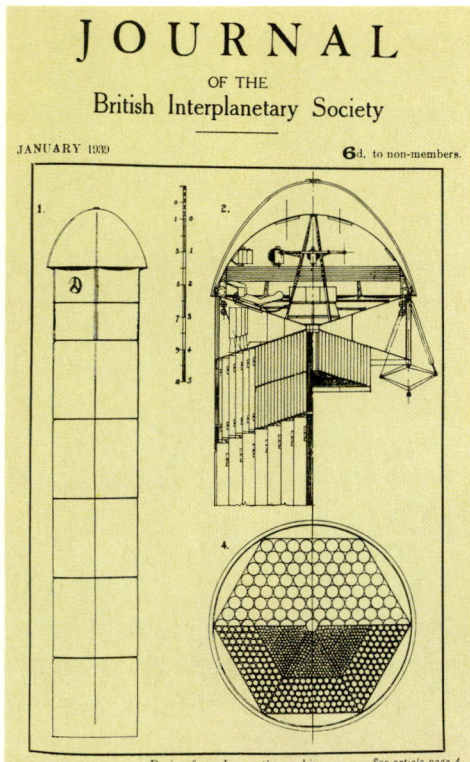

JOURNAL
OF THE
British Interplanetary Society

JANUARY 1939   6d. to non-members.

Design for a Lunar Space-ship.   See article page 4.

A lunar spacecraft proposed by the British Interplanetary Society. The British Interplanetary Society was founded in October 1933. Between February 1937 and the end of 1938, they studied the possibility of a six stage lunar spacecraft consisting of 2490 solid fuel rockets. This was to have 168 large rockets for each of the first five stages (upper part in section 4), 450 average sized rockets and 1200 small rockets for the sixth stage (lower part of the cross section shown in 4). The rocket was to be 32 metres high, 6 metres in diameter and have a launch mass of more than a thousand tonnes.

It was planned to have a cabin for a crew of 2 or 3 men. It was fitted with a liquid fuel rocket propulsion system to descend to the Moon and then return to Earth (Smithsonian Institution).

A test performed by the American Rocket Society, Midvale, New Jersey, 1941. From the end of the 1930s, Midvale was mainly used to test James H. Wyld's rocket motors which were fitted with a closed cooling system. A bottle of compressed nitrogen, shown in the foreground of the photograph, was used to pressurise the fuel reservoir.

Along with other members of the American Rocket Society, Wyld formed a new company in 1941, called Reaction Motors. It started by producing a series of rocket engines (Smithsonian Institution).

The German A3 and A5 experimental rockets. The A3 rocket (on the left) was 7·6 metres high, with a diameter of 0·76 metres and an initial mass of 740 kilograms. It was the first German rocket to be fitted with gyroscopes controlling the ailerons and exhaust jet deflectors. The fuel (ethanol) tank surrounded the combustion chamber and the exhaust, keeping them both cool. A supplementary tank containing nitrogen kept up the pressure in the two fuel tanks.

In comparison with the A3, the A5 (on the right) was more compact. It had a reinforced structure and an improved guidance and control system. The combustion chamber was shorter and the ailerons and the jet deflectors larger.

The A3 rocket in 1937. In this picture, the A3 rocket is about to be tested at Kummersdorf. Part of the body has been removed to show the ethanol tank.

In the autumn of 1937, three A3 rockets were launched from Griefswalder Oie Island, in the Baltic off Peenemünde. The three flights ended in failure due to a malfunction in the guidance system (Deutsches Museum, Munich).

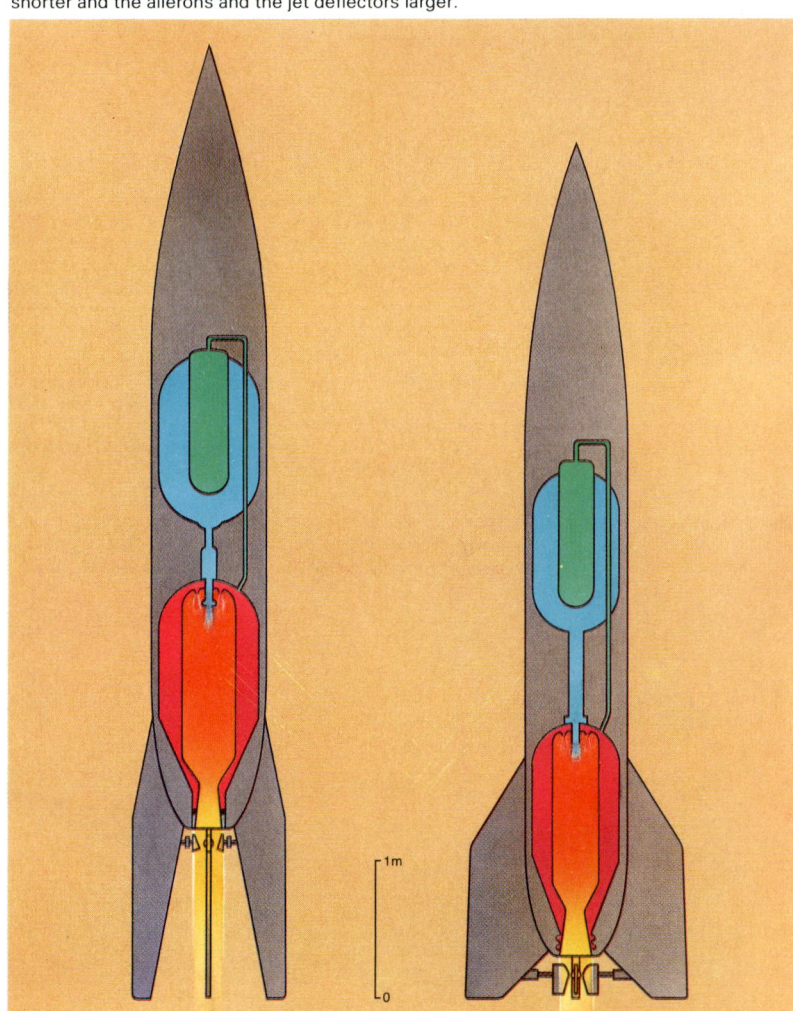

political ones. The Treaty of Versailles had imposed severe restrictions on Germany as far as armaments were concerned. However, there was no clause forbidding them from developing and producing missiles, and so the German military seized the opportunity.

In January 1930, the Reichwehr set up an experimental centre at Kummersdorf-West, in the Berlin suburbs. Between 1930 and 1932, this site was used for tests on solid fuel military rockets which were the forerunners of the famous Nebelwerfer rockets.

Becker and Dornberger followed with interest the work of the VfR which was being carried out a few kilometres from Kummersdorf. In the spring of 1932, they visited Nebel, Riedel and von Braun and, as a result, an agreement was signed. For a fee of 1000 Reichsmarks, Nebel would launch a Repulsor rocket at Kummersdorf. The rocket launch in July was only a partial success. However, the German army decided to support Nebel's work provided that he was more scientific in his approach and that his rocket tests were carried out less publicly. Nebel strongly objected to this proposal and all discussions were suspended. However, Becker was convinced that rockets would be important in the future. He approached the young von Braun with an offer. The German army would fund his thesis and, in exchange, he would carry out theoretical work on the combustion of liquid fuel rockets. The tests resulting from this work would be performed at Kummersdorf. Von Braun accepted the offer and began work on 1 November 1932, helped by the mechanic Heinrich Grünow. By the end of 1932, Germany had thus taken a decisive step towards the possession of rocket technology. Although originally taken by the military, this step eventually led to man's conquest of space.

Less than three months after he began his work, von Braun devised the first liquid oxygen and alcohol engine. It delivered a thrust of just over one kilonewton for 60 seconds. A second engine, which was cooled by the circulation of the alcohol fuel and not water as in previous models, was built six months later. It produced a thrust three times greater than the first model. Von Braun's progress had been exceptionally fast. After a series of successful static trials, a rocket could be envisaged.

The first rocket to be built at Kummersdorf was called the A1 (Aggregate 1). A 3 kilonewton thrust liquid oxygen and alcohol engine was used to make a rocket weighing 150 kilograms. Although the static trials looked very promising, the maiden flight was not a success. A delay in the ignition of the rocket engines caused the first A1 to explode. Shortly afterwards it was shown that modifications to the structure were necessary to make the rocket more stable.

The modified rocket was called A2. Shortly before Christmas 1934, two A2 rockets called Max and Moritz were launched from Borkum Island, in the North Sea. Both vertical flights went off without a hitch, attaining heights of about 2·5 kilometres. At Kummersdorf, everyone felt optimistic and the future looked promising. The effect of the successful launches was to swell the number of people working for von Braun and Dornberger, as well as to increase funding for their activities. Several months before the December success Klaus Riedel came to join the people working at Kummersdorf, and other members of the VfR transferred later.

It was soon decided to begin work on a new engine which would have superior performance to the A2 rocket. The liquid oxygen and alcohol engine would be improved to deliver a thrust of 16 kilonewtons. It would fire for 45 seconds, almost three times as long as the A2 rocket. The speed of the exhaust gases would exceed 2 kilometres per second. Moreover, this new rocket, the A3, would be guided using instruments situated at the rear of the fuselage and jet deflectors in the cone of the exhaust.

Work began on this rocket in 1935. During the same year, another very important event

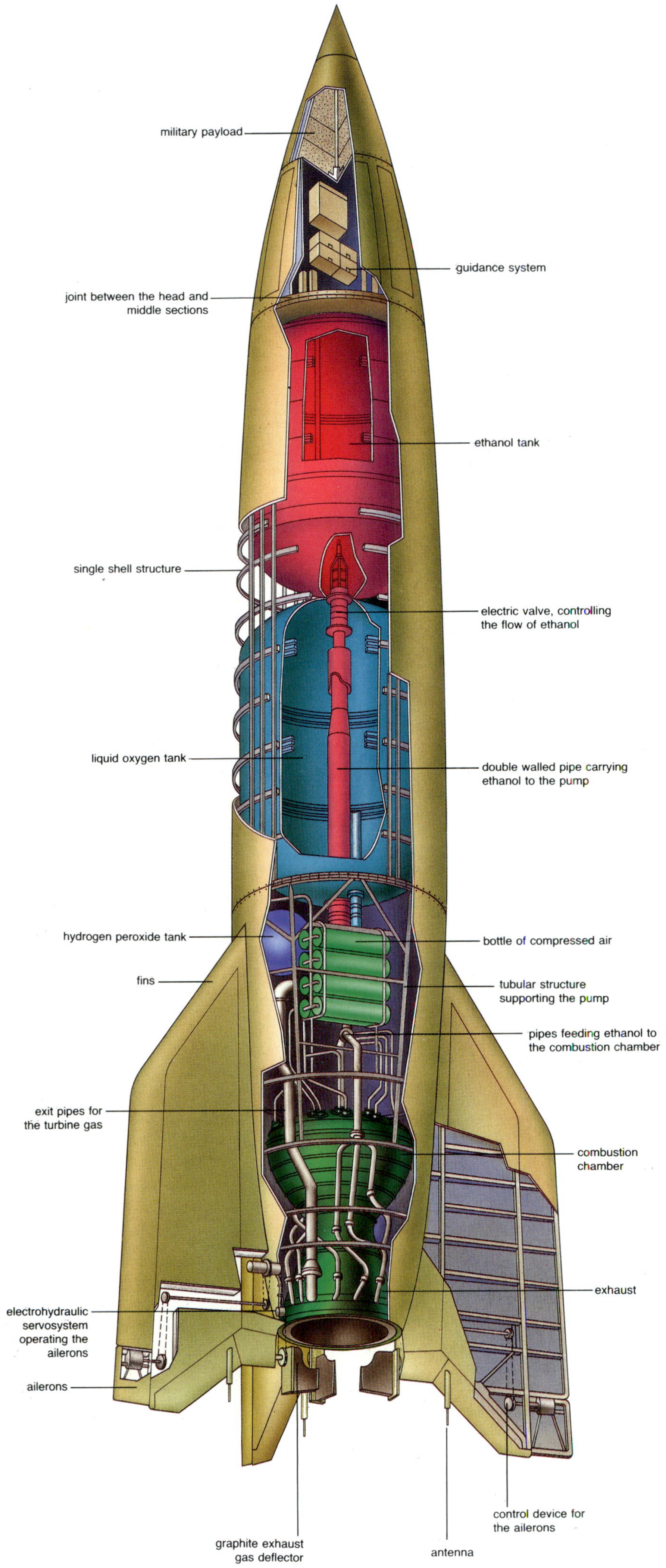

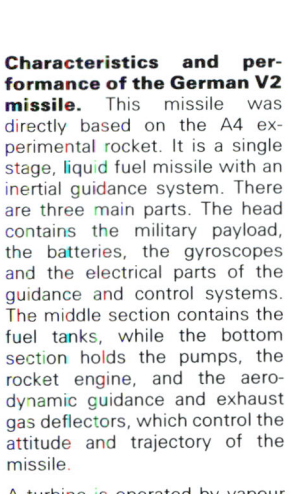

military payload

guidance system

joint between the head and middle sections

ethanol tank

single shell structure

electric valve, controlling the flow of ethanol

liquid oxygen tank

double walled pipe carrying ethanol to the pump

hydrogen peroxide tank

bottle of compressed air

fins

tubular structure supporting the pump

pipes feeding ethanol to the combustion chamber

exit pipes for the turbine gas

combustion chamber

electrohydraulic servosystem operating the ailerons

exhaust

ailerons

graphite exhaust gas deflector

antenna

control device for the ailerons

length : 14 metres	thrust at take off : 250 kilonewtons
diameter of body : 1.65 metres	acceleration at take off : 0.9 g
diameter including the fins : 3.55 metres	acceleration at end of combustion : 5 g
mass at take off : 12 900 kilograms	combustion time : 65 seconds
mass of military payload : 1000 kilograms of which 750 kilograms are explosives	altitude at end of combustion : 22 kilometres
	speed at end of combustion : 1600 metres per second
	impact speed : from 900 to 1100 metres per second, supersonic
mass of ethanol : 3965 kilograms	apogee : from 80 to 90 kilometres
mass of liquid oxygen : 4970 kilograms	range : 320 kilometres
ratio of the fuel mixture : 0.81	

The first launch of the A4 rocket. On 13 June 1942, the first experimental A4 rocket was launched from Peenemünde. A fault in the fuel supply caused the immediate destruction of the rocket (Deutsches Museum, Munich).

Characteristics and performance of the German V2 missile. This missile was directly based on the A4 experimental rocket. It is a single stage, liquid fuel missile with an inertial guidance system. There are three main parts. The head contains the military payload, the batteries, the gyroscopes and the electrical parts of the guidance and control systems. The middle section contains the fuel tanks, while the bottom section holds the pumps, the rocket engine, and the aerodynamic guidance and exhaust gas deflectors, which control the attitude and trajectory of the missile.

A turbine is operated by vapour from the dissociation of hydrogen peroxide which in turn operates the liquid fuel supply pumps.

Preparing for the first successful launch of an A4 rocket, on 3 October 1942. The rocket is sitting on the launch pad of the number 7 complex at Peenemünde, surrounded by a protective circular embankment nearly 10 metres high. The uppermost cover has not yet been put into place, and some of the guidance and control systems are visible.

The fuels were transported in tankers and stored outside the protective embankment; one of these tankers is visible on the left (Deutsches Museum, Munich).

Sergei Pavlovich Korolev (1907 to 1966)

Korolev made an enormous contribution to the development of astronautics and his name has been linked with most of the great achievements at the dawn of the space era. These include the first artificial Earth satellite (1957), the first photographs of the dark side of the Moon (1959), the first manned spaceflight (1961), the first space walk (1965), the first planetary probe to land on Venus (1966), and the first soft landing of a lunar probe (1966).

Sergei Pavlovich Korolev was born on 12 January 1907, at Zhitomir, in the Ukraine. In 1924 he completed his secondary school studies at Odessa, moving on to the Polytechnic Institute at Kiev and then the Higher Technical College at Moscow, where he obtained his aeronautic engineering degree in 1929. He then spent one year working in a research laboratory in the aeronautics industry.

When he was eighteen, Korolev built his first glider. He frequently went to Koktebel, in the Crimea, the mecca of unaided flight enthusiasts who held national competitions there every year. At Koktebel, he showed various gliders which he had built during his free time. The most remarkable of these were Krasnaia Zvenda (Red Star) which he first used for aerobatics in 1930 and the two man glider, SK 9 (1935), which incorporated a liquid fuel rocket motor.

In 1930, Korolev left the flying school and gave up aviation so that he could devote all his time to rockets. He met the great Soviet physicist, Fridrikh Tsander, who was also passionate about interplanetary spaceflight.

From 1932, Korolev then directed the Moscow group studying the principles of propulsion by rocket engines (MosGIRD). There, the first Soviet liquid fuel rockets and winged engines were built and tested. In 1940, the one man rocket glider, RP 318–1, based on the SK 9, was flight tested. Later, during the Second World War (1941 to 1945) Korolev spent time improving the performance of military planes, equipping them with fine adjustment, liquid fuel rockets.

In 1946 Korolev was asked to direct the work being carried out on long range ballistic rockets. The first trials took place in the autumn of 1948. Numerous improvements and modifications were made until 1956, when the first strategic missile carrying a nuclear warhead formed part of the weapons available to the Russian army. In August 1957, the first two stage intercontinental ballistic missile was successfully launched.

Korolev's dream of the conquest of space suddenly became a real possibility. In fact, alongside work on the ballistic missile, a launcher for artificial satellites was being developed. The first ever satellite, Sputnik 1, was launched on 4 October 1957 and under Korolev's impetus, Soviet space exploration programmes to the Moon, Venus and Mars using automatic space probes were developed.

However, it was with manned spaceflight that Korolev saw his most cherished dream become a reality. Between 1949 and 1955, rockets containing recoverable capsules were regularly being launched. In some cases, the capsules contained animals, so that their reactions to spaceflight could be studied. At the end of the 1950s, preparations for manned spaceflight began in earnest. In 1960 and 1961, several satellites were put into orbit with animals on board. These flights were very successful in that they allowed scientists to resolve biological questions and also to improve the spaceship's systems.

On 29 April 1961, Yuri Gagarin carried out a flight lasting 108 minutes around the Earth. The era

A meeting at MosGIRD, in 1931. Korolev is sitting on the left, Tsander is standing to the right, and Boris Cheranovsky is the man smoking a cigarette. The first job given to the MosGIRD in Moscow was outlined in a contract dated 18 November 1931. This was between Ossoaviakhim, an organisation in charge of financing aeronautical, chemical and defence research, and Tsander who had just built the OR 2 rocket motor, with a thrust of 490 newtons. Korolev and Cheranovsky modified it to fit on one of Cheranovsky's gliders, the BICh 11. Tsander's engine would never be used in flight, but a modified version was used on the GIRD X (Tsiolkovsky Museum, Kaluga; photograph Smithsonian Institution).

of manned spaceflight had begun. In the same year, Guerman Titov orbited the Earth for 25 hours. For each of these flights, Korolev played an active part in the preparations. He was even involved in the flight of the first female cosmonaut, Valentina Tereshkova, in 1963, and the first space walk by Aleksei Leonov in 1965.

Korolev joined the Communist Party in 1953. He won the Lenin prize in 1957 and was elected to the Academy of Sciences in 1958. He was twice made a hero of socialist work (1956 and 1961). Korolev died in January 1966. As a last homage to this remarkable man, the urn containing his ashes was placed in the Kremlin wall, in Red Square, Moscow, and his house became a museum.

Boris V. Rauchenbakh

The GIRD X. On 25 November 1933, in the Nakhibino Forest near Moscow, the GIRD X was launched to a height of almost 80 metres, before it turned over and came to land about 150 metres from the launch site. It was the first Soviet liquid fuel rocket and was originally conceived by Tsander at MosGIRD, which was directed by Korolev. In the photograph below, taken just before the launch, Korolev is standing on the extreme left. This rocket was 2·2 metres high and 0·18 metres in diameter; it had a launch mass of 29·5 kilograms. It was fuelled by liquid oxygen and ethanol, fed under pressure to the combustion chamber. It developed a thrust of 700 to 800 newtons, for 22 seconds according to some sources or for 12 to 13 seconds according to others. The Soviet drawing of the rocket, below, shows the structure of GIRD X. From top to bottom, there is the folded parachute, the liquid oxygen tank, the nitrogen tank used to maintain the fuel pressure, the ethanol tank and the motor which was cooled by circulating liquid oxygen.

The GIRD X represented an important step in the history of Soviet rockets. It was the starting point for other more successful rockets launched between 1935 and 1937. It can also be described as the ancestor of the rocket which launched Sputnik 1 (left: Tsiolkovsky Museum; photography, Smithsonian Institution; right: Novosty Press Agency).

The R7 intercontinental ballistic missile. In 1954 Korolev began work on the intercontinental ballistic missile, the R7. It was based on Mikhail Tikhonravov's design incorporating several clusters of rocket stages. For this missile, Valentin Glushko built the rocket engines, RD 107 and RD 108, which were fuelled by liquid oxygen and paraffin oil, and had the unusual design of four combustion chambers. The first R7 was launched on 21 August 1957. Six weeks later, the space launcher version put the first artificial Earth satellite into orbit. This launcher, constantly being uprated, has become the workhorse of the Russian space programme.

This photograph, taken towards the end of the 1950s at the Baikonur Cosmodrome, shows the original version of the ICBM R7. It was 33 metres high, about 10·3 metres in diameter, and had a launch mass of 300 tonnes. Its maximum range was about 7400 kilometres (rights reserved).

occurred. General Becker was so satisfied with the way that the work was progressing that he put to Hitler a proposal for the development of long range ballistic missiles. The new chancellor was impressed with the project, and provided a large grant.

Also in 1935, von Braun and his team were working on a rocket motor, fuelled by liquid oxygen and alcohol, which produced a thrust of nearly 3 kilonewtons. This was to be used to help aeroplanes to take off. Successful tests were carried out in the spring of 1937, using a Heinkel He 112 plane. Activity at Kummersdorf increased to such an extent that the launch site became too small to cope, and a new site had to be found.

Peenemünde, the centre for new weapons

The group from Kummersdorf arrived at Peenemünde, on the Baltic Sea, in April 1937. Von Braun, then twenty-five years old, became the technical director of the Army Rocket Research Centre. From 1937 to 1944, much military research and many rocket developments were carried out at Peenemünde. Problems related to aerodynamics, propulsion and guidance had to be solved. Considerable time and effort was spent building launch tunnels, wind tunnels and testbeds, and by the end of the war several thousand engineers and rocket specialists were working at the site. On the one hand, the Luftwaffe were building several types of air-to-air, ground-to-air and ground-to-ground missiles. On the other, the Wehrmacht were working on ground-to-ground missiles using the V2 rocket, which was given the operational name A4.

Following satisfactory flight tests of the A3, in 1938 the military expressed a wish for a missile to carry a tonne of explosives a distance of 300 kilometres. Thus it was that the A4 came into existence. Initial calculations showed that this rocket would weigh more than 12 tonnes and would need an engine capable of producing a thrust of the order of 250 kilonewtons. This represented an enormous leap in the performance expected of a rocket. Between the A3 and the A4, an intermediate rocket had to be built. This was the A5, used to test the necessary modifications. During its first vertical flight in 1939, the A5 reached a height of 12 kilometres, a considerable altitude for that period.

On 13 June 1942, the first launch of the A4 was a failure. On 16 August, a second launch took place. Although this was not a complete success, the rocket performed remarkably. This was the first time that a vehicle built by man had broken the sound barrier. The third launch on 3 October 1942 proved a complete success. For one minute, the engine delivered the expected thrust. It reached an altitude of 80 kilometres and its range was more than 190 kilometres.

Less than a month later, the A4 rocket went into production, a few kilometres from Peenemünde. It was later transferred to the centre of Germany, where the SS took control. In 1944 and 1945 more than five thousand A4 rockets, which became known as the V2 (Vergeltungswaffe 2: second reprisal weapon) were built. On 6 September 1944, the first operational V2 missile fell on Paris. Two days later the V2 rocket offensive against the South of England began.

Rocket technology went through a period of expansion. Many types, designed exclusively for military use were developed in Germany. These include the Enzian, Rheintochter, Schmetterling, Rheinbote and Wasserfall missiles, and the A9/A10 project. The technology required to design and build rocket aeroplanes also improved, and several examples of operational rocket planes appeared during the last few months of the war.

During the war years the Americans were not idle. Although they did not reach the same standard as the Germans, their researchers made real progress with the development of

A V2 missile on its launcher. From the autumn of 1944, the V2 rockets were launched from camouflaged mobile trailers in France and Holland, fixed launch pads being too vulnerable to attack. The missiles were mounted on cradles and raised vertically by hydraulic jacks.

This photograph was taken in the test complex number 7 at Peenemünde. The conical jet deflector, visible below the fins, was fixed to the missile (Deutsches Museum, Munich).

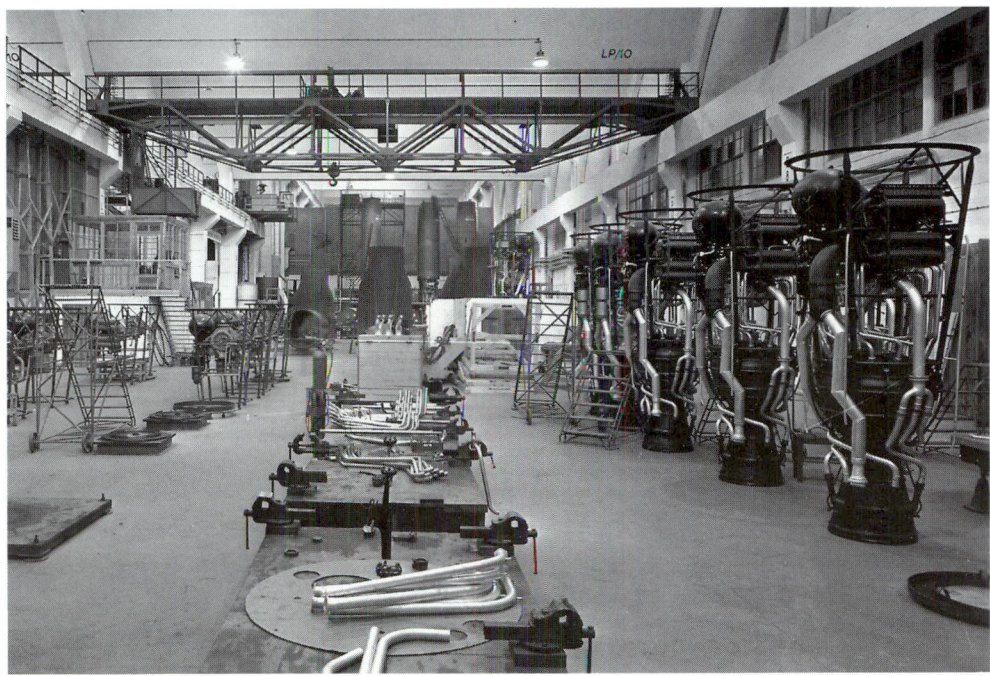

The A4/V2 assembly hall at Peenemünde in 1944. This hall is where both research and assembly of the V2 missiles was carried out. Complete engines are lined up on the right of the photograph (Deutsches Museum, Munich).

Launching a rocket from a submarine. During the summer of 1942, the Germans began testing solid fuel rockets, 21 centimetres in diameter, which could be carried by submarines. These rockets were intended to be launched, while the submarine was submerged, from ramps mounted on the bridge of the class IXC U Boat. Their exhausts were sealed by a diaphragm, and an ignition system was developed which would operate under water. Although these tests were successful, they were not followed up (Deutsches Museum, Munich).

The anti-aircraft missile, Enzian. This missile, built by Messerschmitt, was powered by a liquid fuel rocket, with four solid fuel rockets helping take-off. At launch the missile weighed 1·5 tonnes, was 3·5 metres long and was fitted with glider wings with a span of 4 metres. It was radio controlled and could fly up to 15 kilometres altitude.

Twenty-five Enzian missiles were launched between the beginning of 1944 and the end of the war. Of these, one third reached their targets (Deutsches Museum, Munich).

Wernher von Braun (1912 to 1977)

Wernher Magnus Maximilian von Braun was born on 23 March 1912 in Wirsitz, in the province of Posen, Germany. He was the second of three sons born to Magnus Freiherr von Braun and his wife Emmy von Quisdorp. His father was a *Landrat*, or provincial councillor, one of the founders of the Deutsche Rentenbank (the German Savings Bank) and, in 1931 and 1932, was Minister for Agriculture in the Weimar Republic.

Wernher von Braun showed an early inclination to science and music, generally inheriting his mother's cultural interests rather than his father's preoccupation with business, finance, and politics. In 1923, he entered the famed French school in Berlin, but did not do well there. He moved in 1928 to the progressive Herman Leitz school, where his performance improved greatly.

In 1930, he entered the Technische Universität in Charlottenburg and began an apprenticeship in the *Borsigwerke*, where locomotives were manufactured. At this time he also became fascinated with the idea of space travel and rocketry, having met Hermann Oberth, Willy Ley, Rudolf Nebel and Johannes Winkler, and read of the exploits of men such as Max Valier and his rocket powered automobile. He soon became a member of the Verein für Raumschiffahrt (VfR, the Society for Space Travel) and participated in its experiments at the Raketenflugplatz in Berlin. It was largely through his association with this amateur group that he was to become dedicated to rocketry and eventually to space travel. In 1931, he broadened his engineering background at the Federal Institute of Technology, in Zurich. The following year he returned to Germany to receive his bachelor of science degree in engineering.

On 1 November 1932, von Braun signed a contract with the Ordnance Department of the German Army to conduct research on rockets as military weapons. He came under the influence of Captain Walter Dornberger and, with a grant from the army, entered the Friederichs-Wilhelms Universität. He obtained his doctorate two years later for his dissertation, a theoretical and practical study of the problems of liquid fuel rocket engines.

Once out of the university, his time was fully committed to rocket research at the army's Kummersdorf artillery range, outside Berlin. Von Braun began in earnest the work that would occupy him for the next 43 years and bring him fame throughout the world.

His first effort for Dornberger was not at all auspicious. He refined an earlier rocket engine developed by the VfR which, within seconds of ignition on the night of 21 December 1932, exploded. Nevertheless several colleagues from the VfR soon joined him, working at Kummersdorf and forming the nucleus of his rocket team.

The earliest rocket developed by the small team was the A1, which weighed 150 kilograms, burnt liquid oxygen and ethanol, and produced a thrust of 3 kilonewtons, equivalent to 300 kilograms. In 1934, because of instability, this primitive rocket was redesigned and renamed the A2. Two such missiles were launched in December, from Borkum Island in the Baltic Sea proving the concept of the gyroscopic control of relatively large rockets.

By 1935, von Braun and his team, now 80 strong, carried out static firings of rocket engines with thrusts up to five times as great. Dornberger decided that Kummersdorf would soon be inadequate for testing the larger rockets already on the drawing board. As a result, the army entered into negotiations with the newly established Luftwaffe to build a joint research and testing centre. This had to be in a remote part of the country, for reasons of security. Also, it had to be in a relatively level area, so that the rockets could be tracked by radar and cameras over long distances and rocket propelled aircraft could more easily take off and land.

Von Braun's mother suggested that an area near her childhood home might be worth consideration. It was not far from Anklam, a small town at the mouth of the river Peene (Peenemünde), some 140 kilometres north of Berlin, on Usedom Island in the Baltic Sea. After visiting the site, Dornberger agreed that it was the perfect location. For less than a million Reichsmarks, the site was bought from the town of Wolgast and construction work started immediately.

But research continued at Kummersdorf as the clouds of war were again gathering over Europe. In March 1939, staff remaining at Kummersdorf received a visit from Adolf Hitler. After extensive briefings on the potential of the rocket as a weapon, Hitler observed at first hand static firings of various rocket engines.

With the advent of advanced facilities at Peenemünde for the design, testing and launching of large rockets, Dornberger knew that the time had come for the development of an operational military missile. This was to be the A4. To carry a one tonne warhead over a distance of 360 kilometres, its engine had to produce a hundred times greater thrust than the A1 rocket did. It would become better known as the V2 rocket.

As work proceeded on the V2 and other rocket weapons, such as an anti-aircraft missile, von Braun's team grew to nearly six thousand. Activity peaked in 1942, and the A4 was successfully launched for the first time on 3 October. However, it was another two years before the weapon was unleashed on London. On 17 August 1943, Peenemünde was raided by 600 Royal Air Force bombers. Although the physical destruction was relatively light, nearly 800 people were killed.

On 15 March 1944, von Braun was arrested by the Gestapo for speaking openly of using rockets for space travel when he should have been praising the weapon that would win the war for Germany. Having spent several weeks in prison at Stettin, it was only by the personal intervention of Albert Speer, the Minister of Armaments, and Hitler himself that von Braun was released to the custody of General Dornberger and allowed to return to his duties at Peenemünde.

Facing the inexorable advance of the Soviet army from the east, von Braun realised early in 1945 that Peenemünde must be evacuated. With the British and Americans to the west, von Braun and his team had no option but to move south to Thuringia and to resume operations near the underground factory where the V1 and V2 missiles were made, at Niedersachswerfen near Nordhausen. There he attempted to organise an operation similar to that at Peenemünde.

However, in the chaotic final weeks of the war, and with communications all but impossible, von Braun broke his arm in a car accident and had to spend much of his time in hospital. On 2 May 1945, with his brother Magnus, several other engineers and General Dornberger, he surrendered to the Forty-fourth Infantry Division of the US Army.

In the autumn of 1945, von Braun and some 120 of his engineers signed contracts for six months of consultancy work with the US Army. With six colleagues, he arrived at Fort Strong, in Boston, on 20 September. After a few days in Washington being briefed by Ordnance Department officers on his new duties, von Braun left for Fort Bliss, Texas, near the Mexican border, where he remained for five years.

At Fort Bliss, and at the newly established White Sands Missile Range some 130 kilometres to the north in the desert of New Mexico, von Braun was soon joined by the remaining members of his team. They were disappointed at not being able to improve on the rocket technology which they had developed during the previous decade. Instead, they were called upon to help assemble and check V2 rockets before firing at the White Sands Proving Ground to train American soldiers.

It was then that von Braun began writing his first book, *Das Marsprojekt*, a mixture of fact and speculation which dealt with a voyage to Mars in the not too distant future.

By 1949, the Army Ordnance Corps realised that the facilities at Fort Bliss would not be sufficient for a major research and development programme in long range military rockets. A review of available installations revealed that the Redstone Arsenal in Huntsville, Alabama, was both available and ideal. So the group began moving from Texas in April 1950 and, within eight months, 130 Germans and 300 other personnel had joined von Braun there. The long range surface-to-surface missile which von Braun and his team designed was the Redstone. With a range and payload no greater than those of the V2, the first Redstone was launched from Cape Canaveral, in Florida, on 20 August 1953.

A dream realised. In the upper photograph, taken at the beginning of the 1950s, von Braun is examining a mock up of a launcher designed to serve an orbiting space station, where a rocket would be built and then launched to the Moon. This giant launcher, 81 metres tall, 19·8 metres in diameter at the base and with a launch mass of 6350 tonnes, had three recoverable stages, the first two using parachutes and the third fitted with wings and fins, similar to the space shuttle (collection of F. I. Ordway III).

The photograph in the centre, taken on 31 January 1958, shows William H. Pickering, Director of the Jet Propulsion Laboratory, James A. Van Allen, who became famous for discovering the radiation belts around the Earth, and Wernher von Braun at a press conference at the National Academy of Sciences. This was held after a Juno I rocket put the first American satellite, Explorer I, successfully into orbit (US Army, collection of F. I. Ordway III).

The lower photograph was taken on 16 July 1969, just after the successful launch of Apollo 11. Both joy and relief are clearly seen in the faces of Charles W. Mathews, Associate Administrator for Manned Space Flights, Wernher von Braun, George E. Mueller, Administrator for Manned Space Flights and General Samuel C. Phillips, Director of the Apollo Program (NASA, collection of F. I. Ordway III).

Von Braun then turned his thoughts to a subject that had been absolutely forbidden when he was developing the V2, namely space exploration by rockets – military rockets. On 15 September 1954, he submitted a report to his commander and friend, Colonel Toftoy, entitled 'A minimum satellite vehicle based on components available from missile developments of the Army Ordnance Corps'. In it, von Braun proposed launching a satellite weighing two kilograms using the Redstone rocket as the first stage and clusters of small, solid fuel rockets, called Loki, as upper stages. He felt that the project could be realised in two years. This report became the basis for a joint satellite programme involving the US Army and the US Navy, later referred to as Project Orbiter. In the end, however, it was not pursued since an all Navy plan, Project Vanguard, was chosen instead.

In the summer of 1955, von Braun's team – by now American citizens – were ordered to design and build a liquid fuel missile, later named Jupiter, that could carry a payload of almost a tonne over a distance of 2500 kilometres. To do this, the Army Ballistic Missile Agency (ABMA) was formed at Redstone Arsenal, on 1 February 1956, under Major General John B. Medaris. The highlight of that year came on 20 September, when a three stage Jupiter C test rocket reached an altitude of almost 1000 kilometres and a range of 5000 kilometres.

On 31 May 1957, von Braun witnessed the first launching of the full Jupiter missile from Cape Canaveral. Then, on August 8, another Jupiter C was launched into space to test a scale model of the nosecone that would protect the atomic warhead of an Intermediate Range Ballistic Missile (IRBM) as it reentered the Earth's atmosphere. Von Braun and his fellow engineers were proving that they had the rockets that could give America the lead in space.

The shattering news that the Soviets had orbited Sputnik 1 on 4 October 1957, coupled with the knowledge that the Vanguard programme was not without its technical difficulties, led Secretary of Defense Neil McElroy to order the ABMA team to prepare two satellites and rockets for launching them by March 1958. It did not take von Braun and his associates both at ABMA and at the Jet Propulsion Laboratory of the California Institute of Technology that long. In fact, they were ready by late January with a Juno 1 rocket, a Jupiter C with a solid fuel fourth stage added, and a small satellite payload. However, Army headquarters in Washington and the White House did not want any news of the attempted launching to be made public in case it should fail.

After several delays because of high winds above Cape Canaveral, the Juno 1 rocket lifted off at 22.48 Local Time on 31 January 1958. Wernher von Braun was unable to witness this historic event, as he was in Washington to speak to the media once the satellite was in orbit around the Earth. Von Braun waited nervously in the Pentagon with an equally nervous Dr William Pickering, Director of the Jet Propulsion Laboratory. Eventually, telemetry signals from the small satellite were received, proving that America's first satellite, Explorer 1, was orbiting the Earth.

Other American successes followed. Explorer 3, instrumented to support the findings of Explorer 1, was launched on 26 March 1958. On 3 March 1959 the Juno 2 launch vehicle, which consisted of a Jupiter IRBM first stage and three Juno 1 upper stages sent Pioneer 4, a 7 kilogram interplanetary probe, on a trajectory that passed the Moon by at a distance of 60 000 kilometres and continued into an orbit about the Sun. Seven months later, another Juno 2 placed the 42 kilogram Explorer 7 satellite into Earth orbit to measure radiation in space.

On 15 August 1958, von Braun realised a long held ambition, the design of an extremely powerful rocket with a first stage thrust of over five meganewtons. However, the project had to be carried out with minimum funding, and rapidly. The concept was to use a cluster of available rocket engines, propellant tanks and pumps. In other words, flight tested Redstone and Jupiter missile components were used to construct the first stage of what later became known as the Saturn 1 launch vehicle. At that time, however, the huge rocket was confined to static firing in a tower, and was never launched.

Von Braun's enthusiasm was soon dampened by rumours that ABMA's Development Operations Division might be taken from the Army to become part of the newly established National Aeronautics and Space Administration (NASA). In December 1958, the Army agreed to release the Jet Propulsion Laboratory (JPL) to NASA, but announced that it would retain ABMA intact.

On January 20, 1959, von Braun was honoured by President Dwight D. Eisenhower, who bestowed on him the Distinguished Federal Service Medal. Despite this award, morale at ABMA dropped severely as the year progressed. Rumours that the Development Operations Division would be transferred to NASA were confirmed on 14 January 1960, when it was officially announced that von Braun's group would become the George C. Marshall Space Flight Center (MSFC) and would remain at Huntsville's Redstone Arsenal. This new Center, opened on 1 July 1960, was given responsibility for developing all rocket launching vehicles for NASA. It took over the Redstone Mercury, the Juno 2, the Atlas based Centaur and Agena B upper stages, various Saturn configurations, and the F 1 liquid propellant rocket engine. By the end of 1960, the team at von Braun's new centre had orbited its first spacecraft for NASA, the 40 kilogram Explorer 3 scientific satellite, using the Juno 2 vehicle.

On 25 May 1961, President John F. Kennedy's speech to Congress galvanised the USA into action for a vast new scientific and technological endeavour. 'Now is the time to take longer strides', he said, 'time for a greater new America, time for this nation to take a clearly leading role in space achievement which in many ways may hold the key to our future on Earth... I believe that this nation should commit itself to achieving the goal of landing a man on the Moon and returning him safely to Earth by the end of the decade.'

With this objective of manned lunar exploration, soon to become known as the Apollo programme, activity at MSFC increased. Opinion was divided, however, between the various NASA centres as to how best to accomplish the task. Von Braun and his colleagues preferred a technique known as 'Earth orbital rendezvous'. This foresaw the launching of a Saturn 5 rocket into orbit about the Earth. It would have a tank containing some 95 tonnes of liquid oxygen aboard. Another Saturn 5 would be launched into orbit, with the spacecraft astronauts and the required liquid hydrogen. The two rockets would rendezvous, link, and then the astronauts would pump the liquid oxygen aboard. Thus refuelled, they would travel on to the Moon.

An alternative mode called 'lunar orbital rendezvous' was proposed by John Houbolt and his colleagues at NASA's Langley Research Center. This idea was not original; it had occurred earlier to such space pioneers as Hermann Oberth in Germany and several members of the British Interplanetary Society. Lunar orbital rendezvous certainly sounded simpler and less expensive. A single Saturn 5 rocket would launch a two part spacecraft into orbit about the Moon. There it would separate, with two crew members descending to the lunar surface in one part while their fellow astronaut circled the Moon in the other. Having finished their exploration, the men on the Moon would rejoin their orbiting companion and discard the lunar 'taxi'. It was calculated that such a scheme would save over 4 tonnes in the weight of the spacecraft alone. Some members of von Braun's team considered this too risky. However, von Braun urged them to study the proposal in greater detail – he had an open mind. When it became apparent that the technique was feasible, von Braun accepted it and, as a NASA Center director, began endorsing it. In the end, the lunar orbital rendezvous procedure was adopted.

Because of the size and complexity of the Saturn 5 launch vehicle, it became impossible for the Marshall Center to continue its efforts at managing the several other NASA rocket projects mentioned above. Thus, the Agena B and Centaur stages were transferred to other agencies, and von Braun concentrated on the Saturn 5.

On 9 November 1967, the very first Saturn 5 rocket blasted off from the launch pad at Cape Canaveral, Florida, on an almost perfect maiden flight. Amid all the shouting and congratulations, Wernher von Braun turned to his friend Arthur Rudolph, the Saturn 5 project manager, and said: 'I would never have believed that it could happen.' Other Saturn 5 launches followed, sending Apollo spacecraft around the Moon in late 1968 and the spring of 1969 and, beginning with Apollo 11 on 16 July 1969, onto the Moon itself.

When the manned lunar landing programme ended with Apollo 17 in December 1972, the von Braun team turned its efforts to Skylab, the first US space station. But von Braun was no longer with his teammates, for in 1970 he had moved from Huntsville to Washington to become NASA's Deputy Associate Administrator in charge of advanced planning. After two years in that capacity, he foresaw an uncertain future for NASA. This was a factor in his resignation, two years later, and his subsequent acceptance of a position as Vice President for Engineering and Development at Fairchild Industries in Germantown, Maryland. His initial interest there focused on the Applications Technology Satellite (ATS 6), for which Fairchild was prime contractor to NASA. In his view, that project was an excellent example of how space technology benefited practical applications on Earth.

Von Braun made a number of presentations to government leaders in Spain, Iran, Brazil, Venezuela and Indonesia to explain how advances in satellite communications, as demonstrated by ATS 6, could help developing nations. He directed Fairchild's Strategic Planning Group and was instrumental in winning initial contracts in energy development in connection with the US Department of Energy's coal gasification programme. He also sponsored the establishment of a corporate community laboratory that led to the development of small, inexpensive Earth receiving stations for satellite communications. Von Braun also played a key role in involving Fairchild Industries in NASA's space shuttle programme, and he devoted extensive time and energy to the organisation and growth of the National Space Institute.

His health deteriorating, von Braun retired on 31 December 1976. Early in 1977, President Gerald Ford awarded him the National Medal of Science. Wernher von Braun died in Alexandria, Virginia, on 16 June 1977, survived by his wife, three children, and two brothers.

Frederick I. Ordway III
and Mitchell R. Sharpe

The A4b. Static tests on the A4b experimental rocket, shown on the left, began in the summer of 1944; the first launch on 27 December was a failure. This rocket was fitted with large fins which should have doubled its range.

The photograph, taken on 24 January 1945 on the test complex number 10 at Peenemünde, shows an A4b rocket just before its first successful flight later on the same day. A military version of the A4b was never constructed (Deutsches Museum, Munich).

The Me 163. Germany was the first country to develop rocket planes. The Messerschmitt Me 163A fighter plane above began gliding flight tests in May 1941. It was then fitted with a liquid fuel Walter engine. In the autumn of the same year it began powered flight tests. It reached speeds of 965 kilometres per hour, outstripping the performance of propeller driven fighters of the same period which obtained speeds of only around 560 kilometres per hour. An improved version, the Me 163B, was constructed using a more powerful engine and rockets to assist take-off. About 300 of these were built and put into service in the last few months of the Second World War. In spite of their reduced range (about 10 minutes) these planes attacked so quickly that the Allies' machine guns were useless against them (rights reserved).

The JATO rockets. During the Second World War, the US developed several solid and liquid fuel rocket engines to assist a plane taking off. These rockets, called JATO (Jet Assisted Take-Off), were mainly used on bombers and heavy seaplanes. This photograph shows the first flight test of this type of rocket plane, on 12 July 1941, at March Field, California. An Ercoupe light aircraft was fitted with 6 JATO rockets, each capable of delivering a thrust of 125 newtons for 12 seconds (Smithsonian Institution).

The first American rocket plane, the MX 324/334. The Northrop MX 324/334 was designed as a 'flying wing', 9·75 metres in diameter and 3·70 metres long. The pilot lay flat, to lessen the effects of acceleration on his body. This photograph of the non-powered version, the MX 324, was taken in April 1944, shortly before the first gliding flight test. The powered version (MX 334) flew for the first time on 5 July 1944. It was fitted with an Aerojet XCAL 200 engine, fuelled by nitric acid and monoethylaniline, and produced a thrust of 900 newtons. Other flight tests were carried out but, at the end of the war, the programme came to be abandoned (Northrop).

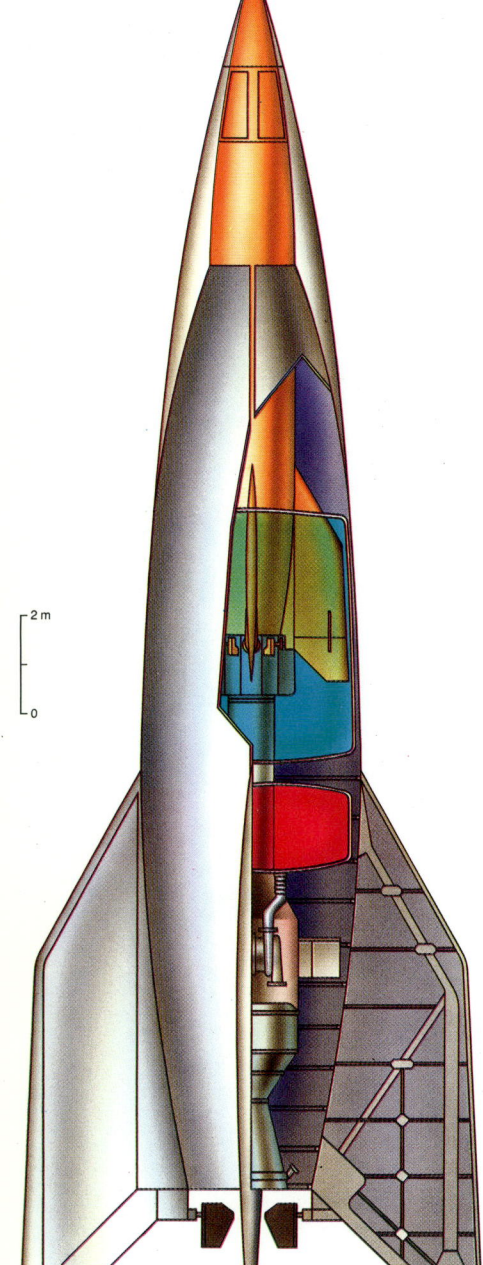

One of the last projects at Peenemünde (left). This was an A9/A10 two stage rocket, with a mass of 85 tonnes at launch, designed using the expertise that had been acquired with the V2 missile. The second stage (A9) section was in fact a slightly modified V2, but the first stage (A10) had a thrust of nearly 1·8 meganewtons. Due to lack of time, the A9/A10 never reached the operational phase, but it was the first intercontinental missile project. It had been planned to use it to bombard New York from the French Atlantic coast. Its efficacy was, however, quite low, with respect to its cost. It was not fitted with a nuclear warhead, but with a tonne of ordinary explosive, so its effect would have been more psychological than destructive.

The A9/A10 project led to the realisation that space exploration was possible. The engineers at Peenemünde conceived the A11, an A9/A10 rocket fitted with a third stage. This would have been powerful enough to put a man into orbit. There was also the possibility of an A12 stage with a thrust of 10 meganewtons. This four stage rocket would have been capable of placing 27 tonnes into orbit.

Tiny Tim (right). The biggest of the air-to-ground missiles of the Second World War was the American 'Tiny Tim'. It was 3·15 metres long, weighed 580 kilograms and carried 150 kilograms of TNT. Its main purpose was to destroy Japanese fortifications, and it was used against Okinawa in the autumn of 1944. This photograph was taken during tests in the Mojave desert, in California (PPP).

Soviet rockets. Soviet groups that had been working on rockets during the 1930s were transferred at the beginning of the Second World War to begin work on the Katyuska. These solid fuel rockets carried explosive charges. They were launched from ramps which were either fixed or mobile. The absence of recoil and simplicity were the prinipal advantages of these rockets over shells fired frcm cannons.

Their efficiency was further increased by firing the 8 centimetre diameter model from multitube rocket launchers. Their firing power was enormous. Some 16 to 48 Katyuska could be launched simultaneously from one vehicle, making them formidable saturation weapons (APN).

The WAC Corporal rocket probe. This rocket was conceived by the Jet Propulsion Laboratory at Pasadena, California. It was a liquid fuel rocket, which carried a scientific payload weighing more than 11 kilograms to an altitude of 70 kilometres.

The project chief was Frank Marina, who is pictured above with one of these rockets, 30 centimetres in diameter and 4·9 metres tall. On take-off it was boosted by two solid fuel boosters based on the Tiny Tim engine (Smithsonian Institution).

rocket engines for aircraft. The MX 324/334 was the first American rocket plane, and was tested in July 1944. In 1941 members of the American Rocket Society formed Reaction Motors, a company which went on to play an important role in establishing American technology. Also worthy of mention is the experimental rocket programme begun in 1944 by the Artillery Command. The WAC Corporal rocket was based on a solid fuel booster and a nitric acid/aniline rocket engine. It was tested at White Sands, New Mexico, in the autumn of 1945, and in March 1946 reached a maximum altitude of 72·4 kilometres.

In the Soviet Union, work on the space applications of rockets was somewhat curtailed during the Second World War. The Soviets concentrated on developing solid fuel rockets (Katyuska) for military purposes and to assist the take-off of planes.

Occupied France did not carry out any real research. However, Colonel Jean-Jacques Barré pursued Esnault-Pelterie's work in secret, in Lyon, and built a liquid oxygen and petrol rocket, called the EA 41. Tests on this rocket could not, however, take place until after the liberation of France in 1944.

Jacques Villain

An Ohka Japanese suicide plane. During the Second World War, the Japanese used ground-to-air barrage rockets, non-guided bombs boosted by solid fuel rockets, and radio controlled ground-to-air missiles.

The most famous and most sinister weapon was, however, the Ohka suicide plane. Conceived in 1943, it went into service in April 1945, inflicting heavy losses on the US Navy. It consisted of a 1200 kilogram bomb, which made up more than half the total mass of the plane. The wooden wings had a span of 5 metres. The fuselage, also made of wood, was 6 metres long, and housed a rudimentary set of controls. The Ohka, a glider, was dropped from an aeroplane, and flown by a Kamikaze pilot. Three solid fuel rockets provided a thrust of 7·5 kilonewtons for a period of 10 seconds, sending the plane towards its target at about 1000 kilometres per hour. Marines are here examining an Ohka at the Japanese base at Yokosuka, in August 1945 (PPP).

The French EA 41 rocket. The first French liquid fuel rocket was built by Colonel Jean-Jacques Barré during the Second World War, unbeknown to the occupying Germans. Static tests were carried out in 1941, but flight tests had to wait until after the liberation of France. They were finally performed at the Établissement d'expériences techniques de La Renardière, near Toulon.

J.-J. Barré had continued the work started by Robert Esnault-Pelterie. At the beginning of the 1950s he built a rocket, called Eole, fuelled by liquid oxygen. This rocket was tested at the Laboratoire de recherches balistiques et aérodynamiques (LRBA), at Vernon (rights reserved).

The golden age of science fiction
(1918 to 1945)

By 1918, it was clear that the rocket was going to be the means by which man travelled into space. However, science fiction was not content to represent the near future, or something which was believed possible. It strode far ahead of the scientific work being done.

Some writers followed the Tsiolkovsky train of thought, believing that the space age was near at hand and that man must be prepared for it. To a certain extent such authors and scientists depended on each other. In 1927, Hermann Oberth and Willy Ley founded the first society for space travel, the German Verein für Raumschiffahrt, and the same two men were later scientific advisers for Fritz Lang's film *Frau im Mond* (The Woman in the Moon, 1929). It was on this occasion, memorably, that the film makers decided that their astronauts would not wear spacesuits on the Moon as the audience would find it absurd.

Shortly after this, both the American Interplanetary Society and the British Interplanetary Society were founded. In 1939, the British author and Interplanetary Society member,

Arthur C. Clarke, published a famous article entitled 'We can rocket to the Moon – now!'. Five years later, Willy Ley, who emigrated to the USA in 1935, published his book *Rockets: the future of travel beyond the stratosphere*. This became the reference on which all subsequent space science fiction was based.

Space technology provided only a narrow viewpoint, of course, and imaginative literature could go beyond the mere routine of space travel. So, in *The Skylark of Space* (1928), Edward E. 'Doc' Smith invented a type of fiction now known as *Space Opera*. Burroughs' planetary epic now became a galactic epic, with spacecraft flying faster than the speed of light and weapons destroying entire planets.

This type of fiction, although popular, rapidly became repetitive and was soon discredited. Smith was aware of Einstein's theory of relativity, which has always been a thorn in the side of science fiction. Yet writers in general have always felt that there has to be a way of travelling faster than light. As a result, their imagination tends to run away with them, for

example into hyperspace, matter transference, and doors in space (as in *2001*). Lester del Rey, writing after Smith, even claimed to have invented a new pseudoscientific concept in every story he produced.

For all that, some authors were aware of the scientific pitfalls and looked for other, more plausible solutions. Astronauts could be put into hibernation, as in A. E. Van Vogt's novel, *Far Centaurus* (1942). Or they could be sent to the stars in a giant spacecraft, perpetually reproducing themselves until they reach their destination. This formula, first developed in Robert Heinlein's book *Orphans of the Sky* (1942) has proved very popular in the half century since.

All science fiction from this era appears extremely optimistic and invites us to believe in indefinite progress. Essentially, space has ceased to be a magical somewhere, and has become an attainable tomorrow.

Jacques Goimard

The other side of the picture. This set of *Frau im Mond* gives an idea of the scale of work carried out by the Berlin studios while producing this film. The mock up of the rocket was life size, and the 'Méliès style' mountains on the horizon were immense. The ceiling of the studio, with its sunlights, reminds us of *Close Encounters of the Third Kind*. But the astronauts are not wearing spacesuits – much to the annoyance of Oberth, the producers thought that the public would be confused by so improbable an innovation (Cinémathèque française).

The image of the flying city. This idea has hardly altered since Jonathan Swift described it in *Gulliver's Travels* (1726). The key innovations here are the small size, which prevents us from seeing the inhabitants, and the means by which the city is held in the air. There are two types of spacecraft – large, long range ones and small ones used for travelling only inside the city (illustration by Frank R. Paul, for the cover of *Air Wonder Stories*, November 1929, for *Cities in the Air* by Edmond Hamilton; © 1929 Gernsback Publications Inc.).

Heading for the stars. H. G. Wells, the scriptwriter for *Things to Come* produced by William Cameron Menzies and released in 1936, was a great pessimist. However, this film ends on an optimistic note: mankind will save itself by leaving Earth for the stars. At the end of the film, there is an image of a spacecraft starting out on its voyage. Wells imagined a colossal telescope with a video relay. For the first time, the style of the set was futuristic; nowadays it is clear that it was factually correct (Prod./D.B.).

A prophetic illustration of 1931. An astronaut, holding onto his spacecraft with one hand, rescues another astronaut. The same image reappears in *2001*, some four decades later. An artificial death star is firing at another: this concept reappears in *Star Wars*, half a century later. In space wars, the spacesuits become uniforms, a recurring image in science fiction (illustration by Leo Morey on the cover of *Amazing Stories*, August 1931, for *Spacehounds of IPC*, by Edward E. Smith; © 1931 Radio-Science Publications Inc., rights reserved).

A futuristic version of Noah's ark. At the end of the 1930s, science fiction became less serious. Many old myths were rewritten, set in the future. In this picture, animals are entering the ark two by two, but the crowd of people who also want to leave are prevented from doing so by troops (illustration by Howard V. Brown, on the cover of *Startling Stories*, November 1939, for *The Fortress of Utopia* by Jack Williamson; in B. Aldiss, *Science Fiction Art*, 1975; © Sceptre Books, London).

Flash Gordon, **by Alex Raymond.** This cartoon is the best comic strip from the 1930s, and one of the best of its genre since. The theme of struggling against a tyrant was borrowed from the reality of the crusade against fascism. This illustration is taken from the French translation of the comic strip, where Flash was known as 'Guy l'Eclair'. The caption reads 'Overwhelmed by numbers, Guy and Zarkov shoot down several of their opponents before being hit themselves' (from *Robinson*, 11 July 1937; © KFS distr., Opera Mundi).

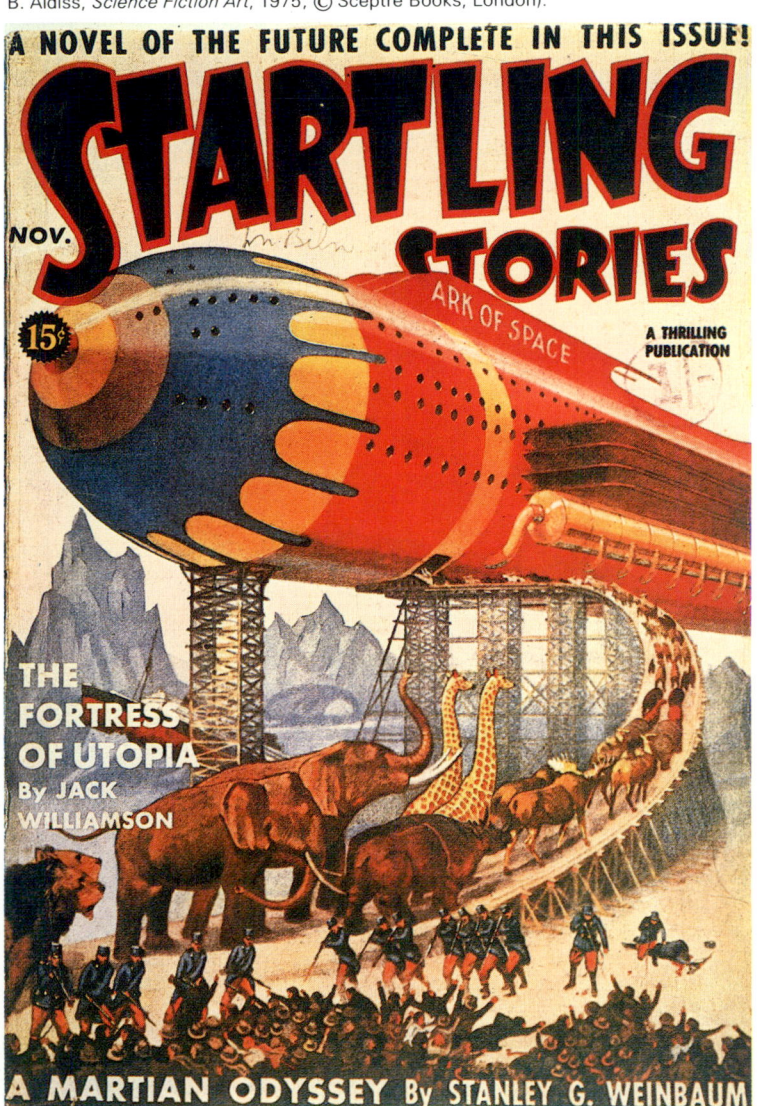

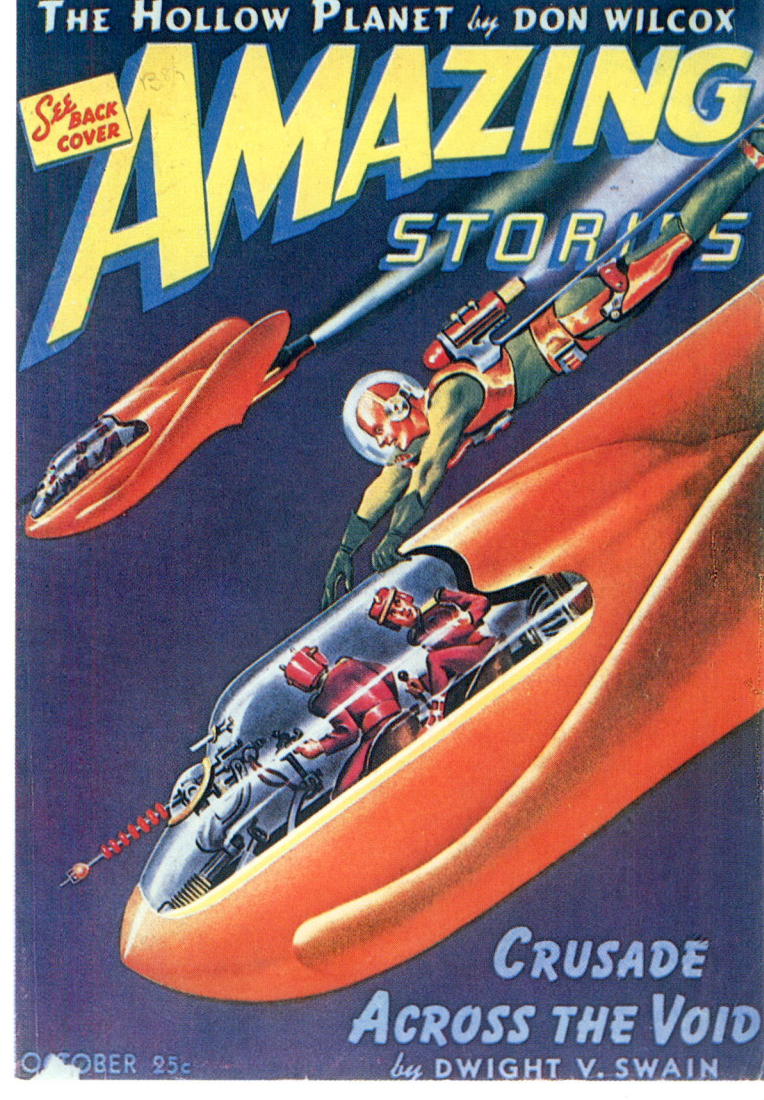

Standardised science fiction. These small spacecraft look like fighter planes after the Second World War. Military astronauts, bearing a strong resemblance to Superman cartoons, wear small rocket packs. Once again, the dream of spaceflight is confronted by the realities of war (illustration by Malcolm Smith, on the cover of *Amazing Stories*, October 1942, for the story *Crusade Across the Void*, by Dwight V. Swain; © 1942 Ziff-Davis Publishing Co., rights reserved).

Prelude to space

Once Germany had been defeated, the Allies set about distributing the spoils of war. Through Operation Paperclip, the Americans recovered all the rockets that were still under construction, the archives at Peenemünde and, most importantly, the men working there themselves. Wernher von Braun, Walter Dornberger and other specialists emigrated to America. Convoys of boats, filled with V1 and V2 rocket motors and various other materials, crossed the Atlantic, an operation carried out at a frenetic speed to prevent the Soviets from obtaining the most well known specialists. They did, even so, acquire a large number of staff in charge of production of the rockets. France also benefited from the bonanza; several V1 and V2 rockets, and about 40 German technicians and engineers, made their way to France in 1946 and 1947. They formed the first state controlled and industrial teams working in this field.

There is no doubt that it was due to the Germans, and in particular the possibilities offered by the V2, that the United States and the Soviet Union were able to start the space and missile race as soon as the Second World War ended. Other European countries did not have comparable budgets and means, so their programmes lagged a few years behind those of the two superpowers.

American developments

From 1945 onwards, both the United States and the Soviet Union began two programmes – one geared to the conquest of space, the second to the development of ballistic missiles. However, although the ultimate aim was to explore space, initial experiments were concerned with the study of the upper atmosphere. Von Braun held on to his youthful dreams of interplanetary voyages, and he proposed a project to construct a manned artificial satellite. However, before this could be realised, a rocket launcher was needed.

The principal groups and organisations were first created. Von Braun's team were installed at Fort Bliss, under the supervision of the US Army, and charged with the job of testing the recovered V2 rockets. The first V2 was launched from American soil on 16 April 1946. For the next six years, the V2 rockets, some of which had been extensively modified, were used for radiation measurements, ionospheric studies, photography of the Earth and so on. These activities, which also involved the US Navy, were coordinated by a commission created on 16 January 1947. This was the V2 Upper Atmospheric Research Panel, directed by James A. Van Allen. At about the same time, the Jet Propulsion Laboratory (JPL) was created; it too went on to play a most important role in the exploration of space.

The US Army, US Navy and US Air Force also maintained their interests in ballistic missiles. In 1946, the US Air Force began an intercontinental ballistic missile project, the MX 774. Several years later this formed the basis of the Atlas missile and launcher. And on 6 September 1947, the Navy fired a V2 from the deck of the aircraft carrier, *Midway*, in order to evaluate the possibilities of using this new type of weapon.

There were also parallel developments in the field of astronautics. In December 1948, James V. Forrestal, the Secretary of State for Defense, revealed that the US was studying the

The legacy of Peenemünde. Under the terms of the Yalta Agreement of 1945, the German region in which some V2 production factories (notably Bleicherode and Nordhausen) were sited was to be placed under Soviet control. A 'V2 special mission' was quickly organised by Colonel Holger N. Toftoy. It was he who was responsible for Operation Paperclip, set up to salvage all the German equipment, send it to Anvers and then New Orleans by ship. The US Army occupied Nordhausen on 10 April 1945. The first convoy left on 22 May and the last on 31 May, the day before the Soviets were due to arrive. In this photograph, an American officer is examining an almost complete V2 rocket in the underground factory at Nordhausen (PPP).

Wernher von Braun and the growth of American astronautics. After negotiations with American intelligence agents, Wernher von Braun joined the forty-fourth Infantry Division of the US Army, on 2 May 1945, at the Austrian village of Reutte. Shortly before this photograph was taken, he had broken his arm in a car accident; on the left is Walter Dornberger.

In September 1945, at the age of 33, von Braun arrived in America and began his second career. Through the US Army, he was involved in the first American ballistic missile programmes, Redstone and Jupiter. The USA used a launcher based on the Jupiter missile to place their first artificial satellite, Explorer 1, into orbit on 31 January 1958. Von Braun's work was then taken over by NASA, so he moved on to become Director of the Marshall Space Flight Center (Keystone).

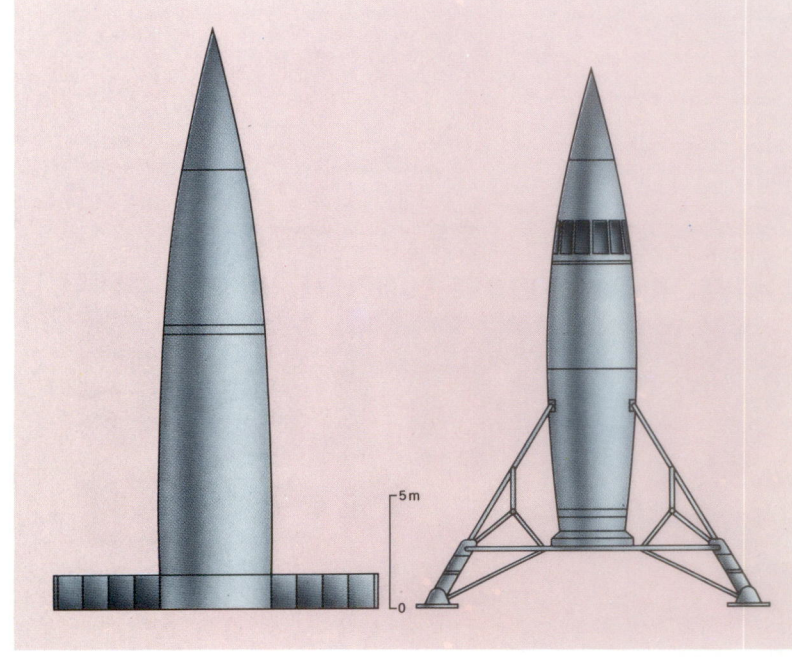

Two early American space projects. The single stage High Altitude Test Vehicle (HATV), on the left, was a project of the US Navy and the Bureau of Aeronautics. It was designed to be placed into orbit, being both a rocket and a satellite. It had nine liquid hydrogen and oxygen engines, capable of producing a thrust of 1·3 meganewtons. Its launch mass was up to 46 tonnes, and it was 25·8 metres high with a maximum diameter of 4·8 metres.

This project was found to be too expensive and was replaced by the Experimental World Cycling Spaceship (EWCS). This programme was paid for by the US Army and Air Force, but the work was carried out in the Rand Division of the Douglas Aircraft aeronautics firm. The three stage launcher (on the right) had a launch mass of 37 tonnes. With liquid hydrogen and oxygen rocket engines, it was capable of placing a 225 kilogram payload into a circular orbit at an altitude of 480 kilometres.

Neither of these projects in the end came to fruition. Thus America missed the opportunity of being the first country to conquer space.

Launching the first American V2 rocket. On 16 April 1946, the first V2, built and adapted by the Americans as part of their Hermes project, was launched from the White Sands Proving Ground, in New Mexico. The observation tower is visible on the left, and the assembly crane and gantry, brought from Germany, are evident on the right. By the end of the Hermes project, on 30 June 1951, 67 V2 rockets had been reconstructed and tested. Most of these had been substantially modified. On 17 December 1946, one of the rockets attained an altitude of 187 kilometres, carrying a scientific payload designed to study cosmic rays and micrometeorites (PPP).

The X1 rocket plane. The Americans soon recognised the potential of rocket planes. On 14 October 1947, Charles E. ('Chuck') Yeager entered the history books as the first man to break the sound barrier. He achieved this in the Bell X1 plane, which was launched from a B29 bomber. The Reaction Motors XLR 11 rocket engine was fuelled by liquid oxygen and ethanol, and delivered a thrust of nearly 27 kilonewtons in steps of about 7 kilonewtons, using its four combustion chambers. The XLR 11 had a long and distinguished career. It was constantly improved, and powered three versions of the X1, the first X15 and the prototype of the M2-F3 reentry glider (PPP).

The Aerobee 150 rocket probe. The development of the Aerobee series can be traced back to the end of the 1940s. The first version, with a mass of about 500 kilograms, could carry about 50 kilograms of scientific instruments to an altitude of 120 kilometres. It was notable at this time because the initial acceleration was provided by a solid fuel rocket delivering a thrust of 83 kilonewtons. An improved version, called the Aerobee Hi, went into service in 1952. This was the forerunner of the Aerobee 150 which appeared at the beginning of the 1960s. The Aerobee 150 was 9·1 metres long and could carry a 70 kilogram payload to an altitude of 270 kilometres. Two more powerful versions, the Aerobee 300 and the Aerobee 350, were produced later (NASA).

A new 'first'. On 20 November 1953, a plane went faster than Mach 2. Called the Douglas D558 11 Skyrocket, it was piloted by A. Scott Crossfield. This photograph was taken immediately after it was launched from a B29 carrier plane. It achieved a speed of 2132 kilometres per hour (Mach 2·005). It was powered by a Reaction Motors LR8 RM6 rocket engine, delivering a thrust of more than 26 kilonewtons.

American rocket planes, and in particular the X15, led to intensive studies in the field of high altitude and high speed flights. This stood the Americans in good stead during the later space shuttle programme (Smithsonian Institution).

The Bumper rocket (left). After mastering the technology required to construct the V2 rocket, the US Army proceeded with eight launchings of the Bumper rocket between 1948 and 1950. It illustrated the close coupling of German and American technology – the first stage was a V2 and the second stage a WAC Corporal. On 24 February 1949, during its fifth flight test, the only one which was completely successful, the second stage reached an altitude of 393 kilometres. This was a record height at that time. The maximum velocity was 8290 kilometres per hour.

This particular Bumper rocket was launched on 2 April 1949. It only achieved an altitude of 50 kilometres due to the premature cut out of the first stage. The seventh and eighth flight tests are famous because they were carried out at a new launch site, Cape Canaveral in Florida (PPP).

The Viking 12 rocket probe (right). On its first flight on 3 May 1949, the American Viking rocket probe reached a height of 80 kilometres. It was propelled by a liquid oxygen and alcohol engine providing a thrust of 91 kilonewtons. On 4 February 1955, a Viking 12 launched from White Sands reached an altitude of 240 kilometres. This rocket weighed 6·7 tonnes, was 12·6 metres high and 1·14 metres in diameter. It was the forerunner of the first stage of the Vanguard rocket launcher (Smithsonian Institution).

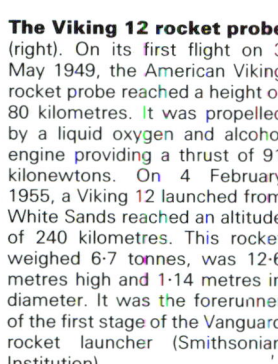

possibilities of launching a satellite. He recommended to Congress that they create a single organisation for studying satellites, work until then carried out by all three armed forces.

An important stage was reached on 24 February 1949, with the successful launch of the Bumper rocket. During the same period, the US Navy was also involved in building upper atmosphere probes. The Viking rocket, conceived in 1946, and inspired by the V2, carried out 14 flights between 1949 and 1957. Its later flights were used to test certain components of the Vanguard launcher. In parallel with the Viking rocket, the US Navy designed and built the Aerobee rocket probe, an improved version of the WAC Corporal.

The next stage of development was the US Army's second generation V2 rocket. In 1950, von Braun's team began work on the Redstone missile. Inspired by the V2 rocket, this was entirely designed and built in the USA. Its first flight test was carried out three years later, and in 1958 it went into service with the American armed forces stationed in Europe. The missile both enabled the Americans to test their knowledge of rocket technology and paved the way for other more ambitious projects.

1955 was an important year. Military chiefs in America received confirmation that the Soviet Union had test fired experimental missiles, so American missile research was intensified. On 1 February 1956, the US Army formed the Army Ballistic Missile Agency (ABMA), and transferred von Braun and his team to it; their task was to carry out the Jupiter programme, to build a missile with a range of 2800 kilometres. On its first flight, on 20 September 1956, Jupiter C, the experimental Jupiter missile flew to an altitude of 1100 kilometres and landed 5475 kilometres from Cape Canaveral, much better than specification.

The US Air Force were also active. Their efforts were directed to the Thor missile, which had the same range as Jupiter and was likewise a single stage missile fuelled by liquid oxygen and paraffin oil (kerosene). However, the Air Force's overall objective was to produce an intercontinental missile. With this purpose in mind, the Atlas programme was started in January 1955. However, it transpired that the problems involved here were much more intractable than those in the medium range missile projects. The Americans began a desperate effort to ensure that they had the best chance of successfully installing a strategic weapons force, so that they would not be left behind the Soviets. Between 1955 and 1958, they were working on no less than seven ballistic missile programmes and two intercontinental cruise missile programmes.

These consisted of the Jupiter missile for the US Army, the Thor, Atlas, Titan I, Titan II, Minuteman I, Snark and Navaho missiles for the US Air Force, and Polaris A1 for the US Navy. The Jupiter, Thor, Atlas and Titan I missiles were all fuelled by liquid oxygen and paraffin oil. The Titan II made use of new fuels such as aerozine 50 and nitrogen peroxide. Minuteman and Polaris used a new powerful solid fuel rocket, and the Snark and Navaho projects involved the development of turbojets and ramjets. The largest of the missiles, the Titan II, weighed 150 tonnes.

The space race begins

By 1955, the space race was in full swing. On 29 July, President Eisenhower announced that plans had been approved for the launch of small satellites as the American contribution to International Geophysical Year (1957 to 1958).

There were then two possible routes by which a nation might develop a launcher. It could adapt ballistic missiles, or develop a launcher using knowledge acquired from rocket probes (notably the Viking and Aerobee probes). The Soviets chose the former method, and were first in space. The Americans chose the latter.

The Redstone missile. With its inertial guidance system, this US Army missile weighed 28 tonnes, and was 21 metres high and 2 metres in diameter. The liquid oxygen and alcohol rocket engine delivered a thrust of 330 kilonewtons for 121 seconds, giving the missile a range of 320 kilometres. Sixteen such missiles were briefly deployed in Europe (Keystone).

Assembly of Atlas missiles. The Atlas missile was the first American intercontinental missile to be built. Both its assembly and preparation for launch were delicate processes because the walls of the fuel tanks were so thin that it was impossible for the missile to be vertical when it was full of the liquid oxygen and paraffin oil fuels. In the assembly hall, the missile was transported in a horizontal position, as shown, and the tanks were pressurised by an inert gas. For operational purposes, the tanks were filled at the last moment, a process that took about fifteen minutes. The missile was then set upright and fired (rights reserved).

An unreliable launcher. The US Navy's Vanguard launcher had three stages. The first, based on the Viking rocket, used liquid oxygen and paraffin oil and had a thrust of 120 kilonewtons. The second stage used nitric acid and asymmetric dimethyl hydrazine (termed UDMH), and the third stage was a solid fuel rocket. This launcher, which had a launch mass of just over 10 tonnes, could put into orbit a payload with a mass of only a few kilograms.

The Americans used Vanguard in their unsuccessful attempt to launch their first satellite on 6 December 1957. The photograph on the right was taken on 17 March 1958 when the Vanguard 1 satellite, with a mass of 1·47 kilograms, was put into orbit, roughly one and a half months after the successful launch of Explorer 1. The unreliability of this rocket brought about its rapid demise. Of eleven launch attempts, eight ended in failure (NASA).

Titan I. This was the first American, two stage, strategic ballistic missile. Titan I was stored in underground silos at several US Air Force bases throughout the USA. It was to be launched from outside the silo, after being hoisted into position. Fuelled by liquid oxygen and paraffin oil, its initial mass was 100 tonnes. It could carry a 3 to 5 megatonne nuclear warhead up to 10 000 kilometres (rights reserved).

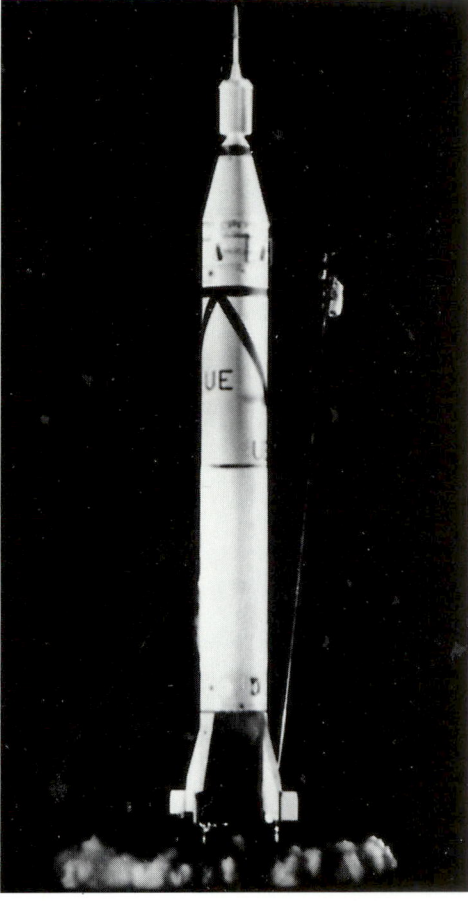

Juno I. Jupiter C was an experimental three stage rocket. The first stage was fuelled by liquid oxygen and hydine, a mixture of diethylene triamine and asymmetric dimethyl hydrazine (UDMH). It delivered a thrust of 369 kilonewtons, and was based on the Redstone missile. The upper two stages were designed by the Jet Propulsion Laboratory, and consisted of clusters of small, solid fuel rockets. There were eleven on the second stage and three on the third stage. After a fourth stage was added, consisting of a single solid fuel rocket, the Jupiter C became the Juno I launcher. It had a mass at launch of just over 29 tonnes and a height of 21·7 metres. The photograph above was taken at the launch of Explorer 1, on 31 January 1958 (PPP).

Characteristics of the four stages of Juno I

stage	first	second	third	fourth
length (m)	17.1	1.08	1.08	1.08
diameter (m)	1.78	0.7	0.3	0.152
mass (kg)	29 000	316	94	28
firing time (s)	155	6	6	6

In fact, the American approach had been decided in June 1954, when the US Army and the US Navy attempted to set up a joint programme to launch small satellites. Von Braun had already demonstrated that a launcher could be developed from parts of existing rockets, but this launcher would only be capable of placing small satellites into orbit. It was the quickest route by which the US could get into space. However, the project, called Orbiter, was turned down in September 1955 and the competing US Navy project (Vanguard) was approved. Based on the Viking rocket, scientific responsibility for Vanguard was given to the National Academy of Sciences while the budget came from the National Science Foundation. The actual work was carried out by the Defense Department, who delegated it to the US Navy. Work began on 9 September 1955. It was for a rocket engine of modest performance compared with its Soviet counterparts. The Vanguard launches ended in a number of failures, however, and it was not until 17 March 1958 that the launcher put a satellite into orbit.

As the first tests on the Vanguard launcher were about to begin, on 23 October 1957, American morale suffered a tremendous blow. For it was on 4 October 1957 that the Soviets successfully placed a satellite into orbit – Sputnik 1.

It was very fortunate that, although not authorised to do so, the US Army and von Braun had done some work towards developing a launcher. They had constructed an experimental unit called Juno I, which was a Jupiter C with a fourth stage. On 8 November 1958, a month after Sputnik 1 had been put into orbit, the Secretary of State for Defense authorised the preparation of two satellites whose launch was initially set for March 1958. Several days later, 3·5 million dollars were made available to the ABMA and the launch date was arranged for 30 January 1958. Explorer 1, the first American satellite was successfully launched on 31 January 1958.

Soviet developments

In the immediate post-war period, the Soviets approached space research in broadly the same way as the Americans, pursuing and developing work that had been done in Nazi Germany. Between 1945 and 1947, the principal Soviet specialists, Sergei Korolev and Valentin Glushko, went to Germany to find out in more detail about the work that had been undertaken.

In 1946, the factories at Nordhausen, where the V2 rockets were produced, were dismantled and taken to the Soviet Union. About 200 German specialists were also moved. They were given the task of designing and constructing a rocket capable of carrying a 3 tonne explosive charge a distance of up to 3000 kilometres.

Over the next seven years little information about Soviet rocketry reached the West. Later it was learnt that considerable importance had been attached to this work on the eastern side of the Iron Curtain, with a great deal of money and resources having been made available. By the end of the 1940s, 13 research groups and some 35 factories were working on rockets.

Also from 1946, the Soviets began studying the possibilities of manned spacecraft. According to *Red Star*, a mouthpiece for the Soviet armed forces (24 January 1980) Mikhail Tikhonravov and his team were studying a space cabin called the VR 190. This would be sent to an altitude of 150 to 200 kilometres by a rocket, though without being put into Earth orbit.

Before these experiments could be carried out, however, it was essential to build a launcher. Korolev was instructed to reconstruct the V2 rocket. He did and the first launch took place on 18 October 1947, from the Kapustin Yar launch site near Volgograd. Then, like the Americans, the Soviets set about improving

Two Soviet rocket probes. Engineers in the USSR, like their US counterparts, were inspired by the performance of German rockets. From 1949, they began exploring the high atmosphere, developing liquid fuel rocket probes. Thus the V2A geophysics rocket (in the foreground of the photograph on the left) bears a striking resemblance to the German V2 rocket. Carrying a 2·2 tonne payload to an altitude of 212 kilometres, it was used to study the uppermost atmosphere and to record the ultraviolet and X ray parts of the solar spectrum. The V5B (in the background of this photograph) carried a payload of 1·3 tonnes to an altitude of 512 kilometres. It was used for astrophysical, geophysical and ionospheric studies. For medical and biological experiments, animals were used. The photograph above shows a V2A which had been specially adapted to carry two dogs into space (Tass).

Véronique, the French rocket probe. After the Second World War, there was also considerable activity on rockets in France. Like the two superpowers, it had benefited, although to a lesser extent, from German technology. Work was directed towards rockets which would assist aircraft to take off, and for this purpose the Societé d'étude de la propulsion à réaction (SEPR), a jet propulsion group was created. Due to the lack of resources and political support, other rocket projects never passed beyond the research stage. It was only with the return to power of General de Gaulle in 1958 and the superpowers' undisguised interest in ballistic missiles, that projects of this type were given any real support.

France also carried out research into rocket probes, the most famous of which was Véronique (shown right). The expertise acquired during this programme and from ballistic rocket research enabled France to become the third space power, on 26 November 1965.

Véronique was designed in 1949 to explore the high atmosphere, and continued in use until 1964. The AGI version, shown in this photograph, was constructed during International Geophysical Year (1957 to 1958). Fuelled by nitric acid and spirit of turpentine, it produced a thrust of 40 kilonewtons. It was capable of carrying a 60 kilogram payload up to 210 kilometres altitude (© SIRPA/ECP Armées France).

their design. From 1949 onwards, geophysical rockets, also based on German technology, were launched.

In 1948, the R1 rocket appeared. It was fitted with an RD 100 engine designed by Glushko, fuelled by liquid oxygen and paraffin oil and delivering a thrust of 245 kilonewtons. This was followed by several other types of rockets whose designs came from Korolev's research groups. In 1949, there was the R2, fitted with an RD 101 engine, which had a thrust of 314 kilonewtons. The R3, which had an intended range of 3000 kilometres, was never constructed. The R4 rocket appeared in 1952 and 1953; it had a nitric acid and paraffin oil engine designed by Aleksei Isayev. Finally there was the R5, which had a range of 1200 kilometres, and was fitted with the RD 103 engine fuelled by liquid oxygen and paraffin oil.

In 1952, Korolev set himself the task of constructing a two stage rocket with a range of 7000 kilometres. His proposal was based on a rocket whose two stages were side by side, not one on top of the other. This rocket was called the R7, or Zemiorka, and was perfected in less than three years. At the beginning, the rocket was intended for military uses; however, it became the Soviet key to space as it was capable of placing 1300 kilograms into a low Earth orbit. On 30 January 1956, several months after the first static firing trials of the engines, the Academy of Sciences decided to use the R7 to launch a satellite. Korolev put Tikhonravov in charge of a section given the task of designing a 'cosmic craft', and several months later the first satellite project, called Object D, began. This satellite had a mass of about 1200 kilograms, of which 200 to 300 kilograms represented scientific instruments. It was to be launched at the end of 1957.

A few months before this, the first launch of the military version of the R7 took place, on 21 August 1957, and the Soviet Union became the first country in the world to possess an intercontinental missile. About ten of these missiles, called the SS 6 Sapwood in the West, became operational, two years before the Americans possessed a similar weapon.

The first space power

Against this background, on 4 October 1957, a long awaited day dawned, and the dreams of many researchers and space enthusiasts were fulfilled. The first artificial Earth satellite was launched from Tyuratam Baikonur: Sputnik 1, a small spherical satellite with a mass of 83 kilograms, transmitted the first 'bleep bleep' sounds from space to the waiting world.

The USSR was at this time significantly ahead of the USA. While the Zemiorka delivered a thrust of 4·4 meganewtons at launch, the American Thor missile, which became operational in 1958, produced a thrust of a mere 765 kilonewtons with its single engine. Korolev's rocket design was most carefully thought out and is still used today, basically because of its simplicity and reliability.

Between 1955 and 1956 Korolev went on to construct four different types of rockets (the R8, V5R, R10 and R11), three of which were experimental rockets. Mikhail Yangel, one of Korolev's students, built a rocket which was tested at the same time as the R7. At the end of the 1950s, Yangel built up a ballistic missile research group at Dniepropetrovsk, and it was from there that Vladimir Chelomei, one of Korolev's rivals and the future designer of the Proton launcher, developed the first ballistic missile to be launched from a submarine in 1955. The Soviets, like their US contemporaries, were building up a huge strategic arsenal.

Jacques Villain

Korolev's famous Zemiorka rocket. This rocket was used by the Soviets to begin both the era of intercontinental missiles, on 21 August 1957, with the SS 6 Sapwood, and the space era, with the R7, on 4 October 1957. The launch mass was about 270 tonnes. The first version of Zemiorka could put about 1·3 tonnes of payload into low Earth orbit.

The first stage consisted of four booster rockets around the central body of the second stage. Korolev chose a large number of small rockets since very powerful engines had not then been designed. All these liquid oygen and paraffin oil rocket engines (RD 107 and RD 108) delivered a thrust of about one meganewton.

At launch all the engines ignited simultaneously. The four boosters delivered their maximum power, while the second stage fired at a reduced level. During the 118 seconds of first stage combustion, their 20 chambers produced a thrust of 4·4 meganewtons. When the boosters separated from the main body, the second stage central engine started burning at full power. Second stage combustion lasted 244 seconds. Fine control of the rocket trajectory was obtained by firing up to twelve small attitude control rockets.

nose cone covering Sputnik 1

central rocket body

liquid oxygen tank

2.95 m

booster

liquid oxygen tank

2.15 m

SS 6. Sapwood intercontinental missile (original configuration)

RD 107 rocket engine

RD 108 rocket engine

paraffin oil tank

small attitude control rockets

3 m

10.3 m

central rocket

R7 launcher

29.2 m

19 m

Optimism turns to doubt
(1945 to 1957)

By the end of the Second World War, rockets had proved their worth. And the whole world, apart from science fiction enthusiasts, was taken by surprise. Science fiction authors, in particular Robert A. Heinlein, presented a coherent picture of life in future centuries, assuming that it would be dominated by the conquest of space, and many writers relied on Heinlein to provide them with the necessary technological information for their novels.

Beyond the limited circle of science fiction fans, the general public became interested in space exploration as they realised that it would soon be a reality. Heinlein was recruited in 1947 by a major publisher to write novels for young people. His readership promptly multiplied ten or twenty times. He maintained the style of his *History of the Future*, and news of his success soon reached Hollywood. In 1950 he became the scriptwriter for the film *Destination Moon*, directed by Irving Pichel, for which Hermann Oberth was the technical adviser. It was adapted from his first book for a younger audience and described, with an almost documentary accuracy, the story of the first lunar voyage. Other technical writers were also involved, including Arthur C. Clarke, who was

made famous by his first novels in which he described artificial satellites (*Islands in the Sky*, 1952), the Moon (*Prelude to Space*, 1951) and even Mars (*The Sands of Mars*, 1951).

Less positively, in 1938, Orson Welles' radio adaption of H. G. Wells' *The War of the Worlds* caused panic, for the public was suddenly terrified of the possibility of an invasion by creatures from Mars.

The flying saucer first appeared in 1947, with the cinema taking up the same theme in such films as *The Thing*, by Christian Nyby, and *The Day the Earth Stood Still*, by Robert Wise. Some sought to find hidden meanings in the fiction, suggesting that the Martian peril was a metaphor for communism, the red peril. Space was evolving into an unfriendly, frightening place.

Heinlein's *History of the Future* competed with Isaac Asimov's *Foundation* cycle (from 1942 onwards). Asimov was concerned with the decline, rather than the infinite growth, of an interstellar empire – although the intelligentsia still played a positive role in his fictional empire. James Blish replied with his *Nomadic Cities* cycle of four books (from 1950 to 1962), in which he imagined that all the cities of the

Earth had been supplied with an antigravity device enabling them to fly. The expansion theme took precedence once more, with humans seeding themselves throughout the galaxy.

Other themes too were repeated, such as space travellers from an alien planet looking for somewhere they could belong. Space became synonymous with fears and uncertainties, and the future of the galaxy became a mystery. In other words, the prophetic vision of science fiction was no longer comforting. Fantasy science fiction flourished, with Mars being given a second lease of life in *The Martian Chronicles* (1950) by Ray Bradbury. The possibilities of interstellar travel let authors imagine all manner of worlds, some fantastic and unexpected, like those of Jack Vance, and others scientifically plausible, as in Hal Clement's *Mission of Gravity* (1953).

By the late 1950s, space as science fiction was being overtaken by events – space exploration was becoming science fact.

Jacques Goimard

Destination Moon. The great astronautics pioneer, Hermann Oberth, was the technical advisor for this film and, twenty years after Lang's *Frau im Mond*, he had the satisfaction of seeing astronauts wearing spacesuits. It took the cinema a long time to admit that space travel should appear realistic. Using special effects, lunar landscapes were miniaturised and the conquest of the Moon was realistically filmed, yet with a reasonable budget. However, the lunar mountains in the background are reminiscent of those in *Frau im Mond*, and are more closely related to fantasy than to realism (Prod./DB).

Science fiction laughs at itself. In 1953, flying saucer fever took hold. Here, an army of anxious extraterrestrials are astounded by the human being who has stepped out of his spaceship. He is small, bald and potbellied, the antithesis of the space heroes found in the rest of science fiction (illustration by Emsh, in *Planet Stories*, 1953; from B. Aldiss, *Science Fiction Art*, 1975; © Sceptre Books, London).

TODAY'S SCIENCE FICTION — TOMORROW'S FACT   FALL 25¢

STARTLING *stories*

A THRILLING PUBLICATION

featuring **SPACEMEN LOST** *a novel by* George O. Smith
and **SIMPLE PSIMAN** *a novelet by* F. L. Wallace

An outdated piece of science fiction. In this 1954 drawing, spacemen are scaling the mountain using climbing equipment dating from thirty years previously. It is interesting that the rockets have slightly sunk into the sand, for a hypothesis of that era was that the Moon was covered by a layer of dust. This illustration by Alex Schomburg dates from the 1950s when science fiction enthusiasts were no longer interested in conquering the Moon, but the general public was (© 1954 Better Books Publications Inc., rights reserved).

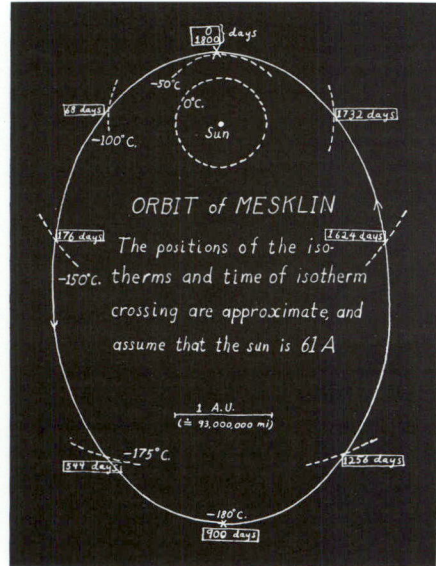

'Hard science fiction'. Hal Clement was a physicist who wrote science fiction from time to time. He imagined a planet called Mesklin, to which he gave fantastic qualities, and his novel, *Mission of Gravity* (1953), was written about it. Clement had taken time to study the scientific reasoning behind his novel, as this unpublished drawing shows (rights reserved).

Forbidden Planet (1956). An Earth spaceship has landed on a distant planet, but this time the travellers are defending themselves against an unknown danger. In the 1950s, space had become an uncertain place. So it was natural that, during space exploration, men were confronted with hostile environments. This picture, inspired by the McCarthy anti-communist witch hunts, comes from a film by Fred Wilcox. It could hardly differ more in tone from Emsh's humorous illustration on the opposite page (Cinestar).

Space and desire. This fantasy illustration is a good example of how science fiction art has developed. The male image of the rocket is travelling through space, symbolised by a desirable woman. The rocket is travelling towards the Milky Way, a symbol once discussed by Sigmund Freud. It has been suggested too that space explorers are, in fact, exploring their intellect – a journey through the mind (drawing by Virgil Finlay, in *Amazing Stories*, 1951; © Ziff-Davis Publishing Co., rights reserved).

Science fiction brought to millions of readers. In 1950, both Hollywood, with *Destination Moon*, and comic strips like Tintin discovered space. This was not a coincidence. The drawing on the cover of *On a marché sur la Lune* (Explorers on the Moon) bears a striking resemblance to those of *Startling Stories*, above left. In his *Adventures of Tintin*, Hergé made no attempt to be original; his lunar mountains are conventional, though the landscape was carefully researched (© Hergé, exclusive rights held by Casterman).

- HERGÉ -

LES AVENTURES DE TINTIN

ON A MARCHÉ SUR LA LUNE

CASTERMAN

The golden age

In the ten years following the Second World War, military requirements dominated all space programmes. The interest shown in space by civil groups appeared later, and its subsequent development even then was closely linked to military requirements. This was because the military were very quick to recognise the destructive potential of combining the power of a rocket with a nuclear weapon.

In 1945, the Soviet Union secretly began studying nuclear and space technology and, in 1948, the Soviet army created a research group to study the possible uses of rockets. Like other countries possessing both military space and nuclear technologies, it only subsequently developed civil applications.

The space race

As part of the International Geophysical Year, both the Americans and the Soviets planned to launch an artificial satellite into orbit around the Earth.

On 26 August 1957, the Soviet Union announced that it had just launched an intercontinental rocket with a range of 8000 kilometres. Nikita Krushchev even declared that 'the age of aeroplanes has given way to that of rockets', an announcement that did not arouse much of a reaction in the West, where it was assumed to be a Soviet bluff. However, on 4 October 1957, Soviet superiority was brought into the full light of day with the launch of Sputnik 1; from then on, there could be no doubt as to the USSR's military and civil technological prowess. Confirming their superiority, the Soviets launched yet another satellite, on 3 November 1957. It weighed 500 kilograms and carried a dog, Laika.

The Americans were taken completely by surprise by the Soviet superiority in space. Fortunately, however, they already had two teams working on satellite launch programmes. The first group, directed by Wernher von Braun, developed the Redstone rocket and a more powerful version, called Jupiter C, which reached an altitude of 1100 kilometres on 20 September 1956. Pleased with this success, von Braun proposed to launch an artificial satellite, but received a formal rejection because the second US team had a similar project in hand. In fact, the US Naval Research Laboratory had been working on the Vanguard project since 9 September 1955.

The Americans prepared to launch their first satellite, Vanguard, on 5 December 1957. Unfortunately, the rocket exploded on the launch site, before the eyes of the assembled world press – the first American attempt to put a satellite into orbit was a failure. Desperate not to be technologically humiliated, the Americans turned to the only person who could help them; in the end it was Wernher von Braun's team that launched the first American satellite, Explorer 1, on 31 January 1958. Although Explorer 1 was small, with a mass of only 14 kilograms, against the 84 kilograms of Sputnik 1, it was responsible for the discovery of the Van Allen radiation belts of energetic charged particles which surround the Earth.

The Soviet Union's response was to launch Sputnik 3, weighing 1·3 tonnes, on 15 May 1958. This satellite was the first automatic scientific space laboratory, an achievement that rapidly made it apparent that satellites could have an important military purpose.

The USSR had once more outstripped the

Sputnik 1. The first artificial Earth satellite was an aluminium sphere, 58 centimetres in diameter, fitted with four antennae and weighing 83·6 kilograms. It had two radio transmitters which sent the famous 'bleep bleep' signals to Earth for 21 days, heralding the start of the space era.

Sputnik 1 contributed to our knowledge of the density, temperature and electron concentration of the uppermost atmosphere and the propagation of radio waves. It was put into an orbit with a perigee of 228 kilometres and an apogee of 947 kilometres. The period of revolution around the Earth was 96 minutes 17 seconds. The low altitude of the perigee caused the satellite to reenter the Earth's atmosphere and burn up on 4 January 1958 (rights reserved).

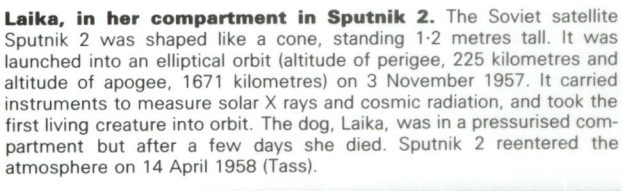

Laika, in her compartment in Sputnik 2. The Soviet satellite Sputnik 2 was shaped like a cone, standing 1·2 metres tall. It was launched into an elliptical orbit (altitude of perigee, 225 kilometres and altitude of apogee, 1671 kilometres) on 3 November 1957. It carried instruments to measure solar X rays and cosmic radiation, and took the first living creature into orbit. The dog, Laika, was in a pressurised compartment but after a few days she died. Sputnik 2 reentered the atmosphere on 14 April 1958 (Tass).

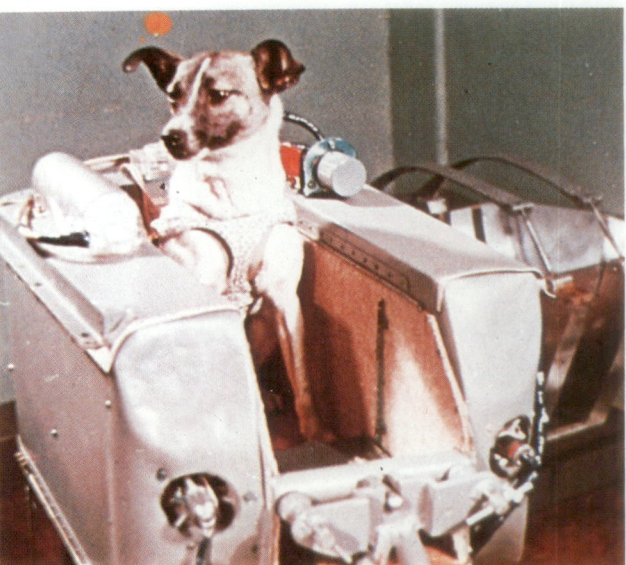

Vanguard 1. In this photograph, engineers are putting the second American satellite, Vanguard 1, onto the third stage of the Vanguard TV4 launcher. It was nicknamed The Grapefruit because of its shape and small size. It was a sphere, 16 centimetres in diameter with a mass of only 1·47 kilograms. Vanguard 1 carried temperature probes and two radio transmitters. These enabled Earth stations to track the satellite to obtain data on the Earth's shape and variations in its gravitational field from variations in the parameters of the satellite's orbit. The satellite was initially placed in an elliptical orbit with perigee at 652 kilometres and an apogee of 3965 kilometres (NASA).

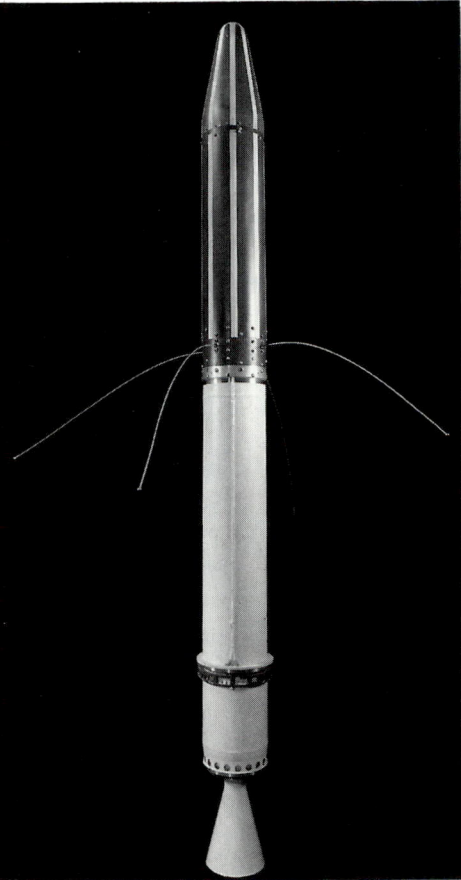

Explorer 1. The first American satellite was launched by a Juno 1 rocket (called Jupiter C at that time) on 31 January 1958. Built by the Army Ballistic Missile Agency and the Jet Propulsion Laboratory, Explorer 1 had a mass of 13·9 kilograms, one sixth of the mass of Sputnik 1. It was 2·03 metres tall and had a diameter of 153 millimetres. It formed the fourth stage of Juno 1; the Sergeant solid fuel rocket and this stage remained attached to the section containing the scientific equipment – the striped upper section in the photograph. The instruments had a mass of 5 kilograms, and included batteries, radio transmitters and Geiger counters. Explorer 1 transmitted scientific data until 23 May 1958. The Van Allen radiation belts were discovered using observations made aboard this satellite. It was in an elliptical orbit, with perigee and apogee at 356 kilometres and 2546 kilometres respectively, and did not reenter the atmosphere until 31 March 1970, burning up over the Pacific (Smithsonian Institution).

The Vanguard programme

TV 3	6 December 1957	failure
TV 3 BU	5 February 1958	failure
TV 4	17 March 1958	put Vanguard 1 into orbit
TV 5	28 April 1958	failure
SLV 1	27 May 1958	failure
SLV 2	26 June 1958	failure
SLV 3	26 September 1958	failure
SLV 4	17 February 1959	put Vanguard 2 into orbit
SLV 5	13 April 1959	failure
SLV 6	22 June 1959	failure
TV4 BU	18 September 1959	put Vanguard 3 into orbit

TV: Test Vehicle (experimental rocket)
SLV: Satellite Launch Vehicle (operational launcher)
BU: Back Up (replacement rocket)
The TV4 BU launcher had a new third stage

USA. There was, moreover, an inescapable political and strategic consequence of the Soviet scientific exploits – for the first time in its history, US territory was vulnerable to attack. American military strategy also had to be altered from one involving massive reprisals to one of gradual retaliation against the aggressor, to avoid resorting immediately to the terrible consequences of nuclear war.

The very way that a nation's defence was organised had to be altered once intercontinental missiles were deployed. It took these missiles only half an hour to reach their targets, compared with the several hours that were required by conventional strategic weapons. The advance warning time had been considerably reduced and it was no longer necessary to wait until there were favourable weather conditions before attacking.

The USSR understood the implications of these changes and, in 1959, created the Strategic Missiles Force which was placed at the head of a hierarchy of military units. The Soviets gave absolute priority to the development of an intercontinental ballistic missile system, to be directed against North America, and a medium range missile system to be directed against Europe.

The US military, for its part, was developing two intercontinental missiles, Atlas and Titan. However, they would not be ready for deployment until the beginning of the 1960s. The Americans had therefore to develop an intermediate range missile to fill the gaps in their defences.

The US Army developed the Jupiter missile, and the US Air Force the Thor rocket. Since they were both medium range missiles, they had to be based in Europe. Thor was based in Great Britain and Jupiter in Italy and Turkey. Their bases were dismantled after the Cuban missile crisis in 1962, following Soviet–American negotiations. Three years later they were replaced by intercontinental Atlas and Titan missiles based on US territory.

In 1963, the Americans constructed networks of radars capable of detecting the trajectories of missiles and determining where their points of impact would be. They began work on the Nike Zeus missile, the forerunner of the anti-missile missiles. In 1965, the Soviets developed their own system for protecting Moscow with Galosh anti-missile missiles. The concept of the Anti-Ballistic Missile defence system has since dominated all discussions on strategic arms limitations.

President Dwight D. Eisenhower wanted America to catch up with the Soviet Union in the space race, and made several political decisions designed to stimulate the American space effort. On 7 November 1957, the President's Scientific Committee was created at the White House and was given the responsibility of devising and coordinating a space programme. On 9 January 1958, the Advanced Research Projects Agency was created, inside the Department of Defense, to coordinate the research of the three armed forces. And, most importantly, on 29 July 1958, President Eisenhower signed the Space Act, which created a space agency, the National Aeronautics and Space Administration, better known as NASA.

The role of NASA was to direct and coordinate all space activities within the USA, and its administrator was made directly responsible to the president. NASA was also allocated all the organisations which were responsible for satellite launches. It was decided to build a new launch centre at Cape Canaveral in Florida. NASA immediately initiated the Mercury programme to launch a manned space capsule, and a post-Mercury programme geared to lunar exploration. It developed a civil space launcher using solid fuels, the Scout rocket, and the Centaur stage using liquid hydrogen and oxygen. Thus it paved the way for rockets powerful enough to put telecommunications and navigation satellites into Earth orbit and send probes to the Moon.

Pioneer 4. This lunar probe was launched by the Americans on 3 March 1959 by Juno II. It passed within 60 000 kilometres of the Moon's surface before going into orbit around the Sun. The probe was shaped like a cone, half a metre high, and with a base diameter of 230 millimetres. It had a mass of just over 6 kilograms. Its external structure was made up of glass fibre; the white bands acted as a passive heat regulator.

Pioneer 4 had a scientific payload consisting of two Geiger counters to investigate the inner and outer Van Allen belts and a rudimentary television camera (Smithsonian Institution).

The first pictures of the dark side of the Moon. The Soviet Luna 3 probe had a mass of 278 kilograms, a height of 1·3 metres and a diameter of 1·2 metres. On 10 October 1959, it transmitted the first pictures of the dark side of the Moon (upper picture, rights reserved; lower picture, USSR Academy of Sciences).

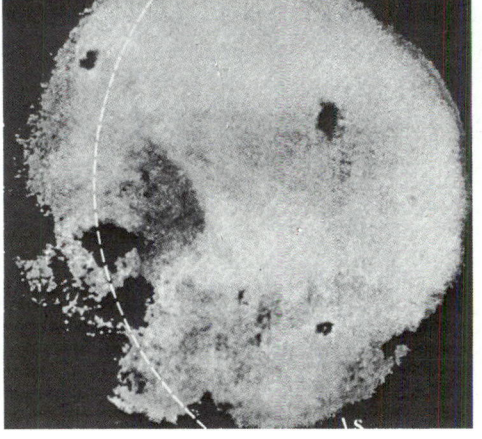

Jupiter C	31 January 1958	put Explorer 1 into orbit
Jupiter C	5 March 1958	failure
Jupiter C	26 May 1958	put Explorer 3 into orbit
Jupiter C	26 July 1958	put Explorer 4 into orbit
Jupiter C	24 August 1958	failure
Jupiter C	22 October 1958	failure
Juno II	16 July 1959	failure
Juno II	14 August 1959	failure
Juno II	13 October 1959	put Explorer 7 into orbit

The Explorer programme

The lunar programmes. The dates given are launch dates.

Successes in the American Ranger programme		
Ranger 4	23 April 1962	lunar impact, but none of the instruments were working
Ranger 6	30 January 1964	lunar impact, but television was not working
Ranger 7	28 July 1964	lunar impact; first high resolution images of the lunar surface as televised pictures
Ranger 8	17 February 1965	lunar impact; images transmitted
Ranger 9	21 March 1965	lunar impact; images transmitted
The Soviet Luna programme		
Luna 1	2 January 1959	did not reach the Moon, but went into orbit around the Sun
Luna 2	12 September 1959	first lunar impact
Luna 3	4 October 1959	passed within 6200 kilometres of the Moon and photographed its dark side
Soft landing programmes; Luna 4 and Luna 8 were both failures		
Luna 9	31 January 1966	first Soviet soft landing
Surveyor 1	30 May 1966	first American soft landing
Luna 13	21 December 1966	second Soviet soft landing
Circumlunar satellite programmes		
Luna 10	31 March 1966	first Soviet lunar satellite
Lunar Orbiter 1	10 August 1966	first American lunar satellite
Luna 11	24 August 1966	success
Luna 12	22 October 1966	success
Lunar Orbiter 2	6 November 1966	second American lunar satellite

The Venera 3 descent probe. This Soviet interplanetary probe was launched on 16 November 1965. On 1 March 1966, it descended into the Venusian atmosphere, making scientific observations on the way.

Though radio communications with this probe were lost during the descent, it became the first terrestrial object to reach the surface of another planet (Associated Press).

Recovering the Discoverer capsule. The American Discoverer military reconnaissance satellites consisted of an Agena stage which had been fitted with a high resolution camera. The film was brought back to Earth in a heat resistant capsule, so that it would survive reentry into the atmosphere. This capsule floated down towards the Earth attached to a parachute, and was recovered in flight by planes trailing long loops. In this photograph, a US Air Force C 119 is seen recovering the capsule of Discoverer 17 on 14 November 1960 (PPP).

The Vostok and Voskhod programmes

Before launches in the manned space programme began, the Soviet Union had only managed to place six payloads in Earth orbit or beyond. The first three Sputniks (from 1957 to 1958) had been launched using the basic SS 6 Sapwood missile. In 1958 the first failures in the lunar programme took place. These missions, together with the three successes in 1959, introduced a new third stage on top of the Sapwood. This was the A 1 or SL 3 vehicle which, as modified, was termed the Vostok rocket.

In April 1958 the Korolev design team finalised the shape of a module to reenter the Earth's atmosphere as a sphere. In August 1958 a feasibility study was submitted, and in November all the options were discussed. It was decided to proceed with a manned orbital mission at the earliest possible date.

The detailed design work on the spacecraft which was to become Vostok began in March 1959. By the end of the year, a prototype was in existence except that no thermal insulation was included.

It was decided that Vostok would take cosmonauts into a low Earth orbit. If the retrorocket failed to fire, it would reenter the atmosphere within ten days, and the cosmonaut would have a chance of survival. As a result, all the Vostok missions carried a full ten days supply of consumables.

In early 1960 the first tests of the descent module had been completed, but the Soviets were not quite ready to try to recover a spacecraft from orbit. The first launch of a Vostok into orbit was on 15 May 1960 when a Korabl Sputnik (capsule satellite) was launched. After four days, when the manoeuvre to take Vostok out of orbit was attempted, the spacecraft was pointing in the wrong direction. Instead of being driven back into the atmosphere, it was propelled into a higher orbit.

A second launch was attempted in July, but the booster failed. The following month a recoverable spacecraft was launched carrying, among other biological specimens, two dogs. Korabl Sputnik 2 was safely recovered after just over a day in orbit. A repeat of the mission was attempted in December, but the descending module entered the atmosphere at the wrong angle and burned up. The final

Towards the stars. This photograph shows Yuri Gagarin sitting in the ejectable seat of his Vostok 1 capsule, just before he became the first man in space. At the height of the Vostok programme, photographs of only the interior of the rocket were distributed. The external configuration was not revealed until 1965 (APN).

Preparing for the launch of Vostok 1. Vostok 1 was launched from an A 1 launcher on 12 April 1961, from Tyuratam Baikonur. At launch, the central body of the rocket and the four booster rockets were all ignited simultaneously. After about two minutes, the boosters separated from the main body and fell back to the Earth. The covering which protected the top of the rocket during its passage through the dense layers of the lower atmosphere were also ejected. About three minutes later, the engine of the third stage was ignited, and used to place the spacecraft into orbit (APN).

The first team of cosmonauts. This photograph was taken at Sochi in May 1961, after Yuri Gagarin's first flight into space. Most of the cosmonauts chosen at the beginning of the 1960s are gathered around Korolev.

In the first row, from left to right, are P. R. Popovich, V. V. Gorbatko, E. V. Khrunov, Y. Gagarin, S. P. Korolev and his wife, who has Popovich's daughter on her lap, E. A. Karpov, who directed the crew of cosmonauts, N. K. Nikitine, the parachute trainer, and E. A. Fedorov, a doctor. In the second row are A. A. Leonov, A. G. Nikolayev, M. Z. Rafikov, D. A. Zaikin, B. V. Volynov, G. S. Titov, G. G. Nelyubov, V. F. Bykovsky and G. S. Shonin. V. I. Filatev, I. N. Anikeyev and P. I. Belyayev are in the third row.

The four cosmonauts who were in the original team and who are not featured here are V. V. Bondarenko, who had died, V. S. Varlamov and A. Y. Kartaskov who had left the team, and V. M. Komarov who was, perhaps, ill (APN).

Vostok and Voskhod cosmonaut trainees. The names of the cosmonauts who actually went into space were released at the time. However, those trained cosmonauts, who were not selected, remained unidentified until the twenty-fifth anniversary of Yuri Gagarin's flight, in April 1986. The assignments shown refer only to the Vostok and Voskhod programmes. Cosmonauts who were subsequently assigned to the Soyuz programme are marked with an asterisk.

Cosmonaut	Assignment(s)
I. N. Anikeyev	none, retired in 1961
P. I. Belyayev (1925–70)	Voskhod 2 commander
V. V. Bondarenko (?–1961)	none
V. F. Bykovsky* (1934–)	Vostok 3 backup, Vostok 5
V. I. Filatev (1925–)	none, retired in 1961
Y. A. Gagarin (1934–68)	Vostok 1
V. V. Gorbatko* (1934–)	Voskhod 2 backup commander (removed following injury)
A. Y. Kartaskov	none, retired in 1960
Y. V. Khrunov* (1933–)	Voskhod 2 backup pilot
V. M. Komarov* (1927–67)	Vostok 4 backup (removed), Voskhod 1 commander
A. A. Leonov* (1934–)	Voskhod 2 pilot
G. G. Nelyubov (?–1966)	Vostok 1 support, retired in 1961
A. G. Nikolayev* (1929–)	Vostok 2 backup, Vostok 3
P. R. Popovich* (1930–)	Vostok 4
M. Z. Rafikov	none, retired in 1962
G. S. Shonin* (1935–)	Voskhod 3 pilot
G. S. Titov (1935–)	Vostok 1 backup, Vostok 2
V. S. Varlamov	none, retired 1960
B. V. Volynov* (1934–)	Vostok 4 backup, Vostok 5 backup, Voskhod 1 backup commander, Voskhod 3 commander
D. A. Zaikin	Voskhod 2 backup commander, retired in 1968 or 1969

Missions of the Vostok programme. The missions shown as KS are the Korabl–Sputnik, Vostok precursor flights. The information presented here is from Soviet sources.

Launch date	Craft	Crew/backup crew	Craft mass (kg)	Orbital parameters Inclination (degrees)	Period (minutes)	Perigee (km)	Apogee (km)	Duration (Days, hours and minutes)			Comments
15 May 1960	KS 1	unmanned	4540	65.0	91.2	312	369	4			recovery not planned
23 July 1960	KS 2 1	2 dogs?	4600?	failed to reach orbit							recovery to be attempted?
19 August 1960	KS 2	2 dogs: Strelka and Belka	4600	65.0	90.7	306	339	1	3	?	first Soviet recovery from orbit
1 December 1960	KS 3	2 dogs: Pchelka and Mushka	4563	65.0	88.5	180	249	1			dog(s) carried and recovered
20 December 1960	KS 4 1	2 dogs?	4600?	failed to reach orbit							dog(s) carried and recovered
9 March 1961	KS 4	1 dog: Chernushka	4700	64.9	88.6	184	249		1	46	dog recovered
25 March 1961	KS 5	1 dog: Zvezdochka	4695	64.9	88.4	178	247		1	45	dog recovered
12 April 1961	Vostok 1	Gagarin/Titov	4725	65.0	89.3	181	327		1	48	first manned space mission
6 August 1961	Vostok 2	Titov/Nikolayev	4731	64.9	88.5	183	244	1	1	18	man in space for a day
11 August 1962	Vostok 3	Nikolayev/Bykovsky	4722	65.0	88.3	181	235	3	22	22	joint flight with Vostok 4
12 August 1962	Vostok 4	Popovich/Komarov or Volynov	4728	65.0	88.4	180	237	2	22	57	passed 6.5 kilometres from Vostok 3
14 June 1963	Vostok 5	Bykovsky/Volynov	4720	65.0	88.3	175	222	4	23	06	joint flight with Vostok 6
16 June 1963	Vostok 6	Tereshkova/Solovyeva	4713	65.0	88.3	181	231	2	22	50	first woman in space
Summer 1964?	Vostok 7	Yegorov/Lazarev?	4750?	mission cancelled							planned week-long mission

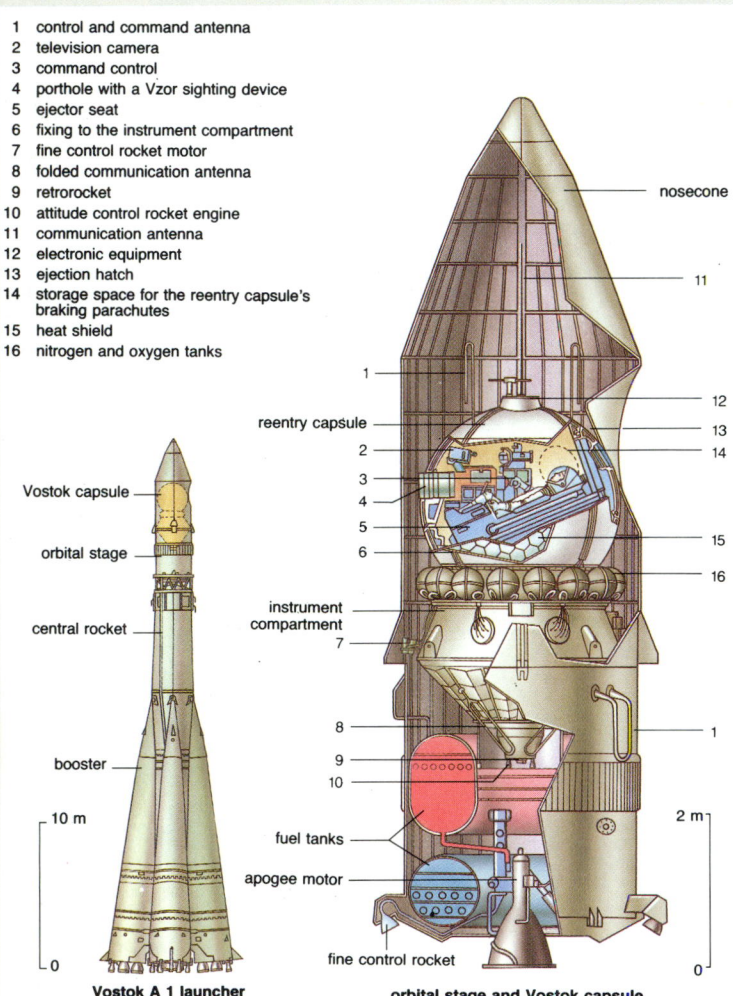

1 control and command antenna
2 television camera
3 command control
4 porthole with a Vzor sighting device
5 ejector seat
6 fixing to the instrument compartment
7 fine control rocket motor
8 folded communication antenna
9 retrorocket
10 attitude control rocket engine
11 communication antenna
12 electronic equipment
13 ejection hatch
14 storage space for the reentry capsule's braking parachutes
15 heat shield
16 nitrogen and oxygen tanks

Vostok A 1 launcher

orbital stage and Vostok capsule

	Mass (tonnes)	Diameter (metres)	Length (metres)	Volume (cubic metres)
Reentry capsule	2.46	2.30	—	5.20
Instrument compartment	2.27	2.43	2.25	—
Complete spacecraft	4.73	2.43	4.40	—

Vostok and its launcher (left). The Vostok spacecraft consisted of two parts – a reentry capsule and an instrument compartment. The cosmonaut lay in a seat which was ejected in the last part of the descent through the atmosphere. He separated from this, returning to Earth by parachute. The seat could also be ejected if there was a problem during the launch, through a small circular opening in the head of the rocket. The retrorocket for taking the spacecraft out of orbit, the TDU 1, was designed in 1959 by Aleksei Isayev and his team. It delivered a thrust of nearly 16 kilonewtons for 45 seconds, and carried 275 kilograms of liquid propellant. The table below the diagram gives parameters of the Vostok spacecraft.

Assembling Vostok 1 (above right). This picture, taken in the assembly hall at Tyuratam Baikonur, shows the reentry capsule being attached to the instrument compartment (APN).

The reentry capsule. The capsule has two circular openings. One is for access (left), and one for the ejector seat; this was guided by rails and ejected by two small, solid fuel rockets (T. Pirard, SIC).

Vostok 1 mission timetable. All times given here are in Universal Time and are based upon Soviet information.

10 April 1961 evening	Gagarin named prime cosmonaut, with Titov his backup
11 April 1961 02.00–04.00	launch vehicle moved to the pad
12 April 1961 02.30	Gagarin and Titov woken up
04.10	Gagarin switches on the Vostok radio transmitter
04.58	Vostok hatch reopened for checking after warning light came on
06.07	launch of Vostok 1
06.12	separation of second stage booster
06.21	separation of third stage in orbit
06.57	Vostok 1 over America
07.25	retrorocket system ignites
07.55	Gagarin lands 26 kilometres south west of Engels, in the Saratov region

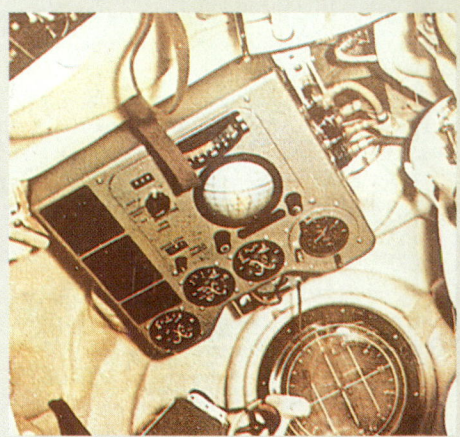

Inside a Vostok capsule. This photograph shows the rectangular control panel available to the cosmonaut. Below this is the porthole fitted with the Vzor sighting device. The rotating globe in the control panel represents the Earth, and it enabled the cosmonaut to know his position at any time. The piloting was automatic, but the cosmonaut could, if necessary, alter the capsule's attitude (APN).

Yuri Gagarin's capsule. Seven kilometres above the Earth, Gagarin ejected from this capsule. At a height of four kilometres, his large parachute opened, as did an even larger parachute attached to the capsule. Both cosmonaut and capsule landed softly, relatively close to each other (APN).

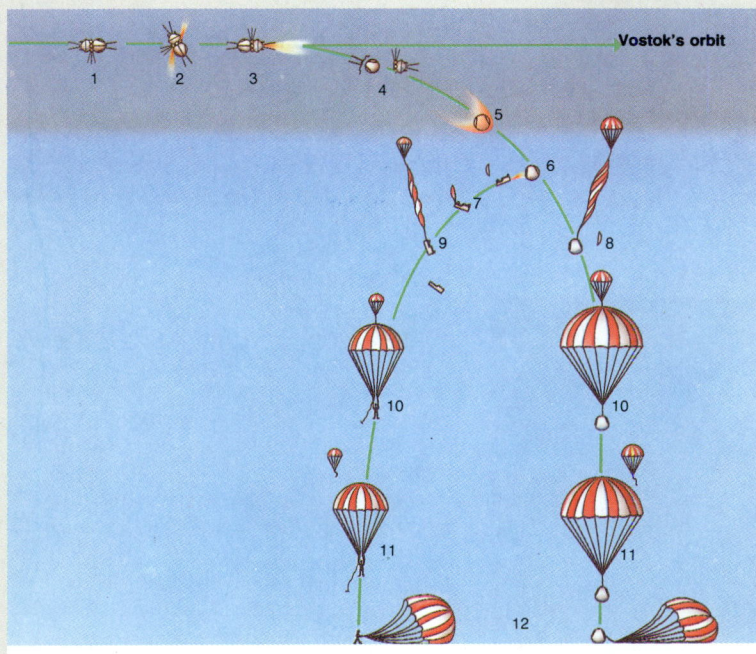

1 configuration of the Vostok spacecraft in orbit
2 rotation manoeuvre
3 retrorocket brings the capsule out of orbit
4 reentry capsule separates from rest of craft
5 reentry into the atmosphere (heating)
6 cosmonaut and seat are ejected through hatch
7 primary parachute opens
8 primary parachute opens (4 km altitude)
9 cosmonaut's main parachute opens and he separates from ejector seat (4 km altitude)
10 main parachute opens
11 descent
12 touchdown

Recovery. The cosmonaut was ejected in the final stages of reentry, because he would have been injured if he had hard landed with the remainder of the craft. (The addition of retrorockets or a larger parachute would have made the capsule too heavy for the A 1 launcher). The cosmonaut was ejected at an altitude of 7 kilometres, parachutes down, and was travelling at only about 5 metres per second when he hit the ground. The capsule from the spacecraft landed nearby, travelling at about twice that speed.

flight of the year failed to reach orbit after problems with the third stage, but the descent craft was recovered, with its biological payload.

In early 1961 the first three man Vostoks were delivered to the Tyuratam-Baikonur launch site. The first two, each with a lone dog on board, were launched on single orbit missions, as direct precursors to the first manned space mission.

The first manned spaceflights

During 1959 the Soviet authorities began to recruit military pilots for their manned space programme. The initial screening of candidates began in October, and by February 1960 the final selections had taken place. On 14 March 1960, the first training session of twenty potential cosmonauts was conducted. During May 1960 six cosmonauts were chosen specifically to train for Vostok missions. By January 1961 Bykovsky, Gagarin, Nelyubov, Nikolayev, Popovich and Titov made up this group.

The very first manned space mission began at 06.07 Universal Time on 12 April 1961 when an SL 3 booster was launched from Tyuratam-Baikonur, carrying Yuri Gagarin aboard Vostok 1. After one orbit, he reentered the Earth's atmosphere and, at an altitude of seven kilometres, ejected to make a parachute landing. The successful flight of Vostok 1 allowed the Soviets to add another 'first' to their list of space successes – the first man in space. Gagarin became an international hero.

Korolev wanted a three orbit mission to follow Gagarin's flight, but he was persuaded to fly a man in space for a full day. In August 1961, Vostok 2 was launched with Titov aboard, and it was on this flight that the spectre of space sickness occurred for the first time. Titov was disoriented for most of his day in orbit, suffering from the equivalent of motion sickness on Earth.

In August 1961 Komarov joined the group of cosmonauts. After being assigned as the back up crew member for Vostok 4, Komarov fell ill, to be replaced by Volynov.

Early in 1962 another group of cosmonauts began training, a group of five women. More than 25 years after the event, the group was identified as being T. D. Kuznetsova, V. L. Ponomareva, I. B. Solovyeva, V. V. Tereshkova and Z. D. Yorkina. Originally they were recruited for a single Vostok flight but, apart from Tereshkova who left after her mission in space, the team was not disbanded until 1969.

There was a break of a year before new manned missions took place, but from then on events moved fast. On consecutive days in August 1962 and using the same launch pad, Vostok 3 and Vostok 4 were launched, carrying Nikolayev and Popovich respectively. At almost the same orbital altitude, the two spacecraft passed within 6·5 kilometres of each other. Vostok 3 remained in orbit for four days and Vostok 4 for three.

The final flights of the Vostok programme took place in June 1963. First, Bykovsky was launched on Vostok 5, and completed a flight of nearly five days, still the longest one man space mission. However, his flight was overshadowed when Valentina Tereshkova was launched in Vostok 6 to become the first woman in space. She remained in orbit for three days, although there were persistent reports that she was unwell during her flight.

Korolev was meanwhile studying other flight options. One was to build up a space train with unmanned rocket modules to take payloads into high orbits. The other, conceived at the same time, called for a three

A Voskhod spacecraft during assembly. This is probably Voskhod 2. The instrument compartment is based on the Vostok one, as is the capsule but modified to hold two or three men. The cylindrical unit above the capsule contains the rescue retrorocket. The structure surrounding the lower part of the instrument compartment is used to attach it to the orbital stage of the SI 4 launcher (APN).

The Voskhod crew. Feoktistov, Komarov and Yegorov are here about to board their spacecraft. Since the capsule was very small, the three cosmonauts were unable to wear spacesuits. They had to rely solely on the pressurised spacecraft for their survival (rights reserved).

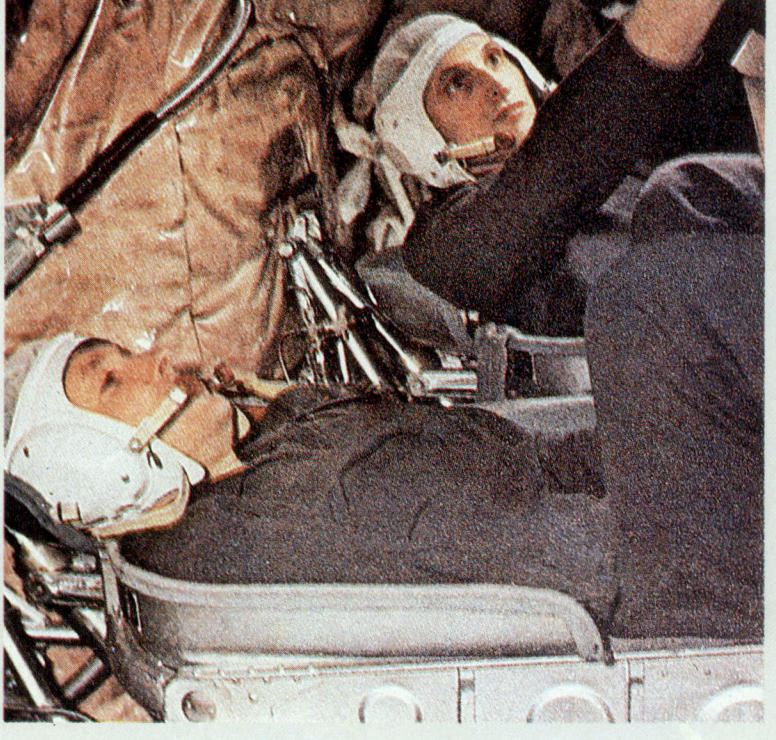

Shonin and Volynov in the Voskhod 3 capsule. These two cosmonauts were photographed during training for the Voskhod 3 mission. It should have lasted for two weeks, but was cancelled at the beginning of 1966 (rights reserved).

spacecraft Soyuz complex to be assembled by two or three men. A Soyuz rocket module would be launched, and then a series of Soyuz craft would supply propellant to it. When it was fully fuelled, a Soyuz manned capsule would be launched and would dock with it. The combined spacecraft could then send men to the Moon.

At the end of 1963, the ambitious Soyuz programme was redirected to a single spacecraft mission, and the gap which resulted in the manned programme was filled by a series of uprated Vostok missions, called Voskhod.

The Voskhod programme

In March 1964 the first Voskhod training group was formed, consisting of Komarov and Volynov, together with a group of five scientists comprising newcomers K. P. Feoktistov, B. B. Yegorov, V. G. Lazarev, A. Sorokin and G. Katys. The aim of the first Voskhod mission was to launch a spacecraft carrying three cosmonauts into space for at least 24 hours.

Because Voskhod was simply a modification of the Vostok craft, only a single precursor mission was required for Voskhod 1. This was Cosmos 47, launched just eight days before the manned spacecraft. In order to allow three men to sit in the modified Vostok cabin, the ejector seat was discarded, and the cosmonauts stayed in their craft down to the ground. Voskhod was too heavy to be launched on the SL 3 booster, and therefore the Soyuz SL 4 booster with a payload capacity of more than seven tonnes was used.

Voskhod 1 was successfully flown with Komarov, Feoktistov and Yegorov. However, a more daring mission was called for on the next flight. A new training group consisting of Belyayev, Gorbatko, Khrunov and Leonov had been selected in April 1964 for the second Voskhod. Gorbatko, however, was replaced by Zaikin after illness.

A single precursor flight to Voskhod 2 was flown. Announced as Cosmos 57, this would seem to have been a test of the extendable airlock and the pressurisation system. But something went wrong – hours after launch, Cosmos 57 disintegrated.

Despite this setback, Voskhod 2 followed within a month carrying Belyayev and Leonov. During the first orbit, Leonov put on a spacesuit and prepared for the first spacewalk. He entered the extendable airlock and, after shutting the inner hatch, depressurised the airlock and opened the outer hatch. Leonov tumbled in space for 12 minutes, but problems arose when he tried to enter the airlock because, during his spacewalk, his spacesuit had expanded. When he finally managed to close the outer hatch, Leonov had been in the vacuum of space for 20 minutes.

When the time for reentry came after 24 hours in orbit, the main retrorocket failed to ignite. The backup retrorocket mounted on the front of Voskhod was used on the next orbit, but it meant that Voskhod 2 descended a long way off the planned course. Landing in a forest, the cosmonauts were not found by the recovery teams for a full day.

Following the Voskhod 2 mission, up to four further manned missions were considered. A training group of Volynov and Shonin with new recruits Shatalov and Beregovoy was formed in April 1965 for a two week flight which was probably scheduled for late 1965 or early 1966. A precursor mission is thought to have failed to reach orbit in July 1965 but, before the end of the year, the planned Voskhod 3 mission was scrapped in order to give attention to the new Soyuz spacecraft.

Launch date	Craft	Crew/backup crew	Craft mass (kg)	Orbital parameters				Duration			Comments
				Inclination (degrees)	Period (minutes)	Perigee (km)	Apogee (km)	(Days, hours and minutes)			
6 October 1964	Cosmos 47	unmanned	5300?	64.8	90.0	177	413	1			Voskhod 1 test
14 October 1964	Voskhod 1	Komarov/Volynov Feoktistov/Katys Yegorov/Lazarev	5320	64.8	90.0	177	408	1	00	17	first three man space mission
22 February 1965	Cosmos 57	unmanned	5600?	64.8	91.1	175	512				disintegrated in orbit
18 March 1965	Voskhod 2	Belyayev/Gorbatko or Zaikin Leonov/Khrunov	5682	64.8	90.9	173	498	1	02	02	first EVA by Leonov; manual landing completed
2 July 1965	Cosmos ?	2 dogs?	5700?	possible launch failure							Voskhod 3 precursor
Late 1965	Voskhod 3	Volynov/Shatalov Shonin/Beregovoy	6000?	mission cancelled							planned two week manned mission
22 February 1966	Cosmos 110	2 dogs: Veterok and Ugolek	5700?	51.9	95.3	187	904	22			biological mission

Missions of the Voskhod programme. The information presented here is from Soviet sources.

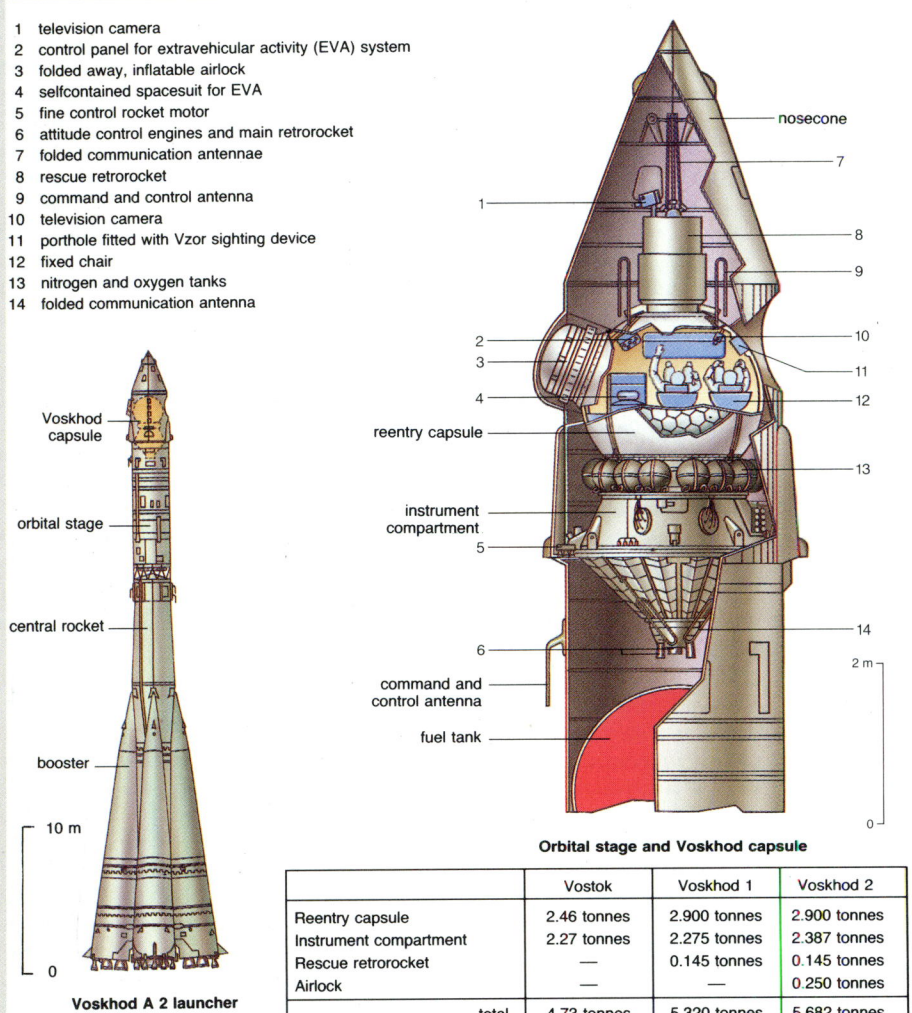

1 television camera
2 control panel for extravehicular activity (EVA) system
3 folded away, inflatable airlock
4 selfcontained spacesuit for EVA
5 fine control rocket motor
6 attitude control engines and main retrorocket
7 folded communication antennae
8 rescue retrorocket
9 command and control antenna
10 television camera
11 porthole fitted with Vzor sighting device
12 fixed chair
13 nitrogen and oxygen tanks
14 folded communication antenna

nosecone

Voskhod capsule

orbital stage

central rocket

booster

Voskhod A 2 launcher

reentry capsule

instrument compartment

command and control antenna

fuel tank

Orbital stage and Voskhod capsule

	Vostok	Voskhod 1	Voskhod 2
Reentry capsule	2.46 tonnes	2.900 tonnes	2.900 tonnes
Instrument compartment	2.27 tonnes	2.275 tonnes	2.387 tonnes
Rescue retrorocket	—	0.145 tonnes	0.145 tonnes
Airlock	—	—	0.250 tonnes
total	4.73 tonnes	5.320 tonnes	5.682 tonnes

The Voskhod spacecraft and its launcher. The central body and boosters were identical to the SL 3, but the SL 4 had a longer and more powerful orbital stage. It was later used on the Soyuz, Soyuz T and Soyuz TM missions. The main retrorocket on the Voskhod capsule was the TDU 1 used in the Vostok missions. The 43 kilogram solid fuel rescue retrorocket delivered a thrust of 120 kilonewtons for 2 seconds. Voskhod was 5 metres long and 2·43 metres in diameter. The table compares the main parameters of the Voskhod spacecraft with those of Vostok.

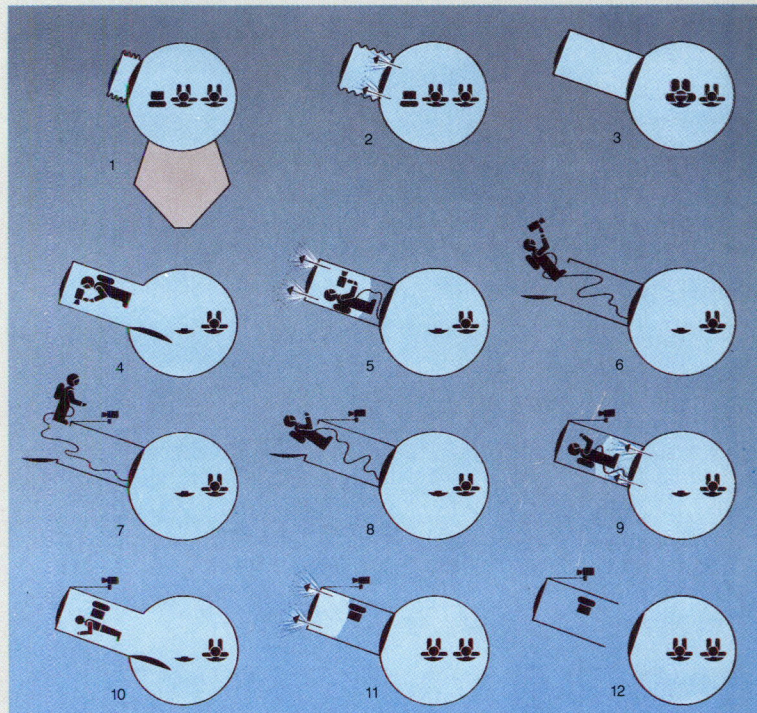

1 configuration of Voskhod 2 before Leonov's spacewalk
2 deploying and pressurising the airlock
3 Leonov dons his selfcontained spacesuit
4 Leonov opens the hatch and enters the airlock with a portable television camera
5 he closes the hatch and plugs in the telemetry and communication cable; then he depressurises the airlock
6 Leonov opens the exit hatch and enters space
7 he attaches the television camera to the edge of the airlock and performs his spacewalk
8 Leonov reenters the airlock
9 he closes the hatch and repressurises the airlock
10 he removes the selfcontained spacesuit and opens the hatchway to the reentry capsule
11 he closes the hatchway and depressurises the airlock
12 the airlock is ejected

Leonov's first spacewalk. The drawing above shows the different phases of a spacewalk. Below are two photographs showing Leonov leaving the airlock (a televised picture) and in space (left, rights reserved; right, APN).

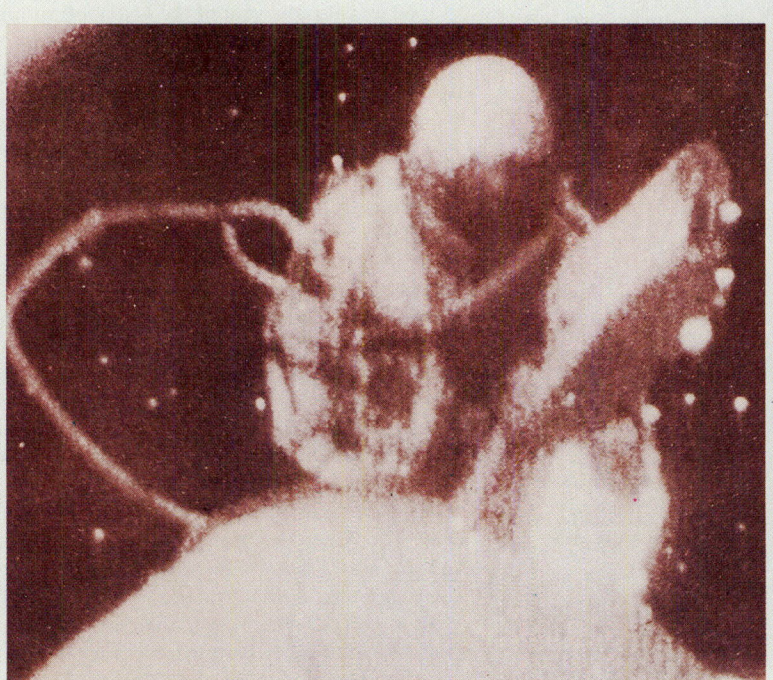

Also in July 1965 two journalists, Y. Golovanov and Y. Letunov, began preliminary training for a spaceflight. This was probably to be a brief, two man mission, with a military pilot and one journalist, the other acting as backup. A second, longer Voskhod mission was planned and three medical doctors, Y. A. Illyin, A. S. Kisilev and Y. A. Senkevich, were selected in 1965 to begin training for two weeks in space. Regrettably the flight was cancelled within a few months of the training beginning. A final Voskhod mission was launched in February 1966, but instead of men it carried two dogs in orbit for 22 days.

The Vostok and Voskhod programmes gave the Soviet Union a number of significant space 'firsts' and, despite western reports to the contrary, they were completed without any flight fatalities. The missions gave the Soviet Union a solid foundation upon which to build their next manned space programme – Soyuz.

Phillip S. Clark

Echo 1A. In this photograph the first telecommunications satellite, Echo 1A, is shown undergoing an inflation test. The satellite was a sphere, 30 metres in diameter, the skin of which was made of Mylar, coated on both sides with aluminium. Echo 1A was launched on 12 August 1960, by a Thor-Delta rocket. Radio waves emitted from the Earth were simply reflected by this metal coated sphere which acted as a passive retransmitter (NASA).

The X15 rocket plane. This photograph was taken on 9 November 1961, just after the plane was launched from a B52 bomber. Robert White piloted the plane to a speed of 6585 kilometres per hour (Mach 6·04) and to an altitude of 31 kilometres.

On 22 August 1963, Joe Walker took the X15 3 to the frontier of space, to an altitude of 108 kilometres. The knowledge acquired with this plane was crucial when designing the space shuttle (NASA).

Manned space missions showing launch dates

Date	Astronaut	Spacecraft	Notes
12 April 1961	Yuri Gagarin	Vostok 1	first spaceflight (1 orbit)
5 May 1961	Alan B. Shepard	Mercury Freedom 7	suborbital flight
21 July 1961	Virgil I. Grissom	Mercury Liberty Bell 7	suborbital flight
6 August 1961	Guerman Titov	Vostok 2	first flight longer than 24 hours (17 orbits)
20 February 1962	John H. Glenn	Mercury Friendship 7	first American orbital flight (3 orbits)
24 May 1962	M. Scott Carpenter	Mercury Aurora 7	(3 orbits)
11 August 1962	Andriyan Nikolayev	Vostok 3	first twinned flight, with Vostok 4 (64 orbits)
12 August 1962	Pavel Popovich	Vostok 4	first twinned flight, with Vostok 3 (48 orbits)
3 October 1962	Walter M. Schirra	Mercury Sigma 7	(6 orbits)
15 May 1963	L. Gordon Cooper	Mercury Faith 7	(22 orbits)
14 June 1963	Valery Bykovsky	Vostok 5	flight twinned with Vostok 6 (81 orbits)
16 June 1963	Valentina Tereshkova	Vostok 6	first woman in space; flight twinned with Vostok 5 (48 orbits)
12 October 1964	Vladimir Komarov Konstantin Feoktistov Boris Yegorov	Voskhod 1	first three man crew in space (16 orbits)
8 March 1965	Paval Belyayev Aleksei Leonov	Voskhod 2	first spacewalk (17 orbits)
23 March 1965	Virgil I. Grissom John W. Young	Gemini 3	first manual orbital manoeuvres (3 orbits)
3 June 1965	James A. McDivitt Edward H. White	Gemini 4	spacewalk (62 orbits)
21 August 1965	L. Gordon Cooper Charles Conrad	Gemini 5	first spaceflight lasting a week (120 orbits)
4 December 1965	Frank Borman James A. Lovell	Gemini 7	first long spaceflight (13 days, 206 orbits); with Gemini 6
15 December 1965	Walter M. Schirra Thomas P. Stafford	Gemini 6	group flight with Gemini 7 (17 orbits)
16 March 1966	Neil A. Armstrong David R. Scott	Gemini 8	first manual docking with an Agena rocket stage (6 orbits)
3 June 1966	Thomas P. Stafford Eugene A. Cernan	Gemini 9	spacewalk (45 orbits)
18 July 1966	John W. Young Michael Collins	Gemini 10	docking and spacewalk (43 orbits)
12 September 1966	Charles Conrad Richard F. Gordon	Gemini 11	docking and spacewalk (44 orbits)
11 November 1966	James A. Lovell Edwin E. Aldrin	Gemini 12	orbital docking and first work carried out during a spacewalk (59 orbits)

On 14 September 1959, the Soviet Luna 2 probe crashed onto the Moon's surface. Before it was destroyed, however, it provided the scientific community with a wealth of information. It also showed the Americans that the Soviets were skilled at correcting the orbits of spacecraft during flight. Three weeks later, on 4 October 1959, the anniversary of Sputnik 1's launch, the Soviets launched Luna 3, which went into a lunar orbit and photographed the dark side of the Moon for the first time.

On 12 February 1961, they launched the first interplanetary probe, Venera 1, which passed within 100000 kilometres of Venus before going into orbit around the Sun. Then came Venera 2, launched on 12 November 1965, which passed within 24000 kilometres of Venus. Venera 3 was launched on 16 November 1965 and crash landed onto the surface of Venus on 1 March 1966. This spacecraft made the first contact between Earth and another planet.

During the period from 1960 to 1965, the USA and the USSR inaugurated nearly all their major satellite programmes. The Soviets sent three probes to Venus and eight to the Moon. Beginning on 16 March 1962, they used the two stage Cosmos rocket to launch 103 scientific satellites in the Cosmos series. Between 1958 and 1960 the Americans launched two Pioneer space probes, and put thirty-nine satellites into orbit about the Earth. Of these, 15 were scientific satellites, 14 were technological, and 10 applications satellites. Seven of the applications satellites were for military purposes, for reconnaissance, navigation and telecommunications.

The development of observation, surveillance and early warning satellites at the beginning of the 1960s without doubt helped to prevent a military conflict between the two superpowers. From then on a surprise attack was no longer possible. The first American satellites of the Discoverer series, launched in 1959, took photographs and then returned the film to Earth in a recoverable capsule; the capsules were 'caught' by aeroplanes as they parachuted back to Earth. In the more advanced Samos series of satellites, the photographs were transmitted to Earth using radio waves. Most notably during the 1962 Cuban crisis, the Americans used military observational satellites to monitor the deployment of Soviet missiles.

To avoid a surprise attack, especially from intercontinental ballistic missiles, the Americans also developed Midas satellites. These detected the infrared radiation given off by the exhaust gases from a missile. The first such satellite was launched on 24 May 1960. The Russians meanwhile had developed similar devices in their military satellites of the Cosmos series.

1960 was also the year of the first applications satellites. The first meteorological satellite, Tiros 1, was launched on 1 April 1960. From its observations the temperatures of clouds could be deduced, and with observations of cloud motions too, it became possible to make better long term weather forecasts. Ten Tiros satellites were ultimately launched between 1960 and 1965, each incorporating improvements over its predecessors. The first navigational satellite, Transit 1, was launched on 13 April 1960. It could determine the position of specialised equipment on the Earth's surface to within 400 metres. And the era of telecommunications began on 12 August, when the metal coated balloon Echo 1A was launched. This reflected radio waves transmitted from the Earth.

All these satellites had both military and civil uses. The Americans were encouraged by their success, and generally felt that they had overcome their initial disadvantage.

Then, on 15 May 1960, the Soviet Union launched Sputnik 4. It weighed 4·5 tonnes and was the forerunner of the Vostok manned spacecraft; once more the USSR had taken a lead in space.

The first man in space

Another surprise occurred almost a year later, on 12 April 1961, when Yuri Gagarin was launched into space aboard Vostok 1. The rocket weighed 1·4 tonnes and was launched from the Tyuratam-Baikonur base north west of the Aral Sea. After orbiting once around the Earth, Gagarin returned safe and sound. This totally automatic space mission was a complete success. Gagarin was given a memorable welcome home in Moscow and became an international hero.

Thus, just at the moment when the Americans thought that they had caught the Soviets up, Yuri Gagarin catapulted the world into the next phase of the space era.

The Americans replied with the brief ballistic flight of Alan B. Shepard. His 15 minute flight took place on 5 May 1961, using a Redstone rocket and the Mercury Freedom 7 capsule. Shepard manually tested the stabilisation and reentry capabilities of his capsule so his flight was by no means simply a repeat of Gagarin's.

Later the same month, on 25 May 1961, President John F. Kennedy announced, in a message to Congress, that the USA had decided that an American would walk on the Moon before the end of the decade. Thus it was that the Apollo programme was initiated. This required a much increased technological and industrial effort, and NASA's budget was substantially enhanced. Between 1961 and 1962 its budget doubled, only to double again between 1962 and 1963. The Department of Defense's space budget was similarly increased.

NASA's work force increased from 16000 in 1960 to over 33000 by 1965. The race was now focused on the Moon, and the Americans were determined to be first. Their overall plan was to build a three man Apollo spacecraft, but to begin with they planned an intermediary craft, the two man Gemini spacecraft. The objective of the Gemini programme was to put two men in space, and to enable them to dock with another space vehicle and walk in space. The Titan rocket was developed to launch this 4 tonne spacecraft.

The Americans repeated their suborbital flight with Virgil I. Grissom's trip on 21 July 1961. He used the Redstone rocket, the more powerful Atlas rocket not yet being operational, and the Mercury Liberty Bell 7 capsule. However, Grissom's flight nearly turned into a tragic disaster when the capsule started to sink after splashdown, and the astronaut had to swim away from it. On 13 September 1961, a capsule containing a dummy was put into orbit and then recovered. A similar experiment was repeated on 29 November with a chimpanzee aboard. Pleased with these successes, the Americans put their first astronaut, John H. Glenn, into orbit, some 10 months after Yuri Gagarin's feat. On 20 February 1962, launched by an Atlas rocket, Glenn completed three orbits around the Earth in the Mercury Friendship 7 capsule.

In the meantime, Guerman Titov had completed 17 orbits of the Earth on 6 August 1961 on board Vostok 2. His was the first spaceflight to last more than 24 hours, demonstrating for the first time that it was safe for man to live in space. A year later, on 12 August 1962, Pavel Popovich, in Vostok 4, and Andriyan Nikolayev, in Vostok 3, launched the previous day, passed in space within 6·5 kilometres of each other. The Soviets showed in this way that it was possible for one spacecraft to intercept another, a success which had particular implications for military satellite programmes.

The continuing space race

The two superpowers carried on trying to achieve 'space firsts' throughout the 1960s, with the USA putting considerable effort into achieving President Kennedy's objective. Three further Mercury flights took place. Scott

Carpenter completed three orbits of the Earth on 24 May 1962, in Mercury Aurora 7, during which time he studied the effects of weightlessness on liquids. However, his capsule landed 400 kilometres from the planned touchdown point where recovery ships were waiting.

On 3 October 1962, Walter M. Schirra carried out a spaceflight which was entirely piloted from his Mercury Sigma 7 capsule. This economised on the amount of fuel carried, enabling him to perform additional manoeuvres. And on 15 to 16 May 1963, L. Gordon Cooper completed a flight lasting more than 24 hours in the Faith 7 capsule. In both of these flights the astronauts landed within 10 kilometres of the recovery vessels, illustrating to the world that the Americans had improved their techniques for bringing astronauts safely back from space.

On 10 July 1962, the USA launched its first experimental telecommunications satellite, Telstar. The Americans once more felt optimistic about their space programme. The Mercury programme was terminated, the Gemini programme began, and a year later, on 26 July 1963, the USA became the first country to put a satellite into a geostationary orbit with Syncom 2. Syncom 3 was launched into geostationary orbit in 1964, and the Americans used it that year to retransmit the Olympic games from Tokyo. This success led to the creation of the international telecommunications organisation, Intelsat. It was Intelsat that controlled the first satellite used for communications by telephone, Early Bird, launched on 28 July 1965.

On 16 June 1963 Valentina Tereshkova became the first woman in space. In Vostok 6 she completed a three day spaceflight with Valery Bykovsky, who has been launched two days earlier in Vostok 5. As with Vostok 2 and Vostok 3, theirs was not a piloted rendezvous; the flight was entirely ballistic and depended on accurate launching.

The Soviets followed this up with a new three man spacecraft, Voskhod 1, launched on 12 October 1964. The first crew consisted of Vladimir Komarov, Konstantin Feoktistov and Boris Yegorov. But their automatic systems broke down on this occasion and the spacecraft landed more than 1500 kilometres from the arranged place. It took several hours to recover the astronauts. On 18 March 1965, Voskhod 2 was launched, carrying a two man crew, Pavel Belyayev and Aleksei Leonov. The latter left the spacecraft and completed the first ever spacewalk, demonstrating in the most direct way possible that a human being could adapt to the environment of space.

The Americans tested Gemini 1 and Gemini 2 without crews, and then, on 23 March 1965, they used a Titan II rocket to launch Gemini 3. The crew of Virgil I. Grissom and John W. Young used the capsule's instruments to modify the orbit manually and the Americans began to display their superiority in matters of electronic equipment, with their ability in particular to miniaturise instruments.

On 3 June 1965, James A. McDivitt and Edward H. White were put into orbit on board Gemini 4. White became the first American to walk in space. During his 21 minute spacewalk, he used a small propulsion unit to manoeuvre himself.

At this point the number of American spaceflights increased rapidly. On 21 August 1965, the Gemini 5 mission achieved a number of firsts. It was the second trip into space for L. Gordon Cooper, and he and Charles Conrad became the first astronauts to spend more than seven days in Earth orbit. They had fuel cells which, for the first time, provided enough electrical energy for long duration flights.

One of the major objectives of the American space programme was to dock two spacecraft, a necessary requirement for Apollo. The Saturn V rocket could put an Apollo spacecraft with a lunar module into Earth orbit. This combination would then leave terrestrial orbit to be put in a lunar orbit. There, the lunar module would detach itself from the Apollo spacecraft, leav-

continued on p. 60

The first man in space. Yuri Gagarin on the journey to Vostok 1's launch pad on 12 April 1961. Behind him, also in a spacesuit, is his 'back up', Guerman Titov; G. G. Nelyubov is standing (APN).

The American response. Six weeks after Yuri Gagarin's successful flight, President Kennedy gave this message to Congress, on 25 May 1961: 'I believe that the aim of this nation should be to land a man on the Moon and return him safely to Earth before the end of the decade.' Thus was the Apollo programme launched (NASA).

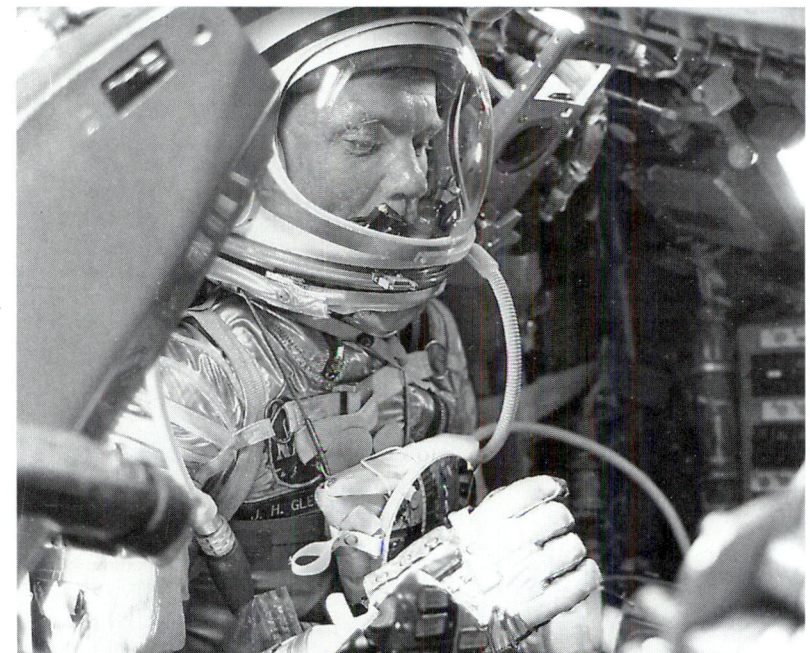

In pursuit of the American goal. On 20 February 1962, John H. Glenn became the first American to orbit the Earth – he completed three orbits in his Mercury Friendship 7 capsule, in a flight lasting nearly 5 hours. The USA had found a new hero.

Glenn's flight was the beginning of a long series of American successes, which were only interrupted by the Apollo 1 tragedy on 27 January 1967. Soviet supremacy in space was slowly eroded thereafter (NASA).

The Gemini 7 mission. On 4 December 1965, Frank Borman (in front) and James A. Lovell stepped onto the gangway leading to the lift in the launch tower of the Titan II launcher. As the photograph shows, they were wearing light spacesuits which could be removed during a spaceflight which was to last fourteen days. The two men were carrying apparatus to provide them with oxygen and keep their spacesuits cool until they could be connected to the capsule's life support systems.

Borman and Lovell, on Gemini 7, and Thomas P. Stafford and Walter M. Schirra aboard Gemini 6 performed the first space rendezvous in history. This success, along with Borman and Lovell's long duration flight augured well for the success of the Apollo missions (NASA).

The Mercury programme

Directed by the National Aeronautics and Space Administration (NASA), Mercury was America's first manned spaceflight programme (1958 to 1963). The prime objectives of the project were to put a man into orbit, to observe his reactions, and to recover him safely. To this end, 25 test and flight missions were made, employing 20 spacecraft, 24 launch vehicles, four animals, and six astronauts. Not one passenger or pilot was lost.

At Cape Canaveral, on 5 May 1961, Alan B. Shepard lay in the Freedom 7 capsule as the Mercury Redstone 3 rocket boosted the spacecraft to a speed of 8300 kilometres per hour, a trajectory apex of 187 kilometres, and a horizontal 'downrange' distance of 486 kilometres. He withstood an acceleration of 6g during launch and of 12g during landing. In his 15 minute flight, during which he was weightless for five minutes, Shepard operated the control jets to rotate the spacecraft about its three axes, and observed landmarks through his window. Recovery, using helicopters and ships, was easily effected.

Virgil I. Grissom, in Liberty Bell 7, piloted the second suborbital mission on 21 July 1961. After landing in the sea and awaiting helicopter pickup, the hatch blew, the spacecraft sank and Grissom had to swim for his life.

On 20 February 1962, John H. Glenn, aboard Friendship 7, became the first American to orbit the Earth. Boosted to 28000 kilometres per hour, Glenn made three orbits of the Earth, operating the controls with ease and finding weightlessness pleasant. During his spaceflight, Glenn reported that he saw gleaming particles that he called 'fireflies'.

Medical problems prevented Donald K. Slayton from piloting the next mission and it was M. Scott Carpenter who, on 24 May 1962, flew Aurora 7 for three orbits. Operations were similar to Glenn's flight, and Carpenter established that the 'fireflies' were crystals from the attitude control jets. At the end of the mission he fired the reentry rockets late so that Aurora 7 overshot the landing zone by 380 kilometres, but a safe recovery was still achieved.

A longer flight duration was one of the goals for Walter M. Schirra on 3 October 1962, when he piloted Sigma 7 for six orbits to a Pacific, rather than an Atlantic, landing. Careful use of the attitude control fuel produced excellent results and qualified the vehicle to fly longer and farther. Nearly nine hours of weightlessness caused blood to accumulate in the pilot's legs, raising medical worries.

An improved Mercury capsule was ready in 1963 and, on 15 May, L. Gordon Cooper in Faith 7 made 22 orbits, landing the next day in the Pacific. Cooper operated the spacecraft systems, ate, slept, observed and performed simple experiments. He proved a pilot's worth in space when an electrical short circuit forced him to carry out many reentry and landing control tasks manually; he landed with pinpoint accuracy in the recovery zone.

Moves were afoot to enable Mercury to rendezvous in space, and the flights were to proceed with Alan Shepard flying the Mercury-Atlas 10 rocket. NASA Administrator James E. Webb, however, concluded that all that was possible had been learned from Mercury, and so, on 12 June 1963, he announced the end of the programme.

James M. Grimwood

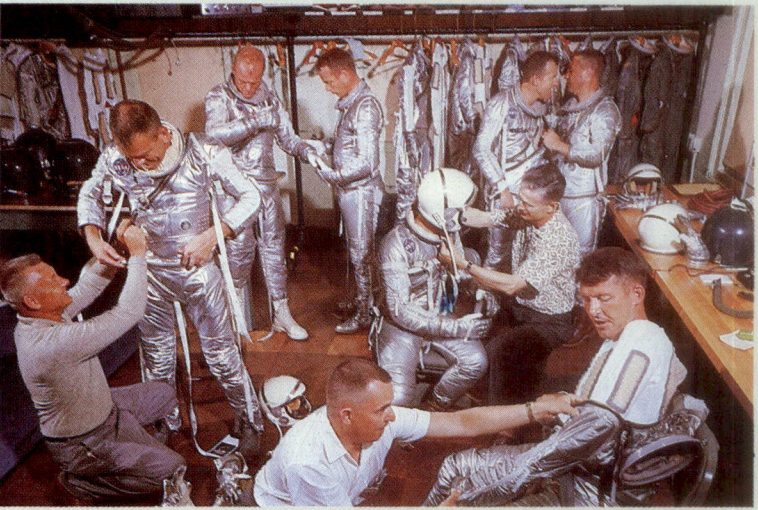

The Mercury programme team. On 9 April 1959, NASA announced the names of the seven US Air Force pilots who had been chosen as astronauts for the Mercury programme. They continued flying F106 fighters to maintain their skills and spent a considerable time liaising with rocket, capsule and spacesuit designers and builders. They were submitted to a rigorous training programme, involving periods spent in a centrifuge, where they were subjected to very high accelerations, and in flight simulators. They also practised desert and sea landings. All this qualified them for suborbital flights. The men seen in spacesuits here are, from left to right, Donald K. Slayton, John H. Glenn, M. Scott Carpenter, Alan B. Shepard (wearing a helmet), L. Gordon Cooper, Virgil I. 'Gus' Grissom and, in the foreground, Walter M. Schirra (Ralph Morse for *Life*/Colorific).

Mercury manned spaceflights

Mission and crew	Date	Flight time	Orbits	Significant events
MR3, Freedom 7 Alan B. Shepard	5 May 1961	15 minutes 22 seconds	first suborbital flight	
MR 4, Liberty Bell 7 Virgil I. Grissom	21 July 1961	15 minutes 37 seconds	second suborbital flight	
MA 6, Friendship 7 John H. Glenn	20 February 1962	4 hours 55 minutes	3	first orbital flight
MA 7, Aurora 7 M. Scott Carpenter	24 May 1962	4 hours 56 minutes	3	initiated spaceflight experiments
MA 8, Sigma 7 Walter M. Schirra	3 October 1962	9 hours 13 minutes	6	developed techniques for long duration missions
MA 9, Faith 7 L. Gordon Cooper	15 to 16 June 1963	34 hours 20 minutes	22	met objective to spend more than one day in space

MR: Mercury Redstone; MA: Mercury Atlas.

The three types of rocket launcher used in the Mercury programme. Far left, the Little Joe launcher with a Mercury capsule on top is launched, on 4 November 1959, from Wallops Island, Virginia. This launch was used to test the safety tower and the recovery parachute system. Little Joe, specially designed for the Mercury programme, was 15 metres tall and 2 metres in diameter. It had eight solid fuel rockets which could deliver a thrust of over 1 meganewton, and could carry a 1·8 tonne payload on a ballistic orbit to a height of more than 160 kilometres. Two rhesus monkeys, Sam and Miss Sam, each took part in a flight to test their reactions when subjected to accelerations of several times that at the Earth's surface, 1g. In fact, Sam experienced 14·8g on 4 December 1959.

On 5 May 1961, a Mercury Redstone 3 (MR 3) launcher, based on the liquid fuel ballistic missile Redstone, carried Alan B. Shepard in his Freedom 7 capsule on the first manned suborbital flight (centre). Prior to this, the Redstone rocket had been used to test the capsule in a suborbital flight. On 31 January 1961, Ham, another chimpanzee, was subjected to a thrust of nearly 350 kilonewtons from the launcher and an acceleration of 11g at lift off. The capsule reached a height of 253 kilometres and was recovered 679 kilometres from the launch site. During reentry, the deceleration reached 14·7g.

The only launcher which was used for Mercury manned spaceflights was the Atlas missile, which produced a thrust at lift off of 1·6 meganewtons. Apart from being used to test the capsule, the rocket tested the heat shield which would protect the capsule during reentry into the atmosphere. These flights also proved the 16 tracking stations in a worldwide network. On 29 November 1961, a Mercury Atlas 5 (MA 5) rocket was launched from Cape Canaveral carrying the chimpanzee, Enos. This completed two orbits of the Earth as the final part of the test phase.

The photograph on the right shows the MA 6 rocket carrying John H. Glenn into space for the first manned orbital flight, on 20 February 1962 (NASA).

Early studies. The concept of a space vehicle, fitted with sails, was abandoned in 1957 in favour of a blunt capsule which would reenter the atmosphere ballistically. This sketch of the capsule still attached to its rocket was made in May 1958. The protective covering has just been ejected to reveal the portholes and to enable the antennae to be deployed. The two cylindrical devices house the parachutes. The astronaut would be able to control the retrorockets to bring the capsule out of orbit, and to reenter the atmosphere. Apart from this, he was a passenger with only a few tasks to undertake.

The test configuration of the Mercury capsule was chosen after tests, most of which were carried out at the NASA Langley Research Center, on life size replicas (drawing by Caldwell C. Johnson, rights reserved).

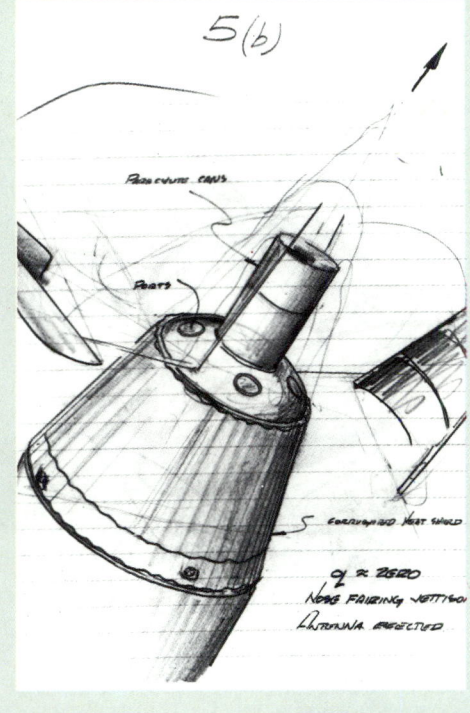

The Mercury capsule. The Mercury capsule was shaped like a truncated cone, with a maximum diameter of 1·89 metres, a minimum diameter of 0·81 metres, and a cylindrical part on top. For the first part of the journey, the capsule was surmounted by a rescue tower consisting of a three nozzle solid fuel rocket which could deliver a thrust of 130 kilonewtons for 1 second. It would be used to separate the capsule from the rocket in case of a rocket failure shortly after launch. If all went well the tower would be ejected, unused, after the Atlas motors had been jettisoned.

The total height, including the tower and the rockets attached to the heat shield was 7·91 metres. The mass was 1·94 tonnes at launch, 1·36 tonnes in orbit, and 1·13 tonnes at touchdown.

The capsule had three walls. The two internal ones, 0·25 millimetres thick, were made of titanium, with the external wall being 0·41 millimetres thick. The external wall had a matt black covering, designed to radiate away the heat produced during reentry.

The capsule contained pure oxygen, at a pressure of 340 millibars, about one third of normal atmospheric pressure. If it were holed in space, the astronaut would be saved by his spacesuit.

Eighteen small hydrogen peroxide thrusters were used to control the capsule's attitude either manually or automatically. The thrusts produced could vary between 4·4 and 107 newtons.

The beryllium heat shield was not removable on the suborbital flights, but was so on the orbital flights. Attached to this shield were six solid fuel rockets: three were to separate the capsule from the launcher and three to bring it out of orbit. Each could give 4·4 newtons of thrust for 10 seconds.

After the reentry phase, at an altitude of 6·4 kilometres, a parachute with a diameter of 1·8 metres opened. This stabilised the capsule and slowed it down to a speed of 76 metres per second. Then the main parachute, with a diameter of 19·2 metres, opened at 3 kilometres altitude. There was also a reserve parachute.

Just before impact, the heat shield detached itself from the base of the capsule. This released a balloon which filled with air and helped reduce the deceleration to 15*g* at touchdown. By filling itself with water, this also acted as an anchor in heavy seas.

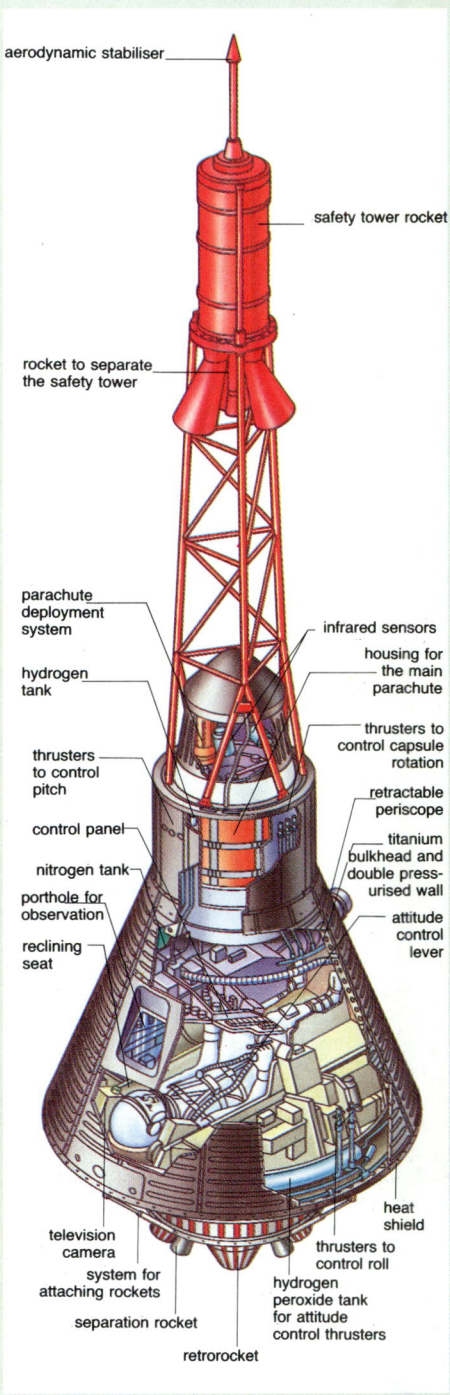

aerodynamic stabiliser

safety tower rocket

rocket to separate the safety tower

parachute deployment system

hydrogen tank

thrusters to control pitch

control panel

nitrogen tank

porthole for observation

reclining seat

infrared sensors

housing for the main parachute

thrusters to control capsule rotation

retractable periscope

titanium bulkhead and double pressurised wall

attitude control lever

television camera

system for attaching rockets

separation rocket

heat shield

thrusters to control roll

hydrogen peroxide tank for attitude control thrusters

retrorocket

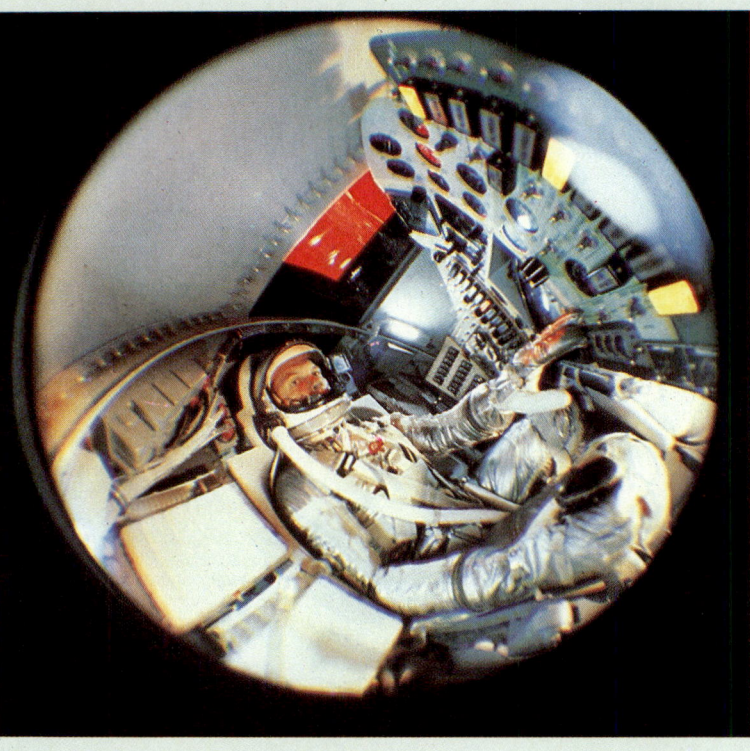

John Glenn training. A procedures monitor, later called a Mercury simulator, was used to plan the astronaut's programme once he was in space. He then practised all the necessary manoeuvres. An operator outside the unit could simulate all the conditions which the astronaut might have to face. The simulator could also be linked to the flight control centre, so that the astronaut and the ground staff could become used to working together as a team.

To help him survive the enormous accelerations, the astronaut lay on a reclining seat which moulded itself around him. Above his head was a porthole, fitted with a Sun filter. There was also a periscope to enable the astronaut to see outside (Ralph Morse for *Life*/Colorific).

Recovering Alan Shepard (right). The trajectory of Freedom 7 returning from its 15 minute suborbital flight was so accurate that the recovery helicopters were able to watch it for a full five minutes. Alan Shepard and the capsule were separately hoisted aboard a helicopter and taken to the aircraft carrier *Lake Champlain* in an 11 minute operation (NASA).

The Cape Canaveral control centre during John Glenn's flight. In the foreground is the console of the director general of operations. To the right, is the director of the tracking network. On the next row are the flight director and his assistant. Other individuals are responsible for the tracking and telemetry network, and for monitoring the operation of the capsule's different systems.

The screen in the distance shows the track of the capsule as it orbited the Earth. The circles represent the ranges of the different tracking stations. It was easier to communicate with Friendship 7 during the first orbit than the second and third, when it was sometimes out of range (rights reserved).

The Gemini programme

Long duration spaceflights and spacecraft rendezvous were requirements for Apollo, the American programme for a manned lunar landing in the 1960s. The Mercury programme alone could not provide sufficient experience to achieve this goal, and so the Gemini programme was approved in December 1961 to bridge the gap.

Mercury's ballistic design was retained, but not its capsules. Gemini systems were made in the form of modules for easy access, and consumables such as fuel, water and oxygen were stored in sections to be discarded prior to landing. A two man crew sat in a cockpit that had controls, instrument panels and ejector seats resembling those of military aircraft.

A Titan II missile was chosen to launch the 3·6 tonne spacecraft into orbit. The first stage thrust Gemini to 60 kilometres altitude where a second stage ignited to complete the orbit insertion.

Most of the Gemini systems were qualified in ground tests. Among these systems were small rocket engines to alter the orbital path, a radar to aid the rendezvous with an Agena vehicle from another Atlas launch, and a fuel cell to supply the electricity required during long duration missions. A paraglider was planned for returning to dry land, but its development could not be finished in time so Gemini relied on parachutes to land on water just as Mercury capsules had done.

Two unmanned flights were made. Gemini 1 lifted off from Cape Canaveral, Florida, on 8 April 1964. The flight, which lasted for 64 orbits, provided launch stress data as well as training for the tracking network teams. The following year, Gemini 2 tested systems from liftoff, on 19 January 1965, to spacecraft recovery.

Firstly, on 23 March 1965, Virgil I. Grissom and John W. Young were launched from Cape Canaveral and made three orbits in Gemini 3, firing thrusters to alter the orbital path for the first time. The reentry control system caused the landing to be some 80 kilometres short of the planned zone in the Atlantic.

Long duration spaceflight was the goal of the next two Gemini missions. Gemini 4 pilots James A. McDivitt and Edward H. White endured four days' weightless flight, allaying medical concerns that had previously been expressed. During the mission, White emerged from the spacecraft and propelled himself with a hand held, gas filled rocket gun. After 62 orbits, they landed on 7 June 1965.·The eight day Gemini 5 mission, with L. Gordon Cooper and Charles Conrad aboard, experienced a fuel cell problem limiting the availability and use of electrical

The Gemini spacecraft. This drawing shows the main parts of the spacecraft. The capsule (A) was fixed to the Titan II rocket launcher by an adapter with two sections. These were the deorbiting system (B) and the resource compartment (C).

A removable heat shield, made of titanium, steel and beryllium, formed the base of the capsule. Each astronaut had a hatch, fitted with a porthole, which was sufficiently big for him to perform spacewalks. The uppermost section contained the rendezvous radar, which was ejected to enable the main parachute, with a diameter of 25·6 metres, to be deployed during reentry.

The deorbiting system had four retrorockets, each with a thrust of 11 kilonewtons, as well as six of the eight 400 newton thrusters for rendezvous and docking manoeuvres.

The resource compartment contained water and oxygen tanks, batteries and fuel tanks for the different attitude control and orbital manoeuvre thrusters. This unit also housed the remaining two orbital manoeuvre thrusters and four pairs of attitude control thrusters, each with a thrust of 110 newtons.

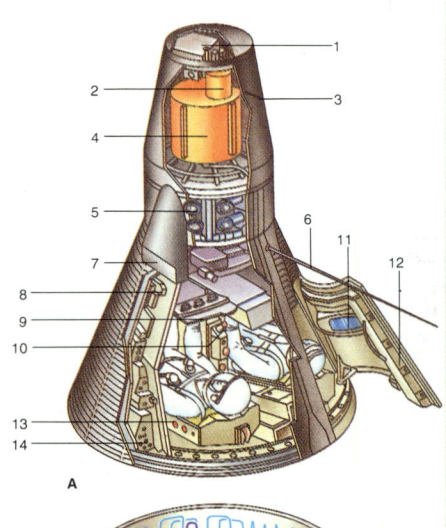

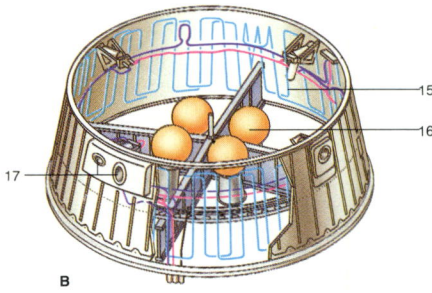

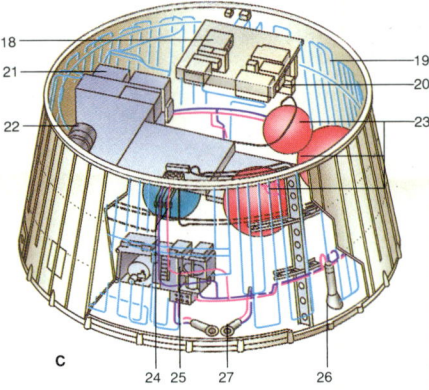

A Capsule
1 orbital rendezvous radar
2 parachute deployment system
3 orbital docking system
4 main parachute
5 16 thrusters to control attitude during reentry
6 high frequency antenna
7 horizon sensors
8 electrical equipment
9 control panel
10 control lever
11 porthole
12 hatchway for spacewalks
13 ejectable seat
14 inertial guidance system

B Deorbiting system
15 cooling system
16 four solid fuel retrorockets
17 six thrusters for orbital manoeuvres

C Resource compartment
18 instruments
19 cooling circuits
20 communications devices
21 batteries
22 drinking water tanks
23 monomethylhydrazine fuel tank (helium pressurised)
24 nitrogen peroxide fuel tank (helium pressurised)
25 pumps for the cooling system
26 two thrusters for orbital manoeuvres
27 eight thrusters for the orbital attitude control system

	capsule	adaptor
minimum diameter (metres).....	0.98	2.29
maximum diameter (metres)....	2.29	3.05
length (metres)........................	3.66	2.29
total length (metres)................	5.74	
mass in orbit (tonnes).............	3.4	
mass at touchdown (tonnes) ...	2.2	

The first space rendezvous in history. On 15 December 1965, at an altitude of 260 kilometres, this photograph of Gemini 7 carrying Frank Borman and James Lovell was taken by Tom Stafford, the co-pilot with Walter Schirra on board Gemini 6. The Sun is shining on the white adaptor ring of Gemini 7 and the Earth below. Circular rendezvous antennae are visible on the nose. The two spacecraft flew together for four orbits, and came as close as 300 millimetres to each other.

The Gemini 6 and 7 missions showed that man could survive long periods in space and that space rendezvous were feasible, and paved the way for the future successes of the Apollo mission (NASA).

Gemini manned spaceflights

Mission and crew	Date	Flight time	Orbits	Significant events
Gemini 3 Grissom & Young	23 March 1965	4 hours 53 minutes	3	first two man orbital flight
Gemini 4 McDivitt & White	3 to 7 June 1965	97 hours 56 minutes	62	first spacewalk
Gemini 5 Cooper & Conrad	21 to 29 August 1965	190 hours 55 minutes	120	long duration flight
Gemini 7 Borman & Lovell	4 to 18 December 1965	330 hours 35 minutes	206	long duration, rendezvous
Gemini 6 Schirra & Stafford	15 to 16 December 1965	25 hours 51 minutes	16	rendezvous with Gemini 7
Gemini 8 Armstrong & Scott	16 March 1966	10 hours 41 minutes	6.6	rendezvous, first docking
Gemini 9 Stafford & Cernan	3 to 6 June 1966	72 hours 21 minutes	45	rendezvous, spacewalk
Gemini 10 Young & Collins	18 to 21 July 1966	70 hours 47 minutes	43	rendezvous, docking, spacewalk
Gemini 11 Conrad & Gordon	12 to 15 September 1966	71 hours 17 minutes	44	rendezvous, docking, spacewalk
Gemini 12 Lovell & Aldrin	11 to 15 November 1966	94 hours 35 minutes	59	rendezvous, docking, spacewalk

The Titan II launcher. On launch pad 19 at Cape Kennedy, the Titan II launcher and the Gemini 3 capsule with Grissom and Young aboard undergo a flight simulation a few days before the actual flight. The erection tower, here being removed, contained various work platforms and, at the top, a white room through which the astronauts walked when boarding their spacecraft. The umbilical tower (right) keeps the launcher and spacecraft supplied with liquid fuel and electricity before launch. The different nozzles and cables are removed at the last moment after the erection tower has been completely lowered.

power. Although many activities were curtailed, the crew managed to rendezvous their spacecraft with an imaginary target. They landed after making 120 Earth orbits.

Gemini 6 should have made a rendezvous with an Agena vehicle, but on 25 October the latter exploded during the launch, leaving Walter M. Schirra and Thomas P. Stafford without a target. NASA decided to launch the 14 day Gemini 7 on 4 December, with Frank Borman and James A. Lovell, and to send Gemini 6 later to rendezvous with them. An initial try failed when the Titan II rocket shut down almost immediately after ignition, leaving Schirra and Stafford on the pad. However, three days later, on 15 December, they were launched for a meeting in orbit with Borman and Lovell. Schirra manoeuvred his craft to record the first rendezvous between two manned space vehicles.

Gemini had achieved its fundamental goals, but NASA contended that five more flights set for 1966 were still needed. With Agena's ailments cured, Neil A. Armstrong and David R. Scott in Gemini 8 docked with their target on 16 March. A stuck thruster caused the spacecraft to pitch and yaw for many minutes at high speed. Swift action by the crew halted the violent motions, but so much fuel had been used up that the mission

had to be curtailed. Gemini 8 ended with a Pacific Ocean splashdown.

After an Atlas booster failed to launch an Agena target vehicle, Gemini 9 pilots Tom Stafford and Eugene A. Cernan tried to dock with a substitute target, but failed as the launch shroud was still attached. However, on 18 July 1966, John Young and Michael Collins, in Gemini 10, docked with an Agena and used its engine to push the combination to just over 750 kilometres altitude. During extravehicular activity (EVA), Collins retrieved an experiment package on the Agena. In a similar mission, Gemini 11 pilots Charles Conrad and Richard F. Gordon reached and docked with an Agena in the first orbit after launch, using its engine to rise to an altitude of 1400 kilometres. Although physically taxing, EVA was a major task too for Gemini 12, which followed two months later, on 11 November 1966.

Gemini proved that man could survive and operate in the space environment for at least two weeks, and that one vehicle could find and successfully dock with another. Most crucially of all, both astronaut and flight control crews gained the experience they needed to prepare for the Apollo missions.

James M. Grimwood

The recovery of Gemini 8 (above). After their premature return to Earth, Neil Armstrong (right) and David Scott had to wait for three hours until a helicopter arrived to transfer them to the US destroyer *Mason* in the Pacific Ocean. The Mercury capsules had landed vertically, but the Gemini capsules were suspended at two points from the parachute and landed horizontally. Frogmen from the helicopter placed an inflatable collar around the capsule to ease its removal from the sea. The astronauts opened their hatches, were hoisted aboard helicopters and taken to the recovery fleet. For most of the flights, except during spacewalks when one of the hatches remained open, the astronauts' vision was restricted to two portholes (NASA).

Inside the Gemini capsule (left). Compared with the Mercury capsule, which fitted snugly around the astronaut, there was a little improvement, but each astronaut still had only 0·76 cubic metres of free space. The two portholes separated the three main control panels for the instruments, indicators, gauges and ignition switches (© Farell Grehan/Wheeler/Cosmos).

The docking targets of the Gemini capsules. A normal rendezvous and docking mission during the Gemini programme began with the launch of an Atlas and Agena rocket from pad 14 at Cape Kennedy.

The lower photograph shows the Agena stage that was the target of Gemini 10. The rocket motor nozzle is visible on the right, while the docking system is on the left. A transponder at the end of a deployable pole received signals from the Gemini's rendezvous radar during the docking manoeuvre.

The photograph on the left, taken by David Scott, shows the Agena docking ring as Neil Armstrong guides the capsule towards it. They were only about 600 millimetres apart at the time. The first space docking took place on 16 March 1966, about 5 hours and 4 minutes after the launch of Gemini 8 (NASA).

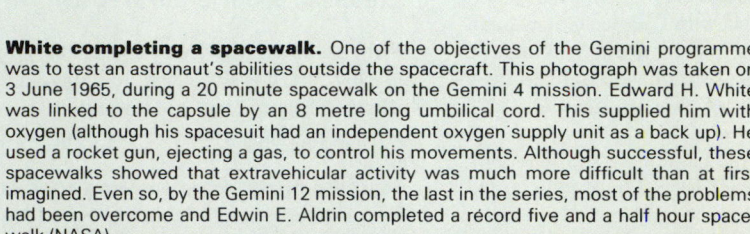

White completing a spacewalk. One of the objectives of the Gemini programme was to test an astronaut's abilities outside the spacecraft. This photograph was taken on 3 June 1965, during a 20 minute spacewalk on the Gemini 4 mission. Edward H. White was linked to the capsule by an 8 metre long umbilical cord. This supplied him with oxygen (although his spacesuit had an independent oxygen supply unit as a back up). He used a rocket gun, ejecting a gas, to control his movements. Although successful, these spacewalks showed that extravehicular activity was much more difficult than at first imagined. Even so, by the Gemini 12 mission, the last in the series, most of the problems had been overcome and Edwin E. Aldrin completed a record five and a half hour spacewalk (NASA).

Saturn I. The successful first trial of the Saturn I rocket, on 27 October 1961, marked the beginning of more than 11 years of launches in the Apollo programme. In the trial, only the first stage, S I, of the launcher was operational, the S IV and S V stages being filled with 91 tonnes of water. The test was used to study the aerodynamics and performance of the entire rocket (NASA).

Testing the F 1 rocket engine. Five F 1 rockets provided the propulsion for the first stage of the Saturn V rocket. The first version delivered a thrust of 6·7 meganewtons, and this was subsequently improved to 6·8 meganewtons. Constructed by the Rocketdyne division of the Rockwell International Corporation, they remained the most powerful rocket engines ever built for more than a quarter of a century. Only in 1987, were they surpassed by the engines of the Soviet Energia heavy launcher (Rockwell International).

ing an astronaut behind, and land the other two crew members on the Moon. For the return trip the lunar module would rejoin the Apollo spacecraft, and when both were back in Earth orbit they would carry out manoeuvres to reenter the atmosphere and land. The Gemini programme was designed to practise these important, yet delicate, space rendezvous manoeuvres and the success of the Apollo programme depended on mastering the techniques.

NASA did not have sufficient equipment to carry out a full docking between spacecraft so they organised a space rendezvous between two Gemini spacecraft. On 4 December 1965, Gemini 7 was launched carrying Frank Borman and James A. Lovell; they spent a fortnight in space, the equivalent of the maximum duration of a lunar mission. Gemini 6 was launched a week later, on 11 December, from the same launch pad, carrying Thomas P. Stafford and Walter M. Schirra. Gemini 6 performed all the necessary orbital adjustments and came to within two metres of Gemini 7. The two spacecraft then proceeded to perform a succession of separation and approach manoeuvres.

The Americans successfully completed a full docking procedure on 16 March 1966, when David R. Scott and Neil A. Armstrong in Gemini 8 docked with the upper stage of an Agena rocket vehicle, which had been placed ready in space.

The docking was a complete success. However, shortly afterwards there was a failure in one of the thrusters of the orientation system of the Gemini spacecraft and the two craft went into an uncontrolled spin. The astronauts managed to regain control of their spacecraft but used up nearly all their fuel reserves in the process, and were forced to return immediately to Earth. This demonstrated only too clearly that, despite numerous successes, the slightest malfunction in space could have disastrous consequences.

The Gemini 9 mission, launched with Thomas P. Stafford and Eugene A. Cernan on 3 June 1966, failed to rendezvous with the Agena target, because the latter had not completely disengaged from its carrier rocket. The mission was, however, a partial success because Cernan was able to perform a spacewalk which lasted more than two hours.

After the difficulties the Americans had encountered in these missions, they were forced to improve their equipment. On 18 July 1966, Gemini 10, with John W. Young and Michael Collins aboard, as a result performed a perfect docking with an Agena target. On 12 September 1966, Gemini 11, with Charles Conrad and Richard F. Gordon, repeated the docking and then used the Agena's propulsion units to raise the two vehicles to an altitude of 1370 kilometres.

The last flight in the Gemini programme took place on 11 November 1966. On board Gemini 12 were James A. Lovell and Edwin E. Aldrin, Aldrin making an extensive spacewalk during the course of the flight which made it possible to plan for repair work outside a spacecraft in the future.

During the Gemini programme, the Americans thus launched ten successful manned flights over two years. During the same period, the Soviets launched only one Voskhod rocket. The USA had, in short, successfully mastered the techniques which would land them on the Moon as part of the Apollo programme.

To fulfil its Apollo objectives, NASA decided to construct a new rocket called Saturn. It appeared in the end as several models, each one more powerful than its predecessor. The initial Saturn I rocket had two stages, and was used during flight tests of unmanned Apollo modules. For the first manned flights which orbited the Earth, NASA used the Saturn IB rocket which could place 17 tonnes into orbit. For lunar missions, the Saturn V rocket, five times more powerful than the Saturn I, was required. Saturn V had three stages and stood 110 metres high; it had a launch mass of 100 tonnes and could send 40 tonnes towards the Moon.

The launcher test programme was 100% successful. Between 1961 and 1965, the Americans launched nine Saturn I rockets and, in January 1964, successfully placed 17 tonnes in Earth orbit. This achievement was followed by four launches of Saturn IB between 1966 and 1968, and two launches of Saturn V in 1967 and 1968. After these successes, NASA developed plans for manned Apollo spacecraft, with the aim of landing a man on the Moon in 1969.

Parallel to the programme of Gemini missions and tests on the Saturn rockets, the Americans continued to send probes to the Moon, to make measurements in preparation for a lunar landing. Between 1964 and 1965, the Ranger probes sent back many photographs of the Moon, and then, on 2 June 1966, Surveyor 1 made a successful soft landing, using its equipment to analyse the soil content. Lunar Orbiter 1 was launched a few months later, on 10 August 1966, and went into orbit around the Moon. It took photographs and made scientific measurements to help scientists determine the best landing sites for Apollo.

Meanwhile, the Soviets continued with their own space programme. On 3 February 1966, they sent Luna 9 to the Moon, where it became the first probe to perform a soft landing. It photographed the lunar surface and transmitted the results back to Earth. The Luna 10 probe followed on 31 March 1966. It went into orbit around the Moon and its observations were used to choose an eventual Soviet landing site.

Between 1961 and 1966, the Americans and Soviets had together carried out 22 manned missions in space without loss of life. Just as men were beginning to feel complacent about 'space routine', however, there occurred two terrible accidents on board new spacecraft, which affected both the Gemini and the Voskhod programmes. On 27 January 1967, there was a fire in the Apollo spacecraft during a training session, whilst it was still on the ground. The three astronauts on board, Virgil I. Grissom, Edward H. White and Roger B. Chaffee, were killed. Only three months later, on 24 April 1967, the cosmonaut Vladimir Komarov was killed during the landing of his capsule, Soyuz 1. As a result, both American and Soviet programmes were delayed while problems with the new equipment were rectified.

European cooperation in space

With so much activity in space, the Americans and the Soviets came to dominate the world in the space race. Yet it was now this very supremacy which Europe was preparing to contest.

Most European space activities have taken place as international ventures. Faced by the large scale programmes of the USA and USSR, European countries decided early on that it would be expedient to pool resources and expertise. This cooperation occurred only in large civil programmes because the political consequences of military space programmes made cooperation in this area impossible.

The idea of European cooperation in space stemmed originally from a British military space programme. In 1955, the De Havilland group were investigating a medium range missile, Blue Streak. The engine design was contracted to Rolls Royce under the terms of licences bought in the USA. In 1957, the Royal Aircraft Establishment then developed a rocket called the Black Knight, which was used to study the effects of reentry into the atmosphere. The combined use of these two rockets prompted the British government to consider the possibility of constructing a civil launcher of moderate size.

When deciding whether or not to launch a national space programme, the British naturally considered whether such a commitment was really necessary. There had been long delays in the Blue Streak programme, and it was finally suspended in 1960. But, to conserve the benefits of its research, the British government offered the use of the Blue Streak rocket to its European neighbours. At a conference in Strasbourg in January 1961, Britain and France suggested creating a European organisation to oversee the construction of a European rocket. This would have a Blue Streak first stage, a second stage consisting of the French Coralie rocket, and a third stage consisting of a German rocket.

Thus it was that the Europa rocket programme came to be launched during a meeting of the newly established European Launcher Development Organisation (ELDO) on 29 February 1964. The Europa programme proved, however, very complicated and poorly organised and there was one failure after another. Not a single Europa rocket ever functioned perfectly, as one of the three rocket stages was always defective.

Britain in the end renounced the European launcher and requested the USA to place its satellites into orbit. However, the UK did participate in another European organisation, the European Space Research Organization (ESRO), created on 20 March 1964 to develop scientific satellites and to coordinate European space technologies. The first satellites to be constructed by European companies were accordingly launched by American rockets, whilst Europe developed its own launcher.

A third organisation, the Conférence européenne de télécommunications par satellites (CETS), was created around the same time, on 22 May 1963. Its task was to ensure the development of European communications satellites, and to negotiate with the USA to establish a worldwide network of telecommunications satellites.

These three organisations were coordinated by the European Space Conference which brought together all the individual ministers responsible for space research. On 20 December 1972, in the light of its continuing failure, the Europa programme was suspended by the European Space Conference.

ELDO and ESRO were then merged, on 1 April 1974, to form the European Space Agency (ESA). Within this new agency France took financial and technical responsibility for developing a heavy launcher, called Ariane. This programme was based on France's experience with satellite launchers, and the entire European space programme has benefited from it since.

French activities in space

As early as 1949, France became involved in rocket construction with the creation of the Laboratoire de recherches balistiques et aérodynamiques (the Aerodynamics and Ballistics Research Laboratory), to develop and test prototypes of military missiles. Early research led to the development of the liquid fuel rocket, Véronique, which was inspired by the German V2 rockets. While France's space programme was less spectacular than the American and Soviet programmes, over time not only Véronique but also rocket probes and solid fuel rockets were developed. These led to strategic

Europa II and Véronique. On 5 November 1971, at Kourou in French Guiana, Europa II was launched (right). Two and a half minutes after take-off the rocket exploded, in effect marking the end of the Europa programme. The European space programme had to go back to square one and start again.

Work began on the French liquid fuel rocket, Véronique, in 1950. Many versions were produced, the last of which, Véronique 61, went into service in 1964. A Véronique 61 rocket at Hammaguir in the Sahara is shown on the far right. It had a launch mass of 1·93 tonnes, and could carry a scientific payload of 60 kilograms to an altitude of 315 kilometres (right: CSG Kourou; far right: © SIRPA/ECP Armées France).

Ranger 3. Ranger 3, launched on 26 January 1962, was America's first attempt to obtain high resolution pictures of the Moon's surface and perform scientific measurements there. The sphere 630 millimetres in diameter visible at the top of the probe contained a seismometer designed to survive an impact on the Moon's surface at a speed of up to 50 metres per second. In the end, Ranger 3 passed more than 36 000 kilometres from the Moon due to a launcher malfunction (JPL/NASA).

Surveyor 3's success. Surveyor 3's shovel has here put a sample of lunar soil onto one of its shock absorbing feet to provide better conditions for the camera to examine it. Surveyor 3, launched on 17 April 1967, landed on the Moon on 19 April. Like its predecessor, Surveyor 1, it provided assurance that the lunar surface could support the weight of the lunar module (NASA).

The Apollo 1 tragedy. During a ground test at Cape Kennedy, Florida, on 27 January 1967, Virgil I. Grissom, Edward H. White and Robert B. Chaffee perished in a fire in the command module of Apollo 1. Although the exact cause of the fire has never been established, the tragedy led to the spacecraft being completely redesigned (NASA).

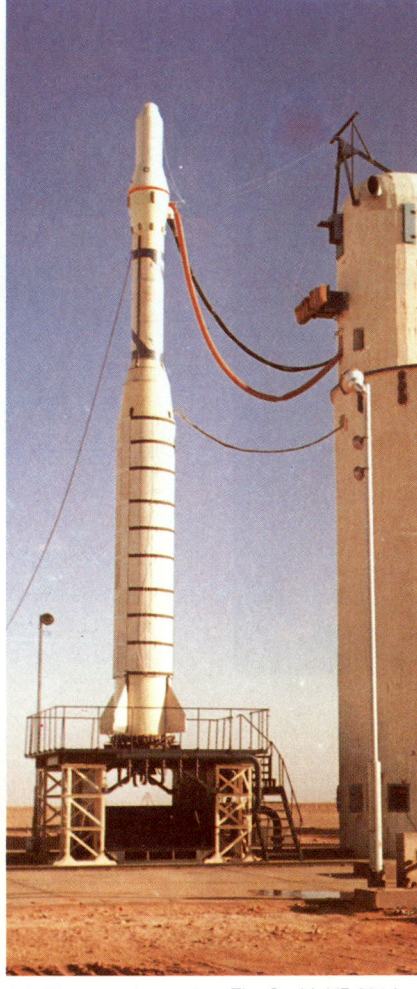

Emeraude, Saphir, Diamant A (from left to right). The experimental rocket VE 121 (Véhicule expérimental) Emeraude was launched for the first time on 17 June 1964; it consisted of a single operational stage and an inert stage which simulated the VE 111 L Topaze solid fuel rocket. It was 17·9 metres tall, had a launch mass of 18·2 tonnes, and a Vexin rocket engine powered by nitric acid and turpentine spirit. On the ground it delivered a thrust of 275 kilonewtons. Emeraude was used to develop a first stage liquid fuel rocket engine and to test the separation of the different stages.

The Saphir VE 231 had an Emeraude rocket as its first stage and a Topaze rocket as its second stage. Saphir was launched for the first time on 5 July 1965, and was used to test guidance systems and to study the effects of reentry into the atmosphere on military warheads.

Diamant A was the first French launcher. It consisted of a Saphir rocket and a third stage, filled with 640 kilograms of isolane, which was capable of delivering a thrust of up to 53 kilonewtons (© SIRPA/ECP Armées France).

The French D1A (Diapason) satellite. The D1A was used as a testbed for a number of new components; although not carrying any scientific instruments, it was used to make geodetic measurements. Here it is pictured, at Hammaguir in the Sahara, just before its launch by a Diamant A rocket on 17 February 1966 (© SIRPA/ECP Armées France).

weapons with nuclear warheads and to the Diamant and Ariane rockets used as civil launchers of scientific satellites.

An industrial infrastructure had to be created if France was going to develop a space programme based on the new technologies. Research and production by different groups were coordinated by the Société d'études et de réalisation d'engins balistiques (SEREB: Ballistic Rockets Research and Development Group), founded in 1959. The objective of this programme was to develop relevant technologies, especially in the fields of propulsion for large missiles and in inertial guidance.

In the civil sector, the French government established the Centre nationale d'études spatiales (CNES: National Centre for Space Studies), on 19 December 1961; its task was not only to develop a civil launcher but also to implement France's space policy. The CNES developed electronic techniques, such as telemetry and telecommunications, and coordinated the industrial activity necessary to build its designs. It also had overall responsibility for launches from French space centres.

In the 1960s, the SEREB developed a series of rockets named after precious stones for both military and civil programmes. The Agate rocket was first launched in 1961. A civil launcher was then constructed out of an Agate rocket with a Rubis rocket used as a third stage. This was used in a suborbital flight to test the D1 prototype satellite on 5 June 1965.

In 1965, the Emeraude rocket was tested and so was the first stage of the Saphir rocket (Emeraude plus Topaze). The Saphir was used to examine the effects on nuclear warheads of reentering the Earth's atmosphere, to perfect a reliable guidance system, and to establish the basis for a civil launcher, the Diamant. This was provided with three stages, the first two being the Saphir rocket, the third stage being used to place a satellite into orbit. The Diamant itself was 19 metres high and had a launch mass of 18 tonnes; on 26 November 1965, at Hammaguir in the Sahara, it put a French satellite, the 42 kilogram A1, into orbit on its first trial. France thus became the third space power.

The first French scientific satellite was FR 1, used to study the ionosphere, which was launched on 6 December 1965 by an American Scout launcher. Only ten weeks later, on 17 February 1966 at Hammaguir a Diamant rocket launched the D1A satellite (Diapason) for making geodetic measurements using the Doppler effect, and for testing CNES's tracking network.

So it was that the dream of conquering space became a reality in 1957 with the launch of Sputnik 1. The ensuing successes of the American and Russian space programmes constitute perhaps the second scientific revolution of the twentieth century; after successfully harnessing the power of the infinitely small, the atom, man turned his attention to the infinitely large – his own Universe – perhaps destined to be his last, and greatest, adventure.

Claude Carlier

Twenty years in space

The space shuttle era. The lower photograph, taken on 29 July 1985, shows the space shuttle Challenger being launched from the Kennedy Space Center carrying Spacelab 2 in its cargobay. This was the nineteenth space shuttle launch. Six months later, the failure of a joint on one of the solid fuel rockets destroyed Challenger, killing the seven crew members. The upper photograph shows the Soviet shuttle on its Energia launcher in October 1988, just before its first launch on 15 November (above: APN; below: NASA).

From Apollo to Buran. The table on the right is a chronological list of some of the most important space ventures that followed the initial flights of man in space (see p. 54). It highlights some of the technological developments made in the first two decades of the conquest of space.

Date	Country	Event
30 October 1967	USSR	first space rendezvous and automatic docking of two unmanned spacecraft, Cosmos 186 and Cosmos 188
9 November 1967	USA	Apollo 4 mission; first Saturn V launch
15 to 21 September 1968	USSR	first lunar orbit, followed by return to Earth, by the Zond 5 spacecraft
11 to 22 October 1968	USA	Apollo 7 mission; tested the command and service modules in an Earth orbit (crew: Walter M. Schirra, Don F. Eisele and Walter Cunningham)
21 to 27 December 1968	USA	Apollo 8 mission; first manned circumlunar mission (crew: Frank Borman, James A. Lovell and William A. Anders)
15 to 17 January 1969	USSR	first docking between two manned spacecraft, Soyuz 5 (crew: Aleksei Eilseyev, Boris Volynov and Evgeny Khrunov) and Soyuz 4 (Vladimir Chatalov)
3 to 13 March 1969	USA	Apollo 9 mission; tested lunar module in Earth orbit (crew: James A. McDivitt, David R. Scott and Russell L. Schweickart)
18 to 26 May 1969	USA	Apollo 10 mission; tested lunar module in circumlunar orbit (crew: Thomas P. Stafford, John W. Young and Eugene A. Cernan)
16 to 24 July 1969	USA	Apollo 11 mission; first man on the Moon (crew: Neil A. Armstrong, Edwin E. Aldrin and Michael Collins)
31 July 1969	USA	Mariner 6 transmitted the first high resolution images of the surface of Mars
11 February 1970	Japan	first Japanese satellite, put into orbit by a Japanese launcher (Lambda 4S)
11 to 17 April 1970	USA	Apollo 13 mission failed (crew: James A. Lovell, Fred W. Hayes and John L. Swigert)
24 April 1970	China	first Chinese satellite put into orbit by Chinese launcher (Long Walk 1)
12 to 24 September 1970	USSR	for the first time, an automatic probe, Luna 16, brings back samples of lunar material to Earth
17 November 1970	USSR	Luna 17 puts the first remote control vehicle (Lunokhod 1) on the Moon's surface
19 April 1971	USSR	launch of the first (unmanned) space station, Salyut 1
7 to 29 June 1971	USSR	launched on board Soyuz 11, Georgy Dobrovolsky, Vladislav Volkov and Viktor Patsayev occupied Salyut 1, but did not survive the return journey to Earth
28 October 1971	UK	first British satellite put into orbit by a British launcher (Black Arrow)
13 November 1971	USA	Mariner 9 goes into orbit around Mars
5 January 1972	USA	President Nixon takes the decision to construct the space shuttle, already in the design stage
23 July 1972	USA	launch of the first Earth resources remote sensing satellite (ERTS A), subsequently renamed Landsat 1
7 to 19 December 1972	USA	Apollo 17 mission, the last of the Apollo programme (crew: Eugene A. Cernan, Ronald E. Evans and Harrison H. Schmitt)
14 May 1973	USA	launch of the Skylab space station
25 May 1973	USA	Skylab is manned for the first time by Charles Conrad, Joseph P. Kerwin and Paul J. Weitz
3 December 1973	USA	for the first time a space probe, Pioneer 10, comes within reach of Jupiter
29 March 1974	USA	Mariner 10 becomes the first space probe to visit Mercury
3 December 1974	USA	Pioneer 11 passes close to Jupiter
15 to 24 July 1975	USA/USSR	joint Apollo–Soyuz mission, with the Soyuz 19 crew (Aleksei Leonov and Valeri Kubasov) and the Apollo crew (Thomas P. Stafford, Donald K. Slayton and Vance D. Brand)
22 October 1975	USSR	first black and white pictures of the surface of Venus are transmitted by the landing probe Venera 9
20 July 1976	USA	Viking 1 lands on Mars
3 September 1976	USA	Viking 2 lands on Mars
12 August 1977	USA	first free flight of the space shuttle Enterprise
5 March 1979	USA	Voyager 1 passes close to Jupiter
9 July 1979	USA	Voyager 2 passes close to Jupiter
1 September 1979	USA	Pioneer 11 passes close to Saturn
24 December 1979	Europe	first launch of Ariane
18 July 1980	India	first Indian satellite put into orbit by an Indian launcher (SLV 3)
12 November 1980	USA	Voyager 1 passes close to Saturn
12 April 1981	USA	launch of the first space shuttle Columbia
20 August 1981	USA	Voyager 2 passes close to Saturn
1 March 1982	USSR	first colour images of the surface of Venus are transmitted by the Venera 13 probe
28 November to 8 December 1983	USA/Europe	first flight of the European Spacelab, on board the space shuttle Columbia
24 January 1986	USA	Voyager 2 passes close to Uranus
26 January 1986	USA	the space shuttle Challenger explodes
20 February 1986	USSR	launch of the new Mir orbiting space station
March 1986	USSR/Europe/Japan	Halley's comet is observed by five space probes: two Soviet, Vega 1 and Vega 2; one European, Giotto; and two Japanese, Sakigake and Suisei
13 March 1986	USSR	Mir is boarded for the first time (Leonid Kizim and Vladimir Solovyev)
15 May 1987	USSR	first launch of the new Energia heavy launcher
15 June 1988	Europe	first launch of Ariane IV
29 September 1988	USA	space shuttle launches resume with Columbia
15 November 1988	USSR	first Soviet shuttle launch, Buran
4 May 1989	USA	space shuttle Atlantis launched carrying the Magellan spacecraft to visit Venus
25 August 1989	USA	Voyager 2 passes close to Neptune
18 November 1989	USA	launch of first satellite to study radiation from 'big bang' origin of the Universe
20 January 1990	USA	the space shuttle returns the Long Duration Exposure Facility to Earth after six years in orbit
24 January 1990	Japan	Muses A satellite launched to the Moon

Towards the 21st century

Sputnik 1 was at once a tremendous triumph for the whole of humanity and an enormous challenge to the Americans. The space race that ensued became a feverish pursuit, and it seemed that fact had almost overtaken fiction.

Was that really so? In only forty years, science fiction had advanced so far that it was no longer concerned·with putting a man on the Moon or, except for Arthur C. Clarke, with artificial satellites. All the indications were that futuristic stories were losing their popularity. In 1962, the English author, J. G. Ballard, branched into another area and began exploring philosophy, using science fiction only as a background.

The three main themes of science fiction, space travel, the galactic empire and the alien planet, now became steadily less important. The new science fiction dealt more with characters, as in Cordwainer Smith's books or Frank Herbert's *Destination: Void* (1966). The empire became the place where power was exerted according to the desires of man, as in Cordwainer Smith or in *Dune* by Frank Herbert (1963–5). The alien planet became a unique place, where the alien was encountered on home territory. Stanilas Lem, in his books *Solaris* (1961) or *The Invincible* (1965), dealt with the theme of escaping from great danger, in this case a heavily armed spacecraft. Peaceful and respectable anthropology appeared in *The*

Left Hand of Darkness (1969) by Ursula Le Guin and *The Fifth Head of Cerebus* (1972) by Gene Wolfe. Here the exterior surroundings became an extension of interior feelings: science fiction became introspective and space became the backdrop against which the characters acted out their parts.

During this period of literary change, the old stalwarts of science fiction were badly received. Robert Heinlein published his last children's book in 1958, and halted for a period of reflection. *Stranger in a Strange Land* (1961) concerned the first man to be born on Mars and his return to Earth, the planet on which the book is set. *The Moon is a Harsh Mistress* (1965) is about the Moon's war of independence, a mirror of the American War of Independence. All this was a far cry from the early days of colonisation fever; there were crises, a return to self reliance and a severing of roots. Heinlein's books were noticeably less reflective than those of modern day authors. Pierre Boulle, who was younger than Heinlein and became disillusioned earlier, wrote *The Planet of the Apes* (1963). This was the same type of personal allegory: no matter where you go in the Universe, the only individual you can count on is yourself.

In Arthur C. Clarke, Stanley Kubrick recognised the ideal collaborator for the film *2001: A Space Odyssey*, which came out in 1968, a year before a man finally reached the

Moon. This was essentially two films in one. On the one hand, there was the glossy epic describing daily life in space, with its events and dangers, on the other, an introspective film ending with the question: is the desire to conquer space which haunts all astronauts just an allegory for the desire for death, a wish to be lost in the infinite? The public went to see the 'first' film because they were enthusiastic about the Apollo programme, and were disturbed by the 'second'. Clarke subsequently developed the theme further in *Rendezvous with Rama* (1973), a story about an empty spaceship which yoked together metaphysics and technology in the same way.

The cinema was enthralled by success in the space race, and a number of straightforward action films including *Silent Running* (1971), *The Wild Planet* (1973), *Star Wars* (1977), *Alien* (1979) and *Outland* (1981) also appeared. The common theme which runs through all these is the strangeness of space and the potential terrors it holds. The cinema in the 1970s and 1980s thus restored epic space adventure as it had been in the 1940s and 1950s.

Now the gap between the visual mass media and literature, which is subject to less constraints, is widening all the time. The true successes of *2001: A Space Odyssey* will accordingly be found in the novel alone.

Jacques Goimard

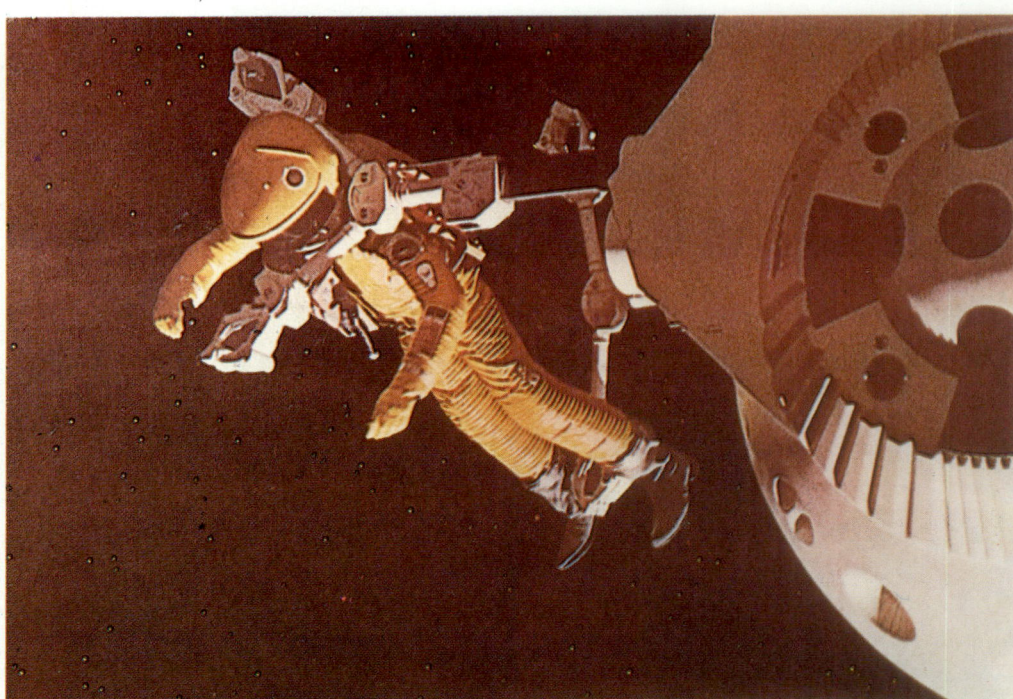

2001: A Space Odyssey. One of the astronauts has been killed by the computer which controls his capsule. In this film, the astronauts as well as their machines have to confront space, and the computer, Hal, acquires a defective personality. The surviving astronaut tries to recover the body, contrary to the tradition of maritime novels where corpses are abandoned to the sea. The image presented gives the corpse the appearance of a puppet with broken strings. For Kubrick, man is as grotesque in space as he is on the Earth (Cinestar).

Space, as the reflection of the inner life. This drawing by Virgil Finlay, one of great illustrators of science fiction, is comparable in its sexual implications to the picture on p.47, top right. But in this drawing the rocket, instead of being directed towards a feminine figure, has arrived, and the giant woman is holding it in her hand. It is the reverse of *King Kong*; flames are shooting upwards and the unfortunate astronaut is no match for female desire. Space is represented as the place where the inner life evolves and eventually becomes a nightmare (© *Fantastic Adventures*, Ziff-Davis Pub Co, rights reserved).

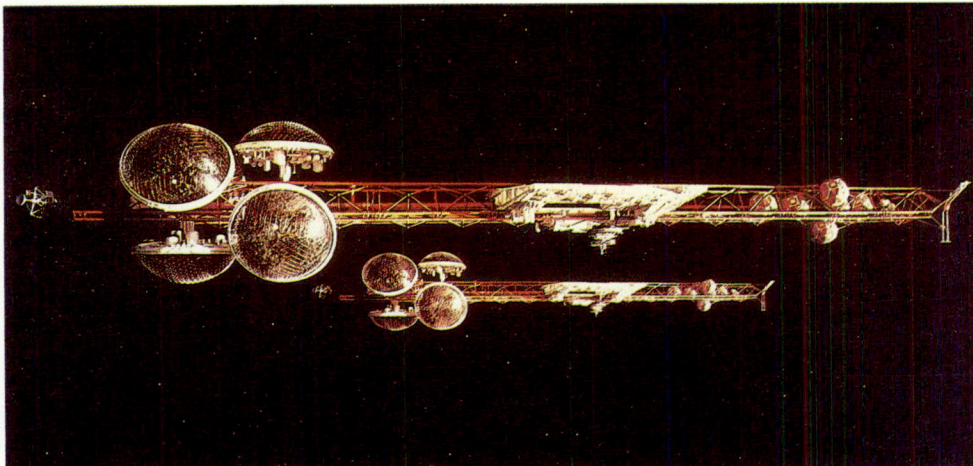

Silent Running. This ecologically sound superproduction was the child of the US hippy movement. It was directed, in 1971, by Douglas Trumbull who was responsible for the special effects in *2001: A Space Odyssey.* All vegetation has disappeared from the Earth, but a forest has been preserved in a spacecraft. It is a new Noah's ark. The depressing fact about the film is that the spacecraft has no destination; this is an orbiting museum immobile in the Universe. The large solar energy collectors also have a marked ecological significance (Prod./DB).

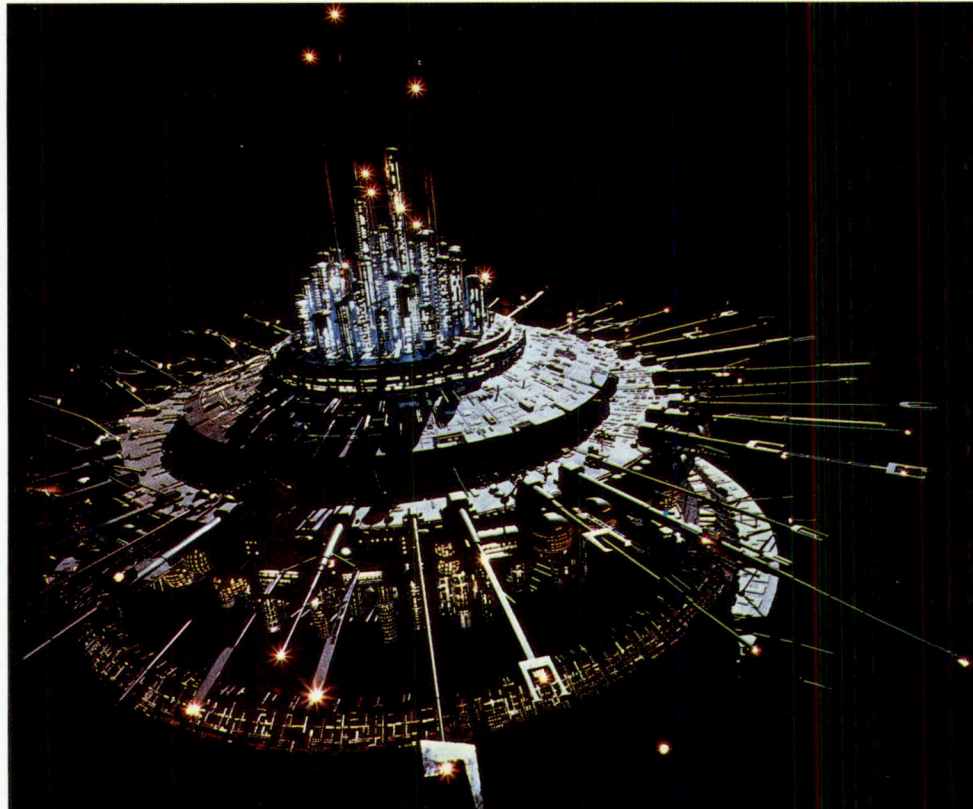

Close Encounters of the Third Kind. The Unidentified Flying Object (UFO) at the end of Steven Spielberg's film (1977) resembles a space city. The baroque character of 1970s spacecraft stems from the idea that future spacecraft will not have to adjust to the constraints of aerodynamics, because they will be constructed in the space vacuum out of extremely tough materials which have not yet been developed. Here, the UFO is about to turn over in order to observe the Earth. Spielberg uses this image to express an idea dear to him on film, that man's familiar reference frame, the horizontal, has no relevance in space (Prod./DB).

The artificial planet in *Star Wars.* The death star is the ultimate version of this archetype of science fiction. The artificial planet used by the military has a dark metallic tint, and is designed around three necessities: walls for defence, openings for launching projectiles for attack, and finally satellites for making observations (model by Ralph McQuarrie; Prod./DB).

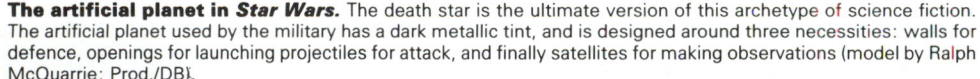

A purely aesthetic spacecraft. After *2001: A Space Odyssey,* it was realised that illustrators could develop spacecraft designs which were purely aesthetic in their intentions. This is true of *Alien* (1979). In this illustration by Colin Hay, the dark openings to the interior of the ship create an impression of escape, reinforced by the number of luminous points inside. It is not space which is infinite here, but the spacecraft (© Colin Hay, *Man From Maybe,* Young Artists).

Preparing the set of *Alien.* A reconnaissance mission returning to Earth stops at an unknown planet and discovers a strange sight; the space explorers do not know whether it is a cemetery or an incubator. Their visit awakens a 'thing' which travels with them in their spacecraft and murders the crew, one by one. The idea that space contains mortal dangers dominates this science-horror film by Ridley Scott (D. Cameron/Sygma).

At an altitude of 4·4 kilometres and a speed of Mach 0·8, the solid fuel boosters of the first Ariane III rocket (flight V 10, on 4 August 1984) are jettisoned over the mouth of the Kourou river in French Guiana (Aérospatiale).

Orbits and trajectories

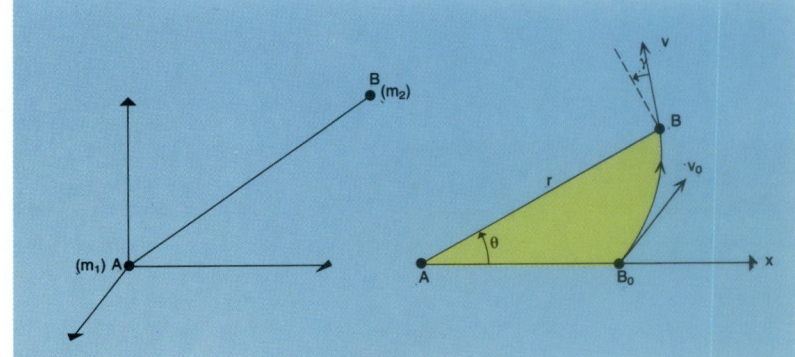

Going into space implies an understanding of all the laws of physics relating to motion within the space system. Before dealing with questions related to the orbits and trajectories of satellites and probes, some definitions of the terms to be used are, however, necessary.
– An orbit is a trajectory which is periodically repeated.
– A trajectory is the path traced out by a moving body.
– An interplanetary trajectory is, therefore, the resultant trajectory determined by the Sun and the interaction of the body, the space probe, with all other members of the solar system, that is the planets.
– A launch trajectory is the path taken, for example, by a rocket which has been launched from the Earth's surface.
– A reentry trajectory is the path taken by a space shuttle on its return to the Earth from a mission in space.

More specifically, the motion, or movement, of the body's centre of gravity constitutes its trajectory. Movement about the centre of gravity, that is rotation, which governs its attitude at any instant does not have to be calculated, except for manoeuvres performed by rotating satellites. Here, for example, their attitude may need to be corrected before changing the apogee, or highest point, of their orbit.

Space mechanics is based on celestial mechanics, and is closely related to classical mechanics. As in Galilean and Newtonian mechanics, the subject is based on a three dimensional Euclidian space, with time as the independent parameter. There is a particular reference frame, in which an object, which is not subjected to any force, is either at rest or moving with a constant velocity in a straight line. This is sometimes called the Galilean frame of reference.

Fundamental laws of motion

In an inertial, or Galilean, frame of reference, the applied force F is proportional to the product of the mass m of the particle and the acceleration a. Put mathematically, $F = ma$. This fundamental law is one of Newton's three laws of motion. In a non-Galilean frame of reference, for example on the surface of the rotating Earth, the absolute acceleration a_a is the sum of three accelerations. These are the relative acceleration, the acceleration due to the Earth's gravitational force, g, and that due to the Coriolis force associated with the Earth's rotation, which depends upon latitude.

When the two particles of mass m_1 and m_2 are separated by a distance d, they experience a mutually attractive force. This is expressed by Newton's law of attraction, that $F = Gm_1m_2/d^2$. Here G is the fundamental gravitational constant. Numerically, $G = 6.672 \times 10^{-14}$ cubic metres per second per second per kilogram.

Global and local geodetic systems have been derived so that measurements of a satellite's position may be expressed and related to the positions of certain ground stations. These positions are known with respect to the 'geoid', where the geoid is defined as an equipotential surface of the rotating terrestrial gravity field. This geoid can be approximated by a reference ellipsoid, or the surface of a calm, non-tidal ocean, which is much simpler to use. However, this may be several tens of metres out from the

vertical position of the true geoid because the materials making up the Earth's crust and the mantle below have different densities.

Finally, it is necessary to link the times of measurements carried out in different parts of the globe. There are actually two independent ways of defining the time. One, which is Universal Time, is based upon the Earth's rotation, the other, Atomic Time, on atomic line spectra for which masers are used.

There are some perturbations which affect the elliptical orbit of a satellite about the Earth. There are two categories of perturbation.
– Those of a gravitational origin, for example those due to the Moon and Sun or to the choice of a non-inertial frame of reference, or to tidal phenomena.
– Those not of gravitational origin, such as atmospheric friction, or direct or indirect solar radiation pressure.
Such perturbations cause a satellite's orbit to change slightly.

Orbital prediction and measurement

Orbital prediction means predicting the evolution of the parameters of a satellite's orbit by taking account of the perturbing forces acting upon the satellite. There are two main ways of doing this.

Analytical methods enable us to represent and interpret each cause of the perturbations. We can therefore directly derive the satellite's position as a function of time. Such methods are included in the computer programs on board satellites or the space shuttle.

It is often impossible to integrate analytically all the perturbations. In this case, we use numerical integration to arrive closer to the exact description of the satellite's orbit with each successive integration. The problem with numerical integration is usually the long time that it takes to carry out the calculation, and also the computer's rounding off and truncation errors which may have disastrous cumulative effects.

The central problem is to know, over a period of time, the successive positions of a satellite. Measurements may be of the angle, the distance, or the speed between the satellite and one or several tracking stations on the Earth's surface. Angular measurements can be carried out optically, say by using a telescope or special camera. To obtain distances, we measure the time that it takes for a laser or a radar signal to travel to and from the satellite. Measurements of the Doppler shift of the frequency of radio waves transmitted by the satellite give the speed of the satellite.

Some satellites need to have their orientation, or attitude, adjusted in orbit. Before that can be done, the position of their three axis reference frame has to be known with respect to

The first orbital velocity.
This table gives the lowest horizontal velocity required to put an object into a circular orbit. Given the symbol v_1, this only depends on the altitude, h, where the object is released. The same is true of the period of revolution around the Earth, the orbital period T. A geostationary satellite has an orbital period of one sidereal day, 23 hours and 56 minutes, which is the Earth's rotation period measured with respect to the distant stars rather than the Sun. As the Earth rotates, the satellite always stays above the same point on the surface.

h (kilometres)	v_1 (metres per second)	T (minutes)
150	7814	87.49
200	7789	88.34
300	7726	90.52
500	7613	94.62
1 000	7350	105.1
2 000	6898	127.2
5 000	5919	201.3
10 000	4933	347.7
35 786*	3075	1 436 = 23 hr 56 min

* Altitude of a geostationary satellite in the Earth's equatorial plane.

h (kilometres)	v_2 (metres per second)
0	11 180
200	11 010
400	10 840
1 000	10 390

The second orbital (escape) velocity.
For a certain horizontal velocity, called the second orbital velocity v_2, the object has sufficient velocity to escape the Earth's gravitational pull. Its trajectory is then parabolic. For all velocities between the first and second orbital velocities, the object remains a satellite of the Earth. It can be shown mathematically that v_2 is $\sqrt{2}$ times greater than v_1.

The two body problem and the N body problem. The movement of a particle B, of mass m_2, with respect to particle A, of much greater mass m_1, is a two body problem. If we consider a system whose axes are parallel to the Cartesian axes, but whose origin is at A, we have the situation as shown in the left diagram above. By applying Newton's laws of motion and his inverse square law of attraction between two point masses, we can conclude that the force acts along the line joining the two bodies. The motion takes place in a plane, and equal areas (in green) are swept out by the line AB in equal intervals of time. This is one of Kepler's laws of planetary motion, illustrated on the right of the diagram above. The trajectory described by point B is a conic, of which A is one of the foci.

The trajectory of a particle P, of mass m, about a central body O, of mass M, in the presence of perturbing bodies, of masses m_1 and m_2, is the N body problem. This applies, for example, to the orbit of a satellite around the Earth, which is perturbed by the Moon and the Sun. The particle's acceleration is now the sum of two terms. The first takes into account the attraction of the central body and is dealt with by considering the two body problem. The second term makes the equations of celestial mechanics very complicated and, as yet, no analytical theory exists to describe this motion.

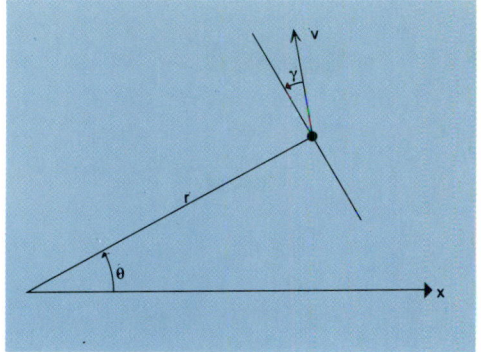

Mathematical descriptions of a satellite orbit. Using initial conditions of the radial position from the centre of the Earth r, velocity v and direction of motion in terms of the angle γ to the perpendicular to the radial direction, and with θ being the angle between the position vector and the reference x axis, an equation can be written for the orbit. This is
$$e^2 = \sin^2\gamma + [1 - r(v^2/\mu)]^2\cos^2\gamma,$$
where e is the eccentricity of the orbit and μ is a constant which is defined as G times the mass of the Earth.

There are three possible solutions to this equation. For e less than unity (e<1) and v<$\sqrt{(2\mu/r)}$, the trajectory is an ellipse. For e = 1, and v = $\sqrt{(2\mu/r)}$, the trajectory is a parabola. Finally, when e is greater than unity (e>1) and v>$\sqrt{(2\mu/r)}$, the trajectory is a hyperbola. These are Keplerian orbits.

The case where e = 0 is obtained when v = $\sqrt{(\mu/r)}$. This is the speed required for a circular orbit about the Earth, and γ is therefore zero. The velocity $\sqrt{(2\mu/r)}$ is called the escape velocity. It is the minimum velocity required by an object to escape from the gravitational force of the attraction of the body. For the Earth, the escape velocity is about 11 kilometres per second.

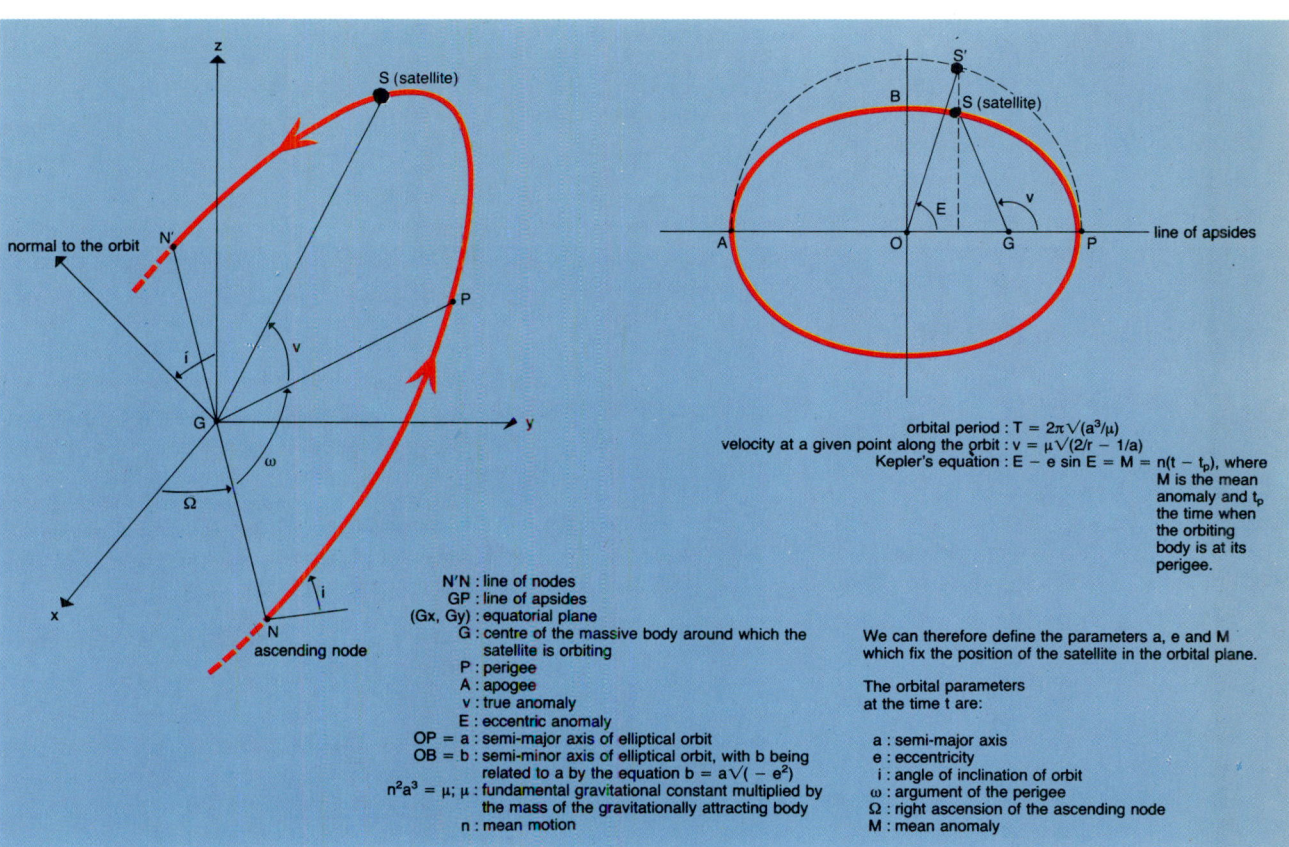

orbital period : $T = 2\pi\sqrt{(a^3/\mu)}$
velocity at a given point along the orbit : $v = \mu\sqrt{(2/r - 1/a)}$
Kepler's equation : $E - e\sin E = M = n(t - t_p)$, where M is the mean anomaly and t_p the time when the orbiting body is at its perigee.

N'N : line of nodes
GP : line of apsides
(Gx, Gy) : equatorial plane
G : centre of the massive body around which the satellite is orbiting
P : perigee
A : apogee
v : true anomaly
E : eccentric anomaly
OP = a : semi-major axis of elliptical orbit
OB = b : semi-minor axis of elliptical orbit, with b being related to a by the equation $b = a\sqrt{(-e^2)}$
$n^2a^3 = \mu$; μ : fundamental gravitational constant multiplied by the mass of the gravitationally attracting body
n : mean motion

We can therefore define the parameters a, e and M which fix the position of the satellite in the orbital plane.

The orbital parameters at the time t are:

a : semi-major axis
e : eccentricity
i : angle of inclination of orbit
ω : argument of the perigee
Ω : right ascension of the ascending node
M : mean anomaly

---

a fixed reference frame. Their attitude has to be accurately known before orbital corrections can be performed because the jets of the thruster rockets have to be correctly aligned before they are used.

For satellites in low Earth orbits, reference directions can be associated with the Earth's magnetic field, the Sun, the Moon, the stars, accelerometers on the satellite or inertial control measurements. In the case of spin stabilised satellites, directional sensors 'lock on to' objects such as the Earth, Sun or a bright star, while satellites which are stabilised about three axes require a large field of view terrestrial sensor or a solar sensor.

In the geometric method of determining a satellite's attitude, the directions measured in the satellite's reference frame are matched to theoretical models which provide values in the inertial frame of reference. The alternative, or dynamic, method is based upon modelling the evolution of the angles measured by different sensors during the satellite's orbital motion. It requires taking a group of measurements for about 20 minutes, and telemetering these to a ground station for analysis and interpretation.

Orbits for remote sensing satellites

Satellites in a near Earth polar orbit, such as the US Landsat or French SPOT Earth observation satellites, produce two types of data. They observe the Earth either in a multispectral mode (three colour bands) in the visible and near infrared part of the spectrum, with a resolution of the order of 20 metres, or in a panchromatic mode (a wider spectral band), with a spatial resolution of the order of 10 metres. The SPOT satellite can alter its viewing angle to increase the frequency of observations

of a given region and also to obtain stereoscopic images.

There are several operational constraints on a remote sensing mission. On the one hand the viewing geometry must remain the same; the orbit is as circular as possible and the orbital eccentricity is kept low (e < 0.002). The altitude chosen, which for SPOT was 820 kilometres, is a compromise between providing images over most of the Earth's surface and obtaining good spatial resolution. To be able to compare images of the same area taken in different seasons and to account for the sensitivity of the cameras to solar light reflected by the Earth's surface and atmosphere, the lighting conditions have to remain constant. For this reason, remote sensing satellites are generally put into a Sun synchronous orbit. For this

$$\frac{d\Omega}{dt} = \dot{\Omega} = 0.98565 \text{ degrees per day.}$$

The orbital nodes maintain a near constant solar time. The satellite always crosses the equatorial plane at the same local time, so that the ascending node is often near 10.00 Local Time, to an accuracy of ± 15 minutes.

Also, the whole globe has to be imaged and some areas have to be regularly viewed. This is done by arranging that, over a certain number of days – in SPOT's case 26 days – the satellite completes a whole number of orbits (369) and thus passes over the same site at the same time of day each month. It is this special orbital cycle which keeps the satellite in phase with the Earth. In order that SPOT views the same zone within its observing track width of 108 kilometres every five days, a sub-cycle of 5/26 orbits per day was established. So that regions can be filmed repeatedly, SPOT is at an altitude of 820 kilometres where it completes 14 + (5/26) orbits per day. The complete orbital cycle

thus lasts 26 days and a grid with 369 orbits is constructed.

SPOT's orbital parameters were therefore chosen as follows. The right ascension of the descending node, Ω_D, was set at 12.30 Local Time, so that the best lighting conditions for viewing, avoiding specular reflection phenomena, were achieved. So that the satellite always passes over the same zone at almost exactly the same height, the perigee is very close to the North pole. This means that e = 0.0011 and ω = 90 degrees. For a Sun synchronous orbit, a = 7200.5 kilometres and i = 98.7 degrees.

The main orbital perturbations which have to be taken into account are those related to the gravitation of the Earth, the Sun and the Moon, and atmospheric friction. The principal effects are a reduction of the semi major axis a due to atmospheric friction. This causes a drift in the period and therefore a phase difference with respect to the reference grid. There is also a secular drift in the orbital inclination i due to the lunar–solar gravitational potential. Finally, the eccentricity e of the orbit evolves due to the terrestrial gravitational potential, to solar radiation pressure and to atmospheric friction.

Corrections to the orbital parameters can be made using orbital manoeuvres. Errors in the inclination i, caused by the launcher, may need to be corrected. For SPOT 1, the precision of Ariane's injection made such a correction unnecessary. Changes in inclination during the satellite's lifetime also have to be corrected for. This is done once a year to maintain the orbital phasing. To modify i without modifying the longitude of the node, a thrust has to be exerted on the satellite normal to the nodal plane. A correction of 0.1 degrees can be obtained by having a 15 newton jet operating for 13

Orbital parameters. Positions in space are described by three axes, x, y and z at right angles to each other, centred on the origin at G, the origin of the gravitational force. The x, y plane is the ecliptic plane, if we are interested in planetary movements or the motion of an interplanetary probe about the Sun. Sun at G. It is the Earth's equatorial plane if we are interested in a satellite in orbit around the Earth. The ascending node corresponds to the position of the orbiting body at the point of intersection between the plane of the orbit and the ecliptic plane. The orbital plane intersects the ecliptic plane along the line GN, called the line of nodes. Thus a satellite orbiting the Earth crosses the equatorial plane at N in the direction of increasing z. Hence, N is termed the ascending node. The orbital plane is inclined at an angle i to the equatorial plane. The angle between Gx and GN is called the right ascension of the ascending node (Ω). In the orbital plane, the angle ω between GN and GP fixes the position of the perigee P, where r has its minimum value. This angle is called the argument of the perigee.

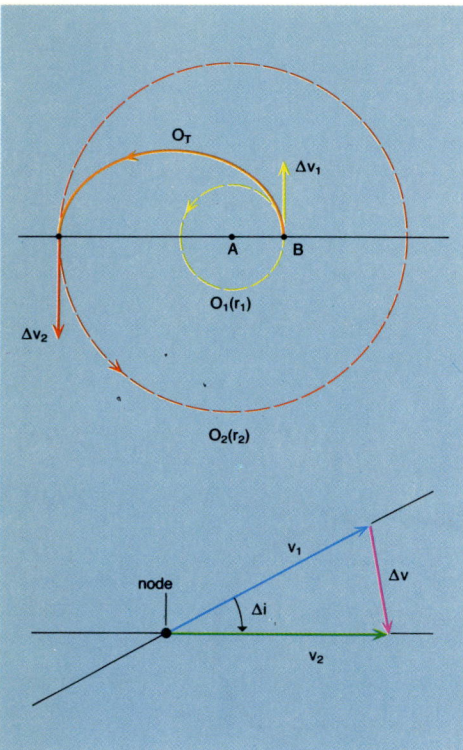

Changing the orbit of a satellite. Orbital corrections, or manoeuvres, are a crucial feature in space missions involving applications satellites. This is because the satellite's orbit may have to be corrected for inexact orbital injection by the launching rocket, for drifts in its orbital parameters, or for removing it from a temporary 'parking' orbit. The corrections are effected by firing a rocket at the correct time and with the correct impulse.

The figure above illustrates the so-called Hohmann's transfer orbit used to transfer a satellite from the orbital plane O_1 to O_2. The transfer orbit O_T (shown in orange) has to be tangential to both the orbits O_1 (shown in yellow) and O_2 (shown in red). The change, or increment, of the satellite's velocity, $\triangle v_1 + \triangle v_2$, is obtained from the formula

$$v = \sqrt{\left[\mu\left(\frac{2}{r} - \frac{1}{a}\right)\right]}.$$

This is the minimum value which will enable the orbit to be changed. To alter the orbital inclination (lower left diagram), a manoeuvre is performed when the satellite is at one of the nodes, and the change in velocity $\triangle v = 2v \sin (\triangle i/2)$.

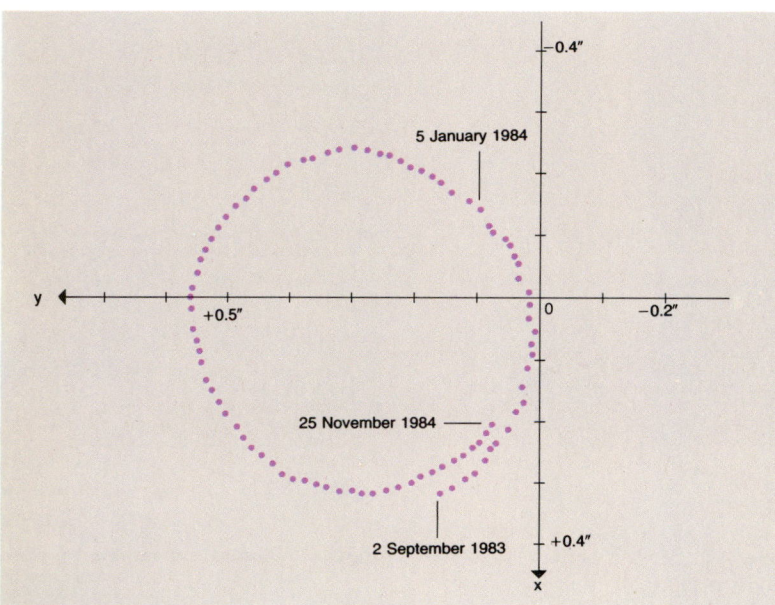

The Médoc 2 experiment. This experiment was to study the slightly changing position of the geographic North Pole, and to measure the variations of the x and y coordinates of the pole. Satellite velocity measurements, obtained using the Doppler effect, of the American Transit satellites were made from tracking stations in seven countries.

Data treatment was performed on the six orbital parameters (a, e, i, ω, Ω and M), two scaling factors representing solar radiation pressure and atmospheric friction (k_f and k_p), the times of different satellites passing over the ground stations, and the required x and y coordinates of the pole. The calculations were carried out every two days and included, on average, 80 satellite passes over the 15 stations participating in the experiment and 2500 measurements. Good agreement was found between these results and those obtained by other techniques such as classical astrometry and very long baseline interferometry. The diagram above shows the movement of the Earth's North Pole, plotted every five days, each dot the mean uncertainty of the measurement. Each mark on the axes represents 0·1 of an arcsecond, which is about 3 metres on the surface of the Earth.

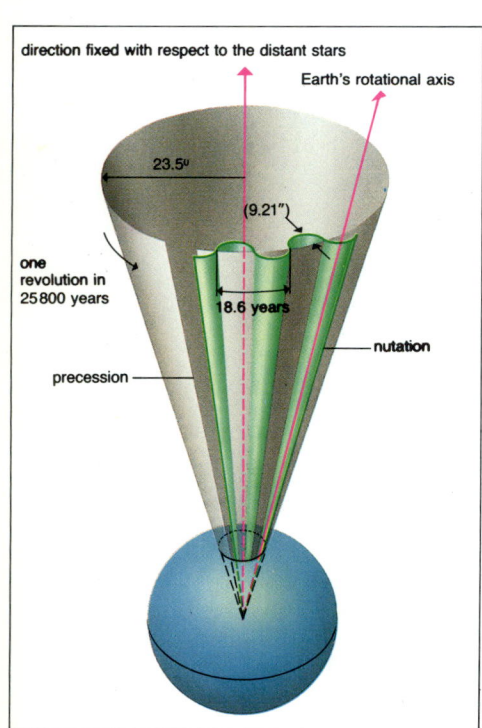

Movements of the Earth's rotational axis. The Earth can be considered as a solid body, an ellipsoid of revolution. The axis of rotation precesses, describing a cone whose half angle is 23·5 degrees. Each complete precessional revolution takes 25 800 years. As the Earth moves around its rotational axis it also experiences a 'wobble', the phenomenon of nutation. This wobble has a tiny amplitude (9·21 arcseconds, or about 30 metres) and a relatively short period (18·6 years).

minutes, though this long thrust does also cause alterations to other parameters.

To change the parameters a, e or ω, manoeuvres are performed by one or two tangential thrusts. They are carried out on the same day each week. The orbit of SPOT is calculated every 12 hours, and a 30 day prediction is made of the mean parameters (a, e, i, ω, Ω and M) and also of the coefficient due to atmospheric friction.

Geostationary orbits

There are many commercial uses of satellites in geostationary orbit; these are reviewed in detail on pp. 230–53. A geostationary orbit is an equatorial orbit with an orbital period equal to the sidereal period of the Earth's rotation, 86 164·1 seconds. A satellite launched into such an orbit appears to have a fixed position in the Earth's reference frame, and its antennae can be permanently pointed in the same direction, for example towards a particular European country. The geostationary orbit is usually defined by the longitude of the satellite's position, for example so many degrees West of the Greenwich meridian, which does not change.

Difficulties are encountered, not only in placing the satellite in the correct orbit but also in keeping it there because there are a number of perturbations with different sources which tend to modify its orbit. Corrections to this type of orbit are carried out in two distinct phases. First, the satellite is put into the correct orbit, a process which generally takes between 20 and 25 days. Then, it has to be kept in this orbit, usually for longer than 7 years, a procedure that is termed 'station keeping'.

Putting the satellite into the correct orbit involves many operations related to moving the satellite from the initial orbit into which it is put by the rocket launcher to the desired circular equatorial orbit at a height of 36 000 kilometres. First of all, the launch plan is studied. This is a graph of the possible 'launch windows' over the year, taking into account all the restrictions on the orbit, such as the number of ground stations 'visible' to the satellite, the apogee number chosen for changing from transfer orbit to geostationary orbit, and so on. It also includes restrictions on the launcher and on the orientation and performance of the satellite itself.

Calculations on the manoeuvres to be made during these operations are then carried out. For example, the necessary increase in the satellite's velocity to achieve the new apogee has to be deduced. Deciding on the time and the optimal direction, taking account of the launcher's precision, and the orbital and

attitude corrections, is the next step. Then the duration of firing of the apogee motor, about 50 seconds, has to be specified; the correct attitude with respect to all three axes has to be ensured. Orbital corrections, to longitude, drift and inclination, may also be needed depending on the precision with which these different manoeuvres have been performed.

Once the satellite is in the correct geostationary orbit, that orbit must be maintained by the so-called 'station keeping' procedure. There are three major processes which affect a satellite in geostationary orbit. These are changes of the orbital inclination under the gravitational attraction of the Sun and the Moon, alterations of the semi-major axis and the mean longitude under the effect of the Earth's gravitational field, and changes of eccentricity due to solar radiation pressure.

The inclination is altered by applying an impulse using a small thruster rocket normal to the orbital plane. A radial impulse alters the mean longitude, and a tangential impulse, parallel to the satellite's velocity, modifies the eccentricity and the drift.

In this way, the satellite is kept close to its optimal position. The success of any mission depends on the satellite remaining within a fraction of a degree of the correct longitude and orbital inclination.

The criteria for optimisation are as follows: the consumption of fuel aboard the geostationary satellite must be minimised; operational commands must be as straightforward as possible, and not too frequent; and there must be back up systems for added reliability.

The annual requirement for keeping the satellite in an orbit with the correct inclination is a total velocity increment of about 50 metres per second. There are several strategies for performing these corrections. For the Télécom 1 satellite, there was the choice of combining the East–West and North–South corrections into the same two week cycle. A repetitive cycle like this simplifies the controllers' task of maintaining the satellite in tip top condition.

Interplanetary trajectories

There are a number of methods which can be used when calculating interplanetary trajectories. The most commonly used rely on numerical integration of the equations of motion of the spacecraft. Others make use of more restrictive hypotheses and produce a good approximation of the space probe's motion. One such concept is the 'sphere of influence', that is the zone around a planet where the perturbing forces due to the other planets can

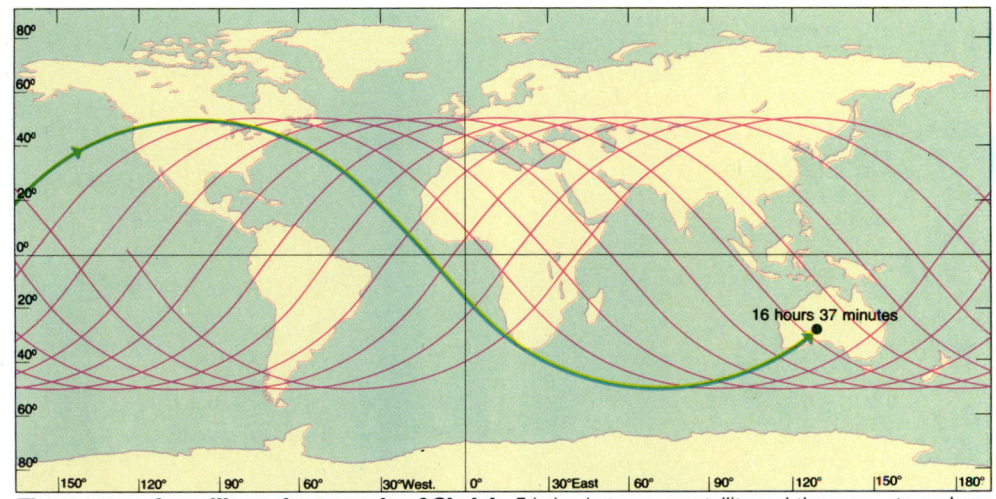

The reentry of satellites: the example of Skylab. Friction between a satellite and the upper atmosphere near perigee causes the semi major axis of the orbit to decrease. The lower the original orbit, the greater this decrease is. First, there is the orbital phase (pink orbits), where the frictional force is much less than the gravitational force, at altitudes above 120 kilometres; then an atmospheric phase (green, partial orbit), where the frictional forces are so great that they cause the satellite to return to Earth. It is difficult to predict the exact time when this will happen. This is due to insufficient knowledge about the atmosphere, to the possibility of magnetic storms, which cause sudden and considerable increases of the density of the upper atmosphere, and to the satellite's attitude which is sometimes difficult to control.

The diagram above shows the last orbits of the American space station, Skylab, which reentered the Earth's atmosphere on 11 July 1979. The last orbital manoeuvres were aimed at causing Skylab to renter over an uninhabited, oceanic area. When it finally did come down, some pieces of Skylab landed in Australia, while the rest burnt up in the atmosphere.

	Advantages	Disadvantages
Numerical integration	• quick to use • complex forces can be taken into account • easy to change the model of forces being considered • very accurate	• the information is only true for a limited interval • treats all perturbations together • difficult to identify causes and effects • requires many calculations
Analytical methods	• long term accuracy, with qualitative and quantitative indications over a much longer period than that for which theoretical methods have the required precision • possible to analyse the different perturbations • fewer calculations are necessary	• preparatory work of defining the problem mathematically and solving it takes a long time • complex forces, such as atmospheric friction, have to be simplified causing some loss of accuracy

The major advantages and disadvantages of using numerical or analytical methods of orbital prediction

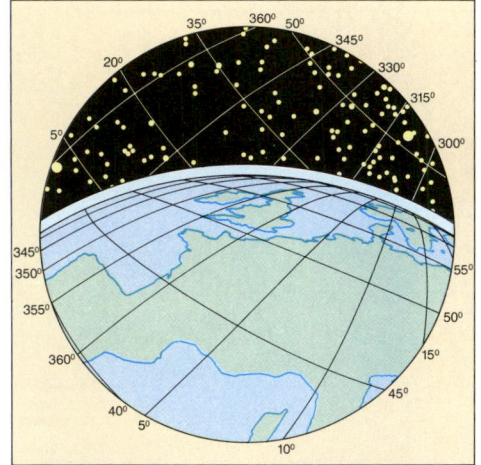

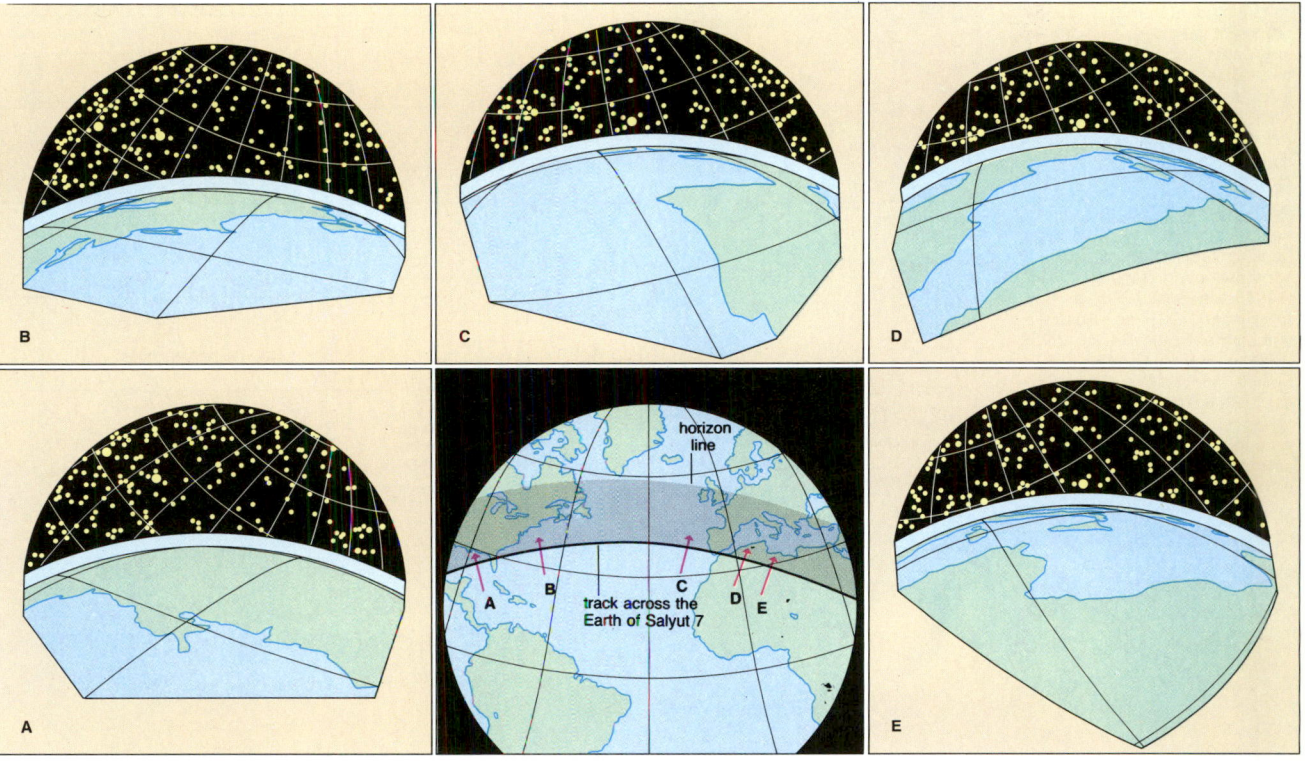

Obtaining information on attitude and orbit for photography from space. During the flight of the French cosmonaut Jean-Loup Chrétien on Salyut 7, a Soviet space station, photographs of the Earth were taken through a porthole. On his return to Earth, Chrétien tried to identify the visible stars as a function of position along the orbit. A computer programme was devised to simulate, in real time, the different stars in view from a manned spacecraft. The diagram above shows an instantaneous field of view, while those on the right show different fields of view for different positions along the orbit, and therefore as a function of time (CNES).

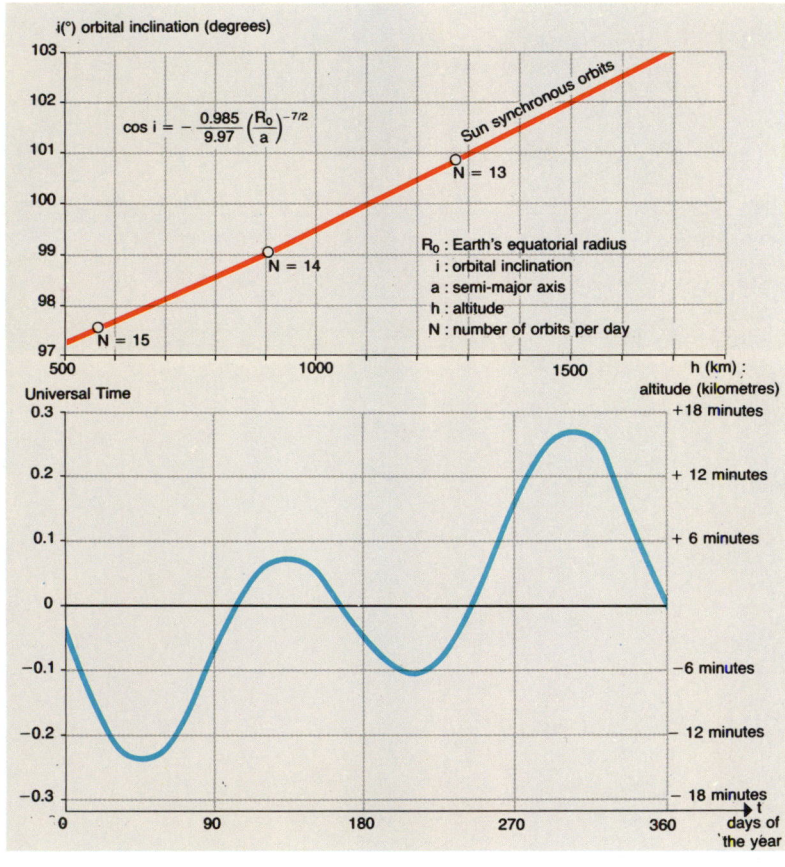

$$\cos i = -\frac{0.985}{9.97}\left(\frac{R_0}{a}\right)^{-7/2}$$

R_0 : Earth's equatorial radius
i : orbital inclination
a : semi-major axis
h : altitude
N : number of orbits per day

The relation between orbital altitude and inclination for a Sun synchronous orbit. On the left, the equation of time shown in the lower graph illustrates the fluctuation of the Earth's rotation about the Sun, because the Earth's orbit around the sun is an ellipse rather than a circle. The equation gives the difference between the mean and true apparent movements of the Earth about the Sun through one year.

The first orbits of the SPOT 1 remote sensing satellite. The satellite was launched by an Ariane rocket into a near polar orbit of the Earth at an altitude of 820 kilometres. Successive tracks of SPOT move towards the West. They are shown in green for the descending tracks and in red for the ascending ones. The interval of time between two points along the orbit is 10 minutes, and the orbital period is close to 100 minutes.

The ranges of the different tracking stations on the Earth's surface are represented in blue. Communications between the satellite and the ground station should be possible when the satellite is within these regions.

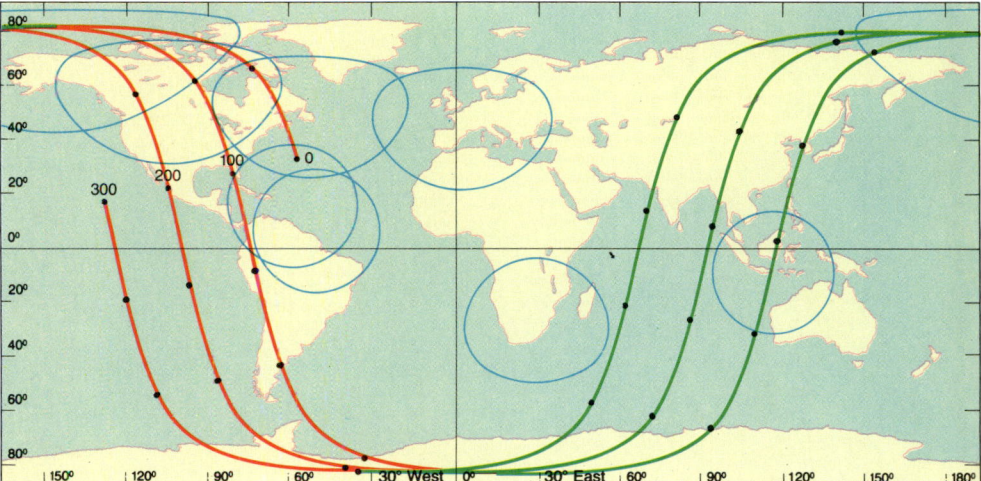

Going into space

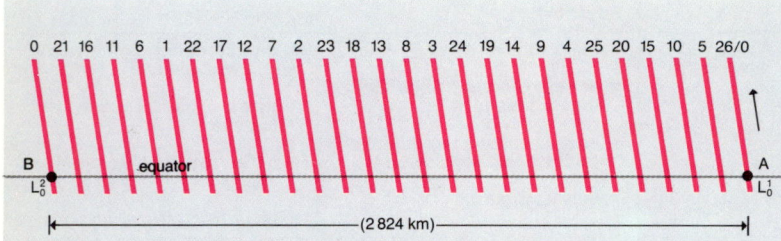

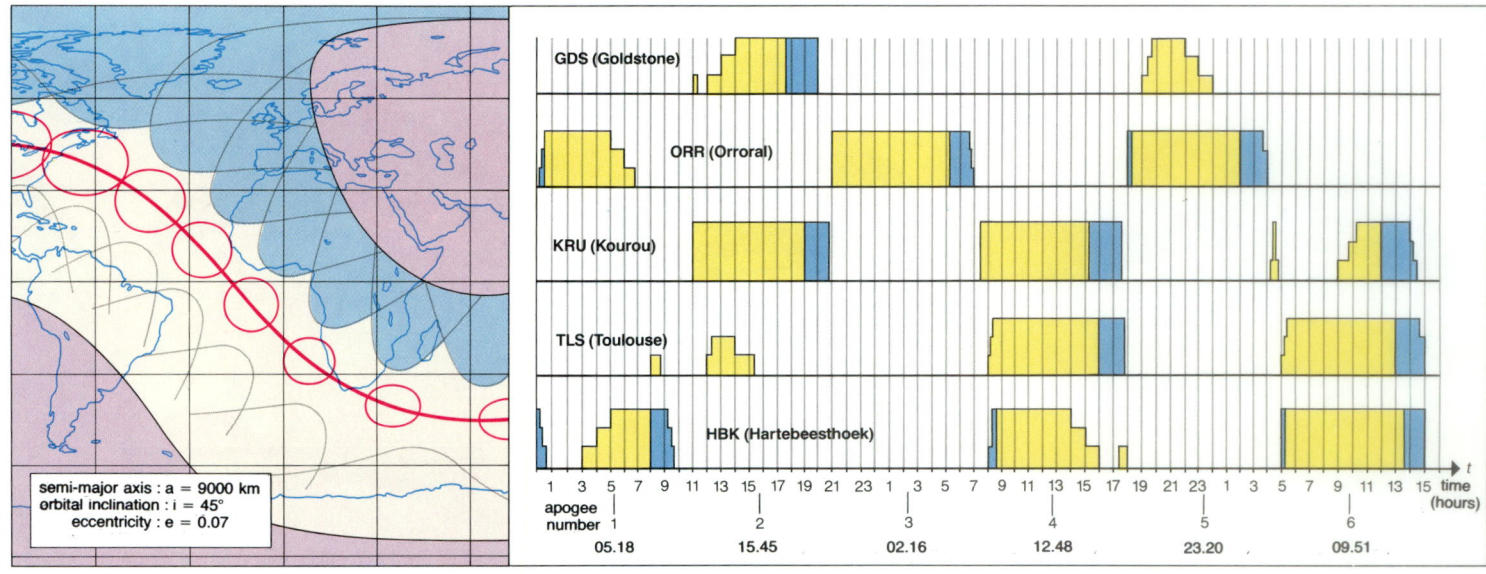

Diagram showing SPOT 1's ascending nodes along the equator. On a particular day, the satellite crosses the equator at longitude A. One orbit, or about 100 minutes later, it crosses the equator some 2824 kilometres, or 14·2 degrees of longitude, to the West, at B. The pink bands show the equatorial crossing points on each day, the pattern repeating exactly every 26 days. It is evident that there are five intervals between orbits on successive days, for example, days 1 and 2, or days 3 and 4.

Diagram showing how SPOT 1 was put into the correct orbit (right). Putting any satellite into a specified position in space is a delicate process. Critical moments in this case included the separation of both the Swedish Viking satellite and the SPOT 1 satellite from the third stage of the Ariane rocket launcher, as well as various corrections to SPOT 1's attitude which followed. The Attitude and Orbit Control System (AOCS) carefully performed many tasks in a specialised plan, and the outcome was monitored by tracking stations around the Earth.

Plan for a satellite in geostationary transfer orbit. For instruments with downwards viewing, areas bounded in pink can be studied from this satellite orbit. For sideways viewing instruments, the blue regions can be scanned. However, there are inaccessible zones (shown in lilac), where a ground station is below the satellite's horizon, and data cannot be received.

On the operational document (far right), the geometric visibilities are shown in yellow for the tracking stations required for a geostationary transfer orbit. NASA networks (GDS in California and ORR in Australia) complement those of the CNES (KRU in French Guiana, TLS in France, and HBK in South Africa). Blue regions represent times when it is impossible for ground stations to work with the satellite, as it is below their visibility horizons.

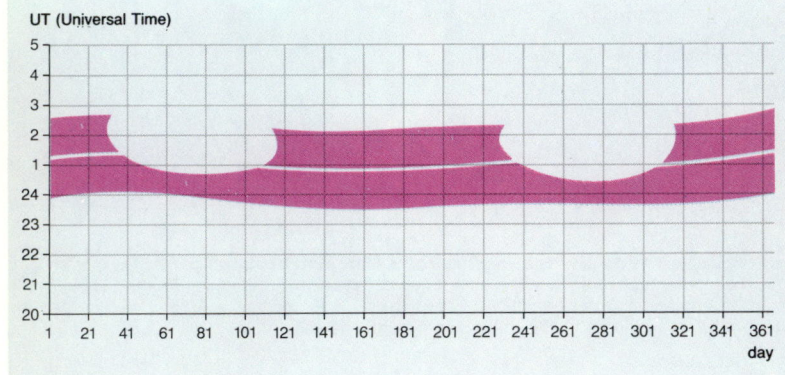

A plan of possible 'launch windows' for a geostationary satellite. All the various launch constraints are established for each day of the year, and the pink regions show the times and dates when a launch is feasible. This diagram actually applies to the French Télécom 1 satellite which was launched on 8 May 1985.

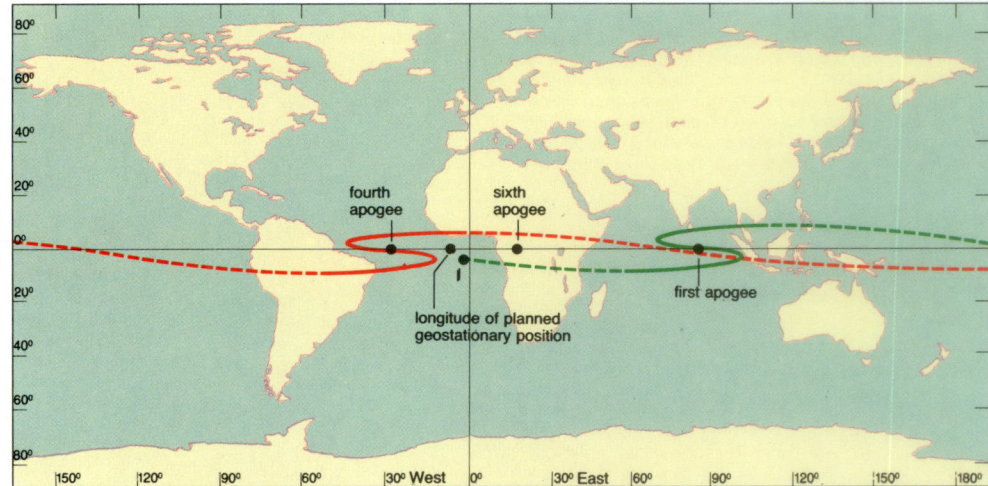

Télécom 1's transfer orbits. Télécom 1 was injected by an Ariane rocket, at the point I. It was then raised to the desired apogee which took about 5 hours 30 minutes. The red and green lines represent the tracks of the satellite across the Earth. The track forms an S shape because, at the apogee, the velocity is less than the Earth's rotational speed.

Since the final stationing point was to be at 8 degrees West longitude, it was sensible to choose the fourth (or sixth) apogee for making the orbit circular. This minimised the time spent in the transfer orbit.

be neglected. The movement of the spacecraft therefore follows a Keplerian orbit.

Numerical integration can be applied to the case of a space probe moving in the Earth–Sun system. In this system there are libation points, called Lagrangian points. If a free object is placed at one of these points, with zero velocity, it is in equilibrium under the action of the forces of gravitational attraction by the Sun and the Earth and the centrifugal force due to its rotation. It therefore remains at that point, suspended in space. There is such a point some 1·3 million kilometres from the Earth towards the Sun – an ideal place from which to study the Sun and the solar wind.

A space probe can of course overcome the force of a planet's gravitational attraction. This is equivalent to the probe leaving the planet's sphere of influence and travelling to an infinite distance. In order to do this, the probe must be given the correct speed v > √(2μ/r) where μ is the fundamental gravitational constant, G, multiplied by the mass of the planet, and r is the distance between the probe and the centre of the planet. If the space probe's velocity exceeds this value, it will move in a hyperbolic trajectory at the edge of the sphere of influence.

A classical interplanetary flight therefore has three phases. There is a planetocentric phase, where the probe has to have a sufficient velocity to escape from the planet from which it starts, normally the Earth. Then there is a heliocentric phase during which the probe moves under the influence of the Sun's gravitation alone. Thirdly, there is the approach phase to the target planet on a hyperbolic trajectory.

Planning an interplanetary flight, such as the US Pioneer or Voyager programmes, always begins by building up a launch plan. The dates of Earth departure and planet arrival are considered. Within these broad parameters, various other constraints must be taken into account, including the launcher's performance, the arrival conditions, and 'visibility' from ground stations, both for trajectory control and for the reception of data via radio.

During the approach to the target planet, the orbital elements are calculated and refined several weeks before the probe's arrival. By making small corrective firings of rocket thrusters, the inclination and the shape of the hyperbola can be modified slightly.

Gravitational assistance, or swing by, can also be used in the approach. This increases the probe's velocity and changes the direction of its motion considerably without having to supply additional energy in the form of rocket fuel. The principle was used to particular effect during the recent tour of the outer planets made by the Voyager spacecraft.

Jean-Pierre Carrou

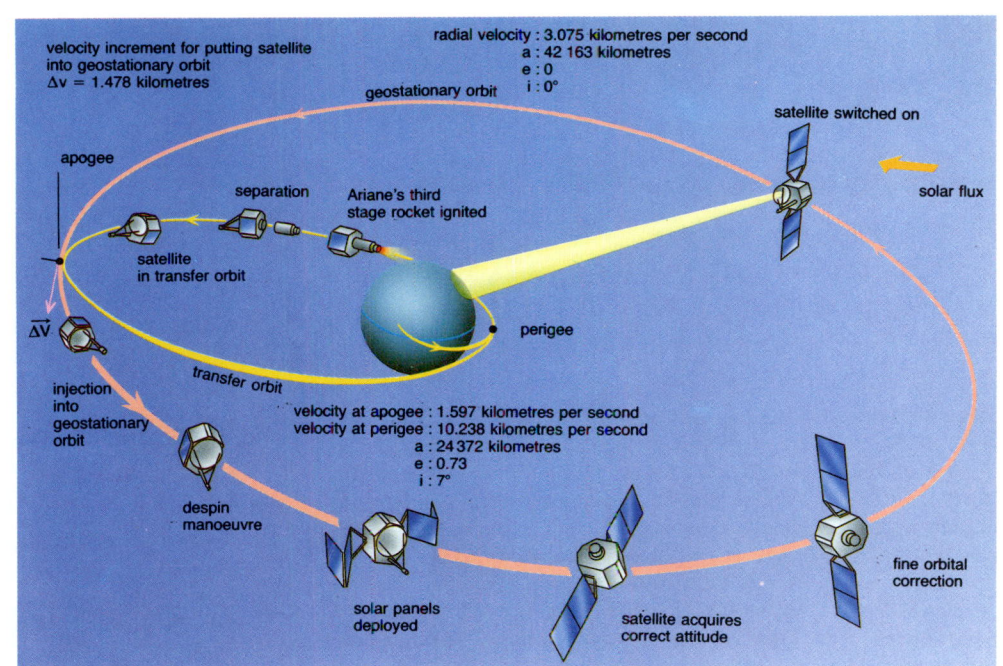

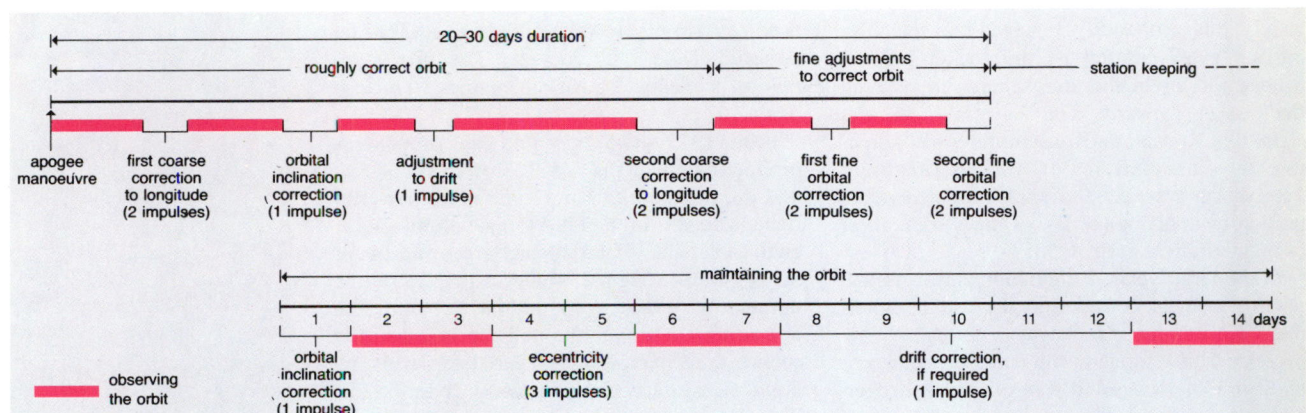

Corrections applied to the orbit of Télécom 1. The diagram above shows the sequence of orbital alterations made to put the satellite into its correct orbit. After firing the rocket motor, at apogee on the fourth transfer orbit, two phases can be distinguished. During the 'coarse' orbital correction, initial differences in longitude and errors acquired during orbital manoeuvres are corrected, so that the satellite is very close to its final station. Then 'fine' orbital corrections take place to keep the satellite accurately in its predetermined orbit. Placing a satellite into the desired geostationary orbit often takes between 20 and 30 days.

The lower of the two diagrams above illustrates the cycle which keeps the satellite in its correct geostationary orbit. This 14 day cycle simplifies the job of ground personnel who would otherwise always be calculating the next set of corrections. The lifetime of a geostationary satellite is, at present, between 7 and 10 years, and is tending to increase.

Gravitational deflection of a space probe by a planet. Placing a space probe in orbit around the target planet can be carried out by making a velocity decrease at the perigee of the hyperbola. Landing on the target planet is treated as an orbital rendezvous. When making a soft landing, as in the Apollo lunar missions, or when returning the American space shuttle to Earth, it is necessary carefully to control the final trajectories so that, for example, the heat generated on reentry into the atmosphere is not too large. The deceleration for a manned spacecraft and the impact velocity onto the planet's surface must not be too great either.

The diagram illustrates the orbit of a space probe moving at high velocity near a planet. The closer that this hyperbolic orbit is to the planet the greater will be the angular deflection, θ, of the probe. Such swing bys were most effective during the Voyager missions.

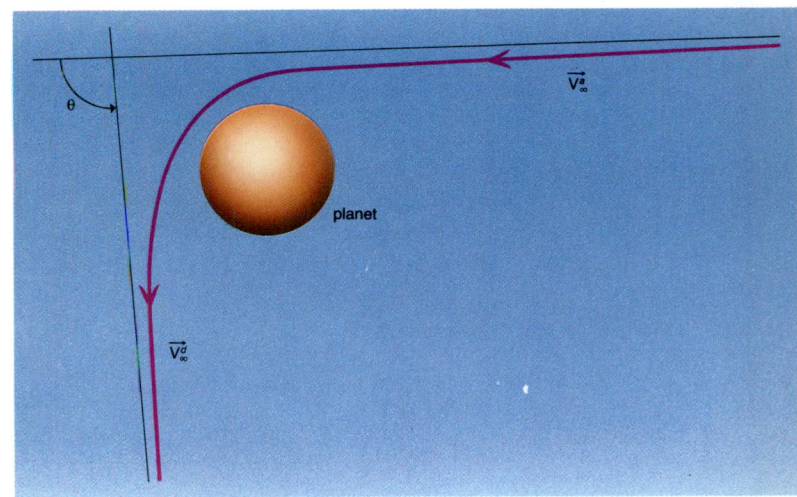

Propulsion

Although it was not until 4 October 1957 that the first artificial satellite was put into orbit around the Earth, rockets had been used long before that date. Before the 1920s, rockets were small, had solid fuel engines, and were in use principally by the military or for entertainment. The combustion gases escaped through a rudimentary hole at the back of the rocket, rather than through a specially shaped nozzle.

Until the middle of the nineteenth century no one really understood the principles on which the rocket and its engine operated. It was widely, but erroneously, believed that the combustion gases emitted by the rocket pressed against the air in the atmosphere, so pushing the rocket forward. The Soviets, however, claim that Konstantin Konstantinov, who directed the manufacture of rockets in Saint Petersburg, succeeded in explaining a rocket's motion by applying the law of the conservation of momentum as early as 1857.

In the latter years of the nineteenth century, scientists began considering the use of liquid fuel. Konstantin Tsiolkovsky, in particular, professed his interest in the conquest of space, and, in 1903, suggested using liquid hydrogen and liquid oxygen as combustible propellants.

From the beginning of the twentieth century the four pioneers of astronautics, the Russian Tsiolkovsky, the German–Rumanian Hermann Oberth, the American Robert H. Goddard and the French Robert Esnault-Pelterie, laid the theoretical and experimental foundations of rocket propulsion. In 1922, Oberth advocated the use of the alcohol–liquid oxygen combination for the first stage of a rocket, with a second stage of liquid oxygen and hydrogen. Goddard's work around the same time marked the beginning of a period of experimentation. In about 1920, he turned away from the use of solid fuels because they could not be used to reach the highest altitudes, and concentrated thereafter on liquid propellants. On 6 December 1925, he performed the first test on an engine fuelled by liquid oxygen and petrol, and on 16 March 1926 this engine powered the first flight of a rocket using liquid fuels.

In the 1930s, in the USA, the USSR, Germany and France, several experimental rocket engines, most of them using liquid oxygen, were designed and built by individuals or small groups of rocket enthusiasts. It was the Germans who first recognised the potential of rockets for military use, constructing the V2 at Peenemünde from 1937 (pp. 35–9). This was the first liquid fuel engine to become operational, and it solved for the first time the intrinsic problems of feeding fuel to the combustion chamber, cooling the engine, and stabilising the combustion process. At the end of the Second World War, the V2's liquid oxygen and ethanol engine was the most powerful in the world. Its thrust of 250 kilonewtons made missiles, and also space launchers, suddenly seem a real possibility.

It was also at this time that rockets were first used to help planes take off, using JATO (Jet Assisted Take Off) rockets. The first aeroplanes propelled by rocket engines were also made.

From 1945 onwards, liquid fuel propellants predominated in the USSR and in the USA, and the race to build more and more powerful rockets began. In the USA, single motor rocket engines capable of producing larger and larger thrusts were designed, while in the USSR the number of motors was multiplied. Until the beginning of the 1960s, ballistic missiles and rocket launchers were fuelled exclusively by liquid fuels, particularly kerosene (paraffin oil) and liquid oxygen. The maximum thrust obtained by such motors approached, and even exceeded, 1 meganewton.

In 1963, however, the Titan II missile went into service in the USA. This was the first missile to use nitrogen peroxide and aerozine, two liquids which were much easier to store than the fuels used hitherto. At this point the rocket industry also began the development of solid fuels for ballistic missiles. Such fuels have the advantages that they can be stored for much longer periods and that they burn for short periods (up to four minutes), but with a much smaller specific impulse than liquid fuels. Enormous solid fuel booster rockets produced the huge thrust needed for the Titan IIIC rocket launcher to blast off in 1965.

In 1962, another new type of rocket engine appeared with the Atlas Centaur launcher. This was the low temperature, or cryogenic, engine using the liquid hydrogen and oxygen combination advocated by Tsiolkovsky at the beginning of the century. With a larger specific impulse, it produced a thrust of 60 kilonewtons and could be reignited in flight. It is still in service today.

The Apollo programme and the Saturn V launcher produced great advances, increasing the thrusts produced by both the kerosene and

The Soviet ORM 65 engine. Designed and constructed in 1936, this was one of the best rocket engines of the era (ORM stands for Opytnyj Raketnyj Motor, or experimental rocket engine). The steel combustion chamber, with a diameter of 100 millimetres, was fed with the fuel (paraffin oil, or kerosene) and the oxidant (nitric acid), there being three radial injectors for each. The neck of the nozzle had a diameter of 23 millimetres. The motor was cooled by circulating the fuel between the inside and outside walls. The pressure in the chamber reached 2·5 megapascals, the speed of the exhaust gas was 2·1 kilometres per second and the specific impulse lasted for 210 seconds. The engine weighed 14·3 kilograms, and could produce a thrust 480 to 1720 newtons.

Between 1937 and 1938, the ORM 65 underwent about thirty fixed firing tests. It was then fitted to the RP 318-1 rocket glider built by Korolev. This engine, slightly reshaped, was first used in flight in 1940, piloted by Vladimir Pavlovich Fedorov. The ORM 65 was also fitted to a 212 type rocket, again designed by Korolev, flight tested in 1939.

cross section of rocket engine at a–b

kerosene supply

nitric acid supply

expanded view of the cooling system in the side of the nozzle

cross section of rocket nozzle at c–d

1 nitric acid injector
2 kerosene injector
3 neck of the nozzle
4 spark plug
5 vehicle fixing point
6 annular pipe for kerosene
7 cooling system for combustion chamber
8 combustion chamber
9 nozzle

Propulsion characteristics of early rockets

Rocket	Put into service	Number of stages	Fuel used in first stage		Number of motors in first stage	Thrust of first stage (kilonewtons)
			Oxidant	Fuel		
V2	Germany, 1944	1	liquid oxygen	ethanol	1	250
Private A	USA, 1944	1	solid fuel		1	4
WAC Corporal	USA, 1945	1	nitric acid	aniline	1	7
Viking	USA, 1949	1	liquid oxygen	alcohol	1	91
Redstone	USA, 1953	1	liquid oxygen	alcohol	1	330
Jupiter C	USA, 1956	3	liquid oxygen	hydine	1	369
Thor	USA, 1957	1	liquid oxygen	kerosene	1	670
Jupiter	USA, 1957	1	liquid oxygen	kerosene	1	670
Vanguard	USA, 1957	3	liquid oxygen	kerosene	1	120
Zemiorka	USSR, 1957	2	liquid oxygen	kerosene	5[1]	4400
Juno I	USA, 1958	4	liquid oxygen	hydine	1	369
Atlas B	USA, 1958	1, 5[2]	liquid oxygen	kerosene	3[2]	1600
Juno II	USA, 1958	4	liquid oxygen	kerosene	1	670
Titan I	USA, 1959	2	liquid oxygen	kerosene	2	1330

[1] Four RD 107 rocket motors and one RD 108. Each motor had four combustion chambers.
[2] Atlas B consisted of one main rocket motor and two other motors jettisoned in flight.

One of Goddard's last rockets (left). Based on his numerous theoretical studies and experiments, Goddard took out no less than 214 patents on rockets and rocket components.

The rocket pictured here on its launch tower was built in 1940 at Goddard's research centre at Roswell, New Mexico. It formed part of a series of 24 rockets which incorporated the most recent improvements in rocket motors, pumps and turbines. The rockets were 6·70 metres tall and 0·46 metres in diameter. Their mass was from 85 to 110 kilograms when empty, and they carried 65 kilograms of liquid oxygen and 51 kilograms of petrol (gasoline). The longest firing time was 43·5 seconds, achieved on 11 June 1940 during a static test. The greatest thrust was registered on 6 January 1941, also during a ground test. Only two launches took place, the programme being interrupted by the entry of the USA into the Second World War. Goddard himself is seen in the top right of the photograph, during preparation for a test (B. Anthony Stewart, © National Geographical Society).

The gigantic F1 rocket engine of Saturn V (right). One of the requirements of the Apollo programme was a colossal launcher, and so the Saturn V rocket was built. Its first stage consisted of five F1 engines fuelled by liquid oxygen and paraffin oil (kerosene), providing a total thrust of 33·8 meganewtons at lift-off. The F1 was the biggest and most powerful rocket engine ever built.

Here Wernher von Braun is seen in front of the enormous F1 nozzles of a Saturn V rocket preserved by the Alabama Space and Rocket Center in Huntsville.

Several statistics on the performance of this engine bear witness to the great technological challenge that it offered. Fuel was fed to the combustion chamber at a rate of almost three tonnes per second; a single turbo pump weighed just over one tonne and delivered 55 000 horse power. To produce such a large amount of power in a combustion chamber of such relatively small volume, scientists had to push their knowledge of the behaviour of materials at high temperatures and pressures to the limit. The key factor governing their success was the use of superalloys.

The F1 nozzle was 5·79 metres tall and its diameter was 3·81 metres. The F1 itself had a dry weight of 8·38 tonnes. At sea level it developed a thrust of 6·77 meganewtons, with combustion lasting for 150 seconds; the pressure and temperature inside the combustion chamber reached 7·7 megapascals and 2800 degrees celsius, respectively. This engine was one of the first to have a turbogenerator which burnt the same fuels as the rocket motor itself, consuming in all about 2% of the total volume of liquid fuel (Alabama Space and Rocket Center, Huntsville, Alabama).

liquid hydrogen types of engine. The F1 kerosene engine of the first stage of the Saturn rocket produced about 6·8 meganewtons of thrust, and the J2 liquid hydrogen engine of the second and third stages produced a thrust of 1 meganewton.

The reusable space shuttle developed in the USA at the beginning of the 1970s does not involve any revolutionary new fuels. It uses solid fuel booster rockets for launch purposes and cryogenic liquid propellants for the shuttle itself. These boosters broke records, however. Each carries 500 tonnes of ammonium perchlorate and aluminium fuel, and has a thrust of nearly 11·8 meganewtons. Yet the mass of each booster rocket is relatively small, requiring only about 10 tonnes of special composite materials.

There are in addition three cryogenic Space Shuttle Main Engines (SSME). Their performance has been improved with respect to their predecessor, the J2 engine of Saturn V, with the thrust enhanced from 1·02 to 2·09 meganewtons. The efficiency of propulsion has also been improved, particularly by making the gases which operate the turbopumps burn also.

Jacques Villain

The V2 rocket engine (below). The German V2 missile became operational in 1944, and was the forerunner of all strategic ballistic missiles and space launchers. The liquid fuels commonly used by launchers today trace their origins back to the V2 engine, which used liquid oxygen and ethanol. These were drawn from tanks at 125 litres per second, using turbopumps, into the 18 injection heads at the top of the combustion chamber. The turbopump consisted of a two stage turbine, powered by hydrogen peroxide, which rotated at a temperature of 425 degrees celsius, and of two centrifugal pumps, one for the oxygen and one for the ethanol. The turbine was of 500 horse power, and the two pumps, mounted on the same shaft, turned at 4300 revolutions per minute. In order to survive the high temperatures produced by the combustion, the motor was cooled by ethanol circulating between the inner and outer walls of the combustion chamber and by the flow of a thin layer of ethanol between the inner wall and the propulsion jet. The 400 kilogram motor produced a thrust of 250 kilonewtons, equivalent to 650 000 horse power. The pressure in the chamber reached 1·5 megapascals and the specific impulse lasted 210 seconds.

The photograph shows an example of one of the last V2s to be constructed, which is preserved in the Vernon establishment of the Société européenne de propulsion. From right to left are evident the end of the liquid oxygen tank, the combustion chamber, and the nozzle, fitted with graphite fins, which enabled the direction of the missile to be controlled by deflecting the exhaust gas jet (SEP).

The Soviet RD 107 rocket engine (right). This engine, developed between 1954 and 1957, was fitted as the first stage of the intercontinental missile SS Sapwood as well as to the Zemiorka launcher. It used liquid oxygen and kerosene as fuels. A single turbopump fed fuel into the four combustion chambers, the pressure in which reached 5·85 megapascals. The total thrust was 1 meganewton, and the specific impulse lasted 314 seconds. The dry weight of the engine was 1·27 tonnes and it was 2·86 metres high. Apart from the four chambers which provided the principal thrust, there were two much smaller, steerable rocket engines, called vernier motors, used to pilot the rocket (J. Villain).

Propulsion

The rocket engine

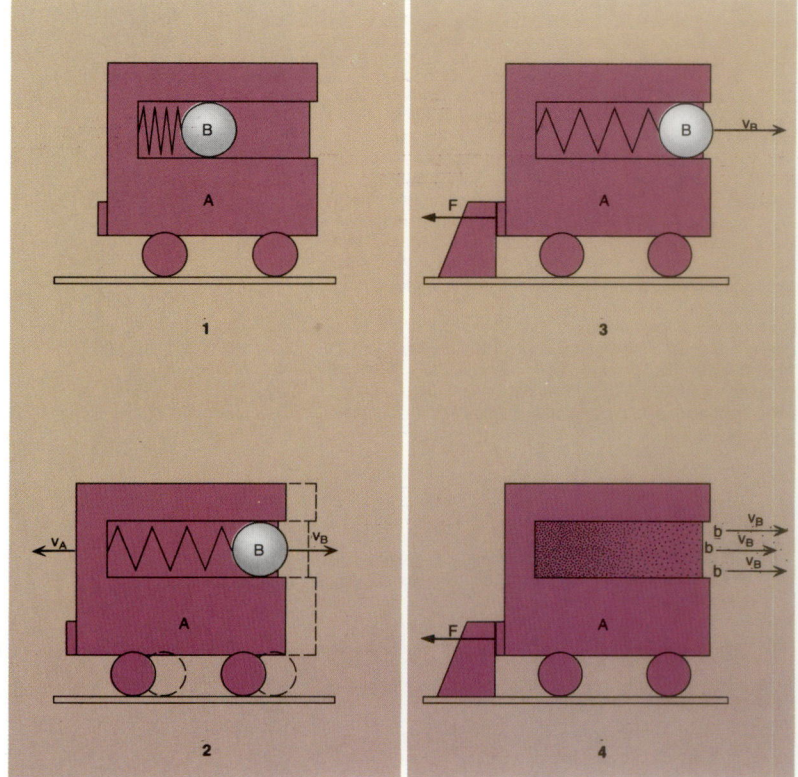

Although the principle of the reaction engine was demonstrated in antiquity and although black gunpowder rockets were used in China in the thirteenth century, the physical principles behind their operation were not fully understood until recently. An understanding of Newton's laws, in particular the law of action and reaction, is needed above all.

Rocket engines propel the vehicle not only up through the Earth's atmosphere but also through the cosmic vacuum. Such engines are propulsion systems where the propulsive force is obtained either by varying the momentum (the product of the mass and its velocity) of the system itself or by varying the momentum of the surrounding fluid. In the first case, matter is ejected from the engine at a certain relative velocity, and a fraction of the original system's mass is lost to the surroundings; this is rocket propulsion, or self propulsion. In the second case, there is also an acceleration of matter, but this matter comes from the medium external to the engine; this is a reaction engine. There are also some systems which employ both concepts together, called mixed propulsion systems.

As far as reaction engines are concerned,

there are three types of primary energy source. These are chemical reactions, nuclear reactions, and external radiation (such as the Sun, or lasers). Energy is usually transferred within the system as electrical energy.

A rocket engine generates a force, termed the thrust, by ejecting at high speed part of its own mass. It does this, at high temperature and pressure, by burning two different fuels which are carried separately in the propulsion unit. An engine will have a better performance when it produces a given thrust by ejecting a smaller mass, and a parameter called the specific impulse characterises its performance.

The propulsion systems most commonly used for space applications are chemical energy rocket engines. For this purpose a high thermal energy is generated by the chemical reaction of combustion. The gases produced in the combustion chamber pass through a convergent–divergent nozzle, termed a Laval nozzle, which transforms as much of the randomly directed thermal motion as possible into the directional motion of the exhaust gases.

Marcel Pouliquen

Propulsion by reaction. A simple way of explaining the principle of a reaction engine is to take the example of a small truck A, which is free to move on a flat horizontal surface. The truck is fitted with a spring which can move a solid mass B. Initially the truck is stationary, the spring is compressed, and the solid mass B is stationary (see diagram 1). Ejection of the mass B at a velocity v_B, to the right, when the compressed spring is released, produces, by reaction, a movement of the truck to the left at a velocity v_A (diagram 2). This phenomenon is an example of Newton's third law, which states that if a system A exerts a force F on a system B (action), then, at the same time, the system B exerts an identical force on the system A, but in the reverse direction (reaction). This law is also known as the principle of action and reaction, that 'action and reaction are equal and opposite'. In this example the action of A on B is obtained through the intermediary of the spring.

To find the value of the velocity v_A acquired by the truck, the principle of the conservation of momentum (the product of the mass of a body and its velocity) is applied, according to which the momentum of an isolated system remains constant. Neglecting the friction between the components of the system, and the masses of the spring and the wheels, this principle shows that

$$m_A v_A = m_B v_B$$

where m_A and v_A are the mass and the velocity of the truck, respectively, and m_B and v_B are the mass and velocity of the solid mass B. When m_A is much greater than m_B, then v_A is much less than v_B. When a cannon is fired, the recoil corresponds to the reaction produced by the high speed ejection of the cannon ball which is equivalent to the solid mass B.

Returning to the experiment with the truck, this time preventing all movement to the left by placing a vertical wall in front of the truck (diagram 3), we can measure the force F exerted on the wall as mass B is ejected. This is the force generated by the spring.

To obtain a certain force for a longer period of time, the single solid mass B can be replaced by millions of small particles b, each moving to the right at the velocity v_B (diagram 4). This illustrates the principle of a rocket's operation.

Energy source	Mass source	Examples
Internal	internal	• cold gas propulsion systems • chemical propellants • nuclear propulsion systems • electric propulsion using a nuclear generator or a chemical battery • photon propulsion from a nuclear generator or a chemical battery
	external	• electrical propulsion of submarines • nuclear propulsion of ships and submarines • turbojets • ramjets
	mixed	• ramjet rockets
External	internal	• propulsion by fluids heated by solar energy • laser propulsion
	external	• sailing ships, gliders • solar sails
	mixed	?
Mixed	internal	• electrical propulsion (ionic, thermoelectric, or magnetohydrodynamic)
	external	• steam train • steam ship • car • turboprop aircraft • turbojet aircraft • ramjets
	mixed	• bypass rocket

The available propulsion systems, showing different types of energy source and mass source. Several examples of each type of system, with internal or external sources of mass and of energy, are presented. For simplicity, nuclear and chemical propulsion, and the solar sail, have been classified under internal–internal and external–external respectively although, strictly speaking, the mass of the photons involved is zero.

Mass ejected	Energy source		
	Chemical reaction	Nuclear reaction (fission or fusion)	External radiation
External fluid	• turbojet • ramjet	• nuclear turbojet • nuclear ramjet	• pulsed laser
External fluid + internal fluid	• bypass rocket • turbojet rocket • liquid air rocket	• nuclear turbojet with chemical afterburn	
Internal fluid	• rocket • electric propulsion with a chemical battery	• nuclear thruster • electrical thruster with nuclear generator	• laser • propulsion by fluid heated by solar radiation
Zero mass		• photon thruster with nuclear generator	• solar sail

Propulsion by reaction systems for different types of mass ejected and different types of energy source. The sources of a vehicle's mass and energy may be either internal, external, or mixed, or may involve massless photons.

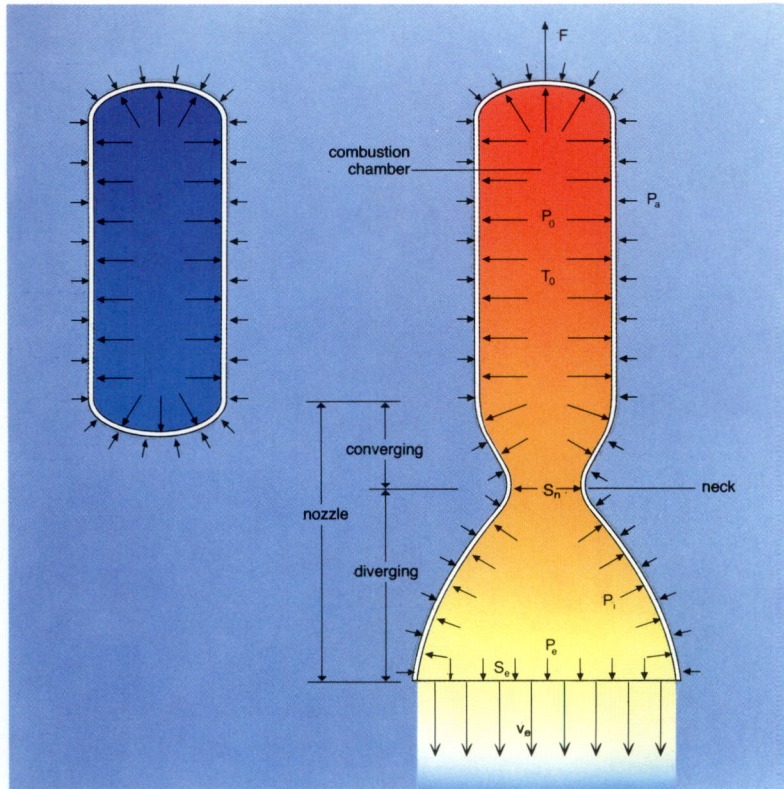

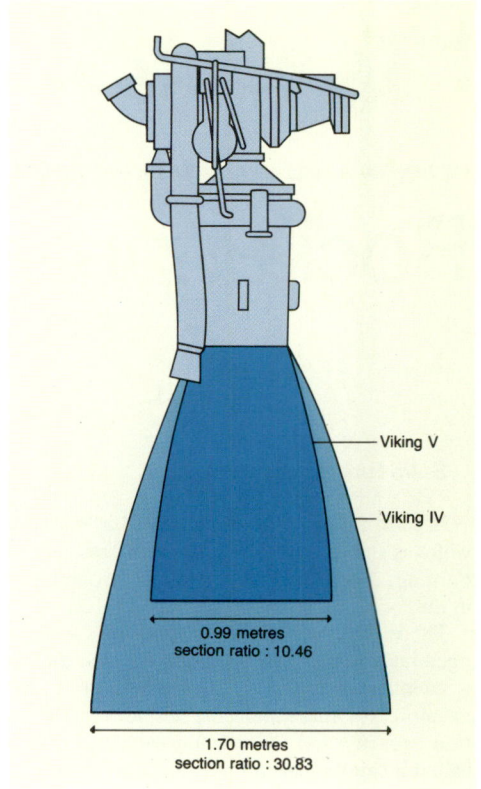

Viking V

Viking IV

0.99 metres
section ratio : 10.46

1.70 metres
section ratio : 30.83

Optimising the nozzles. A nozzle is not designed for a specific propulsion system but for the altitude at which it has to operate. At the Earth's surface, at the atmospheric pressure of sea level (100 kilopascals, or 1000 millibars), the discharge of exhaust gases is limited by the separation of the jet from the nozzle wall. In the cosmic vacuum, this physical limitation does not exist. Therefore there have to be two different types of engines and nozzles, those which propel the first stage of launcher through the atmosphere, and those which propel subsequent stages or control the orientation of spacecraft in the vacuum of space.

The figure to the right shows the difference between the nozzles of two engines with similar values of thrust and combustion pressure. One operates from ground level – this is the Viking V rocket engine on the first stage of Ariane. The other, the Viking IV rocket engine of the second stage of Ariane, operates in the space vacuum. Viking V's thrust is 624 kilonewtons at sea level and 695 kilonewtons in a vacuum. The specific impulse is from 248·2 to 280·9 seconds. The thrust of the Viking IV rocket engine is 713 kilonewtons, with a specific impulse of 295·6 seconds.

To improve the performance of rocket engines, nozzles which can be extended in flight could be used.

Thrust. Physically speaking, thrust is the result of pressure, that is the force per unit area, which is exerted on the wall of the propulsion chamber.

On the left, above, is shown a hermetically sealed chamber, filled with gas at a certain pressure. The forces exerted on the chamber are due to atmospheric pressure on the outside walls and to the pressure of the gas on the inside walls. If the two pressures are equal, then the pressure forces on the outside and the inside are equal and opposite, and the resultant pressure force will be zero. The chamber will accordingly remain stationary.

On the right, above, is shown a chamber with an opening, the nozzle, through which gas can escape. The pressure distribution is now asymmetric; the pressure within the chamber varies little, but the pressure near the nozzle decreases somewhat. The forces due to gas pressure on the bottom of the chamber are now no longer compensated for from the outside. The resultant force F due to the internal and external pressure difference, the thrust, is opposite to the direction of the gas jet. It pushes the chamber upwards.

To create high speed exhaust gases, the necessary high temperature of combustion is obtained by using a very energetic fuel and by having the molecular weight of the exhaust gases as low as possible. Using such a criterion, hydrogen is very desirable as a fuel. It is also necessary to reduce the pressure of the gas as much as possible inside the nozzle by adopting a large section ratio. The section ratio is defined as the area of the exit section S_e divided by the area of the neck section S_n.

The thrust F is the resultant of the forces due to the pressures exerted on the inner and outer walls by the combustion gases and the surrounding atmosphere, taking the boundary between the inner and outer surfaces as the cross section of the exit of the nozzle. Applying the principle of the conservation of momentum gives

$$F = q\,v_e + (P_e - P_a)\,S_e$$

where q is the rate of the ejected mass flow, P_a the pressure of the ambient atmosphere, P_e the pressure of the exhaust gases and v_e their ejection speed. The thrust is specified either at sea level or in a vacuum.

The maximum thrust occurs when $P_e = P_a$. It is thus $F = q\,v_e$, and the nozzle is said to be adapted. When P_e is less than P_a, the nozzle is under-extended. When the opposite is true, it is over-extended.

Temperatures, pressure and gas flow in a rocket engine. This diagram indicates values of the different parameters in a modern rocket engine, in this case the cryogenic HM7B engine built by the Société européenne de propulsion. Temperatures are given in degrees absolute, or kelvin (K), pressures in kilopascals (kPa), fuel flow rates in kilograms per second (kg/s), and velocities in metres per second (m/s). The combustion chamber and the neck of the nozzle are cooled by the flow of the liquid hydrogen into the engine. The diverging part of the nozzle is cooled by a secondary flow of hydrogen which escapes, without combustion, through tiny nozzles at the edge of the main nozzle.

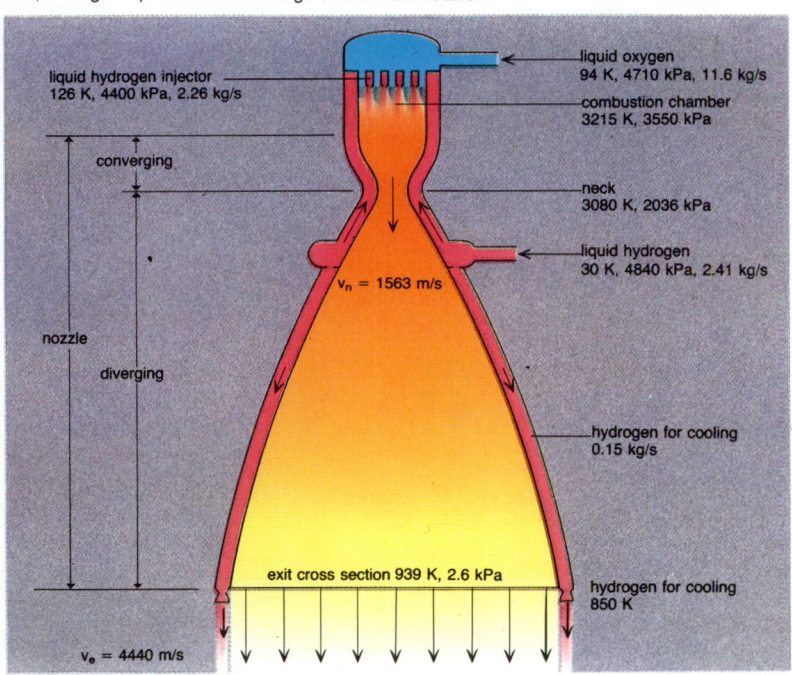

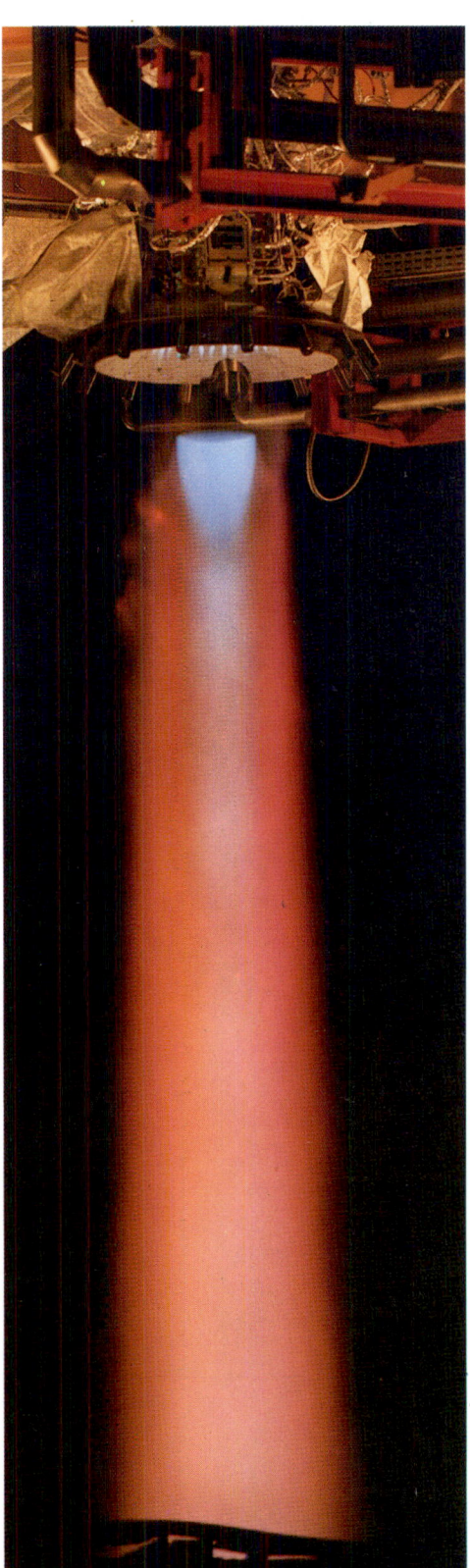

Specific impulse and propulsive thrust. The specific impulse of a rocket, I_{sp}, is the ratio of the thrust F to the flow rate of the weight ejected, that is the product of the acceleration due to gravity at ground level, g_0, and the rate of mass flow (q)

$$I_{sp} = F/q\,g_0.$$

In the International System of Units (SI), F is expressed in newtons and q in kilograms per second; $g_0 = 9·81$ metres per second per second. The specific impulse is therefore a time, expressed in seconds. When the thrust and the flow remain constant throughout the burning of the fuel, the specific impulse is the time for which the rocket engine provides a thrust equal to the weight of fuel consumed.

For a given engine, the specific impulse has different values on the ground and in the space vacuum because the ambient pressure is involved in the expression for the thrust. It is therefore important to state whether the specific impulse is the value at the Earth's surface or in the vacuum of space. For an adapted nozzle, the specific impulse on the ground is equal to v_e/g_0. It is, consequently, about one tenth of the speed (in metres per second) at which the exhaust gases are ejected.

However, there are a number of losses within a rocket engine, the main ones being related to the inefficiency of the chemical reaction (combustion) process, to losses due to the nozzle, and to losses due to the pumps. Overall, the losses affect the efficiency of the specific impulse. This is the ratio of the real specific impulse (on the ground, or in the space vacuum) and the theoretical specific impulse obtained with an ideal nozzle from gases coming from a complete chemical reaction.

The photograph on the left shows the testbed of Ariane's third stage, fitted with a cryogenic HM7 engine. In a vacuum, this engine develops a thrust of 61·7 kilonewtons over 570 seconds. Its specific impulse in a vacuum is 442·6 seconds, and it consumes 14·17 kilograms of fuel per second (SEP).

Propulsion

Rocket propellants

Solid fuels

A solid fuel is a dense combustible material which is stable at ordinary temperatures. When burning, it produces energy in a controlled way in the form of a gas at high temperatures.

There are two families of solid fuels – homogenous and composite. A homogenous fuel is a chemical compound. In nitrocellulose, for example, the same molecule has both an oxidation capacity and a reduction capacity, and is called a simple base homogenous fuel. Double base homogenous fuels usually consist of nitrocellulose and nitroglycerine, to which a plasticiser has been added to provide a certain mechanical resistance. Chemical stabilisers will also have been added so that the fuels can be stored for longer, and can survive changes of atmospheric temperature and humidity. A chemical to regulate the speed of combustion may also be included.

There are two ways to make homogenous fuels. Small fuel blocks with diameters of less than 250 millimetres and lengths less than 1 metre are generally extruded in a press. Alter-natively, they are made by casting them from grains pumped from a nitroglycerine solvent.

These fuels do not usually have specific impulses which are greater than about 210 seconds under standard conditions of use. They have densities, or masses per unit volume, of the order of 1·65 tonnes per cubic metre and their surface combustion speeds lie between 8 and 32 millimetres per second. Their main asset is that they do not produce traceable fumes. This type of fuel is therefore usually used in tactical weapons. It is also chosen sometimes for larger rocket launchers to perform subsidiary functions such as jettisoning spent parts and separating one stage from another.

Modern composite fuels are heterogenous powders (mixtures) which use a crystallised or finely ground mineral salt as an oxidant, and which form a compound with mechanical cohesion. Other compounds are sometimes added to the main ingredients to make the powder easier to manufacture. In these products, the oxidant constitutes between 60 and 90% of the mass of the fuel, and is often ammonium perchlorate. This has many good qualities – it has a high

Launching a rocket using different types of fuel. Rocket fuels are classified according to their state – solid, liquid, gaseous, or hybrid (a mixture of liquid and solid). They may also be specified according to their storage temperatures – cryogenic (at extremely low temperatures), at normal ground temperatures, or at high temperatures (for example, a hot water engine).

It is not uncommon for a spacecraft to be launched with a rocket whose engines use different types of fuel. Thus the American Titan III E Centaur launcher, photographed above during the launch of Voyager 1 on 5 September 1977, uses three fuel types. Two solid fuel engines act as a zero stage, the first and second stages use a storable, liquid fuel (nitrogen peroxide and hydrazine) and the top stage, the Centaur D1 T, uses a cryogenic, liquid oxygen and liquid hydrogen fuel (NASA).

The geometry of solid fuel blocks (below). There are two main types of solid fuel blocks used in the space industry. These are cylindrical blocks, with combustion at a front, or surface, and cylindrical blocks with internal combustion. In the first case, the front of the flame travels in layers from the nozzle end of the block towards the top of the casing. In the second, more usual case, the combustion surface develops along the length of the central channel; sometimes the channel is star shaped to moderate the growth of this surface.

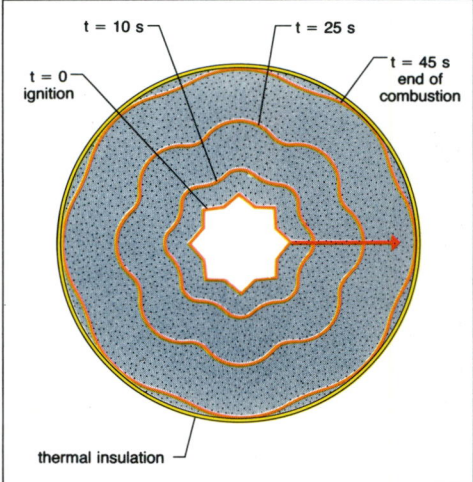

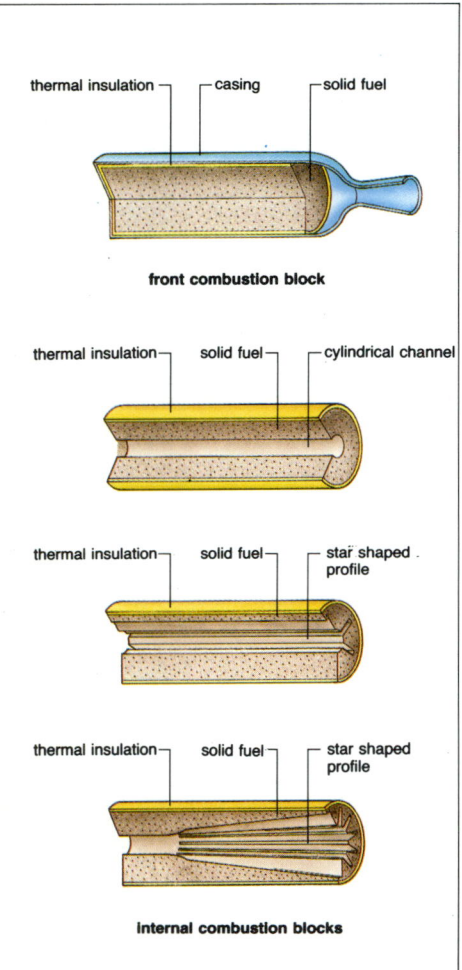

	Nitrocellulose	Nitroglycerine	Plasticiser	Other
French fuel	66.0%	25.0%	8.0%	1.0%
Balistite (USA)	51.5%	43.0%	1.0%	4.5%
Soviet cordite	56.5%	28.0%	4.5%	11.0%

The mass composition of several common solid fuels for rockets. All solid fuels used to have the consistency of powder, like the first fuel ever used, black gunpowder. Nowadays they have the consistency of rubber.

The growth of a combustion surface in a block with a star shaped channel (left). Here, the fuel burns in parallel layers. In this example the initial profile is an eight pointed star. With time measured in seconds, successive positions of the front of the flame are shown in orange. The block has a diameter of 800 millimetres.

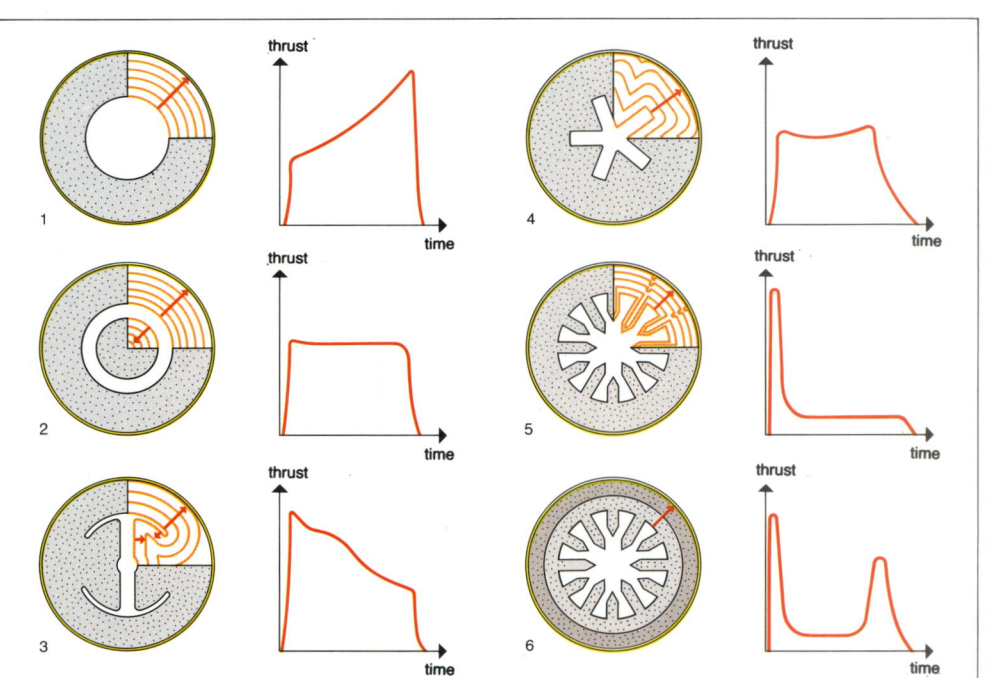

Growth of the thrust for different internal combustion solid fuel blocks. The arrows indicate the progression of the front of the flame, from inside to out. Fuel blocks with a cylindrical channel (1) develop their thrust progressively. Those with a channel and also a central cylinder of fuel (2) produce a relatively constant thrust, which reduces to zero very quickly when the fuel is used up. Fuel in a block with a 'double anchor' profile (3) produces a decreasing thrust. The five pointed star profile (4) develops a relatively constant thrust which decreases slowly to zero as the end of the fuel is used up. The 'cog' profile (5) produces a strong thrust initially, followed by an almost constant lower thrust. A fuel block (6) which contains two different powders develops a strong thrust initially, followed by a moderate thrust, and then a new strong thrust when the second fuel starts to burn near the end of the combustion period.

Characteristics of the fuels used for the US space shuttle

Aluminium	16%
Ammonium perchlorate	70%
Plastic (polybutadiene)	14%
Density, or mass per unit volume	1715 kilograms per cubic metre
Specific impulse	262 seconds
Speed of combustion (pressure: 7 megapascals)	8.8 millimetres per second

concentration of oxygen, it is stable, and cheap to produce.

The fuel itself is aluminium. An organic substance is added to make the solid fuel pliable and to ensure the mechanical homogeneity of the block. Up to 1962, polyvinyl chloride was used as the plastic base for powder fuels. Then polyurethane or polybutadienes were used to make blocks which could either be inserted into the engine or stuck to the chamber walls. However, large fuel blocks can now be manufactured, and the space shuttle uses 500 tonne blocks in its booster engines.

The shape of the fuel block for the rocket is chosen with the particular type of mission that it is required for in mind. Since the combustion of the block progresses from its free surface, as this surface grows, geometrical considerations determine whether the thrust increases, decreases or stays constant.

Each block of solid fuel is carefully checked for deformations that could allow harmful fissures – or even ruptures – to form during storage. These would usually cause an uncontrolled growth in the combustion surface, causing excessive pressure to build up and premature failure of the engine in a spectacular fashion.

The solid fuels used today are easier to store than liquid fuels. Nevertheless, they have one major disadvantage. Once the block has been ignited, it is impossible to stop the combustion; it ceases only when all the fuel has been used.

Jean-Michel Villetorte

Liquid fuels

The most common liquid fuels involve two types of liquid, a fuel proper and an oxidant, stored separately in the liquid state in tanks.

A good fuel is one with a high specific impulse or – and this amounts to the same thing – one with a high speed of exhaust gas ejection. This implies a high combustion temperature and exhaust gases with small molecular weights. However, for the fluids used on space vehicles, there is another important parameter which has to be taken into consideration: the density, or mass per unit volume, of the fuel. Since the mass at lift off is limited, using a low density fuel means that larger fuel tanks are required and therefore that the pressurised tanks will weigh more. Storage temperature is also important. A fuel which requires a low storage temperature – a cryogenic fuel – will have to be thermally insulated, and this too which will increase the mass of the launcher.

The toxicity of the compound is likewise important. Safety hazards would exist when handling, transporting, or storing a highly toxic compound and there could be the possibility of atmospheric pollution during ground tests or in flight. For this reason, in spite of its high performance, the highly toxic substance fluorine has been abandoned by all space nations except for the USSR. A fluorine compound is used, for instance, in the top stage of one of the Soviet launchers, the RD 107 rocket engine, which produces a thrust of 10 kilonewtons. Nitrogen peroxide is also very poisonous, though it can be used with great care, and hydrazine and the related UDMH are dangerous to living tissue. Some fuels are very corrosive too, but materials that are resistant to certain fuels have been identified for use in space technology.

If they spontaneously catch fire on contact, two fuels are said to be hypergolic. This property can be useful because it removes the need for an auxiliary system to cause ignition. Fluorine is hypergolic with all combustibles, while nitric acid and nitrogen peroxide are hypergolic with hydrazine and UDMH. Conversely, however, oxygen is not hypergolic with any commonly used fuel.

Hybrid fuels

Hybrid fuel engines represent an intermediate group between solid and liquid fuel engines. One of the substances here is solid, usually the fuel itself, while the other, usually the oxidant, is liquid. The liquid is injected into the solid, whose fuel reservoir also serves as the combustion chamber. The main advantage of such engines is that they have a high performance, similar to that of a solid fuel, but that combustion can be moderated, stopped or even restarted. However, it remains difficult to make use of this promising concept for very large thrusts, and hybrid fuel engines are rarely built.

A new family of propellants is currently being developed. These are fuels for ramjet rockets which use atmospheric oxygen as the oxidant mixed with primary reducing gases produced by burning a fuel that is low in oxygen. The specific impulses available from this type of propulsion system are very high, up to 1500 seconds, but they require highly complex engines. They can, moreover, only be used where atmospheric oxygen is present.

Marcel Pouliquen

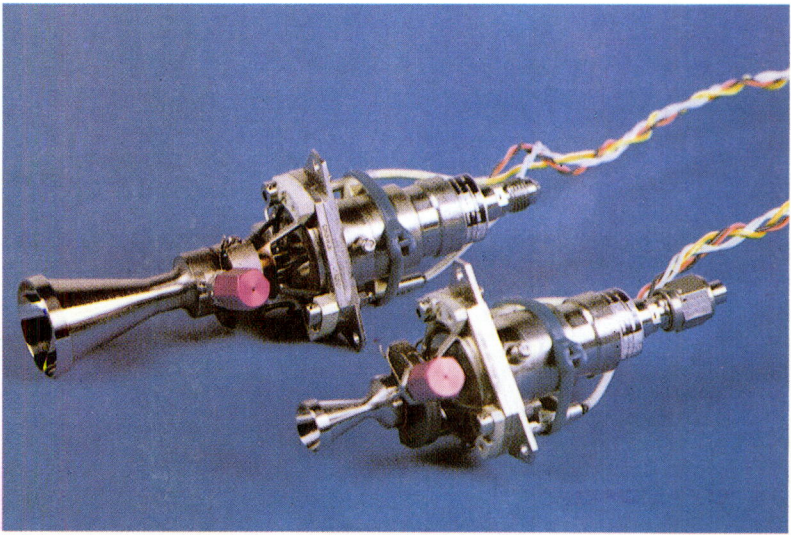

Catalytic decomposition engines. These rocket engines use a single liquid fuel which decomposes into hot gas in the presence of an appropriate catalyst. The most frequently used liquid is hydrazine, a colourless liquid which has physical properties similar to those of water, but is very toxic and unstable at high temperatures. Such engines have a pressurised hydrazine tank, a supply pipe with an injection valve, and a finely ground catalyst placed in a compartment just before the propulsion chamber.

When hydrazine decomposes it produces nitrogen, ammonia and hydrogen. Temperatures of about 1200 kelvin are obtained and, in a vacuum, the specific impulse is about 230 or 240 seconds. Such engines produce thrusts of between a few newtons and several hundred newtons and they are widely used to control the attitude of satellites and the roll of the upper stages of rocket launchers.

The photograph above shows two hydrazine catalytic decomposition engines developed by the Societé européenne de propulsion. In a vacuum, they develop thrusts of 3·5 and 15·4 newtons respectively and their specific impulses are both near 230 seconds. They have been used on the SPOT, GEOS and Exosat satellites amongst others (SEP).

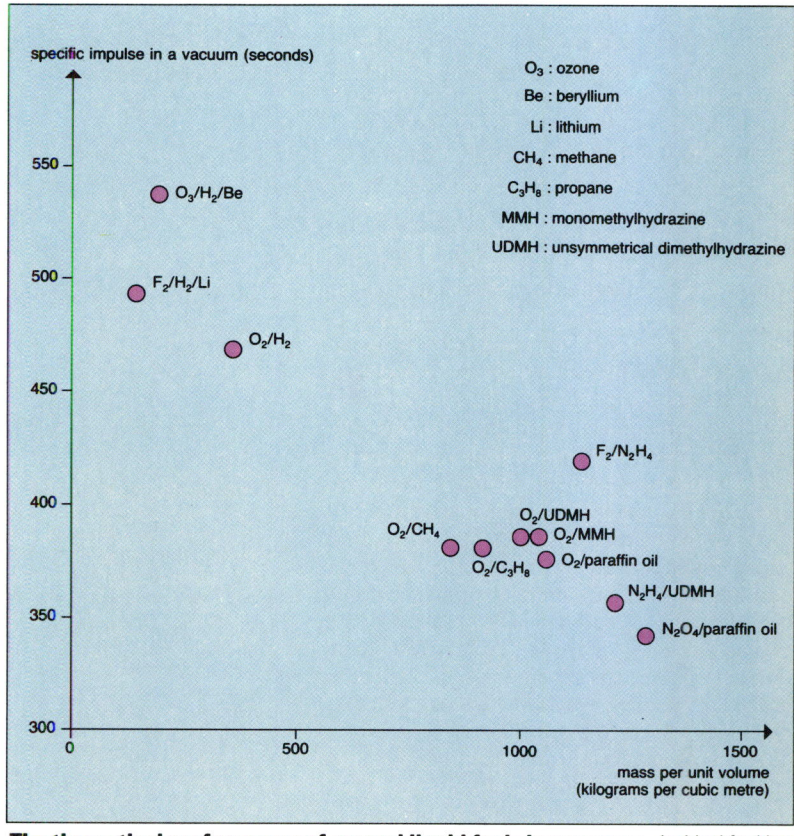

The theoretical performance of several liquid fuels in a vacuum. An ideal fuel has a high mass per unit volume and a high specific impulse but, if the combustion products have too high a molecular weight, the ejection speed of the gases is limited. Such considerations explain the distribution of points on the graph above, where the data correspond to a pressure of 20 megapascals in the combustion chamber and to a section ratio of the nozzle of 100. The O_2/H_2 couplet has a high specific impulse but a low mass per unit volume; its low storage temperature requires large fuel tanks fitted with thermal insulation, which are very heavy.

Within the family of fuels which can be stored on the ground or in space, the best seem to be the fluorine/hydrazine (F_2/N_2H_4) pair and $O_2/UDMH$, and it is these which are used on the upper stages of some Soviet launchers. The US is planning to use oxygen and methane (O_2/CH_4), or oxygen and propane (O_2/C_3H_8), on its future launchers. These have many advantages such as ease of introduction, cheapness, lack of pollution, and good performance.

Various properties of liquid fuels

	oxidant					fuel		
	nitric acid	nitrogen peroxide	oxygen	fluorine	hydrogen	kerosene (paraffin oil)	hydrazine	UDMH
Chemical formula	HNO_3	N_2O_4	O_2	F_2	H_2	$CH_{1.953}$	N_2H_4	$N_2H_2(CH_3)_2$
Molecular weight (atomic mass units)	63	92	32	38	2		32	60
Temperature of freezing point (°C)	−41.6	−11.2	−218.8	−219.5	−258.76	−50	1.53	−57.2
Temperature of boiling point at sea level (°C)	84.1	21.15	−183	−188	−252.76	distillation from 180 to 255	113.5	63.1
Density (kg/m³)	1504	1434	1140	1505	71	800	1004	785

Propulsion

Solid fuel rocket engines

A solid fuel rocket engine produces its thrust by ejecting the products of combustion of a solid fuel. It consists of a casing containing the fuel, one or more nozzles, a system to control the direction of thrust in order to steer the rocket, and an ignition device. Sometimes there is also a device to halt combustion.

The bottom of the cylindrical casing has an elliptical cross section designed to withstand the stresses generated. This casing also acts as the combustion chamber and, for this reason, it has to be able to the withstand the combustion pressure (usually between 5 and 10 megapascals) as well as high temperatures (3000 degrees celsius for 1 to 2 minutes). To assist in these respects there is usually some form of internal thermal insulation. At the rear of the structure is the nozzle, a vital part of the equipment required to transform the energy produced by the combustion into kinetic energy to lift the rocket.

Rocket engines are designed so as to minimise their mass whilst ensuring that the structure can withstand the stresses of launch, and use high performance materials such as special steels or fibre glass impregnated with epoxy resin. Such glass fibres have now been replaced by an aramide fibre, Kevlar, with carbon fibres producing exceptional strength. Their specific resistance, that is the ratio of their resistance to failure to the mass per unit volume, is five to six times greater than that of available steels.

As for the thermal insulation and the coating which modifies the growth of the block's combustion surface, new materials (principally rubber containing silicon) have replaced the original, heavier materials. Apart from their protective role, these substances overcome problems caused by deformation in both the fuel block and the structure.

The most important component in the entire engine is the nozzle. It is the focal point of all the most advanced technologies because a design or construction error would cause the mission to fail. All the hot exhaust gases, under pressure, pass through the nozzle. Its particular shape, which has been carefully designed, must be able to withstand extreme thermal and mechanical forces or its performance will be altered. The first materials to be used for the nozzles of solid fuel rocket engines were refractory metals such as tungsten and polycrystalline graphites. The high mass per unit volume of these substances and their low resistance to heat pulses lasting a few seconds have led to them being replaced by composite materials and by compounds based on phenolic resins. There have in turn been design problems with this family of materials because of the discharge of gases caused by pyrolysis of the resin. A new generation of composites has now been developed, consisting of materials reinforced and moulded with carbon, and known as carbon–carbon composites.

The engine is ignited by means of small pyrotechnic devices containing powders which ignite when an electrical current is passed

Integrating the Mage 2 apogee motor in the ECS satellite. The European Mage 2 apogee engine was designed to put satellites, weighing from 500 to 675 kilograms and launched by Ariane, into geostationary orbit. It was used for the first time on 18 June 1983 with the ECS 1 geostationary satellite.

Such satellites are first put into an elliptic transfer orbit by their launchers. When the satellite passes near apogee, the apogee motor is fired to give the satellite enough speed to change the elliptic orbit into a circular, geostationary orbit at an altitude of 36 000 kilometres. At the end of the combustion period the empty rocket engine remains attached to the satellite.

The Mage 2 is 1·5 metres long, its maximum diameter 0·8 metres and its mass about 40 kilograms. Its nominal fuel payload is between 400 and 490 kilograms. The combustion time is 43·7 seconds and the maximum thrust is 45·5 kilonewtons. The specific impulse of the fuel is 293·9 seconds, and that of the engine 292·6 seconds (SEP).

The technology of a solid fuel rocket engine. This diagram shows the principal elements of a solid fuel rocket engine such as the Mage 2 apogee motor: a cylindrical structure, a cylindrical block of solid fuel, a layer of thermal insulation between the fuel and the walls, a fixed nozzle and an ignition device.

The solid fuel, containing aluminium, is moulded directly into the cylinder and baked at 80 degrees celsius. The nozzle, made of a carbon–carbon composite, is fixed to the casing by a ring made of titanium alloy. An aluminium diaphragm isolates the fuel from all types of external pollution.

The ignition system consists of an explosives box fitted with two detonators and four pyrotechnic fuses.

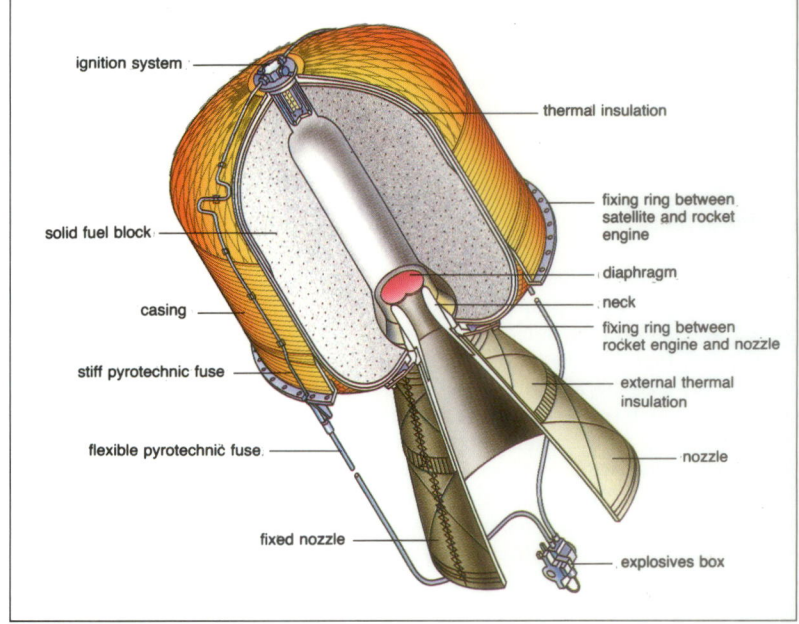

ignition system — thermal insulation — fixing ring between satellite and rocket engine — diaphragm — neck — fixing ring between rocket engine and nozzle — external thermal insulation — nozzle — explosives box — fixed nozzle — flexible pyrotechnic fuse — stiff pyrotechnic fuse — casing — solid fuel block

through them. The fuel burns, causing an increase in pressure which heats the surface of the fuel block sufficiently to ignite it.

Sometimes it is also necessary to decrease the thrust of the rocket engine very quickly. This is done by opening 'escape' holes using other pyrotechnic devices. These holes are situated in the front of the engine so that the gases escaping through them produce a thrust in the opposite direction to that through the main nozzle.

Jean-Michel Villetorte

The Rita 1 rocket engine (below). The French Diamant BP4 rocket launcher had a short lived career and was used only three times. Developed in 1971, it was capable of placing 200 kilograms into an orbit at 300 kilometres altitude.

Rita 1, the engine for the launcher's second stage, was originally designed as part of the French military programme. Its casing, wound in glass fibre, was 1·5 metres in diameter and contained a 4 tonne block of composite solid fuel whose cylindrical profile was machined after cooling. The nozzle was not adjustable, so that the direction of the thrust was controlled by injecting freon, pressurised by nitrogen. These two fluids were contained in annular tanks around the nozzle. The servo valves, installed on the nozzle, are operated hydraulically to control the flow of freon.

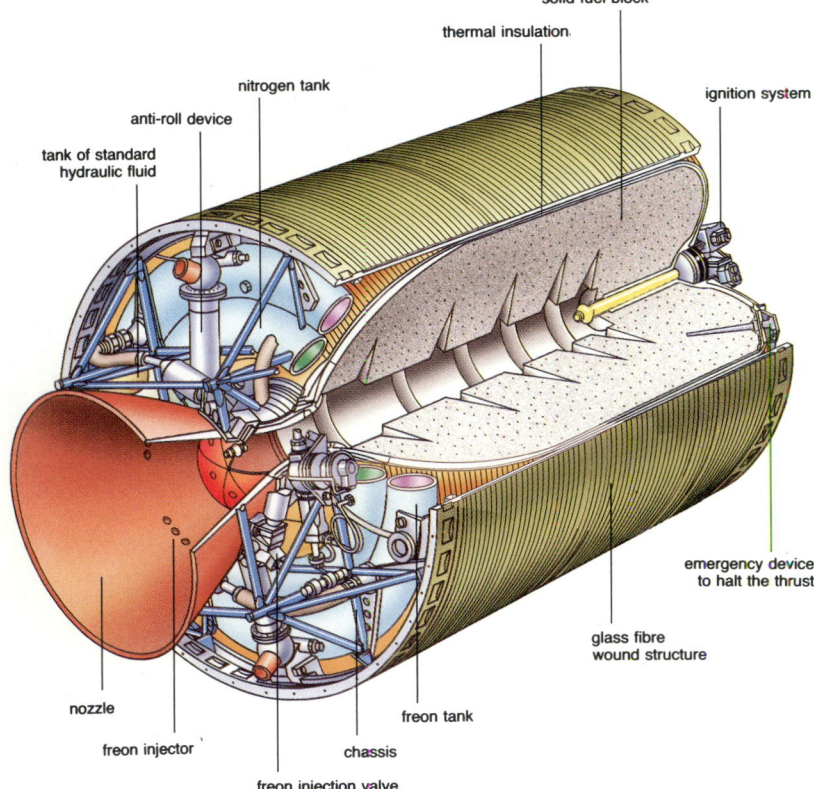

- solid fuel block
- thermal insulation
- nitrogen tank
- anti-roll device
- ignition system
- tank of standard hydraulic fluid
- nozzle
- freon injector
- freon injection valve
- chassis
- freon tank
- glass fibre wound structure
- emergency device to halt the thrust

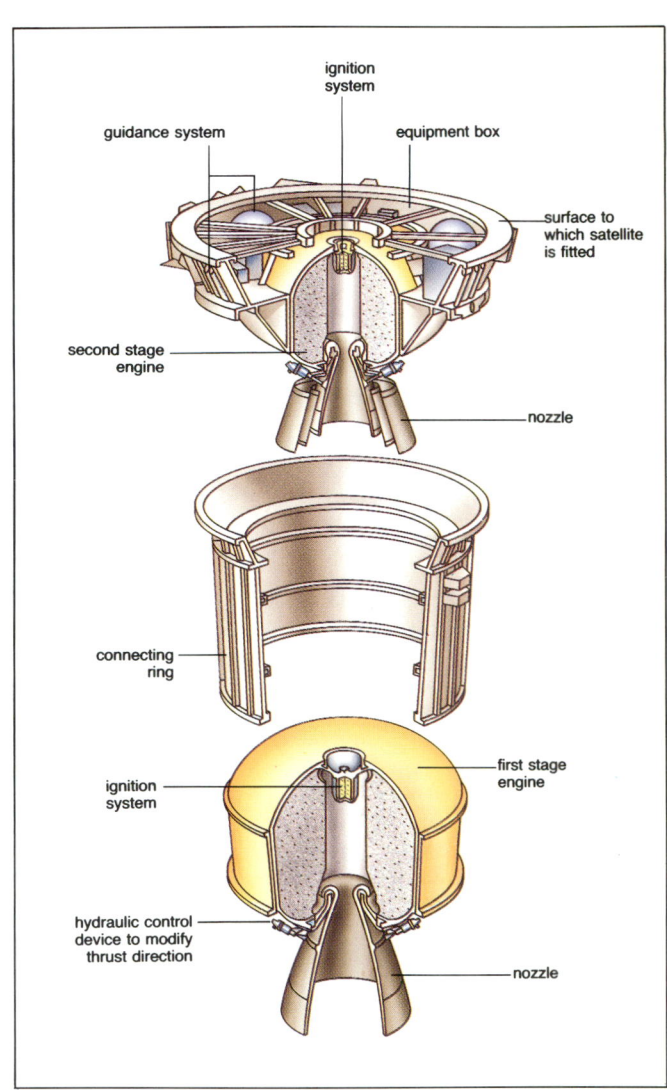

- ignition system
- guidance system
- equipment box
- surface to which satellite is fitted
- second stage engine
- nozzle
- connecting ring
- ignition system
- first stage engine
- hydraulic control device to modify thrust direction
- nozzle

The Inertial Upper Stage (IUS) for the space shuttle (right). As the space shuttle can only reach low Earth orbit, Boeing created an intermediate launcher, the IUS, to put a satellite into a geostationary orbit or prepare it for an interplanetary mission. The IUS consists of two solid fuel engines, the larger measuring 2·3 metres in diameter and weighing 10 tonnes, the smaller measuring 1·6 metres in diameter and weighing 3 tonnes. The maximum diameter of the launcher is 2·9 metres and its length exceeds 5·2 metres.

The casing is made of wound Kevlar. Each nozzle is moved by a hydraulic arm, and the nozzle of the second stage can be extended after the first stage engine has been used and jettisoned. This extendable nozzle keeps the overall length of the launcher to a minimum.

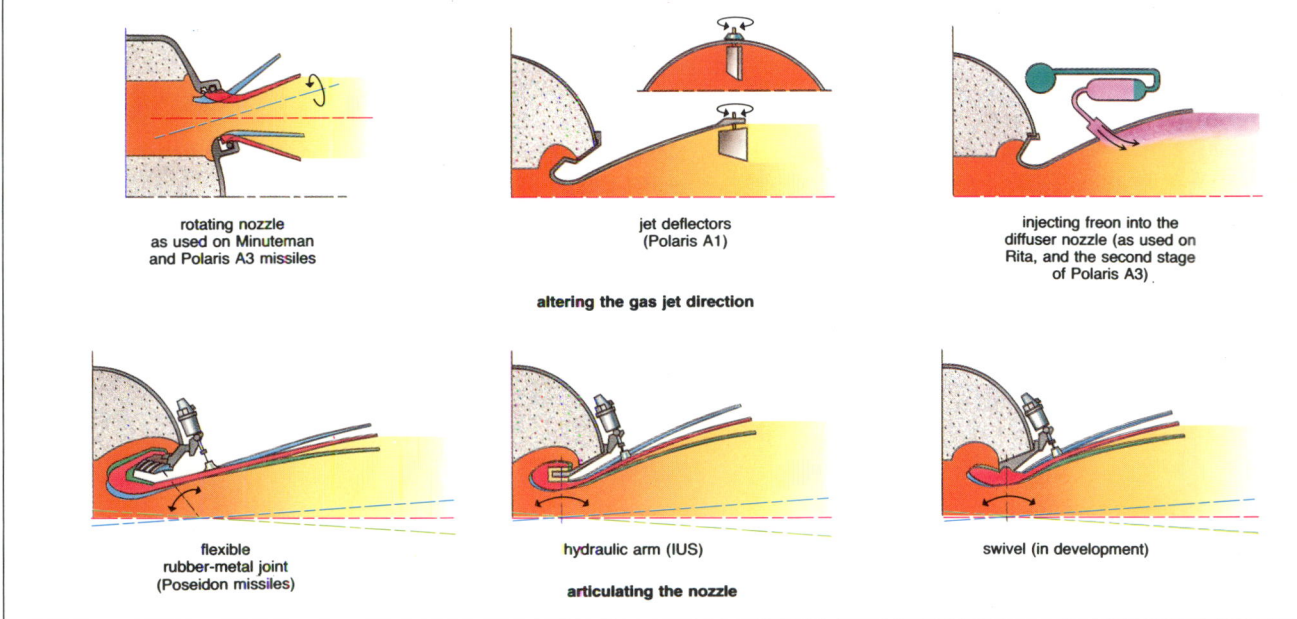

- rotating nozzle as used on Minuteman and Polaris A3 missiles
- jet deflectors (Polaris A1)
- injecting freon into the diffuser nozzle (as used on Rita, and the second stage of Polaris A3)

altering the gas jet direction

- flexible rubber-metal joint (Poseidon missiles)
- hydraulic arm (IUS)
- swivel (in development)

articulating the nozzle

Systems which control the direction of thrust (right). In order to guide the launcher, the direction of the thrust may need to be altered for each of its stages. In a solid fuel engine, this is done by changing the direction of the gas jet or by using articulated nozzles.

Boosters for the US space shuttle. Developed in the 1970s, the space shuttle is assisted at take-off by two of the biggest rocket booster engines ever built. These were constructed by the American company, Morton Thiokol, and are designed to be used ten times. After they have been jettisoned from the space shuttle, they parachute back to Earth, where they are recovered from the sea. Each stage is 45·5 metres long, has a diameter of 3·6 metres and weighs 586 tonnes. The casing consists of eleven metallic segments which are joined together – it was the failure of just such a joint which caused the explosion of Challenger on 28 January 1986. The 500 tonnes of composite solid fuel in each booster produces a thrust of about 11·8 meganewtons, which is equivalent to eleven Boeing 747s at take-off.

The photograph to the left shows this enormous engine ready for a firing on the static testbed of the Morton Thiokol company at Wasatch, Utah (Morton Thiokol).

Propulsion

Liquid fuel rocket engines

Liquid fuel rocket engines are more complicated than solid fuel engines, but they do have several advantages. They use more energetic fuels which are often cheaper than solid fuels. They are more flexible in use, since they can be turned on and off as desired, and the direction of thrust can be varied. They function for a long time providing that the chamber is kept cool and are very reliable despite their complexity.

Controlling the direction of thrust of a liquid engine is usually done by incorporating hydraulic or electrical controls to orient the whole engine or the propulsion chamber alone.

The propulsion chamber can be supplied with fuel by pressurising the fuel tanks, though this limits the combustion pressure to 1 or 1.5 megapascals; the fuel tanks would otherwise have to be very strong and would require a large mass. This type of fuel supply system is accordingly most suitable for small orbital transfer engines and attitude control engines on board spacecraft.

If fuel is to be pumped into the chamber, however, the reservoirs need be only slightly pressurised. They will consequently have a small mass and the combustion pressure can be raised again. A number of different types of pumps can be used. Electrical motors are suitable if only moderate power is required, and if electricity is available; they can be adapted for both spacecraft and satellites in Earth orbit.

Turbopump engines on the other hand take up to 10 years to develop and have to undergo many ground tests before they can be put into service. In the case of the Vulcan cryogenic engine to be used on the Ariane V launcher, several hundred tests are planned.

Some turbopumps, for example the main hydrogen turbopump of the space shuttle (SSME) engines, require vast amounts of power. The engines, and particularly their propulsion chambers, also have to be able to withstand severe mechanical forces. Coupling between the acoustic resonance frequencies and the combustion frequencies could cause catastrophic failure, and work is in progress to try to understand and model such phenomena. Baffles and acoustic cavities are now often installed inside the combustion chamber to reduce such effects.

Because of the high combustion temperatures, the choice of materials for the walls of the propulsion chamber poses a severe technical problem. This can be solved in several ways, for example by constructing an efficient cooling system through the circulation of one of the fuels inside a double wall before injecting it into the combustion chamber, or by insulating the wall from the combustion gases by injecting a fuel layer between them. Alternatively, the inner wall of the combustion chamber may be made out of a refractory or ablating material – though this limits the lifetime of the chamber – or the nozzle may be used as a radiator.

Marcel Pouliquen

The main engines of the American space shuttle. The space shuttle main engines (SSMEs) each produce a thrust of 2.09 meganewtons in a vacuum, with a specific impulse of 455 seconds. Each engine burns 470 kilograms of liquid hydrogen and oxygen per second under a pressure of 20.5 megapascals. The use of liquid hydrogen and the extremely high pressure make these engines the most advanced in existence. Such advanced technology has posed many challenging problems since development was initiated in 1973, and the lifetime of these first engines designed to be reused in space has remained limited. In fact, certain components have to be replaced after each flight. The SSME engines are ignited at take-off and have to survive a rough ride during each mission because the burning of the enormous, solid fuel boosters causes extremely high levels of acoustic and thermal vibration. The photograph above shows the propulsion chamber of the space shuttle Columbia during maintenance work (NASA).

The two main types of rocket engine using liquid fuels. The large majority of liquid fuel rocket engines use one or other of these two engine types. In the engine shown on the left below, hot gases at 900 to 1000 degrees kelvin coming out of a vaporiser are greatly accelerated in the turbine because the downstream pressure is low, almost that of the surrounding medium. Liquid fuels are fed into this vaporiser by diverting some of the flow to the main propulsion chamber. The fuel itself is used to cool the combustion chamber before being injected into it. This type of engine is the more common because all the components can be built and tested separately before the engine is assembled and tested in its entirety. The main disadvantage is that the gas which drives the turbine is not burnt, and this causes a small loss in performance.

In the two stage combustion engine illustrated on the right below, all the fuel circulates around the combustion chamber to cool it. Some of this is then burnt with some of the oxidant in a precombustion chamber where the temperature is raised to almost 1000 degrees kelvin. These gases drive the turbine and stream into the main chamber. There they are mixed with the rest of the oxidant and postcombustion takes place. The development of this type of engine, such as the SSME, takes a long time, is fraught with problems and its production costs are high. However, it is a high performance engine which produces high combustion pressures, from 20 to 30 megapascals.

The Russian RD 253 rocket engine. Probably the first rocket engine to be built using the two stage combustion process, this was developed between 1961 and 1965. The first stage of the Proton rocket launcher is equipped with six of these engines and the RD 253 is still one of the most advanced rocket engines using liquid fuels (nitrogen peroxide and UDMH). It produces a thrust of 1.7 meganewtons in a vacuum, with a specific impulse exceeding 320 seconds. When in operation it has to withstand extremely high pressures, more than 40 megapascals in the fuel supply circuits, 24 megapascals in the precombustion chamber and 15 megapascals in the main propulsion chamber. It has a mass of 1.28 tonnes, of which 400 kilograms is the propulsion chamber. The diameter of the widest part of the nozzle is 1.5 metres (SEP).

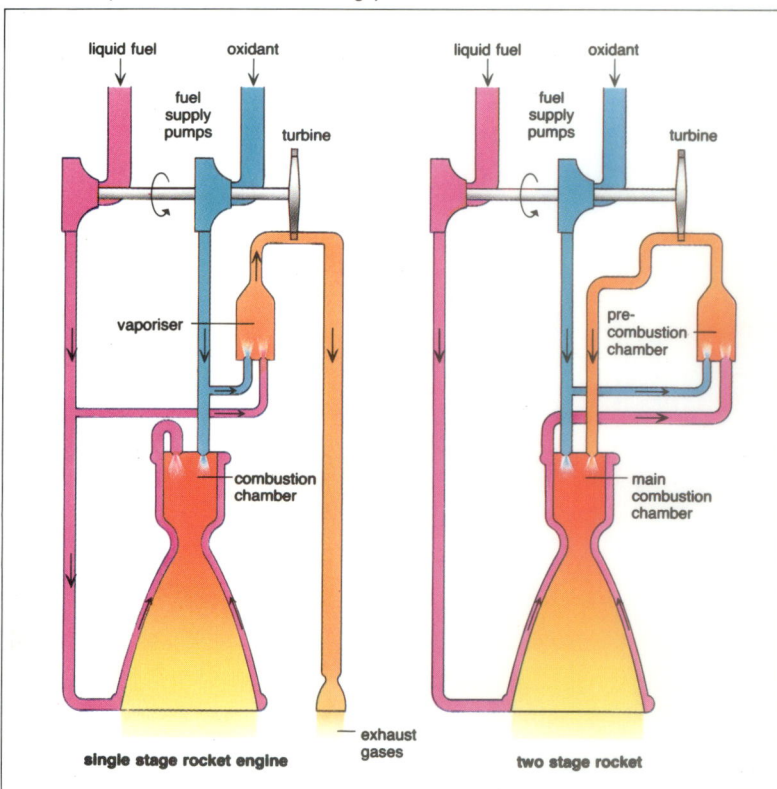

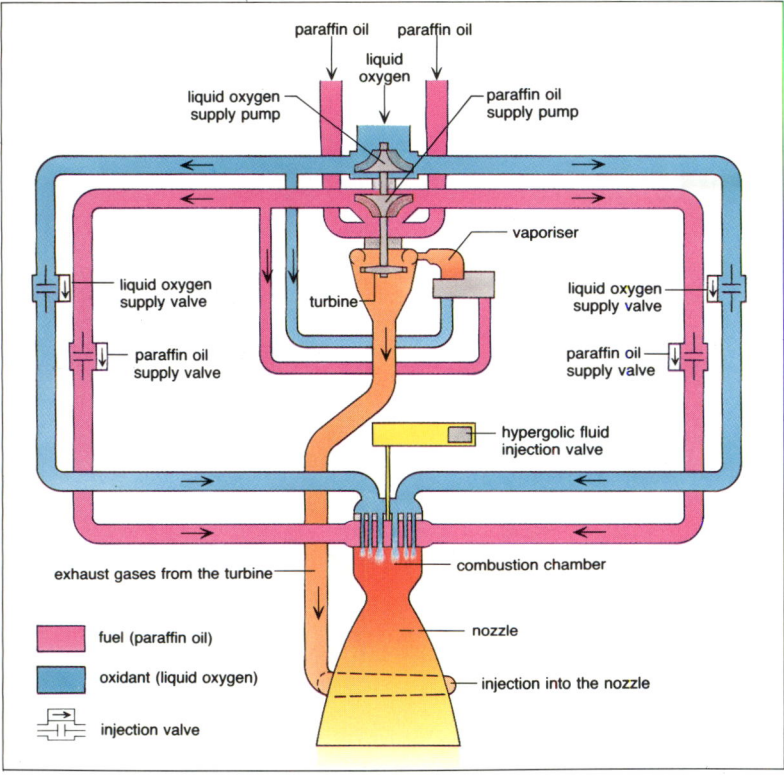

Schematic diagram of the F1 engine used on the Saturn V rocket. This engine of the more common, single stage type has only one turbopump. On the same shaft there is a liquid oxygen centrifuge pump with a single entry and double exit pipe, a paraffin oil (kerosene) pump with double entry and double exit pipe, and a single turbine with one vaporiser. Fuel in the propulsion chamber is ignited by injecting into the paraffin oil a little fluid which makes the paraffin oil and the liquid oxygen burn. The injector at the top of the chamber is shaped like a disc with thousands of vertical holes arranged in concentric circles.

The combustion chamber and the upper part of the nozzle are cooled by the circulation of paraffin oil through pipes around them. The lower part of the nozzle consists of a double walled skirt in which the cooler gases from the turbine circulate around a large annular pipe. These gases are injected into the nozzle through a number of small slits, creating a layer of cool gas which protects the lower nozzle.

Schematic diagram of the French Viking VI rocket engine used with Ariane IV (below). The Viking engines are single stage, but with the vaporiser operating at a very high combustion temperature so that it cannot directly operate the turbine. The gases are therefore cooled by the injection of water, which is also used to keep the fuel tanks pressurised.

Three pumps and the two stage turbine are mounted on a single shaft which rotates at a speed of 9600 revolutions per minute. At the exit of the pumps a small fraction of the UDMH fuel and the nitrogen peroxide is sent with all the water to the vaporiser. However, 97·6% of the gas which passes through the pumps goes to the cylindrical injector and is burnt in the combustion chamber at a pressure of 5·44 megapascals and a temperature of 3100 degrees kelvin. Some 15% of the flow of UDMH spreads out in a layer from the base of the injector, thus protecting the nozzle from the heat of the combustion gases.

The engine can be extinguished by decreasing the control pressure to close the valves. When the amount of either fuel has been depleted, this immediately causes the engine to cut out (source: SEP).

French Viking rocket engines. Viking V engines are here seen in one of the assembly halls of the Vernon establishment of the Société européenne de propulsion (SEP). The Viking V is the engine fitted to the first stage of all versions of the Ariane launcher. In a vacuum it develops a thrust of 678 kilonewtons; nitrogen peroxide is burnt at a rate of 160 kilograms per second, and 87 kilograms of a mixture of hydrazine hydrate and UDMH fuel is consumed per second. In a vacuum, the engine's specific impulse is 280 seconds.

The Viking VI engine is very similar, and is fitted on Ariane IV. The Viking IV engine, with an increased nozzle discharge rate, is used as the second stage on all versions of Ariane (SEP).

The injector of a Viking rocket engine. An injector is subjected to severe mechanical and thermal stresses. Because, at a certain combustion pressure and a certain mixture ratio, combustion instabilities may develop which could cause the destruction of the engine, the construction of the injector has to be most carefully monitored. In this photograph the characteristics of the 1152 injection holes in an injector for a Viking engine are being checked (SEP).

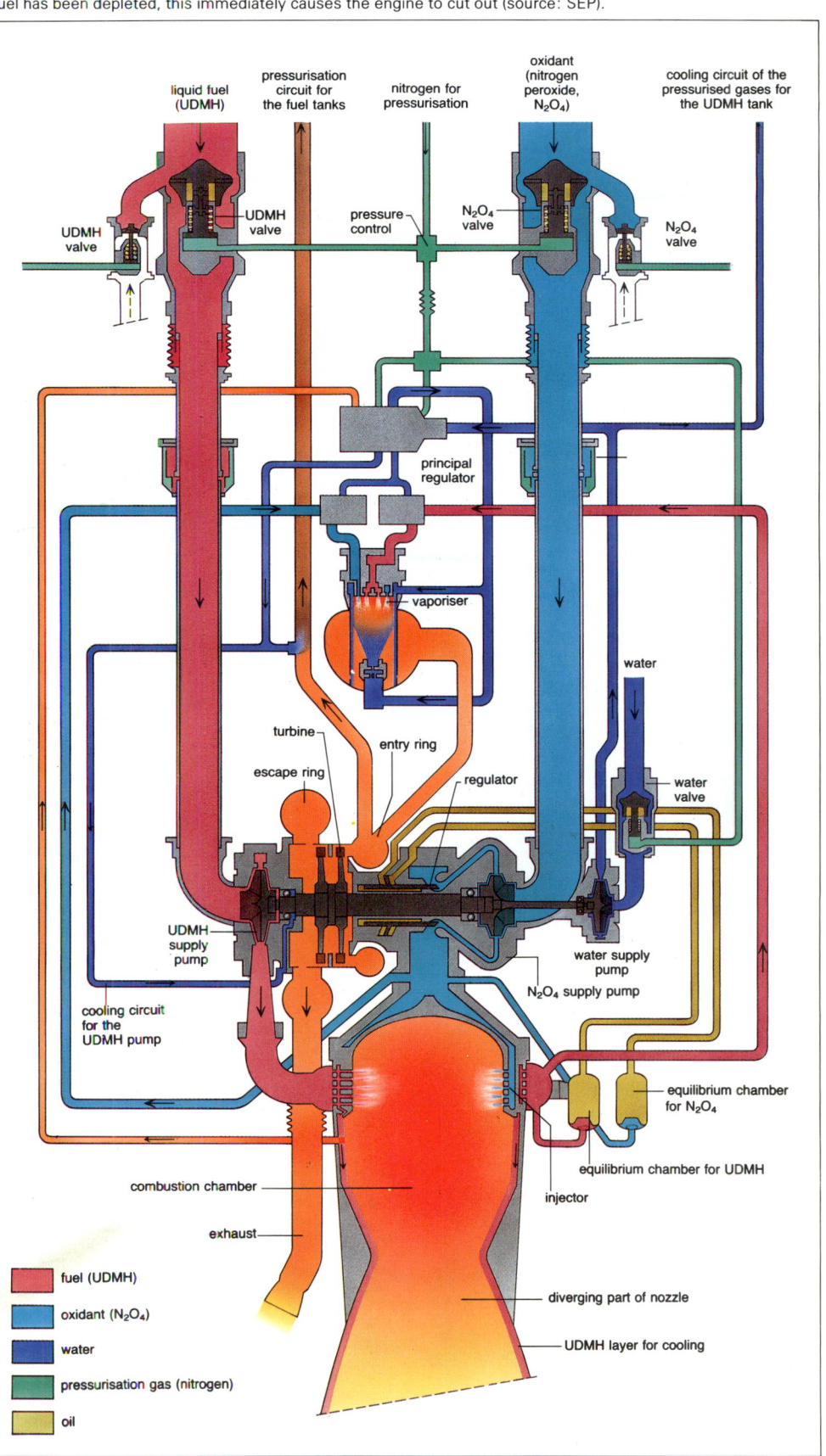

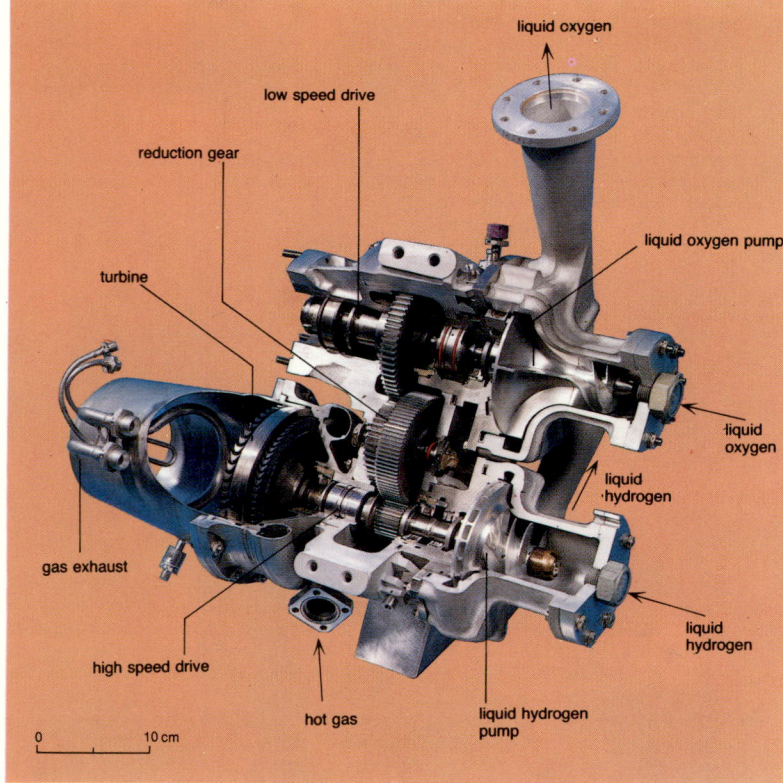

The turbopump of the French HM7. This model, based on a turbopump designed for the HM4 engine in 1964, has a mass of 30 kilograms and delivers a power of 410 kilowatts to the turbine shaft, which turns at a rate of 60 500 revolutions per minute. The liquid hydrogen centrifuge pump is mounted directly onto the turbine shaft. Hydrogen flows through the pump at a rate of 37 litres per second and at a pressure of 0·3 to 5 megapascals. The oxygen pump is driven at 13 000 revolutions per minute by means of a two stage gear train. It increases the pressure of the liquid oxygen from 0·2 to 5 megapascals. The gears are lubricated by the circulation of hydrogen gas containing fine droplets of tributylphosphate.

The two stage turbine shown above is driven by a flow of hot gases (hydrogen and steam) produced by combustion. A large excess of hydrogen has the effect of keeping the gas temperature relatively low to protect the turbine blades. After passing through the turbine, the gases escape into the vacuum of space through a nozzle at the exit of the exhaust system. The rotational speed of the pump is controlled by regulating the hydrogen flow (SEP).

The propulsion unit of the HM7 engine (below). This combustion chamber was designed and developed by the German company, MBB–Erno. It has three sections – the main injector, the combustion chamber and the nozzle.

The injector on top of the combustion chamber turns the liquid oxygen into gas and mixes it with the hydrogen gas. The fuels are burnt in the combustion chamber at a pressure of 3·55 megapascals. The chamber design, patented by MBB, is the same as that used for the SSME. The combustion gases have a temperature of more than 3000 degrees kelvin, and the walls and neck of the chamber, made of extremely pure copper, are kept cool by the circulation of hydrogen (at only 30 to 100 degrees kelvin) from the pump.

The nozzle extending from the neck is cooled by the flow of cold hydrogen (only about 0·130 kilograms per second) running through 242 pipes, each of 4 millimetres diameter, cut into the jointed soldered spirals which constitute the nozzle. After being heated to more than 1000 degrees kelvin, the hydrogen is ejected without combustion by 726 tiny nozzles at the bottom of the diffuser nozzle, and a supplementary thrust is produced. These nozzles are shown in enlarged detail bottom right (SEP).

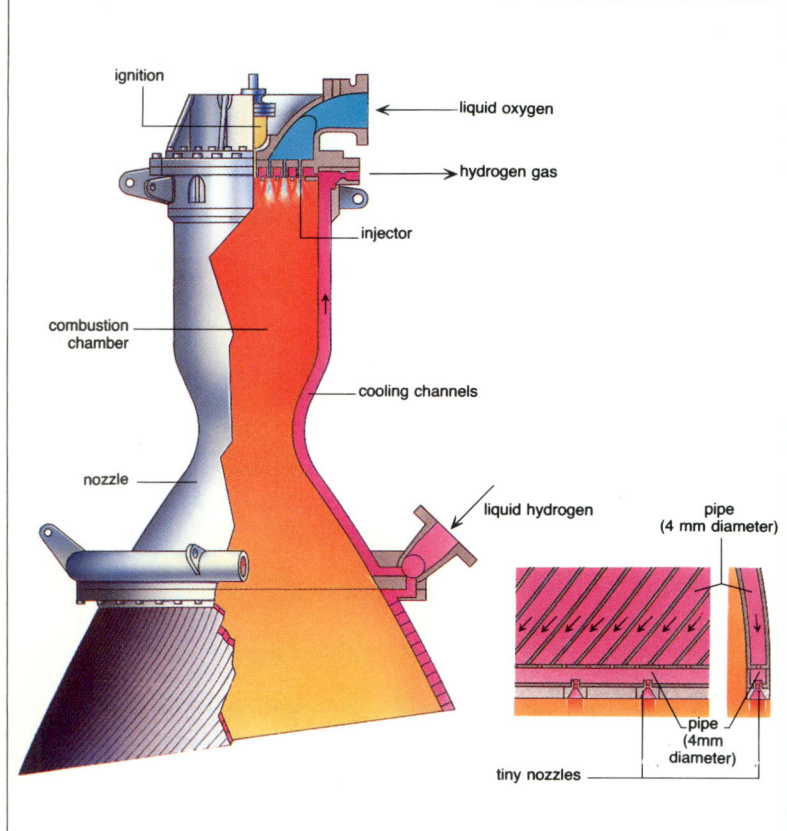

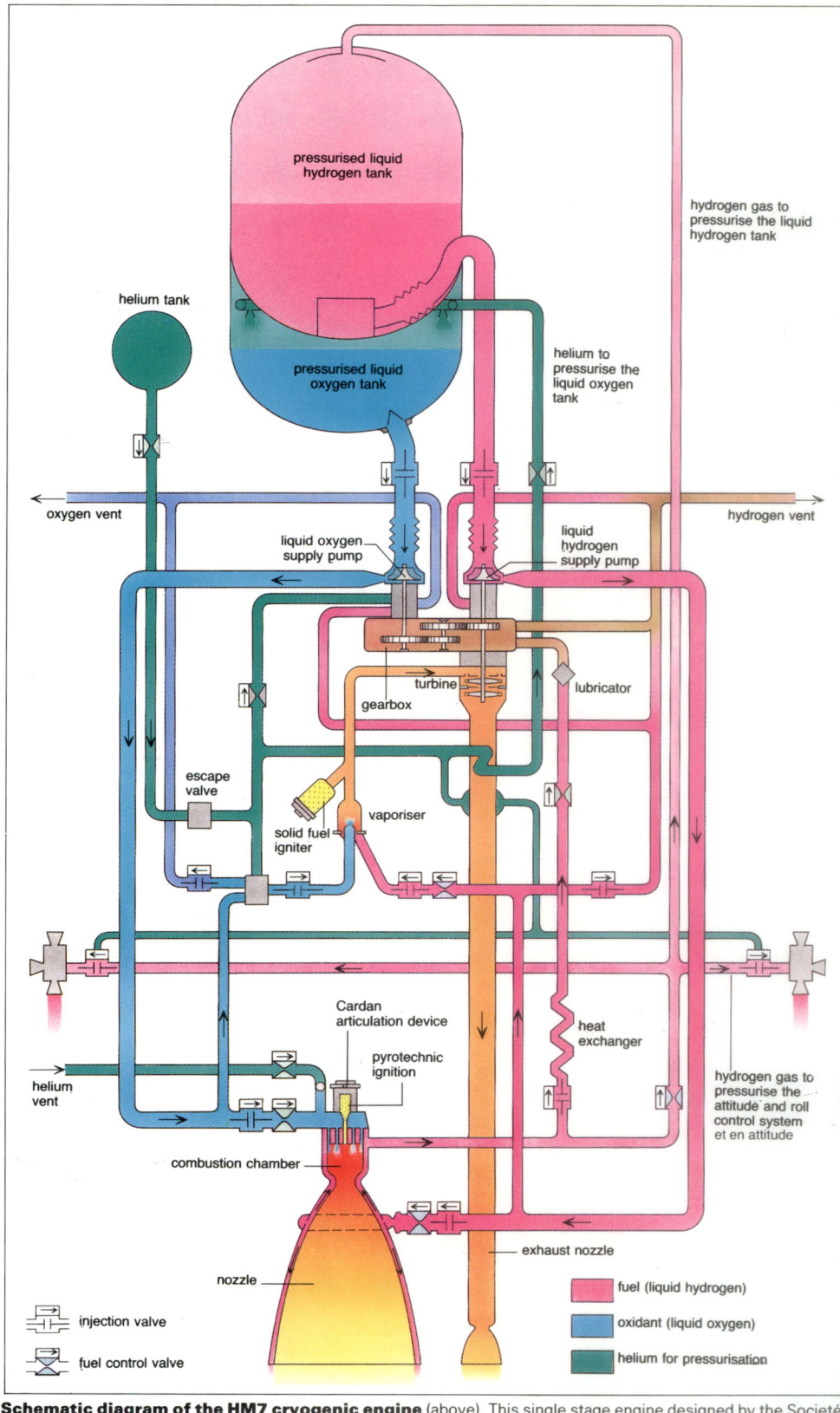

Schematic diagram of the HM7 cryogenic engine (above). This single stage engine designed by the Societé européenne de propulsion is based on the first cryogenic engine, the HM4. This had a thrust of 40 kilonewtons and was developed and tested between 1962 and 1969. Work began on the HM7 engine in 1973 and was completed in 1979. It was first used on the third stage of the Ariane launcher on 24 December 1979.

The original HM7A, used on Ariane I, produced a thrust of 61 kilonewtons in a vacuum and had a specific impulse of 442·4 seconds. The improved HM7B version was developed for the Ariane III and Ariane IV launchers. Improving the expansion rate through the nozzle increased the specific impulse by 4·5 seconds. This engine has a mass of 170 kilograms, its height is 1·90 metres and the diameter of the exit of the nozzle is almost 1 metre.

This schematic diagram shows the arrangement of the H8 propulsion unit and illustrates the complexity of the liquid hydrogen and oxygen propulsion system. The Cardan articulation device and hydraulic controls enable the HM7 to control the pitch and roll of the third stage. The unit supplies hydrogen gas to pressurise the liquid hydrogen tank and the roll control; it also reheats the helium which is used to pressurise the liquid oxygen tank and the pneumatic command system.

At take-off, the fuels are ignited in the propulsion chamber by an explosive ignition device in the centre of the injector. Simultaneously, the vaporiser is ignited and the turbines switched on after the pumps have been cooled. The ignition devices contain blocks of solid fuel which burn for 3 to 4 seconds (SEP).

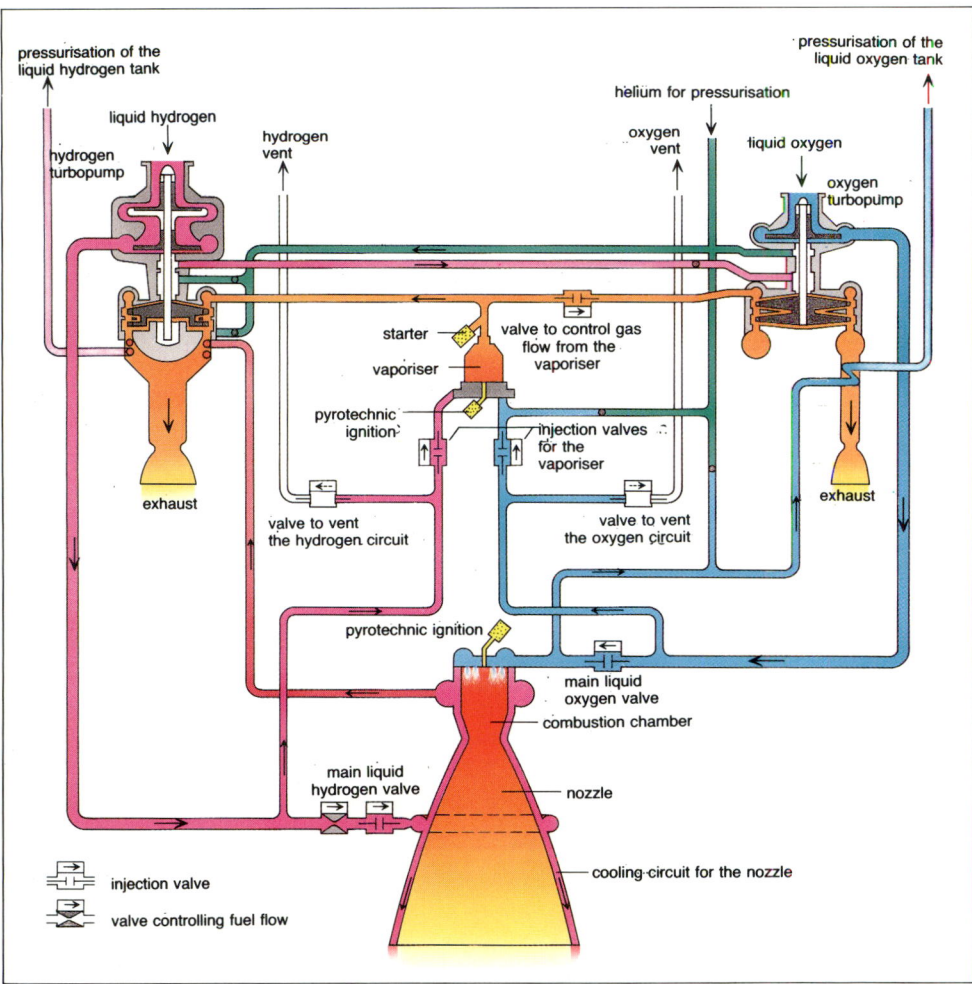

pressurisation of the liquid hydrogen tank

liquid hydrogen

hydrogen turbopump

hydrogen vent

pressurisation of the liquid oxygen tank

helium for pressurisation

oxygen vent

liquid oxygen

oxygen turbopump

starter

vaporiser

valve to control gas flow from the vaporiser

pyrotechnic ignition

injection valves for the vaporiser

exhaust

exhaust

valve to vent the hydrogen circuit

valve to vent the oxygen circuit

pyrotechnic ignition

main liquid oxygen valve

combustion chamber

main liquid hydrogen valve

nozzle

cooling circuit for the nozzle

injection valve

valve controlling fuel flow

Schematic diagram of the Vulcan cryogenic engine. The Vulcan engine (or HM 60) shown to the left was designed for the central stage of the Ariane V launcher; in a vacuum it delivers a thrust of 1 meganewton, with a specific impulse of 433 seconds.

The engine was developed for ESA under European collaboration, with SEP as the main contractor. With a height of 3·18 metres and a mass of 1·1 tonnes, it has a Cardan articulation device to change the angular motion of the engine in order to control the pitch and roll of the central stage after Ariane V's solid fuel boosters have been jettisoned.

Fuel for the single stage Vulcan engine is pumped by two independent turbopumps fitted vertically. The 200 kilogram liquid hydrogen pump consists of a two stage centrifuge pump, preceded by an axial pump, rotating at 35 000 revolutions per minute. This pump is driven by a two stage, 12 megawatt turbine mounted on the same shaft. Liquid hydrogen flows through the pump at a rate of 560 litres per second and a pressure of 17 megapascals. The single stage liquid oxygen turbopump works at 13 000 revolutions per minute, and oxygen flows through it at a rate of 177 litres per second, the power being 2·8 megawatts, at a pressure of 13 megapascals. The two turbines are driven in parallel by gas at 900 degrees kelvin flowing at 8 kilograms per second from a single radial injection generator operating at a combustion pressure of 8 megapascals. After passing through the turbines, these gases are ejected separately by two nozzles situated at the end of the exhaust nozzle.

The fuels are injected into the combustion chamber by 516 coaxial injectors, where they are burnt under a pressure of 10 megapascals. The flow of liquid hydrogen from the turbopump (about 35 kilograms per second) enters the propulsion chamber via an annular distributor. Most of this liquid circulates in the cooling channels in the walls of the neck of the nozzle and the combustion chamber itself. This regenerative cooling prevents the wall temperature from exceeding 600 degrees kelvin. Part of the hydrogen flow (about 1·75 kilograms per second) is diverted to tubes in the diffuser nozzle to cool it. It escapes into the exit section of the nozzle and contributes to the overall thrust.

The turbopumps are switched on, and the gas generator and the combustion chamber are lit, using pyrotechnic cartridges (SEP).

Schematic diagram of the space shuttle main engine (SSME). The two main pumps of the SSME supply the fuels and control the pressure levels in the precombustion chambers and in the propulsion chamber itself. The two precombustion chambers function under high pressure (nearly 34 megapascals), but at a moderate temperature which is suitable for the turbines. This is obtained by using much of the hydrogen flow from the pump, and by limiting the oxygen flow. After driving the turbines, the hydrogen rich gas from the precombustion chambers is injected into the main combustion chamber where postcombustion with the remainder of the oxygen takes place.

The power from the two turbopumps is considerable, nearly 50 megawatts for the hydrogen pump and 20 megawatts for the oxygen pump. To optimise the turbine efficiency, a high rotational speed, which keeps the size and mass to a minimum, is required. This is why there are booster pumps in front of each of the main pumps. Their job is to supply the main pumps with gas at a moderate pressure (2 to 3 megapascals) to avoid the speed of rotation of the main pumps being limited by cavitation phenomena. The booster pumps on the oxygen side are driven by a hydraulic turbine, and on the hydrogen side by a gas turbine (pure hydrogen). Because these precombustion chambers receive only a small amount of the oxygen, there is a pressure pump on the shaft of the main pump, the exit pressure of which is about 50 megapascals.

The SSME has a very elaborate regulation system. This has to vary the thrust between 60 and 110% of its nominal value and control the fuel mixing ratio in the precombustion and main chambers in real time using information from sensors measuring pressure, flow and temperature, and other data from proportional valves.

A microprocessor, with two spares for safety, is installed in the engine and acts a sequencer (for starting or stopping), regulator and safety device. To obtain the necessary high level of reliability, some other important functions are also duplicated, notably the ignition systems and the commands to the main valves.

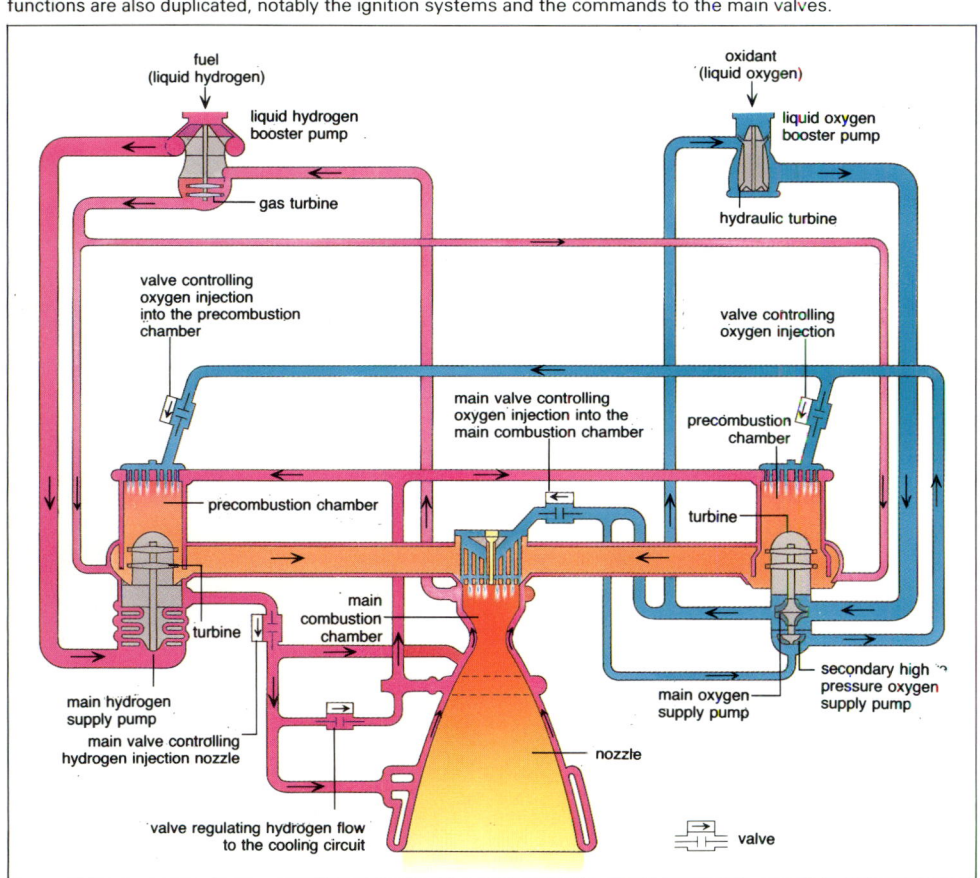

fuel (liquid hydrogen)

oxidant (liquid oxygen)

liquid hydrogen booster pump

liquid oxygen booster pump

gas turbine

hydraulic turbine

valve controlling oxygen injection into the precombustion chamber

valve controlling oxygen injection

main valve controlling oxygen injection into the main combustion chamber

precombustion chamber

precombustion chamber

turbine

main combustion chamber

turbine

main hydrogen supply pump

main valve controlling hydrogen injection nozzle

valve regulating hydrogen flow to the cooling circuit

nozzle

main oxygen supply pump

secondary high pressure oxygen supply pump

valve

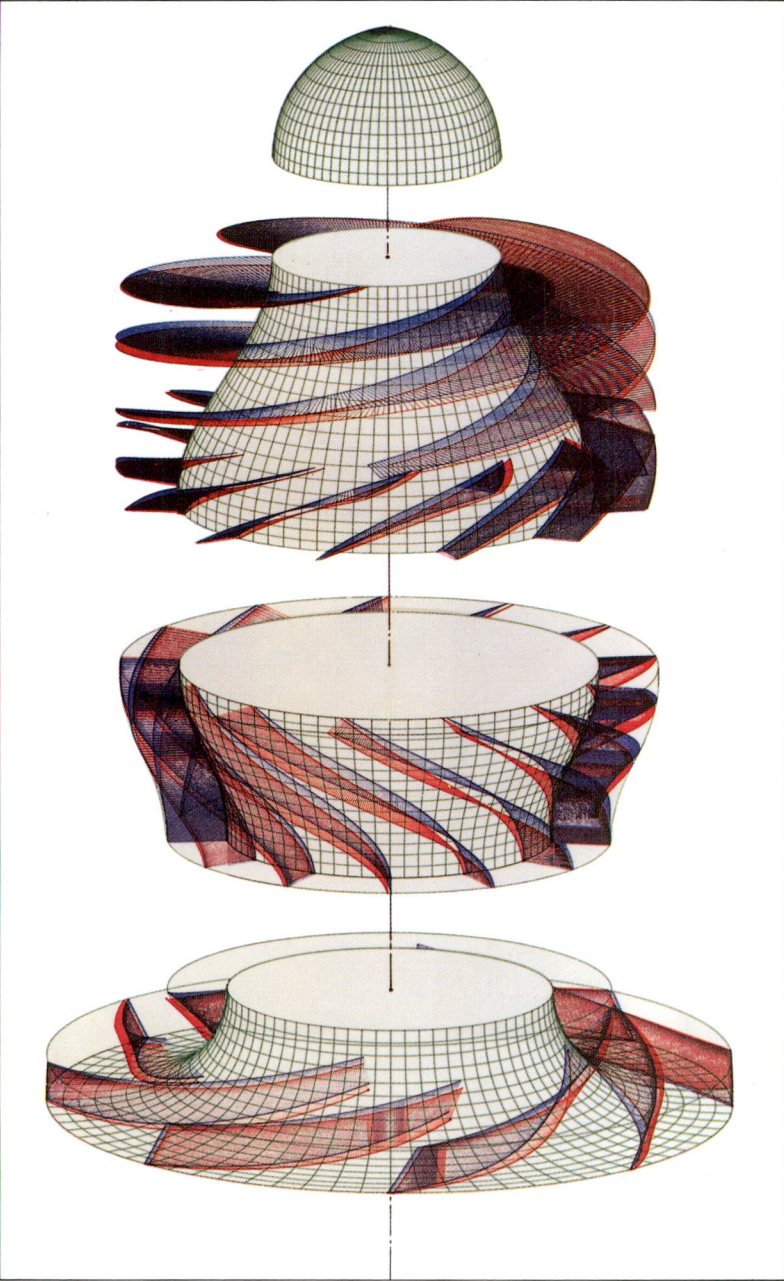

Computer aided design. Until recently, rocket engines were designed and developed in a relatively empirical fashion. The complex phenomena involved, such as combustion, flow through the pumps, and deformation of the structures are, however, becoming better understood as design techniques become more sophisticated. New programs and improved numerical methods in particular have enabled better designs to be constructed using computers. The diagram above illustrates how the design of a turbopump can be built up by computer. The liquid hydrogen pump is designed to take into account not only the real flow of the fluids but also the mechanical and thermal properties of the rotating parts; related programs also describe the shapes of the various parts to be made (SEP).

Propulsion

Rocket engines of the future

There are numerous possible ways in which rocket engines could be built using the reaction principle. At the present time, however, only solid or liquid fuel rocket engines have a sufficiently high thrust to weight ratio (greater than unity) to allow them to be used for vertical take-off launchers.

The designs for single stage horizontal take-off launchers are still based on the combination of an air breathing engine and a rocket engine. An example is the British Horizontal Take-Off and Landing (HOTOL) project (see page 119). During the first phase only the fuel will be carried by the vehicle, the oxidant being atmospheric oxygen. The specific impulse should be of the order of 1500 to 2000 seconds. Beyond a certain altitude, where the air becomes too rarified, a pure rocket mode will be used to obtain the altitude and speed needed to put the vehicle into orbit. This type of very complex engine will, however, only be possible after advances in materials science and artificial intelligence; it will also require considerable funding and extensive testing.

Between 1960 and 1972 the Americans devoted much time and effort to developing a nuclear powered engine for a rocket, the Nuclear Engine for Rocket Vehicle Application (NERVA). It had a thrust of 900 kilonewtons in a vacuum and was to be used to power a manned vehicle to Mars. In 1968 and 1969, an experimental model was built which had a thrust of about 300 kilonewtons for a pressure of 3·1 megapascals. It was ground tested, but the project was abandoned a few years later; this type of engine has a high specific impulse, ranging from 700 to 1200 seconds, but its safety has been questioned.

Research has been carried out into electric rocket engines since the end of the 1950s, and test versions have produced very high performances with specific impulses of from 5000 to 20 000 seconds.

However, as yet they have not been much used. Whilst they may eject either plasma or ions, the required electric power and corresponding engine mass that this entails have limited viable models to thrusts of only several millinewtons to several newtons. Over the next decade or so, it is, however, planned to use such engines to control the attitude of satellites or spacecraft.

Testing a rocket engine. In this photograph a jet of high temperature hydrogen gas is being ejected from the nozzle of a nuclear fission propulsion unit during a fifteen minute ground test carried out on 3 February 1966 in the Nevada desert. The white column evident in the centre is due to water vapour condensing on the liquid hydrogen supply pipe to the fuel tank, the tank itself standing on tall metal columns (NASA).

The principle of electric propulsion units. In arc jet or resistance propulsion units the propellant fluid (such as hydrazine, nitrogen or hydrogen) is heated using a ring shaped electric arc or a resistance heater. The heated gas is then released from the nozzle. Current projects to design arc jet units aim to produce thrusts of several tens of newtons, but they require about a megawatt of electrical power. The specific impulses are about 600 to 1000 seconds, but for hydrogen specific impulses of the order of 3000 seconds have been produced. Electrical resistance propulsion units are being researched with the aim of using them to control the attitude of the American space station. Using hydrazine, they can reach temperatures of 2500 degrees kelvin; the thrusts produced are of the order of 5 newtons using powers of several kilowatts.

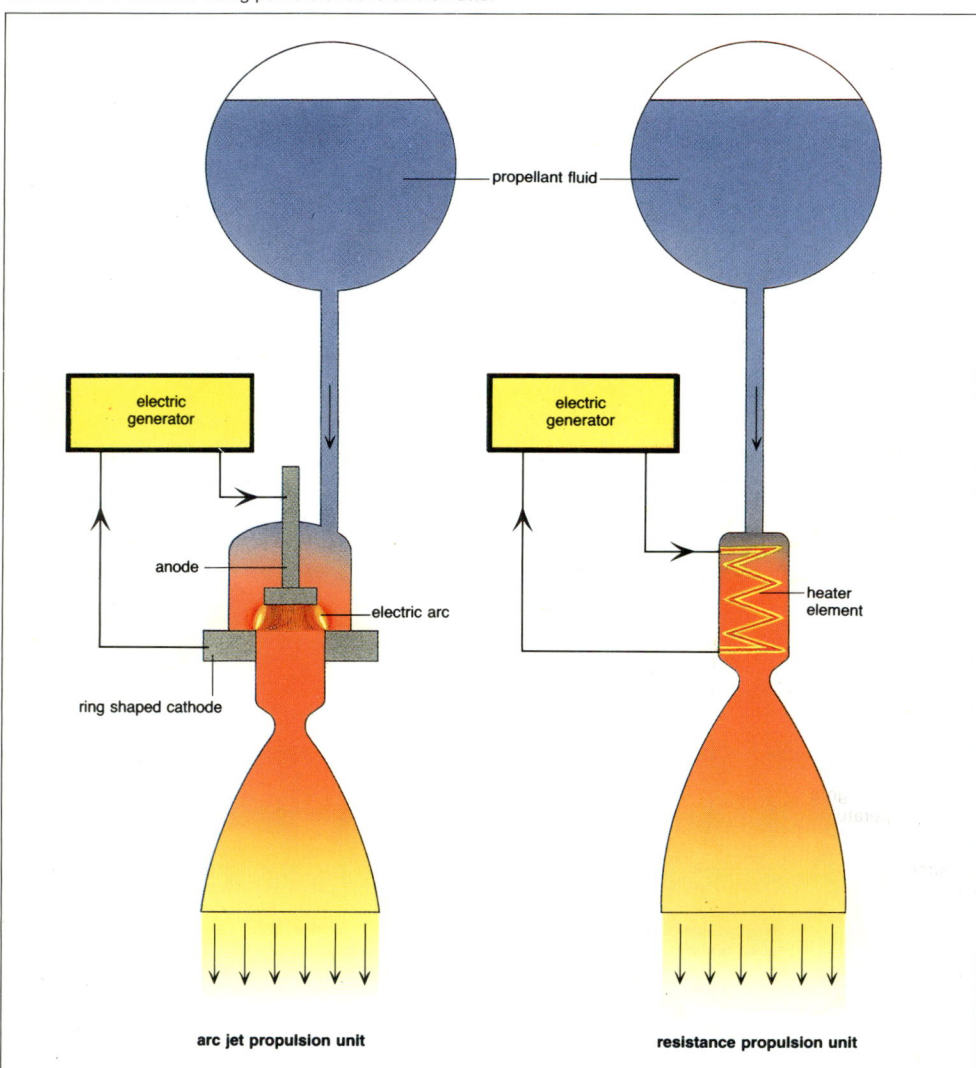

arc jet propulsion unit   resistance propulsion unit

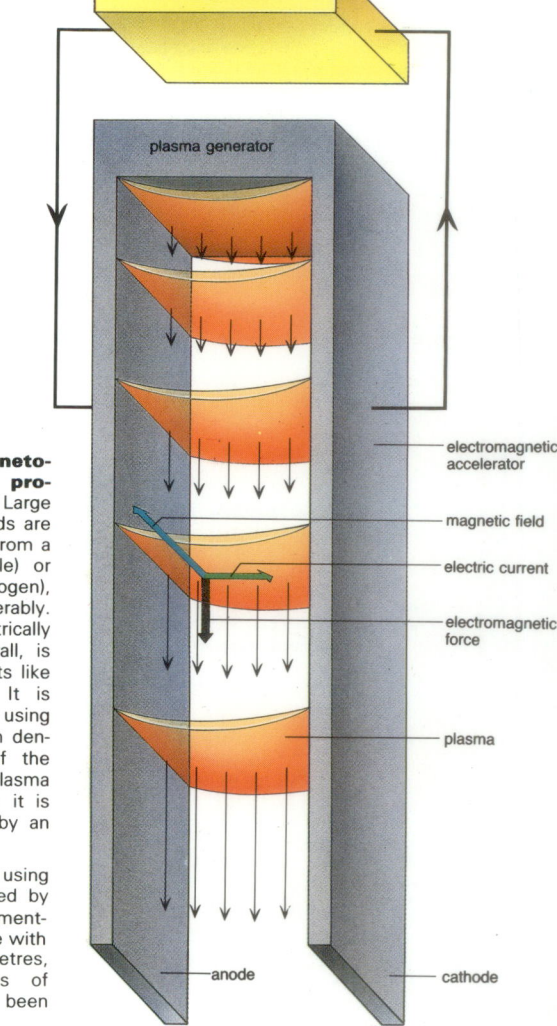

The principle of magneto-hydrodynamic (MHD) propulsion units (right). Large electric and magnetic fields are used to create a plasma from a solid (Teflon, for example) or from a gas (argon or hydrogen), and to accelerate it considerably. A plasma is an electrically charged gas which, overall, is electrically neutral and acts like an electrical conductor. It is created by heating matter using the discharge from a high density electric arc. Part of the kinetic energy of the plasma comes from the heating; it is then accelerated further by an electromagnetic field.

A pulsed propulsion unit using Teflon has been developed by the USA and used experimentally in space. With a device with a typical size of 25 millimetres, thrusts of several tens of micronewtons have been produced.

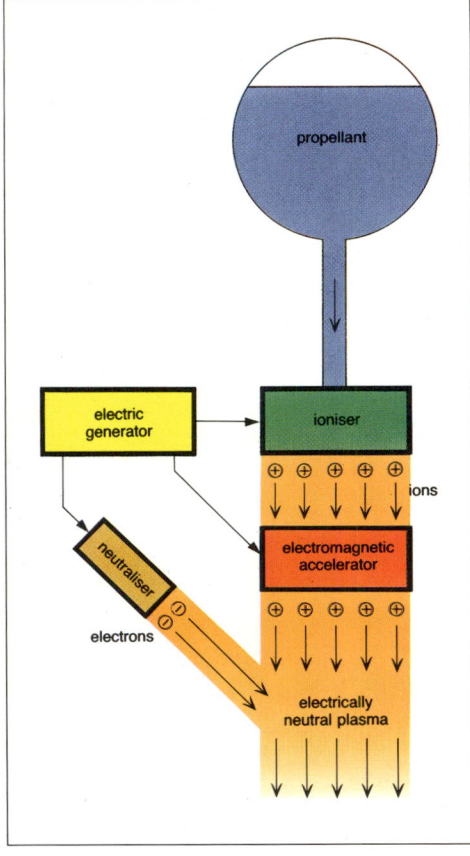

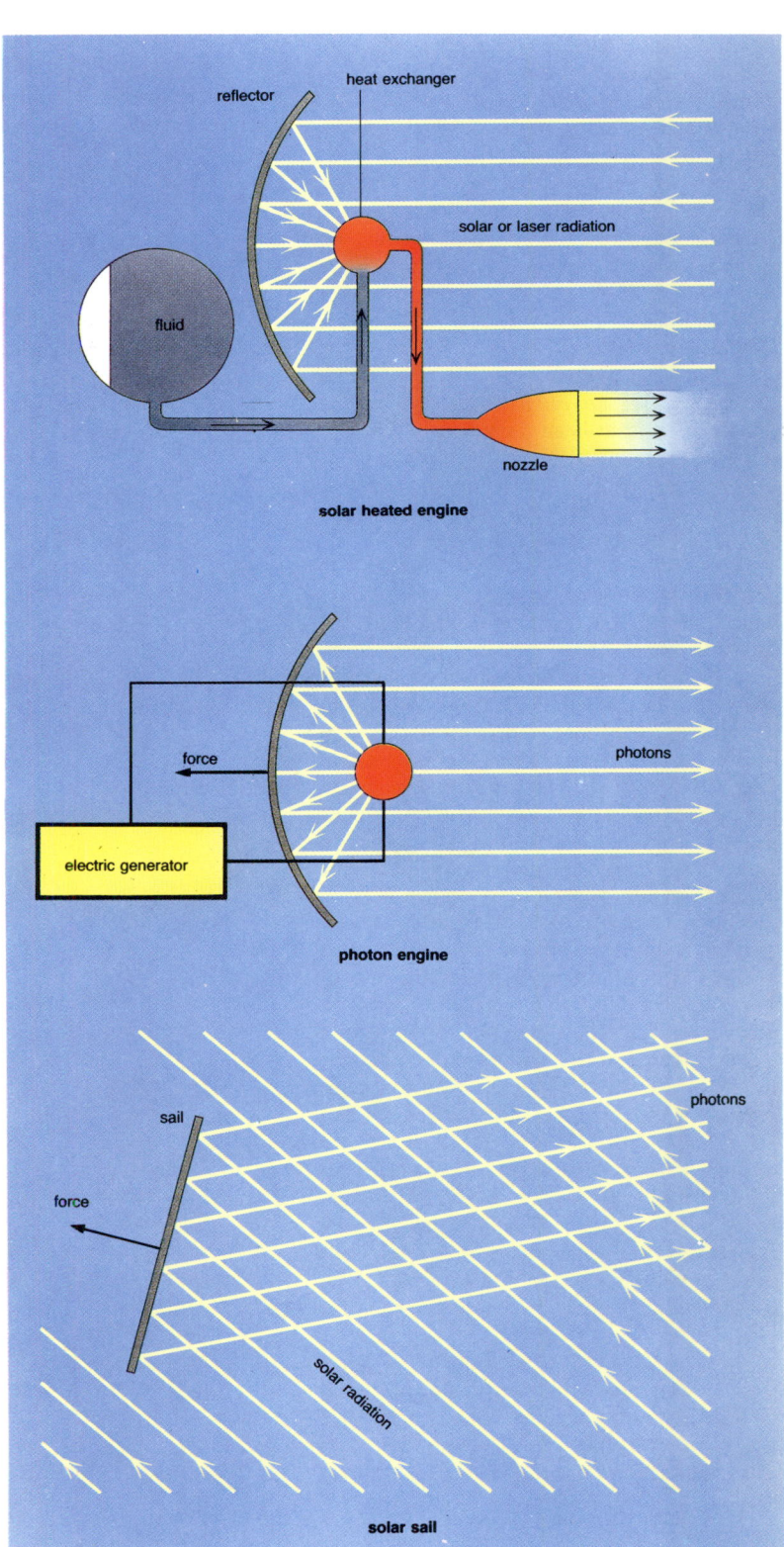

Ion thrusters (left). The propellant fluid (usually caesium, mercury or a rare gas) is first ionised by removing some of the atomic electrons. The positively charged particles (positive ions) are then strongly accelerated by an electric field. To avoid the engine structure becoming charged, the particle beam is neutralised by injecting a beam of electrons. This type of engine produces specific impulses of between 5000 and 10 000 seconds, but the thrusts produced are only several newtons to several hundreds of newtons.

A field effect ion thruster (above). This engine was developed by the Société européenne de propulsion, under contract to the European Space Agency. The principle on which it operates depends on the action of a liquid (in this case caesium), subjected to a strong electric field and then ionised and accelerated. A high voltage (10 kilovolts) is required to produce a sufficiently strong local electric field to create a slight curvature across the surface of the liquid. To do this, the caesium passes through a slit 1·2 micrometres in width and 80 millimetres long. Each engine produces a thrust of 2·5 millinewtons, with specific impulses of 5000 to 6000 seconds. It is planned to use such engines to make satellite orbital corrections or to modify the orbit slowly.

Other types of rocket engine have also been considered as future possibilities, but at present they are no more than ideas. One direction to move would be towards free radical or photon propulsion units. Free radicals, such as atomic hydrogen, will theoretically give very high performance but there remains the tremendously difficult problem of fuel storage; magnetic walls at temperatures close to absolute zero have been proposed as a possible solution. Whilst photons, whose mass is zero, travel at the speed of light, they do transfer momentum. A rocket could therefore operate, in principle, by ejecting photons. Unfortunately, to create a thrust of 1 newton an energy of more than 300 megawatts is needed so such an engine is not in practice viable. Some theoreticians believe that a photon engine working on matter and antimatter, the contact between which would produce energy as light, is also possible; the problem here is, of course, how to store the antimatter.

Amongst all the concepts which use radiation, the solar sail deserves a special mention, because its feasibility does not demand the solution of any fundamental physics problem. Many solar sail projects have been proposed since the beginning of the 1980s for orbital transfers or missions in deep space, but this time the overwhelming problem is the immense surface area of sail required and the difficulties of manoeuvring the spaceship with the equipment in place.

Marcel Pouliquen

The principle of the nuclear engine (left). This diagram illustrates the principle behind the Nuclear Engine for Rocket Vehicle Application (NERVA). A turbine driven pump draws liquid hydrogen from the tank and feeds it into the cooling circuit of the propulsion nozzle and the casing around the reactor. In this way the hydrogen is heated and injected into the upper part of the heart of the fission reactor; the thrust is obtained by ejecting the hot hydrogen through an ordinary nozzle. The low atomic weight of the hydrogen (which is partially dissociated) makes for an effective thrust and the unit produces specific impulses of 700 to 1200 seconds.

Fusion nuclear generators are also being researched, but, at their present stage of development, it seems unlikely that they will come into use except in the long term.

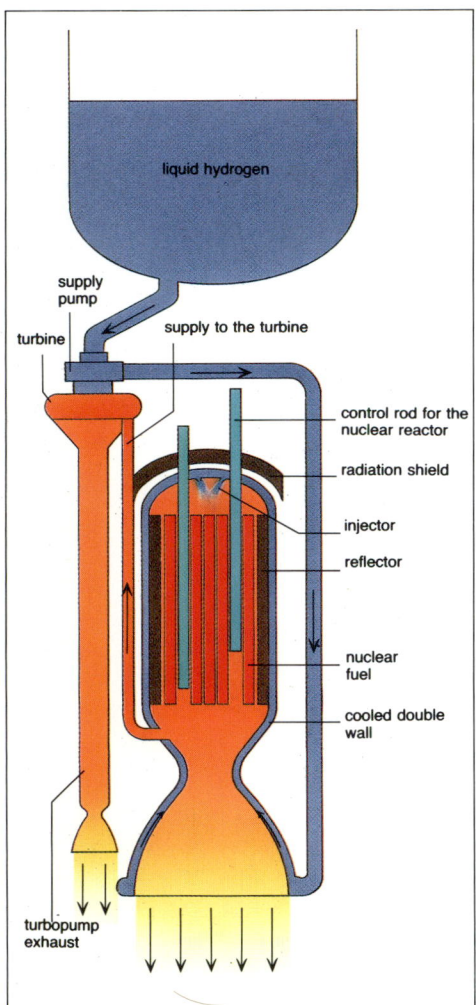

The principles of rocket engines using light (right). Three possible types of engines which use light radiation are illustrated.

In the solar heating (or laser) engine, the radiation is collected and concentrated using a reflector. A fluid (for example, hydrogen) is heated by passing it through a heat exchanger and then ejected at high temperatures through a nozzle.

In the photon engine, an electrical source is used to create the photons at the focus of a large mirror; an enormous amount of electrical power is, however, required.

The solar sail makes use of the pressure caused by solar radiation. Near to the Earth, the flux of this radiation is 1·37 kilowatts per square metre, and a sail of about 2 square kilometres placed perpendicular to this beam of sunlight would produce a thrust of about 40 newtons.

Rocket launchers

The rocket launcher's task is to put a satellite of a certain mass into the desired orbit. To do this, the launcher has to have the necessary thrust and specific impulse to give the satellite, at a given point in space (the injection point), a velocity of the correct magnitude and direction. At an altitude of 200 kilometres, the minimum velocity required by a satellite for it to go into orbit is 7·8 kilometres per second; such a satellite will be in a circular orbit.

In general, a satellite is injected at the perigee of its orbit. At this point, the lowest point of its orbit, the satellite has its greatest velocity but, equally, suffers the greatest atmospheric drag.

The performance of a rocket launcher has to be defined very precisely. In fact, the speed at perigee determines the altitude of the apogee (the point on the orbit furthest from the centre of the Earth), and even slight differences between the required and actual velocities at perigee cause significant differences in apogee altitude. In order to put a satellite into a geostationary transfer orbit, for example, the velocity at perigee has to be 10·25 kilometres per second. The Ariane launcher can inject satellites into orbit with velocities to within 5 metres per second of this value, an indication of the precision that is essential. A particular satellite also has to be injected into its orbit at a certain inclination to the Earth's equatorial plane. For a geostationary satellite the ideal inclination is close to zero degrees.

A launcher's performance reflects its ability to put light, or heavy, payloads into certain orbits. It is calculated numerically using a powerful computer by integrating the equations of motion which depend upon the forces acting on the launcher. The result is a certain trajectory for a certain payload mass.

The calculations show that it is impossible to produce a single stage launcher capable of producing enough velocity to put a satellite into orbit. The mass of the structure has to be at least 10% of the total mass at launch and this means that the mass of fuel is almost 90% of the launch mass. The simplest mission can thus only be accomplished by launchers which have two stages, the first being jettisoned once combustion is over. This eliminates a now superfluous structural mass and enables a high performance second stage to put the small satellite into orbit.

The ideal arrangement for a multistage launcher is for the ratio between the velocity increase and the specific impulse of each stage to equal that of the next stage. Thus, for a two stage launcher designed to achieve a low Earth orbit, the first stage will use liquid fuels with a specific impulse of near 300 seconds, while the second stage will be cryogenic with a specific impulse of 450 seconds. This requires the first stage to furnish a velocity of 3·8 kilometres per second and the second stage 5·7 kilometres per second. The total masses of the two stages would then be 79% and 19% of the launch mass respectively if the empty mass of these two stages represented 10% of the total mass. The payload would be only 2% of total mass at lift off.

The number of stages of a launcher is therefore a compromise between propulsive efficiency (which requires the largest number of stages possible) and technical complexity, mass and cost which increase as the number of stages increases. A three stage rocket is often the best compromise.

Jean-Claude Bouillot

The Energia launcher. On 15 May 1987, the USSR launched its first Energia heavy launcher from the cosmodrome at Baikonur. This launcher, with two recoverable stages, has a launch mass of 2400 tonnes, of which 2000 tonnes are fuel. It can place a payload of more than 100 tonnes into low Earth orbit (at 250 kilometres altitude), 18 tonnes into geostationary orbit, 32 tonnes into a lunar orbit, and send 28 tonnes towards Mars. Energia is also used to launch the Soviet space shuttle, Buran (see p. 299) (APN).

The principles of a rocket launcher. At the moment of launch (1), a single stage launcher will have a mass M_0. Its rocket engine delivers a constant thrust F, for the time T of combustion. At an instant t (2), the mass of the launcher is M, which is less than M_0, its velocity is v, and the value of its instantaneous acceleration is a = F/M. One second later (3), the mass has become $M - (q + q')$, where q and q' are the respective masses of fuel and oxidant lost per second. The speed and instantaneous acceleration are both increased, from v to v_1 and from a to $a_1 = F/(M - q - q')$, respectively.

The increase in the velocity $\triangle v$ furnished by the launcher is given by integrating the acceleration with respect to time from the beginning to the end of combustion (4) when the final velocity v_f is reached. Using the simplified hypothesis of constant thrust,

$$\triangle v = F \int_0^T (1/M)dt = -v_e \int_{M_0}^{M_1} dM/M$$

since the thrust F is equal to the product of the velocity v_e with which the exhaust gases are ejected and their rate of mass loss. Thus $F = v_e \, dM/dt$. The ejection speed is equal to the product of the specific impulse, I_{sp}, with the value of the gravitational acceleration, g

$$\triangle v = g \, I_{sp} \int_{M_0}^{M_1} dM/M = g \, I_{sp} \ln (M_0/M_1)$$

The term $\ln (M_0/M_1)$ is the natural logarithm of the ratio of the total mass of the launcher at the beginning of combustion (M_0) to the mass at the end of combustion (M_1).

Strictly speaking, this formula is only applicable to orbital manoeuvres once the satellite has been placed in orbit. Its use during the launch phase is an approximation because of drag during the rocket's motion up through the atmosphere.

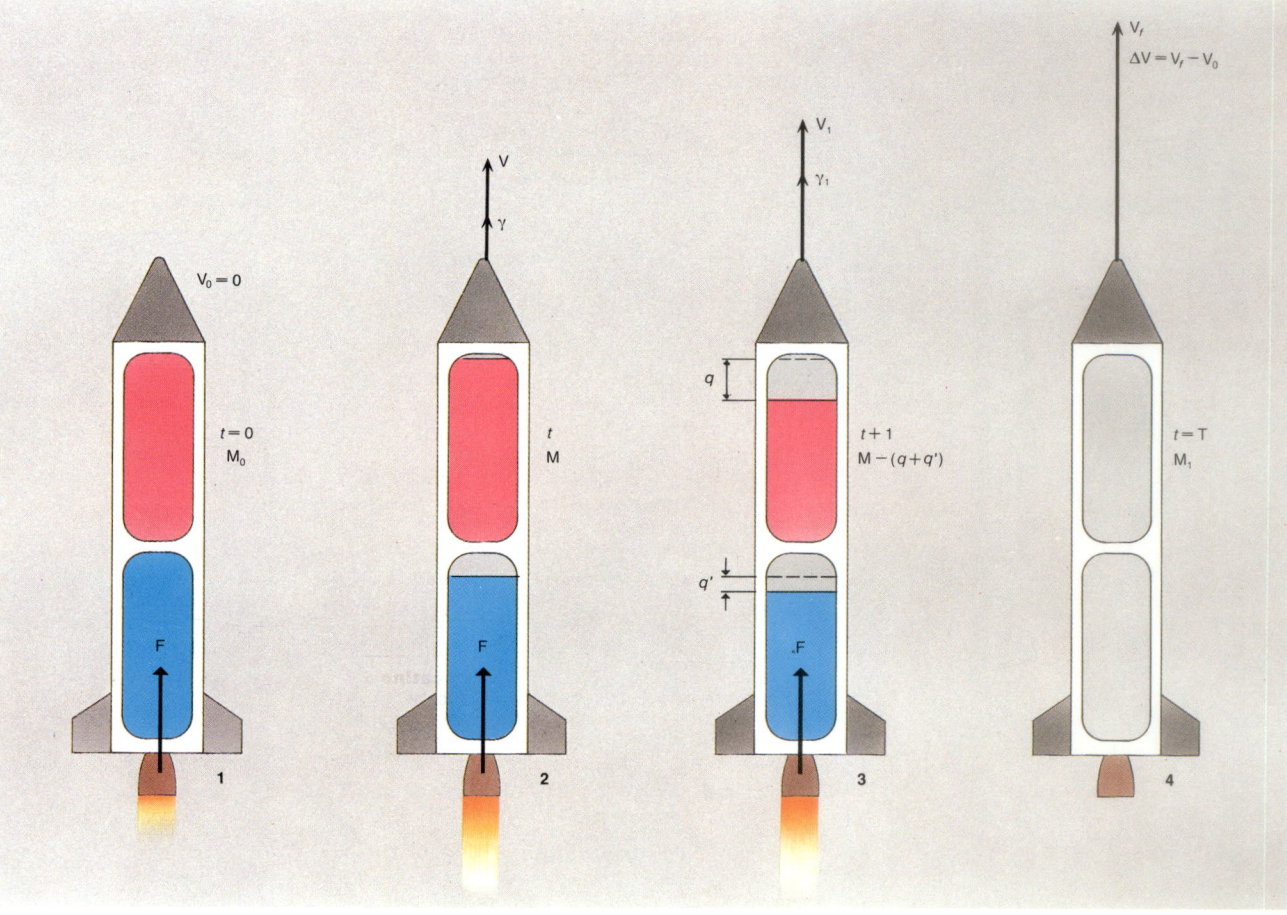

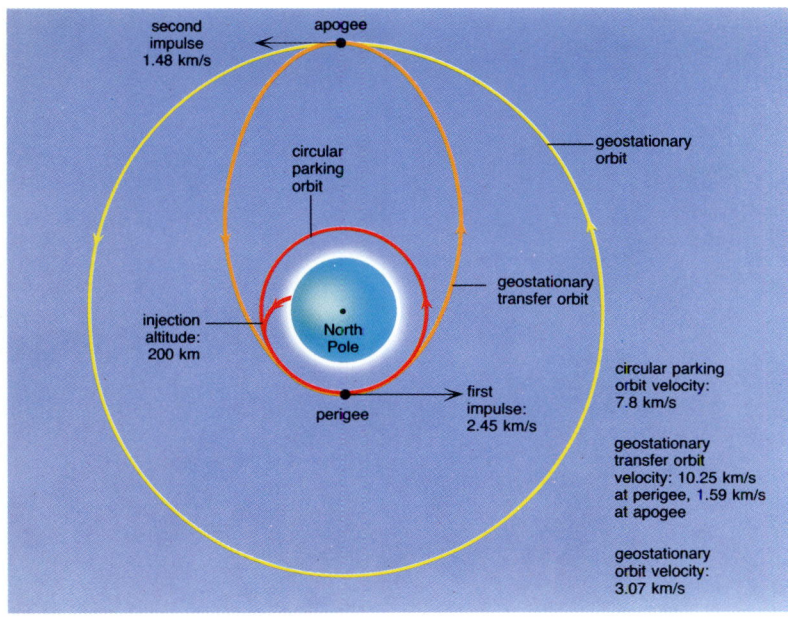

The procedure for putting a satellite into orbit. The diagram on the left is drawn in the Earth's equatorial plane. The launcher first puts the payload into a low altitude, circular orbit around the Earth (shown in red). If the satellite is only going to spend a short period at this altitude, then an altitude near 200 kilometres is chosen as being above almost all the atmosphere, making atmospheric drag insignificant.

The kinetic energy of the satellite determines the nature of the trajectory. At an altitude of 200 kilometres a horizontal velocity of 7·8 kilometres per second produces a circular orbit. Between 7·8 and 11·0 kilometres per second, the orbit will be elliptical. The perigee remains at 200 kilometres, but the altitude of apogee increases; the velocity corresponding to a geostationary transfer orbit (shown in orange, with an apogee at 35 800 kilometres) is 10·25 kilometres per second. The escape velocity is 11·0 kilometres per second, when the trajectory becomes a parabola and the satellite has just enough energy to overcome the Earth's gravitational pull.

The diagram shows the procedure for putting a satellite into geostationary orbit in the most energy efficient way. This is done by transferring it from a low Earth orbit (a circular parking orbit) to a geostationary orbit via an orbit called a Hohmann's transfer orbit. The first firing of the engine gives a thrust which alters the orbit to an elliptical one, with a perigee of 200 kilometres and an apogee at 35 800 kilometres. This is the so-called geostationary transfer orbit. A second engine firing, at the apogee, gives the thrust necessary to transform the orbit into a circular geostationary orbit (shown in yellow). The velocity changes required are at 2·45 and 1·48 kilometres per second, respectively, for orbits in the equatorial plane. Fine orbital corrections are then performed by small, on board engines called thrusters which put the satellite into exactly the right orbit. They position it at the correct longitude and then maintain this orbit for several years.

Launch azimuth and orbital inclination. The velocity at the satellite injection point is the vector sum of the velocity supplied by the launcher and the velocity of the Earth's rotation. The useful component of the latter is the product of the velocity of the Earth at the equator (464 metres per second) with the cosine of the angle between launch azimuth and the East. This explains the difference in performance of a launcher for equatorial and polar orbits. The desired inclination of the orbit determines the azimuth of the launch from a launch site at a given geographic latitude.

The satellite's trajectory cuts the equatorial plane at a point whose longitude is 90° to the East of the launch site and the satellite can then be injected into its geostationary orbit. The final rocket stage is relit as it passes over the equator to achieve the orbit that is required.

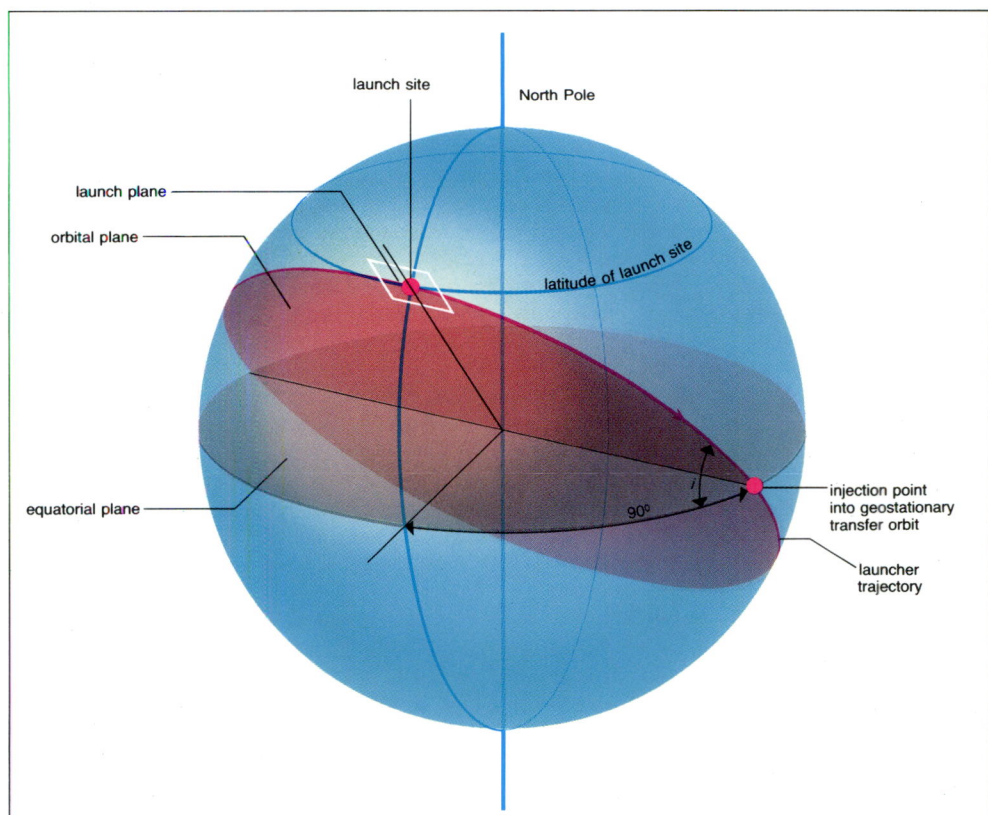

The performance of the Ariane 44 L launcher. The performance of a rocket launcher can be expressed graphically in performance curves, the horizontal axis of which shows the altitude of the apogee on a logarithmic scale while the vertical axis gives the mass of the payload that can be put into that orbit. Each curve represents a different altitude at perigee, and curves of the same colour have the same orbital inclination angle. The general shape of each group of curves varies significantly from one launcher to another, reflecting the number of stages and the performance of each stage. The performance curves for the space shuttle, a two stage launcher where the mass of the empty second stage (the orbiter itself) is very large, shows a rapid decrease in performance as the altitude, or the inclination, increases. By contrast, Ariane, a three stage rocket launcher, whose third stage is very light, has the performance characteristics shown. The addition of a supplementary fourth stage has the effect of further increasing the level of performance for very high altitude orbits.

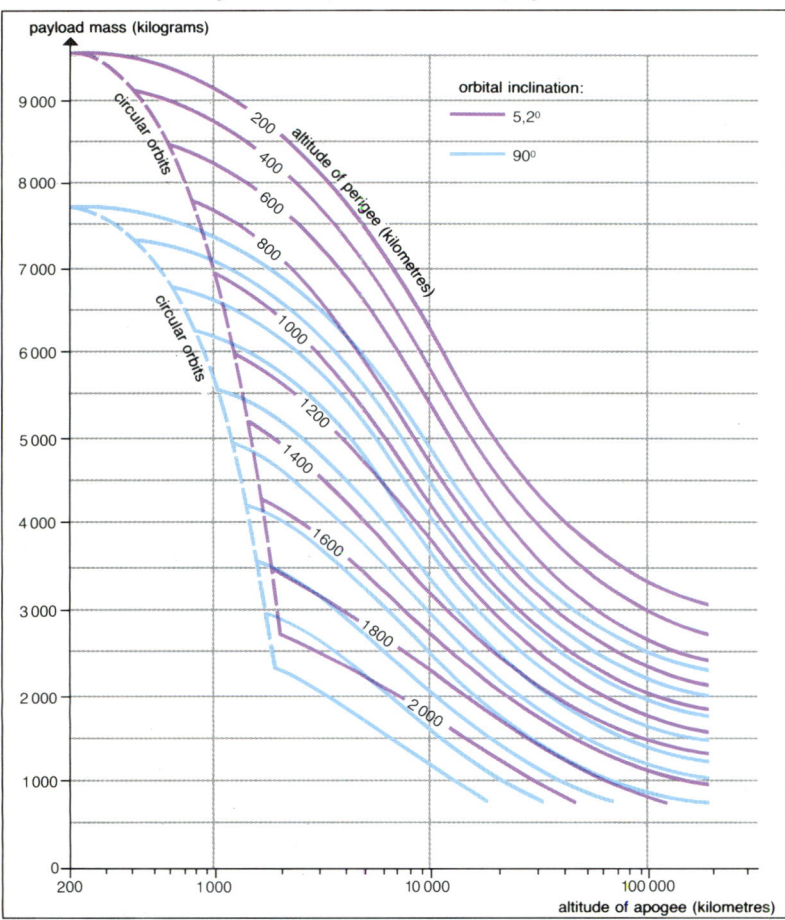

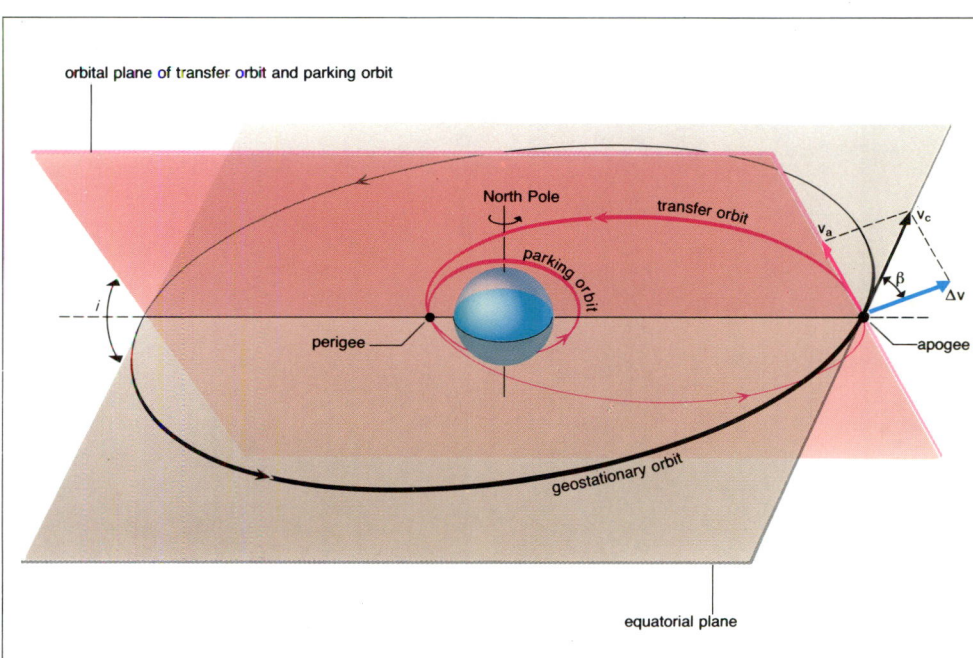

Locating the perigee and apogee. Geostationary satellites orbit in the equatorial plane. This orbit is made circular at the apogee of the transfer orbit, at a point where the orbital transfer plane intersects the Earth's equatorial plane. The perigee of the orbital transfer plane is also in the equatorial plane. The increase in speed required, $\triangle v$, is

$$\triangle v = \sqrt{(v_a^2 + v_c^2 - 2 \, v_a v_c \cos i)}$$

where v_a is the velocity at apogee (1·59 kilometres per second), v_c is the circular velocity (3·07 kilometres per second) and i is the inclination. The angle β of the velocity increment with respect to the equatorial plane is given by the relation $\sin \beta = v_a \sin i / \triangle v$. The apogee motor has to be pointed in the correct direction before it is fired to make this crucial manoeuvre.

Rocket launchers

Ariane IV, a conventional launcher

In many respects, the European rocket launcher Ariane IV is typical of conventional launchers. It has the same basic elements as Ariane I to III, but has been adapted for commercial use, especially for putting satellites into geostationary transfer orbits.

The decision to develop Ariane IV was taken in 1981 in response to the growing demand by commercial organisations for a launcher that could put greater masses into orbit and could also be adapted for different payload masses. Ariane IV can launch several satellites from one launcher. Like its predecessors, it is a three stage launcher, the first two stages using liquid fuels, the third a cryogenic rocket engine. All versions of Ariane IV have the same three stages and payload housing, but the head of the rocket and the double launch system depend on the requirements of a particular mission.

The increase in thrust at take-off is due to extra assistance from solid or liquid fuel booster rockets. The number and type of these engines vary according to which of the six versions of Ariane IV is being used. The payload mass which can be placed into a geostationary transfer orbit by Ariane 40, the smallest version which has no boosters, is 1·9 tonnes. The largest version, Ariane 44 L, is capable of putting 4·2 tonnes of payload into a geostationary transfer orbit thanks to its four liquid fuel boosters.

The production of operational launchers, their commercialisation and their launches is under the control of the company Arianespace, part of the French Centre national d'études

spatiales (CNES). Other industrial manufacturers and thirteen banks are also involved in the programme.

Preparing for launch

The Ariane IV rocket is launched from the Space Centre in French Guiana, the Centre spatial guyanais (CSG). Consecutive launches can be carried out with an interval of only one month between them. Ariane IV requires all the facilities that are available there, including preparation bays for the payload, logistic installations, meteorological stations, radars, telemetry and radar tracking stations, and the control centre itself. Apart from this tracking station, radar tracking stations at Natal (Brazil), on Ascension Island and at Libreville (Gabon) are used.

Launch preparations normally take about three years to complete. They begin with detailed documented information to ensure compatibility between the launcher and the payload. Particular attention is paid to dynamic compatibility, which is verified using computer models.

The actual launch operations begin with the arrival of the payload and its control panel, at least two months before the planned launch date. In special sterile halls, teams of engineers sent by the industrial companies which built the satellites carry out the final stages of assembly and testing. The different rocket stages arrive at Cayenne by ship about five weeks before the launch and go on to the CSG by road. The first stage is erected and fixed to the launch pad

continued on p. 94

The first launch of Ariane IV. The first successful launch of Ariane IV, in the 44 LP version, took place on 15 June 1988. The first commercial mission of the new launcher, in the same version, occurred on 11 December 1988.

Ariane IV is the successor to Ariane II and Ariane III. It has an improved performance and an extension to its modular options, and the payload volume has been increased. The capacity of the fuel tanks on the first stage has also been enlarged. There are liquid fuel booster rockets and a family of redesigned heads which house the satellites (ESA).

---

capacity for a geostationary transfer orbit (altitude of perigee, 200 kilometres; altitude of apogee, 36 000 kilometres; orbital inclination, 7 degrees; argument of perigee, 178 degrees)

58.4 m

44.9 m

third stage H 10

interstage skirt — 37.8 m / 35.0 m

second stage L 33

interstage skirt — 26.9 m / 23.6 m

first stage L 220

0

| 1.9 t | 2.6 t | 3.0 t | 3.1 t | 3.7 t | 4.2 t |

| **Ariane 40** | **Ariane 42 P** | **Ariane 44 P** | **Ariane 42 L** | **Ariane 44 LP** | **Ariane 44 L** |
| no boosters | two solid fuel boosters | four solid fuel boosters | two liquid fuel boosters | two solid fuel and two liquid fuel boosters | four liquid fuel boosters |

The family of Ariane IV launchers. Within a family of launchers the basic launcher is exactly the same, but each member of the family has added boosters to increase the payload capacity, maximising the launcher's performance for the mission that is being undertaken.

In the diagram on the left, the six versions of Ariane IV are shown, each with payload capacity for a geostationary transfer orbit indicated. Ariane 44 L carries 228 tonnes of fuel in its first stage tanks. For Ariane 40, 42 L and 42 P, the fuel amounts are 168 tonnes, 201 tonnes and 218 tonnes respectively.

The larger capacity heads are usually used with more powerful versions. The maximum rocket height of 58·4 metres corresponds to a short Système porteur externe pour lancement double Ariane (SPELDA), that is the Ariane Double Launch System, using an external carrier and a long head, or a long SPELDA and a short head.

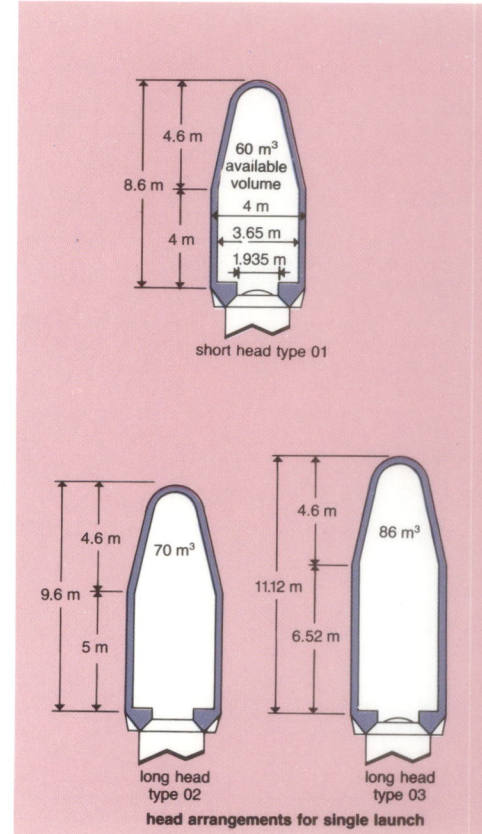

4.6 m

60 m³ available volume

8.6 m

4 m

3.65 m

4 m

1.935 m

short head type 01

4.6 m

70 m³

9.6 m

5 m

long head type 02

4.6 m

86 m³

11.12 m

6.52 m

long head type 03

head arrangements for single launch

The first stage of Ariane IV and a liquid fuel booster. On the right is a photograph taken in the Aérospatiale integration building at Mureaux in France. The L 220 stage of the first Ariane IV is being loaded into the container which will transport it to the space centre in French Guiana. The photograph above shows the liquid fuel boosters being assembled at the MBB–Erno plant at Bremen, West Germany. The Viking VI engine is mounted on a yellow, three armed thrust frame (right: Aérospatiale; above: MBB–Erno).

The gyrolaser inertial tracking system. The advantages of the gyrolaser inertial tracking system over a gyroscope inertial tracking system is that there are none of the moving parts which make the latter relatively delicate and fragile. The gyrolaser systems are more robust, more reliable, require less electricity and also have a faster response.

The gyrolaser uses light in two beams from a single laser which travel in opposite directions around a path between mirrors and converge on a detector. In the absence of any movement, the two parts of the beam have the same frequency. When the equipment is rotated, there is an increase in the frequency of one of the beams and a decrease in the frequency of the other. When the two beams are mixed a fringe pattern is observed, the fringe separation depending on the angular velocity.

A complete tracking system has three gyrolasers of this type for the three axes of rotation. It is mounted directly on the structure, and logic circuits are used to process and act upon the data. The gyrolaser tracking system used on Ariane IV was the first to be used on a space launcher (SFENA).

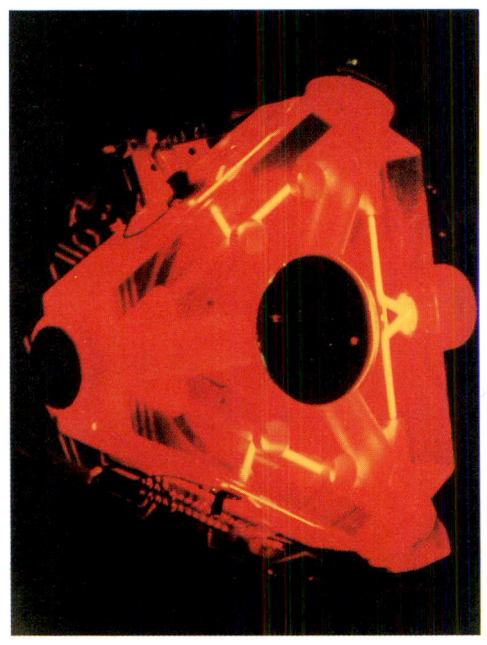

Trial separation of the Ariane IV head. The two halves of the Ariane head separate when an explosive device breaks the rivets holding the two parts together. The head is a lightweight, flexible structure made of aluminium alloy coated with carbon fibre.

Tests on the splitting head are here being performed in ESA's large space simulator in the Netherlands. This can simulate conditions of separation in space such as the vacuum and solar radiation but not, unfortunately, microgravity conditions.

The development of Ariane IV introduced many structural parts made out of carbon fibre. The interstage skirt between stages 2 and 3 was made by Fokker (Holland), the payload housing by CASA (Spain), the SPELDA by British Aerospace and the head by Contraves (Switzerland). The main advantage of carbon fibre is its lightness and its ability to withstand large mechanical forces. Thus the mass of the head of Ariane IV is almost identical to that of Ariane III, which is much smaller (Contraves).

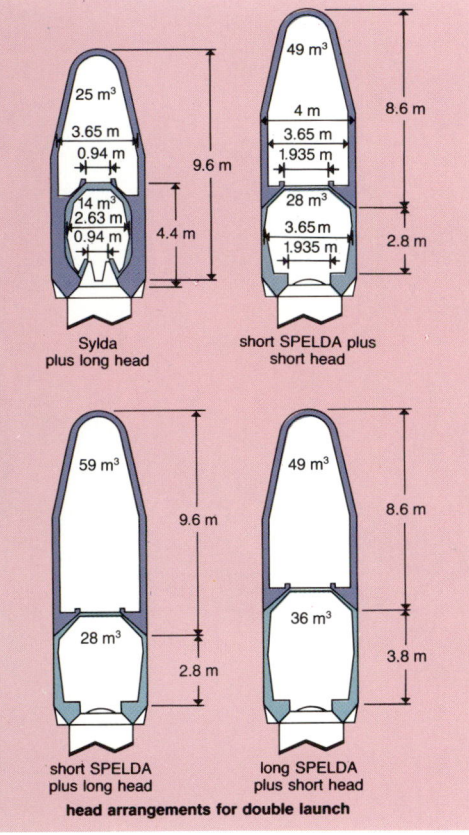

Sylda
plus long head

short SPELDA plus
short head

short SPELDA
plus long head

long SPELDA
plus short head

head arrangements for double launch

The heads and double launch systems of Ariane IV. The head protects the payload and the payload housing against humidity, wind and dust during launch preparations. It also protects the satellite during the journey through the lower atmosphere, in particular against aerodynamic heating by friction with the atmosphere.

The heads consist of a lower cylindrical part and an upper conical part with a rounded nose. Three types are available, of which two are standard; the type 03 head is only available on special request.

To launch two satellites using a single Ariane rocket, the Système de lancement double Ariane (Sylda), that is the Ariane Double Launch System, which was originally developed for Ariane III, can be used. This ovoid structure made of carbon fibre has, however, the disadvantage of limiting the diameter of the satellite which can be launched to 2·63 metres.

A SPELDA (Système porteur externe pour lancement double Ariane, or Ariane Double Launch System Using an External Carrier) has been developed specifically for Ariane IV. Placed between the payload housing and the head, it will take the same maximum diameter of satellite as the head itself (3·65 metres). Two types of SPELDA are available: the short one is for use with one or other of the standard heads, while the long one is for use only with the short head. The short head has a mass of 350 kilograms and the long one a mass of 400 kilograms.

Going into space

A The L220 first stage of Ariane IV
This stage is 23.6 metres tall and has a mass of 17.28 tonnes when empty. The L 220 first stage carries 228 tonnes of nitrogen peroxide and UH25 liquid fuel in two stainless steel tanks, 3.8 metres in diameter, linked by an intertank skirt which covers a water tank with a capacity of 8.2 cubic metres. In flight, the tanks are kept at a pressure of 500 kilopascals by gas produced in the vaporisers linked to the engines. There are four Viking V engines, which at sea level deliver a total thrust of 2.7 meganewtons.

1 Viking V engine
2 exhaust nozzle for the gas from the turbine (two per engine)
3 pump to supply water to the vaporiser (one per engine)
4 control device (two per engine)
5 vaporiser for turbopump (one per engine)
6 hydraulic control of engine orientation
7 valve for oxidant supplied to the engine
8 fuel tank (UH25)
9 system to control tank pressurisation
10 thrust frame
11 cruciform structure supporting the booster fixing arms
12 booster fixing arms (four)
13 arms to fix launcher to the launch pad (four)
14 engine shield
15 pipe supplying fuel to the engine
16 thermal ring
17 connections for liquid fuel booster
18 water supply pipe for the Viking V engine (four)
19 water supply pipe for a liquid fuel engine
20 pipe supplying oxidant to the engine
21 upper steel frame
22 exterior electrical cabling
23 attachment for different pipes
24 pressurisation pipe for the fuel tank
25 water tank
26 intertank skirt (aluminium alloy)
27 forward fixing points for a liquid fuel booster
28 steel frame
29 nitrogen peroxide tank
30 reinforced structure at the forward fixing points for the boosters
31 ring to attach exterior electrical cabling
32 pressurisation pipe for the nitrogen peroxide tank
33 forward skirt (aluminium alloy)
34 first stage separation rockets (eight)
35 conical interstage skirt (aluminium alloy)
36 inspection door (three)

B Solid fuel booster
The solid fuel boosters, whose height exceeds 11 metres, each consist of a steel cylindrical casing 1.07 metres diameter in which there is a block of polybutadiene with a mass of 9.5 tonnes. One of these boosters delivers a thrust of 625 kilonewtons. The fixed nozzle is inclined at an angle of 12° with respect to the axis of the engine in order to orient the thrust direction towards the launcher's centre of gravity. The operating time of 30 seconds is chosen so that the separation of the solid fuel boosters takes place before the supersonic part of the flight.

37 casing
38 solid fuel block
39 nozzle
40 lower fixing point
41 separation mechanism (spring loaded)
42 upper fixing point
43 electrical connectors
44 charge and equipment box

C Liquid fuel booster
The liquid fuel boosters burn for 135 seconds. Their thrust at sea level (587 kilonewtons) is slightly less than the thrust of the solid fuel boosters. Each liquid fuel booster consists of two stainless steel tanks, 12.5 metres in diameter, containing 38 tonnes of nitrogen peroxide and UH25. These tanks are pressurised by hot gas produced by a vaporiser linked to the engine and cooled by water drawn from a common tank in the first stage. The Viking VI engine has a short nozzle to optimise its performance in the atmosphere, and closely resembles those which are used in the first two stages of Ariane.

The liquid fuel booster engine is inclined at an angle of 9° with respect to the axis of the launcher. The upper part of the engine has a conical head to improve its aerodynamic performance. Its total height is 18.6 metres and its mass, when empty, is 4.5 tonnes.

45 Viking VI engine
46 gas exhaust from the turbine
47 turbopump to supply the engine with nitrogen peroxide
48 turbopump to supply the engine with UH25 fuel
49 pump to supply the vaporiser with water
50 tank pressurisation control
51 gas pressurisation pipe
52 pressurisation pipe for the nitrogen peroxide tank
53 pressurisation pipe for the UH25 fuel tank
54 pressurisation valve for use on the ground
55 fuel valve controlling tank filling
56 fuel supply pipe
57 nitrogen peroxide supply pipe
58 water supply pipe
59 shield
60 three armed thrust frame
61 rear skirt (aluminium alloy)
62 steel frame
63 UH25 fuel tank
64 fixing ring for pipes
65 central skirt (aluminium alloy)
66 booster separation rockets (six)
67 nitrogen peroxide tank
68 rear fixing points
69 forward fixing points (two)
70 forward skirt (aluminium alloy)
71 conical head (aluminium alloy)

D The L 33 second stage
The L 33 second stage was designed around the Viking IV engine, which produces a thrust of 755 kilonewtons in a vacuum. The structure is made out of a light alloy and includes two fuel tanks each with a diameter of 2.6 metres. They each contain 34 tonnes of fuel, UH25 and nitrogen peroxide. There is a toroidal shaped reservoir containing 800 kilograms of water below the tanks. The fuel tanks are pressurised by cold gases so there is a spherical tank containing helium within the forward skirt. The Viking IV engine has a long nozzle which is steerable to control the pitch of the launcher; an auxiliary gas ejecting device controls the rolling motion of the launcher. An interstage skirt, made of a light alloy, joins the first and second stages together; it contains a small explosive device which causes the two stages to separate. The separation rockets on the lower part of the second stage and the retrorockets on the forward skirt of the first stage ensure that the stages move apart safely after the first stage has been jettisoned. The L 33 stage is 11.4 metres tall and its mass, when empty, is 3.26 tonnes.

72 Viking IV engine
73 Cardan nozzle orientation control (two)
74 exhaust nozzle for gas from turbine
75 nitrogen peroxide turbopump
76 UH25 fuel turbopump
77 control device
78 fixing between rocket engine and thrust frame (Cardan articulation)
79 toroidal shaped water tank
80 nitrogen peroxide supply pipe
81 fuel supply pipe
82 rear skirt (aluminium alloy)
83 electric cabling
84 thruster to control roll
85 separation rockets (four rockets and two retrorockets)
86 conical thrust frame
87 charge and equipment box
88 steel harness
89 UH25 fuel tank
90 helium pressurisation pipe for tanks
91 detector for fuel gauge
92 nitrogen peroxide tank
93 tank for helium used to pressurise the other tanks (three)
94 helium valves and pressurisation system
95 entry pipe for pressurisation gas
96 fixing ring for pipes
97 forward skirt (aluminium alloy)
98 diaphragm
99 interstage skirt (aluminium alloy)

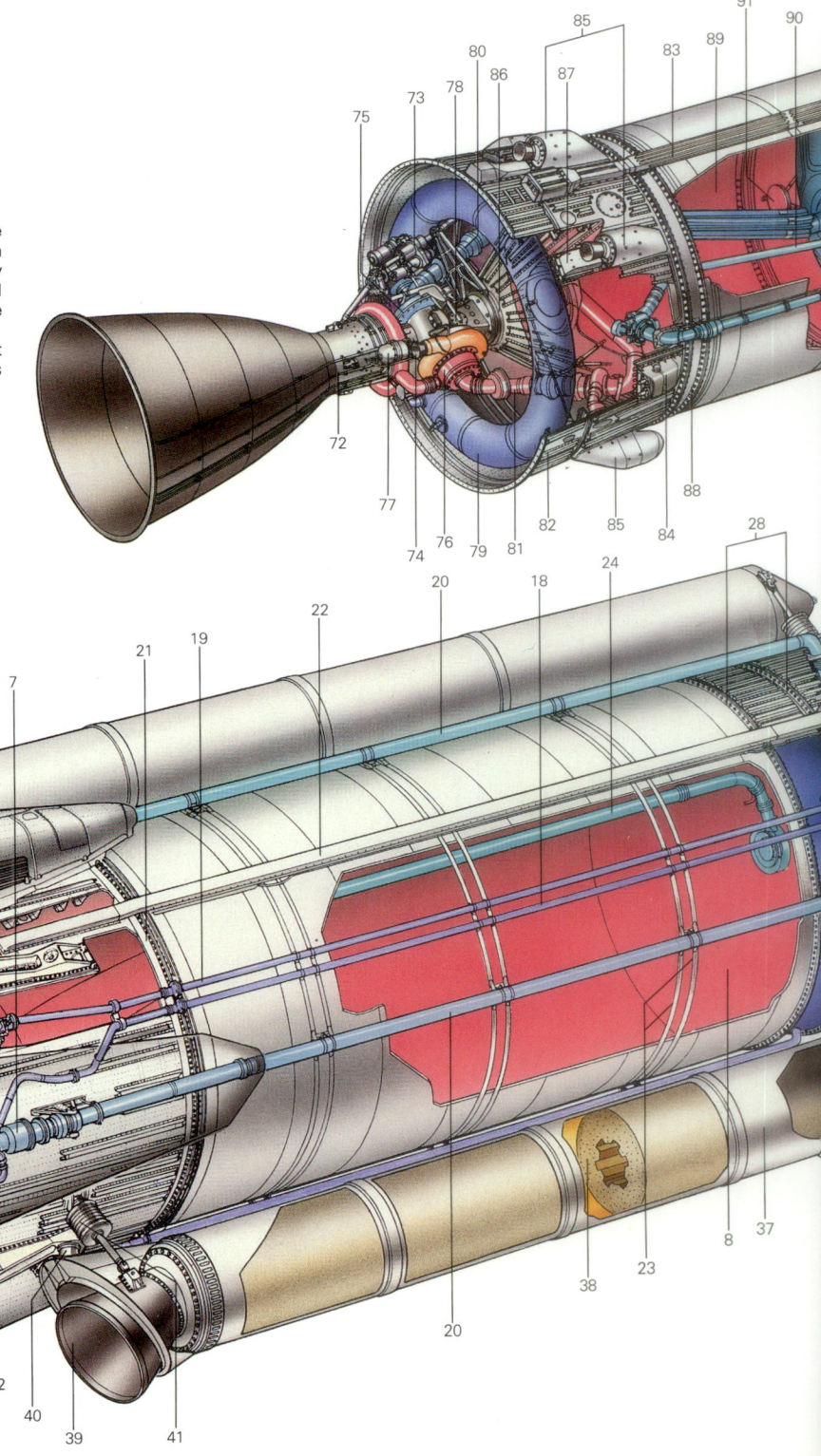

E The H 10 third stage

The H 10 third stage contains 10.6 tonnes of liquid oxygen and hydrogen in tanks separated by a common wall. To limit the transfer of heat between the two fuels which are stored at very different temperatures, the common wall is, in fact, a double wall consisting of an evacuated honeycomb made of phenolic resin. The oxygen tank is pressurised by helium gas and the hydrogen tank is pressurised by hydrogen gas. In a vacuum, the HM 7B engine produces a thrust of 63 kilonewtons. It is fixed on a conical engine frame and the launcher's pitch and yaw are controlled. The rolling motion is regulated by an auxiliary system which ejects hydrogen gas through small nozzles. At the end of combustion this system also acts to orient the satellites and finally rotates them at the desired spin rate. The H 10 stage is 9.9 metres high and its empty mass is 1.25 tonnes. The system for separation from the third stage is the same as that used to separate the first and second stages. The linking structures are all made of light alloy, with the exception of the interstage skirt between the second and third stages which is made of carbon fibre.

100 HM 7B rocket engine
101 exhaust nozzle for gas from the turbine
102 Cardan articulation joint (two)
103 oxygen supply pipe
104 tank for helium used for pressurisation
105 helium pressurisation pipe
106 conical thrust frame (aluminium alloy)
107 aluminium tank containing liquid oxygen
108 separation rockets (four)
109 hydrogen supply pipe
110 telemetry system
111 equipment box for destruction charge
112 jets to control attitude and rolling
113 steel harness for payload housing
114 electric cabling
115 anti-vibration device
116 aluminium tank containing liquid hydrogen
117 external thermal insulation
118 rear skirt (aluminium alloy)
119 anti-cavitation device

F The payload housing

Perhaps the most important part of the launcher is the payload housing, situated at the upper end of the third stage. Made of carbon fibre, this contains the satellites to be launched and the launcher's computer. Two inertial tracking systems aid the guidance systems: one is a conventional platform stabilised by gyroscopes, the other a gyrolaser system used as a back up. Accelerometers mounted on the tracking system detect the launcher's motion about the three perpendicular axes, and the computer integrates the observations to calculate the instantaneous velocity and position of the launcher. The guidance computer program calculates, at each and every instant, the trajectory that must be followed to obtain the desired injection point. Instructions about the necessary corrections are transmitted to the automatic guidance systems which also control the launcher's motion about the three axes. Further, the computer ensures that the correct flight sequence, including separation of the stages and engine ignition, is followed. The system also has radar beacons which are interrogated during the flight by radars on the ground to plot the trajectory in real time. A telemetry system transmits more than 600 parameters about the launcher to ground stations and these are transmitted in real time to the launch base. Some are processed during the flight to analyse the launcher's performance. Finally, there is a remote control, self destruct system to be used only if the launcher becomes a threat to populated areas of the world.

120 annular platform
121 control electronics units
122 removable external panels
123 diaphragm
124 internal cone
125 external cone
126 communications antennae

SPELDA, head and payload arrangement
127 short SPELDA
128 top of SPELDA's truncated cone
129 pyrotechnic separation device
130 lower pay load adaptor
131 lower payload (Eurostar satellite)
132 long head
133 pyrotechnic head separation rivets
134 upper payload adaptor
135 upper payload (Olympus satellite)

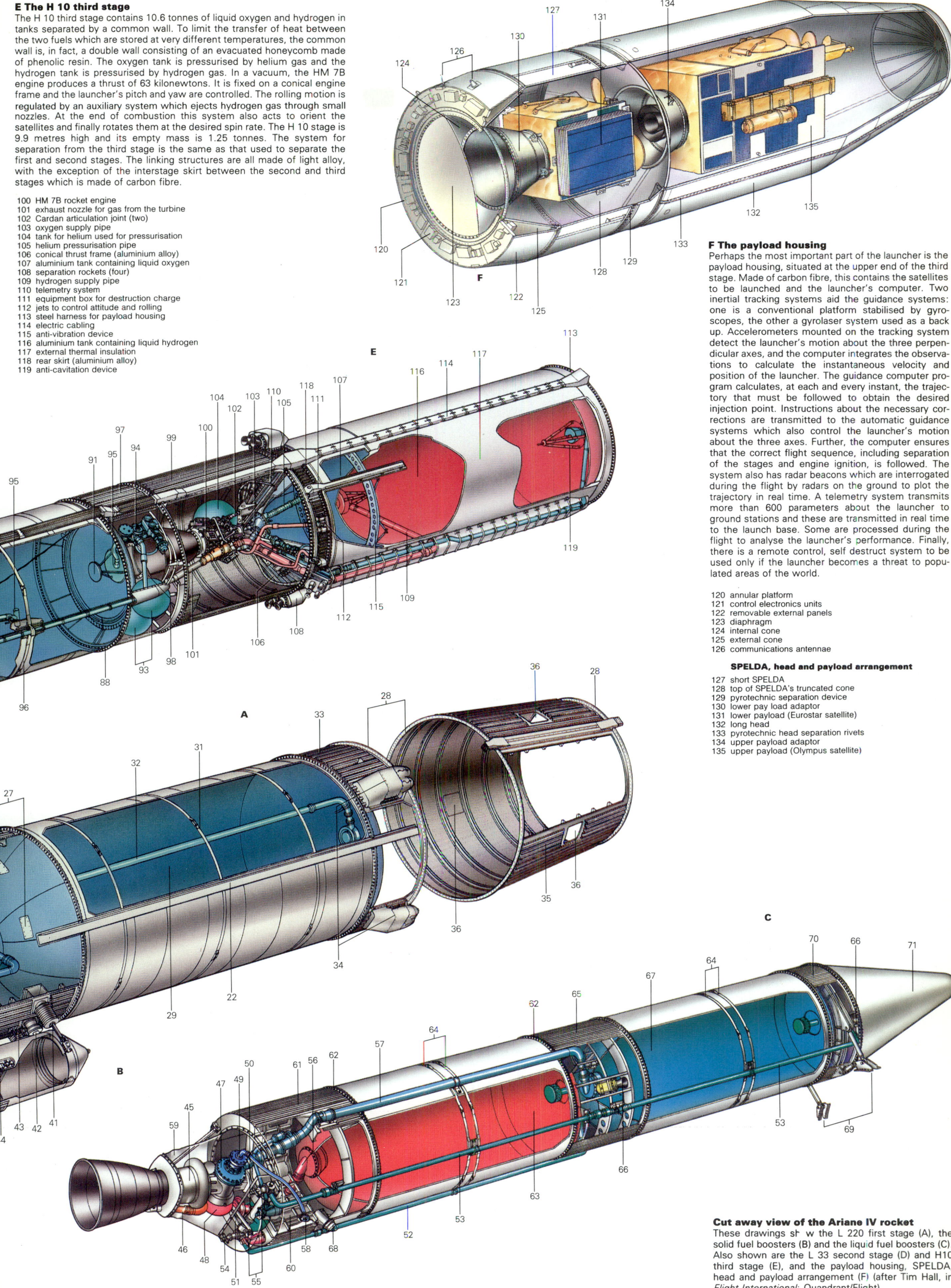

Cut away view of the Ariane IV rocket
These drawings show the L 220 first stage (A), the solid fuel boosters (B) and the liquid fuel boosters (C). Also shown are the L 33 second stage (D) and H10 third stage (E), and the payload housing, SPELDA, head and payload arrangement (F) (after Tim Hall, in *Flight International*; Quandrant/Flight).

which moves between the assembly area and launch area. Whilst this phase is carried out in the assembly area another launcher may be in the final stages of launch. The second stage is added and then the third stage; all stages are then connected electrically. Finally, the payload housing is installed on top of the third stage and tests on the entire electrical circuitry are carried out.

About two weeks before the actual launch, the Ariane IV rocket is moved to the launch site. The payloads undergo their final flight preparations, the fuel tanks are filled and the apogee boost motor is installed. The two satellite payloads are assembled, one in the SPELDA and the other above it. They are then placed in the head where all contact with the environment is avoided so that everything remains very clean. The head is then placed in a special container, transported to the launch site, and mounted on and connected up to the launcher.

The final preparation phase begins with a run through the launch sequence, during which all systems at the CSG are activated and tested. After a meeting, where it is formally confirmed that there are no reasons why the launch should be postponed, the countdown sequence finally begins.

The countdown for an Ariane 44 LP launch

The launch has to be performed within a certain interval of time, termed a 'slot', which suits the satellites from all points of view. Countdown begins at T−30 hours, where T is the time of blast off. The first event is the filling of the nitrogen peroxide tanks, and then the

The Ariane launch site in French Guiana. Ariane IV can only be launched from the launch site shown in the foreground. The launch pad itself has a mass of 500 tonnes and rolls along a perfectly horizontal railway track. A hydraulic transmission tractor produces the very smooth motion required. Behind is the launch tower for earlier Ariane rockets.

Once the launch pad is in position over the exhaust gas pit, the large protection enclosure on the right rolls along to cover the launcher. It is 80 metres high and weighs about 3000 tonnes. When the launch is about to happen, it moves away to a distance of 90 metres.

The launcher photographed here, Ariane IV, on flight 22 on 15 June 1988, is linked to an 'umbilical' tower (left) by cables and nozzles which are disconnected at the moment of lift off. In particular, there are two cryogenic arms for fuel for the third stage (Bernard Paris/Arianespace).

The cryogenic arms. On each side of the third stage there are two valves which link the cryogenic (low temperature) fluids in the tanks on the ground to the rocket via umbilical connections and hinged arms attached to the launch tower. One such system transfers liquid oxygen and liquid helium, and the other transfers liquid hydrogen and gaseous helium. These arms are disconnected just a few seconds before ignition (Bernard Paris/Arianespace).

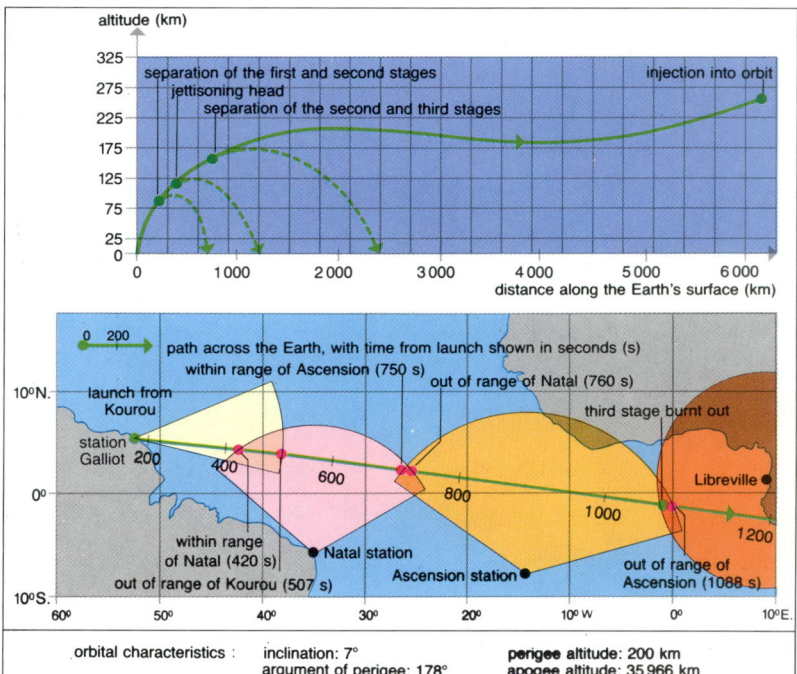

orbital characteristics : inclination: 7°   perigee altitude: 200 km
argument of perigee: 178°   apogee altitude: 35 966 km

Flight profile of Ariane 44 L. The launcher's trajectory shown in the upper diagram above is determined by a computer which takes into account the most recent data received on the mass of the launcher and its payload. This flight profile illustrates the importance of the third stage, which provides half the total velocity given to the payload. Its low thrust is applied over a very long trajectory so that the payload arrives at the equator at the end of the combustion phase.

Information recorded aboard the Ariane IV launcher is transmitted to tracking stations, as shown in the lower diagram, and is used to monitor the launcher's progress and flight path. The data received is immediately transmitted by satellite to the ground control centre at Kourou, French Guiana, which analyses flight parameters in real time.

The launcher's radar beacons are interrogated by radars at Kourou, at Natal in Brazil, and on Ascension Island. A supplementary tracking station has been constructed in Gabon, and a station in Kenya can also be used for missions which have very long final manoeuvres.

UH25 fuel tanks in the first two stages and the liquid fuel boosters. This is done automatically under pressure from storage tanks situated some hundreds of metres away from the launch site. The tanks are overfilled and adjustments are then made. The fuels are kept at a low temperature throughout so that the maximum amount possible can be put on board.

Next, T−12 hours and 45 minutes, preparations are made to withdraw the protective enclosure, the access doors are closed and the gangways removed. Direct access to the launcher is no longer possible. At T−6 hours and 45 minutes, the enclosure is removed and the inertial tracking systems are aligned. At T−6 hours, helium is pumped through the third stage to remove all traces of humidity. The CSG tests all its systems and, at T−3 hours and 35 minutes, filling of the third stage tanks with liquid hydrogen and oxygen begins. This is finished at T−1 hour and 40 minutes; during this period the tanks of the first and second stages are pressurised as required for flight. Following a final test of the ground control's connections to the launcher, the last safety devices preventing the accidental firing of the pyrotechnic circuits are removed.

Finally, with all going according to plan, at T−6 minutes the synchronised launch sequence begins. The computers at the ground control and on the launch pad are synchronised, and the electricity supply is changed from external mains to internal batteries.

At T−4.9 seconds an automatic sequencer takes over. This controls the opening of the arms which supply fluids to the third stage and ignites the first stage engines and the liquid fuel boosters. If everything is working correctly, the order to open the restraining hooks is given, and the solid fuel boosters are ignited. Some 3·4 seconds after ignition Ariane IV lifts off and ascends vertically for 7 seconds before altering course slightly. If an error is detected during this final sequence, the restraining hooks are automatically kept in place and the launcher is made safe before the launch is attempted again.

Jettisoning the solid fuel boosters. The photographs below show the moment at which the solid fuel boosters are jettisoned from Ariane IV; they were taken by a camera attached to one of the boosters. On the lowest photograph, at an altitude of 7·5 kilometres, the boosters have just been released. The shield of the propulsion compartment has been blackened by their fumes and the nozzles of the Viking engines have reached red heat. The other solid fuel booster is visible between the nozzles. In the middle photograph the first stage has moved away and, in the upper photograph, the second solid fuel booster has almost burnt itself out.

To jettison the boosters, small explosive devices are fired, releasing the fixing devices between the first stage and the boosters. These consist of powerful spiral springs compressed between the two parts. The solid fuel boosters land within the vicinity of the launch site. However, the liquid fuel boosters which are jettisoned after 150 seconds land in international waters about 400 kilometres east of the launch site. It was initially decided that they should be parachuted back to Earth for reuse, but this was later deemed uneconomic. Recovery from the sea is not only costly but difficult as the engines have to be tracked by radar, located, and hoisted on board ship before being transported back to Europe for a complete strip down and reassembly. The cost of the supplementary operations renders the advantages marginal. Moreover, should the recovery mission fail, the cost savings completely disappear (Aérospatiale).

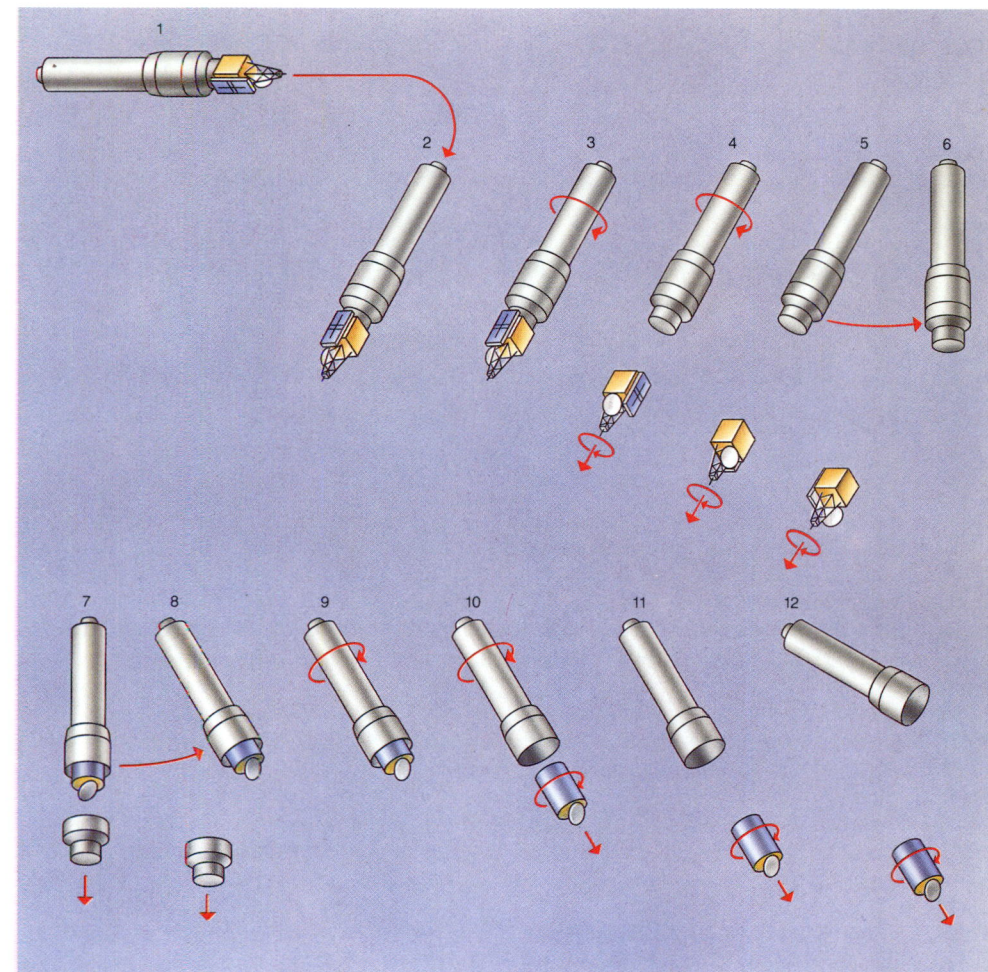

The separation sequence of satellites in a double launch. The attitude and roll control system points the third stage and payload in the desired direction for the upper satellite in the SPELDA (1, 2) and, if necessary, starts it rotating at a rate of, say, 10 spins per minute (3). The computer then commands the separation of the upper satellite by releasing, using small explosives, the restraining bands which attach the satellite to the SPELDA (4). The rotation of the third stage is then reduced to zero (5) and is pointed in the correct direction for the lower satellite. It begins spinning, and the satellite separates itself from the SPELDA (6, 7, 8, 9, 10). Finally, the third stage is reoriented (11, 12) and travels in a direction designed to avoid any risk of collision with either of the satellites.

The first stage and the liquid fuel boosters burn for three and a half minutes, during which time they each consume 250 kilograms of fuel per second. The solid fuel boosters are jettisoned several kilometres from the launch site after burning for 30 seconds. The liquid fuel boosters burn for 150 seconds, falling back into the Atlantic Ocean after travelling about 400 kilometres. When the fuels for the first stage have been used up, acceleration is reduced and there is a dramatic reduction in thrust. Detection of this change initiates the separation of the stages at an altitude of about 70 kilometres, when the rocket's velocity has reached 2·8 kilometres per second. Several seconds after separation, the computer commands the valves of the second stage engines to open. This ignites the second stage while the first stage begins a ballistic trajectory and breaks up.

The head is jettisoned at an altitude of about 110 kilometres during the combustion of the second stage engines. The engines are turned off when the inertial tracking system detects that the required velocity increase has been attained. The computer then commands the jettisoning and separation of the second and third stages. Altitude is now 135 kilometres and the velocity is 5·4 kilometres per second.

Finally, the computer orders the ignition of the third stage which will burn for more than 12 minutes. When the inertial tracking system detects the required speed, these engines are switched off. There will be about 250 kilograms of unburnt fuel remaining, which can be used to make trajectory corrections. The attitude control system remains active and takes charge of the separation of the satellites. Separation accomplished, the launcher's mission has come to a successful end. It only remains to make a thorough examination of the telemetry data recorded on the launcher's performance before the next flight.

Jean-Claude Bouillot

Rocket launchers

The space shuttle: a reusable system

A conventional rocket launcher represents a waste of expensive technological resources, and so the idea of a recoverable, reusable launcher is very attractive. There were therefore two main factors which led to the eventual development of recoverable systems: the need for crews of astronauts and scientifically valuable equipment to be returned safely to Earth, and the requirement that this be done as cheaply as possible.

Crews, equipment and samples could return safely and economically to Earth in space capsules; it could also become desirable to return other expensive elements of the launchers, such as rocket engines, for reuse. However, it is not easy to quantify the economic advantages of following this course of action, as it requires a sizeable increase in the mass of the launcher. For a given payload, this substantially increases the launcher's size, and consequently its manufacturing cost and the cost of its operation. In fact, the ratio of the payload mass put into orbit to the total mass at take-off is 1·35% for the US space shuttle compared with 2·8% for the Ariane rocket, a reflection of the very different design concepts involved.

The American space shuttle programme, the major programme to follow Apollo, has been the object of much conceptual research by different contractors since its beginnings in 1971. One of the original proposals consisted of an orbital vehicle on top of the first stage of a Saturn V rocket, but this was abandoned due to the cost of the non-reusable stage. Most of the other concepts relied on the idea of a two stage vehicle, both stages of which could be recovered.

The enormous development costs were kept down both by reducing the size of the vehicle and by putting the fuel tanks on the outside; new tanks would be required for each flight. Further, the first stage reusable engines were replaced by solid fuel booster rockets which would be only partially reusable. The plans were put out to tender, and the contract was won by Rockwell International.

The American space shuttle is a partially reusable launcher consisting of a space plane, the orbiter; the External Tank (ET) which contains the fuel, liquid hydrogen, and the oxidant, liquid oxygen, used by the main engines during the launch phase; and the Solid fuel Rocket

The space shuttle, Discovery. On 24 January 1985, the space shuttle, Discovery, was launched from the Kennedy Space Center on a military mission. This photograph was taken just as the solid fuel rocket boosters were ignited. The three Space Shuttle Main Engines (SSME) were ignited 3·8 seconds earlier (NASA).

The External Tank (ET)

1 safety valve for liquid oxygen tank
2 liquid oxygen tank
3 anti-vibration partition
4 anti-vortex siphon
5 intertank section

6 forward fixing point for SRB
7 umbilical connection point
8 forward fixing point to orbiter
9 liquid hydrogen tank
10 liquid oxygen pipe

11 interior structure
12 pressurisation pipe for liquid hydrogen tank
13 rear fixing points to the orbiter and fuel delivery pipes
14 anti-vortex siphon

The External Tanks and the Solid fuel Rocket Boosters (left). The External Tank (ET) is made out of aluminium by Martin Marietta. It is 47 metres long, has a diameter of 8·4 metres and an empty mass of 33·5 tonnes. It is used to supply fuel to the three main engines (SSME) of the orbiter. The liquid oxygen and liquid hydrogen fuel tanks have a capacity of 550 cubic metres and 1500 cubic metres, respectively. The support structure contains pipes between the tanks and the orbiter through which the liquid hydrogen flows at 3100 litres per second.

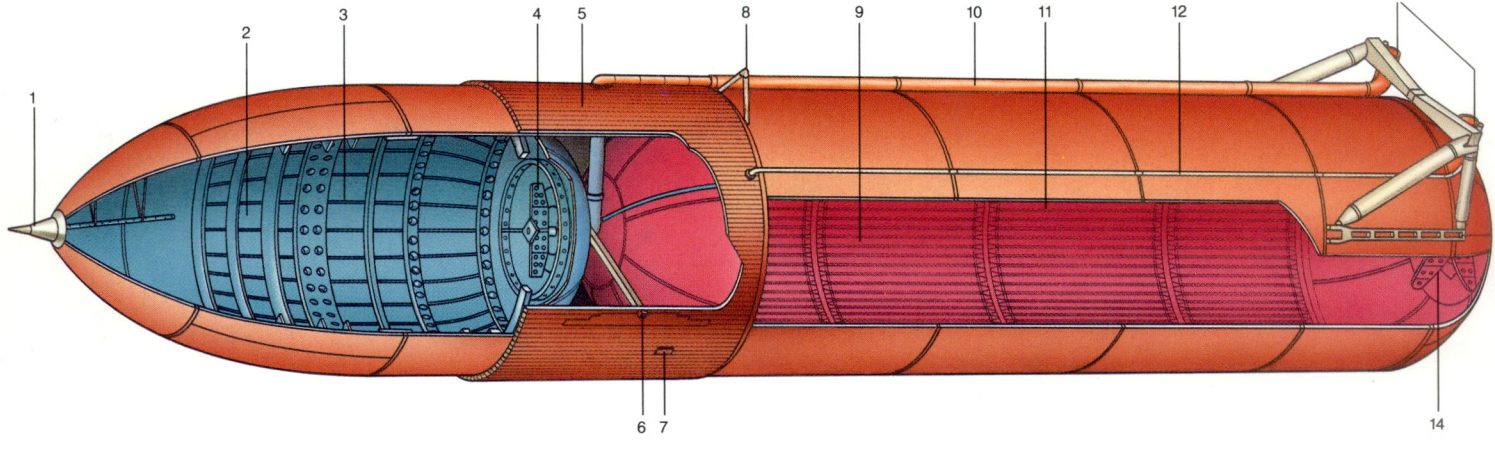

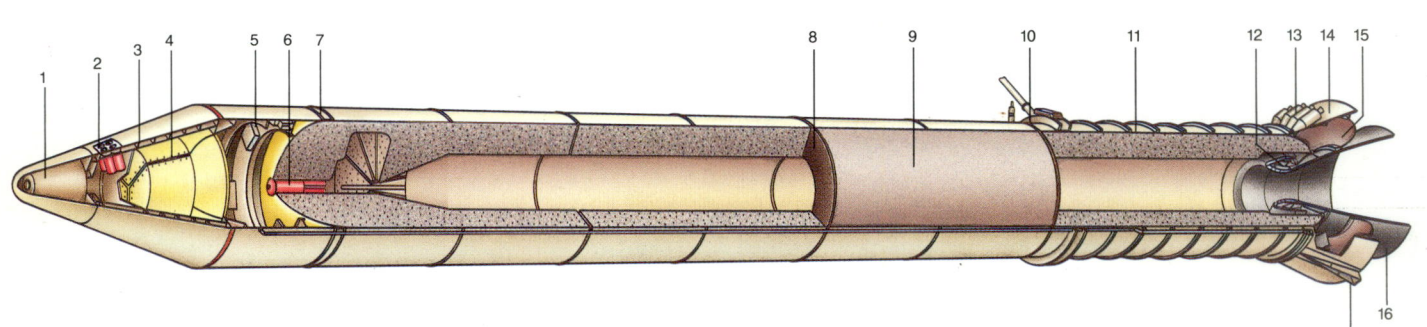

Two Solid fuel Rocket Boosters (SRBs) assist the space shuttle to take off. When empty they have a mass of 83 tonnes each; each contains 503·6 tonnes of solid fuel (polybutadiene) in a metallic casing 3·7 metres in diameter. Built by Morton Thiokol, their length is 45·5 metres. They are constructed in four sections which are independently moulded and then assembled. The joints between the two parts have to be completely tight. The rupturing of one of these joints, the so called O rings, was the cause of the devastating Challenger space shuttle accident on 28 January 1986.

Each SRB produces a thrust of 15 meganewtons at take-off and, thereafter, an average thrust of 13·15 meganewtons during the 120 seconds of combustion. Parachutes placed in their heads enable them to return to Earth and to be recovered from the sea.

Solid fuel Rocket Booster (SRB)

1 primary parachute
2 forward separation rockets
3 flotation system
4 principal parachutes (three)
5 platform for electronic equipment
6 pyrotechnic ignition

7 fixing harness to the ET
8 joint between solid fuel segments
9 solid fuel segment (four per engine)
10 fixing harness to the ET including interconnecting cables
11 solid fuel block

12 articulated joint for nozzle
13 rear separation rockets
14 skirt
15 thermal insulation
16 diffuser nozzle
17 anchor point between SRB and launch pad

10 m

5

0

Going into space

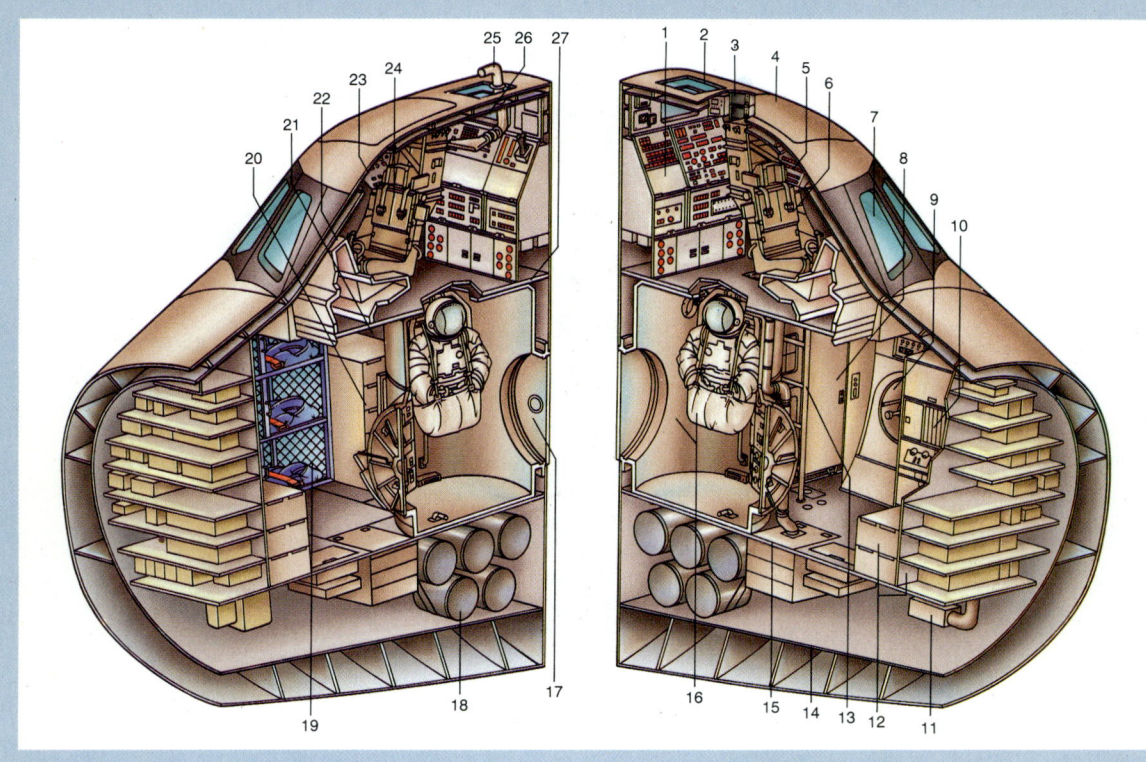

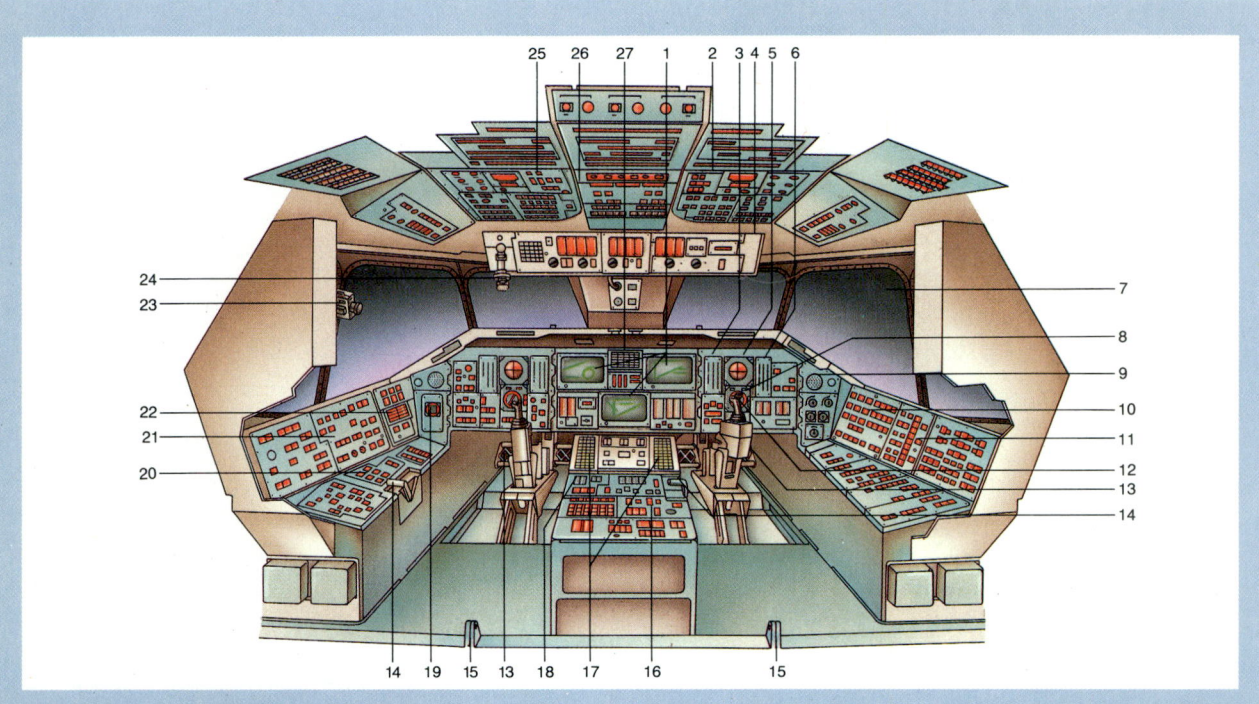

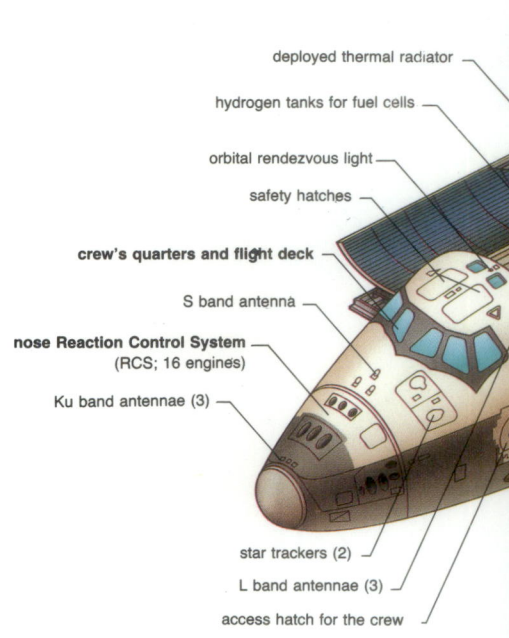

deployed thermal radiator
hydrogen tanks for fuel cells
orbital rendezvous light
safety hatches
crew's quarters and flight deck
S band antenna
nose Reaction Control System
(RCS; 16 engines)
Ku band antennae (3)
star trackers (2)
L band antennae (3)
access hatch for the crew

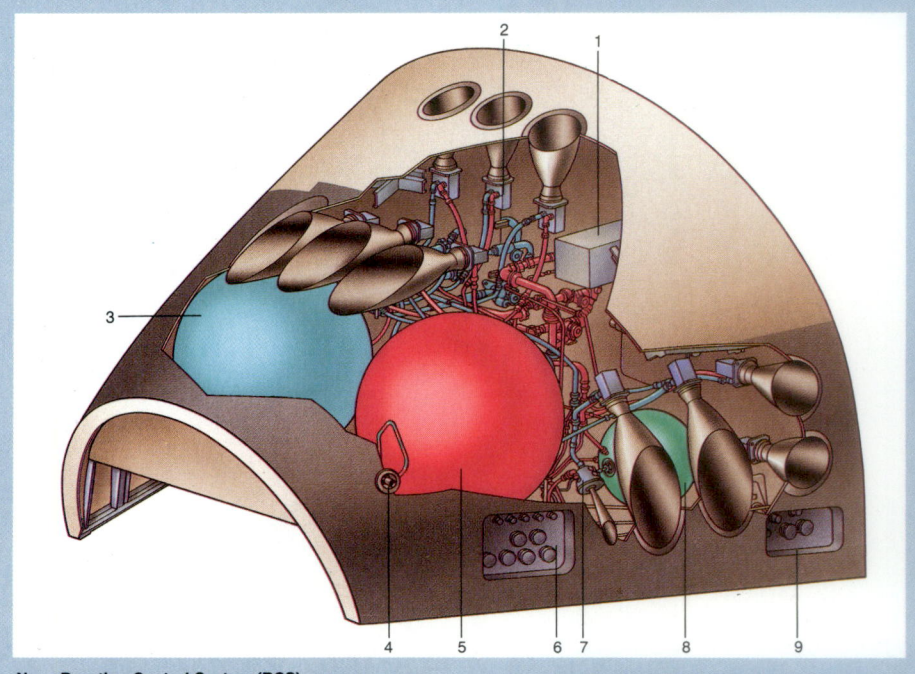

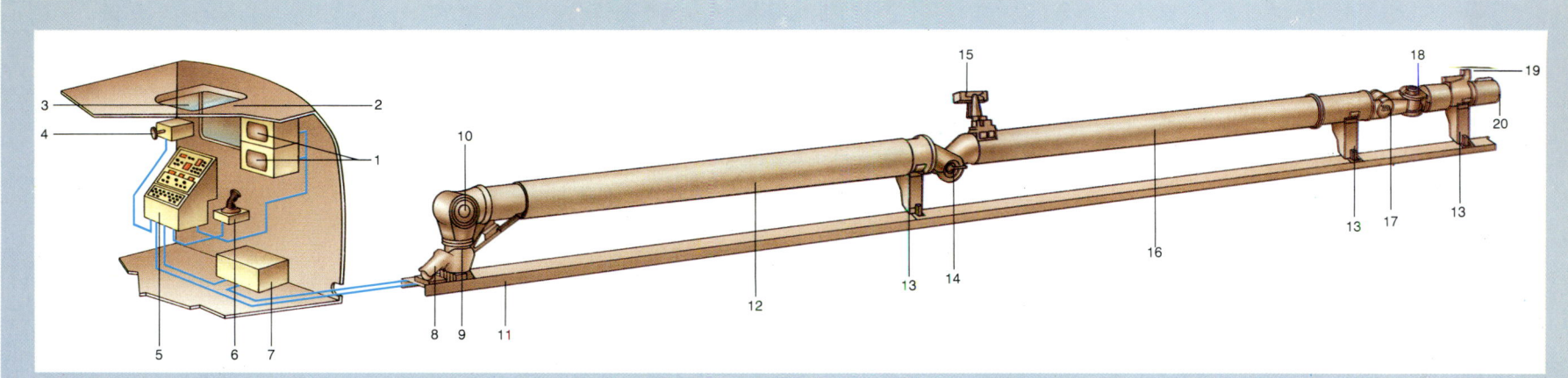

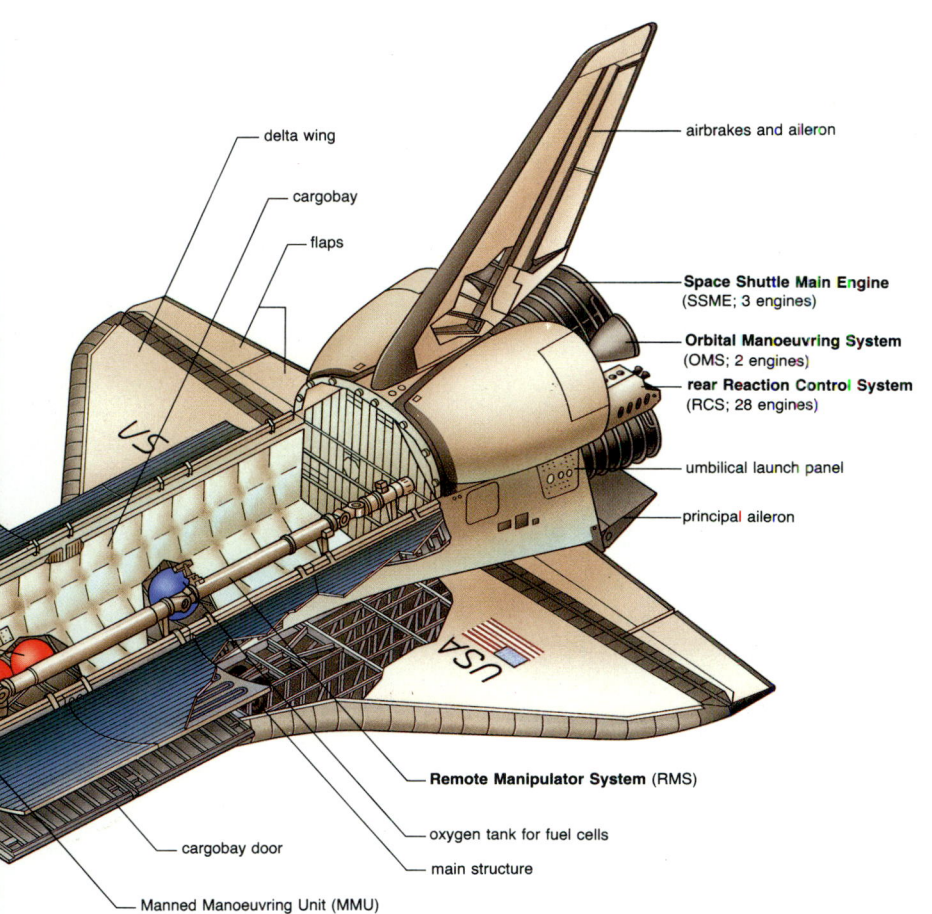

delta wing

cargobay

flaps

airbrakes and aileron

Space Shuttle Main Engine (SSME; 3 engines)

Orbital Manoeuvring System (OMS; 2 engines)

rear Reaction Control System (RCS; 28 engines)

umbilical launch panel

principal aileron

Remote Manipulator System (RMS)

oxygen tank for fuel cells

main structure

cargobay door

Manned Manoeuvring Unit (MMU)

Control system for the Remote Manipulator System (RMS)

1. control via closed circuit television
2. cargobay window
3. upper window
4. RMS control joystick
5. control console
6. control joystick for rotation of arm
7. computer
8. system for extending the arm
9. shoulder joint (twisting)
10. shoulder joint (pitching)
11. RMS support beam
12. upper arm (6.7 metres)
13. support and fixing screw
14. elbow joint (pitching)
15. television camera
16. lower arm (6.7 metres)
17. wrist joint (pitching)
18. wrist joint (twisting)
19. television camera and light
20. end of arm and grappling hook

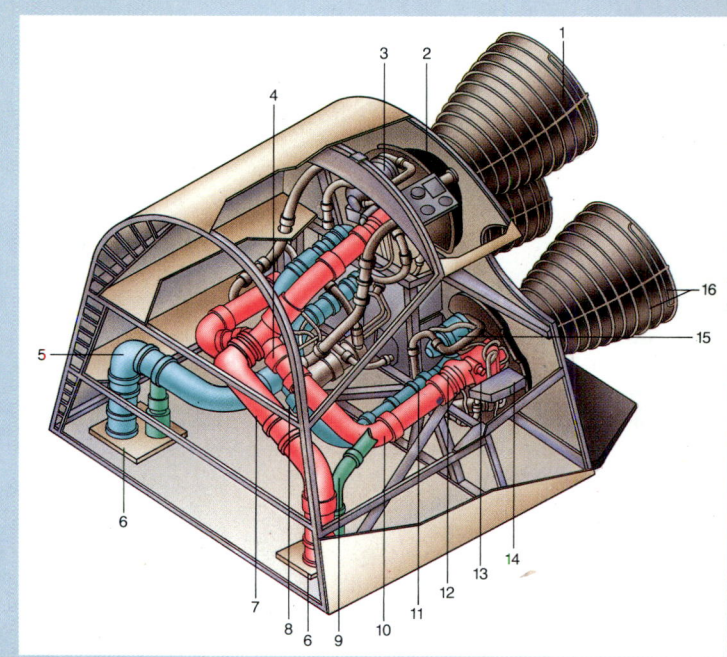

Space Shuttle Main Engines (SSMEs)

1. diffuser nozzle
2. heat shield
3. SSME engine (thrust: 1.7 meganewtons at sea level)
4. main fuel supply valve
5. main liquid oxygen supply
6. detachable umbilical connectors between orbiter and ETs
7. main fuel supply
8. main oxygen supply valve
9. pressurisation of the fuel tank
10. main fuel supply to one engine
11. main oxygen supply to one engine
12. engine joint
13. precombustion chamber and fuel turbopumps
14. device for orienting engines (2 Cardan suspensions, with twist control of ±10.5°, and pitch control of ±8.5°)
15. precombustion chamber and oxygen turbopumps
16. spiral pipes of diffuser nozzle's cooling system

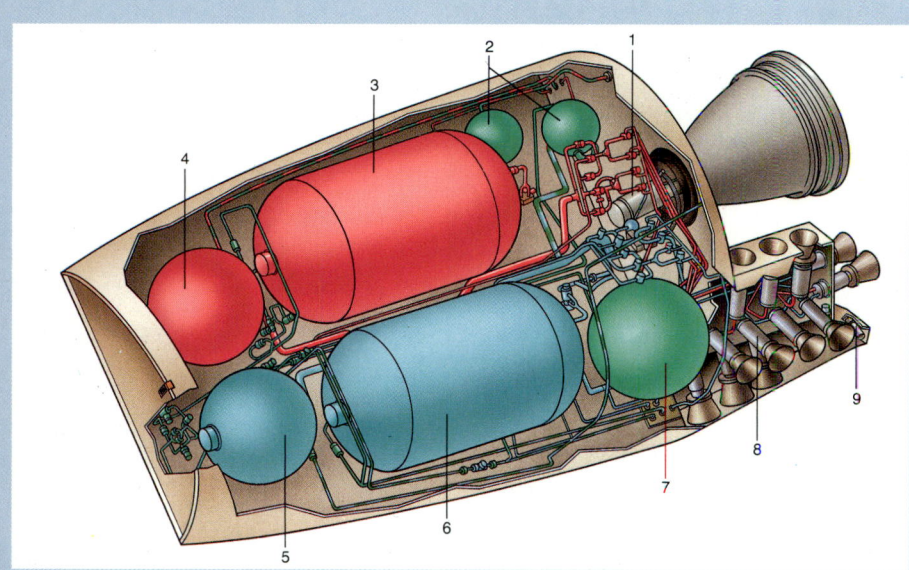

OMS and rear RCS systems (port side)

1. OMS engine (thrust of 27 kilonewtons in a vacuum)
2. helium tank, for pressurising fuel tanks in RCS system
3. MMH fuel tank for OMS engine
4. MMH fuel tank for RCS system
5. nitrogen peroxide tank for RCS system
6. nitrogen peroxide tank for OMS engine
7. helium tank, for pressurising fuel tanks in OMS engine
8. main RCS engine (12 engines of 3.87 kilonewtons each)
9. fine control RCS engine (2 engines of 110 newtons each)

The space shuttle orbiter. The orbiter's structure has five main parts – the forward fuselage, the mid fuselage, the rear fuselage, the vertical tailplane, and the wings.

The forward fuselage contains the nose Reaction Control System (RCS) and the crew's quarters. The cargobay is the main part of the mid fuselage; it contains the payload and the Remote Manipulator System (RMS). The rear fuselage contains the three main engines (SSMEs) and also the port and starboard units, each containing a rear RCS and an Orbital Manoeuvring System (OMS).

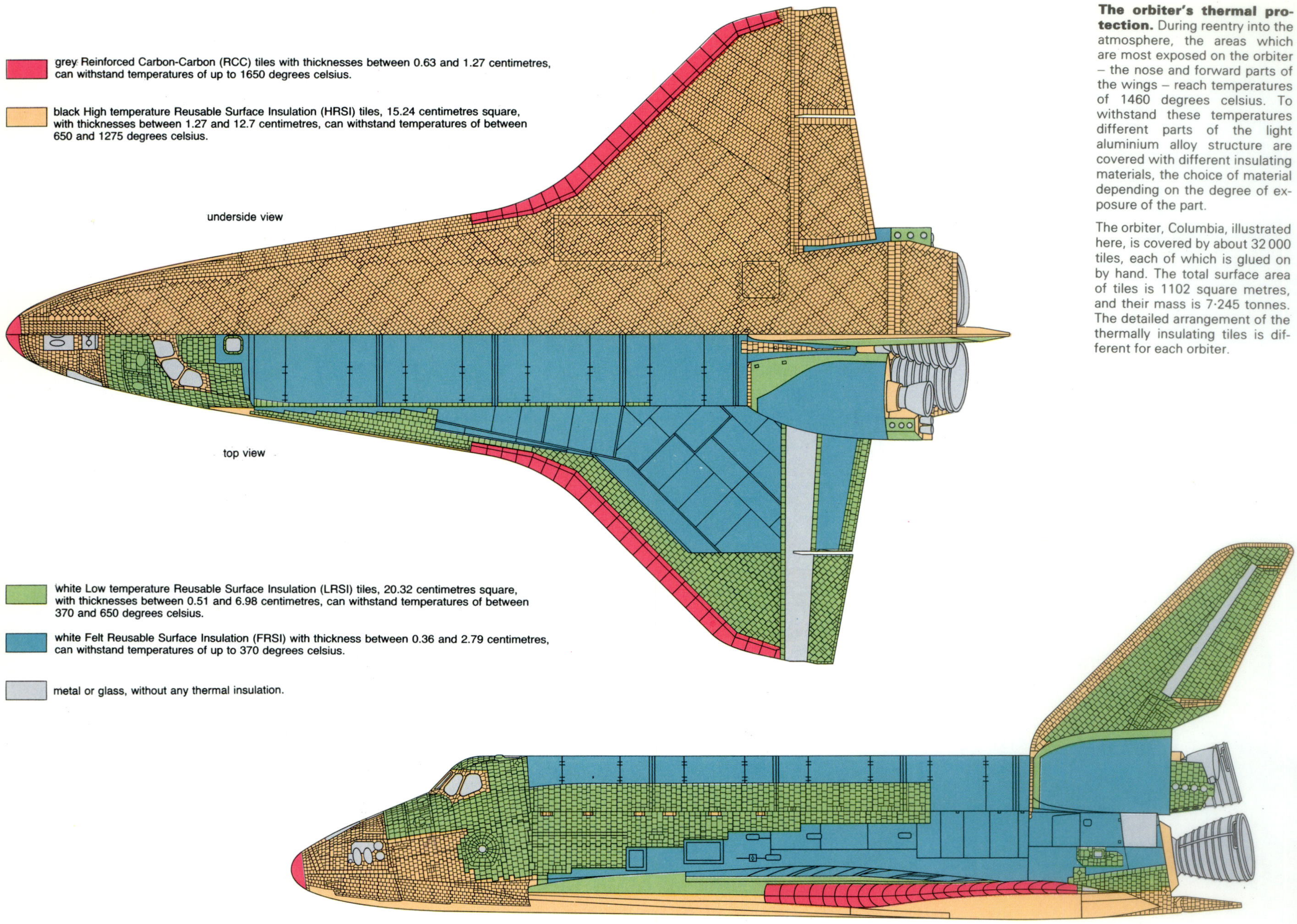

grey Reinforced Carbon-Carbon (RCC) tiles with thicknesses between 0.63 and 1.27 centimetres, can withstand temperatures of up to 1650 degrees celsius.

black High temperature Reusable Surface Insulation (HRSI) tiles, 15.24 centimetres square, with thicknesses between 1.27 and 12.7 centimetres, can withstand temperatures of between 650 and 1275 degrees celsius.

underside view

top view

white Low temperature Reusable Surface Insulation (LRSI) tiles, 20.32 centimetres square, with thicknesses between 0.51 and 6.98 centimetres, can withstand temperatures of between 370 and 650 degrees celsius.

white Felt Reusable Surface Insulation (FRSI) with thickness between 0.36 and 2.79 centimetres, can withstand temperatures of up to 370 degrees celsius.

metal or glass, without any thermal insulation.

The orbiter's thermal protection. During reentry into the atmosphere, the areas which are most exposed on the orbiter – the nose and forward parts of the wings – reach temperatures of 1460 degrees celsius. To withstand these temperatures different parts of the light aluminium alloy structure are covered with different insulating materials, the choice of material depending on the degree of exposure of the part.

The orbiter, Columbia, illustrated here, is covered by about 32 000 tiles, each of which is glued on by hand. The total surface area of tiles is 1102 square metres, and their mass is 7·245 tonnes. The detailed arrangement of the thermally insulating tiles is different for each orbiter.

Boosters (SRB). The orbiter carries the crew and the payload (in the cargobay) and is completely recoverable. The ET is used for only one flight. The boosters, however, are recovered from the sea after descending by parachute and are refitted for later flights.

The orbiter is a combination of a launcher, a plane and a manned spacecraft. It is shaped like a delta-winged plane, with a wingspan of 23·79 metres; it is 37·24 metres long and 17·25 metres high, and its mass when empty is 75 tonnes. The orbiter is made out of aluminium alloy which is covered with thermal insulation. The insulation tiles for the upper parts of the wings and the fuselage are flexible, while hard silica tiles are used on the bottom of the wings and the lower part of the fuselage. The nose, the leading edge of the wings and the undercarriage are covered with reinforced carbon tiles.

The three Space Shuttle Main Engines (SSMEs) are at the back of the orbiter, along with the two Orbital Manoeuvring System (OMS) engines. The SSMEs, developed by the Rocketdyne company, are the most complex rocket engines ever to have been built. They are also the most powerful cryogenic liquid fuel engines constructed to date. They operate at a high pressure for good performance both on the ground and high above the Earth.

The turbines are driven by gases at high pressure generated in a precombustion chamber. After passing through the turbines, these gases are then injected into the main combustion chamber. This operates at a pressure of 20·7 megapascals for a nominal thrust level of 2·09 meganewtons in a vacuum. The thrust from the engine can be adjusted down to 65% of the nominal value during the supersonic phase of the flight, and up to 109% for certain missions where a higher performance is required.

Manned Manoeuvring Unit (MMU). The MMU enables an astronaut to move about around the orbiter or to rendezvous with other space vehicles. It is like an armchair, 1·25 metres high, 0·83 metres wide, and 1·21 metres deep when its arms are deployed to the maximum, and its mass, when empty, is 102 kg. The MMU fixes onto the back of a spacesuit in two places. It has 24 small nozzles each of which produces a thrust of 7·6 newtons by ejecting nonpolluting nitrogen contained in two high pressure tanks. The astronaut has two manual controls so that he can turn freely in all directions and move at speeds of about 20 metres per second. There is enough nitrogen in the tanks for the astronaut to travel several times around the orbiter or to make two return trips between the orbiter and another space vehicle. The nitrogen tanks are usually refilled on the ground, but the operation can also be accomplished on the orbiter.

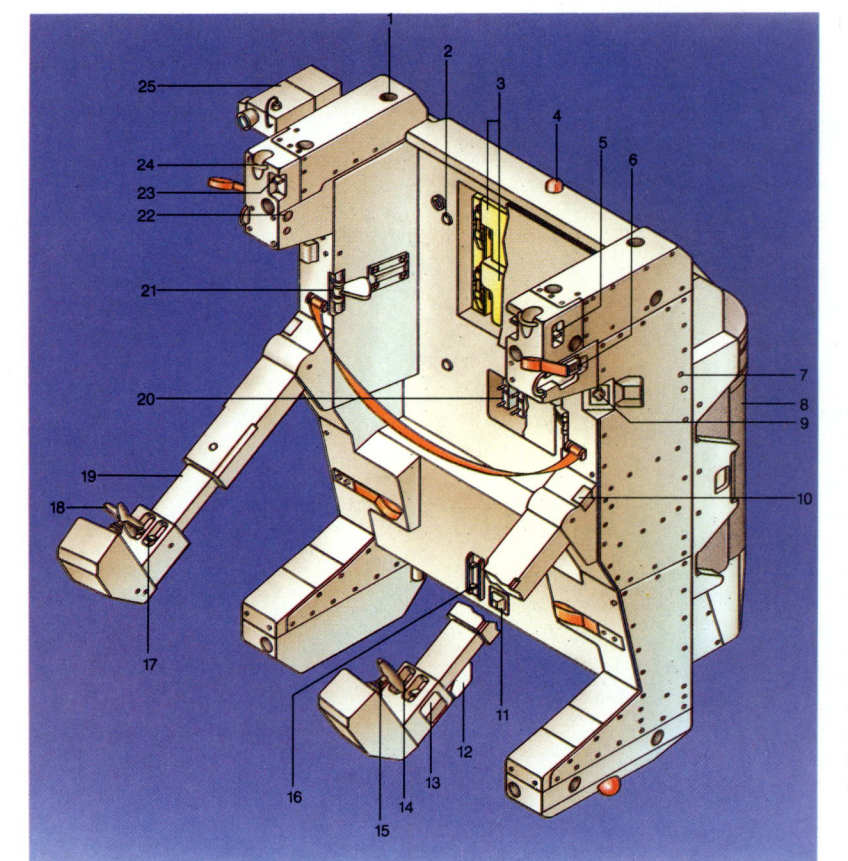

1 nozzle for nitrogen jet (24 small thrusters, each with a thrust of 7.6 newtons)
2 point of contact between the MMU and the spacesuit (four)
3 silver-zinc batteries (16.8 volts, 752 watts)
4 position light (three)
5 switch for the position lights
6 valve for refilling the fuel tank (two)
7 point for fixing auxiliary equipment (three on each side)
8 fuel tank, made of aluminium reinforced with Kevlar (two tanks each containing 5.9 kilograms of nitrogen gas)
9 knob to control the flow during refilling with nitrogen gas
10 arm deployment clip (two)
11 external electrical connector
12 joystick to control the angle of the arm
13 joystick to control the length of the arm
14 switch for the three gyroscopes
15 joystick to control the movement of the MMU
16 exterior electrical switch
17 switch for the navigation and propulsion system
18 joystick to control rotation
19 adjustable arm (two)
20 safety fuses (eight)
21 system to fix the spacesuit to the MMU (two)
22 fuel tank manometer (two)
23 main electrical switch (two)
24 ring to remove the spacesuit from the MMU (two)
25 automatic television camera

After the ET has been jettisoned, the OMS is used to put the orbiter into its final orbit, and subsequently to take it out of orbit, that is to deorbit it. Each of the two OMS engines can produce a thrust of 27 kilonewtons, using monomethylhydrazine (MMH) and nitrogen peroxide. These engines can increase the velocity of a fully laden orbiter by 305 metres per second. Supplementary fuel tanks can be added if a higher orbit is desired.

The Reaction Control System (RCS) uses the same fuels. It consists of three groups of twelve engines and two fine control, or vernier, engines. One group of thrusters is at the front, and one at each side of the rear of the fuselage.

The central part of the orbiter consists of the cargobay, where the payloads are carried. It has a diameter of 4·56 metres and a length of 18 metres, enough room therefore for a coach or Greyhound bus. Two doors enable the cargobay to be completed emptied in space. These doors are opened once the shuttle is in orbit, and their inside walls are covered with radiators to direct excess heat produced by the orbiter's systems away into space. The payloads are attached at the back of the cargobay, and the Remote Manipulator System (RMS) is fixed along the port side. The RMS, designed and built by a Canadian firm, Spar Aerospace, is 15 metres long and has three hinged joints so that its tip can move in all directions (with six degrees of freedom). Television cameras monitor its movement which is controlled by an astronaut from the upper flight deck of the crew's quarters; the control console is adjacent to the cargobay window. The RMS is invaluable when deploying or recovering payloads in space, and when building structures outside the space shuttle. A second arm can be mounted symmetrically, and operated independently.

The front part of the orbiter contains the crew's living and working quarters. It is split into two parts, the upper flight deck where the pilot performs his duties and where the control systems are, and an intermediate deck comprising the sleeping bunks, galley, washroom, avionics systems and the pressurised airlock allowing access to space. A lower flight deck contains various pieces of equipment such as water pumps and air purification systems. This volume (71·5 cubic metres) contains all that up to seven astronauts need for missions lasting up to 10 days.

Fuel cells consume oxygen and hydrogen to produce the electrical energy required by the orbiter and its crew. Each cell produces power of between 2 and 7 kilowatts continuously; this can be increased to 12 kilowatts for short periods of time. The total amount of energy available is 1530 kilowatt hours on each space mission. During the ascent phase, hydraulic energy controls the main SSMEs; during reentry, it controls the flaps, airbrakes, landing gear and the wheel brakes. Three Auxiliary Power Units (APUs) operated only during the launch and reentry phases of the mission supply the necessary energy.

The orbiter's avionics systems are very complex, and are centred on five multipurpose computers. Different guidance systems cover the various stages of the mission, from the rocket launcher (inertial navigation), to orbital navigation (star sensors) and aeroplane navigation (Tactical Air Navigation (Tacan) or Microwave Scan Beam Landing System (MSBLS)), as well as manual piloting. The flight control system has both manual and autopilot modes of operation.

The orbiter's life support system controls the crew's working and living environment, including treating the air by filtering out carbon dioxide, and controlling the cabin temperature.

Jean-Claude Bouillot

Extra Vehicular Activity (EVA). An astronaut's EVA forms a momentous, yet normal, part of his work aboard the orbiter. It involves several systems. The airlock is the link between the interior of the space shuttle and the exterior environment, the vacuum and the radiation of space. It is a cylinder 2·1 metres long and 1·6 metres in diameter, with two airtight bulkheads. Depending on the mission, it can be placed in the orbiter's cabin, in the cargobay, or in the tunnel joining the orbiter to a manned module (for example, Spacelab) placed in the cargobay. The astronaut who intends to carry out EVA uses an Extravehicular Mobility Unit (EMU) which includes a spacesuit, an independent life support system, display and command modules, and also, as this photograph shows, a Manned Manoeuvring Unit (MMU). This enables the astronaut to move about in space, and carries enough tools to allow him to work effectively.

The astronaut's spacesuit is made from layers of Nylon, Dacron and Kevlar. Together with its subsystems it weighs 39 kilograms and should last about 15 years. The independent life support system has a volume of 0·2 cubic metres and a mass of 73 kilograms. This is attached to the back of the upper part of the spacesuit and enables an astronaut to spend up to 7 hours outside the shuttle. It contains oxygen, rechargeable silver–zinc batteries, water for the cooling system and an air treatment system. There is a display and command system on the front of the spacesuit. This gives the astronaut information on the operational state of the life support systems, and enables him to talk with the crew inside the shuttle who are monitoring his progress. EVA usually also involves the Remote Manipulator System (RMS) which is seen at the top right of this picture. The RMS is operated from a console on the orbiter's upper flight deck (NASA).

The Payload Assist Module—Delta (PAM-D) System. Developed by McDonnell Douglas, this is kept in the cargobay and used to put satellites into orbit from the space shuttle. It consists of a solid fuel rocket engine capable of placing a satellite of 1·25 tonnes into a geostationary transfer orbit. The system is spring released near perigee of the desired orbit once the orbiter has been oriented correctly as shown in the diagram below right. The satellite perigee engine system is spin stabilised by first rotating it on a table situated in the lower part of the cradle. The moment of separation is chosen so that the perigee engine is fired up to 45 minutes after separation as it passes over the equator. In this way the rocket's exhaust gases do not pollute the cargobay or any other payloads in it.

The photograph below left shows the PAM-D launch of the Telesat 1 satellite on 10 April 1985 from the space shuttle, Discovery. The white blankets are for thermal insulation (NASA).

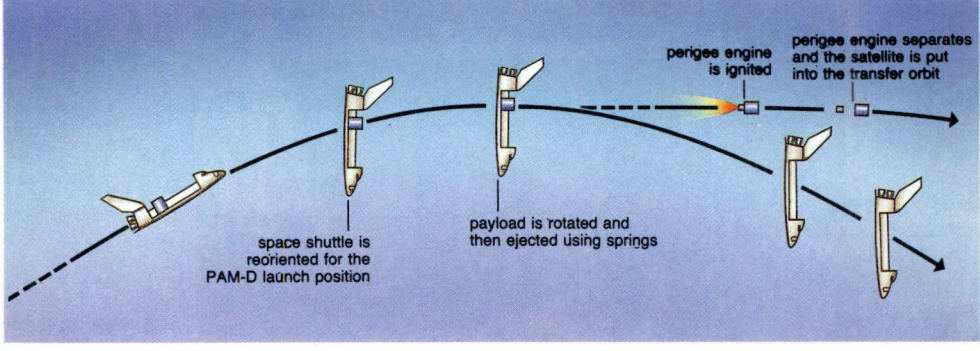

space shuttle is reoriented for the PAM-D launch position

payload is rotated and then ejected using springs

perigee engine is ignited

perigee engine separates and the satellite is put into the transfer orbit

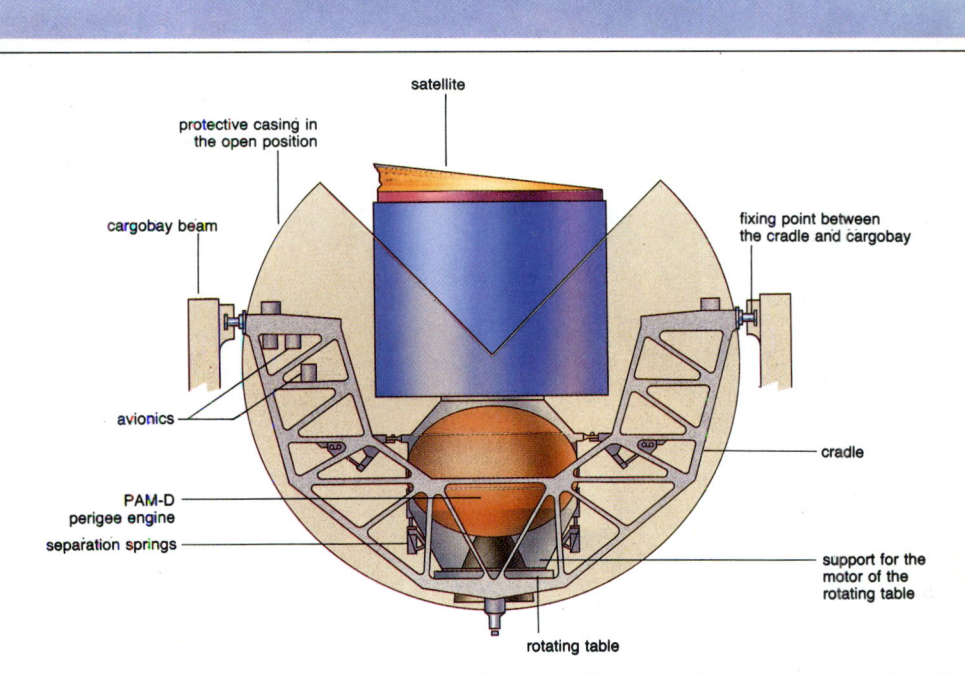

satellite

protective casing in the open position

cargobay beam

fixing point between the cradle and cargobay

avionics

cradle

PAM-D perigee engine

separation springs

support for the motor of the rotating table

rotating table

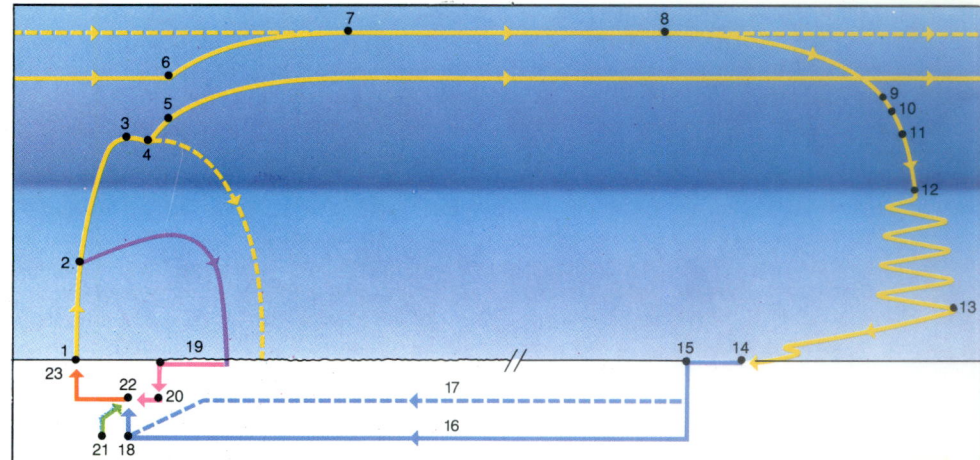

1 In the final stages of the countdown, all three main rocket engines are ignited by t−3.8 seconds; the two boosters are ignited at t=0 and the space shuttle lifts off at t+2.64 seconds

2 The two SRBs are jettisoned at t+2 minutes 7 seconds at an altitude of 45 kilometres when the space shuttle is travelling at Mach 4.5

3 The orbiter reaches an altitude of 130 kilometres at t+6 minutes 30 seconds and its velocity is Mach 15; it starts to descend

4 The SSMEs cut out at t+8 minutes 38 seconds; 16 seconds later, the ET is jettisoned at an altitude of 120 kilometres

5 The two OMS engines are ignited at t+9 minutes to put the orbiter into a low elliptical orbit; they burn for 3 minutes 24 seconds

6 After half an orbit, the OMS engines are reignited at t+45 minutes 58 seconds to put the orbiter into a circular orbit

7 The OMS engines burn for only 36 seconds and the orbiter is now in a circular orbit at an altitude of at least 185 kilometres; any manoeuvres to be made by the orbiter are carried out using the RCS engines

8 After a space mission lasting between 5 and 30 days, the cargobay doors are closed again and the RCS engines rotate the orbiter into the reentry position

9 The OMS engines are ignited an hour and a quarter before touchdown time (tt) to deorbit the shuttle; they burn for 6 minutes

10 At tt−52 minutes the orbiter prepares for reentry

11 The reentry phase commences at tt−30 minutes at an altitude of 122 kilometres at Mach 22.4; the angle of reentry lies between 28 and 38 degrees

12 The orbiter experiences its maximum temperatures at tt−20 minutes at an altitude of 70 kilometres at Mach 19.6

13 The orbiter glides back to Earth, having made four 'S shaped' circuits, from an altitude of 25 kilometres at Mach 2.5

14 The orbiter lands at a velocity of 345 kilometres per hour

15 The first operations on return from space, including decontamination and fuel removal, are carried out on the runway

16 The orbiter is towed back to the launch preparation centre

17 If the landing is not made at the next launch site, the orbiter is carried there on the back of a Boeing 747 aircraft

18 The new payload is installed at the preparation centre

19 The two boosters are recovered

20 After being restored and reassembled, the booster rockets are taken to the shuttle assembly hall

21 The new ET is delivered to the shuttle assembly hall

22 The ET, the two SRBs and the orbiter are mounted vertically onto the 'crawler' (the mobile launch platform) in the shuttle assembly hall

23 The crawler takes the space shuttle to the launch area and the countdown for the next mission can begin

t: time zero for the countdown procedure, just 2.6 seconds before lift off
tt: touchdown time

Space shuttle mission timetable. The phases numbered in bold type relate to the photographs (NASA).

7

7

15

13

22

17

Rocket launchers

The USA

Until the middle of the 1950s, the main interest shown by the USA in rockets was military. The first satellite launchers were accordingly based on short range missiles. The US Navy's artillery missile, Redstone, formed the basis of the small three stage launcher, Vanguard, and the first US satellite was put into orbit by the US Army's Jupiter C rocket in February 1958.

The fact that the three American armed forces and the aeronautical construction industry all developed missiles independently meant that there were many missiles available for space applications. The Vanguard rocket, which always had a small launch capacity, was soon replaced by the Scout rocket. This was developed from the middle of 1958 by Vought under a joint contract with NASA and the Department of Defense to produce an effective launcher from existing products. All its stages used solid fuel; it went into service in 1960 in a three stage version, and a four stage version was subsequently produced.

The US developed both intermediate range ballistic missiles (IRBM) with a range of 2400 kilometres and intercontinental ballistic missiles (ICBM) with a range of 6000 kilometres. In the first category, the US Army had the Jupiter, and the US Navy the (solid fuel) Polaris, while the US Air Force developed the Thor rocket. Both the Jupiter and the Thor used the same Rocketdyne engine, operating on liquid oxygen and paraffin oil (kerosene) with a thrust of 712 kilonewtons. Their designs were very similar, and both had successful maiden flights in 1957 within a few months of each other. The Jupiter, built by Chrysler, had a short life, whereas the Thor rocket was the forerunner of the large Thor Delta family of launchers; later called the Delta rocket, this became NASA's standard medium range launcher. After several impressive developments it is still in service today, more than 30 years after its first flight.

The long range missiles developed during the same period also gave rise to launchers. The Convair Atlas, a single stage missile fuelled by liquid oxygen and paraffin oil, had the unique feature of jettisoning its main engines in flight; constructed out of light metallic components, it could place 1·5 tonnes into a low Earth orbit. Another intercontinental missile, the Titan, developed by Martin Marietta for the US Air Force, was a two stage rocket which used storable liquid fuels, nitrogen peroxide and UDMH. The first successful flight of the Atlas rocket took place in 1957, and that of the Titan in 1959. The Atlas became NASA's heavy launcher for unmanned missions with the addition of Agena upper stages and, more importantly, from 1963 onwards the Centaur stage; the Centaur was the first upper stage to use liquid hydrogen and liquid oxygen. The Atlas rocket was involved in a number of American 'firsts', including their first manned orbital flight.

The Scout family of launchers. The Scout launcher, constructed by the LTV Aerospace and Defense Company, is a lightweight, four stage solid fuel launcher. Since 1960, over a hundred examples have been built of the nine different versions; the ninth version, Scout G1, went into service in 1979. The payload housing is situated above the third stage. The head itself has a diameter of 0·86 metres and a useful volume of 1 cubic metre.

The Scout can be launched by both NASA and the US Department of Defense at the Wallops Island Flight Center for medium inclination (38°) orbits; at the Western Test Range, Vandenberg in California, for missions in polar orbits; or from the equatorial platform of San Marco, established by Italy off the coast of Kenya. The Scout rocket is still used by the US Navy to launch its Transit navigational satellites.

NASA used the Scout launcher to promote international cooperation and, as a result, twenty small European scientific satellites were launched free of charge, with the sole proviso that the Americans could share in the scientific results. Five of these launches were carried out for ESRO, the forerunner of ESA, and fifteen for various European countries.

The photograph on the right shows the one hundred and third launch of a Scout on 27 June 1983, from Vandenberg. The photograph on the far right shows the configuration of the payload in the head of the rocket, when two US navigational satellites, called Oscar, were launched from Vandenberg on 2 August 1985 (LTV Corporation).

The Titan was the specialised launcher of the US Air Force, and so was used primarily as a military launcher. Its robust structure allowed it to have large solid fuel boosters attached, substantially increasing its capacity, so it became the intermediate heavy launcher between the Atlas and the Saturn. It had Agena and Centaur upper stages and, later, the Transtage. This uses fuels which can be reignited, enabling the launcher to inject satellites directly into geostationary orbits. Titan's military programme has been to place large observation satellites into orbit, considerably increasing the US Air Force's reliability and decreasing its susceptibility to radio interference. Titan III had its maiden flight in 1964, and the 34D version is still in service today. The space shuttle boosters are based on the Titan III design.

The range of Saturn launchers is the only one which has been developed purely for the civil market. Although it is true that the original research was carried out by Wernher von Braun and the military, from 1958 the development of Saturn I was undertaken at NASA's Marshall Space Flight Center at Huntsville, Alabama. It was subsequently manufactured by Chrysler. The second stage S IV was built by McDonnell Douglas and powered by a Rocketdyne J2 liquid oxygen and liquid hydrogen engine.

Work began on the Saturn V launcher in 1957. Its maiden flight occurred on 9 November 1967 when it placed 126 tonnes into orbit. Its last flight took place more than five years later, on 14 May 1973, when it put Skylab into orbit.

Jean-Claude Bouillot

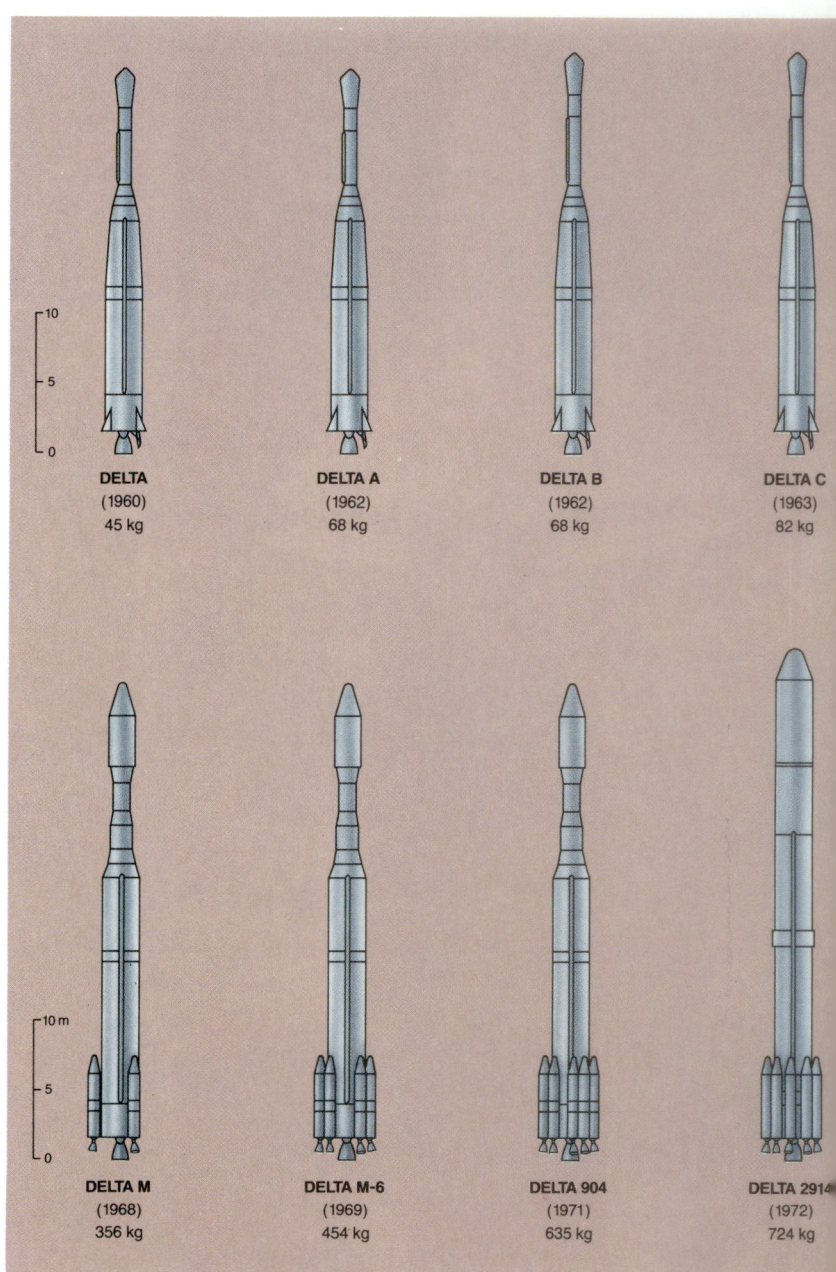

DELTA (1960) 45 kg   DELTA A (1962) 68 kg   DELTA B (1962) 68 kg   DELTA C (1963) 82 kg

DELTA M (1968) 356 kg   DELTA M-6 (1969) 454 kg   DELTA 904 (1971) 635 kg   DELTA 2914 (1972) 724 kg

Inclination	Payload mass (kilograms)								
38°	59	76	87	103	122	143	185	193	208
90°	45	59	68	80	94	116	148	156	166
2,9°						151	198	203	220

Version	First stage	Second stage	Third stage	Fourth stage
Scout X-1 (1960)	Algol IC	Castor I	Antares I	Altair I
Scout X-2 (1962)	Algol ID	Castor I	Antares II	Altair I
Scout X-3 (1963)	Algol IIA	Castor I	Antares II	Altair I
Scout X-4 (1964)	Algol IIB	Castor I	Antares II	Altair II
Scout A-1 (1965)	Algol IIB	Castor II	Antares II	Altair II
Scout B-1 (1965)	Algol IIB	Castor IIA	Antares IIA	Altair IIIA
Scout D-1 (1972)	Algol IIIA	Castor IIA	Antares IIA	Altair IIIA
Scout F-1 (1974)	Algol IIIA	Castor IIA	Antares IIB	Altair IIIA
Scout G-1 (1979)	Algol IIIA	Castor IIA	Antares IIIA	Altair IIIA

The evolution of the Scout launcher. The first Scout was launched on 1 July 1960. Since then its performance has been constantly improved. The table above gives the increase in the payload mass which can be put into a circular orbit at an altitude of 555 kilometres, for various orbital inclinations. These are 2·9° (equatorial orbit, launched from San Marco), 38° (launched from Wallops Island) and 90° (launched from Vandenberg).

Principal characteristics of the Scout G1 launcher. The launch mass of this rocket, which stands 23 metres high, is 21·7 tonnes. The casings of the first and second stage engines are made of steel, while that of the third stage is made of Kevlar, and the fourth uses glass fibre and epoxy resin. The Scout was the first solid fuel launcher to put a payload into orbit, and it has a very high success rate (95%). Between 25 September 1967 and 11 October 1975, there were 37 consecutive successful flights.

Stage	Height (metres)	Diameter (metres)	Total mass (tonnes)	Mass of solid fuel (tonnes)	Thrust in a vacuum (kilonewtons)
First (Algol IIIA)	9.07	1.14	14.215	12.712	484
Second (Castor IIA)	6.19	0.79	4.433	3.724	285
Third (Antares IIIA)	2.18	0.76	1.394	1.286	83
Fourth (Altair IIIA)	1.48	0.51	0.301	0.273	26

The Delta launcher. This is NASA's basic launcher, based on the Thor medium range missile with upper stages from the Vanguard rocket. From 1960 to 1982, 34 different versions appeared as the launcher was improved and adapted to suit both the changing market and the desire to put larger payloads into orbit. Production was practically suspended when NASA decided to encourage the use of the space shuttle as a launcher, but the rocket is still built for military purposes.

Several versions of the Delta launcher are illustrated on the left alongside details of their launch capacity for a payload put into a geostationary transfer orbit. The launcher has a first stage using liquid oxygen and paraffin oil, a second stage using liquid fuels with the payload housing above it, and, if the mission requires, a third, solid fuel stage.

The last version of the Delta, the 3920/PAM, was 35·35 metres tall with a uniform diameter of 2·4 metres. Following the usual designation, the first number represents the type of first stage, the second, the number of boosters, the third the type of second stage, and the last the nature of the third stage. In the case of the Delta 3920/PAM, the first stage is the Extended Long Tank Thor, standing 22·4 metres tall, containing 80·3 tonnes of fuels propelling a Rocketdyne RS 27 engine, and producing a thrust of 912 kilonewtons, using nine Castor 4 boosters. Each of these is 1 metre in diameter and contains 9·4 tonnes of solid fuel. At take-off, six of them are ignited at the same time as the first stage; the other three are ignited when the first six have burnt out. The first stage burns for 224 seconds. The second stage contains 6 tonnes of liquid fuel for an Aerojet rocket engine. This stage is placed inside a cylindrical skirt which remains attached to the first stage when it separates from the rocket. The second stage burns for 430 seconds.

Above this stage is a spin table which is activated before the separation and ignition of the third stage. In the 3920/PAM, the third stage is replaced by the Payload Assist Module–Delta (PAM-D), which is also the perigee propulsion system used from the space shuttle, and which burns for 85 seconds.

The payload housing is integrated with the second stage and an inertial guidance system. After the engine has finished burning, the second stage continues to guide the launcher; it is not jettisoned for another 11 minutes, after the Payload Assist Module has been spun up.

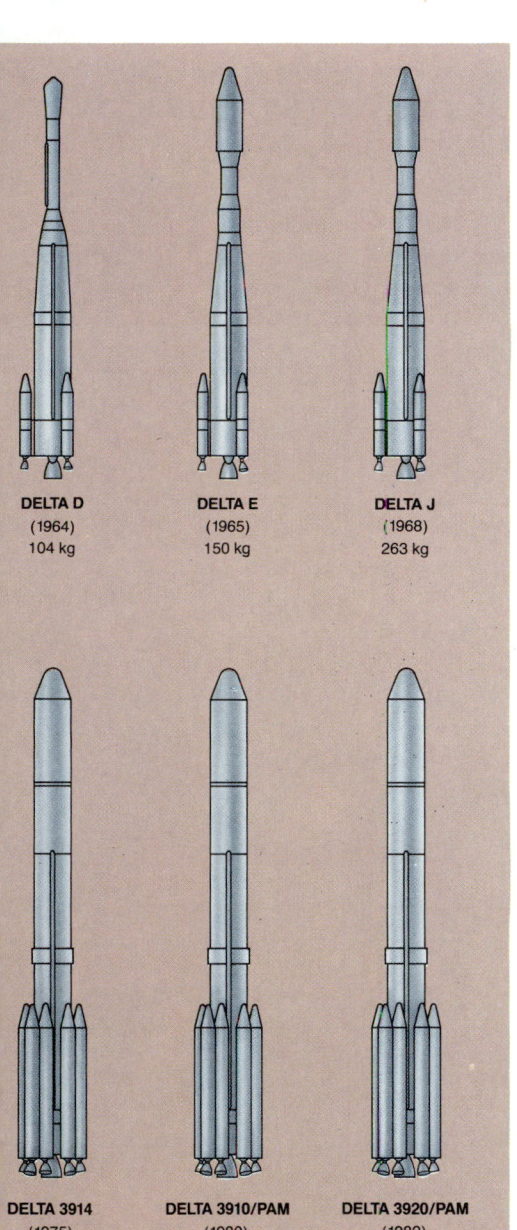

DELTA D (1964) 104 kg — DELTA E (1965) 150 kg — DELTA J (1968) 263 kg

DELTA 3914 (1975) 954 kg — DELTA 3910/PAM (1980) 1 154 kg — DELTA 3920/PAM (1982) 1 312 kg

The Delta 3914. The Delta launcher has had an exceptional success rate. There have been only 11 failures out of 177 launches and a series of 43 consecutive successes since 1977. It has also been associated with several space 'firsts', in particular the launches of the first geostationary satellite, Syncom 1, in 1963, the first Intelsat satellite, Early Bird, in 1965, several satellites in the Explorer series, the Pioneer interplanetary probes, the Intelsat II and III satellites, and a number of Sun synchronous satellites in the TIROS and Landsat series.

The Delta launcher contributed much to the growth of the European space interest by launching ESRO's satellites as well as those of different individual nations. For example, Delta rockets launched HEOS A for ESRO in 1968, four Skynet satellites for the UK from 1969 to 1974, the scientific satellite TD 1 for ESRO in 1972, and the Franco-German Symphonie telecommunications satellites in 1974 and 1975. In 1975, Delta launched ESA's scientific satellite Cos B, and the scientific satellite GEOS. The experimental telecommunications satellite OTS 1 (Orbital Test Satellite) was to have been put in orbit in 1977. However, during the same year Meteosat was successfully launched, and GEOS 2 and OTS 2 were launched using Deltas in 1978. The European scientific satellites IRAS and Exosat were also successfully launched, in 1982 and 1983 respectively, by Delta launchers.

The photograph on the right was taken on 11 May 1978, at Cape Canaveral, during the launch of ESA's first telecommunications satellite OTS 2 by a Delta 3914 (ESA).

The Atlas launcher. The Atlas ballistic missile was transformed into the SLV 3 (Standardized Launch Vehicle). Its original design was a one and a half stage rocket, with a diameter of 3·05 metres, propelled by three liquid oxygen and paraffin oil (kerosene) engines; the central engine develops a thrust of 267 kilonewtons and the two enormous lift-off engines each produce a thrust of 840 kilonewtons. In addition, there are two small vernier engines each generating a thrust of 2·3 kilonewtons. All five engines are ignited at take-off. After 157 seconds, the lift-off engines and their frame are jettisoned, considerably reducing the launcher's mass. The launcher then continues its ascent under power from the central engine, steered by the two vernier engines. The Atlas can be used with a number of upper stages, notably with the liquid fuel Agena stage, built by Lockheed. The SLV 3A version can put 1·23 tonnes into a geostationary transfer orbit, or, with the OV 1 solid fuel stage, two 1·23 tonne satellites into a low Earth, circular orbit. In the SLV 3D version, it can also use the cryogenic Centaur stage. The last version of the launcher to be built, the Atlas G/Centaur D 1A, can put 2·36 tonnes into a geostationary transfer orbit. The total height of this vehicle is 42 metres and it weighs about 163 tonnes at take-off.

Nearly 600 Atlas rockets in various versions have been built, of which about 500 have been launched since 1957. Outdated missiles have been transformed into the Atlas F version and used for launching payloads into low Earth orbits. Amongst the many launches performed by Atlas, the most notable was that of the Mercury capsule containing John Glenn, the first American to orbit the Earth, in February 1962.

The photograph on the left shows the launch of the Mariner IV interplanetary probe, on 28 November 1964, using an Atlas Agena rocket. One of the two lift-off engines is clearly evident, as are flames from the tiny vernier engine making an angle to the launcher's axis. This SLV 3A version stands 36 metres tall (NASA).

The Atlas Centaur (right). The first flight of an Atlas Centaur rocket took place in 1962. By the beginning of 1986, 65 Atlas Centaurs had been launched, with only ten failures. Of these ten, six can be directly attributed to the Centaur stage. This is because a launch from Cape Canaveral requires a ballistic phase and then reignition of the engines as the vehicle crosses the equator, an intricate procedure for a cryogenic stage.

Amongst the missions carried out with an Atlas Centaur rocket are the scientific Mariner 6, 7 and 9 missions to Mars, Pioneer 10 and Pioneer 11 towards the edge of the solar system, and Pioneer Venus. The photograph (right) shows the launch of Surveyor 5 towards the Moon, on 8 September 1967 (NASA).

The Centaur stage. The Centaur stage is constructed by the same company which produces the Atlas, namely the Convair division of General Dynamics. It is a cryogenic rocket with a structure that is similar to the Atlas. Made of ultrathin steel sheets, only 0·36 millimetres thick, it has to be stored under pressure to prevent deformation.

The photograph above shows the assembly of Atlas Centaur launchers in the General Dynamics factory at San Diego, California. Two Centaur stages are visible in the foreground; the second one is being fitted with two Pratt & Whitney RL 10 engines, each producing a thrust of 73·5 kilonewtons, which can be reignited during the flight.

This rocket was initially conceived as a test programme before the development of the large cryogenic upper stages of the Saturn rockets. It has also been used as an upper stage for a Titan rocket, for the launch of the German solar probes, Helios, the Martian Viking probes, and Voyager. The Centaur stage was also chosen by NASA as an upper stage to be launched from the space shuttle. A large diameter version was developed for a launch planned for 1986, but this was abandoned after the Challenger accident (General Dynamics).

Heads and payloads for the Atlas Centaur rocket launcher. There are three types of heads which can be used, the largest of which is needed for major telecommunications satellites. In addition, there is a double launch system which is capable of placing two satellites of 1·1 tonnes into a geostationary transfer orbit. Dimensions are given in metres.

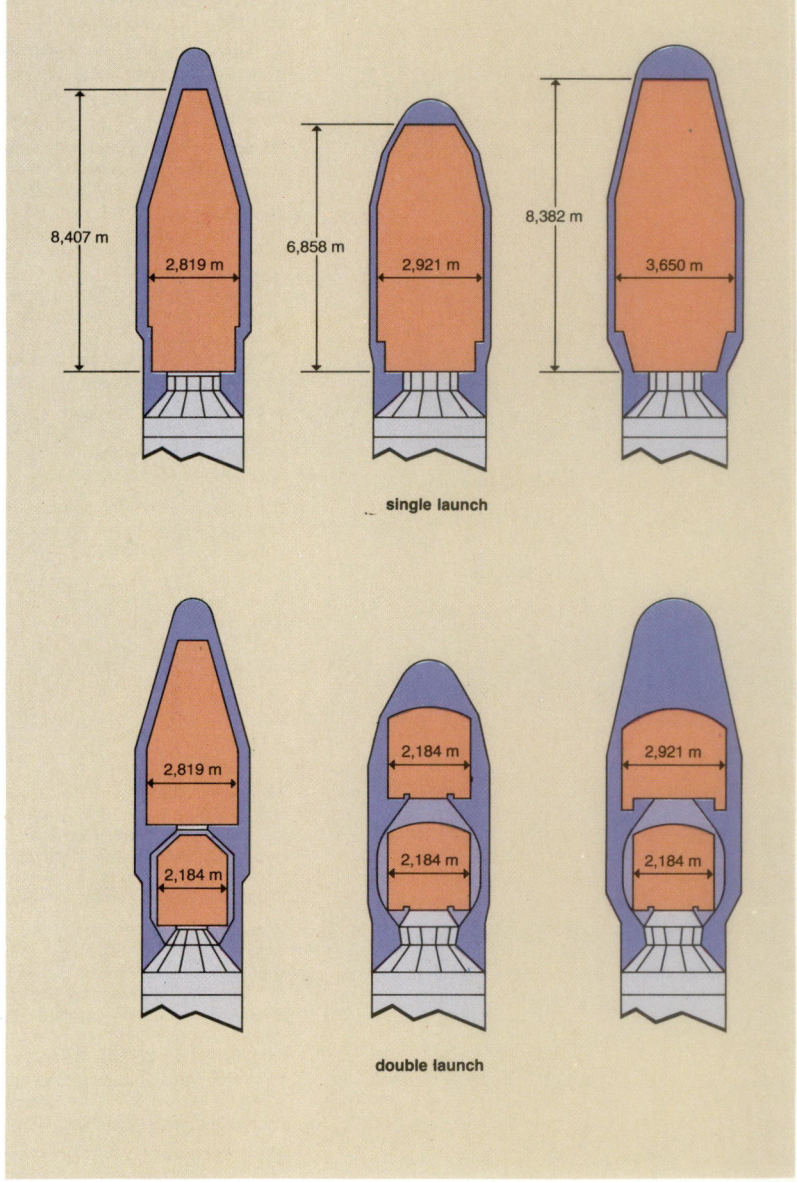

single launch

double launch

The Titan launcher. The Titan launcher originated in a ballistic missile programme begun in 1955, the first Titan II missile being launched in 1962. The Titan is basically a two stage vehicle using liquid fuels (UDMH and aerozine 50). In 1962, Martin Marietta began work to convert the missile into a launcher, the Titan III, which also had two boosters. There have been several versions of this rocket, the most recent being the Titan 34D.

The Titan has been used exclusively by the military as a heavy launcher, for example for the US Air Force's large military reconnaissance satellites. The Titan III Centaur configuration has, however, been used for some scientific missions.

The Titan III lifts off using only its boosters, which burn for 2 minutes 10 seconds before they are exhausted and the first stage engines are ignited. This means that the nozzles on the first stage can be designed to function in the space vacuum, improving their overall performance. The second stage is ignited immediately the first stage fuel has been consumed.

The Titan III has never been used for commercial missions despite recent proposals, notably by Intelsat. All its versions have had a high success rate, with the exception of the new Titan 34D version which had two consecutive failures in August 1985 and April 1986.

The photograph on the left was taken during the launch of the Voyager 2 spacecraft by a Titan III E Centaur in 1977. The launcher's very large head, with a diameter of 4·3 metres, dominates the photograph. The journey of Voyager 2 through the solar system culminated in dramatic photographs of Neptune and its moon, Triton, in August 1989 (NASA).

Configurations of the Titan 34 launcher (right). The basic components of the Titan 34 launcher are, from bottom to top, a liquid fuel stage flanked by two solid fuel boosters, an upper stage, and a head. The different combinations of these components enable the launcher to be adapted to accomplish a wide variety of missions. All types of orbits are possible, from a low Earth orbit to an interplanetary trajectory. Dimensions are in metres.

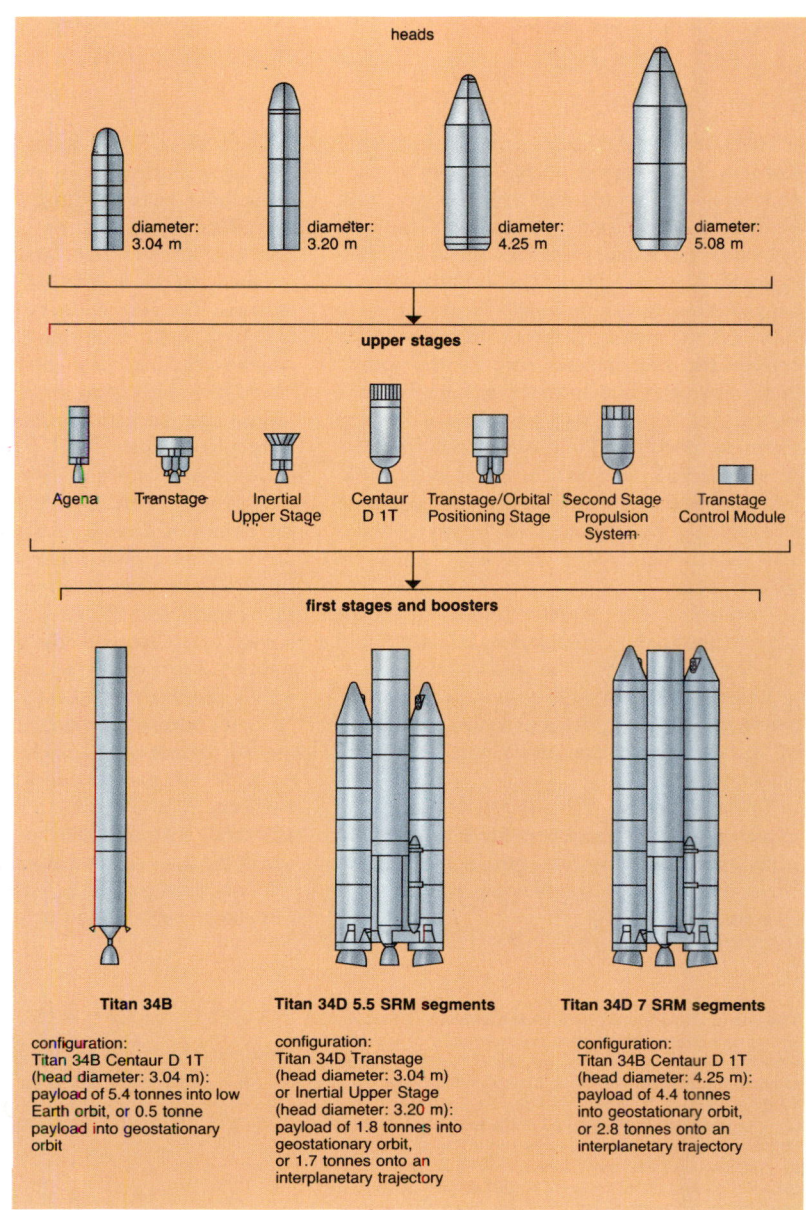

Titan 34D (left). This version of the Titan used two solid fuel boosters, each requiring five and a half 194 tonne segments of solid fuel. Each segment burns for 2 minutes. Guidance is performed by injecting nitrogen peroxide into the nozzle. The first stage has a diameter of 3·05 metres and is 22·25 metres tall. It carries 118 tonnes of fuel (nitrogen peroxide and UDMH) and is propelled by two rocket engines each delivering a thrust of 1·2 meganewtons. The second stage has the same diameter as the first, and carries 30 tonnes of fuel (nitrogen peroxide and UDMH); its thrust is 450 kilonewtons. In this version the third stage is the Inertial Upper Stage (IUS), a solid fuel stage developed for the space shuttle to replace the liquid fuel Transtage.

The Titan 34D has a take-off mass of 760 tonnes and can put 1·9 tonnes into a geostationary orbit and 12·5 tonnes into a polar orbit at 180 kilometres altitude. A new version, the Titan 34D 7, is currently being developed. This consists of lengthened boosters containing seven segments of solid fuel (Martin Marietta).

The Saturn launcher. The Saturn V launcher has a well deserved place in the history books. Even on its last mission, as a two stage version, in 1973, it was the heaviest and most prestigious of all conventional launch vehicles. It was the launcher of the greatest manned missions and the one which enabled man to walk on the Moon.

There are in fact three members of the Saturn family. The Saturn I, used for technological purposes, was composed of an S I first stage and an S IV second stage with six RL 10 engines (engines from the Centaur stage). Ten launches, all of which were successful, took place between 1961 and 1966, though four did not need the second stage. The Saturn IB was a new version of the Saturn I rocket, having a new first stage, the S IB, and a completely new cryogenic second stage based on the H2 engine, the S IVB. This 600 tonne launcher could place 20 tonnes into a low Earth orbit and was used nine times, five times for manned flights – the Apollo, Skylab and Apollo–Soyuz missions.

The Saturn V had the Saturn IVB stage as a third stage and two new lower stages: the first stage, S IC, contained 2140 tonnes of fuel for five F1 engines, each producing a thrust of 7 meganewtons; the second stage (S II) had five J2 engines. The Saturn V was used thirteen times and had a 100% success rate. Ten of its flights were for manned missions.

The photograph (right) shows the Saturn IB launcher chosen for the Apollo–Soyuz mission in 1975, the last time that a Saturn launch took place (NASA).

The USSR

The father of Soviet rocketry, Sergei Korolev, has summed up his country's space philosophy by stating that 'rockets are both weapons and instruments of science.' This indicates how the military and civil sectors overlap in Soviet space activities. The military share is hard to estimate, but probably lies around 60 to 70% of the total. Strategic considerations explain the predominant role of the armed forces in the space industry which, in turn, means that research into launchers is kept as secret as possible. The Soviets publish little information on their launchers and most of the information that is available has been obtained by analysing observations made by spy satellites and by comparing the data with American space systems.

Throughout its three decades of space activity, the Soviet Union has remained faithful to a strategy geared to the systematic conquest of near Earth space with a view to its permanent occupation by man, and to the exploration of distant space, the Moon and Venus in particular.

This strategy has throughout depended on improving existing launchers by using different versions of the same launcher, adding higher performance upper stages, and adopting the concept of modularity.

The scale of Soviet space activities is impressive. Low altitude, Sun synchronous or polar orbits have been used for telecommunications, surveillance, meteorology, Earth observation and anti-satellite test satellites, and also for manned flights in the Salyut and Mir space stations. The geostationary or 12 hour elliptical (Molniya) orbit is occupied principally by telecommunications and observation satellites. There have also been numerous interplanetary probes and spacecraft visiting other planets.

At present the USSR has a large range of non-reusable launchers, which can be split into four groups. As the Soviets have never revealed the names of their launchers, space experts in the West have given them the letters A, C, D and F. These launch automatic payloads, such as Cosmos and Progress, manned craft like Soyuz, or elements of the Salyut or Mir space stations. There is a fifth family, the B launchers, with a relatively small launch capability which have not been used since 1977. The C launcher was its replacement and this, along with the F launcher, has carried out nearly all the military missions. The Proton D launcher, the most powerful Russian launcher, is the only one which did not originate in a ballistic missile. It is not only used to put the Salyut, Modulny, and Mir space station modules into low Earth orbit,

The Proton launcher. Since 1965, the D, or Proton, launcher has put all Soviet heavy satellites, including the Salyut and Mir space stations, into orbit. It has throughout been launched from the Tyuratam space centre.

The Soviets began to promote Proton as a commercial launcher in 1988, in particular for the new generation of Inmarsat satellites. They offered to launch the satellites at a price of $24 million each, cheaper than both the US space shuttle and Ariane.

One advantage of the Proton launcher is that, unlike its rivals, it can place satellites directly into geostationary orbit. This obviates the need for an apogee motor (rights reserved).

The main families of Soviet launchers. The main Soviet launchers shown here are members of five different families, the A, B, C, D and F launchers. The most famous is the A, or Soyuz, launcher. Based on Sergei Korolev's Zemiorka rocket, this consists of four first stage boosters fixed to a central body, the second stage, with upper stages varying according to the type of mission. Each booster has an RD 107 liquid fuel (paraffin oil and liquid oxygen) rocket engine with four combustion chambers and four nozzles; two vernier engines are used to steer the launcher.

The RD 107 operates at a pressure of 6 megapascals and delivers a thrust of 1·02 meganewtons in a vacuum with a specific impulse of 314 seconds. The central body is fitted with a RD 108 engine which has a thrust of up to 960 kilonewtons in a vacuum and a longer combustion time than the RD 107. In its A2 configuration, the launcher was first used in the Voskhod flights at the beginning of the 1960s. It was fitted with a third stage which enabled it to put a maximum payload of 7·5 tonnes into a low Earth orbit. This stage was fitted with a liquid fuel engine which produced a thrust of 300 kilonewtons in vacuo for a specific impulse of 285 seconds. The A2 rocket is still used today to launch most of the Cosmos satellites and all the Soyuz spacecraft. The A2e version has a fourth stage for interplanetary missions. Because the Soviet launch sites are at high latitudes, the fourth stage can also be used to put a payload into orbit in the equatorial plane.

The B, or Cosmos, launcher is based on the two stage SS 4 Sandal missile. Between 1962 and 1973, this was mainly used in the B1 version for scientific and military missions. It could place from 280 to 600 kilograms into a low orbit around the Earth. After 144 successful missions it was replaced by the C launcher. Also called the Cosmos launcher, the C launcher is based on a medium range ballistic missile, the SS 5 Skean. This has a reignitable second stage and can reach very high orbits. It has a capacity of from 500 to 1500 kilograms in a low orbit. Since 1964, it has mainly been used for military missions and for multiple launches of three, five and now eight small satellites.

The D, or Proton, launcher is the only Soviet rocket not based on a military launcher. It was conceived at the beginning of the 1960s by Vladimir Chelomey, and its configuration (see right) and performance were long kept secret. The latest information indicates that the first stage consists of a central nitrogen peroxide tank, surrounded by six UDMH tanks, each with an RD 253 engine designed to produce a thrust of about 1·07 meganewtons in vacuo with a specific impulse of greater than 320 seconds. The second stage is fitted with four Semien Kosberg engines, each producing a thrust of 610 kilonewtons. This launcher can put 20 tonnes into low Earth orbit, from which the payload can be launched into a geostationary orbit or onto a trajectory to a planet of the solar system.

The launchers of the F series have two basic stages, and a third stage which depends on the type of mission. They are based on the intercontinental ballistic missile SS 9 Scarp. The F1r version could be used in an anti-satellite, or 'satellite killer', programme, or for ocean surveillance (drawings by Charles P. Vick, © 1987).

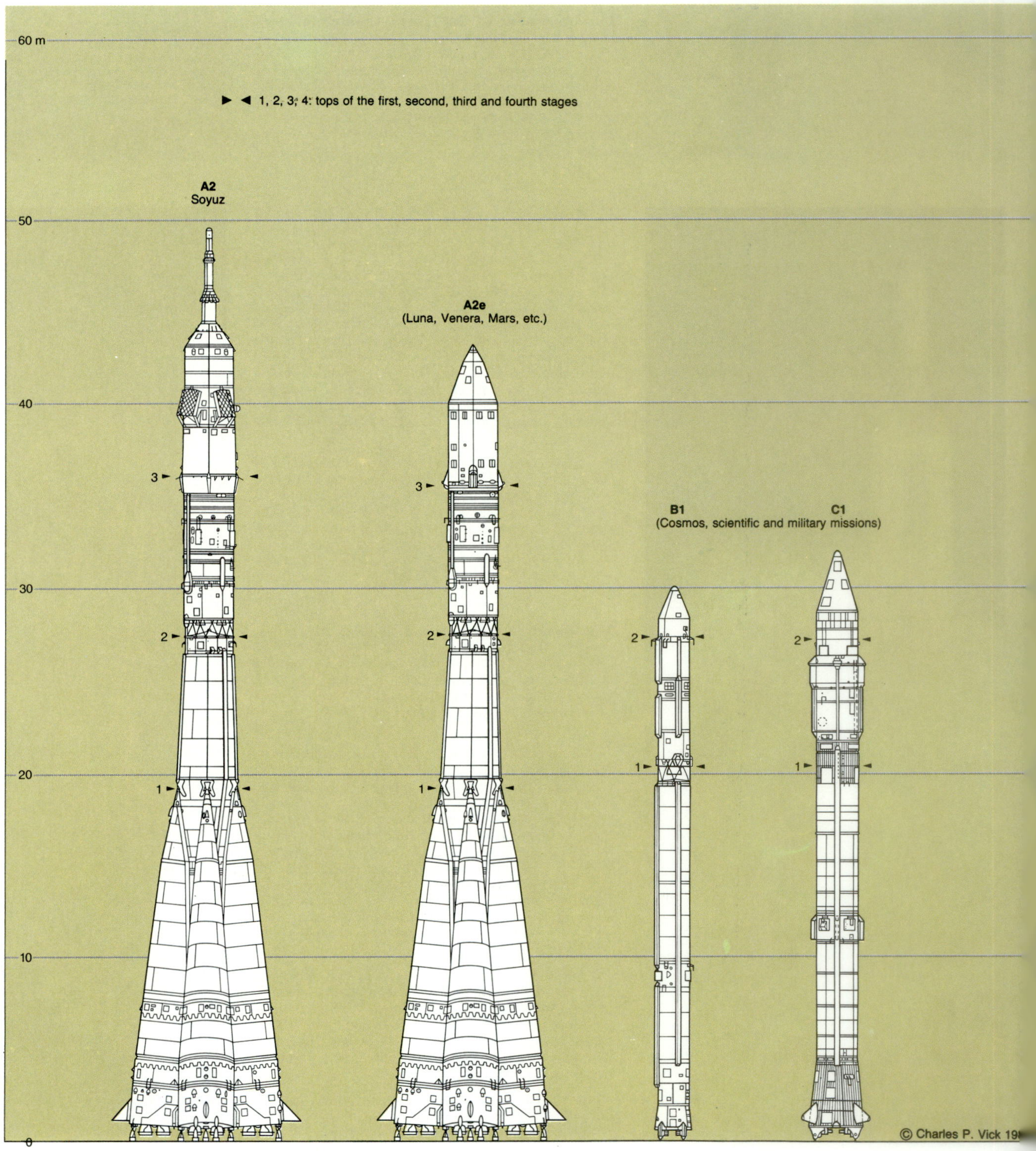

► ◄ 1, 2, 3, 4: tops of the first, second, third and fourth stages

A2 Soyuz

A2e (Luna, Venera, Mars, etc.)

B1 (Cosmos, scientific and military missions)

C1

© Charles P. Vick 198

but also to launch satellites into geostationary orbit and probes on to interplanetary trajectories (notable examples are Luna 24, and Venera 11 and 12).

All these rockets are very reliable, but they are slowly being replaced by a new generation of launchers capable of fulfilling such Soviet space ambitions in the 1990s as orbital missions around the Moon and flights to Mars and Venus. There are in addition three new non-reusable launchers. The Energia was tested on 15 May 1987, and there is also a shuttle look alike, called Buran, and a mini-shuttle. Furthermore, it is possible that the new Modulny space station module docked with Salyut 7 could be used to put cosmonauts into appropriate transfer orbits.

The different approaches to space policy in the USSR and the USA are apparent in the differences between the Soviet and American launchers. The Americans have always used very sophisticated systems, whilst the Soviets have kept things as simple as possible, while exploiting all their systems to the maximum.

The Soviets have also built and launched between six and seven times as many rockets as the Americans. However, the number of opera-

The A, or Soyuz launcher. This photograph shows how the Soyuz 31 and its A2 launcher are taken from the assembly buildings to the launch site at Baikonur.

Soyuz uses the first stage of the intercontinental SS 6 Sapwood missile developed by Sergei Korolev after the Second World War. This formed the basis of the A launcher (also called the R7, or Zemiorka) which launched Sputnik 1 on 4 October 1957 and later Sputnik 2 and Sputnik 3. Upper stages were then added to it, so that it could be used to take Soviet crews to Soyuz spacecraft already in orbit. It is the only Soviet launcher used today for manned flights, and is the best known of all Soviet launchers (ADN).

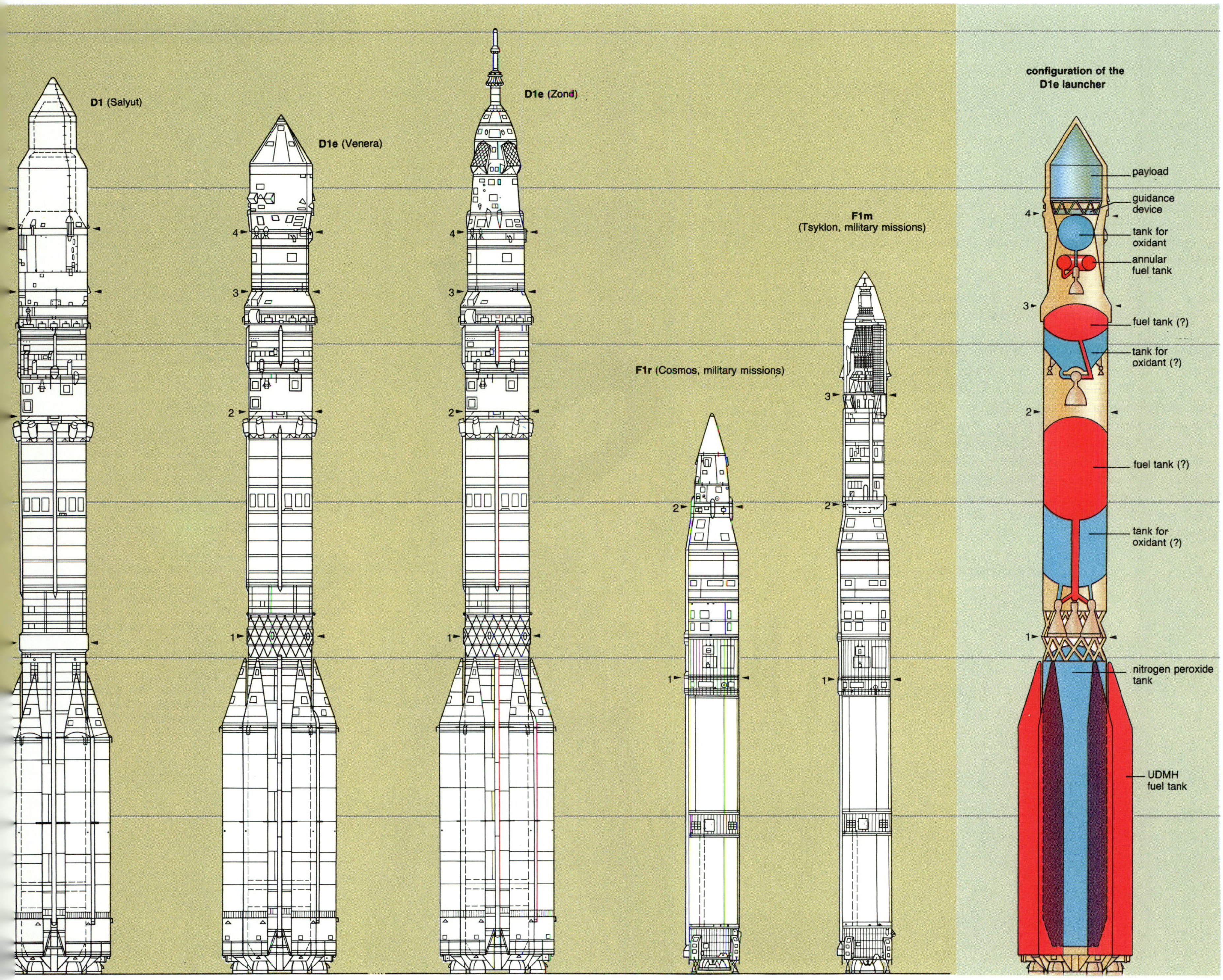

D1 (Salyut)

D1e (Venera)

D1e (Zond)

F1m (Tsyklon, military missions)

F1r (Cosmos, military missions)

configuration of the D1e launcher

- payload
- guidance device
- tank for oxidant
- annular fuel tank
- fuel tank (?)
- tank for oxidant (?)
- fuel tank (?)
- tank for oxidant (?)
- nitrogen peroxide tank
- UDMH fuel tank

The A2 launchers. The A2 launchers are transported to the launch site by a diesel locomotive and are erected on the launch pad (above, left). The launcher is surrounded by arms and service towers (above, centre) which move away at the moment of liftoff. All the rocket engines are ignited at once (right). The four booster rockets separate from the central body after burning for 118 seconds. Then the second stage rocket is ignited and burns for 244 seconds at full power, being guided by four small rocket engines.

The central body of the Soyuz launcher is 28 metres long, with a diameter of 3 metres. The diameter of the launcher plus its stabilisers is 10·3 metres. In these photographs the payloads are, from left to right, Soyuz T2 (launched in June 1980), Soyuz T6 (June 1982) and Soyuz T5 (May 1982) (Tass).

tional satellites that the two superpowers have at any given time is roughly the same because the Soviet payloads tend to have much shorter lifetimes.

It is possible that with the new generation of Soviet launchers, especially the Proton launcher, the USSR will in the future be able to offer commercial launches on the world market. The creation of the civil Glavkosmos agency bears this out. This new agency works closely with all the relevant Soviet ministries and administrations. In the 1990s it will be responsible for coordinating Soviet space activities in the fields of science, technology and agriculture. It will also manage commercial aspects of space, such as the sale of Soviet rockets, and manned spaceflights. A clear distinction is thus being made between the Soviet civil and military space operations.

Marie-Claude Canivet

The C launcher. The C or Cosmos launcher was developed by Mikhail Yangel and replaced the B launcher only after 144 successes. The only rocket launcher which has been launched from all three Soviet space centres, it is still being launched from Plesetsk and Kasputin Yar. The first stage uses two liquid fuel RD 216 engines, and has a diameter of 2·44 metres; it is about 19·3 metres tall. The second stage (right) is transported separately and assembled vertically onto the first stage (below, right). The second stage is about 7·9 metres long with a diameter of about 2·4 metres (right: APN; below, right: rights reserved; below: Tass).

Launchers and space shuttles currently being developed. In 1967, it was announced in the West that a new generation launcher, the G launcher, was being developed by the USSR. More powerful than the Saturn V, it would have been capable of putting 150 tonnes into a low Earth orbit. However, at the end of 1969, three catastrophic launch failures led the Soviets to abandon this design completely.

The new launcher that followed, Energia, can launch a large space station and should be able to place 100 tonnes into a low Earth orbit. The first stage alone is 61 metres tall. Four SL X16 boosters using liquid oxygen and paraffin oil (kerosene) are attached to a central cryogenic rocket fuelled by liquid oxygen and hydrogen. The thrust produced at take-off would be about 30 meganewtons.

The Soviets also have two reusable shuttles. A J1 'mini-shuttle', weighing about 15 tonnes, could be used to transport five or six cosmonauts and cargo between the ground and the space station. It might replace the Soyuz spacecraft and could be used for military missions requiring rapid intervention.

A two stage version of the Energia launcher, the 4K, could be used to launch the larger Soviet shuttle, Buran. This is similar in size to the American space shuttle but, instead of two solid fuel boosters and three rocket engines to assist take-off using liquid fuel stored in a huge external tank, the Russian shuttle has rocket engines, mounted on a central tank, which are jettisoned in flight. It is basically a glider, but with small engines on either side of the orbiter's tail section. These give it manoeuvrability and facilitate landing.

The first Buran was launched, without a crew, on 15 November 1988. The mass of this shuttle and its Energia launcher at take-off is more than 2000 tonnes for a 30 tonne payload carried in the shuttle's cargobay (drawings: Charles P. Vick, © 1987).

Energia and Buran. This photograph, taken in October 1988, shows the Buran space shuttle and the Energia heavy launcher assembled horizontally. They are being taken by four locomotives to the launch pad at Baikonur.

Buran is 16·45 metres high and 36·4 metres long, and has a wingspan of 23·9 metres. Its cargobay is 18·3 metres long, with a diameter of 4·7 metres. Its mass empty is 62 tonnes, while the maximum mass at launch is 105 tonnes and the maximum mass at touchdown 82 tonnes. The shuttle can carry up to 30 tonnes of payload at launch, with as much as 20 tonnes being returned to Earth.

Buran has two larger rocket engines which are used to put it into the correct orbit. Several of the smaller attitude control engines are visible as yellow dots at the front and rear of the fuselage (APN).

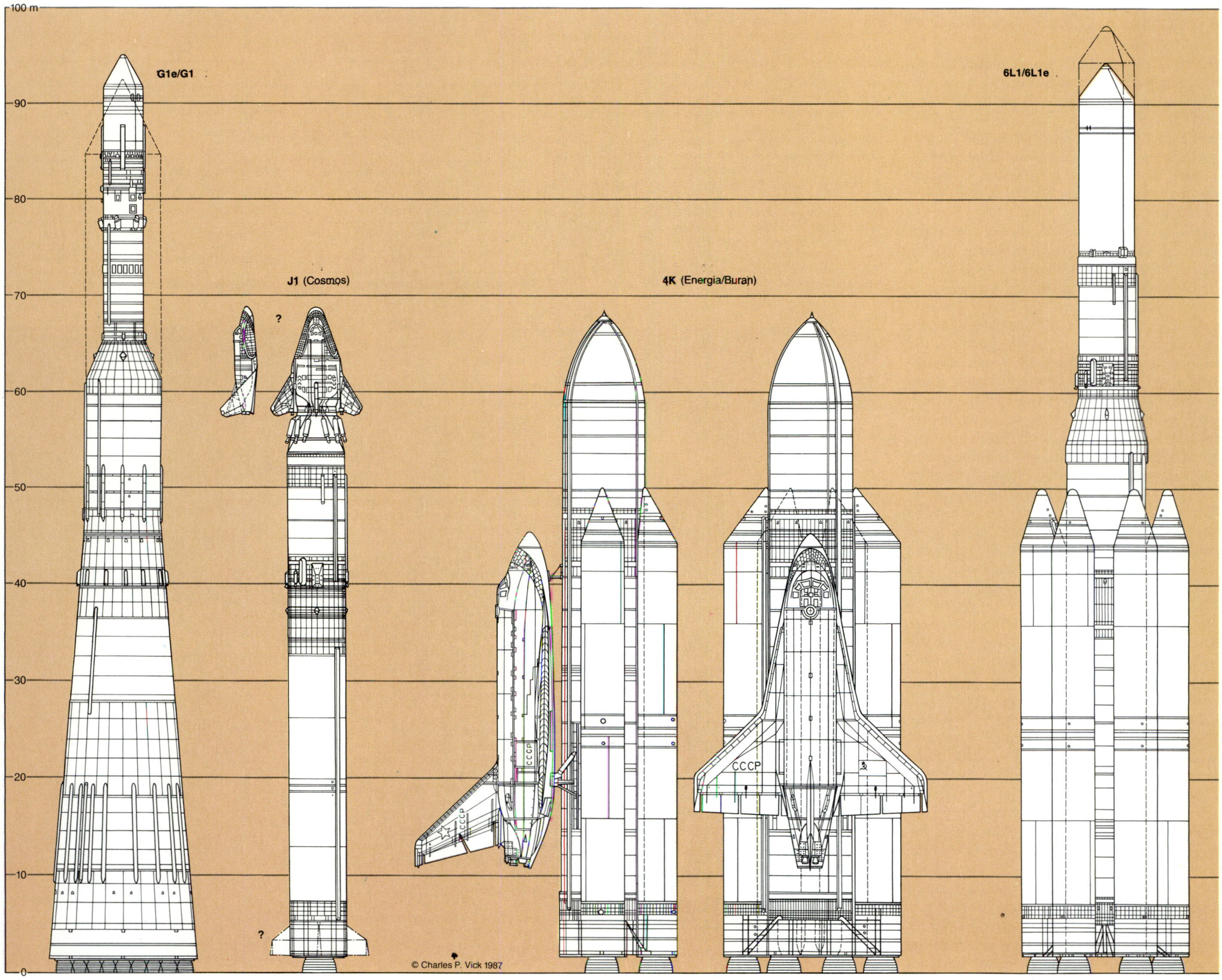

© Charles P. Vick 1987

Europe

The USA and the USSR were not alone in initiating research programmes into solid or liquid fuel rocket engines after the Second World War. Two European countries, Great Britain and France, also started similar programmes. Great Britain began work on a solid fuel rocket which culminated in the Skylark rocket. This was initially planned as a contribution to the International Geophysical Year (1957 to 1958). However, over four hundred examples of the 12 versions were ultimately launched. The last version had three stages and could launch a payload of 135 kilograms to an altitude of 800 kilometres, or a maximum payload of 350 kilograms onto a lower trajectory.

In the field of liquid fuel engines, the Royal Aircraft Establishment (RAE) entrusted the development of a single stage experimental missile (the Black Knight rocket) to the Saunders Roe Company. This missile was propelled by the Gamma Mark 201 engine, developed by Rolls Royce and fuelled by hydrogen peroxide and paraffin oil (kerosene). The first test flight of this missile, in 1958, was a complete success. Between 1960 and 1965, there was a two stage version, which had the more powerful Gamma Mark 301 for the first stage and a solid fuel rocket for the second stage. In 1964, the British Ministry of Aviation also decided to develop a light launcher, called Black Arrow, from the Black Knight missile.

As far as defence was concerned, Britain decided not to develop its own strategic missiles and, in 1950, acquired a licence from the USA to produce one of the first versions of the Atlas missile. The design was adapted and built by De Havilland, with a Rolls Royce rocket engine, and given the name Blue Streak.

Following the rapid development of large solid fuel boosters, Britain abandoned Blue Streak in 1961 because of the difficulties that were experienced operating liquid fuel missiles. Instead, they offered it to the rest of Europe as the first stage of a launcher which came to be known as Europa.

During the same period, France too began work on an independent programme. In the field of solid fuel propulsion, Sud-Aviation and ONERA successfully developed a large range of rockets from Bélier, Centaure, Dragon, Dauphin and Eridan on the one hand to Tacite and Texus on the other. In parallel, the Laboratoire de recherches balistiques et aérodynamiques (LRBA: Ballistic and Aerodynamic Research Laboratory) of the armed forces ministry began work on liquid fuel rocket engines in conjunction with Nord-Aviation. Initial research was centred on the development of an engine with a thrust of 70 kilonewtons fuelled by nitric acid and spirit of turpentine. This was first used to power the Véronique rocket, then the more powerful Vesta; it led eventually to a much more powerful engine, the Valois, with a thrust of 200 kilonewtons, using fuel supplied under pressure.

The Societé pour l'étude et la réalisation d'engins balistiques (SEREB: Ballistic Missiles Research and Construction Group) of the armed forces ministry then began a programme to construct missiles. The Valois engine was chosen to power the heaviest stage, the VE 121, which contained 12 tonnes of fuel. Two solid fuel stages, containing 2200 and 650 kilograms of fuel, were also developed. These three stages were combined in pairs to produce the Rubis, Topaze and Emeraude rockets of the so-called 'jewel' series. Numerous tests were carried out at Hammaguir in the Sahara. Apart from the contribution which this programme made to the development of ballistic missiles, it also led to a launcher, the Diamant, the maiden flight of which took place from Hammaguir in 1962.

France was also involved in the Europa programme, being responsible for the development of the second stage launcher, Coralie. This used

the more powerful fuel mix of nitrogen peroxide and UDMH, and had four 70 kilonewton rockets. The development in turn led to the more powerful Vexin engine producing a thrust of 350 kilonewtons which was fitted to the L17 first stage of the Diamant B launcher. The success of the Vexin engine led the LRBA to develop a prototype engine, containing turbopumps, which produced a thrust of 400 kilonewtons. This was the forerunner of the Viking engine now fitted to the first two stages of the Ariane launcher.

In the 1960s, the ministry of the armed forces and later the CNES entrusted to the Societé pour l'étude de la propulsion par réaction (SEPR: Reaction Engine Research Group) a programme to develop a liquid hydrogen and liquid oxygen engine. This project reached the stage where ground tests were performed, and the prototype engine produced a thrust of 40 kilonewtons before the programme was halted. The success of the enterprise ultimately enabled France to develop the HM 7 engine fitted to Ariane's third stage.

Jean-Claude Bouillot

The Diamant launcher. The French Diamant launcher had a liquid fuel first stage and two solid fuel upper stages. The first two stages were guided, and the third stage was oriented and spin stabilised. The payload housing, placed above the P4 rocket, was of the same diameter as the rocket. A tilting ring, attached to the housing, was used to steer the third stage and the satellite by ejecting cold gas during the ballistic phase after the rocket engine had stopped burning. Once the desired altitude and attitude had been achieved, the third stage was spun up, separated, and the engine ignited.

The Diamant B P4's head was based on that of the Black Arrow. Three versions of this launcher were built, each with a greater capacity than the previous version: Diamant A (four launches, all successful), Diamant B (five launches, of which the last two were failures), and Diamant B P4 (three launches, all successful). The Diamant B P4, the last of the Diamant launchers, is featured in the photograph on the right. The three rockets were all launched in 1975. On 6 February the geodetic satellite, Starlette, was put into orbit. On 17 May, two scientific satellites, D5A and D5B, Castor and Pollux, were launched and, on 27 September, the ultraviolet astronomy satellite, D2B (Aura), was put into orbit (rights reserved).

	Diamant A	Diamant B	Diamant B P4
First stage	VE 121: 12.6 tonnes of fuel	L17: 17 tonnes of fuel (nitrogen peroxide and UDMH)	
Second stage	P2.2: 2.2 tonnes of isolane solid fuel		P4: 4 tonnes of solid fuel
Third stage	0.645 tonnes of solid fuel	P0.68: 0.685 tonnes of isolane solid fuel	
Head diameter	0.65 metres	0.80 metres	1.38 metres
Capacity	40 kilograms into an elliptical orbit of 500 by 2000 kilometres	80 kilograms into a circular orbit at 500 kilometres altitude	120 kilograms into a circular orbit at 500 kilometres altitude

The principal characteristics of the three Diamant launchers

Black Arrow (left). This British launcher, built by Saunders Roe under contract to the Ministry of Technology, was based on the Black Knight ballistic missile. Four Black Arrows were built and launched from Woomera, Australia, between June 1969 and October 1971. The second flight, a successful suborbital test, put the British Prospero satellite into orbit. In July 1973, however, the British government decided to abandon the programme.

The Black Arrow was characteristically squat. It was only 13 metres tall and the diameter of the first stage was 2 metres. The first two stages contained 13 and 3 tonnes of liquid fuel (hydrogen peroxide and paraffin oil) respectively.

The turbopump engines were manufactured by Rolls Royce. Gamma 8, the first stage engine, had eight steerable nozzles, to guide the rocket, while Gamma 2, the second stage engine, had two Cardan articulated nozzles. The solid fuel third stage was designed around a Waxwing engine. This consisted of a metallic casing containing 318 kilograms of solid fuel, and was spin stabilised. The payload housing was situated between the two tanks on the second stage (© SIRPA/ECP Armées France).

Ariane launchers I to IV. In July 1973, the governments of Europe formally accepted a French proposal to develop a heavy launcher to replace the Europa III. France agreed to fund two thirds of the programme, and CNES became the main contractor. The maiden flight, on 24 December 1979, was a complete success; the launcher was passed as being fit for service on 20 December 1981, after four flights, three of which were successful.

In 1977, the council of ESA approved a plan to improve the launcher, and as a result two new versions, Ariane II and Ariane III, were developed. Both have similar configurations to the later Ariane IV rocket.

After six development flights, Arianespace took over responsibility for the production, commercialisation and launching of all operational Ariane rockets.

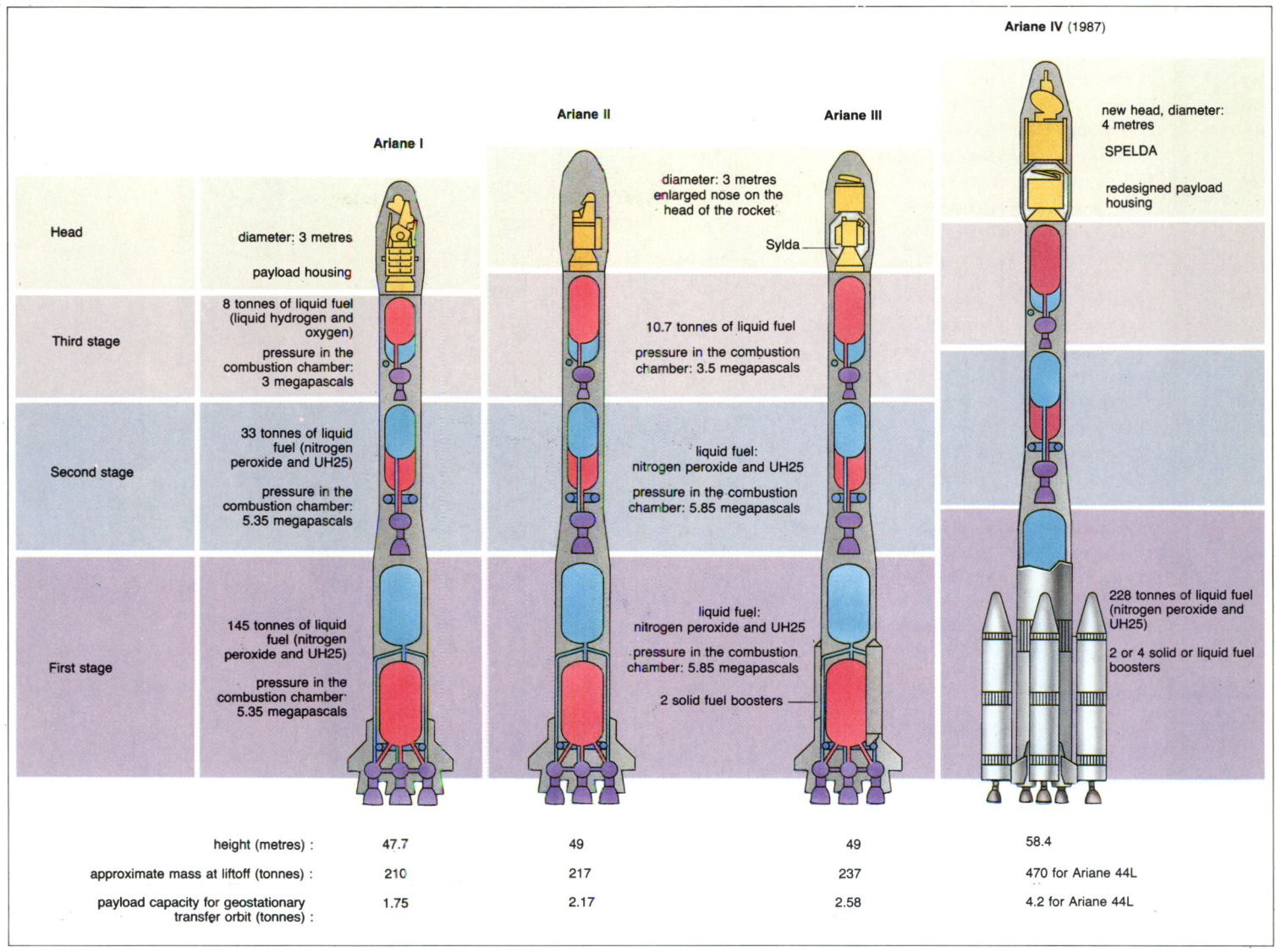

Ariane IV (1987)

Ariane I

Ariane II

Ariane III

				new head, diameter: 4 metres
Head	diameter: 3 metres		diameter: 3 metres enlarged nose on the head of the rocket	SPELDA redesigned payload housing
	payload housing		Sylda	
Third stage	8 tonnes of liquid fuel (liquid hydrogen and oxygen) pressure in the combustion chamber: 3 megapascals		10.7 tonnes of liquid fuel pressure in the combustion chamber: 3.5 megapascals	
Second stage	33 tonnes of liquid fuel (nitrogen peroxide and UH25) pressure in the combustion chamber: 5.35 megapascals		liquid fuel: nitrogen peroxide and UH25 pressure in the combustion chamber: 5.85 megapascals	
First stage	145 tonnes of liquid fuel (nitrogen peroxide and UH25) pressure in the combustion chamber 5.35 megapascals		liquid fuel: nitrogen peroxide and UH25 pressure in the combustion chamber: 5.85 megapascals 2 solid fuel boosters	228 tonnes of liquid fuel (nitrogen peroxide and UH25) 2 or 4 solid or liquid fuel boosters
height (metres):	47.7	49	49	58.4
approximate mass at liftoff (tonnes):	210	217	237	470 for Ariane 44L
payload capacity for geostationary transfer orbit (tonnes):	1.75	2.17	2.58	4.2 for Ariane 44L

	Ariane I	Ariane II	Ariane III	Ariane IV
Boosters			2 P7.3: 7.3 tonnes of solid fuel	0, 2 or 4 solid or liquid fuel rockets
First stage	L145: 145 tonnes of liquid fuel (nitrogen peroxide and UH25)			L220
Second stage	L33: 33 tonnes of liquid fuel (nitrogen peroxide and UH25)			
Third stage	H8	H10: 10.7 tonnes of liquid fuel (liquid hydrogen and oxygen)		
Head diameter	3 metres	3 metres (double cone shaped)		3.65 metres

Principal characteristics of the Ariane launchers

Europa I and II. Work began on the Europa I launcher in 1962 within the European Launcher Development Organisation (ELDO). The first stage consisted of a British ballistic missile constructed under licence from the USA, Blue Streak. The second stage was a French Coralie rocket. The third stage, Astris, was constructed by West Germany. Belgium, the Netherlands and Italy also contributed to the programme. Ten flight tests were performed from Woomera in Australia on different combinations of the three stages. However, the complete launcher was never launched.

After 1967, following a French suggestion, the Europa launcher was transformed into a geostationary satellite launcher, by equipping it with a two stage, solid fuel apogee and perigee system and launching it from Kourou. This rocket, known as Europa II, was used to launch the Franco-German Symphonie telecommunications satellites, but the first launch on 5 November 1971 was a failure. The programme was eventually cancelled in March 1973 to make way for the burgeoning Ariane programme.

The photograph on the left shows the launch of Europa I on 12 June 1970; this was a 'qualification' launch. The photograph above shows Coralie stages being assembled at Aérospatiale's establishment at Mureaux (left: ELDO; above Aérospatiale).

Erecting Ariane III's second stage flight V17. All three stages are erected in the same way. First, the top covering the transport container is removed. This container, which also serves as an erection frame, is hoisted into the required vertical position by a large crane. The rocket stage is then lifted free of the container, which is removed by a second crane. Another large crane removes the rest of the container, and the stage is taken to the launch pad or to the lower stage, where it is fixed and connected up.

The second stage of Ariane III, still partially in its container, is here being placed onto the first stage in the preparation hall at the space centre in French Guiana (rights reserved).

Going into space

No.	Type	Date	Payload	Observations
L01	I	24 December 1979	technological capsule (CAT)	
L02	I	23 May 1980	CAT + Oscar 9 + Firewheel	launch failure
L03	I	19 June 1981	CAT + Apple + Meteosat 2	
L04	I	20 December 1981	CAT + Marecs A	
L5	I	10 September 1982	Marecs B + Sirio 2	launch failure
L6	I	16 June 1983	ECS 1 + Amsat P 3B	
L7	I	19 October 1983	Intelsat V F7	
L8	I	5 March 1984	Intelsat V F8	
V9	I	23 May 1984	Spacenet I	first launch by Arianespace
V10	III	4 August 1984	Télécom 1A + ECS 2	
V11	III	10 November 1984	Spacenet 2 + Marecs B2	
V12	III	8 February 1985	Arabsat + Brasilsat 1	
V13	III	8 May 1985	Télécom 1B + G Star 1	
V14	I	2 July 1985	Giotto	
V15	III	12 September 1985	Spacenet 3 + ECS 3	launch failure
V16	I	22 February 1986	SPOT + Viking	
V17	III	28 March 1986	Brasilsat 2 + G Star 2	
V18	II	3 May 1986	Intelsat V F14	launch failure
V19	III	16 September 1987	Aussat K3 + ECS 4	
V20	II	21 November 1987	TV Sat 1	
V21	III	11 March 1988	Spacenet 3R + Télécom 1C	
V23	II	17 May 1988	Intelsat V F13	
V22	IV	15 June 1988	Meteosat P2 + Amsat 3C + PAS 1	44 LP version

Ariane launches up to mid 1988

Some recent Ariane launches

11 December 1988	double launch of Skynet 4B + Astra 1A
27 January 1989	Intelsat V F15
6 March 1989	Meteosat 4 + Japanese communications satellite
2 April 1989	last launch by an Ariane II: Scandinavian telecommunications satellite
5 June 1989	Japanese + West German satellites
12 July 1989	Olympus 1 launched by an Ariane III
8 August 1989	Hipparcos satellite launched
22 February 1990	an Ariane IV carrying two Japanese communications satellites exploded 101 seconds after take-off

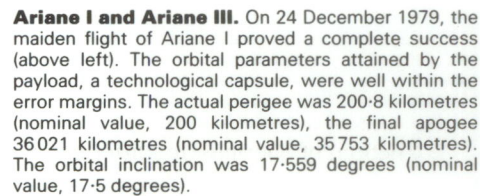

Ariane I and Ariane III. On 24 December 1979, the maiden flight of Ariane I proved a complete success (above left). The orbital parameters attained by the payload, a technological capsule, were well within the error margins. The actual perigee was 200·8 kilometres (nominal value, 200 kilometres), the final apogee 36021 kilometres (nominal value, 35753 kilometres). The orbital inclination was 17·559 degrees (nominal value, 17·5 degrees).

Ariane III was launched for the first time on 4 August 1984 (above right). One of the two new rocket boosters is very evident (left: ESA; right: © CSG, Kourou).

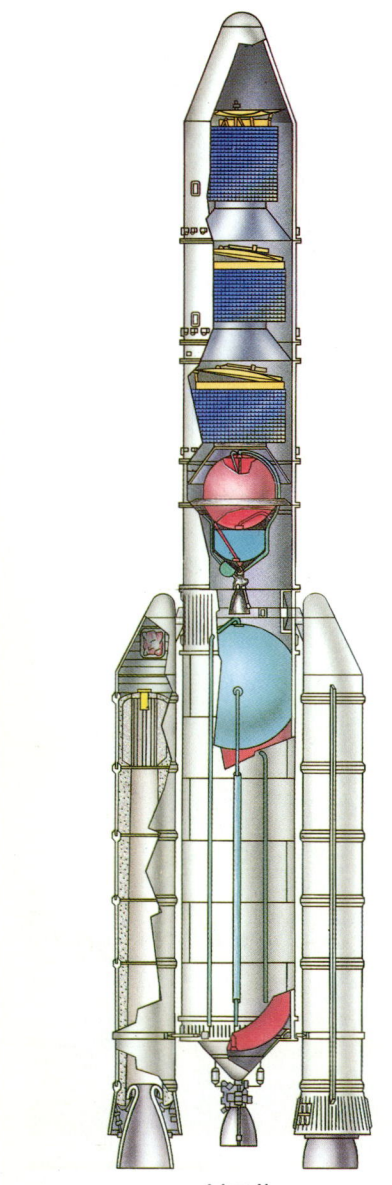
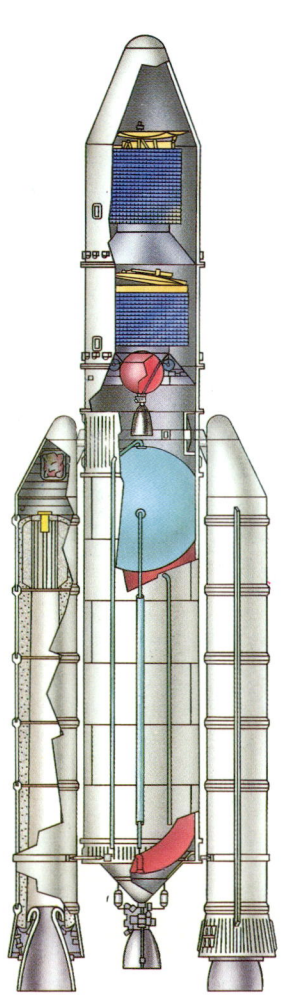
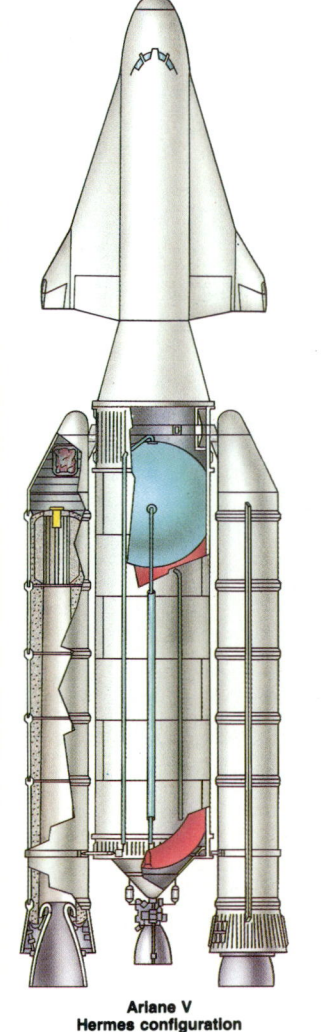

Ariane V
L5 configuration
(triple launch)

Ariane V
L5 configuration

Ariane V
Hermes configuration

Ariane V. Over the years, both the diameters and masses of satellites have increased. The demand for reliable launchers has also grown. CNES began work on its new launcher in 1977 and ESA took the project over in January 1986. From Kourou, Ariane V will be able to put a payload of 15 tonnes into a low Earth orbit, and a payload of 6·8 tonnes into a geostationary transfer orbit. It will also be able to put sections of the European space station into orbit, and could transport crews to it in Hermes.

Part of Ariane V is like its predecessors. It has a cryogenic stage, the H155, which contains 155 tonnes of liquid hydrogen and liquid oxygen stored in a single fuel tank with a partition wall. This tank is 25 metres tall and 5·4 metres in diameter. The H155 stage is propelled by an HM60 Vulcan engine which produces a thrust of 800 kilonewtons at ground level and 1·07 meganewtons at altitude. The liquid fuel engine is ignited, and its performance checked on the ground, before the boosters are lit and liftoff occurs. The two solid fuel boosters weigh 230 tonnes and produce 5·5 meganewtons of thrust.

The upper part of the Ariane V launcher varies according to the mission requirements. It may carry an L5 liquid fuel stage for low Earth orbit or for geostationary missions. Alternatively, it could carry a Hermes shuttle with its own rocket engines. For unmanned missions there is a head with the same diameter (5·4 metres) as the shuttle's cargobay. This can be used for different types of single, double or triple launches, and its length can be varied to suit all types of satellite.

Hermes

With strong support being provided by France, the European Space Agency has initiated the Hermes transport system for taking men and cargo into orbit. In the future the project will enable Europe to have an independent mode of transport to and from a space station.

The Hermes programme has several key elements. The most important is the space plane itself, which is to be launched on the top of an Ariane V rocket. There will also be a flight control centre, a mission centre, and a special Hermes unit built at the Ariane V launch centre in French Guiana. Special installations will be established to overhaul and prepare the space plane for its next flight, and crew training and preparation centres will also be required.

The space plane will land either on existing runways, such as those built for large aircraft, or on specially constructed ones. It will be transferred from one site to another by a special carrier plane. In Europe, the Hermes landing site will be at Istres in Bouches du Rhône, France.

Hermes will mainly be used as a means of transport to and from the space station. It will be able to take equipment into space, and to take astronauts to carry out maintenance and repair work on objects in low Earth orbit. Scientific experiments may also be put into orbit during unmanned flights.

ESA has entrusted parts of the development programme and the construction of Hermes to different companies within those member countries participating in the programme. Aérospatiale (France) is the main contractor, with Avions Marcel Dassault as the main subcontractor for the aeronautics. Hermes equipment, subsystems and structures will be tested throughout the development phase at centres such as those of Intelspace in Toulouse, IABG at Munich, and Estec in the Netherlands. In addition, several European wind tunnels will be involved in designing the optimum shape of the space plane.

Two development and assembly models will be built, while an operational model will evaluate all the mechanical, electrical, computer and fluid systems. Full tests will simulate the conditions likely to be experienced by the two flight models of Hermes when in orbit. These models and mockups will all be assembled and integrated at Toulouse.

Francis Klefstad-Sillonville

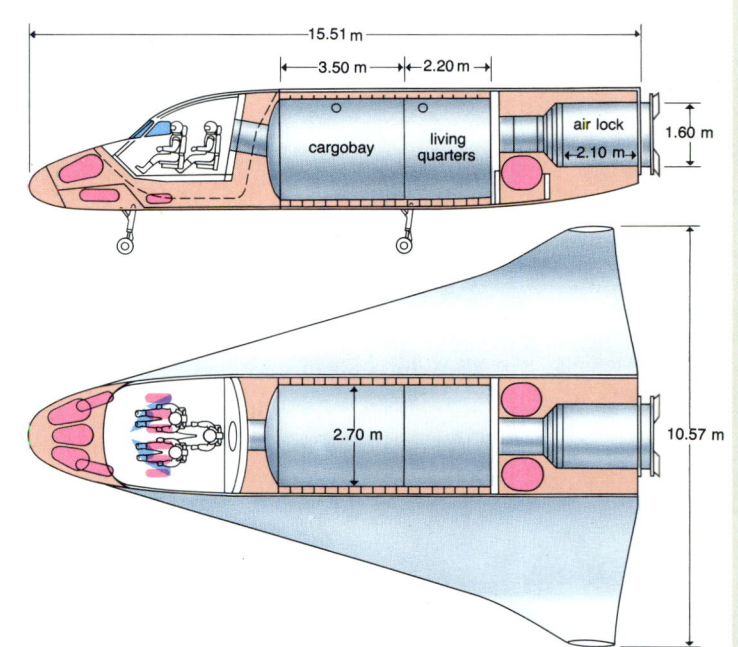

Hermes design characteristics. This space plane has a fairly short fuselage, with a diameter of 3·50 metres and a length of 15·5 metres, attached to a swept back, delta wing. The fuselage does not have a tailplane; instead, the wing tips are cambered upwards and fitted with control surfaces. There is a further control surface at the rear of the fuselage. The manned cabin at the front of the fuselage is ejectable during a launch or reentry emergency, and would parachute down to Earth. The pressurised payload cargobay is in the centre. There are more living quarters at the rear of the fuselage, joined to the cabin by a tunnel. The docking mechanism, the airlock, the fuel tanks and the plane's own engines are also at the rear. When empty, Hermes weighs about 14 tonnes and, at take-off on Ariane V, about 20 tonnes. Then Hermes is attached to the Ariane V launcher by means of a conical adapter which is the L5B propulsion stage, carrying about 5 tonnes of fuel.

Hermes will be able to propel itself in space using several liquid fuel (nitrogen peroxide and MMH) engines delivering thrusts of between 200 and 2000 newtons. These will enable the plane to reach the altitude of the space station and carry out approach manoeuvres. At the end of the mission, they give the plane the correct velocity to come out of orbit. There are also some small rocket nozzles in the nose and in the rear to orientate the plane in space as required. Electrical energy is supplied by two hydrogen and oxygen fuel cells, and two lithium batteries.

Thermal control of the pressurised module and of the subsystems which produce heat will be performed by circulating fluids. Most of the radiators will be inside the cargobay doors, and will radiate energy into space when the doors are open. Passive thermal protection will take the usual form of flexible, padded blankets. Hermes will also have a remote control arm to move payloads away from the space plane or hook itself to an orbiting structure. This arm will be stored under the cargobay doors and controlled from the cabin.

The space plane will be fitted with several computers, all with back up systems, to facilitate its orientation, guidance and control during automatic flight. The reentry phase of the spaceflight will be entirely automatic, the final landing manual. Hermes is fitted with a telemetry system so that the crew can see at a glance the state of all the subsystems. Each crew is expected to have three members, a commander, a copilot and a scientist (Aérospatiale).

Materials for the structure and thermal protection. The structure of Hermes is constructed from various metals (light alloys, titanium and beryllium, for example) with the addition of carbon fibre composites. The fuselage and cargobay doors will all be made out of materials able to withstand temperatures of at least 200 degrees celsius. All the principal structures have passive thermal protection against the temperature increase caused by air friction during reentry. The parts which get hottest are the nose, the leading edges of the wings and the control surfaces. To withstand maximum temperatures of between 1500 and 1900 degrees celsius, these will be made out of a silicon carbide ceramic or carbon fibres set in a carbon matrix. Next hottest to these regions are zones subjected to temperatures of about 1200 degrees celsius, mainly the inner edges of the wings. These will be of silicon based ceramics, the outside of which will be tiled. The upper parts of the fuselage will reach a temperature of only about 500 degrees celsius; they will be covered in a protective material made of silicon fibre, with threads of quartz. The inner part of the space plane will be protected from the outside by insulating materials sandwiched between the ceramic tiles and the primary structure. Here the insulating material will consist of alternate layers of materials chosen to reflect and absorb heat.

The series of computer images below simulate the heating of the plane during reentry. The temperatures increase from pale blue to red (Avions Marcel Dassault–Breguet Aviation Espace).

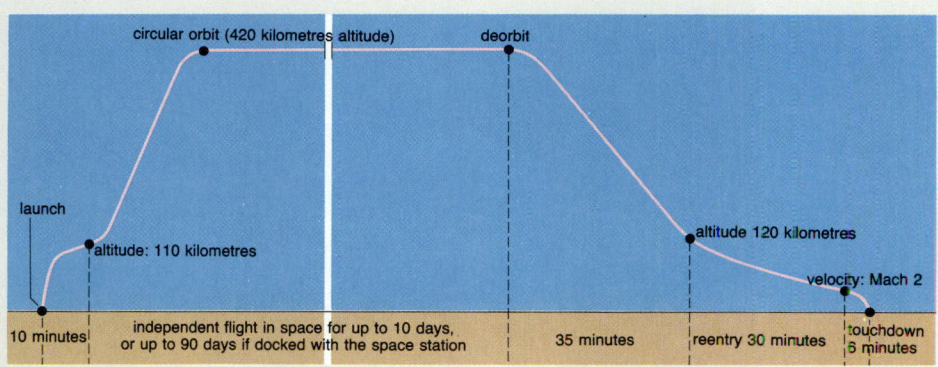

Flight plan of a Hermes mission. At time T_0, Ariane V's cryogenic engine is fired; the two solid fuel boosters are ignited and Ariane V lifts off. At $T_0 + 2$ minutes, combustion finishes and the two solid fuel boosters separate from the main rocket. The cryogenic engine ceases to function and is separated at $T_0 + 10$ minutes, at an altitude of 110 kilometres. The L5B stage is then ignited. Seventy seconds later it separates, and Hermes begins its independent flight in space. The cargobay doors can then be opened.

Hermes is injected into an orbit with a perigee of 110 kilometres and an apogee of 420 kilometres altitude. It slowly rises into a circular orbit at 420 kilometres, by short bursts of engine fire over a period of some tens of hours, and then docks with the space station. After finishing its mission, Hermes once more goes into its own flight routine. It undocks from the space station, withdraws its remote control arm and closes its cargobay doors. The engine is fired to bring it out of orbit at an exact point on its trajectory, about 70 minutes before the anticipated landing time. The space plane reenters the Earth's atmosphere under automatic flight control. Once the landing runway is in sight, the commander takes control and guides the plane down manually.

Expected performances of the Hermes space plane

	Principal mission	Secondary missions	
	service of orbital module	service in low orbit	automatic flight or servicing of other orbital stations
Orbit: altitude inclination	460 kilometres 28.5 degrees	276 kilometres 98.6 degrees	300 to 500 kilometres 5 to 60 degrees
Duration	11 days	7 days	7 to 28 days
Crew	3	3	2 or 3
Payload: mass volume	3 tonnes 18 cubic metres (diameter: 2.7 m; length: 3.5 m)	2 tonnes 18 cubic metres	less than 2.5 tonnes variable (but less than 18 cubic metres)

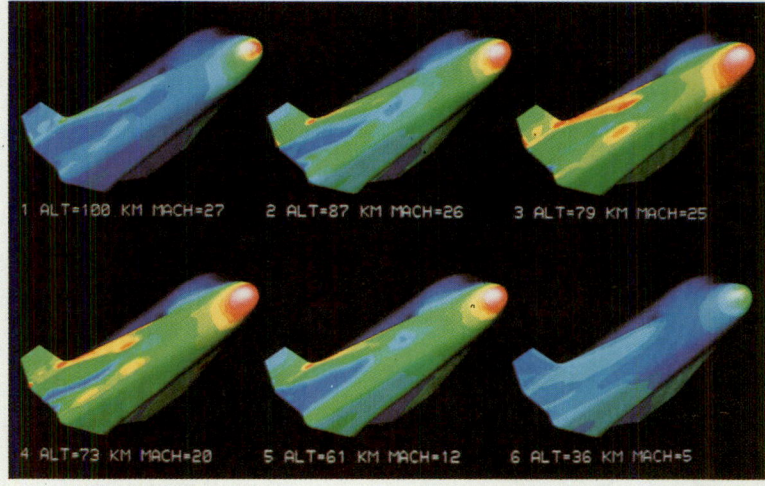

China, Japan and India

The USA, the USSR and Europe are not alone in having launchers. China and Japan have had a number of successes in this field, while India too, has a rocket launcher and Brazil is developing a one.

The first Chinese success was in April 1970 with the CZ1 launcher (the CZ stands for Changzheng, a reference to Mao Zedong's 'Long March'). This was based on a missile developed with assistance from the USSR. The launcher weighed 82 tonnes at take-off and had two liquid fuel stages and one solid fuel stage; it could put a 300 kilogram payload into orbit at an altitude of 440 kilometres.

From 1974 onwards, the Chinese have used the CZ2 launcher, which had its first successful flight in November 1975. The CZ2, also based

on a missile, could put 2·2 tonnes into a low Earth orbit. The CZ3 launcher was based in turn on the CZ2 with the addition of a reignitable cryogenic third stage. This launcher was designed for geostationary missions. Though its first flight in January 1984 was only partially successful as the third stage did not reignite, a totally successful flight took place in April 1984 (see also p. 337).

In Japan, the Institute of Space and Astronautical Sciences (ISAS) at the University of Tokyo developed a family of rockets and, at the end of the 1960s, constructed a four stage, solid fuel launcher, the Lamda 4S. Its first successful flight took place in February 1970. This was in turn improved to produce the Mu launcher. In August 1985, the last version, the M3 III, launched the 125 kilogram Suisei probe to Halley's comet (p. 337).

At the beginning of the 1970s, shortly after its creation, the Japanese space agency (Nasda) decided to develop a launcher for civil and commercial satellites. For reasons of cost and effi-

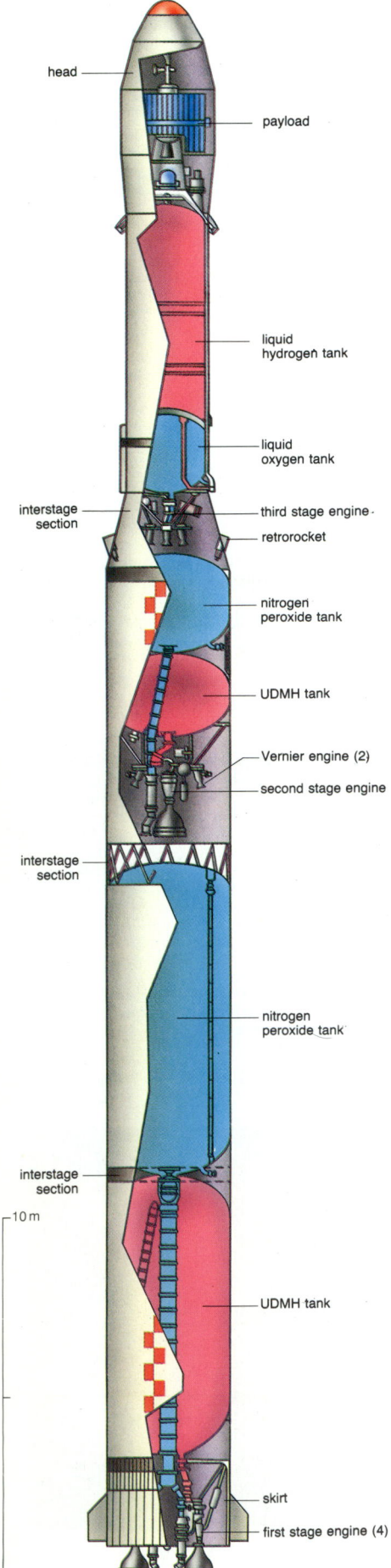

head
payload
liquid hydrogen tank
liquid oxygen tank
interstage section
third stage engine
retrorocket
nitrogen peroxide tank
UDMH tank
Vernier engine (2)
second stage engine
interstage section
nitrogen peroxide tank
interstage section
UDMH tank
skirt
first stage engine (4)
10 m
0

Launching a CZ2 rocket from the space centre at Jiuquan. The first successful flight of the Chinese CZ2 launcher, which is rather similar to the US Titan II, was made in November 1975. Several configurations of this launcher, which can put from two to four satellites into a low Earth orbit, have been tried. In its most basic version (see the photograph on the right of the launch carried out on 21 October 1985), it can carry a payload of 3·9 tonnes into a circular orbit at 200 kilometres altitude with an orbital inclination of 28·5°. A more developed version équipped with the McDonnell Douglas PAM D perigee engine can put a satellite into a geostationary transfer orbit at 28° inclination.

The most powerful version of the CZ2 with two large capacity tanks and from four to eight liquid fuel boosters, has been offered on the international launcher market. The four booster version can place a payload of 9 tonnes into a circular parking orbit for a geostationary mission. The payload can be increased to as much as 16 tonnes on the eight booster version (MOA).

	CZ1	CZ2	CZ3
Number of stages	3	2	3
Diameters (metres): first stage second stage third stage	2.25 2.25 2.25	3.35 3.35 —	3.35 3.35 2.25
Total height (metres)	29.45	32.57	43.25
Mass at take-off (tonnes)	81.6	191	202
Payload (kilograms)	300 (circular orbit, altitude: 440 km; inclination: 70°)	2200 (circular orbit, altitude: 200 km; inclination: 63°)	3800 (circular orbit, altitude: 200 km; inclination: 90°) or 1370 into geostationary transfer orbit

The Chinese CZ launchers

The CZ3 launcher. This rocket has three liquid fuel stages (see the diagram on the left). It has the same first two stages as the CZ2, which use nitrogen peroxide and UDMH. The first stage has four rocket motors, each delivering a thrust of 700 kilonewtons. The second stage is powered by a single engine of the same type and guided by two Vernier rocket engines.

The CZ3 launcher, which is used for geostationary transfer orbits, carries 6 tonnes of fuel and has a cryogenic third stage with four combustion chambers, each producing 45 kilonewtons of thrust.

The Long March 3 launchers blast off from Xichang, in the south of China. The photograph on the right shows the only launch site at Xichang. The imposing service tower stands 76 metres tall, taller than the launcher itself so that it will be able to accommodate future generations of larger rockets. The launcher is mounted, prepared and then launched next to this structure. The experimental STW1 telecommunications satellite seen on top of the launcher, and not yet covered by the head, was successfully launched on 8 April 1984 (MOA).

ciency, a licence for the first stage was bought from the American company McDonnell Douglas; the second stage was developed in Japan and the third stage was bought from America. The NI launcher was launched seven times between 1975 and 1982, five missions in all being successful. A more powerful version called the NII has been successfully launched on six occasions since 1981.

On 13 August 1986, the first launch of the Japanese HI put the 685 kilogram Experimental Geodetic Satellite (EGS) into a circular orbit at an altitude of 1500 kilometres and with an orbital inclination of 50°. The HI has a cryogenic second stage, 10·32 metres tall, propelled by an LE5 engine of 105 kilonewtons thrust and with a specific impulse of 370 seconds over two operating phases. It replaces the second stage of the NII launcher. For geostationary missions, the HI is equipped with a third stage containing 1·9 tonnes of solid fuel, which burns for 67 seconds.

Nasda is also developing an HII launcher, with two cryogenic stages, which should be ready by 1993. This will be able to put a 2 tonne payload into a geostationary orbit. The first stage will have a 1 meganewton thrust engine, and two solid fuel boosters each containing 59 tonnes of fuel. The second stage will be very similar to the engine on the HI second stage.

India launched her four stage, solid fuel launcher, the SLV3 (Satellite Launch Vehicle), for the first time on 18 July 1980. It put the 40 kilogram Rohini 1 satellite into a circular orbit at an altitude of 400 kilometres. An improved version, the Augmented SLV, should subsequently have put a 150 kilogram payload into orbit, but there was a failure during its first launch in 1986 and the launcher was abandoned. The PSLV (Polar SLV) will be the first Indian launcher with two liquid fuel stages. In the early 1990s, India should also have a single stage, cryogenic launcher capable of putting a 2 tonne payload into a geostationary orbit (the GSLV).

Jean-Claude Bouillot

Characteristics of the Japanese launchers

		M3 SII	NI	NII	HI	HII
Payload (kilograms)	into geostationary orbit		130	350	550	2000
	into circular orbit	770 (250 km; inclination: 31°)	800 (1000 km; inclination: 30°)	1600 (1000 km; inclination: 30°)	2200 (1000 km; inclination 30°)	7500 (1000 km; inclination: 30°)
Dimensions (metres)	total height	28.2	33	35	40	48
	diameter of first stage	1.41	2.4	2.4	2.4	4
	diameter of head	1.6	1.6	2.4	2.4	4
Launch mass (tonnes)		61	90	135	140	255
Fuels	first stage	solid fuel	liquid fuel (LO$_2$/RJ1)[1]	liquid fuel (LO$_2$/RJ1)	liquid fuel (LO$_2$/RJ1)	liquid fuel (LO$_2$/LH$_2$)[2]
	second stage	solid fuel	liquid fuel (N$_2$O$_4$/A50)[3]	liquid fuel (N$_2$O$_4$/A50)	liquid fuel (LO$_2$/LH$_2$)	liquid fuel (LO$_2$/LH$_2$)
	third stage boosters [number]	solid fuel solid fuel [2]	solid fuel solid fuel [3]	solid fuel solid fuel [9]	solid fuel solid fuel [9]	— solid fuel [2]
Guidance system		radio	radio	inertial	inertial	inertial

1 LO$_2$: liquid oxygen; RJ1 paraffin oil (kerosene) – 2 LH$_2$: liquid hydrogen – 3 N$_2$O$_4$: nitrogen peroxide; A50: aerozine 50

The Japanese M3 SII and NII launchers. The photograph on the left shows the last launch of the Mu launcher (M3 SII) from Kagoshima on 19 August 1985. It was carrying the Suisei space probe to Halley's comet. This launcher was the last built by Nissan for ISAS, and consisted of three solid fuel stages and two boosters. Each booster contained 4 tonnes of solid fuel and the three stages contained 34·7, 13·1 and 3·59 tonnes respectively. A fourth stage with 420 kilograms of solid fuel could be added.

The NII 7 launcher illustrated below right was launched on 12 February 1986 from the base at Tanegashima to place the 350 kilogram broadcasting satellite BS 2b (Yuri 2b) into a geostationary orbit. The NII is a replica of the American Delta 2914 launcher. The first two stages and the integration of the third stage were carried out under licence by Mitsubishi Heavy Industries; the boosters were made by Nissan (left: ISAS; right: Nasda).

The Indian Polar Satellite Launch Vehicle (PSLV). With a launch mass of 274 tonnes and a total height of 44 metres, the PSLV can place a 1 tonne payload into a Sun synchronous polar orbit at an altitude of 900 kilometres. The first stage has a central propulsion system which uses 129 tonnes of solid fuel and six small boosters, each with 9 tonnes of solid fuel. The second stage will have a 600 kilonewton thrust Vikas engine, based on the Viking engine of the Société européenne de propulsion (SEP). The third stage will use 7 tonnes of solid fuel, the fourth liquid fuel using two 7 kilonewton thrust engines.

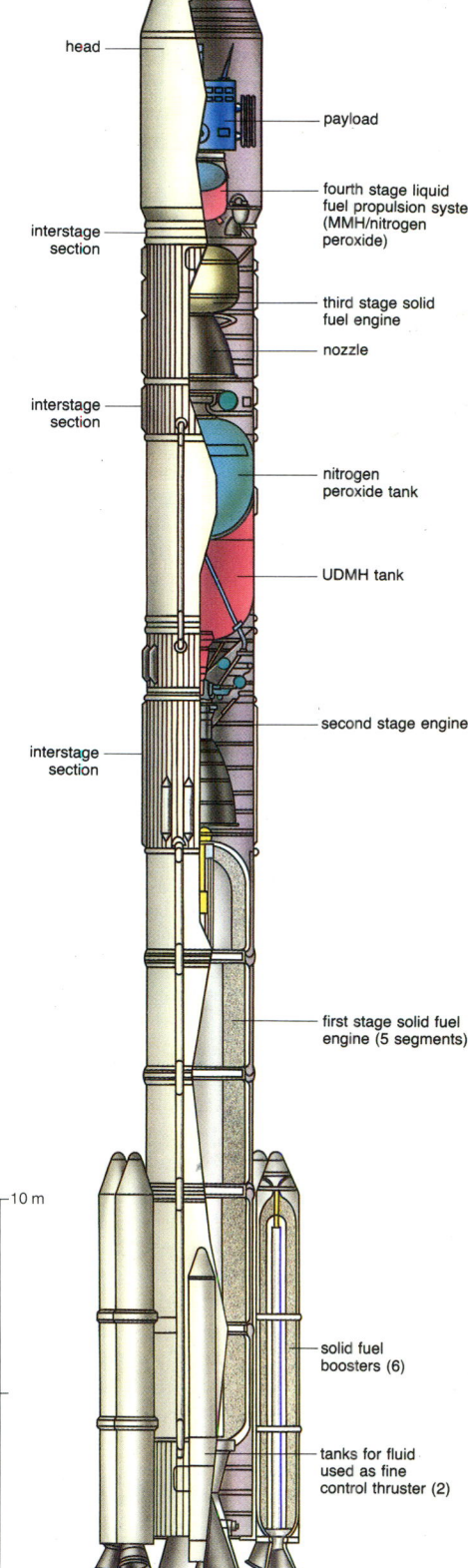

head

payload

fourth stage liquid fuel propulsion system (MMH/nitrogen peroxide)

interstage section

third stage solid fuel engine

nozzle

interstage section

nitrogen peroxide tank

UDMH tank

interstage section

second stage engine

first stage solid fuel engine (5 segments)

10 m

solid fuel boosters (6)

tanks for fluid used as fine control thruster (2)

0

117

Rocket launchers

Space vehicles of the future

The Sänger concept. The first ever theoretical research into a single stage reusable launcher with horizontal take-off and landing took place in Germany between 1937 and 1942. It was conducted by Eugen Sänger, an engineer and physicist, assisted by the mathematician Irene Brendt. Their secret document, dated August 1944, *Über einen Raketenantrieb für Fernbomber* (A rocket drive for a long range bomber), described a long range bomber driven by a rocket engine and piloted by a single man. The (modern) artist's model above illustrates its design. It was to be 28 metres long, with a wingspan of 15 metres and a total mass at take-off of 100 tonnes. Characterised by a wingspan with a triangular profile and sharp leading edges, it would be propelled by liquid oxygen and petrol (gasolene). The engine would have a one meganewton thrust and would be cooled by circulating water.

The Sänger plane was to be accelerated to a velocity of Mach 1·5 by a solid fuel, rocket driven sledge, along a monorail, 3 kilometres long. It would then detach itself and take off at an angle of 30°. The rocket engine would be ignited at an altitude of about 1·7 kilometres, providing the plane with a maximum velocty of 6 kilometres per second on a trajectory rising to an altitude of 160 kilometres. The plane would return to Earth in a series of swoops to lose altitude. Below about 40 kilometres it would glide down. Sänger thought that the maximum range would be about half the Earth's circumference so the launcher was given the name 'antipodean'. Ultimately, the project was abandoned in the summer of 1942, because the German military preferred the V1 and V2 missiles as a longterm programme (MBB).

STS 2000. The French company Aérospatiale has been studying various possibilities for a space transport system that would be operational in the twenty-first century. In terms of advances in propulsion techniques, the constraints of possible delays, costs and the performance required, several types of vehicles are possible. These would include a single stage launcher using rocket engines, a combined air breathing/rocket propulsion unit, or a two stage air breathing/rocket propulsion system such as that illustrated below.

The development of rocket launchers is motivated by the search for better and better performance. This depends essentially on three things – reliability, flexibility and cost. Present launchers are therefore constantly being adapted and improved to meet the demanding requirements of the space market.

Scientists and technologists aim above all to improve the efficiency of the launchers, that is to increase the ratio of their payload mass to their launch mass. Such research can be divided into four categories – structure, propulsion, avionics and multiple launches. Basic structures can be lightened by making them out of composite materials. Improvements in modelling the behaviour of materials have also led scientists to reduce margins of uncertainty and thus to improve safety coefficients. Some gains can be made by increasing the pressure in combustion chambers, by using extending nozzles or by adopting thermodynamic cycles with higher efficiencies. Beyond this, the miniaturisation of electronic components of the avionics systems has had the effect of reducing both their mass and the energy they consume, while fibre optic cabling and more efficient power sources have helped lighten the launcher. Multiple launches need heavier launchers, but the cost of one heavy launcher is of course much less than the cost of two (or more) small launchers.

In the longer term it seems likely that reusable single stage launchers will be developed. However, this more ambitious approach, an impossibility until now, still requires several fundamental decisions relating to the launch mode (whether horizontal or vertical), the need for radically new propulsion systems, and the necessity for space vehicles to be manned.

Horizontal take-off would greatly simplify the infrastructures required for launch, and would require a much smaller initial thrust; it has been estimated that a thrust equal to half the launch mass would produce sufficient acceleration. On the other hand, for the wing loading at launch to remain acceptable, the wing area would have to be much greater than that required for landing because the launch mass would be about ten times as big as the returning mass. This, in turn, would require an increase in the structural mass; the same is true for the landing gear.

The search for improved performance in propulsion systems has led scientists and engineers to consider using atmospheric oxygen as an oxidant whilst the launcher is in flight through the Earth's atmosphere, so reducing the launch mass by carrying much less oxygen on board. However, for this to be a viable proposition, the engines have to operate for as long and over as great a velocity range as possible. Such engines would be much more complicated than those at present. The best known engine, the turbojet, is limited to velocities of the order of Mach 3. The ramjet may be able to reach higher velocities, but its engine needs to be primed and this requires a greater initial velocity.

Maximum velocities are also limited by the temperature of the air sucked into the engine. It may be possible to overcome this limitation by first cooling the air in a heat exchanger with the fuel. In any case, variation in the velocity and density of the air makes intakes with adjustable areas absolutely essential. At high Mach numbers, the surface area of these intakes may need to be more than half the total midship area of the frame of the space plane, a requirement that would generate considerable air resistance. The practical development of such engines is not imminent, however, so the possibilities of a single stage orbiting vehicle remain for the present a matter for speculation.

There is also an ongoing and lively debate between supporters of unmanned flights and those who feel that human beings have something special to contribute to spaceflight. This is a central dispute when considering the relative advantages and disadvantages of a launcher such as Ariane or the American space shuttle. It frequently centres on the tragic Challenger accident. It is generally agreed that astronauts are of little use during the launch, reentry and landing phases; they are, moreover, at risk during these phases, which can never be guaranteed 100% safe. Yet astronauts are essential for many operations in space so it is tempting to involve them also in the transport phase. Perhaps the best solution is a compromise, with two launchers, one for manned and one for unmanned missions. A crew, of course, requires very complicated life support and safety systems, which further complicate an already complex space vehicle and reduce the payload mass which can be carried. For this reason, a system which can be used for both manned or unmanned missions – though theoretically a good idea – may prove technically unrealistic.

Space launchers are often associated with supersonic planes similar to the American transatmospheric vehicle, the Orient Express. However, aeronautics interest in these systems is doubtful. As far as military applications are concerned, these launchers are very vulnerable because of their lack of manoeuvrability, though they could in theory be used to replace ballistic missiles. As far as civil applications are concerned, the cost, and therefore the practicality, are difficult to estimate because the necessary infrastructures have no equivalents in commercial aviation. Commercial development would accordingly be extremely risky.

It is in the end very difficult to speculate on the space transport of the future. It can, however, be expected that new discoveries will enable the vast amounts of energy required for propulsion to be stored in a smaller mass and smaller volume than ever before.

Jean-Claude Bouillot

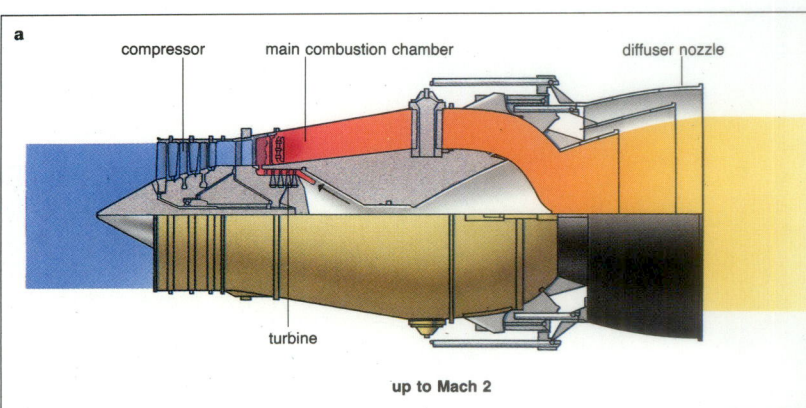

a | compressor | main combustion chamber | diffuser nozzle | turbine

up to Mach 2

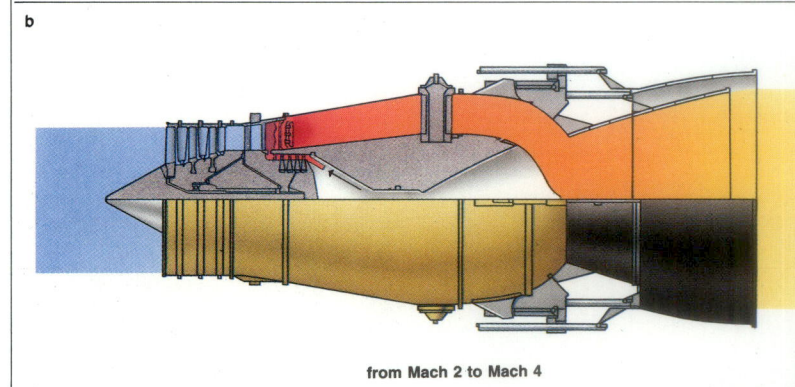

b

from Mach 2 to Mach 4

Requirements for a single stage launcher to put 15 tonnes into low Earth orbit. The curves below illustrate two fundamental parameters, the specific impulse and the structural index, for the performance of a single stage launcher near to non-reusable launchers in performance. The structural index is the ratio of the mass which is put into orbit to the launch mass. For a single stage launcher, this includes the mass of the empty vehicle itself; this mass is greater if the vehicle is to return to Earth. The structural indices for a single stage launcher are generally greater than those shown; the British Hotol, for example, would have an index of about 0·21. The specific impulses shown here correspond to the values of the best cryogenic engines operating *in vacuo*: 445 seconds for the American space shuttle and 470 seconds for the Rocketdyne Advanced Space Engine (ASE). The real values for a single stage launcher have to take into account the operational phase through the atmosphere, and are therefore somewhat lower. Fundamentally, the graph shows that it is not possible to construct a single stage reusable launcher without a propulsion system which produces a specific impulse much greater than that available with conventional chemical propulsion.

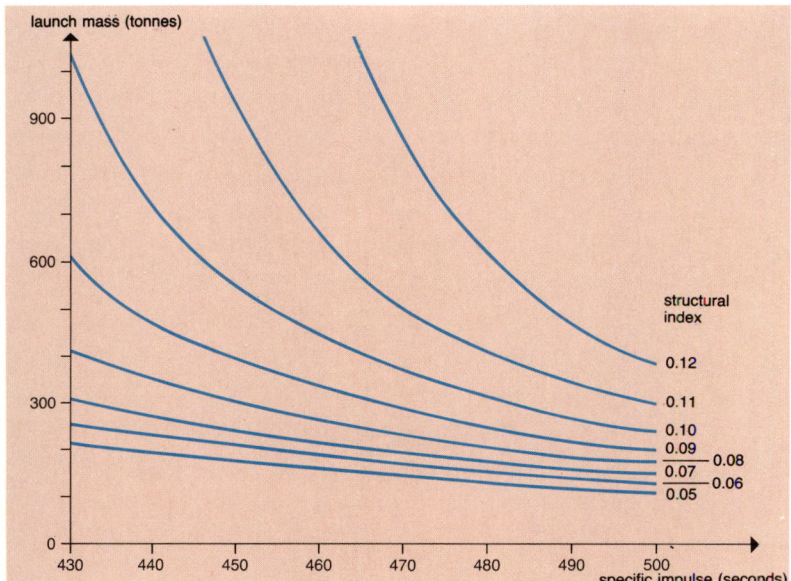

Combined engines. The main types of air breathing/rocket engines are the turbojet and the ramjet. In the turbojet, the air is compressed before entering the combustion chamber where it mixes with the fuel and burns. The gas which is produced drives the turbine attached to the compressor; it then escapes, creating the thrust. In the ramjet, the compressor is replaced by the dynamic pressure of the air entering the system at supersonic velocities. The air has to be slowed to subsonic speeds before entering the combustion chamber, and this causes very high temperatures around the air inlets as the velocity increases. This could be avoided by the air passing through the ramjet at supersonic speeds, though combustion can then become unstable.

No one propulsion system can cover the whole range of speeds required during a space launch. Combined engines which use different propulsion systems in different operational modes, yet with the same mechanical components have therefore to be considered. The diagrams below illustrate an engine currently being studied at SNECMA in France and consisting of a turborocket/ramrocket with three operational modes – turborocket, ramrocket, or rocket. Such an engine could propel a rocket from launch into orbit by using atmospheric oxygen up to an altitude of 35 kilometres and a speed of Mach 7. The air flow and nozzle position could be varied to suit the three operational modes.

The turborocket has a turbine-driven compressor which burns a mixture of liquid hydrogen and liquid oxygen. Atmospheric oxygen is compressed and used in the main combustion chamber to burn the excess fuel (post combustion). The combustion gases, at a temperature of 2600 degrees celsius expand down the converging–diverging nozzle controlling the thrust. This has a short diffuser nozzle for speeds of up to Mach 2 (a), and a medium length nozzle for up to Mach 4 (b). The ramjet mode is put into operation between Mach 4 and Mach 7 (c). The compressor now rotates because of the air flowing through it so that air is burnt with the hydrogen in the main combustion chamber. The spent gases flow down the converging–diverging nozzle in the extended position. The rocket engine takes over at Mach 7 (d), burning a mixture of liquid hydrogen and liquid oxygen. The gas now expands down the diffuser nozzle, the neck part having been moved back to block the entrance to the converging part of the nozzle (SNECMA).

American transatmospheric space vehicles. One week after the Challenger accident, President Ronald Reagan announced the beginning of a $500 million research programme into a transatmospheric vehicle (the X30). The artist's impression, above, may bear little resemblance to the final product.

The programme is essentially concerned with developing the basic techniques needed to build a propulsion system, to produce the necessary structural materials and thermal protection, and to provide high performance three-dimensional computer simulations of the aerodynamics. All the major American constructors are involved in the programme, which will be an important step in the development of a new generation of launchers (rights reserved).

Hotol. The ambitious British project, Hotol (Horizontal Take-Off and Landing), is a recoverable launcher, the brainchild of British Aerospace, its still classified propulsion system being built by Rolls Royce. This probably consists of a cryogenic rocket engine, supplied with atmospheric oxygen which has been liquified in a heat exchanger with the liquid hydrogen on board.

Hotol will have a launch mass of about 200 tonnes, its empty mass will be about 33 tonnes, and it will be 56 metres long. To reduce the mass of the landing gear and to initiate the supply of air to the engine it will take off from a chariot accelerated by a solid fuel engine. Atmospheric air will be used up to a velocity of Mach 5 and an altitude of about 30 kilometres. Then the mission will continue in the conventional rocket mode. Hotol should be able to put 7 tonnes into a low Earth orbit, and it may be able to take a crew compartment in its cargohold. Its aerodynamic shape enables it to land on a conventional runway (British Aerospace).

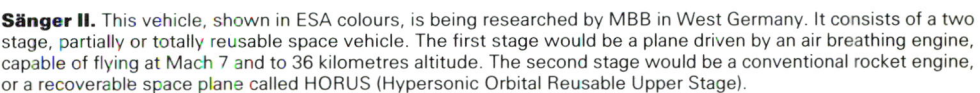

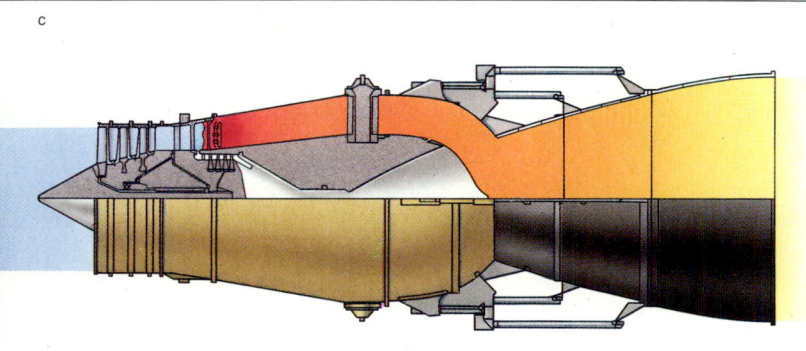

from Mach 4 to Mach 7

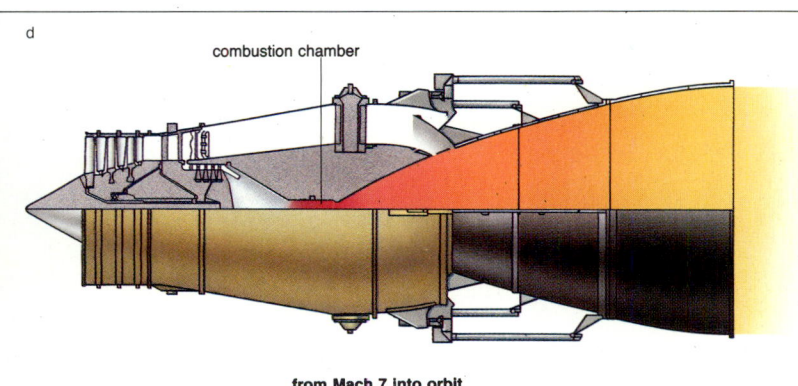

combustion chamber

from Mach 7 into orbit

Sänger II. This vehicle, shown in ESA colours, is being researched by MBB in West Germany. It consists of a two stage, partially or totally reusable space vehicle. The first stage would be a plane driven by an air breathing engine, capable of flying at Mach 7 and to 36 kilometres altitude. The second stage would be a conventional rocket engine, or a recoverable space plane called HORUS (Hypersonic Orbital Reusable Upper Stage).

Being a single stage vehicle, its performance would not be too spoilt by an eventual decrease in propulsive efficiency or by an increase in mass. On the other hand, the two assembled stages would produce a sizeable aerodynamic resistance. This is detrimental during the air breathing phase, and would require a greater initial thrust. Like Hotol, Sänger II and HORUS would use conventional runways (MBB).

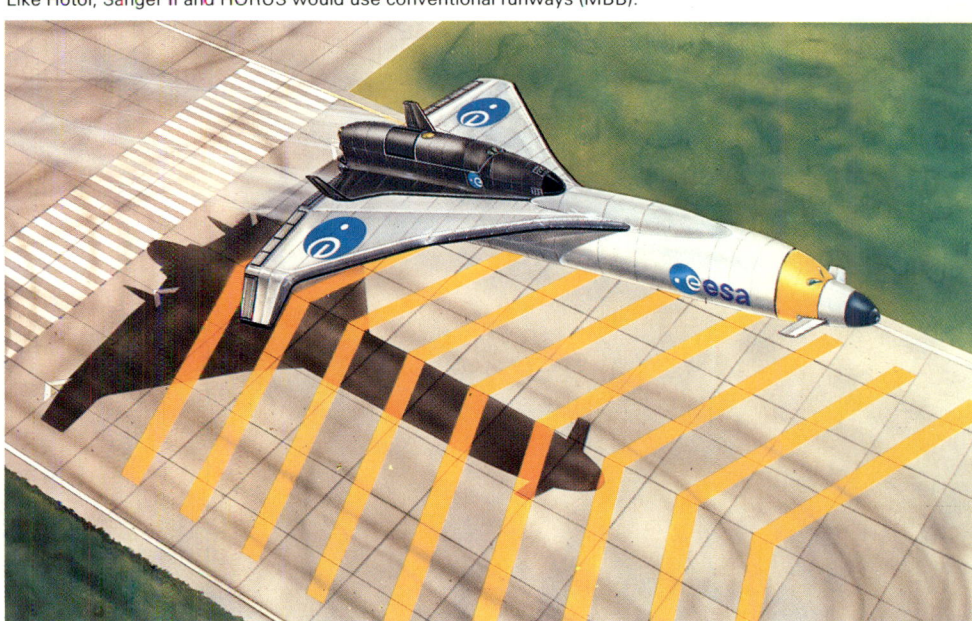

Space centres

A centre for launching vehicles into space has to satisfy many requirements. The choice and layout of the launch centre depend on considerations of safety, profitability, accessibility, infrastructure, and geological as well as political stability.

Safety is the primary consideration when choosing a site from which to launch rockets. Populated areas have to be avoided because of the terrible consequences that would follow an accident involving burning fuels. Such considerations point to three types of suitable site. Sand deserts or ice plains look feasible as it would be simple to find recoverable parts, but they have the inconvenience of extremes of temperature and unpleasant working conditions. Coasts and islands offer vast open and uninhabited areas for rockets to pass over. Problems with these sites relate principally to high levels of humidity, violent cyclones and often intractible difficulties with tropical insects. The space centre also needs good air and sea links, both for communications and access, with sufficient manpower and logistic facilities available to establish the centre. An isolated area, lacking such resources, would require massive investment to turn it into a suitable site.

Likely profitability, taking both geographical and economic factors into account, is usually the deciding factor when choosing a site. The closer the site is to the equator, the more the Earth's rotation helps the rocket for launches to the East. A geostationary satellite launched from the French space centre at Kourou (French Guiana, at 5° North) can thus be 10% heavier than one launched by the same rocket from Cape Canaveral (in Florida, at 28° North). This means that an identical satellite launched from Kourou can carry much more fuel,

extending its operational life considerably. The positioning of the Kourou Space Centre, on the coast of South America, means that it is possible to launch geostationary satellites towards the East and polar satellites towards the North to put a satellite into a Sun synchronous orbit.

As regards stability, the site has to be built on good soil with a rock base to protect it from seismic shocks and potentially severe earthquakes. It also has to be built at a site where the government will not prevent the management from exploiting the centre to the full.

Once the site has been chosen, a layout appropriate to the types of launches to be performed has to be planned. Basically, a space centre needs a technical centre, a launch complex and a control centre. Work begins as soon as the launcher parts arrive. They may arrive by sea (as at Cape Canaveral, Tanegashima, or Kourou), by rail (as at Baikonur, Plesetsk, Kapustin Yar, or Vandenberg), or by road (as at Wallops Island, Kagoshima, Jiuquan, and Xichang). The satellites themselves are often transported by air.

At the technical centre, all parts of the launch vehicle and the payload are assembled, checked using sophisticated computer systems, and prepared for launch. Once the launcher has been configured for flight at the launch complex, the countdown operations begin. These include filling the fuel tanks and pressurising them, starting the synchronised sequence of computer checks, and finally igniting the rocket engines.

The launch complex is one of two basic types. A fixed launch pad means that the launcher has to be assembled, prepared, tested and launched from the same spot. Mobile towers, with platforms, move to and from the launch site allowing access to the launcher at different heights.

The cosmodrome at Baikonur. Baikonur is the largest space centre in the world. It is situated on the arid steppes of Kazakstan where construction work began in the summer of 1955. The imposing concrete structures with metal towers built on 45 metre deep foundations, the service and assembly buildings, the antennae, the communication systems and the roads all had to be built from nothing. Today, this space centre is still used for the Soyuz and Progress launchers (APN).

Cape Canaveral. At Cape Canaveral, close to the Kennedy Space Center, the US Air Force controls complex 40 and complex 41, the bases from which the most powerful members of the Titan III family are launched. Complex 40 is used for Department of Defense satellite launches, whilst complex 41 was used in the 1970s by NASA to launch interplanetary space probes. Titan Centaur rockets sent the two West German Helios probes to the Sun, the Viking 1 and 2 probes to Mars, and the Voyager 1 and 2 probes to the far reaches of the solar system from here.

Titan III rockets were prepared for launch from a mobile platform, towed on rails from a 23 storey building called the Vertical Integration Building, (VIB) to the Solid Motor Assembly Building (SMAB) where their solid fuel engines were fitted. The rockets were then taken to launch complex 40 or 41 to be fitted with upper stages (NASA).

The design is relatively simple, but only five or six launches per year can be carried out from a fixed launch pad. A mobile launch pad, on the other hand, enables twice as many space vehicles to be launched each year, because one vehicle can be assembled whilst another is in the final stages of preparation for launch. In this case, there will be two distinct areas of operation, one for the integration of the vehicle and its payload, and one for the final preparations for launch. These are linked by rail or by a special road so that the rocket and its launch pad can be taken from the assembly halls to the launch site itself.

Théo Pirard

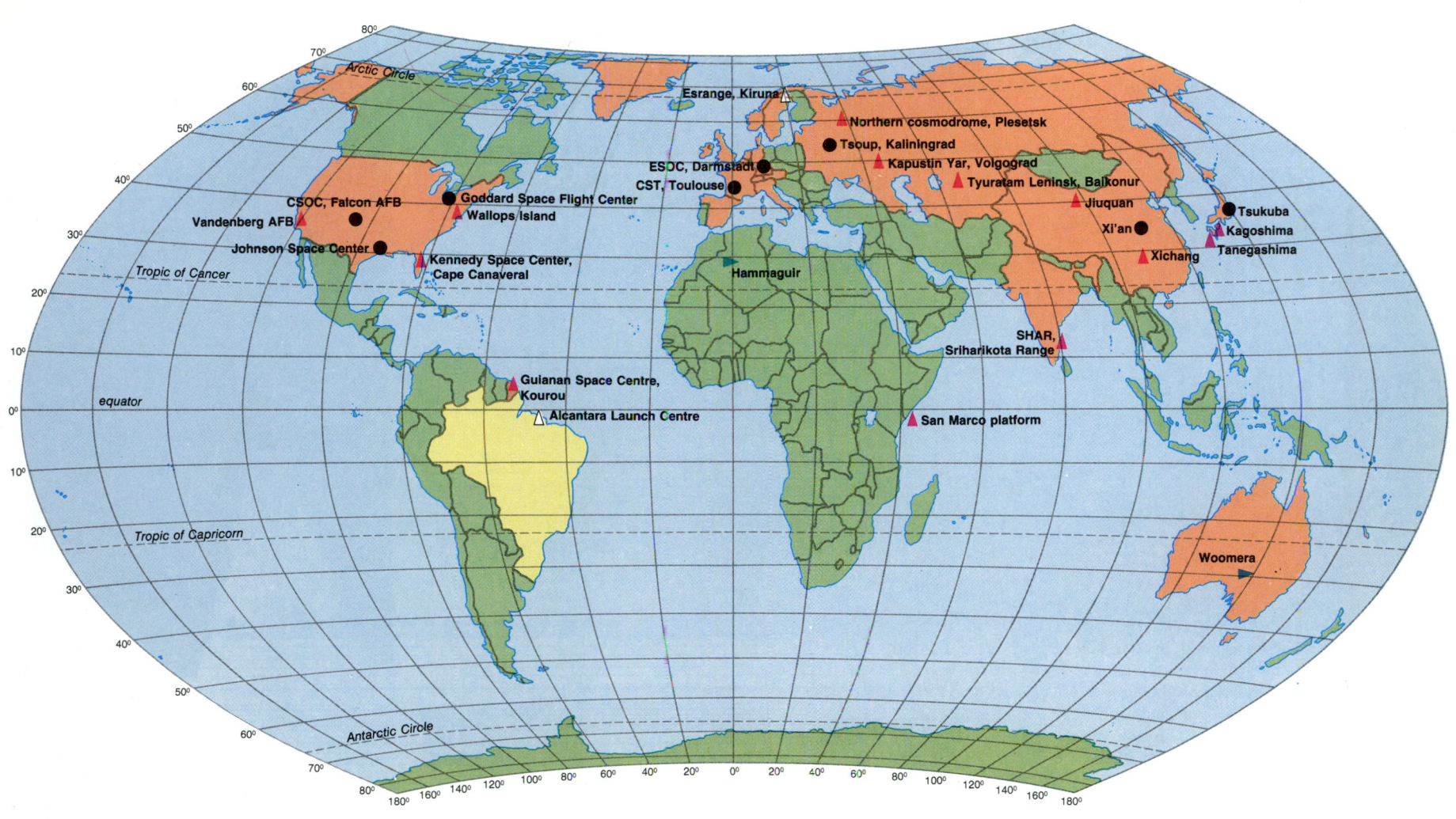

Launch centres and control centres around the world. Of the nineteen space launch centres around the world, fifteen are still in use. One is being built in Brazil (shown in yellow on the map) and another is planned in Sweden, within the Arctic Circle. Countries which have launched satellites are shown in light brown. Countries shown in green have not yet launched satellites and are not planning to do so in the near future, although Pakistan, Argentina, Indonesia and Zaire have shown interest in sending up satellites in the longer term.

▲ operational launch centre
▶ launch centre no longer in use
△ launch centre under construction
● space control centre

■ successful satellite launches
■ satellite launch in preparation
■ satellite launches neither performed nor intended

Satellite launch centres of the world

Launch bases (latitude, longitude)	Organisation responsible (country)	First launch (satellite)	current level of activity, notable launches (number of successful launches between 1957 and 1985)
Tyuratam Leninsk, or Baikonur cosmodrome (45°55'N, 63°20'E)	Ministry of Defence/Academy of Sciences (USSR)	4 October 1957 (Sputnik 1)	launch of manned spacecraft, interplanetary space probes and geostationary satellites (693 launches)
Cape Canaveral AFS (28°30'N, 80°33'W)	US Air Force/NASA (USA)	1 February 1958 (Explorer 1)	launches of military and civil satellites, manned spacecraft, interplanetary space probes and geostationary satellites (329 launches)
Vandenberg AFB (34°42'N, 120°33'W)	US Air Force/SAMTO and NASA (USA)	28 February 1959 (Discoverer 1)	currently used to launch military satellites into polar orbits; second launch base for the US space shuttle (467 launches)
Wallops Island (37°52'N, 75°28'W)	NASA Goddard Space Flight Center (USA)	16 February 1961 (Explorer 9)	oldest launch site in the USA, still used to launch rocket probes; uses Scout launcher for small satellites (19 launches)
Kapustin Yar, or Volgograd cosmodrome (48°30'N, 45°46'E)	Ministry of Defence/Academy of Sciences/Intercosmos (USSR)	16 March 1962 (Cosmos 1)	first Russian space centre to launch interplanetary space probes and small scientific and technological satellites; tests of small scale models of the space plane (82 launches)
Hammaguir/Colombia Bechar (30°48'N, 3°20'W)	CIEES/CNES (France)	26 November 1965 (A1 'Asterix')	test centre in the Sahara, used for launches of early French liquid fuel rockets, notably the Diamant (4 satellite launches)
Plesetsk, or Northern cosmodrome (62°52'N, 40°42'E)	Ministry of Defence/Academy of Sciences (USSR)	17 March 1966 (Cosmos 112)	base used to launch secret military satellites; most active launch centre in the world (1056 launches)
San Marco platform (2°56'S, 40°12'E)	CRA/University of Rome (Italy)	26 April 1967 (San Marco 2)	Scout rockets launched from this platform for NASA (8 launches)
Kennedy Space Center (28°30'N, 80°36'W)	NASA (USA)	9 November 1967 (Apollo 4)	complex 39 specially designed to launch Saturn V rocket for missions to the Moon and adapted to launch the space shuttle (41 launches)
Woomera Range (31°35'S, 136°50'E)	WRE/ELDO/British Department of Trade and Industry (Australia)	29 November 1967 (Wresat)	launch site for missile and rocket probes Europa and Black Arrow as well as an Australian satellite (2 launches)
Kagoshima Space Centre (31°15'N, 131°05'E)	ISAS/University of Tokyo (Japan)	11 February 1970 (Ohsumi)	scientific and technological satellites and rocket probes research centre; two interplanetary space probes launched in 1985 (16 launches)
Guianan Space Centre at Kourou (5°14'N, 52°46'W)	CNES/ESA/Arianespace (France)	10 March 1970 (Dial)	base for launches to East and to North, mostly geostationary satellites; commercial exploitation by Arianespace (18 launches)
Jiuquan SLC (40°50'N, 100°02'E)	Ministry of Defence/MOA (China)	24 April 1970 (SKW1/Tungfanghung)	experimentation centre for Chinese missiles; currently used for CZ2 rocket launches (13 launches)
Tanegashima Space Centre (30°24'N, 130°58'E)	Nasda (Japan)	9 September 1975 (ETS1/Kiku1)	launch site for civil and commercial satellites, usually into geostationary orbit; to be enlarged in the 1990s (13 launches)
SHAR/Sriharikota Range (13°47'N, 80°15'E)	ISRO (India)	18 July 1980 (Rohini RS1)	island centre used for rocket tests; experiments with rocket probes and to launch Indian satellites (3 launches)
Xichang SLC (27°58'N, 102°13'E)	MOA (China)	29 January 1984 (STW1)	remote centre specially built to launch satellites into geostationary and polar orbits; capable of launching CZ3 rockets (2 launches)
Under construction in the 1990s			
Alcantara Launch Centre (2°24'S, 44°24'W)	Ministry of Aeronautics/COBAE/CTA (Brazil)	planned for early 1990s	under construction; possible to launch in all directions for scientific and commercial missions (Orbita company)
Esrange, Kiruna (67°53'N, 21°04'E)	Swedish Space Corporation (Sweden)	during the 1990s	in the Arctic Circle for launching rockets, for control and utilisation of satellites; examining feasibility of launching small satellites into polar orbits

Space centres

Launch sites

The USA

In the USA, the Pentagon and NASA are responsible for all space launch complexes. Since the USA has a considerable coastline, all space launches now take place over the Atlantic or the Pacific Oceans. However, during the 1940s, the desert in New Mexico was considered to be the ideal place for carrying out experiments with bombs and rockets. The test centre at White Sands was used by the US Army to test fire V2 rockets, but the proximity of Mexican cities prevented it from being used to launch satellites. The federal authorities accordingly chose the coasts of California and Florida for testing rockets. During the 1950s, the US Air Force set up two specialised bases to launch medium range and intercontinental missiles: the Eastern Test Range at Cape Canaveral and the Western Test Range at Vandenberg Air Force Base (AFB).

The USA, like the USSR, has a total of three launch sites. When NASA was created in 1958 it was given access to military bases; then, in the 1960s, it built its own facilities for the Apollo lunar exploration programme. It later took control of Wallops Island in Virginia and developed it as a launch site for small satellites.

Cape Canaveral Air Force Station (AFS) is situated near a marshy island which is a nature reserve for a number of protected animals. Until 1950 it was a largely uninhabited area full of reeds, mosquitoes, alligators, and snakes. Only in July 1948 was this wild region chosen over sites in Texas, California and Georgia as the site for an experimental base for American rockets. Problems associated with the area are the humidity and the number of hurricanes; the advantages are the isolated position, accessibility from the sea and possibility of siting linked tracking stations on the Bahamas, Antigua and Ascension Island.

On 24 July 1950, a two stage Bumper 7 rocket was launched to inaugurate what is now the most famous launch site in the world. Between Cape Canaveral in the south and Merritt Island in the north, several launch pads were built along the Atlantic coast as the missile and launcher programmes intensified. Cape Canaveral's famous history began, however, with a major disaster. On 6 December 1957, two months after the successful launch of Sputnik 1, the Vanguard launcher with its satellite payload exploded in full view of television cameras. Yet in the years that followed, NASA used the Redstone, Thor, Atlas and Titan missiles, converted into rocket launchers, to achieve many successes, including manned spaceflights in the Mercury and Gemini capsules. The same launch site was used to put a man on the Moon. Unfortunately, the 6000 hectares of the military base at Cape Canaveral were not enough to assemble, test and prepare the giant Saturn V rockets used for the Apollo programme. After constructing complexes 34 and 37 for launching the Saturn I and IB rockets, NASA took over an additional 35000 hectares on Merritt Island immediately to the west in 1962.

It took four years to build the installations required for complex 39 at the NASA Kennedy Space Center. It was from here that man went

The crawler (below). The crawler, one of the most powerful vehicles in the world, has a maximum speed of 1·6 kilometres per hour on its eight enormous tank tracks. Two 2750 horse power diesel engines drive four 1 megawatt generators which power 16 electric motors. This photograph shows the Saturn V launcher, Apollo 14 and the umbilical tower being transported to pad 39A. The unit weighs 8165 tonnes, about 2700 tonnes for the crawler itself and over 5400 tonnes for the rocket and the umbilical tower. The crawler is also used to transport the space shuttle from the VAB to one of the two launch areas at complex 39 (NASA).

Filling the space shuttle's External Tank (right). The gantry covers the top of the rust coloured External Tank (ET) when filling it with almost two million litres of liquid fuels in the last few hours before launch. The gantry withdraws to the side of the service tower just two minutes before liftoff (NASA).

to the Moon. Skylab and its occupants were launched from here, as were the astronauts destined to rendezvous with the cosmonauts aboard a Russian Soyuz. Most space shuttle launches have also been from here.

The space complex is enormous, the assembly and launch areas being located some distance apart. The launcher is mounted on a platform inside the VAB (Vehicle Assembly Building) and then transported to the actual launch site on the 'crawler', a giant, slow moving platform. The two launch areas, 39A and 39B, are as much as six kilometres from the VAB and the Launch Control Center (LCC).

Near the Kennedy Space Center are complexes 40 and 41, used from 1965 for launching Titan III rockets. An artificial island had to be created nearby for the Vertical Integration Building (VIB) in which four Titan III launchers could be assembled simultaneously.

The main buildings at the Kennedy Space Center (right). The Vehicle Assembly Building (VAB) is the imposing structure in the centre left of the photograph. It covers a ground area of 3·25 hectares, is 218 metres long and 158 metres wide, and has a height of 160 metres. Two space shuttles can be assembled here at once.

The Launch Control Center (LCC) is the four storey building with the large windows in front of the VAB. It has four control rooms, two of which are for space shuttle launches. In the background, the landing runway stretches out for 4·5 kilometres; it is 91 metres wide and the concrete is half a metre deep at the centre. Using a microwave landing system, shuttles can land here whatever the weather. However, landing is more difficult than at Edwards Air Force Base in California because of variable cross winds near the ocean's edge.

On the right of the VAB, the crawler is taking a space shuttle and its launcher towards pad 39A; a mobile launch tower used for the Saturn V and IB rockets can be seen behind (NASA).

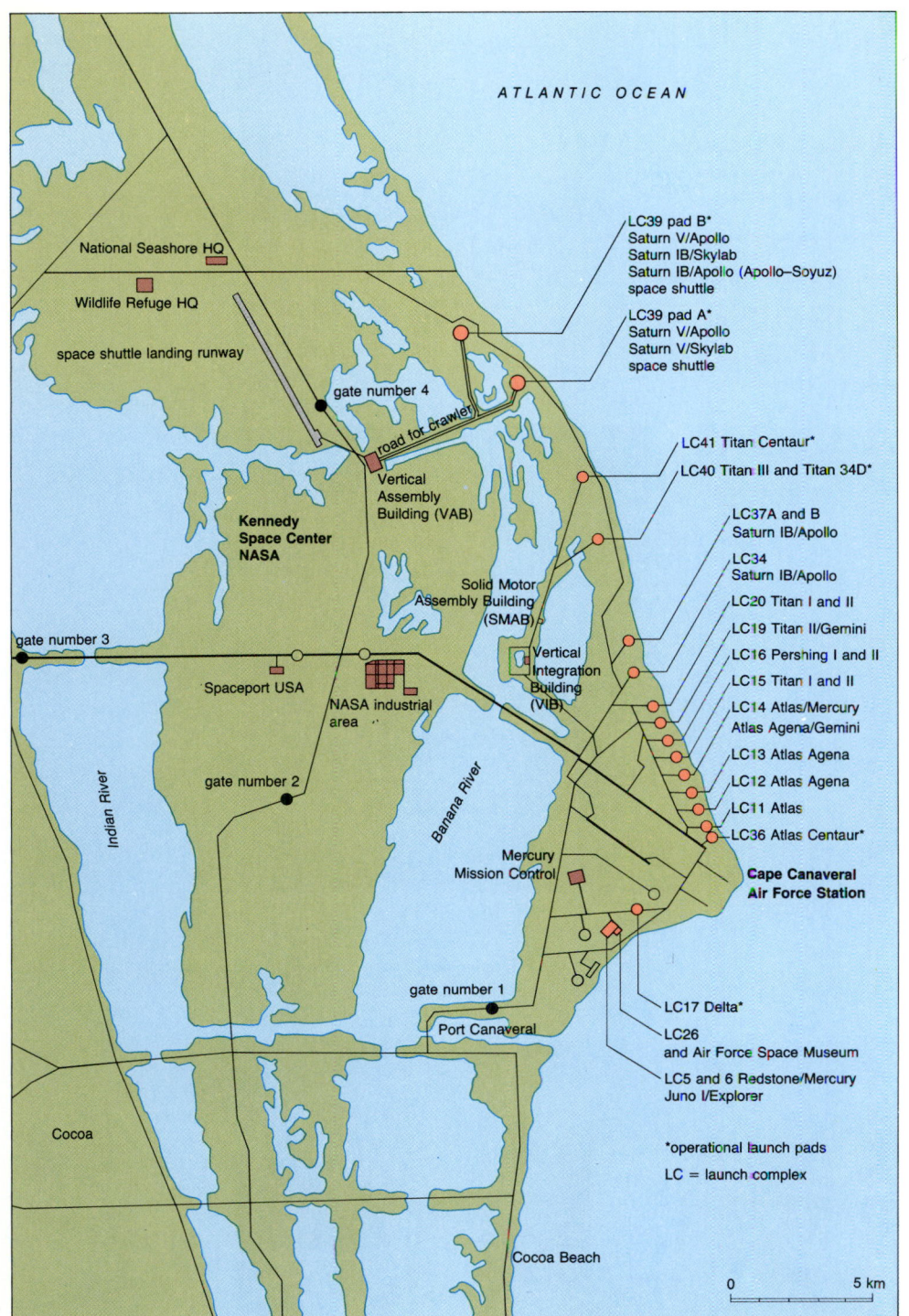

LC39 pad B*
Saturn V/Apollo
Saturn IB/Skylab
Saturn IB/Apollo (Apollo–Soyuz)
space shuttle

LC39 pad A*
Saturn V/Apollo
Saturn V/Skylab
space shuttle

LC41 Titan Centaur*
LC40 Titan III and Titan 34D*

LC37A and B
Saturn IB/Apollo

LC34
Saturn IB/Apollo

LC20 Titan I and II
LC19 Titan II/Gemini
LC16 Pershing I and II
LC15 Titan I and II
LC14 Atlas/Mercury
Atlas Agena/Gemini
LC13 Atlas Agena
LC12 Atlas Agena
LC11 Atlas
LC36 Atlas Centaur*

LC17 Delta*
LC26
and Air Force Space Museum
LC5 and 6 Redstone/Mercury
Juno I/Explorer

*operational launch pads
LC = launch complex

0   5 km

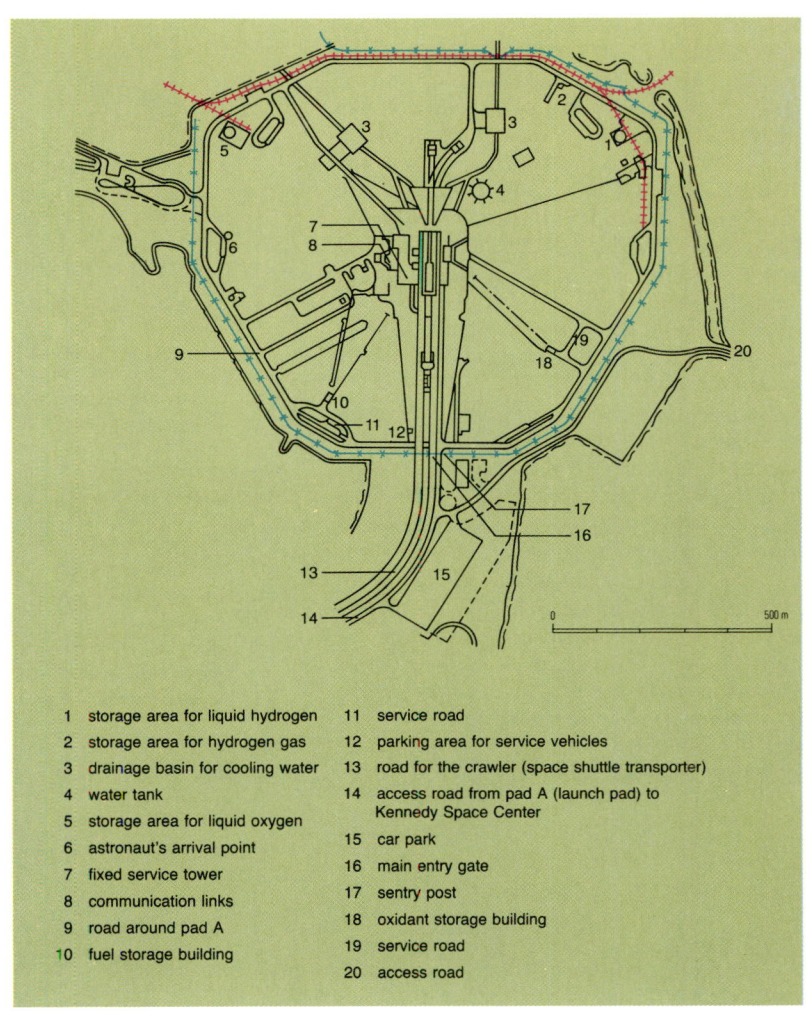

1	storage area for liquid hydrogen	11	service road
2	storage area for hydrogen gas	12	parking area for service vehicles
3	drainage basin for cooling water	13	road for the crawler (space shuttle transporter)
4	water tank	14	access road from pad A (launch pad) to Kennedy Space Center
5	storage area for liquid oxygen	15	car park
6	astronaut's arrival point	16	main entry gate
7	fixed service tower	17	sentry post
8	communication links	18	oxidant storage building
9	road around pad A	19	service road
10	fuel storage building	20	access road

Maps of the Kennedy Space Center at Cape Canaveral. The launch facilities at Cape Canaveral grew out of the lagoons and swamps; concrete and metal soon covered the region. Now only launch complexes 36 (Atlas Centaur), 39 (space shuttle), and 40 and 41 (Titan III) are still operational. At the Kennedy Space Center, the launch pad at complex 39A is the most famous of all. This was used for nine Apollo missions to the Moon and the first twenty-one missions of the space shuttle.

The neighbouring towns of Cocoa Beach and Titusville knew a boom in the 1960s. They are still popular with tourists, but their popularity waxes and wanes with the changing activities at Cape Canaveral Air Force Station and the NASA Kennedy Space Center.

The plan directly above shows details of pad A and launch complex 39 (NASA).

American launch sites. Due to their ideal positions on the Pacific and Atlantic coasts, these two space centres carry out all US space launches. The Kennedy Space Center in Florida launches satellites into geostationary orbit and initiates lunar missions, and interplanetary space probes. The Vandenberg Air Force Base (AFB) is used for satellites launched into near polar orbit. The space shuttle can be launched from both sites (NASA).

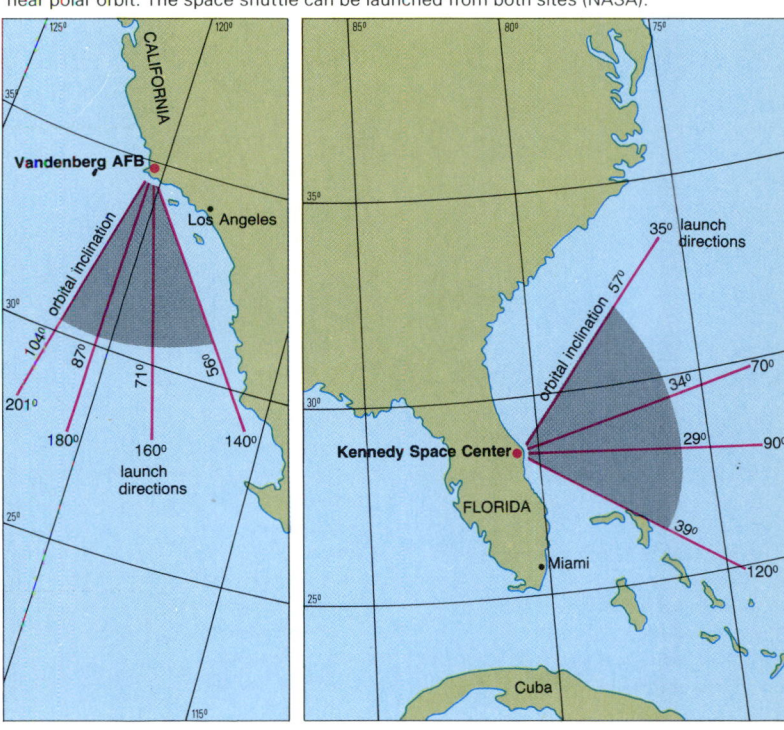

Going into space

The Vandenberg Air Force Base is principally used by the US Military. It is situated amongst the hills bordering the Pacific Ocean, almost halfway between Los Angeles and San Francisco. In all it covers some 40 000 hectares, being served both by an airport and the Southern Pacific Railroad. There are about 50 launch pads here, of which half are silos for liquid fuel or solid fuel missiles. The most important complex of the Space And Missile Test Organization (SAMTO) is located at the southern end of the base. The Shuttle Launch Complex 6 (SLC6) is used for missions requiring a polar orbit.

The Wallops Island Flight Facility in the state of Virginia is now part of the NASA Goddard Space Flight Center. This modest launch base of some 2500 hectares in all is spread over three sites. Between 1945 and 1985, over 13 000 rockets were launched for scientific and technological experiments; in particular, the four stage, solid fuel Scout rocket launched about 20 small satellites from here. Only recently, in September 1986, did NASA hand the installations at Wallops over to the private company, Space Services Inc. of America, which is now responsible for launching commercial payloads using Conestoga solid fuel rockets.

Théo Pirard

1 landing runway
2 centre for mating the space shuttle to its transport plane (a Boeing 747)
3 missile tests and space systems research and management centre
4 flight crew's quarters; medical services and preparation for flight in space
5 computer systems for verification and control of the space shuttle's ground support systems
6 logistics centre; management, and replacement of materials and support systems
7 maintenance and verification centre for the space shuttle; inspection and repair of the shuttle, both inside and out
8 centre for overhaul and assembly of the solid fuel booster rockets
9 Launch Control Center; command and control of all operations up to launch
10 space shuttle area
11 treatment and storage centre for External Tanks, transported by barge from Lousiana
12 recovery centre for the solid fuel boosters; dismantling operations
13 storage area for toxic fuel
14 base control centre
15 supply office
16 support complex for spacecraft
17 administration buildings
18 Minuteman missile preparation buildings

other launch complexes:
A Minuteman III (silos)
B Bomarc
C Thor Delta (SLC2)
D Titan II
E rocket probes (PALC B)
F Thor Agena; Atlas F Agena D (SLC3W)
G Atlas Agena; Atlas F (SLC3E)
H Atlas Agena; Titan IIIB Agena D (SLC4W)
I Atlas Agena; Titan IIID (SLC4E)
J Scout (SLC5)

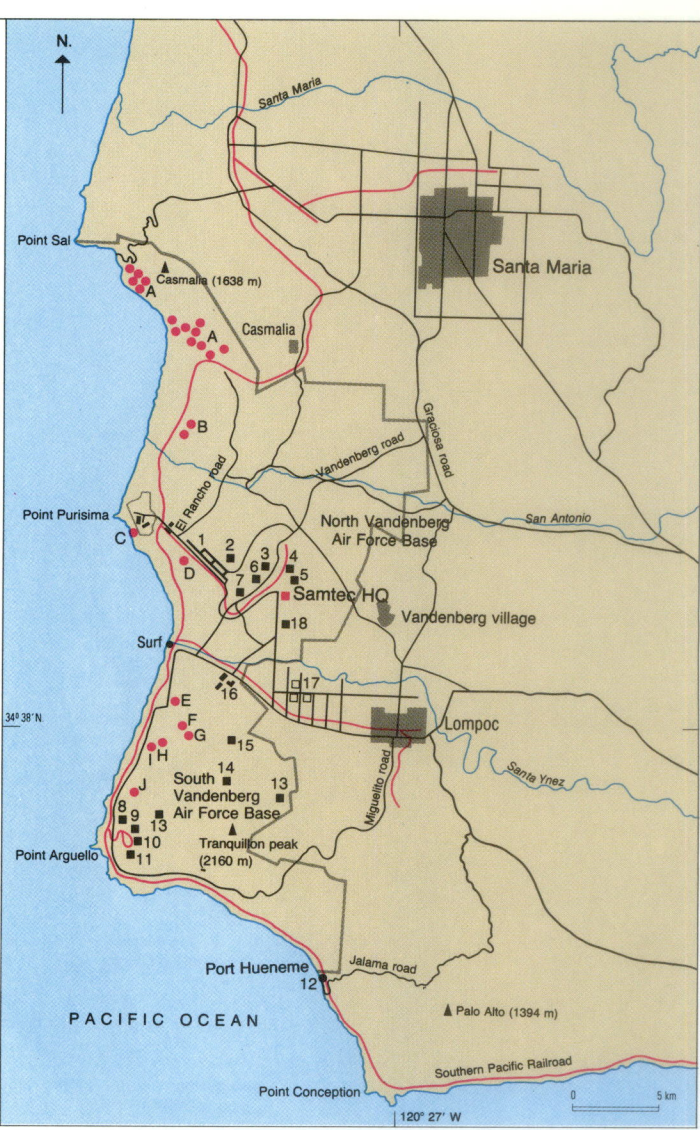

Vandenberg military base. The impressive Shuttle Launch Complex SLC6 (above) on the coast of California was designed to launch four space shuttles each year on military and polar missions; it was originally part of the installations planned in the 1960s for the Military Orbiting Laboratory programme. In March 1985, the space shuttle Enterprise was launched from Vandenberg.

On the left of the photograph, USAF initials identify the Shuttle Assembly Building which covers the space shuttle during its mounting on the launch pad. On the right, the white Mobile Service Tower, with a mass of 7500 tonnes, allows access to the different parts of the shuttle. Also evident in the photograph are the shuttle's rust coloured external tank, the two solid fuel boosters, and the gantry which carries the fuel supply pipes (Martin Marietta).

Wallops Island space centre. The Wallops Flight Facility, a map of which is shown on the left, is a modest base. Its main use is for launching rocket probes into the upper atmosphere for scientific or technological experiments on meteorology, ionospheric physics, solar physics, astronomy and biological research.

The Black Brant X rocket shown below has three stages and is 33 metres long. It is here being prepared on launch pad 0 at Wallops Island for a mission to study the polar cusps of the Earth's magnetosphere (NASA).

1 radio transmitter	12 launch pad number 3
2 tracking radar	13 administration building
3 atmospheric physics measurements laboratory	14 technical services for maintenance and safety
4 radars	15 close tracking radar
5 bridge	16 weather tower
6 installation for dynamic balancing of rocket	17 old port
7 payload test area	18 launch pad and blockhouse number 2
8 launch pad number 5	19 assembly building number 1
9 weather tower	20 launch pad number 1
10 launch pad number 4	21 liquid storage area
11 blockhouse number 3	22 launch pad number 0

Japan

Two government funded organisations run Japan's space activities. They are the Institute of Space and Astronautical Science (ISAS), financed by the Ministry of Education, whose work is of a scientific nature; and the National Space Development Agency of Japan (Nasda), based within the Prime Minister's Office, which is concerned with the practical applications of space activities. Since 1963 ISAS has used the space centre at Kagoshima to launch solid fuel Mu rockets. Nasda prepared a launch complex on the island of Tanegashima some five years later. The two sites are about a hundred kilometres apart.

The space centre at Kagoshima, in the south of Kyushu, covers 71 hectares of picturesque, verdant and hilly land. At 220 metres above sea level, the Mu launch facilities form the most important part of the base. The three or four stage launcher is assembled and checked here, and its satellite payload is attached in a 43 metre high tower near the blockhouse. At an altitude of 277 metres, the buildings where the Kappa and Lambda rockets are prepared are clustered together.

After five attempts, between September 1966 and February 1970, Japan succeeded in putting its first satellite into orbit from Kagoshima using the Lambda 4S (improved) rocket. The control centre, tracking and telemetry station and payload preparation area are situated on the Nagatsubo plateau, 320 metres above sea level. On 24 January 1990, a Muses A satellite was successfully launched towards a lunar orbit from the same site.

Nasda's space centre at Tanegashima, just south of Kyushu, covers 860 hectares of an island with 43 000 inhabitants, about 1000 kilometres from Tokyo. Two launch pads have been constructed in the south of the island on either side of a picturesque cove. The Takesaki pad is used for solid fuel TT500 A rockets carrying microgravity experiments in recoverable capsules in preparation for the Spacelab J1 mission. The Osaki pad, which covers 40 hectares, is used for satellite launches. The NI, NII and HI launchers, built under licence in Japan from the first stage of the American Thor Delta rocket, are assembled here under a mobile service structure. In February 1977, this pad became the third in the world from which geostationary satellites could be launched. Most of Nasda's launchers are used to put telecommunications, meteorological and broadcasting satellites into geostationary orbit.

With the arrival of the HI rocket, the Tanegashima centre was adapted to cope with cryogenic rocket engines. A more powerful version, the HII, is currently being developed, and should be ready in the 1990s. A new complex will be built on the Yoshinobusaki site, a kilometre from the HI complex, to accommodate it. The HII launch site will have separate assembly and launch areas, linked by a railway, and an HII rocket could if necessary be launched every six weeks. The only practical drawback is the Japanese offshore fishing season which means that launches from Kagoshima and Tanegashima can only take place during January and February, or July and August.

Théo Pirard

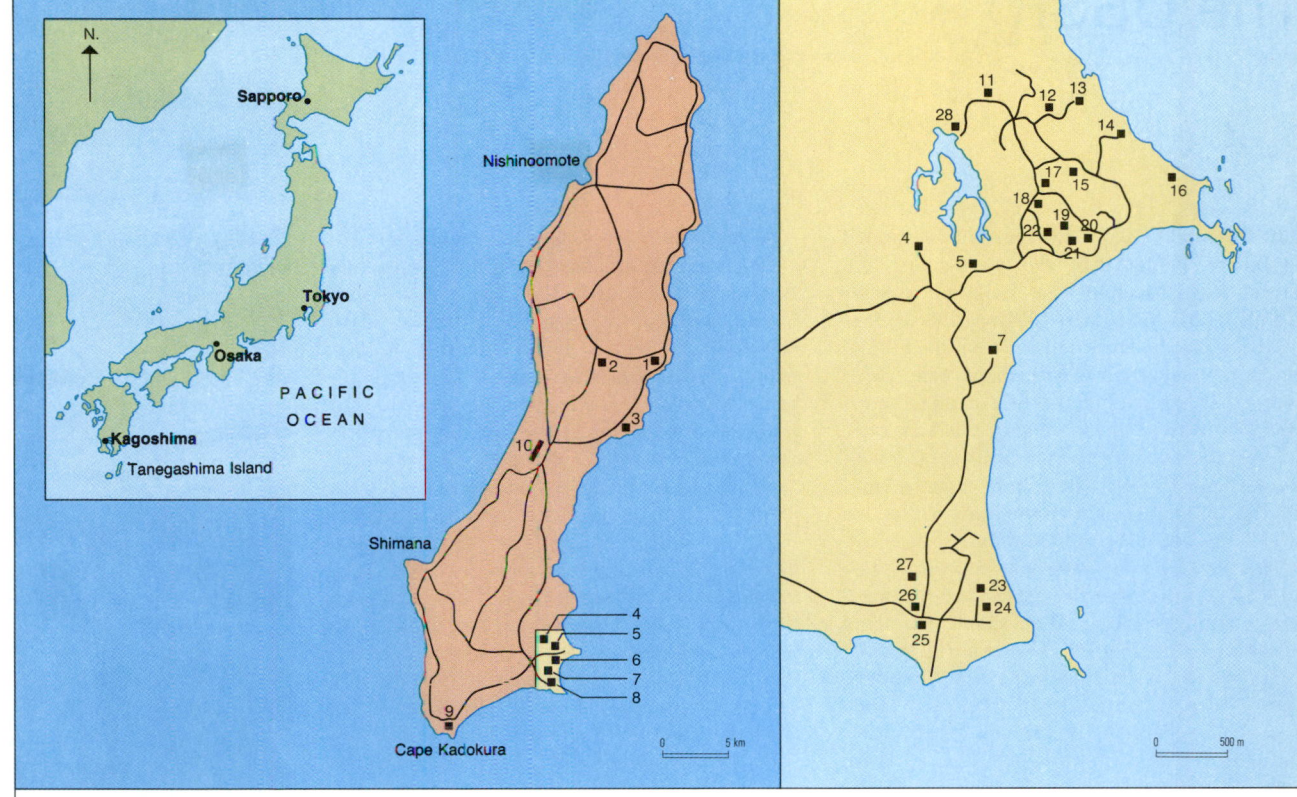

1	Nogi radar station	11	power station
2	Nakawari boresite tower	12	spin test building
3	Masuda tracking station	13	storage area for solid fuel
4	Nakanoyama telemetry station	14	static test firing
5	control centre	15	storage area for liquid fuel
6	Osaki launch site	16	HII launch pad, under construction
7	optical station	17	rocket assembly building number 2
8	Takesaki launch site	18	rocket assembly building number 1
9	optical station	19	blockhouse
10	Tanegashima airport	20	NI launch pad

21	storage area for liquid fuel
22	meteorological observation tower
23	launch pad number 1
24	launch pad number 2
25	exhibition hall
26	meteorological station
27	administration building
28	water supply

Tanegashima launch centre. The space centre at Tanegashima is the largest launch complex in Japan. Satellites are launched from the northern site at Osaki, and rockets from Takesaki to the south. Up to 1984, 86 rockets and 13 NI and NII launchers were launched from here. It is currently used to launch Japan's civil and commercial satellites and, in the future, will be the launch site for the powerful HII launcher (Nasda).

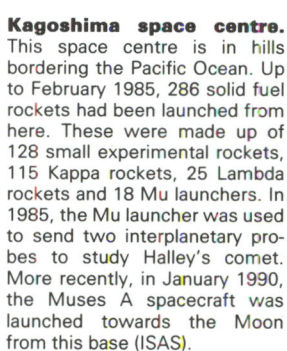

Kagoshima space centre. This space centre is in hills bordering the Pacific Ocean. Up to February 1985, 286 solid fuel rockets had been launched from here. These were made up of 128 small experimental rockets, 115 Kappa rockets, 25 Lambda rockets and 18 Mu launchers. In 1985, the Mu launcher was used to send two interplanetary probes to study Halley's comet. More recently, in January 1990, the Muses A spacecraft was launched towards the Moon from this base (ISAS).

The USSR

In October 1957, the Soviets launched Sputnik 1, inaugurating the world's first and largest civil spaceport, the Baikonur cosmodrome. Thirty years later, nearly 2000 satellite launches have been carried out from the USSR. At present, nearly 100 spaceflights take place every year, an average of two satellites each week. In order to maintain such a launch rate, the Soviets have three cosmodromes, each with several launch sites, where both launcher and satellite preparations can be standardised so procedures become almost routine.

The Baikonur cosmodrome, which is also used for testing intercontinental ballistic missiles, is south of the city of Kazakhstan, some 2000 kilometres from Moscow, near the town of Tyuratam. In the middle of the 1980s, the new service town of Leninsk had 50 000 inhabitants, mostly engineers and technicians, and their families. Living conditions are extreme, with temperatures of 50 degrees celsius in summer and −40 degrees celsius in winter. The climate is very dry, with sand storms or even snow storms, and there is little natural vegetation. The area around the city is, however, irrigated by canals so that it is very green, and every cosmonaut is invited to plant a tree before going into space. From photographs taken by the Landsat and SPOT remote sensing satellites, it appears that Baikonur covers an area that is nearly half the size of Belgium. The greatest single asset of the site is that the Sun shines for more than 300 days a year.

Because of the corrosive effect of the sand, the Soviets have adopted the technique of horizontal launcher assembly and payload integration in immense air-conditioned halls. Once the payload has been put in place, the launch vehicle is transported, still in the horizontal position, to the launch pad. The French delegation at Baikonur for the final preparations for the Franco-Soviet Soyuz T6 mission in June 1982 reported that it took only an hour to transport the launcher, weighing around 310 tonnes, from the assembly halls to its place on the launch platform. Only one or two days are needed for flight verification and for filling the fuel tanks prior to launch.

Soyuz and Progress launchers are prepared in a long assembly building, called the Montachno Ispytatelnyy Korpus (MIK). The biggest installations, with gantries standing 80 metres high, are used for Proton or Salyut launchers. A completely new complex is required for the cryogenic launchers, which will be able to put payloads of between 15 and 100 tonnes, or the Soviet space shuttles, into orbit. Large landing runways, under construction, have also been identified from photographs taken from space.

The Volgograd cosmodrome near Kapustin Yar, on the banks of the Volga, is the oldest of the Soviet rocket launch sites. It has been used since 1947 to test medium range missiles and to launch rocket probes. It was originally believed that the Russians launched the first Sputnik satellites from here. However, it was not in fact until the Cosmos programme began in March 1962 that the site was used to put satellites into orbit. From the Volgograd cosmodrome, Vertikal scientific rockets are launched, as are Cosmos and Intercosmos satellites weighing up to 1 tonne. From here, between June 1982 and December 1984, there were four launches of a scaled down model of the Soviet space shuttle. This splashed down into either the Indian Ocean or the Black Sea after completing one revolution of the Earth.

The Plesetsk, or Northern, cosmodrome is the most active space centre in the world – one satellite can be launched every week. However, it is also the most secret space centre in the world, being mainly used for strategic military missions; the *Kosmonavtika Encyclopedia*, published in Moscow in 1985, devoted only nine lines to it. On clear nights, it is, however, possible to see the glowing exhausts of rockets launched at Plesetsk from both Sweden and Finland. Several scientific satellites, for example the Bulgarian satellite Intercosmos 1300, have been launched from here. Only in August 1981 were photographs published showing launch preparations at Plesetsk. They were reminiscent of the procedures followed at Baikonur, but within a more pleasant northern landscape of pine and silver birch forests.

Théo Pirard

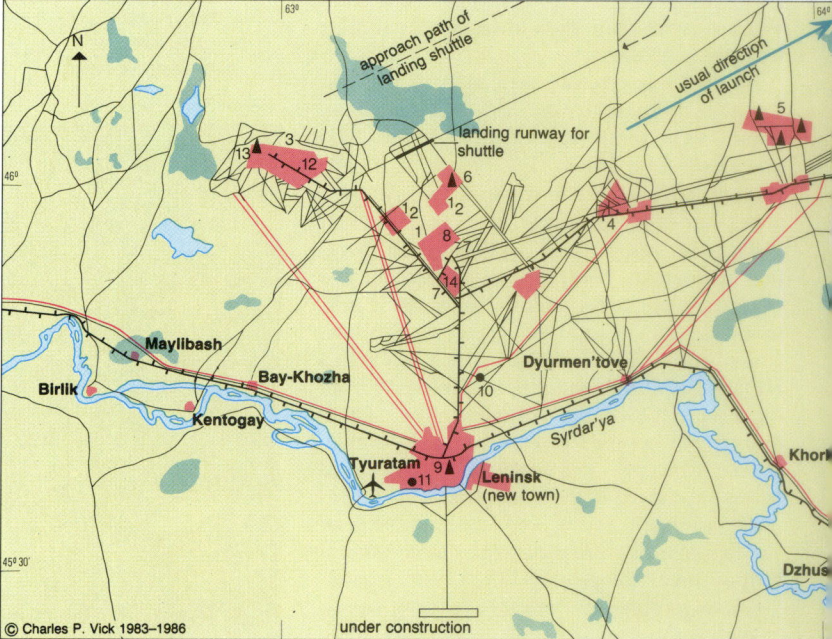

Transporting the Soyuz launcher by rail. Two days before its planned launch date, the A2 launcher with its Soyuz capsule, a total empty mass of 31·5 tonnes, is transported by rail to one of the launch pads at the Baikonur cosmodrome (near right). This most proven of all Soviet launchers is taken out of the MIK building after being assembled in the horizontal position. The raising over the launch pit, of the rocket, with 20 large and 12 small rocket engines on its first stage, takes at least an hour (far right) (APN).

A launch pad at the Baikonur cosmodrome. The Vostok and Soyuz launch platform (left) consists of a rectangular paved area with a circular hole of 16 metres diameter in the middle. During a launch, the hot exhaust gases escape under the paved area into a 45 metre deep basin.

For final prelaunch checks and fuelling, the rocket is partially enclosed between two high structures. The umbilical pole, the two towers, the rocket and the four pylons which support it over the hole together weigh about 1000 tonnes.

Each of the three launch pads is based on the Sputnik launch system, and more than 200 launches have been performed. However, on 26 September 1983, one launch pad was seriously damaged after the launcher for the Soyuz T10 mission exploded about 90 seconds before lifting off. The crew of Vladimir Titov and Gennady Strekalov had just enough time to activate their emergency ejection system, at the top of the rocket, which saved them from certain death (APN).

The MIK assembly building (right). The different parts of the Soyuz rocket launcher are brought from industrial sites throughout the USSR to the assembly hall of the Baikonur cosmodrome. This massive building has a floor area of more than 11 000 square metres.

The photograph shows the final preparation phase of a Soyuz launcher. The third stage and the payload are being put into place (centre foreground). The second stage, clustered around the first, is seen at the top left of the picture (APN).

Moving an Intercosmos rocket to the Volgograd cosmodrome (left). The Volgograd cosmodrome was the first Soviet space centre to be opened to the West, during an Intercosmos programme to launch small scientific satellites. Launchers, based on medium range missiles, are prepared in the horizontal position, transported by rail and then launched from silos (APN).

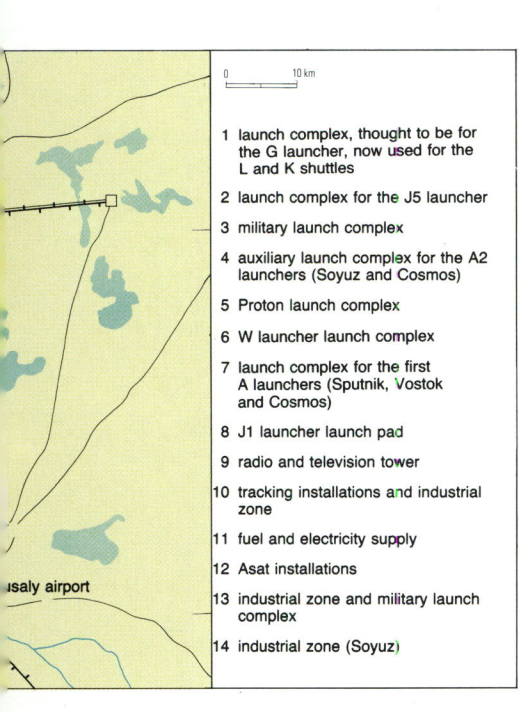

1 launch complex, thought to be for the G launcher, now used for the L and K shuttles
2 launch complex for the J5 launcher
3 military launch complex
4 auxiliary launch complex for the A2 launchers (Soyuz and Cosmos)
5 Proton launch complex
6 W launcher launch complex
7 launch complex for the first A launchers (Sputnik, Vostok and Cosmos)
8 J1 launcher launch pad
9 radio and television tower
10 tracking installations and industrial zone
11 fuel and electricity supply
12 Asat installations
13 industrial zone and military launch complex
14 industrial zone (Soyuz)

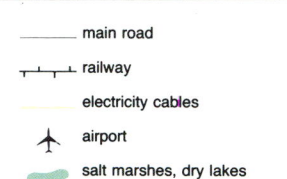

—— main road
—⊢⊢⊢— railway
—— electricity cables
✈ airport
salt marshes, dry lakes

© Charles P. Vick 1983-1986

1 base headquarters
2 V2 monument
3 high frequency antenna
4 guard post
5 radars
6 telemetry station
7 horizontal assembly building
8 press centre
9 C1 launch pad
10 B1 launch silos
11 Vladimirovka airport
12 Achtubinsk airport
13 main airport at Kapustin Yar
14 early installations for launching V2, R1, R2 and R3 rockets
15 other installations for the launch of rockets

Soviet cosmodromes. Maps of the cosmodromes at Baikonur (above left), Volgograd (above right) and Plesetsk (right) were prepared by Charles P. Vick using photographs taken by Landsat satellites, together with other information available in Soviet publications, official photographs, films, documentaries and visitors' reports.

Plesetsk is both the most active and the most secret of the three Soviet cosmodromes. In March 1966, when the first satellite, Cosmos 112, was launched from a site near the Arctic Circle, the Soviet authorities did not announce the inauguration of a new cosmodrome. It was Geoffrey E. Perry and his students at Kettering Grammar School, in England, who analysed and calculated the orbit of Cosmos 112 and subsequently announced the existence of the military complex at Plesetsk (Charles P. Vick).

The main installations seem to be concentrated around the city of Kochmas and along the Yemtsa river. It is thought that there are a number of ICBM installations between Plesetsk, Obozerskiy and Sredmerenga.

△ old launch pads for IRBM/ICBM and Cosmos
▲ Sputnik, Cosmos, Soyuz, A2, A2e and Molniya launch pads
▲ ICBM installations
■ new ICBM installations
1 Obozersky South East airport
2 Sel'co airport
3 Plesty airport
4 industrial zone

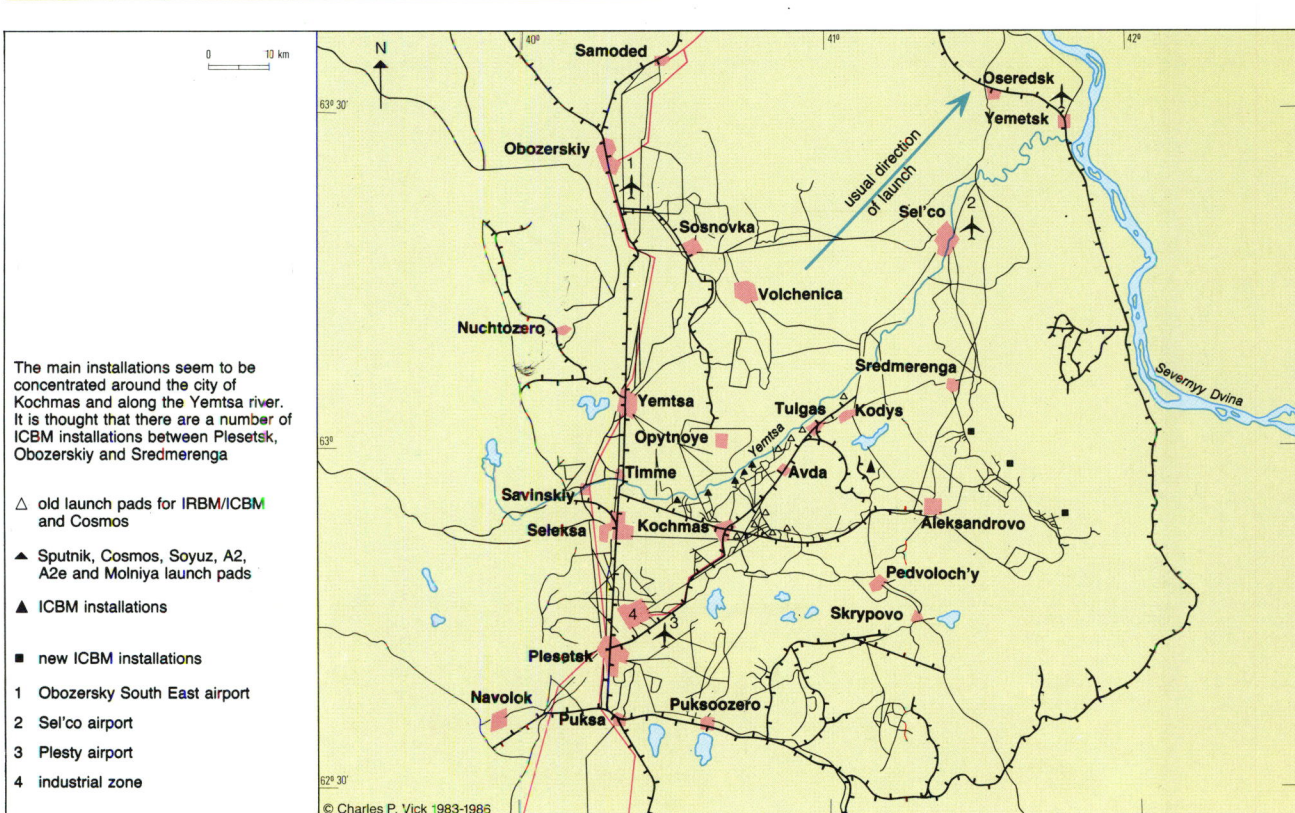

© Charles P. Vick 1983-1986

Europe

Europe early on showed a desire to investigate space alongside the two superpowers. France went to work in the Sahara, establishing the Centre interarmées d'essais d'engins spéciaux (CIEES: Armed forces' special vehicles test centre) at its base at Colomb-Béchar on the Hammaguir plateau. The launch pad and installations erected here in 1959 covered only 160 hectares, but the field of fire extended over a thousand kilometres. Hammaguir was used to launch small satellites until the beginning of 1967. There were four successful launches of the three stage Diamant launchers from here. Following the Franco-Algerian Evian Treaty, however, France agreed to evacuate the Sahara on 1 July 1967, and it subsequently established a new space centre, this time in South America, at Kourou in French Guiana.

The European Launcher Development Organisation (ELDO) used the base at Woomera (Australia) to launch the multinational Europa rocket. Managed by the Weapons Research Establishment (WRE, Australia), Woomera was used principally as a missile test centre, and it was from here that Australia used a modified Redstone missile, called the Sparta, to launch a small scientific satellite (Wresat) into a near-polar orbit in November 1967. The second satellite to be launched from the base, in October 1971, used the British Black Arrow launcher.

In the meantime, it had been decided to build the Europa 2 launcher, designed to put a satellite into geostationary orbit from the Centre spatial guyanais (CSG, Guianian Space Centre). The CSG, situated at Kourou about 70 kilometres north-west of Cayenne, required a large investment to build bridges, roads, a power station, a freshwater pumping station and a modern city for at least 4000 inhabitants. There were, however, many advantages in building a space launch centre at this point on the coast. Above all, the site was near the equator, allowing satellites to be launched favourably both towards the East for the geostationary orbit and towards the North for near polar orbits. It was also well sheltered from cyclones.

The largest industrial establishment in French Guiana, the CSG has two parts. Near

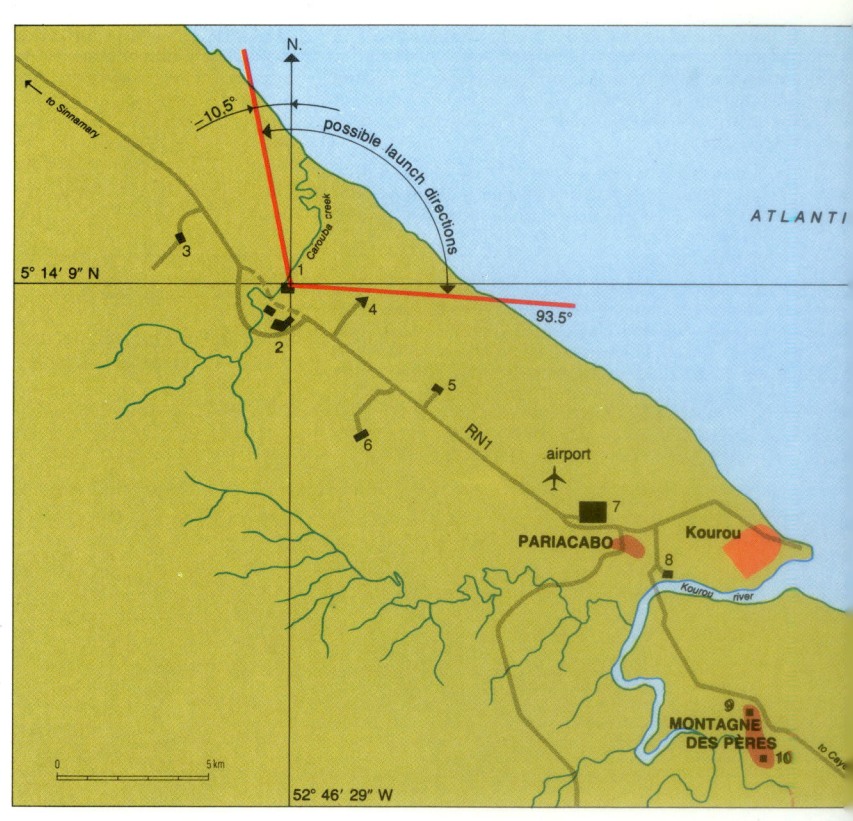

An Ariane III rocket being towed to the umbilical tower for the seventeenth Ariane launch. The first Ariane III rocket was launched on 30 January 1986. Standing on the moving platform, and towed by a MAN diesel locomotive, it takes the launcher an hour to move the 950 metres between the preparation area and the launch zone. Once it is in position on the launch pad next to the 74 metres tall umbilical tower, it is covered by a mobile service and monitoring enclosure for protection. This metal structure, weighing 3000 tonnes, also moves on rails (ESA).

The Europa rocket at Woomera. During the 1960s, Britain and Europe had a satellite launch site at Woomera, Australia. Ten launches were carried out by ELDO as part of the Europa programme, but none of them succeeded in putting a satellite into orbit. However, Australia successfully used the same site to launch its own satellite, Wresat, on 29 November 1967, making use of a modified American Redstone missile as a launcher (WRE, Salisbury).

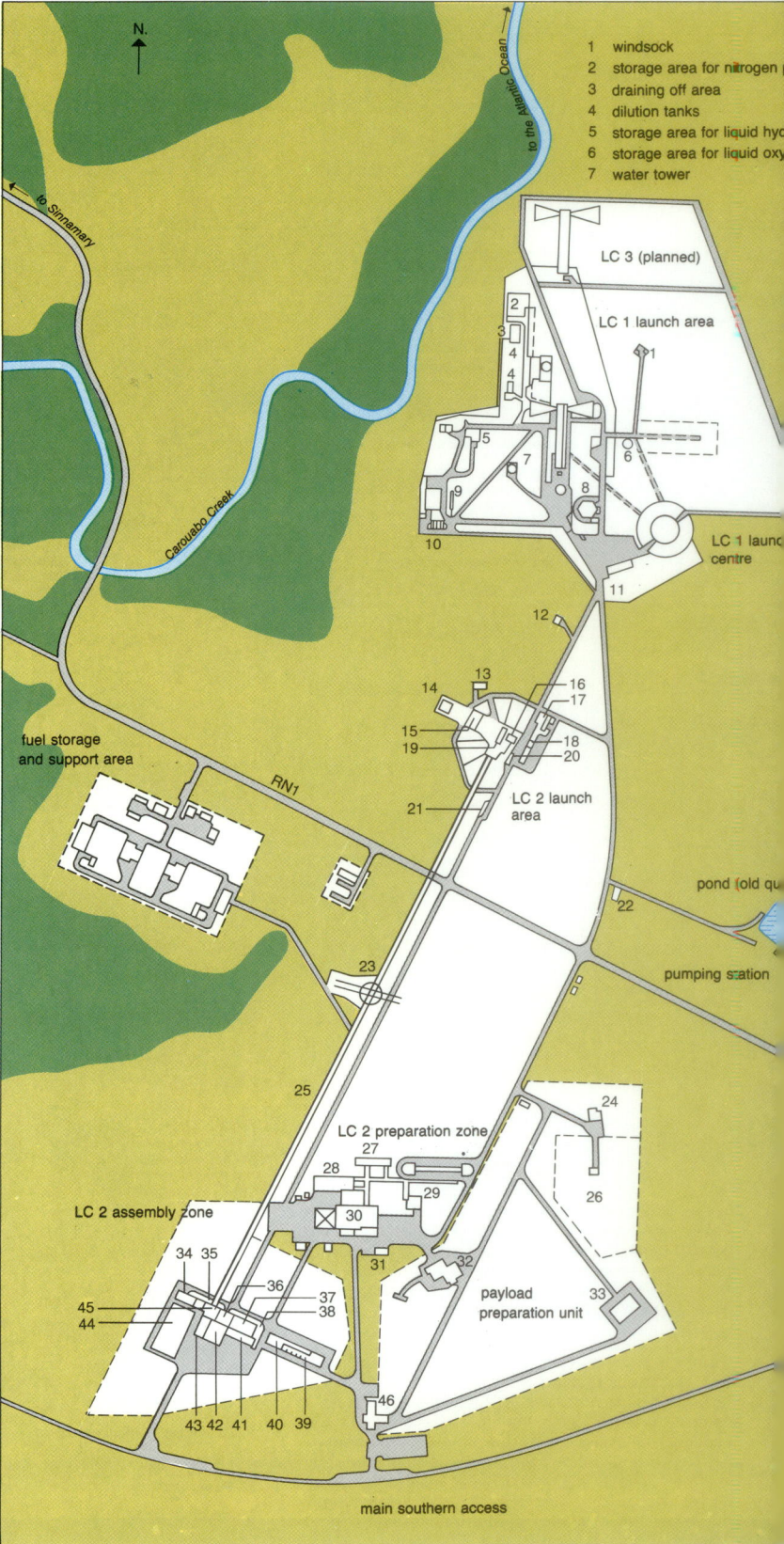

1 windsock
2 storage area for nitrogen
3 draining off area
4 dilution tanks
5 storage area for liquid hydrogen
6 storage area for liquid oxygen
7 water tower

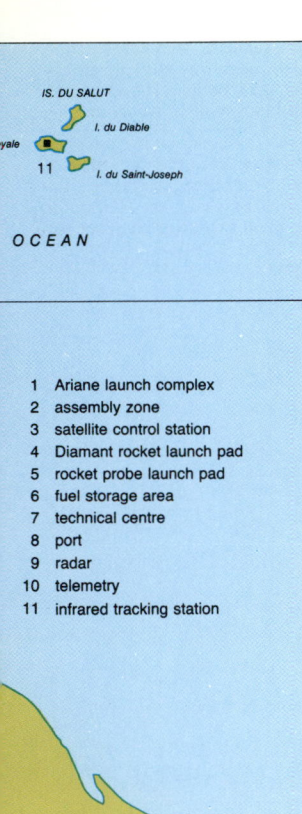

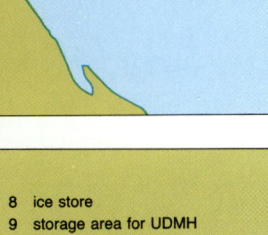

OCEAN

IS. DU SALUT
I. du Diable
11
I. du Saint-Joseph
Royale

1 Ariane launch complex
2 assembly zone
3 satellite control station
4 Diamant rocket launch pad
5 rocket probe launch pad
6 fuel storage area
7 technical centre
8 port
9 radar
10 telemetry
11 infrared tracking station

8 ice store
9 storage area for UDMH
10 sound insulated building
11 support building
12 liquid hydrogen tank
13 tank
14 entrance to enclosure
15 service and protection enclosure
16 umbilical tower
17 fresh air inlet
18 sprinklers (in case of fire)
19 solid structure (beneath the rocket)
20 fuel supply pipes
21 liquid oxygen
22 security building
23 turntable
24 solid fuel engines
25 railway track for launcher
26 radiography building
27 offices
28 shops
29 documentation building
30 assembly hall
31 emergency generator
32 payload balancing
33 payload preparation
34 fluid production
35 mechanics
36 assembly region
37 launch centre 2
38 firing chamber
39 airconditioning plant
40 power plant
41 offices
42 laboratory for launchers
43 erection hall
44 storage area for gas and fuel
45 assembly dock
46 safety and control centre

RN 1
to Kourou

0   200 m

Pariacabo is the technical centre, with buildings for management and administration, clean rooms and satellite preparation services, data reception and processing systems, and the launch control centre. North of Pariacabo, launch installations spread to either side of the main road (RN1). This is the rocket launch site itself, Ariane launch complexes (LC) 1 and 2. It includes assembly halls and a meteorological station as well as tracking radars.

The Ariane rocket is assembled vertically on the flight pad within an air-conditioned mobile tower. High up on this there is a clean room for preparing the payload and installing it. About 200 metres from the LC 1 launch site is positioned a reinforced blockhouse for the personnel and countdown control equipment. The countdown itself lasts 28 hours.

The LC 2, planned in 1980, is designed to accommodate the new Ariane IV launchers as well as Ariane II and III. It became operational on 1 August 1985. Its key feature is the separation of the launcher preparation area and the actual launch site at which the payload is mounted, final checks are carried out, and the fuel tanks are filled. The system of vertical assembly of the launcher on a mobile platform is retained, these elements together enabling the CSG to double the number of Ariane launches per year.

Both LC 1 and LC 2 were constructed for the European Space Agency (ESA), with France's CNES as the main contractor. The installations are rented, used and maintained by a commercial space transport company, Arianespace. It was Arianespace that carried out the first completely commercial launch of a telecommunications satellite on 22 May 1984.

Two other European countries and members of the European Space Agency have launch centres, but they are not as large as the CSG. In the 1960s, Italy put two offshore platforms into service off the Kenyan coast. From San Marco, Scout rockets and small satellites are launched; Santa Rita, located some 500 metres distant, is the site from which final control and launch surveillance is carried out. This unique launch complex is the property of the University of Rome's Centro ricerche aerospaziali (CRA: Aerospace Research Centre).

In northern Europe, Sweden plans to be able to launch polar orbiting satellites in the 1990s. The Swedish Space Corporation (SSC) is currently developing Esrange, 40 kilometres from Kiruna, inside the Arctic Circle. Inaugurated in 1966, Esrange was the property until July 1972 of the European Space Research Organisation. It is particularly well equipped to prepare and launch rockets for studying the aurora borealis, for conducting microgravity experiments, and for controlling satellites in orbit.

Théo Pirard

The Guianan Space Centre. The location of the CSG (Centre spatial guyanais) at Kourou, and its facilities, are shown in the maps on the left. Ariane rockets have been launched from only two launch complexes, from LC 1 in the 1960s and 1970s and from LC 2 during the 1980s. When LC 2 was constructed, RN 1, the main road from Kourou to Sinnamary, had to be diverted to the south. At the beginning of the 1990s, ESA and Arianespace are planning to start using LC 3.

The precise trajectory of the rocket launchers is calculated from observations made by six radars and an infrared tracking system on île Royale using eight computers at the control centre at the CSG and at two forward tracking stations (CNES).

The Italian launch platform, San Marco. In 1964, the Aerospace Research Centre (CRA) at the University of Rome anchored a floating base from which small satellites could be launched into equatorial orbits in the sea off Kenya. The San Marco platform, which weighs 3000 tonnes and measures 90 by 27 metres, is shown above; the nearby San Rita platform houses the control and information centre (LTVAC, PR & A).

Satellite testing and preparation at the Guianan Space Centre. The payload preparation rooms are situated on the edge of the Ariane launch complexes LC 1 and LC 2. There are two clean rooms in the technical centre, as well as buildings for checking and preparing the solid fuel rocket engines, and buildings from which the satellites are fuelled. In the lefthand photograph below, two technicians, wearing protective clothing, are filling the Indian Apple satellite with hydrazine, a highly toxic fuel. Once testing, verification for flight, and fuelling have taken place, the satellite is transported in a payload container to the launch pad, as shown in the central photograph. It is then taken to the assembly tower and placed under the payload head.

The righthand photograph shows the double payload of Ariane's eleventh launch, which took place on 10 November 1984. Clearly seen are the payload housing, a lightweight structure called the Sylda (système de lancement double d'Ariane or Ariane double launch system), and the American Spacenet 2 satellite (left and right: ESA; centre: Estec).

China

China has two sites from which it launches its CZ (Changzheng, or Long March) launchers, one in the north in a desert region, the other in a valley between mountains in the south. Both centres are accessible by road, railway and aeroplane, so that parts manufactured in Shanghai and Beijing arrive in good condition at the launch sites.

The Jiuquan Space Launch Centre, near Shuangzhengzi, on the edge of the Gobi desert, has been used since the end of the 1960s for experiments on Chinese missiles; Earth observation satellites supplied with recoverable capsules are regularly launched from here. Jiuquan's Long March 2 complex has two launch pads, both of which are served by the same enclosure, in all some 50 metres tall. The two stage launchers and payloads are taken to the launch complex on lorries and are integrated vertically on fixed launch pads.

In contrast, the Xichang Space Launch Centre in the province of Sichuan nestles amongst mountains. The Chinese Ministry of Astronautics authorised its construction in 1980 for the launch of satellites into geostationary and polar orbits. There is a single launch site with a striking metal tower 76 metres high. Long March 3, which measures 44·6 metres, is mounted, prepared and launched beside this structure.

Théo Pirard

Jiuquan Space Launch Centre. This space centre is on the edge of the Gobi desert in northern China. Since 1970, the complex has been used to launch Chinese scientific and Earth observation satellites.

The two stage Long March 2 launchers and payloads are brought to the site by lorry, as in the upper photograph on the left. The lower left photograph shows the launch of a Long March 2 (CZ2) rocket, on 21 October 1985, which put an observation satellite with a recoverable capsule into orbit. The capsule was returned to Earth five days later (MOA).

A map of the Jiuquan Space Launch Centre.

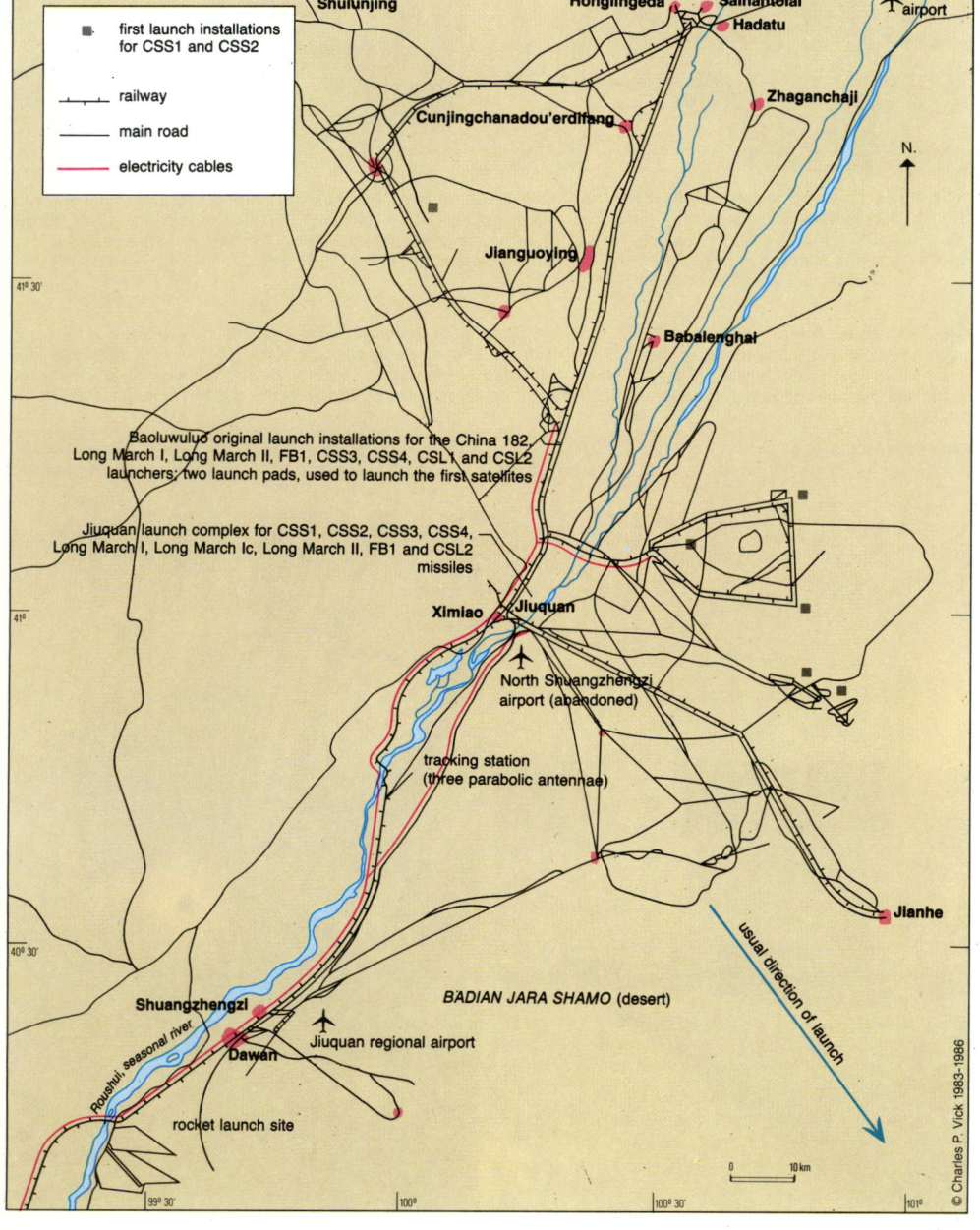

The launch pad at the Xichang Space Launch Centre. The Long March 3 (CZ3) launcher is prepared on a single launch site, whose imposing metal tower, shown in the upper photograph, is 76 metres tall. A crane at the top of the service tower here hoists the third, cryogenic stage into position on top of the lower two stages. The satellite, without a protective covering, is then placed at the very top of the rocket.

In the lower photograph, the experimental telecommunications satellite STW1 is being fitted to the rocket head after integration on top of the launcher (MOA).

India and Brazil

The Indian Space Research Organisation (ISRO) expects to be completely independent, producing all its own satellites and rocket launchers, by the year 2000. Since the 1960s, the Thumba Equatorial Rocket Launching Station (TERLS) on the west coast of India has been involved in international rocket launches. ISRO founded the Sriharikota High Altitude Range (SHAR) on the island of Sriharikota about 100 kilometres north of Madras from which to launch more powerful rockets and satellites. The first rockets were launched from SHAR in October 1971.

The site covers an area of 14 500 hectares in a wooded region which is subject to monsoons. It is equipped with rocket engine testbeds, a technical centre for preparing payloads, and tracking and computer equipment, and was further enlarged by ISRO in 1985. The launchers ASLV (Augmented Satellite Launch Vehicle) and PSLV (Polar SLV) are assembled here and prepared vertically in a mobile tower 40 metres high and weighing 600 tonnes.

Théo Pirard

The Alcântara launch centre under construction in northern Brazil. Brazil has begun work on a launch centre on the edge of the Amazon forest and the Atlantic Ocean. The Centro de lançamento de Alcântara de l'IAE (Instituto de actividades espaciais) covers a humid, wooded area of 52 000 hectares. Before construction could begin, the local Indian population of about 6000 people had to be moved and rehoused in new villages. The centre is well sited, being close to the equator and capable of launches both to the East and to the North like the Guianan Space Centre at Kourou (ministerio da Aeronautica).

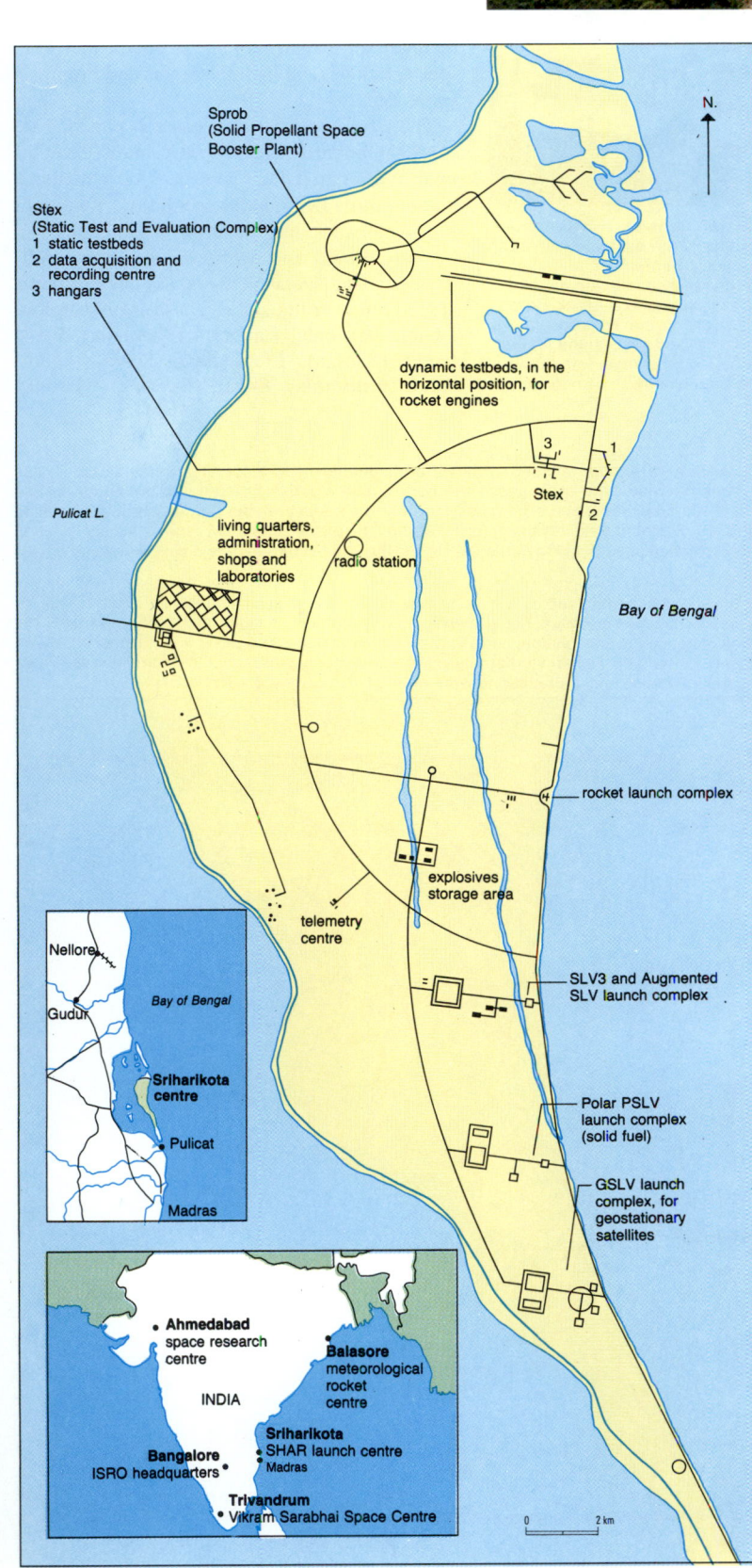

The Sriharikota High Altitude Range (SHAR). This range is on the island of Sriharikota, off the coast of the province of Andhra Pradesh. It is the largest site in India for launching satellites and rockets, though the ISRO also has launch sites at Trivandrum and Balasore.

The SLV3 launchers with four solid fuel stages are assembled horizontally in an air-conditioned hangar, as illustrated in the photograph below. Four SLV3s have been launched, and three satellites have been successfully put into orbit. The upper photograph shows the Augmented SLV launcher on the launch pad with its payload, the Sross scientific satellite (Stretched Rohini Satellite Series) (ISRO).

Space centres

Control centres

Whilst satellite launch centres are very publicly involved in the success or failure of space missions and regularly appear in the news, control centres operate continuously and quietly in the background. When the launch centres have successfully performed their tasks, control centres take over and monitor the satellite or space station for the rest of its mission. They receive radio signals from the space vehicle and monitor its operational state and behaviour. They give it commands and check that they are understood and executed so that the space mission is successful – their role, in short, is absolutely vital, particularly if the flight is manned.

The control centre has computers to process the data received from the vehicle and, most importantly, it is able to work in real time so that it can react quickly to any situation which may arise. For this, it relies on a system of Tracking, Telemetry and Command stations (TT&C stations).

The ideal situation would be to have enough tracking stations around the world to provide global coverage. However, since no such network is available, Data Relay Satellites (DRS) in geostationary orbits are used to collect and retransmit data. The American system is called

The operations room in the Kaliningrad space control centre. This enormous control room is used for manned Soviet spaceflights and is probably the best known part of Tsoup at Kaliningrad, near Moscow. The photograph was taken on 1 September 1978 during the flight of Soyuz 29, Salyut 6 and Soyuz 31. The central screen shows the trajectory of the orbiting vehicles, and the zones covered by seven terrestrial tracking stations (black circles; at Yevpatoria, Tbilisi, Dzhusaly, Kopalshevo, Ulan Ude, Ussuriyisk and Petropavlovsk) and five marine tracking stations (white circles) provided by a fleet of specialised ships in the Atlantic Ocean, the Pacific Ocean and the Mediterranean Sea. The screen on the lower left shows a photograph of the three coorbiting spacecraft. The upper right screen shows cosmonauts on Soyuz 29 and Soyuz 31 (APN).

the Tracking and Data Relay Satellite system (TDRS system) while the Soviets use the Cosmos satellites in geostationary orbits which form their Satellite Data Relay Network (SDRN).

It is essential that the ground stations can receive the satellite's radio signals free from interference. This is ensured by the regulations of the International Telecommunications Union (ITU) which coordinates the use of radio signals in the different frequency bands: VHF (around 140 and 270 megahertz), UHF (towards 400 and 900 megahertz), L band (from 1·4 to 1·8 gigahertz), S band (around 2 gigahertz), C band (4 to 6 gigahertz), Ku band (11 to 14 gigahertz), and Ka band (20 and 30 gigahertz).

The Soviet Union has the advantage of size when communicating with its spacecraft. Nevertheless, it also has a fleet of scientific ships, named after cosmonauts who have died, which are equipped with antennae of all types and sizes. It can, in addition, call on several control centres to cope with the large number of Soviet satellites. The best known of these is Tsoup (Tsentr Oupravlienia Poliotom) at Kaliningrad, 50 kilometres from Moscow. Tsoup was established in 1970 and now employs 2500 engineers and technicians. It is permanently responsible for communications with manned spaceflights using the Salyut and Mir space stations, and with the Soyuz and Progress spacecraft.

The USA has three main control centres. The NASA Goddard Space Flight Center (GSFC), near Washington DC, controls space missions and monitors US scientific satellites. From here the Americans also manage installations on Wallops Island and a dozen other Spacecraft Tracking and Data Network (STDN) stations spread out over the globe. These are Ascension Island, Bermuda, Canberra (Australia), Fairbanks (Alaska), Fresnedillas (Spain), Goldstone (California), Guam (Oceania), Hawaii,

The network of S band tracking stations used by the CNES. In 1977, the CNES decided to modernise its satellite tracking network, to equip it to operate in the S band (2 gigahertz) and to make it compatible with American, Swedish and Japanese networks. There are now three operational stations, at Aussaguel (near Toulouse, France), Kourou (French Guiana) and Hartebeesthoek (South Africa). Data relay satellites transmit information to the operations centre at Toulouse (COR: Centre d'opération réseau) which also serves as the operational orbit centre (COO: Centre d'orbitographie opérationnel). The network also relies on cooperation with other stations such as Goldstone, Greenbelt and Fairbanks (USA), Malindi (Kenya), Xian (People's Republic of China), Katsuura (Japan) and Canberra and Perth (Australia). So that it can track satellites in polar or Sun synchronous orbits, the CNES intends to bring two new stations into service in the early 1990s. They are at Saint-Pierre and Miquelon (off Newfoundland, Canada) and on one of the Kerguelen Islands in the southern Indian Ocean.

The map below shows the zones covered by the different ground stations operating in the S band. These correspond to an antenna sited at 5° above the horizon and a satellite orbiting at an altitude of 800 kilometres. The red lines show the orbit across the Earth's surface of the Sun synchronous satellite SPOT 1, in the first 24 hours after its launch from Kourou. The dashed line shows the satellite's injection point into orbit after being launched towards the North; the interval between two successive red dots is 10 minutes.

The number of ground stations used by a satellite depends on the mission and the different 'critical' or 'routine' phases within that mission. For example, a critical phase includes the launch, the first few orbits, the time of apogee motor ignition, and all orbital manoeuvres. When SPOT 1 was launched, seven stations (Kourou, Greenbelt, Fairbanks, Katsuura, Hartebeesthoek, Aussaguel and Kiruna) were used, yet during its routine phase only four stations were needed (J. M. Lesecq, CNES/CST).

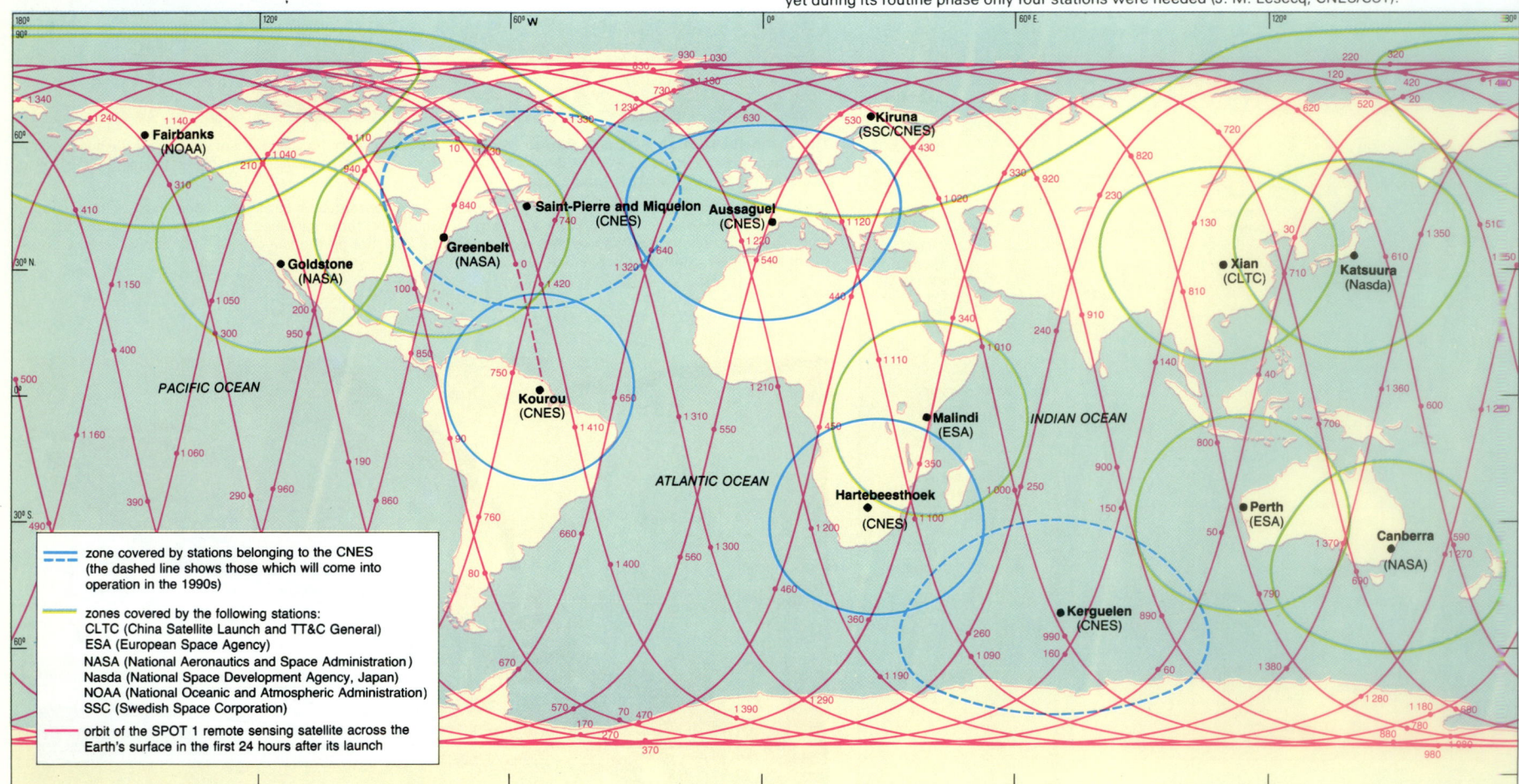

zone covered by stations belonging to the CNES (the dashed line shows those which will come into operation in the 1990s)

zones covered by the following stations:
CLTC (China Satellite Launch and TT&C General)
ESA (European Space Agency)
NASA (National Aeronautics and Space Administration)
Nasda (National Space Development Agency, Japan)
NOAA (National Oceanic and Atmospheric Administration)
SSC (Swedish Space Corporation)

orbit of the SPOT 1 remote sensing satellite across the Earth's surface in the first 24 hours after its launch

Merritt Island (Florida), Quito (Ecuador), Rosman (North Carolina) and Santiago (Chile).

For its manned flights around the Earth and to the Moon, NASA has the Mission Control Center (MCC) at the Johnson Space Center (JSC). This centre was built in 1961 at Clear Lake City in the suburbs of Houston, Texas, and spreads out over 648 hectares. It is used for astronaut training, and for the planning and execution of NASA's manned missions. The MCC has two identical control rooms, one above the other so that, even if one fails, the mission will not be lost. The MCC maintains contact with the space shuttle in orbit via the centre at White Sands in New Mexico and the TDRS system of data relay satellites.

The Consolidated Space Operations Center (CSOC) was constructed under the Cheyenne mountains by the US Air Force at the Falcon AFB in Colorado. This centre is used to control satellites belonging to the Department of Defense and also to monitor the space shuttle when it is on a military mission. The CSOC employs nearly 3000 people and provides backup and assistance to the Satellite Test Center (STC) located in Sunnyvale, California. It operates in close cooperation with the Norad (North American Air Defense Command) system which monitors all spacecraft launched into space. It is assisted by a network of stations around the globe, on several of the Pacific islands, in Greenland (at Thule), Alaska (Clear), and in Turkey, Italy and the UK.

Europe has two principal satellite control centres. The Toulouse Space Centre (CST: Centre spatial de Toulouse), employs more than 1500 people and is the main CNES establishment; it is the French equivalent of NASA's Goddard Space Flight Center. CST manages the TT&C network of CNES, which has been using the S band since 1984. In all it has five control rooms: the specialised control centre (CCS: centre de contrôle spécialisé) for Télécom 1 telecommunications satellites; the CCS for direct broadcasting satellites; the CCS Export for non French satellites; the mission control centre (CCM: centre de contrôle et de mission) for SPOT remote sensing satellites; and the CCM for the Sarsat–Cospas system of satellite search and rescue.

ESA directs the European Space Operations Centre (ESOC) at Darmstadt, West Germany. This employs 600 people. It has a main control room as well as specialised rooms devoted to European satellites. It manages the Estrack network, with VHF tracking stations at Redu (Belgium), Kourou (French Guiana), Malindi (Kenya), Carnavon (Australia): S band stations at Odenwald (West Germany) and Villafranca (Spain); and a Ku band station at Fucino (Italy). ESOC was in the public eye most notably on the night of 13 and 14 March 1986, when the European Giotto probe observed the nucleus of Halley's comet.

In Asia, the number of tracking and control centres is increasing as Japan, India and China develop their space activities. In Japan, Nasda manages the Tsukuba Space Centre about 60 kilometres from Tokyo, with out-stations at Katsuura, Kagoshima, and on the islands of Tanegashima, Okinawa, Christmas and Ogasawara.

The Chinese Ministry of Astronautics, via the intermediary of the China Satellite Launch and TT&C General (CLTC), exploits a network with its main control centre at Xian. This utilises stations spread throughout China from Beijing, Jiuquan and Xichang to Yibin and Gueiyang, as well as two suitably equipped ships (*Yuanwang 1* and *Yuanwang 2*) located in the Pacific Ocean.

In India, ISRO has its Istrac network, with TT&C stations operating in the S band at Trivandrum, Bangalore (the main centre), Lucknow, and in the Bay of Bengal on the islands of Sriharikota and Nicobar.

Théo Pirard

The *Cosmonaut Vladimir Komarov*. One of the jewels of the Soviet fleet of space vehicle tracking ships, this ship was constructed in the naval shipyards at Kherson in 1966, and fitted out at Leningrad in 1967. It was named after the cosmonaut Vladimir Komarov who was killed in April 1967 during a test flight of the Soyuz 1 spacecraft. It has a crew of about a thousand and is generally at anchor in the Cuban port of Havana (APN).

The Jupiter room of the space control centre at Kourou. This main building of the technical centre at the Guianan Space Centre (CSG: Centre spatial guyanais) is pictured above. Its layout is shown on the right. It contains the control centre and the computers to monitor and control all the operations such as launch, tracking, telemetry, rescue and weather pertaining to an Ariane mission. From this room, those responsible for Ariane and their guests can maintain a general view of all the operations in progress and of the performance of the installations (ESA/CSG).

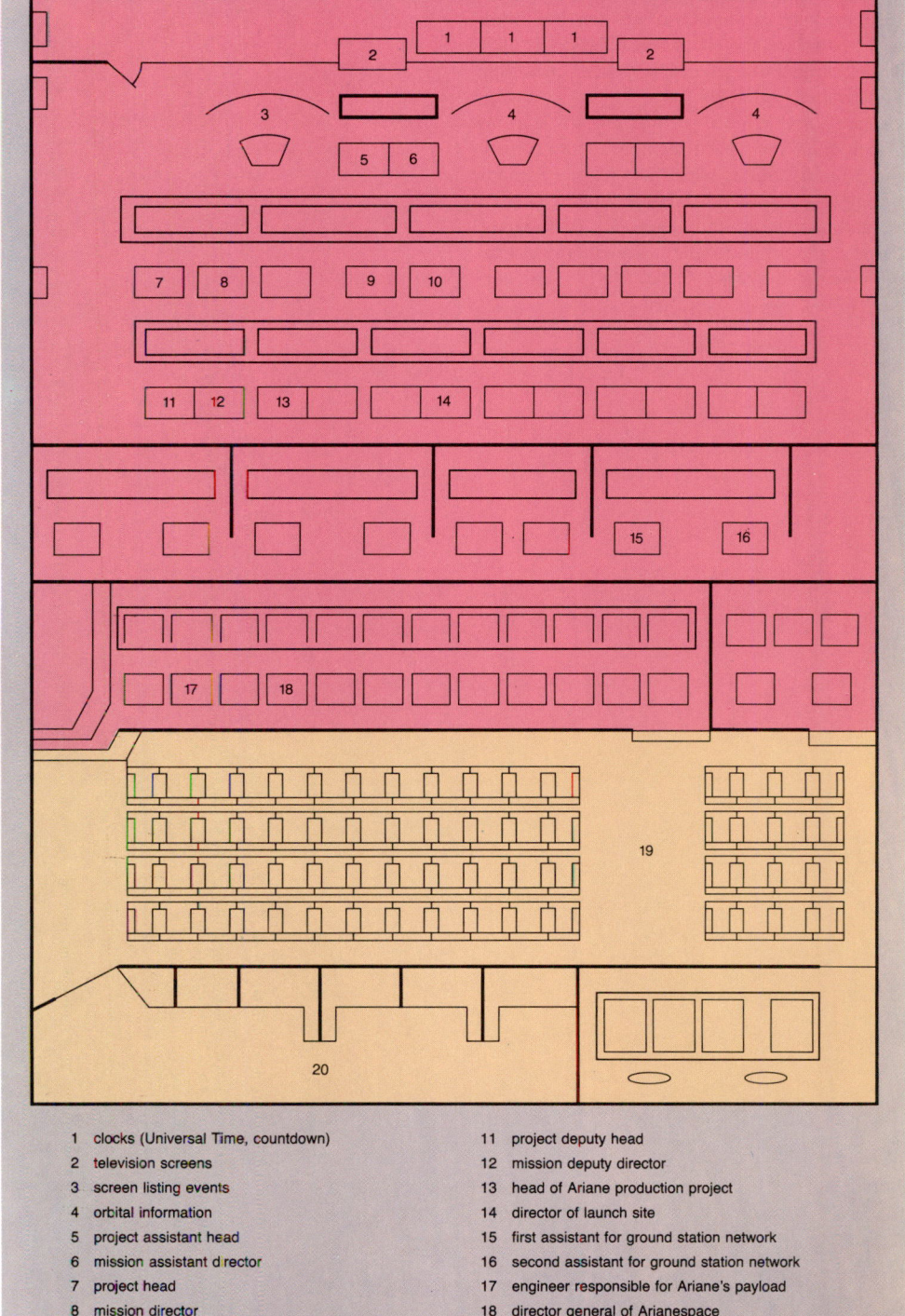

1 clocks (Universal Time, countdown)	11 project deputy head
2 television screens	12 mission deputy director
3 screen listing events	13 head of Ariane production project
4 orbital information	14 director of launch site
5 project assistant head	15 first assistant for ground station network
6 mission assistant director	16 second assistant for ground station network
7 project head	17 engineer responsible for Ariane's payload
8 mission director	18 director general of Arianespace
9 head of mission	19 guest room
10 director of operations	20 press room

Satellite systems

Arthur C. Clarke, in 1945, proposed using a geostationary satellite 36 000 kilometres above the Earth as a relay for telecommunications. As he pointed out then, the most effective way of communicating thousands of kilometres around the Earth is by using an orbiting satellite.

The telecommunications satellite developed over the years since this acute prediction is the most important economic application of space to have been invented so far. More than half the transoceanic and transcontinental telephone conversations that take place today are routed via satellites, and the growth rate of such communications has in recent years been in the region of 30% per year. Communications costs have decreased at the same rate.

As is most clearly indicated by satellite communications, all satellite applications require a close working relationship between the satellites themselves and ground installations. Satellites belonging to a particular system, including replacement satellites, and their tracking, telemetry and remote control ground stations all belong to the 'space segment' of a mission. The ground stations which are responsible for running the satellite's mission by themselves are called the 'ground segment'. Both space segment and ground stations are equally crucial to a mission's success.

Alexandre Dauguet

The Arabsat control station at Dirahb. A satellite is controlled from the ground using tracking, telemetry and command stations which receive information on the state of the satellite, and transmit commands to it, to control both its passage and the way it functions in space. The performance of these stations can be characterised by their antennae and their amplifiers. As regards the antennae, the size of the parabolic dish determines the gain of the system. The antennae themselves are used both to transmit and to receive radio signals. Powerful amplifiers are required on the transmit side, while the receivers have to be sensitive, low noise devices. There is usually a data processing centre, with several powerful computers, at each station. To obtain the high level of reliability which is essential, several stations are used for the same satellite, thus forming a control network.

In this photograph of the tracking station at Dirahb, the lefthand antenna is used for high speed tracking, with great precision in all directions; the righthand antenna has a much simpler, low speed tracking system, with limited precision; it operates over a relatively small range of angles (Aérospatiale).

The antenna at the Lhasa station. The ground station at Lhasa, Tibet, has a 12 metre diameter dish, and forms part of a network of five ground stations belonging to the Chinese Ministry of Post and Telecommunications.

Three such stations are already operating, at Lhasa, Guanzhou and Hohhot. The programme has been operational since 1986, using Intelsat telecommunications satellites (Spar Aerospace Limited).

The Meteosat system. The European Meteosat system provides a good example of the complex dialogue which takes place between a satellite and ground stations. An Earth observation satellite, such as Meteosat, is also a telecommunications satellite. It records images of the cloud cover, in the visible and infrared parts of the spectrum, and transmits them to the main data collection station at Darmstadt, in West Germany.

These images are corrected and then transmitted as facsimile messages back to the satellite, which retransmits them to other comparable ground stations in countries involved in the programme. In addition, the satellite collects much useful data from automatic ground stations, including weather observations made from buoys, aircraft or balloons, all termed Data Collection Platforms (DCPs). It retransmits them via Darmstadt to a powerful computer in the UK or France, which uses them to develop weather forecasts.

Meteosat can also relay data from sister satellites, in particular the American GOES meteorological satellite.

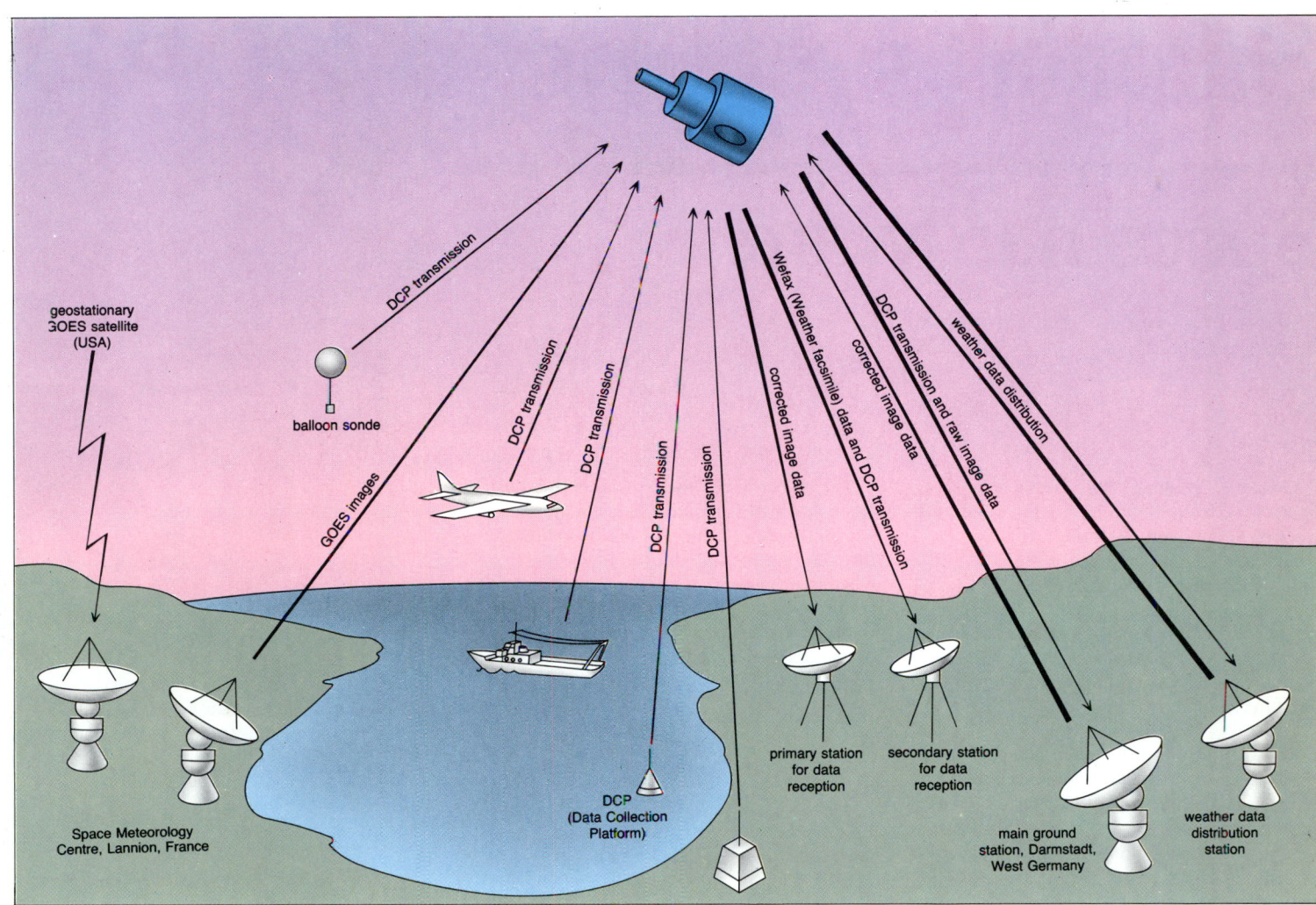

The different satellite systems. There are three different types of satellite – scientific, civil, and military.

The upper righthand diagram shows an example of a scientific satellite, the Infrared Space Observatory (ISO). The ISO programme was conceived by ESA to make observations in infrared astronomy. This satellite, to be launched in the early 1990s, is essentially a telescope placed inside a cryostat, a container rather like a large Thermos or Dewar flask designed to keep the payload temperature at −270 degrees celsius, or 3 degrees kelvin.

Meteosat, shown on the right, is an Earth observation satellite. This programme is run by a European organisation called Eumetsat, founded in 1983. Meteosat observes the distribution of clouds over Europe, Africa and the Atlantic Ocean from a geostationary orbit, both in the visible (wavelengths 0·5 to 0·9 microns) and the infrared (10·5 to 12·5 microns). These images are captured using a radiometer with a high performance, whose resolution on the ground is 2·5 kilometres in the visible (5000 lines per image) and 5 kilometres in the infrared (2500 lines per image). A complete image is obtained every 30 minutes, the line scanning ensured by rotating the satellite about its axis, at 100 revolutions per minute.

Telecommunications satellites are the most important of all commercial satellites. The Eutelsat satellite shown in the photograph above is to be used in the early 1990s for telephone, television broadcasting, data transmission and business links for 26 European countries. Its mass is close to 1 tonne. It will be stabilised with respect to its three axes, and its antennae (twin polarisation, with shaped and reconfigurable beams) will always face the Earth. The solar panels are rotated in the opposite direction and always face the Sun. They supply 3 kilowatts of electrical power during the satellite's lifetime from a 22·4 metre span. The payload consists of sixteen 50 kilowatt transponders (Ku band) with a minimum life of 7 years (Aérospatiale).

Satellite systems

Space hardware

Generally speaking, there are six subsystems which have to carry out different allotted functions aboard a space platform. These are:
– structural and mechanical
– thermal control
– propulsion in orbit
– production, storage and distribution of energy
– attitude and orbital control
– telemetry, remote control and on-board data treatment

The platform itself links the launcher to the satellite payload, acts as a support for all the electronic equipment carried, and serves as a protective screen against energetic radiation, dust and micrometeorites in space. Its mass is often between 7% and 10% of the total satellite mass at launch.

Because the cost of a launch into geostationary orbit is so high, about £10,000 or $17000 per kilogram, lightness of structure is a basic requirement. Current technology is therefore exploited to the limit in order to reduce the structural mass to a minimum. Use is made of ultralight, yet strong, materials such as aluminium alloys, magnesium, titanium, beryllium, carbon or Kevlar fibres and, still more commonly, composite materials. The sophisticated design of the structure relies heavily on computer simulations made during the design stage when complicated sets of experiments involving static and dynamic tests subject the platform to stresses and accelerations similar to those that will be encountered during the mission.

Although the structure must be light, and the costs of developing the necessary materials kept affordable, other conditions also need to be considered. There are, for instance, mechanical accelerations and vibrations, which are particularly important during the launch phase, and thermal cycles which operate on the structure throughout the satellite's lifetime. The satellite is subjected to large temperature differences as the Sun is regularly eclipsed by the Earth. It is also stressed by extreme temperature gradients across the platform, with temperatures often of several hundred degrees celsius on the side facing the Sun and several tens of degrees below zero celsius on the shaded face. The space environment itself generates other potentially damaging effects. These include energetic charged particle radiation, bombardment by cosmic dust particles and effects of being in the space vacuum, such as degassing from the surfaces, evaporation and even the decomposition of the materials.

Still more severe are the restrictions on the platform's mechanisms necessary to ensure that the various functions required on board are satisfied in space. Such processes as the separation of the satellite from the launcher, the deployment and orientation of the solar panels or telescopic rods, the fine pointing of the antennae and the operation of the rotating parts all have to work reliably. The effects of friction are particularly difficult to predict, even though progress has been made in recent years in producing equipment which is designed to function in the space environment.

The object of the thermal control subsystem is to maintain temperature limits between which the equipment will operate throughout the desired lifetime of the satellite. It also ensures a reasonable temperature distribution throughout the space structure. This is essential to retain dimensional stability, without warping or bending, and to maintain the alignment of critical pieces of equipment.

The structure of Intelsat 5. The satellite's platform consists of a frame which supports different pieces of equipment such as the mechanical and electronic systems, antennae and solar panels. The upper photograph shows the structure of the telecommunications satellite, Intelsat 5. The structure itself weighs only 140 kilograms, although the total mass of the satellite is greater than 1 tonne.

A small mass is one of the most important requirements when designing space platforms. Complex technology and ultralight materials are therefore used throughout. The structure of Intelsat 5 consists of carbon fibre tubing and honeycomb panels as illustrated in the lower photograph; the cellular structure is made of aluminium and sandwiched between two layers of carbon (Aérospatiale).

Thermal control of satellites. The techniques employed to control a satellite's temperature, that is its thermal regulation, are either active or passive. Passive techniques include having surfaces which either reflect or absorb radiation that is produced internally or generated by an external source such as the Sun.

The photograph, below left, shows the superinsulation being installed on the SPOT satellite. This consists of multiple layers of insulation made of capton, a very strong, light plastic, on which a reflecting metallic layer has been deposited. Used in conjunction with selective solar reflectors, these are transparent to the infrared radiation passing outwards from the spacecraft.

Active thermal regulation systems include remote controlled heaters, systems of flaps which can be opened to expose the outer part of the radiator, and heat pipes. The heat pipes on the direct broadcasting satellite TDF1 are visible in the righthand photograph below. These enable the heat produced in the power amplifier and transponder circuits (four tubes of 50 watts each) to escape to the radiators on the sides of the satellite that face North and South (Aérospatiale).

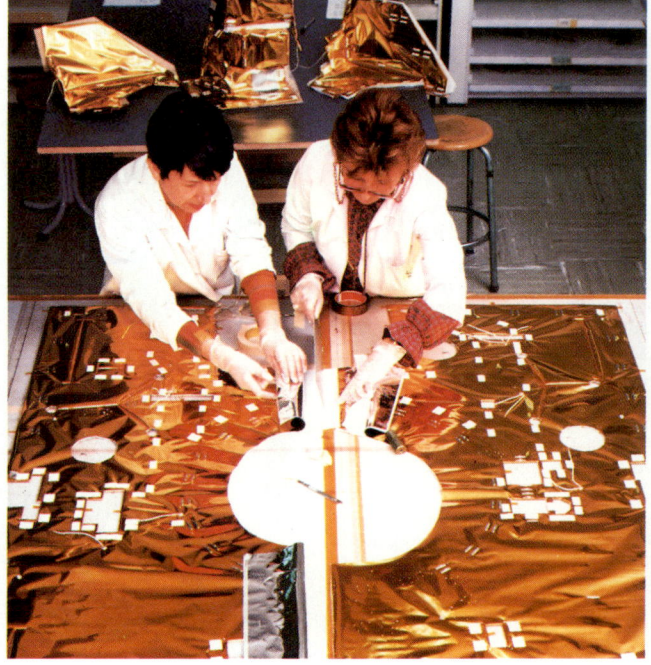

For most of the electronic equipment, the operational temperature limits are from −10 degrees celsius to +40 degrees celsius. This range is narrower for some components such as batteries (0 to +20 degrees celsius), and wider for others, for example for solar cells (from −190 to +60 degrees celsius) or components which dissipate a considerable amount of energy such as power amplifiers (from −10 to +80 degrees celsius).

Thermal control on the Earth is usually performed by heating or cooling, using a stable reference point such as the ambient temperature. This is not possible in space. The temperature of a system and its component parts is regulated by heat exchange through radiation and conduction, with no convection present except during the pre-launch phases. Thermal control technology is accordingly dominated by heat exchange caused by radiation.

There are fundamentally three sources of radiation external to the spacecraft. Firstly, the Sun is equivalent to a black body, a perfect radiator radiating at 5760 kelvin (almost 5500 degrees celsius) whose flux at the Earth's orbit is 1370 watts per square metre. Some 40% of this energy is in the visible part of the spectrum, and some 50% in the infrared. About 30% of incident solar radiation is reflected back into space by the Earth's atmosphere, particularly its clouds.

Secondly, the Earth and its atmosphere acts like a black body radiating at 250 kelvin (−23 degrees celsius), predominantly in the infrared. The flux of this radiation is quite large for low Earth orbits (about 150 watts per square metre), and low in the geostationary orbit.

Thirdly, there is space itself, acting like a thermal sink, the opposite of a source of thermal radiation at a temperature close to absolute zero (0 kelvin).

Inside the space platform, there are in addition many internal heat sources, because no piece of equipment is 100% efficient. For example, travelling wave amplifiers used for direct broadcasting have a nominal power of 200 or 250 watts, but they are only 30 or 40% efficient. A satellite with only one such amplifier has to dissipate some 150 watts of internal heat.

Design of the thermal control system also makes extensive use of computer models. These are constructed by dividing the satellite up into many thousands of isothermal (constant temperature) nodes (pieces of equipment or structural elements) linked together by radiation and conduction. In order to keep each piece of equipment within the prescribed temperature limits whatever the external conditions, the following procedures are applied:

– the satellite is shaded as much as possible from changes of radiation from the Sun, as happens during a solar eclipse when the satellite passes behind the Earth at night. This is done by using highly reflective coatings and multilayer thermal protection called super-insulation.

– selective reflectors are arranged so that the internally produced energy, which is mostly in the infrared, dissipates towards the outside without allowing external energy in.

– wherever possible, the hottest parts of the satellite subsystems (for example power amplifiers) are attached to the inside of an outside wall, highly thermally conducting heat pipes being used to convey the excess heat to the outside.

The Sun/space vacuum simulation chamber is the most important device available to scientists and engineers on the ground who are developing thermal control systems for use in space. With walls cooled by liquid nitrogen and a simulated source of solar illumination, the conditions found in orbital flight can be reproduced in a volume of several cubic metres. Although such installations are very expensive, there are now four in Europe, at Estec, Farnborough, Munich, and Toulouse. Life size models of satellites or of large individual subsystems can be tested inside them.

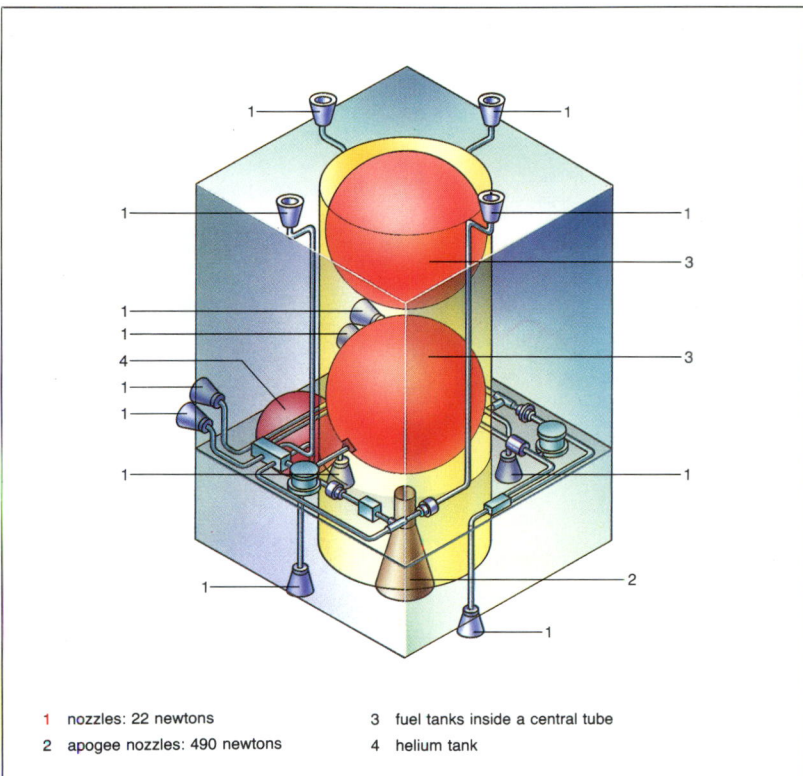

1 nozzles: 22 newtons
2 apogee nozzles: 490 newtons
3 fuel tanks inside a central tube
4 helium tank

The Arabsat propulsion system. This propulsion system can produce both the apogee impulse (a thrust of 490 newtons) and the orbital and attitude control impulses (from a dozen nozzles, each with 22 newtons of thrust). It uses a fuel mix of MMH/N₂O₄ (monomethylhydrazine and nitrogen peroxide), contained in spherical fibreglass tanks (Aérospatiale).

The propulsion systems are used to change the satellite's velocity during all the manoeuvres necessary in its lifetime. These may be major manoeuvres such as moving the satellite from a transfer orbit to its final geostationary orbit, a shift that requires a velocity increase of up to 1·8 kilometres per second provided by the apogee motor. Smaller adjustments are performed throughout the operational life of the satellite to maintain its desired position and attitude. Keeping a satellite in the correct geostationary orbit, for instance, requires an equivalent velocity increase of about 50 metres per second every year. The rocket engines needed for this use liquid fuel to produce a thrust of from 1 to 20 newtons. The most common such rocket motor uses catalytically decomposed hydrazine to produce a gas ejection speed of about 2 kilometres per second. There is also a much simpler, cold gas propulsion system, invaluable for scientific satellites, which allows freon, propane or even nitrogen, compressed to 200 or 300 atmospheres, to escape through electronically controlled thrusters. In this case gas ejection speeds do not exceed 1 kilometre per second.

Also available is an electric propulsion system, termed an ion thruster, which produces a high gas ejection speed (more than 28 kilometres per second) but only a small thrust (5 to 10 micronewtons). This works by extracting ions from a substance such as mercury and accelerating them through a potential difference of several thousand volts. This type of propulsion will be particularly useful in the future for interplanetary probes or satellites with a very long lifetime.

Deployable solar generators. High performance solar generators used in space may have either a rigid or a flexible structure. The former, producing powers of up to 30 watts per kilogram, are made of a number of rigid, yet jointed, panels which can be folded in on themselves during the launch phase. The deployment mechanisms for a pair of panels are necessarily synchronised; they are operated by gentle springs so that all movements are slow and smooth. This type of generator is often found on telecommunications satellites which require up to 6 kilowatts.

The flexible solar generator structure, used on satellites such as SPOT and shown in the photograph below, achieves a performance of about 40 to 50 watts per kilogram up to a power of several kilowatts. The individual solar cells and their wires are glued to a sheet of plastic which is folded like an accordion during the launch phase. This is deployed in orbit by a series of pantographs, or jointed levers, operated by springs working at a constant velocity of only 4 centimetres per second (Aérospatiale).

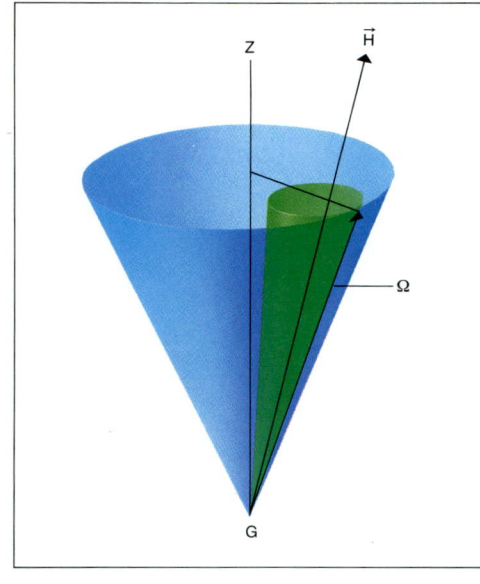

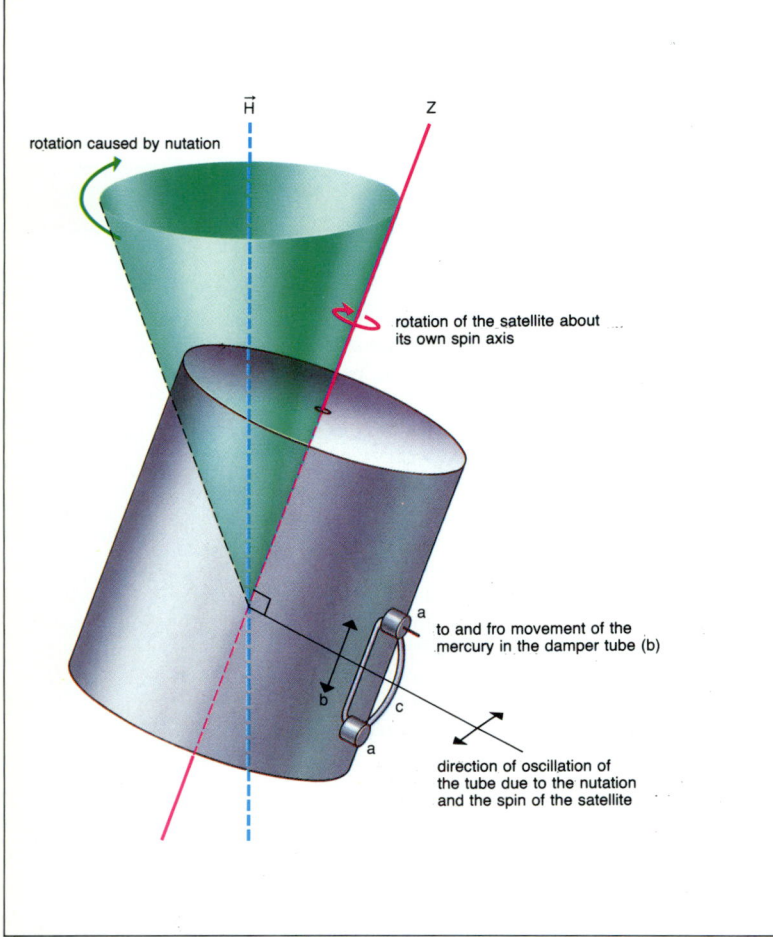

rotation caused by nutation

rotation of the satellite about its own spin axis

to and fro movement of the mercury in the damper tube (b)

direction of oscillation of the tube due to the nutation and the spin of the satellite

The principle of the passive nutation damper. Two small, sealed reservoirs, containing mercury (a), linked by a narrow tube, lie parallel to the satellite's spin axis. If there is no nutation, the spinning motion has the effect of dividing the mercury equally between the two reservoirs and filling the tube (b). The tube (c) then equalises the pressure in both reservoirs to the pressure of saturated mercury vapour.

If there is some nutation, the tube oscillates about an axis perpendicular to the satellite's spin axis. The mercury goes to and fro along the tube (b), dissipating energy by friction so that the angle of nutation tends towards zero. In practice, it is reduced to an angle of only one arcsecond.

Every satellite requires electrical energy, and this energy has, of course, to be generated, stored and distributed. Several varieties of generator may be used, capable of supplying just one watt or several kilowatts, depending on the mission. One type is the isotopic nuclear generator, sometimes used for military missions or missions distant from the Sun. However, spaceborne generators generally use solar energy, of which there is an abundant and free supply in space except during periods in which the satellite is eclipsed by the Earth. At the Earth's orbit around the Sun, the solar constant, the flux of solar energy available, is 1·37 kilowatts per square metre. A typical generator composed of an array of photovoltaic cells on a solar panel has a return of just over 10%, so the area of solar panels necessary to produce a given amount of electrical power can readily be determined for a three-axis stabilised satellite whose panels always face the Sun. Against this, in the case of spinning satellites covered by solar panels, it is necessary to increase that area by a factor of about 4. It must also be borne in mind that the performance of the solar cells may degrade by about 30% during the satellite's lifetime.

The most commonly used solar cells are silicon diodes 2 centimetres square. These are linked together to form the complex network of connections in series and in parallel necessary to generate the voltage and power required. Other types of photovoltaic cells, made for instance of gallium arsenide, will undoubtedly be used in the future.

There are two other essential components in a satellite's power system, the batteries and the regulators. The batteries have basically to store enough energy for the satellite to function during eclipses. The most commonly used, of nickel–cadmium, can last up to seven years. However, these are slowly being replaced by nickel–hydrogen batteries which are both lighter and have a lifetime of more than ten years. A complicated system of transformers and voltage regulators supplies the energy as it is required, regardless of variations in the incident solar flux and other changes.

A satellite's orbital motion is subject to a number of perturbations deriving from both external sources (such as aerodynamic, magnetic, and solar radiation pressure, and gravitational forces) and from internal sources (such as the movement of mechanical parts or liquid fuels). Such perturbations have the effect of modifying the satellite's orbit and attitude. For a mission to be successful, therefore, an orbital control system and an attitude control system are essential. Orbital control refers to the regulation of the movement of the satellite's centre of gravity by making appropriate velocity corrections. The attitude of a satellite can then be defined as the orientation of the satellite's axes through the centre of gravity with respect to the stars, which are considered to be fixed points.

Attitude measurements are made by attitude sensors. There are three types of these – inertial sensors (gyroscopes or laser rings), optical sensors (stellar, solar or terrestrial sensors, working in the visible or in the infrared), and electromagnetic sensors which measure the direction or polarisation of a wave emitted by a groundbased beacon or the orientation of the Earth's magnetic field.

Attitude control, or stabilisation, can then be either passive or active. One example of the passive mode is gravity gradient stabilisation, a system which uses a large mass attached to the end of a telescopic rod to orient this axis along the vertical, all the resulting pendulum-like oscillations being damped out by means of magnetic hysteresis. In magnetic stabilisation, a small but powerful magnet orients itself like a compass needle along the direction of Earth's magnetic field. The most common passive stabilisation system remains, however, the gyroscope. Here the satellite itself spins like a top about an axis which tends to describe a conical shape. This has to be cancelled out by a nutation damper, which may operate by the movement of liquid in a ring shaped tube. The spin axis drifts under the influence of external perturbations, and is corrected by applying small thrusts; the impulses that are required are usually calculated on the ground and relayed to the satellite by remote control.

Active stabilisation modes for a satellite are more sophisticated. Here the three most common ways of achieving the desired attitude are the reaction wheel, the flywheel and mass ejection. In reaction wheel stabilisation, a heavy solid disc is rotated by a motor about its axis, in the opposite direction to the movement of the satellite. Three reaction wheels are used, one for each axis.

For stabilisation using a flywheel, the principle is similar to spin stabilisation, but with one great advantage – the outer body does not rotate. This technique can therefore be used, for example, to maintain the position of antennae always pointing towards the Earth.

Finally, there is stabilisation by the ejection of mass through attitude correction rocket engines which operate continuously. This obviously consumes much fuel or compressed gas, and can only be used on short missions. Yet such small rocket engines have to be used from time to time even during a mission on which attitude is principally maintained by reaction wheels or a flywheel.

During any mission, a large number of measurements made using sensors have to be transmitted to ground stations using telemetry. Telemetry and remote control commands constitute the satellite's telecommunications service system. These two elements are now being merged as the microcomputer becomes a standard feature on satellites and comes to be used to organise data and to code and decode messages. Telemetry transmitters have been allocated frequencies in the VHF band (from 136 to 138 megahertz) or in the S band (up to 2 gigahertz). Their signals are either frequency modulated or pulse code modulated. The command signals are also transmitted in the VHF or S band, through they sometimes use the telecommunications repeater frequency (at 4 gigahertz).

One further function associated with a satellite's telemetry and remote control system is a transmitting beacon using tone modulation. From this, ground stations can pinpoint the satellite's position and velocity using precise measurements of angle and distance.

Alexandre Dauguet

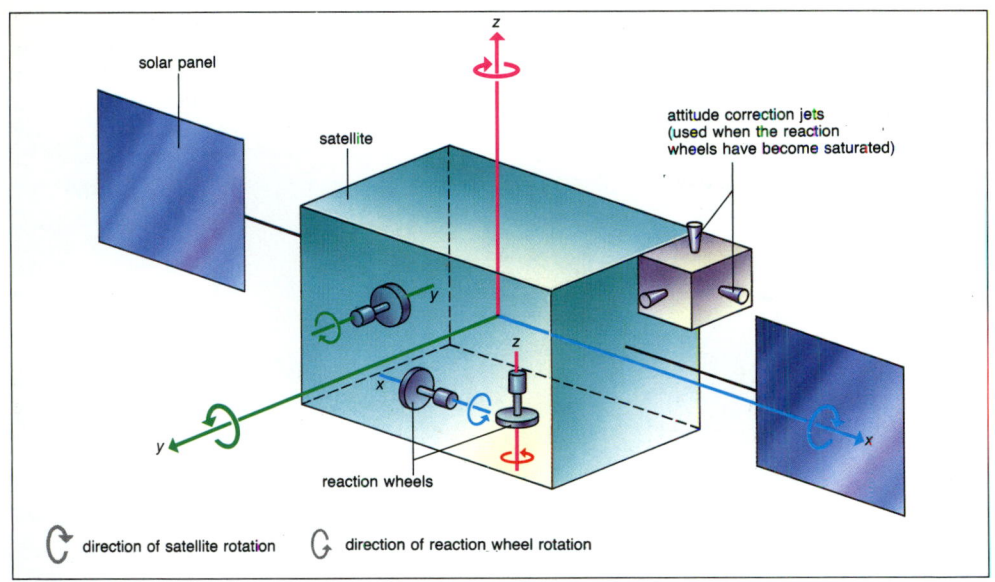

Using reaction wheels to control a satellite's attitude. A reaction wheel with a large moment of inertia can be rotated about its axis by a servomotor (see upper diagram on the left). If an error in the orientation of the satellite about this axis is detected by an optical or electromagnetic sensor, the wheel is driven in the opposite direction until the error is removed.

On the SPOT remote sensing satellite, for example, there are three reaction wheels like the one in the photograph above. The resulting accuracy of the attitude control system is to within 0·025 of a degree, or 1·5 arcminutes (Aérospatiale).

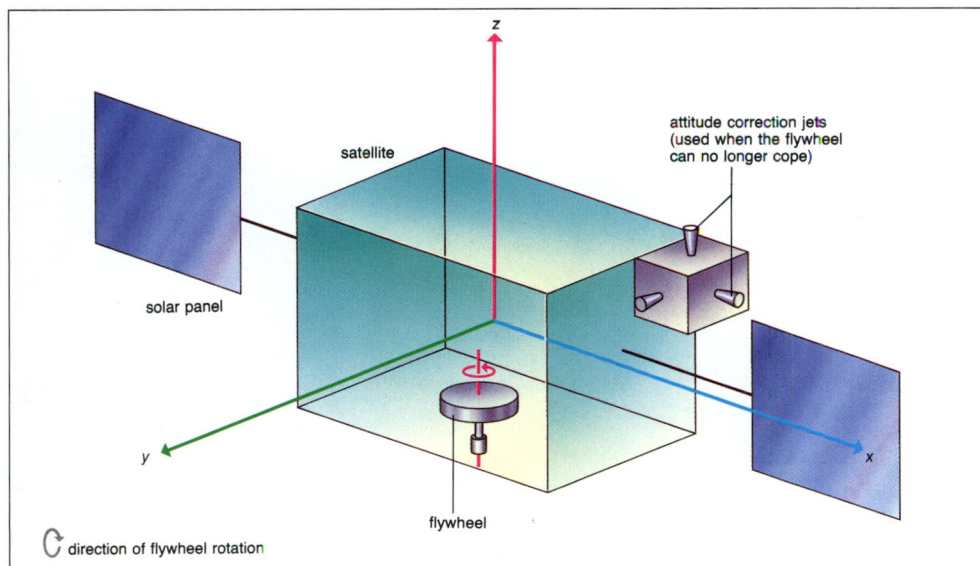

Using a flywheel for attitude control. Shown in the diagram on the left is a flywheel with a large moment of inertia which is made to rotate at high speed (20 000 revolutions per minute). In the absence of perturbations, it keeps a fixed direction in space (North-South, for example). This direction is only slightly changed by small perturbing forces, and constitutes the principle of gyroscopic stabilisation.

The orientation of the satellite with respect to this axis can be measured, for example by an infrared sensor which calculates the local horizontal to an accuracy of about 0·1 degrees. This can then be controlled by the electric servomotor driving the flywheel.

Eventually, small perturbing effects, such as those due to solar radiation pressure, cause an unacceptable difference. Corrective impulses have then to be applied periodically from small jets directed along the three axes, x, y and z.

The principle of telemetry, remote control and localisation used in Arabsat. Because operation has to be reliable at all times, two identical systems are built in. These are the main system (1), and a complete back up system (2), an arrangement achieved either by doubling every component involved (for example, transmitters and receivers) or by making use of a part of the payload (for example, the telecommunications subsystem) which can also transmit telemetry and remote command data.

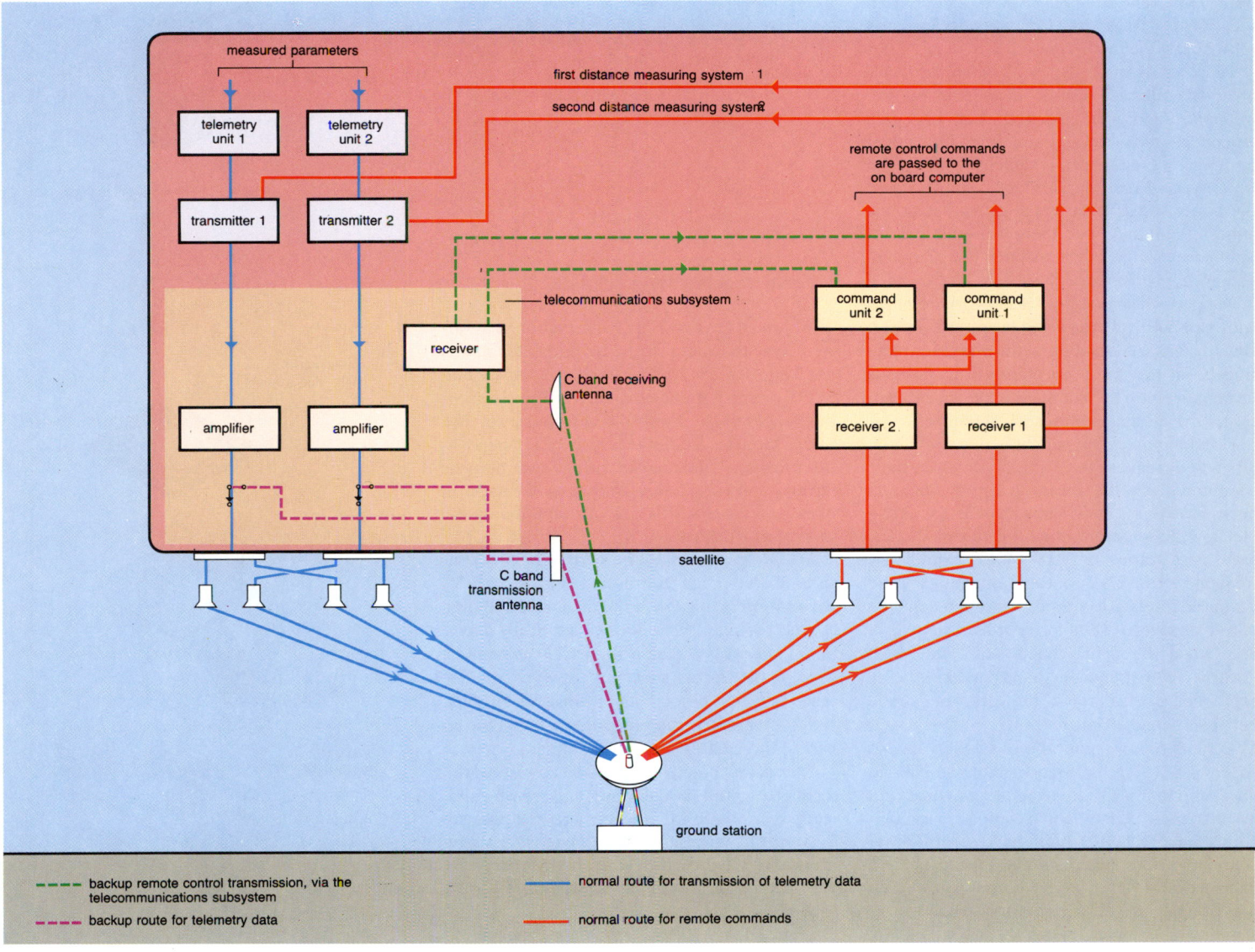

Satellite systems

Payload integration

Telecommunications payloads

Telecommunications and broadcasting satellites transmit radio signals between different parts of the Earth's surface and even between satellites themselves, and propagation distances are considerably increased because of the removal of terrestrial obstacles. In the case of ground to ground communication via a geostationary satellite, a one way signal propagates over 72 000 kilometres in a quarter of a second.

Satellites nonetheless have to be equipped with very sensitive, high gain, long life amplifiers, substantial antennae with as large a gain as possible, and powerful transmitters. All this equipment needs to be chosen in accordance with the very strict weight and bulk considerations that pertain to satellite borne equipment and the amount of power the individual elements will consume.

Besides having antennae for transmission and for reception, a telecommunications or broadcasting satellite has another subsystem of 'repeaters'. These amplify radio signals from the Earth, transpose the frequencies, and rebroadcast them.

There are various types of antennae available, the ultimate choice depending on the frequency and gain required. For low gain antennae, such as are required for global coverage, a simple horn is sufficient. This is the usual type of receiving antenna used, because the power transmitted by the ground station is almost unlimited, but there is some risk of interference from other systems. For high gain antennae, sophisticated systems have been developed which combine a network of horns with parabolic reflectors and even radio lenses. By judicious combination of the phases of radio signals at the horn aperture, it is possible instantaneously to reconfigure the beam pattern, or polar diagram, of such antennae.

Telecommunication satellites use amplifiers, filters and frequency shifters, all of which have benefited from the recent progress made in microwave electronics. They include, for example, low noise receivers (using tunnel diodes, and parametric or transistor amplifiers), frequency mixers, power amplifiers and advanced filters. The output stages can deliver a power of several watts for broadcasting over a very wide frequency band and with high linearity. New frequency bands are also being exploited, particularly in the little used band between 20 and 30 gigahertz.

A modern communications satellite has to cope with several thousand telephone calls at once, and Intelsat V, for example, can deal with as many as 25 000 conversations simultaneously. Such satellites often have several other communications functions also, being able to handle digital data transmission and television broadcasting as well as telephone calls.

A payload module on the SPOT remote sensing satellite. Two identical High Resolution Visible (HRV) cameras make up the payload on board SPOT at an altitude near 820 kilometres. The entire HRV camera measures 1·6 metres by 1·1 metres by 2·5 metres, and weighs 242 kilograms.

In the focal plane of a spherical mirror, whose focal length is 1·082 metres with an aperture of f 3·5 is a line of 6000 detectors which are swept electronically. The resulting image corresponds to a field of view 4·8 degrees wide, or 60 kilometres across on the Earth's surface.

The motion of the satellite along its orbit provides the image's second dimension, using the so-called pushbroom technique. The images obtained have the remarkable resolution of 20 metres on the ground, in the multispectral (colour) mode, and 10 metres in the black and white mode. They can be converted into numerical data (that is digitised), recorded and retransmitted to the ground at a rate of 50 million bits per second (Matra).

Assembling a telecommunications satellite. The sequence diagram on the right shows the different stages of integration of the Arabsat telecommunications satellite. The systems were constructed in different factories and then integrated to form a communications module (the payload) and a service module (the platform). These two modules were mounted separately onto a U shaped structure and then assembled.

Earth observation payloads

Although the first Earth observation missions were essentially for scientific purposes, it was not long before satellites such as Landsat and SPOT opened up the commercial phase by selling images of the Earth taken from space. The SPOT satellite, for instance, produces images in three colour bands in the visible and the near infrared, and also takes panchromatic images in black and white with a spatial resolution on the ground of 10 metres.

SPOT's payload has two parts. The first consists of two High Resolution Visible (HRV) cameras weighing 242 kilograms and standing 2·5 metres high. When looking vertically down, SPOT observes a region that is 117 kilometres wide on the Earth's surface. Moreover, the distance between two tracks on successive orbits, 108 kilometres at the equator, ensures that no part of the Earth's surface is forgotten.

The second part of the payload consists of the telemetry and data recording and transmission equipment; on SPOT, this includes the capacity to store 132 megabits of data. Data can then be transmitted to the Earth at a rate of 25 megabits per second, using an X band transmitter at around 8·2 gigahertz.

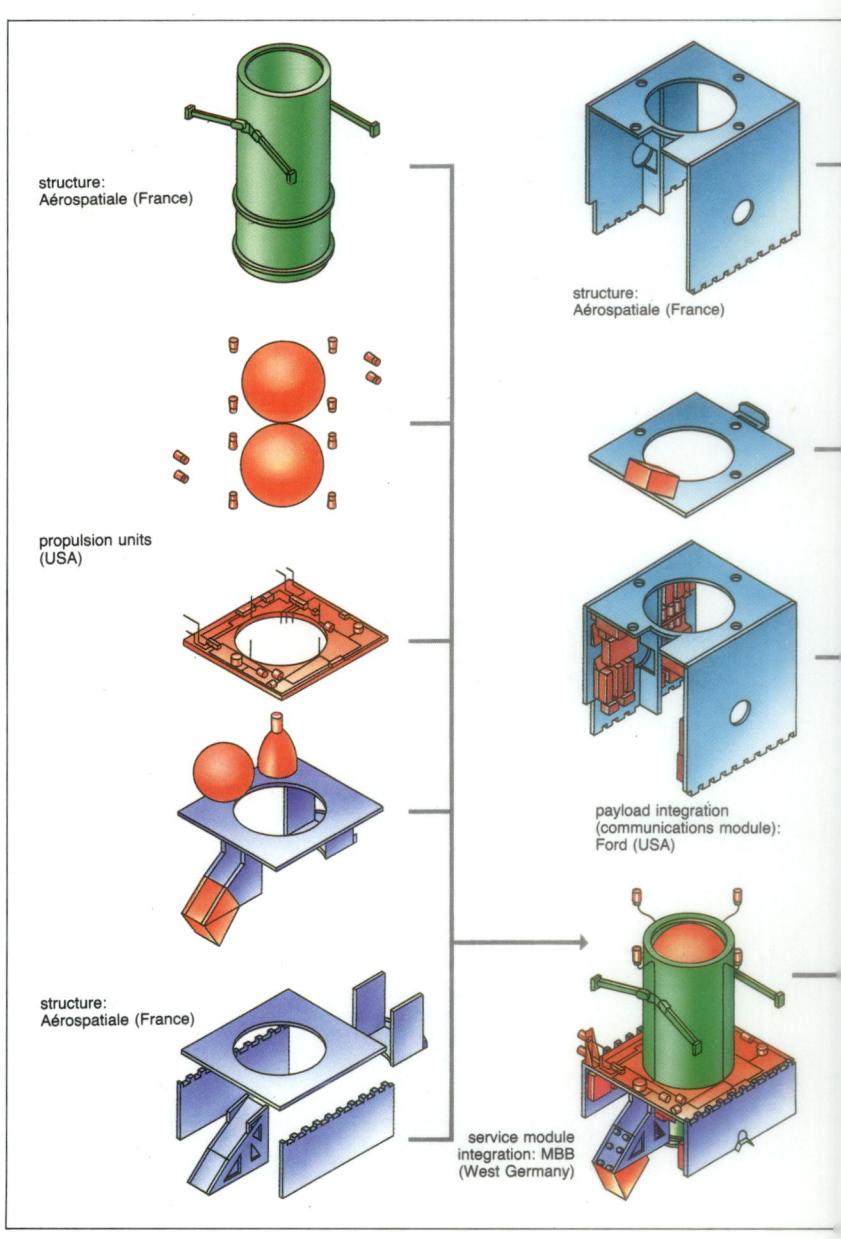

structure:
Aérospatiale (France)

propulsion units
(USA)

structure:
Aérospatiale (France)

structure:
Aérospatiale (France)

payload integration
(communications module):
Ford (USA)

service module
integration: MBB
(West Germany)

The Meteosat radiometer. Europe's geostationary meteorological satellite, Meteosat, has a high resolution radiometer (shown in the photograph above), sophisticated data processing techniques, and telecommunications transmitters and repeaters in the VHF and S bands.

The radiometer is used as a camera, and consists essentially of a telescope with a 40 centimetre diameter mirror. It has a set of detectors sensitive to visible radiation (at wavelengths in the range 0·5 to 0·9 microns), the near infrared (from 10·5 to 12·5 microns) and the far infrared (at 57 to 71 microns in the water vapour absorption band). The detectors scan as the satellite rotates, the different lines of the image being created by an oscillating mirror (Matra).

Satellite integration

Few modern technologies require the same consistently high level of reliability as satellites. There must be no noticeable decrease in the performance of the subsystems since no repair or maintenance work can usually be carried out during the seven to ten year operational life of the satellite.

A production line working on more than ten satellites at once is extremely rare, so the satellite industry is like a specialised craft industry. However, families of satellites can be developed using identical subsystems which can be built together, other subsystems being built to order, to suit a specific mission. Each subsystem can be built in a different factory, the finished satellite ultimately being assembled in an integration and test hall, usually by the project's main contractor.

Integration and test procedures require the greatest care, and working conditions are kept as sterile as possible; numerous measuring and checking procedures have been developed to ensure that breakdown of the equipment in space is as unlikely as possible, and most methods used for testing individual subsystems are computerised. Besides the test system in the integration hall, there is another close to the launch pad, making several thousand vital measurements in the last few seconds of the countdown to launch.

Alexandre Dauguet

Matra's satellite integration hall at Toulouse. This large centre is used for the construction, integration and testing of satellites. After the different modules have been assembled, the satellite is subjected to a series of mechanical and electrical checks, followed by a series of tests to see how it will cope with the space environment. Only then is it prepared for launch.

The SPOT 1 satellite, seen in the foreground of the photograph above, spent two weeks in a vacuum simulator where it was subjected to temperature extremes cycling between −10 to +50 degrees celsius to test the quality of the equipment. The satellite then spent another 15 days undergoing flight tests before being transported to Kourou on a Boeing 747 for final, pre-launch electrical tests (F. Watbled/Matra).

Satellite integration procedures. The photograph below shows the communications module of the direct broadcasting satellite, TDF 1, being joined to its service module. Clean rooms are essential for such tasks to increase the reliability of the equipment on long life satellites by reducing the risks of electrostatic, mechanical, chemical and even biological contamination. The personnel who work in these rooms wear special protective clothing (Aérospatiale).

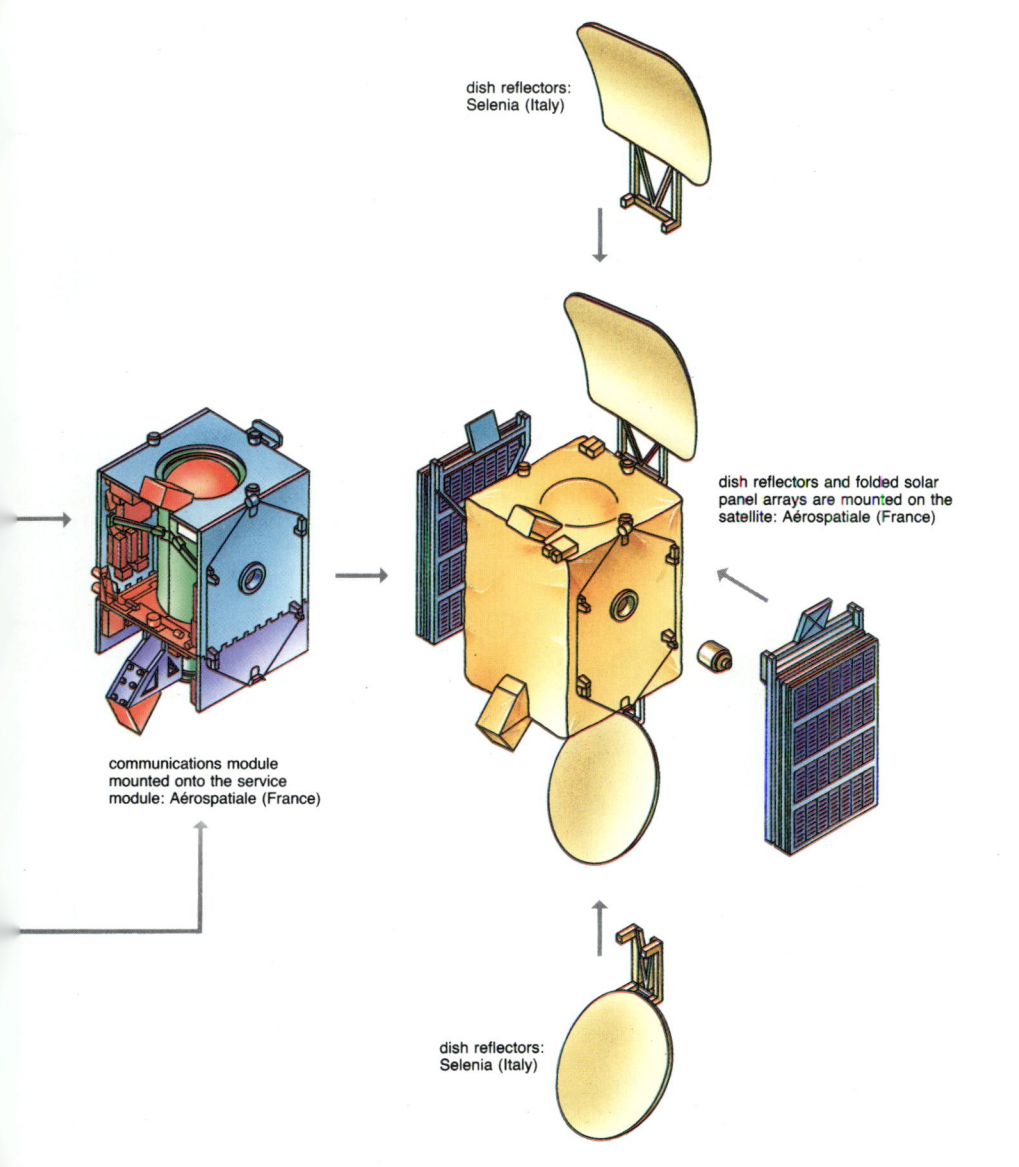

dish reflectors: Selenia (Italy)

dish reflectors and folded solar panel arrays are mounted on the satellite: Aérospatiale (France)

communications module mounted onto the service module: Aérospatiale (France)

dish reflectors: Selenia (Italy)

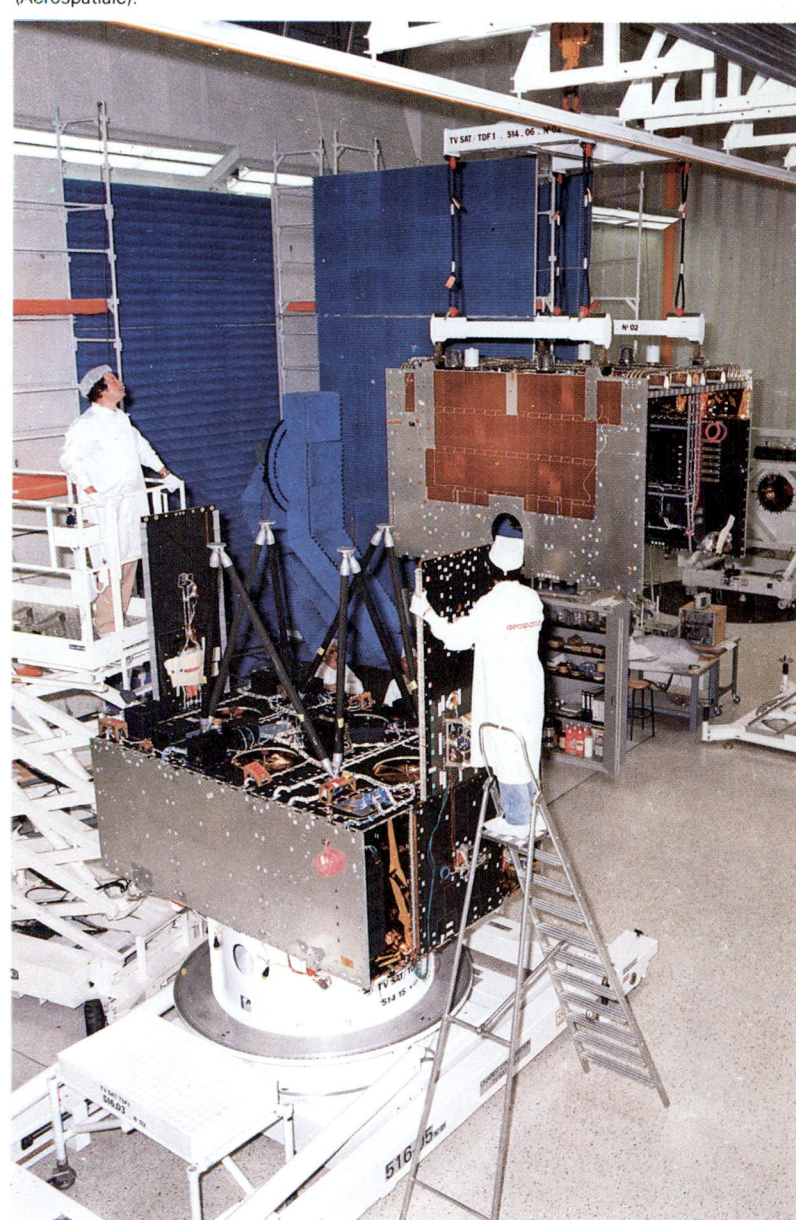

Satellite systems

Ground stations

The A group dish at Pleumeur-Bodou, France. There are several C group (14·5 metre diameter) and A group (32·5 metre diameter) dishes on the site at Pleumeur-Bodou, which belongs to the French Post Office and Telecommunications service. They operate mainly with the Intelsat satellites (Thomson-CSF).

Ground stations for the space segment

The scientific personnel responsible for the launcher are also responsible for the satellite until after the last rocket stage has burnt out and the satellite has separated from the launcher. The transfer orbit, apogee manoeuvres and final positioning in the correct geostationary location are all supervised by the launch control centre. A different control centre is then used during the satellite's operational phase, once it is successfully in orbit.

A series of ground stations track the satellite, with the minimum number of 'blind' periods possible. Such stations accurately locate the satellite, receive its telemetry signals, send remote control commands, monitor the payload's health and make the necessary calculations for any correction manoeuvres. These ground stations comprise the Tracking, Telemetry and Command (TT&C) station network.

There are several world networks of TT&C stations. Those belonging to NASA, the CNES and the European Space Agency form the international telecommunications network, Intelsat. They are all independent but cooperate continuously with one another. The CNES stations operating at 2 gigahertz, for example, have dishes 11 metres in diameter and transmit at a power adjustable between 100 watts and 1 kilowatt. All receivers of radio signals transmitted by a satellite require a high signal to noise ratio.

The totality of messages from the TT&C station network is relayed to the satellite's operational control centre. This is responsible for mapping the satellite's orbit and determining its attitude. A computer calculates the necessary corrections, formulates commands, and transmits this information to the network so that it can be relayed to the satellite.

Ground stations for the Earth segment

The stations which form the Earth segment are those telecommunications centres which exploit the data the satellite has collected and transmitted down to Earth. They are well equipped with antennae for transmission and reception, and all necessary radio apparatus. The most striking aspects of these stations are their antennae; these vary considerably in type and appearance depending on their required function. A network of dipoles is chosen for the lower frequencies and parabolic dishes for higher frequencies, and dimensions can vary greatly depending on the desired gain.

The biggest antennae are those designed to receive either the lowest frequencies or the weakest transmissions. The largest dishes have diameters of 70 metres and are used to track space probes investigating distant parts of the solar system; in contrast, dishes with diameters of less than 1 metre are used for the domestic reception of satellite television channels. Telecommunications stations normally have dishes with diameters between 2 and 32 metres.

The international organisation, Intelsat, uses three types of antennae. Those in the A group have diameters of 32 metres, operate at 4 to 6 gigahertz and are used for transatlantic communications. The B group dishes have diameters of 11 metres and use the same frequencies, but are cheaper and have a smaller capacity. Antennae of the C group, with diameters between 14 and 19 metres, are used for frequencies between 11 and 14 gigahertz. Regional systems, such as Arabsat, or national ones, such as the French Télécom 1, use 10 metre diameter dishes for direct communication links and 3 metre dishes for the mobile links used for video or data transmission.

All receivers have to be of advanced design because the satellite signal is very weak. The first amplifiers operated at extremely low temperatures (−268 degrees celsius, or 5 kelvin). However, it is now possible to obtain very high signal to noise ratios using parametric amplifiers which operate at room temperature, and – most recently – low noise transistors.

Station transmitters also vary according to usage, with power ranges that can be altered between 25 watts and 5 kilowatts according to need. Two major families of power amplifiers are in use – wide band amplifiers, with travelling wave tubes, and narrow band amplifiers using klystrons.

In addition to the necessary receivers and transmitters, data processing centres have been established to deal with all the information received from scientific and observation satellites. Large amounts of data are stored at such establishments, and very sophisticated image processing techniques can now be carried out. False colour images, for example, or high definition images of cartographic quality may be the commercial end products.

Alexandre Dauguet

A mobile transmission and reception station for Télécom 1. The development of this new type of station, which has a 2 metre diameter dish and is mobile and easily dismantled and reerected, has been extremely rapid. In the USA and Canada it is used to transmit television programmes to centres which then distribute them via cable to private users or companies, usually hotels. In France, one of the aims of Télécom 1 is to transmit data which travel along telephone lines, for example linking computers, facsimile machines, or video conferences. The small size of the unit means that it can easily be assembled on roofs (Thomson-CSF).

A reception station for a direct broadcasting satellite. Parabolic dishes less than 1 metre in diameter are relatively cheap and less prone to being blown out of line than larger dishes.

Other recent developments in the field of domestic receivers have included the introduction of flat receivers which can be fitted to the roofs of houses or blocks of flats (Jacques Pierre; photograph, Seditas).

The hazards of space debris

Despite the vastness of near Earth space, the millions of natural and man made objects within some tens of thousands of kilometres of the Earth pose a threat to both manned and unmanned satellites. During the early years of the space age, when preparations were underway for trips to the Moon and extended manned missions in Earth orbit, measurements of the natural meteoroid environment were made. It was, however, determined that these small particles present no significant risk. The probability of a collision between a satellite with a cross sectional area of 1 square metre and a meteoroid 1 millimetre in diameter, the smallest particle with the potential for causing catastrophic damage, is only once every 100 years in low Earth orbit. A much smaller meteoroid is believed to have struck the Soviet Salyut 7 space station in July 1982, scaring the crew but leaving no damage other than a 4 millimetre crater in one of the station's portholes.

Of greater concern now is the growing number of pieces of artificial debris in Earth orbit; although fewer in number, these are typically much larger and much longer lived. Given average impact velocities of 10 kilometres per second compared with 15 to 20 kilometres per second for meteoroids, man made debris already exceeds meteoroids as a cause of spacecraft failure.

Artificial debris can be created in three ways. The most obvious is when items in space are discarded after they have served their intended purpose. Old satellites, spent rocket stages, sensor covers, deployment mechanisms, and even gloves and screwdrivers come into this category. The firing of solid fuel upper stages like those used for geosynchronous missions can put tonnes of very fine particles of aluminum oxide into orbit, and many spacecraft returning from long stays in space show evidence of numerous aluminum oxide impacts. The longterm effects of minute debris on large scientific instruments, such as the Hubble Space Telescope, may accordingly be severe.

A second, largely invisible source of space debris comes from deteriorating satellites. Under the extreme radiation and thermal conditions of space, spacecraft thermal blankets and solar cells come apart over time and paint peels off. New space debris fragments continue to be formed, for instance, from the remains of the Pageos balloon launched in 1966; the aluminised mylar material used has apparently become brittle with age.

The third, and most serious, debris threat to the near Earth environment comes from the fragmentation of satellite payloads and rocket bodies. Between 1961 and the beginning of 1988, more than 100 breakups were observed, involving 92 parent satellites. The consequences of such events could be great. Approximately half of the more than seven thousand objects being tracked by sensitive NORAD radars originated from satellites breaking up, and a third of the nineteen thousand manmade objects catalogued since the launch of Sputnik 1 are known to have originated from satellite breakup.

Satellites can disintegrate for a variety of reasons. On average, one satellite per year destroys itself due to a malfunction of its propulsion system. Although infrequent, such events are of particular concern because energetic explosions can propel thousands of particles with diameters greater than 1 millimetre into near Earth space. In fact, the inadvertent breakups of just seven US Delta second stage rockets account for a third of all man made debris; these occurred up to three years after a successful mission, and were traced to a poor fuel tank design which allowed residual propellants to mix explosively. Such upper stages are now restarted after satellite deployment to consume the remaining fuel. In the same way, and in line with its high launch rate, the Soviet Union too suffers occasionally from catastrophic upper stage launch failures, as occurred with Cosmos 1305 in 1981 and Cosmos 1423 in 1982.

A large number of satellites have also been destroyed intentionally, and anti-satellite (ASAT) tests by both superpowers have been responsible for nearly a thousand catalogued pieces of debris. Three Soviet ASAT targets have also violently fragmented, although apparently not as the direct result of ASAT engagements. In 1966 a Saturn upper stage was deliberately overpressurised and exploded to demonstrate its engineering specifications; however, because of the low altitude of the test, all the debris produced reentered the Earth's atmosphere within three weeks and did not contribute to the longterm pollution of space.

Unfortunately, the cause of almost half of all satellite breakups is unknown. This is due in part to the lack of data available and in part to a reluctance on the part of some satellite owners to acknowledge the events. For instance, the mysterious and violent breakup of Cosmos 1275, a navigation satellite, at an altitude of about 1000 kilometres, occurred just seven weeks after its launch; this satellite was in the most densely populated region of near Earth space, and may well have been struck by space debris. Such a hypervelocity collision would have created hundreds of thousands, or even millions, of new debris fragments, the actual number depending upon the mass of the colliding object. Some 300 fragments from Cosmos 1275 that are bigger than 10 centimetres have been detected by NORAD radars more than four years after the breakup. Above a height of 1000 kilometres, anything smaller is invisible.

A particular debris problem exists in the geostationary orbit, almost 36000 kilometres above the equator. Although the number of objects known to be in near geostationary orbits amounts to only several hundred, the 'density' of spacecraft here is high compared with that of low altitude satellites. Collision probabilities in geostationary orbit are fortunately still considered minimal since all the satellites are moving in the same direction at low relative velocities. However, though no breakups are known to have occurred in the geostationary orbit, at such altitudes the NORAD surveillance system is still incapable of detecting objects less than 1 metre across.

Knowledge of the true debris environment is thus essential to engineers designing large permanent space stations. NASA is currently conducting a number of experiments aimed at increasing understanding of the space debris environment, and present estimates of the debris population suggest that a permanent space station could expect an impact by a dangerous, 1 centimetre particle approximately once every 200 years.

Nicholas L. Johnson

Almost lost in space. The metal structure visible in the centre of the photograph became separated from the space shuttle Challenger during the extravehicular activity made on 9 February 1984 by Bruce McCandless and Robert L. Stewart. It was later recovered to avoid the possibility of subsequent collision with a satellite (NASA).

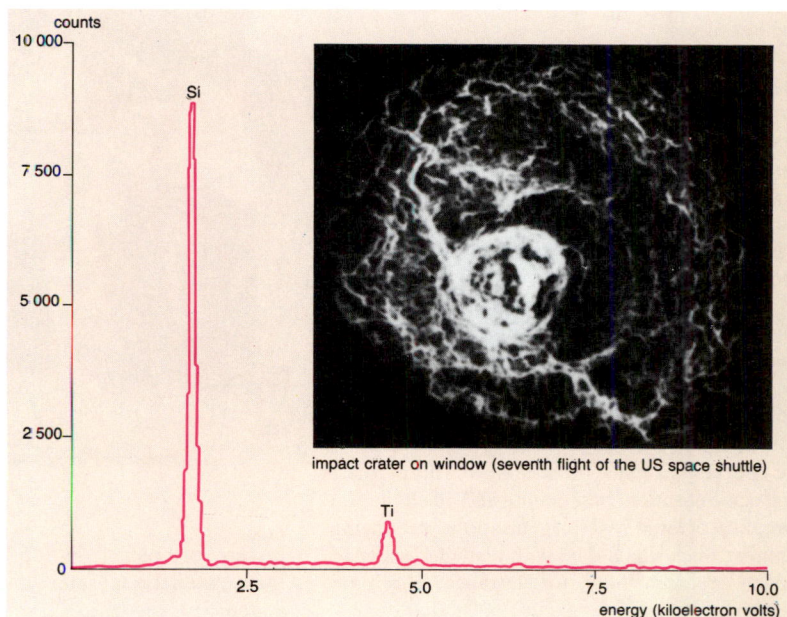

impact crater on window (seventh flight of the US space shuttle)

The impact crater caused by a fleck of paint. Millions of microscopic pieces of artificial debris are in orbit about the Earth. On the morning of their fourth day in space, the crew of the seventh space shuttle mission reported a 4 millimetre crater on the surface of one of the shuttle windows. Laboratory examinations of the crater after return to Earth revealed traces of titanium oxide, aluminum, carbon and potassium. The particle that is believed to have made the crater is a 0·2 millimetre diameter fleck of paint from a satellite.

Solar radiation can break down the bonding agent in spacecraft paints, and many small particles will be released. A particle 1 centimetre in diameter could cause much more serious damage to the shuttle and could in turn endanger the lives of the crew (NASA).

Man made debris in space. The average rate of satellite breakup has increased noticeably since 1980 as the blue curve below shows. Fortunately, the average number of detectable pieces of debris associated with each incident has diminished, resulting in an overall lower rate of growth for artificial debris (red curve). During the five year period from 1981 to 1985, 32 satellites are known to have broken up; of these 3 were American and 29 Soviet satellites. Only 3 events could be attributed to propulsion-related causes; 17 are believed to have been deliberate and the causes of 12 are unknown.

The number of pieces of catalogued debris is not, however, always equivalent to the detectable debris. In the case of Cosmos 1405, which broke up on 20 December 1983, only 31 pieces of debris have been catalogued, though more than 130 objects were detected during a special analysis of data acquired using a very sensitive radar.

If the creation of debris in Earth orbit is not curbed, the Earth could in time become enveloped by a sheath of debris (From N. L. Johnson et al., History of On-Orbit Satellite Fragmentations, Colorado Springs, Colorado, 1986).

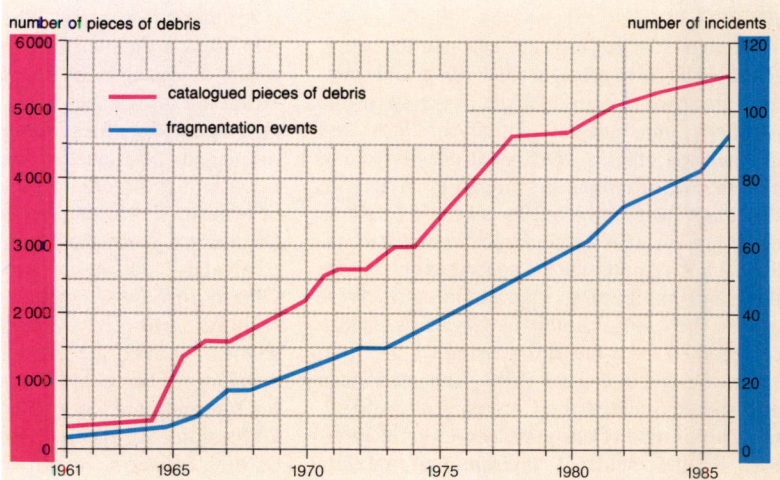

Space agencies

From the first, space programmes have had strong political elements by their very nature. Any nation which has the ability to build and launch satellites into space is demonstrating not only its power but also its place at the forefront of the development of new technologies. Satellite telecommunications alone represent a market worth thousands of millions of dollars, and space meteorology and remote sensing of the Earth's resources are having a profound effect on the economic development of the world. In the future, the economic impact of industrial activities that can only effectively be carried out in the weightlessness of space may be just as great.

For these reasons, a number of countries have established specialised agencies for coordinating activities in space. Other countries have undertaken considerable space programmes without basing them on specifically developed institutions, but some at least are now finding it necessary to create a central organisation which can coordinate all the projects under development.

Against this trend, countries which formerly had well defined space administrations are now feeling the need to decentralise and let the users have more control. A prime example here is telecommunications where there has been a strong move towards the commercial realisation of operational space programmes. This increasing specialisation has manifested itself in the breakup of large space organisations, producing smaller ones which deal with a single aspect of space research like, for instance, maritime telecommunications.

Several examples are presented here to illustrate how the different space institutions and programmes have evolved into their current state.

National organisations

The most prestigious national space organisation is undoubtedly the American National Aeronautics and Space Administration (NASA). Created on 1 October 1958 to meet the challenge raised by the Soviets when they launched their first artificial satellite on 4 October 1957, NASA was established specifically to ensure that the USA became the leader in the space race. It took up where the old National Advisory Committee for Aeronautics (NACA, created in 1915) left off. However, a key feature of NASA is that it is constitutionally responsible for civil and peaceful activities alone, all military space programmes coming under the aegis of the Department of Defense (DOD).

Though it also has an aeronautics wing, NASA's basic purpose is to develop and demonstrate space systems in flight. It is responsible for both unmanned scientific satellites and manned spaceflights. NASA has a lesser role to play in civil programmes, though it carried out the basic work which has since led to the development of telecommunications, meteorological and remote sensing space systems. Once these systems became operational, they were made the responsibility of groups which represented the users of the systems.

At the beginning of 1968, the American government created the Communication Satellite Corporation (Comsat) to represent its interests in the field of international satellite telecommunications. In addition, a number of

private companies in the USA now possess their own national satellite telecommunications systems.

The National Oceanic and Atmospheric Administration (NOAA) is responsible for the meteorological satellite systems that observe the Earth's atmosphere from space for weather forecasting purposes. NASA meanwhile has continued to supply the means for launching operational satellites and pursuing research into future generations of civil satellites. As the number of space activities has increased and more systems have become operational, the USA – the nation, par excellence, of the market and free enterprise – has encouraged the private sector to participate in new space programmes. This participation has mostly occurred to date in the lucrative field of telecommunications. A law is in place to govern the privatisation and exploitation of the results obtained by Earth observation satellites, and one company, the Earth Observation Corporation (Eosat), is now responsible for pursuing all Earth observation satellite programmes which were formerly run by NASA and then managed by NOAA.

In marked contrast, the USSR has never published a detailed description of the way in which it organises its space programmes. The Academy of Sciences has a very visible role in civil space activities, however, and enjoys a privileged position in the Soviet hierarchy because it is directly responsible to the Council of Ministers. At the heart of the Academy, the Institute of Space Research (IKI) in Moscow is particularly active on an international level. Other institutes, notably the Vernadsky Institute with its laboratory of planetary studies, collaborate with the IKI, and the Academy of Sciences has now created a Council for International Cooperation in the Study and Utilisation of Space (Intercosmos) to help develop cooperation with Western Europe.

Some individual Soviet ministries are also interested in using space. The ministry responsible for the mercantile marine has, for instance, created an organisation, called Morsviazsputnik, which is responsible for satellite marine telecommunications as part of the international Inmarsat organisation.

Most recently, the Soviet Union has created another space organisation, called Glavkosmos, to develop a commercial side to Soviet space activities. Glavkosmos will be able to take largely independent decisions on space matters and act as the spokesman for both Soviet industries and the countries with which the USSR wishes to cooperate. Very much in line with recent developments in Eastern Europe, the decision to establish Glavkosmos seems to spring from a new desire to increase flexibility in international dealings.

In Japan, the Space Activities Commission (SAC) has the job of coordinating space activities. Created in 1968, it is the supreme administration on space matters, attached to the Prime Minister's Office and able to make recommendations on the definition, detailed development, and budgeting of Japanese space policy. The Science and Technology Agency (STA) provides the secretariat to the SAC and, through its Research Coordination Bureau (RCB), is responsible for policy planning in the fields of space science and technology, for developing international cooperation and for promoting the use of space. The STA also controls the National Space Development Agency (Nasda), created in October 1969 to take responsibility for practical applications in space. It is principally Nasda that develops satellites and launchers, especially for communications, direct broadcasting and Earth observations. The same agency has related responsibilities for the launching, tracking and control of satellites, the reception and processing of data from remote sensing satellites, and the overall promotion of scientific experiments in space.

The Japanese Institute of Space and Astronautical Science (ISAS), created in April 1981, has over the last decade taken over activities previously undertaken by the University of Tokyo in the field of space sciences. It is particularly concerned with research and development into scientific satellites and launchers. A complementary agency, the National Space Laboratory (NSL), linked to the STA, is in charge of fundamental research in the space sciences.

The administrative organisation regulating posts and telecommunications, which was formerly responsible for satellite telecommunications, has recently been deregulated. As a result, several Japanese industrial companies are now constructing operational telecommunications satellites which will eventually be managed by private companies.

Finally, the Ministry of International Trade and Industry (MITI) is trying hard to increase the access that Japanese industry has to space techniques, particularly in the fields of microgravity.

China too has made considerable progress in the realisation of its space programme in recent years, above all in the field of launchers. The Ministry of Aeronautics (MOA) is responsible for most space activity, and in particular for the series of Long March rockets. There is, however, no clear distinction between the organisations which are responsible for planning the programmes and the industries which carry them out. According to MOA, some 100 000 people in China work in the aerospace industry.

Among developing countries, it is India which has best managed to assimilate the possible contribution that space technology can make to its economic development. The prime minister is directly responsible for all space activities, although the Indian National Committee for Space Research (INCRS) has been in existence since 1962. In 1965, an Indian Space Research Organisation (ISRO) was created in addition by the Ministry for Atomic Energy to support India's ambitious space programme. Other Indian institutions involved in space activities include the Ministry of Telecommunications, the Tata Institute of Fundamental Research and the National Remote Sensing Agency (NRSA).

Western European countries decided early on to pool their resources and work together on space programmes under the guidance of the European Space Agency (ESA). Several countries have national programmes besides, and some even have their own specialised institutes for such purposes. These institutes are generally responsible for that country's participation in the wider European programme.

In France, the Centre national d'études spatiales (CNES, National Space Research Centre) was created in 1961 to provide France with the framework to carry out both its national programme and its European commitments in the space field. Largely responsible for the European Ariane launcher programme, it is accountable to the government ministry responsible for research and industry. The CNES also manages bilateral space programmes developed independently between France and other countries.

An important aspect of the CNES is its ability to create privately owned subsidiary companies to develop commercially oriented space projects. Thus, although the remote sensing satellite SPOT 1 was developed and launched by the CNES, a private company, SPOT-Image, created by the CNES, is now responsible for marketing the images obtained, both in France and abroad. SPOT-Image also carries out negotiations for the installation of receiving stations capable of receiving SPOT images throughout the world.

In much the same way, the CNES is working with the French PTT (Post, Telephone and Telecommunications) organisation to build a system of telecommunications satellites for domestic use – the so-called Télécom programme. These satellites are managed by the PTT. At the same time, the CNES is also working with Télédiffusion de France (TDF) on a direct broadcasting satellite programme.

France has the largest national space agency in Europe. However, as its space activities diversify, some elements are becoming more commercial and some are being privatised. An increasing number of public and private bodies are thus no longer dependent on the CNES for their activities in space.

West Germany has had an aeronautics research establishment for many years, and this has steadily widened its field of interest to include space. Although this establishment, the Deutsche Forschungs- und Versuchsanstalt für Luft und Raumfahrt EV (DFVLR), is financed from public funds, it remains independent of the government; it advises the Ministry of Research and Technology (BMFT) which takes the actual decisions on programme development. In the space domain, the DFVLR's most important establishments are at Porz-Wahn (Bonn) and Oberpfaffenhofen (Munich).

Other countries have space programmes which either do not depend on a central agency, or which pass its development functions to committees or commissions which meet only periodically. For example, in Great Britain, space work is carried out by more general organisations with aerospace concerns like the Royal Aerospace Establishment at Farnborough, or by industry.

Even over the last few years, however, a number of countries have established permanent and specifically space oriented bodies. In particular, Great Britain founded the small British National Space Centre (BNSC) in 1985, and Italy likewise has decided to create its own national space agency. These two organisations are in charge of coordinating space activities both nationally and internationally.

Three other European countries – Sweden, Austria and Spain – have space agencies: the Swedish Space Corporation (SSC); the Austrian Solar and Space Agency (ASSA); and in Spain, the Comisión nacional de investigación del espacio (Conie/INTA), at present the subject of a major reorganisation programme. Outside Europe, Argentina has its National Commission for Space Research (CNIE), Pakistan its Commission for Research into Space and the High Atmosphere (LAPAN), and Indonesia the Indonesian National Institute for Aeronautics and Space.

International organisations

International organisations, which may have either a global or a regional perspective, are generally only involved in specific aspects of the space industry. They may, for instance, be regulatory bodies or bodies involved with only one function, such as telecommunications satellites.

The United Nations itself has specialised agencies which deal with space issues. The UN Committee for the Peaceful Uses of Space was founded at the beginning of the space era and now has members from 59 countries who meet at least once a year; it also has two subcommittees, one juridical and one scientific. This committee has been responsible for the international space treaties which are in existence today and this legislative work, on a world scale, is one of the UN's greatest successes.

The UN General Secretary has a Space Division charged with the task of helping countries which are in the process of developing space techniques. Beyond this, the UN has other specialised agencies which are particularly involved in space matters. The International Telecommunications Union coordinates the use of frequencies by satellites to avoid interference, and regulates the positions of direct broadcasting satellites in the geostationary orbit. The World Meteorological Organisation is responsible for promoting the use of meteorological satellites, and the Food and Agriculture Organisation (FAO) studies and supports the use of space techniques for predicting harvests, water and weather conditions.

Ever since the launch of the first telecommunications satellites, it has been clear that an international organisation would be needed to coordinate them. In 1973 North America and Western Europe created the International Telecommunications Satellites Organisation (Intelsat), its declared objective to supply to all countries, on a commercial basis and without discrimination, the reliable, high quality space sector that was needed by international public telecommunications services.

Already in 1971, the Soviet Union and Eastern European countries had created an organisation called Intersputnik, which is similar in fundamental terms to Intelsat. About 20 countries are linked into this telecommunications system through Soviet Molniya satellites.

To improve maritime communications an organisation called Inmarsat has also been established. It operates space systems which link ship to shore and ship to ship, its ultimate origin lying within the International Maritime Organisation, part of the UN, which includes all the major maritime powers, including the USSR.

The European Space Agency (ESA) was founded in Paris on 30 May 1975, by 11 Western European countries; its origins lie in two organisations which were created in 1964, the European Space Research Organisation (ESRO) and the European Launcher Development Organisation (ELDO). ESA is the largest international agency that deals with science and technology in space, and its member states have developed a longterm policy which in time will enable Europe to become the third space power, after the USA and the USSR.

ESA's basic objective is cooperation between member countries for purely peaceful purposes. It organises research and development which often lead to operational systems being established. These include, most notably, Eutelsat, Eumetsat and Arianespace.

The European Telecommunications Satellites Organisation (Eutelsat) joins together the telecommunications administration of 26 European countries. It manages the European Communication Satellites (ECS) system which operates only over Europe, and is responsible for both communication and satellite television broadcasting (p. 248).

The European Meteorological Satellite Organisation (Eumetsat) links together the weather services of 15 European countries; it is responsible for managing an operational weather satellite system, built by ESA, which goes under the name Meteosat (p. 232).

Arianespace is a private French commercial company whose shareholders are the CNES and the group of companies involved in the construction of the Ariane launcher. Arianespace is responsible for the production and marketing of satellite launchers developed by ESA; it is the first private company in the world to be responsible for launchers. The activities of Arianespace are governed by the Convention on the International Responsibility for Damage caused by Space Objects which states that a country remains responsible for space activities initiated within its boundaries, even when they are carried out by private companies.

The space agencies and structures which have been created to develop space activities around the globe are thus now used mainly to define and regulate space policy. In addition, they control large scale programmes such as the construction of a space station, the planning of planetary expeditions, or the development of new technology.

Jean Arets

145

This computer enhanced photograph was constructed from 102 images taken by the Viking Orbiter 1 probe, in the red and blue parts of the visible spectrum. It shows the surface of Mars, cut in half by the massive canyon of Valles Marineris. To the west there are three large volcanoes on the plateau of Tharsis. From bottom to top these are Arsia Mons, Pavonis Mons and Ascraeus Mons. The spatial resolution of this remarkable image is about 800 metres, and the colours have been enhanced for the best effect (Alfred S. McEven, USGS).

Exploring the Universe

Images from space

Producing images of views from space is one of the most important parts of many space programmes, whether they be planetary missions, or Earth observation programmes with astronomical, or meteorological, remote sensing or military applications.

Most of the instruments used to make such images have the same three basic elements. These are an optical system (for example a sequence of lenses) to focus the light, a shutter to control the exposure time, and a medium (for example photographic film or an electronic system) to record the image.

Two basic physical concepts, which may be expressed as questions, determine the optimum design of these instruments. The first of these is the spatial resolution – what is the smallest detail that has to be distinguishable? The second is the spectral sensitivity – over what range, or ranges, of the electromagnetic spectrum are the observations to be made?

The images with the highest resolution are obtained using photographic film, but this presupposes that there is a way to return the exposed film to Earth for processing. Such familiar space imaging is currently used by military reconnaissance satellites, the rolls of film being sealed in a capsule which returns to Earth, is slowed down by the atmosphere, and is recovered after parachuting to the ground. By this method a spatial resolution on the ground of about 10 centimetres is possible with satellites flying in low Earth orbit at about 200 kilometres altitude.

As far as lunar exploration is concerned, however, only the American Apollo lunar missions and the Soviet Zond probes have been able to return film to the Earth for processing. Other Earth observation satellites and the American Lunar Orbiter probes have processed the film on board and then scanned them with a light beam. This converts the images into electrical signals which can be sent by telemetry to terrestrial stations. The signals can then be decoded to recreate the photographs.

A Vidicon television camera system has also been used in space, mainly for planetary exploration. Here the image is focused onto a photoconductor which causes the intensity of the electron beam discharged from an electron gun to vary with the intensity of the light. The values of the intensity are converted into digital information and transmitted directly to Earth. Such a system was used on the Ranger, Mariner, Viking and Voyager probes. Mostly recently, however, the image has been structured as a succession of tiny square elements called pixels (picture elements); such digital results can be subjected to advanced processing techniques like image enhancement or false colour imaging.

Another alternative is a Charge Coupled Device (CCD) array consisting of an arrangement of many small, square photosensitive cells onto which the light is focused. Each CCD cell creates an electrical charge which varies with the intensity of the incident light; the entire array accordingly forms an area of pixels carrying digital data which can be processed by computer. The Landsat and SPOT remote sensing satellites, the Galileo planetary probe and the recently launched Hubble Space Telescope all use this method of imaging.

Radar imaging from satellites provides clear images of the topography of the Earth or planets at night, even when the surface is hidden by clouds. A radar beam using long wavelength radio waves that can penetrate the cloud cover is emitted by the satellite in the direction of the region to be studied; it is then scattered at different angles depending on the shape of the topographic relief, and reflected back to a receiver aboard the satellite.

This method is used for remote sensing, for example by the Seasat satellite, the space shuttle's Synthetic Aperture Radar, and Cosmos 1870. The technique has been and will continue

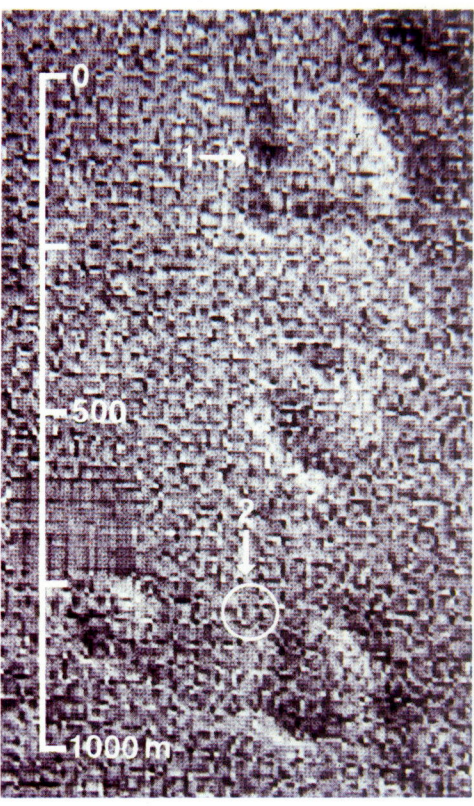

The spectacular results of image processing. Built up of thousands of pixels, or picture elements, the illustration on the left is part of an image taken by the Viking 2 probe of Viking 1's landing site on Mars (at 22·483° N, 47·968° W). Near the top, the arrow (1) points to the crescent shaped crater caused by the ejection of the thermal shield which protected the probe during its descent into the martian atmosphere. The shield was jettisoned at an altitude of 6 kilometres, just before the probe's parachute opened completely.

Although it cannot definitely be seen here, the circle (2) shows the uncertainty zone, with a diameter of 80 metres, in which the probe is to be found. Each pixel represents an area of 7·70 square metres of the martian surface. Since the maximum diameter of the probe was about 3 metres, it must lie within a single pixel.

The impact crater (1) was discovered in 1987 by Olivier de Goursac and James B. Garvin, working at the NASA Goddard Space Flight Center (NASA/JPL Promospace).

Colour enhancement of the surface of Mars. Several different images were recorded through different filters by the Viking 2 lander and then sent back to Earth. From these records obtained on the martian surface, and by knowing the passband of the carefully calibrated filters that were used, a computer was able to build up an image of the surface in true colour. Any fault noticed later could be corrected by algorithms introduced into the reconstruction program.

Each Viking landing station was fitted with two cameras, mounted 80 centimetres apart and viewing the landscape from a height of 1·3 metres in order to show the relief. These cameras had a small rotating mirror, which reflected light from a minute portion of the landscape below into red, green and blue photosensitive cells, so building up one vertical line, or sample, in a picture that contains 512 pixels. The camera optics then step slightly, and the mirror sweeps an adjoining portion of the landscape from top to bottom to obtain the next sample. Using continual repetition of the sequence, a complete colour panorama is built up by superposition of the images in the three different colours.

The wide angle panorama below, which is almost 2000 pixels across, covers an azimuth of 230 degrees. It was taken by the Viking 2 lander on 18 August 1979, or the 1050th martian day to have passed since the probe landed at 47·97° N, 225·1° W, on 3 September 1976. One martian day is 24 hours 39 minutes 35 seconds long, and there are 668·6 days in one martian year. The picture was taken just after local noon (martian time), 25 days before the martian spring equinox. Ice is evident as the white substance, in the shadow of the rocks, which has not yet been melted by the Sun. The prevailing surface temperature is −70 degrees celsius, thought it will rise to −30 degrees celsius at the same time in summer.

In the foreground, from left to right, can be seen the spacecraft itself, the mechanism for extending the spade which collected ground samples and next to it on the martian soil, the protective cylinder which covered the spade during the journey to Mars. Also evident are the UHF antenna, with its red cable; the large grey, protective cover of the radio isotope generator (bearing the American flag); and two small colour testcards.

The sky is pink coloured, turning to yellow nearer the Sun. The soil is a rich red-brown colour, particularly where it has been dug. The shadows on the surface are very distinct; this indicates that the amount of dust in the atmosphere which diffuses the sunlight decreases with the approach of spring (NASA/JPL Promospace).

1

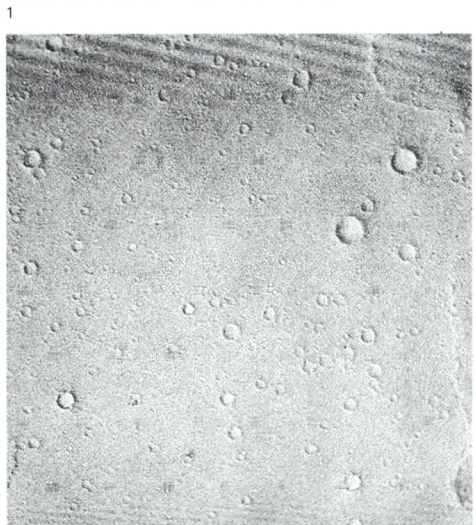

3

6

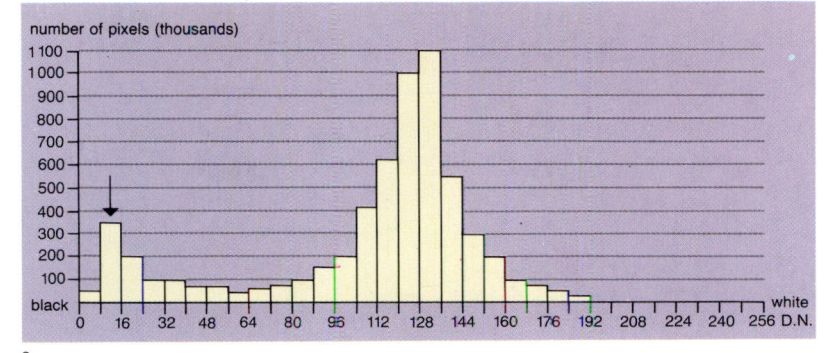

number of pixels (thousands)

2

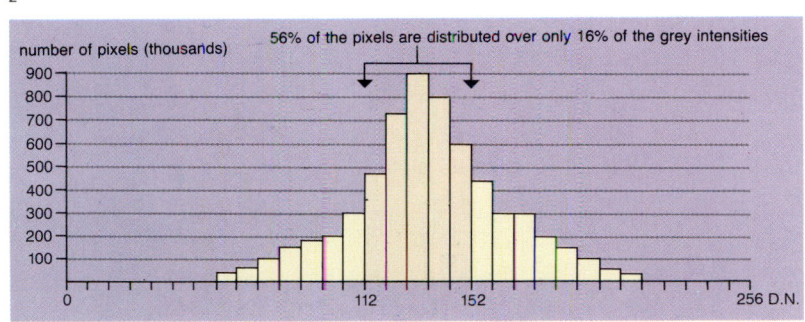

56% of the pixels are distributed over only 16% of the grey intensities

number of pixels (thousands)

4

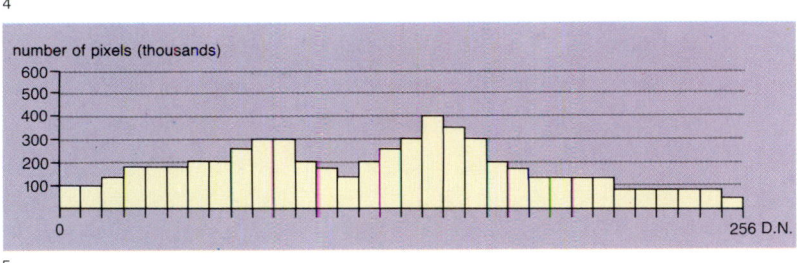

number of pixels (thousands)

5

to be used to penetrate the cloud cover of Venus (from, for example, the Soviet Venera 15 and Venera 16, and the American Magellan probe), and to study Titan, the largest of Saturn's moons in the course of the joint American and European Cassini project.

Computer techniques have in addition revolutionised space imaging in the last 25 years. In 1964 the Vidicon on Mariner 4 obtained 200 by 200 pixels per image with 64 possible grey (light) levels for each pixel, and it took eight and a half hours to transmit each picture back to the Earth. For Galileo's CCD array, there are 800 by 800 pixels per image, 256 grey levels per pixel, and a CCD camera which is 100 times more sensitive to light than the Vidicon camera. And in real time, it took only 40 seconds to transmit the whole picture back to Earth.

Olivier de Goursac

Image processing. All remote sensing images produced, for example, by a CCD camera or radar are stored in digital form. This enables them to be computer processed. An image is a two dimensional grid each of its elements is a pixel (or picture element) whose coordinates are known and whose light intensity has a DN (Digital Number) value. The coordinates of the pixels and their DN numbers describe the image as rows, called lines, and columns called samples. There are usually 256 brightness levels per pixel (level 0 is black and level 255 white). As an example, an image from the Viking probe to Mars is composed of almost 2000 by 512 pixels. Each image with 256 (or 2 to the power of 8) grey levels therefore represents almost 10 million bits of information to be stored in the memory before processing.

Before any processing can take place, the raw image is first examined (see 1 top left). All obvious defects, such as missing lines, overexposure at the corners due to the camera's optical system, and regular noise that has entered during transmission to the Earth, are removed. A histogram of the image's DN values is established by the computer (see 2 above). The most obvious defects appear as a peak near the centre of the histogram. Missing lines and noisy results are replaced by values made by taking the average DN of adjacent lines, and the black corners are removed by a computer program which takes into account the progression of the darkening. The computer then compensates for any calibration faults in the camera.

Geometrical corrections are also important for remote sensing and planetary studies. By knowing the viewing angle of the camera and the position of the satellite or space probe at the instant that the image was made, it is possible to move all the pixels so as to eliminate distortions due to the angle of view. A corrected image, as if taken from the vertical, is thus produced. A good example of this type of corrected photograph is shown above left (3). The corrected histogram for this is the central figure above (4), which shows how the abnormal peaks have been reduced.

Images can be enhanced once the pictures have been corrected. One of the most commonly used processes is the stretch process, used to increase the contrast of the image. In fact, the histogram for the corrected image (4) shows that the distribution of the grey levels (DN) is uneven, and is concentrated into one peak. This makes the image a dull grey, without contrast, so it requires further computer processing to give more detail. To increase the contrast, the higher DN values have to be stretched out (DN 112 to 152 for the example shown in histogram 4). This dominant zone is thus stretched over the 256 intensities of grey in the histogram to increase the overall contrast. A new histogram (5 above) is produced on which the main peak has been stretched out until it has almost disappeared. The final image (6, on the left) shows the result of this process; the rectangular box marked top right shows the landing site of Viking 1.

Other image processing is possible using, for example, digital computer filters, which emphasise brightness differences between adjacent pixels, or make the image sharper, thereby producing more detail. It is also possible to replace pixels from one image with ones taken from an earlier picture. In this way, scientists can see what changes have occurred since the first picture was taken (NASA/JPL Promospace).

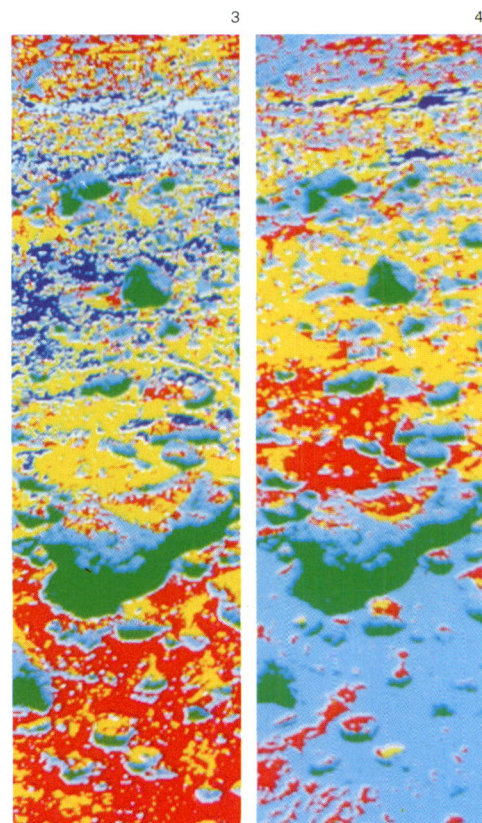

1 2 3 4

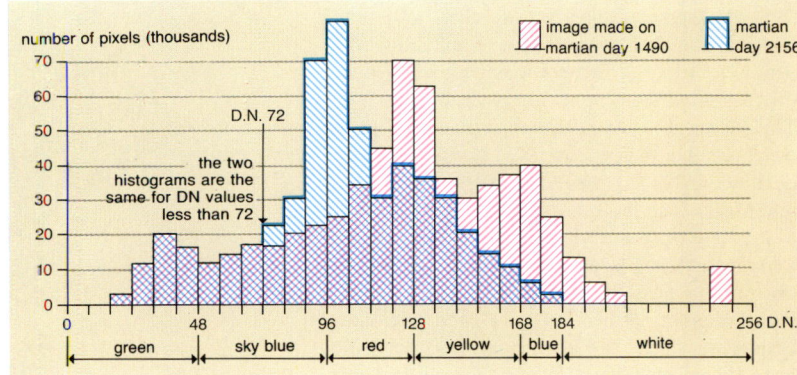

number of pixels (thousands)

image made on martian day 1490   martian day 2156

D.N. 72

the two histograms are the same for DN values less than 72

green   sky blue   red   yellow   blue   white

False colour image processing. In false colour processing those pixels which have the same DN value are given an arbitrary colour. This technique is used, for example, to differentiate between different types of terrain, or to show changes which are not perceptible to the naked eye. Thus, in the pictures on the left, false colour treatment has been used to show the effects of a dust storm on Mars. Images 1 and 2 were taken of the martian surface by the Viking 1 lander on two days almost exactly one martian year apart. During this year, there was a dust storm, and the false colour treatment highlights its effects on the landscape. The grey intensities (DN values) are coded, from dark to light, in green, sky blue, red, yellow, blue and white as shown in the DN histogram above, for the images obtained on martian day 1490 and day 2156.

The histogram peak on day 2156 is to the left of that on day 1490, demonstrating that the surface has been considerably disturbed between the two photographs. The false colour treatment confirms this: practically all the colours on the images of day 2156 (4) have moved down one level of colour; for example, immediately in front of the probe, in the foreground, the red in 3 has become sky blue in 4. This shows that the storm blew the surface layer of light coloured dust into the atmosphere, revealing darker rock beneath (James B. Garvin and Olivier de Goursac).

Exploring the solar system

Mercury

The purpose of the American Mariner 10 mission was to explore Mercury. It was exceptionally successful on several counts. Apart from all the photographs taken and the measurements made, this was the first time that a space probe had flown past two planets and used the gravitational field of one to help it reach the other. (Later, this technique was also successfully used by the Voyager probes.) In addition, Mariner 10 is the only space probe to date to have used the solar sail technique, and the only one to have flown past the same planet several times. It was the only mission ever to have been directed towards Mercury, and no more are planned.

Mercury itself is one of the most mysterious of the nine planets in the solar system. It is very difficult to observe from the Earth and, before Mariner 10 arrived there, only its physical and orbital parameters were known with any certainty. The radius of Mercury is 2439 kilometres, its mean density 5440 kilograms per cubic metre. Its sidereal period of revolution is 87·97 days, and the period of rotation about itself, that is to say one day on Mercury, is 58·65 Earth days. Other information, such as the properties of its surface, and its possible magnetic field were completely unknown. A probe to fly past Mercury accordingly seemed to be an essential part of any coherent space programme.

The idea of this mission to Mercury came about almost by accident in 1962. A student from the University of Los Angeles doing a project at the Jet Propulsion Laboratory realised that, once every 10 years, the relative positions of Venus and Mercury were such that a space probe launched from the Earth towards Venus would be deviated and accelerated by the venusian gravitational field and shot towards Mercury. This would save both time and fuel and, as a consequence, would allow the probe to carry a heavier payload with more instruments than would otherwise be possible. This favourable arrangement of planetary positions was due to occur in 1973. It was therefore decided, in 1969, to send a mission to Venus and Mercury in the same year.

A probe from the Mariner series comparable to one which had already been successfully used on martian missions was chosen. Once it had been adapted, Mariner 10 weighed 504 kilograms, of which 79·4 kilograms were scientific instruments. It had a hydrazine propulsion unit for carrying out trajectory corrections, with a 20 kilogram reserve of fuel. The space probe's attitude was maintained by a gyroscope and sensors which tracked Canopus and the Sun; attitude modifications were made using small nitrogen jets mounted at the tips of the solar panels. The electrical energy was supplied by two steerable solar panels measuring 2·69 metres by 0·97 metres.

Communications between the probe and the Earth were maintained by a low gain antenna and, more importantly, a high gain antenna (a parabolic dish measuring 1·37 metres in diameter) which was always kept pointed towards the Earth. The probe transmitted on

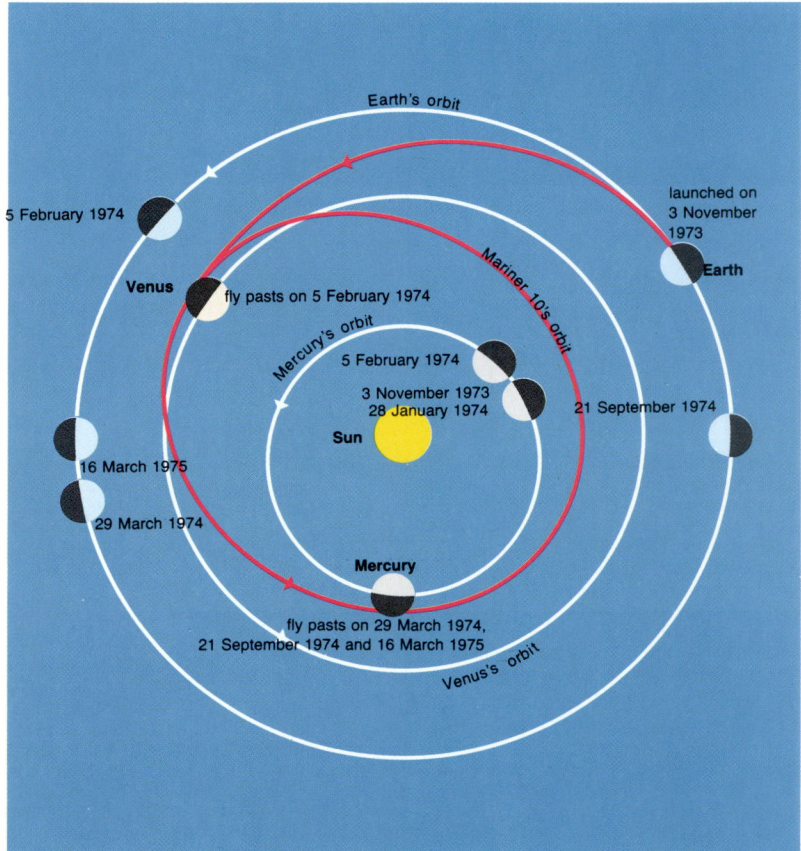

The trajectory of Mariner 10. Mariner 10's trajectory was both unusual and highly successful. This space probe was launched from the Earth on 3 November 1973 towards Venus, which it passed on 5 February 1974. The velocity and angle of the trajectory were chosen so that it would fly over Venus at an altitude of about 5000 kilometres; as the probe passed over, its heliocentric velocity was sufficiently reduced to place the probe in an elliptical solar orbit, with carefully calculated parameters. The orbital period was exactly twice that of Mercury so the two orbits were tangential at about 69 million kilometres from the Sun.

The launch date was chosen so that Mercury and the probe would be at this tangential point at the same moment, an arrangement which is only possible once every 10 years. With such an orbit, Mariner 10 and Mercury pass close to each other every 176 days and Mariner 10 regularly crosses the dark face of Mercury, a cycle that will endure for eternity. Scientific observations were, however, only made on the first three fly pasts.

The structure of the Mariner 10 probe. Mariner 10 has two radio antennae: a low gain antenna and a high gain antenna which is always directed towards the Earth. The instruments used to study Mercury include a high frequency radar (X band), two ultraviolet spectrometers, two television cameras, plasma detectors, and two magnetometers situated at the end of a long rod so that they will not be affected by the space probe's own magnetic field.

The star tracker fixes on the bright star Canopus to maintain the probe's orientation in space. This is essential because the high gain telemetry antenna always has to face the Earth and the optical instruments must view the planet being studied. The solar panels are steerable and, apart from supplying energy, can be used as 'solar sails'.

Nitrogen nozzles attached to the tips of the panels are used to change the probe's orientation. In the diagram below, the main hydrazine propulsion unit is not visible.

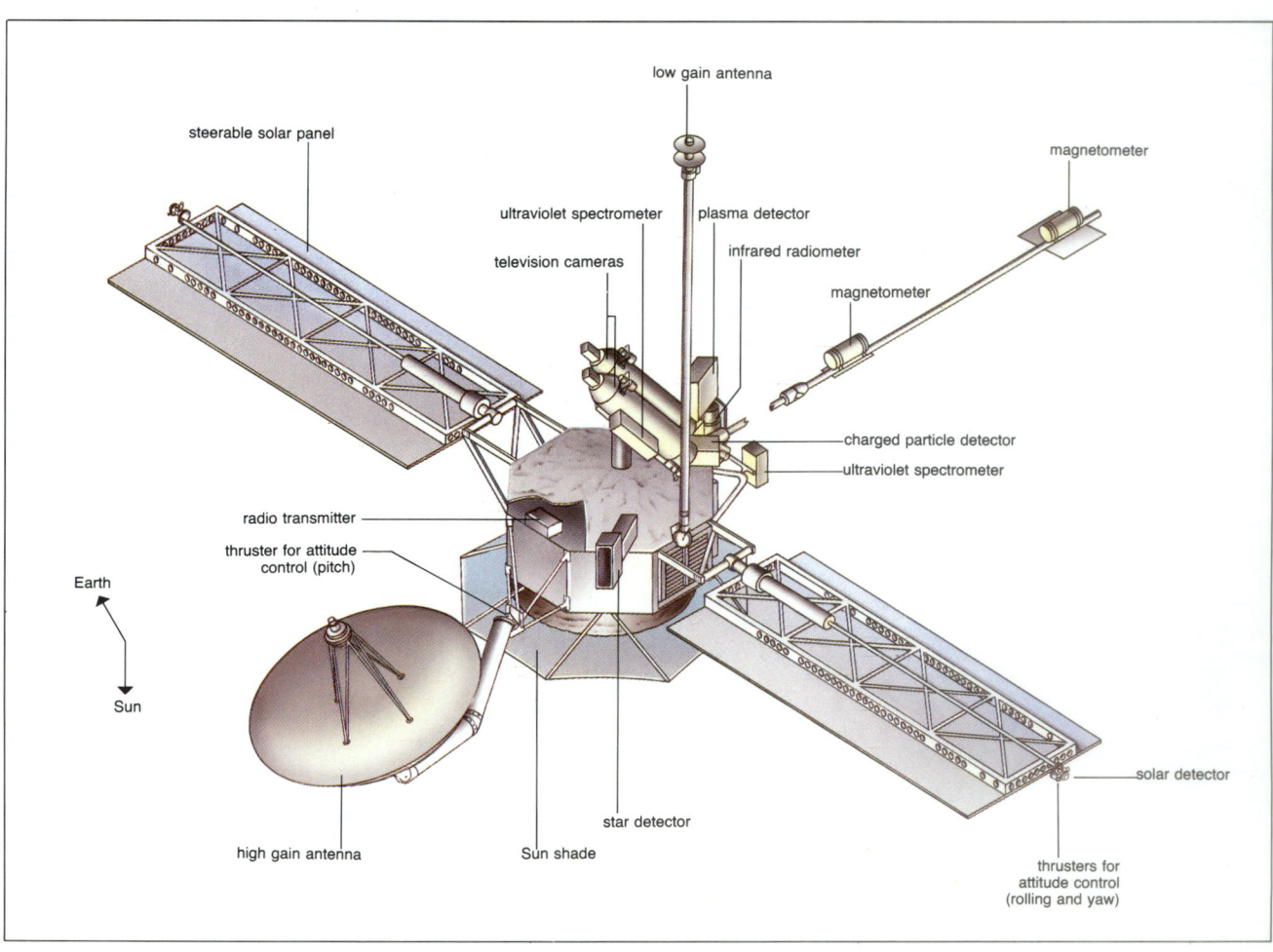

two frequencies, 2295 and 8415 megahertz, and received commands from the Earth on 2113 megahertz. Besides being used for communication purposes, the radio transmissions gave the probe's exact position; from this the physical parameters (mass, moment of inertia, and so on) of the planets visited could be deduced. The frequencies were such, moreover, that propagation was modified as the probe passed through the atmosphere and ionosphere and was occulted first by Venus, and then by Mercury.

Mariner 10 carried five principal scientific experiments. An infrared radiometer was to be used for determining Mercury's surface temperature and the thermal properties of its surface materials. The rate at which the ground cooled as night fell, for example, provided information on the porosity of the surface materials. An ultraviolet spectrometer was included to measure ultraviolet emissions from possible atmospheric gases, and to provide an estimate of pressure and an analysis of chemical composition. A magnetometer was to investigate the possible magnetic field around the planet. Two charged particle and plasma detectors were to study the solar wind and to establish whether Mercury had radiation belts like the Earth's. Finally, there were two identical television cameras, each with a focal length of 1·5 metres.

These cameras posed most of the technical problems, due mainly to the rather high relative speed between the probe and Mercury and the trajectory imposed by celestial mechanics. It was essential that the transmission system could operate at a rate of 117 kilobits per second if the pictures were to be of reasonable quality (that is, to have a spatial resolution of 1 to 2 kilometres). However, the systems which were available at the time – those built for the Mars missions – could only transmit at a rate of 12 kilobits per second. Modifications were made to the receiving antennae of NASA's Deep Space Network to cope with the high data rate, the last improvements only three days before the launch.

On 4 November 1973, Mariner 10 was put into a parking orbit around the Earth at an altitude of 188 kilometres by an Atlas Centaur rocket. The third stage engines of the Atlas Centaur then injected Mariner 10 into an orbit about the Sun.

The 17 months that the probe was in service were peppered with incidents that only its robust materials and the ingenuity of its technicians were able to overcome. Though the camera heating systems broke down, for instance, the cameras, which were designed to operate at +10 degrees celsius, were found to operate perfectly well at −30 degrees celsius. Similarly, if the trajectory corrections had been perfect, the probe would have flown over Venus at the height necessary to send it on its way to Mercury. However, the gyroscope of the attitude control system did not function very well and a large amount of nitrogen had to be consumed. To prevent the mission from coming to a premature end, the technicians therefore experimented with the solar panels and used the solar wind to blow the probe back onto the right course. The concept of the solar sail was proved and precious nitrogen saved.

The probe passed closest to Venus on 5 February 1974, 5800 kilometres above the surface; it took more than 3000 photographs as it passed by. It first flew over Mercury, on 29 March 1974, 705 kilometres above the dark side of the planet, taking photographs of the sunlit side during both the approach and departure phases. The trajectory of the probe around the Sun was chosen so that it passed by Mercury every 176 days. This trajectory was then adjusted so that during its second fly past the probe would not rephotograph the same areas. On 21 September 1974 it accordingly flew 48 069 kilometres above the South pole of Mercury. On its third passage the probe made a careful study of Mercury's magnetic field, passing on 16 March 1975 only 327 kilometres above

the nighttime face. Eight days later, the final reserves of nitrogen were used up and Mariner 10 ceased to be manoeuvrable. It was no longer able to orient itself correctly with respect to the Sun's radiation; its internal temperature rose and the fragile electronics were destroyed. In this way Mariner 10 died and became a new planet taking 176 days to travel around the Sun.

The Mariner 10 probe collected a colossal amount of information. This was the first mission to study the extraordinary circulation of clouds on Venus, and it provided much new information on Mercury's atmospheric pressure, surface temperature, and magnetic field. These latter results were completely unexpected and led to serious discussions of the origin of planetary magnetism. Most important of all, it was discovered that Mercury's surface, although heavily cratered by meteorite bombardment, had remained intact for three thousand million years, due to the small amount of internal planetary activity.

Pierre Thomas

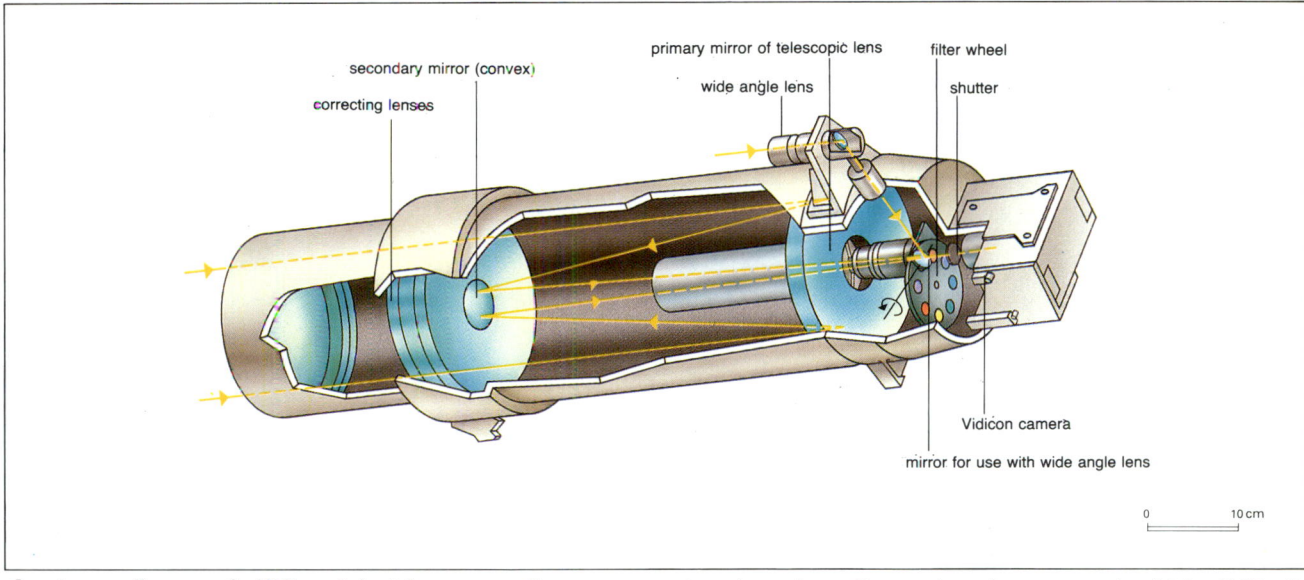

A cut away diagram of a Vidicon television camera. Two cameras were each fitted with a wide angle lens, a telescopic lens and a wheel of different filters (blue, ultraviolet, orange and visible). The observations made in the ultraviolet revealed the structure and motion of the venusian atmosphere. Every 42 seconds an image measuring 9·6 by 12·35 millimetres, comprised of 700 lines and 832 pixels in each line, was obtained. The best resolution of the images was 30 metres, but the spatial resolution was usually between 1 and 2 kilometres.

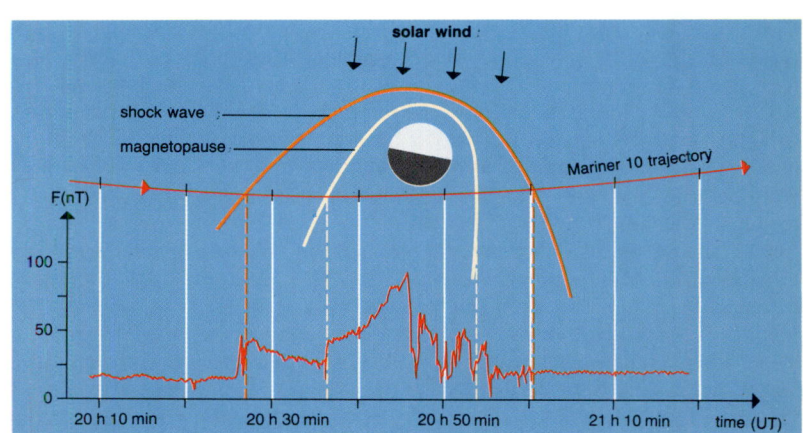

Recording the magnetic field during the flypast of Mercury. During Mariner 10's passage over Mercury, the magnetic field was recorded continuously and transmitted to Earth in real time. The upper part of the diagram shows the trajectory of the probe on 29 March 1974, between 20.10 and 21.20 Universal Time (UT).

The lower part of the diagram shows the variation of the magnetic field (F) along the trajectory, over the same interval of time. Until 20.26 UT, the magnetic field (F) was normal for the region 70 million kilometres from the Sun, and equal to about 20 nanoteslas (nT). Between 20.26 and 21.00 UT this field increased to 100 nanoteslas, showing variations characteristic of crossing a magnetosphere. At 21.00, the field returned to normal. With other recordings, these results enabled the geometry of Mercury's magnetosphere and shock wave to be discovered (after N. F. Ness *et al.*, 1974).

The landscape of Mercury in the Antoniadi Dorsum region (27° N, 30° W). This spectacular photograph obtained by Mariner 10 shows a typical mercurian landscape which, with its innumerable meteorite craters, strikingly resembles the lunar landscape. The large crater in the lower righthand corner has a diameter of 55 kilometres. There is also an escarpment (A–B in the photograph), which could be indicative of tectonic activity in the geologic past (NASA).

Exploring the solar system

Venus

Soviet missions

The Soviets began their scientific exploration of Venus in 1967 with the Venera 4 probe. This was the second time that a probe had successfully flown over Venus, the first being the American Mariner 4 probe of 1962 which transmitted invaluable information on the venusian atmosphere back to Earth. Venera 4 and Mariner 5 were together responsible for the discovery of Venus's hydrogen corona, or outer atmosphere. Venera 4 also had a descent module which dropped through the atmosphere, making the first *in situ* measurements of its chemical composition, pressure and temperature. The planetary orbits in fact are such that space probes to Venus may be launched every 19 months; as many as fifteen Soviet probes have accordingly reached Venus since 1967.

The vertical profiles of temperature and pressure were measured both on the night side of the planet (Veneras 4, 5, 6 and 7) and the day side. Although the early probes used simple techniques to analyse the chemical composition of the atmosphere, Venera 9 was the first probe to carry a mass spectrometer; later probes still used gas chromatographs. The abundance and isotopic composition of rare gases in the low venusian atmosphere, as well as the concentrations of the main constituents, were all successfully determined.

Each Venera probe had two parts, which separated several days before their arrival at Venus. One was the spherical descent module, the other essentially a telecommunications relay probe which went into planetary orbit.

The Venera 8 probe, launched in March 1972, initiated studies of the surface of Venus. This was not an easy task, the pressure at ground level being about 100 atmospheres and the temperature about 450 degrees celsius. Conditions severely restricted the methods of surface analysis used. A gamma spectrometer, which was improved on subsequent trips, determined the radioactivity of surface rocks. In addition, panoramic photographs were taken from several landing sites by Venera 9 to Venera 14, and a large part of the venusian surface was mapped using radar techniques by Venera 15 and Venera 16 which were placed in orbit around the planet in October 1983.

The Venera programme was in particular credited with the discovery of low frequency radio wave emissions (Venera 11 and Venera 14) and seismic activity (Venera 13 and Venera 14). On Venera 13 and Venera 14, and also on the later Vega missions, direct analysis was made of samples taken from the venusian soil using X ray fluorescence.

In June 1985, the Vega probes also put into the venusian atmosphere two balloons equipped with instruments for analysing aerosols and motions of the atmosphere. These balloons made one third of a revolution about Venus at an altitude of 54 kilometres.

The Vega orbiting probe, which came into use in 1984, was very different from its predecessors on the Venera missions; in particular, it had a reinforced protective cover because it was going to be used to examine Halley's comet at close quarters. In flight it was stabilised in all three axes, with the solar panels perpendicular to the Sun and an antenna permanently pointing towards the Earth.

Surface topography

The thick cloud layer over Venus has always prevented direct observation of the planet's surface. At the end of the 1950s, progress in detection techniques in radio astronomy meant that scientists had established the presence of radio emissions with wavelengths of some tens of centimetres. Identified with thermal radiation from the ground, this suggested that the surface temperature of Venus was of the order of 450 degrees celsius. The origin of these signals remained controversial until the Mariner 2 probe made observations of the venusian disc in December 1962, and showed that the surface temperature was indeed this high; the finding was confirmed by the later Venera missions.

Venera 15 and Venera 16 mapped the northern hemisphere, completing the altimetric measurements carried out by the American Pioneer Venus probe. Analysis of these maps has shown that the venusian surface, like the Earth's, is strongly influenced by volcanic activity (with, for example, craters) and by tectonic activity (with characteristic mountain formations). However, because there is less erosion and the surface is better protected from meteorites by the atmospheric layer, Venus' surface is much less modified than the Earth's. It is consequently ideal for investigating the geological evolution of the planets.

The Venera 9, 10, 13 and 14 probes transmitted photographs from their landing sites in the Beta Regio, a region of high plains with few mountains, the probes landing more than a thousand kilometres apart. The black and white photographs of the Venera 9 and 10 probes were taken by panoramic cameras, with a horizontal field of view of 180°. In contrast, the Venera 13 and 14 probes each had two identical colour cameras, so that they could view the whole, 360° panorama. Subsequent examination of the photographs has enabled scientists to divide the surface rock into three categories – ground rock, rock fragments (larger than 1 centimetre) which have broken off the ground rock, and gravel. A comparative study of the morphology and albedo of venusian rocks has shown in addition that they are very similar to terrestrial basalt lava flows, indicating that there were very active volcanoes on Venus in the past.

One of the other basic aims of the Venera 13 and Venera 14 missions was to analyse the venusian soil by measuring the X ray spectrum of a sample of rock irradiated by appropriate radioactive sources. These sources were chosen so as to ensure good excitation of the X ray fluorescence from magnesium to iron in the sample taken. The composition of the venusian soil measured in this way was found to be strikingly similar to terrestrial basalts; the main oxides were found to be silicon dioxide, or sand (45%), aluminium oxide (16%) and magnesium oxide (11%).

The Venera 8, Venera 10 and Vega probes incorporated a spectrometer for measuring the gamma radiation from the ground to give an indication of its natural radioactive elements (uranium, thorium and potassium). The advantage of this method was that it did not require a

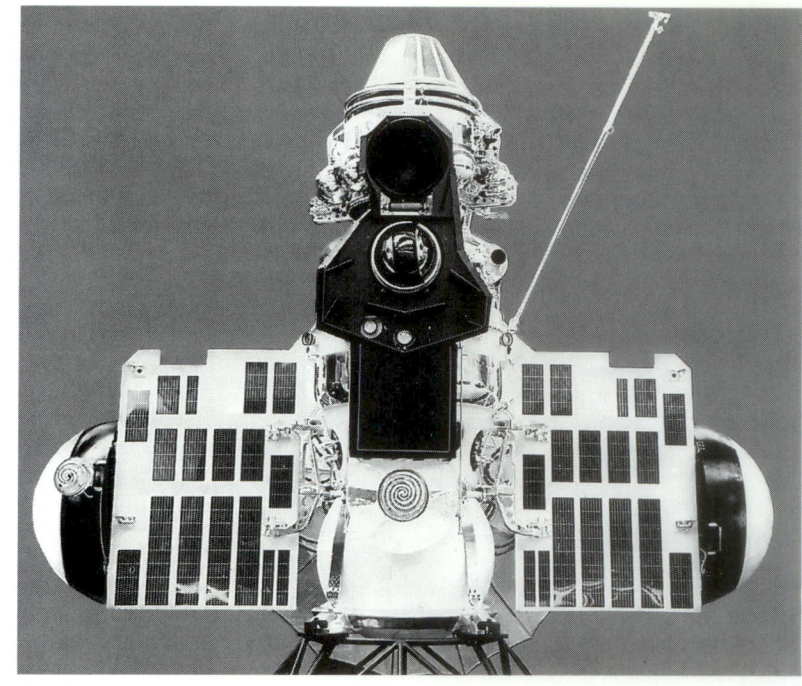

The Venera 3 probe. This Soviet probe consists of an orbital module and a descent module. The descent module, at the base of the structure, is spherical and is provided with an instrument compartment; above it is the body of the orbital probe, with solar panels, transmission antennae, and directional sensors. The rocket engine for making trajectory corrections is at the top, while a magnetic field sensor is fixed to the tip of the rod. The large parabolic dish for transmitting data back to the Earth is just visible behind the probe. The descent module itself is destroyed as the unit penetrates the atmosphere (Tass).

The Vega landing probe (opposite, right). In this picture, the Soviet Vega probe is being inserted into the lower half of the reentry sphere. This sphere, 2·4 metres in diameter, protects the probe from heat as it enters the venusian atmosphere; it is jettisoned at an altitude of 63 kilometres.

From bottom to top are seen a ring-shaped impact absorber designed to minimise the effects of impact with the ground at a likely velocity of 30 kilometres per hour; a sealed spherical compartment containing the instruments, which is capable of surviving high pressures (10 megapascals); an airbrake; and a spiral shaped antenna for transmitting data, surrounding a compartment capable of withstanding pressures of up to 1 megapascal. This holds scientific instruments for analysing the atmosphere. On the right of the central compartment is the ultraviolet spectrophotometer and the cylindrical cover protecting the chromatograph (APN).

Venera 15 and Venera 16. Both these probes were used mainly for mapping Venus's northern hemisphere with a radar operating at a wavelength of 8 centimetres. They did not have a descent module. The solar panels, deployed on either side of the unit as in all Venera probes, the parabolic dish for data transmission to the Earth, and some key elements of the radar system are evident (APN).

sample to be taken, nor necessitate the detector's removal from its sealed compartment; the measurements could be taken through the walls. The detectors were crystals which sparkled when bombarded with gamma radiation, their light being recorded by a photomultiplier. On Venera 9 and Venera 10, a device measured the radiation from a source outside the probe after it had been diffused by the rock, and used the results to estimate the surface density at 2·8 tonnes per cubic metre. The scientific results on the radioactive content of the rocks and their density overall support the theory that the rock was of volcanic origin.

The atmosphere and clouds of Venus

As early as 1932 it was discovered by observing the absorption bands in the near infrared part of the spectrum that carbon dioxide was present in Venus's atmosphere. Subsequent progress in spectroscopy has helped to identify other molecules. By 1967, the year in which the Venera 4 space probe first penetrated the venusian atmosphere, carbon dioxide, carbon monoxide, hydrochloric acid and hydrofluoric acid had already been identified with certainty. During its descent, Venera 4 established the main constituents to be carbon dioxide (97%) and nitrogen (3%).

More sophisticated mass spectrometry and gas chromatography were not used until Venera 9. However, spectroscopic observations made from the Venera space probes enabled the vertical distribution of trace species such as hydrogen and helium in the atmosphere to be deduced. The clouds of Venus were also studied using spectroscopic and polarisation measurements in the 1960s. The exact nature of the aerosols, composed of droplets of sulphuric acid which make up the clouds, was not definitely established until 1973, however, when it was confirmed by *in situ* measurements.

One of the most interesting phenomena discovered in the 1950s, and established with precision in 1966 by analysing numerous photographs taken in the ultraviolet, was the rapid rotation of the atmosphere, with a period of about 5 days. However, Venus itself turns about its own axis much more slowly – the venusian day is 243 Earth days long. One of the objectives of the Vega mission was therefore to study the little understood motions of the atmosphere by means of a balloon probe moving at an altitude of about 50 kilometres.

Some gases in the venusian atmosphere are produced by radioactive decay in the crust and then outgassed at a rate which depends on the tectonic activity, whereas others come directly from the supersonic solar wind. Their isotopic composition was measured by the probe. Gas chromatography was also used to measure the amounts of minor constituents such as hydrogen, oxygen, water vapour, hydrogen sulphide, carbonyl sulphide and krypton, in an atmosphere composed mainly of carbon dioxide and 3% nitrogen.

The Vega probes were fitted with a mass spectrometer to analyse aerosols collected from the cloud layer near an altitude of 50 kilometres during the descent phase. These were collected on a filter and then heated to vaporise them after the entrance valve had been sealed. The pyrolysis products were analysed using a quadrupole mass spectrometer. The results obtained by this method agreed with those obtained by X ray fluorescence and gas chromatography, demonstrating that the clouds are composed mostly of sulphur and chlorine compounds. The concentration of sulphur, which occurs as droplets of sulphuric acid created photochemically from sulphur dioxide, is several milligrammes per cubic centimetre.

Probe	Launch date	Arrival date	The mission
Venera 1	12 February 1961	19 May 1961	planned closest approach of 99 800 kilometres; contact lost at 7 million kilometres
Venera 2	12 November 1965	27 February 1966	closest approach 23 950 kilometres; data not transmitted to the Earth
Venera 3	16 November 1965	1 March 1966	planned to impact surface; destroyed by venusian atmosphere at 32 kilometres altitude, and data not transmitted to the Earth
Venera 4	12 June 1967	18 October 1967	impact (presumed) on the night side; 94 minutes of transmission during descent
Venera 5	5 January 1969	16 May 1969	impact (presumed) on the night side; penetrated more deeply than Venera 4
Venera 6	10 January 1969	17 May 1969	as above
Venera 7	17 August 1970	15 December 1970	night side landing; survived 23 minutes on the surface
Venera 8	27 March 1972	22 July 1972	day side landing; 50 minutes of radio transmission from the surface
Venera 9	8 June 1975	23 October 1975	day side landing; first photographs of the surface; one probe left in orbit (perihelion 1560 kilometres; orbital period of 48 hours 18 minutes)
Venera 10	11 June 1975	26 October 1975	day side landing; photographed surface; one probe in orbit (perihelion 1620 kilometres; orbital period of 49 hours 23 minutes)
Venera 11	9 September 1978	25 December 1978	day side landing; possible detection of emissions; orbiting probe
Venera 12	14 September 1978	21 December 1978	as above
Venera 13	30 October 1981	1 March 1982	day side landing; first chemical analysis of ground by X ray fluorescence; orbiting probe
Venera 14	4 November 1981	5 March 1982	as above
Venera 15	2 June 1983	10 October 1983	in polar orbit (altitude from 1000 kilometres to 65 000 kilometres); radar cartography
Venera 16	7 June 1983	14 October 1983	as above
Vega 1	15 December 1984	11 June 1985	day side landing, left balloon probe in cloud layer; probe continued to Halley's comet
Vega 2	21 December 1984	15 June 1985	as above

Soviet missions to Venus

Diagram representing the descent of the Vega probe. Two days before it entered the atmosphere, the descent module containing a landing probe and a balloon separated from the fly past module, Vega. It was slowed down by the atmosphere and then opened its parachute on the night side of the planet. The balloon, equipped with a package of scientific instruments left the upper half of the sphere at 63 kilometres altitude and continued to free fall, slowed down by a group of parachutes. It then inflated with helium when it arrived at the dense cloud layer, at 54 kilometres altitude.

At the same time, the Vega landing probe left the lower half of the sphere and continued towards the ground under the braking power of its own parachute. It passed through the different cloud layers and opened its main parachute at a height of 47 kilometres. It then continued in free fall, braked aerodynamically, and landed softly (at 30 kilometres per hour) after about 65 minutes.

When balloon probes were put into the venusian atmosphere on 11 and 15 June 1985 (by Vega 1 and Vega 2), it was the first time that a balloon had flown in any atmosphere other than the Earth's. These balloons drifted longitudinally around the atmosphere for 46 hours until their batteries ran out. At an average speed of 70 metres per second, they completed one third of a complete revolution around Venus while the scientific experiments on board measured the temperature, pressure, and vertical wind, and the incident and backscattered solar radiation. The data were sent directly back to Earth and received by an international network of 20 radio telescopes. These telescopes were also able to measure the coordinates and velocity of the balloons using the technique of long baseline interferometry.

The landing probes supplied data on the physical and chemical characteristics of the venusian atmosphere, and on the chemical composition of the clouds and the ground. The scientific experiments functioned for a period of 20 minutes after the probe landed, the scientific data being transmitted to the Earth by way of the fly past probe.

In the diagram, distances are measured in kilometres, km; temperatures, T, are in degrees celsius, °C; and pressures, P, are in megapascals, PMa.

Descent diagram labels:
- entry into the atmosphere (altitude: 125 km)
- drogue parachute deployed (altitude: 64 km)
- opening of main parachute and jettisoning of lower half of sphere (altitude: 63 km)
- upper hemisphere stabilises itself (altitude: 63 km; T: −25 °C; P: 50 hPa)
- opening of first parachute of balloon deployment system (altitude: 61 km)
- opening of main parachute of balloon deployment system (altitude: 55 km)
- positioning the balloon probe (altitude: 54 km; T: 30 °C; P: 0.04 MPa)
- descent using parachute
- balloon deployed and inflated (altitude: 54 km)
- separation of balloon and inflation unit from parachute (altitude: 53 km)
- ballast jettisoned (minimum altitude: 50 km)
- main parachute jettisoned (altitude: 47 km; T: 97 °C; P: 0.2 MPa)
- probe in free fall
- landing (T: 450 °C; P: 10 MPa)

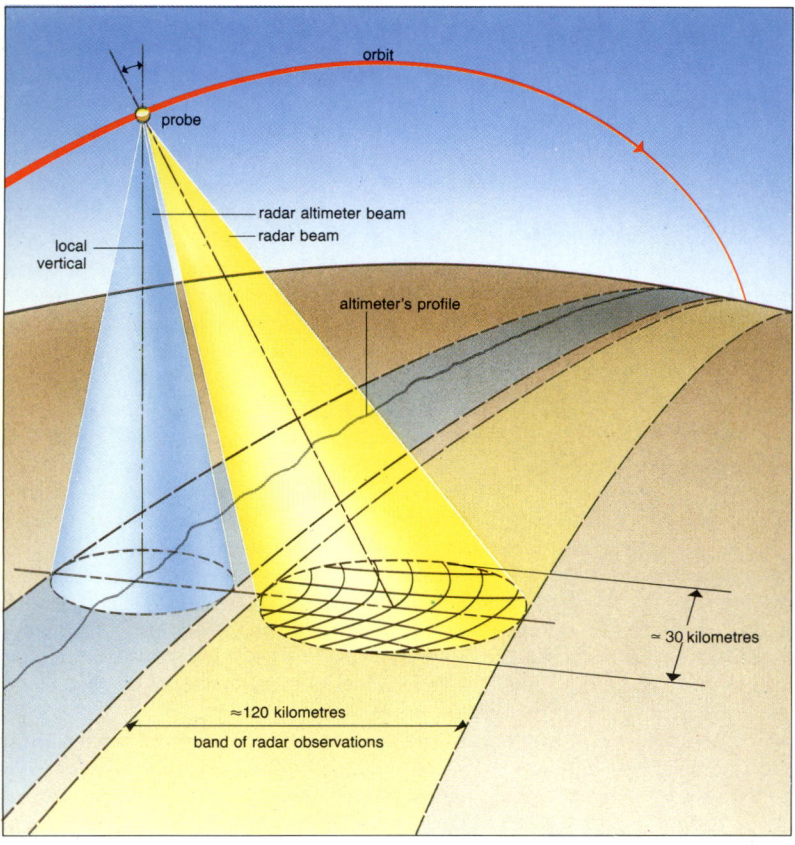

Radar mapping of Venus by Venera 15 and Venera 16. The probes were placed into an elliptical polar orbit, of 62 degrees inclination, with an orbital period of 24 hours, an aphelion of 65 000 kilometres and a perihelion of 950 kilometres. The measuring device was a Synthetic Aperture Radar operating at a wavelength of 8 centimetres and scanning a region 120 kilometres wide for mapping purposes. There was also a radar altimeter to give an accurate measurement of altitude from 950 to 2000 kilometres. As illustrated in the diagram on the left, the axis of the altimeter antenna was pointed to the centre of the planet, and the radar axis made an angle of about 10 degrees with this. The planet rotates once every eight months (243 days) and so the area observed was displaced by 1.5 degrees of longitude each time the probe passed overhead. This is equivalent to a distance of 80 kilometres at a latitude of 60 degrees. The radar altimeter provided a cross section of the altitude of a region three days before it was actually mapped by the radar because of the angle that the radar beam made to the vertical. In all it took eight months for the radars to map the whole of the northern hemisphere above 30 degrees latitude, an area of 125 million square kilometres.

Two acquisition and processing methods called 'band' and 'image' methods were used to make images of the surface. The intensity of the radar signal depends on the angle between the incident wave and the normal to the surface element. Slopes which face the probe appear light coloured, and those which face away appear dark.

The 'Band' method of radar imaging. The image above, constructed in real time, is read in three frequency bands, covering about 15% of the grid, so that the superposition of eight consecutive partial images is sufficient to fill the observed band. The map shown here, obtained by adding together bands obtained by the Venera 15 and Venera 16 probes, is of a region of plains (Atlanta Planitia). Meteorite craters and mountain belts are visible (APN).

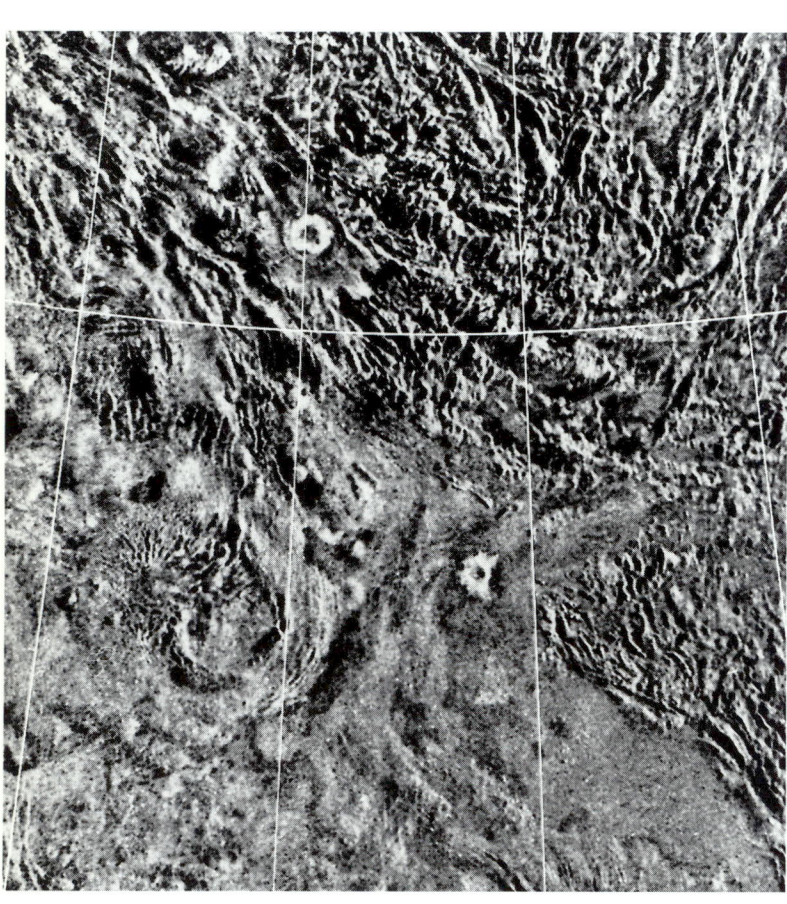

The 'Image' method of radar imaging. Every 0·3 seconds, the time that it takes for the radar beam to move forward a distance as great as its width, some 2500 readings are made of its signal. These are processed on Earth using Fourier analysis. The radar delay time is split into 127 time elements and the Doppler shift into 31 frequency elements defining 4000 points in the field of view. Each image is reconstructed with a resolution of the order of a kilometre and the partial repetition of images is then used to improve their quality. Illustrated on the left is the combination of images, obtained by the Venera 15 and Venera 16 probes, of a region of tectonic deformation situated to the south of the Freya mountains. It is of a region some 700 kilometres by 800 kilometres. North is at the top. Two ejection craters, which have a central dark mountain and a very bright, asymmetric region around them, stand out (APN).

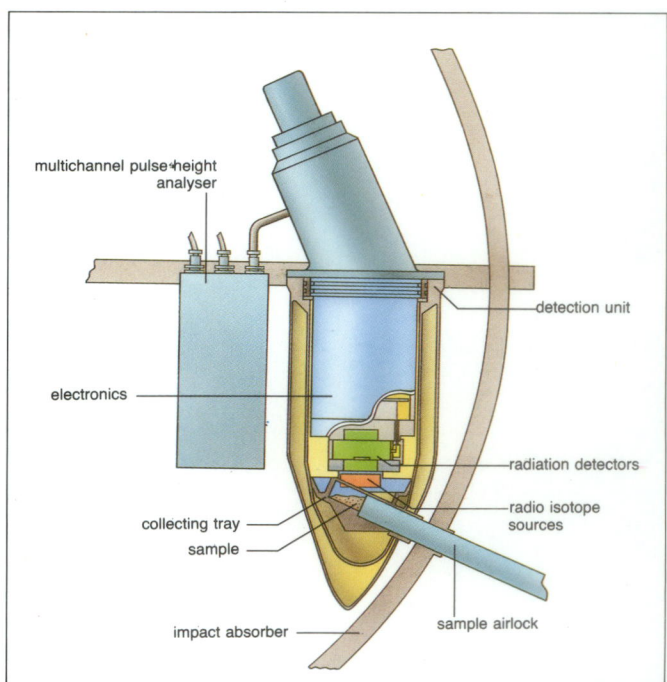

The Vega instrument for ground analysis using X ray fluorescence. This device removes a sample of 1 cubic centimetre from a depth of 3 centimetres and places it in a chamber. The venusian atmosphere is pumped out and the sample is then transferred through an airlock onto a collecting tray. The radioisotope sources (two of iron 55 and one of plutonium 238) irradiate the sample whose fluorescence is recorded by detectors in the lower compartment of the unit. The alpha particle radiation of the plutonium 238 excites light elements such as magnesium, aluminium and silicon. The X radiation from the iron 55 excites the heavier elements like potassium and calcium, while X rays from the plutonium 238 excite the even heavier elements such as manganese and iron. Proportional counters detect the fluorescence. After the signal has been amplified, it is examined by a pulse height analyser in which the results are stored and regularly transmitted to Earth.

Photographing Venus at ground level. Venera 9, 10, 13 and 14 cameras used two mirrors to scan the surface of Venus from a height of 90 centimetres at an angle of 50 degrees to the probe's horizontal plane. The total field of view was 40 degrees by 180 degrees. An optical system directed light towards the detector, where it was converted into a video signal.

Both the nearby ground and the distant horizon (in the upper corners of the photographs) are seen in the photograph below taken by Venera 13. Also visible are the circular base of the impact absorber and its triangular edge which stabilised the probe as it descended through the atmosphere. From right to left are the rectangular testcard for checking colour, the camera's lens cap and the articulated arm of the dynamic penetrometer, a device used to measure the hardness of the soil (Soviet Academy of Sciences).

The gas chromatograph on Vega's landing probe. Gas chromatography was used for the first time by the Soviets in 1978 on the Venera 11 and Venera 12 probes. Later improvements to the chromatograph design increased the range of gas species which could be analysed and also improved the sensitivity of the detectors.

A sample of gas to be analysed is mixed with a carrier gas and then injected into a column filled with an appropriate absorbent. The retention time in the column depends on the element. Apart from being used for identification, the gas chromatograph also provides an absolute measure of the abundance of the different elements. An electron capture detector was installed on Venera 13 and Venera 14 in 1981, in addition to the neon ionisaton detector, to measure the amount of oxygen without first having to separate it from the complicating argon.

In this gas chromatograph placed aboard Vega, helium is used as a carrier gas, except for the column of the electron capture detector for which pure nitrogen is used. The gases analysed included water vapour, carbon dioxide, hydrogen sulphide, carbonyl sulphide and sulphur dioxide (rights reserved).

Studying the optical properties of aerosols produces information on their dimensions, shape, concentration and refractive index which complements the chemical analysis. Venera 9 and Venera 10 carried out the first measurements using nephelometry, a technique of directing a light beam into the atmosphere and collecting the backscattered light. The optical analysis system used on the Vega probes was more complicated. Besides the nephelometer there was an aerosol analyser for measuring the optical properties of particles carried by a fine gas jet into the instrument. This experiment showed that there were two main cloud layers between 47 and 63 kilometres altitude, with higher aerosol concentrations between 47 and 51 kilometres and between 55 and 63 kilometres. Most aerosol particles had sizes of less than a micron (one micrometre). It was found that there were about 10 000 such particles per cubic centimetre.

The Vega missions also released balloon probes in the venusian atmosphere. One balloon was dropped from each of the descent probes and drifted nearly one third of the way round the planet at an altitude of about 54 kilometres.

Typical vertical wind speeds of between 1 and 2 metres per second were measured, indicating the importance of vertical displacements in the cloud layer. Combined with temperature information and measurements of the horizontal winds at speeds of up to 100 metres per second, these data provided much fundamental information on the circulation of the venusian atmosphere. Even the topography of the ground was shown to have influenced the motion of the Vega 2 balloon probe.

Éric Chassefière

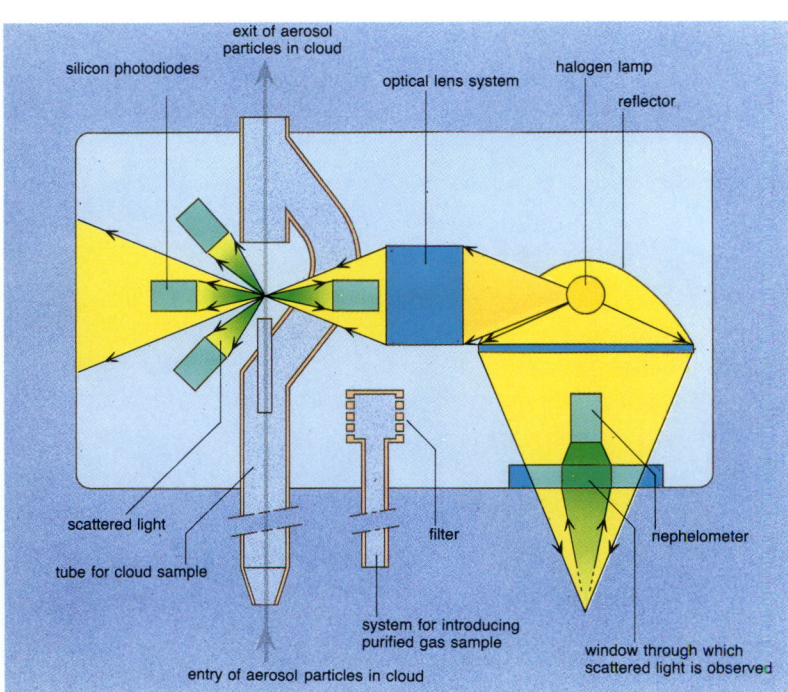

The optical instruments for measuring aerosols on the Vega probe. Light from a halogen lamp is focused onto a tiny volume (1 cubic millimetre) in which the light scattered by an aerosol particle is measured. The aerosol is injected into this volume by a fine gas jet and collected from the cloud layer by a vertical tubular structure (on the left of the above diagram) at an altitude between 63 and 47 kilometres. The light is reflected to the front, sides and back of the instrument, and is picked up by four silicon photodiodes. The signals obtained are analysed using a 64 channel pulse height analyser to find the size distribution of small (aerosol) particles in the venusian clouds.

Another instrument, termed a nephelometer (on the right of the diagram), is in the same sealed compartment and uses the same halogen light source. It measures, through a window, the light scattered through a sample of atmosphere a few centimetres below. Switching the light off periodically enables the background illumination to be measured, and this has to be deducted from the measurements.

The Vega balloon instrumented probe. Shown on the right is the instrumented probe which is 1·2 metres tall and has a mass of 6·9 kilograms. It is attached to the balloon, which is filled with helium, by a 13 metre long cable.

From top to bottom are the antenna, the meteorological instruments, the radio system, the power supply system, and the aerosol instrument. All outside parts were coated with a substance to resist the corrosive action of sulphuric acid in the venusian clouds. There are two temperature sensors, or thermistors, and a pressure sensor which is a quartz crystal whose resonant frequency depends on the external pressure. A specially designed propeller gauge measures the vertical wind speed, the rotation of the propeller being detected by the interruption of two light beams. There is a light detector to observe the ambient light intensity and lightning, if any, next to the pressure sensor; this is a silicon photodiode operating at visible and near infrared wavelengths. At the base is the nephelometer which measures the light backscattered by the atmosphere below at a wavelength of 930 nanometres.

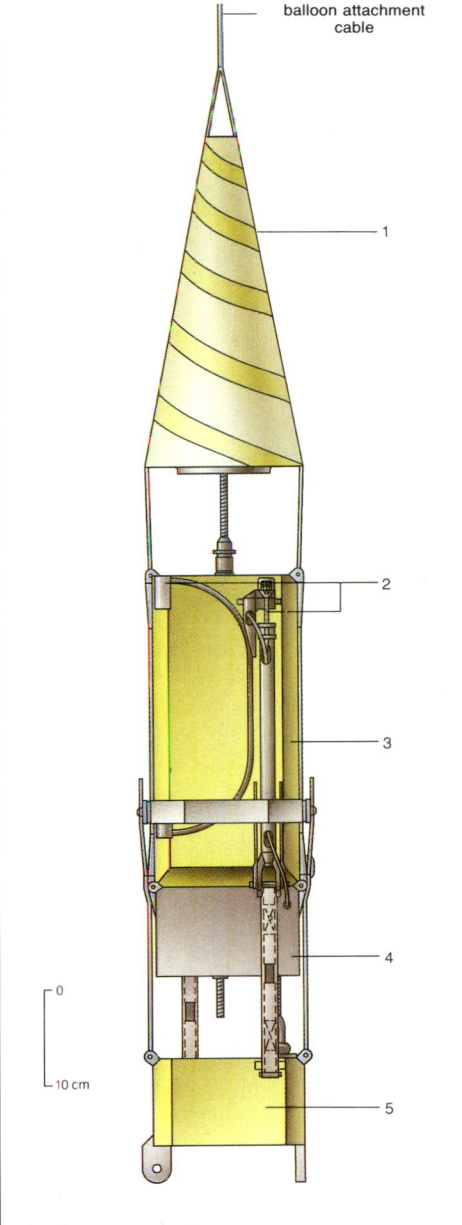

1 **antenna**
spiral antenna mounted on a cone

2 **scientific equipment**
temperature sensors (from 0 to +70 degrees celsius)
pressure sensor (from 2000 to 15 000 hectopascals)
wind gauge (from 0 to 20 metres per second)
light detector

3 **radio device**
5 watt transmitter at a wavelength of 18 centimetres

4 **data processing device**
collects and processes the data coming from the scientific equipment

5 **batteries**
and nephelometer

155

American missions

Mariner 2

Man's first direct exploration of the planets in the solar system using space vehicles began with the planet Venus almost thirty years ago. Three of these early missions were conducted as part of the US Mariner series.

On 27 August 1962, at 06.58 Universal Time, an Atlas Agena rocket lifted off from the US Air Force Eastern Test Range at Cape Canaveral, Florida, carrying the NASA spacecraft designated Mariner R2. The spacecraft had been in storage at the Cape as a standby for its twin, Mariner R1, destroyed after 293 seconds of flight on 22 June 1962 as the result of a booster guidance error. Mariner 2 was injected onto its planned interplanetary trajectory 26 minutes 3 seconds later; the mission destined to result in the first planetary encounter by a spacecraft was underway.

The Mariner 2 spacecraft weighed 212·9 kilograms, including a scientific payload of 23·6 kilograms. Its resemblance to the Lunar Ranger spacecraft was emphasised by the superstructure carrying the omnidirectional antenna and mountings for most of the scientific instruments. The electronics packages were housed in a structure with the variable opening louvres for thermal control which were to become a familiar feature of subsequent Mariner spacecraft. The spacecraft was powered by 2·27 square metres of solar panels producing up to 250 watts and charging a silver–zinc battery. Attitude control of the three-axis stabilised spacecraft was via a cold gas system which used the Earth and Sun as celestial references; maintaining the roll axis pointed at the Sun provided maximum illumination of the solar panels and simplified the thermal control problem. Continuous communications with the Earth were maintained using the high gain antenna.

Mariner 2's instruments were in two groups designed respectively to make measurements of the interplanetary medium and the planet Venus. In the first category were a magnetometer, charged particle detectors, a solar plasma spectrometer, and a cosmic dust detector; in the second, a two channel microwave radiometer and an infrared radiometer observing in the carbon dioxide band.

On 14 December 1962 at 19.59 Universal Time, the spacecraft passed by Venus, on the sunlit side, at a distance of 34 632 kilometres. About an hour earlier, the radiometers had begun their three scans across the disc, one on the dark face, one along the terminator and one on the sunlit side. The results showed an almost uniform temperature, and unmistakable limb darkening at both microwave and infrared wavelengths; this latter observation established that the previously observed high temperatures (around 700 kelvin) originate at, or very near, the venusian surface. Other experiments demonstrated that Venus's intrinsic magnetic field, if indeed one existed, must be less than one tenth of the Earth's.

Mariner 5

The Mariner Venus 1967 mission was authorised by NASA in December 1965 to make further use of hardware built in support of the Mariner 4 mission to Mars, launched a year earlier. Only modifications necessary to meet Mariner Venus primary objectives were made, and only a single launch attempt was planned. This ultimately took place on 14 June 1967 from Cape Kennedy, Florida, using an Atlas Agena rocket.

The Mariner 5 spacecraft weighed 245 kilograms, including a 22·4 kilogram scientific payload. As was the case with previous Mariners, three-axis attitude stabilisation was used, the Sun and the star Canopus serving as the attitude references. Up to 450 watts of

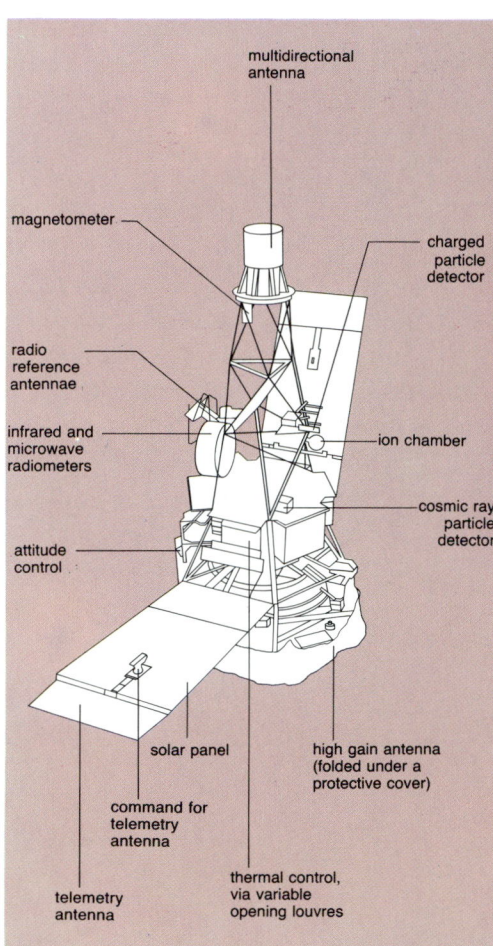

Mariner 2. Mariner 2's design, shown on the left, was based on the Lunar Ranger probe. Apart from the communications antennae and the central computer system, the spacecraft carried scientific instruments to make measurements in the interplanetary medium and the region around Venus. This first spacecraft to visit Venus is shown, complete and ready to be taken to the launch pad, in the photograph on the right (NASA/JPL).

power was provided by four solar panels with a total area of 4 square metres, and a silver–zinc battery was used, as in Mariner 2. An ultraviolet photometer was on board, as was a solar plasma probe, a magnetometer, a trapped radiation detector, and a dual frequency radio receiver.

At 17.35 Universal Time on 19 October 1967, Mariner 5 came as close as 4094 kilometres to the surface of Venus. The encounter sequence stored in the spacecraft's computer had been initiated from the NASA Deep Space Network tracking station at Woomera, Australia, some 15 hours earlier. The principal scientific results on this occasion included the definition of the planet's equatorial radius as 6053 kilometres ± 4 kilometres. Carbon dioxide was shown to be the main constituent of the atmosphere (at more than 85%), and the high surface temperature (700 kelvin) was verified. The surface pressure was also estimated to be very high (100 bars). There was considerable scientific interest in Venus's unique interaction with the solar wind, in which the absence of an intrinsic magnetic field coupled with the presence of a well developed ionosphere produces a unique, comet-like interaction region.

Mariner 10

Unlike Mariners 2 and 5, scientific investigations of Venus were not the sole, nor even the priority, objective of the Mariner 10 mission. This time, by using the gravitational energy of Venus, the spacecraft's heliocentric velocity was reduced by 4·41 kilometres per second, thereby allowing a Mercury encounter to be achieved with a launch energy only two thirds of that which would otherwise have been required.

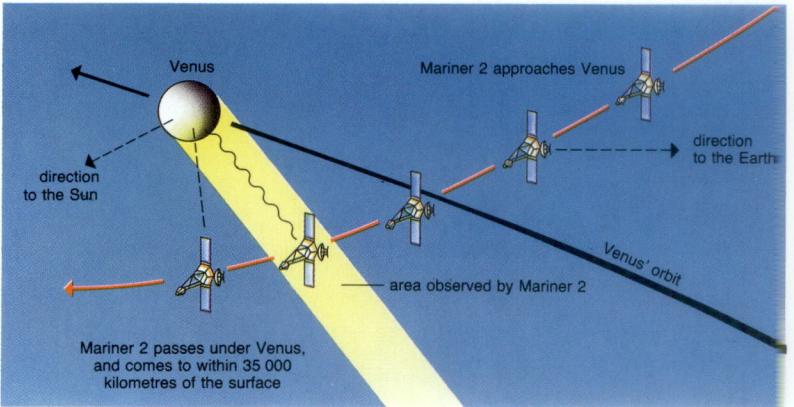

The launch took place on 2 November 1973 from Cape Kennedy, using an Atlas/Centaur launch vehicle. The Mariner 10 spacecraft used earlier Mariner design and hardware, with new configurations for the solar panels, temperature controls, flight data and antennae. Mariner 10 also featured a large sunshade and a thermal protection cover for its hydrazine rocket motor. The solar panels were rotatable about their long axes to reduce solar heating near perihelion. With a total area of 5·2 square metres, they produced 584 watts at Venus and 496 watts at Mercury, and used a rechargeable nickel–cadmium battery.

The 79·7 kilogram scientific complement consisted of a charged particle telescope, two triaxial fluxgate magnetometers, a scanning electrostatic analyser, an electron spectrometer, an infrared radiometer, an extreme ultraviolet spectrometer, a radio transmitter and a telescope with a Vidicon imaging system; television images of Venus were used to search for structure in the clouds.

Mariner 2's flypast of Venus. Mariner 2's flight sequence was planned for the observation of Venus. Flight manoeuvres were controlled using NASA's Central Computer and Sequencer subsystem with a crystal controlled oscillator. Telemetry data were transmitted by phaseshift keying with a repeating pseudonoise code for synchronisation.

Four antennae were carried: a multidirectional antenna mounted on the superstructure for mid course trajectory correction, a high gain antenna and two telemetry antennae. The rate of data transmission was only 33·33 bits per second near the Earth, and 8·33 bits per second during the interplanetary and Venus observation phases of the mission.

Contact with the Earth was lost on 3 January 1963, when the probe was about two million kilometres distant.

Mariner 10's Venus encounter occurred at 17.01 Universal Time on 5 February 1974, at a closest approach distance of 5785 kilometres from the solid surface. Earlier, the charged particle, plasma and magnetic field instruments on the spacecraft had measured the characteristics of the downstream solar wind, improving knowledge of this unique ionospheric interaction around Venus. High resolution imaging of the limb from equator to pole showed very thin haze layers in the stratosphere, indicating great stability at these levels.

Shortly after its closest approach, the spacecraft passed behind Venus and a dual frequency radio occultation experiment was conducted. The results extended those obtained by Mariner 5, showing four distinct temperature inversions of heights between 56 and 63 kilometres; the electron number densities in both the daytime and the nighttime ionosphere were established also.

Ultraviolet imaging of Venus's atmosphere showed vertical convection at the equatorial subsolar point, and zonal flow in equatorial belts feeding spiral streaks leading to higher latitudes and to polar vortices.

For the first time these provided a determination of atmospheric circulation in the upper troposphere and lower stratosphere of Venus.

James A. Dunne

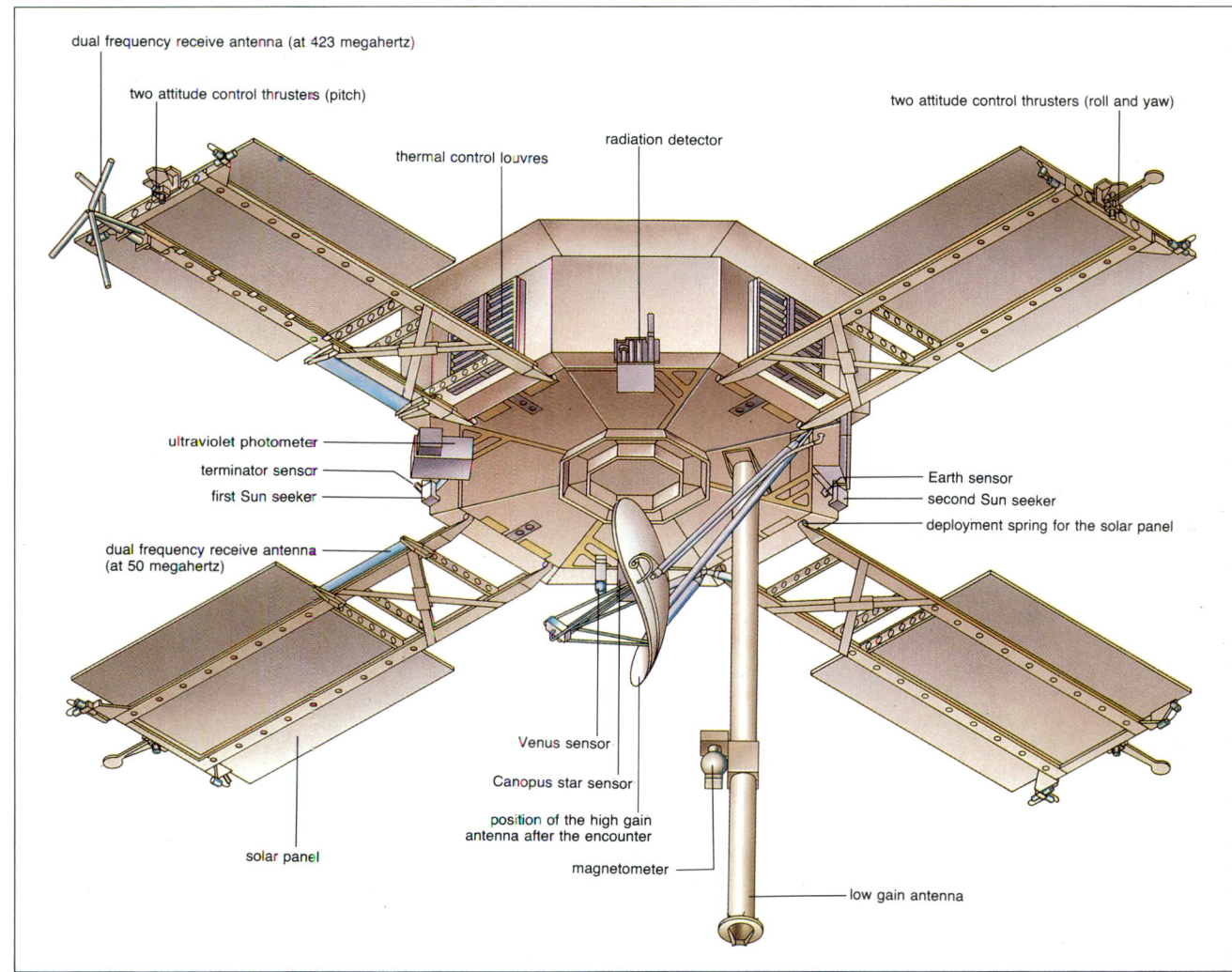

Mariner 5. Based on the design of Mariner 4, Mariner 5 had to take into account changes in the relative positions of the Sun and Earth; the flight attitude of the spacecraft was consequently inverted, and the solar panels were reversed.

Mariner 5's scientific payload consisted of five instruments, shown on the diagram above, with a total mass of 22·4 kilograms. An ultraviolet photometer measured radiation at the atomic resonance of hydrogen and oxygen (at wavelengths of 121·6 and 130·4 nanometres respectively). The solar plasma detector (not visible in this diagram) was a dish shaped,

electrostatic analyser; the helium vapour magnetometer was a three axis instrument; and the radiation detectors used Geiger tubes to record high energy electrons and protons. Finally, there was a four channel spectrometer used to observe protons and alpha particles (helium nuclei). In addition, a dual frequency radio wave receiver was available to study propagation effects and to deduce the average electron density in interplanetary space and in the venusian atmosphere. Radio waves with frequencies of 49·8 and 423·3 megahertz were transmitted by the 49·2 metre dish antenna at Stanford University, California.

Mariner 10. Mariner 10 was similar in design to the Mariner 6 and Mariner 9 craft used for the exploration of Mars. Although the 79·7 kilograms of scientific equipment was originally designed with the exploration of Mercury in mind, researchers at the NASA Jet Propulsion Laboratory made adjustments to adapt it to Venus's characteristics. A wide angle optical system produced images in the near ultraviolet using a slow scanning television camera system. These were used to study the detailed cloud structure.

Another technique developed especially for this Venus mission was the high gain antenna pointing system. This compensated for atmospheric curvature during the occultation period, enabling results to be obtained for several minutes after the occultation began and several minutes before it ended.

The ultraviolet spectrometer was able to detect small amounts of atomic hydrogen, helium, carbon and oxygen in the upper atmosphere. It obtained an exospheric temperature of about 400 kelvin (NASA).

The atmosphere of Venus. This remarkable photograph of Venus was taken by Mariner 10 on 6 February 1974 at a distance of 760 000 kilometres. Individual pictures were analysed and treated by computers at NASA's Jet Propulsion Laboratory and then reassembled as a mosaic by the Astrogeological Division of the US Geological Survey at Flagstaff, Arizona. As the photographs were taken in the ultraviolet part of the spectrum, the blue is not true to the actual colour – a dazzling white.

This particular photograph is of the venusian atmosphere, where the clouds contain a substance which absorbs in the ultraviolet part of the spectrum. Such images can be used to build up a dynamic model of the atmosphere, showing its circulation; particularly evident is the vortex (whirlpool) visible over Venus's South pole (NASA).

Pioneer Venus missions

Although the Pioneer Venus spacecraft, Pioneer Venus 1 and 2, were launched three months apart, in May and August 1978, they encountered Venus only five days apart, on December 4 and December 9 1978. Prior to that time, the planet had been the target for thirteen spacecraft, of which three were American and ten Soviet. Five of these missions were strictly flybys of the planet, while eight either entered the atmosphere or landed. The American Pioneer Venus missions were nonetheless unique in many ways. Most importantly, Pioneer Venus 1 was the first spacecraft to orbit the planet while Pioneer Venus 2 was the first mission to have more than one atmospheric probe.

The Pioneer Venus Orbiter carried 12 scientific experiments designed to study Venus and its environment. The aspects chosen included the structure and dynamics of the solar wind's interaction with the ionosphere and upper atmosphere; the composition and structure of the ionosphere and the upper atmosphere; the physical and thermal structure of the venusian clouds; upper atmospheric winds and turbulence; and the topography of the surface of Venus.

The spacecraft were inserted into a highly elliptical orbit around the planet Venus, with a 24 hour period. Closest approach (periapsis) was only 150 kilometres above the surface, while the furthest distance reached (apoapsis) was 66 900 kilometres. This orbit was chosen so that the spacecraft could obtain both closeup and distant global views of the planet.

The Pioneer Venus Multiprobe Mission consisted of one large and three small entry probes. The four probes were separated from their carrier before the planetary encounter and were targeted to enter the atmosphere at different latitudes and longitudes. In this way, a variety of meteorological regimes was sampled on the nightside and dayside, and in the equatorial, mid latitude and polar regions. The large probe (the Sounder Probe) contained seven scientific instruments, whereas the identical small probes each carried three experiments. These addressed such important issues as the composition, temperature and pressure structure of the lower atmosphere, the vertical structure and composition of the venusian clouds, and the global scale of the winds extending from the surface to cloud altitudes. The Multiprobe carrier itself also carried two experiments to measure, *in situ*, characteristics of the ionosphere and atmosphere as the carrier entered and burned up in the upper atmosphere.

The Pioneer Venus Orbiter completed its nominal mission in August 1979, 243 days after orbit insertion on 4 December 1978. The spacecraft continues in operation today, however, with most of its 12 scientific instruments still operating. In an extended mission, it is exploring the various regions of Venus's environment over a complete 11 year cycle of solar activity. The orbiter should continue to collect valuable scientific data until mid 1992, when it will enter Venus's upper atmosphere and be burnt up.

The Pioneer Venus Multiprobe Mission was completed in two and a half hours on 9 December 1978, during which time each of the four probes entered the upper atmosphere and completed one hour descents to the surface. They were destroyed upon impact. The large probe was deployed on a parachute for a slow descent through the clouds of Venus; the parachute was jettisoned beneath the clouds to permit the probe to fall freely, and more rapidly, to the surface. The three small probes went from the top of the atmosphere to the surface in free fall, while the carrier entered and burned up in a matter of minutes.

The Pioneer Venus Orbiter and Multiprobe Missions produced many important scientific results, the most celebrated being:
– a global topographic map of the surface of Venus showing rolling plains punctuated by two features of continental scale, Aphrodite Terra and Ishtar Terra, and several volcanic regions
– evidence for lightning, intriguingly associated with volcanic features in Aphrodite Terra

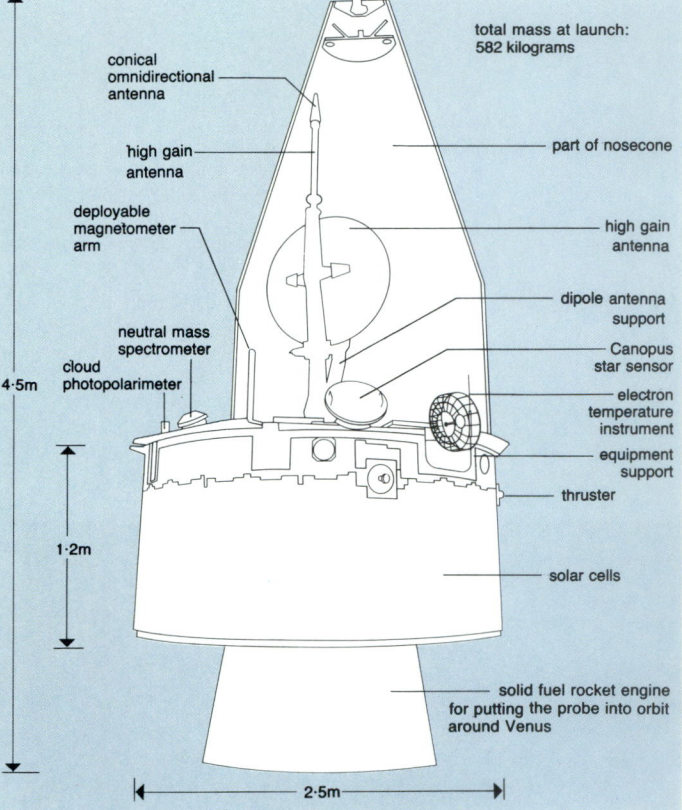

total mass at launch: 582 kilograms

conical omnidirectional antenna

high gain antenna

deployable magnetometer arm

neutral mass spectrometer

cloud photopolarimeter

4.5m

1.2m

part of nosecone

high gain antenna

dipole antenna support

Canopus star sensor

electron temperature instrument

equipment support

thruster

solar cells

solid fuel rocket engine for putting the probe into orbit around Venus

2.5m

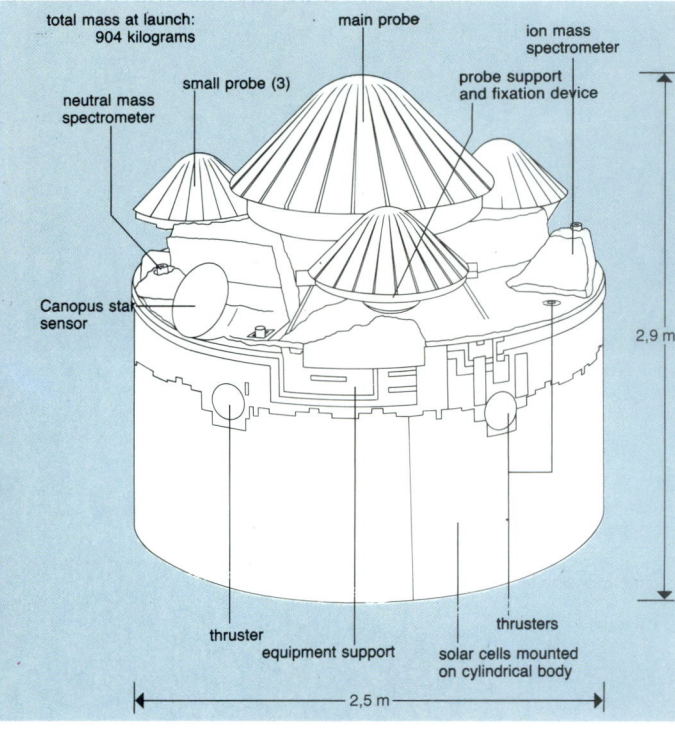

total mass at launch: 904 kilograms

main probe

ion mass spectrometer

small probe (3)

probe support and fixation device

neutral mass spectrometer

Canopus star sensor

2.9 m

thruster

equipment support

thrusters

solar cells mounted on cylindrical body

2.5 m

Pioneer Venus 1 and Pioneer Venus 2. The photograph of Pioneer Venus 1 (far left) was taken on 18 May 1970, two days before its launch from the Kennedy Space Center in Florida. In the lower left photograph, Charles Hall, who was in charge of the Pioneer Venus programme, is standing next to Pioneer Venus 2.

The cylindrical structures of the two probes, covered in blue solar cells, were 2·5 metres in diameter and 1·2 metres high. The parabolic dish of Pioneer Venus 1 was replaced by four probes on Pioneer Venus 2.

The Pioneer Venus 1 orbiter had twelve instruments, of which most are still functioning today. Three examined emissions from the ionosphere while a further three analysed the atmosphere. Another instrument examined gamma radiation coming from the galaxy, and a photopolarimeter sent back pictures of the clouds; a magnetometer was also carried. There was a special radar designed to continue the mapping of Venus begun by Venera 9 and Venera 10, and a plasma analyser and an electric field detector designed to study the interaction between the ionosphere and the solar wind.

Pioneer Venus 2 was designed to drop four probes into the venusian atmosphere and to become, itself, a fifth probe. This operation was performed at an altitude of between 150 and 115 kilometres. The main body, with its two mass spectrometers, analysed the composition of the upper atmosphere. One spectrometer measured the concentration and composition of neutral particles in the high atmosphere, while an ion mass spectrometer analysed the composition of the ionosphere and the concentration of charged particles. Not being protected against the intense heat, the main body disintegrated 64 seconds after it reached an altitude of 115 kilometres (NASA).

- strikingly small temperature contrasts near the surface, both from day to night and from equator to pole
- rapid zonal winds at cloud altitudes, but gentle surface breezes
- compared with the Earth and Mars, enhanced concentrations of certain noble gases in the lower atmosphere
- peculiar size distributions of particles in the venusian clouds
- vertical cloud structure, consisting of three layers, across the entire planet
- comet-like interaction of the solar wind with the ionosphere and upper atmosphere
- confirmation of scientific observations made by previous missions; these include a high surface temperature (730 kelvin), a high surface pressure (95 bars), sulphuric acid clouds, a scarcity of water anywhere on the planet or in its atmosphere, the absorption of solar energy mainly in the clouds, and little, if any, intrinsic magnetic field of planetary origin.

The US Magellan Mission, successfully launched aboard the space shuttle Atlantis on 4 May 1989, now promises to extend the Pioneer Venus Radar Mapper results to much smaller features on the surface.

Lawrence Colin

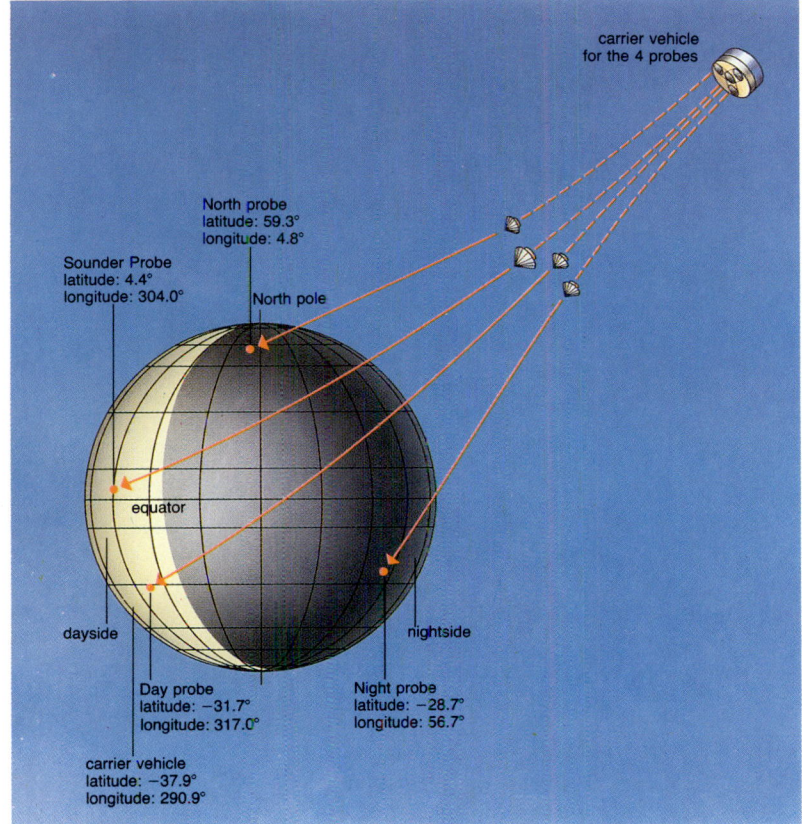

Trajectories of the Pioneer Venus 2 probes. As it approached Venus, Pioneer Venus 2 launched its four probes towards different parts of the planet. The main probe, called the Sounder Probe, was situated on the spin axis of the space vehicle. Some 24 days before it penetrated Venus's upper atmosphere, the vehicle was reoriented, so that this axis coincided with the desired trajectory into the atmosphere. The Sounder Probe was then launched. The vessel's trajectory was altered so as to head it towards the centre of Venus, and the small probes were launched 4 days later, 20 days before the probe was due to reach the planet. The vehicle's spin enabled the small probes to separate and follow different trajectories to achieve their varying objectives on Venus.

The three small probes were called by names corresponding to their points of entry into the venusian atmosphere. North entered the night side, Day landed at mid latitudes near the Sounder Probe (the only probe to have a parachute), as did Night. The scientific payloads were carefully chosen so that the same parameters could be compared at different latitudes and local times on Venus. There has been no other planetary mission of such sophistication to date.

The Sounder Probe of Pioneer Venus 2. This probe was approximately 1·5 metres in diameter, with a mass of 315 kilograms. The front part consisted of an aerodynamic heat shield; the walls were pressure resistant, and the back covering was carefully made out of titanium, to protect it against the high temperatures encountered without making it too heavy. The casing was 73·2 centimetres in diameter. The drawing on the right is a cutaway view showing its internal structure and the layout of the various systems. The scientific instruments were placed on the front panel.

In the lefthand drawing, the apertures for the instruments can be seen. A parachute was used to slow the Sounder Probe down after it had entered the atmosphere at a supersonic speed, and the heat shields were jettisoned when the parachute was released. The parachute was ejected when the probe was just above the cloud layer and it then fell freely towards the surface. The four probes took about 60 minutes to descend.

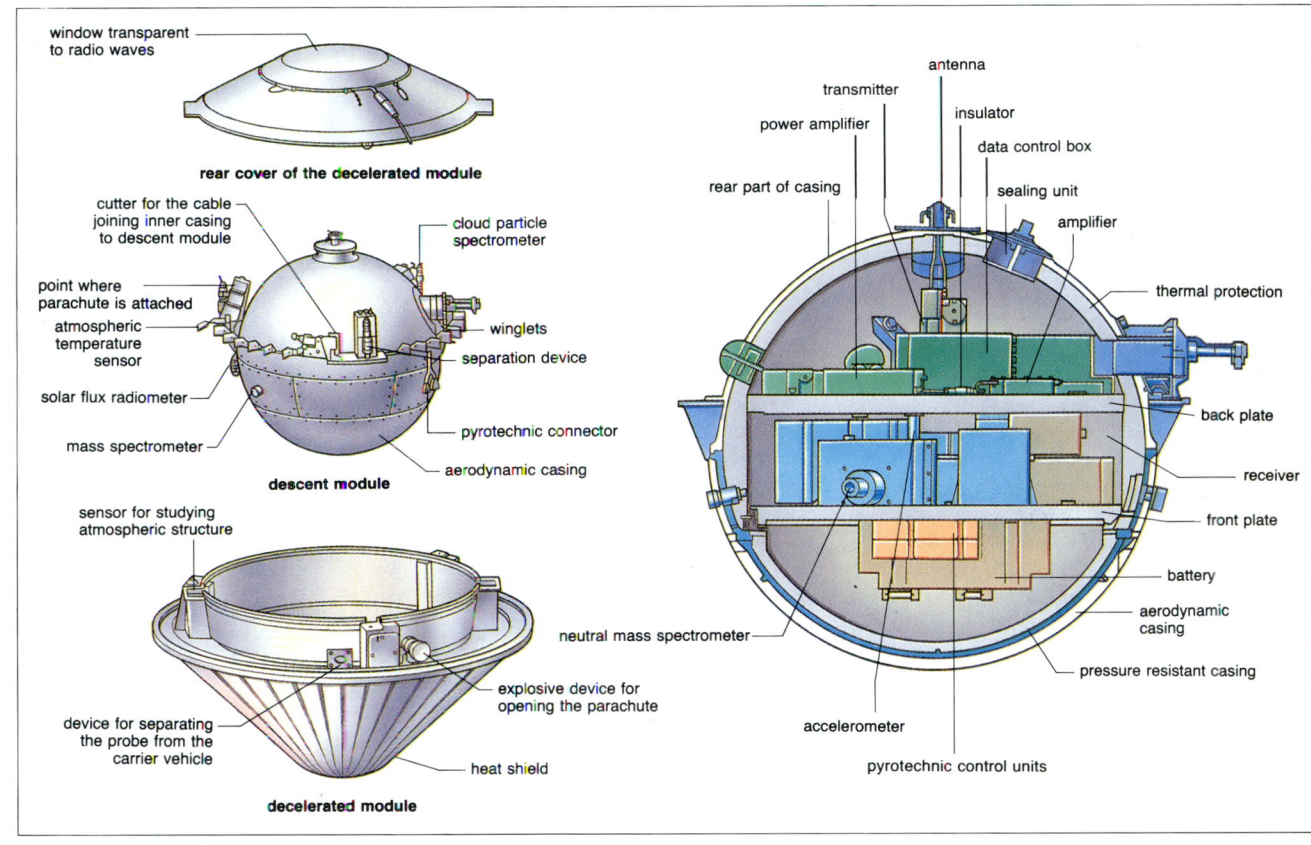

The small probes of Pioneer Venus 2 These three small identical probes were carefully constructed to withstand the enormous pressures and temperatures of Venus's atmosphere. Each probe, made in two parts out of titanium, had a mass of 18 kilograms and a diameter of 46 centimetres. The average thickness of the walls was 3 millimetres.

The lefthand drawing is a cutaway view of the probe, showing its internal structure, the layout of the systems and the three scientific instruments. These are a nephelometer for measuring the properties of the cloud particles, a device for measuring the atmospheric pressure and temperature, and a radiometer measuring both incoming solar energy and outgoing infrared energy as a function of depth through the atmosphere.

The righthand drawings show the pressure resistant casing and also the descent module made from a resin which would protect the probe as it entered the atmosphere at supersonic speed. Unlike the Sounder Probe, these remained intact until the moment of impact with the surface of Venus.

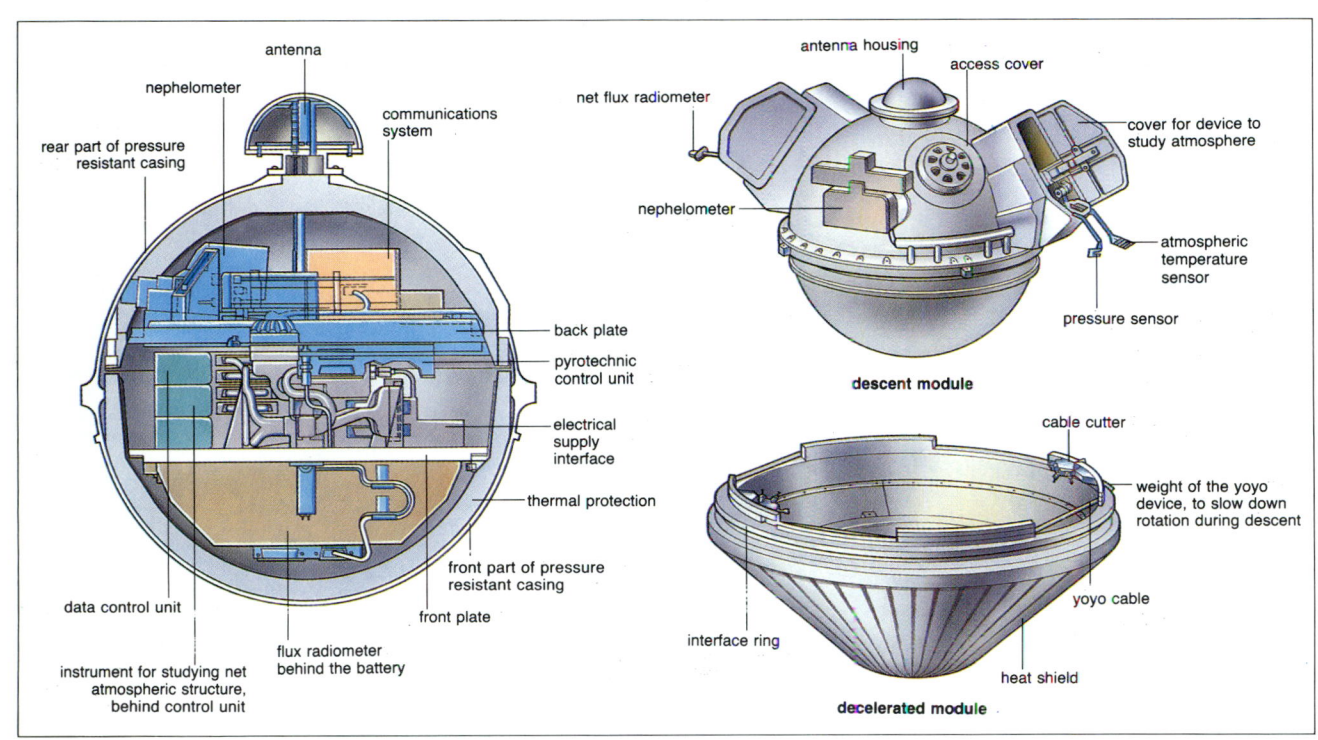

Exploring the solar system

Unmanned lunar missions

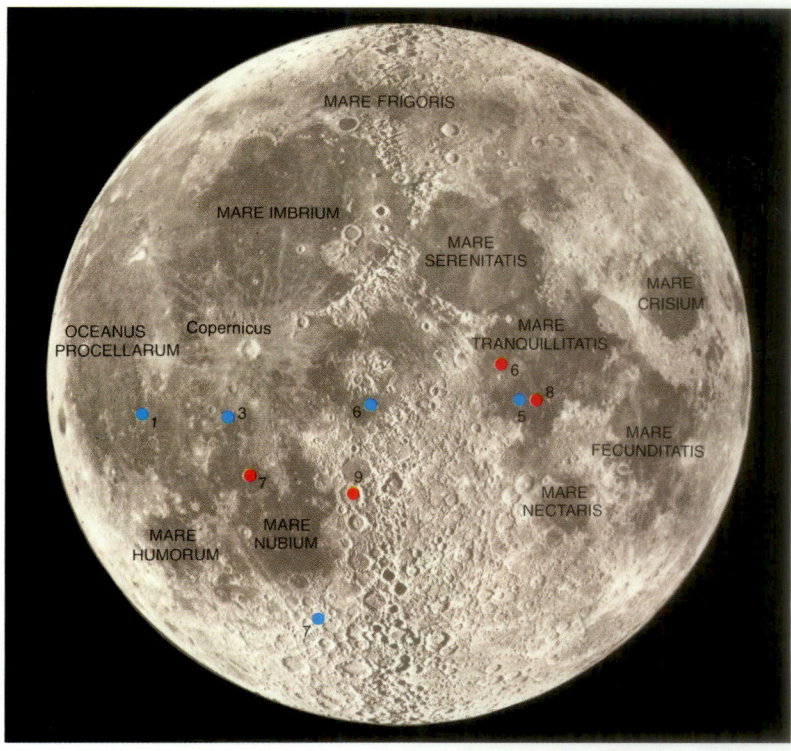

landing sites: ● Ranger ● Surveyor

The Surveyor and Ranger landing sites on the Moon. Three of the nine spacecraft in the Ranger series sent back 17 267 pictures of the lunar surface before they crashed into it. The Surveyor probes were more successful, with five soft, controlled landings. They sent back more than 86 000 images, a vast quantity of information on the nature of the surface (Lick Observatory).

American programmes

The moon was a primary goal for space exploration even before the National Aeronautics and Space Administration (NASA) was established. President Dwight D. Eisenhower approved Department of Defense plans for a lunar probe programme in March 1958, and both the Air Force Ballistic Missile Division and the Army Ballistic Missile Agency were assigned to develop probes. Their objective was to place a payload in the vicinity of the Moon, with scientific instruments designed to measure the energetic radiation, temperature and micrometeorite distribution. Space Technology Laboratories joined the Air Force in designing the Thor Able launch vehicle and its payloads for Moon exploration. However, the Air Force failed to put any of its three probes onto a lunar trajectory during 1958 because of launch vehicle problems.

On 1 October 1958, the new civilian space agency, NASA, assumed responsibility for the lunar probe programme, but delegated its authority back to the Air Force and Army. The Army and Jet Propulsion Laboratory team failed to put their first small conical probe onto a lunar trajectory in 1958, and a second probe in 1959 did not pass close enough to the Moon for its instruments to record any data on the near, or cis, lunar environment.

Project Ranger was then established as a response to the increasing scientific interest in the Moon and the successful lunar investigations of the Soviet Union. The design of the spacecraft was first suggested during studies conducted at the Jet Propulsion Laboratory (JPL) in California, where advanced planners were considering lunar and planetary missions for NASA's new Vega launch vehicle. When Vega was cancelled in favour of the Atlas Agena B launch vehicle in late 1959, the design group at JPL was directed to adapt its lunar spacecraft and experiments to suit such a launcher. Lunar photography was considered to be the prime objective since it would support future manned lunar landings and provide valuable scientific data.

The Ranger programme originally called for two lunar probes and three impact missions. The first two 306 kilogram spacecraft were to be launched into highly elliptical Earth orbits that would take them near the Moon to study the cislunar environment. Their eight scientific instruments were to measure the radiation and magnetic field and serve as a test for the new, hexagonally shaped, solar powered spacecraft.

Because of launch vehicle failures, Ranger 1 and 2 were boosted into only low Earth orbits in 1961, reentering the atmosphere shortly afterwards. The next two Rangers, equipped with television camera systems, impacted the Moon in early 1962, but their ability to transmit lunar images by radio had been impaired. Ranger 5

missed the moon by 725 kilometres that same year. In an attempt to simplify the mission and ensure a successful lunar impact complete with photographs, the next Ranger spacecraft was designed to carry a television system but no other experiments. However, Ranger 6, too, failed to return any data before it crashed onto the Moon in 1964.

NASA Headquarters accordingly directed JPL to terminate its advanced Ranger activities, which had called for a spacecraft that would survive a hard landing, and conduct a thorough investigation into their troubled programme. An increased number of design and hardware reviews, revised schedules, closer monitoring of subcontractors, and more intense participation by NASA Headquarters personnel led thereafter to highly successful missions for Ranger 7, 8, and 9. In 1964 and 1965, they returned over 17 000 high quality images of the lunar surface from three different locations, namely the Sea of Clouds, the Sea of Tranquility, and the crater Alphonsus. These were studied in detail by scientists looking for the first Apollo lunar landing sites. Only budgetary cuts and plans for more sophisticated lunar orbiting and landing missions prompted NASA to terminate the Ranger programme after the third successful mission.

Four years before, on 25 May 1961, NASA had been given the task of landing a man on the Moon and returning him safely to Earth by President John F. Kennedy. Unmanned lunar exploration projects to assist NASA with its Apollo programme of manned landings gained a higher priority as result, and the Lunar Orbiter programme was born.

A project called Surveyor was approved by NASA headquarters in 1960, and planned as a two part undertaking. An orbiter would be used for lunar reconnaissance and a lander for surface exploration. However, a series of problems, with the development of the Centaur launch vehicle and with Ranger, along with increasing demands from the Office of Manned Space Flight for information on the lunar surface that would help find suitable landing sites for Apollo, led NASA to look for an alternative to the Surveyor orbiter. The requirements of an orbiter only mission, using a new lightweight probe, were formulated at NASA's Langley Research Center by 1963.

The 385 kilogram Lunar Orbiter was to carry a photography system developed by Eastman Kodak, and three scientific experiments sponsored by NASA Langley and the Jet Propulsion Laboratory, JPL. These were on selenodesy (the lunar equivalent of geodesy), meteoroid detection and radiation measurement.

Lunar Orbiters 1 to 5, launched by Atlas Agena D rockets, were all successful missions conducted in 1966 and 1967. They returned

Unmanned American missions to the Moon

Project	Launch date	Comments
Pioneer 1	11 October 1958	failed to reach velocity required for lunar trajectory
Pioneer 2	8 November 1958	failed to reach velocity required for lunar trajectory
Pioneer 3	6 December 1958	failed to reach velocity required for lunar trajectory
Pioneer 4	3 March 1958	did not pass close enough to Moon for instruments to function
Able 4	26 November 1959	unsuccessful and final launch of Air Force lunar probes
Ranger 1	23 August 1961	injected into low Earth orbit due to launch vehicle failure
Ranger 2	18 November 1961	injected into low Earth orbit due to launch vehicle failure
Ranger 3	26 January 1962	missed Moon by 37 000 kilometres; some useful radiation data received
Ranger 4	23 April 1962	hit Moon as planned but no data received; possible failure of central computer and sequencer
Ranger 5	18 October 1962	missed Moon by 725 kilometres; on board power failure; some useful gamma ray data received
Ranger 6	30 January 1964	hit Moon as scheduled but no data received because of TV system failure
Ranger 7	28 July 1964	successful impact; transmitted 4316 images
Ranger 8	1 February 1965	successful impact; transmitted 7137 images
Ranger 9	21 March 1965	successful impact; transmitted 5814 images
Lunar Orbiter 1	10 August 1966	transmitted 207 images of Apollo target sites; impacted surface on 29 October 1966
Lunar Orbiter 2	6 November 1966	transmitted 211 images of Apollo target sites; impacted surface on 11 October 1967
Lunar Orbiter 3	4 February 1967	transmitted 211 images of Apollo and Surveyor target sites; 28% of planned images not taken due to readout system malfunction; impacted surface on 9 October 1967
Lunar Orbiter 4	4 May 1967	transmitted 193 images; photographed southern polar region; impacted surface on 6 October 1967
Lunar Orbiter 5	1 August 1967	transmitted 212 images; completed coverage of far side of Moon; impacted surface on 31 January 1968
Surveyor 1	30 May 1966	landed on 2 June 1966 in the Ocean of Storms; returned over 10 000 images and selenological data; primary mission ended on July 13; communications re-established until January 1967
Surveyor 2	20 September 1966	crashed onto surface on 22 September due to a malfunction of vernier engine
Surveyor 3	17 April 1967	landed on 19 April; returned 6315 images and soil sample data; functioned until early May
Surveyor 4	14 July 1967	crashed onto Moon 2.5 minutes before scheduled landing; unknown malfunction
Surveyor 5	8 September 1967	landed on 10 September in the Sea of Tranquility; returned 18 000 images and data on lunar surface radar and thermal reflectivity; telemetry signal lost on 16 September
Surveyor 6	7 November 1967	landed on 9 November in the Sinus Medii; returned 29 500 images and data on touchdown dynamics and surface; spacecraft restarted and moved 3 metres; signal lost on 14 December
Surveyor 7	7 January 1968	landed on 9 January in the Tycho crater; returned 21 274 images; signal lost on 20 February

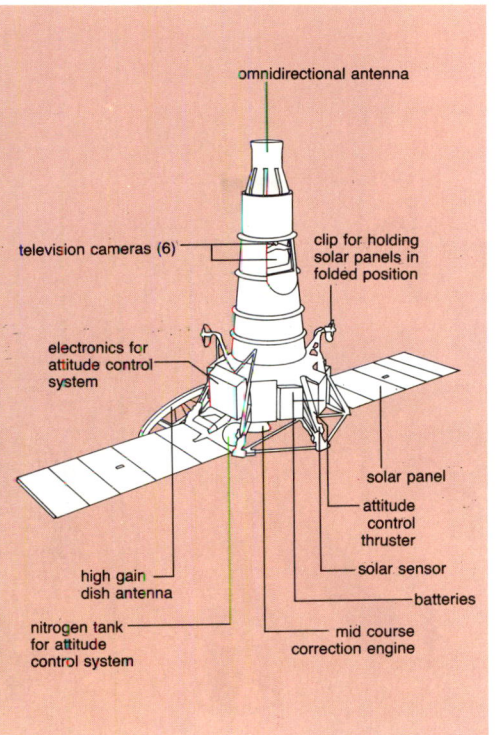

The Ranger space probes. Built around a hexagonal structure, these each had a mass of 355 kilograms. They were 3·6 metres tall, with a wingspan of 5·2 metres when the solar panels were deployed, and were equipped with six Vidicon television cameras, two of them with wide fields of view. These filmed the surface at altitudes from 1400 kilometres down to 0·8 kilometres.

Ranger 7, shown on the left, was the first successful probe in the series. It transmitted 4316 high resolution images back to the Earth before crashing into the Moon at Mare Cognitum at a speed of 9334 kilometres per hour (NASA).

The Lunar Orbiter probes and their photographic coverage of the Moon's surface. These space probes orbited at an altitude of about 40 kilometres; from their television pictures of the lunar surface, the first detailed maps were made of the dark side of the Moon. The last two lunar probes of the series were placed in polar orbits.

Four solar panels produced a power of 375 watts for these probes which had two distinct parts. The lower part was a compartment containing the fuel tanks and a small rocket engine, the upper part a platform supporting the main equipment. The probe measured 5·6 metres by 3·7 metres, with the antennae and solar panels deployed, and had a mass of 385 kilograms. All the Lunar Orbiters carried an imaging system, plus scientific instruments produced by NASAs Langley Research Center and Jet Propulsion Laboratory. These were to detect meteorites and energetic radiation, and to make geodetic measurements of the Moon. (A. Humbert-Droz)

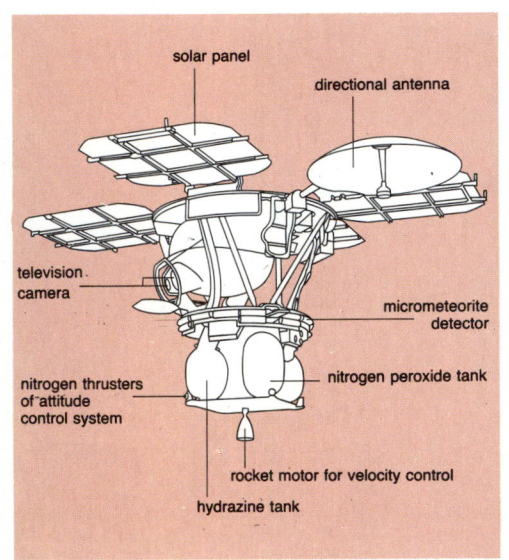

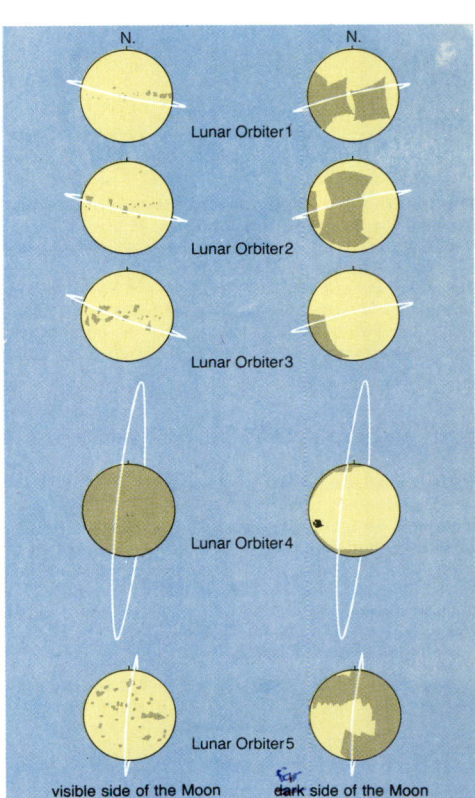

The Surveyor probes which landed on the Moon. The triangular aluminium structure of a Surveyor probe contained two compartments of instruments, a column supporting the solar panel, and a high gain antenna. The base contained a solid fuel retrorocket, three fine control (Vernier) rocket motors, a shock absorber and three shock resistant feet.

The model in the photograph shows the Surveyor probe in its landing position on the Moon; the feet are deployed, giving a width of 4·2 metres and a height of 3 metres for a mass of 283·5 kilograms. The retrorocket, which decelerates the probe, is not visible; it is positioned in the central part of the structure (Hughes Aircraft Company).

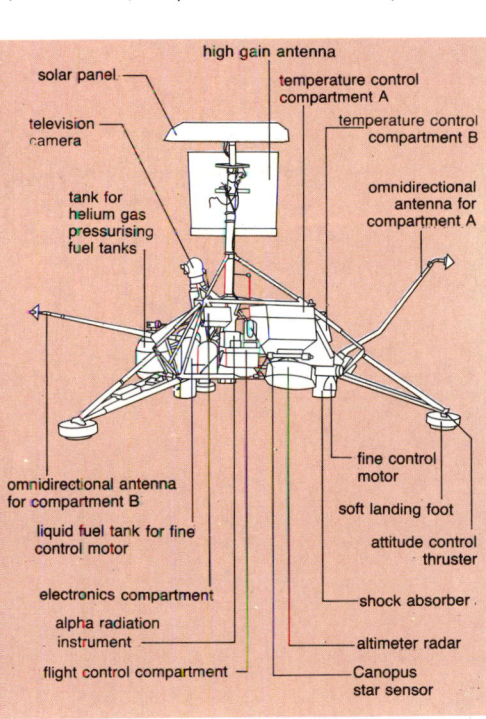

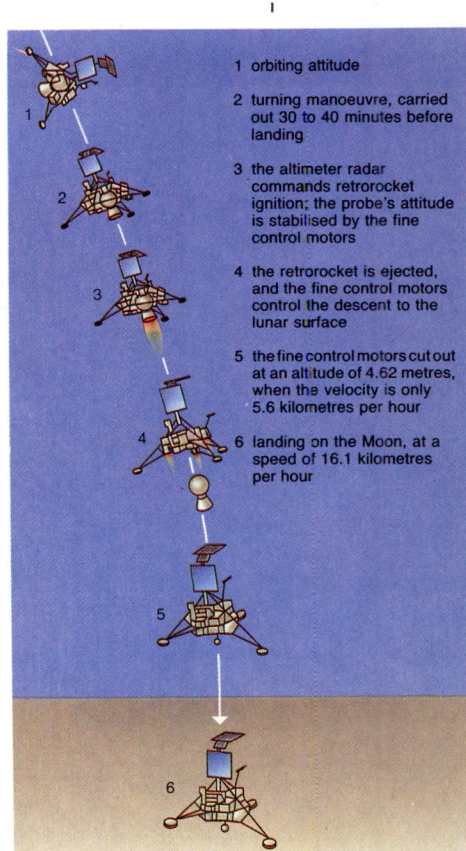

1 orbiting attitude

2 turning manoeuvre, carried out 30 to 40 minutes before landing

3 the altimeter radar commands retrorocket ignition; the probe's attitude is stabilised by the fine control motors

4 the retrorocket is ejected, and the fine control motors control the descent to the lunar surface

5 the fine control motors cut out at an altitude of 4.62 metres, when the velocity is only 5.6 kilometres per hour

6 landing on the Moon, at a speed of 16.1 kilometres per hour

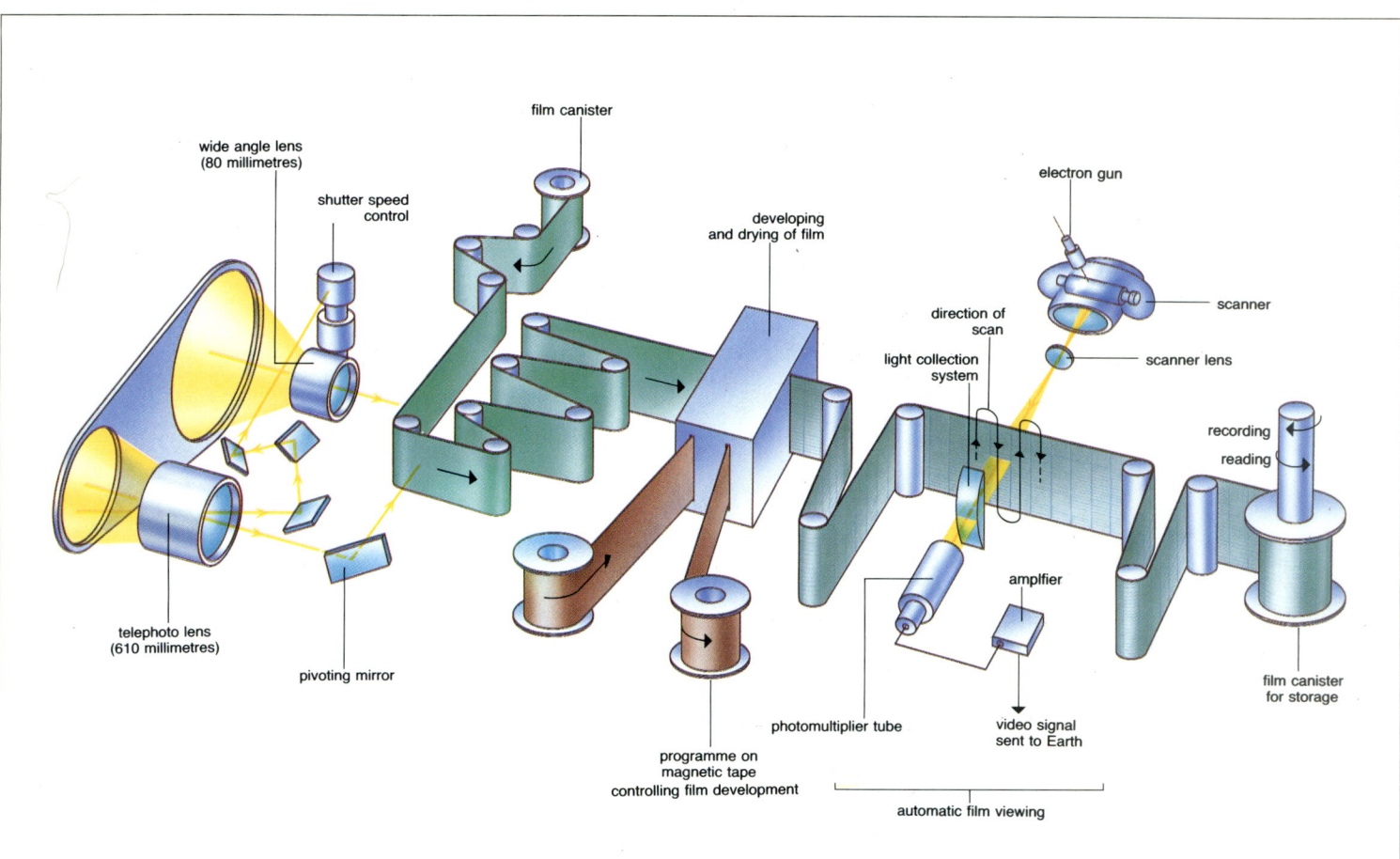

wide angle lens
(80 millimetres)

shutter speed
control

film canister

developing
and drying of film

electron gun

direction of
scan

scanner

light collection
system

scanner lens

recording

reading

telephoto lens
(610 millimetres)

pivoting mirror

amplfier

film canister
for storage

photomultiplier tube

video signal
sent to Earth

programme on
magnetic tape
controlling film development

automatic film viewing

The imaging system from the Lunar Orbiter probes. Using two lenses, these probes could simultaneously take pictures of the Moon's surface at high and medium resolutions. The telephoto lens (610 millimetres focal length) and the wide angle lens (80 millimetres focal length) had a resoluton of about 1 metre and 8 metres respectively.

Unlike the Ranger probes, the photographic system on the Lunar Orbiter probes, which was developed by the Eastman Kodak Company, developed and then scanned the exposed photographic film. The data were then transmitted to the Earth as a video signal.

The landing sites selected by the Lunar Orbiter probes for the Apollo missions. Photographs of the Moon's surface were used to identify safe landing sites for the Apollo missions. The two photographs on the right were taken in November 1966 by Lunar Orbiter 2. The region shown on the left was retained as a possible site for a future landing, but the one on the right was rejected because of the numerous craters (NASA).

Photograph obtained by Lunar Orbiter 4. This vertical photograph, taken on 19 May 1967 from 2900 kilometres altitude, was obtained as the space probe made its twenty-first orbit about the Moon. It shows a region near 50 degrees North latitude, North being at the top to the North East of the Mare Imbrium. The oblique shape crossing the mountainous zone is the Vallis Alpes. It had never been observed with such precision from the Earth (NASA).

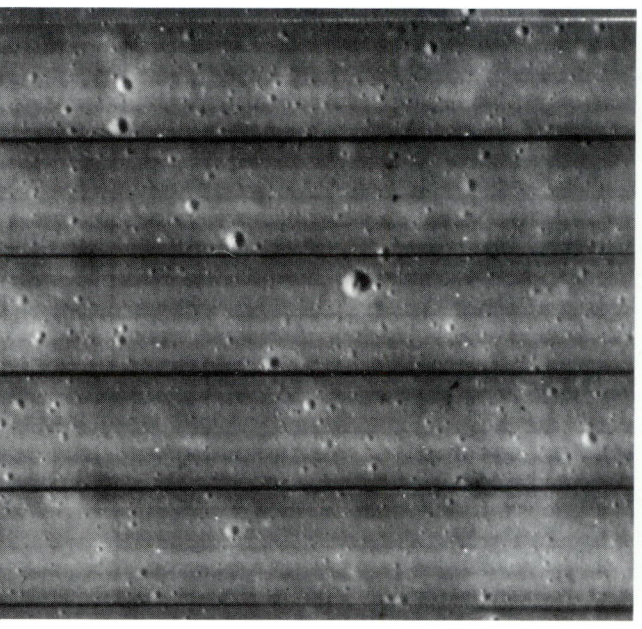

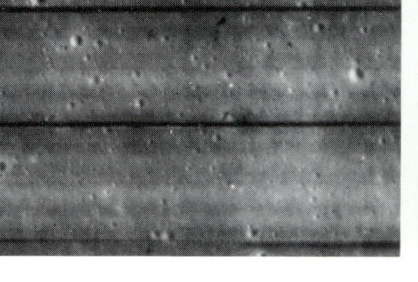

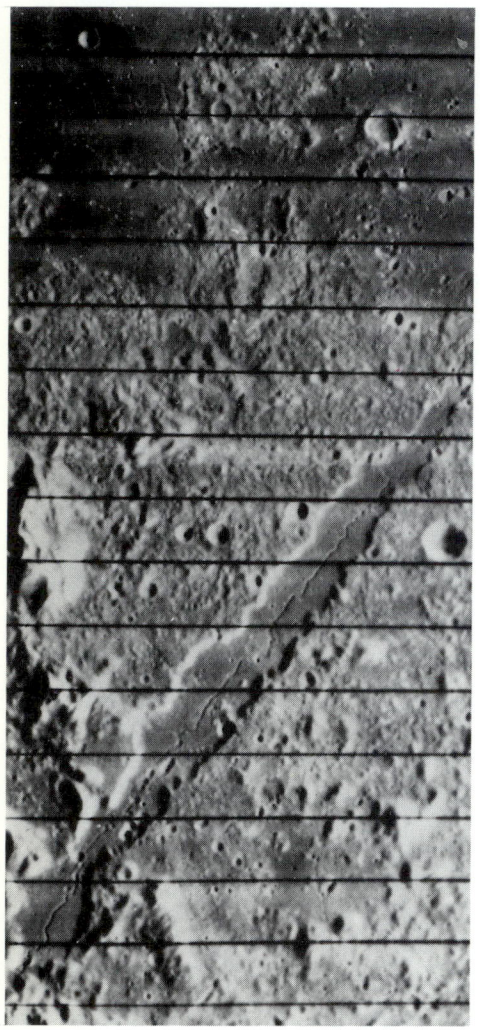

Oblique view taken by Lunar Orbiter 3. This picture of the lunar surface was taken on 22 February 1967 by the wide angle camera. The Kepler crater (centre below) is situated in the Oceanus Procellarum at 8 degrees North, 38 degrees West. The crater is about 32 kilometres in diameter and more than 1·5 kilometres deep (NASA).

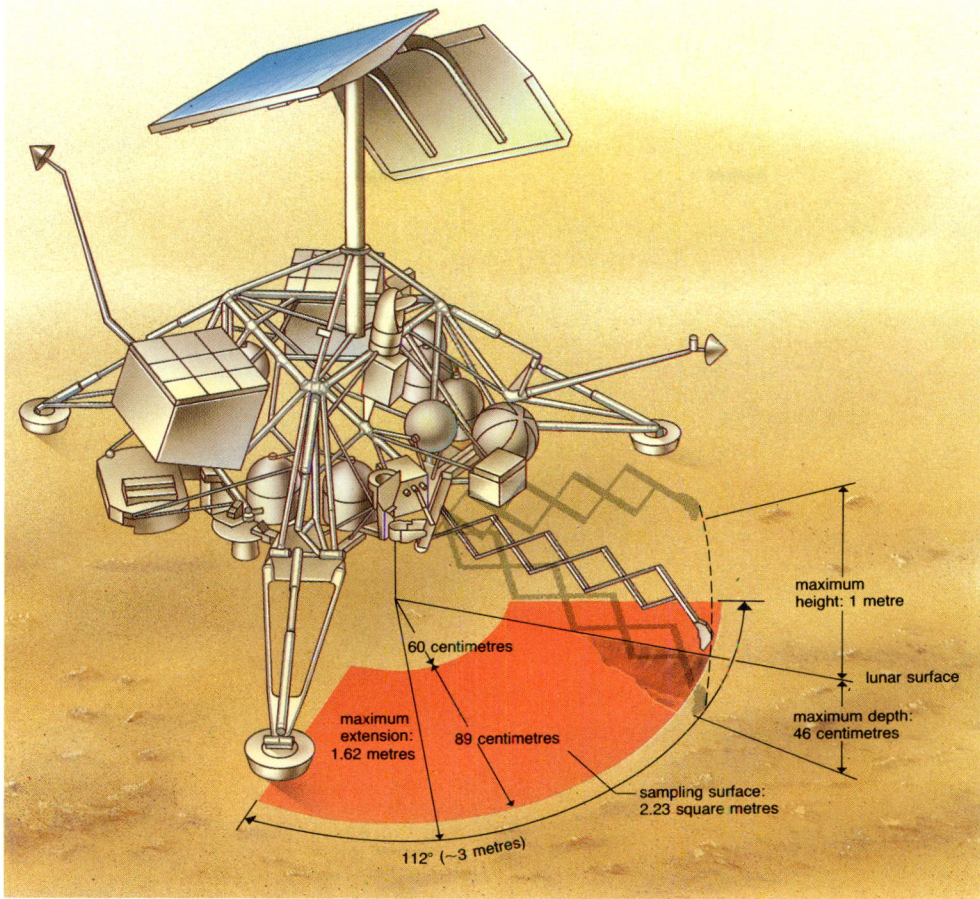

The configuration of the Surveyor probes after landing. This diagram demonstrates the operation of a Surveyor craft on the lunar surface. The probes were equipped with a television camera, a system for collecting samples from the regions shown in orange, and an alpha radiation instrument for analysing the composition of the lunar soil.

Surveyor 6 was moved 3 metres from its original landing site after eight days by firing the vernier rocket motors for 2·5 seconds.

Panorama of the Surveyor 7 landing site. Surveyor 7 landed on the Moon on 9 January 1968 at 40·9 degrees South, 11·4 degrees West, to the North West of Tycho crater. This region of great scientific interest was outside the research zones for future Apollo missions.

The photograph on the right shows the soil near the probe, with the sample collector digging a trench and the alpha radiation instrument (left) being lowered to the lunar surface. The picture immediately below is a photomosaic; the rocks in the foreground were 6 metres from the probe (right: NASA; below: JPL/NASA).

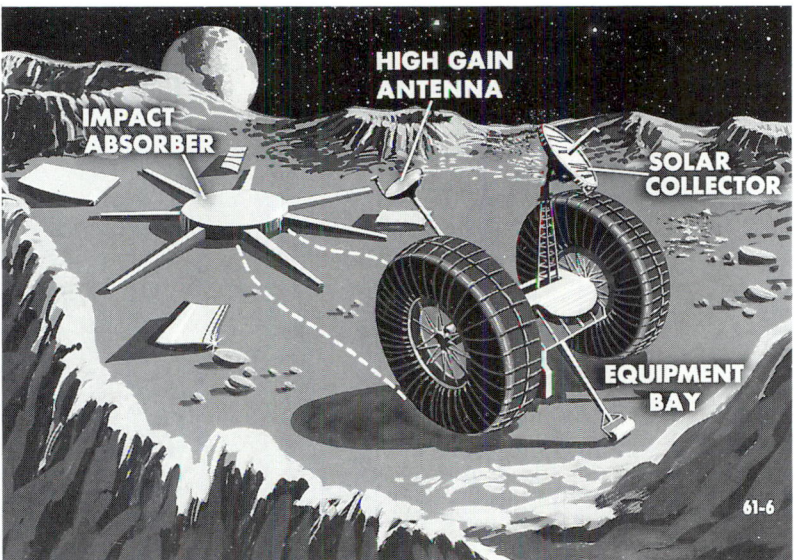

The Prospector project. This was to be the last lunar exploration project performed by US unmanned probes. It was to move over a 48 kilometre radius from the landing site, collecting samples, and transmitting detailed images of the Moon's surface.

The first Prospector probes were to have been launched in 1965 and 1966. However, when the US Congress decided to reduce NASA's budget for 1963, this third generation of automatic lunar probes was abandoned (NASA).

hundreds of high resolution photographs of the Moon that were much better than those returned by Ranger. By the end of the third mission, the Apollo programme's requirements of the Lunar Orbiter had been met. Besides locating possible landing sites, other areas of the moon had been photographed, and by the end of the project a broad systematic survey had been accomplished which included the Moon's far side.

Although not pursued as an orbiter and lander design as its originators had intended, the Surveyor project was continued as a lander only spacecraft in support of the manned Apollo programme from 1966 to 1968. In its initial configuration, the Surveyor soft lander would have carried several scientific instruments to the Moon, but weight constraints and the growing importance of the Apollo programme eliminated most of Surveyor's scientific objectives. Before men could be sent on a lunar expedition, spacecraft designers needed more information on the moon's crust and its mechanical structure, its soil, magnetic properties, and radar and thermal reflectivity. Equipped with a television camera, sampling scoops, magnetic footpads, and an alpha radiation instrument, Surveyor's purpose was now to supply the manned spacecraft designers with these critical data.

In early 1961, NASA chose Hughes Aircraft's proposal for a Surveyor lander and began mission planning at JPL for seven lunar flights, the first of them planned for launch using an Atlas Centaur rocket in 1963. Unfortunately, there were repeated delays with the launch vehicle so that NASA had to postpone the first mission. Surveyor's designers also had to pare down the spacecraft's size so that it was compatible with Centaur's capabilities, reducing an original 1124 kilograms with a 156 kilogram payload to a 953 kilogram spacecraft with 52 kilograms of instruments. Although it was 1966 before Atlas Centaur was operational, the new booster launched all seven Surveyors successfully.

Surveyor 1 landed on the Moon on 2 June 1966, three days after it had started its journey from the Eastern Test Range. Transmitting more than 10 000 high quality images, it remained operational until the following January. Trouble with the vernier engines caused the second lander to crash onto the Moon, but Surveyor 3, with added features, returned an abundance of data in April 1967. In addition to more than 6000 photographs, information on the composition and surface bearing strength of the lunar crust was obtained as the television camera focused on a surface sampler which dug trenches in the soil.

Surveyor 4 failed later in 1967; minutes before it was due to land, something went wrong and the spacecraft either exploded or crashed onto the lunar surface. The last three Surveyor missions, in late 1967 and early 1968, all returned thousands of images, however, and supplied invaluable data on chemical elements in the soil, on touchdown dynamics, and on the magnetic properties of the lunar surface.

One additional unmanned lunar exploration project was seriously considered by NASA during the early 1960s. This was Prospector, weighing some 2270 kilograms, to be launched by a Saturn I rocket. Prospector was intended to rove across the Moon, gathering samples, depositing instrumented packages, transmitting close up images of the lunar surface, and detonating explosive charges at various points for seismic studies. Regretably, it succumbed to budget cuts in 1963.

Linda Neuman-Ezell

Soviet programmes

The Soviets began studying the Moon, using automatic space probes, in January 1959 when Luna 1 was launched. Luna 1 passed within 6000 kilometres of the Moon's surface, making measurements on the field and charged particles. In the 27 years that followed, 22 space probes were launched to construct an atlas of the dark side of the Moon.

During the initial stage of Moon exploration, the space probes discovered that there was no notable lunar magnetic field or radiation belt (Luna 1 and Luna 2). The dark side of the Moon (Luna 3 and Zond 3) was photographed, soft landings were performed, and some television pictures were transmitted to Earth. The lunar surface appeared to be firm enough to support impacting probes and the movement of moving vehicles such as Lunokhod (Luna 9 and Luna 13). Cislunar space was examined with respect to charged particle radiation and meteorites, and the chemical composition of Moon rock was discovered to be similar to terrestrial basalts (Luna 10, Luna 12 and Luna 14). The data gathered by the early probes were, however, essentially qualitative or, at best, semi quantitative.

In the second stage of lunar exploration, the gravitational and magnetic fields near the Moon, and the radiation and meteorite environment on the surface and in circumlunar space were investigated. These studies were realised using the Luna 14, Luna 19 and Luna 22 space probes and the Lunokhod 1 and Lunokhod 2 vehicles. Magnetic data were interpreted to give information on the electrical conductivity distribution and temperature of the Moon's mantle under the Mare Serenitatis (Sea of Serenity), down to a depth of several hundred kilometres. When this was combined with the results of similar measurements made by Apollo 16, scientists were able to conclude that, at a depth of between 200 and 400 kilometres, the Moon's mantle is colder under the mare than under the adjacent continental regions. This could be a consequence of intense basaltic volcanic activity under the mare at this depth.

Other Lunokhod investigations led to a clear understanding of the morphology of the lunar surface, and of its physical and mechanical properties and chemical composition. Observations of the albedo of the lunar rock in the region North West of the Sea of Showers and on the western coast of the Sea of Serenity helped in particular to increase understanding of impact and explosion on the Moon, and of the way meteorite impacts cause the formation of new impact craters and simultaneously destroy older craters.

The chemical composition and albedo of the lunar soil demonstrated the essentially basaltic character of the lunar mare, with a decrease in the iron content and an increase in the aluminium content over a continental region.

Finally, in the third stage of Soviet lunar exploration, the Luna 16, 20 and 24 probes brought back a fraction of a kilogram of rock samples from the Moon. All of these were obtained from the eastern hemisphere of the visible side of the Moon. They were taken from near the landing sites of Luna 16 (in the Sea of Fertility), of Luna 20 (in the continent of Apollonius) at a depth of 40 centimetres, and at a depth of 2 metres at Luna 24's landing site (in the Sea of Crises). The Moon's surface was disturbed as little as possible during the sample's removal and packing into a container for return to Earth. The samples were examined in the USSR and pieces were then sent to researchers in other countries, both in the East and West. Most of the samples were of friable rocks with a grain size of less than 200 microns, but a few had a grain size between 0.5 and 2.3 millimetres. These larger particles were used mainly for studies in mineralogy and petrography, and for geochemical research. They showed that the Sea of Fertility was rich in titanium basalts,

which are thought to have crystallised about 3·6 billion (thousand million) years ago. The geochemical analysis of the basalts in the Sea of Crises revealed links with the rock in the lunar subsoil from the base rock of most basalts on the Moon. The crystallisation ages of basalts studied in the Sea of Crises vary between 3·3 and 3·5 billion years, while rocks in the continent of Apollonius, found between the Sea of Crises and the Sea of Fertility, prove to be rich in feldspar (anorthite). The isotopic age of these rocks is of the order of 4 to 4·4 billion years.

Besides the debris of primary magma rocks, all the Luna rock samples brought back included a large quantity of secondary formations such as glasses, scoria (volcanic rocks like clinkers), agglutinates and debris from the coarse grained breccia bedrock. These were formed out of the bedrock under the action of meteorite bombardment, the breccia exploding on impact.

Alexander Bazilevsky
and Larissa Moskaleva

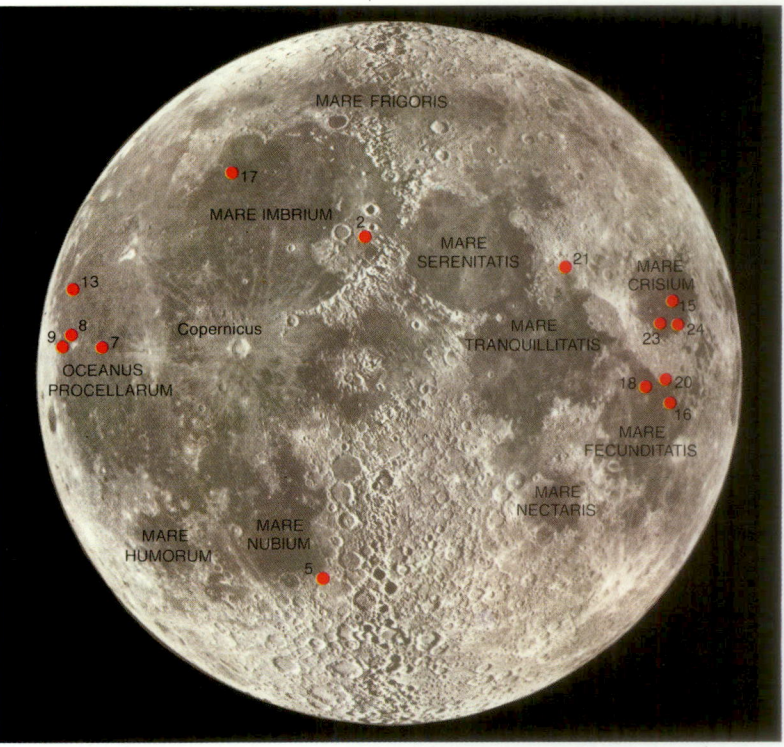

● Luna landing sites

Map of the Luna probe landing sites. The landing sites are generally spread out in the region near the Moon's equator, which is well lit compared with the dark polar regions. Luna 2 was the first probe to land on the Moon, but Luna 9 was the first to perform a soft landing. In total, 14 unmanned Soviet probes have landed on the Moon. Two of these missions, Luna 17 and Luna 21, left Lunokhod vehicles which could move around on the surface (Lick Observatory).

The unmanned Luna and Zond missions

Probe	Launch date	Key results from each mission
Luna 1	2 January 1959	measured the characteristics of cosmic and circumlunar space; established for the first time that the Moon had no appreciable magnetic field of its own
Luna 2	12 Sept 1959	first powered flight of a spacecraft from the Earth to the Moon; lack of appreciable magnetic field confirmed
Luna 3	4 October 1959	dark side of the Moon photographed for the first time
Luna 4	2 April 1963	examined the technical problems posed by lunar exploration
Luna 5	9 May 1965	tested a soft landing system for the Moon
Luna 6	8 June 1965	flight trajectory missed the planned trajectory and the probe found itself on a heliocentric orbit
Zond 3	18 July 1965	photographed the dark side of the Moon
Luna 7	4 October 1965	studied a soft landing system for lunar landings
Luna 8	3 Dec 1965	studied a soft landing system for lunar landings
Luna 9	31 January 1966	first soft landing on the Moon; first panoramic pictures of the lunar surface, with a resolution of 1 millimetre were transmitted to Earth
Luna 10	31 March 1966	first probe put into a circumlunar orbit; examined cislunar space, with particular reference to the radiation and meteorite environment; first evaluation of the chemical composition of the top layer of the Moon's surface using gamma radiation
Luna 11	24 August 1966	probe went into orbit around the Moon and made radio-astronomical observations of the Sun and Moon; examined radiation and meteorite environment around the Moon, and the Moon's gravitational field
Luna 12	22 October 1966	probe photographed the lunar surface from its lunar orbit and made a detailed study of the Moon and circumlunar space
Luna 13	21 Dec 1966	soft landing on the Moon; transmitted panoramic views of the landscape; examined the density and solidity of the lunar soil
Luna 14	7 April 1968	probe placed in circumlunar orbit; studied the gravitational field of interplanetary and circumlunar space
Zond 5	15 Sept 1968	probe flew over the Moon, at a minimum distance of 1960 kilometres, and then returned to Earth
Zond 6	10 Nov 1968	probe flew over the Moon and then returned to Earth with pictures of the lunar surface
Luna 15	13 July 1969	experiments with new unmanned navigational systems on a probe in orbit around the Moon
Zond 7	8 August 1969	probe flew over the Moon and then returned to Earth with pictures of the lunar surface
Luna 16	12 Sept 1970	soft landing on the Moon, in the Sea of Fertility; after drilling into the Moon's surface, the probe brought rock samples back to Earth
Zond 8	20 October 1970	probe flew over the Moon and then returned to Earth with pictures of the lunar surface
Luna 17	10 Nov 1970	soft landing on the Moon, in the region of the Sea of Showers; put a remote controlled vehicle on the Moon, Lunokhod 1 which carried out scientific experiments for 10.6 months with a range of 10 kilometres, taking televised panoramic views of the lunar surface and studying the chemical composition and physical and mechanical properties of the lunar rock
Luna 18	2 Sept 1971	examined unmanned methods of circumlunar navigation and landing on the Moon's continental surface
Luna 19	28 Sept 1971	probe in orbit around the Moon to study the gravitational and magnetic fields, cosmic radiation and the density and flux of meteorites
Luna 20	14 February 1972	soft landing in the continental region of Apollonius, situated between the Sea of Fertility and the Sea of Crises; after drilling into the lunar surface, the probe returned rock samples back to Earth
Luna 21	8 January 1973	soft landing on the Moon, in the Sea of Serenity, put Lunokhod 2 on the surface; for 4 months, it carried out scientific studies over a range of more than 37 kilometres, transmitting televised panoramic views of the lunar surface and studying the lunar rock
Luna 22	29 May 1974	probe put into circumlunar orbit; took television pictures of the surface, measured the gravitational field and the radiation and meteorite environment
Luna 23	28 October 1974	experiments and tests with new construction and equipment elements; programme only partly successful due to the deterioration of the sample gathering equipment
Luna 24	9 August 1976	soft landing on the Moon, in the Sea of Crises; took rock samples and returned them to the Earth

The Luna 2 probe. Luna 2 was launched on 12 September 1959. Moving at a speed of 3·3 kilometres per second in a plane inclined at 60 degrees to the equator, it was the first man made vehicle to land on another planet.

Luna 2 weighed 390·2 kilograms and resembled Luna 1 in appearance; the only difference was a slight modification to the magnetometer, improving its sensitivity. The measurements made by this probe during its descent confirmed the absence of an appreciable magnetic field and also the absence of lunar radiation belts.

To commemorate the occasion of the first landing of a man made object on the Moon, Luna 2 carried two small spheres, 9 and 15 centimetres in diameter. These broke on impact into small pentagonal elements carrying the emblem of the Soviet Union (Moklestov, APN).

The Luna 1 probe on the A1 launcher. On 2 January 1959, the first vehicle built by man to escape from the Earth's gravitational influence was launched by the Soviet Union.

Luna 1, also called Mechta, was launched straight onto a lunar trajectory without first going into a terrestrial orbit. The spherical probe, 120 centimetres in diameter, resembled Sputnik 1 which was launched 15 months earlier. Luna 1 weighed 361·3 kilograms; its interior was pressurised to 1·3 atmospheres and kept at a temperature of 20 degrees celsius.

About 34 hours after its launch, the probe passed above the Moon's surface at a distance of 6000 kilometres and became the first terrestrial object to go into orbit around the Sun. All communications with the probe ceased after 62 hours, 597 000 kilometres from the Earth.

During its passage over the Moon, Luna 1 discovered that there was no appreciable magnetic field around the Moon (rights reserved).

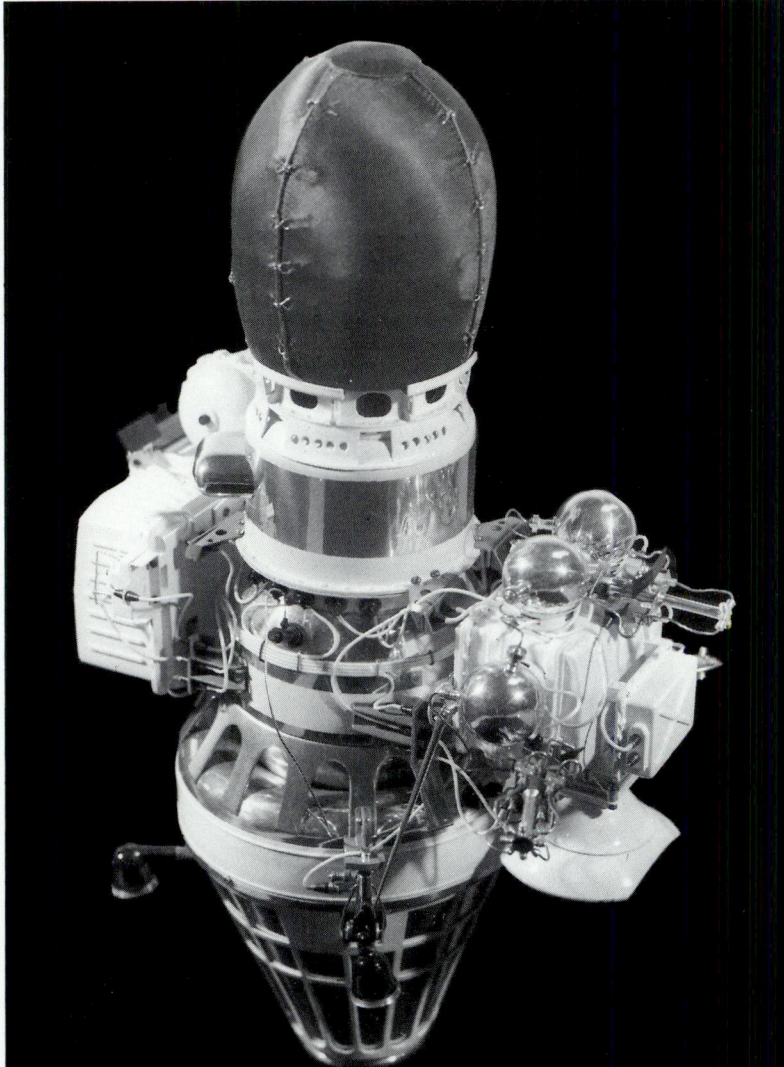

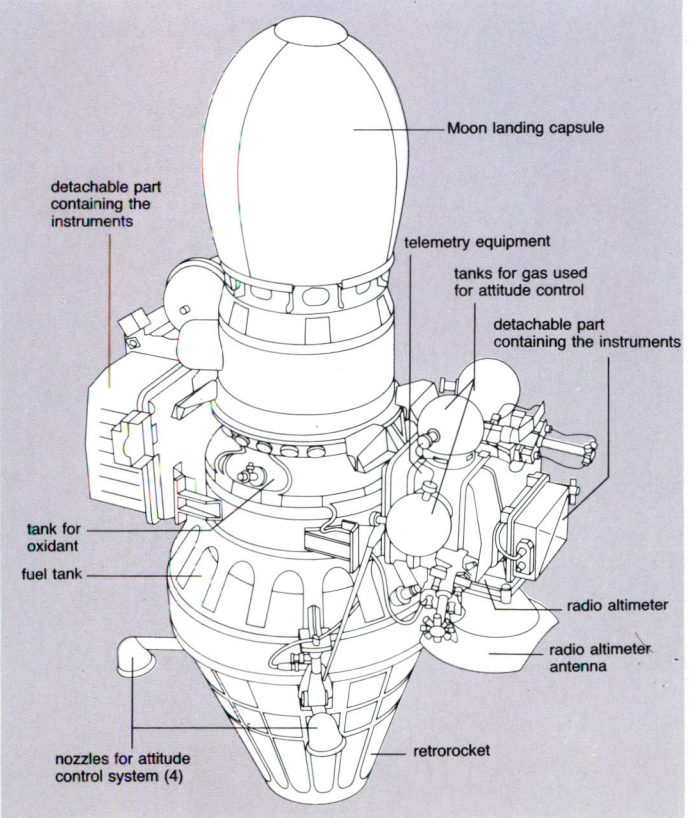

The Luna 9 probe. On 31 January 1966 the Soviet Union launched the first lunar probe to make a successful soft landing on the Moon. Three days after launch it became the first probe to transmit panoramic pictures of the lunar surface.

The mission began with Luna 9 being put into a terrestrial transfer orbit; as it passed over the Soviet Union, the propulsion stage was reignited to put the probe onto a trajectory towards the Moon. Some 75 kilometres from the surface, the radar and navigation equipment were jettisoned for the descent phase. Just before impact, the landing capsule separated itself from the probe to bounce, roll across the ground, and — thanks to the ballast in its base — finally right itself in the correct position. Once it had been stabilised, the capsule opened its four panels like petals to reveal its television equipment and to allow it to move its antennae. Luna 9 stopped transmitting to the Earth on 7 February, when its batteries ran down (APN).

Luna 10's trajectory. Luna 10, the first probe to be put into a circumlunar orbit, examined the radiation and meteorite environment of circumlunar space. It weighed 1·6 tonnes and was 4 metres long.

First of all, the probe was put into a terrestrial parking orbit, at an altitude of 250 kilometres and an orbital inclination of 51·9 degrees. It was shifted to a translunar orbit on 1 April 1966 and, when nearly at the Moon, reoriented to prepare it for the manoeuvre into a lunar orbit.

Luna 10 sent scientific information back to the Earth for 56 days. On 30 May 1966, after 460 orbits of the Moon, communications ceased owing to exhaustion of the chemical batteries.

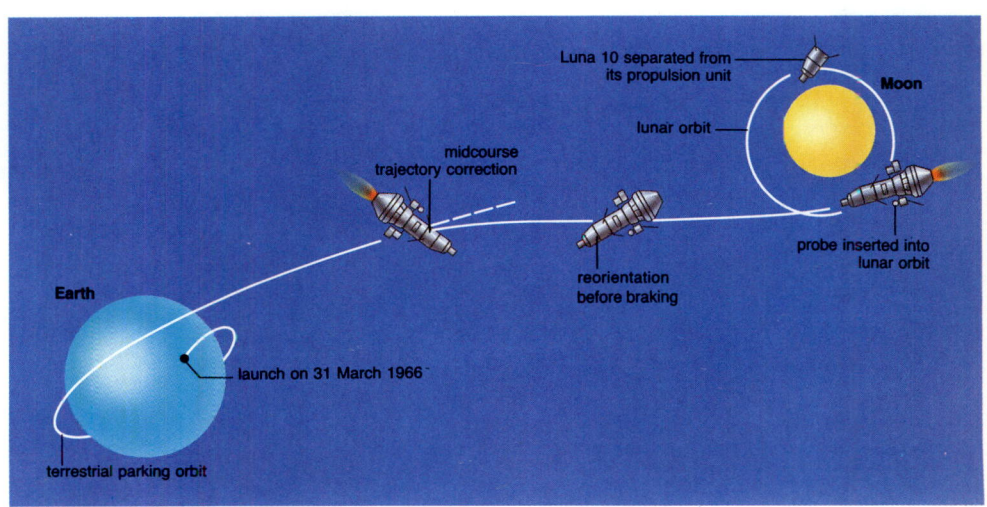

Part of a panoramic picture of the Moon's surface taken by Luna 13. On 22 December 1966, Luna 13 was launched from the base at Tyuratam, in the USSR. On 24 December, the probe was reoriented, 70 kilometres above the Moon's surface, and the retrorockets were ignited. Two minutes later, Luna 13 landed successfully about 400 kilometres from Luna 9; four minutes later, the capsule opened and radio transmissions began. Once the panels had opened, the two mechanical arms were free to move. One arm was fitted with a device for penetrating the Moon's surface, the other with an instrument to measure radiation and determine the consistency and density of the soil.

The photographic equipment used for the visual exploration of the Moon was similar to that on Luna 9. The camera weighed 1·3 kilograms and used 2·5 watts of power. Inclined at an angle of 16 degrees to the horizontal, the camera had a resolution of 2 millimetres at a distance of 1·5 metres. As with Luna 9, a complete panorama (360 degrees) took about 100 minutes to make. On this section of the picture, the shadow cast by the landing capsule is clearly visible (APN).

Luna 16. During its mission, Luna 16 (shown on the right) became the first unmanned probe to return a sample of rock from the Moon to Earth.

The probe weighed 1·88 tonnes when it landed on the Moon. The descent module had liquid fuel tanks, a variable thrust propulsion system, two low thrust propulsion units, an impact absorber system and instrument compartments. The instruments included attitude and other control systems, a radio transmitter and a thermal regulation system.

The photograph below shows the core sample taken by Luna 16. The drilling reached a depth of 35 centimetres, the sample weighing 101 grams. The capsule was returned to Earth on 24 September, some 80 kilometres South West of the town of Dzezkazgan in the Soviet Republic of Kazakhstan (right: Tass; below: APN).

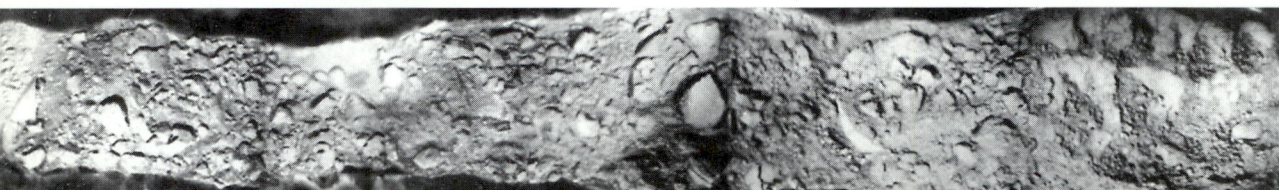

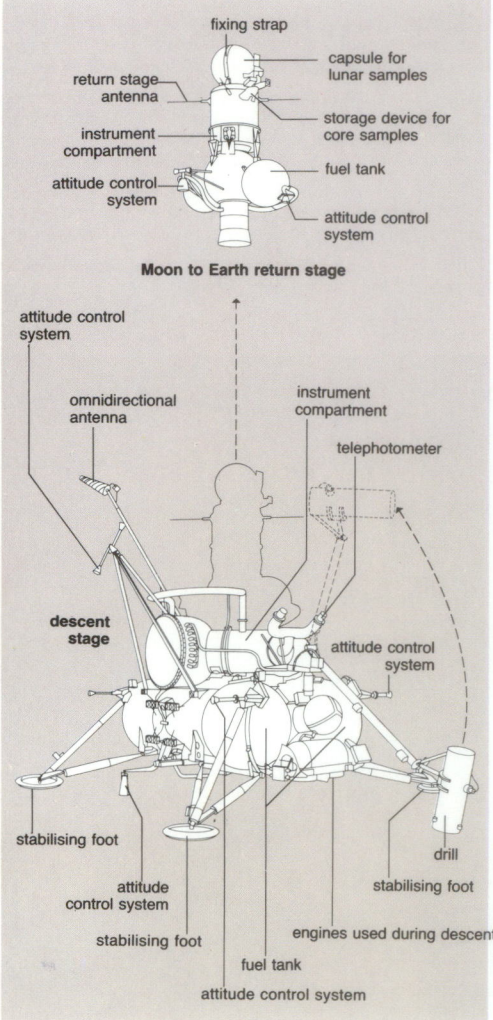

fixing strap
capsule for lunar samples
return stage antenna
storage device for core samples
instrument compartment
attitude control system
fuel tank
attitude control system

Moon to Earth return stage

attitude control system
omnidirectional antenna
instrument compartment
telephotometer
descent stage
attitude control system
stabilising foot
drill
attitude control system
stabilising foot
stabilising foot
engines used during descent
fuel tank
attitude control system

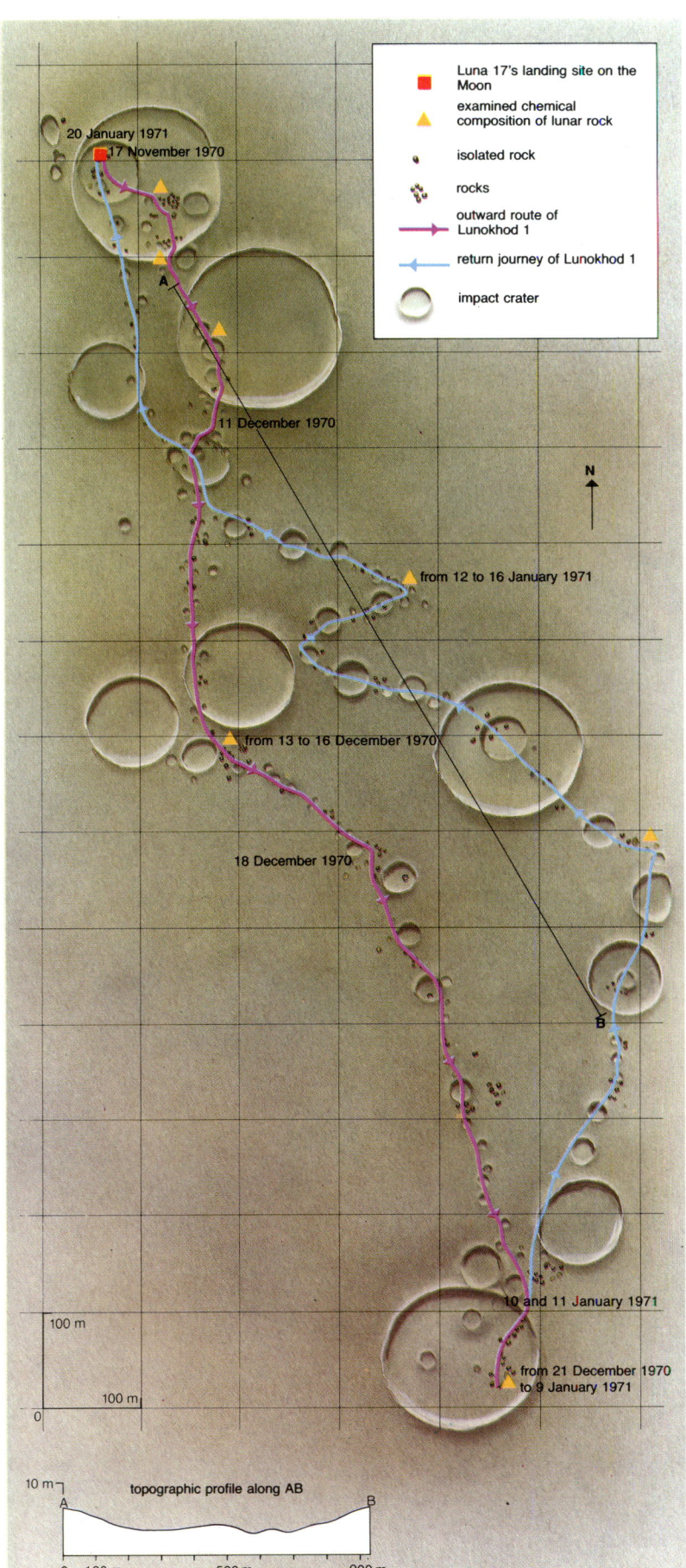

The Luna 20 return capsule. This return capsule brought samples from the Moon back to Earth, protecting them during the journey, in particular during the passage through the Earth's atmosphere. The casing was made of metal with a special surface to protect it from extreme temperatures.

In the capsule's various compartments were the hermetically sealed cylinder containing the core sample, a parachute system, automatic devices such as the batteries and radio transmitters, and two balloons (visible on the photograph) filled with gas to ensure that the probe landed the right way up.

The Luna 20 capsule landed on 25 February 1972 on an island in the River Karlinger, some 40 kilometres North of Dzezkagan, during a snowstorm (APN).

The Luna 17 and Lunokhod 1 mission. The Luna 17 probe consisted of a lunar landing module similar to Luna 16, and the Lunokhod 1 vehicle. Although its travels on the Moon were controlled from Earth, Luna 17 was thus responsible for the first mobile scientific laboratory in the history of astronautics.

Lunokhod 1, shown in the photograph on the far left, p. 166, was designed to perform scientific and technical research on the Moon's surface, while roving quite considerable distances from the landing probe. Weighing 456 kilograms, it had a chassis mounted on eight metallic wheels. The instrument compartment carried the scientific instruments, the control and electrical supply systems, and the thermal regulation system for the television systems and other automatic devices. The upper part of the compartment, which had a lid, acted as a radiator for thermal regulation. During the night, this lid was closed to protect the instrument compartment from excessive heat loss; during the day, it was opened to enable excess heat to escape. Solar cells were arranged on the inside.

On the front part of the compartment and along its sides were the television cameras. Also attached to it were the antennae, a laser corner reflector and the radio isotope heat source for the thermal regulation system.

Luna 17 reached the Moon on 17 December 1970 and landed near the Sea of Showers at 38° 17' North, 35° West. Lunokhod's research programme came to an end on 4 October 1971. The photograph on the left was taken on 25 January 1971 and shows the tracks left by Lunokhod 1 as it moved across the Moon's surface.

Lunokhod travelled a total of 10·45 kilometres and examined an area of 50 hectares; the map above shows the route followed between 17 November 1970 and 19 January 1971. It transmitted 210 panoramic pictures and more than 20 000 photographs of the lunar surface back to the Earth. Studies were also made of the physical and mechanical properties of the lunar surface at 500 points, analysing its chemical composition at 25 of them (Tass).

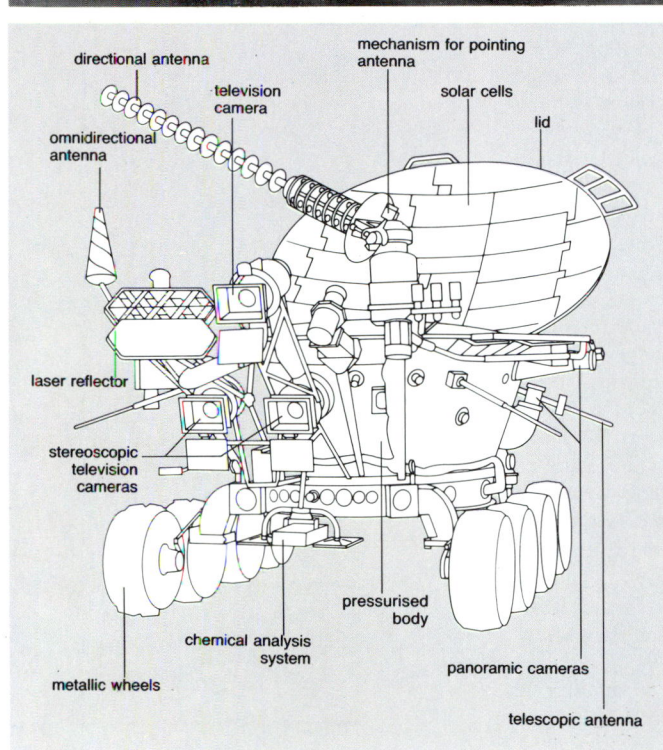

The Lunokhod 2 vehicle of the Luna 21 mission. This improved version of Lunokhod 1 was 7·21 metres long and 1·6 metres wide. The vehicle weighed 84 kilograms more than Lunokhod 1. It had a supplementary television camera at the front above the pressurised compartment; the much greater field of view assisted the Earthbound controllers considerably.

After the soft landing, Lunokhod 2 began exploring the Sea of Showers for a period of ten and a half months. During this time it took 8000 television pictures and 86 panoramic photographs. It also carried out several hundred mechanical and chemical tests on the lunar rock (APN).

Exploring the solar system

The Apollo programme

Organisation

From the dawn of the space age in 1957, many in the United States saw manned flights to the Moon as a means of demonstrating technological prowess. The National Aeronautics and Space Administration (NASA) was created, on 1 October 1958, the Mercury programme was initiated simultaneously, and the Apollo programme followed shortly after.

Even before NASA's formation, committees had studied what should be done in space and, already in 1959, one group was focusing on manned circumlunar flight. Thereafter, the various NASA research establishments accelerated activities geared to that goal: the Langley Research Center in Virginia studied structures and materials; the Lewis Research Center in Ohio experimented with liquid oxygen and liquid hydrogen propulsion systems; the NASA Marshall Space Flight Center in Alabama analysed proposed launch vehicles; and the Ames Research Center in California studied problems related to navigation to the Moon. The Space Task Group in Virginia coordinated these studies, and in July 1960 NASA outlined the proposed Apollo programme to industry. On 25 October 1960, three aerospace firms (Convair Astronautics, General Electric, and Martin Marietta) were awarded study contracts, all later reporting that the proposed mission was feasible.

In January 1960, President Dwight D. Eisenhower directed NASA to accelerate what was then called the 'superbooster programme' (Saturn I), but by December he was found unwilling to commit the nation to a circumlunar project costed at $38 million. George M. Low, among others in NASA, concluded that the agency had been mistaken in promoting a circumlunar mission; a manned landing should be the objective.

Politics affected the issue early in 1961. When John F. Kennedy became president, his science adviser criticised both the Mercury programme and NASA management. A month later President Kennedy appointed James E. Webb to head NASA. Three events, occurring in rapid succession, followed shortly afterwards. On 12 April 1961, Yuri Gagarin orbited the Earth in a Vostok spacecraft, and five days later 1600 American-trained Cuban exiles failed in the Bay of Pigs invasion of Cuba. Spurred on by these setbacks, Kennedy aimed to 'get America moving', identifying space as the obvious arena for regaining the technological edge. Finally, on 5 May 1961, Alan B. Shepard successfully made a Mercury suborbital flight to the nation's acclaim and relief. President Kennedy had the necessary base for a national commitment and, on 25 May 1961, sent to Congress the message 'that this nation should commit itself to achieving the goal, before this decade is out, of landing a man on the Moon and returning him safely to the Earth'.

No project could have been more difficult and challenging, and some 18 months passed before clear plans were laid. Several radical schemes were proposed; in one, an astronaut would even land, establish a base and wait on the Moon until the capability was developed to bring him home.

More serious studies involved one of three modes: direct flight to the Moon, rendezvous in Earth orbit, and rendezvous in lunar orbit. Direct flight, using a series of rocket stages and discarding them at points in the journey, was seen as the most uncomplicated way to get to the Moon and back. A landing could be made either vertically or horizontally, with a propelled stage provided for the return to Earth. After determining that a booster to provide a thrust of 53 meganewtons would be required, however, enthusiasts for a direct flight to the Moon became disenchanted and themselves turned to rendezvous schemes.

When President Eisenhower approved the acceleration of the Saturn rocket programme, the team led by Wernher von Braun at the NASA Marshall Space Flight Center took charge of development. This involved clustering eight Redstone rocket engines into a single stage to produce a thrust of 5·8 meganewtons.

The Saturn rocket had no mission at that stage, and von Braun naturally sought to remedy the situation. Since the vehicle was not powerful enough for a direct flight to the Moon, a rendezvous in Earth orbit was proposed for which as many as 15 Saturns would be launched. Rendezvous would be effected, and a launch vehicle put together for a direct flight to the Moon and a lunar landing. However, this plan was deemed initially to be too dangerous and difficult, and von Braun's team was unable to win the necessary support.

Proponents of a rendezvous in lunar orbit, where a spacecraft was sent to the lunar surface and returned to a mother ship orbiting the Moon, presented almost unbelievable claims for the low weight of the equipment required. The lunar lander, with one pilot, was to be a small flying platform. Those in favour of the direct flight concept were attracted to the idea of not landing the entire spacecraft on the Moon because it reduced the need for a large launch vehicle.

To prove the rendezvous technique, NASA initiated the Gemini programme in December

Accomplishing the dream of the millennium. By 197? two astronauts in spacesuits with equipment and several tens of kilograms of samples, were travelling across the Moon at speeds of up to 17 kilometres per hour.

On 31 July 1971, on their first Extra Vehicular Activity, commander David R. Scott of the Apollo 15 mission photographed James B. Irwin, the pilot of the Lunar Module, checking the lunar exploration vehicle (lunar rover) at the landing site in the Apennines. This was near Mount Hadley, which can be seen in the background to the North East.

A navigation system on the rover enabled the astronauts to know at any instant their position with respect to the Lunar Module. On the Earth, the lunar rover weighed 209 kilograms; on the Moon, it weighed one sixth of this (NASA).

Diagram showing how early concepts for a lunar visit evolved. From a NASA document dated 1963, this diagram shows four versions of the lunar module adapted for landing on the Moon after a direct flight from Earth. From left to right are the designs of May 1960, July 1961, December 1961 and April 1962; the fifth version (July 1962) corresponds to the rendezvous in lunar orbit procedure that was finally chosen. The section with the large windows was planned to separate from the command module and descend towards the Moon's surface.

Four of these versions were equipped with a rocket safety tower (at the top). This could be used in case of a launcher malfunction to eject the command module from the launcher during the first few minutes of flight. This tower would be jettisoned, unused, once the initial launch phase had taken place without incident.

The early versions of the command module (below) were equipped with aerodynamic surfaces to guide the module during reentry into the Earth's atmosphere. The final module (lower right) did not have these (NASA).

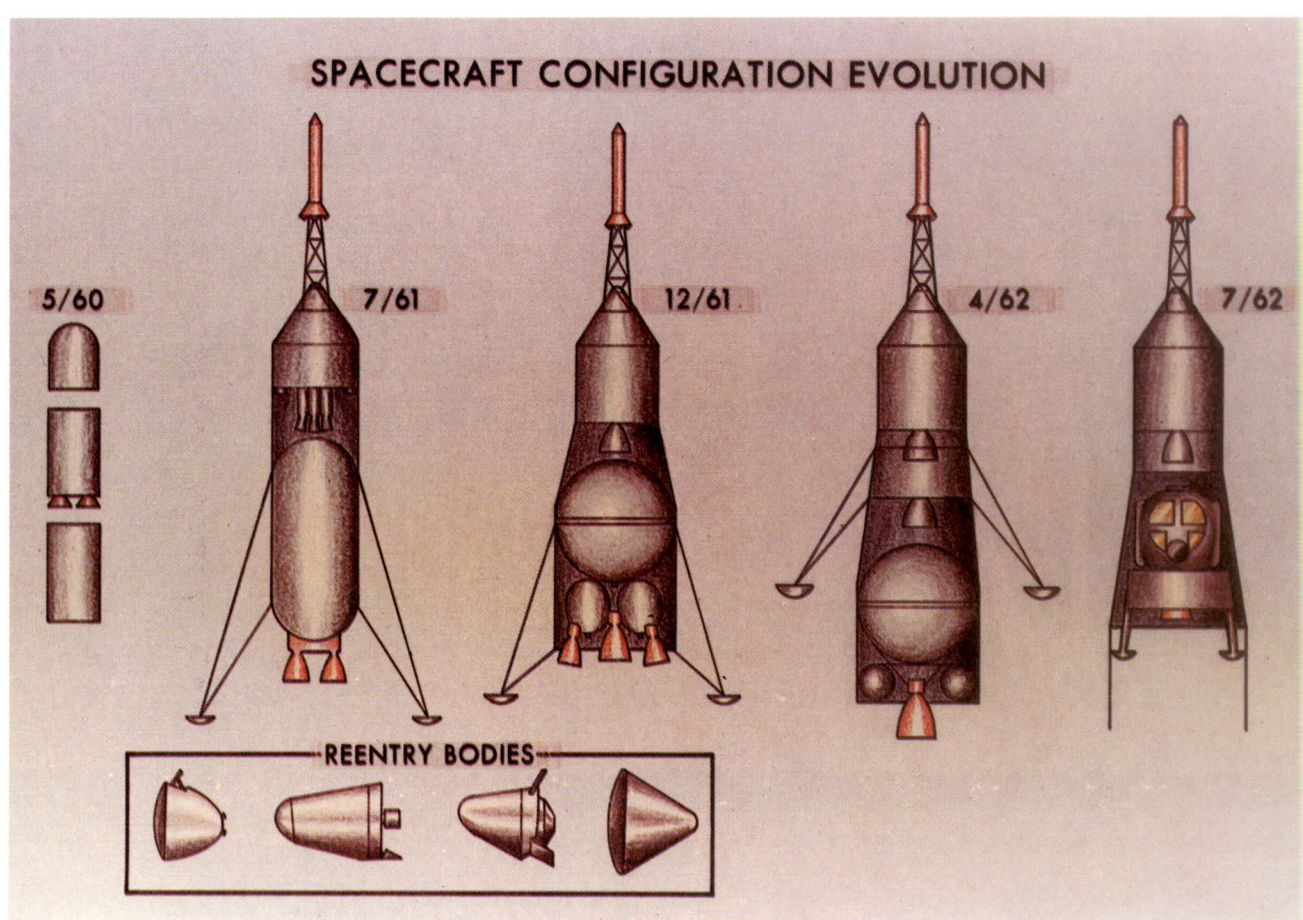

SPACECRAFT CONFIGURATION EVOLUTION

5/60   7/61   12/61   4/62   7/62

REENTRY BODIES

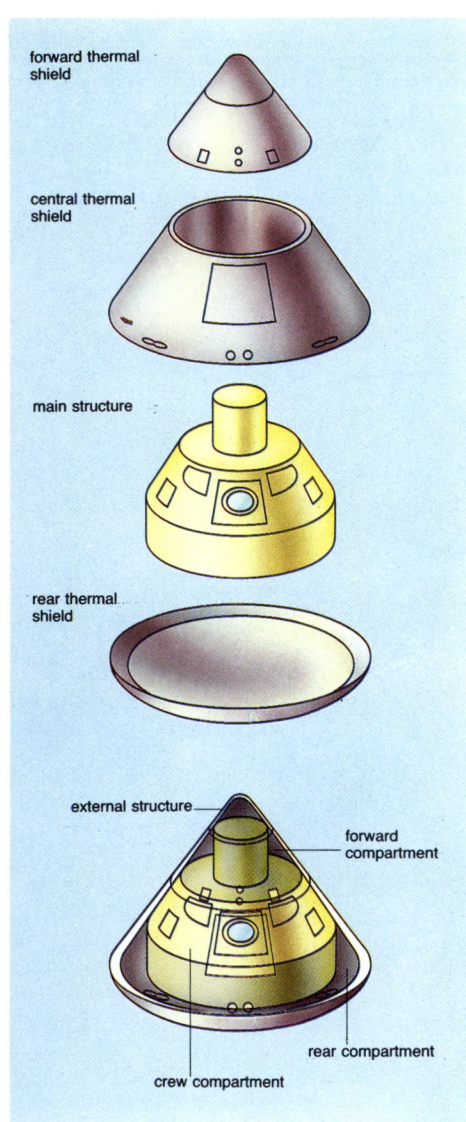

forward thermal shield

central thermal shield

main structure

rear thermal shield

external structure

forward compartment

rear compartment

crew compartment

The structure of the command module (left). The command module was constructed so that its different compartments were surrounded by three thermal shields protecting the interior from heat generated during reentry into the Earth's atmosphere and from radiation encountered in space (NASA).

The Command and Service Module (CSM). The Command Module (CM), seen on the right, was supplied with oxygen, water (a by product of the fuel cells which provided power), coolant, fuel, and electricity by the Service Module (SM). The SM had one main engine, of 97 kilonewtons thrust, to perform trajectory corrections and carry out orbital manoeuvres near the Moon. Sixteen small thrusters, grouped together in fours and each producing a thrust of 445 newtons (two groups are visible in the photograph), were used during the flight to the Moon to control the vehicle's attitude. Before reentry into the Earth's atmosphere, the SM was jettisoned; the CM finished the return journey using its own attitude control systems, fuel and oxygen reserves (NASA).

The Mercury and Gemini capsules, and Apollo Command Module. The one man Mercury capsule (top left) was 1·89 metres in diameter at the base and 2·92 metres high. For the two man Gemini capsule (centre left) these values were increased to 2·29 metres and 5·79 metres. For the three man Apollo Command Module the base diameter was 3·91 metres and the height of the truncated cone 3·05 metres (NASA).

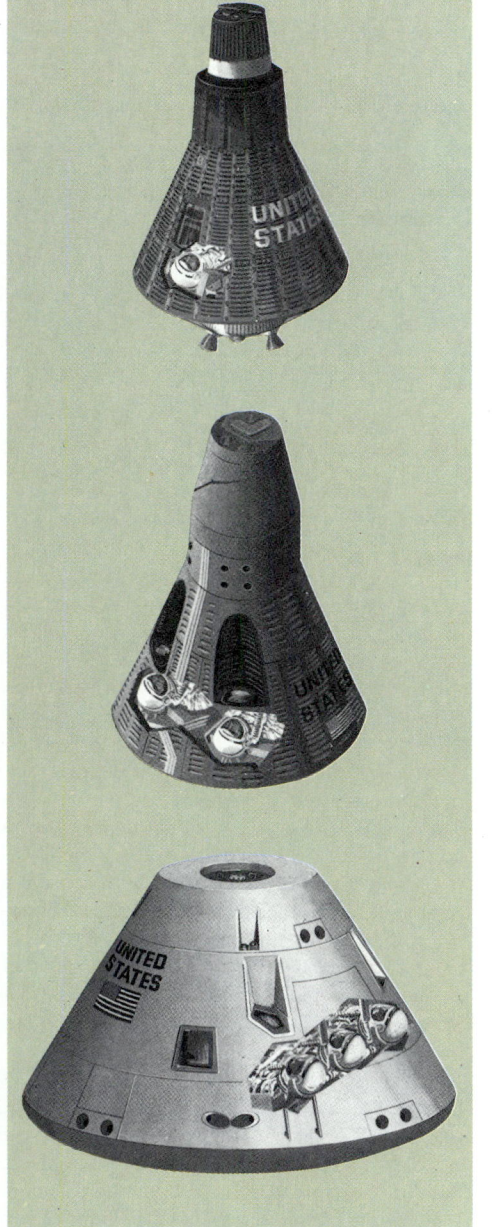

The lunar vehicle. On the right below, the Command Module (CM), the Service Module (SM) and the Lunar Module (LM) are drawn separately; on the left, they are shown in the configuration used for the journey to the Moon.

The two large windows planned for the LM in 1962 have been replaced by two small, triangular windows. The 1962 design had two ways of docking the CM. The square door was to be used by the astronauts during Extra Vehicular Activities on the Moon; a platform and ladder were added to facilitate descent to the Moon's surface (NASA).

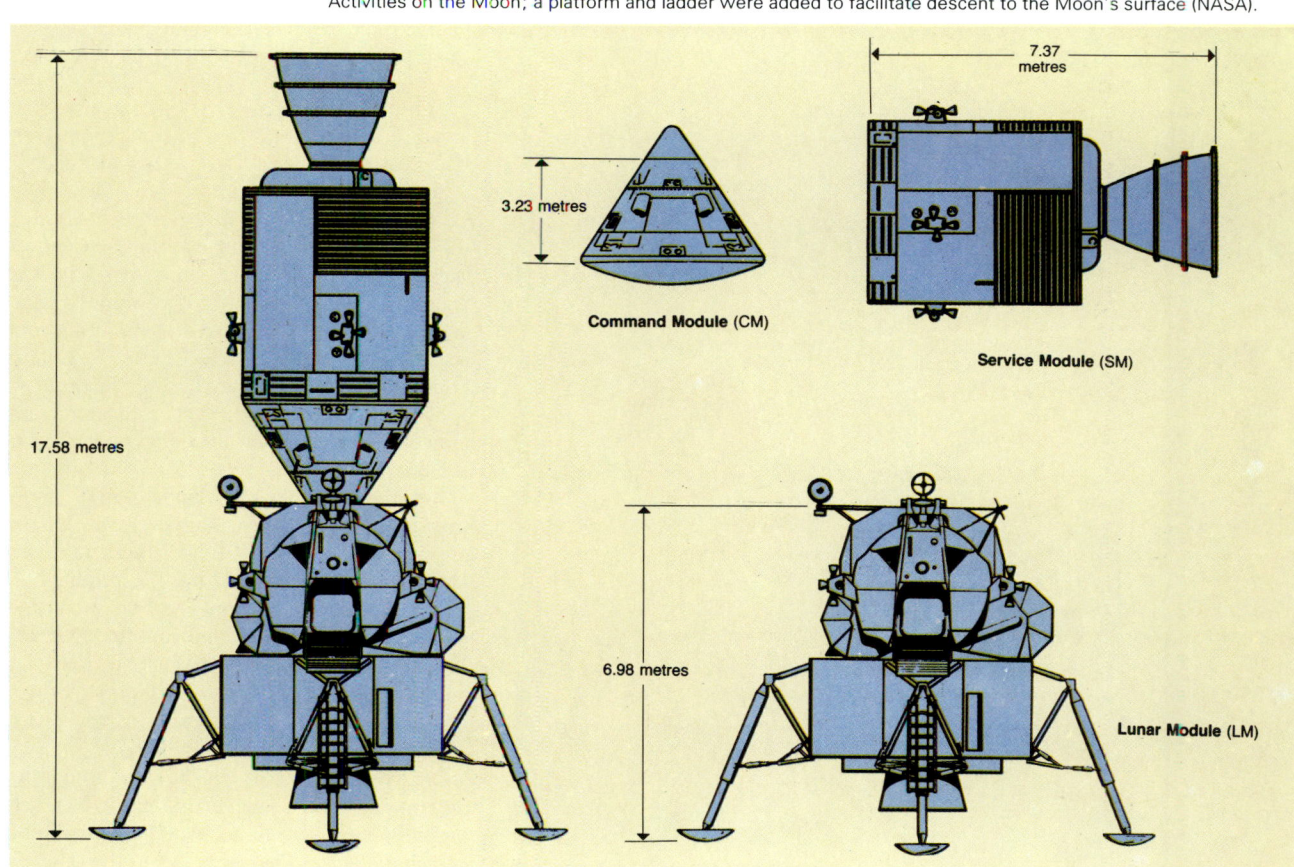

7.37 metres

3.23 metres

Command Module (CM)

Service Module (SM)

17.58 metres

6.98 metres

Lunar Module (LM)

The command console in the Lunar Module. In 1964, engineers concluded that the astronauts would survive the shock of landing on the Moon better if they were horizontal; previous seating arrangements were changed accordingly. The mission commander was on the left, the Lunar Module pilot on the right (NASA).

The Lunar Module with its landing legs folded. The photograph below shows the Snoopy Lunar Module (LM) used on the Apollo 10 mission in 1969. So that the LM would fit inside the adaptor to the Saturn S IVB stage, the legs were folded inwards. The total mass was kept low by covering most of the LM with thin layers of metallised plastic to protect it from large temperature differences (NASA).

The Lunar Module. The diagram below left shows the configuration of the Lunar Module (LM) in the adaptor of the Saturn S IVB stage. In the drawing on the right, the circular docking section of the Command Module (CM) to the Lunar Module is visible on top of the LM. The small rectangle visible above the triangular window is the rendezvous window. Assisted by radar information, the commander of the CM and the pilot of the LM could observe the CM visually in order to make a perfect rendezvous and docking. Twelve of the sixteen attitude control thrusters are visible, in groups of four, on the reentry stage. Each of these delivered a thrust of 445 newtons. The reentry stage was powered by a single rocket engine producing a constant thrust of 15·7 kilonewtons. The thrust of the descent engine could be varied between 5 and 47 kilonewtons (NASA).

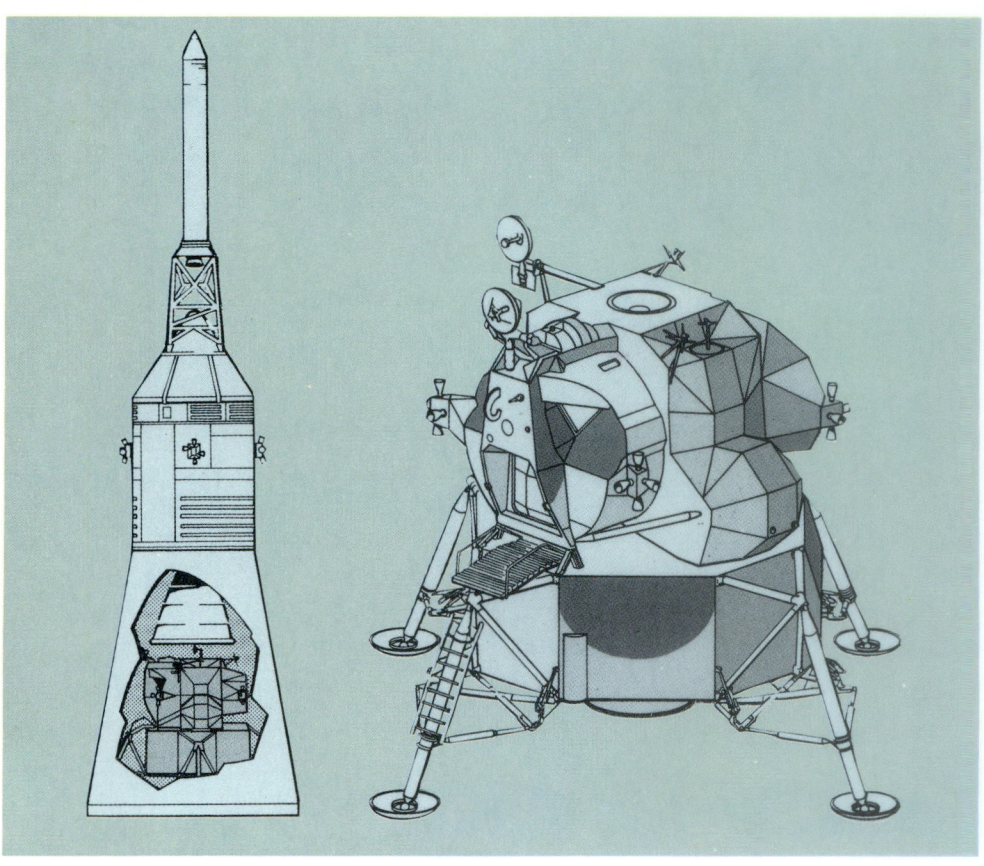

1961. Gemini managers soon proposed adding a rendezvous in lunar orbit, but the Administrator of NASA, James E. Webb, ruled that Gemini should not compete directly with Apollo.

On 11 July 1962 NASA announced that a rendezvous in orbit about the Moon would be the way forward. Whilst awaiting this decision, Webb had directed that contracts should be placed with industry for those vehicles which were least likely to alter in the event of a change of plan. The Apollo command ship fell in this category. The Manned Spacecraft Center, in Houston, Texas, chose a modified Mercury design with a base diameter of 3·9 metres, as against 1·9 metres for Mercury. Since Apollo had to attain 40 000 kilometres per hour to escape from the Earth's gravitational pull, the spacecraft was to be provided with a heat shield to protect it against frictional heat produced when moving through the atmosphere, as well as a radiation shield. This design was presented to industrial bidders in July 1961, and a contract was awarded the following November to North American Aviation, in Downey, California.

Several subsystem contracts for the Apollo Command Module were also agreed. One of the subsystems, for guidance and navigation, was of prime importance since very little was known about navigating to the Moon; in fact more study had been given to landing a probe on Mars. In the event, the Charles S. Draper Laboratory at the Massachusetts Institute of Technology built a prototype subsystem, and the contract for its production was awarded to AC Spark Plug.

Attempts to develop the launch vehicle under contract met with delays. However, the two primary rocket engines, the F1 and J2, were already being developed; the F1, producing a thrust of 6·7 meganewtons, had been contracted to Rocketdyne of California in 1959. The J2, developing a thrust of 890 kilonewtons, was an unconventional engine using liquid hydrogen fuel, for which a year later Rocketdyne also won the contract.

In November 1961, a NASA committee determined that, whatever the mode of reaching the Moon were to be, Apollo needed a big launch vehicle. Thus was born the massive

Saturn V launcher consisting of five F1 engines in the first stage, five J2 engines in the second stage, and one J2 engine in the third. By January 1962, this configuration had been formally adopted. The Boeing Aircraft Company of Seattle, Washington, won the first stage contract, North American Aviation the second stage, and Douglas Aircraft of California the third stage. NASA retained the Saturn I programme to prove the cluster concept and to flight test the spacecraft; an improved version, the Saturn IB, was to be employed in Earth orbital operations.

Having drafted detailed specifications for the Lunar Module, NASA awarded the construction contract to Grumman Aircraft, New York, on 7 November 1962. It was, of course, a very different task for designers to plan a craft whose operations were to be beyond the Earth's atmosphere. Visibility was important and the pilots had to be close to the two rather small triangular windows to afford a wide view. There were to be two hatches, the front hatch, with a porch, being used for access to and from the surface of the Moon. The top hatch was to be used for docking with the Command Module.

Since the Lunar Module had to land on and take off from the Moon, it was designed as a two stage vehicle, the descent stage serving as the 'launch pad' for the ascent stage. This decision was easily made in principle; the practical difficulty lay in producing a rocket engine of variable thrust for the descent. Both Rocketdyne and Space Technology Laboratories (STL) worked on an engine that operated at a maximum of 47 kilonewtons thrust and a minimum of 5 kilonewtons. Rocketdyne injected an inert gas into the fuel flow to achieve a reduction in thrust, while STL employed pressure fed control valves to regulate the flow of propellant in much the same way as the head of a shower regulates water flow. NASA ultimately chose the STL descent engine for the production vehicle.

NASA itself began in 1958 with a staff of 8000. By the time Apollo was approved in 1961, that figure had doubled, and by 1967, at the peak of the test and qualification phase of the Apollo programme, it had doubled again. Increases of personnel in the space industry as a whole also reflected the NASA trend; from 36000 in 1960, the total number of people employed had risen to 377000 in 1965.

Amongst the most 'visible' NASA staff were the astronauts. The seven men chosen in April 1959 were called the Mercury astronauts; nine more were added in September 1962, and a further 14 in October 1963. From this 30 man corps, a total of 16 flew in Gemini and four trained for a flight. This provided the Apollo programme with a number of crewmembers with experience of spaceflight; the remaining crew came from six scientist astronauts selected in June 1965, and 19 pilots picked in April 1966.

It was also apparent that the Apollo programme required a field centre to handle spacecraft design, testing and checkout, and to provide astronaut training. The facilities needed included a vacuum chamber to test both spacecraft and crew in a simulated space environment, a centrifuge to put a three man Apollo crew through the accelerations experienced during a rocket launch, and buildings in which to house spaceflight simulators. These requirements prompted NASA to establish the Manned Spacecraft Center in Houston, Texas; a mission control center was later added. Although flight control for the Mercury programme was at the Florida launch site, NASA reasoned that the prime requirement was for good communications, making it best to place mission control, spacecraft engineers and backup astronauts all in the same place. To allay fears that astronauts might return organisms which could cause disease (pathogens) from the lunar surface, a lunar receiving laboratory with quarantine facilities for crew and lunar samples was also constructed at Houston.

The NASA Kennedy Space Center was allocated the task of assembly, checkout and launch of the Saturn Apollo vehicles. A Vehicle Assembly Building (VAB) was constructed to house the Saturn V launcher and the Apollo spacecraft mounted on top of it. A crawler vehicle transported the 110 metre tall Apollo stack vertically from the VAB to the launch complex.

By 1965, all the facilities required for the Apollo programme were therefore in place and, by 1967, their value was proven.

Missions to the Moon

Believing that the Moon's surface was a sea of dust, some scientists predicted that any lunar lander would sink. It was not until 1966, when Surveyor 1 demonstrated that the surface could support the 13·6 tonne Lunar Module, that this theory was proved wrong.

From 1963, assessments were made of the pilot activities and vehicle operations necessary to land two astronauts and their scientific equipment on the near Earth side of the Moon. By 1966, the mission had come to be seen as composed of nine phases or segments. These were launch, Earth parking orbit, injection towards the Moon (over Hawaii), lunar orbit, Lunar Module descent, lunar surface stay, Lunar Module ascent, lunar orbit rendezvous and return to Earth for a landing in the Pacific Ocean. Fuel capacity and safety considerations initially limited the lunar landings to the maria a few degrees of latitude on either side of the lunar equator, but vehicle improvements later afforded landings outside that zone.

Without the rapid development of both computer and communication technology, Apollo would have been impossible. Mission control in Houston maintained, through its world wide tracking network, essentially continuous voice contact with the astronauts, as well as telemetry contact to assess the behaviour of the spacecraft's systems. To assure good communications throughout the astronaut's stay on the lunar surface, three 64 metre diameter antennae were spaced equidistantly around the Earth, at Goldstone in California, at Madrid in

Assembling the lunar payload. In this photograph the Command Module, Service Module and the adaptor which contained the Lunar Module are being assembled on the Instrument Unit. Fitted above the Saturn S IVB stage, this is the electronic brain of the launcher; it controlled all three of Saturn V's engines (NASA).

Spain, and at Canberra in Australia. There were therefore only a few periods when communications were lost as the spacecraft went behind the Moon.

Scientific interest in the Apollo programme came relatively late. Interested technologists were swamped with engineering problems, and scientists were generally content to fly experiments on unmanned satellites. Thus although NASA established a Manned Space Flight Experiments Board in 1963, it was only in 1965 that a group of scientists made proposals for what astronauts should actually do on the Moon. Uppermost in their minds was the aim of bringing back lunar soil and rock samples; they also suggested that an Apollo lunar surface experiments package (ALSEP) be put on the surface to measure the Moon's topographical and geophysical characteristics, and that a roving vehicle to range far from the landing site be provided. In March 1966, NASA contracted with Bendix, in Michigan, to develop four ALSEPs for the early Apollo lunar landing missions. It was, however, 1968 before a lunar rover, built by Boeing Aircraft, could be added to the programme.

Spacecraft designers chose a shirt sleeve environment for much of the mission, as they believed pilots wearing pressure suits could not operate systems so effectively. Spacesuits were worn during critical phases, such as the launch, with hoses hooked to the on board supplies of oxygen, water and coolants in the Command and Lunar Modules. When venturing onto the lunar surface, the astronauts were to attach a 'back pack', or an 'Extravehicular Mobility Unit' (EMU), with the same supplies for life support plus radio equipment to talk to each other and to mission control in Houston. If more than one Moon walk were planned, the

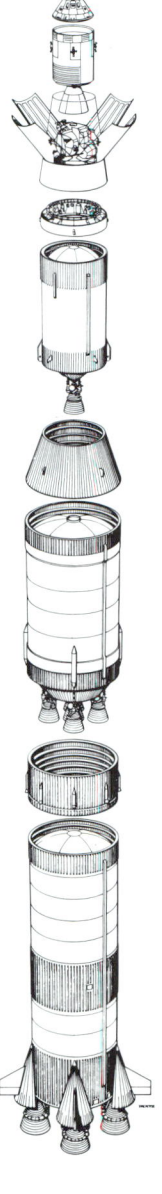

Launchers developed for the Apollo programme. The solid fuel launcher called Little Joe II (below left) produced a thrust of about 1·5 meganewtons. It could propel the Command Module and its safety tower to a height of some tens of kilometres. Tested at the White Sands Missile Range, it was used to check that the rocket on the safety tower (which produced a thrust of 650 kilonewtons) was capable of ejecting the Command Module from the launcher in case of an accident on the launch pad or during the initial flight phase.

The two stage Saturn I launcher had eight H1 engines fuelled by liquid oxygen and paraffin oil (kerosene), which produced a total thrust of 6·7 meganewtons. The second S IV stage had six RL10 engines which operated on liquid hydrogen and liquid oxygen and delivered a thrust of 400 kilonewtons. The Saturn I was used to test the arrangement of groups of rocket engines and also the separation and ignition of the upper stage in flight.

The Saturn IB rocket was fitted with an improved version of the H1 engines which increased the thrust of the first stage to 7·1 meganewtons. The second S IVB stage was quite different from the S IV stage because it was propelled by a single J2 engine fuelled by liquid hydrogen and oxygen and producing a thrust of 890 kilonewtons. This launcher was used to test the CM on flights in Earth orbit.

The Saturn V was the launcher used on the Apollo Moon missions. Its first S IC stage had five F1 engines delivering a total thrust of 33 meganewtons. The S II and S IVB used J2 engines, there being five on the S II and one on the S IVB stage. The drawing on the right shows the different elements of the Saturn V rocket and lunar vehicle. In its launch configuration, the launcher weighed more than 2700 tonnes (Deutsches Museum, Munich).

Figure labels (centre diagram, left to right):

Little Joe II — 27.13 metres — Command and Service Modules, SI stage

Saturn I — 57.91 metres — Command and Service Modules, Instrument Unit, S IV stage, SI stage

Saturn IB — 68.27 metres — Command and Service Modules, Instrument Unit, S IVB stage, S IB stage

Saturn V — 110.64 metres — Command and Service Modules, Instrument Unit, S IVB stage, S II stage, S IC stage

Scale markings: 100 m, 75, 50, 25, 0

Assembling the first stage of the Saturn V rocket. The first stages of the Saturn IB and Saturn V rockets were assembled in a factory at Michoud, to the east of New Orleans. This photograph shows the S IC stage of the Saturn V, with a diameter of 10 metres and a length of 42 metres. Assembly was carried out in a building whose roof, made all in one piece, covered an area of 10 hectares. This roof had a very high span under which the rocket stage could be erected. After assembly, the S IC stage was taken to a quay where it was put on a barge. This took it up the Pearl River to the Mississippi Test Facility where it underwent firing tests (NASA).

The F1 engine. The photograph on the left shows the F1 rocket engine being subjected to tests at Edwards Air Force Base in California. The picture below gives some impression of how enormous it was. During the launch, the five F1 engines of Saturn V's first stage consumed 15 tonnes of fuel per second (Rockwell International-Rocketdyne Division).

The packhorse of the Apollo missions. A modified Boeing B377 Stratocruiser christened Super Guppy, remarkable for its cavernous double lobed fuselage, was used to transport many of the huge components required for the Apollo programme. Here it is seen being loaded with a Saturn V payload housing to be transported to the Kennedy Space Center (NASA).

The crawler. This was a platform moving on tracks like a tank which was used to transport the Saturn Apollo vehicles and their umbilical launch tower from the Vehicle Assembly Building at the Kennedy Space Center to one of the two launch sites at complex 39. Situated on Merritt Island, which lies next to Cape Canaveral, the launch sites were 5·6 kilometres away. The crawler has been likened to a steel sandwich with First World War tanks at each corner. It had a mass of 2950 tonnes and could carry a load of up to 5900 tonnes. It was driven by 16 electric motors which were fed by generators driven by two 2750 horse power diesel engines. The motors drove four bogies with two tracks each; each track then consisted of 57 rollers, each weighing 900kg (NASA).

The final stages of assembly. The various parts of the Saturn V rocket and the Apollo spacecraft are assembled in the Vehicle Assembly Building at the Kennedy Space Center. In this enormous building, 160 metres tall, 218 metres long and 158 metres wide, four complete vehicles can be assembled at the same time in order to maintain a tight launch schedule. This photograph shows the vehicle used for the Apollo 6 mission, which took place in April 1968 (NASA).

The arrival of an S II stage at the Kennedy Space Center (left). The S IC and S II stages travelled by sea, as shown on the left, from the Mississippi Test Facility up the Gulf of Mexico and along the coast of Florida to the Kennedy Space Center. This S II rocket stage for the Apollo 14 mission has just arrived at the quay near the Vehicle Assembly Building (NASA).

The journey to the launch site. At the Kennedy Space Center the crawler moves the lunar vehicles out of the Vehicle Assembly Building and travels along a special road, at a speed of only 1·6 kilometres per hour, to the launch site. In order to support masses of more than 9200 tonnes on this road, millions of cubic metres of sand and mud were excavated and replaced by fine gravel and compact aggregates.

The mobile launch platform can be seen in the photograph on the right, with the umbilical launch tower and an Apollo Saturn V rocket. The platform transports the Saturn V rocket in the vertical position from the Vehicle Assembly Building (on the left of the photograph) to the launch site. The platform carries computers linked to the launch control centre, and also has a hole of 196 square metres in its centre through which the launcher's exhaust flames escape.

The Apollo Saturn V rocket, standing 110 metres tall, is kept vertical by four arms attached to the launch tower. This also has nine arms at various levels to supply the vehicle with electricity, fuel and compressed air; these arms automatically withdraw between ignition and take-off.

The building with windows in the foreground is the launch control centre. Here personnel from NASA and other involved parties work on 400 consoles, taking decisions concerning all of Apollo's systems, recording data and, finally, giving the order to lift off (NASA).

The training programme. In this photograph, taken on 19 June 1969, Neil Armstrong is pictured at the command console of the Lunar Module simulator. He is training for his flight on the Apollo 11 mission. The simulator operators prepare various scenarios for the crews, including realistic noises, movements and conditions that they would expect to encounter during the spaceflight. There is also a simulator for the Command Module. Each crew spent 140 hours in the Lunar Module simulator and 180 hours in the Command Module simulator (NASA).

EMUs were to be recharged from Lunar Module supplies.

In 1962, contracts were given to International Latex for the spacesuit and to Hamilton Standard for the EMU, the latter having responsibility for managing the system as a whole. This arrangement did not, however, continue as the prototype proved unsatisfactory. The use of Gemini spacesuits was planned for the early Earth orbiting Apollo missions, but after NASA took over management of the Apollo spacesuit and EMU development in 1965, International Latex and Hamilton Standard were able successfully to produce the products needed.

The Apollo pilots faced a variety of difficult tasks. First, they had to fly two totally different space vehicles, each with systems – for example, for navigation and guidance – peculiar to its particular role. Unless the pilots could operate these systems effectively, they might crash attempting a landing on the Moon or even 'bounce' from the top of the atmosphere into endless space on return to Earth. Second, if a subsystem malfunctioned, the pilots had also to know which redundant system could be employed to save the mission. Besides crawling in and out of the vehicles, the astronauts spent hundreds of hours in spaceflight simulators that afforded them the cues, views and problems entailed in a lunar mission, from launch right through to the eventual return to Earth. To simulate a touchdown on the Moon's surface, a Lunar Landing Training Vehicle (LLTV), built by Bell Aerospace and dubbed the 'flying bedstead', was employed.

The astronauts studied celestial and lunar navigation, and went through survival training in the Panamanian jungle, geological field trips to areas that simulated the lunar surface, and water exercises that simulated the process of pilot recovery. A one sixth gravity ($0.167\,g$) trainer allowed them to get the feel of walking on the lunar surface wearing the suit and backpack. It also helped them to judge their ability to pull the ALSEP or the lunar rover from the equipment bays in the Lunar Module's descent stage.

Before attempting to fly a crew, 19 launch tests were made between October 1961 and July 1966. Ten involved the Saturn I rocket, four to prove that its engines could be clustered in a single stage, one to demonstrate the separation and ignition of an upper stage, and the other five to launch models of the Apollo Command Module. Six tests were made to ensure that the rocket motor of the launch escape system could pull the spacecraft away from the launch vehicle either on the pad or during launch. Since the first crew were to be boosted by a Saturn IB rocket, three of these were launched between February and July 1966; after the third mission, Apollo Saturn (AS) 203, the vehicles were rated as being capable of supporting a crew.

On 27 January 1967, Virgil I. Grissom, Edward H. White, and Roger B. Chaffee practised launch simulation for a 14 day Earth orbiting mission, AS 204. They had spent a trouble plagued training year, as the Command Module flight simulator was almost constantly out of order. They had seen their spacecraft delivery date delayed, chiefly because the environmental control system had to be replaced. And there were problems even in January, as Grissom complained that the environment smelled like sour milk. An emergency egress test was scheduled, but the pilots regretably did not reach that point; a sudden flash fire in the cabin led to their tragic deaths.

Faulty wiring and poor workmanship were suspected as being the cause, but the source of ignition was never found. NASA ordered the contractor to work on an improved spacecraft, and a mechanically operated hatch rapidly replaced bolted inner and outer hatches. Another significant change was the air which the astronauts breathed on the launch pad: a mix of 60% oxygen and 40% nitrogen at normal pressure were substituted for the pure oxygen atmosphere that was previously used.

The Apollo programme had suffered a terrible tragedy, but there were positive portents. All component parts, except the Lunar Module (LM), had come together at the Cape, and had been assembled in the Vehicle Assembly Building (VAB). The crawler had hauled the spacecraft and launch vehicle stack the five and a half kilometres to Launch Complex 39 for a final checkout before the mission.

Apollo 4 was successfully launched on 9 November 1967. The Saturn V first stage produced a thrust of 33 meganewtons, and the second and third stages ignited in sequence to put the spacecraft into orbit about the Earth.

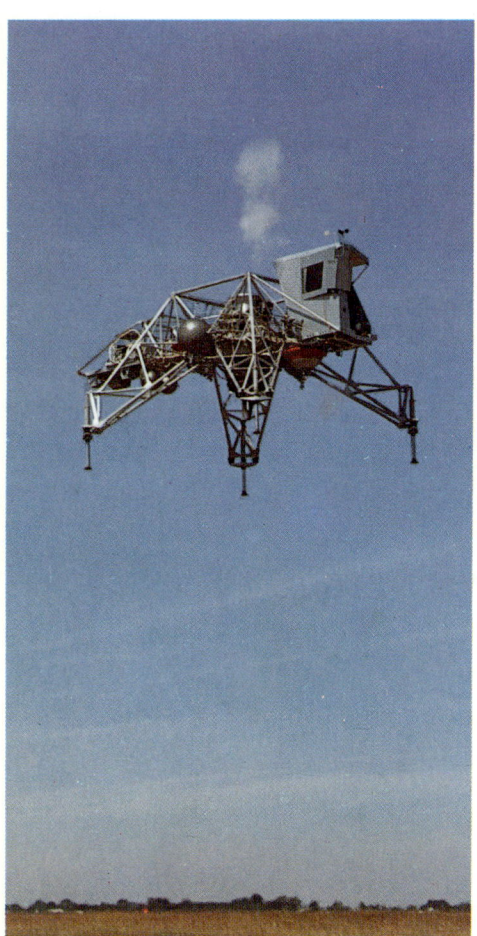

The training vehicle for the Moon landing. This unusual piece of machinery, nicknamed the 'flying bedstead', is here photographed at the US Air Force Base at Ellington, Texas, several kilometres to the north of the Manned Spacecraft Center at Houston. It gave the Lunar Module crews an experience of the last 150 metres of free flight before they made contact with the Moon.

In 1968, the training vehicle broke down twice; Neil Armstrong was forced to evacuate the vehicle and land by parachute on one of these occasions. The vehicle was then nearly scrapped. However, the astronauts insisted on using it and Armstrong was able to obtain sufficient training before the launch of Apollo 11 in July 1969 (NASA).

During the mission, the S IVB rocket was fired again to propel the spacecraft to an altitude of 1680 kilometres where it separated. The Service Module (SM) propulsion system, with a thrust of 97 kilonewtons, then accelerated the spacecraft to a speed of 39 600 kilometres per hour to simulate a return from the Moon. The heat shield and parachute recovery systems operated perfectly.

Two months later, the LM was ready for a critical test in the Apollo 5 mission. Launched by a Saturn IB rocket into Earth orbit on 22 January 1968, the variable thrust descent engine operated successfully. One test measured the effects of firing the ascent engine through the descent stage 'launch pad', showing the concept to be feasible; the engine started and stopped as programmed. Since the LM had no heat shield, the craft burned up on reentry into the Earth's atmosphere.

Launched on 4 April 1968, Apollo 6 was intended to be a dress rehearsal. It proved in the event notably unsuccessful; because of interrupted fuel flow to the F1 engines, the Saturn V first stage 'bounced' for 30 seconds, two of the five J2 engines in the second stage failed to ignite, and the S IVB third stage had to fire longer than planned to put the spacecraft into orbit. When flight controllers attempted to restart the third stage to simulate injection into a lunar orbit, it refused to respond.

The crew of Walter M. Schirra, Donn F. Eisele and R. Walter Cunningham trained for over a year for the next manned mission, Apollo 7. Launched on 11 October 1968 by a Saturn IB rocket, this was to be the maiden cruise of the improved spacecraft, its 11 day flight longer than that planned for the early lunar landing missions. The crew proved on this occasion that the SM engine could propel the spacecraft from the S IVB stage, turn over, and simulate rendezvous and docking with an LM. The engine fired accurately eight times, boding well for its use, not only to go in and out of lunar orbit but also to make course corrections on the journey to and from the Moon. The fuel cell electrical system, foodstuffs and the arrangements for periods of work, rest and sleep were also tested.

George Low of NASA subsequently suggested that a crew should be sent on a circumlunar mission in December 1968. This was a daring flight. On 21 December 1968, after a

Training for recovery after splashdown. In the pictures on the left taken on 20 November 1968, the crew of the Apollo 9 mission (James A. McDivitt, Russell L. Schweickart and David R. Scott) are seen practising for their recovery after splashdown. In the upper picture, McDivitt is preparing to join Schweickart and Scott on board the life raft.

Just after the splashdown the reentry module had a tendency to turn over, tipping the pilots upside down and submerging the exit hatch; this happened in fact to the crew of the Apollo 7 mission (Walter M. Schirra, Donn F. Eisele and R. Walter Cunningham). The craft was righted again by inflating three air bags in the Instrument Unit of the reentry module, along with the landing parachutes.

In the lower picture, James A. McDivitt, the commander of the Apollo 9 mission, is being hoisted from a life raft to a helicopter during a training exercise. During the Gemini programme, medical personnel believed that astronauts who had spent a long time in space would not be able to hang on to the recovery ring, shaped like a horse's collar, to be winched aboard the helicopter. In the Apollo programme, therefore, the astronauts simply sat on the device to be winched up (NASA).

The Mission Control Center. This photograph shows one of the two control rooms in the Mission Control Center of the Manned Spacecraft Center at Houston. After the Saturn V rocket was launched, flight control passed from the launch centre in Florida to the Mission Control Center.

The men in the foreground are sitting at the consoles from which the doctor in charge of the flight monitors the health of the crew and directs all the medical activities. The people next to them are sitting in front of the consoles for communications between the crew and the ground. On the other side of the aisle are consoles belonging to the engineers in charge of the different spacecraft systems.

Whilst activity in the operational control room is highly visible, it represents only part of the activities during a mission. The operational control room is surrounded by technical support rooms, one of which is visible in the photograph, whose personnel monitor all the flight activities. If a system on the spacecraft stops working, these personnel use an identical piece of equipment to see if they can resolve the problem. They then transmit their results to the mission director (NASA).

Training for Extra Vehicular Activity. The photograph on the left, taken on 18 June 1969, shows Aldrin and Armstrong, except for the protective screen on the visor in full spacesuits, training for their Moon walk.

The Apollo spacesuit had three layers: a double layer of material on the inside for comfort, a double wall of nylon covered in rubber, and an exterior layer of nylon to help keep the spacesuit's shape. Supple joints were planned for the shoulders, elbows, thighs, knees and ankles. Channels in the internal surface allowed oxygen to pass to the helmet, for respiration, for demisting the visor and for keeping the astronaut cool.

The EMU provided the astronauts with eight hours of oxygen. It contained a cartridge of lithium hydroxide which filtered the air before putting it back into circulation. It also carried the communications and telemetry circuits; an antenna is visible at the top.

For Extra Vehicular Activity, a 17 layer protective spacesuit was donned. It consisted of two layers of nylon coated with Neoprene, and seven layers of aluminised plastic film resistant to high temperatures separated by six layers of insulating 'Beta' material. Beta fibres are non-flammable, but also fragile and irritating to the skin. Coating each fibre with Teflon and providing the astronauts with close-fitting pants they could wear beneath made the suits altogether more comfortable. (NASA).

The launch of a Saturn V rocket. In this photograph can be seen the blazing trail of the Saturn V rocket for the Apollo 8 mission as it blasted off into space from Launch Complex 39 at the Kennedy Space Center. During this, the third flight of a Saturn V rocket, and the first manned flight to escape from the Earth's gravitation, Frank Borman, James A. Lovell and William A. Anders were put into a lunar orbit. They became the first men to visit another celestial body. Less than three minutes after liftoff, the first S IC stage stopped burning and fell back to Earth. Two seconds later, the S II stage was ignited and burnt for more than six minutes, during which time the safety tower was jettisoned. The S IVB stage was then ignited and burnt for more than two minutes to put the spacecraft into a terrestrial orbit with the third stage still in place. After one and a half orbits of the Earth and after all the systems had been checked, the S IVB directed the spacecraft on a trajectory towards the Moon. The spent rocket was then itself jettisoned (NASA).

Extra Vehicular Activity. Tests were made on the Lunar Module (LM) in Earth orbit during Apollo 9's mission in March 1969. Russell L. Schweickart, wearing the Apollo spacesuit designed for walking on the Moon, left the spacecraft and stood on the platform of the LM. His spacesuit included a gold optical filter on the visor and, in the picture below, an image of the LM is reflected in this. James A. McDivitt, who was in the LM throughout, anchored Schweickart with a nylon cord to prevent him floating off into deep space and being lost. (NASA).

The Lunar Module as it approached the Moon. Michael Collins, who remained in the Command Module (Columbia) of Apollo 11, visually inspected and photographed the Lunar Module, named Eagle, containing Neil Armstrong and Edwin Aldrin. He did this to ensure that the impact absorber was correctly deployed and that all was ready for the descent to the Moon (NASA).

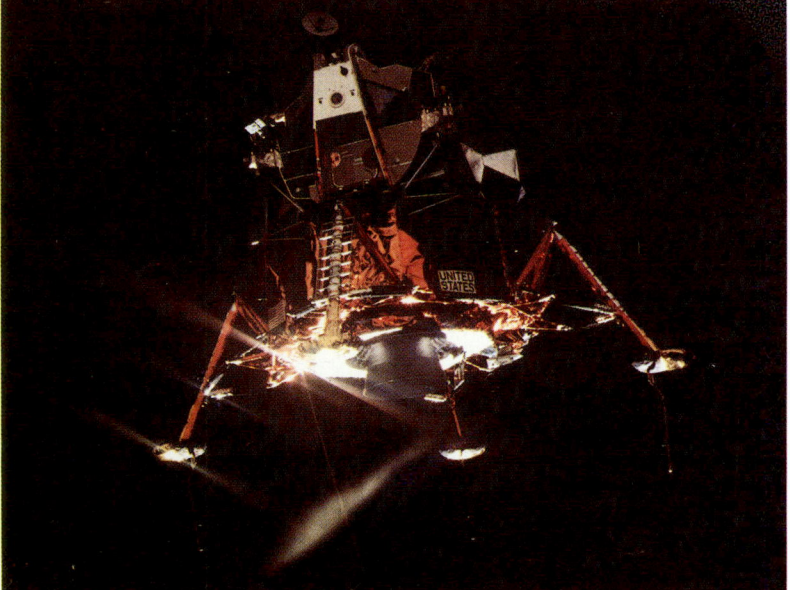

perfect launch and one and a half orbits of the Earth in which to check systems, Frank Borman, James A. Lovell and William A. Anders heard the words: 'you are go for TLI (trans lunar injection)'. The S IVB rocket then fired and accelerated to 10 800 kilometres per second. After separating, Borman found formation flying with the S IVB easy. On the afternoon of 23 December, Apollo 8 crossed into the region where the Moon's gravitational pull was greater than that of the Earth. Next day, the SM engine fired to slow the craft and put it into an orbit about 110 kilometres above the lunar surface. On Christmas Day, after 10 orbits of the Moon, the engine fired again for the return to Earth. Landing in the Pacific Ocean was on 27 December. It was on this flight, through the medium of television, that millions of people in almost 100 countries saw the Moon's stark, lifeless and rugged surface, and heard the crew compare it so memorably with Earth's fragile, wispy, blue and white beauty.

As 1969 dawned, worries mounted about meeting the goal of a manned landing before the decade was out. Two critical Lunar Module test flights remained. Before attempting a lunar landing, NASA had to put the LM through its paces, first in Earth orbit and then in lunar orbit. So it was, on 3 March 1969, that James A. McDivitt, David R. Scott and Russell L. Schweickart in Apollo 9 pulled away from the S IVB rocket, rotated their spacecraft, and moved forwards and docked with the LM. They then extracted the lunar lander from its adaptor atop the S IVB rocket. The SM engine was fired, but the docked vehicles withstood the shock, and maintained their position.

For convenience of communications, the CM was named Gum Drop and the LM Spider. McDivitt and Schweickart crawled into Spider, opened the front hatch and Schweickart backed out onto the porch. Later, Spider's pilots flew 185 kilometres away from Scott in Gum Drop; they then released the descent stage and fired the ascent engine to rendezvous with Gum Drop once again. Within two hours, Spider and Gum Drop had docked successfully.

On 18 May 1969, Thomas P. Stafford, John W. Young, and Eugene A. Cernan travelled in Apollo 10, reaching the Moon on 21 May. Stafford and Cernan prepared Snoopy for a close visit to the surface and the next day undocked from Charlie Brown. The descent engine operated at from 10 to 40% of its maximum performance to lower the lander to within 15 kilometres of the Moon's surface; they noted smooth landing areas and reported that the lighting conditions presented no problems of visibility. Before discarding the descent stage, a switching error caused Snoopy to lurch wildly. Stafford, however, regained control and fired the ascent engine to rendezvous successfully with Charlie Brown.

Although Apollo 10 came close to the lunar surface, there were still many problems connected with landing a 13·6 tonne vehicle there. Some worried that the lander might topple. Others wondered what, if anything, bulkily suited men could do on the Moon that was worthwhile. And some considered that only one astronaut should get out of the lander. All this time a crew was training for the mission; and when a session on ALSEP deployment went badly, the long-standing plan to take a package of scientific instruments to the Moon came close to being cancelled.

Neil A. Armstrong, Michael Collins and Edwin E. Aldrin ultimately set out for the Moon in Apollo 11 on 16 July 1969. Four days later, Armstrong and Aldrin crawled into Eagle, leaving Collins in Columbia. Armstrong dodged a field of lunar boulders before setting Eagle down in the Sea of Tranquility. He stopped the engines, and positioned control switches ready for a rapid take-off, should that be necessary. Satisfied that all was well, the crew donned their backpacks. Armstrong backed through the hatch, stood on the porch and climbed down the ladder. Millions watched

on television as he took a first step 'for mankind' onto the lunar surface. He described the soil and rocks as he gathered samples. Aldrin soon joined him, and they drew a small ALSEP from the equipment bay. Aldrin set up a laser ranging retroreflector so that a laser beam fired from the Earth could measure the Earth–Moon distance extremely accurately. He then installed a passive seismometer to record moonquakes and meteor hits, and collected soil and rocks.

Both astronauts found that a loping gait was a pleasant, if ungainly, way of getting around in one sixth gravity conditions. After two and a half hours on the lunar surface, and with 22 kilograms of samples, they climbed into Eagle, rested and then took off on 21 July to rendezvous with Columbia. Arriving back at the Earth on 24 July, all three astronauts donned biological isolation garments; they were flown to Houston, and put into quarantine for 30 days.

After this triumphant success and following further discussions, NASA managers relaxed the schedule for the next mission to the Moon. They allowed for two walks of nearly four hours, ranging up to a kilometre from the landing site. The Ocean of Storms was picked for this, a site some 2000 kilometres West of Eagle's landing site, where an unmanned Surveyor III had touched down nearly three years earlier.

Charles Conrad, Richard F. Gordon and Alan L. Bean had a frightening moment in Apollo 12 when, on 14 November 1969, lightning struck during the first minute of their flight. After coasting to the Moon, Conrad and Bean, in Intrepid, left Yankee Clipper and landed only 163 metres from Surveyor. During their first walk, they gathered samples, set up an antenna for transmitting data to the Earth, and deployed an array of experiments, including a full ALSEP and a solar wind composition experiment. On the second walk, they continued gathering samples, photographed part of the Ocean of Storms and collected parts of Surveyor. With 34 kilograms of soil and rocks, Conrad and Bean soon joined Gordon in Yankee Clipper. Intrepid was then purposely crashed onto the Moon, producing reverberations recorded by the seismometer and transmitted to Earth.

Targeted for Fra Mauro, 320 kilometres East of the Apollo 12 landing site, Apollo 13, with James Lovell, Fred W. Haise and John L. Swigart aboard, headed for the Moon on 11 April 1970. Fifty-six hours after launch, an oxygen tank in the SM exploded, destroying not only the engine but also consumables for the CM, Odyssey. The spacecraft was left with only minimal supplies. Since the SM engine could not be fired, a contingency plan was drawn up and a flight trajectory planned to take the CM around the Moon and return it to Earth. The descent engine of the LM was fired to make the necessary course corrections.

The Apollo 13 emergency was serious, since more than three days were required for the return to Earth. The crew crawled into the LM Aquarius and carefully rationed its electrical and oxygen supplies to survive the ordeal. Later, they returned to the CM, turned on its power, and separated from Aquarius for Odyssey's reentry into Earth's atmosphere an hour later, landing on 17 April just 6·5 kilometres from the recovery ship.

Although the lunar rover was not available when Alan B. Shepard and Edgar D. Mitchell were with Antares on Fra Mauro during the Apollo 14 mission, from 31 January to 9 February 1971, they did have a 'rickshaw' for carrying tools and samples. On their first Moon walk, of about five hours, they deployed the second full ALSEP, and a number of new items. Explosive charges were planted in a line, and 13 of the 21 fired; another experiment involved a launcher that fired four grenades after Shepard and Mitchell had departed to join Stuart A. Roosa in Kitty Hawk. The second moon walk, almost

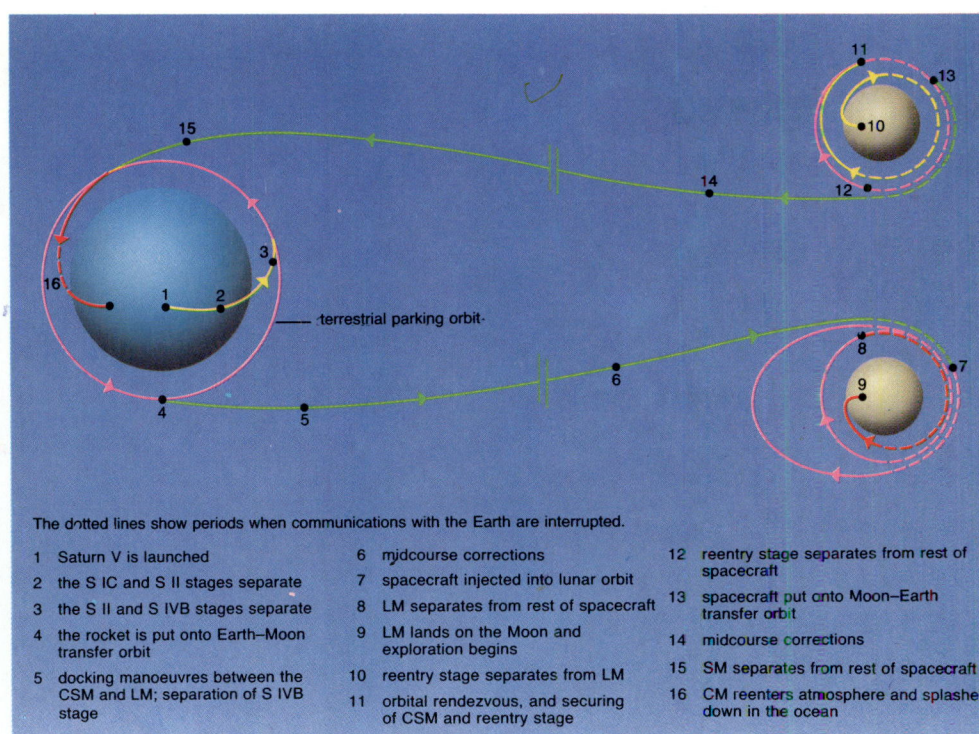

The dotted lines show periods when communications with the Earth are interrupted.

1 Saturn V is launched
2 the S IC and S II stages separate
3 the S II and S IVB stages separate
4 the rocket is put onto Earth–Moon transfer orbit
5 docking manoeuvres between the CSM and LM; separation of S IVB stage
6 midcourse corrections
7 spacecraft injected into lunar orbit
8 LM separates from rest of spacecraft
9 LM lands on the Moon and exploration begins
10 reentry stage separates from LM
11 orbital rendezvous, and securing of CSM and reentry stage
12 reentry stage separates from rest of spacecraft
13 spacecraft put onto Moon–Earth transfer orbit
14 midcourse corrections
15 SM separates from rest of spacecraft
16 CM reenters atmosphere and splashes down in the ocean

The flight profile of an Apollo mission.

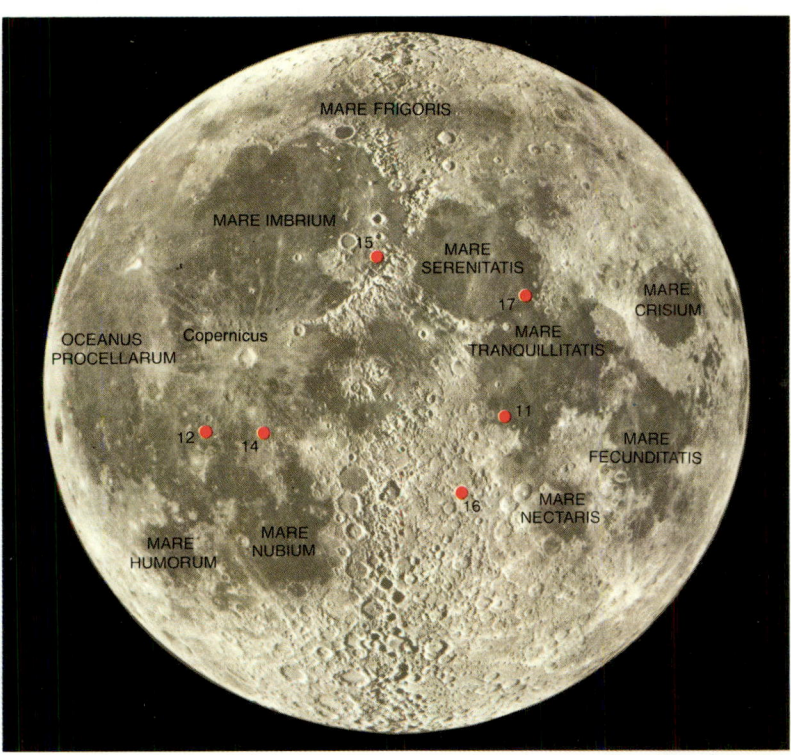

● landing sites for Apollo missions

The Apollo landing sites. For Apollo missions 7 to 13, the landing sites were all clustered around the Moon's equator because of the limited capacity of even the Saturn V rocket. After the F1 engines on the S IC stage had been improved, the rocket was able to carry more fuel This in turn enabled it to travel further North or South on the Moon, and to carry a vehicle for lunar exploration, the lunar rover, on Apollo missions 15, 16 and 17 (Lick Observatory).

as long, aimed for the rim of Cone Crater to obtain samples that had splashed up from the crater bottom when a meteoroid struck; these were believed to be older lunar material. This time, they pulled the cart, but found that landmarks were less distinguishable than on Earth so that they missed their target within the time allowed. During the two walks together, the astronauts nonetheless gathered 42 kilograms of material for scientists to examine.

Apollo 15, from 26 July to 7 August 1971, saw David Scott and James B. Irwin with Falcon at Hadley Plain, near the Apennine Mountains at 25 degrees latitude North, far outside the equatorial zone of earlier landings. They spent about 77 hours on the surface, nearly a quarter of this on walks and rides. On the first of three forays, they used a battery powered rover. Limited to a distance of 10 kilometres from Falcon in case they had to walk back, they travelled at 8 kilometres per hour up and down slopes of as much as 25 degrees. A television camera on the rover, operated either by the crew or by mission control in Houston, provided a visual record of their activities. Besides putting out experiments, Scott and Irwin also collected 77 kilograms of materials to be loaded into Endeavour when they rejoined Alfred M. Worden. Before leaving lunar orbit, the crew deployed a satellite.

Apollo 16, from 16 to 27 April 1972, aimed for the rocky, hilly Descartes region south west of the Sea of Tranquility. John Young and Charles M. Duke, who spent three days there, confirmed that there were many rocks close to Orion's landing spot. Commenting that the area was 30% rock covered, with 70% being small craters, they drove the rover and, on the second outing, climbed Survey Ridge and Stone Mountain; by the end of their third period on the rover, they had travelled 27 kilometres. While at South Ray Crater, they remarked that the sharp boulders strewn around the rim area resembled those at a crater in Nevada where they had trained. Later, Thomas K. Mattingly helped to transfer 97 kilograms of Moon material from Orion into Casper for the return to Earth.

Hardware problems caused a post midnight

launch of the Apollo 17 mission, which took place from 7 to 19 December 1972, but Eugene Cernan and Harrison H. Schmitt, a geologist and the only scientist to fly in the Apollo programme, nonetheless landed Challenger safely in the Taurus Littrow Valley, between the Seas of Serenity and Tranquility. On this, the final mission in the Apollo series, they stayed on the surface for 75 hours, gathered 116 kilograms of samples, and travelled 35 kilometres during three periods of walking and riding, a total exploration time of 22 hours. Schmitt became particularly excited when he discovered orange soil at Shorty Crater that might have resulted from comparatively recent vulcanism, 100 million years ago.

A camera on the parked lunar rover, operated by mission control in Houston, obtained television coverage of Challenger's take-off to rejoin Ronald E. Evans in the CM America. After firing the SM engine for the trans Earth injection manoeuvre, Evans crawled out of the CM and retrieved a camera that had been mapping the lunar crust while Cernan and Schmitt were on the moon.

Apollo's lunar missions had ended, but aspects of the Apollo programme now took on other forms as America's manned spaceflight activities refocused on Earth orbiting operations. The third stage of the Saturn V rocket was made habitable and fitted with equipment to support three men in a space laboratory called Skylab. Three different crews were launched by Saturn IB rockets and sent in Apollo CMs to Skylab during 1973 and 1974; and in 1975, a Saturn IB launched three men in an Apollo CM to rendezvous and dock with the two man crew of a Soyuz spacecraft for the Apollo–Soyuz Test Project.

The astonishing successes of the Apollo programme remain nonetheless imprinted for ever on our collective memory. As the historian Arthur Schlesinger has written: 'the twentieth century will be remembered, when all else is forgotten, as the century when man burst his terrestrial bonds'.

James M. Grimwood

Apollo manned missions

Mission and crew	Launch date and duration	Vehicles	Accomplishments
Apollo 7 Walter M. Schirra, Donn F. Eisele and R. Walter Cunningham	11 October 1968 260 hours 8 minutes 58 seconds	Saturn IB Command and Service Modules (CSM)	first manned test of spacecraft; first test of improved spacecraft; first use of Apollo suits; first live TV coverage from space
Apollo 8 Frank Borman, James A. Lovell and William A. Anders	21 December 1968 147 hours 42 seconds	Saturn V CSM	first manned flight to escape Earth's gravity; first manned flight to the Moon; first manned Saturn V launch
Apollo 9 James A. McDivitt, David R. Scott and Russell L. Schweickart	3 March 1969 241 hours 54 seconds	Saturn V CSM Gum Drop Lunar Module (LM) Spider	first lunar vehicle configuration flight; first Apollo ExtraVehicular Activity (EVA); first LM docking
Apollo 10 Thomas P. Stafford, John W. Young and Eugene A. Cernan	18 May 1969 192 hours 3 minutes 23 seconds	Saturn V CSM Charlie Brown LM Snoopy	separation and docking of LM and CSM in lunar orbit; low altitude visual and photographic assessment of candidate lunar landing sites
Apollo 11 Neil A. Armstrong, Michael Collins and Edwin E. Aldrin	16 July 1969 195 hours 18 minutes 35 seconds	Saturn V CSM Columbia LM Eagle	first manned lunar landing and lunar surface EVA; first acquisition of lunar soil samples for return to Earth
Apollo 12 Charles Conrad, Richard F. Gordon and Alan L. Bean	14 November 1969 244 hours 36 minutes 25 seconds	Saturn V CSM Yankee Clipper LM Intrepid	demonstrated precision landing; first deployment of major scientific experiments; first acquisition of sample from an earlier spacecraft (Surveyor 3)
Apollo 13 James A. Lovell, John L. Swigert and Fred W. Haise	11 April 1970 142 hours 54 minutes 41 seconds	Saturn V CSM Odyssey LM Aquarius	after an explosion in the Service Module, the LM was successfully used as a 'lifeboat' during return to Earth
Apollo 14 Alan B. Shepard, Stuart A. Roosa and Edgar D. Mitchell	31 January 1971 216 hours 1 minute 59 seconds	Saturn V CSM Kitty Hawk LM Antares	first manned landing in lunar highlands; extensive lunar surface EVA
Apollo 15 David R. Scott, Alfred M. Worden and James B. Irwin	26 July 1971 295 hours 11 minutes 53 seconds	Saturn V CSM Endeavour LM Falcon	first exploration of lunar mountain and rille area; first use of lunar rover; first launch of a subsatellite in lunar orbit
Apollo 16 John W. Young, Thomas K. Mattingly II and Charles M. Duke	16 April 1972 265 hours 51 minutes 5 seconds	Saturn V CSM Casper LM Orion	exploration of lunar highlands and Cayley formation; first use of the Moon as an astronomical laboratory
Apollo 17 Eugene A. Cernan, Ronald E. Evans and Harrison H. Schmitt	7 December 1972 301 hours 51 minutes 59 seconds	Saturn V CSM America LM Challenger	longest Apollo mission; longest lunar stay; longest total lunar EVA time; longest distance travelled in lunar rover during one EVA; greatest amount of lunar samples returned; longest time in lunar orbit

The first men on the Moon. Neil Armstrong photographed Buzz Aldrin (far left) as he stepped backwards out of Eagle to join him on the Moon, 18 minutes after taking his own first footsteps on the Moon. All the concerns of the mission were centred on this task, and so Apollo 11 did not carry much scientific equipment; a small box contained a seismic experiment and a laser reflector, weighing a total of 77 kilograms. One of the aims of the seismic equipment was to gather data to investigate the structure of the Moon, and in particular to determine whether it had a core and a mantle like the Earth. To this end, the impacts of meteorites and the lunar seismic waves which they caused were measured. Stations in Arizona, Texas and California directed laser beams at the reflector, enabling scientists to measure the exact distance between the Earth and the Moon.

The photograph (near left) was taken on 20 July by Armstrong and shows Aldrin preparing to spread out some scientific equipment. The camera on the right was taking stereoscopic photographs of the lunar surface (NASA).

Returning to the Command and Service Module. The photograph (near right) taken by Michael Collins shows Eagle's return stage which was due to rendezvous and dock with the Columbia Command Module. After docking and opening the door between the two craft, Neil Armstrong and Edwin Aldrin carefully loaded the samples they had gathered. The return stage of the Lunar Module was then jettisoned, and they prepared to ignite the engine on the Service Module ready for the return journey to Earth. They landed safely on 24 July 1969 (NASA).

Tracks across the Moon's surface. Alan B. Shepard and Edgar D. Mitchell here look back at the tracks left by their equipment rickshaw leading to Antares, their Lunar Module during the Apollo 14 mission to Fra Mauro. On one occasion, being short of time, Shepard and Mitchell carried the rickshaw between them and made their journey in leaps and bounds to avoid having to leave equipment and samples behind (NASA).

Mission	Time spent on the Moon/ Duration of ExtraVehicular Activities (EVA)	Samples taken
Apollo 11	22 hours/2 hours 35 minutes	22 kg
Apollo 12	32 hours/7 hours 45 minutes over two EVAs	34 kg
Apollo 14	34 hours/9 hours 24 minutes over two EVAs	42 kg
Apollo 15	67 hours/18 hours 35 minutes over three EVAs	77 kg
Apollo 16	71 hours/20 hours 15 minutes over three EVAs	97 kg
Apollo 17	75 hours/22 hours 4 minutes over three EVAs	116 kg

Extra Vehicular Activity. The table to the left shows the time (in hours, h) spent on the Moon, the length of time (in hours and minutes, h and min) spent outside the Lunar Module (LM) and the weight of samples taken (in kilograms, kg). The duration of a particular EVA is counted from the time that the LM cabin is depressurised to the time that it is repressurised; during this time the astronauts breath only the oxygen circulating in their spacesuits.

After a perfect landing, the LM Orion of the Apollo 12 mission was 163 metres from the Surveyor 3 probe (shown on the left) which had landed some two and a half years previously. Charles Conrad, photographed by Alan L. Bean, has his left hand on the arm supporting the shovel for taking samples and his right hand on the probe's television camera. Both parts were brought back to Earth.

On the right David R. Scott is surrounded by experiments and the device for drilling into the Moon. The red bands on his helmet and legs identify him as the commander of the Apollo 15 mission (NASA).

Scientific experiments. In April 1972, John Young, the commander of the Apollo 16 mission, put in place equipment for seismic experiments in the Descartes region.

In the foreground, the lunar magnetometer is linked by a cable to the radio isotope generator, which supplies it with electrical energy. This generator was developed and supplied by the American Commission on Atomic Energy; it produced the energy required to power the ALSEP experiments and maintain the temperature of the equipment during the 340 hour lunar night when temperatures dropped to −207 degrees celsius. In all the Apollo missions which involved landing on the Moon, such generators were used to supply up to 74 watts of electricity. In later years, they were used to supply energy to scientific experiments at the lunar landing sites (NASA).

The return of the Apollo 17 mission. On 17 December 1972, the day after the separation of the return stage from the Lunar Module of the Apollo 17 mission, Challenger, Ronald E. Evans went outside the module to recover the cartographic camera and other scientific equipment installed on the Service Module (right). This hour long trip was necessary because the Service Module was jettisoned before reentry into the Earth's atmosphere. Evans was linked to the spacecraft by a supple pipe which supplied him with oxygen and also prevented him floating off into space.

During this last Apollo mission, a small satellite was put into lunar orbit to gather information on the charged particles and magnetic fields found in circumlunar space (NASA).

Splashdown. The unfurling of these three orange and white parachutes, each with a 26 metre diameter, marked the final stages of an Apollo mission. At the end of the Apollo 15 mission, on 7 August 1972, one of the parachutes did not open and the astronauts did not have a very soft landing in the Pacific Ocean, though none of them was hurt. The precise cause of this failure was never discovered (NASA).

A geologist on the Moon. Harrison H. Schmitt, the pilot of the Apollo 17 Lunar Module, is the only scientist to have visited the Moon. A geologist by training, he is seen here examining an enormous piece of broken rock in the Taurus Littrow valley, in December 1972. Schmitt estimated that the rock had descended about 1·5 kilometres down a slope in the North Massif.

Eugene A. Cernan, the commander of this last Apollo mission, took a series of photographs, including the one above, which were assembled into a panorama, accurately showing the layout of the valley. The lunar rover has been parked on the other side of the rock, out of sight (NASA).

Exploring the solar system

Mars

Mars, the red planet, has always captured man's imagination and, since the alleged discovery of martian canals by Giovanni Schiaparelli in 1877, science fiction has consistently maintained the idea that some sort of life form exists on this planet. The scientific community remained unconvinced, but it is not, however, surprising that, at the beginning of the space era, Mars became a priority for planetary exploration.

The Americans had the first success when, on 14 July 1965, Mariner 4 passed over the surface of Mars at an altitude of just under 10 000 kilometres. The spacecraft had travelled 523 million kilometres in 228 days. The flypast took 30 minutes and the probe then rapidly left the planet; radio contact was lost on 1 October 1965.

Mariner 4 carried a magnetometer, a cosmic dust detector, an ionisation chamber, a telescope for studying cosmic radiation, a radiation detector, a solar plasma detector and a television camera. Only the camera was used exclusively for examining Mars, the other

The martian landscape. This colour image was made by one of the two cameras on the Viking Lander 2 in the Utopia Planitia region, on 5 April 1978. It is the result of combining three recordings obtained by sweeping 564 vertical lines, each of 512 pixels, in three colours – blue, green and red. The distance to the surface varies from 1·7 metres to infinity, and corresponds to the range of elevations shown on the left of the image (EL); this varies from −60 degrees (at the foot of the probe) to 0 degrees (the camera's horizon). As well as the landscape, one of the probe's three feet is seen (at the lower right), as is the protective cover of the sampling device (20 centimetres long) which was ejected after landing (NASA/JPL).

Exploratory missions to Mars. Over 11 years from 1962 to 1973, the Soviets sent eight probes towards Mars. The results of these missions did not reach expectations and none of the soft landing attempts succeeded. However, three of the four orbiting probes transmitted scientific data. The USA had eight Mars missions between 1964 and 1975. Of these, only two were failures – Mariner 3 and Mariner 8.

Probe	Launch date	Objectives and main results
Mars 1 USSR	1 November 1962	flypast; failure, radio communications ceasing on 21 March 1963, at 106 million kilometres from the Earth; probably passed within 193 000 kilometres of Mars on 19 June 1963
Mariner 3 USA	5 November 1964	flypast and study of the interplanetary medium; failure as head protecting the probe during launch not ejected
Mariner 4 USA	28 November 1964	flypast and study of the interplanetary medium; probe (identical to Mariner 3) passed within 9780 kilometres of the martian surface on 14 July 1965 and transmitted the first pictures of the planet
Mariner 6 USA	24 February 1969	flypast; successful trajectory correction; probe passed within 3330 kilometres of the martian surface on 31 July 1969; transmitted 76 images back to Earth; measured structure and composition of the martian atmosphere
Mariner 7 USA	27 March 1969	flypast; probe identical to Mariner 6; successful midcourse trajectory correction; probe passed within 3518 kilometres of the martian surface on 5 August 1969; transmitted 159 images of the surface back to Earth
Cosmos 419 USSR	10 May 1971	orbital probe and landing probe; failure – the probes could not be placed into a transfer orbit for Mars as they did not separate from the launcher
Mars 2 USSR	19 May 1971	orbital probe placed into martian orbit on 27 November 1971, at an unknown distance; a scientific capsule was ejected on the same day, before the probe went into orbit; it might have landed at 40° South, 47° East; results unknown
Mars 3 USSR	28 May 1971	orbital probe placed into martian orbit on 2 December 1971, at an unknown distance; as with Mars 2, a scientific capsule was released which landed at 45° South, 158° West; transmissions ceased 20 seconds after landing for an unknown reason
Mariner 8 USA	9 May 1971	orbital probe; launch failure
Mariner 9 USA	30 May 1971	orbital probe put into orbit around Mars on 13 November 1971, at an altitude of 1390 kilometres; transmitted 7329 images of the surface back to Earth; all experiments functioned as planned; mission ended on 27 October 1972
Mars 4 USSR	21 July 1973	orbital probe failed to go into orbit around Mars; probe passed within 2200 kilometres of the planet
Mars 5 USSR	25 July 1973	orbital probe went into orbit around Mars on 2 February 1974 (orbital period of 25 hours); probe functioned for 20 orbits – it had been planned to use it as a relay probe
Mars 6 USSR	5 August 1973	orbital probe went into orbit 1500 kilometres above Mars; landing probe descended to the surface (24° South, 25° West); transmitted atmospheric measurements during the descent, but transmissions ceased 0.3 seconds before landing
Mars 7 USSR	9 August 1973	orbital probe mission identical to Mars 6; following an error in the trajectory, landing probe passed within 1300 kilometres of the surface (landing planned for 50° South, 28° West)
Viking 1 USA	20 August 1975	orbital probe placed into orbit on 19 June 1976; sent more than 25 000 images back to Earth; measured the gravitational field, studied atmospheric water vapour and made a thermal map of the surface; ceased operating in 1980. Lander probe touched down on Mars on 20 July 1976, at 22.4° North, 48° West, in the Chryse Planitia region; sent back more than 1600 images of the surface; performed the first *in situ* analysis of the martian surface; ceased functioning in November 1982
Viking 2 USA	9 September 1975	orbital probe placed into martian orbit on 7 August 1976; mission and experiments identical to Viking 1; transmitted more than 15 000 images of the surface to Earth; operations ceased on 25 July 1978. Lander probe touched down on Mars on 3 September 1976, at 48° North, 45.7° East, in the Utopia Planitia region; transmitted more than 1300 images; ceased functioning in 1980

Orbits of Mars and the Earth. The orbit of Mars about the Sun is more elliptical than that of the Earth. The two orbits are closest at perihelion, when they are closest to the Sun (the Sun–Earth distance is 152 million kilometres, and the Sun–Mars distance is 207 million kilometres), and furthest apart at aphelion, that is when the two planets are furthest from the Sun. At perihelion, the Earth and Mars are 55 million kilometres apart and, at aphelion, they are 103 million kilometres apart.

The diagram below shows the relative positions of the Earth and Mars at the time of the Mariner 4 launch (28 November 1962), and at the time the probe flew over Mars (14 July 1965). Mariner 4's trajectory was typical of the martian probes. The two stages separated 254 seconds after launch. The probe was first placed onto an elliptical transfer orbit. After unfolding its solar panels, it was then oriented using the star Canopus and started on its interplanetary voyage. On 5 December 1964, a trajectory correction of 0·25 degrees was made to reduce the margin of error and prevent the probe from crashing onto the martian surface.

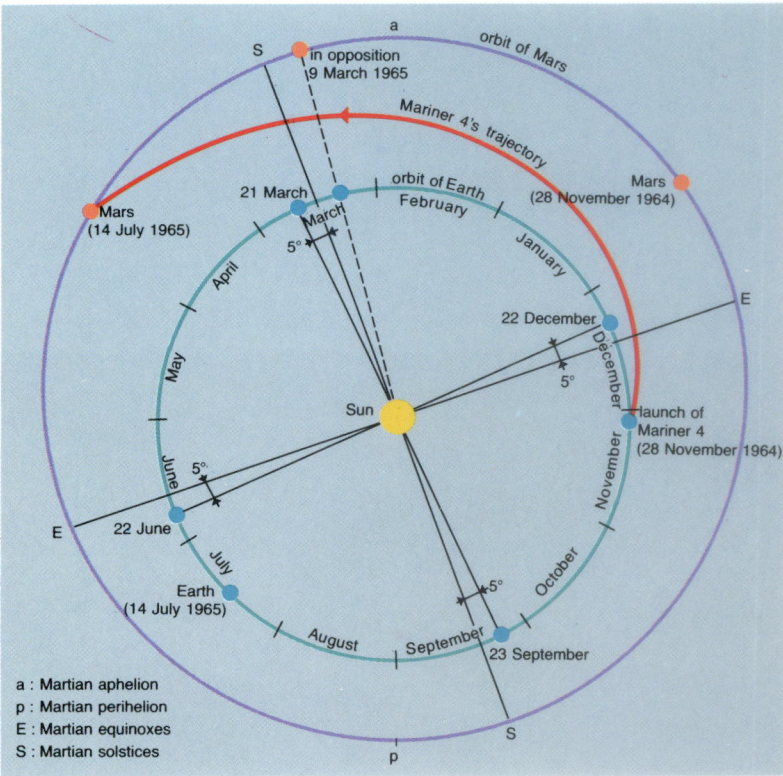

a : Martian aphelion
p : Martian perihelion
E : Martian equinoxes
S : Martian solstices

Longterm variations of the distance between the Earth and Mars. When the Earth is situated between the Sun and Mars, the planets are said to be in opposition, and when the Sun lies between the two planets they are said to be in conjunction. The conditions for observing Mars from the Earth are best when the planets are in opposition; this is when the planets are closest to one another and the martian surface is well illuminated.

The Earth takes 365 days to travel around the Sun, while Mars takes 687 days. A martian year is therefore nearly twice as long as an Earth year, placing the Sun, Mars and the Earth in opposition about every 780 days. This succession of oppositions with a period of about 26 months (shown in the diagram on the right) is used when determining the best launch dates for space probes to Mars.

Since Mars' period of revolution is not exactly twice the Earth's, there are also still more favourable oppositions, when the Earth to Mars distance is shorter and when Mars is near its perihelion. Such oppositions occur about once every 16 years.

instruments being included primarily to make measurements on the charged particles, magnetic fields and dust found in the inner solar system. However, the instruments also made important observations as they passed near the planet. The magnetometer, for instance, showed that, if Mars had a magnetic dipole moment, it was less than three ten thousandth's that of the Earth's; this result indicates that Mars does not have a metallic core (of iron and nickel) which produces a planetary magnetic field by dynamo action.

The structure of the martian atmosphere was evaluated using occultation measurements of the radio signals transmitted by Mariner 4. Shortly after the probe arrived at Mars, it passed behind the planet and the telemetry signals could no longer be received at the Earth. Just before it disappeared, the radio signals were refracted by the atmosphere. These perturbations, changes of the phase and amplitude of the radio signals, provide a model of the atmospheric density and temperature as a function of altitude. The surface atmospheric pressure was estimated to be about 5 millibars.

The Mariner 4 mission also sent back the first pictures of the martian surface. A single television camera recorded 22 images, the best of which had a resolution of 3 kilometres. To the general disappointment of all concerned there was little contrast in these images, despite computer enhancement. However, the images showed more than 300 meteorite craters with a size distribution between that of the lunar continents and seas; this result caused scientists to conclude that Mars was in many respects very similar to the Moon. This idea persisted throughout the Mariner 6 and Mariner 7 programmes until the images sent back by Mariner 9 forced a rethink.

No mission to Mars was planned for the 1967 launch slot, and it was not until 1969 that NASA began two new experiments. Mariner 6 was launched on 24 February 1969 by an Atlas Centaur rocket, and only a month later Mariner 7 lifted off.

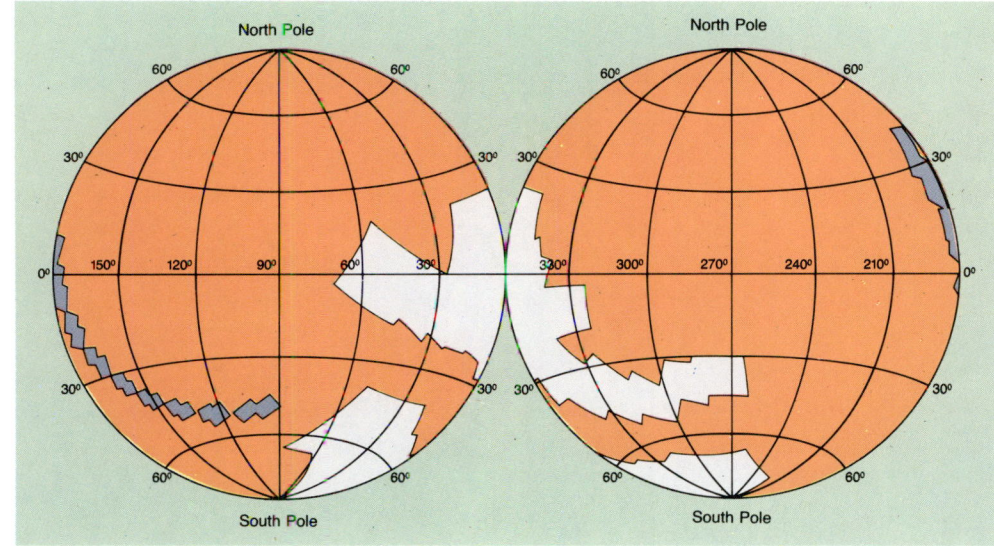

The main regions of Mars photographed by Mariner 4, Mariner 6 and Mariner 7. The region covered by the 22 images from Mariner 4 are shown in dark grey. These were taken as the probe flew over Mars and so represent the probe's track across the martian surface, crossing the equator and extending from 37° N, 183° W to 50° S, 89° W.

The regions photographed by Mariner 6 and Mariner 7 are shown in white.

On 1 August 1969, Mariner 6 passed very close to Mars. Some 50 hours before the flypast, and more than a million kilometres from Mars, the high resolution camera was pointed at the planet and began transmitting a sequence of 33 images, relayed in all over a period of 20 hours. A second sequence of filming took place some 300 000 kilometres from the planet. The flypast took place this time on 31 July 1969 and lasted 30 minutes; the probe passed within 3431 kilometres of Mars and the two cameras recorded 25 images of the equatorial zone between 10 degrees West and 265 degrees West.

As Mariner 6 was flying over Mars, Mariner 7 was still several million kilometres away from the planet though its radio signals were no longer being received at the Earth. After several attempts, a new signal was received, but this time it was partially distorted; the spacecraft seemed to have peculiar movements, and the radio signals were not being correctly beamed towards Earth. The spacecraft was

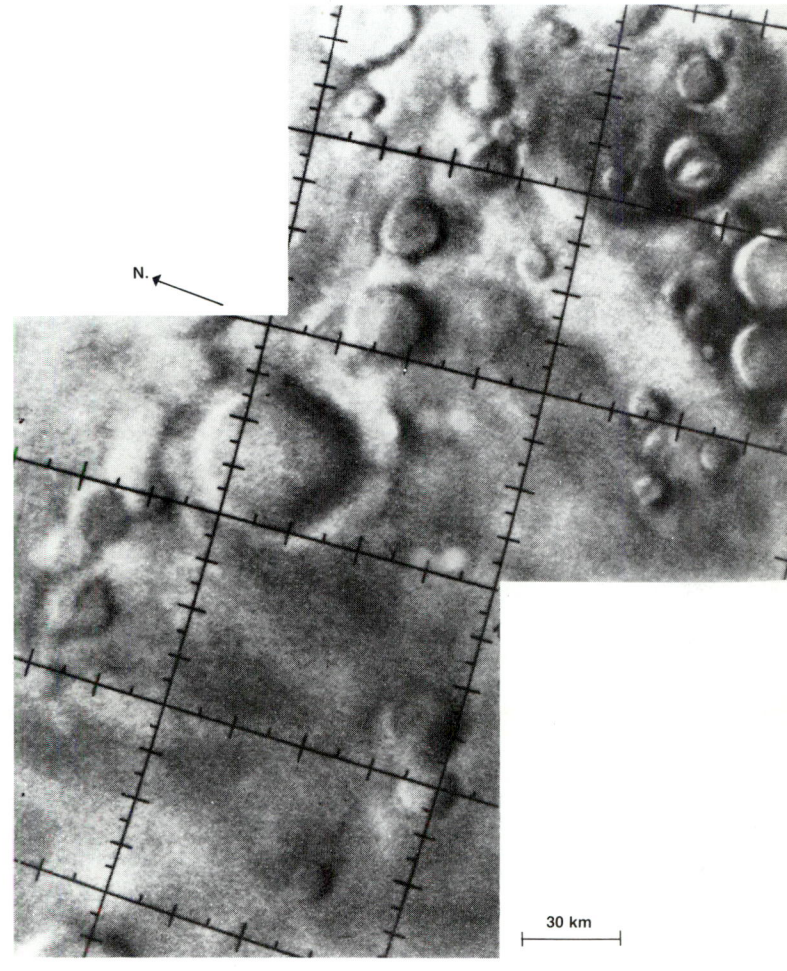

N.

30 km

Two of the images made by Mariner 4. The overlapping photographs shown to the right cover a region in the southern hemisphere (47° S, 141° W). They show a number of meteorite craters, of which the largest, in the centre, is approximately 50 kilometres across (NASA/JPL).

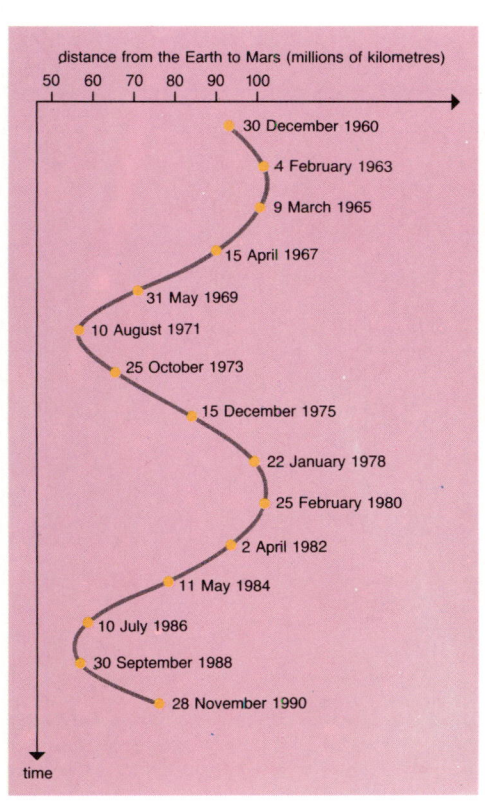

distance from the Earth to Mars (millions of kilometres)

50 60 70 80 90 100

30 December 1960
4 February 1963
9 March 1965
15 April 1967
31 May 1969
10 August 1971
25 October 1973
15 December 1975
22 January 1978
25 February 1980
2 April 1982
11 May 1984
10 July 1986
30 September 1988
28 November 1990

time

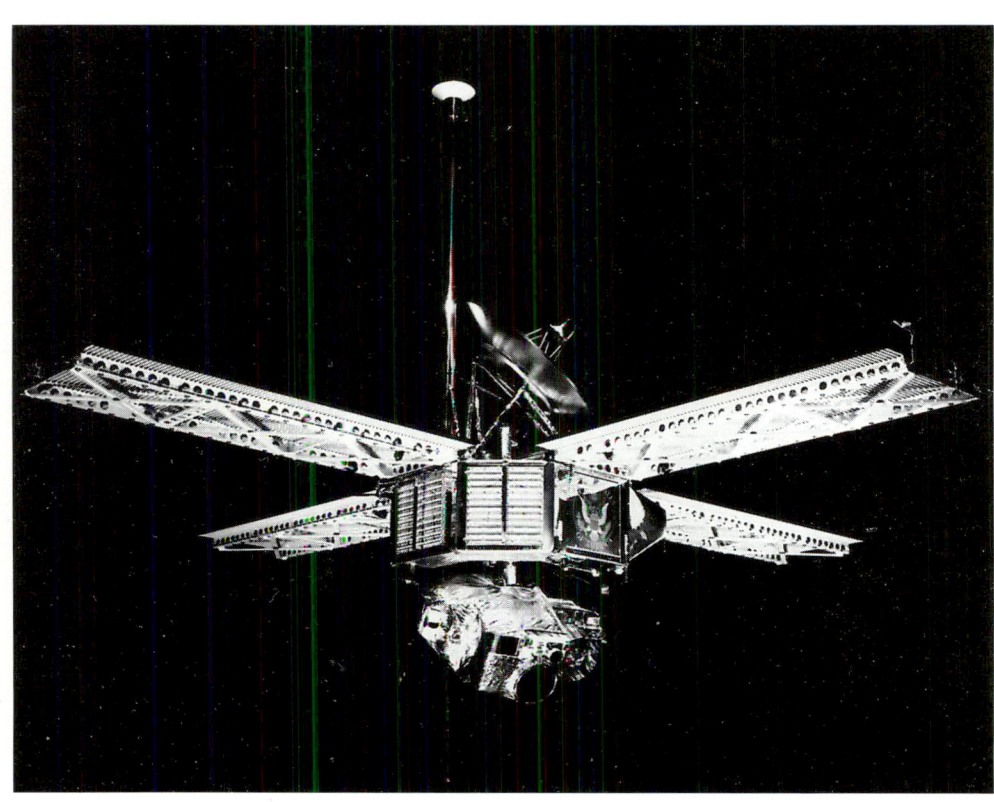

Mariner 6 and Mariner 7. Mariner 6 and Mariner 7 belonged to the same generation of spacecraft as Mariner 3 and Mariner 4, but they were much improved. The mass was increased from 260 to 380 kilograms, and the mass of scientific instruments was tripled. The instruments were completely new, and included infrared and ultraviolet spectrometers for studying the composition of the atmosphere, an infrared radiometer designed to measure surface temperature, and two television cameras. These cameras had different fields of view and different spatial resolutions (NASA).

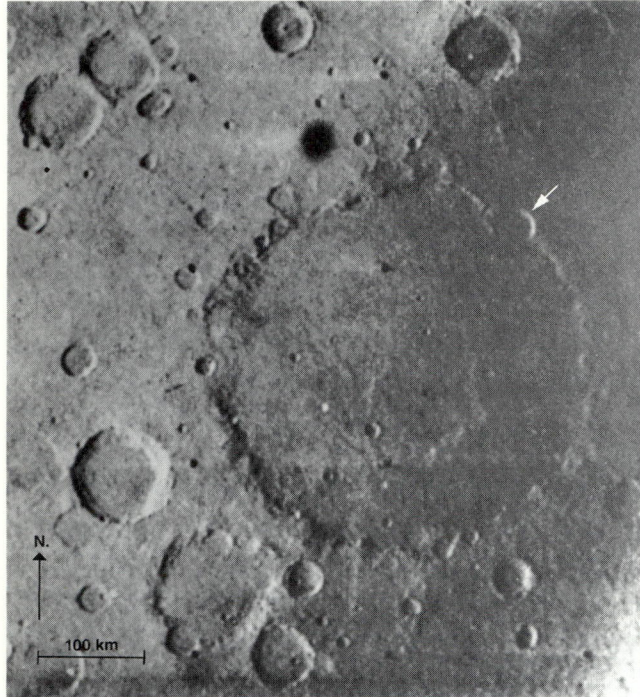 

Two images taken by Mariner 6. These two images were taken in the southern hemisphere, in the Sinus Sabeus region (15° S, 345° W). The lefthand picture was acquired using the low resolution camera, the right-hand one – of part of the same area – with the high resolution camera; the North East edge of the large crater is indicated by the arrows. On the upper right of the opposite page is an image made by Mariner 9 of the same area. These two images, like those taken by Mariner 4, revealed the existence of numerous meteorite impact craters (NASA/JPL).

reoriented with respect to Canopus using several commands, and these irregular movements fortunately stopped.

Mariner 6's images of the southern polar region showed some very interesting features, so Mariner 7 was then reprogrammed to make high resolution images of the same area during its final approach to the planet. Most of the images transmitted by the two spacecraft showed that the surface was covered with craters, supporting the view that Mars was very similar to the Moon. However, several new features, including rocky outcrops, appeared on some of the images, and measurements made using the infrared spectrometer confirmed that carbon dioxide was one of the principal components of the atmosphere. Other absorption bands were found which could indicate an abundance of solid carbon dioxide in the polar caps; ultraviolet spectrometer observations confirmed this hypothesis and showed that nitrogen represented at least 1% of the martian atmosphere.

Initially, the Mariner 8 and Mariner 9 programme was planned to photograph 70% of the martian surface, to study its topography and temperature, and to gather information on its composition and that of the atmosphere. To achieve these objectives, six categories of experiments were devised: imaging, infrared and ultraviolet spectrometric studies, infrared radiometry, occultation in the S band and celestial mechanics. A wide angle camera was developed to photograph the whole area with a resolution of about 1 kilometre. In addition, a camera with a much smaller field of view capable of taking pictures with a resolution of about 100 metres was to be included. It was planned to use variations of surface atmospheric pressure to measure the topography of the martian landscape, while infrared radiometry was to be used to deduce the ground temperatures and obtain information on the physical properties of the ground rock.

The programme intended to use Mariner 8 as a reconnaissance probe to make a general survey of the planet; Mariner 9 would then examine promising areas in more detail. The first probe was to be placed in a near polar orbit with an altitude at closest approach (periastre) of 1250 kilometres. The second was to go into a slightly inclined orbit, with an orbital period of 20 hours 30 minutes so that every five days the probe would pass over the same point. This second orbit was designed to detect variations caused by the seasons or by winds, to study the atmosphere using measurements made on the limb of the planet, and to photograph the two satellites of Mars, Phobos and Deimos.

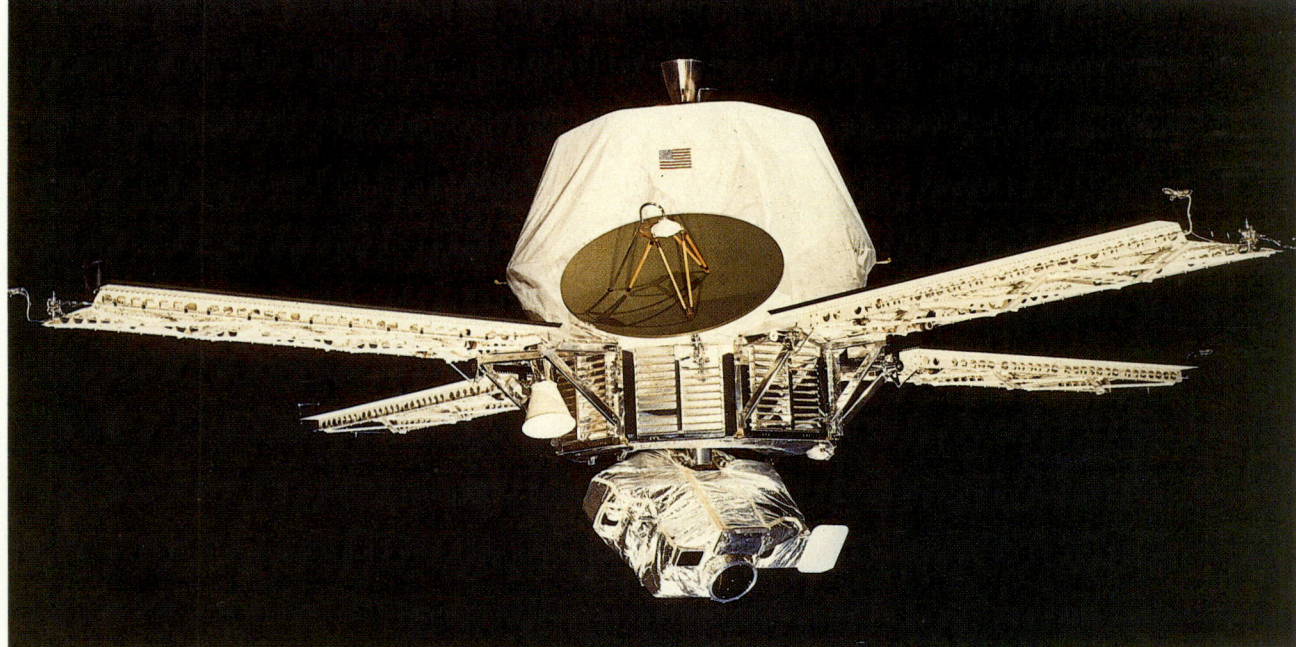

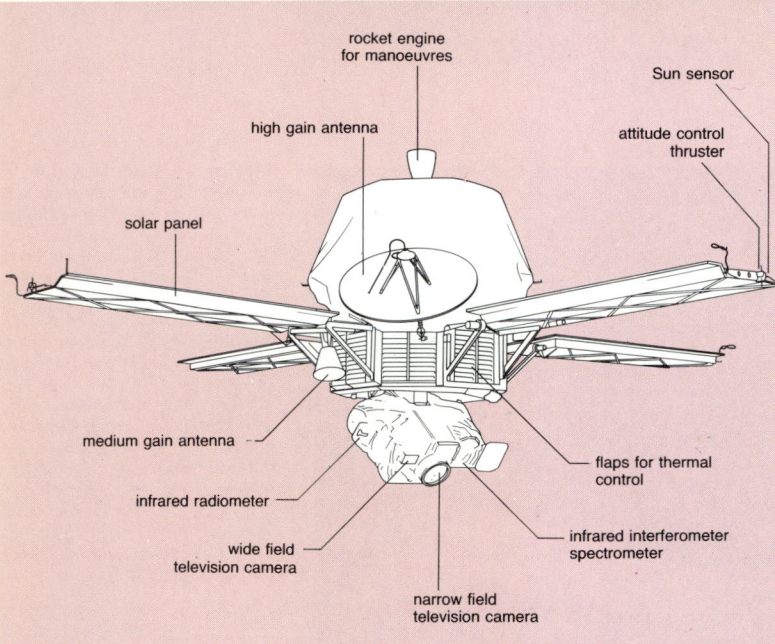

The Mariner 9 spacecraft. Although similar to their predecessors, Mariners 8 and 9 had rocket engines which could give them a velocity of 1·7 kilometres per second to put them into orbit around Mars, whilst still leaving enough fuel to perform orbital manoeuvres. The on board computer could be reprogrammed daily to fulfil the mission requirements, initially planned for 90 days.

The Deep Space Network (DSN), spread over four continents, received the data and relayed instructions to the probes. Data processing treatment was carried out on board the spacecraft, in particular by filtering and improving the images before transmission.

The photograph above was taken at the Jet Propulsion Laboratory in California and shows the four solar panels which supplied electricity to the probe and also the scientific instruments located on the probe's orientable platform (NASA/JPL).

Mariner 9 instruments. The diagram below illustrates the different parts of the electromagnetic spectrum observed by each instrument.

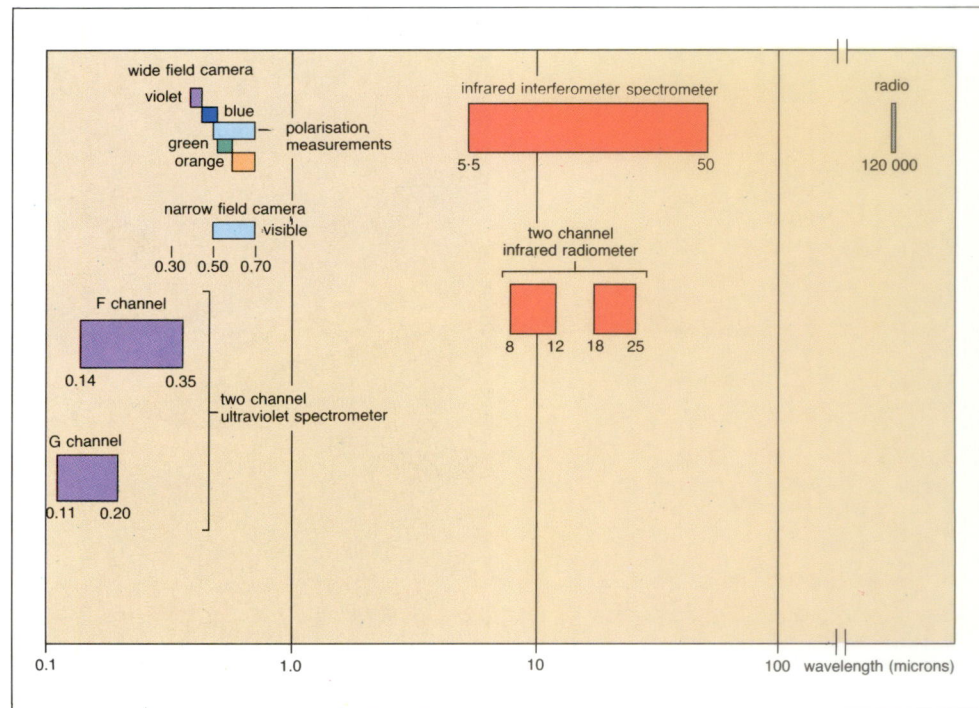

	Orbital period	Periastre (kilometres)	Orbital inclination
Planned	12 h	1350	65.0°
After being inserted into orbit	12 h 34 min 1 s	1398	64.4°
After first correction, orbit number 4	11 h 58 min 14 s	1387	64.4°
After second correction, orbit number 94	11 h 59 min 28 s	1650	64.4°

Mariner 9's main orbital parameters.

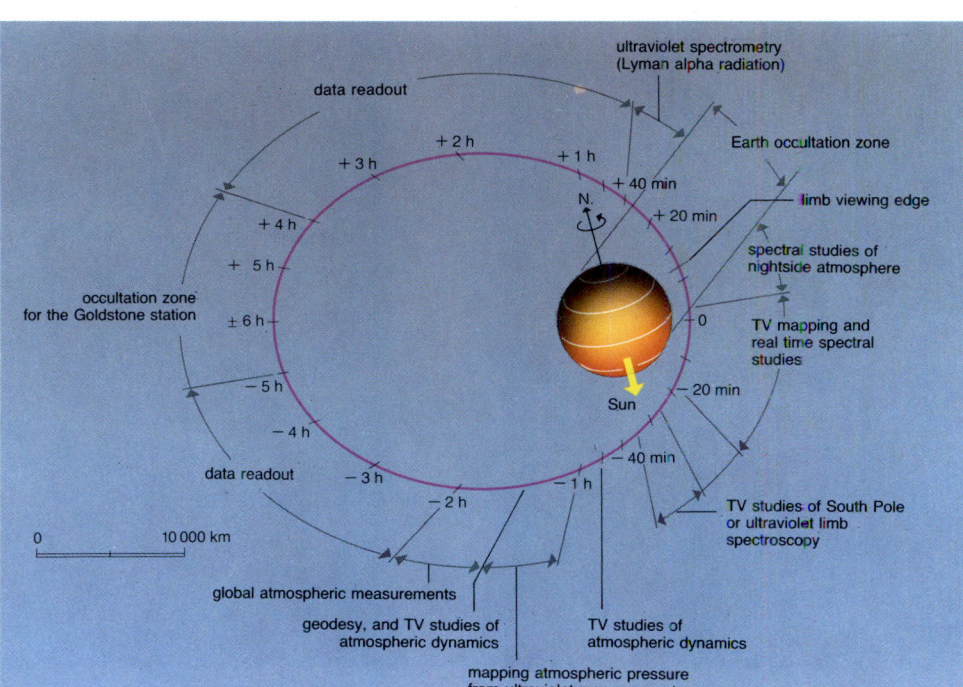

Key scientific operations during a Mariner 9 orbit. Shown to the left are the different studies carried out at different points on the spacecraft's orbit around Mars. Times (in hours, h, or minutes, min) are shown relative to the time of closest approach (periastre).

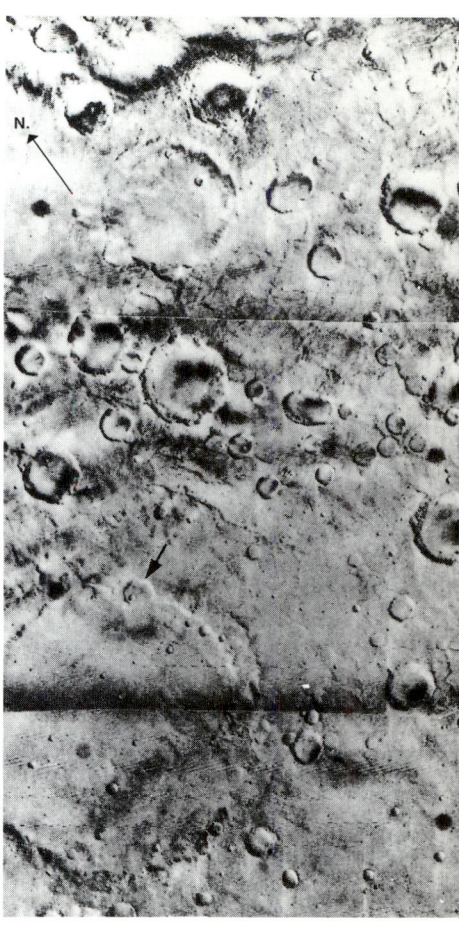

Images taken by Mariner 9. This photograph was made from three images taken, during orbit 145, of the same region in the southern hemisphere of Mars as those acquired earlier by Mariner 6 and shown on p. 182. The arrow indicates the region that is common to all three images (NASA/JPL).

Processing an image made by Mariner 9. The 'raw' images recorded by the probe (MTC–MTVS, for Mission Test Computer–Mission Test Video System) are processed to give 'improved' images (TVRDR, for Television Reduced Data Record) at the Image Processing Laboratory (IPL) of the Jet Propulsion Laboratory (JPL, NASA/California Institute of Technology) at Pasadena in California.

The series of MTS–MTVS images below illustrates the different stages of image processing obtained by the narrow field, high resolution camera on Mariner 9. Each processing stage is illustrated by the histograms of the data used (data input) and of the film output. The images are subjected, from left to right, to improvements in contrast, to geometric corrections and finally to shadow reductions. The information on the right of the image describes the conditions during filming, as well as the main corrections performed afterwards.

A Reduced Data Record (RDR) image consists of 800 scanned lines (instead of 700 in an MTVS image), and each line contains 950 pixels (instead of 832). However, the 9 bit coding of each pixel is preserved; each pixel can take an intensity (or brightness) value of between 0 (black) and 511 (white) (NASA/JPL).

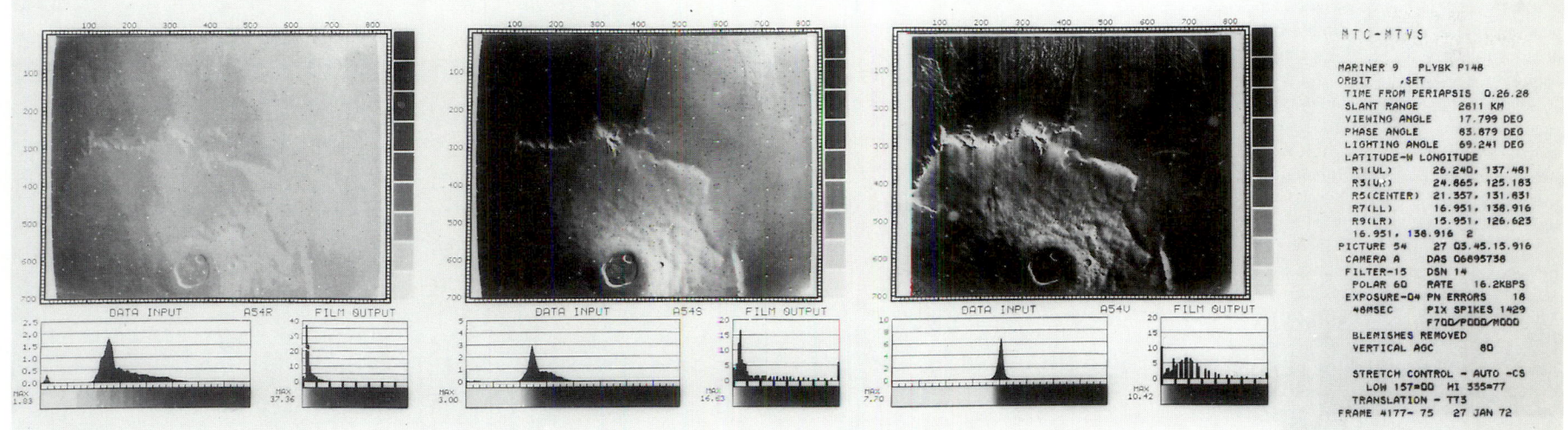

The Soviet Mars programme. On the left is a photograph of the Mars 3 craft; the later Mars 5 was almost identical.

The image of the martian surface on the right was taken by a high resolution camera in the southern hemisphere, near 35° S, 38° W (APN).

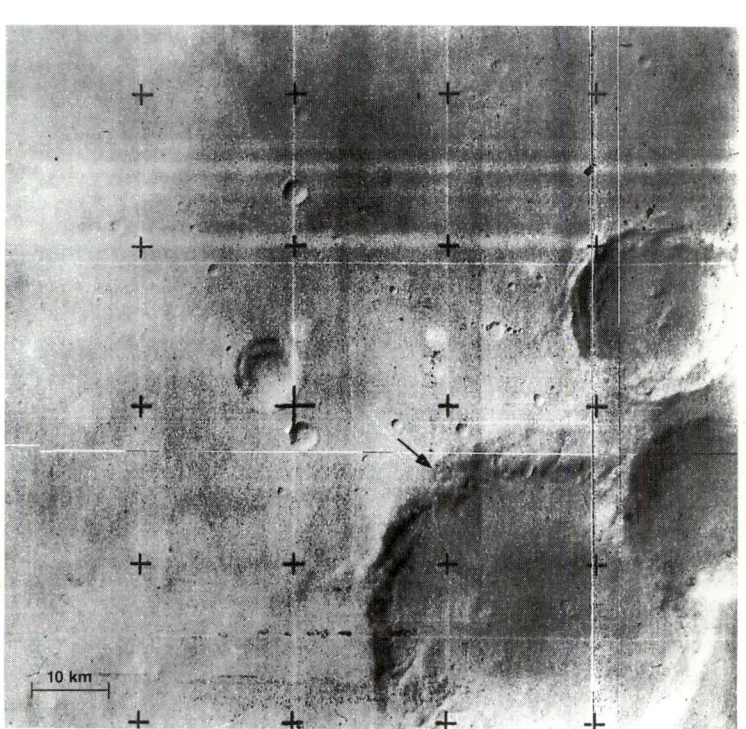

Mariner 8 was launched on 9 May 1971. Unfortunately the second stage of the Atlas Centaur launcher did not function and the probe fell back into the Atlantic Ocean, 1500 kilometres from Cape Kennedy. Mariner 9 was, however, successfully launched on 30 May 1971. Following a trajectory correction, six days after launch, the probe was placed into a transfer orbit which would take it to Mars in 161 days – two weeks before the Soviet Mars 2 and Mars 3 probes were due to arrive – at the end of a journey of 400 million kilometres.

At the end of September 1971, Mariner 9's instruments were activated to test the pointing capability of the platform and calibrate the cameras; on this occasion, images of Saturn and Mars were transmitted to the Earth. At the same time, observations made on Earth revealed that a dust storm was blowing up in the southern hemisphere of Mars. This storm continued to develop over the next few weeks, and, on 10 November 1971, some 800 000 kilometres from the planet, the spacecraft began filming it at the rate of one image per hour. The images transmitted showed the martian surface to be completely hidden by dust in the atmosphere. In spite of these unfavourable conditions, however, several images made just before the probe went into orbit showed the southern polar cap of Mars and several dark regions in the northern hemisphere, in the region around Nix Olympica.

When it was 2740 kilometres from Mars, Mariner 9 was reoriented and the retrorockets ignited for 915·6 seconds. The probe was then decelerated and put into orbit around the planet. The operation was performed automatically using an accelerometer which calculated the best speed for going into orbit and for cutting out the engines.

After this operation, the spacecraft disappeared behind the planet for 36 minutes. When it reappeared, it was confirmed that Mariner 9 was in orbit as expected; four orbits later, the engines were reignited for 6 seconds to make an orbital correction.

Several images were obtained during each orbit of Mars, allowing the evolution of the storm to be followed. By orbit 64 the southern hemisphere had cleared sufficiently for systematic photographic coverage to begin. Unexpected features in Mars' gravitational field slowly altered the periastre (the martian equivalent of perigee at the Earth) and reduced the time available for transmitting data to the Earth. The distance from the Earth to Mars was also slowly increasing, and it proved necessary during orbit 94 to enlarge the orbit, raising the distance to the periastre to 1650 kilometres. This improved conditions for transmitting results to the Earth and also increased the field of view of the cameras.

During orbit 100, the programme to photograph Mars systematically began in earnest. The atmosphere was still not as clear as scientists would have liked, but the quality and distribution of photographs was satisfactory. New features, such as lava flows, volcanic structures around Nix Olympica and, more surprisingly, an extraordinary canyon, Valles Marineris, stretching for nearly 5000 kilometres close to the equator, were discovered.

By 9 March 1972, the initial programme of photography was complete. After a period of inactivity from mid March to 8 June, the probe was then reactivated to finish photographing the northern hemisphere and obtain the best possible images to help scientists choose suitable landing sites for the Viking probes.

The Mariner 9 mission finally came to an end on 27 October 1972, having obtained 7329 images during 697 orbits around Mars. During a manoeuvre to repoint the probe towards the Earth, the tank of fuel for the attitude control engines was emptied. The last commands to be issued to the spacecraft from Earth were to close down the radio transmission system to avoid interference with other experiments in space.

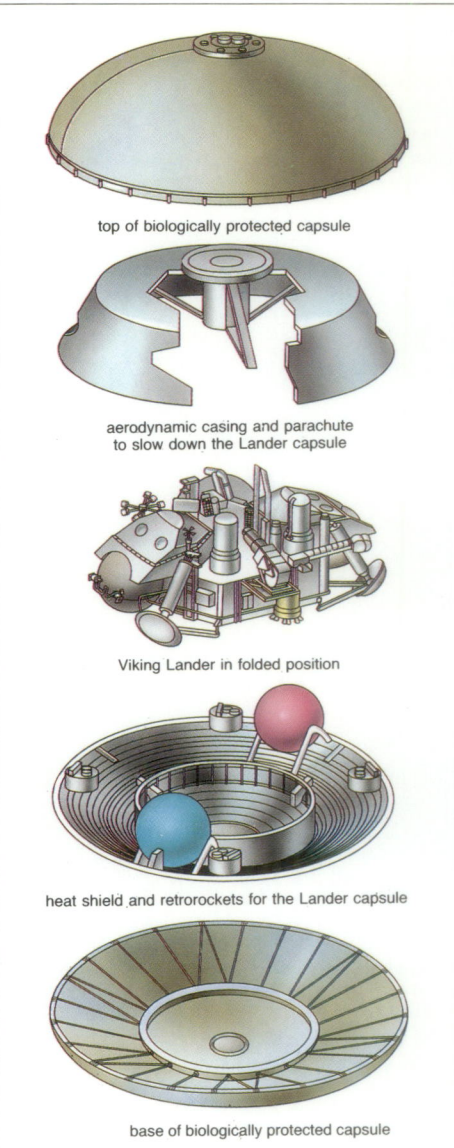

top of biologically protected capsule

aerodynamic casing and parachute to slow down the Lander capsule

Viking Lander in folded position

heat shield and retrorockets for the Lander capsule

base of biologically protected capsule

A Viking spacecraft in its launch configuration. The photograph above shows a Viking probe ready to be put into the nosecone of the Titan III Centaur rocket. The solar panels have been folded against the sides of the Viking Orbiter. This has the Viking Lander, a cutaway diagram of which is shown on the far right, sitting on top of it. The entire unit is covered in a biologically protecting shroud (NASA).

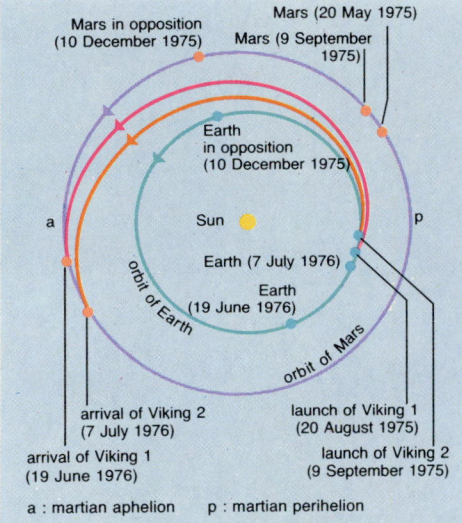

The trajectories of the two Viking probes (above left). The Viking spacecraft were launched from the Earth to Mars in 1975; their journeys took over a year, more than twice as long as Mariner 9 did. To economise on energy and rocket fuel, NASA's engineers chose a trajectory which went half way round the Sun, as shown in the diagram above.

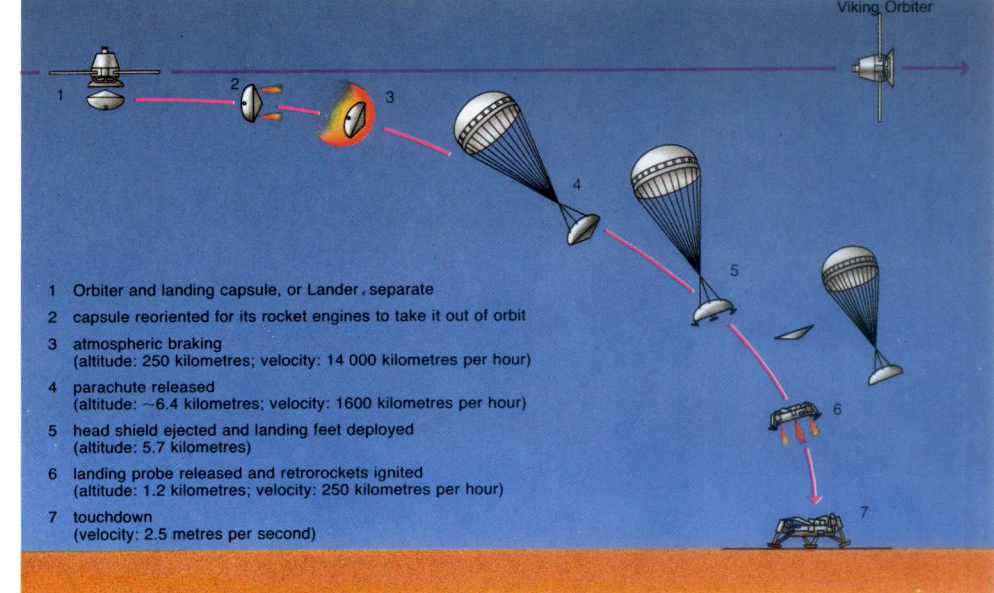

1 Orbiter and landing capsule, or Lander, separate

2 capsule reoriented for its rocket engines to take it out of orbit

3 atmospheric braking (altitude: 250 kilometres; velocity: 14 000 kilometres per hour)

4 parachute released (altitude: ~6.4 kilometres; velocity: 1600 kilometres per hour)

5 head shield ejected and landing feet deployed (altitude: 5.7 kilometres)

6 landing probe released and retrorockets ignited (altitude: 1.2 kilometres; velocity: 250 kilometres per hour)

7 touchdown (velocity: 2.5 metres per second)

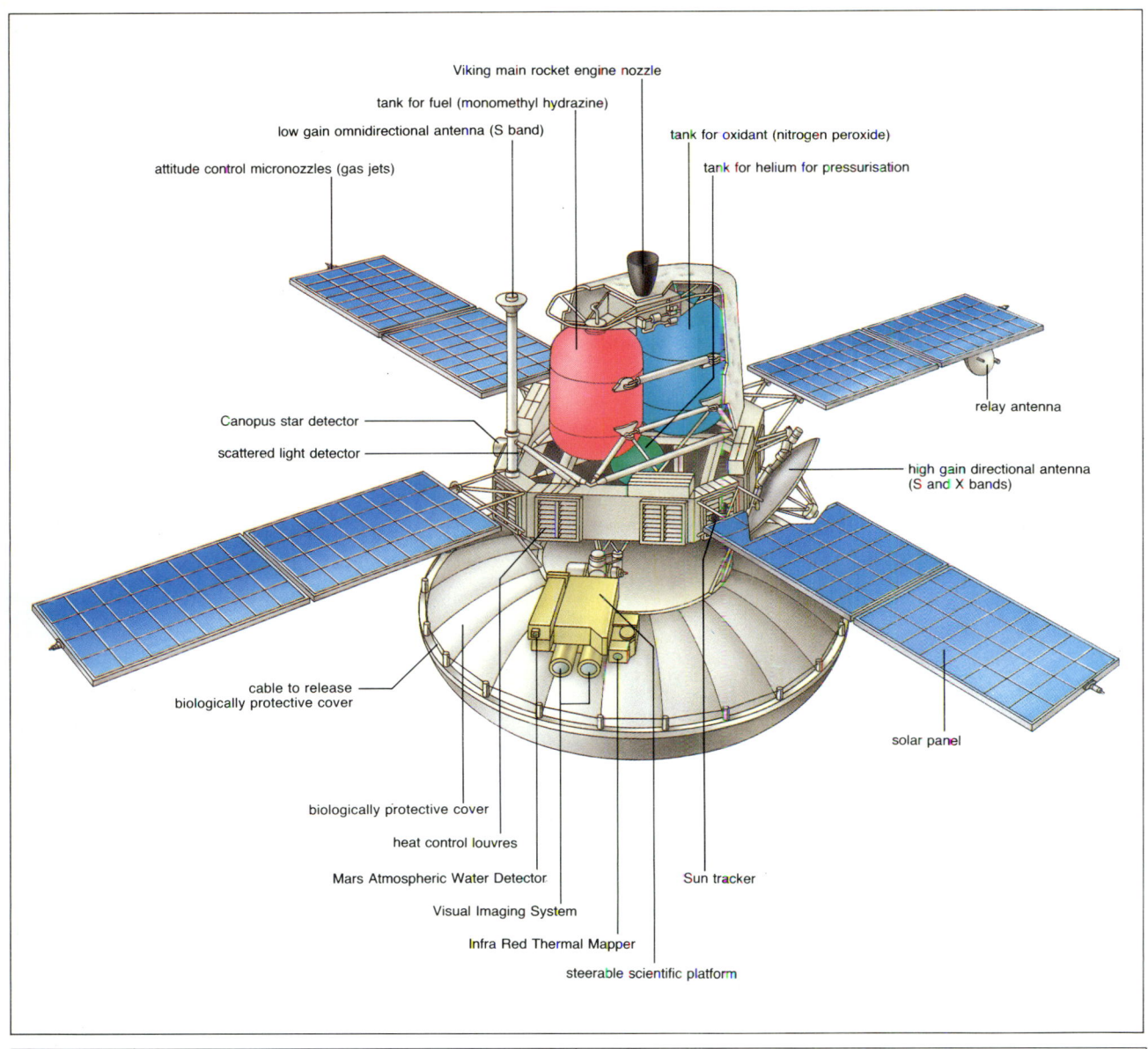

Viking main rocket engine nozzle

tank for fuel (monomethyl hydrazine)

low gain omnidirectional antenna (S band)

tank for oxidant (nitrogen peroxide)

attitude control micronozzles (gas jets)

tank for helium for pressurisation

Canopus star detector

scattered light detector

relay antenna

high gain directional antenna (S and X bands)

cable to release biologically protective cover

solar panel

biologically protective cover

heat control louvres

Mars Atmospheric Water Detector

Sun tracker

Visual Imaging System

Infra Red Thermal Mapper

steerable scientific platform

The Viking spacecraft. Of the several functions of these probes, perhaps the most important was to transport the landing capsules or Viking Landers. The spacecraft also observed the martian surface, chose the most suitable landing sites, studied the martian atmosphere in relation to features on the landscape, and finally relayed to Earth the data transmitted by the Landers on the martian surface.

The scientific payload consisted of a Visual Imaging System (VIS), an Infra Red Thermal Mapper (IRTM) and a Mars Atmospheric Water Detector (MAWD).

These three systems were placed on a platform which could be oriented so that any point on the martian surface could be examined while the Orbiter itself was still facing the Sun. In this way the solar panels, with a total surface area of 15 square metres, received the maximum amount of solar radiation they needed to produce 620 watts of electricity. Two rechargeable batteries supplied an extra 30 ampere hours, and UHF, S band and X band communications systems relayed data to ground stations.

The VIS consisted of two identical cameras. Each had a Cassegrain telescope, a wheel containing six different filters and a Vidicon tube. The field of view was about 1·5 degrees by 1·7 degrees, to cover a region on the surface that was 41 kilometres by 46 kilometres, for a periastre distance of 1500 kilometres. An image was produced every 8·96 seconds.

The IRTM was a 28 channel radiometer operating in the infrared. It consisted of four telescopes, each supplied with a set of filters and seven detectors sensitive to a certain part of the spectral domain. The thermal emissivity of the surface was measured in four spectral bands and seven detectors observed the reflected sunlight in the visible and infrared. Another detector measured the radiation in the carbon dioxide band in order to find the temperature of the stratosphere.

The third system, the MAWD, was an infrared spectrometer operating at five wavelengths around the water vapour absorption band (at a wavelength of 1·38 microns). The MAWD measured the proportion of incident solar radiation passing through the atmosphere, and from this determined the amount of water vapour that this radiation had passed through. By comparing the measurements made at the five wavelengths, the atmospheric pressure at the level where the absorption occurred could be calculated, and the average altitude where the water vapour was to be found could be deduced. In the MAWD, the radiation was focused by a small telescope onto a diffraction grating of 12 000 lines per centimetre. The field of view corresponded to a 0·12 degree by 0·92 degree rectangle, or to a distance on the ground of 3 kilometres by 24 kilometres from an altitude of 1500 kilometres.

Viking Orbiter 1			Viking Orbiter 2		
Date	Orbit	Operations	Date	Orbit	Operations
19 June 1976	0	elliptical orbit (period: 24 hours; apoastre: 33 000 kilometres; periastre: 1513 kilometres; orbital inclination: 39 degrees)	7 August 1976	0	elliptical orbit (period: 24 hours; apoastre: 30 033 kilometres; periastre: 1519 kilometres; inclination: 80 degrees)
20 July 1976	92	Viking Lander 1 touched down	3 September 1976	25	Viking Lander 2 touched down
12 February 1977	235	orbit synchronised with Phobos	20 December 1976	123	periastre lowered to 789.2 kilometres
24 March 1977	263	periastre lowered to 297 kilometres	9 October 1977	418	orbit synchronised with Deimos
20 July 1979	1120	periastre increased to 357 kilometres	23 October 1977	432	periastre lowered to 290 kilometres
7 August 1980	1485	command issued from Earth to cease operations	25 July 1978	706	stopped working due to power failure

The separation manoeuvre of the Viking Lander from the Orbiter. After several orbits, the Lander separated from the Orbiter, in the manner shown on the left. It then followed an elliptical trajectory to the martian surface.

Descent of Viking Lander through the martian atmosphere. During their descent towards the martian surface, the two Viking Landers made *in situ* measurements of the martian ionosphere and atmosphere. Three instruments were used, the Retarding Potential Analyzer (RPA), the Upper Atmosphere Mass Spectrometer (UAMS) and the Lower Atmospheric Experiment (LASE).

The RPA measured the ionospheric photoelectrons, the ionospheric electron temperature, and the composition, concentration and temperature of the positive ions. It also observed the interaction between the solar wind and the upper atmosphere.

The UAMS analysed the molecular composition of the atmosphere for all electrically neutral gases with a molecular weight of less than, or equal to, 50. It also measured their isotopic abundance. The most common neutral species is carbon dioxide (CO_2); nitrogen (N_2) amounts to only 6% of the amount of carbon dioxide found, and molecular oxygen (O_2) only 0·3%.

The LASE established the variation of atmospheric density, pressure and temperature from an altitude of 90 kilometres down to the surface.

A Viking image of Mars. This low resolution image, obtained by the Viking 1 Orbiter, covers an area of the martian surface around the Olympus Mons volcano.

Such images are made by scanning 1056 lines, each line comprising 1182 pixels, each of 7 bits. Having been transmitted to the Earth, each image is processed digitally to improve its quality. Several preliminary treatments are carried out; missing pixels are generated by averaging the eight adjacent pixels, errors are eliminated, and corrections applied.

The final image consists of 1056 horizontally scanned lines; each line is made up of 1204 pixels, each of 8 bits (NASA/JPL).

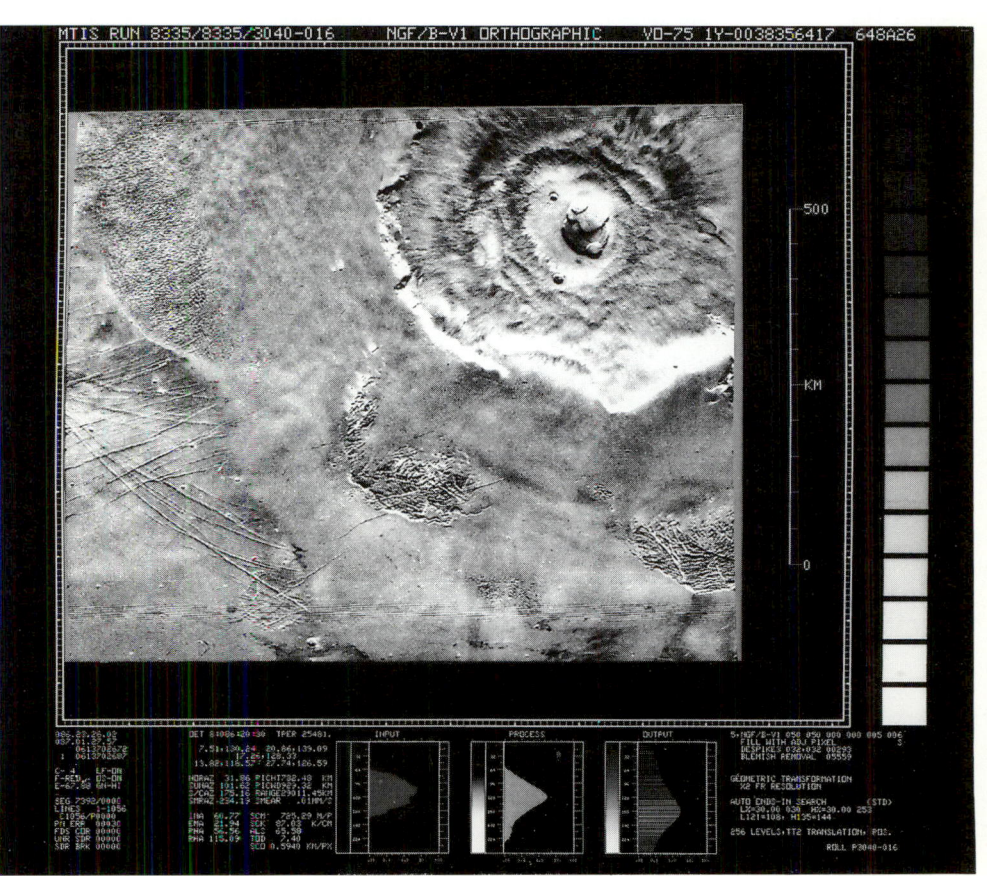

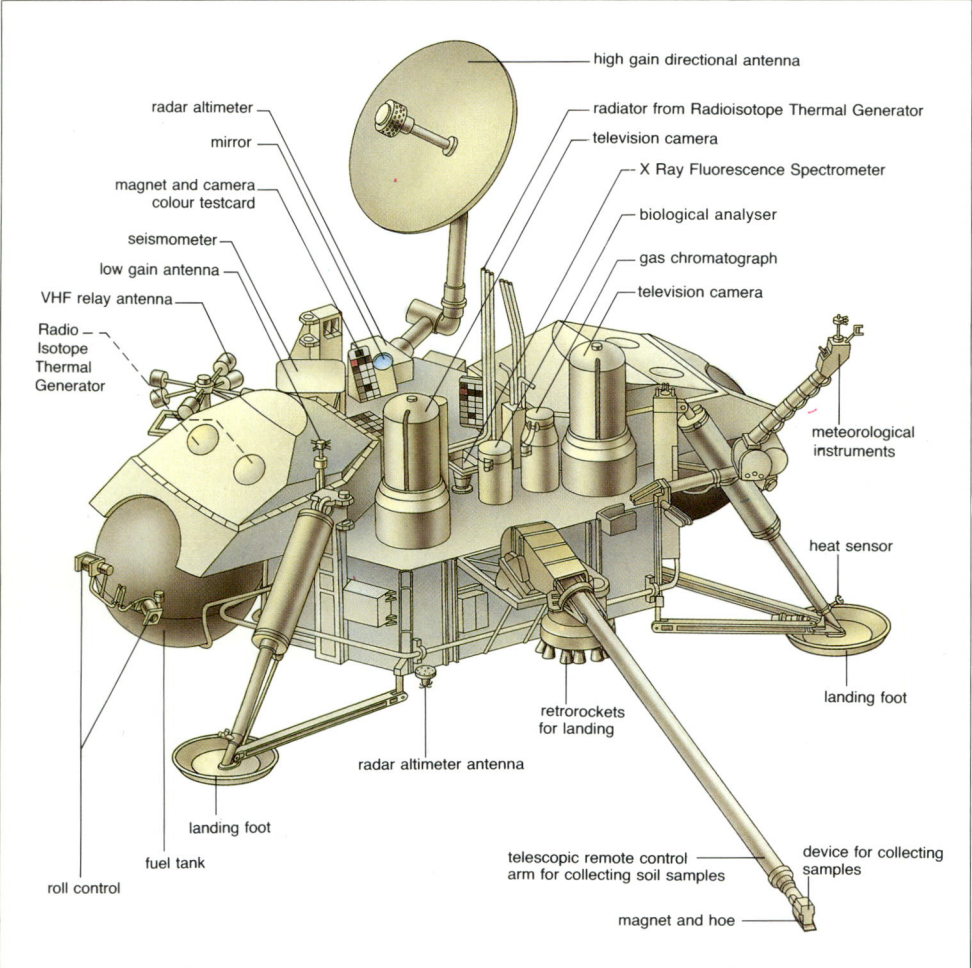

high gain directional antenna
radar altimeter
mirror
radiator from Radioisotope Thermal Generator
television camera
magnet and camera colour testcard
X Ray Fluorescence Spectrometer
seismometer
biological analyser
low gain antenna
gas chromatograph
VHF relay antenna
television camera
Radio Isotope Thermal Generator
meteorological instruments
heat sensor
landing foot
retrorockets for landing
landing foot
radar altimeter antenna
landing foot
fuel tank
telescopic remote control arm for collecting soil samples
device for collecting samples
roll control
magnet and hoe

The Viking Landers. The drawing on the left illustrates the configuration of one of the two martian landing probes and their scientific instruments. Once these had landed on Mars, they began a long series of operations which included observing the landscape, examining the environment, analysing the composition of the soil, making meteorological observations, carrying out seismic studies and searching for organic materials and life forms. The programme lasted in all for about one martian year.

All the operations were regulated by an on board computer – the Guidance Control Sequencing Computer (GCSC). Three units then controlled the scientific data: these were the Data Acquisition and Processing Unit (DAPU), a digital memory and a recorder.

Most of the electrical energy (35 watts) for the mission was provided by the Radioisotope Thermal Generator (RTG), which used plutonium 238. In addition, there were four nickel–cadmium batteries that could provide an auxiliary source of power (70 watts) as and when required.

The physical properties of the soil were studied using relatively simple techniques. The hardness of the ground was measured, for instance, by examining how much the Lander's feet had sunk into it. Two pairs of magnets separated out magnetic minerals from the rest of the samples, while other magnets on the cover of the RTG captured magnetic dust. These experiments showed that the martian ground is relatively hard and, in several places, consists of a crust which is several centimetres thick. This covers a more solid layer.

Meteorological measurements (temperature, pressure and wind speed and wind direction) were made twelve times a day by sensors on top of a pole erected after the landing. The temperatures were measured by three thermocouples. They showed that the daily temperature ranged from −85 degrees celsius as the Sun set to −29 degrees celsius at midday. Wind speeds of up to 8 metres per second were recorded during the day.

The soil composition was analysed to discover which chemical elements were present and to identify their molecular composition. An X Ray Fluorescence Spectrometer (XRFS) was used to establish the presence of iron, calcium, aluminium and titanium in the samples, a Gas Chromatograph Mass Spectrometer (GCMS) to analyse the molecules present and to search for the presence of either organic or inorganic gases. The GCMS did not find organic molecules present in any quantity of more than one part per million, but it showed that a small amount of water was associated with certain minerals. The GCMS established that the proportion of argon 36 to argon 40 was much less in the martian atmosphere than in the terrestrial atmosphere, so demonstrating that outgassing on Mars happened at a much slower rate than on Earth (NASA).

The biological experiments. The Viking Landers each carried three experiments, shown diagrammatically on the right, to search for traces of organic materials and evidence of life on Mars.

The first, the Pyrolitic Release Experiment (near right), analysed the gas produced by heating soil samples. This relied on the fact that life forms are based on carbon atoms and that living organisms fix carbon compounds in the atmosphere by photosynthesis. The samples were incubated under artificial light for five days, during which time they were kept under martian conditions, but supplied with carbon dioxide doped with carbon 14. The samples were then heated to a temperature of 650 degrees celsius in order to release all organic materials. Helium gas was introduced into the chamber to transfer the resulting vapour into the column of a gas chromatograph. The carbon monoxide and carbon dioxide were then separated by a filter while the rest of the volatile products were analysed by a radiation detector to identify the carbon 14 which could have been fixed by any organic matter. To remove the possibility of uncertainty, a part of the sample was sterilised at a temperature of 160 degrees celsius for three hours to destroy all possible organic material before it was subjected to the incubation period and pyrolysis. The radioactivity measurements were then compared. If the same values were obtained, there could then have been no organic materials fixing carbon on Mars; if the measurements made on the sterilised part of the sample showed less carbon, organic material could have been present.

The isotope Labeled Release Experiment (centre right) was based on the concept of assimilation of organic molecules such as amino acids by microorganisms in the soil. The gas resulting from this process would contain part of the carbon present in the organic molecules. In the experiment, samples were placed in an incubator in the martian atmosphere with a little added water containing nutrients (formates, lactates, and amino acids) labelled with the carbon 14 isotope. If an increase in the radiation in the atmosphere was measured during the experiment, it could be expected to have resulted from the emission of carbon 14 gas produced through the assimilation of the nutrients by microorganisms in the samples.

The third experiment, the Gas Exchange Experiment (far right) was based on the principle of exchanges between living material and the atmosphere, and the presence of nutrients in the soil. The sample was placed in a porous container within an incubator, half of which held a mixture of carbon dioxide, krypton and helium, and half of which contained a mixture of nutrients. During the experiment, samples of the gaseous mixture were analysed by the gas chromatograph, to detect any increase in the concentrations of carbon dioxide, methane and nitrogen which would indicate that the nutrients had been assimilated by living organisms in the soil sample.

Unfortunately, none of the three experiments produced sufficiently clear cut results to prove, without ambiguity, the presence of organic matter or organisms in the samples analysed.

A calendar showing the main phases of the Viking mission

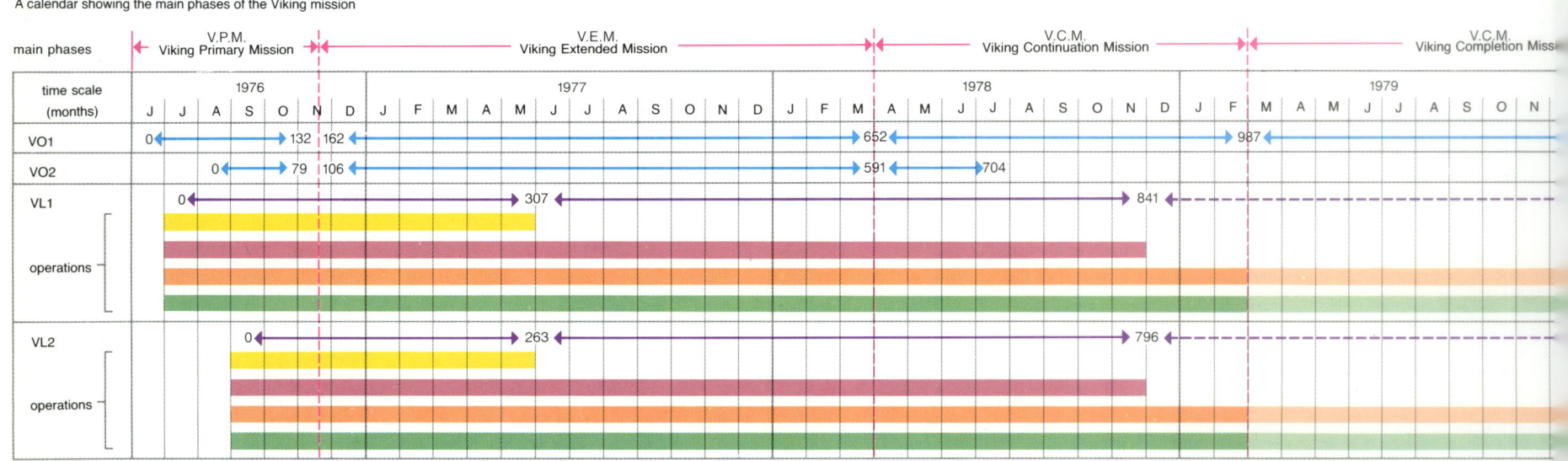

main phases	V.P.M. Viking Primary Mission	V.E.M. Viking Extended Mission	V.C.M. Viking Continuation Mission	V.C.M. Viking Completion Mission

time scale (months)	1976 J J A S O N D	1977 J F M A M J J A S O N D	1978 J F M A M J J A S O N D	1979 J F M A M J J A S O N
VO1	0 → 132 | 162		652 ←	987 ←
VO2	0 → 79 | 106		591 ← 704	
VL1	0	307 ←	841 →	
operations				
VL2		0	263 ←	796 →
operations				

scientific tasks on the surface of Mars:

biological and molecular analysis (soil and atmosphere)

inorganic analysis

For the Viking Orbiters (VO) the numbers are orbit numbers
For the Viking Landers (VL) the numbers are solar martian days (24 hours 39 minutes 25 seconds)

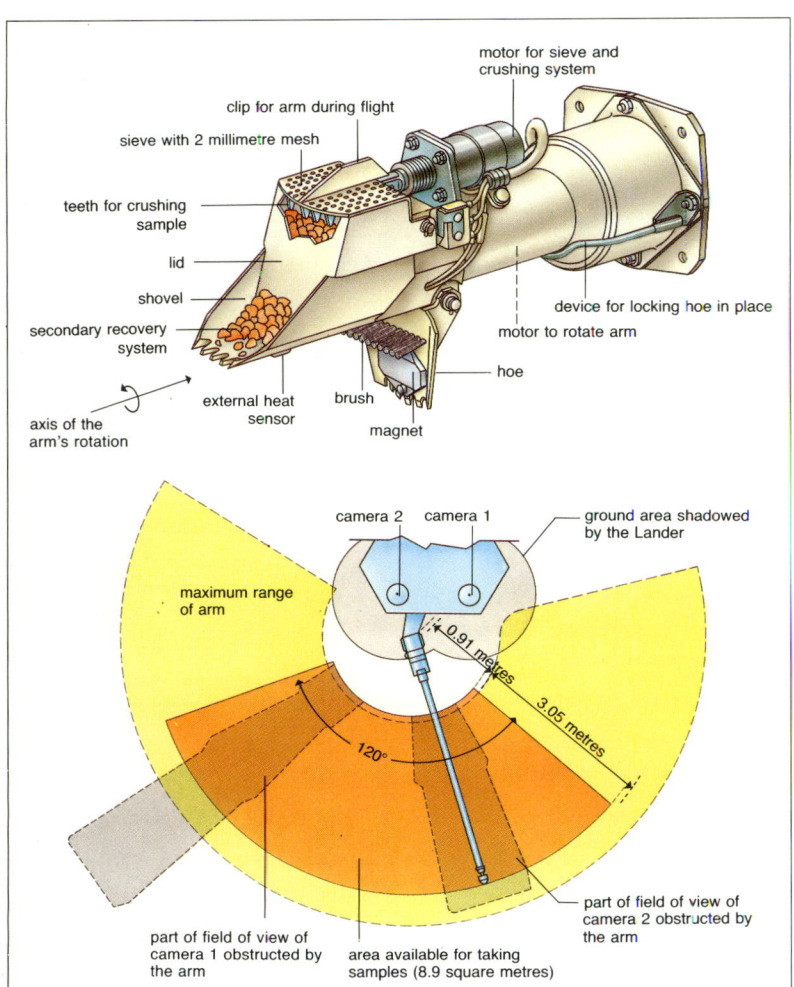

The Viking system for taking soil samples. The two Viking Landers had a device, shown diagrammatically on the left, for gathering soil samples and transferring them into the on-board analysis equipment. This was a shovel at the end of an articulated arm, 3 metres long, that could also dig channels and take samples from a depth of several centimetres.

Labels (upper diagram):
- clip for arm during flight
- motor for sieve and crushing system
- sieve with 2 millimetre mesh
- teeth for crushing sample
- lid
- shovel
- secondary recovery system
- axis of the arm's rotation
- external heat sensor
- brush
- magnet
- hoe
- motor to rotate arm
- device for locking hoe in place

Labels (lower diagram):
- camera 2
- camera 1
- ground area shadowed by the Lander
- maximum range of arm
- 0.91 metres
- 3.05 metres
- 120°
- part of field of view of camera 1 obstructed by the arm
- area available for taking samples (8.9 square metres)
- part of field of view of camera 2 obstructed by the arm

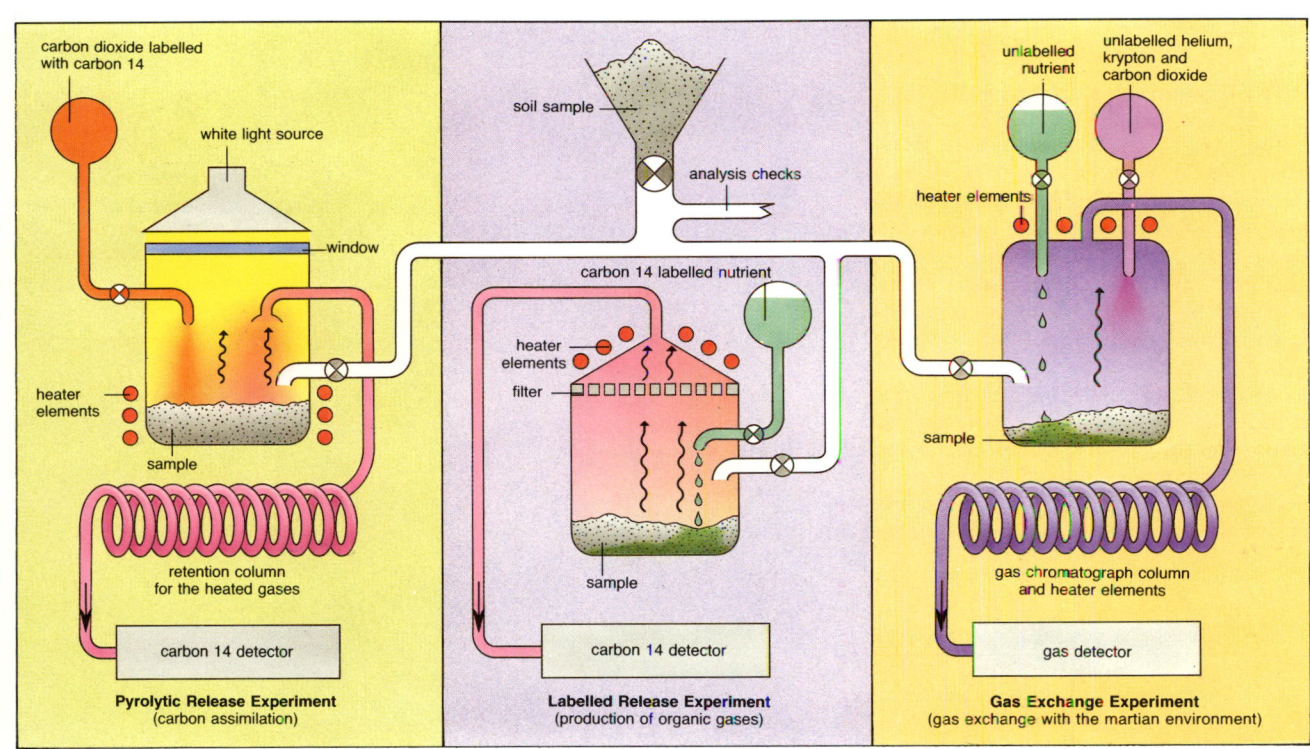

Pyrolytic Release Experiment (carbon assimilation)
- carbon dioxide labelled with carbon 14
- white light source
- window
- heater elements
- sample
- retention column for the heated gases
- carbon 14 detector

Labelled Release Experiment (production of organic gases)
- soil sample
- analysis checks
- carbon 14 labelled nutrient
- heater elements
- filter
- sample
- carbon 14 detector

Gas Exchange Experiment (gas exchange with the martian environment)
- uniabelled nutrient
- unlabelled helium, krypton and carbon dioxide
- heater elements
- sample
- gas chromatograph column and heater elements
- gas detector

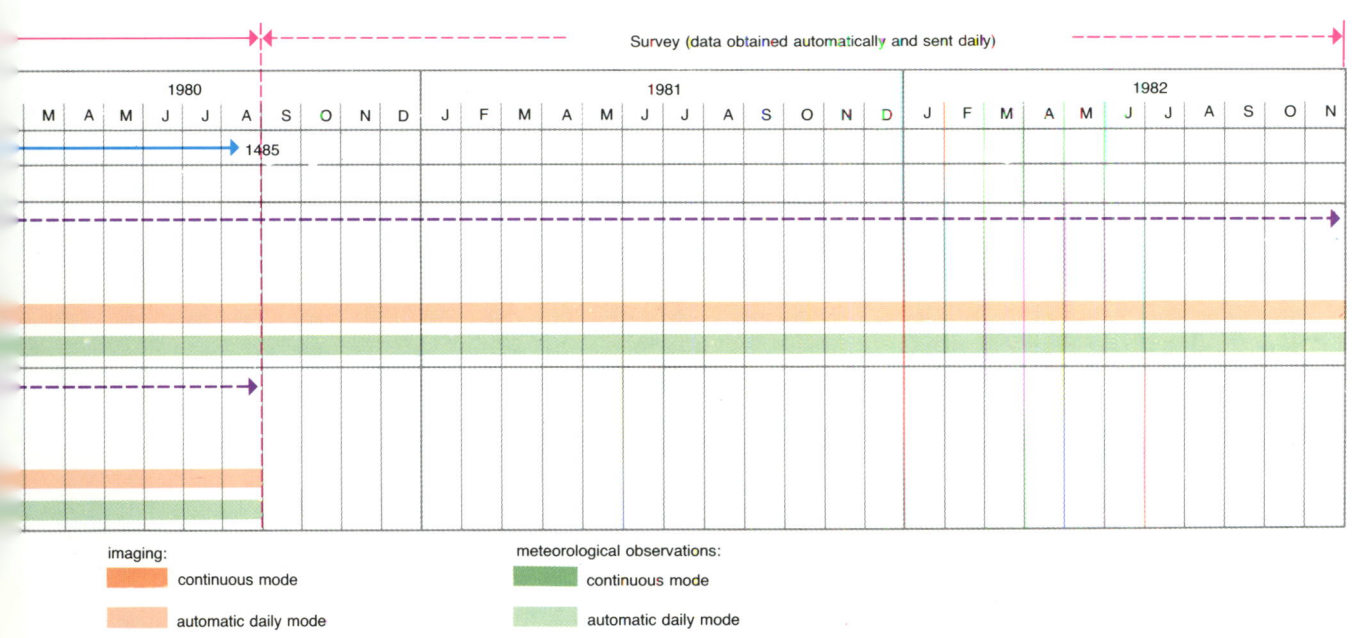

Survey (data obtained automatically and sent daily)

1980	1981	1982
M A M J J A S O N D	J F M A M J J A S O N D	J F M A M J J A S O N

1485

imaging:
- continuous mode
- automatic daily mode

meteorological observations:
- continuous mode
- automatic daily mode

The Soviets launched three probes to Mars in 1971 and four in 1973. Mars 2 and Mars 3, launched on 19 and 28 May 1971, respectively, were about five times heavier than Mariner 9; the Soviet spacecraft were also on a slightly different trajectory to that of the American spacecraft and arrived at Mars two weeks later.

On 27 November 1971, just before being put into orbit around Mars, Mars 2 released a scientific capsule which was designed to land in the region of Hellas Planitia. Mars 3 performed the same operation on 2 December. For the landings, the probes used parachutes at high altitudes and retrorockets during the final descent phase. Radio contact was lost with the Mars 3 landing probe 20 seconds after landing, for reasons unknown. It was postulated that the probe had been buried in a thick layer of dust, or been blown off course by violent winds and smashed against rocks. Although the orbiters themselves appeared to be functioning well, the images received from them did not show any surface detail because of the dust storm.

The Soviets decided to use the launch slot in 1973 to try to perform a successful landing on Mars. Conditions were less favourable than during other opposition phases and so the scientific payload was split on this occasion between four probes, to provide each payload with more power. The orbiting probes, Mars 4 and Mars 5, reached their target in March 1974, but one of the retrorockets on Mars 4 failed and it did not go into orbit. Mars 5 was successfully put into orbit, with a period of 25 hours and a periastre of 1500 kilometres; it operated for 20 orbits, and scientific data were gathered for 10 of these. However, the Soviets failed to land Mars 6 and Mars 7. Mars 7 missed the planet altogether. Mars 6 successfully descended towards the surface in the region north east of the Argyre basin, but three seconds before it landed, radio contact was lost.

Each of these orbiting probes had 14 instruments. Two television cameras made 70 images of the surface, with resolutions varying from 1 kilometre down to 100 metres. Spectroscopic measurements indicated a small amount of water vapour in the air, and the magnetometer on Mars 5 confirmed earlier measurements made by Mars 2 and Mars 3 indicating that the magnetic field was of the order of 30 nanoteslas. This is to be compared with the Earth's field which varies from about 30000 to 60000 nanoteslas at the surface. Although the mass spectrometer did not operate properly, the presence of an inert gas, probably argon, was also indicated.

Mars 7 was the last probe sent to Mars by the Russians. In the meantime, the Americans had embarked on the ambitious Viking programme, initiated in 1968, three years before Mariner 9 blasted off. Each of the two Viking missions was to consist of an Orbiter and a Lander, to be launched by a Titan III Centaur rocket.

Viking 1 was successfully launched on 20 August 1975, and Viking 2 on 9 September 1975. After arriving at Mars – Viking 1 on 19 June 1976 and Viking 2 on 7 August 1976 – the two spacecraft were put into orbit around the planet, initially in almost synchronous orbits. These were then modified so that very high resolution images of the martian surface, with 1 pixel being only 10 metres, could be obtained. Phobos and Deimos, two moons of Mars were also observed.

The Viking Lander 1 touched down on 20 July 1976 in the Chryse Planitia, at 22·4° North, 48° West; Viking Lander 2 touched down on 3 September 1976, in Utopia Planitia, at 48° North, 45·7° West. Once on the ground it was planned that each probe would function for about 60 days; in fact, their missions lasted very much longer and they provided an extraordinary amount of data on conditions in the martian environment. Yet so far the biological experiments have neither proved nor definitely disproved the idea that life exists on Mars.

Philippe Masson

Exploring the solar system

The giant planets

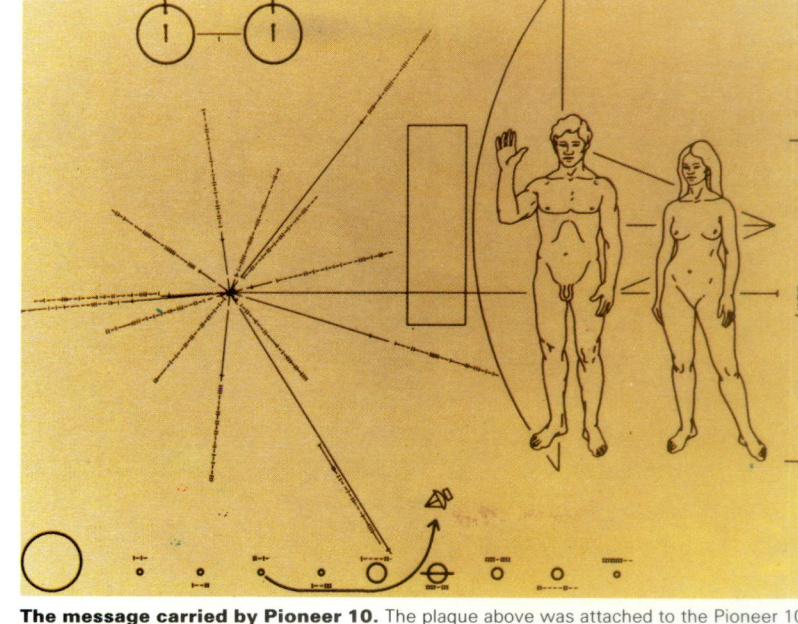

The message carried by Pioneer 10. The plaque above was attached to the Pioneer 10 spacecraft. Its purpose was to indicate to any extraterrestrials who might intercept it that the spacecraft was launched from the Earth. A man and a woman show what the inhabitants of Earth look like, in proportion to the scale of Pioneer's antenna; the man has his arm raised in a sign of peace and welcome.

On the left, the lines represent the positions of 14 pulsars with respect to the Sun. The symbols along these lines represent their periods on the date that Pioneer 10 was launched. The frequency of atomic hydrogen has been indicated in the top left as the reference. Since the period of a pulsar increases slightly with time, this would enable another civilisation to calculate the time that had elapsed since the spacecraft began its journey.

At the bottom of the diagram, the Sun and the planets are represented, along with Pioneer 10's trajectory, as it left Earth, passed by Jupiter, and carried on its way to the edge of the solar system.

The drawing was engraved on aluminium and covered in a layer of gold. It was attached to the antenna support in a place where it would best protected from erosion by cosmic dust. In size it measures 152 × 299 millimetres (NASA)

Humanity has long known of the existence of the planets, though it was not possible to study them in any detail until the advent of suitable instruments in the Renaissance. In 1609, Galileo constructed the world's first telescope, and with it observed the surface of Jupiter and several of its moons, and discovered the rings that surround Saturn.

Some 350 years later, with the advent of the space age, the solar system could be explored directly. This exploration began close to home, with visits to the Moon and nearby planets such as Venus and Mars. In time, however, desire for further knowledge led researchers inexorably to the giant planets of Jupiter and Saturn, and beyond to Uranus, Neptune and Pluto.

These giant planets were explored as part of two ambitious American space programmes, Pioneer and Voyager. Each of these missions had two spacecraft – Pioneer 10 and Pioneer 11, and Voyager 1 and Voyager 2 – designed from the first to be sent to the outermost reaches of the solar system.

It was in 1969 that the Pioneer mission was approved by Congress. Its main objectives were to explore the interplanetary medium beyond Mars, to examine the asteroid belt, and then to explore the region around Jupiter with Pioneer 10 and around Saturn with Pioneer 11. One of the most important aims was also to study the magnetospheres of the giant planets; after flying past, the spacecraft were to carry on towards the edge of the solar system.

Pioneer 10 and Pioneer 11 were launched from Cape Canaveral on 2 March and 5 April 1973, respectively. The launch window was chosen paying particular attention to the relative alignment of the planets in the 1980s when Pioneer 11 would be passing close to both giant planets. This programme was designed as a reconnaissance mission for a more ambitious later project, called the Grand Tour. However, budget restrictions led in the end to this being modified, with the result that the Voyager programme was devised. Two Voyager spacecraft were to visit Jupiter and Saturn to examine their magnetospheres and moons, paying particular attention to Titan, Saturn's largest moon. They were ultimately launched from Cape Canaveral on 20 August and 5 September 1977. Voyager 2 left first and arrived at Jupiter on 9 September 1979; Voyager 1 followed a shorter trajectory and arrived at Jupiter on 5 March 1979.

The Pioneer mission

The two Pioneer spacecraft were identical. They each carried a system for monitoring their instrumentation and for transmitting data back to Earth; they were also able to receive commands from Earth to modify their mission programmes. In flight, both spacecraft were stabilised by spinning them around axes that always pointed towards the Earth.

Pioneer 11's payload consisted of 12 instruments, seven of them for studying charged particles and magnetic fields. Two more instruments were for studying cosmic dust particles: the first observed the impact of very small (one microgram) dust grains, while the second measured the light scattered by somewhat

The scientific instruments on board Pioneer 11

Instruments	Experimental objectives
Magnetometer	measure the magnetic field in interplanetary space and near Jupiter and Saturn
Plasma analyser	measure the density and velocity of the solar wind
Charged particle detector	study the composition of charged particles from the Sun or the galaxy, and particles captured by Jupiter's magnetosphere
Cosmic ray telescope	study the spectrum of galactic and solar cosmic radiation
Geiger counter	study charged particles in the radiation belts around Saturn and Jupiter
Trapped radiation detector	measure the energies of electrons and protons trapped in the magnetic field of Jupiter and Saturn
Asteroid and meteorite detector (malfunction)	detect small interplanetary bodies by the solar radiation which they reflect
Meteorite detector	detect meteorites by impact
Radio transmitter for Deep Space Network	use celestial mechanics to find mass of Jupiter and its Galilean moons, and of Saturn, its rings and Titan
Ultraviolet photometer	observe scattered ultraviolet solar radiation, and ultraviolet radiation emitted by hydrogen and helium in interplanetary space and in the atmospheres of Jupiter and Saturn
Photopolarimeter	study zodiacal light, and light from the stars in the galaxy
Infrared radiometer	observe infrared radiation emitted by Jupiter and Saturn
Radio transmitter for Deep Space Network	carry out occultation experiments (S band) to determine ionospheric structure of Jupiter and Saturn

larger grains. The other three were remote sensing instruments designed to study Jupiter and Saturn and the latter's rings and moons.

Once assembled, the Pioneer probes had a mass of 258 kilograms, of which just 30 kilograms comprised scientific instruments. Launched by an Atlas Centaur rocket to reach a cruising speed of 51 500 kilometres per hour, each probe followed a curved trajectory which took it a thousand million kilometres around the Sun, from the Earth to Jupiter. The first part of the journey provided information on the radiation belts around the Earth and the risks facing the spacecraft when they arrived at Jupiter. The probes also spent six months passing through the asteroid belt from which they escaped intact in spite of the risk of being hit by a cosmic stone or lump of rock.

The Jupiter element in the programme began on 26 November 1973. About 6·4 million kilometres from Jupiter the instruments recorded a sudden change from interplanetary conditions to those caused by Jupiter's magnetic field. Several of the instruments became saturated. Pioneer 10 ultimately cruised past Jupiter at a distance of 130 000 kilometres above the clouds on 3 December 1973, just as Pioneer 11 was emerging from the asteroid belt. Pioneer 11 was programmed to pass closer to Jupiter, at a distance of 43 000 kilometres, on 2 December 1974, and performed just as planned; although the spacecraft's performance was affected by Jupiter's radiation belts, excellent photographs were taken of the North pole which had never before been observed from the Earth.

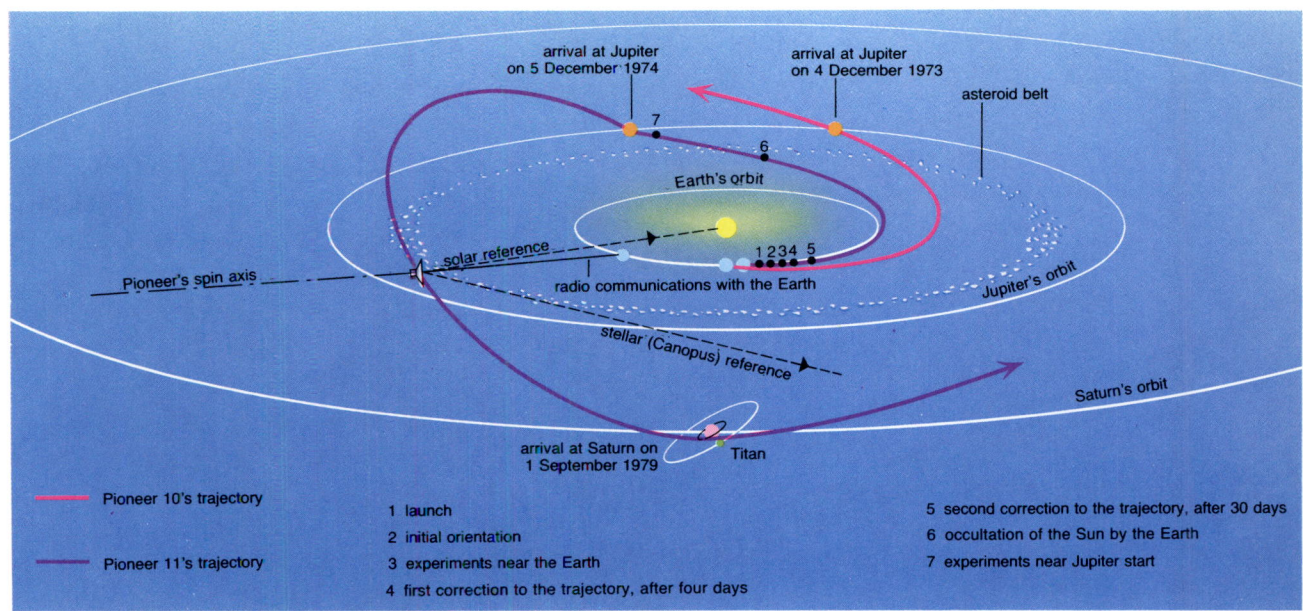

The trajectories of Pioneer 10 and Pioneer 11.

After passing Jupiter, the two spacecraft carried on with their routine measurements of the interplanetary medium. Pioneer 10 travelled towards the edge of the solar system, while Pioneer 11 was directed towards Saturn, using Jupiter's gravity to put it on the right course. It reached Saturn in September 1979, more than six years after launch. It then followed a trajectory that will eventually take it out of the solar system altogether.

Pioneer 11. The Pioneer 11 spacecraft, photographed on the left and shown diagrammatically below, consisted of a hexagonal compartment, 36 centimetres high, whose sides measured 71 centimetres; on one of these sides was a package containing most of the scientific experiments. On the main body was located a high gain antenna, with a dish which measured 2·74 metres in diameter and 46 centimetres deep, a low gain antenna, and two 3 metre arms, at an angle of 120 degrees, which had radioisotope thermal generators of electricity at their ends. The magnetometer used to measure the magnetic field in space was at the end of a 6·6 metre long rod maintained at an angle of 120 degrees to the two other arms.

During the mission, the axis of the high gain antenna was kept oriented towards the Earth to facilitate communications. The spacecraft was, in addition, stabilised by spinning it about this axis like a gyro-

scope. This rotation, the spacecraft's attitude and velocity were controlled by three pairs of small thrusters, which could be operated either continuously or in short bursts.

The temperature in the interior of the scientific payload compartment was kept at between −23 to −38 degrees celsius. The thermal control system was able to adjust the temperature to cope with the effects of moving away from the Sun and passing through the shadow of the Earth, Jupiter or Saturn. It also provided protection against the heat from of the third stage and the radio isotope (plutonium 238) thermal generators.

The excess energy produced was used to charge a battery, brought into play when the instruments were operating in a mode requiring more energy than the generators could provide. Excess energy could also be dissipated into space by way of blades attached to the fission generators (NASA).

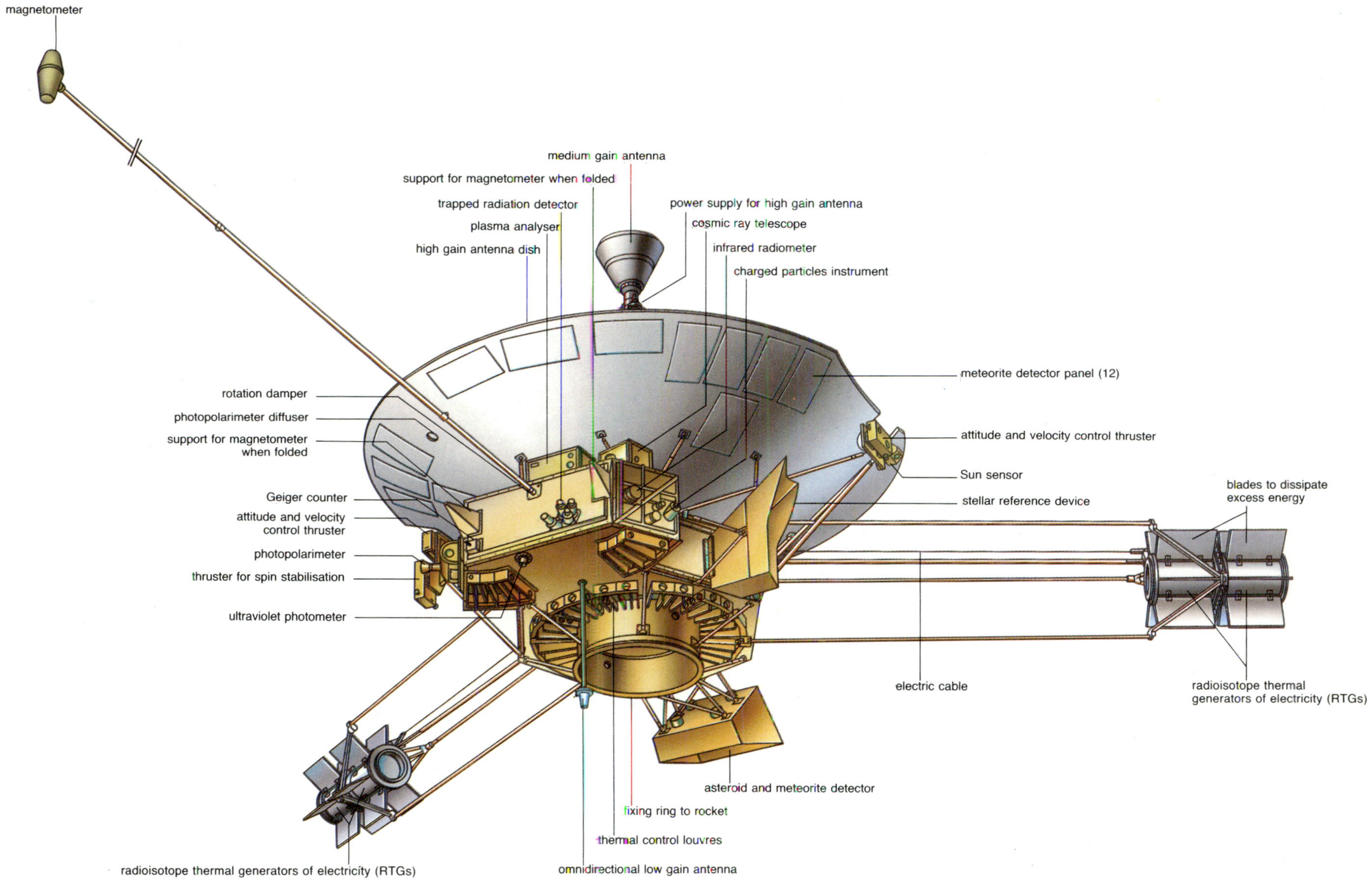

magnetometer

medium gain antenna
support for magnetometer when folded
trapped radiation detector
plasma analyser
high gain antenna dish

power supply for high gain antenna
cosmic ray telescope
infrared radiometer
charged particles instrument

rotation damper
photopolarimeter diffuser
support for magnetometer when folded

meteorite detector panel (12)

attitude and velocity control thruster
Sun sensor
stellar reference device

blades to dissipate excess energy

Geiger counter
attitude and velocity control thruster
photopolarimeter
thruster for spin stabilisation
ultraviolet photometer

electric cable

radioisotope thermal generators of electricity (RTGs)

asteroid and meteorite detector

fixing ring to rocket
thermal control louvres
omnidirectional low gain antenna

radioisotope thermal generators of electricity (RTGs)

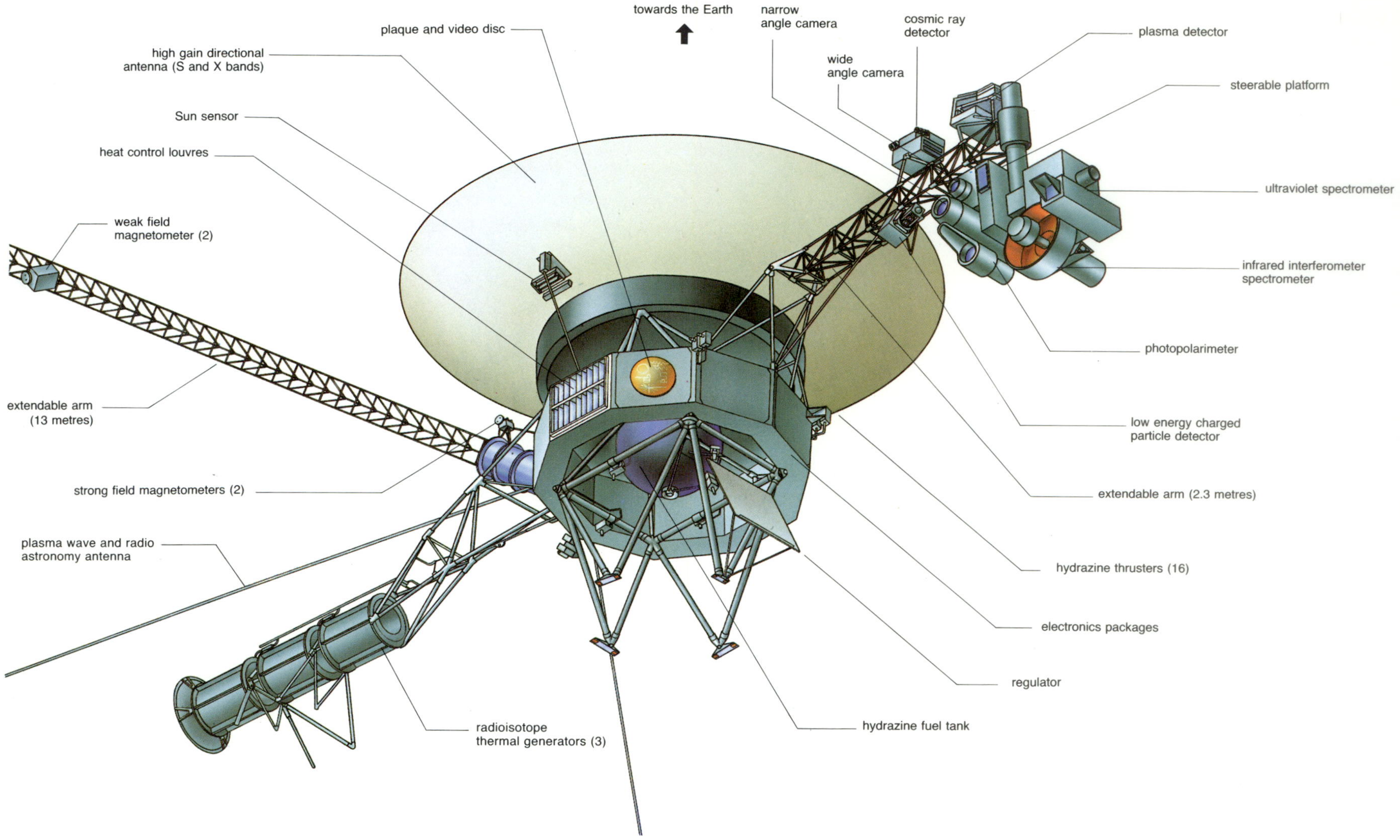

The Voyager spacecraft diagram with labels:

- plaque and video disc
- high gain directional antenna (S and X bands)
- Sun sensor
- heat control louvres
- weak field magnetometer (2)
- extendable arm (13 metres)
- strong field magnetometers (2)
- plasma wave and radio astronomy antenna
- radioisotope thermal generators (3)
- towards the Earth
- narrow angle camera
- wide angle camera
- cosmic ray detector
- plasma detector
- steerable platform
- ultraviolet spectrometer
- infrared interferometer spectrometer
- photopolarimeter
- low energy charged particle detector
- extendable arm (2.3 metres)
- hydrazine thrusters (16)
- electronics packages
- regulator
- hydrazine fuel tank

The Voyager spacecraft. The two Voyager probes were identical, each with a mass of 815 kilograms, and designed around a 10 sided compartment containing electronic control and command systems. The high gain parabolic antenna, 3·7 metres in diameter, was mounted on tubular poles. The radioisotope thermal generators providing electricity and all the scientific instruments were also placed at the ends of extendable arms.

The spacecraft were stabilised by gyroscopes, and there were 16 thrusters for manoeuvres and attitude control. The orientation and trajectory of the spacecraft were maintained with respect to the Sun, the star Canopus and an internal reference system linked to the gyroscopes (NASA).

The Voyager spacecraft and its instruments. Each Voyager spacecraft had 11 instruments, which were either for making *in situ* measurements or for remote sensing. Magnetic fields, charged particles, cosmic rays and the electrically charged gas, or plasma, were observed both in interplanetary space and in the magnetospheres of Jupiter, Saturn and Uranus. Five optical, remote sensing instruments were mounted on a platform which could be pointed in nearly all directions, yet with great precision. There were two cameras (one wide angle and one telephoto) with Vidicon imagers, a Michelson interferometer, an ultraviolet spectrometer and a photopolarimeter. The other remote sensing instrument received and analysed natural radio emissions emanating from the magnetospheres around Jupiter, Saturn and Uranus. The Voyager to Earth radio link was also used for making scientific measurements, the signal being modified by the planet's atmosphere and the rings around Saturn and Uranus. A detailed analysis of the spacecraft's trajectory enabled scientists to calculate the mass of the planet and its moons as the spacecraft passed by.

Three radio isotope (plutonium 238) nuclear generators supplied 450 watts of electrical power to the instruments and other systems (see the diagram above). This power decreased by about 2% per year. A parabolic dish antenna, 3·7 metres in diameter, was used for communications between the probe and the Earth and was always kept facing Earth. The spacecraft maintained its orientation in space using the Sun and stars for reference. Stored in its computer memory was the position of the Earth, with respect to the Sun, for each part of its mission.

The main scientific experiments on board the Voyager probes

Instruments	Experimental objectives
Cosmic ray detector	measure energy spectrum and particle composition of cosmic rays and energetic particles in the outer planets' magnetospheres
Television cameras	photograph planets and their moons at high resolutions and from angles that are impossible from the Earth; film atmospheric motions
Infrared interferometer spectrometer	measure planetary reflectivity (or albedo); measure atmospheric composition and temperature profiles; deduce composition and physical characteristics of surfaces of moons and Saturn's rings
Low energy charged particle detector	obtain energy spectrum and composition of low energy charged particles in the outer planets' magnetospheres and in interplanetary space
Magnetometers	measure planetary and interplanetary magnetic fields
Photopolarimeter	investigate atmospheric methane, ammonia, molecular hydrogen and aerosols; derive composition and physical characteristics of the moons' surfaces and Saturn's rings
Planetary radio astronomy and plasma wave antenna	observe planetary radio emissions and plasma resonances in planetary magnetospheres; observe in planetary magnetospheres interactions between waves in plasma and charged particles; measure electron density
Plasma detector	derive energy spectrum of ions and electrons in solar wind and of charged particles trapped in the planets' magnetospheres
Radio transmitter	deduce physical properties of planetary atmospheres and ionospheres; derive mass, density and gravity fields of planets and their moons; investigate the structure of Saturn's rings
Ultraviolet spectrometer	obtain information on atmospheric composition (hydrogen and helium) and thermal structure of upper atmospheres of outer planets; observe hydrogen and helium in interplanetary and interstellar space

The Pioneer results

The two Pioneer spacecraft made measurements in the interplanetary medium and observed the zodiacal light throughout their journeys into space. In addition, as they passed through the asteroid belt, they showed that it contained far fewer small sized particles than had previously been thought – an important result for the future of space exploration in the solar system beyond the orbit of Mars.

Despite the new data that the probes supplied about interplanetary space, the most eagerly awaited information to come from the Pioneer spacecraft related to the giant planets. The mission confirmed, for instance, that Jupiter emitted twice as much energy as it received from the Sun, and therefore has a significant internal source of energy. It was also shown that Jupiter's magnetic field was two thousand times stronger than the Earth's, the axis of the magnetic field being some 11 degrees off the rotational axis and off centre by about 10 000 kilometres. Measurements were made on the inner and outer magnetosphere, and Jupiter's famous red spot was shown to be a meteorological phenomenon.

The mission to Saturn was equally successful. Pioneer 11 observed the rings as they had never been seen before, and a new ring was even discovered, ring G. Yet the most important discovery concerned the magnetic field. The planet is now believed to have a core consisting of heavy elements, about the same size as the Earth's but three times as heavy; however, for Saturn, it is not the core that produces the magnetic field, but electric currents flowing in the metallic mantle. Other studies were able to confirm that Saturn is the only planet with a magnetic axis almost exactly in line with its rotational axis.

As Pioneer 11 passed by, it also discovered new moons near the rings. Observations in the infrared part of the spectrum revealed temperatures of about 100 kelvin in Saturn's atmosphere and for its rings; these results imply that, like Jupiter, Saturn emits more energy than it receives from the Sun – probably about two and a half times as much.

The imaging systems took some remarkable pictures, but their results were soon outclassed by the images obtained by the Voyager spacecraft, launched some two years before Pioneer 11 arrived at Saturn.

The Voyager missions

The Voyager spacecraft were more sophisticated than the Pioneers. With a mass of 815 kilograms, they each had a central body with a diameter of 3·7 metres, to which the radio antenna, and three arms were attached. Communications between the Earth and the spacecraft were made with the antenna always being pointed to the Earth; the 23 watt transmitters sent radio signals over a thousand million kilometres to be received by ground stations with very large dish antennae.

Visiting Jupiter and Saturn. The diagrams on the right give the Voyager 1 trajectory (in red) and the Voyager 2 trajectory (in blue) near Jupiter (upper part) and Saturn (lower part). They are shown in the equatorial planes of the planets and in planes perpendicular to these. The Voyager 1 and 2 spacecraft passed Jupiter on 5 March 1979 and 9 July 1979, and Saturn on 12 November 1980 and 26 August 1981, respectively. The orbiting moons, or satellites, are drawn to a much larger scale than the planets. The minimum distances of the flypasts are indicated by the dotted lines, the times before and after the flypasts being noted, in hours, on the spacecraft trajectories. The data tables show data relevant to the time of closest approach in hours, h, and minutes, min, and the distance in kilometres, km, between the probe and the centre of mass of each of the objects in question.

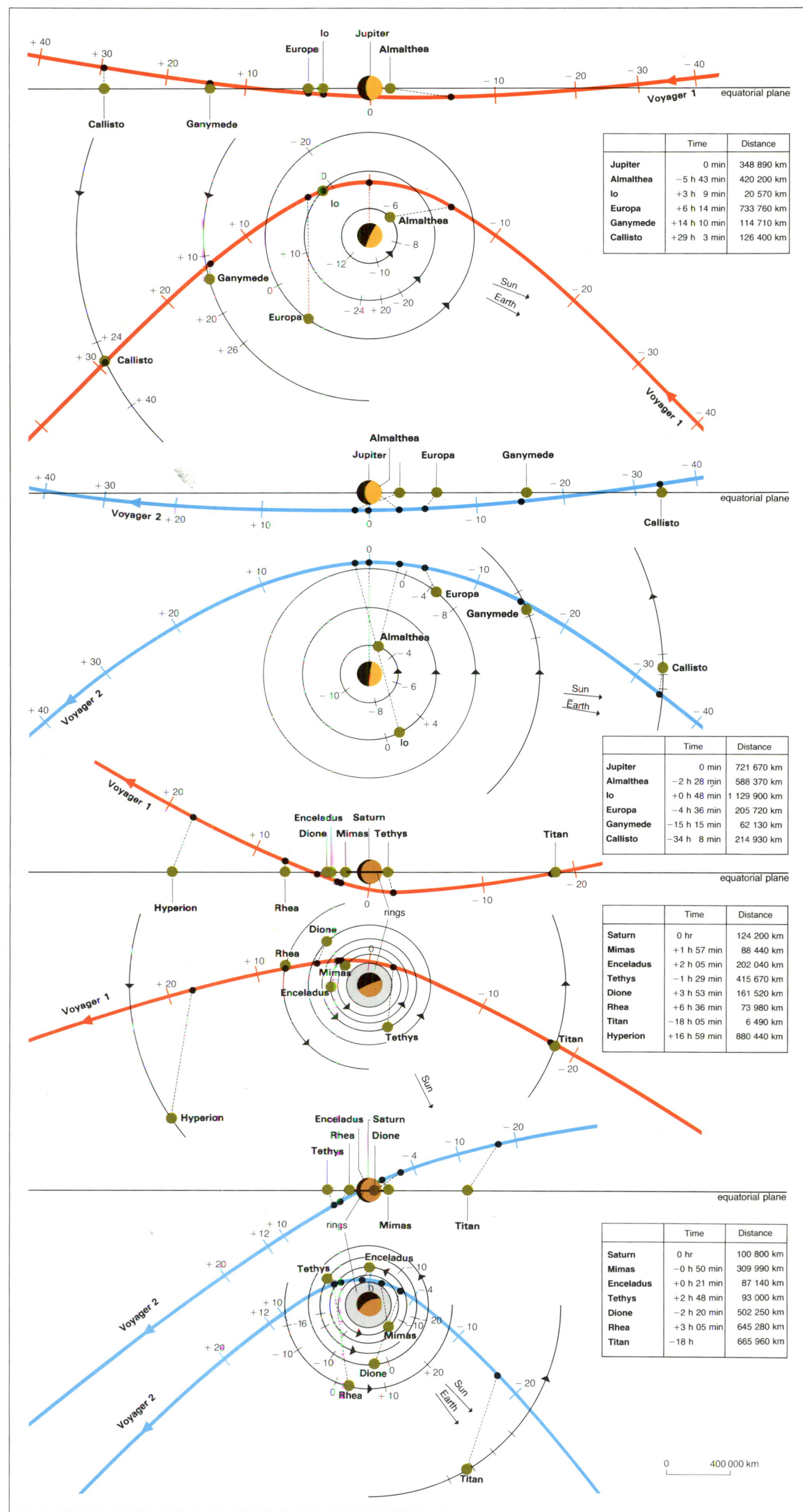

	Time	Distance
Jupiter	0 min	348 890 km
Almalthea	−5 h 43 min	420 200 km
Io	+3 h 9 min	20 570 km
Europa	+6 h 14 min	733 760 km
Ganymede	+14 h 10 min	114 710 km
Callisto	+29 h 3 min	126 400 km

	Time	Distance
Jupiter	0 min	721 670 km
Almalthea	−2 h 28 min	588 370 km
Io	+0 h 48 min	1 129 900 km
Europa	−4 h 36 min	205 720 km
Ganymede	−15 h 15 min	62 130 km
Callisto	−34 h 8 min	214 930 km

	Time	Distance
Saturn	0 hr	124 200 km
Mimas	+1 h 57 min	88 440 km
Enceladus	+2 h 05 min	202 040 km
Tethys	−1 h 29 min	415 670 km
Dione	+3 h 53 min	161 520 km
Rhea	+6 h 36 min	73 980 km
Titan	−18 h 05 min	6 490 km
Hyperion	+16 h 59 min	880 440 km

	Time	Distance
Saturn	0 hr	100 800 km
Mimas	−0 h 50 min	309 990 km
Enceladus	+0 h 21 min	87 140 km
Tethys	+2 h 48 min	93 000 km
Dione	−2 h 20 min	502 250 km
Rhea	+3 h 05 min	645 280 km
Titan	−18 h	665 960 km

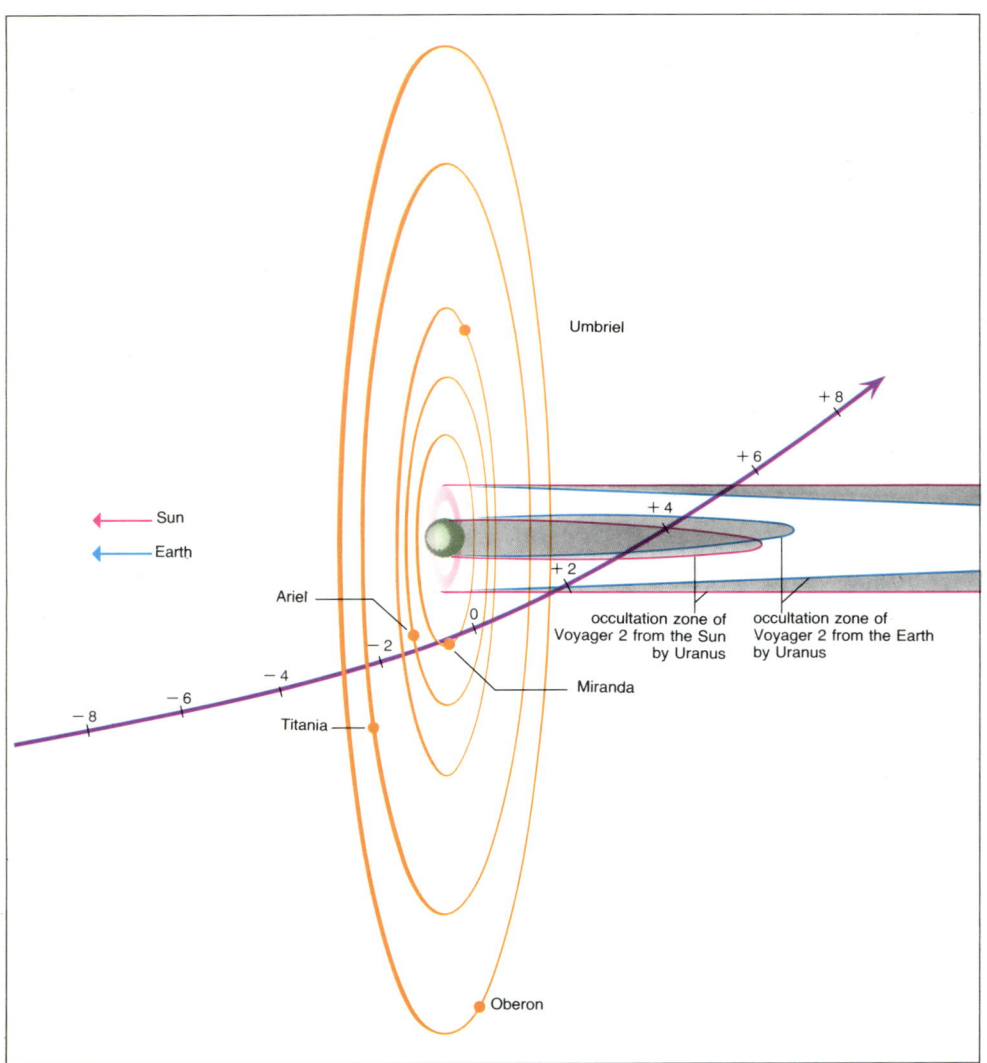

Saturn, its rings, and two of its moons, Tethys and Dione. Saturn has an elaborate system of rings and also 17 moons; the surfaces of the moons all exhibit a high proportion of ice to rock, between 50 and 90%. As Voyager passed by, it discovered that the rings were composed of thousands of small rings of ice particles, whose spatial density is influenced by the moons and by the prevailing magnetic field. Their thickness is only about 1 kilometre.

On this image, the shadow of the rings on the planet is clearly seen (JPL/NASA).

Voyager 2's trajectory past Uranus. This diagram showing Voyager 2's path as it passed close to Uranus is drawn in the plane of the spacecraft's trajectory. The position of the moons is shown at the time, in hours, corresponding to time zero, the time of closest approach, at a distance of 107 000 kilometres from the centre of the planet. The shadow (or occultation) zones of the Sun and the Earth are shown for the planet and for the planetary ring system.

Twenty-four hours before the flypast, Voyager 2 was 1·2 million kilometres from Uranus. The detail of the cloud layers started to become visible twelve hours later, and the equatorial cloud bands could be seen six hours before closest approach. Soon after, some detail was becoming visible on the rings. The probe passed through Miranda's orbit one hour and ten minutes before the time of closest approach, at a distance of only 12 700 kilometres.

Eight hours after passing Uranus, Voyager 2 set its course for Neptune, which it reached on 25 August 1989.

The dish for receiving radio signals from Voyager at Canberra, Australia. This 64 metre diameter dish is one of the three giant dishes in NASA's Deep Space Network. The other two are at Goldstone, California, and near Madrid, in Spain. The dishes are spread over the globe so that they can maintain continuous contact with interplanetary spacecraft such as Pioneer and Voyager. The network is managed by the Jet Propulsion Laboratory of the California Institute of Technology (JPL/NASA).

Voyager's steerable platform. This platform is equipped with various instruments for making high quality images of the giant planets and their moons. On the top left is the wide angle camera with a field of view of 3 degrees. The narrow angle camera is below it; its field of view is 0·4 degrees. Each camera has several filters: for the wide angle unit, these filters are in the violet, blue, green, orange, and yellow bands (with a wavelength of 589 nanometres, for sodium) and at the 541 nanometres and 618 nanometres methane absorption bands.

Below the cameras is the interferometer spectrometer, with its large mirror, operating at wavelengths between 4 and 50 microns (micrometres) to probe the atmospheres. The ultraviolet spectrometer, on the right, observes Jupiter's and Saturn's atmosphere and aurorae. The photopolarimeter is on the left, in a recess. It was designed to measure the amount of light and its polarisation to study the surfaces of the moons and the rings, but has never worked well enough to provide useful data (JPL/NASA).

Io, in front of Jupiter. This remarkable Voyager image shows Jupiter's volcanic moon, Io, with the swirling atmosphere below.

Voyager passed each of the Galilean moons on 5 and 6 March 1979, observing all four of them. These moons are similar to small planets. Europa and Io are almost the same size as the Earth's Moon, whilst Ganymede and Callisto are larger, only a little smaller than Mars. They move in almost circular orbits, and interact strongly with energetic charged particles and the plasma of Jupiter's magnetosphere. During its passage, Voyager discovered two more moons, bringing the number now known to 16 (NASA).

Miranda as observed by Voyager 2. Voyager's trip to Uranus obtained the first detailed images of its moons. Miranda is the moon closest to the planet, and is both heavily cratered and stressed (JPL/NASA).

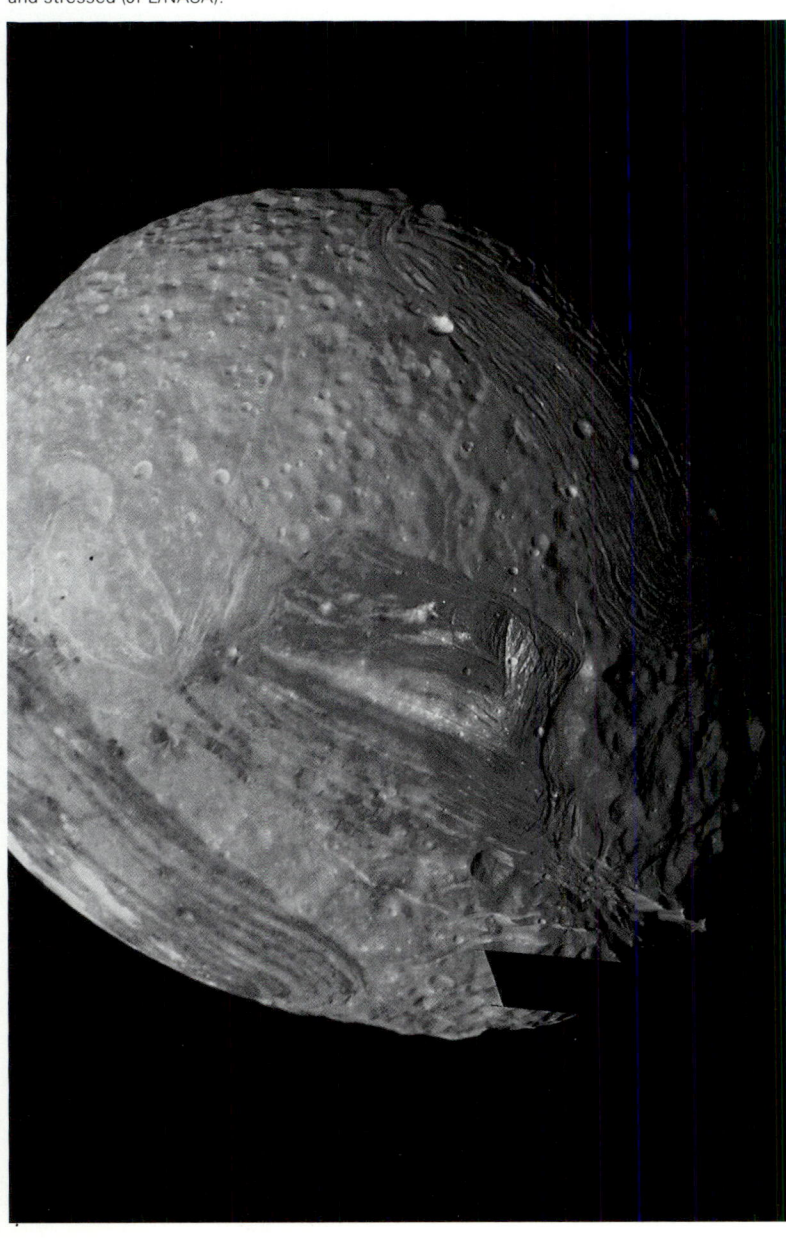

The Voyager probes transmit data to the Earth at a maximum rate of 115 200 bits per second, a hundred times faster than the Pioneer probes did. The transmission rate can be varied to suit the mission's requirements, and the spacecraft also have a digital recorder with a capacity of 500 million bits.

Each Voyager spacecraft has three 400 watt nuclear generators of electricity. The spacecraft are controlled by the Attitude and Articulation Control Subsystem (AACS), the Flight Data Subsystem (FDS) and the Computer Command Subsystem (CCS). The spacecraft are, moreover, sophisticated enough to detect errors and make corrections before the Earth based controllers know anything about them; they are the most complex space vehicles that have ever been built.

Each Voyager spacecraft was launched by a Titan Centaur rocket. During the first phase, the Titan stage placed the Voyager Centaur system into a low Earth orbit. The Centaur and another small rocket then provided the Voyager spacecraft with enough energy to begin its journey to Jupiter. Travelling at 52 000 kilometres per hour, they reached the lunar orbit in less than 10 hours, a journey that took the Apollo missions three days.

Each spacecraft followed a long curved trajectory to Jupiter after taking nearly nine months to pass through the asteroid belt. After 16 months in flight, Voyager 1 was close enough to begin observing the planet Jupiter on 4 January 1979, although it was still 60 million kilometres away. Even at this distance, the image quality was better than anything that had ever been obtained by a telescope on Earth.

The Voyager spacecraft had several scientific objectives, but the one which seized most people's imagination was the powerful imaging of the giant planets. The imaging system was composed of two television cameras, each fitted with a range of filters; one camera was fitted with a wide angle lens with a field of view of 3 degrees, the other with a narrow angle lens of 0·4 degrees field of view. Black and white images were produced every 48 seconds, and colour images were obtained by combining the monochrome pictures taken with different filters. Such a picture of Saturn was received every three minutes.

During the approach phase, observations were carried out to examine the atmospheric circulation and changes in Jupiter's red spot. Programmes to observe the moons of Jupiter were also activated, using ultraviolet and infrared spectrometry, photopolarimetry and imaging.

Voyager 1 passed closest to Jupiter on 5 March 1979, 280 000 kilometres from the planet. Even though the spacecraft was then subjected to intense bombardment by high energy charged particle radiation in the magnetosphere, it continued to observe Jupiter for another six weeks. During this time, Voyager 2 also entered its observation phase, passing within 645 000 kilometres of the planet on 9 September 1979. It followed a different trajectory to Voyager 1 to avoid the intense radiation belts and obtain complementary observations.

After the flypast, the two spacecraft used Jupiter's gravity to place themselves on a trajectory towards Saturn. Voyager 1 reached its goal on 12 November 1980, passing within 140 000 kilometres of the planet above the South pole. Hundreds of images were made with the two cameras, and the polarimeter and the ultraviolet and infrared spectrometers were used to examine the rings. Measurements on the charged particles and magnetic fields began particularly early, in mid October, in an attempt to calculate the size of Saturn's magnetosphere. The distances involved meant that some of the pictures had to be recorded before being transmitted by radio, and the radio signal took a staggering hour and a half to reach the Earth.

The day before the flypast, Voyager 1 passed within 4000 kilometres of Titan, and later on passed other moons – Tethys, Mimas, Enceladus, Dione and Rhea.

Nine months later, on 22 August 1981, Voyager 2 also reached Saturn and used the planet's gravity in the same way to put itself on a trajectory towards Uranus. Uranus was ultimately reached on 24 January 1986, Voyager 2 flying over the planet at a distance of 81 000 kilometres above the cloud layer. After four years of silence, the spacecraft was reactivated and delivered precious information on this strange world, hurtling past at a speed of 75 000 kilometres per hour. Its orbit was then directed towards Neptune, which it reached on 25 August 1989.

The Voyager results

The two Voyager spacecraft have supplied an astonishing amount of information about the giant planets. They made, for instance, detailed observations of the jovian atmosphere enabling scientists to determine the meteorological characteristics of the red spot and the anticyclonic winds which are associated with it. A very strong ultraviolet emission from Jupiter, which indicated temperatures in excess of 1000 kelvin, was also measured.

The spacecraft examined the planets' moons, and Voyager 1 passed very close to Io whilst it was undergoing volcanic eruptions and ejecting sulphur and sulphur dioxide. Much more is now known about Europa, Ganymede and Callisto too: all are heavily cratered or fractured moons, evolving or frozen by the weather.

Around Saturn, Voyager 2 discovered a myriad of small rings, composed of thousands of millions of ice and dust particles, and confirmed earlier indications that Saturn and Jupiter had a similar hydrogen and helium composition.

Seventeen moons were examined, the smallest being 20 kilometres in diameter and the largest, Titan, 5140 kilometres. Titan appears as an orange sphere, with an opaque atmosphere, the composition of which could be similar to the Earth's primitive atmosphere. Other of the moons turned out to be inhospitable, frozen worlds.

Continuing on its journey, Voyager 2 then visited Uranus, sending back images of its moons which showed them also to be very strange worlds, especially Miranda, which is geologically active. Ten small moons were examined in addition to the five larger ones – Miranda, Ariel, Umbriel, Titania and Oberon – the diameters of which, ranging from 300 kilometres to 1600 kilometres, were accurately measured for the first time. Voyager 2 measured the length of a day on Uranus, 16 hours 48 minutes, and found clear evidence of a magnetic field; its intensity was similar to the Earth's, but the magnetic axis made an angle of 55 degrees with the rotational axis. Uranus also proved to be surrounded by an ultraviolet halo resulting from shocks between high speed electrons and hydrogen atoms.

While Voyager 1 travelled into outer space, Voyager 2 continued on its journey towards Neptune, which it successfully observed on 25 August 1989. A system of rings was discovered, and it was found too that the magnetic field axis is strongly tilted away from the rotational axis. The probe went to within 5000 kilometres of Neptune itself, passing only 25 000 kilometres from its large moon, Triton. High cirrus clouds and a large dark spot were seen on Neptune, while Triton's surface looked strikingly blotchy; this is probably due to the sublimation of methane ice by the weak sunlight.

Such images and results provide a fitting climax to the Voyager 2 mission. Voyager 2's final act, in spring 1990, was to transmit images looking back across the span of the entire solar system.

Nathalie Cabrol

Exploring the solar system

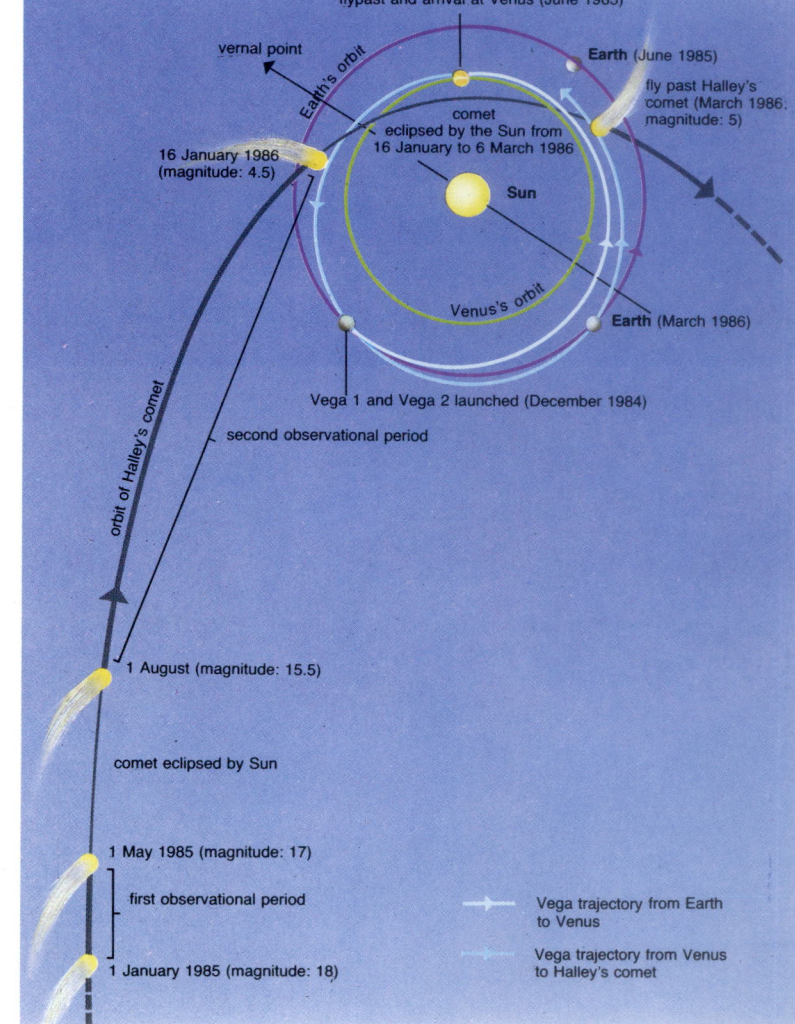

NUCLEUS OF COMET HALLEY
HALLEY MULTICOLOUR CAMERA
COMPOSITE OF 60 IMAGES

Sun

Comets

Since the beginning of time, mankind has regarded comets as heavenly bodies portending change, whether for good or evil. Careful scientific observations in this century have, however, revealed their true nature and provided remarkable information about the formation of the solar system.

Since the creation of the solar system, cometary bodies have existed in the Oort cloud, at its very edges. There, they have changed only little because of their relatively small sizes and the very low temperatures. When a star passes close to the Oort cloud, it changes the gravitational force and this causes a number of comets to be ejected into the inner solar system. There they can be trapped forever or put into elliptical orbits under the effect of gravitational forces caused by a giant planet. In the most fundamental way, scientific interest in comets therefore stems from the fact that their physical and chemical properties are characteristic of the primitive nebula out of which the solar system was formed.

The objective – Halley's comet

There was unprecedented mobilisation in the scientific community as Halley's comet became due to pass near the Sun in 1986. The comet reappears periodically, about every 76 years; the first known sighting was in 240 BC, and Halley himself observed it in 1682. Each time the comet has passed, its journey has been well documented so that its trajectory has become accurately enough known for space probes to be sent to fly past it.

Now, however, *in situ* measurements could be made for the first time. A flotilla of five space probes was planned to examine Halley's comet at close quarters. The Soviet Vega 1 and Vega 2 probes, the Japanese Suisei and Sakigake probes, and the European Giotto probe had complementary missions and payloads coordinated between the European Space Agency, the Soviet Intercosmos Agency, NASA, and the Japanese ISAS. In addition to these specially designed probes, other scientific spacecraft and astronomical experiments already in existence were used for observation, and about 800 scientists from 40 different

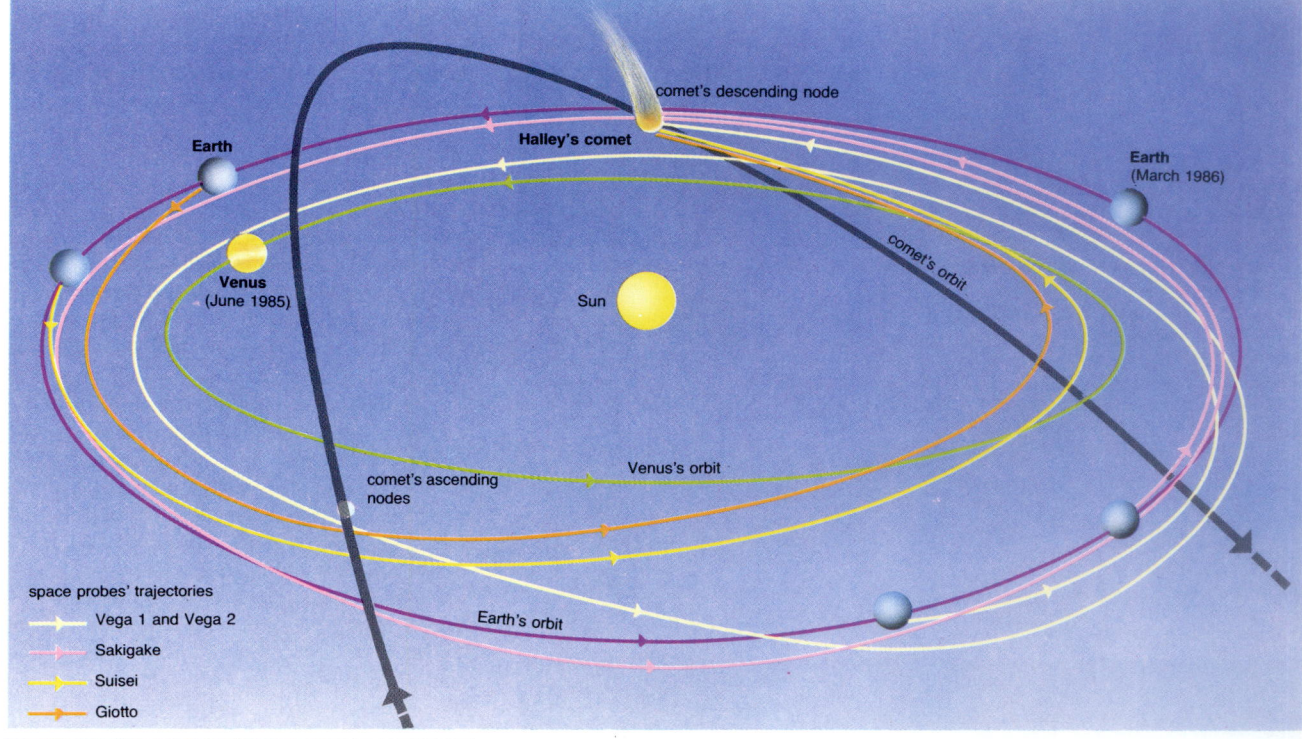

Probe	Date (1986)	Flypast Distance (km)	Relative velocity (km/s)
Vega 1	6 March	8890	79.2
Vega 2	9 March	8030	76.8
Sakigake	11 March	6 990 000	—
Suisei	8 March	151 000	73
Giotto	14 March	605	68.4

The missions to fly past Halley's comet. The schematic diagram above, drawn looking down on the ecliptic plane, shows the different trajectories taken by the space probes to reach Halley's comet. The comet was moving in the opposite direction to the probes, and so the relative velocity between probes and comet was very high, 70 kilometres per second (km/s) or more.

The ESA space probe Giotto obtained the image of Halley's comet at the top of the page, assembled from 60 different images at this close encounter. The most brilliant parts are jets of dust, coming from the nucleus. The outline of the dark side of the comet, the side facing away from the Sun, is clearly visible as is its elongated shape, measuring 14 kilometres by 7 kilometres (rights reserved).

The Vega mission. The two Soviet Vega probes were launched in December 1984, their first task to drop two landing probes on Venus and to analyse the planet's atmosphere and surface. They then continued their journey towards Halley's comet, in the manner shown in the diagram to the right. The brightness of the comet at different times is described using the stellar magnitude scale.

The aims of the mission were to obtain pictures of the comet's nucleus, to identify its dimensions, nature and albedo, to analyse the physical chemical processes taking place in the comet's tail, to determine the composition of the gas and the dust at different distances from the nucleus, and, finally, to examine the interaction of the solar wind with the comet's ionosphere and atmosphere.

The instruments for measuring the plasma were activated two days before the flypast, the data being stored aboard the probe and relayed, at a low rate, during periods of visibility. The centre of flight operations was at Evpatoria in the Crimea, but the data transmitted in real time were also received at the Institute of Space Research in Moscow. The telemetry signals were received by the 70 metre diameter dish at Evpatoria and the 64 metre diameter dish at Medvezy Ozera, near Moscow.

During the postcomet encounter trials, it was found that several instruments had been damaged, and that the power from the solar panels had been reduced by 50%, probably because solar cells had been destroyed by cometary dust.

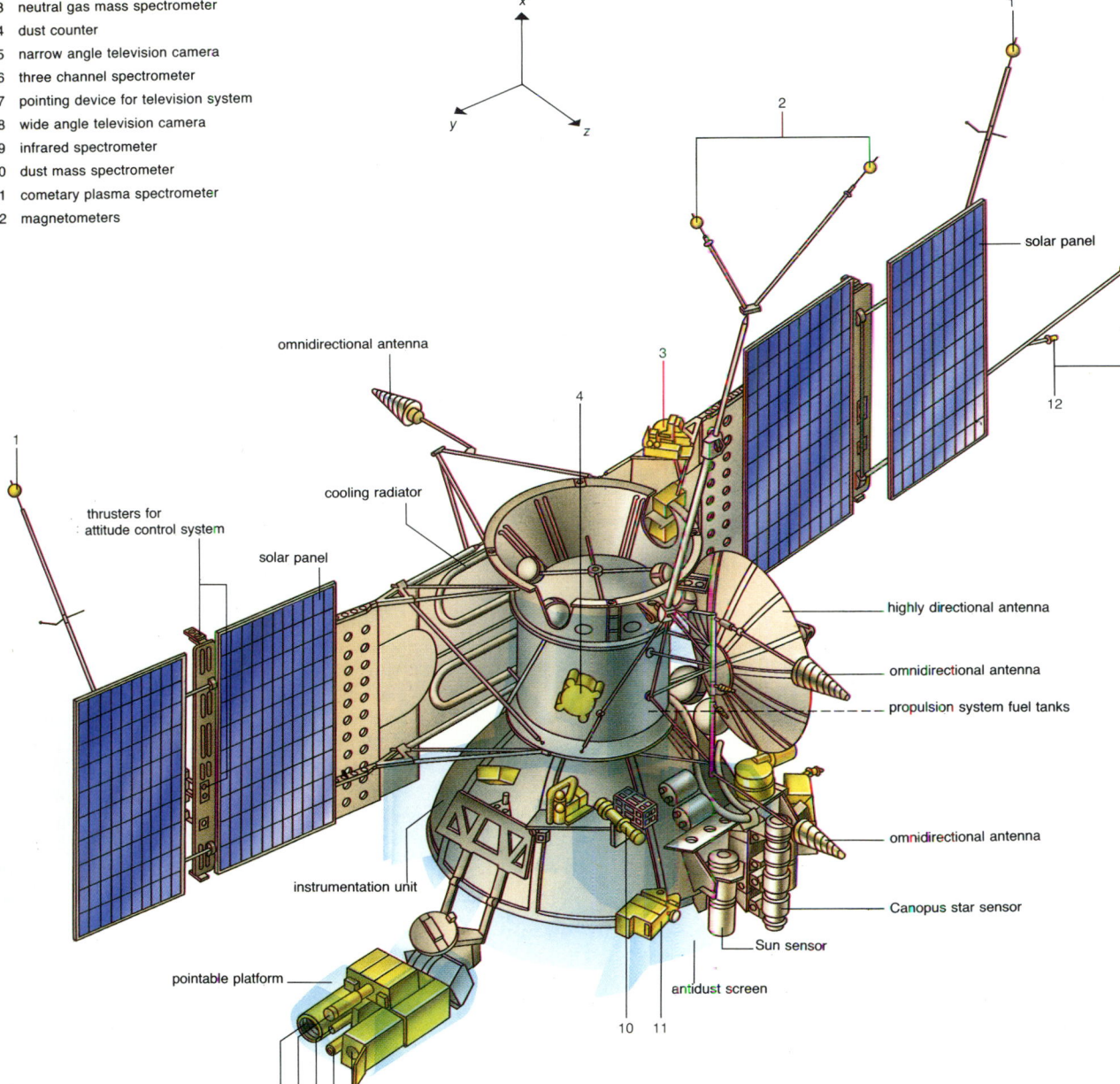

1 plasma amd wave analyser
2 plasma and wave analyser
3 neutral gas mass spectrometer
4 dust counter
5 narrow angle television camera
6 three channel spectrometer
7 pointing device for television system
8 wide angle television camera
9 infrared spectrometer
10 dust mass spectrometer
11 cometary plasma spectrometer
12 magnetometers

solar panel

omnidirectional antenna

thrusters for attitude control system

cooling radiator

solar panel

highly directional antenna

omnidirectional antenna

propulsion system fuel tanks

omnidirectional antenna

instrumentation unit

Canopus star sensor

Sun sensor

pointable platform

antidust screen

countries, working as the International Halley Watch, coordinated telescopic observations made around the world by both professional and amateur astronomers.

Although the five space probes were launched on different dates, between December 1984 and August 1985, they all passed Halley's comet within a week of one another. The comet was then at its descending node, that is crossing the ecliptic plane, and was also most active, having passed through perihelion on 9 February 1986. The space probes were travelling at velocities of about 30 kilometres per second and the comet had a velocity of about 40 kilometres per second, but in the opposite direction. The relative velocity of probe to comet was thus about 70 kilometres per second or 250 000 kilometres per hour.

The Vega mission

The international Vega mission (or Venera–Galleya, the Russian for Venus–Halley) was a mission to both Venus and Halley's comet, using two unmanned space probes, Vega 1 and Vega 2. The Soviet Union was responsible for the probes and for launching them, but France, West Germany, Austria, the USA and all the nine Eastern European countries in Intercosmos were involved in the scientific programme and in providing parts of the payload. The two Vega probes were launched from Baikonur Tyuratam on 15 and 21 December 1984, and arrived at Venus in June 1985. Both dropped a balloon into the atmosphere, and then made use of Venus's gravity to launch themselves onto a trajectory towards Halley's comet.

The two Vega probes were the first to fly past, on 6 and 9 March, and their results enabled the comet's motion to be calculated with precision. Its location was pinpointed by using a television system to measure its position with respect to the Vega probes, the positions

The configuration of the Vega probes during the flypast of Halley's comet. The identical Vega 1 and Vega 2 probes were 2·9 metres high, with a mass of about 2·5 tonnes, excluding the Venus landing probe which had an additional mass of 2 tonnes. This landing probe is not visible on either of the pictures below.

During the launch phase, the solar panels and the steerable platform were folded inwards. The solar panels were deployed and locked into position about 30 minutes after launch, but the platform was not unfolded until 20 days before the flypast of Halley's comet after final trajectory corrections had been made.

The probes were stabilised about all three axes, with the y direction towards the Earth. The attitude control system consisted of jets of cold nitrogen gas and most of the thrusters were on the solar panels. Trajectory corrections were made by firing a rocket engine.

There were three categories of instruments making up the scientific payload. Depending on the nature of the measurements, they were located in three different regions. Instruments for making electro-magnetic measurements were attached to the tip of an arm away from the perturbations caused by the rest of the space probe; instruments for making *in situ* measurements were attached directly to the probe's body; optical instruments, which needed to be accurately pointed (to within 5 arcminutes) at the comet's nucleus, were placed on the stabilised platform. This explains why the Vega probes, which were based on the earlier Venera craft, had a controllable platform (lower right) containing a television camera, a three channel spectrometer, and an infrared spectrometer. Because of the high relative speed of the probe and comet, and their orientation with respect to the platform, the optical instruments also had an antidust screen which is not shown on this photograph.

Each of the Vega probes carried 209 kilograms of scientific payload, of which 61 kilograms was located on the platform. Data transmission to the Earth was by analogue telemetry, or by slow, direct or recorded digital telemetry transmitted at 3072 bits per second. Rapid direct telemetry, transmitted at a speed of 65 536 bits per second was used to protect against possible destruction of the probe by cometary dust. It took in all 10 minutes for a radio signal to travel from Halley's comet to the Earth (below left: rights reserved; right: APN).

Instrument	Scientific objectives	Mass (kg)	Participating countries
Optical instruments			
TV system	make images of nucleus and inner coma; two CCD cameras (fields of view 0.43° by 0.57° and 3.5° by 5.3°)	32	USSR, Hungary, France
Infrared spectrometer	detect infrared emission from nucleus to determine its dimensions, temperature and emissivity	18	France
Three channel spectrometer	observe emissions from nucleus and coma	14	France, Bulgaria, USSR
In situ measurements of cometary dust			
Dust mass spectrometer	find dust composition in terms of elements present	19	West Germany, USSR, France
Dust counter	derive dust flux and mass spectra (mass>10^{-16} grams)	2	USSR
Dust counter	derive dust flux and mass spectra (mass>10^{-16} grams)	4	USSR
Dust detector	derive dust flux and mass spectra (mass>1.5×10^{-13} grams)	3	Hungary, USSR, West Germany
Dust detector	detect large pieces of dust	2	USSR
In situ experiments to analyse gas, plasma and fields			
Neutral gas mass spectrometer	find composition of neutral gases	7	West Germany, USSR, Hungary
Cometary plasma spectrometer	observe ion composition and energy spectrum of ions and electrons	9	Hungary, USSR, West Germany
Particle analyser	make energy and flux measurements on accelerated cometary ions	5	Hungary, USSR, West Germany
Magnetometer	observe magnetic field	4	Austria, USSR
Plasma and wave analyser	observe plasma waves (0.01 to 1 hertz), variations in ion flux	5	Poland, Czechoslovakia, USSR
Plasma and wave analyser	observe plasma waves (0 to 300 kilohertz), plasma density and temperature	3	France
Pointable platform	point optical instruments at nucleus	82	Czechoslovakia
		209	

Scientific payload carried by the Vega probe

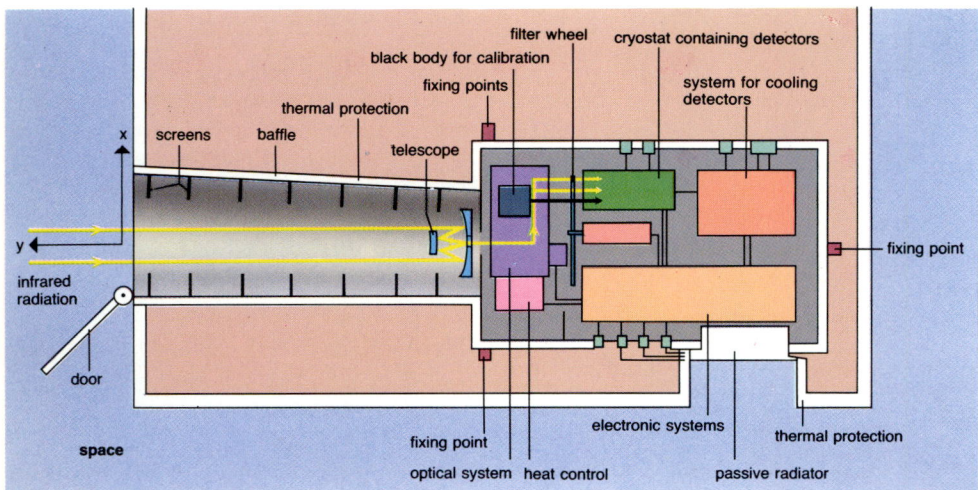

The infrared spectrometer aboard Vega. The infrared spectrometer, shown diagrammatically above, made observations at wavelengths between 2·5 and 12 microns. Its purpose was to identify the most common molecules which escaped from the nucleus of Halley's comet and to measure their abundance, as shown in the spectrum (below). It also measured the temperature of the nucleus for the first time, detecting an emitting region with a temperature of 400 kelvin; this temperature is consistent with the nucleus being a substance covered with a black insulating substance, rather like tar.

of the Vega probes in turn being calculated using NASA's Deep Space Network (DSN). The long baseline interferometry used meant that Giotto's trajectory could be calculated to within ±40 kilometres of the comet's nucleus. The data on the Vega probes' trajectories were transmitted directly from Moscow to the European Space Agency's establishment at Darmstadt in West Germany.

Giotto

Giotto was the first interplanetary mission attempted by the European Space Agency. It was also the first scientific satellite launched by Ariane, and the fourteenth flight of Ariane V. Launched by an Ariane I rocket on 2 July 1985, the probe took its name from the Florentine painter Giotto di Bandone who observed the comet in 1301 and included it in his group of frescoes, *The Adoration of the Magi*, which decorates the inside of the chapel in the Arena at Padua.

Although it was a most ambitious mission, Giotto passed safely to within 605 kilometres of the comet's core on 14 March 1986. During the eight month journey, the spacecraft's systems were tested and fine orientation and trajectory corrections carried out. Several dummy runs were then performed to prepare for the encounter with the comet. The objective was to pass within 600±40 kilometres of the nucleus on the sunward side, the ±40 being the remaining margin of uncertainty about the comet's position following the Vega flypasts. From the camera's observations, closest approach occurred on 14 March 1986 at 3 minutes and 2 seconds past midnight UT, at a distance of 605±8 kilometres from the nucleus.

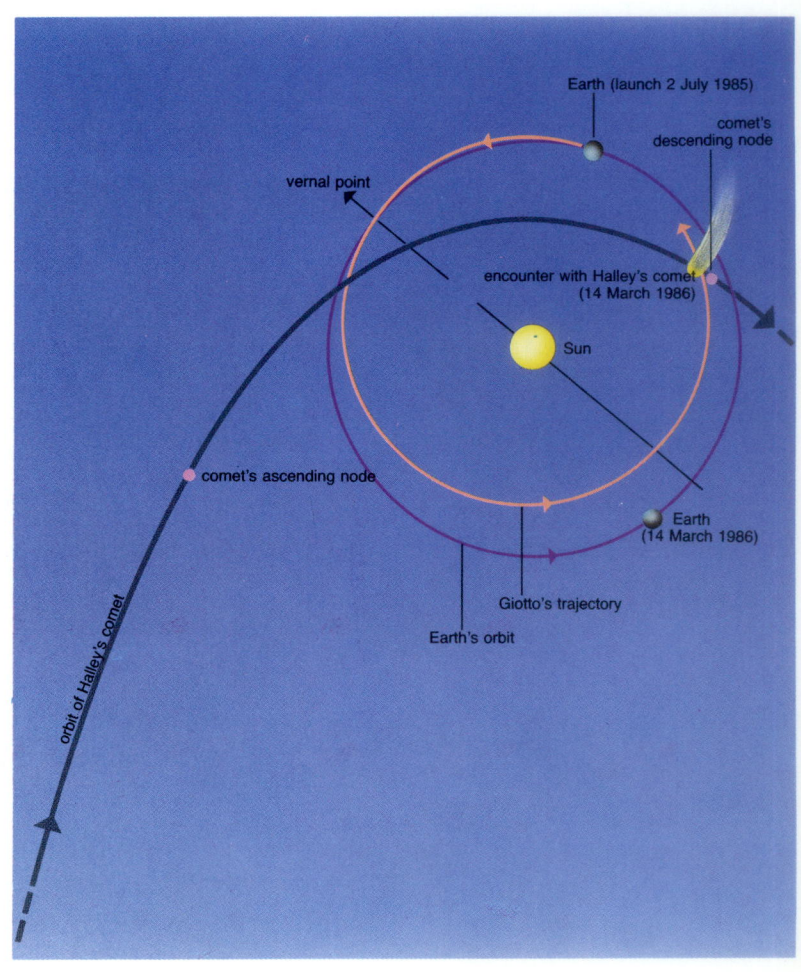

The Giotto mission (below). The Giotto spacecraft was launched on 2 July 1985 from the Guianan Space Centre at Kourou, by an Ariane I launcher. After three revolutions in a geostationary transfer orbit around the Earth, it was put onto a trajectory around the Sun (a heliocentric orbit). After a number of trajectory corrections, it passed close to Halley's comet on 14 March 1986.

The four hours of data collected during the flypast were transmitted in real time. They were received at the Parkes station in Australia, using a dish antenna, 64 metres in diameter, and at the DSN station at Carnavon, also in Australia. Both stations were also used to transmit commands to the Giotto spacecraft.

Fourteen seconds before the moment of closest approach, it is thought that Giotto was hit by an enormous jet of dust from the nucleus. The impact altered the spacecraft's direction of motion by 0·9 degrees, manifesting itself as a nutational movement; the probe began turning around a new axis with an amplitude of 0·9 degrees and a period of 16 seconds. For the 32 minutes that it took the nutational damper to reduce the attitude deviation to its nominal value of about 0·3 degrees, the precise pointing of the high gain antenna towards the Earth could not be maintained. During this time, the experiments were exposed to cometary dust, resulting in damage to the camera's baffle and mirror, and parts of the plasma analysers and mass spectrometers. Some of the probe's sub-systems – the baffle of the star sensor, the thermal regulator and the solar panels – were also damaged by dust during the flypast itself.

Sakigake and Suisei

Developed by ISAS, the two Japanese spacecraft sent to study Halley's comet were the first interplanetary spacecraft constructed by the Japanese. After their launch from the space centre at Kagoshima, they were named Sakigake, or scout, and Suisei, comet.

The two probes were also similar. Their mass was limited to 140 kilograms, so they could not carry a large number of experiments

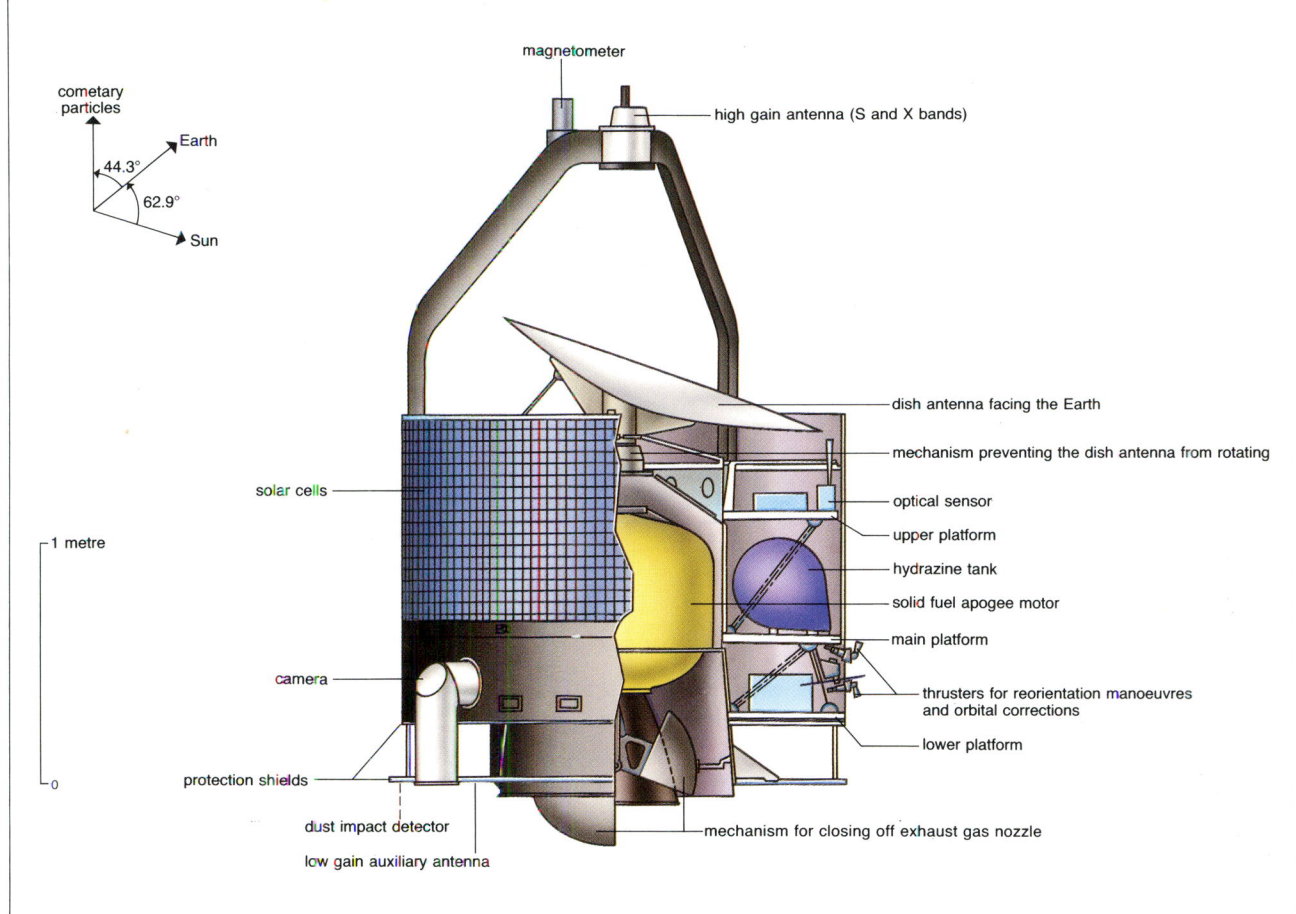

The Giotto spacecraft. The spacecraft, shown diagrammatically above, was cylindrical and was spin stabilised at 15 turns per minute. A tripod mounted on one end supported the magnetometer and supplied power to the antenna. Mounted on the other side of the probe was a high gain parabolic dish, inclined at 44·3 degrees to the rotational axis to keep it pointing at the Earth during the encounter; this operated in either the S band (reception at 2·1 gigahertz and transmission at 2·3 gigahertz) or the X band (8·4 gigahertz).

The total mass of the spacecraft was 960 kilograms at launch; however, by the time it arrived at Halley's comet it weighed only 574 kilograms, the apogee motor having been used and the hydrazine fuel consumed during trajectory alterations and midcourse correction. Only 9 kilograms of the 69 kilograms of hydrazine available had in the end to be used because the probe had been put into the heliocentric orbit so accurately.

A double walled shield protected the lower face of the Giotto spacecraft, and was pointed towards the comet during the encounter.

The photograph to the right shows the Giotto probe, which was made by British Aerospace, just prior to undergoing testing in the solar simulator belonging to Intelspace at Toulouse (ESA).

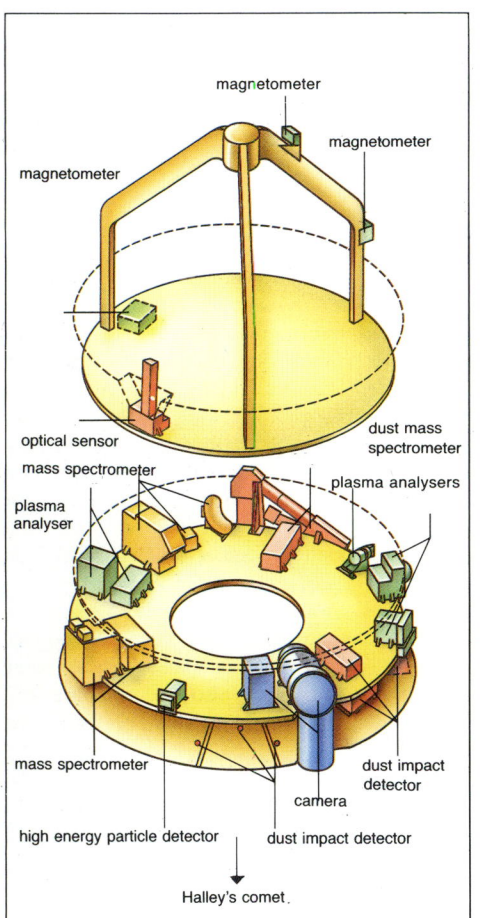

The payload carried by Giotto. One of the main aims of the Giotto mission was to examine the nucleus of Halley's comet and, for this reason, Giotto passed very close. It was specially designed to carry a total of 59 kilograms of instruments, mostly on the lower platform. There were ten *in situ* experiments involving, for example, mass spectrometers, impact detectors and measurement of the plasma and fields around the comet. A break down of Giotto's payload is given in the table below.

All the data were transmitted in real time at a speed of 40 kilobits per second; no data were stored on board. In the drawing to the left are shown the camera (in blue), mass spectrometers for studying the cometary gases (yellow), dust detectors (red), and plasma instruments (green).

Instrument	Scientific objectives	Mass (kg)	Participating countries
Camera	make images of the nucleus and inner coma with 'small field' CCD camera (resolution of 11 metres at 600 kilometres)	13.5	West Germany, France, Italy, Belgium, USA
Neutral gas mass spectrometer	find composition of neutral gases in atomic mass units: 1 to 36 amu, 1 to 57 amu and 9 to 89 amu	12.7	West Germany, Switzerland, France, USA
Ion mass spectrometer	find ion composition using two spectrometers	9.0	Switzerland, West Germany, USA
Dust mass spectrometer	observe flux and composition of dust: 3×10^{-6} to 5×10^{-11} grams	9.9	West Germany
Dust impact detector	dust flux and mass distribution using three detectors: 6×10^{-17} to 6×10^{-16} grams; $>10^{-10}$ grams; 10^{-10} to 10^{-1} grams	2.3	West Germany, France, USA
Plasma analyser	find three dimensional ion velocity distribution in electronvolts: 10 eV to 20 keV; derive flux, mass and velocity distribution of ions	4.7	Great Britain, Italy, West Germany
Plasma analyser	obtain electron velocity distribution in three dimensions: 10 eV to 30 keV; find composition of cold ions: 10 to 50 amu and 50 to 203 amu	3.2	France, West Germany, USA
High energy particle analyser	measure flux of electrons and accelerated ions ≥20 keV	1.0	USA, Ireland, West Germany
Magnetometer	measure magnetic field	1.4	West Germany, USA, Italy
Optical sensor	observe brightness of comet in four continuum bands (dust) and four discrete emission bands	1.3	France, USA
		59.0	

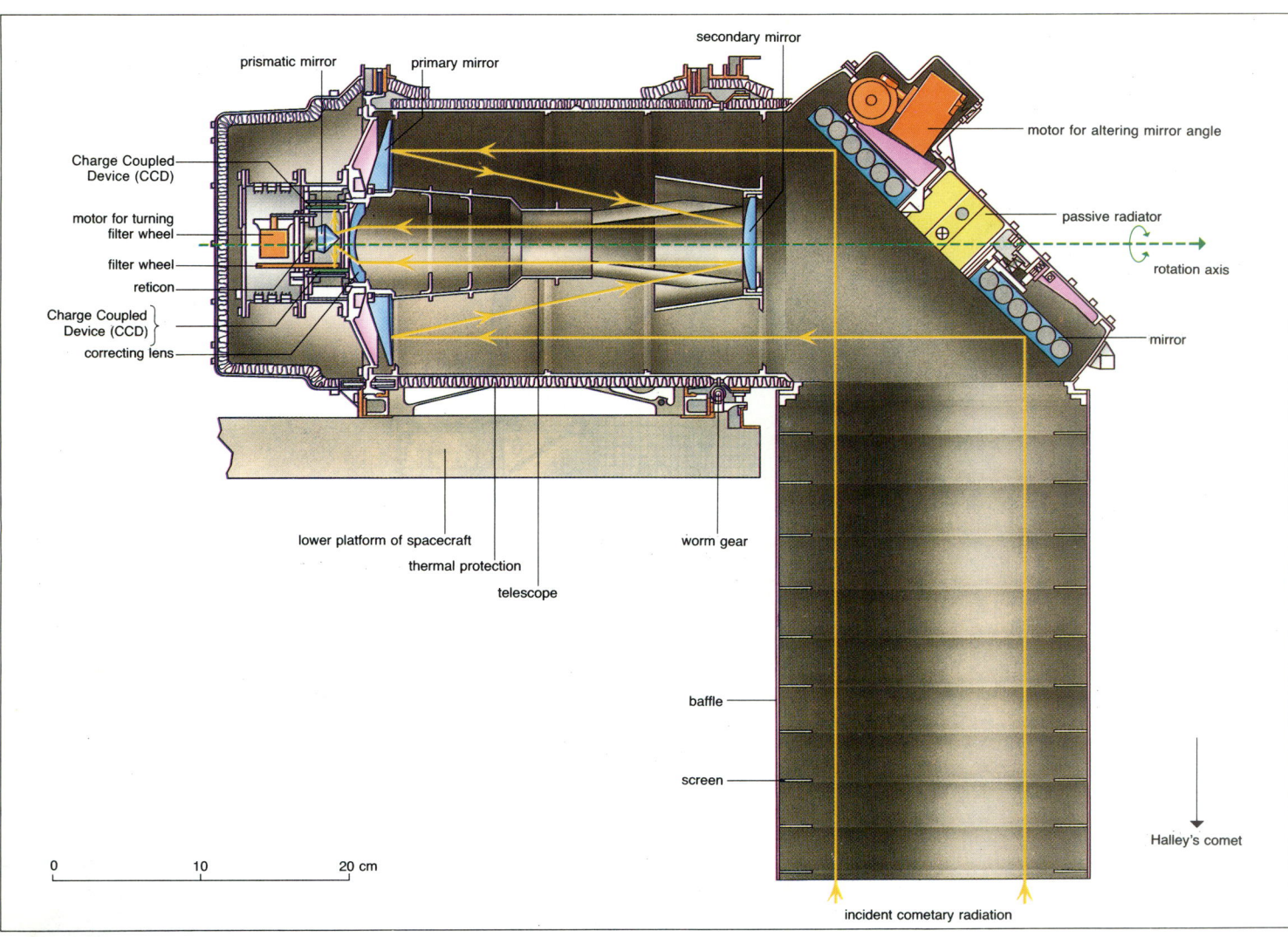

prismatic mirror
primary mirror
secondary mirror
Charge Coupled Device (CCD)
motor for turning filter wheel
filter wheel
reticon
Charge Coupled Device (CCD)
correcting lens
motor for altering mirror angle
passive radiator
rotation axis
mirror
lower platform of spacecraft
thermal protection
telescope
worm gear
baffle
screen
Halley's comet
incident cometary radiation
0   10   20 cm

The multicolour camera carried by Giotto. This camera (pictured centre left) obtained images of the central part of the coma and, in particular, of the nucleus and dust jets which it ejected. The camera consisted of a Ritchey–Chrétien telescope, with a focal length of 1 metre and an aperture of f7·7.

The detection system had four channels; it used two charge coupled devices (CCDs) split into two sections, each one placed behind a diaphragm fixed to a slit. The lines were swept by rotating the spacecraft, and the exposure time varied from 6 milliseconds at the beginning (when the direction of the comet was approximately the same as the direction of the axis of rotation), to 57 microseconds when the spacecraft was closest to Halley's comet (when the axes were perpendicular to each other). The field of view for each of the channels was 0·5 degrees by 0·36 degrees, and the geometric resolution (one pixel) was 11 metres at the distance of closest approach. Three of the measuring channels were fitted with fixed filters (blue, red and visible), and the fourth channel had 11 different filters on a wheel, as shown in the diagram on the left.

The camera was controlled by three microprocessers, which calculated, in real time, the relative trajectory of Giotto with respect to the brightest part of the comet. It had a mass of 13·5 kilograms and used 12 watts of power. The camera supplied high definition images up to 14 seconds before the time of closest approach (ESA).

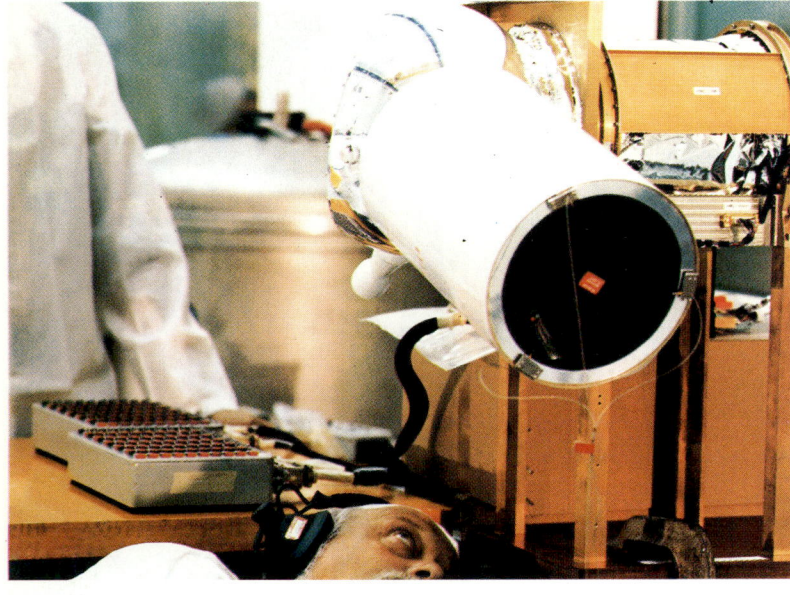

Giotto's encounter with Halley's comet. Giotto passed closest to Halley's comet on 14 March 1986, at 0 hours 3 minutes 2 seconds ± 1 second Universal Time (UT), at a velocity of 68·4 kilometres per second and at a distance of 605±8 kilometres from the nucleus.

The high gain antenna, a parabolic dish, sent the data back to the Earth in real time. Fourteen seconds before the actual moment of closest approach the probe was knocked slightly off course by a jet of dust. This damaged some of the subsystems and prevented the spacecraft from transmitting its final set of data as it flew past for reception at the Earth.

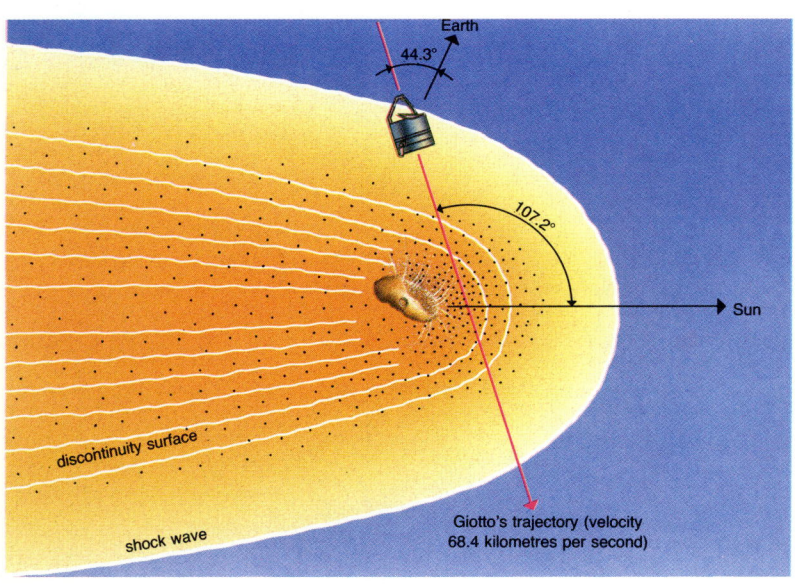

Earth
44.3°
107.2°
Sun
discontinuity surface
shock wave
Giotto's trajectory (velocity 68.4 kilometres per second)

or much protection against impacts from cometary dust and they did not approach Halley's comet as closely as Vega or Giotto. Their main purpose was to gather information on the solar wind, at the time when the other spacecraft were flying by the comet, and also to observe the overall activity of the cometary activity – that is the production of water molecules, ions and jets. Passing between the comet and the Sun, Sakigake measured the solar wind in some detail as planned, while Suisei observed the cometary coma and the interaction between the solar wind and the cometary ions.

A month and a half after launch, the three experiments carried by Sakigake were activated. For the next year, they measured the parameters of the solar wind and correlated these with the behaviour of the comet's tail. The imaging device on Suisei was activated rather later, in September 1985. After several fruitless attempts to observe the comet Giacobini Zinner at the moment the International Cometary Explorer (ICE) spacecraft flew past, it detected the hydrogen corona around Halley's comet from mid November 1985 until the time of its closest approach. Since the data transmission rate was limited, this experiment was then abandoned in favour of one to measure the interaction between cometary ions and the solar wind. Suisei was hit at this point by two particles of dust, whose mass was

estimated to be several milligrams, but luckily survived without damage.

Other observations of Halley's comet

In addition to the five purpose built probes which visited Halley's comet, five other spacecraft were used to make relevant observations.

NASA's International Sun Earth Explorer (ISEE 3), renamed the International Cometary Explorer (ICE), was moved from its Lagrange point between the Sun and Earth and, after several manoeuvres, was put into a heliocentric orbit to fly past the Giacobini Zinner comet on 11 September 1985. It flew to within a distance of 7000 kilometres of the comet and then travelled on to Halley's comet which it passed on 28 March 1986, at a distance of 35 million kilometres. Measurements were made of plasma, magnetic fields and waves to complement the measurements made by the other spacecraft. ICE was also to compare the electromagnetic environments of the two different comets.

The ultraviolet spectrometer on board the Pioneer Venus spacecraft in orbit around Venus examined the hydrogen cloud around Halley's comet, making observations as the comet passed through perihelion in February 1986 at a time when it was not visible from the Earth.

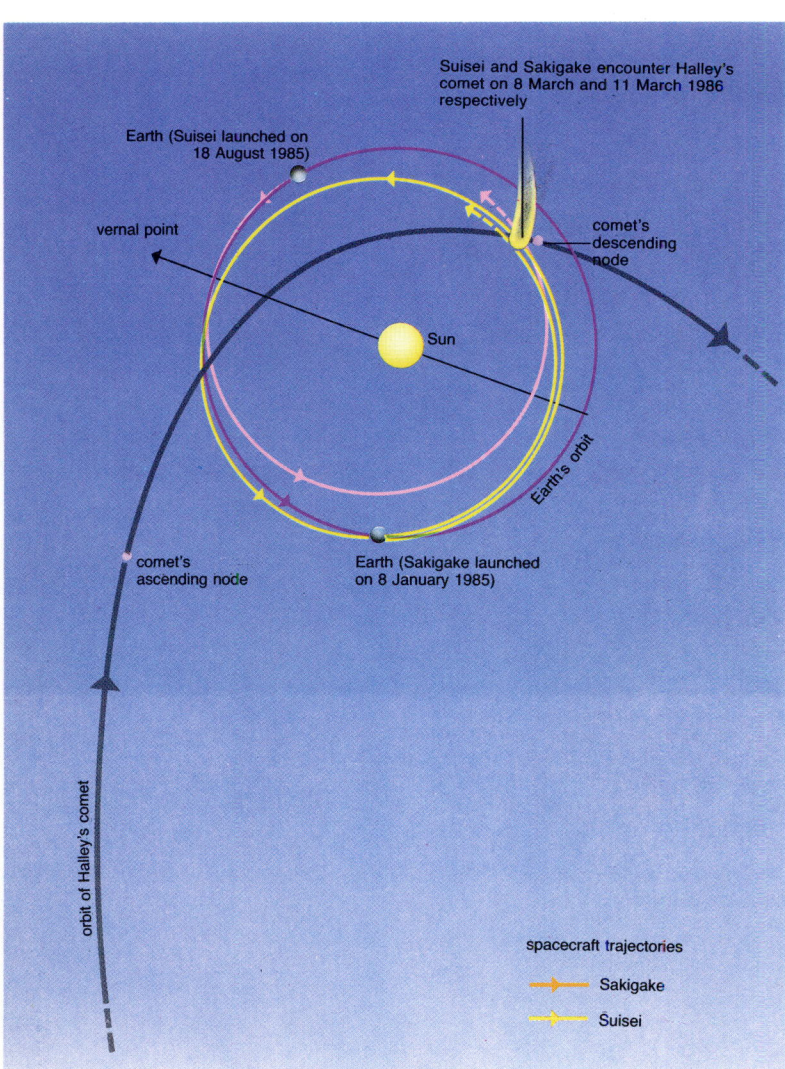

The Sakigake probe. The two Japanese probes sent to Halley's comet were spin stabilised at 6·3 turns per minute. As shown on the right, they were cylindrical in shape, with a diameter of 1·4 metres and a height of 0·7 metres. On top they had a non-spinning, high gain antenna, 0·7 metres in diameter. On the Suisei probe, the spin rate was reduced by 0·2 turns per minute when the ultra-violet imaging system was in operation.

The probes were very similar in design and concept and, including the 13 kilogram payload, they weighed 139 kilograms at launch. The outside of the cylinder was covered with solar cells which provided a maximum power of 100 watts (ISAS).

The Japanese Sakigake and Suisei missions. The orbits of these two spacecraft which visited Halley's comet are shown diagrammatically on the left. Sakigake was placed so accurately in its heliocentric orbit at launch that only two small corrections were necessary before it passed between the comet and the Sun on 11 March 1986, at 4 hours 17 minutes 51 seconds UT, at a minimum distance of 6·99 million kilometres. The planned distance had been 7 million kilometres. The Suisei probe too was in an almost perfect heliocentric orbit at launch. However, a trajectory correction was made to reduce the distance of closest approach from 200 000 to 151 000 kilometres on 8 March 1986, at 13 hours 5 minutes 49 seconds UT.

Spacecraft	Experiment	Instrument	Scientific objectives
Sakigake	magnetic field	triaxial magnetometer, resolution better than 0.1 nanoteslas	measure interaction between interplanetary magnetic field and Halley's comet
	plasma waves	10 metre dipole antenna; coil observing wave magnetic fields	measure plasma waves and natural radio emissions to examine interaction between comet and solar wind
	plasma	Faraday probe	measure solar wind ion temperature, ion density, speed and direction
Suisei	imaging	ultraviolet imaging camera (field of view 1.85 degrees by 1.96 degrees)	measure amount and distribution of hydrogen in coma (Lyman alpha radiation) to examine emission of water
	plasma	spherical electrostatic analysers, measuring ion and electron energy spectrum	examine interaction between cometary ions and solar wind

The scientific payload carried by Sakigake and Suisei

NASA's International Ultraviolet Explorer (IUE) spacecraft was also used to investigate ultraviolet emissions originating from the comet, and, from 11 September 1985 until mid July 1986, conducted some 280 hours of observation. This programme became more important after the Challenger accident, because one of the payloads lost then was Astro 1, which was specifically designed to observe Halley's comet in the ultraviolet. The measurements made by the IUE showed that the production of gas varied considerably between all the comets studied.

NASA's Solar Maximum Mission (SMM) satellite used its coronograph to follow the evolution of Halley's comet in the visible spectrum during the six weeks surrounding its passage through perihelion, except between 1 and 11 February 1986. During that period, the comet's proximity to the Sun in relation to the viewing direction from the Earth meant that it was impossible to observe from the Earth or from satellites observing the Earth.

Lastly, a French instrument on board the Soviet Salyut 7 space station took dust samples as the Earth passed through the stream of dust left behind Halley's comet; these were eventually brought back to Earth in August 1986 for analysis.

Josette Runavot

Trajectory of the US spacecraft ICE. This spacecraft, launched on 12 August 1978, was originally called the International Sun Earth Explorer 3 (ISEE 3) and was one of three satellites designed to investigate solar terrestrial physics. It was renamed the International Cometary Explorer (ICE) before it left the L1 Lagrange point between the Earth and Sun. After a series of manoeuvres illustrated in the diagram below, it was put into a heliocentric orbit. It then examined the Giacobini Zinner comet on 11 September 1985, and Halley's comet on 28 March 1986. The ICE spacecraft will return to the vicinity of the Earth in the year 2013.

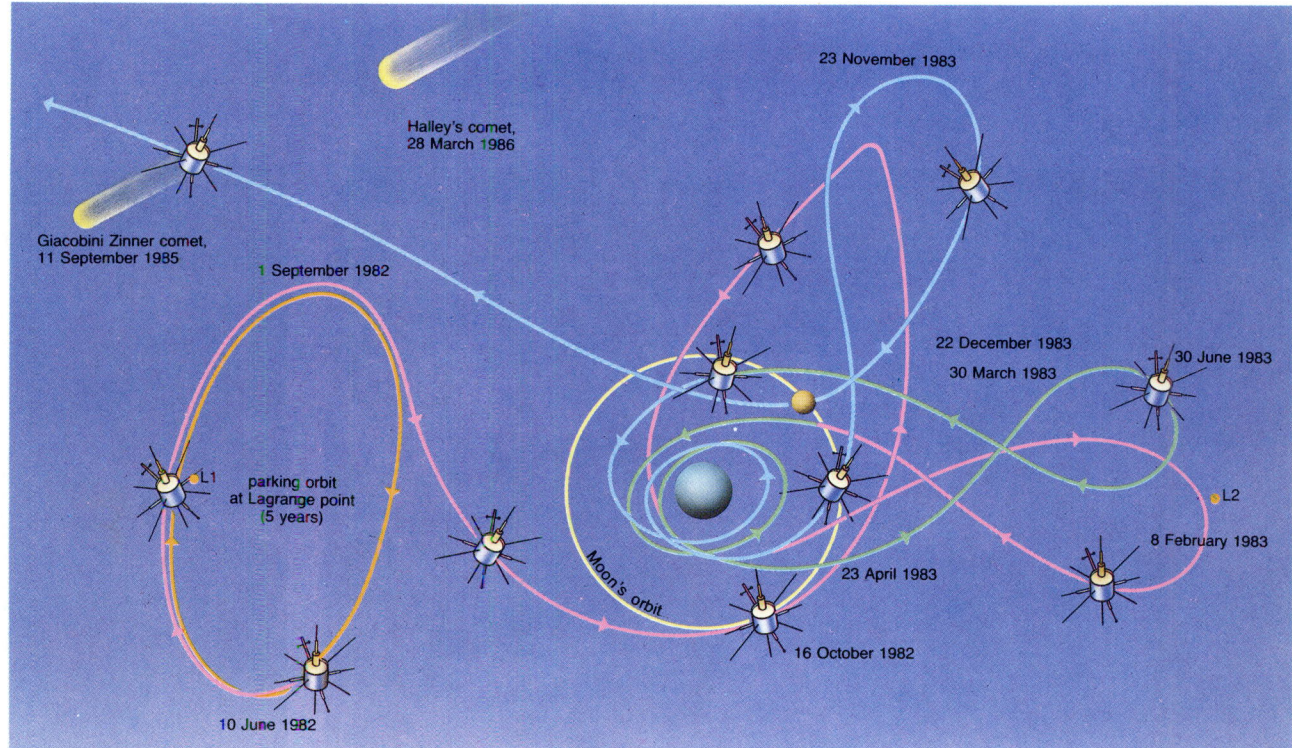

Exploring the solar system

The latest developments

Unmanned missions

Magellan (Venus Radar Mapper). The main objective of this mission is to map Venus's surface, which remains permanently hidden underneath thick cloud cover, using a Synthetic Aperture Radar. The polar orbit was chosen so that the probe can obtain a resolution of several hundred metres over all the planet's surface, a considerable improvement on the results obtained by the Venera 15 and Venera 16 spacecraft, which had a resolution of 1 to 2 kilometres over the northern polar region only (JPL/NASA).

Despite the Challenger accident early in 1986 and its repercussions on NASA's planetary programme, the major objectives for solar system exploration programmes over the next 20 years, based on the technical advances made and the scientific data acquired during the space age, have already been agreed.

Nearly all the planets and moons of the solar system have now been visited by spacecraft. The USA and the USSR have launched many spacecraft to the planets, and only Pluto remains unexplored. The surfaces of the Moon, Mars and Venus have all been examined by unmanned landers, and nearly 500 kilograms of rock samples from the Moon have been brought back to Earth. In March 1986, Halley's comet too was visited by five spacecraft launched by the European Space Agency, Japan and the USSR.

For the next two decades of solar system exploration, the objectives will be to observe, at close quarters, objects which have never been visited by spacecraft, and to increase the data on the planets and their moons which have already been visited. A mission to Pluto and its companion, Charon, would be long and complex because of their unusual orbits in the solar system, and no visits are planned for the foreseeable future.

The solar system also contains innumerable small bodies – asteroids and comets – and this is where the next period of space exploration will begin. The difference between comets and asteroids lies in their properties and their position in space. Most comets have come from Oort's cloud, at the edge of the solar system,

several thousand astronomical units from the Sun (one astronomical unit is the distance from the Sun to the Earth). Only when a passing star causes a gravitational disturbance is one or more of these objects ejected towards the Sun to become an observable comet.

Asteroids on the other hand are confined to orbits close to the Sun, mostly between the orbits of Mars and Jupiter. They are the constituents of a planet which did not develop properly due to the proximity of Jupiter and have been left as planetesimals, subject to the effects of collisions amongst themselves and to gravitational perturbations caused by the nearby planets, particularly Jupiter. These bodies probably have very different sizes and compositions due to the different stages of their internal evolution; for this reason, one of the most interesting characteristics of asteroids is their diversity.

The two moons of Mars, Phobos and Deimos are both considered to be asteroids and Phobos has been the subject of a recent Soviet mission. It is the nearest moon to Mars and also the largest, an irregular shaped body with a typical size of 20 kilometres. On 7 and 12 July 1988, the Soviets launched two 6·2 tonne probes to Mars from the Baikonur cosmodrome, their main objective being for one of them to fly very close to Phobos in April 1989. Unfortunately, all contact with one probe was lost on 1 September 1988 after an erroneous command had been sent, while radio contact with the other broke down on 27 March 1989 as it approached Phobos. The loss was due to an on board computer failure.

NASA's longterm plans. Shown to the right is a list of NASA's longterm planetary programmes as agreed in 1983. There were four priority missions – Venus Radar Mapper (Magellan), the Mars Observer, the Cometary Rendezvous and Asteroid Flyby (CRAF), and Cassini, a mission to Titan, Saturn's large moon. The first two programmes are already in progress.

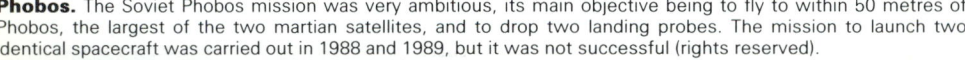

Phobos. The Soviet Phobos mission was very ambitious, its main objective being to fly to within 50 metres of Phobos, the largest of the two martian satellites, and to drop two landing probes. The mission to launch two identical spacecraft was carried out in 1988 and 1989, but it was not successful .

Planetary Observer. This spacecraft, based on two Earth observation satellites, could perform a number of missions in the inner solar system at a relatively small cost. The first such mission which has been planned is the Mars Observer, which will be put into a polar orbit around Mars (RCA/Astro-Space Division).

Galileo. This mission to Jupiter, designed to make a detailed study in the light of the information sent back by the Voyager spacecraft, will carry a probe designed to investigate Jupiter's atmosphere. The orbiting probe will observe the four Galilean moons, explore the ring system and the small moons discovered by Voyager. It will also map very powerful phenomena occurring in the jovian magnetosphere (Hughes Aircraft Co.).

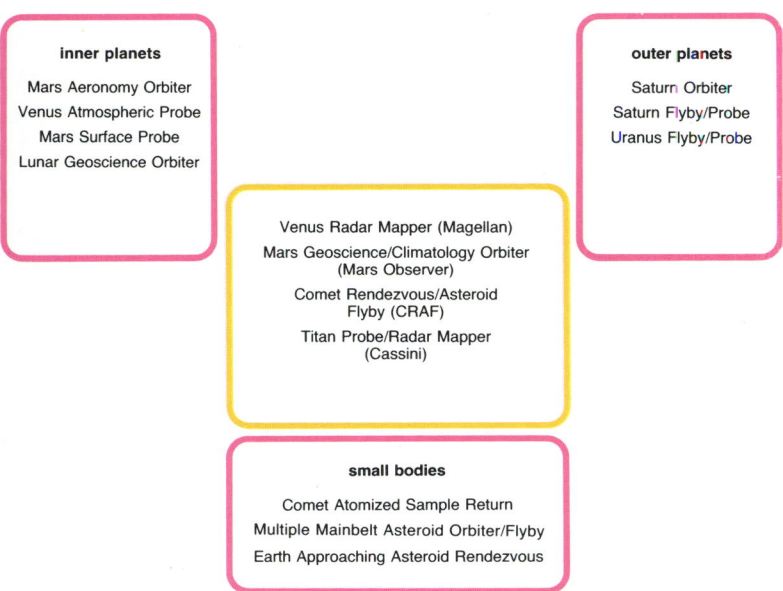

inner planets
Mars Aeronomy Orbiter
Venus Atmospheric Probe
Mars Surface Probe
Lunar Geoscience Orbiter

outer planets
Saturn Orbiter
Saturn Flyby/Probe
Uranus Flyby/Probe

Venus Radar Mapper (Magellan)
Mars Geoscience/Climatology Orbiter (Mars Observer)
Comet Rendezvous/Asteroid Flyby (CRAF)
Titan Probe/Radar Mapper (Cassini)

small bodies
Comet Atomized Sample Return
Multiple Mainbelt Asteroid Orbiter/Flyby
Earth Approaching Asteroid Rendezvous

The European Space Agency: 'Horizon 2000'. In 1985, ESA redefined its long term scientific programme. Four major projects, the 'cornerstones', shown in red in the diagram below, have been selected. Their development will continue independently of the normal selection of payloads by direct competition, the smaller projects shown in blue and yellow. The first cornerstone mission, on solar terrestrial physics, has already begun. This programme will study the Sun from the Solar and Heliospheric Observatory (Soho), placed at the Lagrange point between the Sun and Earth. It will also use the Cluster mission to study the plasma environment around the Earth. In this mission four satellites will be launched into the same orbit in the mid 1990s.

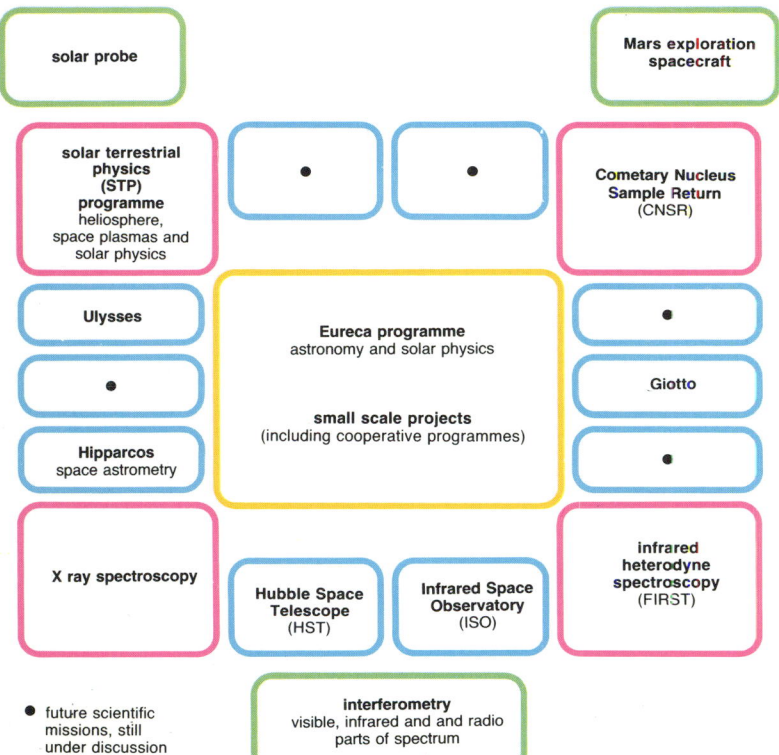

solar probe

Mars exploration spacecraft

solar terrestrial physics (STP) programme
heliosphere, space plasmas and solar physics

Cometary Nucleus Sample Return (CNSR)

Ulysses

Eureca programme
astronomy and solar physics

Giotto

Hipparcos
space astrometry

small scale projects
(including cooperative programmes)

X ray spectroscopy

Hubble Space Telescope (HST)

Infrared Space Observatory (ISO)

infrared heterodyne spectroscopy (FIRST)

• future scientific missions, still under discussion

interferometry
visible, infrared and and radio parts of spectrum

The distance of closest approach to Phobos should have been about 100 metres, or even less, and the relative velocity about 1 metre per second. During the mission, a detailed analysis was to have been made also of Phobos's surface by taking close-up images and recording infrared spectra. A particularly ambitious experiment planned was to direct an ion beam at Phobos's surface to pulverise it, and to aim a laser beam at the surface and vaporise it; mass spectrometer observations of the ions emitted would have given information on the elements and isotopic composition of the surface.

As far as the asteroids and comets are concerned, there are broadly three strategies which can be adopted to examine them – a close flypast, a rendezvous mission and a sample taking exercise. The first method is the simplest and was used, for instance, to study Halley's comet in March 1986.

Amongst the different projects of this type under consideration, the most advanced is the Vesta programme. This joint programme between France and the USSR plans to launch, in 1994, two interplanetary probes which will be built by the CNES and ESA. Each will fly past three or four objects, say, three asteroids of different families and one comet. During each encounter, the instruments carried by the probe will measure the mass and density of the object, its surface mineral composition and its topography; it will also photograph the surface using an electronic camera. The probes will carry mass spectrometers so that they can analyse dust as they pass through interplanetary space and examine the dust associated with the individual objects being studied.

The second method, that of making a rendezvous with the asteroid or comet, consists of putting a probe in orbit about the object of interest. The main difficulty here is to find objects sufficiently slow in relative velocity to allow the probe to go into orbit. NASA has a project of this type, called Comet Rendezvous and Asteroid Flyby (CRAF), at a great distance from the Sun (about 5 astronomical units). The nucleus of the comet is not very active at this point; for the next three years, the space probe could monitor changes in the comet's activity as its distance from the Sun decreased. NASA is considering Temple II, Kopff or Wild II as target comets, the rendezvous to take place in 1999, 2001 and 2003 respectively, after voyages of four to seven years, depending on the type of trajectory used.

The third method – the most ambitious of all – consists of removing samples from a comet's nucleus and bringing them to Earth for analysis. The European Space Agency has called this project Cometary Nucleus Sample Return (CNSR), or Rosetta, and established it as one of the cornerstones of its long term 'Horizon 2000' programme. In support of this way of proceeding are the advances that have been made by analysing extraterrestrial matter, whether from the Moon or as a meteorite in the laboratory. Isotope analyses can, for example, be performed on individual grains, enabling the samples to be dated. Missing isotopes indicate the processes which accompany the formation or evolution of the parent bodies, and is possible to detect organic components, even at very low concentrations, and also to search for the presence of complex molecules in an attempt to reconstruct primordial extraterrestrial organic chemistry. The challenge remains the extreme technical problems of sampling deep into a comet's nucleus and preserving the samples (grains, ices and organic compounds) during the return journey to Earth.

In the next two decades, new missions are also planned to Venus, the Moon, Mars, Jupiter and Saturn.

Venus is surrounded by a cloud layer which is completely opaque to visible radiation. Several Soviet probes have landed on the surface, taken photographs and succeeded in analysing the soil despite a pressure of 95 atmospheres and temperatures exceeding 450 degrees celsius. Although the data indicate that the surface is similar to the Earth's ocean floor, material similar to a continent has not yet been found. Radar mapping by the American Pioneer Venus Orbiter has also revealed the existence of mountainous regions, though no traces of tectonic plates have been detected. Maps of the northern polar icecap, made by the Russian Venera 15 and Venera 16 probes, show in addition small circular structures more likely to be caused by volcanic eruptions than by meteorite impacts. The current priorities are therefore to understand the internal behaviour of Venus by studying high resolution images of the surface structures. NASA in particular has a venusian orbiting probe programme, called Magellan, which will map the entire surface of Venus at a resolution of several hundred metres; this was successfully launched on 4 May 1989 aboard the space shuttle Atlantis.

Since the marvellous success of the Apollo manned missions, no spacecraft have been sent to the Moon; over the years, work has continued to evaluate all the data and samples taken on these missions, but much remains to be done. The next stage of lunar exploration may well be establishing bases on the Moon for exploiting its resources. Scientists and engineers from several space agencies are working on the problems of producing energy, or synthesising oxygen and water, so that communities can survive in this hostile environment. In the short term, it is also planned to observe the Moon at high latitudes. NASA, ESA, Russia and Japan are all planning lunar polar satellites because, as the Moon rotates, a probe in polar orbit can map the entire surface.

Most information acquired so far about Mars has been provided by Mariner 9, Viking 1 and Viking 2. Although Mars is now a geologically inactive planet, in the past it was subjected to a long period of intense internal activity; the giant volcanoes and vast network of canyons bear witness to this. Amongst the scientific objectives of future missions to Mars are therefore an understanding of its tectonic and volcanic characteristics, as well as an investigation into its hydrological cycle. Several observations have pointed to the existence of water on Mars. Water could have been responsible for violent rivers in the past and, today, could explain an apparent layer of permafrost at a shallow depth. A specific intention is to return samples to Earth by the end of the century.

As part of the Soviet programme for exploring Mars, several missions have been planned for the middle and late 1990s. These will include placing several modules into orbit around Mars which will release balloons, launch penetrators and drop rolling vehicles onto the surface. The aim here is to obtain a precise description of the surface in various places so that well documented samples can be taken, probably by a mobile vehicle, and returned to Earth. This programme could also involve cooperation with France.

NASA is continuing to develop plans for the Mars Observer programme, which will orbit Mars in a polar orbit at 300 kilometres altitude and make a high resolution analysis of the

long as the energy reserve is diminishing all the time.

The Cassini project is designed to study Saturn and its environs. A joint project between NASA and ESA, this involves the development of an orbital probe for studying Saturn, its rings, and its moons with the exception of Titan. A separate probe is being designed and developed by ESA to study Titan.

Japan is planning programmes to investigate the seismology of the Moon, with penetrators, and the interaction of the solar wind with the venusian atmosphere. It is also developing a comet sample return mission.

All the agencies which develop and launch interplanetary spacecraft are responsible for managing the projects, but their success depends on the scientific payload which is usually constructed by a number of different countries. International projects are now becoming the norm as far as large space programmes are concerned; as a result engineers and scientists from many countries have to work together to build and integrate the instruments, and exploit and analyse the data.

Whilst it is true that the space community was badly shaken by the Challenger accident, the need for programmes to explore the Earth's environment and the solar system beyond is not

CRAF and Cassini. These two NASA missions are planned to use the Mariner Mark II spacecraft, which is designed around a number of modules.

CRAF (on the left) is designed to rendezvous with a comet and to observe it at close quarters, examining both the atmosphere and the nucleus for several years. The probe will include a 'penetrator', the green conical device between the two tanks in the foreground. This will be dropped by the probe and will implant itself in the comet's surface, to make *in situ* analyses.

Cassini (on the right) is designed to study Saturn, its ring system and Titan, the largest of its moons. On one side of the spacecraft is a landing probe, which will be dropped into Titan's atmosphere; this will be constructed by ESA (JPL/NASA).

whole of the surface, including the polar caps. The first of the Planetary Observer probes planned, it is to be launched in the early 1990s.

The Galileo programme, also devised by NASA, consists of an orbiting spacecraft designed to study Jupiter, its rings and moons over a period of several years. In addition, it will release a probe into the jovian atmosphere which will analyse the different layers up to a pressure of several atmospheres. It was planned initially to launch Galileo in 1983 using the space shuttle, so the probe is now ready and awaiting its launch. In this type of mission, far from the Sun, the energy source is nuclear; an isotope with a relatively short lifetime has been chosen, so the launch must not be delayed too

in dispute. Planned launch dates have had to be altered, however. Some launches have been delayed for years, and others have had to be abandoned altogether.

Realising the importance of understanding how the Earth evolved, and how we may be changing the environment of our planet, we are slowly coming to understand our place in the Universe. The increasing knowledge of the planetary objects in the solar system around the Earth, which were created at the same time, from the same primeval cloud, is teaching us profound lessons about the Earth itself and our role on it.

Jean-Pierre Bibring and Yves Langevin

Return to the Moon

Astronauts will return to the Moon in the next century, not to stay for just a few days as on the Apollo missions, but to remain for several months or even longer. On the Apollo missions, only 24 astronauts visited the Moon and, of these, only 12 actually walked on the surface. The human presence on the Moon to date has lasted less than two weeks in total. In the future, however, people will live in colonies on the lunar surface and begin to exploit its resources.

Some 40% of the lunar rock is actually oxygen. Because rocket engines use about 6 kilograms of oxygen for every kilogram of hydrogen burnt, a return to the Moon could tap its oxygen supply. If very long term plans are to include colonising the solar system (Mars, the asteroids and so on) from Earth orbit, it is clearly more efficient to extract the oxygen reserves from the Moon than from the Earth where they weigh six times as much. In fact, only 5% of the energy required to put a certain mass into a low Earth orbit from the Earth would be needed to put the same mass into the same orbit from the Moon. From this point of view, then, a Moon base for extracting oxygen from the rock would be a very sound concept, even if the actual extraction process would be very difficult to achieve.

Meteorite bombardments have, however, pulverised the top layer of the Moon's surface so that the particles which make up the lunar soil are microscopic. They would not therefore have to be crushed before being processed. The likely procedure would be to remove the lunar soil to a depth of perhaps 10 metres, and send it directly to an extraction plant which would use solar generated electricity as its power supply. Although only present in small quantities, hydrogen could also be extracted from the lunar soil, by heating it using solar reflectors and then processing it to remove the oxygen. The Moon's other natural resources include silicon (20% of the lunar soil), which could be used to make the photovoltaic cells essential for solar panels. There is also aluminium (14%) and iron (4%), which would both be useful for building space structures.

Other possibilities open to people living on the Moon include setting up radio telescopes. On the dark side of the Moon, protected from radio interference from the Earth by 3500 kilometres of lunar rock, they would be very sensitive. Ordinary optical telescopes would also have the advantage of being free from the atmospheric conditions which make good quality, Earthbound observations so difficult to obtain. Physiological experiments on the human body, genetic engineering, and potentially dangerous tests on microorganisms and viruses could also be carried out on the Moon, under conditions of complete security.

The first colony of Earth people on the Moon would always be sure of prompt help from the Earth in the case of serious damage to their base as they were establishing themselves. The lunar base would also be an excellent way of investigating the possibility of survival in a closed environment, a useful exercise when considering, for instance, whether to colonise Mars. As the Moon is only a light second from the Earth, scientists on the Moon could easily use computing systems on the Earth, thereby minimising the cost of building and maintaining computer systems on the Moon to analyse the results of experiments.

The technology required to build a base on the Moon would not in fact be very different from that being developed for orbiting space stations such as the Russian Mir station and the future international space station. For example, the pressurised, cylindrical modules needed as living quarters on the Moon's surface could be assembled in near Earth (circumterrestrial) space. Life in the base would not be so very different from the way that astronauts live in space stations, and the ExtraVehicular Activity (EVA) needed now for repairing satellites or assembling structures in orbit would become EVA for mining purposes on the Moon.

Studies by NASA have shown that it is not unreasonable to expect a lunar population of about a thousand people by the year 2040. The fundamental aim of these new colonies would in time be to make themselves completely independent of Earth, to ensure their own survival. In fact, astronauts on the Moon would be no more isolated than their counterparts at Antarctic bases, which can be totally cut off for six months of the year or more. The colonies of this New World would therefore in time be free to develop their own regional identities and social life.

Humanity has always been able to adapt to new environments and the Moon now holds the promise of becoming a new frontier, an eighth continent.

Olivier de Goursac

Constructing the lunar base. This artist's impression shows how cargo lunar modules might bring the elements for a base to the Moon. Some of these have already been positioned and buried to shield them from harmful solar radiation. They are then pressurised and prepared as the astronauts' living quarters. In the distance, a mining company has already begun removing the surface rock to extract oxygen. This is stored in large tanks, before being sent to low Earth orbit .

2061: lunar colonists watch the return of Halley's comet. One of the colonists points to the famous comet which last visited the Earth 76 years before. The Earth, in the black lunar sky, appears four times larger from the Moon than the Moon does from the Earth (William K. Hartmann).

2020: destination Mars

The next phase of martian exploration will be the installation of colonies on Mars. For political reasons, or more simply just in the spirit of adventure, space scientists now believe that humans will visit Mars at the beginning of the twenty-first century.

Despite the success of the Mariner and Viking missions, there are still mysteries about Mars which remain unsolved, above all the question of whether life exists. It may be that there is an oasis on Mars, where life could in principle develop, or where there exist fossils of a primitive life form which came to nothing in the past because of an increasingly unfavourable climate. If there is life on Mars today, it could be hidden in the large subterranean lakes, which are believed to exist or be buried beneath polar ice.

We can expect that these uncertainties will be removed before humans arrive on Mars. There could be awful consequences if astronauts from Earth were contaminated by a martian virus against which mankind would have no defence. Planetary expeditions have, moreover, to respect the international rules established to make sure Mars is not itself contaminated with terrestrial bacteria; these might destroy any indigenous life which may exist there. It is for this reason too that the Viking probes were sterilised before they were sent to the red planet. The destruction of any life which might exist on Mars would mean a wait until the nearest stars can be visited before any encounter with a different life form would be possible.

The water which once flowed on Mars is now either frozen in the polar ice caps or fixed as permafrost in the subsoil. It is possible, however, that water exists as a liquid at depth, and that this could be used to support life. Certainly the discovery of large quantities of water in certain regions on Mars, in the easily exploitable form of ice near the surface or liquid at great depths, would enable mankind to contemplate colonising the planet.

Colonising Mars would be an immense technological challenge. But it would give a major boost to astronautics, because of the new technologies which would have to be developed. These would include the need for cheap, heavy launchers to put parts of martian spacecraft into terrestrial orbit, and new ways of producing cheap energy which do not require heavy or bulky equipment in space or on Mars. There will need to be new technologies to help people to live in space, including food production and the recycling of waste and water.

Also necessary will be a technology to enable astronauts to exploit the natural martian resources, and to help them to live and work

there, for example by extracting water and producing liquid carbon monoxide fuel and liquid oxygen to make the return from Mars possible. Space medical science will also need to solve the problems of long duration flights, including the development of surgical techniques in weightlessness.

The first missions to Mars are already planned. A manned interplanetary spacecraft will be built in Earth orbit out of three identical pieces; at the same time, an unmanned cargo-craft will leave for Mars, carrying two landing craft with the payloads necessary to create the first martian base.

A year and a half after the first interplanetary spacecraft leaves the Earth, an identical one would be constructed in Earth orbit and launched towards Mars with a relief crew. Having successfully completed its mission in the meantime, the first spacecraft would return to Earth. It would dock with an international space station and be serviced ready to return to Mars; two years later, it would be sent on the third mission.

On arrival at Mars, the second spacecraft would drop three manned shuttles, which would land near the base, followed by two other landing cargos. Once the replacement had taken place, eight of the twelve astronauts who arrived two years earlier would enter the three shuttles, which by then would have been refuelled. They would lift off towards the second interplanetary spacecraft and begin the journey back to Earth, leaving the four astronauts remaining to help the new crew enlarge the base. Two new cargos would be dropped and assembled on the base.

Every two years, the original installation would increase. As spacecraft are improved, they will take more men, women and materials to the planet, until such a time as a human colony is properly established.

At least 80 flights of the space shuttle, or its equivalent, will be needed for the construction of an interplanetary spacecraft, martian space shuttles and all the necessary equipment. The high costs of the programme, of the same order as the total cost of the Apollo programme, are therefore likely in time to prompt space agencies to establish an international project. This would have the desirable effect of speeding up the conquest of the red planet using an international team.

Five centuries ago, Christopher Columbus set off on a journey into the unknown, and discovered the New World. Today, a comparable, and equally challenging, journey is under way to explore the solar system.

Olivier de Goursac

An astronaut on Mars in 2020. In this simulation an astronaut is shown placing a commemorative plaque on the old Viking space probe which arrived on Mars in 1976. Mars's two moons, Phobos and Deimos, are rising above the martian horizon (Promospace/Computer Video film, Paris).

The first interplanetary voyage. The first interplanetary spacecraft may well consist of three identical elements assembled in Earth orbit, and arranged in a starlike configuration. The spaceship will rotate to create an artificial gravity of about one third of the Earth's, and the journey from the Earth to Mars will take about six months.

On arriving at the red planet, three martian shuttles will separate from the three spacecraft elements. After being slowed down by the martian atmosphere, parachutes will open and the shuttles, in the final landing phases, will use their engines as retrorockets. The now unmanned spacecraft will then fire its engines to return it to Earth, two and a half years later.

The disparity in the lengths of the journeys is explained by celestial mechanics; on the outward journey, the spacecraft will gain time because it will benefit from the Earth's orbit around the Sun at a speed which is greater than that of Mars. However, on the return journey, it will have to go one and a half times around the Sun in order to catch the Earth up. As it approaches the Earth, it will ignite its engines to put it on a trajectory to rendezvous with a space station where it will be repaired (Michael W. Carroll).

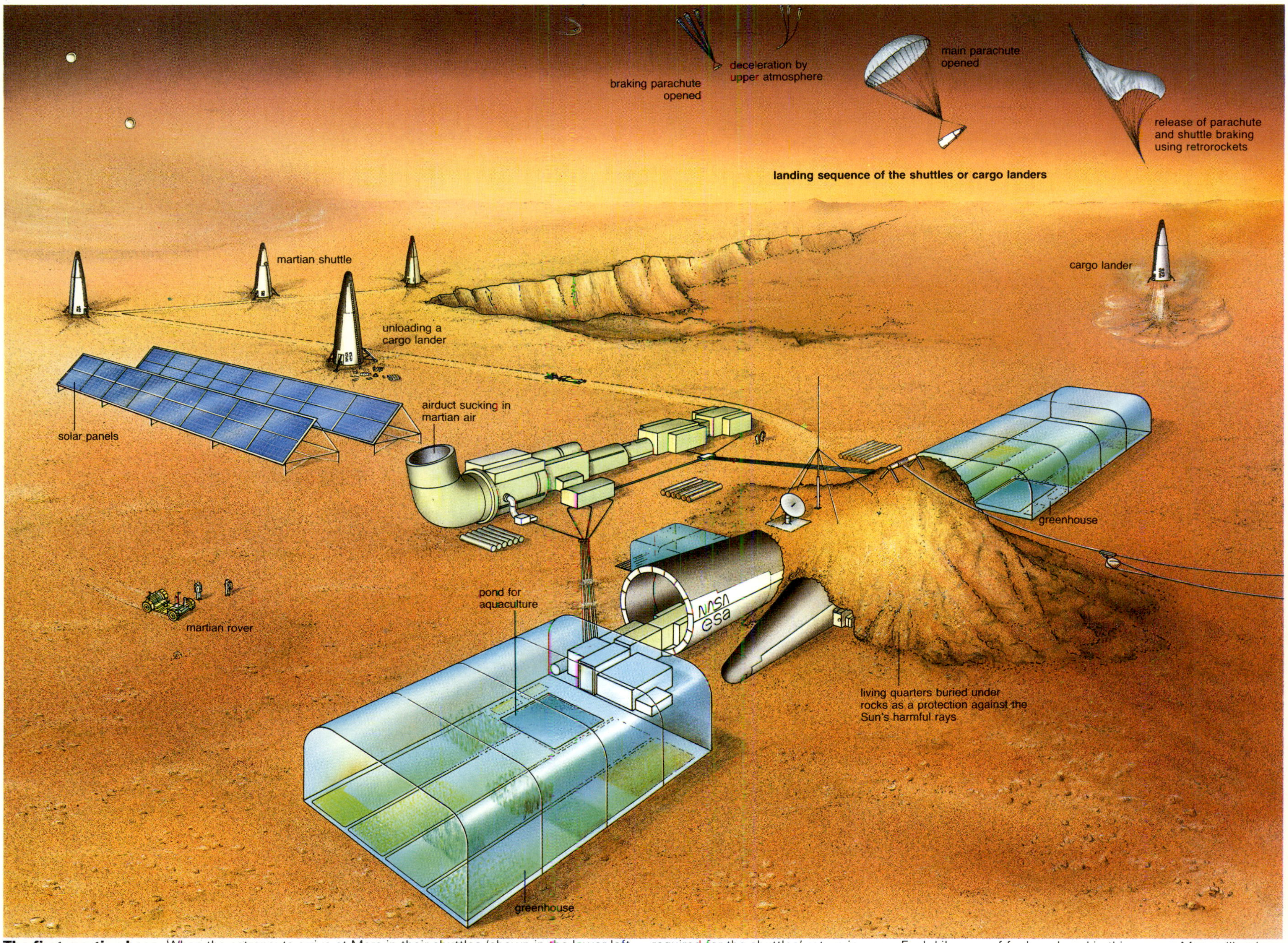

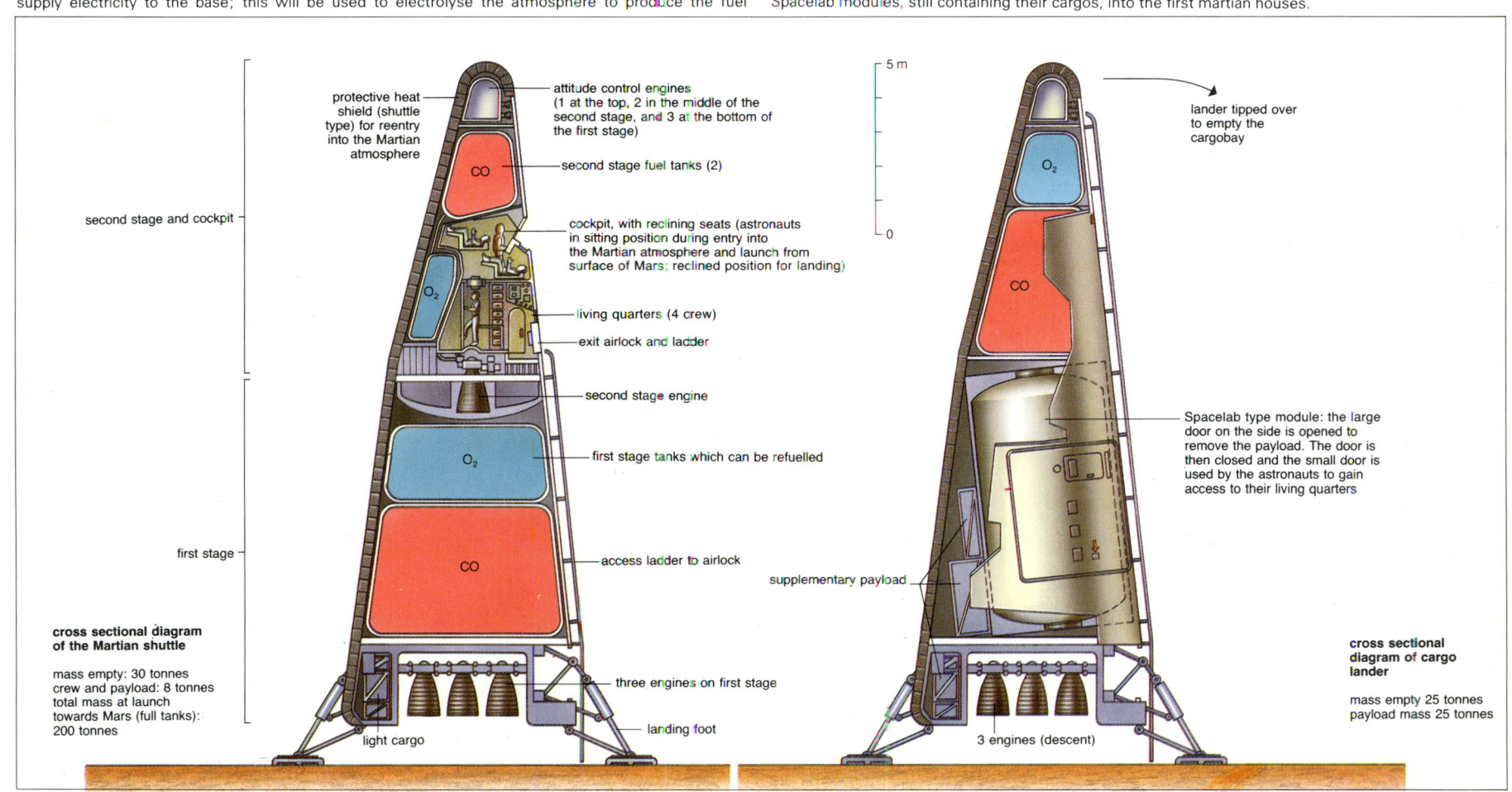

landing sequence of the shuttles or cargo landers

braking parachute opened

deceleration by upper atmosphere

main parachute opened

release of parachute and shuttle braking using retrorockets

martian shuttle

cargo lander

unloading a cargo lander

solar panels

airduct sucking in martian air

greenhouse

martian rover

pond for aquaculture

living quarters buried under rocks as a protection against the Sun's harmful rays

greenhouse

The first martian base. When the astronauts arrive at Mars in their shuttles (shown in the lower left diagram), they will transmit a signal to the unmanned spacecraft with the exact coordinates of their landing site. The spacecraft will then release two cargo landers (lower right diagram) which will land near the shuttles.

The astronauts will empty them, lie them on their sides, and pull them to the site they have chosen, where they will be assembled head to tail. The interior will be equipped rather like a Spacelab module, designed for living.

The astronauts will then have five essential tasks to perform. They will install a solar power station to supply electricity to the base; this will be used to electrolyse the atmosphere to produce the fuel required for the shuttles' return journey. Each kilogram of fuel produced in this way on Mars will reduce the mass of fuel to be sent from the Earth to Mars by about 10 kilograms. When compared with other fuel mixes, the carbon monoxide/oxygen (CO/O$_2$) combination is not so efficient (the specific impulse is only 260 seconds) but it could be produced in large quantities on Mars, at the rate of several hundred kilograms per day. Following the solar power station, a backup electric generator will be installed using a nuclear source to compensate for reduced solar radiation during prolonged dust storms. A module for dehumidifying the air will also be required to produce the water needed by the base. Two greenhouses will be built to use conventional aeroponic and hydroponic cultures, and an aquaculture unit will be constructed to enrich the water supplied to the plants. Finally, the astronauts will convert the two Spacelab modules, still containing their cargos, into the first martian houses.

protective heat shield (shuttle type) for reentry into the Martian atmosphere

attitude control engines (1 at the top, 2 in the middle of the second stage, and 3 at the bottom of the first stage)

second stage fuel tanks (2)

cockpit, with reclining seats (astronauts in sitting position during entry into the Martian atmosphere and launch from surface of Mars; reclined position for landing)

living quarters (4 crew)

exit airlock and ladder

second stage engine

first stage tanks which can be refuelled

access ladder to airlock

three engines on first stage

landing foot

light cargo

second stage and cockpit

first stage

cross sectional diagram of the Martian shuttle

mass empty: 30 tonnes
crew and payload: 8 tonnes
total mass at launch towards Mars (full tanks): 200 tonnes

CO

O$_2$

O$_2$

CO

5 m

0

lander tipped over to empty the cargobay

O$_2$

CO

Spacelab type module: the large door on the side is opened to remove the payload. The door is then closed and the small door is used by the astronauts to gain access to their living quarters

supplementary payload

3 engines (descent)

cross sectional diagram of cargo lander

mass empty 25 tonnes
payload mass 25 tonnes

Science in space

The experimental techniques used in space by geophysicists and astronomers have undergone a radical transformation in recent years. This is so whether we wish to investigate the Earth, in particular its crust or core, the oceans, the inner and outer atmosphere, or the Sun and planets in our solar system, or the Universe itself. The ability to make measurements in space has enabled us to study the entire Earth and its atmosphere. For the first time, we have been able to measure radiation from the Universe which is partially or totally absorbed by the atmosphere.

The discoveries resulting from space research in these disciplines fit within the framework of knowledge acquired during centuries of theoretical reflection and observations made here on Earth. Space research has certainly added a new dimension, but groundbased experiments and those in space remain complementary; they need to be developed concurrently.

Science in space is sometimes confused with its applications, such as mapping and meteorology. In these areas, which are continually evolving, it is not easy to distinguish between fundamental and applied research. However, for the astronomer or the geophysicist, 'science in space' has a well defined meaning. It is using space techniques to gain fundamental knowledge about the world on which we live, about near space (the Earth, the Sun, the planets and interplanetary space) or about far space (the stars, the galaxies and the Universe).

This section covers the contributions made by space research to Earth sciences (geology, oceanography and the study of the ionised environment of the Earth), solar physics and the study of interplanetary space, and finally to astronomy and astrophysics. As this last area is already covered by a companion volume, *The Cambridge Atlas of Astronomy*, only the experimental techniques will be described here; the other sections will also discuss the most important discoveries.

Roger Gendrin

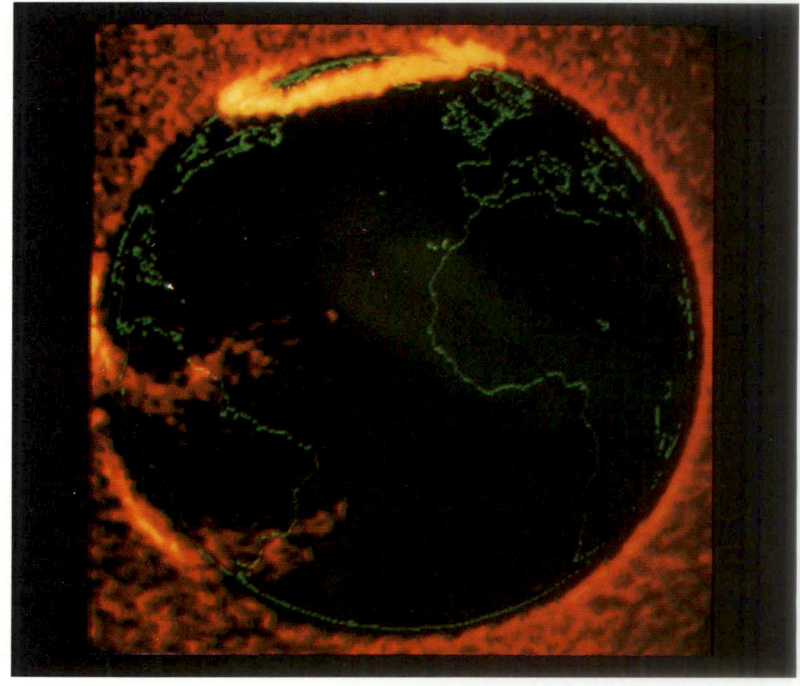

The Earth crowned. This false colour photograph was taken in the far ultraviolet (118 to 165 nanometres) part of the spectrum on 16 February 1982, by the US satellite Dynamics Explorer 1, at an altitude of about three Earth radii, when it was in the Earth's shadow. The picture shows the hidden splendour of the Earth, the setting for electromagnetic interactions between energetic charged particles and the Earth's neutral atmosphere.

The brilliant ring of light around the North polar region is the aurora borealis. It is always present, but its brightness varies as the magnetosphere responds to variations of the solar wind. The aurora is caused by energetic electrons from the tail of the magnetosphere which move along the Earth's magnetic field lines into the upper atmosphere. On either side of the equator there is a less intense and transient emission, called the red arc. This is caused by the precipitation, into the uppermost atmosphere, of energetic protons trapped in the Earth's radiation belts.

Finally, surrounding the entire globe there is an even weaker radiation field called the geocorona. This phenomenon is caused by the resonant scattering of Lyman-alpha radiation from the Sun. This emission only occurs at altitudes higher than 200 kilometres above the surface of the Earth (outlined in green, after the photograph was taken, and showing the outlines of the continents). The atmosphere at lower altitudes strongly absorbs radiation in the ultraviolet, and so the limb of the Earth appears black (Prof. L. Frank, University of Iowa).

Fundamental and applied research: satellite charging. All bodies which are placed in a plasma in thermal equilibrium acquire a negative electric charge. The negative potential of the object depends on the plasma temperature. At altitudes of 300 to 500 kilometres, the average kinetic energy of the plasma is low (less than 1 electronvolt) and satellites become only weakly charged. At high altitudes (for example that of a geostationary satellite), and more importantly during magnetic storms, the thermal kinetic energy of the ambient plasma is very large and the satellite acquires a high potential with respect to it. The greatest recorded potential is of the order of −20 kilovolts.

A high potential in itself is not dangerous. However, when the satellite is illuminated by the Sun, the situation is complicated by the many photoelectrons released from the satellite by the light. In the ionosphere where the ambient plasma is relatively dense (10^4 to 10^5 per cubic centimetre), the photoelectron flux is usually negligible compared with the flux of electrons from the plasma to the satellite. By contrast, the ambient plasma in the magnetosphere is of such a low density (0·1 to 10 per cubic centimetre) that the photoelectron flux dominates. Thus, the potential of the illuminated side of the satellite tends to be slightly positive.

If the satellite body is not a uniform conductor, there will be a potential difference between the sunlit side and the dark side of the satellite. In the ionosphere these potential differences are negligible. In the magnetosphere they are large enough to cause damaging electrical discharges through the satellite. These have occurred on several large and complex commercial satellites, principally those in geostationary orbit. They manifest themselves by huge transient currents in the electrical circuits which cause non-telecommanded changes in the operating format, or even the destruction of vital circuit elements. These problems have been reduced by judicious design of the conducting (metallic) and insulating (dielectric) parts of the satellite surface, by making a detailed model of the surface conductivity, by careful earthing and by shielding of sensitive elements.

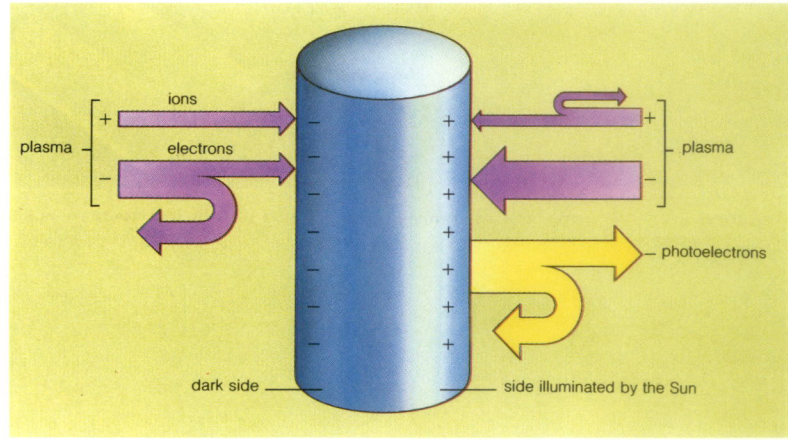

A spectacular contribution of space techniques: anomalies in the ocean gravity field derived from altimetric mapping of the geoid. The position of the geoid over the oceans can be determined directly from satellite height measurements. On this map the differences between the real and theoretical (uniform geoid) gravity values are shown for a reference ellipsoid, with a major axis of 6378·137 kilometres and a minor axis of 6356·752 kilometres. The quantity is an acceleration, $\triangle g$, and is measured in milligals (10^{-5} metres per second squared). For the smaller scale variations, the close correlation with the ocean depth provides an explanation for most of the anomalies. Thus, ocean ridges, subduction zones, and fracture zones can be clearly seen.

Unfortunately the surface gravitational field is not so well known for the large continental areas, except in Western Europe, North America, North Australia and South Africa where many groundbased gravimetric measurements have been made. A new set of space experiments is planned between 1993 and 1996 to complete the mapping of the Earth's gravitational field (rights reserved).

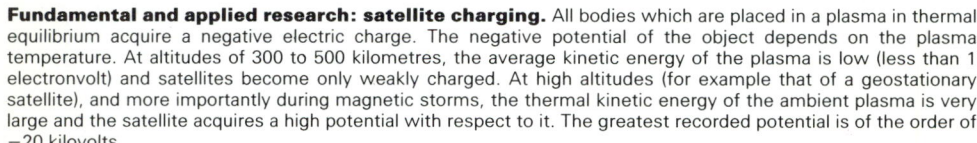

| $\triangle g \geqslant 20$ | $0 \leqslant \triangle g < 20$ | $-20 \leqslant \triangle g < 0$ | $-100 \leqslant \triangle g < -20$ | $\triangle g < -100$ | **?** continental or other land area |

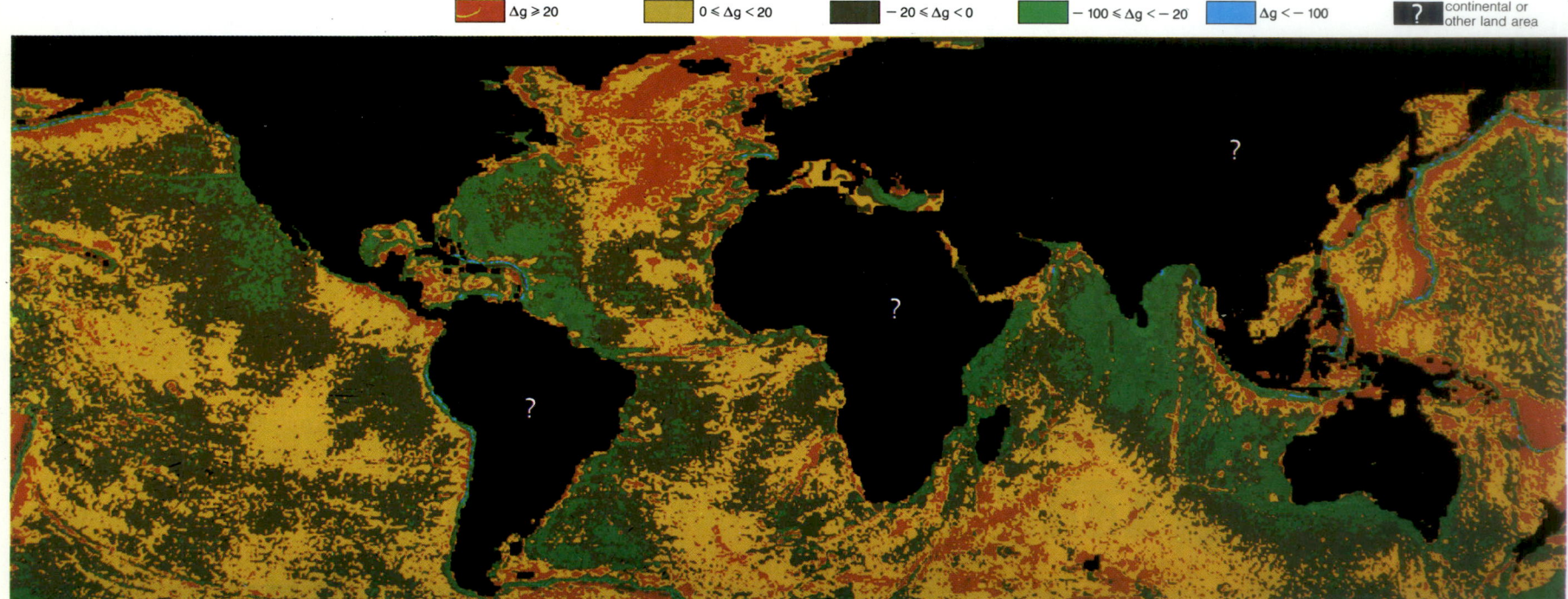

Science in space

Space research and internal geophysics

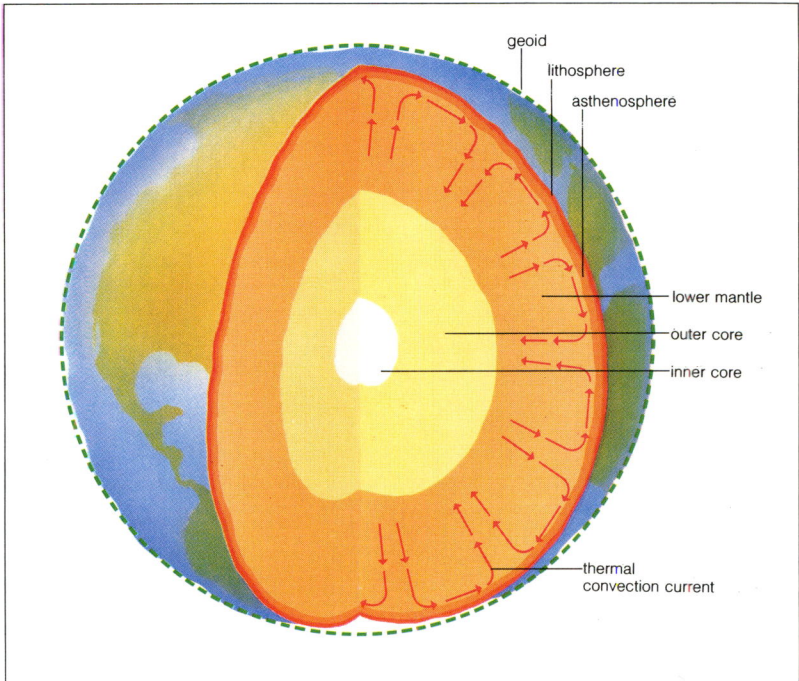

The Earth: its shape and internal structure. Our planet can be thought of as a sphere of average radius 6370 kilometres, revolving around a polar axis. Better still, it can be modelled as an ellipsoid (drawn in green). The major axis of the ellipsoid is 6378·137 kilometres and the minor axis is 6356·752 kilometres, ignoring local variations in the topography. This ellipsoid is close to being one of the possible equilibrium shapes of a fluid in rotation. However, it is different from this by several tens of metres. This poses an, as yet, unsolved question – what mechanism keeps the Earth in shape?

The average surface of the oceans, disregarding some oceanographic effects, is an equilibrium surface on which the sum of the gravitational potential and the potential caused by the centripetal force is constant. This shape can be defined mathematically and is called the geoid. It is the reference equipotential for the measurement of altitudes, and its surface differs by as little as ± 100 metres, at most, from the ellipsoid.

Seismology has provided information about the internal structure of the Earth, which has five main regions. The lithosphere, which includes the crust and part of the outer mantle, is solid and rigid. Plate tectonic movements cause the continents to move by up to a few millimetres per year. The lithosphere deforms elastically under the action of mountains, sediments and icecaps. The asthenosphere, which is just below the lithosphere in the outer mantle, behaves as a fluid and allows the crust to deform and move above it. The lower mantle is the location of creep phenomena (the 'flow' of solid matter) and thermal convection, which is believed to cause the movement of plates on the Earth's surface. The outer core is liquid, and is composed mainly of iron, with some nickel (2%) and iron sulphide. Electric currents, driven by dynamo action, flowing in it are the source of the Earth's magnetic field. The inner core is solid, probably an alloy of iron and nickel.

These days, we regard space geodesy as being concerned with studies from space of the average shape of our planet, its internal structure, its rotational motion and the tidal oscillations of the seas. In antiquity, geodesy was defined as the science of measurement of the Earth. For a long time, however, it was confined to surveying and local mapping. Geodesy gained its current reputation when it attacked the problem of measuring the separation between points on the Earth's surface over greater and greater distances, then looking at the significance of these measurements in relationship to the irregularities of the Earth's gravity field. It also considers the origins of the spatial, if not the temporal, variations in this field in as much detail as modern techniques allow. As in related studies, measurements are made at a distance, using artificial satellites. These give a more accurate global perspective and improve the quality of the study. Space geodesy has now become a very precise tool which is used in many Earth sciences such as geodynamics, interior geophysics and oceanography.

The gravitational field, shape, rotation and structure of the Earth

The shape of the Earth, globally or locally, is determined by measuring the distances and angles of a large network of triangles set up on the Earth's surface. Simple geometry is used to determine the shape of these triangles, the coordinates of their apices being calculated in a suitable Earth based coordinate system. This reference system can itself be defined in terms of fundamental points or external reference points like the stars, and from a physical model of the movement and rotation of the Earth. The highest level of precision is limited, in the geocentric reference system, by the apparent gravity field and its irregularities. The apparent gravity is defined as the sum of the gravitational attraction and the centripetal acceleration due to the Earth's rotation. Almost all geodesic measurements are related to the Earth's gravitation. For example, to use a theodolite, one of the axes must be aligned with the local vertical, which is parallel to the local gravitational field line, and perpendicular to the equipotential surface passing through the point being considered. Thus, in order to make these measurements correctly, the local apparent gravitational field must be known. The apparent gravity vector and, in particular, its magnitude vary from one point to another on the Earth's surface. This is because the planet is not spherical (the distance from the Earth's centre to the surface decreases from the equator to the poles), because the centripetal effect is not constant (it is zero at the poles), and also because of variations in the Earth's composition and the thermomechanical state of the planet's interior.

The shape of the Earth is defined by a surface coincident with the mean theoretical surface of the oceans, ignoring the effects of tides, changes in atmospheric pressure, winds, stormy seas and currents. This theoretical surface is called the geoid. To a first approximation it is the free surface of a fluid in rotation, corresponding to the state of the Earth at its formation. It can be shown to be an oblate spheroid of revolution with equatorial symmetry. Early measurements (for example those made two and a half centuries ago by Pierre Bougner and Charles de la Condamine, in Peru and Lapland, on the lengths of meridional arcs) used an ellipsoid to represent the shape of the Earth. Departures from the geoid, the altitude of which is measured relative to such an ellipsoid, reveal irregularities in the gravitational potential and thus the existence of inhomogeneities within the Earth. The large scale variations are due essentially to density anomalies deep in the Earth's interior. Small scale variations reflect the presence of anomalies within the crust, for example, related to the local topography. An artificial satellite moving in the Earth's gravitational field suffers greater orbital perturbations when it is in a relatively low altitude orbit. A wealth of information about the interior of the Earth can be obtained from studies of the Earth's gravitational field. We can therefore appreciate the importance of observing satellite trajectories. Nevertheless, the usefulness of this information is limited as there is no mathematically unique solution to this inversion problem. Thus, geodesy has to be used in conjunction with other geophysical information provided by seismic surveys or by the measurement of heat flux.

Studying the Earth's rotation is an important part of geophysics. The spatial and temporal variations of the axis of rotation and of the angular velocity, recorded in space or with respect to the Earth's crust, reflect variations of an elastic nature, dissipative phenomena and electromagnetic effects at the boundary between the Earth's core and the mantle. This is a second area in which space techniques have made a sizeable contribution. The orbit of the satellite can act as an external frame of reference if the forces which perturb the orbit can be modelled; this is altogether easier if the satellite is in a high orbit. Since the observations of the satellite orbit are made on Earth, it is the movements of the tracking stations with respect to the orbit which are observed.

Methods, instruments and satellites

High altitude satellites can be observed from points on the Earth's surface that are far apart. They can therefore be used to extend classical geodesy. Such objects near the zenith are good targets for triangulation from the Earth's surface. Most importantly these measurements are less sensitive to the effects of atmospheric refraction which are a problem when observing satellites at low angles of elevation. Artificial satellites, and even the Moon, have acted as geodetic targets for more than fifteen years. They constitute targets which are simultaneously visible from points which, sometimes, are thousands of kilometres apart. Because the satellites obey the laws of celestial mechanics, they yield fundamental information on the Earth's gravitational field.

Since the beginning of the space era several different techniques have been used to observe

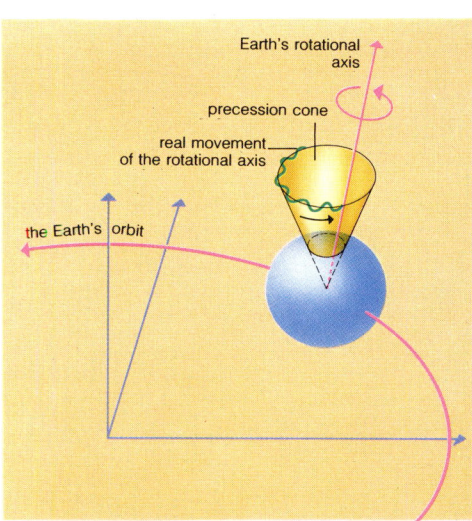

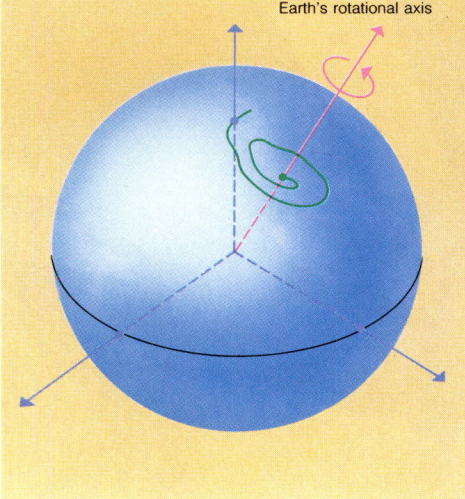

The Earth's rotation. In the upper diagram, the movement of the Earth's rotational axis in space is shown as seen by an external observer. The Earth spins like a top with a period of revolution (with respect to the ecliptic and mean revolution of the Earth around the Sun) of 26 000 years, and various nutations with periods between 18·5 years and 10 days. The axis precesses around the normal to the ecliptic plane, describing a cone in space of half angle 23 degrees 27 minutes. The nutations are of small amplitude, about 0·0001 arcseconds to 17 arcseconds. These amplitudes reflect the variations in density within the Earth, the mechanical (elastic) behaviour of the different layers, and the fluidity of the outer core.

In the lower diagram, the movement of the rotational axis is shown in the Earth's frame of reference; it is very small, lying within a square of side less than 20 metres and exhibiting annual variations, superimposed on a 430 day cycle named after Chandler. This cycle reveals the global elasticity of the planet in addition to diverse fluctuations due to the atmosphere, to electromagnetic coupling at the core–mantle interface, and to oceans. These same effects also influence the speed of the Earth's rotation. Moreover, the Earth's angular velocity of rotation exhibits a steady decrease due to the tides and the evolution of the Earth–Moon system. The fractional change is presently estimated at -3×10^{-8} per century.

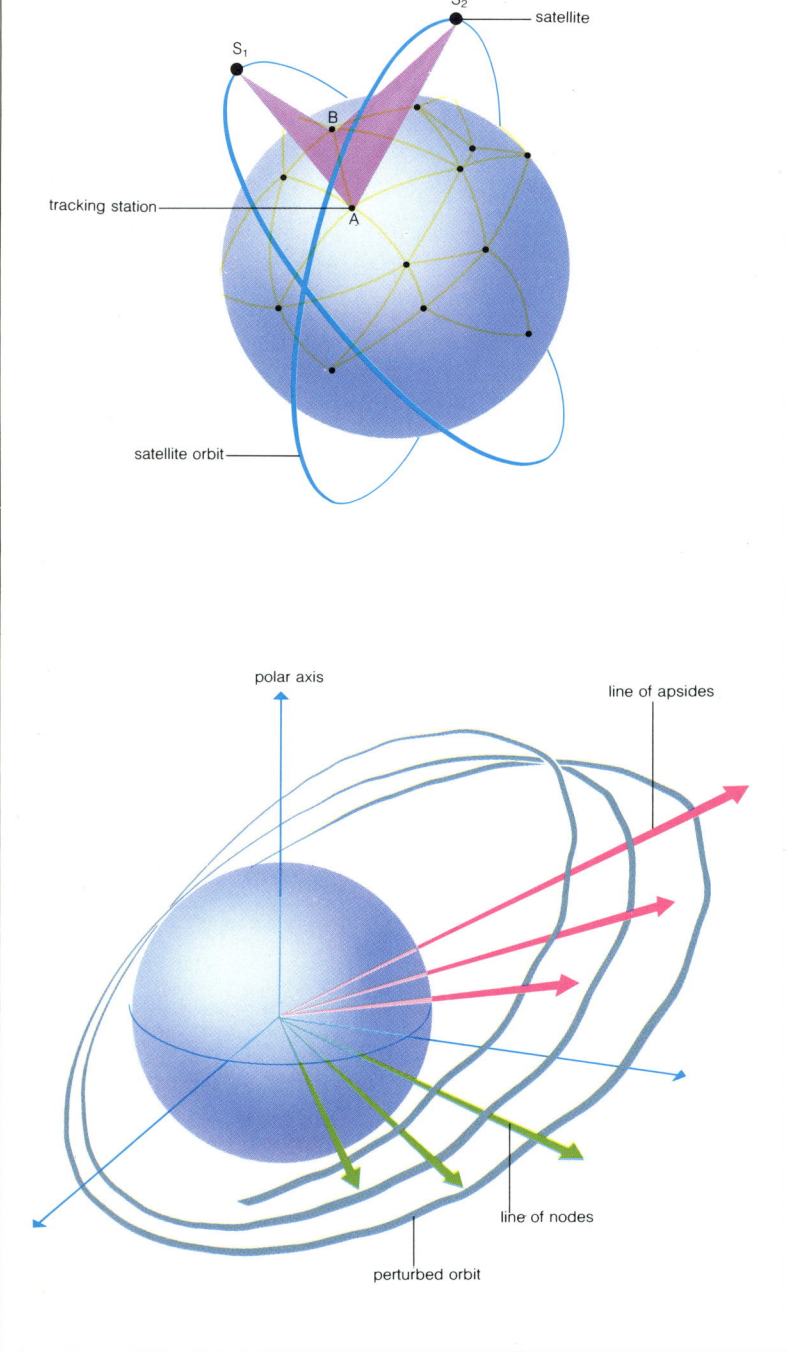

Instruments which observe geodetic satellites (above). Since 1960 a dozen Baker–Nunn cameras have been installed around the world by the Smithsonian Astrophysical Observatory. They have been used as the basic network for making observations of geodetic satellites. Using a Schmidt optical telescope, of large aperture and wide field, these cameras benefit from having a four axis mounting which compensates for the regular diurnal motion of the Earth. By rotating the equipment around an axis which is at right angles to the mean orbital plane, the satellite is followed as it is photographed. If the camera moves with the satellite, the image of the satellite appears sharp and the stars appear as trails (interrupted by time markers). Measurements are made on the photographic negative. The topocentric direction of the satellite is then reproduced with respect to the stars (whose positions are taken from a catologue), with an accuracy of 1 arcminute to 3 arcminutes.

A new French technique was introduced at the end of 1964; its accuracy revolutionised geodesy. This used lasers to measure the distances between a ground station and the satellite. A light signal is sent up to a satellite fitted with total internally reflecting corner prisms. The light is reflected back to the station where it is received through a telescope, pictured above. The travel time, there and back, is measured to within about 0·1 nanosecond, and gives the distance accurate to a few centimetres. Today there are more than twenty laser stations, identical to the French one at CERGA in the Alpes-Maritimes, distributed around the world and some are mobile. The same technique has been carried out on the Moon, using reflectors left during various American and Russian missions. (R. Fut>ally).

Irregularities in the Earth's gravitational field illustrated by the shape of the geoid (below). The geoid is defined as an equipotential surface, a contour of constant terrestrial weight, $W = U + C$; here U is due to gravity alone and C is the centrifugal potential. This surface, on which W is constant, can also be defined as the average level of the oceans, being naturally extended into the continental zones by its mathematical definition. The centrifugal force C varies smoothly with latitude and is responsible for the polar flattening of the geoid. Thus the holes and humps in the geoid surface are caused by variations in U only.

This map was taken from the Franco-German model GRIM 3-L1; the variations in the shape of the Earth are shown by the contours on the geoid. The height is calculated with respect to a reference ellipsoid (major axis: 6378·137 kilometres; minor axis 6356·752 kilometres). Of particular interest are the 'holes' around Sri Lanka (−105 metres), Tibet (−65 metres) and the Antarctic (−55 metres), and the 'humps' around Iceland (+70 metres) and New Guinea (+75 metres). This map shows the large scale variations (greater than 500 kilometres), which were detected by analysing the perturbations of satellite orbits. Without doubt their origin is deep within the Earth.

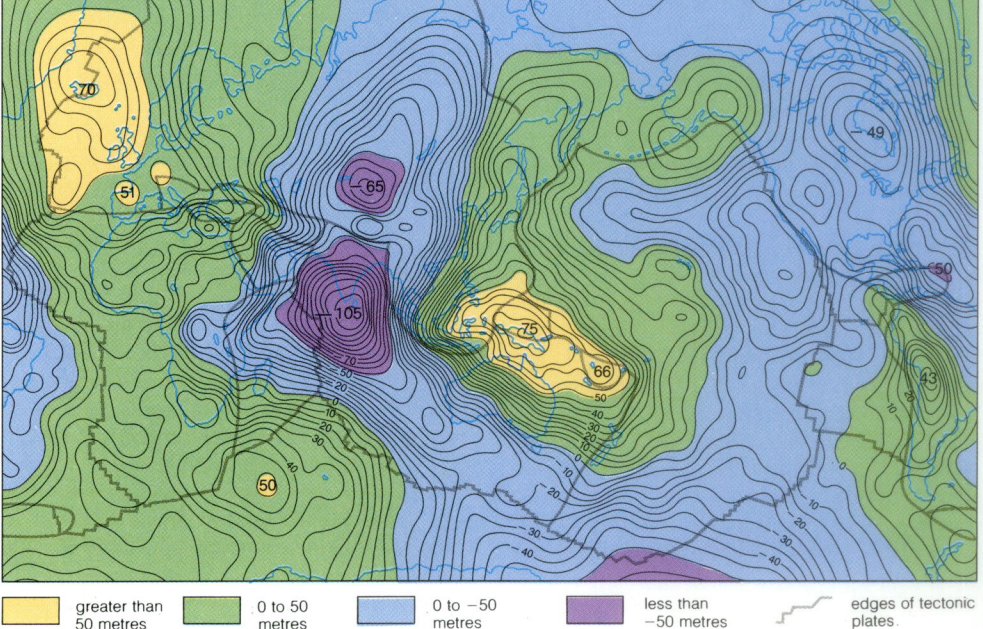

greater than 50 metres	0 to 50 metres	0 to −50 metres	less than −50 metres	edges of tectonic plates

Principal methods of space geodesy (above). Geometric geodesy (upper diagram) uses quasisimultaneous observations and only requires an approximate knowledge of the satellite's orbit. The satellite is used as a distant mirror to link points which are 1000 kilometres or more apart. In this example there are two tracking stations, A and B, following the satellites S_1 and S_2. The intersection of the planes ABS_1 and ABS_2 gives the direction of AB in space. In practice, many observations are made to reduce the statistical errors of the measurements. By repeating these measurements from other stations, a polyhedron of directions is obtained. The scale is obtained by measuring the length of one of the sides, for example by using laser ranging techniques.

Dynamic geodesy (lower diagram) measures and interprets perturbations of the satellite's orbit. The structure of the Earth's interior causes satellites to have complicated orbits, not the simple ellipses predicted by theory for the motion of two point masses. The mean orbital plane rotates about the polar axis (motion embodied by the line of nodes). The mean major axis of the trajectory (a continually distorting ellipse), or the line of apsides, rotates in the mean plane; this motion can be faster or slower than that of the ideal unperturbed trajectory. Added to these effects, which increase with time, are the quasiperiodic perturbations whose amplitudes depend on the irregularities of the Earth's gravitational potential and on the mean trajectory itself. Besides this, the satellite orbit is perturbed by friction in the high atmosphere (perceptible up to an altitude of 3000 kilometres), by solar radiation pressure, tides, and sometimes by the magnetic field. Analysing these perturbations enables us to establish parameters of these forces as well as the coordinates of the stations which are tracking the satellites.

Measuring irregularities of the geoid by space altimetry over the oceans. The average surface of the oceans can be mapped by a radar altimeter aboard a satellite. Since the orbit is derived from observations made on Earth, at each instant the vector joining the satellite to the centre of the Earth can be calculated. The satellite is stabilised along the local vertical and the radar operates in this direction. The measurement corresponds to the distance between the satellite and a point on the ocean along this line. The distance between the centre of the Earth and the average surface of the oceans is found by vector subtraction, as is the height of this surface with respect to that of a reference ellipsoid.

NASA carried out the first altimetric experiment in 1974 aboard Skylab 4, followed by two more projects. The first, between 1975 and 1978, used an altimeter (with an accuracy of 0·50 metres to 1·20 metres) aboard the satellite Geos 3. The second with an improved altimeter (10 centimetres accuracy) was installed on the satellite Seasat (pictured on the left). This was launched in June 1978 and, unfortunately, functioned for only three months (NASA).

Determining the geopotential by space gradiometry (opposite, on the right). The mapping of fine variations in the terrestrial potential can be obtained from measurements of the gravitational gradients (in three directions) made aboard a single satellite. These are the second derivatives of the gravitational potential.

Inside the satellite, ultrasensitive accelerometers measure the gravity at points A and B. Treating the instrument as a gradiometer, the measurements give the gravitational gradient in the direction AB. This quantity is an acceleration per unit length. In SI units, it is measured in metres per second squared per metre $(m/s^2/m)$, or in other words in reciprocal seconds squared (s^{-2}). The unit currently employed is the eötvös, where $1 E = 10^{-9} s^{-2}$. The sensitivity achieved so far for a satellite orbiting at 200 kilometres above the Earth's surface is 10^{-2} to 10^{-3} E, which represents a remarkable technological feat.

Measurements with the sensitivity and accuracy described above can be made using a gradiometer consisting of eight or more accelerometers. These measure small changes in electrical capacitance.

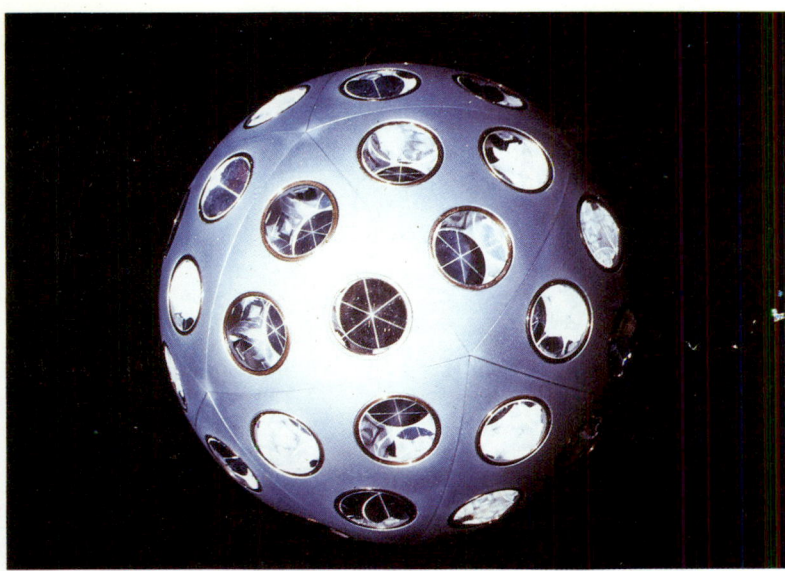

Specialised satellites like Starlette. These very dense satellites are spherical and covered by reflectors. Lasers are used to measure the distances from stations on the Earth to the satellites.

The French satellite, Starlette, in the photograph above, was launched on 6 February 1975 from Kourou in French Guyana, aboard an Ariane rocket. It is a sphere, 24 centimetres in diameter, with a mass of 47 kilograms, and is covered by 60 reflectors. The inclination of its orbit around the Earth is 50 degrees, and its altitude varies between 810 kilometres and 1105 kilometres (perigee and apogee, respectively). This satellite has contributed significantly to the improvement of models of the Earth's gravitational field. Both long term average values and temporal variations due to the tides within the Earth, which acts as an elastic solid, and the oceans have been studied.

The American satellite, Lageos, is very similar to Starlette, but much bigger. It was launched on 4 May 1976 by NASA and placed in an almost circular orbit at an altitude of 5950 kilometres, at an angle of 110 degrees to the equator. Lageos is a sphere, of 60 centimetres diameter and mass 408 kilograms, covered by 426 laser reflectors. The high altitude of this target enables the separation of points on the Earth as far as 10 000 kilometres to be measured with great accuracy (50 centimetres). The temporal variation of distance between tracking stations situated on different tectonic plates has been derived, confirming the theory that tectonic plates move on a time scale as short as a decade. Large undulations of the geoid (wave lengths of 2000 kilometres or greater) have been measured to within a few centimetres (R. Futually).

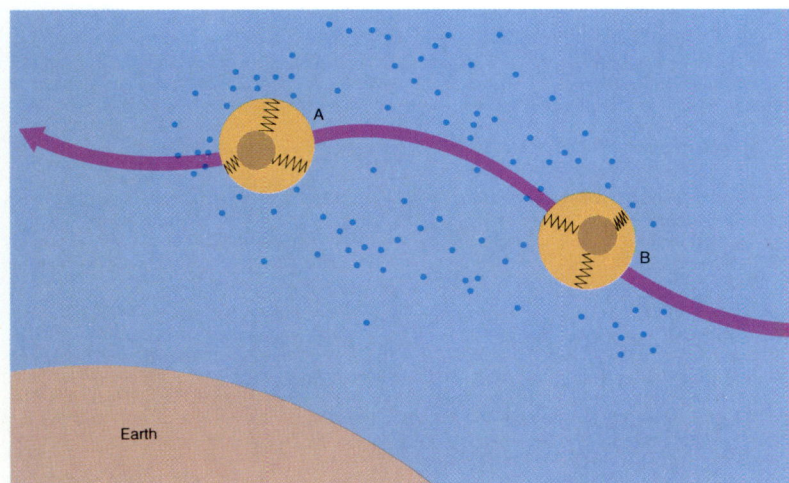

Direct measurements of the gravitational potential using two satellites (above). If two almost identical satellites are tracked along the same low altitude orbit (about 160 kilometres altitude), the variations in their radial velocity can be found. These variations are approximately proportional to the relative variations of the gravitational potential at the altitude of the satellites. The blue dots represent the atmosphere; its braking effect is compensated by a special system built around the triaxial accelerometer in each satellite.

The American Geopotential Research Mission (GRM) is a similar experiment, with a planned start in 1996. The two satellites involved will be 50 to 300 kilometres apart. The leading satellite will also be equipped with ultrasensitive magnetometers. These will measure variations in the Earth's magnetic field originating in the crust.

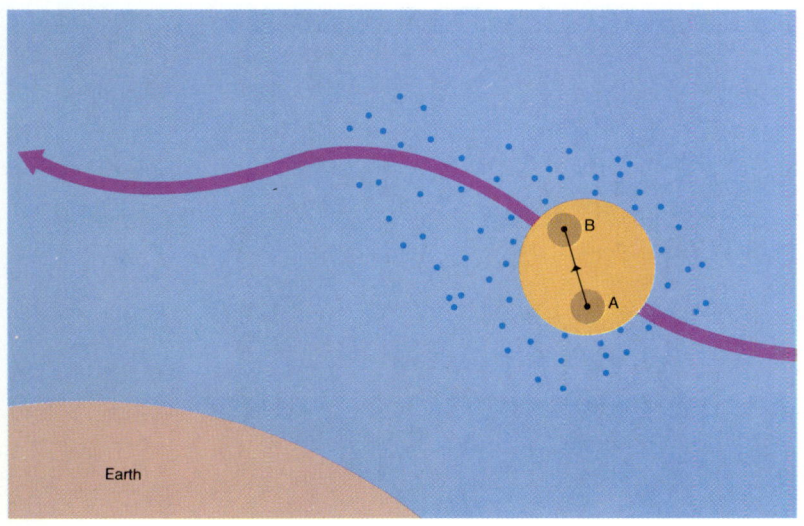

satellites from the ground. Photography of the satellite and stars at a precise moment in time can be used to give the direction of the tracking station–satellite vector in the Earth's cartesian coordinate system. This technique is used to find the purely geometrical location of the stations. When the directions of the station network have been determined, forming polyhedra, the scale is calculated by measuring at least one of the sides, either on the Earth or using a satellite. The accuracy of the distance measurements was between one and two metres in 1967 but is now down to only a few centimetres. Many modern satellites are used in the study of space geodesy. Others like Starlette and Lageos have been specially designed to make full use of the accuracy of laser stations. The Doppler effect can be used to measure the radial velocity of a satellite (equipped with a stable transmitter) along the line of sight. These differences in distance also allow us to calculate the quasigeometric position of the stations. Distance measurements made from four stations can be used to locate the position of one of the stations if the coordinates of the other three are known. This is done by centring spheres on the three reference stations whose radii correspond to the measured distance to the fourth station. The fourth station then lies at the point where the three spheres intersect. In the case of Doppler measurements, it is the intersection of hyperboloids which is used to find the position of the station. The difficulty with these techniques is the need to programme simultaneous observations of the same satellite from several stations.

The easiest way to locate a tracking station is to use several satellites, visible at the same time. This is the principle of the Global Positioning System which will use up to 18 satellites, at an altitude of 20 000 kilometres. At present six of the satellites are in orbit.

A different method of analysis is the dynamic method, where all the unknowns are treated. These are the parameters describing the geopotential (spherical harmonics), the coordinates of the tracking stations and the basic elements (coordinates and speeds) of the observed satellites at given instants in time along a particular arc of each trajectory. Obviously these calculations are complex, but they do exploit all the measured quantities. Any satellite is considered as a test body placed in the gravitational field of the planet, and the laws of physics allow us to relate its movement to all the forces which act on it and to the initial conditions. Analysing orbital perturbations measured from the Earth is a problem of inversion in celestial mechanics. The forces other than those due to the Earth's gravitation must all be modelled. Gravitational forces due to the Moon, the Sun, tides, and forces due to atmospheric friction and solar radiation pressure, cause perturbations to the satellite's orbit. Thus the technique becomes even more complex and several satellites have to be used in order to separate out the different unknowns.

Towards better resolution: space altimetry

All the methods discussed in the previous section have led to global geodetic models. The first such models were constructed by the Americans from 1965 onwards. Current models have been developed independently by a group at the NASA Goddard Space Flight Center and by a Franco-German team. Modern representations of the geopotential include about 1350 parameters (with the coordinates of more than a hundred stations), and the holes and humps of the geoid have been resolved on a scale down to about 500 kilometres.

A new measurement technique appeared in 1975. This is satellite altimetry over the oceans. The average surface of the seas is now known to great accuracy (about 10 centimetres), with a spatial resolution of only some tens of kilometres at latitudes between 65 degrees

South and 72 degrees North. The surface of the geoid may be determined by modelling from the topography of the ocean surface. In geophysics this difference can often be neglected, but it is now being studied by oceanographers. The gravitational field of the oceans is well documented, thanks to satellite altimetry using radar, and the results of this direct mapping are impressive. An extraordinary correlation has been found with the topography of the seabed. This allows us to measure with some precision the thermal and mechanical properties of the lithosphere as well as its evolution. New experiments are being planned by various space agencies to investigate the polar regions, to improve the density of observations and to improve the accuracy to a few centimetres. Early in the 1990s the European Space Agency will launch the Earth Remote Sensing (ERS 1) satellite, followed by ERS 2 later in the decade. The Franco-American project, Topex–Poseidon, is scheduled for launch in 1992. These satellites will carry other instruments to study the surface of the seas. They will mark an important step forward in space oceanology.

Some revolutionary projects

The accuracy of geoid models differs considerably for different regions of the Earth and depends on the fineness of the scale being used. At the longest wavelengths (2000 to 10 000 kilometres), the accuracy is several centimetres to several tens of centimetres. For shorter wavelengths (20 to 2000 kilometres), there is a dearth of information. This is due to a lack of gravimetric observations in remote areas, such as high mountains, the Antarctic, the equatorial forests, Russia and China, because of their inaccessibility. Space methods, very different to those already described, are being developed to fly on board specialised satellites to be launched in the 1990s. The first concept, studied by NASA since 1975, consists of measuring the radial velocity between two satellites with an accuracy of the order of ten microns per second, and deducing the relative differences in the gravitational potential. The second idea has been studied in the USA and in France since 1982. It is a gradiometric method, measuring the derivatives of the gravitational field aboard a satellite. In all cases the altitude of the satellite has to be as low as possible, below 200 kilometres altitude, to optimise the detection of smaller scale gravitational anomalies. Thus a propulsion system is required to enable it to stay in orbit for at least six months. One or other of the approaches will provide a complete map of the gravitational anomalies with a precision of 10^{-5} metres per second squared at a resolution of 100 kilometres. It is expected to link these experiments with a mission to measure the Earth's magnetic field. The American satellite, Magsat, measured the magnetic field with a spatial resolution of about 600 kilometres in 1979. However, the geophysicists investigating this field also require observations with improved resolution.

Without doubt, interpreting the variations in both the gravitational and magnetic potentials of the Earth is very important for the progress of all the Earth sciences. It will lead to a better understanding of phenomena such as topographic loading in the continental regions (isostasy), the systematic study of large sedimentary basins and modelling the thermal convection in the Earth's mantle on a medium scale. Oceanographers will be able to separate the variation of sea level from that of the geoid, using altimetry. Studies of ocean currents and their seasonal variations will be possible. Finally, there will be an improvement of at least an order of magnitude in the derivation of satellite trajectories, of benefit in many fields of application.

Georges Balmino

Science in space

The ionised environment of the Earth

The study of the ionised environment of the Earth has its own separate niche within the disciplines which rely upon space techniques. Its very existence was only discovered at the beginning of the twentieth century. Guglielmo Marconi (1901) and Oliver Heaviside (1902) experimentally confirmed the existence of ionised layers in the upper atmosphere. Behaving as electrical conductors, these reflect radio waves with frequencies of up to about 20 megahertz. As a result of observational and theoretical studies, two Norwegian scientists, Olaf Birkeland (1867–1917) and Carl Størmer (1874–1957) hypothesised that charged particles, electrons or protons, emanating from the Sun or the cosmos, are guided by the Earth's magnetic field to precipitate into the high atmosphere. At altitudes above about 100 kilometres, they give rise to the aurora in polar regions.

Unfortunately, groundbased radars can only probe the ionosphere below its peak, the region of maximum electron density which is situated at 250 to 300 kilometres altitude. The mysterious particles which precipitate in the auroral regions do not penetrate down to the altitudes (about 30 kilometres) reached by stratospheric balloons. This is why the introduction of rockets and, above all, satellites has been so welcomed by those scientists working on topics in external geophysics or geospace who were keen to investigate the hidden world. It is why, throughout the first decade of the space era, experiments were almost exclusively confined to the study of this region – the magnetosphere. This is the region of space around the Earth where the geomagnetic field, rather than pressure or gravity, provides the dominant controlling force.

The Earth's magnetic field and the magnetospheric cavity

Although it was not the first discovery made by satellites (it was necessary to wait until the 1960s when satellite apogees increased to 100 000 kilometres), we must begin by introducing the concept of the 'magnetospheric cavity'. On the one hand, this allows us to define the region of space under discussion and, on the other, it provides a framework for the geomagnetic field. The magnetospheric cavity plays a key role in organising and controlling all the phenomena within this region.

Like Jupiter, Saturn, Uranus and, to a lesser degree, Mercury, the Earth is a magnetised planet. Electric currents flow inside the Earth's molten core to cause the geomagnetic field, which spreads far from the Earth. If the Earth were placed in a vacuum, at great distances its field would be like that of a giant bar magnet whose axis was almost exactly that of the Earth's rotational axis. The solar wind, composed of electrons and protons and travelling away from the Sun at a speed between 300 and 1000 kilometres per second, acts as an electri-

cally conducting medium. At a distance of about ten Earth radii (64 000 kilometres) from the Earth, where this moving conductive medium comes into contact with the Earth's magnetic field, electric currents flow. They prevent the charged particles in the solar wind from penetrating into the Earth's magnetic field, and also prevent the geomagnetic field from spreading out into interplanetary space. A cavity forms. This is compressed on the sunward side and stretched out a long distance, away from the Sun in the antisolar direction. This tail of the magnetosphere is similar to a comet's tail. The boundary between the magnetosphere and solar wind is called the magnetopause. This is contained within an outer shell, a thin transition region, bounded by the Earth's bow shock. This shock front forms in the supersonic solar wind ahead of the obstacle in its flow, the magnetosphere. The structure of the magnetic field lines inside the magnetospheric cavity is not at all like those of a bar magnet. This distortion was postulated in 1932 by the British geophysicist, S. Chapman (1888–1970).

Experiments in space have enabled us to verify the conclusions of detailed theories about the interaction of the solar wind with the magnetosphere. Measurements of intensity and orientation of the field, using magnetometers on board satellites, have confirmed the very marked distortion of the field in the magnetospheric tail and its compression on the dayside of the Earth.

Charged particles in the magnetosphere

One of the most fascinating discoveries of the early years of the space era was that of the radiation belts (or van Allen belts after one of the two scientists who discovered them). This 'radiation' is, in fact, due to energetic charged particles, high energy electrons and protons (between a fraction and several tens of millions of electronvolts) which populate the Earth's magnetosphere, hardly penetrating the atmosphere. We say that these particles are trapped by the magnetic field.

There are some high energy particles (several million electronvolts or more) which do collide with the atmosphere and even with the Earth itself. These are the cosmic rays which originate in the distant Universe. The aurora borealis is caused by charged particles from the Sun, with energies of a few kiloelectronvolts or more, striking the top of the atmosphere. They excite atmospheric atoms and molecules which then emit their characteristic light. The process is the natural analogue of a television set in operation.

The techniques of detecting these particles and measuring their charge, mass, energy or pitch angle distribution have been much improved since the first instruments sent aloft aboard early Soviet and American satellites.

Firing a rocket at Terre Adélie. Rocket experiments are indispensable for making *in situ* measurements at heights of between 40 kilometres (the maximum altitude of stratospheric balloons) and 200 kilometres (the lowest practical satellite orbit). This photograph shows the launch of a Dragon rocket, in 1967, from the French base of Dumont d'Urville in Terre Adélie, Antarctica. French research scientists measured the electric fields and the charged particle fluxes between 100 kilometres and 300 kilometres altitude whilst there were magnetic disturbances over the polar caps.

The variation of electron and ion density with height. Above 80 kilometres altitude, collisions between atoms and molecules are extremely rare. Ions and electrons, formed by the solar photoionisation of molecules and atoms, are not immediately removed by recombination. An electrically charged gas, termed a plasma, is created. This has the important property of reflecting electromagnetic (radio) waves.

The diagram, below, shows the diurnal variation in composition of the plasma, during conditions of minimum solar activity at middle latitudes. Each molecular or atomic species has a different height distribution, the lightest atoms being most common at the greatest altitudes. The time constants of photodissociation, photoionisation and recombination depend upon height. The number of electrons per cubic centimetre always equals the number of positive ions per cubic centimetre.

The diagram also shows how a different photochemical species is associated with each layer in the ionosphere (NO^+ for the D layer, O_2^+ for the E layer and O^+ for the F layer). At night, there is no photoionisation and so recombination partially destroys the ionosphere, in particular the lower layers. A transient E layer, named 'sporadic E', is produced under certain special conditions.

Prior to the 1960s, groundbased measurements were made of the electron density using classical ionospheric sounders. With this technique it was impossible to measure beyond the 'F2 layer peak' at a height near 300 kilometres. The Americans (at Arecibo, in Puerto Rico, and Chatanika in Alaska) and Europeans (at Saint-Santin, in France, and Tromsø in Norway) extended these studies using incoherent scatter radars. These sophisticated radars make measurements above and beyond the F2 peak, not only of the plasma density but also of other characteristics of the ionospheric plasma, such as the ionic and electronic temperatures, the velocity of the ions with respect to the neutrals and even the ionic composition.

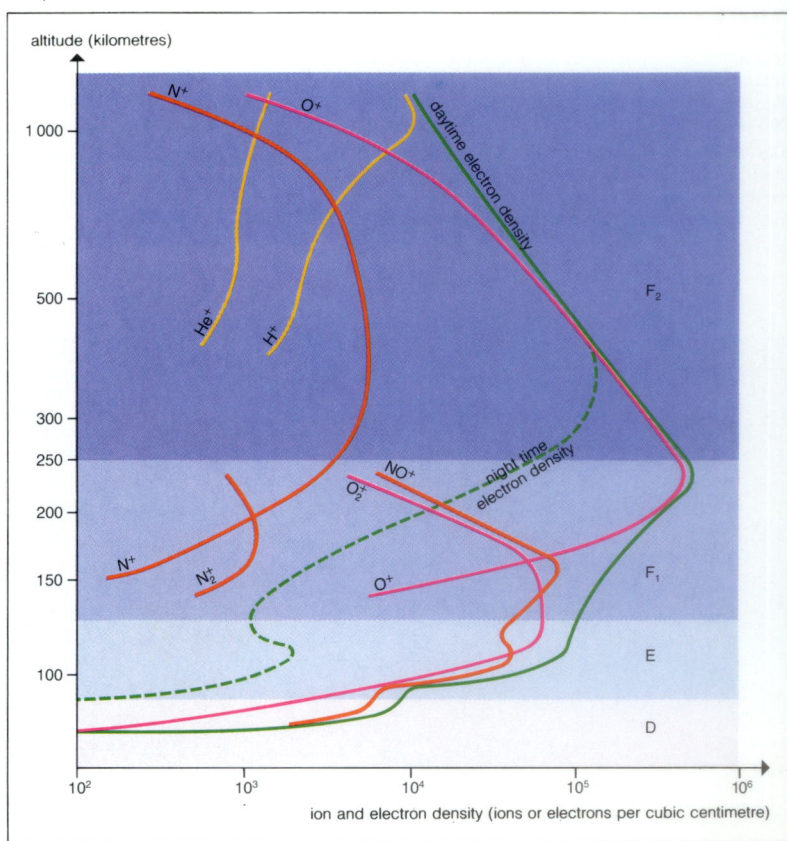

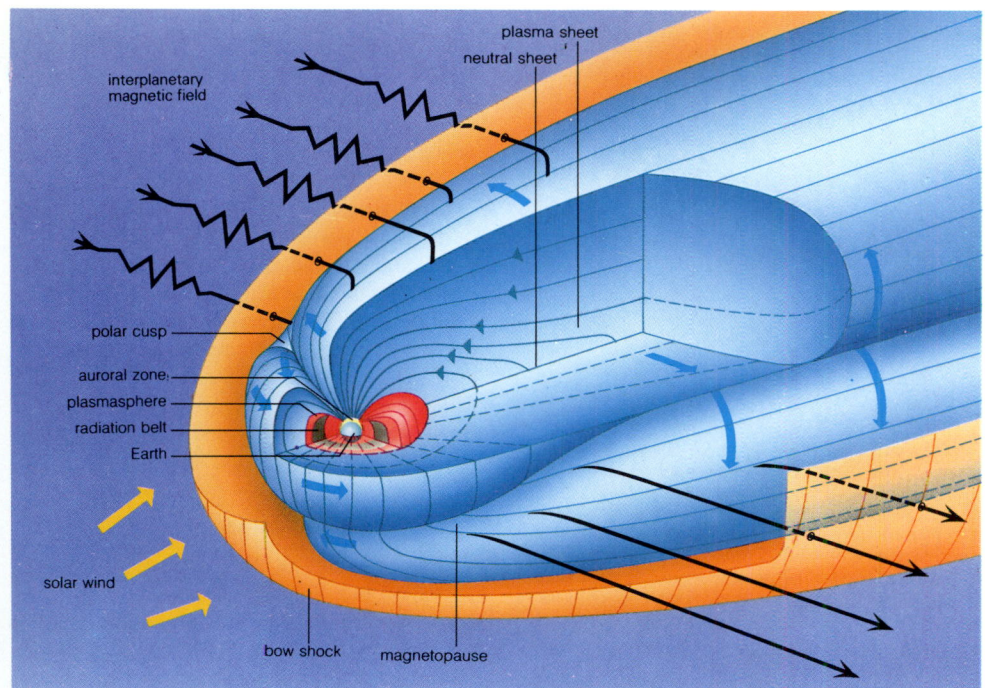

The structure of the magnetosphere. Above is a three dimensional schematic diagram of the Earth's magnetosphere. The charged particles of the solar wind are diverted by the Earth's magnetic field. Their speed is typically about 400 kilometres per second (from left to right in the picture). The magnetopause separates the region where particles from the solar wind dominate from that where the Earth's magnetic field is predominant. Electric currents (bold blue arrows), which flow on the magnetopause, reinforce the magnetic field inside the magnetospheric cavity and almost completely nullify it outside. Since the relative speed of the solar wind with respect to the magnetosphere is much greater than that of either sound waves or magnetohydrodynamic waves, both of which propagate in the solar wind, a shock wave is created in front of the cavity. This is termed the bow shock; it is the outer boundary of the region shown in orange above.

Inside the magnetosphere there is a zone populated by low energy charged particles. These diffuse up from the ionosphere and fill the plasmasphere. High energy charged particles stem from cosmic rays; these constitute the radiation belts and are shown in red and green. The high latitude regions are the auroral zones and polar caps; they are linked to the tail of the magnetosphere by magnetic field lines (shown in blue).

There are two regions where charged particles from the solar wind have direct access to the magnetosphere. These are both on the dayside, and they are called the north and south polar cusps. These are the two points on the magnetopause where the magnetic field is weak.

Finally, the solar wind itself carries a weak magnetic field from the surface of the Sun. These magnetic field lines can, in certain circumstances, join up with those from the Earth. This phenomenon is called magnetic reconnection and gives rise to disturbances in the magnetosphere.

Charged particles in the magnetosphere (both diagrams below). Electrically charged particles moving in a magnetic field have complex orbits. In the Earth's magnetic field, the trajectory of a charged particle is made up of three parts (upper diagram):
a spiralling motion along the field line;
a bouncing motion, to and fro from North to South and back, along the field line between two 'mirror' points;
a drift in longitude, caused by the non-uniformity (gradient and curvature) in the magnetic field with positively charged particles drifting westwards, and negatively charged ones eastwards.

The lower diagram represents contours for the fluxes of trapped particles of different energies. The flux J is expressed as the number of particles per square centimetre per second. These figures are meridional cross sections since particle drifts populate all longitudes. Higher energy particles are concentrated in regions nearer the Earth. Electrons of lower energy populate regions further from the Earth.

These discoveries were made by numerous satellites between 1960 and 1980. A detailed description of the fluxes of particles, of all energies, is now well established at all geocentric distances and at all pitch angles. (The pitch angle is the angle between the velocity vector of a charged particle and the magnetic field vector.)

Experimental evidence of the magnetopause and the Earth's bow shock (below). The upper figure drawn in the Earth's frame of reference shows the data gathered by several satellites of the Explorer, Mariner and Pioneer series in very elliptical orbits. In the ecliptic plane the x-axis is towards the Sun and the y-axis is towards dawn. The red and yellow dots indicate the positions of the bow shock and the magnetopause respectively, detected at different crossings of these boundaries. The black lines show the calculated positions of these boundaries, for typical solar wind conditions.

On crossing these boundaries, an instrument aboard a satellite records a sharp variation in the total intensity, F, of the magnetic field. Examples of this are given in the two lower figures. The measurements come from the Pioneer 6 probe whose orbit was approximately along the y-axis. In the lower lefthand figure there is a sharp discontinuity in the field shortly before 13 Earth radii. Just before this discontinuity, corresponding to the magnetopause, the field is double the dipole field value that it should have if the magnetic field were due only to the Earth. The solar wind compresses the field lines, and theoretical calculation shows that at the discontinuity the field strength ought to be doubled. The lower righthand figure is of the same trajectory as it passes through a second discontinuity corresponding to the bow shock. Beyond this is the solar wind, which carries a weak magnetic field of solar origin. Its strength is between 2 and 10 nanoteslas, small compared to that of the Earth's magnetic field, which is 300 000 and 600 000 nanoteslas at the equator and the poles, respectively.

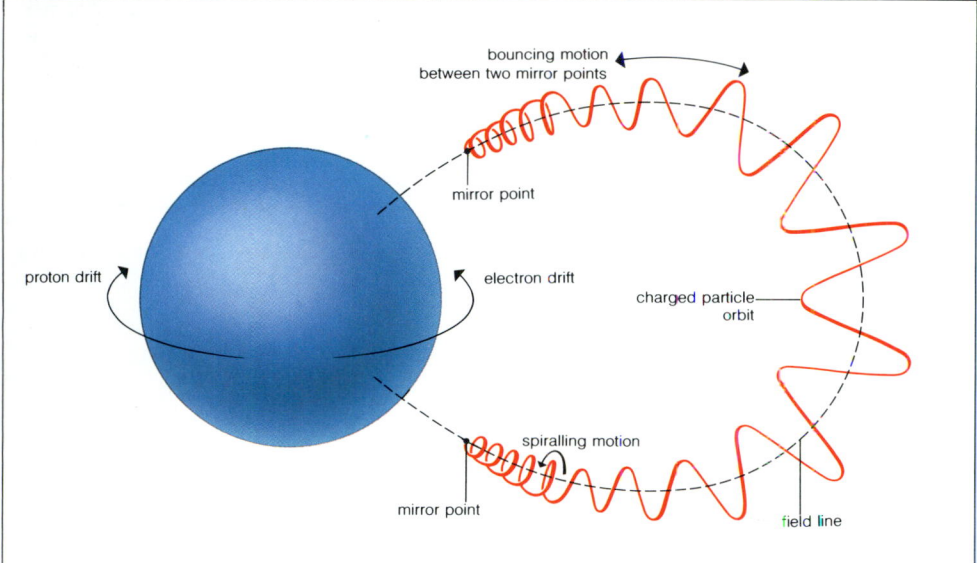

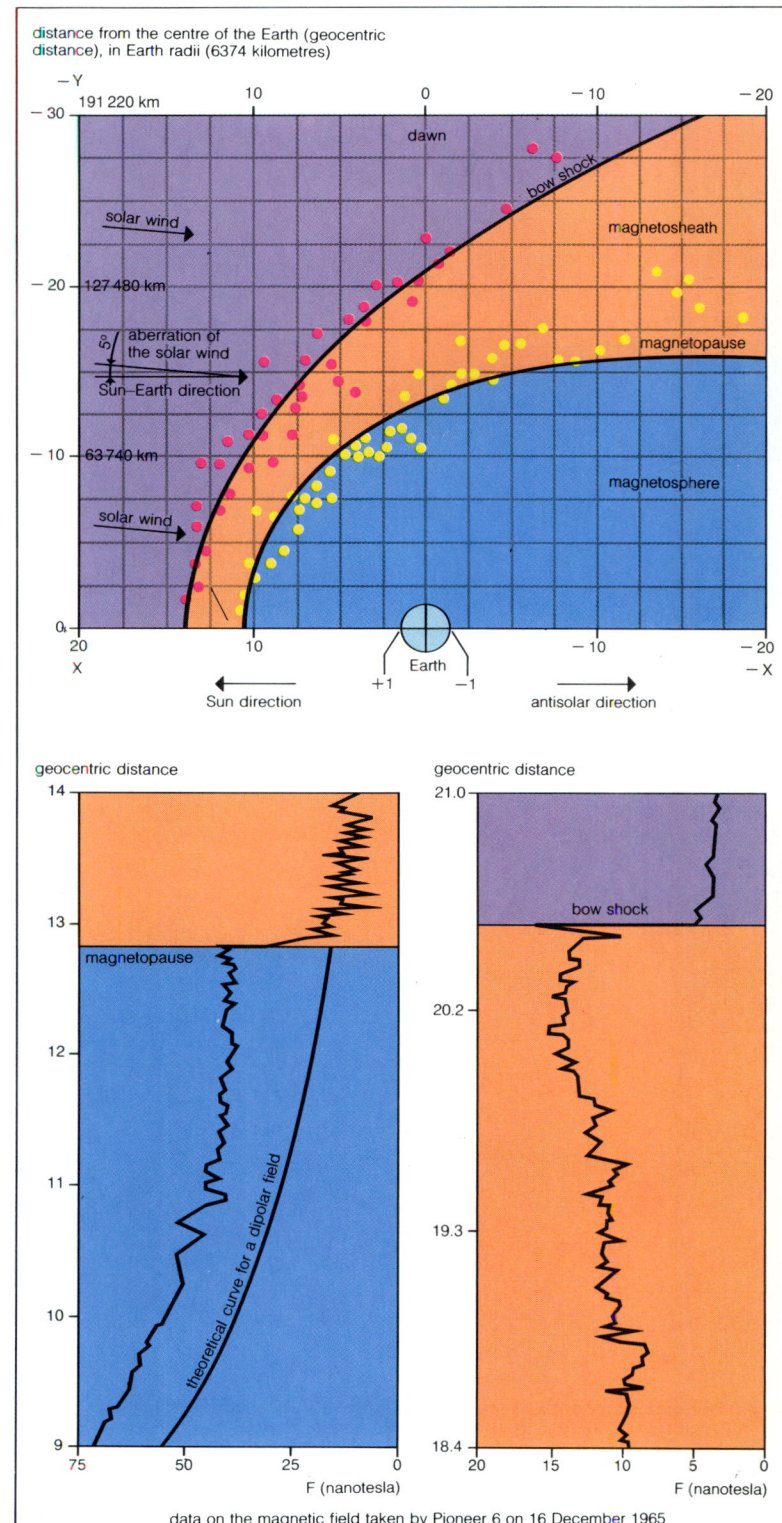

data on the magnetic field taken by Pioneer 6 on 16 December 1965

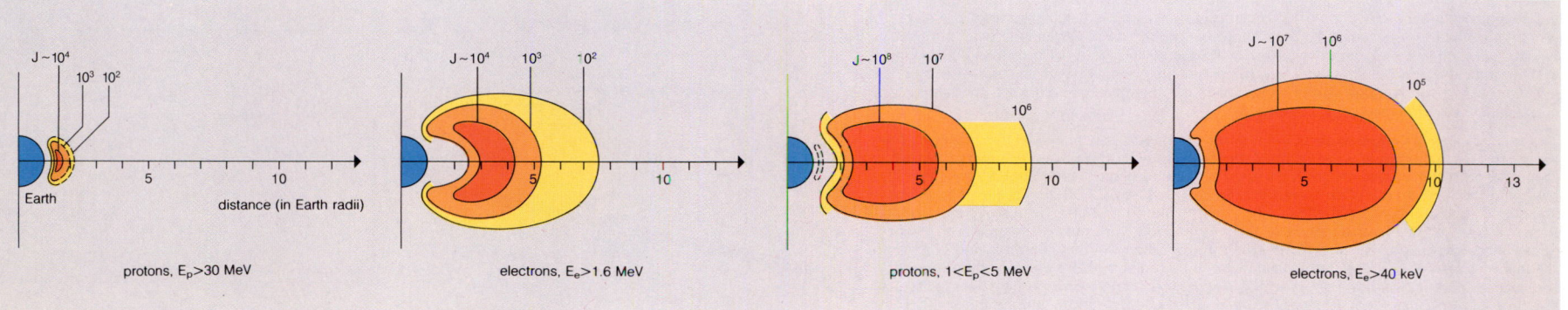

protons, $E_p > 30$ MeV

electrons, $E_e > 1.6$ MeV

protons, $1 < E_p < 5$ MeV

electrons, $E_e > 40$ keV

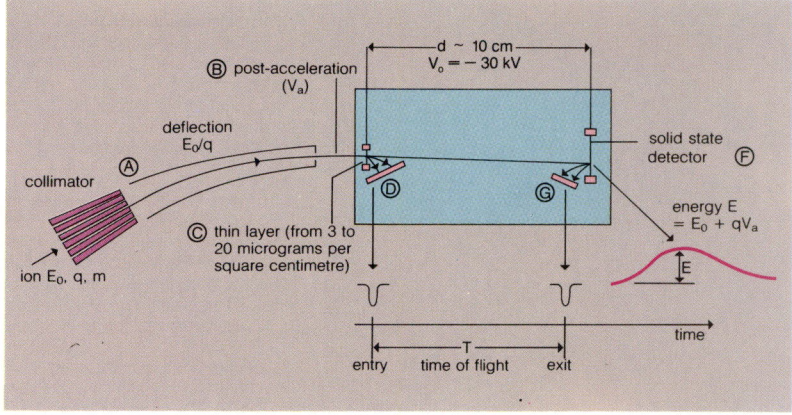

They make use of knowledge acquired in the fields of nuclear physics and optical electronics and, in certain cases, have also led to new techniques themselves. There is continual development in both methods of analysis and presentation of data, for use on satellites and on Earth.

Understanding the characteristics of these particles – particularly their distribution in space and movement in time, and especially with respect to changing solar and geomagnetic activity – is very important for the future development of space technologies. Indeed, we need to be able to estimate accurately the damage which charged particles cause to electronic devices already in space and their possible effects on the health of astronauts.

Charged particle detectors. There have been great advances in particle detection techniques since the beginning of the space era. Initially limited to basic Geiger counters, these techniques were improved by using methods devised for research in nuclear physics. These include mass and energy spectrometers, in which the charged particles are deflected by electric and magnetic fields, or interaction with matter to measure the energy of the incident particles, and measurement of the time of flight of a charged particle between two fixed points to derive its velocity. One of the major challenges facing researchers and engineers has been to adapt these methods for use at lower energies than those encountered in nuclear physics.

The photograph (left), which is of historic interest, shows the Geiger counter designed by Prof. J. A. van Allen, of the University of Iowa. This was sent aloft aboard the Explorer 1 satellite launched on 31 January 1958. Although following Sputnik 1, which was launched on 4 October 1957, it was this satellite which discovered the Earth's radiation belts.

The diagram (above) shows the principle of the 'time of flight' spectrometer. An electrostatic analyser (A) measures the ratio E_0/q, where E_0 is the incident energy of the particle and q its charge. Later acceleration (B) by a potential difference V_a increases the energy of the ions to the value $E = E_0 + qV_a$, allowing improved detection and resolution at lower energies. The incident ions pass through a thin layer (C), of width a few microns, which becomes the source of secondary electrons. These electrons are picked up by the detector D and are used to define the entry time of the ions into the measuring chamber E, of length d. A solid state detector F detects the secondary electrons emitted as the ions pass through the thin layer at G, thus defining the exit time of the ions; it also measures the total energy E. From these three quantities (E_0/q, d/T and E), m, E_0 and q can be deduced (Dr P. Wilken, Max Planck Institute, Lindau).

The thermal plasma

Less spectacular than energetic charged particles, but no less important in terms of space applications, was the discovery of a thermal component of the plasma in the outer regions of the magnetosphere (at 5 or 6 Earth radii). This is the high altitude continuation of the ionospheric plasma. Its temperature corresponds to energies of between a fraction of an electronvolt and several electronvolts. It is called the thermal plasma. As in the ionosphere, it is composed of equal numbers of electrons and ions. The ions are principally those of hydrogen but, in certain circumstances, in the outer ionosphere, helium or oxygen ions form a significant fraction of the plasma.

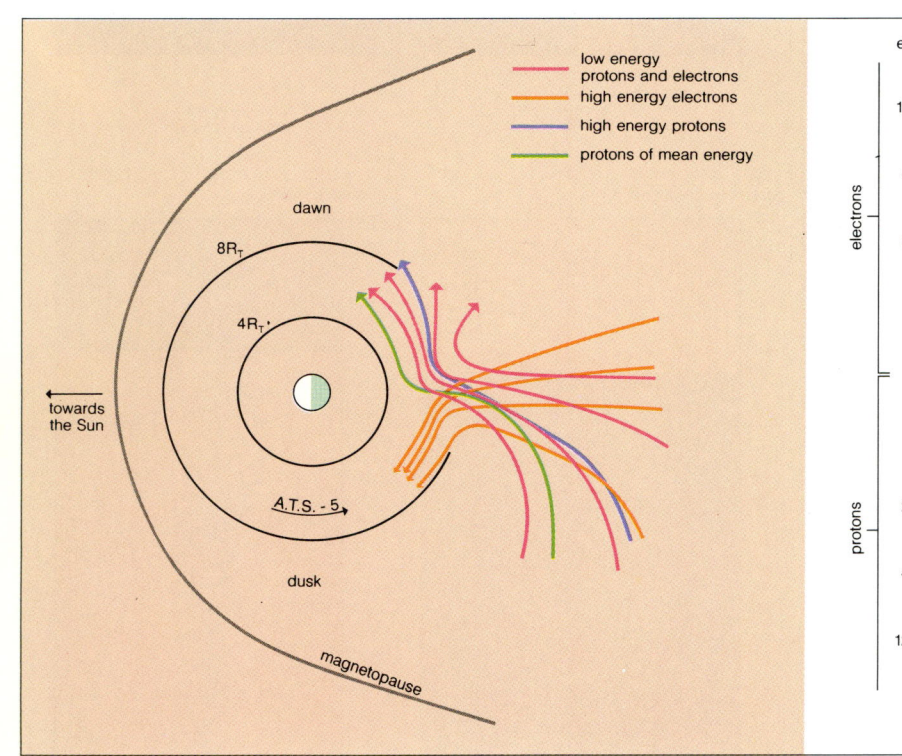

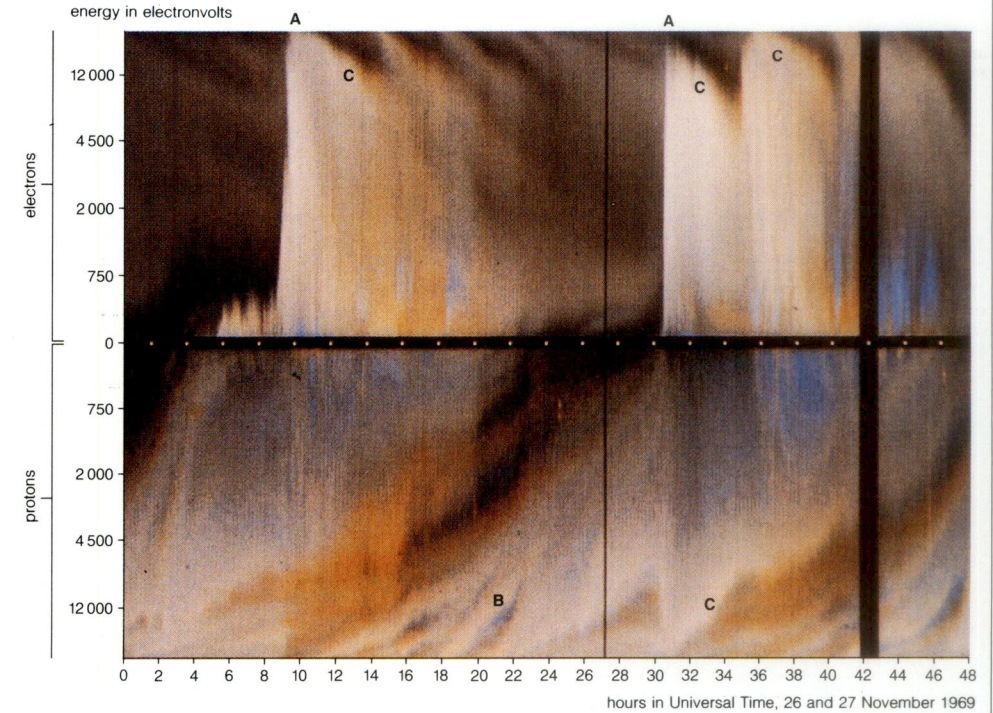

Diagnostic measurements of the thermal plasma. When the plasma temperature is relatively high, greater than several million degrees, the average thermal energy is a few hundred electronvolts. Under these conditions, charged particle detectors can be used. However, the temperature of the ionospheric plasma or of the plasmasphere are low, 2000 to 15 000 degrees kelvin or about 0·2 to 1·5 electronvolts, and other methods – such as Langmuir probes and resonance probes – are required.

Langmuir probes, which are often used in the laboratory, consist of a small sphere which is raised to a potential V when placed in the plasma. The current I, collected by the sphere, is measured as a function of V (upper figure). When V is negative, a weak ionic current is measured; because these ions are much heavier than the electrons their thermal velocity is much smaller, and the ion flux to the sphere is much less than the electron flux. When V is positive, there is a strong electron current. The electron temperature can be deduced from the shape of the characteristic V(I). The electron density n_e is calculated from the electron temperature and the saturation current. Langmuir probes work particularly well in rocket or low altitude satellite experiments, because the electron density to be measured is much greater than the photoelectron density generated in the vicinity of the satellite by solar radiation. At greater altitudes care must be taken, but the measurements are still valid where n_e exceeds 3 electrons per cubic centimetre.

The second class of probes exploits the resonant frequencies which exist in a plasma. When the plasma is excited by a wave of the same frequency as the plasma frequency, which is proportional to the square root of n_e, a large amplitude electrostatic field is observed. The lower figure is of a relaxation sounder like that used on GEOS (Europe's geostationary scientific satellite), ISEE (International Sun Earth Explorer) and the Swedish Viking satellite. An oscillator excites a long aerial, up to 100 metres long, with pulses of variable frequency. There is no response from the plasma until the excitation frequency equals one of its own resonant frequencies. These frequencies are the harmonics of the electron gyrofrequency, the plasma frequency and the upper hybrid frequency. These probes are extremely precise. Their measurements are not affected by the cloud of photoelectrons around the satellite nor by electrostatic charging phenomena which often affect particle detectors.

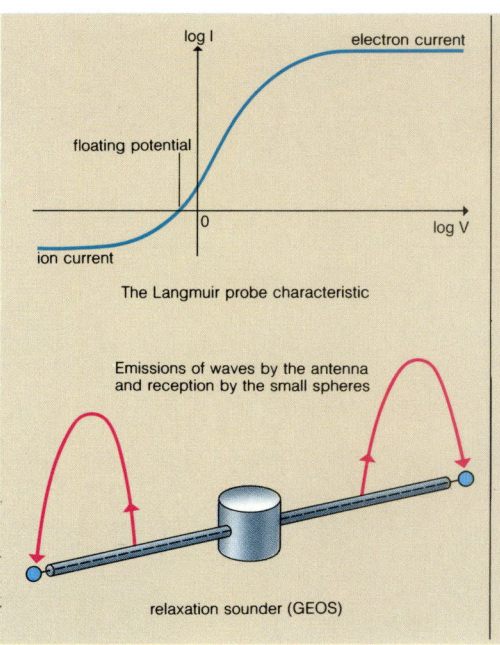

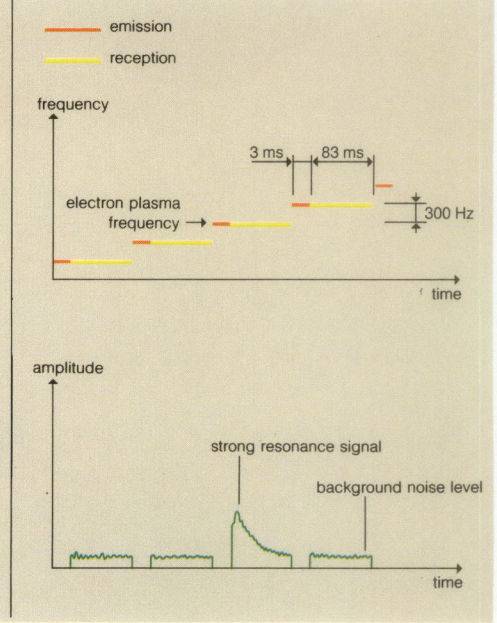

The distribution of thermal plasma in the magnetosphere (on the right). Beyond the peak of the ionosphere, at an altitude of about 300 kilometres, the electron density decreases with distance, but not simply exponentially. Measurements of whistlers observed on the Earth have provided density estimates to geocentric distances of 5 Earth radii. Only with the advent of satellites have precise measurements been possible. The electron density exceeds 100 electrons per cubic centimetre in the plasmasphere, but beyond the plasmapause it becomes very low, less than a few electrons per cubic centimetre. This boundary, the plasmapause, is not fixed; it moves towards lower latitudes as geomagnetic activity, characterised here by the planetary magnetic index K_p averaged over 24 hours, increases. The measurements on the upper graph were taken by the satellite ISEE 1.

The plasmapause boundary is asymmetric, with a 'bulge' towards 18.00 Local Time. The second figure gives relaxation sounder results from the European GEOS 2 satellite whose geostationary orbit enabled measurements of the variation of electron density with Local Time to be taken at a constant geocentric distance of 6·6 Earth radii.

Visualising charged particle data (photograph and drawing opposite, on the left). A three dimensional representation is necessary to illustrate the temporal variation of charged particle fluxes, as observed by satellites. The x-axis represents time, the y-axis particle energy and the observed flux is shown by the shading. This spectrograph is of data, on two consecutive days, recorded by the US geostationary satellite ATS 5 situated at a longitude of 105 degrees West. Increasing energies of electrons and protons are shown in opposite directions, away from the zero energy dots on the central horizontal axis; the extremes of the axes correspond to energies of the order of 50 kiloelectronvolts. Particles moving along the geomagnetic field are shown in blue, with those moving in the perpendicular direction being in orange. Regions of intense flux on the spectrograph are due to electrons. Events such as A correspond to the satellite crossing a particle injection boundary situated near the local midnight meridian, that is at 07.00 Universal Time, taking account of the longitude.

The effects of electric and magnetic fields on the trajectories of charged particles depend to a certain extent on where they enter the fields and on their energy. This is illustrated in the diagram on the left, for a particular dawn to dusk electric field. High energy protons drift to the West, whilst low energy protons and electrons of all energies drift towards the East. Higher energy particles drift faster than those of lower energies. Therefore the 10 kiloelectronvolt protons observed in the afternoon between 19.00 and 24.00 Universal Time, shown as B, are not mixed with low energy particles. At times, shown as C, high energy electrons and protons are recorded. Such spectrograms allow us to deduce the spatial and temporal properties, and energies, of charged particle injection into the magnetosphere during magnetic substorms (Prof. C. McIlwain, University of San Diego, California).

Magnetospheric convection (on the right). The solar wind flowing past the magnetosphere causes an electric field E to develop inside the magnetosphere. The field is directed from the dawn side to the dusk side of the magnetopause. The corresponding electric potential difference between the two sides usually lies between 60 and 150 kilovolts.

The joint influence of this electric field and the Earth's magnetic field B causes the thermal plasma in the tail of the magnetosphere to drift towards the Sun. Near the Earth, however, the plasma is pulled around the Earth. The trajectory of the thermal plasma in the equatorial plane is shown in the upper figure.

The convective movement of thermal plasma at ionospheric altitudes is illustrated in the lower diagram, as observed from above the North Pole at latitudes greater than 60 degrees; Local Time is marked on the circumference of the outer ring. Two cells of plasma convection are evident, with the plasma moving in a direction away from the Sun at very high latitudes across the polar cap. This motion relates to the existence of auroral source regions in the distant magnetosphere. Measurements made by satellites or taken on Earth using enormous ionospheric radars in Alaska, Greenland and Scandinavia have improved our understanding of the relationships which exist between the electric field, the ionospheric conductivity, and the movement of the ionospheric and magnetospheric plasma.

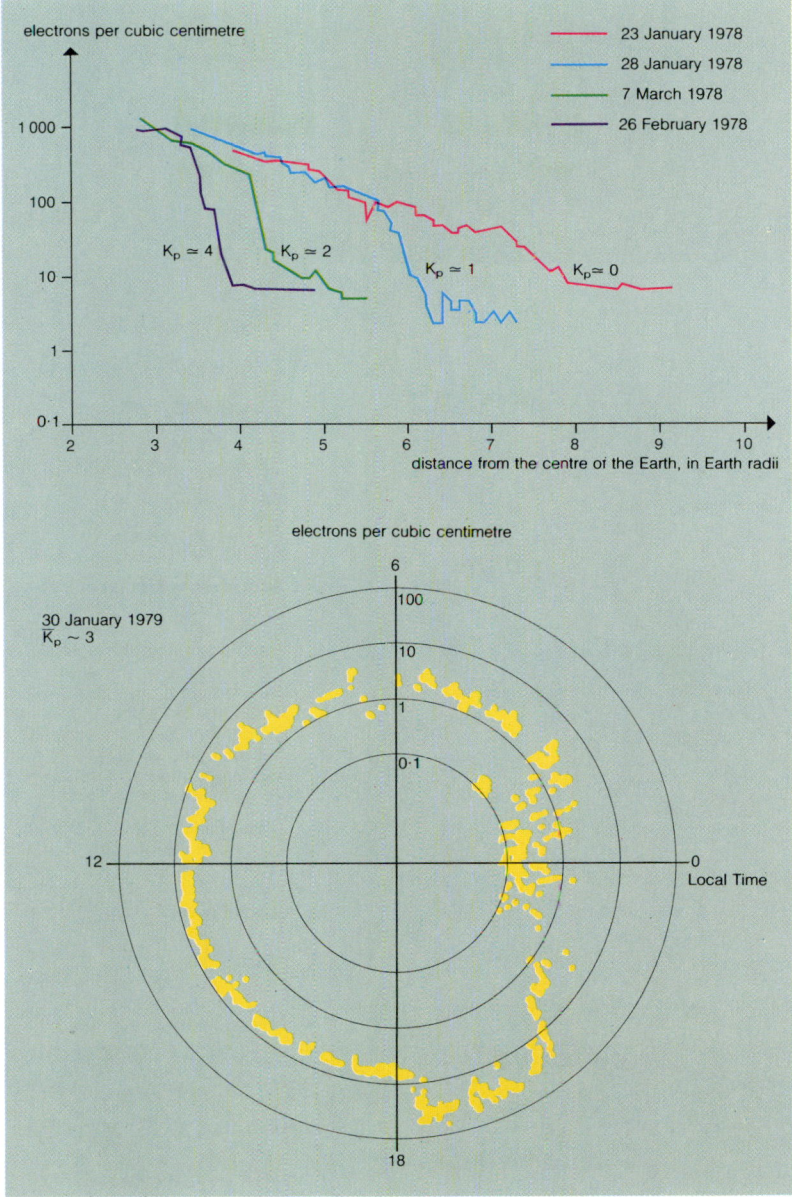

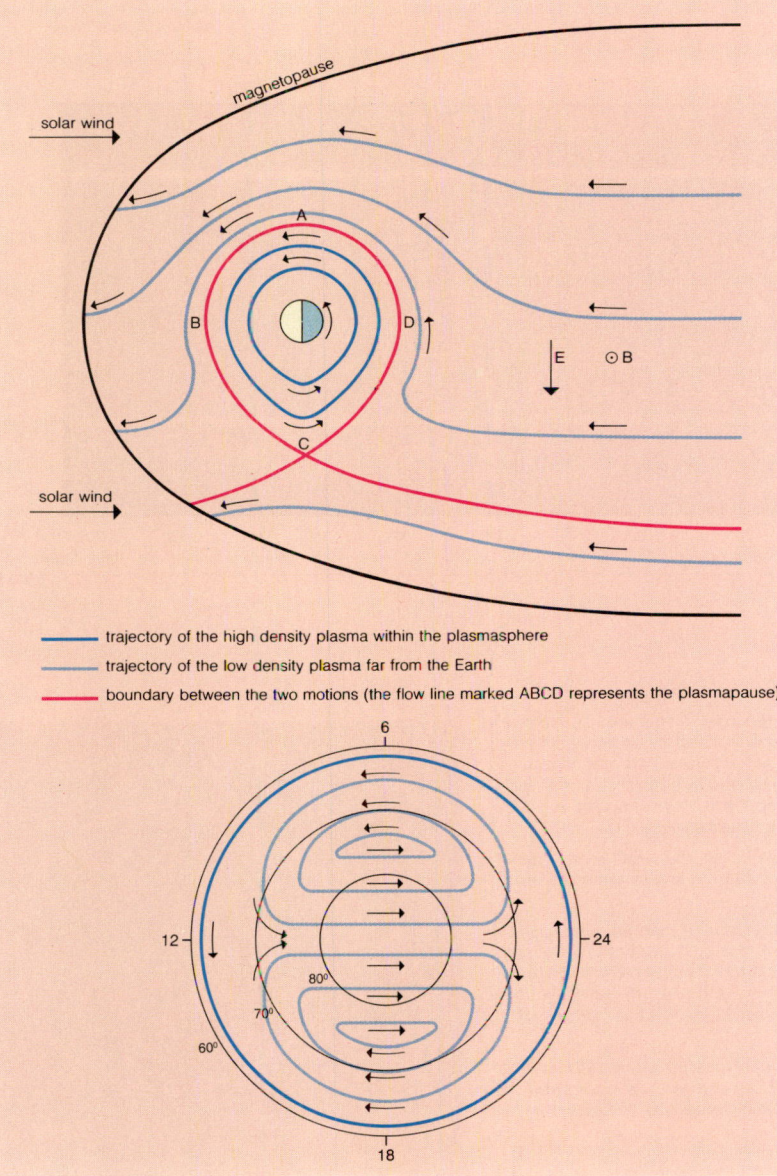

trajectory of the high density plasma within the plasmasphere

trajectory of the low density plasma far from the Earth

boundary between the two motions (the flow line marked ABCD represents the plasmapause)

The existence of this plasma, whose density is too great to be explained by hydrostatic equilibrium under the action of gravity and pressure gradient forces, was first suggested by Dr L. R. Owen Storey in 1953, based on his studies of the propagation of audio frequency radio waves called whistlers. The advent of satellites has made *in situ* measurements of the plasma possible, using instruments such as Langmuir probes, very low energy particle detectors and active experiments, all exploiting the plasma's response to probing or excitation by electric fields.

The thermal plasma occupies a well defined volume of space, called the plasmasphere. In general it has a density which is greater than 50 electrons per cubic centimetre. Beyond the plasmasphere, the density is extremely variable and may be less than one electron per cubic centimetre. The boundary between these two regions is a geomagnetic field aligned surface called the plasmapause.

Although the thermal plasma has a low energy, it plays an important role in determining the electric charge on Earth orbiting satellites. Its absence, coupled with large increases in the energetic charged particle flux, such as occur during magnetic storms, has often been the cause of large electric fields, which in turn cause electronic instruments in space to fail.

The electric field and large scale plasma convection in the magnetosphere

A dynamo is created by the rapid movement of the highly conducting solar wind past the Earth's magnetic field, not forgetting the weak magnetic field associated with the solar wind itself. An electric potential difference is generated between the dawn and dusk sides of the magnetosphere, which is of the order of 60 to 150 kilovolts. In the equatorial plane, in the Earth's frame of reference, there is a weak associated electric field, of the order of several tenths of a millivolt per metre. It is somewhat stronger at ionospheric altitudes over the polar caps, of the order of several millivolts per metre. Under the combined action of the electric and magnetic fields on the one hand and the effects of the Earth's rotation on the other, the thermal plasma can only move along certain flow lines.

For a long time the ability to measure such weak electric fields in space presented great technical difficulties, and it is only recently that reliable data have been obtained. This has been done by combining several instrumental techniques on the same satellite.

Waves in the magnetosphere

The Earth's magnetosphere contains several species of charged particles with a broad range of energies. It is also criss-crossed by waves of many types and frequencies. Whereas some radio waves reach the Earth from a source in the near or distant Universe (planetary, solar or galactic emissions), others come from the region around the Earth, a natural source of intense radio wave emissions. Some of these emissions can be observed from the Earth; others can only be detected from satellites. This is because the ionosphere or plasmasphere reflects electromagnetic waves with frequencies less than about 10 megahertz, or because electrostatic waves only propagate a short distance from their source. Whilst we can consider these waves as a whole, their spectrum extending from some tens of millihertz to several megahertz, they are neither emitted in a continuous fashion, nor are they observable in all regions of space, nor at the same time. Each type of wave has its own characteristic propagation, with a certain phase velocity and group velocity which depends on the two principal parameters governing the medium: plasma density and the intensity of the magnetic field.

Exploring the Universe

Measuring the electric field (right). The most commonly used method to find the electric field consists of measuring the potential difference between two conducting spheres immersed in the plasma and placed symmetrically on either side of the body of the satellite, a distance 2L apart. If V is the potential difference measured, then $E = V/2L$. The distance 2L is chosen for the sensitivity that is required, which depends on the region being studied. The spheres are placed either on the ends of rigid arms (which limits L to between 5 and 7 metres) or on the ends of flexible coaxial cables (with L from 20 to 100 metres), which unwind under the action of the centrifugal force of the spinning satellite. The first method is often used on rockets because the ionospheric electric field is intense (from 5 to 50 millivolts per metre). The second is better on magnetospheric satellites, because the electric field is very weak (from 0·1 to 3 millivolts per metre).

Preamplifiers are placed inside the two spheres. Their internal impedance is very great (about 10^{12} to 10^{13} ohms), much larger than the resistance of the ambient plasma. This prevents a decrease in instrument response at high frequencies due to the large capacitance of the connecting cables between the sphere and satellite. An example of such a system is shown in the 'exploded' view of the system, which represents part of that used on the GEOS satellite (Dr A. Pedersen, European Space Technology Centre, Noordwijk, Holland).

Also employed on the same satellite was an extremely original method of measuring E. It involved measuring the displacement of the arrival point of a 1 kiloelectron-volt beam of electrons, emitted by a small on board accelerator. Under normal circumstances these electrons would have a circular orbit, with a radius of around 1 kilometre at the geostationary orbit, perpendicular to the magnetic field B; they would come back to their starting point. Under the influence of an electric field, E, the electrons return to a point that is slightly displaced from this. According to the strength of the field, E, one or other of four electron guns is used. This method, developed by the Max Planck Institute, Garching, cuts out the local parasitic effects generated by the cloud of photoelectrons around the satellite or by fluctuations in the potential of the satellite.

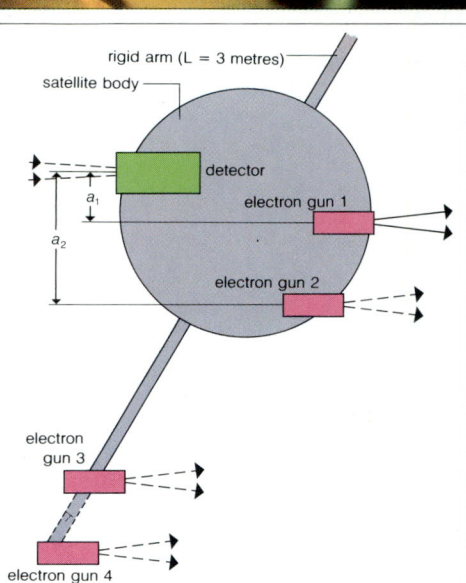

rigid arm (L = 3 metres)
satellite body
detector
electron gun 1
a_1
a_2
electron gun 2
electron gun 3
electron gun 4

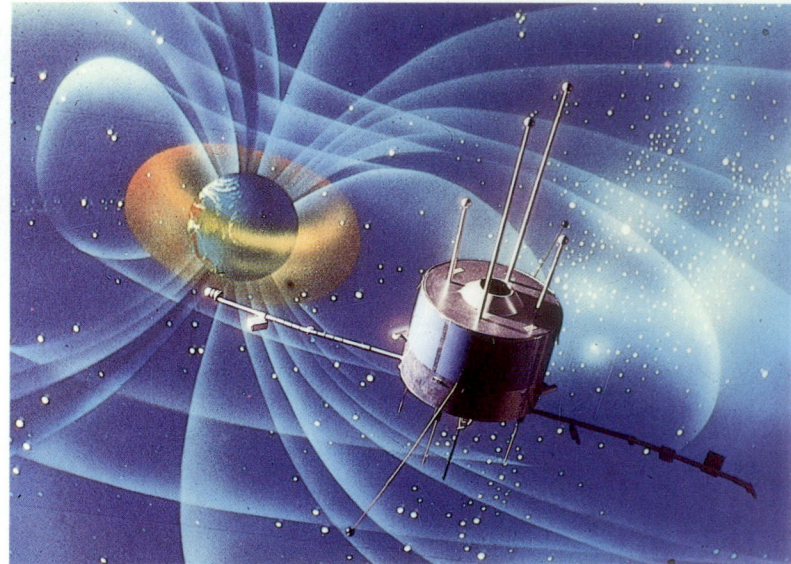

Satellites which study the environment (above and on the right). The satellites, Viking, GEOS and ISEE, which study the Earth's magnetospheric environment, have similar designs. As they are not power hungry, there are no solar panels. Solar cells are spread over the external surface of the satellite. The satellite is spin stabilised. It has long antennae in the equatorial plane to measure the electric field. The third component of the electric field is obtained either from one or more antennae mounted parallel to the rotational axis (Viking and GEOS, upper picture) or by an antenna placed at 45 degrees to this axis (ISEE, the picture on the right). In the first two cases, the length of the antenna is limited (so that it does not affect the rotational stability of the satellite); this reduces the sensitivity of the experiment. The shorter jointed rigid arms carry equipment which need to be far from the central body, such as the magnetometer or thermal plasma detectors.

The Swedish satellite, Viking, was launched in February 1986, with a perigee of 800 kilometres and apogee of 14 000 kilometres. The GEOS 2 satellite, of the European Space Agency, was launched in April 1978 into a geostationary orbit at an altitude of 36 000 kilometres. The ISEE 1 satellite (ESA and NASA combined) was launched in October 1977; its perigee was 700 kilometres and its apogee was 140 000 kilometres (ESA).

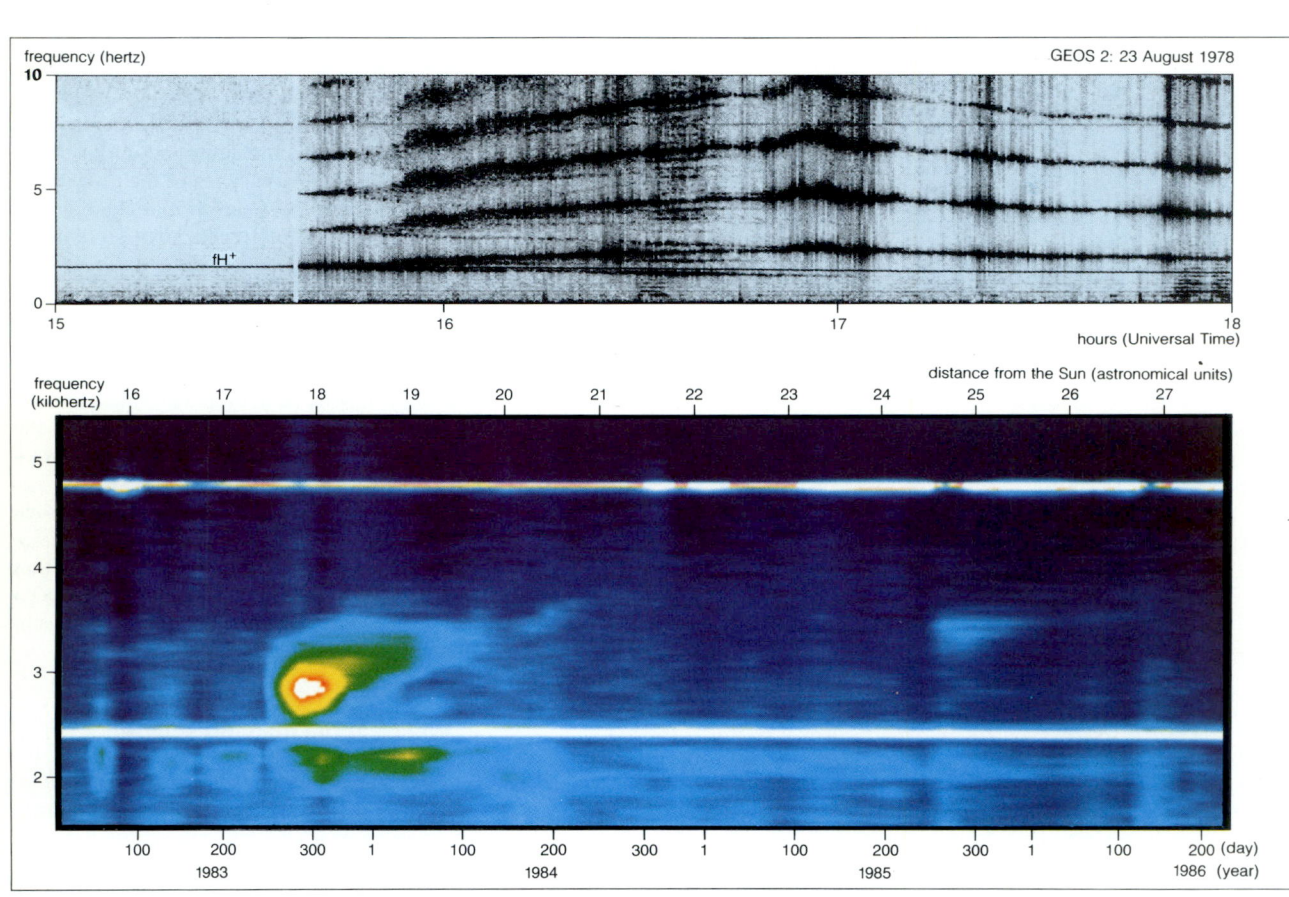

The observation of natural electromagnetic waves in space (left). The Earth's environment, and that of the other planets and the solar wind, are all sources of natural electromagnetic emissions which can be very intense. A 'frequency–time' graph is used to represent these emissions, where time is along the x-axis and frequency along the y-axis. The intensity of the signal at a given instant is represented by the darkness (in black and white pictures) or is colour coded.

These signals can be emitted over a very wide frequency range (measured in hertz, kilohertz or megahertz), depending on their origin. The upper plot corresponds to a signal in the Earth's magnetosphere recorded by the geostationary satellite, GEOS 2. The lower record shows signals detected in the distant solar wind using the Voyager 1 spacecraft.

The upper graph is of harmonic emissions where the fundamental has been excited at the proton gyro-frequency (of the order of 1 hertz, indicated by the line marked fH$^+$ on the figure). This emission lasted about one hour. It most probably originated from an anomaly in the angular velocity distribution of protons with energies of several tens of kiloelectronvolts.

The second example corresponds to a signal observed over more than two months at a frequency of around 3 kilohertz. It is thought that this signal was caused by the heliopause, that is the boundary between the intergalactic medium and the solar wind, at a distance of nearly a hundred astronomical units (Dr W. S. Kurth, University of Iowa).

Reception of electromagnetic signals at conjugate points. Two points situated on the Earth's surface on the same geomagnetic field line are said to be geomagnetically conjugate. Certain electromagnetic waves are guided by these field lines. Part of their energy is reflected by the ionosphere and the wave returns in the opposite direction. The other part carries on to the Earth where it is detected. This phenomenon is often accompanied by dispersion; signals with different frequencies propagate at different speeds.

For radio waves of very low frequencies (between 1 and 10 kilohertz), the time taken to travel from one hemisphere to the other is of the order of 1 second. At ultra low frequencies (from 0·2 to 5 hertz), it is of the order of 1 minute.

The example on the right is of ultra low frequencies. The amplitudes of magnetic oscillations were recorded as a function of time on 25 October 1964 at two conjugate stations, Kerguelen (in the Indian Ocean) and Sogra (USSR). A series of wave packets was observed which had a central frequency in the region of 1 hertz and a period (time to make the return journey) of the order of 2.5 minutes. The two wave trains, showing a striking similarity, were recorded with a time lag of about 75 seconds at the two stations.

Groundbased observations of these signals provide extremely useful information on the distribution of the thermal plasma in the magnetosphere. They can also be interpreted to derive the characteristics of energetic charged particles which give rise to natural wave emissions.

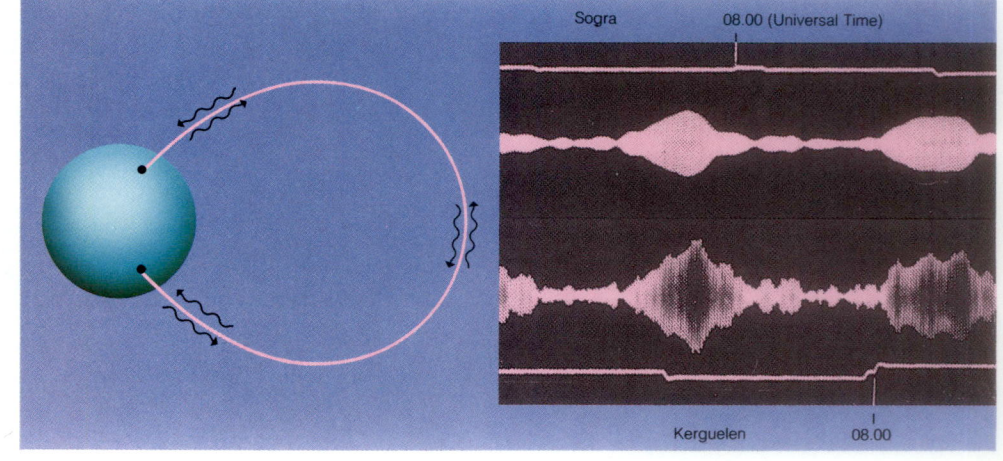

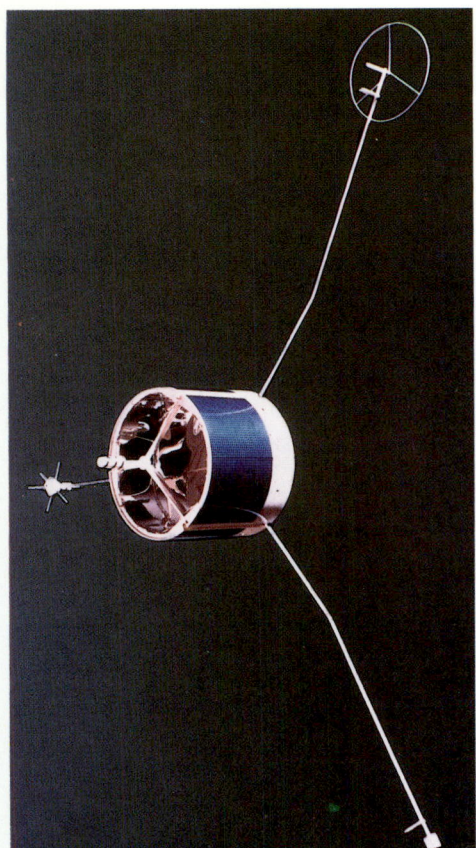

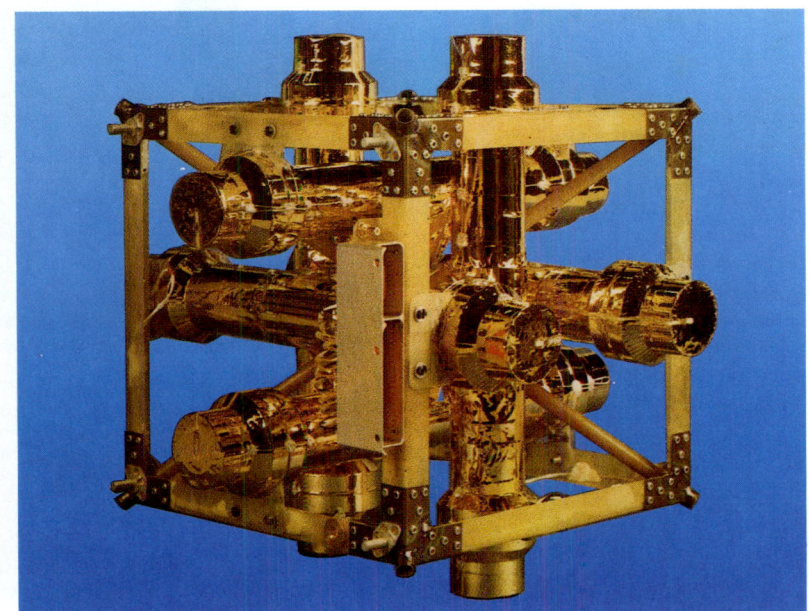

Antennae of the GEOS 2 satellite for measuring alternating magnetic fields (below). Fluctuations in the magnetic field are picked up by small antennae (about 25 centimetres). Depending on which frequency band is being studied, they are made of mu-metal (from 0·1 to 50 hertz) or ferrite (from 0.1 to 10 kilohertz) cores and two electric coils, one of which provides feedback to stabilise the gain and flatten the frequency response. The European geostationary satellite, GEOS 2, launched in 1978 had six antennae to measure the three components of the field in the two frequency bands.

Another probe, Ulysses, which was designed to measure the distant solar wind and whose launch was delayed by the Challenger accident, has only two orthogonal antennae. These will measure the fields between 0.1 and 1000 hertz.

care has to be taken in screening cables and in the general design and layout of equipment such as power converters and telemetry encoders.

The polar aurorae

The phenomenon of the polar aurorae is explained by the impact of charged particles, precipitating along the Earth's magnetic field lines, with oxygen and nitrogen atoms or molecules in the atmosphere at altitudes between 100 and 200 kilometres. The impact raises the atoms and molecules to an excited state. When they decay, the excited atoms and molecules emit light rays of a well defined and characteristic wavelength. This is the light seen by the naked eye or by cameras sensitive to visible or ultraviolet light.

This phenomenon can only be seen at certain places, at high latitudes. It is seen where there is a transition from closed, dipolar geomagnetic field lines to field lines which stretch down the geomagnetic tail. This discontinuity allows charged particles which normally accumulate in the tail of the magnetosphere to be suddenly accelerated and precipitated into the Earth's atmosphere during magnetic storms.

The region of this precipitation over the two solar regions is called the auroral oval. This oval is slightly off centre with respect to the Earth's magnetic pole because of the compression of the field lines on the dayside and their extension on the nightside. The existence and structure of the auroral ovals were first recognised and described from groundbased observations made at several stations during the International Polar Year of 1932 and the International Geophysical Year of 1957 to 1958. The instruments used were photometers adapted to the different wavelengths of the emissions and 'all sky' cameras with fish-eye lenses aimed at the zenith. These instruments, or their improved versions, are still used at numerous Arctic and Antarctic stations.

The most important contribution of space techniques to this study is to give a truly global view of the phenomenon. Further, they allow *in situ* measurements to be made of the charged particle flux or of the intensity of the associated waves of the aurora.

This brief summary of the knowledge acquired by studying the ionised environment of the Earth using space techniques shows how important research in this area is. After all, the magnetosphere is the only cosmic plasma, that is to say of very large scale and without direct collisions between particles, which is accessible from Earth. Likewise, phenomena such as the reconnection between two magnetic fields of opposite polarities, the penetration of two colliding plasmas with different characteristics, and phenomena such as the creation of filamentary structures are met in ever larger scales throughout the Universe (for example, stars, star clusters, and galaxies). A detailed knowledge of the mechanisms which cause these plasma phenomena is essential to our understanding of the Universe.

Both experimental and theoretical research has been made possible by links with other scientific disciplines such as astrophysics, plasma physics, nuclear physics and computer studies. The different disciplines work together to produce new experimental techniques, for example particle counters and plasma devices, and new theories which are applicable to several plasmas. These studies should be pursued, and they surely will be. Continuous surveillance of the interplanetary medium, disturbances in which cause nearly all magnetospheric perturbations, and of the deep magnetosphere, where the precursors of these perturbations arise, is also required. The installation on all commercial satellites of small instruments to make this surveillance possible would help to solve such problems.

The aurora australis, photographed from the space shuttle Challenger. The accounts of travellers and explorers who went to Scandinavia and the Antarctic in the eighteenth century are full of descriptions of this spectacular phenomenon, the aurora borealis and aurora australis. At night, in the sky at high latitudes, colourful, luminous and moving shapes are often seen. These have been given evocative names such as arcs, curtains, rays and veils.

This photograph was taken on board Challenger by Robert F. Overmyer, commander of the Spacelab 3 mission which lasted from 29 April to 6 May 1985. During this flight the team was able to observe an aurora australis when the craft was midway between Australia and the Antarctic; the cloud cover was moonlit. The blue-green band and the red rays represent the aurora whereas the atmospheric airglow is indicated by the brownish band visible above the terrestrial horizon (NASA).

The effect of solar activity on the lifetime of satellites. There are times, eleven years apart, during which the sun is more 'active' than usual. There is an increase in solar ultraviolet radiation and in the precipitation of charged particles in the auroral regions. Further, there is an increase in the density and temperature in the outermost layers of the Earth's atmosphere. Increases in solar activity cause satellites in low orbits to have shorter operational lifetimes. The prediction of satellite lifetimes and the monitoring of solar activity are operational necessities to twentieth century man.

Predictions and observations of the apogee and perigee of the satellite Magsat are shown in the figure below. In November 1979, it was predicted that there would be considerable solar activity, the maximum of which would have a Wolf sunspot number, R=200, and that the deceleration effect would cause the satellite to burn up in the atmosphere in March 1980. However, in February 1980 it was confirmed that the maximum value of R was 160. Consequently, the satellite's orbit was not affected as much as was expected. A new prediction was made that it would burn up in the month of June; this is precisely what happened.

For certain types of waves, the ionic component (for example the relative amounts of He^+ and H^+) also plays a role. As there are large variations of this from one point to another in space, only numerical ray tracing techniques enable us to locate the source from the points of observation. For a large number of natural electromagnetic emissions, the magnetic field lines act as a sort of waveguide. They are so effective that the source and points of observation can be regarded as two geomagnetically conjugate points.

The source of these waves is related to the temporary presence in some parts of the magnetosphere of energetic charged particles which are not in thermal equilibrium with the ambient plasma. To understand the mechanisms which control the origin of the waves, it is necessary to use complex satellites on which there are different types of instruments to measure all the parameters of the environment (both fields and particles) at all frequencies and energies.

Special antennae have been designed which can observe these low intensity waves in space. The sensitivity of the antennae is high, so the manufacturers have to pay special attention to the 'electromagnetic cleanliness' of the satellite. The electric currents which flow in numerous satellite circuits cause harmful interference to the reception of weak signals. Great

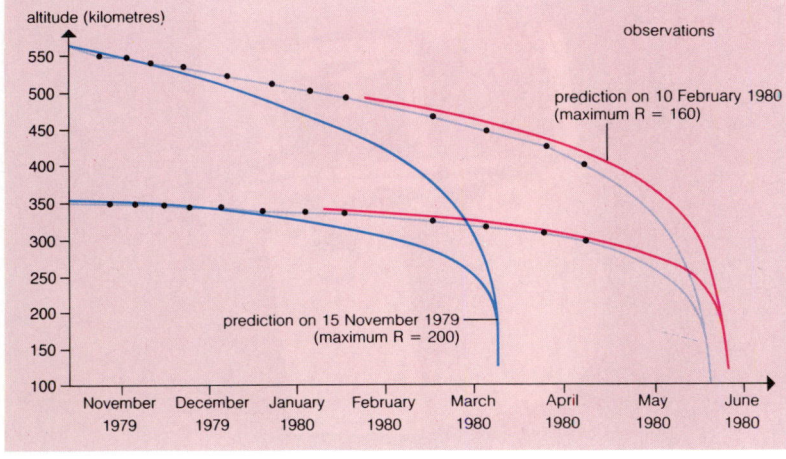

Roger Gendrin

Science in space

Solar physics

Astronomical observations in space are made above the ozone layer. Situated between 10 and 40 kilometres above the Earth, this protects all life at the Earth's surface by filtering out harmful ultraviolet rays from the Sun, the first celestial body to be studied in the space era. On 10 October 1946, at White Sands in New Mexico, the US Naval Research Laboratory successfully launched a V2 rocket. Reaching an altitude of 160 kilometres, it carried a solar spectrograph with an entry window, two millimetres in diameter, made of lithium fluoride. For the first time the solar spectrum was recorded in the ultraviolet part of the spectrum down to a wavelength of 200 nanometres. Following the improvement of pointing and lock-on techniques, and of instrumentation, the quality of the spectra produced from rockets improved to such an extent that, by 1970, the angular resolution had increased to one second of arc and the spectral resolving power to 3×10^4. During the same period, rockets enabled the solar spectrum to be measured at X ray and even gamma ray wavelengths.

At the beginning of the 1960s, a systematic study of the Sun was initiated, using satellites from the Orbiting Solar Observatory series (OSO 1 to OSO 8, between 1962 and 1975). This project was followed by the Apollo Telescope Mount (ATM) of Skylab (1973–1974) and the Solar Maximum Mission (SMM) satellite. This scheme, coordinated by NASA, was exclusively concerned with the Sun. Other experiments designed to study Sun–Earth relationships flew aboard other American satellites such as those of the Explorer, Orbiting Geophysical Observatory (OGO) and Atmospheric Explorer (AE) series.

Other countries also studied the Sun using instrumentation aboard satellites. For example, France put solar experiments on board the D2A and D2B satellites at the beginning of the 1970s, the UK launched Ariel 5, the USSR put a solar telescope on board Salyut 4 in 1975 and Japan launched the Hinotori satellite in 1981 with the sole purpose of studying X ray and gamma ray emissions during solar eruptions.

In 1987, the European Space Agency (ESA), in cooperation with NASA, launched an invitation for the construction of solar instruments for SOHO (Solar and Heliospheric Observatory) which will be put into orbit towards the middle of the 1990s. This satellite forms part of the vast International Solar Terrestrial Physics (ISTP) programme.

The Sun and observational constraints

The Sun has a mean angular diameter of 32 arcminutes (1 arcsecond corresponds to about 725 kilometres on its surface). The average distance from the Sun to the Earth is 150 million kilometres; light takes approximately 500 seconds to travel from the Sun to the Earth. The Sun derives its energy from nuclear reactions within its core at temperatures of several million degrees. The rotation of the internal solar plasma creates a magnetic field by dynamo action. Magnetic field lines cross a turbulent convection zone and emerge from the surface to create structure in the external solar atmosphere. The electron temperature, which is in the region of 4200 kelvin, increases

to more than a million degrees in the outer layers of the corona. The majority of emissions in the solar atmosphere are at wavelengths of less than 200 nanometres. They are the emission lines of various elements which have been ionised several times and which emit in the ultraviolet. Solar structures are essentially unstable and have lifetimes which range from a few seconds (eruptions), to tens of seconds or a few minutes (for example magnetic loops and spicules) and several hours or days (chromospheric cells, coronal holes and active regions).

Studying the Sun and understanding solar phenomena require observation. Collecting and interpreting data brings in knowledge acquired in the laboratory and theoretical or semi-empirical models. As it is impossible to alter local conditions on the Sun to carry out controlled experiments, the correct physical interpretation of phenomena will depend on the quality of observations.

An instrument which makes solar observations consists essentially of a photon collector of variable angular resolution and a light analyser, for example a spectrograph or filter, to separate out the contributions of the different spectral wavelengths. These are related to different parameters of the solar atmosphere, such as temperature, density, and velocity.

The observational quality depends on the pointing accuracy and stability of the platform which supports the instruments. Within the OSO series, the pointing stability increased from 1 arcminute to 1 arcsecond. For comparison, the ensemble constituting the Apollo Telescope Mount was also stabilised at 1 arcsecond. The SMM satellite had a stabilisation of 1 arcsecond along all three axes. The satellite D2A, D2B and Hinotori were stabilised by rotation around the Sun–satellite axis with a precision of the order of several arcminutes to several tens of arcminutes.

Instrumentation

Instrumentation can be specified once the wavelength to be studied, and the scientific objectives to be fulfilled, have been defined. Even today there have been only a few solar observations made in the infrared. In the visible band (400 to 800 nanometres), there are two types of instrument which are unique to space – coronographs which remove the light scattered by the solar atmosphere and other instruments which cut out atmospheric turbulence. These have high angular resolution; they measure solar energy and its rapid variations. On the Earth, except during solar eclipses by the Moon, coronographs are limited by light diffusion to observations of only a few arcminutes at the solar edge. In space it is possible to create an artificial eclipse using an external occultor. This allows an area of several solar radii to be observed. Observations of areas near the solar surface are improved by having the occultor as far from the instrument as possible (several metres or tens of metres). To make these observations, the lenses which are used have highly polished surfaces and have excellent uniformity. Because the coronal intensity is very weak (at 7 solar radii it is about 10^{-10} of the solar intensity), scattering by dust along the light paths becomes critical.

The Solar Maximum Mission (SMM) satellite seen from the space shuttle during repairs in 1984. The SMM satellite of 2315 kilograms was launched by NASA on 14 February 1980 atop a Delta rocket. There are seven instruments on board, all pointed at the Sun with a precision of 1 arcsecond along all three axes. These are a monitor of the solar constant, a visible polarising coronograph (from 446 to 638·5 nanometres), an ultraviolet spectrometer (from 115 to 360 nanometres), a soft X ray polychromator (from 0·14 to 2·24 nanometres), a hard X ray image spectrometer (from 3·5 to 30 kiloelectronvolts), a hard X ray spectrometer (from 20 to 260 kiloelectronvolts), and a gamma ray spectrometer (0·3 to 9 megaelectronvolts and from 10 to 100 megaelectronvolts).

This satellite was launched at the solar maximum, its chief mission being to study active solar regions and eruptions. The observational instruments were chosen to cover as much of the spectrum as possible, and also to study the parts of the spectrum containing spectral lines of highly ionised elements in the heart of the solar eruptions. The high temperatures, greater than 10 million degrees there, cause X and gamma rays to be emitted. These eruptions released into the solar atmosphere disturb the lowest chromospheric and photospheric layers. They project large amounts of plasma into interplanetary space and generate different sorts of waves. After operating successfully for two years, the guidance systems and several instruments began to malfunction.

The SMM satellite programme included a maintenance and refurbishment mission by the space shuttle. This took place in 1984. In 1987, this satellite was still operational and the majority of the experiments were still functioning; in 1989, it reentered the earth's atmosphere (NASA).

The satellites OSO 1, 7 and 8 (below, at the bottom of the page and on the bottom right, respectively). The OSO (Orbiting Solar Observatory) satellites each consist of one part which rotates, creating stability about one axis, and one part oriented relative to the Sun which contains the solar panels. OSO 1 to 6 are identical while OSO 7 and 8 are much bigger. The stability of OSO 1 was 1 arcminute; for OSO 8 this had improved to 1 arcsecond. The first satellites of the series were pointed at the Sun. From OSO 4 (1965) onwards, the satellites were able to scan the solar surface, as a television scans, and so form solar images in the wavelengths studied by the instrumentation.

The instruments placed in that part of the satellite pointed at the Sun have taken excellent images of solar phenomena in the outer layers of the solar atmosphere, from the chromosphere to the corona. Experiments which did not require high angular resolution were placed in the permanently spinning outer wheel (NASA).

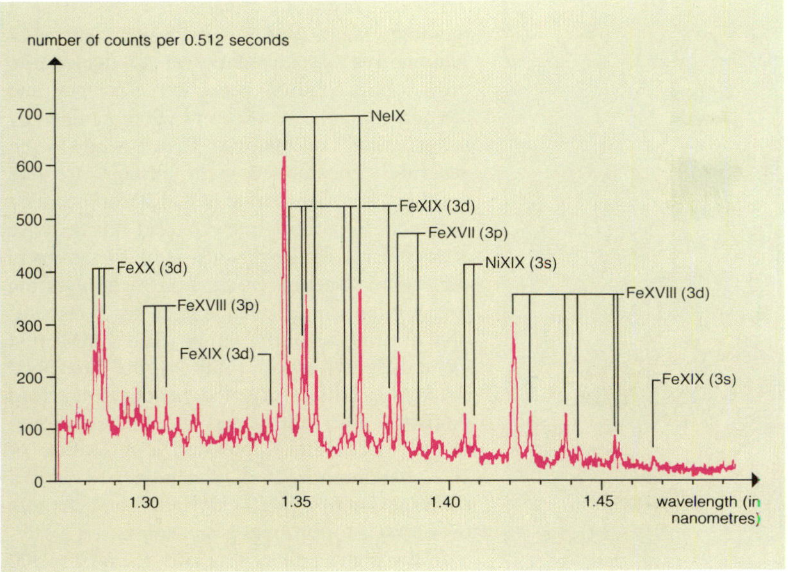
number of counts per 0.512 seconds
700
600
500
400
300
200
100
0
NeIX
FeXIX (3d)
FeXVII (3p)
NiXIX (3s)
FeXX (3d)
FeXVIII (3p)
FeXIX (3d)
FeXVIII (3d)
FeXIX (3s)
1.30
1.35
1.40
1.45
wavelength (in nanometres)

The spectrum of a solar eruption. This spectrum in the region of soft X rays was obtained on 25 August 1980 by the Flat Crystal Spectrometer on the Solar Maximum Mission (SMM) satellite. The lines in the spectrum come from highly ionised elements which emit at temperatures of several million degrees. Fe XIX, for example, is an iron atom which has been ionised 18 times, that is, it has lost 18 electrons. The instrument has an angular resolving power of about 14 arcseconds and a resolving power of 10^4 (SERC Rutherford Appleton Laboratory/Lockheed).

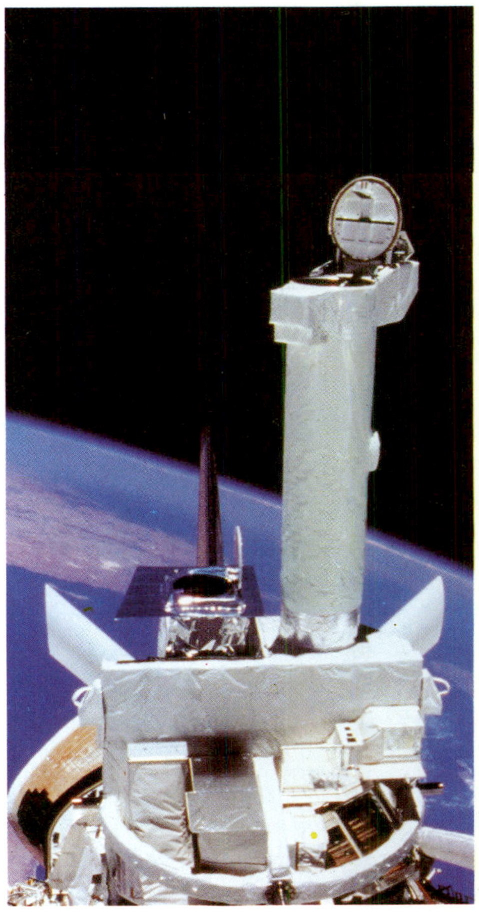

Solar instruments from the Spacelab 2 mission in the open hold of the space shuttle Challenger in July 1985. NASA's Spacelab 2 mission consisted of a group of four solar instruments mounted on the Instrument Pointing System (IPS). Furnished by the European Space Agency, this was being used for the first time. In spite of several initial operational difficulties, it produced a stability which was better than 1 arcsecond for the several hundred kilograms of instrumentation. The solar experiments consisted of:
– a visible telescope, 30 centimetres in diameter, with an internal image stabilising system which had an angular resolution of better than 0.5 arcseconds
– a tunable filter, coupled with some polarisers, to measure small scale magnetic structures;
– a spectrometer for the absolute callibration of solar flux measurements in the ultraviolet, with wavelengths between 120 and 300 nanometres;
– a 30 centimetre telescope, coupled with a high resolution spectrograph (500 nanometres and 1 arcsecond), recording simultaneously on film the spectrum along a solar radius (960 arcseconds) in the band from 117 to 170 nanometres;
– a low angle of incidence telescope, coupled with a grazing incidence spectrograph, with 11 detectors simultaneously recording selected rays from 15 to 130 nanometres. This experiment has a resolution of 15 arcseconds. It enables us to measure the intensity ratio of strong lines, in the field of view, and to deduce the abundance of helium in the solar atmosphere and the density of the corona (NASA).

Orbiting Solar Observatory (OSO) satellite characteristics

Satellite	Launch date	Weight (kg)	Stabilisation (arcminutes, ′, or arcseconds, ″)	Instruments pointing at the Sun
OSO 1	March 1962	206	±1.25′ (azimuth) ±3′ (elevation)	no scanning (X and gamma rays, and interplanetary dust)
OSO 2	February 1965	245	±39″ (azimuth) ±18″ (elevation) scanning 40′ by 40′	1 ultraviolet spectrometer, 1 white light coronograph and 1 X ray telescope–spectroheliograph
OSO 3	March 1967	284	±15″ (azimuth and elevation) no scanning	1 X ray spectrometer and 1 ultraviolet spectrometer
OSO 4	October 1967	274	±16″ (azimuth) ±25″ (elevation) scanning 38′ by 39′	1 ultraviolet spectrometer, 1 X ray spectrometer and 1 X ray spectroheliograph
OSO 5	January 1969	281	±26″ (azimuth) ±40″ (elevation) scanning 40′ by 42′	1 ultraviolet spectrometer, 1 spectroheliograph and 1 X ray spectrometer
OSO 6	August 1969	289	±1″ scanning 7′ by 6.6′ and 45′ by 44′	1 ultraviolet spectrometer–spectroheliograph and 1 X ray spectroheliograph
OSO 7	September 1974	635	±1″ scanning 7′ by 6.6′ and 45′ by 44′	1 X ray and extreme ultraviolet spectrometer and 1 white light and extreme ultraviolet coronograph
OSO 8	June 1975	1052	±1″ scanning 2.7′ by 2.5′ and 44′ by 44′	1 ultraviolet spectrometer and 1 visible and ultraviolet polychromator

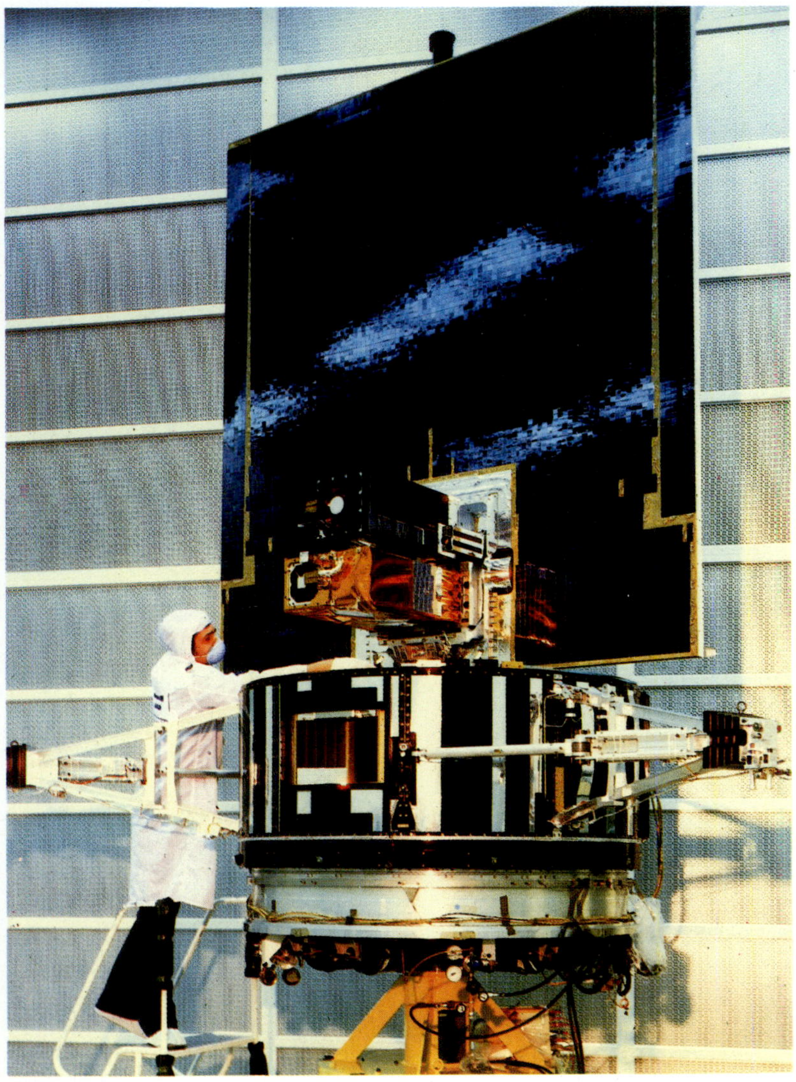

Turbulence in the Earth's atmosphere limits the angular resolution that can be achieved to about 1 arcsecond. Under certain conditions it may be possible to obtain 0·2 arcseconds for short intervals of time. In space the limitation to angular resolution is due to the pointing accuracy and the optical diameter (the diffraction limit is equal to $1{\cdot}22\,\lambda/\alpha$, where λ is the wavelength and α is the optical diameter, for a perfect telescope with a circular aperture). Thus the visible telescope mounted on Skylab 2 was able to obtain, over a period of several hours, images of solar granulations at 500 nanometres with a resolution of better than 0·5 arcseconds. It is envisaged that a large aperture telescope, with an internal stabilising system, will be capable of resolving 0.1 arcseconds, which corresponds to about 70 kilometres on the Sun's surface. The Solar Spatial Telescope, which was ratified by NASA in 1980, consists of a telescope with an aperture of 1·25 metres capable of resolving 0·1 arcseconds at a wavelength of 500 nanometres.

Another consequence of atmospheric turbulence is to limit the photometric quality of integrated intensity observations over the solar disc (the so-called 'solar constant'). Since the beginning of the twentieth century, careful measurements have been made of this solar constant in order to try to relate its variations to fluctuations in the Earth's climate. It is only now that measurements can be made beyond the atmosphere that variations of about 0·1% have been reliably detected. Aboard the SMM satellite was an active cavity radiometer which uses, as a reference, a carefully temperature controlled cavity. It obtained an absolute measurement of the solar constant to 0·1%, with a relative measurement to better than 10^{-5}. It was found that sunspots reduced the solar constant by up to 0·2%. Oscillations in the overall brightness of the Sun were also found. This last result is important because it leads to the new subject of solar seismology. The interior of the Sun can be investigated from the period and intensity of resonant waves which exist within its internal layers, and their relation to radial oscillations of the Sun's surface which have speeds of several tens of centimetres per second. The European Space Agency, with NASA, is planning the Solar and Heliospheric Observatory (SOHO) to study these phenomena in the 1990s.

Exploring the ultraviolet region of the Sun's spectrum was the first objective of space experiments, observing at shorter wavelengths than is possible from the Earth's surface. For wavelengths near 100 nanometres, aluminium coated optics are used; these are protected by either magnesium fluoride or lithium fluoride. Great care has to be taken with these hygroscopic substances when handling them on Earth. In space, these coatings deteriorate with time. This is generally attributed to pollution by hydrocarbon or silicon compounds, outgassing from the vehicle's surface, which decompose under the influence of solar ultraviolet rays.

In this spectral region, open detectors (without windows) of the channeltron type are used. Recently, arrays of microchanneltrons, fixed side by side, have been produced; they can provide information in two dimensions.

In the extreme ultraviolet or X ray region (from 30 nanometres down to a few nanometres), normal incidence optics can be used. In fact the classic mirror coating materials (gold, platinum and tungsten) do not reflect such short wavelength radiation. To obtain reflection grazing incidence is used. Instead of using the parabola, hyperbola or ellipse at nearly normal incidence, as in the Cassegrain and Gregorian telescopes, Wolter I and II telescopes use optical surfaces at grazing incidence, the angle of incidence being chosen so as to give maximum reflection of the chosen wavelength. Thus an angle of incidence of about 1 degree is appropriate for a wavelength of several tenths of a nanometre, while an angle of incidence of 10 degrees easily covers the region from 10 to 50 nanometres. One of the major difficulties of this type of telescope is the great length of optical material that is necessary to obtain useful collecting areas. Thus practical constraints on the dimensions, the weight and the quality of the polishing of the surfaces of telescopes in space have limited their angular resolutions to less than 2 arcseconds, with significant aberrations in a point image. Improvements are being made, and in a few years these telescopes should have a resolution of 1 arcsecond or better.

There are two important technical developments which may significantly improve observations in the future. One is the design and preparation of multilayered Fabry–Perot reflection filters. The other concerns two dimensional detectors; arrays of Charge Coupled Devices (CCDs) are known to be sensitive to X rays.

The Japanese satellite Hinotori (meaning firebird) launched in 1981 to observe the Sun during the maximum of its 11 year cycle of activity. The Hinotori satellite is spin stabilised (to 1.0 ± 0.5 degrees) and it carries instrumentation to make measurements of X radiation and solar gamma rays (from 2.0 to 6.7 megaelectronvolts). It consists of a Bragg crystal spectrometer which has a resolution of 4.2 femtometres (where 1 femtometre equals 10^{-15} metres) in the band from 0.183 to 0.189 nanometres (ISAS).

For X rays, at wavelengths less than 2 nanometres (a photon of wavelength 1.24 nanometres has an energy of 1 kiloelectronvolts), both photon collection efficiency and adequate angular resolution can be obtained by using grille collimators. These need to be accurately positioned with respect to one another, and a resolution of 8 arcseconds can be obtained. Separating the different spectral rays is done using Bragg crystals. Here the atoms in the crystal structure create a diffraction grating for X rays which is analogous to a classical optical transmission grating. The SMM Flat Crystal Spectrometer (built by the Lockheed Palo Alto Laboratory, the SERC Rutherford Appleton Laboratory and the Mullard Space Science Laboratory) attained a resolution of 10^{-5} nanometres at 0.18 nanometres with a combination of 3 Si(III) crystals. The detectors used were proportional gas counters.

In the highest energy regions, from 20 to 300 kiloelectronvolts for X rays, and from 300 kiloelectronvolts to 9 megaelectronvolts for gamma rays, the sources on the Sun are transient and discrete, appearing only during solar eruptions. The collimator is very basic, consisting only of a tube. The CsI and NaI detectors, combined with a CsI (Na) crystal, are mounted in anticoincidence, enabling the distribution of the radiation to be determined.

Philippe Lemaire

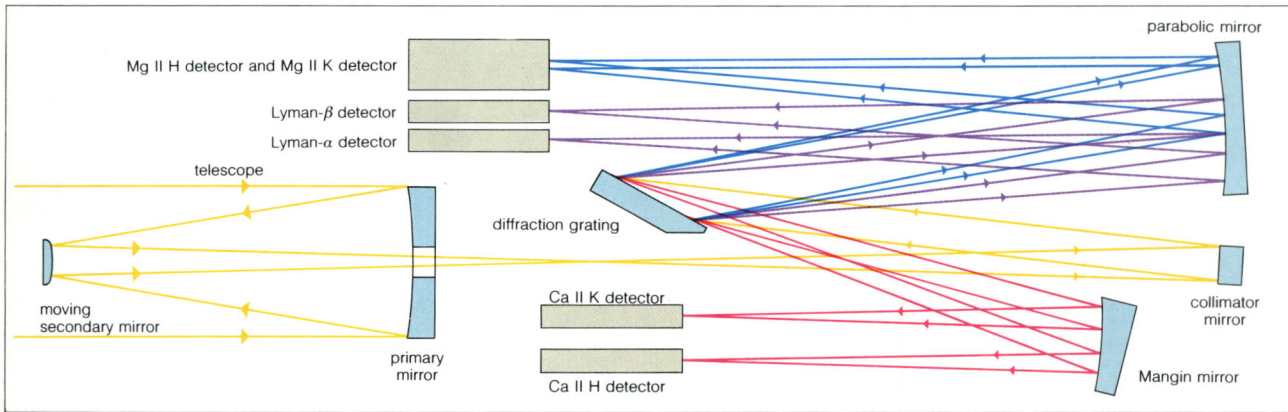

The optical principle of the multiray ultraviolet spectrometer on the OSO 8 satellite (Laboratoire de Physique Stellaire et Planetaire, LPSP, in Paris). A Cassegrain telescope, 16 centimetres in diameter with a focal length of 3 metres, forms an image of the Sun. A parabolic mirror, the collimator mirror, creates a beam of parallel light. This is intercepted and diffracted by a flat grating which separates the light into its monochromatic components in several orders. Part of the monochromatic beams from the grating is collected and focused by a Mangin mirror (a lens where the back face is a reflector) onto two photomultipliers to detect Ca II H and K radiation (at 396.9 and 393.5 nanometres). The other part of the monochromatic beams is collected and focused by a parabolic mirror onto a Mg II H and K (279.6 and 280.3 nanometres) detector, a hydrogen Lyman-β (102.5 nanometres) detector and a hydrogen Lyman-α (121.6 nanometres) detector.

Spectral scanning occurs simultaneously in all six lines by rotation of the flat grating. This gives a resolution of 2 picometres (0.002 nanometres) in five of the lines and a resolution of 6 picometres in the Lyman-β line.

The telescope has its own internal scanning system. The secondary mirror is rotated and scans a field of 64×64 arcseconds in steps of either 1 or 0.5 arcseconds. The best angular resolution obtained by such an instrument is about 1 arcsecond.

To enable this instrument to be used in the spectral region from 100 to 400 nanometres, all the optical surfaces have to be coated with a layer of aluminium protected by a thin layer (several tens of nanometres) of lithium fluoride. Because this coating is very sensitive to humidity, mounting and integration has to take place in an artificially dry atmosphere before flight (LPSP, CNRS).

Optical principle of the ultraviolet spectrometer and polarimeter (UVSP) on NASA's SMM satellite (NASA Goddard Space Flight Center and Marshall Space Flight Center). This instrument is very similar to the University of Colorado ultraviolet spectrometer on OSO 8.

In the Gregorian telescope, the focus of the primary mirror is before the secondary mirror, which is elliptical. This gives a solar image at the second focus of the ellipse. The telescope is 12 centimetres in diameter and has a focal length of 1.8 metres. The solar image is formed on the slit of the spectrometer. The beam passing through the slit is collected and then reflected as a parallel beam by a concave mirror. It is then diffracted by the plane grating and the parallel monochromatic beams which result are refocused by a section of the same concave mirror onto the exit slits. Four photomultipliers analyse the subsequent beams. Spectral scanning is performed by rotating the plane grating; this produces a maximum resolution of 2 picometres in the region of 115 to 180 nanometres. At the entrance of the spectrometer there is a polarimeter which works partly by polarisation on reflection and partly by the action of a birefringent crystal, MgF_2.

The telescope possesses its own system of scanning, by rotating the secondary mirror. It can cover a field of 4×4 arcminutes in steps of 1 arcsecond (corresponding to the narrowest slit). The Gregorian system allows a diaphragm to be placed at the focus of the primary mirror which limits the field of view to 8×8 arcminutes. This reduces the flux intercepted by the small surface of the secondary mirror by a factor of 12 (NASA GSFC).

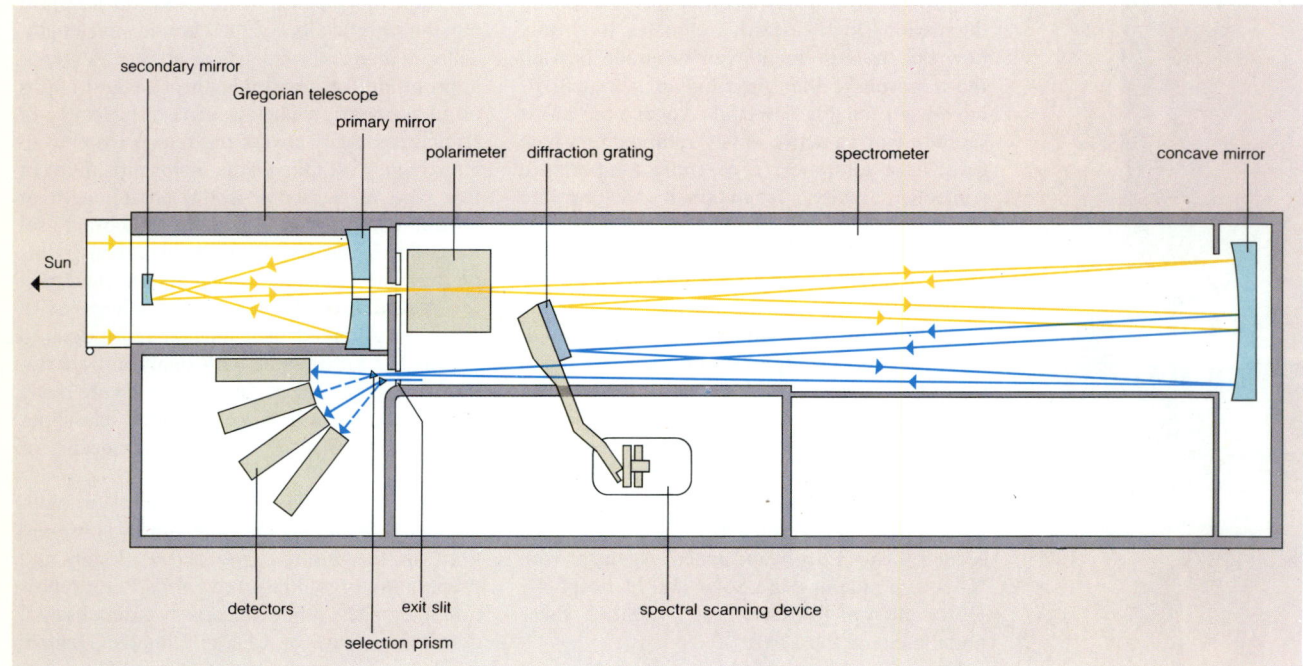

The optical principle of the grazing incidence spectrometer. Such an instrument aboard the space shuttle for the Spacelab 2 mission in 1985 made measurements of the abundance of different species, particularly helium, in the solar corona. The Wolter I grazing incidence telescope uses a parabolic section and a hyperbolic section which are aligned to give a solar image 5 millimetres in diameter on the slit of the spectrometer.

The spectrometer consists of a single, grazing incidence concave grating in the Rowland mounting. Here the entry slit, the exit slits and the grating traced on a spherical mirror lie on a circle whose diameter is equal to the radius of curvature of the sphere. The spectral dispersion occurs in the plane of this circle. At the back of the exit slits there are 11 windowless channeltron detectors for lines with wavelengths between 15 and 125 nanometres. Wavelength scanning is done by rotating the grating, and a photodiode placed in the zero order position of the grating, which thus acts like a mirror, allows this rotation to be controlled. To scan the solar image, the entry slit moves in a direction perpendicular to the plane of dispersion produced by the spectrometer and the telescope moves in the dispersion plane.

Contamination of the optical surfaces is reduced by opening a door at the telescope entrance only after several hours in orbit. Then the surfaces of both the Shuttle and the instruments carried had outgassed into the vacuum environment of space (SERC Rutherford Appleton Laboratory and Mullard Space Science Laboratory of University College, London).

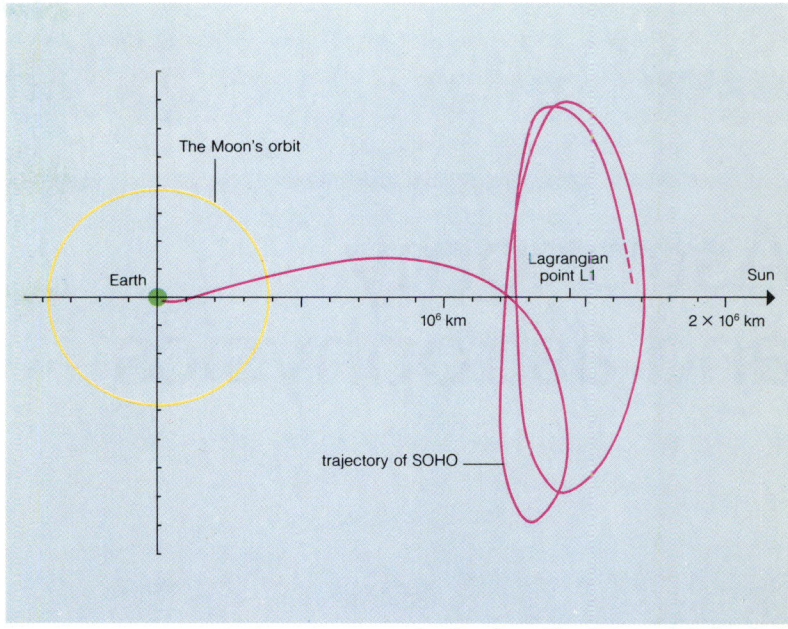

Trajectory of the SOHO probe towards the Sun. The Solar and Heliospheric Observatory (SOHO), being developed by ESA and NASA, should be launched in the middle 1990s. Its mission is to study the solar corona, and the structure and internal dynamics of the heart of the Sun's photosphere, using helioseismological methods.

With all three axis stabilised, the instruments aboard SOHO will continually point at the Sun. The diameter of the probe is 3·7 metres, with a height of 3·6 metres; its mass is about 1350 kilograms, with 650 kilograms of useful, scientific payload, and about 140 kilograms of propellant for controlling the spacecraft's orientation.

The trajectory of the satellite will be around the L1 Lagrangian point about 1·5 million kilometres from the Earth towards the Sun. The spacecraft will always be in the solar wind and outside the Earth's magnetosphere (ESA, Estec).

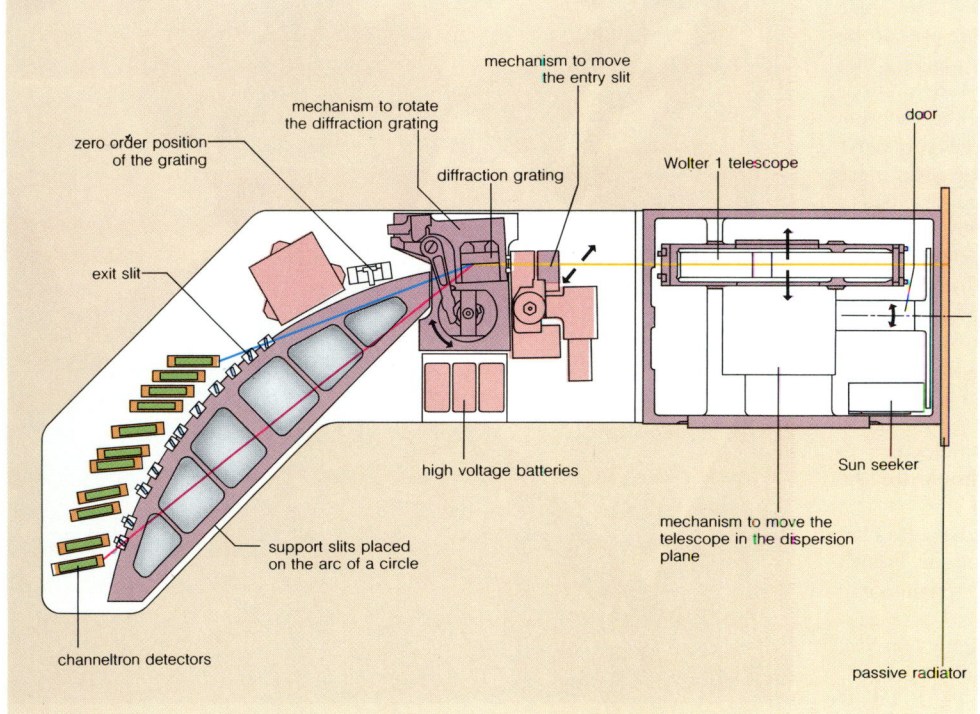

Optical principle of the grille collimator used by the X ray imaging spectrometer on the SMM satellite. The collimator consists of ten plates, each divided into 576 subcollimators. Each plate has four grilles. The alignment of the image obtained by the alignment of each subcollimator is a function of the relative positions of the grilles. Between 3·5 and 30 kiloelectronvolts, a resolution of 8 × 8 arcseconds is obtained for a field of diameter of 160 arcseconds and a resolution of 32 × 32 arcseconds for a diameter 384 arcseconds. The detector is made of 450 tiny proportional counters, with beryllium and aluminium filters to separate different spectral bands. (Space Research Laboratory, Utrecht, and the Department of Space Research, University of Birmingham).

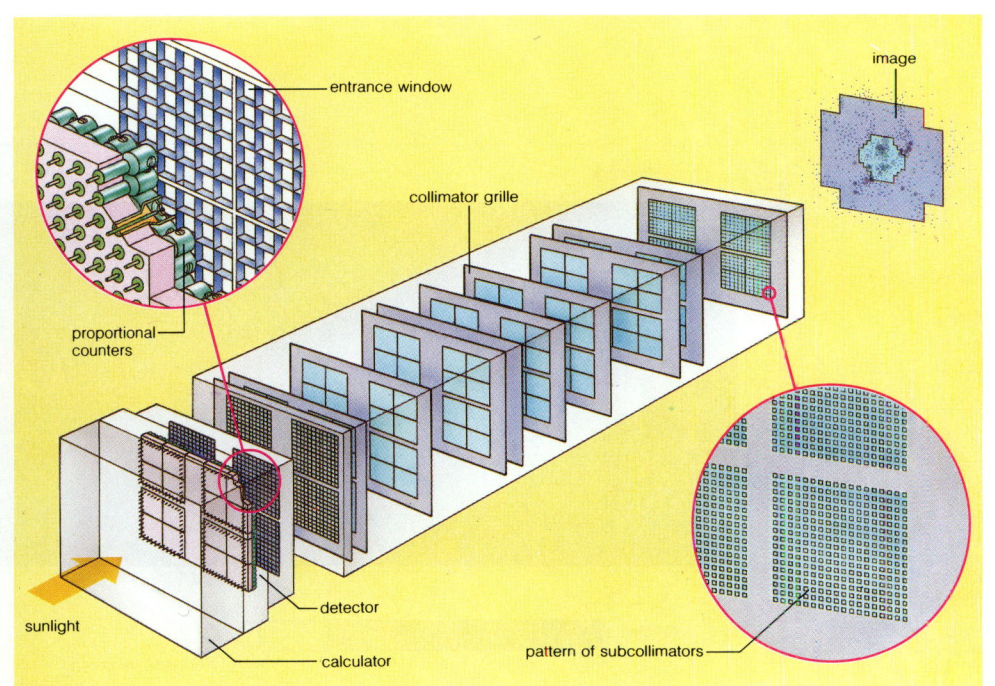

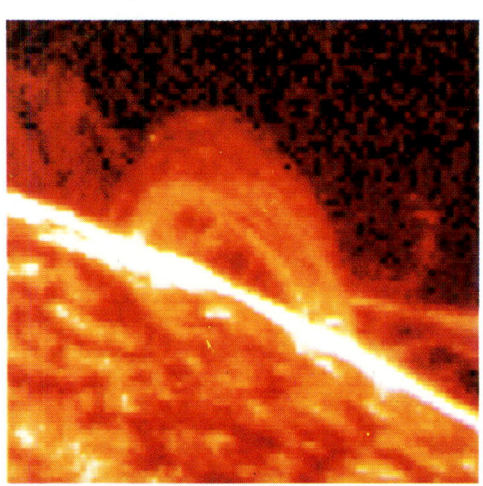

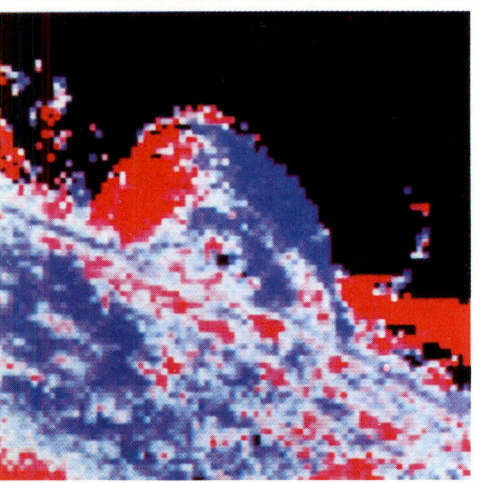

The solar limb and a prominence observed on 17 March 1980 by the ultraviolet polarimeter and spectrometer (UVSP) on the SMM satellite. The phenomenon observed in the CIV line, at a temperature of 100 000 degrees kelvin, is shown in the upper image. The lower image shows the velocity of plasma in the solar prominence, with ascending velocities in red and descending velocities in blue (NASA).

Science in space

Astronomy and astrophysics

Hipparcos

Work began on the European astrometric satellite in 1980. It was to be placed in a geostationary orbit and used to measure the precise position of some 100 000 selected stars brighter than thirteenth magnitude. In addition, the satellite was to observe each of the stars more than a hundred times during its two and a half year mission.

The main aim of the mission was to produce a uniform, whole sky stellar catalogue suitable for detailed astrometric and astrophysical studies. This would be a considerable improvement on the accuracy of existing catalogues, with absolute rather than relative parallaxes, a relatively dense reference network and uniform coverage across the sky. The selected stars were chosen so as to provide a basic reference frame against which all celestial objects, detected in different wavebands, could be identified. Scientists planned to use changes of the positions of stars within the reference frame to measure stellar distances and the dynamics of the solar system and of our galaxy.

The Tycho experiment was to involve making a fivefold increase in the precision of measurements of trigonometric parallaxes, compared with Earth-based observations. A very much greater number of stars would also be observed.

The satellite was designed to make about eleven revolutions about its spin axis (perpendicular to the two viewing directions) every 24 hours. Thus, any given star lying on an appropriate great circle would cross the telescope's preceding field of view in a little more than 20 seconds, and then again for the same time 20 minutes later as the following field of

view sweeps the same area of sky. The angle between the spin axis and the Sun was to be maintained at 43 degrees. It was planned that the spin axis would describe 6·4 revolutions about the Sun in 1 year, the satellite's motion being controlled by cold nitrogen gas thrusters.

Four independent scientific consortia were established for this astrometric mission. Stars to be observed were first selected by the Input Catalogue Consortium. The astrometric data from Hipparcos will be analysed by the Northern Data Analysis Consortium (NDAC) and the Fundamental Astronomy by Space Techniques (FAST) Consortium. These consortia will carry out their work in parallel to provide a full and independent cross check on the intermediate and final astrometric catalogues. A fourth consortium will be responsible for the Tycho catalogue.

Hipparcos was launched by an Ariane rocket on 9 August 1989 from Kourou in French Guiana. The apogee motor failed to ignite and so the satellite could not be placed in a geostationary orbit but stayed in a highly elliptical orbit. The mission has been partially salvaged, and another ground station in Perth (West Australia) has been equipped to receive data from Hipparcos. Unfortunately, even so, only 40% of the observations made will be recorded at a ground station. The accuracy of the measurements will therefore suffer greatly.

ESA officials are discussing an Hipparcos 2 mission which could be built at a third of the cost of the original mission and be ready to launch in half the time.

Brian G. Taylor

Hipparcos was launched on 9 August 1989, from Kourou, French Guiana, into a highly elliptical transfer orbit, by Ariane. Its Mage 2 apogee motor, however, failed to ignite, so it could not be transferred into the desired geostationary orbit. Hipparcos can make measurements from its present orbit, but with less than the desired accuracy. Each of the selected stars is observed as it passes through the field of view of the instruments.

The accuracy of Hipparcos' measurements will depend on the magnitude and ecliptic coordinates of the stars observed. Variations in the accuracy as a function of stellar magnitude will be minimised by selecting observation times carefully (ESA).

Hipparcos programme: Primary experiment
Number of stars: 100 000
Limiting stellar magnitude* brightness: 13
Accuracy (stars brighter than magnitude 9)*:
– positions: 0.002 arcseconds** (this compares with the current best of 0.04 arcseconds)
– proper motions: 0.002 arcseconds per year (comparable with the best motions available after 50 years of ground-based observation)
– parallaxes (absolutes, not relative): 0.002 arcseconds (present 0.01 arcseconds for bright stars)
Systematic errors less than 0.001 arcseconds
Northern and southern celestial hemispheres

Hipparcos programme: Tycho experiment
Number of stars: 400 000 or more
Limiting stellar magnitude* brightness: 10 to 11
Accuracy (stars brighter than magnitude 10):
– positions: 0.03 arcseconds**
– magnitudes: 0.05 magnitudes in blue and visible
Number of observations: about 100 photometric observations for each star during the mission

* Stellar magnitude. A bright star, for example Polaris, has a magnitude of 2. A star 100 times less bright than Polaris is defined as of magnitude 7, and another star 100 times fainter is of magnitude 12. The faintest star that can be seen with the naked eye has magnitude 6, while the faintest star visible with binoculars is of ninth magnitude.
** Measurement of angles. Dividing the circumference of a circle into 360 equal parts, the angle subtended at the centre by one such part is 1 degree. Each arcdegree is subdivided into 60 arcminutes and, within each arcminute, there are 60 arcseconds.

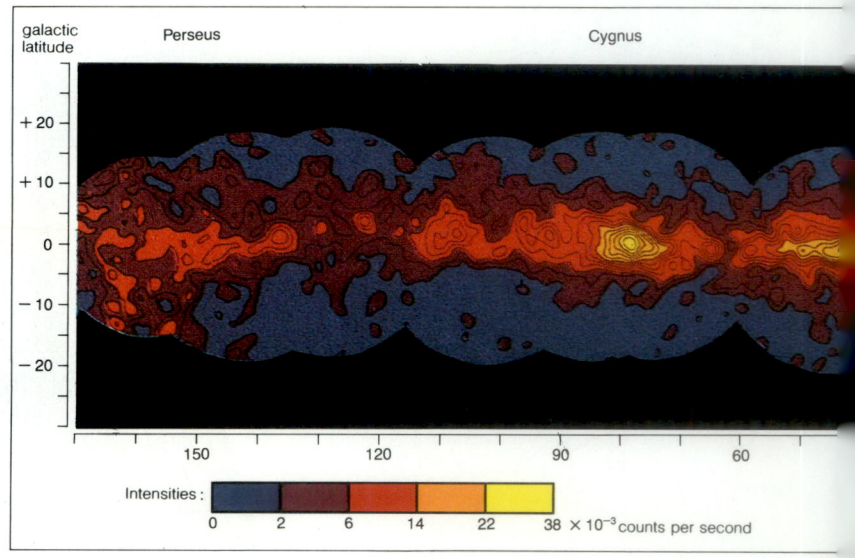

Cos B and gamma ray astronomy

The Cos B satellite was launched from NASA's Western Test Range by a Thor Delta vehicle on 9 August 1975. Its scientific mission was to study in detail sources in the Universe of extremely energetic (greater than 30 million electronvolts) gamma radiation. Its objectives were to investigate the angular structure and energy spectrum of gamma ray emission from the galactic plane, to measure the flux and energy spectrum of radiation from high galactic latitudes, believed to be of extragalactic origin, and to examine known or postulated point sources of gamma radiation, to determine the energy spectrum of all such sources, and to search for time variations in the intensities of the sources. An ancillary objective was to study the longterm variability of X ray sources.

The duration of the mission was originally expected to be two years. In fact, Cos B was finally switched off on 25 April 1982, having worked successfully for 6 years and 8 months. It was found that damage to the solar cells by the Earth's radiation belts was less than had been supposed. The photovoltaic power generation system remained healthy to the end of the satellite's life. The batteries, on the other hand, became virtually unserviceable and long eclipses resulted in total power loss. However, since the periods of eclipse were short, the overall effect on the mission was negligible. The satellite reentered the Earth's atmosphere on 6 January 1986.

The Cos B satellite was a cylinder, 1·4 metres in diameter and 1·1 metres long. It carried a single large experiment, the design and building of which were the responsibility of a consortium of research laboratories in Europe.

During 1985, this consortium completed the final calibrations and data reduction, and released the Cos B data set to the scientific community. Magnetic tapes of the data set have been issued to some 25 institutes as well as to the Centre Données Stellaire Strasbourg, who have agreed to further distribute the data set on request.

In the 1990s, NASA's Gamma Ray Observatory (GRO) will carry four large gamma ray instruments of broader energy coverage than Cos B, and with much improved sensitivity. With a mass of about 1·5 tonnes, any one of these will dwarf the Cos B satellite!

Brian G. Taylor

The Cos B satellite undergoing thermal testing in a vacuum chamber at Estec. The Cos B satellite is a cylinder, 1·4 metres in diameter and 1·2 metres long. It has a total mass of 230 kilograms, of which 120 kilograms is the scientific payload.

The satellite's polar orbit was chosen to provide the satellite with long, uninterrupted periods of observation. The perigee is at 350 kilometres and the apogee at 100 000 kilometres. It has an orbital period of 37 hours 10 minutes, giving an observational time of 30 hours outside the van Allen belts.

The telescope is positioned at the centre of the satellite. Placed around it are the solar and terrestrial albedo detectors, for measuring the satellite's orientation, the tank for nitrogen which controls the rotation, a reservoir containing neon used for flushing out the telescope's spark chamber, and several electronic units (Estec).

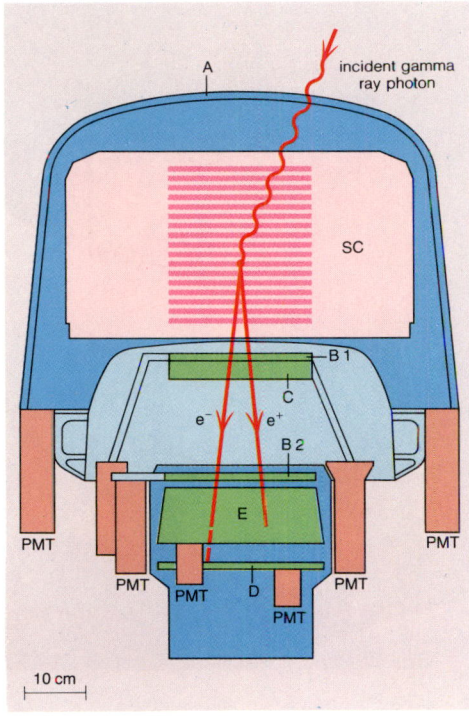

Cut-away diagram of the telescope. The spark chamber (SC), used for detecting gamma rays, is the most important part of Cos B's payload. It contains neon and 17 thin plates. The scintillation counter A also acts as a protective layer. When charged particles (cosmic rays) strike the counter, a device activates the spark chamber. The incident gamma ray photon penetrates the spark chamber and is converted into an electron positron pair in the plates. The charged particles continue their journey towards the B_1, C and B_2 detectors, ionising the gas as they go.

A high voltage is applied between the plates; sparks appear, defining the trajectories of the charged particles, and so the path of the incident gamma ray can be calculated. The electron energy is measured using a calorimeter (D and E); this is almost equivalent to the energy of the incident photon. There are several photomultipliers (PMTs) which transform the photoelectrons into an electric signal. The overall angular resolution lies between 2 and 5 degrees.

Gamma ray image of the Milky Way produced by Cos B. The different colours represent the intensities of the celestial gamma radiation. The maxima are found near the galactic centre where there are remains of supernovae. Examples are evident in the constellations of Cygnus and Perseus (ESA).

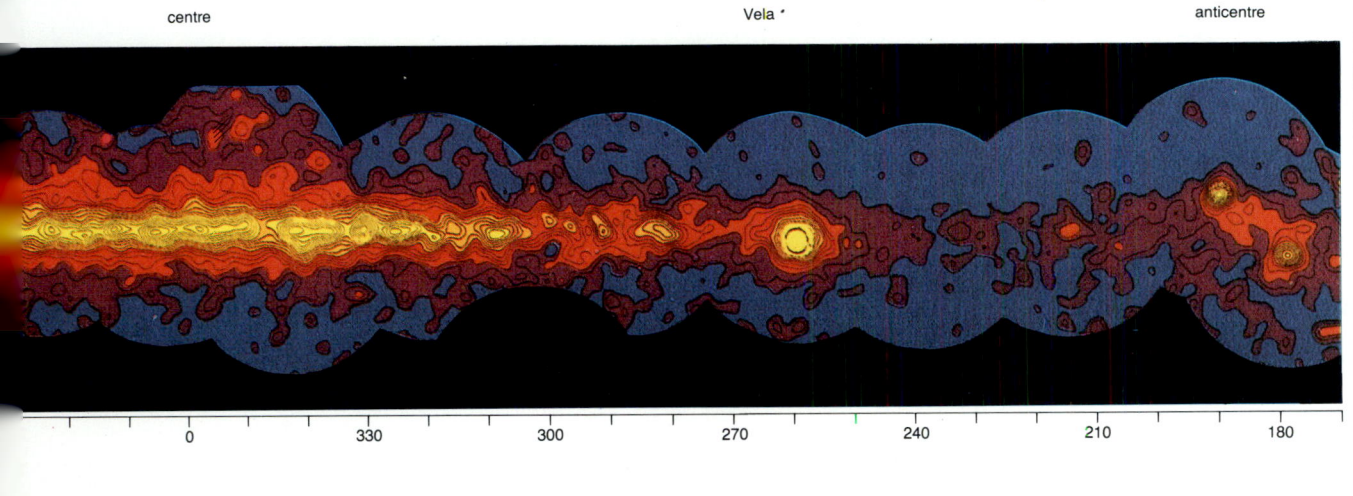

X ray astronomy

In the early 1970s, the Universe was explored at X ray wavelengths (the photons typically having energies from 1 to 10 kiloelectronvolts) by the NASA UHURU and the UK Ariel V satellites. Almost 400 X ray sources were found. These satellites, both launched by Scout rockets, were spin stabilised. They carried scanning (by virtue of the spinning satellite) non-imaging, gas filled proportional counters. X ray source positions were determined to something better than one arcdegree, making the task of unambiguously identifying such objects with their optical or radio counterparts exceedingly difficult. None the less, some identifications were made and it was soon recognised that the technique of X ray astronomy was the key to unlocking the mysteries surrounding the death of stars at, or near the end of, their evolutionary sequence. By recording X rays, astrophysical plasmas heated to some tens of millions of degrees, either as a result of a catastrophic event (such as a supernova) or through the conversion of gravitational energy to heat as material fell onto a highly condensed object (a white dwarf, a neutron star, or black hole), were being observed.

The sensitivity of these early missions was such that X ray sources down to one thousandth of the strength of the Crab nebula could be detected. A major step forward in X ray astronomy was brought about by the development of the imaging telescope. This enabled images of the sky to be made at resolutions better than 1 arcminute, or even better than 1 arcsecond, depending on the quality of the mirror, the dimensions of the telescope, etc.

Two major missions with imaging telescopes have been undertaken, NASA's Einstein and ESA's European X ray Observatory Satellite (Exosat), while the German mission Röntgen satellite (Rosat) is currently ready for launch. Two major facility class missions are planned for the 1990s, NASA's AXAF and ESA's 'high throughput X ray spectroscopy mission'.

The basic configuration of the telescopes flown on all these missions – known as the Wolter 1 type geometry – is, first, a paraboloid X ray mirror and then a confocal, coaxial hyperboloid X ray mirror to focus the X rays. Beams of X rays can be reflected, and hence focused, by making only very shallow angles (of the order of 1 degree) to the special mirrors; X rays are absorbed, and not reflected, by a normal mirror. Hence these telescopes are often referred to by the term 'grazing incidence'.

The NASA Einstein spacecraft, originally known as the High Energy Astrophysics Observatory B (HEAO B) was launched in November 1978, and remained operational until April 1981. It was placed in a 28 degree inclination orbit by an Atlas-Centaur vehicle. During its lifetime it performed over 5000 pointed observations. The Einstein mirror system comprised four nested surfaces with optical diameters of up to half a metre. The focal length was 3·4 metres. The sensitivity was a thousand times greater than previously achieved with UHURU.

The European Exosat observed X rays at energies from 40 electronvolts to some 40 kiloelectronvolts, far beyond the range of imaging telescopes. It had a large area, narrow field proportional counter array and a gas scintillation spectrometer.

The 500 kilogram satellite was launched by a Delta rocket from Vandenberg in California on 26 May 1983 into a highly eccentric orbit. The initial apogee height was some 190 000 kilometres, with the apogee being above the Earth's north polar regions. Of the 90 hour orbital period, over 72 hours could be used for observations while the spacecraft was beyond the Earth's radiation belts. This meant that unprecedented long periods of observation could be undertaken. Exosat operations terminated with a failure of the attitude control

system in April 1986, with satellite reentry following in May 1986. Some 2000 pointed observations had been undertaken.

Surprisingly, perhaps, an all-sky survey to a level of sensitivity far better than that achieved by UHURU or Ariel V will not be undertaken until the launch of the German satellite Rosat. This will carry two imaging telescopes. It will be placed in a low earth orbit (at 430 kilometres altitude) with an inclination of 57 degrees. The survey will be a thousand times more sensitive than UHURU's, the whole sky being surveyed once in six months. The source location accuracy will be about 1 arcminute, and it is expected that some 500 000 X ray sources will be detected.

Two major missions are planned to be undertaken in the late 1990s. The NASA Advanced X ray Astrophysics Facility (AXAF) will have a single telescope system of about 10 metres focal length for studies at high resolution. The proposed European mission will have three telescope systems of 8 metres focal length, with a much greater collecting area. Both missions are expected to be operated for 10 years.

Brian G. Taylor

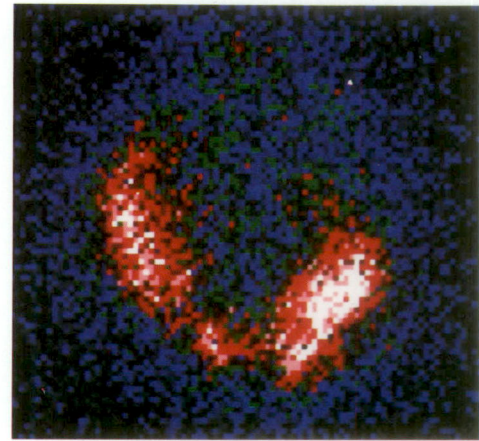

The Cassiopeia A supernova, observed by Exosat (right). When a supernova explodes, it releases a large quantity of high temperature gas (40 million degrees) which emits X rays. These X ray emissions provide information on the physical characteristics of the interstellar medium, the distribution of heavy elements in interstellar space and the nature of the star which exploded.

The galactic remains of the Cassiopeia A supernova relate to an explosion which happened about 300 years ago (Estec).

Artist's impression of the planned AXAF satellite. In the 1990s, NASA plans to launch the Advanced X ray Astrophysics Facility satellite (AXAF). The satellite will carry a telescope with a focal length of 10 metres to produce high resolution images (1 arcsecond). It will be in a low Earth orbit, like the Hubble space telescope.

A second mission will be ESA's X ray Multi-Mirror Mission (XMM) with its high throughput X ray spectrometer. It will have four telescopes with a focal length of 8 metres and with a much greater collecting area, but reduced angular resolution (30 arcseconds). The instruments will enable rapid spectrophotometry and high resolution spectroscopy to be carried out. XMM will make observations from a highly eccentric orbit like Exosat's.

These missions should have an observational lifetime of about 10 years (NASA).

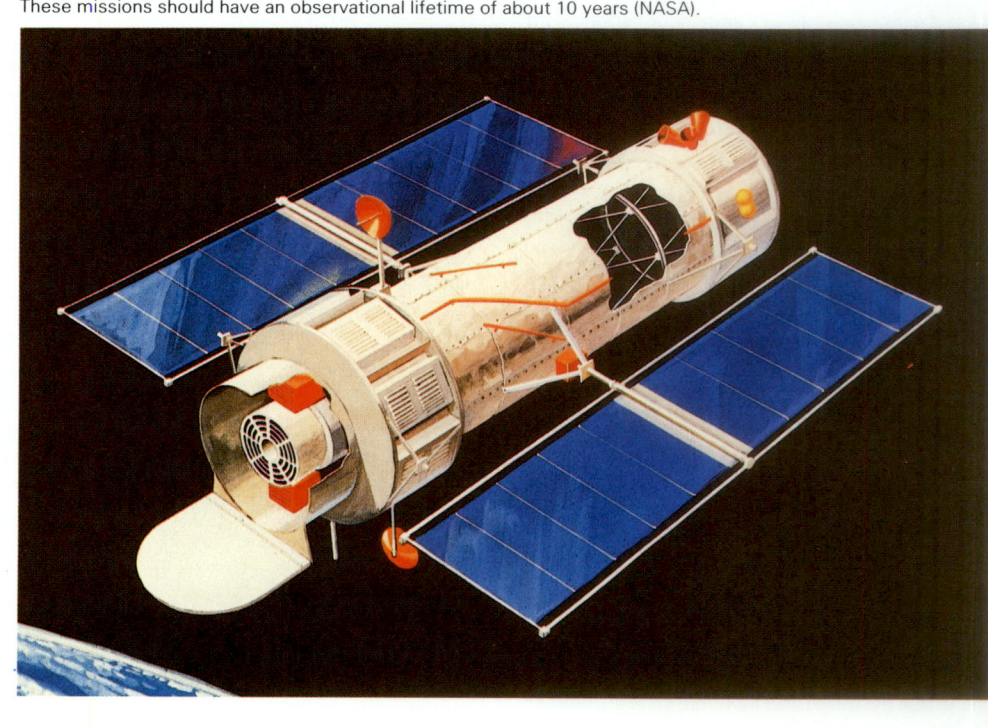

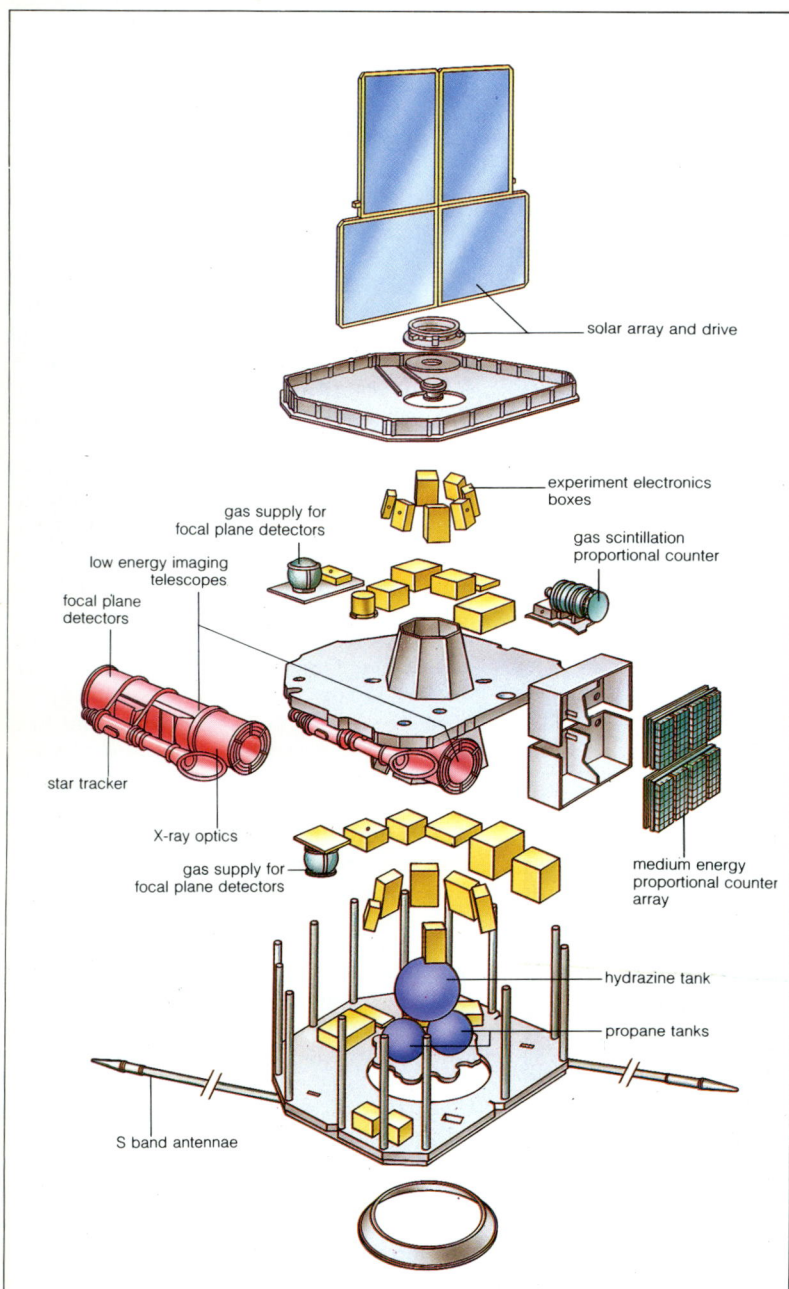

Exosat. This European X Ray Observatory Satellite (photograph, above, and drawing left) was designed by ESA to study X rays with energies between 0.04 and 40 kiloelectronvolts. This 500 kilogram satellite was launched by a Delta rocket on 26 May 1983 from the US base at Vandenberg. The payload consisted of two imaging telescopes with Wolter 1 optics, a gas proportional counter, a scintillation counter, a star tracker, two high resolution electronic cameras, a filter wheel to select the X rays and a diffraction grating used for high resolution spectroscopy.

The attitude control system broke down and all work with the satellite ceased on 6 April 1986. During its 1045 days of operation, 2000 observations were transmitted from the satellite to the Exosat Observatory at the European Space Operations Centre (ESOC) in Germany. Numerous celestial objects, including planets, stars, quasars, neutron stars, black holes, active galaxies, star clusters and supernovae, were located and observed (Estec).

Ultraviolet astronomy

The atmosphere is completely opaque to ultraviolet light, at wavelengths less than about 300 nanometres. However, it is in this part of the electromagnetic spectrum that many celestial bodies emit most of their energy. This is true for hot stars (that is young and massive stars, or degenerate white dwarves), supernovae, planetary nebulae, quasars and other exotic astronomical objects. In fact, most of the astrophysically important electron transitions in atoms give rise to emission and absorption lines in the ultraviolet. The best example of this is the line, at 121·6 nanometres, of atomic hydrogen, the most abundant element in the Universe.

The space era has enabled scientists to examine the ultraviolet sky from beyond the atmosphere. This research began in the 1960s with brief rocket flights and was followed a decade later by three satellites, purpose built for studying ultraviolet astronomy. The American–Dutch ANS satellite and the European Space Agency's TD1 satellite scanned the heavens, but because of their relatively low sensitivity they could only detect relatively bright stars. Furthermore, they had a low resolving power and could not make real spectroscopic observations. The American satellite, Copernicus, however, had a high resolving power. It observed the sharp ultraviolet lines which are emitted from clouds of interstellar gas when they absorb nearby starlight. This most successful satellite has completely altered our understanding of the interstellar medium where stars are born. Unfortunately, it can measure only the brightest stars.

Scientists had long felt the need to have a proper ultraviolet observatory in space to study sources, including those faint ones situated outside our galaxy. Their plans were fulfilled with the launching of the International Ultraviolet Explorer (IUE) satellite, a collaboration between NASA, SERC (in Britain) and ESA, on 26 January 1978, from Cape Canaveral, Florida, by one of NASA's Thor-Delta rockets.

The satellite is in a geosynchronous orbit above the Atlantic. Its altitude varies from 27 600 kilometres at perigee to 43 950 kilometres at apogee. The satellite remains continually in view from the east coast of the United States. Between 10.00 and 12.00 UT it is visible from Europe. It is controlled, for 16 hours per day, from the NASA Goddard Space Flight Center. European astronomers have access to IUE for the remaining 8 hours, from ESA's station at Villafranca near Madrid. This division of observational time reflects the relative financial contributions of the United States and Europe to the project.

The scientific instrumentation on board IUE consists of a telescope to collect light from stars, spectrographs over the whole range of ultraviolet wavelengths from 120 to 320 nanometres, and detectors. The primary mirror of the telescope measures only 45 centimetres in diameter. This is very modest in size compared with the giant telescopes on Earth which have apertures of 4 metres or more. However, the lack of atmosphere enables the performance of IUE to rival its earthly counterparts operating in the visible part of the spectrum.

The detectors are similar to television cameras. Photons of ultraviolet light are transformed into a cascade of electrons, which strike a phosphor target. 'Holes' of positive charge are created whose intensity is proportional to the intensity of the incident beam. Little by little the charges accumulate during the exposure. When the exposure is completed the target is 'read', that is it is scanned by a narrow beam of electrons which fill the positive 'holes'. At each position of the beam, or pixel, the negative charge required to neutralise the positive charges created by the stellar radiation is measured. Thus, a numerical image of 768 by 768 pixels is obtained and transmitted to Earth as a radio telemetry signal. This is displayed on a television screen where astronomers can examine it at their leisure. It takes 8 minutes to read and transmit a picture, and the exposure time depends on the brightness of the star being observed. The star Eta in Ursa Major, for example, is very bright, and requires an exposure time of less than 1 second, while the integration time needed for a quasar of stellar magnitude 17 can be up to 16 hours. After each reading, the phosphor target is uniformly illuminated using tungsten lamps and then read with an unfocused beam to erase all traces of the previous display. The camera is then ready for the next observation.

The IUE is a most successful astronomical satellite. It has given rise to more than a thousand articles in specialist astronomical journals and a wealth of fundamental discoveries. Its operational flexibility is largely responsible for its success. Another incontrovertible factor is its longevity. IUE continues to function at nearly full capacity, although its design lifetime was only 3 years. IUE was the only ultraviolet observatory until the Hubble space telescope was launched in May 1990 by the space shuttle. Even now it continues to be of service to the scientific community, complementing the Hubble space telescope, for example by observing variable stars.

Jean Clavel

The 4.17 metres tall International Ultraviolet Explorer (IUE) satellite during integration tests at the NASA Goddard Space Flight Center in 1977. The shiny metal coating is to reflect away a large fraction of the solar light and therefore to protect the satellite against excessive heat. The thermal equilibrium of the satellite is controlled from the Earth using an array of thermistors, heat pipes and radiators. Particular care is taken with the telescope and its spectrographs to avoid deterioration by thermal distortion of the optical surfaces.

The long tube contains the telescope. It is protected from light from the Sun, Earth and Moon. Also evident are two of the solar panels which provide the satellite with electricity. The octagonal body of the satellite contains other scientific instruments, such as the spectrographs and cameras and all their associated electronics. At launch, the total mass of the satellite was 644 kilograms, of which 122 kilograms was scientific instrumentation. At the bottom is the apogee motor which propelled IUE into its geosynchronous orbit. (NASA).

An ultraviolet spectrum of the star RR Telescopii obtained by IUE. This ultraviolet spectrum was obtained using the high resolution mode of IUE, and is as it appeared on the console of the station near Madrid. The parallel bands show different orders containing adjacent segments of the spectrum, each one covering a region of about 2 nanometres. They form a circle, 25 millimetres in diameter, which is an image of the phosphor target of the camera. The different colours represent the different intensities of stellar ultraviolet radiation. On the right hand side is a scale in arbitrary units, red representing the strongest intensities, while black shows a complete absence of signal. The red spots correspond to reference spectral lines listed in the laboratory. (ESA).

The Hubble space telescope

The main objective of the Hubble Space Telescope (HST) project is to place a 2·4 metre diameter astronomical telescope and its associated instrumentation in low Earth orbit (altitude 600 kilometres) at 28·5 degrees inclination and to maintain it over a 15 year period as an international observatory. The Space Telescope was successfully launched by the space shuttle in May 1990.

The mission is largely a NASA programme; ESA's contribution to the project consists of three elements. These are the Faint Object Camera, the solar arrays which provide power to the spacecraft, and staff at the Space Telescope Science Institute in Baltimore, Maryland. In return for this contribution, European astronomers will be guaranteed a minimum of 15% of the Space Telescope's observing time.

The Hubble Space Telescope, shown in the cut away diagram below, has a mass of 11 tonnes and is over 13 metres long. The main body has a diameter of some 4·3 metres and, with the solar panels deployed, is 12 metres across. The HST carries a 2·4 metre, f/24 Ritchey–Chrétien Cassegrain telescope. The two mirrors of the telescope, coated with aluminium and magnesium fluoride, are capable of focusing light with wavelength between about 115 nanometres (UV) and 1 millimetre (microwave).

Groundbased telescopes rarely provide better than 2 arcseconds resolution, except under the very best 'seeing' conditions. The 0·02 arcsecond resolution of the HST is expected to detect objects as weak as 28th magnitude compared with about 25th magnitude achievable from the ground. Thus the Space Telescope will observe objects up to 20 times fainter (and often more distant) than can be seen from the ground. Being above the absorbing atmosphere, it can observe in the ultraviolet and infrared regions of the spectrum. Also it will detect rapid variations in light unobservable from the ground due to atmospheric scintillation.

The HST is so sensitive that it cannot make observations when pointed within 50 degrees of the Sun, 30 degrees of the Moon, 80 degrees of the bright limb of the Earth or 5 degrees of the dark limb. These celestial constraints, together with other operational constraints, mean that the time available for observing is only about 30%.

An important aspect of the Hubble Space Telescope is its modular design. All scientific instruments and many of the critical spacecraft subsystems are designed such that they can be repaired or replaced by an astronaut. The space shuttle is expected to visit the HST approximately every three years. Hence it will be possible to refurbish or replace various instruments as they fail or become obsolete during the planned 15 year lifetime of this observatory in space.

Brian G. Taylor

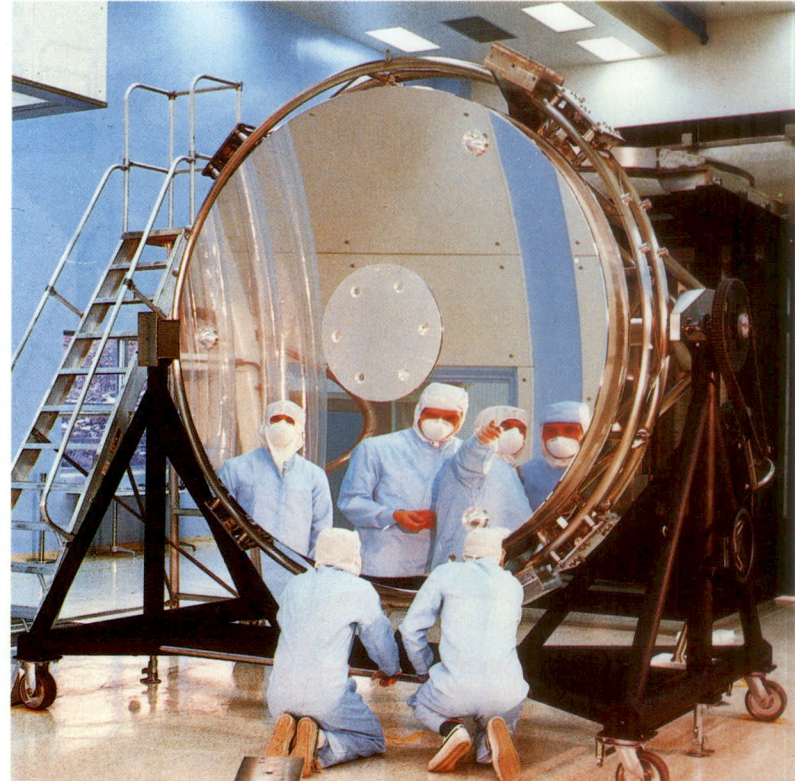

The first generation instruments for the Hubble Space Telescope

Instrument	Wavelength coverage (nanometres)	Dynamic range (stellar magnitudes)
Wide Field/Planetary Camera (WF/PC)	115–1100	9.5–28
Faint Object Camera (FOC)	120–600	15–28
Faint Object Spectrograph (FOS)	115–800	19–26
High Resolution Spectrograph (HRS)	115–320	≤19
High Speed Photometer (HSP)	120–800	0–24

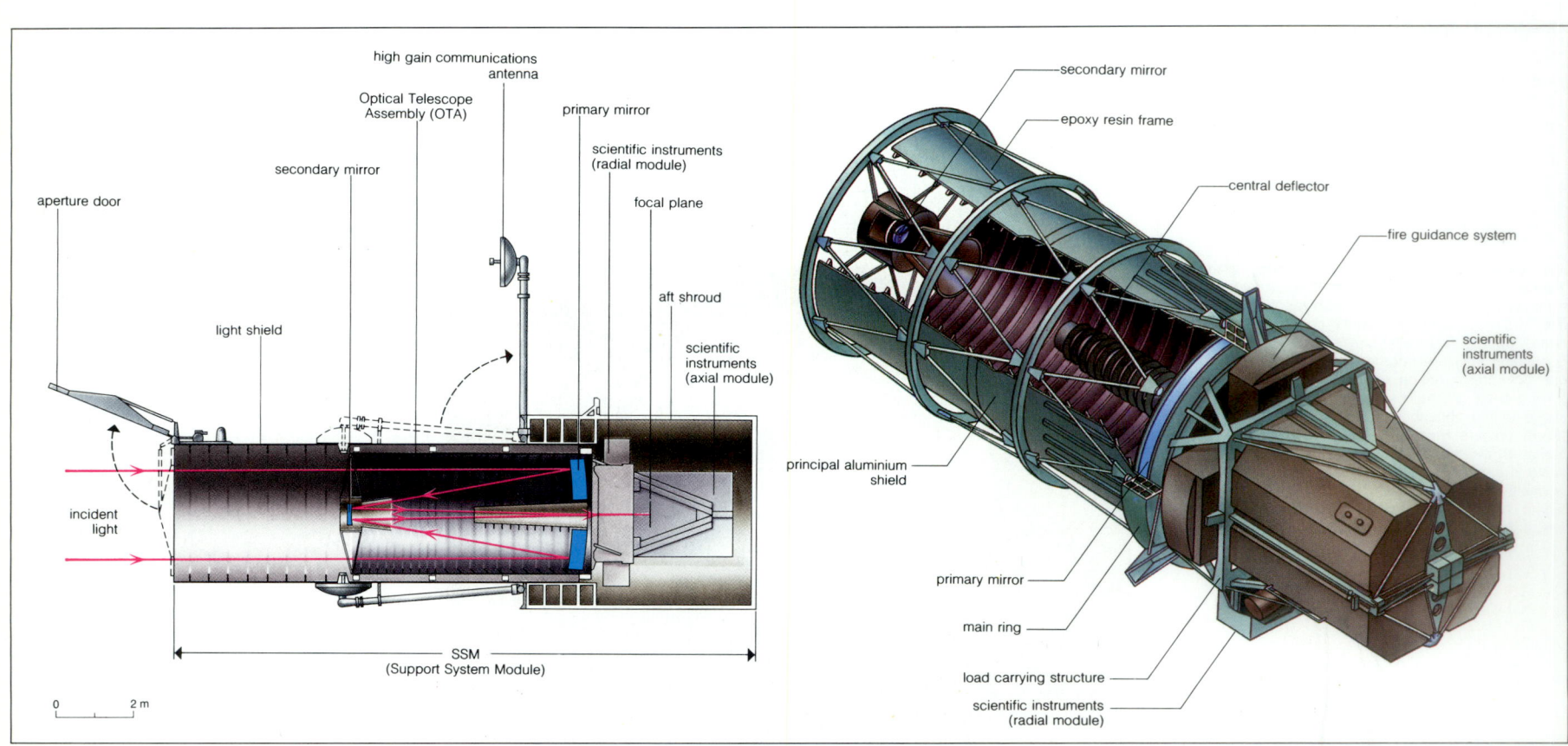

Artist's impression of the Hubble Space Telescope (left). The space observatory consists of three parts: the Optical Telescope Assembly (OTA), the Scientific Instruments (SI) and the Support System Module (SSM) which carries the other two parts. The SSM is 13·16 metres long, 4·26 metres in diameter and has a mass of 11 tonnes. It houses both the telescope and the scientific instruments. Its purpose is to protect the equipment, to supply electricity from the solar panels, to store and transmit data to Earth via communications satellites, to maintain thermal control and to control the fire guidance systems (NASA).

1 high gain antenna
2 aperture door
3 light shield
4 steerable solar panels
5 aft shroud

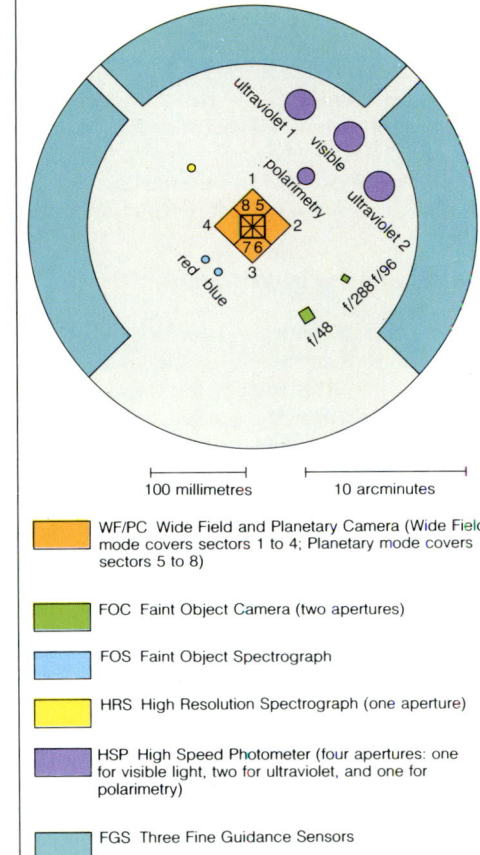

100 millimetres   10 arcminutes

WF/PC Wide Field and Planetary Camera (Wide Field mode covers sectors 1 to 4; Planetary mode covers sectors 5 to 8)

FOC Faint Object Camera (two apertures)

FOS Faint Object Spectrograph

HRS High Resolution Spectrograph (one aperture)

HSP High Speed Photometer (four apertures: one for visible light, two for ultraviolet, and one for polarimetry)

FGS Three Fine Guidance Sensors

The Fine Guidance Sensors (FGSs) are located at the outermost edge of the HST focal plane. They consist of Koester-prism interferometers, read by photomultipliers. During an observation, these devices will 'lock on' to pre-selected guide stars in the vicinity of the target and assist in keeping the telescope steadily pointed at the target to within an accuracy of 0·007 arcseconds. However, since only two FGS interferometers are needed to point the spacecraft at any given time, the third spare FGS is free to carry out relative astrometry with respect to the guide stars within its field of view. An accuracy of less than 0·002 arcseconds will be achieved. Such an accuracy would enable parallax determinations of the Hyades and Pleiades clusters as well as several RR Lyrae and Cepheid variable stars. Extrasolar planets could, perhaps, be detected through their perturbations on their parent stars. Interferometric studies will also be carried out, giving information on whether the star being observed is a multiple or extended star.

The High Speed Photometer (HSP) is the simplest of the first-generation Space Telescope instruments. It contains no moving parts and consists of four image-dissector tubes, a photomultiplier and more than fifty focal-plane filter/aperture combinations. The complete telescope must be pointed so that the light passes through the desired aperture and filter. The HSP also has polarimetric capabilities at ultraviolet wavelengths. It can operate in a rapid read out mode at a time resolution of better than 20 microseconds. The dynamic range of the HSP at 0·1% photometric accuracy is impressive, from 0 to 24 magnitude.

The primary mirror of the Hubble Space Telescope (left). The primary mirror is a feat of engineering. It consists of a piece of special glass (92·5% silica and 7·5% titanium dioxide), with a small coefficient of thermal expansion. It has a mass of 740 kilograms, a diameter of 2·4 metres and a thickness of 30 centimetres. It took two years to polish this mirror so that it gives the greatest possible spatial resolution. In this photograph, taken at the Perkin-Elmer Corporation, at Wilton, Connecticut, the mirror is being examined by technicians before being integrated into the telescope (NASA).

The Hubble Space Telescope (left). The Support System Module (SSM) carries the optical telescope and scientific instruments. The red arrows show the path followed by light entering the instrument. It strikes the primary mirror (which has a diameter of 2·4 metres) and is reflected towards the secondary mirror (30 centimetres diameter). This mirror reflects the light which is then focused behind the primary mirror (at 1·5 metres from its front surface) through a 60 centimetre diameter hole cut in the centre of the mirror.

The five scientific instruments (two cameras, two spectrographs and a photometer) then convert the images into useful data.

The Optical Telescope Assembly includes the telescope, its structure, the thermal control system and the fine guidance optical control sensors. The light shields are used to eliminate stray light (from the Sun, Earth or Moon) so that extremely low intensity objects can be observed.

The High Resolution Spectrograph (HRS). This has two 512 element Digicons, one for the range 115 to 170 nanometres, the other for 115 to 320 nanometres. The HRS has three levels of resolving power for objects down to 19th, 16th and 14th magnitudes.

The HRS will mainly be used to study stars in our own Galaxy. Its spectral resolution capabilities will enable detailed determination of photospheric abundances as well as studies of stellar chromospheres and the loss of mass by stars via stellar winds. Interstellar absorption lines will also be extensively studied using HRS spectra.

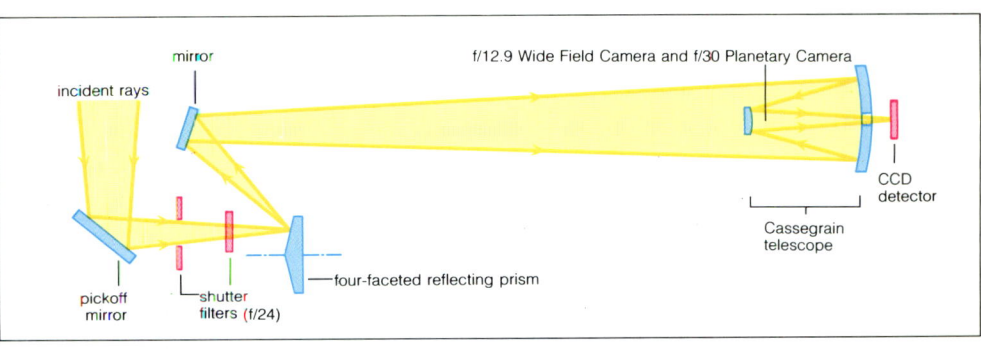

Diagram of the Wide Field/Planetary Camera (WF/PC). This is capable of operating in two modes: a 'Wide Field' f/12·9 mode having a 2·7 by 2·7 arcminute field of view, and a higher magnification f/30 'Planetary' mode having a 1·2 by 1·2 arcminute field of view. The detectors are two sets of four 800 by 800 pixel CCD chips. The size of the CCD pixels is 15 microns corresponding to a sampling resolution of 0·1 and 0·04 arcseconds for the Wide Field and Planetary Camera modes respectively. It is equipped with a large bank of filters, prisms and polarisers for spectrophotometry, slitless spectroscopy and polarimetry.

Diagram of the Faint Object Camera (FOC). This has four basic modes: direct imaging at f/48, f/96 and f/288 as well as in a 20 by 0·1 arcsecond spectrographic mode. Whereas the WF/PC provides a slightly undersampled image of a 'wide' region of the sky, the FOC is designed to exploit the unique imaging capability of the Space Telescope fully. It will give images with pixel sizes of 0·04, 0·02 or 0·008 arcseconds. The imaging photon counting detectors comprise a hot, bialkali photocathode at the input to convert the light quanta into electrons, a three stage intensifier tube (with an electron gain of 10^5) electromagnetically focusing the electron cloud onto an output, scintillating phosphor and a scanning television camera viewing the output phosphor. A microprocessor digitises the analogue TV camera signal and determines the location, size and amplitude of each scintillation event. The fields of view in the three nominal imaging modes are 22 by 22, 11 by 11, and 4 by 4 arcseconds respectively. Whereas the WF/PC operates best at longer wavelengths, the FOC is most sensitive in the blue and ultraviolet spectral region. The photon counting FOC is limited to objects fainter than 20th magnitude.

WF/PC and FOC images of Jupiter and Saturn are expected to be of comparable quality to the Voyager fly-by pictures, and images of the outermost planets will be comparable to the best groundbased images available today. Attempts to detect extrasolar planets directly will be carried out using the coronographic facilities of the FOC. Cepheid variables will be detectable out to distances of the Virgo cluster. This will lead to a vast improvement in the determination of the cosmic distance scale. The tenfold increase in angular resolution will be extremely important in studying new galaxies.

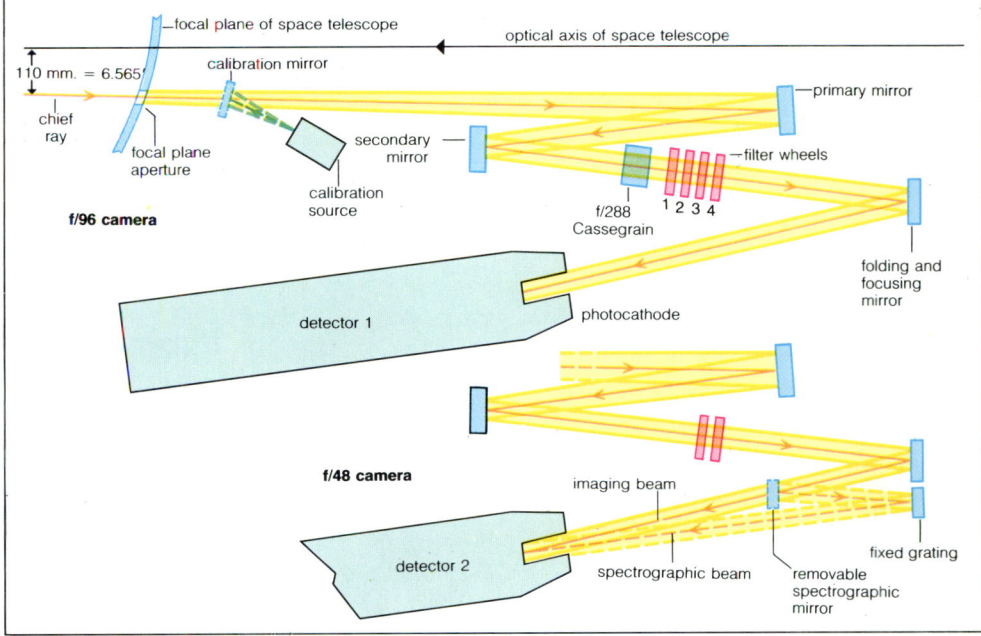

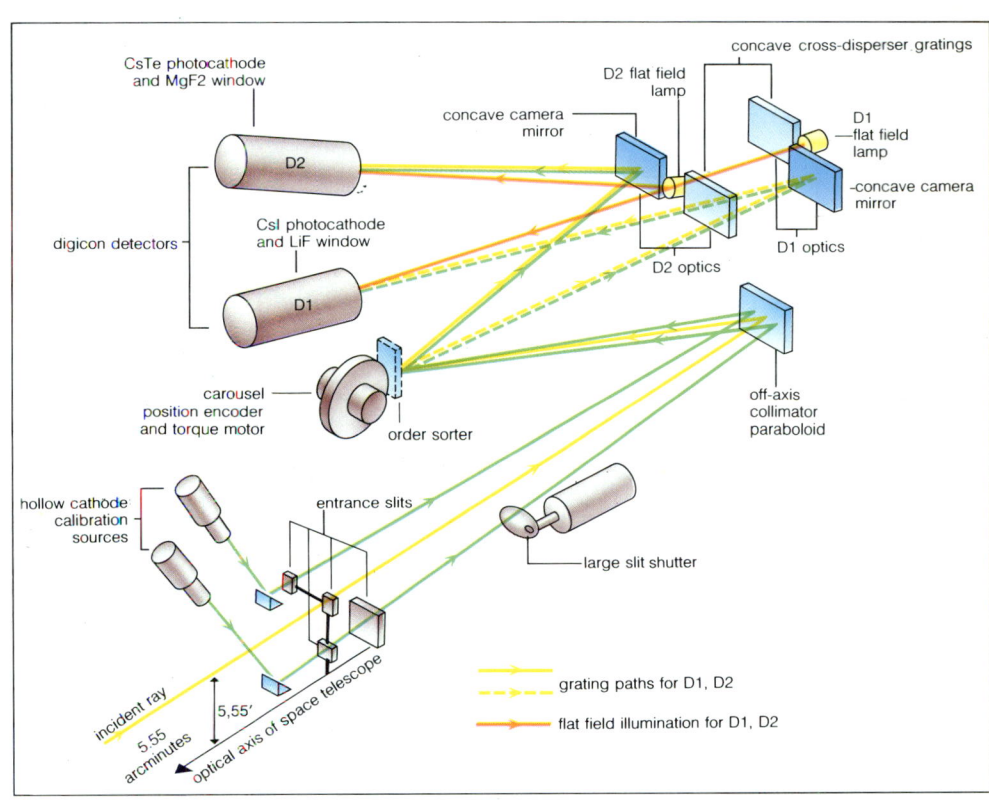

Infrared astronomy

The infrared part of the electromagnetic spectrum may, for astronomical purposes, be considered to cover the range from a few microns to several hundred microns. It is in this band that cool objects and material (at 15 to 300 degrees kelvin) radiate the bulk of their energy. The band also contains a rich variety of atomic, ionic, molecular and solid state spectral features. It is of special interest that the birth of stars and the formation of planetary systems can best be observed at infrared wavelengths. Apart from a few 'windows' at the shorter wavelength end, the Earth's atmosphere absorbs most infrared radiation, forcing infrared astronomers to use space techniques. In 1983, the InfraRed Astronomical Satellite (IRAS), a joint project between NASA, the Netherlands Agency for Aerospace Programs (NLVR) and the British Science and Engineering Research Council (SERC) performed the first scientific, all-sky survey in the infrared. The European Space Agency is currently developing the Infrared Space Observatory (ISO) for launch in the mid 1990s. NASA is studying the Space Infrared Telescope Facility (SIRTF) for possible launch towards the end of the century.

A major feature of a mission in IR astronomy is that the telescopes themselves and their detector systems must be cooled cryogenically to just a few degrees kelvin. They must be colder than the matter being observed if the astronomical signal is not to be overwhelmed by the infrared radiation of the instrumentation itself.

IRAS and the all-sky survey

The IRAS satellite was launched by a Delta vehicle from Vandenberg in California on 25 January 1983. The cooled, telescope-aperture cover was ejected when in orbit. By the end of its mission, IRAS had surveyed 95% of the celestial sphere with at least two successive orbit scans.

Some 60% of IRAS orbital time was given over to scanning to carry out the survey. However, it was possible to hold the satellite pointed to a selected region of sky where there were interesting IR sources, and to perform a detailed (about 1 degree) raster scan of the region. The remaining 40% of the mission was spent in this pointed mode, with several thousand regions being observed.

The Infrared Space Observatory (ISO)

With the availability of the pioneering all-sky survey from IRAS, the next logical step is to examine the sources of infrared radiation in

Characteristics of the InfraRed Astronomical Satellite (IRAS)

Mechanical	overall length	3.6 metres
	diameter	2.2 metres
	mass at launch	1076 kilograms
Cryogenic	coolant	superfluid helium
	bath temperature	1.805 K
	focal plane temperature	2.5 K
	baffles temperature	10 K
	sunshade temperature	100 K
	outer shell temperature	195 K
	helium at launch	475 litres, 71.6 kilograms
	end of cryogen	22 November 1983
Optical	telescope	2 mirror Ritchey–Chrétien
	aperture	57 centimetres
	focal length	5.5 metres
	plate scale	1.6 millimetres per arcminute
	focal ratio	f/9.6
	mirror material	beryllium

The InfraRed Astronomical Satellite (IRAS). The infrared telescope is cryogenically cooled by liquid helium contained in a cryostat. This schematic cut-away shows the three major elements, the spacecraft platform at bottom, the cryostat and the baffle/sunshade system, and the deployed solar array.

In the focal plane of the telescope there are 62 detectors covering the wavelength range 8 to 120 microns in four bands. Key elements of the detector system are cryogenically cooled JFET preamplifiers. Besides the main survey instrument, the focal plane contained a low resolution spectrometer and a chopped photometric channel, the former for recording the infrared spectrum of bright sources during scanning, the latter intended to make high resolution maps of individual sources (Estec).

Orbital characteristics of IRAS. The near-polar orbit was chosen so that the orbital plane precessed by about one degree of arc per day, just matching the Earth's orbital motion around the Sun. The satellite was orbiting the Earth near the terminator, the boundary between day and night, and the telescope was kept pointing roughly 90 degrees away from the Sun. For the all-sky survey the telescope's pointing direction was maintained near the zenith such that the sky was scanned, the infrared sources crossing the focal plane at the rate of 3·85 arcminutes per second or 6 millimetres per second. Each element in the main detector array swept over a strip of sky about 5 arcminutes wide.

To confirm the detection of a celestial source, it had to be seen by two detector elements the appropriate number of seconds apart, and then again on the next orbit. Subsequent reexamination of the same region of sky, weeks or months later, gave further confirmation.

Infrared emission of the celestial sphere viewed by IRAS. This picture is dominated by emission (yellow and red) in the galactic plane. The blank curved areas indicate those parts of the sky not surveyed (Estec).

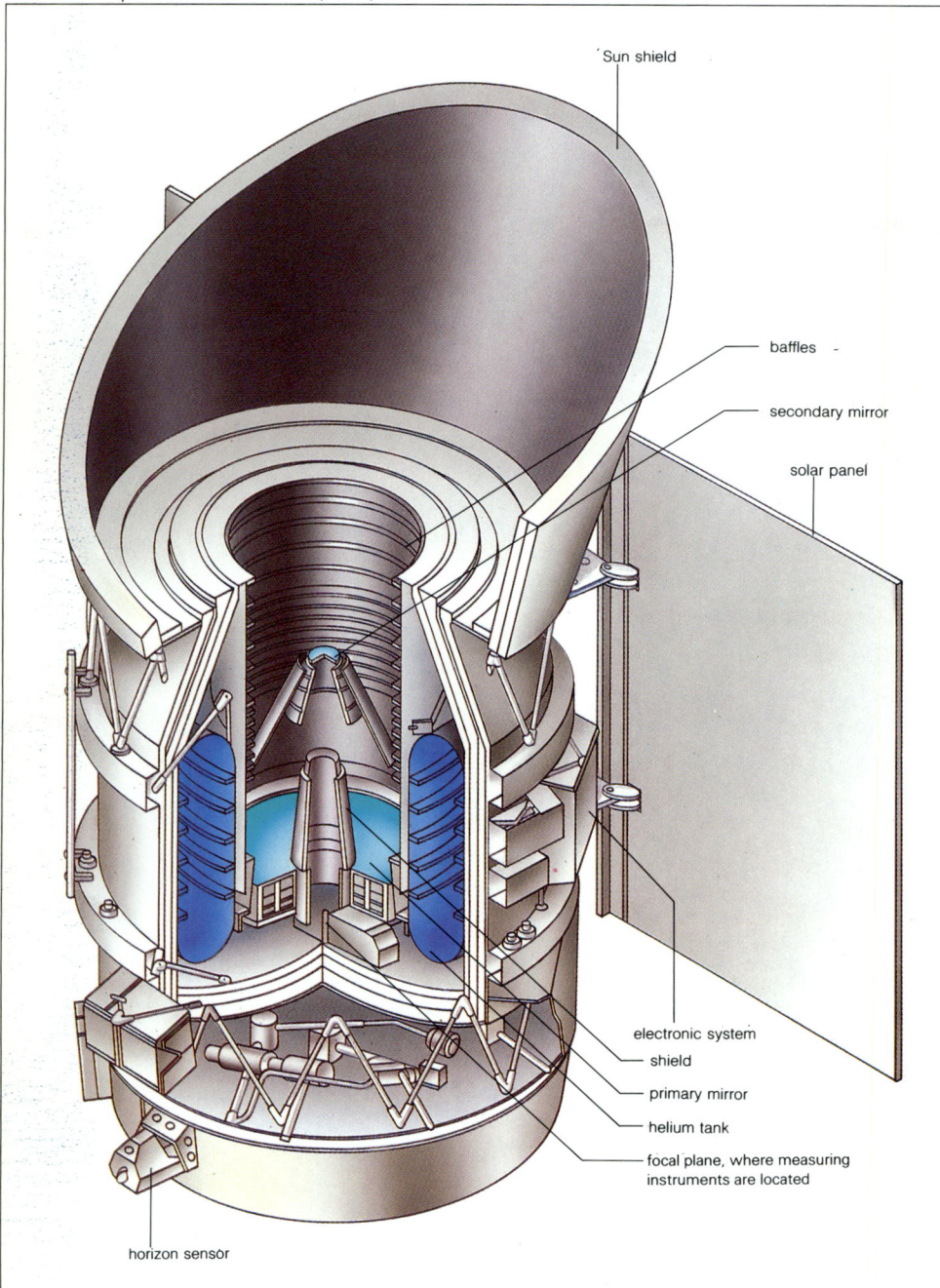

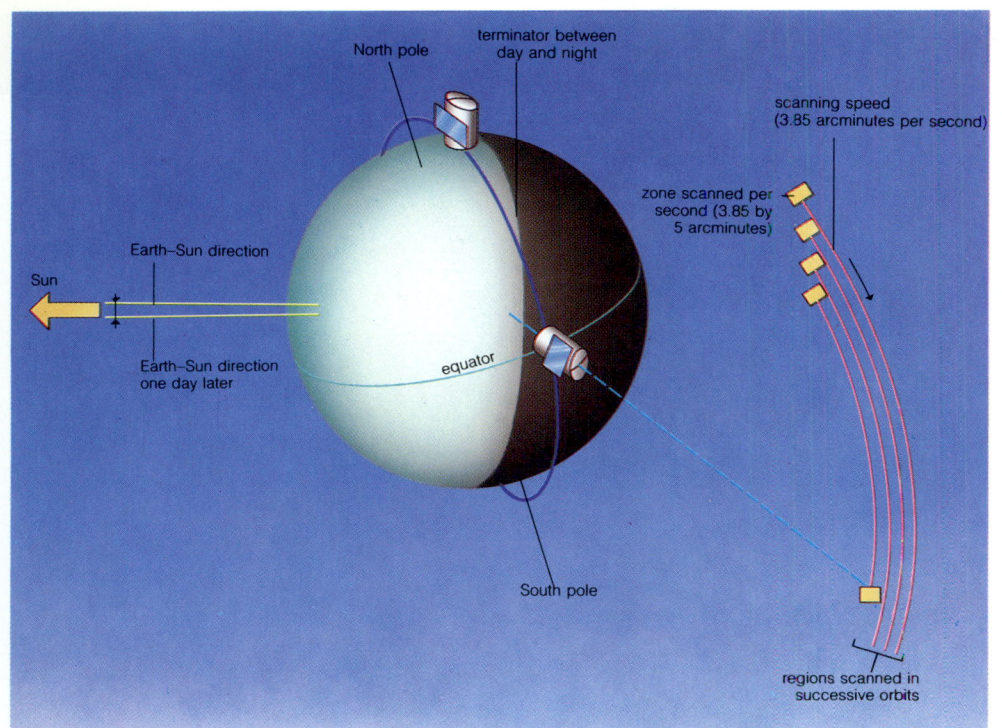

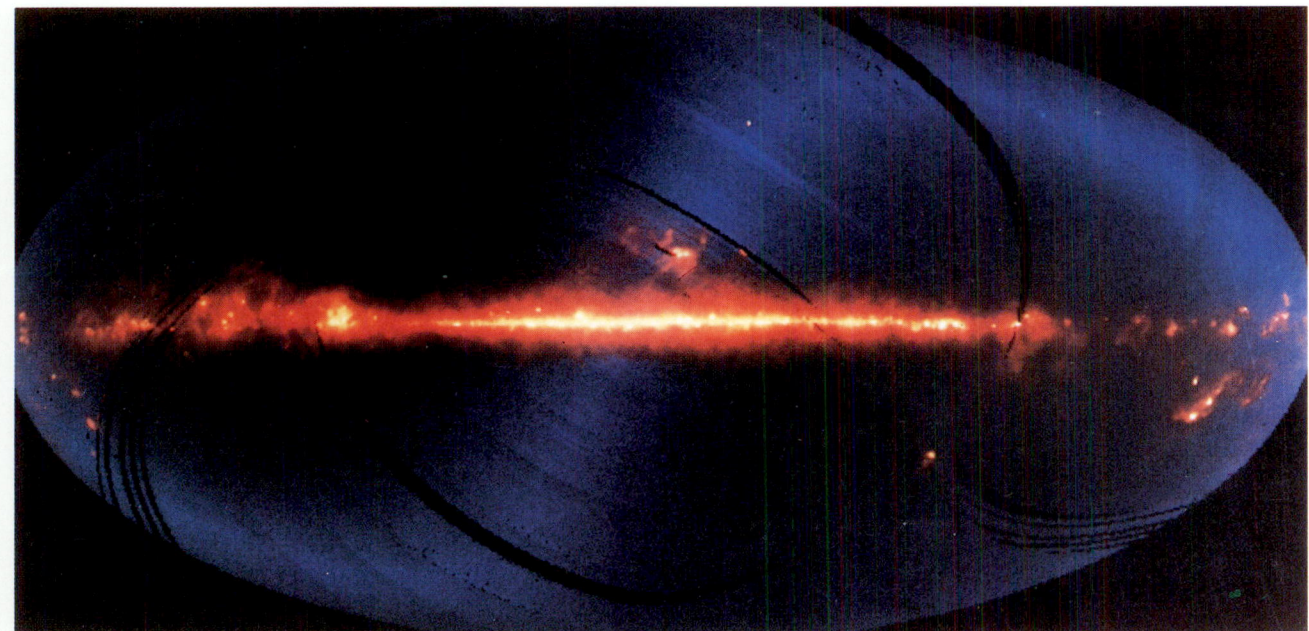

much more detail. For this, a telescope which can be held pointing to a source for long periods and which is equipped with instruments of higher spatial and spectroscopic resolution, and with higher sensitivity, is required. Such a mission is ESA's ISO.

Astronomical objects in the solar system, right out to the most distant extragalactic sources, will be observed. Its cryogenically-cooled telescope will have four scientific instruments, which together will permit imaging, and photometric, spectroscopic and polarimetric observations, at wavelengths from 3 to 200 micrometres. The telescope is a Ritchey–Chrétien configuration with an effective aperture of 60 centimetres. The optical quality of its mirrors is adequate for diffraction limited performance at a wavelength of 5 micrometres. Stringent control of stray light, particularly from bright infrared sources outside the telescope's field of view, is necessary in order to ensure that the sensitivity is not degraded. This is accomplished by imposing viewing constraints and by means of the sunshade and the Cassegrain and main baffles.

The instrument complement of ISO consists of a camera, an imaging photopolarimeter and two spectrometers. Photometric, spectroscopic, and imaging observations will be made at various spatial and spectral resolutions from 3 to 200 micrometres. The four instruments will view adjacent areas of the sky, and only one instrument will be active at a time.

Extension of the IR band to submillimetre wavelengths

At wavelengths longer than a hundred microns or so, yet shorter than those wavelengths at which groundbased radio astronomy is practical, lies the submillimetre band of the electromagnetic spectrum. Technological advances now allow radio astronomy methods to be used in this band. Coherent receivers using the superheterodyne technique provide spectral resolutions of the order 10^6 at submillimetre (about 300 gigahertz) wavelengths. These receivers are coupled to a telescope or dish antenna of about 10 metres diameter. Unlike receivers making observations at IR wavelengths, they do not require cooling. The detector elements of the receivers do, however, require cryogenic cooling. The ESA longterm plan for space science calls for such a submillimetre astronomy mission to be realised towards the end of the century.

Brian G. Taylor

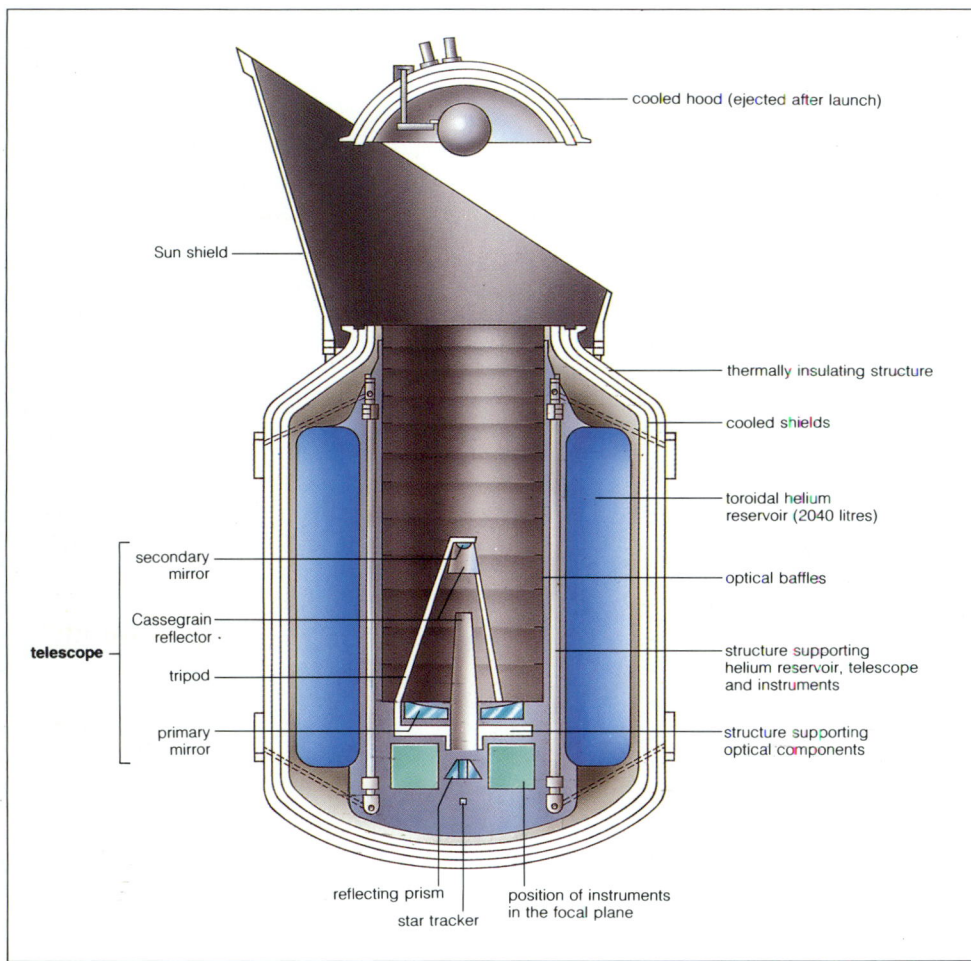

Diagram of the Infrared Space Observatory (ISO). The satellite is to be 5·2 metres high, 2·3 metres wide and will weigh around 2·3 tonnes. It will be launched by an Ariane IV vehicle into a highly eccentric orbit with a period of 24 hours.

The basic spacecraft functions are provided by a service module. These include the solar array mounted on the sunshield and subsystems for thermal control, data handling, power conditioning, telemetry, and attitude and orbit control. The last provides the three-axis stabilisation, to an accuracy of a few arcseconds, needed for the mission.

The payload module is essentially a large cryostat. Inside the vacuum vessel is a tank filled with about 2000 litres of superfluid helium, which will provide a life of at least 18 months. Some of the infrared detectors directly coupled to the helium tank are at a temperature of around 2 degrees kelvin. Apart from these, all other units are cooled using the cold boil-off gas from the liquid helium. This is first routed through the optical support structure, where it cools the telescope and the scientific instruments to a temperature of 3 to 4 degrees kelvin. The gas is then passed along the baffles and radiation shields before being vented to space. Mounted on the outside of the vacuum vessel is a sunshield, which prevents the Sun from ever shining directly on the cryostat.

The scientific instruments are mounted on the opposite side of the optical support structure to the primary mirror, each one occupying an 80 degree segment of the cylindrical volume available. The 20 arcminute unvignetted field of view of the telescope is distributed radially to the four instruments by a pyramid mirror. Each experiment receives a 3 arcminute unvignetted field, centred on an axis at an angle of 8·5 arcminutes to the main optical axis.

During the mission of the space shuttle Discovery, in November 1984, the telecommunications satellite Palapa B2 was recovered by two astronauts and brought back to Earth. This Indonesian satellite was launched in February 1984, but failed to reach its planned orbit, due to a failure of the rocket on the Payload Assist Module (PAM).

In this photograph, Joseph P. Allen is at the end of the remote controlled arm attached to the shuttle, preparing to recover the satellite, whilst Dale A. Gardner remains in the vicinity of the space shuttle. (NASA).

Living with space

Satellite applications

Meteorology

In 1959, the small Explorer 7 satellite was launched by the United States. It carried the first spaceborne meteorological experiment, consisting of a radiometer designed and built by Professor Verner Suomi of the University of Wisconsin. The radiometer had two hemispheres to detect radiative energy (bolometers). One was painted black to absorb all wavelengths, and the other was painted white to reflect all the solar energy and receive only terrestrial infrared radiation. The imbalance between incoming solar energy and outgoing terrestrial radiation, which depends strongly on latitude, is the driving force of the atmospheric heat engine. It is this which provides energy for the developing weather systems.

The TIROS (Television and Infra-Red Observation Satellite) series of satellites followed. TIROS 1, launched on 1 April 1960, was the first satellite to record, in the visible and the infrared, the development of cloud formations over the Earth's surface using a vidicon camera system. All ten satellites in this series, launched between 1960 and 1963, were placed in similar near polar, Sun synchronous orbits at a mean altitude of 900 kilometres. The orbital period is about 100 minutes. TIROS 8 was the first ever Automatic Picture Transmission (APT) satellite to send cloud images as radio telemetry signals.

A number of technological developments were incorporated into the new Environmental Sciences Services Administration (ESSA) programme. The first nine satellites of this programme, launched between 1966 and 1969, were fitted with advanced vidicon cameras. These produced high quality images from high orbits, in the region of 1600 kilometres altitude. In 1970, the Improved TIROS Operational Satellite (ITOS 1) and the first three-axis stabilised satellite of the US National Oceanographic and Atmospheric Administration (NOAA) series were launched. The TIROS satellites were spin stabilised around the principal axis of rotation, at a relatively low rate (100 revolutions per minute). This is necessary because of the small but finite time during which the cameras must be stationary with

An eruption of Mount Etna. Smoke from this volcano was photographed by the TIROS N satellite on 4 August 1979. It forms a unique sort of cloud, consisting of ash and particles less than a millimetre in size. Water vapour in the atmosphere condenses on these particles and droplets of water are formed. The 'cloud chimney' from the crater rises at an angle due to the north west wind. Then it comes into contact with a horizontal inversion layer which prevents it from rising higher into the atmosphere. Diffusion causes the plume to spread out.

The inversion layer marks the transition between the 'free' atmosphere at high altitudes and the frictional boundary layer near the ground. Both natural and man made pollution become trapped in the relatively stagnant region below the inversion layer. When this layer descends to ground level, mist is produced. In areas of high pollution, this turns to smog. Volcanic emissions can alter the climate. Although much smaller than the eruption of Krakatoa in Indonesia in 1883, clouds due to recent eruptions of Mount Agung in Indonesia (1963), Mount St Helens in the United States (1980) and El Chichon (1982) in Mexico obscured the sky over large areas, lowering the temperature at the Earth's surface. (CMS, Lannion).

Weather systems. The European meteorological satellite, Meteostat F2, is positioned in a geostationary orbit over the Atlantic and records the development of weather systems. The image below is of a weather system building up just to the west of Europe. It consists of a spiral of clouds around the 'eye' of the storm, a region of low atmospheric pressure. The winds blow in an anticlockwise direction around the low in the Northern hemisphere, and in a clockwise direction in the Southern hemisphere.

This weather system, photographed on 18 September 1983, is typical for this region. An enormous vortex covers a large part of the north Atlantic and moves towards the east. Ahead of this weather system is a wide ribbon of clouds, spreading out towards the east. The rear part of this ribbon is marked by a discontinuity in the clouds, called a cold front. This is followed by clouds which have the appearance of a leopard's skin. This is the most active part of the weather system, consisting of progressively heavier rainfall as it advances, and strong gusty winds (ESA).

respect to the Earth in order to obtain good quality cloud images. However, at such rates the gyroscopic effect is insufficient to prevent a slow drift of the satellite's rotational axis. Several technological developments, notably the inertial wheel, have led to satellites being stabilised along all three axes. In this way, pitching, rolling and yawing motions are minimised.

New techniques in visible and infrared imagery radiometry were incorporated in ITOS instruments. ITOS carried the first Advanced Very High Resolution Radiometer (AVHRR). This took photographs in the visible and infrared regions of the spectrum with a resolution of about one kilometre. This represents an optimum spatial resolution. It is sufficient for all cloud formations to be identified, even local low cloud systems such as form in stable layers in San Francisco Bay. Only military satellites, such as in the US Defense Meteorological Satellite Program (DMSP), have better spatial resolution.

Another major development was of satellite instruments to derive the vertical temperature profile of the atmosphere. These results complement the profiles obtained from balloon borne radiosondes released from the Earth's surface. All the results are used in large computer models of atmospheric behaviour to make weather forecasts.

Soviet satellites in the Cosmos series are similar to those of the ESSA series. These are launched into orbits whose inclination to the equatorial plane is determined by the positions of the launch site and the tracking stations. After a time, the Cosmos satellites move into a Sun synchronous orbit. Since 1967, Cosmos 144 and Cosmos 156 have formed the basis of the meteorological system, termed Meteor. They carry vidicon cameras and infrared radiometers, but they do not have an APT system.

The NASA Nimbus series is used to test new technologies, and sensors developed and tested on Nimbus have been incorporated into the NOAA series. The first Nimbus satellite, launched in 1964, was devoted to cloud imaging techniques in the visible and infrared. Taken on a cloudless day, one of its first clear images showed the west of the European continent, with the coasts of Great Britain, France and Spain being defined. Nimbus 4, launched in April 1970, carried the first spectrometers capable of carrying out vertical sounding. In December 1972, Nimbus 5 carried an improved version which included microwave cameras capable of 'seeing' through the cloud layer. The instruments carried on Nimbus 6 form the basis of all the microwave and infrared sounding devices found on NOAA satellites since the TIROS N satellite in 1978.

Historically, the geostationary satellite programme dates back to 1966 and 1967 when the Application Technology Satellites (ATS 1 and 3) were launched by NASA. They carried the Visible Infrared Spin Scan Radiometer (VISSR). Several meteorological satellites were put into geostationary orbit around 1977. These included US GOES (Geostationary Observational Environmental Satellites) East and West, GMS 1 by Japan, Meteostat F1 by Europe and Insat by India. Others have since been launched to maintain an operational capability. In the future, on geostationary satellites with Vertical Atmospheric Sounding (VAS), imaging and vertical sounding techniques will be integrated.

Space techniques in meteorology

A satellite acts as the 'third eye' of the meteorologist. This is an excellent analogy, considering the eye's field of view, visual acuity and sensitivity to visible sunlight. But the satellite improves on the human eye, by seeing vast areas of the Earth's surface. It sees with the high resolution of a telescope. It can explore regions of the spectrum beyond the visible, notably in the infrared. A satellite's ability to observe at night is just as important as its day vision, because the satellite spends as long on the night as on the day side of the Earth. Electronic vidicon cameras have been improved, with dual scanning by optical cells in both the visible and infrared domains. The high resolution, dual channel radiometer, Advanced Very High Radiation Radiometer (AVHRR), is the first camera which has the same resolution (about one kilometre) in both the visible and infrared.

Making observations on the cloud cover is similar to remote sensing of detail of the Earth's surface. Clouds reveal movements in the atmosphere. Using geostationary satellite images, winds can be deduced from the movements of individual clouds. These have to be coupled with information on the altitude of the tracer cloud. In the absence of a radar altimeter to observe clouds from above, satellite infrared observations are used to calculate the temperature of the top of the cloud.

A meteorological satellite can 'see' down through the atmosphere, in a technique called remote sounding. The atmosphere, consisting of a mixture of gases, is transparent to wavelengths in the visible region. It is relatively opaque to wavelengths from the ultraviolet to gamma rays, and to microwaves with

Using satellites to study global weather patterns. The upper image was obtained on 13 March 1986 by the European geostationary satellite Meteosat F2. It shows the meteorological coupling between the Northern and Southern Hemispheres. At temperate latitudes the scene is dominated by powerful weather systems moving from West to East. Systems in the Northern Hemisphere rotate in an anticlockwise direction, whereas those in the Southern Hemisphere, often call the 'roaring forties', rotate clockwise. At tropical latitudes, where easterly winds dominate, there is a marked contrast between the large rain systems near the Gulf of Guinea and the cloudless zone above the Sahara.

The lower image was taken by US geostationary satellite GOES East on 8 August 1980. It shows hurricane Allen in the Northern Hemisphere during the second stage of its development. Born off the African coast, it passed to the south of Martinique, then over the south of Haiti and Cuba before dying out over the coast of Texas on 11 August.

The satellite observes the movement of the eye of the hurricane. Around this calm region is a vertical wall of cloud and maximum rainfall. Weather satellites are the most efficient means of forecasting the behaviour of such potentially dangerous weather systems. (above: Meteosat Images, ESA; below: Weather Centre, Lannion, France).

frequencies down to about 100 gigahertz. The infrared absorbing properties of some molecules in the atmosphere, such as oxygen and carbon dioxide, make remote sounding possible.

The infrared radiation which emerges from the top of the atmosphere to be measured by a satellite carries information on the absorption by all atmospheric layers piled one on top of the other. These individual absorptions depend only on the temperature, if the fractional concentration of the absorbing gas is independent of altitude, as it is in the case of carbon dioxide. Thus by inverting a number of radiative measurements, in different narrow spectral bands, these temperatures can be calculated to find the vertical temperature profile. By combining these two parameters, temperature and pressure, the vertical profile of the mass density of the atmosphere can be obtained.

The key requirement for mathematical models of the atmosphere and for meteorological forecasting is a knowledge of the large scale mass density and wind distributions, discussed in the previous section. Traditionally, meteorologists have used a worldwide network of 8000 surface weather observation stations and 500 stations which carry out balloon borne radiosonde ascents of packages instrumented to measure pressure, temperature and humidity. Weather ships stationed on the oceans are no longer used, because of the high operational costs associated with them. Surface stations and meteorological buoys transmit their data to satellites for onward transmission. These ways of collecting and distributing data are supplemented by systems like Argos (cf. *Navigation* pp. 254–7) which give the geographical position of the station transmitting the data.

International cooperation

The World Meteorological Organisation (WMO), based in Geneva, coordinates programmes concerned with the collection and treatment of meteorological data worldwide. The WMO does not forbid more local agreements. For example, in Europe there is an agreement between the European Centre for Medium Range Forecasting near Reading (Great Britain) and Eumetsat which manages the Meteosat programme. Furthermore, there is international coordination between the various geostationary satellite programmes (United States, Europe, Soviet Union, Japan and India) to standardise procedures. The large field of view from a satellite and the continuity of high standard observations ideally complement the network of stations distributed irregularly – with enormous gaps in the oceans – over the Earth's surface.

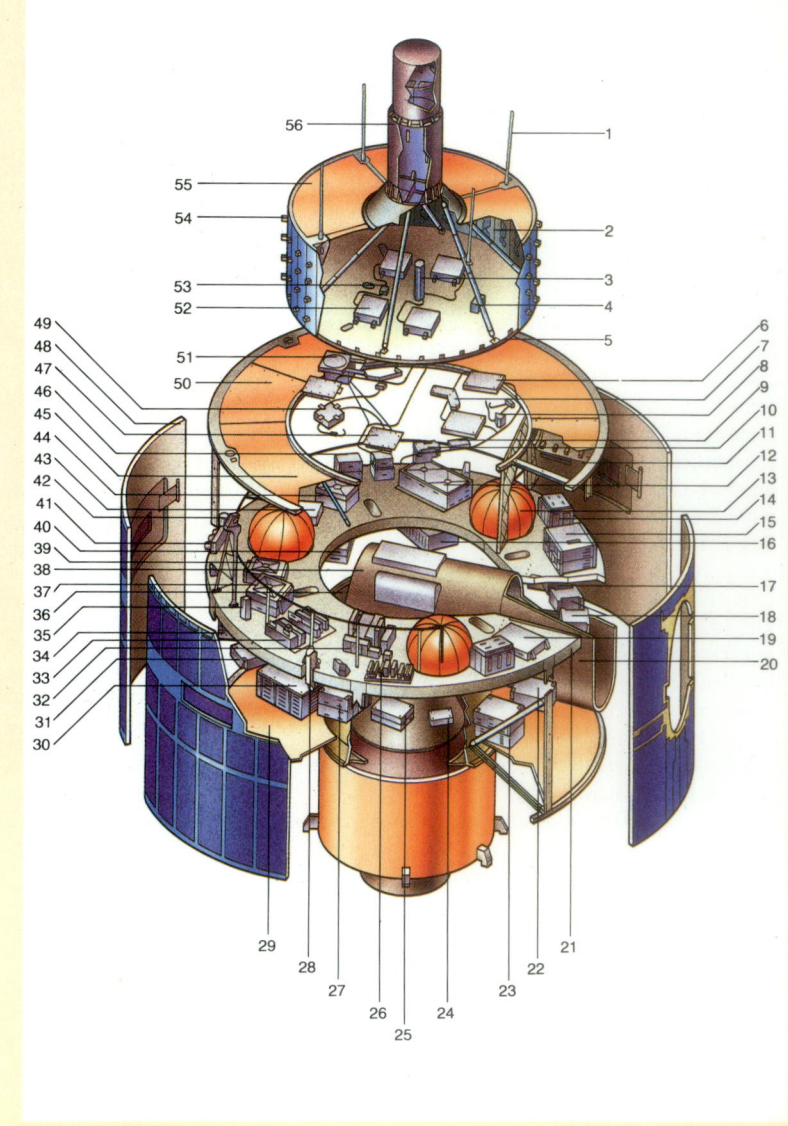

The Meteosat programme. In 1972, eight members of the European Space Research Organisation embarked on a programme to develop preoperational meteorological satellites (Meteosat). ESA constructed these satellites, and two models (F1 and F2) were successfully launched in 1977 and 1981.

The satellites were launched from the Kourou Space Centre in French Guiana, and placed in a geostationary transfer orbit. The Mage apogee motor, using solid fuel propellant, was used to position them. Meteosat is at a geographic longitude of 0 degrees, and its orbit has a maximum inclination of 0·8 degrees to the equatorial plane. Meteosat F1 operated successfully from November 1977 to November 1979, when there was a fault in the secondary power supply system and the radiometer stopped working. Since then it has only been able to collect data transmitted to it from the ground. Meteosat F2 has outlived its planned life of June 1984, but is still operating in a satisfactory manner, although the data collection equipment broke down shortly after launch.

On 24 May 1983, a convention signed in Geneva created an international organisation, Eumetsat. Its purpose was to set up a network of meteorological satellites based on the Meteosat programme. Eumetsat will construct and maintain the meteorological operational satellite systems, at the end of the preoperational Meteosat programme. In the operational Meteosat programme for the 1990s, three satellite launches are planned.

Claude Honvault

1	VHF antenna	6	UHF power amplifier
2	S band feeder network	7	UHF power amplifier switch
3	four channel transmission switch	8	UHF duplexer
4	hybrid network	9	S band receiver filter
5	UHF and S band transponder platform	10	S band preamplifier

A sandstorm in the Sahara.
This photograph, taken on 12 March 1982 by Meteosat F2, shows a sandstorm in the form of circulation around a vortex, or low pressure centre, the central 'eye' of the storm. Not only does the wind carry air particles, it also carries sand (Meteosat F2, CMS).

Research in meteorology

Meteorological research has two main aims which complement each other. These are to observe atmospheric phenomena and to understand the mechanisms responsible for them through research based on theoretical models.

In the 1930s, a Norwegian, Jakob Bjerknes, constructed a descriptive theory which classified the apparently random shapes of the most active clouds into a scheme involving fronts. Such fronts represent boundaries in the atmosphere. Rainclouds accumulate on their front edge and unstable clouds gather on their back edge. Satellites have confirmed the validity of the theory. They have also revealed a number of peculiarities about the arrangement of the cloud mass on the leading edge of the front. Similarly, satellites have provided new data on the birth and behaviour of tropical cyclones. Therefore, these days we can use remote sensing to measure the distribution of winds and the intensity of cyclones and typhoons.

A major area of space research concerns the observation and understanding of climatic changes. Recent experiments are focused on the oceans, because they can 'force' the climate. They have an enormous capacity to store heat and to transfer it from one place to another. Currents such as the Gulf Stream move polewards huge amounts of thermal energy which are eventually transferred to the atmosphere.

The importance of sea surface temperature measurements was made brutally clear in 1973 and in 1982 and 1983. El Niño is a current in the Pacific ocean, called 'Christ child' by Peruvian fishermen as it appeared to them during the month of the nativity. In El Niño events, warm waters replace the cold upwelling water which provides an essential food resource for the region in the form of anchovies. The temperature of the sea surface rose by as much as 5 degrees celsius. Satellites and groundbased observational networks were able to record these effects (causing climatic changes far beyond the initial area of disturbance).

Thus, the Earth's climate can change. But the climate would be expected to remain the same if the radiative properties of the Sun and Earth did not alter. For the mean temperature of the atmosphere and the surface to be the same the average reflectivity, or albedo, of the Earth, averaged over all regions of the sky, whether they are clear or cloudy, must not change. However, a reduction of cloud cover and, therefore, a reduction of the planetary albedo will cause an increase in the penetration of solar radiation and increased heating at the surface. In turn this will cause an increase in evaporation from ocean surfaces. The consequence of this will be an increase in the amount of water vapour in the atmosphere. This will condense to form clouds, and compensate for the initial deficiency. This is an example of a self stabilising change which is termed negative feedback by engineers.

The long term objective of such research is to predict the climate and its changes, whether they are natural or man made. This work is of great socio-economic importance; it is absolutely vital for the world of tomorrow.

Future programmes

Development in the space applications of meteorology, climatology and the environment will continue throughout the 1990s, and it is expected that microwave technology will have an important part to play. Since microwaves can penetrate cloud cover, they will be used to complement signals from infrared sensors. The Advanced Microwave Sounding Unit (AMSU) is designed to produce a vertical temperature profile and a water vapour profile; the latter will be used to make rain forecasts. The possibilities are further increased by radiating microwaves from space vehicles. This method, which is

The Japanese meteorological system. In the early 1970s, Japan decided to participate in the Global Atmospheric Research Program (GARP) proposed by the World Meteorological Organisation (WMO) by contributing a geostationary meteorological satellite (GMS). In 1977, the first GMS satellite was launched and started taking pictures from geostationary orbit above the western Pacific (140 degrees East longitude). Even during its initial checkout, the satellite was acclaimed as valuable by keeping track of the typhoons then approaching Japan. GMS 2 and GMS 3 were launched in 1981 and 1984, respectively, to continue these observations. GMS 4 is scheduled for launch soon.

GMS and GMS 2 were financed by the Japanese National Space Development Agency (NASDA). The cost of GMS 3 and GMS 4 was shared by the Japan Meteorological Agency (JMA) and NASDA. The satellites were built in the USA, by the Hughes Aircraft Company, with NEC of Japan acting as the main contractor to NASDA.

The satellite, controlled at JMA's Meteorological Satellite Centre in the suburbs of Tokyo, scans the Earth's full disc in 25 minutes, in the visible and infrared bands simultaneously. Rays enter through the sun shaded oval opening. The camera, called VISSR (Visible and Infrared Spin Scan Radiometer), has its optical axis along the axis of symmetry.

The satellite relays ground-processed image data to many user stations and also relays meteorological observation data from unmanned data collection platforms (DCPs). The Space Environment Monitor (SEM) installed on the satellite measures energetic particles coming from the Sun and trapped in the Earth's magnetosphere.

An antenna cone to which three antennae are rigidly attached forms a despun portion of the satellite. The outer diameter of the solar panel measures 2·15 metres. (NASDA).

Akira Kikuchi

The two families of meteorological satellites, in geostationary and polar orbit. The two types of meteorological satellites complement each other well. Satellites in a geostationary orbit at an altitude of 36 000 kilometres have the same period of rotation as the Earth – one day. They thus remain above a certain point on the Earth. The geostationary satellites view a wide band of latitudes to the north and south of the equator. However, they cannot encompass the polar regions at all and their field of view is very distorted at high latitudes. Other satellites in polar orbit, at altitudes between 600 kilometres and 1600 kilometres, repeatedly observe the polar regions. Their low altitude favours good spatial resolution on the ground and in the atmosphere. They are also used as relay transmitters over the horizon, and to collect and store data for redistribution.

The US TIROS and NOAA satellites and the Soviet Meteor satellites are at an altitude of about 800 kilometres. They observe up to 1500 kilometres on either side of the subsatellite path. The two satellites of the NOAA series provide meteorological data for the whole globe every six hours.

The satellite network in 1987 consisted of five geostationary satellites in a ring around the equator – GOES East and West, Meteosat F2, Insat 1B and GMS 3. Thus five parts of the world are well covered meteorologically – North and South America, the Caribbean and the Pacific, by GOES East and West, with Europe and Africa by Meteosat, part of Asia and the Indian Ocean by Insat, and south east Asia, the west Pacific and Australia by the Japanese satellite. It also included satellites in near polar orbits, NOAA 9 and NOAA 10, and up to three satellites in the Meteor series, only one of which is shown in the diagram.

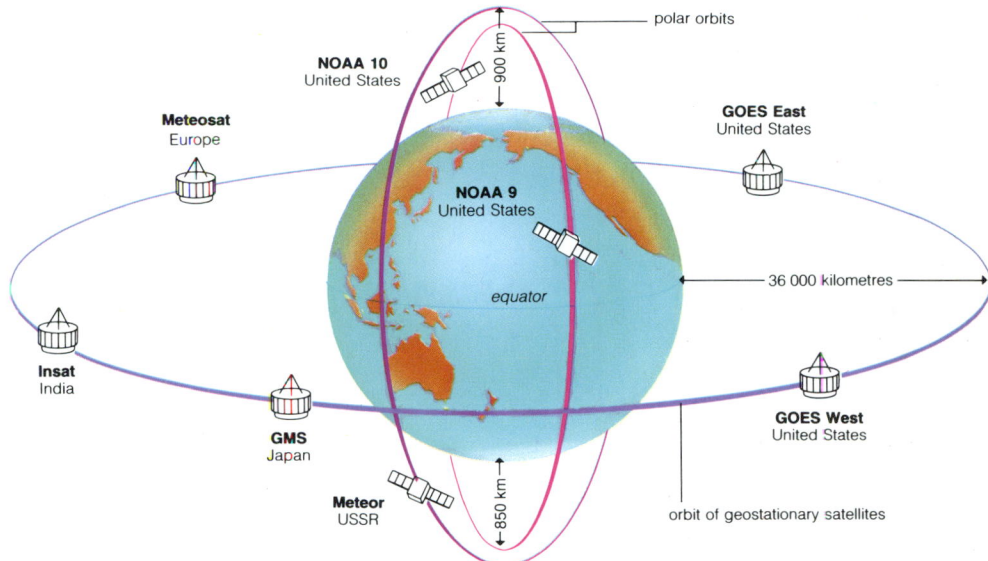

rather like radar, quite literally 'probes' the atmosphere.

Microwave technology will be used to investigate climatic change. For studies of ocean-atmosphere coupling, it enables sea surface temperature to be measured accurately and, using a microwave scatterometer and an altimetric radar, allows the wave state of the surface to be estimated. These parameters provide indirect measurements of the surface winds and ocean currents.

Internationally agreed scientific programmes will evaluate changes in global energy and in the amounts of water vapour and condensed water in clouds and rainfall. At present, rainfall measurements are made using rain gauges at thousands of weather stations. However, indirect measurements can be obtained from satellite-borne radiometers such as the Electrically Scanning Microwave Radiometer (ESMR) and the Scanning Multichannel Microwave Radiometer (SMMR). The Special Sensor Microwave Imager (SSMI), the first operational microwave radiometer, will be capable of estimating rainfall of up to 10 millimetres per hour; above this limit, clouds are almost completely opaque to the radiation. Since it is more usual to have vertical clouds, it is nonetheless possible to obtain a correlation between cloud depth and intensity of rainfall.

The meteorological satellites of tomorrow bristle with instruments such as radars and radiometers to monitor the environment as well as the weather. All levels of the Earth's atmosphere will come under surveillance: there is a growing desire to protect our planet and its natural environment, illustrated notably by the Vienna and Montreal agreements on protecting the ozone layer and recent international initiatives on the danger of global heating through the burning of fossil fuels and tropical deforestation – the so-called greenhouse effect.

Adelin Villevieille

Thermal mapping. This image of Africa was built up over the period from 17 to 23 June 1982. It is based on data from the radiometer of Meteosat F2 which is sensitive to thermal infrared radiation emitted by the Earth's surface at wavelengths between 10·5 and 12·5 microns. Clouds are opaque at these wavelengths. Thus, to avoid false values caused by cloud cover, the image was built up over the period of a week, at the rate of two images per day taken at 12.00 and 15.00 Universal Time. Each point on the image corresponds to the radiometric maximum, or maximum temperature, taken from the fourteen readings.

The image clearly shows the different climatic zones of the continent.

These are expressed as different temperatures of the Earth's surface. The extreme north and south are the coldest regions; white (below 23 degrees celsius) across the north of Europe, with blue, yellow and green (up to 26 degrees celsius) across mid-Europe and South Africa. Red, ochre, brown and black correspond to the hottest climatic zones (above 27 degrees celsius); while the Mediterranean region is shown in red and ochre, brown and black delineate the Sahara and Arabian deserts. The humid, mid-tropical region is represented by bands, running from east to west, of dark red, light red, green and yellow; these show a decrease in temperature towards the equator (Meteosat F2, CMS).

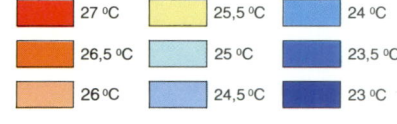

27 °C	25,5 °C	24 °C
26,5 °C	25 °C	23,5 °C
26 °C	24,5 °C	23 °C

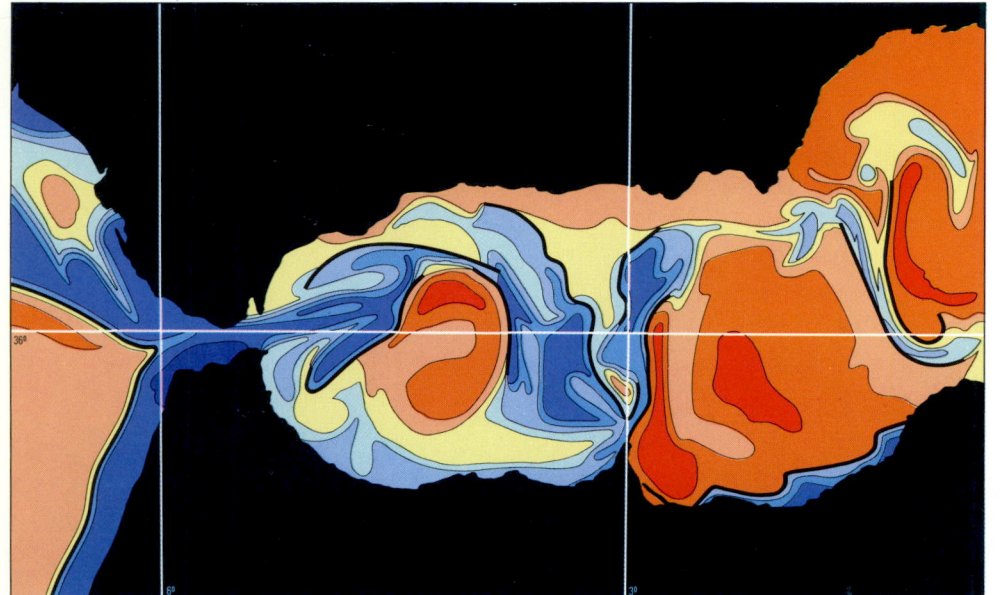

Eddies in the Mediterranean Sea. Infrared imaging from a meteorological satellite is used to construct this map of surface temperature variations. The image on the left is part of the Mediterranean Sea between Spain, the Straits of Gibraltar and Morocco. The currents through the Straits of Gibraltar form well defined layers, with return flows, and air currents in this region are diverted by the mountains. Because the sea surface temperature is a key parameter governing the exchange of heat from the water surface to the atmosphere, there are semi-permanent sea eddies associated with marked temperature differences. The Algerian coast and the western Mediterranean are susceptible to the formation of wind eddies, which make the weather seem unpredictable.

On a global scale, the interaction between the sea and atmosphere is important in determining the climate. International experiments such as the Tropical Ocean/Global Atmosphere (TOGA) programme seek to clarify the way in which heat fluxes originating in the equatorial oceans are organised. (NOAA, Washington).

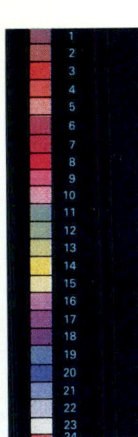

The colours 1 to 24 correspond to decreasing temperatures, from 60 degrees celsius (saturation of the signal) to less than 15 degrees celsius. The range of colours from 13 to 17 corresponds to temperatures from 25 degrees celsius to 21 degrees celsius.

The Meteor system. This Soviet meteorological system has been in operation since 1967. It was replaced in 1975 by an improved version with two or three Meteor II satellites in orbit round the Earth at about 900 kilometres altitude. During one revolution each satellite gathers information over one fifth of the globe. There are three ground stations, at Moscow, Novosibirsk and Khabarovsk, to receive and treat the satellite data. A third generation satellite, Meteor III, was launched in October 1985.

The photograph shows one of the receiving antennae at the Novosibirsk station (APN).

Mikhail Chernichov

Near polar orbiting meteorological satellites					
Satellite	Launch date	Weight (kg)	Perigee (km)	Apogee (km)	Orbital inclination (°)
United States					
TIROS 1	1 April 1960	119	796	867	48.3
TIROS 2	23 November 1960	126	717	837	48.5
TIROS 3	12 July 1961	129	854	937	47.8
TIROS 4	8 February 1962	129	817	972	48.3
TIROS 5	19 June 1962	130	680	1119	58.1
TIROS 6	18 September 1962	127	783	822	58.2
TIROS 7	19 June 1963	136	713	743	58.2
Nimbus 1	28 August 1963	376	422	932	98
TIROS 8	21 December 1963	118	696	878	58.5
Nimbus 2	15 May 1964	413	1100	1181	100
TIROS 9	22 January 1965	145	806	2967	96.4
TIROS 10	2 July 1965	145	848	957	98.6
ESSA 1	3 February 1966	145	800	965	97.9
ESSA 2	28 February 1966	131	1561	1639	101
ESSA 3	2 October 1966	159	1593	1709	101
ESSA 4	26 January 1967	131	1522	1656	102
ESSA 5	20 April 1967	159	1556	1635	101.9
ESSA 6	10 November 1967	131	1622	1713	102.1
ESSA 7	16 August 1968	159	1646	1691	101.7
ESSA 8	15 December 1968	131	1622	1682	101.8
ESSA 9	26 February 1969	159	1637	1730	101.9
Nimbus 3	14 April 1969	575	1070	1131	99
ITOS 1	23 January 1970	310	1648	1700	102
Nimbus 4	8 April 1970	675	1093	1107	107
NOAA 1	11 December 1970	310	1422	1472	101.9
NOAA 2	15 October 1972	340	1438	1458	99.8
Nimbus 5	11 December 1972	768	1089	1102	99
NOAA 3	6 November 1973	340	1502	1512	101.9
NOAA 4	15 November 1974	340	1447	1461	101.6
Nimbus 6	12 June 1975	827	1092	1104	99.9
NOAA 5	29 July 1976	340	1504	1518	102.1
TIROS N	13 October 1978	1418	849	864	102.3
Nimbus 7	24 October 1978	907	943	953	99
NOAA 6	27 June 1979	?	807.5	823	98.74
NOAA 7	23 June 1981	?	845	879	98.9
NOAA 8	28 April 1983	?	850	875	98.8
NOAA 9	12 December 1984	1030	810	875	99.1
NOAA 10	17 September 1986	1030	850	875	98.8
NOAA 11	24 September 1988	1030	850	875	98.9
China					
Fengyun 1	7 November 1988	?	881	904	99.1
Fengyun 2	September 1990	?	?	?	?
USSR					
30 Meteor I satellites from 1969 to 1978 with 3 or 4 launches per year					
Meteor II 01	11 July 1975	?	900	900	81
Meteor II 15	5 January 1987	?	950	973	82.5
Meteor II 16	18 August 1987	?	954	974	82.5
Meteor II 17	30 January 1988	?	947	973	82.5
Meteor II 18	28 February 1989	?	951	974	82.5
Meteor III 01	24 October 1985	?	1227	1251	82.6
Meteor III 02	26 July 1988	?	1198	1221	82.5

Geostationary satellites (period = 24 hours; apogee = perigee = 36 000 kilometres; inclination = 0°)			
Satellite	Launch date	Weight (kg)	Position
United States			
SMS 1	17 May 1974	627	75° W
SMS 2	6 February 1975	630	115° W
GOES 1	16 October 1975	293	90° W
GOES 2	16 June 1967	?	105° W
GOES 3	16 June 1968	?	replaced GOES 1
GOES 4	9 September 1980	?	135° W
GOES 5	22 May 1981	?	75° W
GOES 6	28 April 1983	834	107.9° W then 135° W
GOES 7	26 February 1987	834	75° W
Europe			
Meteosat 1	23 November 1977	720	0.73°
Meteosat 2	19 June 1981	720	0°
Meteosat 3	15 June 1988	720	0°
Meteosat 4	6 March 1989	720	0°
Meteosat 5	1990	?	
Japan			
GMS F1	14 July 1977	303	160° E
GMS F2	11 August 1981	296	120° E
GMS 3	3 August 1984	296	140° E
India			
Insat 1A	10 April 1982	580	74° E
Insat 1B	30 August 1983	580	74° E
Insat 1C	1 July 1988		
Insat 2	1990		

Source: J. Maclure, NOAA; Nasda, Paris, and BSI, Paris

235

Satellite applications

Remote sensing

Wise management of a nation's natural resources calls for a system to make surveys of resources such as air, water, fauna and flora, and the surface of the soil and subsoil. The system should survey and record changes in each of these resource types, whether the changes are of natural or man made origin. The aim is to detect, evaluate and predict changes, particularly those of a negative or dangerous nature. Examples here are soil erosion, floods, droughts and various kinds of pollution. In this way, changes of lifestyle, regional developments, and the impact of large projects such as the construction of dams or irrigation systems, mining, and communications networks, can be pursued without causing irreparable damage to the environment.

Information can be gathered by a number of conventional methods, such as terrain surveys using aerial photography and statistical studies of groundbased measurements. Such work is generally very costly to operate and is not being updated rapidly enough. Thus it is practically impossible to achieve a complete and homogenous survey of an entire country. Besides this, in some countries with a low population, remote areas are sometimes inaccessible to conventional methods of study.

Observation by satellite, or remote sensing, using aerial photography and measurements of the terrain, enables homogenous observations to be made over vast regions – several thousand square kilometres are covered in the same image. The whole Earth is accessible to satellite observations, regardless of the geography or climate of the region. New types of measurements can be repeated periodically, allowing changes to be identified. Data can be evaluated using computers, and geographically coded so that they may be compared with groundbased data.

The repetitive nature of satellite orbits increases the possibility of obtaining images unobscured by clouds, and of revealing changes in the environment. Since the orbits are often Sun synchronous, the images are obtained at the same local time so that, over a period of a few weeks, the angle of the Sun and the shadows remain the same. This makes it easier to identify changes. Computer technology is ideal for treating and analysing satellite data which can then be integrated with other categories of information.

Remote sensing satellites such as the US Landsat and the French SPOT satellite are used for topographic and geological mapping and mineral exploration. They provide useful data on agricultural resources which can be used for predicting harvests, evaluating forests and deserts, managing water resources and coastal regions, analysing environmental impact studies and evaluating the damage caused by natural disasters.

Gérard Brachet
and Jeffrey Maclure

Using satellites to observe fires. The photograph of western Siberia above was taken by the Soviet satellite Meteor. It covers the area to the south of the Tazonskoye peninsula, between the Gulfs of Obskaya and Tazonskoye. The plumes of smoke from fires are clearly visible. (APN).

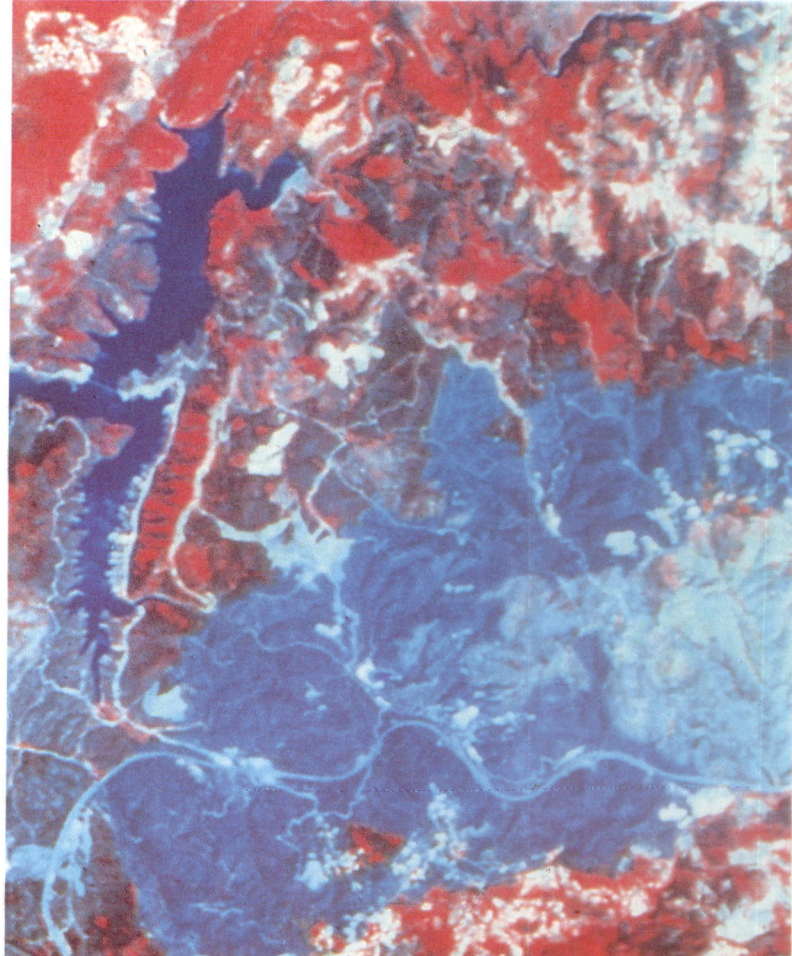

Satellite view of a forest fire. The image on the right, taken by SPOT 1, shows the devastation caused by forest fires in south east France in July 1986. It covers 8 by 10 kilometres of the Massif du Tanneron, which is about thirty kilometres north west of Cannes. Light blue represents regions destroyed in previous years. To the left of this, the mid-blue area is the region destroyed between 25 and 29 July 1986 by the fire which even crossed the autoroute. The dark-blue region on the left is an artificial lake, Saint-Cassien (CNES).

Landsat observations

Synoptic photographs of the Earth taken during early manned spaceflights, the growth in the use of high altitude multispectral imagery from aircraft, and the success of American meteorological satellite programmes in the 1960s combined to stimulate land remote sensing by satellite. In 1966, the Department of the Interior in the USA requested the National Aeronautics and Space Administration (NASA) to study the feasibility of developing and launching a polar-orbiting satellite to aid in Earth resource assessment and management. After four years of research, development and consultation, NASA completed the formulation of technical specifications for the first experimental Earth Resources Technology Satellite (ERTS 1). On 23 July 1972, ERTS 1, which was subsequently renamed Landsat 1, was launched to survey the Earth's land surface on a systematic, repetitive and continuing basis. Landsat 1 was followed on 22 January 1975 by Landsat 2. These two satellites were joined in Earth orbit by Landsat 3 on 5 March 1978.

Landsat 1 operated until 6 January 1978, and was considered a major success; although expected to function for one year, it had worked well for over five years. Landsat 2 ceased operating on 27 July 1983, more than one year after the launch of Landsat 4 on 16 July 1982. Technical difficulties with Landsat 4 led to an early launch of Landsat 5 on 1 March 1984. Landsat 3 subsequently was retired on 7 September 1983. The Landsat 4 and 5 satellites continue to provide a variety of useful data.

The Landsat system remained an experimental NASA programme until 1983. The system was then declared operational and its management was turned over to the National Oceanic and Atmospheric Administration (NOAA). The Land Remote-Sensing Commercialization Act of 1984 authorised a phased commercialisation, the first step of which was the Government contract awarded in 1985 to the Earth Observation Satellite Company (Eosat) for the day-to-day operation of the Landsat 4 and 5 system. Eosat will also commercially develop the inter-

national market for Landsat data products and services. Further, Eosat will deliver, operate and manage a follow-on Landsat 6 and 7 Earth observation system.

Technology

The Landsat system has both a space segment and a ground segment of operation. The space segment consists of the satellite platform, on board imaging instrumentation, initial data processing, and relay to ground receiving stations. The ground segment of the Landsat system is made up of activities dedicated to the control of the satellite, data reception at ground stations, and data and information processing, analysis and dissemination.

Landsats 1, 2 and 3 carried a MultiSpectral Scanner (MSS) sensor system which was capable of imaging at 80 metre resolution in four spectral bands. In addition to the MSS, Landsats 1 and 2 also utilised a 3 band, 80 metre resolution Return Beam Vidicon (RBV) sensor. Their capabilities were later enhanced on Landsat 3, with a 25 metre resolution panchromatic system.

Two changes in instrumentation payload accompanied a new spacecraft design in the transition to the Landsat 4 and 5 system. The first change in instrumentation involved the sensors and the type of data transmitted: both Landsat 4 and 5 continued to carry MSS sensors, but the RBV system was abandoned and replaced by the functionally advanced seven band, 30 metre resolution Thematic Mapper (TM). The second change involved the use of on board tape recorders. The Landsat 1, 2 and 3 series carried data tape recorders that were employed in instances when data for a region were desired, but the satellite was not in line-of-sight transmission range of an appropriately equipped ground receiving station. Data recorded would be stored in orbit until such time that ground reception facilities were available. By contrast, the Landsat 4 and 5 system

Example of geological (mineral exploration) applications of Landsat data. Above is a Landsat Thematic Mapper colour composite image (using bands 1, 4 and 7) of the Muscat region in the Sultanate of Oman. Spectral contrasts in the short wavelength infrared band sharply delineate a folded limestone terrain that plunges under massive dark ophitic rock. Volcanic units within the ophitic formations (appearing as lighter shades of grey-purple) contain sulphide deposits which may hold economically exploitable concentrations of copper, zinc and lead. The data are from a single quadrant of a Landsat scene collected on 28 January 1986. (Earth Observation Satellite Company, Eosat).

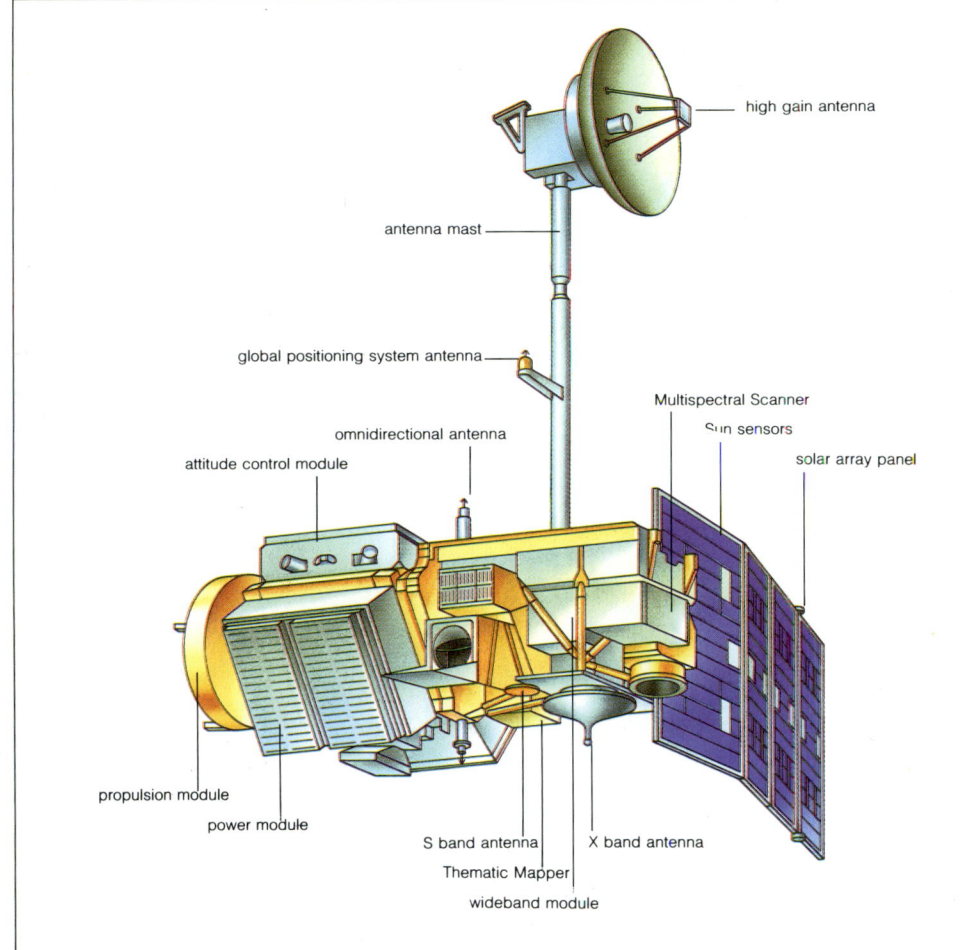

The Landsat 4 and 5 spacecraft. Their mass is 2 tonnes, length 4 metres, and width 2 metres; the high gain antenna diameter is 1·8 metres, and the antenna mast height 3·7 metres. The solar array, with an area of 13·6 square metres, generates 2 kilowatts of electrical power.

Example of land use and agricultural applications of Landsat data. Pictured is an image of the New Orleans, Louisiana, area in the United States. The data are a combination of Thematic Mapper bands 2, 4 and 5 from a single quadrant of a Landsat scene collected on 16 September 1982. The built up areas appear in shades of blue; agricultural areas are visible as polygonal shapes of green, yellow and orange. The structure of the wetlands to the southeast of the city is well defined (Earth Observations Satellite Company, Eosat).

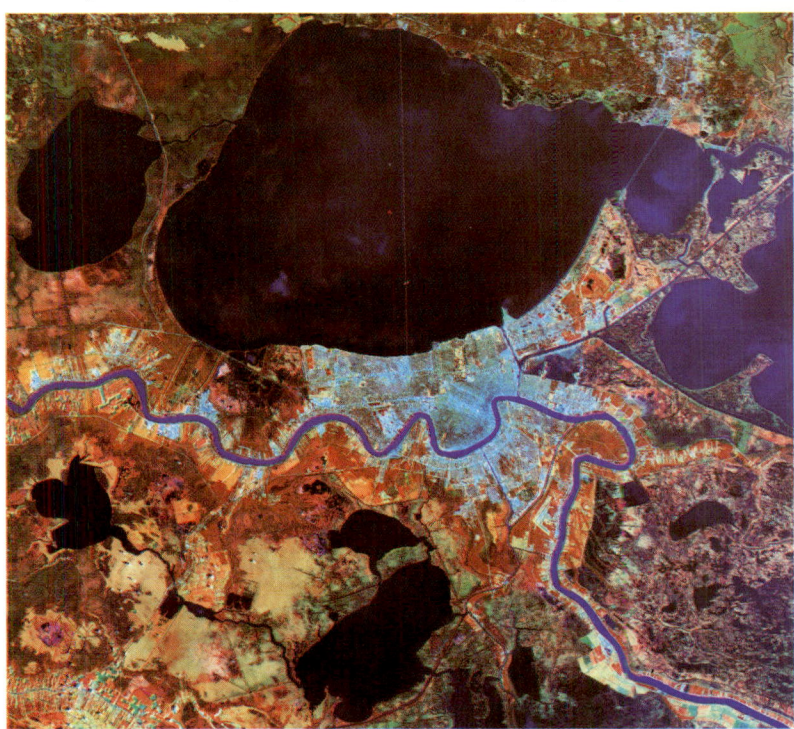

Comparison of Landsat Thematic Mapper (TM) and MultiSpectral Scanner (MSS) image characteristics. From Landsat data collected on 15 May 1984, enlarged images centred on the twin desert cities of Buraimi, Oman, and Al Ain, Abu Dhabi, are shown. The image on the left is a Thematic Mapper colour composite at 30 metres resolution using bands 2, 3 and 4. The image on the right is a MultiSpectral Scanner colour composite at 80 metres resolution using spectrally similar bands 1, 2 and 4 (Earth Observation Satellite Company, Eosat).

Comparison between the Landsat and SPOT systems
(after T. Pirard, Space Information Centre, January 1986)

Characteristics	Landsat		Satellite Pour l'Observation de la Terre (SPOT)	
Operator	Eosat Company (Lanham, Maryland, USA)		SPOT Image (Toulouse, France)	
Start	27 September 1985		April 1986	
Satellites/launch date (planned minimum lifetime)	Landsat 4/16 July 1982 (3 years) Landsat 5/1 March 1984 (3 years) Landsat 6 Landsat 7		SPOT 1/12 January 1986 (2 years) SPOT 2 SPOT 3 SPOT 4	
Orbit – altitude inclination Equatorial crossing time Orbit repeat cycle	700 kilometres 98.2 degrees 09.40 Local Time 16 days		832 kilometres 98.7 degrees 10.30 Local Time 26 days or 2.5 days	
Sensor swathe width	185 kilometres		117 kilometres or 2 at 60 kilometres	
Sensor type	Multi Spectral Scanner (MSS)	Thematic Mapper (TM)	High Resolution Visible multispectral	High Resolution Visible panchromatic
Spectral bands (wavelengths in micrometres)	0.5–0.6 0.6–0.7 0.7–0.8 0.8–1.1	0.45–0.52 0.52–0.60 0.63–0.69 0.76–0.90 1.55–1.75 10.40–12.50 2.08–2.35	0.50–0.59 0.61–0.68 0.79–0.89	0.51–0.73
Resolution	80 metres	30 metres	20 metres	10 metres
Ground segment status	MSS data only	MSS data and TM data	Operational	Planned
Data receiving stations in the following countries	Argentina Australia Indonesia Japan Spain (Canaries) South Africa Sweden	USA Brazil Canada China India Italy Pakistan Saudi Arabia Thailand	Brazil Canada France India Japan Pakistan Spain (Canaries) Sweden Thailand	Australia China Ecuador Indonesia Israel Saudi Arabia South Africa

Example of bathymetric applications of Landsat data. Landsat MultiSpectral Scanner data were collected over the Persian Gulf off the Abu Dhabi coast on 30 November 1972. The upper part is a standard colour composite of MultiSpectral Scanner bands 1, 2 and 4. In the lower part, data from the water area have been processed to map increasing water depths as colours trending from red to blue/black (Earth Observation Satellite Company, Eosat).

The French SPOT programme

was designed to fly without on board data tape recorders. Instead, these satellites could image remote regions and relay the data from orbit to a set of NASA geosynchronous communications satellites, called the Tracking and Data Relay Satellite System, and then to ground.

In a near polar, Sun synchronous orbit at an altitude of 705 kilometres, the Landsat 4 and 5 satellites circle and image the Earth in 185 kilometre wide swathes every 99 minutes. Each satellite makes 15 complete orbits in a 24 hour time period and images the entire Earth every 16 days. Resource and environmental data are collected, coded and transmitted to ground stations in the United States and around the world. Data downlinked from space are demodulated and recorded on magnetic tape in preparation for standard data processing into computer compatible tapes (CCTs) and photo imagery.

Applications

Earth observation from space has four significant advantages over other methods of resource inventory. First, satellites can monitor vast areas more quickly and more economically than can conventional ground survey or aerial photogrammetric techniques. Secondly, the repetitive orbital perspective increases the chances of cloud-free imagery and can reveal slowly changing or radically altered environmental conditions. Thirdly, orbits are Sun synchronous so that each scene is imaged at the same time (09.40 mean Local Time) everywhere: as a result, the Sun angle and ground shadow in the imagery remain nearly the same for several weeks which helps to detect, update and monitor changes in ground conditions. Finally, computer technology can be applied to the processing and analysis of the digital data.

Applications of Landsat data and information include agricultural inventories, monitoring and prediction of yields, forest and rangeland assessment, geological investigation and mineral exploration, urban and rural land use planning, water resources planning and management, coastal zone management, environmental analysis and impact assessment, and disaster warning and damage assessment.

The promise of technical improvements, such as new sensor instrumentation and modular, serviceable platforms in space, will intensify the important role of satellite remote sensing. The Landsat programme has pioneered the global technology of land remote sensing and, in concert with others in the international community, will continue to assist in the management of planet Earth.

Jeffrey Maclure

The origin of the SPOT programme

In the field of remote sensing, as in the area of rocket launchers, France was ahead of its partners in Europe. As early as in 1974 the Centre Spatial de Toulouse was planning an observational satellite. By December 1976, this project had advanced sufficiently for the CNES to propose to its partners in ESA that this should be carried out. Their reaction was very lukewarm, apart from Sweden which showed great interest, because of the cloudiness of the European skies. France therefore decided to make the project a national one, and, in 1977, embarked on the high resolution, multispectral Satellite Pour l'Observation de la Terre (SPOT) project with the participation of those European states who wanted to invest in this technology. Sweden and Belgium each contributed 4% of the cost of the programme. SPOT itself was successfully launched on 22 February 1986.

All Earth observation satellites require a special orbit. This type of space mission imposes a large number of constraints on the choice of the optimum orbit.

In the first instance, the orbit is chosen to be circular, at a constant height above the Earth's surface. This ensures that all images possess the same characteristics, regardless of the region being observed. In reality, there will be small height differences, because the Earth is not spherical. (The Earth's radius is more than 20 kilometres larger at the equator than at the poles).

Secondly, in order for the satellite to be capable of taking photographs of the whole Earth, the orbit must also be near polar. The Earth rotates inside this orbit and the satellite is able to cover the whole world in a certain period of time. An observational cycle period is created by arranging for the satellite to complete a certain number of orbits in the same time that the Earth completes a different number of rotations. Thus SPOT, orbiting at an altitude of 832 kilometres at the equator, completes 14 + 5/26 revolutions per day. The observational cycle is therefore 26 days or, more precisely, 26 Earth rotations.

For SPOT, the maximum distance between the tracks is 108 kilometres (at the equator), and the total field of view, with both cameras angled vertically downwards, is 117 kilometres. The field of view is slightly wider than the track width, to prevent any part of the Earth's surface being missed during the satellite's observational cycle. Every 26 days, the whole of the Earth's surface has been photographed.

Another requirement is that the orbit plane makes a constant angle with the Sun, so that observations of a given point, taken on different dates, can be compared. It is only possible to make detailed comparisons of images if the light conditions are very similar. To achieve this the images must be taken at approximately the same local time, and so the satellite is also

The first pictures of Paris taken by SPOT. The upper picture taken on 10 March 1986 is a multiband picture centred on the city of Paris and extending some 30 kilometres east and west, that is from Nogent-sur-Marne to Nanterre. The centre of Paris, dotted with red marks, corresponding to open green spaces – the Bois de Boulogne on the left and the Bois de Vincennes on the right are easily identifiable. The southern region, particularly the region of Meudon and Saint-Cloud, is rich in such open spaces. In the north the most important green area corresponds to the cemetery of Aubervilliers.

The lower picture is a panchromatic image taken simultaneously but with the spatial resolution increased to 10 metres. This example of 2·5 by 5 kilometres covers the west of Paris, from the Bois de Boulogne to the Jardin des Tuileries and from the Parc Monceau to the Champ de Mars. The urban part which stands out is on the right bank of the Seine. The Champs Elysées is clearly visible and, from the Etoile to the Bois de Boulogne, the most striking road, because of its exceptional width, is that of the Avenue Foch. At the bottom of the image the dark shadow of the Eiffel tower can be seen crossing the Seine (CNES).

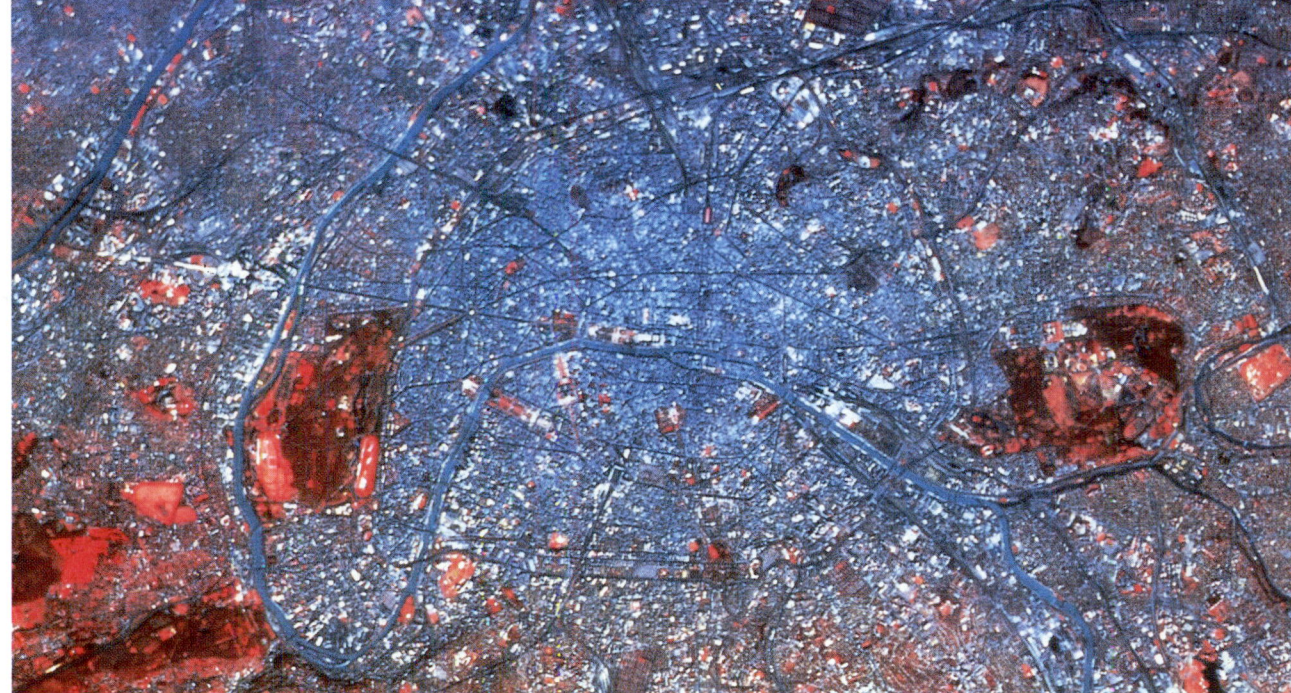

Living with space

placed in a Sun synchronous orbit. Since SPOT orbits at an altitude of 832 kilometres, Sun synchronism is achieved by inclining the orbital plane at 98·7 degrees to the equatorial plane.

As part of its cycle, the satellite passes over the equator, from north to south, at 10.30 Local Time on 15 June, every year. The time that the satellite passes over a given region is kept within 15 minutes of its nominal time, regardless of the length of the year. The satellite remains within 5 kilometres of its original tracks. The entrance mirrors to SPOT's High Resolution Visible (HRV) cameras can be angled up to 27 degrees off the vertical, with respect to the orbital plane. There are two reasons for doing this. First, important areas can be photographed more frequently at the expense of less interesting regions. Secondly, three dimensional images can be built up. In reality, this means that any region lying within a 950 kilometres wide corridor centred on the satellite's track can be photographed.

SPOT's telescopes are 2·5 metres long and weigh 250 kilograms. They have a resolution of 10 metres. Once light enters the optical system, it contributes to the image. In other words, 'filming' takes place.

One of two things happens to the data gathered by the satellite. If the satellite is 'visible' to a ground receiving station, data are transmitted directly to it. If the satellite is not visible to such a reception station, then the information is stored on magnetic tape to be transmitted to one of the European stations (at Toulouse in France and Kiruna in Sweden) as soon as they come into sight. Data transmission, at 8 gigahertz, takes place while the satellite is within the 'visibility circle' of a receiving station. This circle has a radius of about 2500 kilometres, corresponding to the satellite being at an angle of 5 degrees above the horizon. On the Earth, space image reception stations (SRIS) pick up the telemetry signal from the satellite, demodulate it and record it.

SPOT's platform contains all the instruments of the control subsystem which are vital to the success of the mission. This keeps the satellite in its correct orbit, stabilising it about three axes. It also manages the telemetry system and programmes the payload, using an on-board computer, whose memory is accessed by remote control from the ground.

The Sun synchronous, circular orbit of Earth observation satellites places certain constraints on the subsystems which operate the payload. For example, the electrical subsystem has to operate throughout the rapidly changing pattern of day and night of the orbit – 65 minutes of day followed by 35 minutes of night. The satellite has batteries to provide enough power for the satellite to keep operating during its night period. During the day period, the batteries are recharged by equipment which supplies electricity to the other instruments. The precision of the satellite's stabilising system determines the quality of the images produced. The stabilising gyroscope mechanism has to ensure that any rotational movements are less than a thousandth of a degree per second. The position of the Sun and of Earth's horizon are also measured. Sensors detect transitions between space, which is cold, and the warm Earth to adjust the satellite's attitude about its axes of roll and pitch. A computer analysing these data calculates the true attitude and angular velocity of the satellite. It then calculates the corrections required to the satellite's orbit. Larger orbital corrections are made with small hydrazine booster jets.

Marketing SPOT images

While detailed plans were being drawn up in the late 1970s for the SPOT satellite, market studies were commissioned, paying particular attention to cartographic applications and to the American market. They confirmed that the programme was financially viable, bearing in mind the small market for other Earth observation satellite (Landsat) data. They concluded that it was vital to have clear a policy on the services available from SPOT. It was decided to have a single group responsible for marketing and distributing the images. That group would have sole responsibility for dealing with users, taking charge of all legal, technical and economic aspects of data distribution.

As a result of market studies, a policy group proposed that image distribution should be carried out on a strictly commercial basis, and not subsidised at all. Image distribution and marketing is therefore carried out by a special body, Spot Image, created in 1982.

The French government has confirmed that it intends to continue with the SPOT programme, by putting four SPOT satellites in all into orbit by the end of the century.

The latest satellite, Spot 4, will belong to a new generation of satellites with a longer operational life-time (5 years), improved performance and better filming capabilities with its high resolution visible and infrared (HRVIR) instrument.

Gérard Brachet

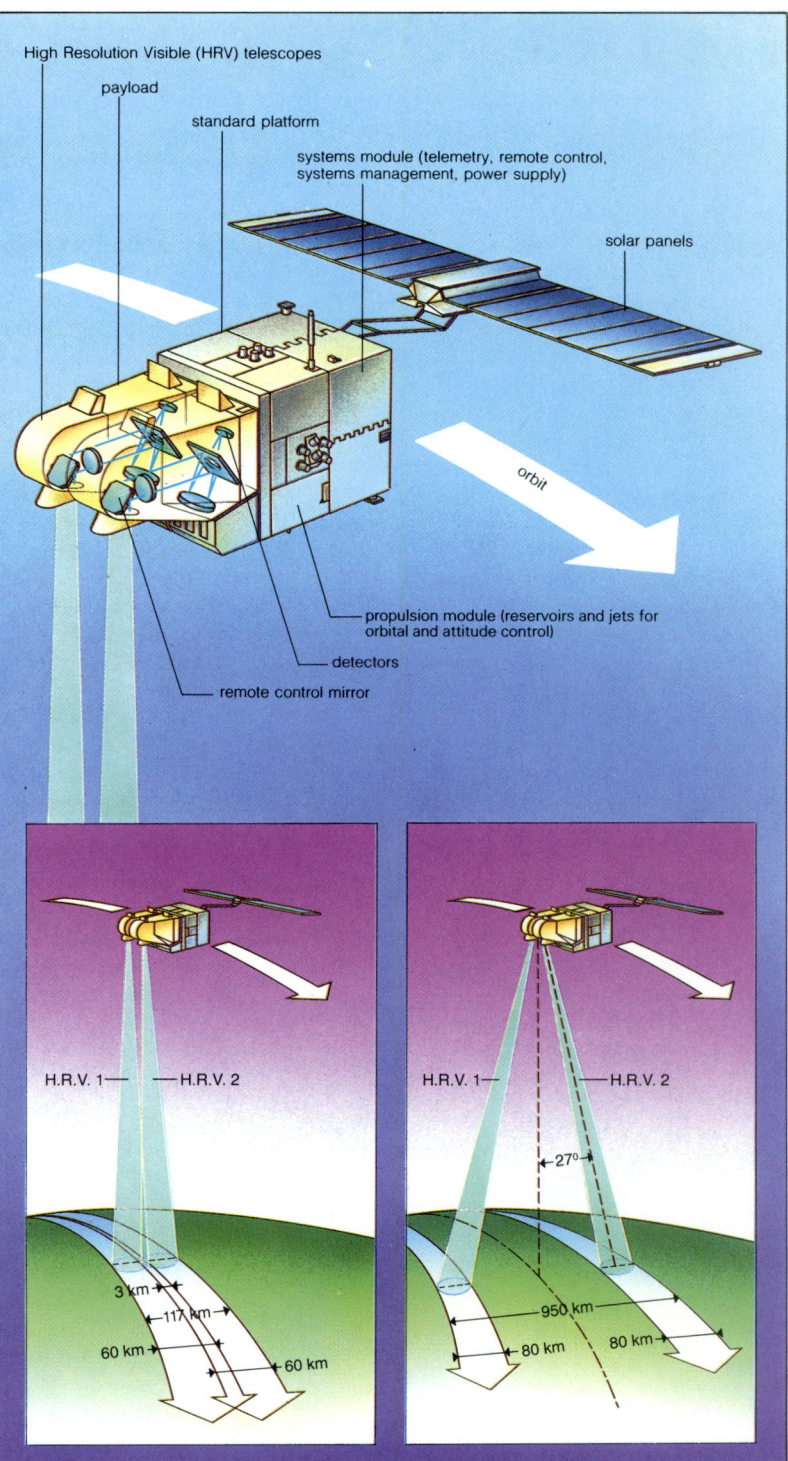

The Spot system. The payload on board the SPOT satellite consists of two identical High Resolution Visible (HRV) instruments and several devices which record data onto magnetic tape or transmit them directly to the Earth. Each instrument covers a width of 60 kilometres on the ground vertically below the satellite. When both HRV instruments point downwards, the total field of view is 117 kilometres wide, as there is a 3 kilometre overlap of the individual fields of view. They have a resolution of 10 to 20 metres, and can produce topographic maps at a scale of 1:100 000, with the desired geometric precision, and thematic maps on a scale of 1:25 000.

The satellite takes measurements in four wavelength bands, split into two spectral modes:
– The XS multiband mode consists of three wavelength bands – green (0·5 to 0·59 microns), red (0·61 to 0·68 microns) and the near infrared (0·79 to 0·89 microns). They cover the spectral response of chlorophyll, which peaks in the green, and also has a response to near infrared, radiation which is not visible to the human eye.
– The panchromatic (P) mode takes measurements in the wavelength band from 0·51 to 0·73 microns, with 10 metres resolution on the ground. It is used to obtain geometrically sharp images.

The width of the area observed by the instruments varies between 60 kilometres in the nadir and 80 kilometres when they are angled at 27 degrees to the vertical. A sequence of 'filming' can include a succession of panchromatic or multiband modes, and changes to the viewing angle of each instrument.

A region on the equator can be imaged 9 times during the 26 day orbit repetition cycle, or 126 times per year. At a latitude of 45 degrees, the same region can be observed 12 times during one observational cycle, with an interval of from 1 to 4 days between observations, or 176 times per year. This short time is very useful for studying rapidly changing phenomena, such as crop ripening. Also it increases the possibility of acquiring high quality images of regions which often have cloud cover, for example the tropics. Images taken at different angles are used to build up three dimensional pictures. These can be combined with the high quality panchromatic images to produce excellent maps.

The HRV telescopes consist of a line of six thousand tiny photodiodes (each 13 by 13 microns) at the focus of the instrument. These convert the light signal into an electrical one. Each detector analyses an element, of length 10 metres, say, along the field of view. Light from this sample enters the detector during the time that it takes the satellite to travel 10 metres (1·3 milliseconds). The signal is amplified and then digitised.

The amount of data passing through the satellite is very large. For a resolution of 10 metres it is 2·4 million bits per second. The satellite can transmit on the two channels simultaneously, choosing between two panchromatic and two multiband channels – there are six possible combinations.

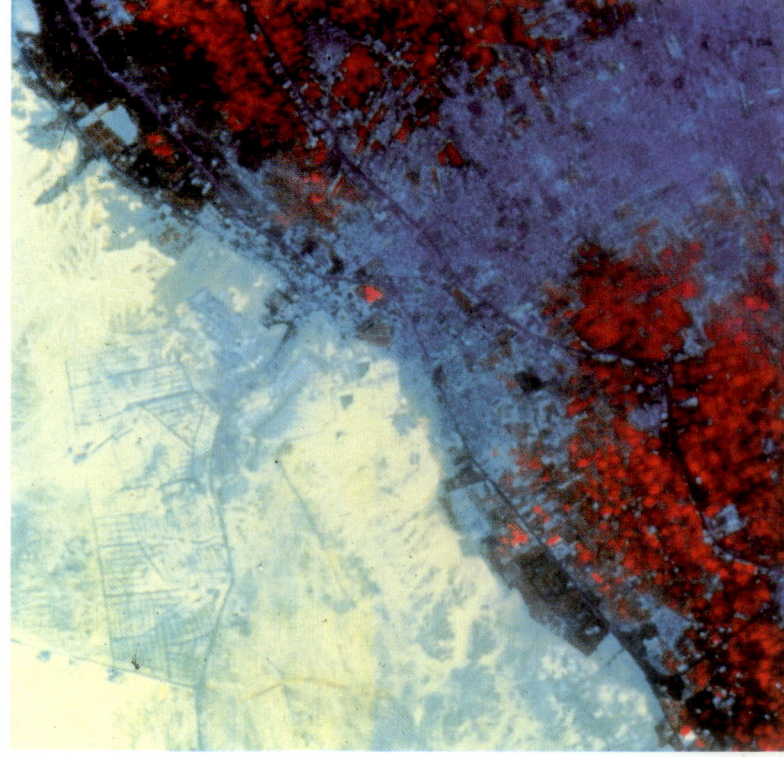

Cairo and the pyramids. This SPOT image covers an area of 10 by 10 kilometres at the head of the Nile delta. Cairo is the bluish area on the right of the picture, and the plateaux of the Libyan desert stretch away to the west. To the south-west of the city are the three pyramids at Giza – Khufu, Kephren and Menkaure. To the west of the pyramids, the geometrical pattern on the desert was caused by archaeological excavations (CNES).

Johannesburg (South Africa). The uppermost picture is of an agricultural zone (10 by 10 kilometres) near Johannesburg. There is a marked contrast between the arid regions and the red, circular, irrigated regions (CNES).

The Nakuru region. The multiband SPOT image (in the middle) is an enlargement of a region in Kenya, in the Great African Rift Valley. The rift valley is sandwiched between escarpments which tower 800 to 1000 metres above it. On the western escarpment, the forested areas are shown in bright red. They are being cut down and the land is being used for agricultural purposes. Areas of the forest which have been cultivated are shown in pink amongst the bright red forested areas. Continuing deforestation is likely to cause a severe lack of fuel in the future (CNES).

The petroleum terminal on Kharg Island. The photograph on the left is an enlargement of an image made on 21 March 1986 of the terminal on Kharg Island (Iran). This 5 by 5 kilometre zone is essential to the economy of Iran. Some of the storage tanks appear to have been hit by Iraqi bombs, and a tanker on the left of the picture appears to have run aground. This photograph illustrates both the possibilities and the limitations of using Earth observation satellites to observe strategically important sites. It is easy to detect the large scale structure, but much higher resolution is necessary to pick out the detail of these buildings (CNES).

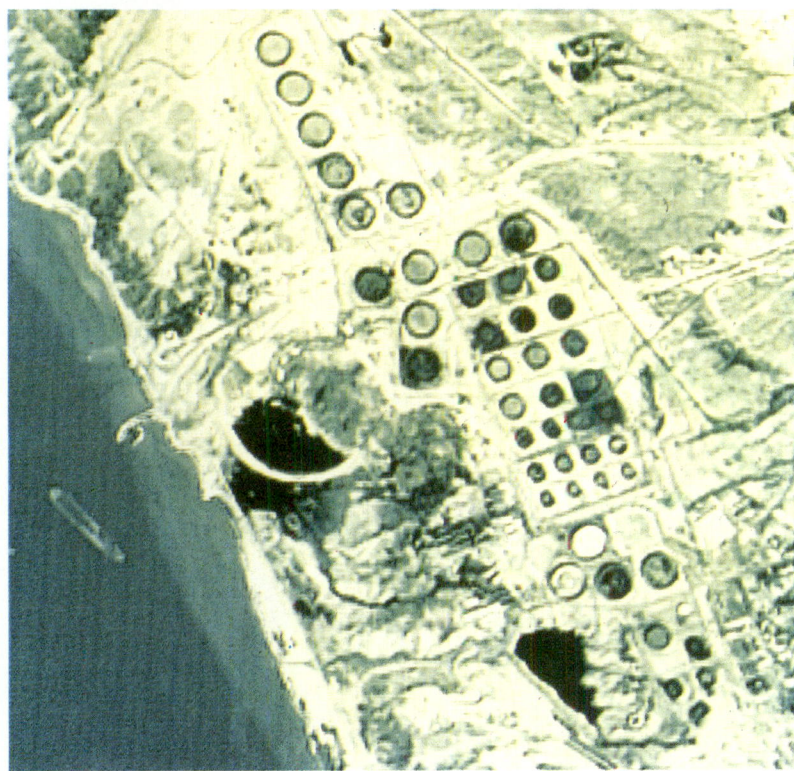

Oceanography

Remote sensing in oceanography was pioneered in studies of the Gulf Stream by an airborne bolometer, sensitive to infrared radiation in the range between 8 and 13 micrometres. The edge of the Gulf Stream and its meandering mesoscale features were detected. This investigation led the way to rapid sea surface temperature mapping, using airborne radiation thermometers over large ocean areas.

The launch of the meteorological satellite TIROS 2 on 23 November 1960, equipped with infrared radiometers, opened up routine mapping of sea surface temperatures, on a global scale, in regions not heavily covered by clouds. The sensors on these operational weather satellites, being designed to study the atmosphere, mean that oceanographic observations such as sea surface temperature and ice conditions are by-products.

Sensors dedicated to studies of the ocean have been flown on aircraft and in experimental satellites, such as the Nimbus series of satellites. The first dedicated ocean satellite, Seasat, was launched on 26 June 1978. Unfortunately, the lifetime of this satellite was only 100 days, while Nimbus 7, launched in October 1978, was operational for 8 years. In spite of its short life time, Seasat demonstrated that active and passive microwave sensors can operate independently of the weather conditions and during both night and day. The wind velocity, ocean surface and internal waves, major current systems, ocean eddies, frontal boundaries and ice can all be studied. In the 1990s several ocean satellites are planned. The use of such satellite systems coupled with *in situ* oceanographic investigations, as well as numerical modelling in research and operational modes, is a demanding challenge for the world's scientific marine communities.

Principles

Remote sensing utilises electromagnetic radiation classified by its frequency in cycles per second (or hertz) or, equivalently, by its wavelength. Although the electromagnetic spectrum spans over 24 orders of magnitude, remote sensing is restricted to using the nine orders of magnitude from 10^6 to 10^{15} hertz, going from radio waves to ultraviolet light. The emission or the reflection of electromagnetic radiation from the ocean surface allows remote sensing sensors to derive properties of the sea or ice surfaces, such as temperature and roughness.

Surface temperature. Sea surface temperature is established from measurements made in two radiation bands, from 3 to 4 and 10 to 12 micrometres, where the atmospheric absorption is small. When proper atmospheric corrections during cloud free conditions have been carried out, the sea surface temperature at 1 kilometre resolution can be estimated absolutely to within 1 degree, while relative differences of a tenth of a degree can be detected.

At the longest wavelengths in the microwave band, the atmosphere has little effect, causing radiation from the sea surface to be dominant. For example, the Scanning Multichannel Microwave Radiometer (SMMR) on the Nimbus 7 and Seasat records at wavelengths of 0·81, 1·4, 2·8 and 4·6 centimetres; the major contribution from the sea surface is in the 4·6 centimetres region. The sea surface temperature can be retrieved to an absolute accuracy of one degree kelvin on a global scale.

The disadvantage of this technique is that the receiving antennae at these wavelengths have poor spatial resolution, about 150 kilometres. Furthermore, no information is obtained within 300 kilometres of the coast, due to the effects of land in the sidelobe patterns of the antenna.

Surface and internal waves. The two prime sensors for measuring surface waves and swells are the radar altimeter and the Synthetic Aperture Radar (SAR). These active sensors transmit short radar pulses toward the Earth and receive the signal reflected from the surface. Significant wave height, defined as the height of the highest one third of the waves, can be derived from the shape of the reflected signal from the altimeter with an accuracy of about 20 centimetres. Using Seasat data, global pictures of significant wave height and ocean swell height can be calculated.

Currents. The height from the altimeter to the ocean surface is found by measuring the travel time of the radar pulse from the sensor to the surface and back. Seasat measurement indicated an accuracy of 10 centimetres. Coupled with precise orbital information, obtained by tracking the satellite, about 50 centimetres for Seasat, global information about ocean current systems can be derived. The height of the ocean surface is greater on the outside curves of its motions.

Ice. Several passive and active sensors can be used to give information about the ice edge position, ice concentration, type and floe size distribution. Meteorological satellites give visible and infrared information, on a 1 kilometre scale, of the ice edge position. Remote sensing satellites such as SPOT give photographic information with a resolution as good as 10 metres, allowing the ice floe distribution to be studied. The limitation of these sensors is that they require cloud-free conditions, which occur infrequently at the outer edges of the polar ice. However, all weather passive microwave radiometers, for example the Scanning Multichannel Microwave Radiometer (SMMR) on Nimbus 7, has been used to estimate ice concentrations to an accuracy of better than 5%. The microwave emission from first year (1 metre thick) ice and from hard multiyear ice (3 to 4 metres thick) is different, allowing estimates of the fraction of multiyear ice to be made to 15%. During the melting season, wet snow becomes the important emitter, making discrimination of the ice type difficult. The spatial resolution is again poor, of the order of 25 to 50 kilometres.

The SAR offers high resolution observations of ice edge position, ice concentration, ice type discrimination and ice floe distributions. In addition, promising studies are underway to allow the SAR to be used for ice type discrimination during the difficult melt season. This is based on texture and roughness, with the first year ice being smoother than the rougher multiyear ice.

Applications and future prospects

Remote sensing from aircraft and satellites has demonstrated that oceanographic and meteorological variables can effectively be retrieved on a global scale. Such results have importance for weather and climate, offshore operations, aquaculture, ship routing and defence. The emitted or reflected radiation from the coastal and ocean areas only give information about the surface. Such observations must be complemented by subsurface measurements made from buoys and ships.

The linking of remote sensing results to geophysical models is very important. The physical condition of large systems such as the ocean and atmosphere can only be described effectively with mathematical models. Today such models are the basis for global operational weather and wave forecasting, for storm surge prediction and ice forecasting. Furthermore, model simulations can be very useful when planning large field experiments. They are

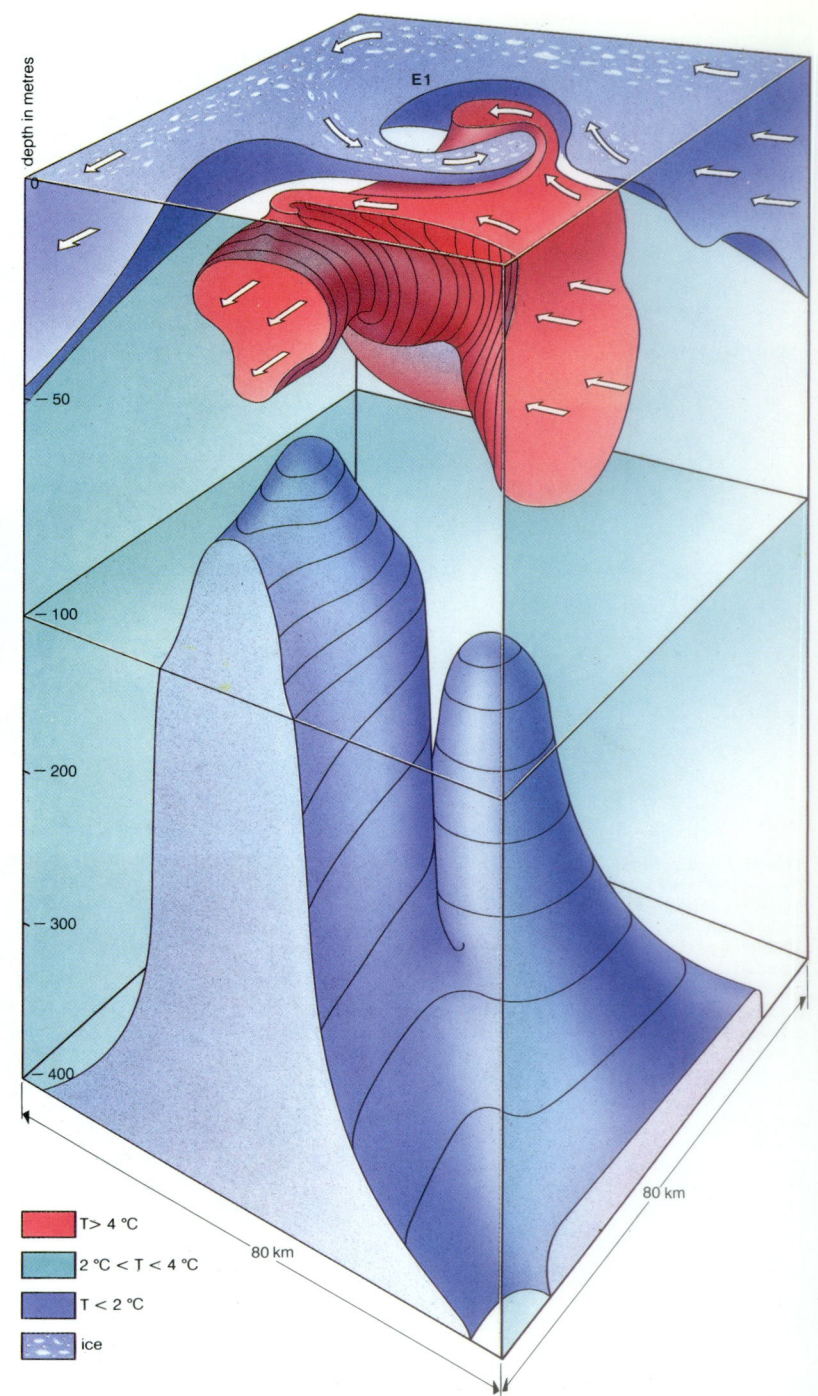

depth in metres

E1

— 50

— 100

— 200

— 300

— 400

80 km

80 km

■ T > 4 °C

■ 2 °C < T < 4 °C

■ T < 2 °C

░ ice

0   10 km

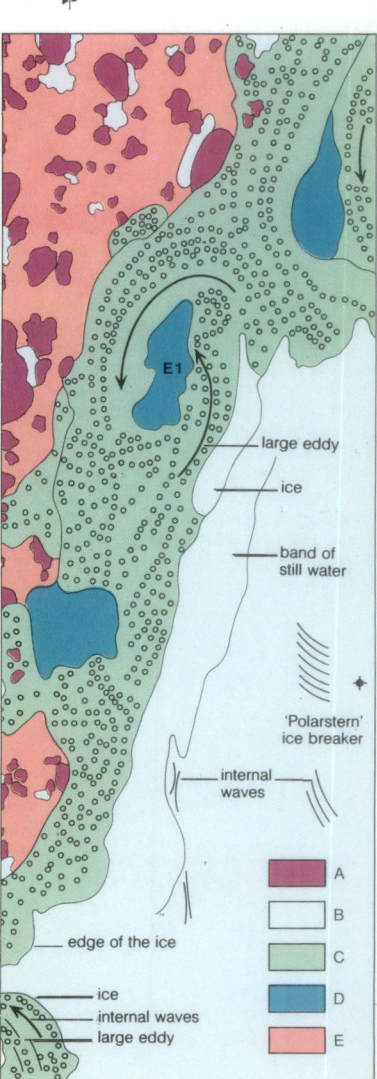

E1

large eddy

ice

band of still water

'Polarstern' ice breaker

internal waves

edge of the ice

ice

internal waves

large eddy

■ A

□ B

■ C

■ D

■ E

necessary for analyses after the experiment. To initialise and verify models, remote sensing data sets are essential, in particular from regions with sparse observations such as the polar regions. The large amount of remote sensing observations can best be used if combined with computer models.

The world oceanographic community will enter the space age in the 1990s. Several ocean satellites will be launched equipped with all weather, day and night, passive and active microwave sensors. The international scientific community is, with NASA and ESA as lead agencies, planning future experiments on the next generation of polar orbiters, a component of the space station. These offer the opportunity for space shuttle servicing. Such an observing programme is needed to identify man made changes in a naturally varying system.

Ola M. Johannessen

Other Earth observation programmes

Quite a few other countries and agencies are developing their own Earth observation or remote sensing systems. In 1982, members of the European Space Agency approved plans for the construction of ERS 1 (the first ESA Remote Sensing Satellite) which is primarily concerned with studying coastal regions and collecting meteorological data from all over the globe. The satellite is due to be launched in 1990. Another satellite belonging to the same series, ERS 2, should be launched later in the 1990s. It will carry a scatterometer to measure wind speeds and directions, and a radar altimeter to measure significant ocean wave heights and to collect data on ocean currents. It will also carry a Synthetic Aperture Radar (SAR) to build up images of the ocean surfaces and a scanning radiometer to measure the sea surface temperature. This satellite will use the same platform as the SPOT programme.

The National Space Development Agency (NASDA) of Japan has its own Earth observation programme. On 18 February 1987 an N2 launcher was used to put the experimental Maritime Observation Satellite (MOS) into orbit. It has several radiometers, including the

Multispectrum Electronic Self Scanning Radiometer (MESSR), the Visible and Thermal Infrared Radiometer (VTIR) and the Microwave Scanning Radiometer (MSR).

India launched an experimental Earth observation satellite, Bhaskara 1, in 1979, and is currently developing a programme of Earth observation satellites, the first of which, IRS 1A, was launched by the Soviets in 1988. Canada is developing an all weather radar satellite, to help exploit natural resources. It should be launched in the 1990s.

In the Soviet Union, there is an overlap between civil and military missions. Earth observation is carried out from the Salyut stations and the Cosmos series of satellites. The Cosmos satellite launched on 25 July 1987 was the biggest remote sensing satellite (more than 15 tonnes) ever to be placed in orbit. Some satellites of the Meteor II series are equipped with multispectral cameras adapted for remote sensing. Since July 1987 the Soviet Union has been selling its remote sensing data through its intermediary, Soyuzcarta.

Gérard Brachet

The Marginal Ice Zone Experiment. To the left is shown the three dimensional distribution of ocean temperature obtained by combining remote sensing observations of an ice-ocean eddy off Greenland. The subsurface data were obtained by two research vessels over a 4 day period in July 1984. The blue colour in the upper layer represents the polar water with temperature less than 2 degrees celsius, while the red colour is Atlantic water with a temperature above 4 degrees celsius. Ice is shown by the white spots, while the blue colour at depths below 100 metres represents water with a temperature below 2 degrees celsius. The mean movement of the ice and water, indicated by arrows, shows the westward drift in the northern domain, and the sudden cyclonic turn southward at the edge of the East Greenland Current. Significant dome structures appear beneath the surface layer, indicating that the vertical depth of the eddies exceeds 500 metres. The abundance of eddies along the ice edge enhances melting by up to 2 kilometres per day.

The black and white picture below is a mosaic image collected by the Environmental Research Institute of Michigan (ERIM) and the Canadian Center of Remote Sensing (CCRS) L band (1·2 GHz) SAR system on 5 July 1984. On the radar image, bright zones represent ice while the dark zones are ice-free water. The large eddy (E1) is clearly visible on the data with 3 metre resolution. The interpretation (lower right) of the SAR mosaic reveals that large individual floes (A), polynyas and ice-free ocean areas (B), areas with 30% ice concentration, and 10 to 500 metre floes (C), areas with 80% ice concentration and up to 6 kilometre floes (E) are clearly delineated in the image. The average floe sizes for areas C, D and E are 125 metres, 150 metres and 1 kilometre, respectively. The dots in area C indicate increased local ice concentrations due to surface currents (O. M. Johannessen).

Characteristics of the MOS and ERS systems

Characteristics	MOS system			ERS system		
Country or agency Satellite (launch date)	Japan[1] MOS 1 (19 February 1987)			ESA ERS 1 (1991) ERS 2 (1993)		
Orbit: altitude inclination local time repeat cycle across the equator	908 kilometres 99.1 degrees 10.00 to 11.00 17 days			777 kilometres 98.52 degrees 10.15 15 1/3 days or every 3 days[2]		
Type of radiometer	MESSR	VTIR	MSR	AMI	radar altimeter	ATSR
Width of area scanned	100 to 185 km	1500 km	317 km	80 km[3] 5 km[4] 500 km[5]	1 to 20 m	500 km
Spectral bands	0.51 to 0.59 microns 0.61 to 0.69 microns 0.73 to 0.80 microns 0.80 to 1.10 microns	0.5 to 0.7 microns 6.0 to 7.0 microns 10.5 to 11.5 microns 11.5 to 12.5 microns	23.8 GHz 31.4 GHz	5.3 GHz 5.3 GHz 5.3 GHz	13.5 GHz	3.7 microns 11 microns 12 microns
Resolution	50 m	900 m (visible) 2700 m (IR)	23 to 32 km	30 m	50 km	10 cm to 40 cm	1 km

MOS: Maritime Observation Satellite; ERS: ESA Remote Sensing Satellite; MESSR: Multispectrum Electronic Self Scanning Radiometer; VTIR: Visible and Thermal Infrared Radiometer; MSR: Microwave Scanning Radiometer; AMI: Active Microwave Instrument; ATSR: Along Track Scanning Radiometer.

1 Japan is also developing an Earth Resources Satellite, which will be launched in 1992
2 ERS can view at an oblique angle, increasing the number of times that important areas can be filmed, at the expense of less important areas
3 Synthetic Aperture Radar (SAR)   4 Waves   5 Winds

Photograph of the first Indian Earth observation satellite (IRS 1). This photograph of the Indian Remote Sensing satellite was taken before simulation trials, at Intespace, Toulouse in February 1987. IRS 1 weighs 950 kilograms and will be launched by the Soviet Union into a Sun synchronous polar orbit at an altitude of 904 kilometres. The satellite will take photographs in the visible and the near infrared, with a resolution of 30 metres. India is planning to use the satellite to help evaluate its natural resources and to map previously uncharted land. Prior to IRS 1, the Indian Space Research Organisation (ISRO) launched two experimental satellites, Bhaskara 1 and 2.

Satellite applications

Telecommunications

Telstar. Developed by the American Telephone & Telegraph Company, Telstar made history in August 1962 with the first transatlantic live television transmissions. Spherical in shape, only 90 centimetres in diameter and with most of its surface covered in solar cells, Telstar was injected into an elliptical orbit inclined at 45 degrees to the equatorial plane. With an orbital period of 157 minutes and an apogee of 5640 kilometres, it was possible to communicate via Telstar for about twenty minutes at a time between Pleumeur Bodou in France, Goonhilly Downs in England and Andover, Maine in the USA, where large steerable antennae had been built (Telefocus, British Telecom).

History

The idea of using satellites as microwave radio relay stations was first expounded in 1945 by Arthur C. Clarke, a member of the British Interplanetary Society then serving in the Royal Air Force. Some twelve years were to elapse before the first Sputnik was placed in orbit and seventeen years before he saw the practical realisation of his concept. This was the Telstar satellite, a commercial venture and, at that time, the most recent episode in a long and exciting history of telecommunications going back to the introduction of the electric telegraph by Cooke and Wheatstone in 1837. This was followed by the signal codes of Morse and the invention of the telephone by Alexander Graham Bell in 1876.

It was during this period that Maxwell deduced that electrical disturbances could produce effects at a distance. He predicted that electromagnetic energy would travel in the form of waves at the speed of light. In 1887, by means of induction coils and spark gaps, Hertz produced secondary sparks some 1·5 metres away from the source, thereby confirming one aspect of Maxwell's theory. No one, however, saw any practical application until the end of the century when Marconi began a series of experiments and demonstrations which were to lead not only to the development of wireless telegraphy but also to the establishment of the first company in history to design, produce and sell radio apparatus on a commercial basis. Fleming's investigations of one way current effects between electrodes in a vacuum and De Forest's invention of the triode amplifier led to a succession of thermionic valves and electronic tubes. These greatly accelerated the development of radio and telecommunications between the two World Wars. The invention of the transistor and the remarkable developments in solid state electronics since that time bring us to the point where radio receivers and transmitters are now able to operate routinely in space some 36 000 kilometres above the earth's surface and for years on end.

As well as combining communications with astronautics, Clarke's main achievement was his proposal to use artificial satellites in a particular stable orbit where they would appear to be stationary above the Earth. He proposed to communicate with them at frequencies greater than 50 megahertz. At this time there was no direct evidence that radio waves could travel from Earth to outer space, and return. All that was known with certainty was that shorter wavelengths were not reflected back to the Earth by the ionosphere, and herein lies an interesting distinction between the ideas of Clarke and Marconi. The basis of Marconi's work rested initially on his intuition, and later on the knowledge, that radio waves could be propagated over the horizon and half way round the world by refraction or reflection. Clarke relied on the proposition that high frequency radio waves would in fact penetrate the ionosphere in both directions.

Satellites as radio relay stations in space

Until the middle 1960s, long distance transoceanic telecommunications were limited to high frequency (HF) radio services of poor quality and variable reliability. There were only a few point-to-point submarine telephone cables of relatively low capacity. Overland it was a different story. Chains of microwave line-of-sight links were used for long distance backbone routes across countries and continents. Such systems have considerable potential because radio waves at these frequencies can be focused into narrow beams with parabolic reflectors, thereby conserving transmitter power. At the same time, these reduce the risk of interference with other communications systems. They also have a considerably greater capacity to carry information because a much larger bandwidth is available at these high frequencies.

At 4 gigahertz, for example, several thousand voice circuits and one or two television channels can be accommodated. This is a physical

Communications satellites in geostationary orbit. With the help of a long time exposure, Paul Maley of the Rockwell Shuttle Operations Company obtained this photograph of seven American domestic communications satellites in geostationary orbit. Taken from Brazos Bend near Houston in Texas, USA, towards the end of 1985, the picture shows the reflected sunlight from the seven satellites as white dots, with the stars appearing as white lines due to the movement of the Earth with respect to the stellar background during the course of the exposure.

From left to right, the satellites and their positions (given in degrees East longitude), all within an 8 degree arc of the geostationary orbit, are as follows: A. Galaxy 3 Hughes Aircraft Company 266·7°; B. SBS 3 Satellite Business Systems 265·2°; C. Telstar 3A American Telephone & Telegraph 264·2°; D. SBS 2 Satellite Business Systems 263·2°; E. Westar 4 Western Union & Hughes 261·2°; F. SBS 1 Satellite Business Systems 261·1°; G. SBS 4 Satellite Business Systems 259·2°.

The advantages of geostationary communications satellites are such that this unique orbit is in danger of overcrowding. Congestion is not uniform over the entire orbit because certain positions are more suitable for satellites providing services to individual countries, continents or between continents. The most crowded parts are, therefore, from 50 to 90 degrees East longitude over the Indian Ocean, from 0 to 35 degrees West longitude over the Atlantic Ocean, and from 85 to 135 degrees West longitude over the North American continent.

Radio interference between satellites has so far been avoided by the International Telecommunications Union (ITU). This regulates both the position and the operating frequencies of every satellite either operating in geostationary orbit or planning to use this orbit (P. D. Maley).

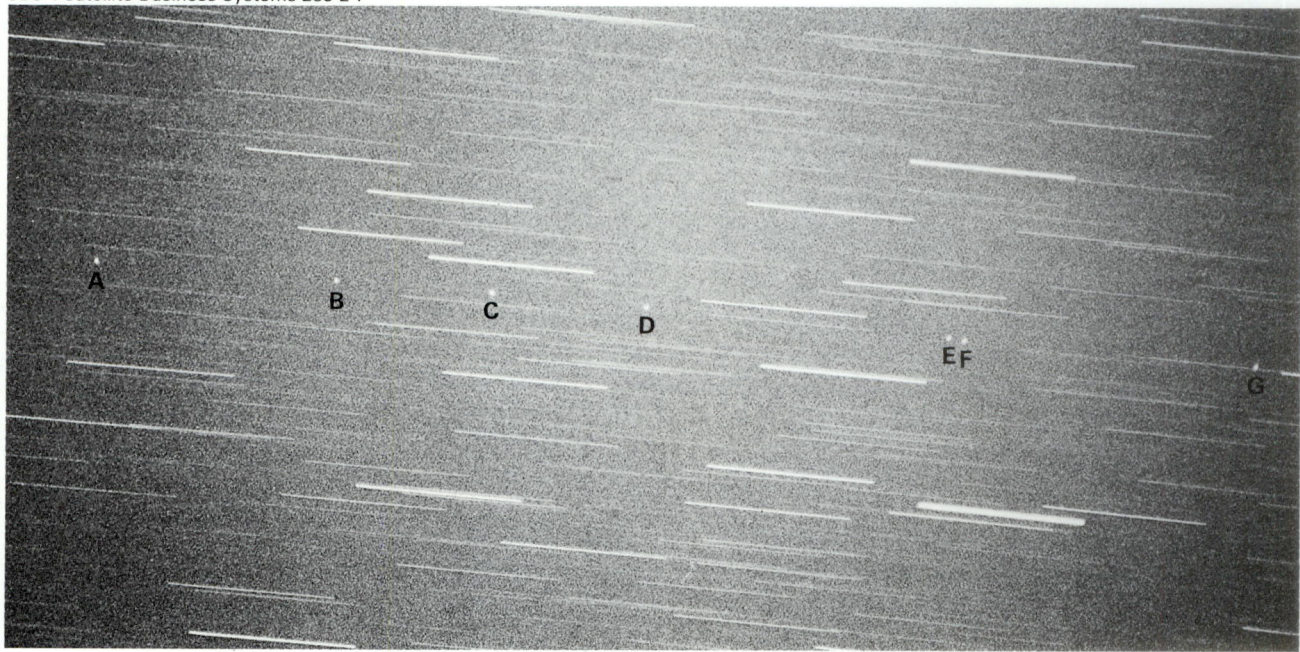

impossibility with HF radio systems. The main disadvantage is the fact that, having formed the radio waves into a narrow beam (rather like that of a searchlight), the receiving end of the link must be within sight of the transmitter. Consequently aerials have to be mounted at intervals of 50 to 100 kilometres on tall buildings or towers to overcome the effect of the curvature of the Earth. This restricts their use to overland routes or, occasionally, across short stretches of water. These limitations disappeared virtually overnight with the advent of geostationary satellites. In effect such satellites raised the height of the tower so that only one relay station was needed, for example, to link Europe and North America, or Africa and the Far East.

Early developments in the USA

As early as 1951 the United States Army used the Moon, a natural satellite, as a passive reflector for communications experiments. It also launched the first man made object to transmit human voice signals from space. This was Project SCORE (Signal Communication by Orbiting Radio Equipment), an Atlas missile stripped of all unnecessary equipment but carrying a special radio transmitter and tape recorder. The complete vehicle was injected into orbit in December 1958. It broadcast prerecorded messages including a Christmas greeting from President Dwight D. Eisenhower. Two years later, the Army launched its Courier repeater satellite into low Earth orbit at a height of about 1000 kilometres. This was used to record telex, facsimile and voice messages transmitted from the ground when the satellite was in view in readiness for transmission back to Earth when interrogated later by other ground stations.

The next significant conceptual step in the direction of practical satellite communications

was taken in 1955 when John R. Pierce first suggested the use of unmanned satellites for space telecommunications. His analysis ranged from passive reflectors, including balloons, to active radio transponders in low, intermediate and geosynchronous orbits. The idea of using balloons in space for communications purposes had also occurred to other people, but it was Pierce who drew these ideas together and pursued the concept with NASA. His reward came in May 1960 with the launching of Echo, an inflatable aluminised plastic balloon, some 30 metres in diameter, into a near circular low Earth orbit. There it was used for many years for passive communications experiments. The success of these experiments focused attention on the potential of space communications. In turn this led to increased activity by industry, government departments and communicators on both sides of the Atlantic, with particular attention being paid to systems of satellites in low orbit.

In the United States the American Telephone & Telegraph Company developed Telstar as a private venture, while NASA supported the development of Project Relay. Both satellites were designed as active repeaters in low Earth orbit to test the feasibility of transatlantic telecommunications via broadband microwave radio equipment in space. Solar cells on the body of the satellite were used as the primary source of electrical power. The immediate technical success of Telstar and the commercial attributes of Relay added realism to the many contemporary proposals for low altitude multi-satellite systems intended to provide worldwide broadband communications networks.

None of these materialised, however, because in parallel with the development of Telstar and Relay, H. Rosen and colleagues at the Hughes Aircraft Company had decided that satellites in geostationary orbit were the only practical longterm solution. Starting with

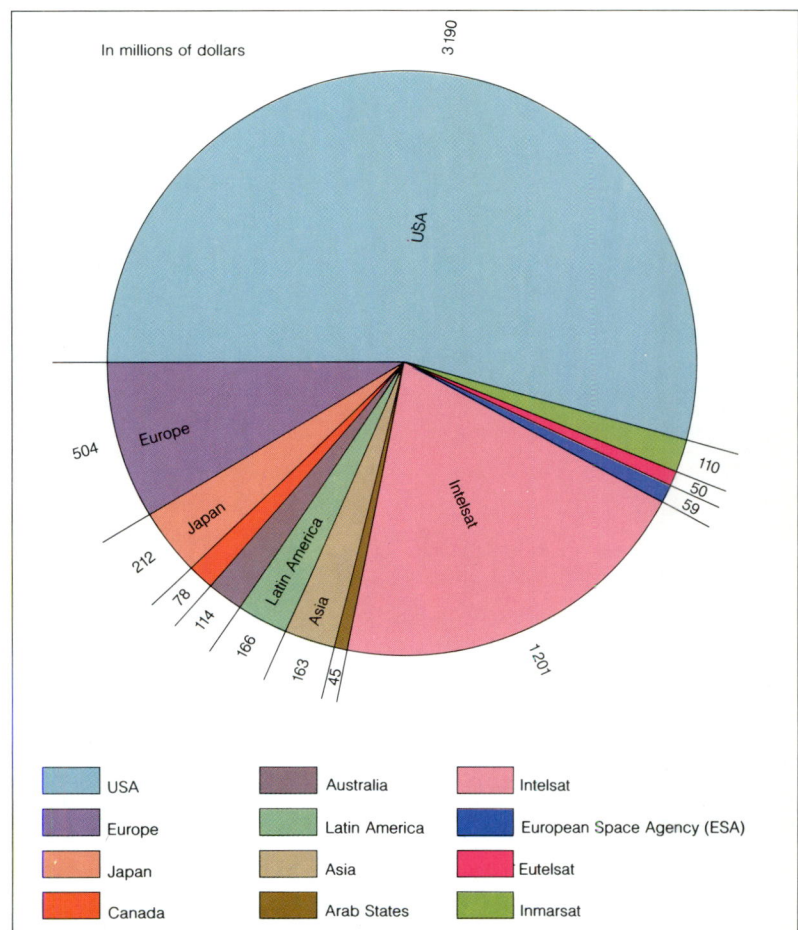

The space telecommunications market: estimates for 1985–1989. The chart (top right) shows a 1985 projection of market shares.

The table (bottom right) shows the market share of the major Western consortia (Eurospace, Paris 1988).

Commercial satellite market (5.075 million US dollars in 1986)		Satellite (number)
Hughes Aircraft (USA)	1.155	ATT (3), Westar (4), Galaxy (3), SBS (5), Aussat (3), Satmex (2), Anik C (3), Palapa (3)
Ford Aerospace (USA)	1.131	Intelsat V (15), Insat (4), CS 2 (2)
Radio Corporation of America, taken over by General Electric in 1986 (USA)	1.097	Satcom Ku (3), Satcom C (6), G Star (4), Spacenet (4), Panamsat (1), Astra (1), STC (2), ASC Amsat (2)
MBB Erno (West Germany)	0.426	DFS (3), TV Sat (2)
British Aerospace (GB)	0.378	ECS (5), Marecs (3)
Aérospatiale (France)	0.287	TDF (2), Arabsat (3)
Matra (France)	0.271	Télécom 1 (3)
Spar Aerospace Ltd. (Canada)	0..246	Anik D (2), SBTS (2)
General Electric (USA)	0.084	BS 2 (2)

The civil telecommunications satellite industry. Civil telecommunications satellites form a major part of the commercial sector of the space industry. In this diagram, the areas of the squares represent the shares of satellite launches between 1980 and 1986, while interconnecting lines represent cooperation agreements between different companies. The hexagonal shapes represent different satellites and the circles different consortia. This diagram includes only satellites made jointly by two or more companies; it does not include satellites built by a single company.

American industry controls nearly three quarters of the international satellite market (*Espace mondial 1986,* Euroconsult).

André Lebeau

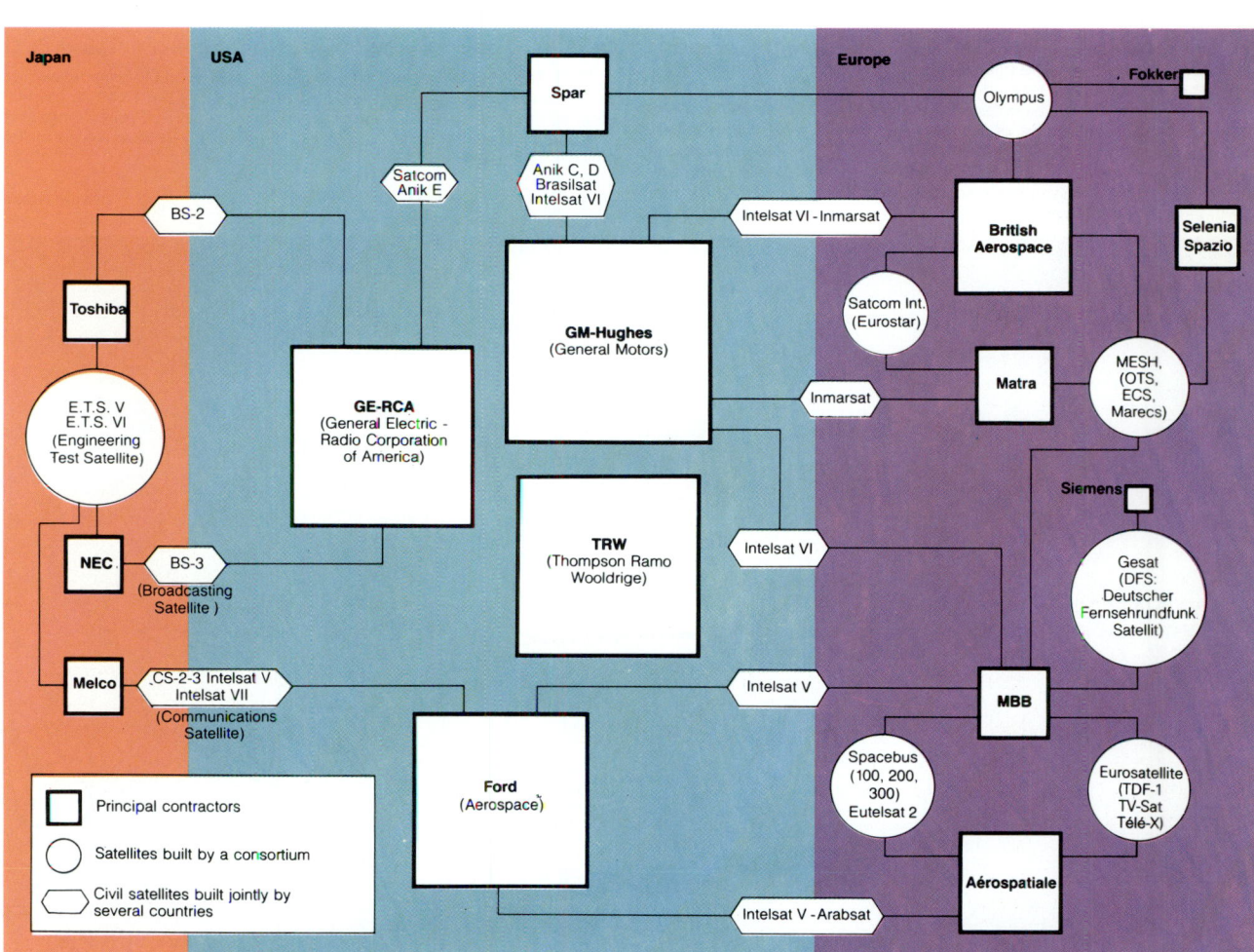

The telecommunications centre at Fucino, Italy. Incongruous as it may seem, there is both an historic and a scientific connection between the prominent objects in this photograph. These modern dishes are satellite communications and control antennas operated by the Italian Space Communications Centre at Fucino, near Rome, for organisations such as ESA, Inmarsat and Intelsat. The older structure in the foreground is the stern part of the celebrated steam yacht *Elettra* from which G. Marconi conducted many of his wireless experiments in the early part of the twentieth century.

It is the transmission of radio waves that is the common link – it is at the heart of all space communications, and the person most commonly associated with the invention of radio and its subsequent development is Marconi. He began experimenting with spark gap transmitters as early as

1894. These experiments led, in due course, to a system of radiotelegraphy which he demonstrated initially at close range and later over increasingly longer distances. In 1896 he moved to England where, with the help of his cousin J. Davis, he formed the Wireless Telegraph and Signal Company. By the turn of the century, Marconi had established wireless communications across the Channel to France over a distance of about fifty kilometres. His most sensational achievements were the historic wireless telegraphy messages across the Atlantic Ocean from England to Newfoundland in 1901, to Brazil in 1910 and then, much later, in 1918, half way round the world to Australia. During this period, and as a direct result of his work, many commercial and government wireless stations were established throughout the world (Telespazio).

The Symphonie programme. The first European telecommunications satellite programme was the military Skynet programme in Great Britain. The first civil programme was a joint venture between France and West Germany. The design, development and construction of the satellites was carried out by a consortium of German and French industries, namely Messerschmitt Bölkow Blohm (MBB), Siemens and AEG-Telefunken, and Aérospatiale, Thomson-CSF and Société anonyme des télécommunications (SAT). The first Symphonie satellite was launched on 19 December 1974, using an American Thor-Delta rocket from the Kennedy Space

Centre. The second Symphonie satellite was launched on 27 August 1975.

In 1977, Symphonie 1 was positioned above the Indian Ocean to allow the Indian Space Research Organisation (ISRO) to carry out tests as foundations for their own satellite telecommunications system. Some companies involved in the construction of Symphonie went on to be involved in the Intelsat V programme (CNES).

Alain Dupas

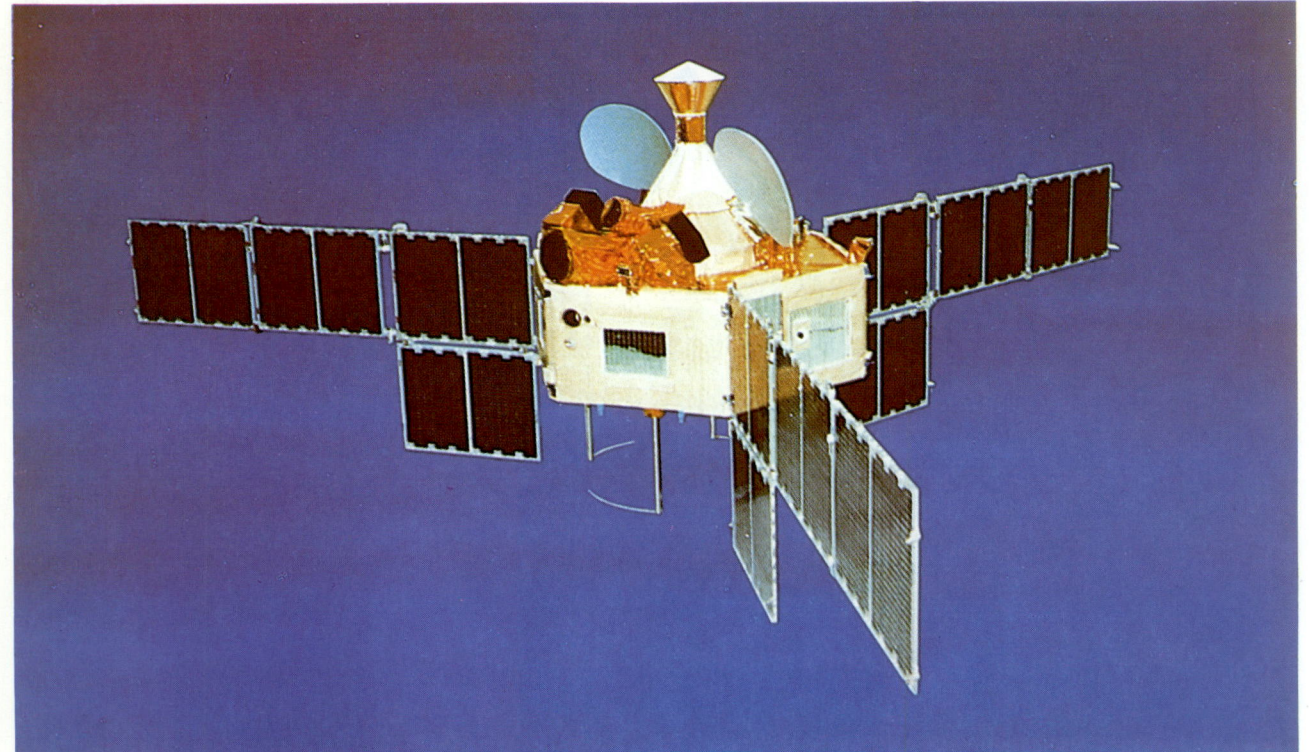

private funds and then through a NASA programme, they developed a satellite called Syncom which could be placed in a 24 hour orbit by available launch vehicles. This was achieved by reducing the weight to less than half that of Telstar or Relay, by incorporating an extra rocket stage within the satellite itself, and by adopting the compromise of an orbit inclined to the equator whilst retaining the 24 hour, geosynchronous, period.

In this way a Thor-Delta rocket could be used to place the satellite in a highly elliptical orbit with apogee at synchronous altitude. After separation, and when the satellite was at apogee, the internal motor could be fired to circularise the orbit. Thus Syncom 1 was launched in February 1963 into a 33 degree inclined orbit, although radio contact was lost soon after it attained the desired position. Syncom 2, launched into a similar 28 degree geosynchronous orbit in June of that year was immediately successful. However, because of its orbital inclination, it appeared, from the ground, to move in a daily figure of eight pattern. Syncom 3, the last of the series, was injected into a more nearly equatorial orbit. It was used during the opening ceremonies of the Tokyo Olympic Games for live television transmissions. This design concept proved to be so successful that it became the basis for a whole family of international and domestic communications satellites.

European developments and the European Space Agency

A number of European countries in the early 1960s were involved in space research. However, the projects were mostly unrelated and only indirectly concerned with satellite communications. A pattern of cooperation did emerge at this time, however, largely because of common membership of the European Launcher Development Organisation (ELDO), the European Space Research Organisation (ESRO) and CETS, the European Conference on Satellite Communications. By 1966 these organisations had joined the European Space Conference as the forum for determining space policy and institutional structures. It was ten years before the Conference, in April 1975, formally adopted the Convention which finally established the European Space Agency as a legal entity. Funded studies of regional communication satellite systems were first conducted by ESRO in conjunction with industry in 1968. Their purpose was to meet European needs as defined by the Conference of European Postal and Telecommunications Administrations (CEPT) and the European Broadcasting Union (EBU).

It became evident by 1970 that advanced technologies would be needed if the European system were to be competitive with contemporary terrestrial networks. Thus, in order to make up for lost time, ESRO embarked on a 'Support Technology Programme' to develop transponders to operate at frequencies greater than 10 gigahertz. ESRO also aimed to develop digital telephony and time division multiple access techniques, spot beam antennae, and the critical elements of three-axis satellite stabilisation and orbital control systems. In parallel, a group of interested member states subscribed in 1972 to an optional telecommunications programme starting with an Orbital Test Satellite (OTS). This was a forerunner of the European Communications Satellite (ECS) and a commercial European regional system. The fruits of this programme can be seen in satellites now being used by both the European Telecommunications Satellite Organisation Eutelsat and the International Maritime Satellite Organisation Inmarsat in their operational systems.

Molniya satellite orbits and the USSR

Domestic requirements for communications at high northern latitudes, for which satellites in geostationary orbit were originally considered to be unsuitable, largely influenced the development of communication satellites in the Soviet Union. Additional satellites in polar orbits would have provided full global cover but spacecraft in highly inclined and highly eccentric orbits offered a more elegant solution. Satellites in 12 hour, 63 degree inclined orbits, with perigee at about 500 kilometres and apogee at about 40 000 kilometres, for instance, appear to linger for several hours at a time over a large part of the Earth's surface while they move slowly towards and away from apogee. Conversely, only a few hours will elapse as they pass rapidly through perigee on the other side of the world. Hence, it is not surprising that the USSR, with its vast territory extending northwards from mid latitudes to Arctic regions and straddling all of Asia and half of Europe, was the pioneer in the development of communications satellites for this particular orbit. Molniya 1, launched in April 1965 with three-axis stabilisation, Sun pointing solar cell arrays and steerable Earth pointing antennae, was the first operational satellite of this kind. Within two days of this 1600 kilogram satellite being placed in orbit, black and white television programmes were transmitted from Moscow to Vladivostok, an achievement which was followed six months later by experimental colour television transmissions between Moscow and Paris.

International satellite systems and organisations

The commercial potential of satellite communications was recognised at an early stage in the United States. Backed by a national policy which stressed technological leadership and the sharing of benefits with other nations, NASA was able to advance the state of the art very rapidly by placing research and development contracts with industry. Its role in seeking international cooperation in communications experiments via US satellites undoubtedly brought the realisation of global communication satellite systems one step nearer. The next step was the creation in 1962 of the US Communications Satellite Corporation, Comsat. Its purpose was to establish a global communications satellite system, preferably in cooperation with other countries. In Europe, where the general level of satellite technology was, at that time, far below that of the United States, the pace was much slower and opinions were divided. Some saw commercial advantages in joining a Comsat system, others sought to maintain traditional worldwide links through a predominantly European satellite network. Discussions with the United States during 1962, however, concentrated attention on international ownership and highlighted the need for a common European approach. Many bilateral and multilateral discussions then ensued. These eventually led to eleven countries signing intergovernmental agreements in August 1964 setting up an Interim Communications Satellite Committee, Intelsat, to procure a communications satellite system which could be shared by all nations and of which the space segment would be jointly owned by the signatories. The agreements also made provision for establishing a permanent organisation. This would reflect the maturing technological developments in other parts of the world as well as the experience gained in the operation of the interim system. This objective was achieved in 1973 when definitive arrangements entered into force following several years of negotiations between active and potential members. During the intervening period, Intelsat had become the dominant carrier for international telecommunications. It carried two thirds of all overseas telephone and data communications and almost all live transoceanic television transmissions.

From the outset, Intelsat has consistently sponsored the development of satellite communications technology. It has commissioned

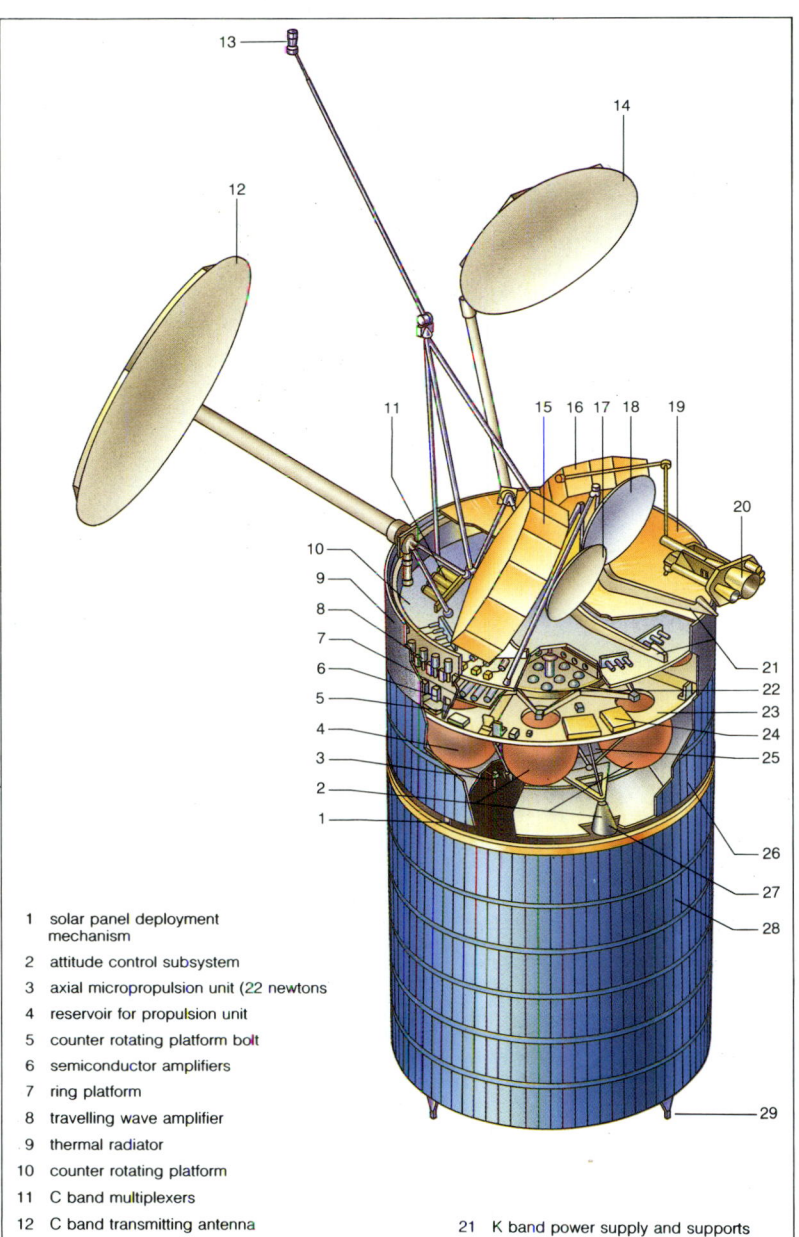

1	solar panel deployment mechanism
2	attitude control subsystem
3	axial micropropulsion unit (22 newtons
4	reservoir for propulsion unit
5	counter rotating platform bolt
6	semiconductor amplifiers
7	ring platform
8	travelling wave amplifier
9	thermal radiator
10	counter rotating platform
11	C band multiplexers
12	C band transmitting antenna
13	telemetry and command omnidirectional antenna
14	receiving antenna
15	power supply for C band transmitter
16	power supply for C band receiver
17	K band narrow beam (east) antenna
18	K band narrow beam (west) antenna
19	heat shield
20	communication and telemetry horn antennae
21	K band power supply and supports
22	batteries
23	electronic system platform
24	digital electronic circuits
25	central tube
26	forward solar panels
27	apogee propulsion unit (489 newtons)
28	rear solar panels
29	solar panels bolt

The Intelsat VI satellite. All Intelsat satellites, except for the Intelsat V series, have been spin stabilised. All have been powered by solar cells and all have operated in the geostationary orbit.

Intelsat I, otherwise known as Earlybird, was a 40 kilogram satellite launched from Cape Kennedy by NASA in April 1965. It had a capacity equivalent to 240 voice circuits for point-to-point communications between large antennae. Also, to make best use of the limited power available, its antenna covered the northern hemisphere only. Intelsat II, a bigger satellite with more than twice the power, provided the same capacity in both hemispheres and with multipoint operations over both the Pacific and Atlantic Oceans. With its mechanical de-spun Earth-pointing antenna, Intelsat III provided a significant increase in capacity, together with improved multiple access. The third flight model, brought into service over the Indian Ocean in July 1969, finally realised the pioneers' dreams of a global communications satellite service. The next step was Intelsat IV, with spot beams to concentrate the radiated power over land areas rather than the sea. Intelsat IVA extended this concept and doubled the capacity by dual polarisation and frequency re-use techniques.

Breaking with tradition, Intelsat V is a modular three-axis stabilised satellite, with deployable solar cell panels to face the Sun. It has fully steerable spot beam antennae with dual polarisation and frequency re-use, together with additional transponders operating at 11 and 14 gigahertz. Some flight models carry maritime communication subsystems which are leased to Inmarsat. The new Intelsat VI satellites will be the largest commercial satellites ever to be built. They have multibeam antennae, automatic station keeping, and time division multiple access switching of circuits in the satellite.

The decision to use geostationary satellites for commercial purposes was taken soon after the formation of the Interim Intelsat Organisation in 1964. This was a far reaching decision, considered by many at the time to be a technical and economic risk. In the event, however, the concept of a few satellites with relatively simple ground stations proved to be an enduring one, resulting in the rapid growth of both the number of members and satellite capacity. Membership now stands at 110. The number of countries served, either directly or indirectly, is over 150, having grown from 15 in 1965 to 100 in 1973 at the time of the definitive Intelsat agreements. The corresponding number of communications paths between Earth stations has also grown, from only one in 1965 to about 300 in 1973 and to more than 1700 in 1985 (AMRT).

The Olympus satellite. This is the first of a new generation of multipurpose, high power geostationary satellites developed by the European Space Agency. The initial emphasis is on communications services ranging from high density trunk telephony, to business, data and mobile communications, and radio and television broadcasting. ESA has defined the primary objectives for the Olympus spacecraft. First it is to be a platform that can exploit the full potential of a three-axis stabilised spacecraft. Second, it is a means of providing direct broadcast services to European nations. Third, it is a test vehicle for new communications services in the 11 to 14 and 20 to 30 gigahertz frequency bands.

Similar to the ESA Orbital Test Satellite (OTS) concept which was a forerunner of ECS, Marecs and Skynet IV (a British military satellite), Olympus 1, which was launched in July 1989, is in effect a pre-operational satellite. Potential users can carry out operational tests in orbit prior to proceeding with production models to meet their specific requirements. Modular construction ensures flexibility. There are, for example, three antenna panels, two equipment panels, a propulsion module, a service module and steerable flexible solar cell arrays which can be partially deployed and Sun oriented in the transfer orbit.

Olympus in its current configuration has a mass of 2·3 tonnes in transfer orbit and a solar array power of 2·9 kilowatts. It has two independently steerable spot beams for high power communications at 20 or 30 gigahertz, and a steerable group of five spot beams for space switched, time division multiple access to small ground terminals. It also has a television broadcast payload with a fixed spot beam for use by Italy and a steerable spot beam for European Broadcast Union pilot services (British Aerospace).

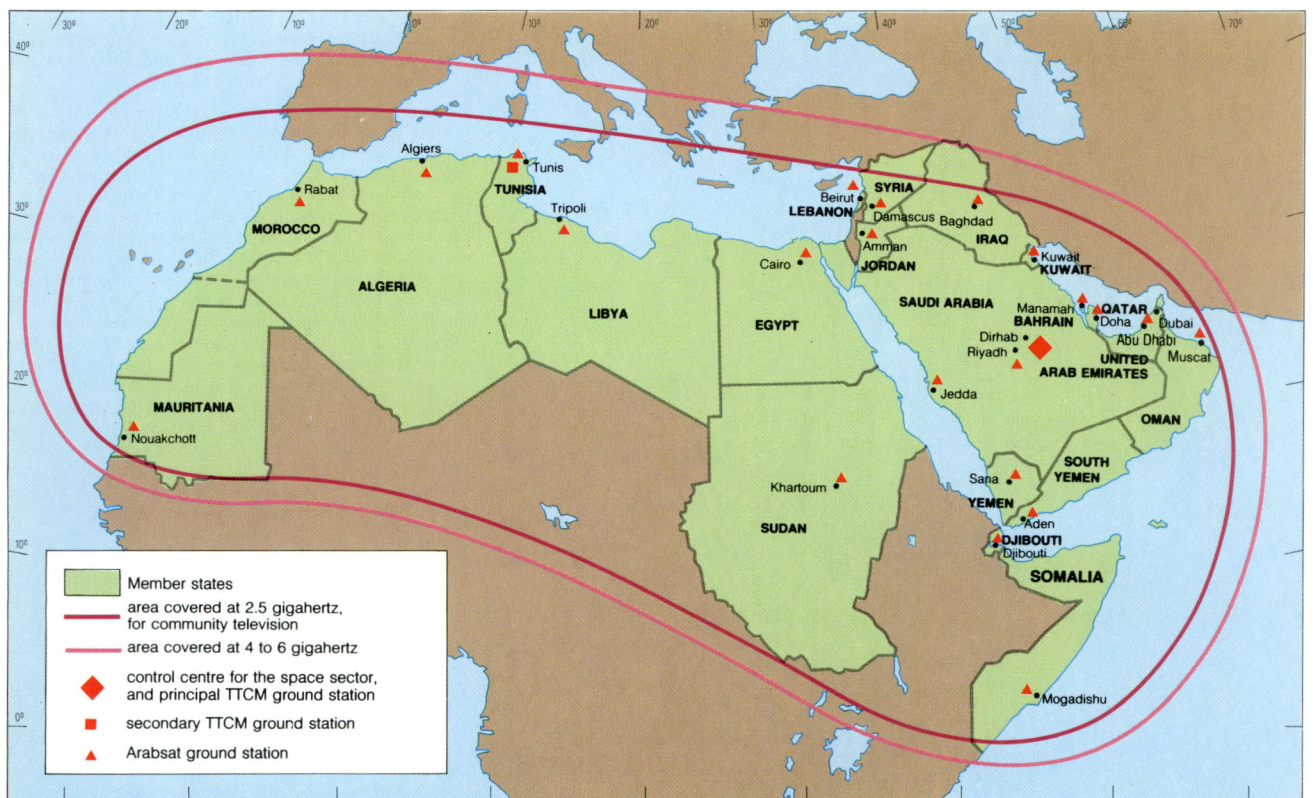

Member states
area covered at 2.5 gigahertz,
for community television
area covered at 4 to 6 gigahertz

◆ control centre for the space sector,
and principal TTCM ground station
■ secondary TTCM ground station
▲ Arabsat ground station

The Arab Satellite Communications Organisation (ASCO). This is a special agency of the Arab League. It came into force in December 1976 charged with the definition, procurement and operation of a satellite system to improve domestic and regional communications. There were two priorities. The first was to establish reliable telecommunications and television distribution links between the Arab member states. The second was to establish a community television broadcast service to remote and rural areas, with particular emphasis on education, information and culture. A further objective was to encourage the exchange of radio and television programmes between public broadcasters in member countries.

The overall Arabsat system is intended to complement existing and future terrestrial networks as well as other international communications satellite systems. It has a ground segment consisting of several different types of Earth station operating at 4 to 6 gigahertz in the C band or 2500 to 2690 megahertz in the S band, according to members' needs. The space segment, consisting of satellites and a master control network, is jointly owned with satellite control being exercised through one of two telemetry, tracking, command and monitoring (TTCM) stations. The primary station is located near Riyadh in Saudi Arabia and there is a secondary one near Tunis.

The first operational satellites, Arabsat 1A and 1B were launched during 1985 into geostationary orbits above the equator, at 19 and 26 degrees East longitude. These, plus Arabsat 1C, launched in 1990, were procured through open tender from an international consortium led by Aérospatiale and supported by the Ford Aerospace and Communications Corporation and several leading European companies.

Eutelsat. Eutelsat, the European organisation for telecommunications satellites, was formed in 1977 by several telecommunications groups. Eutelsat achieved permanent status in August 1985, when an inter-governmental agreement signed by the 26 member countries of the EC came into force. It is responsible for the design, construction, launch, operation and maintenance of the European regional satellite systems.

Following a pre-operational test phase with the OTS satellite, Eutelsat began the commercial phase of the first generation of ECS satellites in October 1983. The satellites were built and launched by the European Space Agency. Eutelsat F1 was launched by Ariane in June 1983, Eutelsat I F2 in August 1984, Eutelsat I F3 in September 1985 (launch failure), Eutelsat I F4 in September 1987 and Eutelsat I F5 in July 1988. The second generation of satellites, Eutelsat II, are being constructed by a European consortium led by Aérospatiale (France) and the launch phase will begin in the 1990s. The third generation of satellites and a semi-direct broadcasting satellite called Europesat are already being studied.

The Eutelsat I satellites (called ECS, in the pre-operational phase) have 14 repeaters (12 on the first) operating in the 11 to 14 gigahertz and 12 to 14 gigahertz (for the first satellite) frequency ranges. They deliver a power of 20 watts. Eutelsat II satellites have 16 repeaters in the operational phase (as opposed to 10 on the Eutelsat I satellites), delivering a power of 50 watts. Eutelsat uses four satellites in orbit (increasing to seven in September 1992) and provides Eutelsat members with telephone services, data treatment, business links and the distribution of television programmes. Thus 17 television channels and nine radio channels are transmitted via Eutelsat satellites apart from the Eurovision network (two repeaters have been rented by the European Broadcasting Union for 10 years). The reception of the television programmes is used by cable networks or people with small parabolic dishes, about 90 centimetres in diameter when they are situated at the centre of the West, East and Atlantic SPOT beams (60 centimetres for Eutelsat II). Twenty exchanges control the international telephone traffic, Eurovision and business links (source: Eutelsat).

Philippe Binet

six distinct marques of satellite in an unbroken programme of development and commercial operation. These range from the 40 kilogram Earlybird in 1965 to the 3·9 tonne Intelsat VI in 1989. A new generation of satellites, Intelsat VII will come into service in the 1990s. Three of these are expected to be launched by Ariane IV and two others by Atlas.

Regional systems

As needs arose and technology developed indigenously in other countries and regions, so new satellite systems and organisations began to emerge. The USSR used Molniya satellites for domestic communications as early as 1965. However, it was not until 1970, because of increasing telecommunications traffic between Comecon countries, that the Soviet Union promoted the formation of the Intersputnik international satellite communications organisation. Once formed, Intersputnik began leasing transponders in 1971 on Molniya satellites and later, from 1979, on Gorizont geostationary satellites.

Intersputnik was followed by three regional satellite systems established with international approval during the early 1980s. These were the Indonesian Palapa B launched in June 1983, designed to carry international traffic between remote Earth stations in ASEAN countries (Association of South East Asian Nations), the European Eutelsat system using OTS, Telecom 1 and ECS satellites, and the Arab League countries' Arabsat. The international convention which conferred legal status on the European Telecommunications Satellite Organisation (Eutelsat) came into force in September 1985. By working jointly with the European Space Agency, Eutelsat had gained more than four years operational experience with OTS 2 by the time that the first ECS satellite was launched in October 1983. The Arabsat system, with more than three quarters of its members also subscribing to Intelsat and operating Earth stations in the global system, is used primarily for domestic and intraregional communications.

As with the Intelsat organisation, both Eutelsat and Arabsat have the responsibility for developing, establishing and operating a jointly owned space segment in which all members participate financially. Their nominated telecommunications entities individually procure and operate the Earth stations which make up the ground segment.

National systems

From the earliest days, communications satellite systems have been seen to offer many advantages for national services as well as for transoceanic and intercontinental links. The reason for embarking on a national satellite system may be, as in Canada, India, Indonesia and the USSR, that it would be difficult or economically impossible for telecommunications services to be achieved in any other manner. It could be, as in the United States, that satellite systems offer a more cost effective way of increasing broadband capacity in the national networks. Another consideration is the speed at which satellite systems can be implemented compared with the laying of cables or the building of towers and masts for microwave line-of-sight radio relay networks. The reasons behind a decision are many, embracing geographic, demographic, social, industrial and economic factors, and the balance will differ widely from country to country. The telecommunications requirements of a rural community in a developed country may be very little different from those in the urban and metropolitan areas of a less developed country. The need for community information and educational television in villages may well take precedence over the general pro-

area covered by the multiuser business telecommunications system (12 to 14 gigahertz)

Eurovision television broadcasting to European networks.

Atlantic beam
West of Europe beam
East of Europe beam

narrow beams (11 to 14 gigahertz): telephone and telegraph, position of repeaters for television broadcasts

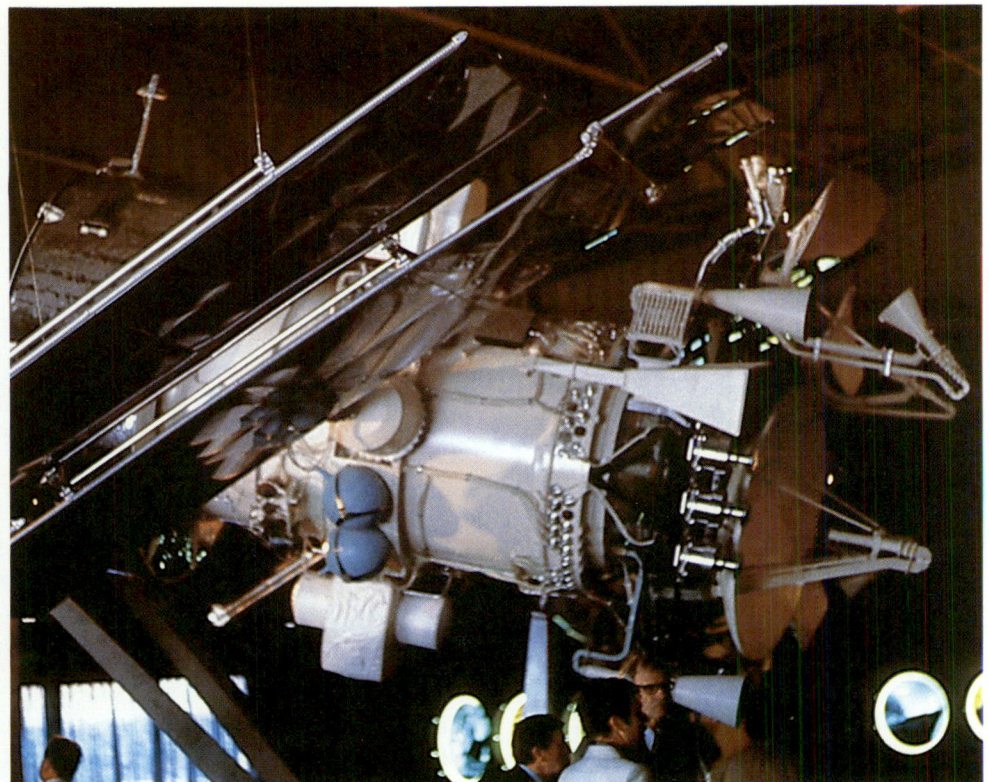

The Gorizont satellite. Soviet geostationary satellites have been used since 1979 for radio and television distribution, telephony, telegraphy and for the transmission of newspaper page facsimiles and meteorological charts.

As part of its long term planning for space communications, the USSR in 1976 registered plans with the International Frequency Registration Board for ten positions in the geostationary orbit. Four of these locations are now occupied by one or two Gorizont satellites. Those now at 14 degrees West and 53 degrees East longitude are known as Statsionar 4 and 5 (Intersputnik network for the Atlantic and Indian Ocean regions).

When Intersputnik was formed in 1971, the nine founder members leased transponders on Molniya satellites. Growth in membership, the Olympic Games in Moscow and a general increase in the level of international traffic was such that, by 1980, five 15 watt Gorizont transponders were needed. Three were on Statsionar 4, one for telecommunications, and two for television and radio, plus two on Statsionar 5, one for telephony and telex, and one for radio and television.

Membership of Intersputnik now stands at fourteen nations, including Afghanistan, Bulgaria, Cuba, Czechoslovakia, the German Democratic Republic, Hungary, the Lao People's Democratic Republic, Mongolia, North Korea, Poland, Syria, the USSR, Vietnam, and the Yemen People's Democratic Republic. To establish continuous communications, Cosmos 1700, with Louch repeaters, was placed in geostationary orbit in October 1985. Cosmos 1897 succeeded it in 1987 (A. Dupas).

Country	System or series	First launch
Arab League	Arabsat	1985
Australia	Aussat	1985
Brazil	SBTS	1985
Canada	Télésat (Anik A to D)	1972
China	STW 2 CBSC	1986 1988
France	Télécom 1	1984
India	Insat 1, Insat 2	1983, 1990
Indonesia	Palapa	1976
Italy	Italsat	1990
Japan	CS 2, CS 3	1983, 1988
Mexico	Morelos	1985
Soviet Union	Molniya 1 Molniya 2 Molniya 3 Radouga	1965 1975 1974 1975
United States	Westar Satcom Comstar SBS Galaxy Telstar 3 Spacenet G Star ASC Amsat Panamsat	1974 1975 1976 1980 1983 1983 1984 1985 1985 1988
West Germany	DFS (Deutsche Fernsehrundfunk Satellit) DFS 1, DFS 2, DFS 3	1987, 1989, 1990

National telecommunications satellite systems

Japanese Telecommunications. In 1973, Japan decided on a plan for Communication Satellites (CS) for domestic telecommunications experiments. The CS 1 satellite was manufactured by Mitsubishi Electric Corporation (MELCO) and Ford Aerospace and Communications Corporation (FACC) under contract from the Japanese National Space Development Agency (NASDA). Launched by a Delta rocket in 1977, it was located at 135 degrees East longitude. The K and C band communications experiments were conducted by the Radio Research Laboratory and Nippon Telegraph and Telephone Corporation (NTT) until 1984.

The CS 2 (CS 2a and CS 2b) satellites are the first operational communications satellites (spin stabilised, with despun antennae) developed by NASDA. MELCO/FACC were the main contractor for the satellite system and Nippon Electric Company (NEC) made the satellite transponders. Both satellites were launched by the Japanese N II launch vehicle in 1983, and stationed at 132 and 136 degrees East longitude respectively. They are now being used, for domestic K and C band telecommunications, by NTT and other users.

The CS 3 satellites, successors to the CS 2, were launched in September 1988 by the H I rocket to accommodate the increased communications demand and to enhance Japanese autonomous satellite technology.

Fumio Otsuki

vision of telephones and similar services in those same villages. If the traffic and capacity requirement is relatively small, leasing transponders on another nation's satellite can be the most economic way of setting up a domestic space segment. This can be on a permanent basis or as a means of gaining operational experience before procuring a dedicated satellite. Thus, some forty countries have, to date, leased the equivalent of nearly sixty Intelsat transponders since Algeria first leased capacity in a spare satellite in 1975.

Mobile, emergency and military communications

The Intelsat Global System demonstrated how satellite communications can be provided at affordable cost. This and the other systems so far discussed have all been limited to providing links, nationally or internationally, between fixed points. Initially these links were between very large Earth stations serving national networks but, in the course of time, there has been a steady trend towards smaller stations – still in fixed locations – serving local area networks. In the process, however, a whole new vista of applications has appeared. None of these was previously possible, or even conceivable, without the use of satellites. The most notable is the current ability to communicate via space using small mobile terminals on ships, aeroplanes and land vehicles. Experimental demonstrations of mobile communications were first made with Syncom 2 in 1963, then within the NASA-ATS satellite programme, followed by the US military in 1969 with narrow band UHF channels in Tacsat.

The development of mobile satellite services has been much slower than that of the fixed services. To date, only maritime satellite services have reached operational status. Regular telecommunications with ships at sea via satel-lite were first made in 1976 by the Marisat organisation, a consortium of US international common carriers. A similar interest for maritime satellite communications was also expressed in Europe based, at that time, on the European Space Agency's Marots and Marecs satellites as the prospect of an International Maritime Satellite Organisation (Inmarsat) became a reality. By 1979 Inmarsat was a legal entity, with an objective to procure, establish and operate a space segment for the provision of high quality voice, telex and data communications between coastal Earth stations and ships at sea.

Following negotiations with the European Space Agency and with the Comsat-Marisat organisation, Inmarsat introduced its first operational system in February 1982. This was officially inaugurated in London by Marconi's widow in recognition of his work and efforts at the turn of the century which introduced a new era of 'wireless' ship to shore radio communications. At this point, Inmarsat took over all leases on Marisat capacity. It gradually augmented them as new and greater capacity became available on two entire Marecs satellites leased from the European Space Agency and on Maritime Communications Subsystems on several Intelsat V satellites.

Apart from conventional telecommunications services to ships and offshore platforms, Inmarsat is also mandated to provide facilities for the transmission of real time management and operations data, accurate navigational information, radio medical assistance, and search and rescue (SAR) messages.

Communications services from aircraft, via space, became operational in February 1989 with the inauguration of British Airways Skyphone, following modification to the Inmarsat convention at the end of 1985. The development of direct services to vehicles and persons on land has yet to be fully exploited, but with

The Marecs B2 satellite during integration with the Ariane rocket. Marecs (Maritime European Communications Satellite) was built for ESA by a consortium of European industries headed by British Aerospace. Two satellites are rented by Inmarsat, giving more than fifty telephone and telex circuits with ships in the Atlantic and Indian oceans. For the first time, the world has high quality voice and telex ship to ship or ship to shore links.

The second generation satellites, Inmarsat II, are also being built by a group of ten companies headed by British Aerospace. Each satellite will have at least 250 circuits, with an expected lifetime of at least seven years.

In cooperation with the International Civil Aviation Organisation (ICAO) and the International Air Transport Association (IATA), a 1 megahertz wide band reserved for Inmarsat will offer two aeronautical services. One is narrow band transmission for the crew. The other is a voice and data transmission service for the crew and passengers (ESA).

the prospect of broadband fibre optic links replacing satellites for fixed station services, satellite communications with mobiles is an area ripe for development. Examples of current interest include the European Space Agency's Prosat project, the Canadian M Sat programme, and the dozen or so applications made in 1985 to the US Federal Communications Commission. These last seek to establish services such as voice communications between dispatchers and fleets of vehicles, ships and aircraft over a wide area, or two way communications between subscribers and the public telephone networks. Other examples are control messages and data acquisition to and from remote sensors in automatic weather stations, rivers, lakes, pipelines, lighthouses, etc., or data acquisition from on board computers on mobiles and one way paging services to individuals travelling in land vehicles, aircraft and ships.

Various armed forces are also interested in communicating with units all round the world. Military communications satellites were introduced for such purposes by the United States during the late 1960s and by the United Kingdom and NATO in the early 1970s. Both satellite and communications technologies developed quickly during this period, with the result that the quality and reliability of military communications over long distances was greatly improved. As technology developed still further, so the requirement widened to embrace a variety of tactical and strategic purposes.

Until recently the majority of protected military satellite communications were effected in a shared SHF band in the range from 7·25 to 8·4 gigahertz. There are allocations for the military in the region of 20 and 44 gigahertz, but these frequencies have not yet been fully exploited. The crowded state of the SHF band, the large bandwidth potential at EHF and the relative freedom from interference by non-military users in the same band, coupled with the potential for smaller and lighter antennae and radio

equipment, are such that military communications satellites regularly operating at higher frequencies cannot be long delayed. Inevitably, there are attendant disadvantages of working at EHF. These include increased cost, the need for more precise antenna pointing, and excessive attenuation through the atmosphere, particularly at low angles of antenna elevation at the ground terminal. This latter effect is most noticeable with communications between geostationary satellites and Earth terminals (whether fixed or mobile) at high latitudes. For this reason alone, if not for overcrowding in the geostationary orbit, an increased use of military communications satellites in the Molniya type of inclined elliptic orbit can be foreseen.

Prospects for the future

We have seen that satellite communications have advanced very rapidly over the last 25 years. The first step was to put satellites into geostationary orbit. Later their communications capacity rapidly increased as did their radiated power.

Such trends will continue, particularly at higher operating frequencies, with higher gain, multibeam and contoured beam antennae on spacecraft, higher transmitter powers and improved receiver sensitivities, and more and more on board processing and switching between separate multiple steerable beams.

Strenuous technical and political efforts will be needed to conserve and make more efficient use of the radio frequency spectrum, for example by increasing the number of times that frequencies can be reused within a satellite. The congestion in geosynchronous orbit and in the radio spectrum will also be relieved, in due course, by direct radio and optical communications between satellites so as to form a very broadband 'ring main' or 'trunk loop' around the orbit.

John C. Leeming

The Mobile Satellite (M Sat) system. The basic objective of this satellite is to supply, for renting, reliable and mobile communications links for all rural and remote regions of Canada, including a maritime zone of 200 miles. Voice communications services are being replaced by digital transmissions.

Ultra High Frequency (UHF) bands will be used for links to mobile terminals. Super High Frequency (SHF) bands will link ground stations and the control centre in order to minimise energy requirements.

The data transmission service will use a band of 5 kilohertz, at rates of 2·4 kilobits per second. Other services include data acquisition and command transmission, long distance radio paging, vehicle location and one way emergency calls.

Different antennae are envisaged depending on the particular application and geographic position. The simplest will have a 4 decibel gain and will not be steerable. More expensive will be electronically steerable models, with a gain of up to 10 decibels (Ministry of Communications, Ottawa).

Robert W. Breithaupt,
Pierre M. Boudreau and Hugh M. Reekie

Satellite applications

Direct broadcasting

Unlike telecommunication satellites which, for the last 20 years, have relayed signals around the globe, a direct broadcasting satellite permits users to receive directly the signals which it retransmits. For this sort of satellite, the antenna has to remain pointed at a certain area at all times, and transmitting techniques have to be more sophisticated. However, the satellite has only a limited amount of electrical power at its disposal. Thus the dimensions of the region on the Earth served by the transmitting antennae is smaller than all the countries in the European Economic Community. However, reception across the whole area is possible with parabolic dishes about 90 centimetres in diameter.

Broadcasting satellites are especially suitable for regions which either lack a good communications network or are far from large urban centres, and for developing countries where programmes have to be transmitted over great distances. These satellites also have a niche in developed countries where the choice of programmes is limited by the lack of frequencies for conventional broadcasting transmitters or where cable networks are not being introduced quickly enough.

The birth and development of European broadcasting

At the end of the 1960s, West Germany and France were faced with a number of technical challenges which stimulated an examination of the possibilities of satellite broadcasting. At that time there was no international agreement on the frequencies and positions in geostationary orbit that such satellites require. However, from August 1975 to July 1976, the Satellite Instructional Television Experiment (SITE) project took place in India, using the American telecommunications satellite ATS 6 (Application Technology Satellite). Direct broadcasting trials were begun in Canada in 1976, using the satellite Hermès, and in Japan in 1978 with the satellite Yuri.

In the late 1970s, West Germany and France joined forces in the successful Symphonie programme. In September 1980, a Franco-German project group, commissioned by the Centre National des Etudes Spatiales (CNES), Deutsche Forschungs- und Versuchsanstalt für Luft- und Raumfahrt (DFVLR), the German Post Office and TéléDiffusion Français (TDF) began work in Munich.

Interests in the consortium were split, with 54% going to German industry and 46% to French industry.

The Eurosatellite consortium consists of ANT-AEG, ATES, Aérospatiale and MBB, all of which hold 24%, and the Belgian company ETCA which holds 4%. The four parent companies subcontract work out. The third level of contracts involve such companies as Crouzet, Matra, Sagem, Erno, Saft, Teldix, Dornier, ETCA, Saab and Ericsson.

Hermann Strub

Technical characteristics

The satellites, each weighing about 2150 kilograms at launch, are designed so that the acceleration forces at launch are spread throughout the structure. Carbon fibre struts within the communications module transmit the strain acting on the tower to the propulsion module structure.

Some equipment in the satellite can only function within a narrow temperature range. So, when the satellite enters the Earth's shadow at night, a Thermal Control Electronics (TCE) system operates to keep the equipment warm. This can also be controlled from the ground.

Coarse pointing of the satellite is carried out using the solar and infrared sensors, an inertial wheel and thrusters. An on board computer and the Interface and Security Electronics (ISE) system link the detectors with the actuators. They carry out orbit and attitude corrections during both the transfer and geostationary orbital phases. If there is a malfunction, corrections can also be programmed from the ground control centre to enable the satellite to function automatically. The fine pointing of the satellite is carried out by the antenna orientation mechanism.

The satellite's power is provided by 43 200 solar cells, each of which measures 21 by 40 millimetres. These are fixed to eight solar

Engineering model for Symphonie. The engineering model of a satellite enables technologists to test the structure and to verify the mathematical model of its structural properties. Apart from this, tests are made on the ability of the layers of heat insulating material to withstand the mechanical forces of launch. To do this, the engineering model has to resemble the flight model as closely as possible. It includes the antenna tower reflectors and solar panels, which are identical to those of the flight version, and which are sensitive to vibrations. All other pieces of equipment are replaced with dummy parts, although their dimensions, masses and centres of gravity correspond to those of the real components. Only one of the four panels of solar cells is fitted with real cells. About 200 strain gauges and accelerometers are joined by cables to recorders.

The model is subjected to mechanical vibrations of variable amplitude, with frequencies up to 100 hertz. It is further subjected to acoustic energy with frequencies from 30 to 8000 hertz. These are representative of what the satellite will encounter during launch. Finally, shock tests are carried out and physical parameters of the satellite such as the position of the centre of gravity and the moments of inertia with respect to the three axes, are measured. All these experiments are later repeated on the flight model itself. (Aérospatiale).

Pointing the transmitting antennae. A fundamental requirement of the satellite's attitude and orbital control system is that the transmitting antenna must remain pointed at the region that it is to serve with a precision of a fraction of a degree. Alignment errors due to mechanical and thermal deformations which are present are eliminated by observing infrared beacons on the Earth. (CNES).

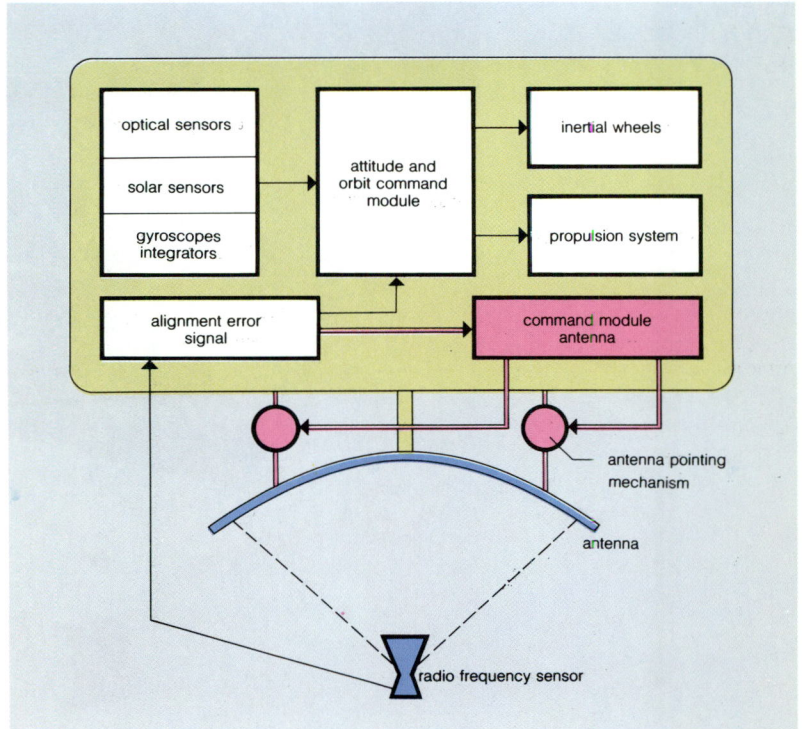

panels measuring 1·56 by 3·63 metres. The 4·7 kilowatts available is transmitted to the power supply system in the main body of the satellite by Bearing And Power Transmission Assembly (BAPTA) revolving contacts.

The satellite measures 7·2 metres from the exterior of the adaptor to the outer edge of the S band antenna and its base measures 1·6 by 2·4 metres. The span of the solar panels is 19·2 metres.

In order to guarantee continuous uninterrupted broadcasting, the German Post Office and TDF have each commissioned second satellites. Almost identical to the first Symphonie satellites, these were to be launched in 1989.

In August 1983, Eurosatellite signed a contract with the Swedish Space Corporation to build a broadcasting satellite, Tele X, for the whole of Sweden. The subsystems of this satellite are identical to those of Symphonie. The payload consists of three television channels, and three channels, one of which is held in reserve, for video and digital communications.

For the future, many nations have plans for direct broadcasting satellites which are well advanced. They are examples of space technology of direct benefit to millions.

Bernhard Fabis

Propulsion system. This photograph shows the underneath of a Symphonie satellite and its apogee motor. The nozzle is covered by a protective red cover which will be removed just before launch.

On either side of the nozzle are helium reservoirs, maintained at high pressure. A regulator valve reduces the helium pressure to 17·5 bars (17·5 times atmospheric pressure). This is then fed to the fuel reservoirs, propelling it into the combustion chamber. Two of the four reservoirs behind the black panel contain 393 kilograms of monomethyl hydrazine (MMH), and

two contain 645 kilograms of nitrogen peroxide. Heat insulating material is attached by white Velcro strips to the underside of the satellite.

The rows of rivets on the edges and the outer shell form part of the ring adaptor, which holds the satellite to the rocket motor. After the third stage of the Ariane rocket launcher has fired, the satellite separates from the adaptor. This then falls into the atmosphere with the third stage where it burns up (MBB Erno).

The satellite communications module. In the photograph, this part of a Symphonie satellite lies on a handling device during preparations for thermal tests in a vacuum to simulate conditions in space. The reflecting surfaces are subjected to simulated solar radiation.

At the front is the Earth panel, so called because it always faces towards the Earth, and six heat collectors (three white and three black) (Aérospatiale).

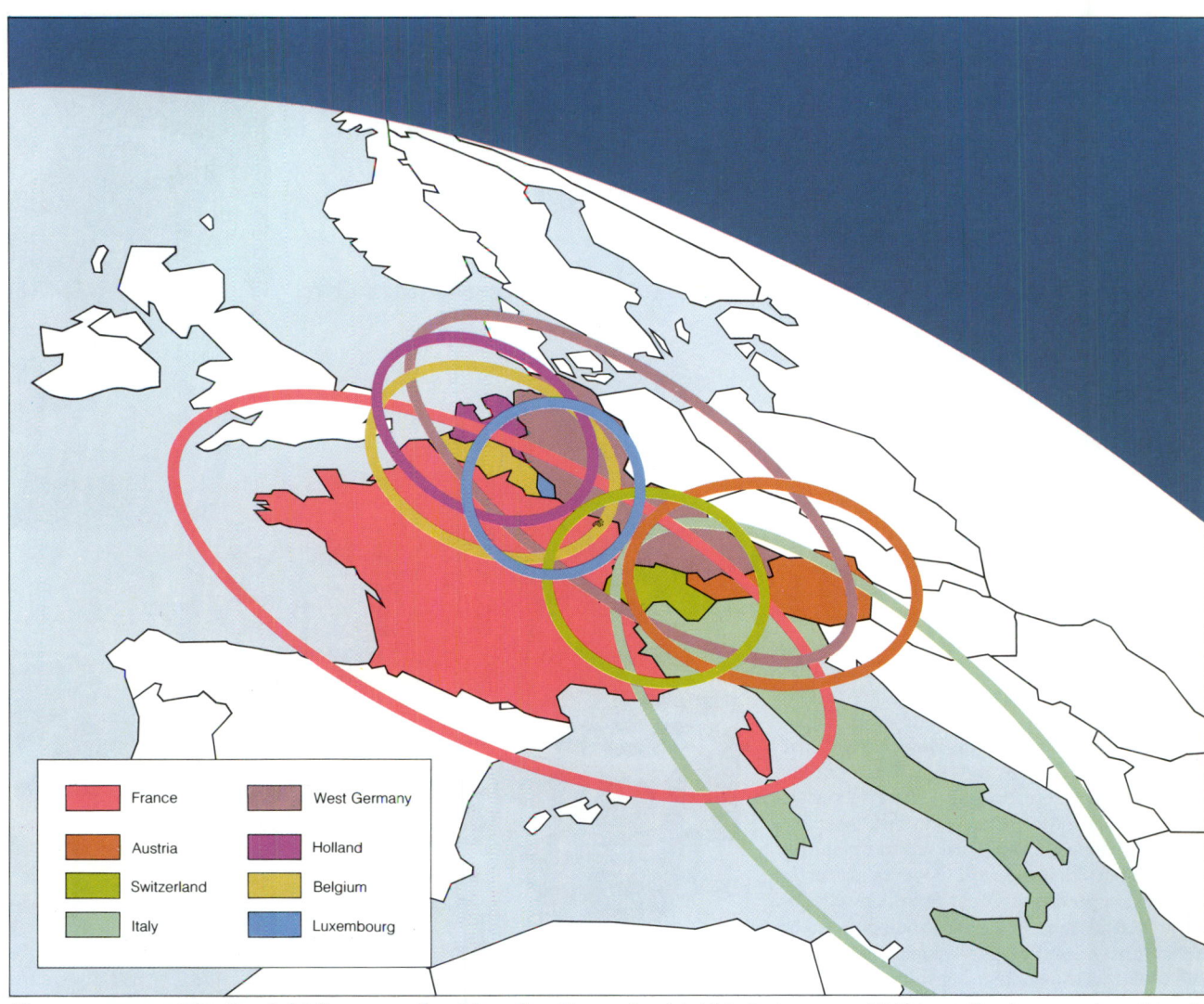

The areas covered by the eight European direct broadcasting satellites. This map illustrates the optimum coverage provided by the Symphonie satellites as well as each area covered by geostationary satellites at 19 degrees West belonging to six other European countries. The area covered by each satellite is much greater than the national area. The Spanish, Irish, Portuguese and British satellites in preparation will be placed at a longitude of 31 degrees West. To receive transmissions from these satellites, would-be viewers in Europe will have to point a second dish in this direction (World Administrative Radio Conference).

Legend:
- France
- Austria
- Switzerland
- Italy
- West Germany
- Holland
- Belgium
- Luxembourg

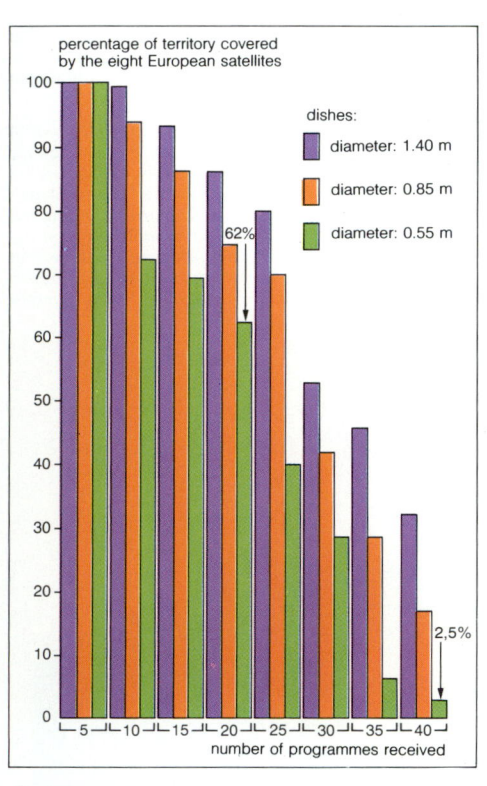

percentage of territory covered by the eight European satellites

dishes:
- diameter: 1.40 m
- diameter: 0.85 m
- diameter: 0.55 m

62%

2,5%

number of programmes received

The coverage of Europe by eight geostationary satellites at 19 degrees West. Television viewers in Europe are able to receive a number of broadcasts from satellites, depending on geographical location and the size of their receiving dish. For example, around Strasbourg, in an area corresponding to 2·5% of the total European territory, satellite broadcasts from Austria, Belgium, France, Holland, Italy, Luxembourg, West Germany and Switzerland can be received. This represents a maximum of forty programmes which can be received at any time using a dish with a diameter of 55 centimetres.

The diagram above shows the percentage of the total European territory covered by the eight European countries, for receiving dishes of different diameter. For example, twenty programmes can be received by a dish with a diameter of 55 centimetres over 62% of the area of these countries (WARC).

The educational perspective. Direct broadcasting by satellite is one of the space programmes being developed by the Indian Space Research Organisation (ISRO). It has been in operation for over a decade. With the Satellite Instructional Television Experiment (SITE) programme, educational programmes were run on agriculture, hygiene, health and family planning via the ATS 6 satellite. These programmes were received by 2400 villages in six Indian states.

Insat 1A, launched on 10 April 1982 by a Delta rocket, broadcast programmes to rural communities. It broke down 147 days after its launch, and was replaced by Insat 1B which was launched by the space shuttle Challenger on 30 August 1983 (ISRO).

Direct broadcasting satellites

Satellite name	Country	Launch date	Total power radiated (decibel/watts)	Frequency band (megahertz)	Transmitted frequency (gigahertz)	Radiated power (watts)
CTS Hermès (Communications Test Satellite)	Canada	1976	59.5	85	11.7 to 12.2	200
Ekran Stationary T	USSR	1976	50	25	0.714	300
BS 2a (Broadcasting Satellite)	Japan	1986 1984	55	13.5	11.7 to 12.2	100
BS 2b		1986				
BS 2x		1989				
TV Sat 1 (non-functioning)	West Germany	1987	65.6	27	11.7 to 12.2	230
TV Sat 2		1989				
TDF 1	France	1988	63.9	27	11.7 to 12.2	260
TDF 2		1989				
Olympus	Europe (ESA)	1989	27	27	11.7 to 12.2	230
Tele X	Sweden	1989	60	40 or 85	11.7 to 12.2	230
STC (Satellite Television Corporation)	USA	1989	54 to 57	16	11.7 to 12.2	220

Satellite applications

Navigation

Mankind has long looked to the heavens to help him navigate from one position on the Earth to another. His earliest experiences have probably been lost. However, history does record a number of ancient navigators using positions of the Sun, Moon and stars to help them travel across the seas. For example, Minoan seamen during the Bronze Age navigated between Crete and Egypt for trading purposes. Herodotus tells that the Phoenicians used the North Star, Polaris, to find their way between Phoenicia and Cornwall to obtain tin. Homer states that the wise Goddess instructed Odysseus to keep the Great Bear constellation on his left hand as he crossed the open sea on his return from Calypso's Island. Even the Bible tells us of people using stars to navigate. St Matthew's gospel records that men who studied the stars were led by one star to the birthplace of Jesus. Chapter 27 of the Acts of the Apostles indicates that mariners used the Sun and the stars as guides for finding North, South, East and West.

Three key devices were invented and perfected to improve navigation considerably. These were the magnetic compass, the sextant and an accurate seagoing chronometer. The magnetic compass was probably first used in about the twelfth century, and it allowed seamen to determine North when weather obscured the celestial bodies. The evolution of the sextant made the Sun and the stars considerably more useful to mariners. Whenever the Sun and stars were visible, the sextant could be used to measure their elevation angles very precisely, to determine latitude: however, they could not accurately measure longitude. At the earth's spin rate, a one minute error in time can make as much as a 28 kilometre error in East–West position. By the seventeenth century the best clocks could keep time to an accuracy of one or two minutes over several days when on dry land. When placed on a ship with wide variations in temperature and pressure, these clocks either stopped or became too erratic for accurate navigation.

With the discovery of the new world and an increase in world trade in the eighteenth century, more and more ships were taking long voyages at sea. This larger traffic increased the number and severity of maritime disasters, many of which were caused by navigation errors. Britain was the first nation to take positive action to curb these disasters. An act of parliament established the British Board of Longitude, a study group composed of the finest scientists in the British Isles. After much debate, the board decided to offer a prize of £20 000 to anyone who could develop a workable method of finding a ship's longitude to within 50 kilometres after a six week transoceanic voyage. After many impractical proposals over several decades, the prize was finally claimed by an English cabinet maker with little formal education. John Harrison successfully developed a marine chronometer which was nearly as accurate as the best land-based clocks. In 1761 his son, William, sailed

The Global Positioning System (GPS) Satellite Assembly Line. It takes a large number of satellites to form the operational constellation; depending on the actual lifetime of the satellites, it will also take many additional satellites over several years to maintain the operational constellation. In the past, satellites for other programmes have been bought in ones, twos or small numbers. However, GPS provided a unique opportunity to set up a satellite assembly line. The US Congress allowed the Department of Defense (DOD), through a unique funding arrangement, to procure the 24 satellites required initially, plus four spares.

The picture shows the clean room assembly line at the manufacturing plant where seven satellites are being built. The satellites in the foreground are having their wiring harnesses installed. Installation of the various electronic boxes has started on the raised satellite at the centre back. Once these are all installed, the satellite will be thoroughly checked.

It will then have the exterior installed, and move to the system testing chamber. This was specially built to accomplish system tests on the completed GPS satellites. These are either shipped to the launch site or put into storage to await a launch date.

To help satisfy the requirement for small Global Positioning System (GPS) user equipment, the US Defense Advanced Research Project Agency (DARPA) is developing a hand held GPS user set. A mock-up of that set is shown at the top. It is called the mini-GPS receiver, or the 'Virginia Slims', after a packet of cigarettes. The antenna for the set is shown as the round gold device in the upper right corner; the display and controls are on the lower portion. The electronics in the set will take advantage of advanced electronic circuits developed in the Very High Speed Integrated Circuits (VHSIC) programme (top, Magnavox; bottom, Rockwell Space System Division).

Navigating with Transit. Transit satellite orbits form a birdcage around the Earth. With this type of orbit satellites will be visible anywhere on the Earth several times per day. At the poles, a satellite will be seen on each orbit. At the equator, a user will have to wait longer on average for a satellite to become visible.

In order to calculate his position, the Transit user must receive two pieces of information from the satellite. The first is the navigation message. This gives the location of the satellite as a function of time. The second piece is the Doppler shift in the stable frequency of the satellite transmitter, due to the relative motion between the satellite and the user's receiver. To obtain a 'position fix', the user must relate his position to the known satellite location. This relationship is established by measuring the Doppler shift, which is a unique function of the observer's position and motion relative to the satellite location.

At the first observation, t_1, the received frequency f_{R1} is above the transmitted frequency because the satellite is moving toward the receiver. When the satellite is directly overhead as shown between t_3 and t_4, the user will receive exactly the same frequency that is being transmitted because the satellite is neither moving toward nor away from the observer. Conversely, at t_6 he will be receiving a lower frequency because the satellite is moving away from him. This information is processed in a microcomputer to find the user's latitude and longitude.

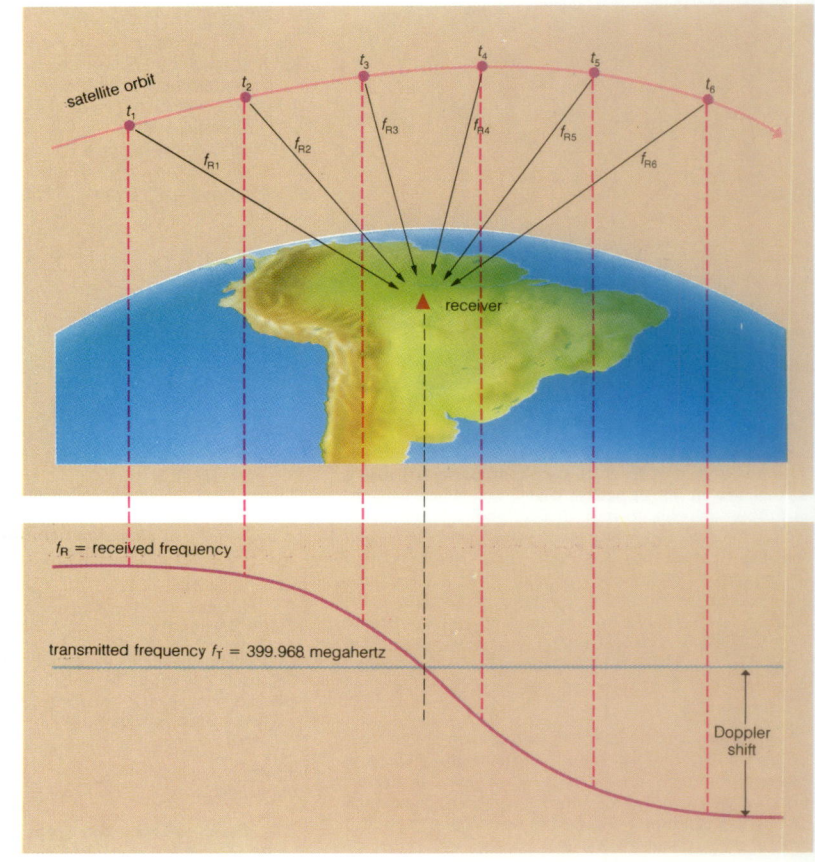

f_R = received frequency

transmitted frequency f_T = 399.968 megahertz

Doppler shift

from London to Jamaica with an error of 30 kilometres after the six week voyage.

Sextant readings timed by precise marine chronometers were the only reliable means of position fixing for the next two centuries. In fact they are still used today; however, radio navigation techniques are more commonly employed. Radio navigation is a method of position finding by receiving radio signals broadcast from multiple transmitters and using triangulation techniques to determine position. The development of radio navigation systems started in World War II to help improve bombing accuracy. Loran-C (Long Range Navigation) and Omega, which employ families of low frequency (LF) or very low frequency (VLF) radio transmitters around the globe, are typical of today's groundbased radio navigation systems. Higher frequency signals would yield greater accuracy; however, the signals are blocked by mountains and will not bend over the horizon. Low frequency signals do not have these problems; however, their accuracies are not as good. The solution to this dilemma is to move the transmitters into space aboard Earth orbiting satellites. This allows the use of accurate, high frequency signals and still allows coverage of wide areas.

Transit and Navstar – the Global Positioning System (GPS)

The genesis of satellite navigation really started with Sputnik in 1957. Scientists from the Applied Physics Laboratory of Johns Hopkins University used a single ground station to measure the frequency of the radio signals from Sputnik I. They noted an apparent frequency variation, known as the Doppler frequency shift. This phenomenon is caused by the relative velocity between the transmitter and an observer. Radio signals move at the speed of light; however, when a transmitter is moving toward an observer, more waves will be measured by the observer because each successive wave will have a slightly smaller distance to travel to the observer. Therefore, the observer will measure more waves per unit of time, thus indicating a higher frequency. Conversely, when a transmitter is moving away from an observer, the observer will measure a lower frequency. Using careful Doppler measurements, the scientists were able to determine the entire satellite orbit. It did not take them long to realise that this process could be reversed – a navigator's position could be determined by measuring the Doppler shift of a satellite radiating a fixed frequency signal with an accurately known orbit. This idea became the basis for Transit.

During the late 1950s and early 1960s nuclear submarines were being developed and deployed. An accurate worldwide navigation system was needed to update the inertial navigation units of these submarines. The coincidence of this need and the emerging satellite technology led to the development of the Transit programme which was initially funded in 1958. Several major tasks were required to make Transit an operational system. Among these were developing satellites, modelling of the Earth's gravity field to permit accurate determination of satellite orbits, developing equipment to determine navigation results, and establishing ground stations to monitor and control the satellites. These tasks were all completed and Transit was declared operational in January 1964. In July 1967, Transit was released for commercial use.

The Transit system is operated by the US Navy Astronautics Group headquarters at Point Mugu, California, with three remote tracking stations in Maine, Minnesota and Hawaii. These stations monitor the satellites to determine each satellite's position and to project each orbit. These projections are used to update the satellites' navigation message. This message permits the user to calculate the satel-

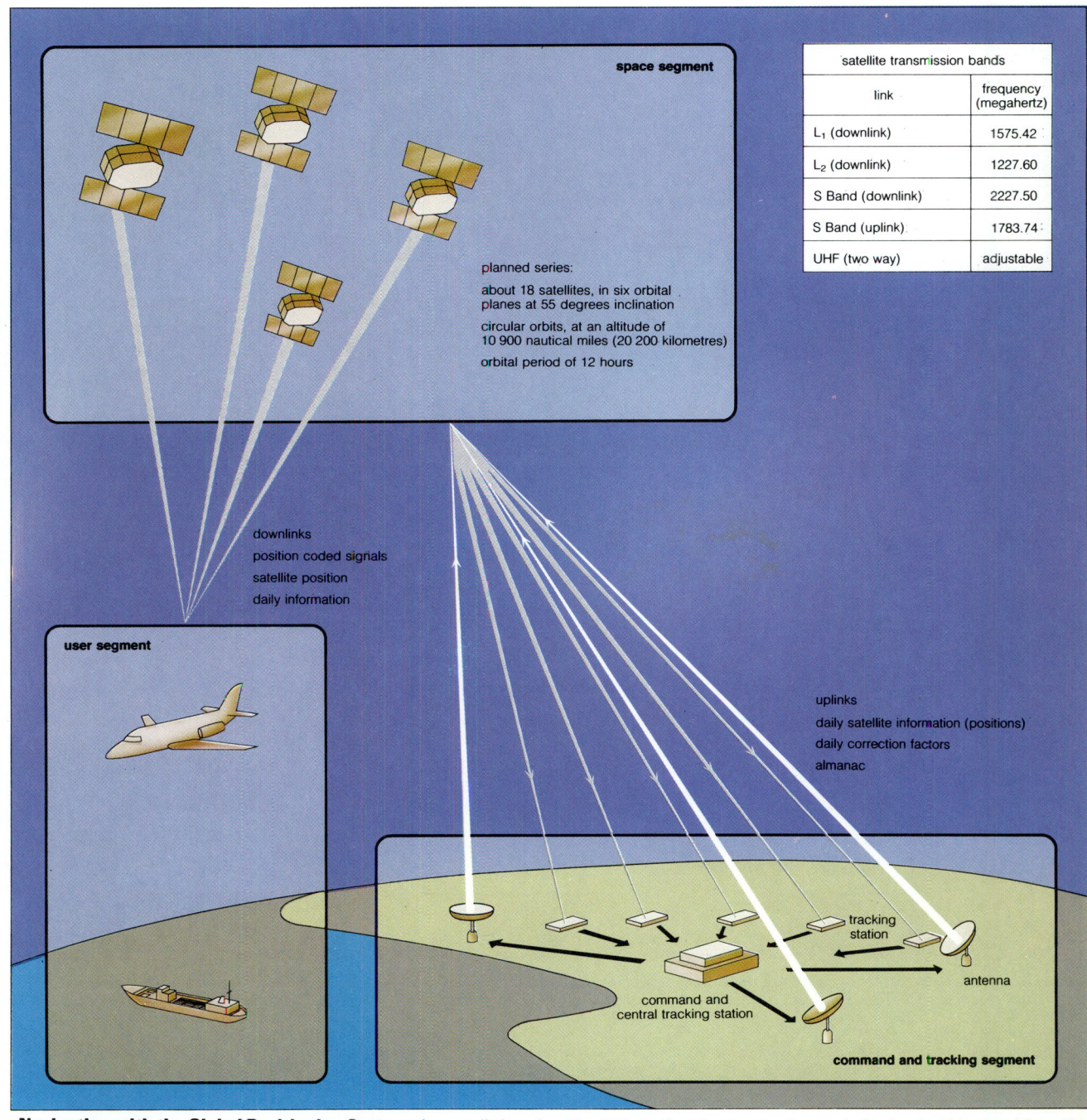

satellite transmission bands	
link	frequency (megahertz)
L₁ (downlink)	1575.42
L₂ (downlink)	1227.60
S Band (downlink)	2227.50
S Band (uplink)	1783.74
UHF (two way)	adjustable

Navigation with the Global Positioning System. A constellation of satellites broadcast signals to an unlimited number of users, who receive and process them to determine their location and velocity, and the time.

This diagram illustrates a hypothetical civil navigation system. The user equipment on board the aircraft broadcasts a signal to satellites which in turn relay it to a central control facility. The central facility transmits the signal back to the user and/or to his headquarters. With such a system the user equipment and satellites are simpler and cheaper. The system monitors use and charges a user for services provided just like a telephone company.

The diagram also summarises the three major segments of the Global Positioning System (GPS). These are the space, control and user segments. The operational constellation of 24 satellites are to be placed in six planes, with four satellites each and with an orbital inclination of 55 degrees. The orbit altitude is almost 20 000 kilometres and the period 12 hours.

The GPS satellites have several transmission bands. Links 1 and 2 provide the coded ranging signals, satellite position information and the almanac data from which the users determine their position, velocity and time. An S Band downlink to the control segment reports on the satellite's health, giving status data, and there is an uplink for giving commands to the satellites. The control segment consists of a master control station, five monitor stations and three uplink command stations. The purpose of this segment is to monitor the accuracy of the satellites' downlink data, and to update the navigation messages and the atomic clocks on the satellites.

The satellite carries four caesium or rubidium atomic clocks whose accuracy is plus or minus one second over 300 000 years. Only one of the clocks operates at a given time, the others providing back up. When the first clock fails, another one will take over. The two solar panels shown on either side of the satellite generate the electrical power needed to run the satellite. They rotate to maintain an optimum angle to the Sun.

lites' positions as a function of time. The satellites broadcast signals at two frequencies (150 and 400 megahertz) to help correct for ionospheric time delays, although a less accurate position can be calculated using only one frequency. Some of the more important uses of Transit are surveying, fishing, private and commercial maritime uses, offshore oil exploration, and drifting buoys. Transit is expected to be operational well into the 1990s until it is replaced by the Global Positioning System (GPS).

Despite the success of the Transit programme, both the US Navy and Air Force wanted a spacebased navigation system that would overcome the weaknesses of the Transit system. Both services worked on separate programmes until April 1973 when the two were combined. The resulting programme was called the Navstar (Navigation Satellite for Time and Ranging)/ Global Positioning System. When this system is fully deployed, it will have five major advantages over the Transit system. It will be more accurate. A user will not have to wait for a satellite to pass overhead. A position fix can

be obtained in a much shorter time. An accurate fix can be obtained on a moving platform, and a user can calculate his velocity very accurately.

The Global Positioning System (GPS) has completed the research and development phase, and is in production. It is being developed in three different segments – the space, control, and user equipment segments. The space segment will provide navigation and timing information to the user. The operational satellites are expected to be in orbit by the early 1990s, and will be launched primarily by the Delta II rocket. The purpose of the control segment is to monitor and update the satellites' navigation data and atomic clocks. It consists of a master control station, five monitor stations and three uplink stations. This segment has already been completed. The user's equipment will receive the navigation and timing information from the satellites and calculate his position and velocity, and also the time of the observation. Besides the Department of Defense, there are several commercial

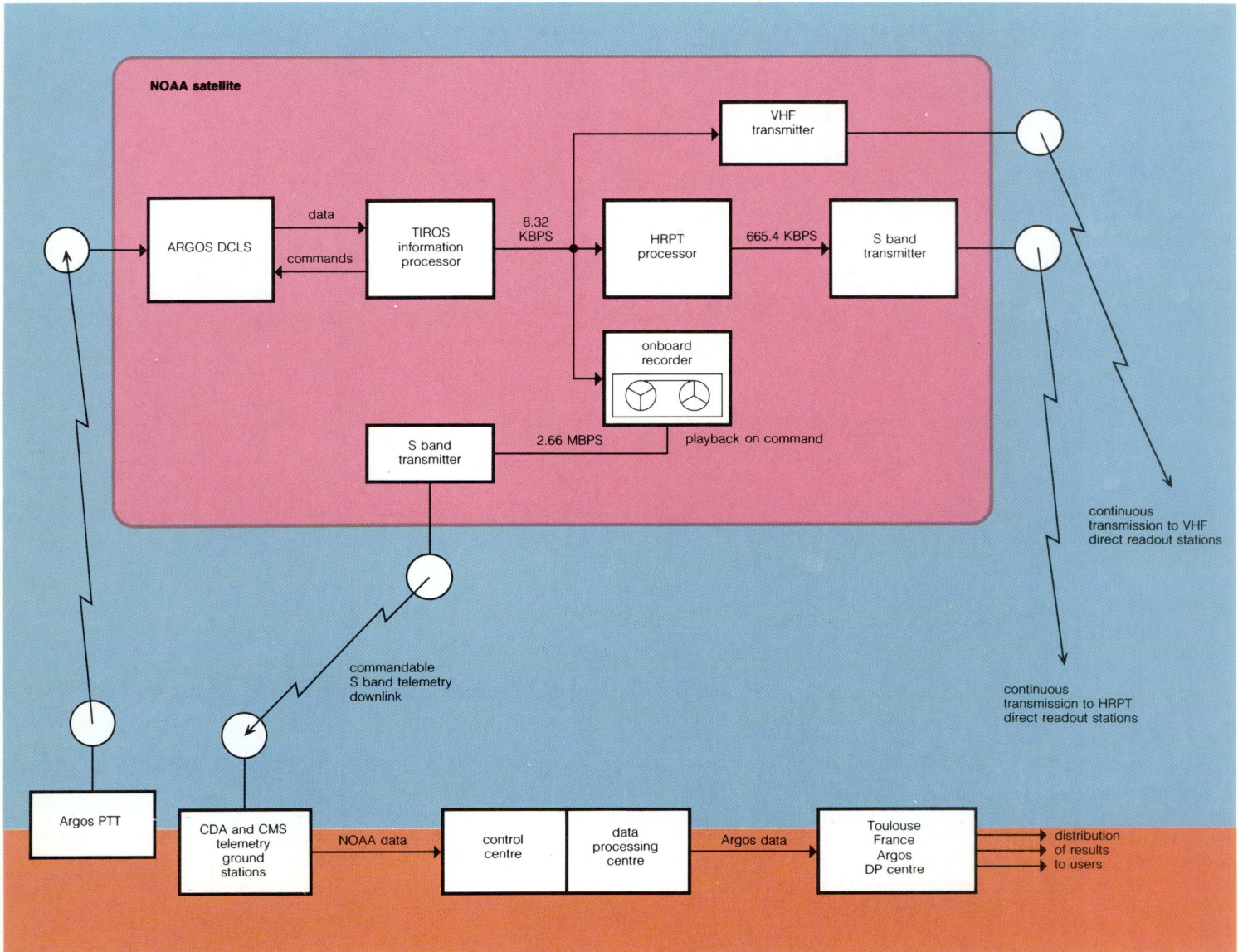

Diagram illustrating the flow of Argos data. Data from the Argos Platform Transmitter Terminals (PTT) on the Earth's surface are transmitted by radio, or uplinked, to a NOAA (TIROS) satellite. The satellite Data Collection and Location System (DCLS) processes the PTT data to generate telemetry data which includes PTT identification, sensor data, measured frequency, and time and date of measurement. The frequency and time data will eventually be used to determine the platform location. The data then move into the TIROS Information Processor (TIP) where they are combined with the other TIROS information. The Argos data are allocated 720 bits per second of the total TIROS downlink of 8 320 bits per second. The data are then transmitted in one of three different ways, by VHF, by S Band, or recorded on board for later playback on command. The data using Argos follows the third method.

When a satellite is visible to one of the two Command and Data Acquisition (CDA) stations, one on Wallops Island, Virginia, USA, and one at Gilmore Creek, Alaska, USA, or to the Centre de Météorologie Spatiale (CMS) at Lannion, France, it is commanded to transmit its telemetry data via the S Band downlink. When the data are received they are sent to the NOAA control and data processing centres in Suitland, Maryland, USA, where the Argos data are stripped off and sent to the Argos Data Processing (DP) Centre in Toulouse, France. This centre performs sensor data processing and location calculations in parallel. When the two operations for a given telemetry flow are over, the complete results are brought together in files. Each file contains the output data from one PTT. These data are then distributed to Argos users. Using Argos, the Global Telecommunications System is the primary method for the exchange of meteorological data.

organisations developing and producing GPS user equipment for various applications. When it is operational, GPS promises to have many thousands of users, and it is expected that new uses will be found for several years to come.

The Argos system

The Transit and GPS are navigation systems in that they use instantaneous (real time) satellite position data to help a user to travel from one location to another. Another satellite system uses positioning data to report where the user has been. This system, called the Argos system, provides the locations of fixed and moving platforms, and the collection of environmental data. It is a cooperative program between the Centre National d'Etudes Spatiales (CNES) of France, the National Aeronautics and Space Administration (NASA) and the National Oceanic and Atmospheric Administration (NOAA), both of the USA. The Argos system has four parts. There are Data Collection Platforms (DCPs) for land and sea applications called Platform Transmitter Terminals (PTTs). NOAA TIROS satellites (Television and InfraRed Observation Satellites) in polar, circular, Sun synchronous orbits at approximately 850 kilometres altitude receive messages transmitted by the PTTs and retransmit them to ground stations. The ground

system consists of telemetry acquisition and processing stations and a processing centre at Toulouse, France. Finally, there is a results distribution system.

The theory for determining the Argos PTT locations is the same as for Transit; it uses Doppler shift information. However, the implementation is somewhat different. For Transit, the user determines his location by observing the Doppler shift of the signal received from the satellite. Argos uses the Doppler shift of the signal from the PTTs as received by the satellites. Each Argos platform transmits PTT encoded messages at regular intervals on a 401·65 megahertz uplink. Messages transmitted by the various platforms within satellite visibility are selected for processing on a random access basis. The satellite Data Collection and Location System (DCLS) computes the Doppler effect on the receive frequency and generates the Argos telemetry message which includes PTT identification number, sensor data, measured frequency, and time and date of measurement. Approximately 8·6% of the TIROS downlink is reserved for Argos data. Each time that a satellite is within visibility of one of the three receiving stations it transmits the recorded data down. These data are then forwarded to the Argos Data Processing Centre in Toulouse via a permanent link. This processing centre operates continuously to provide the user with PTT sensor and location data which

are distributed to the customer by many different communications methods. The accuracy of the location data is dependent primarily on the PTT altitude, transmitter frequency stability, and platform movement. With good PTT frequency stability, the location accuracy is to better than 1 kilometre. A movement of 1 metre per second can lead to an additional error of up to 300 metres.

Argos is used for a variety of environmental studies, ranging from the measurement of the physical, chemical or biological properties of the Earth's surface, rivers, lakes, oceans and the atmosphere. Marine PTTs are used on drifting buoys, ships, ice buoys and moored buoys for collecting data on weather, currents, winds, waves and many other parameters. Land PTTs are used for weather, snow, hydrological, volcanic and seismic data.

PTTs have been developed for balloons to study weather, physical and chemical properties of the atmosphere, and even to track long duration manned balloon flights, for example the flight of Double Eagle V from Tokyo, Japan, to San Francisco, USA. In another interesting application, J.-L. Etienne used Argos to maintain a daily check on his position during his solo journey to the North Pole.

One of the biggest challenges to Argos users is to develop a PTT for animal tracking. Some of the technical problems that have been encountered are the short duration of satellite

The Sarsat–Cospas ground station network. The Sarsat–Cospas programme is an international system of satellites for search and rescue (SAR). It includes the American NOAA programme, the Russian merchant navy, the Canadian defence and communications ministries and CNES in France.

The ten Sarsat–Cospas stations use the data provided by the four satellites currently in use (three Russian Cospas satellites and the American NOAA 9) in near polar orbits with a period of about 100 minutes. Two transmission frequencies are used. On the frequency of 121·5 megahertz, continuous distress signals are relayed by the satellite to a ground station, where the exact position of the stricken vessel is calculated from the observed Doppler shift of the signal between the satellite and the vessel. The 406 megahertz signal from the satellite carries a code which identifies the vessel (boat or plane) in distress, as well as information on the nature of the problem. Several hundred people have already been saved thanks to this system (CNES, Novosty Press Agency).

visibility, high pressure and mechanical forces, short battery lives, and weight. Perfecting a PTT for this use is a continuing project.

Future programmes

For the future of satellite navigation, there appear to be three trends. These are the reduction in size of the user equipment, the exploitation of positioning and navigation data, and the proliferation of spacebased navigation systems. As the electronics industry continues to produce smaller circuit boards or chips, the size of user receivers will continue to shrink. With this size reduction there will also be increased reliability, reduced power and cooling requirements, and decreased costs. For example, the initial GPS user equipment in the 1970s was contained in large racks of equipment weighing a few hundred kilograms. By the early 1980s the GPS manpack weighed eight kilograms. In the late 1980s there are several development programmes that are reducing this weight considerably, to less than half a kilogram. This size reduction also allows a satellite navigation unit to be placed in an existing navigation system, such as an inertial navigation system. This will allow a navigator to use the best capabilities of each type of system to meet his requirements.

These improvements will, in turn, make satellite navigation equipment much more accessible to a larger number of users. With a much larger population using satellite navigation, new uses will be developed. For example, railways are using satellite navigation data to develop a modern traffic management system that will replace a system that has been in effect

for over a hundred years, making trains safer and more efficient. Differential satellite navigation data can help blind people move from place to place. A GPS receiver could even be put in an artillery shell to help guide it to its target.

The third trend in the future will be the proliferation of satellite navigation systems. Whilst the above discussion has concentrated on Transit, GPS and Argos, several other navigation systems are being developed. They all use either the same basic effect as Transit or GPS, but the implementation may be considerably different. The USSR is developing a Global Navigation Satellite System (Glonass) that is very similar to GPS. They have announced an intention to have a 24 satellite constellation that would provide worldwide three dimensional coverage and provide 100 metre accuracy to civil users. A commercial development within the USA is called the Geostar Satellite System. Here the user transmits a signal to three geosynchronous satellites which in turn relay the signals to a ground station. The ground station calculates the position, velocity and time of the user and sends it back to the user and/or to users at another location. Some of the advantages of this type of system for the commercial user are that the satellites and the user equipment are much simpler than for a system like GPS. The system can also provide two way digital communications services, and a user can be charged for his exact use of the system.

In Europe, two navigation satellite system concepts have been proposed. The European Space Agency's concept is called Navigation Satellite (Navsat), and Germany has proposed a system called Global Radio Navigation System (Granas). After much discussion,

Granas has been combined with Navsat and the resulting system is managed by ESA. The Navsat system will be similar to both GPS and Glonass, but it will be a civil system controlled by a civil agency. The Navsat concept calls for a mix of geosynchronous equatorial and highly elliptical orbits. The navigation payload can either be included as a secondary payload on another satellite or it can be carried on its own dedicated satellite. In addition, the Navsat signal will be compatible with the GPS signal in order to provide a timely health warning capability for the GPS.

Two other systems using position and location data are Starfix and the Search and Rescue Satellite (Sarsat). Starfix is a commercial system that uses known, fixed Earth reference stations which send timing signals, via satellites with known orbital parameters, to users. The users then calculate their positions. The Sarsat system carries relay equipment for signals from emergency locator beacons. A cooperative programme between the USA, France and Canada, it operates in cooperation with the USSR's Cospas system. The purpose of this programme is to improve search and rescue operations by the satellite-aided pinpointing of emergency locator beacons, carried on aircraft, ships or used in special applications. It has already saved several hundred lives.

In summary, the future of satellite navigation is indeed bright. A user has the promise of inexpensive, reliable equipment. He will have several systems to choose from, depending upon his particular objectives. In addition, new uses of position and navigation data promise to make the world a better place in which to live.

Phillip J. Baker

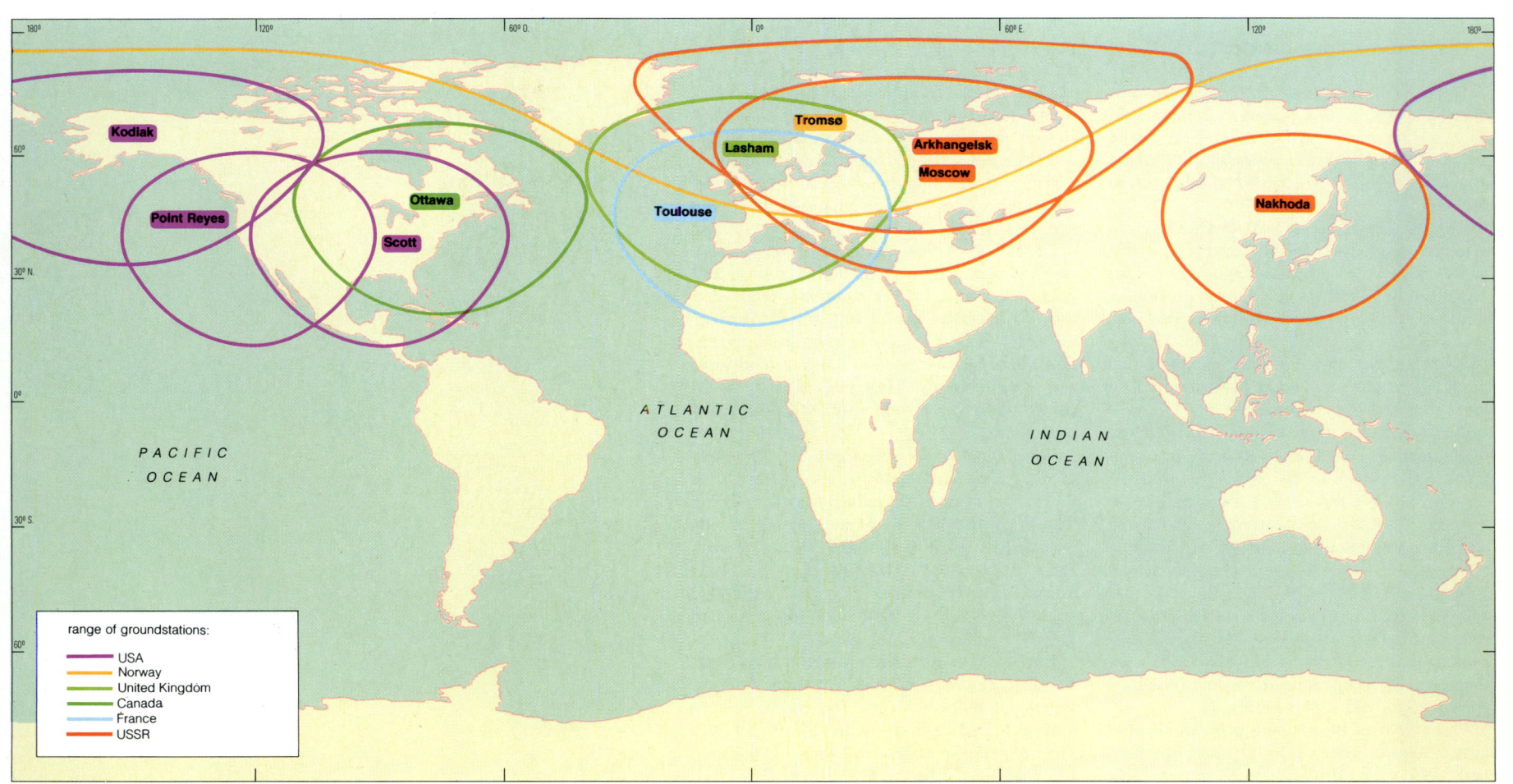

Man in space

Astronaut training

Training Soviet cosmonauts. Manned operations outside the Soviet Mir space station are becoming more and more frequent. Cosmonauts are trained for such activities in a large swimming pool, simulating conditions of weightlessness. At the beginning of the 1980s, a new training pool was built specifically for this purpose, at Star City, in Moscow. The pool is 20 metres in diameter and 12 metres deep. The cosmonauts, wearing modified spacesuits, train at a depth of about 5 metres. This provides the best longterm simulation of weightlessness. The cosmonauts learn to move around in the simulated weightless environment and to perform tasks similar to the work they will carry out in space. This involves either repairs or attaching devices, such as dust collectors, to the outside of the spacecraft. They can also install supplementary solar panels or metal frames, and weld or plate, using an electron beam (APN).

Marie-Rose Cukierman

In this section, we take a look at how American and European astronauts are trained for space shuttle missions. Soviet cosmonaut training, of both national and international crews for missions to the Mir space station, is touched upon in the caption for the photograph shown on the right.

The European Astronaut Centre

In March 1989 work began on the European Astronaut Centre (EAC) near Cologne in West Germany. This centre will eventually be responsible for the selection, recruitment and training of European astronauts and for naming the crews for different missions.

Other European astronaut facilities are planned. The Crew Training Complex (CTC) is at Cologne, where there will be Columbus simulators, medical facilities and other training equipment. The Hermes Training Complex (HTC) will be at Toulouse, France. The Pilot Training Facility (PTF) will be at Brussels, Belgium, in the same complex as a Hermes simulator and an aircraft landing simulator. There will be a large swimming pool to practice extravehicular activities at the Water Immersion Facility (WIF) at Marseille, France. Lastly, there is the Hermes Robotic Arm (Hera) which will be sited at Estec in Noordwijk, Holland.

In addition, European astronauts will be trained in Houston, Texas, for missions to the Freedom space station, and in Turin, Italy, where many of the devices used in space are constructed.

Andres Ripoll

The Johnson Space Center

The crew of the American space shuttle normally consists of five people – commander, pilot, and three mission specialists, all of whom are NASA astronauts. Occasionally, additional mission specialists or payload specialists are assigned.

Pilot astronauts serve as both shuttle commanders and pilots. Mission specialist astronauts have the overall responsibility for coordinating shuttle operations, including experiment and payload operations. Payload specialists are primarily professionals in the physical and life sciences, or technicians skilled in the operation of unique equipment taken into space on a particular mission.

Phase One of the training is orientation and flight training. Activities begin with an orientation course given by the management at the Johnson Space Center (JSC). Pilot candidates undergo T 38 jet aircraft training and flying checkout, physiological training, and training for survival in water. Mission specialists attend T 38 ground school to facilitate the transition from passenger to crewmember. Mission specialists also receive physiological training, survival training, and training in ejection/parasail, communications, navigation, cross country, crew coordination, and T 38 systems.

Phase Two of the training programme consists of a wide variety of lectures and briefings, and work using textbooks and shuttle flight operations manuals. These latter cover shuttle systems including guidance, navigation and control, data processing, instrumentation, electrical and environmental systems, and tracking techniques. Flight operations cover aerodynamics for ascent and reentry, and orbital mechanics with regard to working in space near the space shuttle and rendezvous. Mission operations include flight planning, integration of the payloads carried – such as Spacelab, the Payload Assist Module (PAM), and the Inertial Upper Stage (IUS) rocket – ground support, and mission rules. Also studied are space physiology, medicine, Earth observations and photography, astronomy and star identification, planetary science, space physics, atmospheric science, materials science, geology and oceanography. Manned spaceflight concepts cover shuttle and space station design.

Phase Three is participation in flight activities, simulations, meetings and other activities. These include working at the Kennedy Space Center (KSC) in Florida, making public relations appearances, and becoming involved with crew support and test environments.

After these three phases of training, some candidates are chosen to become astronauts. They then have a very busy training schedule in preparation for space flight. Before being assigned to a particular flight, astronauts become part of the pilot pool for further training in small groups. The Single System Trainer (SST) allows a potential astronaut to interact with the space shuttle controls and displays, though these trainers can only simulate some shuttle systems.

An advanced phase of training is then conducted in the Shuttle Mission Simulator (SMS). All pilots and missions specialists awaiting mission assignment are trained in ascent, orbit and reentry skills using this high fidelity simulator. The SMS uses actual flight computers and software, duplicates the spacecraft interior and has cockpit hardware. The crew workstation controls, displays, and communication systems replicate the flight systems. Computer generated scenes and hidden speakers provide audio-visual cues.

Pilot pool training also covers the avionics system (guidance, navigation and control, and data processing), orbiter systems (caution and warning, electrical power system, environmental control and life support system, communications and instrumentation, and propulsion), and crew systems (photography and closed circuit television, habitability, and emergency procedures).

Other types of training teach the astronauts to work under conditions of weightlessness. A KC 135 jet aircraft is modified for this training. The Weightless Environment Training Facility (WETF), an eight metres deep water tank with full scale mockups of the orbiter payload bay, airlock and payloads, provides controlled neutral buoyancy in water to simulate zero gravity for extravehicular activity (EVA).

Because pilot astronauts land the space shuttle much like an aircraft on a runway, conventional and modified aircraft are used to practice approach and landings. The KC 135 jet provides experience in handling heavy aircraft and the modified Grumman Gulfstream II aircraft, designated the Shuttle Training Aircraft (STA), simulates the landing characteristics of the orbiter.

When assigned to a particular flight crew, an astronaut becomes part of a very formal training programme. Crews are usually named for a specific flight about one year before the planned launch date. With flights at frequent intervals, several crews will be in training at the same time.

Shuttle flight crews train for an average of 16 to 25 hours per week, over eleven weeks, at the SMS. This high fidelity replica of the orbiter flight deck forward station seats the commander, pilot and two mission specialists. It is mounted on a moving platform and tilt-frame assembly with six degrees of freedom. The simulator is rotated by its maximum of 90 degrees for a realistic simulation of the effects of g-forces encountered during launch. An onset motion cue is given to duplicate the actual acceleration associated with a certain manoeuvre in space.

A crew's training is evaluated at least three times during its progress. Before flight, NASA and the payload customers formally review the final flight procedures, the training and simulation plans, and flight rules developed to support the flight.

Training is also given in the areas of flight operations, crew systems and extravehicular activity (EVA) needed for a specific flight. Such flight specific operations might include payload deployment or retrieval or proximity operations and rendezvous. Specific training is given for Spacelab, PAM, IUS, the attached payloads, the middeck experiments, and for the detailed objectives of that particular flight. Each crewmember is also trained as a back up for another crewmember to guard against illness or other such emergency.

Payload specialists begin specialised payload experiment training about two years before the expected launch date. This takes place at universities, government institutes or industrial facilities. About six months before launch, they join the JSC for training with other crewmembers in matters such as shuttle systems, crew operations and emergency procedures.

About eleven weeks before launch, the crew begins the flight specific integrated simulations. The SMS is linked to the Mission Control Center (MCC) and with a simulated version of the tracking station network. This final phase of the training can also include the payload customers' control centres. It prepares for the real space flight and ensures complete integration between the flight crew and the ground control teams.

Between their simulator sessions, the crewmembers also practice activities related to the mission, such as deploying and retrieving satellites, carrying out extravehicular activity (EVA), and operating experiments. They are also trained in celestial navigation, in the details of the experiments to be carried out and in gathering the necessary scientific data.

Prior to the Challenger accident, shuttle astronaut training took at least five years to complete. Since then, the training period has extended to eight years or more. There are countless numbers of people who dream of flying in space but, of the thousands of applicants, only twelve to fifteen are accepted for the three phase training programme. Most of those who undergo training eventually become astronauts.

Bethene E. McNealy

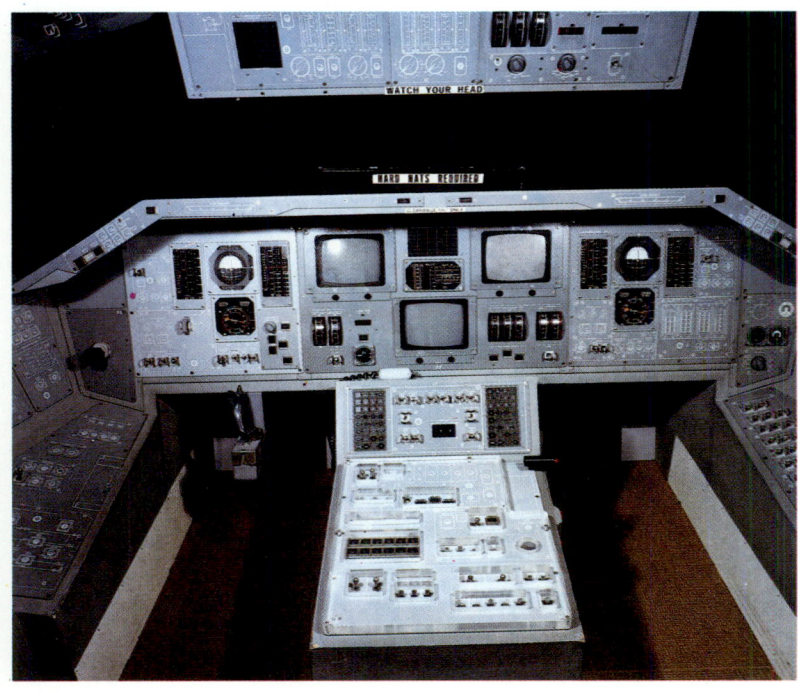
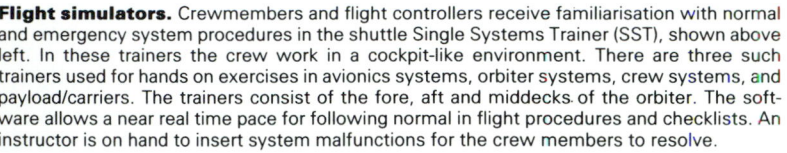

Flight simulators. Crewmembers and flight controllers receive familiarisation with normal and emergency system procedures in the shuttle Single Systems Trainer (SST), shown above left. In these trainers the crew work in a cockpit-like environment. There are three such trainers used for hands on exercises in avionics systems, orbiter systems, crew systems, and payload/carriers. The trainers consist of the fore, aft and middecks of the orbiter. The software allows a near real time pace for following normal in flight procedures and checklists. An instructor is on hand to insert system malfunctions for the crew members to resolve.

The Shuttle Mission Simulator (SMS), above right, is the prime training simulator for shuttle crew training. It is a high fidelity simulator capable of flight crew training in all phases (ascent, orbit, deorbit and entry to the Earth's atmosphere, and payloads) of the mission from 30 minutes prior to launch to landing. The SMS can simulate both normal operations and malfunctions of every support and avionics subsystem on the shuttle. The picture shows astronauts John Young and Robert Crippen during training for the first shuttle mission.

The SMS is a complex device which includes a large computer, several minicomputers, five shuttle computers, simulation interfaces, several stations for instructors, both fixed and moving crew stations, and a multiplicity of image display devices. Both crew station simulations can be run simultaneously and independently of each other. The simulation of subsystems is provided by mathematical models. The SMS software is designed to perform and respond just like the actual space shuttle vehicle. The SMS can also be interfaced with a network simulation system (NSS) and Mission Control Center (MCC) to conduct integrated simulations.

The photograph on the right shows the aft station of the fixed SMS. This simulator is the most critical element of the shuttle training programme. It is used to train crewmembers to use the Remote Manipulator System (RMS) for payload bay operations and payload handling. As with the forward station simulators, 'out of the window' views are provided by high quality digital image generation systems (NASA).

Man in space

Skylab

Born out of the need to know man's capability for living in space, the orbiting laboratory Skylab resulted from a compromise between technology, costs, and social and political interests. Its shape derived from Gemini and Apollo hardware. Its launch into space on 14 May 1973 was marred by a mishap to a micrometeorite shield and solar panel which posed a severe threat to its very existence. Manned by its adventurous crews, Skylab was to survive both this and many other problems until, five years later, it suffered a fiery death.

As its mission unfolded, the usefulness of Skylab was gradually revealed. It was a space station with immense capabilities for increasing our understanding of the physical and physiological behaviour of man in space, of the Universe, the Sun, the Earth and its environment, and of the science of microgravity. Moreover, it fostered an educational interest in space activities through the participation of students and an increased public awareness of the benefits of manned spaceflight.

To some, Skylab was plagued with problems. But to others it was a vindication of the role of man in space. Its main achievement, of great significance for the future of space exploration and exploitation, was evidence that man could survive for extended periods of time, working effectively in this new habitat and outside in the hostile environment of space.

Scientifically, Skylab was a great success. New information was acquired about physical processes occurring on the Sun, particularly solar flares. It demonstrated the importance of new technologies for studies of Earth resources and for material processing. Lessons were learned that would be applied to the design of future space stations. Further, it fired the imagination of the whole world.

A space station emerges

In the planning which led to Skylab, considerable effort was spent in developing a space station from the used third stage of the Saturn V rocket, called the Saturn IVB. Fixtures installed prior to launch in this stage and an attached docking module were to be used by astronauts to construct the primary element of a space station. After the Apollo 11 lunar landing, when it became evident that a Saturn V was available to launch Skylab, this idea was discarded. However, the concept of forming a station from the Saturn IVB persisted.

The Saturn IVB Orbital WorkShop (OWS) was divided into two areas – the lower area was the living quarters, the upper level a large domed cavity for storage and for experiments. Two airlocks, one of which was to prove invaluable in the rescue of Skylab, were installed in the wall of the OWS. Scientific instruments could be mounted outside the airlocks and exposed to space conditions without affecting Skylab's internal environment.

Electric power was provided by the OWS and the Apollo Telescope Mount (ATM) solar arrays. Each system could produce five kilowatts. Additional power was available from the Command and Service Module (CSM) batteries. All the electric power was regulated

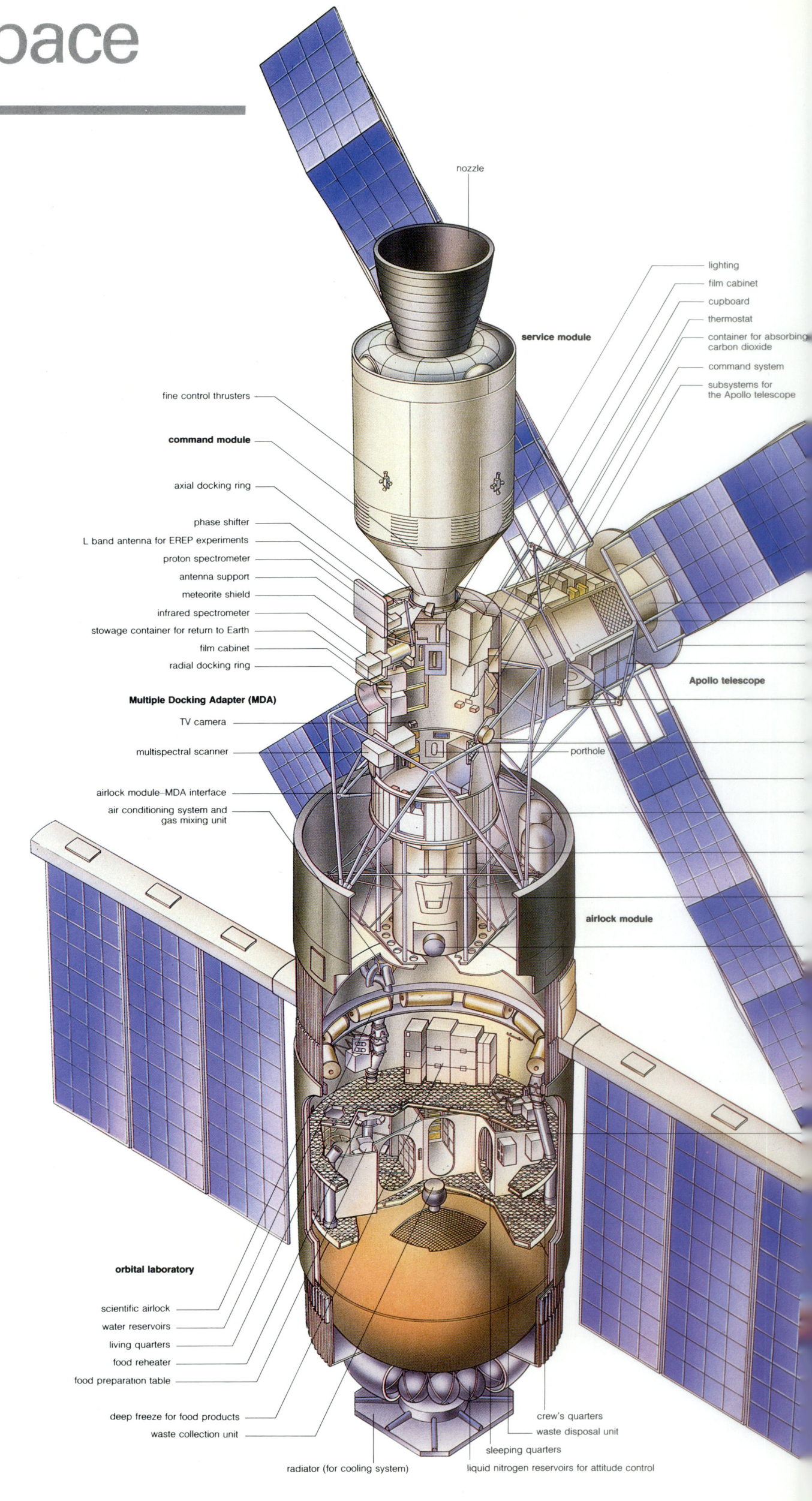

from the Airlock Module (AM). The capability of using power from either of the arrays was to be the single most important factor in the post-launch rescue of Skylab. With electric power from the ATM arrays, flight controllers at Houston were able to maintain Skylab until the first crew succeeded in releasing the remaining OWS array.

In the earlier space station designs, the Multiple Docking Adapter (MDA) was to have a number of ports for crew docking and for attaching separately launched instrument payloads. For Skylab only two ports were retained – the axial port for normal crew docking and the radial port for a rescue vehicle. The large volume of the MDA was put to good use for experiments including the Command and Display Console for the ATM, the Earth Resources Experiment Package (EREP), the Material Processing Facility, experiment storage, and a film vault. At times, all three crewmembers operated experiments from the MDA.

In an earlier version of the plan, the solar experiments were to have been mounted in the Service Module of an Apollo spacecraft. This accounts for the name Apollo Telescope Mount – while the acronym ATM was something of an anomaly for Skylab, it was retained. Throughout the planning for the ATM, instrument pointing accuracy and contamination were continuing concerns. Observations made by the instruments themselves were used to fine point the entire telescope system. Contamination problems were solved by minimising and controlling the venting of gases from Skylab.

Left over from the Apollo lunar programme, the four Command and Service Modules (CSM) used for the Skylab programme were essentially

radiator

work platform

sun shield

battery and thermal regulator

inertial gyroscope for attitude control

footrest and grip

solar panel

oxygen reservoir

electronic units

airlock for extravehicular activities (Gemini)

environment control system

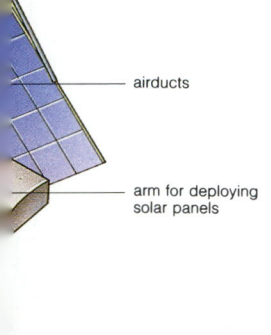

airducts

arm for deploying solar panels

solar panel

Skylab in orbit at the end of the first mission. This photograph, taken by the crew of the first mission as they prepared to return to Earth, shows the Multiple Docking Adaptor (MDA) and the Apollo Telescope Mount (ATM). Skylab, with one of its solar panels and micrometeorite shield gone, orbits majestically, protected from the Sun's heat by its makeshift parasol. At the bottom of the MDA, below the axial docking port, are the antennae for the EREP scatterometer, altimeter and radiometer.

The ATM was formed with an outer structure (3·3 metres in diameter and 3·6 metres in height) and an interior canister which housed eight telescopes. The canister was attached to a gimballed ring which could rotate for polarisation experiments and for loading of film by the crew. The Skylab attitude control system provided pointing accuracies of six arcminutes. The ATM pointing system met the difficult requirement of maintaining pointing accuracy to within 2·5 arcseconds for 15 minutes. Three large control moment gyros mounted to the outer structure provided the primary attitude control.

The instruments included a white light coronograph, a X ray spectrographic telescope, an ultraviolet scanning polychromator spectroheliometer, an X ray telescope, an extreme ultraviolet spectroheliograph, an ultraviolet spectrograph, and a hydrogen alpha telescope (NASA).

Skylab. (left) The main part of Skylab was the Orbital WorkShop (OWS), an unused Saturn IVB some 14·7 metres long and 6·6 metres in diameter. Deployable solar arrays were attached to the OWS which was protected by a micrometeorite shield. Also attached to the OWS was the Airlock Module (AM), the heart of Skylab. Ten kilowatts of electric power, environmental conditions, and the reception and transmission of data were controlled from here.

Hinged to the AM, and deployed in orbit, was the Apollo Telescope Mount (ATM) with its huge 30 metre long solar array panels. The Multiple Docking Adaptor (MDA) was attached to the AM. It provided ports for the crew of three to enter Skylab from the Command and Service Module (CSM) and contained crew operated panels for the acquisition of solar data by the ATM and Earth data by the Earth Resources Experiment Package (EREP). The entire Skylab was mounted for launch atop the Saturn V rocket. An Instrument Unit (IU), between the OWS and the AM, controlled the ascent of the Saturn V and the deployment of Skylab; it was designed to function for 7·5 hours and then to remain passive throughout the mission. With a volume of 330 cubic metres, the mass of this space station was 82 tonnes.

Much of the crew's time was spent in the lower level of the OWS. Here the crew relaxed, ate their meals, slept and collected data for medical experiments. Each crew-member had a separate sleeping compartment, essentially a sleeping bag hung on a wall, with a private area. An entertainment locker in the compartment contained personal reading and writing materials and a tape player. The washroom and toilet (termed the Waste Management Compartment) had a special function: the body's waste products were collected and processed for return to Earth for medical studies.

Water tanks near the top of the dome housed 2·7 tonnes of water for the crews. Air blowers circulated air, via ducts, throughout Skylab. The temperature was maintained at 20 degrees celsius by passive coatings on the exterior of the WorkShop and by the use of heaters. The area under the micrometeorite shield was painted black to absorb heat. Because the shield was lost just after launch, the black coating caused a near disaster as the OWS temperatures rose to intolerable levels (NASA).

Skylab with its sun shield. This photograph, taken by the second crew as they departed from Skylab to return to Earth, shows the sail which they installed over the parasol deployed by the first crew. Concern that ultraviolet radiation would degrade the parasol materials and the existence of hotspots in the WorkShop led to the decision to instruct the second crew to deploy the sail. Using 17·5 metre poles which they assembled from eleven sections, astronauts Garriott and Lousma erected a large V structure over the OWS. The poles were attached to the ATM truss. Attaching the sail to a continuous loop of 'clothes line' running the length of the poles, they hoisted the 7·4 metre by 6·8 metre sail over the existing parasol. The lines were then secured to outriggers at the corners of the ATM. The sail, the largest structure deployed in space, corrected the temperature problems still remaining after the parasol was deployed, and lowered temperatures in the WorkShop to near normal levels (NASA).

unchanged. Three were used to ferry the crews. After docking with Skylab, the CSM was dormant while waiting to ferry the crew back to Earth. The fourth CSM was intended for use as a rescue mission in the event that the ferry vehicle became unusable for any reason. The rescue vehicle was modified to carry five astronauts. However, the rescue capability was limited by the availability of suitable launch opportunities. If the first crew needed to be rescued, it would be 48 days, an intolerable time, before the rescue team could reach Skylab. For the second crew, this time was reduced to 28 days, still too long to be effective. Only for the final crew would a rescue launch vehicle be in a state of readiness. Even then, the minimum time for rescue was 10 days. During the second manned mission, a leak in the Service Module control system gas tanks prompted initiation of a rescue mission. Fortunately, it was not needed.

Talking to Skylab astronauts was a new experience for flight controllers on the ground. Voluminous, detailed schedules and instructions had to be transmitted to the crew each day. Normally, Skylab flew in an inertially stabilised mode, with its solar arrays and ATM pointing towards the Sun. For Earth orientation, needed for EREP, it had to be reconfigured for three-axis stabilisation. While this was accomplished by on board computers, the computer commands had to be sent to Skylab by the controllers.

During the mission the flight controllers were severely taxed by attitude manoeuvres made increasingly difficult by malfunctioning control moment gyros and rapidly depleting control gas supplies. During the manned phases, almost all of the data acquired were stored on magnetic tape or in the form of film which they returned to Earth at the end of the mission. While Skylab was unmanned, only one of the ATM experiments was equipped to operate and return data via the downlink. However, controllers continued to monitor Skylab's vital subsystems in order to maintain its health so that it was ready for the next crew.

Use of two of the three voice communication channels was to prove controversial. During the mission, the crew's conversations were recorded on magnetic tape for later playback to the ground stations. Another channel was for private conversations between the crew and their physicians on the ground or family members. NASA's policy of protecting the confidentiality of these channels was strongly disputed by the news media, but was not changed.

Skylab missions

The Saturn V launch appeared to be flawless, but it was soon learned that a major mishap had occurred. While this was investigated and alternatives for rescuing Skylab were studied, the first crew of Charles Conrad, Joseph Kerwin and Paul Weitz trained for their new role as rescuers. Delayed several times, they finally lifted off on 25 May 1973. Whilst the launch of the second crew was to have occurred on 15 August 1973, concern about Skylab prompted moving the launch forward to 28 July. Alan Bean, Owen Garriott and Jack Lousma remained in orbit for 59 days, twice the time of the first crew's stay in space. The final crew of Gerald Carr, Edward Gibson and William Pogue entered Skylab on 16 November 1973. This mission was also scheduled for 56 days, although

options existed to increase this. After several extensions, the last crew left Skylab on the 84th day of their mission.

Only minutes after the launch of the Saturn V, air pressure tore off the micrometeorite shield surrounding the OWS. As the shield separated, it broke the latches on one of the OWS solar arrays, which apparently deployed and was blown away. The shield, which was tightly held to the OWS at launch, was designed to be deployed in orbit to stand 0·15 metres away from it. Micrometeorites striking and penetrating the shield would thus lose most of their energy before reaching the OWS wall. Without the shield, flight controllers were immediately confronted with the problem of rising temperatures inside the WorkShop which threatened to damage the food and film carried aboard. Although electric power from the ATM was more than sufficient to maintain Skylab at a low level of operation, it was inadequate to carry out the planned experiments. Unless the temperature could be lowered and the remaining solar array deployed, Skylab's mission would be severely curtailed.

During the following two weeks, both the ingenuity and the forbearance of the entire Skylab team were taxed to the limit. While flight controllers wrestled to reduce the interior temperatures, engineers strove to build and test fabric covers which could be erected using special tools to save Skylab. An ingenious idea, a parasol which could be deployed by the crew from the Scientific Airlock, was a prime candidate.

A larger sail-like cover, which would require a strenuous and risky deployment by crewmembers outside Skylab, was a back up. Releasing

Skylab mission profile. The illustration below depicts the mission profile for the Skylab programme. The first manned mission lasted 28 days. The next mission was planned to occur three months following the first and to last 56 days. The length of the mission was chosen so as to provide opportunities for studies of the effects of longer periods of weightlessness on the crew. While the last mission was also planned for 56 days, a decision was made, as the mission progressed, to extend its duration to 84 days. In between crew visits, Skylab was placed in a 'storage mode' with its solar arrays pointing towards the Sun (NASA).

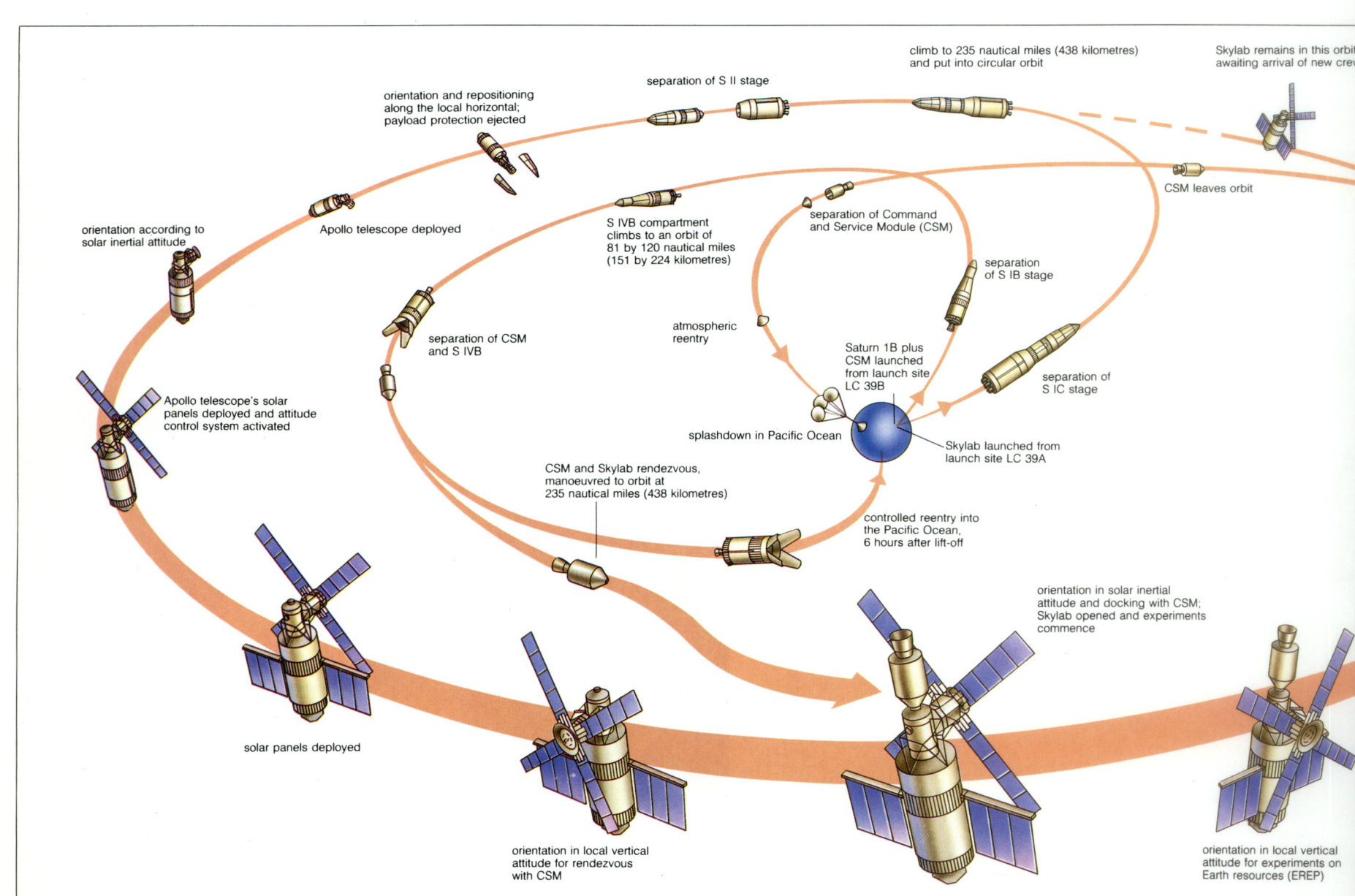

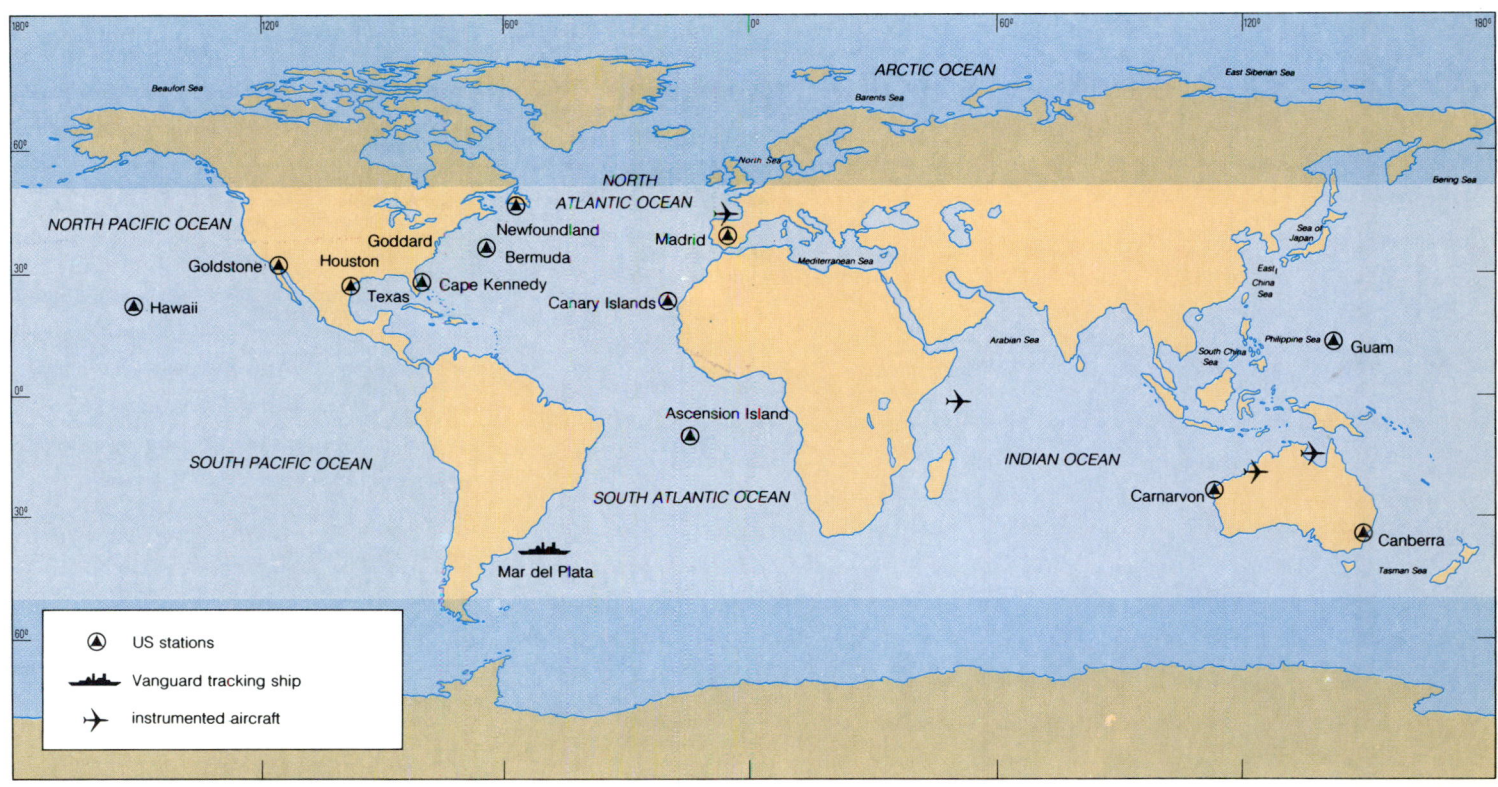

Skylab ground coverage. With its 50 degree orbital inclination, all regions of the Earth with latitudes up to 50 degrees were covered by Skylab's orbital track. This inclination was chosen to support the Earth Resources Experiment Package (EREP). Almost 75% of the Earth's land area and 90% of the world's population lie within this region. At a 438 kilometre altitude, Skylab passed over the same point on the ground every five days.

The EREP instruments included film cameras, imaging sensors and a pointable spectrometer for studies of land use, agriculture, and geology. An L band radiometer was tested for the detection of soil moisture. A microwave scatterometer and altimeter provided the first information from space on ocean waves and sea surface topography.

Tracking and data acquisition for Skylab were provided by eleven ground stations, an airborne relay, and one ship of the NASA Space Tracking and Data Network (STDN). Communication with Skylab was generally limited to 28 minutes in each 93 minute orbit, with an average contact time of 6·5 minutes per station. In addition to real time telemetry, two hours of tape recorded data could be played back ('dumped') to a ground station in 5·5 minutes.

Skylab data received at a ground station were passed through the STDN at the Goddard Space Flight Center, Maryland, to the Mission Control Center in Houston, Texas. Processed telemetry data and film, samples, specimens, notes and crew log books were given to investigators for scientific analysis (NASA).

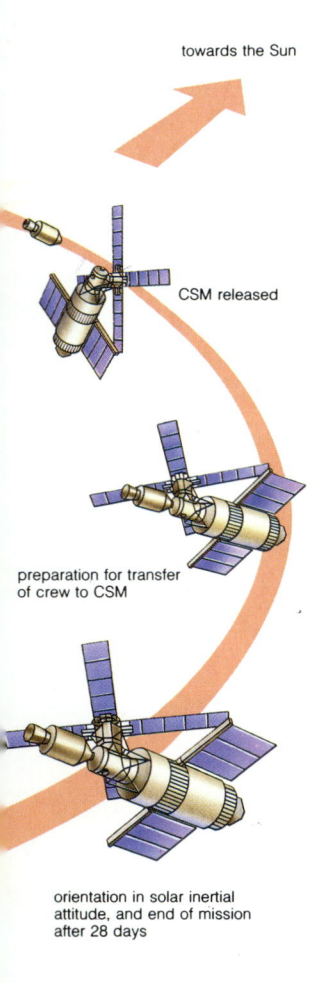

towards the Sun

CSM released

preparation for transfer of crew to CSM

orientation in solar inertial attitude, and end of mission after 28 days

CSM = Command and Service Module

the stuck solar array would be equally risky, since there were no foot restraints or hand holds to assist the astronauts.

On arriving at Skylab, the first crew deployed the parasol. The temperatures in the OWS immediately began to fall and, as indicated by ground tests, the food had not spoiled. However, based on the results of such tests, the crew took additional film and medical kits with them as a precaution.

Later in the first mission, astronauts Conrad and Kerwin performed a spacewalk in order to free the stuck solar array. Using cable cutters mounted on the end of an eight metre pole, Kerwin locked on to a 'strap' of metal from the, now lost, micrometeorite shield which was preventing array deployment. Conrad attached a cable to the array. After the strap was cut, it took the physical efforts of both astronauts to pull the array free; the sudden release of the array sent them flying into space held only by their umbilical lines.

The crew performed spacewalks regularly to replace film in the ATM experiments. During these trips, they often installed or retrieved experiment packages which needed exposure to space. They found the views of the Earth, the sky, and the Moon exhilarating. During the final mission, the appearance of Comet Kohoutek provided yet another opportunity for the crew to venture outside in order to photograph it.

One of the more difficult tasks for the final crew was the attempt to repair the EREP antenna. The antenna, designed to rotate in pitch and roll, stopped operating during the second mission. Faulty potentiometers were suspected. Armed with tools and bypass cables, astronauts Pogue and Gibson removed covers and cleaned the potentiometers. When this failed to correct the problem, they inserted a pin to restrain the pitch gimbal and connected the bypass cable. This restored the roll motion. Once again, the Skylab mission had demonstrated the capability of man to repair electromechanical equipment in space.

Living in Skylab

Skylab has been compared with an average house in terms of its size. The interior volume far exceeded that of Gemini and Apollo, and was even greater than that of the Soviet Salyut space station. Habitability was a major concern of its designers. The advice of industrial design experts was sought, and a pale yellow paint with bright accents was chosen for the interior. Lights were relocated and noise suppression techniques were used. So the Skylab environment was relatively hospitable. The living quarters and the Earth viewing window were pleasant for the crew. However, the food was a continuing source of complaint, particularly the pre-planned menu. Food that did not stay in the tray, or reconstituted packages which exploded, presented formidable housekeeping problems. Sleeping was difficult for most astronauts because of noise, and the toe-to-nose ventilation which was used. However, the three piece suit worn by the crew worked well.

The euphemistically termed Waste Management Compartment was difficult to use and often did not work. It was also noisy and, when used during the sleep period, disturbed the other crew members.

Moving large bulky objects in Skylab was no problem, but small tools and parts easily floated away, carried by the air currents. These smaller items could be retrieved at the filter in front of the return air ducts.

The crew's day was intended to include eight hours each of work, relaxation, and sleep, with one day off each week. But this was not to be. Wearied by continuing problems with Skylab itself and the complex work schedules developed by flight planners, the crews often fell behind schedule. The planners, spurred on by anxious experimenters, strove to raise the performance of the crews by assigning increasingly more work. During each mission the relationship between mission planners and crews became strained at times, and conferences were needed to resolve the problems. However, the

The effects of acceleration on astronauts. A chair which tilted, or rotated at up to 30 revolutions per minute, was used for investigating motion sickness as the astronaut moved his head while being rotated. Special devices were used to measure visual space orientation in two dimensions as well as the crewmember's ability to judge his orientation.

Calibrated with known weights, the seat was oscillated back and forth to measure the crewman's weight each day (NASA).

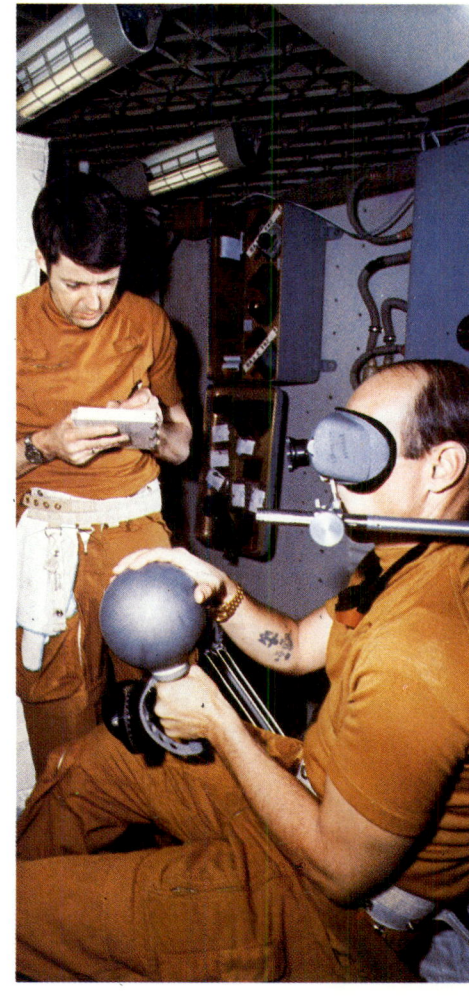

Living with space

Mission	Experiment number	Type of experiment	Project leader and centre	Description
1	S 015	effect of weightlessness on individual human cells	Dr P. O. Montgomery Dallas County Hospital (Texas)	aim: to examine the effects of weightlessness on living cells means: microscope camera, samples data: films of the growth of tissues in a culture and analysis of tissue cultures after the flight
2	S 071	circadian rhythm; *Perognathus* (mouse)	Dr Robert G. Lindberg Northrop Corporate Laboratory (California)	aim: to examine the effects of weightlessness on physiological rhythms means: six mice in a dark cage data: body temperature, and degree of activity
2	S 072	circadian rhythm; *Drosophila ampelophila* (fruit fly)	Colin S. Pittendrigh Stanford University (California)	aim: to examine the effects of weightlessness on the daily production cycle of fruit fly chrysalides means: four groups of flies in thermally controlled containers; synchronised light pulses to operate photodetectors data: detecting the emergence of fruit flies from chrysalides by photoelectric cells
1	ED 31	behaviour of bacteria and bacterial spores	Robert L. Staehle University of Rochester (New York)	aim: to examine the effect of weightlessness on the survival rate, growth and mutation of bacteria and spores data: culture during the flight, and tests on the ground afterwards
2	ED 32	*in vitro* studies of certain immunological phenomena	Todd A. Meister Jackson Heights (New York)	aim: to study the effects of weightlessness on antibodies means: microscope slides fixed with acetic acid and photographed data: the slides themselves, and photographs
3	ED 41	performance of motor responses	Kathy L. Jackson Houston (Texas)	aim: to examine the modifications to, and competence of, the crew's motor responses means: tests using an electronic board, and putting shapes into holes data: timing the test
2	ED 52	formation of spider's webs in weightlessness	Judith S. Miles Lexington (Massachusetts)	aim: to examine the effects of weightlessness on the construction of a spider's web and on its structure means: spider, living in a glass container data: photographs
3	ED 61	growth of plants in weightlessness	Joel G. Wordekemper West Point (Nebraska)	aim: to examine the growth of rice grains in space and on the Earth; to examine the effects of light as a substitute for gravity data: photographs
3	ED 62	orientation of a plant embryo in weightlessness	Donald W. Schlack Downey (California)	
2	ED 63	cytoplasmic flux in weightlessness	Cheryl A. Pelitz Littleton (Colorado)	aim: to examine the effects of weightlessness on the intra- and inter-cellular cytoplasmic movement means: cells of pondweed leaves data: microscopic observations

Biological experiments (above) and medical experiments (below) on board Skylab

Mission	Experiment number	Type of experiment	Project head and centre	Description
1, 2 and 3	M 071	mineral equilibrium	Dr G. D. Wehon US National Institute of Health, Bethesda (Maryland)	aim: to collect data on the effects of weightlessness on muscles and the skeleton data: body weight; absorption of solids and liquids; urinary flow; faeces and vomit; blood samples, before and after flight
1, 2 and 3	M 073	biological analysis of body fluids	Dr Carolyn S. Leach NASA/Johnson Space Center (Texas)	aim: to examine the effects of weightlessness on endocrinometabolic functions data: body weight; absorption of solids and liquids; urinary flow; blood samples, before and after flight
1, 2 and 3	M 074	measuring the mass of specimens	Dr William E. Thornton NASA/Johnson Space Center (Texas)	aim: to determine the faecal mass, the mass vomited and the food residues data: measuring known masses for calibration, and measuring faecal masses and food residues for medical experiments
1, 2 and 3	M 078	measuring bone minerals	Dr J. M. Vogel US Public Health Service	aim: to examine the effects of weightlessness on bone minerals data: gamma ray examination, before and after the flight, on heel and forearm bones
1, 2 and 3	M 092	negative pressure on the lower body	Dr Robert L. Johnson NASA/Johnson Space Center (Texas)	aim: to examine how the cardiovascular system adapts to weightlessness, and to obtain information on the body's condition during the return to Earth means: negative pressure, used to simulate the effects of hydrostatic pressure in the blood in a 1 g gravity field data: blood pressure; cardiac rhythm; temperature; vector cardiogram; change of leg volume; body weight
1, 2 and 3	M 093	vector cardiogram	Dr Newton W. Allebach US Naval Aerospace Medical Institute (Florida)	aim: to examine cardiac alterations during the flight means: harness with eight electrodes; exercise bicycle data: vector cardiograph, using measurements of potential, at rest and also before and after eating (measurements performed before and after flight)
1, 2 and 3	M 111	cytogenetic studies of blood	Dr Lillian H. Lockhart University of Texas, Medical Branch, Houston	aim: to examine chromosome aberrations in leucocytes (white blood corpuscles); to examine the genetic effects of spaceflight data: periodic blood samples, before and after flight
1, 2 and 3	M 112	*in vitro* aspects of human immunity system	Dr Stephen E. Ritzmann University of Texas, Medical Branch, Houston	aim: to analyse modifications of cellular and humoral immunity by studying proteins in the blood plasma and corpuscles, and the transformation and synthesis of DNA and RNA by the lymphocytes means: equipment to sample the blood during the flight, and a centrifuge machine data: blood samples taken before, during and after the flight; comparison with a control group on the ground
1, 2 and 3	M 113	blood volume, and lifetime of red corpuscles	Dr Phillip C. Johnson, Jr. Baylor University School of Medicine, Waco (Texas)	aim: to examine the effects of weightlessness on the plasma volume and quantity of red corpuscles means: injection of four radio-isotope tracers into the crew and a control group; blood samples taken during the flight data: blood samples taken before, during and after the flight
1, 2 and 3	M 114	metabolism of red corpuscles	Dr Charles E. Mengel University of Missouri School of Medicine	aim: to look for possible metabolic and/or membranaceous changes in red corpuscles data: blood samples taken before, during and after the flight
1, 2 and 3	M 115	effects of weightlessness on the blood	Dr Stephen L. Kimsey NASA/Johnson Space Center (Texas)	aim: to examine the physico-chemical parameters of the blood, in order to study the equilibrium between its different components data: blood samples taken before, during and after the flight
1 and 2	M 131	human vestibular function	Dr Ashton Graybiel US Naval Aerospace Medical Institute	aim: to test the susceptibility to travel sickness; to understand the effects of weightlessness on the body's gravity receptors; to test changes in the sensitivity of semi-circular canals in the ears means: a rotating chair; apparatus for detecting calcium build up in the inner ear; a reference sphere and magnetic pointer; reading aloud data: threshold of perception of rotation; sickness symptoms when moving; determining orientation
1 and 2	M 133	sleep patterns	Dr J. D. Frost, Jr. Baylor University School of Medicine, Waco (Texas)	aim: to evaluate the quantity and quality of sleep during spaceflight means: electroencephalograph (EEG and electro-oculograph (EOG); a helmet containing electrodes data: EEG and EOG monitoring before, during and after the flight
1, 2 and 3	M 151	studying time and movement	Dr Joseph F. Kubis Fordham University (New York)	aim: to examine adaption to weightlessness by comparing the time taken and movement made for identical tasks data: photographing activities of the crew, before and during the flight
1, 2 and 3	M 171	metabolic activity	E. L. Michel NASA/Johnson Space Center (Texas)	aim: to examine the metabolic effects of weightlessness on the metabolic efficiency during mechanical work; evaluating the efficiency on the exercise bicycle means: work measured by the bicycle (number of turns per minute); measuring oxygen absorption, and respiration of carbon dioxide; vital capacity; respiratory quotient; cardiac rhythm; blood pressure; vector cardiogram; weight, and body temperatures
1, 2 and 3	M 172	measuring the astronaut's body mass	Dr W. E. Thornton NASA/Johnson Space Center (Texas)	aim: demonstrating the technique, and supplying data for medical experiments means: springs; chair mounted on flexible pivot data: calibration before flight; measuring known masses; calculating the weight of the crew members daily

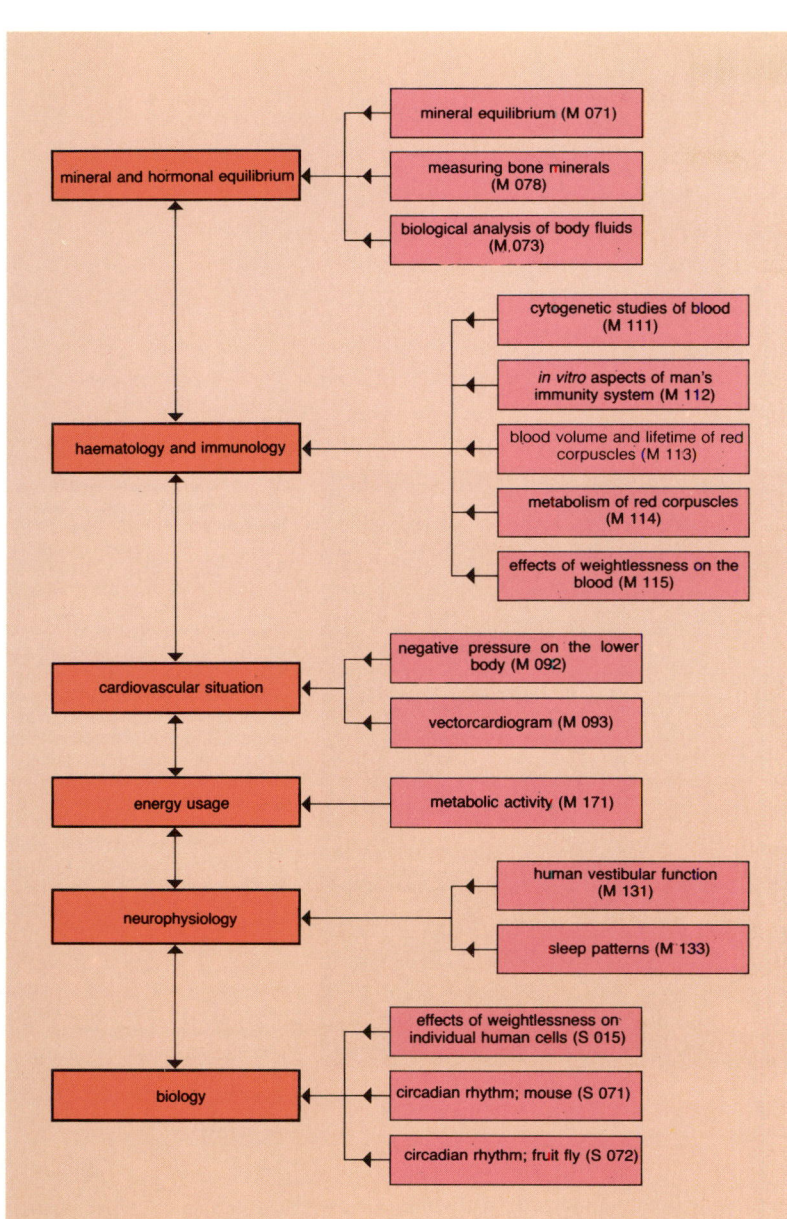

planning bore fruit: Skylab acquired about twice as much data as was planned.

Medical and biological experiments

Experiments on Gemini and Apollo had revealed that the heart rate of astronauts was lowered by not having to work against gravity. Bone calcium and other minerals were found to be expelled at a surprising rate. In addition, many of the crew experienced nausea. These earlier missions were short, mostly less than fourteen days, so it would be interesting to learn what would happen on longer missions. Would weakening of the heart muscles lead to heart failure upon return to Earth? Would calcium loss permanently weaken the bones? Could exercise overcome muscle deterioration? Did rapid head movements cause nausea, and which medicine was effective in combating it? The Skylab medical experiments were designed to seek answers to questions such as these. The crews found it difficult to adjust to some of the experiments. However, they were generally effective in that the crews on the longer dura-

Flow chart showing the main areas of the biological and medical studies performed on board Skylab. Before long duration manned flights can be planned, man's ability to adjust to the rigours of space has to be tested. Therefore a number of biological and physiological experiments were planned, especially on the human circadian rhythm.

This flow chart shows each main area of study and the main experiments performed on board Skylab (NASA).

tion missions found it relatively easy to return to their pre-launch condition.

The Mineral Balance Experiment presented the crew with other problems. This experiment required an accurate assessment of both food intake and waste products – hence, the prescribed food menu. Any leftover food had to be weighed before it was discarded. However, the experiment proved that calcium loss continued even on the longer missions and in spite of the crew taking exercise.

Since earlier missions had shown that body fluids tend to move upward in space, imparting a 'puffy eye' appearance and distended veins, considerable time was spent measuring and photographing body shape.

Overall, the Skylab medical experiments revealed no physiological changes, other than motion sickness and the bone calcium loss, which would preclude much longer flights. The long duration of the Skylab missions was ideal for such biological experiments. Tissue cultures of living human cells were maintained and observed to study the functioning of cells in weightlessness.

Mice and fruit flies were carried on board to study changes in their circadian rhythms. Housed in the Apollo Service Module, in their own environmentally controlled package, the body temperature and activity of the six mice were to be monitored and telemetered to Earth. In the experiments four separate groups of fruit fly pupae were to be exposed to a flash of light at different times to stimulate the emergence of adult flies and determine whether weightlessness affected the daily rhythm mechanism. Unfortunately, a power failure occurred in the Module early in the mission terminating the experiment.

Spider and plant experiments were submitted by students. The *Araneus diadematus*, a spider which consumes its web each day, was studied to observe the effects of weightlessness on web formation. The growth of rice seedlings was studied to determine the effects of the lack of gravity and the stimulation effects of light as a substitute for gravity. Other student experiments included microscopic observations of intracellular cytoplasm in plant leaf cells, the reaction of antibodies to foreign substances, and studies of the growth of bacteria and bacterial spores.

The Demise of Skylab

At the end of their mission, and before they departed from Skylab, the final crew boosted it into a higher orbit. A controlled reentry using the Service Module engines had been considered, but this was evaluated as being too risky for the crew. Later, as Skylab's orbit decayed, plans were developed for a Space Shuttle mission to attach a rocket stage in order to boost Skylab to a safe altitude. In early 1979, Skylab's systems were reactivated to control its attitude and minimise atmospheric drag. But it soon became apparent that the Shuttle, with its many development problems, would not be ready in time to save Skylab. While most of the abandoned space station would be consumed by the heat of reentry into the atmosphere, several parts, including the heavy lead film vaults, would not. Fearful of the prospect of loss of life and damage to property, it was decided to try and control the impact zone, so minimising the risk to highly populated areas. Flight controllers, including some who had laboured five years earlier to save Skylab, now had the problem of bringing it down. A 'funeral' in the Indian Ocean was decided upon. Skylab reentered the atmosphere on 11 July 1980. As Skylab failed to breakup as expected, the impact area moved eastwards, showering an area of low population near Perth, Australia, with debris. No lives were lost and few observed the demise of the world's first space station.

Thomas L. Fischetti

International cooperation in space. On 15 July 1975, the Saturn IB and the Apollo CSM, with a crew of three, blasted off on what was to be the last flight for both systems. The mission was to rendezvous with the crew of the Soyuz.

Shortly thereafter, the Apollo crew of Thomas Stafford, Vance Brand and Donald Slayton manoeuvred to extract the docking adaptor from the launch vehicle and proceeded to join Soyuz. Two days later, the Apollo (right) and Soyuz (left) spacecraft linked up and, for the next few days, the American and Russian crews visited each other's craft. At an altitude of 225 kilometres, they carried out life science and material processing experiments. Of the 28 experiments planned for Apollo, five were conducted jointly with the Soyuz crew of Alexei Leonov and Valeri Kubasov.

After undocking, the crews used each other's spacecraft to perform experiments to measure the density of atomic oxygen and nitrogen using an ultraviolet radiation absorption technique. With the Apollo CSM occulting the solar disc, the Soyuz crew photographed the solar corona. After once again testing the docking system, the Apollo and Soyuz spacecraft parted to continue their separate missions. The Soyuz craft returned to Earth on 21 July.

During their nine day mission, the Apollo crew observed and photographed surface features of the Earth and measured its gravity field. They also studied the near Earth atmosphere (NASA).

Man in space

Soyuz–Salyut–Cosmos

Spaceflight has evolved through a number of logical steps. The first series of Soviet spacecraft, Vostok, were designed to test the ability of human beings to adapt to weightlessness. Vostok flights were therefore planned to be relatively short in duration. The next step was to design larger, multipurpose spacecraft capable of longer duration flights.

The Soyuz spacecraft

The Soyuz programme was conceived as this next step in manned spaceflight. Development began in 1962, and the first unmanned craft was launched in 1966. Manned spacecraft were launched from 1967 onwards.

The first Soyuz spacecraft weighed 6·38 tonnes, including its payload. Successive spacecraft, including present day ones, all weigh 6·8 tonnes. Until 1971, Soyuz carried a crew of three; later spacecraft had room for only two. Each Soyuz spacecraft consists of three main sections – an orbital compartment, a recovery capsule and an instrument and flight equipment module. These three compartments are joined together, but can be separated from each other by small explosive charges.

The recovery capsule is situated in the central part of the spacecraft. It is pressurised and is used by the cosmonauts during launch and insertion into orbit, space manoeuvres and return to Earth. The outermost parts of the spacecraft are covered by a special refractory coating for reentry into the Earth's atmosphere.

Inside the recovery module are the cosmonauts' seats. They are specially designed to help the cosmonauts withstand the great forces which they experience, especially during reentry. The capsule also contains the flight control instruments for the return, radio equipment, a life support system and parachutes. The rocket motors used for the return flight to Earth and the soft landing retrorockets are mounted on the exterior of this part of the spacecraft.

The shape of the capsule has been designed to create an aerodynamic lift force during the reentry phase. Thus, by altering the position of the capsule's centre of gravity, the descent trajectory is modified and the force exerted on the cosmonauts is reduced by a factor of about two compared with those which they would experience in a direct descent. The capsule has three portholes. Two, one on either side of the instrument panel, are used for naked eye observations and for photography. The third, fitted with an optical sight, is next to the control panel.

The orbital compartment is the most spacious part of the spacecraft. Cosmonauts carry out scientific experiments and rest in the orbital compartment which also contains the equipment for recycling and purifying the air, so necessary for their work in space. This compartment is also used as an airlock, when making spacewalks. It is connected to the recovery capsule by another airlock.

For the outward journey to the orbiting Salyut space station, there is a docking collar fitted to the upper part of the orbital compartment. This acts as a shock absorber during docking. The ring creates a rigid (and, since Soyuz 10, an airtight) joint between the two

spacecraft. Further, it enables the spacecraft to separate and move apart.

Behind the reentry module, the third compartment contains the spacecraft's propulsion systems. The pressurised part of this section contains chemical batteries for power, the heat regulation system, telemetry and radioguidance instruments, the attitude control system, and the on board computer. The non-pressurised part contains the rocket engines, the propellant tanks and the retrorockets which enable the spacecraft to be manoeuvred. The solar panels, antenna systems and the star trackers for the attitude control system are also situated in this module.

Part of the docking equipment is situated in the airlock which joins the equipment and reentry modules. This is where the spacecraft's centre of gravity is located.

Inside the pressurised compartment, the cosmonauts live without wearing spacesuits. The air temperature, humidity and composition are regularly monitored and kept at the same level in both the orbital compartment and the descent module. The results are fed to the on board surveillance system and are displayed on the instrument panel.

The cosmonauts have manual control of the small rocket motors thus enabling them to carry out docking manoeuvres and to rotate the spacecraft about its centre of gravity at a controlled rate. The spacecraft pilot can simultaneously see the Earth's surface and the horizon. Further, he can observe the stars and orient the spacecraft so that the solar panels always face the Sun.

The systems and other automatic devices on board Soyuz were devised to give the crew as much time as possible to carry out their pre-arranged schedule of scientific experiments.

Between April 1967 and May 1981, forty Soyuz spacecraft were launched, of which three were unmanned. On 5 June 1980 the first Soyuz T2 was launched, marking the beginning of a new series of manned spacecraft. Although the Soyuz T craft is very similar in appearance to the original Soyuz spacecraft, its systems have

been extensively modified, including a new navigation system and integral computer. Rapid calculations can be made relating to the flight trajectory; the spacecraft automatically selects the series of orbital adjustments which allows for optimum fuel efficiency and carries these out. All the computer's information and calculations are displayed for the cosmonauts. The result has been to increase flight precision, as well as the reliability and flexibility of manoeuvres, during both the period in orbit and the descent.

V. V. Kovalenok and A. S. Ivanchenkov on board Soyuz 29. On 15 June 1978, Soyuz 29 took Vladimir Kovalenok and Alexander Ivanchenkov to the orbiting space station, Salyut 6. The cosmonauts established a new space endurance record by spending 140 days in space. They made semiconductors and grew crystals in a special oven, and studied both the ultraviolet spectra of certain stars and the stratospheric ozone layer. During this period, two international crews were taken to Salyut 6. Piotr Klimouk (USSR) and Miroslav Hermaszewski (Poland) were there from 27 June to 5 July 1978, followed by Valery Bykovski (USSR) and Sigmund Jähn (East Germany) from 27 August to 3 September 1978. The Progress 2, 3 and 4 cargo-craft brought them fresh supplies of fuel, water, food and various equipment. This flight, lasting more than four months, marked an important step towards very long duration spaceflights (Tass).

The Soyuz T2 spacecraft launched at Baïkonour. Yuri Malychev and Vladimir Aksenov were the first crew to fly on board the modified Soyuz T spacecraft. Although the exterior of Soyuz T2, launched on 5 June 1980, is the same as its predecessors, there is a much more powerful computer in the orbital compartment which allows the cosmonauts more free time. In fact, the computer's two terminals, with their video displays and data banks, perform calculations which would otherwise occupy cosmonauts during manoeuvres. When Soyuz T2 was 180 metres from Salyut 6, Malychev and Aksenov carried out docking procedures. Separation of the descent module from the spacecraft was also carried out under manual control after a four day space mission (APN).

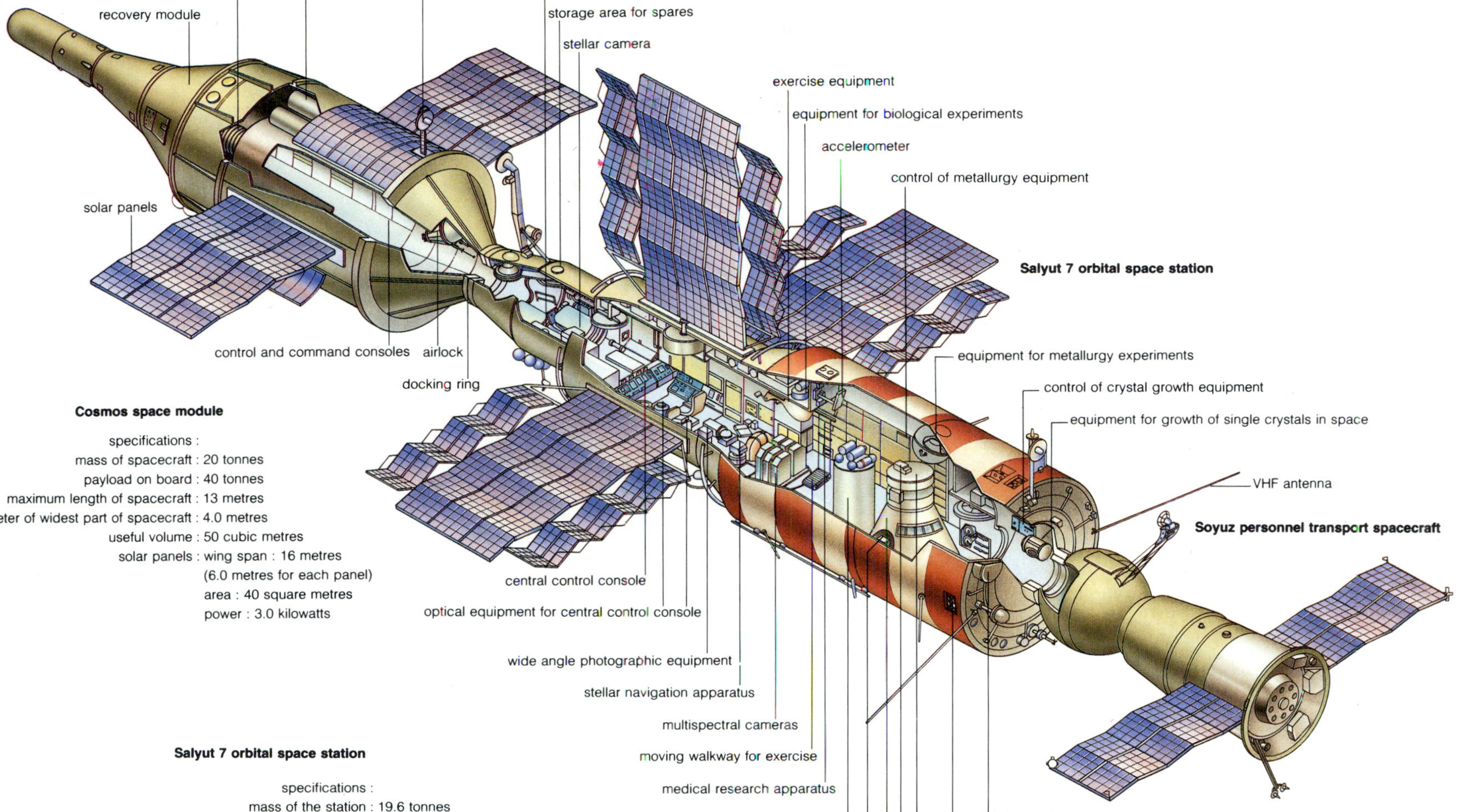

Cosmos space module

airlock at entrance to recovery module

propellant tanks

docking system antenna

recovery module

sextant

storage area for spares

stellar camera

exercise equipment

equipment for biological experiments

accelerometer

control of metallurgy equipment

solar panels

Salyut 7 orbital space station

control and command consoles   airlock

equipment for metallurgy experiments

docking ring

control of crystal growth equipment

equipment for growth of single crystals in space

VHF antenna

Soyuz personnel transport spacecraft

Cosmos space module

specifications :

mass of spacecraft : 20 tonnes

payload on board : 40 tonnes

maximum length of spacecraft : 13 metres

diameter of widest part of spacecraft : 4.0 metres

useful volume : 50 cubic metres

solar panels : wing span : 16 metres

(6.0 metres for each panel)

area : 40 square metres

power : 3.0 kilowatts

central control console

optical equipment for central control console

wide angle photographic equipment

stellar navigation apparatus

multispectral cameras

moving walkway for exercise

medical research apparatus

shower

four channel spectrometers

orbital correction system

attitude control unit

compartment for scientific equipment

gamma ray telescope

submillimetre radio telescope

Salyut 7 orbital space station

specifications :

mass of the station : 19.6 tonnes

payload on board : 2.0 tonnes

maximum length of space station : 15 metres

maximum diameter of space station : 4.1 metres

useful volume : 90 cubic metres

solar panels : wingspan : 17 metres

(7 metres for each panel)

area : 60 square metres

power : 4.0 kilowatts

Orbital Cosmos – Salyut 7 – Soyuz complex

orbital parameters :

altitude : 200–350 kilometres

angle of inclination of orbital plane to equatorial plane : 51.6 degrees

orbital period : approx 89 minutes

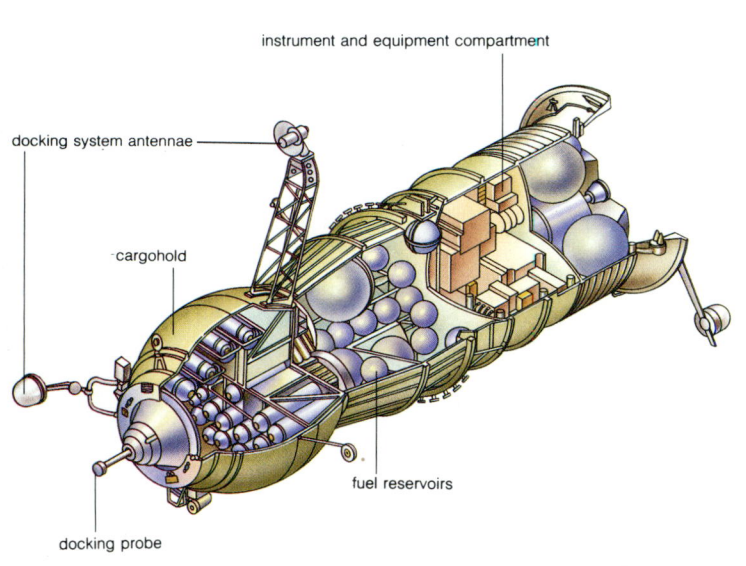

instrument and equipment compartment

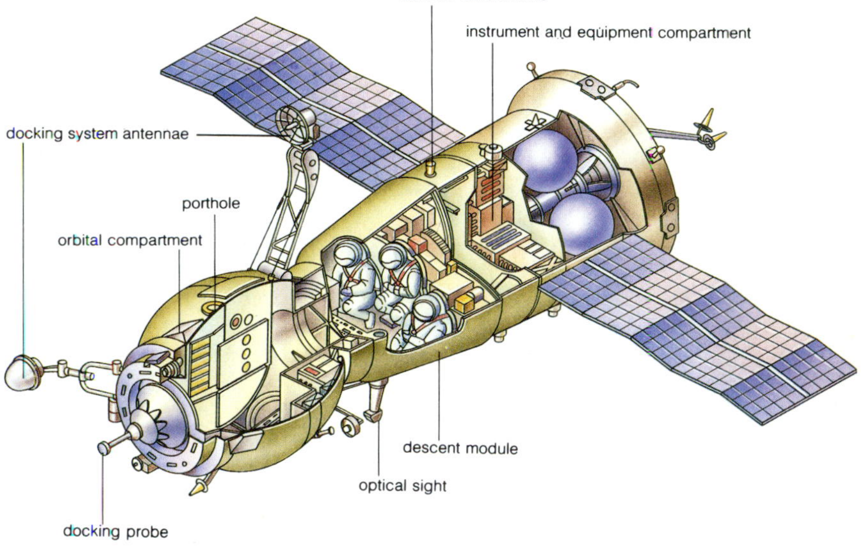

attitude control units

instrument and equipment compartment

docking system antennae

docking system antennae

porthole

orbital compartment

cargohold

descent module

fuel reservoirs

optical sight

docking probe

docking probe

Progress unmanned cargocraft

specifications :

mass of spacecraft : 7.2 tonnes

payload on board : 2.3 tonnes

(split between cargohold, up to 1 300 kilograms,

and the fuel reservoirs, up to 1 000 kilograms)

maximum length of the spacecraft : 7.9 metres

maximum diameter of the airlocks : 2.2 metres

solar panels wing span : 10.6 metres

type of launcher : Zemiorka

duration of independent flight : up to 3 days

duration of flight when docked with the orbiting

space station : up to 30 days

Soyuz personnel transport vessel

specifications :

crew : 2 or 3 people

mass of spacecraft : 6.8 tonnes

mass of descent module : 3.0 tonnes

length of spacecraft : 7.0 metres

maximum diameter : 2.7 metres

mass of payload brought from Salyut : 50 kilograms

solar panels wing span : 10.6 metres

type of launcher : Zemiorka

duration of independent flight : up to 3 days

duration of flight when docked with the orbiting

space station : up to 100 days

267

Living with space

The engines have also been redesigned. On the Soyuz T spacecraft the approach and orbital correction motors as well as the docking and attitude control system units are fuelled by the same propellants. The result is a common system for storing and distributing fuel and therefore for using up practically all the fuel on board. To further reduce the amount of fuel used, the descent module is separated from the spacecraft before the retrorockets are ignited.

The Salyut orbital space station

From its early days, the main aim of the Soviet space programme has been the construction of large, permanently manned space stations orbiting the Earth. The first Salyut orbiting space station was launched in April 1971, less than ten years after the first manned spaceflight. Since the beginning, the basic design has been an unmanned Salyut space station, placed in orbit, and a transport spacecraft to ferry the crew to it. The crew pass directly from the transport spacecraft to the station via an airlock. After docking, the Soyuz–Salyut complex has a mass of almost 26 tonnes, and a length of 23 metres.

The orbital part of the space station is launched without a protective covering. Only certain exterior elements, such as the solar panels, portholes and antennae, have individual covers which detach themselves after the space station has passed through the dense layers of the atmosphere.

The orbital station has three compartments. Two of them, the work compartment and the airlock are pressurised. The crew live in the work compartment and nearly all the station's equipment is located there. The third, non-pressurised compartment contains all the machinery including the fuel reservoirs, the attitude control and navigation systems, and the orbital correction rocket motors.

Salyut can alter its position to facilitate docking with a cargo transport vessel. It can modify its orbit or flight trajectory, and can alter its attitude and maintain this automatically so that,

The shower on Salyut 7. Anatoli Berezovoy and Vladimir Lebedev were the first cosmonauts to use Salyut 7. They left the Earth on 13 May 1982 on Soyuz. T5 and spent 190 days in space. During their long stay in space, the cosmonauts particularly appreciated being able to take a shower (APN).

for example, the solar panels are perpendicular to the Sun's rays for maximum efficiency.

The work compartment contains research instruments and machinery as well as the station's systems, separated from the living area by sliding panels which can be removed. This module also contains the central control panel and consoles. Apparatus for both physical exercise and medical examinations, and a device which simulates the force of gravity, are also found here.

Salyut 2 was put into orbit on 3 April 1973 to test new systems and apparatus. The data gathered were used to improve subsequent space stations, enabling them to remain in operation for longer. Many improvements were made with Salyut 3. A new electric gyroscope stabilised it along its trajectory. Some new bat-

teries and a high performance heat regulation system were tested. In addition a water recycling plant was used in space for the first time. A recoverable module was included, so that the results of work carried out could be brought back to Earth.

On Salyut 4, the automatic orientation and navigation systems were changed. More powerful solar panels, which automatically adjust their position to face the Sun, were included. Salyut 4 was put into orbit on 26 December 1974 and functioned for two years. The first crew to spend time on board were A. Goubarev and G. Gretchko who spent 30 days there. The second crew, P. Klimouk and V. Sevastianov, spent 31 days on board.

Salyut 5 was launched in June 1976. V. Volynov and V. Jolobov spent 49 days on

Scientific experiments on board the Salyut 6 and 7 orbital space stations

The first Soviet experiment involving space technology was carried out in 1969 on board Soyuz 6. It involved the electrical soldering of metals in zero gravity. Since then, this work has played an important part in maintenance, repair and improvement of equipment. Cosmonauts also manufacture in space certain materials, such as alloys or single crystals, which are either very difficult or very expensive to make in the 1g environment on Earth.

Under the weightless conditions of space, cosmonauts produce top quality silicon and germanium crystals for semiconductors for the electronics industry. Metallurgical experiments have also generated great interest. Alloys such as cadmium–mercury–selenium and cadmium–mercury–tellurium have been produced in space. The coating of metals and other materials by evaporation under a vacuum was first tested on Salyut 6. The pre-programmed evaporator on Salyut 7 has been used to develop many new coatings and has become indispensable for

repair work. Optical lenses and components for use in lasers have also been manufactured in space.

Another area which is being developed is space biotechnology. Experiments on board Salyut 7 have demonstrated that it is possible to produce biological preparations at a rate that is ten times greater than is possible on Earth. Orbital research into the manufacture of medicines and other pharmaceutical preparations by electrophoresis in space continues today. The products should be up to 20 times purer and more active than those manufactured on Earth.

Purer and more homogenous substances are demanded as developments are made in science and technology. The cost of producing these on Earth is becoming more and more expensive. At the same time, transport costs for the Earth–space–Earth round trip are decreasing.

Space medicine has made enormous progress during the 25 years of manned spaceflight. The results of cardiovascular tests on cosmonauts are immediately transmitted to ground control and also displayed on the screen of Salyut's computer. Results obtained during long spaceflights

suggest that the human body is capable of adapting to life in space. Even longer spaceflights are therefore being planned.

Cosmonauts use equipment such as multispectral cameras, wide angle cameras and four channel spectrometers to observe the Earth's surface and so acquire information on its natural resources. To give an idea of the importance of these observations, the data are used by some four hundred establishments and administrations in the USSR. They map different types of land use, geology and vegetation in different regions of the Soviet Union. They predict harvests, list available grazing land and locate new sources of subterranean water and mineral or petroleum deposits. Space observations can monitor the migration of shoals of fish. They are also invaluable to meteorologists, helping them to make accurate weather forecasts, to study the formation of hurricanes and cyclones and to investigate air pollution.

Immense regions can be mapped from space. Salyut 7 takes four to five minutes to map a region which, using aerial photography, would require 18 to 24 months.

Soviet Bureau of Information

board. They were relieved by V. Gorbatko and Y. Glazkov. This was the last of this generation of orbiting space station. Designed using experience gained from previous versions, it was in turn the forerunner of later stations.

The Salyut–Soyuz orbiting space complexes

When Salyut 6 was launched on 29 September 1977, it marked an important step towards the construction of permanent orbiting space stations. Its construction was rather different and it had provision for more diverse scientific research. Equipped with two docking ports, it could receive two spacecraft at once. Thus more than two people could be on board at any one time and new equipment and materials could be delivered to the station when required. Two people could leave the station and go into space together. The propulsion unit could be refuelled in flight. The total mass of the orbiting complex, comprised of the station and two spacecraft, was 32·9 tonnes with a volume of 100 cubic metres. It was 29 metres long and the maximum span of the solar panels was about 17 metres.

Salyut 6 consisted of five compartments, three of which were pressurised (the communication airlock, the work module and an interconnecting chamber). The other two compartments contained scientific instruments and space station systems. During the launch to orbit phase, the folded solar panels, the optical devices of the orientation system and the compartment containing the scientific instruments were protected. Selfcontained spacesuits were designed for Salyut 6, a shower cabin was built and the air in the inhabited modules was ionised.

The Soyuz design was adapted to produce an unmanned 'space freighter' or cargo spacecraft, called Progress. It consists of three separate modules – a cargo hold, with docking port, a compartment with fuel tanks and gas bottles, and a navigation and control system compartment. It supplies the space station complex with food, fuel and instruments. A Progress spacecraft can deliver up to 1·3 tonnes of freight, including up to a tonne of fuel.

During the nearly five year life of Salyut 6, the station was inhabited for about two years. A total of sixteen Soyuz and four Soyuz T spacecraft docked with the station. The five main long stay crews were joined by eleven short stay crews, of which eight had international crewmembers. A total of twenty-seven cosmonauts, including six who made return journeys, stayed on board. About 22 tonnes of freight were delivered by twelve Progress spacecraft. Some 1600 different experiments and observations were carried out in the fields of astronomy, medicine, biology and technology.

Even before Salyut 6 went out of service, Salyut 7 was launched. Improvements included two portholes, made of a new material which allowed ultraviolet radiation through.

Since the length of time spent in space by the cosmonauts was increasing, particular attention was paid to their comfort and to the interior conditions of the spacecraft. In response to a request by the cosmonauts, the bulky seats were replaced by lighter ones which could be dismantled and moved around as required.

The solar panels had a greater capacity which could be further increased during the flight. The apparatus for medical inspections was also improved. For example, the results from electrocardiograph tests were simultaneously transmitted to ground control and displayed on the station's computer screen. The portholes were partially protected from being damaged by micrometeorites by exterior flaps. New spacesuits were developed for sorties into space.

The period of time spent by crews on board Salyut 6 increased from 96 days to 140, 175 and finally 185 days. The first crew to stay on board Salyut 7 (Anatoli Berezovoy and Valentin Lebedev) set a new world record by spending 211 days and 9 hours, or approximately 7 months, in orbit. Later flights lasted 150 and 237 days. Four crews visited the long stay cosmonauts. A total of 21 cosmonauts have stayed on board Salyut 7, with two international crews – Jean-Loup Chrétien (of France) in 1982, and R. Charma (of India) in 1984. Svetlana Savitskaïa made two trips and Vladimir Djanibekov three.

For the first time, the crew was altered during flight. Djanibekov and V. Savinykh left Earth on 6 June 1985; they were joined by A. Volkov, V. Vassioutine and G. Gretchko. Gretchko returned with Djanibekov, while the other three remained on board Salyut 7.

Whilst the orbiting space station was in operation, the cosmonauts had to carry out routine maintenance and repair work, both to the exterior and the interior of the complex. Djanibekov and Savinykh were forced to dock with Salyut 7 under manual control because the station did not respond to command signals from their spacecraft. This was due to a malfunction in one of the solar panels, so the cosmonauts spent their first few days aboard working in temperatures of less than zero degrees celsius and breathing air with a low oxygen content.

Salyut 7 was the last of the second generation orbiting space stations. The first of the third generation, called Mir, or Peace, was launched on 20 February 1986.

Running parallel to these developments, Cosmos 929 was launched on 17 July 1977. It was an improved transport spacecraft, destined to replace the Progress vehicle. In 1981, Cosmos 1267 docked with Salyut 6, taking control of the attitude and stabilisation functions. On 10 March 1983, Cosmos 1443 docked with Salyut 7 in order to change the space station's orbit. Cosmos 1443 consists of a descent module, to return freight to Earth, and an orbital unit. This design provides the cosmonauts with more space which can be used as a supplementary laboratory. Once the recovery module has separated, the latter can remain attached to the orbiting complex or fly independently, under autopilot.

Salyut 7 and Soyuz T5 seen from Soyuz T6. This is how Salyut 7 appeared to the first French astronaut Jean-Loup Chrétien who was aboard Soyuz T6, launched on 24 June 1982. With Vladimir Djanibekov and Alexander Ivantchenko, he boarded Salyut 7 where Anatoli Berezovoy and Valentin Lebedev had been living for more than a month on 25 June 1982. The second crew stayed on board for seven days. During this period, they carried out observations for astronomy and astrophysics research, and also some medico-biological and technological experiments (APN).

Spacecraft or space station	Crew members	Launch date	Flight duration	Remarks
Soyuz 1	V. M. Komarov	23 April 1967	1 day 2 hours 48 minutes	Retroparachute failed to open, causing cosmonaut to be killed
Soyuz 2	unmanned	25 October 1968	about 3 days	
Soyuz 3	G. T. Beregovoy	26 October 1968	3 days 22 hours 51 minutes	Soyuz 3 approached Soyuz 2
Soyuz 4	V. A. Chatalov	14 January 1969	2 days 23 hours 21 minutes	First docking of two piloted spacecraft: two cosmonauts, Elisseïev and Khrounov, walked
Soyuz 5	B. V. Volynov	15 January 1969	3 days 54 minutes	through space to enter the other spacecraft
	A. S. Elisseïev			
	E. V. Khrounov			
Soyuz 6	G. S. Chonine	11 October 1969	4 days 22 hours 43 minutes	Flight mission: first attempts at soldering in space
	V. N. Koubassov			
Soyuz 7	A. V. Filipchenko	12 October 1969	4 days 22 hours 40 minutes	
	V. N. Volkov			
	V. V. Gorvatko			
Soyuz 8	V. A. Chatalov	13 October 1969	4 days 22 hours 51 minutes	
	A. S. Elisseïev			
Soyuz 9	A. G. Nikolaïev	1 June 1970	17 days 16 hours 59 minutes	This flight marked the beginning of working in space under weightless conditions
	V. I. Sevastianov			
Soyuz 10–Salyut 1	V. A. Chatalov	23 April 1971	1 day 23 hours 46 minutes	Adjustment of an improved docking bay between the spacecraft and the orbiting Salyut
	A. S. Elisseïev			space station, but no cosmonauts entered the orbiting station
	N. N. Roukavichnikov			
Soyuz 11–Salyut 1	G. T. Dobrovolsky	16 June 1971	23 days 18 hours 22 minutes	The orbiting space station was manned for the first time: the cosmonauts died on the return
	V. N. Volkov			journey due to a sudden loss of pressure in the cabin
	V. I. Patsaïev			
Soyuz 12	V. B. Lazarev	27 September 1973	1 day 23 hours 16 minutes	After the Soyuz 11 accident, new life support equipment was tested
	O. G. Makarov			
Soyuz 13	P. I. Klimouk	18 December 1973	7 days 20 hours 56 minutes	Astrophysical observations are made, and the Earth is photographed
	V. V. Lebedev			
Soyuz 14–Salyut 3	P. R. Popovich	13 July 1974	15 days 17 hours 30 minutes	The cosmonauts boarded the orbiting station (not docking with Salyut 2, launched in June
	Y. P. Artioukhine			1974)
Soyuz 15	G. V. Sarafanov	26 August 1974	2 days 12 minutes	The first return to Earth during the night
	L. S. Demine			
Soyuz 16	A. V. Filipchenko	2 December 1974	5 days 22 hours 24 minutes	Trial run with a modified Soyuz capable of docking with the American Apollo spacecraft
	N. N. Roukavichnikov			
Soyuz 17–Salyut 4	A. A. Goubarev	11 January 1975	29 days 13 hours 20 minutes	The cosmonauts boarded the orbiting station
	G. M. Grechko			
Soyuz 18/1	V. G. Lazarev	5 April 1975	21 minutes	suborbital flight
	O. G. Makarov			
Soyuz 18–Salyut 4	P. I. Klimouk	24 May 1975	62 days 23 hours 20 minutes	The cosmonauts board the orbiting station
	V. I. Sevastianov			
Soyuz 19	A. A. Leonov	15 July 1975	5 days 22 hours 31 minutes	Docking and transfer of crew between Soyuz 19 and Apollo
	V. N. Koubassov			
Soyuz 20	unmanned	17 November 1975	about 92 days	
Soyuz 21	B. V. Volynov	6 July 1976	49 days 6 hours 24 minutes	The cosmonauts board the orbiting station
	V. M. Jolobov			
Soyuz 22	V. F. Bykovsky	15 September 1976	7 days 21 hours 52 minutes	The spacecraft was modified to enable the crew to photograph the Earth
	V. V. Aksenov			
Soyuz 23	V. D. Zoudov	14 October 1976	2 days 7 minutes	Docking between the spacecraft and space station failed
	V. I. Rojdestvensky			
Soyuz 24–Salyut 5	V. V. Gorbatko	17 February 1977	17 days 17 hours 26 minutes	The cosmonauts board the orbiting station
	Y. N. Glazkov			
Soyuz 25	V. V. Kovalenok	9 October 1977	2 days 45 minutes	The planned manual docking failed
	V. V. Rioumine			
Soyuz 26–Salyut 6–Soyuz 27	Y. V. Romanenko	10 December 1977	96 days 10 hours	Cosmonauts board the space station and the return is made on Soyuz 27: Progress 1
	G. M. Grechko			resupplies the orbiting complex
Soyuz 27–Salyut 6–Soyuz 26	V. A. Djanibekov	10 January 1978	5 days 22 hours 59 minutes	The cosmonauts board the orbiting station: they return to Earth on Soyuz 26
	O. G. Makarov			
Soyuz 28–Salyut 6	A. A. Goubarev	2 March 1978	7 days 22 hours 16 minutes	First international crew (USSR and Czechoslovakia)
	V. Remek			
Soyuz 29–Salyut 6–Soyuz 31	V. V. Kovalenok	15 June 1978	139 days 14 hours 48 minutes	The cosmonauts board the orbiting station and return on Soyuz 31: Progress 2, 3 and 4
	A. S. Ivanchenkov			resupply the orbiting complex
Soyuz 30–Salyut 6	P. I. Klimouk	27 June 1978	7 days 22 hours 3 minutes	Second international crew (USSR and Poland)
	M. Hermaszewski			
Soyuz 31–Salyut 6–Soyuz 29	V. F. Bykovsky	26 August 1978	7 days 20 hours 49 minutes	Third international crew (USSR and East Germany), who return aboard Soyuz 29
	S. Jähn			
Soyuz 32–Salyut 6–Soyuz 34	V. A. Liakhov	25 February 1979	175 days 36 minutes	Cosmonauts board the space station and return on Soyuz 34: Progress 5, 6 and 7 resupply
	V. V. Rioumine			the orbiting complex
Soyuz 33	N. N. Roukavichnikov	10 April 1979	1 day 23 hours 1 minute	Fourth international crew (USSR and Bulgaria): following a malfunction on the spacecraft,
	G. Ivanov			docking with Salyut 6 did not take place
Soyuz 34	unmanned	6 June 1979	75 days	
Soyuz T	unmanned	16 December 1979	100 days 9 hours 30 minutes	The mission tested the ability of Soyuz to sustain prolonged spaceflight
Soyuz 35–Salyut 6–Soyuz 37	L. I. Popov	19 April 1980	184 days 20 hours 12 minutes	Cosmonauts board the orbiting space station and return to Earth on Soyuz 37: Progress 8, 9
	V. V. Rioumine			and 11 resupply the orbiting complex
Soyuz 36–Salyut 6–Soyuz 35	V. N. Koubassov	26 May 1980	7 days 20 hours 46 minutes	Fifth international crew (USSR and Hungary)
	B. Farkas			
Soyuz T2–Salyut 6	Y. V. Malychev	5 June 1980	3 days 22 hours 20 minutes	First manned spaceflight of the new spacecraft: manual docking with Salyut 6
	V. V. Aksenov			
Soyuz 37–Salyut 6–Soyuz 36	V. V. Gorbatko	23 July 1980	7 days 20 hours 42 minutes	Sixth international crew (USSR and Vietnam)
	Pham Tuan			
Soyuz 38–Salyut 6	Y. V. Romanenko	18 September 1980	7 days 20 hours 43 minutes	Seventh international crew (USSR and Cuba)
	A. Tamayo Mendez			
Soyuz T3–Salyut 6	L. D. Kizim	27 November 1980	12 days 19 hours 28 minutes	Cosmonauts board the orbiting station: Progress 11 resupplies the orbiting complex
	O. G. Makarov			
	G. M. Strekalov			
Soyuz T4–Salyut 6	V. V. Kovalenok	12 March 1981	74 days 17 hours 37 minutes	Cosmonauts board the space station: Progress 12 resupplies the orbiting complex
	V. P. Savinykh			
Soyuz 39–Salyut 6	V. A. Djanibekov	22 March 1981	7 days 20 hours 42 minutes	Eighth international crew (USSR and Mongolia)
	J. Gourragtcha			
Soyuz 40–Salyut 6	L. I. Popov	14 May 1981	7 days 20 hours 42 minutes	Ninth international crew (USSR and Rumania)
	D. Prunariu			
Soyuz T5–Salyut 7–Soyuz T6–Soyuz T7	A. N. Berezovoy	13 May 1982	211 days 9 hours 5 minutes	Cosmonauts board space station, and return on Soyuz T7: Progress 13, 14, 15 and 16
	V. V. Lebedev			resupply the orbiting complex
Soyuz T6–Salyut 7–Soyuz T5	V. A. Djanibekov	24 June 1982	7 days 21 hours 51 minutes	Tenth international crew (USSR and France): cosmonauts return on Soyuz T6
	A. S. Ivanchenkov			
	J. L. Chrétien			
Soyuz T7–Salyut 7–Soyuz T5	L. I. Popov	19 August 1982	7 days 21 hours 52 minutes	Second woman in space
	A. A. Serebrov			
	S. E. Savitskaïa			
Soyuz T8	V. G. Titov	12 April 1983	2 days 18 minutes	No docking with Salyut 7 following a failure of the manœuvreing systems
	G. M. Strekalov			
	A. A. Serebrov			
Soyuz T9–Salyut 7–Cosmos 1443	V. A. Liakhov	27 June 1983	149 days 10 hours 46 minutes	Cosmonauts carry out assembly work outside the space station: Progress 18 resupplies the
	A. P. Alexandrov			orbiting complex
Soyuz T10–Salyut 7–Soyuz T11–Soyuz T12	L. D. Kizim	8 February 1984	236 days 22 hours 49 minutes	Cosmonauts board the space station and return on Soyuz T11: during their stay in space,
	V. A. Solovev			the cosmonauts receive two crews and four supply craft, make six sorties into space
	O. Y. Atkov			totalling 22 hours 10 minutes; Progress 19, 20, 21, 22 and 23 resupply the station
Soyuz T11–Salyut 7–Soyuz T10	Y. V. Malychev	3 April 1984	7 days 21 hours 41 minutes	Eleventh international crew (USSR and India): the cosmonauts return on Soyuz T10
	G. M. Strekalov			
	R. Charma			
Soyuz T12–Salyut 7	V. A. Djanibekov	17 July 1984	11 days 19 hours 14 minutes	Cosmonauts board the space station: for the first time a woman works outside in space for
	S. E. Savitskaïa			3 hours 45 minutes
	I. P. Volk			
Soyuz T13–Salyut 7–Cosmos 1669	V. A. Djanibekov	16 June 1985	V. Djanibekov: 112 days 3 hours 12 minutes V. Savinykh: 168 days 3 hours 51 minutes	Important work is done to repair both the interior and exterior of Salyut 7, working in space for 5 hours: Progress 24 resupplied the station
	V. P. Savinykh			
Soyuz T14–Salyut 7–Cosmos 1686	V. V. Vassioutine	17 September 1985	A. Volkov and V. Vassioutine: 64 days 21 hours 52 minutes G. Grechko: 8 days 21 hours 31 minutes	This flight was cut short after V. Vassioutine became ill
	A. A. Volkov			
	G. M. Grechko			
Soyuz T15–Mir	L. D. Kizim	13 March 1986	125 days	Cosmonauts board the new Mir space station: on 15 May 1986 they transfer to Salyut 7 and return to Mir on 27 June 1987: the cosmonauts make two sorties into space, totalling 8 hours 30 minutes
	V. A. Soloviev			
Soyuz TM	unmanned	21 May 1986	9 days	Cosmonauts dock with the space station Mir: Progress 25 and 26 resupply Mir

Space flights made by the Soyuz spacecraft and the Salyut space station to May 1986 (Novosty press releases)

The Soyuz T9 – Salyut 7 – Cosmos 1443 complex. Cosmos 1443 docked with the uninhabited Salyut 7 station on 10 March 1983, carrying a payload of more than three tonnes. Soyuz T9 and the cosmonauts Vladimir Liakhov and Alexander Alexandrov docked with the station on 28 June 1983. On 14 August 1983 Cosmos 1443 undocked from the orbiting complex. The separation and subsequent movement of the cargocraft was controlled by the cosmonauts. Inside the descent module were various samples and films to be returned to Earth. Two days later, Soyuz T9 separated from Salyut 7, and docked at the port vacated by Cosmos 1443.

The two cosmonauts stayed on board Salyut 7 from 23 June to 23 November 1983, carrying out an extensive programme of scientific and technological research. They carried out two spacewalks in order to install two supplementary solar panels on the exterior of Salyut 7 to increase the station's power capacity and to practise assembly methods in the vacuum of space. The cosmonauts spent a total of 5 hours and 45 minutes outside the space station.

Upper picture: A Soyuz T9 solar panel as seen from Salyut 7 (APN). Lower picture: Flight engineer Alexander Alexandrov moves supplies from Cosmos 1443 to Salyut 7, after docking with the orbiting complex in Soyuz T9. The photograph was taken by flight commander Liakhov (Tass).

Cosmos 1686, launched in 1985, was as big as Salyut 7. It could be used as a space cargo ship, an interorbital tug, and research and manufacturing laboratories. Cosmos 1686 was equipped with its own solar panels so that it did not depend on Salyut 7 for any of its power.

Spacecraft such as these will be indispensable for the construction of vast, orbiting space stations in the future.

Nikolai Kardachev

The first woman to leave the space station complex. On 25 July 1984, Svetlana Savitskaïa went outside Salyut 7, more than 300 kilometres above the Earth, and carried out some difficult technological operations which had never been attempted before. She has been involved in the cosmonaut programme since 1982, and has made two trips into space. In August 1982 she accompanied Leonid Popov and Alexander Serebrov when they visited Anatoli Berezovoy and Valentin Lebedev on board Salyut 7. In July 1984, Savitskaïa flew in Soyuz T12, with V. A. Djanibekov and I. P. Volk, and docked with Salyut 7. She worked in space with Djanibekov, testing a new tool capable of cutting, soldering and brazing metal plates, as well as changing the surfaces of different metals. This is a prelude to construction work on future orbiting complexes. At the end of these tests, the equipment and samples were brought back into the station airlock. The samples were panels of different materials, which had been fitted to the outside wall of Salyut 7 at an earlier date, in order to study the effects of prolonged exposure to the extremes of the space environment (APN).

Man in space

The American space shuttle programme

The third shuttle flight (Columbia) in March 1982. The scientific aim of this flight was to study plasma physics in space, solar physics, astronomy and aspects of the life sciences. The crew used the remote control arm, made in Canada and shown in the top righthand corner of the photograph, to make *in situ* space plasma measurements to study the interaction of the orbiter with its environment. Sensors on the end of the remote control arm were used to produce a map of the plasma and electromagnetic fields around the orbiter (NASA).

When Neil Armstrong stepped onto the Moon's surface on 20 July 1969, he achieved the objective set by President John F. Kennedy in 1961 – to put the first man on the Moon, and to return him safely to Earth by the end of the decade.

The Americans spent about two years considering what form the civil space programme should take after the completion of the Apollo and Skylab missions. They decided that the natural progression would be for the development of a permanently manned orbiting space station and a reusable launch vehicle. Plans for the space station were formulated, but then dropped owing to financial constraints.

The reusable launch vehicle was originally intended to ferry crew and equipment between Earth and the space station. In time the aims of the project were modified. The result was the American space shuttle project, which was announced to the American people by President Richard Nixon on 5 January 1972.

The space shuttle, or orbiter, is designed to carry out three tasks. First, it is an orbiting space laboratory. Experiments lasting up to a week can be carried out either inside the laboratory at a pressure of one atmosphere or outside in the vacuum of space. Second, the shuttle can carry commercial payloads. It is used to place satellites into low altitude orbit, or into a transfer orbit if they are designed to be geostationary satellites. The shuttle's third mission is to carry out maintenance in orbit, to repair and resupply satellites in space, or bring them back to Earth.

After a sequence of twenty-four successful flights, the space shuttle Challenger exploded soon after launch on 28 January 1986, killing the crew of seven. President Ronald Reagan immediately indicated that this tragic accident would not radically alter American space policy, but that private enterprise would take over missions with a commercial emphasis, NASA retaining its interest in scientific and military space projects. There were thereafter no further space shuttle flights until September 1988.

In 1972, when Europe was considering its space strategy for the next ten years, the USA offered the opportunity to participate in the shuttle programme. The Europeans were particularly interested in the 'tug' initially planned to carry out manned or unmanned rendezvous between the orbiter and other objects orbiting in space. When this project was abandoned, Europe instead concentrated on designing and constructing Spacelab. This was to be a laboratory carried in the space shuttle's cargo bay, increasing the number of experiments requiring control by astronauts which could be carried out on short flights.

Spacelab's design is modular in order to allow greater flexibility of use. It can consist of a long or short pressurised module and one or more equipment carrier, or pallet. Spacelab has provided Europe with the opportunity of becoming familiar with the problems of living and working in space, before embarking on more ambitious projects. Both the planned American space station (Freedom) and the European component, called Columbus, will utilise modules similar to those of Spacelab and space platforms similar to Eureca. These space platforms will orbit the Earth at some distance from the space station and will be visited periodically by astronauts to ensure that they are functioning correctly and to carry out maintenance work. Once the space station is in operation, the space shuttle will revert to its original function – that of a reusable launch vehicle.

Michel Bignier

The seventh shuttle flight (Challenger) in June 1983. Besides the two communications satellites deployed on this mission – Telestat F for Canada and Palapa B1 for Indonesia – the shuttle carried the free-flying satellite SPAS 01 and a package of scientific experiments in materials science, OSTA 2 developed by the Federal Republic of Germany. This unusual photograph of the Challenger was taken with a 70 millimetre camera carried aboard SPAS 01. Challenger's Remote Manipulator System (RMS) can be seen in an extended, upright position in the upper left corner of the cargo bay, as can the pallet carrying the scientific package OSTA 2 and the empty cradle which held Telestat F and Palapa B1.

OSTA 2 was developed jointly by NASA and the West German Bundesministerium für Forschung und Technologie (BMFT). The American element comprised three experimental samples heated and resolidified under controlled conditions. The German contribution, in three Get Away Special (GAS) containers, included studies of fluid mechanics, transport phenomena and metallurgy, as well as the development of an X ray observational technique. The longest investigation required about 84 hours of processing time in the zero gravity environment (NASA).

The accelerating advance of science and technology in space over the past 30 years has produced increasing demands from the commercial, scientific and military communities for accommodation in space vehicles. During this period, there has been a considerable growth in the space capabilities of different nations as well as an evolving trend in space technology towards economies in launch and orbital operations. Because of this the NASA Space Transportation System and its prime component, the space shuttle or orbiter, emerged in the late 1970s, with the first launch taking place in 1981.

Accommodation for space payloads

The orbiter is designed to accommodate a wide variety of scientific, commercial and military equipment destined for spaceflight. The many requirements of such equipment define the necessary environment, the instrument racks and pallets, the electrical power, thermal control, further rockets or upper stages, and other support facilities. They also determine the phasing of experiments, crew involvement, orbital parameters and instrument pointing requirements. Items destined for flight are aggregated into payloads. Missions are planned by combining payloads that require similar orbits, subject to the availability of space, weight and other related considerations.

There are dedicated payloads, such as the Spacelab missions, which involve many experiments carried out by astronauts using instruments on pallets. There are also payloads of free flying satellites that are launched from the orbiter, often accompanied in turn by other attached payloads. Since even the larger, dedicated or mixed payloads often do not completely fill the orbiter's cargo bay, several small, economical payload carriers are included to utilise fully all available flight opportunities. These include the Hitchhiker and Get Away Specials (GAS), and the orbiter's middeck storage lockers.

Hitchhiker payloads are accommodated as secondary payloads in the cargo bay on a space available basis, as late as six to eight months prior to launch. The type of equipment best suited for Hitchhiker not only fits within modest resource and space allocations but also does not require fine pointing or access to the orbiter's computers.

Accommodation for self-sufficient experiments is provided by GAS carriers in the payload bay and by the locker compartments located in the orbiter middeck, which normally contain the crew's food, clothing and equipment. While basic services are limited, these allow relatively simple, exploratory and 'proof-of-concept' experiments to be conducted before more elaborate equipment is developed.

Although the orbiter is primarily a space vehicle for scientific research and development, its design allows for commercial applications. For example, free flying satellites can be launched from the orbiter by the Payload Assist Module (PAM). This consists of an upper stage with a spin platform for placing satellites in higher orbits. It is carried in the orbiter's cargo bay. Additional upper stages are available to extend these capabilities for heavier satellites and higher orbits. The Inertial Upper Stage (IUS) has a built in guidance and propulsion system for stability and flight control. This can place payloads of about 2·3 tonnes into geosynchronous orbit. A liquid propellant booster, known as the Centaur Upper Stage, had been designed for launching spacecraft on planetary missions. However, as a result of the Challenger accident, development of the Centaur booster has been dropped.

A key feature of the orbiter is the Remote Manipulator System (RMS). Developed and built in Canada, the RMS is essentially a robot copying the human arm. It has joints at the 'shoulder', 'elbow' and 'wrist', ending in a device called the 'end effector' that can handle payloads. The arm is operated by the crew from the aft flight deck of the orbiter. Combining the RMS with the crew's ability to work in the cargo bay in so-called 'extra-vehicular activity' (EVA) mode, an entirely new capability has emerged for retrieving, repairing and servicing satellites.

Radio communications with the orbiter are maintained through the Mission Control Center at the NASA Johnson Space Center (JSC) near Houston, Texas. Communications with other free flying satellites in Earth orbit go through the NASA Goddard Space Flight Center in Greenbelt, Maryland, near Washington, DC. Communications with Spacelab or other payloads attached to the orbiter are maintained through the Payload Operations Control Center (POCC) at either the Johnson Space Center or the Marshall Space Flight Center at Huntsville, Alabama.

The missions

Twenty-four space missions had been flown with NASA's four orbiters, Columbia, Challenger, Discovery and Atlantis, prior to the ill fated flight of Challenger on 28 January 1986. Space shuttle flights resumed on 29 September 1988, when Discovery successfully lifted off carrying its five member crew into orbit at the start of a four day mission. The mission proved that the numerous changes to the solid rocket booster and the orbiter itself worked well. Also, the astronauts deployed the second Tracking and Data Relay Satellite (TDRS), which is vital for communications in future manned and unmanned Earth orbital missions.

Earlier successful missions included a series of orbital flight tests with some scientific payloads, the deployment of communications or free flying scientific satellites, some military payloads, and several demonstrations of the orbiter's unique servicing and repair capabilities. The table opposite lists all these flights, with their respective main payloads and the purposes of the different missions. Emphasis here is placed on a few selected missions that represent the various types of payloads flown and the different types of on orbit operations.

The first four orbiter flights were made in Columbia and were designated the Orbital Flight Test (OFT) programme. The primary purpose was to evaluate Columbia's performance in the space environment. Two of these flights carried the first scientific payloads mounted in Columbia's cargo bay. These were the Space and Terrestrial Applications payloads called OSTA 1, flown on the second orbital test flight in November 1981, and OSS 1, a Space Science payload flown on the third test flight in March 1982.

Experiments selected for the OSTA 1 mission laid stress on the environmental sciences, fitting within the constraints of the tests planned for the OFT programme. They included remote sensing of Earth resources, environmental quality, ocean conditions, meteorological phenomena and life sciences.

OSTA 1 was the first demonstration of the orbiter's capability as a space research platform. Its experiments included the Shuttle Imaging Radar A (SIR A), a side looking synthetic aperture radar that maps terrestrial features; the Feature Identification and Location Experiment (FILE), a group of sensors and electronic systems designed to develop techniques to make data gathering by Earth resources satellites more efficient; and a radiometer for making remote measurements of atmospheric pollution. The SIR A antenna sends and receives microwave radiation to create maplike images of the Earth's surface. On this flight, SIR A recorded a 50 kilometre wide image along Columbia's ground track. Similar airborne radar systems have uncovered ancient Mayan canals, and have flown on an ocean surveying satellite (Seasat) to study

Flight	Launch date	Orbiter	Principal payload	Mission
1	12 April 1981	Columbia	test materials	flight test
2	12 November 1981	Columbia	test materials OSTA 1	flight test Earth observation
3	22 March 1982	Columbia	test materials OSS 1	flight test astronomy
4	27 June 1982	Columbia	test materials military	flight test military
5	11 November 1982	Columbia	SBS C Telesat E	communications communications
6	4 April 1983	Challenger	TDRS A	communications
7	18 June 1983	Challenger	SPAS 01 OSTA 2 Telesat F Palapa B1	deployment, recovery, material sciences materials sciences communications communications
8	30 August 1983	Challenger	PDRS (remote control arm) Insat 1B	flight test communications
9	28 November 1983	Columbia	Spacelab 1	scientific, multidisciplinary
10	3 February 1984	Challenger	SPAS 01 A Palapa B2 Westar 6	deployment, recovery, material sciences communications communications
11	6 April 1984	Challenger	LDEF 1 solar observatory	scientific, multidisciplinary recovery, repairs
12	30 August 1984	Discovery	OAST 1 SBS D Telstar 3C Syncom IV 2	solar power, structural dynamics communications communications communications
13	5 October 1984	Challenger	OSTA 3 LFC ERBS ORS	Earth observation Earth observation atmospheric research demonstration of fuelling in orbit
14	8 November 1984	Discovery	Palapa Telesat H Syncom IV 1	recovery of Palapa B2 and Westar 6 communications communications
15	24 January 1985	Discovery	military	military
16	12 April 1985	Discovery	Telesat 1 Syncom IV 3	communications communications
17	29 April 1985	Challenger	Spacelab 3	scientific, multidisciplinary
18	17 June 1985	Discovery	Spartan 1 Marelos A Arabsat 1B Telstar 3D	astrophysics communications communications communications
19	29 July 1985	Challenger	Spacelab 2	scientific, multidisciplinary
20	27 August 1985	Discovery	Aussat 1 ASC 1 Syncom IV 4	communications communications communications repairs to Syncom IV 3
21	3 October 1985	Atlantis	military	military
22	30 October 1985	Challenger	Spacelab D1	scientific, multidisciplinary
23	26 November 1985	Atlantis	EASE/ACCESS Morelos B Satcom KU 2 Aussat 2	space structures communications communications communications
24	12 January 1986	Columbia	MSL 2 Satcom KU 1 GAS unit	material sciences communications scientific, multidisciplinary
26	29 September 1988	Discovery	TDRS C	communications
27	2 December 1988	Atlantis	military	military
28	13 March 1989	Discovery	TDRS D	communications

Successful missions performed by NASA orbiters up to March 1989

Recent and planned missions for the space shuttle

Astronomy	automatic: Hubble Space Telescope Gamma Ray Observatory
	attached to the Orbiter: Astro 1, 2 high energy astrophysics laboratories
Earth sciences	automatic: Upper Atmosphere Research Satellite Laser Geodynamics Satellite
	attached to the Orbiter: atmospheric physics laboratory tethered satellite system Shuttle radar wide angled Michelson–Doppler imaging interferometer
Interplanetary exploration	automatic (interplanetary probes): Galileo Ulysses Magellan
Microgravity sciences	attached to the Orbiter: Spacelab J (Japanese Spacelab Mission) SLS 1, 2, 3, 4 (life sciences laboratories 1, 2, 3, 4) IML 1, 2, 3 (international life sciences and materials in microgravity laboratories 1, 2, 3) United States Microgravity Laboratories 1, 2, 3, 4 United States Microgravity Pallets 1, 2, 3, 4

ocean wave patterns and ice flows. Such remote sensing helps to delineate faults and other geological formations. It may eventually locate oil and other mineral deposits.

FILE was designed to make remote sensing instruments such as the SIR A more efficient by activating them only under the right conditions for taking data. On this mission, the experiment attempted to characterise scenes as either vegetation, water, snow or clouds, or bare ground, using the ratio between visual red reflectance and near infrared reflectance. Further data collection in a certain category was suppressed after a given number of scenes had been acquired. The experiment's system consisted of a sunrise sensor, two television cameras, a decision making electronics unit, a buffer memory, a tape recorder, and a 70 millimetre camera. The radiometer experiment package consisted of an electro-optical sensor, an electronics module, a digital tape recorder, and an aerial camera. This operated successfully during data acquisition and calibration.

On the third orbital test flight, Columbia carried the OSS 1 payload. Instruments checked many factors that could not be tested on Earth, but which might affect future scientific observations from the orbiter. These included the response of the orbiter and payload to extreme thermal variations, the effects of a 'cloud' of particles and gases from the orbiter itself, and the degree of electrical charging of the spacecraft. The OSS 1 experiments covered the disciplines of astronomy, space plasma physics and space life sciences.

This mission was primarily a thermal test for flights in several different attitudes with respect to the Sun. The objective was to register the response to the most extreme differences of temperature that might be encountered on later flights. In addition, one unit on a pallet, the Thermal Canister Experiment, demonstrated a technique of keeping tight temperature control for instruments in the orbiter's payload bay.

During this flight, Columbia kept its nose toward the Sun for 60 hours, its attitude fixed with respect to the Sun, with the pallet and its payload remaining entirely in the shade and bitter cold. Then, for 34 hours, Columbia kept its tail facing the Sun, rolling as it circled the Earth. The bottom of the craft always faced the Earth, again leaving the payload bay cold. Two experiments were operated in both of these attitudes: these were the Plasma Diagnostic Package and the Shuttle Induced Atmosphere Experiment. Then, for 26 hours, Columbia moved with the payload bay always facing the Sun, keeping it fully exposed to the solar heat. This attitude was necessary for data gathering by the Solar Ultraviolet Spectral Irradiance Monitor and by the Solar Flare X Ray Polarimeter Equipment. The Thermal Canister Experiment and the Vehicle Charging and Potential Experiment were carried out with the orbiter in any attitude. So was the Plant Lignification Experiment, which studied the way in which seedlings made their first growth in a weightless environment. This was carried inside the pressurised orbiter middeck. All other experiments were mounted on a Spacelab pallet in the cargo bay.

Flight 4 was the last of the orbital test series. On the fifth shuttle flight, NASA began providing space transportation services for commercial and international customers. Many were for putting communications satellites into a low Earth orbit where they would be deployed from the orbiter and transferred into geosynchronous orbit. On 12 of the orbiter's 24 successful flights, a total of 23 communications satellites were deployed for several private US firms and six other nations. As the numbers

The tenth space shuttle flight (Challenger) in February 1984. Aboard this Challenger flight were the Indonesian satellite Palapa B2, the US Western Union Company's WESTAR 6 and West Germany's SPAS 01A. Both Palapa B2 and WESTAR 6 used the Payload Assist Module (PAM), which consists of a spin platform and an upper stage rocket, to reach higher orbits. The two satellites did not reach these orbits due to a malfunction in the PAM. However, both were recovered and returned to Earth by Discovery in November 1984.

In this photograph, astronaut Bruce McCandless is seen demonstrating the Manned Maneuvering Unit (MMU) a few metres away from Challenger. The nitrogen propelled, hand controlled MMU allows the astronaut to move in space without the restrictive tethers worn by earlier spacewalkers (NASA).

The eleventh space shuttle flight (Challenger) in April 1984. The eleventh orbiter flight, again with Challenger, was a showcase demonstration of the crucial role of the crew in space, the so called on orbit operations. On this flight, a free flying, retrievable satellite called LDEF (Long Duration Exposure Facility) was deployed, and a defunct NASA spacecraft, the Solar Maximum Satellite, was recovered for repair.

The LDEF is a passive satellite that carries materials for exposure to the space environment for long periods. LDEF 1 is still in orbit. In the photograph on the left, LDEF 1 is suspended from the Remote Manipulator System (RMS) high above the Gulf of Mexico prior to its release in space.

The Solar Maximum Satellite carried instruments for observing the Sun. Its attitude control system failed nine months after launch. This satellite was recovered by the Challenger's crew, successfully repaired, and returned to orbit where it resumed solar observations. In the photograph on the right, the Solar Maximum Satellite is seen after its capture by the RMS, temporarily docked aboard Challenger where repairs were made by astronaut James van Hoften. His feet are anchored on a work station that is moved by the Remote Manipulator System. The electronics component and an attitude control system module were replaced in less than an hour. This mission finally came to an end when the satellite burnt up in the upper atmosphere in December 1989 (NASA).

suggest, up to three communications satellites were launched per mission.

All but three of the 23 communications satellites were successful. Two failures were caused by Payload Assist Module (PAM) malfunctions, and the third (Syncom IV 3) by a short circuit that prevented the firing of the satellite's own propulsion system. Syncom IV 3 was repaired in orbit, after which it was successfully placed in its geostationary orbit.

On the fifth flight, two communications satellites were deployed, namely SBS C (Satellite Business Systems) and Telesat E (for Canada). The Tracking and Data Relay Satellite (TDRS A) was launched on the sixth shuttle flight, the first flight of Challenger. A malfunction in the IUS upper stage resulted in TDRS A being placed in a highly elliptical orbit. After a thorough assessment of its systems, the TDRS A was eventually moved to its proper geosynchronous orbit using its small thruster motors over a period of several weeks. TDRS A was the new link in NASA's communications network and the first in a series of satellites planned to replace the NASA ground tracking network.

The seventh flight of the orbiter took place in June 1983, with Challenger carrying a mixed payload into space. Aboard Challenger were OSTA 2, a German satellite called SPAS 01 with microgravity experiments onboard, a Canadian commercial satellite (Telesat F) and an Indonesian communications satellite called Palapa B1. Unlike its predecessor, OSTA 2 also had a microgravity payload.

Analysis of more than 50 experiments on Skylab and other spacecraft suggests that the space environment holds promise for materials processing. Products whose quality depends on the nature of their crystalline state, such as semiconductors, and specialised composites which separate by gravity induced convection on Earth are examples here. OSTA 2, the first

major materials processing payload aboard the orbiter, was operated following the launch of the commercial satellites. The OSTA 2 instrument package was mounted on a different pallet known as the Multi Purpose Experiment Support Structure (MPESS), a bridge-like structure crossing the orbiter's cargo bay.

This mission was a cooperative effort between NASA and the West German Ministry for Research and Technology. Its objective was to perform materials processing experiments in the microgravity space environment that allowed in-flight monitoring of phenomena, sample production and a postflight analysis of the samples produced. The OSTA 2 payload consisted of the US Materials Experiment Assembly (MEA) which contained three experiment furnaces in which the samples were heated and resolidified under controlled conditions. The German contribution, packaged in three GAS canisters and known wryly to all as the *Materialwissenschaftliche Autonome Experimente unter Schwerelösigkeit* (MAUS), included studies of fluid dynamics, transport phenomena, metallurgy, and an X ray observational technique.

The mission was one of the first cooperative international research projects to be conducted on the orbiter. Besides providing apparatus for the investigation of materials processing, scientists from each country shared experimental data and exchanged analytical information about crystal growth, the containerless production of glass and metallurgical processes in space.

On the eighth flight on 30 August 1983, the RMS was flight tested and a communications satellite (INSAT 1B) was deployed for India. Flight number nine, in November 1983, was the first Spacelab mission. On flight 10 in February 1984, a mixed payload consisting of SPAS 01A and two communications satellites were flown

The twelfth space shuttle flight (Discovery) in August 1984. Flight 12 was Discovery's first mission. Three communications satellites, SBS D (Satellite Business Systems), Telstar 3 C (AT&T) and Syncom IV 1 (Hughes Aircraft Company), were all successfully deployed.

Discovery also carried the OAST 1 payload, which consisted of a solar power panel to investigate the characteristics of large structures in space and to measure the performance of solar cells. In this photograph, the solar power array is fully deployed. It extends about 30 metres above Discovery's cargo bay. When retracted, the array folds into a package that is only about 18 centimetres thick (Smithsonian Institution/Lockheed Corporation, 1985).

The thirteenth space shuttle flight (Challenger) in October 1984. Flight 13 in the series was the sixth space mission for Challenger. Its payload consisted of the Earth viewing experiments of OSTA 3, a stereo photographic system called the Large Format Camera, NASA's Earth Radiation Budget Satellite for deployment, and the Orbital Refueling System destined for its first flight test. Several of the OSTA 3 experiments had been flown previously, on flight 2. These were a synthetic aperture radar for observing the Earth's land and sea surface, an instrument designed to characterise surface features, and a radiometer for measuring air pollution.

In the photograph on the left (below), the antenna for the imaging radar, in its folded position, is in the left foreground. Astronauts David Leestma (left) and Kathryn Sullivan are at the far end of the cargo bay as they test

the Orbital Refueling System. The Large Format Camera is to David Leestma's left.

The Earth Radiation Budget Satellite (ERBS), a free flying satellite designed for launch by the orbiter, is shown here (below right) being deployed by the Remote Manipulator System on 5 October 1984. The colourful patterns surrounding ERBS were reflections from objects inside Challenger's flight deck on the window through which the photograph was taken. The free flying ERBS satellite contains its own systems for attitude control, electrical power generation and storage, thermal control, orbital adjustments and communications. Instruments measure the solar energy input to, and that reflected by, the Earth and its atmosphere. ERBS also contained instruments to investigate the distribution of aerosols and trace gases in the atmosphere (NASA).

The eighteenth space shuttle flight (Discovery) in June 1985. Three communications satellites were aboard Discovery on this flight. They were Morelos A (Mexico), Arabsat 1B (Arab Satellite Communications Organisation) and Telstar 3D (AT&T). Discovery also carried a retrievable, free flying satellite called Spartan 1.

In this photograph, Arabsat 1B is seen emerging from Discovery's cargo bay. Spartan 1 is in the foreground awaiting deployment by the Remote Manipulator System (RMS). It accommodated smaller scientific payloads, in a class previously flown on sounding rockets. Much longer observation periods are possible in orbit than from a rocket (NASA).

aboard Challenger. The communications satellites, Palapa B2 for Indonesia and WESTAR 6 for the US Western Union Company, were unsuccessful due to a malfunction in the Payload Assist Modules. Both satellites were recovered and returned to Earth by Discovery on the fourteenth flight in the series in November 1984.

In April 1984, on the eleventh orbiter flight, Challenger carried a free flyer called the Long Duration Exposure Facility (LDEF), a satellite designed to be deployed and then retrieved on a later flight. Retrievable free flyers like this offer several advantages to the investigator. They are unaffected by disturbances and contamination from orbiter and payload activities, and they can carry out viewing programmes independent of the pointing requirements of other experimental payloads in the orbiter's cargo bay.

LDEF, one of NASA's free flyers, was designed to orbit the Earth, unpowered, carrying large panels or trays of materials that engineers and scientists need to expose to the space environment. It is suited to studying the durability of materials in space for future satellites and for the space station. It is also a good vehicle for flying passive experiments, such as in cosmic ray astronomy. At the end of its five year mission, the LDEF was retrieved and returned to Earth in December 1989 by the space shuttle, Colombia. LDEF was originally designed so that old panels can be replaced with new ones, so this free flyer can be placed in orbit once again. After it was successfully

deployed for the first time, the orbiter and its crew demonstrated their ability to retrieve, repair, and redeploy a malfunctioning satellite with the capture and repair of the Solar Maximum Mission spacecraft.

Launched by a Delta vehicle on 14 February 1980, the Solar Maximum Mission was the source of very detailed information about the Sun. For the first nine months of the planned two year mission, the satellite collected data for scientists at NASA's Goddard Space Flight Center in Greenbelt, Maryland, and for ground based observatories around the world.

Nine months after the Solar Maximum satellite was launched, its attitude control system failed and precision pointing at the Sun was lost. The instruments on board the satellite had investigated hundreds of solar flares, and numerous discoveries had been made. There were many reasons for repairing the satellite and extending its mission. First of all, it was the only solar observatory in orbit. Secondly, successful repair would reactivate the $77 million satellite at an estimated one quarter of its replacement cost, and would extend the observatory's operational life for several years. Finally, based on knowledge gained from nine months of prior solar observations and three years of data analysis, scientists were anxious to extend the Solar Maximum satellite's operational period.

The Solar Maximum Repair Mission began in April 1984, when the satellite's orbital altitude had decayed to 491 kilometres. Initial attempts by an astronaut, using the Manned Maneuvering Unit (MMU) to dock with the satellite and to stop its rotation, failed. The docking attempts gave the satellite uncontrollable roll, pitch and yaw. Later, NASA Goddard Space Flight Center staff were able to stabilise the satellite using its own attitude control systems. It was then secured by the orbiter's Remote Manipulator System and placed on the flight support system located in the orbiter payload bay.

The Attitude Control System module was removed from the satellite by one of the astronauts, and replaced with a new unit. The entire module replacement took less than an hour. The old module was secured on the lower starboard side of the flight support system and returned to Earth.

The main electronics box of the Coronograph-Polarimeter was replaced successfully, even though it was not designed for servicing, and the faulty unit was also returned to Earth. After the repairs were completed, the Solar Maximum satellite was checked and redeployed successfully. The orbiter landed two days later on 14 April 1984.

The Solar Maximum Repair Mission demonstrated that the orbiter, together with its crew, has the unique capability to retrieve and service satellites, and that multimillion dollar spacecraft may no longer need to be abandoned because of subsystem failures or other hardware problems.

On 30 August 1984, the twelfth orbiter mission was launched. The payload for this mission was composed of three communications free flyer satellites plus OAST 1, a mission for the Office of Aeronautics and Space Technology. Experiments mounted on the MPESS across Discovery's cargo bay consisted of systems aimed at investigating solar energy and large space structures technology. These are vital to NASA's evolving Space Station programme.

Past satellites and spacecraft, such as Skylab, were equipped with large, rigid, solar arrays for electrical power generation. These earlier arrays were heavy, bulky and expensive. They weighed approximately eight times as much as the OAST 1 solar array and cost approximately twice as much. After they were deployed in space they could not, as a general rule, be restowed. OAST 1 was the first demonstration in space of a large, lightweight, solar array capable of being restowed after deployment in space. The solar array 'wing' was extended and

retracted several times and extensive data were gathered on its performance.

The OAST 1 experiments demonstrated two advanced methods of acquiring, processing and analysing the vibrational characteristics of large space structures. One method used the orbiter's closed-circuit television cameras to obtain stereo views of white circles imprinted on the solar array wing. Data were reduced by triangulation to study the vibrational deflections of the array. The other method used an adaptation of star tracking techniques to track special reflectors also located on the array.

Data on the performance of various types of solar cells were obtained during the mission. After the mission, results were compared after the facility had been flown again on a balloon.

Challenger returned to space for the sixth time on 5 October 1984, fully laden with scientific instruments and payloads. It was the thirteenth orbiter mission, and the first having seven crewmembers. It was a 'first' in several ways, with a Canadian payload specialist, a spacewalk by an American woman and a crewman flying on his fourth orbiter mission. It was the first space mission to demonstrate satellite refuelling in space, and the first flight to reenter over the eastern United States. The major payloads flown on the mission included NASA's Earth Radiation Budget Satellite (ERBS), the OSTA 3 payload, a Large Format Camera and Canadian scientific experiment packages known as CANEX. Also aboard the Challenger was a movie camera, flown in the crew cabin along with a handheld device called the Radiation Monitoring Equipment. The Aurora Photography Experiment and several battery powered devices to measure gamma radiation were also flown for the first time. Eight GAS canisters were mounted in the cargo bay, activated by crewmembers at various times during the mission.

OSTA 1, which flew on the second orbiter mission in November 1981, provided a clear demonstration of the orbiter's role as a research platform for observing phenomena on the Earth's surface. On this flight, three of the OSTA 1 experiments were reflown. These were a modified SIR A, FILE and the Measurement of Air Pollution from Satellites (MAPS) radiometer. These were joined by the Large Format Camera (LFC) to make up the Earth viewing payload.

On the 1981 flight, radar images of about 10 million square kilometres of the Earth's surface had been obtained by SIR A. SIR B, the modified version flown on the OSTA 3 mission, had a longer, higher gain antenna that folded up during launch and landing. It could also be adjusted to look in various directions. SIR B also transmitted digital data during the flight via the Tracking and Data Relay Satellite (TDRS) system.

The MAPS radiometer gathered data over more than 800 000 kilometres of the orbiter's flight path. Using thermal radiation coming up from the atmosphere, the instrument measured the concentration of carbon monoxide in the troposphere with acceptable accuracy and repeatability. Changing one of the carbon monoxide cells to a nitrous oxide cell enabled atmospheric temperatures to be found and the data reduction process to be refined. The LFC provides the capability of making detailed maps of large areas of the world. The lens, coupled with a 23 by 45 centimetres image area, makes possible wide angle coverage with little radial distortion and high geometric fidelity. Each frame acquired by this camera covers an area on the Earth's surface of 169 by 338 kilometres. Excellent quality, stereoscopic images were obtained.

Making its first flight on this mission was equipment to test the Orbiter Refueling System (ORS), with two astronauts performing an EVA or spacewalk into the payload bay to install the hydrazine servicing tool. From inside the cabin, the astronauts later transferred fuel through the tool connection, demonstrating the orbiter's capability to refuel satellites in orbit in order to extend their life in space.

Also aboard Challenger was the Earth Radiation Budget Satellite (ERBS) with its Sun-viewing instrument. This measured the short wavelength incident radiation from the Sun, reflected sunlight and the long wavelength radiation emitted by the Earth and its atmosphere. An accompanying sensor measured the attenuation of sunlight through the atmosphere and mapped the distribution of aerosols, nitrogen dioxide and ozone. By determining seasonal and geographic variations in the Earth radiation budget, scientists hope to predict longterm variations in climate and to assess climatic perturbations.

ERBS was the first NASA satellite specifically designed and engineered for an orbiter launch. It contains operational subsystems for attitude control and determination, electrical power generation and storage, thermal control, thrusters to adjust its orbit, and communication and data handling through the Spacecraft Tracking and Data Network (STDN) or TDRS.

The movie camera captured such scenes as the operation of the SIR B antenna and the spacewalk. These on orbit shots may be seen in the film *The Dream is Alive*. It also led to the dramatic films *To Fly* and, more recently, *Hail Columbia!*

The fourteenth orbiter flight was made with Discovery in November 1984. Two communications satellites were aboard for deployment, the Canadian Telesat H and Syncom IV 1 for the Hughes Company. This was also a retrieval mission. Palapa B2 and WESTAR 6, which had failed to reach a transfer orbit earlier in the year, were successfully recovered and returned to Earth.

Flight 15 was a secret military mission aboard Discovery. Flight 16 with Discovery, in April 1985, deployed Telesat 1 and Syncom IV 3. US Senator Jake Garn flew as a payload specialist on this mission and performed several life sciences and materials sciences experiments. On the seventeenth flight late in April 1985, Spacelab 3 flew aboard Challenger.

The eighteenth orbiter flight was made with Discovery in June 1985. Three communications satellites, Morelos A (Mexico), Arabsat 1B (Arab Satellite Communications Organisation) and Telstar 3D (AT&T), were successfully launched. Also flown on this mission was Spartan 1, a free flying satellite which was retrieved at the end of the mission. The Spartan concept is to place modest, sounding rocket types of experiments into Earth orbit to obtain longer observational periods. Spartan 1 was designed to provide astronomers with an opportunity to observe X rays emanating from clusters of galaxies and to explore the centre of our galaxy, the Milky Way. It contained its own attitude control system for pointing instruments at chosen celestial objects or at a particular area of the Sun's surface. The observations were automatically stored on a tape recorder for subsequent analysis.

In July 1985, on orbiter flight 19, Challenger flew its eighth mission with Spacelab 2 aboard. On the twentieth orbiter flight, Discovery carried three communications satellites, Aussat 1 (an Australian Communication Satellite), ASC 1 (for the American Satellite Company) and Syncom IV 4 (a Hughes Geosynchronous Communications Satellite). All were successfully launched. Also, the Syncom IV 3 was successfully repaired on orbit. In October 1985, Atlantis flew the twenty-first mission carrying a military payload. The twenty-second flight, launched the same month, carried the West German Spacelab D1 mission.

Currently, the US is moving towards establishing a permanent presence in space with the development and operation of a space station. Its components must be lightweight for transport into orbit, yet durable and strong. Since the station will be maintained permanently in orbit, it must be made with parts designed for replacement or easy servicing and repair by astronauts. Construction methods must be efficient as crews are only able to work 'outside' in space for a limited time before returning to a module with a controlled environment. Aspects of working effectively in microgravity must also be thoroughly explored and practised before any large structure can be erected in orbit.

In preparation for permanent space construction, NASA developed two structures for assembly by astronauts working in the payload bay of the orbiter. These were the Experimental Assembly of Structures in EVA (EASE) and the Assembly Concept for Construction of Erectable Space Structures (ACCESS). The first EASE/ACCESS mission was flown aboard Atlantis in November 1985 on the twenty-third orbiter flight. Also aboard were three communications satellites, Morelos B (Mexico), Aussat 2 (Australia) and Satcom KU 2 (RCA).

The twenty-fourth and last successful flight of the orbiter was made with Columbia early in January 1986. The payload for this mission consisted of the Materials Science Laboratory (MSL 2) and Satcom KU 1. The MSL 2 payload elements consisted of a carrier bridge mounted across the cargo bay and three materials science experiments. The carrier system provided structural support, electrical power, thermal control, an accelerometer measurement package, and data recording. US Congressman Bill Nelson flew as a payload specialist on this flight. He also conducted several materials sciences and life sciences experiments.

The twenty-fifth space shuttle mission came to an abrupt and tragic end with the Challenger accident on 28 January 1986. After a gap of two years and nine months, missions were restarted with the flight of the Discovery orbiter on 29 September 1988.

Future missions

Over the next few years, the orbiter will continue to carry scientific experiments into space and to launch free flying scientific, commercial, and military satellites. On board scientific activity will include Spacelab missions as well as other attached scientific payloads and retrievable experiment carriers, such as LDEF and the Multi Purpose Equipment Support Structure (MPESS).

There will be a trend towards using space laboratories that are dedicated to particular scientific disciplines. Examples here are Earth observations, astronomy, materials science, life sciences, astrophysics and space plasma physics. Dedicated facilities will incorporate experimental hardware in standard modules and pallets which are not taken apart after each flight, as is now the practice. Keeping the main experiments together between missions avoids the considerable time and large costs associated with disassembly and reintegration of the components. Major scientific missions planned in the pre space station era are given in the table at the foot of page 273.

In the early 1990s, orbiters will be needed to construct and service the space station Freedom. Some 20 flights will be required in the construction phase over a three year period. This should lead to Man Tended Capability (MTC) of a space station in a low inclination orbit in the late 1990s. At least one unmanned platform is planned in polar orbit. Another, in the same orbit as the manned space station, is being considered. Such platforms will provide permanent facilities for observing the Earth, for investigating plasma phenomena, and for conducting astrophysics investigations.

It is expected that, until the availability of the permanent space station, many new scientific experiments and instruments will be flown aboard the orbiters to test and develop them.

Robert H. Benson

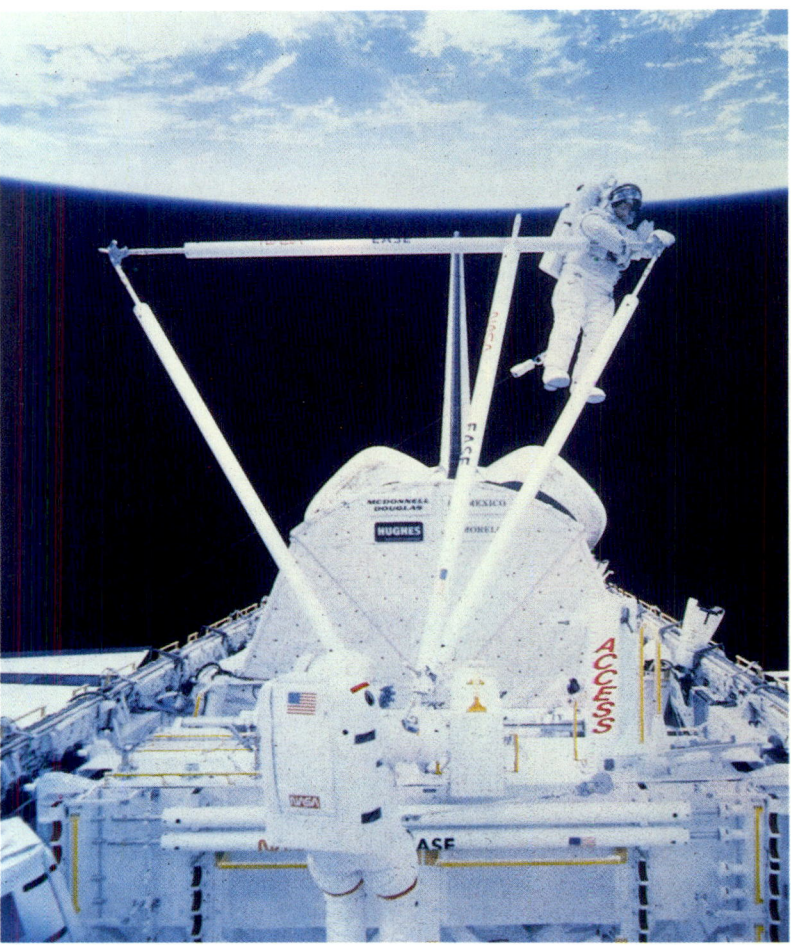

The twenty-third space shuttle flight (Atlantis) in November 1985. This was the first flight of the orbiter Atlantis. Three communications satellites, Morelos B (Mexico), Aussat 2 (Australia) and Satcom KU 2 (RCA) were successfully deployed by Atlantis' crew. In the photograph above, Morelos B rises from the cargo bay for subsequent transfer into geosynchronous orbit. The remainder of this mission was devoted to demonstrating space construction techniques essential for the space station programme. The Experimental Assembly of Structures in EVA (EASE) and the Assembly Concept for Construction of Erectable Space Structures (ACCESS) are seen in the cargo bay forward of Morelos B. Astronaut Jerry Ross is assembling elements of EASE with astronaut Sherwood Spring in the foreground. In the lower photograph Ross is attached to the end of the Remote Manipulator System working on the components of ACCESS, which extends from Atlantis' cargo bay high above the Gulf of Mexico (NASA).

Man in space

Spacelab and the space shuttle

The space shuttle is a launch system for putting a variety of payloads into low Earth orbits. As such, it lacks the full capability for detailed research investigations. The additional capability required is supplied by Spacelab. This unique space laboratory is an integral part of the space shuttle, being taken to orbit and returned to Earth in the large cargo bay of the orbiter. It remains in the payload bay, with the bay doors open, during a mission, its orientation being determined by the orbiter itself. The crew are housed in the orbiter cabin and spend their off duty time there, working in Spacelab only during their duty periods. With a flight duration of up to ten days the orbiter/Spacelab combination may be regarded as a short stay space station.

In many ways Spacelab provides a new dimension for space research. It not only extends the habitable volume of the shuttle but also supplies the experimenter with many of the tools that he uses in a groundbased laboratory. It is a member of the advanced Space Transportation System (STS). Like the space shuttle itself, it is reusable. In fact, Spacelab has been designed to be used for up to fifty flights. On its return to Earth, the equipment carried may be changed or modified for its next flight. This means that a certain phenomenon may be further studied using different techniques or a completely new topic may be investigated.

Spacelab is the first purpose built space laboratory. It draws on the many lessons learned during the performance of experiments in previous space vehicles, particularly Skylab. It ensures that an experimenter's equipment is suitably housed, thermally controlled and supplied with power. The experimenter can plan to use specialised devices, such as an airlock or instrument pointing system, and the data to and from the experiment are suitably handled.

Spacelab was developed in Europe, with European funds, under the auspices of the European Space Agency (ESA) acting on behalf of its member states. The design, development and manufacture of Spacelab were carried out under the prime contractorship of the German company MBB–Erno. The responsibilities of MBB–Erno included project management, system engineering and the integration and check out of the many parts of Spacelab produced throughout Europe. Cocontractors of the Spacelab team, and their main responsibilities in the programme, were as follows:

Aeritalia (Italy)	pressurised module
British Aerospace (United Kingdom)	pallet
Fokker (Netherlands)	airlock
Matra (France)	command and data management

The instrument pointing system (IPS). As part of the Spacelab programme, ESA undertook to develop and produce the Instrument Pointing System to improve on the pointing accuracy and stability available with the orbiter. The deadband of the orbiter system is 0·1 degrees per axis. The IPS gives three-axis attitude control, with a pointing accuracy of 1 or 2 arcseconds in the two axes perpendicular to the line of sight and about 18 arcseconds in roll about the pointing axis.

The IPS, with a total weight of 1180 kilograms carried on a pallet, can point instruments weighing up to 2000 kilograms. Torques are applied when three star sensors in a package mounted on the body of the instrument to be pointed detect a drift. The IPS is extremely sensitive to outside disturbances. Crew motion and thruster firing have to be kept to a minimum during use.

A crewmember uses the keyboard and data display unit to call up computer software packages for the planned IPS operation.

The photograph above shows the first flight of the IPS, as part of the Spacelab two mission. After initial teething troubles, the system worked perfectly and in most cases to better than its design specification. During the mission, the IPS was used to point three experiments at the Sun. These were the coronal helium abundance instrument, an ultraviolet telescope and the ultraviolet spectral irradiance monitor (ESA).

	Configurations using module	Pallet-only configurations
Payload mass (kilograms)	up to 4900 (long module)	up to 8000
Volume available for experimental equipment (cubic metres): pressurised	7.6 (short module) 22.2 (long module)	
non-pressurised	about 33.5 per pallet	
Pallet mounting area (square metres)	about 17 per pallet	
Electrical power (28 volts DC, 115/200 volts at 400 hertz AC): average (kilowatts) .... peak (kilowatts) .... total energy (kilowatt hours)	3–4 8–9 about 400	4–5 10 about 600
Thermal control (kilowatts): module atmosphere .... cooling for rack-mounted equipment .... experiment heat exchanger .... cold plates (each 50 centimetres × 40 centimetres)	2.7 4.5 4 1	— — 4 1–8
Experiment support computer with central processing unit ...	64 000 (64k) core memory of 16 bit words 320 000 operations per second	
Data handling: real time through orbiter (Ku band) .... storage in high data rate recorder .... total capacity	up to 50 million bits per second up to 32 million bits per second 38 thousand million bits	
Data display: data display unit .... keyboard	999-symbol, 3-colour display on 12-inch diagonal screen alpha-numeric keys, plus 25 function keys	Similar units available in the aft flight deck of the orbiter
Instrument Pointing System (mounted on pallet)	arcsecond pointing accuracy in three axes, for up to 3000 kilograms. 3 metre diameter payloads	

The resources available for experiments on Spacelab. The table lists the mass, space, power, computers and data handling capabilities that Spacelab experimenters can plan to use. Two configurations are possible, either with a manned module or using only pallets directly exposed to the space environment (after David Shapland and Michael Rycroft, *Spacelab – Research in Earth Orbit*, Cambridge University Press, 1984).

The first Spacelab mission (SL 1). The photograph shown above left was one of the first views that the SL 1 crew had from orbit. It was taken from the window in the rear of the aft flight deck of the orbiter. The Spacelab module, with its thermal protective coating can just be seen at the bottom. The Earth's curvature and cloud pattern are clearly visible.

The SL 1 flight commenced with lift off at 16·00 GMT on 28 November 1983 from the Kennedy Space Center, Florida. The flight, also identified as STS 9, was completely successful and lasted 10 days, 7 hours and 45 minutes. Orbital activities were carried out at an altitude of 240 kilometres in an orbit inclined at 57 degrees. Columbia landed at Edwards Air Force Base at 23·47 GMT on its 167th orbit. The crew consisted of John Young (Commander), Brewster Shaw (Pilot), Drs Owen Garriott and Robert Parker (mission specialists) and Drs Ulf Merbold and Byron Lichtenberg (payload specialists). Dr Merbold, an ESA scientist astronaut, was the first non-American to fly on the shuttle and the first ESA member to fly in space.

The principal objective of the flight – the proof of Spacelab's performance – was achieved in all respects. Some 350 sensors located throughout the module and pallet measured such quantities as temperature, structural deformation, acceleration, pressure, radiation levels and acoustic environment. The results obtained, together with the satisfactory operation of the subsystems and the very low leak rate of air from the module showed Spacelab to be a reliable and safe place to perform space experiments. A joint ESA–NASA payload was carried. Seventy-one experiments, with 58 from Europe, 12 from the USA and 1 from Japan, comprised the payload. The experiments were representative of a wide variety of disciplines and included astronomy, solar physics, space plasma physics, Earth's atmosphere and Earth observations, materials sciences, life sciences and technology.

A major facility carried in the Spacelab module during the SL 1 flight was the Materials Science Double Rack (MSDR). It included several furnaces as well as the fluid physics module. In all, 30 experiments were to be performed in the MSDR, but due to an electrical problem two of the experiments were not operated. In the photograph (above right), Dr Ulf Merbold is seen inserting a sample, contained in a special cartridge, for treatment in the gradient heating furnace. Other facilities on board were NASA life sciences experiments and ESA's metric camera and microwave remote sensing instrument for observing the Earth's surface The total experiment payload was 2785 kilograms. This mass was divided equally between NASA and ESA, and each Agency shared the power and crew time available. In addition 860 kilograms of sensor equipment was used to verify Spacelab's performance. A vast amount of data was returned and analyses are continuing even now. Highlights included first-rate pictures of the Earth's surface, the observation of Marangoni convection effects in fluids, information on trace species in the upper atmosphere, the growth of large protein crystals and observations that led to new theories on the mechanisms by which humans balance (ESA).

AEG-Telefunken (Federal Republic of Germany)	electrical power distribution
Dornier Systems (Federal Republic of Germany)	environment control and life support; also instrument pointing system (IPS)
SABCA (Belgium)	igloo and utility bridge
Bell Telephone (Belgium)	electrical ground support equipment
Kampsax (Denmark)	computer software
Sener (Spain)	mechanical ground support equipment

The actual work was distributed amongst the participating States according to their financial contributions to the programme. Since the latter was optional, each member state's contribution depended on its means and particular interest in the programme. The leading contributors were the Federal Republic of Germany (54·9%), Italy (15·6%), France (10·3%) and the United Kingdom (6·5%). Austria and Switzerland were also valued partners in the programme.

The main design and development phase proceeded through the 1970s with each cocontractor and supporting subcontractor producing a contribution to the Spacelab system. The final assembly and test of all these parts was performed by the prime contractor at a specially built integration hall in Bremen.

It was a true joint venture, with NASA giving technical assistance as needed, and developing certain peripheral hardware items, such as the access tunnel, and arranging some crew training facilities. The total programme, from the early studies to the design, development and production, cost about three quarters of a billion dollars. The programme spanned a period from 1972 to 1983 and resulted in the delivery to NASA of one flight unit and one engineering model. This latter was identical in all respects to the flight unit but had not been subjected to the stringent tests required for spaceflight.

The Spacelab system

Spacelab is of modular construction. Its size and capability may be changed by choosing from the elements that make up the total system. In addition, certain equipment may be included or excluded so that the form of Spacelab used best fits the requirements of a particular mission. It may then be used for man tended experiments in low Earth orbit. Spacelab is a flexible system. Three basic configurations are possible – module only, module plus pallet, and pallets only.

The module is constructed of aluminium alloy and is pressurised. An inside pressure of one atmosphere ensures that the crew work in an Earthlike environment. Experiments are housed in standard racks which are provided with electrical power and data lines. Air ducts in each rack provide cooling for the electronic equipment. The work bench has storage facilities, a filing cabinet, writing paper and waste disposal units.

The first double rack also contains a control centre for monitoring and controlling the Spacelab subsystems and experiments. A keyboard and visual display system are used to link crew and equipment.

Each single rack is 56 centimetres wide. It can support 290 kilograms of equipment and a double rack can take twice that. Single and double rack structures weigh 42 and 59 kilograms respectively. The racks are shaped at the top so that they fit the contours of the module, being firmly attached to the floor and overhead structure. Special cooling equipment can be installed in the double rack next to the control centre. Large equipment that cannot be accommodated in the racks is placed on the Spacelab floor (centre aisle).

The racks are designed to accept normal laboratory 48 centimetre wide trays. There is a total of ten single racks per module segment. Thus a long module has ten racks, four double and two single, on each side.

The U-shaped pallets outside the space laboratory are of conventional aircraft con-

The Spacelab SL 2 mission. The principal objective of the SL 2 mission was the verification of the pallet only mode of Spacelab operation and of the sophisticated Instrument Pointing System (IPS). The configuration consisted of three pallets, arranged as a two pallet train and a single pallet with an igloo. The pallets supported equipment for 11 of the total of 13 experiments performed on the mission. The total payload mass was around 5 tonnes.

This flight, designated as STS 51/F, took place between 29 July and 6 August 1985. The duration was 7 days 22 hours and 45 minutes. The orbital inclination was 50 degrees and the flight altitude 320 kilometres. The crew of seven was Gordon Fullerton (commander), Roy Bridges (pilot), Drs Story Musgrave, Anthony England and Karl Henize (mission specialists) and Drs Loren Acton and John Bartoe (payload specialists). A lower than planned orbit was reached due to an orbiter main engine malfunction. However, the main scientific objectives, to obtain scientific data in the visible and ultraviolet parts of the solar spectrum, together with much other information on atmospheric physics, plasma and high energy physics, infrared astronomy and life sciences, were achieved.

The photograph shows the SL 2 payload integrated on the pallets. The large sphere in the foreground is a cosmic ray detector and the circular (orange) dish is an infrared telescope. Immediately behind this are twin X ray telescopes. A plasma diagnostics package is between the IR and X ray telescopes; to the left the IPS and its associated solar radiation detectors can be seen near the orbiter cabin (NASA).

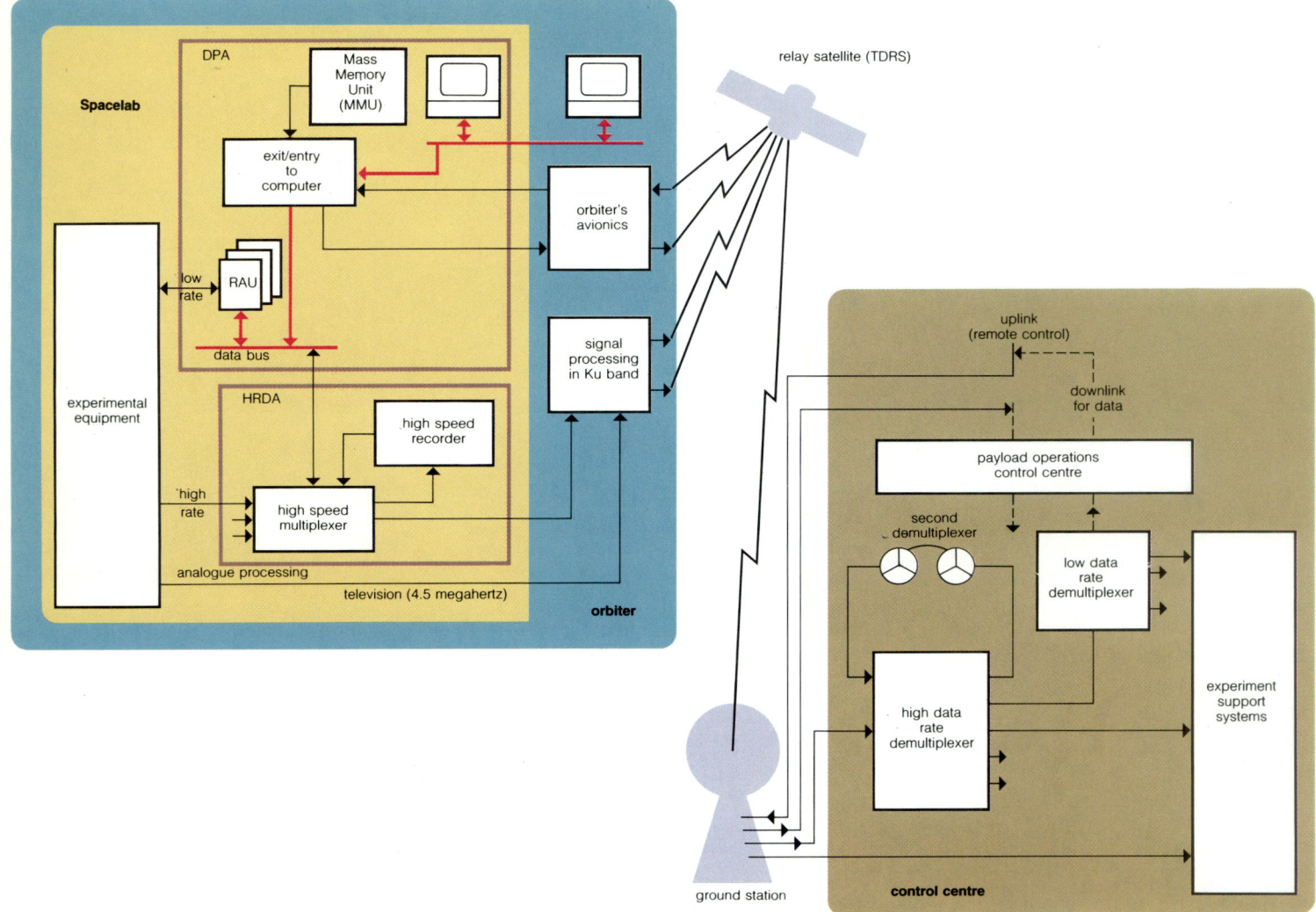

Command and data management subsystem. The CDMS functions come under two broad categories, the processing of low speed data or the processing of high speed data. The former is referred to as the Data Processing Assembly (DPA) and the latter as High Rate Data Assembly (HRDA). The DPA handles experiment commands and data acquired at relatively low rates (up to about 60 kilobits per second).

Both types of data are provided to the experiment or subsystem by a Remote Acquisition Unit (RAU). The RAU produces on/off commands, timing information and a variety of input and output channels. RAUs are located near the experiments and also near subsystem elements. The data are processed by the computers for transmission, display or storage as directed either automatically or semiautomatically, by the intervention of a crewmember through the keyboard.

The high rate data stream is produced by sampling from 16 sources with data rates of up to 16 megabits per second or up to 50 megabits per second from only one source. The data may be transmitted in real time or stored on board on the High Data Rate Recorder (HDRR). This latter is particularly useful when the TDRSS satellites are not visible. Real time transmission to the ground can be at up to 50 megabits per second. On the ground, the high speed data go through a reverse process, using a demultiplexer, to recover their original configuration.

The subsystems and experiments are controlled by two different computers, whose programmes are loaded into and stored by a digital tape recorder termed the Mass Memory Unit (MMU) (diagram after David Shapland and Michael Rycroft, *Spacelab – Research in Earth Orbit*, Cambridge University Press, 1984).

struction. Each 3 metre element can support up to 3 tonnes. When used in the two or three pallet train configuration the nominal total load carrying capability is limited to 5 tonnes. The basic frame, which has a mass of 590 kilograms, is covered by 24 honeycomb sandwich panels, each of which can support 50 kilograms per square centimetre. Larger masses must be accommodated so that the loads may be distributed by 'hard points' of which there are 24 per pallet. These hard points are located at the intersection of the circular and longitudinal members of the basic frame. Each pallet provides electrical power, data lines and cooling.

In the pallet only mode, the essential subsystems, such as computers and data handling equipment which are normally contained in the core segment, are housed in an 'igloo'. The igloo is a cylinder 1·1 metres in diameter mounted on the front frame of the first pallet. It has a usable volume of 2·2 cubic metres and provides a pressurised and thermally controlled environment for the equipment.

A pallet is used to mount the Instrument Pointing System (IPS). This complex system was developed as part of the Spacelab programme. It provides one arcsecond pointing for instruments weighing up to 3 tonnes.

A limited amount of work related to Spacelab can be carried out in the aft flight deck of the orbiter. Computer terminals and up to about 750 watts of power are available there. The Spacelab crew maintain voice contact among themselves, with the orbiter crew and with the groundbased experimenters by means of a specially designed intercom system. There is also a closed circuit television system. Experiments may be controlled from the module, the

aft flight deck of the orbiter, or from the ground. Moreover, unique data transfer links and the on board crew permit the groundbased experimenter to be an intimate part of his experiment.

Because the position of the centre of gravity of the orbiter/Spacelab combination is dictated by the requirements for reentry and landing, Spacelab is placed towards the rear of the orbiter cargo bay. The total weight of a loaded Spacelab must not exceed 14·5 tonnes.

Spacelab subsystems

Electrical power distribution. Electrical power is an essential requirement for most experiments. Spacelab provides it in a form similar to that in a laboratory on Earth. The power comes from one of the orbiter's fuel cells. This uses the interaction of oxygen and hydrogen to generate electricity amounting to 7 kilowatts, nominally at 28 volts DC. The Spacelab subsystem converts this power into a form that can be conveniently used by the experiment. Thus, electrical power is provided as stabilised 28 volts DC and 115 volts single phase AC or 200 volts three phase AC at a frequency of 400 hertz, which is normal for an aircraft.

Electrical power is also supplied to experiments located in the centre aisle and airlock, and to experiment equipment attached to the 'high quality' window. Power for interior lighting of the module and other low power requirements, such as caution and warning signals, is also provided.

The total amount of electrical energy available, regardless of the power level at which it is used, depends on the amount of reactants avail-

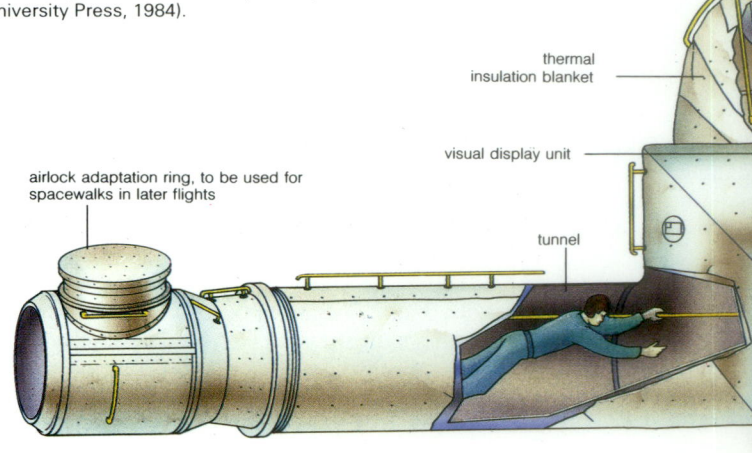

thermal insulation blanket

visual display unit

tunnel

airlock adaptation ring, to be used for spacewalks in later flights

able in the orbiter fuel cells. This is stored in tank sets or 'energy kits' which provide about 840 kilowatt hours of electrical energy. Additional energy may be obtained by adding further energy kits, but the associated mass of about 740 kilograms per kit must be carried into space and so is not available for experimental payloads.

Command and data management. During a flight, it is important that data be acquired from, and that commands be sent to, the experiments and the subsystems on board Spacelab. The actual path for the transmission of Spacelab data is through the orbiter communications system and then, via the Spaceflight Tracking and Data Network (STDN) by S band, or the Tracking and Data Relay Satellite System (TDRSS) by Ku band, to a ground station. The on board control of the data flow together with other important functions such as

Inside the Spacelab module. The view inside the Spacelab 1 module illustrates the spacious interior in which the crew perform the experiments.

The airlock and high quality window are easily identified in the module roof as are the equipment racks and Spacelab floor. The latter is important for two reasons. Once in orbit, it is psychologically desirable to have a reference 'down'; on the ground, experiment equipment must be integrated into the module with a firm floor. The Spacelab design, therefore, provides an interior layout which is both practical for many tasks before launch and convenient for working under the microgravity conditions of space.

The control centre rack with its keyboard and data display unit can be seen on the right. The centre aisle supports equipment used for life sciences experiments. At the foot of the racks are foot restraints which may be folded down in flight. The yellow rods, attached to the racks, are fixed hand rails to aid crew movement and provide body stabilisation under weightless conditions in space. The Materials Sciences Double Rack (MSDR) facility, used by many experimenters, is on the left. On the rear end cone of the module can be seen one of the portable fire extinguishers and portable oxygen assemblies that are part of the normal safety equipment (NASA).

data display, data recording, and the monitoring and control of the subsystems and experiments, is the function of the Command and Data Management Subsystem (CDMS).

The subsystem and experiment data handling are computer controlled. Three identical computers are carried by Spacelab. One is dedicated to the subsystems, one to the experiments and the third is a backup for either. Each computer is a general purpose CIMSA 125 MS. The computer memory is 64K, that is 64 000 words, each of 16 binary digits, or bits. The crew-to-computer interface is by means of a keyboard that resembles that of a normal typewriter. The alphanumeric keys, supplemented by a further 25 function keys, generate instructions that are recognised by the operating system software. The associated data display unit presents selected information for verification and monitoring by the crew.

For the payload, the overall operating system that controls standard functions such as data collection from the experiment Remote Acquisition Units (RAUs) is the Experiment Computer Operating System (ECOS). This provides a set of standard operating services such as distribution of time and orbiter supplied navigation data for the experiments.

Due to rapidly advancing technology in this area, the CDMS is being updated to provide a larger memory and to ensure decentralised handling of the data.

Environmental control. The crewmembers need an environment that is conducive to performing their tasks well. Further, the experiments may be exposed to deep space so that they cool down, or to the Sun so that they heat up. Some experiments may generate heat. Since most experiments only operate within a relatively narrow range of temperatures, their operating environment must accordingly be thermally controlled.

The interior of the module is maintained at one atmosphere pressure, the air content being similar to that on Earth, mainly oxygen and nitrogen, and purified. The temperature is about 22 degrees celsius and the relative humidity is around 50 per cent. Within the module, air and water are used as coolants. On the pallet, freon cooled cold plates are used, the system being able to cope with up to eight standard cold plates. Thermal 'capacitors', using melting wax are also used to absorb sudden, heavy heat loads.

Passive thermal control techniques, using insulation blankets and special surface coatings, are also employed, particularly for the Spacelab outer surfaces and individual experiments which produce significant amounts of heat.

Crew systems. The main man/Spacelab interface is effected through the crew station and habitability subsystem. This is centred on the workbench which is located in the core segment for activities of a general nature. Lighting throughout the module can be dimmed, and emergency lighting can be maintained in the event of power loss.

Foot restraints and hand rails are situated throughout the module to help the crewmembers perform their tasks efficiently. Outside the module and on the pallet there are hand rails to assist a crewmember engaged in ExtraVehicular Activity (EVA).

All controls and displays have been designed so that they can be operated and observed conveniently. The most important and frequently used controls are in the most easily reached positions. The position which man automatically assumes under weightless conditions has been evaluated in water tanks. The results, together with photographs taken during the Skylab missions, have been used in the design of the control centre rack and, particularly, in establishing an optimum arrangement of controls and indicating instruments.

Safety is an important factor in any manned system. A caution and warning subsystem, in

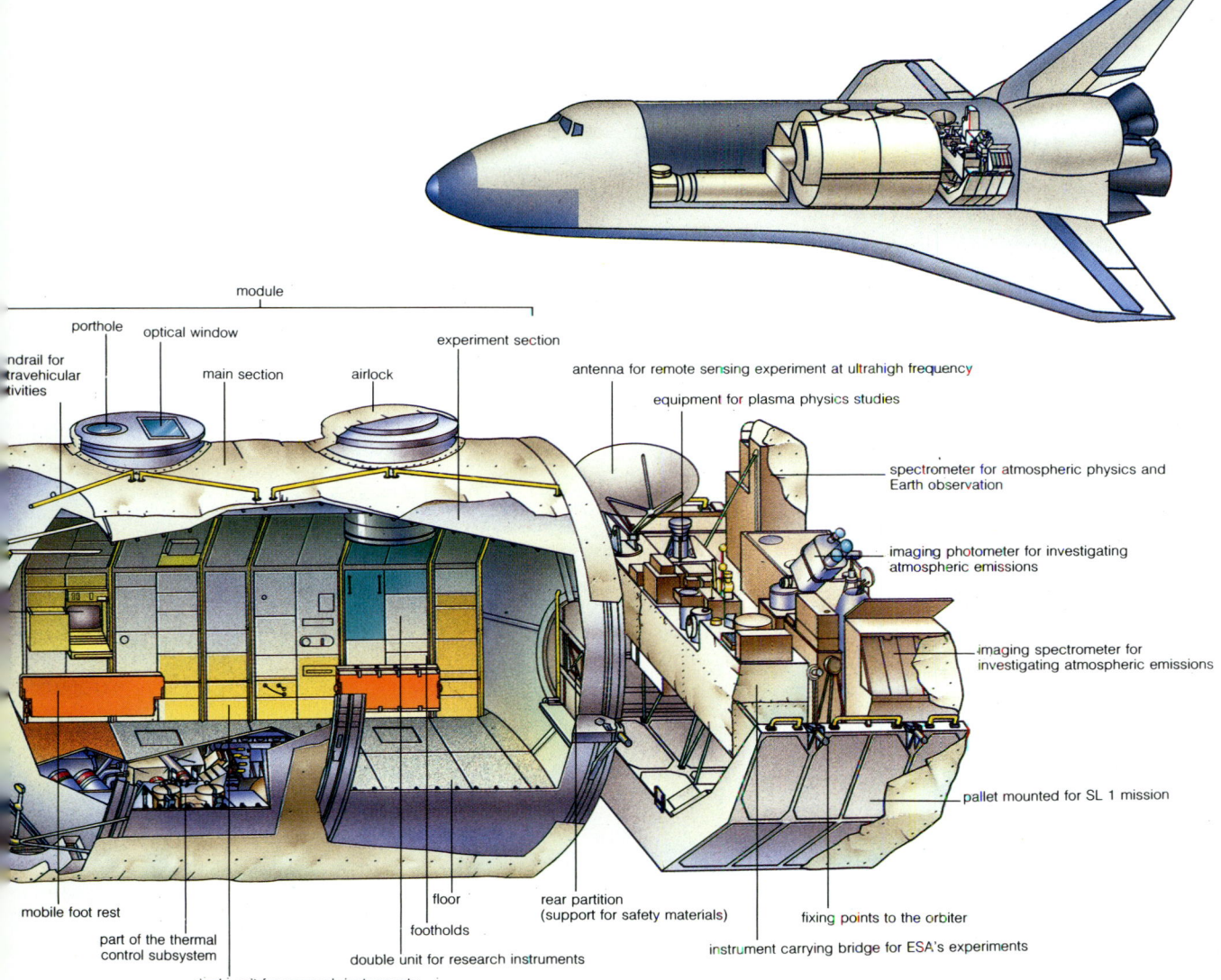

module

porthole · optical window · experiment section

handrail for extravehicular activities · main section · airlock

antenna for remote sensing experiment at ultrahigh frequency

equipment for plasma physics studies

spectrometer for atmospheric physics and Earth observation

imaging photometer for investigating atmospheric emissions

imaging spectrometer for investigating atmospheric emissions

pallet mounted for SL 1 mission

mobile foot rest

part of the thermal control subsystem

single unit for research instruments

double unit for research instruments

floor

footholds

rear partition (support for safety materials)

fixing points to the orbiter

instrument carrying bridge for ESA's experiments

Spacelab – its principal design features. Spacelab consists of two essential parts – the module and the pallet. The pressurised module is the manned laboratory whereas the pallet acts like a platform, permitting the instruments attached to it to be exposed to space conditions. The module is cylindrical in shape, with a diameter of 4 metres. It consists of either one or two 2·7 metres long segments enclosed between end cones. A short module has an overall length of 4·3 metres and a long module 7 metres. The pallet element consists of up to five sections, each 3 metres long and 4 metres wide.

Spacelab fits inside the cargo bay of the orbiter as shown. It is held by keel fittings at the bottom and attach fittings (or trunnions) at the sides. The crew reach the module from the orbiter cabin through a tunnel which is 1 metre in diameter. During flight the entire Spacelab surface is covered by a thermal insulation blanket to reduce heat flow to and from the laboratory.

The pressurised core segment contains the Spacelab subsystems and also has 8 cubic metres available for experiment equipment. The experiment segment is dedicated solely to experiments and provides a further 14·6 cubic metres for housing equipment. The core segment has a high quality window, for accurate optical measurements, and a viewport for observing events outside. The size of the window is 41 centimetres by 56 centimetres, while the viewport is circular with a diameter of 30 centimetres. If required, an airlock can be carried in the experiment segment. This is 1 metre in diameter and 1 metre high. It supports equipment of up to 100 kilograms attached to a small table. Power, lighting and data handling connections are available to airlock experiments.

Experimental equipment is delivered to NASA's integration and launch site at Kennedy Space Center in Florida. Parts of the payload, or even full payloads, might have been pre-integrated elsewhere. For instance, for European payloads, the pre-integration may have taken place at an ESA centre or at a central national facility. The NASA operations are carried out in the Operations and Checkout (O&C) building. These include joining the equipment to the appropriate parts of Spacelab, such as racks or storage containers, and to essential support elements such as RAUs. Integration involves checking and testing all the experiments so that they work together as a whole. When integration has been satisfactorily completed, the payload is put into the Spacelab and the module and pallet segments are joined. The Spacelab segments are prepared in parallel with the payload and parts that have already flown will have been refurbished. The full Spacelab system is then checked, using Spacelab's own support subsystems. After further tests, Spacelab is placed in a specially designed and environmentally controlled canister for transport to the Orbiter Processing Facility (OPF) where it meets the orbiter for the first time. Once launch aboard the space shuttle has been carried out, the cargo bay doors are opened, exposing instruments on the pallets to the space environment. The scientist astronauts enter Spacelab from the orbiter via a tunnel. At the end of the mission, the cargo bay doors close and the space shuttle returns to Earth (ESA).

the form of a master alarm and display of the relevant data to the orbiter and spacelab crew station, provides an indication of dangerous situations. The equipment carried includes fire alarms, portable fire extinguishers and portable oxygen systems.

Applications of Spacelab

Spacelab is an ideal platform for studying phenomena that can be adequately observed over a flight of up to 10 days and where a manned presence is beneficial. Spacelab's vantage point above the atmosphere, and the near weightless conditions that prevail within the vehicle, can be used to the full. Since the payload weight and volume capability is so great, large instruments using more than one technique or different parts of the electromagnetic spectrum may be used simultaneously.

The three main uses of Spacelab are as a research laboratory, as an observation platform and as a development testbed. A fourth potential application, beyond the initial basic research programmes, may be as a limited production facility in space. In a general sense, the experience gained with the operation of Spacelab and its experiments will be extremely advantageous for the eventual use of the space station.

Some typical examples of Spacelab as a laboratory can be cited, but these are by no means exhaustive. In astronomy, large telescopes and cameras, using film if necessary, can view stellar objects and galaxies from above the Earth's atmosphere. Solar physics can be pursued using specialised instruments to study the Sun's surface or the variation of the Sun's radiated output, 'the solar constant'. Instruments in Spacelab in high inclination orbits can be used to study the Earth's plasma environment *in situ*. Observations of the Earth may be made with visual and microwave instruments. Such remote sensing techniques can be developed for operational satellites. In the microgravity environment of Spacelab, basic materials sciences, fluid physics and life sciences processes may be studied. The environment and facility offered by Spacelab is particularly useful for such experiments. The payload specialist in attendance can use his skills in performing the experiments. He may even act as a test subject in certain life sciences investigations. In the area of technology experiments, Spacelab is ideally suited because of the presence of man and the fact that equipment can be brought back to Earth for further evaluation.

Mention should be made here of the highly successful technique used for the operation of Spacelab experiments. Thanks to the real time voice and video links which use the Tracking and Data Relay Satellite System (TDRSS), the groundbased experimenter can partake in the performance of his experiment, directly influencing the way in which it is carried out. Although the total mission is controlled from the Mission Operations Control Room (MOCR), the hub of the experimenter's involvement is the Payload Operations Control Centre (POCC). Experimental data can also be recorded, both on board and on the ground, for later analysis.

Spacelab missions

To date, four Spacelab missions have been carried out. These are Spacelab 1, using Columbia (28 November to 8 December 1983), Spacelab 2 using Challenger (29 July to 6 August 1985), Spacelab 3 using Challenger (29 April to 6 May 1985) and the German Spacelab mission D 1, also using Challenger (30 October to 6 November 1985). All launches were from the Kennedy Space Center, Florida, and the landings took place at Edwards Air Force Base, California. These flights both established the Spacelab concept and returned a prodigious amount of scientific data. Further uses of the Spacelab for NASA, ESA and individual

The Spacelab SL 3 mission. This photograph illustrates the installation of the tunnel connecting the Challenger cabin to the Spacelab module in preparation for the SL 3 flight. The 1 metre diameter flexible tunnel and supporting struts are covered with insulating blankets for thermal control. The thermal tent of Spacelab is seen to the right. Two getaway special (GAS) containers, attached to the inside of the cargo bay, are in the centre foreground. The yellow rails assist the crew on spacewalks.

The Spacelab configuration used for the first operational flight of Spacelab, the SL 3 or 51B flight, was a long module plus a palletlike structure called the Mission Peculiar Experiment Support Structure (MPESS). A 57 degree inclination orbit, at an altitude of 350 kilometres, was chosen. The crew were Robert Overmyer (commander), Frederick Gregory (pilot), Drs Don Lind, Norman Thagard and William Thornton (mission specialists), with Drs Taylor Wang and Lodewijk van den Berg (payload specialists).

This mission carried out 12 investigations in five scientific disciplines – materials sciences, life sciences, fluid mechanics, atmospheric science and astronomy, the experiment payload being about 2·5 tonnes. Apart from the reflight of the Very Wide Field Camera from SL 1 all experiments went well. The results included the growth of mercury iodide crystals, the study of liquid drops in microgravity, the composition and variability of the upper atmosphere, the observation of aurorae and measurement of the composition and energy of cosmic rays. Twenty-four rats and two monkeys were carried and a new animal facility was tested in life sciences work (NASA).

The Spacelab D 1 mission. The D 1 mission was the first in a series of German Spacelab missions, all sponsored by the German Federal Ministry of Research and Technology. The flight took place over the period from 30 October to 6 November 1985. Designated as STS 61A, the orbit was inclined at 57 degrees and the flight altitude was 325 kilometres. The truly international crew consisted of Hank Hartsfield (commander), Steve Nagel (pilot), Jim Buchli and Drs Bonnie Dunbar and Guion Bluford (mission specialists), all Americans, and Drs Ernst Messerschmid and Reinhard Furrer from Germany and Dr Wubbo Ockels of ESA, the three Europeans being payload specialists.

The total payload weight was 2·7 tonnes carried within a long module and on a simple support structure in place of a true pallet. The principal objectives were concerned with the behaviour of materials in the microgravity environment but the 76 experiments on board included some on life sciences, fluid physics and navigation. The bulk of the experiments came from Germany, but NASA and ESA were also well represented. Major facilities on board were the Materials Science Double Rack (MSDR) with a new set of experiments on melting and solidification under microgravity conditions, a Biorack for biological studies, a vestibular 'sled' and a fluid physics module. The space sled and the Biorack are multiuser facilities for life scientists. The sled, which moves along a rail fitted to the module floor, can apply a precise acceleration to a human subject sitting on a special seat. The Biorack contains incubators held at various temperatures, a freezer and a glove box. Experiments are performed with biological specimens in a controlled environment in the Biorack.

The photograph shows Reinhard Furrer (left) and Wubbo Ockels during a less serious moment in the Spacelab module. Ockels tries to solve the enigma of the egg of Columbus. The puffy facial appearance of the payload specialists is due to the redistribution of blood from the lower body due to the absence of gravity (DFVLR).

Flight number	Date Orbiter	Inclination Altitude	Flight duration Crew size	Payload
35	1 March 1990 Columbia	28.5° 352 km	10 days 7	Igloo + 2 Pallets (ASTRO-01)
40	7 June 1990 Columbia	39° 296 km	8 days 7	Long Module (SLS-01)
42	1 November 1990 Columbia	33.4° 324 km	7 days 7	Long Module + 1 Pallet (DOD)
45	21 February 1991 Columbia	28.5° 296 km	10 days 7	Long Module (IML-01)
47	2 May 1991 Atlantis	57° 250 km	7 days 5	Igloo + 2 Pallets (ATLAS-01)
48	1 July 1991 Discovery	44° 296 km	7 days 7	Long Module (SL-J)
52	19 December 1991 Columbia	57° 296 km	10 days 7	Long Module + Support Structure (SL-D2)
54	30 March 1992 Columbia	28.5° 296 km	10 days 7	Long Module + Support Structure (USML-01)
57	11 June 1992 New Orbiter	57° 250 km	7 days 5	Igloo + 2 Pallets (ATLAS-02)
58	16 July 1992 Columbia	39° 296 km	8 days 7	Long Module (SLS-02)
59	13 August 1992 Discovery	28.5° 352 km	7 days 7	Igloo + 2 Pallets (ASTRO-02)
62	22 October 1992 Columbia	28.5° 296 km	10 days 7	Long Module (IML-02)

Spacelab related flights manifested for the near future
(from Payload Flight Assignments, January, 1989)

Biorack and Anthrorack. The two life sciences facilities illustrated here are typical of the multiuser equipment that will be used in Spacelab during the 1990s. The upper photograph shows mission specialist Dr Bonnie Dunbar working in the glove box of the ESA-supplied Biorack during the D1 flight. The Biorack will be part of the payload for the International Microgravity Laboratory (IML 1) whose objective is to support research in the areas of cardiovascular–pulmonary adaptation to weightless conditions, sensor motor functions and metabolic processes. The IML 1 activities will extend the baseline data gathered with Biorack during the D1 mission. The IML investigations will involve the study of mechanisms of proliferation and differentiation of cells and small organisms in a low gravity environment. The glove box is used to minimise the risk of contamination of sensitive biological specimens.

The lower photograph is of a mockup of the double rack Anthrorack facility developed by ESA for human physiological research, treating the whole human body as a system. It consists of an ergometer, an echo cardiograph and various physiological measuring devices. A computer system permits storage, display and transmission of data. In the photograph the echograph display screen is seen at the top. There is a TV monitor for visual display of physiological parameters, the respiratory monitoring system to its right. The black data display unit and alphanumeric keyboard is evident, as are the seat and pedals of the leg ergometer apparatus, at the bottom. It will first be used during the German D2 mission late in 1991 (above, NASA, below Aérospatiale).

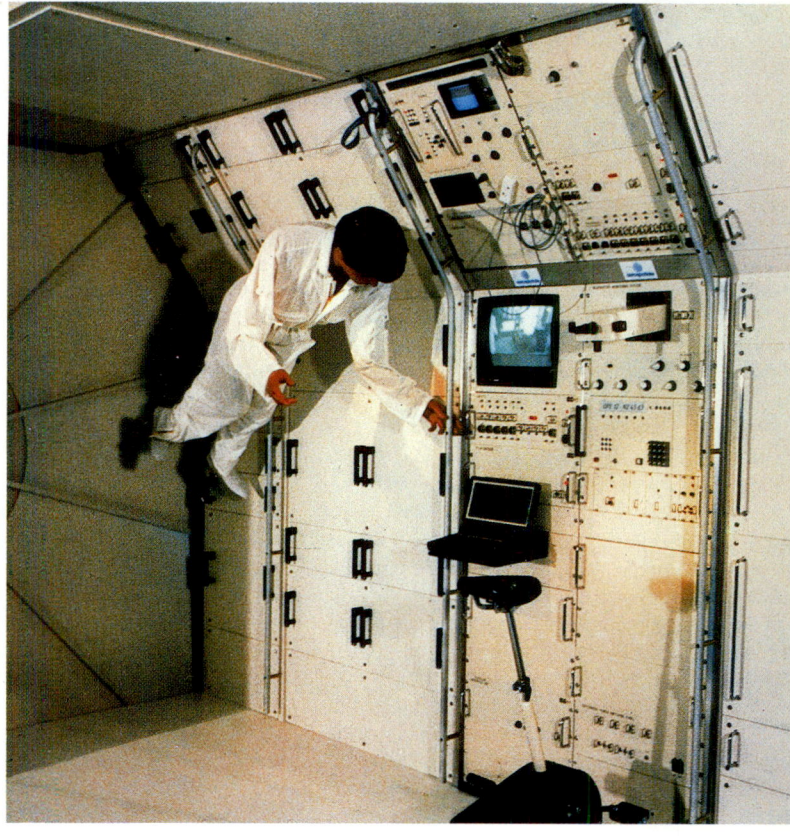

countries are planned now that shuttle flights have resumed.

The SL 1 flight at the end of 1983 was the space baptism of Spacelab. It was essentially a flight verification of the long module plus pallet mode. However, a secondary objective was to demonstrate the usefulness of Spacelab for experimentation in various disciplines. The flight was a tremendous success and both objectives were handsomely fulfilled.

The SL 2 mission, which actually took place after SL 3, proved the remaining Spacelab elements. In the pallets only mode, this flight proved the igloo and Instrument Pointing System (IPS). At the same time, large amounts of important data on the Earth's atmosphere, the Sun and other astronomical targets were obtained from the pallet mounted instruments.

The SL 3 mission was devoted mainly to investigations in the materials, fluid, and life sciences, so the flight path was optimised to ensure the best possible microgravity environment and the payload specialists were experts in these fields. Again, a vast amount of important scientific data was returned.

The German D 1 mission also concentrated on microgravity sciences. For the first time, the POCC was situated outside the US, at Oberpfaffenhofen in West Germany.

The outlook for Spacelab

Information on the planned Spacelab missions for 1990 to 1992 is given in the table above.

The ASTRO 01 mission will observe astronomical objects in the ultraviolet part of the spectrum using a number of coaligned instruments pointed by the IPS. ASTRO 02 should be launched in August 1992.

The life sciences will be served through the Space Life Sciences (SLS) Laboratory series, two of which are scheduled in NASA's manifest. Some 25 experiments on SLS 01 will study the biomedical problems of human spaceflight and plant development in microgravity.

The experiment operators will be skilled in the life sciences discipline and the crew themselves will act as test subjects. It is possible that animals will also be used.

The International Microgravity Laboratory (IML) represents a major international venture in the materials and life sciences, permitting participating states to use each other's facilities. If the US experimenters wish to use a non-US facility the latter is launched free of charge by NASA. This is the first of a series of international microgravity science laboratories. The IML 02 and IML 03 flights will follow at about 20 month intervals. The USA is also planning a microgravity laboratory for launch in 1992.

Originally called the Environmental Observation Missions (EOM), the Atmospheric Laboratory for Applications and Science (ATLAS) programme will commence early in the 1990s. The experiments aboard will include US, European and Japanese experiments to study the Earth's atmosphere, the terrestrial plasma environment, deep space and the Sun. It will include reflights from previous Spacelab missions. The Spacelab J flight will carry the Japanese First Materials Processing Test (FMPT), a forerunner of Japan's materials science investigations, and will be devoted to the microgravity sciences.

The second flight of the German Spacelab research programme (D2) is scheduled for the beginning of the 1990s. This flight includes many repeats from the D1 mission, the aim being to improve understanding of the basic principles of certain aspects of materials and life sciences. Participants will include experimenters from Germany, ESA, NASA, France and Japan. A third mission (D3) for research under microgravity conditions is also planned.

A further series of microgravity experiments is envisaged with the US Microgravity Laboratory (USML). The first mission is planned for March 1992.

David J. Shapland

Man in space

Life sciences in a microgravity environment

There is little doubt that the ubiquitous force of gravity has dictated both the internal and the external forms of life on Earth in ways which are, at the same time, both dramatic and subtle. Gravity not only preceded life on Earth, but has also been a pervasive and stable companion of evolution through the eons of the existence of life, whatever its form. An organism's ability to sense gravity, to interpret correctly the relationship between gravity and its position, and to make the physical adjustments necessary to prevent damage in a threatening situation frequently determines whether the organism will survive to maturity. The relationship between gravity and life is so intimate that, before the advent of spaceflight, no one could predict how, or even whether, any particular biological process would function if gravity were absent. With the passage of time and the accumulation of data, a new field of scientific research, space life sciences, has been born.

Historical background

Biomedical research. Mankind, like every other organism on the Earth, is completely adapted to the normal gravitational force which exists at the surface of our planet (termed 1g). There are only a very few moments during most of our lives on Earth when this force does not act on the body (e.g. during some sports activities such as jumping on a trampoline, or when flying in an airplane during a parabolic trajectory), but the duration of such exceptions is extremely short, of the order of seconds. During a spaceflight, however, the effective force of gravity decreases to a thousandth, or even a millionth, of its value at the Earth's surface. Scientists term this reduced gravitational environment, where objects are nearly weightless, 'microgravity'.

Investigating life and the adaptation of biological systems in such an altered environment is both highly interesting and extremely important. This is particularly true if mankind is to ever journey for long periods in space. Biomedical research in space is primarily devoted to studying the body's responses to various stimuli in order to understand the physiological mechanisms underlying those responses. Space medicine, on the other hand, is dedicated to developing the means of protecting mankind from being harmed while in space as well as following the return to Earth.

The biomedical problems associated with exposures to microgravity for periods of days, or perhaps weeks, can be divided into three main groups. These are:
(1) functional neurophysiological changes or disorders caused by modified sensory input during spaceflight;
(2) cardiovascular deconditioning caused by the effects (mostly related to hormonal and autonomic adjustments) of the shift towards the head of body fluids, which occurs upon entering microgravity;

(3) so-called negative training effects, generally showing the opposite effects on muscle tissue, bones, etc., to those which are observed during endurance training of an athlete.

The cause of the latter effects is that, during weightlessness, no great effort is exerted to maintain normal posture, as would be necessary if gravity were present, so the normal strains of muscles and bones required for movement are practically absent. Moreover, the energy needed for movement is markedly reduced in space.

The neurophysiological adjustments take place very rapidly (within minutes to hours) following entry into the microgravity environment of space, as does the fluid shift within the body. The secondary, hormonal, adjustments occur somewhat more slowly (within hours to days). The negative training effects continue to take place over a considerable period of time (weeks to months). There are, of course, additional complicating interactions which occur between the three major effects described here.

Even in the early flights of the Soviet Vostok series, a phenomenon appeared which has never been completely explained – space motion sickness, today sometimes called the space adaptation syndrome. In later flights, it became obvious that about 50 percent of all humans entering space suffer from this disorder within the first hours or days of flight. Its name was derived from sea sickness, since it involved some of the same symptoms such as nausea, vomiting, and reduction of performance. It now appears that this disorder is connected with the functional neurophysiological adjustments occurring within the body during the first few hours and days of spaceflight.

A second striking phenomenon became apparent in those early flights. During a stay in space, the body always lost some of its fluid. Then, upon returning to the gravitational pull at the surface of the Earth, the crewmembers had problems standing without fainting. Doctors call this type of problem 'orthostatic insufficiency' (or orthostatic intolerance). The symptoms of the disorder include an extremely low heart rate, sweating, and loss of consciousness. They are normally caused by a temporarily insufficient blood supply to the brain. Today, this problem can be connected to the headward shift of body fluids which occurs when humans spend time in microgravity environments.

With the limited payload capability of the early Soviet and US spacecraft, most of the biomedical and medical studies aimed at understanding the problems associated with spaceflight could only be conducted before and after the mission. Thus, only limited progress could be made in solving these early medical problems. For example, in the American Mercury programme (lasting from May 1961 to May 1963), inflight measurements were restricted to continuous monitoring of the heart and respiratory rates, and measurements of blood

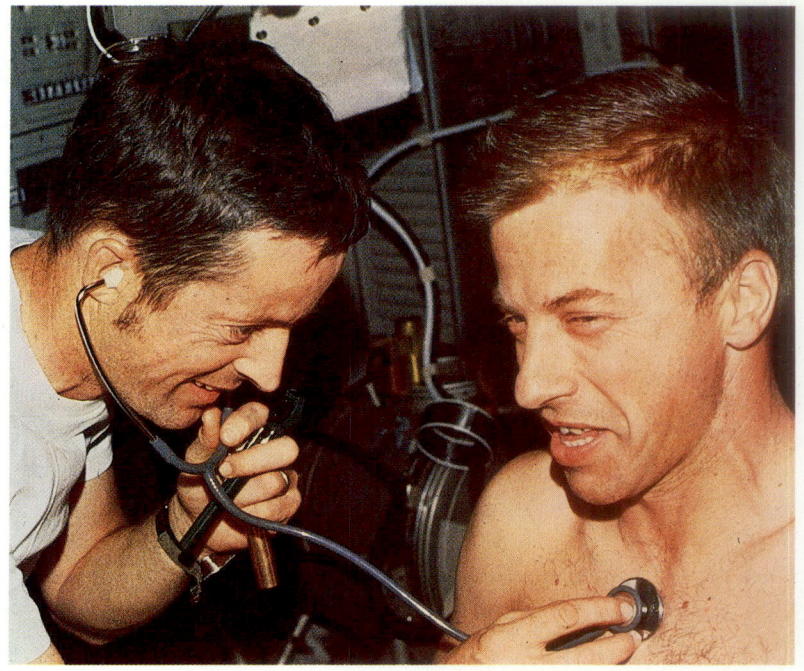

Physical examination on US Skylab mission. US scientist astronaut Joseph P. Kerwin, a doctor, uses a stethoscope to check the heartbeat of fellow astronaut Paul J. Weitz on the Skylab space station during the 28 day Skylab 2 mission. Skylab was utilised for three manned missions during 1973 and 1974, the longest of which lasted for nearly three months. Nine astronauts flew in space aboard these missions and the biomedical data collected on these nine subjects are among the most comprehensive data sets ever collected in space (NASA).

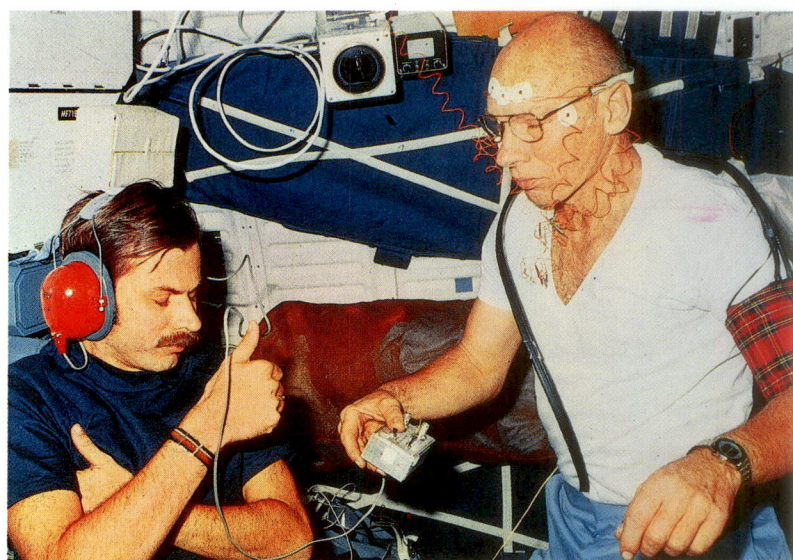

Audiometric tests on board Challenger. During the Challenger mission from 30 August to 5 September 1983, William E. Thornton (on the right in the photograph) conducted a series of hearing tests on another astronaut, Dale A. Gardner. His hearing thresholds in space were compared with those on Earth (NASA).

American flight echocardiograph study. American astronaut Rhea Seddon, a doctor, applies a blood pressure cuff to US Senator E. J. (Jake) Garn in the middeck area of the space shuttle Discovery.

During this mission, which orbited the Earth for seven days in April 1985, Senator Garn flew as a payload specialist. Among his duties on this flight was participation in a biomedical study using echocardiography with Dr Seddon. In addition, Senator Garn and Dr Seddon conducted a number of other medically oriented studies (NASA).

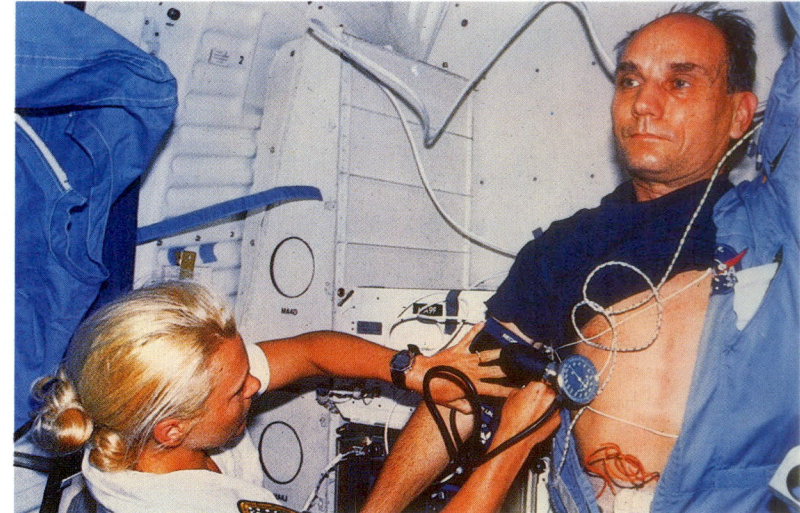

pressure and body temperature. Photographs of the astronaut's face were taken at intervals of 12 seconds. During this early period, spurred on by the difficulty in obtaining biomedical data during spaceflight, very powerful techniques were developed to simulate different elements of the microgravity environment on Earth using bed rest and water immersion.

Why is observation of the face interesting during exposure to microgravity? The face looks somewhat different compared to its appearance on Earth, mainly some years younger, due to the fluid shift phenomenon. Standing on the earth, in an upright position, about 0·7 litres of blood and 1·5 litres of water is found in the legs. These fluids are located partly in the blood vessels and partly in the interstitial spaces. The reduced gravity of spaceflight removes the water from the legs. Most of the water is shifted to those areas of the body where the distension of the blood vessels and also of the interstitial tissue spaces is greater. Therefore, in a microgravity environment, we find more body fluids in the lungs, the heart, and also in the face.

The blood shift also causes a second severe impact on the human body. The atria of the heart contain receptors which are part of the system for the control of blood volume. If a person drinks one litre of water, this will be absorbed via the intestine and will add one litre to the blood volume, which is usually approximately five litres. This additional volume causes the distensible parts of the circulatory system to stretch. The receptors located in this area inform the kidneys, via neural and hormonal loops, to excrete more water until the volume is normal. This is a biological analogue of a servomechanism. Moreover, the salt concentration and, through this, the osmotic pressure of the body fluids is controlled by similar feedback loops. Since these volume receptors are just stretch receptors, they cannot distinguish whether the stretching is caused by drinking or by the microgravity induced blood shift from the peripheral to the central parts of the circulatory system. A persisting blood shift – as happens during spaceflights – activates the servo loop in an almost inadequate way, leading to severe disorders of the system. Furthermore, it seems that the mechanism of hormonal adjustment of the blood electrolytes also impairs the transformation of energy in the muscles and, as a consequence, the capacity for exercise.

If we follow up the historical development of biomedical research under microgravity during the last 25 years, we may state different objectives. In the beginning – at least for the American programmes – the main problem was whether a human being was able to tolerate seven days of weightlessness without being harmed. Project Mercury was designed specifically to establish man's ability to survive in the space environment, and it did exactly that. From a biomedical point of view, the main value of the two suborbital and four orbital missions was the many medical concerns related to spaceflight which were either dispelled or verified. Project Gemini, which involved 10 manned flights between 1965 and 1966, was important because the data gathered served as the foundation on which to construct the biomedical experiments for later missions of longer duration. The biomedical data gathered during the Apollo missions confirmed and extended the Gemini results. But the available time for biomedical studies on the operationally complex missions was severely limited.

The Soviets instituted the long running Soyuz programme in 1967, two years after the last Voskhod flight. The objective of the programme was to provide a multipurpose spacecraft which could be employed in connection with an Earth-orbiting space station. During the early Soyuz missions, before the availability of a space station, the level of medical monitoring and experimentation was not much different from that of the US programme. None of the

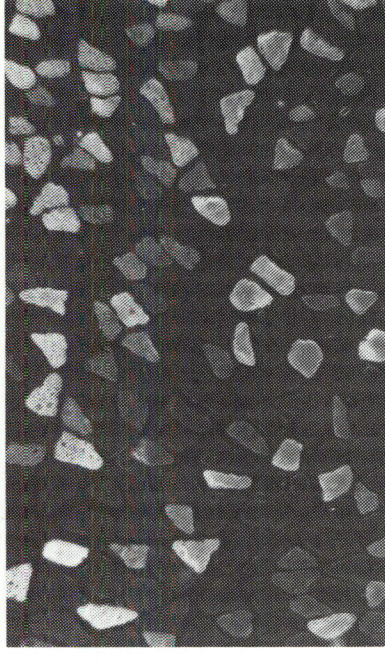

Morphological and biochemical changes in the muscles of rats in space. Spacelab 3, flown in May 1985, provided valuable insights into muscle atrophy induced by zero gravity conditions. Flight rats were exposed to seven days of microgravity and control animals remained on earth in simulated flight cages. Hindlimb muscles were studied some 16 hours after the flight. Marked atrophy of the muscles was noted, especially in the soleus and extensor digitorum longus, muscles that are normally related to postural and weight bearing limbs. Atrophy of these muscles was indicated by a decrease in muscle fibre area from 25 to 35%. Overall, the histochemical properties of flight muscles shifted from slow twitch toward those of fast twitch muscle fibres (i.e. from oxidative toward glycolytic metabolism). Under the microscope, this is indicated by the increase in ATPase staining for the space rats, shown in the righthand photograph. These results are consistent with Earthbased models of disuse and previous biosatellite findings (NASA).

A French study of balance on board Discovery. In June 1985, the French payload specialist Patrick Baudry participated in a study involving equilibrium and vertigo as part of a cooperative project between NASA and the Centre National d'Etudes Spatiales (CNES).

The objective of this French designed investigation on the space shuttle was to obtain data during spaceflight relating to the balance system's response to conditions of near weightlessness (NASA).

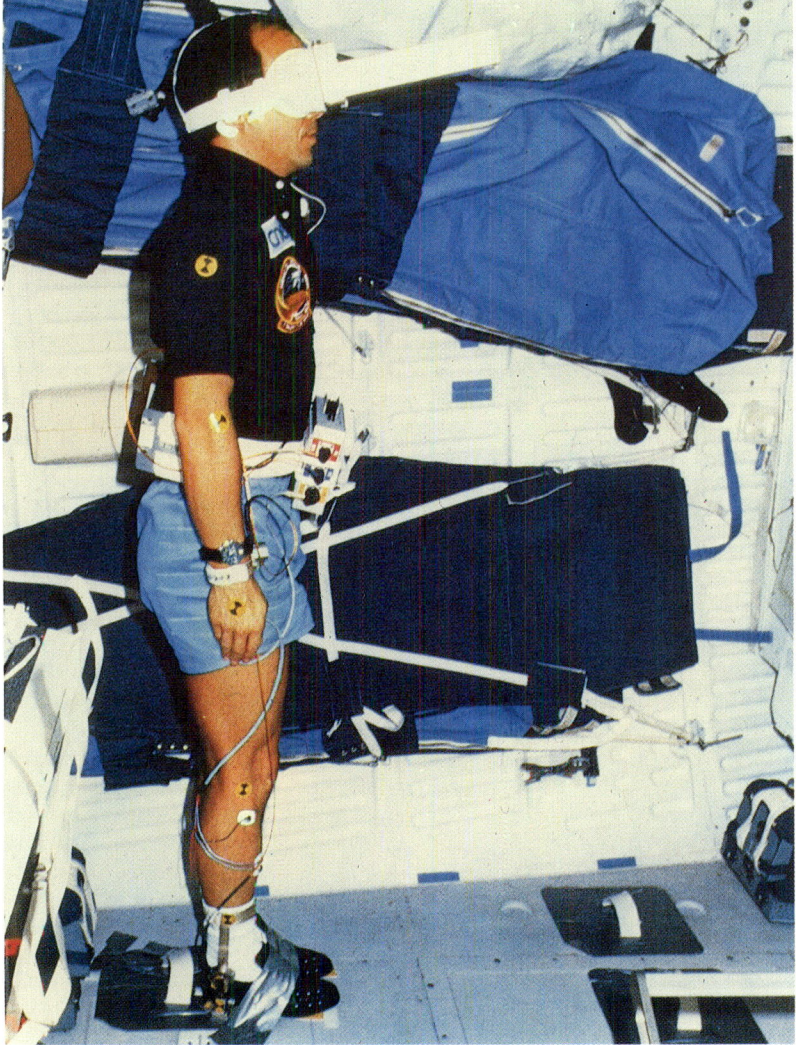

cosmonauts participating in these missions demonstrated unusual or unexpected physiological changes, except for the fact that, after the 18 day flight of Soyuz 9, the two crewmembers demonstrated a pronounced orthostatic intolerance and had to be carried from their spacecraft after landing. Full postflight readaptation to gravity took at least 11 days. This experience, which subsequently turned out to be anomalous, gave rise to concern about the outlook for longterm manned space missions and led to a vigorous search for countermeasures to halt cardiovascular deconditioning in the next phase of the Soviet programme.

The Soviets launched their first orbital station, Salyut 1, in 1971, but the first and only crew to utilise that station died during reentry because of a valve malfunction. Two years later, Salyut 2 was launched, but it was evidently damaged during launch and was never occupied. Salyut 3, 4 and 5 were all successfully used by a large number of crews for increasingly longer periods, up to two months. Salyut 6, which was utilised for manned missions from 1977 to 1981, represented a new generation of orbital station. It was indeed a fullscale orbiting research laboratory, and was visited by 27 cosmonauts participating in 15 separate missions. The next station, Salyut 7, was launched in 1982 and remained in service until 1986.

On these stations, Soviet cosmonauts remained in space for over eight months (237 days on Salyut 7) and returned safely to Earth. A great deal of biomedical data has been gathered, particularly related to the effects of longterm spaceflight. Various countermeasures have been developed which help to combat the deleterious effects of spaceflight on crewmembers so they can readily readapt on their return.

Biological research. Given the uncertainty that existed in the days before manned orbital flights on how biological processes would function without gravity, it is not surprising that biological experimentation in space preceded man's first visit to that environment. Bacteria, fungi, various cell cultures, plants, dogs, and monkeys all flew in space before a human did. In 1961 the first man in space carried a package containing bacteria with him. Mice journeyed with man to the Moon, and back, in 1972. Man has continued to carry ever more complicated scientific investigations of biological significance on the spacecraft that he uses. In addition, both the United States and the Soviet Union have flown dedicated biological satellites (Biosatellite and Cosmos series), though the Soviet Union alone has carried out regular flights of such spacecraft every two or three years. Many of the early biological experiments in space were crude by scientific standards, being designed to address the capability to survive and function in the space environment. As data from these early flights accumulated and were analysed, it became clear that there were no great biological surprises. Spaceflight, in general, turned out to be surprisingly benign and tolerable. Cellular effects were subtle, and thus difficult to detect. However, at the level of more complex organisms, with developed systems for sensing and maintaining their orientation with respect to gravity, there were significant effects. Thus, for both plant and animal systems, the key scientific questions became:

(1) how does the organism perceive gravity?
(2) how is that information transmitted to a site capable of responding to the perception?
(3) how does the responding site process the information and control the response?

In addition, it became increasingly clear that a key question concerned the role of gravity in an organism's life cycle. Does the influence of gravity extend even into the initial days or hours of life? How does gravity affect the development of a seed or embryo, or the maturation and behaviour of the organism? Such questions formed the basis for many of the studies of the 1980s.

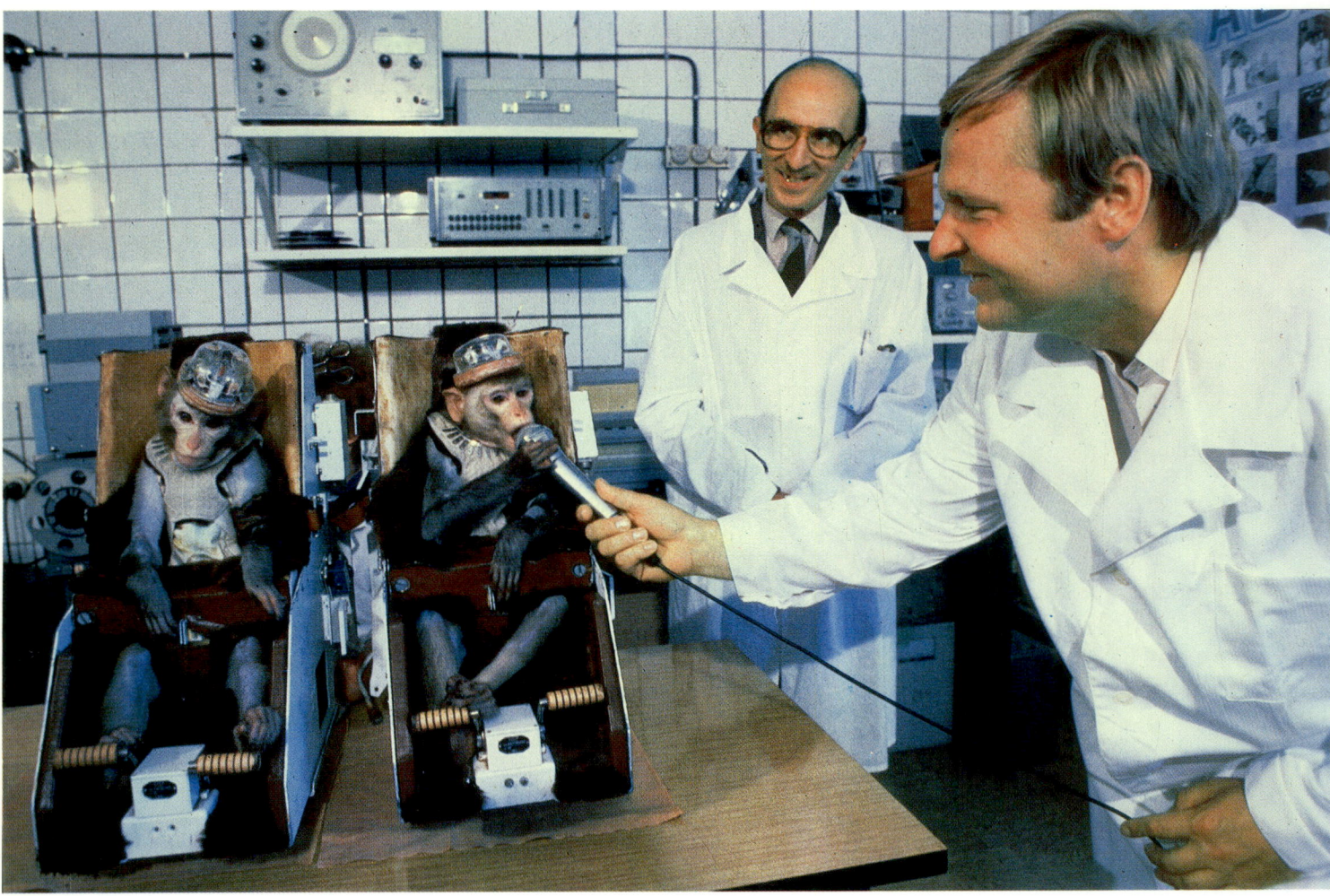

A biological experiment on board Cosmos 1667. Two monkeys, 1500 fish and flies, 10 newts and several rats were put into orbit on 10 July 1985 for one week on board Cosmos 1667. Also carried were some grains of maize and some crocuses.

The aim of the mission was to study how living organisms adapt to weightlessness, especially during the initial period of orbital flight. A world first occurred during this flight: some rats were born in space.

The countries involved in the programme were the USSR, Bulgaria, USA, France, Hungary, Poland, East Germany, Rumania and Czechoslovakia. In this photograph, Oleg Gazenko, the director of the Institute of Biology and Medicine in Moscow, is helping with a television 'interview' with the two monkeys, Verny (meaning Faithful) and Gordy (Proud), after their first flight in space (APN).

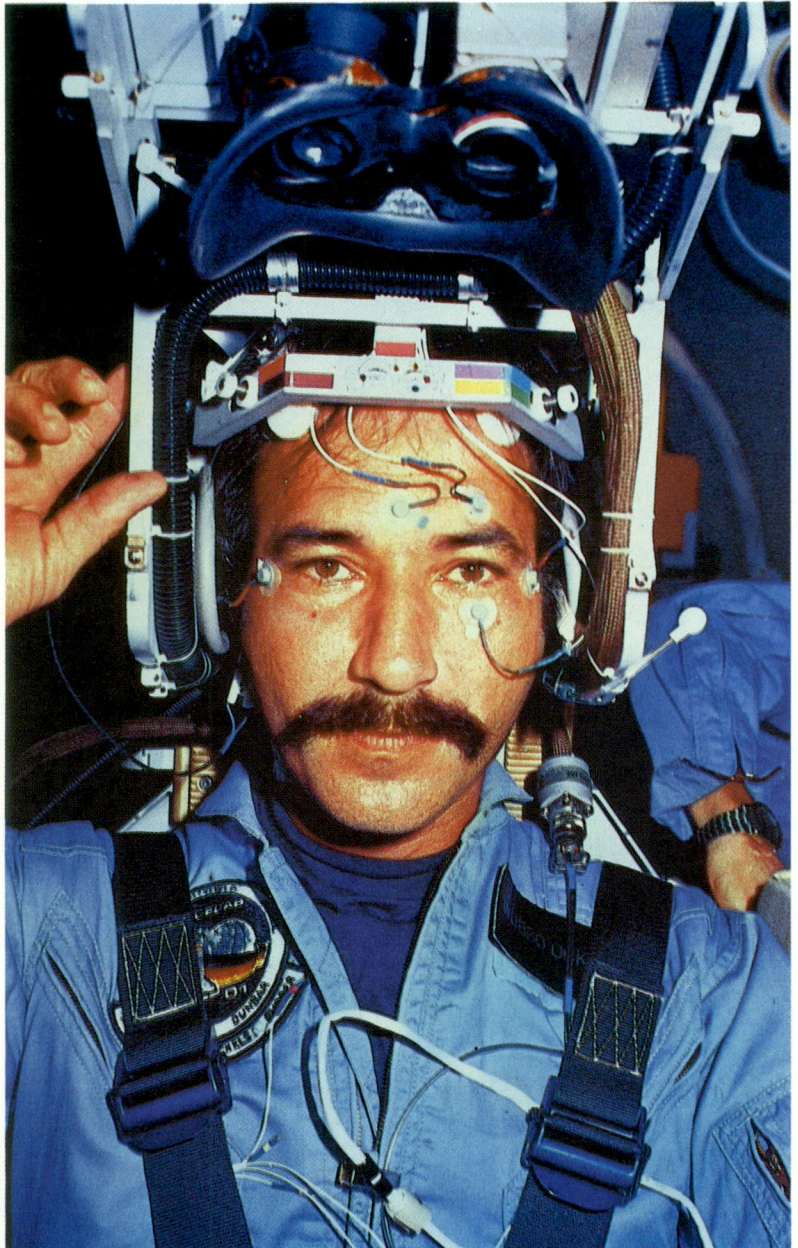

Use of the vestibular sled helmet on board Spacelab. The vestibular sled, a research facility designed and built by the European Space Agency (ESA) to fly within the Spacelab module, first flew in space on the space shuttle mission sponsored by the German Federal Ministry of Research and Technology and known as the D1 (Deutschland 1) mission. This lasted from 30 October to 6 November 1985. Dutch payload specialist Wubbo J. Ockels prepares here to lower the eyegear portion of a specially designed helmet which, with sensors on his face and forehead, measures and monitors his physiological reactions while riding on the sled (NASA).

Current status

The United States and Europe. The first orbital flight of NASA's space shuttle, on 12 April 1981, together with the first flight of a special research facility, the Spacelab, on 28 November 1983 (on the ninth shuttle flight) marked the beginning of a new era in space life sciences research. In particular, the European scientific community now had the opportunity to participate more fully in manned space research. The Spacelab system, developed by the European Space Agency (ESA) includes as one component a cylindrical pressurised laboratory module carried in the cargo bay of the shuttle. This laboratory module carries multiple racks, each containing the dedicated hardware necessary for special groups of experiments. It also provides the power distribution, a computerised data collecting system, and other features necessary for the management of the various experiment racks. The total system, therefore, is highly versatile and can be assembled for each mission according to its specific scientific objectives. With Spacelab, the transition from pre- and postflight experimentation only to real and comprehensive inflight research seems to be at least technically complete. A disadvantage compared with Skylab, or with the Soviet stations, is that the present maximum mission duration of 10 days for the shuttle is obviously not sufficient for detailed studies of long duration adaptation processes. Such studies will only be possible in the US programme after the launch of NASA's space station in the mid 1990s. This will include, besides a US laboratory, a Japanese laboratory and a European laboratory (Columbus), all of them equipped in a similar way to Spacelab.

The first Spacelab mission, carried out in 1983, was a remarkable success. It conclusively demonstrated that high quality inflight research was feasible. Sixteen life sciences experiments from both US and European researchers were part of the payload for the mission. Spacelab investigations of the involuntary rapid eye movements (nystagmus) resulting from irritation of the ear canals with water, at a different temperature from the temperature of the body, yielded information which has necessitated changes in the information contained in physiology textbooks. The so-called caloric nystagmus

indeed occurs in space so the classic explanation involving thermal convection due to density gradient differences must be incorrect.

Ballistocardiographic studies, central venous pressure measurements, red blood cell kinetics experiments, studies related to the response of the immune system, endocrine studies, radiation studies, and investigations concerned with the ability to discriminate various masses in microgravity were all performed on the same mission, as were a number of basic biological experiments.

Spacelab has demonstrated its unique versatility. As a result of this mission, it is also clear that a comprehensive and complicated scientific programme requires scientists in Spacelab who are able to understand the goals of the investigations. They must be able to carry out and, under certain conditions, modify the different experimental steps. One of the payload specialists on such missions is therefore often an expert in biology or medicine.

The second flight of the Spacelab laboratory module took place in May 1985 and had, as its major payload element, the largest group of animals ever to fly in space with humans, including 24 laboratory rats and two squirrel monkeys. Although the primary purpose of the flight was to test the hardware designed for carrying the animals into space, several significant research investigations were also undertaken. Postflight analysis demonstrated that there were substantial decreases in the masses of the postural muscles and weightbearing bones in the rats. The otolith organs in the rats (composed of tiny crystals containing calcium) did not decalcify as expected, but, instead, may have grown new crystals. The heart muscle of the rats which flew in space was structurally altered. The production of interferon by the spleen was severely inhibited postflight, and growth hormone production was suppressed after the flight as well. One of the monkeys exhibited some symptoms associated with space motion sickness. In all, the mission produced dramatic results whose complete interpretation awaits further studies on the ground and in space.

The last Spacelab mission, before the terrible accident of Challenger on 28 January 1986, was the D1 mission. Funded by the Federal Republic of Germany, and controlled as far as

Plant investigations on Spacelab 2. Two miniature greenhouses, called plant growth units, were flown on the Spacelab 2 mission in July and August 1985. These two greenhouses contained 4 day and 10 day old pine seedlings (far left), mung bean seeds (middle) and oat seeds (left). Studies were made of the growth of the plants and the process of lignification in space. Lignin, a structural polymer that makes up 30% of plant tissue, is a woody substance in plants. It allows plants to grow and stand upright despite the downwards pull of gravity on Earth. Results from these studies indicate that plants can grow in space, but that the amount of lignin produced during spaceflight is reduced. In addition, the germination success of mung beans and oats was found to be comparable with that obtained on Earth, but root orientation of germinating mung beans was not normal, with 29% of the roots of the young seedlings protruding above the supporting root medium (NASA).

Human responses to spaceflight. The experiments for SLS 10 and SLS 20 were carefully chosen to reflect the interdisciplinary nature of spaceflight adaptation prevalent at the time that the investigations were proposed. A highly simplified view of this understanding of the human adaptation to spaceflight is shown. Although some of the interconnections are speculative, several broad ideas clearly emerge. First, a number of physiological systems exhibit gross disturbances in weightlessness, including the cardiovascular, fluid-electrolyte, erythopoietic, musculoskeletal and metabolic systems. Secondly, these disturbances appear to be attributed to several major effects of weightlessness, including the redistribution and loss of body fluids due to an absence of hydrostatic forces, a degeneration of loadbearing musculoskeletal tissues due to an absence of deformation forces, and a longterm change of the metabolic state as reflected in diet, oxygen consumption and energy storage. Thirdly, the most significant and consistent consequences of these fundamental changes include a change in body composition (loss of body weight, body fluids and electrolytes), blood volume loss and alteration of blood biochemistry, cardiovascular deconditioning (decreased orthostatic tolerance, and degraded exercise performance upon return to the 1g environment), atrophy of musculoskeletal tissue (loss of calcium, potassium and nitrogen), and shortterm vestibular disturbances (including space sickness). Fourthly, the time required to achieve a new state appropriate for zero gravity conditions is different for each major physiological system, as indicated grossly by the width of the interconnecting lines in the figure. Fifthly, there is a high degree of interaction between the major subsystems, indicating that a true understanding of these responses requires a rigorous interdisciplinary approach (NASA).

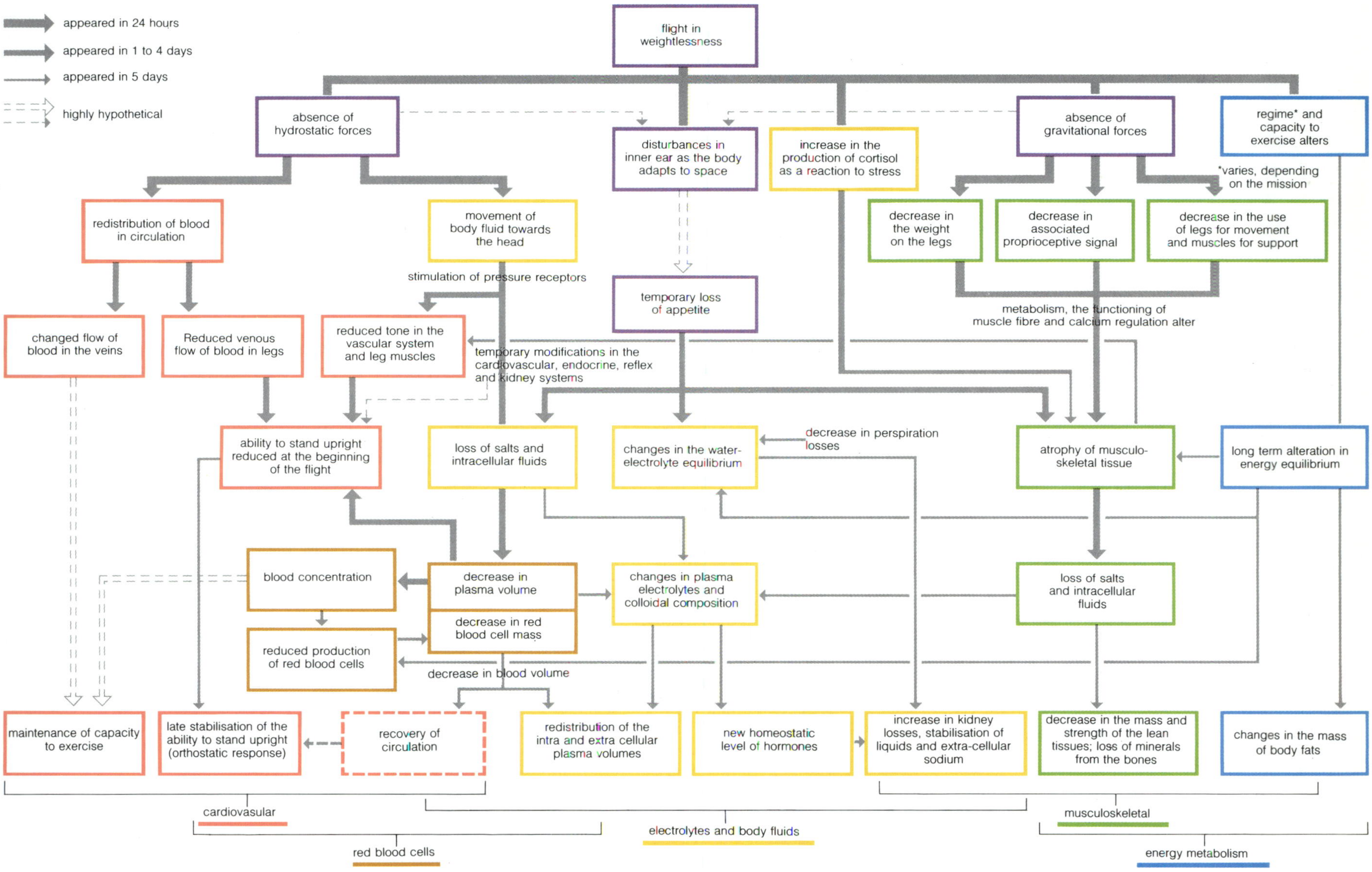

Flowchart

Legend:
- appeared in 24 hours
- appeared in 1 to 4 days
- appeared in 5 days
- highly hypothetical

flight in weightlessness

- absence of hydrostatic forces
- disturbances in inner ear as the body adapts to space
- increase in the production of cortisol as a reaction to stress
- absence of gravitational forces
- regime* and capacity to exercise alters

*varies, depending on the mission

- redistribution of blood in circulation
- movement of body fluid towards the head
- decrease in the weight on the legs
- decrease in associated proprioceptive signal
- decrease in the use of legs for movement and muscles for support

stimulation of pressure receptors

- changed flow of blood in the veins
- Reduced venous flow of blood in legs
- reduced tone in the vascular system and leg muscles
- temporary loss of appetite

metabolism, the functioning of muscle fibre and calcium regulation alter

temporary modifications in the cardiovascular, endocrine, reflex and kidney systems

- ability to stand upright reduced at the beginning of the flight
- loss of salts and intracellular fluids
- changes in the water-electrolyte equilibrium
- decrease in perspiration losses
- atrophy of musculo-skeletal tissue
- long term alteration in energy equilibrium

- blood concentration
- decrease in plasma volume
- decrease in red blood cell mass
- changes in plasma electrolytes and colloidal composition
- loss of salts and intracellular fluids
- reduced production of red blood cells

decrease in blood volume

- maintenance of capacity to exercise
- late stabilisation of the ability to stand upright (orthostatic response)
- recovery of circulation
- redistribution of the intra and extra cellular plasma volumes
- new homeostatic level of hormones
- increase in kidney losses, stabilisation of liquids and extra-cellular sodium
- decrease in the mass and strength of the lean tissues; loss of minerals from the bones
- changes in the mass of body fats

Categories:
- cardiovasular
- red blood cells
- electrolytes and body fluids
- musculoskeletal
- energy metabolism

the payload was concerned from the German Space Operations Centre near Munich, this mission was a logical continuation of the Spacelab programme with both improved instrumentation and important new investigations. Participants included a large number of investigators from different European countries, as well as from the United States. A US–Canadian team and a German team shared a very sophisticated ESA device, the vestibular sled. This consists of a movable seat, which is mounted on a rail fixed to Spacelab's floor, and control electronics mounted in two racks. The seat on the sled can be oriented in any of the three orthogonal directions allowing a thorough investigation of the interrelationships between motion and neurophysiological responses. A special helmet with an integrated infrared eye movement recording system, as well as a device allowing stimulation of the optical system by special visual patterns, enabled the investigators to learn how the brain 'computes' and coordinates its different sensory inputs. Other experimental approaches extended the experiences of the first Spacelab mission, and introduced new techniques. For example, the adaptation of the intraocular pressure induced by the shift towards the head of fluid in the body in microgravity was measured. Measurements were also made of body impedance, a technique yielding additional information on the redistribution of body fluids. Other investigations were concerned with problems of illusion associated with microgravity.

A second major ESA developed hardware element, the Biorack, was also part of the payload of the D1 mission. This device consists of a set of constant temperature incubators fitted with small centrifuges capable of maintaining a variety of specimens at Earth gravity (1g) while in space. Such a device is critical for the exact determination of the effects of microgravity on samples of interest. Important investigations concerned with human lymphocyte activation, the growth rate of *paramecium*

Fertilisation in the sea urchin. This photomicrograph illustrates the process of sperm penetration into a sea urchin egg. Sperm DNA appears violet and the microfilaments forming at the egg surface are red. The sea urchin egg is a classic model in developmental biology, and new probes, such as those used here to visualise the process of sperm penetration, have been developed to enable a depth of investigation that was previously impossible. It is now possible to explore the influence of gravity on fertilisation and early cell division processes. Such studies are ideal candidates for future Spacelab projects (NASA).

tetraurelia, gravity sensitivity of cellular systems, radiation levels in the Biorack, embryogenesis and aging of fruit flies (*Drosophila melanogaster*), and the embryogenesis and organogenesis of the stick insect (*Carausius morosus*) were all conducted using the ESA Biorack. The perception of gravity by plants, differentiation of cells, geotropism and other topics were the subjects of studies in other facilities included on the D1 mission. In all, this Spacelab mission demonstrated clearly that gravity has a significant effect even on cellular systems.

The Soviet Union. The Soviet Mir space station was launched on 19 February 1986. Soviet space work has followed a straight and persistent course over the last 20 or so years, with each spacecraft being an improved version of its predecessor. Spectacular effects are not part of the Soviet programme. The Mir station replaces the Salyut 7 station which has been in space since 1982. Although of the same size as Salyut 7, Mir does not carry the same large array of scientific equipment as the earlier Soviet stations. Instead, Mir is considered to be the future living quarters of a comprehensive space station complex. The large number of docking ports on Mir will permit this. Dormitories, dining rooms and a psychologically designed environment will provide more privacy and comfort than in any spacecraft before. This last is an important issue, since a longterm lack of privacy can cause social stress and lead to both psychological and medical disorders. A state of longterm stress can also have a confounding negative impact on physiological parameters being used for research into the effects of microgravity. Equipment for exercise, including a bicycle and a treadmill, are aboard so that the crew may keep as fit as possible.

The Soviet Union is intending to add another module to the Mir space station in the mid 1990s, which will be devoted to life sciences, in particular the physiological effects of long stays in space.

Expectations for the 1990s

Future Spacelab research. The next Spacelab flight, which is scheduled in 1990 to carry an extensive payload for space life sciences investigations, is a NASA mission dedicated entirely to life science research (all of the Spacelab missions discussed earlier were shared by several other sciences). This mission, called Spacelab Life Sciences 1 (SLS 01), is by far the most complicated life sciences mission yet planned. Mission objectives include the completion of interdisciplinary studies of both the physiological responses which occur rapidly upon entering a microgravity environment and the known problems related to one week's stay in space and return to Earth. Although research animals (laboratory rats) will fly on this mission, the emphasis will be on human studies.

A second mission devoted entirely to life sciences, Spacelab Life Sciences 2 (SLS 02), is scheduled for 1992. This mission will complete many of the studies begun on SLS 01, and will devote a major portion of the mission to research using both squirrel monkeys and laboratory rats. It is expected that further NASA Spacelab missions will be devoted entirely to the life sciences, and that the SLS series will continue for some time, at least until a comparable laboratory is available aboard the space station.

An interdisciplinary mission, called International Microgravity Laboratory 1 (IML 01), scheduled for 1991, will contain significant US, Canadian and European studies in the life sciences. The payload will include ESA's Biorack as well as a sophisticated set of equipment to investigate plant behaviour in microgravity. Also on board will be a rotating chair which will be used to investigate neurovestibular functions in space. The International Microgravity Laboratory series of missions is designed to

allow various members of the international scientific community to fly investigations in a cooperative manner on the Spacelab. Further missions in this series are expected during the 1990s.

The SLS and IML series will be equipped with a joint NASA/CNES experiment on Rhesus monkeys, and also a centrifuge of 1·8 metres diameter.

The IML 01 mission will be followed by a Spacelab mission known as Spacelab J, because the Japanese government has purchased nearly one half of the resources of the Spacelab facility for their use. The Japanese intend to fly a significant number of life sciences investigations on that mission. The US also intends to fly at least two major investigations in the life sciences area, one related to developmental biology using frogs' eggs and the other related to human performance in microgravity.

Scheduled for launch in 1991 is the German D2 Spacelab mission. As was the D1 mission, D2 will be a mixture of experiments on materials sciences and life sciences. The vestibular sled will be replaced by a newly developed ESA device, the Anthrorack, a sophisticated multipurpose apparatus designed to study human physiological changes in microgravity. Anthrorack contains elements for cardiovascular, respiratory, blood and hormonal research, at rest and using defined exercise stimuli elicited by a bicycle ergometer. This provides the opportunity to elucidate the adaptation of these systems in a detailed way, and to extend the measurements made on previous missions. In addition, as on D1, a number of other facilities will be flown, including both plant and animal experiments. A study group has been established to examine the feasibility of a third German mission, D3, but it is still too early to provide details.

Eureca. Eureca is the acronym for the European Retrievable Carrier. It is an unmanned platform, designed to provide longterm untended stays in space and a gravitationally less contaminated environment than Spacelab. It is operated like a satellite in a free flying mode away from the space shuttle. In fact, the only task of the shuttle is to launch Eureca in an orbit of approximately 300 kilometres altitude, and to catch it again for return to Earth. Eureca's own propulsion system will carry it up to an operational altitude of 500 kilometres where it will stay for a period of six to nine months. Thus, Eureca will provide prolonged flight durations, retrievability and reusability. As it is unmanned, life science experiments will be restricted to botanical and microbiological investigations. A number of Eureca flights are planned before the NASA space station with the European Columbus module becomes available.

US space station. Plans are underway to launch an international space station complex called Freedom using the space shuttle to place the numerous elements into orbit and to resupply the station once it is operational. The initial configuration will consist of at least five elements, each larger than a Spacelab module. These elements are a habitability module for the crew to live in, a logistics module to house supplies, and three laboratory modules supplied by the US, Europe and Japan. Plans also include permanent occupancy of the station by the last half of the 1990s.

With the construction of this station, researchers in the life sciences will finally be able to address some of the critical questions that face man if he is ever to journey on longterm missions away from the vicinity of Earth.

Jürgen Stegemann, Ronald J. White and Joel I. Leonard

Twinned tadpoles. On Earth, gravity's effects may be studied using a centrifuge to produce gravitational forces higher than normal. In this picture, twinned tadpoles of the African Clawed Frog, *Xenopus laevis*, were produced as a result of perturbing the normal gravity vector by centrifuging during the period between fertilisation and the first cell division. Such studies on Earth clearly demonstrate that gravity does have an effect on development (NASA).

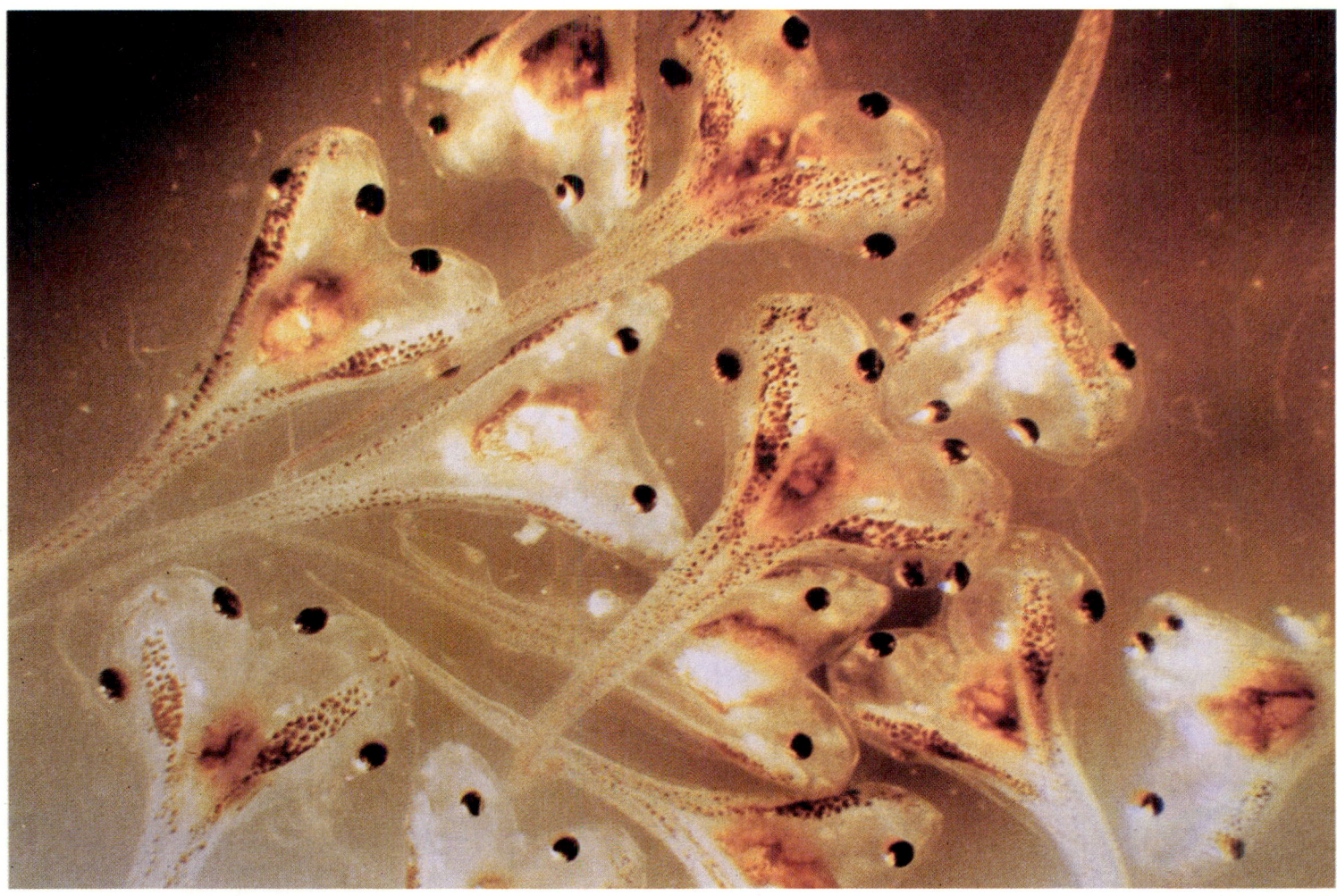

Overview of the major science activities on SLS 01 and SLS 02. The research selected for the first dedicated Life Sciences Spacelab (SLS) missions will be unlike any previous research conducted in the US space programme and quite different from any conducted in traditional terrestrial laboratories. Although originally conceived for a single flight, 24 experiments have been integrated into activities spanning two dedicated Spacelab flights and parts of several others. Just as space adaptation is highly interdependent on a number of body systems, it was recognised that the next generation of life sciences experiments must also emphasise the interdisciplinary aspects of biomedical space research. The figure indicates, by colour, the important issues to be addressed, including cardiovascular/cardiopulmonary, renal/endocrine, vestibular, haematological, immunological, muscular, bone and gravitational aspects. There are definite advantages in conducting an entire suite of investigations at the same time, using common subjects and highly trained scientist astronauts. Also, human and animal studies will be tightly coupled; an important objective is to qualify the rat and the monkey as suitable animal models to provide insight into human responses. This synergistic approach, in which the total scientific yield is greater than the sum of that of the individual components, represents an efficient use of resources. More importantly, it provides a means of making the broadest possible scientific attack on complex and interrelated biomedical phenomena (NASA).

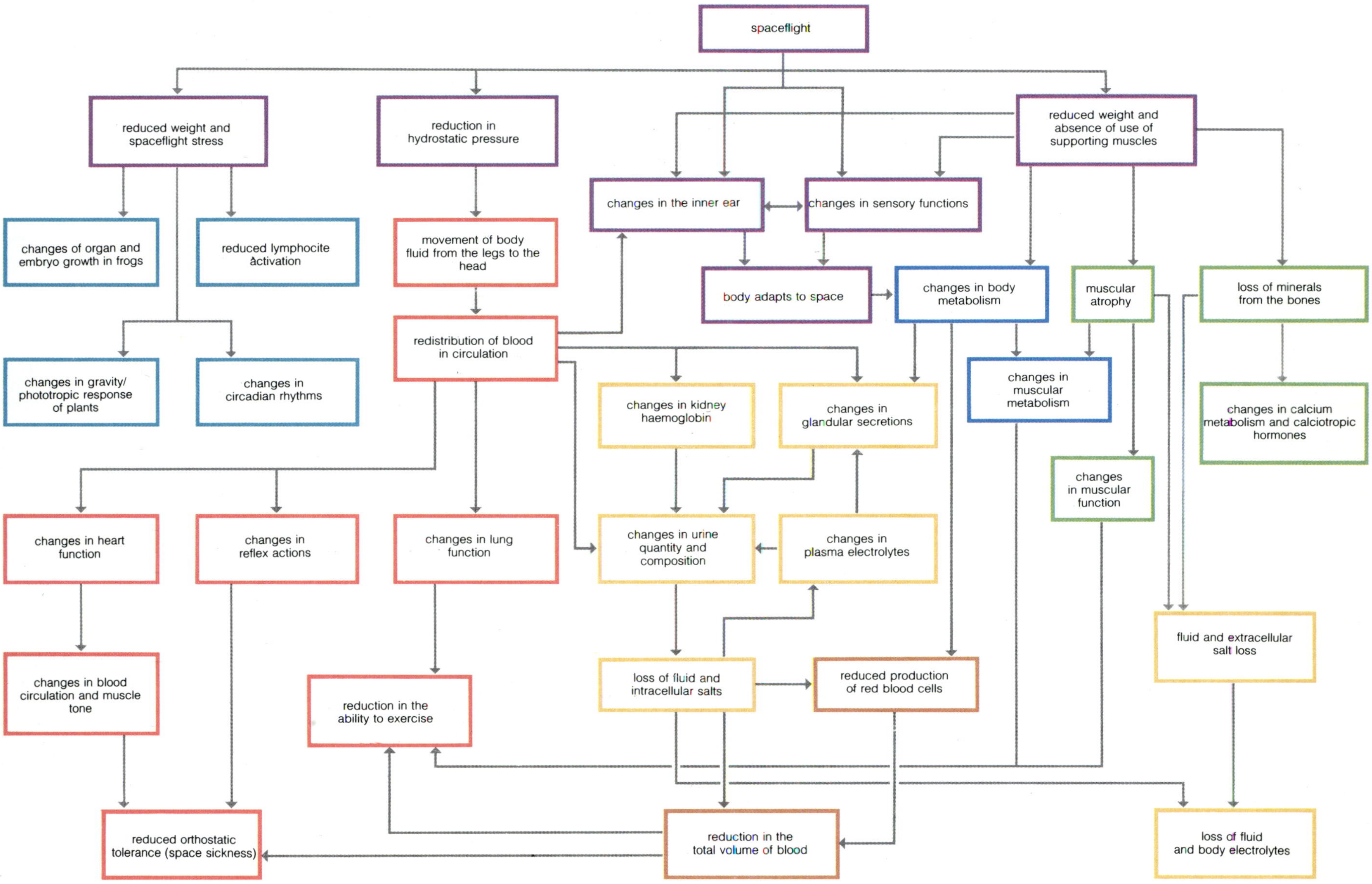

Man in space

Materials science in microgravity

Research into the behaviour of materials in microgravity environments is one of the most recent subjects in space research. Work in this area began in earnest once space laboratories were in orbit around the Earth and essentially gravity free conditions could be obtained for a few hours, days or even weeks.

A brief history

The USSR carried out the first experiment in materials science on board the Soyuz 6 spacecraft which was launched on 11 October 1969. It consisted of soldering using an electron beam. In the Apollo programme of the early 1970s, the Americans systematically evaluated the possibilities that microgravity opened up in the field of materials science. Experiments were carried out on the solidification front of molten bodies and on the separation of biological substances using electrophoresis.

Both the Soviets and the Americans developed research programmes on the fundamental physics of fluids, notably on convection and the behaviour of free surfaces, on the solidification of metals and semiconductors and on containerless processing techniques that are only possible in space. Skylab, the American orbiting laboratory, carried out 21 materials science experiments and in 1975 the USSR embarked on a vast programme of experiments using the Salyut space stations. In July 1975, the two superpowers agreed on a joint project, the Apollo–Soyuz Test Project (ASTP). The Soviet part of this involved producing germanium and composite semiconductors.

Preparations for long duration experiments in space have generally involved short experiments, lasting between five and ten minutes, on board rockets in ballistic trajectories. In 1975, the West Germans carried out their first rocket flight as part of the *Technologische Experimente unter Schwerelösigkeit* (Texus) programme. Its success has been followed up with several launches per year. Other nations, sometimes working collaboratively, have also carried out materials science research in the microgravity environment.

A permanent space station orbiting the Earth is a basic requirement for countries wishing to produce various materials with a commercial value under microgravity conditions. The Soviet Union has made considerable progress in this direction, starting with the Salyut space stations and then the Mir space station launched at the beginning of 1986. The Americans have used the space shuttle as a laboratory and also Spacelab, built in Europe by ESA under German supervision and designed to fit into the shuttle's cargo bay. The field of materials science has also benefited from three Spacelab missions, in December 1983, May 1984 and October 1985.

Microgravity

Weightlessness is a state which can only be attained for a few seconds on Earth, during the free fall of a body from the top of a tall tower.

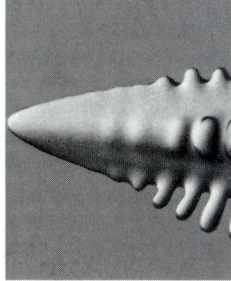
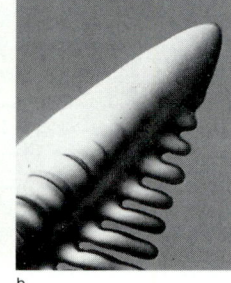
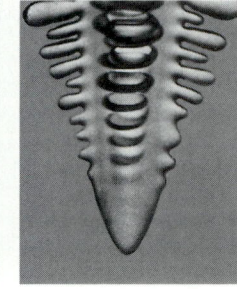
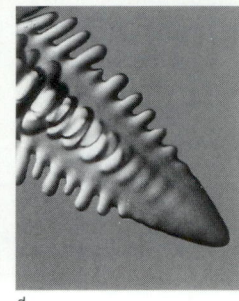

a   b   c   d

↓ acceleration due to gravity

125 micrometres

Dendritic growth. The internal structure of metals is often made up of crystals which, when magnified greatly, resemble fir trees. These crystals are called dendrites. Their shape determines the physical characteristics of a material, and in particular its strength. In a microgravity environment, dendritic growth can be observed unhampered by phenomena such as thermal convection. For experimental studies it is convenient to use molten transparent substances such as succinonitrile, as shown in the upper photograph above. (P. R. Sahm, A. Ecker).

The formation of the tip of the dendrite controls the overall symmetry and the spacing between branches. Convection, caused by gravity, modifies the tips considerably, as shown in the lower four photographs. In each of these, the acceleration due to gravity is directed downwards. These individual dendrites, formed at different angles to the gravity vector, have quite different tip structures. (M. E. Gliksman).

Apart from this, everything which happens on Earth is influenced by gravity.

Astronautics has opened up the field of research in gravity free or, more precisely, microgravity conditions. However, to put rockets into space at all, several problems had first to be solved. These included the behaviour of fluids – liquid fuels for the rockets – in partially empty reservoirs. The behaviour of batteries also had to be understood. When these are used, heat is released and the internal state of the battery is altered, though the temperature remains constant.

Early research experiments carried out in microgravity utilised a 'free fall tower'. Objects were subjected to a few seconds of weightlessness, depending on the height of the tower, when they were dropped down 'free fall chutes'. Ballistic rockets subsequently provided conditions of weightlessness for between five to ten minutes. Finally, manned and unmanned spacecraft and space stations provide days or even months of microgravity conditions.

True weightlessness is not achieved in orbit around the Earth, for a variety of reasons. These include the complex shape and rotation of the satellite or space station, atmospheric drag which varies according to the altitude of the orbit, the movement of astronauts inside the space station and the operation of equipment which causes vibrations. Thus complete weightlessness, or zero gravity, does not exist. The condition is one of microgravity. The acceleration due to gravity at the Earth's surface, g, is equal to 9·81 metres per second squared. In orbit, under microgravity conditions, the acceleration is typically of the order of $10^{-4}\,g$.

In a state of weightlessness, there is no separation between substances with different densities and the surrounding fluid. For example, in space the bubbles in champagne would not rise to the surface and the pulp in a bottle of fruit juice would not settle at the bottom. Equally, there is no natural convection, as found in clouds or when milk disperses in a cup of coffee, when there is no gravity. Warmer and lighter fluids, whether they be gases or liquids, do not rise upwards, nor do colder and heavier layers sink downwards. Whereas bodies move about freely in space, and fluids take the form of droplets, on Earth bodies are attracted towards the centre of the Earth and fluids spread themselves as thinly as possible across the available surface.

All these phenomena involve fluid substances, in a liquid or gaseous state. Such systems are particularly interesting when there is a change of state, such as from liquid to gas, as in boiling, or from liquid to solid, as the result of freezing.

The only way to remove the effects of the Earth's gravity on various fluid processes is to conduct experiments in gravity free conditions. Three processes which depend on gravity – separation, convection and surface tension – have already been described. There are in addition other, more subtle, processes which require the elimination of such gross phenomena before they can be studied. Space provides the ideal laboratory for such experiments.

Materials science experiments aboard Spacelab. The experiments carried out during Spacelab's first German mission (D1) between 30 October and 6 November 1985 represent a cross section of the work being done in the field of materials science.

Research topic	Experiment number	Experiment title	Researcher	Affiliation
Capillarity	WL FPM 04 WL FPM 06 WL FPM 08	Hydrodynamics of floating zones The adhesive force between liquid layers The behaviour of liquids in partially filled containers	J. Da Riva J. F. Padday J. P. B. Vreeburg	University of Madrid (Spain) Kodak Ltd., Harrow (United Kingdom) Nationaal Lucht-en-Ruimtevaart Laboratorium (NLR), Amsterdam (Holland)
Marangoni effects	PK HOL 03 PK MKB 00 WL FPM 07 WL FPM 01 WL FPM 05 PK HOL 01	The movement of bubbles due to thermal gradients Marangoni convection in an open container Marangoni currents Marangoni convection in liquids and gases Convection caused by surface tension The displacement of bubbles by chemical effects	D. Neuhaus D. Schwabe L. Napolitano A. A. H. Drinkenburg J. C. Legros A. Bewersdorff	Deutsche Forschungs- und Versuchanstalt für Luft- und Raumfahrt (DFVLR), Cologne (West Germany) University of Giessen (West Germany) University of Naples (Italy) University of Groningen (Holland) University of Brussels (Belgium) DFVLR, Cologne (West Germany)
Diffusion	WL HTT 00 WL GHF 01 PK IDS 00 WL IHF 05 ME GPRF 2 WL GHF 07 ME SAAL	Diffusion in melting metals Thermal diffusion, the Soret effect Diffusion in saline liquids Homogeneity of glass The diffusion of molten zinc in molten lead Thermal diffusion of cobalt in tin Containerless cooling of glass	K. H. Kraatz J. Dupuy W. Merkens G. H. Frischat R. B. Pond J. P. Praizey D. E. Day	Technische Universität, Berlin (West Germany) University of Lyon (France) Rheinisch Westfälische Technische Hochschule (RWTH), Aachen (West Germany) Technische Universität, Clausthal-Zellerfeld (West Germany) Marvalaud Inc., Westminster (USA) Centre d'Etudes Nucléaires (CEN), Grenoble (France) University of Missouri-Rolla (USA)
Critical point phenomena	MD HPT 00 PK HOL 02	Heat capacity studies Density distribution and phase separation at the critical point	J. Straub H. Klein	Technische Universität, Munich (West Germany) DFVLR, Cologne (West Germany)
Dynamics of the solidification front	PK HOL 04 MD GFQ 01 MD GFQ 02 WL GHF 02 WL GHF 04 MD ELI 04 WL IHF 09	Boundary layer phenomena during solidification of molten transparent bodies Diffusion at the phase separation surface Convection caused by solidification Cellular morphology in tellurium–lead alloys Dendritic solidification of aluminium–copper alloys Solidification of indium–antimony and nickel–antimony eutectic alloys Solidification of eutectic alloys	A. Ecker H. M. Tensi S. Rex B. B. Billia D. Camel G. Müller Y. Malmejac	RWTH, Aachen (West Germany) Technische Universität, Munich (West Germany) RWTH, Aachen (West Germany) University of Marseille (France) CEN, Grenoble (France) University of Erlangen–Nuremberg (West Germany) CEN, Grenoble (France)
Crystal growth	WL MHF 01 WL MHF 04 WL GHF 03 MD ELI 01 WL MHF 02 WL MHF 03 MD ELI 02 MD ELI 03 WL GHF 05 WL GHF 06 ME GPRF 4 ME GPRF 5 WL CRY 00	Silicon crystal production by molten zone technique Crystallisation of a silicon bubble Growth of doped indium–antimony Growth of semiconductors Using heat treatment to produce gallium–antimony crystals Using heat treatment to produce cadmium–tellurium crystals Using heat treatment to produce lead–tin–tellurium crystals Crystallisation of cadmium–tellurium by molten zone method Chemical growth of germanium/germanium–iodine Growth in the evaporation phase of germanium–iodine Growth by evaporation of semiconductor alloy crystals Growth of semiconductors Production of protein crystals	A. Croll H. Kölker C. Potard K. W. Benz K. W. Benz R. Schönholz M. Harr M. Bruder J. C. Launay J. C. Launay H. Wiedemeier R. K. Crouch W. Littke	University of Freiburg (West Germany) Wacker Chemie, Munich (West Germany) CEN, Grenoble (France) University of Stuttgart (West Germany) University of Stuttgart (West Germany) University of Freiburg (West Germany) Battelle Inst., Frankfurt (West Germany) University of Freiburg (West Germany) University of Bordeaux (France) University of Bordeaux (France) Rensselaer Polytechnic Institute, Troy (USA) Langley Research Center (USA) University of Freiburg (West Germany)
Composite materials	WL IHF 01 WL IHF 02 WL IHF 06 WL IHF 08 WL FPM 03 WL FPM 02 ME GPRF 3 WL IHF 04 WL IHF 03 WL IHF 07	The separation of non-miscible liquids Clay particles in a copper solidification front Behaviour of particles at melting and solidification fronts Melting and solidification of composite metallic materials Mixing and separation of transparent fluids Dynamic and fluid phase separation of bubbles Miscibility of interstitial materials Oswald maturation in metals Thin layer technology Thin layer technology of cast iron	H. Ahlborn J. Pötschke D. Langbein A. Deruyttere D. Langbein R. Naehle H. S. Gelles H. F. Fischmeister H. Sprenger H. Sprenger	University of Hamburg (West Germany) Krupp Forschungsinstitut, Essen (West Germany) Battelle Inst., Frankfurt (West Germany) University of Louvain (Belgium) Battelle Inst., Frankfurt (West Germany) DFVLR, Cologne (West Germany) University of Columbus (USA) Max Planck Institut, Stuttgart (West Germany) MAN Society, Munich (West Germany) MAN Society, Munich (West Germany)

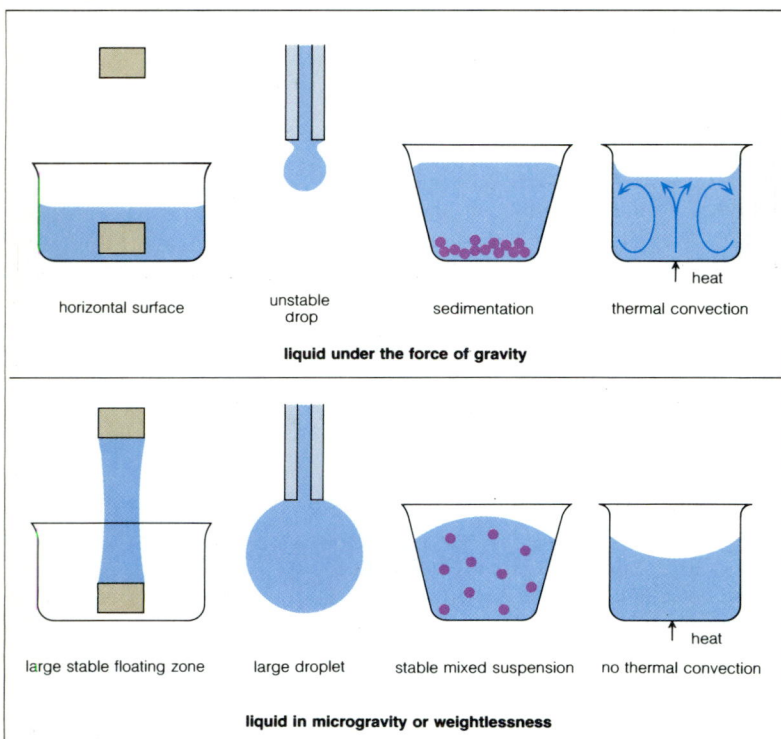

horizontal surface   unstable drop   sedimentation   thermal convection

heat

liquid under the force of gravity

large stable floating zone   large droplet   stable mixed suspension   no thermal convection

heat

liquid in microgravity or weightlessness

Liquid bodies in conditions of weightlessness. Under microgravity conditions it is possible to create long stable fluid bridges whereas on Earth the normal force of gravity causes them to collapse under their own weight. Very large diameter droplets can be produced in microgravity. Heavier particles do not sink to the bottom of a solution and no stable suspensions can be created. There are no convection currents and, as a consequence, there is no transport of mass or heat (ESA).

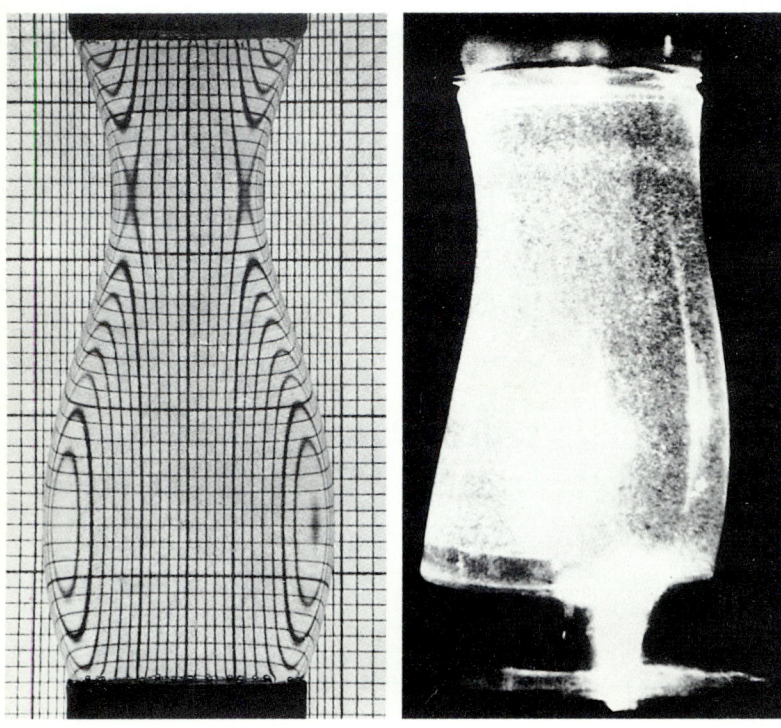

A floating zone in silicone oil, under microgravity. The force of gravity causes a bulge to form in the lower half of the zone which finally splits in two at the 'neck' as illustrated in the lefthand picture. In microgravity, the behaviour of these large zones can be observed under the effects of vibrations and rotation.

The righthand picture of a similar zone, rotated about its longitudinal axis, was taken during the Spacelab 1 mission. This research is relevant to the production of certain crystals in space (J. Da Riva).

Convection at a boundary, or Marangoni convection. Marangoni, a nineteenth century Italian physicist, considered the convection currents which develop at the surface of a fluid as the result of a temperature gradient or a concentration gradient. In the terrestrial laboratory, this process is completely eliminated by convection due to gravity and associated with density differences in the fluid. This type of Marangoni convection was the subject of one experiment on the first Spacelab mission at the end of 1983.

Convection due to variations in volume, during changes of state. Solidification and evaporation are usually accompanied by changes in volume. When, for example, aluminium is cooled, there is a volume change of about 7% at the solidification point. There is in fact an additional flow of fluid during solidification, which is independent of gravity.

Diffusion is a process in which a temperature and/or a concentration gradient causes atoms to be displaced, until equilibrium is achieved. Fick's laws of diffusion provide a quantitative description of this process.

Essential points in materials research

The study of the behaviour of materials in gravity free situations can be separated into four main topics – fluid physics, the technology of thin layers, materials science and production techniques. Fundamental research is being carried out on an international scale, with a certain amount of competition between East and West.

Solidification in weightlessness

It is particular new materials which form the basis of all technological improvements. Experiments in weightlessness have helped not only to improve traditional materials, making the most of production techniques on Earth, but also to introduce new products into the terrestrial laboratory from the laboratory in space.

The process which controls the production of materials is solidification. This determines the internal structure of the material sample and therefore its mechanical and electrical properties.

A researcher needs to be able to control the solidification process in order to carry out detailed experiments. These are difficult, either on Earth or in space, because liquid metals are opaque. In a groundbased laboratory, both convection due to buoyancy and sedimentation have to be recognised and eliminated. Under conditions of weightlessness, solidification is solely a diffusion process, if Marangoni convection is eliminated by judicious experimental design.

The dynamics of the solidification front. As solidification takes place, atoms move from the liquid to the solidification front where the temperature or concentration gradient is the key parameter. It governs whether the solidification front is smooth, cellular or dendritic and thus determines the micro- and macro-structure of the material. Dendritic growth is particularly interesting since dendrites can give materials their unique physical and electrical properties. Experiments are carried out in terrestrial and space laboratories on the cooling of pure opaque metals and eutectic metals, as well as on the fusions of transparent organic materials.

Composite materials. Liquid–solid mixtures are interesting for the study of the dispersion of one material within a certain liquid. The central problem is the integration of foreign particles into the solidification front in a regular manner. Such research is difficult to carry out on Earth as these particles either rise to the surface or sink to the bottom. It may be possible to keep

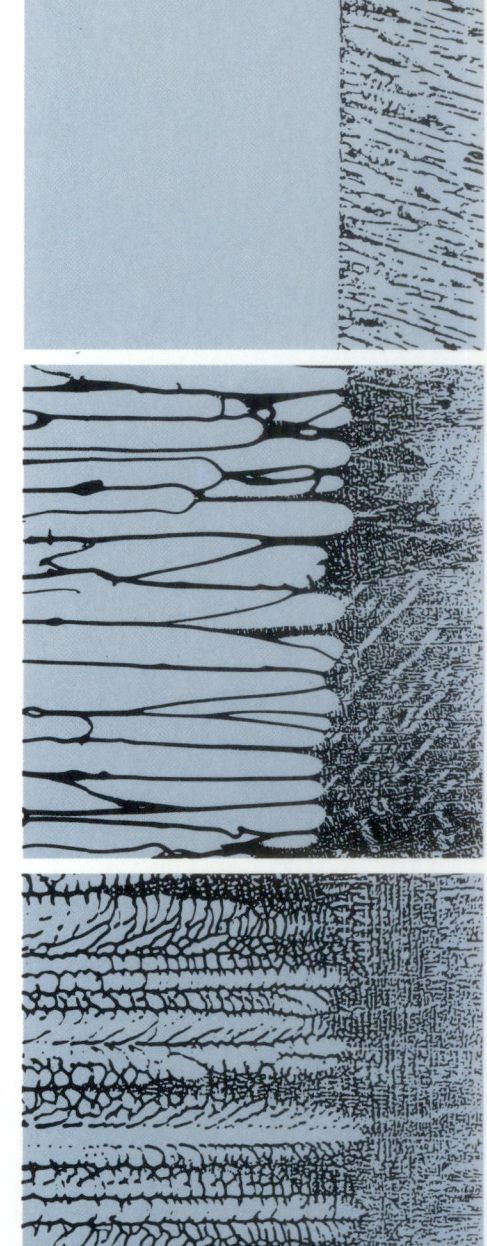

Different types of solidification front. To make it possible to study the solidification front in molten metal, the sample is rapidly cooled by plunging it into oil or water. Convection affects the internal structure of the substance being cooled. These photographs show the three basic structures that form at the edge of the solidification front. From top to bottom, these are smooth-walled, cellular and dendritic structures.

In microgravity, it is only diffusion which causes atoms in the molten substance to move towards the solidification front. The substance becomes dendritic in structure (H. M. Tensi).

them in suspension by applying an external magnetic field, but this alters the viscosity of the liquid mixture and raises a whole new set of questions that need to be answered. In space experiments, all these difficulties are avoided.

Mixtures of liquids, also called non-miscible alloys, have been created in weightless conditions since the beginning of solidification experiments in space. The 'imperfect' alloys of aluminium–lead or aluminium–indium have a certain technical interest. When these alloys are created under microgravity conditions, the different components mix together very well above a certain temperature which, for the examples cited, is 800 degrees celsius. However, they separate out during cooling for thermodynamic reasons, and forces at the surface cause separation, even in gravity free conditions.

This unexpected result has spawned a new series of theoretical and experimental studies. Today, the most important questions concern the motion and separation of one liquid within another caused by a temperature gradient in the liquid mixture (the Marangoni effect considered above).

Single crystals. The production of perfect single crystals for use in the semiconductor and opto-electronics industries is based on research into the dynamics of the solidification front and into composite materials. The solidification front should be a smooth, slightly convex curve into the cooling mixture, on the one hand; on the other, small amounts of a particular material should be evenly distributed throughout the crystal at the atomic level. In this way, a silicon crystal can be 'doped' with minute amounts of germanium, to produce a semiconductor with desired characteristics.

The usual process for producing a crystal on Earth and in space is to build it up by pulling a seed crystal through the molten liquid at a well defined speed. The diameter and length of the crystal are limited by gravity in the Earthbound laboratory and by forces occurring at the separation surface in space. Experiments are carried out in space on the physics of fluids, particularly on these floating zones and their stability and different modes of oscillation, and on Marangoni convection at the surface.

Doping of semiconductors. Although silicon of sufficient quality is produced in terrestrial laboratories for use in semiconductors, new materials such as gallium arsenide, mercury cadmium telluride and lead tin telluride present technological challenges. Here, success owes much to experiments made under conditions of weightlessness where the effects of the different constituents having different densities are minimised.

Technical processes in weightlessness

All processes which are influenced in any way by gravity can essentially be removed in microgravity conditions. For example, work can be carried out on the fusion and solidification of large volumes of metals by containerless processing.

Solidification of a molten liquid placed in a container often occurs on the wall of the container. If there is no such seed formation, then the solution solidifies into a vitreous substance, where the atoms are arranged irregularly. By contrast, in a crystal the atoms are arranged in a regular pattern which constitutes the crystal structure.

Such vitreous metals, or amorphous metals with a non-crystalline structure, are technologically important because their electrical and mechanical properties are usually better than those of the same metal having a crystalline structure. Unfortunately, however, in the terrestrial laboratory rapid solidification produces only amorphous powders or thin strips of non-crystalline metals. These have to be recon-

Protein crystal production. Early experiments on the growth of large protein crystals in microgravity yielded very promising results. Crystals were produced with volumes much greater than those produced on Earth. Medical and pharmaceutical researchers have displayed a great interest in these crystals, because they can be structurally analysed in detail using X rays.

The upper picture is of lysozyme proteins (bacteria found in milk and tears) which are a thousand times larger than normal. The length of one side of the crystals is about 1 millimetre. The lower photograph is of galactosidase beta proteins, 27 times greater than normal size. The length of the needle-shaped crystal is about 0·6 millimetres.

These results were obtained during the German Spacelab D1 mission. The experimental apparatus consisted of a block of acrylic glass, with different compartments containing the different proteins (W. Littke and C. John).

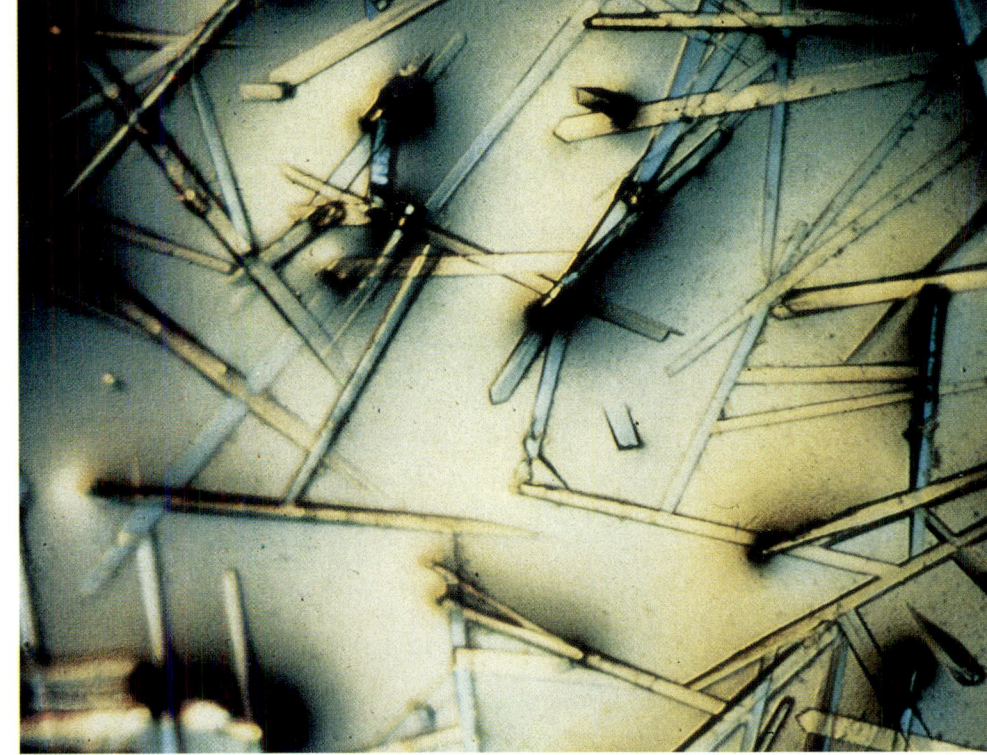

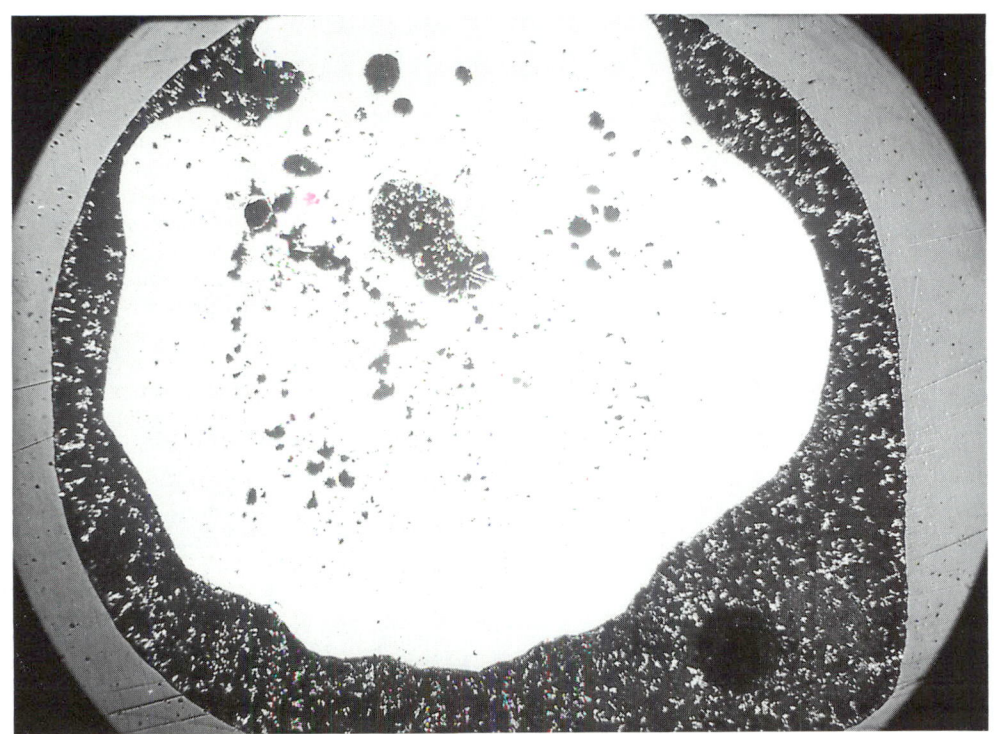

Alloys. Some metal alloys separate during cooling and solidification because of the different densities of the component metals. Although it was expected that separation would not occur in weightless conditions, that it does occur is evident in the picture on the left. Taken during the Space Processing Application Rocket 4 (SPAR 4) flight in 1976, this shows the structure of an aluminium–indium alloy. The indium has accumulated on the outer edge of the sample and the aluminium is in the centre. The separation is caused by the Marangoni effect, that is the displacement of one liquid in another due to temperature differences (K. Löhberg and H. Alborn).

Producing semiconductors. Better semiconductors are produced in microgravity. Under such conditions, heating and the distribution of one material in another are carried out uniquely by diffusion processes. Thus, a much more even distribution of the doping element in a semiconductor is attained. This is responsible for the high quality of the semiconductor and the regular crystal structure. Molten samples in a quartz phial form a free surface diffusion zone. Imperfect semiconductors are produced when currents occur at the surface and cause striations. This happens both on Earth and in space. Experiments on the first Spacelab mission in 1983 and on the German D1 mission in 1985 revealed striations caused by the irregular distribution of the doping material.

The upper photograph shows a solid tellurium sample doped with gallium–antimony produced in a terrestrial laboratory. It contains a large number of defects.

The lower photograph, taken at a much greater magnification, is of the same type of semiconductor, produced on board Spacelab during the D1 mission. Under conditions of weightlessness, the distribution of the doping material is much more homogeneous (K. W. Benz).

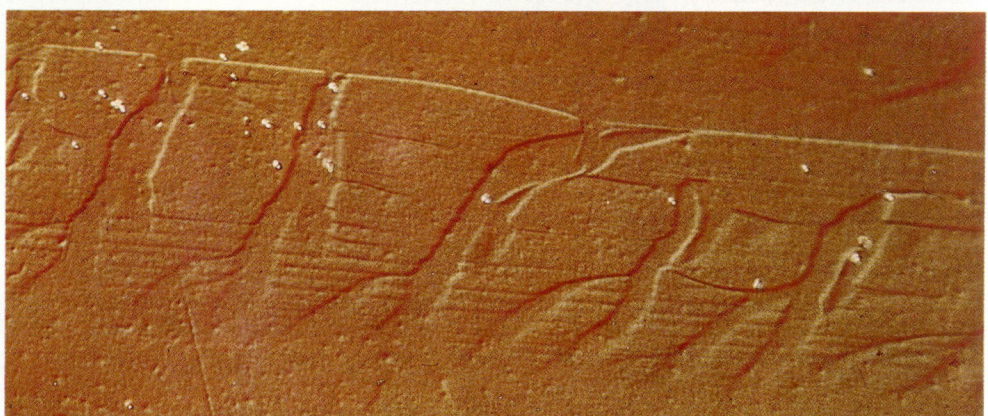

stituted to produce samples of larger volume. Containerless processing in a microgravity environment enables scientists to study the processes of seed formation and to produce larger samples of amorphic material whose technical characteristics can then be studied.

Containerless processing can also be used with thin film technology. For example, a piece of iron can be cast into the desired shape on Earth and covered in a thin ceramic layer about 10 microns thick. The iron is then reheated in microgravity, the ceramic layer retaining the shape of the object. When it has resolidified into its original shape, the mechanical strength is much improved.

It is not just techniques involving molten metals which have benefited from weightlessness. Biological substances can also be produced in space. Large single organic crystals of ribosomes and enzymes are formed by crystallising aqueous solutions. Their structures can be analysed by X ray crystallography.

Cellular fusion and division were studied on the Apollo–Soyuz Space Test Project (ASTP) in July 1975. The aim was to examine whether or not the electrophoresis technique for separating biological samples was more effective in weightlessness than on Earth. The tests were conclusive – weightlessness improved the technique. The first experiments on cellular fusion in space produced an output which was ten times better than on Earth.

Specialised research equipment and the presence of man in space

In materials science research in space, not only are data obtained but also samples are produced which can be returned to Earth. Many different types of equipment are required, and these may be either automatic or astronaut controlled. The former are often placed on board recoverable space platforms, such as Eureca, or on ballistic rockets. The latter are adapted for manned space laboratories. Human intervention may be necessary to conduct materials

science experiments in space. An astronaut can record the appearance of a sample, its colour, shape and so on, as an experiment proceeds. However, he is detrimental to the environment of weightlessness, as the level of microgravity is not so perfect when an astronaut is moving about performing tasks required by the mission schedule.

On the other hand, human presence in space is essential when man himself is the object of medical research. Man in space has already proved his value because human skill and intelligence cannot yet be matched by any machine. When the unexpected happens in the new world of weightlessness, man can use his judgement to rescue the situation. He can even develop and improve automated processes.

For the future, what is indisputable is that much more research on materials science under weightless conditions needs to be carried out.

Herman Strub,
Gottfried Greger and Rainer Jansen

Thin film technology. Here a piece of cast iron, in this case a turbine blade, is cast in the usual way on Earth, and then coated in a thin protective coat a few microns thick. This piece is then heated and recast in weightlessness. The protective coating preserves the exterior shape of the object which is then subjected to containerless processing. The objective is to improve the structural quality. Once the object has resolidified, the protective coating can be removed and the object used as intended (MAN).

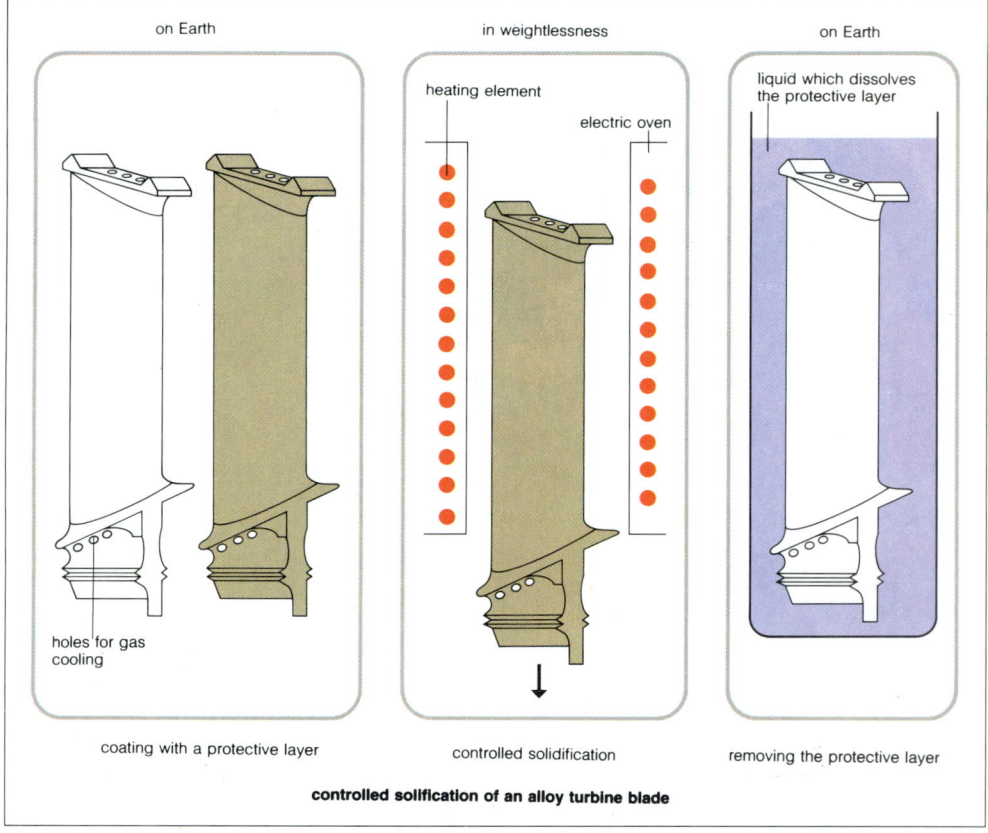

controlled solification of an alloy turbine blade

The commercial aspect

Some research carried out in the fields of physics, chemistry, materials science, biology and medicine has now reached the stage where it can be transferred to industrial applications. However, it is difficult to involve commercial companies in space activities, when all such commercial investments are risky, and when it is clear that there will be no profit for at least another 10 years.

Some preparations for industrial involvement have been made by government bodies. These may also plan other services, such as cheaper space flights or tax benefits, to encourage commercial exploitation in space.

The potential market has been analysed by advisory committees in different countries with respect to the longterm possibilities. It has been estimated that, by the year 2000, large sums will have been spent on manufacturing goods in microgravity, especially by the pharmaceutical industry. However, such estimates were made before the Challenger accident slowed the space programme, and a number of American companies have now backed out of their projects with NASA. Both public and financial organisations understand that a number of projects which were still at the planning stage will not be carried out for a long time. Some of them were even conceived as part of the space station programme.

The main aim of the commercial exploitation of space is the future production of extremely high quality materials. Naturally, the costs will be very high because of the transport and specialised equipment involved. But, in addition, terrestrial production techniques may be improved. And pure, homogeneous materials produced in space could serve as a reference for terrestrial production techniques and research.

In America, companies such as General Motors, John Deere & Co and the 3M Corporation are studying the commercial possibilities of materials produced in microgravity. The 3M Corporation is particularly interested in crystal and thin film technology. Space Industries Inc., are carrying out work to design and build an automatic space platform with a manned module, which would enable other companies to carry out work in space. Most of these companies hold longterm cooperation agreements with NASA. An agreement was also signed between McDonnell Douglas and the pharmaceutical group Johnson & Johnson on the production of extremely pure biological materials using electrophoresis. However, in October 1985, Johnson & Johnson formally withdrew from the agreement.

A British company, North Industrial Systems, is interested in long duration automated experiments in microgravity. During the *Space Commerce 86* exhibition in Montreux, this firm offered Europe sole access to an unmanned recoverable capsule. This would be put into orbit by an appropriate launch vehicle and, after completing experiments in a prearranged time period, would return to Earth.

A German company, Intospace, which was created in October 1985, offered European countries a choice of different rocket flights to carry out experiments in microgravity. Intospace is composed of a number of space companies, banks, and large as well as small industrial enterprises from West Germany; Belgium, Holland, France, Italy, Sweden, Switzerland, Spain and the United Kingdom. Intospace plans to develop the market for industrial exploitation of microgravity in space, with particular respect to processes and materials. It also proposes to act as an intermediary, to play a consultancy role, to develop apparatus and to carry out experiments.

In Japan, several industrial enterprises, helped by the government, joined together to form the Space Utilisation Promotion Organisation in 1986. This includes the Japan Space Utilisation Promotion Centre (JSUPC) and the Space Technology Corporation (STC) which represent nearly all of Japan's industry as well as the universities and national research institutes. These organisations prepare microgravity experiments on materials for future flights and carry out market studies on the commercial aspect of space products.

Most of these companies are not only involved in developing production techniques, but also in market studies to decide which materials are likely to be a commercial success, and in automated production techniques for the future. At present, Japan has sold only one 'made in space' product – latex spheres, 10 microns in diameter. On Earth, gravity makes it impossible to manufacture these balls to the correct size and exactly spherical. They are used in the calibration of devices such as filters, membranes and microscopes.

The commercial exploitation and manufacturing of high quality goods in space should eventually affect production and transport costs, and this in turn will affect the market. A space station should also help to reduce costs, as the equipment used for experimentation and production will be permanently installed, making frequent return journeys into space with equipment superfluous.

Herman Strub

One aspect of commercial development: an oven with reflecting walls. This oven was used in 1985, during the Spacelab D1 mission, in experiments on the production of crystals. In the future, it will be used to produce extremely pure crystals for a commercial market (Dornier).

A sample of the estimated costs involved in materials science research in space (1987 values, after R. Jansen)

	KC 135	Mikroba	Texus	MAUS	Spacelab	Eureca
Type of mission	on board an aircraft: cost for 6 hours (120 parabolic flights)	using a balloon for transport: cost for one launch	on experimental rockets: cost for one launch	automatic payload: transport by space shuttle	European manned laboratory: transport by space shuttle	transport by space shuttle: mission in the 1990s
Length of time in weightlessness	less than 1 minute	about 1 minute	5 minutes	1 to 7 days	7 days	several weeks, up to 6 months
Types of experiments	physics of fluids		solidification of materials and crystal production			
Preparation for the experiments on Earth	0.3	0.3	1.6	0.45	41	15
Scientific equipment on board	0.3	0.5	2.6	0.50	80	30
Integration of the payload		0.2	0.4	0.25	72	50
Launch costs	0.6	0.3	0.9	0.02	169	55
Running costs of the experiments		0.2	0.5		40	20
Total (in millions of Deutsche Marks)	0.66	1.5	6.0	1.22	402	170 (estimate)

Texus: Technologische Experimente unter Schwerelosigkeit.
MAUS: Materialwissenschaftliche Autonome Experimente unter Schwerelosigkeit.
Eureca: European Retrievable Carrier.

Man in space

The Mir orbital space station

Mir (which means 'peace' in Russian) is the third generation Soviet orbiting space station. Launched on 20 February 1986, it is equipped with an entirely new docking system which has six ports, thus enabling a more complex space station to be created in space. When completed, this will be both extremely versatile and permanent. The space station will be capable of receiving manned Soyuz TM spacecraft, unmanned Progress cargocraft and modules carrying scientific equipment or supplies.

A description of the Mir space station

The work compartment is connected to the docking compartment by an airlock. Only these two modules are pressurised. The third compartment contains two 300 newton rocket motors which are used during orbital manoeuvres and thirty-two 14 newton rocket motors which are used to make small adjustments about the three axes of rotation. It also contains the fuel reservoirs, the heat control system and a docking unit.

A directional antenna, mounted on the outside of the propulsion compartment, forms part of the satellite relay communications link with Earth. The satellite relay is necessary because any space station component in a low orbit, at an altitude of several hundred kilometres, can only communicate directly with Earth while it is passing over terrestrial bases or ships spread out over the oceans. At present, a semipermanent communications link has been set up with Mir, via geostationary relay satellites. Information can now be transmitted almost without interruption. This stable link is important, because it enables the computers on board Mir to form part of an Earth–space station network. As a result, the station's system and scientific experiments can be much more automated.

The docking compartment is fitted with a central collar, along the longitudinal axis of the station and four other collars, situated perpendicular to this axis (see illustration, right). The outside surface of this compartment is thermally insulated. The specialised modules and the cargocraft dock with the central docking collar and then a remote control arm transfers them to one of the side docking rings. If manual docking has to take place, the cosmonauts use the antenna of the radio system for approach manoeuvres, with the help of television cameras, navigation lights and controls for reciprocal orientation. The docking compartment also contains the air control and heat regulation systems of the space station, the radio and television links and the electric power supply system.

Inside the work compartment, the walls, floor and ceiling are painted in different colours to help the crew to orient themselves. The solar panels, radio antenna and the handrails used by the cosmonauts during work outside the station are fitted to the exterior of this unit. The narrowest part of the work compartment, which has a diameter of 2·9 metres, contains the crew's main work console. From here the crew monitor and control the space station systems. Attached to the floor are various instruments, the command desk and monitoring equipment, optical sights for orientation, the stellar attitude control and navigation instruments, radio and television apparatus, communications and electrical equipment and two chairs for the cosmonauts. These last are a sort of 'saddle stool' which would be very uncomfortable on Earth, but in zero gravity they can be sat upon without the cosmonaut having to be strapped down.

The largest part of the work compartment, with a maximum diameter of 4·2 metres, is designed for maximum comfort. There are two cabins, one on the port and one on the starboard sides, where crewmembers can eat, sleep and make observations through the portholes. Sitting on a foldaway seat in front of a small desk, the cosmonaut may read or write. Sleeping bags are fixed in an upright position to the side walls of the cabin.

The space refectory, on the starboard side, can accommodate up to four people at once. At the back of the station is an airlock which is fitted with a passive docking device. The cosmonauts enter the space station via this airlock at those times when docking is made at this end.

remote control antenna

telemetry antenna

rendezvous antenna

red navigation light

The Mir orbital space station. This photograph of the Mir space station was taken in the assembly room of the cosmodrome at Baïkonour. The station was launched on 20 February 1986 by a Proton rocket vehicle (A. Pouchkaryov).

The cut-away illustration, above right, shows the orbital configuration of Mir. It consists of a multiple docking module, a work compartment and a propulsion compartment. Mir is the first part of a future permanent orbiting complex which will have enough facilities to cope with several missions at once. In fact, from 1990, supplementary modules, each designed for a specific purpose, will be added to the multiple docking module. The orbital complex, with four specialised modules, a Soyuz TM and a Progress cargocraft, all accessible via airlocks, should weigh about 115 tonnes.

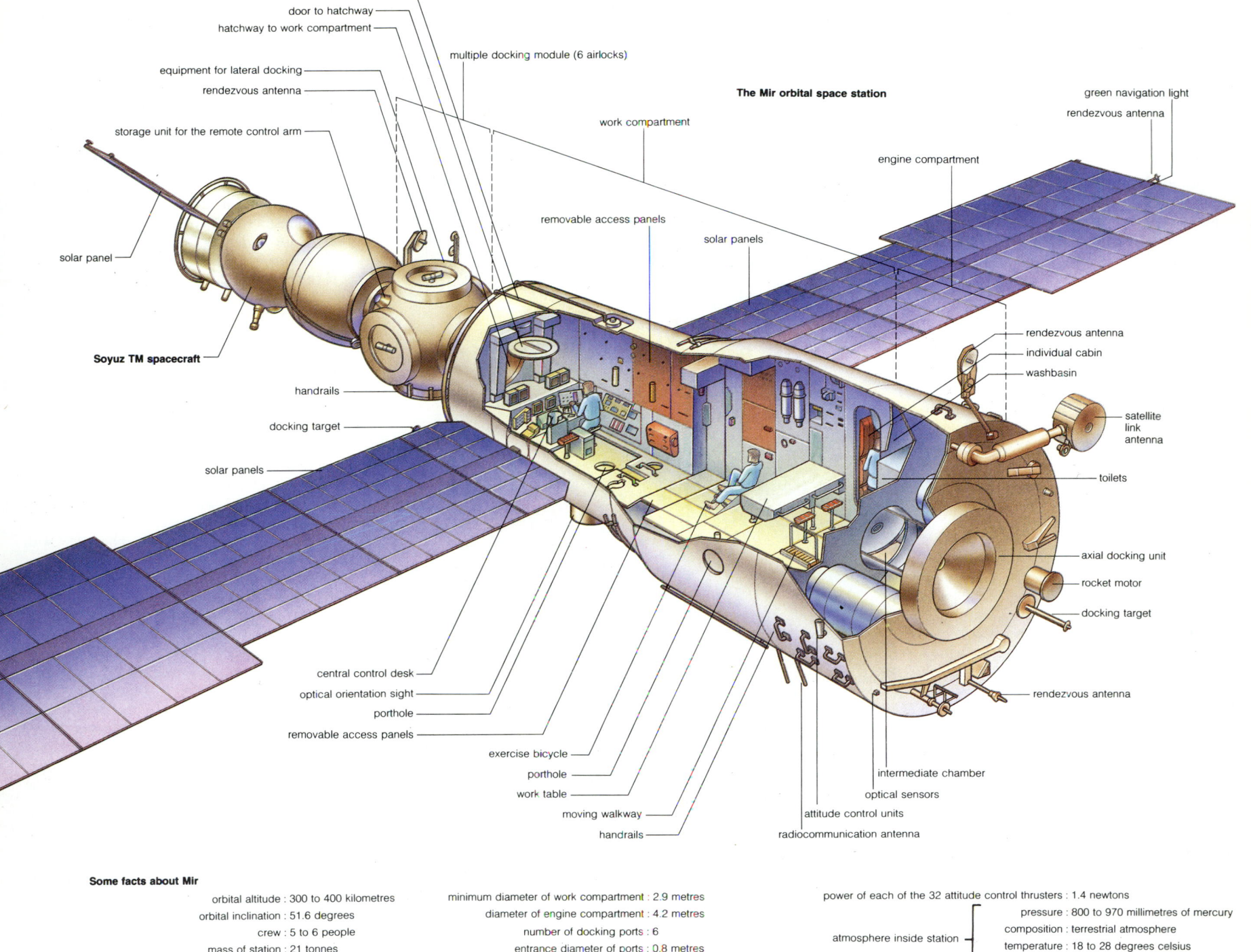

handrails for cosmonauts working outside the station

door to hatchway

hatchway to work compartment

multiple docking module (6 airlocks)

equipment for lateral docking

rendezvous antenna

The Mir orbital space station

green navigation light

rendezvous antenna

storage unit for the remote control arm

work compartment

engine compartment

removable access panels

solar panels

solar panel

rendezvous antenna

individual cabin

washbasin

Soyuz TM spacecraft

satellite link antenna

handrails

docking target

toilets

solar panels

axial docking unit

rocket motor

docking target

central control desk

optical orientation sight

porthole

removable access panels

rendezvous antenna

exercise bicycle

porthole

work table

intermediate chamber

optical sensors

moving walkway

handrails

attitude control units

radiocommunication antenna

Some facts about Mir

orbital altitude : 300 to 400 kilometres	minimum diameter of work compartment : 2.9 metres	power of each of the 32 attitude control thrusters : 1.4 newtons
orbital inclination : 51.6 degrees	diameter of engine compartment : 4.2 metres	
crew : 5 to 6 people	number of docking ports : 6	
mass of station : 21 tonnes	entrance diameter of ports : 0.8 metres	
length : 13.1 metres	surface area of each solar panel : 38 square metres	
maximum diameter of work compartment : 4.2 metres	wingspan of station with panels fully extended : 29.7 metres	

atmosphere inside station
- pressure : 800 to 970 millimetres of mercury
- composition : terrestrial atmosphere
- temperature : 18 to 28 degrees celsius
- relative humidity : 30 to 70%
- voltage (DC) : 28.6±0.5 volts

It contains docking instruments, the water supply, radio instruments, various other systems and the toilet unit.

The station is kept in the correct position either automatically or under manual control, using a computerised flight system consisting of optical sensors, visual orientation instruments, gyroscopes, and an array of logic switches and convertors.

Low powered thruster rockets can move the space station with respect to its centre of mass, but have little effect on its orbit. The two more powerful motors at the back of the station are able to make considerable adjustments to the orbit. Fuel is fed to the motors by means of compressed gas. The USSR has planned to make it possible to refuel Mir from cargoships using fuel lines connected by hydraulic links mounted on the outside of the docking module.

An array of solar panels and batteries automatically keep the space station supplied with energy. The solar panels cover an area of 76 square metres, which is about 25 square metres more than those used on Salyut 7. The gallium arsenide solar panels are kept oriented perpendicular to the incident solar radiation by an automatic control system. After docking takes place between a transport craft and Mir, the two craft form a single power supply network.

The thermal regulation system has the ability to both increase and decrease the temperature. It automatically maintains the air temperature

near 20 degrees celsius. The cosmonauts themselves have to decide whether or not to turn on the radiators, airconditioning or fans. The crew make daily checks on the air temperature and humidity in all the compartments and cabins. Another system regulates the composition of the air in the space station.

The water drunk by crews on board Mir – about two litres per cosmonaut per day – is delivered in ten litre containers by Progress cargocraft. Silver ions are added to the water on Earth, in order to sterilise it, and in this condition it remains safe for up to one year. The station is also fitted with a system which recycles water from the atmosphere. It is similar to that on board Salyut 7, but more powerful.

An exercise bicycle and rolling walkway have been installed for the cosmonauts to exercise their muscles. The space station also contains 'Pingvine' (penguin) and 'Tchibis' (peewit) suits, which stimulate blood circulation (cf. *Life sciences in a microgravity environment* pp. 284–9).

Several fully equipped laboratory modules can be docked to Mir. Thus, complete systems can be sent out to the station, as opposed to isolated pieces of apparatus. Each module has its own specialised design. For example, there is a workshop module for the production of technological materials, an observatory module for astrophysics, a laboratory module for biological

research, a pharmacy module for the production of medicines and so on. Crewmembers are responsible for maintaining the modules in good working order.

As Mir is transformed into a large orbital complex, a new approach and docking system for the transport vessels has come into operation. When a manned transport craft or a cargocraft approached the Salyut stations, it was the Salyut station itself, using retrorockets, that was aligned with the axis of the incoming spacecraft, and performed all the docking manoeuvres. Now it is the transport craft which, as it approaches from 100 metres away, carries out docking manoeuvres with Mir.

The space station automatically makes orbital adjustments after a long period of 'free flight' – that is flight without any particular orientation. Flight instructions are issued by the on board computer, using data obtained by various sensors. The orientation system, which does not require fuel, uses a gyro stabiliser system. The flywheel in this acts as a 'reference point' relative to which the station moves using its thruster rockets. To further reduce fuel consumption, gyrostabilisers will be installed in each of the other modules, to perform most of the orientation manoeuvres of the space station. This will reduce the number of refuelling operations carried out on the spacecraft.

The electric power supply on Mir is an improvement on that of Salyut 7. Mir has a constant power supply of $28 \cdot 6 \pm 0 \cdot 5$ volts. This has made the electronic, electrical and radio equipment more reliable so that, in some cases, voltage regulators are no longer necessary. There is about 9 kilowatts of power available on board.

The heat control unit has undergone considerable modification. Instead of the usual coils, piping has been installed which is more reliable and efficient. Each of the science modules is fitted with its own heat control system, so that each can be kept at a non-standard temperature if that is required by the experiments which they contain.

The first missions

The first cosmonauts to board Mir were Leonid Kizim and Vladimir Soloviev. They were launched from Baikonur on board Soyuz T 15 on 13 March 1986. Once on board the cosmonauts ran a series of checks on the equipment and Mir's systems. They unloaded equipment which arrived on Progress 25 (on 21 March) and Progress 26 (on 27 April). They filmed the Earth, set up a communications link with Earth via the geostationary satellite Loutch (Cosmos 1700) and ran checks on the seven on board computers.

Fifty days after their arrival at Mir, the cosmonauts left and joined Salyut 7–Cosmos 1686 on 6 May 1986. This was the first time that a crew had transferred from one space station to another. Both cosmonauts were very well acquainted with this space station because they had been part of the team which set a new world record of 237 days, in 1984, for the length of time spent in space. On this later occasion, the cosmonauts spent five very busy days on board Salyut 7.

On 25 June 1986, Soyuz T 15 separated from Salyut 7 and, two days later, it redocked with Mir. The cosmonauts brought with them a large number of things from Salyut 7, including the results of experiments and studies, films, photographs and equipment such as a camera, a spectrometer and medical instruments.

Before leaving Mir, the two cosmonauts put the station 'to bed' until February 1987. After spending a total of 125 days in space, the cosmonauts returned safely to Earth on 16 July 1986. The descent module of Soyuz T 15 landed 55 kilometres north-east of the town of Arkalsk, in Kazakhstan.

On 16 January 1987, the Progress 27 cargo-craft was launched from the cosmodrome at Baikonur. It docked with Mir on 18 January 1987, at 10.27 Moscow Time. The approach, coming alongside and docking of the two craft, was carried out using the automated equipment in both craft, under ground control. Progress 27 docked at Mir's aft airlock. It was transporting fuel and other perishable materials, necessary for the maintenance of Mir, as well as food and water for the crew who had not yet arrived. Yuri Romanenko and Alexander Laveïkine arrived, in Soyuz TM2, on 6 February 1987, on a long duration mission. Their first task was to empty Progress 27 and prepare Mir to receive a specialised module. The cosmonauts tested the space station systems and apparatus, both in automatic and manual control modes. During this mission the Earth–space station–Earth satellite relay link was put into operation.

Mir's evolution progressed one stage further with the arrival of a specialised module, about 13 metres in length. This was an astrophysical observatory, called Kvant ('Quantum'). As planned, it docked at Mir's longitudinal collar, and the remote control arm moved it to one of the lateral docking rings. Kvant weighs about 20·6 tonnes and contains an automated propulsion unit for berthing with the station, and a scientific laboratory which is 5·8 metres long and 4·15 metres in diameter. The laboratory notably contains the Röntgen International Observatory, weighing 800 kilograms, which consists of the Soviet Glazar ultraviolet telescope and four X ray spectrometer telescopes

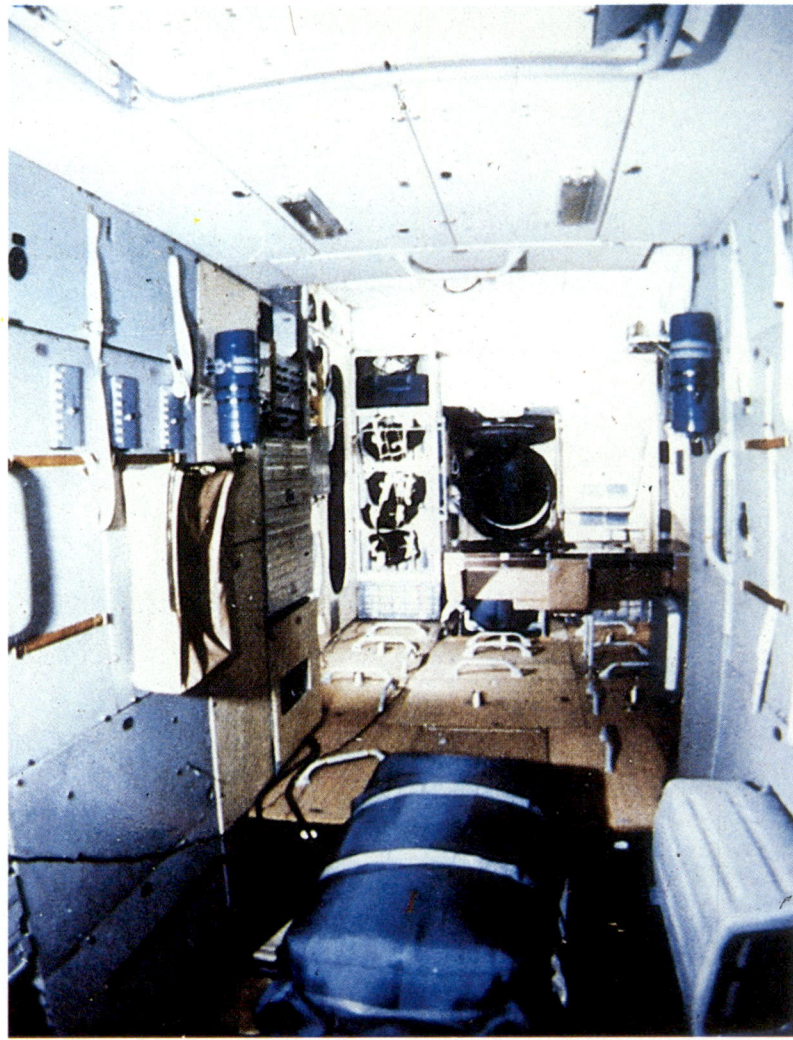

The interior of Mir's work compartment. The work compartment is the central element of the space complex. The upper photograph is what Yuri Romanenko and Alexander Laveïkine saw when they boarded Mir through the forward airlock on 7 February 1987. At the back of the compartment the aft airlock is visible. It is used by visiting crews and supply ships. Near the airlock is a rest area used by crews who spend a long time on board Mir. Amongst other things there are two individual cabins, a shower, some exercise equipment and toilets which are visible to the left of the airlock.

The photograph on the left shows one of the individual cabins. A sleeping bag is attached to the near wall, in an upright position. Cosmonauts drift off to sleep whilst admiring the Earth through a porthole.

The central command console is shown below. It controls the ship's systems. Above the two computer screens is the airlock which links this compartment with the multiple docking unit (IKI Intercosmos, APN).

(one Soviet, one from Great Britain and Holland, one from West Germany and one provided by the European Space Agency). These telescopes, operating in their dedicated module, make long duration observations without prejudicing the rest of Mir's programme. The module also contains apparatus to produce biological substances in space.

The orbiting space station Mir is not limited solely to astrophysical research. The programme also includes remote sensing and medical research on man's ability to adapt to weightlessness. There are plans to produce extrapure biological substances, in particular thymazine and interferon, and to grow crystals in the near future.

Yuri Romanenko spent 326 days in space and his spectacular readaption to life on Earth confirmed the possibility of long duration flights. Following heart problems, Romanenko's colleague, Alexander Laveikine, was however replaced by Alexander Alexandrov, a member of the twelfth international crew (USSR–Syria) which spent a week on board Mir in July 1987. The other two members of this crew were Alexander Viktorendo and Mohmand Fares (Syria).

On 23 December 1987 V. Titov and M. Manarov joined Mir from Soyuz TM 4 to replace Romanenko and Alexandrov, who returned to Earth on 28 December 1987 with Anatoli Levchenko. Their year long programme included astrophysical research using the Kvant laboratory module, various remote sensing and technological experiments, medical examinations and biological research. In addition, they completed three spacewalks and were host to three international crews. In June 1988 Alexander Soloviov, Viktor Savinykh (Bulgaria) and Alexander Alexandrov spent a week aboard Mir. In August of the same year, A. Mohmand (Afghanistan), Vladimir Liakhov and Velery Poliakov boarded Mir from Soyuz TM 6. Poliakov, a doctor, investigated the health of the long duration crew.

On 26 November 1988 Soyuz TM 7 carried Alexander Volkov, Sergei Krikalev and Jean-Loup Chrétien (France) to Mir. After 26 days, Chrétien returned to Earth with V. Titov and M. Manarov, leaving his two cosmonaut colleagues and the doctor on board. A. Volkov, S. Krikalev and V. Poliakov returned to Earth on 27 April 1989, leaving Mir to fly unmanned until the arrival of another crew.

In the future two more specialised modules will be attached to Mir. One will allow cosmonauts to move independently during extra-vehicular activity, and the other will be used for the industrial production of crystals and for biotechnical research.

Nikolai Kardachev

Man in space

The Soviet space shuttle

The Soviet space shuttle has been named 'Buran', which means 'snowstorm' in Russian. Its basic design is that of a plane without the horizontal tail fin, but provided with a triangular wing system at the base of the fuselage, similar to the space shuttle. Unlike the American shuttle, Buran does not have its own launch system: this is why it is always associated with the Energia launcher (see page 111).

The most interesting feature of Buran is its autopilot system. The shuttle can fly unmanned (for instance in the vicinity of a space station) for seven days in the first, exploitation phase and up to thirty days subsequently. However, it can also be piloted by a crew from a pressurised cabin (of 70 cubic metres volume), situated in the forward compartment which also contains the autopilot systems for the orbital, descent and landing phases of the mission.

Buran's central compartment is similar in shape to that of the American space shuttle. It can take up to 30 tonnes of payload and can open into space. The rear compartment contains the propulsion system. There are two main rocket engines each of 8·8 tonnes, thirty-eight 380 kilogram attitude control systems and eight 20 kilogram precision thrusters. For the fine control of Buran's orbit, there are two rings of engines, one at the front of the fuselage in front of the cabin and one at the rear of the tail compartment. These use a fuel mix of oxygen and paraffin oil (kerosene) to place the shuttle into the correct orbit, to alter this orbit and to

make manoeuvres around the space stations it is designed to serve.

The control system has more than fifty subsystems, controlled by four interchangeable computers and an additional external memory. All control operations are carried out automatically. The computer also monitors all the subsystems and, in the event of failure, can bring reserve subsystems into operation.

One of the most important features of the shuttle is that it can remain in permanent contact with the Earth via relay satellites in specially chosen orbits.

The critically designed aerodynamic shape of Buran enables it to perform a piloted descent into the atmosphere, to move laterally 2000 kilometres with respect to its initial track, and thus to land safely. The 38 000 heat resistant tiles on the fuselage are made from a beryllium and titanium–nickel alloy, which can withstand temperatures of up to 1600 degrees celsius. The tiles can be used for several missions before they need to be replaced.

The Buran missions

On 15 November 1988, the Buran made its first automatic flight in space, without a crew. The flight lasted 205 minutes, enough time to complete two orbits of the Earth. Scientists were able to test Buran's launch by Energia, its entry into orbit (with correct orientation and

stabilisation), the descent phase, reentry into the atmosphere, and touchdown.

The flight was monitored by the Kaliningrad control centre near Moscow and also by ships anchored in the Pacific and Atlantic Oceans. The Soviet space shuttle landed at a speed of 340 kilometres per hour at an aerodrome near its launch site, the Baikonur cosmodrome. Other such aerodromes in Russia are planned.

Comparable test flights were planned for 1989 and a piloted flight will shortly be carried out, under the control of Y. Volk, and including Y. Cheffer, R. Stankravicius, V. Sultanov, M. Tolboyev, S. Treviatsky and V. Zabolotsky. No military missions have been planned for Buran as yet.

Up to two launches per year are likely, although the number of piloted flights or unmanned flights has not yet been decided. The autopilot system can be used when it is essential to carry out very delicate experiments in space which would be disturbed by the presence of cosmonauts.

Like the American space shuttle, Buran can launch satellites, even on unmanned flights, and return defunct satellites to Earth. These satellites can then be refitted and relaunched. Buran can also put into orbit a large piece of equipment such as an optical telescope with electronic image recording. It is a huge step forward.

Yuri Semionov

Touchdown. Buran lands, after its first unmanned flight on 15 November 1988, on the aerodrome near Baikonur. This is the only landing strip of its type, measuring 5 kilometres by 80 metres. Some of the heat resistant tiles on the fuselage were burnt during the first mission (APN).

Man in space

Space platforms: Eureca

The Europeans have been planning a recoverable space platform since 1980, three years before the first Spacelab flight. This type of platform, representing the next stage in the development of Spacelab, is unmanned. However, astronauts will visit it from time to time in order to change experiments and carry out maintenance work. Long duration experiments can be carried out, and the level of microgravity is even less than on board a manned spacecraft. This is of particular advantage in materials science and life sciences. The electrical power available to the payload will also be increased to several kilowatts.

The platform will be launched by the space shuttle, carrying experiments lasting between several weeks and months. Another space shuttle will rendezvous with the platform and collect the results of the experiments, deposit new experiments and perform any necessary maintenance work. The next stage will be Low Earth Orbit (LEO) platforms which, as the name suggests, will be in low terrestrial orbit. They will be even more powerful and no time limit will be set on the duration of each experiment. The payloads will be replaced and returned to Earth, and maintenance will be carried out while the platform remains in orbit.

Preliminary studies were begun by the Europeans in 1981 on the first generation of recoverable satellite platforms. In April 1982, as a result of this study, the European Space Agency decided to build a platform called Eureca (European Retrievable Carrier), to be launched at the beginning of the 1990s.

Nine countries are participating in this project, and their financial commitments are as follows:

West Germany	53·66%
Italy	17·33%
France	17·31%
Belgium	3·68%
Spain	2·80%
United Kingdom	2·10%
Holland	1·50%
Switzerland	1·00%
Denmark	0·62%

The cost amounts to 273 million European Currency Units (ECUs), which is equivalent to $220 million (January 1986). This includes development of the platform and a nucleus of payload for research into microgravity, the costs of integration and flight tests, the launch costs and recovery of equipment after flight tests.

When the programme was approved, it was decided that subsequent developments should

aim to make Europe an independent space power. Current work therefore includes the second generation of space platforms, which will be launched by the Ariane V rocket and maintained in space by Hermes, the proposed French space shuttle, and will orbit alongside the future international space station complex. It will contain a wide range of experiments and installations in the fields of research in microgravity, space sciences, Earth observations and resource studies. It will require human intervention only for repair work, and for replacing the payload, filling the fuel tanks and recovering the test-tube samples.

When final decisions were made to develop Eureca, European and American industries took the initiative to design and build competitive platforms. Thus the MBB–Erno group in West Germany developed and launched two versions of the Shuttle Pallet Satellite (Spas). This was deployed some 200 metres from the shuttle and recovered by the same shuttle before returning to the Earth. In the USA, Teledyne-Brown, in an agreement with NASA, developed Spartan. Unfortunately, Spartan was destroyed in the Challenger accident. Fairchild, another American company, began work on the second generation of space platform, capable of carrying 4 tonnes of payload and having about

Eureca (European Recoverable Carrier). A structure, made of carbon fibre tubing, divides Eureca into cubic units, of side length 0·7 metres, with each containing different pieces of apparatus. The platform's command, measurement and control systems are also placed in this part of the structure. The payload, of up to 1 tonne, is placed in this front part of the structure so that it is easily accessible.

There is a single power unit which stores and supplies electricity to both the platform's systems and the payload. The two solar panels and the four 40 ampere hour batteries supply several kilowatts of continuous power to Eureca, even during the eclipse period. During its period on board the space shuttle, the shuttle's own systems supply about 200 watts to the platform, to prevent some of the results (in the form of samples) from being destroyed. The heat regulation system is based on that used aboard Spacelab. The temperature in the platform and payload is kept constant, by a freon pump.

The experiments carried by Eureca are very sensitive to mechanical disturbances. During operation of the platform's orientation and orbital command system, the accelerations felt by the experiments never exceed 10^{-5} g. This system also carries out the support operations which allow rendezvous and docking with the shuttle.

For communications, both uplink and downlink, S band frequencies (2230 megahertz) are used during a mission. A magnetic bubble memory, using very advanced technology, stores data, during the eclipse period and also during the voyage back to Earth, for later processing (ESA).

Subsystems

1	cold plate
2	docking system
3	antennae
4	electronics unit
5	electronics unit
6	gyroscopes
7	reservoir (hydrazine)
8	reservoir (hydrazine)
9	reservoir (hydrazine)
10	radiator
11	reservoir (hydrazine)
12	stirrup arm
13	stirrup
14	solar panels
15	reservoir (hydrazine)
16	electronics unit
17	electronics unit
18	electronics unit
19	vernier of the Attitude and Orbital Control Subsystem (AOCS) and the accelerometer
20	booster for the Orbital Transfer Subsystem (OTA)
21	electronics unit
22	reservoir (gaseous nitrogen)
23	reservoir (gaseous helium)

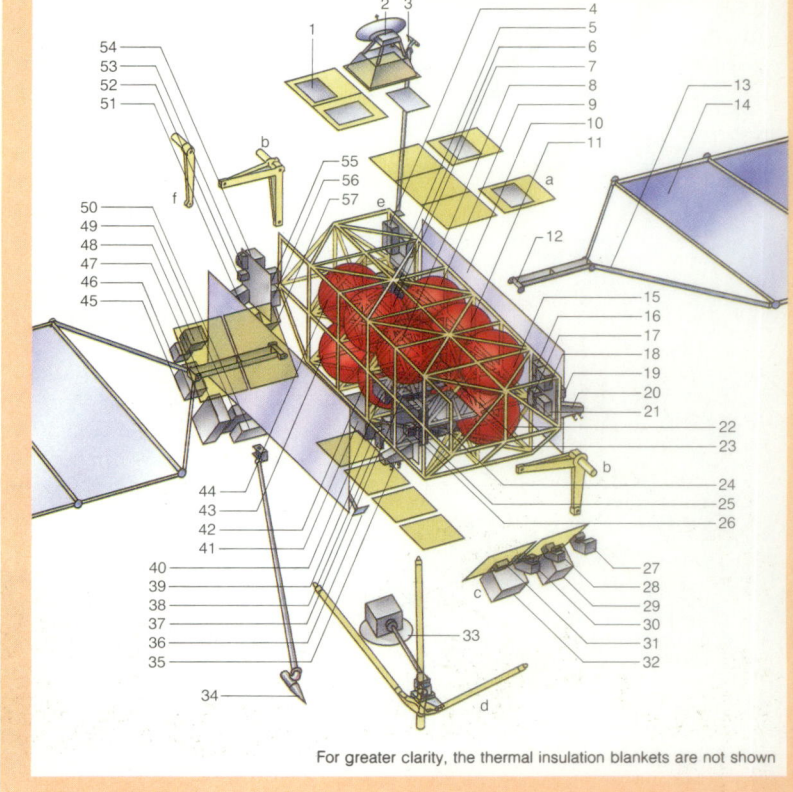

For greater clarity, the thermal insulation blankets are not shown

Eureca: scenario of a mission. Eureca is deployed by a space shuttle at an altitude of about 300 kilometres, using the remote manipulator system. The separation of the platform and the space shuttle takes place at a relative speed of 0·15 metres per second. This operation is controlled and monitored visually, up to a distance of about 90 metres, and Eureca's own propulsion system is not utilised. It is only used at larger distances, for safety's sake.

The next stages of the platform's operation are tests by the European Space Operations Centre (ESOC) at Darmstadt, in West Germany, via the intermediary of the space shuttle and NASA's Johnson Space Center at Houston, or directly by ESA ground stations, such as Maspalomas (Canary Islands), Kourou (Guyana) or Malindi (Kenya).

After this verification, Eureca's propulsion system – consisting of two thruster arrays containing 20 newton gas jets and a reservoir for 620 kilograms of hydrogen, pressurised by helium – places it in its operational orbit, at an altitude of 525 kilometres, for six months. At the end of this period the platform is manoeuvred to a dormant orbit of 500 kilometres altitude. It waits in this orbit for a period of up to three months for a second shuttle to rendezvous with it for between two to three days.

When the platform achieves its rendezvous point, the antennae and solar panels retract and the systems are switched off. The shuttle carries out the last phase of approach, from when the platform is 15 kilometres below and 35 kilometres in front of it. It should be noted that Eureca has enough fuel to readopt its sleeping orbit at 525 kilometres for another six months and then repeat the rendezvous procedure, if the first one fails (ESA).

24	electronics unit for gyroscope
25	Remote Acquisition Unit (RAU)
26	verniers belonging to the AOCS
27	gyroscopes
28	infrared detector
29	electronics unit
30	infrared detector
31	connector for data buses
32	data processing computer
33	interorbit communication assembly
34	antenna
35	orbital transfer boosters
36	solar detector
37	electronics unit
38	battery control unit
39	power supply feeders
40	freon pump
41	battery
42	reservoir (gaseous nitrogen)
43	reservoir (gaseous nitrogen)
44	reservoir (hydrazine)
45	electronics unit
46	microgravity measurement system
47	thermal control subsystem
48	electronic system for the deployment arm
49	orbital control computer
50	orbital control computer
51	orbital transfer boosters
52	verniers belonging to the AOCS
53	connector
54	electronics unit
55	electronics unit
56	electronics unit
57	electronics unit

Structure

a	equipment support panels
b	mounting for the edge of the orbiter's cargo bay
c	equipment support plate
d	Longeron fitting
e	carbon fibre struts
f	handling fitting

3500 watts of power available. This platform would be put into a low Earth orbit by the shuttle and it would be repaired, serviced and its payload replaced in orbit. This project was based on industrial investment and, despite a 'shared knowledge' agreement with NASA, was suspended in 1985 due to a lack of paying customers.

European and American industry has, however, now agreed under certain conditions to finance the construction of a second platform, identical to Eureca, called Amica (Autonomous Microgravity Industrial Carrier) and to privatise use of the two platforms. After 1991, it should be possible to have one flight per year using alternate platforms.

When they were approached in 1982, possible European users responded favourably to the idea of building and using the Eureca platform. Apart from the obvious advantage of being able to return samples to Earth, it has been predicted that, due to its reusable nature, this platform will significantly increase the profitability of missions for numerous payloads and, as a consequence, increase the number of flights.

Different disciplines place different demands on the platform. Materials science research experiments require two to three weeks of microgravity. In life sciences experiments, incubators and containers need to continue functioning, to ensure the survival of biological substances, even during the phases of mounting and recovering the samples. In general, one or two weeks is sufficient for metallurgy and fluid physics experiments; however, a number of processes in crystal growth require up to two months. The growth of large crystals in space demands that ovens and chambers function continuously, consuming large amounts of energy.

Measurements to be made in atmospheric physics include such parameters as the composition, temperature and motion of air masses, as a function of geographic coordinates (latitude and longitude), altitude, Local Time and season. It is then possible to evaluate longterm trends over a period of years. However, experi-

Orbit:	
altitude	525 kilometres
inclination	28.5 ± 1 degrees
Duration of mission:	
operational	6 months
inactive	3 months
Theoretical life	5 missions or 10 years
Rotation cycle:	
from recovery of previous platform to launch of new platform	18 months
dormant period	< 12 months
Mass:	
total in orbit	4200 kilograms
payload	1000 kilograms
Volume:	
available for the payload	8.5 cubic metres
Energy:	
provided by the solar panels	5000 watts
at the peak	1500 watts
available for the payload	1000 watts
Thermal regulation	a ring of liquid freon (1000 watts) multilayer insulation
Data management:	
memory capacity	128 kilobits per second
Rate of data treatment and transmission:	
high speed	256 kilobits per second
low speed	2 kilobits per second
average speed for payload	1.5 kilobits per second
The conditions of microgravity as a function of the level of vibrations of the platform, in hertz (Hz) (g is the gravitational acceleration)	$10^{-5}\,g$ at < 1 Hz $10^{-3}\,g$ at > 100 Hz

Characteristics of Eureca A

ments lasting several months can provide sufficient geographic coverage at reasonable altitudes. Further developments include making localised measurements using powerful instruments and developing new technologies suitable for future long duration missions.

Astronomy is the main subject to be studied during missions with unmanned platforms such as Eureca. Observation runs require at least one month in order to gain the maximum value from a mission. Other disciplines, such as cryogenics (low temperature science), find that Eureca's operational diversity – in particular the choice of orbit and inclination – and the amount of power available offer interesting research possibilities. For Earth observations work, Eureca is more correctly described as a testbed than an operational satellite system.

As space activities in many scientific fields

evolve towards profit making and industrial applications, new technologies are introduced. Solutions have to be found to problems of assembly, maintenance and upkeep of large space platforms, which need to remain in service for long periods of time. The solution will be to develop robots and remote handling equipment to ensure that the platform remains a profitable and flexible piece of machinery.

Eureca's final task may be to test, and validate, technologies which will be used in the construction of future large orbiting space stations. For instance, the platform may be used for rendezvous and docking trials, and to test robotic systems. It could also be used to test the quality of materials assembled by robots under microgravity conditions.

Robert Mory

Man in space

The orbiting space station Freedom

The space station Freedom is an international cooperative project dedicated to creating an orbiting laboratory for the conduct of science, the development of new technologies and the stimulation of commerce. It will provide a facility in space to service and repair experiments and spacecraft. Ultimately, it will function as a transportation way station from which spacecraft can depart to geosynchronous orbit and beyond. The lessons learned from living and working on the station – in life sciences, technology development and assembly of large structures – are essential to future long duration human spaceflight. Before we return to the Moon or visit Mars, we must learn how to adapt to the unique environment of space.

The space station Freedom is the next logical step in the human exploration and utilisation of space. For science, Freedom offers a pressurised laboratory for multidisciplinary research, as well as platforms for instruments to look out at the universe and back toward the Earth. For technological development, Freedom will be a testbed for evaluating technologies, procedures and design approaches for future space systems. For exploration, Freedom represents the establishment of a permanently manned outpost in space, a way station to more distant destinations.

The space station will be international in character. The United States is developing it as part of its national strategy to explore and use the environs of space. With the elements provided by the partners – Canada, Japan and nine members of the European Space Agency – the station will be far more effective than it would have been had each partner proceeded individually. The partners too, will further their own civil space programmes through participation.

Freedom will encourage private sector involvement in space activities. There will be two kinds of commercial opportunities on Freedom. The first will be the chance to perform privately funded research on board the station: research aimed at creating new commercial products. The second type of opportunity will be to provide new systems or services for the station, for example the supply of logistics processing. Such commercial opportunities will be numerous as the station evolves.

The programme is making significant progress and has received strong support from both the US Congress and the President. The main contractors are at work, the international negotiations have been completed and agreements signed, and the management structure is in place. Detailed preliminary design and development have begun.

In many respects, Freedom is similar to the early waterway, railroad and highway projects funded in the United States over the last century. The station is an essential piece of space infrastructure that will allow future generations continued access to space and its opportunities. Like other infrastructure projects, the station is not an end in itself, but rather, a means to an end. Like its predecessors, it is not without technical and economic risk. No progress is ever made without incurring some risk, and Freedom is an essential part of the future.

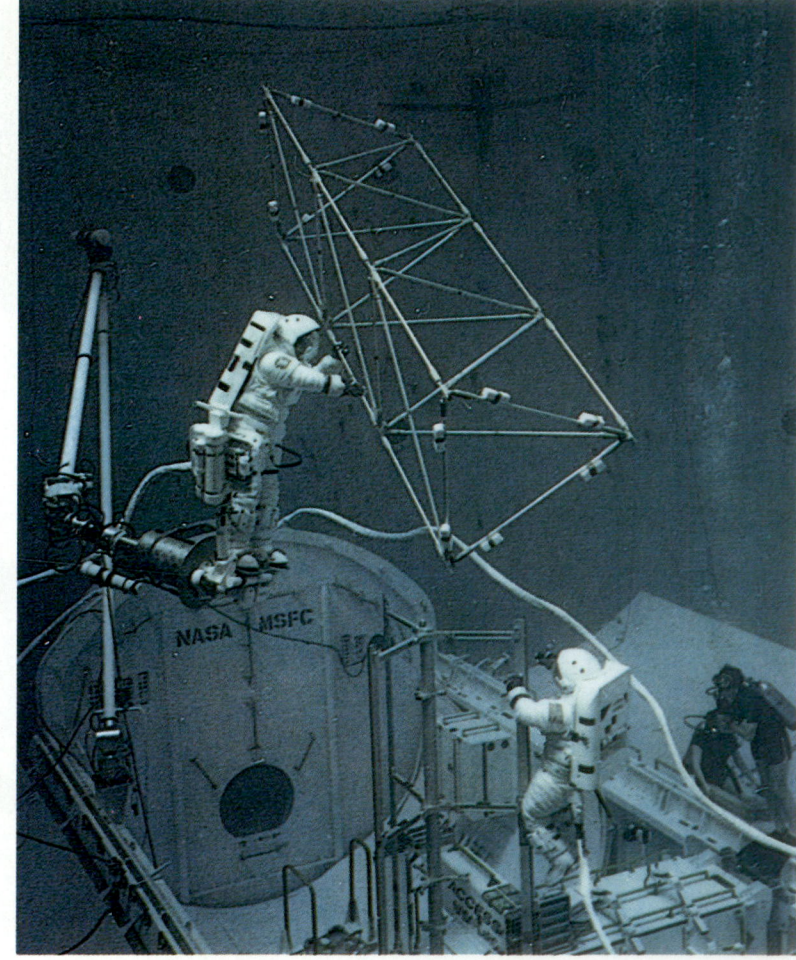

Astronauts in a swimming pool practise handling structures for the space station. The NASA training pool in Houston, Texas, simulates the weightless conditions in Earth orbit for astronauts preparing for their space experience (NASA).

Programme history

The space station programme formally began after President Reagan's State of the Union address in January 1984. Early planning, however, was started shortly after Reagan first came into office. In 1982, NASA formally established the Space Station Task Force to define the necessary preliminary requirements. This definition process was directed toward identifying potential user needs on a space station, and developing configuration concepts that would meet these and other requirements. In parallel, prospective international partners

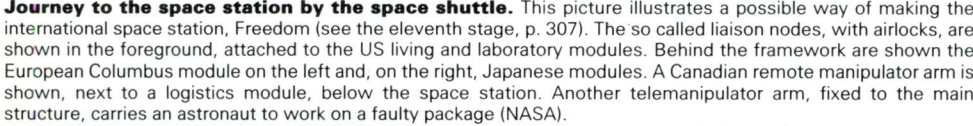

Journey to the space station by the space shuttle. This picture illustrates a possible way of making the international space station, Freedom (see the eleventh stage, p. 307). The so called liaison nodes, with airlocks, are shown in the foreground, attached to the US living and laboratory modules. Behind the framework are shown the European Columbus module on the left and, on the right, Japanese modules. A Canadian remote manipulator arm is shown, next to a logistics module, below the space station. Another telemanipulator arm, fixed to the main structure, carries an astronaut to work on a faulty package (NASA).

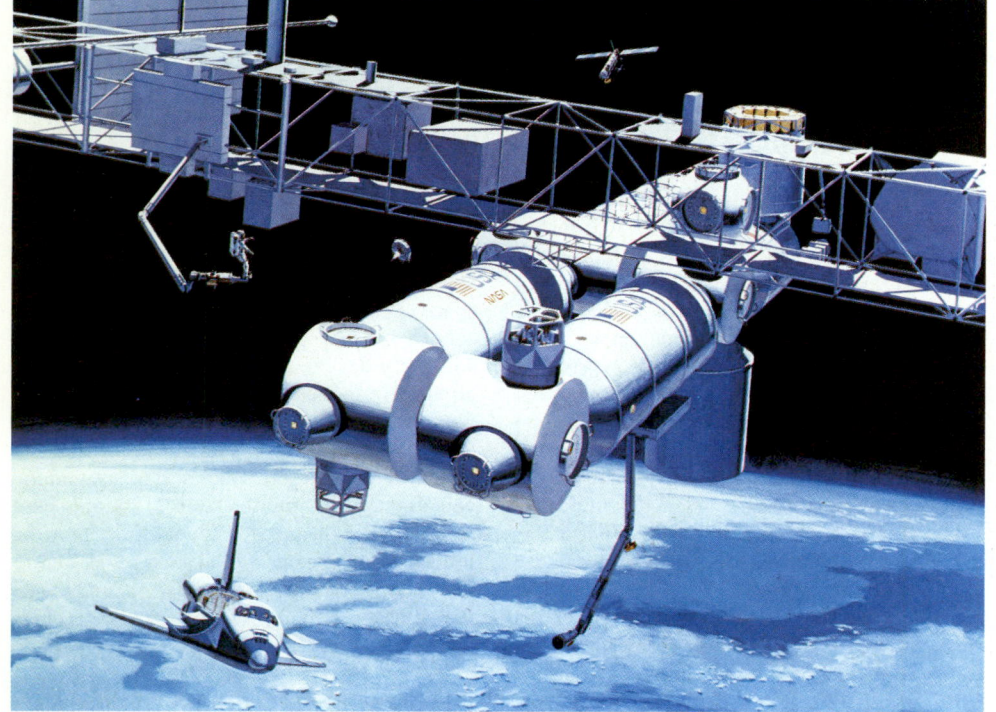

Main characteristics of the polar platform (late 1990s)

Parameters	Description	Comments
Dimensions	approximately 9 metres × 2.8 metres diameter	deployed solar panels: span approximately 10 metres
Mass	from 5500 kilograms to 5900 kilograms 1750 kilograms	at launch net payload at launch
Propulsion	hydrazine	16 to 24 engines of 15 to 20 newtons thrust
Orbit	approximately 822 kilometres	Sun synchronous, circular, 98° inclination
Orientation	0.1% accuracy over the three axes	accuracy of maintaining the track across the ground: ±1 kilometre
Use	Earth observations	
Attitude control	according to the local vertical and pitch, roll and yaw motions	
Transmission speed	300 megabits per second X band direct or 400 megabits per second with the Data Relay Satellite (DRS)	
Power used by payload	approximately 2 kilowatts	average daily requirement
Launcher	Ariane IV or V	double launch possible with Ariane V
Orbital lifetime	4 years	enough fuel for 6 years

began doing similar work. In April 1983, NASA Administrator James Beggs briefed President Reagan on the preliminary directions of the programme; presidential approval followed nine months later.

The announcement of the programme, and the invitation to American friends and allies to participate, was a key message of President Reagan's State of the Union Address that year, and the President clearly sought to evoke the image of John F. Kennedy's speech of 24 years earlier, the speech which effectively began the US manned space programme.

In 1984, the programme began in earnest. The Task Force on Scientific Uses of the Space Station (TFSUSS) was established to define precisely what resources would be needed on the station, and how they would be used. An early reference configuration, named the Power Tower was selected from a field of five potential concepts. The Power Tower appeared to meet several key requirements: it supplied 75 kilowatts of electrical power, it could have the capability to service spacecraft, it allowed both Earth, solar and sky viewing, it could evolve to accommodate future missions and technologies, and it would be inherently stable in flight.

The management structure for the programme also began to be defined in 1984. In a change away from NASA's traditional methods, the programme was divided up into four work packages, and assigned to four different NASA centres. Previously, responsibility for an entire programme had been given to just one centre, so the new method created a structure for closer cooperation within NASA.

Undertaking the definition of the configuration was a complex process requiring the balancing of many competing objectives as well as the many needs of users. In particular, the designers have had to take into account the operating costs associated with the facility. The station's thirty year period of operations make these costs a central concern. For this reason, early emphasis was placed on designing systems that require relatively simple logistics, and can be easily and efficiently serviced on-orbit. Prevailing over all other considerations was a concern for the safety of the crew and the station as a whole.

In June 1984, memoranda of understanding (MOU) were signed with Japan, Canada and the European Space Agency to enable cooperation during the next phase of configuration definition, Phase B. The following year negotiations began on a more detailed set of MOUs that would cover the hardware design, and the development and operational phases of the programme (referred to as Phases C/D/E). These negotiations were completed three years later, in late 1988.

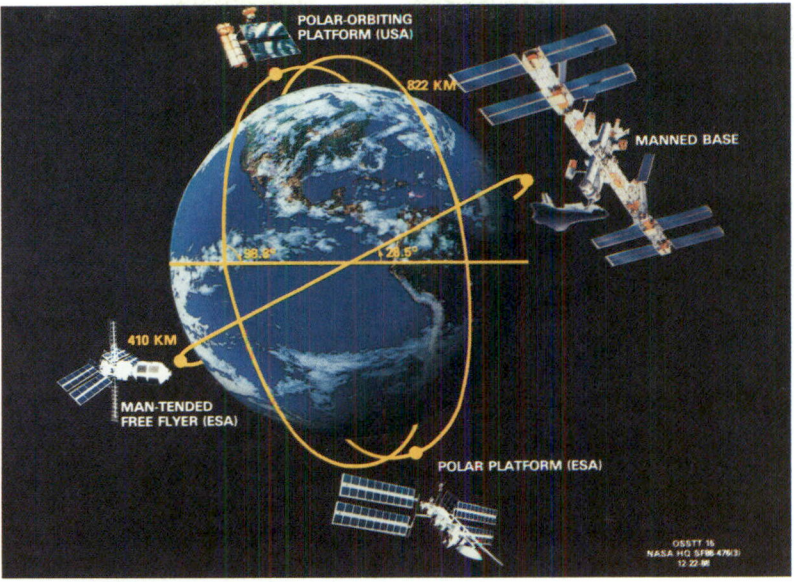

The space station Freedom. This NASA document of 22 December 1988 shows the positions of the different components of the planned orbiting space station. Freedom will be put into orbit by the space shuttle at an altitude varying from 180 to 500 kilometres. The American and European platforms will be in polar orbit at an altitude of 822 kilometres (NASA).

The Orbital Manoeuvring Vehicle (OMV). This 'space tug' carries satellites and equipment into different orbits around the Earth. This structure of relatively small mass is piloted automatically. In this cutaway diagram, the spherical fuel tanks are shown. Rocket thrusters control the speed and direction of the vehicle's motion (NASA).

During 1985 and 1986, the efforts to define the station's design requirements continued. The emphasis on user needs forced a replacement of the Power Tower with the Dual Keel configuration in mid 1985. The Dual Keel was chosen because its mass was distributed much more evenly than that of the Power Tower, considerably improving the microgravity environment of the station; other refinements were also made for safety and operational reasons. The Dual Keel featured a rectangular truss structure with four pressurised modules attached to a horizontal beam truss.

Following the Challenger accident in early 1986, as part of an overall safety reassessment, greater safety constraints were placed on the use of crew in spacewalks or extravehicular activity (EVA). This change, in addition to the prospect of fewer yearly shuttle flights and greater weight restrictions per flight, initiated changes to the configuration and assembly sequence that reduced the amount of EVA needed during assembly and maintenance.

After a full scale cost review in early 1987, the Dual Keel configuration was subsequently scaled down to a single horizontal beam with four pressurised modules (two supplied by the United States, the other two by Japan and ESA). The planned electrical power level was also reduced from 87·5 kilowatts to 75 kilowatts. In essence, NASA adopted a phased approach to the station, identifying a smaller basic configuration, with plans for another phase as new missions for the station were identified.

Requirements definition work was largely completed in late 1988. Design and develop-

The polar platform. Proposed by the UK, this is one of the three parts of the Columbus programme. Such a polar platform would observe the Earth's atmosphere and oceans, its land surface, and the charged particle environment of the platform. The platform could be placed in a Sun synchronous orbit at a height of 822 kilometres. This is high enough for data transmission to a Data Relay Satellite (DRS), yet not too high for observations to be made of the Earth's surface with good spatial resolution (MBB-Erno).

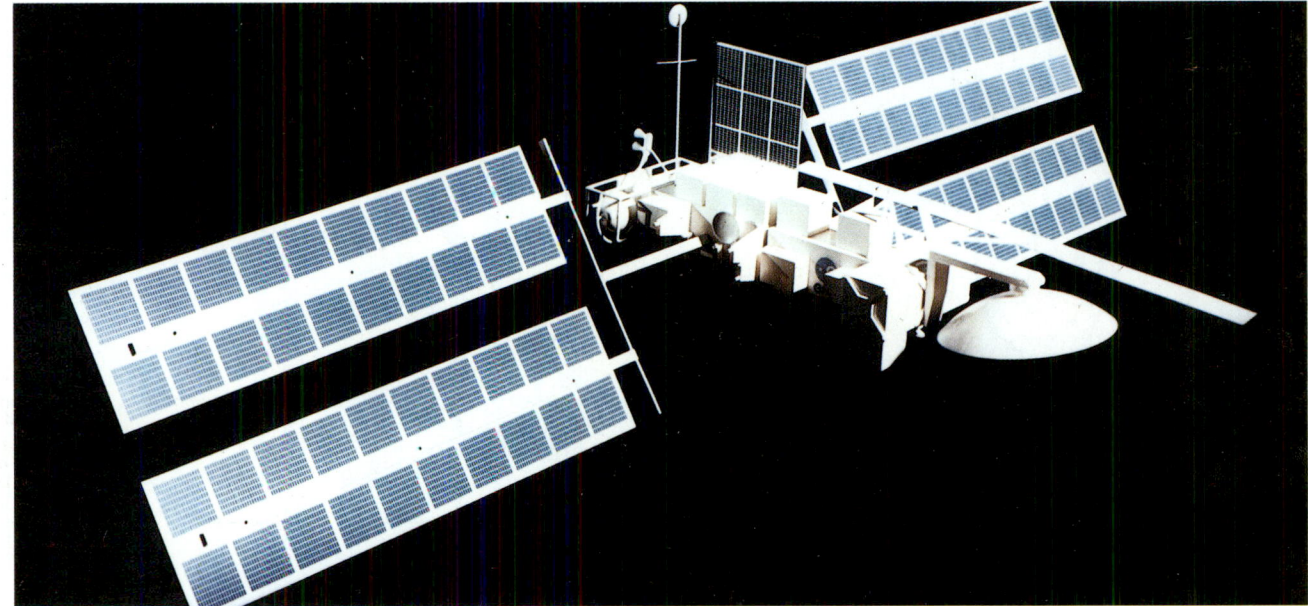

Living with space

Concentrating the Sun's rays to provide power for the space station. This artist's view shows the space station from an unusual angle. In the foreground is illustrated a mirror made up of 19 hexagons, each of which is formed of six triangular facets. The focused solar energy is converted to electric energy, via a turbine which uses helium and xenon, in a Closed Brayton Cycle (CBC) engine (NASA).

Resupplying the space station at stage 8. The table on the right details the expected requirements of the space station in its stage 8 configuration (see page 306). It shows the volumes and masses which must be transported to the station and those which need eventually to be returned to Earth; these are the volumes required for the laboratory module and the crews' living quarters. Requirements for Columbus and the Japanese Experiment Module (JEM) are not included (NASA).

Category	Resupply			Return		
	Mass (kg)	Volume (m³)	Density (kg/m³)	Mass (kg)	Volume (m³)	Density (kg/m³)
Crew and station equipment:						
pressurised	37 300	2 074	18.0	33 939	1 710	19.8
unpressurised	6 400	704	9.1	6 400	704	9.1
fluids	3 180	62		0	0	
propellants	5 000	80		0	0	
subtotal	51 880	2 920		40 339	2 414	
Payload equipment:						
pressurised	43 690	1 966	22.2	41 953	1 942	21.6
unpressurised	36 620	4 611	7.9	36 616	4 611	7.9
fluids	3 220	71		1 532	24	
propellants	14 830	237		0	0	
subtotal	98 360	6 885		80 101	6 577	
Total	150 240	9 805		120 440	8 991	

Arrangement of the service and equipment module. This pressurised module provides supplementary living space for the orbital station. It will remain attached to the space station between space shuttle visits and be used to store food and other perishable materials. On its return to Earth, it will carry the results and materials from laboratory experiments as well as waste. The structural design of two other unpressurised service and equipment modules has not yet been decided (NASA).

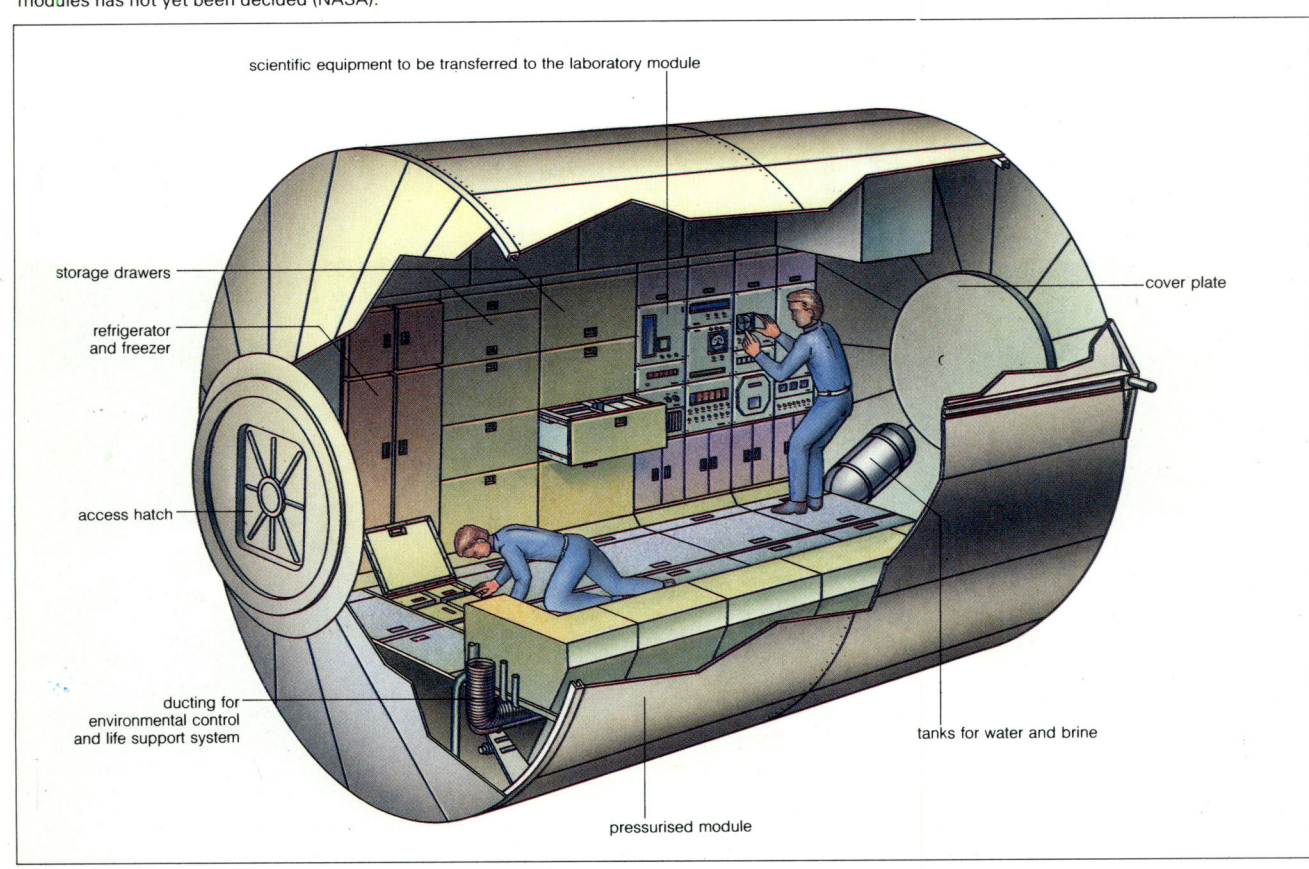

ment of the station's hardware has begun. The integrated design for the station's many components and systems will be reviewed in mid 1990, and again in 1992. Thereafter, hardware construction will begin. On-orbit assembly of the station will begin in early 1995. Early manned-tended operations will begin in late 1995, when the US polar platform will be launched, and one year later the station will be permanently manned. The international elements will be delivered into orbit in 1997, and the station will be complete by 1998.

The space station Freedom

The space station Freedom includes a manned station and an unmanned co-orbiting platform in a 28·5 degree orbit, and two polar orbiting platforms. The manned station will be developed by the United States, with extensive European, Japanese and Canadian participation. The polar orbiting platforms will be developed by the United States and the European Space Agency (ESA). In addition, ESA will, as part of its Columbus programme, develop a co-orbiting platform, called the Man Tended Free Flyer (MTFF).

Freedom was designed with the needs of scientific and commercial users in mind. Space transportation considerations, as well as engineering and technological factors therefore played a key role in the development of the configuration. The result described here best meets those requirements and considerations.

The space station is able to meet a diverse set of requirements and objectives because its design combines a pressurised environment on the manned base, and a truss structure to accommodate many payloads with free flying platforms to gain a different perspective on the Earth and its environment. This assorted set of hardware will allow researchers from around the world to pursue a diverse set of scientific disciplines and research.

The manned base will consist of four pressurised modules, mounted together on a 145 metre long transverse boom flying perpendicular to the station's velocity vector. The station will operate at an altitude ranging from 280 to 500 kilometres in a 28·5 degree inclination orbit. ESA's Man Tended Free Flyer, a pressurised, 7 metre long laboratory, will be in a similar orbit. The US and ESA polar platforms, operating in a sun synchronous orbit at near 90 degrees inclination 822 kilometres from Earth, will be unmanned satellites dedicated to a variety of Earth observation missions.

Major elements and systems of the manned station

At the centre of the station will be four pressurised cylindrical modules. Each of these will be about 10 to 13 metres long and 4 metres in diameter, the maximum allowable diameter of a space shuttle payload. One of the modules, the habitation module, will house a crew of up to eight people. The other three will be laboratories. The modules will be pressurised at sea level pressure (1 bar or 14·7 pounds per square inch) and will provide a shirt sleeve environment for the crew. Each module will be able to accommodate up to 42 cubic metres of payloads and equipment. The interior of the modules will be oriented like Spacelab, with a floor and ceiling, and payloads and work stations lining the walls. By giving an up–down reference, this orientation will help the crew avoid space sickness.

The laboratories will be used for fluid physics, microgravity materials and life sciences research, and materials processing. The station is being designed to have a mean acceleration equivalent to about one millionth that on Earth at the centre of the station's mass. This will enable the crew to perform microgravity research in a weightless environment much improved over that of the shuttle. These laboratories will be particularly well suited to

The Canadian contribution

Canada has acquired considerable expertise in the field of remote manipulation. Following the great success of the Canadarm, designed for the American space shuttle, an agreement was signed between Canada and the USA to give Canada the responsibility for constructing the Mobile Servicing System (MSS) for the Freedom space station. In addition to the space component, there will be simulation units and control centres situated in Canada. The MSS will have a major role to play in the assembly, maintenance and movement of pieces of equipment around the space station, in the deployment and recovery of satellites and in back up for astronauts during extravehicular activity. It will also be used to hold the space shuttle against the space station during the loading and unloading of the cargo bay.

An important feature of the MSS will be the Remote Manipulator System (RMS), an improved version of the Canadarm. It will be 17·6 metres in length, approximately the same size as the original arm. A separate specialised manipulator equipped with two arms, each two metres long, will be used for very delicate work such as repairing electronic circuits and pipes belonging to the fuel and cooling systems. It will be attached either to the RMS or to one of the interfaces along the side of the space station.

Spar Aerospace is the prime contractor of the MSS programme, with dozens of other Canadian enterprises and university research teams being involved, including Canadian Astronautics Ltd (CAL), SED Systems and CAE Electronics.

It is hoped that in the future Canada will produce an all weather Remote Sensing System for the polar platform which will be built in conjunction with the space station. This installation will be based on the Radarsat system.

Canada has become a supplier of specialised equipment as well as a potential user of the space station for scientific and industrial research. Canada's technological expertise includes space instruments and materials, telecommunications satellites, and remote sensing systems. Space mechanisms, such as robots and Remote Manipulator Systems (RMSs), space structures, solar panels and computer equipment are also made in Canada. In addition Canada has experience in all the basic space sciences and space medicine.

Visible on the artist's impression to the right are, in the upper left, the test antenna, and below it, the attached experiment packages, bearing the word, Canada. On the right is a satellite undergoing maintenance work; the Dextrous Manipulator is below it, with a robotic retrieval and maintenance system at the end of it. At the base of the arm is a mobile platform. The two cylinders on either side of the base of the arm are a storage unit for satellite spare parts and the Orbital Maneuvering Vehicle (OMV) in its garage. Just above the OMV (centre left) is a berthing fixture for the Robotic Servicer System (RSS). Above this is a thermal shield folded back to reveal some satellite spare parts. The MSC work station is situated above the other storage unit. Finally, there are three solar panels.

Commercial ventures

In 1982 Canada began preliminary studies on the advantages of involvement in an international space programme. The main objectives were to examine how this would affect the universities, industry and the Canadian government. This study was carried out by Spar Aerospace and Philip A. Lapp Associates under contract to the Canadian National Research Council (CNRC). It concluded that both the public and private sectors would benefit from any involvement.

Canadian experts proposed several possible experiments on space physiology, and in particular on man's ability to adapt to the space environment. In 1984, a second stage was proposed, including experiments in the life sciences. Carried out on the space station, these would involve more experiments on the body's ability to adapt to space, and studies on calcium loss and muscle atrophy suffered by astronauts who spend long periods in space.

Artist's impression of the Mobile Servicing Centre (MSC) visiting the international space station (NASA).

In November 1984, the CNRC contracted six companies to examine the commercial possibilities of Canadian users of the space station for such purposes as producing new materials in space (semi-conductors, ceramics, glasses, metals and alloys) for industrial use, and pharmaceutical and biological products. In a separate contract Currie, Coopers and Lybrand were asked to study the commercial and economic benefits of Canada's involvement in the space station programme. It was only in 1988 that the government established the Canadian Space Agency (CSA).

Michel Giroux

Two 1980s mock-ups of the space station living quarters. The lefthand photograph shows the interior of the module designed by Rockwell International, the righthand picture the one designed by the McDonnell-Douglas Corporation. The design by the Boeing Corporation that was eventually chosen was for eight astronauts. A mock-up of this can be found at the Marshall Center at Huntsville, Alabama (NASA).

experiments requiring this low level of gravity, extensive crew interaction, and long periods of time.

The four pressurised modules will be linked together through tunnel-like structures, called resource nodes. These nodes, will serve as passageways and as the command and control centres for space station systems and communications. Two of the nodes will have viewing towers, called cupolas, to allow the crew to direct and view all external activities.

Space station supplies will be carried back and forth on the shuttle in logistics carriers which will attach to one of the nodes between shuttle flights. The pressurised version of these carriers will provide additional space inside the station complex.

There will be two types of robotic devices on the truss assembly to provide servicing capability. The US Flight Telerobotic Servicer (FTS) will be a highly automated device capable of precise manipulations in space. It will be used for both routine and hazardous tasks outside the modules, thus reducing the time the

continued on p. 311

Living with space

Sequence of events during construction of a space station. In each stage of the assembly of the space station, its complexity grows with the additional equipment, shown as the manifest, brought from Earth. Up to the fourteenth stage, there is only a single structure, which is 155 metres in length (along the y-axis). From the fifteenth stage, a dual keel configuration is apparent. The dimension of the keel is 105 metres (along the z-axis) (NASA).

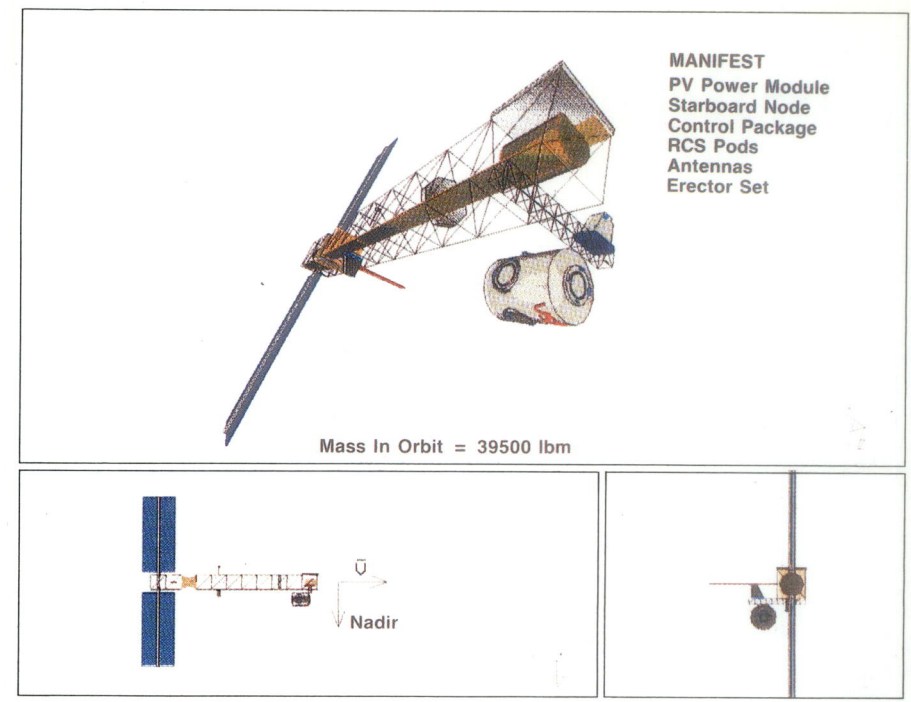

MANIFEST
PV Power Module
Starboard Node
Control Package
RCS Pods
Antennas
Erector Set

Mass In Orbit = 39500 lbm

First stage
Mass in orbit = 17.9 tonnes

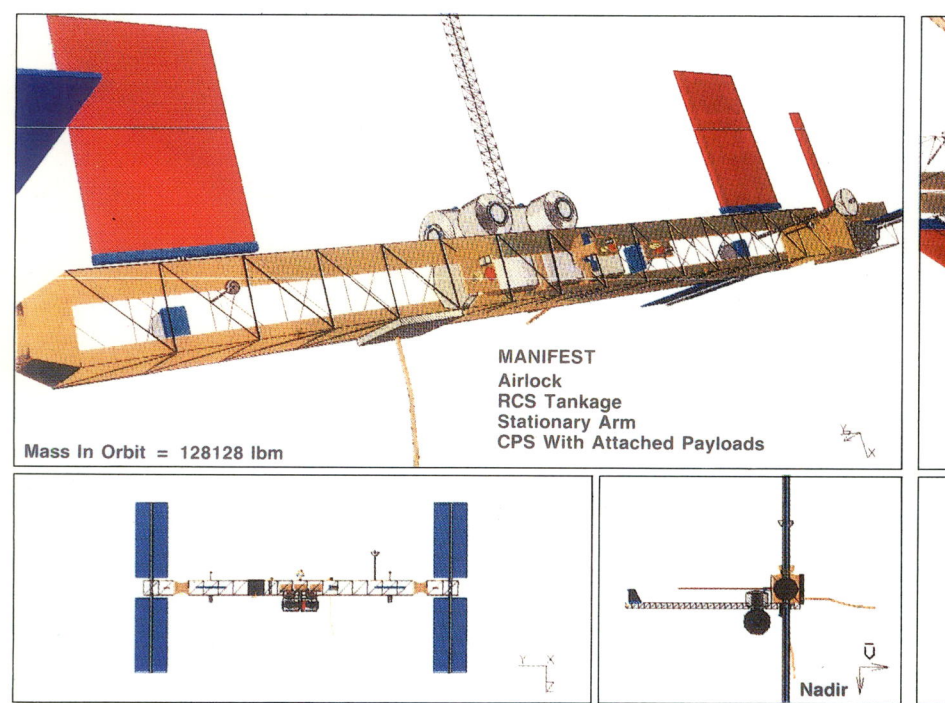

MANIFEST
Airlock
RCS Tankage
Stationary Arm
CPS With Attached Payloads

Mass In Orbit = 128128 lbm

Fourth stage
Mass in orbit = 58.1 tonnes

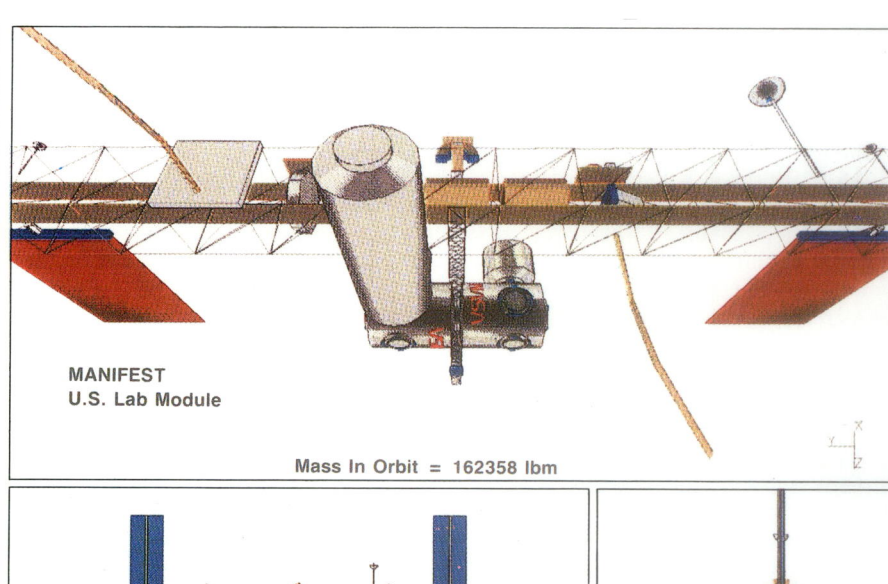

MANIFEST
U.S. Lab Module

Mass In Orbit = 162358 lbm

Fifth stage
Mass in orbit = 73.6 tonnes

Eighth stage
Mass in orbit = 126.3 tonnes

Ninth stage
Mass in orbit = 140.4 tonnes

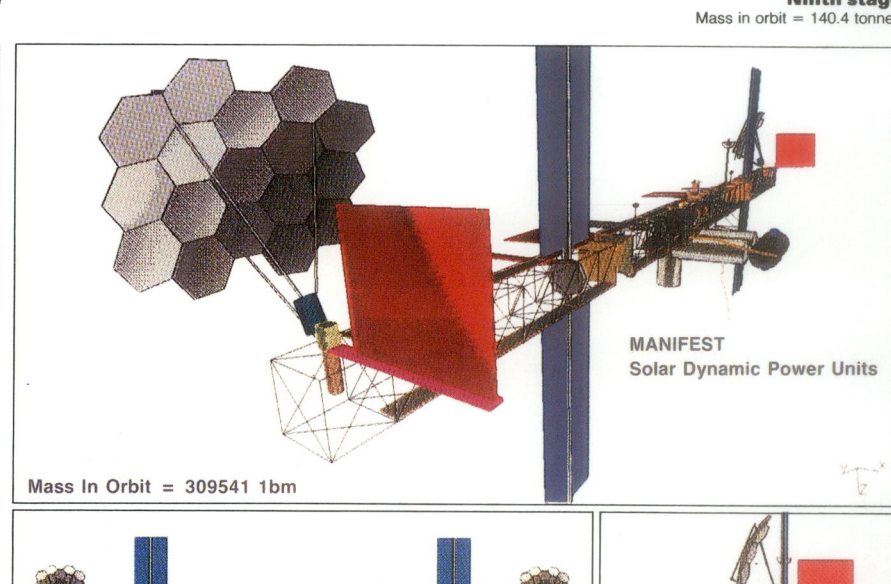

MANIFEST
Logistics Module
Crew

Mass In Orbit = 278569 lbm

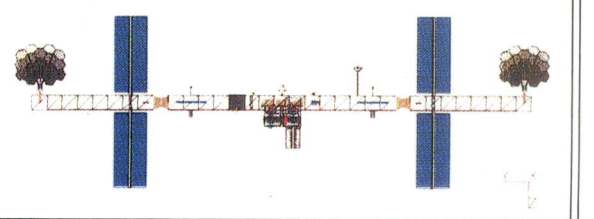

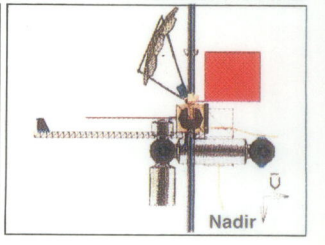

MANIFEST
Solar Dynamic Power Units

Mass In Orbit = 309541 1bm

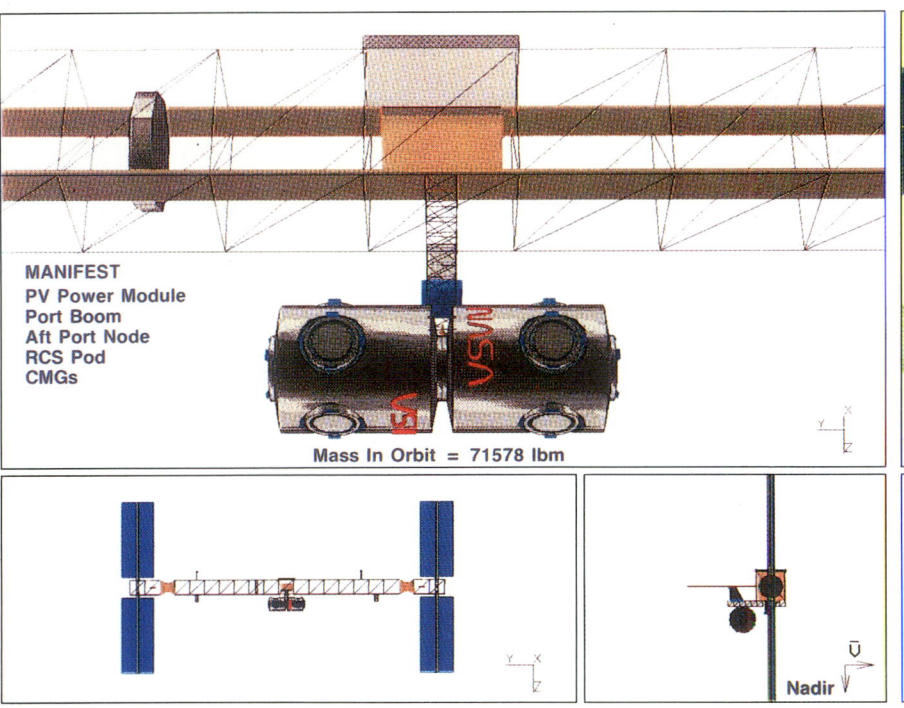

MANIFEST
PV Power Module
Port Boom
Aft Port Node
RCS Pod
CMGs

Mass In Orbit = 71578 lbm

MANIFEST
Thermal System Raditors
Transporter Upgrade and Arm
RCS Tankage
Airlock
Attended Payloads

Mass In Orbit = 100,326 lbm

Nadir

Second stage
Mass in orbit = 32.5 tonnes

Third stage
Mass in orbit = 45.5 tonnes

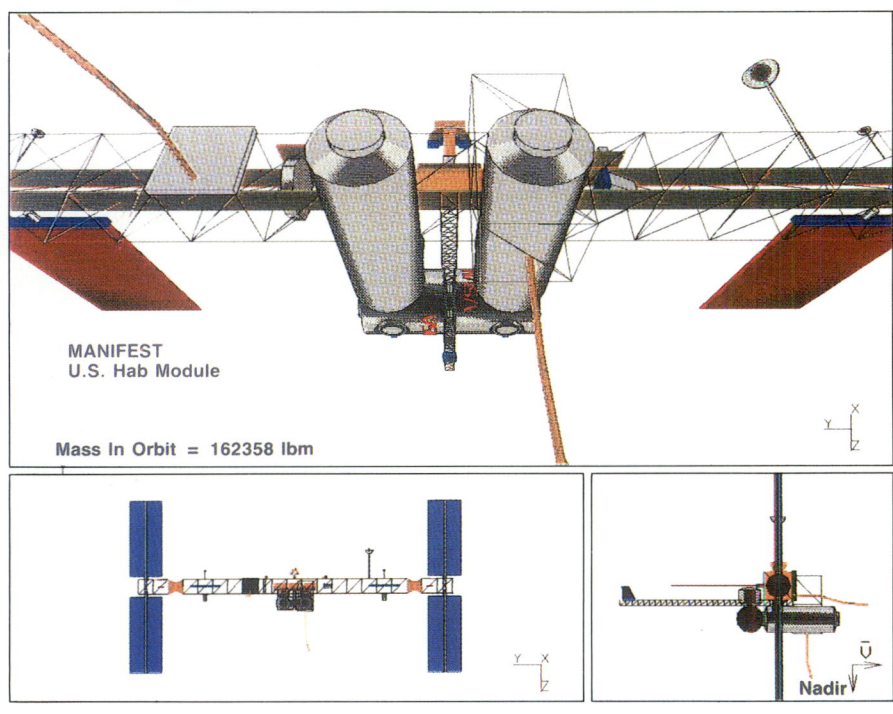

MANIFEST
U.S. Hab Module

Mass In Orbit = 162358 lbm

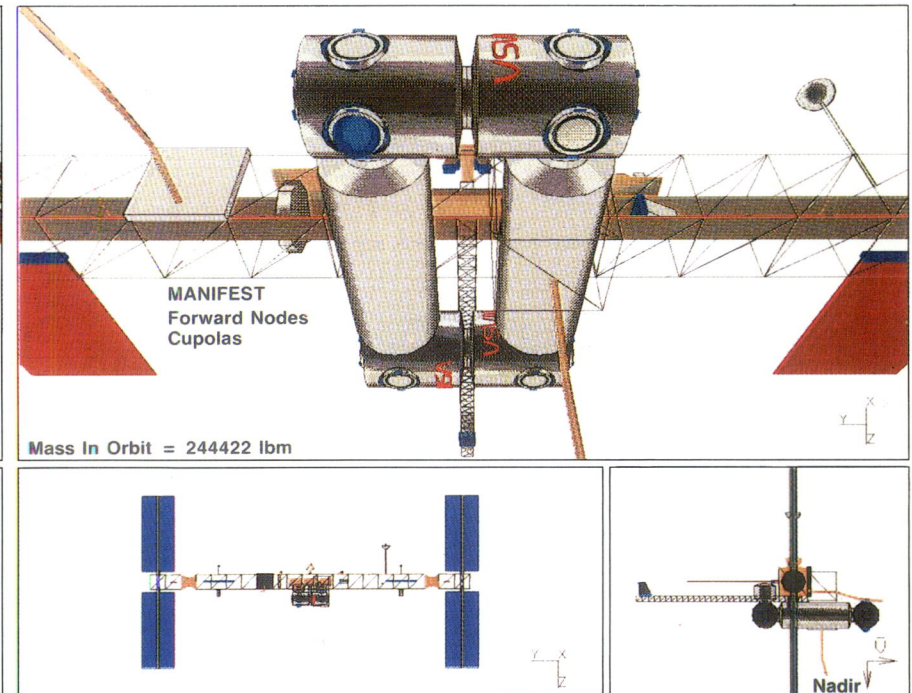

MANIFEST
Forward Nodes
Cupolas

Mass In Orbit = 244422 lbm

Nadir

Nadir

Sixth stage
Mass in orbit = 73.6 tonnes

Seventh stage
Mass in orbit = 110.9 tonnes

Tenth stage
Mass in orbit = 156.8 tonnes

Eleventh stage
Mass in orbit = 176.2 tonnes

MANIFEST
JEM Module
Exposed Facility #1

Mass In Orbit = 345671 lbm

MANIFEST
ESA Module

Mass In Orbit = 3875545 lbm

Nadir

Nadir

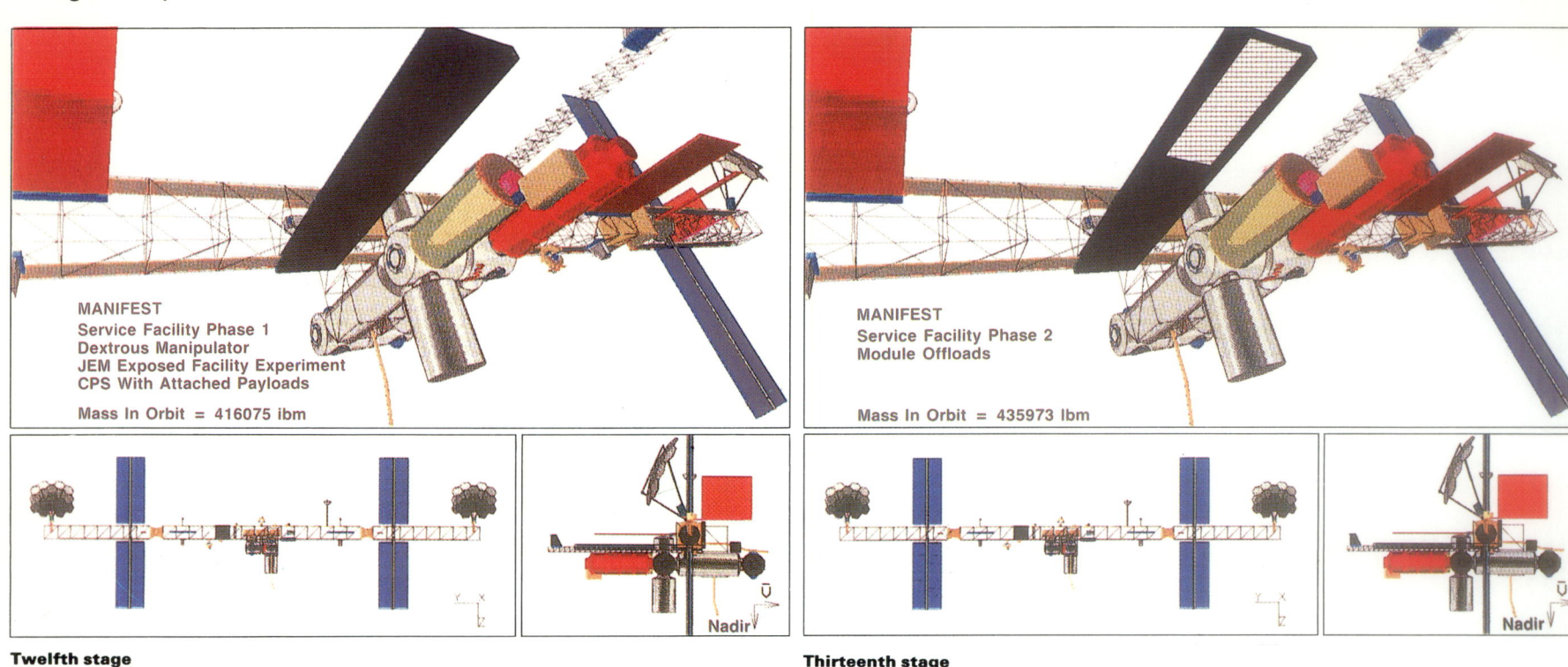

MANIFEST
Service Facility Phase 1
Dextrous Manipulator
JEM Exposed Facility Experiment
CPS With Attached Payloads

Mass In Orbit = 416075 ibm

Twelfth stage
Mass in orbit = 188.7 tonnes

MANIFEST
Service Facility Phase 2
Module Offloads

Mass In Orbit = 435973 lbm

Thirteenth stage
Mass in orbit = 197.8 tonnes

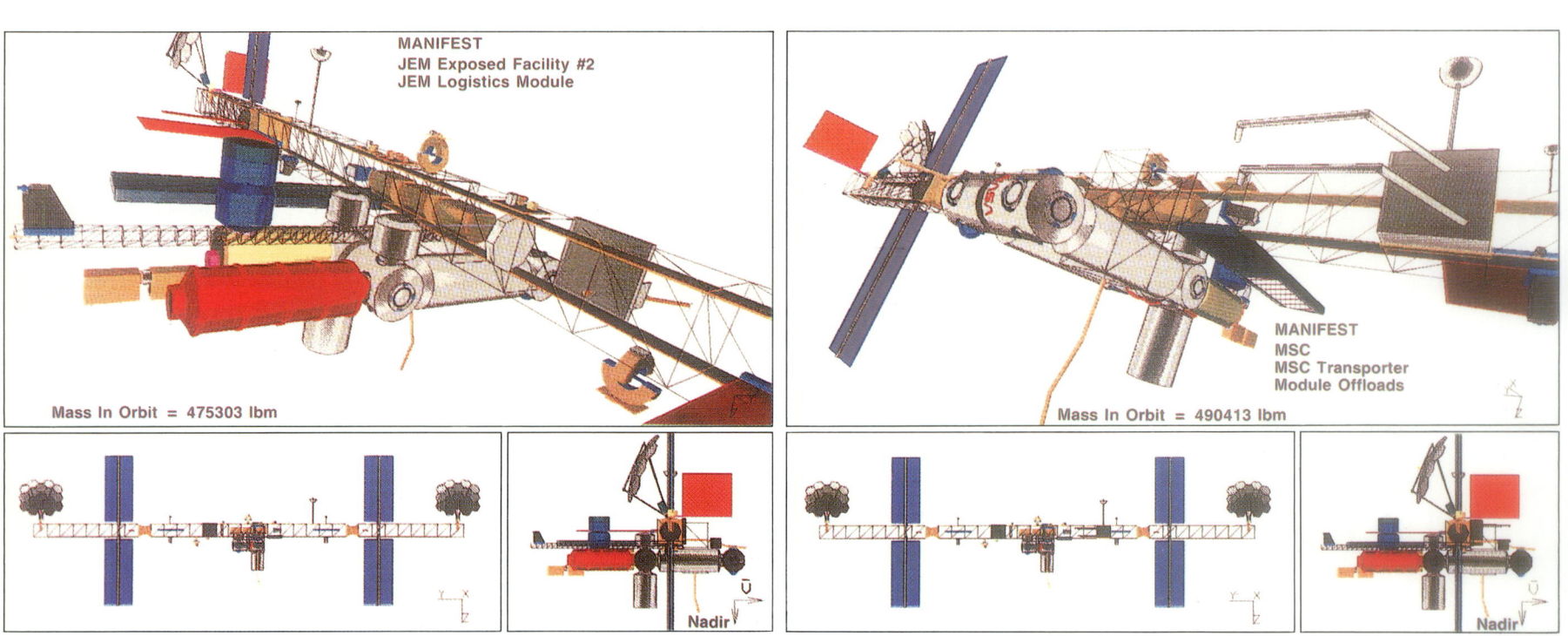

MANIFEST
JEM Exposed Facility #2
JEM Logistics Module

Mass In Orbit = 475303 lbm

Fourteenth stage
Mass in orbit = 215.6 tonnes

MANIFEST
MSC
MSC Transporter
Module Offloads

Mass In Orbit = 490413 lbm

Fifteenth stage
Mass in orbit = 222.4 tonnes

Sixteenth stage
Mass in orbit = 236.0 tonnes

Seventeenth stage
Mass in orbit = 247.4 tonnes

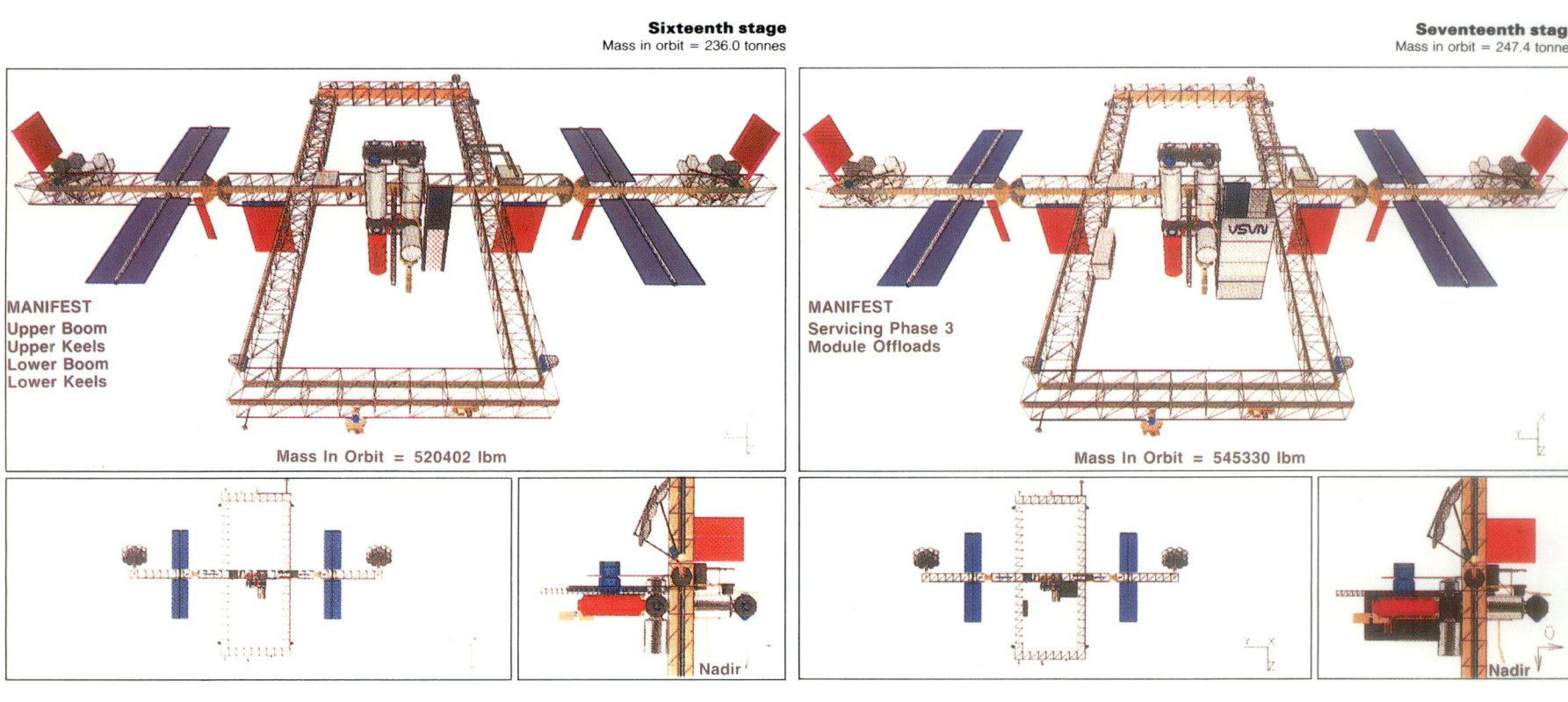

MANIFEST
Upper Boom
Upper Keels
Lower Boom
Lower Keels

Mass In Orbit = 520402 lbm

MANIFEST
Servicing Phase 3
Module Offloads

Mass In Orbit = 545330 lbm

Japan's contribution

Japan's contribution to NASA's international space station will be to develop the Japanese Experiment Module (JEM), an attached multipurpose research and development laboratory module. The rationale for Japanese participation in the programme is to acquire highly advanced technology, to advance next generation science and technology, to expand the human frontier into space, to enhance industrial activities in space, and to contribute to international cooperation. The Japanese National Space Development Agency (NASDA) implements the JEM design and development activities. Technical issues have been coordinated between NASA and NASDA to ensure JEM's compatibility with the space station.

JEM consists of three major elements, a Pressurised Module (PM) with the scientific/equipment airlock and dedicated remote manipulator arm, an Exposed Facility (EF), and an Experiment Logistics Module (ELM). JEM has seven functional subsystems. These are for structure and mechanisms, electrical power, communications and control, thermal control, environmental control and life support for the crew of two, experiment support, and manipulator subsystems. Since JEM is an attached module, it receives its primary resources and services from the space station, including electrical power and heat rejection, crew living quarters, air, and data relay to and from the ground.

JEM is being designed, developed and operated to suit the requirements of users from various disciplines. The JEM payload accommodation concept covers missions for Earth observations, scientific observations, communications experiments, material processing, life sciences, including biotechnology, and technology development.

The Pressurised Module (PM) provides a shirt sleeve environment for the crew to perform research activities for materials processing, life sciences and biotechnology. The PM is a cylindrical shell of aluminium alloy and has a semimonocoque structure. Shields protect the PM from micrometeorites and similar space debris. The PM has a stowage space roughly equivalent to 24 standard double racks: ten double rack spaces are reserved for the payload installation and four double rack spaces for mission payload storage. Major functional subsystem components for JEM operations and control are installed in the floor and ceiling sections.

The Exposed Facility (EF) accommodates experiments for Earth observations, scientific observations, technology development and communications missions requiring the unique space environment, as well as those for materials processing missions which must be conducted on the EF for safety and other reasons. The EF has a box-type structure made of carbon fibre reinforced plastic material. The Experiment Exchange Unit (EEU) is the standard method of accommodating payloads or of providing storage space on the EF.

The Experiment Logistics Module (ELM) provides the JEM logistics transport and storage support, and consists of pressurised and exposed sections. The pressurised section is a cylindrical structure of aluminium alloy and functions, in case of emergency, as a rescue vehicle for transferring the crew to the space station itself. The exposed section serves both as a carrier of and as a storage place for gas bottles and specimens used for experiments.

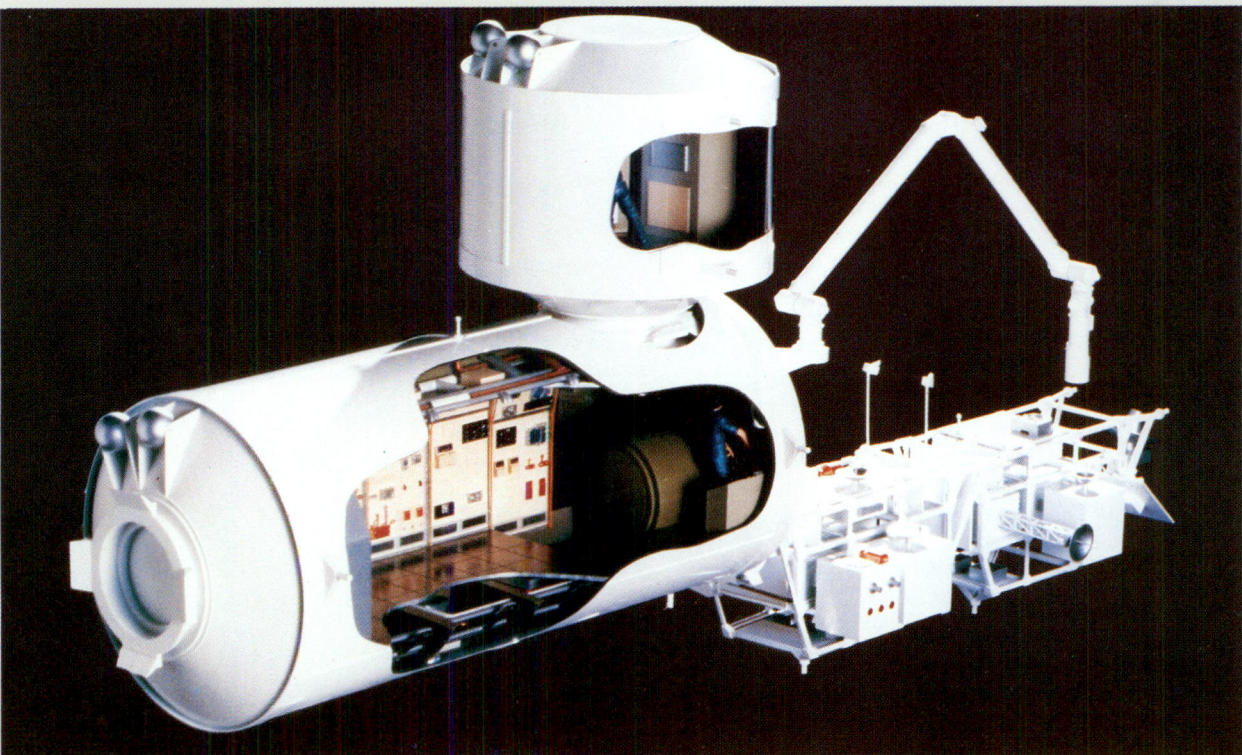

Artist's impression of the Japanese Experiment Module (JEM). This shows the JEM, a space laboratory attached to the space station, consisting of a central Pressurised Module (PM), an Exposed Facility (EF), and an Experiment Logistics Module (ELM), as well as the scientific/equipment airlock and local remote manipulator arm. The crewmember inside the PM operates the arm to support experiments which require the unique space environment, such as a vacuum or a wide field of view for observing the Earth and the Universe. The berthing mechanism at the left hand end of the PM attaches the JEM to the space station (NASDA).

Inside the JEM. The JEM design studies are carried out not only with mere drawings but also a full size mockup, shown below. Identifying the man–machine interface, rack and utility installation, and other aspects critical to a manned spacecraft, this allows engineers to carry out effective and efficient design procedures. This photograph shows the internal layout of the PM (NASDA).

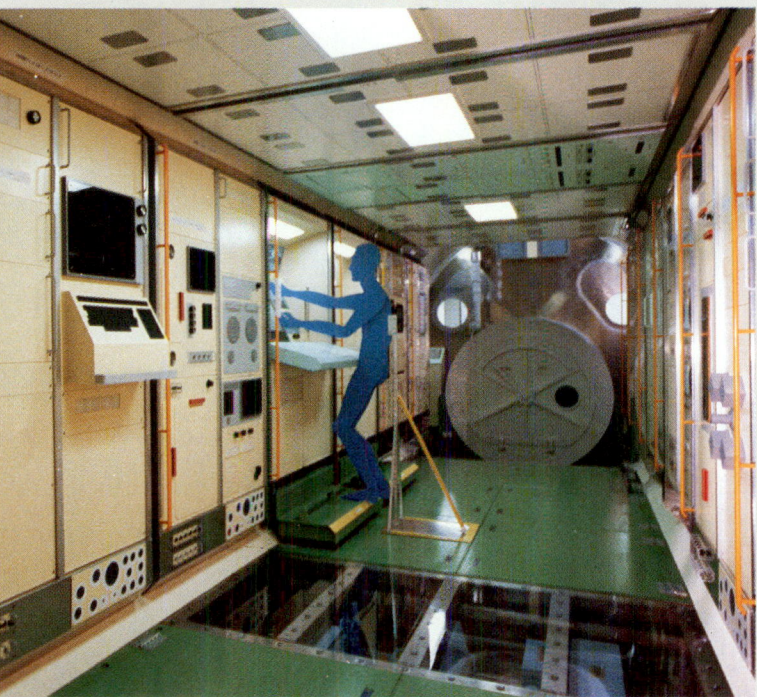

During 1985 and 1986 NASDA worked on the preliminary phase of JEM's design and development programme. This involved establishing a basic shape, identifying the appropriate technology and specifications, and planning the development programme. The process began in 1987 with the aim of producing a fully operational flight prototype and ground support stations. It is hoped that JEM will be launched in 1997.

Masafumi Miyazawa

JEM specifications

	Pressurised Module (PM)	Experiment Logistics Module (ELM)		Exposed Facility (EF)	
		pressurised section	exposed section	EF 1	EF 2
Structure	cylindrical	cylindrical	box	box	
Dimensions (metres)	10 × 4	4 × 4	4.5 × 2.0 × 4.3	4.0 × 1.4 × 2.5	
Dry weight (tonnes)	11.7	3.5	0.8	1.9	1.3
Launch weight (tonnes) (includes payload weight)	15.7	8.5	4.8	1.9	1.3
Payload/storage volume (cubic metres)	17/7	0/14	0/12	10/2 (Experiment Exchange Unit)	
Electrical power (kilowatts)	6 (housekeeping), 9 (mission)				
Data transfer (megabits per second)	32 (maximum)				
Microgravity	10^{-5} to 10^{-6} g				
Gas supply	Air, N_2, Ar, He, Kr, O_2, CO_2				
Gas treatment	NH_3, Cl_2, H_2O, CO_2				
Vacuum vent	5×10^{-4} torr				
Data management	data acquisition, processing, storage, and transmission				

Columbus

In January 1985 ESA began feasibility studies on a European component for the US Freedom space station. The outcome, unveiled in March 1987, was a proposal for the Columbus programme. This consists of three elements: a four segment pressurised laboratory called Columbus attached to the space station, an automatic two segment laboratory with its own resources module, and a European polar platform.

The first element to become operational when it docks at the heart of the US space station in the late 1990s will be the pressurised laboratory. This central position is the best place for microgravity experiments. The four segment module, similar in design to Spacelab, will be used both as a laboratory and as living quarters for the crew. Next will come the polar platform for Earth observation and meteorological applications (pp. 302–3); this will be placed in a near polar orbit at an altitude of about 822 kilometres. The final stage will be Man Tended Free Flyer (MTFF), which will have two pressurised segments and a resource module. The MTFF, now known as the Columbus laboratory, will be completely autonomous though it will co-orbit with the space station.

The European countries involved in the Columbus programme have contributed in the following proportions: West Germany 38%; Italy 25%; France 13·8%; Spain 6%; UK 5·5%; Belgium 5%; Holland 1·3%; Denmark 1%; Sweden 1%; Norway 0·4%. The total currently reaches only 97%, so adjustments will be required during the first production phases of the programme.

The cost of the space part of the Columbus programme was estimated in 1986 at 2400 thousand million ECUs, this budget being intended to cover the development and construction of all three elements. Italy is in charge of building the pressurised laboratory, while West Germany has responsibility for the resource modules for the polar platform, for the MTFF and for integrating the MTFF. The UK or France will be responsible for the polar platform itself, and France will organise the data management system for the entire programme.

Columbus is one of the European Space Agency's long term programmes. Others include the development of Ariane V, a more powerful rocket launcher than its predecessors, and research into the Hermes space plane, a possible payload for Ariane V.

Mario Deleo and Hermann Strub

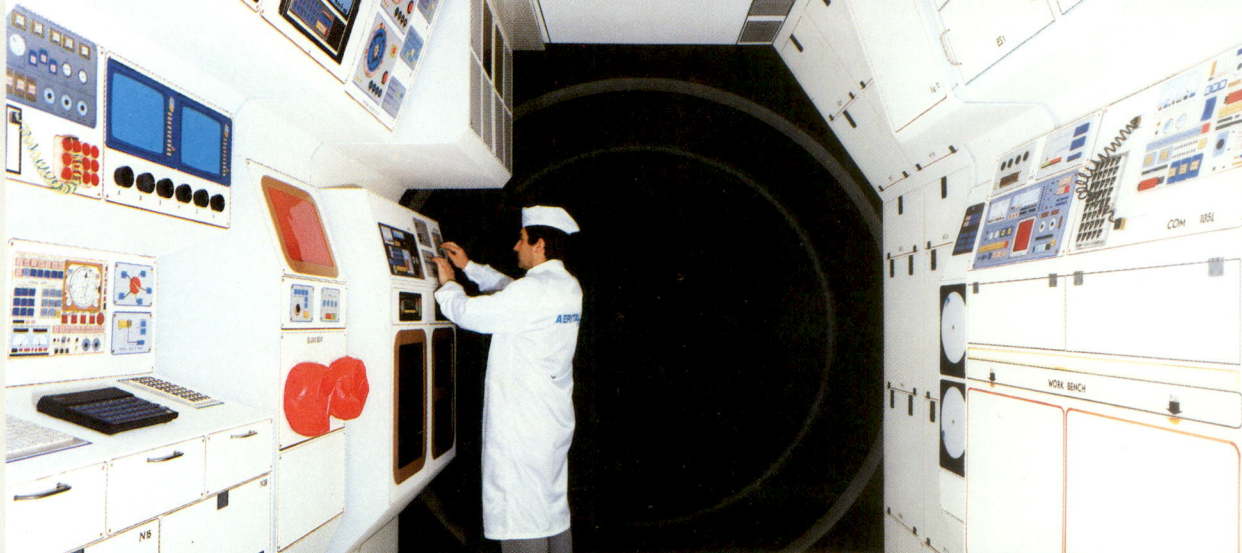

The pressurised laboratory. These two photographs show the exterior and interior of the full size mockup of the Columbus pressurised module, developed by Aeritalia in conjunction with various European companies, including Selenia (Italy) and Matra (France).

NASA proposed that the pressurised module of the Columbus system should be permanently installed in the orbiting station. ESA agreed to this in 1988, and devised a utilisation programme for the module which was compatible with their own experiments and those of the orbiting complex. The dimensions of the module are also compatible with the Ariane V launcher. Three segments are visible in the upper photograph, but the final version will have four (Aeritalia).

The Man Tended Free Flyer. The table below lists the main characteristics of the two segment pressurised module and the resources module of the MTFF. A cost effective modular design was chosen so that the subsystems of the resources module could also be used for the MTFF and for the polar platform. Electricity for solar generators will be stored using an array of nickel-hydrogen batteries and transmitted as a direct current (DC at 120 volts) to the payload. The resources module will regulate the temperature of the system, using both radiant and reflective surfaces and cooling circuits. Data transmission to stations on the Earth will be via a Data Relay Satellite (DRS). The module will be fitted with thrusters and suitable instruments to enable it to alter its position and orbit.

The MTFF is intended to have a 180 day cycle. It is hoped that it will one day become an integral part of an independent European space station.

Hermann Strub

Principal characteristics of the Columbus pressurised module, attached to the space station

Parameters	Description	Observations
Dimensions	about 12.8 metres × 4.4 metres for four segments	to be determined
Mass	about 14 000 kilograms	payload not included (up to 10 000 kilograms)
Orbit	that of the space station	
Transmission speed: downlink	100 megabits per second continuous	combined vocal and video
uplink	25 megabits per second	combined vocal and video
Payload power	12 kilowatts	
Microgravity	$10^{-5}\,g$ for a frequency less than 1 hertz	situated on the module's longitudinal axis
Uses	materials sciences, physics of fluids, life sciences	compatible with the microgravity specifications
Equipment	up to 43 units of payload	
Crew	2 astronauts	enough room for three people
Maintenance	by the American shuttle, every 90 days	

Parameters	Description	Observations
Dimensions	approximately 12.4 metres × 4.4 metres	length of deployed solar panels: 55 metres
Total mass	18 400 kilograms	at launch
Payload	2000 kilograms	at launch
possible payload	2000 to 5000 kilograms	automatic or remote controlled
Fuel capacity	2700 kilograms	1200 kilograms at launch
Loading capacity	10.5 cubic metres	up to 23 pallets for the payload
Electrical power: total	9 kilowatts	
payload	4 kilowatts	on average
Transmission speed: downlink	100 megabits per second maximum	2 megabits continuously
uplink	2.5 megabits per second maximum	1 megabit continuously
Microgravity	$10^{-6}\,g$ for a frequency less than 1 hertz	lowest value in free flight
Crew	2 astronauts	only during servicing
Orbit	350 to 460 kilometres, 28.5° inclination	same orbit as the space station for major service every 3 years

crew must spend outside and increasing their safety. It is planned that the FTS will be used to help assemble the station truss, install external equipment and tackle maintenance activities.

The Canadian mobile servicing system (MSS) will also be an automated tool used for transportation about the station. It will also help perform assembly, and routine servicing, of station elements and scientific payloads. The MSS will consist of a remote manipulator system (RMS) similar to the one on the space shuttle, attached to a US-built mobile transporter moving along the truss. Either the FTS or another automated robotic device will be attached to the end of the RMS at any time, depending on the task being accomplished.

Station propulsion will be supplied by a series of thrusters using hydrogen and oxygen as fuel, these materials being derived from water on the station. The propulsion system will keep the station at the appropriate altitude and attitude.

Electrical power will be generated by four 10·5 metre wide by 27 metre long photovoltaic solar arrays located at either end of the truss assembly. These panels will be able to move to track the Sun as the station orbits around the Earth. When the station is in the Earth's shadow, power will be stored in hundreds of nickel–hydrogen batteries. Initially, the station will produce an average of 75 kilowatts of power. Potentially, however, solar dynamic technology could be added to increase this level to between 125 and 175 kilowatts.

Freedom will have several systems vital to space station operations, including thermal control, fluids distribution, environmental control and life support, communications, guidance and navigation, and data management. Each of these systems will contribute to maintaining the health of the crew and the operability of the station. Communications and tracking and the data management system will be particularly important to space station users monitoring experiments from the ground.

The station will also have a variety of crew accommodation, collectively called man systems. These include crew health care, food management, cleaning equipment, personal hygiene, mobility aids and restraints, lighting and storage. There will also be an extravehicular activity (EVA) system to allow crew members to work safely outside the station. This latter system will include a serviceable space suit and associated life support hardware.

Space station Freedom and its associated platforms

The US and ESA polar platforms will be self contained free flying spacecraft in a polar orbit. The platforms will have a set of instruments designed to perform Earth, biological, geological and oceanographic observations. They will also be suitable for upper and lower atmospheric research, solar observations and plasma physics measurements.

The US polar platform may be planned to be serviceable via a robot on an unmanned launch vehicle. It will also be designed to use, where practical, components being designed for the manned base. Use of common parts could allow some cost savings. The US platform, 13·4 metres long and 3·3 metres in diameter, will have many systems similar in function to those on the manned base. ESA's platform, which is slightly smaller, will attempt to utilise common components used on the MTFF. The MTFF will be a co-orbiting unpressurised laboratory for long duration microgravity experiments that need only periodic crew presence; its fields of study will include fluid physics, life and materials sciences.

Space station Freedom: the management approach and budget

In order to use fully the relevant NASA expertise, experience and facilities available at its space centres, NASA has divided the

Type	Number	Location	Major function
Fixed, command and control	2	Living module, and command and control module (HSO)	primary operator interface to subsystems and to utilities
	1	Laboratory module (MPL)	
	1	Columbus (ESA)	
	1	JEM	
Portable	6	As required in MPL, HSO	multipurpose services
Extravehicular activity	2	Extravehicular Mobility Unit (EMU)	provide EVA activity with procedure displays and simple commands
Maintenance	1	MPL	troubleshooting and repair
Health maintenance facility	1	HSO	health-related activities

Number and type of workstations on board the space station

Artist's impression of the space station Freedom. Attached to the main lattice structure are several modules (shown in white), the robotic Mobile Servicing System and enormous panels of solar cells which will provide up to 75 kilowatts of electrical power. A co-orbiting space shuttle is shown about to return an astronaut crew to Earth (NASA).

station's hardware development into four work packages. These are divided between four of NASA's centres – Marshall Space Flight Center in Huntsville, Alabama; Johnson Space Center in Houston, Texas; Goddard Space Flight Center in Greenbelt, Maryland; and Lewis Research Center, in Cleveland, Ohio. Management and integration of the entire programme will be accomplished by the Space Station Programme Office, located near Washington DC.

The Marshall and Johnson Space Centers are responsible for most of the work related to the pressurised modules and their related systems, and oversee the work package contractors, Boeing and McDonnell-Douglas, respectively. The Lewis Research Center will, with the help of General Electric Corporation, develop the power systems necessary to run the station, and the Goddard Space Flight Center will focus on

developing the US polar platform, the accommodation for the station's attached payloads, and the Flight Telerobotic Servicer. Rockwell International/Rocketdyne is the contractor for this element in the programme.

The involvement of several centres, contractors and the international partners necessitates strong central management control. To meet the challenge of integrating the activities of so many different groups, NASA has established a strong headquarters organisation in Washington DC (Level I) and a central programme office in Reston, Virginia just outside Washington. With the assistance of three separate contractors, the Reston office will perform the systems engineering and integration necessary to ensure that all the pieces of the station will work together once assembled. It will also assert control over the programme budget to ensure that the station is developed on time and within its budget.

After two years of rephased budgets caused by constraints placed on the programme by an overall effort to deal with the US government deficit, the programme was funded at a level of $900 million in 1989. This budget enabled NASA to make strong progress in the design of space station systems and components, and maintain its planned hardware delivery schedule. NASA is requesting $2·05 billion in 1990, funding that will pay for the thousands of engineers needed to begin the extensive development and testing of hardware and software planned in the next three years.

Using Freedom

The space station Freedom will provide an extensive set of resources for a host of users over the thirty years of its lifetime. These resources include space inside pressurised laboratories, accommodation mounted along the truss assembly, greater electrical power and data handling capability than any other spacecraft to date, various fluid and other utilities,

The Orbital Transfer Vehicle (OTV). The illustration above shows one of the most recent designs for the OTV, produced by NASA's Marshall Center, at Huntsville in Alabama. A possible use could be to move a satellite from a low Earth orbit into a geostationary orbit (NASA).

and extensive crew time devoted to users. Crew interaction with experiments will be particularly valuable because it will permit new avenues of research as results are assessed and new technologies are incorporated.

In addition to crew involvement, advancing computer technologies and the extensive data transmission capabilities available on the station will enable scientists in their home institutions to interact directly with their payloads in orbit as well as with other scientists all over the United States. This new 'tele-science', will allow greater interaction and

return on a given space experiment than ever before.

The primary uses of the laboratories in the early years of station operations are anticipated to be in the life and materials sciences. Basic research in physics, technology development and materials production are also expected. Space station researchers will take advantage of the extremely low gravity levels to grow large, defect-free crystals not usually possible on Earth. This activity may eventually lead to the development and production of new, superfast semiconductor crystals. Scientists will also use the station to investigate phenomena normally masked by gravitational effects, continuing, for instance, research on the effects of gravity on plant growth.

Life sciences research on the station may lead to the development of new pharmaceuticals, as well as to a much better understanding of the effects of gravity and weightlessness on human physiology. It is known that astronauts typically lose calcium, muscle mass and strength when in space for extended periods. Understanding of how to prevent or mitigate these effects will be essential before manned space exploration missions are undertaken. At the same time, such studies will lead to better understanding of living organisms generally, which in turn may lead to new medical discoveries.

Payloads attached to the truss will cover a wide array of scientific disciplines. Plasma physics experiments will improve our understanding of the Earth's interaction with particles coming in from space. Telescopes and other astronomy sensors will be dedicated to better understanding the structure and origins of the Universe. Still other observation payloads will be pointed toward the Earth. The station's orbit is particularly suited to making extended observations of the atmosphere in the tropics near the equator, the source of most of the Earth's weather. Since it will fly over a majority of the world's rain forests, the station will also provide data on the environmental effects of deforestation in these areas. This data, coupled with information derived from the many sensors on the polar platforms, will greatly enhance our understanding of the Earth's physical environment.

Planning is also underway to put instruments on the truss to provide data on the behaviour of large space structures such as the station. This information will allow improvement of current structural models, support future evolution of the station's configuration, and enable better design of other space structures.

Many of the station's scientific uses will require years of operation to achieve full results. Others will require only weeks or months, but even these activities can be accomplished with relative efficiency, since a succession of experiments can be supported by a single instrument. Samples can be returned to Earth for analysis, and later experiments modified in response to the findings. This flexibility and room for creativity is expected to serve as a catalyst for a wide variety of new sciences and technologies. Because of the quick turnaround in experiment results, the space station is expected to be very useful to graduate students and others involved in education.

Evolution of the space station

The space station Freedom will be the place where the United States and its international partners learn to live and work productively in space for long periods of time. Thus, the station's configuration must be able to grow and evolve as new missions and requirements are identified. For example, the station could provide increased support to the 'Mission to Planet Earth', the programme being undertaken to advance understanding of the nature of the Earth's environment. It could also function as a way station for missions to Mars or back to the Moon, or other destinations in the solar system. It could likewise serve as a base for industrialis-

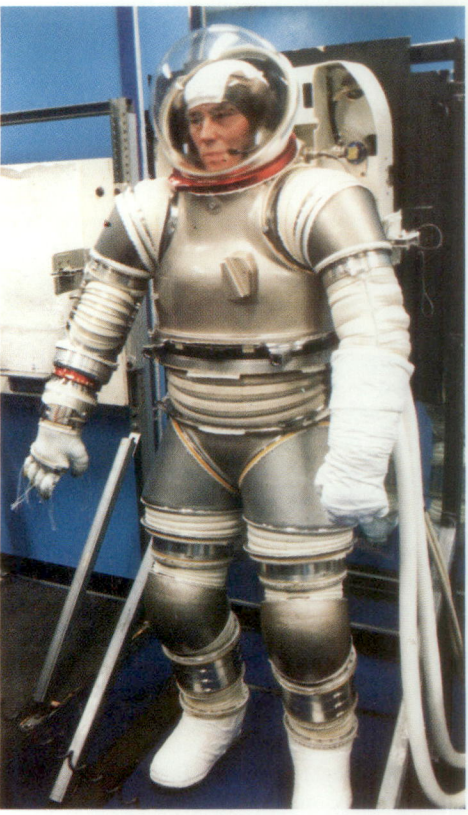

A space station astronaut's spacesuit. Astronaut Jerry Ross models a prototype spacesuit for EVA in the space station era. It has to be light, flexible and give effective protection from the hazards of space (NASA).

ing space. Such missions represent a broad range of potential paths for Freedom. They would require additions to the station's power generation capability, pressurised volume and crew. They could create the need for the development of additional co-orbiting platforms, fuel storage facilities, and satellite servicing capabilities. If we decide to pursue manned exploration of the solar system, the means to build the necessary spacecraft would have to be added to the station's basic structure. Freedom's current configuration is being designed to accommodate the addition of these new functions as well as new technologies as the need for them is identified.

The evolution of the space station will be a primary focus for international cooperation and commercial participation in the programme. The agreements signed between the United States and its partners call for coordination of all future evolution plans. Evolution will also provide the commercial sector with new opportunities to provide future space station related facilities.

The space station Freedom programme will provide many benefits, both tangible and intangible, to the United States and its partners. Not only does it provide the infrastructure to advance scientific knowledge, but the station will also enable us to explore our solar system. The programme will strengthen leadership in space and enhance international cooperation; Freedom is truly the next logical step in man's exploration of his world and the universe of which he is a part.

Margaret B. Edwards and Noah Rifkin

Man in space

Hermes

One of the European Space Agency's (ESA) objectives in the 1990s is the development of the European space plane. Its purpose will be to transport astronauts and materials between the Earth and Columbus, the European element of the international space station which is scheduled to be in use after 1995. It will also be used during maintenance of Columbus' different units and large low orbit European platforms like Eureca. The space plane will ensure Europe's independence in the space race, and enable European science and industry to be competitive in the world market. The name of the vehicle has been taken from the Greek god, Hermes, the winged messenger.

The low orbit of Hermes will be invaluable. It will benefit various scientific fields (particularly fluid physics, life sciences and materials sciences), civil applications (such as thematic observation of the Earth's surface and weather forecasting) and commercial interests (notably those producing pharmaceutical, chemical and biological materials and semiconductors).

Detailed studies are being carried out on the space plane, principally in France, under the aegis of the Centre National d'Etudes Spatiales (CNES), with ESA's guidance. The next phase will be the development of the space plane and the necessary infrastructure on Earth. The first experimental flight should take place after 1995, and it is anticipated that the plane will be in full operational use at the end of the 1990s.

Fourteen members of ESA have agreed to finance the project, under the central direction of ESA. This principally consists of guaranteeing participating countries an industrial return corresponding to the level of their financial contribution.

A provisional model has been built up of the participation of various countries in the Hermes programme, based on the political wishes of the relevant governments, during the preparatory phase. The financial involvements are as follows:

France	43·5%
West Germany	27%
Italy	12·1%
Belgium	5·8%
Spain	4·5%
The Netherlands	2·2%
Switzerland	2%
Sweden	1·3%
Ireland	0·6%
Austria	0·5%
Canada	0·45%
Denmark	0·45%
Norway	0·2%

The exact financial contributions will be decided by an industrial organisation created for the purpose before the beginning of the development phase.

All the big European space and aeronautical enterprises will be involved (for more details, see *The World Space Industry*, p. 327). In the various European countries, the companies involved include:

France	Aérospatiale, Avions Marcel Dassault and Matra
West Germany	MBB-Erno, ANT and Dornier
Italy	Aeritalia
The Netherlands	Fokker
Sweden	Saab
Spain	CASA and Sener
Canada	Spar Aerospace Limited
Belgium	ETCA
Switzerland	Contraves

The unanimous support of industrial concerns is important, as it will enable Europe to independently develop and master technologies related to the exploitation of space.

The first estimation of the cost in European Currency Units in 1987 came to 4500 million ECUs, which is roughly equivalent to $4000 million. This programme includes building two space planes, two test flights in 1998 and the development of the necesary back up systems on Earth. This estimate does not include the transport costs of the payload, maintenance operations, the facilities where the payload is prepared and controlled, operational flight tests and the programme's management costs.

Final decisions have not yet been made on how much it will cost to use Hermes during its operational phase. However, the price should include only a tiny proportion of the costs related directly to the mission – the cost of launchers and launching, maintenance of the craft between flights and its adaption to different missions.

Since Hermes has a wide variety of tasks to perform, it is essential to calculate the optimal division of work between the astronauts and the automatic systems and robots. Hermes will be able to transport crews, comprising two pilots and two other astronauts, and provisions such as water, clothes and food. It will recover materials produced in the laboratories by automatic production units and resupply fuel for the propulsion units and the raw materials for experiments. Further, it will replace or add to crews so that other experiments or essential maintenance may be carried out on the space station and orbiting platforms. Finally, it will be used in missions to repair faulty equipment and to carry out assembly or towing operations in orbit.

Hermes should carry up to 3 tonnes of payload to a circular orbit of altitude 410 kilometres inclined at 28 degrees. The space plane is also equipped with sophisticated service equipment, such as a remote control arm, a pressurised container and a wide range of tools.

Equipment on board a spacecraft is standardised, and in modular form to facilitate resupply and maintenance operations in orbit. The large platforms are composed of modules whose dimensions and mechanical and electrical interfaces are designed to optimise their reliability, and also to allow for human intervention or intervention using the remote control arm. In addition, during all operations there must be a high degree of coordination between the ground stations responsible for the different elements of Columbus and the Ariane V launcher. Examples here are coordination between the centre where the payload is prepared and integrated into Hermes, the astronaut training centre, the centres in Europe and at Kourou responsible for maintenance and integration of Hermes, the flight and mission control centres, the communication facilities with European geostationary Data and Relay Satellites, the landing and emergency landing sites and also the life-saving equipment such as ships and aircraft.

As with the American space shuttle, it is planned to use Hermes in a maintenance, servicing and intervention role. Other missions have been postulated. For example, the space plane may be used to retrieve and mend unmanned satellites, and to demonstrate new technologies or experiments on equipment installed in the cargohold or cabin. It could also maintain and service non-European orbiting space complexes, or even attempt a lifesaving rescue mission.

The Hermes project is undoubtedly ambitious but, if successful, it will provide Europe with great technological and industrial potential. The objective of the programme is to design a space plane capable of responding to the future complexity of orbital operations, including human involvement. The developers must also be responsible for increasing the flexibility of orbital operations, whilst keeping costs down to an acceptable level. Most important of all, Hermes should provide Europe with an independence in all areas of space research and applications.

Guy Valentiny

Hermes in space. Hermes will be launched by Ariane V, which will place it in an intermediate orbit. It will then perform its rendezvous and docking procedure with the Columbus orbiting laboratory at an altitude of 410 kilometres.

The docking mechanism is situated at the rear of the pressurised 25 cubic metre cargobay. The internal service operations, which take place inside the pressurised part of the composite Hermes–Columbus orbital laboratory can then begin. The external service operations are performed with the help of a remote control arm, which is carried by Hermes and can reach all the elements of the laboratory's resource module. In certain cases, the astronauts will also be involved in external operations. In the first version of the autonomous and inhabitable laboratory, Hermes will have to make at least two visits per year.

Once its task is over, Hermes will separate itself and begin its descent into the atmosphere. It will glide to the Earth's surface, land on a runway like a conventional plane – the sites which have been proposed are Istres (France) and Kourou (French Guiana) – where the fluids (fuel and the liquid oxygen and hydrogen) and the cargo will be removed. A transporter plane will then carry Hermes back to its base (David Ducros, CNES).

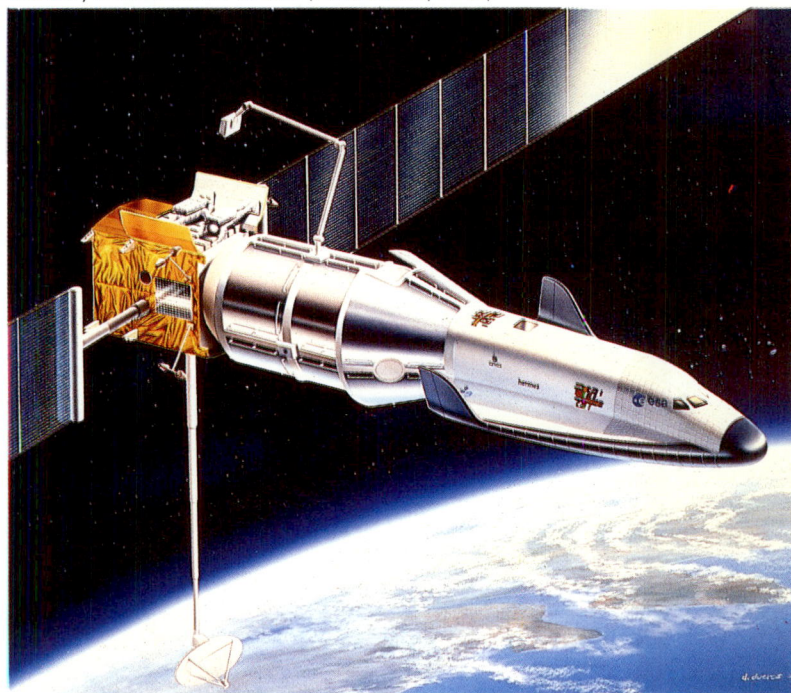

Man in space

Future space voyages

By the beginning of the twenty-first century, the world's space powers will find themselves in the position of explorers who have established a reliable bridgehead to a virgin territory, wondering what riches it contains and how best to exploit them.

The bridgeheads, installed on the edge of the cosmos, will be none other than space stations orbiting the Earth. They will be used for scientific and technical research and as support vehicles for other satellites and platforms in Earth orbit. Totally dependent on Earth, they will be served by conventional heavy lift launch vehicles which will be at least partially reusable like the space plane. The space stations will be very expensive to put into orbit, and their industrial products will be limited to those high value substances which will benefit from production under conditions of microgravity. By the year 2000, it is not unreasonable to expect that between 20 and 100 people will be living in space, professional astronauts spending periods of between three and six months there. The space stations may serve as the departure point for a manned mission to the Moon or to Mars. These expeditions, made either by a single country or by several cooperating countries, will be carried out in the same spirit as were the Apollo flights. However, they will take much longer to complete and may even involve establishing small semipermanent scientific bases.

Hopes of the advanced exploitation and colonisation of space do not rely on traditional disciplines, nor on the uncertain promises of microgravity. It may be possible to exploit another space resource, namely solar energy. Above the Earth's atmosphere, the flux of solar energy is 1·4 kilowatts per square metre. This energy could be converted into electricity and transmitted down to Earth as a microwave beam, with an overall efficiency of approaching 10%. The main problem is the size of the orbiting station. A mass of 50 000 tonnes is needed in geostationary orbit and a surface area of 50 square kilometres. To fulfil all the world's basic electricity needs, it would be necessary to construct 10 to 20 of these stations per year. However, the subsequent price of electricity could finance the whole operation. The manufacture of many such space solar power stations would inevitably require the extraction of extraterrestrial materials, from the Moon or asteroids in favourable orbits. The energy required to transport material from the Moon's surface, or from nearby asteroids, to space stations in low or geostationary orbit is much less than from the Earth's surface. However, for this to be economically viable, the level of space activities will have to be sufficient to justify constructing the necessary means to extract and process these minerals in space.

The Earth–space–Moon system could therefore become an industrial complex. Other new techniques might involve large transport vehicles, using electric propulsion systems to transfer material between terrestrial and lunar orbits or electromagnetic accelerators to make cheap launchings from the Moon's surface. Further, liquid oxygen could be extracted from lunar minerals and used as fuel for rockets travelling between the Earth and Moon or other parts of the solar system.

Permanently manned stations on the Moon could house mine workers and factory workers. These habitats could then evolve into space colonies, with workers living with their families to form an incipient space population.

During the first stages of space colonisation, man made structures could be put at the Lagrange points, gravitational equilibrium points in the Earth–Moon system. These structures would rotate to provide the artificial gravity which is considered essential for human well being in space. Such systems have to be selfsufficient. Space colonies would therefore need to be productive ecosystems, based on recycling, intensive farming and animal husbandry.

Alain Dupas

The spaceport. At the Lagrange point this spaceport could serve as the springboard for voyages to Mars and other planets (Robert McCall, US National Commission on Space, Bantam Books Inc.).

Robots assembling a space solar power station. A 5 gigawatt solar power station could consist of flat panels of silicon photocells over an area of fifty square kilometres. An antenna one kilometre in diameter fixed to the end of one solar panel would beam energy to the Earth. In the drawing above of a trellis of girders, a robot, equipped with remote control arms, itself on the end of another remotely controlled arm, is seen attaching a panel (NASA).

A toroidal space station: a future space city? In a toroidal rotating space station artificial gravity is created by spinning the structure. It contains living quarters, agricultural areas and factories, in a tube of a circular section of 130 metres in diameter. The toroid itself is 1·8 kilometres in diameter.

The space colony will benefit from the continuous free supply of solar energy, via an array of mirrors. The principal mirror, fixed above the city, will reflect light to secondary mirrors placed in the central core and in the peripheral ring. A day/night cycle will be created in the living quarters and in the agricultural areas, whilst other sections of the colony will be permanently illuminated (Chelsey Bonestell, Bonestell Space Art).

The Soviet Union

The Soviet Union has already begun work on the construction of orbital complexes, which will be permanently inhabited by about 10 men. These space complexes will be composed of up to ten units in the first instance. Mir is the first stage. In the medium term, the Soviet Union is looking into the possibilities of creating orbital cities, inhabited by about 100 people. These complexes should remain in service for several decades. They will be composed of modules which can be added, detached, or altered independently and then reattached to the space station.

Energy will be provided by a powerful solar power station. Efficient transport between different space cities will be the responsibility of 'space taxis'. The Soviets plan to build a six person version, but later versions could carry up to twelve. These transfer vehicles between two orbits will be used by crews of maintenance specialists. It will also be necessary to return to Earth a variety of products which have been produced in the different space cities. The USSR is also considering the possibility of a space depot where unmanned craft could have maintenance or repair work carried out. These installations are all designed with the same basic precept: that space exploitation should always be profitable, whilst ensuring the safety and comfort of the people involved.

In the long term, Soviet objectives are directed towards the creation of space colonies in terrestrial or lunar orbits, and towards Mars. The Soviets plan to build lunar orbiting stations, which will then be secured to the Moon's surface and used as telecommunications relay units. These orbiting stations will have crews of between 10 and 12 people. The first ones will be prefabricated on Earth and transported to low Earth orbit where they will be assembled. Interorbital tugs will place them in lunar orbit, and lunar transport craft will take them to the Moon's surface. It is simpler and more profitable to construct some laboratories and factories on the Moon, to exploit technologies which on the Earth are either impractical or very difficult. In addition, lunar soil contains many riches. Iron, titanium, aluminium and beton (a kind of concrete) are all found on the Moon, and could be used to build permanently manned bases. Inhabitable units, including agricultural and farming areas, would then be constructed.

Nikolaï Kardachev
and Marie-Rose Cukierman

The first space city, at the beginning of the twenty-first century. This drawing of an orbiting city shows spherical metallic structures clustered around a central core. All the spherical modules would be inhabited.

Vast solar panels capture the Sun's energy, and feed it to the solar power station. Attached to the axis of the structure is the immense parabolic antenna of a radiotelescope. Maintenance and repair of manned and unmanned bases in space presupposes a new means of transport which can readily serve the different orbital installations. Large cargocraft will continue to be used as Earth–space–Earth transporters. Crews will travel into space aboard lighter reusable craft, such as the one in the drawing which represents the Soviet space shuttle (A. Leonov, A. Sokolov).

The orbiting solar power station. This drawing shows a solar power station in a terrestrial orbit. The linear dimensions of the panels may be anything up to several kilometres (A. Sokolov).

The first stage in the creation of space cities. Amongst other plans, the Soviets intend to construct space cities which will be able to support up to 10 000 people. They will be about 0·5 kilometres in diameter and built of aluminium and glass. In order to achieve this objective by the end of the next century a lot of progress has to be made in the realm of space science and technology.

Stretching from the centre of the structure to the inhabited units will be solar panels feeding a central solar power station. The hemispherically shaped inhabited units will have an atmosphere which includes reconstituted oxygen, and will be rotating to create artificial gravity. The cities will be linked to enormous mirrors at the periphery of the complex. These will provide light to agricultural units (A. Sokolov).

The United States

Predicting the future of activities in space is never easy. There is the problem that programme funding from the Federal Government can never, in real terms, be relied upon to be held or increased at a consistent level. Added to this, the loss of the Challenger space shuttle and her crew has caused a deceleration in the immediate programme as the systems are reviewed and extensive extra safety factors are taken into consideration.

In 1986 a report was prepared by the United States National Commission on Space. The Commission recommended that the United States should substantially increase investment in its space technology base. This would mean a threefold rise in NASA's technology budget, which would increase this item from 2% to 6% of the total annual NASA appropriation. This growth would permit the necessary acceleration of work in many critical technical fields such as space propulsion, robotic construction, high performance materials, artificial intelligence and the processing of non-terrestrial materials.

The Commission also recommended that a special emphasis be placed on intelligent autonomous systems. Cargo trips beyond the lunar distance should be made by unmanned vehicles. The first roving vehicles on the Martian surface would be unmanned. Processing plants for propellants from the materials on asteroids, Phobos or Mars would run unattended. To support these complex, automated, remote operations, a new generation of robust, fault tolerant, and pattern recognising automata is needed. Such automata must employ new computers, sensors, and diagnostic and maintenance equipment that can avoid accidents and can repair failures. These systems must be capable of taking the same commonsense corrective actions that a human operator would take. These developments by NASA should also have broad application to US industry in the twenty-first century.

The Commission further recommended demonstration projects in seven critical technological areas:
– flight research on aerospace plane propulsion and aerodynamics
– advanced rocket vehicles
– aerobraking for orbital transfer
– long duration, closed ecosystems
– electric propulsion systems
– nuclear electric space power
– space tethers and artificial gravity

Highway to space

The two most significant contributions that the US Government could make to opening the space frontier would be to ensure the continuity of launch services and to reduce drastically transportation costs within the solar system. The current design of the space shuttle will become obsolete by the turn of the century. There will be a strong need for reliable, economical launch vehicles to provide flexible, routine access to low Earth orbit for cargo and passengers at greatly reduced cost. A complementary system will be needed for cheap transport from low Earth orbit to geostationary orbit and to the Moon. To reduce the cost of space operations at the earliest possible opportunity, the Commission recommended that three major space transport needs be met by the end of the century. These transport system requirements are:
– cargo transport to low Earth orbit
– passenger transport to and from low Earth orbit
– roundtrip transfer beyond low Earth orbit

For cargo transport, it will be necessary to have a new vehicle in operation by the year 2000 with the goal of achieving operation costs of approximately $400 per kilogram delivered to orbit.

For passenger transport, there would need to be two competing developments for the follow on to the shuttle programme. These would be either an advanced reusable rocket vehicle, or an airbreathing aerospace plane. These piloted vehicles could carry both passengers and compact cargo. Accordingly, the Commission proposed an intensive technology base programme for the late 1980s and the early 1990s in order to provide critical engineering data on both systems so that the United States could make a sound selection by 1992 at the earliest. Key technologies include computational fluid dynamics, dual fuel rocket propulsion, supersonic combustion ramjet engines, high performance materials, structures, aerodynamics, thermal shielding and launch automation.

The airbreathing hypersonic propulsion has broad potential for a number of applications in the next century including intercontinental passenger transport, low cost orbital transport and a wide range of defence missions. The Commission therefore supported a major national commitment to achieve early flight research with an experimental aerospace plane. It also believed that, in the next century, a passenger transport system should be developed and operated privately for routine non-military operations between Earth and low Earth orbit.

For destinations beyond Earth orbit, a new transfer vehicle will be required. In the coming era of fully reusable Earth to orbit vehicles, the needs of government and industry reliably to place expensive satellites beyond low Earth orbit will require new spacebased 'workhorse' vehicles designed for flexibility through modular systems. Basic components should be capable of being linked, or provided with propellant capacity, for higher energy missions. They should be capable of transporting both cargo and people, be reusable, employ aerobraking, and be adapted to in-orbit servicing, maintenance, test and repair. A transfer vehicle will be required to lift large payloads to geostationary orbit, to move payloads and crews to lunar orbit, to land payloads on the lunar surface, and to travel beyond the Earth Moon system when required. The international space station may be a critical pacing item. The transfer vehicle should be designed for return to a low Earth orbit spaceport using aerobraking.

The recommendation of the Commission that the US space station programme be kept on schedule for an operational capability by 1994 looks increasingly unlikely to be achieved. This will cause cost overruns which could further seriously delay activities in orbit and would delay the development of the spacebased robotic transfer vehicle. However, given time, the space station will happen and the *Bridge between Worlds* will be initiated.

The next three critical space facilities required are:
– an Earth spaceport
– a variable gravity research facility
– a lunar surface outpost

These facilities will be evolutionary versions of the space station. A geostationary orbit (GEO) space station is not included in the Commission's programme. It is reasonable to assume that, by the time it is required, American industry would be able to construct it with private financing and NASA's technical assistance. A GEO space station is an excellent candidate for the first major commercial servi-

Tethers in space in the 21st century. Diagonally across this picture is an Earth Spaceport with a transfer vehicle being deployed at one end by a tether and a passenger transport vehicle being deployed at the other end in a similar manner.

Tethers capitalise on the fundamental dynamics of bodies moving through central gravity and magnetic fields. They can even provide a pseudo force field in deep space where none exists. Energy and momentum can be transferred from a spacecraft being lowered on a tether below the orbital centre of mass to another spacecraft being raised on a tether above it by applying the principle of conservation of angular momentum of mass in orbit. Upon release, the lower spacecraft will fly to a lower energy level, since it is in a lower energy orbit, while the upper will fly to a higher apogee. Thus, for example, a shuttle departing from a space station can tether downward and then release, reentering the atmosphere without firing its engines, while transferring some energy and momentum to a transfer vehicle leaving the station upward bound for geostationary orbit or the Moon. The result is significant savings of propellants for both vehicles. Since the process of transfer and storage of energy and momentum are reversible, outgoing vehicles can be boosted by the slowing of incoming vehicles. This can be applied in Earth orbit, in a lunar transfer station, or even in a two piece elevator system of tethers on Phobos and Deimos that could greatly reduce requirements for propellants for the colonisation of Mars.

Variable gravity research. Bottom right is a Variable Gravity Research Facility that will be used to determine the longterm effects of weightlessness and radiation on human beings in space. Early research using the space shuttle is urgently needed to help answer some critical questions. For example, what rotation rates are comfortable or tolerable for humans experiencing normal Earth gravity simulated by rotation? What gravity level is needed to prevent the deleterious effects of less than Earth gravity? We suspect that the answer will turn out to be much less than 1g, but experiments are needed to establish how much less. If one sixth gravity is adequate, then longterm habitation on the Moon will be practicable; if one third gravity is adequate, then humans can inhabit the surface of Mars.

What are the effects of return from low g to Earth gravity? In addition to physiological studies, the variable gravity research facility should support basic research on the effects of low gravity in many scientific disciplines. Thus, it will be available for studies of physics, chemistry, and biology in space. This facility will also be needed for longterm testing of the synthetic biospheres that will support life on voyages to Mars and on the surfaces of the Moon and Mars.

The most economical way to conduct the necessary long duration experiments will probably be to rotate a habitation module connected to a counterweight at the end of a cable. In a variable gravity research facility, the rotation rate and the gravity level will be independently variable through control of the tether length and rotation rate. Earlier experiments will have established the upper limit of rotation rates that are comfortable for most people. We expect the limit to be in the range from 1 to 10 revolutions per minute (Robert McCall).

Space science objectives for the year 2000

- identification of the 'missing' matter that makes up 90% of the mass of the Universe
- detection of gravitational waves
- discovery of source of huge energies in exploding galaxies
- image of the immediate surroundings of a black hole at the centre of our galaxy, the 'Milky Way'
- discovery of amino acids in the Uranian ocean
- recovery of supernova debris from comet ice
- identification of methane volcanoes on Pluto
- discovery of first planet outside the solar system
- detection of signal from extraterrestrial intelligence
- monthly solar flare predictions accurate to within hours
- understanding of links between solar activity and the Earth's environment
- image of the Earth's entire radiation belt
- monthly hurricane predictions accurate to within 12 hours and 170 kilometres
- accurate predictions of earthquakes to within 24 hours and 80 kilometres
- operation for a year within a synthetic biosphere
- bone thinning in astronauts halted with treatment applicable to people on Earth
- production of perfect gallium arsenide crystals in space station
- thirty day weather forecasts now 95% accurate
- exploration of Mars and Venus

ces venture in space. An orbital manoeuvring vehicle (OMV, a 'space harbour tug') will be required by the time that the space station comes into being, and is already being developed by NASA. The variable gravity research facility is required within the next 20 years in order to understand the required artificial gravity levels necessary for long duration flights well in advance of human travel to Mars. As the programme continues to evolve during the twenty-first century, there will be an evolutionary growth of the initial space station into the first spaceport. Future spaceports will be developed beyond Earth orbit, for example at the L1 Lagrangian point, in lunar orbit, and eventually in orbit around Mars. Outposts may be established on the surface of the Moon as well as on Mars, and perhaps on its two moons.

US National Commission on Space

© *Pioneering the Space Frontier*, Report of the US National Commission on Space, Bantam Books, New York 1986

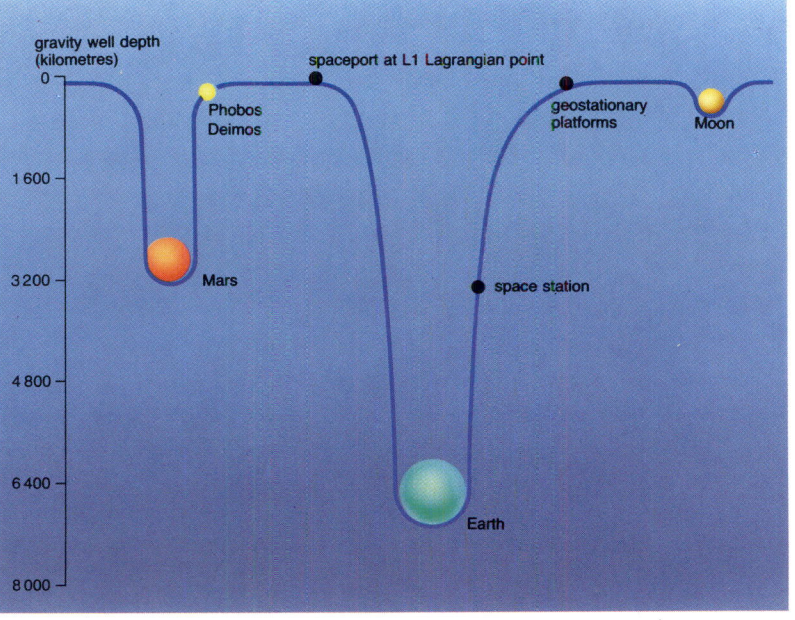

The Earth's gravity well. To lift payloads in the Earth's gravitational field and place them in orbit, we must expend energy. This is first generated as the energy of motion – hence the great speeds (11 kilometres per second) that rockets must attain. As rockets coast upwards after firing, their energy of motion converts, according to Newton's laws, to the energy of height. In graphic terms, to lift a payload entirely free of the Earth's gravitational pull, we must spend as much energy as if we were to haul that payload against the full force of gravity that we feel on Earth to a height of 6400 kilometres. To reach the nearer goal of low Earth orbit, where rockets and their payloads achieve a balancing act, skimming above the Earth's atmosphere, we must spend about half as much energy. This is still equivalent to climbing a mountain 3200 kilometres high. Once in 'free space', the region far from the planets and their moons, we can travel many thousands of kilometres for only a small expenditure of energy. There exist five points in the Earth Moon system where spaceports can be placed without expending a great deal of energy. These are the so called Lagrangian points, points free of any gravitational attraction to the Earth. Three are located on the lunar orbit, at 60, 180 and 300 degrees from the Earth Moon axis. Two are on the Earth Moon axis, one between the Earth and the Moon and the other beyond the Moon. Certain points (L_1, L_2, L_3) will be preferred stopover points on the Earth Moon route (US National Commission on Space).

Space highways. The diagram on the right shows the space transport system of the future clearly divided into two domains. The first concerns connections between the Earth and the space stations or spaceports in low Earth orbit, which consist of hypersonic aircraft or heavy reusable launchers. The second plies routes between low orbits and higher orbits (geostationary, lunar, etc.) where the spaceports, variable gravity research laboratories and lunar or martian bases are located. This will be done by orbital transfer vehicles capable of returning to their original space base. For the return trip, the transfer vehicles could 'aerobrake' by friction with the upper layers of the atmosphere (US National Commission on Space).

Earth orbiting spaceport (lower right). In the foreground is an aerospace plane and the Earth spaceport. The spaceport is receiving cargo from a cargo transport vehicle (lower lefthand corner). In the background, a two stage transfer vehicle is returning to the Earth spaceport from the Moon (Robert McCall).

Two transfer vehicles aerobraking. In the drawing below, two transfer vehicles with ceramic heat shields slow down before final manoeuvres to join up with their port of call station. Aerobraking like this provides an impulse manoeuvre that gains some 2 kilometres per second on return from geostationary orbit (Robert McCall).

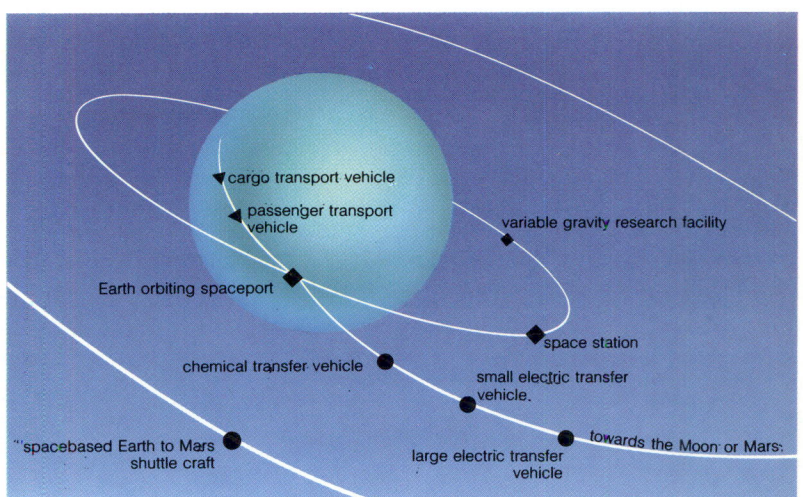

Future of transport in the solar system. The chart on the right outlines the phased approach to achieving low cost access to the solar system. The *Highway to Space* starts with economical new cargo and passenger transport vehicles, adding a transfer vehicle for destinations beyond low Earth orbit. These three systems should become operational in conjunction with an orbital spaceport by the end of this century.

In the following five years, the *Bridge between Worlds* would support initial robotic lunar surface operations, followed by a permanent outpost to support astronaut operations.

In ten more years, the space bridge would be extended out to Mars for detailed robotic exploration followed by a Mars outpost for human activity. To achieve this the US National Commission on Space recommended that the phased space transport network outlined in the chart be developed and placed in operation. It starts with simple components, but evolves over time into a system of spaceports, bases and connecting transport systems that will open the space frontier for large scale exploration, science and the initiation of economic development. Resources will be utilised where they are found to minimise the need for them to be transported from Earth (US National Commission on Space).

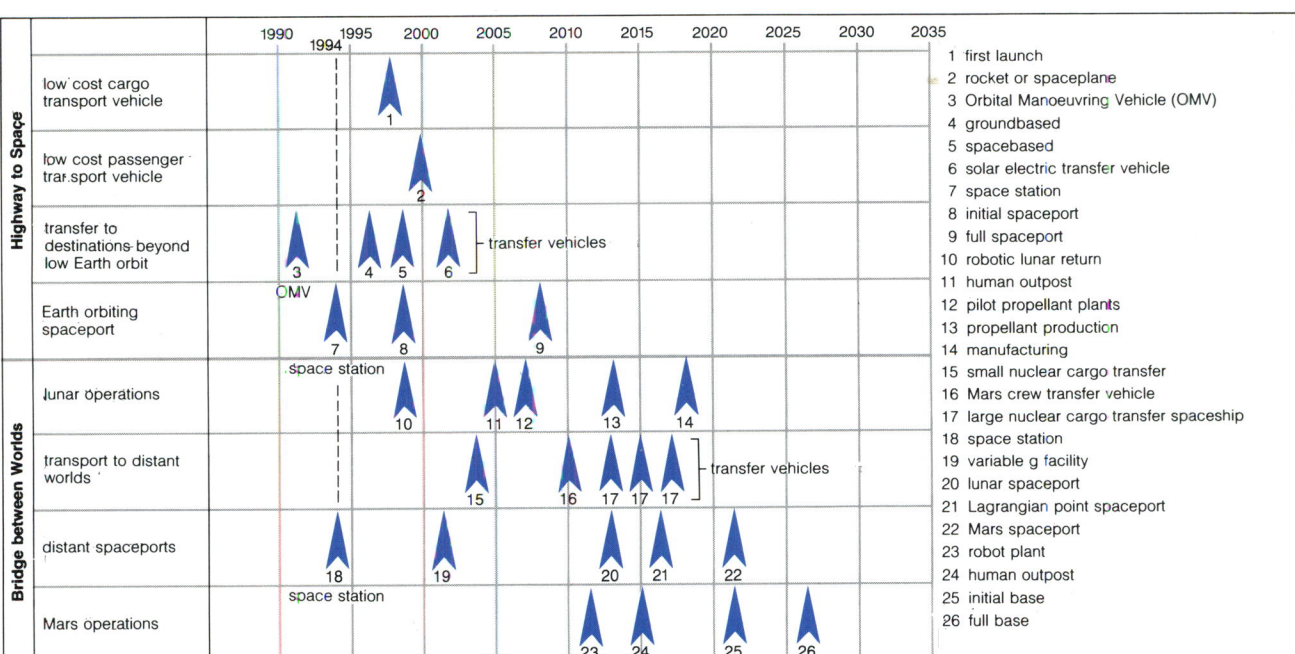

1 first launch
2 rocket or spaceplane
3 Orbital Manoeuvring Vehicle (OMV)
4 groundbased
5 spacebased
6 solar electric transfer vehicle
7 space station
8 initial spaceport
9 full spaceport
10 robotic lunar return
11 human outpost
12 pilot propellant plants
13 propellant production
14 manufacturing
15 small nuclear cargo transfer
16 Mars crew transfer vehicle
17 large nuclear cargo transfer spaceship
18 space station
19 variable g facility
20 lunar spaceport
21 Lagrangian point spaceport
22 Mars spaceport
23 robot plant
24 human outpost
25 initial base
26 full base

Industry and space

The main space laboratories

Man's access to space in the past twenty years has led to new developments in several research areas, including studies of the Universe, exploration of the solar system and analysis of phenomena in microgravity. Other research, specifically linked to man's presence in space, has led to the creation of new disciplines such as space biology and physiology. Research into the effects of microgravity is essential if we intend to have permanently manned space stations. Many laboratories carry out experiments in this field (*Life sciences in microgravity* pp. 284–9, *Materials sciences* pp. 290–5, and *The world space industry*, pp. 326–37).

Personnel at scientific and industrial laboratories are faced with a large number of constraints when they are designing experiments to be sent into space. These include the conditions to which instruments are subjected, such as the space vacuum, thermal variations in orbit, and the very severe mechanical forces and vibrations during launch. Researchers are always trying to improve their equipment, sub-systems and components which all have to be thoroughly tested for the space environment. Experiments are generally run by remote control, and data are received by telemetry.

The experiments have to be designed to minimise the possibility of failure. The necessity of carrying out repair work in orbit will be one of the economic problems facing future space stations.

The mirror for an ultraviolet astronomy telescope. This mirror, which has a diameter of 1 metre, was constructed for an astronomy experiment in the far ultraviolet. Its surface is coated with iridium, which is highly reflecting at short wavelengths.

The experiment was a joint project between the University of Tübingen in West Germany and the Space Science Laboratory at the University of California at Berkeley. It was launched on board one of NASA's Aries rockets from White Sands in New Mexico (University of Tübingen).

Research subject	Main laboratories	Examples of cooperation
External geophysics, ocean and atmospheric studies, X ray astronomy, planetology	ISAS (Institute of Space and Astronautical Science), Tokyo	Canada, ESA (Spacelab), USA, Great Britain
External geophysics	Radiowave research laboratory, Tokyo, University of Rikkyo, University of Tamagawa, University of Tokyo	
External geophysics, ocean and atmospheric studies, X ray and infrared astronomy	University of Nagoya	USA, Great Britain
External geophysics, X ray astronomy	Electronics Department, University of Kyoto	USA, Great Britain
External geophysics, planetology, ocean and atmospheric studies	Tohoku University, University of Tokyo	
Ocean and atmospheric studies, X ray astronomy	University of Rikkyo	USA, Great Britain
Ocean and atmospheric studies	University of Tsukuba, Water Research Institute, University of Nagoya, University of Tokyo	
X ray astronomy	University of Osaka, University of Utsunomiya, University of Tokyo	
Cosmic ray astronomy	University of Kobe, Institute of Cosmic Ray Research, Tokyo	
Planetology	Geophysical Research Laboratory, Tokai	

Some Japanese laboratories involved in space research (CNES)

Some Soviet laboratories involved in space research (CNES)

Research subject	Main laboratories	Examples of cooperation
External geophysics, gamma ray, X ray and infrared astronomy, planetology, solar studies	Institute of Space Research of the Academy of Sciences (IKI), Moscow	France (Vega, Phobos, Granat, Gamma 1, Aureol 3, Interball), Great Britain, Holland, West Germany (Kvant), Switzerland (Phobos), Sweden (Vega, Interball, Phobos)
Planetology	Chemical Institutes, Vernadsky	Finland (Phobos, Interball), Austria (Phobos, Vega), Poland, Hungary, East Germany, Czechoslovakia, Bulgaria, France (Phobos, Vega)
External geophysics	Izmiran Institute of Radiowave Propagation and Terrestrial Magnetism, Apatity Institute of Polar Geophysics	Bulgaria, Hungary, Poland, Czechoslovakia, France
Ocean and atmospheric studies	Hydrometeorological Service	France (Meteor)
Ultraviolet and visible astronomy	Observatories in the Crimea and Burakan	France, Switzerland
X ray astronomy, space geodesy, solar studies	Lebedev Institute, Academy of Sciences	Poland, Czechoslovakia, France
X ray and gamma ray astronomy	Moscow Institute of Physics and Engineering	France (Gamma 1)
Gamma ray astronomy	Leningrad Institute of Physics and Technology, Nuclear Physics Research Institute, University of Moscow	Poland, France

Space research has been a feature of many scientific institutes since the beginning of the 1960s. Then many universities specialising in astronomy and all types of geophysics realised the enormous contribution which studies from space would bring to their fields, and so diversified their studies to embrace space experiments. Some nations even went so far as to create laboratories and institutes specifically for the purpose.

For an experiment to be carried out in space at all, the high initial investment must be made. Industrial subcontracts are let and appropriate management methods used, and the teams involved must have access to substantial human and material resources.

The USA, the USSR and Japan have the means to support space exploration by providing space vehicles or even interplanetary probes to their space laboratories. The other nations of the world can become involved by taking part in joint missions. As for European laboratories, they rely on the European Space Agency (ESA) which gives space research a higher priority than space exploration, and therefore spends most of its funds in this area.

The USA (p. 321), USSR and Japan have a lot of money available for space research and so support projects working in most areas. The USSR and the other communist countries support space research via their science academies. Important space programmes are usually carried out in multi-discipline space research institutes and a large amount of money is placed at their disposal. Japan, with no specific geographic or political alliances, organises its space budget so as to spend a large part of it on building better and better satellites of all types.

Beyond this, a large number of institutes and university establishments are involved in carrying out experiments and interpreting data. European countries, whose priorities are split between science and applications, have the opportunity to send experiments into space either as part of an ESA programme or as part of a bilateral agreement, usually with the USA or the USSR. European countries which do not have large space budgets tend to specialise in one scientific area. It is only the larger European nations – France, Great Britain and West Germany, where a significant fraction of the Gross National Product (GNP) is allocated to space research – that are able to diversify.

Space research and industry

In space research scientists try to measure phenomena which are difficult to observe, using methods at the cutting edge of advanced technology. Fundamental research pushes to the extremes. For example, ultraviolet or gamma ray detectors measure individual photons, but their performance is limited by the amount of noise present. Thus, whilst achieving the highest performance possible, they are far from perfect. Advanced detectors or other new instruments developed for space research purposes may find applications in other areas of industry. This is why many industries are involved in space programmes. Modern techniques used by space scientists such as sophisticated logic and data systems or ultrasensitive stellar sensors have unquestionably helped to improve other technologies.

Geneviève Debouzy

Country	Research subject	Main laboratories	Examples of cooperation
France	external geophysics; X ray, gamma ray and infrared astronomy; planetology	Centre of Space Radiation Studies (CSER), Toulouse	ESA (GEOS, ISEE 1 and 2, Ulysses, Giotto, ISO); USSR (Granat, Gamma 1, Aureol 3, Prognoz, the Interball programme)
	external geophysics; planetology	Laboratory of Physics and Chemistry of the Environment (LPCE), Orléans	ESA (Spacelab); Sweden (Viking); USSR (Aureol 3, Interball, Vega, Phobos)
	external geophysics; ocean and atmospheric studies	Environmental Physics Research Centre (CRPE), Issy-les-Moulineaux, Saint-Maur-des-Fossés	Great Britain (ATRS); ESA (GEOS, Giotto); Sweden (Viking); USSR (Aureol 3, Interball)
	infrared, visible and UV astronomy; planetology	Space Astronomy Laboratory (LAS), Marseille	Great Britain; USSR (observatory in Crimea); ESA (ISO)
	infrared, cosmic ray and gamma ray astronomy	Astrophysical Service (CEA), Saclay	ESA (Ulysses, ISO); USA (HEAO 3); USSR (Granat, Gamma 1)
	infrared astronomy; solar studies; planetology	Stellar and Planetary Physics Laboratory (LPSP), Verrières-le-Buisson	ESA (Giotto); USSR (Vega, Phobos); USA (OSO 8)
	external geophysics; planetology; infrared and UV astronomy	Space Research Laboratory, Paris-Meudon Observatory	ESA (ISEE, Ulysses, ISO); USSR (Vega, Phobos)
	ocean and atmospheric studies; planetology	Aeronomy Service, Verrières-le-Buisson	ESA (Giotto); USA (UARS); Canada; USSR (Vega, Phobos)
	geodesy	Space Geodesy Research Group (GRGS), Toulouse-Grasse	ESA (Hipparcos)
	ocean and atmospheric studies	Laboratory for Dynamical Meteorology, Palaiseau	USSR (Meteor)
Great Britain	external geophysics; ocean and atmospheric studies; X ray, infrared, visible and UV astronomy; solar studies; planetology	Rutherford Appleton Laboratory (RAL); Mullard Space Science Laboratory (MSSL), London	ESA (ERS 1, Exosat, Giotto, ISO, Spacelab); USA (HST, IRAS); Japan (Astro C); West Germany (AMPTE, Rosat); Sweden (Viking)
	external geophysics; planetology	University of Sussex; Imperial College, London	West Germany (AMPTE); ESA (Ulysses, Giotto)
	ocean and atmospheric studies	University of Oxford; National Meteorological Office; National Physical Laboratory; University College of Wales, Aberystwyth	ESA (ERS 1, Eureca); USA (UARS)
	ocean and atmospheric studies; visible and UV astronomy	Queen's University, Belfast	ESA (IUE)
	space geodesy	University of Aston; Royal Aircraft Establishment	
	space geodesy; visible and UV astronomy	Royal Greenwich Observatory	ESA (IUE)
	X ray, visible and UV astronomy	University of Birmingham	ESA (Exosat, IUE); West Germany (Rosat); USSR (Kvant)
	X ray astronomy	University of Leicester; Imperial College, London	Japan (Astro C)
	infrared, visible and UV astronomy	Royal Observatory, Edinburgh	ESA (IUE, ISO); USA; Holland (IRAS)
	gamma and cosmic ray astronomy	University of Southampton; University of Bristol	Italy (balloons)
	infrared astronomy	Queen Mary College; University College, London	ESA (ISO)
Italy	external geophysics; cosmic, gamma, X ray and infrared astronomy	CNR, Frascati	ESA (GEOS, ISEE, Exosat, ISO); Great Britain
	space geodesy; ocean and atmospheric studies; infrared astronomy	CNR, Florence	
	space geodesy	Geophysics Institute, Trieste	
	visible and UV astronomy	Systems Studies Centre, Turin	ESA (Hipparcos)
	X ray astronomy	University of Palermo	ESA (Exosat); France
	cosmic, gamma and X ray astronomy	CNR, Milan	Great Britain
	ocean and atmospheric studies; cosmic, gamma, X ray and infrared astronomy	CNR, Bologna	Great Britain; ESA (ISO)
The Netherlands	external geophysics; X and gamma ray astronomy; planetology	ESTEC (European Space Technology Centre), Noordwijk	ESA (GEOS, Exosat); USA (GRO); USSR (Salyut, Kvant)
	space geodesy	Space Geodesy Observatory, Kootwijk	
	cosmic and gamma ray, UV, visible and infrared astronomy; solar studies	Space Research Organisation Netherlands (SRON), Utrecht	ESA (Hipparcos, Ulysses, IRAS, ISO, Eureca); USSR (Kvant)
	cosmic and gamma ray astronomy	SRON, Leiden	USA; West Germany (GRO)
	infrared astronomy	SRON, Groningen	ESA (IRAS, ISO)
West Germany	ocean and atmospheric studies; planetology	Cologne Meteorological and Geophysical Institute; University of Wuppertal; Bonn Institute of Astrophysics	ESA (Giotto); USA (Voyager, Galileo)
	ocean and atmospheric studies	Meteorological Institutes at the Universities of Berlin and Munich; Max-Planck Institute, Heidelberg	
	external geophysics; UV, visible, infrared and X, gamma and cosmic ray astronomy; planetology	Institute of Extraterrestrial Physics and Astrophysics at the Max-Planck Institute, Munich	Great Britain (AMPTE); ESA (Exosat, ISO, Ulysses); NASA (Gamma Ray Observatory, Galileo)
	infrared, visible and UV astronomy	Institute of Astronomy, Heidelberg	ESA (IUE)
	X ray, visible and UV astronomy	Institute of Astronomy, Tübingen	ESA (IUE, Exosat); USSR (Kvant)
	visible and UV astronomy	Observatories at Hamburg and Bonn	ESA (Hipparcos, IUE)
	cosmic and gamma ray astronomy	University of Siegen	
	solar studies; planetology	University of Freiburg	ESA (Giotto)
	planetology	Max-Planck Institute, Heidelberg; Physics and Astronomy Faculty, Bochum; Institute of High Frequency and Very High Frequency Techniques, Bochum	ESA (Giotto); NASA (Galileo)
	external geophysics; UV and visible astronomy; planetology	Brunswick Institute of Meteorology and Geophysics	USA (Galileo); Great Britain (AMPTE)
	external geophysics; gamma and cosmic ray astronomy; planetology	Institute for Aeronomy, Max-Planck Institute, Lindau	ESA (Spacelab, Ulysses, Giotto); NASA (Galileo)
	external geophysics; cosmic radiation; planetology	Institute of Applied Nuclear Science, Kiel	ESA (ISSE, Ulysses); NASA (Galileo)

Some European laboratories involved in space research. All these countries are members of ESA, which explains why this table contains many references to ESA's programmes (CNES)

Country	Research subjects	Main laboratories	Examples of cooperation
Argentina	external geophysics	Physics department at the Space Centre, San Miguel	
	ocean and atmospheric studies	Space Centre, San Miguel	
	infrared astronomy	Institute of Astronomy and Space Physics (IAFE)	
	solar studies	(IAFE)	
Austria*	external geophysics; planetology	Institute of Space Research, Austrian Academy of Sciences; Institute of Communication and Wave Propagation, Technical University, Graz; Research Centre, Graz	ESA (Spacelab); Norway (University of Bergen); USSR (Phobos)
	space geodesy	Department of Satellite Geodesy	
	external geophysics; ocean and atmospheric studies	Technical University, Graz	
Belgium*	ocean and atmospheric studies	Institute of Space Aeronomy, Brussels; Institute of Astrophysics, Liège; Royal Meteorological Institute of Belgium	ESA, France (Spacelab); Great Britain
	space geodesy	Royal Observatory, Belgium	
	visible and UV astronomy; planetology	Institute of Astrophysics, Liège	ESA (Hipparcos, Giotto)
Brazil	external geophysics	National Institute of Space Research (INPE)	USA
	space geodesy	INPE	
	gamma ray astronomy	INPE	France
Canada	external geophysics; astronomy	Space science group, University of Calgary; Hertzberg Institute of Astrophysics; National Research Council (NRC)	Sweden (Viking); Japan (Exos D)
	external geophysics	University of Victoria; Radioscience Centre, Western University, Ontario	
	external geophysics; ocean and atmospheric studies	University of Saskatchewan	
	ocean and atmospheric studies	University of York	USA; France (UARS)
	space geodesy	Memorial University of Newfoundland	
Denmark*	external geophysics	Danish Space Research Institute (DSRI), Lyngby; Danish Meteorological Institute, Copenhagen	ESA (GEOS); Sweden (Viking)
	space geodesy	Institute of Geodesy	
	visible and UV astronomy	Observatory of the University of Copenhagen	ESA (Hipparcos); West Germany
	cosmic and gamma ray astronomy	DSRI, Lyngby	ESA (Eureca); France; USA (HEAO 3)
Spain*	ocean and atmospheric studies	Meteorological and neutral atmosphere group, CONIE (Comisión National de Investigacion del Espacio); Institute of Astrophysics, Andalusia	
	astronomy	Department of Space and Earth Physics, University of Barcelona	
	astronomy	ground station, Villafranca	ESA (IUE)
	cosmic and gamma ray astronomy	Corpuscular Physics Laboratory, Barcelona	
Finland*	external geophysics; planetology	Finnish Meteorological Institute, Oulu	Sweden (Viking); USSR (Phobos, Interball)
	external geophysics	Physics Department, University of Oulu	Sweden (Viking)
	space geodesy	Finnish Institute of Geodesy	
India	external geophysics; ocean and atmospheric studies	Physical Research Laboratory, Ahmedabad	
	space geodesy	Physical Research Laboratory, Geodesic and Research Branch of the Survey of India	
	cosmic, gamma and X ray astronomy	Tata Institute of Fundamental Research, Bombay	Canada; USSR
	ocean and atmospheric studies	Vikram Sarabhai Space Centre, Trivandrum; Andhra (Waltair) University; Indian Institute of Tropical Meteorology	
Norway*	external geophysics	Physics Laboratory, University of Bergen; Observatory at the University of Tromsø; Electronics Division of the National Defence Research Establishment	USA; Sweden (Viking); Canada; ESA (Spacelab)
	solar studies; external geophysics	Institute of Astrophysics, University of Oslo	Canada; USA (NRL)
Sweden*	external geophysics	Institute of Geophysics, Kiruna; Royal Institute of Technology, Stockholm; Ionospheric Observatory, Uppsala	USSR (Prognoz, Interball, Phobos); ESA (Ulysses, Giotto)
	ocean and atmospheric studies	Department of Meteorology, University of Stockholm	Canada; Great Britain; West Germany
	space geodesy; planetology	Space Observatory, Onsala	USSR (Vega)
	visible and UV astronomy; planetology	Lund Observatory	ESA (Hipparcos, Giotto); West Germany; NASA (Galileo)
	infrared, visible and UV astronomy	Stockholm Observatory	ESA (Hipparcos, ISO)
Switzerland*	external geophysics; ocean and atmospheric studies	Institute of Physics, University of Bern	USA (ISEE 3)
	ocean and atmospheric studies; visible and UV astronomy	Geneva Observatory	USSR (Observatories in Crimea and Armenia)
	space geodesy	Institute of Astronomy, University of Bern	
	solar studies	Davos Observatory; Zurich Institute of Astronomy	USSR (Phobos)

A worldwide sample of space research laboratories. The countries marked with an asterisk are members of the European Space Agency. This explains why ESA often appears in the fourth column

The United States

Throughout the United States there are numerous space research laboratories which have been created under different circumstances and have different objectives. In many instances the laboratories are those of individual Principal Investigators (PIs) who have submitted proposals in response to NASA's announcements of opportunity, programme solicitations, etc., and who have been competitively selected to undertake major research projects. One such example would be the development and fabrication of the faint object spectrograph, to be used on the space telescope at the University of California at San Diego. Another class of laboratory would include those institutes established to pursue focused research projects. Examples here would include the Lunar and Planetary Institute in Houston, Texas, and the Space Telescope Science Institute in Baltimore, Maryland.

There can be a similar arrangement at a university, where several PIs are supported for research projects which are closely related. Examples would include the space processing portion of the Materials Processing Center at the Massachusetts Institute of Technology. Other government agencies, such as the National Science Foundation and the Department of Defense through its related agencies such as DARPA, AFOSR, etc., sponsor individual investigators and institutes in both the basic and the applied space sciences and technology.

Recently, however, space research institutes have been established with a unique (at least in the context of government supported research) objective in mind. Rather than conducting contract research to support the objectives of the government agency directly, these new institutes have been established to allow the private sector to direct the activities. The remainder of this section discusses these new institutes, known as Centers for the Commercial Development of Space or CCDS.

Centers for the Commercial Development of Space

The CCDS are funded by NASA, but with substantial corporate and state resources also. The overall objective of the CCDS is to stimulate capital investment in space by US industry. The table on this page summarises the philosophy of operation of the CCDS and gives, for comparison, the equivalent philosophy of projects sponsored by the Office of Space Science and Applications (OSSA). The research projects supported by OSSA are reviewed by scientists expert in the field – that is the scientific peer review process. There are significant differences between the two classes of research programmes.

The CCDS programme was one of the first initiatives undertaken by NASA's Office of Commercial Programs (OCP). NASA has provided initial funding for five years, after which the Centers are expected to be self sustaining. Two programme solicitations were released in 1985 and 1986, and 46 proposals were collectively received. Nine CCDS were selected for establishment; these are listed in the table at the top of p. 322.

In 1987, a third program solicitation occurred to which there were 26 responses. Of these, seven were selected, as shown in the lower table on p. 322.

There are many research disciplines represented in the CCDS. While over half are in microgravity materials processing, such as biotechnology, metal alloy solidification, and crystal growth, there are substantial activities in other commercially promising fields such as remote sensing and the study of materials in the space environment.

Two of the first CCDS had spaceflight programmes before their establishment as a CCDS and were fortunate to obtain results prior to the Challenger tragedy. The University of Alabama at Huntsville flew four experiments using a Get Away Special (GAS) Canister on shuttle flight 61 C in January 1986. An earlier version of this activity, an atomic oxygen experiment, was positioned in the aft section of the cargo bay during the eighth shuttle flight. The experiments were of a preliminary nature, designed with a view to checking hardware operations for the various experiments.

Item	Centers for the Commercial Development of Space (CCDS)	Office of Space Science and Applications (OSSA)
Objective	research towards commercially viable space projects	innovative space research and development
Funding and review process	'leveraging' of NASA funds with corporate and other (non-NASA) resources, and technical review of projects	NASA funding, and scientific peer review
Beneficiary	industry	scientific community, predominantly academics
Results	built upon the industrially useful database	builds up the fundamental and technical databases

Comparison between CCDS and OSSA (NASA)

Preparing an experiment on the growth of crystal proteins. This experiment was installed in a unit on the mid deck of the space shuttle during the 61 C flight in January 1986. The astronaut is examining the phials of crystals obtained by gas diffusion (NASA).

The atomic oxygen experiment. This experiment was performed by the University of Alabama on shuttle flight STS 8, launched on 8 August 1983 (NASA).

NASA's Lewis Research Center. This aerial view shows the Lewis Research Center at Cleveland, Ohio. This centre is for NASA's use and does not form part of OSSA or of CCDS (NASA).

Living with space

The University of Alabama group at Birmingham also conducted some experiments on shuttle flights. These experiments, which involved the growth of protein crystals, only required low power so they could be performed in the shuttle mid deck. The photograph on the previous page shows an astronaut working on the experimental package on shuttle flight 61 C. The crystals obtained were found to be larger and of a higher quality than those obtained under similar processing conditions on Earth.

Members of two CCDS, those at the University of Houston and at the University of Alabama at Huntsville, have also been involved in the discovery of a material that is superconducting at temperatures above those of liquid nitrogen.

It is too early to determine the effectiveness of the CCDS in terms of contributing to the ultimate objective, namely that of 'stimulating capital investment in space'. It is even premature to judge their technical accomplishments in terms of the quality of research and its relevance to corporate interests.

Nevertheless, the CCDS have had success in capturing the interests of American industry, especially the non-aerospace industry. The CCDS are already providing an invaluable service to NASA in generating possible industrial requirements for future projects such as the space station. To date, the level of activity and energy demonstrated by the individual CCDS programmes clearly suggests that the majority will be successful in creating an industrial constituency for furthering commercial space activities.

William A. Oran

CCDS	Research areas	Corporate affiliates
Battelle Laboratories, Columbus, Ohio Director: Frank Jelinek	catalyst processing, crystal growth, multiphase material processing in glasses and ceramics	Rockwell, Lockheed, General Electric, E.I. DuPont & Co., Amoco, Hercules, PPG Industries
Vanderbilt University, Nashville, Tennessee Director: Robert Bayuzick	containerless processing of aluminium, nickel, niobium, and other alloys, directional solidification of aluminium and immiscible alloys, alloy casting	Alcoa, Armco, Cabot, Engelhard, General Electric, General Motors, GTE, Lockheed, Special Metal, Teledyne Wah Chang
Institute for Technology Development, Hancock County, Mississippi Director: Carl Schueler	remote sensing of renewable resources, hazard planning with remote sensing	Geo Information Services, Geo Decisions Inc., Synercom, Hutson Chemical
University of Alabama, Huntsville Director: Charles Lundquist	vapour crystal growth, organic crystal growth, effect of the space environment on materials, electrodeposition, polymer processing	Boeing, Celanese, Deere and Co., Martin Marietta, McDonnell Douglas, Teledyne Brown, Wyle Labs.
University of Alabama, Birmingham Director: Charles Bugg	protein crystal growth	Schering, Proctor and Gamble, Dow, E.I. DuPont de NeMours & Co., Upjohn, Merck Pharm., McDonnell Douglas
University of Wisconsin, Madison Director: John Bollinger	robotic and autosystems, robot manipulator system, automatic grip research	Astronautics, Automated Systems, Delco, Johnson Controls, Madison Kipp, Phyto Farms, Pierson Products, Silicon Sensors, Snap on Tools, Sundstrand Corps.
University of Texas, Houston Director: C. W. Chu	epitaxy of a molecular beam using the slipstream vacuum of a spacecraft	Rockwell, AT&T, Perkin Elmer, Wyle Labs.
University of Ohio, Columbus Director: Ivan Mueller	satellite mapping in real time	Destek, General Electric, Synercom, Ohio Farm Bureau, Gas Research Institute
Clarkson Postdam University, New York Director: William Wilcox	liquid and vapour phase crystal growth, research into theoretical models of crystal growth	Barnes Engineering, Boeing, Grummann, Rockwell, Spectrum Development, Dantec Electronics, Westinghouse

Centers for the commercial development of space (NASA)

New CCDS selected since spring 1987

CCDS	Research areas
Auburn University	space power
Texas A&M University	space power
University of Tennessee	space propulsion
Case Western Reserve University	materials and structures in space
University of Colorado	biotechnology
Pennsylvania State University	life processes in space
University of Michigan	automation and robotics

The Langley Research Center at Hampton, Virginia. Researchers are constructing a trellis of graphite-epoxy resin rods using a mobile workunit. This system will eventually be used by two astronauts in spacesuits to construct large structures in space.

An astronaut will be positioned on either side of the workunit, which will move, acting like a space assembly line. It will be installed either in the shuttle's cargo bay or nearby as an independent payload. This mock-up is being used to test the astronauts' ability to build complicated large structures in space using the simplest possible devices (NASA).

Money spent on microgravity research (BMFT)

	1982	1983	1984	1985	1986	est 1987
National Aeronautics and Space Administration (NASA) Bureau of science and space applications (millions of dollars)[1]:						
life sciences		56	58	62	66	75
materials research in space		22	24	27	31	44
European Space Agency (ESA) Microgravity research programme (life sciences and materials sciences) Eleven countries involved: Belgium, Denmark, France, Italy, the Netherlands, Norway, United Kingdom, West Germany, Spain, Sweden, Switzerland (millions of ECUs)[2]:						
phase 1	6	13	16	12	1	1
phase 2	—	—	—	10	31	29
phase 3 (beginning in 1989)	—	—	—	—	—	5
Bundesministerium für Forschung und Technologie (BMFT) Microgravity research programme (life sciences and materials science) (millions of DMs):						
use of space laboratories[1]	35	38	40	44	46	78
launch costs	24	35	61	62	36	39
Centre national d'études spatiales (CNES) Microgravity research programme (millions of francs)[3]		18	25	31	37	60

1 The costs include preparing the experiments on Earth, performing them in space, the necessary materials and equipment, the training and organisation of astronauts, health measures in flight and finally processing the results; launch costs are not included.
2 These costs include the construction of the experimental materials and part of the launch but not the scientific preparation of the experiments in laboratories.
3 These costs include preparing the experiments on Earth and the development and construction of experimental materials; launch costs are not included.

322

Industry and space

Technological spinoff

In the 30 years of its existence, the US National Aeronautics and Space Administration (NASA) has provided the people of the world with closeup views of the Moon and the planets beyond. Technological advances in aeronautical design, materials fabrication and electronic microminiaturisation have led to unsurpassed scientific breakthroughs in space. In the Space Act of 1958 the US Congress also made NASA responsible for providing 'the widest practicable and appropriate dissemination of information concerning its activities and results thereof'. As a result, NASA has transferred its aerospace technology to an estimated 30 000 'spinoff' applications in fields as diverse as electronics, materials, biomedicine and computer science.

NASA actively facilitates such a 'technology transfer process' by disseminating a wide variety of information which heightens the awareness of potential users to the latest NASA technologies. In addition, NASA maintains a geographically distributed network of centres to assist industrial and government clients. In its applications engineering programme, NASA collaborates with industry, government agencies, universities, and other public sector and private organisations to reengineer existing aerospace technologies to help solve problems encountered on Earth.

NASA has formalised these activities in its Technology Utilization Program. Staff located at each of NASA's nine centres help coordinate many of the programme's activities.

NASA also supports nine Industrial Applications Centers (IACs) and a Scientific and Technical Information Facility to assist government and industrial clients with information retrieval and technical support.

Another important part of this network is the Computer Software Management and Information Center (COSMIC) located at the University of Georgia. COSMIC collects, stores and distributes NASA developed software at low cost to industry, government agencies and other organisations. NASA computer programs have helped others with such diverse tasks as computer aided design, structural analysis, design of fluid systems, electronic circuit design and company management inventories.

NASA has a contract with the Research Triangle Institute (RTI) in the State of North Carolina to operate a NASA Technology Applications Team. Its purpose is to assist industry and public sector organisations in developing applications engineering projects. This multidisciplinary group of engineers and scientists works closely with NASA and with industry, redesigning and reengineering aerospace technology to develop projects for terrestrial application. The team has helped initiate spinoff projects in electronics, bioengineering, rehabilitation, materials, automation and robotics.

There are five phases to this process, with decisions being made at the end of each phase on whether or not to go on to the next stages. These are:

Define the problem and match with NASA technology. NASA technology transfer agents work to identify problems of widespread significance that may be solved by applying aerospace technology. The problems are documented and distributed to engineers and scientists at their respective centres.

Analyse possible solutions to these problems. Possible solutions are returned by the NASA engineers to the technology transfer agents and then to the problem originator for evaluation. Factors such as technical feasibility, development costs, potential for commercial success and estimated final product costs help NASA and the originator of the problem decide whether or not to proceed with the applications engineering project.

Develop partnerships and a project plan. NASA, the problem originator and the manufacturer next develop a plan for the commercialisation of the new product or process. Issues addressed in the project plan include the responsibilities of the various participants, schedules and milestones, and costs for engineering design, hardware development and evaluation. Possible sources of joint funding and any patent or licence requirements must also be considered.

Implement project. NASA helps to implement the project plan, and provides technical and management assistance as needed.

Commercialisation. The goal of a successful applications engineering project is the commercialisation of the new product or process. This ensures not only the solution to the original problem but also the greatest dividend on the investment in aerospace research and development.

NASA's Technology Utilization Network. This map shows the Technology Utilization Network, the original plans for which were laid down in 1976, in the form that it was completed in 1989 (NASA).

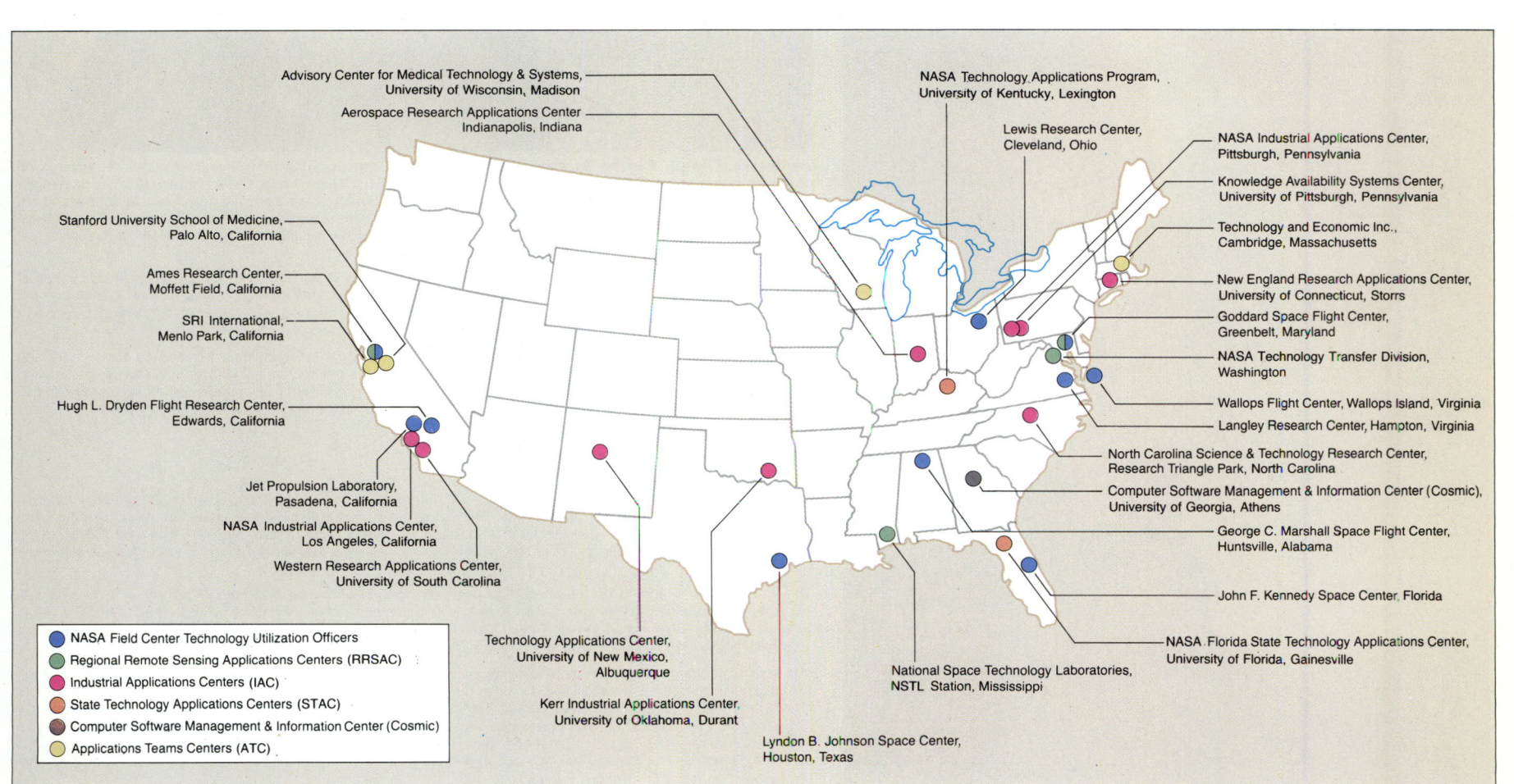

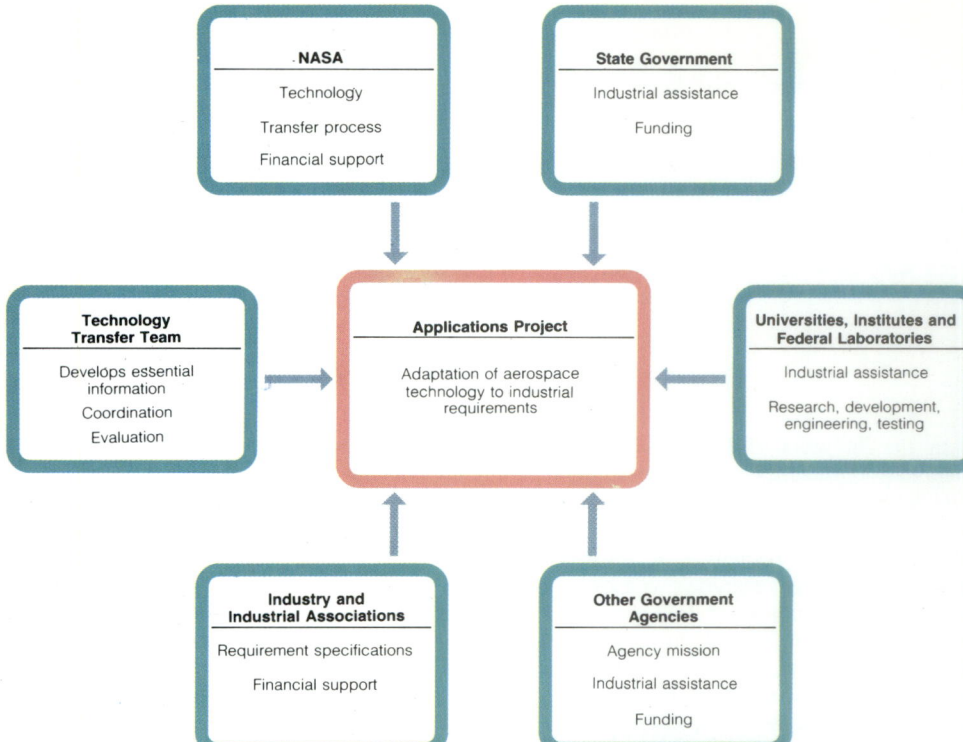

The transfer of space technology to industry. NASA technology transfer agents work with manufacturers, industry associations, government agencies, and public and private organisations to identify problems of widespread significance that may be solved by applying the results of aerospace technology. NASA contributes technology, management support and funding to applications engineering projects. Universities, institutions and government laboratories may either initiate a new product concept or contribute research, engineering development or testing facilities to an applications project. Government agencies often initiate or financially support projects that are related to their charters. Manufacturers and industry associations are essential for specifying new product concepts and then for supporting the development, testing and marketing of the spinoff product or process. The Applications Team, under contract to NASA, develops the essential information, coordinates the project relationships, and provides consultation and management support during the course of the project. All elements of this network are critical to the success of the technology transfer (NASA).

The discovery of a pre-Inca civilisation using remote sensing. NASA's National Space Technology Laboratories (NSTL) and Colorado University at Boulder used remote sensing techniques to find a pre-Inca civilisation in the Peruvian jungle. A map was drawn up using data obtained over the site in the Rio Abiseo national park from the satellite and a reconnaissance plane. A successful expedition to the site followed soon after. The photograph above is of a bas relief, in stone, which is typical of those found in the Gran Pajaten area in this way (NASA).

An interior lining for the Statue of Liberty. A protective coating that originated in NASA research on corrosion resistant materials was used in a recent project to restore New York's Statue of Liberty for its centenary. Tests of the exterior skin of the statue showed little damaging wear, so it was decided to clean the copper and not to apply an exterior protective film. However, a primer coating manufactured by Inorganic Coatings Inc. and known as IC 531 was used on the interior structure of the statue to help provide protection against the corroding salt spray, fog and atmospheric pollution present in New York City harbour.

IC 531 traces its origins to work done by the NASA Goddard Space Flight Center to develop a protective coating of potassium silicate for the gantries and other launch structures at NASA's Kennedy Space Center. Located on the Atlantic coast of Florida, these structures are subjected to constant salt spray and fog, as well as hot rocket exhausts and the thermal shock created by rapid temperature changes during a space launch.

IC 531 is water based, non-toxic, non-flammable, and has no organic emissions. Bonding to steel in only 30 minutes, the coating leaves a very hard ceramic finish with superior adhesion and abrasion resistance. It is applied with standard equipment. Tests on other structures in severe environments around the world have shown that IC 531 has excellent long term corrosion resistance properties. Thus this NASA technology spinoff should help Lady Liberty enjoy many more anniversary celebrations (NASA).

Continuous casting of steel. NASA advances in materials technology have played an important role in improving the continuous casting of steel, a process that is less time consuming and less labour intensive than the more conventional batch casting. A manufacturer of continuous casters brought two materials related problems to the attention of the NASA/RTI Applications Team and the NASA Lewis Research Center. These were abrasion and thermal shock.

The first problem occurs in the upper portion or moulding area of the casting train where there is considerable erosion of the moulding surface. To accomplish low abrasion and high heat transfer at this surface, NASA's Lewis Research Center is providing arc jet sprayed metal composite materials which have excellent strength, thermal conductivity stability, and wear resistance in spacecraft applications.

The second problem presented to NASA engineers was surface failures in the large casting train rollers. Such failure results from the thermal cycling between the temperatures of the steel and roller cooling regions. NASA has coated test rollers with a high nickel alloy developed at the Lewis Research Center. This material was originally designed for nosecones of rockets that would exceed Mach 8 in the atmosphere. The manufacturer is conducting tests in a commercially operating plant and, based on the results, expects to fit new casters with the improved surfaces. Considerable financial savings are expected when both materials applications are transferred to continuous casting trains (J. Launois, Rapho).

Alternative energy. Many NASA spinoffs have contributed to solving environmental pollution and energy supply problems. The solar panels shown here are manufactured by Independent Utility Systems (IUS), Oklahoma, using a polycarbonate material that resists ultraviolet radiation. This was developed by the Jet Propulsion Laboratory for spacecraft sensor assemblies. A NASA information base search also provided information about a French company with experience in the use of a metal graphite compound for brushes for IUS motors. Solar driven water pumps based on this technology have been applied in Pakistan, Egypt and Thailand. Solar powered refrigeration units are used in remote medical clinics in India, South America and North Africa.

The NASA Lewis Research Center has been active in several solar energy projects designed to assist remote regions of countries where power is not readily available. Those who have benefited to date include a community in Tunisia and rural health clinics in Ecuador, Guyana, Kenya and Zimbabwe (NASA).

Fabric roofing materials. Designed to look like a tent city, Saudi Arabia's Haj Terminal in Jeddah is a rest stop for pilgrims bound for Mecca. Made of a NASA spinoff material, it is the world's largest fabric structure.

There are many areas of aerospace technology with potential for spinoff applications. Two examples of successful technology transfer projects, the Programmable Implantable Medication System (PIMS) and the Power Factor Controller (PFC), are discussed here.

Diabetes, a disease that destroys the body's ability to control its blood sugar, afflicts up to 1% of the population. Patients currently manage the disease by injecting prescribed doses of insulin. Scientists believe that a more reliable control of blood sugar levels in diabetics may help prevent some serious complications including heart disease, kidney malfunction and blindness. In an effort to develop a method for the improved control of blood sugar levels, the PIMS is being developed to deliver microlitres of insulin automatically to the body at schedules set by the doctor. The patient will operate a control unit which gives additional insulin, depending on diet or exercise during the day, if it is needed.

NASA experience in microminiaturised, low power electronics was applied to the PIMS's programming unit and the pump circuitry. Telemetry originally developed for small astronomy satellites was essential. The small pump capable of delivering doses of medication of only one millionth of a litre traces its origin to technology used in the Mars Viking spacecraft.

The PIMS performed well in longterm animal studies. It was first implanted in humans in November 1986. NASA scientists expect PIMS to improve the quality of life of diabetics significantly, and they anticipate that the unit can be used in the treatment of other diseases as well.

Another example of a successful technology transfer project is the PFC, a device developed in the mid 1970s by Frank Nola, an engineer at NASA's Marshall Space Flight Center, to conserve energy in alternating current motors. These motors are designed to operate at a fixed maximum voltage. They waste power when the load on the motor is reduced but the supply voltage stays constant. The PFC plugs into the motor and continuously monitors the load by sensing shifts in the relationship between voltage and current. Energy savings of typically 25% result when the PFC senses a light load and then reduces the voltage to the minimum needed.

Another spinoff of the PFC has been the development of a solid state motor starter which electronically regulates the starting current and running voltage of alternating current motors. An integrated circuit has been developed to reduce onto one chip most of the circuitry of the original PFC.

Henry J. Clarks

Fabric roofing traces its origins to a material developed for early astronaut spacesuits. NASA requested Owens Corning Fiberglass Corporation to help develop a material that was durable, noncombustible, and yet thin, light and flexible. Glass fibre yarn that was woven into a fabric and coated with Teflon (also a NASA spinoff), a product of DuPont Company, was the result. These materials have been adapted for heavier applications in construction engineering. Fabric structures require fewer interior supports than conventional roofs, thus freeing more floor space. For example, in the Haj Terminal two identical structures with multitented fabric roofs span more than 50 acres each. Fabrics may be designed with high reflectivity (typically 75% of sunlight is reflected) and their transluscence (transmitting 10% of daylight) allows shadowless natural light to fill the under-roof area. The typical fabric roof, weighing only one thirtieth of a conventional roof of the same size, may be supported by a network of cables or by air pressure.

Fibreglass fabric as a permanent covering has been in service since the early 1970s. It is used in structures all over the world, including the Schlumberger Cambridge Research Ltd. building in Great Britain, animal enclosures at the North Carolina Zoological Park and Boston's Franklin Park Zoo, and many sports and recreation centres, such as in Pontiac, Michigan, and Vancouver (NASA).

Prosthetic urinary sphincter. Urinary incontinence is the inability to control bladder function. It is severely debilitating to those who have spinal cord injuries or who are incontinent as a result of diabetes, congenital defects or complications resulting from surgery.

After defining the problems with medical researchers, the NASA/RTI Applications Team identified technology that has led to the development of a simple, reliable prosthetic urinary sphincter. This enables people who are incontinent to control their bladder function. The NASA technology match was found in a valve system originally developed for use in experiments by the Viking lander in which precise volumes of reagents were put into Martian soil samples. This valve technology was an improvement over previous sphincter designs whose hydraulic control system often failed. The current sphincter, designed for both males and females, has a two chamber inflatable cuff placed around the urethra, a selfsealing storage system, a check valve mechanism and a valve fluid reservoir. When the sphincter system is implanted, the valve and bulb assembly is accessible through the skin to open and close the urethra (NASA).

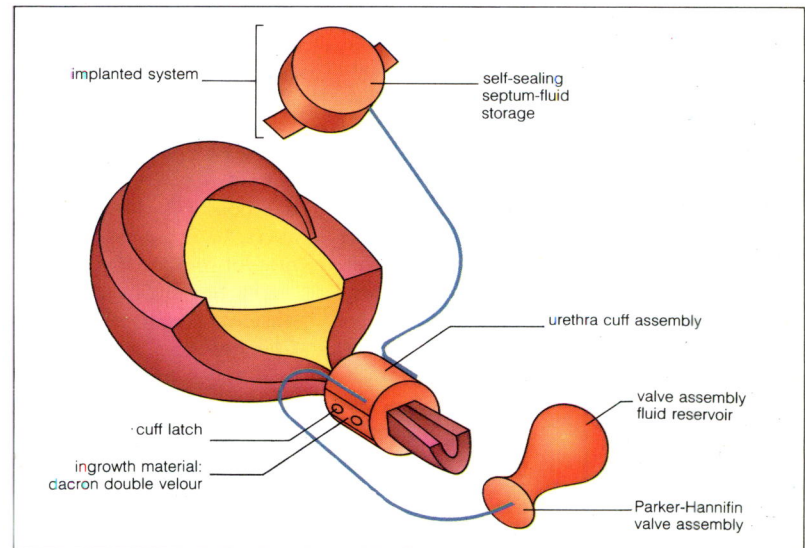

Industry and space

The world space industry

During the development of space technology, as in all major technologies, industry plays two important roles. First of all it acts as a reservoir, accumulating knowledge and preserving it for the future. Secondly, it is the sector which coordinates the interaction between the forces of supply and demand. Supplies determined by economic considerations may not match the technological demands, and the analysis of both is of paramount importance in the space industry, and in its future.

Nor is it the case that space technology is a single subject – it is an amalgamation of many technologies. For example, solar cells were originally developed to provide electrical energy for satellites, and they are being used more and more on Earth.

The space industry covers three major categories: the construction of launchers and satellites, their operation and the varied uses of their data. The first two categories are those which indicate the development of space applications in industry. The infrastructure, on the other hand, requires other forms of specialised knowledge. In market terms, the systems used for satellite support, such as the network of ground stations which track and receive signals from a telecommunications satellite, are frequently the dominant element.

Technical developments have tended to make the difference between these three categories much less clear than they once were. Orbital transport motors, reusable parts of spacecraft, space stations and so on have blurred the distinction between satellites and launchers. Moreover, further down the line, support services have been created to exploit space products such as the images furnished by remote sensing satellites.

Due to the nature and number of space systems involved, the aeronautics industry and the electronics industry have played equal parts in developing the world space industry. There is, however, a marked bias on the part of the aeronautics industry towards the launcher sector. It is also the rule that no one industry is involved in space products. Space activity occurs as a branch of the more traditional industries, and it is very seldom that this branch is profit making.

The complex and strict requirements of a space mission cause the space industry to be very careful in its technical preparations. This work is usually reflected in the high final cost. However, space contracts confer prestige upon companies because it is in the detailed design and thorough testing of a space system (not merely in having the necessary technology) that the essence of success in space is concentrated.

In the West, space technology is developed on the basis of a relationship between the state and industry in which political wishes are subject to market forces. Space activities represent the first time in history that a civil technology has confronted the state with its involvement in what was previously a military reserve. Space technology carries major economic stakes, but the initial investments required are too great and the returns too distant for it to be left unattended in a free market. Thus political involvement often gives the operational part of a space programme to a government agency, created specifically for this purpose – NASA for the USA, ESA for Europe, CNES for France and Nasda for Japan. The one sector in which the free market has become dominant is telecommunication satellites.

It is a fact that the growth of a nation's space industry is generally the result of its government's space policy. Most Western countries are now preoccupied with trying to make their space industries independent, and this is why much emphasis is placed on the development of a space transport system.

The industrial development of launchers obviously preceded that of satellites. The first launchers were simply ballistic rocket motors to which an extra stage, containing the payload, had been added. US launchers of this type include Jupiter, Thor, Atlas and Titan. Thus the launcher industry grew out of the ballistic rocket engine industry which in itself represented a diversification of the aeronautics industry. Usage of the term 'aerospace industry' emphasises the close relationship between designers of modern aircraft, missiles, rocket motors and space launchers.

In Europe, the leading aerospace companies are Aérospatiale and Matra in France, MBB and Dornier in West Germany, British Aerospace in Great Britain, Aeritalia in Italy and Saab-Scania in Sweden. For satellites, however, the situation is quite different. Because the electronics involved are more important than the launchers, large electronics companies have been able to assume the role of experts. In Britain, for example, these include Marconi Space and Defence Systems, and Plessey; in West Germany, Siemens. In Japan, on the other hand, where the relative number of electronics firms involved is much greater, the three major firms are Melco (Mitsubishi Electric Corporation), Toshiba and NEC (Nippon Electric Company).

The straightforward distinction between electronics firms and aerospace firms belies a far more complicated reality. In fact, each company possesses a large range of technical skills. Some companies specialise in telecommunications or Earth observation payloads; the French company, CIT-Alcatel is an example. Other companies, in contrast, may produce a single component, such as a battery or attitude sensors; these are specialist suppliers.

The American space industry dominates the market in the western world, yet both Europe and Japan have created independent space industries. In the West, these are the only two bodies which are capable of competing with the USA. By contrast, Canada's space policy does not aim to make its space industry independent, nor does it include the development of launchers. Its objective is to develop civil programmes for social and economic benefit.

The Soviet Union collaborates with several western countries on some space projects. China too has entered the commercial market by selling space on its 'Long March' launchers. Although it is difficult to predict how successful this venture will be, it has been boosted by the crisis in space transport systems in the West following the Challenger accident.

André Lebeau

The world space effort. The diagrams show the amount of money spent in the space industry in 1985. This consists solely of the cost of satellites and launchers; associated services on the ground or groundstations are not included.

The amount of money spent by Europe on space is $1000 million, which is double the amount spent by the Japanese, and about a sixth of what NASA spends. The amount of money spent by the military in Japan and Europe is small, but military expenditure represents more than half the American space programme. In the Canadian budget, there is no money spent on the development of launchers, and research is completely oriented towards civil programmes. Canada is the only country where industrial expenditure ($145 million) exceeds that from public funds.

China's space budget has multiplied substantially since 1985, fivefold between 1987 and 1989 (Euroconsult, *World Space Industry Survey* 1988).

The European space effort. Money spent in the space industry is unevenly distributed throughout Europe. The amount of public money is 40 times greater in France than in Denmark. Obviously, the size of each country plays a part in determining the funds spent but, even considering the Gross National Product (GNP), the disparity is still large. The proportion of the GNP invested by France is 0·1% while it is only 0·01% for Spain. These differences have a direct effect on the evolution of the space industry in the different countries.

In the same way, the percentage of public money available for the European Space Agency (ESA) is very variable from country to country. It constitutes the most important part of the space budget for the seven countries least involved in Europe's space industry, yet less than half of the public money available goes to ESA from countries such as France, West Germany and Sweden. These variations are due to the different policies followed by the governments of different countries.

Some fifty firms represent about 70% of Europe's industrial activity. In 1977 they employed 10 500 people and, in 1984, 18 000 people, a growth of 71%. The growth in different countries is, of course, not directly comparable. France and Sweden have experienced the most rapid growth, related to the large percentage of their GNP which is devoted to the development of space activities (Euroconsult, *World Space Industry Survey. Ten Years Outlook*, 1988).

The symbol ‰ in the figures means parts per thousand.

AEG: Allgemeine Elektrizitäts Gesellschaft
ANT: Allgemeine Nachrichtentecnik GmbH
    (Space Communications Systems)
Ates: Alcatel Espace
BAe: British Aerospace
BADG: British Aerospace Dynamics Group
BTMC: Bell Telephone Manufacturing Company
CASA: Construcciones Aeronauticas, SA
    (Sociedad Anónima)
CIR: Compagnie Industrielle Radioélectrique
CNES: Centre National d'Etudes Spatiales
ELDO: European Launcher Development Organisation
ERS: Earth Resources Satellite
ESA: European Space Agency
ESD: Electronique Serge Dassault
ESRO:* European Space Research Organisation
ETCA: Etudes Techniques et Constructions
    Aérospatiales SA (Société Anonyme)
FIAR: Fabbrica Italiana Apparecchiatene
    Radioelectriche, SpA (Società per Azione)
FNH: Fabrique Nationale Herstal SA
GTE: Telecommunicazioni: General Telephone
    Electronics, Telecommunicazioni, SpA
HSA: Holland Signaal Apparatuur
HSD:* Hawker Siddeley Dynamics
INTA: Instituto Nacional de Técnica Aeroespacial
ISRO: Indian Space Research Organisation
LSat: Large Satellite
MAN: Maschinenfabrik Augsburg-Nürnberg AG
    (Aktien Gesellschaft)
MBB–Erno: Messerschmitt–Bölkow–Blohm GmbH–Erno
MCS: Marconi Communication Systems
MESH: Matra, Erno, Saab and HSD
MOA: Ministry of Astronautics
MSDS: Marconi Space and Defence Systems Ltd
NASA: National Aeronautics and Space Administration
Nasda: National Space Development Agency of Japan
ÖRS: Österreichische Raumfahrt- und Systemtechnik
Saab–Scania Ab: Svenska Aeropol Aktiebolag–
    Scania Ab
SABCA: Société Anonyme Belge de Constructions
    Aéronautiques
SAT: Société Anonyme des Télécommunications
SEL: Standard Elektrik Lorenz
SEP: Electronique Européene de Propulsion
SNIA–BPD: Società di Navigazione Italiana ed
    Applicazione – Bompieni, Parodi, Defino
Snias:* Société Nationale Industrielle Aérospatiale

*These companies and organisations no longer function.

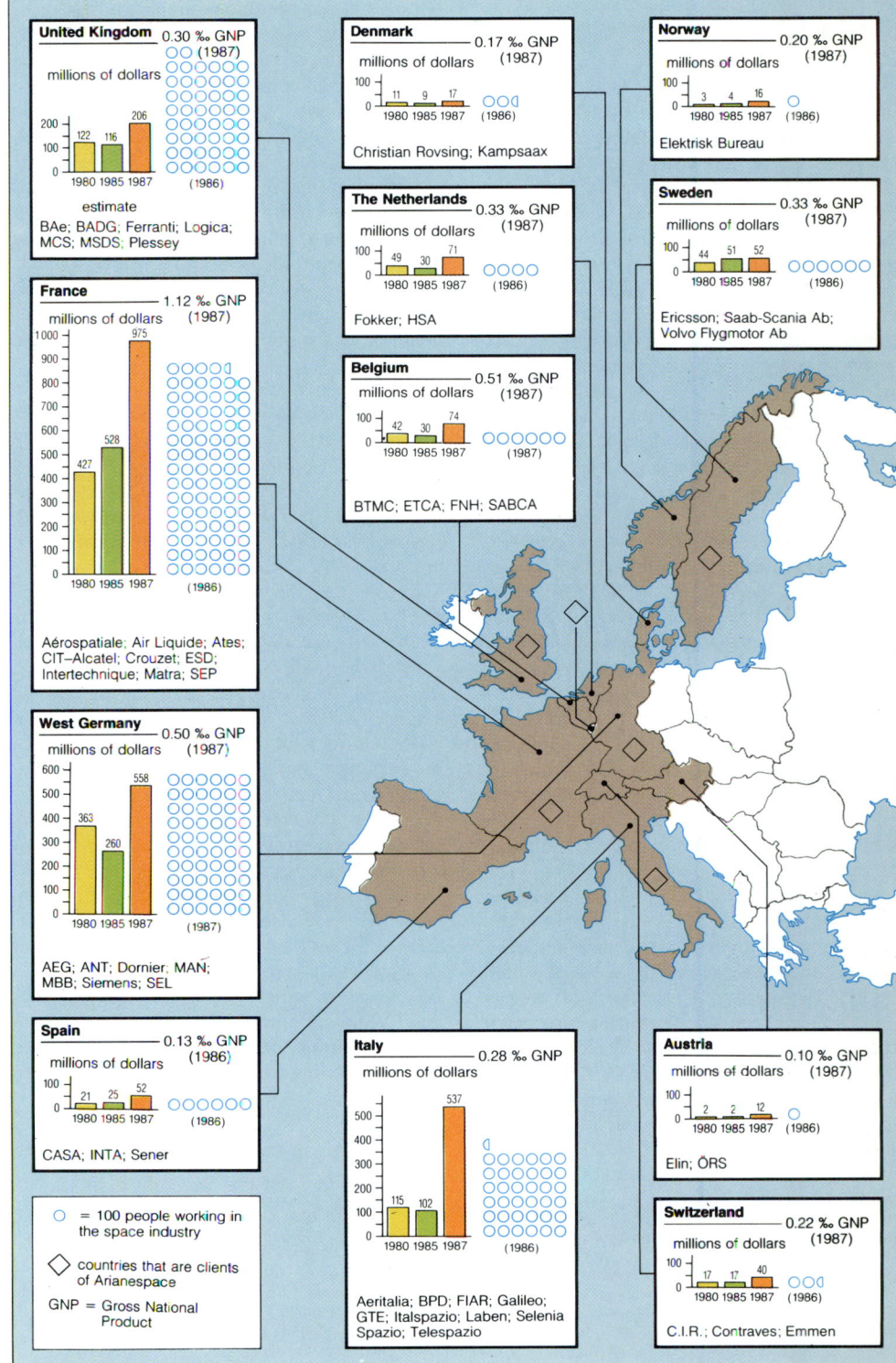

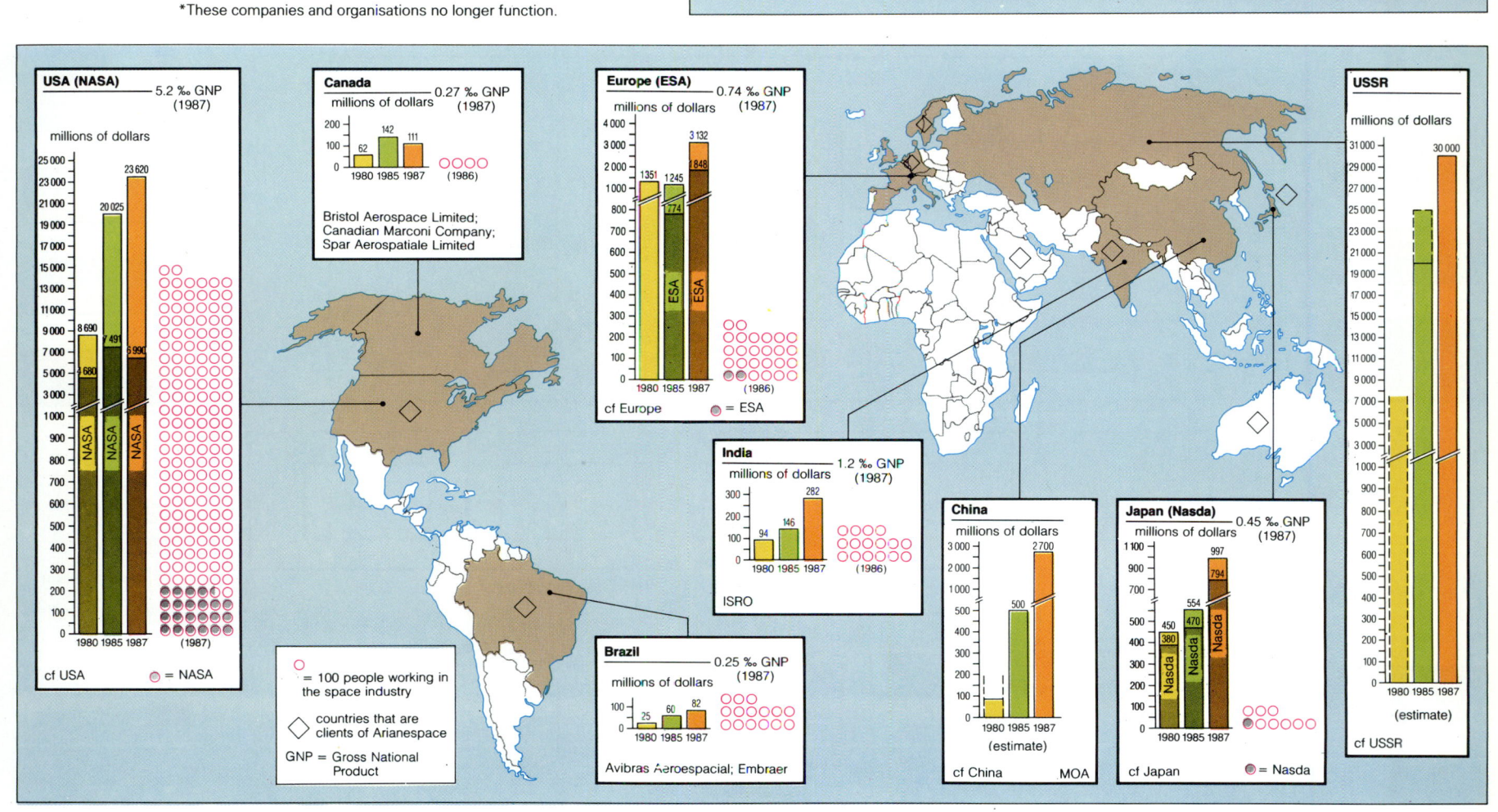

Europe

The creation of a large scale space industry in Europe capable of competing on the world market began as a modest venture in 1962 and has been gaining momentum ever since. There have been three distinct periods of growth. The first was from 1962 to 1970, when Europe acquired the basic know how. From 1970 to 1977, Europe became less dependent on others and, since 1977, has been developing its own operational and commercial programmes.

During the first phase of development, each European country pursued its own space policy, and there was no overall strategy for the whole of Europe. To describe this period, it would be necessary to deal with each country individually. France, however, deserves a special mention as the most 'space conscious' of all the European countries.

France has devoted much time and money to becoming the European leader in this field. Following work carried out by the army, the Centre national d'etudes spatiales (CNES), created in 1962, began work on a small rocket launcher, the Diamant ('Diamond'), and on scientific satellites. The selection of competent and space motivated industries, led to two companies, Matra and Aérospatiale, being given the powers of main contractors. The industrial production of launchers was based on the industrial structure built up by the military to construct ballistic rockets, and has remained the same ever since.

Most work has taken place on a national level. However, the first non-scientific civil satellite, the Symphonie telecommunications satellite, was the result of a collaboration between France and Germany. Also around 1962 two European organisations were created. They were the European Space Research Organisation (ESRO) and the European Launcher Development Organisation (ELDO), designed essentially to build large rocket launchers.

Under these conditions the second phase of development began – a concerted effort to make Europe an independent space power. The most important event was the creation of the European Space Agency (ESA) in 1975, the result of a merger between ESRO and ELDO. The size of the European programme forced industrial groups to adapt to the 'fair returns' principle, in which ESA provides work for each country in proportion to the amount of money it receives from them. Without this constraint, the net effect would be that the less developed countries would subsidise the further advancement of the more developed, an intolerable situation.

After accepting this, ESA had to create international industrial groupings in order to coordinate projects with the greatest possible efficiency. In pursuing this policy, ESRO and later ESA have relied on three European consortia upon which Europe's industrial capacity in space has been built. These are MESH, Cosmos and Star.

In the case of the Ariane launchers, the reverse process occurred. The contributions from each country were adjusted to match the work carried out by its industrial groups at the beginning of the programme in the middle 1960s.

The third phase of the European space industry was marked by the growth of the organisation under the pressure of requirements for reasonable operational running costs and for commercial competition. Satellite construction was restructured into two groups, Eurosatellite and Satcom International. In the case of launchers, a European firm, Arianespace, was created to design a commercially viable product. The development of a new space transport system, Ariane V, Hermes and Columbus, is now being carried out within the framework of the groups which were instituted during the second phase of European development.

André Lebeau

Arianespace: an example of commercialisation

The European programme to build a heavy launcher (under ELDO) resulted in a launch failure and the programme was terminated in 1972. Nevertheless, the experience pinpointed fundamental errors which had to be avoided so that future European technical collaborations would be successful.

In the USA military expertise had been used to develop three families of rocket launchers. These were the Scout (equivalent to the Diamant), the Thor-Delta (to put 1·1 tonnes into the geostationary transfer orbit) and the Atlas Centaur (1·7 tonnes into the geostationary transfer orbit). An estimate of the potential market, based on the rapid development of space telecommunications, suggested that by the mid 1980s, Europe would need to be carrying out two to four launches per year.

For this reason, in 1973 France proposed the Ariane programme to its European partners. Its proposals were based on studies made by the CNES, and the objective was to be able to launch satellites of the Atlas Centaur group by the year 1981. The project was to make maximum use of all the technical knowledge that had been acquired over the years, and to provide Europe with an independent rocket launcher, most notably for the field of space telecommunications. France agreed to finance two thirds of the programme under the aegis of ESA with the CNES being the main contractor.

Shortly after this the world situation changed quite dramatically. The USA had underestimated the future role of conventional launchers (Expendable Launch Vehicles), and concentrated on making a commercial success of a unique product, the space shuttle. Intelsat (the International Telecommunication Satellite company) wanted to have access to two launcher companies and so it presented itself to Ariane as a client.

The weight and volume of the payload increased and, even before the launch of

The eight principal companies involved in the Ariane launcher programme. The group of companies, shown on the right is the largest European industrial organisation in the space industry. The importance which each government attaches to developing an independent European launcher is illustrated by the relative proportions of the shareholders. French companies own 58·48% of shares (34·0% is owned by the Centre nationale d'etudes spatiales, CNES), so France controls the company. Other countries have the following percentages of shares: West Germany, 19·6%; Belgium, 4·40%; Italy, 3·60%; Great Britain, 3·17%; Switzerland, 2·70%; Spain, 2·50%; Sweden, 2·40%; Holland, 2·20%; Denmark, 0·70%; Ireland, 0·25%. The shareholders are enterprises which specialise in aerospace products, banks and even private investors (Arianespace, 1988).

The structure of the European space industry. At first, the European Space Research Organisation (ESRO) organised European industry into consortia – Cosmos, Star and MESH (Matra, Erno, Saab and HSD) in order to apply to the industries the concept of 'juste retour', or 'fair (financial) returns'. From 1975 onwards, the European Space Agency (ESA) grouped various companies together to work on large projects including the Ariane launcher, the Spacelab orbiting laboratory, the experimental direct broadcasting satellite LSat (Large Satellite), later called Olympus, and the Earth Resources Satellite (ERS 1). Further small companies have been created to market ESA's products. For example, Eurosatellite, Aérospatiale, MBB, Alcatel Espace, AEG, ANT, ETCA were created to deal with the long standing

consortia of Cosmos and Star. Satcom International, British Aerospace and Matra are linked to MESH, and there is also Arianespace.

In the satellite sector these structures show how European industry has adapted itself to the limitations of international cooperation, to the problem of receiving fair returns for investment in development programmes, and to competition in the international market. These companies only partially solve the problems of duplication of skills in the major companies (AIAA, Euroconsult, Eurospace).

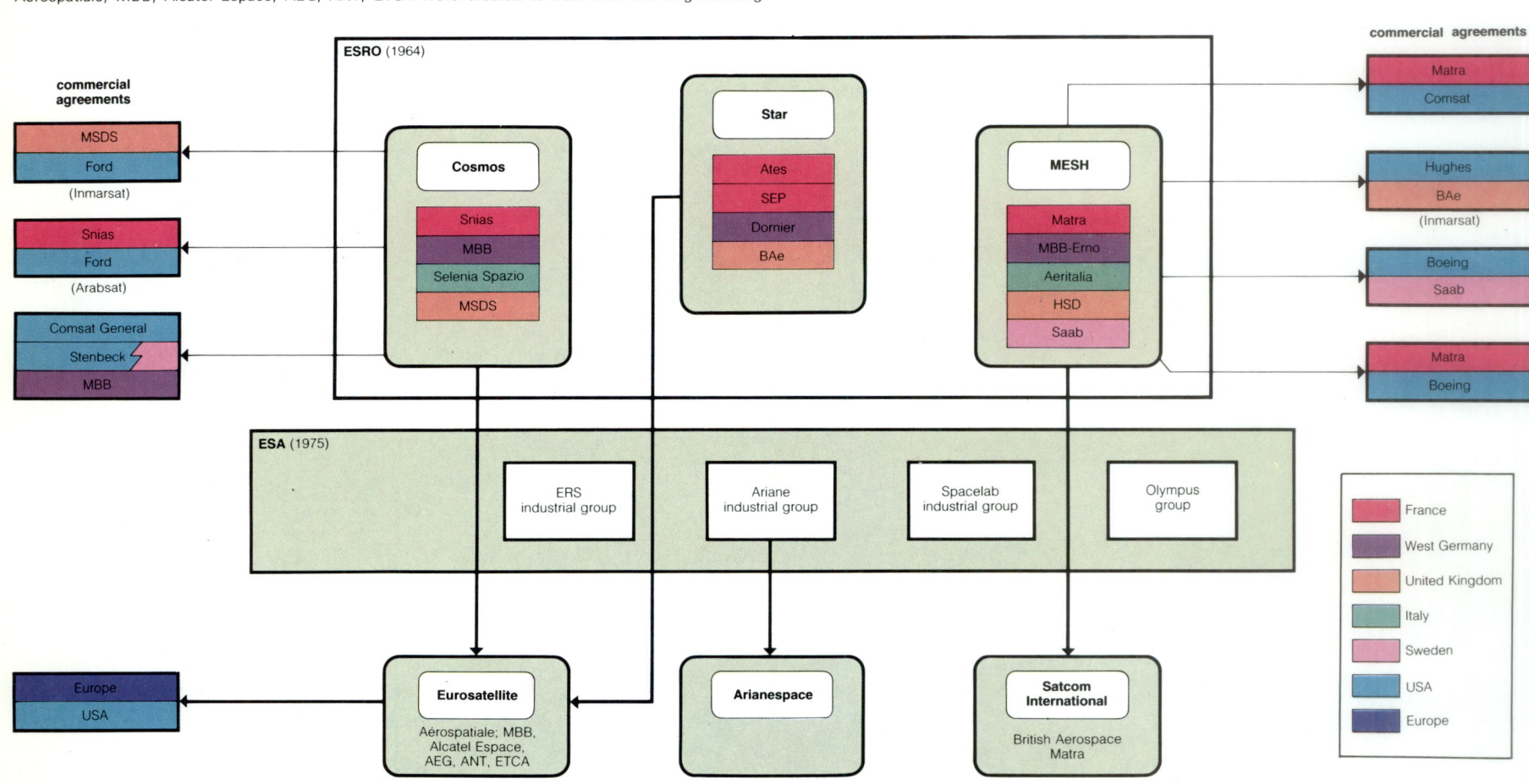

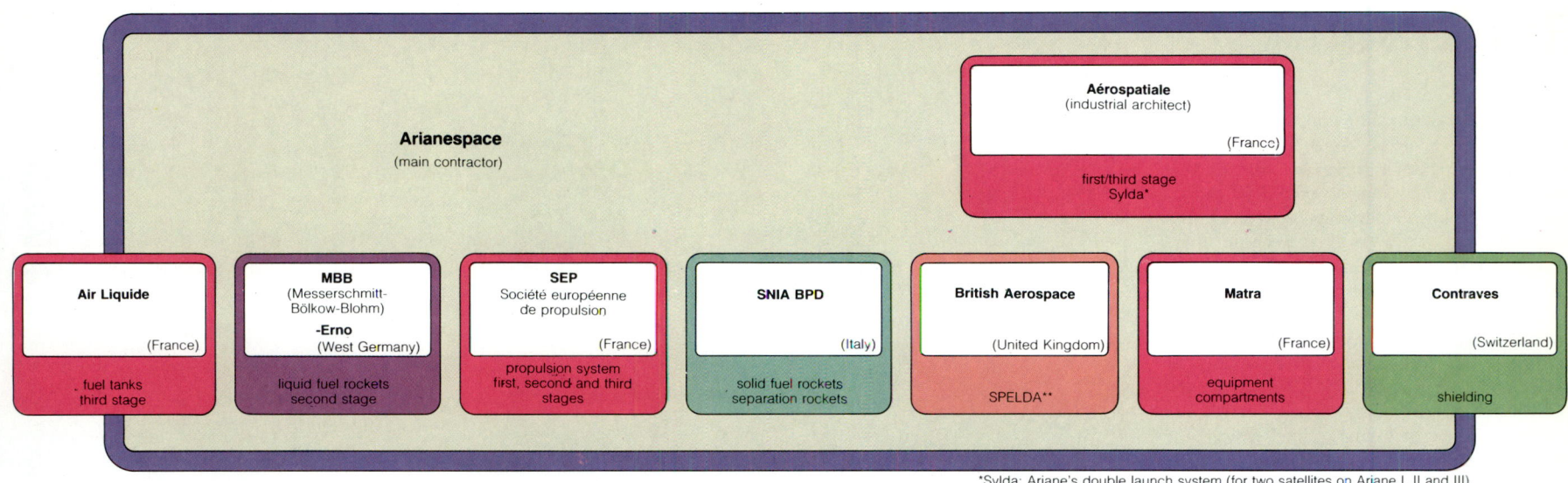

Arianespace
(main contractor)

Aérospatiale
(industrial architect)
(France)
first/third stage
Sylda*

Air Liquide
(France)
. fuel tanks
third stage

MBB
(Messerschmitt-Bölkow-Blohm)
-Erno
(West Germany)
liquid fuel rockets
second stage

SEP
Société européenne
de propulsion
(France)
propulsion system
first, second and third
stages

SNIA BPD
(Italy)
solid fuel rockets
separation rockets

British Aerospace
(United Kingdom)
SPELDA**

Matra
(France)
equipment
compartments

Contraves
(Switzerland)
shielding

*Sylda: Ariane's double launch system (for two satellites on Ariane I, II and III).

**SPELDA: external carrying structure, for launching two satellites on Ariane IV.

Ariane I, a more powerful version, Ariane III, was being designed and developed. Ariane III had the extra capability of performing two launches. The commercial launch services market grew, and to cope with this Arianespace was created on 26 March 1980. Arianespace is a public limited company, whose shareholders consist of European industrial companies involved in the Ariane project, large banks and the CNES. Arianespace is the company responsible for the production, finance and launching of operational Ariane launchers, developed by ESA, as well as the operations related to the launching of satellites.

On 24 December 1979, the first Ariane I was launched. This marked the beginning of Europe's independence in the field of rocket launchers. The date of the 'first commercial space transport line', the inauguration of Arianespace, was 22 May 1984.

As the needs of the commercial market evolved, it was necessary for yet another change at Arianespace. In the same spirit of adaptability which was behind the creation of Ariane I and Ariane III, a new model, Ariane IV, was designed. It used essentially the same technology but, by combining the number and nature (powder or liquid fuel) of propulsion units or boosters, it can facilitate six different variations of payload. This is a most cost effective way of responding to different needs. The second launch stage was adapted to fit Ariane IV, thus reducing the delay between two launches and increasing the number of launches per year.

In January 1985, during the ministerial summit in Rome, members of ESA agreed on the development of a new and even more powerful launcher, Ariane V. This launcher should be more reliable and have a higher performance than its predecessors and should keep Ariane at the forefront of the international market into the twenty-first century.

Following losses in the world space insurance market (see pp. 340–43), Arianespace set up a subsidiary insurance company in 1985. The aim of this company is to offer a guarantee against the risks of launch failures at the time the launch contract is signed. This company (S3R) has had a promising start and should be able to offer more clients the opportunity to obtain 'all risks cover'.

Following the dramatic and tragic explosion of the space shuttle on 28 January 1986, President Ronald Reagan outlined a new space policy. On 15 August 1986, he ordered the transfer of commercial satellite launchings from NASA's responsibility to the private sector, and the return to using conventional launchers for this task. Paradoxically, this American about turn vindicates the choice made by Europe in the 1970s.

Ariane's commercial success is based on:

First, the industrial network across Europe. Ariane is a splendid example of European cooperation which simultaneously maintains continuity and the innovative capacity and ability to adapt. Some fifty launchers are being built by eight thousand people throughout Europe.

Second, the Ariane launchers. The last Ariane I launcher was used on 21 February 1986 to put the French satellite SPOT (Satellite d'Observation de la Terre) and the Swedish satellite Viking (a scientific satellite to investigate auroral physics) into orbit. The Ariane IV launcher was successfully launched at the end of 1987 and during 1988. This is based on Ariane III, but the size of the tanks on the first rocket stage have been increased and more powerful boosters have been installed. A large order for 50 Ariane IV rocket launchers from European companies was placed in February 1989. This historic contract covers a period of about 10 years during which the Ariane V launcher will be introduced.

Third, the space centre at Kourou in French Guiana. This site, chosen in 1965 by the CNES, is remarkably close to the equator. It thus provides the best conditions for placing satellites into geostationary orbit. It is one of the most modern launch space complexes in the world. Launch campaigns at Kourou are also very short because the rendezvous between satellite and launcher need only be eight or nine days before the launch date.

There is a growing market for civil satellites for telecommunications, data transmission, direct broadcasting, navigation or positioning, Earth observation, meteorology and hydrography. There is also a need to launch scientific satellites or interplanetary probes such as Giotto.

Arianespace forecasts an increase in production rate to enable eight launchings per year by 1990. This represents some twelve to fourteen satellites being put into orbit per year. Ariane's commercialisation of space extends from Europe towards the USA and the rest of the world. In 1986 and 1987, for example, contracts were signed with Canada, India and Japan.

Arianespace also faces international competition. Japan intends to launch its new rocket, HII, in 1992. This should quickly pass into the industrial phase with regular launches. The Soviet Union will probably continue to be constrained by political factors related to the transfer of advanced technology from the West since some 80% of all commercial satellites are built in the USA. China will, no doubt, continue to develop its programme.

A space transport policy is a longterm policy. Large investments are important, as are the technological risks. It is necessary to accept failures and above all to strive to overcome such difficulties. With a return in terms of industrial turnover already more than three times the development investment made by the contributing states and an order book worth more than £200 million, Arianespace is in a good position.

One of the major assets of the Ariane programme is, without doubt, its ability to adapt to changing world situations and to retain a high level of competence and continuity throughout its programme. This will be even more important in the future.

Frédéric d'Allest

Space companies are now detaching themselves from public institutions. They are setting up subsidiary companies to deal with the sales side of the business. In France, one such company is Prospace which has dealt with the promotion of space products and services since 1979. Another, Spot Image, distributes images from the SPOT remote sensing satellite, while Intospace in West Germany provides industry with access to microgravity conditions.

Europe has made valiant efforts at overcoming difficulties associated with international bureaucratic structures and those related to the changeover from public to private funding. It has demonstrated considerable flexibility when dealing with different economic systems. At the same time, however, there is some weakness in this European industrial organisation. There is in particular a strong national feeling in the civil satellite industries which is related to the lack of a coherent European policy on the telecommunications satellite sector. The absence of a significant military component in the European space programme may also be a contributory factor.

André Lebeau

The USSR

The USSR is pursuing the most extensive space programme in the world. The statistics of its space programme illustrate this beyond doubt. In 1986, for example, the USSR carried out 114 successful launchings, compared with 12 for the rest of the world. Every year about 100 carrier rockets place about 500 tonnes of payload into low Earth orbit.

This activity relies on strong economic performance and a governmental policy which provides vast human and material resources. The Americans have officially estimated that 600 000 people are employed in the Soviet space sector and that between 1·5 and 2% of the Gross National Product (GNP) is allocated to space activities. They have also calculated that the Soviets spent $2·5 billion dollars on space experiments in 1985, a figure compatible with this percentage of the GNP and similar to the American space budget.

Independent estimates made in France have put the cost of Soviet launchers, satellites, space probes and manned spacecraft at $1 billion per year. To this amount has to be added the development costs of new systems, such as a launcher of large payloads, a 'space shuttle', a new generation of planetary probes, and so on, as well as the running costs of the programme. By this method, a figure for the space budget similar to the American estimate is reached.

This Soviet programme has very different technical priorities from those of Western programmes. In the first place, it is characterised by the extended use of basic space designs. The same principles are employed to design today's carrier rockets as put Sputnik 1 into orbit thirty years ago. The Soyuz space station likewise has undergone several modernisations, but it is still used by cosmonauts a quarter of a century after studies were first made on it by Sergei Korolev at the Experimental Studies Bureau (OKB, or Opytnoie Konstrouktorskoie Biuro).

The second major difference is the size of a production series. More than 1100 launchers have been based on the Sputnik launcher series. There have been more than 700 recoverable military and civil satellites based on the Vostok rocket which carried Yuri Gagarin into space in 1961. The Soyuz series of spacecraft, and the recoverable satellites based on it, have numbered about a hundred.

There is also considerable standardisation of equipment. For example, the command console from Soyuz was adapted with very few modifications to fit the Salyut stations. The booster jets of the orbital manoeuvre subsystem used for the first generation of interplanetary probes are also found on the current Molniya telecommunications satellites.

The Soviet space programme has used technologically simple rocket engines wherever possible. The reliability of their space engines has increased, enabling complex missions such as the Vega probes to Venus and Halley's comet to have been successful. This technical progress, coupled with considerable industrial resources, should permit the USSR to embark upon extremely ambitious programmes in the future. These might include launching very large space stations as the successors to Mir, or sending men to the Moon or even Mars.

Alain Dupas

One of the halls in Star City. Star City, near Moscow, was created in 1960 as a cosmonaut training centre. One of the most important halls in the centre contains mockups of the Soviet space stations and spacecraft. Astronauts use them to prepare for their missions. In this photograph, mockups of Salyut 7 and Mir are seen. Since 1982 the astronaut training programme has been run by Boris Volynov, like the director of the centre, General Chatalov, a former cosmonaut.

The main purpose of the Soviet space stations is for research, but their use for economic purposes is increasing. For example, cameras have been installed for remote sensing. A specialised Earth observation module is available for Mir. Furthermore, work which benefits from the microgravity conditions in space will also be increased by the addition of specialised modules. These will be the forerunners of small space factories which will be in orbit in the vicinity of the Soviet space stations (APN).

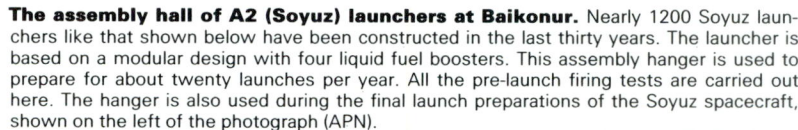

The assembly hall of A2 (Soyuz) launchers at Baikonur. Nearly 1200 Soyuz launchers like that shown below have been constructed in the last thirty years. The launcher is based on a modular design with four liquid fuel boosters. This assembly hanger is used to prepare for about twenty launches per year. All the pre-launch firing tests are carried out here. The hanger is also used during the final launch preparations of the Soyuz spacecraft, shown on the left of the photograph (APN).

The Proton (D) rocket launcher used for commercial launchings. The Proton launcher is used by the USSR to launch geostationary satellites. In the future it will be available to foreign clients, through the civil space organisation, Glavkosmos, and the import export company, Licensinvorg.

This four stage heavy launcher, with the addition of an apogee motor, can place a 2·2 tonnes geostationary satellite directly into its prearranged orbit. It is thus of the same calibre as the European launcher, Ariane IV, and the American rocket, Titan III. These will be the main competitors on the commercial launch market in the early 1990s.

Glavkosmos is asking about $45 million to launch a payload which is less than half the amount charged for an Ariane IV or Titan III. However, satellites built in the West, which contain components or subsystems of a 'sensitive' technological nature, cannot at present be launched by the USSR.

Nevertheless, the Soviet offer to launch foreign satellites illustrates the new commercial policy of the USSR. Other systems and services have also been proposed. These include the Soyuz launcher, for putting 7·5 tonnes of payload into low Earth orbit; the Intercosmos rocket, for placing several tonnes of payload in a suborbital flight; the possibility of putting payloads on board recoverable satellites or space stations; and the possibility of buying satellites such as Gorizont telecommunications satellites. The objective of this exercise is to bring foreign currency into the country and, at the same time, to gain prestige by demonstrating the advanced nature of the Soviet space industry (APN).

The political organisation of the Soviet space economy

The political organisation of the Soviet space programme can be pieced together fairly accurately. The broad outline of the policy is decided at the highest level within the Communist Party of the Soviet Union, by the Central Committee and the Politburo. One member of the Politburo is responsible for both the defence sector and the space sector. During the period when Leonid Brezhnev was Secretary General, this post was held by Dmitri Oustinov, who died in 1985. He was responsible for the initial development of the Soviet missile and space engines industry at the end of the 1950s and the beginning of the 1960s. One of the secretaries of the Central Committee is also responsible for the space and defence industries. The space policy is decided by the department of defence industries and the science department of the Central Committee. Their outlines are put into operation at governmental level. The president of the Council of Ministers controls a group of ministers and the State Committees. Several of the latter (such as the State Committee for Science and Technology, and the State Planning Committee, Gosplan) play important roles in defining and inaugurating the Soviet space programme. The powerful military and industrial commission (VPK, Voyenno-Promychlennaia Komissya) is in charge of allocating funds to the defence and space industries. In 1985, the USSR announced the creation of a company, Glavkosmos, which is part of the State Committee involved with coordinating civil programmes. Directed by Alexander Dounaev, Glavkosmos will play an important role in international negotiations with Russia's scientific or commercial space partners.

The development of different types of spacecraft comes under the aegis of the Ministry for General Engineering Projects (MGEP). This ministry was created in 1965 and was directed by Oleg Baklanov from 1983 to 1988. For the previous seventeen years it was directed by Sergei Afanassiev. The MGEP has the same structure as the Ministry of Aircraft Production (MAP). The major similarity between the two ministries, is the office of experimental construction (OKB), which is both a design office and a factory for building prototypes.

There are four principal offices:
– The OKB founded by Sergei Korolev and based near Moscow was the originator of the first Soviet intercontinental rocket (called the SS 6 by the Americans). This rocket was the forerunner of the large rockets needed to launch Sputnik, Vostok and Soyuz. Today, this OKB specialises in the construction of the orbiting space stations, Salyut and Mir, and the transport spacecraft, Soyuz and Progress. It is now directed by Yuri Semionov.
– The OKB founded by Mikhail Yangel is based near Dniepropetrovsk. It is responsible for the Soviet intercontinental missile programmes, the SS 9 and the SS 18, as well as for developing some of the scientific satellites of the Cosmos and Intercosmos series.
– The OKB founded by Vladimir Chelomei, near Plesetsk, is responsible for the Proton launcher programme, missiles like the SS 19, satellites of the Proton series, the space stations Salyut 3 and Salyut 5, and heavy modules used in the Mir space station programme.
– The fourth OKB, the Gazodinamitcheskaia Laaboratoria (GDL), was directed by its founder, Valentin Glouchko, until early 1989. It is developing powerful liquid fuel rocket motors at its laboratories in Leningrad.

In addition, there is a series of specialised OKBs established to develop lunar and planetary probes (under the direction of V. M. Kovtunenko), meteorological satellites (founded by Andronik Issofian), geostationary telecommunications satellites (directed by Mikhail Rechetnev), recoverable reconnaissance satellites (directed by Dmitri Kozlov, and situated at Kouibychev), upper stage boosters for launchers (founded by Kosberg at Voronej, and directed by Alexander Konopatov), and orbital manoeuvre engines (founded by A. M. Issaiev).

The specifications of missiles, launchers and space engines are drawn up in the Central Ideas Bureau of the MGEP, under the direction of a 'constructor in chief'. This person, who is responsible for ensuring that the programmes are carried out, has overall control of them. A council of principal constructors, which has existed since the time of Sergei Korolev, has a role which can be compared to that of the constructors in chief. The MGEP also includes technical institutes, whose function is to carry out research and development work in order to improve rocket and space engine technologies. The Central Institute for Scientific Research into General Engineering, directed by Vassili Michine since 1972, has an important role in developing future space programmes. Until the beginning of 1989, the person in overall charge of these programmes was Valentin Glouchko, with V. Goubanov being responsible for Energia and Y. Semionov in charge of Buran.

The Soviet Academy of Sciences, which has the same rank as a ministry, is responsible for defining and carrying out scientific and technical research programmes. Several of its institutes are responsible for conceiving and then developing and running scientific experiments. The most famous of these is the Institute of Cosmic Research (IKI, Institout Kosmicheskikh Issledovaniy) in Moscow, which until 1988 was directed by Roald Z. Sagdeev. Since then the Director has been Alex A. Galeev. The Institute of Applied Mathematics also plays an essential role. It was created by Mstislav Keldych, a scientist who along with the engineer Sergei Korolev was instrumental in initiating the Soviet space programme. The Institute of Applied Mathematics is responsible for all the theoretical and ballistic calculations required by the different space programmes in the USSR. The Academy of Sciences contains a committee, called Intercosmos, which is responsible for all the scientific programmes carried out in collaboration with other countries of the Eastern bloc. Intercosmos' importance appears to have decreased with the creation of Glavkosmos. The Academy of Sciences is also responsible for the fleet of ships which track orbiting spacecraft.

There are some institutes, which do not depend on either the MCMG or the Academy of Sciences, but still carry out important work relevant to the development of new space systems. This is the case for the Central Institute of Aero-Hydrodynamics (TsAGI) which is closely associated with the Soviet space shuttle or space plane projects. TsAGI (Tsentralny Aeroguidrodinamicheski Institut) comes under the Ministry of Aeronautical Construction.

Outside the MGEP, the Ministry of Defence plays an equally fundamental role. The Soviet armed forces are not content just to use military satellites, which constitute the majority of payloads launched. They are also involved in other aspects of space experiments. This has had two results, first, to ensure that large space installations and launch bases are built and, second, to control all the strategic missiles which carry out the launches and to take responsibility for the payloads until they are placed in orbit. The air force controls the astronaut training centre, and is also responsible for recovering manned spacecraft returning from space.

Alain Dupas

The men responsible for the Soviet space programme. After the success of the Vega interplanetary probes to Halley's comet, a reception was held at the Kremlin, on 18 March 1986. To celebrate the occasion, all the top people responsible for the Soviet space programme were invited to meet Mikhail Gorbachev. From left to right they are M. V. Zimianine, secretary to the Central Committee of the Communist Party; L. N. Zaikov, a member of the Politburo, and also a secretary to the Central Committee; A. I. Dounaev, director of Glavkosmos; R. Z. Sagdeev, director of the Institute of Cosmic Research; E. P. Velikhov, vice-president of the Academy of Sciences; Mikhail Gorbachev; V. M. Kovtunenko, director of the Bureau of Studies into Interplanetary Probes, an ex-president of the Academy of Sciences; A. P. Alexandrov, and the ballistics expert on the Vega project, J. A. Mozzhorine (Tass).

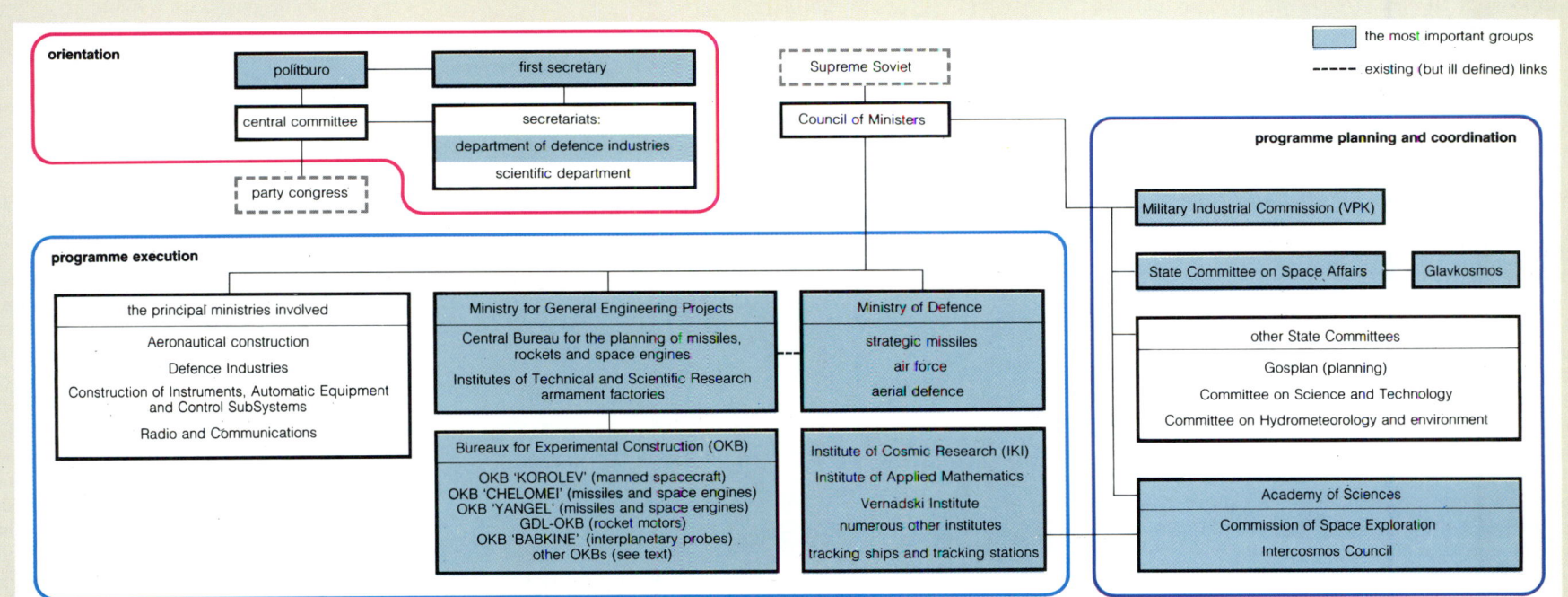

The USA

The creation of the National Aeronautics and Space Administration (NASA) in 1958 focused attention on rocket technology that had been developed primarily for military purposes, but came to be adapted by NASA and its contractors for civil space applications. All the so-called expendable launchers – Delta, Atlas and Titan – were developed in this way. Indeed, Vanguard, planned to be the first American satellite, had originally been scheduled for launch by a rocket developed specifically for military applications. However, after the launcher failed, the first US satellite, Explorer I, was put into orbit by the Jupiter rocket developed by the Army.

The forerunner of today's satellite communications industry, a rudimentary communication device called SCORE (Signal Communication by Orbiting Radio Equipment), was launched in 1960 by an Air Force Atlas rocket. And the first two phases of the US manned space programme, Mercury and Gemini, depended on the Army Redstone and the Air Force Atlas and Titan rockets for their launches.

It is therefore difficult to separate military and civil space development in the early decades of spaceflight. Indeed, until the mid 1970s the only space industry that generated any significant revenue was that created by government contracts. Government agencies hired industrial firms to design and manufacture launchers and spacecraft to fulfil both military and civil government space requirements.

This aspect of space industry continues today to be by far the main source of revenue for those companies which comprise the US industrial capability in this field. The only other major revenue source is satellite communications, both satellite and ground station hardware and communications services (voice, data, television and facsimile).

There are, however, several new areas of space industrial development on the horizon. For example, the Remote Sensing Commercialization Act initiated the transfer of the government supported Earth observations programme, Landsat, to a private corporation called Eosat. This was created jointly by Hughes and RCA (Radio Corporation of America).

Jerry Grey

Marketing satellite launchers

In the 1960s and 1970s, NASA used the Atlas, Atlas Centaur, Delta and Scout rockets to launch scientific satellites and commercial communications satellites into orbit. The Department of Defense (DOD) was primarily involved in the development of military communications satellites.

The communications satellite business, as it evolved in the United States, started with Early Bird. This, the first successful geosynchronous communications satellite, was developed jointly by NASA and AT & T (American Telephone and Telegraph Company). Subsequently, the International Telecommunications Satellite Organisation (Intelsat) was formed to stimulate and develop the international use of communications satellites.

Marketing launch services then was fairly straightforward because the US had a monopoly in the market. These early launches were offered at a price equivalent to the additional cost of the launch for the communications satellite customer. As the market developed and the demand for communications satellite launches increased, the US Government adopted a pricing policy that required the communications satellite customer to pay all reasonable costs associated with developing and maintaining the expendable launch vehicle (ELV) capability. These costs included the cost of maintaining the launch facilities and the asso-

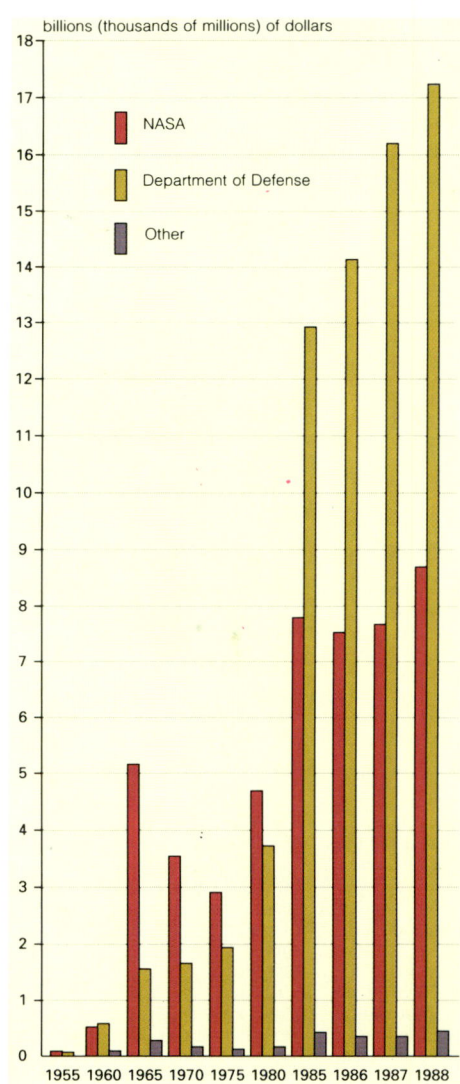

American federal space budgets. Most industrial space activity in the USA is in the form of federal contracts for equipment and services put out to industry and universities. The extremely rapid growth in military procurement in recent years is particularly evident (*Aerospace Facts & Figures*, Aerospace Industries Association, 1987–88).

The growth of American space expenditure from 1974. NASA was responsible for most of the money spent on space contracts until 1981. During this year, military spending outstripped it. By 1982, military spending overtook the combined expenditure of NASA and the commercial sector which had begun in 1979 (Euroconsult, *World Space Industry Survey. Ten Years Outlook*, 1988).

ciated mission control centre and, where appropriate, the costs of analysing launch failures. It was during this period that the communications satellite insurance industry grew out of the need to reduce the cost risk associated with the uncertainties of spacebased operations.

The space shuttle. The space shuttle was conceived from the start as a reusable launcher that would substantially bring down the cost of launching satellites. The intent was to make space more accessible to all space users, both in industry and in government. The early shuttle pricing policy was based on the goal of recovering from all users their fair share of the full operating costs of a twelve year programme. To establish the base price, NASA estimated the cost associated with twelve years of Space Transportation System (STS) shuttle operations and divided this cost by the expected number of flights in the period. Adjustments were made for each market segment, depending upon NASA's relationship with the user. Discounts were allowed for ESA and its member nations because they participated in the development of Spacelab (see pp. 278–83). The DOD price was adjusted to account for NASA's use of the launch facilities at the USAF Vandenberg Air Force Base. Commercial and foreign organisations were charged a fee for the use of Government facilities and services. In short, adjustments were made to account for the different markets to be served by the space shuttle, but with all users paying their fair share.

Unlike the early ELVs, one shuttle flight could launch several satellites and a wide variety of tasks could also be undertaken in orbit. It was necessary, therefore, to develop the concept of both standard and optional services which the shuttle could provide for both satellite and Spacelab users, and to offer the lowest possible base price. It is important to point out here that all the terms and conditions for a shuttle launch were developed in a conservative and monopolistic environment. Perhaps for this reason the launch agreements, financial restrictions, penalty fees for schedule adjustments, operational constraints and documentation requirements were not so oriented towards the customer as they later became. The ELVs were being phased out because it was judged that the cost of maintaining both expendable and reusable launch capabilities would be excessive. To encourage ELV users to transfer to the shuttle, a 10% price reduction was offered for the first three years of operation. Intelsat was the first to accept the offer and endured the arduous negotiation of the first launch service agreement. Within three years of the signing of the Intelsat agreement, 70% of the communications satellite market had reserved flights on the space shuttle.

A presidential directive, dated 11 February 1988, authorised the Department of Defense to acquire non-reusable launchers from the Titan IV, Atlas II and Delta II Series. This change has had the effect of decreasing NASA's military market.

Arianespace. The semi-private Arianespace ended NASA's monopoly in the communications satellite launch market and changed its approach to marketing launches using the shuttle. Arianespace's focused efforts to penetrate NASA's communications satellite market were successful and, to remain competitive, both NASA and Arianespace quickly moved to a less than full operations cost pricing. Where appropriate, both NASA and Arianespace allocated costs to their governments' base. However, the loss of the space shuttle Challenger and its impact in the USA on the development of commercial launchers for communications satellites arrested the competition with Arianespace. The loss of an Ariane IV rocket on 22 February 1990, when it exploded 101 seconds after take-off has changed the picture again.

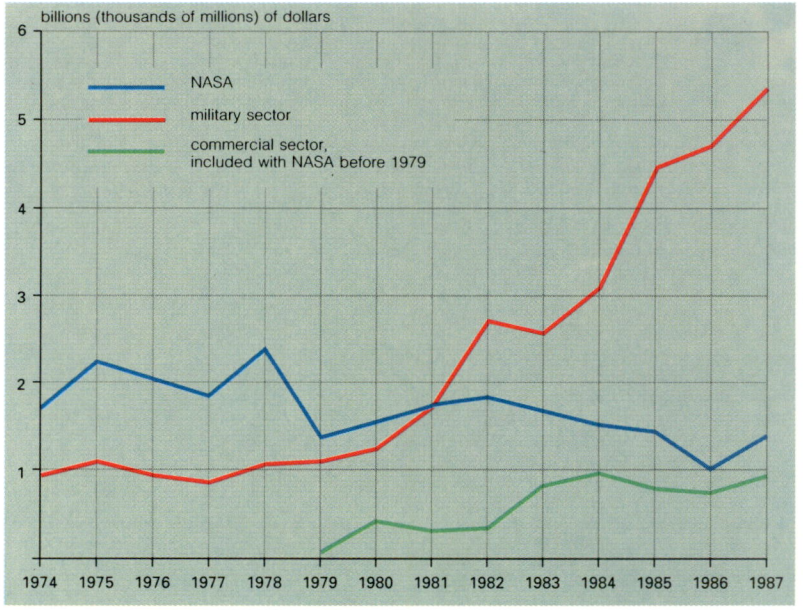

The production of American launchers capable of putting satellites into geostationary orbits. The space industry had its heyday in the 1960s, with three different types of rockets – Atlas, Titan and Delta. It has decreased since, in proportion to the reductions in the US civil space budget, and as the importance of the space shuttle has increased.

This graph does not include the 33 Saturn rockets launched between 1961 and 1975 (Euroconsult, *World Space Industry Survey. Ten Years Outlook*, 1988).

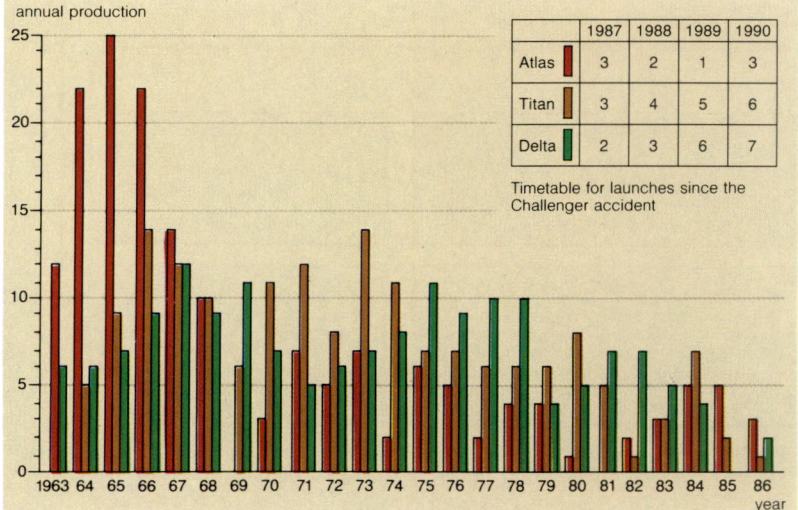

	1987	1988	1989	1990
Atlas	3	2	1	3
Titan	3	4	5	6
Delta	2	3	6	7

Timetable for launches since the Challenger accident

Additional factors influenced the market's decision to use one launcher rather than the other. These were the perception of the reliability of the launcher, the confidence that the users had in the launch schedule, and the ease of accommodating customer requirements.

Marketing the shuttle was difficult because NASA's charter was not primarily focused on the objective of making the shuttle cost effective. The shuttle programme supported many projects involving international scientific research. It supported the DOD for national security, and it supported a continuing role in developing space technology. Such factors led to a highly complex and often conflicting set of objectives for it and NASA. Marketing the shuttle to such diverse users involved many compromises not found in a typical industrial marketing programme with the sole objective of making, and retaining, satisfied customers.

Chester M. Lee

Other commercial activities

Several companies have committed themselves to another potentially significant area of space industry, by providing services to both commercial and government users. By far the most widely publicised of such services is space transportation – putting spacecraft into orbit. McDonnell Douglas designed and built the Payload Assist Modules (PAMs) to boost spacecraft from the shuttle's altitude to geosynchronous transfer orbits. Boeing Aerospace developed the Inertial Upper Stage (IUS), with US Air Force support, to transport large shuttle launched payloads such as the Tracking and Data Relay Satellite, and large interplanetary scientific spacecraft like Galileo and Ulysses (studies over the solar pole). Galileo was successfully launched using Atlantis on 18 October 1989; it will travel to Jupiter via Venus. General Dynamics manufactured the high performance cryogenic Centaur upper stage rocket. This is used in the Titan IV vehicle to launch the biggest military payloads into their prescribed orbits.

Another activity generating revenue for the space industry is payload integration, that is preparing commercial satellites for launch by making sure that all interface requirements with the launch vehicle are properly met.

The segment of space industry with by far the greatest potential, however, is space manufacturing. Although still in its early research phase, there is ample evidence that the processing of certain products in the virtual absence of gravity or in the essentially infinite volume of nearly perfect vacuum, conditions available only in the space environment, offer significant market opportunities. Under conditions of microgravity, crystal growth, the separation of complex fluid mixtures, the solidification of mixed liquids, and the containerless melting and alloying of metals proceed without the complications such as convection and sedimentation which occur in the presence of gravity. Thus, a degree of purity that is unobtainable in the omnipresent gravity at the Earth's surface is achieved in space.

In some cases the microgravity environment available in space allows materials that cannot be made at all on Earth to be manufactured. The 3M Company, for example, has demonstrated the growth of organic crystals whose use in computer chips could significantly reduce their size and increase computer speed correspondingly.

The vacuum obtainable in the wake of a shield towed by the shuttle or a space station permits the vapour deposition of ultrapure, flaw free electronic materials. These could be used for making high electron mobility transistors which might be able to boost computing speeds by perhaps a thousand times over those achieved in present microprocessors.

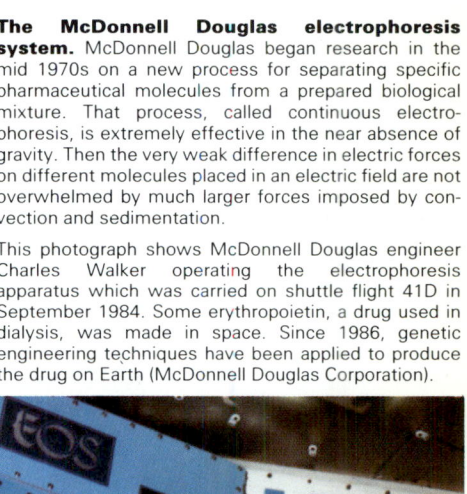

One of the accessories designed to increase the electrical power available to the space shuttle. The Solar Array Flight Experiment (SAFE) is a flexible structure capable of producing 12·5 kilowatts of power from solar radiation (NASA).

The McDonnell Douglas electrophoresis system. McDonnell Douglas began research in the mid 1970s on a new process for separating specific pharmaceutical molecules from a prepared biological mixture. That process, called continuous electrophoresis, is extremely effective in the near absence of gravity. Then the very weak difference in electric forces on different molecules placed in an electric field are not overwhelmed by much larger forces imposed by convection and sedimentation.

This photograph shows McDonnell Douglas engineer Charles Walker operating the electrophoresis apparatus which was carried on shuttle flight 41D in September 1984. Some erythropoietin, a drug used in dialysis, was made in space. Since 1986, genetic engineering techniques have been applied to produce the drug on Earth (McDonnell Douglas Corporation).

The Indian satellite INSAT 1B. The triple purpose INSAT 1B satellite, built for India, is shown during final assembly operations at Ford Aerospace & Communications Corporation's Western Development Laboratories Division in Palo Alto, California. Unique among satellites, INSAT 1B combines telecommunications, television broadcasting and meteorological services in one spacecraft. INSAT 1B was successfully launched by mission specialists from Challenger during the eighth mission of the space shuttle on 31 August 1983 (Ford Aerospace & Communications Corporation).

Although not precisely space industry, an important use of the space environment is for research applicable to Earth bound manufacturing operations. The John Deere Company, for example, has used microgravity research to improve the processes by which it makes cast iron for its farm tractors and other heavy machinery. Both NASA and the European Space Agency have strongly emphasised this indirect, but extremely important, industrial use of spacebased research facilities.

The greatest potential for using the space environment, however, lies in the development and manufacture of chemical catalysts. Used in extremely small quantities, these are absolutely essential for the manufacture of many industrial chemicals. Because the physico-chemical mechanisms by which catalysts work are not at all well known, new catalysts cannot be devised by any systematic analytical process. They are largely developed by trial and error. Further, because catalysts themselves do not participate in the chemical reactions they accelerate, they are generally composed of materials with very low reaction rates. It therefore takes a long time both to experiment with them and to manufacture them. Effects such as sedimentation and convection, which are induced by gravity, accordingly make catalyst research and manufacture extremely difficult and expensive, and often prevent the required degrees of purity being obtained.

As yet, however, there is no manufacturing industry in space. The only space made products marketed to date have been tiny, monodisperse latex spheres. These are used for calibrating electron microscopes and other laboratory instruments, clearly a highly limited market. A great deal of research and testing must be undertaken before marketable products can be identified, evaluated, and put in production.

The primary need for at least the next decade, is for orbital test facilities of various types. NASA and other organisations have conducted brief tests using samples dropped from towers, which give about four seconds of microgravity time. Aircraft flying parabolic paths offer about 30 seconds in a microgravity environment. And for a number of years rocket

Living with space

Martin Marietta's space station design. In 1987 NASA invited tenders from a selection of space station constructors. This picture shows the design produced by Martin Marietta. Other companies who submitted designs included Boeing Aerospace, General Electric, McDonnell Douglas, RCA and Rockwell International. Designs from the first three companies together with Rocketdyne, a division of Rockwell, were finally accepted (NASA).

experiments in the US SPAR programme and the West German Texus programme have offered up to about six minutes of microgravity during a rocket's period above the atmosphere.

Manned microgravity environments in space have an acceleration due to gravity that is one thousandth of that at the Earth's surface (10^{-3} g). Such values pertain in shuttle mid deck lockers and payload bay racks. The facilities available include the Materials Services Laboratory, the Materials Experiment Assembly, the Experiment Apparatus Container, Spacelab racks, panels, and pallets (including the Spacelab itself) and 'Get Away Special' (GAS) canisters. NASA's Long Duration Exposure Facility (LDEF) and the European Eureca spacecraft offers similar environments, of approximately 10^{-5} g.

In the more distant future, extensive longterm microgravity facilities on the space station will offer values of 10^{-3} to 10^{-4} g, with station tended 'free flyers' going down to perhaps 10^{-6} g.

In the next century there may be prospects for a power satellite, in which large arrays of solar photovoltaic cells in orbit would generate electric power to be beamed down to Earth continuously. Space station operations and a lunar base to extract and manufacture materials are essential ingredients of such future large scale space projects. They could make the world less dependent on both fossil and nuclear fuels with their environmental dangers.

Although there is no way to make accurate projections of future space industry revenues, it is quite evident that they will eventually be substantial. The question is not really how much, but how soon. McDonnell Douglas Astronautics have been investing heavily in pharmaceutical manufacture in space since 1976, but are not likely to generate their first return on that investment until a decade and a half later. In 1986 their entire investment was written off due to a loss of the entire market for the first space-manufactured drug – erythropoietin – to groundbased genetic technology competitors.

Hence the companies that are investing today are not likely to survive unless they are able to carve out a small profitable area or, like 3M, have other product lines whose revenues will sustain the necessary research until the expected large markets develop.

Nonetheless longterm prospects are excellent. From past experience we know that research in wholly new environments will eventually lead to new product opportunities. It is likely that, with the space station operating in the mid 1990s, the research opportunities so essential for the development of a space manufacturing industry will occur.

Jerry Grey

Examples of NASA contracts in USA (Euroconsult)

Company	Main space programmes	Total NASA contracts (millions of dollars)		
		1975	1980	1987
Rockwell International Corp.	prime contractor for space shuttle and GPS/Navstar navigation satellites	682	1273	1610.2
Martin Marietta Corp.	shuttle external tank, Manned Manoeuvring Unit (MMU) for extravehicular activity (EVA), prime contractor for Viking to Mars	130	233	325.9
Lockheed Space Operations Co.	maintenance of shuttles and their ground segment at Kennedy Space Center and Vandenberg Air Force Base	–	–	323.3
Morton Thiokol Inc.	advanced propulsion systems, including shuttle solid fuel boosters	29	79	286
McDonnell Douglas Corp.	Delta launcher, Payload Assist Module type apogee motors, integration of shuttle payloads, including Spacelab	125	160	285
GE–RCA Corp. (General Electric–Radio Corporation of America)	telecommunications, TV broadcasting, weather and ACTS satellites	40	32	225.4
USBI (United Space Boosters Inc., a subsidiary of United Technologies Corp.)	shuttle solid fuel boosters	–	43	183
Boeing Co.	Inertial Upper Stage (IUS), Swedish Viking scientific satellite	44	45	174.8
United Technologies Corp.	solid fuel boosters for military Titan 34D, satellite propulsion systems	36	75	165.6
Allied Bendix Aerospace	electronic and microelectronic systems, expert systems and software	76	97	142
TRW Inc. (Thompson Rano Woodridge)	scientific satellites, military and civilian telecommunications satellites, research and development on space weapons	34	42	124.5
Ford Aerospace & Communications	communications and weather satellites, management of Department of Defense space control centre	29	48	119.9
Lockheed Missiles & Space Co.	military early warning satellites and telecommunications satellites	–	47	107.9
IBM (International Business Machines)	on board and ground data processing systems	54	84	72
General Dynamics Corp.	Atlas Centaur launcher, Centaur upper stage	85	46	25.4

Canada's commercial successes

Canada was quick to recognise the possibilities of space technologies. It was responsible for the Remote Manipulator System (RMS) fitted to the American space shuttle (see photograph, right) and has now turned its attentions towards satellite telecommunications with the aim of reducing the cost of communicating with its rural and outlying areas. Anik A, the first generation of domestic satellites was launched in 1972. It was followed by the Anik B series (in 1978), Anik C (1982, 1983 and 1985), Anik D (1982 and 1984) and Anik E (1990). Canada also had to develop a groundbased system to cope with the new technology. In May 1986, the Canadian government launched a new telecommunications programme, the M Sat programme, in which fourteen companies are involved.

The M Sat system will provide the following services:
– vocal radiocommunications between a central region and Canadian aircraft and ships;
– a two way telephone service between vehicles equipped with M Sat terminals, linked through the telephone network, a telephone service designed for Canadians living outside existing telephone networks;
– a data transmission service for use in locating mobile vehicles, and for gathering data from small stations all over Canada about, for example, pollution, pipelines, alarm systems and lighthouses;
– a one way SOS system for Canadian aircraft and ships.

The first generation of M Sat consisting of a single satellite and a ground segment will have a control and communications centre, access stations, exchanges and 65 000 mobile terminals. It will require an investment of 500 million dollars from Telesat Canada and other relevant industries. The companies expect a return of more than 2000 million dollars from customers using the first two generations of satellite and Canadian industry expects to export 1000 million dollars worth of products relating to the M Sat system in the 1990s.

Canada is also involved in some of ESA's major programmes, such as the Olympus satellite launched in July 1989, and the ERS 1 remote sensing programme.

Robert W. Breithaupt, Pierre M. Boudreau
and Hugh M. Reekie

The 'Canadarm'. Work began on the Canadarm in 1974, and it was first used aboard the space shuttle, Columbia, on 12 November 1981. This arm was also used in August 1985, by astronauts on Discovery when repairing the Syncom IV 3II satellite. The project has given Canada great expertise in the field of robotics and Canada will be responsible for a similar system for the orbiting space station, Freedom. This will consist of the Mobile Servicing System (MSS) which includes the Remote Manipulator (RMS) and the American Flight Telerobotic Servicer (FTS) (NASA).

Japan

Japan's space development programme has been actively supported by the nation's space industry since 1955 when the University of Tokyo started research on solid fuel rockets. Following the development of various types of sounding rockets, Japan's first satellite launch vehicle, the four-stage solid propellant launch vehicle Lambda 4S, was developed and put Japan's first satellite, Ohsumi, into orbit on 11 February 1970.

The space development programme at the University of Tokyo was subsequently reorganised as the Institute of Space and Astronautical Science (ISAS), which developed a fully fledged launch vehicle, Mu 4S. Further improvements made to the launch vehicle led to the completion of the Mu 3S II. Successful Mu launches promoted Japan's scientific satellite programme. A total of 17 experimental and scientific satellites had been launched from the ISAS Kagoshima Space Centre by the end of 1988. Two of these satellites, Sakigake and Suisei, were put into orbit around the Sun in 1985 to explore Halley's comet. On 25 January 1990, a Muses A satellite was successfully launched from the Kagoshima Space Centre. The satellite went into orbit round the Moon on 19 March 1990.

In 1960, the National Space Activities Council (NSAC) was established in the Prime Minister's Office. In 1968, the Space Activities Commission (SAC) was set up to succeed NSAC. In 1969, the National Space Development Agency of Japan (Nasda) was founded as a special corporate entity. Its primary responsibility is to implement practical applications of space developments solely for peaceful purposes, whereas ISAS carries out activities in the field of space science. Nasda has developed satellites for various practical applications and

also the N I launch vehicle with technical assistance from the United States. Japan's first geostationary satellite, ETS II, was launched by the N I launch vehicle from Nasda's Tanegashima Space Centre on 23 February 1977.

The N II launch vehicle, an upgraded version of the N I, was subsequently developed and has been used to launch eight satellites since 1980. To further improve its launch capabilities, Nasda developed the H I launch vehicle in 1986, featuring a liquid oxygen/liquid hydrogen second stage and a solid propellant third stage. To meet the expected needs of the 1990s, Nasda started development of the H II launch vehicle, which is capable of putting satellites weighing around two tonnes in geostationary orbit at low cost and with high reliability.

By the end of 1988, Nasda had launched 24 satellites, 21 from its Tanegashima Space Centre and three from NASA's Kennedy Space Center. The Muses A satellite was launched from the Kagoshima Space Centre in March 1990. This satellite is intended to go into an orbit which circles both the Earth and the Moon.

Industrial activities in Japan related to space date back more than thirty years. The utilisation of space is now drawing greater attention from other industrial sectors. Various new companies and business groups have recently been set up with the aim of commencing business activities in the fields of satellite communications and the industrial uses of space.

The fundamental direction of Japan's space programmes is toward the development and accumulation of autonomous technology on a world-class level while striving to promote international cooperation. Along this line, the two tonne class high performance satellite ETS VI and H II launch vehicle are scheduled to be developed by 1992. ERS 1, an earth resources satellite being developed jointly by the Ministry of International Trade and Industry (MITI) and Nasda, will be launched in 1992 by the H I

Company	Major products
Fujitsu Ltd	satellite communications equipment data processing systems and equipment material processing in space
Hitachi Ltd	Earth station system for Earth observation satellite measuring equipment for satellite and rocket large size space simulation chamber
Ishikawajima-Harima Heavy Industries Co. Ltd	rocket propulsion systems for N II, H I and H II attitude control systems experimental equipment for material processing in space
Japan Aviation Electronics Industry Ltd	inertial guidance system fuel quantity guaging system inertial sensor
Kawasaki Heavy Industries Ltd	experimental geodetic satellite launch facilities for N and H rockets nose fairing for H II

Mitsubishi Electric Corporation	communications satellites
	observation satellites:
	  Ionosphere Sounding Satellite (ISS)
	  Earth Resource Satellite (ERS 1)
	satellite communications Earth stations

Mitsubishi Heavy Industries Ltd	N I, N II, H I and H II vehicles rocket launchers and test equipment rocket chambers
Mitsubishi Precision Co. Ltd	guidance and control systems inertial navigation systems fly wheel
Mitsubishi Space Software Co. Ltd	system engineering service software development

NEC Corporation	scientific satellites
	observation satellites:
	  Geostationary Meteorological Satellite (GMS)
	  Marine Observation Satellite (MOS)
	satellite communications Earth stations

NEC Aerospace Systems Ltd	systems engineering software development
Nippon Oil & Fats Co. Ltd	solid rocket propellant pyrotechnics
Nissan Motor Co. Ltd	sounding rockets L and M launch vehicles solid rockets for N I, N II, H I and H II
Toshiba Corporation	broadcasting satellites subsystems, components and parts for spacecraft software for satellite systems

Major Japanese space companies (Society of Japanese Aerospace Companies, 1989)

Japanese space budget. The graph below shows the relatively late entry of Japan into space, the rapid growth from 1972 to 1977, and the slow increase since then. Japan's expenditure is about 0·04% of GNP which is comparable to the most committed European countries (UK, Sweden, West Germany).

Nasda controls most government funding (68·1% in 1988); but ISAS (14% in 1988) retains its independence, developing and operating the Mu solid fuel launchers from its own launch centre for scientific satellites. Other government agencies include the Ministry of International Trade and Industry (MITI), the Ministry of Transport (MOT) and the Ministry of Posts and Telecommunications (MPT) (Nasda).

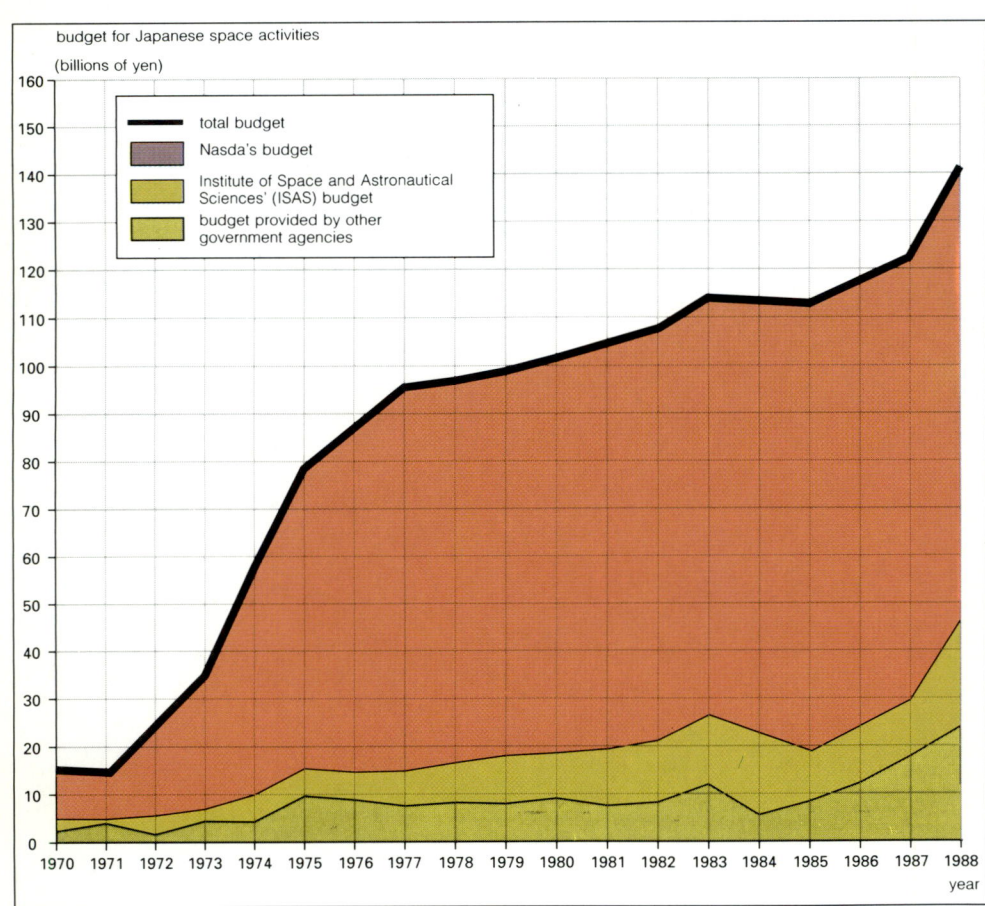

budget for Japanese space activities
(billions of yen)

- total budget
- Nasda's budget
- Institute of Space and Astronautical Sciences' (ISAS) budget
- budget provided by other government agencies

Satellite	Mass (kg)	Orbital altitude (km)	Launch vehicle	Launch date
ISS b	141	1220	N I4	16 February 1978
BSE	350	geostationary, 110° E	Delta 140	8 April 1978
ECS	130	failed	N I5	6 February 1979
ECS b	130	failed	N I6	22 February 1980
ETS IV	638	transfer orbit	N II1	11 February 1981
GMS 2	296	geostationary, 120° E	N II2	11 August 1981
ETS III	385	1000	N I7	3 September 1982
CS 2a	350	geostationary, 132° E	N II3	4 February 1983
CS 2b	350	geostationary, 136° E	N II4	6 August 1983
BS 2a	350	geostationary, 110° E	N II5	23 January 1984
GMS 3	303	geostationary, 140° E	N II6	3 August 1984
BS 2b	350	geostationary, 110° E	N II7	12 February 1986
EGS	685	1490	H I1	13 August 1986
JAS 1	50	1500	H I1	13 August 1986
MOS 1	740	909	N II8	19 February 1987
ETS V	550	geostationary, 150° E	H I2	27 August 1987
CS 3a	550	geostationary, 132° E	H I3	19 February 1988
CS 3b	550	geostationary, 136° E	H I4	16 September 1988
GMS 4	400	geostationary	H I	1989

ISS: Ionosphere Sounding Satellite; GMS: Geostationary Meteorological Satellite; CS: Communications Satellite; BSE: Broadcasting Satellite for Experimental Purposes; ECS: Experimental Communications Satellite; BS: Broadcasting Satellite; EGS: Experimental Geodetic Satellite; JAS: Japan Amateur-radio Satellite; MOS: Marine Observation Satellite.

Japanese application satellites, 1978 to 1989 (SJAC, 1989)

Japanese scientific satellites, 1970 to 1989 (SJAC, 1989)

Satellite	Mass (kg)	Orbital altitude (km)	Launch vehicle	Launch date
Ohsumi	24	337–5151	L4 S5	11 February 1970
TS Tansei	63	990–1110	M4 S2	16 February 1971
SS1 Shinsei	66	870–1870	M4 S3	28 September 1971
SS2 Denpa	75	250–6560	M4 S4	19 August 1972
TS Tansei II	56	288–3236	M3 C1	16 February 1974
SS3 Taiyo	86	260–3140	M3 C2	24 February 1975
TS Tansei III	130	791–3813	M3 H1	19 February 1977
SS5 Kyokko	126	636–3977	M3 H2	4 February 1978
SS6 Jikiken	90	227–30 051	M3 H3	16 September 1978
SS4 Hakucho	90	545–577	M3 C4	21 February 1979
TS Tansei IV	185	521–606	M3 S1	17 February 1980
SS7 Hinotori	180	576–644	M3 S2	21 February 1981
SS8 Tenma	216	497–503	M3 S3	20 February 1983
Sepac	participation in the first Space lab mission			28 November 1983
SS9 Ohzora	210	357–878	M3 S4	14 February 1984
TS Sakigake	138	heliocentric	M3 SII1	8 January 1985
SS10 Suisei	125	heliocentric	M3 SII2	19 August 1985
SS11 Ginga	420	505–673	M3 SII3	5 February 1987
SS12 Akebono	294	270–10 500	M3 SII4	22 February 1989

TS: Test Satellite; SS: Scientific Satellite; Sepac: Space Experiments with Particle Accelerators.

Satellite	Mass (kg)	Orbital altitude (km)	Launch vehicle	Launch date
SS13 Muses A	190	lunar flyby probe	M3 S II	1990
SS14 Solar A	420	550–600	M3 S II	1991
SS15 Astro D	420	550–600	M3 S II	1993
SS16 Muses B	300	1000–10 000	M3 S II	1993
MOS 1b	740	909	H I	1990
BS 3a	550	geostationary	H I	1990
BS 3b	550	geostationary	H I	1991
ERS 1	1400	570	H I	1991
Geotail	750	apogee of 1 600 000	space shuttle	1991
ETS VI	2000	geostationary	H II	1992
GMS 5	340	geostationary	H II	1993

SS: Scientific Satellite; MOS: Marine Observation Satellite; BS: Broadcasting Satellite; ERS: Earth Resources Satellite; Geotail: Magnetosphere Research Satellite; ETS: Experimental Test Satellite; GMS: Geostationary Meteorological Satellite.

Japanese satellite launch schedule, 1990 to 1993 (SJAC, 1989)

Research into space materials. This photograph, taken at the research centre at Kamakura, shows a researcher conducting studies on the surface of crystals grown by epitaxy. In the space vacuum, certain chemical components of the materials used evaporate. In some cases, the vapour condenses on the surface of optical systems or structures needing careful thermal control, thereby reducing their efficiency. Another problem is the damage caused by an electrostatic discharge through the vapour (Mitsubishi Electric Corporation).

Microsoldering at Mitsubishi Electric. This photograph, taken in the white room at Kamakura, shows where electronic subsystems are assembled. Different components are connected without using solder, making them reliable and keeping the mass to a minimum, an important consideration for space equipment (Mitsubishi Electric Corporation).

launch vehicle. In 1993, the Space Flyer Unit (SFU), an unmanned multipurpose reusable platform now being developed by ISAS, MITI and Nasda, will be launched by the H II launch vehicle and will be retrieved by the US space shuttle.

Both ISAS and Nasda are actively participating in various international cooperative programmes. To promote further utilisation of space, Nasda is planning to conduct the First Material Processing Test (FMPT) aboard a space shuttle. A total of 34 experiments will be carried out by one of the three Japanese payload specialists, who were selected in 1985 and have been trained in Japan and by NASA.

Japan has decided to participate in the international manned space station programme, Freedom, and will supply the Japanese Experiment Module (JEM). This is expected to foster and promote the growth of the space industry in Japan in the coming years.

Michiyoshi Shiraishi

China

Little known either inside or outside China until recently, the Beijing based Great Wall Industrial Corporation (GWIC) suddenly became a competitor with the major space agencies when China announced, in October 1985, that it would launch satellites for international customers. Operating within the Ministry of Aerospace Industry, GWIC reportedly charges at least 15% less than the rates offered by its foreign counterparts. By the end of 1987, about 30 foreign companies had asked GWIC to help them launch or recover satellites. They came from more than 20 countries including the United States, Australia, Brazil, the Federal Republic of Germany, France, Great Britain and Belgium.

Up until early 1989, China had twice successfully launched 'piggy back' satellites for overseas customers, but that is still short of the goal of up to four launches each year for foreign nations. However, GWIC has signed an agreement to launch Sweden's Freja satellite, two communications satellites for Australia, and Asiasat 1 which, as Westar 6, was recovered by the American space shuttle. This was successfully launched on 9 April 1990, using a Long March 3 rocket.

In August 1987, representatives of Matra from France were given two microgravity experimental devices that had orbited for five days in a Chinese satellite. The sealed French devices were rushed to Beijing after the return satellite – called FSW 1 – had been retrieved two days earlier in central Sichuan province, in the south west of China. The satellite had been launched into orbit by a Long March 2 rocket from the Jiuquan Space Launch Centre in the north west province of Gansu.

While its prime business is to conduct space flights, GWIC also deals in broadcast and communications equipment, electronics instruments and medical apparatus.

Up to the end of 1988, China had launched 25 satellites, including four geostationary telecommunications satellites, and retrieved all 11 of the satellites intended for retrieval. This 100% success rate is regarded as strong evidence of GWIC's reliable technological performance.

GWIC currently produces two types of launch vehicle. These are as follows.

– Long March 2 (CZ 2): this is a two stage, liquid fuel rocket, 32·57 metres long, 3·35 metres in diameter, with a mass of 191 tonnes at lift off; it can put a 2·5 tonne satellite into low

Earth orbit (see p. 116). An updated version of this launcher will soon enter service. With the addition of four liquid fuel boosters, the new Long March 2 rocket will be capable of putting 8 tonne satellites into orbit. The first Long March 2, launched in the late 1960s, had to be destroyed because a fault in its automatic control system made it veer off course during ascent. The rocket has since performed extremely well.

– Long March 3 (CZ 3): this is a three stage rocket, 43·25 metres long, 3·35 metres in diameter, with a lift off mass of 202 tonnes and a payload capability of 1·4 tonnes; it can put satellites into geostationary orbit. The third stage uses hydrogen and oxygen as fuels, and so requires cryogenic facilities at the launch site. An improved version of the Long March 3 is being developed. It will be powerful enough to put 2·5 tonne satellites into geostationary orbit.

The most powerful member of the Long March series of rockets is Long March 4 (CZ 4). This three stage rocket, 41·9 metres long, 3·35 metres in diameter, with a mass of 300 tonnes, can put satellites into Sun synchronous orbit. It was first used in 1988 to launch China's first meteorological satellite.

GWIC has three launch sites. Of the two already mentioned, the Jiuquan site is used for launching low Earth orbiting satellites with Long March 2 rockets, while the Sichuan province site of Xichang is used to launch geostationary satellites by Long March 3 rockets. Long March 4 rockets are launched from Taiyuan in Shanxi province in North China.

A telemetry and tracking network has the Weinan Control Centre near Xi'an as its nerve centre. In the case of a launch from Xichang, the satellite is tracked by the landbased control network for 460 seconds. After that, tracking is done by a ship in the Pacific Ocean. For the time being, this network can only track a satellite for one third of its orbit.

The several formal launch orders received so far show that GWIC is competitive. Apart from the low prices for its launching services, GWIC has the support of China's state insurance company, which charges lower premiums for its service. It is also keen to make business as easy as possible for its customers. GWIC has, for example, made arrangements with China's customs agency to allow foreign satellites to enter China without inspection. Foreign customers can take their payload to the launch site using their own personnel. GWIC requires only mechanical and dynamic information about a customer's satellite, such as its weight and moment of inertia, but not detailed information about its technical performance.

Chen Gengtao

Industry and space

Financing space activities

Contrary to scientific research and space exploration, which are entirely government funded, certain activities involving space technologies (such as launch vehicles, telecommunications, remote sensing and doubtless, in the future, space manufacturing) offer possibilities of making a profit. The question then arises as to whether they should be publicly or privately financed.

Space from the investors' point of view

An investment is generally made on the basis of a comparative analysis of four parameters. These are the amount of money needed; the period that will elapse between the time the investment is made and the time the returns appear; the size of the returns and how they are distributed over the years during which the investment is productive; and the risks incurred. The profitability is then determined by weighing the first three parameters against the risks.

However, on all four of these counts, any space enterprise is exceptional.

First, the sums to be invested over the initial years need to be very large, even when an existing system is to be bought. The most elementary communications systems, with two satellites in orbit and a spare on the Earth, costs at least 300 million dollars; and the ground equipment costs three to five times that much. For more advanced generations of satellites, or those used for industrial manufacture in space, the expenditures for research and development are considerably greater.

Secondly, at least three years elapse between the initial investment and the initial profits. This is the time needed to build and install a satellite using relatively well established technology. This time increases with the level of technological innovation and sophistication, and can reach as much as a decade for manufacturing systems in space.

Finally, the financial returns are closely related to three categories of risks. The first is market related. Does the demand actually exist, and has it been correctly evaluated? The second relates to all those technical worries that could be summed up by the single question – 'will it work?' Here it must be admitted that, except for the telecommunications sector, the answers to these questions are not yet very definite, because of lack of experience. Also, launch systems cannot be guaranteed to put a satellite into orbit, and the only recourse is to take out expensive insurance (see Space insurance, p. 340). The third type of risk relates to government policies. It concerns the administrative procedures and launch vehicle priorities, standards and approval of the products and services offered, and the size of government orders.

The role of government

Even though the use of space for profit goes along with a shift toward private sources of investment, all the major space programmes have been financed mainly by public funds through national space agencies (such as NASA in the USA, or CNES in France) or international agencies (such as ESA). Whether the programme is announced as being private in advance (as with the marketing of Ariane launch vehicles by Arianespace since 1980, or the sale by Spot Image of pictures from the French remote sensing satellite SPOT) or after the fact (like the sale of the first generation American remote sensing system Landsat to private concerns in 1985, or the forthcoming sale of the German Texus materials science rocket research programme), the transfer of responsibilities from the public to the private sector involves only the operation of the systems, never the initial investments.

More generally speaking, public expenditure on contracts for scientific or application programmes has made it possible for companies in the space sector to reach sufficient technological maturity to enter the market on their own. Governments provide funds for research and development before industry becomes involved in the field of space manufacture.

Governments also play a financial role as owners or customers of telecommunications and weather satellites, such as the international Intelsat and Eutelsat organisations. These consist of telecommunications organisations across the world and in Europe, respectively. Inmarsat is the international organisation for maritime communications and Eumetsat the body responsible for weather data over Europe.

Finally, governments support space activities in other ways, in particular through export credits, loan facilities, guarantees to lending organisations and the participation by national banks in the capital investment of companies like Arianespace and Spot Image.

Methods of funding

Internal versus external financing. Internal financing refers to purchasing a system from funds generated by a sponsor's activities outside space research, from accumulated funds, in the case of a government from hard currency reserves, or, for international organisations such as Intelsat, from capital contributions from member states or commercial owners.

External financing on the other hand means obtaining funds from sources outside the sponsoring organisation. This can be done by borrowing from banks, or through investment by other companies or individuals. This is usually necessary when the needs to build a system are far in excess of the buyer's ability to generate the required funds. The basis for external financing is the economic viability of the project, the sponsor's overall business profitability, or, in the case of a government, the ability to obtain tax revenues in hard currency.

Usually, the stronger the sponsor, the less relationship there is between the structure of the financing and the economic characteristics of the system. For example the US government or General Motors borrows for many projects under the same fund raising activity. Before 1980, with the exception of the initial capitalisation of the Communications Satellite Corporation, virtually all of the space systems were financed internally.

Construction financing. This refers to obtaining the funds necessary to build a system. A satellite buyer must pay for the satellite to be delivered to the launch site, the launch vehicle necessary to put the satellite into its appropriate orbit, the insurance cost, and the cost of the financing. This latter item is important because it takes up to three years to build a satellite.

Construction financing usually takes the form of investments or loans which are made during the two to three year construction period. The loans are then repaid over the life of the satellite. Because this is generally within the period over which a lender will be willing to accept repayment, the loans could finance the entire life of a satellite. Generally, however, a borrower will want to take advantage of lower cost funds available through tax oriented financing. In that case, the construction financing loans will be repaid through the proceeds of a permanent financing.

Permanent financing. This refers to the use of funds obtained through other means to repay the construction loans. Among the techniques used are:

Sale of capacity: the sale of rights to use parts of a system that the sponsor does not expect to use for long periods of time. The profit margin from the sale is then used to repay the construction loans for that part of the system that the sponsor will use. If parts are sold to different users, the technique is often called condominium financing. The profit margin is obtained from the ownership by an operator of the right to provide satellite service from a particular orbit location. Depending on the satellite power and the number of transponders, the cost per transponder after launch for a typical communications satellite can be up to six million dollars. If a user obtains the right to use a transponder over the lifetime of the satellite, the transponder is deemed to have been 'sold'. The owner of the satellite can then accept monthly payments over the life of the satellite, in which case the satellite owner is financing the user. However, the owner can sell the obligation of a user to a bank and use the proceeds to repay part of the construction loan, or accept a cash payment from the user which will also repay the construction loan. Examples of this type of transaction are the sale of transponders by Hughes Communications Inc. and Western Union Corporation.

Leasing or renting transponder space: the rights to use a portion of a system's bandwidth can be provided to a user on a monthly basis. In effect, a user is financed by the owner of the satellite. Capacity is leased in this way by the Radio Corporation of America (RCA), Western Union, Intelsat and many others.

Leasing (sale and leaseback): the rights to the satellite for its useful life are sold to a financing institution; the previous owner of the rights then rents use of the system. This technique is used to reduce financing costs. Expense is reduced because the new owner can obtain tax benefits that the original owner could not use. The effective cost to the sponsor is reduced somewhat by those benefits. This technique has also been popular because an owner who builds a system and generates revenue may not receive

The Viking satellite. The photograph shows the Viking Satellite being delivered from SAAB Space to the Swedish Space Corporation. This satellite was designed to study the ionosphere and the magnetosphere. The launch by the Ariane III rocket on 22 February 1986 enabled Sweden to join the select club of countries which have designed and launched their own satellite. This feat showed that Swedish industry could work in very advanced technologies.

Financing came from both State and private concerns. The Swedish Board for Space Activities defined the project which was managed, under contract, by the Swedish Space Corporation. The Industry Ministry is responsible for the space budget, which enjoys additional grants from the Ministry of Research and Education. In recent years, Sweden has increased her participation in the European Space Agency. The major private firms concerned are Saab Space, Ericsson and Volvo (Saab Space).

Olof Nordling

the same tax benefits as a buyer who can generate the same revenue. The sale and leaseback technique enables the equilibration of this situation by allowing a sale price to be increased to an equivalent retail value as determined by independent appraisers. Companies that have employed these techniques are General Telephone Electronics (GTE), American Telephone & Telegraph Co. (AT&T), Satellite Business Systems, and the Radio Corporation of America (RCA).

Sources of financing

Venture capital. This is direct investment in new companies. The form of investment is usually equity or a form of debt that will be converted ultimately to equity. An initial investment is usually followed by several more at staged intervals. Investment is usually made in amounts of less than five million dollars. Because the amounts are relatively small, this type of investment is usually not suitable for satellite purchases.

Suppliers of venture capital are private investors, banks and corporations with investment funds; and, in Europe, governments that have funds that aid in economic development. Surprisingly few space oriented investments have been able to obtain venture financing. Successful examples are Geostar Inc, Private Satellite Network Inc, Space Services Inc, and Scott Science and Technology.

Banks and institutional debt market. This market has the capacity to support the largest known commercial projects. Funds are usually supplied by small groups of large publicly or government owned banks and insurance companies. Users of this type of support tend to have the ability to repay loans from activities other than the satellite; they are usually financially strong companies or governments. Banks have in this way financed the acquisition of satellites by Australia's telecommunications organisation.

Export finance. This is a special case of the debt market where industrialised countries provide credit support in the form of loan guarantees to commercial banks and/or direct loans at

below commercial market rates to countries who have foreign exchange limitations. These agencies also support exports to companies in the form of credit or political risk insurance to enable commercial bank financing. Mexico and Indonesia have used this method to buy satellites from the United States, as has Brazil to purchase launch services from Arianespace.

Publicly owned debt and equity. In this case, debt obligations and equity are sold to the public. This is an international market with the capacity to finance virtually any known commercial activity. However, these markets are less flexible than the institutional debt markets. This makes the market tend more toward financing ongoing, rather than new, activities. (One notable exception was the 200 million dollar initial equity financing of the Communication Satellite Corporation in 1963.) Examples of companies that use this type of financing are AT&T, RCA, Ford Aerospace and Hughes Communications, Inc.

Customer progress payments. This financing is usually provided by the ultimate buyer who, in turn, obtains funds from banking or public sources. This is the principal form of financing used by governments for the procurement of large systems.

Limited partnerships, joint ventures and closely held corporations. These are forms of organisations where corporations and governments with corporations join together to form operating companies that need large amounts of capital but entail substantial business risk. Examples are Arianespace, Satellite Business Systems before sale to MCI, American Satellite Co. before sale to Contel, Inc., and the domestic satellite venture in Japan with Hughes Aircraft, Mitsui and C. Itoh.

Research and development limited partnerships. This is a type of organisation where high income people join in a partnership to develop a technology and sell it to a company which will then use it in its line of business. The incentives to the investors are royalties from the use of the technology and income tax benefits obtained from financing research and development. The

limited partnership was used in the development of Orbital Sciences Corporation's upper stage rocket motor used in conjunction with the space shuttle.

Joint endeavour agreements. This is an agreement by NASA to provide transportation on the space shuttle in exchange for a share in the revenues of the research and development space activity.

Project finance. This is a method where banks and others make loans and investments to a special purpose company based on revenue contracts obtained before the system is built. This technique, used in producing oil refineries, mines and energy sources, is appropriate when the capital needed for the project strains or exceeds the financial capacity of the builder. It has been tried many times but has been unsuccessful in space activities. The reasons have been that the ultimate users have not been willing to enter into contracts early in the long construction period, nor have insurance sources been willing to offer longterm commitments for launch insurance.

What future for private financing?

The need for finance in the future will ever be on the increase, particularly for new applications, higher payload costs, and higher insurance costs. However, if these needs continue to exceed the limits of the risk capital market, they must stay within the limits of the public and banking markets. It is most likely that the initial high risk investments will be those made directly by governments through the purchase of technology development such as the US Strategic Defense Initiative and the European Eureka projects.

Internal financing should still be widely used in the future. If insurers or governments manage to set up a structure that can offer insurance for the duration of the construction time and lifetime of a space system, project financing techniques could play a major role.

Jerome Simonoff

Industry and space

Space insurance

The early days

In the late 1960s and early 1970s, a space insurance industry was created. Space commercialisation was in its infancy. There were valid doubts on the insurance of space risks, so underwriters were persuaded only slowly to enter the field of launch insurance; launches during this period were generally not insured at all. As time progressed, the underwriters became braver, or the brokers more persuasive. The hardware was apparently reliable, and insurance rates dropped to such a degree that it became attractive for spacecraft owners to consider full insurance without deductibles.

When the European Space Agency Orbital Test Satellite (OTS) was launched in September 1977, it carried full insurance (at a value of 29 million dollars). The launch was a failure, and the Delta 3914 launch vehicle and the spacecraft were totally destroyed. This first major loss payment more than consumed the space insurance premiums accrued to that date. In February 1979 the Japanese ECS spacecraft was lost due to the collision of the third stage of the N 2 launch vehicle with the spacecraft. The claim amounted to some 14 million dollars.

A much larger loss occurred in December 1979, when the RCA Satcom 3 spacecraft, launched on a Delta rocket, was lost due to an apparent malfunction of the apogee kick motor built into the spacecraft. The loss to the market in this case was 77 million dollars. Nevertheless, the underwriting market was not excessively discouraged; it remained in place, and even grew over the period as a whole.

The next major loss did not happen for over two years, despite a significant number of launches in the interim. The Indian telecommunications and meteorological spacecraft Insat 1A failed in orbit following various operational difficulties, and finally fuel depletion. Although this was an in orbit failure, 70 million dollars were paid out by the underwriters under the launch policy which, traditionally, was arranged to include a period for spacecraft commissioning.

It might have been supposed that, by the end of 1982, with accumulated losses in excess of 200 million dollars, the underwriting market would have paused to reflect, and to examine launch risks. That this was not the case is perhaps a reflection of the general optimism existing in the whole industry. 1982 saw a number of launch risks being placed at very low rates. Launch rates on Ariane in the particular case of Intelsat fell below 8% of the insured value, while rates on the space shuttle fell to 6% or below. Even the second loss of an Ariane vehicle, on the occasion of the fifth launch, did not significantly dampen enthusiasm; the Marecs B spacecraft lost on this Ariane launch was insured for 20 million dollars. This second Ariane loss was due to the failure of a third stage turbopump, whereas the first loss (on the second launch) had been due to a combustion instability in the first stage.

Recent history

In February 1984 two spacecraft were left in low Earth orbit from the same shuttle launch. Both Westar 6 and Palapa B2 suffered the same failure; the perigee stage exit cone separated some seconds into the burn, leading to hot gases causing the motor rear domes to fail. In both cases the burn time was sufficient to place the satellites into low elliptical orbits, with perigees close to the shuttle orbit, and with apogees of around a thousand kilometres. The total insured value, some 180 million dollars, was paid by the underwriters, who then assumed title to the spacecraft. In subsequent protracted negotiations between NASA, Hughes as the spacecraft vendor, and the underwriters, a recovery plan was devised. Late in 1984, both spacecraft were recovered on a single shuttle mission, and then resold. Westar 6 was refurbished and relaunched as Asiasat by a Long March III rocket in March 1990 while Palapa B2, as B2R, will be launched by a Delta rocket.

Later in 1984 the Intelsat F9 spacecraft was lost due to a malfunction of the Centaur stage of the Atlas Centaur launch vehicle. This was considered to have originated in an oxygen tank rupture, which led to attitude loss during the coast phase and the inability to restart the Centaur engine. The loss was 102 million dollars.

It might have been hoped that three major losses in one year would, in some way, lead to a subsequent loss free period, if only because the losses surely pointed to a need for caution. That was not to be. A further four major losses occurred in 1985, of which three were insured. Syncom IV 3 failed to function following deployment from the space shuttle. It was yet again left in low Earth orbit, from which it had to be retrieved and activated manually on a subsequent shuttle mission.

The Syncom IV 3 spacecraft subsequently worked correctly, and reached the proper orbit. However, the claim for 85 million dollars lodged prior to its retrieval was paid as one of the conditions for the effort, and the underwriters stood to recoup only a part of the loss payment over a period of years. The total loss of Syncom IV 4, following a successful launch

Catastrophic launch failure of OTS 1. The Orbital Test Satellite (OTS) project of the European Space Agency was intended to demonstrate the ability of European industry to produce high performance telecommunications satellites. Two spacecraft were ordered, and the launch of OTS 1 was first attempted early in 1977. The launch campaign was terminated when one of the Castor IV 'strap on' solid rocket motors attached to the Delta launch vehicle broke loose on the pad due to defective attachment fittings, and hit the first stage of the vehicle. The solid rocket motor and the first stage were both replaced, and the spacecraft was finally launched in September 1977. The flight lasted about 55 seconds, when one of the strap on motors ruptured the first stage. This subsequently led to the break up of the vehicle, a huge explosion, and the total loss of the spacecraft. Subsequent enquiries showed that, in all probability, a defective solid propellant mix was the cause of the loss (NASA).

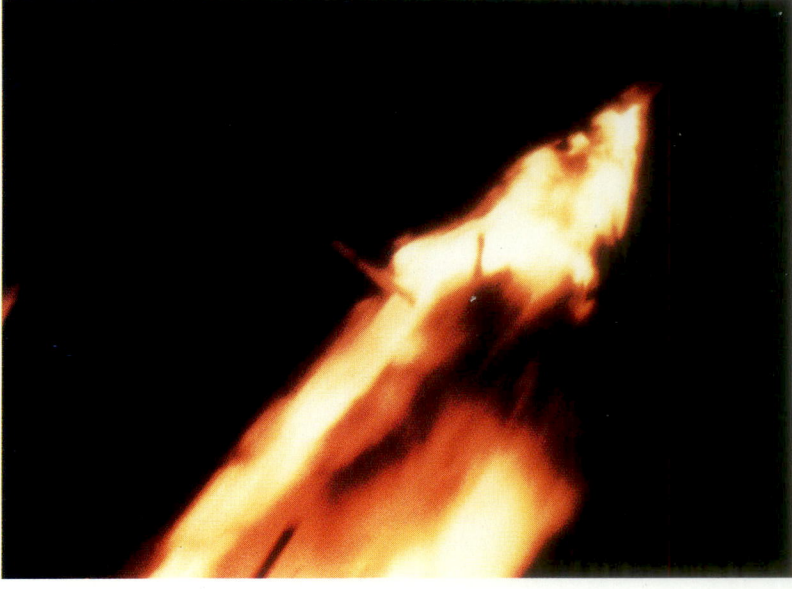

into the right orbit and a few days of operation, cost the underwriters a further 84 million dollars. The cause of the failure was apparently the disconnection of the antenna from the repeater.

The fifteenth flight of Ariane III in 1985 carried two insured payloads, Spacenet 3 for the General Telephone and Electric Co. (GTE) and ECS 3 for the European Space Agency. Their total value was approximately 167 million dollars. When the Ariane third stage failed to ignite due to valving problems, the loss was total.

Late in 1985 a military payload was lost when the Titan vehicle failed. Several possible causes were identified but no single explanation of the cause seems to have been identified. The next vehicle in the series was launched, virtually unmodified, in 1986. It, too, was lost. This time the cause was the burning through of the casing of a solid strap on motor. Three further notable launch failures occurred in 1986. The loss of Challenger on 28 January, the later loss of the GOES spacecraft aboard a Delta rocket, and the loss of Intelsat F14 on the eighteenth Ariane III launch in May.

The Challenger tragedy was the subject of an exhaustive enquiry. This revealed that one of the strap on solid fuel rocket motors had burnt through at a joint, causing flames to lick the external tank as well as rupturing that tank as the rocket broke free. It was concluded that the joint design was defective, and was known to have been less than perfect, and that the launch should not, moreover, have taken place after such a cold night.

The second Tracking and Data Satel-

Recovery of the Palapa B2 satellite. The failure of the McDonnell Douglas perigee stages on both Westar 6 and Palapa B2 left these spacecraft in low Earth orbit, a situation never seriously contemplated previously. After considerable technical evaluation, and in collaboration with the new owners, the insurance underwriters, a recovery plan was devised. This culminated in the recovery of both spacecraft. From on board the space shuttle Discovery, Joseph Allen and Dale Gardner, two mission specialists, performed spacewalks on 12 November 1984 to rescue the Palapa B2 satellite (NASA).

Intelsat F9 launched by an Atlas Centaur rocket. The loss of the Intelsat F9 spacecraft in June 1984 was due to a failure in the Centaur stage. An oxygen tank ruptured. Had this launch succeeded, it would have been the twentieth successive successful launch for vehicles of this family. The spacecraft was left in low Earth orbit, complete with apogee kick motor. Having separated from the Centaur rocket, it was later put into a reentry orbit, recovery being deemed to be dangerous and unjustified.

A subsequent launch in March 1987, which had been authorised despite poor weather conditions, was also a failure when the rocket was struck several times by lightning as it ascended (NASA).

lite, TDRS 2, was lost along with Challenger. However, it was not insured for the launch risk, and no property insurance existed for the hardware of either the shuttle or the payload. Following twenty-four successful shuttle flights, it might rather callously be construed that there was a 4% loss rate; shuttle only insurance cover had been available at 5% prior to the loss.

The loss of the geostationary GOES spacecraft followed 43 straight successes of the Delta launch vehicle, the last failure having been that of OTS in 1977. The cause of the failure seems to have been electrical, perhaps a wiring harness, but to have a failure after so many successes raises questions of quality control and procedures.

In summary, from 1977 to 1986, the total losses due to launch and commissioning malfunctions exceeded 900 million dollars. The corresponding insurance premiums were somewhat in excess of 500 million dollars.

The underwriters

As the number of failures mounted, particularly from 1984 to 1986, the insurance underwriting community became increasingly concerned about the risks entailed in space ventures. Even with a tried and tested launch system, changes are continually made, so that each launch vehicle will carry some items for the first time.

It may be of interest to review the attitudes of the main space underwriters over this period, both as an indication of attitudes and opinions and as a guide to the likely course of the market in the future. The first space insurances were largely prepared by aviation underwriters in London, at Lloyds and by the companies. In the early 1980s there were three main Lloyds leaders and a principal company lead. By 1986 only two of the previous Lloyds leaders remained in the business while the previous company lead was out of the business entirely so far as any new insurance was concerned.

There is little doubt that the London market capacity had halved from its peak, falling from over 60 million dollars per risk to under 30 million dollars from 1983 to 1986. This trend

stemmed, interestingly, not only from disillusionment with the space business but from the abundance of non-space, high risk businesses from which underwriters could choose. This was not to the benefit of space activities.

The European markets for space insurance were relatively large in the early 1980s, and remained so to a remarkable degree considering the circumstances. European underwriters became increasingly selective in risk acceptance and increasingly demanding in terms of technical visibility. In summary, the total capacity in continental Europe has amounted to some 40 million dollars, and has not shown great signs of contraction.

The situation in the United States has been more complex. In the early 1980s a significant number of underwriters with large capacity were available to underwrite space risks, plus a host of smaller facilities. The total capacity per risk probably exceeded 60 million dollars at the peak. More recently this has been reduced to perhaps little more than 30 million dollars via the elimination of the smaller markets, and the dissolution of more than one major facility. By 1986 two underwriters alone represented the only major sources of underwriting capacity in the United States. In one case, the underwriter has attempted to restructure the insurance of space risks, and has taken the position that failures arising during the commissioning of a spacecraft following a proper launch should be the responsibility of the spacecraft manufacturer. This position has now changed. The smaller markets are taking up the slack and the maximum US capacity is now about 70 million dollars.

In summary, therefore, the risk capacity per launch went from a maximum of far in excess of 100 million dollars in 1983, to rather less than 100 million dollars in 1986, and has now built up to about 200 million dollars in 1989.

The future is clouded by the many catastrophic losses between 1984 and 1986. With such a loss of technical confidence, either underwriting results have to show a major improvement so as to keep the 'traditional' market in place, and even to grow as past losses are recovered, or other risk management and risk sharing schemes have to evolve. There

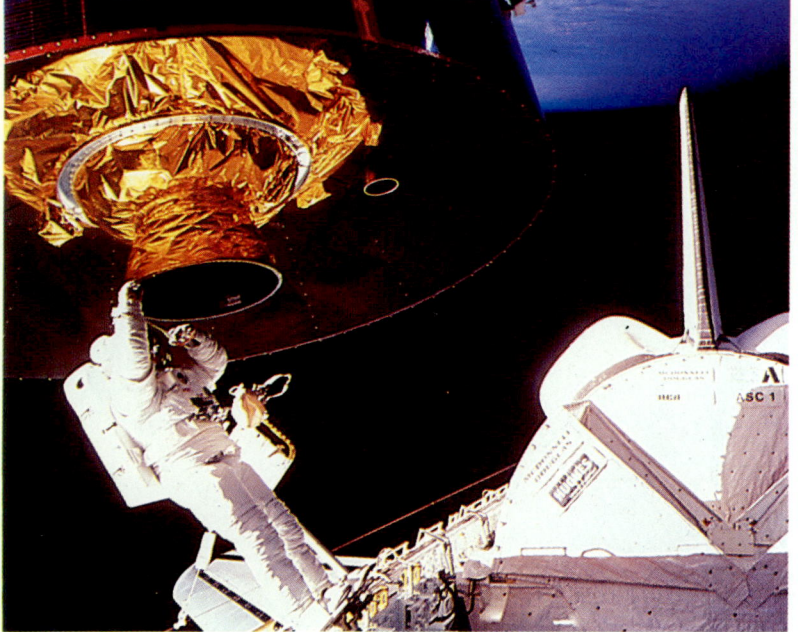

The repair of Syncom IV 3 in orbit. Syncom IV 3, otherwise known as Leasat 3, could not be activated following deployment from the space shuttle. The launching team made repeated attempts to activate the separation switch manually, but to no avail. On a subsequent mission, which also deployed Syncom IV 4, a 'jump-start' kit was attached to the spacecraft by the astronauts. This was successful; the perigee motor was duly ignited, the desired orbit was attained and the spacecraft was put into service (NASA).

Year of accident	Satellite	Cause	Result
1984	Westar 6	Pam D exit cone failure	recovery by another space shuttle
	Palapa B2	Pam D exit cone failure	
	Intelsat F9	Centaur failure	destruction
1985	Arabsat 1	In orbit malfunction	
	Telesat Anik D	In orbit malfunction	
	Syncom IV3	Separation malfunction	reduced performance, in orbit repair
	Syncom IV4	In orbit malfunction	
	Spacenet 3	Ariane third stage failure	destruction
	ECS 3		
	Military	Titan failure multiple causes	destruction
1986	TDRSS	Challenger loss due to solid fuel booster rocket failure	total destruction
	Military	Titan failure	destruction
	GOES	Delta first stage motor shutdown	destruction
	Intelsat	Ariane third stage failure	destruction
1987	Eutelsat F14	Centaur failure	destruction
	TV Sat 1	Solar panel failure	loss of satellite
1988	Télécom 1B	attitude control failure	loss
	Insat 1C	power supply failure	loss
	G Star III	wrong orbit because of satellite malfunction	

Space losses between 1984 and 1988 (Inspace Insurance)

The loss of Challenger. Early in 1986 Challenger was lost and all the crew of seven perished. The failure was due to the burning through of a seal at a joint between the segments of one of the solid rocket boosters. This was felt to be due to a combination of deficiencies of design, misunderstanding the behaviour of insulating putty and joint dynamics, and low air temperatures. As always with Failure Review Boards, the whole system was examined in fine detail, and doubt was cast on many non failure related items. The delay to the space shuttle programme exceeded two and a half years. However, since September 1988, all three orbiters, Columbia, Discovery and Atlantis, have made successful flights (NASA).

have been several initiatives in this latter direction, and Arianespace has offered a relaunch guarantee to be paid in advance via a surcharge on the launch service price.

Major American space companies have followed suit. Prior to the loss of Challenger, NASA had offered a marginal cost relaunch guarantee. There had also been an initiative by one group, including departments of the US government, to consider provision of a government backed (re)insurance facility, in order to promote space commercialisation. This is now considered superfluous.

The problem has been and will remain that commercial insurance capacity could hardly be expected to keep up with the existing, let alone the projected, demand. A double launch on an Ariane III or IV rocket could involve aggregate values for the two spacecraft of over 200 million dollars, perhaps reduced by 30% via the Arianespace relaunch guarantee. A triple commercial payload on a space shuttle, even with the marginal cost relaunch policy, could involve an insured value of 1000 million dollars. These are for single risks, and could not have been insured easily for Ariane or at all for the shuttle. It is for this reason that a Memorandum of Understanding was signed with NASA in December 1985 so as to provide up to 350 million dollars of coverage per bay. The rate projected, from main engine ignition through to deployment of the individual payloads was between 5% and 6% of the insured value. However, this is still only under discussion.

The future

The future direction for space insurance is hard to define given the many variables of launch capabilities and schedules, of future successes and failures, of user demand and of market reaction to events. It will take time to rebuild the confidence of users of the space shuttle, or of the Ariane, Atlas, Delta or Titan launch vehicles.

Against this background the Chinese have been aggressively marketing the Long March 3 launch vehicle, and have found customers. However, the vehicle is relatively new and the

Underwriting market	Maximum underwriting capacity per risk (millions of dollars)
U.S. domestic...............	70
Lloyds, and companies at Lloyds	40
European continent	76
Japan, Australia	6
Total maximum	192

Estimated market capacities
The actual capacity or participation that each underwriter offers on a given risk is normally less than the maximum amount shown (Inspace Insurance).

Loss history of commercial telecommunications satellites between 1977 and 1988 (Euroconsult)

Year of loss	Satellite	Insured value (millions of dollars)
1977	OTS	29
1979	ECS	14
	Satcom 3	77
1982	Insat 1A	70
	Marecs B	20[1]
1983	Satcom 2	9
1984	Palapa B2	75
	Westar 6	105
	Intelsat F9	102
1985	Leasat F4[2]	84
	Spacenet 3	85[1]
	ECS 3	85[1]
	Anik D2	5
	Intelsat F6/7	3
1986	Intelsat F14	82[1][3]
1988	G Star 3	77
	Insat 1C	72
	Total	994

1 Attributable to Ariane (total $272 million).
2 Leasat 3, later recovered, has not been calculated.
3 Estimate.

Year	Premiums	Losses	Cumulative premiums	Cumulative losses	Underwriting balance
1968 to 1977	31	29	31	29	+2
1978	8	0	39	29	+10
1979	13	91	52	120	−68
1980	7	0	59	120	−61
1981	29	0	88	120	−32
1982	52	90	140	210	−70
1983	80	0	220	210	+10
1984	107	288.5	327	498.5	−171.5
1985	162	336.5	489	835	−346
1986	56	84	545	919	−374

The premiums and losses for all launches from 1968 to June 1986 (all figures in millions of dollars). The estimated gross premiums exclude no claims bonuses, and they do not reflect the anticipated recovery of 130 million dollars for Leasat, Palapa and Westar losses (Inspace Insurance, 1987).

insurance prospect is clouded, not only by the lack of a flight record of sufficient span but also by the possible intervention of the Peoples Insurance Company of China. Of course, such an intervention could ease the situation if, as with Arianespace, the conventional space insurance market is not to be used to any degree.

So far as Russia is concerned, the Proton rocket is available, and has been for years, but its use is bedevilled by political considerations. The Japanese H2 rocket is still not proven.

However, the major nations will wish to exploit space for reasons of prestige, and in some cases of national security and commerce. This is why the western nations have supported the international space station initiative of the United States.

The current population of communications satellites is ageing and will require replacement. Despite trends towards the greater use of groundbased communications such as fibre optics for point to point communications, there remain distributed services that can best be provided via satellite. There will thus be a growing need to supply and launch telecommunications satellites.

As the commercial exploitation of space grows, so will the demand for insurance, since the financing of commercial ventures can only go ahead if insurance is available.

Brian Stockwell

The launch of Intelsat F14.
The loss of the Intelsat F14 spacecraft on the eighteenth Ariane III launch in 1986 was the second loss for Intelsat out of 13 launches. It was due to a failure of the oxygen and hydrogen third stage Ariane rocket. Thereafter, a major test effort was carried out to explore and define the performance boundaries of the ignition system. Successful modifications have meant that, until the Ariane IV explosion in January 1990, the Ariane rocket enjoyed several launches without mishap (NASA).

The military dimension

Space policies: the world stage

Space territory

When Sputnik 1 was placed into orbit on 4 October 1957, lawyers were forced to redefine the boundaries of space. With the onset of aviation, countries extended their national boundaries to encompass the air space above them. It then became international law that all the air space above a country where aeroplanes fly would be the exclusive property of that country.

With the birth of spaceflight, how could this type of boundary be extended into space? It could be projected upwards to an altitude where it is technically possible to ensure control of that space. However, such a limit depends on the performance of advanced space planes and their engines. Alternatively, it could be projected to an arbitrary height such as 100 kilometres. When the first artificial satellite was placed into orbit it was necessary to find yet another definition. The limit between national and international space is now fixed by the altitude of the lowest orbit in which a satellite can be placed to complete at least one Earth orbit. This is some 120 to 160 kilometres above the Earth's surface.

Extending into space the proposals adopted by the United Nations (UN) concerning the non-militarisation of the Antarctic, President Eisenhower put a motion before the General Assembly of the UN on 22 September 1960 to the effect that celestial bodies could not be the object of even tentative national appropriation, nor be used in any way as a theatre of war; that no nation should put weapons into orbit which could cause massive destruction; that all launches of spacecraft should be controlled by the UN; and that a programme of international cooperation should be established which would encourage the peaceful use of space and involve all the countries of the United Nations. In the year before, on 22 December 1959, the General Assembly of the UN had unanimously supported a similar proposal: 'It is in the interests of humanity to limit itself to peaceful uses of space which will benefit all the people of the World regardless of the state of their economic or scientific development'.

Military aspects of space

Between the first journeys of men into space in 1961 and the signing of the Space Treaty in 1967, the two superpowers and, to a lesser extent, France and Great Britain, proceeded to explore beyond the Earth's atmosphere. However, neither the USA nor the USSR restricted itself solely to peaceful activities. Both superpowers carried out work for civil purposes while adding a new dimension to their military prowess. And once the trajectories of experimental ballistic rockets reach altitudes of 1200 to 1500 kilometres, is it not true to say that space has been militarised? When Nikita Krushchev, as Secretary General to the Communist Party, announced in August 1957 that his country had detonated ballistic missiles that were capable of crossing the ocean, he put the

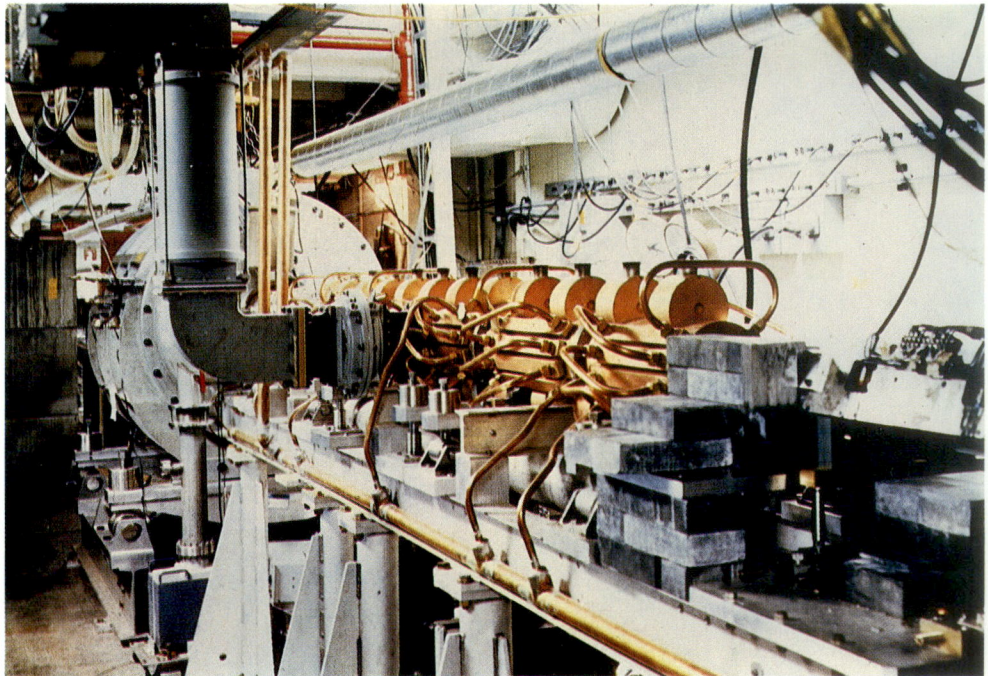

final nail in the coffin of the solely peaceful use of outer space. Henceforth space became a theatre of military operations.

On 27 January 1967, in Moscow, London and Washington, the UN Outer Space Treaty was signed. It was essentially the same as the resolutions passed by the UN on 17 March 1963. Whilst prohibiting countries from placing nuclear weapons and all massively destructive weapons in orbit around the Earth, it did not mention the military usage of space. It was too late to prevent that. The USA was studying a space plane, the forerunner of the space shuttle. The Soviet Union was experimenting with orbital bombardment in order to attack American defence installations from the rear, and beginning a long series of trials on anti-satellite satellites. Nowadays, spy photography, electronic surveillance, monitoring international agreements, surveying the migration of people around the world, mapping terrain to ensure the accuracy of ballistic rockets, strategic communications, and maritime navigation from space are all carried out in accordance with the guidelines of the 1967 Outer Space Treaty.

The American plan to build a space shield (Strategic Defense Initiative, SDI) has reopened the controversy over the use of space for military purposes. For these reasons, the Soviet Union asked the Secretary General of the UN to draw up 'a treaty prohibiting the use of weapons in extra-atmospheric space, and from space directed against the Earth … items in space are not to be used for any offensive means'. Obviously this text excludes all military uses of space that are already in existence, but it would prevent a nation from placing anti-satellite and anti-missile satellites into orbit. The current Geneva disarmament negotiations are marked by the deep opposition of the Soviets to the American SDI project. While Mikhail Gor-

bachev has accepted that work can be carried out in the laboratory, he is steadfastly opposed to trials in space and the deployment of space weapons.

France too has remained concerned about retaining the deterrent effect of her weapons. Interviewed on 12 June 1984, at the UN conference on disarmament, the French representative declared that a situation in which the two superpowers would look to avoid all counter-attacks, without being absolutely sure of achieving it, would be fraught with danger. 'France would like to see a limit on anti-satellite systems, and a prohibition on the deployment of directed energy weapons in space, for a renewable period of five years…. We refuse to accept the introduction of more and new weapons into space, which would create serious risks and destabilisation and cause the arms race to start once more on a new and dangerous path'. He was supported by the Soviets, and opposed by the Americans. But can a middle-ranking nuclear power really respond otherwise?

The SDI initiative

For the past forty years, the most powerful countries in the world have held the belief that peace is maintained by having so many weapons that no one would dare to make the first attack. However, there is no rational relation between the advantages of a nuclear war and the massive destruction that it would cause. The major powers feel secure from a war aimed at their territory or threatening their sovereignty, but nuclear weapons do nothing to prevent other wars from being waged. And these countries are not safe from economic wars, social instability encouraged from the outside, subversion, terrorism and so on.

A laser beam used as an anti-satellite weapon. Researchers are studying the feasibility of using lasers and energetic particle beams in space as weapons against ballistic missiles. They could also be used as anti-satellite weapons. The Outer Space Treaty of 1967 banned the placing of nuclear weapons in space, and the Partial Test Ban Treaty of 1963 banned nuclear explosions (or at least put a partial ban on space trials). However, there is no agreement banning or limiting non-nuclear anti-satellite weapons, even though proposals have been submitted to the United Nations.

Several types of short wavelength lasers have been tested in the laboratory. In addition, trials with the free electron laser operating at microwave frequencies have been quite successful. However, much more work is required to build a suitable laser operating in the visible region. In this photograph, a high power microwave laser, operating in the near infrared, is pulsed by an electron beam from a particle accelerator at the National Laboratory at Los Alamos, USA (Sygma).

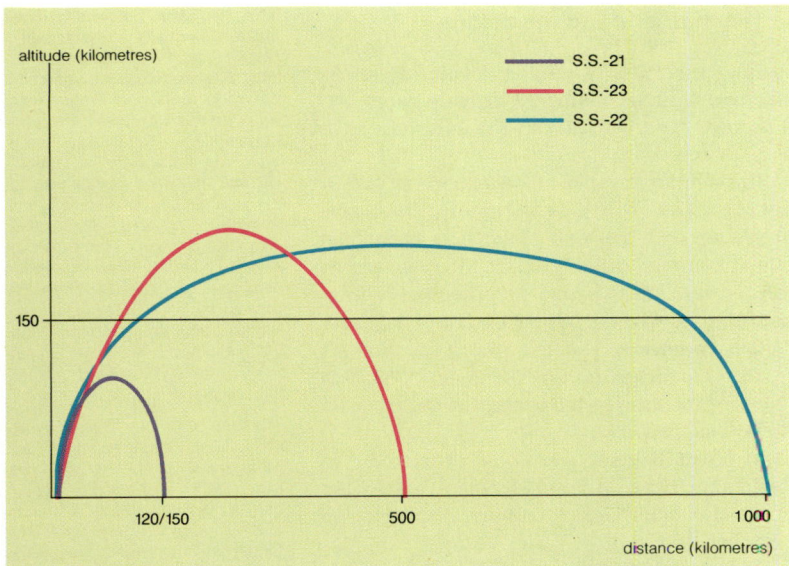

The trajectories of ballistic weapons which threatened the European members of NATO in the 1980s. Technically, the trajectories of nuclear warheads launched by Soviet SS 22 and SS 23 missiles are not low orbit trajectories, since their highest points are above 150 kilometres altitude. Warheads launched by the SS 20 have a maximum range of 4500 kilometres, and other projectiles have a range of up to 10 000 kilometres. To avoid detection the target is chosen and the trajectory calculated a little after launch. The Washington treaty of December 1987 eliminated these weapons.

However, at a relatively small cost of only about 10% of total military expenditure, nuclear arms have at least imposed a no war status quo between rival nations who previously fought over frontiers and decided the fate of the people who lived there. President Reagan, on 23 March 1983, aroused surprise and worry by proposing the SDI to find the means of destroying enemy weapons before they reach their target. The President believed this to be a morally sound proposition, because it destroys arms without destroying humans, and therefore he hoped to gain support from most Americans and non-nuclear countries. He vowed to remove the Soviet superiority in strategic arms and destructive power, and sought to improve the prestige of American laboratories. Finally, he wanted to prepare for the strategic and space future of America, as well as leading the scientific world of tomorrow.

Yet the SDI programme will change the existing geopolitical order and all governments will have to rethink their policies for defence and security. What would happen, for instance, to the Anti-Ballistic Missiles (ABM) Treaty of 1972? This American–Soviet agreement, signed on 26 May 1972 in Moscow, offers the populations of each of the two signatory countries as hostages to increase the probability of dissuading both countries from using nuclear arms. Some countries which do not share the American vision are afraid that the net result of the SDI programme will be an increase in space militarisation, which would stimulate a new arms race and lead to attempts at disarmament being abandoned. Moreover, the disparity of military capabilities between the superpowers and the rest of the world would be further increased.

Even before the American Secretary of State for Defence proposed to 'eighteen allied and friendly countries', in March 1984, a share of the research necessary to build such a shield, Great Britain had displayed some interest in President Reagan's SDI project. After negotiations, an agreement was signed between the two countries on 6 December 1985 and a special office was installed, at the Ministry of Defence, to coordinate work between British firms and Universities.

On 18 December 1985, Bonn announced that negotiations were in progress which would determine the work carried out by German institutes and firms. The German–American agreement was signed on 27 March 1986. In April 1986, the Italian government decided to allow Italian firms to work on the project if they so desired, but announced there were no political implications. Ten Italian firms formed a consortium, CITES (Conzorzio Industrie

Tecnologia e Spazio) to negotiate for a number of contracts on the SDI project.

The participation of the State of Israel in research and development related to the SDI project had unexpected effects on the attitudes of the USA and Western Europe. When deploying twenty-four SS 21 units in Syria, the Soviets were obviously not expecting a reaction from Israel so strong that it would echo throughout the rest of the World. Shimon Peres explained to the Americans that, in the future, Israel's military installations would be under considerable threat from these rockets, and that their firing range was accurate enough to paralyse Tsahal, the Israeli army, in one salvo. This shocked the United States. It was discovered that NATO armies were in the same situation, and that it was futile to try and defend allies in the Old World with conventional weapons. This was because they were now vulnerable where the weapons were stored to one attack by the Soviet SS 21 missiles. After this incident, there was revived interest in studies for a more specifically European defence system.

As regards disarmament, America's allies have all declared that they are in favour of the Soviet–American dialogue on strategic arms limitations (SALT I, signed in Moscow on 26 May 1972, and SALT II, signed in 1979), the ABM treaty, the Vienna negotiations on the limitation on the presence of armed forces in Europe, and the work of the Stockholm conference. Governments in NATO are well aware that the Soviets only conform to treaties when they do not affect their policies or strategies. Whereas the signing of the SALT I treaty triggered an increase of armaments in the East, the Americans instituted an arms freeze. However, it is recognised that even if these agreements are contravened by Moscow, they still impose certain constraints on the growth of arms. They are a step in the right direction for world peace.

Prospects for nuclear disarmament

A joint communiqué, issued on 22 January 1984, announced that the Soviet–American dialogue on arms reduction, which had been suspended for the last few months of 1983, had been resumed. Since then, the two superpowers have followed two strategies. One is the public declaration, intended for public opinion, the other the more cautious statement, issued by experts after more sober deliberations. The most interesting and surprising propositions come from the initial declaration. The dossier presented at Geneva by Mikhail Gorbachev at the beginning of November 1985, contained concessions, most of which were more apparent than real, each concession demanding disarmament but letting the Soviets maintain a stronger position. Moscow proposed a 50% reduction in strategic carriers, and stabilisation in the number of nuclear warheads held by each country at 6000. Of these, 3600 would be for long range ballistic missiles, submarine launched missiles and bombers. All cruise missiles with a range of greater than 600 kilometres would be eliminated, and there would be a halt on the research and development of new missiles, whatever their nature.

The American counter proposal also included a reduction in strategic arms, but it took a strong line against the amount of Soviet conventional weaponry. It suggests that on both sides the number of warheads mounted on long range missiles should be reduced to 4500, of which 3000 should be in missile silos. The launch capacity for a strike of strategic rockets should be reduced by 50%. Each side should only be allowed 1500 cruise missiles and the number of bomber planes should be less than 350. Finally, mobile missiles and the deployment of new large missiles should be forbidden. It also includes the provision that America should be allowed to continue work on SDI, and the Soviets be invited to join in the

research. Where Western Europe is concerned, the USA suggested bringing the number of SS 20 missiles into line with the number of Pershing and Cruise missiles already installed in Europe, 140 in all, and keeping the total at that.

Against these complicated proposals, discussed over a number of years, Mikhail Gorbachev suggested a set of counter proposals which were more spectacular. He accepted without question the 'zero option' proposal. In Europe there should be no SS 20s and no Pershing II or cruise missiles. Further, there should be a reduction of strategic rockets, on site verification of disarmament measures and a reduction in conventional weapons.

In October 1986, Mikhail Gorbachev and Ronald Reagan met in Reykjavik, Iceland. The American President refused to alter his position on the SDI project. He insisted on continuing work on the project, and the two sides could not agree on the reduction of strategic weapons. However, they did agree to remove all nuclear weapons from Europe. Both Helmut Schmidt of West Germany and Valéry Giscard d'Estaing of France were also in favour of the zero option, although this agreement was not, on the whole, popular with America's European allies. In reality, Western Europe was being asked to relinquish the ultramodern, accurate and minimally destructive American weapons, which could therefore be justifiably used, whilst the Soviet Union was being asked to remove the SS 20 missiles, which were already old, inaccurate and soon due to be dismantled. Also, after long debate, another 'zero option' was added. All short range nuclear weapons (with a range between 500 and 1000 kilometres) would be withdrawn from Europe. The Soviets would only remove their SS 22 missiles, whilst the Allies (notably the West Germans) would lose their American Pershing IA's.

Following the only partial success of the Reykjavik summit, President Reagan and Premier Gorbachev met again in Washington DC, in December 1987. This was an historic occasion which ended with the signing of the Intermediate range Nuclear Forces (INF) Treaty on 8 December. This treaty consisted of the double zero option, and called for the complete elimination of Long Range INF missiles (from 1000 to 5500 kilometres) and Short Range INF missiles (from 500 to 1000 kilometres). It also included very detailed verification procedures. Ronald Reagan insisted that the agreement would not prevent him from being able to continue with the SDI programme. However, the summit was considered a great success, and the US Senate finally ratified the agreement in mid 1988.

Negotiators from both countries then began working on the Strategic Arms Reduction Talks (START), aimed at promoting stability and halving the nuclear arsenal. A final superpower summit between President Reagan and Premier Gorbachev was held in Moscow from 29 May to 2 June 1988. This meeting did not achieve as much as was hoped, and the START Treaty was not ready to be signed. The human rights issue clouded the main discussions about weapons. The Russians surprised the Americans by suggesting even more free access for verification. However, both sides agreed to work on the INF Treaty, and there was an all round increase in confidence. Amongst the more modest accords signed were a five to ten year extension of cooperation on the peaceful uses of outer space.

The US presidential elections prevented any further superpower summits for a while. When President George Bush took up office he included in his political agenda further superpower summits on arms control and other issues. One was held in the Mediterranean in December 1989 and another in the spring of 1990.

Pierre M. Gallois

Europe

General policy

In the future, people will live permanently in space at altitudes of several hundred kilometres. They will work there, live out their lives in microgravity conditions, leave the station, assemble experimental structures in the near vacuum of space, and observe the Earth in minute detail. These space activities may not be wholly peaceful. Space adds a new dimension to conflict problems. Where there is latent or suppressed antagonism, or where there is armed confrontation, all tactical developments can be carefully monitored from space. Space, just like the land, the seas and the sky, is a region where mankind can either cooperate or fight.

For many years, European space ambitions have been maintained to a greater or lesser degree, and ambitious projects have been announced. Their end result has, however, remained ambiguous. All projects have a scientific or commercial dimension, but military aspects cannot be overlooked. The excellent images available from the 'commercial' SPOT satellite can be used to maintain surveillance of the Soviet Union or, indeed, any other country. Is there any reason why the Europeans should

not use their expertise in space to view countries in the same way that they themselves are viewed?

The French government makes no secret of its activities. In 1992, it plans to launch an Earth observation system, based on four Sun synchronous satellites, one of which will be launched every three years. Each of these four Hélios satellites will be equipped with a high power telescope with a very high resolution, similar to that on American observational satellites. France is also planning a venture with Great Britain to place a system of communication satellites into orbit which will be for the sole use of the armed forces. These will be operational in the early or mid 1990s.

This 'militarisation' of space will not undermine world peace. Unlike the two superpowers, which have many military satellites, Western Europe can only place a limited number into orbit. And such satellites will be so vulnerable that, in times of war, the armed forces will not be able to use them. At the very most, the neutralisation of these satellites will serve to alert the nations to the imminence of a great peril.

However, for the ordinary affairs of state, space allows us to 'see, hear and communicate' around the globe. Satellites in fact help governments to conduct their affairs well.

Pierre M. Gallois

The methods and the means

Since the 1970s, a decade devoted to scientific and basic technological developments, the European launcher and satellite industries have both matured significantly.

The military has played an important role in initiating the civil space sector. In France the first four civil 'Diamant' launchers were built under contract to the Minister for Armaments. They were based on experimental rocket motors used when designing nuclear missiles for defence purposes. The first French satellite, A1 Asterix, launched on 26 November 1965, was built for the army, which expected the launcher to be a success.

In Great Britain, a national programme to build the 'Black Arrow' launcher, led to the successful launch of a satellite (Prospero) in October 1971.

The Ariane rocket launcher is based on a number of military developments. The French armed forces developed excellent guidance and piloting systems, and the British developed sophisticated navigation equipment for their fighter planes. Ariane's inertial guidance systems make use of these techniques to carry out accurate satellite launchings.

The development and subsequent industrialisation of an operational launcher has been a civil enterprise, carried out chiefly by the European Launcher Development Organisation (ELDO), from 1962 to 1972. But the Europa rocket was not a success. From 1973 to 1979, the European Space Agency (ESA) took this over and developed Ariane. By 1986, three launchers, Ariane I, II and III, were available to Europe. They are equally capable of putting into orbit military information or telecommunications satellites, thus fulfilling the medium term objectives of the European programme. In 1988, Ariane IV successfully launched 4·2 tonnes of payload into a geostationary transfer orbit. It can put 5 tonnes into a low Earth orbit, extending even further the programme's launch capabilities.

From 1995, the civil market will have altered and Ariane IV will be replaced by a new launcher Ariane V. This will be capable of placing 8 tonnes into a geostationary orbit and 16 tonnes into low Earth orbit (around 400 kilometres altitude). Ariane V will also be able to transport the space plane, Hermes (cf. *Hermes* p. 313).

(cf. *Hermes* p. 313).

Skynet IV satellites. The Skynet IV satellite programme was commissioned in 1981 by the British Ministry of Defence to complete and then replace earlier versions of the same series. When Skynet IA was launched in 1969, it was the first operational military satellite in Europe.

The design of Skynet IV is similar to ESA's European Communications Satellite (ECS); they are both based on a modular design. They are used by the British armed forces for long distance strategic links, links between small mobile terminals for terrestrial operations, communications with ships, and for transmission despite electronic jamming, with unpredictable levels of demand which may change rapidly. All these needs can be satisfied by using signal processors in Ultra High Frequency (UHF) and Super High Frequency (SHF) bands and by improving the terrestrial sector of the communications link. It consists of two UHF repeaters, which cover the zone visible to the satellite and an Extremely High Frequency (EHF) repeater for experimentation. The mass of the satellite at launch is 1·3 tonnes.

British Aerospace is the prime contractor for the project. Marconi Space and Defence Systems is responsible for the telecommunications payload and for building the control ground station. The first Skynet IVB should have been launched by the space shuttle, but its launch was delayed due to the Challenger accident on 28 January 1986. It was finally launched on 10 December 1988 by Ariane IV. The second and third Skynet IV satellites will be launched later. The control ground station is at Oakhanger (UK) and was inaugurated in May 1986 (British Aerospace).

The military communications system 'Syracuse'. Besides establishing data links and telephone communication networks between France and its overseas territories, the two Télécom I satellites, each weighing 1·2 tonnes at launch, carried the space component of a military communications system, Syracuse. This uses two of the twelve channels between 7 and 8 gigahertz available on each satellite. The military part of the satellite is protected against jamming and intrusion, and all communications are protected from interception.

The two satellites, Télécom IA and Télécom IB, were launched by Ariane III in August 1984 and May 1985, respectively. Télécom IC was launched in March 1988 to replace Télécom IB. The Syracuse system includes ground stations on French territory (on the right), which ensure that communications between mobile stations (on ships, on the land and on aeroplanes) are protected. Thus ships of the French navy (bottom right) equipped with the Syracuse system are able to travel from Réunion to the Antilles, and over the whole Atlantic, whilst retaining secure telephone, telegraph and data links with France. A mobile Earth station (centre) can be transported by plane. It enables troops outside the country quickly to establish reliable links with France (Alcatel-Espace).

The satellites

In Great Britain, the Royal Aircraft Establishment (RAE) has been carrying out work on space and geostationary satellites since the beginning of the 1960s. The first European military telecommunications satellite, Skynet I, was launched by an American rocket in November 1969. Since then, three other Skynet satellites have been launched, although the programme was suspended in 1971. In 1981, a decision was made to construct three satellites of the Skynet IV series. Great Britain also uses satellite links for military purposes and has reception stations on Earth for the army, navy and air force.

France's military telecommunications system, called Syracuse, has been operational since 1985.

To gather information, the Europeans rely on civil remote sensing satellites, such as the American Landsat system and more recently the French SPOT system. These satellites only partially fulfil the military's requirements. France expects to put its Hélios system into operation in the early 1990s. This will use the same platform as the civil satellite SPOT which has been operational since 22 February 1986. Technological progress in the fields of optical, radar and infrared observations has been very promising. Advanced sensors, signature analysis techniques and improvements in reliability and resistance to jamming have all been developed. Europe has the knowledge and ability to build systems to replace the French Hélios system at the beginning of the next century.

Satellite launch and tracking facilities

Even though Europe has no operational surveillance system of space activity, France, Italy, Great Britain and West Germany all possess the means to launch and follow the trajectories of satellites and to 'listen' to them.

France has several centres for its space and ballistic programmes. The two most important of these are the test centre at Landes, where strategic ballistic missiles are fired, and the space centre at Kourou, in French Guyana, which is used by the European Space Agency. These stations are equipped with modern optical equipment and large radar and telemetry antennae, which were mostly built by the French nationalised industry. France also has a military test building, 'Henri-Poincaré', which is used for recording telemetry and tracking ballistic rockets.

Italy is able to launch satellites from the San Marco Space Centre, a platform in the sea off Kenya, and has its own remote sensing programme. It has also built receiving, telemetry and tracking stations.

Great Britain possesses good capabilities, allowing it to monitor space activities at the Australian launch site at Woomera. It also has a large early warning radar station integrated into the American Norad (North American Aerospace Defence) network, which can track objects having low orbits.

Finally, the European Space Agency is able to track satellites at different points over the globe from its ground station at Darmstadt in West Germany. This station forms part of the European Space Operation Centre (ESOC).

Anti-missile and anti-satellite space weapons

Directed energy weapons. This type of weapon is characterised by its ability to strike a target with either microwaves, laser beams or electrically charged or neutral particles at speeds close to that of light. This particular principle is used in the SDI programme. The advantage of this type of weapon is that the shortest time possible elapses between a ballistic missile being fired upon and destroyed. It is viable over distances of up to several thousands of kilometres and can also be used against satellites.

Only the concepts involved in laser weapons have any real credibility. There are many difficulties to overcome before they can be built in practice. Of the other proposed types of weapons, microwave beams require an antenna which is prohibitively large in order to strike the target with sufficient energy. Neutron beams can only be used at altitudes of less than 100 or 150 kilometres. And charged particle beams are affected by the Earth's magnetic field in a way that cannot be accurately predicted so their aim is always going to be poor.

The lasers which may be operable in space are chemical lasers such as hydrogen fluoride, HF (wavelength = 2·6 microns), deuterium fluoride, DF (wavelength = 3·8 microns) and iodine (wavelength = 1·3 microns). Equally, excimer lasers such as krypton fluoride, KrF (wavelength = 0·5 microns) or free electron lasers could be used. The main advantage of chemical lasers is that they do not require electrical power supplies. Excimer lasers emitting in the near ultraviolet are also very efficient, as are electron lasers which have the advantage of emitting radiation over a large area.

The major constraint on a spacebased laser weapon is the amount of energy which is required to operate it. This is some tens of megawatts for continuous lasers, and megajoules or tens of megajoules for pulsed lasers.

In Europe, only France and West Germany have sizeable research programmes into high energy lasers. The following results have been obtained so far. A carbon dioxide (CO_2) gas laser (at 10·6 microns) produced a power of 300 watts at the Marcousis laboratory (a part of the CGE, the French General Electric Company). A power of 15 kilowatts was obtained with a DF–HF chemical laser during joint work by the CGE, the SEP (Société Européenne de Propulsion) and ONERA (Office National d'Etudes et de Recherches Aérospatiales). An iodine laser also produced a power of 150 watts at ONERA. At the University of Orsay, near Paris, a free electron laser operated in 1983 using electrons circulating in the storage ring.

In West Germany, notable results have been obtained with a CO_2 combustion chemical laser in the laboratories of the firm MBB (Messerschmitt–Bölkow–Blohm). A power of about one hundred watts was obtained using a device fuelled by a benzene and nitrogen oxide mixture.

Kinetic energy weapons. This type of weapon includes anti-missile and anti-satellite weapons based on work carried out on tactical and ballistic missiles.

France acquired all the technology necessary to build such missiles fired from the ground or from planes, using its industrial experience in building ballistic missiles and target guided tactical missiles. Other European nations (Great Britain, West Germany and Italy in particular) have also sufficiently advanced technology to construct such missiles.

Other kinetic energy weapons include the electromagnetic cannons envisaged by the Americans as part of the SDI programme. Although Europe possesses the ability to make all these weapons, there are no plans to build such systems at present.

Daniel Pichoud

The USSR

General policy

The exploration and utilisation of space policies of the Soviet Union are based on two important principles. These are that all countries have the same rights to space, and that the use of space should have entirely peaceful purposes.

Since the beginning of the space era, the Soviet Union has kept to these principles. An initiative by the USSR resulted in the 1967 Space Treaty, which regulates the activities of countries involved in the exploration and use of space beyond the Earth's atmosphere, including the use of the Moon and other celestial bodies. This treaty states the principles of equality and the right of all countries to explore and use space in a way which is beneficial and in the interests of all countries, regardless of the level of their scientific and economic development. The treaty also emphasises that the results which are obtained should be made available to all peoples. It indicates that space is open to all people (article 1), that there should be no discrimination and that space activities should be carried out in the interests of peace, international security and the development of cooperation. All activities should conform with international law and with the UN Charter (article 3).

The bans and limitations outlined by international law include the prohibition of all military activity in certain regions, in particular circumlunar space, where there is a ban and limitation of use on certain types of weapons and military space systems. At present, there is no global ban on military activities in the rest of space, including near Earth space.

Amongst the early measures which were designed to limit the militarisation of space, the Soviet Union considers the undertaking of the signatories of the 1967 Space Treaty not to 'place into circumterrestrial orbit any engine armed with a nuclear weapon or any weapon capable of massive extermination, and to not deploy weapons in space by any other means' (article 4) to be most important. All nuclear tests as well as all nuclear explosions in space are illegal under article 1 of the 1963 Partial Test Ban Treaty. This prohibits nuclear weapons tests in the atmosphere, in space and under water. This regulation has been respected by the signatories and also by China and France who have not yet signed.

The convention which came into force on 5 October 1978 banned all military action in the natural medium and prohibited the use of weapons systems for military purposes in space and directed from space against the Earth. All these regulations indicate that strict controls are being formulated under international law concerning the military use of space.

Claims by the Americans that the proposed Strategic Defense Initiative (SDI) would render nuclear weapons 'obsolete and inoperable', and that it would 'therefore reinforce strategic stability and reduce the arms race', have been shown to be without foundation by researchers from the Soviet Union and from other countries, including neutral and non-aligned nations such as India, Sweden and Argentina. The USA, unlike the USSR, has refused to agree either to a moratorium on nuclear tests or to a ban on the first use of nuclear weapons. On the contrary, the US is increasing its first strike capacity which lends credence to the view that the SDI project is primarily a means to ensure that the Americans will have the power of first strike.

Some Americans consider that the creation of such an anti-missile system will mark the turning point in strategic thought 'from dissuasion by intimidation to dissuasion by invulnerability'. However, there is nothing in this system which guarantees absolute protection

The SS 9 missile. The Soviet intercontinental missile, which the Americans call the SS 9 (Strategic System 9), was displayed for the first time at Red Square in Moscow on 7 November 1967 in the procession celebrating the October Revolution.

It is 35 metres long, weighs about 20 tonnes and is equipped with a six jet rocket. The SS 9 forms the basis of the space launcher which is exten-sively used in experiments by the Soviet military. This launcher, which is called 'F' by the Americans, is used by the orbital missile (FOBS) that the Soviets tested between 1967 and 1971. It is also used to launch the oceanic surveillance satellites of the Rorsat series, and anti-satellite satellites. A recent version, the F2, was used to launch photographic reconnaissance satellites and meteorological satellites (V. Yegorov, Tass).

against ballistic missiles. To offer the power of retaliation against this anti-missile weapon system, new weapons are going to appear. Alongside their construction and deployment, strategic offensive weapons already in place will be updated. Furthermore, the creation of an anti-missile system with a space component will lead to a growth in strategic nuclear arms, and in particular to long range, low altitude cruise missiles which operate over land or sea.

A space anti-missile weapon is also an anti-satellite weapon. It therefore has a destabilising effect on the strategic equilibrium. This depends on the confidence that a country has in its control, surveillance and warning systems which put various Earth orbiting satellites into operation in case of a missile attack.

If tests on a space weapon were to take place, even if it were not later deployed, the Anti-Ballistic Missile (ABM) Treaty of 1972, signed by the Americans and the Soviets, would have been violated. In fact, article 1 of this treaty stipulates that the signatories agree not to deploy an anti-missile defence system which protects their country and not to carry out the work necessary to construct this type of defence. Furthermore, article 5 states that the parties involved will not create nor experiment nor deploy ABM systems or components in the air, in space or in mobile terrestrial silos.

By embarking on the SDI initiative, the Americans have violated this treaty, and established a stumbling block to arms limitations talks. President Gorbachev has emphasised that a Soviet response would be more efficient, less expensive and more quickly put into operation. However, this retaliation would not necessarily involve space; the many counter measures that exist are described in reports written by the Committee of Soviet Researchers for Peace and Against Nuclear Weapons.

Mikhail Gorbachev's proposals made on 15 January 1986 put forward a different response. Instead of introducing anti-missile weapons which would destabilise the military strategic equilibrium in Europe, he proposed to free the European continent from all tactical and strategic nuclear weapons. The first step in achieving this would be to create a 'non-nuclear corridor' between NATO countries and those of the Warsaw Pact, as the Palme commission

proposed to the two superpowers in its statement in February 1986.

The creation of a non-nuclear zone in the North of Europe and in other regions would be part of the same process of reducing the numbers of conventional weapons proposed by the USSR. It would also help to increase the threshold of security in Europe.

The creation of a large scale anti-missile system could undermine all hopes of reaching an agreement to limit and reduce strategic weapons. The Soviet Union believes that some encouraging steps have been made in the direction of controlling military usage of space. In this way the treaty limiting anti-missile systems also prohibits the creation, testing and deployment of anti-missile systems with a space component. The provisional treaty signed in 1972 established a basis for the USA and the USSR to limit the number of intercontinental ballistic missile launch silos. This led to a reduction in the military usage of space.

The Strategic Arms Limitations Talks II (SALT II) agreement came into force in 1979 when both the superpowers agreed that they would neither create, experiment nor deploy the means to place nuclear or other massively destructive weapons, including orbital missiles, in orbit around the Earth. Such an agreement would furnish a supplementary guarantee with respect to the ban on massively destructive weapons in space.

During 1985 the Soviets drew up a new set of proposals which would prevent the arms race being extended into space. These proposals banned all recourse to force in space and all aggression directed against the Earth from space. They created guarantees that space vehicles could not constitute a military menace to other countries, so improving the security of these countries.

The Soviet Union also invited the USA to engage in bilateral negotiations in order to prevent the militarisation of space. To facilitate this, it announced a unilateral moratorium on the launching of anti-satellite weapons. In June 1984, the Soviet Union proposed to the USA a moratorium, based on mutual reciprocity and dating from the beginning of arms talks, on the testing and deployment of space weapons. Other countries could also adopt such measures.

The Soviet–American negotiations on nuclear and space weapons began in March 1985. The Soviet Union proposed a ban on offensive space weapons and a significant reduction (about 50%) in the nuclear weapons which are able to reach the territories belonging to both the USA and the USSR.

On 15 January 1986, Mikhail Gorbachev outlined the Soviet programme for the total and universal withdrawal of nuclear weapons between that date and the year 2000. The Americans and Soviets were to agree not to create, experiment with, or deploy offensive space weapons.

In June 1986, the USSR submitted for international scrutiny a three stage programme advocating joint action to keep space activities peaceful. It proposed the establishment before the year 2000 of the foundations of political, juridical and organisational structures to keep the 'star peace'. To establish this programme, the Soviet Union proposed that the UN create the World Space Organisation (WSO). This would be in charge of ensuring that only peaceful work was carried out in space and would ensure that space treaties were adhered to. It would also be responsible for drawing up agreements to prevent the arms race from spreading into space.

Evgeni P. Velikhov,
Andrei A. Kokochine
and Alexei A. Vassiliev

The methods and the means

The Soviet military space effort is directed towards collecting and communicating information, in a role supportive to the armed forces but without assuming an aggressive element. The first stage of this task is to gather a variety of strategic and tactical information on the military installations, troop movements, equipment and military manoeuvres of other countries. This surveillance is carried out using photographs from satellites, electronic monitoring devices, radar platforms to observe the oceans, and early warning satellites to monitor tests and missile firings. This alone constitutes more than half the Soviet space launchings which take place every year. The second military use of space in order of importance is communications, followed by navigation and geodesy.

Beyond these traditional applications, the USSR has carried out a programme which aimed, by the end of the 1960s, to make operational a special orbital missile. This would have been capable of making a nearly complete revolution around the Earth in a low orbit before finding its target. This programme, of which there is no equivalent in the USA, was called the Fractional Orbit Bombardment System (FOBS). It is not known whether its experimental success was followed by deployment. Two trials were made between 1968 and 1983 of anti-satellite satellites carrying non-nuclear weapons. They are at least part of the reason why the Americans decided to develop the Anti-Satellite (Asat) weapon at the end of the 1970s. This is a comparable weapon which can destroy enemy satellites in orbits below 2000 kilometres altitude.

About two thirds of Soviet satellites are used for military purposes. However, this does not mean that two thirds of the Soviet space effort relates to military programmes. Most Soviet military satellites are part of large series which cost much less than the corresponding civil programmes such as manned space flight and scientific missions. The funds devoted to Soviet military and civil space projects are in fact closely comparable.

The use of recoverable reconnaissance satellites

The photographic observation satellite programme constitutes the largest part of the

The surveillance of conflict zones throughout the world. The Russians use photographic reconnaissance satellites to survey and evaluate the military installations of other countries, and also to monitor conflict zones. Such satellites are thus used for strategic and tactical purposes.

One example of how a reconnaissance satellite is put into operation during a crisis is the mission of Cosmos 1489. On 10 August 1983, the town of Faya Largeau in Chad was invaded by Libyan troops. The same day, the Soviets put into orbit Cosmos 1489, a Vostok photographer. It passed over the conflict zone on 11, 12 and 13 August, on the trajectories shown in the upper map.

Another example detailed in the lower map is that of Cosmos 1630, a multicapsule reconnaissance Soyuz. This monitored the fighting of the 'war of the cities' in the Iran–Iraq conflict at the end of March 1985 (Nicholas L. Johnson, *The Soviet year in space 1985*, Teledyne Brown Engineering, Colorado Springs, 1986). Alain Dupas

Soviet space programme. Work began in 1962 when Cosmos 4 was put into orbit. Since then more than 600 such satellites have been launched from the cosmodromes at Baikonur, in Central Asia, and Plesetsk. Since the mid 1970s just over forty of these satellites have been launched each year. In comparison, the USA launches only a few of this type of satellite each year.

The reason for the disparity is technical. The Soviets prefer to use recoverable reconnaissance units which fly for a few weeks and then bring their films back to Earth to be developed and interpreted. This procedure allows the Soviets to produce pictures of excellent quality using traditional cameras. However, in order to maintain continuous surveillance, they need to make many launches per year.

In contrast, the Americans bring back to Earth only a few very high quality pictures (those with a resolution of about 10 centimetres, at an altitude of 150 kilometres) in recoverable capsules.

The use of manned spacecraft

The Soviet reconnaissance satellites, unlike the American ones, are based on their first manned spacecraft. By their very nature these had a recoverable cabin. Most such space vehicles are based on the first rocket to take a man into space, the Vostok. This weighs 5 tonnes and has a spherical recoverable cabin weighing more than 2·3 tonnes. There are several variants of the Vostok photographer, which produce high, medium and low resolution photographs (HR, MR and LR respectively). Technical improvements over a number of years have extended the durations of these spacecraft missions from 4 or 5 days to 8 days, and finally to 12 or 13 days.

The MR version, with an orbit of 350 to 400 kilometres altitude, is the one which has been most used since the middle 1980s. A civilian version of the Vostok photographer has been officially in use since 1980, for two week remote sensing missions. It flies at an altitude of about 250 kilometres in an orbit whose inclination is about 82·3 degrees. It is equipped with a multispectral camera called the SA 34. This simultaneously films in five different wavebands, producing pictures of 180 kilometre square regions with a resolution of 15 to 20 metres. Its images are comparable with those produced by the French SPOT system which transmits its pictures back to Earth like a television.

The HR version, based on the Soyuz spacecraft, weighs 7 tonnes, and usually orbits at altitudes between 170 and 400 kilometres. It contains two recoverable capsules in addition to the principal cabin which can be returned during the flight. It can deliver back to Earth pictures from three sessions of filming during and at the end of a mission which can last one or two months. This satellite is also equipped with solar panels, whereas the Vostok design uses chemical batteries as an energy source.

The Soyuz photographer which flew for the first time in 1975 represented a considerable technological advance. Another type of reconnaissance satellite appeared in 1983, marking an even greater step forward. This weighs about 7 tonnes and has a lifetime of several months, with a record 238 days logged in space in 1986. In all likelihood it transmits its photographs by radio telemetry like American satellites. These images are probably sent to the USSR in real time using relay satellites, the analogues of NASA's TDRS, which the Soviets now place in geostationary orbits.

In 1985, the Soviets launched 34 photographic observation satellites. There were seven civil models, nine Vostok MR, seven Vostok HR, ten Soyuz HR and one long lifetime advanced model. For the first time, the Soviets carried out continuous surveillance of the world, using a battery of six reconnaissance

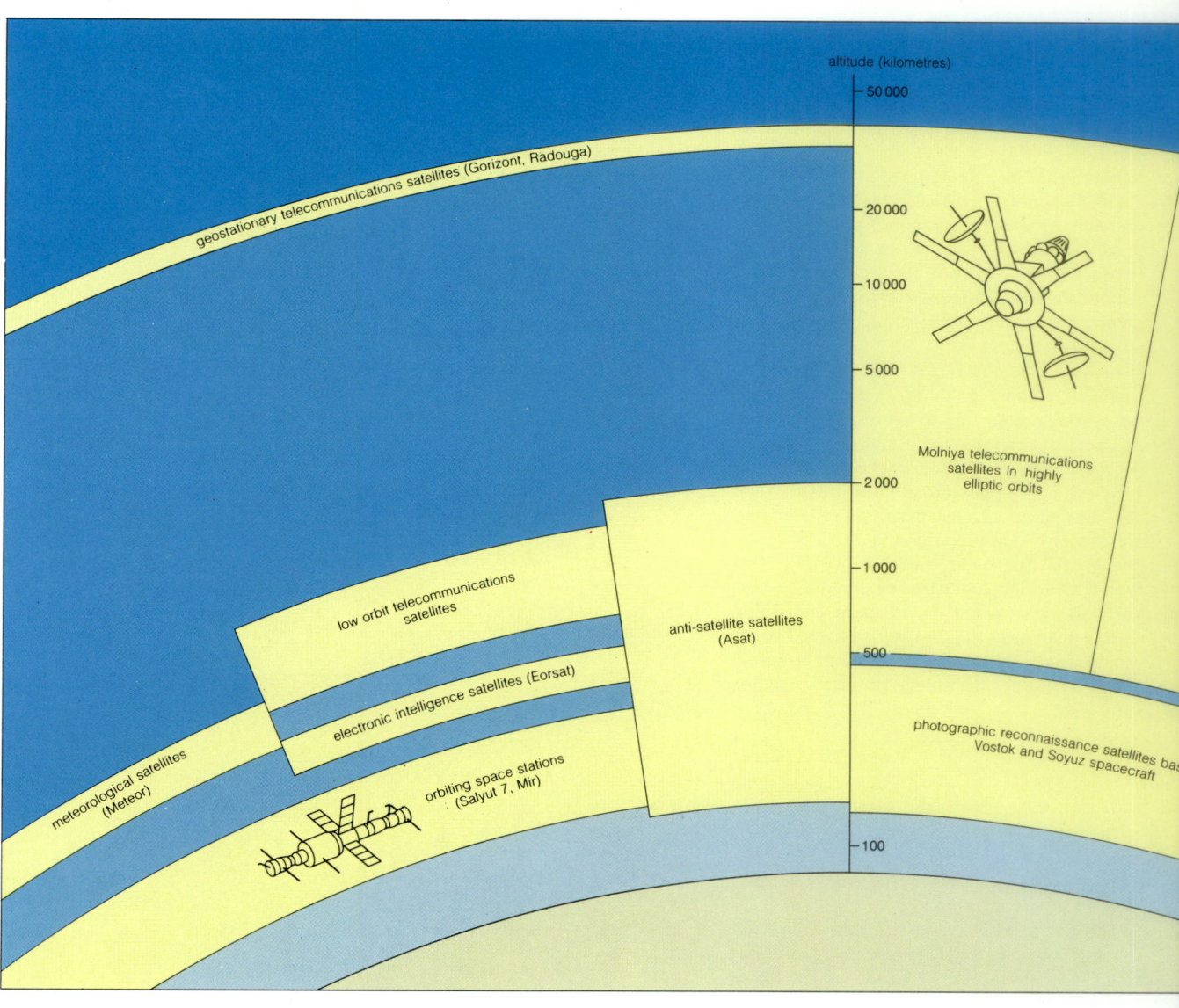

Low orbital navigation satellites. The Soviet navigation satellite is of the same design, whether for civilian or military use. Cylindrical in shape, and with a height and diameter of about 2 metres, it has a mass of about 700 kilograms. A long rod on the top of the satellite stabilises it, using the gradient of the gravity field, in an orbit near 1000 kilometres altitude.

The Soviets have called the civil system 'Tsikada'. It can be distinguished from the military system by the different wavebands it uses, although both systems transmit in the region of 150 to 400 megahertz. The Cospas lifesaving system is also carried (A. Dupas).

The number of missions of reconnaissance satellites between 1962 and 1985 (opposite, on the right). Photographic reconnaissance is the most important military space application in the USSR, whether it is measured by the number of missions or the total satellite mass involved. After rapid growth in the 1960s, the number of launches has remained fairly constant since 1975 at about 35 launches per year or 3 launches per month on average.

Until 1965, all the reconnaissance satellites were launched from the cosmodrome at Baikonur, in Central Asia. Since 1966 a cosmodrome in the north of Russia, at Plesetsk, has also been used. It is from there that most of the Soviet photographic reconnaissance satellites have been launched in the past 15 years (Nicholas L. Johnson, *The Soviet Year in Space 1985*, Teledyne Brown Engineering, Colorado Springs, 1986).

Reconnaissance satellites. Since 1975, the USSR has used a new type of high resolution reconnaissance satellite based on the Soyuz spacecraft design shown in the drawing below.

According to the British observer, Phillip S. Clark, the photographic equipment is installed in the orbital compartment in the front, and the cabin is replaced by an array of recoverable capsules. This procedure has increased the lifetime of these reconnaissance missions to one or two months (Phillip S. Clark, *Spaceflight*, June 1983).

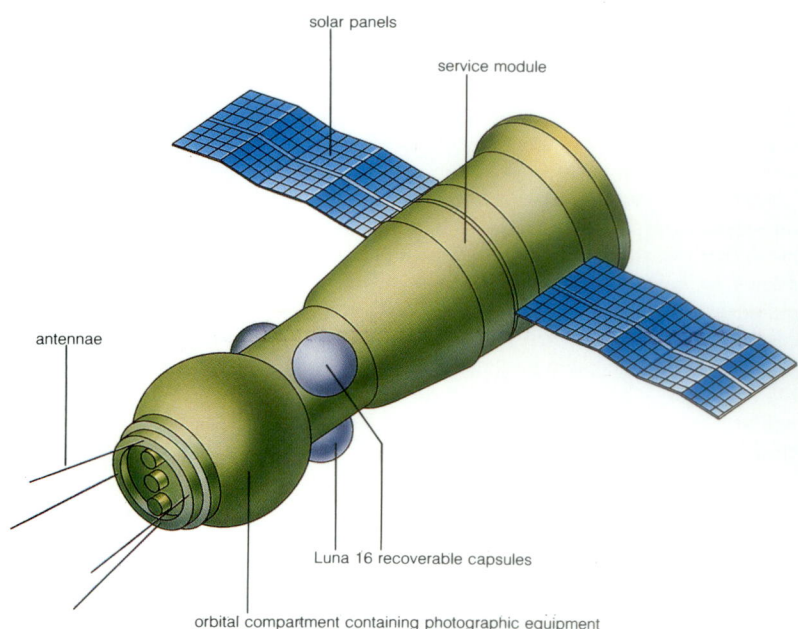

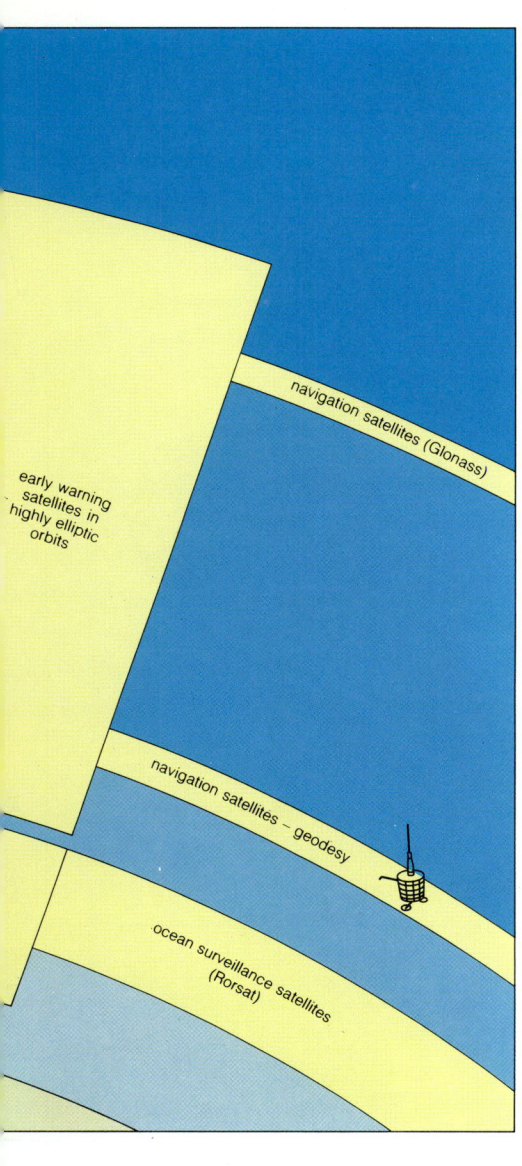

Different types of Soviet spacecraft suspected of military activity. Certain functions, such as reconnaissance photography, electronic intelligence and advanced warning, are carried out by military spacecraft only. Navigation, meteorology and telecommunications satellites in geostationary orbits are joint military and civil missions.

Manned orbital stations are used for visual and photographic observations, and for technological experiments, but their military involvement is for the moment marginal. Such satellites have been classified in the diagram according to the altitude of their orbits (Nicholas L. Johnson).

satellites. The cumulative number of days of observation per year was 940. Although they have a number of advanced rocket engines available, the Soviets have shown no signs of radically reducing the number of launches per year; their policy is apparently to increase their observational capacity.

Nuclear powered radar satellites

Apart from photographic reconnaissance missions, the Soviets devote much effort to ocean surveillance. For this task they use two sorts of satellites which carry out coordinated missions. These are radio surveillance satellites and satellites equipped with active radars. The former are similar to the American Electronic Intelligence (Elint) satellites which record radio signals coming from the countries they are flying over; these are then located and identified, for example from radars, or messages are intercepted. Similar to the American Electronic Ocean Reconnaissance Satellite (Eorsat), they are used to determine the position of ships which do not take the precaution of maintaining radio silence while the satellite is passing overhead. The Soviet satellites, with a mass of 1 tonne, are at an altitude of about 450 kilometres, and an orbital inclination angle of 65 degrees. While the system is operational, there are two or three satellites simultaneously in the same orbit, each covering the same area at intervals of several tens of minutes.

The radar satellites represent a class of space vehicles which do not exist in America. They are equipped with pulsed radars whose only task is to locate targets. They are very different from the Synthetic Aperture Radar (SAR) technique which is used on civil ocean remote sensing satellites in America (Seasat), in Europe (ERS 1), in Canada (Radarsat), in Japan (MOS 1) and even in Russia (some Cosmos satellites).

These Soviet spacecraft use a nuclear reactor to supply some tens of kilowatts of electrical power. The Americans have only carried out one experiment in space using a nuclear reactor and have never used this type of power source in an operational system. The situation may alter, however, at the end of the century if the SP 100 project comes to fruition.

A pulsed radar requires a lot of power. It could only work for a short period of time on chemical batteries. The power could not be provided by photocells, since it would require more than 100 square metres of solar panels which are clumsy and difficult to orient. A nuclear reactor has the double advantage of being compact and providing a continuous supply of energy. However, the use of such technology is not without risk. There is in particular the danger that a reactor containing nuclear fuel will return to Earth and cause a major catastrophe. To compensate for this, and the added fact that the Radar Ocean Reconnaissance Satellite (Rorsat) must operate at low altitudes for its radar to be effective, the Soviets have developed a complicated operational procedure. After several months, the nuclear reactor separates from the satellite and is sent to an altitude of about 1000 kilometres by its own small solid fuel rocket boosters. It was precisely this action which enabled nations in the West to identify Rorsat's power supply.

When operational, two Rorsats follow each other at an interval of twenty minutes, in the same orbit inclined at 65 degrees to the equator. Their observations are always coordinated with those of the two or three Eorsats, whose orbital planes make an angle of 145 degrees to the trajectory of the Rorsat. A group of five ocean surveillance satellites have been in operation since August 1985 when NATO carried out major naval exercises, Ocean Safari 1985.

The US Department of Defense (DOD) considers that Rorsats represent a serious danger in times of conflict. This is because they are able to communicate the positions of US and allied

warships directly to their own vessels, which could then attack them with missiles. This analysis makes Rorsat the prime target for the American Asat system if it is ever put into operation.

Despite launching many Eorsats and Rorsats, the Soviet space ocean surveillance system is not yet operational. Its development has been marred by two accidents. The nuclear reactors of Cosmos 954, in 1978, and Cosmos 1402, in 1982, were not sent into the very upper atmosphere, but instead fell back to Earth. The effects on the environment were fortunately quite limited. After the first accident, the Soviets had already modified the reactor, in case it should disintegrate in the atmosphere and parts of it unexpectedly return to Earth. Although the usage of nuclear reactors in low orbits is very hazardous, this has not prevented the Soviets from actively continuing with their plans to put Rorsat into operation.

Independently of the Eorsat satellites, the Soviets have been using electronic intelligence satellites. Their task is to monitor all radio signals coming from the land or sea. These satellites weigh about 5 tonnes and orbit at altitudes of about 650 kilometres at an angle of 83 degrees to the equator. The operational system consists of six active satellites in pairs with orbital planes at 60 degrees to each other. In addition, in 1984, the Soviets began testing heavier satellites with masses estimated at between 6 and 8 tonnes. These are placed in orbits at altitudes of 850 kilometres, with an inclination of 71 degrees.

Low orbit telecommunications satellites

Whereas the American armed forces use almost exclusively geostationary satellites for communication purposes, the Soviets use a system of satellites orbiting at less than 1500 kilometres altitude. These record signals of interest as they pass over the transmitter and then retransmit the message when they pass over the USSR.

One satellite system consists of about 24 small satellites, each weighing less than 100 kilograms. These are launched in clusters of eight to an altitude of about 1450 kilometres, the orbits all being in the same plane inclined at 74 degrees to the equator. The second system consists of three satellites weighing nearly half a tonne each. These are in a 74 degree inclination orbit at 800 kilometres, and the three orbital planes are inclined at 120 degrees to each other.

Apart from these satellites, it is difficult to identify with confidence the telecommunications satellites used by the Soviet armed forces. The USSR has the Molniya satellites which complete an elliptical orbit every 12 hours reaching a height of 42 000 kilometres at very high latitudes over the northern hemisphere. The Molniya satellites have the advantage that they are high above the horizon when seen from the northern parts of Russia. They are cheap to launch from the Soviet cosmodromes, though they are difficult to keep on the correct orbit. There are two generations of this type of satellite in use today. The Molniya 1 series is an operational system composed of eight satellites moving in planes at 45 degrees to each other. The Molniya 3 series consists of four satellites moving in orbital planes inclined at 90 degrees to each other. Western observers believe that the older of the two systems is primarily used for military purposes.

Geostationary satellites

There are four types of geostationary telecommunications satellite in use at present. These are Gorizont (teledistribution and international communication links), Raduga (communications inside the USSR), and Ekran (teledistribution), plus Cosmos platforms used as links with satellites and space stations. This

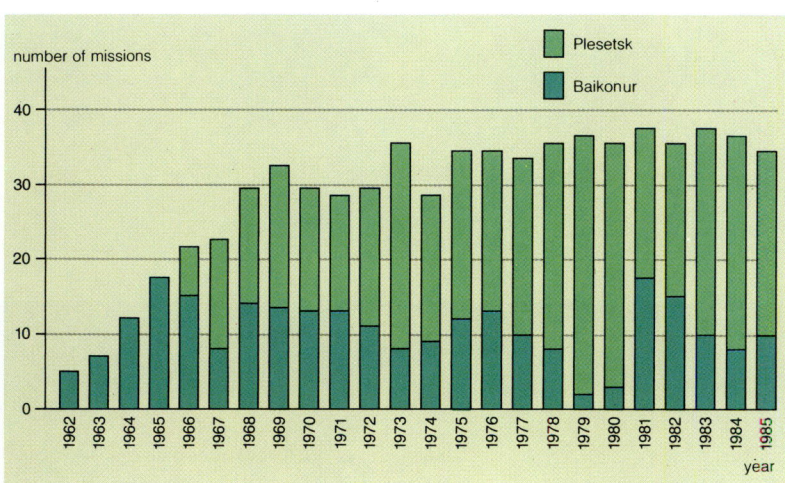

The number of reconnaissance satellites in orbit in 1985. Although Soviet reconnaissance satellites have increasingly long lifetimes, the Soviets have not reduced their annual number of launchings. The total length of observation is therefore increasing year by year. In 1985, for the first time, Soviet photographic satellites were launched throughout the year. For a brief period, six satellites were even in orbit at once (Nicholas L. Johnson).

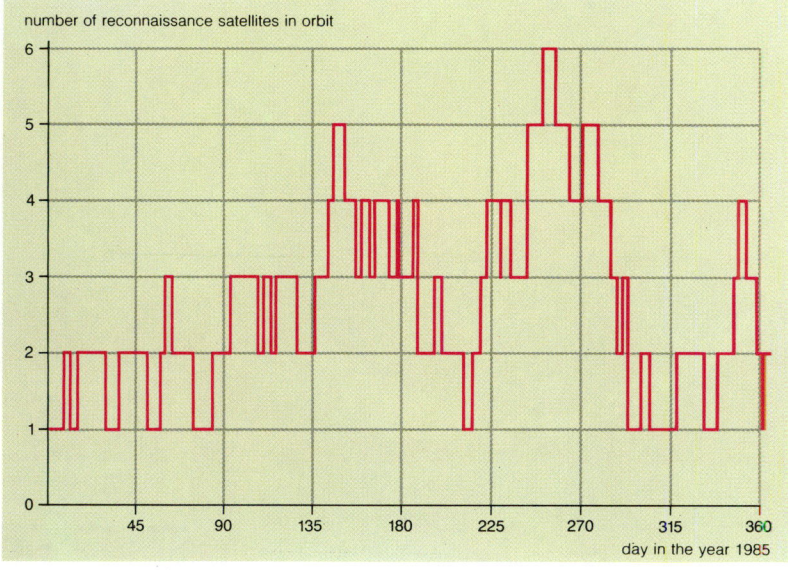

Living with space

last system is equivalent to the American TDRS system, and is apparently called Loutch by the Soviets. The USSR has announced to the International Telecommunications Union (ITU) that it would like to use a geostationary system called Gals working at the frequencies allocated to the USSR by the international board, for military and government purposes. The longitudes of the orbits of the Gals would be the same ones as for the Raduga satellites. However, it is not known whether the Gals system will be specialised or Radugas equipped with military repeaters. Alongside this, the Soviet armed forces have access to repeaters on the civil Raduga satellites and the Gorizonts (or the Molniya 3).

Satellites are also used to detect, as early as possible, enemy missile launches, and to acquire such information on them as the launch site, nature of the missile and information on the trajectory. For this, the Soviets use a satellite system based on the Molniya series which detects the infrared radiation produced by the rocket's exhaust fumes. They are a very important part of the military's space activities. This type of continuous space surveillance of land and maritime regions from where enemy missiles may be launched is carried out in order that retaliation can take place as soon as possible. The more effective the radar coverage is, the swifter the response. The Soviet early warning satellite system consists of nine satellites in orbits similar to those of the Molniyas whose planes are separated by angles of 40 degrees.

Navigation is another area where it is difficult to distinguish between Soviet military and civilian systems. Satellites reaching 1000 kilometres altitude, in orbits inclined at 83 degrees to the equator, use the Doppler effect to provide an accurate location to within 100 metres. Western observers have identified two arrays of these satellites. The first essentially military system is based on six satellites which have orbital planes inclined at about 30 degrees to each other. The second system is civilian and consists of four satellites with orbital planes inclined at 45 degrees to each other.

It is difficult to make the same distinction for the space navigation system Glonass, the most recent and modern system. This comprises satellites orbiting at 19000 kilometres altitude, completing one revolution every 12 hours with orbits inclined at 65 degrees to the equator. These satellites are launched in clusters of three by the most powerful Soviet rocket, the Proton, called SLX 16 by the Americans. They are obviously equipped with atomic clocks and, while operating, can give an instantaneous positioning to within a few metres. In 1986, the Glonass network consisted of several groups of three satellites orbiting in planes angled at 120 degrees to each other. This was not yet sufficient for the system to be fully operational over the whole globe.

Orbital missile tests

Apart from the systems that have already been described, some of the civil systems are also used to gather information for the armed forces. For example, the meteorological 'Meteor' satellites and the Cosmos satellites used for ocean and icecap surveillance are equipped with Synthetic Aperture Radar (SAR). Similarly, the crews on the Salyut or Mir space stations observe and photograph the Earth, and carry out different technological experiments at the request of the military.

Even if most of the military space programmes are devoted to support roles, there have been less peaceful uses. Between 1966 and 1971, the USSR carried out 16 trials of orbital missiles. They were intercontinental rockets, whose military payload was placed in a very low orbit at about 150 kilometres altitude, completing about three quarters of an orbit, some 30000 kilometres before descending towards their target. This trajectory is very unusual for

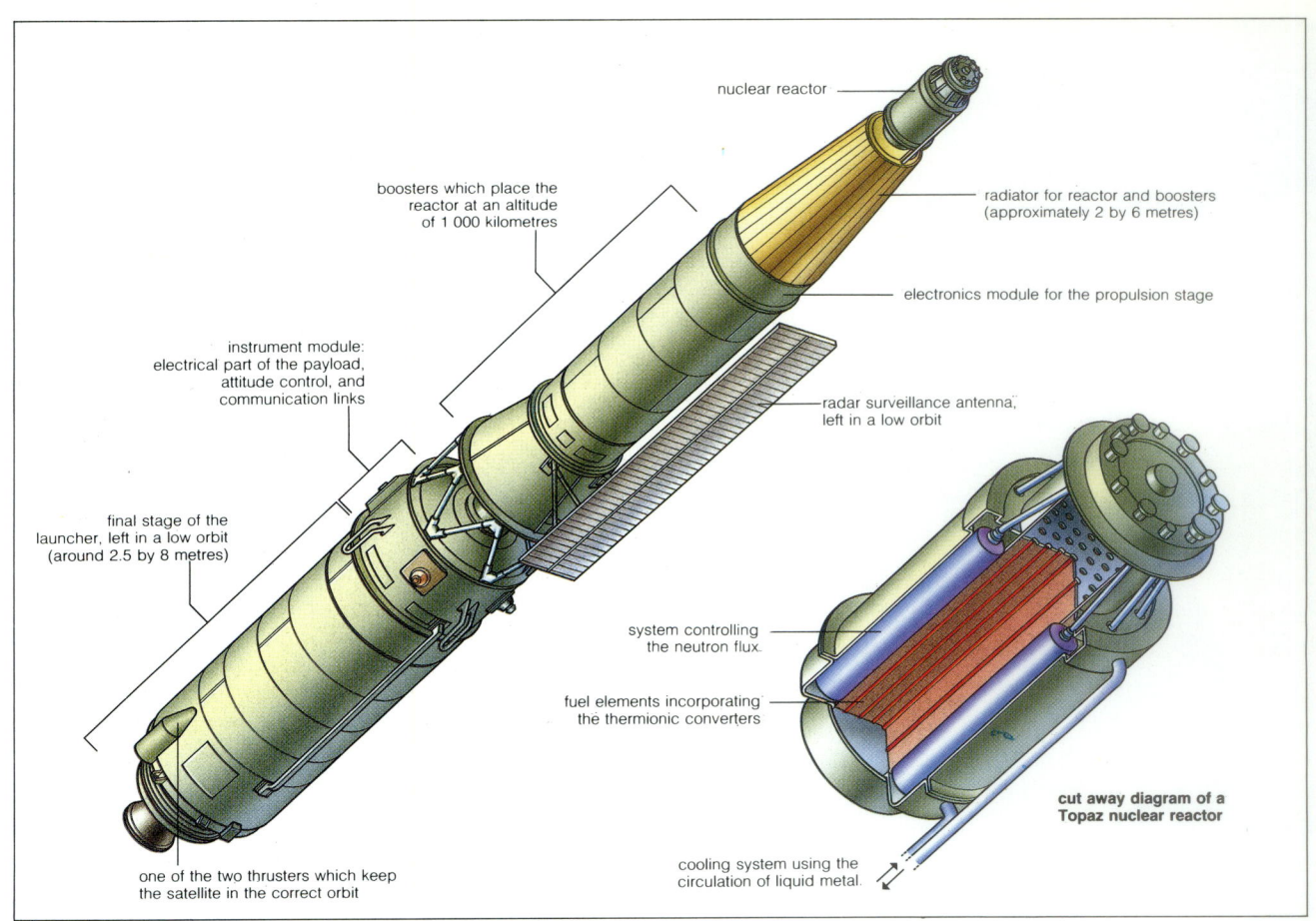

nuclear reactor

boosters which place the reactor at an altitude of 1 000 kilometres

radiator for reactor and boosters (approximately 2 by 6 metres)

electronics module for the propulsion stage

instrument module: electrical part of the payload, attitude control, and communication links

radar surveillance antenna, left in a low orbit

final stage of the launcher, left in a low orbit (around 2.5 by 8 metres)

system controlling the neutron flux.

fuel elements incorporating the thermionic converters

cut away diagram of a Topaz nuclear reactor

one of the two thrusters which keep the satellite in the correct orbit

cooling system using the circulation of liquid metal.

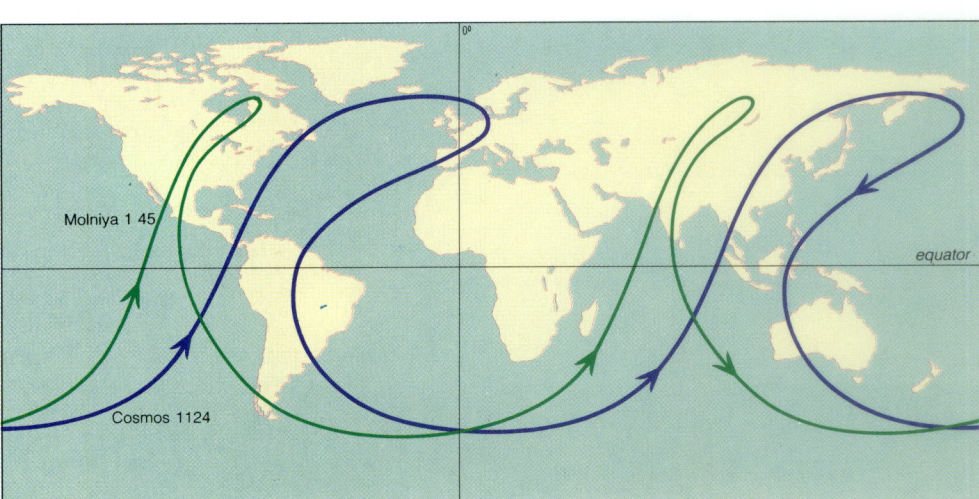

Molniya 1 45

Cosmos 1124

equator

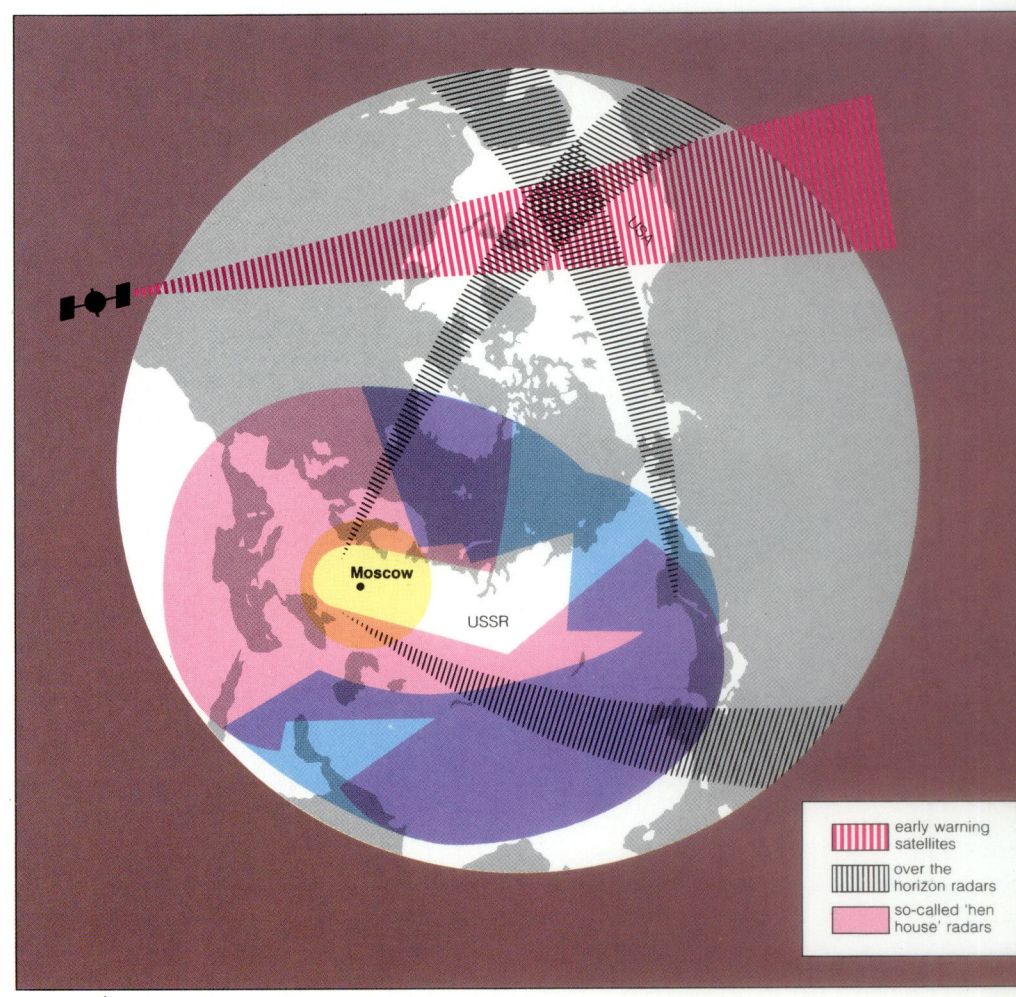

Moscow

USSR

early warning satellites

over the horizon radars

so-called 'hen house' radars

Rorsat satellites. The Soviet ocean surveillance satellites that the Americans call Rorsat are the first satellites to obtain their electrical power from a nuclear reactor. This is situated at the front of the vehicle, and in all likelihood is a small very strongly enriched, uranium reactor of the Topaz design. This contains about 50 kilograms of uranium 235 and provides about 10 kilowatts of power to the satellite. (This type of reactor is able to supply up to 100 kilowatts of power). The heat from the reactor is turned into electricity by thermionic diodes. The radar's antenna is probably along the length of the satellite, as shown in the diagram. The low power ion thrusters are used almost continuously to keep the satellite in its low orbit at 250 kilometres altitude. At the end of its surveillance mission, the reactor detaches itself from the satellite and is propelled to a higher orbit at 1000 kilometres. This is to avoid the premature falling back to Earth of radioactive material (D. R. Woods, 1984).

long range missiles, which normally fly at between 1000 and 1500 kilometres altitude, before descending towards their target at the end of a journey which has usually not exceeded some 10 000 kilometres. The object of such a system is, without doubt, to approach the USA from the South, avoiding detection by the large radars which cover the North of America. The SS 9 missiles are put into orbit under the codename of Cosmos.

These orbital missiles, which constitute the FOBS (Fractional Orbit Bombardment System) system, appear to have remained operational until the end of the 1970s, when their final dismantling was decided in the Strategic Arms Limitations Talks (SALT II). These agreements were not formally ratified, but were respected by both parties until 1986. The FOBS programme is most certainly contrary to the 1967 Space Treaty, which prohibits placing massively destructive weapons into orbit; it actually puts nuclear warheads into orbit.

The anti-satellite satellite programme

While the age of orbital missile tests appears to have passed, the same cannot be said of anti-satellite (Asat) satellites. Though suspended since 1982, Asat programmes could conceivably be resumed if required. About fifty satellites

were launched during the Asat programme: three small satellites were used to calibrate the radars on Earth, seventeen satellites acted as targets in several experiments, and there were twenty interceptors. The interceptors were manoeuvrable satellites weighing 5 tonnes launched by SS 9 intercontinental missiles. Depending on the experiment, they were guided towards their target by radar or infrared detectors. They generally cruised at very high speeds towards their targets and destroyed them by firing a shower of small projectiles. The interceptions were carried out during the first or second revolution of the Asat satellite, at altitudes between 160 and 1500 kilometres. Taking into account the short lifetime of these missions, the only information available comes from the Americans. These evaluations consider the mission a success if the interceptor reaches within 1 kilometre of its target. According to this criterion, about half the missions were successful.

If it were operational from the Baikonur station, as American sources indicate, then Asat could be used to attack American reconnaissance satellites or the space shuttle, which have low orbits. The navigation and telecommunication satellites which have high orbits would be safe from attack. This system is complex and relies on heavy missiles for its operational capabilities. How does the Soviet Asat

system compare with the American Asat system which launches light missiles from aircraft? The Soviet system was in existence long before the Americans began work in this field and, in retrospect, these tests do not lend much credibility to Soviet peace initiatives against US Asat weapons and the SDI programme.

The position of the USSR with respect to the American SDI programme

The Soviet position on the SDI programme was explained by Marshal S. Akhromeev, who said 'we are not carrying out similar studies in order to produce a similar ABM system. On the contrary, we are working to perfect our early warning systems, our means of control, communication and navigation, and to put into operation a terrestrial anti-ballistic missile defence system which does not contravene the ABM Treaty, which we have always rigorously observed'.

The ABM Treaty of 1972 does not prohibit research, development or deployment of groundbased anti-ballistic missile weapons. The situation is, however, less clear for directed energy weapons (lasers and particle beams) because they cannot be considered to be a simple modernisation of anti-missile missiles. There is no reason to disbelieve Marshal Akhromeev when he states that the USSR is not interested in building a Soviet 'ABM space system'. Soviet experts seem to prefer terrestrial bases and envisage installing a non-space replica using multiple warheads, for example, rather than deploying a space ABM device. It is therefore reasonable to suppose that there will be no Soviet SDI programme.

It is therefore reasonable to think that the Soviet military space programme is less extensive than the American military programme and does not necessarily contain a programme that is comparable with SDI. However, the future situation depends very much on the result of negotiations on limiting Asat weapons, ABM systems and strategic weapons more generally. Account also has to be taken of the launch possibilities of the giant rocket Energia, which came into operation on 15 May 1987, and of the Soviet shuttle which is planned for the early 1990s.

Alain Dupas

The orbits of early warning satellites. Early warning systems have to be able to detect missile launches from the sea or land as soon as possible. The Soviet system for this consists of satellites in orbits like those of the Molniya satellites. Inclined at 65 degrees to the equator, they have a perigee of about 600 kilometres over the southern hemisphere and an apogee at nearly 42 000 kilometres above the northern hemisphere. The orbital period is 11 hours 58 minutes, so the projection of the orbit onto the Earth is identical every day.

This projection is shown on the diagram. During its two revolutions per day, the satellite is only rarely in the southern hemisphere, because it moves more rapidly at low altitudes. It stays over the northern hemisphere for much longer since its speed is much less at high altitudes. Therefore for most of the time it is ideally suited for observing American territory and the Atlantic during one of its revolutions, and China and the Pacific during the other (from *Soviet Space Programs*: US Government Printing Office, Washington, DC).

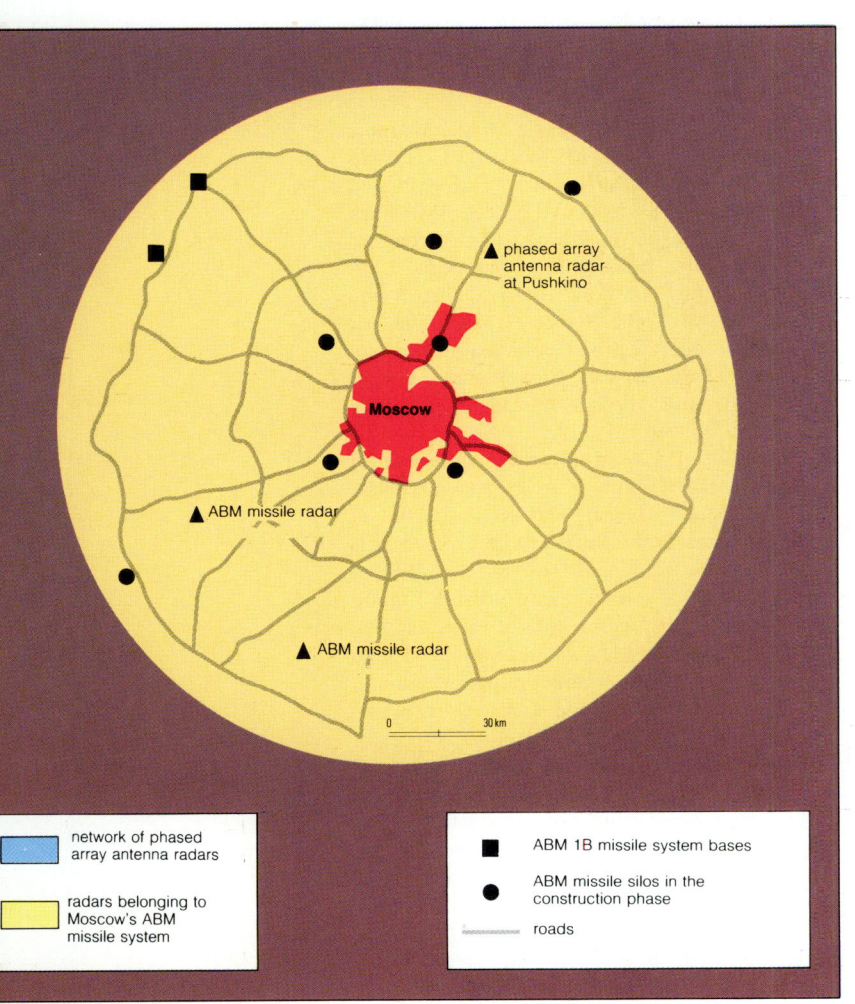

Regions monitored for ballistic missiles and an anti-missile defence map of Moscow. The Soviet Union, like America, has several early warning radar networks, to detect attacks by enemy missiles in low or medium orbits and to acquire information for the guidance of its anti-ballistic missiles (ABMs). Long distance surveillance is carried out by 'over the horizon' radars. Observing over shorter distances are eleven large radars installed around the edge of Soviet territory. The cover is completed by five substantial radars using 'phased array' antennae in which the radar beam is 'steered' electronically. The overlapping cover of the two systems is shown in violet in the diagram. A sixth radar at Kranoyarsk has been the cause of an argument with the Americans because they believe it to be a violation of the 1972 ABM Treaty (cf *International law and space*, p. 368).

The USSR has made full use of the concession in the 1972 ABM Treaty which allowed it to place an anti-missile defence, including up to 100 ABMs, around Moscow. This defence cover consists of a number of launch complexes for 'Galosh' missiles. These can intercept ballistic missiles above the atmosphere. Silos are being built for rapid acceleration missiles which will intercept enemy missiles at lower altitudes and, therefore, at a later time. The Muscovite system includes a modern network of 'phased array' antenna radars installed at Pushkino, and several guidance and detection radars (from *Soviet Military Power*, Department of Defence, Washington DC, 1985).

Caption labels on map:
phased array antenna radar at Pushkino
Moscow
ABM missile radar
ABM missile radar
0   30 km

Legend:
network of phased array antenna radars
radars belonging to Moscow's ABM missile system
■ ABM 1B missile system bases
● ABM missile silos in the construction phase
roads

The USA

General policy

The United States is becoming increasingly dependent on space systems for national security, since the official military view is that space is a region, like the land, sea and air, within which military operations may be conducted.

The military has had an active role in space since the beginning of the space age. Even before that time, the US Naval Observatory, the nation's oldest space-oriented institution, was established by Congress in 1842. It has played a leading role in astronomy and in developing methodologies for precise measurement of the Earth's motion and coordinates.

Space is having a profound effect on the strategy of warfare. A recent US Government study of military space activities noted that 'military strategists throughout history have known the importance of taking and holding the high ground'. Space, termed the ultimate high ground, offers an immensely strategic vantage point from which the US political and military leadership can command, control, and communicate with the military forces that will deter or wage war in the future.'

The potential use of space by the military is, however, far greater than as a mere vantage point for command, control and communications. Some observers believe that an analogy may be drawn between the evolution of the helicopter for combat missions and that of spacecraft. The helicopter was first introduced to the Korean War battlefield as a speedy means of transport for high level commanders. Its use to evacuate wounded directly from the battlefield to field hospitals was soon recognised, causing the Air Force to design the famed UH 1 'Huey' for this purpose. Years later, though, during the Vietnam War, the Huey was credited with saving thousands of lives through its medical evacuation role. However, this use was greatly overshadowed by its successful application as a transporter of troops and cargo, as a command and reconnaissance platform, and as a mount for both defensive and offensive weapons. Today, entire Army divisions are based on helicopters and the fire support which they provide, and some opine that the sophisticated antitank helicopter will render tank warfare obsolete.

The military's application of developing space technology so far appears to be similar to its development and application of rotary wing technology. US Defense Secretary Caspar Weinberger announced in February 1987 a revision of US military space policy, superseding the previous Defense Department policy statement on space issued in 1982. The many significant advances in space technology that had been accomplished in the 1980s resulted in a need to refocus the military's efforts to keep pace with developments. The military effort was now therefore to be more directed toward providing deterrence or defence against enemy attack, ensuring that the forces of hostile nations cannot prevent the US from using space, and enhancing US military operations by utilising space systems.

While the revised policy statement maintains that military space activities will comply with the national arms control policy, it also directs the services to plan for responses in the event that other parties 'break out' from existing arms control treaties (see pp. 366–9). The 1987 policy statement outlines four specific military functions in space. *Space support* includes those functions needed to deploy and maintain military equipment and personnel in space, that is launching and deploying vehicles in space, maintaining and sustaining space vehicles while in orbit, and recovering space vehicles. Space related support operations which improve the

The Flexible Lightweight Agile Guided Experiment (FLAGE), a Kinetic Energy Weapon (KEW). On 20 April 1986, a FLAGE flight vehicle directly impacted a 1·12 metre diameter aluminum sphere at an altitude of 2·3 kilometres (12 000 feet). This experiment on kinetic energy weapon technology achieved the guidance accuracy required for a non-nuclear intercept of an incoming warhead within the atmosphere. In a second test on 27 June 1986, a ground launched FLAGE destroyed a target moving at more than three times the speed of sound. The FLAGE, which was launched 22 seconds after the target was released from an aircraft (shown), used its on board radar guidance system to lock onto the target. The vehicle guided itself to the point of impact by firing 216 tiny azimuthally mounted solid rocket motors. These successful experiments demonstrated the technologies necessary for the guidance, manoeuvring and destruction of longer range kinetic energy weapons (US Department of Defense).

effectiveness of terrestrial and spacebased forces are categorised as *force enhancement*. This includes such activities as global communications, surveillance of the Earth for meteorological, early warning and treaty verification, surveillance of space to track debris and to control traffic, and navigation. *Space control* ensures freedom of action for friendly activities, while limiting or denying the enemy's freedom of action. Anti-satellite and space system protection are elements of space control. Finally, *force application* includes all combat operations conducted from space. The deployment of technologies and systems developed under the Strategic Defense Initiative (SDI) would be considered a force application function.

Charles D. Odorizzi

The methods and the means: US military organisation

By the mid 1980s, the military services had become increasingly dependent on the support provided by systems in space and the number of space systems had multiplied to the point that a reorganisation of effort was necessary. In September 1985, the Defense Department activated the United States Space Command to coordinate all military space assets that were previously operated and maintained separately by the three services. With headquarters at Peterson Air Force Base, Colorado, it has responsibilities in three of the four military functions in space, namely space support, space control and force enhancement. It also has a contingency mission to perform the fourth, force application, if and when the applicable technology is developed and systems are fielded. The unified command exercises its responsibilities through its two component commands, the US Air Force and Navy.

The US Air Force. The Air Force Space Command operates and manages 28 missile warning and space defence facilities around the globe. The missile warning network includes both spacebased and groundbased sensor systems. These systems track and predict the impact of intercontinental ballistic missiles (ICBMs) and sea launched ballistic missiles (SLBMs) targeted on the North American continent. The sensor systems also provide about 25 000 satellite observations each day to the Space Surveillance Center located just south of Colorado Springs. The Satellite Early Warning System, a spacebased system, provides the first information on newly launched ballistic missiles, as it constantly monitors known ballistic

missile launch areas, as well as the open seas, from orbit.

The Ballistic Missile Early Warning System (BMEWS), one of the groundbased sensor systems, uses mechanical motion to steer the radar beams. Fixed radar detection arrays scan the area just above the horizon. More detailed information on objects so detected is then provided by large steerable, parabolic dish antennae. A BMEWS is located at Thule Air Force Base, Greenland, and at Clear Air Force Base, Alaska. An additional BMEWS located at Fylingdales in the United Kingdom is operated by the Royal Air Force. Another groundbased system uses thousands of dipole antennae to aim the radar beam electronically, by accurately phasing the energy emitted from the radar's surface to detect objects in space. Phased array radar systems are far superior to mechanically driven systems because they can direct radar beams into several directions at once, switch targets in only a few milliseconds, and provide a greater amount of tracking data. Phased array radars are in operation at Shemya Air Force Base, Alaska, Cavalier Air Station, North Dakota, and Eglin Air Force Base, Florida. Another, at Thule Air Force Base, Greenland, was completed in 1987 to replace the BMEWS radar there.

The Sea Launched Ballistic Missile Warning System uses radars in the PAVE PAWS (Position Acquisition Vehicle Entry Phased Array Warning System) to detect SLBMs. Such radars are located at Otis Air Force Station, Massachusetts; Beale Air Force Base, California; Robins Air Force Base, Georgia; and Eldorado Air Force Station, Texas. The Air Force also operates the Groundbased Electro-optical Deep Space Surveillance system (GEODS) and another mechanical tracking radar.

Four GEODS sites are now operational, at Choejong-San, South Korea, Socorro, New Mexico, Maui, Hawaii, and on the island of Diego Garcia in the Indian Ocean. Another is planned to be located in Portugal. The GEODS consists of three telescopes, two with a 1 metre diameter and a 2 degree field of view, and one with a 380 millimetre diameter and a 6 degree field of view. Weather data are provided to all of the military services and civilian users by the Defense Meteorological Satellite Program. Global visual and infrared cloud imagery and other specialised meteorological oceanographic and solar geophysical data are collected by two satellites which continuously orbit the Earth at 800 kilometres altitude. The information is received at Fairchild Air Force Base, Washington, and Loring Air Force Base, Maine, and then processed at Offut Air Base, Nebraska.

The control of operational spacecraft and the

The different phases of the trajectory of a ballistic missile. Achieving an effective ballistic missile defence depends on the ability to attack a ballistic missile in all four phases of its trajectory – boost, post boost, mid course and final. An effective ballistic missile defence also requires sensors to observe the attack, interceptors to destroy the ballistic missiles and warheads, and battle management system elements to operate the whole system efficiently.

The most important capabilities of a ballistic missile defence include
– Attacking the missile in its boost phase. In addition to destroying the booster, this will eliminate several nuclear warheads and many decoys designed to defeat defences in the later stages of flight.
– Intercepting the missile in mid course flight. Entirely outside the atmosphere, this offers the defender the longest reaction time, up to 20 or 30 minutes. The intercept weapons may be either spacebased or groundbased; however, they must be complemented by the capability for the early identification of non-threatening objects and the continuing attrition of threatening reentry vehicles to minimise the pressure on the final defence system. Failure to start the defence before mid-course could result in a ten to several hundred fold increase in the number of objects.
– Attacking the ballistic missile several times throughout its flight to the target. This gives the defence a high degree of effectiveness while avoiding the difficult design requirements and potential catastrophic failure modes of a single layer of defence.

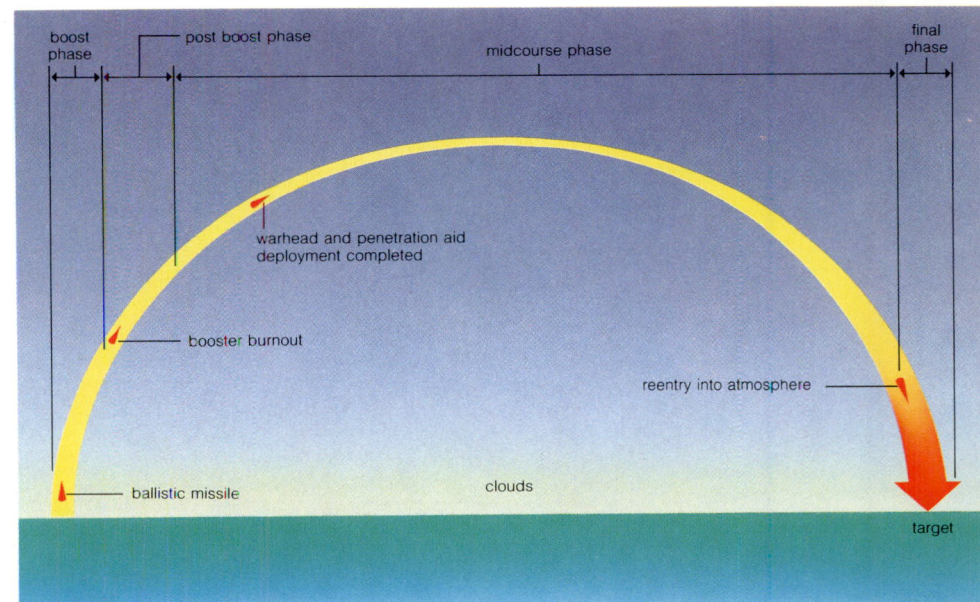

A Ballistic Missile Early Warning System (BMEWS) site. This stationary radar detection array continually scans the sky a few degrees above the horizon for initial sightings of ballistic missiles. The information is passed to a steerable dish radar antenna that provides more detail. This array is located 20 kilometres north of the US Air Base at Thule, Greenland. The BMEWS, designed and built in the 1960s, is reportedly not capable of providing adequate defence against multiple reentry vehicles, decoys or chaff (US Department of Defense).

A PAVE PAWS Radar Site. This is an aerial view of the PAVE PAWS (Precision Acquisition Vehicle Entry Phased Array Warning System) radar at Otis Air Force Base, Massachusetts. The phased array radar beam is steered electronically, rather than mechanically as in the BMEWS (US Department of Defense).

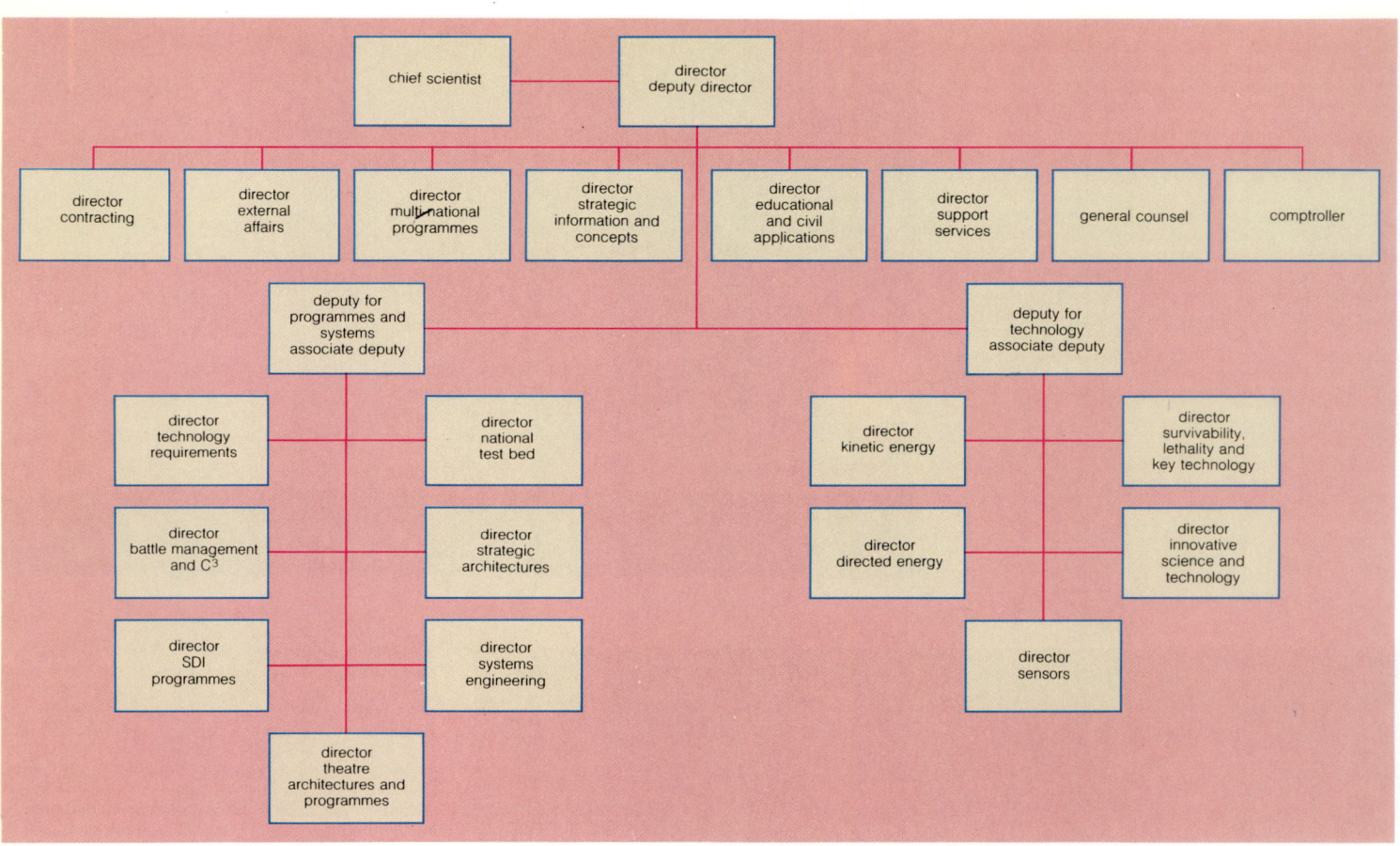

The current organisational structure of SDIO, the Strategic Defense Initiative Organization. This is an advanced technology programme formed in the USA in 1984 from a collection of ongoing research and development projects. It is an independent defence agency whose director reports directly to the Secretary of Defense. Initially, the SDIO was organised with only 80 military and civilian personnel but it was soon apparent that it was undermanned. The SDI programme is very ambitious, and intensive research of many technologies has to be examined in short periods of time. The staff increased to 226 in 1986 (US Department of Defense).

planning, managing and control of all military space shuttle flights is carried out from Falcon Air Force Station, near Peterson Air Force Base in Colorado. The satellite operations complex is organised to track, receive telemetry from, and command orbiting spacecraft in conjunction with the Air Force Systems Command Satellite Test Center at Onijunka Air Force Station, California. The military space shuttle complex will provide flight planning, flight readiness and flight control for all military space shuttle missions, and will be compatible with the NASA Johnson Space Center at Houston, Texas. In fact, the complex will provide a backup capability to the Johnson Space Center in the event of a control failure which would prevent NASA from continuing shuttle flight operations.

The US Navy. The Navy is the principal tactical user of space sensors, and is becoming increasingly reliant on satellites for surveillance, environmental monitoring, communications and navigation. The responsibility for these systems belongs to the Naval Space Command, whose headquarters are at Dahlgren, Virginia. It has two major subordinate organisations, the Naval Astronautics Group at Point Mugee, California, and the Naval Space Surveillance Center at Dahlgren.

The former is responsible for operating Transit (see pp. 254–9), the multiple satellite constellation that provides precise navigation data to government, commercial and other users. First launched in 1959, the Oscar and Nova satellites of the Transit system provide two dimensional position fixes to more than 56 000 ship, submarine, and landbased receivers located around the world. Transit is supported by a ground network of a computational facility at Point Mugee and four tracking and control stations at Prospect Harbor, Maine; Rosemont, Minnesota; Wahiawa, Hawaii; and Point Mugee.

The Navstar Global Positioning System (GPS) will replace Transit in the 1990s. Navstar is designed to be an all weather, worldwide, satellite based positioning system, with 18 primary satellites. Four of these will provide accurate, three dimensional location and velocity data to users in the air, at sea and on land.

The Naval Space Surveillance System provides reports on space objects by predicting where satellites will be in the future. The system consists of three transmitters which emit a 'fence' of radio energy approximately 9000 kilometres long and 28 000 kilometres into space. Satellites penetrating the fence cause the radio energy to be reflected back to one or more of six receiver stations. The satellites are precisely located when at least two of the receivers record the intersecting angles of the reflected radio beam.

The US Army. The US Army Space Agency was established in August 1986 at Peterson Air Force Base, with a complement assigned to the Johnson Space Center. It plans Army participation and operates systems in support of national space programmes. However, the Army has been active in space since the end of World War II. It developed America's first modern rocket, the Redstone, built and launched the first US satellite, Explorer I, and provided the boosters that launched the first US astronauts into space.

During the late 1950s and early 1960s, however, the Army's missions in space were either transferred to other military services or cancelled. Army interest in space was rekindled only in the 1980s when the Army Space Agency was charged with assisting Army forces in determining and coordinating requirements for space support. Future plans call for the agency to command the evolving space and strategic defence elements, and to augment the Air Force's satellite control efforts.

The Strategic Defense Initiative

In March 1983, President Ronald Reagan announced the Strategic Defense Initiative, a joint service, multibillion dollar research and technology programme, 'to find ways to provide a better basis for deterring aggression, strengthening stability, and increasing the security of its [US] allies.' Formally chartered as a Defense Agency in April 1984, the SDI programme became President Reagan's priority defence programme. Reasons cited for the new initiative included the fact that recent advances in defensive technologies warranted a new evaluation of ballistic missile defence as a basis for a safer form of deterrence. The possibilities for maintaining security by means of an enhanced ability to deter war through an increasing capability to defend against attack, rather than by depending on the theory of Mutual Assured Destruction (MAD), were considered to deserve serious exploration. The premise of the Reagan administration was that the technical information gained from five to seven years of basic SDI research and the projected expenditure of 26 billion dollars would, by the early 1990s, be available to President George Bush and permit his administration to make an informed decision on whether or not to develop and deploy a defence dominant deterrence strategy. Both President Bush and Vice-President Dan Quayle have reaffirmed that the US will not be left defenceless against ballistic missiles.

In addition to sponsoring new research programmes, the SDI programme consolidated and expanded several efforts that were being conducted separately by the various services and by the Defense Advanced Research Projects Agency (DARPA). The SDI programme initially focused on the exploitation of advances already made in several technologies.

The basic structure considered for fielding such SDI capabilities as may be developed is known as a multitiered, or layered, defence. Military strategists first defined the concept of layered defence in the 1960s, but it lay dormant as the resources to research the concept were not available. In the 1980s, computer and weapons technology had advanced to the point that attention was again focused on the concept. A multitiered defence is actually a series of defences. It consists of multiple strikes using both spacebased and groundbased techniques on an attacking ballistic missile in each of the four phases of its trajectory, namely boost, post boost, mid course (or ballistic) and final. The major uncertainties in achieving a successful attack against a layered defence system and the penalties of failure are a significant disincentive to any potential aggressor.

Specific SDI research efforts are organised in the five areas of Surveillance, Acquisition, Tracking and Kill Assessment (SATKA); Directed Energy Weapons (DEW) technology; Kinetic Energy Weapons (KEW) technology; Systems Analysis and Battle Management (SA/BM); and Survivability, Lethality and Key Technologies (SLKT).

SATKA research identifies and validates the various sensors needed for surveillance, acquisition, tracking, discrimination and kill assessment of enemy ballistic missiles, from launch to warhead reentry and detonation (that is, from 'birth to death'). The programme has three areas. These are technology base development (infrared sensors, laser radars,

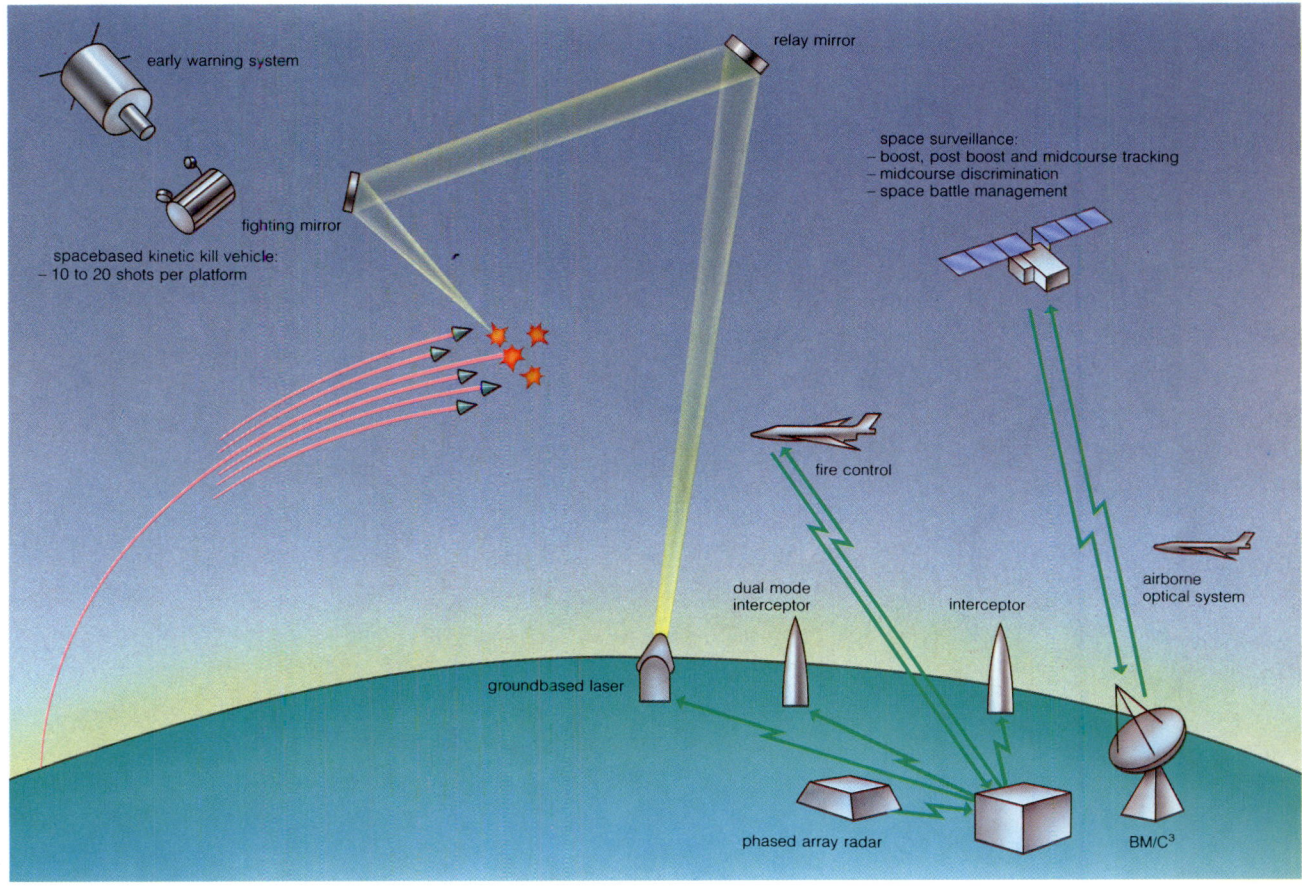

A regional defence system. The infrastructure required for regional defence against ballistic missiles is different from that designed for strategic defence in that the short range ballistic missiles have shorter flight times, lower trajectories and greater warhead variety than the intercontinental ballistic missiles.

Since the short range missiles never leave the atmosphere, they are not vulnerable to spacebased interceptors; however, they are vulnerable to groundbased defensive systems because of their low velocities. Such systems could be directed by airborne sensors throughout most of their flight. The short flight times of tactical ballistic missiles require fast acquisition, tracking, discrimination and reaction which, in turn, require great sensor sensitivity and fast data processing. Most short range systems are single warhead missiles which carry no decoys. However, an added burden is placed on the discrimination function if these missiles do have 'penetration aids'.

microwave radars, interactive discrimination and signal processing); data collection and measurements; and technology integration experiments for the various phases of the trajectory.

DEW technology research concerns directed energy systems that could destroy large numbers of enemy rocket boosters and their payloads in the few minutes that the missiles are in their boost phase. It can also discriminate between decoys and warheads.

KEW technology research focuses on the interception and destruction of ballistic missiles with groundbased and/or spacebased conventional weapons. The interceptors may be guided or unguided projectiles, and may be launched by rocket boosters, missiles or hypervelocity guns on the ground or in space.

Research conducted by the Battle Management/Command, Control and Communications (BM/C^3), now called the Command Center/ System Operation and Integration Functions (CC/SOIF), seeks to develop and experimentally to validate a responsive, reliable, durable and cost effective CC/SOIF system. To constitute an effective multitiered defence against ballistic missile attacks, the CC/SOIF system must process information from surveillance satellites, airborne sensors and ground radars, and then pass that information to 'battle managers'. These identify targets and communicate target assignments to space and groundbased weapons.

SLKT research examines whether or not to develop and deploy a particular strategic missile defence system. Specifically, the objectives are to develop the technology base necessary to ensure that the strategic defence force elements will survive in hostile environments, together with appropriate materials and structures, methods of power generation and launch vehicle concepts.

As part of SLKT research, two Space Power Experiment Aboard Rockets (SPEAR) satellites were launched in December 1987 and mid 1989. These were designed to investigate the use of high electrical power in low Earth orbit. Also in late 1989, a device built by General Electric was launched to test the use of nuclear power sources in space.

International agreements

From the outset, the US government has maintained that military endeavours in space, particularly the SDI, will comply with applicable international agreements. The United States is a signatory to three space related treaties which affect US military space policy. These are the Treaty between the United States and the Union of Soviet Socialist Republics on the Limitation of Anti-Ballistic Missile Systems (the Anti-Ballistic Missile [ABM] Treaty); the Treaty on the Principles Governing the Activities of States in the Exploration and Use of Outer Space, Including the Moon and Other Celestial Bodies (the Outer Space Treaty); and the Treaty Banning Nuclear Weapon Tests in the Atmosphere, in Outer Space, and Under Water (the Partial Test Ban Treaty).

The ABM Treaty was signed by President Richard Nixon and Soviet General Secretary Leonid Brezhnev in May 1972. The purpose of the treaty (see pp. 366–9) was to prohibit US and Soviet deployment of a nationwide ABM system, leaving each party vulnerable to attack by the other. The treaty also prohibits the development, testing and deployment of sea, air, and mobile landbased ABM systems. Under the treaty, however, new systems 'based on other physical principles' can be developed. This article in effect provides the basis for SDI.

The treaty also allows each party to have an ABM deployment site to protect either its capital or an ICBM (Inter Continental Ballistic Missile) field and to carry out research, for example on different ABM systems, including spacebased systems. The Soviets chose to defend Moscow (see pp. 352–3), and an ABM system now operates around their capital. The United States chose to defend an ICBM field, but the Safeguard system was dismantled in the 1970s before it was completed.

The Outer Space Treaty, signed in January 1967, by the United States, the United Kingdom and the Soviet Union, deals with the use of outer space for peaceful purposes. 'Peaceful' is understood to mean non-aggressive, rather than non-military, so such non-aggressive military uses of space as communication satellites are allowed under the treaty. Weapons in space are, however, prohibited. The signatories must 'not place in orbit around the Earth any objects carrying nuclear weapons or any other kinds of

The Delta 181 payload. This was a very successful technology validation experiment sponsored by the SD10 Kinetic Energy Weapons programme. A twin spacecraft payload, launched on 8 February 1988, made critical space observations and actually performed a space intercept. The payload on the Delta rocket is shown during the installation of its shroud on Pad 17 at Cape Canaveral (US Department of Defense).

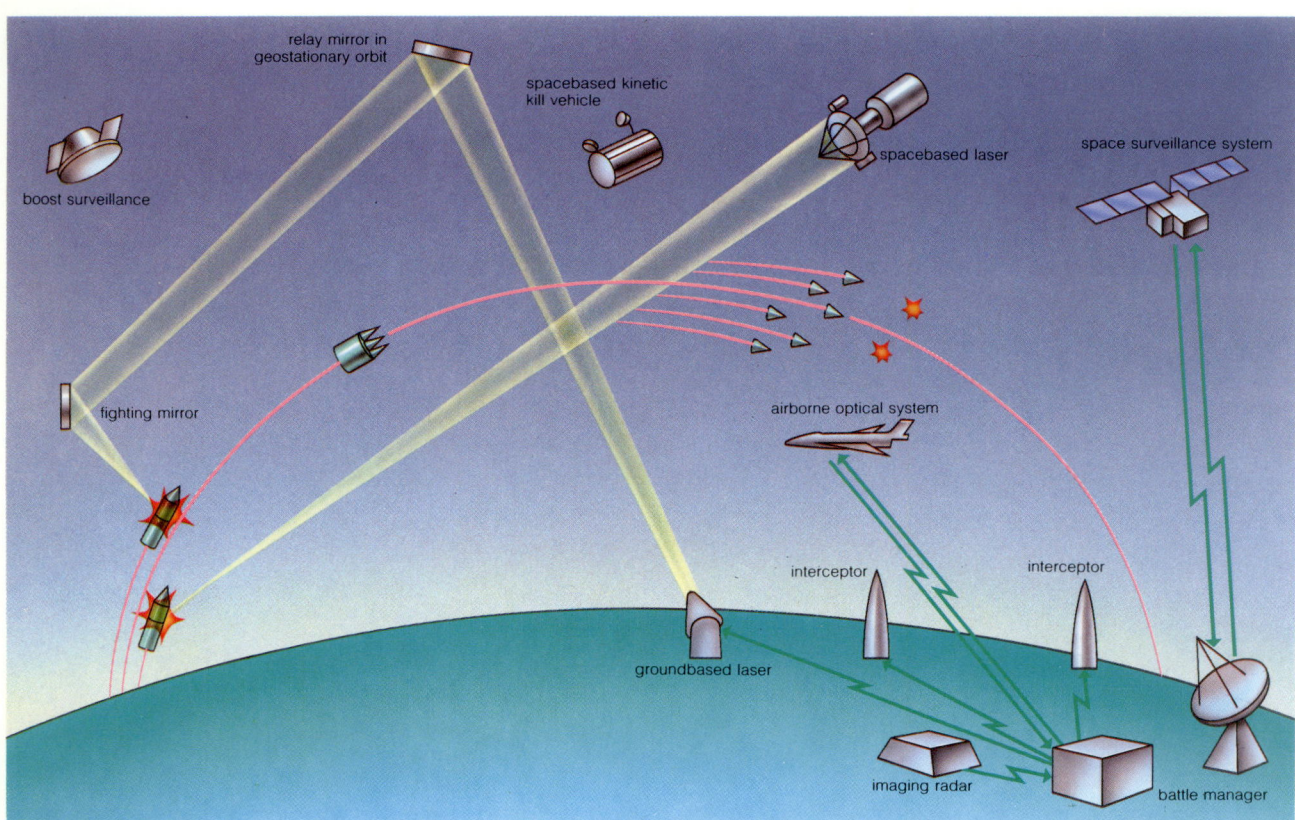

Ground and spacebased defences. A Space Based Kinetic Kill Vehicle (SBKKV) defence system is augmented by directed energy weapons. Among directed energy weapons, some high energy lasers are able to counter threats before they reach space, thereby increasing the 'engagement time'. A spacebased laser, or alternatively a groundbased laser with spacebased relay and fighting mirrors, could be used.

weapons of mass destruction, or install such weapons in outer space in any other manner'. The Outer Space Treaty therefore prohibits in outer space the deployment and testing of nuclear powered laser ABM systems, the testing or use of groundbased kinetic energy weapons (KEW) with nuclear warheads, and the deployment and testing of any kind of spacebased ballistic missiles with nuclear warheads. The Treaty, however, does not prohibit other non-nuclear ballistic missiles or ballistic missile defence (BMD) technologies, such as space, ground, and airbased conventional lasers, spacebased particle beams, space, ground, and airbased KEW with conventional warheads, antitactical ballistic missiles (ATBMs), space shuttles, or heavy lift vehicles.

It should also be noted that the prohibition of weapons testing in outer space is confined to the Moon and the other celestial bodies. The prohibition does not apply to tests in Earth orbit.

The Partial Test Ban Treaty, signed by the United States and the Soviet Union in 1963, prohibits 'test explosions of nuclear weapons' so as 'to put an end to the contamination of man's environment of radioactive measures.' The treaty specifically prohibits the parties to carry out or participate in 'any nuclear explosion, at any place under its jurisdiction or control.' However, not all BMD technologies are nuclear. Furthermore, the Test Ban Treaty prohibits only nuclear weapon test explosions (or any nuclear explosion), not testing. Accordingly, some BMD technologies are permitted under the treaty.

Charles D. Odorizzi
and Amy K. Bodnar

A spacebased laser. One example of a directed energy weapon (DEW) is the spacebased laser. In development since the late 1970s, this has the capability to intercept ballistic missiles in their boost phase, before they can deploy their warheads or decoys. It could engage ballistic missiles launched from anywhere on the Earth or sea, as well as intermediate range ballistic missiles. Furthermore, because the beams of some types of laser can penetrate the atmosphere down to the height of cloud tops, such weapons may be able to provide some defence against aircraft, cruise missiles and tactical missiles.

Electromagnetic Launchers. An Electromagnetic Launcher (EML) is a kinetic energy device that can accelerate projectiles, or 'bullets', to ultrahigh velocities using electric and magnetic energy, as opposed to rockets which use chemical energy as a propellant. In a strategic defence system, an EML would propel a projectile against ballistic missiles and/or reentry vehicles. Velocities for EML projectiles of approximately 70 000 kilometres per hour are considered to be plausible, while chemical rockets are inherently limited to values of less than 22 000 kilometres per hour.

The photograph below shows a Department of Defense EML in California. It has fired a plastic projectile weighing 0·14 kilograms at a velocity of 11 000 kilometres per hour, or 3 kilometres per second. This penetrated a steel sheet 2·5 centimetres thick (US Department of Defense).

A Kinetic Energy Weapon (KEW). This artist's impression shows the Homing Overlay Experiment (HOE), en route to intercept a ballistic missile beyond the Earth's atmosphere. The metal ribs on the non-explosive warhead of the interceptor, approximately 2 metres long, are wound around the neck of the HOE vehicle during flight. The ribs unfurl seconds before the vehicle collides with the target to destroy it.

In June 1984, the HOE, a kinetic energy weapons research project, proved the capability of a non-nuclear interceptor to destroy an incoming ballistic missile outside the Earth's atmosphere. The closing speed of the interceptor and target, over 30 000 kilometres per hour, resulted in the target being demolished. Such kinetic energy weapons could be an essential part of a multilayered defence system (US Department of Defense).

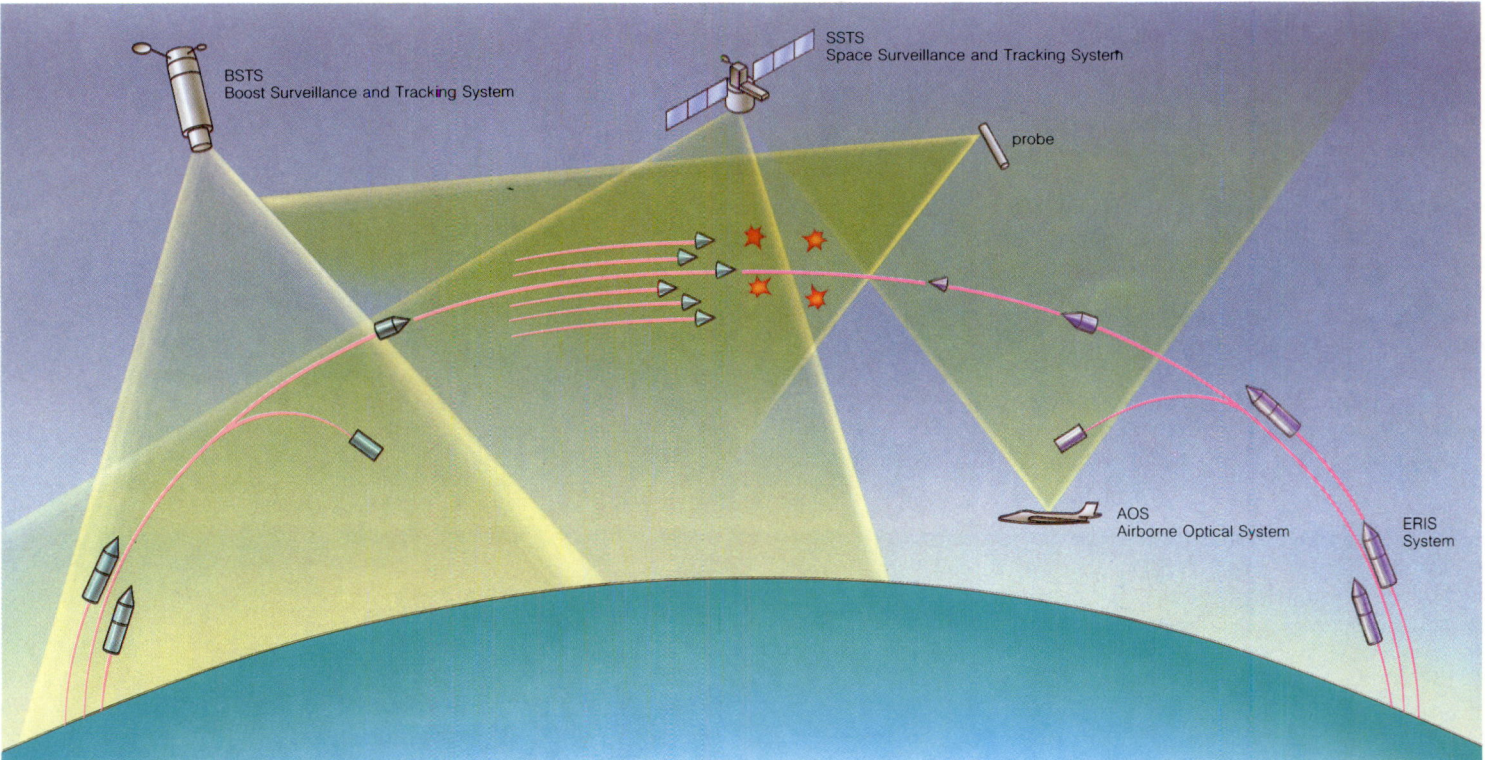

The concept of mid course (ballistic phase) defence. Nuclear warheads launched aboard ballistic missiles would run the gauntlet of early detection and tracking before being intercepted by a kinetic energy weapon (KEW, on the right). This destroys warheads in space by physical impact. The missiles, on the left, are detected by the Boost Surveillance and Tracking System (BSTS), and then by either the Space Surveillance and Tracking System (SSTS), a sensor probe, or an airborne optical system (AOS). (US Department of Defense).

International law and space

General features

Space law, or the jumble of international and national rules governing the space activities of various countries, international organisations and private industry, has been evolving since 1957 when the General Assembly of the United Nations created the Committee on the Peaceful Uses of Outer Space (COPUOS). One of its sub-committees was instrumental in drawing up a body of space law governing the peaceful exploration and utilisation of outer space. The scientific and technical sub-committee is involved in promoting international cooperation on space projects. Other international organisations, for example, the International Telecommunications Union (ITU), have also been involved in these processes.

The evolution of space law

The development of a comprehensive set of laws governing space activities has taken place in two distinct phases. The initial phase began in 1959, when the Space Committee was created, and ended in 1975. During this period, the chief principles of space law were set down and numerous international organisations were created or began working in space research. It was the era when the two superpowers worked separately to develop the same technologies. The period from 1975 to the present day is marked by a diversification of objectives on the part of these nations. The regulations drawn up by the Space Committee are very complicated, but there are underlying principles which govern specific aspects of space utilisation. The complexity is essentially due to the profound growth of space activity in the early years of the space age. The benefits of space exploitation have resulted in a new economic order being established, and East–West relations have been affected.

Today, new trends have contributed to the diversification of space law. National regulations, which complement international laws, have been instituted to control internal affairs, notably in the USA. These govern the affairs of private industries which want to make use of space in the manner authorised in the 1967 Outer Space Treaty. In addition, the militarisation of space by the extension of the arms race to include space and the new perspective generated by the almost permanent presence of man in space will modify the context in which space law is written. The fact that, within each country, launch capacity has been developed under government auspices, has conferred a large degree of central control upon space activities. International cooperation has also encouraged the sharing of the benefits of space technology.

Today, space law has achieved a certain maturity. It remains distinguishable from other sections of international law, such as maritime law and air law. However, the overall principles of international law still apply, as stated in article 1, paragraph 2, and article 3 of the 1967 Outer Space Treaty. These stipulate that the exploration and utilisation of space should conform to the general regulations of international law.

The non-appropriation of space

Contrary to the premises on which other aspects of international law have been established, and unlike the laws governing inner space, sea and air, space law is not constructed on the territorial concept of state sovereignty. Article 2 of the 1967 Outer Space Treaty states that 'outer space including the Moon and other celestial bodies must not be the object of national appropriation by the proclamation of sovereignty nor by usage nor by occupation nor by any other means'. The uniqueness of space law has not, however, always been accepted. For example, some nations denounce the 'economic appropriation' by the major space powers of certain portions of outer space and yet, paradoxically, claim sovereign rights over geostationary orbits of great use for telecommunications satellites. The absence of the notion of national sovereignty is the major difference between space law and the laws governing the sea, the air and the Antarctic continent.

Article 1, paragraph 1, of the Outer Space Treaty of 27 January 1967 states that the exploration and utilisation of outer space is the privilege of all humanity. However, only the natural resources of the Moon and other celestial bodies have been declared the 'common inheritance of all mankind' by article 5 of the Accord, of 18 December 1979, governing the activities of countries on the Moon and other celestial bodies. It is planned that, when it becomes possible to exploit these natural resources, each country will establish internal regulations governing this activity. This ceremonial treaty therefore has no application at present and is only supported by a few countries. This contrasts with the large number of countries which have ratified the 1967 Outer Space Treaty.

The freedom to explore and use space

The principle of being free to explore and use outer space is underlined in article 1, paragraph 2, of the 1967 Outer Space Treaty which declares that 'outer space, which includes the Moon and other celestial bodies can be freely explored and used by all countries'. This is the natural consequence of the policy of non-appropriation of space. The principle was the result of an optimistic and fruitful vision of the use of space, and an acceptance of certain responsibilities by each State making use of this freedom. Article 1 of the treaty imposes certain obligations on the nations which take part in such activities. For example, the exploration and utilisation of space should be in the interests of all peoples, whatever the stage of their economic or scientific development. Also, space should be explored and utilised freely in conditions of equality and in conformity with international law. All regions of celestial bodies should be freely accessible and nations should facilitate and encourage international cooperation in the matter of scientific space research. Reference to encouraging international cooperation is also repeated in four other articles of the treaty (articles 3, 9, 10 and 11).

The stipulations of international cooperation

Article 9 of the 1967 Outer Space Treaty includes a description of the obligations related to the negative consequences of certain space activities which may have harmful conse-

The thirtieth convention of COPUOS, from 1 to 11 June 1987, at New York. Following the launch of Sputnik 1 in 1957, the United Nations created a committee to deal with space issues. Its first meeting was in 1959. Because of procedural disagreements, it was three years before a permanent committee was created. The Committee on the Peaceful Uses of Outer Space (COPUOS) held its first meeting on 2 November 1961, after it was agreed that members should be equally split between countries in the West, socialist countries and developing countries; decisions were to be by consensus.

The first working meeting of the committee, which all the member states attended, took place in March 1962. Since then the committee has met yearly. In June 1987, it discussed the methods and means of using space for peaceful purposes and satellite remote sensing. Also considered were nuclear power as an energy source for spacecraft, the boundary between air space and space beyond the atmosphere, and the use of the geostationary orbit.

In the photograph, from left to right, are Adigun A. Abiodun, Department of Political and Security Council Affairs (DPSCA); Vasily S. Safronchuk, Under-Secretary General (DPSCA); Peter Jankowitsch (Austria), Chairman; Vladimir Kopal, head of the division on outer space (DSPCA) and Committee Secretary; N. Jasentuliyana, assistant head (DSPCA) and Deputy Secretary to the Committee; and Henrique Rodrigues Valle (Brazil), reporter. (Yukata Nagata, United Nations).

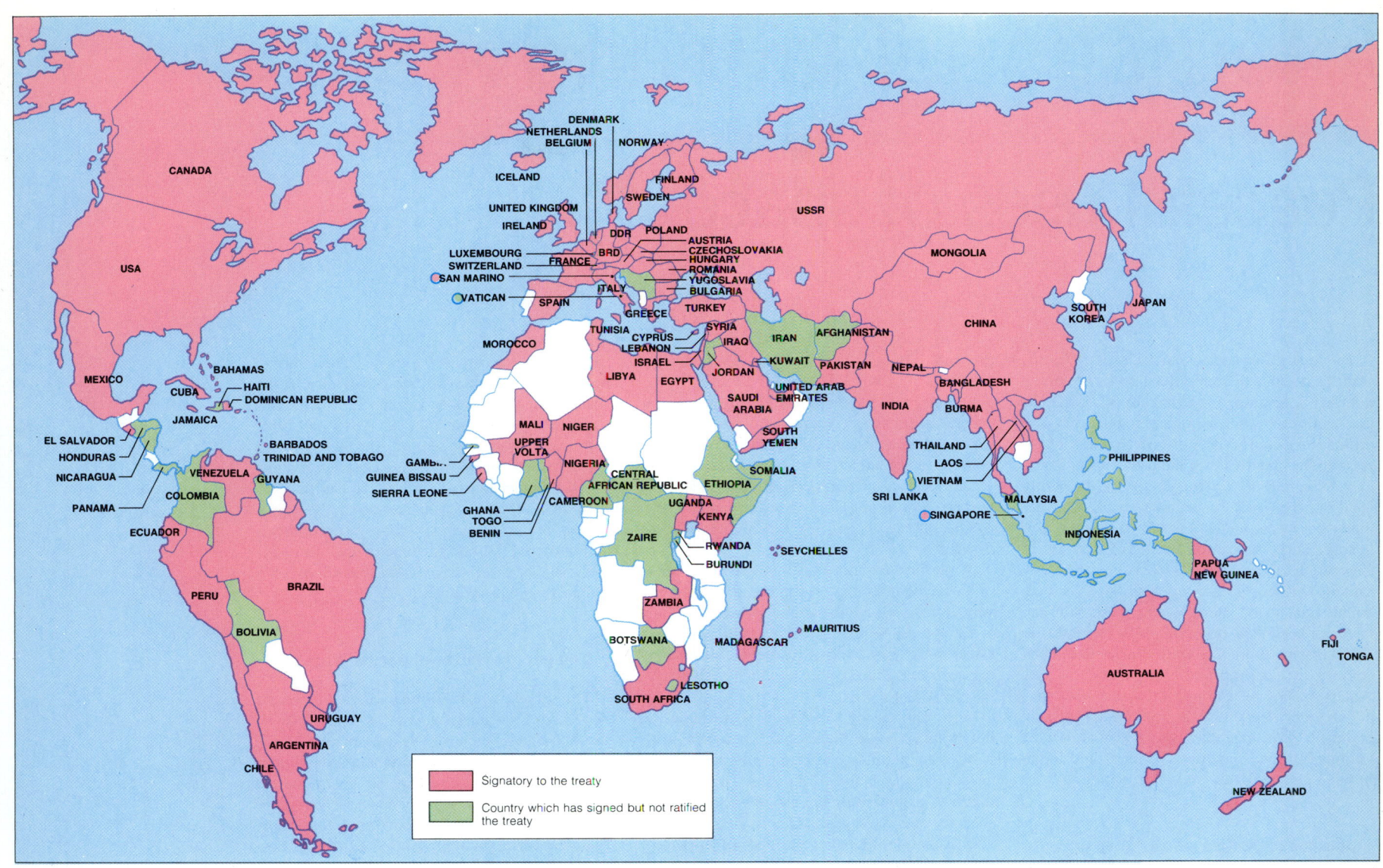

Signatory to the treaty

Country which has signed but not ratified the treaty

quences for other nations or for the planet as a whole. It stipulates that countries should conduct their space activities taking due account of the interests of all the other signatories. Countries are requested to carry out their space activities with care to avoid the introduction of extra-terrestrial substances which may contaminate or modify the terrestrial environment.

Article 5 of the treaty deals with international cooperation, assigning to astronauts the role of 'representatives of all mankind'. Countries must be prepared to provide assistance in the event of an accident or emergency landing on their territory, or in the event of a splashdown on the high seas. For such landings or splashdowns, the return of the astronauts and their vehicle to their own country should be carried out promptly and in all security. During space activities, the astronauts of one country should be prepared to provide assistance to astronauts of other nations which have signed the treaty.

The arrangements concerning the safety and return of astronauts and the return to Earth of other objects launched into space are the subject of a supplementary agreement signed on 22 April 1968. Moreover, nations which signed the 1967 Outer Space Treaty are requested to inform the Secretary General of the UN, the public and the international scientific community of the nature and purpose of their activities, the location where they are being carried out and the results, wherever this is feasible. The Secretary General of the UN has the task of distributing information as and when he receives it.

The convention on the registration of objects launched into space, signed on 14 January 1975, was the result of the general wish of the international community to be aware of the space activities of other countries. This convention states (article 2) that when an object is placed into Earth orbit or beyond, the launch state must register it with the appropriate authority. Each registered State must supply the Secretary General of the UN (article 4) with information such as the name of the launch country, or

countries, an appropriate description or registration number of the space vehicle, the date and territory or place of launch, the main parameters of the orbit, and the general function of the space object.

Other requests for active cooperation have been instituted, for example to encourage the tracking of space vehicles (article 10 of the 1967 Outer Space Treaty). Also 'all materials and space vehicles found on the Moon and other celestial bodies will be accessible under the conditions of reciprocity to other signatories of the 1967 Treaty'.

International responsibility

A very important component of space law concerns the responsibilities of groups working in space activities. Each country monitors work carried out within it, especially that by non-government groups. If there is an incident, there are automatic rights of compensation to the victim.

This responsibility is outlined in article 7 of the 1967 Outer Space Treaty. This states that the country which launches, or intends to launch, an object into outer space and the country whose territory or installations are used to launch the vessel are both internationally responsible for damage caused by the launch vehicle or the spacecraft or by components of it. The convention on the international responsibility for damage caused by space objects was signed on 29 March 1972. At an international level, absolute responsibility, without exception, was placed on the launch state. This obliges that nation to make compensation for all damage caused by a space vehicle to the Earth's surface or to objects in flight (article 2). The amount of compensation is determined by the cost of restoring the claimant (a person, country or international organisation) to its original condition before the accident happened (article 12).

Partial non-militarisation of space

The conditions of article 4 of the 1967 Outer Space Treaty only limit the placing of nuclear weapons or massively destructive weapons into space. They do not prohibit other military uses of space, except those on the Moon or other celestial bodies, which are banned under article 4. Other international agreements complement these regulations, but they are still not sufficient to prevent the arms race from spreading into space.

Olivier de Saint-Lager

The Outer Space Treaty of 27 January 1967. This treaty governs the outer space activities of nations which wish to explore and make use of space, the Moon and other celestial bodies. International space law is very different from other international laws. It is based on a humanist and pacifist philosophy and on the principles of the non-appropriation of outer space, and the freedom that all nations have to explore and use space.

A very large number of countries signed this agreement, including those from the western alliance, the eastern block and non-aligned countries. The map shows the world position in December 1986. Since then Antigua and Barbuda, Equatorial Guinea and Sri Lanka have become parties to the treaty (United Nations).

Peaceful uses of space

The Space Committee of the United Nations, with its legal sub-committee, and the International Telecommunications Union (ITU) are the key bodies which formulate regulations governing the peaceful uses of outer space. These regulations may relate to the use of space (such as placing nuclear reactors in space), to purely legal matters (such as defining and setting the limits on space, and international cooperation in space under article 1 of the 1967 Outer Space Treaty) and to resources (such as geostationary satellite orbits). Other applications, such as commercial space launches and space stations, have not been considered as yet by any international organisation. Laws are drawn up in each country as appropriate (for example, the American law on commercial space launches, 30 October 1984), or negotiated by several countries (for example, the participation of various European countries, Canada and Japan in the American space station programme).

Sources of nuclear power in space

In January 1978, radioactive debris from the Soviet Cosmos 954 satellite, which had disintegrated, fell onto Canadian territory. As a result, when the Space Committee convened in 1979, it discussed the question of nuclear energy sources in space in order to formulate an international law on the subject.

Today, the debate revolves about five points submitted to the legal sub-committee and presented by Canada in 1986. These are as follows:

– nations intending to launch space objects carrying nuclear energy sources should carry out a safety assessment, and the authorities should be notified of the launch as early as possible;
– there should be a general directive and a set of criteria outlining the safe usage and potential risks related to the use of nuclear energy sources;
– the authorities should be notified in the event of an accidental falling back to Earth of a space vehicle carrying a nuclear energy source;
– aid should be given to countries which are affected by the debris of a space vehicle carrying a nuclear energy source which accidentally falls back to Earth;
– there should be conditions governing the operating responsibilities of the launch country.

In spite of differences of opinion over the necessity, the nature and the priorities of regulations governing the use of nuclear energy sources, most countries support their use, provided that scientific interest does not jeopardise the health of people and their environment.

In January 1983, there was another incident involving a Cosmos satellite carrying a nuclear energy source. The Soviet Cosmos 1402 accidentally fell back to Earth. Following this incident, the UN recommended that a standard procedure of international notification be instituted. In 1986, the legal sub-committee agreed on an improved draft of the text of the notification procedure of 1983. It recommended that information about the space vehicle should be made available at an increased rate as the time when the satellite is expected to reenter the atmosphere approaches. Also in 1986, agreement was reached on the question of mutual aid in the event that an object carrying a nuclear energy source falls back to Earth.

In 1988, Cosmos 1900 reentered the atmosphere, but an automatic safety system immediately isolated the nuclear reactor and pushed it into a higher orbit where it will remain until the radioactivity has decayed.

The geographic boundary of space

The subject which has been debated most by the Space Committee is 'what is, and where is, the boundary of space?' There are two bodies of opinion. One side supports an unambiguous 'geographic' boundary, at a given height between air space and outer space. The regions above and below this boundary are governed by two very different sets of laws. Countries possess sovereign rights over the air space above them, whereas mankind is free to explore and make use of all outer space. The other side supports a 'functional' boundary between the two zones, believing that the governing principle should be whether the activity could be classed as a 'space activity' or not. This controversy has been debated for a number of years, owing to the absence of a scientific criterion for defining the boundary, for

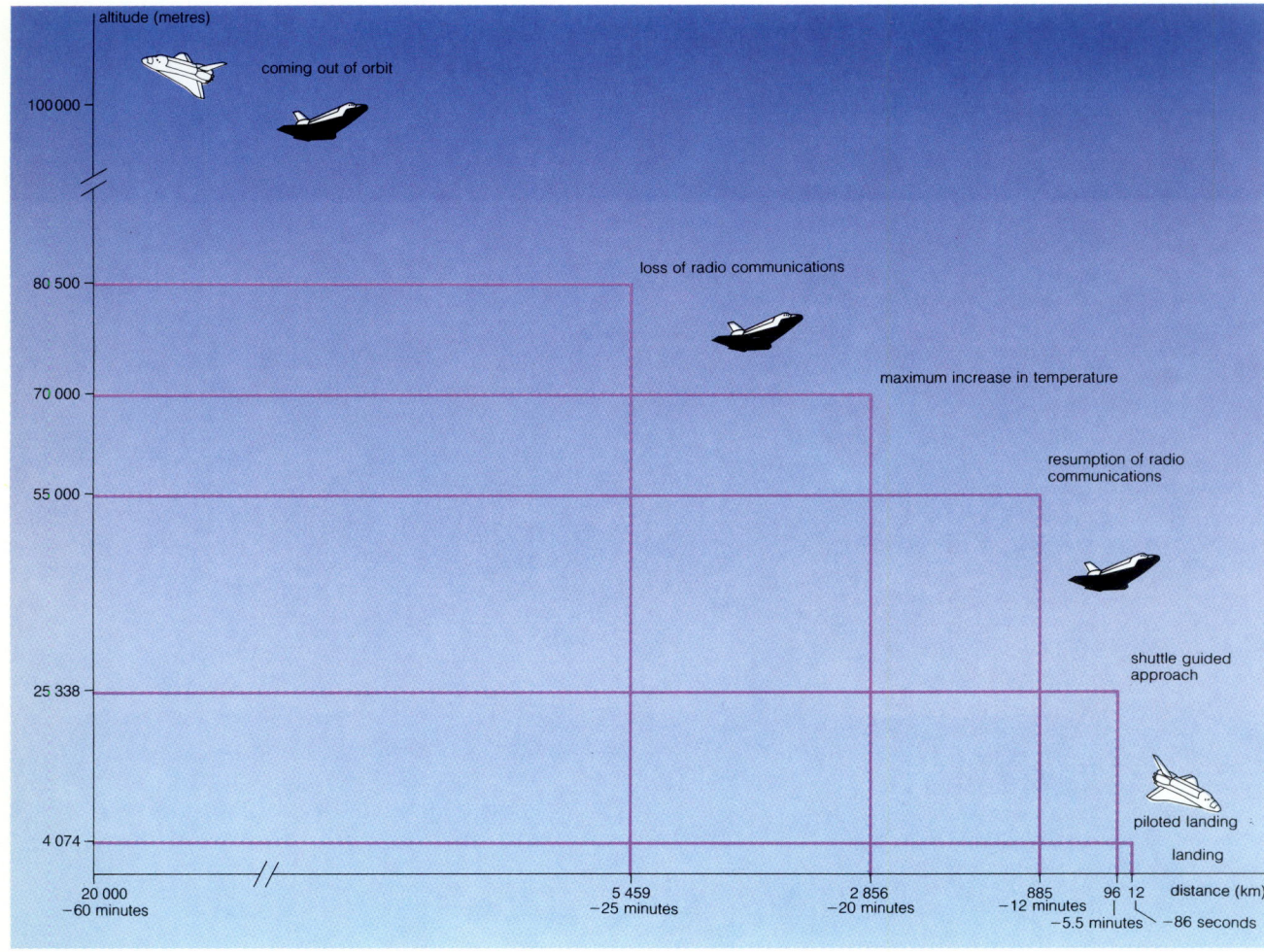

Defining the boundaries of air space, using the space shuttle as an example. Some nations support the proposition of instituting an arbitrary boundary, at 100 kilometres altitude, between air space and outer space. Countries exercise sovereign control over the air space above them, while outer space is governed by the freedom to explore and use it. Unfortunately a boundary of this type will hinder the freedom of passage of space vehicles, especially on their return to Earth. If this boundary is accepted, then a space vehicle such as the space shuttle, which flies for several thousand kilometres below this limit, will have to obtain permission from all the countries that it flies over to use their air space.

There is no scientific or legal justification why this limit should be set at 100 kilometres, and many countries are therefore opposed to it. On the other hand, functional altitude limits will be useful in the future when dealing with specific questions, such as the regulations governing the approach of aerospace vehicles.

instance, a change in gravity or the composition of the atmosphere.

The supporters of the concept of a geographic boundary insist that it is necessary for space law to have a fixed zone of authority, beginning at an arbitrary yet agreed height below which countries can exert all their sovereign rights. The supporters of a functional boundary believe that a geographical boundary is an inappropriate limit because space law already covers areas beneath the geographic limit. There are for instance regulations on the responsibilities of space nations, on the safety of astronauts, on the registration of space vehicles and on the sharing of knowledge. Furthermore, they believe that it would have a serious effect on the rights of passage of spacecraft flying below this level. This restriction on the 'rights of passage' would be particularly serious if the boundary were set at a high altitude, say 100 kilometres. In this case, launch countries would have to request authorisation to fly over neighbouring countries and this could eventually lead to tolls being payable. Aerospace vehicles, such as the American space shuttle, would be most affected because, during their return to Earth, they fly for several thousands of kilometres below 100 kilometres altitude.

The nations which do not support a geographical boundary also believe the compromise suggestion of the 'rights of innocent passage' for space vehicles below the 100 kilometre level to be unsuitable because it would have a negative effect on all space activities above this limit. Neighbouring countries could still try to exert sovereign rights over returning space vehicles and restrictive practices would evolve.

A geographical boundary would serve to decrease the authority of space law, or at least to modify it where space activities happen to occur in another country's air space. Below the boundary, the principle of freedom to explore and make use of space would be restricted by the whims of the country whose air space was being used.

This is why the notion of 'space activities' is a better way of defining what should be governed by space law. In the future, regulations or laws governing space vehicles at low altitudes could be devised as and when the need arises.

The geostationary orbit

The question of ownership of geostationary orbits was raised by a group of equatorial countries, and outlined in the Declaration of Bogota (Columbia) of 3 December 1976. The unique characteristic of this orbit is that satellites have the same period of rotation as does the Earth and so remain fixed above a given point on the Earth's surface. This type of orbit is much used by telecommunications and meteorological satellites. Some of the equatorial nations believe that they should be able to exert full rights of sovereignty over geostationary orbits, since they represent a natural resource. Some claim ownership over the geostationary orbits which project down onto their territory, and have requested economic remuneration from countries which use this 'sovereign natural resource'.

The majority of countries do not recognise the validity of these claims and rely on article 2 of the 1967 Outer Space Treaty: 'Outer space cannot be the object of national appropriation by claims of sovereignty, nor by the means of use or occupation, nor by any other means.'

Most countries consider, further, that these claims, made under the name of justice or the law governing developing countries, would only benefit a small number of countries. These few countries, simply because of their geographical location, would have rights which are not available to all those other developing countries not situated on the equator. The principle of equal rights for all countries to use these geostation-

ary orbits and the frequency bands allocated to space radiocommunications was, moreover, established by the International Telecommunications Union (ITU) in 1971. The operating procedures of this regulation are examined during the world conferences of the ITU.

Space remote sensing

Earth observation from space for non-meteorological civil purposes has been under discussion at the Space Committee of the UN for a long time. A consensus of principles on the subject was submitted to the committee in 1984 by Austria. This was confirmed on 3 December 1986 by the UN General Assembly.

The geostationary orbit: a limited natural resource

'When using frequency bands for space radio communications, members should be aware that the frequencies available for, and the orbits of, geostationary satellites are a limited natural resource. To this end they should be used in the most efficient and economic manner, conforming to the guidelines laid down in the radio communications regulations. This should enable different countries, or groups of countries, to have reasonable access to this orbit and these frequencies. Members should also be aware of the special needs of developing countries and the geographic situation of others.'

This principle, drawn up in 1971, and introduced in 1973 into the International Convention on Telecommunications, prompted members of the International Telecommunications Union (ITU) to arrange a World Administrative Conference on Space Radio Communications. This was termed the Conference on the Utilisation of Geostationary Orbits and Planning Services which use this orbit. The first session took place in Geneva from 8 August to 15 September 1985.

Richard E. Butler

Such a consensus is important because remote sensing from space is a very important future technology, which has only been in its operational and commercial phase for a short time. There are many positive results to be gained from developing it much further.

The debate revolves around four key issues concerning the distribution of images obtained from satellites.

The freedom to film seems to be well established, although there are no strict regulations governing it. This principle is supported by article 1, paragraph 2, of the 1967 Outer Space Treaty: 'outer space can be freely explored and used by all'. In addition, there are some bilateral Soviet–American agreements (the 1972 ABM Treaty), which establish in a limited and indirect manner the same right. The two nations will not interfere with each other's national means of observation. For a long time, however, some member countries have contested this freedom, demanding so-called sovereign rights of nations over information relating to their natural resources.

In spite of this controversy it seems unlikely that these demands will be met. Today, it is a piece of history that a number of countries tried to limit filming by Earth observation satellites, by an agreement favouring the observed country. The guidelines on space remote sensing contain no restrictions of this type. The civil use of remote sensing is naturally limited by the resolving power of the imaging system; there is, simply, a limit to the fineness of quality of the pictures.

The second problem is that of acquiring prior authority from the observed country for the distribution of data to a third country. This question is different from the first one, and was until recently the subject of debate by the Space Committee. Before the Brazilian proposition in 1982, this demand formed the hard core of opposition in all negotiations on the subject by the contesting countries, supported by the Eastern block. For the first time in 1982, Brazil, a large developing country, officially denounced the need for a country to authorise the distribution of information on itself. Brazil, however, added the proviso that the observed country should have access to the relevant data before it is passed on to a third country. This demand, like the question of prior authority, was not finally included in any agreed regulations.

The third problem concerns the conditions in which a country should have access to data about its territory. Developing countries would like access under preferential conditions to data on their land. This request would replace the need for a country to authorise the distribution of data on its territory. The argument was, however, not accepted by western countries. It was reworked into another requirement that, for the remotely observed country, non-discriminatory access at reasonable prices should be given for remote sensing data relevant to that country. In the case of primary or treated data, that is data which have been subjected to the minimal treatment necessary to render them usable, the observed countries have access as soon as they are produced, under non-discriminatory conditions and at reasonable prices. For analysed data, or data which have been further treated to render them more useful, the country has access under the same conditions, taking into account the needs and interests of developing countries, while they are available to and in the possession of the nation which carried out the remote sensing from space or on the Earth.

The last problem concerns the international responsibility of countries which carry out remote sensing. The 1967 Outer Space Treaty and the convention on the responsibility of space nations of 1972 does not contain any specific guidelines on this. In fact space law only covers the responsibilities of space activities carried out in space. It does not cover those activities carried out in space with respect to the Earth, such as remote sensing.

The Eastern block has insisted for a long time that there should be specific references in space law to the distribution of data. Developing countries have shown more flexibility in this area, although this demand was included in the 1982 Brazilian document. The aim of the Soviet Union is to make it possible for states to have some say in what happens to data acquired by a country, or private company within that country, about their own territory. Countries in the West refuse to accept this condition before they distribute data. This increase in the responsibilities of countries who carry out remote sensing was not, in the end, incorporated into the tenets of the 1967 Outer Space Treaty nor the convention on the responsibility of space nations of 1972.

Olivier de Saint-Lager

Direct broadcasting and the United Nations' Committee on Space

After much negotiation, the United Nations voted on a list of recommendations concerning direct broadcasting by satellite on 19 November 1982. Western delegates found the text too restricting, and either voted against or abstained.

The main bone of contention was whether or not prior consent from the receiver country was needed before an international direct broadcasting service could be set up. Delegates were split into two camps, those who supported the freedom of information and those who upheld the sovereignty of the state.

An International Telecommunications Union ruling states that, for national coverage, the satellite beam should have the minimum width necessary for total coverage of the country. However, since the beam is ellipsoidal, there will be inevitable overlaps into adjacent countries.

Three arguments were presented as to why gaining prior permission was not feasible. First, it is technically impossible to avoid broadcasting from space into neighbouring countries. Secondly, it is, in practice, impossible to differentiate between programmes which are purely national and those which have an international flavour. And, thirdly, juridical groups would have to be set up to monitor and control those programmes which might morally, socially or politically be thought liable to corrupt the population of a neighbouring country.

Similar problems confront radio broadcasting. In 1972, UNESCO produced guidelines concerning the use of radio to promote the free circulation of information, education, and the development of cultural exchanges. These state in relation to radio broadcasting from satellites that the sovereignty and equality of countries should always be respected. The broadcasts should be apolitical and every effort should be made to check the truth of the information broadcast. Cultural programmes should respect cultural differences, and the rights of all people to preserve their cultural heritage. All nations should try to gain the prior permission of other countries receiving their satellite broadcasts. These guidelines are based, for example, on the United Nations Charter, the Universal Declaration on the Rights of Man, the European Convention on the Rights of Man, and the International Pact relating to civil and political rights passed by the UN General Assembly on 16 December 1966. All these documents, including UNESCO's declaration, have tried to find a balance between freedom of information and the need for a country to protect its identity and legitimate interests.

A final argument against an excessive set of rules concerning broadcasts aimed at neighbouring countries is that such transmissions can always be jammed by the receiving country. Commercial investors would in such circumstances be discouraged by the lack of a guaranteed broadcasting service.

Olivier de Saint-Lager

Space radio communications

Before discussing the use of space for radio communications, an area of continuing development, it is necessary briefly to review the origins of international legislation relating to the use of radio frequencies. International legislation governing the use of the radio frequency spectrum originated at the first International Radio Telegraph Conference held in Berlin in 1906. This designated specific frequencies for the maritime mobile service, the first service to use radio communications.

In view of the increasing number of users, the International Radio Telegraph Conference held in Washington in 1927 decided to draw up a frequency band allocation table. It was recommended that this should be applied to obtain orderly use of the spectrum. The Bureau of the International Telegraph Union, which later became the International Telecommunication Union (then based in Berne and, since 1948, in Geneva) was required to compile and update the 'list of frequencies'.

In 1947 the ITU Plenipotentiary Conference, having regard to expanding radio communications requirements, decided to make the observance of the Table of Frequency Allocations obligatory, each sovereign state submitting evidence of its use of each frequency and its proposed use of a new frequency.

It was also decided that this information would be transmitted to an independent body, the IFRB (International Frequency Registration Board), a quasijudicial body of the ITU. The board currently consists of five independent members elected or reelected by the Plenipotentiary Conference who serve, not as representatives of their respective countries or of a region, but as custodians of an international public trust.

The procedures adopted for terrestrial services in 1947 in the Radio Regulations annexed to the International Telecommunications convention govern the use of the radio frequency spectrum and the geostationary orbit. They may be broadly subdivided into acts of notification (by the administration) and (by the IFRB) acts of examination, for conformity with the Table of Frequency Allocations and other regulations concerning the avoidance of interference. These procedures were refined in 1959 and again twenty years later.

It was, of course, with the launching of

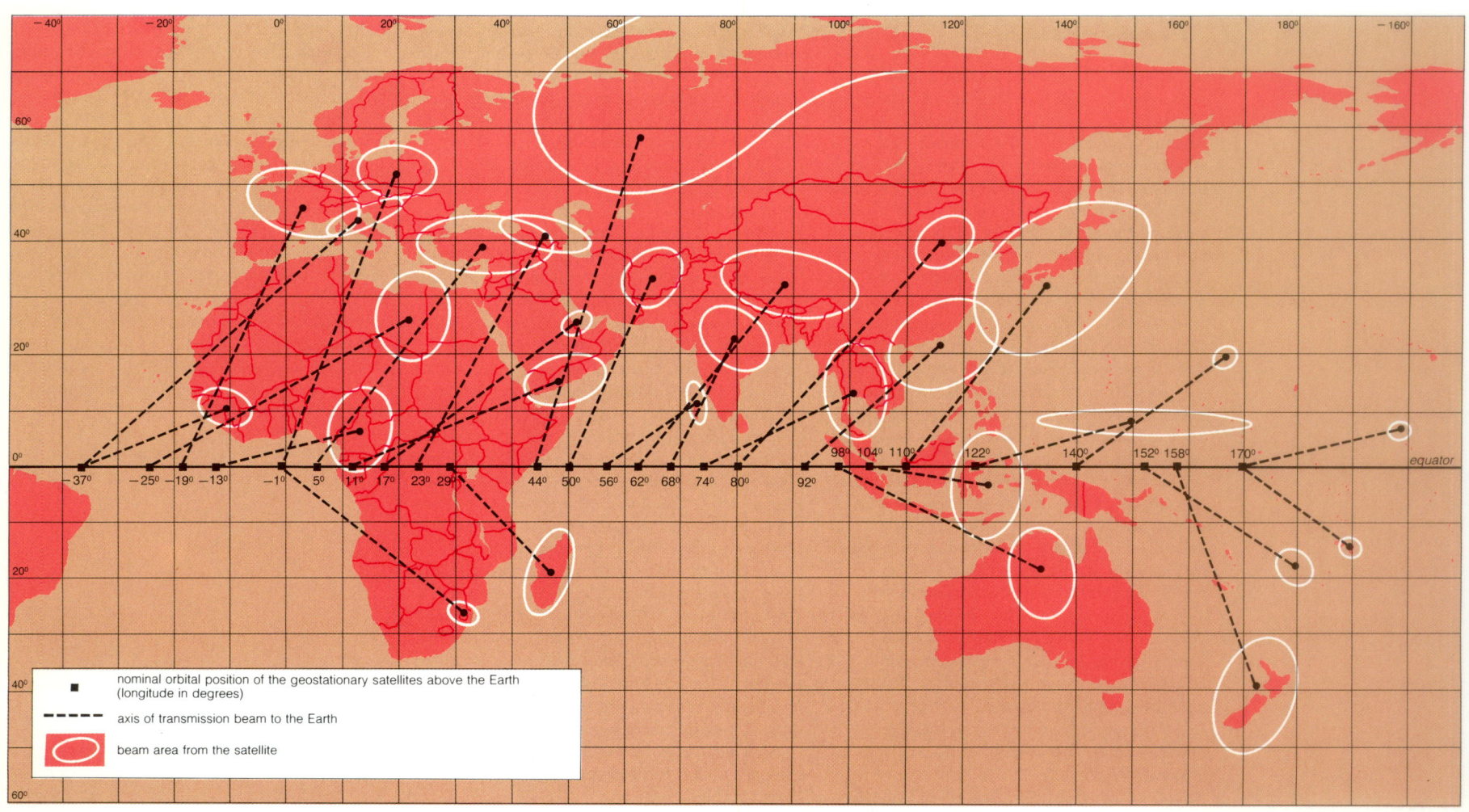

- ■ nominal orbital position of the geostationary satellites above the Earth (longitude in degrees)
- - - - - axis of transmission beam to the Earth
- ⬭ beam area from the satellite

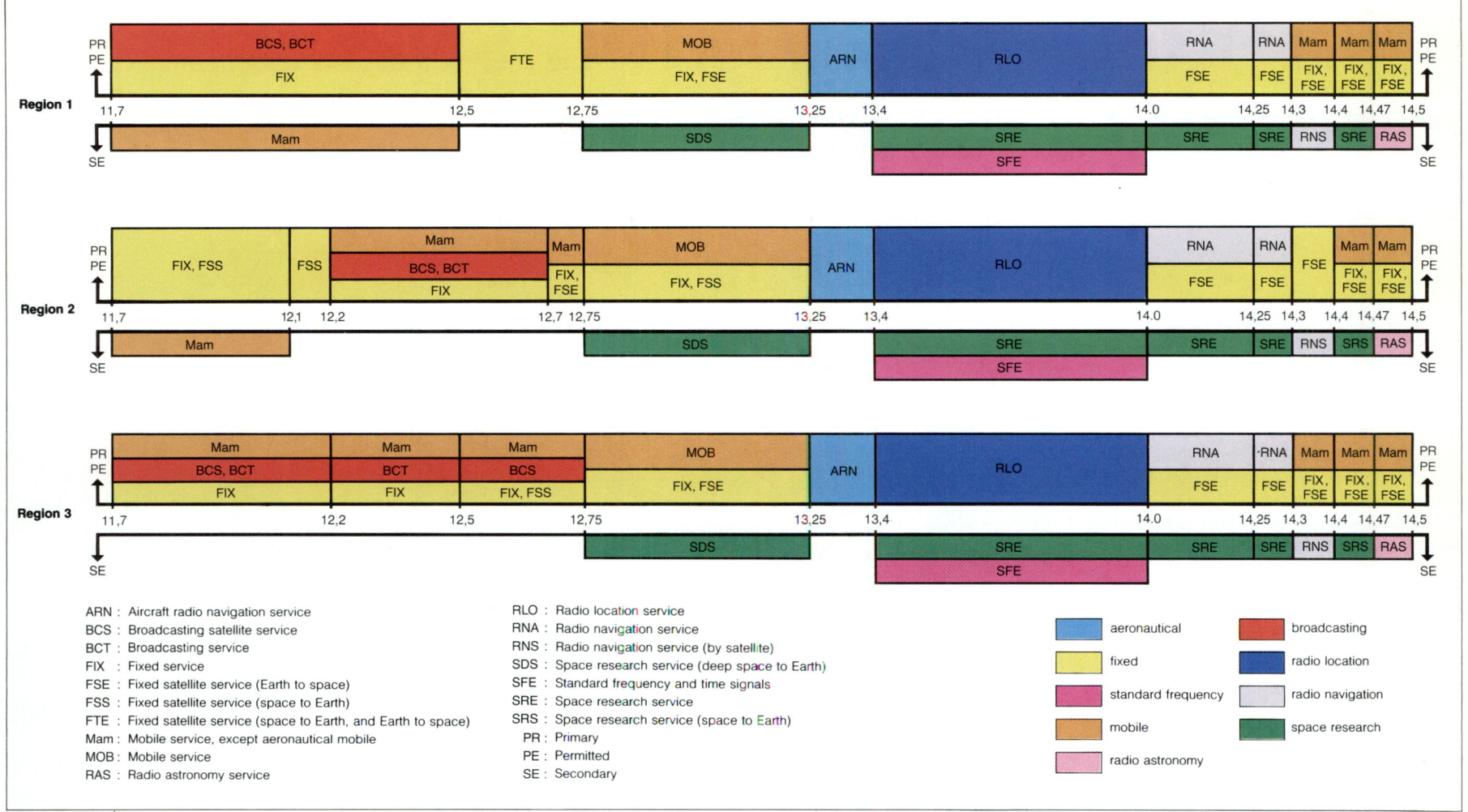

Frequency allocations between 11·7 and 14·5 gigahertz. This diagram shows the different frequency bands used by radio communications satellites in geostationary orbit for different purposes. Region 1 covers Africa, Europe and the USSR; Region 2, the Americas; and Region 3, Asia and Oceania (ITU).

The law on the peaceful uses of the geostationary orbit for communications. The International Telecommunications Union (ITU) organised the World Conference on Satellite Broadcasting in 1977 in Geneva. The following ranges of frequencies for broadcasting were established: Region 1 (Africa, Europe and USSR) from 11·7 to 14·5 gigahertz; Region 3 (Asia and Oceania) from 11·7 to 12·7 gigahertz. The conference decided on a spacing of 19·18 megahertz between channels, providing 40 channels in the 11·7 to 14·5 gigahertz band (and 25 channels in the other), with a safety band at the upper and lower limits.

The map opposite shows the nominal positions of the geostationary satellites for channel 1 in Regions 1 and 3, as well as the zones to which they broadcast. The size of the zone depends on the width of the transmission beam.

Decisions about Region 2 (the Americas) were made in 1983 at a regional conference (ITU).

Sputnik I by the USSR on 4 October 1957 that the practical use of space radio communications began. In 1959 the International Radio Consultative Committee (CCIR), which, of the Union's four permanent organs, is the one responsible for radio studies and standardisation, established a special study group. Its purpose was to examine the systems used in space telecommunications and to start collecting the data necessary for space radio communications legislation.

It was also in 1959 that the ITU World Radio Conference, convened to carry out an overall revision of the Radio Regulations, allocated specific frequency bands to the space services. However, the 1963 Space Radiocommunication Conference was the first world conference with an agenda devoted specifically to space. It constituted an important landmark in the legislation governing the use of space radio communications, marking the transition between research and experiment on the one hand and space telecommunications as an everyday reality on the other.

This Conference radically revised the Radio Regulations by extending the basic philosophy and provisions, which had stood the test of time in governing the use of terrestrial radio services, to services using space techniques. Provision was made for frequency bands for fixed, meteorological, mobile and other radio services using space techniques, and for tracking, telemetry and telecommand. Also covered were a series of technical criteria and regulatory provisions, including the compulsory coordination among the Union's member countries of the use of the radio spectrum and the geostationary satellite orbit before stations were put into service. The provisions also specify the rights and obligations of member countries in both these areas.

In addition to these actions, the Conference recognised 'that all Members of the Union have an interest in and right to an equitable and rational use of frequency bands allocated for space communications'. It also recommended 'to all ITU Members that the utilisation and exploitation of the frequency spectrum for space communication be subject to international agreements based on principles of justice

and equity permitting the use of sharing of allocated frequency bands in the mutual interest of all nations'. Further, the Conference pointed out that 'the use of satellite transmission for direct reception by the general public of sound and television broadcasts may be possible in the future'. It urged the CCIR to expedite its studies on the technical feasibility of broadcasting from satellites.

After 1963, the ITU proceeded step by step, building gradually on past experience. For example, it had to deal with problems arising from the use of space communications, affecting the terrestrial telecommunications network and concerned, for instance, with circuit switching and tariffs. Both of these are dealt with by one of the Union's permanent organs, the International Telegraph and Telephone Consultative Committee (CCITT).

By 1971, space communications had made such prodigious advances that it was necessary to review completely the existing regulations. The World Administrative Conference on Space Radio Communications greatly extended the scope of ITU regulations concerning space. Its work included such fundamental matters as revising the philosophy used in arriving at definitions of radio communications services so that the relationship between space and terrestrial services was more evident. Another innovation was the setting up of a procedure for the coordination of geostationary satellite systems.

The 1971 Conference drew up regulations governing the use of the geostationary orbit for direct (sound and television) satellite broadcasting. It decided that stations in the broadcasting satellite service should be established and operated in accordance with the agreements and associated plans adopted by world or regional administrative conferences, as the case might be. It also adopted a most important principle concerned with national coverage and reception in individual homes.

In 1977 the World Broadcasting Satellite Administrative Radio Conference drew up the first such plan. This relates to the broadcasting satellite service and takes account of the requirements expressed by the countries of Europe and Africa (ITU Region 1) and of Asia

and Oceania (ITU Region 3). Planning for Region 2, the Americas, was carried out in 1983, thus completing the world plan.

The World Administrative Radio Conference convened in 1979 to revise the whole of the Radio Regulations recast several provisions relating to space radio communications, including the allocation of frequency bands to the services using space techniques, together with technical criteria and limits. Procedures for the advance publication of information on satellite networks and the coordination and notification of frequency assignments to stations in the space service were reviewed and refined.

In order to secure rational and efficient use of both the frequency spectrum and the geostationary satellite orbit, the notion of a period of validity of frequency assignments to satellites was introduced on an experimental basis.

The first session of the World Administrative Radio Conference on the Use of the Geostationary Satellite Orbit and the Planning of Space Services Utilising It took place in 1985. Its main task was to decide which space services (fixed, mobile, meteorological, Earth exploration, etc.) and frequency bands were to be planned. It also had to draw up technical criteria and planning principles and methods for the use of the geostationary orbit by the service planned. A second session took place in 1988.

Thus, year by year, telecommunications law, just one of many aspects of man's use of outer space, is being developed. Cooperation exists between the ITU and other United Nations specialised agencies involved in the use of space, such as the World Meteorological Organisation (WMO), UNESCO, the International Maritime Organisation (IMO) and the International Civil Aviation Organisation (ICAO).

Finally, attention should also be drawn to the complementary nature of the activities of the United Nations Committee on the Peaceful Uses of Outer Space and the ITU's important work in the development and establishment of space law.

Richard E. Butler

Legal aspects of the military use of space

Since the beginning of the space age, over two thousand military satellites have been launched, amounting to about 70% of all satellites. Their functions include communications, navigation, meteorology, electronic intelligence, detection of nuclear explsosions, early warning of missile attack and reconnaissance. While at present only the United States and the Soviet Union possess a full range of operational military satellites, Britain has launched military communications satellites, China has a modest reconnaissance satellite programme, and France is now developing a reconnaissance satellite.

The function of the existing operational military satellites is not to attack or destroy hostile targets but rather to support military operations and planning on the ground. In view of their importance in the strategic systems of both the United States and the Soviet Union, it is not surprising that these satellites are tempting military targets. Both the United States and the Soviet Union have programmes to develop space weapons.

The first developmental work on weapons for use in space began with anti-satellite weapons, sometimes referred to as killer or interceptor satellites, designed to destroy enemy military satellites. While that work was proceeding, President Ronald Reagan, in 1983, announced the Strategic Defence Initiative (SDI), a programme to develop a system to defend the United States against nuclear missile attack, based on advanced space technology including spacebased lasers and particle beam weapons. Proposals for such advanced weapons have caused the programme to be popularly called 'Star Wars'. A feasibility study and scientific research phase is under way at a cost of about 17 billion dollars up to 1988; since the inception of the programme, however, plans for advanced spacebased weapons have gradually given way to more conventional groundbased systems. Studies indicate that an operational system designed to provide such a defence, if it proves feasible, might cost of the order of 800 billion dollars.

The current importance of military space technology is indicated by the funding allocated to such programmes. The United States military space budget now substantially exceeds the civilian space budget of the National Aeronautics and Space Administration (NASA). Currently, the United States government spends annually about 13 billion dollars on military space activities, including 4 billion dollars on SDI, compared with about 11 billion dollars on civilian space activities. Soviet space expenditures are assumed to be comparable or somewhat larger.

Many nations have expressed the fear that the development of these new military space systems will adversely affect both civilian space programmes and international security, and will initiate a new phase of the arms race. Arms control negotiations on nuclear armaments and space weapons are now a major issue between the United States and the Soviet Union. Bilateral negotiations between the two superpowers have been going on in Geneva since March 1985, and multilateral discussions on the prevention of an arms race in outer space are taking place in the United Nations Con-

ference on Disarmament (CD), the main forum for multilateral arms control negotiations for more than twenty years. The United Nations Committee on the Peaceful Uses of Outer Space (COPUOS) is also concerned with this issue.

A number of legal principles concerning space activities and disarmament are contained in existing international legal agreements. Specific provisions relating to space are contained both in international treaties and in bilateral agreements between the United States and the Soviet Union.

International treaties

Established before the space age began, the principles contained in the United Nations Charter were subsequently declared, by the 1967 Outer Space Treaty, to apply to space activities.

Article 2 of the Charter prohibits the use of force or the threat of use of force in international relations. In general, an attack on a satellite or other space activity of another state would therefore be prohibited. It has also been suggested that the introduction into space of anti-satellite weapons or the deployment of spacebased weapons directed at targets on Earth could be considered a threat of force and should therefore also be prohibited. The generality of this principle and its frequent violation in other contexts, however, undermine its effectiveness here.

Article 51 of the Charter recognises the right of self defence against armed attack. Some writers, including those from the socialist countries, maintain that this provision applies only to situations where an actual armed attack has occurred, and not to preventive measures

against an anticipated attack. Other writers, notably from the United States, have argued that anticipatory self defence should be included within the ambit of this provision and should be recognised as a right, especially in view of the short delivery times of modern nuclear weapons.

While there is agreement that interference with the operation of certain satellites or military systems that are recognised by bilateral arms control agreements as contributing to security and stability would be in breach of the UN Charter, no consensus exists as to whether an attack on space weapon systems that might be considered threatening would be covered under the right of self defence.

In 1958, the United Nations General Assembly, in its first resolution relating specifically to outer space, unanimously recognised that space should be used for peaceful purposes only and expressed the wish that national rivalries should not be extended into this new field. While this desire was subsequently repeated in other space related resolutions, the 1963 Declaration of Legal Principles Governing the Activities of States in the Exploration and Use of Outer Space, which was the blueprint for the subsequent Outer Space Treaty, contained no specific provisions addressing the military implications of space activities.

In 1966, the General Assembly adopted the Treaty on Principles Governing the Activities of States in the Exploration and Use of Outer Space, including the Moon and Other Celestial Bodies, more commonly called the Outer Space Treaty. This treaty, which came into force in 1967 and has been ratified by 88 countries, contains the fundamental principles of international law governing space activities.

The Outer Space Treaty establishes the general principle that the use of outer space

Signing the Outer Space Treaty. On 12 January 1967, the Outer Space Treaty was signed in the capitals of the three depository governments, the USSR, the United Kingdom and the United States. Shown here, signing the treaty at the White House in Washington, is the Soviet Ambassador to the US, Anatoly F. Dobrynin. Seated to his left are Sir Patrick Dean, British Ambassador to the UN, Arthur J. Goldberg, US Ambassador to the UN, Dean Rusk, US Secretary of State, and US President Lyndon B. Johnson. The treaty was subsequently ratified by 88 countries and forms the basis of international space law.

The treaty was the result of negotiations carried out in the United Nations in 1966. In June 1966, draft treaties were submitted by both the United States and the Soviet Union. These were considered during two sessions of the legal sub-committee of the Outer Space Committee and most, but not all, of the provisions were agreed. The disputed provisions concerned the international observation of space flights and lunar stations, notification of space activities to the UN, legal responsibilities relating to intergovernmental space organisations, and the use of military 'installations' and 'equipment' on the Moon. Informal negotiations eventually brought agreement on these issues also, and the General Assembly, in December 1966, unanimously adopted the final draft treaty. A number of delegations noted, however, that the treaty left questions such as the complete demilitarisation of outer space still unresolved (United Nations).

'shall be carried out for the benefit and in the interests of all countries', a provision that has been interpreted to mean that outer space should not be used for military purposes, or at least not for 'aggressive' purposes. It has been argued, however, that some military space activities are essentially peaceful in nature and contribute to international security and that the framers of the Outer Space Treaty would have expressly banned military activities had it been their intention to do so. Furthermore, at the time of the negotiation and conclusion of the treaty, both major space powers were already using satellites for reconnaissance and other military support functions, clearly indicating that it was not the general understanding that such activities were to be prohibited.

The United States government and others have therefore argued that military uses of outer space for maintaining national security must be considered as being legal. In particular, they have argued that since the proposed ballistic missile defence system being studied in the SDI programme is meant to be a defensive system to be used if a nuclear attack occurs, it is 'non-aggressive' and is thus not counter to the interests of other countries. They also argue that whatever is not expressly prohibited by the treaty is permissible and lawful.

Socialist writers, on the other hand, argue that military activities by their nature imply an underlying threat of violence, and cannot be in the interests of all countries.

The only article that deals directly with the permissible scope of military activities in space is article 4. This establishes a clear prohibition against placing 'nuclear weapons or other weapons of mass destruction' in Earth orbit or in outer space, or installing them on celestial bodies. While the term 'weapons of mass destruction' is not defined in the treaty, it is generally considered to include chemical and biological weapons capable of severe and extensive damage or injury, as well as nuclear weapons. In general, the space weapons proposed in recent years, such as lasers and particle beam weapons, are considered to be point or target specific weapons intended to destroy individual objects, not indiscriminate weapons of mass destruction, and are thus not prohibited.

Article 4 further specifies that the Moon and other celestial bodies are to be used 'exclusively for peaceful purposes', but the meaning of the phrase 'peaceful purposes' in this context has been a subject of disagreement. One view is that 'peaceful purposes' exclude only 'aggressive' uses of outer space such as the use of space weapons while permitting 'non-aggressive' military activities, including intelligence gathering. The other view holds that 'peaceful purposes' excludes all military activities.

Finally, another provision of the Outer Space Treaty directs nations to 'undertake appropriate international consultations' before proceeding with any activity that might cause 'potentially harmful interference with the activities of other States in the peaceful exploration and use of outer space'. Some have argued that states developing anti-satellite weapons should do so only after 'appropriate international consultations'. However, the vague wording of this provision reduces its value as an effective arms control measure.

In practical terms, it should be noted that the prohibitions of the Outer Space Treaty do not expressly cover either the existing Soviet and American anti-satellite systems or the proposed ballistic missile defence system, any of which require the use of nuclear warheads to destroy their targets. However, one type of weapon that is being studied as part of the SDI programme, an X ray laser system powered by a small nuclear explosion, could be prohibited under article 4 of the Outer Space Treaty if it were placed in orbit, as opposed to being launched when needed. It has also been argued that these are not weapons of mass destruction and could be considered to be nuclear powered

Date of entry into force	Number of parties	Treaty	Relevant provision
10 October 1963	116	**Partial Test Ban Treaty, 1963** Treaty Banning Nuclear Weapon Tests in the Atmosphere, in Outer Space and Under Water	Article 1 prohibits any test of nuclear weapons, or any other nuclear explosion, *inter alia*, in outer space
10 October 1967	90	**Outer Space Treaty, 1967** Treaty on Principles Governing the Activities of States in the Exploration and Use of Outer Space, including the Moon and Other Celestial Bodies	Article 4 prohibits the placing in orbit around the earth of nuclear weapons and other weapons of mass destruction. Article 9 requires states to avoid activities that would cause potentially 'harmful interference' with the peaceful exploration and use of outer space by other states
3 October 1972	USA and USSR	**ABM Treaty, 1972** Treaty between the United States of America and the Union of Soviet Socialist Republics on the Limitation of Anti-Ballistic Missile Systems	Article 5 prohibits the development, testing or deployment, *inter alia*, of spacebased anti-ballistic missile (ABM) systems. Article 12 states that both parties are not to interfere with national technical means of verification
3 October 1972	USA and USSR	**SALT I accord** Interim Agreement between the United States of America and the Union of Soviet Socialist Republics on Certain Measures with Respect to the Limitation of Strategic Offensive Arms	Article 5 states that both parties are not to interfere with national technical means of verification
15 September 1976	35	**Registration Convention, 1975** Convention on the Registration of Objects Launched into Outer Space	Article 4 requires launching states to furnish the Secretary General of the United Nations with information on their launchings, such as designation and general function
5 October 1978	54	**ENMOD Convention, 1977** Convention on the Prohibition of Military or any Hostile Use of Environmental Modification Techniques	Article 2 prohibits the deliberate manipulation of natural processes, *inter alia*, in outer space
Signed on 18 June 1979 but not in force yet. Both parties have nevertheless agreed to honour the provisions of the treaty as long as the other party does likewise		**SALT II accord** Treaty between the United States of America and the Union of Soviet Socialist Republics on the Limitation of Strategic Offensive Arms	Article 9 prohibits the development, testing or deployment of nuclear weapon systems or other weapons of mass destruction in an orbit around the Earth, including fractional orbital missiles. Article 15 reiterates the principle of non-interference with national technical means of verification
1 January 1984	157	**ITU Convention** International Telecommunication Convention	Article 35 obliges parties to avoid harmful interference with radio services or communications systems of other parties. Article 38 states that members retain their entire freedom with regard to military radio installations
11 July 1984	7	**Moon Treaty, 1979** Agreement Governing the Activities of States on the Moon and Other Celestial Bodies	Article 3 prohibits the threat or use of force or any other hostile act on the Moon or the use of the Moon to commit any such act in relation to the Earth, the Moon, spacecraft, the personnel of spacecraft or man made space objects

Treaties and agreements relevant to military uses of outer space

weapons, as distinct from nuclear weapons. They might therefore not be covered by the prohibition on 'nuclear weapons and other weapons of mass destruction'.

The Treaty Banning Nuclear Weapons Tests in the Atmosphere, in Outer Space and under Water was, in 1963, the first multilateral treaty with provisions relating to the use of weapons in outer space. It bans 'any nuclear weapon test explosion or any other nuclear explosion' in outer space. In addition to its primary purpose, the treaty also prohibits the testing or use in space of X ray or gamma ray lasers powered by nuclear explosions as proposed for ballistic missile defence in the SDI programme. The likelihood of illegal testing of nuclear weapons in outer space remains remote, due to the devastating effects on satellites of the electromagnetic pulse that is induced by the gamma rays from nuclear explosions and can overload and destroy electronic circuits.

While the 1975 Convention on Registration of Objects Launched into Outer Space does not deal directly with military activities in outer space, it establishes a mandatory registration, with the Secretary General of the United Nations, of space objects launched into orbit and beyond. Each launching state must provide specific information concerning the objects launched into outer space, including the 'general functions of the space object'. However, the permissive nature of this provision enables countries to give a minimum of information on the functions of their space objects. No space mission has ever been reported as having a military function.

The 1977 Convention on the Prohibition of Military or Any Other Hostile Use of Environmental Modification Techniques prohibits the hostile use of environmental modification techniques, including those that affect the outer space environment, as a means of

Sources of nuclear energy in space. This photograph was taken on Great Slave Lake in Northern Canada during the search for debris from the Soviet Cosmos 954 satellite. The debris was scattered over a distance of 800 kilometres stretching from the south east to the north west in an orbit in January 1978.

The uncontrolled reentry of a satellite carrying a nuclear power generator made the international community realise the need to make laws governing the use of nuclear reactors in space. To date, the work of the United Nations Space Committee has led to the production of a text concerning the notification of the uncontrolled reentry of a satellite carrying a nuclear reactor, the information which must be included when notifying the authorities, and the help to be given to the countries affected by such an incident (Canadian Armed Forces).

Deploying a Tracking and Data Relay Satellite (TDRS) from the space shuttle. The great majority of military space missions to date have been support missions rather than space weapons missions. Military support functions provided by satellites include communications links and meteorological observations similar to those provided by civilian satellites, photographic observation of military facilities and activities, detection of missile launchings and tracking of missiles, detection of nuclear explosions, interception of radio communications, and analysis of electronic signals from radar systems and other electrical and electronic equipment.

The NASA Tracking and Data Relay Satellite (TDRS), shown here being deployed from the space shuttle, is an advanced type of communication satellite that can track other satellites in lower orbits and relay data from them to a central receiving station at White Sands, New Mexico. The TDRS System allows the control of satellites and reception of their data all around the Earth without depending on receiving and tracking stations operating in other countries.

Some military missions, notably the reconnaissance satellites used for observing strategic missile facilities, are part of the 'national technical means of verification' recognised and protected in the bilateral SALT I and SALT II Treaties. Military support missions, especially systems designed for verification of arms control agreements, are widely considered to be stabilising factors in international relations since they can reduce the probability of conflict due to accident or miscalculation. There is a feeling, however, that a total demilitarisation of outer space would be beneficial since all military satellites can contribute to warmaking efforts. Even the space shuttle could be used in an anti-satellite role (NASA).

by satellites launched subsequently. The convention, however, specifies that countries retain their entire freedom with regard to military radio installations, providing that they do not interfere with registered systems. While frequency bands are reserved for 'government' (that is military) use, most military satellites are not registered. The bands are therefore not internationally coordinated and published, but also are not protected against interference. Some writers have called for the mandatory inclusion of military satellites in the ITU's coordination and registration system, to provide a means for the control and regulation of military space activities.

Bilateral arms control agreements

The Treaty Between the USA and the USSR on the Limitation of Anti-Ballistic Missile Systems (the ABM Treaty) was the most important of the four agreements concluded during the bilateral Strategic Arms Limitation Talks (SALT I) held between 1969 and 1972. In negotiating the ABM Treaty, the United States and the Soviet Union adopted the doctrine of deterrence. This assumes that each state will be discouraged from launching a nuclear attack on the other if it knows that the other will be able to launch an equally effective counter attack. In order to minimise the pressures of technological change and its destabilising effect on the strategic balance, the United States and the Soviet Union agreed not to deploy anti-ballistic missiles except under the very limited conditions set forth in the treaty.

The most important provision of the treaty is the agreement 'not to develop, test or deploy ABM systems or components which are seabased, airbased, spacebased or mobile land-

destruction, damage or injury to other states. The convention does not bar all environmental modification techniques for military or hostile purposes, only those which have 'widespread, long lasting or severe effects', terms that are not defined in the convention. While massive nuclear explosions in space could be said to have widespread effects, the convention has limited importance in the current discussions of military space activities.

The 1979 Agreement Governing the Activities of States on the Moon and Other Celestial Bodies reiterates and clarifies the principles of the Outer Space Treaty to the effect that the threat or use of force or any other hostile act or threat of hostile act on or around the Moon or other celestial body is prohibited.

It also prohibits use of the Moon for committing any such act or for engaging in any such threat in relation to the Earth or other celestial bodies, spacecraft, the personnel of spacecraft, or man made space objects. It reaffirms that states are not to place in orbit around or in other trajectory to or around the Moon or other celestial body objects carrying nuclear weapons or weapons of mass destruction, or place or use such weapons on or in the Moon. The Moon Treaty, although more specific in its provisions relating to the Moon, did not change the substance of the obligations concerning the denuclearisation of outer space as provided for in the Outer Space Treaty.

Since radio communications are vital for all space activities, the International Telecommunication Convention is worthy of note. The International Telecommunications Union (ITU) is responsible for the equitable and rational allocation of radio frequencies for all space activities, and for ensuring that the radio spectrum is used in such a manner as to avoid harmful interference. In accordance with the Radio Regulations which form part of the convention, the use of radio frequencies by satellites is to be coordinated through, and registered by, the ITU. The coordination process is designed to ensure that registered frequency assignments are not interfered with

Anti-satellite neutral beam weapons. Substantial progress has been made since 1985 in the research associated with ion sources that can be used as the first stage of a neutral particle beam device. They are being used to study the feasibility of using neutral particle beams to destroy the important electronic circuits that might be found on a ballistic missile. The Oak Ridge National Laboratory has produced large ion beam currents lasting up to 5 seconds.

Shown here is an ion beam accelerator for the neutral particle beam experiment at the Los Alamos National Laboratory in New Mexico. The White Horse Advanced Test Stand has met an initial goal of producing an ion beam using a radio frequency quadrupole accelerator, the second stage of a neutral particle beam device. This acceleration technique, which was first developed by Soviet scientists, may make low weight, space-based neutral particle beam weapons feasible (Sygma).

based' with the exception of a single landbased system within a radius of 240 kilometres of each country's capital.

Assurance of treaty compliance was to be provided by each state's 'national technical means of verification'. The latter include satellites, aircraft and ground systems, with high resolution cameras for observing ground facilities, radar for tracking missile tests, and sensitive radio receivers for intercepting communications.

The prohibition on development and the lack of mention of research raises the question of where research ends and development begins. The most often cited interpretation is that the prohibition on development applies to activities after a component moves from the laboratory stage to the field testing stage. The provision for assurance of compliance by 'national technical means of verification' further supports the interpretation of 'develop' as referring to field testing as opposed to laboratory development, since 'national technical means of verification' cannot detect laboratory activities. The Soviet Union has argued, however, that research should also be considered as being prohibited under the treaty.

The United States argues that research is generally permitted under the ABM Treaty and that, since the SDI is defined as a research programme, it is therefore permitted. No clear statement has been made by the United States as to the point at which the ABM Treaty might have to be amended to allow the development of ballistic missile defence technologies to continue.

A further difficulty arises from the fact that the distinction between anti-satellite weapons and ballistic missile defence systems is not always clear. For the purposes of the ABM Treaty, 'an ABM system is a system to counter strategic ballistic missiles or their elements in flight trajectory'. Therefore, anti-satellite weapons would be prohibited by the ABM Treaty if they were also capable of destroying strategic ballistic missiles or warheads. The development, testing or deployment of anti-satellite weapons of lesser capability would not be covered by the treaty.

The definition of an ABM system is accompanied by a statement which refers to such systems as 'currently consisting of' ABM missiles, ABM launchers and ABM radars. This specifies that, in the event that ABM systems 'based on other physical principles' are created in the future, specific limitations of such systems and components are to be the subject of consultations. While the SDI programme is studying technologies based on other physical principles, such as lasers and particle beams, there is no agreement as to the precise implications of this provision for new types of weapons that might be created.

Finally, while the treaty is of unlimited duration, each party has the right to withdraw on six months notice, 'if it decides that extraordinary events related to the subject matter of this Treaty have jeopardised its supreme interests'. The requirement that the party choosing to abrogate the treaty must specify, in its notice of withdrawal, the reasons for its action still gives wide latitude to both parties in the selection of such reasons.

The Interim Agreement Between the USA and the USSR on Certain Measures with Respect to the Limitation of Strategic Offensive Arms (SALT I) contains verification provisions that state that the parties shall use 'national technical means of verification' to monitor adherence to the limitations on the numbers of strategic ballistic missiles as stipulated in the agreement. The agreement further provides that each party shall not interfere with the other's national technical means of verification. While the agreement thereby provides some measure of protection to reconnaissance and other intelligence gathering satellites used to monitor treaty compliance, it does not restrict the development, testing or deployment of anti-

Testing the Miniature Homing Vehicle (MHV) anti-satellite weapon from an F 15 fighter. As part of the Anti-Ballistic Missile (ABM) Treaty of 1972, the USA and the USSR agreed not to develop, test, or deploy anti-ballistic missile systems, whether based in the sea, atmosphere or space. The USA interpreted this treaty as enabling it to carry out research in this field and maintained that the Soviets were doing exactly the same thing. The USA developed an anti-satellite weapon called the Miniature Homing Vehicle (MHV), consisting of several stages which detached from each other, and the parent F 15 fighter plane, at certain altitudes.

The MHV is a small vehicle which, when powered by its own rocket engines, follows an ascending trajectory and cuts across the target satellite's orbit. The missile is guided by infrared sensors and destroys the satellite by collision; the MHV does not carry any explosives and is not designed to destroy just the electronic circuits of the target.

This tracking system in space has the advantage of being very mobile. Within a few hours, the same F 15 fighter plane can make several anti-satellite attacks.

This MHV test was performed on 13 September 1985. According to the SDIO (Strategic Defense Initiative Organization) the MHV programme has since been shelved (Sygma).

satellite systems capable of attacking such satellites. Legal protection is offered only to systems used to verify the SALT I agreement. It does not cover other intelligence gathering or other military support satellites.

The Limitation of Strategic Offensive Arms (from SALT II) is generally respected by both sides. Along with the limitations on the numbers of strategic missiles, SALT II prohibits the development, testing or deployment of 'systems for placing into Earth orbit nuclear weapons or any other kind of weapons of mass destruction, including fractional orbital missiles'. This provision was included to ban Fractional Orbital Bombardment Systems (FOBS), missiles that are put into orbit, travel the long way around the Earth rather than taking the more direct trajectory of ballistic missiles, and then descend onto the target, thus subjecting the enemy to incoming warheads from all directions and complicating the problem of missile defence.

Proposals for preventing an arms race in outer space

Some new arms control measures in outer space have been proposed in recent years both by governments and by non-governmental organisations. In 1981, the Soviet Union submitted to the United Nations a draft treaty that would prohibit the stationing of weapons of any kind in outer space, including on 'reusable manned space vehicles', and would ban interference with space objects other than those carrying weapons. The draft was criticised for its specific mention of a reusable manned space vehicle, taken to be the United States space shuttle, as well as for not banning the development, testing and ground deployment of the existing anti-satellite systems.

A revised Soviet draft treaty, introduced in 1983, would prohibit the use or threat of force in outer space and the atmosphere and on Earth through the use, as instruments of destruction, of space objects in orbit around the Earth, on celestial bodies or stationed in space. The parties would also undertake not to test or create new anti-satellite systems and to destroy existing systems in their possession. The draft treaty would also prohibit interference with the normal functioning of space objects and the use of spacebased systems as means to destroy targets on Earth, in the atmosphere or in space, a provision which would cover spacebased ballistic missile defence systems.

A proposal made in 1983 by the American Union of Concerned Scientists was aimed particularly at limiting anti-satellite weapons. This draft treaty contained an undertaking not to destroy, damage or change the flight trajectory of any space object. It also prohibits the deployment of weapons, but only 'in orbit around the Earth' and therefore does not limit groundbased ballistic missile defence systems.

Most recently, in 1988, the Soviet Union submitted proposals to the United Nations calling for the establishment of a World Space Organisation. This would ensure that space was used for exclusively peaceful purposes and would verify compliance with international agreements to prevent an arms race in space.

Although important measures establishing certain limitations on space weapons have been taken, the existing body of international law contains serious loopholes rendering it unable to prevent present trends towards an arms race in outer space. A number of additional arms control measures covering space weapons have been proposed in intergovernmental fora and by non-governmental organisations to close these loopholes. While it is not yet too late to prevent an extension of the arms race into outer space, research and development on new weapons are proceeding and time is running short. Once operational weapons are deployed, the political obstacles to limiting or banning such weapons will be much greater. Increased involvement by more countries in peaceful space activities should strengthen the international political will to keep outer space free from armed conflicts.

Nandasiri Jasentuliyana

Further reading

FROM DREAM TO REALITY

General

J.P. Allen, *Entering space: an astronaut's odyssey*, London: Orbis 1986.
D. Baker, *The history of manned space flight*, New York: Crown 1985.
D. Baker, *The rocket: the history and development of rocket and missile technology*, New York: Crown 1978.
N. Booth, *The encyclopedia of space*, London: Brian Trodd 1990.
W. von Braun, F.I. Ordway III and D. Dooling, *Space travel: a history*, New York: Harper & Row 1985.
W. von Braun and F.I. Ordway III, *The rocket's red glare: an illustrated history of rocketry through the ages*, Garden City, NY: Anchor Press 1976.
K. Gatland, *The illustrated encyclopedia of space technology*, London: Salamander 1989.
R.C. Hall (ed), *Essays on the history of rocketry and astronautics*, 2 volumes, Washington, DC: NASA 1977.
W. Ley, *Rockets, missiles, and men in space*, New York: Viking 1968.
H.E. Newell, *Beyond the atmosphere: early years of space science*, Washington, DC: NASA 1980.
A. Wilson, *The eagle has wings: the story of American space exploration 1945–1975*, London: British Interplanetary Society 1982.

The rocket – from East to West

J.R. Partington, *A history of Greek fire and gunpowder*, Cambridge: Heffer 1960.
Fang-Toh Sun, 'Rockets and rocket propulsion devices in ancient China', *Journal of Astronautical Sciences* 29 iii (1981), 289–305.
R.S. Westfall, *Never at rest: a biography of Isaac Newton*, Cambridge: Cambridge University Press 1980.
F.H. Winter, 'On the origin of rockets', *Chemistry* 49 ii (1976), 8–12.
F.H. Winter, 'The rocket in India from ancient times to the nineteenth century', *Journal of the British Interplanetary Society* 32 (1979), 467–71.
F.H. Winter, 'A new look at early Chinese rocketry, 1200s–1900', *Astronautics History* (December 1982), 522–9.
F.H. Winter and M.R. Sharpe, 'Edward Mourrier and his rockets in peace and war', *Spaceflight* (November 1974), 427–9.

KONSTANTIN EDVARDOVICH TSIOLKOVSKY (1857 to 1935)
M.S. Arlazorov, *K.E. Tsiolkovsky*, Moscow 1967 (in Russian).
K.E. Tsiolkovsky, *Collected works*, Washington, DC: NASA 1965.
M.K. Tikhonravov (ed), *K.E. Tsiolkovsky: works on rocket technology*, Washington, DC: NASA 1965.

The Pioneers

N.J. Bowman, *Handbook of rockets and guided missiles*, Chicago: Perastadion 1957.
B. Collier, *The battle of the V-weapons 1944–1945*, Morey, Yorkshire: Elmfield 1976.
H. Gartmann, *The men behind the space rockets*, New York: David McKay 1956.
R.C. Hall (ed), *Essays on the history of rocketry and aeronautics*, NASA, CP: NASA 2014 1977.
B. Johnson, *The secret war*, New York: Methuen 1978.
D. Lasser, *The conquest of space*, New York: Penguin 1931.

I.A. Slukhai, *Russian rocketry. A historical survey*, NASA: NASA TT F-426 1968 (translated from the Russian).
F.H. Winter, *Prelude to the space age. The rocket societies: 1924–1940*, Washington, DC: Smithsonian Institution Press 1983.

ROBERT HUTCHINGS GODDARD (1882 to 1945)
C.M. Deutherty, *Robert Goddard: trail blazer to the stars*, New York: Macmillan 1964.
E.C. Goddard and G.E. Pendray (eds), *The papers of Robert H. Goddard* (3 volumes), New York: McGraw-Hill 1970.
R.H. Goddard, *The autobiography of Robert Hutchings Goddard, father of the space age. Early years to 1927*, Worcester, Mass: St Onge 1966.
F.H. Winter, 'Celebrating Goddard's centenary', *Spaceflight* (April 1983), 154–6.

HERMANN OBERTH (1894 to 1989)
H. Oberth, 'My contribution to astronautics', F.C. Durrant III and G.S. James (eds), *First steps towards space*, Washington, DC: Smithsonian Institution Press 1974.
E. Roth-Oberth, 'The Hermann Oberth museum', *Spaceflight* (May 1980), 199–201.
E.J. Sellner, 'Hermann Oberth', *Spaceflight* (May 1980), 197–8.
H.B. Walters, *Hermann Oberth, father of space travel*, New York: Macmillan 1962.

ROBERT ESNAULT-PELTERIE (1881 to 1957)
L. Blosset, 'Robert Esnault-Pelterie', F.C. Durrant III and G.S. James (eds), *First steps towards space*, Washington, DC: Smithsonian Institution Press 1974.
R. Esnault-Pelterie, *L'Astronautique*, Paris: Lahure 1930.

SERGEI PAVLOVICH KOROLEV (1907 to 1966)
P.T. Astashenkov, *Academician S.P. Korolev. Biography*: Air Force Systems Command, Foreign Technology Division, translation FTD-HC-23-542-70, March 1971.
J.E. Oberg, 'Korolev and Kruschev and Sputnik', *Spaceflight* 20 (1978), 144–50.
Y.V. Biryukov, 'S.P. Korolyev and the development of Soviet rocket engineering to 1939', F.C. Durrant III and G.S. James (eds), *First steps towards space*, Washington, DC: Smithsonian Institution Press 1974.

WERNHER VON BRAUN (1912 to 1977)
A.S. Bédini, W. von Braun and F.L. Whipple, *Moon, man's greatest adventure*, New York: Abrams 1971.
E. Bergaust, *Wernher von Braun*, Washington, DC: National Space Institute 1976.
W. von Braun, *The Mars project*, Urbana: University of Illinois Press 1953.
W. von Braun, *First men to the moon*, New York: Holt, Rhinehart & Winston 1960.
W. von Braun, *Space frontier*, New York: Holt, Rhinehart & Winston (rev. edn) 1971.
W. von Braun and F.I. Ordway III, *New worlds. Discoveries from our solar system*, Garden City, NY: Anchor Press/Doubleday 1979.
E. Stuhlinger, 'Dr Wernher von Braun. Biography', E.A. Steinhoff (ed), *The eagle has returned*, San Diego: Univelt 1976.

Through the eyes of authors

B.W. Aldiss, *Billion year spree: the true story of science fiction*, New York: Doubleday 1973.
B.W. Aldiss, *Science fiction art*, London: New English Library 1975.

B. Ash (ed), *The visual encyclopedia of science fiction*, New York: Harmony 1977.
M. Ashley (ed), *The history of the science fiction magazine. Part 1: 1926–1935*, London: New English Library 1974; *Part 2: 1936–1945*: New English Library 1975; *Part 3: 1946–1955*, Chicago: Contemporary Books 1977.
J. Baxter, *Science fiction in the cinema*, London: Zwemmer 1970.
L. Del Rey, *The world of science fiction: the history of a subculture*, New York: Ballantine 1979.
E. Emme (ed), *Science fiction and space futures: past and present*, San Diego: Univelt 1963.
R. Freedman, *2000 years of space travel*, New York: Holiday House 1963.
A. Frewin, *One hundred years of science fiction illustration: 1840–1940*, London: Jupiter 1971.
A. Gaul, *Complete book of space travel*, New York: World 1956.
D. Gifford, *Science fiction film*, London: Studio Vista 1971.
R.L. Green, *Into other worlds*, New York: Abelard-Schuman 1958.
J. Gunn, *Alternate worlds: the illustrated history of science fiction*, Englewood Cliffs, NJ: Prentice-Hall 1975.
P. Haining (ed), *The fantastic pulps*, London: Victor Gollancz 1975.
R. Holdstock (ed), *Encyclopedia of science fiction*, London: Octopus Books 1978.
W. Johnson (ed), *Focus on the science fiction film*, Englewood Cliffs, NJ: Prentice-Hall 1972.
D. Kyle, *The illustrated book of science fiction ideas and dreams*, London: Hamlyn 1977.
D. Kyle, *A pictorial history of science fiction*, London: Hamlyn 1977.
P. Leighton, *Moon travellers*, London: Oldbourne 1960.
S.J. Lundwall, *Science fiction: an illustrated history*, New York: Grosset & Dunlap 1977.
J. McHugh and L. Harris, *Journey to the moon*, Millbrae, Calif: Celestial Arts 1974
S. Moskowitz, *Explorers of the infinite*, New York: World 1963.
S. Moskowitz (ed), *Under the moons of Mars*, New York: Holt, Rhinehart & Winston 1970.
P. Nicholls (ed), *The science fiction encyclopedia*, New York: Dolphin/Doubleday 1979.
M. Nicholson, *Voyages to the moon*, New York: Macmillan 1948.
F.I. Ordway III, 'Collecting literature in the space and rocket fields', *Space Education* (September 1982), 176–82.
J.R. Parish and M.R. Pitts, *The great science fiction pictures*, Metuchen, NJ: Scarecrow Press 1977.
R.M. Philmus, *Into the unknown: the evolution of science fiction from Francis Godwin to H.G. Wells*, Berkeley: University of California Press 1970.
F.K. Pizor and T.A. Comp (eds), *The man in the moon and other lunar fantasies*, New York: Praeger 1971.
F. Rottensteiner, *The science fiction book: an illustrated history*, London: Thames & Hudson 1975.
D.H. Tuck, *The encyclopedia of science fiction fantasy* (3 vols), Chicago: Advent 1974, 1978, 1982.
D. Wingrove (ed), *The science fiction source book*, London: Longman 1984.
H. Wright, H. Wright and S. Rapport (eds), *To the moon: a distillation of the great writings from ancient legend to space exploration*, New York: Meredith 1968.

Prelude to space

M.H. Armacost, *The politics of weapons innovation: the Thor-Jupiter controversy*,

New York: Columbia University Press 1969.
J. Baar and W.E. Howard, *Polaris: the concept and creation of a new and mighty weapon*, New York: Harcourt, Brace & World 1960.
E. Beard, *Developing the ICBM: a study in bureaucratic politics*, New York: Columbia University Press 1976.
N.J. Bowman, *Handbook of rockets and guided missiles*, Chicago: Perastadion 1957.
R.L.F. Boyd and M.J. Seaton (eds), *Rocket exploration of the upper atmosphere*, London: Pergamon 1954.
W. Bridgeman and J. Hazard, *The lonely sky*, New York: Holt 1955.
E. Burgess, *Guided weapons*, New York: Macmillan 1957.
M. Caiden, *Rockets and missiles, past and future*, New York: McBride 1954.
J.L. Chapman, *Atlas: the story of a missile*, New York: Harper 1960.
C. Coombs, *Skyrocketing into the unknown*, New York: Morrow 1954.
F.K. Everest Jr, *Fastest man alive*, New York: Dutton 1958.
R.P. Hallion, *Supersonic flight: the story of the Bell X-1 and Douglas D-558*, London: Macmillan 1972.
H. Harper, *Dawn of the space age*, London: Sampson Low, Marston & Co 1946.
J. Hartt, *Mighty Thor*, New York: Duell, Sloan & Pearce 1961.
D.K. Huzel, *Peenemünde to Canaveral*, Englewood Cliffs, NJ: Prentice-Hall 1962.
C.G. Lasby, *Project paperclip: German scientists and the cold war*, New York: Atheneum 1971.
W. Ley, *Conquest of space*, New York: Viking Press 1949.
W.R. Lundgren, *Across the high frontier*, New York: Morrow 1955.
J. McGovern, *Crossbow and overcast*, New York: Morrow 1964.
J.B. Medaris, *Countdown for decision*, New York: Putnam 1960.
H.E. Newell Jr, *High altitude rocket research*, New York: Academic Press 1953.
H.E. Newell Jr, *Sounding rockets*, New York: McGraw-Hill 1959.
F.I. Ordway III and R.C. Wakeford, *International missile and spacecraft guide*, New York: McGraw-Hill 1960.
G.E. Pendray, *The coming age of rocket power*, New York: Harper 1945.
M.W. Rosen, *Viking rocket story*, New York: Harper 1955.
C. Ryan (ed), *Across the space frontier*, New York: Viking Press 1952.
J.G. Vaeth, *200 miles up*, New York: Ronald 1955.
J.A. Van Allen (ed), *Scientific uses of earth satellites*, Ann Arbor: University of Michigan Press 1956.
A. Wilcox, *Moon rocket*, London: Thomas Nelson 1946.
A. Wilson, 'Jupiter C/Juno I. America's first satellite launcher', *Spaceflight* 3 i (January 1981), 12–17.

The golden age

J. Bergman, *Ninety seconds to space: the X-15 story*, Garden City, NY: Doubleday 1960.
C.R. Bergwin and W.T. Coleman, *Animal astronauts: they opened the way to the stars*, Englewood Cliffs, NJ: Prentice-Hall 1963.
M. Caidin, *Rendezvous in space*, New York: Dutton 1962.
M. Caidin, *Red star in space*, New York: Crowell-Collier 1963.
M. Chester and S.B. Kramer, *Discoverer: the story of a satellite*, New York: Putnam 1960.

P.E. Cleator, *An introduction to space travel*, New York: Pitman 1961.

K.W. Gatland, *Astronautics in the 60s*, New York: Wiley 1960.

J.M. Gavin, *War and peace in the space age*, New York: Harper 1958.

B. Harvey, *Race into space: the Soviet space programme*, Chichester: Ellis Horwood.

L.F. Hubert and P.E. Lehr, *Weather satellites*, Waltham, Mass: Blaisdell 1967.

J.R. Killian Jnr, *Sputnik, scientists, and Eisenhower*, Cambridge, Mass: MIT Press 1977.

C.R. Koppes, *JPL and the American space program: a history of the Jet Propulsion Laboratory*, New Haven: Yale University Press 1982.

A.A. Needell, *The first 25 years in space*, Washington, DC: Smithsonian Institution Press 1983.

J.E. Oberg, *Red star in orbit*, New York: Random House 1981.

G.V. Petrovich (ed), *The Soviet encyclopedia of spaceflight*, Moscow: Mir 1969.

J. Popescu, *Russian space exploration: the first 21 years*, Henley-on-Thames: Gothard House 1979.

E. Riabchikov, *Russians in space*, New York: Doubleday 1971.

M.R. Sharpe, *Satellites and probes*, London: Aldus 1970.

W.R. Shelton, *American space exploration*, Boston, Mass: Little, Brown 1967.

A. Shternfield, *Soviet space science*, New York: Basic Books 1959.

A.L. Sobel, *Space: from Sputnik to Gemini*, New York: Facts on File 1965.

K.R. Stehling, *Project Vanguard*, New York: Doubleday 1961.

J.A. Van Allen, *Origins of magnetospheric physics*, Washington, DC: Smithsonian Institution Press 1983.

M. Vassiliev and V.V. Dobronravov, *Sputnik into space*, London: Souvenir 1958.

T. Wolfe, *The right stuff*, New York: Farrar, Straus & Giroux 1979.

THE VOSTOK AND VOSHKOD PROGRAMMES

I.G. Borisenko, *In outer space*, Moscow: Machinostroenie 1974.

I.G. Borisenko, *Space launches and finishes*, Moscow: Znanie 1975.

N. Daniloff, *The Kremlin and the cosmos*, New York: Alfred A. Knopf 1972.

Y. Gagarin, *Road to the stars*, Moscow: Foreign Languages Publishing House 1962.

V. Lebedev and Y. Gagarin, *Survival in space*, New York: Bantam 1969.

M.R. Sharpe, *Yuri Gagarin, first man in space*, Huntsville, Alab: Strode 1969.

W. Shelton, *Soviet space exploration: the first decade*, New York: Washington Square Press 1968.

P.L. Smolders, *Soviets in space*, New York: Taplinger 1974.

T.M. Wilding-White, *Jane's pocket book of space exploration*, New York: Collier 1976.

G.E. Wukelic, *Handbook of Soviet space science research*, New York: Gordon & Breach 1968.

THE MERCURY PROGRAMME

M.S. Carpenter et al., *We seven*, New York: Simon & Schuster 1962.

I.D.Ertel and J.M. Grimwood, 'Mercury program – the pioneers of US spaceflight', *Above and beyond: the encyclopedia of aviation and space sciences*, Chicago: New Horizons Publishers 1968.

L.S. Swenson Jr, J.M. Grimwood and C.C. Alexander, *This new ocean: a history of Project Mercury* (The NASA History Series), NASA: NASA SP-4201 1966.

THE GEMINI PROGRAMME

V. Grissom, *Gemini: a personal account of man's venture into space*, New York: Macmillan 1968.

G. Gurney, *Walk in space: the story of Project Gemini*, New York: Random House 1967.

B.C. Hacker and J.M. Grimwood, *On the shoulders of Titans: a history of Project Gemini*, NASA: NASA SP-4203 1977.

I. Stambler, *Project Gemini*, New York: Putnam 1964.

GOING INTO SPACE

Orbits and trajectories

G.W. Collins II, *The foundations of celestial mechanics*, Tucson: Pachart Publishing House 1989.

P.R. Escobal, *Methods of astrodynamics*, Huntingdon, NY: R.E. Krieger 1979.

S. Herrick, *Astrodynamics* (2 vols.), New York: Van Nostrand Reinhold 1971.

D. King-Hele, *Satellites and scientific research*, London: Routledge & Kegan Paul 1960.

J.P. Marec, *Optimal space trajectories*, Amsterdam: Elsevier/North Holland 1979.

W.T. Thomson, 'Introduction to space dynamics', New York: Dover 1986.

Propulsion

J.D. Clark, *Ignition: an informal history of liquid rocket propellants*, New Brunswick, NJ: Rutgers University Press 1972.

P.S. Clark, 'The Scarp Program', *Spaceflight* 23 (May 1982).

P.S. Clark, 'Soviet launchvehicles: an overview', *Spaceflight* 23 (May 1982).

J.L. Sloop, *Liquid hydrogen as a propulsion fuel, 1945–1959*, Washington DC: NASA SP-4404 1978.

THE ROCKET ENGINE

N. Barrere et al., *Rocket propulsion*, Amsterdam: Elsevier 1960.

H.H. Koelle, *Handbook of astronautical engineering*, New York: McGraw-Hill 1961.

G.P. Sutton, *An introduction to the engineering of rockets* (5th edition), New York: Wiley-Interscience 1986.

ROCKET PROPELLANTS

F.A. Warren, *Rocket propellants*, New York: Reinhold 1958.

SOLID FUEL ROCKET ENGINES

A. McDonald, *Design evolution of the space shuttle solid fuel rocket motors*, AIAA 85-1265: 21st AIAA/SAE/ASME/ASEE Joint Propulsion Conference 1985.

P.F. Mella, *A detailed thermal analysis of a large solid propellant rocket nozzle*, AIAA 85-1169: 21st AIAA/SAE/ASME/ASEE Joint Propulsion Conference 1985.

LIQUID FUEL ROCKET ENGINES

D. Altman et al., *Liquid propellant rockets*, Princeton, NJ: Princeton University Press 1960.

M.F. Pouliquen, 'HM60 Cyrogenic rocket engine for future European launchers', *Journal of Spacecraft and Rockets* 21 no. 4 (1984).

ROCKET ENGINES OF THE FUTURE

G.R. Brewer, *Ion propulsion – technology and applications*, New York: Gordon & Breach 1970.

R.G. Jahn, *Physics of electric propulsion*, New York: McGraw-Hill 1968.

E.A. Stuhlinger, *Ion propulsion for space flight*, New York: McGraw-Hill 1964.

Rocket launchers

H.H. Koelle, *Handbook for astronautical engineering*, New York: McGraw-Hill 1961.

G. Warwick, 'Satellite launcher directory', *Flight International* (January 1986) 29–34.

A. Wilson (ed), *Interavia space directory*, London: Interavia 1991.

ARIANE IV, A CONVENTIONAL LAUNCHER

J. Moxon, 'Ariane 4: Europe's launcher grows', *Flight International* (May 1985) 40–6.

I. Naddeo-Souriau, *Ariane. Le pari européen*, Paris: Hermes 1986.

A. Souchier and P. Baudry, *Ariane*, Paris: Flammarion 1986.

THE SPACE SHUTTLE: A REUSABLE SYSTEM

H. Allaway, *The space shuttle at work*, Washington, DC: NASA 1979.

J.P. Allen, *Entering space: an astronaut's journey*, New York: Stewart, Tabori & Chang 1984.

J.L. Grey, *Enterprise*, New York: Morrow 1979.

K.M. Joels and G.P. Kennedy, *The space shuttle operator's manual*, London: Macmillan 1983.

R.M. Powers, *The world's first spaceplane*, Harrisburg, Pa: Stackpole 1979.

Report of the Presidential Commission on the Space Shuttle Challenger accident (5 vols.), Washington, DC: Presidential Commission on the space shuttle Challenger accident 1986.

M. Smith, *An illustrated history of the space shuttle. US winged spacecraft, X-15 to Orbiter*, Newbury Park, Calif: Haynes 1986.

W. Stockton and J.N. Wilford, *Spaceliner: the New York Times report on the Columbia's voyage into tomorrow*, New York: Times Books 1981.

THE USSR

S.G. Alexandrov and R.Y. Federov, *Soviet satellites and spaceships*, Moscow: 1961 (translated from the Russian).

P.S. Clark, 'The Sapwood launch vehicle', *Journal of the British Interplanetary Society* 34 (1981), 437–43.

P.S. Clark, 'Soviet launch vehicles: an overview', *Journal of the British Interplanetary Society* 35 (1982), 51–7.

P.S. Clark, 'The Sapwood launch vehicle revisited', *Journal of the British Interplanetary Society* 35 (1982), 79–81.

C. Durney, 'Proton – an alternative launch system', *Space Policy* (February 1985).

N.L. Johnson, *Handbook of Soviet manned space flight*, San Diego: Univelt 1980.

C.S. Sheldon II, *Review of the Soviet space program*, New York: McGraw-Hill 1968.

A.J. Zaehringer, *Soviet space technology*, New York: Harper 1961.

EUROPE

H. Massey and M.O. Robbins, *History of British space science*, Cambridge: Cambridge University Press 1986.

D.R. Samson (ed), *Development of the Blue Streak satellite launcher*, New York: Pergamon 1963.

CHINA, JAPAN, INDIA

'International launch vehicle', *Aviation Week and Space Technology* (9th March 1987) 164.

SPACE VEHICLES OF THE FUTURE

G.Y. Anderson, D.P. Bencze and B.W. Saunders, 'Ground tests confirm the promise of hypersonic propulsion', *Aerospace America* (September 1987) 38–42.

C.J. Cohen, W.B. Olstad, D.W. Patterson and R. Salkeld, *Space transportation systems 1980–2000*, New York: American Institute of Aeronautics and Astronautics 1979.

'High work to space', *Pioneering the space frontier: report of the US National Commission on Space*, Washington, DC: US National Commission on Space 1985.

Space centres

C.D. Benson and W.B. Faherty, *Moonport: a history of Apollo launch facilities and operations*, Washington, DC: NASA History Series 1978.

'Le centre spatial guyanais', *La Recherche spatiale* 13 nos. 4 and 6, Paris: CNES 1974.

The Kennedy Space Center: NASA Kennedy Space Center 1974.

The RAE table of Earth satellites 1957–1982, London: Macmillan 1983.

J.A. Shortal, *A new dimension. Wallops Island flight test range: the first fifteen years*, NASA: NASA RP-1028 1978.

W.R. Shelton, *Countdown: the story of Cape Canaveral*, Boston, Mass: Little, Brown 1960.

J. Southall, *Woomera*, Sydney: Angus & Robertson 1962.

Satellite ground systems

D.L. Dalglish, 'An introduction to satellite communications', London: Peter Peregrinus 1989.

M. Long. 'World satellite almanac: the complete guide to satellite transmission and technology', Indianapolis: Howard W. Sams 1987.

The hazards of space debris

D.J. Kessler, 'Sources of orbital debris and the projected environment for future spacecraft', *Journal of Spacecraft and Rockets* 18 no. 4 (1981), 357–60.

R.C. Reynolds, N.H. Fischer and E.E. Rice, 'Man-made debris in low earth orbit – a threat to future space operations', *Journal of Spacecraft and Rockets* 20 no. 3 (1983), 279–85.

Space agencies

F.W. Anderson Jnr, *Orders of Magnitude: a history of NACA and NASA, 1915–1980* (2nd edn), NASA Washington, DC: NASA SP-4403 1981.

R. Kerrod, *The illustrated history of NASA: an anniversary edition*, London: Prion 1986.

EXPLORING THE UNIVERSE

Images from space

R. Greeley, *Planetary landscapes*, London: George Allen & Unwin 1985.

K.W. Kelley, *The home planet*, Reading, Mass: Addison-Wesley 1988.

Baxter Art Gallery, *25 years of space photography*, Pasadena: California Institute of Technology 1985.

Exploring the solar system

H. Couper and N. Henbest, *The planets*, London: Pan 1990.

P. Moore, *Mission to the planets*, London: Cassell 1990

MERCURY

M.E. Davies, S.E. Dwornik, D.E. Gault and R.G. Strom, *Atlas of Mercury*, NASA, Washington, DC: NASA SP-423 1978.

B. Murray and E. Burgess, *Flight to Mercury*, New York: Columbia University Press 1977.

R.G. Strom, *Mercury, the elusive planet*, Cambridge: Cambridge University Press 1987.

VENUS

● SOVIET MISSIONS

D.M. Hunten, L. Colin, T.M. Donahue and V.I. Moroz (eds), *Venus*, Tucson: University of Arizona Press 1983.

N.L. Johnson, *Handbook of Soviet lunar and planetary exploration (section III: 'Exploration of Venus', 133–75)*, San Diego: Univelt 1979.

Y. Surkov, *Exploration of the terrestrial planets from spacecraft*, Chichester: Ellis Horwood 1990.

● AMERICAN MISSIONS

E. Burgess, *Venus – an errant twin*, New York: Columbia University Press 1985.

D.M. Hunten, L. Colin, T.M. Donahue and V.I. Moroz (eds), *Venus*, Tucson: University of Arizona Press 1983.

I. Newland, *First to Venus: the story of Mariner II*, New York: McGraw-Hill 1963.

H.J. Wheelock (ed), *Mariner mission to Venus*, New York: McGraw-Hill 1963.

UNMANNED LUNAR MISSIONS

● AMERICAN PROGRAMMES

C.T. Leondes and R.W. Vance (eds), *Lunar missions and exploration*, New York: John Wiley & Sons 1964.

E. Levin, D.D. Viele and L.B. Eldenkamp, 'The lunar orbiter missions to the Moon', *Scientific American* 218 no. 5 (1968), 58–78.

W. Ley, *Ranger to the Moon*, New York: New American Library 1965.

J.F. McCauley, *Moon probes*, Morristown, NJ: Silver Burdett 1969.

H.M. Schurmeier, R.L. Heacock and A.E. Wolfe, 'The Ranger missions to the Moon', *Scientific American* 214 no. 1 (1966), 52–67.

● SOVIET PROGRAMMES

N.L. Johnson, *Handbook of Soviet lunar and planetary exploration*, San Diego: Univelt 1979.

THE APOLLO PROGRAMME

T. Alexander, *Project Apollo: Man to the Moon*, New York: Harper 1964.

N. Armstrong, M. Collins and E.E. Aldrin Jr, *First on the Moon*, Boston, Mass: Little, Brown 1970.

S.A. Bedini, W. von Braun and F.L. Whipple, *Moon: man's greatest adventure*, New York: Abrams 1971.

C.D. Benson and W.B. Faherty, *Moonport: a history of Apollo launch facilities and operations (The NASA History Series)*, NASA, Washington, DC: NASA SP-4204 1978.

R.E. Bilstein, *Stages to Saturn: a technological history of the Apollo/Saturn launch vehicles (The NASA History Series)*, NASA, Washington, DC: NASA SP-4206 1980.

P.J. Booker, G.C. Frewer and G.K.C. Pardoe, *Project Apollo: the way to the Moon*, London: Chatto & Windus 1970.

C.G. Brooks, J.M. Grimwood and L.S. Swenson Jr, *Chariots for Apollo: a history of manned lunar spacecraft (The NASA History Series)*, NASA, Washington, DC: NASA SP-4205 1979.

M. Collins, *Carrying the fire: an astronaut's journey*, New York: Farrar, Straus & Giroux 1974.

C. Coombs, *Project Apollo mission to the Moon*, New York: Morrow 1965.

H.S.F. Cooper Jr, *Apollo on the Moon*, New York: Dial Press 1969.

H.S.F. Cooper Jr, *Thirteen: the flight that failed*, New York: Dial Press 1973.

E.M. Cortright (ed), *Apollo expeditions to the Moon*, NASA, Washington, DC: NASA SP-350 1975.

W. Cunningham, *The all-American boys*, New York: Macmillan 1977.

D. Dooling, 'The evolution of the Apollo spacecraft', *Spaceflight* (March 1974), 82–8.

F. El-Baz and D.M. Warner (eds), *Apollo–Soyuz test project*, NASA, Washington, DC: NASA 1979.

E.C. Ezell and L.N. Ezell, *The partnership: a history of the Apollo–Soyuz test project (The NASA History Series)*, NASA, Washington, DC: NASA SP-4209 1978.

G. Farmer and D.J. Hamblin, *First on the Moon: a voyage with Neil Armstrong, Michael Collins, Edward E. Aldrin Jnr*, Boston, Mass: Little, Brown 1970.

R.P. Hallion (ed) *Apollo: ten years since Tranquillity Base*, National Air and Space Museum, Washington, DC: Smithsonian Institution Press 1979.

W.G. Holder, *Saturn Five: the Moon rocket*, New York: Messner 1968.

K.M. Joels, *Apollo to the moon: a dream of centuries*, National Air and Space Museum, Washington, DC: Smithsonian Institution Press 1982.

A.S. Levine, *Managing NASA in the Apollo era*, NASA, Washington, DC: NASA 1982.

R.S. Lewis, *Appointment on the Moon*, New York: Viking Press 1968.

J.M. Logsdon, *The decision to go to the Moon: Project Apollo and the national interest*, Cambridge (Mass) and London: MIT Press 1970.

H. Mazursky, G.W. Colton and F. El-Baz (eds), *Apollo over the Moon: a view from orbit*, NASA, Washington, DC: NASA 1978.

C. Murray and C. Bly Cox, *Apollo: the race to the Moon*, London: Secker & Warburg 1989.

E. Rabinowitch and R.S. Lewis (eds), *Man on the Moon*, New York: Basic Books 1969.

N. Ruzic, *The case for going to the Moon*, New York: Putnam 1965.

S.R. Taylor, *A post-Apollo view*, New York: Pergamon 1975.

S.R. Taylor, *A lunar perspective*, Houston: Lunar and planetary Institute 1982.

The Apollo spacecraft: a chronology (The NASA History Series), NASA, Washington, DC: NASA SP-4009. *Vol I*, I.D. Ertelmand and M.L. Morse, *Through November 7, 1962*, 1969; *Vol II*, M.L. Morse and J.K. Bays, *November 8, 1962–September 30*, 1964, 1973; *Vol III*, C.G. Brooks and I.D. Ertel, *October 1, 1964–January 20, 1966*, 1976; *Vol IV*, I.D. Ertel, R.W. Newkirk and C.G. Brooks, *January 21, 1966–July 13, 1974*, 1978.

H. Young, B. Silcock and P. Dunn, *Journey to Tranquillity*, Garden City, NY: Doubleday 1970.

MARS

R.V. Arvidson, A.B. Binder and K.L. Jones, 'The surface of Mars', *Scientific American* 238 iii (1978), 76–89.

E. Burgess, *To the red planet*, Irvington: Columbia University Press 1978.

M.H. Carr, *The surface of Mars*, New Haven: Yale University Press 1981.

E.C. Ezell and L.N. Ezell, *On Mars: exploration of the red planet 1958–1978 (The NASA History Series)*, NASA, Washington, DC: NASA SP-4212 1983.

N.H. Horowitz, 'The search for life on Mars', *Scientific American* 237 v (1977), 52–61.

J.N. James, 'The voyage of Mariner IV', *Scientific American* 214 iii (1966), 42–52.

N.L. Johnson, 'Exploration of Mars', *Handbook of Soviet lunar and planetary space exploration*, section IV, San Diego: Univelt 1979.

R.B. Leighton, 'The photographs from Mariner IV', *Scientific American* 214 iv (1966), 54–68.

R.B. Leighton, 'The surface of Mars', *Scientific American* 222 v (1970), 26–41.

R.B. Leighton et al., 'Mariner 6 and 7 television pictures: preliminary analysis', *Science* 166 no. 3901 (1969), 49–67.

W. Ley, *Mariner IV to Mars*, New York: New American Library 1966.

F. Miles and N. Booth, *Race to Mars*, London: Macmillan 1988.

B.C. Murray, 'Mars from Mariner 9', *Scientific American* 228 i (1973), 48–69.

T.A. Mutch (ed), *The geology of Mars*, Princeton, NJ: Princeton University Press 1977.

J.B. Pollack, 'Mars', *Scientific American* 233 iii (1975), 107–17.

C. Sagan, 'Mars: the view from Mariner 9', *Astronautics and Aeronautics* 10 ix (1972), 26–41.

R.S. Sloan, 'The scientific experiments of Mariner IV', *Scientific American* 214 v (1966), 62–72.

A.E. Smith, *Mars: the next step*, Bristol: Adam Hilger 1989.

'Viking', special edn *Science* 143 no. 4255 (1976); special edn *Science* 194 no. 4260 (1976); special edn *Science* 194 no. 4271 (1976).

THE GIANT PLANETS

J.K. Beatty, 'Voyager 2's triumph', *Sky and Telescope* 72 iv (1986) 336–43.

E. Burgess, *By Jupiter. Odysseys to a giant*, New York: Columbia University Press 1982.

R.O. Fimmel, J. Van Allen and E. Burgess, *Pioneer: first to Jupiter, Saturn and beyond*, NASA, Washington, DC: NASA SP-446 1980.

G. Hunt and P. Moore, *Atlas of Uranus*, Cambridge: Cambridge University Press, 1989.

R.P. Laeser, W.I. McLaughlin and D.M. Wolff 'Engineering Voyager 2's encounter with Uranus', *Scientific American* 255 v (1986), 34–43.

E.D. Miner, *Uranus: the planet, rings and satellites*, Chichester: Ellis Horwood 1987.

'Mission systems', special edn *Journal of the British Interplanetary Society* 38 x (1985).

P. Moore, *The planet Neptune*, Chichester: Ellis Horwood 1988.

'Pioneer Saturn', special edn *Science* 207 no. 4429 (1980), 400–53.

'Pioneer Saturn', special edn *Journal of Geophysical Research* 85 (1980), 5651–958.

M. Poynter and A.L. Lane, *Voyager: the story of a space mission*, New York: Athenaeum 1981.

'Voyager 1 mission to Jupiter', special edn *Nature* 280 (1979), 725–806.

'Voyager 1 mission to Saturn', special edn *Nature* 292 (1981), 675–755.

'Voyager 2 mission to Saturn', special edn *Science* 215 (1982), 499.

'Voyager 2 mission to Uranus', special edn *Science* 233 (1986), 39.

COMETS

'Encounters with Comet Halley. The first results', special edn *Nature* 321 no 6067 (1986), 259–368.

J.W. Mason, *Comet Halley – investigations, results, interpretations*, Chichester: Ellis Horwood 1989.

R. Reinhard, 'The Giotto encounter with comet Halley', *Nature* 321 (1986), 313–18.

R. Reinhard and B. Batrick (eds), *The Giotto mission. Its scientific investigations*, Noordwijk: ESA SP-1077 1986.

R. Reinhard and B. Batrick (eds), *Space missions to Halley's Comet*, Noordwijk: ESA SP-1066 1986.

THE LATEST DEVELOPMENTS

● UNMANNED MISSIONS

Project Galileo: the Phoenix rises', *Sky and Telescope* 123 iv (1987), 359–61.

P.S. Clark, 'The soviet Mars programme', *Journal of the British Interplanetary Society* 39 i (1986), 3–18.

D.H. Collins and S.L. Miller, 'Comet rendezvous: the next stage in cometary exploration', *Journal of the British Interplanetary Society* 39 vi (1986), 263–72.

M. Littmann, *Planets beyond: discovering the outer solar system*, New York: John Wiley & Sons 1988.

T.R. McDonough, *Space: the next twenty-five years*, New York: John Wiley & Sons 1989.

M. Neugebauer, 'Comet rendezvous – the next step', *Sky and Telescope* 73 iii (1987), 266–70.

C.M. Yeates et al., *Galileo: exploration of Jupiter's system*, NASA, Washington, DC: NASA SP-479 1985.

● 2020: DESTINATION MARS

E.C. Ezell and L.N. Ezell, *On Mars: exploration of the red planet. 1958–1978*, NASA, Washington, DC: NASA SP-4212 1984.

J.E. Oberg, *Mission to Mars*, New York: New American Library 1983.

J.E. Oberg, *Pioneering the space frontier*, Report of the US National Commission on Space, New York: Bantam Books 1986.

Science in space

United Nations, *The World in space: a survey of space activities and issues*, Englewood Cliffs, NJ: Prentice-Hall 1982.

SPACE RESEARCH AND INTERNAL GEOPHYSICS

G. Balmino, 'Present status and future improvements in measuring the gravity field of the earth and planets', A.J. Anderson and A. Cazenave (eds), *Space geodesy and geodynamics*, 19–54, London: Academic Press 1986.

THE IONISED ENVIRONMENT OF THE EARTH

S.I. Akasofu and Y. Kamide (eds), *The solar wind and the Earth*, Dordrecht: Reidel 1990.

W.N. Hess, *The radiation belt and magnetosphere*, London: Blaisdell 1968.

L.J. Lanzerotti, C.F. Kennel and E.N. Parker (eds), *Solar system plasma physics*, Amsterdam: North Holland Publishers 1979.

J.G. Roederer, *Dynamics of geomagnetically trapped particles*, Berlin: Springer-Verlag 1970.

SOLAR PHYSICS

R.G. Athay, *The solar chromosphere and corona: quiet sun*, Dordrecht: Reidel 1976.

R. Giovanelli, *Secrets of the Sun*, Cambridge: Cambridge University Press 1984.

S. Mitton, *Daytime star: the story of our Sun*, London: Faber 1981.

D.G. Wentzel, *The restless Sun*, Washington, DC: Smithsonian Institution Press 1989.

ASTRONOMY AND ASTROPHYSICS

M.W. Friedlander, *Cosmic rays*, Cambridge, Mass: Harvard University Press 1989.

R. Giacconi (ed), *X-ray astronomy with the Einstein satellite*, Boston, Mass: Reidel 1980.

M. Longair, *Alice and the space telescope*, Baltimore: Johns Hopkins University Press, 1989.

J. Mathers and G. Longanecker, *Cosmic background explorer (Cobe)*, NASA, Washington, DC: NASA 1980.

W.H. Tucker, *The star-splitters: the high energy astronomy laboratories*, NASA, Washington, DC: NASA 1984.

W.H. Tucker and R. Giacconi, *The X-ray universe*, Cambridge, Mass: Harvard University Press 1985.

LIVING WITH SPACE

Satellite applications

D.R. Sloggett, *Satellite data: processing, archiving and dissemination*, (2 volumes), Chichester: Ellis Horwood 1989.

METEOROLOGY

J.G. Vaeth, *Weather eyes in the sky: America's meteorological satellites*, New York: Ronald 1965.

W.K. Widger Jr, *Meteorological satellites*: Holt 1966.

REMOTE SENSING

P.J. Curren, *Principles of remote sensing*, Harlow: Longman 1985.

R. Harris, *Satellite remote sensing: an introduction*, London: Routledge & Kegan Paul 1987.

W.G. Rees, *Physical principles of remote sensing*, Cambridge: Cambridge University Press 1990.

R.S. Scorer, 'Satellite as microscope', Chichester: Ellis Horwood 1990.

LANDSAT OBSERVATIONS

P.K. Charles, 'Mapping and remote sensing education requirements in developing countries', Washington, DC: *Proceedings of the American Society of Photogrammetry and Remote Sensing* 1986.

R. Colwell (ed), *Manual of remote sensing*, vols I and II (2nd edn), Falls Church, Va: American Society of Photogrammetry 1983.

NASA, *Linking remote sensing technology and global needs*, Washington, DC: US GPO June 1987.

NASA, *Earth system science: a program for global change*, NASA: January 1988.

OCEANOGRAPHY

N.M. Mognard, 'Swell propagation in the North Atlantic Ocean using Seasat altimeter', T. Allen (ed), *Satellite microwave remote sensing*, London: John Wiley & Sons 1983.

R.H. Stewart, *Methods of satellite oceanography*, London: University of California Press 1985.

TELECOMMUNICATIONS

J.E. Allnutt, *Satellite-to-ground radiowave propagation*, London: Peter Peregrinus 1989.

J.B. Gantt, *United States space policy, law and regulation – three key issues*, New York–Washington: Space Publ. Communication and Broadcasting vol. 6 1988.

K.W. Gatland, D. Dooling et al., 'Voices from the sky', *The illustrated encyclopedia of space technology*, London: Salamander Books 1981.

L. Jaffe, *Communications in space*: Holt 1966.

D.M. Jansky, *World atlas of satellites*, Dedham, Mass: Artech House 1983.

G. Maral and M. Bousquet, *Satellite communications systems*, Chichester: John Wiley & Sons 1986.

G.E. Muller and E.R. Spangle, *Communication satellites*: John Wiley & Sons 1964.

J.R. Pierce, *The beginnings of satellite communications*, San Francisco: San Francisco Press 1968.

D.W.E. Rees, *Satellite communications: the first quarter century of service*, Chichester: John Wiley & Sons 1990.

L. Solomon, *Telstar*, New York: McGraw-Hill 1962.

DIRECT BROADCASTING

B.J. Evans, *Satellite communications systems*: IEE 1987.

R.L. Douglas, *Satellite communications technology*, Englewood Cliffs, NJ: Prentice-Hall 1988.

NAVIGATION

N. Ackroyd and R. Lorimer, *Global navigation: a GPS user's guide*, London: Lloyds 1990.

M.A. Rothblatt, *Radiodetermination satellite services and standards*, Norwood, Mass: Artech House 1987.

S.D. Thompson, *Everyman's guide to satellite navigation*, Annapolis, Md: Arinc Research Corporation 1985.

Man in space

ASTRONAUT TRAINING

'Astronaut selection and training', *NASA information summaries*, Washington, DC: PMS-019 December 1986.

R. Kerrod, *The illustrated history of man in space*, London: Prion 1989.

J. Simms and M. Sterling, *The flights before the flight: an overview of shuttle astronaut training*, Boston, Mass: AIAA Flight Simulation Technology Conference 14–16 August 1989.

SKYLAB

W.D. Compton and C.D. Benson, *Living and working in space. A history of Skylab (The NASA History Series)*, NASA: NASA SP-4008 1983.

C. Ezell and L.N. Ezell (eds), *The partnership, a history of the Apollo–Soyuz test project*, NASA: NASA SP-4209 1978.

R.W. Newkirk and I.D. Ettel, *Skylab. A chronology (The NASA History Series)*, NASA: NASA SP-4011 1977.

SOYUZ – SALYUT – COSMOS

P. Smolders, translated M. Powell, *Soviets in space: the story of Salyut and the Soviet approach to present and future space travel*, Guildford London: Taplinger Publishing Company 1973.

THE AMERICAN SPACE SHUTTLE PROGRAMME

B. Lichtenberg, 'A new breed of space traveller' *New Scientist* 103 no. 1418 (1984).

NASA, *Science in orbit. The shuttle and Spacelab experience: 1981–1986*, Washington, DC: US Government Printing Office 1988.

SPACELAB

NASA, *Science in orbit. The shuttle and Spacelab experience: 1981–1986*, Washington, DC: US Government Printing Office 1988.

D. Shapland and M. Rycroft, *Spacelab: research in Earth orbit*, Cambridge: Cambridge University Press 1984.

LIFE SCIENCES IN A MICROGRAVITY ENVIRONMENT

G.H. Grampton, *Motion and space sickness*, New York–Washington: CRC Press 1989.

R. Harding, *Survival in space*, London: Routledge 1989.

R.S Johnston and L.F. Dietlein (eds), *Biomedical results of Apollo*, NASA, Washington, DC: NASA SP-368 1975.

C. Lewis, 'Space life sciences', *Soviet space programs: 1981–1987*, Washington, DC: US Senate Committee on Commerce, Science and Transport report 1988.

A.E. Nicogossian and J.F. Parker, *Space physiology and medicine*, NASA SP-447, Washington, DC: US Government Printing Office 1989.

H.I. Shipman, *Humans in space: 21st century frontiers*, New York: Plenum 1989.

MATERIALS SCIENCE IN MICROGRAVITY

H. Hamacher and R.J. Naumann, *Materials sciences in space*, Heidelberg: Springer-Verlag 1986.

NASA, *Science in orbit. The shuttle and Spacelab experience: 1981–1986*, Washington, DC: US Government Printing Office 1988.

National Research Council, *Industrial applications of the microgravity environment*, Washington, DC: NRC 1988.

● THE COMMERCIAL ASPECT

'Commercialisation of space', special edn *Aviation Week and Space Technology*, New York: McGraw-Hill 25 June 1984.

FUTURE SPACE VOYAGES

NASA, *Beyond earth's boundaries*, NASA, Washington, DC: NASA 1989.

J. Grey, *Reach heads in space*, New York: Macmillan 1983.

Launch options for the future: Congress of the United States, Office of Technology 1988.

● THE SOVIET UNION

Glavkosmos, *The USSR in outer space, the year 2005*, Moscow: Kosmos 1989.

● THE UNITED STATES

J. Allen, *Entering space: an astronaut's odyssey*, New York: Tabori & Chang 1984.

I. Bekey and H. Daniel (eds), *Space stations and space platforms – concepts, design, infrastructure, and uses*, New York: American Institute of Aeronautics and Astronautics 1985.

J. Botkin et al., *Global stakes – the future of high technology America*, New York: Penguin Books 1984.

US National Commission on Space, *Pioneering the space frontier*, New York: Bantam Books, May 1986.

Industry and space

THE MAIN SPACE LABORATORIES – THE UNITED STATES

NASA, *Science in orbit. The shuttle and Spacelab experience: 1981–1986*, Washington, DC: US Government Printing Office 1988.

US Office of Technology Assessment, *International co-operation and competition in civilian space activities*, Washington, DC: Office of Technology Assessment 1985.

TECHNOLOGICAL SPINOFF

T.W. Halstead and P.A. Dupour, *Biological and medical experiments on the space shuttle 1981–1985*, NASA, Washington. DC: NASA 1986.

NASA, *Spinoff*, Washington, DC: US Government Printing Office, annually since 1986

THE WORLD SPACE INDUSTRY

● EUROPE

Euroconsult, *World space industry survey. Ten year outlook*: Paris 1988.

International co-operation and competition in civilian space activities, Washington, DC: Office of Technology Assessment, Congress of the United States 1985.

● THE USSR

P.S. Clark, 'Soviet space activity, 1985–1986', *Journal of the British Interplanetary Society* 40, 203.

N. Johnson, *Soviet space program 1980–1985*, San Diego: Univelt 1987.

● THE USA

Federal policy and commercial space development, Dallas: National Center for Policy Administration 1987.

D.E. Koelle, *Commercialisation of space activities*, London: Astronautica Acta, Pergamon Press 1988.

● JAPAN

FEO (Federation of Economic Organizations), *Space in Japan 1988–1989*, Tokyo 1988.

SJAC (The society of Japanese Aerospace Companies Inc.), *Aerospace industry in Japan 1989–1990*, Tokyo 1989.

Brandin and Harrison, *The Technology War, a case for competitiveness*, New York: John Wiley & Sons 1987.

FINANCING SPACE ACTIVITIES

US Department of Commerce, *Space commerce and industry assessment*, Washington, DC: May 1988.

SPACE INSURANCE

J.B. Gantt, 'United States space policy, law and regulation. Three key issues', *Communication and Broadcasting* 6 (1988), 188–94.

The military dimension

SPACE POLICIES: THE WORLD STAGE

D. Jacquelyn and R.P. Pfaltzgraff, *Strategic defense and extended deterrence*, Washington, DC: Pergamon-Brassey's 1986.

F. Long, *Weapons in space*, New York: AAAS 1986.

M. Long, *World satellite*, New York: Commtek Publishing Co. 1985.

D. Mikheyev, *The Soviet perspectives on the strategic defense initiative*, Washington, DC: Pergamon-Brassey's 1987.

● EUROPE

R. Richardson, 'Exploiting space in peace and war', *Journal of Social, Political and Economic Studies* 14 ii (1989).

● THE USSR

E. Velikhov and A. Kokoshin, 'Avoiding a new round in the militarization of outer space: an urgent problem and goal', SIPRI (ed), *Space weapons. The armed control dilemma*, 185–92, London–Philadelphia: Taylor & Francis 1984.

V. Glouchko, *Soviet Cosmonautics: questions and answers*, Moscow: Novosty 1989.

P. Stares, *The militarization of space: US policy 1945–1954*, New York: Cornell University Press 1985.

● THE USA

T.L Heyns, *Understanding US strategy: a reader*, Fort McNair, Washington, DC: National Defense University Press 1983.

J. Logsdon and R. Williamson, 'US Access to space', *Scientific American* 260 iii (March 1989).

Office of Technology Assessment, *Launch options for the future*, Washington, DC: US Government Printing Office July 1988.

T.G. Paterson, *Major problems in American foreign policy*, Lexington, Mass: D.C. Heath & Company 1984.

J.F. Reichart and S.R. Sturm, *American defense policy*, Baltimore: Johns Hopkins University Press 1982.

W.J. Durch, *National interests and the military use of space*, Cambridge, Mass: Ballinger Publishing Company 1983.

C.R. Whelan, *Guide to military space programs*, Arlington, Va: Pasha Publications 1984.

International law and space

GENERAL FEATURES

J.B. Gantt, 'United States space policy, law and regulation. Three key issues', *Space Communication and Broadcasting* vol. 6, 189–94, Washington, DC: 1988.

G.C.M. Reijen and W. de Graaff, *The pollution of outer space, in particular of the geostationary orbit*, Dordrecht: Martinus Nijhoff 1989.

PEACEFUL USES OF SPACE

C.Q. Christol, *The modern international law of outer space*, New York: Pergamon Press 1982.

M.L. Smith, *International regulation of satellite telecommunications after the space WARC*, Montreal: McGill University 1989.

Space Communication and Broadcasting, Amsterdam (North Holland): Elsevier Science Publishing Company, thrice yearly since 1983.

University of Mississippi, *Journal of Space Law*, Jackson, Miss: three issues per year since 1973.

R.L. White, *The law and regulation of international space communication*, Norwood, Mass: Artech House 1988.

LEGAL ASPECTS OF THE MILITARY USES OF SPACE

N. Jasentuliyana, *Maintaining outer space for peaceful uses*, Tokyo: United Nations University 1984.

N.L. Johnson and D.S. McKnight, *Artificial space debris*, Malabar: Orbit Book Company 1987.

T. Karas, *The new high ground. Strategies and weapons of space-age war*, New York: Simon & Schuster Inc. 1983.

P. Stares, *Space and national security*, Washington, DC: Brosleys Institution 1988.

G. Zhukov and Y. Kolosov, *International space law*, Moscow: Praeger 1984.

Glossary and index

The glossary and index that follows is deliberately selective but it includes all the major names and concepts found in the *Encyclopedia*. To avoid unnecessary duplication, glossary entries have been integrated; not every entry found below is therefore followed by a page reference.

Figures in italics refer to illustrations and captions.

378

382

inside the module can be controlled. This allows the study of biological, physiological and physiochemical reactions under variable acceleration, or gravity.

VEGA. Soviet interplanetary probe 152, *152*, 153, *153*, 155, *155*, 194, *194*, 195, *195*, 196, *196*, 197.

VENERA. Soviet missions to Venus 49, 54, *63*, 152, *152*, 153, *154*, 155, 159.

VENUS. Planet 54, 150, 151, 152–5, 156–9, *159*, 194, *200*, 201.

VENUS RADAR MAPPER. US interplanetary probe 200, 201.

VENUSIAN ATMOSPHERE 149, *151*, 153, *153*, 154, 155, 156, 157, *157*, 158, *158*, 159, *159*, 196, 201.

VEREIN FÜR RAUMSCHIFFAHRT. German astronautics company *23*, 27, *27*, 28, *28*.

VERNE, Jules (1828–1905) *21*, 22, *22*, 28.

VERNIER MOTOR. For fine adjustment of attitude 45, 98, 99, 296, 297, *297*, 301.

VÉRONIQUE. French rocket 45, *45*, 60, 61, *61*, 112.

VESTA. Franco-Soviet programme 201, 202.

VESTIBULAR MECHANISM. Balance mechanism of humans via the inner ear. 285, 288, *289*.

VESTIBULAR SLED. Apparatus designed by the European Space Agency and installed onboard the German Spacelab mission D1. It enables linear accelerations in three axes to be applied to study the response of the vestibular organ to precisely defined stimuli. *282*, 286, *286*.

VfR.
See **VEREIN FÜR RAUMSCHIFFAHRT.**

VIB (Vertical Integration Building) *120*, 122.

VIKING. Rocket motor *83*, *92*.

VIKING. Swedish satellite *77*, *212*, *214*, *339*.

VIKING. US Martian orbital or landing probes *146*, *147*, *180*, 184, *184*, *185*, *204*; **Viking 1** *63*, *149*, 187, 204; **Viking 2** *63*, *148*, 187.

VIKING 12. US rocket probe 42, *43*.

VIKTORENKO, Alexander 299.

VIS (Visual Imaging System) *185*.

VOICE COMMUNICATIONS 174, 244—50, 335.

VOLGOGRAD. Soviet cosmodrome 126, 127, *127*.

VOLYNOV, Boris Valentinovich (born in 1934) *50*, 52.

VOSKHOD. Soviet manned spacecraft 52, 53, *53*, 55.

VOSTOK. Soviet manned spacecraft 50–2, 54, *54*, 55, *55*, 266, 351.

VOYAGER. US space probe *63*, *107*, *190*, 191, *192*, 193, *193*, 200, 202.

VTIR (Visible and Thermal Infrared Radiometer). 243, *243*.

V2 MISSILE. *23*, *33*, *35*, 36, 37, *38*, 39, 42, 43, 45, 74, *75*, 109.

VULCAN. Cryogenic engine for Ariane V rocket 82, *85*.

VULCANISM 152, 153, 164, 201, 202, *230*.

WAC CORPORAL. Early US rocket probe 39, *39*, 43.

WALLOPS ISLAND. NASA rocket launching base *121*, 122, *124*, 256, *256*.

WASSERFALL. German missile 36.

WATER SUPPLY IN MANNED SPACECRAFT *258*, 269, 296, 297, 299.

WATERLOO. 16.

WEATHER FORECASTS 223, 234, 235, 243.

WEBB, James E. 56, 170.

WEIGHTLESS ENVIRONMENT TRAINING FACILITY (WETF). System at the NASA Johnson Space Cen-

ter, a water tank eight metres deep inside which a life size mock-up of the hold and airlock of the space shuttle has been reconstructed to practise extravehicular activity. It has a pressurisation system for astronauts' suits, a medical centre, and closed circuit television. 258.

WEIGHTLESSNESS. State when a mass no longer has a weight, as it is not subject to any gravitational acceleration. 54, *258*, 259, *264*, 265, *265*, 283, 284, 289, 290, 291, 292, 293, *295*.

WEINAN. Chinese control centre 337.

WEINBERGER, Caspar (born in 1917) 354.

WEITZ, Paul (born in 1932) 262.

WELLES, Orson (1915–1985) 46.

WELLS, Herbert George (1866–1946) 22, 24, 41.

WESTAR. Series of American telecommunications satellites operated by the Western Union Telegraph Company. The first of the series was launched in 1974, followed by a second generation of Hughes satellites in 1982. They are used in the United States for distributing television programmes to cable networks. 244, 245, 274, 276, 337.

WETF (Weightless Environment Training Facility) 258.

WHEATSTONE, Charles (1802–1875) 244.

WHISTLERS. Radio signals from lightning propagated through the magnetosphere. 213.

WHITE, Edward H. (1930–1967) 54, 55, 58, 59, 60, 61, 175.

WIDE BAND CAPACITY. This refers to a communications channel where the transmitted signal occupies a relatively wide band of frequencies, ie has a wide bandwidth. For instance, a television channel requires a 7 megahertz (MHz) bandwidth whilst a telephone line needs only a narrow bandwidth of 3 to 4 kilohertz.

WINKLER, Johannes (1897–1947) *23*, 27, *27*, 29.

WISE, Robert (born in 1914). Film director 46.

WMO (World Meteorological Organisation). United

Nations organisation based in Geneva, responsible for all aspects of meteorological activity (including international telecommunications). 145, 232, 365.

WOHNRAD. *29*.

WOMEN IN SPACE 271.

WOOMERA. Launch site in Australia *112*, *121*, 128, *128*.

WORCESTER. Robert H. Goddard's launch site 24, 25, *25*.

WORLD CONFERENCE FOR RADIOCOMMUNICATIONS 365.

WRESAT. Scientific satellite 128, *128*.

WUBEI ZHI. Chinese military treaty *11*.

X15. US rocket plane *43*, *54*.

XICHANG SITE. Launch site in South West China used for Long March III launchers. 116, 130, *130*, 337.

X1. US rocket plane *43*.

X RAYS. Quanta of short wavelength electromagnetic radiation. 153, 216, 218, 219, 221, 222, *222*, 272, 276, 277, 304.

YANGEL, Mikhail Kouzmich (1911–1971). Soviet rocket engineer.

YEGOROV, Boris Borisovich (born in 1937) 52, *52*, 55.

YOUNG, John W. (born in 1930) 54, 58, 60, 176, *177*, *179*, 279.

YURI. Japanese satellite 251.

ZAIKIN. 52.

ZEMIORKA. Soviet rocket 44, 45, *45*, 48.

ZOND. Soviet probes *164*.

Authors

Frédéric d'Allest
Chairman and Managing Director, Arianespace, Evry;
President, Locstar, Evry

Jean Arets
Head of International Affairs, European Space Agency
(ESA), Paris

Phillip J. Baker
Colonel, US Air Force;
Former Military Assistant, Department of Defense,
Washington DC

Georges Balmino
Director, International Gravimetrics Bureau, French
National Centre for Space Research (CNES), Toulouse

Hans Barth
Director, Hermann-Oberth Museum, Feucht

Alexander Bazilevsky
Doctor of geological and mineral sciences, Moscow

Robert H. Benson
Director, Flight Systems Division, Office of Space Science
and Applications, NASA, Washington DC

Jean-Pierre Bibring
Assistant lecturer, University of Paris XI, Orsay

Michel Bignier
President, French National Academy of Air and Space,
Paris; Member, International Academy of Astronautics

Philippe Binet
Head of Documentation and Public Affairs, Eutelsat, Paris

Amy K. Bodnar
Senior editor, Techedit Inc., Burke, Virginia

Pierre M. Boudreau
Deputy Regional Director, Canadian Ministry of
Communications, Moncton, New Brunswick

Jean-Claude Bouillot
Head of Orbital Intervention, French National Centre for
Space Research (CNES), Evry

Gérard Brachet
Chairman and Managing Director, Spot Image, Toulouse

Robert W. Breithaupt
Director-General, Communications Research Centre,
Ottawa

Richard E. Butler
Secretary-General, International Telecommunications
Union, Geneva

Nathalie Cabrol
Lecturer in physical geography, University of Paris I

Marie-Claude Canivet
Project engineer, Solid rocket boosters Ariane V, French
National Centre for Space Research (CNES), Evry

Claude Carlier
Director, Centre for the History of Aeronautics, University
of Paris I

Jean-Pierre Carrou
Head of Mathematical Astronautics, Space Centre,
Toulouse

Eric Chassefière
French National Centre for Scientific Research (CNRS),
Verrières-le-Buisson

Michail Chernichov
Journalist, *Moscow News*, Moscow

Chen Gengtao
Managing editor, *China Features*, Beijing

Phillip S. Clark
Specialist in Soviet and Chinese space programmes;
Computer scientist, GEC Avionics Ltd., Rochester,
Kent

Henry J. Clarks
Director, Technology Utilization Division, NASA,
Washington DC;
Acting director, Commercial Development Division, NASA,
Washington DC

Jean Clavel
Deputy Director, International Ultraviolet Explorer
Observatory, Madrid

Lawrence Colin
Project scientist, Pioneer Venus programme;
Head, Space Science Division, Ames Research Center,
NASA, California

Pierre Contensou
Armaments engineer;
Former president, Aeronautics and Astronautics Association
of France;
Member of the Academy of Sciences, Paris

Marie-Rose Cukierman
Journalist and editor, Soviet Information Bureau, Paris

Alexandre Dauguet
Deputy director, External Affairs and Communications, and
Ballistics and Space Systems divisions, Aérospatiale, Les
Mureaux

Geneviève Debouzy
Head of Science Division, Univers;
Programme supervisor, French National Centre for Space
Research (CNES), Paris

Mario De Leo
President, Dataspazio, Rome;
Former chief Italian delegate to European Space Agency
(ESA)

James A. Dunne
Head, Science Requirements and Operations Planning team,
Galileo programme;
Jet Propulsion Laboratory, Pasadena, California

Alain Dupas
Senior lecturer, University of Paris XI, Orsay;
Director of Programme Planning, French National Centre
for Space Research (CNES), Paris

Margaret B. Edwards
Policy analyst, Office of Space Science, NASA, Washington
DC

Bernhard F. Fabis
Divisional Head, German Research Institute for Air and
Space, Cologne

Terence T. Finn
Director of Policy and Planning, Office of Space Flight,
NASA, Washington DC

Thomas L. Fischetti
Former program manager, Skylab, NASA, Washington DC;
President, Technology Management Consultants Inc., Silver
Spring, Maryland

Pierre M. Gallois
Air Commodore;
Vice-president, International Institute of Geopolitics, Paris

Chantal M. Gauthier
Engineer, M Sat programme, Canadian Ministry of
Communications, Ottawa

Roger Gendrin
Head of research, French National Centre for Scientific
Research (CNRS);
Director, Research Centre for Physics of Terrestrial and
Planetary Environments, French National Centre for
Telecommunications Research (CNET), Issy-les-Moulineaux

Michel Giroux
Adviser on European space affairs at the Canadian
Embassy, Paris

Jacques Goimard
Assistant lecturer, University of Paris I

Olivier de Goursac
President, Promospace, Paris;
President, Planetary Surfaces Working Group, International
Association of Planetology, Brussels

Gottfried Greger
Ministerial adviser to the Federal Department of Research
and Technology, Bonn

Jerry Grey
Director of Science and Technology Policy, American
Institute of Aeronautics and Astronautics, Washington DC

James M. Grimwood
Historian, Johnson Space Center, NASA, Houston, Texas

Claude Honvault
Project leader, Meteosat programme, European Space
Agency (ESA), Paris;
Head of Support Systems, European Space Operations
Centre (ESOC), Darmstadt

Rainer Jansen
Consultant to Spacelab-1 mission;
Deputy Research Director, German Federal Department for
Research and Technology, Bonn

Nandasiri Jasentuliyana
Deputy Director, Outer Space Affairs Division, United
Nations, New York

Ola M. Johannessen
Director, Nansen Remote Sensing Centre, Bergen;
Professor, Geophysical Institute, University of Bergen

Nicholas L. Johnson
Scientific consultant, Teledyne-Brown Engineering,
Colorado Springs, Colorado

Nikolai Kardachev
Deputy Director, Institute of Space Research, Soviet
Academy of Sciences;
Corresponding member of the Soviet Academy of Sciences,
Moscow

Akira Kikuchi
Chief engineer, Earth Observation Satellite Group,
Japanese National Space Development Agency (Nasda),
Tokyo

Francis Klefstad-Sillonville
Senior armaments engineer;
Assistant Director, Hermes programme, Aérospatiale,
Blagnac

Andrei A. Kokochine
Historian and Assistant Director of the American and
Canadian Institute at the Soviet Academy of Sciences,
Moscow;
Vice-president, Soviet Committee for Peace

Ivan S. Korochentsev
Director, Museum of Astronautics, Moscow

Yves Langevin
Head of Research, Centre for Nuclear Spectroscopy and
Mass Spectrometry, French National Centre for Scientific
Research (CNRS)

Christian Lardier
Member of Cosmos Club of France, Paris;
Associate editor, *Aviation Magazine International*, Paris

André Lebeau
Lecturer in space technology and programmes,
Conservatoire National des Arts et Métiers (CNAM), Paris
Director, French National Meteorological Office, Paris

Chester M. Lee
Executive Vice-president, Spacehab Inc., Washington DC

John C. Leeming
Space consultant;
Former Director of Policy and Programmes, British
National Space Centre, London

Philippe Lemaire
Head of Research, Laboratoire de physique stellaire et
planétaire, French National Centre for Scientific Research
(CNRS), Verrières-le-Buisson

Joel I. Leonard
Senior program scientist, Lockheed Corporation,
Washington DC

Jeffrey Maclure
International Affairs Officer, National Environmental
Satellite, Data and Information Service, National Oceanic
and Atmospheric Administration (NOAA), US Department
of Commerce, Washington DC

Bethene E. McNealy
Senior Engineer, Payload Specialist Training Manager,
NASA Training Division, Johnson Space Center, Houston,
Texas

Philippe Masson
Senior lecturer, University of Paris XI, Orsay

Masafumi Miyazawa
Chief, Rocket Group, Japanese National Space
Development Agency (Nasda), Tokyo

Robert Mory
Project leader, Eureca programme, European Space Agency
(ESA), Paris

Larissa Moskaleva
Lecturer in physical science and mathematics, Moscow

Linda Neuman-Ezell
Deputy Director, Space Science and Exploration
Department, National Museum of Air and Space,
Smithsonian Institution, Washington DC

Olof Nordling
Scientific attaché to the Swedish Embassy, Paris

Charles D. Odorizzi
Major, US Armed Forces;
International Editor, *Armed Forces Journal International*,
Washington DC

William A. Oran
Science consultant, US House of Representatives,
Washington DC

Frederick I. Ordway III
Consultant to the Alabama Space and Rocket Center,
Huntsville, Alabama

Fumio Otsuki
Director, Space Station Group, Japanese National Space
Development Agency (Nasda), Tokyo

Daniel Pichoud
Group Head, Ballistics Division, General Armaments
Delegation, French Ministry of Defence, Paris

Théo Pirard
Professor, Notre-Dame Institute, Jupille-sur-Meuse
Journalist and writer on space affairs

Marcel Pouliquen
Head of research and technology, Société européenne de
propulsion, Paris;
Senior lecturer, Ecole Nationale Supérieure de
l'aéronautique et de l'espace, Paris.

Boris V. Rauchenbakh
Specialist in theoretical mechanics and piloting systems;
Member of the International Academy of Astronautics,
Moscow

Hugh M. Reekie
Engineer, M Sat programme,
Canadian Ministry of Communications, Ottawa

Noah Rifkin
Project manager, Egan Group, Washington DC

Andrés Ripoll
Director-General, European Astronautics Centre, European
Space Agency (ESA), Cologne

Josette Runavot
Engineer, French National Centre for Space Research
(CNES);
Project leader, Venus Halley (Vega) programme, Space
Centre, Toulouse

Olivier de Saint-Lager
Official representative, Legal Affairs Directorate, French
Foreign Ministry, Paris;
Member of International Institute of Space Law

Yuri Semionov
Corresponding member of the Soviet Academy of Sciences,
Moscow;
Senior spacecraft construction engineer

David Shapland
Consultant and former Public Affairs Director for Spacelab/
Eureca programme, European Space Agency (ESA), Paris

Mitchell R. Sharpe
Historian, Alabama Space and Rocket Center, Huntsville,
Alabama

Michiyoshi Shiraishi
Deputy general manager, Nissan Motor Co., Tokyo

Jerome Simonoff
Vice-president and Technology Initiatives Manager,
Citicorp, New York

Jürgen Stegemann
Director, Department of Physiology, Deutsche
Sporthochschule, Cologne

Brian Stockwell
President, Corroon and Black Inspace Inc., Washington DC

Hermann A. Strub
Director, Space Affairs, German Federal Department for
Research and Technology, Bonn

Brian G. Taylor
Astrophysics adviser, Space Science Department, European
Space Research and Technology Centre (Estec), Noordwijk
(Netherlands)

Pierre Thomas
Lecturer, Ecole Senior Normale Supérieure, Lyon

US National Commission on Space
Charged by US Congress to determine the aims of space
exploration in the 21st century, Washington DC

Guy Valentiny
Chief of Bureau, Hermes applications, European Space
Agency (ESA), Paris

Alexei A. Vassiliev
Head of department, American and Canadian Institute,
Soviet Academy of Sciences, Moscow;
Member, Soviet Peace Committee

Evgeni P. Velikhov
Vice-president, Soviet Academy of Sciences, Moscow;
President, Soviet Peace Committee

Jacques Villain
Head, Scientific and Technical Information Bureau, Société
européenne de propulsion, Paris

Jean-Michel Villetorte
Engineer;
Scientific and Technical Information Bureau, Société
européenne de propulsion, Saint-Médard-en-Jalles

Adelin Villevieille
Former Director, Ministry of the Environment, Paris

Ronald J. White
Chief program scientist, Life Sciences Division, NASA,
Washington DC